Britannica
REFERENCE
ENCYCLOPEDIA

ENCYCLOPÆDIA
Britannica®

Encyclopædia Britannica, Inc.
Chicago • London • New Delhi • Paris • Seoul • Sydney • Taipei • Tokyo

Encyclopædia Britannica

Photo credits. *Front cover:* © dmussman/Fotolia; (inset, left to right) AP; © Outdoorsman/Fotolia; © Gino Santa Maria/Fotolia; © Corbis. *Back cover:* © Ronnie Howard/Fotolia; (inset, left to right) © Beboy/Fotolia; © ktsdesign/Fotolia; © Andrei Kazarov/Fotolia.

Contents

Foreword

"Utility [i.e., usefulness] ought to be the principal intention of every publication. Wherever this intention does not plainly appear, neither the books nor their authors have the smallest claim to the approbation of mankind."

So began the author's Preface to the First Edition of *Encyclopædia Britannica* in 1768. These words have guided Britannica editors ever since and, accordingly, influenced the development of the *Britannica Reference Encyclopedia*.

The *Britannica Reference Encyclopedia* is a unique selection of essential articles from the *Britannica Concise Encyclopedia* made with the readers of India in mind. Its nearly 800 pages and approximately 7,500 articles cover basic topics in world history, geography, the sciences and technology, religion, the arts, and sports and entertainment. With its special emphasis on South and Southeast Asia, the *Britannica Reference Encyclopedia* also highlights the rich heritage and landscape of India, from languages, arts and culture, customs and beliefs to Indian cities and states.

Encyclopædia Britannica is the oldest continuously published reference work in the English language. The first edition, referred to above, was published in Edinburgh, Scotland, between 1768 and 1771. Between 1768 and 2012 a total of 15 print editions were published.

In 1981 the company published what very likely was the first electronic encyclopedia, a text-only version of *Encyclopædia Britannica* for LexisNexis subscribers. In 1994 the first encyclopedia on the Internet, *Britannica Online*, appeared. Print and, in some cases, electronic versions of *Encyclopædia Britannica* have been available in the Japanese, Turkish, Chinese, Korean, Polish, and Hungarian languages, as well as related encyclopedias in French, Greek, Spanish, and Portuguese.

Today the editors of Encyclopædia Britannica are pleased to present the *Britannica Reference Encyclopedia*, in one handy and information-packed volume. We hope that consulting it for basic facts and information will become part of your daily life and also inspire you to explore the wealth of knowledge in the *Encyclopædia Britannica* online database.

Dale H. Hoiberg
Senior Vice President and Editor
Encyclopædia Britannica, Inc.

Explanatory Notes

Alphabetization. The articles are alphabetized word by word, with further alphabetizing letter by letter within a word. A "word" is here defined as a unit of one or more characters set off from other words by spaces, dashes, hyphens, or other symbols. Entry titles consisting of more than one word are arranged in alphabetical order of the succeeding words. Titles with identical spellings are arranged in the order (1) persons, (2) places, and (3) things. The following list illustrates the word-by-word principle:

horn
Horn, Cape
Horn of Africa
hornbill
horned owl

Further alphabetization rules include the following: (1) Diacritics, apostrophes, dashes, periods, and ampersands are ignored in alphabetization. (2) Names of monarchs and popes that are identical except for the Roman numeral following the name are ordered numerically. (3) Names beginning with *Mac-* and *Mc-* are ordered literally, all names beginning with *Mac-* preceding (by a number of pages) all names beginning with *Mc-*. (4) Entry headwords beginning with numbers are alphabetized as if they were spelled out.

Entry headword style. Variant spellings or versions of the encyclopedia's entry headwords are printed in boldface type when they are in common use; more obscure variants are printed in ordinary roman type. No effort has been made to be exhaustive in listing variants.

Several italicized terms are used to discriminate among the variants. The label *or* simply indicates a common alternative name or spelling. The label *orig.* precedes the birth name of a person who is entered under a name that was adopted or acquired subsequently. When a person's original surname is different from the name in the principal headword, the entire birth name is given, not enclosed in parentheses. The label *known as* precedes a common way of referring to a person that may never have had formal status. The label *formerly* indicates an older and generally discarded name for an entity, usually a geographical locale. The label *officially* indicates a formal or legal version of a name. The label *in full* precedes a fully spelled-out version of a name that is usually encountered in its shorter form. A label consisting of a language name precedes a native version or spelling of a name or term.

Biographical entry headwords in particular may employ parentheses in several ways. Parentheses may enclose portions of a person's name that are rarely used, a person's original given name or names, a later addition such as a title, or translations of titles or epithets.

Odin *or* **Wotan**
Latvia *officially* **Republic of Latvia**
OCR *in full* **optical character recognition**
Magellan, Strait of *Spanish* **Estrecho de Magallanes**
Odysseus *Roman* **Ulysses**
Doctorow, E(dgar) L(aurence)
Hughes, (James Mercer) Langston

Romanization of languages. Words from languages that do not use the Western (Roman) alphabet generally reflect the spellings most commonly seen in English-language contexts.

Chinese names are almost always transcribed according to the Pinyin system. Where a Chinese name or term appears as a headword, the older Wade-Giles spelling is given as an *or* variant. Place-names and biographical names on Taiwan, however, are generally listed in their Wade-Giles spelling, with the Pinyin spelling as a variant. A few Chinese names widely used in English (e.g., Confucius) retain their traditional English spelling.

Japanese names and terms are generally transcribed according to the Hepburn system.

Arabic names and terms generally follow the best-established Western usage. Except in a few well-established Western transliterations, the *l* in the article *al-* or *el-* ("the") is not assimilated to a following consonant (thus, we employ the spelling *Hārūn al-Rashīd*, not *Hārūn ar-Rashīd*), even though such assimilation reflects Arabic pronunciation and is sometimes encountered in English sources.

Place-names generally follow the system employed by the U.S. Board on Geographic Names.

Territorial boundaries. In articles and maps indicating disputed territories and geopolitical boundaries, the attribution of sovereignty or administrative subordination to any specific area does not imply recognition of the status claimed by an administering power.

Abbreviations

AD	anno Domini		Mass.	Massachusetts
Adm.	Admiral		Md.	Maryland
Ala.	Alabama		Me.	Maine
Amer.	American		mi	mile(s)
Ariz.	Arizona		Mich.	Michigan
Ark.	Arkansas		Minn.	Minnesota
BC	before Christ		Miss.	Mississippi
C	Celsius		ml	millilitre(s)
c.	circa		mm	millimetre(s)
Cal.	California		Mo.	Missouri
Capt.	captain		Mont.	Montana
cc	cubic centimetre(s)		mph	miles per hour
cent.	century, centuries		N	North
cm	centimetre(s)		N.C.	North Carolina
Co.	Company, County		N.D.	North Dakota
Col.	Colorado, Colonel		NE	northeastern
Conn.	Connecticut		Neb.	Nebraska
Corp.	Corporation		Nev.	Nevada
cu	cubic		N.H.	New Hampshire
D.C.	District of Columbia		N.J.	New Jersey
Del.	Delaware		N.M.	New Mexico
Dr.	Doctor		NW	northwestern
E	East		N.Y.	New York
e.g.	exempli gratia (for example)		Okla.	Oklahoma
est.	estimate, estimated		Ore.	Oregon
Eth.	Ethiopia		oz	ounce(s)
F	Fahrenheit		Pa.	Pennsylvania
fl.	flourished		Ph.D.	Doctor of Philosophy
Fla.	Florida		Pres.	President
ft	foot, feet		Queen.	Queensland
g	gram(s)		r.	reigned, ruled
Ga.	Georgia		Rev.	Reverend
Gen.	General		R.I.	Rhode Island
Gov.	Governor		S	South
i.e.	id est (that is)		S.C.	South Carolina
Ill.	Illinois		S.D.	South Dakota
in.	inch(es)		SE	southeastern
Ind.	Indiana		Sen.	Senator
Jr.	Junior		sq	square
K	Kelvin		St.	Saint
Kan.	Kansas		SW	southwestern
kg	kilogram(s)		Tenn.	Tennessee
km	kilometre(s)		UN	United Nations
kph	kilometres per hour		U.S.	United States
Ky.	Kentucky		Va.	Virginia
La.	Louisiana		vs.	versus
lb, lbs	pound, pounds		Vt.	Vermont
m	metre(s)		W	West
M.A.	Master of Arts		W.V.	West Virginia
Maj.	Major		Wash.	Washington
			Wisc.	Wisconsin
			Wy.	Wyoming

A

Aachen, French AIX-LA-CHAPELLE, City (pop., 2007 est.: 258,770), western Germany, southwest of Cologne. It was inhabited by Romans in the 1st century AD. A center of Carolingian culture, and the second city of Charlemagne's empire, it was the site of his great palace. The cathedral built by Charlemagne *c.* 800 saw the coronation of most German kings of the 10th–16th century; his chapel, with his tomb, remains as part of the larger Gothic cathedral today. Aachen was part of France 1801–15. It is famous for its many spas.

abalone, Any of several marine snail species (genus *Haliotis*, family Haliotidae), found in warm seas worldwide. The outer surface of the single shell has a row of small holes, most of which fill in as the animal grows; some remain open as outlets for waste products. Abalones range from 4 to 10 in. (10–25 cm) across and up to 3 in. (8 cm) deep. The largest is the 12 in. (30 cm) abalone (*H. rufescens*). The shell's lustrous, iridescent interior is used in ornaments, and the large muscular foot is eaten as a delicacy. Commercial abalone fisheries exist in California, Mexico, Japan, and South Africa.

Abalone (Haliotis)
Jacques Six

Abbas, Mahmoud, also called ABU MAZEN (b. 1935, Zefat, Palestine [now in Israel]), Palestinian leader. Abbas earned a law degree from the University of Damascus and a doctorate in history from Moscow State University. In the late 1950s he was one of the founders of Fatah, which spearheaded the Palestinian armed struggle and dominated the Palestine Liberation Organization. In the 1990s Abbas shaped Palestinian negotiating strategy in peace talks that led in 1993 to the Oslo Accords, in which Israel and the Palestinians extended to each other mutual recognition and which called for Israel to cede some authority over the West Bank and Gaza Strip to the Palestinians. He briefly served as prime minister of the Palestinian Authority in 2003 and was elected its president in 2005.

abbey, Complex of buildings housing a monastery or convent under the direction of an abbot or abbess, serving the needs of a self-contained religious community. The first abbey was Monte Cassino in Italy, founded in 529 by St. Benedict of Nursia. The cloister linked the most important elements of an abbey together. The dormitory was often built over the dining hall on the eastern side of the cloister and linked to the central church. The western side of the cloister provided for public dealings, with the gatehouse controlling the only opening to the outer, public courtyard. On the southern side of the cloister were a central kitchen, brewery, and workshops. The novitiate and infirmary were housed in a building with its own chapel, bathhouse, dining hall, kitchen, and garden. In the 12th–13th century, many abbeys were built throughout Europe, especially in France.

abbreviation, Shortened form of a written word or phrase used in place of the whole. Abbreviations began to proliferate in the 19th century and have been prevalent since; they are employed to reduce the time required for writing or speaking, especially when referring to the myriad new organizations, bureaucratic entities, and technological products typical of industrial societies. An abbreviation can now easily become a word, either as an initialism in which the letters are pronounced individually (e.g., TV or FBI) or as an acronym in which the letters are combined into syllables (e.g., scuba, laser, or NAFTA).

ʿ**Abduh, Muḥammad,** Egyptian religious scholar, jurist, and liberal reformer. As a student in Cairo, he came under the influence of Jamāl al-Dīn al-Afghānī. He was exiled for political radicalism (1882–88); he began his judicial career when he returned to Egypt. He rose from judge to muftī (legal counselor) in 1899. In his *Treatise on the Oneness of God,* he argued that Islam was superior to Christianity because it was more receptive to science and civilization. He liberalized Islamic law and administration, promoting considerations of equity, welfare, and common sense, even when this meant disregarding the literal texts of the Qur'ān.

Abdul Kalam, A(vul) P(akir) J(ainulabdeen) (b. Oct. 15, 1931, Rameswaram, India), Indian president (2002–07). After graduating from the Madras Institute of Technology, Kalam played a leading role in the development of India's missile and nuclear weapons programs. He planned a program that produced a number of successful missiles, helping earn him the nickname "Missile Man." Beginning in the early 1990s, he also served as scientific adviser to the government, and his prominent role in India's 1998 nuclear weapons tests established Kalam as a national hero. In 2002 the Hindu nationalist (Hindutva) National Democratic Alliance nominated Kalam, a Muslim, to succeed outgoing President K.R. Narayanan. Kalam easily won the elections in 2002, and in the largely ceremonial post he sought to use science and technology to transform India into a developed country. In 2007 he was succeeded by Pratibha Patil, the country's first woman president.

Aberdeen, City, council area (pop., 2001: 212,125), and commercial port on the North Sea, eastern Scotland. It constitutes the council area of Aberdeen, an enclave within the surrounding council area of Aberdeenshire, which was also the name of the historic county of which Aberdeen was the seat. Situated at the mouths of the Rivers Dee and Don, it is the chief port of northern Scotland. It was a royal burgh from the 12th century and a Scottish royal residence in the 12th–14th centuries. It supported Robert the Bruce in wars for Scottish independence, and for a time it was the headquarters of Edward I. From the 1970s Aberdeen developed rapidly as the principal British centre of the North Sea oil industry and its associated service and supply industries.

Abhidhamma Pitaka, Third and latest collection of texts comprising the Pali canon of Theravada Buddhism. The first two collections, Sutta Pitaka and Vinaya Pitaka, are attributed to the Buddha. Abhidhamma Pitaka texts are ascribed to later disciples and scholars; they deal with ethics, psychology, and epistemology.

The ruins of Fountains Abbey, a Cistercian monastery founded in the 12th century, near Ripon, North Yorkshire, England
Andy Williams

Abidjan, Largest city (pop., 2005 est.: 3,576,000) and chief port of Côte d'Ivoire. Abidjan was a rail terminus from 1904; after its lagoon was opened to the sea to create a port (1950), the city became the financial centre of French West Africa. Though it was once the country's capital and remains its seat of government, the official capital was moved to Yamoussoukro in 1983. Abidjan has a museum of traditional Ivorian art, a national library, and several research institutes.

abnormal psychology, or PSYCHOPATHOLOGY, Branch of psychology. It is concerned with mental and emotional disorders (e.g., neurosis, psychosis, mental deficiency) and with certain incompletely understood normal phenomena (such as dreams and hypnosis). The chief tool used in classifying psychological disorders is the American Psychiatric Assn.'s *Diagnostic and Statistical Manual of Mental Disorders* 4th edition (*DSM-IV*).

abolitionism (*c.* 1783–1888) Movement to end the slave trade and emancipate slaves in western Europe and the Americas. The slave system aroused little protest until the 18th century, when rationalist thinkers of the Enlightenment criticized it for violating the rights of man, and Quaker and other evangelical religious groups condemned it as un-Christian. Though antislavery sentiments were widespread by the late 18th century, they had little immediate effect on the centres of slavery themselves—the West Indies, South America, and the southern U.S. In 1807 the importation of African slaves was banned in the U.S. and the British colonies. Slavery was abolished in the British West Indies by 1838 and in the French possessions 10 years later. In the 11 Southern states of the U.S., however, slavery was a social and economic institution. American abolitionism laboured under the handicap that it threatened the harmony of North and South in the Union, and it also ran counter to the U.S. Constitution, which left the question of slavery to the individual states. The abolitionist movement in the North was led by agitators such as William Lloyd Garrison, founder of the American Anti-Slavery Society, writers such as John Greenleaf Whittier, former slaves such as Frederick Douglass, and Harriet Beecher Stowe. The election of Abraham Lincoln, who opposed the spread of slavery to the West, marked a turning point in the movement. Convinced that their way of life was threatened, the Southern states seceded from the Union, which led to the American Civil War. In 1863 Lincoln (who had never been an abolitionist) issued the Emancipation Proclamation, which freed slaves held in the Confederate states; the 13th Amendment to the U.S. Constitution (1865) prohibited slavery throughout the country. Slavery was abolished in Latin America by 1888. In some parts of Africa and in much of the Islamic world, it persisted as a legal institution well into the 20th century.

abortion, Expulsion of a fetus from the uterus before it can survive on its own. Spontaneous abortion at earlier stages of pregnancy is called miscarriage. Induced abortions often occur through intentional medical intervention and are performed to preserve the woman's life or health, to prevent the completion of a pregnancy resulting from rape or incest, to prevent the birth of a child with serious medical problems, or because the woman does not believe she is in a position to rear a child properly. The drug RU-486, if taken within a few weeks of conception, will trigger a miscarriage. Up to about 19 weeks of pregnancy, injections of saline solutions or hormones may be used to stimulate uterine contractions that will expel the fetus. Surgical removal of the contents of the uterus may be performed in the second trimester or later. Intact dilation and extraction procedures may occur in the third trimester; sometimes critically referred to as "partial-birth abortions," they have been very controversial. Other abortion procedures include manual vacuum aspiration (extraction by manual syringe) and dilation and suction curettage (extraction by machine-operated suction), both of which can be performed in early pregnancy. The social acceptability of abortion as a means of population control has varied from time to time and place to place throughout history. It was apparently a common method of family limitation in the Greco-Roman world, but Christian theologians early and vehemently condemned it. It became widely accepted in Europe in the Middle Ages. Severe criminal sanctions to deter abortion became common in the 19th century, but in the 20th century those sanctions were gradually modified in many countries. In the U.S. the 1973 *Roe* v. *Wade* decision had the effect of legalizing abortion during the first three months of pregnancy; states were able to implement restrictions on access to abortion after the first trimester, though within constraints set by the courts. Since that decision, there has been a fierce debate between supporters and opponents of a liberalized abortion policy.

Abraham (fl. early 2nd millennium BC), First of the Hebrew patriarchs, revered by Judaism, Christianity, and Islam. Genesis tells how Abraham, at 75, left Ur with his barren wife, Sarai (later Sarah), and others to found a new nation in Canaan. There God made a covenant with him, promising that his descendants would inherit the land and become a great nation. Abraham fathered Ishmael by Sarah's maidservant Hagar; Sarah herself bore Isaac, who inherited the covenant. Abraham's faith was tested when God ordered him to sacrifice Isaac; he was prepared to obey but God relented. In Judaism he is a model of virtue, in Christianity he is the father of all believers, and in Islam he is an ancestor of Muhammad and a model (in Sufism) of generosity.

abrasives, Sharp, hard materials used to wear away the surface of softer, less resistant materials. Abrasives are indispensable to the manufacture of the highly precise components and ultrasmooth surfaces required in the manufacture of automobiles, airplanes and space vehicles, mechanical and electrical appliances, and machine tools. Abrasives may be natural (e.g., diamond, corundum, emery) or synthetic (e.g., silicon carbide or Carborundum, synthetic diamond, alumina—a synthetic form of corundum). They range from the relatively soft particles used in household cleansers and jeweler's polish to diamonds.

abscess, Localized collection of pus in a cavity in the deeper layers of the skin or within the body, formed from tissues broken down by white blood cells (leukocytes) in response to inflammation caused by bacteria. A wall develops, separating the thick yellowish pus from the extracellular fluid of nearby healthy tissues. Rupture of the abscess allows the pus to escape and relieves swelling and pain. Treatment consists of cutting into the wall to drain the pus and giving antibiotics. If infective contents enter the bloodstream, they may be carried to remote tissues, seeding new abscesses.

absolute zero, Temperature at which a thermodynamic system has the lowest energy, 0 kelvin (K). It corresponds to $-459.67°$F ($-273.15°$C) and is the lowest possible temperature theoretically achievable by a system. A gas at constant pressure contracts as the temperature is decreased. A perfect gas would reach zero volume at absolute zero. However, a real gas condenses to a liquid or a solid at a temperature higher than absolute zero. At absolute zero, the system's molecular energy is minimal and none is available for transfer to other systems. The Kelvin temperature scale has absolute zero as its zero point, and its fundamental unit is the kelvin.

absolution, In Christianity, a pronouncement of forgiveness of sins made to a person who has repented. This rite is based on the forgiveness that Jesus extended to sinners during his ministry. In the early church, the priest absolved repentant sinners after they had confessed and performed their penance in public. During the Middle Ages, it became the custom for priests to hear confession and grant absolution privately. In Roman Catholicism penance is a sacrament, and the priest has the power to absolve a contrite sinner who promises to make satisfaction to God. In Protestant churches, the confession of sin is usually made in a formal prayer by the whole congregation, after which the minister announces their absolution.

absolutism, Political doctrine and practice of unlimited, centralized authority and absolute sovereignty, especially as vested in a monarch. Its essence is that the ruling power is not subject to regular challenge or check by any judicial, legislative, religious, economic, or electoral agency. Though it has been used throughout history, the form that developed in early modern Europe (16th–18th century) became the prototype; Louis XIV is seen as the epitome of European absolutism. Religious authority was assumed by the monarch, who became the head of the church as well as the state, on the basis that the right to rule came from God.

Abū Bakr (b. *c.* 573, Mecca, Hejaz, Arabian Peninsula—d. Aug. 23, 634, Medina), One of the close Companions of the Prophet Muhammad and the first Muslim caliph. Some Muslim traditions say he was the first male convert to Islam after Muhammad. He became caliph after Muhammad's death in 632, and during his two years in that office he consolidated central Arabia under Muslim control, engaging in the wars of apostasy (*riddah*). He also realized the urgency of expanding the regions under Muslim control in order to maintain peace among Arab tribes.

Abu Dhabi, Arabic ABŪ ẒABY, City (pop., 2005 est.: 633,136), capital of Abū Ẓaby emirate and national capital of the United Arab Emirates. It occupies most of the small island of Abū Ẓaby, which is connected to the mainland by a bridge. Settled in 1761, it began to develop rapidly following the discovery of petroleum in 1958; oil royalties revolutionized Abu Dhabi's political and economic position, and it has grown into a modern city and regional hub.

Abu Simbel, Site of two temples built by Ramses II in the 13th century BC. The area, at the southern frontier of pharaonic Egypt, lies near the present-day border between Egypt and The Sudan. The temples were unknown to the outside world until their rediscovery in 1813. The larger temple displays four 66-ft (20-m) seated figures of Ramses; the smaller was dedicated to Queen Nefertari. When the reservoir created by the building of Aswan High Dam threatened to submerge the site in the early 1960s, an international team disassembled both temples and reconstructed them 200 ft (60 m) above their previous site.

Sandstone figures of Ramses II in front of the main temple at Abu Simbel near Aswān, Egypt.
© Spectrum Colour Library/Heritage-Images

Abū Ẓaby, or ABU DHABI, Largest constituent emirate (pop., 2005 prelim.: 1,292,119) of the United Arab Emirates. Bounded to the north and west by the Persian Gulf, to the south and southwest by Saudi Arabia, and to the east by Oman, it has an area of 28,210 sq mi (73,060 sq km). It has numerous offshore islands, and internally it partially surrounds Dubayy and has a short boundary with Al-Shāriqah (Sharjah). Since the 18th century the Āl Bū Falāḥ, a clan of the Banū Yās confederation, has held power. In 1761 they found wells of potable water at the site of Abu Dhabi city, and they made their headquarters there from 1795. In the 19th century territorial conflicts with Muscat (Masqaṭ) and Oman and with the ancestors of the Saʿūd dynasty (which now rules Saudi Arabia) led to border disputes that have remained largely unsettled. Abū Ẓaby signed an agreement with Great Britain in 1892, placing its foreign affairs under British control. When Britain withdrew from the Persian Gulf in 1968, the emirate and the other Trucial States formed the United Arab Emirates. Its rich oil fields make it and Dubayy the federation's two most prosperous emirates.

Abuja, City (pop., 2003 est.: 452,000), federal capital of Nigeria. Construction of the city, at a site chosen for its healthful climate and central location about 300 mi (480 km) northeast of Lagos, began in 1976 under the architect Tange Kenzo. It officially replaced Lagos as the capital in 1991.

Abydos, Sacred city, one of the most important archaeological sites of ancient Egypt. It was an area of royal cenotaphs of the first two dynasties and later a pilgrimage centre for the worship of Osiris. The pharaohs, including Thutmose III and Ramses III, embellished the temple to Osiris, and some pharaohs had cenotaphs at Abydos. The temple of Seti I, one of the most beautiful, has helped decode Egyptian history: in a long gallery is a relief, the so-called Abydos list of kings, showing Seti and his son Ramses making offerings to the cartouches of 76 dead predecessors.

Abyssinian cat, Breed of domestic cat, considered more similar to the sacred cat of ancient Egypt than any other living cat. It is lithe and has slender legs and a long, tapering tail. Its short, finely textured coat is ruddy reddish brown, with individual hairs distinctively ticked, or tipped, with bands of black or brown. The nose is red, and the tail tip and backs of the hindlegs are black. The Abyssinian is affectionate and quiet, though generally shy with strangers.

acacia, Any of the approximately 800 species of trees and shrubs that make up the genus *Acacia*, in the family Fabaceae. Acacias are native to tropical and subtropical regions of the world, particularly Australia and Africa. Sweet acacia (*A. farnesiana*) is native to the southwestern U.S. Acacias have distinctive, finely divided leaflets, and their leafstalks may bear thorns or sharp spines at their base. Their small, often fragrant, yellow or white flowers have many stamens apiece, giving each a fuzzy appearance. On the plains of southern and eastern Africa, acacias are common features of the landscape. Several species are important economically, yielding substances such as gum arabic and tannin, as well as valuable timber.

Académie Française, Literary academy in France. The Académie Française was established by Cardinal Richelieu in 1634 to maintain standards of literary taste and to establish the literary language. In modern times it has endeavoured (somewhat absurdly) to purify French of foreign loanwords. Its membership is limited to 40. Despite its conservatism, most of France's great writers, including Pierre Corneille, Jean Racine, Voltaire, and Victor Hugo, have been members.

Academy Awards, Annual awards of merit in the U.S. presented by the Academy of Motion Picture Arts and Sciences. The Academy was formed in 1927 by Louis B. Mayer and others to raise the standards of film production, and its first awards were presented in 1929. The awards (nicknamed Oscars) recognize excellence in acting, directing, screenwriting, and other activities related to film production.

acanthus, Any of the more than 3,500 plant species that make up the family Acanthaceae, of the mint order (Lamiales). Acanthus are found mostly in tropical and subtropical regions. Most are herbaceous plants or shrubs that grow in tropical rainforests; some are climbers (vines) or trees. Acanthus have simple leaves arranged in opposite pairs on the twigs and enlarged cells called cystoliths in streaks or protuberances in the vegetative parts. The bisexual flowers are bilaterally symmetrical and usually crowded together in clusters. Individual flowers are enclosed by leaflike bracts, which are often coloured and large. Acanthus are mainly of horticultural interest and include some ornamentals.

Acapulco, in full ACAPULCO DE JUÁREZ, City and port (pop., 2000: 619,253), southwestern Mexico. Situated on a deep semicircular bay, it has the best harbour on Mexico's Pacific coast. It was discovered by Hernán Cortés in 1531, and a settlement was founded in 1550. Until 1815 it was a main depot for Spanish colonial fleets going to the Far East. It has become a major international resort for tourists attracted by its scenic beauty, climate, and excellent beaches.

acceleration, Rate of change of velocity. Acceleration, like velocity, is a vector quantity: it has both magnitude and direction. The velocity of an object moving on a straight path can change in magnitude only, so its acceleration is the rate of change of its speed. On a curved path, the velocity may or may not change in magnitude, but it will always change in direction, which means that the acceleration of an object moving on a curved path can never be zero. If velocity is stated in metres per second (m/s) and the time interval in seconds (s), then the units of acceleration are metres per second per second (m/s/s, or m/s^2).

acclimatization, Any of numerous gradual, long-term responses of an individual organism to changes in its environment. The responses are more or less habitual and reversible should conditions revert to an earlier state. These criteria differentiate acclimatization from homeostasis; from growth and development (which cannot be reversed); and from evolutionary adaptation (which occurs in a population over generations). Acclimatization can occur in anticipation of a change and enable organisms to survive conditions beyond their natural experience. Examples include adaptations to seasonal changes and adjustments to changes in altitude.

accordion, Portable musical instrument that uses a hand-pumped bellows and two keyboards to sound free reeds, small metal tongues that vibrate when air flows past them. The keyboards on either side of the bellows effectively resemble individual reed organs. The right-hand keyboard plays the treble line or lines. Most of the keys on the left-hand (bass) keyboard sound three-note chords; "free-bass" accordions permit the playing of single-note lines. A prototype accordion, using buttons rather than keys, was patented in Berlin in 1822 by Friedrich Buschmann (also inventor of the harmonica). The instrument gained wide popularity in dance bands and as a folk instrument.

account receivable, Any amount owed to a business as the result of a purchase of goods or services from it on a credit basis. Although the firm making the sale receives no written promise of payment, it enters the amount due as a current asset in its books. Accounts receivable constitute a major portion of the assets of many companies, and they may even be sold or pledged as collateral to obtain loans.

accounting, Systematic development and analysis of information about the economic affairs of an organization. The actual recording and summarizing of financial transactions is known as bookkeeping. When the data thus produced are abstracted in reports (usually quarterly or annually) for the use of persons outside the organization, the process is called financial accounting. Three reports are typically generated in financial accounting: the balance sheet, which summarizes the firm's assets and liabilities; the income statement, which reports the firm's gross proceeds, expenses, and profit or loss; and the statement of cash flow, which analyzes the flow of cash into and out of the firm. The creation of reports (usually monthly) for internal planning and decision-making is called managerial accounting. Its aim is to provide managers with reliable information on the costs of operations and on standards with which those costs can be compared, to assist them in budgeting.

Accra, Capital and largest city (pop., 2001 est.: 1,551,200) of Ghana, on the Gulf of Guinea. When the Portuguese first settled on the coast in 1482, the site was occupied by the Ga people. Three fortified trading posts were built 1650–80 by the Danes, the Dutch, and the British. The Danes and Dutch left the region in 1850 and 1872, respectively, and in 1877 Accra became the capital of the British Gold Coast colony. The city became Ghana's administra-

tive, economic, and educational centre after the country gained its independence in 1957. Tema, 17 mi (27 km) east, has taken over Accra's former port functions.

acetaminophen, also called PARACETAMOL, Drug used to relieve mild headache or muscle and joint pain and to reduce fever. An organic compund, it relieves pain by inhibiting prostaglandin synthesis in the central nervous system and reduces fever by acting on the temperature-regulating centre of the brain. Unlike aspirin, it has no anti-inflammatory effect. It also is much less likely to irritate the stomach and cause peptic ulcers, is not linked with Reye syndrome, and can be taken by persons using anticoagulants or allergic to aspirin. Overdosages can cause fatal liver damage. Common brand names around much of the world are Tylenol and Panadol.

Achaean League, 3rd-century BC confederation of towns of Achaea, an area in the northern Peloponnese of ancient Greece. Twelve cities had joined together by the 4th century BC to combat piracy, but they disbanded after the death of Alexander the Great. Ten cities renewed the league in 280 BC, later admitting non-Achaean cities to defend themselves against Macedonia, then Sparta, and finally Rome. Rome dissolved the league after defeating it in 146 BC. Later a smaller league was formed that existed into the Roman imperial age.

Achebe, (Albert) Chinua(lumogu) (b. Nov. 16, 1930, Ogidi, Nigeria), Nigerian Igbo novelist. Concerned with emergent Africa at its moments of crisis, he is acclaimed for depictions of the disorientation accompanying the imposition of Western customs and values on traditional African society. *Things Fall Apart* (1958) and *Arrow of God* (1964) portray traditional Igbo life as it clashes with colonialism. *No Longer at Ease* (1960), *A Man of the People* (1966), and *Anthills of the Savannah* (1988) deal with corruption and other aspects of postcolonial African life. *Home and Exile* (2000) is in part autobiographical, in part a defense of Africa against Western distortions.

Achilles, In Greek mythology, the bravest and strongest of the Greek warriors in the Trojan War. Because his mother dipped him into the River Styx, he was invulnerable except at the heel by which she held him. During the war against Troy Achilles took 12 nearby cities, but after a quarrel with Agamemnon he refused further service. He allowed his beloved cousin Patroclus to fight in his armor, and when Hector slew Patroclus, Achilles returned to battle, killed Hector, and dragged his body around the walls of Troy. Homer mentions Achilles' funeral but not the circumstances of his death; the later poet Arctinus relates that Paris killed Achilles with an arrow guided by Apollo.

acid, Any substance that in water solution tastes sour, changes the colour of acid-base indicators (e.g., litmus), reacts with some metals (e.g., iron) to yield hydrogen gas, reacts with bases to form salts, and promotes certain chemical reactions (e.g., acid catalysis). Acids contain one or more hydrogen atoms that, in solution, dissociate as positively charged hydrogen ions. Inorganic, or mineral, acids include sulfuric acid, nitric acid, hydrochloric acid, and phosphoric acid. Organic acids include carboxylic acids, phenols, and sulfonic acids. Broader definitions of acids cover situations in which water is not present.

acid rain, Any precipitation, including snow, that contains a heavy concentration of sulfuric and nitric acids. This form of pollution is a serious regional environmental problem in many large urban and industrial areas. Automobiles, certain industrial operations, and electric power plants that burn fossil fuels emit the gases sulfur dioxide and nitrogen oxide into the atmosphere, where they combine with water vapour in clouds to form sulfuric and nitric acids. The highly acidic precipitation from these clouds may contaminate lakes and streams, damaging fish and other aquatic species; damage vegetation, including agricultural crops and trees;

damage soils; and corrode the outsides of buildings and other structures (historic monuments are especially vulnerable). Though usually most severe around large urban and industrial areas, acid precipitation may also occur at great distances downwind of the source of the pollutants.

acne, Inflammatory disease of the oil glands of the skin. Acne vulgaris, probably the most frequent chronic skin disorder, results from an interplay of hereditary factors, hormones, and bacteria, beginning in the teen years when overactive sebaceous glands are stimulated by high levels of androgens. Its primary lesion, the blackhead, may be open or closed; it consists of a plug of skin oil (sebum), cell debris, and microorganisms in a hair follicle. Acne has four grades of severity, with increasing degrees of spread, inflammation, pustule formation, and scarring. Methods of treatment vary from skin medication to antibiotics and hormones; many cases eventually resolve spontaneously.

Aconcagua, Mount, Mountain, western Argentina, on the Chilean border. Located in the Andes Mountains at an elevation of 22,831 ft (6,959 m), it is widely considered the highest peak in the Western Hemisphere. It is of volcanic origin but is not itself an active volcano. The summit was first reached in 1897.

aconite, Any member of two genera of perennial herbaceous plants of the buttercup family: *Aconitum* (monkshood or wolfsbane), consisting of summer-flowering poisonous plants, and *Eranthis* (winter aconite), consisting of spring-flowering ornamentals. The dried tuberous root of *A. napellus* was formerly used as a sedative and a painkiller.

acoustics, Science of production, control, transmission, reception, and effects of sound. Its principal branches are architectural, environmental, musical, and engineering acoustics, and ultrasonics. Environmental acoustics focuses on controlling noise produced by aircraft engines, factories, construction machinery, and general traffic. Musical acoustics deals with the design and use of musical instruments and how musical sounds affect listeners. Engineering acoustics concerns sound recording and reproduction systems. Ultrasonics deals with ultrasonic waves, which have frequencies above the audible range, and their applications in industry and medicine.

acrobatics, Art of jumping, tumbling, and balancing. The art is of ancient origin; acrobats performed leaps, somersaults, and vaults at Egyptian and Greek events. Acrobatic feats were featured in the commedia dell'arte theatre in Europe and in jingxi ("Peking opera") in China. The later use of apparatuses such as poles, tightropes, and flying trapezes made acrobatics a major attraction in circus performances. Its popularity increased in the 20th century with such performers as the Flying Wallendas.

acromegaly, Growth and metabolic disorder in which the skeletal extremities enlarge when a pituitary gland tumor causes overproduction of growth hormone after maturity. It is often associated with pituitary gigantism. Acromegaly is characterized by gradual enlargement of hands and feet, exaggeration of facial features, skin thickening, and enlargement of most internal organs, along with headaches, excessive sweating, and high blood pressure. Acromegalic individuals are likely to develop congestive heart failure, muscle weakness, joint pain, osteoporosis, and often diabetes mellitus and visual problems, including blindness. If treatment with surgery and/or radiation fails, then hormone therapy is used. Treatment can cause hormone deficiency, necessitating hormone replacement therapy; spontaneous events may also cause hormone deficiency.

acropolis, (Greek: "city at the top") Central, defensively oriented district in ancient Greek cities, located on the highest ground and containing the chief municipal and religious buildings. The renowned Athens Acropolis (5th century BC), atop a craggy walled hill, is home to four main edifices—the Propylaea, Parthenon, Ere-

chtheum (Ionic temple noted for its caryatid porch), and Temple of Athena Nike—all built from white marble plentiful in the region.

The Acropolis, Athens.
© Neil Setchfield—Lonely Planet Images/Getty Images

acting, Art of representing a character on a stage or before a camera by means of movement, gesture, and intonation. Acting in the Western tradition originated in Greece in the 6th century BCE; the tragedian Thespis is traditionally regarded as founder of the profession. Aristotle defined acting as "the right management of the voice to express various emotions" and declared it a natural gift that he doubted could be taught. Acting declined as an art in the Middle Ages, when Christian liturgical drama was performed by craft guilds and amateurs. Modern professional acting emerged in the 16th century with Italy's commedia dell'arte troupes. It flourished during the era of William Shakespeare. Not until the 18th century, however, was acting considered a profession to be taken seriously, through the efforts in England of the actor-manager David Garrick and the talents of actors such as Sarah Siddons, Edmund Kean, and Henry Irving. Modern acting styles have been influenced by Konstantin Stanislavsky's emphasis on the actor's identification with his role and by Bertolt Brecht's insistence on the objectivity and discipline of the actor. The Stanislavsky method was adopted in the U.S. by Lee Strasberg and Stella Adler (1901–92) and is the basis of most contemporary training, which features the cultivation of emotional and sense memory, physical and vocal training, and improvisation.

Actium, Battle of (31 BC) Naval battle off Acarnania, Greece, between Octavian (later Augustus) and Mark Antony. With 500 ships and 70,000 infantry, Antony camped at Actium, between the Ionian Sea and the Ambracian Gulf. Octavian, with 400 ships and 80,000 infantry, cut Antony's line of communication from the north. Desertion by allies and a lack of supplies forced Antony to act. Outmaneuvered on land, he followed Cleopatra's advice to attack Octavian at sea. Antony's larger fleet included his own and Cleopatra's ships. In the heat of battle Cleopatra fled with her galleys, and Antony followed with a few ships. His fleet surrendered immediately, his army a week later. Octavian's victory left him undisputed ruler of the Roman world.

actuary, One who calculates insurance risks and premiums. Actuaries compute the probability of the occurrence of such events as birth, marriage, illness, accidents, and death. They also evaluate the hazards of property damage or loss and the legal liability for the safety and well-being of others. Usually employed by insurance companies, actuaries set premium rates based on statistical studies, establish underwriting procedures, and determine the amounts of money required to assure the payment of benefits.

acupressure, or SHIATSU, Alternative-medicine practice in which pressure is applied to points on the body aligned along 12 main meridians (pathways), usually for a short time, to improve the flow of vital force (qi). Though often referred to by its Japanese name, shiatsu, it originated in China thousands of years ago. A single point may be pressed to relieve a specific symptom or condition, or a series of points can be worked on to promote overall well-being. Some studies suggest that acupressure can be effective for certain health problems, including nausea, pain, and stroke-related weakness. Risks are minimal with cautious use.

acupuncture, Medical technique in which needles are inserted into the skin and underlying tissues, devised in China before 2500 BC. One or more small metal needles are inserted at precise points along 12 meridians (pathways) in the body, through which the vital life force (qi) is believed to flow, in order to restore yin-yang balance and treat disease caused by yin-yang imbalance. Acupuncture appears to relieve pain and is used as an anesthetic for surgery. Theories to explain its effects include stimulation of release of natural opiates, blockage of pain-signal transmission, and a placebo effect.

Adam and Eve, In the Judeo-Christian and Islamic traditions, the parents of the human race. Genesis gives two versions of their creation. In the first, God creates "male and female in his own image" on the sixth day. In the second, Adam is placed in the Garden of Eden, and Eve is later created from his rib to ease his loneliness. For succumbing to temptation and eating the fruit of the forbidden tree of knowledge of good and evil, God banished them from Eden, and they and their descendants were forced to live lives of hardship. Cain and Abel were their children. Christian theologians developed the doctrine of original sin based on the story of their transgression; in contrast, the Quran teaches that Adam's sin was his alone and did not make all people sinners.

Adams, John (b. Oct. 30, 1735, Braintree, Mass.—d. July 4, 1826, Quincy, Mass., U.S.), U.S. politician, first vice president (1789–97) and second president (1797–1801) of the U.S. After graduating from Harvard College in 1755, he practiced law in Boston. In 1764 he married Abigail Smith. Active in the American independence movement, he was elected to the Massachusetts legislature and served as a delegate to the Continental Congress (1774–78), where he was appointed to a committee with Thomas Jefferson and others to draft the Declaration of Independence. In 1776–78 he was appointed to many congressional committees, including one to create a navy and another to review foreign affairs. He served as a diplomat in France, the Netherlands, and England (1778–88). In the first U.S. presidential election, he received the second largest number of votes and became vice president under George Washington. Adams's term as president was marked by controversy over his signing of the Alien and Sedition Acts in 1798 and by his alliance with the conservative Federalist Party. In 1800 he was defeated for reelection by Jefferson and retired to live a secluded life in Massachusetts. In 1812 he overcame his bitterness toward Jefferson, with whom he began an illuminating correspondence. Both men died on July 4, 1826, the Declaration's 50th anniversary. John Quincy Adams was his son.

John Adams, oil painting by Gilbert Stuart, 1826; in the National Collection of Fine Arts, Washington, D.C.

Courtesy of the Smithsonian American Art Museum (formerly National Museum of American Art), Washington, D.C.

Adams, John Quincy (b. July 11, 1767, Braintree, Mass.—d. Feb. 23, 1848, Washington, D.C., U.S.), Sixth president of the U.S.

(1825–29). He was the eldest son of John Adams, second president of the U.S., and Abigail Adams. He accompanied his father to Europe on diplomatic missions (1778–80) and was later appointed U.S. minister to the Netherlands (1794) and to Prussia (1797). In 1801 he returned to Massachusetts and served in the U.S. Senate (1803–08). Resuming his diplomatic service, he became U.S. minister to Russia (1809–11) and to Britain (1815–17). Appointed secretary of state (1817–25), he was instrumental in acquiring Florida from Spain and in drafting the Monroe Doctrine. He ran for the presidency in 1824 against three other candidates; none received a majority of the electoral votes, though Andrew Jackson received a plurality. By constitutional design, the selection of the president went to the House of Representatives, where Adams was elected after receiving crucial support from Henry Clay, who had finished third in the initial balloting. He appointed Clay secretary of state, which further angered Jackson. Adams's presidency was unsuccessful; when he ran for reelection, Jackson defeated him. In 1830 he was elected to the House, where he served until his death. He was outspoken in his opposition to slavery; in 1839 he proposed a constitutional amendment forbidding slavery in any new state admitted to the Union. Southern congressmen prevented discussion of antislavery petitions by passing gag rules (repealed in 1844 as a result of Adams's persistence). In 1841 he successfully defended the slaves in the *Amistad* mutiny case.

Adam's Peak, Mountain, southwestern Sri Lanka. Standing

7,360 ft (2,243 m) high, it is sacred and a place of pilgrimage to Buddhists, Muslims, and Hindus. On its summit, it has a large hollow, 5.3 ft (1.6 m) long, that is venerated as the footprint of Buddha, Adam, and Shiva, respectively. Many pilgrims of all faiths visit the peak every year.

Adam's Peak, southwestern Sri Lanka.
Ed Lark—Artstreet

Adana, City (pop., 2000: 1,091,000), south-central Turkey, on the Seyhan River. An agricultural and industrial centre and one of Turkey's largest cities, it probably overlies a Hittite settlement that dates from *c.* 1400 BC. Conquered by Alexander the Great in 335–334 BC, it was later a Roman military station. It came under the rule of the ʿAbbāsid dynasty at the end of the 7th century AD and changed hands intermittently until the late 14th century, when it fell into the hands of the Ramazan dynasty, a Turkmen group that remained influential even after the city's conquest by the Ottoman Empire in 1516. Adana's prosperity has long derived from the fertile valleys behind it and its position as a bridgehead on the trade routes connecting Anatolia and the Arabian Peninsula.

adaptation, In biology, the process by which an animal or plant becomes fitted to its environment. It is the result of natural selection acting on inherited variation. Even simple organisms must be adapted in many ways, including structure, physiology, and genetics; movement or dispersal; means of defense and attack; and reproduction and development. To be useful, adaptations must often occur simultaneously in different parts of the body.

Addis Ababa, Capital and largest city (pop., 2007 est.: 3,100,000) of Ethiopia. It lies on a plateau in the country's geographic centre at an altitude of about 8,000 ft (2,450 m). The city was founded as the capital in 1887 because of the unsatisfactory location of the former capital, Entoto. Addis Ababa was the capital of Italian East Africa 1935–41. It has become the national centre for higher education, banking and insurance, and trade. Several international organizations have their headquarters there, including the Organization of African Unity. In recent decades it has suffered unrest and extensive damage as a result of the country's political instability.

Adelaide, City (pop., 2004 est.: 1,124,315) and capital, South Australia. Adelaide lies at the base of the Mount Lofty Ranges on the Torrens River, near its harbour facilities at Port Adelaide. Founded in 1836, it was incorporated in 1840 as Australia's first municipal government. Its rise as an agricultural marketing centre and the proximity of natural mineral deposits contributed to its economic growth. It is an industrial centre and has petroleum refineries as well as connections by pipeline to natural gas fields. Landmarks include the University of Adelaide, Parliament House, Government House, and two cathedrals.

Aden, Seaport city (pop., 2004 prelim.: 580,000), southern Yemen, on the Gulf of Aden. It was a principal terminus of the spice road of western Arabia for about 1,000 years before the 3rd century AD. It then became a trading centre under Yemeni, Ethiopian, and Arab control. The Ottoman Empire captured the city in 1538, and the British (who established a garrison there around 1800) governed it from India (1839–1937). It grew in importance as a coaling station and transshipment point after the opening of the Suez Canal. It was made a crown colony in 1937, incorporated in the Federation of South Arabia (1963–67), and served as the capital of South Yemen until that republic's merger with North Yemen in 1990.

Aden, Gulf of, Arm of the Indian Ocean between the Arabian Peninsula and Somalia. To the west, it narrows into the Gulf of Tadjoura; its eastern limit is the meridian of Cape Guardafui. In these terms it is about 550 mi (885 km) long; geologically, it extends a total of 920 mi (1,480 km), to the eastern limits of the continental shelf beyond the Khuriyyā Muriyyā islands to the north and the island of Socotra to the south. Its marine life is rich in quantity and variety. Its coastline lacks large-scale fishing facilities but supports many fishing towns, as well as the major ports Aden and Djibouti.

Adenauer, Konrad (b. Jan. 5, 1876, Cologne, German Empire—d. April 19, 1967, Rhöndorf, W.Ger.), German statesman, first chancellor of the Federal Republic of Germany (West Germany). Elected to the Cologne city council (1906), he served as the city's lord mayor (1917–33). He was elected to the Prussian Staatsrat (state council) in 1920 and served as its speaker (1928–33). He lost his posts when the Nazis came to power, and in 1944 he was sent to a concentration camp. As World War II drew to a close, he played an important role in the formation of the Christian Democratic Union. As chancellor from 1949, Adenauer stressed individualism under the rule of law. His fear of Soviet expansion made him a strong supporter of NATO. He worked hard to reconcile Germany with its former enemies, especially France. He retired his post in 1963.

Konrad Adenauer.
©Karsh/Woodfin Camp and Associates

adenoids, or PHARYNGEAL TONSILS, Mass of lymphoid tissue, similar to the (palatine) tonsils, on the back wall of the nasal pharynx. If the adenoids become infected in childhood, their inflammation can obstruct nasal breathing and sinus drainage (promoting sinusitis) and block the eustachian tubes that connect to the middle ear (setting the stage for otitis). Surgical removal of enlarged or infected adenoids is frequently recommended.

adenovirus, Any of a group of spheroidal viruses, made up of DNA wrapped in a protein coat, that cause sore throat and fever in humans, hepatitis in dogs, and several diseases in fowl, mice, cattle, pigs, and monkeys. An adenovirus develops within the nucleus of an infected cell. In humans, adenoviruses, like cold viruses, may cause infections of the upper respiratory tract, the eyes, and frequently the lymph nodes. Like cold viruses, adenoviruses are often found in inactive infections in clinically healthy persons. Because only a few adenoviruses commonly cause illness in humans, vaccines against them are possible.

Adi Granth (Punjabi: "First Book") Sacred scripture of Sikhism. Composed of nearly 6,000 hymns of the Sikh Gurus and Hindu and Islamic saints, it is the central object of worship in all gurdwaras (temples). It is ritually opened and closed daily and is read continuously on special occasions. First compiled in 1604 by Arjan, it included his own hymns and those of his predecessors and the devotional songs of saints. In 1704 the last Guru, Gobind Singh, added more hymns and decreed that after his death the Granth would take the place of the Guru. Written mostly in Punjabi or Hindi, it contains the *Mul Mantra* (basic prayer), *Japji* (the most important scripture, written by Nanak), and hymns arranged according to the ragas in which they are to be sung.

administrative law, Law regulating the powers, procedures, and acts of public administration. It applies to all public officials and public agencies. As distinguished from legislative and judicial authority, administrative authority entails the power to issue rules and regulations based on statutes, grant licenses and permits to facilitate the conduct of government business, initiate investigations of and provide remedies for complaints or problems, and issue orders directing parties to conform to governing statutes or rules. An administrative-law judge is a government official with quasi-judicial powers, including the authority to conduct hearings, make findings of fact, and recommend resolution of disputes concerning the agency's actions.

adobe, Handmade sun-dried bricks formed from a mixture of heavy clay and straw found in arid regions. As a building material, adobe dates back thousands of years and is found in many parts of the world. Molds for shaping the bricks were brought to the New World by the Spanish. Excellent insulating properties make adobe an ideal material for both dwellings and ovens; home interiors retain heat in winter and stay cool in summer. The adobe buildings at Taos, N.M., are typical of Native American pueblo dwellings.

adolescence, Period of life from puberty to adulthood (roughly ages 12–20) characterized by marked physiological changes, development of sexual feelings, efforts toward the construction of identity, and a progression from concrete to abstract thought. Adolescence is sometimes viewed as a transitional state, during which youths begin to separate themselves from their parents but still lack a clearly defined role in society. It is generally regarded as an emotionally intense and often stressful period.

Adonis, In Greek mythology, a youth of remarkable beauty, the favorite of Aphrodite. As a child he was put in the care of Persephone, who refused to allow him to return from the underworld. Zeus ruled that he should spend a third of the year with Persephone, a third with Aphrodite, and a third on his own. He became a hunter and was killed by a boar. In answer to Aphrodite's pleas, Zeus allowed him to spend half the year with her and half in the underworld. Mythically, Adonis represents the cycle of death and resurrection in winter and spring. He is identified with the Babylonian god Tammuz.

adoption, Act of transferring parental rights and duties to someone other than the adopted person's biological parents. The practice is ancient and occurs in all cultures. Traditionally, its goal was to continue the male line for the purposes of inheritance and succession; most adoptees were male (and sometimes adult). Contemporary laws and practices aim to promote child welfare and the development of families. In the latter part of the 20th century, there was a relaxation of traditional restrictions on age differences between adoptive parents and children, on the parents' minimum income level, on the mother's employment outside the home, and on placements across religious and ethnic lines. Single-parent adoptions and adoptions by same-sex couples also became more acceptable. Beginning in the 1970s, a growing adoptees-rights movement in the United States called for the repeal of confidentiality laws in most states that prevented adoptees as adults from viewing their adoption records, including their original birth certificates.

Adriatic Sea, Arm of the Mediterranean Sea, lying between Italy and the Balkan Peninsula. It is about 500 mi (800 km) long, with an average width of 110 mi (175 km), a maximum depth of 4,035 ft (1,324 m), and an area of 50,590 sq mi (131,050 sq km). The Italian coast is relatively straight and continuous, having no islands, but the Balkan coast is full of islands, generally running parallel to the shore. The Strait of Otranto at its southeasterly limit links it with the Ionian Sea.

adulthood, Period in the human life span in which full physical and intellectual maturity have been attained. Adulthood is commonly thought of as beginning at age 20 or 21. It includes middle age (commencing around age 40) and old age (from about age 60). Physically, it is characterized by the peaking (around age 30) and gradual decline of bodily functioning; the postpeak phase includes diminished acuity of the senses, reduction in muscular and skeletal mass, buildup of cholesterol in the arteries, weakening of the heart muscle, and diminished production of hormones. Some slowing in the rate of central-nervous-system processing also begins with middle age, but it is generally compensated for by an increased capacity to retain practical information and apply accumulated cultural knowledge. In old age, most individuals experience a significant decline in physical capacity, and many eventually also suffer impaired mental function.

Advaita (Sanskrit: "Nondualism") Most influential school of Vedanta. It originated with Gaudapada's 7th-century commentary on the Mandukya Upanishad. Gaudapada builds on the Mahayana Buddhist philosophy of emptiness, asserting that there is no duality; the mind, awake or dreaming, moves through maya (illusion). The mind's ignorance conceals the truth that there is no becoming and no individual soul or self (jiva), only a temporary delineation from the atman (all-soul). In the 8th century Sankara developed Advaita further, arguing that the world is unreal and that the Upanishads teach the nature of Brahman, the only reality. The extensive Advaita literature influences modern Hindu thought.

Advent, In the Christian calendar, the first season of the church year, a period of preparation for the birth of Jesus. Advent begins on the Sunday nearest to November 30 and continues until Christmas. Viewed as a penitential season, it is also considered a time of preparation for the Second Coming of Christ. The origin of Advent is unknown, but it was observed as early as the 6th century. In many countries it is celebrated with popular customs such as the lighting of Advent candles.

Adventist, Member of any of a group of Protestant churches that arose in the U.S. in the 19th century and believe that the Second Coming of Christ is close at hand. Adventism was founded during a period marked by millennialism by William Miller (1782–1849), a former U.S. army officer, who asserted that Christ would return to separate saints from sinners and inaugurate his 1,000-year kingdom on earth sometime in the year before March 21, 1844. After that date passed, Miller and his followers set a new date, Oct. 22, 1844. The "Great Disappointment" was followed by a Mutual Conference of Adventists in 1845. Those who persisted concluded that Miller had misinterpreted the signs and that, though Christ had begun the "cleansing of the heavenly sanctuary," he would not appear until he had completed that task. These Millerites founded the Seventh-Day Adventists in 1863; other Adventist groups include the Evangelical Adventists and the Advent Christian Church. Seventh-Day Adventists observe Saturday as the Sabbath and avoid eating meat and using narcotics or stimulants.

advertising, Techniques and practices used to bring products, services, opinions, or causes to public notice for the purpose of persuading the public to respond in a certain way. Weekly newspapers in London first carried advertisements in the 17th century; by the 18th century such advertising was flourishing. The first advertising agencies were established in the 19th century to broker for space in newspapers, and by the early 20th century agencies were producing the advertising message itself, including copy and artwork. Most advertising promotes goods for sale, but similar methods are used in public service messages to promote causes, charities, or political candidates. In many countries, advertising is the most important source of income for the media through which it is conducted. In addition to newspapers, magazines, and broadcast media, advertising media include direct mail, billboards and posters, transit advertising, the Internet, and promotional items such as matchbooks or calendars. Advertisers attempt to choose media that are favoured by the advertisers' target audience.

Aegean civilizations, The Bronze Age civilizations that arose and flourished *c.* 3000–1000 BCE in the region bordering the Aegean Sea. They include Crete, the Cyclades, the Greek mainland south from Thessaly, including the Peloponnese, and Macedonia, Thrace, and western Anatolia. The most significant were the Minoan and Mycenaean civilizations. The term also sometimes refers to Neolithic civilizations in the same region *c.* 7000–3000 BCE.

Aegean Islands, Greek islands in the Aegean Sea, particularly the Cyclades, Sporades, and Dodecanese groups. The Cyclades consist of about 30 islands. The Dodecanese, or Southern Sporades, include Kálimnos, Kárpathos, Cos, Léros, Pátmos, Rhodes, and Sími. The Sporades, or Northern Sporades, include Skyros, Skópelos, and Skíathos.

Aegean Sea, Arm of the Mediterranean Sea, lying between Greece and Turkey. About 380 mi (610 km) long and 186 mi (300 km) wide, it has a total area of some 83,000 sq mi (214,000 sq km) and a maximum depth of 11,627 ft (3,543 m). The straits of the Dardanelles, the Sea of Marmara, and the Bosporus connect it with the Black Sea. The Aegean was the cradle of the great early civilizations of Crete and Greece. Thíra, one of its numerous islands, has been linked with the legend of Atlantis.

Aeneas, Mythical hero of Troy and Rome. He was the son of Aphrodite and Anchises, a member of Trojan royal family. According to Homer, he was second only to his cousin Hector in defending Troy during the Trojan War. Virgil's *Aeneid* tells of Aeneas's escape after Troy's fall, carrying his elderly father on his back, and of his journey to Italy, where his descendants became the rulers of Rome.

Aeolian harp, Stringed instrument played by the wind (named for the wind god Aeolus). It is usually a long, narrow, shallow box with soundholes and 10 or 12 strings strung lengthwise between two bridges. The strings are of the same length but different thicknesses and are all tuned to the same pitch; the wind makes them vibrate in successively higher harmonics. The harp may be hung, or set horizontally under a window sash. The first known Aeolian harp was constructed *c.* 1650 by Athanasius Kircher (1601–1680).

aerobics, System of physical conditioning for increasing the efficiency of the body's intake of oxygen. Aerobic exercises (e.g., running, jogging, swimming, dancing) stimulate heart and lung activity. To produce a benefit, aerobic training must raise the heart rate (pulse) to the exerciser's target level for at least 20 minutes and include at least three sessions a week. The concept of aerobics was pioneered by Kenneth H. Cooper and popularized in his books *Aerobics* (1968) and *The Aerobics Way* (1977).

aerospace engineering, Field concerned with the development, design, construction, testing, and operation of airplanes and spacecraft. The field has its roots in balloon flight, gliders, and airships, and in the 1960s it was broadened to include space vehicles. Principal technologies are those of aerodynamics, propulsion, structure and stability, and control. Aerospace engineers in academic, industrial, and government research centres cooperate in designing new products. Flight testing of prototypes follows, and finally quantity production and operation take place. Important developments in aerospace engineering include the metal monocoque fuselage, the cantilevered monoplane wing, the jet engine, supersonic flight, and spaceflight.

aerospace medicine, Branch of medicine, pioneered by Paul Bert, dealing with atmospheric flight (aviation medicine) and space flight (space medicine). Intensive preflight simulator training and attention to design of equipment and spacecraft promote the safety and effectiveness of humans exposed to the stresses of flight and can prevent some problems. The world's first unit for space research was established in the U.S. in 1948. Physicians trained in aerospace medicine are known as flight surgeons.

Aeschylus (b. 525/524—d. 456/455 BC, Gela, Sicily), Greek tragic dramatist. He fought with the Athenian army at Marathon (490) and in 484 achieved the first of his many victories at the major dramatic competition in Athens. He wrote over 80 plays, but only 7 are extant; the earliest of these, *Persians*, was performed in 472 BC. Other plays that survive are the *Oresteia* trilogy (*Agamemnon, The Libation Bearers*, and *The Eumenides*), *Seven Against Thebes, The Suppliants*, and *Prometheus Bound*. Considered the father of Greek tragic drama, he added a second actor to the performance, an innovation that enabled the later development of dialogue and created true dramatic action. He was the first of the three great Greek tragedians, preceding Sophocles and Euripides.

Aesop, Supposed author of a collection of Greek fables, almost certainly a legendary figure. Though Herodotus, in the 5th century BC, said that he was an actual personage, "Aesop" was probably no more than a name invented to provide an author for fables centring on beasts. Aesopian fables emphasize the social interactions of human beings, and the morals they draw tend to embody advice on how to deal with the competitive realities of life. The Western fable tradition effectively begins with these tales. Modern editions list some 200 Aesopian fables.

Aestheticism, Late 19th-century European arts movement that centred on the doctrine that art exists for the sake of its beauty alone. It began in reaction to prevailing utilitarian social philosophies and to the perceived ugliness and philistinism of the industrial age. Its philosophical foundations were laid by Immanuel Kant, who proposed that aesthetic standards could be separated from morality, utility, or pleasure. James McNeill Whistler, Oscar Wilde, and Stéphane Mallarmé raised the movement's ideal of the cultivation of refined sensibility to perhaps its highest point. Aestheticism had affinities with French Symbolism and was a precursor of Art Nouveau.

Aetolian League, Federal state of ancient Aetolia in central Greece, probably based on a looser tribal community. A leading power by *c.* 340 BC, the Aetolian League resisted invasions by Macedonia in 322 and 314–311, expanded into Delphi, and allied with Boeotia *c.* 300. It fended off the Gauls in 279 and formed an alliance with Macedonia (*c.* 270–240). The league's power in central Greece was confirmed with the defeat of the Boeotians (245). From the late 3rd century Aetolia began to lose power and territory to Macedonia, culminating in the sacking of the league's federal capital, Thermum, by Philip V in 220. The league then allied with Rome against Macedonia and defeated Philip at Cynoscephalae (197). Rome later forced it into a permanent alliance (189) that cost it territory, power, and independence.

affective disorder, also called MOOD DISORDER, Any of several mental disorders characterized by dramatic changes or extremes of mood. The major affective disorders include bipolar disorder—which may include manic and depressive episodes—and major depressive disorder. Among the symptoms of manic episodes are elevated, expansive, or irritable moods, with hyperactivity, pressured (rapid and forced) speech, and inflated self-esteem. Depressive episodes and major depressive disorder are characterized by dejected moods, lack of interest in life, sleep disturbances, agitation, and feelings of worthlessness or guilt.

Afghan hound, Breed of dog developed as a hunter in the hill country of Afghanistan. It was brought to Europe in the late 19th century by British soldiers returning from the Indian-Afghan border wars. It hunts by sight, and in Afghanistan it has been used to pursue leopard and gazelle. Its high, wide hipbones are well adapted to rough country. It stands 24–28 in. (61–71 cm) high and weighs 50–60 lbs (23–27 kg). It has floppy ears, a long topknot, and a long silky coat of various colours.

Afghan hound
Sally Anne Thompson/EB Inc.

Afghan wars, Series of wars in Afghanistan during the 19th, 20th, and early 21st centuries. In the 19th century Britain twice invaded Afghanistan (the first and second Anglo-Afghan Wars; 1839–40 and 1878–80). The British were unable to fully subdue the country, and the third Anglo-Afghan War (1919) led to its full independence. The outbreak of civil war in 1978 led to an invasion by the Soviet Union the following year (the Afghan War). For the next 10 years the Soviets supported the communist government against a coalition of Islamic insurgents, the mujahideen, who toppled the regime in 1992. A group of disaffected fighters known as the Taliban had taken control of most of the country by 1996. The ensuing stalemate was broken in 2001 when the U.S. overthrew the Taliban for supporting international terrorism.

Afghanistan, officially ISLAMIC STATE OF AFGHANISTAN, Country, south-central Asia. Area: 252,072 sq mi (652,864 sq km). Population: (2011 est.) 26,442,000. Capital: Kabul. About two-fifths of the people belong to the Pashtun ethnic group; other ethnic groups include Tajiks, Uzbeks, and Ḥazāra. Languages: Pashto, Persian (both official). Religions: Islam (official; predominantly Sunni); also Zoroastrianism. Currency: afghani. Afghanistan has three distinctive regions: the northern plains are the major agricultural area; the southwestern plateau consists primarily of desert and semiarid landscape; and the central highlands, including the Hindu Kush, separate these regions. Afghanistan has a developing economy based largely on agriculture; its significant mineral resources remain largely untapped because of the Afghan War of the 1980s and subsequent fighting. Traditional handicrafts remain important; woolen carpets are a major export. Afghanistan is an Islamic republic with two legislative bodies; the president is head of both state and government. The area was part of the Persian Achaemenian Empire in the 6th century BCE and was conquered by Alexander the Great in the 4th century BCE. Hindu influence entered with the Hephthalites and Sāsānians. Islam became entrenched during the rule of the Ṣaffārids, *c.* 870 CE. Afghanistan was divided between the Mughal Empire of India and the Ṣafavid empire of Persia until the 18th century, when other Persians under Nādir Shāh took control. Britain fought several wars in the area in the 19th century. From the 1930s the country had a stable monarchy, which was overthrown in the 1970s. Marxist reforms sparked rebellion, and Soviet troops invaded. Afghan guerrillas prevailed, and the Soviets withdrew in 1989. In 1992 rebel factions overthrew the government and established an Islamic republic. In 1996 the Taliban militia took power in Kabul and enforced a harsh Islamic order. The militia's unwillingness to extradite extremist leader Osama bin Laden and members of his al-Qaeda militant organization following the September 11 attacks in 2001 led to military conflict with the U.S. and allied nations, the overthrow of the Taliban, and the establishment of an interim government.

Africa, Second largest continent on Earth. It is bounded by the Mediterranean Sea, the Atlantic Ocean, the Red Sea, and the Indian Ocean and is divided almost equally by the Equator. Area: 11,717,370 sq mi (30,348,110 sq km). Population (2001 est.): 816,524,000. Africa is composed largely of a rigid platform of ancient rocks that underlies vast plateau regions in the interior. Its average elevation is about 2,200 ft (670 m), but elevations range from 19,340 ft (5,895 m) at Mount Kilimanjaro to 515 ft (157 m) below sea level at Lake Assal. The Sahara, the world's largest contiguous desert, occupies more than one-fourth of the total land area. The continent's hydrology is dominated by the Nile River in the north, the Niger River in the west, and the Congo River in central Africa. Less than one-tenth of the land area is arable, while nearly one-fourth is forested or wooded. The peoples of Africa probably speak more languages than those of any other continent. Arabic is predominant from Egypt to Mauritania and in The Sudan. Northern Africans speak a family of languages known as Afro-Asiatic. The vast majority of sub-Saharan peoples speak Bantu languages of the Niger-Congo family, while smaller numbers in central Africa speak Nilo-Saharan languages and in southern Africa Khoisan languages. Peoples of European descent are found mostly in the south; Dutch (Boer) migrations began in the 17th century, and the English first settled in what is now Kenya and Zimbabwe in the 19th century. Africa as a whole is a developing region. Agriculture is the key sector of the economy in most countries. Diamond and gold mining are especially important in the south, while petroleum and natural gas are produced particularly in the west. Most African governments are controlled by the military or a single party. Many legal systems combine laws introduced by European powers during the colonial era with traditional law, though North African countries derive many laws from Islam. African leaders have sought to develop a pan-African approach to the continent's political and military affairs through the Organization of African Unity and its successor, the African Union. Africa is widely recognized as the birthplace of humankind. Archaeological evidence indicates that the continent has been inhabited by humans and their hominid forebears for some 4,000,000 years or more. Anatomically modern humans are believed to have appeared about 100,000 years ago in the eastern region of sub-Saharan Africa. Somewhat later these early humans spread into northern Africa and the Middle East and, ultimately, to the rest of the world. Africa's first great historical kingdom, Egypt, arose along the Nile c. 3000 BC and flourished for nearly 3,000 years. The Phoenicians established a colony at Carthage and controlled the western Mediterranean for nearly 600 years. While northern Africa was dominated by the Romans for several centuries, the first known empire in western Africa was Ghana (5th–11th century AD). Muslim empires included those of Mali (c. 1250–1400) and Songhai (c. 1400–1591). In eastern and central Africa the emphasis was on trade with Arabia, and several powerful city-states, including Mogadishu and Mombasa, were established. The Portuguese explored the western coast in the 15th century. Before the late 19th century, Europe showed little interest in colonizing Africa, but by 1884 European countries had begun a scramble to partition the continent, and by 1920 much of it was under colonial rule. Anticolonial sentiment developed gradually, becoming widespread after 1950, and one by one the colonies became independent, the last in 1990. Political instability, refugee problems, famine, and AIDS are the chief problems facing the continent at the start of the 21st century.

Africa, Proconsular Roman province. It was founded after Rome defeated Carthage in 146 BC and was subsequently extended to include Numidia and the northern part of modern Libya. Between 30 BC and AD 180, other parts of northern Africa, including Cyrenaica and Mauretania, became part of the Roman Republic and Empire. In the 5th century the region was taken by the Vandals, though areas were later reconquered by the Byzantine (Eastern Roman) Empire; the Muslims conquered the area in the late 7th century.

African languages, Languages indigenous to Africa that belong to the Niger-Congo, Nilo-Saharan, Khoisan, and Afro-Asiatic language phyla. Africa is the most polyglot continent; estimates of the number of African languages range from 1,000 to more than 1,500. Many have numerous dialects. Distinctions in tone play a significant role in nearly all sub-Saharan languages. Contact between people who do not speak the same language has necessitated the development of lingua francas such as Swahili in East Africa, Lingala in the Congo River basin, Sango in the Central African Republic, and Arabic across much of the Sahel.

African lily, or LILY OF THE NILE, Perennial evergreen herbaceous plant (*Agapanthus africanus*) of the Alliaceae family, native to Africa. In summer, long stalks bear many funnel-shaped flowers. The attractive, thick, dark green leaves are sword-shaped. There are many varieties, some with white or purple flowers and others with patterned leaves. If grown in a climate with frost, they must be kept in containers and moved indoors to survive the cold weather.

African religions, Indigenous religions of the African continent. The introduced religions of Islam (in northern Africa) and Christianity (in southern Africa) are now the continent's major religions, but traditional religions still play an important role, especially in the interior of sub-Saharan Africa. The numerous traditional African religions have in common the notion of a creator god, who made the world and then withdrew, remaining remote from the concerns of human life. Prayers and sacrificial offerings are usually directed toward secondary divinities, who are intermediaries between the human and sacred realms. Ancestors also serve as intermediaries. Ritual functionaries include priests, elders, rainmakers, diviners, and prophets. Rituals are aimed at maintaining a harmonious relationship with cosmic powers, and many have associated myths that explain their significance. Animism is a common feature of African religions, and misfortune is often attributed to witchcraft and sorcery.

African violet, Any plant of the genus *Saintpaulia*, of the gesneriad family, especially *S. ionantha*. African violets are native to high elevations in tropical eastern Africa. They are small, hairy, usually stemless herbaceous plants with crowded, long-stalked leaves. The violet, white, or pink flowers bloom most of the year. They are popular houseplants, and hundreds of varieties have been developed, including half-sized miniatures.

Afrikaans language, Germanic language of South Africa. It was developed from 17th-century Dutch by descendants of European settlers, indigenous Khoisan-speaking peoples, and African and Asian slaves in the Dutch colony at the Cape of Good Hope. It differs from Dutch in its sound system, in some grammatical simplification, and in vocabulary. Afrikaans is spoken as a first language by close to six million South Africans and as a second or third language by several million more; there are also about 150,000 Afrikaans speakers in Namibia. Standard Afrikaans was formally separated from Dutch and made an official language in South Africa in 1925; it is one of 11 official South African languages.

Afro-Asiatic languages, formerly HAMITO-SEMITIC LANGUAGES, Family of about 250 languages spoken in North Africa, parts of sub-Saharan African, and the Middle East. It includes such languages as Arabic, Hebrew, Amharic, and Hausa. The total number of speakers is estimated to be more than 250 million. The major branches of Afro-Asiatic are Semitic, Berber, Egyptian, Cushitic, Omotic, and Chadic. Berber languages are spoken by perhaps 15 million people in enclaves scattered across North Africa from Morocco to northwestern Egypt and in parts of the western Sahara. Cushitic consists of some 30 languages spoken by more than 30 million people in northeastern Sudan, Eritrea, Ethiopia, Somalia, Djibouti, Kenya, and a few areas of northeastern Tanzania. Omotic, formerly classified as part of Cushitic, is a cluster of perhaps more than 30 languages spoken by 2–3 million people, most of whom live near the Omo River in southwestern Ethiopia. Chadic comprises about 140 languages (most of which are poorly known to linguists), spoken in northern Nigeria, southern Niger, southern Chad, and northern Cameroon; except for Hausa, it is likely that no individual Chadic language has more than half a million speakers.

Agamemnon, In Greek legend, the son of Atreus, brother of Menelaus, and king of Mycenae and commander of the Greek forces that attacked Troy. By his wife, Clytemnestra, Agamemnon had a son, Orestes, and three daughters. When Paris carried off Menelaus's wife, Helen, Agamemnon called on the Greeks to unite in a war of revenge against the Trojans. Artemis sent a calm or contrary winds to prevent the Greek fleet from sailing, and Agamemnon sacrificed his daughter Iphigeneia to appease the goddess. After the Trojan War he returned home, where he was killed by his wife and her lover, Aegisthus. His murder was avenged by Orestes. These events formed the basis of Aeschylus' great dramatic trilogy the *Oresteia.*

agave family, Family Agavaceae of the lily order (Liliales), comprising more than 700 species of short-stemmed, often woody plants found in tropical, subtropical, and temperate areas. They have narrow, lance-shaped, sometimes fleshy or toothed leaves, which are clustered at the base of the plant. Most have large flower clusters. The fruit is a capsule or berry. Plants of the genus *Agave* are important primarily for the fibres obtained from their leaves. Sisal hemp, from *A. sisalana,* is the most valuable hard fibre. Some species of *Agave* contain a sap that is fermented to produce the intoxicating drinks known as tequila, pulque, and mescal. Many species of yucca are popular as ornamentals; other ornamentals in the agave family include plants of the genera *Dasylirion, Nolina, Cordyline, Dracaena,* and *Sansevieria.*

Agent Orange, Mixture of herbicides. It contains approximately equal amounts of esters of 2,4-D (2,4-dichlorophenoxyacetic acid) and 2,4,5-T (2,4,5-trichlorophenoxyacetic acid) and trace amounts of dioxin. About 13 million gallons were sprayed by U.S. military forces onto Vietnam's forests and crops during the Vietnam War, with the dual purpose of destroying cover for enemy movements and destroying food sources. Exposure to Agent Orange has been blamed for an abnormally high incidence of miscarriages, skin diseases, cancers, birth defects, and malformations among Vietnamese and of cancers and other disorders in U.S., Australian, and New Zealand servicemen and their families.

Agincourt, Battle of (October 25, 1415) Battle resulting in the decisive victory of the English over the French in the Hundred Years' War. In pursuit of his claim to the French throne, Henry V invaded Normandy with an army of 11,000 men in August 1415. The English took Harfleur in September, but with their forces cut in half by battle and disease, they resolved to return to England. At Agincourt they were cornered by a French army of 20,000–30,000 men, including many mounted knights in heavy armor. On a cramped battlefield where the superior French numbers offered little advantage, Henry made skillful use of his lightly equipped, mobile archers. The French were disastrously defeated, losing over 6,000 men, while the English lost fewer than 450.

aging, Gradual change in an organism that leads to increased risk of weakness, disease, and death. It takes place in a cell, an organ, or the total organism over the entire adult life span of any living thing. There is a decline in biological functions and in ability to adapt to metabolic stress. Changes in organs include the replacement of functional cardiovascular cells with fibrous tissue. Overall effects of aging include reduced immunity, loss of muscle strength, decline in memory and other aspects of cognition, and loss of colour in the hair and elasticity in the skin. In women the process accelerates after menopause.

Agnon, S.Y., orig. SHMUEL YOSEF HALEVI CZACZKES (b. July 17, 1888, Buczacz, Galicia, Austria-Hungary—d. Feb. 17, 1970, Reḥovot, Israel), Israeli writer. Born into a Polish Galician family, Agnon settled in Palestine in 1907 and chose Hebrew as his literary language. *The Day Before Yesterday* (1945), perhaps his greatest novel, examines the problem facing the Westernized Jew who immigrates to Israel. Other works include the novels *The Bridal Canopy* (1919) and *A Guest for the Night* (1938). He is regarded as one of the greatest modern Hebrew novelists and short-story writers. In 1966 he and Nelly Sachs shared the Nobel Prize for Literature.

agnosticism, Doctrine that one cannot know the existence of anything beyond the phenomena of experience. It is popularly equated with religious skepticism, and especially with the rejection of traditional Christian beliefs under the impact of modern scientific thought. T.H. Huxley popularized philosophical agnosticism after coining the term agnostic (as opposed to gnostic) in 1869, to designate one who repudiated traditional Judeo-Christian theism but was not a doctrinaire atheist. Agnosticism may mean no more than the suspension of judgment on ultimate questions because of insufficient evidence, or it may constitute a rejection of traditional Christian tenets.

agora, In ancient Greek cities, an open space serving as an assembly area and backdrop for commercial, civic, social, and religious activities. Use of the agora varied in different periods. Located in the middle of the city or near the harbor, it was often enclosed by public buildings, colonnades containing shops, and stoas for protection from sun and bad weather. The highest honor for a citizen was to be granted a tomb in the agora.

Agra, City (pop., 2001: 1,275,134), west-central Uttar Pradesh state, India. It was founded by Sikandar Lodi in the early 16th century on the Yamuna River southeast of Delhi and was intermittently the Mughal capital. The city fell successively to the Jats and the Marathas in the late 18th century and finally to the British in 1803. It is the site of the Taj Mahal and the imperial tomb of Akbar.

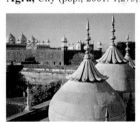

The Pearl Mosque (Moti Masjid) and the fort at Agra, Uttar Pradesh, India.
Picturepoint

agricultural revolution, Gradual transformation of the traditional agricultural system that began in Britain in the 18th century. Aspects of this complex transformation, which was not completed until the 19th century, included the reallocation of land ownership to make farms more compact and an increased investment in technical improvements, such as new machinery, better drainage, scientific methods of breeding, and experimentation with new crops and systems of crop rotation. The agricultural revolution was an essential prelude to the Industrial Revolution.

agriculture, The active production of useful plants or animals in ecosystems that have been created by people. Agriculture may include cultivating the soil, growing and harvesting crops, and raising livestock. Agriculture was independently developed in many places, including the Middle East, East Asia, South Asia, and the Americas. The earliest evidence for agriculture has been found in the Middle East and dates to between 14,500 and 12,000 BP. Early cultivars include wild barley (Middle East), millet (China), and squash (the Americas). The domestication of many animals now considered to be livestock occurred during roughly the same period, although dogs were domesticated considerably earlier. Slash-and-burn land-clearing methods and crop rotation were early agricultural techniques. Steady improvements in tools and methods over the centuries increased agricultural output, as did mechanization, selective breeding and hybridization, and, beginning in the 20th century, the use of herbicides and insecticides.

agrimony, Any plant of the genus *Agrimonia*, of the rose family, especially *A. eupatoria*. This species is a herbaceous, hardy perennial native to Europe but widespread in other northern temperate regions, where it grows in hedge banks and the borders of fields. Its leaves yield a yellow dye. The leaflets are oval with toothed margins; the small, stalkless yellow flowers are borne in a long terminal spike. The fruit is a tiny burr. *A. gryposepala*, a similar species, is widespread in the U.S.

agrochemical, Any chemical used in agriculture, including chemical fertilizers, herbicides, and insecticides. Most are mixtures of two or more chemicals; active ingredients provide the desired effects, and inert ingredients stabilize or preserve the active ingredients or aid in application. Together with other technological advances, including tractors, mechanical harvesters, and irrigation pumps, agrochemicals have increased the per-acre productivity of regions such as the Great Plains by 200–300% since the 1930s. Their long-term effects on the environment and the stability of agricultural systems that use them are hotly debated.

agronomy, Branch of agriculture that deals with field crop production and soil management. Agronomists generally work with crops that are grown on a large scale (e.g., small grains) and that require relatively little management. Agronomic experiments focus on a variety of factors relating to crop plants, including yield, diseases, cultivation, and sensitivity to factors such as climate and soil.

Agulhas, Cape, Cape, southernmost point of the African continent. Its name, Portuguese for "needles," may refer to the jagged rocks and reefs there that have wrecked many ships; another explanation attributes the name to observations by Portuguese navigators that their compass needles showed no magnetic deviation there. The cape's meridian of 20°E is the official boundary between the Indian and Atlantic oceans.

ahimsa (Sanskrit: "noninjury") Fundamental ethical virtue of Jainism, also respected in Buddhism and Hinduism. In Jainism ahimsa is the standard by which all actions are judged. It requires a householder observing the small vows (*anuvrata*) to refrain from killing any animal life. An ascetic observing the great vows (*mahavrata*) is expected to take the greatest care not to injure any living substance, even unknowingly. To do so interrupts that being's spiritual progress and increases one's own karma, delaying liberation from the cycle of rebirth. In the 20th century Mohandas K. Gandhi extended ahimsa into the political sphere as satyagraha.

Ahmadabad, or AHMEDABAD, City (pop., 2001: metro. area, 4,525,013), Gujarat state, west-central India. It is located on the Sabarmati River 275 mi (440 km) north of Mumbai (Bombay). Founded in 1411 by Sultan Aḥmad Shah, Ahmadabad reached its height later that century but subsequently declined. It was revived under Mughal emperors in the 17th century and came under British rule in 1818. With the opening of cotton mills in the mid-19th century, it became India's largest inland industrial centre. The city is associated with Indian nationalism; Mohandas K. Gandhi's political agitation began there in 1930. In 2001 the city was struck by a violent earthquake that took many lives.

Aḥmadiyyah, Islamic sect, founded in India in 1889 by Mīrzā Ghulām Aḥmad. It holds that Jesus feigned death and resurrection and escaped to India and that jihad is a peaceful battle against nonbelievers. Following the death of Ghulām Aḥmad's successor (1914), the Aḥmadiyyah split. The Qadiani, based in Rabwah, Pak., recognize Ghulām Aḥmad as a prophet; they are zealous missionaries, preaching Aḥmadi beliefs as the one true Islam. A Lahore-based sect regards Ghulām Aḥmad merely as a reformer and seeks to make converts to Islam generally. The term Aḥmadiyyah is also used to describe various Sufi orders, particularly that founded by Aḥmad al-Badawī (d. 1276). One of the most popular orders in Egypt, it has branches throughout the Islamic world.

Ahura Mazda, Supreme god of ancient Iranian religion, especially Zoroastrianism. Ahura Mazda was worshiped by Darius I and his successors as the greatest god and the protector of the just king. Zoroaster taught that Ahura Mazda created the universe and maintains the cosmic order, and that the history of the world consists of the battle between two spirits he created—the beneficent Spenta Mainyu and the destructive Angra Mainyu. The Avesta identifies Ahura Mazda himself with the beneficent spirit and represents him as bountiful, all-knowing, and the creator of everything good. In late sources (from the 3rd century), Zurvan ("Time") is the father of the twins Ormazd (Ahura Mazda) and Ahriman (Angra Mainyu), who in orthodox Mazdaism (Zoroastrianism and Parsiism) reign alternately over the world until Ormazd's ultimate victory.

AIDS, in full ACQUIRED IMMUNODEFICIENCY SYNDROME, Transmissible disease of the immune system caused by HIV. AIDS is the last stage of HIV infection, during which time the individual develops frequently fatal infections and cancers, including *Pneumocystis carinii* pneumonia, cytomegalovirus (CMV), lymphoma, and Kaposi sarcoma. The first AIDS cases were identified in 1981, HIV was isolated in 1983, and blood tests were developed by 1985. According to the UN's 2004 report on AIDS, some 38 million people are living with HIV, approximately 5 million people become infected annually, and about 3 million people die each year from AIDS. Some 20 million people have died of the disease since 1981. Sub-Saharan Africa accounts for some 70 percent of all HIV infections. Rates of infection are lower in other parts of the world, but the epidemic is spreading rapidly in eastern Europe, India, South and Southeast Asia, Latin America, and the Caribbean.

ailanthus, Any of the flowering plants that make up the genus *Ailanthus*, in the quassia family (Simaroubaceae), native to eastern and southern Asia and northern Australia and naturalized in subtropical and temperate regions elsewhere. Ailanthus leaves alternate along the stem and are composed of multiple leaflets arranged along an axis. The most familiar species is the tree of heaven.

air, Mixture of gases constituting the earth's atmosphere. Some gases occur in steady concentrations. The most important are molecular nitrogen (N_2), 78% by volume, and molecular oxygen (O_2), 21%. Small amounts of argon (Ar; 1.9%), neon (Ne), helium (He), methane (CH_4), krypton (Kr), hydrogen (H_2), nitrous oxide (N_2O), and xenon (Xe) are also present in almost constant proportions. Other gases occur in variable concentrations: water vapour (H_2O), ozone (O_3), carbon dioxide (CO_2), sulfur dioxide (SO_2), and nitrogen dioxide (NO_2). Air also contains trace amounts of ammonia and hydrogen sulfide. The variable constituents are important for maintaining life. Water vapour is the source for all forms of precipitation and is an important absorber and emitter of infrared radiation. Carbon dioxide is necessary for photosynthesis and is also an important absorber and emitter of infrared radiation. Ozone in the stratosphere is an effective absorber of ultraviolet radiation from the Sun but at ground-level is a corrosive pollutant and a major constituent of smog.

air-cushion vehicle, or HOVERCRAFT, Vehicle supported above the surface of land or water by an air cushion, produced by downwardly directed fans, enclosed within a flexible skirt beneath the hull. The concept was first proposed by John Thornycroft in the 1870s, but a working model was not produced until 1955, when Christopher Cockerell solved the problem of keeping the air cushion from escaping from under the vehicle, and formed Hovercraft Ltd. to manufacture prototypes. Problems with skirt design and engine maintenance have restricted the vehicle's commercial application; today hovercraft are used mainly as ferries.

air force, Military organization that has the primary responsibility for conducting air warfare. The air force must gain control of the air, support ground forces (e.g., by attacking enemy ground forces), and accomplish strategic-bombing objectives. Its basic weapons platforms are fighters, bombers, attack aircraft, and early warning and control aircraft. Since the mid-20th century, some air forces have also been responsible for land-based nuclear missiles as well as nuclear-armed bombers. The army and naval branches of a state's armed forces may also operate aircraft.

air mass, In meteorology, a large body of air having nearly uniform conditions of temperature and humidity at any given altitude. Such a mass has distinct boundaries and may extend hundreds or thousands of miles horizontally and sometimes as high as the top of the troposphere. An air mass forms whenever the atmosphere remains in contact with a large, relatively uniform land or sea surface long enough to acquire its temperature and moisture properties. The Earth's major air masses all originate in polar or subtropical latitudes. The middle latitudes constitute essentially a zone of modification, interaction, and mixing of the polar and tropical air masses.

aircraft carrier, Naval vessel equipped with a platform that allows airplanes to take off and land. Takeoffs are facilitated by the use of catapults or by a ramp at the end of the flight deck. For landing, aircraft are fitted with retractable hooks that engage arresting wires on the deck, or they are built with vectored-thrust engines that allow them to be landed vertically. Britain's Royal Navy developed the first true aircraft carrier near the end of World War I, and carriers played leading roles in World War II naval engagements such as the Pearl Harbor attack and the Battles of Midway and the Coral Sea. The largest modern carriers are 1,000-ft (300-m) nuclear-powered vessels of the U.S. Navy, which can carry 100 jet aircraft. Other types include the light carrier, equipped for anti-submarine warfare and ground attack, and the helicopter carrier, intended for conducting amphibious assault.

airplane, Fixed-wing aircraft that is heavier than air, propelled by a screw propeller or a high-velocity jet, and supported by the dynamic reaction of the air against its wings. An airplane's essential components are the body or fuselage, a flight-sustaining wing system, stabilizing tail surfaces, altitude-control devices such as rudders, a thrust-providing power source, and a landing support system. Beginning in the 1840s, several British and French inventors produced designs for engine-powered aircraft, but the first powered, sustained, and controlled flight was only achieved by Wilbur and Orville Wright in 1903. Later airplane design was affected by the development of the jet engine; most airplanes today have a long nose section, swept-back wings with jet engines placed behind the plane's midsection, and a tail stabilizing section. Most airplanes are designed to operate from land; seaplanes are adapted to touch down on water, and carrier-based planes are modified for high-speed short takeoff and landing.

airport, Site and installations for the takeoff and landing of aircraft. Early airports were open grass-covered fields, called landing fields, that allowed a pilot to head directly into the wind to aid a plane's lift on takeoff and to decrease its speed on landing. In the 1930s heavier airplanes required paved runway surfaces. Larger planes needed longer runways, which today can reach 15,000 ft (4,500 m) to accommodate the largest jet aircraft. Air traffic is regulated from control towers and regional centres. Passenger and cargo terminals include baggage-movement and passenger-transit operations.

ʿĀʾishah (bint Abī Bakr) (b. 614, Mecca, Arabia—d. July 678, Medina), Third wife of Muhammad. The daughter of his supporter Abū Bakr, she became Muhammad's favourite wife. Left a childless widow at 18, she became politically active during the reign of the third caliph, ʿUthmān ibn ʿAffān, leading the opposition that resulted in his murder in 656. She led an army against his successor, ʿAlī, who defeated her in the Battle of the Camel. She was allowed to live her remaining years quietly in Medina and is credited with transmitting more than a thousand Ḥadīth.

Aix-en-Provence, City (pop., 2006 est.: 142,534), southeastern France. Founded as a military colony by the Romans *c.* 123 BC, it was the scene of the defeat of the Teutons by Marius in 102 BC. Visigoths, Franks, Lombards, and finally Muslim invaders from Spain successively plundered the town. As the capital of Provence, it was a centre of culture during the Middle Ages; it became part of France in 1486. It is now a residential suburb of Marseille; its industries include tourism, food processing, and the manufacturing of electrical machinery.

Aix-la-Chapelle, Treaty of (Oct. 18, 1748) Treaty that ended the War of the Austrian Succession. The treaty, negotiated largely by Britain and France, was marked by the mutual restitution of conquests, including the fortress of Louisbourg (in Nova Scotia) to France and Madras (now Chennai; in India) to England. It preserved Maria Theresa's right to the Austrian lands, but the Habsburgs were weakened by Prussia's retention of Silesia. The treaty did not resolve any issues in the commercial colonial struggle between England and France and thus did not lead to a lasting peace.

Akal Takht, Chief centre of religious authority for Indian Sikhs, located in Amritsar opposite the Golden Temple. It also serves as the headquarters of the Akali Party. Since the line of Gurus came to an end in 1708, the Sikh community has settled religious and political disputes at meetings in front of the Akal Takht. In the 20th century local congregations began to pass resolutions on matters of Sikh doctrine and rules of conduct; disputed resolutions may be appealed to the Akal Takht. It was badly damaged during the assault on the Golden Temple by the Indian army in 1984 and had to be rebuilt.

Akbar, in full ABŪ AL-FATḤ JALĀL AL-DĪN MUḤAMMAD AKBAR (b. Oct. 15, 1542, Umarkot, Sind, India—d. 1605, Agra), Greatest of the Mughal emperors of India (r. 1556–1605). Akbar, whose ancestors included Timur and Genghis Khan, ascended the throne as a youth. Initially his rule extended only over the Punjab and the area around Delhi. The Rajput raja of Amber (Jaipur) acknowledged his suzerainty in 1562, and other Rajput rajas followed suit. Akbar included Rajput princes and other Hindus in the highest ranks of his government and reduced discrimination against non-Muslims. He continued his conquests, taking Gujarat in the west (1573) and Bengal in the east (annexed in 1576). Toward the end of his reign he conquered Kashmir (1586) and moved south into the Deccan. Administratively, he strengthened central power, establishing that all military officers and civil administrators were to be appointed by the emperor. He encouraged scholars, poets, painters, and musicians, making his court a centre of culture. He had Sanskrit classics translated into Persian and was enthusiastic about the European paintings presented to him by Jesuit missionaries. His reign was often portrayed as a model by later governments—strong, benevolent, tolerant, and enlightened.

Akhmatova, Anna, orig. ANNA ANDREYEVNA GORENKO (b. June 23, 1889, Bolshoy Fontan, near Odessa, Ukraine, Russian Empire—d. March 5, 1966, Domodedovo, near Moscow), Russian poet. She won fame with her first poetry collections (1912, 1914). Soon after the Revolution of 1917, Soviet authorities con-

Anna Akhmatova.
Novosti Press Agency

demned her work for what they perceived as its narrow preoccupation with love and God, and in 1923, after the execution of her former husband on conspiracy charges, she entered a long period of literary silence. After World War II she was again denounced and expelled from the Writers Union. Following Joseph Stalin's death in 1953, she was slowly rehabilitated. In her later years she became the influential centre of a circle of younger Russian poets. Her longest work, *Poem Without a Hero*, is regarded as one of the great poems of the 20th century. Regarded today as one of the greatest of all Russian poets, she is also admired for her translations of other poets' works and for her memoirs.

Akita, Breed of working dog that originated in the mountains of northern Japan. In 1931 the Japanese government designated the breed as a national treasure. It is a powerful, muscular dog with a broad head, erect pointed ears, and a large curved tail carried over the back or curled against the flank. Colours and markings vary, including all-white, brindle, and pinto. All but the white akitas bear a distinct mask (dark area around the muzzle). Males stand 26–28 in. (66–71 cm) high, females 24–26 in. (60–66 cm).

Akkadian language, or ASSYRO-BABYLONIAN LANGUAGE, Semitic language spoken in Mesopotamia in the 3rd–1st millennia BC. It is known from a great many inscriptions, seals, and clay tablets in cuneiform writing. Akkadian supplanted Sumerian as the major spoken language of southern Mesopotamia by 2000 BC and about this time split into an Assyrian dialect spoken in the northeast and a Babylonian dialect spoken in the south. Akkadian died out as a vernacular in the first half of the 1st millennium BC, being effectively replaced by Aramaic in Mesopotamia, though it continued to be written until about the 1st century AD.

'**Akko,** or ACRE, Seaport town (pop., 2004 est.: 45,600), northwestern Israel. First mentioned in an Egyptian text from the 19th century BC, it was long a Canaanite and Phoenician city. After its conquest by Alexander the Great (336 BC), it was a Greek polity (called Philadelphus), and for several centuries it was part of the Roman Republic and Empire. The city was being ruled by the Turkish Seljūq dynasty when the Crusaders captured it in 1104 and renamed it St. Jean d'Acre. It was the last capital of the Crusades, falling in 1291. Except for brief intervals, it was under the rule of the Ottoman Empire from 1516 until British forces took it in 1918. It was part of Palestine under the British mandate and became part of Israel in 1948, when most of its Arab inhabitants fled. Notable structures include the Great Mosque and the Crypt of St. John. It is the burial place of Bahā' Ullāh, the founder of the Bahā'ī faith.

Aksum, or AXUM, Ancient kingdom, northern Ethiopia. At its apogee (3rd–6th century AD), Aksum merchants traded as far as Alexandria and beyond the Nile River. The modern town of Aksum, once the kingdom's capital, is a religious centre best known for its antiquities. It has long been regarded as a holy city for the Ethiopian Orthodox church; according to tradition, King Menilek I, son of Solomon and the Queen of Sheba, brought the Ark of the Covenant there from Jerusalem. Aksum's antiquities have made it a tourist centre.

al-Khwārizmī, Arabic in full MUḤAMMAD IBN MŪSĀ AL-KHWĀRIZMĪ (b. *c.* 780, Baghdad, Iraq—d. *c.* 850), Muslim mathematician and astronomer. He lived in Baghdad during the golden age of Islamic science and, like Euclid, wrote mathematical books that collected and arranged the discoveries of earlier mathematicians. His *Al-Kitāb al-mukhtaṣar fī ḥisāb al-jabr wa'l-muqābala* ("The Compendious Book on Calculation by Completion and Balancing") is a compilation of rules for solving linear and quadratic equations, as well as problems of geometry and proportion. Its translation into Latin in the 12th century provided the link between the great Hindu and Arab mathematicians and European scholars. A corruption of the book's title resulted in the word *algebra*; a corruption of the author's own name resulted in the term *algorithm*.

alabaster, Fine-grained gypsum that has been used for centuries for statuary, carvings, and other ornaments. It normally is snow-white and translucent but can be artificially dyed; it may be made opaque and similar in appearance to marble by heat treatment. Florence, Livorno, Milan, and Berlin are important centres of the alabaster trade. The alabaster of the ancients was a brown or yellow onyx marble.

Alaskan malamute, Sled dog developed by the Malemiut, an Eskimo group. It is a strongly built dog with a broad head, erect ears, and a plumelike tail carried over its back. Its thick coat is usually gray and white or black and white, the colours frequently forming a caplike or masklike marking on the head. It stands 23–25 in. (58–64 cm) tall and weighs 75–85 lbs (34–39 kg). Characteristically loyal and friendly, it has served on expeditions to the Antarctic.

albacore, Large oceanic tuna (*Thunnus alalunga*) that is noted for its fine flesh. The streamlined bodies of these voracious predators are adapted to fast and continuous swimming. They occur in both the Atlantic and Pacific oceans and migrate long distances. The bluefin tuna is also sometimes called albacore.

Albania, officially REPUBLIC OF ALBANIA, Country, Balkan Peninsula, southeastern Europe. Area: 11,082 sq mi (28,703 sq km). Population: (2011 est.) 3,196,000. Capital: Tirana (Tiranë). Language: Albanian (official). Albanians comprise two major subgroups: Gegs (Ghegs) and Tosks. Religions: Islam, Christianity. Currency: lek. Albania may be divided into two major regions: a mountainous highland and, to the west, an Adriatic coastal lowland that contains the country's agricultural lands and most of its population. Albania has a developing free-market economy that until 1991 was shaped by a socialist system of state ownership. The country is a unitary multiparty republic with one legislative house. The head of state is the president, and the head of government is the prime minister. The Albanians are descended from the Illyrians, an ancient Indo-European people who lived in central Europe and migrated south by the beginning of the Iron Age. The Gegs settled in the north and the Tosks in the south, along with Greek colonizers. The area was under Roman rule by the 1st century BCE; after 395 CE it became part of the Byzantine Empire. Turkish invasion began in the 14th century and continued into the 15th; though the national hero, Skanderbeg, was able to resist them for a time. After his death (1468) the Turks consolidated their rule. The country achieved independence in 1912 and was admitted into the League of Nations in 1920. It was briefly a republic (1925–28), then became a monarchy under Zog I, whose initial alliance with Italy deteriorated into that country's invasion of Albania in 1939. After the war a socialist government under Enver Hoxha was installed, and gradually Albania cut itself off from the nonsocialist international community and eventually from all other countries, including China, its last political ally. By 1990 economic hardship had fomented antigovernment demonstrations that led to the election of a noncommunist government in 1992 and the end of Albania's international isolation. In the late 20th and early 21st centuries, Albania continued to experience economic uncertainty and ethnic turmoil, the latter involving Albanian minorities in Serbia and Macedonia.

Albanian language, Indo-European language spoken by five to six million people in Albania, Kosovo, western Macedonia, and enclaves elsewhere, including southern Italy and southern Greece. There are two main dialect groups, Gheg (Geg) in the north, including Kosovo and Macedonia, and Tosk in the south. Albanian is the only extant representative of a distinct branch of Indo-European, whose pre-Roman Balkan ancestry is uncertain. The earliest written attestation is from the 15th century, though a standard orthography using the Latin alphabet was not adopted until 1909. The core vocabulary of Albanian is native, though in the course of its history it has absorbed many loanwords from Greek, Latin, Balkan Romance languages, Slavic languages, and Turkish.

albatross, Any of more than a dozen species of large seabirds (family Diomedeidae). Albatrosses are among the most spectacular gliders of all birds; in windy weather they can stay aloft for hours without flapping their wings. They drink seawater and usually eat squid. Albatrosses come ashore only to breed, in colonies typically established on remote oceanic islands. Adults of common species attain wingspans of 7–11 ft (200–350 cm). Albatrosses live long and may be among the few birds to die of old age. They were once held in awe by seamen, who held that killing one would bring bad luck.

albedo, Fraction of light reflected by a body or surface, commonly used in astronomy to describe the reflective properties of planets, natural satellites, and asteroids. "Normal" albedo (the relative brightness of a surface when illuminated and observed from directly above) is often used to determine the surface compositions of satellites and asteroids. The albedo, diameter, and distance of such objects together determine their brightness.

Albert, Lake, Lake, east-central Africa. Lying at an altitude of 2,021 ft (616 m), it is 100 mi (160 km) long and has an average width of about 20 mi (32 km). In the southwest, the Semliki River brings into the lake the waters of Lake Edward; at its northeastern corner, just below Murchison Falls, it receives the Victoria Nile from Lake Victoria. In 1864 the lake's first European visitor, Samuel Baker, named it after Queen Victoria's consort. Initially part of Uganda, it now forms part of the Uganda-Congo border.

Albigensian Crusade (1209–29) Crusade called by Pope Innocent III against the heretical Cathari of southern France. The war pitted the nobility of northern France against that of southern France, and it eventually involved the king of France who established his authority over the south. The Crusade ended with the Treaty of Paris (1229), which took away the independence of the southern princes and largely destroyed the culture of Provence. The Crusade caused much devastation and injustice, which Innocent came to regret, but did not bring about the extirpation of the Albigensian heresy (named for its center in the town of Albi, France). The heresy lingered on into the 13th–14th centuries and became the object of the Inquisition.

albinism, Absence of the pigment melanin in the eyes, skin, hair, scales, or feathers. It arises from a genetic defect and occurs in humans and other vertebrates. Because they lack the pigments that normally provide protective coloration and screen against the sun's ultraviolet rays, albino animals rarely survive in the wild. Humans have long intentionally bred certain albino animals (e.g., rabbits) for their appearance. There are two primary forms of the condition in humans: oculocutaneous albinism and ocular albinism. In the former, the affected person has milk-white skin and hair. In both forms, the iris of the eye appears pink, the pupil red. Vision abnormalities such as astigmatism, nystagmus (rapid involuntary oscillation of the eye), and photophobia (extreme sensitivity to light) are common. Oculocutaneous albinism occurs throughout the world in about one in 20,000 persons; the ocular form occurs in about 1 in 50,000 persons.

alcazar, Spanish ALCÁZAR, Form of military architecture of medieval Spain, generally rectangular with defensible walls and massive corner towers. Inside was an open space (patio) surrounded by chapels, salons, hospitals, and sometimes gardens. The finest surviving example from the Moorish period is Sevilla's Alcázar Palace; begun in 1181 under the Almohads and continued by the Christians, it exhibits both Moorish and Gothic features, including a decagonal brick tower, the Torre del Oro.

Toledo alcazar, 14th century, renovated 16th century, severely damaged during the Spanish Civil War and later restored.
© Getty Images

Alcmaeon, or ALCMEON, In Greek mythology, the son of the seer Amphiaraus. The seer had been persuaded by his wife to join the expedition of the Seven Against Thebes. On realizing that he would die, he charged Alcmaeon and his other sons with avenging his death. Alcmaeon led the sons of the seven in the destruction of Thebes and then obeyed his father's injunction to kill his mother, a crime for which the Furies drove him mad. He was purified by King Phegeus of Psophis, whose daughter he married but subsequently killed. Following the advice of an oracle, he settled on an island at the mouth of the Achelous River, where he married again, but was killed by Phegeus and his sons.

alcohol, Any of a class of common organic compounds that contain one or more hydroxyl groups ($-OH$) attached to one or more of the carbon atoms in a hydrocarbon chain. The number of other substituent groups (R) on that carbon atom make the alcohol a primary (RCH_2OH), secondary (R_2CHOH), or tertiary (R_3COH) alcohol. Many alcohols occur naturally and are valuable intermediates in the synthesis of other compounds because of the characteristic chemical reactions of the hydroxyl group. Oxidation of primary alcohols yields aldehydes and (if taken further) carboxylic acids; oxidation of secondary alcohols, ketones. Tertiary alcohols break down on oxidation. Alcohols generally react with carboxylic acids to produce esters. They may also be converted to ethers and olefins. Products of these numerous reactions include fats and waxes, detergents, plasticizers, emulsifiers, lubricants, emollients, and foaming agents. Ethanol (grain alcohol) and methanol (wood alcohol) are the best-known alcohols with one hydroxyl group. Glycols (e.g., ethylene glycol, or antifreeze) contain two hydroxyl groups, glycerol three, and polyols three or more.

Alcoholics Anonymous (AA), Voluntary fellowship of people suffering from alcoholism who seek to become and stay sober through mutual self-help by meeting in local, independent groups to share their common experience. Anonymity, confidentiality, and understanding of alcoholism as a disease free members to speak frankly. Many consider AA to be the most successful method of coping with alcoholism; participation raises the chances of success of other treatments. Its 12 steps to recovery include acknowledgment of the problem, faith in a "higher power" as understood by each individual, self-examination, and a desire to change for the better and to help others recover. Begun in 1935 by two alcoholics, AA has grown to some 2 million members worldwide. Similar organizations for abusers of other substances and for habitual gamblers and debtors are based on its principles.

alcoholism, Excessive habitual consumption of alcoholic beverages despite physical, mental, social, or economic harm (e.g., cirrhosis, drunk driving and accidents, family strife, frequently missing work). Persons who drink large amounts of alcohol over time become tolerant to its effects. Alcoholism is usually considered an addiction and a disease. The causes are unclear, but there may be a genetic predisposition. It is more common in men, but women are more likely to hide it. Treatment may be physiological (with drugs that cause vomiting and a feeling of panic when alcohol is consumed; not an effective long-term treatment), psychological (with therapy and rehabilitation), or social (with group therapies). Group therapies such as Alcoholics Anonymous are the most effective treatments. Suddenly stopping heavy drinking can lead to withdrawal symptoms, including delirium tremens.

Alcott, Louisa May (b. Nov. 29, 1832, Germantown, Pa., U.S.—d. March 6, 1888, Boston, Mass.), U.S. author. Daughter of the reformer Bronson Alcott, she grew up in Transcendentalist circles in Boston and Concord, Mass. She began writing to help support her mother and sisters. An ardent abolitionist, she volunteered as a nurse during the American Civil War, where she contracted the typhoid that damaged her health the rest of her life; her letters, published as *Hospital Sketches* (1863), first brought her fame. With the huge success of the autobiographical *Little Women* (1868–69), she finally escaped debt. *An Old-Fashioned Girl* (1870), *Little Men* (1871), and *Jo's Boys* (1886) also drew on her experiences as an educator.

Louisa May Alcott, portrait by George Healy; in the Louisa May Alcott Memorial Association collection, Concord, Mass.
Courtesy of Louisa May Alcott Memorial Association

alder, Any of about 30 species of ornamental shrubs and trees in the genus *Alnus*, of the birch family, found throughout the Northern Hemisphere and western South America on cool, wet sites. Alders are distinguished from birches by their usually stalked winter buds and by cones that remain on the branches after the small, winged nutlets are released. Alders have scaly bark, oval leaves that fall without changing colour, and separate male and female flowers (catkins) borne on the same tree. Some familiar North American alders are the red alder (*A. rubra* or *A. oregona*); the white, or Sierra, alder (*A. rhombifolia*); and the speckled alder (*A. rugosa*). Alder wood is fine-textured and durable, even under water; it is useful for furniture, cabinetry, and lathe work and in charcoal manufacture and millwork. Alders' spreading root systems and tolerance of moist soils lend them to planting on stream banks for flood and erosion control.

Alder (Alnus glutinosa)
Earl L. Kubis/Root Resources

Aleppo, Arabic ḤALAB, City (pop., 2004 est.: 1,975,200), northwestern Syria. Syria's largest city, it is about 30 mi (48 km) from the Turkish border. Lying at the crossroads of great commercial routes, it has long been inhabited and is first mentioned at the end of the 3rd millennium BC. It subsequently came under the control of many kingdoms, including the Hittites (17th–14th centuries BC). Controlled by the Persian Achaemenian dynasty in the 6th–4th centuries BC, it soon came under the control of the Hellenistic Seleucid dynasty, under which it was renamed Beroea. It was absorbed into the Roman Empire in the 1st century BC and it prospered for several centuries. In AD 637 it was conquered by the Arabs, under whom it reverted to its old name, Ḥalab. The city successfully defended itself from the Crusaders (1124), fell to the Mongols (1260), and finally was incorporated into the Ottoman Empire (1516). Modern Aleppo is an industrial and intellectual centre rivaling the Syrian capital, Damascus. Its historic structures were designated a UNESCO World Heritage site in 1986.

Alexander the Great, or ALEXANDER III (b. 356 BC, Pella, Macedonia—d. June 13, 323 BC, Babylon), King of Macedonia (336–323) and the greatest military leader of antiquity. The son of Philip II of Macedonia, he was taught by Aristotle. He soon showed military brilliance, helping win the Battle of Chaeronea at age 18. He succeeded his assassinated father in 336 and promptly took Thessaly and Thrace; he brutally razed Thebes except for its temples and the house of Pindar. Such destruction was to be his standard method, and other Greek states submitted meekly. In 334 he crossed to Persia and defeated a Persian army at the Granicus River. He is said to have cut the Gordian knot in Phrygia (333), by which act, according to legend, he was destined to rule all Asia. At the Battle of Issus in 333, he defeated another army, this one led by the Persian king Darius III, who managed to escape. He then took Syria and Phoenicia, cutting off the Persian fleet from its ports. In 332 he completed a seven-month siege of Tyre, considered his greatest military achievement, and then took Egypt. There he received the pharaohs' double crown, founded Alexandria, and visited the oracle of the god Amon, the basis of his claim to divinity. In control of the eastern Mediterranean coast, in 331 he defeated Darius in a decisive battle at Gaugamela, though Darius again escaped. He next took the province of Babylon. He burnt Xerxes' palace at Persepolis, Persia, in 330, and he envisioned an empire ruled jointly by Macedonians and Persians. He continued eastward, quashing real or imagined conspiracies among his men and taking control to the Oxus and Jaxartes rivers, founding cities (most named Alexandria) to hold the territory. Conquering what is now Tajikistan, he married the princess Roxana and embraced Persian absolutism, adopting Persian dress and enforcing Persian court customs. By 326 he reached the Hyphasis in India, where his weary men mutinied; he turned back, marching and pillaging down the Indus, and reached Susa with much loss of life. He continued to promote his unpopular policy of racial fusion, a seeming attempt to form a Persian-Macedonian master race. When his favourite, Hephaestion (324), died, Alexander gave him a hero's funeral and demanded that divine honours be given at his own funeral. He fell ill at Babylon after long feasting and drinking and died at age 33. He was buried in Alexandria, Egypt. His empire, the greatest that had existed to that time, extended from Thrace to Egypt and from Greece to the Indus valley.

Alexandria, Arabic AL-ISKANDARIYYAH, City (metro. area pop., 2006: 4,110,015) and chief seaport, northern Egypt. It lies on a strip of land between the Mediterranean Sea and Lake Maryūṭ (Mareotis). The ancient island of Pharos, whose lighthouse was one of the Seven Wonders of the World, is now a peninsula connected to the mainland. Alexandria's modern harbour is west of the peninsula. The city was founded in 332 BCE by Alexander the Great and was noted as a centre of Hellenistic culture. Its library (destroyed in the early centuries CE) was the greatest in ancient times; a new library was opened in 2002. The city was captured by the Arabs in CE 642 and by the Ottoman Empire in 1517. After a long period of decline, caused by the rise of Cairo, Alexandria was revived commercially in the 19th century when Muḥammad

ʿAlī joined it by a canal to the Nile River and introduced the production of cotton. Modern Alexandria is a thriving commercial community; cotton is its chief export, and important oil fields lie nearby. Cultural institutions include the Museum of Alexandria and the Bibliotheca Alexandrina.

Alexandria, Library of, Most famous library of classical antiquity. It was part of the Alexandrian Museum, a research institute at Alexandria, Egypt. The museum and library were founded and maintained by a succession of Ptolemies from the early 3rd century BC. The library aspired to the ideal of an international library—incorporating all Greek literature and also translations into Greek—but it is uncertain how close this ideal came to being realized. A bibliography of the library compiled by Callimachus, lost in the Byzantine period, was long a standard reference work. The museum and library were destroyed in civil war in the late 3rd century AD; a subsidiary library was destroyed by Christians in AD 391.

alfalfa, Perennial, clover-like legume (*Medicago sativa*). It is widely grown primarily for hay, pasturage, and silage. It is known for its tolerance of drought, heat, and cold, and for its improvement of soil by nitrification due to bacteria associated with its roots. The plant, which grows 1–3 ft (30–90 cm) tall, develops numerous stems that arise from a much-branched crown at soil level, each bearing many three-leaved leaflets. Its long primary root—as long as 50 ft (15 m) in some plants—accounts for its unusual ability to tolerate drought. Its remarkable capacity for regeneration of dense growths of new stems and leaves following cutting makes possible as many as 13 crops of hay in one growing season. Alfalfa hay is very nutritious and palatable, high in protein, minerals, and vitamins.

Alfred, known as ALFRED THE GREAT (b. 849—d. 899), King of Wessex (871–99) in southwestern England. He joined his brother Ethelred I in confronting a Danish army in Mercia (868). Succeeding his brother as king, Alfred fought the Danes in Wessex in 871 and again in 878, when he was the only West Saxon leader to refuse to submit to their authority and was driven from the kingdom to the island of Athelney. He defeated the Danes at the Battle of Edington (878) and saved Kent from another Danish invasion in 885. The next year he took the offensive and captured London, a success that brought all the English not under Danish rule to accept him as king. The conquest of the Danelaw by his successors was enabled by his strategy, which included the construction of forts and a naval fleet and the reformation of the army. Alfred drew up an important code of laws and promoted literacy and learning, personally translating Latin works by Boethius, Pope Gregory I, and St. Augustine of Hippo into Anglo-Saxon. The compilation of the Anglo-Saxon Chronicle was begun under his reign.

algae, Members of a group of mostly aquatic photosynthetic organisms that defy precise definition. They range in size from the microscopic flagellate *Micromonas* to giant kelp that reach 200 ft (60 m) in length. Algae provide much of Earth's oxygen, serve as the food base for almost all aquatic life, and provide foods and industrial products, including petroleum products. Their photosynthetic pigments are more varied than those of plants, and their cells have features not found among plants and animals. The classification of algae is changing rapidly because new taxonomic information is being discovered. Algae were formerly classified into three major groups—the red, brown, and green seaweeds—based on the pigment molecules in their chloroplasts. Many more than three groups are now recognized, each sharing a common set of pigment types. Algae are not closely related to each other in an evolutionary sense. Specific groups can be distinguished from protozoans and fungi only by the presence of chloroplasts and by their ability to carry out photosynthesis; these specific groups thus have a closer evolutionary relationship with the protozoa or fungi than with other algae. Algae are common on "slimy" rocks in streams and as green sheens on pools and ponds. Use of algae is perhaps as old as humankind; many species are eaten by coastal societies.

algebraic geometry, Study of geometric objects expressed as equations and represented by graphs in a given coordinate system. In contrast to Euclidean geometry, algebraic geometry represents geometric objects using algebraic equations (e.g., a circle of radius r is defined by $x^2 + y^2 = r^2$). Objects so defined can then be analyzed for symmetries, intercepts, and other properties without having to refer to a graph.

algebraic topology, Field of mathematics that uses algebraic structures to study transformations of geometric objects. It uses functions (often called maps in this context) to represent continuous transformations. Taken together, a set of maps and objects may form an algebraic group, which can be analyzed by group-theory methods. A well-known topic in algebraic topology is the four-colour map problem.

Algeria, officially PEOPLE'S DEMOCRATIC REPUBLIC OF ALGERIA, Country, North Africa. Area: 919,595 sq mi (2,381,741 sq km). Population: (2011 est.) 36,649,000. Capital: Algiers. Most of the population is ethnically and linguistically Arab, with a large Amazigh minority. Languages: Arabic (official), Tamazight (national), French. Religion: Islam (official; predominantly Sunni). Currency: Algerian dinar. Algeria has the largest land area on the continent. The coastline has numerous bays, and the country's rivers are small and generally seasonal. Northern Algeria is mountainous and is crossed from east to west by the Atlas Mountains; its highest point, elevation 7,638 ft (2,328 m), is Mount Chélia. In central and southern Algeria is much of the northern Sahara. Algeria has a developing economy based primarily on the production and export of petroleum and natural gas. After achieving independence, the country nationalized much of its economy but since the 1980s has privatized parts of the economy. Algeria is a multiparty republic with two legislative bodies; its head of state is the president, and its head of government is the prime minister. Phoenician traders settled there early in the 1st millennium BCE; several centuries later the Romans invaded, and by 40 CE they had control of the Mediterranean coast. The fall of Rome in the 5th century led to an invasion by the Vandals and later to a reoccupation by the Byzantine (Eastern Roman) Empire. The Islamic invasion began in the 7th century; by 711 all of northern Africa was under the control of the caliphs of the Umayyad dynasty. Several Islamic Amazigh empires followed, most prominently the Almoravid (c. 1054–1130), which extended its domain to Spain, and the Almohad (c. 1130–1269). The Barbary Coast pirates menaced Mediterranean trade for centuries; their raids served as a pretext for France to enter Algeria in 1830. By 1847 France had established military control over most of the region and by the late 19th century had instituted civil rule. Popular protest against French rule resulted in the bloody Algerian War (1954–61); independence was achieved following a referendum in 1962. Beginning in the early 1990s, Islamic fundamentalist opposition to secular rule led to an outbreak in civil violence between the army and various Islamic extremist groups.

Algiers, Arabic AL-JAZĀʾIR, French ALGER, City (pop., 2004 est.: 1,790,700), chief seaport and capital of Algeria. Located along the Bay of Algiers and first settled by Phoenicians, it was later ruled by the Romans. It was destroyed by the Vandals in the 5th century AD but revived under a Berber dynasty in the 10th century. When the Spanish threatened it in the early 16th century, the local emir appealed to the Ottoman corsair Barbarossa, who expelled the Spanish and placed Algiers under the rule of the Ottoman Empire. Algiers became the major base for the Barbary Coast pirates for 300 years; their activities were greatly curtailed in 1815 by an American force led by Stephen Decatur. The French took the city in 1830 and made it headquarters for their African colonial empire. In World War II (1939–45) it became the Allied headquarters in northern Africa and for a time the provisional capital of France. In the 1950s it was the focal point in the drive for Algeria's independence; after independence, Algiers grew as the country's political, economic, and cultural centre.

Ali, Muhammad, orig. CASSIUS (MARCELLUS) CLAY (b. Jan. 17, 1942, Louisville, Ken., U.S.),

U.S. boxer. Cassius Clay took up boxing at the age of 12 and rose through the amateur ranks to win the Olympic light heavyweight crown in 1960. His first professional heavyweight title win was against Sonny Liston in 1964. After defending the title nine times between 1965 and 1967, he was stripped of it for refusing induction into the armed forces following his acceptance of the teachings of the Nation of Islam. It was then that he changed his name to Muhammad Ali. In 1974 Ali regained his title after defeating the former champion Joe Frazier and the then-current champion

Muhammad Ali (right) fighting Ernie Terrell, 1967.
UPI/Bettmann Archive

George Foreman. He lost to Leon Spinks in 1978 but later that year regained the title a third time, becoming the first heavyweight champion ever to do so. He retired in 1979, having lost only three of 59 fights. Attempted comebacks in 1980 and 1981 failed. Throughout his career Ali was known for his aggressive charm, invincible attitude, and colourful boasts, often expressed in doggerel verse. "I am the greatest" was his personal credo. Ali's later years have been marked by physical decline. Damage to his brain, caused by blows to the head, has resulted in slurred speech, slowed movement, and other symptoms of Parkinson disease.

Alicante, City (pop., 2001: 284,580), southeastern Spain, located on Alicante Bay of the Mediterranean Sea. It was founded as a Greek colony in 325 BC and was captured in 201 BC by the Romans, who called it Lucentum. After being ruled by the Moors (718–1249), it was later incorporated into the kingdom of Aragon in 1265. The city was besieged by the French in 1709 and by the Federalists of Cartagena in 1873. Its economy is based on tourism and the export of wine and produce.

alienation, In the social sciences context, the state of feeling estranged or separated from one's milieu, work, products of work, or self. The concept appears implicitly or explicitly in the works of Émile Durkheim, Ferdinand Tönnies, Max Weber, and Georg Simmel but is most famously associated with Karl Marx, who spoke of workers being alienated from their work and its products under capitalism. In other contexts the term alienation, like anomie, can suggest a sense of powerlessness, meaninglessness, normlessness, social isolation, or cultural- or self-estrangement brought on by the lack of fit between individual needs or expectations and the social order.

alkaloid, Basic organic compounds of plant origin, containing combined nitrogen. Alkaloids are amines, so their names usually end in "ine" (e.g., caffeine, nicotine, morphine, quinine). Most have complex chemical structures of multiple ring systems. They have diverse, important physiological effects on humans and other animals, but their functions in the plants that produce them are poorly understood. Some plants (e.g., opium poppy, ergot fungus) produce many different alkaloids, but most produce only one or a few. Certain plant families, including the poppy family (Papaveraceae) and the nightshade family (Solanaceae), are particularly rich in them. Alkaloids are extracted by dissolving the plant in dilute acid.

Allah (Arabic: "God"), Standard Arabic word for God, used by Arab Christians as well as by Muslims. According to the Qurʾān, Allah is the creator and judge of humankind, omnipotent, compassionate, and merciful. The Muslim profession of faith affirms that there is no deity but God and emphasizes that he is inherently one: "nothing is like unto him." Everything that happens occurs by his commandment; submission to God is the basis of Islam. The Qurʾān and the Ḥadīth contain the 99 "most beautiful names" of God, including the One and Only, the Living One, the Real Truth, the Hearer, the Seer, the Benefactor, and the Constant Forgiver.

Allahabad, ancient PRAYAG, City (pop., 2001: metro. area, 1,042,229), south-central Uttar Pradesh state, northern India, on the Ganges (Ganga) and Yamuna rivers. An ancient holy city sacred to Hindu pilgrims, it is the site of the Pillar of Ashoka (erected *c.* 240 BC). The Mughal emperor Akbar founded the present-day city in 1583; it was ceded to the British in 1801. Allahabad was the scene of a serious outbreak in the 1857 Indian Mutiny. As the home of the Neh-

Tomb at Allahabad, Uttar Pradesh, India.
Frederick M. Asher

ru family, it was later a centre of the Indian independence movement. It is the site of the Jami Masjid (Great Mosque) and the University of Allahabad.

allegory, Work of written, oral, or visual expression that uses symbolic figures, objects, and actions to convey truths or generalizations about human conduct or experience. It encompasses such forms as the fable and parable. Characters often personify abstract concepts or types, and the action of the narrative usually stands for something not explicitly stated. Symbolic allegories, in which characters may also have an identity apart from the message they convey, have frequently been used to represent political and historical situations and have long been popular as vehicles for satire. Edmund Spenser's long poem *The Faerie Queen* is a famous example of a symbolic allegory.

allele, Any one of two or more alternative forms of a gene that may occur alternatively at a given site on a chromosome. Alleles may occur in pairs, or there may be multiple alleles affecting the expression of a particular trait. If paired alleles are the same, the organism is said to be homozygous for that trait; if they are different, the organism is heterozygous. A dominant allele will override the traits of a recessive allele in a heterozygous pairing. In some traits, alleles may be codominant (i.e., neither acts as dominant or recessive). An individual cannot possess more than two alleles for a given trait. All genetic traits are the result of the interactions of alleles.

allergy, Exaggerated reaction by the body to foreign substances that are harmless to most people. Those substances, called allergens or antigens, may include pollens, drugs, dusts, foods, and other items. Immediate allergic reactions result from genetic predisposition or sensitization by previous exposure. Blood vessels dilate and bronchial air passages constrict. A severe reaction (anaphylaxis) can obstruct breathing and may be fatal. Delayed allergic responses (e.g., contact dermatitis) appear 12 hours or more after exposure. Avoiding allergens and taking antihistamines can prevent or treat allergies. When avoidance is not feasible and antihistamines do not relieve symptoms, desensitization can be attempted.

alliance, In international politics, a union for joint action of various powers or states. Examples include the alliance of the European powers and the U.S. against Germany and its allies during World War II and the alliance of the NATO states against the Soviet Union and its allies during the Cold War. Many alliances rest on the principle of collective security, through which an attack on one member is considered an attack on all members. Major alliances formed after World War II include the ANZUS Pact, the Arab League, ASEAN, the Organization of American States, the Southeast Asia Treaty Organization, and the Warsaw Pact.

Alliance for Progress, International development program. Initiated by the U.S. and joined by 22 Latin American countries in 1961, it aimed to strengthen democratic government and promote social and economic reforms in Latin America. The program, which provided loans and aid from the U.S. and the international financial community, built some schools and hospitals, but by the early 1970s it was widely viewed as a failure. Significant land reform was not achieved, population growth outstripped gains in health and welfare, and the U.S. willingness to support military dictators to prevent communism from gaining a foothold sowed distrust and undermined the reforms the Alliance was intended to promote.

Allied Powers, or ALLIES, Nations allied in opposition to the Central Powers in World War I or to the Axis Powers in World War II. The original Allies in World War I—the British Empire, France, and the Russian Empire—were later joined by many other countries, including Portugal, Japan, and Italy. Other nations joining the Allies, including the U.S. after 1917, were called Associated Powers, a term emphasized by Pres. Woodrow Wilson to preserve the U.S.'s free hand in the war. In World War II the major Allied Powers were Britain, France, the Soviet Union, the U.S., and China. More generally, the Allies included all the wartime members of the United Nations, the 1942 signatories to the Declaration of the UN.

alligator, Either of two species of long-snouted reptiles constituting the genus *Alligator* (family Alligatoridae, order Crocodilia). Alligators differ from crocodiles in snout shape and tooth placement. Living in large bodies of water such as lakes, swamps, and rivers, these lizardlike carnivores use their powerful tail for defense and swimming. The eyes, ears, and nostrils, located on top of the long head, project above the water's surface. Alligators dig burrows in which they shelter from danger and hibernate in cold weather. The once-endangered American alligator of the southeastern U.S. may grow to 19 ft (5.7 m) long but usually ranges from 6 to 12 ft (1.8 to 3.7 m) long. The Chinese alligator of the Chang (Yangtze) River region, which grows to 5 ft (1.5 m), is critically endangered.

*Alligator (*Alligator mississippiensis*)*
P. Morris/Woodfin Camp and Associates

alliteration, or HEAD RHYME, Repetition of consonant sounds in two or more neighbouring words or syllables. A frequently used poetic device, it is often discussed with assonance (the repetition of stressed vowel sounds within two or more words with different end consonants) and consonance (the repetition of end or medial consonants).

allium, Any plant of a large genus (*Allium*) of bulbous, onion- or garlic-scented herbs of the Alliaceae family, including the onion, garlic, chive, leek, and shallot. *Allium* species are found in most regions of the world except the tropics and New Zealand and Australia. Some are cultivated as ornamental border plants.

allocation of resources, Apportionment of productive assets among different uses. The issue of resource allocation arises as societies seek to balance limited resources (capital, labour, land) against the various and often unlimited wants of their members. Mechanisms of resource allocation include the price system in free-market economies and government planning, either in state-run economies or in the public sectors of mixed economies. The aim is always to allocate resources in such a way as to obtain the maximum possible output from a given combination of resources.

Allosaurus, Large carnivorous dinosaur of a group similar to the tyrannosaurs, found as fossils primarily in Late Jurassic rocks of North America. It weighed 2 tons (1,800 kg) and grew to 35 ft (10.5 m) long. Its well-developed tail, half of its total body length, probably functioned as a counterbalance for the body. *Allosaurus* walked on its two hind limbs and probably used the much smaller forelimbs for grasping. Equipped with powerful, flexible jaws, allosaurs likely preyed on medium-sized dinosaurs; they were possibly scavengers that hunted in groups. Some related allosaurs (*Giganotosaurus, Carcharodonotosaurus*) may have been larger than *Tyrannosaurus rex*.

allspice, Tropical evergreen tree (*Pimenta dioica*) of the myrtle

*Allspice (*Pimenta dioica).
J.E. Cruise

family, native to the West Indies and Central America and valued for its berries, the source of a highly aromatic spice. Allspice was so named because the flavour of the dried berry resembles a combination of cloves, cinnamon, and nutmeg. It is widely used in baking. The name is applied to several other aromatic shrubs as well, including Carolina allspice (*Calycanthus floridus*), Japanese allspice (*Chimonanthus praecox*), and wild allspice, or spicebush.

alluvial deposit, Material deposited by rivers. It consists of silt, sand, clay, and gravel, as well as much organic matter. Alluvial deposits are usually most extensive in the lower part of a river's course, forming floodplains and deltas, but they may form at any point where the river overflows its banks or where the flow of a river is checked. They yield very fertile soils, such as those of the deltas of the Mississippi, Nile, Ganges and Brahmaputra, and Huang (Yellow) rivers. They contain most of the world's supply of tin ore, as well as, in some regions, gold, platinum, and gemstones.

Almagest, Astronomical and mathematical encyclopedia compiled *c.* AD 140 by Ptolemy. It served as the basic guide for Arab and European astronomers until the 17th century. The name derives from the Arabic for "the greatest." Its 13 books cover such topics as the geocentric (Earth-centred), or Ptolemaic, model of the solar system; eclipses; the coordinates and sizes of certain fixed stars; and the distances to the Sun and the Moon.

Almaty, formerly ALMA-ATA, City (pop., 2008 est.: 1,324,739), southeastern Kazakhstan. Formerly the capital of Kazakhstan, it lost its capital status in 1995 to Aqmola (now Astana). The modern city was founded in 1854, when the Russians established a military fortification on the site of the ancient city of Almaty, destroyed by the Mongols in the 13th century. With the coming of the railroad in 1930, its population grew rapidly. In World War II (1939–45), heavy industry expanded widely as factories were evacuated to the site from European Russia. The city remains a major industrial centre.

aloe, Any shrubby succulent plant of the genus *Aloe,* in the family Asphodelaceae. Native to Africa, most of the 200 or so species have a rosette of leaves at the base but no stem. Several are cultivated as ornamentals. The juice of some species, especially the popular potted plant known as true aloe (*Aloe vera*), is used as an ingredient in cosmetics, as a purgative, and as a treatment for burns.

alphabet, Set of symbols or characters that represent language's sounds in writing. Each character usually represents a simple vowel, a diphthong (two vowels), or one or two consonants. A writing system in which one character represents a whole syllable is called a syllabary. The first alphabet is believed to have been the North Semitic, which originated in the eastern Mediterranean region between 1700 and 1500 BC. Alphabets that arose in the next 500 years included the Canaanite and Aramaic, from which the modern Hebrew and Arabic alphabets descended, and the Greek (ancestor of the Latin alphabet), considered the first true alphabet because it includes both consonants and vowels. Scholars have attempted to establish an exact correspondence between each sound and its symbol in new alphabets such as the International Phonetic Alphabet.

Alpine skiing, Class of competitive ski events consisting of speed events (the downhill and the supergiant slalom) and technical events (the slalom and giant slalom). Speed events are contested in single runs down longer, steeper, faster courses, with fewer turns than those featured in the technical events. Alpine skiing was first included in the Olympic Games in 1936.

Alps, Mountain system, south-central Europe. The Alps extend in a crescent about 750 mi (1,200 km) from the Mediterranean coast between France and Italy to Vienna and cover more than 80,000 sq mi (207,000 sq km). Several peaks rise above 10,000 ft (3,000 m); the highest is Mont Blanc. The Alps form a divide between the Atlantic Ocean, the Mediterranean Sea, and the Black Sea and give rise to several major European rivers, including the Rhône, Danube, and Po. Glaciers cover about 1,500 sq mi (3,900 sq km), mostly at elevations above 10,000 ft (3,000 m). The Saint Gotthard Pass is one of the Alps's notable tunnels. Grenoble, Innsbruck, and Bolzano are major Alpine cities.

Altai Mountains, Russian ALTAY, Chinese ALTAY SHAN, Mongol ALTAYN NURUU, Mountain system, Central Asia. The range extends about 1,200 mi (2,000 km) in a southeast-northwest direction from the Gobi Desert to the West Siberian Plain, through parts of China, Mongolia, Russia, and Kazakhstan. The highest point is the Russian peak Belukha, 14,783 ft (4,506 m) in elevation. The mountains are the source of the Irtysh and Ob rivers and are notable for their mining and hydroelectrical potential.

Altaic languages, Group of more than 50 languages, comprising the Turkic, Mongolian, and Manchu-Tungus subfamilies. Altaic languages are spoken across Eurasia by more than 140 million people (the overwhelming majority of whom speak Turkic languages). Most scholars consider Altaic itself to be a family, of proven genetic relationship, though a minority attribute similarities in the languages to borrowings and areal convergence. The Uralic and Altaic language families were once believed to form a superfamily, but reliable sound correspondences have not been demonstrated, and the numerous similarities between the two are now attributed to areal influences.

Altamira, Cave near Santander, northern Spain, famous for its magnificent prehistoric paintings and engravings. The paintings, dating to 14,000–12,000 BC, were first described in 1880. Altamira cave is 890 ft (270 m) long. The roof of the main chamber is covered with paintings, chiefly of bison, in vivid red, black, and violet. Other figures, in a simpler style, include wild boars, horses, and a hind, as well as eight engraved anthropomorphic figures and various handprints and hand outlines. Engraved artifacts and other material remains suggest that the site may have been a centre for seasonal gatherings.

alternating current (AC), Flow of electric charge that reverses periodically, unlike direct current. It starts from zero, grows to a maximum, decreases to zero, reverses, reaches a maximum in the opposite direction, returns again to zero, and repeats the cycle indefinitely. The time taken to complete one cycle is called the period, and the number of cycles per second is the frequency; the maximum value in either direction is the current's amplitude. Low frequencies (50–60 cycles per second) are used for domestic and commercial power, but frequencies of around 100 million cycles per second (100 megahertz) are used in television and of several thousand megahertz in radar and microwave communication. A major advantage of alternating current is that the voltage can be increased and decreased by a transformer for more efficient transmission over long distances. Direct current cannot use transformers to change voltage.

alternation of generations, In biology, alternation of a sexual phase (gametophyte) and a nonsexual phase (sporophyte) in the life cycle of an organism. The two phases, or generations, are often distinct in structure and sometimes in chromosome makeup. Alternation of generations is common in algae, fungi, mosses, ferns, and seed plants. The character and extent of the two phases vary greatly among different groups of plants and algae. During the course of evolution, the gametophyte stage has been progressively reduced. Thus in higher (vascular) plants, the sporophyte is the dominant phase; in more primitive, nonvascular plants the gametophyte is dominant. Among animals, many invertebrates (e.g., protozoans, jellyfish, flatworms) have an alternation of sexual and asexual generations.

altitude sickness, or MOUNTAIN SICKNESS, Acute reaction to a change from low altitudes to altitudes above 8,000 ft (2,400 m). Most people gradually adapt, but some have a severe reaction that can be fatal unless they return to low altitude. Normal adaptations to the reduced oxygen at high altitude (e.g., breathlessness, racing heartbeat) are exaggerated; other manifestations include headache, gastrointestinal upsets, and weakness. Pulmonary edema is quickly reversed with oxygen and evacuation to a lower area.

alto, or CONTRALTO, Voice or register that extends approximately from the F below middle C to the second D above it. The second-highest part in four-part music, it is normally sung by women. The name derives from *contratenor altus,* the part above the tenor part. It is used for some instruments that play principally in the alto range (alto saxophone, alto flute, etc.).

aluminum, Metallic chemical element, chemical symbol Al, atomic number 13. A lightweight, silvery white metal, it is so reactive chemically that it always occurs in compounds. It is the most abundant metallic element in Earth's crust, chiefly in bauxite (its principal ore), feldspars, micas, clay minerals, and laterite. It also occurs in gemstones, such as topaz, garnet, and chrysoberyl; emery, corundum, ruby, and sapphire are crystalline aluminum oxide. Aluminum was first isolated in 1825, became commercially available in the late 19th century, and is now the most widely used metal after iron. Its surface oxidizes at once to a hard, tough film, deterring further corrosion. Uses include building and construction, corrosion-resistant chemical equipment, auto and aircraft parts, power transmission lines, photoengraving plates, cookware and other consumer goods, and tubes for ointments and pastes. Important compounds include alums; alumina (aluminum oxide), useful as corundum and as a carrier for many catalysts; aluminum chloride, a widely used catalyst for organic syntheses; and aluminum hydroxide, used to waterproof fabrics.

Alzheimer disease, Degenerative brain disorder. It occurs in mid-to-late adult life, destroying neurons and connections in the cerebral cortex and resulting in significant loss of brain mass. Three stages of the disease are recognized: preclinical, mild cognitive impairment, and Alzheimer dementia, which is the most common form of dementia among older persons. Some 35.6 million people worldwide were living with dementia in 2010. Alzheimer disease progresses from short-term memory impairment to further memory loss; deterioration of language, perceptual, and motor skills; mood instability; and, in advanced stages, unresponsiveness, with loss of mobility and control of body functions. Death ensues after a disease course lasting 2–20 years. Originally described in 1906 by the German neuropathologist Alois Alzheimer (1864–1915) with reference to a 55-year-old person and regarded as a presenile dementia, Alzheimer disease is now recognized as accounting for much of the senile dementia once thought normal with aging. The 10% of cases that begin before age 60 appear to result from an inherited mutation. Early detection is based on the presence of biomarkers (physiological changes specific to or indicative of a disease) and on diagnostic imaging, with visualization of neuritic plaques and neurofibrillary tangles in the brain providing evidence of the disease. No cure has been found. Most treatment targets the depression, behavioral problems, and sleeplessness that often accompany the disease.

amanita, Any mushroom of the genus *Amanita*, containing about 500 species, some of which are poisonous to humans. Among the deadliest of all mushrooms are the large, white destroying angels (*A. bisporigera*, *A. ocreata*, *A. verna*, and *A. virosa*), which are found in forests during wet periods in summer and autumn. The green or brown death cap (*A. phalloides*), also deadly, is found in woods in summer or early autumn. The poisonous fly agaric (*A. muscaria*), found in pastures and fields in summer, was once used as a fly poison. Common edible species include *A. caesarea*, *A. rubescens*, and *A. vaginata*.

Fly agaric (Amanita muscaria)
Larry C. Moon/Tom Stack & Associates

amaranth family, Family Amaranthaceae, which contains about 60 genera and more than 800 species of herbaceous plants and a few shrubs, trees, and vines, native to tropical America and Africa. Globe amaranth (*Gomphrena*) and cockscomb (*Celosia*) are cultivated as ornamentals. The large genus *Amaranthus* contains the ornamentals love-lies-bleeding (*A. caudatus*) and Joseph's-coat (*A. tricolor*), as well as many weedy plants known as pigweed, especially *A. retroflexus*. Some *Amaranthus* species are tumbleweeds, and some are potential high-protein grain crops.

Amarāvatī sculpture, Style of sculpture found in the Andhra region of southeastern India. It flourished there from about the 2nd century BC to the end of the 3rd century AD, during the rule of the Sātavāhana dynasty. Carved in relief on greenish-white limestone, these sculptures depict events in the life of the Buddha. The compositions are dynamic, sensuous, and dramatic, with overlapping figures and diagonals suggesting depth. The style spread from the Amarāvatī ruins west to Mahārāshtra Pradesh, to Sri Lanka (Ceylon), and to much of South Asia. The Amarāvatī stupa was one of the largest in Buddhist India; it was largely destroyed in the 19th century by building contractors to make lime mortar.

Amarna, Tell el-, Ancient city, Egypt. Located midway between Thebes and Memphis on the Nile River, it was built in the 14th century BC by the Egyptian king (pharaoh) Akhenaton, who moved his subjects there in order to found a new monotheistic religion. Artifacts discovered there in the 19th century included hundreds of cuneiform tablets. Archaeological finds of the late 20th century included sculptures and paintings.

amaryllis family, Family Amaryllidaceae of the order Aspergales, containing about 59 genera and at least 800 species of perennial herbaceous plants, found mostly in tropical and subtropical regions and prized for their showy flowers, which are borne on smooth, hollow stalks with few or no leaves. Many species are cultivated as garden ornamentals. Many tropical lilylike plants also belong to the family, including the genera *Haemanthus* (Cape tulip, or blood lily), *Alstroemeria* (Peruvian lily), and *Hippeastrum*. Some are grown as houseplants.

Amaterasu (Omikami), In Shintō, the sun goddess from whom the Japanese royal family traditionally claims descent. She was given domain over heaven while her brother, the storm god Susanoo, was set to rule over the sea. The two produced children together, but Susanoo began to behave rudely and destructively, and Amaterasu withdrew in protest into a cave, plunging the world into darkness. She was lured out by the other gods and goddesses, and a rope was placed over its entrance to prevent her return. Her chief place of worship is the Grand Shrine of Ise, Shintō's most important shrine.

Amazon, In Greek mythology, a member of a race of women warriors. One of the labours of Heracles was to obtain the girdle of the Amazon queen Hippolyte. In another tale, Theseus attacked the Amazons, and they responded by invading Attica, where they were defeated; Theseus married the Amazon Antiope. In ancient Greek art, Amazons resembled Athena (with weapons and helmet) and later Artemis (in a thin dress girded high for speed).

Amazon River, Portuguese RIO AMAZONAS, River, northern South America. It is the largest river in the world in volume and in area of drainage basin; only the Nile River of eastern and northeastern Africa exceeds it in length. It originates within 100 mi (160 km) of the Pacific Ocean in the Peruvian Andes Mountains and flows some 4,000 mi (6,400 km) across northern Brazil into the Atlantic Ocean. Its Peruvian length is called the Marañón River, and the stretch of river from the Brazilian border to the mouth of the Negro River is the Solimões River. Its more than 1,000 known tributaries rise in the Guiana Highlands, the Brazilian Highlands, and (principally) the Andes; 7 of these are longer than 1,000 mi (1,600 km), and the Madeira River exceeds 2,000 mi (3,200 km). The Amazon can accommodate large freighters as far upriver as the city of Manaus, Braz., 1,000 mi (1,600 km) from the Atlantic. The first European descent was made by Francisco de Orellana in 1541–42; he is said to have given the river its name after reporting battles with tribes of women, whom he likened to the Amazons of Greek legend. Pedro Teixeira achieved the first ascent in 1637–38, but the river remained little explored until the mid-19th century. Many indigenous peoples originally lived along the river, but they moved inland as exploring parties and raiders sought to enslave them. The river was opened to world shipping in the mid-19th century; traffic increased exponentially with the coming of the rubber trade, which reached its height *c.* 1910 but soon declined. Its basin encompasses the world's most extensive rainforest and is home to an extraordinary diversity of birds, mammals, and other wildlife. Since the 1960s the effects of economic exploitation on the region's ecology and the destruction of the rainforest have generated worldwide concern.

amenorrhea, Lack of menstruation. Signs of primary amenorrhea (failure to start menstruating by age 16) include infantile reproductive organs, lack of breasts and pubic hair, dwarfism, and deficient muscle development. In secondary amenorrhea (abnormal cessation of cycles once started), the genitals atrophy and pubic hair diminishes. Not itself a disease, amenorrhea reflects a failure in the balance among the hypothalamus, pituitary gland, ovaries, and uterus; tumours, injuries, or diseases of these can lead to amenorrhea. Other causes include systemic diseases, emotional shock, stress, hormone over- or underproduction, anorexia nervosa, absence of ovaries or uterus, pregnancy, lactation, and menopause. Infrequent menstruation or amenorrhea not resulting from organic disease is not harmful.

American Civil War, or CIVIL WAR, or WAR BETWEEN THE STATES (1861–65) Conflict between the U.S. federal government and 11 Southern states that fought to secede from the Union. It arose out of disputes over the issues of slavery, trade and tariffs, and the doctrine of states' rights. In the 1840s and '50s, Northern opposition to slavery in the Western territories caused the Southern states to fear that existing slaveholdings, which formed the economic base of the South, were also in danger. By the 1850s abolitionism was growing in the North, and when the antislavery Republican candidate Abraham Lincoln was elected president in 1860, the Southern states seceded to protect what they saw as their right to keep slaves. They were organized as the Confederate States of America under Jefferson Davis. The Northern states of the federal Union, under Lincoln, commanded more than twice the population of the Confederacy and held greater advantages in manufacturing and transportation capacity. The war began in Charleston, S.C., when Confederate artillery fired on Fort Sumter on April 12, 1861. Both sides quickly raised armies. In July 1861, 30,000 Union troops marched toward the Confederate capital at Richmond, Va., but were stopped by Confederate forces in the Battle of Bull Run and forced to retreat to Washington, D.C. The defeat shocked the Union, which called for 500,000 more recruits. The war's first major campaign began in February 1862, when Union troops under Ulysses S. Grant captured Confederate forts in western Tennessee. Union victories at the battles of Shiloh and New Orleans followed. In the East, Robert E. Lee won several Confederate victories in the Seven Days' Battles and, after defeat at the Battle of Antietam, in the Battle of Fredericksburg (December 1862). After the Confederate victory at the Battle of Chancellorsville, Lee invaded the North and engaged Union forces under George Meade at the momentous Battle of Gettysburg. The war's turning point in the West occurred in July 1863 with Grant's success in the Vicksburg Campaign, which brought the entire Mississippi River under Union control. Grant's command was expanded after the Union defeat at the Battle of Chickamauga, and in March 1864 Lincoln gave him supreme command of the Union armies. He began a strategy of attrition and, despite heavy Union casualties at the battles of the Wilderness and Spotsylvania, began to surround Lee's troops in Petersburg, Va.. Meanwhile William T. Sherman captured Atlanta in September, set out on a destructive march through Georgia, and soon captured Savannah. Grant captured Richmond on April 3, 1865, and accepted Lee's surrender on April 9 at Appomattox Court House. On April 26 Sherman received the surrender of Joseph Johnston, thereby ending the war. The mortality rates of the war were staggering—there were about 620,000 deaths out of a total of 2.4 million soldiers. The South was devastated. But the Union was preserved, and slavery was abolished.

American Indian, or NATIVE AMERICAN, or AMERINDIAN, or INDIGENOUS AMERICAN, Any member of the various aboriginal peoples of the Western Hemisphere, with the exception of the Eskimos (Inuit) and the Aleuts. Though the term "Native American" is today often preferred to "American Indian," particularly in the U.S., many Native American peoples continue to prefer American Indian (or Indian). In Canada the name First Nation is preferred. The ancestors of the American Indians were nomadic hunters of northeast Asia who migrated over the Bering Strait land bridge into North America probably during the last glacial period (11,500–30,000 years ago). By c. 10,000 BC they had occupied much of North, Central, and South America.

American Indian languages, Languages spoken by the original inhabitants of the Americas and the West Indies and by their modern descendants. They display an extraordinary structural range, and no attempt to unite them into a small number of genetic

groupings has won general acceptance. Before the arrival of Columbus, more than 300 distinct languages were spoken in North America north of Mexico by an estimated population of two to seven million. Today fewer than 170 languages are spoken, of which the great majority are spoken fluently only by older adults. A few widespread language families (Algonquian, Iroquoian, Siouan, Muskogean, Athabaskan, Uto-Aztecan, Salishan) account for many of the languages of eastern and interior North America, though the far west was an area of extreme diversity. It is estimated that in Mexico and northern Central America (Mesoamerica), an estimated 15–20 million people spoke more than 300 languages before Columbus. The large Otomanguean and Maya families and a single language, Nahuatl, shared Mesoamerica with many smaller families and language isolates. More than 10 of these languages and language complexes still have more than 100,000 speakers. South America and the West Indies had an estimated pre-Columbian population of 10–20 million, speaking more than 500 languages. Important language families include Chibchan in Colombia and southern Central America, Quechuan and Aymaran in the Andean region, and Arawakan, Cariban, and Tupian in northern and central lowland South America. Aside from Quechuan and Aymaran, with about 10 million speakers, and the Tupian language Guaraní, most remaining South American Indian languages have very few speakers, and some face certain extinction.

American Revolution, or UNITED STATES WAR OF INDEPENDENCE (1775–83) War that won political independence for 13 of Britain's North American colonies, which formed the United States of America. After the end of the costly French and Indian War (1763), Britain imposed new taxes and trade restrictions on the colonies, fueling growing resentment and strengthening the colonists' objection to their lack of representation in the British Parliament. Determined to achieve independence, the colonies formed the Continental Army, composed chiefly of minutemen, to challenge Britain's large, organized militia. The war began when Britain sent a force to destroy rebel military stores at Concord, Mass. After fighting broke out on April 19, 1775, rebel forces began a siege of Boston that ended when American forces under Henry Knox forced out the British troops under William Howe on March 17, 1776. Britain's offer of pardon in exchange for surrender was refused by the Americans, who declared themselves independent on July 4, 1776. British forces retaliated by driving the army of George Washington from New York to New Jersey. On December 25, Washington crossed the Delaware River and won the battles of Trenton and Princeton. The British army split to cover more territory, a fatal error. In engaging the Americans in Pennsylvania, notably in the Battle of the Brandywine, they left the troops in the north vulnerable. Despite a victory in the Battle of Ticonderoga, British troops under John Burgoyne were defeated by Horatio Gates and Benedict Arnold in the Battle of Saratoga (Oct. 17, 1777). Washington quartered his 11,000 troops through a bleak winter at Valley Forge, where they received training from Frederick Steuben that gave them victory in Monmouth, N.J., on June 28, 1778. British forces in the north thenceforth chiefly concentrated near New York. France, which had been secretly furnishing aid to the Americans since 1776, finally declared war on Britain in June 1778. French troops assisted American troops in the south, culminating in the successful Siege of Yorktown, where Charles Cornwallis surrendered his forces on Oct. 19, 1781, bringing an end to the war on land. War continued at sea, fought chiefly between Britain and the U.S.'s European allies. The navies of Spain and the Netherlands contained most of Britain's navy near Europe and away from the fighting in America. The last battle of the war was won by the American navy under John Barry in March 1783 in the Straits of Florida. With the Treaty of Paris (Sept. 3, 1783), Britain recognized the independence of the U.S. east of the Mississippi River and ceded Florida to Spain.

American Samoa, officially TERRITORY OF AMERICAN SAMOA, Unincorporated U.S. territory, south-central Pacific Ocean. It includes the islands of Tutuila (the largest, with over two-thirds of the territory's land area and almost all of its population), Aunuu, Rose, Swains, and the Manua group. Area: 77 sq mi (200 sq km). Population: (2011 est.) 66,700. Capital: Fagatogo (legislative and judicial); Utulei (executive) (both part of Pago Pago urban agglom., on Tutuila). Languages: Samoan, English (both official). Religion: Christianity (mostly Protestant; also Roman Catholic, other Christians). Currency: U.S. dollar. Most of the islands are rocky, formed from extinct volcanoes, and are surrounded by coral reefs. Tutuila and the islands of Manua are dominated by central mountain ranges. Fishing and tourism are major industries, but the U.S. administration is the main employer. The great majority of the population is of Samoan ancestry. The islands were probably inhabited by Polynesians 3,000 years ago. Dutch explorers became the first Europeans to visit the islands in 1722. Missionaries began arriving in the islands in the 1830s. The U.S. gained the right to establish a naval station at Pago Pago in 1878, and the U.S., Britain, and Germany administered a tripartite protectorate in 1889–99. In 1899 Britain and Germany renounced their claims over the eastern islands. The high chiefs ceded the eastern islands to the U.S. in 1904. American Samoa was administered by the U.S. Department of the Navy until 1951 and afterward by the Department of the Interior. Its current constitution was approved in 1967, and in 1978 the territory's first elected governor took office.

America's Cup, Most prestigious trophy in international yachting competition. First offered under another name in Britain in 1851, the cup was won easily by the *America* from New York and subsequently became known as the America's Cup. The America's Cup race, held about every four years, is between one defending vessel and one challenging vessel; each must be designed and built in the country it represents. The 22.6-mi (36.4-km) racecourse is divided into eight legs. The U.S. completely dominated the competition until 1983, when it was defeated by Australia. New Zealand won the Cup in 1995 and retained it in 2000 by defeating a challenger from Italy in the first competition without a U.S. participant.

americium, Synthetic radioactive chemical element, chemical symbol Am, atomic number 95. The fourth transuranium element discovered, it was first produced in 1944 from plutonium-239 in a nuclear reactor. The isotope americium-241 has been prepared in kilogram quantities and is used in a variety of measuring applications that utilize its gamma radiation. Its most familiar use is in household smoke detectors.

amethyst, Transparent, coarse-grained variety of quartz that is valued as a semiprecious gem for its violet colour. It contains a little more iron oxide (Fe_2O_3) than any other variety of quartz, and its colour probably arises from this iron content. Heating removes the colour or changes it to the yellow of citrine; most commercial citrine is made in this manner. Notable deposits are found in Brazil, Uruguay, Ontario, and North Carolina. The birthstone for February, amethyst is usually faceted with step cuts or emerald cuts but also has been used since ancient times for carved intaglios.

White-tipped amethyst from Guerrero, Mexico
Lee Boltin

amino acid, Any of a class of organic compounds in which a carbon atom has bonds to an amino group ($-NH_2$), a carboxyl group ($-COOH$), a hydrogen atom ($-H$), and an organic side group (called $-R$). They are therefore both carboxylic acids and amines. The physical and chemical properties unique to each result from the properties of the R group, particularly its tendency to interact with water and its charge (if any). Amino acids joined linearly by peptide bonds in a particular order make up peptides and proteins. Of over 100 natural amino acids, each with a different R group, only 20 make up the proteins of all living organisms. Humans can synthesize 10 of them (by interconversions) from each other or from other molecules of intermediary metabolism, but the other 10 (essential amino acids: arginine, histidine, isoleucine, leucine, lysine, methionine, phenylalanine, threonine, tryptophan, and valine) must be consumed in the diet.

Amish, Member of a conservative Christian group in North America known as the Old Order Amish Mennonite Church. The Amish originated in 1693–97 as followers of the Mennonite elder Jakob Ammann (1644?–*c.* 1730) in Switzerland, Alsace, and Germany. He taught that lying was grounds for excommunication (which meant being shunned by all other Mennonites), that clothing should be uniform and beards untrimmed, and that the state church should be avoided. Migration to North America and assimilation eliminated the Amish in Europe. They settled in Pennsylvania in the 18th century. After 1850 they split into "Old Order" (traditional) and "New Order" (now the Mennonite churches). Old Order Amish now live in Pennsylvania, Ohio, Indiana, Iowa, Illinois, and Kansas. Adults are baptized and admitted to formal church membership at age 17 to 20. Services are in Pennsylvania Dutch (a German dialect) and some English. Though similar in theology to Mennonites, Amish wear modest, old-fashioned clothing and generally reject modern technology, including automobiles and telephones.

Amitabha, Japanese AMIDA, Saviour deity worshiped by followers of Pure Land Buddhism in Japan. According to the *Sukhavati-vyuha-sutra* (Pure Land sutra), the monk Dharmakara vowed many ages ago that once he attained buddhahood, all who believed in him and called upon his name would be born into his paradise (the Pure Land) and reside there until achieving nirvana. The cult of Amitabha came to the forefront in China *c.* 650 and then spread to Japan, where it led to the formation of the Pure Land and True Pure Land sects. In the Tibet Autonomous Region of China and in Nepal, Amitabha is regarded as one of the five eternal buddhas (rather than as a saviour), who manifested himself as the earthly Buddha Gautama and as the bodhisattva Avalokitesvara.

Great bronze Amida (Daibutsu) at Kamakura, Japan, 1252.
Gavin Hellier—Robert Harding Picture Library/Getty Images

Amman, City (pop., 2004 est.: 1,036,330), capital of Jordan. It lies 25 mi (40 km) northeast of the Dead Sea. Amman is by far the largest city of Jordan. Fortified settlements have existed in the area from remote antiquity; the earliest date from the Chalcolithic Period (*c.* 4000–3000 BCE). As Rabbah, it became the capital of the Ammonites. It was conquered by Egypt's Ptolemy II (Ptolemy Philadelphus), who renamed it Philadelphia, a name it retained through Roman times. Taken by the Arabs in 635 CE, it later went into decline and subsequently disappeared. In 1878 the Ottoman Empire resettled it. When the British established the country of Transjordan in 1921, Amman became its capital. Its modern development was furthered by the independence of Transjordan in 1946. Along with the rest of Jordan (the country's name from 1949), Amman has had to absorb a large number of Arab refugees that fled Palestine during the Arab-Israeli wars.

ammonia, Colourless, pungent gas composed of nitrogen and hydrogen, chemical formula NH_3. Easily liquefied by compression or cooling for use in refrigerating and air-conditioning equipment, it is manufactured in huge quantities. Ammonia is made by the Haber-Bosch process. Its major use is as a fertilizer, applied directly to soil from tanks of the liquefied gas. Also employed as fertilizers are salts of ammonia, including ammonium phosphate and ammonium nitrate (the latter used in high explosives as well). Ammonia has many other industrial uses as a raw material, catalyst, and alkali. It dissolves readily in water to form ammonium hydroxide, an alkaline solution familiar as a household cleaner.

amnesia, Loss of memory as a result of brain injury or deterioration, shock, fatigue, senility, drug use, alcoholism, anesthesia, illness, or neurotic reaction. Amnesia may be anterograde (in which events following the causative trauma or disease are forgotten) or retrograde (in which events preceding the trauma or disease are forgotten). It can often be traced to a severe emotional shock, in which case personal memories (in effect, identity) rather than such abilities as language skills are affected. Such amnesia seems to represent an escape from disturbing memories and is thus an example of repression; these memories can generally be recovered through psychotherapy or after the amnesic state has ended. Amnesia may occasionally last for weeks, months, or even years, a condition known as fugue.

amnesty, In criminal law, a sovereign act of oblivion or forgetfulness (from Greek *amnestia,* "forgetfulness") granted by a government, especially to a group of persons who are guilty of (usually political) crimes in the past. It is often conditional upon the group's return to obedience and duty within a prescribed period.

Amnesty International (AI), International human rights organization. It was founded in 1961 by Peter Benenson, a London lawyer who organized a letter-writing campaign calling for amnesty for "prisoners of conscience." AI seeks to inform the public about violations of human rights, especially abridgments of freedom of speech and religion and the imprisonment and torture of political dissidents. It actively seeks the release of political prisoners and the support of their families when necessary. Fifty years after its founding, its members and supporters were estimated to number three million people in some 150 countries. Its first director, Seán MacBride, won the 1974 Nobel Prize for Peace, and AI itself won the award in 1977.

amniocentesis, Surgical insertion of a hollow needle through the abdominal wall into the uterus of a pregnant female to extract fluid from the amniotic sac for analysis of fluid and fetal cells. This can reveal the fetus's sex (important when sex-linked genetic disease is possible), chromosomal disorders, and other problems. First performed in the 1930s, amniocentesis is generally done under local anesthesia in the 15th–17th week of gestation.

amoeba, One-celled protozoan that can form temporary extensions of cytoplasm (pseudopodia) in order to move about. Some amoebas are found on the bottom of freshwater streams and ponds. Others live in the human digestive system; one type causes amebic dysentery in humans. Each amoeba contains a small mass of jellylike cytoplasm with vacuoles and a nucleus. Food is taken in and material is excreted at any point on the cell surface. Amoebas are used extensively in cell research for determining the relative functions and interactions of the nucleus and the cytoplasm.

Amoeba (magnified).
Russ Kinne/Photo Researchers

Amon, or AMEN, Egyptian deity revered as king of the gods. Amon may have originally been one of the eight deities of the Hermapolite creation myth. His cult spread to Thebes, where he became patron of the pharaohs by Mentuhotep I's reign (2008–1957 BCE) and was identified with the sun god Re. Represented as a human, a ram, or both, Amon-Re was worshiped with the goddess Mut and the youthful god Khons. Akhenaton directed his reforms against the cult of Amon, but with little success, and Amon's status was restored in the 14th–13th century BCE. In the New Kingdom, Amon came to be seen as one of a triad with Ptah and Re, and in the 11th–10th century BCE as a universal god who intervened in affairs of state by speaking through oracles.

amortization, In finance, the systematic repayment of a debt; in accounting, the systematic writing off of some account over a period of years. An example of the first meaning is a home mortgage, which may be repaid in monthly installments that include interest and a gradual reduction of the principal. Such systematic reduction is safer for the lender, since it is easier for the borrower to repay a series of small amounts than a single lump sum. In the second sense, a firm may gradually reduce the balance-sheet valuation of a depreciable asset such as a building, machine, or mine. The U.S. government has sometimes permitted accelerated amortization of assets, which encourages industrial development by decreasing a company's tax burden in the years immediately after a purchase.

amphetamine, Organic compound, prototype of a class of synthetic amphetamine drugs (e.g., Benzedrine, Dexedrine, methamphetamine), that stimulates the central nervous system. It was first synthesized in 1887. Amphetamines cause wakefulness, euphoria, decreased fatigue, and increased ability to concentrate. Since they dull the appetite, they have been used for weight reduction. Often called "speed," they are used (often illicitly) to stay awake. In children with attention deficit (hyperactivity) disorder, they have a calming effect, helping them concentrate. Undesirable effects include overstimulation, with paranoia, restlessness, insomnia, tremor, and irritability, and a deep depression when the drug wears off. This, along with rapid development of tolerance requiring increased doses, can lead to drug addiction.

amphibian, Any member of a class (Amphibia) of cold-blooded vertebrate animals that includes more than 6,200 species in three groups: frogs and toads (order Anura), salamanders (order Caudata), and caecilians (order Gymnophiona). Probably evolved from certain fish species of the Early Devonian Epoch (416–397 million years ago), amphibians were the first vertebrates to move from an aquatic environment to land. Most species have an aquatic larval, or tadpole, stage that metamorphoses into a terrestrial adult, but a few species spend their entire life in water. Amphibians are found worldwide, the majority in the tropics.

amphitheater, Freestanding, open-air round or oval structure with a central arena and tiers of concentric seats. The amphitheater originated in ancient Italy (Etruria and Campania) and reflects the entertainment forms popular there, including gladiatorial games and contests of animals with one another or of men with animals. The earliest extant amphitheater is one built at Pompeii (c. 80 BC). Examples survive throughout the former provinces of the Roman empire, the most famous being Rome's Colosseum.

amputation, Removal of any part of the body, usually surgical removal of part or all of a limb. Congenital amputation means lack of a limb at birth. Surgical amputation may be a lifesaving measure to prevent excessive blood loss from injury or to check the spread of infection, gangrene, or malignant soft-tissue or bone tumours. Reconstructive surgery, prompt treatment with blood and plasma, and rehabilitation have made amputation rarer than in the past. Prostheses reduce handicaps for amputees, whose surgery may have been designed with a prosthesis in mind.

Amsterdam, City (pop., 2010 est.: city, 767,457; 2008 est.: metro. area, 1,482,287), western Netherlands. It lies at the head of the IJsselmeer. It is the nominal capital of the Netherlands, whose seat of government is at The Hague. Originally a fishing village, it received its charter as a town in 1306. It joined the Hanseatic League in 1369 and grew steadily in the 14th and 15th centuries. After the decline of Antwerp at the end of the 16th century, Amsterdam became the source of growing Dutch commercial and naval power. It was the centre for the Dutch East India and West India companies and became the leading trade metropolis of Europe. It became part of the Kingdom of Holland, which entered the Kingdom of the Netherlands in 1815. After suffering a partial decline in the 18th century, its prosperity increased when it became connected by canal to the North Sea in the late 19th century. It was occupied by Germany in World War II. After the war Amsterdam became known as a place of tolerance and liberalism. The city is now a major European port and a hub for international finance and trade.

Amu Darya, ancient OXUS RIVER, River, Central Asia. It is one of the longest rivers in Central Asia, 1,578 mi (2,540 km) long measured from the remotest sources of the Panj River; its other headstream is the Vakhsh. It flows west-northwest to its mouth on the Aral Sea. It forms part of Afghanistan's borders with Tajikistan, Uzbekistan, and Turkmenistan and part of Uzbekistan's border with Turkmenistan.

Amundsen, Roald (Engelbregt Gravning) (b. July 16, 1872, Borge, near Oslo, Nor.—disappeared June 18, 1928?, Arctic Ocean), Norwegian explorer, leader of the first group to reach the South Pole. In 1897 he took part in a Belgian expedition that was the first to winter in the Antarctic. In 1903–05 he was the first to navigate the Northwest Passage. He planned an expedition to the North Pole, but, after learning that Robert E. Peary had reached that goal, he set off for the South Pole in 1910. He prepared his trip carefully and in October 1911 set out with four men, 52 dogs, and four sledges. He reached the South Pole in December 1911, one month before Robert Falcon Scott's ill-fated attempt. He returned to Norway and established a successful shipping business. In 1926 he and Umberto Nobile (1885–1978) passed over the North Pole in a dirigible. Amundsen disappeared in 1928 while flying to rescue Nobile from a dirigible crash.

Roald Amundsen, 1923.
UPI/Bettmann

Amur River, Chinese HEILONG JIANG, or HEI-LUNG CHIANG, River, northeastern Asia. The Amur proper begins at the confluence of the Shilka and Argun rivers and is 1,755 mi (2,824 km) long. It flows east-southeast along the Russian-Chinese border to Khabarovsk, Siberia, and then northeast across Russian territory to empty into the Tatar Strait. Among its tributaries are the Zeya, Bureya, and Ussuri rivers. Since the 18th century, Russians have settled to the north of the river and Chinese to the south, a situation that since 1950 has provoked occasional border clashes.

amyotrophic lateral sclerosis (ALS), or LOU GEHRIG DISEASE, Degenerative nervous-system disorder causing muscle wasting and paralysis. The disease usually occurs after age 40, more often in men. Most victims die within two to five years from respiratory muscle atrophy. ALS affects motor neurons; the muscles they control become weak and atrophied, with debility usually beginning in the hands and creeping slowly up to the shoulders. The lower limbs become weak and spastic. Variants include progressive muscular atrophy and progressive bulbar palsy. In

1993 the defective gene that accounts for 5–10% of cases was discovered; it produces an ineffective version of an enzyme that neutralizes free radicals, which destroy motor neurons.

Anabaptist, Member of a movement of the Protestant Reformation characterized by adult baptism. Anabaptists held that infants were not punishable for sin because they had no awareness of good and evil and thus could not yet exercise free will, repent, and accept baptism. Denying the validity of infant baptism, they accepted adult baptism, which was regarded as a second baptism by those outside the group who identified them as Anabaptists (from the Greek for rebaptizers). Confident of living at the end of time, early Anabaptists sought to restore the institutions and spirit of the primitive church. The first adult baptisms took place outside Zürich in early 1525. Most Anabaptists were pacifists and refused to swear civil oaths. Thomas Müntzer advocated a more violent eschatology that called for the overthrow of the rich by the poor and was executed after leading the Thuringian peasant revolt (1525). Another group of Anabaptists, led by John of Leiden, took control of the city of Münster and sought to establish the millennial kingdom. Their excesses led to their violent suppression in 1535 and further persecution and martyrdom of the Anabaptists. Many Anabaptists settled in Moravia, where they stressed the community of goods modeled on the primitive church at Jerusalem. This branch continues as the Hutterite movement, primarily in the western U.S. and Canada. Increasingly persecuted throughout Europe, Anabaptists in the Netherlands and northern Germany rallied under the leadership of Menno Simonsz. and survive as the Mennonites.

anabolic steroid, Steroid hormone that increases tissue growth. Anabolic steroids are given to promote muscle growth and tissue regeneration in, for example, elderly or postoperative patients. Unsupervised use by athletes to build muscle and improve strength can have serious harmful effects, including coronary heart disease, sexual and reproductive disorders, immunodeficiencies, liver damage, stunted growth, aggressive behaviour, susceptibility to connective-tissue injury, and (in females) irreversible masculinization.

anaconda, Either of two South American snake species in the genus *Eunectes* (family Boidae) that constrict their prey. The heavily built giant anaconda, or great water boa, is usually not more than 16 ft (5 m) long but can be longer than 24 ft (7.5 m), rivaling the largest pythons in length. The yellow anaconda is much smaller. Typically dark green with alternating oval black spots, the giant anaconda lives along tropical rivers east of the Andes and in Trinidad. It kills at night by lying in wait in water; it constricts prey as large as young pigs or caimans and occasionally forages in trees for birds. It may bear 75 live young at a time.

Green anaconda (Eunectes murinus).
© Z. Leszczynski/Animals Animals

analgesic, Drug that relieves pain without blocking nerve impulse conduction or markedly altering sensory function. Two classes are defined by the type of pain-relieving action. Opioids (opiates and synthetic narcotics; *see* opium) act on brain receptors to inhibit pain impulses. They may be used for short- or long-term pain relief, usually by prescription, but carry a risk of drug addiction. Nonopioids, used mostly for short-term relief and modest pain, are available without prescription. They include NSAIDs (including aspirin and ibuprofen) and acetaminophen; all act by inhibiting synthesis of prostaglandins, molecules involved in the peripheral perception of pain.

analysis, Field of mathematics that incorporates the methods of algebra and calculus—specifically of limits, continuity, and infinite series—to analyze classes of functions and equations having general properties (e.g., differentiability). Analysis builds on the work of G.W. Leibniz and Isaac Newton by exploring the applications of the derivative and the integral. Several distinct but related subfields have developed, including the calculus of variations, differential equations, Fourier analysis, complex analysis, vector and tensor analysis, real analysis, and functional analysis.

analytic geometry, Investigation of geometric objects using coordinate systems. Because René Descartes was the first to apply algebra to geometry, it is also known as Cartesian geometry. It springs from the idea that any point in two-dimensional space can be represented by two numbers and any point in three-dimensional space by three. Because lines, circles, spheres, and other figures can be thought of as collections of points in space that satisfy certain equations, they can be explored via equations and formulas rather than graphs. Most of analytic geometry deals with the conic sections. Because these are defined using the notion of fixed distance, each section can be represented by a general equation derived from the distance formula.

analytic psychology, Psychoanalytic method of Carl Jung as he distinguished it from that of Sigmund Freud. Jung attached less importance than did Freud to the role of childhood sexual conflicts in the development of neurosis. Moreover, he defined the unconscious to include both the individual's own unconscious and that inherited, partly in the form of archetypes, from his or her ancestors (the "collective unconscious"). He classified people into introvert and extravert types and further distinguished them according to four primary functions of the mind—thinking, feeling, sensation, and intuition—one or more of which predominated in any given person.

anaphylaxis, Severe, immediate, potentially fatal bodily reaction to contact with a substance (antigen) to which the individual has previously been exposed. Often triggered by antiserum, antibiotics, or insect stings, the reaction's symptoms include skin flushing, bronchial swelling (with difficulty breathing), and loss of consciousness. Shock may follow. Milder cases may involve hives and severe headache. Treatment, consisting of injection of epinephrine, followed by antihistamines, cortisone, or similar drugs, must begin within minutes. Anaphylaxis may be caused by extremely small amounts of antigen.

anarchism, Political theory holding all forms of government authority to be unnecessary and undesirable and advocating a society based on voluntary cooperation and free association of individuals and groups. The word was used only pejoratively until Pierre-Joseph Proudhon, now regarded as the founder of anarchism, adopted it in *What is Property?* (1840). The anarchist Mikhail Bakunin clashed with Karl Marx at the First International; when it was dissolved in 1872, Bakunin's followers retained control of workers' organizations in Latin countries such as Spain and Italy. Even anarchists who believed that the transition to a government-free society required violent revolution disagreed on the nature of the transition. Anarcho-syndicalism, which developed in the late 1880s, emphasized labour unions (*syndicats*) and called for general strikes to paralyze the state. In the 19th and 20th centuries, anarchism also inspired experimental communities, including New Lanark in Britain and Brook Farm in the U.S. During the early months of the Spanish Civil War, anarchist militias were in virtual control of much of eastern Spain, where they established hundreds of anarchist collectives. Suppressed as an organized movement by fascism in the 1930s, anarchism reemerged in the 1950s and '60s through its influence on the civil rights movement and the student movements in the U.S. and Europe. The radical ecology movement in the 1970s also was inspired by anarchist ideas. Beginning in 1999, anarchist-led street demonstrations against the World Bank and International Monetary Fund received unprecedented publicity and inspired new anarchist groups, periodicals, and Internet sites. Anarchist themes are reflected in the work of many 20th-century artists, writers, and musicians, including Pablo Picasso, the American poets of the Beat movement, the Spanish Surrealist filmmaker Luis Buñuel, and the American composer John Cage.

Anatolia, or ASIA MINOR, Turkish ANADOLU, Peninsula forming the western extremity of Asia. It is bounded by the Black Sea to the north, the Mediterranean Sea to the south, and the Aegean Sea to the west. Its eastern boundary is generally marked by the southeastern Taurus Mountains. Anatolia is roughly contiguous with the Asian portion of the modern Republic of Turkey. Because of its location at the point where Asia and Europe meet, it has long been the scene of numerous migrations and conquests. It was the original location of the kingdom of Hittites (*c.* 1700–1180 BCE). Later, Indo-European peoples, possibly Thracian, established the Phrygian kingdom. In the 6th century BCE the Persian Achaemenian dynasty came to rule the area; it was conquered by Alexander the Great in 334–333 BCE. Beginning in the 1st century BCE, the area was absorbed into the Roman Republic and Empire. When the empire split in 395 CE, Anatolia became part of the Byzantine Empire. The area endured invasions by Arabs, Turks, Crusaders, Mongols, and the Turkic army of Timur before the Ottoman Empire established full control in the 15th century. From 1923 its history was that of modern Turkey.

ancestor worship, Religious beliefs or practices that involve addressing prayers or offerings to the spirits of dead relatives. It existed among the ancient Greeks, other Mediterranean peoples, and the ancient Europeans; it also plays a major role in traditional African religions. The dead are related to the family, clan, tribe, or village; mythical ancestors may be included. They may be friendly, or they may be displeased and require propitiation. Commemorative ceremonies are sometimes held at graves or monuments and may include prayers, offerings, sacrifices, and festivals of honor. Worship of individual ancestors is common; it may be combined with communal forms of worship, as in the case of the Roman emperor cult. An ancestor whose deeds are heroic may attain the status of a god. In China and Japan, ancestor worship (more accurately, ancestor reverence) has declined with the decline in the size and importance of kinship groups.

Anchorage, Seaport, largest city (pop., 2010: 291,826), and chief commercial centre of Alaska, U.S. It lies at the head of Cook Inlet near the base of the Kenai Peninsula. It was founded in 1914 as a construction camp for the building of a railroad to Fairbanks. It became a key aviation and defense centre in World War II and is now a regular stop on air routes from the U.S. to East Asia. Anchorage experienced rapid population growth in the late 20th century. In 1964 a severe earthquake caused a number of deaths and extensive property damage.

anchovy, Any of more than 100 species of schooling saltwater fishes (family Engraulidae) related to the herring. Anchovies are distinguished by a large mouth, almost always extending behind the eye, and by a pointed snout. Most species live in shallow tropical or warm temperate seas, where they often enter brackish water around river mouths. Adults are 4–10 in. (10–25 cm) long. Temperate species such as the northern and European anchovies are important food fishes; tropical species such as the tropical anchovy, or anchoveta, are important bait fishes.

Anchovies (Engraulis mordax)
Tom McHugh/Photo Researchers

Andaman and Nicobar Islands, Union territory (pop., 2008 est.: 411,000), India. It consists of two groups of islands in the Bay

Andaman redwood on the coast of Cinque Island, south of Rutland Island, Andaman Islands.
© Ashvin Mehta/Dinodia Photo Library

of Bengal about 800 mi (1,300 km) east of the Indian subcontinent and Sri Lanka; the total area is 3,185 sq mi (8,249 sq km). The chief islands are North Andaman, Middle Andaman, and South Andaman (known collectively as Great Andaman), and Little Andaman. The Nicobar group includes Car Nicobar, Camorta (Kamorta) and Nancowry, and Great Nicobar. Of the hundreds of islands that constitute the territory, the number of populated islands of the Andaman group is about double that of the Nicobar group. Port Blair on South Andaman, established by the British in 1858, is the territorial capital.

Andaman Sea, Sea, eastern extension of the Bay of Bengal. Bounded by the Andaman and Nicobar Islands, Myanmar, the Malay Peninsula, and the Strait of Malacca and Sumatra, it covers some 308,000 sq mi (798,000 sq km). Trading vessels have plied the sea since ancient times. Part of the early coastal trade route between India and China, from the 8th century it formed a route between India (and Sri Lanka) and Myanmar. Its largest modern ports are George Town (Malaysia) and Yangôn (Myanmar). A large earthquake-generated tsunami in 2004 inundated many of the sea's coastal areas.

Andean civilization, Complex of aboriginal cultures that evolved in the Andean region of western South America before the arrival of the Spanish conquistadores in the 16th century. Unlike the peoples of the Mesoamerican civilization to the north, none of the aboriginal Andean peoples developed a system of writing, though the Inca devised a sophisticated system of recording numbers. In its level of cultural development and technical expertise in the arts and crafts, however, this civilization constitutes a New World counterpart to those of ancient Egypt, China, and Mesopotamia.

Andersen, Hans Christian (b. April 2, 1805, Odense, near Copenhagen, Den.—d. Aug. 4, 1875, Copenhagen), Danish writer of fairy tales. Though reared in poverty, he received a university education. In his many collections of tales, published 1835–72, he broke with literary tradition and employed the idioms and constructions of spoken language. His stories are imaginative combinations of universal elements from folk legend and include such favourites as "The Ugly Duckling" and "The Emperor's New Clothes." While some reveal an optimistic belief in the ultimate triumph of goodness and beauty (e.g., "The Snow Queen"), others are deeply pessimistic. Part of what makes his tales compelling is the way they identify with the unfortunate and outcast. He also wrote plays, novels, poems, travel books, and several autobiographies.

Hans Christian Andersen.
The Bettmann Archive

Andes Mountains, Mountain system, western South America. One of the great natural features of the globe, the Andes extend north-south about 5,500 mi (8,900 km). They run parallel to the Caribbean Sea coast in Venezuela before turning southwest and entering Colombia. There they form three distinct massifs: the Cordilleras Oriental, Central, and Occidental. In Ecuador they form two parallel cordilleras, one facing the Pacific and the other descending toward the Amazon River basin. These ranges continue southward into Peru; the highest Peruvian peak is Mount Huascarán (22,205 ft [6,768 m]) in the Cordillera Blanca. In Bolivia the Andes again form two distinct regions; between them lies the Altiplano. Along the border of Chile and Argentina, they form a complex chain that includes their highest peak, Mount Aconcagua, which reaches an elevation of 22,831 ft (6,959 m). In southern Chile part of the cordillera descends beneath the sea and forms numerous islands. The Andes are studded with a number of volcanoes that form part of the Circum-Pacific chain known as the Ring of Fire. The Andes mountain system is the source of many rivers, including the Amazon and Pilcomayo.

Andhra Pradesh, State (pop., 2008 est.: 82,180,000), southeastern India. Located on the Bay of Bengal, it is bordered by Tamil Nadu, Karnataka, Maharashtra, Chhattisgarh, and Orissa states. Covering 106,204 sq mi (275,068 sq km), it was created in 1953 and achieved its present-day form in 1956; its capital is Hyderabad. Its name derives from the Telugu-speaking Andhra people, who have long inhabited the area. Many dynasties have flourished there, dating roughly to the 4th century BCE. The area came under British influence in the 17th century. In the 19th century the Andhras played a decisive role in the rise of Indian nationalism. Although the state's economy is primarily agricultural, it also is one of the most industrialized in India.

Andijon, or ANDIZHAN, City (pop., 2000 est.: 336,500), eastern Uzbekistan. Dating to at least the 9th century AD, it was an important trading centre in the 15th century because of its location on the Silk Road. Part of the khanate of Kokand in the 18th century, it was captured by the Russians in 1876. The surrounding area is the most densely populated part of Uzbekistan and the country's main petroleum-producing region.

Andorra, officially PRINCIPALITY OF ANDORRA, Parliamentary coprincipality, southwestern Europe. Area: 179 sq mi (464 sq km). Population: (2011 est.) 85,600. Capital: Andorra la Vella. Lying on the southern slopes of the Pyrenees, it consists of a cluster of mountain valleys whose streams form the Valira River; it is bounded by Spain and France. Much of the population is Spanish or Andorran. Language: Catalan (official). Religion: Christianity (predominantly Roman Catholic; also other Christians). Currency: euro. Andorra's independence is traditionally ascribed to Charlemagne, who recovered the region from the Muslims in 803 CE. It was placed under the joint suzerainty of the French counts of Foix and the Spanish bishops of Urgel in 1278, and it was subsequently governed jointly by the Spanish bishop of Urgel and the French head of state. This feudal system of government, the last in Europe, continued until 1993, when a constitution was adopted that transferred most of the coprinces' powers to the Andorran General Council, which is elected by universal suffrage. Andorra has long had a strong affinity with Catalonia; its institutions are based in Catalonian law, and it is part of the diocese of Urgel (Spain). The traditional economy was based on sheep raising, but tourism grew in importance since the 1950s and became central to Andorra's economy by the early 21st century.

Andorra la Vella, Town (pop., 2001 est.: 20,800), capital of Andorra. It lies near the confluence of the Valira and Valira del Norte rivers. The town long remained relatively isolated from the outside world, but its population began to grow after World War II as tourists began arriving at the nearby sports areas. Because of its country's duty-free status, the town has become a retail shopping centre for other Europeans.

Andrić, Ivo (b. Oct. 10, 1892, Dolac, near Travnik, Bosnia—d. March 13, 1975, Belgrade, Yugos.), Bosnian writer. He established his reputation with *Ex Ponto* (1918), which he wrote while interned for nationalist political activities in World War I. He later served as a Yugoslavian diplomat. Collections of his short stories were published from 1920 onward. Of his three novels, written during World War II, two—*The Bridge on the Drina* (1945) and *Bosnian Story* (1945)—are about the history of Bosnia. He was awarded the Nobel Prize for Literature in 1961.

androgen, Any of a group of hormones that mainly influence the development of the male reproductive system. The main and most active androgen is testosterone, produced by cells in the testes. Androgens produced in smaller quantities, mainly by the adrenal gland but also by the testes, support the functions of testosterone. Androgens cause the normal changes of puberty in boys' bodies and then influence sperm-cell formation, sexual interest and behaviour, and male pattern baldness. Females produce trace quantities of androgens, mostly in the adrenal glands, as well as in the ovaries.

Andromeda Galaxy, or M31, Great spiral galaxy in the constellation Andromeda. It is the nearest spiral galaxy outside the Milky Way Galaxy and one of the few visible to the unaided eye, appearing as a milky blur. About 2 million light-years from Earth, it has a diameter of about 200,000 light-years, which makes it the largest galaxy in the Local Group. For centuries astronomers considered it part of the Milky Way; only in the 1920s did Edwin Hubble determine conclusively that it was a separate galaxy.

anemia, Condition in which erythrocytes are reduced in number or volume or are deficient in hemoglobin. The patient is usually noticeably pale. Close to 100 varieties exist (including aplastic anemia, pernicious anemia, and sickle-cell anemia), distinguished by cause; erythrocyte size, shape, and hemoglobin content; and symptoms. Anemia may result from blood loss; increased destruction, reduced production, or inhibited formation of red cells; or hormone deficiency. Treatment may involve nutrition, toxin removal, drugs, surgery, or transfusion.

anemone, Any of more than 100 species of perennial plants that make up the genus *Anemone*, in the buttercup family, many of which are cultivated for their colourful flowers. Though found throughout the world, anemones are most common in woodlands and meadows of the northern temperate zone. Many varieties of the tuberous, poppylike anemone *A. coronaria* are grown for the garden and florist trade. Popular spring-flowering species include *A. apennina*, *A. blanda*, and *A. pavonina*. Other species, such as the Japanese anemone (*A. hupehensis*, or *A. japonica*), are favourite border plants for autumn flowering. The European wood anemone, *A. nemorosa*, causes blistering of the skin and was once used as an ingredient in medicines. Anemones are also known colloquially as pasqueflowers or windflowers.

anesthetic, Agent that produces a local or general loss of sensation, including pain, and therefore is useful in surgery and dentistry. General anesthesia induces loss of consciousness, most often using hydrocarbons (e.g., cyclopropane, ethylene); halogenated hydrocarbons (e.g., chloroform, ethyl chloride, trichloroethylene); ethers (e.g., ethyl ether or vinyl ether); or other compounds, such as tribromoethanol, nitrous oxide, or barbiturates. Local anesthesia induces loss of sensation in one area of the body by blocking nerve conduction, usually with alkaloids such as cocaine or synthetic substitutes (e.g., lidocaine).

aneurysm, Blood-filled protrusion in the wall of a blood vessel (usually an artery, and particularly the aorta). Disease or injury weakens the wall so that normal blood pressure makes it balloon out. Typically, the two inner layers rupture and the outer layer bulges. In a false aneurysm, all three layers rupture and surrounding tissues hold the blood in place. Symptoms vary with size and location. Aneurysms tend to enlarge over time, and blood-vessel walls weaken with age. Many aneurysms eventually burst, causing serious, even massive, internal bleeding; aortic aneurysm rupture causes severe pain and immediate collapse. Rupture of an aneurysm in the brain is a major cause of strokes. Treatment can

consist of simply tying off a small vessel; more serious aneurysms require surgery to replace the diseased section of artery with a plastic graft.

angel, Primarily in Western religions, any of numerous benevolent spiritual beings who mediate between earth and heaven. They often serve as messengers or servants of God or as guardians of an individual or nation. In Zoroastrianism the *amesha spenta* are arranged in a hierarchy of seven. Judaism and Christianity base their notion of angels on references in the Hebrew scriptures to divine servants and to the heavenly hosts. Two archangels (Michael and Gabriel) are mentioned in the Old Testament and two others (Raphael and Uriel) in the Apocrypha. Angels are mentioned throughout the Christian scriptures, and Christian tradition identifies nine orders of angels. Islam's hierarchy of angels descends from the four throne bearers of God to the cherubim who praise God, the four archangels, and lesser angels such as the *ḥafaẓah* (guardian angels).

Angel Falls, Waterfall, southeastern Venezuela. It lies on the Churún River, a tributary of the Caroní, southeast of Ciudad Bolívar. The highest waterfall in the world, the cataract drops 3,212 ft (979 m) and is 500 ft (150 m) wide at its base. It was named for James Angel, an American who crash-landed his plane nearby in 1937.

Angel Falls (Salto Ángel), La Gran Sabana region of Bolívar state, Venezuela.
G. De Steinheil/Shostal Associates

Angevin dynasty, Descendants of a 10th-century count of Anjou (the source of the adjective Angevin). The Angevin dynasty overlaps with the house of Plantagenet but is usually said to consist of only the English kings Henry II, Richard I, and John. Henry established the Angevin empire in the 1150s when he took control of Normandy, Anjou, Maine, and, through his marriage to Eleanor, Aquitaine. When he became the king of England in 1154, Henry extended the Angevin holdings from Scotland to the Pyrenees. English claims to French territory led to the Hundred Years' War; by 1558 the English had lost all their former French lands.

angina pectoris, Spasm of chest pain, caused when the heart's oxygen demand temporarily outpaces its blood supply, usually because of coronary heart disease. A deep, viselike pain in the heart and stomach area commonly spreads to the left arm. Exertion or emotional stress can bring on angina, obliging the victim to rest until the pain subsides. If rest does not help, drugs can dilate the blood vessels. As heart disease worsens, angina recurs with less exertion.

angioplasty, Therapeutic opening of a blocked blood vessel. Usually a balloon is inflated near the end of a catheter to flatten plaques against an artery's wall. Performed on a coronary artery, angioplasty is a less invasive alternative to coronary bypass surgery in the treatment of coronary heart disease. Complications, including embolisms and tearing, are rare and results are excellent, but plaques tend to build up again after the procedure. Angioplasty is also used to expand a severely obstructed heart valve.

Angkor, Archaeological site, northwestern Cambodia. Located 4 mi (6 km) north of the modern town of Siĕmréab (Siem Reap), it was the capital of the Khmer (Cambodian) empire from the 9th to the 15th century. Its most imposing monuments are Angkor Wat, a temple complex built in the 12th century by King Suryavarman

II, and Angkor Thom, a temple complex built *c.* 1200 by King Jayavarman VII. During the period of great construction that lasted more than 300 years, there were many changes in architecture as the religious focus changed from Hindu to Buddhist cults. After the Tai conquest of the Khmer in the 15th century, the ruined city and its temples were buried in the jungle. When the French colonial regime was established in 1863, the entire site became the focus of scholarly interest. During Cambodia's political upheavals of the late 20th century, there was some war damage, but the major problem was one of neglect. Angkor was designated a UNESCO World Heritage site in 1992.

Angkor Wat, Temple complex in Angkor (now in northwestern Cambodia), the crowning work of Khmer architecture. About 1,700 yards (1,550 m) long by 1,500 yards (1,400 m) wide, it is the world's largest religious structure. Dedicated to Vishnu, it was built in the 12th century by Suryavarman II. The Wat, an artificial mountain originally surrounded by a vast external wall and moat, rises in three enclosures toward a flat summit. The five remaining towers (shrines) at the summit are composed of the repetitive diminishing tiers typical of Asian architecture.

Angle, Any member of a Germanic people who, with the Jutes and Saxons, invaded England in the 5th century AD. According to Bede, their homeland was Angulus, traditionally identified as the Angeln district in Schleswig. They abandoned this area when they invaded Britain, where they settled in the kingdoms of Mercia, Northumbria, East Anglia, and Middle Anglia. Their language was known, even then, as Englisc, and they gave their name to England.

Anglo-Saxon law, Body of legal principles that prevailed in England from the 6th century until the Norman Conquest (1066). It was directly influenced by early Scandinavian law as a result of the Viking invasions of the 8th and 9th centuries and indirectly influenced (primarily through the church) by Roman law. Anglo-Saxon law had three components: laws promulgated by the king, customary practices such as those regulating kinship relations, and private compilations. The primary emphasis was on criminal law, though certain material dealt with problems of public administration, public order, and ecclesiastical matters.

Angola, officially REPUBLIC OF ANGOLA,, formerly PORTUGUESE WEST AFRICA, Country, southern Africa. Its northernmost section of coastland, the Cabinda exclave, is separated from Angola proper by a narrow corridor of Congo territory. Area: 481,354 sq mi (1,246,700 sq km). Population: (2011 est.) 19,618,000. Capital: Luanda. The population is made up of mostly Bantu-speaking peoples; the main ethnic groups are the Ovimbundu and the Mbundu. Languages: Portuguese (official), indigenous languages. Religions: Christianity (mostly Roman Catholic; also Protestant); also traditional beliefs. Currency: kwanza. The country contains several plateau regions, which separate it into three distinct drainage systems. One in the northeast drains into the Congo River basin, and another, in the southeastern sector, drains into the Zambezi system; the remaining drainage, westward into the Atlantic, provides most of Angola's hydroelectric power. About half of the land area is forest; less than 10% is arable. With the exception of the development of the country's substantial petroleum reserves, Angola's economy has long been unable to take advantage of its natural resources because of the devastation caused by the protracted civil war. Angola is nominally a unitary multiparty republic with one legislative house; its head of state and government is the president. An influx of Bantu-speaking peoples in the 1st millennium CE led to their dominance in the area by *c.* 1500. The most important Bantu kingdom was Kongo; south of Kongo was the Ndongo kingdom of the Mbundu people. Portuguese explorers arrived in the early 1480s and over time gradually extended their rule. Angola's frontiers were largely determined by other European powers in the 19th century but not without strong resistance by the indigenous peoples. Resistance to colonial rule led to the outbreak of fighting in 1961, which led ultimately to independence in 1975. Rival factions continued fighting after independence. Although a peace accord was reached in 1994, forces led by Jonas M. Savimbi continued to resist government control until his death in 2002. A lasting peace accord was signed shortly thereafter, ending 27 years of civil war.

Angola made its Olympic debut at the 1980 Summer Games in Moscow.

Anhui, or AN-HUI, conventional ANHWEI, Province (pop., 2002 est.: 63,380,000), east-central China. It is bounded by Jiangsu, Zhejiang, Jiangxi, Hubei, Shandong, and Henan provinces. With an area of 54,000 sq mi (139,900 sq km), it is one of China's smallest provinces; its capital is Hefei. Anhui was the first part of southern China to be settled by the Han dynasty, from *c.* 205 BCE. Well-watered by the Huai and Yangtze (Chang) rivers, it was the empire's major agricultural area for several centuries. Anhui was ruled by the Ming dynasty in the 14th–17th centuries. It was occupied by the Japanese in World War II; after the war the Nationalists held it briefly before the communists took over. It remains a notable agricultural producer.

aniline, One of the most important organic bases, parent substance for many dyes and drugs. Pure aniline is a highly poisonous, oily, colourless liquid with a distinctive odour. First obtained (1826) from indigo, it is now prepared synthetically. It is a weakly basic primary aromatic amine and participates in many reactions with other compounds. It is used to make chemicals used in producing rubber, dyes and intermediates, photographic chemicals, urethane foams, pharmaceuticals, explosives, herbicides, and fungicides as well as to make chemicals used in petroleum refining.

animation, Process of giving the illusion of movement to drawings, models, or inanimate objects. From the mid-1850s, such optical devices as the zoetrope produced the illusion of animation. Stop-action photography enabled the production of cartoon films. The innovative design and assembly techniques of Walt Disney soon moved him to the forefront of the animation industry, and he produced a series of classic animated films, beginning with *Snow White and the Seven Dwarfs* (1937). The Fleischer brothers and the animators at Warner Brothers offered more irreverent cartoons that often appealed to adult audiences. In Europe new animation alternatives to line drawing were developed, including animation using puppets (sometimes made from clay). In the late 20th century computer animation, as seen in the first fully computer-generated animated feature, *Toy Story* (1995), moved the art to a new level.

animé, Style of animation popular in Japanese films. *Animé* films are meant primarily for the Japanese market and, as such, employ many cultural references unique to Japan. For example, the large eyes of *animé* characters are commonly perceived in Japan as multifaceted "windows to the soul." Much of the genre is aimed at the children's market, but *animé* films are sometimes marked by adult themes and subject matter. Modern *animé* began in 1956 and found lasting success in 1961 with the establishment of Mushi Productions by Osamu Tezuka, a leading figure in modern *manga* (Japanese comics). Such *animé* as *Akira* (1988), *Princess Mononoke* (1997), and the *Pokémon* series of films have attained international popularity.

animism, Belief in the existence of spirits separable from bodies. Such beliefs are traditionally identified with small-scale ("primitive") societies, though they also occur in major world religions. They were first competently surveyed by Edward Burnett Tylor in *Primitive Culture* (1871). Classic animism, according to Tylor, consists of attributing conscious life to natural objects or phenomena, a practice that eventually gave rise to the notion of a soul.

anise, Annual herb (*Pimpinella anisum*) of the parsley family, cultivated chiefly for its fruit, called aniseed, which tastes like licorice. Native to Egypt and the eastern Mediterranean region, anise is cultivated throughout the world. Aniseed is used as a flavouring and as a soothing herbal tea. Star anise is the dried fruit of the evergreen tree *Illicium verum* (magnolia family), native to southeastern China and Vietnam. Its flavour and uses are similar to those of anise.

Ankara, formerly ANGORA, City (pop., 2000: 3,203,362), capital of Turkey. Located about 125 mi (200 km) south of the Black Sea, it has been inhabited at least since the Stone Age. Conquered by Alexander the Great in 334 BC, it was incorporated into the Roman Empire by Augustus. As a city of the Byzantine Empire, Ankara fell to the Turks in *c.* 1073, but the Crusader Raymond IV of Toulouse drove them out in 1101. In 1403 it came under the rule of the Ottoman Empire. After World War I (1914–18) Mustafa Kemal

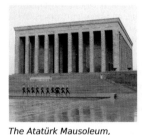

The Atatürk Mausoleum, Ankara, Turkey.
Robert Harding Picture Library

Atatürk made Ankara the centre of resistance to both the Ottomans and the invading Greeks, and it became the capital of the Republic of Turkey in 1923. The modern city is the country's chief industrial centre after Istanbul. Its history is displayed in its Roman, Byzantine, and Ottoman architecture and ruins and in its important historical museums.

Anna Comnena (b. Dec. 2, 1083—d. *c.* 1153), Byzantine historian. Daughter of the emperor Alexius I Comnenus, she conspired with her mother against her brother John II Comnenus; when the plot was discovered, she was forced to enter a convent. There she wrote the *Alexiad*, a biography of her father and a pro-Byzantine account of the early Crusades.

Annan, Kofi (Atta) (b. April 8, 1938, Kumasi, Gold Coast), Seventh secretary-general of the United Nations (1997–2006), who shared, with the UN, the 2001 Nobel Prize for Peace. He was the son of a provincial governor and hereditary paramount chief of the Fante people. He did graduate work at Geneva's Institute for Advanced International Studies and at MIT. He has spent almost his entire career within the UN, beginning at the World Health Organization (1962). As undersecretary-general for peacekeeping (from 1993), he transferred peacekeeping operations in Bosnia from the UN to NATO. Elected in December 1996, he became the first UN secretary-general from sub-Saharan Africa, and he enjoyed a mandate to reform the UN bureaucracy. He criticized the UN's failure to prevent or minimize genocide in Rwanda (1994) and unsettled many by declaring that the UN should address human-rights violations perpetrated by governments against their own people. His priorities included restoring public confidence in the organization and strengthening the UN's activities for peace and development. Annan was appointed to a second term in 2001, and terrorism and global security became major issues following the September 11, 2001, attacks in the U.S. He also oversaw the adoption of a number of reforms, including many institutional and administrative changes, though some measures, such as the expansion of the UN Security Council, were rejected. Annan left office in 2006, succeeded by Ban Ki-moon.

Annapurna, Mountain range, Nepal. It forms a ridge 30 mi (48 km) long and contains four main summits. Annapurna I (26,545 ft, or 8,091 m) was first scaled in 1950 by a French expedition; it was the first peak of more than 26,000 ft (8,000 m) to be ascended to the summit. In 1970 an all-woman Japanese team climbed Annapurna III (24,786 ft, or 7,555 m). See photograph above.

Naudanda village in the Annapurna Range of the Himalayas, Nepal.
Cathy Melloan/EB Inc.

annealing, Treatment of a metal, alloy, or other material by heating to a predetermined temperature, holding for a certain time, and then cooling to room temperature, done to improve ductility and reduce brittleness. Process annealing is carried out intermittently during the working of a piece of metal to restore ductility lost through repeated hammering or other working, if several cold-forming operations are required but the metal is so hardened after the first operation that further cold working would cause cracking. Full annealing is done to give workability to such parts as forged blanks destined for use in the machine-tool industry. Annealing is also done for relief of internal stresses in metal and glass. Annealing temperatures and times differ for different materials and with properties desired; steel is usually held for several hours at about 1,260°F (680°C) and then cooled for several hours.

annuity, Payment made at a fixed interval. A common example is the payment received by retirees from their pension plan. There are two main classes of annuities: annuities certain and contingent annuities. Under an annuity certain, a specified number of payments are made, after which the annuity stops. With a contingent annuity, each payment depends on the continuance of a given status; for example, a life annuity continues only as long as the recipient survives. Contingent annuities such as pension plans or life insurance depend on shared risk. Everyone pays in a fixed amount until the annuity begins; some will not live long enough to receive back all the money they have paid, while others will live long enough to collect more than they have paid.

anodizing, Method of coating metal for corrosion resistance, electrical insulation, thermal control, abrasion resistance, sealing, improving paint adhesion, and decorative finishing. Anodizing consists of electrically depositing an oxide film from aqueous solution onto the surface of a metal, often aluminum, which serves as the anode in an electrolytic cell. In the most common type of anodizing, which uses a 15% sulfuric acid bath, dyes can be introduced into the oxidation process to achieve a coloured surface. Aluminum thus anodized and coloured is used widely in giftware, home appliances, and architectural decoration.

anorexia nervosa, Eating disorder, mostly in young women, characterized by a failure to maintain body weight at a normal level because of an intense desire to be thin, a fear of gaining weight, or a disturbance in body image. Anorexia nervosa typically begins in late adolescence. In women a usual symptom is amenorrhea. A person with anorexia nervosa will often go to great lengths to resist eating in order to lose weight, and medical complications can be life-threatening. Treatment can include psychological and social therapy.

Anschluss (German: "union") Political union of Austria with Germany, which occurred when Adolf Hitler annexed Austria. In 1938 the Austrian chancellor Kurt von Schuschnigg was bullied into canceling a plebiscite on union with Germany, which he expected Austrians to oppose. He resigned his office and ordered the Austrian army not to resist the Germans. The Germans invaded on March 12, and the enthusiasm shown by Austrians persuaded Hitler to annex Austria outright the next day. Though France and Britain protested Hitler's methods, they and other countries accepted the fait accompli.

Anshan, City and territory of ancient Elam, north of modern Shīrāz, Iran. Anshan came to prominence *c.* 2350 BC, but its greatest period was in the 13th–12th century BC, when, as kings of Anshan and Susa, Elamite rulers periodically raided the cities of Babylonia. The area apparently came under the control of the Persians *c.* 675 BC. Its ruins have yielded major finds, including examples of early Elamite writing.

antacid, Any substance, such as sodium bicarbonate, magnesium hydroxide, or aluminum hydroxide, used to relieve the discomfort caused by indigestion, gastritis, and several forms of ulcers. Antacids counteract or neutralize gastric acidity for up to three hours after a single dose. Antacids should be taken when gastric acidity is most likely to be increasing—namely, between one and three hours after each meal and at bedtime.

Antananarivo, formerly TANANARIVE, City (pop., 2001 est.: 1,403,449), capital of Madagascar. Located in central Madagascar Island, and rising to an elevation of 4,694 ft (1,431 m), the city was founded in the 17th century and was controlled by the Merina from the early 1790s until the end of the 19th century. The French made it the capital of their colony when they took control of the region at the end of the 19th century and renamed it Tananarive. The name became Antananarivo after the 1972 revolution. The University of Madagascar (1961) is located there, as are tobacco- and food-processing plants. A railway connects it with Toamasina, the island's chief port.

Antarctica, Fifth largest continent on Earth. Antarctica lies concentrically around the South Pole, its landmass almost wholly covered by a vast ice sheet averaging 6,500 ft (2,000 m) thick. It is divided into two subcontinents: East Antarctica, consisting mainly of a high, ice-covered plateau, and West Antarctica, consisting largely of an archipelago of mountainous islands covered with ice. Its land area is about 5.5 million sq mi (14.2 million sq km). The southern portions of the Atlantic, Pacific, and Indian oceans surround it. Antarctica approximates a circular form, except for the outflaring Antarctic Peninsula and two principal bays, the Ross Sea and the Weddell Sea. East and West Antarctica are separated by the long chain (1,900 mi [3,000 km]) of the Transantarctic Mountains. The ice sheet overlaying the continent represents about 90% of the world's glacial ice. By far the coldest continent, it has the world's lowest recorded temperature, −128.6 °F (−89.2 °C), measured in 1983. The climate supports only a small community of land plants, but the rich offshore food supply sustains penguins, aquatic mammals, and immense seabird rookeries. There are no permanent human inhabitants. The Russian F.G. von Bellingshausen (b. 1778—d. 1852), the Englishman Edward Bransfield (b. 1795?—d. 1852), and the American Nathaniel Palmer (b. 1799—d. 1877) all claimed first sightings of the continent in 1820. The period to *c.* 1900 was dominated by the exploration of Antarctic and sub-Antarctic seas. The early 20th century, the "heroic era" of Antarctic exploration, produced expeditions deep into the interior by Robert Falcon Scott and later Ernest Shackleton. The South Pole was reached by Roald Amundsen in December 1911 and by Scott in January 1912. The first half of the 20th century was also Antarctica's colonial period. Seven countries claimed sectors of the continent, while many other countries carried out explorations. In the International Geophysical Year of 1957–58, 12 countries established more than 50 stations on the continent for cooperative study. In 1961 the Antarctic Treaty, reserving Antarctica for free and nonpolitical scientific study, entered into full force. A 1991 agreement imposed a ban on mineral exploitation for 50 years.

anteater, Any of four species of toothless, insect-eating placental mammals. Found in tropical savannas and forests from Mexico to northern Argentina and Uruguay, anteaters have a long tail, dense fur, a long skull, and a tubular muzzle. Their mouth opening is small, and the tongue is long and wormlike. They live alone or in pairs and feed mainly on ants and termites, which they obtain by inserting their sticky tongue into a nest torn open by the long, sharp, curved claws of their forefeet. The species range in length from 15 in. (37 cm) to 6 ft (1.8 m). Once grouped together, anteaters are now considered as separate from echidnas and pangolins.

antenna, In zoology, one of a pair of slender, segmented sensory organs on the head of insects, myriapods (e.g, centipedes, millipedes), and crustaceans. Antennae of insects, which are movable, are believed to serve as both tactual and smell receptors; in some species, the development of elaborate antennal plumes and brushlike terminations has led to the suggestion that they also serve for hearing. Evidence supports this idea only for the mosquito, whose antennae are attached to specialized structures stimulated by vibrations of the antennal shaft. In social insects (e.g., ants), antennae movements may serve as communication.

anthracite, or HARD COAL, Coal containing more fixed carbon than any other form of coal and the lowest amount of volatile (quickly evaporating) material, giving it the greatest heat value. The most valuable of the coals, it is also the least plentiful, making up less than 2% of all coal reserves in the U.S., with most of the known deposits occurring in the East. Anthracites are black and have a brilliant, almost metallic lustre. Hard and brittle, they can be polished and used for decorative purposes. They are difficult to ignite but burn with a pale-blue flame and require little attention to sustain combustion. In the past they were used for domestic heating, but today they have given way to other sources of energy (e.g., natural gas and electricity).

anthrax, Infectious disease of warm-blooded animals, caused by *Bacillus anthracis*, a bacterium that, in spore form, can retain its virulence in contaminated soil or other material for many years. A disease chiefly of herbivores, the infection may be acquired by persons handling the wool, hair, hides, bones, or carcasses of affected animals. Infection may lead to death from respiratory or cardiac complications (within 1–2 days if acute), or the animal may recover. In humans, anthrax occurs as a cutaneous, pulmonary, or intestinal infection. The most common type, which occurs as an infection of the skin, may lead to fatal septicemia (blood poisoning). The pulmonary form of the disease is usually fatal. Sanitary working environments for susceptible workers are critical to preventing anthrax; early diagnosis and treatment are also of great importance. In recent decades, various countries have attempted to develop anthrax as a weapon of biological warfare; many factors, including its extreme potency (vastly greater than any chemical-warfare agent), make it the preferred biological-warfare agent. Concerns about anthrax mounted in 2001 after it was found in letters mailed to members of the U.S. government and news agencies.

anthropology, The "science of humanity." Anthropologists study human beings in aspects ranging from the biology and evolutionary history of *Homo sapiens* to the features of society and culture that decisively distinguish humans from other animal species. Because of the diverse subject matter it encompasses, anthropology has become, especially since the middle of the 20th century, a collection of more specialized fields. Physical anthropology is the branch that concentrates on the biology and evolution of humanity. The branches that study the social and cultural constructions of human groups are variously recognized as belonging to cultural anthropology (or ethnology), social anthropology, linguistic anthropology, and psychological anthropology. Archaeology, as the method of investigation of prehistoric cultures, has been an integral part of anthropology since it became a self-conscious discipline in the latter half of the 19th century.

anthurium, Any plant of the genus *Anthurium*, comprising about 825 tropical herbaceous species in the arum family, many of which are popular foliage plants. A few species are widely grown for the florist trade for their showy, long-lasting blossoms;

these include the flamingo lily (*A. andraeanum*), which boasts a salmon-red flower, and the flamingo flower, or pigtail plant (*A. scherzeranum*), which has a scarlet flower.

anti-Semitism, Hostility toward or discrimination against Jews as a religious group or "race." Although the term *anti-Semitism* has wide currency, it is regarded by some as a misnomer, implying discrimination against all Semites, including Arabs and other peoples who are not the targets of anti-Semitism as it is usually understood. In antiquity, hostility to the Jews emerged because of religious differences, a situation worsened as a result of the competition with Christianity. By the 4th century, Christians tended to see Jews as an alien people whose repudiation of Christ had condemned them to perpetual migration. Jews were denied citizenship and its rights in much of Europe in the Middle Ages (though some societies were more tolerant) or were forced to wear distinctive clothing, and there were forced expulsions of Jews from several regions in that period. Developed during the Middle Ages were many of the stereotypes of Jews (e.g., the blood libel, alleged greed, conspiracy against humankind) that have persisted into the modern era. The Enlightenment and the French Revolution brought a new religious freedom to Europe in the 18th century but did not reduce anti-Semitism, because Jews continued to be regarded as outsiders. In the 19th century violent discrimination intensified, and so-called "scientific racism" emerged, which based hostility to the Jews on their supposed biological characteristics and replaced religion as the primary basis for anti-Semitism. In the 20th century the economic and political dislocations caused by World War I intensified anti-Semitism, and racist anti-Semitism flourished in Nazi Germany. Nazi persecution of the Jews led to the Holocaust, in which an estimated six million Jews were exterminated. Despite the defeat of the Nazis in World War II, anti-Semitism remained a problem in many parts of the world into the 21st century.

antiaircraft gun, Artillery piece fired from the ground or shipboard in defense against aerial attack. They were first used in combat in World War I, when field artillery were converted to antiaircraft use by mountings that enabled them to fire nearly vertically. Range finders and searchlights, developed in the 1920s and '30s, increased their effectiveness. Advances in World War II included rapid-firing and automatic weapons, radar for target tracking, and radio-operated fuses. British and U.S. forces used a 40-mm gun that fired ammunition to a height of 2 mi (3.2 km). Heavier guns, up to 120 mm, were used against high-flying bombers. For most of the war, the most effective was the German 88-mm *Fliegerabwehrkanone*; its abbreviated name, flak, became a universal term for antiaircraft fire. With the introduction of guided missiles in the 1950s and '60s, heavy antiaircraft guns were phased out, though lighter radar-guided automatic guns remained effective against low-flying aircraft and helicopters.

antiballistic missile (ABM), Weapon designed to intercept and destroy ballistic missiles. Effective ABM systems have been sought since the Cold War, when the nuclear arms race raised the spectre of complete destruction by unstoppable ballistic missiles. In the late 1960s both the U.S. and the Soviet Union developed nuclear-armed ABM systems that combined a high-altitude interceptor missile (the U.S. Spartan and Soviet Galosh) with a terminal-phase interceptor (the U.S. Sprint and Soviet Gazelle). Both sides were limited by the 1972 Treaty on Antiballistic Missile Systems to one ABM location each; the U.S. dismantled its system, while the Soviet Union deployed one around Moscow. During the 1980s the U.S. began research on an ambitious Strategic Defense Initiative against an all-out Soviet attack, but this effort proved expensive and technically difficult, and it lost urgency with the collapse of the Soviet Union. Attention shifted to "theatre" systems such as the U.S. Patriot missile, which was used with limited effect against conventionally armed Iraqi Scud missiles during the Persian Gulf War (1990–91). In 2002 the U.S. formally withdrew from the ABM treaty in order to develop a defense against limited missile attack by smaller powers or "rogue" states.

antibiotic, Chemical substance that in dilute solutions can inhibit the growth of microorganisms or destroy them with little or no harm to the infected host. Early antibiotics were natural microbial products, but chemists have modified the structures of many to produce semisynthetic and even wholly synthetic ones. Since the discovery of penicillin (1928), antibiotics have revolutionized the treatment of bacterial, fungal, and some other diseases. They are produced by many actinomycetes (e.g., streptomycin, tetracycline) and other bacteria (e.g., polypeptides such as bacitracin) and by fungi (e.g., penicillin). Antibiotics may be broad-spectrum (active against a wide range of pathogens) or specific (active against one, or one class). Drawbacks include activity against beneficial microorganisms, often causing diarrhea; allergies; and development of drug-resistant strains of the targeted microorganisms.

antibody, Molecule in the immune system that circulates in blood and lymph in response to invasion by an antigen. Antibodies are globulins formed in lymphoid tissues by B cells, whose receptors are specialized to bind to a specific antigen. These receptors are copied as antibodies that attack the target antigens by binding to them, either neutralizing them or triggering a complement reaction. Antibodies have widely varying binding sites, providing protection from a wide range of infectious agents and toxic substances. Antibodies derived from the blood serum of infected people or animals are often given in an antiserum for quick immunization against fast-acting toxins or microbes. In 1975 César Milstein and colleagues developed a process for producing specific antibodies in virtually limitless amounts; these monoclonal antibodies can deliver radiation or drugs directly to specific antigens.

Antichrist, Chief enemy of Christ who would reign at the end of time, first mentioned in the epistles of St. John. The idea of a mighty ruler who will appear at the end of time to fight against the forces of good was adapted from Judaism; the Jewish concept in turn had been influenced by Iranian and Babylonian myths of the battle of God and the devil at the end of time. In the Book of Daniel the evil one is a military leader modeled on Antiochus IV Epiphanes, who persecuted the Jews. In several books of the New Testament, the Antichrist is a tempter who works by signs and wonders and seeks divine honors. It was a potent concept in medieval Christianity that received the attention of many commentators including Adso of Montier-en-Der, whose work became the basic medieval treatise on the Antichrist. During the Middle Ages, popes and emperors struggling for power often denounced each other as the Antichrist, and during the Reformation, Martin Luther and other Protestant leaders identified the papacy itself as the Antichrist.

anticoagulant, Substance that prevents blood from clotting by suppressing the synthesis or function of various clotting factors. Anticoagulants are given to prevent thrombosis and used in drawing and storing blood. There are two main types of anticoagulants: heparin and vitamin K antagonists (e.g., warfarin). The latter have longer-lasting effects, interfering in the liver's metabolism of vitamin K to cause production of defective clotting factors. Anticoagulant therapy carries a high risk of uncontrollable hemorrhage.

antifreeze, Any substance that lowers the freezing point of water, protecting a system from the ill effects of ice formation. Antifreezes such as ethylene glycol or propylene glycol commonly added to water in automobile cooling systems prevent damage to radiators. Additives to prevent freezing of water in gasoline (e.g., Drygas) usually contain methanol or isopropanol. Organisms that must survive freezing temperatures use various chemicals to inhibit ice crystal formation in their cells and tissues: glycerol or dimethyl sulfoxide in insects, glycerol or trehalose in other invertebrates (nematodes, rotifers), and proteins in Antarctic fishes.

antigen, Foreign substance in the body that induces an immune response. The antigen stimulates lymphocytes to produce antibodies or to attack the antigen directly. Virtually any large foreign molecule can act as an antigen, including those of bacteria, viruses, parasites, foods, venoms, blood components, and cells and tissues of various species, including other humans. Sites on the antigen's surface fit and bind to receptor molecules on the lymphocytes' surface, stimulating the latter to multiply and initiate an immune response that neutralizes or destroys the antigen.

Antigone, In Greek legend, the daughter born of the incestuous relationship between Oedipus and his mother, Jocasta. After Oedipus had blinded himself in self-punishment, Antigone and her sister Ismene served as his guides, following him into exile. When he died, Antigone returned to Thebes, where her brothers Eteocles and Polyneices were at war. Both were killed, and Creon, the new king, declared that because Polyneices was a traitor, his corpse should remain unburied. Unwilling to let the body be defiled, Antigone buried him; when Creon condemned her to death, she hanged herself. Her story was dramatized by Sophocles and Euripides (in Euripides' version she escapes and joins her beloved, Haemon).

Antigua and Barbuda, Island country, Lesser Antilles, Caribbean Sea. It consists of three islands: Antigua, Barbuda, and Redonda. Area: 171 sq mi (442 sq km). Population: (2011 est.) 91,400. Capital: St. John's (on Antigua). The majority of the population are descendants of African slaves brought in during colonial times. Language: English (official). Religion: Christianity (mostly Protestant; also Roman Catholic). Currency: Eastern Caribbean dollar. The largest of the islands is Antigua (108 sq mi [280 sq km]), which lacks forests, mountains, and rivers and is subject to droughts. The main anchorage is the deepwater harbour of St. John's. Barbuda—25 mi (40 km) north of Antigua, 62 sq mi (161 sq km) in area, and mostly uninhabited—is home to a large bird sanctuary; its only human settlement is Codrington, on the western coast. Redonda, an uninhabited rock (0.5 sq mi [1.25 sq km]), lies southwest of Antigua. Tourism is the mainstay of the country's economy; offshore banking is growing. Christopher Columbus visited Antigua in 1493 and named it after a church in Sevilla, Spain. It was colonized by English settlers in 1632, who imported African slaves to grow tobacco and sugarcane. Barbuda was colonized by the English in 1678. In 1834 the islands' slaves were emancipated. Antigua (with Barbuda) was part of the British colony of the Leeward Islands from 1871 until that colony was defederated in 1956. The islands achieved full independence in 1981.

antihistamine, Synthetic drug that counteracts the effects of released histamine in the body. Antihistamines compete with histamine at one of the three types of histamine receptors, preventing allergic attacks or inflammation. Some antihistamines also prevent motion sickness and vertigo. Drowsiness is a frequent side effect. H_2 antihistamines, which bind to the second receptor type, are used to control gastric-acid secretion and treat peptic ulcers.

Antilles, Greater and Lesser, Two groups of islands in the West Indies, bounding the Caribbean Sea on the north and east, respectively. The Greater Antilles include the largest islands (Cuba, Jamaica, Hispaniola, and Puerto Rico), the Lesser Antilles all being much smaller. The name Antilia originally referred to semimythical lands located somewhere west of Europe across the Atlantic. After Christopher Columbus's discoveries, the Spanish name Antillas was commonly assigned to the new lands; "Sea of the Antilles" in various European languages is used as an alternative name for the Caribbean Sea.

antimatter, Substance composed of elementary particles having the mass and electric charge of ordinary matter (such as electrons and protons) but for which the charge and related magnetic properties are opposite in sign. The existence of antimatter was posited by the electron theory of P.A.M. Dirac. In 1932 the positron (antielectron) was detected in cosmic rays, followed by the antiproton and the antineutron detected through the use of particle accelerators. Positrons, antiprotons, and antineutrons, collectively called antiparticles, are the antiparticles of electrons, protons, and neutrons, respectively. When matter and antimatter are in close proximity, annihilation occurs within a fraction of a second, releasing large amounts of energy.

antimony, Semimetallic to metallic chemical element, chemical symbol Sb, atomic number 51. Of its various allotropes, the most common is a lustrous, bluish, brittle, flaky solid. In nature antimony occurs chiefly as the gray sulfide mineral stibnite, Sb_2S_3. Pure antimony metal has no important uses, but its alloys and compounds are extremely useful. Some antimony alloys have the rare quality of expanding on solidifying; these are used for castings and for type metal. Alloys with lead are used in car batteries, bullets, and cable sheaths. Antifriction alloys with tin and lead (babbitt metals) are used as components of machine bearings. Antimony compounds (valences 3, 4, and 5) are widely used as flame retardants in paints, plastics, rubber, and textiles; others are used as paint pigments.

antinovel, Type of avant-garde novel that departs from traditional novelistic conventions by ignoring such elements as plot, dialogue, and human interest. Seeking to overcome readers' habits and challenge their expectations, antinovelists deliberately avoid any intrusion of authorial personality, preferences, or values. Though the term was coined by Jean-Paul Sartre in 1948, the approach is at least as old as the works of the 18th-century writer Laurence Sterne. Writers of such works include Nathalie Sarraute, Claude Simon, Alain Robbe-Grillet, Uwe Johnson, and Rayner Heppenstall.

Antioch, Turkish ANTAKYA, or HITAY, City (pop., 2000: 144,910), south-central Turkey. Founded in 300 BC by the Seleucid dynasty, Antioch was the centre of the Seleucid power until 64 BC, when it became the capital of the province of Syria under the Roman Republic and Empire. An early centre of Christianity, the city was the headquarters of St. Paul c. AD 47–55. Despite being briefly occupied by the Persians in the 6th and 7th centuries, it remained part of the Byzantine Empire until the Arab invasion of the 7th century. Thereafter it returned to Byzantine rule (969) and was seized by the Turkish Seljūq dynasty (1084) before being captured by the Crusaders in 1098. From 1268 it was ruled by the Mamlūk dynasty, and it was absorbed by the Ottoman Empire in 1517. The city remained under their control until after World War I (1914–18), when it was transferred to Syria. It was made part of the Republic of Turkey in 1939. The economy of the modern town is based on agriculture and light manufacturing.

antipope, In Roman Catholicism, a person who tries to take the place of the legitimately elected pope. Some antipopes were elected by factions in doctrinal disagreements, and others were chosen in double elections arbitrated by secular authorities or picked as third candidates in an effort to resolve such disputes. The earliest of the antipopes appeared in the 3rd century. During the Investiture Controversy, Henry IV appointed an antipope, and several more antipopes claimed the papal office over the next 200 years as a result of disputed elections or further struggles with secular rulers. The principal age of the antipope came after the papal court was moved from Rome to Avignon in the 14th century, an event that led to the Western Schism of 1378–1417. During this era, the popes now considered canonical were elected in Rome, and the antipopes were elected in Avignon.

antiseptic, Any of a variety of agents applied to living tissue to destroy or inhibit growth of infectious microorganisms. An antiseptic's efficiency depends on concentration, time, and temperature. It is most valuable in the disinfection of contaminated wounds or skin surfaces when a wide margin exists between the concentration at which it is germicidal and that at which it is toxic to the body's cells. Many antiseptics destroy specific types or forms of microorganisms (e.g., bacteria but not spores). Among the major families of antiseptics are alcohols, phenols, chlorine and iodine compounds, mercury-based tinctures, certain acridine dyes, and some essential oils. Antiseptics are distinguished from disinfectants, which are germicidal agents used to destroy microorganisms on inanimate surfaces.

antitoxin, Antibody formed in the body in reaction to a bacterial toxin, which it can neutralize. People who have recovered from bacterial diseases often develop specific antitoxins that give them immunity against recurrence. Injecting an animal (usually a horse) with increasing doses of toxin produces a high concentration of antitoxin in the blood. The resulting highly concentrated preparation of antitoxins is called an antiserum. The first antitoxin developed (1890) was specific to diphtheria; today, antitoxins are also used to treat botulism, dysentery, gas gangrene, and tetanus.

antitrust law, Any law restricting business practices that are considered unfair or monopolistic. Among U.S. laws, the best known is the Sherman Antitrust Act of 1890, which declared illegal "every contract, combination…or conspiracy in restraint of trade or commerce." The Clayton Antitrust Act of 1914, as amended in 1936 by the Robinson-Patman Act, prohibits discrimination among customers through prices or other means; it also prohibits mergers or acquisitions whenever the effect may be "to substantially lessen competition." Labour unions are also subject to antitrust laws.

Antony, Mark, Latin MARCUS ANTONIUS (b. *c.* 83—d. August, 30 BC), Roman general. After

Mark Antony, detail of a marble bust; in the Vatican Museum.
Alinari/Art Resource, New York

military service (57–54), he joined the staff of his relative Julius Caesar. He helped Caesar drive Pompey from Italy in 49 and in 44 was made co-consul. After Caesar's assassination, Octavian (later Caesar Augustus) initially opposed Antony but later formed the Second Triumvirate with Antony and Lepidus. Antony helped defeat republican forces at Philippi and took control of Rome's eastern provinces. On a mission to Egypt to question Cleopatra about her loyalty, he became her lover (41–40). He returned to Italy in 40 to settle differences with Octavian, whereupon he received command of the eastern provinces. To strengthen his position, he agreed to marry Octavian's sister Octavia. When relations with Octavian again collapsed, he headed for Syria and sent for Cleopatra for aid. Octavian sent Octavia to him, and, when Antony ordered her back to Rome, a fatal breach opened. The Triumvirate ended in 32, leaving Antony little support in Rome. He divorced Octavia, and Octavian declared war on Cleopatra. Antony lost the Battle of Actium, and he and Cleopatra fled to Egypt, pursued by Octavian. When resistance became futile, they committed suicide.

Antwerp, French ANVERS, Flemish ANTWERPEN, City (pop., 2000 est.: 446,500), capital of Antwerp province, Belgium. One of the world's major seaports, it is located 55 mi (88 km) southeast of the North Sea. Because it lies in the Flemish-speaking part of Belgium, it plays the role of unofficial capital of Flanders. It received municipal rights in 1291 and became a member of the Hanseatic League by 1315. As a distribution centre for Spanish and Portuguese trade, it became the commercial and financial capital of Europe in the 16th century. Following destructive invasions, it went into decline but began to revive after Napoleon's improvement of the harbour *c.* 1803. It was part of the Kingdom of the

Netherlands (1815–30), then was ceded to Belgian nationalists. Its current economic life centres around shipping, port-related activities, and major manufacturing.

antyesti, Hindu funeral rites. They generally involve cremation followed by disposal of the ashes in a sacred river. As soon as possible after death, the body is removed to the cremation grounds, usually on the riverbank. The eldest son of the deceased and a priest perform the final rites. For 10 days, the mourners are considered impure as they perform rites intended to provide the soul of the deceased with a new spiritual body for the next life. At a prescribed date, the bones are collected and buried or immersed in a river.

Anubis, Ancient Egyptian god of the dead, represented as a jackal or as a man with the head of a jackal. In the Early Dynastic period and the Old Kingdom he was preeminent as lord of the dead, but he was later overshadowed by Osiris. Anubis was associated with the care of the dead and was credited with the invention of embalming, an art he first practiced on the corpse of Osiris. Later assigned the role of conducting souls into the underworld, he was sometimes identified in the Greco-Roman world with Hermes.

anxiety, In psychology, a feeling of dread, fear, or apprehension, often with no clear justification. Anxiety differs from true fear in that it is typically the product of subjective, internal emotional states rather than a response to a clear and actual danger. It is marked by physiological signs such as sweating, tension, and increased pulse, by doubt concerning the reality and nature of the perceived threat, and by self-doubt about one's capacity to cope with it. Some anxiety inevitably arises in the course of daily life and is normal; but persistent, intense, chronic, or recurring anxiety not justified by real-life stresses is usually regarded as a sign of an emotional disorder.

ANZUS Pact, officially PACIFIC SECURITY TREATY, Security pact for the South Pacific, signed in 1951 by Australia, New Zealand, and the U.S. (hence its acronym). The U.S. first suggested a pact to Australia in the wake of the U.S.-Japan Security Treaty and fears of Japanese rearmament. The signatories agreed to maintain a consultative relationship for their collective security. In the 1980s New Zealand refused to let ships carrying nuclear weapons dock at its ports; the U.S., refusing to identify its nuclear-armed ships, suspended its treaty obligations to New Zealand in 1986, and the treaty has since been nonoperative with reference to New Zealand.

Apache, North American Indians of the southwestern U.S. Their name comes from a Zuñi word meaning "enemy." Most Apache live on five reservations in Arizona and New Mexico. Culturally, the Apache are divided into Eastern Apache, which include the Mescalero, Jicarilla, Chiricahua, and Lipan, and Western Apache, which include the Cibecue. The Eastern Apache were predominantly hunting and gathering societies, while their Western counterparts relied more on farming. Their ancestors had come down from the north, as is evident from their languages; Apachean languages are distantly related to other Athabaskan languages spoken in Canada. They settled the Plains, but, with the introduction of the horse, they were pressed south and west by the Comanche and Ute. They attempted to befriend the Spanish, the Mexicans, and later the Americans. Beginning in 1861, however, they engaged in a quarter-century confrontation against U.S. military forces. The Apache wars were among the fiercest fought on the frontier. The last ended in 1886 with the surrender of Geronimo. The Chiricahua Apache were evacuated from the West and held successively in Florida, Alabama, and Oklahoma. Apache descendants numbered some 100,000 in the early 21st century.

apartheid (Afrikaans: "apartness" or "separateness") Policy of racial segregation and political and economic discrimination against non-European groups in South Africa. The term was first used as the name of the official policy of the National Party in 1948, though racial segregation, sanctioned by law, was already widely practiced. The Group Areas Act of 1950 established residential and business sectors in urban areas for each "race" and strengthened the existing "pass" laws, which required nonwhites to carry identification papers. Other laws forbade most social contacts between those of European descent and others, authorized segregated public facilities, established separate educational standards, restricted each group to certain types of jobs, curtailed nonwhite labour unions, denied nonwhite participation in the national government, and established various black African "homelands," partly self-governing units that were nevertheless politically and economically dependent on South Africa. These so-called homelands were not recognized by international governments. Apartheid was always subject to internal criticism and led to many violent protests, strikes, and acts of sabotage; it also received international censure. In 1990–91 most apartheid legislation was repealed, but segregation continued on a de facto basis. In 1993 a new constitution enfranchised blacks and other racial groups, and all-race national elections in 1994 produced a coalition government with a black majority. These developments marked the end of legislated apartheid, though not of its entrenched social and economic effects.

Apatosaurus, Genus of giant herbivorous dinosaur, one of the largest land animals of all time. *Apatosaurus* lived between 147 million and 137 million years ago during the Late Jurassic and Early Cretaceous Periods in North America and Europe. It weighed as much as 30 tons and was as long as 70 ft (21 m), including the very long neck and tail. Formerly known as *Brontosaurus* because of incomplete fossil evidence, its head was depicted until 1978 as massive and snub-nosed, with spoonlike teeth; scientists now know the animal had a slender, elongated skull and long, peg-like teeth. Skeletal evidence indicates that, despite their great bulk, apatosaurs were primarily land animals.

Apennines, Mountain range, central Italy. It stretches some 870 mi (1,400 km) from near Savona in the northwest to Reggio di Calabria in the south, its width varying from 25 to 125 mi (40–200 km). Monte Corno is its highest peak, at 9,554 ft (2,912 m). The range is the source of most of Italy's rivers, including the Arno, Tiber, and Volturno.

Apgar Score System, Rating procedure to identify newborns needing life-sustaining medical assistance. It was developed in 1952 by Virginia Apgar (1909–1974). Five signs, keyed to Apgar's name—Appearance (color), Pulse, Grimace (reflex irritability), Activity (muscle tone), and Respiration—measure adaptation to leaving the uterus. The maximum score is 10. If the total score at one and then five minutes after birth is less than 7, the infant is reevaluated every five minutes for 20 minutes or until two consecutive scores of 7 or more are obtained.

aphasia, or DYSPHASIA, Defect in the expression and comprehension of words, caused by damage to the frontal and temporal lobes of the brain. It can result from head trauma, tumour, stroke, or infection. Symptoms vary with the brain area involved, and the ability to put words in a meaningful order may be lost. Speech therapy may be useful. In some cases, improvement may be due to assumption of some language functions by other areas of the brain.

aphid, Any of several species of sapsucking, soft-bodied insects (order Homoptera) that are about the size of a pinhead, with tube-like projections on the abdomen. Serious plant pests, they stunt plant growth, produce plant galls, transmit plant viral diseases, and deform leaves, buds, and flowers. Ants may take care of aphids, protecting them from weather and natural enemies and transferring them from wilted to healthy plants. The ants in turn obtain honeydew, a sweet product excreted by aphids, which the ants retrieve by "milking" the aphids (stroking their abdomens).

aphorism, Terse formulation of any generally accepted truth or sentiment conveyed in a pithy, memorable statement. The term was first used in the *Aphorisms* of Hippocrates, a long series of propositions concerning disease and the art of healing. Aphorisms were used especially in dealing with subjects for which principles and methodology developed relatively late, including art, agriculture, medicine, jurisprudence, and politics, but in the modern era they have usually been vehicles of wit and pithy wisdom. Celebrated modern aphorists include Friedrich Nietzsche and Oscar Wilde.

aphrodisiac, Any of various forms of stimulation thought to arouse sexual excitement. They may be psychophysiological (arousing the senses of sight, touch, smell, or hearing) or internal (e.g., foods, alcoholic drinks, drugs, love potions, medicinal preparations). Most foods traditionally believed to be aphrodisiacs have no chemical components that would have such an effect. In some cases, their reputation may be based on a supposed resemblance to genitalia (e.g., ginseng root, rhinoceros horn). Drugs such as alcohol or marijuana may lead to sexual excitation by lessening the user's inhibitions. Few medical studies have been conducted; the only substances medically recognized as aphrodisiacs are extremely hazardous to the health.

Aphrodite, Greek goddess of sexual love and beauty. She is also associated with the sea and, according to legend, was born of sea foam arising from the genitals of Uranus. Sparta, Thebes, and Cyprus honored her as a goddess of war. Many scholars believe that her cult is Semitic rather than Greek in origin. According to Homer, she was the daughter of Zeus and his consort Dione, and she married Hephaestus but betrayed him with Ares. She had many mortal lovers. Her main centres of worship were on the islands of Cyprus and Cythera and at Corinth. As a fertility goddess, she is associated with Eros, the Graces, and the Horae (seasons). Venus is her Roman counterpart.

Apia, Seaport town (pop., 2001: 38,836) and capital, Samoa. It lies on the northern coast of Upolu Island. Its economy centres on the export of goods to American Samoa. Robert Louis Stevenson is buried at nearby Mount Vaea; Vailima, his former home, is now the residence of the head of state.

Apis, In ancient Egyptian religion, a sacred bull deity worshiped at Memphis. The cult originated at least as early as the 1st dynasty (*c.* 2925–*c.* 2775 BCE). Apis was probably at first a fertility god but became associated with Ptah and also with Osiris and Sokaris, gods of the dead. When an Apis bull died, it was buried with great pomp, and the calf that was to be its successor was installed at Memphis. Apis's priests drew omens from the bull's behaviour, and his oracle had a wide reputation. The worship of Serapis (a combination of Osiris and Apis) probably arose at Memphis in the 3rd century BCE and became one of the most widespread Eastern cults in the Roman Empire.

Apis, bull deity, painted on the bottom of a wooden coffin, c. 700 BC; in the Roemer und Pelizaeus Museum, Hildesheim, Ger.
Bavaria-Verlag

apocalypse, In many Western religious traditions, the period of catastrophic upheaval expected to occur just before the end of the world, when God will come to sit in judgment on humankind. The belief that the world will come to a violent and cataclysmic end exists in Judaism and Christianity as well as in Zoroastrianism. Several of the prophetic works of the Hebrew Scriptures, notably the book of Daniel, include visions of the apocalypse. The book of Revelation (or Apocalypse) gives a dark and dramatic picture of the end of time, when the wicked will be punished and the good will triumph through God's intervention. The approach of the Last Days is expected to be marked by famines, wars, earthquakes, plagues, and other natural disasters, along with signs in the heavens. Today apocalyptic themes are emphasized by various religious groups (e.g., fundamentalist Christians) and have also been taken up by science-fiction writers.

Apocrypha, In biblical literature, works outside an accepted canon of scripture. In modern usage the Apocrypha refers to ancient Jewish books that are not part of the Hebrew Bible but are considered canonical in Roman Catholicism and Eastern Orthodoxy. Among the various books included are Tobit, Judith, Baruch, and the Maccabees as well as Ecclesiasticus and the Wisdom of Solomon. Protestant churches follow Jewish tradition in judging these works apocryphal or noncanonical. The term deuterocanonical is used to refer to works accepted in one canon but not all. Pseudepigrapha are spurious works for which biblical authorship is claimed.

Apollo, Most widely revered of the Greek gods. He communi-

cated the will of his father Zeus, made humans aware of their guilt and purified them of it, presided over religious and civil law, and foretold the future. His bow symbolized distance, death, terror, and awe; his lyre symbolized music, poetry, and dance. As a patron of the arts, he was often associated with the Muses. He was also a god of crops and herds. He became associated with the sun, and was even identified with Helios, the sun god. Also associated with healing, he was the father of Asclepius. By tradition, Apollo and his twin, Artemis, were born at Delos to Leto. Apollo's oracle was established at Delphi; the Pythian Games commemorated his killing (while still an infant) of the serpent Python to take the shrine. His many lovers fared poorly: the fleeing Daphne became a laurel tree; the unfaithful Coronis was shot by Artemis, and Cassandra, who rejected him, was doomed to utter true prophecies no one would believe.

Apollo Belvedere, restored Roman copy of the Greek original attributed to Leochares, 4th century BC; in the Vatican Museum, Rome
Alinari/Art Resource, New York

Apologist, Any of the Christian writers, primarily in the 2nd century, who attempted to provide a defense of Christianity against Greco-Roman culture. Many of their writings were addressed to Roman emperors and were submitted to government secretaries in order to defend Christian beliefs and practices. The Apologists tried to prove the antiquity of Christianity as the fulfillment of Old Testament prophecy, and they argued that the worshipers of the mythological gods were truly godless. They also insisted on the philosophical nature of their faith and its high ethical standards. Greek Apologists include Justin Martyr and Clement of Alexandria. Latin Apologists of the 2nd century include Tertullian.

apology, In literature, an autobiographical form in which a defense is the framework for discussion of the author's personal beliefs. Examples include Plato's *Apology* (4th century BC), in which Socrates answers his accusers by giving a history of his life and moral commitment, and John Henry Newman's *Apologia pro Vita Sua* (1864), an examination of the principles that inspired his conversion to Roman Catholicism.

apoptosis, or PROGRAMMED CELL DEATH, Mechanism that allows cells to self-destruct when stimulated by the appropriate trigger. It may be initiated when a cell is no longer needed, when a cell becomes a threat to the organism's health, or for other reasons. The aberrant inhibition or initiation of apoptosis contributes to many disease processes, including cancer. Though embryologists had long been familiar with the process of programmed cell death, not until 1972 was the mechanism's broader significance recognized. Apoptosis is distinguished from necrosis, a form of cell death that results from injury.

Apostle, Any of the 12 disciples chosen by Jesus. They were Peter, James and John (sons of Zebedee), Andrew, Philip, Bartholomew, Matthew, Thomas, James (son of Alphaeus), Thaddaeus or Judas (son of James), Simon the Cananaean or Zealot, and Judas Iscariot. The 12 were privileged to attend Jesus continually and receive his teaching. Peter, James, and John formed an inner circle and were allowed to witness such events as the Transfiguration and the agony of Jesus at Gethsemane. After the defection and death of Judas Iscariot, Matthias was elected an Apostle. Paul also claimed the title on the ground that he had seen the Lord and been commissioned by him.

Apostolic succession, In Christianity, the doctrine that bishops represent an uninterrupted line of descent from the Apostles of Jesus. This succession gives bishops special powers, including the right to confirm church members, ordain priests, consecrate bishops, and rule over the clergy and church members of a diocese. Clement, bishop of Rome, stated the doctrine as early as AD 95, and it is accepted by Roman Catholic, Eastern Orthodox, Old Catholic, and several other churches. Some Protestant churches maintain that succession is spiritual and doctrinal rather than ritual and historical.

Appalachian Mountains, Mountain system, eastern North America. The Appalachians, among the oldest mountains on Earth, extend almost 2,000 mi (3,200 km) from the Canadian province of Newfoundland and Labrador in the northeast southwestward to Alabama in the U.S. They include the White Mountains in New Hampshire, the Green Mountains in Vermont, the Catskill Mountains in New York, the Allegheny Mountains primarily in Pennsylvania, the Blue Ridge Mountains in Virginia and North Carolina, the Great Smoky Mountains in North Carolina and Tennessee, and the Cumberland Plateau extending from West Virginia to Alabama. Their highest peak is Mount Mitchell in North Carolina.

appeasement, Foreign policy of pacifying an aggrieved nation through negotiation in order to prevent war. The prime example is Britain's policy toward Fascist Italy and Nazi Germany in the 1930s. Neville Chamberlain sought to accommodate Italy's invasion of Ethiopia in 1935 and took no action when Germany absorbed Austria in 1938. When Adolf Hitler prepared to annex ethnically German portions of Czechoslovakia, Chamberlain negotiated the notorious Munich Agreement.

appendix, in full VERMIFORM APPENDIX, Vestigial hollow tube attached to the cecum of the large intestine. The human appendix, usually 3–4 in. (8–10 cm) long and less than 0.5 in. (1.3 cm) wide, has no digestive function. Its muscular walls expel their own mucous secretions or any intestinal contents that enter it. Blockage of the opening may prevent expulsion and cause appendicitis: fluids collect, bacteria propagate, and the appendix becomes distended and inflamed; tissue in the appendix begins to die, and the organ may burst, causing peritonitis. Its symptoms may begin with moderate pain in the upper abdomen, about the navel, or all over the abdomen. Nausea and vomiting may then develop. The pain may shift to the right lower abdomen. Fever is usually present but is seldom high in the early phases. Differentiating acute appendicitis from other causes of abdominal pain requires careful examination. Treatment is removal of the appendix (appendectomy).

Appian Way, Latin VIA APPIA, First and most famous of the ancient Roman roads, running from Rome to Campania and southern Italy. Begun in 312 BC by the censor Appius Claudius Caecus, the road originally ran 132 mi (212 km) to ancient Capua; by 244 BC it extended 230 mi (370 km) to the port of Brundisium (Brindisi) in Italy's heel. Built of smoothly fitted blocks of lava on a heavy stone foundation, the road provided a long-lasting surface for transporting merchandise to these seaports (and thence by ship to Greece and the eastern Mediterranean). Remains can be seen today outside Rome.

applied psychology, Branch of psychology concerned with solving practical problems of human behaviour by using the findings and methods of psychological science. Intelligence testing, legal problems, industrial efficiency, motivation, and delinquency were among the first areas of application in the early 20th century. World Wars I and II fostered work on vocational testing, teaching methods, evaluation of attitudes and morale, performance under stress, propaganda and psychological warfare, and rehabilitation. The aviation and aerospace industries were important for the development of engineering psychology, the study of human-machine relationships. Other areas include consumer psychology, school psychology, and community psychology.

apprenticeship, Training in an art, trade, or craft under a legal agreement defining the relationship between master and learner and the duration and conditions of their relationship. Known from antiquity, apprenticeship became prominent in medieval Europe with the emergence of the craft guilds. The standard apprenticeship lasted seven years. During the Industrial Revolution a new kind of apprenticeship developed in which the employer was the factory owner and the apprentice, after a period of training, became a factory worker. The increasing need for semiskilled workers led to the development of vocational and technical schools in Europe and the U.S., especially after World War II. Some industries in the U.S., such as construction, continue to employ workers in an apprenticeship arrangement.

April Fools' Day, or ALL FOOLS' DAY, First day of April, named for the custom of playing practical jokes on that date. Though it has been observed for centuries in several countries, including France and Britain, its origin is unknown. It resembles the Hilaria festival of ancient Rome (March 25) and the Holi festival of India (ending March 31). The custom of playing April Fools' jokes was brought to America by the British.

Aqaba, Gulf of, Northeastern arm of the Red Sea, between Saudi Arabia and the Sinai Peninsula. It varies in width from 12 to 17 miles (19 to 27 km) and is 100 miles (160 km) long. Its head touches Egypt, Israel, Jordan, and Saudi Arabia. Its only sheltered harbour is Dhahab (Dahab), Egypt; Jordan and Israel created the ports of Al-ʿAqabah and Elat, respectively, as outlets to the Red Sea and the Indian Ocean.

aquarium, Receptacle for maintaining aquatic organisms, either freshwater or marine, or a facility in which a collection of aquatic organisms is displayed or studied. The first display aquarium opened in Regent's Park, England, in 1853. Many of the world's principal cities now have public aquariums as well as commercial ones; other aquarium facilities serve chiefly as research institutions. Regardless of size—whether a small one-gallon jar or a huge million-gallon tank—aquariums must be constructed with care; many substances, especially plastics and adhesives, that are nontoxic to humans are toxic to water-breathing animals. The primary requirement for maintaining aquatic organisms is water quality.

Aquarius (Latin: "Water carrier") In astronomy, the constellation lying between Capricorn and Pisces; in astrology, the 11th sign of the zodiac, governing approximately the period January 20–February 18. It is usually represented as a man pouring a stream of water out of a jug, probably because in ancient times the rising of Aquarius coincided in the Middle East with the annual arrival of floods or rainfall. In the astrological concept called the Great Year—the 25,000-year period it takes the earth to pass through the influence of the entire zodiac—the early 19th century was the beginning of the Age of Aquarius.

aqueduct, Conduit built to carry water from its source to a main distribution point. Ancient Rome's aqueduct system, an extraordinary feat of engineering, brought water to the city from as far as 57 mi (92 km) away. Only a portion of the Roman aqueducts utilized the familiar stone arch; most were underground conduits made of stone or terra-cotta pipe. Modern aqueduct systems employ cast iron or steel.

aquifer, In hydrology, a rock layer or sequence that contains water and releases it in appreciable amounts. The rocks contain water-filled pores that, when connected, allow water to flow through their matrix. A confined aquifer is overlain by a rock layer that does not transmit water in any appreciable amount or that is impermeable. There probably are few truly confined aquifers. In an unconfined aquifer the upper surface (water table) is open to the atmosphere through permeable overlying material. An aquifer also may be called a water-bearing stratum, lens, or zone.

Aquinas, Saint Thomas (b. 1224/25, Roccasecca, near Aquino, Terra di Lavoro, Kingdom of Sicily—d. March 7, 1274, Fossanova, near Terracina, Latium, Papal States; canonized July 18, 1323; feast day January 28, formerly March 7), Foremost philosopher and theologian of the Roman Catholic church. Born of noble parents, he studied at the University of Naples, joined the Dominicans, and taught at a Dominican school at the University of Paris. His time in Paris coincided with the arrival of Aristotelian science, newly discovered in Arabic translation; his great achievement was to integrate into Christian thought the rigours of Aristotle's philosophy, just as the early Church Fathers had integrated Plato's thought in the early Christian era. He held that reason is capable of operating within faith; while the philosopher relies solely on reason, the theologian accepts faith as his starting point and then proceeds to conclusion through the use of reason. This point of view was controversial, as was his belief in the religious value of nature, for which he argued that to detract from the perfection of creation was to detract from the creator. He was opposed by St. Bonaventure. In 1277, after his death, the masters of Paris condemned 219 propositions, 12 of them Thomas's. He was nevertheless named a Doctor of the Church in 1567 and declared the champion of orthodoxy during the modernist crisis at the end of the 19th century. A prolific writer, he produced more than 80 works, including *Summa contra Gentiles* (1261–64) and *Summa theologica* (1265–73).

Aquino, (Maria) Corazon, orig. MARIA CORAZON CO-JUANGCO (b. Jan. 25, 1933, Tarlac province, Phil.—d. Aug. 1, 2009, Makati), President of the Philippines (1986–92). Born into a politically prominent family, she married Benigno Simeon Aquino, Jr. (1932–83), who became the most prominent opponent of Pres. Ferdinand Marcos. Benigno was assassinated in 1983 on his return from exile, and Corazon Aquino became the opposition candidate for president in 1986. Though Marcos was officially reported the winner, there were widespread allegations of voting fraud; high officials in the military supported Aquino, and Marcos fled. As president, Aquino introduced a hugely popular constitution. Over time her popularity declined amid charges of corruption and economic injustice.

Arab, Any member of the Arabic-speaking peoples native to the Middle East and North Africa. Before the spread of Islam in the 630s, the term referred to the largely nomadic Semitic peoples of the Arabian Peninsula; it came to apply to Arabic-speaking peoples from Africa's Mauritanian and Moroccan coasts east to Iraq and the Arabian Peninsula and south to The Sudan after their acceptance of Islam. Traditionally, some Arabs are desert-dwelling pastoral nomads, whereas others live by oases and in small, isolated farming villages. While most Arabs are Muslims, some are Christian. The term has also been used in a political sense by Arab nationalists to describe a greater sociolinguistic or ethnic ideal ("the Arab nation").

Arab-Israeli wars, Series of military conflicts fought between various Arab countries and Israel (1948–49, 1956, 1967, 1969–70, 1973, and 1982). The first war (1948–49) began when Israel declared itself an independent state following the United Nations' partition of Palestine. Protesting this move, five Arab countries—Egypt, Iraq, Jordan, Lebanon, and Syria—attacked Israel. The conflict ended with Israel gaining considerable territory. The 1956 Suez Crisis began after Egypt nationalized the Suez Canal. A French, British, and Israeli coalition attacked Egypt and occupied the canal zone but soon withdrew under international pressure. In the Six-Day War of 1967, Israel attacked Egypt, Jordan, and Syria. The war ended with the Israel occupying substantial amounts of Arab territory. An undeclared war of attrition (1969–70) was fought between Egypt and Israel along the Suez Canal and ended with the help of international diplomacy. Egypt and Syria attacked Israel in 1973 (the Yom Kippur War), but, despite early Arab success, the conflict ended inconclusively. In 1979 Egypt made peace with Israel. In 1982 Israel invaded Lebanon in order to expel Palestinian guerrillas based there. Israel withdrew from most of Lebanon by 1985 but maintained a narrow buffer zone inside that country until 2000.

Arab League, or LEAGUE OF ARAB STATES, Regional organization formed in 1945 and based in Cairo. It initially comprised Egypt, Syria, Lebanon, Iraq, Transjordan (now Jordan), Saudi Arabia, and Yemen; joining later were Libya, Sudan, Tunisia, Morocco, Kuwait, Algeria, Bahrain, Oman, Qatar, the United Arab Emirates, Mauritania, Somalia, the Palestine Liberation Organization, Djibouti, and Comoros. The league's original aims were to strengthen and coordinate political, cultural, economic, and social programs and to mediate disputes; a later aim was to coordinate military defense. Members have often split on political issues; Egypt was suspended for 10 years (1979–89) following its peace with Israel, and the Persian Gulf War (1990–91) also caused deep rifts. In 2011, amid widespread popular uprisings in the Middle East and North Africa, the Arab League supported a no-fly zone in Libya to protect the opposition there from air attack by loyalist forces and suspended Syria's membership over its heavy-handed crackdown against protesters.

Arabian Desert, Desert region, Arabian Peninsula. It covers about 900,000 sq mi (2,330,000 sq km), occupying nearly the entire peninsula. It lies largely within Saudi Arabia but large portions extend into Jordan, Iraq, Kuwait, Qatar, the United Arab Emirates, Oman, and Yemen. Its relief is broken by a number of mountain ranges, with elevations reaching as high as 12,000 ft (3,700 m), and it is bounded on three sides by high escarpments. At least one-third of the desert is covered by sand, including the Rubʿ al-Khali, considered to have one of the most inhospitable climates on Earth. There are no perennial bodies of water, though the Tigris-Euphrates river system lies to the northeast and the Wadi Ḥajr is located to the south, in Yemen. Humans have inhabited the area since Pleistocene times.

Arabian horse, Earliest improved breed of horse, valued for its speed, stamina, beauty, intelligence, and gentleness. Its long history has been obscured by legend, but it was developed in Arabia by the 7th century AD. It has contributed its qualities to most modern breeds of light horses. It is compact and relatively small, with a small head, protruding eyes, wide nostrils, marked withers, and a short back. Its average height is about 15 hands (60 in. [152 cm]), its average weight 800–1,000 lbs (360–450 kg). Though many colours are possible, gray is the most common.

Arabian Peninsula, or ARABIA, Peninsular region, southwest Asia. With its offshore islands, it covers about 1 million sq mi (2.6 million sq km). Constituent countries are Bahrain, Kuwait, Oman, Qatar, United Arab Emirates, Yemen, and, the largest, Saudi Arabia. It is generally arid and is covered almost entirely by the Arabian Desert. The modern economy is dominated by the production of petroleum and natural gas. The world's largest proven reserves of petroleum are in the Arabian Peninsula. It was the focal point for the origins and development of the Islamic faith in the 7th century CE. Political consolidation of the region was begun by the Prophet Muhammad, and it was the centre of the caliphate until 661, when that office passed to the Umayyad dynasty in Damascus. After 1517 much of the region was dominated by the Ottoman Empire, though the peninsula's people, who had remained largely tribal and nomadic, revolted repeatedly until World War I (1914–18), when the Ottoman Empire dissolved. Thereafter, individual nation-states followed their own histories, though many maintained close ties with European powers such as the United Kingdom.

Arabian Sea, Northwestern part of the Indian Ocean, lying between India and the Arabian Peninsula. It has an area of about 1,491,000 sq miles (3,862,000 sq km) and an average depth of 8,970 feet (2,734 m). The Gulf of Oman connects it with the Persian Gulf via the Strait of Hormuz, while the Gulf of Aden connects it with the Red Sea via the Strait of Mandeb. The Indus is the principal river draining into the Arabian Sea. Socotra, Lakshadweep, and other islands lie within it. Chief ports are Mumbai (Bombay), India; Karachi, Pak.; and Aden, Yemen. The sea has been part of the principal trade route between Europe and India for centuries.

Arabic alphabet, Script used to write Arabic and a number of other languages whose speakers have been influenced by Arab and Islamic culture. The 28-character Arabic alphabet developed from a script used to write Nabataean Aramaic. Because Arabic had different consonants than Aramaic, diacritical dots came to be used to eliminate ambiguous readings of some letters, and these remain a feature of the script. Arabic is written from right to left. The letters denote only consonants, though the symbols for $w, y,$ and (historically) the glottal stop do double duty as vowel letters for long $u, i,$ and $a.$ Additional diacritics, representing short vowels (or the lack thereof), case endings, and geminate (duplicate) consonants, are normally employed only for the text of the Qurʾān, for primers, or in instances where the reading might otherwise be ambiguous. Because Arabic script is fundamentally cursive, most letters have slightly different forms depending on whether they occur in the beginning, middle, or end of a word. Non-Semitic languages for which some version of the Arabic alphabet is or is used include Persian, Kurdish, Pashto, Urdu, some Turkic languages, Malay, Swahili, and Hausa. The Maltese language is the only form of Arabic to be written in the Latin alphabet.

Arabic language, Ancient Semitic language whose dialects are spoken throughout the Middle East and North Africa. Though Arabic words and proper names are found in Aramaic inscriptions, abundant documentation of the language begins only with the rise of Islam, whose main texts are written in Arabic. Grammarians from the 8th century on codified it into the form known as Classical Arabic, a literary and scribal argot that differed markedly from the spoken vernacular. In the 19th–20th centuries, expansion of Classical Arabic's stylistic range and vocabulary led to the creation of Modern Standard Arabic, which serves as a lingua franca among contemporary Arabs. However, Arabic speakers, who number roughly 200 million, use an enormous range of dialects, which at their furthest extremes are mutually unintelligible. Classical Arabic remains an important cultural and religious artifact among the non-Arab Islamic community.

Arabic literary renaissance (19th-century) Movement to develop a modern Arabic literature. Inspired by contacts with the

West and a renewed interest in classical Arabic literature, it began in Egypt with Syrian and Lebanese writers who sought the freer environment there, and it spread to other Arab countries as a result of the dismemberment of the Ottoman Empire after World War I and the coming of independence after World War II. Its success in altering the direction of Arabic literature is related to the spread and modernization of education and the emergence of an Arabic press.

arachnid, Any member of the class Arachnida, primarily carnivorous arthropods having a well-developed head, a hard external skeleton, and four pairs of walking legs. Spiders and scorpions have a segmented body, but daddy longlegs, ticks, and mites do not. Arachnids range in size from tiny mites (0.003 in. [0.08 mm] long) to the 8-in. (21-cm) black scorpion of Africa. As arachnids grow, they molt several times. Most are unable to digest food internally; instead, they inject their prey with digestive fluids and suck the liquefied remains. Arachnids are found worldwide in nearly every habitat. Most groups are free-living, but some mites and ticks are parasitic and can carry serious diseases of animals and humans. Venomous spiders and scorpions also may pose a danger to humans. However, most arachnids are harmless and prey on insect pests.

ʿ**Arafāt, Yāsir,** orig. MUḤAMMAD ʿABD AL-RAʾŪF AL-QUDWAH AL-ḤUSAYNĪ (b. August 1929—d. Nov. 11, 2004, Paris, France), Palestinian leader. The date and place of his birth are disputed. A birth certificate registered in Cairo, Egypt, gives Aug. 24, 1929, but some sources support his claim to have been born in Jerusalem on Aug. 4, 1929. He graduated from the University of Cairo as a civil engineer and served in the Egyptian army during the 1956 Suez Crisis. That year, working as an engineer in Kuwait, he cofounded the guerrilla organization Fatah, which became the leading military component of the Palestine Liberation Organization (PLO), which he led from 1969. In 1974 the PLO was formally recognized by the UN, and ʿArafāt became the first leader of a nongovernmental organization to address the UN. In 1988 he acknowledged Israel's right to exist, and in 1993 he formally recognized Israel during direct talks regarding land controlled by Israel since the Six-Day War. In 1994 he shared the Nobel Prize for Peace with Israelis Yitzhak Rabin and Shimon Peres. In 1996 he became president of the new Palestinian Authority.

Aragon, Spanish ARAGÓN, Autonomous community (pop., 2001: 1,204,215), northeastern Spain. Roughly coextensive with the historical kingdom of Aragon, it occupies an area of 18,425 sq mi (47,720 sq km). Its capital is Zaragoza (Saragossa). Mountains, including the Pyrenees, dominate the relief north and south of the Ebro River, which bisects Aragon. Established in 1035 by Ramiro I, the historical kingdom grew as land was retaken from the Moors: Zaragoza, the capital of the Almoravid kingdom, fell to Alfonso I of Aragon in 1118, and the reconquest of present-day Aragon was completed by the late 12th century. In the 13th–15th centuries it came to rule Sicily, Sardinia, Naples, and Navarra. In the 15th century Ferdinand married Isabella of Castile, uniting the kingdoms of Aragon and Castile and forming the nucleus of modern Spain. The old kingdom of Aragon survived as an administrative unit until 1833, when it was divided into provinces. Agriculture, mining, and industry, the latter concentrated at Zaragoza, are economically important.

Aral Sea, Large salt lake between Kazakhstan and Uzbekistan. It once covered some 26,300 sq mi (68,000 sq km) and was the fourth largest inland body of water in the world, but diversion of the waters of the Syr Darya and Amu Darya rivers for irrigation has led to an overall reduction of its surface area by more than half since 1960. Its volume has been reduced drastically, which has led to an increase in salinity. The soil of the dried-up lake bed has been found to contain salts and other toxic substances.

Ararat, Mount, Turkish AĞRI DAĞI, Extinct volcanic massif, eastern Turkey. Located in Ağri province, near the Iranian border, Ararat has two peaks, Great Ararat, at 16,853 ft (5,137 m) the highest point of elevation in Turkey, and Little Ararat, almost 13,000 ft (4,000 m). Ararat is traditionally associated with the mountain where Noah's ark came to rest at the end of the biblical Deluge. A village on its slopes at the site where Noah is said to have built an altar was destroyed in an earthquake in 1840.

araucaria, Any pinelike coniferous plant of the genus *Araucaria* (family Araucariaceae). Found in South America, the Phoenix Islands, and Australia, araucaria trees are magnificent evergreens, with whorled branches and stiff, flattened, pointed leaves. Common species are the monkey puzzle tree and the Norfolk Island pine, often grown as a houseplant. Several species are cultivated on the Pacific coast of the U.S. and in southern Florida.

Arawak, American Indians of the Greater Antilles and South America. The Taino, an Arawak subgroup, were the first native peoples encountered by Christopher Columbus on Hispaniola. The island Arawak were wiped out by disease, but some mainland South American Arawak, who inhabited northern and western areas of the Amazon River basin, survived conquest. At the turn of the 21st century, the Arawak lived mainly in Guyana, where they represented about one-third of the Indian population. Smaller numbers live in Suriname, French Guiana, and Venezuela.

arbitration, Process of resolving a dispute or a grievance outside a court system by presenting it for decision to an impartial third party. Both sides in the dispute usually must agree in advance to the choice of arbitrator and certify that they will abide by the arbitrator's decision. In medieval Europe arbitration was used to settle disputes between merchants; it is now commonly used in commercial, labour-management, and international disputes. The procedures differ from those used in the courts, especially regarding burden of proof and presentation of evidence. Arbitration avoids costly litigation and offers a relatively speedy resolution as well as privacy for the disputants. The main disadvantage is that setting guidelines is difficult; therefore the outcome is often less predictable than a court decision.

arboretum, Place where trees, shrubs, and sometimes herbaceous plants are cultivated for scientific and educational purposes. An arboretum may be a collection in its own right or a part of a botanical garden. Important U.S. arboretums include the Arnold Arboretum of Harvard University (Jamaica Plain, Mass.) and the U.S. National Arboretum in Washington, D.C.

arbovirus, Any of a large group of viruses that develop in arthropods (chiefly mosquitoes and ticks). The name derives from "*arthropod-borne virus*." The spheroidal virus particle is encased in a fatty membrane and contains RNA; it causes no apparent harm to the arthropod host. Arboviruses are transmitted by bites to vertebrate hosts, in which they establish infections and complete their growth cycle; they include the agents responsible for yellow fever and equine encephalitis.

Arc de Triomphe, Largest triumphal arch in the world. A masterpiece of Romantic Classicism, it is one of the best-known monuments of Paris. It stands at the centre of the Place Charles de Gaulle, at the western terminus of the Champs-Élysées. Initiated by Napoleon, designed by Jean-Francʹois-Thérèse Chalgrin, and constructed in 1806–36, the monument is 164 ft (50 m) high and 148 ft (45 m) wide. Decorative relief sculptures celebrating Napoleon's victorious military campaigns were executed on the arch by François Rude, Jean-Pierre Cortot, and Antoine Etex.

arch, Curved structure that spans the opening between two piers or columns and supports loads from above. The masonry arch provides the stepping stone from the post-and-beam system to the evolution of the vault, and was first widely used by the Romans. Its construction depends on a series of wedge-shaped blocks (voussoirs) set side by side in a semicircular curve or along two intersecting arcs (as in a pointed arch). The central voussoir is called the keystone, and the two points where the arch rests on its supports are known as the spring points. An arch can carry a much greater load than a horizontal beam of the same size and material, because downward pressure forces the voussoirs together instead of apart. The resulting outward thrust must be resisted by the arch's supports. Present-day lightweight monolithic (one-piece) arches of steel, concrete, or laminated wood are highly rigid, and thereby minimize horizontal thrust.

archaea, A group of prokaryotes whose members differ from bacteria, the most prominent prokaryotes, in certain physical, physiological, and genetic features. The archaea may be aquatic or terrestrial microorganisms. They exhibit a diversity of shapes, including spherical, rodlike, and spiral forms. In addition, archaea can survive in various extreme conditions, including very hot or salty environments. Some archaea require oxygen, whereas others do not. Some produce methane as an end product; others depend on sulfur for their metabolism. The archaea can reproduce by several mechanisms, including binary fission, budding, and fragmentation. While the archaea share some features with bacteria, genetic studies have indicated that archaea are more closely related to eukaryotes than to bacteria.

archaeology, Scientific study of material remains of past human life and activities. These include human artifacts from the very earliest stone tools to the man-made objects that are buried or thrown away in the present day. Archaeological investigations are a principal source of modern knowledge of prehistoric, ancient, and extinct cultures. The field emerged as an academic discipline in the late 19th century, following centuries of haphazard antiquarian collecting. Among the archaeologist's principal activities are the location, surveying, and mapping of sites and the excavation, classification, dating, and interpretation of materials to place them in historical context. Major subfields include classical archaeology, the study of ancient Mediterranean and Middle Eastern civilizations; prehistoric archaeology, or general archaeology; and historical archaeology, the study of historic-period remains to augment the written record.

archbishop, In Christianity, a bishop who has jurisdiction, but not superiority, over the other bishops in a province as well as episcopal authority in his own diocese. Introduced as an honorary title in the Eastern churches in the 4th century, the office did not become common in Western churches until the 9th century. It is now most widely used in the Roman Catholic and Eastern Orthodox churches. It is more rarely used in Protestant denominations, though the Church of England has archbishops of Canterbury and York, and the Lutheran churches of both Sweden and Finland have an archbishop.

Archean Eon, or ARCHAEAN EON, or ARCHEOZOIC EON, Older of the two divisions of Precambrian time. The Archean begins with the formation of the Earth's crust 4 billion years ago and extends to 2.5 billion years ago, up to the start of the Proterozoic Eon, the second division of the Precambrian Period. The earliest and most-primitive forms of life (bacteria and cyanobacteria) originated more than 3.5 billion years ago in the middle of the Archean Eon (the Archean's alternative name, Archeozoic, means "ancient life").

archery, Sport of shooting with bow and arrow. As the bow began to be replaced by the gun as the principal weapon of warfare and the hunt beginning in the 16th century, it increasingly became a sporting device. By the mid-19th century, many archery clubs had sprung up in England and the U.S. Competitions including target-shooting were held at the Olympic Games in the early 20th century, but were then suspended until 1972. Other varieties of archery include field archery, or roving (a simulation of hunting), and flight shooting (a distance event).

archetype, Primordial image, character, or pattern of circumstances that recurs throughout literature and thought consistently enough to be considered universal. Literary critics adopted the term from Carl Gustav Jung's theory of the collective unconscious. Because archetypes originate in pre-logical thought, they are held to evoke startlingly similar feelings in reader and author. Examples of archetypal symbols include the snake, whale, eagle, and vulture. An archetypal theme is the passage from innocence to experience; archetypal characters include the blood brother, rebel, wise grandparent, and prostitute with a heart of gold.

Archimedean screw, or ARCHIMEDES' SCREW, Machine for raising water, said to have been invented by Archimedes for removing water from the hold of a large ship. One form consists of a circular pipe enclosing a helix and inclined at an angle of about 45°, with its lower end dipped in the water; rotation of the device lifts the water in the pipe. Other forms consist of a helix revolving in a fixed cylinder or a helical tube wound around a shaft.

architecture, Art and technique of designing and building, as distinguished from the skills associated with construction. The practice of architecture emphasizes spatial relationships, orientation, the support of activities to be carried out within a designed environment, and the arrangement and visual rhythm of structural elements, as opposed to the design of structural systems themselves. Appropriateness, uniqueness, a sensitive and innovative response to functional requirements, and a sense of place within its surrounding physical and social context distinguish a built environment as representative of a culture's architecture.

archon, In ancient Greece, the chief magistrate or magistrates in a city-state, from the Archaic period onward. In Athens, nine archons divided state duties: the *archon eponymous* headed the boule and Ecclesia, the polemarch commanded troops and presided over legal cases involving foreigners, the *archon basileus* headed state religion and the Areopagus, and the six remaining archons handled various judicial matters. At first only elected aristocrats could serve, and their term was for life; later, terms were limited to a year. Archons were chosen by a combination of election and lot. In the 5th century BC the authority of the archons declined as elected generals assumed most of their powers.

Arctic Ocean, Ocean centring approximately on the North Pole. Smallest of the world's oceans, it is almost completely surrounded by the landmasses of Eurasia and North America, and it is distinguished by a cover of ice. Lands in it and adjacent to it include Point Barrow in Alaska, the Arctic Archipelago, Greenland, Svalbard, Franz Josef Land, and northern Siberia. The ocean covers about 5,440,000 sq mi (14,090,000 sq km) and reaches a maximum depth of about 18,050 ft (5,502 m). Its marginal seas include the Barents, Beaufort, Chukchi, East Siberian, Greenland, Kara, Laptev, and White seas. Areas within the Arctic Circle were first explored beginning in the 9th century by the Norse. In the 16th–17th centuries explorers searching for the Northwest Passage reached the area; Martin Frobisher discovered the southern part of Baffin Island (1576–78), and Henry Hudson navigated the eastern coast of Hudson Bay (1610–11). Later explorers included Roald Amundsen, Fridtjof Nansen, Robert E. Peary, and Richard E. Byrd. Development of the area's natural resources was spurred by the discovery of oil in Alaska in the 1960s. Virtually all of the Arctic has now been mapped.

Ardennes, or FOREST OF ARDENNES, Wooded plateau region, northwestern Europe. It covers over 3,860 sq mi (10,000 sq km) and includes parts of Belgium, Luxembourg, and the Meuse River valley of France; its average height is about 1,600 ft (488 m). Though half of it is covered with forests, the soil is generally unfertile and supports only heath. It is located in the middle of the heavily populated triangle of Paris, Brussels, and Cologne. During World Wars I and II, the area was the scene of severe fighting in 1914, 1918, and 1944.

Ares, Greek god of war. Unlike his Roman counterpart, Mars, his worship was not extensive. From the time of Homer, he was one of the Olympian deities, the son of Zeus and Hera, but disliked by the other gods. His worship occurred largely in northern Greece. He was associated from early times with Aphrodite, occasionally portrayed as his legitimate wife and at other times his lover. He was accompanied in battle by his sister Eris (strife) and by two of his children by Aphrodite, Phobos and Deimos (Panic and Rout).

Ares, classical sculpture; in the National Roman Museum, Rome
Anderson—Alinari/Art Resource, New York

Argentina, officially ARGENTINE REPUBLIC, Country, southern South America. Area: 1,073,520 sq mi (2,780,403 sq km). Population: (2011 est.) 40,365,000. Capital: Buenos Aires. The people are mostly of European ancestry, especially Spanish, with smaller mestizo, Indian, and Arab populations. Language: Spanish (official). Religions: Christianity (predominantly Roman Catholic; also Protestant); also Islam, Judaism. Currency: Argentine peso. Argentina can be divided into four general regions: the North, the Pampas, Patagonia, and the Andes Mountains. The subtropical plains in the northeast are divided by the Paraná River into Mesopotamia to the east and Gran Chaco to the west and north. The Pampas, south and west of the Paraná, is one of the world's most productive agricultural areas and the country's most populous region. Patagonia lies south of the Colorado River. The Argentine Andes include the continent's highest peak, Mount Aconcagua. Argentina's hydrology is dominated by rivers that include the Paraná, Uruguay, and Pilcomayo, which drain into the Río de la Plata. Argentina has a developing economy based largely on manufacturing and agriculture; it is Latin America's largest exporter of beef and beef products. It is a federal republic with two legislative houses; the head of state and government is the president. Little is known of the indigenous population before the Europeans' arrival. The area was explored for Spain by Sebastian Cabot beginning in 1526; by 1580 Asunción, Santa Fe, and Buenos Aires had been settled. Early in the 17th century it was attached to the Viceroyalty of Peru, but in 1776 it was included with regions of modern Uruguay, Paraguay, and Bolivia in the Viceroyalty of the Río de la Plata, whose capital was Buenos Aires. With the establishment of the United Provinces of the Río de la Plata in 1816, Argentina achieved its independence from Spain, but its boundaries were not set until the early 20th century. In 1943 the government was overthrown by the military; Col. Juan Perón took control in 1946. He in turn was overthrown in 1955. He returned in 1973 after two decades of turmoil. His third wife, Isabel, became president on his death in 1974 but lost power after another military coup in 1976. The military government tried to take the Falkland Islands (Islas Malvinas) in 1982 but was defeated by the British in the Falkland Islands War, with the result that the government returned to civilian rule in 1983. The government of Raúl Alfonsín worked to end the human rights abuses that had characterized the former regimes. Hyperinflation, however, led to public riots and Alfonsín's party's electoral defeat in 1989; his Peronist successor, Carlos Menem, instituted laissez-faire economic policies. In 1999 Fernando de la Rúa of the Alliance coalition was elected president, but his administration struggled with rising unemployment, heavy foreign debt, and government corruption; he resigned later that year, amid antigovernment protests. Under a succession of interim presidents, Argentina experienced one of its worst economic collapses at the beginning of the 21st century. Néstor Kirchner won the 2003 presidential elections and helped to stabilize the economy. Four years later his wife became the country's first elected female president.

argon, Chemical element, chemical symbol Ar, atomic number 18. Colourless, odourless, and tasteless, it is the most abundant of the noble gases on Earth and the one most used in industry. It constitutes about 1% of air and is obtained by distillation of liquid air. Argon provides an inert gas shield in welding and brazing, in light-bulbs and lasers, in Geiger counters, and in the production and fabrication of certain metals. Because a radioactive form of argon is produced by decay of a naturally occurring radioactive potassium isotope, it can be used to date rocks and samples more than 100,000 years old.

Argonauts, In Greek legend, a band of 50 heroes who went with Jason in the ship *Argo* to retrieve the Golden Fleece from the grove of Ares at Colchis. They had many adventures before arriving at Colchis, from which they were eventually forced to flee, pursued by Medea's father, Aeëtes. The *Argo* eventually returned to Jason's home kingdom (Iolcos) and was placed in a grove sacred to Poseidon; Jason died when its prow toppled as he was resting in its shadow.

arhat, or ARAHANT, In Buddhism, one who has gained insight into the true nature of existence, has achieved nirvana, and will not be reborn. Theravada Buddhism regards becoming an arhat as the goal of spiritual progress. It holds that a seeker must pass through three earlier stages before being reborn in a heaven as an arhat. Mahayana Buddhism criticizes the goal of becoming an arhat as selfish and considers the bodhisattva to be a higher goal because the bodhisattva remains in the cycle of rebirths to work for the good of others. This divergence of opinion is one of the fundamental differences between Theravada and Mahayana Buddhism.

aria, Solo song with instrumental accompaniment in opera, cantata, or oratorio. The strophic or stanzaic aria, in which each new stanza might represent a melodic variation on the first, appeared in opera in Claudio Monteverdi's *Orfeo* (1607) and was widely used for decades. The standard aria form *c.* 1650–1775 was the da capo aria, in which the opening melody and text are repeated after an intervening melody-text section (often in a different key, tempo, and metre); the return of the first section was often virtuosically embellished by the singer. Comic operas never limited themselves to da capo form. Even in serious opera, from *c.* 1750 a variety of forms were used; Gioacchino Rossini and others often expanded the aria into a complete musical scene in which two or more conflicting emotions were expressed. Richard Wagner's operas largely abandoned the aria in favour of a continuous musical texture, but arias have never ceased to be written.

Arianism, Christian heresy that declared that Christ is not truly divine but a created being. According to the Alexandrian presbyter Arius (4th century), God alone is immutable and self-existent, and the Son is not God but a creature with a beginning. The Council of Nicaea (AD 325) condemned Arius and declared the Son to be "of one substance with the father." Arianism had numerous defenders for the next 50 years but eventually collapsed when the Christian emperors of Rome Gratian and Theodosius assumed power. The First Council of Constantinople (381) approved the Nicene Creed and proscribed Arianism. The heresy continued among the Germanic tribes through the 7th century, and similar beliefs are held in the present day by the Jehovah's Witnesses and by some adherents of Unitarianism.

Arias Sánchez, Óscar (b. Sept. 13, 1941, Heredia, C.Rica), President of Costa Rica (1986–90, 2006–10). Born to wealth,

Arias became a moderate socialist and worked for the National Liberation Party from the 1960s. He first became president at a time when much of Central America was torn by civil war. His 1987 Central American peace plan, signed by the leaders of El Salvador, Guatemala, Honduras, and Nicaragua, included provisions for cease-fires, free elections, and amnesty for political prisoners. He was awarded the 1987 Nobel Peace Prize. Reelected president in 2006, Arias unsuccessfully mediated the political crisis that rocked Honduras in 2009, following the military ouster of that country's president.

Aries (Latin: "Ram") In astronomy, the constellation lying between Pisces and Taurus; in astrology, the first sign of the zodiac, governing approximately the period March 21–April 19. It is represented by a ram, which is sometimes identified with the Egyptian god Amon. In Greek mythology Aries was identified with the ram that carried the prince Phrixus out of Thessaly to Colchis. Phrixus sacrificed the ram to Zeus, who placed it in the heavens as a constellation. Its golden fleece was later recovered by Jason.

aristocracy, Originally, leadership by a small privileged class or a minority thought to be best qualified to lead. Plato and Aristotle considered aristocrats to be those who are morally and intellectually superior, and therefore fit to govern in the interests of the people. The term has come to mean the upper layer of a stratified group. Most aristocracies have been hereditary, and many European societies stratified their aristocratic classes by formally titling their members, thereby making the term roughly synonymous with nobility.

Aristotle (b. 384, Stagira—d. 322 bc, Chalcis), Greek philosopher and scientist whose thought determined the course of Western intellectual history for two millenia. He was the son of the court physician to Amyntas III, grandfather of Alexander the Great. In 367 he became a student at the Academy of Plato in Athens; he remained there for 20 years. After Plato's death in 348/347, he returned to Macedonia, where he became tutor to the young Alexander. In 335 he founded his own school in Athens, the Lyceum. His intellectual range was vast, covering most of the sciences and many of the arts. He worked in physics, chemistry, biology, zoology, and botany; in psychology, political theory, and ethics; in logic and metaphysics; and in history, literary theory, and rhetoric. He invented the study of formal logic, devising for it a finished system, known as syllogistic, that was considered the sum of the discipline until the 19th century; his work in zoology, both observational and theoretical, also was not surpassed until the 19th century. His ethical and political theory, especially his conception of the ethical virtues and of human flourishing ("happiness"), continue to exert great influence in philosophical debate. He wrote prolifically; his major surviving works include the *Organon, De Anima* ("On the Soul"), *Physics, Metaphysics, Nicomachean Ethics, Eudemian Ethics, Magna Moralia, Politics, Rhetoric,* and *Poetics,* as well as other works on natural history and science.

arithmetic, Branch of mathematics that deals with the properties of numbers and ways of combining them through addition, subtraction, multiplication, and division. Initially it dealt only with the counting numbers, but its definition has broadened to include all real numbers. The most important arithmetic properties (where a and b are real numbers) are the commutative laws of addition and multiplication, $a + b = b + a$ and $ab = ba$; the associative laws of addition and multiplication, $a + (b + c) = (a + b) + c$ and $a(bc) = (ab)c$; and the distributive law, which connects addition and multiplication, $a(b + c) = ab + ac$. These properties include subtraction (addition of a negative number) and division (multiplication by a fraction).

Arjuna, One of the five brothers who are the heroes of the *Mahabharata*. His reluctance to go into battle prompts Krishna, manifested as his friend and charioteer, to deliver the discourse on duty that constitutes the *Bhagavadgita*. An exemplar of skill, duty, and compassion as well as a seeker of true knowledge, Arjuna is a central figure in Hindu myth and theology.

Ark of the Covenant, In Judaism and Christianity, the ornate, gold-plated wooden chest that in biblical times housed the two tablets of the Law given to Moses by God. The Levites carried the Ark during the Hebrews' wandering in the wilderness. Following the conquest of Canaan, it was kept at Shiloh but was sometimes carried into battle by the Israelites. David took it to Jerusalem, and Solomon placed it in the Temple of Jerusalem, where it rested in the Holy of Holies and was seen only by the high priest on Yom Kippur. It is believed to have been captured when Jerusalem fell to the Babylonians in 586 bc, and its subsequent fate is unknown.

Arkhangelsk, or ARCHANGEL, City (pop., 2002: 355,500), northwestern Russia. Located near the mouth of Northern Dvina River, it has a large harbour kept open in winter by icebreakers. The area was settled by Norsemen in the 10th century AD. In 1553 it was visited by the English who were looking for the Northeast Passage. Founded in 1584 as a monastery of Michael the archangel, it became a trading station of the Muscovy Co. It was opened to European trade by Tsar Boris Godunov and flourished as the sole Russian seaport until St. Petersburg was built in 1703. Arkhangelsk was the scene of British, French, and U.S. support of the northern Russian government against the Bolsheviks in 1918–20. During World War II it received convoys of lend-lease goods from Britain and the U.S. (1941–45). It is a major timber-exporting port and has extensive shipbuilding facilities.

Armada, Spanish, Great fleet sent by Philip II of Spain in 1588 to invade England in conjunction with a Spanish army from Flanders. Philip was motivated by a desire to restore the Roman Catholic faith in England and by English piracies against Spanish trade and possessions. The Armada, commanded by the duke of Medina-Sidonia, consisted of about 130 ships. In the weeklong battle, the Spanish suffered defeat after the English launched fire ships into the Spanish fleet, breaking the ships' formation and making them susceptible to the English ships' heavy guns. Many Spanish ships were also lost during the long voyage home, and a total of perhaps 15,000 Spaniards died. The defeat of the Armada, in which Francis Drake played a principal role, saved England and the Netherlands from possible absorption into the Spanish empire.

Armageddon, In the New Testament, the place where the kings of the earth under demonic leadership will wage war on the forces of God at the end of history. Armageddon is mentioned only in the Revelation to John. The name may mean "Mountain of Megiddo," a reference to the city of Megiddo, which held strategic importance in Palestine. Other biblical references suggest Jerusalem as the battle site.

Armenia, officially REPUBLIC OF ARMENIA, Country, Transcaucasia, western Asia. Area: 11,484 sq mi (29,743 sq km). Population: (2011 est.) 3,100,000. Capital: Yerevan. Armenians constitute nine-tenths of the population; there are also small numbers of Azerbaijanians, Kurds, Russians, and Ukrainians. Languages: Armenian (official), Russian. Religions: Christianity (predominantly Armenian Apostolic; also Roman Catholic); also Islam. Currency: dram. Armenia is a mountainous country with an average elevation of 5,900 ft (1,800 m). The Lesser Caucasus ranges stretch across its northern portion, and Lake Sevan lies in the east-central part. Armenia has a dry and continental climate that changes dramatically with elevation. Though the country has become highly industrialized (as a result of the development of hydroelectric power during Soviet rule) and increasingly urbanized, agriculture is still important. Armenia is a unitary multiparty republic with a single legislative body. The head of state is the president, and the head of government is the prime minister. The Republic of Armenia is a successor state to a historical region in Caucasia. Historical Armenia's boundaries have varied considerably, but old Armenia extended over what are now northeastern Turkey and the Republic of Armenia. The area was equivalent to the ancient kingdom of Urartu, which ruled *c.* 1270–850 BCE. It was later conquered by the Medes and Macedonia and still later allied with Rome. Armenia adopted Christianity as its national religion *c.* 300 CE. For centuries the scene of strife among Arabs, Seljūqs, Byzantines, and Mongols, it came under the rule of the Ottoman Empire in 1514–16. Over the next centuries, as parts were ceded to other rulers, nationalism arose among the scattered Armenians; by the late 19th century it had caused widespread disruption. Fighting between Ottomans and Russians escalated when part of Armenia was ceded to Russia in 1828, and it continued through World War I (1914–18), leading to genocide against Armenians. With the Ottoman defeat, the Russian portion became part of a Soviet republic in 1922. Armenia was established as a constituent republic of the U.S.S.R. in 1936. The U.S.S.R. began to dissolve in the late 1980s, and Armenia declared its independence in 1991. In the years that followed, it fought Azerbaijan for control of Nagorno-Karabakh, a conflict that continued despite attempts to settle it. Large numbers of Armenians left the country in the 1990s following an economic downturn, and many stayed away even after the economy began to improve.

Armenian, Armenian HAY, plural HAYK OR HAYQ, Member of an Indo-European people first recognized in the early 7th century BC when they moved into areas of Transcaucasia, Anatolia, and the Middle East that came to be known as Armenia. Armenian history has been one of nearly constant struggles for independence from foreign domination, first from the Medes and Persians, the Seleucid dynasty, and the Roman Republic and Empire and later from the Byzantine Empire, the Seljūq dynasty, the Ottoman Empire, the Ṣafavid dynasty, and tsarist Russia. At the beginning of the 20th century most Armenians were driven from Anatolia or killed by Ottoman forces during the Armenian massacres. The Republic of Armenia was declared in 1990 after being part of the Soviet Union since 1922. More than 3.5 million Armenians live there, and there is an appreciable diaspora in other countries of Transcaucasia, in parts of the Middle East, and in the West. Armenian culture reached an apex in the 14th century, producing highly regarded sculpture, architecture, and fine art. Until the 20th century, Armenians were primarily agricultural; now they are highly urbanized. Traditionally they are either Orthodox or Roman Catholic Christians; Armenia was considered the first Christian state.

Armenian massacres, Murder and expulsion of Turkish Armenians by the Ottoman Empire under Abdülhamid II in 1894–96 and by the Young Turk government in 1915–16. In 1894, when the Armenians began agitating for territorial autonomy and protesting against high taxes, Ottoman troops and Kurdish tribesmen killed thousands. In 1896, hoping to call attention to their plight, Armenian revolutionaries seized the Ottoman Bank in Istanbul. Mobs of Muslim Turks, abetted by elements of the government, killed more than 50,000 Armenians in response. Sporadic killings occurred over the next two decades. In response to Russia's use of Armenian troops against the Ottomans in World War I (1914–18), the government deported 1.75 million Armenians south to Syria and Mesopotamia, in the course of which some 600,000 Armenians were killed or died of starvation.

armour, or BODY ARMOUR, Protective clothing that can shield the wearer from weapons and projectiles. By extension, armour is also protective covering for animals, vehicles, and so on. Prehistoric warriors used leather hides and helmets. Chinese warriors used rhinoceros skin in the 11th century BC, and Greek infantry wore thick, multilayered metal-and-linen cuirasses (armour covering the body from neck to waist) in the 5th century BC. Shirts of chain mail were worn throughout the Roman Empire, and mail was the chief armour of western Europe until the 14th century. Ancient Greeks and Romans used armour made of rigid metal plates, which reappeared in Europe around the 13th century. Plate armour dominated European design until the 17th century, when firearms

began to make it obsolete. It began to disappear in the 18th century, but the helmet reappeared in World War I and became standard equipment. Modern body armour (the bulletproof vest) covers the chest and sometimes the groin; it is a flexible garment reinforced with steel plates, fibreglass, boron carbide, or multiple layers of synthetic fabric such as Kevlar.

arms control, Limitation of the development, testing, production, deployment, proliferation, or use of weapons through international agreements. Arms control did not arise in international diplomacy until the first Hague Convention (1899). The Washington Conference (1921–22) and the Kellogg-Briand Pact (1928) were broken without much fear of sanction. U.S.-Soviet treaties to control nuclear weapons during the Cold War were taken more seriously. In 1968 the two superpowers and Britain sponsored the Nuclear Non-proliferation Treaty (signed also by 59 other countries), which committed signatory countries not to promote the spread, or proliferation, of nuclear weapons to countries that did not already possess them.

Armstrong, Louis (b. Aug. 4, 1901, New Orleans, La., U.S.—d. July 6, 1971, New York, N.Y.), U.S. jazz trumpeter and singer. As a youth in New Orleans, he participated in marching, riverboat, and cabaret bands. A childhood nickname, Satchelmouth, was shortened to Satchmo and used throughout his life. In 1922 he moved to Chicago to join King Oliver's Creole Jazz Band. In 1924 he joined the Fletcher Henderson Orchestra in New York City; the following year he switched from cornet to trumpet and began recording under his own name with his Hot Five and Hot Seven ensembles. In these recordings the prevailing emphasis on collective improvisation gives way to his developing strength as soloist and vocalist. By the time of his "West End Blues" (1928), Armstrong had established the preeminence of the virtuoso soloist in jazz. His vibrant melodic phrasing, inventive harmonic improvisation, and swinging rhythmic conception established the vernacular of jazz music. His powerful tone, great range, and dazzling velocity set a new technical standard. He also was one of the first scat singers, improvising nonsense syllables in the manner of a horn. He became something more than a jazz musician: solo attraction, bandleader, film actor, and international star.

Louis Armstrong.
AP

Armstrong, Neil (Alden) (b. Aug. 5, 1930, Wapakoneta, Ohio, U.S.), U.S. astronaut. He became a pilot at 16, studied aeronautical engineering, and won three Air Medals in the Korean War. In 1955 he became a civilian research pilot for the forerunner of NASA. He joined the space program in 1962 with the second group of astronauts. In 1966, as command pilot of Gemini 8, he and David Scott completed the first manual space docking maneuver, with an unmanned Agena rocket. On July 20, 1969, as part of the Apollo 11 mission, he became the first person to step onto the Moon, proclaiming "That's one small step for [a] man, one giant leap for mankind."

Neil Armstrong, 1969.
NASA

army, Large, organized force armed and trained for war, especially on land. The term may be applied to a large unit organized for independent action or to a nation's or ruler's overall military organization for land warfare. The character and organization of armies have varied through history. At various times armies have been built around infantry soldiers or mounted warriors (e.g., cavalry) or men in machines, and have been made up of professionals or amateurs, of mercenaries fighting for pay or for plunder, or of patriots fighting for a cause.

Arno River, River, central Italy. It is 150 mi (240 km) long, flowing west from the Apennines through Florence and into the Ligurian Sea below Pisa. Near Arezzo it is connected with the Tiber River by its canalized tributary, the Chiani. Subject to disastrous floods, in 1966 it inundated Florence and caused extensive damage.

arrest, Restraint and seizure of a person by someone (e.g., a police officer) acting under legal authority. An officer may arrest a person who is committing or attempting to commit a crime in the officer's presence. Arrest is also permitted if the officer reasonably believes that a crime has been committed and that the person arrested is the guilty party. A court or judicial officer may issue an arrest warrant on a showing of probable cause. Most states restrict or prohibit arrest in civil (noncriminal) cases; an example of occasionally permitted civil arrest is the taking into custody of a debtor who might otherwise abscond. In the U.S., suspects must be warned of their rights when they are arrested. An unlawful arrest is regarded as false imprisonment and usually invalidates any evidence collected in connection with it.

Arrow, Kenneth J(oseph) (b. Aug. 23, 1921, New York, N.Y., U.S.), U.S. economist. He received his Ph.D. from Columbia University and taught principally at Stanford and Harvard. Arrow's books include *Social Choices and Individual Values* (1951). His most striking claim was that, under certain conditions of rationality and equality, a ranking of societal preferences will not necessarily correspond to the rankings of individual preferences, given more than two individuals and alternative choices. In 1972 he shared the Nobel Prize with John R. Hicks.

arsenic, Nonmetallic to semimetallic chemical element, chemical symbol As, atomic number 33. It exists uncombined in two stable (and several unstable) allotropes, one gray and one yellow, but is more often found in nature as the sulfide or oxide. The elemental form is used to form alloys of metals (especially lead), and certain semiconductors are made from crystals of gallium arsenide (GaAs). Arsenious oxide (arsenic trioxide or white arsenic, As_2O_3) is used in pesticides, as a pigment, and as a preservative of hides and wood; this is the poisonous "arsenic" in detective stories. Arsenic pentoxide (As_2O_5) is also used in insecticides, herbicides, metal adhesives, and pigments.

Arsenic (gray) with realgar (red) and orpiment (yellow)
Courtesy of the Joseph and Helen Guetterman collection; photograph, John H. Gerard/EB Inc.

art, also called VISUAL ART, A visual object or experience consciously created through an expression of skill or imagination. The term *art* encompasses diverse media such as painting, sculpture, printmaking, drawing, decorative arts, photography, and installation. The various visual arts exist within a continuum that ranges from purely aesthetic purposes at one end to purely utilitarian purposes at the other. This should by no means be taken as a rigid scheme, however, particularly in cultures in which everyday objects are painstakingly constructed and imbued with meaning. Particularly in the 20th century, debates arose over the definition of *art*. Figures such as Dada artist Marcel Duchamp implied that it is enough for an artist to deem something "art" and put it in a publicly accepted venue. Such intellectual experimentation continued throughout the 20th century in movements such as conceptual art and Minimalism. By the turn of the 21st century, a variety of new media (e.g., video art) further challenged traditional definitions of art. *See* aesthetics; art conservation and restoration; drawing; painting; printmaking; sculpture; photography; decorative arts.

Art Deco, or STYLE MODERNE, Movement in design, interior decoration, and architecture in the 1920s and '30s in Europe and the U.S. The name derives from the Exposition Internationale des Arts Décoratifs et Industriels Modernes in Paris in 1925. Its products included both individually crafted luxury items and mass-produced wares, but, in either case, the intention was to create a sleek and antitraditional elegance that symbolized wealth and sophistication. Influenced by Art Nouveau, Bauhaus, Cubist, Native American, and Egyptian sources, the distinguishing features of the style are simple, clean shapes, often with a "streamlined" look; ornament that is geometric or stylized from representational forms; and unusually varied, often expensive materials, which frequently include man-made substances (plastics, especially bakelite; vita-glass; and ferroconcrete) in addition to natural ones (jade, silver, ivory, obsidian, chrome, and rock crystal). Typical motifs included stylized animals, foliage, nude female figures, and sun rays. New York City's Rockefeller Center (especially its interiors supervised by Donald Deskey), the Chrysler Building by William Van Alen, and the Empire State Building by Shreve, Lamb & Harmon are the most monumental embodiments of Art Deco.

Art Nouveau, Decorative style that flourished in western Europe and the U.S. *c.* 1890–1910. The term was derived in 1895 from a gallery in Paris called L'Art Nouveau. Characterized by sinuous, asymmetrical lines based on plant forms, the style was used in architecture, interior design, graphic art and design, jewelry, and glass. It was international in scope, with celebrated exponents in England (Aubrey Beardsley), Paris (Alphonse Mucha), the U.S. (Louis Comfort Tiffany), Scotland (Charles Rennie Mackintosh), Spain (Antonio Gaudí), and Belgium (Victor Horta). The style did not significantly survive the outbreak of World War I.

Artemis as a huntress, Classical sculpture; in the Louvre, Paris.
Alinari/Art Resource, New York

Artemis, In Greek religion, the goddess of wild animals, the hunt, vegetation, chastity, and childbirth. Artemis was the daughter of Zeus and Leto and the twin sister of Apollo. Accompanied by nymphs, she danced in mountains and forests. She both killed game and, as Mistress of Animals, protected it. Stories of her nymphs' love affairs may originally have been told of the goddess herself, but poets after Homer stressed her chastity. She was known for her unpitying wrath when offended. Artemis may have developed out of Ishtar in the East. Her Roman counterpart was Diana.

artery, Vessel that carries blood from the heart to other parts of the body. Arterial blood carries oxygen and nourishment to tissues; the one exception is the pulmonary artery, which conveys oxygen-depleted blood from the heart to the lungs for oxygenation and removal of excess carbon dioxide. Arteries are muscular, elastic tubes that transport blood under the pressure of the heart's pumping action, which can be felt as the pulse. Large arteries branch off from the aorta and give rise to smaller arteries, down to the threadlike arterioles, which branch into capillaries. An artery wall's inner layer (tunica intima) consists of an endothelial (cellular) lining, a fine connective tissue network, and a layer of elastic fibres. The middle layer (tunica media) is mostly smooth muscle cells. The outer layer (tunica externa) contains supportive collagen fibres.

arthritis, Inflammation of the joints and its effects. Acute arthritis is marked by pain, redness, and swelling. The principal forms are osteoarthritis, rheumatoid arthritis, and septic arthritis. Several forms of arthritis are part of the symptom complexes of autoimmune diseases.

arthropod, Any member of the largest phylum, Arthropoda, in the animal kingdom. Arthropoda consists of more than one million known invertebrate species in four subphyla: Uniramia (five classes, including insects), Chelicerata (three classes, including arachnids and horseshoe crabs), Crustacea (crustaceans), and Trilobita (trilobites). All arthropods are bilaterally symmetrical and possess a segmented body covered by an exoskeleton containing chitin, which serves as both armour and a surface for muscle attachment. Each body segment may bear a pair of jointed appendages. The phylum includes carnivores, herbivores, omnivores, detritus feeders, filter feeders, and parasites in nearly all environments, both aquatic and terrestrial.

Arthurian legend, Body of stories and medieval romances centring on the legendary English king Arthur. The stories chronicle Arthur's life, the adventures of his knights, and the adulterous love between his knight Sir Lancelot and his queen, Guinevere. The legend was popular in Wales before the 11th century, was brought into literature by Geoffrey of Monmouth, and was adapted by other medieval writers, including Chrétien de Troyes, Wace, Lawamon, and Sir Thomas Malory, becoming entwined with legends of the Holy Grail. From Victorian times, when interest in the legend revived, it has figured in major works by Alfred Tennyson (*Idylls of the King*) and T.H. White (*The Once and Future King*). It is uncertain whether Arthur was a historical figure. Medieval sources say he was a 6th-century warrior and champion of Christianity who united the British tribes against the Saxon invaders, died in battle at Camlann *c.* 539, and was buried at Glastonbury.

artichoke, Large, coarse, herbaceous, thistlelike perennial plant (*Cynara scolymus*) of the family Asteraceae. The thick, edible scales and bottom part (heart) of the immature flower heads are a culinary delicacy. The artichoke is native to the Mediterranean and is cultivated extensively in other regions with rich soil and a mild, humid climate. The Jerusalem artichoke is a tuber and does not resemble the artichoke.

articulation, In phonetics, the shaping of the vocal tract (larynx, pharynx, and oral and nasal cavities) by positioning mobile organs (such as the tongue) relative to other parts that may be rigid (such as the hard palate) and thus modifying the airstream to produce speech sounds. Articulators include the tongue, lips, teeth and upper gum ridge, hard and soft palate, uvula, pharyngeal wall, and glottis. Primary articulation refers either to where or how the vocal tract is narrowed or blocked to produce a consonant, or to the tongue contour, lip shape, and larynx height that determine the sound of a vowel. Other articulators may be used to produce a secondary articulation such as palatalization (the front of the tongue approaching the hard palate), glottalization (complete or partial closure of the vocal cords), or nasalization (simultaneous passage of air through the nasal and oral tracts).

artificial heart, Machine or mechanical pump that maintains blood circulation in the human body. The heart-lung machine, a mechanical pump, can maintain circulation for a few hours while the heart is stopped for surgery. It shunts blood away from the heart, oxygenates it, and returns it to the body. No device has yet been developed for total, long-term replacement of the heart; existing artificial hearts reduce the heart's workload by pumping between beats or acting as an auxiliary ventricle and are suitable only as temporary replacements in patients awaiting transplant.

artificial insemination, Introduction of semen into a female's vagina or cervix by means other than sexual intercourse. First developed for animal breeding in the early 20th century in Russia, it is now also used to induce pregnancy in women whose partners cannot impregnate them. The partner's (or other donor's) semen is inserted with a syringe. Though reasonably successful, artificial insemination in humans raises moral issues that are not yet fully resolved. In livestock, deep-frozen semen from a male animal can be stored for long periods without losing its fertility, thus allowing a single bull to sire as many as 10,000 calves a year.

artificial intelligence (AI), Ability of a machine to perform tasks thought to require human intelligence. Typical applications include game playing, language translation, expert systems, and robotics. Although pseudo-intelligent machinery dates back to antiquity, the first glimmerings of true intelligence awaited the development of digital computers in the 1940s. AI, or at least the semblance of intelligence, has developed in parallel with computer processing power, which appears to be the main limiting factor. Early AI projects, such as playing chess and solving mathematical problems, are now seen as trivial compared to visual pattern recognition, complex decision making, and the use of natural language.

artillery, In modern military science, big guns such as cannons, howitzers, or mortars operated by crews and of a calibre greater than 15 mm. The earliest artillery, introduced in the 14th century, were cannons and mortars of bronze, brass, or iron mounted on two-wheeled carriages. Modern artillery dates from the second half of the 19th century, when advances included steel gun barrels, more powerful gunpowders, and piston mountings that held artillery carriages steady during recoil. Both powder and projectile were encased in a shell, which allowed for faster loading. Since World War II, artillery has been ranked as light (up to 105 mm, for support of ground troops), medium (106–155 mm, for bombardment), and heavy (over 155 mm, for attacking rear installations).

Arts and Crafts movement, English social and aesthetic movement of the second half of the 19th century, dedicated to reestablishing the importance of craftsmanship in an era of mechanization and mass production. The name derives from the Arts and Crafts Exhibition Society (1888). Inspired by John Ruskin and other writers who deplored the effects of industrialization, William Morris founded a firm of interior designers and manufacturers to produce handcrafted textiles, printed books, wallpaper, furniture, jewelry, and metalwork. The movement was criticized as elitist and impractical in an industrial society, but in the 1890s its appeal widened and spread to other countries, including the U.S. See photograph on following page.

Aruba, Island, Lesser Antilles, off northwestern Venezuela. Aruba is an autonomous state within the Kingdom of the Netherlands. Area: 75 sq mi (193 sq km). Population: (2011 est.) 102,000. Capital: Oranjestad. The majority of the present-day population is a combination of mostly American Indian, Spanish, Dutch, and African ancestry. Dutch and Papiamentu are the official languages. The principal religion is Roman Catholicism. The currency is the Aruban florin. The formal head of government is a governor appointed by the reigning monarch of the Netherlands. The Council of Ministers, headed by a prime minister, has executive authority and is responsible to a unicameral legislature called

An English room decorated by William Morris in the Arts and Crafts style.
Courtesy of the Victoria and Albert Museum, London, photograph, John Webb

the Staten. Aruba's lack of water severely limits agriculture. The large petroleum-refining complex there, once the island's main employer, reopened after closing in the mid-1980s, but tourism is now the island's economic mainstay. The earliest inhabitants were Arawak Indians, whose cave drawings can still be seen. Though the Dutch took possession of Aruba in 1636, they did not begin to develop it aggressively until 1816. In 1845 it became one of the six Dutch island dependencies in the West Indies to come under collective administration from Curaçao. This grouping was reorganized in 1954 as the Federation of the Netherlands Antilles. In 1986 Aruba seceded from the Netherlands Antilles in an initial step toward independence. In 1994 the government postponed indefinitely a decision on independence.

arugula, or ROCKET, Yellowish-flowered European herbaceous plant (*Eruca vesicaria sativa*), of the mustard family, cultivated for its foliage, which is used especially in salads. The leaves taste sharp and peppery when young and succulent but become bitter with age. A medicinal oil is extracted from the seeds.

Arunachal Pradesh, State (pop., 2008 est.: 1,200,000), extreme northeastern India. Bordered by Bhutan, the Tibet Autonomous Region of China, and Myanmar and Nagaland and Assam states, it occupies 32,333 sq mi (83,743 sq km); its capital is Itanagar. Known under the British Indian government as the North East Frontier Agency, the region became Arunachal Pradesh union territory in 1972 and was granted statehood in 1987. China does not recognize the boundary (the McMahon Line) between it and Arunachal Pradesh. The state incorporates major ranges of the Himalaya foothills and has a rugged terrain. The population consists of many ethnic groups who speak dialects of the Tibeto-Burman languages.

Hillsides cleared for shifting cultivation (jhum) near Along, central Arunachal Pradesh, India.
© Vinay Parelkar/Dinodia Photo Library

arupa-loka, In Buddhism, the "world of immaterial form," the highest of the three spheres of existence in which rebirth takes place. The others are the "fine-material world" (*rupa-loka*) and the "world of feeling" (*kama-loka*). In the *arupa-loka*, existence depends on the stage of concentration attained in the previous life, of which there are four levels: the infinity of space, the infinity of thought, the infinity of nonbeing, and the infinity of neither consciousness nor nonconsciousness. Beings in the *arupa-loka* do not have a material body.

Aryan, Name formerly given to prehistoric people who settled in ancient Iran and the northern Indian subcontinent. Their language is believed to have influenced the Indo-European languages of South Asia. In the 19th century there arose a notion, propagated by the count de Gobineau and later by his disciple Houston Stewart Chamberlain, of an "Aryan race": people who spoke Indo-European, especially Germanic, languages and lived in northern Europe. The "Aryan race" was considered to be superior to all other peoples. Although this notion was repudiated by numerous scholars, including Franz Boas, the notion was seized on by Adolf Hitler and was made the basis of the Nazi policy of exterminating Jews, Roma (Gypsies), and other "non-Aryans." *See also* racism.

asbestos, Any of several minerals that separate readily into long, flexible fibres. Chrysotile accounts for about 95% of all asbestos still in commercial use. The other types all belong to the amphibole group and include the highly fibrous forms of anthophyllite, amosite, crocidolite, tremolite, and actinolite. Asbestos fibre was used in brake linings, insulation, roofing shingles, floor and ceiling tiles, cement pipes, and other building materials. Asbestos fabrics were used for safety apparel and theatre curtains. In the 1970s it was found that prolonged inhalation of the tiny asbestos fibres can cause asbestosis, lung cancer, and/or mesothelioma, all serious lung diseases. The incidence of mesothelioma is most commonly associated with extensive inhalation of amphibole asbestos. In 1989 the U.S. government instituted a gradual ban on the manufacture, use, and export of most products made with asbestos.

asbestosis, Lung disease caused by long-term inhalation of asbestos fibres. A pneumoconiosis found primarily in asbestos workers, asbestosis is also seen in people living near asbestos industries. Fibres remain in the lungs and many years later cause extensive scarring and fibrosis. Shortness of breath and inadequate oxygenation result; advanced cases include a dry cough. There is no effective treatment. The associated increased cardiac effort may induce heart disease. Cigarette smoking greatly exacerbates its symptoms. Lung cancer and malignant mesothelioma are more common with asbestos inhalation and asbestosis.

Ascension, In Christian belief, the ascent of Jesus into heaven 40 days after the Resurrection. The Book of Acts relates that, after several appearances to the Apostles over a period of 40 days, Jesus was taken up in their presence and hidden behind a cloud, a symbol of God's presence. The event is thought to indicate a new relationship between Jesus and God and between Jesus and his followers. The feast of the Ascension is universally observed by Christians, and its celebration emphasizes the kingship of Christ. Since the 4th century, it has been celebrated 40 days after Easter and 10 days before Pentecost.

asceticism, Practice of the denial of physical or psychological desires in order to attain a spiritual ideal or goal. Most religions have some features of asceticism. The desire for ritual purity in order to come in contact with the divine, the need for atonement, and the wish to earn merit or gain access to supernatural powers all are reasons for ascetic practice. Christian hermits and monks, wandering Hindu ascetics, and Buddhist monks all reject worldly goods and practice various forms of self-denial, including celibacy, abstinence, and fasting. Members of the Digambara sect of Jainism practice an extreme form of asceticism that includes the rejection of wearing clothes. Though monasticism is rejected in the Qur'ān, ascetic movements such as *zuhd* have arisen in Islam. Zoroastrianism forbids fasting and mortification.

ASCII, in full AMERICAN STANDARD CODE FOR INFORMATION INTERCHANGE, Data-transmission code used to represent both text (letters, numbers, punctuation marks) and noninput device commands (control characters) for electronic exchange and storage. Standard ASCII uses a string of 7 bits (binary digits) for each symbol and can thus represent $2^7 = 128$ characters. Extended ASCII uses an 8-bit encoding system and can thus represent $2^8 = 256$ characters. While ASCII is still found in legacy data, Unicode, with 8-, 16-, and 32-bit versions, has become standard for modern operating systems and browsers. In particular, the 32-bit version now supports all of the characters in every major language.

Asclepius, Latin AESCULAPIUS, Greco-Roman god of medicine. He was the son of Apollo and the nymph Coronis. He learned the art of healing from the Centaur Chiron. Fearful that Asclepius would make humans immortal, Zeus slew him with a thunderbolt. His cult originated in Thessaly and spread throughout Greece. Because he was said to cure the sick in dreams, the practice of sleeping in his temples became common. Asclepius was often represented holding a staff with a serpent coiled around it.

Asclepius, from an ivory diptych, 5th century AD; in the Liverpool City Museum, England
The Bridgeman Art Library/Art Resource, New York

ASEAN, in full ASSOCIATION OF SOUTHEAST ASIAN NATIONS, International organization established by the governments of Indonesia, Malaysia, the Philippines, Singapore, and Thailand in 1967 to accelerate regional economic growth, social progress, and cultural development and to promote peace and security in the region. Brunei became a member in 1984, Vietnam in 1995, Laos and Myanmar (Burma) in 1997, and Cambodia in 1999. ASEAN became a leading voice on regional trade and security issues in the 1990s; in 1992 member nations created the ASEAN Free Trade Area.

Asgard, In Norse mythology, the dwelling place of the gods. It consisted of 12 or more realms, including Valhalla, home of Odin; Thrudheim, home of Thor; and Breidablick, home of Balder. Each Norse god had his own palace in Asgard. This heavenly region could only be reached from earth via the rainbow bridge called Bifrost.

Ashʿariyyah, School of Muslim theology founded by Abū al-Ḥasan al-Ashʿarī in the 10th century. It supported the use of reason and speculative theology (*kalām*) to defend the faith but was not as extreme in its rationalism as the Muʿtazilah school. Followers attempted to demonstrate the existence and nature of God through rational argument, while affirming the eternal, uncreated nature of the Qurʾān. They were accused by the Muʿtazilah of believing in predestination because they claimed the human capacity for action was only acquired at the very moment of action.

Ashgabat, formerly ASHKHABAD, City (pop., 2002 est.: 743,000), capital of Turkmenistan. It lies in an oasis at the northern foot of the Kopet-Dag Range near the Iranian border. Founded in 1881 as a Russian military fort, it was the capital of Turkmenistan S.S.R. (1924–90). A violent earthquake destroyed the city in 1948; it was rebuilt on the same plan. It is now an industrial, transportation, and cultural centre.

Ashkenazi, Any of the historically Yiddish-speaking European Jews who settled in central and northern Europe, or their descendants. They lived originally in the Rhineland valley, and their name is derived from the Hebrew word *Ashkenaz* ("Germany"). After the start of the Crusades in the late 11th century, many migrated east to Poland, Lithuania, and Russia to escape persecution. In later centuries Jews who adopted the German-rite synagogue ritual were called Ashkenazim to differentiate them from the Sephardic, or Spanish-rite, Jews, from whom they differ in cultural traditions, pronunciation of Hebrew, and synagogue chanting as well as in the use of the Yiddish language (until the 20th century). Today they constitute more than 80% of the world's Jews.

Ashoka, or ASOKA (b. *c.* 304—d. *c.* 232 BC), Last major emperor (*c.* 269–232 BC) of the Mauryan empire in India and a patron of Buddhism. After his bloody conquest of Kalinga in the eighth year of his reign, Ashoka renounced military aggression and resolved to live according to the dharma. He spoke of Buddhism only to fellow Buddhists and adopted a policy of toleration for other religions. He spread Buddhist teachings through inscriptions known as the Rock Edicts and Pillar Edicts. He enjoined officials to be aware of the needs of common people and to dispense justice impartially; dharma ministers were appointed to relieve suffering and look to the special needs of other religions, women, outlying regions, and neighbouring peoples. He erected stupas and monasteries, developed a course of study for adherents, and sent missionaries to Sri Lanka. He is remembered as the ideal Buddhist ruler.

ashram, or ASHRAMA, In Hinduism, any of the four stages of life through which a "twice-born" Hindu ideally will pass. These stages are: the student, who is devoted and obedient to his teacher; the householder, who supports his family and the priests and fulfills duties to the gods and ancestors; the hermit, who withdraws from society to pursue ascetic and yogic practices; and the homeless mendicant, who renounces all possessions and wanders from place to place begging for food. In English the word has come to mean a place for the pursuit of spiritual or religious disciplines, often under a guru.

Ashur, Ancient religious capital of Assyria. It is located on the Tigris River, 60 mi (97 km) south of Mosul, Iraq. The name Ashur was applied to the city, to Assyria itself, and to Assyria's principal god. The capital's seat was originally occupied *c.* 2500 BC. By the late 12th century BC, Ashur was under Assyrian control. Its religious sanctity ensured its continuous upkeep until 614 BC, when it was destroyed by Babylonia. The archaeological site has yielded fortifications, temples, and palaces. It was designated a UNESCO World Heritage site in 2003.

Asia, Largest continent on Earth. It is bounded by the Arctic, Pacific, and Indian oceans. The western boundary, with Europe, runs roughly north-south along the eastern Ural Mountains; the Caspian, Black, Aegean, and Mediterranean seas; the Suez Canal; and the Red Sea. The islands of Sri Lanka and Taiwan and the archipelagoes of Indonesia (excluding New Guinea), the Philippines, and Japan also form part of Asia. Area: 17,226,000 sq mi (44,614,000 sq km). Population (2004 est.): 3,879,659,000. Mountains and plateaus predominate on the continent, with the highest mountains located in Central Asia and north of the Indian subcontinent. Terrain features include Earth's highest peak, Mount Everest, at 29,035 ft (8,850 m), and the lowest natural point, the Dead Sea, at 1,312 ft (400 m) below sea level. The largest of Asia's many arid regions are the Thar and Gobi deserts. It has some of the longest rivers in the world, including the Euphrates, Tigris, Indus, Ganges (Ganga), Yangtze (Chang; the longest river in Asia), Huang He (Yellow), Ob, Yenisey, and Lena. The Caspian, Aral, and Dead seas are major saltwater lakes. About one-fifth of Asia's landmass is arable. Its principal language groups include Sino-Tibetan, Indo-Aryan, Austronesian, Austroasiatic, and Semitic; important singular languages include Japanese and

Korean. East Asia contains three main ethnic groups: Chinese, Japanese, and Korean. The Indian subcontinent is home to a vast diversity of peoples, most of whom speak languages from the Indo-Aryan subgroup of the Indo-European family. Because of the influence of China and the former Soviet Union, the Mandarin Chinese dialect and the Russian language are used widely. Asia is the birthplace of all the world's major religions and hundreds of minor ones. Hinduism is the oldest major religion to have originated in southern Asia; Jainism and Buddhism emerged in the 6th and 5th centuries BC, respectively. Southwest Asia was the cradle of the so-called Abrahamic religions: Judaism, Christianity, and Islam. Daoism and Confucianism, both of which originated in the 6th or 5th century BC, have profoundly influenced Chinese culture and the cultures of surrounding peoples. Asia is marked by great disparities in wealth. A few countries, notably Japan, Singapore, and the oil-rich countries of the Arabian Peninsula, have attained high standards of living; others, such as Bangladesh and Myanmar, are among the poorest. Between these two extremes lie Russia, China, and India. Asia is a land of great cultural diversity, but there are five main cultural influences: Chinese, Indian, Islamic, European, and Central Asian. China has had great influence in East Asia as the source of Confucianism, artistic styles, and the Chinese writing system. Indian influence has been expressed through Hinduism and Buddhism, affecting the Tibet Autonomous Region of China, Indonesia, Cambodia, and Central Asia. Islam spread from its original Arabian home to become important in the Middle East, South Asia, Central Asia, and elsewhere. Members of the earlier human species *Homo erectus* migrated from Africa to East Asia at least one million years ago. One of the earliest civilizations to use writing developed in the Tigris and Euphrates river valleys *c.* 3000 BC. Civilization in the Indus River valley and in northern Syria followed *c.* mid-3rd millennium BC. Chinese urban civilization began with the Shang dynasty (*c.* 1600–1046 BC) and continued under the Zhou dynasty (1046–256 BC). Indo-European-speaking peoples (Aryans) began to invade India from the west *c.* 2000–1500 BC and developed the Vedic religion. A succession of empires and charismatic rulers, including the Macedonian Alexander the Great, spread their political control as far as military power could carry them. In the 13th century AD Genghis Khan and his Mongol successors united much of Asia under their rule. In the 14th century the Turkic warlord Timur conquered much of Central Asia. Muslim Turks destroyed the remnants of the Byzantine Empire in the 15th century. In the 19th century European imperialism began to replace Asian imperialism. Tsarist Russia pushed its political control across Asia to the Pacific Ocean, the British gained control of India and Burma (Myanmar), the French dominated eastern Southeast Asia, the Dutch occupied the East Indies (Indonesia), and the Spanish and later the U.S. ruled the Philippines. After World War II (1939–45), European imperialism steadily disappeared as former colonies gained independence in the second half of the 20th century.

Asimov, Isaac (b. Jan. 2, 1920, Petrovichi, Russia—d. April 6, 1992, New York, N.Y., U.S.), Russian-born U.S. author and biochemist. He arrived in the U.S. at age 3, earned a doctorate from Columbia University, and subsequently taught for many years at Boston University. Before embarking on graduate study, he had already begun publishing his stories. "Nightfall" (1941) is often called the finest science-fiction short story ever written. His *I, Robot* (1950) greatly influenced how later writers treated intelligent machines. A trilogy of novels—*Foundation, Foundation and Empire,* and *Second Foundation* (1951–53)—is widely considered a classic. Asimov's nonfiction science books for lay readers are noted for their lucidity and humour. Immensely prolific, he published more than 300 volumes in all.

Asmara, City (pop., 2002 est.: 500,600), capital of Eritrea. It lies on the northern tip of the Ethiopian Plateau at an elevation of 7,628 ft (2,325 m). Its Red Sea port, Massawa, is 40 mi (65 km) northeast. Formerly a hamlet of the Tigre people, Asmara became the capital of the Italian colony of Eritrea in 1900. It was under British control from 1941 until Eritrea's federation with Ethiopia in 1952 and became the capital of independent Eritrea in 1993. It is an agricultural marketplace.

asparagus, Any plant of the genus *Asparagus* (lily family), which contains about 300 species native from Siberia to southern Africa. The best-known and economically most important species is the garden asparagus (*A. officinalis*), cultivated as a green vegetable for its succulent spring stalks. Several African species are grown as ornamental plants. The poisonous species prized for their delicate and graceful foliage are *A. plumosus* (the feathery asparagus fern, or florists' fern—not a true fern), *A. sprengeri,* and *A. asparagoides.*

aspartame, Synthetic organic compound (a dipeptide) of phenylalanine and aspartic acid. It is 150–200 times as sweet as cane sugar and is used as a nonnutritive tabletop sweetener and in low-calorie prepared foods (brand names NutraSweet, Equal) but is not suitable for baking. Because of its phenylalanine content, persons with phenylketonuria must avoid it. Though it is approved by the U.S. Food and Drug Administration and other regulatory authorities around the world, its safety even for those without the disease remains controversial.

asphyxia, Lack of exchange of oxygen and carbon dioxide due to respiratory failure or disturbance, resulting in insufficient brain oxygen, which leads to unconsciousness or death. Causes include strangulation, drowning, and carbon monoxide poisoning. Breathing in food or fluid can cause obstruction of the airway and pulmonary collapse. Emergency resuscitation usually includes cardiopulmonary resuscitation.

aspirin, Common name of acetylsalicylic acid, an organic compound introduced in 1899. The ester of salicylic acid and acetic acid, it inhibits production of prostaglandins in the body. Its analgesic, fever-reducing, and anti-inflammatory effects make it useful in treating headaches, muscle and joint aches, arthritis pain, and the symptoms of mild fevers and infections. It also has anticoagulant activity and is taken in low doses by coronary heart disease patients to prevent heart attack. Prolonged use may cause stomach bleeding and peptic ulcer, and its use in children with fever has been linked to Reye syndrome. *See also* acetaminophen; ibuprofen; NSAID.

Assam, State (pop., 2008 est.: 29,929,000), northeastern India. With an area of 30,285 sq mi (78,438 sq km), Assam borders the countries of Bhutan and Bangladesh and the states of Arunachal Pradesh, Nagaland, Manipur, Mizoram, Tripura, Meghalaya, and West Bengal; its capital is Dispur. A strong independent kingdom was founded there in the 13th century by invaders from Myanmar (Burma) and China; it reached its zenith in the early 18th century. The British took control in the early 19th century. In the division of India (1947), Assam lost some territory to Pakistan. Beginning in the 1960s, four new states—Nagaland, Meghalaya, Mizoram, and Arunachal Pradesh—were created from land within Assam. The Brahmaputra River valley is its dominant physical feature. The population consists of peoples of Indo-Iranian and Asian descent; the most widely spoken language is Assamese.

Assassin, properly NIZĀRIYYAH, Byname for any member of a sub-sect of Ismāʿīlī Shīʿite Muslims who operated in parts of Iran and Syria from the 11th to the 13th century. The order takes its name from the purported use of hashish to induce ecstatic visions of paradise among its devotees (*hashshāshūn,* "hashish smokers"—whence is derived the English term) before they set out to face martyrdom. The Assassins operated out of series of mountain fortresses and, seeing assassination as a religious duty, engaged in a long campaign of murder against members of the Sunnite community, including numerous officials of the ʿAbbāsid and Seljūq dynasties, and others. The Assassins' power was finally broken by the Mongols, who captured the great Assassin stronghold of ʿAla-mūt in Iran in 1256. The Syrian branch was destroyed by the Mam-lūk Baybars I in 1271–73. Leadership of the Nizārī order continued until modern times in the line of the Aga Khans, a family prominent worldwide as philanthropists and public servants.

assault rifle, Military firearm that is chambered for ammunition of reduced size or propellant charge and has the capacity to switch between semiautomatic and fully automatic fire. Light and portable, yet able to deliver a high volume of fire with reasonable accuracy at modern combat ranges of 1,000–1,600 ft (300–500 m), assault rifles have become the standard infantry weapon of modern armies. Their ease of handling makes them ideal for mobile assault troops crowded into personnel carriers or helicopters, as well as for guerrilla fighters engaged in jungle or urban warfare. Widely used assault rifles are the U.S. M16, the Soviet Kalashnikov (the AK-47 and modernized versions), the Belgian FAL and FNC, and the German G3.

assaying, In chemical analysis, the process of determining proportions of metal, particularly precious metal, in ores and metallurgical products. The most important assaying technique grew largely out of the experiments of the ancient alchemists and goldsmiths. Precious metals tend to occur as scattered particles randomly distributed, so a large sample of ore is required. Such large samples (typically containing gold, silver, and lead) are still most economically assayed by this ancient method, which involves several steps of heating and cooling. More sophisticated recent methods, such as spectrochemical analysis, are not suited to assaying precious metal ores because the samples of the inhomogeneous ore that must be used are larger than the instruments can handle.

assembly language, Type of low-level computer programming language consisting mostly of symbolic equivalents of a particular computer's machine language. Computers produced by different manufacturers have different machine languages and require different assemblers and assembly languages. Some assembly languages can be used to convert the code that programmers write (source code) into machine language (readable by the computer), and have functions to facilitate programming (e.g., by combining a sequence of several instructions into one entity). Programming in assembly languages requires extensive knowledge of computer architecture.

association, In psychology, the process of forming mental connections or bonds between sensations, ideas, or memories. Though discussed by the ancient Greeks (in terms of similarities, contrasts, and contiguities), the "association of ideas" was first proposed by John Locke and subsequently examined by David Hume, John Stuart Mill, Herbert Spencer, and William James. Ivan Pavlov used objective methods to study the phenomenon, resulting in his identification of the conditioned reflex. Within psychoanalysis, the therapist encourages "free association" in order to help identify latent conflicts. Practitioners of Gestalt psychology and others have criticized associationist theories as too all-embracing, while some theorists of cognitive psychology have made it central to their theory of memory.

Assyria, Ancient empire, southwestern Asia. It grew from a small region around Ashur (in modern northern Iraq) to encompass an area stretching from Egypt to Anatolia. Assyria may have originated in the 2nd millennium BC, but it came to power gradually. Its greatest period began in the 9th century BC, when its conquests reached the Mediterranean Sea under Ashurnasirpal II (883–859), and again c. 746–609 BC, during the Neo-Assyrian empire, when it conquered much of the Middle East. Its greatest rulers during the latter period were Tiglath-pileser III, Sargon II, Sennacherib, and Ashurbanipal. Famous for their cruelty and fighting prowess, the Assyrians were also monumental builders, as shown by archaeological finds at Nineveh, Ashur, and Calah. The opulence of Ashurbanipal's court at Nineveh became legendary. Artis-

tically, the Assyrians were particularly noted for their stone bas-reliefs. The kingdom was finally vanquished in 612–609 BC by a coalition of Media and Babylonia (Chaldea).

Astana, formerly (1992–98) AQMOLA, or AKMOLA, or (1961–92) TSELINOGRAD, City (pop., 2004 est.: 510,533), capital of Kazakhstan. Situated on the banks of the Ishim River in north-central Kazakhstan, it was founded in 1824 as a Russian military outpost. The city's importance was enhanced by its location at the junction of the Trans-Kazakhstan and South Siberian railways. It is in the centre of a mineral-rich steppe region. In 1994 the Kazakh government began to transfer the national capital from Almaty to Astana, changing the city's name in 1998.

asteroid, Any of the many rocky small bodies that orbit the Sun mainly in a flat ring, the asteroid belt, between the orbits of Mars and Jupiter. It is thought that the gravitational influence of what became Jupiter kept the asteroids from aggregating into a single planet while the solar system was forming. Also called minor planets, asteroids are smaller than any of the solar system's major planets; only about 30 are more than 125 mi (200 km) across. Ceres is the largest known asteroid. Millions of boulder-sized asteroidal fragments are thought to exist in the solar system. Asteroids or their fragments regularly strike Earth, plunging through the atmosphere as meteors to reach its surface. Asteroids appear to be composed of carbonaceous, stony, and metallic (mainly iron) materials.

asthenosphere, Zone of the Earth's mantle lying beneath the lithosphere, believed to be much hotter and more fluid than the lithosphere. The asthenosphere is thought to extend from about 60 mi (100 km) to about 450 mi (700 km) below the Earth's surface.

asthma, Chronic disease with attacks of shortness of breath, wheezing, and coughing from constriction and mucous-membrane swelling in the bronchi (air passageways in the lungs). It is caused primarily by allergy or respiratory infection. Secondhand smoke can cause asthma in children. Asthma is common and runs in families; predisposition may be hereditary. In established asthmatics, exercise, stress, and sudden changes in temperature or humidity can bring on attacks. Attacks usually last from a half hour to several hours; severe attacks can be fatal. Corticosteroids can control asthma; injections of epinephrine can relieve acute attacks. Prevention involves avoiding exposure to allergens.

astigmatism, Lack of symmetry in the curvature of the cornea or, rarely, the lens of the eye. The unequal curvatures spread light rays, preventing them from being sharply focused at a point on the retina, causing blurring of part of the image. The effect of astigmatism can also be produced by misalignment of the lens. Astigmatic vision is corrected by means of lenses that refract the light rays to the proper degree in the opposite direction of that produced by the defects in curvature.

astrobiology, multidisciplinary field dealing with the nature and existence of and search for extraterrestrial life (life beyond Earth). Astrobiology encompasses areas of biology, astronomy, and geology. The principal areas of astrobiology research can be classified as (1) understanding the conditions under which life can arise, (2) looking for habitable worlds, and (3) searching for evidence of life.

Astrolabe, 11th century.
Oxford Science Archive/
Heritage-Images

astrolabe, Type of early scientific instrument used for reckoning time and for observational purposes. Astrolabes can be traced to the 6th century AD; they came into wide use in Europe and the Islamic world in the early Middle Ages and were adopted by mariners by the mid-15th century. One widely used variety, the planispheric astrolabe, can be regarded as a rudimentary analog computer. It enabled astronomers to calculate the positions of the Sun and prominent stars with respect to both the horizon and the meridian.

astrology, Divination that consists of interpreting the influence of stars and planets on earthly affairs and human destinies. In ancient times it was inseparable from astronomy. It originated in Mesopotamia (*c.* 3rd millennium BC) and spread to India, but it developed its Western form in Greek civilization during the Hellenistic period. Astrology entered Islamic culture as part of the Greek tradition and was returned to European culture through Arabic learning during the Middle Ages. According to the Greek tradition, the heavens are divided according to the 12 constellations of the zodiac, and the bright stars that rise at intervals cast a spiritual influence over human affairs. Astrology was also important in ancient China, and in imperial times it became standard practice to have a horoscope cast for each newborn child and at all decisive junctures of life. Though the Copernican system shattered the geocentric worldview that astrology requires, interest in astrology has continued into modern times and astrological signs are still widely believed to influence personality.

astronomical unit (AU), Length of the semimajor axis of Earth's orbit around the Sun, 92,955,808 mi (149,597,870 km), often defined simply as the average distance from Earth to the Sun. Direct measurement through the parallax method cannot be used for accurate determinations, because the Sun's glare blots out the light of the background stars necessary to make the measurement. The most precise values have been obtained by measuring the distance from Earth to other objects orbiting the Sun. This indirect method requires an accurate proportional mathematical model of the solar system; once the distance to one planet or other object is determined, then the distance to the Sun can be calculated.

astronomy, Science dealing with the origin, evolution, composition, distance, and motion of all bodies and scattered matter in the universe. The most ancient of the sciences, it has existed since the dawn of recorded civilization. Much of the earliest knowledge of celestial bodies is often credited to the Babylonians. The ancient Greeks introduced influential cosmological ideas, including theories about the Earth in relation to the rest of the universe. Ptolemy's model of an Earth-centred universe (2nd century AD) influenced astronomical thought for over 1,300 years. In the 16th century, Nicolaus Copernicus assigned the central position to the Sun, ushering in the age of modern astronomy. The 17th century saw several momentous developments: Johannes Kepler's discovery of the principles of planetary motion, Galileo's application of the telescope to astronomical observation, and Isaac Newton's formulation of the laws of motion and gravitation. In the 19th century, spectroscopy and photography made it possible to study the physical properties of planets, stars, and nebulae, leading to the development of astrophysics. In 1927 Edwin Hubble discovered that the universe, hitherto thought static, was expanding. In 1937 the first radio telescope was built. The first artificial satellite, Sputnik, was launched in 1957, inaugurating the age of space exploration; spacecraft that could escape Earth's gravitational pull and return data about the solar system were launched beginning in 1959.

astrophysics, Branch of astronomy concerned mainly with the properties and structures of cosmic objects, including the universe as a whole. Starting in the 19th century, spectroscopy and photography were applied to astronomical research, making it possible to study the brightness, temperature, and chemical composition of cosmic objects. It was soon realized that the properties of these bodies could be fully understood only in terms of the physics of their atmospheres and interiors. X-ray astronomy, gamma-ray as-tronomy, infrared astronomy, ultraviolet astronomy, and radio and radar astronomy are all basically concerned with extending electromagnetic coverage beyond the visible spectrum to constrain the physical characteristics of astronomical objects.

Asturias, Miguel Ángel (b. Oct. 19, 1899, Guatemala City, Guat.—d. June 9, 1974, Madrid, Spain), Guatemalan poet, novelist, and diplomat. He moved to Paris in 1923 and became a Surrealist under the influence of André Breton. His first major works appeared in the 1930s. He began his diplomatic career in 1946; it culminated in his serving as ambassador to France 1966–70. Asturias's writings combine a Mayan mysticism with an epic impulse toward social protest, especially against U.S. and oligarchic power. In *Men of Maize* (1949), often considered his masterpiece, he depicts the seemingly irreversible wretchedness of the Indian peasant. Other major novels, some of which employ the style of magic realism, are *El Señor Presidente* (1946), a fictional denunciation of Guatemala's dictator; *The Cyclone* (1950); *The Green Pope* (1954); and *The Eyes of the Interred* (1960). He won the Nobel Prize for Literature in 1967.

Miguel Ángel Asturias.
Camera Press/Globe Photos

Asunción, in full NUESTRA SEÑORA DE LA ASUNCIÓN, City (pop., 2002: 512,112), capital of Paraguay. It lies on the Paraguay River near its confluence with the Pilcomayo River. Founded in 1537 by Spanish conquistadores, it replaced Buenos Aires as the headquarters of Spanish colonial activities in eastern South America during the period of the latter's depopulation (1541–80). In 1731 Asunción was the site of one of the first major rebellions against Spanish rule. The city declared independence from Spain in 1811. Today it dominates social, cultural, and economic trends in Paraguay.

Asvaghosa (b. AD 80?, Ayodhya, India—d. 150?, Peshawar), Indian philosopher and poet considered the father of Sanskrit drama. Born a Brahman, he opposed Buddhism until a debate with a Buddhist scholar led to his conversion. Asvaghosa became known as a brilliant orator, and he spoke on Mahayana at the fourth Buddhist council. He is considered India's greatest poet before Kalidasa. Works attributed to him include the *Buddhacarita* ("Life of the Buddha") and the *Mahalankara* ("Book of Glory").

Aswān, City (pop., 2006: 266,013), southeastern Egypt. It lies on the Nile River just north of Lake Nasser. In ancient times it was the southern frontier of pharaonic Egypt. Later known as Syene, it served as a frontier garrison post for the Romans, Ottomans, and British. Modern Aswān is located near the old Aswān Dam (completed 1902) and the Aswān High Dam.

Aswan High Dam, Dam across the Nile River, north of Aswan, Egypt. Built 4 mi (6 km) upstream from the earlier Aswan Dam (1902), it is 364 ft (111 m) high and 12,562 ft (3,830 m) long. Differences with Gamal Abdel Nasser led the U.S. and Britain to withdraw their financial support of the project in 1956, whereupon Nasser turned to the Soviet Union for assistance. The dam, completed in 1970, impounds the reservoir Lake Nasser and controls the annual Nile flood, releasing floodwaters when needed for irrigation; it also enables the production of great amounts of electric power. Its construction necessitated the relocation of the ancient Abu Simbel ruins.

asylum, Protection from arrest and extradition given to political refugees by a country or by an embassy that has diplomatic immunity. No one has a legal right to asylum, and the sheltering state, which has the legal right to grant asylum, is under no obligation to give it. It is thus a right of the state, not the individual. Its traditional use has been to protect those accused of political offenses such as treason, desertion, sedition, and espionage. Beginning in the 20th century, asylum also was granted to those who could demonstrate a significant risk of politically motivated persecution if they returned to their home countries.

Atacama Desert, Cool, arid area, north-central Chile. Extending north from the city of Copiapó, the area runs from north to south for a distance of some 600 to 700 mi (1,000 to 1,100 km) and covers most of the Antofagasta region and the northern part of the Atacama region. Because of its location between low coastal mountains and a higher inland range, the region is meteorologically anomalous. Despite its low latitude, summer temperatures average only about 65 °F (18 °C), and, though heavy fogs are common, the desert is one of the driest regions in the world. Some areas receive heavy rain only two to four times a century. For much of the 19th century, the desert was the object of conflicts between Chile, Bolivia, and Peru; after the War of the Pacific (1879–83), Chile emerged with permanent ownership of sectors previously controlled by Peru and Bolivia. For years before the development of synthetic methods of fixing nitrogen, the desert was a chief source of the world's nitrates.

Atatürk, Mustafa Kemal, orig. MUSTAFA KEMAL (b. 1881, Salonika, Greece, Ottoman Empire—d. Nov. 10, 1938, Istanbul, Tur.), Founder of modern Turkey. Dedicated by his father to military service, he graduated near the top of his class in military school. As a young officer, he was critical of the government of the Ottoman Empire and became involved with the Turkish nationalist Committee of Union and Progress. He nevertheless fought for the government during World War I (1914–18), achieving great success against Allied forces during the Dardanelles Campaign. The eventual Allied victory brought British, French, and Italian troops to Anatolia; appointed to restore order there, he used the opportunity to incite the people against the Allied occupation. Greece and Armenia, territorial beneficiaries of the Ottoman defeat, opposed the Turkish nationalists, but Mustafa Kemal overcame all opposition, and the Republic of Turkey was established in 1923. He was given the name Atatürk ("Father of the Turks") in 1934. He pursued a policy of Westernization and secularization, in which Western styles of dress and appellation were made mandatory, seclusion of women was abolished, and the legal and educational system was overhauled.

ataxia, Inability to coordinate voluntary muscular movements. In common usage, the term describes an unsteady gait. Hereditary ataxias are usually caused by degeneration of the spinal cord, cerebellum, or other parts of the nervous system. The most common is Friedreich ataxia, which begins at ages 3–5, progressing slowly to almost complete incapacity by age 20. There is no specific therapy. Metabolic disorders, brain injuries, and toxins can cause ataxia.

atheism, Critique and denial of metaphysical beliefs in God or divine beings. Unlike agnosticism, which leaves open the question of whether there is a God, atheism is a positive denial. It is rooted in an array of philosophical systems. Ancient Greek philosophers such as Democritus and Epicurus argued for it in the context of materialism. In the 18th century David Hume and Immanuel Kant, though not atheists, argued against traditional proofs for God's existence, making belief a matter of faith alone. Atheists such as Ludwig Feuerbach held that God was a projection of human ideals and that recognizing this fiction made self-realization possible. Marxism exemplified modern materialism. Beginning with Friedrich Nietzsche, existentialist atheism proclaimed the death of God and the human freedom to determine value and

meaning. Logical positivism holds that propositions concerning the existence or nonexistence of God are nonsensical or meaningless.

Athena, or ATHENE, In ancient Greek religion, the goddess of war, handicraft, and wisdom and the patroness of Athens. Her Roman counterpart was Minerva. Hesiod told how Athena sprang in full armour from Zeus's forehead. In the *Iliad* she fought alongside the Greek heroes, and she represented the virtues of justice and skill in warfare as opposed to the blood lust of Ares. She was associated with birds (especially the owl) and the snake, and she was usually represented as a virgin goddess. Her birth and contest with Poseidon for suzerainty of Athens were depicted on the Parthenon. Her birthday festival was the Panathenaea.

The Varvakeion, a Roman marble copy (c. AD 130) of the colossal gold and ivory statue of the Athena Parthenos by Phidias (438 BC); in the National Archaeological Museum, Athens.
Alinari/Art Resource, New York

Athens, Greek ATHÍNAI, City (pop., 2001: 745,514), capital of Greece. It is located inland near its port, Piraeus, on the Saronic Gulf in eastern Greece. The source of many of the West's intellectual and artistic conceptions, including that of democracy, Athens is generally considered the birthplace of Western civilization. An ancient city-state, it had by the 6th century BC begun to assert its influence. It was destroyed by Xerxes in 480 BC, but rebuilding began immediately. By 450 BC, led by Pericles, it was at the height of its commercial prosperity and cultural and political dominance, and over the next 40 years many major building projects, including the Acropolis and Parthenon, were completed. Athens's "Golden Age" saw the works of the philosophers Socrates, Plato, and Aristotle; the dramatists Sophocles, Aristophanes, and Euripides; the historians Herodotus, Thucydides, and Xenophon; and the sculptors Praxiteles and Phidias. The Peloponnesian Wars with Sparta ended in Athens's defeat in 404, but it quickly recovered its independence and prosperity. After 338 BC Athens came under Macedonia's hegemony, which was lifted with the aid of Rome in 197 BC in a battle at Cynoscephalae. It became subject to Rome in 146 BC. In the 13th century Athens was taken by the Crusaders. It was conquered in 1456 by the Ottoman Turks, who held it until 1833, when it was declared the capital of independent Greece. Athens is Greece's principal centre for business and foreign trade. The city's ruins and many museums make it a major tourist destination. It was selected to host the 2004 Olympic Games.

atherosclerosis, or HARDENING OF THE ARTERIES, Chronic disease characterized by abnormal thickening of the walls of the arteries due to fatty deposits (atheromas) of cholesterol on the arterial inner walls. These thicken, forming plaques that narrow the vessel channel (lumen) and impede blood flow. Scarring and calcification make the walls less elastic, raising blood pressure. Eventually plaques may completely block a lumen, or a blood clot (thrombus) may obstruct a narrowed channel. Atherosclerosis of one or more coronary arteries (also called coronary heart disease) can decrease the heart muscle's blood supply, causing angina pectoris. Complete blockage causes heart attack. In the brain, atherosclerosis may result in stroke. Treatments include drugs that reduce the level of cholesterol and fat in the blood, anticoagulants and other drugs that prevent the formation of blood clots, coronary bypass, and balloon angioplasty.

athletics, or TRACK AND FIELD, also TRACK-AND-FIELD GAMES, Variety of sport competitions held on a running track and on the adjacent field. It is the oldest form of organized sports, having been a part of the ancient Olympic Games from *c.* 776 BC to AD 393. Modern events include various sprint and middle- and long-distance races, relay races, hurdling, steeplechase, high jump, pole vault, long jump, triple jump, shot put, discus throw, hammer throw, javelin throw, decathlon, pentathlon, and heptathlon. Cross-country running, marathons, and speed walking, which are rarely held on a track, are usually considered adjuncts of athletics. Events are held indoors and outdoors, and records are kept separately; some events are modified or eliminated for indoor competition.

Athos, Mount, Mountain, northern Greece. Reaching a height of 6,670 ft (2,033 m), it occupies Aktí, a promontory of the Chalcidice Peninsula. It is the site of a semiautonomous republic of 20 monasteries and dependencies (skítes). Organized monastic life began there in 963, when St. Athanasius the Athonite founded the first monastery. By 1400 there were 40 monasteries. Long regarded as the holy mountain of the Greek Orthodox Church, it was declared a theocratic republic in 1927. Its churches and libraries house a rich collection of Byzantine art and ancient and medieval manuscripts.

Atlanta, City (pop., 2010: 420,003), capital of Georgia, U.S. Lying in the foothills of the Blue Ridge Mountains, Atlanta is Georgia's largest city. In 1837 a spot was selected there for a railroad terminus that would serve the southeastern U.S. First named Terminus and later Marthasville, it was given the name Atlanta in 1845. An important supply depot during the American Civil War, it was burned by Union forces under William T. Sherman. Atlanta became the state capital in 1868. As it recovered from the war's destruction, it began to epitomize the spirit of the "New South" in seeking reconciliation with the North. It was the home of Martin Luther King, Jr., and the first major Southern city to elect a black mayor (1970). It is the principal trade and transportation centre of the southeastern U.S.

Atlantic, Battle of the, Contest in World War II between Britain (and later the U.S.) and Germany for the control of Atlantic sea routes. Initially the Anglo-French coalition drove German merchant shipping from the Atlantic, but with the fall of France in 1940, Britain was deprived of French naval support. The U.S. then assisted Britain with the lend-lease program. Early in 1942, the Axis began a large-scale submarine offensive against coastal shipping in U.S. waters, and German U-boats also operated in force along the South Atlantic ship lanes to India and the Middle East. Allied shipping losses were severe, but the Allies succeeded in tightening their blockade of Axis Europe and combating the Axis war on shipping. By mid-1943 the Allies had recovered control of the sea routes.

Atlantic Charter, Joint declaration issued on Aug. 14, 1941, during World War II, by Winston Churchill and Franklin D. Roosevelt. Among the statements made in this propaganda manifesto, signed when the U.S. had not yet entered the war, were that neither the U.S. nor Britain sought aggrandizement and that both advocated the restoration of self-government to peoples forcibly deprived of it. The charter was incorporated by reference in the Declaration of the UN (1942).

Atlantic Ocean, Ocean separating North and South America from Europe and Africa. The second largest of the world's oceans, the Atlantic has an area of 31,830,000 sq mi (82,440,000 sq km). With its marginal seas, including the Baltic, North, Black, and Mediterranean to the east, and Baffin Bay, Hudson Bay, the Gulf of St. Lawrence, Gulf of Mexico, and Caribbean Sea to the west, it covers some 41,100,000 sq mi (106,450,000 sq km). Including these latter bodies of water, its average depth is 10,925 ft (3,330 m); its maximum depth is 27,493 feet (8,380 m) in the Puerto Rico Trench. Its most powerful current is the Gulf Stream.

Atlantis, Legendary sunken island in the Atlantic Ocean west of Gibraltar. The main sources for the legend are two of Plato's dialogues, *Timaeus* and *Critias*. According to Plato, Atlantis had a rich civilization, and its princes made many conquests in the Mediterranean before earthquakes destroyed the island and it was swallowed up by the sea. Plato also supplied a history of its ideal commonwealth, and Atlantis is sometimes imagined as a utopia. The legend may have originated with the eruption *c.* 1500 BC of a volcano on Thíra, which was so powerful that it gave rise to earthquakes and tidal waves.

Atlas, In Greek mythology, the strong man who supported the weight of the heavens on his shoulders. He was the son of the Titan Iapetus and the nymph Clymene (or Asia) and the brother of Prometheus. According to Hesiod, Atlas was one of the Titans who waged war against Zeus, and as punishment he was condemned to hold aloft the heavens.

Atlas Mountains, Mountain system, northwestern Africa. It extends some 1,200 mi (2,000 km) from the Moroccan port of Agadir in the southwest to the Tunisian capital of Tunis in the northeast. It comprises several ranges, rising to various elevations, including the High Atlas in Morocco; the Tell, or Maritime, Atlas, which runs along the coast from Morocco to Tunisia; and the Saharan Atlas in Algeria, located farther inland and running adjacent to the Sahara. Among these ranges are situated numerous plateaus and plains that support diverse ecologies. The system's highest peak is Morocco's Mount Toubkal, elevation 13,665 ft (4,165 m).

atman (Sanskrit: "breath" or "self") Basic concept in Hindu philosophy, describing that eternal core of the personality that survives death and transmigrates to a new life or is released from the bonds of existence. Atman became a central philosophical concept in the Upanishads. It underlies all aspects of personality, as Brahman underlies the working of the universe. The schools of Samkhya, Yoga, and Vedanta are particularly concerned with atman.

atmospheric pressure, or BAROMETRIC PRESSURE, Force per unit area exerted by the air above the surface of the Earth. Standard sea-level pressure, by definition, equals 1 atmosphere (atm), or 29.92 in. (760 mm) of mercury, 14.70 lbs per square in., or 101.35 kilopascals, but pressure varies with elevation and temperature. It is usually measured with a mercury barometer (hence the term barometric pressure), which indicates the height of a column of mercury that exactly balances the weight of the column of atmosphere above it. It may also be measured using an aneroid barometer, in which the action of atmospheric pressure in bending a metallic surface is made to move a pointer.

atoll, Coral reef enclosing a lagoon. Atolls consist of ribbons of reef that may not be circular but that are closed shapes, sometimes miles across, around a lagoon that may be 160 ft (50 m) deep or more. Most of the reef itself is usually below the water surface; around the rim along the top are usually low, flat islands or more continuous strips of low, flat land.

atom, Smallest unit into which matter can be divided and still retain the characteristic properties of an element. The word derives from the Greek *atomos* ("indivisible"), and the atom was believed to be indivisible until the early 20th century, when electrons and the nucleus were discovered. It is now known that an atom has a positively charged nucleus that makes up more than 99.9% of the atom's mass but only about 1/100,000 of its volume. The nucleus is composed of positively charged protons and electrically neutral neutrons, each about 2,000 times as massive as an electron. Most of the atom's volume consists of a cloud of electrons that have very small mass and negative charge. The electron cloud is bound to the nucleus by the attraction of opposite charges. In a neutral atom, the protons in the nucleus are balanced by the electrons. An atom that has gained or lost electrons becomes negatively or positively charged and is called an ion.

atomic bomb, Weapon whose great explosive power results from the sudden release of energy upon the splitting, or fission, of the nuclei of heavy elements such as plutonium or uranium. With only 11–33 lb (5–15 kg) of highly enriched uranium, a modern atomic bomb could generate a 15-kiloton explosion, creating a huge fireball, a large shock wave, and lethal radioactive fallout. The first atomic bomb, developed by the Manhattan Project during World War II, was set off on July 16, 1945, in the New Mexico desert. The only atomic bombs used in war were dropped by the U.S. on Hiroshima on Aug. 6, 1945, and on Nagasaki three days later. In 1949 the Soviet Union tested its first atomic bomb, followed by Britain (1952), France (1960), China (1964), India (1974), and Pakistan (1998). Israel and South Africa were suspected of testing atomic weapons in 1979.

atomic number, Number of a chemical element in the systematic, ordered sequence shown in the periodic table. The elements are arranged in order of increasing number of protons in the nucleus of the atom (the same as the number of electrons in the neutral atom), and that number for each element is its atomic number.

atomic weight, Ratio of the average mass of a chemical element's atoms to $1/12$ the mass of an atom of the carbon-12 isotope. The original standard of atomic weight, established in the 19th century, was hydrogen, with a value of 1. From *c.* 1900 until 1961, the reference standard was oxygen, with a value of 16, and the unit of atomic mass was defined as $1/16$ the mass of an oxygen atom. Oxygen, however, contains small amounts of two isotopes that are heavier than the most abundant one, and 16 is actually a weighted average of the masses of the three isotopes of oxygen. Therefore, the standard was changed to one based on carbon-12. The new scale required only minimal changes to the values that had been used for chemical atomic weights.

atomism, Philosophical doctrine that material objects are aggregates of simpler parts known as atoms. Atomism in the strict sense is characterized by three points: the atoms are absolutely indivisible, qualitatively identical apart from shape, size, and motion, and combinable with each other only by juxtaposition. Atomism is usually associated with realism and mechanism; it is mechanistic because it maintains that all observable changes can be reduced to changes in the configuration of the atoms that constitute matter. It is opposed to holism because it holds that the properties of any whole can be explained in terms of those of its parts.

Aton, or ATEN, In ancient Egyptian religion, a sun god, depicted as the solar disk emitting rays terminating in human hands. The pharaoh Akhenaton (r. 1353–36 BC) declared Aton to be the only god, and in opposition to the Amon-Re priesthood of Thebes, built the city of Akhetaton as the center for Aton's worship, but Aton's religion is poorly understood. After Akhenaton's death, the old religion was restored. See photograph above.

atonality, In music, the absence of functional harmony as a primary structural element. Probably originally a pejorative term applied to music of extreme chromaticism, it has become the most widely used descriptive term for 20th-century music whose connection with tonality is difficult to hear. Arnold Schoenberg and his students Alban Berg and Anton Webern are regarded as the seminal atonal composers; the serialism of their later work is often distinguished from their earlier "free atonality."

atonement, Religious concept in which obstacles to reconciliation with God are removed, usually through sacrifice. Most religions have rituals of purification and expiation by which the rela-

King Akhenaton (left) with his wife, Queen Nefertiti, and three of their daughters under the rays of the sun god Aton, altar relief, mid-14th century BCE; in the State Museums at Berlin
Foto Marburg/Art Resource, New York

tion of the individual to the divine is strengthened. In Christianity, atonement is achieved through the death and resurrection of Jesus. In Roman Catholicism, Eastern Orthodoxy, and some Protestant churches, penance is a sacrament that allows for personal atonement. In Judaism the annual Day of Atonement, Yom Kippur, is the culmination of 10 days centered on repentance.

atrophy, Decrease from previous normal size of the body or a part, cell, organ, or tissue. An organ or body part's cells may be reduced in number, size or both. Atrophy of some cells and organs is normal at certain points in the life cycle. Other causes include malnutrition, disease, disuse, injury, and hormone over- or underproduction.

attention deficit (hyperactivity) disorder (ADD OR ADHD), formerly HYPERACTIVITY, Behavioral syndrome in children, whose major symptoms are inattention and distractibility, restlessness, inability to sit still, and difficulty concentrating on one thing for any period of time. It occurs in about 5% of all schoolchildren, and it is three times more common in boys than in girls. It can adversely affect learning, though many children with ADD can learn to control their behaviour sufficiently to perform satisfactorily in school. It appears to be caused by a combination of genetic and environmental factors. Certain aspects of the syndrome may persist into adulthood. Treatment usually entails counseling and close parental supervision, and it may also include prescription medication.

Attila (d. 453), King of the Huns (434–53, ruling jointly with his elder brother until *c.* 445). He was one of the greatest of the barbarian rulers who assailed the Roman Empire. He and his brother Bleda inherited an empire that stretched from the Alps and the Baltic nearly to the Caspian Sea. The failure of the Romans to pay promised tributes prompted Attila to launch assaults along the Danube in 441 and 443. He murdered his brother in 445 and two years later invaded the Balkan provinces and Greece, a campaign later ended by another peace treaty that exacted heavy damages from the Eastern Romans. He invaded Gaul (451) but was defeated by an alliance of the Roman general Aetius and the Visigoths. His invasion of Italy (452) was ended by famine and plague. His depredations, which seemed to some like divine punishment, earned him the epithet Flagellum Dei ("Scourge of God"). Attila died on his wedding night, possibly murdered by his bride. His sons took control of his empire, which collapsed shortly after Attila's death.

attitude, In psychology, a mental position with regard to a fact or state. Attitudes reflect a tendency to classify objects and events and to react to them with some consistency. Attitudes are not directly observable but rather are inferred from the objective, evaluative responses a person makes. Thus, investigators depend heavily on behavioral indicators of attitudes—what people say, how they respond to questionnaires, or such physiological signs as changes in heart rate. Attitude research is employed by social psychologists, advertising professionals, and political scientists, among others. Public-opinion researchers often attempt to distinguish attitudes from related concepts such as values, opinions, and knowledge.

Auckland, City (pop., 2006: city, 396,000; metro. area, 1,208,091), North Island, New Zealand. Located on Waitemata and Manukau harbours, it is the country's principal port and largest city. Founded in 1840 as New Zealand's capital and named for George Eden, earl of Auckland, it remained the capital until superseded by Wellington in 1865. It is a major manufacturing and shipping centre. A bridge links it with the growing northern shore suburbs and with Devonport, New Zealand's chief naval base.

Augsburg, City (pop., 2002 est.: 257,800), Bavaria, southern Germany. Founded as a Roman colony by Augustus *c.* 14 BC, it was the seat of a bishopric by AD 739. It became an imperial free city in 1276 and joined the Swabian League in 1331. The Fugger and Welser families made the city a major banking and commercial centre in the 15th–16th centuries. The Augsburg Confession was read at the Diet of 1530; the Peace of Augsburg was concluded in 1555; and the League of Augsburg was formed in 1686. The city became part of Bavaria in 1806. It was heavily bombed during World War II. Sites of interest include the Fuggerei (1519), the world's oldest housing settlement for the poor.

Augsburg, League of, Coalition formed in 1686 by Emperor Leopold I, the kings of Sweden and Spain, and the electors of Bavaria, Saxony, and the Palatinate. The league was formed to oppose the expansionist plans of Louis XIV of France prior to the War of the Grand Alliance. It proved ineffective because of the reluctance of some princes to oppose France and the absence of provisions for combined military action.

Augsburg, Peace of, Convention promulgated in 1555 by the Diet of the Holy Roman Empire, which provided the first permanent legal basis for the existence of Lutheranism in addition to Catholicism in Germany. The Diet determined that no member of the empire would make war against another on religious grounds. It recognized just two denominations, the Roman Catholics and the Lutherans, and it stipulated that in each territory of the empire, only one denomination was allowed. However, people were allowed to move to states where their faith was adopted. Despite numerous shortcomings, the accord saved the empire from serious internal conflicts for over 50 years.

Augsburg Confession, Basic doctrinal statement of Lutheranism. Its principal author was Philipp Melanchthon, and it was presented to Emperor Charles V at the Diet of Augsburg on June 25, 1530. Its purpose was to defend the Lutherans against misrepresentations of their teachings and to provide a statement of theology that Roman Catholics might accept. It consisted of 28 articles that outlined Lutheran doctrine and listed abuses that had crept into Western Christendom over the centuries. The unaltered document has remained authoritative for Lutherans, and a heavily revised version by Melanchthon is accepted by some Reformed churches. Translated into English in 1536, it had a major influence on the Anglican Church's Thirty-nine Articles and the Methodists' Twenty-five Articles of Religion.

Augustinian, In the Roman Catholic church, a member of any of the religious orders and congregations whose constitutions are based on the Rule of St. Augustine, including the Hospitallers (Knights of Malta) and the Dominicans. The two main branches of the Augustinians, however, are the Augustinian Hermits and the Augustinian Canons. The former was one of the four great mendicant orders of the Middle Ages, and its members (including Martin Luther) were active in European university life and ecclesiastical affairs. The latter became in the 11th century the first Roman Catholic order to combine clerical status with full common life. The order declined after the Reformation, but it continues missionary, educational, and hospital work. Other notable orders are the Augustinian Recollects (founded in the 16th century) and the Second Order of St. Augustine (1264) for nuns, both still active today.

Augustus, Caesar, or OCTAVIAN, orig. GAIUS OCTAVIUS, later GAIUS JULIUS CAESAR OCTAVIANUS (b. Sept. 23, 63 BC—d. Aug. 19, AD 14, Nola, near Naples), First Roman emperor. Born to a wealthy family, at age 18 he was named adoptive son and heir of his great-uncle Julius Caesar. After Caesar's assassination (44 BC) a power struggle ensued, and several battles later Octavian formed the Second Triumvirate with his chief rivals, Lepidus and Mark Antony. Octavian disposed of Lepidus in 32 and Antony (then allied with Cleopatra) at the Battle of Actium in 31 to become sole ruler. He was anointed *princeps*; the Roman Empire is said to begin with his accession. At first he ruled as consul, maintaining republican administration, but in 27 he accepted the title Augustus and in 23 he received imperial power. His rule (31 BC–AD 14) brought changes to every aspect of Roman life and lasting peace and prosperity to the Greco-Roman world. He secured outlying imperial provinces, built roads and public works, established the Pax Romana, and fostered the arts. He took steps to rectify Roman morality, even exiling his daughter Julia for adultery. When he died, the empire stretched from Iberia to Cappadocia and from Gaul to Egypt. He was deified after his death.

Aung San Suu Kyi (b. June 19, 1945, Rangoon, Burma [now Yangon, Myan.]), Opposition leader in Myanmar (Burma). Daughter of nationalist leader Aung San, she studied in Burma and India and at the University of Oxford. She lived quietly in Britain until 1988, when she returned to Burma. Moved by the brutality of U Ne Win's military regime, she began a nonviolent struggle for democracy and human rights. The 1990 electoral victory of her National League for Democracy was ignored by Ne Win's government, and she was held under house arrest from 1989 to 1995. She subsequently continued her opposition activities and was subject to varying degrees of government harassment, including more periods of house arrest beginning in 2000. She was released from house arrest in 2011 and won a seat in the lower house of the national legislature in 2012. She was awarded the 1991 Nobel Prize for Peace.

aurora, Luminous phenomenon of the upper atmosphere that occurs primarily at high latitudes. Auroras in the Northern Hemisphere are called aurora borealis, or northern lights; in the Southern Hemisphere they are called aurora australis, or southern lights. Auroras are caused by the interaction of energetic particles (electrons and protons) from outside the atmosphere with atoms of the upper atmosphere. Such interaction occurs in zones surrounding the Earth's magnetic poles. During periods of intense solar activity, auroras occasionally extend to the middle latitudes.

Auschwitz, or AUSCHWITZ-BIRKENAU, Nazi Germany's largest concentration camp and extermination camp, located in southern Poland (modern Oświęcim). It consisted of three camps (prison, extermination, and forced labour), established in 1940, 1941 (Birkenau), and 1942. Able-bodied Jewish prisoners were sent to a slave-labour camp, while the aged, the weak, and children and their mothers were killed. Some prisoners were also subjected to medical experiments, conducted by Josef Mengele. The camp was gradually abandoned in 1944–45 as Soviet troops advanced. The total number who died at Auschwitz is estimated at between 1.1 million and 1.5 million, 90% of which were Jews; also among the dead were some 19,000 Roma (Gypsies), who were killed in July

1944, and some 83,000 Poles. Much of the camp was later converted into a museum and memorial. It was designated a UNESCO World Heritage site in 1979.

Austen, Jane (b. Dec. 16, 1775, Steventon, Hampshire, Eng.—d. July 18, 1817, Winchester, Hampshire), English novelist. The daughter of a rector, she lived in the circumscribed world of minor landed gentry and country clergy that she was to use in her writing; her closest companion was her sister, Cassandra. Her earliest known writings are mainly parodies, notably of sentimental fiction. In her six full-length novels—*Sense and Sensibility* (1811), *Pride and Prejudice* (1813), *Mansfield Park* (1814), *Emma* (1815), *Persuasion* (1817), and *Northanger Abbey* (published 1817 but written before the others)—she created the comedy of manners of middle-class English life in her time. Her writing is noted for its wit, realism, shrewd sympathy, and brilliant prose style.

Jane Austen, pencil and watercolour by her sister, Cassandra Austen, c. 1810; in the National Portrait Gallery, London.
Courtesy of the National Portrait Gallery, London

Through her treatment of ordinary people in everyday life, she was the first to give the novel its distinctly modern character. She published her novels anonymously; two appeared only after her death, which probably resulted from Addison disease.

Austerlitz, Battle of (Dec. 2, 1805) First engagement of the War of the Third Coalition and one of Napoleon's greatest victories. In the battle, fought near Austerlitz in Moravia (now Slavkov u Brna, Czech Rep.), Napoleon's 68,000 troops defeated almost 90,000 Russians and Austrians under Russia's Alexander I and Mikhail Kutuzov. Also called the Battle of the Three Emperors, Napoleon's resounding victory forced Austria's Francis I to conclude the Treaty of Pressburg, ceding Venetia to the French kingdom in Italy and temporarily ending the anti-French alliance.

Australia, officially COMMONWEALTH OF AUSTRALIA, Smallest continent and sixth largest country (in area) on Earth, lying between the Pacific and Indian oceans. Area: 2,973,952 sq mi (7,702,501 sq km). Population: (2011 est.) 22,651,000. Capital: Canberra. Most Australians are descendants of Europeans. The largest nonwhite minority is the Australian Aborigine population. The Asian portion of the population has grown as a result of relaxed immigration policy. Language: English (official). Religions: Christianity (mostly Protestant; also Roman Catholic, Eastern Orthodox, other Christians), Buddhism, Islam. Currency: Australian dollar. Australia has three major physiographic regions. More than half of its land area is on the Western Australian plateau, which includes the outcrops of Arnhem Land and the Kimberleys in the northwest and the Macdonnell Ranges in the east. A second region, the Interior Lowlands, lies east of the plateau. The Eastern Uplands, which include the Great Dividing Range, are a series of high ridges, plateaus, and basins. The country's highest point is Mount Kosciuszko in the Australian Alps, and the lowest is Lake Eyre. Major rivers include the Murray-Darling system, the Flinders and Swan rivers, and Cooper Creek. There are many islands and reefs along the coast, including the Great Barrier Reef, Melville Island, Kangaroo Island, and Tasmania. Australia is rich in mineral resources, including coal, petroleum, and uranium. A vast diamond deposit was found in Western Australia in 1979. The country's economy is basically free enterprise; its largest components include finance, manufacturing, and trade. Formally a constitutional monarchy, its head of state is the British monarch, represented by the governor-general. In reality it is a parliamentary state with two legislative houses; its head of government is the prime minister. Australia has long been inhabited by Aborigines, who began arriving at least 50,000 years ago. Estimates of the population at the time of European settlement in 1788 range from 300,000 to 1,000,000. Widespread European knowledge of Australia began with 17th-century explorations. The Dutch landed in 1616 and the British in 1688, but the first large-scale expedition was that of James Cook in 1770, which established Britain's claim to Australia. The first British settlement, at Port Jackson (1788), consisted mainly of convicts and seamen; convicts were to make up a large proportion of the incoming settlers. By 1859 the colonial nuclei of all Australia's states had been formed, but with devastating effects on the indigenous peoples, whose populations declined sharply with the introduction of European diseases. Britain granted its colonies limited self-government in the mid-19th century, and an act federating the colonies into a commonwealth went into effect in 1901. Australia fought alongside the British in World War I, notably at Gallipoli, and again in World War II, preventing Australia's occupation by the Japanese. It joined the U.S. in the Korean and Vietnam wars. Since the 1960s the government has sought to deal more fairly with the Aborigines, and a loosening of immigration restrictions has led to a more heterogeneous population. Constitutional links allowing British interference in government were formally abolished in 1968, and Australia has assumed a major role in Asian and Pacific affairs. During the 1990s there were several debates about giving up its British ties and becoming a republic.

Australian Aboriginal languages, Group of perhaps as many as 500 languages spoken by the 300,000 to 1,000,000 native inhabitants of Australia before the beginning of European conquest in 1788. More than half are now extinct; of the remainder, only about 20, mostly in the North Territory and northern Western Australia, remain in active use by both adults and children. Most Australian languages belong to a single superfamily, Pama-Nyungan, and the remainder, a very diverse group of languages spoken in the Kimberley region of Western Australia and parts of the North Territory, may be remotely akin to Pama-Nyungan.

Australian Aborigine, Any of the indigenous peoples of Australia. The first Australians are estimated to have reached the continent at least 50,000 years ago. At one time there may have been as many as 500 language-named, territorially anchored groups of indigenous Australians. They subsisted as hunters and gatherers. Groups (bands) were formed along the male line (patrilineal descent) and consisted of two or more families. Their lives were centred around a specific site settled by the group's ancestors. The men were custodians of the mythology, ritual, sites, and symbols evoked in the Dreaming. Australian Aborigines are believed to have numbered 300,000–1,000,000 when European colonization began in the late 18th century, but they were devastated by introduced diseases and by the bloody 19th-century policy of "pacification by force." In the early 21st century they were estimated to number more than 400,000. Most aspects of their traditional culture have been severely modified. All Aboriginal peoples have had some contact with modern Australian society, and all are now Australian citizens. At the turn of the 21st century Aboriginal interest in cultural revival was strong.

Australian religion, Religion of Australia's Aborigines, based in the Dreaming. Religion involved living in agreement with the way of life ordained in the Dreaming, through the performance of rituals and obedience to the law. Through dreams and other states of altered consciousness, the living could come into contact with the spiritual realm and gain strength from it; myths, dances, and other rituals bound the human, spiritual, and physical worlds together in a single cosmic order. A child's spirit was held to come from the dreaming to animate a fetus, and a person's spiritual heritage was more important than the bond between a physical parent and child. Sacred art included tjurunga, sand and cave paintings, and paintings on bark.

Australian rules football, Variety of football played between two teams of 18 players. The field is oval, 145–200 yd (135–185 m) long, with four goalposts at each end. A six-point goal is scored when the oval ball is kicked through the two central goalposts. A one-point "behind" is scored when the ball is kicked over the behind line extending between the central and outer goalposts. The game's finest spectacle is the "mark" in which competing players leap, sometimes riding on the back of an opponent, in order to catch the ball directly from the kick of another player. The player making such a catch is awarded a mark, an unhindered kick from behind the spot of the catch. The sport was developed in Melbourne. The Victorian Football League was established in 1896 as the first professional league. It was renamed the Australian Football League in 1990 to reflect the addition of franchises outside of Victoria state.

Australopithecus (Latin: "southern ape"), Genus of extinct hominins that may be ancestral to human beings (*Homo sapiens*). The name *Australopithecus* refers to the first fossils, which were discovered in South Africa. *Australopithecus* lived in much of Africa during the Pliocene (*c.* 5.3–2.6 million years ago [mya]) and Pleistocene (*c.* 2.6 million–11,700 years ago) epochs. These hominins were distinguished from apes by their upright posture and bipedal gait, and their teeth were more humanlike than apelike, but their brains were small and not very different from those of living apes. Five species are recognized: *A. anamensis* (4.2–3.9 mya), *A. afarensis* (3.8–2.9 mya), *A. bahrelghazali* (3.5–3.0 mya), *A. africanus* (3–2.4 mya), and *A. garhi* (2.5 mya). Three "robust" species are now instead classified as *Paranthropus* (2.7–1.3 mya): *P. aethiopicus*, *P. robustus*, and *P. boisei*. *Paranthropus* eventually became extinct, leaving no evolutionary successors.

Lateral view of an Australopithecus africanus skull found at Sterkfontein, S.Af.
Courtesy of the Transvaal Museum, Pretoria, S.Af.

Australasia, or OSTRASIA, Early medieval European kingdom. During the Merovingian dynasty (6th–8th centuries AD), it was the eastern Frankish kingdom and Neustria was the western kingdom. Australasia covered present-day northeastern France and areas of western and central Germany; its capital was at Metz. The region was the power base of the early Carolingian mayors of the palace, one of whom, Pippin III, deposed the last Merovingian king in 751 and founded the Carolingian dynasty. The dynasty's heartland, Australasia, was an important region in the empire established by Charlemagne.

Austria, officially REPUBLIC OF AUSTRIA, Country, south-central Europe. Area: 32,386 sq mi (83,879 sq km). Population: (2011 est.) 8,419,000. Capital: Vienna. The population is predominantly Austrian. Language: German (official). Religions: Christianity (predominantly Roman Catholic; also Protestant and Orthodox); also Islam. Currency: euro. Much of Austria is covered by Alpine regions, including the eastern Alps, where the country's highest point, the Grossglockner, is found. The Bohemian Forest, a highland region, extends north into the Czech Republic. The lowland region, including the Vienna Basin, lies in the east; it supports mainly agricultural activities. The Danube River and its tributaries drain nearly the entire country. Austria has a developed mixed free-market and government-operated economy based on manufacturing and commerce; tourism is also important. Austria is a federal state with two legislative houses. The head of state is the

president, and the head of government is the chancellor. Austria's greatest cultural contribution has been in music. Major cultural figures in other fields include Oskar Kokoschka in art, Sigmund Freud in psychoanalysis, and Ludwig Wittgenstein in philosophy. Settlement in Austria goes back more than 5,000 years. The Celts invaded *c.* 400 BCE and established the kingdom of Noricum. The Romans arrived after 200 BCE and established the provinces of Raetia, Noricum, and Pannonia; prosperity followed, and the population became Romanized. Germanic tribes began invading the area before the fall of Rome in the 5th century CE, after which more Germanic tribes and the Slavs entered the region; they were eventually subdued by Charlemagne, and the area became ethnically Germanic. The distinct political entity that would become Austria emerged in 976 with Leopold I of Babenberg as margrave. In 1278 Rudolf IV of Habsburg (Rudolf I as the king of Germany) conquered the area; Habsburg rule lasted until 1918. While in power, the Habsburgs created a kingdom centred on Austria, Bohemia, and Hungary. The Napoleonic Wars brought about the end of the Habsburg-controlled Holy Roman Empire (1806) and the emergence of the Austrian Empire. The prince von Metternich tried to assure Austrian supremacy among Germanic states, but war with Prussia led Austria to divide the empire into the Dual Monarchy of Austria-Hungary. Nationalist sentiment plagued the kingdom, and the assassination of Francis Ferdinand by a Bosnian Serb nationalist in 1914 triggered World War I, which destroyed the Austro-Hungarian Empire. In the postwar carving up of Austria-Hungary, Austria became an independent republic. It was annexed by Nazi Germany in 1938 and joined the Axis powers in World War II. The republic was restored in 1955 after 10 years of Allied occupation. Austria became a full member of the European Union (EU) in 1995. After a half-century of military neutrality, Austria was one of the few members of the EU that was not a member of NATO at the outset of the 21st century.

Austria-Hungary, or AUSTRO-HUNGARIAN EMPIRE, Former monarchy, central Europe. Austria-Hungary at one time included Austria and Hungary, Bohemia, Moravia, Bukovina, Transylvania, Carniola, Küstenland, Dalmatia, Croatia, Fiume, and Galicia. The so-called Dual Monarchy, formed by the Compromise of 1867, created a king of Hungary in addition to the existing Austrian emperor; though these were the same person, Hungary was granted its own parliament and considerable autonomy. Francis Joseph held both titles from Austria-Hungary's inception until his death in 1916. Up to 1914, the monarchy maintained a precarious balance among its many minorities; that year saw the balance toppled with the assassination of the Austro-Hungarian Francis Ferdinand by a Serbian nationalist that precipitated World War I. With its defeat in that war and revolutions by the Czechs, Yugoslavs, and Hungarians, the monarchy collapsed in 1918.

Austrian school of economics, Body of economic theory developed by several late 19th-century Austrian economists. Carl Menger (1840–1921) published a paper on their new theory of value in 1871. The concept of value was subjective, the source of a product's value being its ability to satisfy human wants. The actual value depended on the utility derived by the consumer from the product in its least important use (marginal utility). The theory was also applied to production and pricing. Other founders of the school included Friedrich von Wieser (1851–1926) and Eugen von Böhm-Bawerk (1851–1914).

Austrian Succession, War of the (1740–48) Group of related wars that took place after the death (1740) of Emperor Charles VI. At issue was the right of Charles's daughter Maria Theresa to inherit the Habsburg lands. The war began when Frederick II of Prussia invaded Silesia in 1740. His victory suggested that the Habsburg dominions were incapable of defending themselves, prompting other countries to enter the fray. The conflict was ended by the Treaty of Aix-la-Chapelle.

Austroasiatic languages, Superfamily of about 150 languages spoken by close to 90 million physically and culturally very diverse people in South and Southeast Asia. Today most scholars believe that it is subdivided into two families, Munda and Mon-Khmer. The present fragmented distribution of Austroasiatic languages is most likely the result of relatively recent incursions by Indo-Aryan, Sino-Tibetan, Tai, and Austronesian-speaking peoples. In prehistoric times Austroasiatic languages most likely extended over a much broader and more continuous area, including much of what is now southeastern China. Other than Vietnamese and Khmer, no Austroasiatic language is an official national language.

Austronesian languages, formerly MALAYO-POLYNESIAN LANGUAGES, Family of about 1,200 languages spoken by more than 200 million people in Indonesia, the Philippines, Madagascar, the central and southern Pacific island groups (except most of New Guinea; *see* Papuan languages), and parts of mainland Southeast Asia and the island of Taiwan. Before European colonial expansion, it had the widest territorial extent of any language family. A primary genetic division in the family separates the Austronesian languages of Taiwan from the remaining languages, which are divided into Western and Central-Eastern Malayo-Polynesian. Western Malayo-Polynesian includes Javanese, which is spoken by about 76 million people—more than a third of all Austronesian speakers. Eastern Malayo-Polynesian includes Oceanic, the best-defined subgroup of Austronesian, comprising nearly all the languages of Polynesia, Micronesia, and Melanesia. Typological generalizations about Austronesian languages are difficult because of their enormous number and diversity, though content words tend to be disyllabic, and vowel and consonant inventories tend to be limited, especially in Polynesian. Written records in scripts of Southeast Asian provenance survive for several languages, including Old Javanese and Cham, the language of the kingdom of Champa.

authoritarianism, Principle of unqualified submission to authority, as opposed to individual freedom of thought and action. As a political system, authoritarianism is antidemocratic in that political power is concentrated in a leader or small elite not constitutionally responsible to those governed. It differs from totalitarianism in that authoritarian governments usually lack a guiding ideology, tolerate some pluralism in social organization, lack the power to mobilize the whole population in pursuit of national goals, and exercise their power within relatively predictable limits.

autism, Neurobiological disorder that affects physical, social, and language skills. First described by Leo Kanner and Hans Asperger in the 1940s, the syndrome usually appears before 2¹/₂ years of age. Autistic infants appear indifferent or averse to affection and physical contact. They may be slow in learning to speak and suffer episodes of rage or panic; they may also appear deaf and display an almost hypnotized fascination with certain objects. Autism is often characterized by rhythmic body movements such as rocking or hand-clapping and by an obsessive desire to prevent change in daily routines. Autistic individuals may be hypersensitive to some stimuli (e.g., high-pitched sounds) and abnormally slow to react to others (e.g., physical pain). The disorder is three to four times more common in males. Though postnatal factors such as lack of parental attention were once blamed, it is now known that autism is the result of abnormalities in the brain structure. About 15–20% of autistic adults live and work independently; "high-functioning" autistic people may have special abilities based on their unusual ability for visual thinking.

autobiography, Biography of oneself narrated by oneself. Little autobiographical literature exists from antiquity and the Middle Ages; with a handful of exceptions, the form begins to appear only in the 15th century. Autobiographical works take many forms, from intimate writings made during life that are not necessarily intended for publication (including letters, diaries, journals, memoirs, and reminiscences) to the formal autobiography. Outstanding examples of the genre extend from St. Augustine's *Confessions* (*c.* AD 400) to Vladimir Nabokov's *Speak, Memory* (1951).

automata theory, Body of physical and logical principles underlying the operation of any electromechanical device (an automaton) that converts information input in one form into another, or into some action, according to an algorithm. Norbert Wiener and Alan M. Turing are regarded as pioneers in the field. In computer science, automata theory is concerned with the construction of robots from basic building blocks of automatons. The best example of a general automaton is an electronic digital computer. Networks of automata may be designed to mimic human behaviour.

automation, Term coined about 1946 by a Ford Motor Co. engineer, used to describe a wide variety of systems in which there is a significant substitution of mechanical, electrical, or computerized action for human effort and intelligence. In general usage, automation can be defined as a technology concerned with performing a process by means of programmed commands combined with automatic feedback control to ensure proper execution of the instructions. The resulting system is capable of operating without human intervention.

automobile, Four-wheeled automotive vehicle designed for passenger transportation and commonly propelled by an internal-combustion engine using a volatile fuel. The modern automobile consists of about 14,000 parts and comprises several structural and mechanical systems. These include the body, containing the passenger and storage space, which sits on the chassis, or steel frame; the internal-combustion gasoline engine, which powers the car by means of a transmission; the steering and braking systems, which control the car's motion; and the electrical system, which includes a battery, alternator, and other devices. Subsystems involve fuel, exhaust, lubrication, cooling, suspension, and tires. Though experimental vehicles were built as early as the 18th century, not until the 1880s did Gottlieb Daimler and Karl Benz in Germany begin separately to manufacture cars commercially. In the U.S., James and William Packard and Ransom Olds were among the first auto manufacturers, and by 1898 there were 50 U.S. manufacturers. Some early cars operated by steam engine, such as those made from *c.* 1902 by Francis E. Stanley and Freelan O. Stanley. The internal-combustion engine was used by Henry Ford when he introduced the Model T in 1908; Ford would soon revolutionize the industry with his use of the assembly line. In the 1930s European manufacturers began to make small, affordable cars such as the Volkswagen. In the 1950s and '60s U.S. automakers produced larger, more luxurious cars with more automatic features. In the 1970s and '80s Japanese manufacturers exported their small, reliable, fuel-efficient cars worldwide, and their increasing popularity spurred U.S. automakers to produce similar models. During a period of stable fuel prices and economic prosperity in the 1990s, sport-utility vehicles (SUVs) and minivans, with their greater cargo and passenger capacities, became highly popular. After the turn of the 21st century, rising fuel prices and concerns about vehicle emissions spurred a rising interest in electric and hybrid-electric automobiles. Some 50 million passenger cars are produced each year worldwide. China and the U.S. are the world's largest automobile markets; annual sales in China surpassed those in the U.S. for the first time in 2009.

automobile racing, Sport practiced in a variety of forms on roads, tracks, or closed circuits. It includes Grand Prix racing, speedway racing (including the Indianapolis 500), stock-car racing, sports-car racing, drag racing, midget-car racing, and karting, as well as hill climbs and rally driving. The International Motor Sports Hall of Fame is located in Talladega, Ala., U.S. There is no central governing body for automobile racing in the U.S. as there is in most other countries.

autonomic nervous system, Part of the nervous system that is not under conscious control and that regulates the internal organs. It includes the sympathetic, parasympathetic, and enteric nervous systems. The first, which connects the internal organs to the brain via spinal nerves, responds to stress by increasing heart rate and blood flow to the muscles and decreasing blood flow to the skin. The second comprises the cranial nerves and the lower spinal nerves, which increase digestive secretions and slow the heartbeat. Both have sensory fibres that send feedback on the condition of internal organs to the central nervous system, information that helps maintain homeostasis. The third division, embedded in the walls of the stomach and intestines, controls digestive movement and secretions.

autopsy, or NECROPSY, or POSTMORTEM, Dissection and examination of a dead body to determine cause of death and learn about disease processes in ways that are not possible with the living. Autopsies have contributed to the development of medicine since at least the Middle Ages. Beyond revealing causes of individual deaths, autopsy is crucial to the accuracy of disease and death statistics, the education of medical students, the understanding of new and changing diseases, and the advancement of medical science.

avalanche, Large mass of material, such as snow or rock debris, that moves rapidly down a mountain slope, sweeping everything in its path. Avalanches begin when a mass of material overcomes the frictional resistance of the sloping surface, often after the material's foundation has been weakened by rains or the snow has been partially melted by a warm, dry wind. Other weather conditions that can lead to avalanches are heavy snowfall and high winds. A common method of avalanche control consists of detonating explosives in the upper reaches of avalanche zones, which intentionally causes the snow to slide before accumulations have become very great.

Avalokitesvara, Chinese GUANYIN, Japanese KANNON, Bodhisattva of infinite compassion and mercy, the most popular of Mahayana Buddhist deities. He is the earthly manifestation of Amitabha, guarding the world between the departure of the historical Buddha, Gautama, and the appearance of the future Buddha, Maitreya. He is the creator of the fourth world, the actual living universe. In China and Japan his gender became ambiguous; he is sometimes called a goddess. For Pure Land Buddhists, he forms a ruling triad with Amitabha and the bodhisattva Mahasthamaprapta. In Tibetan Buddhism, he is thought to be reincarnated in each Dalai Lama in order to preserve buddha-teaching.

Avalokiteshvara, bronze figure from Kurkihar, Bihar, 9th century; in Patna Museum, Patna, Bihar.

avatar, In Hinduism, the incarnation of a deity in human or animal form to counteract an evil in the world. It usually refers to 10 appearances of Vishnu, including an incarnation as the Buddha Gautama and Kalkin (the incarnation yet to come). The doctrine appears in the *Bhagavadgita* in the words of Lord Krishna to Arjuna: "Whenever there is a decline of righteousness and rise of unrighteousness then I send forth Myself."

Averroës, Arabic IBN RUSHD, in full ABŪ AL-WALĪD MUḤAMMAD IBN AḤMAD IBN MUḤAMMAD IBN RUSHD (b. 1126, Córdoba—d. 1198, Marrakech, Almohad empire), Spanish Arabic philosopher. Trained in law, medicine, and philosophy, he rose to be chief judge of Córdoba, an office also once held by his grandfather. His series of commentaries on most of the works of Aristotle, written between 1169 and 1195, exerted considerable influence on both Jewish and Christian scholars in later centuries. While mostly faithful to Aristotle's thought, he endowed the Aristotelian "prime mover" with the characteristics of the Plotinian and Islamic transcendent God, the universal First Cause. In his *Commentary on Plato's Republic* he attempted to apply Platonic doctrines to the contemporary Almoravid and Almohad states.

Avesta, or ZEND-AVESTA, Sacred book of Zoroastrianism. It contains hymns, prayers, and appeals to righteousness ascribed to Zoroaster. The present text was assembled in the 3rd–7th century AD from the remains of a larger body of scripture that was destroyed when Alexander the Great conquered Persia. It has five parts: the *Gathas*, hymns in what are thought to be Zoroaster's own words; *Visp-rat*, containing homages to spiritual leaders; *Vendidad*, the main source for Zoroastrian law; the *Yashts*, 21 hymns to angels and ancient heroes; and the *Khurda avesta*, composed of minor texts.

aviation, Development and operation of aircraft. In 1783 the balloon became the first aircraft to carry humans. Production of a successful glider in 1891 and refinement of the internal-combustion engine led to the first successful engine-powered airplane flight by Wilbur and Orville Wright in 1903. World War I accelerated the expansion of aviation, and in the 1920s the first small airlines began carrying mail and passengers. World War II was another period of innovation in aircraft size, speed, and range. In the late 1940s the jet engine made possible the subsequent development of commercial airlines throughout the world.

Avignon papacy, Roman Catholic papacy during the period 1309–77, when the popes resided at Avignon, France. Elected pope through the machinations of Philip IV of France, Clement V moved the papal capital to Avignon four years later primarily for political reasons. All seven popes of this period were French, as were most of the cardinals, which aroused English and German animosity. During the Avignon papacy the cardinals began to play a stronger role in church government, church and clergy were reformed, missionary efforts were expanded, and popes tried to settle royal rivalries and establish peace. The heavy French influence damaged the prestige of the papacy, however, and in 1377 Gregory XI returned to Rome. The cardinals elected a new pope who took the Avignon seat, becoming the first of a line of antipopes and beginning the Western Schism.

Avignon school, School of late Gothic painting associated with the city of Avignon, Fr., during the Avignon papacy, when many Italian artists worked there. This "school" represents a body of late Gothic painting and not necessarily a single stylistic evolution. Under the direction of Simone Martini, the papal palace of Avignon and secular buildings in nearby towns were decorated with frescoes. The city was one of the channels by which Italian 14th-century art reached France. By the early 15th century Flemish influences had reached the city, consolidating the Italian and northern styles. The Avignon Pietà (*c.* 1460), attributed to Enguerrand Charonton, is the masterpiece of the school. The artistic activity at Avignon greatly influenced French painting in the late 15th and 16th centuries.

Avogadro's number, Number of units in one mole of any substance (defined as its molecular weight in grams), equal to

$6.02214179 \times 10^{23}$. The units may be electrons, atoms, ions, or molecules, depending on the nature of the substance and the character of the reaction (if any).

Avon, River, or UPPER AVON, River, central England. Rising in Northamptonshire, it flows 96 mi (154 km) southwest into the River Severn at Tewkesbury. It is known for its scenic beauty, notably in the Vale of Evesham. Important towns along it include Stratford, where William Shakespeare was born.

AWACS (Airborne Warning and Control System), Mobile, long-range radar surveillance-and-control centre for air defense. Used by the U.S. Air Force since 1977, AWACS is mounted in a specially modified Boeing 707 aircraft, with its main radar antenna affixed to a rotating dome. It can detect, track, and identify low-flying aircraft at a distance of 200 nautical mi (370 km) and high-level targets at much greater distances. It can also track maritime traffic and operate in any weather. The computer system can assess enemy action and track the location and availability of any aircraft within range. Operators of its secure communications system can guide friendly aircraft against enemy planes.

Axis Powers, Coalition headed by Germany, Italy, and Japan that opposed the Allied Powers in World War II. The alliance originated in a series of agreements between Germany and Italy, followed in 1936 by the Rome-Berlin Axis declaration and the German-Japanese Anti-Comintern Pact. The connection was strengthened by the formal Pact of Steel (1939) between Germany and Italy and by the Tripartite Pact signed by all three powers in 1940. Several other countries, including Hungary, Romania, Bulgaria, Croatia, and Slovakia, later allied themselves with the original Axis Powers.

ayatollah, In the Shiite branch of Islam, a high-ranking religious authority regarded by his followers as the most learned person of his age. The ayatollah's authority rests on the infallible imam. His legal decisions are accepted as binding by his personal followers and (in the present day) by the wider community.

Ayodhya, or OUDH, Town (pop., 2001: 49,417), Uttar Pradesh state, northern India. It lies on the banks of the Ghaghara River just east of Faizabad, of which it is now a suburb. Ayodhya in ancient times was one of India's greatest cities. It was the capital of Kosala, as described in the *Ramayana*. Today it is one of the seven holy cities of Hinduism. It became an important Buddhist centre in Buddhism's early years (6th–4th century BCE), and the Buddha is said to have lived there. In the 16th century the Mughal emperor Bābur built a mosque on a site traditionally associated with an ancient Hindu temple marking the birthplace of the god Rama. The storming of the mosque by Hindus in 1990, amid religious tensions, was followed by riots, and the ensuing crisis brought down the government. In 1992 the mosque was demolished by Hindu nationalists, and hundreds of people died in the rioting that subsequently swept through India.

Babri Mosjid ("Mosque of Bābur"), Ayodhya, Uttar Pradesh, India.
Frederick M. Asher

Ayrshire, Breed of hardy dairy cattle that originated in the county of Ayr, Scotland, in the late 18th century. It is considered the only special dairy breed to have originated in the British Isles. Its body colour varies from almost pure white to nearly all cherry red or brown. Exported widely to other countries, it is especially common in Great Britain, the U.S., and Canada.

azalea, Any plant of certain species of the genus *Rhododendron* (heath family), formerly given the generic name *Azalea*. Though some gardeners consider azaleas distinct from rhododendrons, distinguishing characteristics of the two groups are not consistent enough to separate them into two genera. Azaleas typically are deciduous, with flowers that are funnel-shaped, somewhat two-lipped, and often fragrant. Cultivated varieties have been bred from species native to the hilly regions of Asia and North America. Well-known North American kinds include the smooth, or sweet, azalea (*R. arborescens*); the flame azalea (*R. calendulaceum*); and the pinxter flower (*R. periclymenoides*).

Azerbaijan, officially REPUBLIC OF AZERBAIJAN, Country, Transcaucasia, western Asia. Area: 33,436 sq mi (86,600 sq km). Population: (2011 est.) 9,150,000. Capital: Baku. Most residents are of Turkic origin, dating from the 11th century. Later migrations during the Seljūq period brought further groups, including some speaking Persian; Russians are a decreasing minority. Languages: Azerbaijanian (official), Russian. Religion: Islam (mostly Shīʿite). Currency: manat. Azerbaijan is characterized by a variety of landscapes. More than two-fifths of its territory is lowlands, while areas above 5,000 ft (1,500 m) occupy some one-tenth of the total area. The central part of the country is a plain through which flows the Kura River and its tributaries, including the Aras, whose upper course forms part of the boundary with Iran. The Caspian Sea serves Baku as a trade outlet. Agriculture, petroleum refining, and light manufacturing are economically important. Azerbaijan is a unitary multiparty republic with one legislative body; its head of state and government is the president, assisted by the prime minister. Azerbaijan adjoins the Iranian region of the same name, and the origin of their respective inhabitants is the same. By the 9th century CE it had come under Turkish influence, and in ensuing centuries it was fought over by Arabs, Mongols, Turks, and Iranians. Russia acquired what is now independent Azerbaijan in the early 19th century. After the Russian Revolution of 1917, Azerbaijan declared its independence, but it was subdued by the Red Army in 1920 and was incorporated into the Soviet Union. It declared independence from the collapsing Soviet Union in 1991. Azerbaijan has two geographic peculiarities. The exclave Naxçivan (Nakhichevan) is separated from the rest of Azerbaijan by Armenian territory. Nagorno-Karabakh, which lies within Azerbaijan and is administered by it, has a Christian Armenian majority. Azerbaijan and Armenia went to war over both territories in the 1990s, causing many deaths and great economic disruption. Though attempts at mediation were made, the political situation remained unresolved.

Azores, Portuguese AÇORES, Archipelago (pop., 2001: 242,073), northern Atlantic Ocean, constituting an autonomous region of Portugal. Its islands are Flores, Corvo, Terceira, São Jorge, Pico, Faial, Graciosa, São Miguel, and Santa Maria; the capital is Ponta Delgada (on São Miguel). It covers an area of 901 sq mi (2,333 sq km). Subject to earthquakes and volcanic eruptions, the islands lie some 1,000 mi (1,600 km) west of mainland Europe. The uninhabited Azores were reputedly discovered c. 1427 by Portuguese pilot Diogo de Sevilha. Settlement began c. 1432; by the end of the 15th century, all the islands were inhabited and trade with Portugal was well established. They were subject to Spain in 1580–1640, and a famous sea battle between the British and Spanish occurred off Flores in 1591. The Portuguese installed a governor and captain general for the whole group in 1766; the islands were given limited autonomy in 1895. Important air and naval bases were set up there during World War II; in 1951 the U.S. established a NATO base on Lajes.

Azov, Sea of, Inland sea in Europe between Ukraine and Russia. It is connected to the Black Sea by Kerch Strait. About 210 mi (340 km) long and 85 mi (135 km) wide, it occupies an area of 14,500 sq mi (37,600 sq km). With a maximum depth of only about 46 ft (14 m), it is the world's shallowest sea. It is fed by the Don and Kuban rivers, and at their entrance in the Taganrog Gulf, its depth is 3 ft (1 m) or less. In the west lies the Arabat Spit, a 70-mi-

(113–km-) long sandbar that separates the Sea of Azov from the Syvash, a system of marshy inlets dividing the Crimean Peninsula from the Ukrainian mainland.

Aztec, Nahuatl-speaking people who in the 15th and early 16th centuries ruled a large empire in what is now central and southern Mexico. They may have originated on the northern Mexican plateau before migrating to their later location. Their migration may have been linked to the collapse of the Toltec civilization. The Aztec empire, which at its height comprised roughly five to six million people spread over some 80,000 sq mi (200,000 sq km), was made possible by their successful agricultural methods, including intensive cultivation, irrigation, and reclamation of wetlands. The Aztec state was despotic, militaristic, and sharply stratified according to class and caste. Aztec religion was syncretic, drawing especially on the beliefs of the Maya. The Aztec practiced human sacrifice, an activity that sometimes reached mass proportions. The empire came to an end when the Spanish conquistador Hernán Cortés took the emperor Montezuma II prisoner and conquered the great city Tenochtitlán (modern Mexico City).

azulejo, Spanish and Portuguese glazed, polychromed tile produced from the 14th century. Azulejos, which were introduced into Spain by the Arabs during the Moorish occupation, were used in Islamic architecture for facing walls and for paving floors. Early designs were geometric and were about 5–6 in. (13–15 cm) square. In the 15th and 16th centuries Portugal imported the tiles from Spain for use in religious and private buildings, particularly on facades. The Portuguese exported them in the 17th century to the Azores, Madeira, and Brazil, and the Spaniards introduced them to their American colonies. In the 18th century, interiors and exteriors in Puebla, Mex., were covered with azulejos in brilliant colours on a scale unequaled elsewhere.

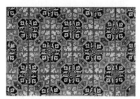

Azulejos from Seville, late 16th century; in the Museum Boymans-van Beuningen, Rotterdam
Courtesy of Museum Boymans-van Beuningen, Rotterdam

B

B cell, One of the two types of lymphocytes (the others being T cells). All lymphocytes begin their development in the bone marrow. B cells are involved in so-called humoral immunity; on encountering a foreign substance (antigen), the B lymphocyte differentiates into a plasma cell, which secretes immunoglobulin.

Baal, God worshiped in many ancient Middle Eastern communities, especially among Canaanites, for whom he was a fertility deity. In the mythology of Canaan, he was locked in combat with Mot, the god of death and sterility; depending on the outcome of their struggles, seven-year cycles of fertility or famine would ensue. Baal was also king of gods, having seized the kingship from the sea god, Yamm. Baal worship was popular in Egypt from the later New Kingdom to its end (1400–1075 BC). The Aramaeans used the Babylonian pronunciation Bel; Bel became the Greek Belos, identified with Zeus. The Old Testament often refers to a specific local Baal or multiple Baalim.

baʿal shem, In Judaism, a title bestowed on men who worked wonders and cures through secret knowledge of the names of God. The practice dates to the 11th century, long before the term was applied to certain rabbis and Kabbalists. They were numerous in 17th- and 18th-century eastern Europe, where they exorcised demons, inscribed amulets, and performed cures using herbs, folk remedies, and the Tetragrammaton. Because they combined faith healing with use of the Kabbala, they clashed with physicians, rabbis, and followers of the Haskala.

Babbage, Charles (b. Dec. 26, 1791, London, Eng.—d. Oct. 18, 1871, London), British mathematician and inventor. Educated at Cambridge University, he devoted himself from about 1812 to devising machines capable of calculating mathematical tables. His first small calculator could perform certain computations to eight decimals. In 1823 he obtained government support for the design of a projected machine with a 20-decimal capacity. In the 1830s he developed plans for the so-called Analytical Engine, capable of performing any arithmetical operation on the basis of instructions from punched cards, a memory unit in which to store numbers, sequential control, and most of the other basic elements of the present-day computer. The forerunner of the modern digital computer, the Analytical Engine was never completed. In 1991 British scientists built Difference Engine No. 2 (accurate to 31 digits) to Babbage's specifications. His other contributions included establishing the modern postal system in England, compiling the first reliable actuarial tables, and inventing the locomotive cowcatcher.

Charles Babbage, detail of an oil painting by Samuel Lawrence, 1845; in the National Portrait Gallery, London.
Courtesy of the National Portrait Gallery, London

Babel, Tower of, In the Hebrew scriptures, a high tower built in Shinar (Babylonia). According to Genesis 11:1–9, the Babylonians wanted to build a tower "with its top in the heavens." Angry at their presumption, God disrupted the enterprise by confusing the languages of the workers so that they could no longer understand each other. The tower was left unfinished and the people dispersed over the face of the earth. The myth may have been inspired by a tower temple located north of the Marduk temple and known as Bab-ilu ("Gate of God").

The Tower of Babel, *oil painting by Pieter Bruegel the Elder, 1563; in the Kunsthistorisches Museum, Vienna.*
Courtesy of the Kunsthistorisches Museum, Vienna

Bābism, Religion that developed in Iran around Mīrzā ʿAlī Muḥammad's claim (1844) to be the Bāb. Its beliefs are set forth in the *Bayān*, a holy book written by the Bāb, which proclaims a universal law in place of all existing religious legal codes. Bābism originated as a messianic movement in Shiʿite Islam. In 1867 the movement split, with the Azalīs remaining faithful to the original teachings of the Bāb and those of his successor Ṣobḥ-e Azal. Most Bābīs accepted the leadership of Ṣobḥ-e Azal's half-brother Bahāʾ Ullāh, and under him the Bahāʾī faith was developed.

baboon, Any of five species of robust monkeys (genus *Papio*) of Arabia and sub-Saharan Africa. Baboons have a large head, cheek pouches, and a long, doglike muzzle. They walk on all fours, carrying the tail in a characteristic arch. They weigh 30–90 lbs (14–40 kg) and are about 20–45 in. (50–115 cm) long, excluding the tail (18–28 in., or 45–70 cm, long). Found mainly in drier savanna and rocky areas, they feed on a variety of plants and animals. Highly social and intelligent, they travel in large noisy troops, communicating by calls. They may destroy crops, and their enormous canine teeth and powerful limbs make them dangerous opponents.

Anubis, or olive, baboon (Papio anubis).
Norman Myers/Photo Researchers

Bābur, orig. ẒAHĪR AL-DĪN MUḤAMMAD (b. Feb. 15, 1483, principality of Fergana—d. Dec. 26, 1530, Agra, India), Emperor (1526–30) and founder of the Mughal dynasty of India. A descendant of Genghis Khan and Timur, he came from a tribe of Mongol origin but was Turkish in language and upbringing. In his youth he tried for 10 years (1494–1504) to gain control of Samarkand, Timur's old capital. Those efforts ended in his losing his own principality in Fergana (modern Uzbekistan), but he consoled himself by seizing and holding Kabul (1504). After four failed attempts, he successfully occupied Delhi (1525). Surrounded by enemy states, Bābur (the name means "Tiger") persuaded his homesick troops to stand their ground, and over the next four years he defeated his foes. His grandson Akbar consolidated the new empire.

Bābur was also a gifted poet and a lover of nature who constructed gardens wherever he went. The *Bābur-nāmeh*, his prose memoirs, has become a world classic of autobiography.

Baby Yar, Large ravine near Kiev, Ukraine, the site of a mass grave of some 100,000 people killed by German Nazi SS squads between 1941 and 1943. Most of the victims were Jews, but some were communist officials and Russian prisoners of war. After the initial massacre of Jews, Baby Yar remained in use as an execution site for Soviet prisoners of war and for Roma (Gypsies) as well as for Jews. It became the symbol of the first stage of killing during the Holocaust and of the massacres by the *Einsatzgruppen* (German: "deployment groups")—the mobile killing units. The site came to world attention after the 1961 publication of Yevgeny Yevtushenko's poem *Baby Yar*. Though a small obelisk and memorial were erected in the 1960s and '70s, not until 1991 was the identity of the Jewish victims recorded on the monument by the newly independent Ukrainian government.

Babylon, Ancient Middle Eastern city. The city's ruins are located about 55 mi (89 km) south of Baghdad, near the modern city of Al-Ḥillah, Iraq. Babylon was one of the most famous cities in antiquity. Probably first settled in the 3rd millennium BC, it came under the rule of the Amorite kings around 2000 BC. It became the capital of Babylonia and was the chief commercial city of the Tigris and Euphrates river system. Destroyed by Sennacherib in 689 BC, it was later rebuilt. It attained its greatest glory as capital of the Neo-Babylonian empire under Nebuchadrezzar II (r. 605–*c.* 561 BC). Alexander the Great, who took the city in 331 BC, died there. Evidence of its topography comes from excavations, cuneiform texts, and descriptions by the Greek historian Herodotus. Most of the ruins are from the city built by Nebuchadrezzar. The largest city in the world at the time, it contained many temples, including the great temple of Marduk with its associated ziggurat, which was apparently the basis for the story of the Tower of Babel. The Hanging Gardens, a simulated hill of vegetation-clad terracing, was one of the Seven Wonders of the World.

Babylonia, Ancient cultural region of the Tigris and Euphrates river system. The area was divided into Sumer (southeast) and Akkad (northwest) when the first Babylonian line of Amorite kings took power after 2000 BC. Largely because of the efforts of Hammurabi (r. *c.* 1792–50 BC), Babylonia gained regional hegemony but declined after his death; the Kassites from the east eventually assumed power (*c.* 1595) and established a dynasty that lasted some four centuries. After Elam conquered Babylonia (*c.* 1157 BC), a series of wars established a new Babylonian dynasty whose outstanding member was Nebuchadrezzar I (r. *c.* 1124–03 BC). Following his rule, a three-way struggle developed for control of Babylonia among Assyria, Aram, and Chaldea, in which the Assyrians ruled the area most frequently (9th–7th century BC). In the 7th–6th century BC the Chaldean Nebuchadrezzar II (605–562 BC) instituted the last and greatest period of Babylonian supremacy, conquering Syria and Palestine and rebuilding Babylon, the capital city. It was conquered in 539 BC by the Persian Achaemenian dynasty under Cyrus II and in 331 BC by Alexander the Great, after which the capital city was gradually abandoned.

Babylonian Exile, or BABYLONIAN CAPTIVITY, Forced detention of Jews in Babylonia following Babylonian conquest of Judah in 598/597 and 587/586 BC. The first deportation may have occurred after King Jehoiachin was deposed in 597 BC or after Nebuchadrezzar destroyed Jerusalem in 586. In 538 BC the Persian Cyrus II conquered Babylonia and allowed the Jews to return to Palestine. Some Jews chose to remain in Babylonia, initiating the Jewish Diaspora. During the Babylonian Exile the Jews maintained their national spirit and religious identity despite cultural pressures in a foreign land, with Ezekiel and other prophets keeping hope alive. Petrarch and other writers designated the Avignon papacy as the Babylonian Captivity in the 14th century, and Mar-

tin Luther used the term in the title of one of his works attacking the papacy and the Roman Catholic church in the 16th century.

Baccarat glass, Glassware manufactured since 1765 in Baccarat, France. The firm originally produced soda glass for windows and industrial use. In 1816 it was acquired by a Belgian manufacturer of lead crystal; since then it has specialized in this type of glass, especially paperweights. Baccarat exhibited works in the important 1925 Exposition des Arts Décoratifs et Industriels Modernes in Paris. Today the company produces tableware in both historical and modern designs.

Bacchanalia, or DIONYSIA, In Greco-Roman religion, any of the festivals of the wine god Bacchus (Dionysus), which probably originated as fertility rites. The most famous Greek festivals included the Greater Dionysia, with its dramatic performances; the Anthesteria; and the Lesser Dionysia, characterized by simple rites. Bacchanalia were introduced from lower Italy into Rome, where they were at first secret, open only to women, and held three times a year. They later admitted men and became as frequent as five times a month. In 186 BC their reputation as orgies led the Senate to prohibit them throughout Italy, except in special cases.

Bach, Johann Sebastian (b. March 21, 1685, Eisenach, Thuringia, Ernestine Saxon Duchies—d. July 28, 1750, Leipzig), German composer. Born to a musical family, he became a superbly well-rounded musician; from 1700 he held positions as singer, violinist, and organist. His first major appointment, in 1708, was as organist at the ducal court at Weimar. This was followed by a six-year stay (1717–23) as kapellmeister at the princely court of Köthen, which was in turn followed by his appointment as cantor at the great church of St. Thomas in Leipzig, where he would remain for the rest of his life. Imbued with the northern German contrapuntal style from early childhood, he encountered the lively Italian style, especially in the works of Antonio Vivaldi, about 1710, and much of his music embodies an immensely convincing melding of the two styles. At St. Thomas he wrote more than 200 church cantatas. His orchestral works include the six *Brandenburg Concertos*, four orchestral suites, and many harpsichord concertos, a genre he invented. His solo keyboard works include the great didactic set *The Well-Tempered Clavier* (1722 and 1742), the superb *Goldberg Variations* (1742), the massive but unfinished *Art of the Fugue* (1749), numerous suites, and many organ preludes and fugues. His surviving choral works include (in addition to the sacred cantatas) more than 30 secular cantatas, two monumental Passions, and the *Mass in B Minor*. His works, never widely known in his lifetime, went into near-total eclipse after his death, and only in the early 19th century were they revived, to enormous acclaim. He was perhaps the most accomplished organist and harpsichordist of his time. Today Bach is regarded as the greatest composer of the Baroque era, and, by many, as the greatest composer of all time.

Bachchan, Amitabh (b. Oct. 11, 1942, Allahabad, India), Indian film actor. Bachchan's first film success was *Zanjeer* (1973); by the end of the 1970s he was something of a cultural phenomenon in India and was regarded as the most popular star in the history of Indian films. He is often compared to such American action stars as Clint Eastwood, although Bachchan's talents also extend to singing, dancing, and comedy. After a brief stint in politics in the mid 1980s, Bachchan gained a new generation of fans in the next decade as host of the television game show *Kaun banega crorepati*, the Indian version of the U.S. and U.K. hit *Who Wants to Be a Millionaire?*

backgammon, Two-person game played by moving counters (called stones) on a board or table, the movement of the counters being controlled by the throw of two dice. The board has four sections (called tables), each marked with six narrow wedges (points) in two alternating colors. Representing the two opposing sides are 15 white and 15 black stones. Stones are moved from point to point in opposite directions according to the number of points shown on the dice. On getting all 15 of his stones into his own home (inner) table, a player may begin "bearing off"—moving his stones to an imaginary point beyond the edge of the board. The player who first bears off all 15 stones wins the game. Backgammon is one of the most ancient board games, dating from 3000 BC.

Bacon, Francis, Viscount St. Albans (b. Jan. 22, 1561, London, Eng.—d. April 9, 1626, London), British statesman and philosopher, father of modern scientific method. He studied at Cambridge and at Gray's Inn. A supporter of the Earl of Essex, Bacon turned against him when Essex was tried for treason. Under James I he rose steadily, becoming successively solicitor general (1607), attorney general (1613), and lord chancellor (1618). Convicted of accepting bribes from those being tried in his court, he was briefly imprisoned and permanently lost his public offices; he died deeply in debt. He attempted to put natural science on a firm empirical foundation in the *Novum Organum* (1620), which sets forth his scientific method. His elaborate classification of the sciences inspired the 18th-century French Encyclopedists, and his empiricism inspired 19th-century British philosophers of science. His other works include *The Advancement of Learning* (1605), *History of Henry VII* (1622), and several important legal and constitutional works.

bacteria, Group of microscopic, single-celled organisms that inhabit virtually all environments, including soil, water, organic matter, and the bodies of multicellular animals. Bacteria are distinguished in part by their morphological and genetic features; for instance, they may have spherical, rodlike, or spiral shapes. They also can be divided into two main groups, gram-positive or gram-negative, based on the structure of their cell wall and their reaction to the gram stain. Many bacteria swim by means of flagella. The DNA of most bacteria is found in a single circular chromosome and is distributed throughout the cytoplasm rather than contained within a membrane-enclosed nucleus. Though some bacteria can cause food poisoning and infectious diseases in humans, most are harmless and many are beneficial. They are used in various industrial processes, especially in the food industry (e.g., the production of yogurt, cheeses, and pickles). Bacteria are genetically distinct from the archaea. As prokaryotic organisms (having no membrane-bound nucleus), they are also distinct from eukaryotes.

badminton, Court or lawn game played with light long-handled rackets and a shuttlecock volleyed over a net. The game is named after the residence of Britain's duke of Beaufort, where it supposedly originated *c.* 1873. Officially sanctioned badminton matches are played indoors to protect the shuttlecock from winds. Play consists entirely of hitting the shuttlecock back and forth without letting it touch the floor or ground. The best-known match is the All-England Championships. Badminton became a full-medal sport at the 1992 Olympics. The world governing body is the International Federation of Badminton in Cheltenham, Gloucestershire, Eng.

Baffin Island, Largest island in Canada and fifth largest island in the world (183,810 sq mi [476,068 sq km]), lying between Greenland and the Canadian mainland. Located west of Baffin Bay and the Davis Strait, it is administered as part of Nunavut territory. It was probably visited by Norse explorers in the 11th century. It was sighted by Martin Frobisher during his search for a Northwest Passage (1576–78). It is uninhabited except for a few coastal settlements. The world's northernmost mines are at Nanisvik. In 1972 Auyuittuq National Park was created on the eastern coast.

Baghdad, or BAGDAD, City (pop., 2011 est.: 6,150,000), capital of Iraq. Located on the Tigris River, the site has been settled from ancient times. It rose to importance after being chosen in 762 CE by Caliph al-Manṣūr (r. 754–775) as the capital of the ʿAbbāsid dynasty. Under Hārūn al-Rashīd it achieved its greatest glory—

reflected in the many tales from *The Thousand and One Nights* that were set there—as one of the world's largest and wealthiest cities. A centre of Islamic civilization, it was second only to the Byzantine capital, Constantinople (modern Istanbul), in trade and culture. The capital was moved briefly to Sāmarrāʾ in 836, after which the city was prone to bouts of political instability. It was sacked by the Mongols under Hülegü in 1258, taken by Timur in 1401, and captured by the Persian Ṣafavid dynasty in 1508. Under the sultan Süleyman I, the city became part of the Ottoman Empire in 1534 and remained so—save for a brief period (1623–38) when it returned to Ṣafavid rule—until the end of World War I (1914–18). It became capital of the kingdom (1920) and then the republic (1958) of Iraq. During the 20th century the city grew greatly in size and population. It was severely damaged during the Persian Gulf War (1990–91) and during the Iraq War (2003–11), when it was occupied by a U.S.-led coalition force.

bagpipe, Wind instrument consisting of two or more single- or double-reed pipes, the reeds being vibrated by wind fed by arm pressure on a skin or cloth bag. The pipes are held in wooden sockets tied into the bag, which is inflated either by the mouth or by bellows strapped to the body. Melodies are played on the fingerholes of the melody pipe, or chanter, while the remaining pipes, or drones, sound single notes. Bagpipes existed by about AD 100. The early bag was an animal bladder or a nearly whole sheepskin or goatskin. Bagpipes have always been folk instruments, but after the 15th century some were used for court music, and others have survived as military instruments. An important related instrument is the Irish union (or uilleann) pipe.

Bahaʾi, Religion founded in Iran in the mid-19th century by Bahāʾ Ullāh. It emerged from Bābism when in 1863 Bahāʾ Ullāh asserted that he was the messenger of God predicted by the Bāb. Before his death in 1892, he appointed his son ʿAbd ol-Bahā to lead the community. The writings of the Bāb, Bahāʾ Ullāh, and ʿAbd ol-Bahā form the sacred literature. Worship consists of readings from scriptures of all religions. Bahāʾī faith proclaims the essential unity of all religions and the unity of humanity. It is concerned with social ethics and has no priesthood or sacraments. Because of its 19 initial disciples, it considers the number 19 sacred, and the calendar consists of 19 months of 19 days (with four additional days). Adherents are expected to pray daily, fast 19 days a year, and keep to a strict ethical code. Bahāʾī has experienced major growth since the 1960s but has been persecuted in Iran since the fundamentalist revolution of 1979.

Bahamas, The, officially COMMONWEALTH OF THE BAHAMAS, Archipelago and state, northwestern edge of the West Indies, lying southeast of Florida and north of Cuba. It consists of about 700 islands and numerous cays. Area: 5,382 sq mi (13,939 sq km). Population: (2011 est.) 360,000. Capital: Nassau (on New Providence Island). The people are of African and European ancestry, a legacy of the slave trade. Language: English (official). Religion: Christianity (mostly Protestant; also Roman Catholic, other Christians). Currency: Bahamian dollar. Chief among the islands, from north to south, are Grand Bahama, Abaco, Eleuthera, New Providence, Andros, Cat, and Inagua; New Providence has most of the population. All are composed of coralline limestone and lie mostly only a few feet above sea level; the highest point is Mount Alvernia (206 ft [63 m]) on Cat Island. There are no rivers. The country's market economy is heavily dependent on tourism, for which gambling is a particular attraction, and on international financial services. Most foodstuffs are imported; refined petroleum and chemicals are significant exports. The U.S. is the major trading partner of The Bahamas. The Bahamas is a constitutional monarchy with two legislative houses; its head of state is the British monarch, represented by a governor-general, and the head of government is the prime minister. The islands were inhabited by Lucayan Tainos when Christopher Columbus sighted them on Oct. 12, 1492. Many scholars believe Columbus landed on San Salvador (Watling) Island, though others contend his first landfall was on

Samana Cay or Cat Island. The Spaniards made no attempt to settle but carried out slave raids that depopulated the islands; when
English settlers arrived in 1648 from Bermuda, the islands were
uninhabited. They became a haunt of pirates and buccaneers, and
few of the ensuing settlements prospered. The islands enjoyed
some prosperity following the American Revolution, when loyalists fled the U.S. and established cotton plantations there. The islands were a centre for blockade runners during the American
Civil War. Not until the development of tourism after World War
II did permanent economic prosperity arrive. The Bahamas was
granted internal self-government in 1964 and became independent
in 1973.

Bahrain, officially KINGDOM OF BAHRAIN, Country, Middle
East, southwestern Asia. Area: 292 sq mi (757 sq km). Population:
(2011 est.) 1,325,000. It occupies an archipelago consisting of
Bahrain Island and about 30 smaller islands lying along the Arabian Peninsula in the Persian Gulf. Saudi Arabia lies to the west
across the Gulf of Bahrain, and the Qatar peninsula lies to the east.
The capital is Manama. Most of the population is Arab. Language:
Arabic (official). Religion: Islam (official). Currency: Bahraini
dinar. Bahrain Island, which is about 30 mi (50 km) long and 10
mi (16 km) wide, accounts for seven-eighths of the country's total
area and, with the islands of Al-Muḥarraq and Sitrah off its northeastern coast, constitutes the population and economic centre of
the country. Since 1986 the main island has been connected to
Saudi Arabia by a 15-mi (24-km) causeway. The highest point of
elevation is Al-Dukhān Hill (440 ft [134 m]). Bahrain has a developing mixed (state and private enterprise) economy based largely
on natural gas and petroleum production and refining. Bahrain is
a constitutional monarchy. The head of state is the king, and the
head of government is the prime minister. The area has long been
an important trading centre and is mentioned in Persian, Greek,
and Roman references. It was ruled by various Arab groups from
the 7th century CE but was then occupied by the Portuguese (1521–
1602). Since 1783 it has been ruled by a family group known as
Āl Khalīfah, though (through a series of treaties) its defense long
remained a British responsibility (1820–1971). After Britain withdrew its forces from the Persian Gulf (1968), Bahrain declared its
independence (1971). It served as a centre for the allies in the Persian Gulf War (1990–91). Since 1994 it has experienced periods
of political unrest, mainly among its large Shīʿite population. Constitutional revisions, ratified in 2002, made Bahrain a constitutional monarchy and enfranchised women; parliamentary elections (the first since 1975) were held in October 2002.

Baikal, Lake, Russian OZERO BAYKAL, Lake, southern Siberia,
Russia, in Asia. With a length of 395 mi (636 km) long and an area
of some 12,200 sq mi (31,500 sq km), it is the largest freshwater
basin in Eurasia. It is also the deepest continental body of water
on Earth (5,315 ft [1,620 m]), containing one-fifth of the fresh
water on Earth's surface. More than 330 rivers and streams flow
into it; on its east it receives the Barguzin and Selenga rivers, and
most of its outflow is through the Angara at the northern end. The
island of Olkhon is in its centre. Plant and animal life are rich and
various; at least 1,500 species are unique to the lake. Growing
industrialization along its shores has produced threatening pollution. In 1996 the Lake Baikal Coastal Protection Zone was designated a UNESCO World Heritage site.

Baku, City (pop., 2003 est.: 1,828,800), capital of Azerbaijan.
Located on the western shore of the Caspian Sea at the sea's best
harbour, Baku has long been inhabited. By the 11th century AD it
was in the possession of the Shirvan shahs, who made it their capital in the 12th century. In 1723 Peter I (the Great) took Baku, but
it was returned to Persia in 1735; Russia recaptured it in 1806. It
was the capital of the short-lived independent state of Azerbaijan
(1918–20) and in 1920 became the capital of the new Soviet republic of Azerbaijan. The basis of Baku's economy is petroleum. The
city's historic centre was designated a UNESCO World Heritage
site in 2000.

balalaika, Russian stringed instrument with a triangular body,
three strings, and movable frets
on its fingerboard. It comes in
six sizes, from piccolo to double
bass. It developed in the 18th
century from the dombra. It has
been primarily a solo folk instrument for accompanying
song and dance, but is also
played in large balalaika orchestras.

*Russian tenor balalaika, 20th
century; in the Metropolitan
Museum of Art, New York City*
Courtesy of the Metropolitan Museum
of Art, New York City, the Crosby
Brown Collection of Musical
Instruments, 1889

balance of payments, Systematic record of all economic
transactions during a given period between residents (including the government) of one
country and residents (including
the governments) of other countries. The transactions are presented in the form of double-
entry bookkeeping. The U.S.
balance of payments, for example, records the various ways in
which dollars are made available to foreigners through U.S.
imports, U.S. tourist spending
abroad, foreign lending, and so
on. These expenditures are
shown on the debit side of the
balance. The credit side shows
the various uses to which for-
eigners put their dollars, including paying for U.S. exports, ser-
vicing debts to the U.S., and the like. Foreign countries may acquire more dollars than they need to spend on U.S. goods and
services and may hold the surplus or purchase gold or securities;
or they may have fewer dollars than they need to purchase U.S.
goods and services, and may acquire additional dollars by transferring gold, selling holdings in the U.S., and so on. Certain forms
of transferring funds (e.g., large outflows of gold) are less desirable as a way of settling foreign debts than others (e.g., transfers
of currency acquired through international trade). The International Monetary Fund helps address problems relating to balance
of payments.

balance of power, In international relations, an equilibrium of
power sufficient to discourage or prevent one nation or party from
imposing its will on or interfering with the interests of another. The
term came into use at the end of the Napoleonic Wars to denote
the power relationships in the European state system. Until World
War I, Britain played the role of balancer in a number of shifting
alliances. After World War II, a Northern Hemisphere balance of
power pitted the U.S. and its allies against the Soviet Union and
its satellites in a bipolar balance of power backed by the threat of
nuclear war. China's defection from the Soviet camp to a nonaligned but covertly anti-Soviet stance produced a third node of
power. With the Soviet Union's collapse (1991), the U.S. and its
NATO allies were recognized universally as the world's paramount military power.

balance of trade, Difference in value over a period of time
between a nation's imports and exports of goods and services. The
balance of trade is part of a larger economic unit, the balance of
payments, which includes all economic transactions between residents of one country and those of other countries. If a nation's
exports exceed its imports, the nation has a favourable balance of
trade, or a trade surplus. If imports exceed exports, an unfavourable balance of trade, or a trade deficit, exists. Under mercantilism a favourable balance of trade was an absolute necessity, but in
classical economics it was more important for a nation to utilize
its economic resources fully than to build a trade surplus. The idea

of the undesirability of trade deficits persisted, however, and arguments against deficits are often advanced by advocates of protectionism.

Balaton, Lake, Lake, Hungary. Southwest of Budapest, it is the largest lake in central Europe, covering 231 sq mi (598 sq km), with a maximum depth of about 37 ft (11 m). It contains two wildlife reserves. While agriculture remains important in the area, the tourist industry has become significant, and resorts, including Siófok and Balatonfüred, have been developed.

bald eagle, Species of sea eagle (*Haliaeetus leucocephalus*) that  occurs inland along rivers and large lakes. Strikingly handsome, it is the only eagle native solely to North America, and it has been the U.S. national bird since 1782. The adult, about 40 in. (1 m) long with a wingspan of 6.5 ft (2 m), is dark brown with white head and tail and yellow beak, eyes, and feet. Bald eagles snatch fish at the water surface, rob osprey of fish, and eat carrion. They nest in lone trees, often on river islands. Though still protected in the U.S., the bald eagle is no longer considered an endangered species.

Bald eagle (Haliaeetus leucocephalus).
Alexander Sprunt, IV

Balder, In Norse mythology, the just and beautiful son of Odin and Frigg. He could be harmed by nothing except mistletoe. Knowing he was invulnerable, the gods amused themselves by throwing things at him. Deceived by Loki, the blind god Höd hurled mistletoe at Balder and killed him. The giantess Thökk, probably Loki in disguise, refused to weep the tears that would have released Balder from the underworld.

Balearic Islands, Spanish ISLAS BALEARES, Archipelago (pop., 2001: 841,669), western Mediterranean Sea, constituting an autonomous community and province of Spain. It occupies an area of 1,927 sq mi (4,992 sq km); its capital is Palma. The most important islands are Majorca, Minorca, Ibiza, Formentera, and Cabrera. Long inhabited, the islands were ruled by Carthage in the 6th century BC, by Rome from *c.* 120 BC, and by the Byzantine Empire from AD 534. Raided by the Arabs, the area was conquered in the 10th century by the Umayyad dynasty at Córdoba. It was reconquered by the Spanish and united with the kingdom of Aragon in 1349. After territorial challenges in the 18th century by the British, the islands came under Spanish rule in 1802. The present-day economy is fueled by tourism.

baleen whale, Any of about 13 species of cetaceans in the suborder Mysticeti. They are distinguished by a specialized feeding structure, the baleen, which strains plankton and small crustaceans from the water. It consists of two horny plates attached to the roof of the mouth. Each plate (as long as 12 ft, or 3.6 m, in the right whale) is composed of parallel slats with fringes that mat together to form a sieve. Other baleen whales are the blue, fin, gray, humpback, and sei whales and the rorqual. Baleen was once used for corset stays and is still used in some industrial brushes.

Balfour Declaration (Nov. 2, 1917) Statement issued by the British foreign secretary, Arthur James Balfour, in a letter to Lionel Walter Rothschild, a leader of British Jewry, as urged by the Russian Jewish Zionist leaders Chaim Weizmann and Nahum Sokolow. The declaration promised the establishment of a homeland for the Jewish people in Palestine that would not disturb the non-Jewish groups already residing there. The British anticipated gaining a mandate over Palestine after World War I (1914–18) and

hoped to win over Jewish public opinion to the side of the Allies. They also hoped that pro-British settlers would help protect the approaches to the Suez Canal, a vital link to Britain's South Asian possessions.

Bali, Island (pop., 2005 prelim.: 4,309,600), Indonesia. Located in the Lesser Sunda Islands, off the eastern coast of Java, it constitutes, with minor adjacent islands, a province of Indonesia. The main towns are Singaraja and Denpasar, the provincial capital. The island is mountainous; its highest peak is Mount Agung (10,308 ft [3,142 m]). Colonized by India in early times and supplemented by émigrés from Java in the 16th century, Bali is the remaining stronghold of Hinduism in the Indonesian archipelago. Visited by the Dutch in the late 16th century, it came under Dutch rule only in the late 19th century. It was occupied by the Japanese in World War II and became part of Indonesia in 1950. Tourism is now one of the mainstays of its economy.

Balinese, People of the island of Bali, Indon. They differ from other Indonesians in adhering to Hinduism, though their culture has been heavily influenced by the Javanese. In Balinese villages each family lives in its own compound, surrounded by earthen or stone walls; all villages have temples and an assembly hall. Balinese religion fuses Hindu Shaivism with Buddhism, ancestor cults, and belief in spirits and magic. Marriage is often limited to members of the same kinship organization, and family relationships are reckoned through the male line.

Balkan League (1912–13) Alliance of Bulgaria, Serbia, Greece, and Montenegro, which fought the first Balkan War against the Ottoman empire. Ostensibly created to limit Austrian power in the Balkans, the league was actually formed at the instigation of Russia to expel the Turks from the Balkans. The league disintegrated when its members quarreled over the division of territorial spoils after their victory in the first Balkan War.

Balkan Mountains, Bulgarian STARA PLANINA, Mountain range, southeastern Europe. It extends east to west across central Bulgaria from the Black Sea to the Serbian border; the highest point is Botev Peak, at 7,795 ft (2,376 m). The range forms the major divide between the Danube River in the north and the Maritsa River in the south. It is crossed by about 20 passes (notably Shipka Pass), several railway lines, and the Iskur River.

Balkan Wars (1912–13) Two military conflicts that deprived the Ottoman Empire of almost all its remaining territory in Europe. In the First Balkan War, the Balkan League defeated the Ottoman Empire, which, under the terms of the peace treaty (1913), lost Macedonia and Albania. The Second Balkan War broke out after Serbia, Greece, and Romania quarreled with Bulgaria over the division of their joint conquests in Macedonia. Bulgaria was defeated, and Greece and Serbia divided up most of Macedonia between themselves. The wars heightened tensions in the Balkans and helped spark World War I.

Balkans, or BALKAN PENINSULA, Peninsula, southeastern Europe. Located between the Adriatic Sea, the Mediterranean Sea, and the Aegean and Black seas, it is inhabited by a variety of linguistic, religious, ethnic, and national groups. It also contains many countries, including Romania, Moldova, Bulgaria, Greece, Albania, and the independent states of the former Yugoslavia—Serbia, Croatia, Slovenia, Macedonia, Bosnia and Herzegovina, and Montenegro—but there is not universal agreement on the region's components. Some define the region in cultural and historical terms and others geographically, though there are even different interpretations among historians and among geographers. From 168 BCE to 107 CE, part of the area was incorporated into Roman provinces, including Epirus, Moesia, Pannonia, Thrace, and Dacia. It was subsequently settled by Slavic invaders, Serbs, Croats, Slovenes, and Slavonized Bulgars, the last of whom were pushed into the Balkan region in the 6th century. It was gradually organized into kingdoms, many of which were overrun by the Ottoman Empire in the 14th–15th century. The factional strife that occurred there throughout the 20th century, provoking the continual breakups and regroupings of different states, introduced the word *balkanize* into English.

ballad, Form of short narrative folk song. Its distinctive style crystallized in Europe in the late Middle Ages as part of the oral tradition, and it has been preserved as a musical and literary form. The oral form has persisted as the folk ballad, and the written, literary ballad evolved from the oral tradition. The folk ballad typically tells a compact tale with deliberate starkness, using devices such as repetition to heighten effects. The modern literary ballad (e.g., those by W.H. Auden, Bertolt Brecht, and Elizabeth Bishop) recalls in its rhythmic and narrative elements the traditions of folk balladry.

ballet, Theatrical dance in which a formal academic technique (the *danse d'école*) is combined with music, costume, and stage scenery. Developed from court productions of the Renaissance, ballet was renewed under Louis XIV, who in 1661 established France's Académie Royale de Danse, where Pierre Beauchamp developed the five ballet positions. Early ballets were often accompanied by singing and incorporated into opera-ballets by composers such as Jean-Baptiste Lully. In the 18th century Jean-Georges Noverre and Gasparo Angiolini separately developed the dramatic ballet (*ballet d'action*) to tell a story through dance steps and mime, a reform echoed in Christoph Willibald Gluck's music. Significant developments in the early 19th century included pointe work (balance on the extreme tip of the toe) and the emergence of the prima ballerina, exemplified by Marie Taglioni and Fanny Elssler. In the late 19th and early 20th centuries, Russia became the centre of ballet production and performance, through the work of innovators such as Sergey Diaghilev, Anna Pavlova, Vaslav Nijinsky, Marius Petipa, and Michel Fokine; great ballets were composed by Pyotr Tchaikovsky and Igor Stravinsky. Since then, ballet schools in Great Britain and the U.S. have elevated ballet in those countries to Russia's level and greatly increased its audience.

Ballets Russes, Ballet company founded in Paris in 1909 by Sergey Diaghilev. Considered the source of modern ballet, the company employed the most outstanding creative talent of the period. Its choreographers included Michel Fokine, Léonide Massine, Bronislava Nijinska, and George Balanchine, and among its dancers were Yekaterina Geltzer, Tamara Karsavina, and Vaslav Nijinsky. Music was commissioned from composers such as Igor Stravinsky, Maurice Ravel, Darius Milhaud, Sergey Prokofiev, and Claude Debussy, and ballets featured stage designs by artists Alexandre Benois, Pablo Picasso, Georges Rouault, Henri Matisse, and André Derain.

ballista, Ancient missile launcher designed to hurl long arrows or heavy balls. The Greek version was basically a huge crossbow fastened to a mount. The Roman ballista was powered by torsion derived from two thick skeins of twisted cords through which were thrust two separate arms joined at their ends by the cord that propelled the missile. The largest could accurately hurl 60-lb (27-kg) weights up to about 500 yards (450 m).

ballooning, Flying in a balloon in competition or for recreation. Sport ballooning began in the early 20th century and became popular in the 1960s. The balloons used are of lightweight synthetic materials (e.g., polyester coated in aluminized mylar) and are filled with hot air or lighter-than-air gas. Balloon races often involve tasks such as changing elevations or landing on or near a target. Competitions are regulated by the Fédération Aéronautique Internationale. The first transatlantic, transcontinental, and transpacific balloon flights were achieved in 1978, 1980, and 1981, respectively. In 1997–98 international teams began competing to become the first to balloon nonstop around the world. This feat was finally accomplished in 1999 by the Swiss psychiatrist Bertrand Piccard (grandson of famed physicist and balloonist Auguste Piccard) and his British copilot Brian Jones, who spent 19 days in the air.

ballroom dance, European and American social dancing performed by couples. It includes standard dances such as the foxtrot, waltz, polka, tango, Charleston, jitterbug, and merengue. Ballroom dance was popularized by Vernon and Irene Castle and Fred Astaire and, later, by Arthur Murray (1895–1991), who established ballroom dance studios throughout the U.S. Ballroom dance contests, especially popular in Europe, feature both amateur and professional dancers.

Baloch, or BALUCH, Any member of a group of tribes speaking the Balochi language and inhabiting the province of Balochistan in Pakistan and neighbouring areas of Iran and Afghanistan. Some 70% of the total Baloch population live in Pakistan, where they are divided into two groups, the Sulaimani and the Makrani. Mentioned in 10th-century Arabic chronicles, they probably came originally from the Iranian plateau. Traditional Baloch are nomads, but settled agricultural existence is becoming more common. They raise camels and other livestock and engage in carpet making and embroidery.

Balochistan, or BALUCHISTAN, Province (pop., 2003 est.: 7,450,000), southwestern Pakistan. Its capital is Quetta (pop., 1998: 560,307). Its landscape includes mountains, notably the Sulaiman and Kithar ranges; barren, flat plains; arid desert; and marshy swamps. In ancient times, it was part of Gedrosia. Alexander the Great traversed it in 325 BC. It was included in the Bactrian kingdom, then was ruled by Arabs from the 7th to the 10th century AD. It was ruled by Persia for centuries, with the exception of a period when it belonged to the Mughal Empire (1594–1638). It became a British dependency in 1876 and a British province of India in 1887. It was made part of Pakistan in 1947–48 and was designated a separate province in 1970. Wheat, sorghum, and rice are staple crops; manufactures include cotton and woolen goods.

Baltic languages, Branch of the Indo-European language family that includes three attested languages, Lithuanian, Latvian, and Old Prussian. They were or are spoken along the eastern and southeastern shore and hinterlands of the Baltic Sea. Medieval chronicles report four other Baltic-speaking peoples in the region, though by the 16th century these peoples had been completely assimilated. Baltic has certain striking features in common with Slavic languages, though the deep divisions within Baltic itself, among other factors, make the hypothesis of a common Balto-Slavic protolanguage difficult to defend.

Baltic religion, Ancient beliefs and practices of the Balts of Eastern Europe. They are believed to give evidence of a common source with Vedic and Iranian religion. The most important Baltic divinities were sky gods: Dievs (the sky), Perkons (the thunderer), Saule (sun goddess), and Meness (moon god). A forest divinity, the Mother of the Forest, was common to all Baltic peoples and was differentiated into goddesses that personified various aspects of nature. Destiny or luck was personified as the goddess Laima, who determined a person's fate at the moment of birth. The dead were thought to revisit the world as good or evil spirits; evil was also done by the devil, Velns, and by a werewolf-like creature known as Vilkacis or Vilkatas. The structure of the world, with the world tree at its center, and the enmity between Saule and Meness are important themes. Festivals marked the summer solstice, the harvest, marriages, and funerals. Worship was conducted at holy groves and small hills; excavations have also revealed circular wooden temples.

Baltic Sea, Sea, northern Europe. An arm of the Atlantic Ocean, connecting with the North Sea, it is about 1,000 mi (1,600 km) long, covers an area of about 149,000 sq mi (386,000 sq km), and has a maximum depth of about 1,500 ft (450 m). It receives the Vistula and Oder rivers and many other rivers. It is enclosed by Denmark, Sweden, Finland, Estonia, Latvia, Lithuania, Poland, Germany, and Russia. It has two large arms, the Gulf of Bothnia and the Gulf of Finland. The modifying effect of the North Atlantic Current is scarcely felt; its waters contain only about one-fourth as much salt as the oceans, and it freezes readily.

Baltic States, Republics of Lithuania, Latvia, and Estonia, situated on the eastern shore of the Baltic Sea. The name has sometimes been used to include Finland and Poland. They were created as independent states in 1917 from the Baltic provinces of Russia, the city of Kovno, and part of the Polish department of Wilno (later Lithuania). With the aid of German and Allied forces, the Baltic states repelled a Bolshevik invasion in 1919. In 1940 they were forcibly occupied by the Soviet Union and incorporated as constituent republics. In 1944 Soviet troops recovered the territory, which had been overrun by German forces in 1941. The Baltic states gained independence on the breakup of the Soviet Union in 1991.

bamboo, Any of the tall, treelike grasses, found in tropical and subtropical to mild temperate regions, that make up the subfamily Bambusoideae, family Poaceae. Bamboos are giant, fast-growing grasses with woody stems. A few species of the genus *Arundinaria* are native to the southern U.S., where they form dense canebrakes along riverbanks and in marshy areas. The woody, hollow, aerial stems grow in branching clusters from a thick rhizome, often forming a dense undergrowth that excludes other plants. All parts of the bamboo are used, for purposes including food, livestock fodder, fine-quality paper, construction materials, and medicines. Bamboos also have ornamental use in landscape gardens.

banana, Fruit of the genus *Musa* (family Musaceae), a gigantic herbaceous plant spread by rhizomes, and one of the most important food crops of the world. The banana is consumed extensively throughout the tropics, where it is grown, and is also valued in the temperate zone for its flavour, nutritional value, and constant availability. Hundreds of varieties are cultivated. Perhaps the most important species is the common banana, *M. sapientum.* The ripe fruit is high in carbohydrates (mainly sugar), potassium, and vitamins C and A, and it is low in protein and fat. Though usually eaten fresh, bananas may also be cooked. The U.S. imports more bananas than does any other country.

band, Musical ensemble that generally excludes stringed instruments. Ensembles of woodwind, brass, and percussion instruments originated in 15th-century Germany, taking on a particularly military role; these spread to France, Britain, and eventually the New World. In the 15th–18th centuries, many European towns had town musicians, or waits, who performed especially for ceremonial occasions in wind bands often consisting primarily of shawms and sackbuts (trombones). In the 18th–19th centuries, the English amateur brass band, largely consisting of the many newly developed brass instruments, took on the important nonmilitary function of representing organizations of all kinds. In the U.S., Patrick Gilmore's virtuoso band became famous in the mid-19th century; his greatest successor, John Philip Sousa, bequeathed a repertory of marches that has remained very popular. The "big band," under leaders such as Duke Ellington and Count Basie, was central to American popular music in the 1930s and '40s. In the rock band, unlike most other bands, stringed instruments (electric guitars and electric bass) are paramount.

Bandar Seri Begawan, formerly BRUNEI TOWN, City (pop., 2001: city, 27,285; 2002 est.: metro. area, 74,700), capital of Brunei. Lying along the Brunei River near its mouth on Brunei Bay, it is a trade centre and river port. Heavily damaged during World War II, it was largely rebuilt; newer buildings include the largest mosque in eastern Asia.

Bandung, City (pop., 2010 est.: 2,394,873), capital of West Java (Jawa Barat) province, Indonesia. It was founded by the Dutch in 1810 on a 2,400-ft (730-m) plateau in the interior of Java. It is surrounded by beautiful scenery. Bandung is the centre of cultural life for the Sundanese, who compose most of West Java's population and differ in customs and language from their Javanese neighbours. It is also a centre for the study and preservation of Sundanese culture and an educational centre.

bandwidth, Measurement of the capacity of a communications signal. For digital signals, the bandwidth is the data speed or rate, measured in bits per second (bps). For analog signals, it is the difference between the highest and lowest frequency components, measured in hertz (cycles per second). For example, a modem with a bandwidth of 56 kilobits per second (Kbps) can transmit a maximum of about 56,000 bits of digital data in one second. The human voice, which produces analog sound waves, has a typical bandwidth of three kilohertz between the highest and lowest frequency sounds it can generate.

Banerjea, Sir Surendranath (b. Nov. 10, 1848, Calcutta, India—d. Aug. 6, 1925, Barrackpore, near Calcutta), Indian statesman, one of the founders of modern India. As a young man, he attempted unsuccessfully to serve in the Indian Civil Service, at the time virtually closed to ethnic Indians. He then became a teacher and founded a college in Calcutta (now Kolkata), which was later named for him. Banerjea attempted to bring Hindus and Muslims together for political action, and for 40 years he put forward a nationalist viewpoint in his newspaper, *The Bengalee.* Twice elected president of the Indian National Congress, he advocated for an Indian constitution on the Canadian model. He was elected in 1913 to two legislative councils and later was knighted (1921); in 1924 he was defeated by an independence candidate, whereupon he retired to write his autobiography, *A Nation in the Making* (1925).

Bangalore, City (pop., 2001: city, 4,301,326; metro. area, 5,701,446), capital of Karnataka state, southern India. It is a cultural meeting place for speakers of the Kannada, Telugu, and Tamil languages. Founded in the 16th century, it became a fief of the Indian ruler Hyder Ali *c.* 1760 but was later taken by the British. It was the headquarters of the British administration 1831–81, when it was restored to the raja of Mysore (now Karnataka). Today, it is one of India's largest cities and an industrial and educational centre.

Attara Kacheri (1864), Bangalore, Karnataka, India.
Spectrum Colour Library—Impact Photos/Heritage-Images

Banghāzī, or BENGHAZI, Coastal city (pop., 2005 est.: 685,367), northeastern Libya. Located on the Gulf of Sidra, it is Libya's second largest city and was once its capital. Founded by Greeks as Hesperides, it received from Ptolemy III the additional name Berenice in honour of his wife. After the 3rd century AD it superseded Cyrene and Barce as the chief city of the region. After its importance waned, it remained a small town until it was extensively developed during the Italian occupation of Libya (1912–42). In World War II it suffered considerable damage before being captured by the British in 1942. It is now an administrative and commercial centre and the site of one of the world's largest desalinization plants.

Bangkok, Thai KRUNG THEP, City (pop., 2000: metro. area, 6,355,144), capital of Thailand. Lying 25 mi (40 km) above the mouth of the Chao Phraya River, it is the country's major port and also its cultural, financial, and educational centre. It was established as the capital of Siam (Thailand) in 1782 by King Rama I. Seized by the Japanese in World War II, it subsequently suffered heavy Allied bombing. In 1971–72 it incorporated several outlying districts to form a single province-level metropolis and has since experienced phenomenal growth. Throughout the city, walled Buddhist temples and monasteries serve as focal points for its religious life.

Bangladesh, officially PEOPLE'S REPUBLIC OF BANGLADESH, Country, south-central Asia. Area: 56,977 sq mi (147,570 sq km). Population: (2011 est.) 142,875,000. Capital: Dhaka. The vast majority of the population are Bengali. Language: Bengali (official). Religions: Islam (official; mainly Sunni); also Hinduism. Currency: taka. Bangladesh is generally flat, its highest point reaching over 1,000 ft (305 m) above sea level. The landscape is characterized by alluvial plains dissected by numerous connecting rivers. The southern part consists of the eastern sector of the Ganges-Brahmaputra delta. The chief rivers are the Ganges (there known as the Padma) and the Brahmaputra (or Jamuna), which unite as the Padma. Though primarily agricultural, the country often is not self-sufficient in food production. The monsoonal rains that occur from May to October produce extreme flooding over much of Bangladesh, often causing severe crop damage and great loss of life. Cyclones in 1970 and 1991 killed some 300,000 and 140,000 Bengalis, respectively. Bangladesh is a unitary multiparty republic with one legislative house; its head of state is the president, and its head of government is the prime minister. In its early years Bangladesh was known as Bengal. When the British left the subcontinent in 1947, the area that was East Bengal became the part of Pakistan called East Pakistan. Bengali nationalist sentiment increased after the creation of an independent Pakistan. In 1971 violence erupted; some one million Bengalis were killed, and millions more fled to India, which finally entered the war on the side of the Bengalis, ensuring West Pakistan's defeat. East Pakistan became the independent country of Bangladesh. Little of the devastation caused by the war has been repaired, and political instability, including the assassination of two presidents, has continued.

Bangui, City (pop., 2003: 622,771), capital of the Central African Republic. A major port on the Ubangi River, it is connected by an extended 1,100-mi (1,800-km) river and rail transport system with the Congolese cities of Pointe-Noire and Brazzaville. Chiefly a commercial and administrative centre, Bangui is also the site of a university and research institutes.

banjo, Plucked stringed musical instrument of African origin. It has a tambourine-like body, four or five strings, and a long fretted neck. The fifth string (if present) is pegged at the fifth fret and acts primarily as a drone plucked by the thumb. In its original form, the banjo had only four strings and lacked frets. Slaves introduced the instrument to the U.S., where it was popularized in 19th-century minstrel shows and thence exported to Europe. It has been an important American folk instrument, especially in bluegrass, and it was used in early jazz.

Banjul, formerly (1816–1973) BATHURST, Seaport (pop., 1993: urban agglomeration, 270,540), capital of The Gambia. Located on the Island of St. Mary in the Gambia River, it is the country's largest city. Founded by the British in 1816 to suppress the slave trade, it subsequently became the capital of the British colony of Gambia. With The Gambia's independence in 1965, it became the national capital. Tourism is of increasing importance, and Banjul serves as a transportation centre with connections to the interior and to Senegal.

bank, Institution that deals in money and its substitutes and provides other financial services. Banks accept deposits and make loans and derive a profit from the difference in the interest paid to lenders (depositors) and charged to borrowers, respectively. They also profit from fees charged for services. The three major classes of banks are commercial banks, investment banks, and central banks. Banking depends entirely on public confidence in the system's soundness; no bank could pay all its depositors should they simultaneously demand cash, as may happen in a panic.

bankruptcy, Status of a debtor who has been declared by judicial process to be unable to pay his or her debts. It also refers to the legal process involved: the administration of an insolvent debtor's property by the court for the benefit of the debtor's creditors. Filing by a debtor is called voluntary bankruptcy; involuntary bankruptcy is declared by the court upon petition by a creditor. The U.S. Bankruptcy Code makes four types of relief available to bankrupt individuals or corporations: liquidation (under Chapter 7), reorganization (Chapter 11), debt adjustment for a family farmer (Chapter 12), and debt adjustment for an individual with a regular income (Chapter 13). Municipalities may file under Chapter 9. Generally, not all debts are paid in a bankruptcy. The court determines which debts are to be repaid, and the debtor is typically granted a discharge of the rest.

Bantam, Former city and sultanate, Java. It was located at the western end of Java between the Java Sea and the Indian Ocean. In the early 16th century it became a powerful Muslim sultanate, which extended its control over parts of Sumatra and Borneo. Invaded by the Dutch, Portuguese, and British, it ultimately recognized Dutch sovereignty in 1684. The city was Java's most important port for the European spice trade until its harbour silted up in the late 18th century. It suffered severely from the eruption of Krakatoa in 1883.

Bantu languages, Group of some 500 languages belonging to the Benue-Congo language branch of the Niger-Congo language family. They are spoken by more than 200 million people in a very large area, including most of Africa from southern Cameroon eastward to Kenya and southward to the southernmost tip of the continent. Twelve Bantu languages, including Rundi (Kirundi), Rwanda (Kinyarwanda), Shona, Zulu, and Xhosa, are spoken by more than 5 million people.

Bantu peoples, Speakers of the close to 500 distinct Bantu languages, numbering more than 200 million and occupying almost the entire southern projection of Africa. The classification is primarily linguistic, for the cultural patterns of Bantu speakers are extremely diverse. Included in the group are the Bemba, Bena, Chaga, Chewa, Embu, Fang, Ganda, Gusii, Hehe, Herero, Hutu, Kagwe, Kikuyu, Luba, Luhya, Lunda, Makonde, Meru, Nyamwezi, Ndebele, Nkole, Nyakyusa, Nyoro, Pedi, Shona, Sotho, Swazi, Tsonga, Tswana, Tutsi, Venda, Xhosa, Yao, Zaramo, and Zulu.

banyan, Unusually shaped tree (*Ficus benghalensis*, or *F. indica*) of the fig genus in the mulberry family, native to tropical Asia. Aerial roots that develop from its branches descend and take root in the soil to become new trunks. The banyan reaches a height of up to 100 ft (30 m) and spreads laterally indefinitely. One tree may in time assume the appearance of a very dense thicket as a result of the tangle of roots and trunks.

baobab, Tree (*Adansonia digitata*) of the mallow family (Malvaceae), native to Africa. The barrel-like trunk may reach a diameter of 30 ft (9 m) and a height of 60 ft (18 m). The large, gourdlike, woody fruit contains a tasty pulp. A strong fibre from the bark is used locally for rope and cloth. The trunks are often excavated to serve as water reserves or temporary shelters. The baobab is grown for its extraordinary shape as a curiosity in areas of warm climate, such as Florida. A related species, *A. gregorii*, occurs in Australia, where it is also called a bottle tree.

baptism, In Christianity, the sacrament of admission to the church, symbolized by the pouring or sprinkling of water on the head or by immersion in water. The ceremony is usually accompanied by the words "I baptize you in the name of the Father, and of the Son, and of the Holy Spirit." Indeed, Christians believe that after his resurrection, Jesus appeared to his disciples and commanded them to baptize in the name of the Father, Son, and Holy Spirit. In the teaching of St. Paul, it signifies the wiping away of past sins and the rebirth of the individual into a new life. Judaism practiced ritual purification by immersion, and the Gospels report that John the Baptist baptized Jesus. Baptism was an important ritual in the early church by the 1st century, and infant baptism appeared by the 3rd century. Roman Catholic, Orthodox, and most Protestant churches practice infant baptism. The Anabaptist reformers insisted on adult baptism after a confession of faith; modern Baptists and the Disciples of Christ also practice adult baptism.

Baptist, Member of a group of Protestant Christians who hold that only adult believers should be baptized and that it must be done by immersion. During the 17th century two groups of Baptists emerged in England: General Baptists, who held that Christ's atonement applied to all persons, and Particular Baptists, who believed it was only for the elect. Baptist origins in the American colonies can be traced to Roger Williams, who established a Baptist church in Providence, R.I., in 1639. Baptist growth in the U.S. was spurred by the Great Awakening in the mid-18th century. The 1814 General Convention showed divisions among U.S. Baptists over slavery; a formal split occurred when the Southern Baptist Convention was organized in 1845 and was confirmed when the Northern (American) Baptist Convention was organized in 1907. African-American Baptist churches provided leadership in the 1960s civil rights movement, notably through the work of Martin Luther King. Baptist belief emphasizes the authority of local congregations in matters of faith and practice; worship is characterized by extemporaneous prayer and hymn-singing as well as by the exposition of scripture in sermons.

bar code, Printed series of parallel bars of varying width used for entering data into a computer system, typically for identifying the object on which the code appears. The width and spacing of the bars represent binary information that can be read by an optical (laser) scanner that is part of a computer system. The coding is used in many different areas of manufacturing and marketing, including inventory control and tracking systems. The bar codes printed on supermarket and other retail merchandise are those of the Universal Product Code (UPC).

Bar Mitzvah, Jewish ritual celebrating a boy's 13th birthday and his entry into the community of Judaism. It usually takes place during a Sabbath service, when the boy reads from the Torah and may give a discourse on the text. The service is often followed by a festive Kiddush and a family dinner on the same day or next day. Reform Judaism substituted confirmation of boys and girls for the Bar Mitzvah celebration after 1810, but many congregations restored the Bar Mitzvah in the 20th century. A separate ceremony for girls, Bat Mitzvah, has been instituted in Reform and Conservative Judaism.

Barbados, Island country, West Indies. The most easterly of the Caribbean islands, it lies about 100 mi (160 km) east of Saint Vincent and the Grenadines. Area: 166 sq mi (430 sq km). Population: (2011 est.) 277,000. Capital: Bridgetown. More than nine-tenths of the population is of African ancestry. Language: English (official). Religion: Christianity (mostly Protestant). Currency: Barbados dollar. Largely covered by a layer of coral, Barbados is low and flat except in its north-central part; its highest point is Mount Hillaby, at 1,115 ft (340 m). There is little surface water. The island is almost encircled by coral reefs. Bridgetown is its only seaport. The economy is based on tourism and sugar, while the offshore financial sector is growing. Barbados is a constitutional monarchy with two legislative houses; its head of state is the British monarch, represented by a governor-general, and the head of government is the prime minister. The island was probably inhabited originally by Arawak and later by Carib Indians. Spaniards may have landed by 1518, and by 1536 they had apparently wiped out the Indian population. Barbados was settled by the English in the 1620s. Slaves were brought in to work the sugar plantations, which were especially prosperous in the 17th–18th century. The British Empire abolished slavery in 1834, and all the Barbados slaves were freed by 1838. In 1958 Barbados joined the West Indies Federation. When the latter dissolved in 1962, Barbados sought independence from Britain, which it gained in 1966.

barbiturate, Any of a class of heterocyclic compounds based on the parent structure, uric acid, and used in medicine. They depress the central nervous system, acting particularly on certain parts of the brain, though they tend to depress the functioning of all the body's tissues. Long-acting barbiturates (e.g., barbital and phenobarbital) are used to treat epilepsy. Intermediate ones (e.g., amobarbital) are used to treat insomnia, short-acting ones (e.g., pentobarbital) to overcome difficulty in falling asleep (one aspect of insomnia), and ultra-short-acting ones (e.g., thiopental sodium) to induce unconsciousness in surgical patients before administration of other anesthetics. Prolonged use of barbiturates may lead to addiction. Sudden withdrawal can be fatal; addicts must be weaned from the drug under medical supervision. Overdoses can result in coma and even death; barbiturates are particularly dangerous, even at normal doses, when combined with alcoholic beverages.

Barbizon school, Group of 19th-century French landscape painters. They were part of a larger European movement toward naturalism that made a significant contribution to realism in French landscape painting. Led by Theodore Rousseau and Jean-François Millet, they attracted a large following of painters who came to live at Barbizon, a village near Paris; most notable of this group were Charles-François Daubigny, Narcisse-Virgile Díaz de la Peña, Jules Dupré, Charles-Émile Jacque, and Constant Troyon. Each had his own style, but all emphasized painting out-of-doors directly from nature, using a limited palette, and creating atmosphere or mood in their landscapes.

Barcelona, Seaport city (pop., 2005 est.: 1,593,075), capital of Catalonia autonomous region, northeastern Spain. Spain's largest port and second largest city, it is the country's principal industrial and commercial centre, as well as a major cultural and educational centre. It is said to have been founded in the 3rd century BC by the Carthaginians or the Phoenicians, and it was later ruled by the Romans and Visigoths. It was captured by the Moors c. AD 715, but it was retaken by the Franks under Charlemagne in 801 and made the capital of the Spanish March (Catalonia). After Catalonia united with Aragon in 1137, Barcelona became a flourishing commercial centre and the rival of Italian ports. In the 19th century it was a cauldron for radical social movements and Catalan separatism. It was the loyalist capital in 1937–39 during the Spanish Civil War; its capture by Francisco Franco brought the collapse of Catalan resistance and Catalonia's reintegration into Spain. Modern Barcelona is known for its handsome architecture, including buildings by Antoni Gaudí. It hosted the 1992 Summer Olympic Games.

bard, Celtic tribal poet-singer gifted in composing and reciting verses of eulogy and satire or of heroes and their deeds. The institution died out in Gaul but survived in Ireland, where bards have preserved a tradition of chanting poetic eulogy, and in Wales, where the bardic order was codified into distinct grades in the 10th century. Despite a decline in the late Middle Ages, the Welsh tradition is celebrated in the annual National Eisteddfod.

Bardeen, John (b. May 23, 1908, Madison, Wis., U.S.—d. Jan. 30, 1991, Boston, Mass.), U.S. physicist. He earned a Ph.D. in mathematical physics from Princeton University. He worked for the U.S. Naval Ordnance Laboratory during World War II, after which he worked for Bell Telephone Laboratories. His work there led to his sharing a 1956 Nobel Prize with William B. Shockley and Walter H. Brattain for the invention of the transistor. In 1972

Bardeen.
Courtesy of University of Illinois at
Urbana-Champaign

he again shared a Nobel Prize, this time with Leon Cooper and J. Robert Schrieffer for developing the theory of superconductivity (1957); this theory (called the BCS theory, for Bardeen-Cooper-Schrieffer) is the basis for all later theoretical work in superconductivity. Bardeen was also the author of a theory explaining certain properties of semiconductors.

Barents Sea, Outlying portion of the Arctic Ocean. Named for the Dutch explorer Willem Barents, it is bounded by the Norwegian and northwestern Russian mainland (south), the Norwegian Sea and Svalbard (west), Franz Josef Land (north), and the Kara Sea and Novaya Zemlya (east). It is 800 mi (1,300 km) long and 650 mi (1,050 km) wide and covers 542,000 sq mi (1,405,000 sq km). Its average depth is 750 ft (229 m), with a maximum depth of 2,000 ft (600 m) in the major Bear Island Trench.

baritone, In vocal music, the most common category of male voice, between the bass and the tenor. Its range is approximately from the second A below middle C to the F above middle C. The term *baritonus* was first employed in 15th-century five- and six-voice part music; when four-part settings became standard, the baritone part was dropped, and natural baritones were forced to develop either their bass or tenor register. Instruments that play principally in the baritone register include the baritone saxophone and the baritone horn.

barium, Chemical element, one of the alkaline earth metals, chemical symbol Ba, atomic number 56. It is very reactive and in compounds always has valence 2. In nature it is found chiefly as the minerals barite (barium sulfate) and witherite (barium carbonate). The element is used in metallurgy, and its compounds are used in fireworks, petroleum mining, and radiology and as pigments and reagents. All soluble barium compounds are toxic. Barium sulfate, one of the most insoluble salts known, is given in a "barium meal" as a contrast medium for X-ray examination of the gastrointestinal tract.

bark, In woody plants, tissues outside of the vascular cambium. The term is also used more popularly to refer to all tissues outside the wood. The inner soft bark is produced by the vascular cambium; it consists of secondary phloem (food-conducting) tissue whose innermost layer transports food from the leaves to the rest of the plant. The layered outer bark contains cork and old, dead phloem. The bark is usually thinner than the woody part of the stem or root.

Barnard's star, Star about six light-years away from the Sun, next nearest the Sun after the Alpha Centauri system, in the constellation Ophiuchus. Named for Edward Emerson Barnard (b. 1857—d. 1923), who discovered it in 1916, it has the largest proper motion of any known star. It is gradually nearing the solar system. The star attracted astronomers' attention in the 1960s when its proper motion was claimed to show periodic deviations attributed to the gravitational pull of two planets. The deviations were later proved to be artifacts of measurement.

Baroque architecture, Architectural style originating in late 16th-century Italy and lasting in some regions, notably Germany and colonial South America, until the 18th century. It had its origins in the Counter-Reformation, when the Catholic Church launched an overtly emotional and sensory appeal to the faithful through art and architecture. Complex architectural plan shapes, often based on the oval, and the dynamic opposition and interpenetration of spaces were favoured to heighten the feeling of motion and sensuality. Other characteristic qualities include grandeur, drama and contrast (especially in lighting), curvaceousness, and an often dizzying array of rich surface treatments, twisting elements, and gilded statuary. Architects unabashedly applied bright colours and illusory, vividly painted ceilings. Outstanding practitioners in Italy included Gian Lorenzo Bernini, Carlo Maderno (1556–1629), Francesco Borromini, and Guarino Guarini (1624–83). Classical elements subdued Baroque architecture in France. In central Europe, the Baroque arrived late but flourished in the works of such architects as the Austrian Johann Bernhard Fischer von Erlach (1656–1723). Its impact in Britain can be seen in the works of Christopher Wren. The late Baroque style is often referred to as Rococo or, in Spain and Spanish America, as Churrigueresque.

Baroque period (17th–18th century) Era in the arts that originated in Italy in the 17th century and flourished elsewhere well into the 18th century. It embraced painting, sculpture, architecture, decorative arts, and music. The word, derived from a Portuguese term for an irregularly shaped pearl and originally used derogatorily, has long been employed to describe a variety of characteristics, from dramatic to bizarre to overdecorated. The style was embraced by countries absorbed in the Counter-Reformation; artworks commissioned by the Roman Catholic church were overtly emotional and sensory. The period's most notable practitioners were Annibale Carracci, Caravaggio, and Gian Lorenzo Bernini. A spectacular example of the Baroque arts is the Palace of Versailles. In music, the Baroque era is usually considered to extend from *c.* 1600 to *c.* 1750, when such significant new vocal and instrumental genres as opera, oratorio, cantata, sonata, and concerto were introduced and such towering composers as Claudio Monteverdi, J.S. Bach, and George Frideric Handel flourished.

barracuda, Any of about 20 species of predaceous marine fishes (family Sphyraenidae) found in all warm and tropical regions and in some more temperate areas. Swift and powerful, barracudas are slender and have small scales, a jutting lower jaw, and a large mouth with many large, sharp teeth. They vary in size from relatively small to 4–6 ft (1.2–1.8 m) long. They are primarily fish eaters. They are popular sport fishes and are caught for food, though in certain seas they may become contaminated with a toxic substance. Bold and inquisitive, they are potentially dangerous to humans when large.

*Barracuda (*Sphyraena*)*
C. Leroy French/Tom Stack & Associates

basalt, Dark igneous rock that is low in silica content and comparatively rich in iron and magnesium. Some basalts are glassy (have no visible crystals), and many are very fine-grained and compact. Basaltic lavas may be spongy or pumice-like. Olivine and augite are the most common minerals in basalts; plagioclase is also present. Basalts may be broadly classified into two main groups. Calc-alkali basalts predominate among the lavas of mountain belts; the active volcanoes of Mauna Loa and Kilauea in Hawaii erupt calc-alkali lavas. Alkali basalts predominate among the lavas of the ocean basins and are also common in mountain belts.

base, In chemistry, any substance that in water solution is slippery to the touch, tastes bitter, changes the colour of acid-base indicators (e.g., litmus paper), reacts with acids to form salts, and promotes certain chemical reactions (e.g., base catalysis). Examples of bases are the hydroxides of the alkali metals and alkaline earth metals (sodium, calcium, etc.; *see* caustic soda) and the water solutions of ammonia or its derivatives (amines). Such substances produce hydroxide ions (OH^-) in water solutions. Broader definitions of bases cover situations in which water is not present.

baseball, Game played with a bat and ball between two teams of nine players (or 10, if a designated hitter bats and runs for the pitcher). Baseball is played on a large field that has four bases laid out in a square, positioned like a diamond, whose outlines mark the course a runner must take to score. Teams alternate positions as batters and fielders, exchanging places when three members of the batting team are put out. Batters try to hit a pitched ball out of reach of the fielding team and complete a circuit around the bases in order to score a "run." The team that scores the most runs in nine innings (times at bat) wins the game. If a game is tied, extra innings are played until the tie is broken. Baseball is traditionally considered the national pastime of the United States. It was once thought to have been invented in 1839 by Abner Doubleday in Cooperstown, N.Y., but it is more likely that baseball developed from an 18th-century English game called rounders that was modified by Alexander Cartwright. The first professional association was formed in 1871; in 1876 it became the National League. Its rival, the American League, was founded in 1900, and since 1903 (except in 1904 and 1994) the winning teams of each league have played a postseason championship known as the World Series. The Baseball Hall of Fame is located in Cooperstown. Professional baseball leagues also exist in several Latin American countries. The champions of leagues in the Dominican Republic, Mexico, Puerto Rico, and Venezuela compete in the Caribbean Series each February. In Asia there are professional baseball leagues in Japan and South Korea and on the island of Taiwan. Japan has two major leagues, the Central and the Pacific, that face off in the Japan Series every October.

Basel, or BASLE, French BÂLE, City (2000: city, 166,558; metro. area, 402,387), northwestern Switzerland. It straddles the Rhine at the point where France, Germany, and Switzerland meet. It was originally a settlement of the Celtic Rauraci tribe. Its university, the first in Switzerland, was founded by Pope Pius II while attending the Council of Basel (1431–49). In 1501 Basel was admitted into the Swiss Confederation. When Desiderius Erasmus taught at the university (1521–29), the city became a centre of humanism and of the Reformation. Primarily German-speaking and Protestant, it is an important trading and industrial city and river port.

Basel, Council of (1431–49) Council of the Roman Catholic church held in Basel, Switz. It addressed the question of ultimate authority in the church and the problem of the Hussite heresy. Its members renewed the decree *Sacrosancta* (issued by the Council of Constance), which declared the council's authority to be greater than the pope's, and voted to receive most Hussites back into the church on terms opposed by the pope. In 1437 Pope Eugenius IV transferred the council to Ferrara to negotiate reunion with the Orthodox church more effectively, but several members remained in Basel as a rump council and declared Eugenius deposed. They then elected a new pope, Felix V, and the renewed schism cost the council its prestige and popular support. On the death of Eugenius, his successor, Nicholas V, obliged the antipope Felix to abdicate, ended the rump council, and brought the conciliar movement to a close.

Bashō, or MATSUO BASHŌ, orig. MATSUO MUNEFUSA (b. 1644, Ueno, Iga province, Japan—d. Nov. 28, 1694, Ōsaka), Japanese haiku poet, the greatest practitioner of the form. Following the Zen philosophy he studied, he attempted to compress the meaning of the world into the simple pattern of his poetry, disclosing hidden hopes in small things and showing the interdependence of all objects. His *The Narrow Road to the Deep North* (1694), a poetic prose travelogue, is one of the loveliest works of Japanese literature.

BASIC, in full BEGINNER'S ALL-PURPOSE SYMBOLIC INSTRUCTION CODE, Computer programming language developed by John G. Kemeny and Thomas E. Kurtz (b. 1928) at Dartmouth College in the mid 1960s. One of the simplest high-level languages, with commands similar to English, it can be learned with relative ease even by schoolchildren and novice programmers. Since *c.* 1980, BASIC has been popular for use on personal computers.

basic Bessemer process, Modification of the Bessemer process for converting pig iron into steel. The original Bessemer converter was not effective in removing the phosphorus from iron made from the high-phosphorus ores common in Britain and Europe. The invention of the basic process in England by Sidney G. Thomas (1850–1885) and Percy Gilchrist overcame this problem; the Thomas-Gilchrist converter was lined with a basic material such as burned limestone rather than an acid siliceous material. The introduction of the basic Bessemer process in 1879 made it possible for the first time for such high-phosphorus ore to be used for making steel.

basic oxygen process, Steelmaking method in which pure oxygen is blown through a long, movable lance into a bath of molten blast-furnace iron and scrap, in a steel furnace with a refractory lining called a converter. The oxygen initiates a series of heat-releasing reactions, including the oxidation of such impurities as silicon, carbon, phosphorus, and manganese; carbon dioxide is released, and the oxidation products of the other impurities form molten slag that floats on the molten steel. The advantages of using pure oxygen instead of air in refining iron into steel were recognized as early as the 1850s, but the process could not be commercialized until the late 1940s, when cheap, high-purity oxygen became available. Within 40 years it had replaced the open-hearth process and was producing more than half of all steel worldwide. Commercial advantages include high production rates, less labour, and steel with a low nitrogen content.

basilica, Originally a secular public building in ancient Rome, typically a large rectangular structure with an open hall and a raised platform at one or both ends. In one type, the central hall was flanked by side aisles set off by colonnades, and the raised platform was enclosed by an apse. The early Christians adopted this type for their churches. In the typical early Christian basilica, the columns separating the nave from the lower side aisles carried either arches or entablatures, above which rose clerestory walls that supported the roof. The long nave came to be crossed just before the apse by a shorter transept, creating the cross-shaped plan that remains a standard church form to the present. "Basilica" is also a title of honor given to a Roman Catholic or Greek Orthodox church distinguished by its antiquity or its role as an international center of worship.

basketball, Court game between two teams of five players. They score by tossing, or "shooting," an inflated ball through a raised hoop, or "basket," located in their opponent's end of the court. A goal is worth two points, three if shot from outside a specified limit. A player who is fouled (through unwarranted physical contact) by another is awarded one to three free-throw attempts (depending on the circumstances of the foul). A successful free throw is worth one point. Invented in 1891 by James A. Naismith at the YMCA Training School in Springfield, Mass., basketball quickly became popular throughout the U.S., with games organized at the high school and collegiate level for both sexes. (For the first game, Naismith used as goals two half-bushel peach baskets, which gave the sport its name.) Women first played the game under a markedly different set of rules. The game developed internationally at a slower pace. The first Olympic basketball contest was held in 1936, and the Fédération Internationale de Basketball Amateur (FIBA) introduced world championships for men and women in 1950 and 1953, respectively. In the U.S., high school and collegiate championship tournaments are traditionally held in March and generate considerable excitement. A men's professional league was organized in 1898 but did not gain much of a following until 1949, when it was reconstituted as the National Basketball Association (NBA). The first women's professional leagues in the U.S. emerged during the 1970s but failed after a year or two. The current Women's National Basketball Association (WNBA), owned by the NBA, was organized in 1997. Club and professional basketball outside the U.S. developed rapidly in the latter part of the 20th century. The Basketball Hall of Fame is located in Springfield.

basketry, Art and craft of making containers and other objects from interwoven flexible fibres such as grasses, twigs, bamboo, and rushes. It is primarily a functional rather than a decorative art. The type of basketry in a given geographic region is determined by the type of vegetation available there. Numerous Asian, African, Oceanic, and Native American cultures have excelled in basketry.

Basque, Spanish VASCO, Member of a people of unknown origin living in Spain and France along the Bay of Biscay and in the western Pyrenees mountains in the region of the Basque Country. About 850,000 true Basques live in Spain and another 130,000 in France. Physically the Basques are similar to other Western European peoples; the Basque language, however, is not Indo-European. The Basques have sought autonomy from Spain since the 19th century. A national government was proclaimed in the Spanish Civil War, which saw the brutal bombing of Guernica (1937). After the war, the government and many Basques went into exile as Francisco Franco abolished their special privileges. The Basque separatist movement was rekindled after Franco's death and the establishment of a liberal Spanish monarchy in 1975. Despite the granting of limited autonomy in 1978, the more militant separatists, including the terrorist ETA (Basque Homeland and Liberty), continued a campaign for complete independence.

Basque Country, Spanish PAÍS VASCO, Euskera EUSKADI, Autonomous community's (pop., 2008 est.: 2,138,453) and historic region, northern Spain. Bounded by the Bay of Biscay, it consists of the provinces of Vizcaya (Biscay), Álava, and Guipúzcoa and has an area of 2,793 sq mi (7,235 sq km). Its capital is Vitoria-Gasteiz. The Pyrenees Mountains separate it from the Basque Country of France. The Basques who inhabit the region have long sought autonomy. A separatist movement succeeded in regaining Basque autonomy in 1936 under the short-lived Republican government, but autonomy was withdrawn by Francisco Franco in 1937. Though limited autonomy was granted in 1979, a campaign of terrorism against the Spanish government continued. Álava is an agricultural region, while metallurgical industry is concentrated around Bilbao.

Basque language, Language spoken by an estimated 1,000,000 Basque people living in the Basque Country of north-central Spain and southwestern France. About 200,000 Basques live in other parts of the world. The only remnant of the languages spoken in western Europe before incursions by Indo-European-speaking peoples, Basque has no known linguistic relatives; linguists call it a language isolate. Its grammar is markedly distinct from that of all other western European languages. Basque is sparsely attested before the 16th century, when the first book in the language was printed (1545), though it has maintained a continuous literary tradition since then.

Baṣrah, Al-, or BASRA, Port and city (pop., 2011 est.: 1,200,000), southeastern Iraq. It lies at the head of the Shaṭṭ Al-ʿArab, about 70 mi (110 km) upstream from the Persian Gulf. Founded in 638 CE, it became famous under the ʿAbbāsid dynasty; in *The Thousand and One Nights* it was the city from which Sindbad the Sailor set sail. In the 17th–18th centuries it became a trading centre. Occupied by the British in World War I (1914–18), the town and port underwent many improvements and grew in importance. After World War II (1939–45) the growth of Iraq's petroleum industry turned Al-Baṣrah into a major refining centre. It suffered heavy damage in the Iran-Iraq War (1980–88) and the Persian Gulf War (1990–91), and in the early 21st century it was a scene of fighting during the Iraq War.

bass, Lowest musical voice or register. In vocal music, its range is approximately from the second E below middle C to middle C itself. A basso profundo emphasizes a lower register, a basso cantante a somewhat higher one. Outside of Russia, the solo bass voice has generally been relegated to certain standard operatic character roles. The lowest-pitched member of most instrumental families is usually called the bass (bass clarinet, double bass, etc.). In Western tonal music, the bass part is usually second in importance only to the melody, being the chief determiner of harmonic movement, a tendency that became particularly notable after the appearance of the basso continuo *c.* 1600.

bassoon, Principal tenor and bass instrument of the orchestral woodwind family. Its mouthpiece has a double reed attached to a curved metal crook, which leads to a narrow conical bore that doubles back on itself (to keep its length manageable). It developed from the older curtal (or dulzian) in the 17th century. An agile instrument with a mild tone, it has a range of $3^1/_2$ octaves, starting at B-flat two octaves below middle C. The contrabassoon, a large metal instrument whose tubing doubles back four times, has a range an octave lower.

Bastille, Medieval fortress in Paris that became a symbol of despotism. In the 17th–18th centuries, the Bastille was used· as a French state prison and a place of detention for important persons. On July 14, 1789, at the beginning of the French Revolution, an armed mob of Parisians captured the fortress and released its prisoners, a dramatic action that came to symbolize the end of the ancien régime. The Bastille was subsequently demolished by the Revolutionary government. Bastille Day (July 14) has been a French national holiday since 1880.

bat, Any member of more than 1,100 species (order Chiroptera) of the only mammals to have evolved true flight. Their wings are evolutionary modification of the forelimbs, with greatly elongated fingers joined by a membrane that extends down the side of the body. Most bats use echolocation to orient themselves and find prey. Found worldwide, they are particularly abundant in the tropics. Wingspreads vary among species from 6 in. (15 cm) to 5 ft (1.5 m). Nearly all species roost during the day (in caves, crevices, burrows, building, or trees) and feed at night. Most are insectivores, consuming enough insects to affect the balance of insect populations. Others feed on fruit, pollen, nectar, or blood (vampire bats). Some may live more than 20 years. The guano of bats has long been used for agricultural fertilizer.

Batak, Any member of any of several closely related ethnic groups of central Sumatra, Indon. The Batak are descendants of a powerful Proto-Malayan people who until 1825 lived in relative isolation in the highlands surrounding Lake Toba in Sumatra. They have their own written language. In their traditional religion, ancestors, plants, animals, and inanimate objects are considered to possess souls or spirits; today about a third of the 3.1 million Batak adhere to traditional beliefs, while the rest profess Christianity or Islam.

Bath, City (pop., 2001: 90,144), southwestern England. Situated on the River Avon, it was founded as Aquae Sulis by the Romans, who were attracted to its hot mineral springs. The Anglo-Saxons arrived in the 6th century AD, followed by the Normans *c.* 1100. In the Middle Ages it was a prosperous centre for the cloth trade. When the Roman baths were rediscovered in 1755, Bath had already revived as a spa; its popularity is reflected in the works of Jane Austen, Richard Brinsley Sheridan, and Tobias Smollett. It was rebuilt and extended in the Palladian style during the 18th century. Bath today retains many of its 18th-century structures.

batik, Method of dyeing textiles, principally cottons, in which patterned areas are covered with wax so that they will not receive colour. Multicoloured effects are achieved by repeating the dyeing process several times, the initial pattern of wax being boiled off and another design applied before redyeing. Wax was applied with bamboo strips in Indonesia, where the technique originated. A small copper pot with a handle and narrow applicator spout for applying the wax came into use in Java by the mid 18th century; a wood-block wax applicator was developed in the 19th century. Dutch traders imported the cloth and the technique to Europe. Today machines for applying wax in traditional Javanese patterns reproduce the same effects as the hand-dyeing process.

battery, Any of a class of devices, consisting of a group of electrochemical cells, that convert chemical energy into electrical energy; the term is also commonly applied to a single cell of this kind. A wet cell (e.g., a car battery) contains free liquid electrolyte; in a dry cell (e.g., a flashlight battery) the electrolyte is held in an absorbent material. Chemicals are arranged so that electrons released from the battery's negative electrode flow through a circuit outside the battery (in the device powered by it) to the battery's positive electrode. The battery's voltage depends on the chemicals used and the number of cells (in series); the current depends on the resistance in the total circuit (including the battery—and thus on electrode size). Multiple batteries may be connected in series (the positive electrode of one to the negative electrode of the next), which increases total voltage, or in parallel (positive to positive and negative to negative), which increases total current. Batteries that are not rechargeable include standard dry cells used in flashlights and certain wet cells for marine, mine, highway, and military use. Car batteries, many kinds of dry cells used in cordless appliances, and batteries for certain military and aerospace uses may be recharged repeatedly.

Bauhaus (German: "House of Building"), (1919–33) Influential, forward-looking German school of architecture and applied arts. It was founded by Walter Gropius with the ideal of integrating art, craftsmanship, and technology. Realizing that mass production had to be the precondition of successful design in the machine age, its members rejected the Arts and Crafts Movement's emphasis on individually executed luxury objects. The Bauhaus is often associated with a severe but elegant geometric style carried out with great economy of means, though in fact the works produced by its members were richly diverse. Its faculty included Josef Albers, László Moholy-Nagy, Lyonel Feininger, Paul Klee, Vasily Kandinsky, and Marcel Breuer. The school was based in Weimar until 1925, Dessau through 1932, and Berlin in its final months, when its last director, Ludwig Mies van der Rohe, closed the school in anticipation of the Nazis' doing so.

Bay of Pigs invasion (April 17, 1961) Abortive invasion of Cuba directed by the U.S. Central Intelligence Agency and carried out by Cuban exiles. The invasion was intended to spark a rebellion that would topple Fidel Castro, whose communist regime was considered a threat to U.S. interests in the region. The invasion began with the bombing of Cuban military bases; two days later a force of about 1,500 landed at several sites along the coast, including the Bay of Pigs. The rebellion never materialized, the invasion force was quickly defeated, and more than 1,100 men were impris-

oned. The result was a huge propaganda victory for Castro and a severe embarrassment for the administration of U.S. president John F. Kennedy.

Bayeux Tapestry, Medieval embroidered tapestry depicting the Norman Conquest. Woven in woolen threads of eight colours on coarse linen, it is about 231 ft (70 m) long by about 20 in. (50 cm) wide. It consists of 79 consecutive scenes, with Latin inscriptions and decorative borders. Stylistically it resembles English illuminated manuscripts. It was probably woven *c.* 1066, within a few years of the conquest, and was possibly commissioned by Odo, bishop of Bayeux, brother of William I (the Conqueror). The most famous of all pieces of needlework, it hung for centuries in the cathedral in Bayeux (Normandy) and now hangs in the tapestry museum there.

English axman in combat with Norman cavalry during the Battle of Hastings, detail from the 11th-century Bayeux Tapestry, Bayeux, France.
Giraudon/Art Resource, New York

beadwork, Ornamental work in beads. In the Middle Ages beads were used to embellish embroidery work. In Renaissance and Elizabethan England, clothing, purses, fancy boxes, and small pictures were adorned with beads. In the 19th–20th century beadwork proliferated in dress decoration. Beads are used as ornamentation on a variety of objects (clothing, masks, weapons, dolls) in many cultures, including the Native American, African, and Oceanic.

bear market, In securities and commodities trading, a declining market. A bear is an investor who expects prices to decline and, on this assumption, sells a borrowed security or commodity in the hope of buying it back later at a lower price, a speculative transaction called short-selling.

Beat movement, American social and literary movement of the 1950s and '60s. It is associated with artists' communities in San Francisco, Los Angeles, and New York. Its adherents expressed alienation from conventional society and advocated personal release and illumination through heightened sensory awareness and altered states of consciousness. Beat poets, including Lawrence Ferlinghetti, Allen Ginsberg, Gregory Corso (1930–2001), and Gary Snyder, sought to liberate poetry from academic refinement, creating verse that was vernacular, sometimes sprinkled with obscenities, but often powerful and moving. Jack Kerouac and William S. Burroughs developed an unstructured, spontaneous, sometimes hallucinatory approach to prose writing that was designed to convey the immediacy of experience. The Beat movement had faded by *c.* 1970, though its influence continued to be felt decades later.

Beatles, British rock group that came to personify the counterculture of the 1960s. Its principal members, all born in Liverpool,

Eng., were Paul McCartney, John Lennon, George Harrison, and Ringo Starr. The group began with the pairing of McCartney and Lennon in 1956; Harrison joined in 1957, and Stu Sutcliffe and Pete Best later. In 1960 they adopted the name the Beatles. In 1962 they signed a recording contract and replaced Best with Starr (Sutcliffe had left the group in 1961). The release in 1962–63 of such songs as "Please Please Me" and "I Want to Hold Your Hand" made them England's most popular rock group, and in 1964 "Beatlemania" struck the U.S. Originally inspired by Chuck Berry, Elvis Presley, Little Richard, and Buddy Holly, among others, their direct, energetic songs kept them at the top of the pop charts. Their long hair and tastes in dress were influential throughout the world, as were their experimentation with hallucinogenic drugs and Indian mysticism and their involvement with the politics of peace. From 1965 to 1967 the Beatles' music rapidly evolved, becoming increasingly subtle, sophisticated, and varied—ranging from ballads such as "Yesterday" to the psychedelic hard rock of "Tomorrow Never Knows." Their public performances ended in 1966. Albums such as *Rubber Soul* (1965), *Revolver* (1966), and *The Beatles* ("White Album," 1968) set new trends in rock. In 1967 they produced *Sgt. Pepper's Lonely Hearts Club Band*, an album novel for its conception as a dramatic whole, use of electronic music, and character as a studio work not reproducible on-stage. They appeared in the films *A Hard Day's Night* (1964) and *Help!* (1965). The group dissolved in 1970. In 1988 the Beatles were inducted into the Rock and Roll Hall of Fame, and Lennon (1994), McCartney (1999), and Harrison (2004) were also inducted as solo performers.

Beauvoir, Simone (Lucie-Ernestine-Marie-Bertrand) de (b. Jan. 9, 1908, Paris, France—d. April 14, 1986, Paris), French writer and feminist. As a student at the Sorbonne, she met Jean-Paul Sartre, with whom she formed a lifelong intellectual and romantic bond. She is known primarily for her treatise *The Second Sex* (1949), a scholarly and passionate plea for the abolition of what she called the myth of the "eternal feminine"; the book became a classic of feminist literature. She also wrote four admired volumes of autobiography (1958–72), philosophical works that explore themes of existentialism, and fiction, notably *The Mandarins* (1954, Prix Goncourt). *The Coming of Age* (1970) is a bitter reflection on society's indifference to the elderly.

Beaux-Arts style, or SECOND EMPIRE STYLE, or SECOND EMPIRE BAROQUE, Architectural style developed at the École des Beaux-Arts in Paris. It enjoyed international dominance in the late 19th century and rapidly became an official style for many of the new public buildings demanded by expanding cities and their national governments. Beaux-Arts buildings are typically massive and have a symmetrical plan with rooms arranged axially, profuse Classicist detail, and pavilions that extend forward at the ends and centre. Among the most admired Beaux-Arts structures is the Paris Opéra.

bebop, or BOP, Jazz characterized by harmonic complexity, convoluted melodic lines, and frequent shifting of rhythmic accent. In the mid-1940s, a group of musicians, including Dizzy Gillespie, Thelonious Monk, and Charlie Parker, rejected the conventions of swing to pioneer a self-consciously artistic extension of improvised jazz, which set new technical standards of velocity and harmonic subtlety. Two genres grew out of bebop in the 1950s: the delicate, dry, understated approach that came to be known as cool jazz, and the aggressive, blues-tinged earthiness of hard bop.

Becker, Gary S(tanley) (b. Dec. 2, 1930, Pottsville, Pa., U.S.), U.S. economist. He studied at Princeton University and the University of Chicago. As a professor at Columbia University and the University of Chicago, he applied the methods of economics to aspects of human behaviour previously considered the domain of sociology and demography. In *Human Capital* (1964) and *A Treatise on the Family* (1981), he advanced the theory that rational economic choices, based on self-interest, govern most human activities, even apparently noneconomic activities such as the formation of families. He won the Nobel Prize in 1992.

Samuel Beckett, 1965.
© Gisèle Freund

Beckett, Samuel (Barclay) (b. April 13?, 1906, Foxrock, Co. Dublin, Ire.—d. Dec. 22, 1989, Paris, France), Irish playwright. After studying in Ireland and traveling, he settled in Paris in 1937. During World War II he supported himself as a farmworker and joined the underground resistance. In the postwar years he wrote, in French, the narrative trilogy *Molloy* (1951), *Malone Dies* (1951), and *The Unnamable* (1953). His play *Waiting for Godot* (1952) was an immediate success in Paris and gained worldwide acclaim when he translated it into English. Marked by minimal plot and action, existentialist ideas, and humour, it typifies the Theatre of the Absurd. His later plays, also sparsely staged, abstract works that deal with the mystery and despair of human existence, include *Endgame* (1957), *Krapp's Last Tape* (1958), and *Happy Days* (1961). In 1969 he was awarded the Nobel Prize.

Becquerel, (Antoine-) Henri (b. Dec. 15, 1852, Paris, France—d. Aug. 25, 1908, Le Croisic), French physicist. His grandfather, Antoine-César (1788–1878), was one of the founders of the field of electrochemistry, and his father, Alexandre-Edmond (1820–91), made important studies of light phenomena. Henri likewise studied phosphorescent materials as well as uranium compounds and employed photography in his experiments. He is remembered for his discovery of radioactivity, which occurred when he found that the element uranium (in a sample of pitchblende) emitted invisible rays that could darken a photographic plate. His 1901 report of a burn caused by a sample of Marie Curie's radium that he carried in his vest pocket led to investigations by physicians and ultimately the medical use of radioactive substances. In 1903 he shared a Nobel Prize for Physics with the Curies. The unit of radioactivity, the becquerel (Bq), is named for him.

bedbug, Any member of approximately 75 species of nocturnal insects (family Cimicidae) that feed by sucking the blood of humans and other warm-blooded animals. The reddish brown adult is broad and flat and less than 0.2 in. (4–5 mm) long. Among the most cosmopolitan of human parasites, they are found in every kind of dwelling. They digest meals slowly; adults have lived for at least a year without food. Though the bite is irritating, it is not known to transmit diseases to humans.

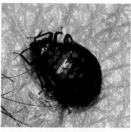

Bedbug (Cimex lectularius) magnified 5 ×
William E. Ferguson

Bedouin, Any member of a community of Arabic-speaking desert nomads of the Middle East. Ethnically, the Bedouin are identical to other Arabs. Bedouin traditionally have made their living by animal husbandry, and social rank among them is determined by the animals that they herd: camel nomads enjoy the greatest status, followed by sheep and goat herders and, finally, cattle nomads. Traditionally, Bedouin would migrate into the desert during the rainy season and return

Bedouin with a young goat in central Qatar
M. Ericson/Ostman Agency

Leaf-cutting bee (Anthidium)
M.W.F. Tweedie—Natural History Photographic Agency/EB Inc.

to cultivated areas during the dry season, but since World War II (1939–45) the governments of many countries have nationalized their range lands, and conflicts over land use have arisen. Many Bedouin have since adopted sedentary ways of life; most, however, retain pride in their nomadic heritage.

bee, Any of some 20,000 insect species belonging to the superfamily Apoidea (order Hymenoptera), including the familiar bumblebee. Adults range in size from about 0.08 to 1.6 in. (2 mm–4 cm). Bees are related to wasps, but, unlike wasps, which can eat other insects, most bees are entirely dependent on flowers for their food. Male bees are usually short-lived and never collect pollen; female bees make and provision the nest and usually have special anatomical structures for carrying pollen. Most species are solitary. The so-called killer bee, an Africanized subspecies of *Apis mellifera*, reached the U.S. from Mexico *c.* 1990; killer bees react quickly and attack in number.

beekeeping, or APICULTURE, Care and manipulation of honeybees to enable them to produce and store more honey than they need so that the excess can be collected. Beekeeping is one of the oldest forms of animal husbandry. Early efforts at collecting the honey required destroying the hive; modern beekeepers use an extractor that empties the cells of the honeycomb without damaging them. To collect honey, beekeepers need a veiled helmet for protection, a tool for cutting comb, and a smoker for tranquilizing the bees. Maintaining the hive includes protecting the colony against diseases, parasites, and predators.

Beer Hall Putsch, or MUNICH PUTSCH (Nov. 8–9, 1923) Unsuccessful attempt by Adolf Hitler to start an insurrection in Germany against the Weimar Republic. On Nov. 8, 1923, Hitler and his men pushed their way into a right-wing political meeting in a Munich beer hall and obtained agreement that the leaders there should join in carrying the "revolution" to Berlin. The next day, some 3,000 Nazis marched toward the Marienplatz but were met by police gunfire. Hitler was subsequently sentenced to five years in prison for treason; he served only eight months, time he spent writing *Mein Kampf.*

Beersheba, City (pop., 2006 est.: 185,300), southern Israel. Historically it marked the extreme southern limit of Palestine, hence the biblical phrase "from Dan to Beersheba" (Dan is in far northern Israel). It fell to the Arabs in the 7th century and to the Ottoman Empire in the 16th century. It was long a watering place for the nomadic Bedouin tribes of the Negev desert. Held by the British from 1917, it became part of Israel in 1948. It has since developed as the administrative, cultural, and industrial centre of the Negev.

beeswax, Commercially useful wax secreted by worker honeybees to make the cell walls of the honeycomb. A bee consumes an estimated 6–10 lbs (3–4.5 kg) of honey for each pound of the wax it secretes in small flakes from glands on the underside of its abdomen. After honey removal, the comb is melted to produce the beeswax, which ranges from yellow to almost black. It is used for candles (often for churches), artificial fruit and flowers, modeling wax, and as an ingredient of furniture and floor waxes, leather dressings, waxed paper, lithographic inks, cosmetics, and ointments.

Beethoven, Ludwig van (baptized Dec. 17, 1770, Bonn, archbishopric of Cologne—d. March 26, 1827, Vienna, Austria), German composer. Born to a musical family, he was a precociously gifted pianist and violist. After nine years as a court musician in Bonn, he moved to Vienna to study with Joseph Haydn and remained there for the rest of his life. He was soon well known as both a virtuoso and a composer, and he became the first important composer to earn a successful living while forsaking employment in the church or court. He uniquely straddled the Classical and Romantic eras. Rooted in the traditions of Haydn and Mozart, his art also encompassed the new spirit of humanism expressed in the works of German Romantic writers as well as in the ideals of the French Revolution, with its passionate concern for the freedom and dignity of the individual. His astonishing *Third (Eroica) Symphony* (1804) was the thunderclap that announced the Romantic century, and it embodies the titanic but rigorously controlled energy that was the hallmark of his style. He began to lose his hearing from *c.* 1795; by *c.* 1819 he was totally deaf. For his last 15 years he was unrivaled as the world's most famous composer. In musical form he was a considerable innovator, widening the scope of sonata, symphony, concerto, and string quartet. His greatest achievement was to raise instrumental music, hitherto considered inferior to vocal, to the highest plane of art. His works include the celebrated 9 symphonies; 16 string quartets; 32 piano sonatas; the opera *Fidelio* (1805, rev. 1814); 2 masses, including the *Missa Solemnis* (1823); 5 piano concertos; a violin concerto (1806); 6 piano trios; 10 violin sonatas; 5 cello sonatas; and several concert overtures.

beetle, Any of at least 250,000 species of insects constituting the order Coleoptera (the largest order in the animal kingdom), characterized by special forewings, called elytra, which are modified into hardened covers over a second pair of functional wings. Beetles occur in almost all environments except Antarctica and the peaks of the highest mountains. Temperate zones have fewer beetle species than the tropics but in greater numbers. The smallest species are less than 0.04 in. (1 mm) long; the largest can exceed 8 in. (20 cm). Most beetles eat either other animals or plants; some eat decaying matter. Some species destroy crops, timber, and textiles and spread parasitic worms and diseases. Others are valuable predators of insect pests. Some beetles are known by other common names (e.g., borer, chafer, curculio, firefly, weevil). Beetles are preyed on by other insects and by bats, swifts, and frogs.

Menachem Begin, 1987.
Ralph Crane/Camera Press from Globe Photos

Begin, Menachem (Wolfovitch) (b. Aug. 16, 1913, Brest-Litovsk, Russia—d. March 9, 1992, Tel Aviv, Israel), Prime minister of Israel (1977–83). He earned a law degree from the University of Warsaw, Pol. During World War II (1939–45) the Soviet authorities sent him to Siberia, but he was soon released to join the Polish army in exile. He escaped to Palestine, where he became leader in 1943 of the Irgun Zvai Leumi (a right-wing underground movement in favour of a Jewish state). From 1948 to

1977 he led the opposition in the Israeli Knesset, except for three years when he sat in the Government of National Unity (1967–70). As head of the Likud party coalition, he became prime minister in 1977. He shared the 1978 Nobel Prize for Peace with Anwar el-Sādāt for negotiations that resulted in the 1979 Israel-Egypt peace treaty. His 1982 invasion of Lebanon turned world opinion against Israel, and he resigned in 1983.

begonia, Any of about 1,000 species (genus *Begonia*) of mostly succulent, tropical or subtropical plants, many with colourful flowers or leaves and used as potted plants indoors or as garden plants. Begonias come in a bewildering array of cultivated varieties. The wax begonia (*B. semperflorens*) is the most popular for use as a summer bedding plant; angelwing begonias are characterized by their tall stems; hairy begonias have feltlike leaves. Most begonias are tender and intolerant of dry conditions; they require protection from strong sunlight.

behaviour genetics, The study of the interaction of heredity and environment insofar as they affect behaviour. The question of the determinants of behaviour, commonly called the "nature-nurture" controversy, was initially investigated by English scientist Sir Francis Galton. A balanced view that recognized the importance of both genetics and environment prevailed in the 1970s. Modern research is focused on identifying genes that affect behavioral dimensions, such as personality and intelligence, and disorders, such as depression and hyperactivity. Two quasi-experimental methods of study, the twin method and the adoption method, are used to quantify the genetic and environmental contributions to an individual's behaviour.

behaviour therapy, or BEHAVIOUR MODIFICATION, Application of experimentally derived principles of learning to the treatment of psychological disorders and the control of behaviour. The concept, which has its roots in the work of Edward L. Thorndike, was popularized in the U.S. by theorists of behaviourism, including B.F. Skinner. Behaviour-therapy techniques are based on the principle of operant conditioning, in which desired behaviours are rewarded. There is little or no concern for conscious experience or unconscious processes. Such techniques have been applied with some success to disturbances such as enuresis, tics, phobias, stuttering, obsessive-compulsive disorder, and various neuroses. Behaviour modification more generally refers to the application of reinforcement techniques for shaping individual behaviour toward some desired end or for controlling behaviour in classrooms or institutional situations.

behaviourism, Highly influential academic school of psychology that dominated psychological theory in the U.S. between World War I and World War II. Classical behaviourism concerned itself exclusively with the objective evidence of behaviour (measured responses to stimuli) and excluded ideas, emotions, and inner mental experience. It emerged in the 1920s from the work of John B. Watson (who borrowed from Ivan Pavlov) and was developed in subsequent decades by Clark L. Hull and B.F. Skinner. Through the work of Edward C. Tolman, strict behaviourist doctrines began to be supplemented or replaced by those admitting such variables as reported mental states and differences in perception. A natural outgrowth of behaviourist theory was behaviour therapy.

Beijing, or PEI-CHING, conventional PEKING, formerly (1928–49) BEIPING, City, municipality with provincial status (pop., 2003 est.: city, 7,699,300; 2007 est.: municipality, 15,810,000), and capital of China. The municipality is bordered by Hebei province and Tianjin municipality and has an area of 6,500 sq mi (16,800 sq km). Lying on a broad plain in northeastern China, the city has been settled since ancient times and has been known by various names. It became the royal residence of Kublai Khan, who in 1272 named it Dadu. It was chosen as the capital of the Ming dynasty (1368–1644) in 1421 and was renamed Beijing, and it remained the capital during the Qing dynasty (1644–1911/12). It suffered heavy damage when it was occupied by European forces in 1860 and 1900. In 1928 the capital was moved to Nanjing, and the name Beiping (Pei-p'ing) was given to the former capital. Nearby, in 1937, the Marco Polo Bridge Incident took place. Beijing's capital status and its name were restored following the communist victory in 1949. It is China's cultural and educational centre. The old Forbidden City contains the former imperial palace, designated a UNESCO World Heritage site in 1987. Abutting it is Tiananmen Square, one of the world's largest public squares. Beijing was the main venue for the 2008 Summer Olympic Games.

Beira, Coastal city (pop., 2007: 436,240), central Mozambique. Situated on the Mozambique Channel at the mouths of the Púngoè and Búzi rivers, it is the chief port for central Mozambique and for landlocked Zimbabwe and Malawi. Founded in 1891 as a trading company's headquarters, it passed to Portuguese administration in 1942 and then to independent Mozambique in 1975. It is the terminus of railways from South Africa, Zimbabwe, Congo (Kinshasa), Zambia, and Malawi.

Beirut, City (pop., 2005 est.: urban agglom., 1,777,000), capital of Lebanon. The country's chief port and largest city, it lies at the foot of the Lebanon Mountains. Initially settled by the Phoenicians, it gained prominence under Roman rule in the 1st century BC. It was captured by the Arabs in AD 635. Christian Crusaders held Beirut (1110–1291), after which it was dominated by the Mamlūk dynasty. In 1516 it fell under the control of the Ottoman Empire. Under a French mandate, it became the capital of the new state of Lebanon in 1920 and capital of an independent Lebanon in 1943. It went on to flourish as the chief banking hub and a major cultural centre of the Middle East. It was severely damaged during the Lebanese Civil War (1975–90), during fighting between Israeli forces and those of the Palestine Liberation Organization in 1982, and during the Israeli siege on Hezbollah in mid-2006. The city slowly began to rebuild after the end of the civil war and again in 2006 after the siege.

Belarus, Country, eastern Europe. Area: 80,153 sq mi (207,595 sq km). Population: (2011 est.) 9,472,000. Capital: Minsk. The population is mainly Belarusian, with Russian, Polish, and Ukrainian minorities. Languages: Belarusian, Russian (both official). Religion: Christianity (predominantly Eastern Orthodox; also Roman Catholic), though about one-half of the people are nonreligious or atheist. Currency: Belarusian rubel. The northern part of the country is crossed by the Western Dvina (Dzvina) River; the Dnieper (Dnyapro) flows through eastern Belarus; the south has extensive marshy areas along the Pripet (Prypyats') River; the upper course of the Neman (Nyoman) flows in the west; and the Bug (Buh) forms part of the boundary with Poland in the southwest. The chief cities, in addition to Minsk, are Homel, Mahilyow, and Vitsyebsk. Agriculture, once the linchpin of the Belarusian economy, has diminished in importance, while manufacturing and the service sector have grown. Belarus is a republic with two legislative houses. Its president is the head of state and effectively the head of government; the prime minister is nominally the head of government but actually is subordinate to the president. Although Belarusians share a distinct identity and language, they never enjoyed political sovereignty before the country's independence in 1991, except during a brief period in 1918. The territory that is now Belarus underwent partition and changed hands often; as a result, its history is entwined with its neighbours'. In medieval times this region was ruled by Lithuanians and Poles. Following the Third Partition of Poland, all of Belarus was ruled by Russia. After World War I the western part was assigned to Poland, and the eastern part became Soviet territory—the Belorussian S.S.R. After World War II the western portion was taken from Poland and integrated into the Belorussian S.S.R. Much of the area suffered radioactive contamination from the Chernobyl accident in 1986, which forced many to evacuate. Belarus declared its independence in 1991 and later joined the Commonwealth of Independent States.

Amid increasing political turmoil in the 1990s, it moved toward closer union with Russia but continued to struggle economically and politically at the start of the 21st century.

Belém, City (pop., 2000 prelim.: metro. area, 1,271,615), northern Brazil. The capital of Pará state, the port of Belém lies on the Pará River in the vast Amazon River delta 90 mi (145 km) from the Atlantic Ocean. It began in 1616 as a fortified settlement; as it gradually became established, it helped consolidate Portuguese supremacy in northern Brazil. It was made the state capital in 1772. It enjoyed prosperity in the late 19th century as the main exporting centre of the Amazon rubber industry. After the rubber era ended in 1912, it continued to be northern Brazil's commercial centre and a main port for Amazon River craft.

Belfast, District, seaport, and capital (pop., 2001: 348,291) of Northern Ireland. On the River Lagan, the site was occupied in the Stone and Bronze ages, and the remains of Iron Age forts can still be seen. Belfast's modern history began in the early 17th century when Sir Arthur Chichester developed a plan for colonizing the area with English and Scottish settlers. Having survived the Irish insurrection of 1641, the town grew in economic importance, especially after a large immigration of French Huguenots arrived after the rescinding of the Edict of Nantes (1685) and strengthened the linen trade. It became a centre of Irish Protestantism, setting the stage for sectarian conflict in the 19th–20th centuries. Fighting was renewed in the 1960s and did not subside until a peace agreement was reached in 1998. The city is Northern Ireland's educational and commercial hub.

Belgium, officially KINGDOM OF BELGIUM, Country, northwestern Europe. Area: 11,787 sq mi (30,528 sq km). Population: (2011 est.) 10,971,000. Capital: Brussels. The population consists mostly of Flemings and Walloons. The Flemings, more than half of the population, speak Flemish (Dutch) and live in the northern half of the country; the Walloons, about one-third of the population, speak French and inhabit the southern half. Languages: Dutch, French, German (all official). Religions: Christianity (predominantly Roman Catholic); also Islam. Currency: euro. Belgium can be divided into several geographic regions. The southeast consists of the forested Ardennes highland, which extends south of the Meuse River valley and includes Belgium's highest point, Mount Botrange (2,277 ft [694 m]). Middle Belgium is a fertile region crossed by tributaries of the Schelde River. Lower Belgium comprises the flat plains of Flanders in the northwest with their many canals. Maritime Flanders borders the North Sea and is agriculturally prosperous; the chief North Sea port is Ostend, but Antwerp, near the mouth of the Schelde, handles more trade. Belgium has minimal natural resources, so the manufacture of goods from imported raw materials plays a major role in the economy, and the country is highly industrialized. It is a federal constitutional monarchy with two legislative bodies; the head of state is the monarch, and the head of government is the prime minister. Inhabited in ancient times by the Belgae, a Celtic people, the area was conquered by Julius Caesar in 57 BCE; under Augustus it became the Roman province of Belgica. Conquered by the Franks, it later broke up into semi-independent territories, including Brabant and Luxembourg. By the late 15th century, the territories of the Netherlands, of which the future Belgium was a part, gradually united and passed to the Habsburgs. In the 16th century it was a centre for European commerce. The basis of modern Belgium was laid in the southern Catholic provinces that split from the northern provinces after the Union of Utrecht in 1579. Annexed by France in 1795, the area was reunited with Holland and with it became the independent Kingdom of the Netherlands in 1815. After the revolt of its citizens in 1830, it became the independent Kingdom of Belgium. Under Leopold II it acquired vast lands in Africa. Overrun by the Germans in World Wars I and II, it was the scene of the Battle of the Bulge (1944–45). Internal discord led to legislation in the 1970s and '80s that created three nearly autonomous regions in accordance with language distribution: Flemish

Flanders, French Wallonia, and bilingual Brussels. In 1993 Belgium became a federation comprising the three regions, which gained greater autonomy at the outset of the 21st century. It is a member of the European Union.

 Belgium made its Olympic debut at the 1896 Summer Games in Athens. The Summer Games were held in Antwerp in 1920.

Belgrade, Serbian BEOGRAD, City (pop., 2002: 1,120,092), capital of the republic of Serbia. Lying at the juncture of the Danube and Sava rivers, it is one of the Balkans' most important commercial and transportation centres. Inhabited by Celts in the 4th century BC, it was later taken by the Romans and named Singidunum. It was destroyed by Huns in the 5th century. In the 11th century it became a frontier town of Byzantium and in the 13th century came under the rule of Serbia. The Ottoman Empire besieged the city in the 15th century, and the forces of Süleyman I finally took it in 1521; it was held almost continuously by the Turks into the 19th century. It became the capital of the kingdom of Serbia in 1867 and, after World War I, of the new Kingdom of Serbs, Croats, and Slovenes (renamed Yugoslavia in 1929). It suffered severely under Nazi occupation (1941–44). It was damaged by NATO bombers in the Kosovo conflict (1999). When federal Yugoslavia fragmented in the 1990s, Belgrade remained the administrative centre of the rump Yugoslav state, which changed its name to Serbia and Montenegro in 2003; the constituent republics became independent countries in 2006.

Belize, formerly (1840–1973) BRITISH HONDURAS, Country, Central America. Area: 8,867 sq mi (22,965 sq km). Population: (2011 est.) 322,000. Capital: Belmopan. Most Belizeans are of mixed ancestry (Maya and Spanish; African and British), with smaller groups of Maya and Garifuna. Languages: English (official), Creole, Spanish. Religion: Christianity (Roman Catholic, Protestant). Currency: Belize dollar. The country is bounded to the north by Mexico, to the east by the Caribbean Sea, and to the west and south by Guatemala. Belize is a land of mountains, swamps, and tropical jungles. The northern half consists of swampy lowlands drained by the Belize and Hondo rivers; the latter forms the boundary with Mexico. The southern half is more mountainous and contains the country's highest point, Victoria Peak (3,681 ft [1,122 m]). Off the coast lies Belize Barrier Reef, the world's second largest barrier reef. Belize is relatively prosperous and has a developing free-market economy with some government participation. It is a constitutional monarchy with two legislative houses; its head of state is the British monarch, represented by a governor-general, and the head of government is the prime minister. The area was inhabited by the Maya (c. 300 BCE–900 CE); the ruins of their ceremonial centres, including Caracol and Xunantunich, can still be seen. The Spanish claimed sovereignty from the 16th century but never tried to settle Belize, though they regarded the British who did as interlopers. British loggers arrived in the mid-17th century; Spanish opposition was finally overcome in 1798. When settlers began to penetrate the interior, they met with Indian resistance. In 1871 British Honduras became a crown colony, but an unfulfilled provision of an 1859 British-Guatemalan treaty led Guatemala to claim the territory, a situation still unresolved. Belize became independent on Sept. 21, 1981. Although Guatemala officially recognized the territory's independence in 1991, a British force, stationed there to ensure the new country's security, was not withdrawn until 1994.

bell, Hollow vessel, usually of metal, that produces a ringing sound when struck by an interior clapper or a mallet. In the West, open bells have acquired a standard "tulip" shape. Though the vibrational patterns of such open bells are basically nonharmonic, they can be tuned so that the lower overtones produce a recognizable chord. Forged bells have existed for many thousands of years. Bells were first cast, or founded, in the Bronze Age; the Chinese were the first master founders. Bells have carried a wide range of cultural meanings. They are particularly important in religious ritual in East and South Asia. In Christianity, especially Russian Orthodoxy, bells have also been used ritually. They have tolled the hours from monastery and church steeples, originally to govern monastic routine and later also to fill a similar role for the secular world.

Bell, Alexander Graham (b. March 3, 1847, Edinburgh, Scot.—d. Aug. 2, 1922, Beinn Bhreagh, Nova Scotia, Can.), Scottish-born U.S. audiologist and inventor. He moved to the U.S. in 1871 to teach the visible-speech system developed by his father, Alexander Melville Bell (1819–1905). He opened his own school in Boston for training teachers of the deaf (1872) and was influential in disseminating these methods. In 1876 he became the first person to transmit intelligible words through electric wire ("Watson, come here, I want you," spoken to his assistant Thomas Watson). He patented the telephone the same year, and in 1877 he cofounded Bell Telephone Co.

Alexander Graham Bell.
Culver Pictures

With the proceeds from France's Volta Prize, he founded Volta Laboratory in Washington, D.C., in 1880. His experiments there led to the invention of the photophone (which transmitted speech by light rays), the audiometer (which measured acuteness of hearing), the Graphophone (an early practical sound recorder), and working wax recording media, both flat and cylindrical, for the Graphophone. He was chiefly responsible for founding the journal *Science*, founded the American Association to Promote Teaching of Speech to the Deaf (1890), and continued his significant research on deafness throughout his life.

Bell, Gertrude (b. July 14, 1868, Washington Hall, Durham, Eng.—d. July 12, 1926, Baghdad, Iraq), British traveler, writer, and colonial administrator. After graduating from Oxford, she journeyed throughout the Middle East. After World War I she wrote a well-received report on the administration of Mesopotamia between the end of the war (1918) and the Iraqi rebellion of 1920 and later helped determine postwar boundaries. In 1921 she helped place a son of the sharif of Mecca, Fayṣal I, on the Iraqi throne. In helping create the National Museum of Iraq, she promoted the idea that excavated antiquities should stay in their country of origin.

Bellow, Saul (b. June 10, 1915, Lachine, near Montreal, Que., Can.—d. April 5, 2005, Brookline, Mass., U.S.), Canadian-born U.S. novelist. Born to an immigrant Russian Jewish family, he was fluent in Yiddish from childhood. His family moved to Chicago when he was nine; he grew up and attended college there and, after some years in New York, returned to teach in Chicago. His works, which make him representative of the Jewish American writers whose works became central to American literature after World War II, deal with the modern urban dweller, disaffected by society but not destroyed in spirit; his originality lay partly in his combination of cultural sophistication and street wisdom. His works include *The Adventures of Augie March* (1953, National Book Award), *Seize the Day* (1956), *Henderson the Rain King* (1959), *Herzog* (1964, National Book Award), *Mr. Sammler's Planet* (1970, National Book Award), *Humboldt's Gift* (1975, Pulitzer Prize), *The Dean's December* (1982), and *Ravelstein* (2000). He won the Nobel Prize for Literature in 1976.

Belmopan, City (pop., 2000: 8,130), capital of Belize. It lies in the Belize River valley, 50 mi (80 km) inland from the former capital, Belize City. After a hurricane did extensive damage to low-lying Belize City, the new capital site was chosen far enough inland to avoid flooding. Construction began in 1966, and Belmopan became the capital in 1970.

beluga, or HAUSEN, Large species of sturgeon (*Huso huso*, or *Acipenser huso*) that inhabits the Caspian and Black seas and the Sea of Azov. It reaches a length of 25 ft (7.5 m) and a weight of 2,900 lbs (1,300 kg), but its flesh and caviar are less valuable than those of smaller species.

beluga, or WHITE WHALE, Species (*Delphinapterus leucas*) of whale found in the Arctic Ocean and adjacent seas, in both deep offshore and coastal waters. It may also enter rivers that empty into far northern seas. A toothed whale with a rounded forehead and no dorsal fin, the beluga is about 13 ft (4 m) long. Born dark blue-gray or blackish, it fades to white or cream at 4–5 years of age. It feeds on fish, cephalopods, and crustaceans and usually lives in groups of five to 10. It has been hunted commercially for its oil, hide, and flesh, and is used in the Arctic as food for humans and dogs.

*Beluga, or white whale (*Delphinapterus leucas*).*
E.R. Degginger/EB Inc.

Ben-Gurion, David, orig. DAVID GRUEN (b. Oct. 16, 1886, Płońsk, Pol., Russian Empire—d. Dec. 1, 1973, Tel Aviv–Yafo, Israel), First prime minister of Israel (1948–53, 1955–63). Introduced to Zionism by his father, Ben-Gurion immigrated to Palestine, then part of the Ottoman Empire, in 1906, hoping to fulfill the Zionist aspiration of building a Jewish state in historic Israel. Expelled by the Ottomans at the outbreak of World War I (1914–18), he traveled to New York, where he married. Following the issuance of the Balfour Declaration, he joined the British army's Jewish Legion and returned to the Middle East. In the 1920s and '30s he led several political organizations, including the Jewish Agency, world Zionism's highest directing body. As Britain became more sympathetic to the interests of the Palestinian Arabs, thereafter restricting Jewish immigration to Palestine, he called on the Jewish community to rise against Britain. However, he again called for Jews to support the Allies during World War II (1939–45), while continuing the clandestine immigration of Jews to Palestine. On the establishment of the State of Israel (1948), he became prime minister and minister of defense. He succeeded in fusing the underground Jewish militias that had fought the British into a national army, which he used successfully to defend against Arab attacks. Unpopular with Britain and the U.S., he found an ally in France—then embroiled in its own war in the Arab world—which helped arm Israel in the period leading to the Suez Crisis (1956). He retired from the premiership in 1963 and from the Knesset (parliament) in 1970.

Ben Nevis, Highest mountain, British Isles. It is located in the Scottish Highlands; its summit, which reaches 4,406 ft (1,343 m), is a plateau of about 100 acres (40 hectares). Snow lies in some parts all year. It consists of a superstructure of volcanic rocks surmounting the ancient schists of the Highlands.

Benavente y Martínez, Jacinto (b. Aug. 12, 1866, Madrid, Spain—d. July 14, 1954, Madrid), Spanish dramatist. His most celebrated work, *The Bonds of Interest* (1907), was based on the Italian commedia dell'arte; his 1913 tragedy *La malquerida* was also popular. During the Spanish Civil War he was detained by the authorities for a time, but he reestablished himself in official favour with *Lo increíble* (1941). One of the foremost Spanish dramatists of the 20th century, he continued to write until the end of his life, producing more than 150 plays. He received the Nobel Prize for Literature in 1922.

Bene-Israel (Hebrew: "Sons of Israel") one of three groups of Jews in India. The origins of the Bene-Israel are uncertain, but because of their observance of certain traditions and lack of observance of others, they are believed to have escaped persecution in Galilee before the 2nd century BCE and to have shipwrecked on the coast of India. Seven couples are believed to have survived, without the benefit of a material culture. Isolated from other Jews, they largely assimilated into India's caste system, though they practiced Jewish dietary laws, circumcised male children on the eighth day, and did not work on Saturday. Present-day Bene-Israel bear a physical resemblance to the Marathi people and speak Marathi and English. Many have emigrated to Israel.

Benedictine, Member of the Order of St. Benedict, the confederated autonomous congregations of monks and lay brothers who follow the Benedictine Rule, created by St. Benedict of Nursia in the 6th century. The Rule spread slowly in Italy and Gaul. By the 9th century it was nearly universal in northern and western Europe, where Benedictine monasteries became repositories of learning, literature, and wealth. The order declined during the 12th–15th century, when it was revived with reforms that limited abbots to fixed terms and required monks to make their vows to the congregation rather than a particular house. The Reformation virtually eliminated Benedictines from northern Europe, and they declined elsewhere. In the 19th century another revival strengthened the order in Europe, especially in France and Germany, and led to the establishment of new congregations worldwide.

Benelux Economic Union, Economic union of Belgium, the Netherlands, and Luxembourg. The three countries formed a customs union in 1948, and in 1958 they signed the Treaty of the Benelux Economic Union, which became operative in 1960. Benelux became the first completely free international labor market and contributed to the establishment of the European Economic Community.

Bengal, Former province, northeastern British India. Generally corresponding to the area inhabited by speakers of the Bengali language, it is now divided between eastern India and Bangladesh. Bengal formed part of most of the early empires that controlled northern India. From the 8th to the 12th century it was under a Buddhist dynasty, and from 1576 it belonged to the Mughal Empire. In the 18th century it was dominated by the nawabs of Bengal; they came into conflict with the British, who had established themselves at Calcutta (now Kolkata) in 1690. By 1764 the British had taken possession, and Bengal became the base for British expansion in India. Bengal was partitioned in 1905, and with the end of British rule in 1947, the western portion formed the Indian states of West Bengal, Bihar, and Orissa. East Bengal went to Pakistan; in 1971 it became Bangladesh. Jharkhand state was created from southern Bihar in 2000.

Bengal, Bay of, Part of the Indian Ocean. Occupying about 839,000 sq mi (2,173,000 sq km), it is bordered by Sri Lanka, India, Bangladesh, Myanmar, and the northern Malay Peninsula. It is about 1,000 mi (1,600 km) wide, with an average depth exceeding 8,500 ft (2,600 m). Many large rivers, including the Godavari, Krishna, Kaveri (Cauvery), Ganges (Ganga), and Brahmaputra, flow into it. The Andaman and Nicobar Islands, the bay's only islands, separate it from the Andaman Sea to the southeast. It has long been crossed by Indian and Malaysian traders; Chinese maritime trading dates from the 12th century. Vasco da Gama led the first European voyage into the bay in 1498.

Bengali language, Indo-Aryan language spoken principally in Bangladesh and the Indian state of West Bengal. Bengali has more speakers—some 190 million—than all but a handful of other languages of the world. Like other Modern Indo-Aryan languages, Bengali has drastically reduced the complex inflectional system of Old Indo-Aryan. It has virtually dropped grammatical gender and fixed stress on the initial syllable of a word or phrase. Bengali was the first of the Indian languages to adopt Western secular literary styles, such as fiction and drama.

Benin, officially REPUBLIC OF BENIN, formerly DAHOMEY, Country, western Africa. Area: 44,310 sq mi (114,763 sq km). Population: (2011 est.) 9,100,000. Capital: Porto-Novo (official), Cotonou (de facto). The Fon people and related groups constitute two-fifths of the population; minorities include the Yoruba, Fulani, and Adjara. Languages: French (official), Fon. Currency: CFA franc. Religions: traditional religions, Islam, Christianity. Extending about 420 mi (675 km) inland from the Gulf of Guinea, Benin includes a hilly region in the northwest, where the maximum elevation is 2,103 ft (641 m). There are plains in the east and north and a marshy region in the south, where the coastline extends about 75 mi (120 km). Benin's longest river, the Ouémé, flows into the Porto-Novo Lagoon and is navigable for 125 mi (200 km) of its 280-mi (450-km) length. Benin has a developing mixed economy based largely on agriculture and operates an offshore oil field. It is a multiparty republic with one legislative house; the head of state and government is the president, who may be assisted by the prime minister. In southern Benin the Fon established the Abomey kingdom in the early 17th century. In the 18th century the kingdom expanded to include Allada and Ouidah, where French forts had been established in the 17th century. By 1882 the French were firmly reestablished in the area, and conflict between the French and Africans ensued. In 1894 Dahomey became a French protectorate; it was incorporated into the federation of French West Africa in 1904. It achieved independence in 1960. Dahomey was renamed Benin in 1975. Its chronically weak economy created problems for the country into the 21st century.

Bentham, Jeremy (b. Feb. 15, 1748, London, Eng.—d. June 6,

Jeremy Bentham, detail of an oil painting by H.W. Pickersgill, 1829; in the National Portrait Gallery, London
Courtesy of the National Portrait Gallery, London

1832, London), British moral philosopher and legal theorist, the earliest expounder of utilitarianism. A precocious student, he graduated from Oxford at age 15. In his *An Introduction to the Principles of Morals and Legislation,* he argued that mankind was governed by two sovereign motives, pain and pleasure. The object of all legislation, therefore, must be the "greatest happiness of the greatest number"; and since all punishment involves pain and is therefore evil, it ought only to be used "so far as it promises to exclude some greater evil." His work inspired much reform legislation, especially regarding prisons. He was also an exponent of the new laissez-faire economics of Adam Smith and David Ricardo. Though a vocal advocate of democracy, he rejected the notions of the social contract, natural law, and natural rights as fictional and counterproductive ("Rights is the child of law; from real law come real rights; but from imaginary laws, from 'law of nature,' come imaginary rights"). He helped found the radical *Westminster Review* (1823). In accordance with his will, his clothed skeleton is permanently exhibited at University College, London.

Benue River, or BÉNOUÉ RIVER, River, western Africa. Rising in northern Cameroon (as the Bénoué), the river flows west across east-central Nigeria (as the Benue). About 870 mi (1,400 km) long, it is the chief tributary of the Niger River and transports a considerable volume of trade.

Benz, Karl (Friedrich) (b. Nov. 25, 1844, Karlsruhe, Baden—d. April 4, 1929, Ladenburg, Ger.), German mechanical engineer who designed and built the first practical automobile powered by an internal-combustion engine. The original car, his three-wheeled *Motorwagen*, first ran in 1885. Benz's company produced its first four-wheeled car in 1893 and the first of its series of racing cars in 1899. Benz left the company in 1906 to form another group with his sons. In 1926 the Benz company merged with the company started by Gottlieb Daimler.

Beowulf, Heroic poem considered the highest achievement of Old English literature and the earliest European vernacular epic. It deals with events of the early 6th century and was probably composed *c.* 700–750. It tells the story of the Scandinavian hero Beowulf, who gains fame as a young man by vanquishing the monster Grendel and Grendel's mother; later, as an aging king, he kills a dragon but dies soon after, honoured and lamented. *Beowulf* belongs metrically, stylistically, and thematically to the Germanic heroic tradition but shows a distinct Christian influence.

Berber, Any member of a community native to the Maghrib who speaks one of various Berber languages, including Tamazight, Tashahit, and Tarifit. Berber-speakers were the original inhabitants of North Africa, though many regions succumbed to colonization by the Roman Republic and Empire and later (from the 7th century AD) to conquest by the Arabs. Berbers gradually accepted Islam, and many switched to Arabic or became bilingual. Berber languages are still spoken in some rural and mountain areas of Morocco and Algeria and by some inhabitants of Tunisia and Libya. Since the 1990s Berber intellectuals have sought to revive interest in the language. The Berber-speaking Almoravid and Almohad dynasties built empires in North Africa and Spain in the 11th–13th centuries.

Bergen, City (pop., 2000 est.: municipality, 229,496), southwestern Norway. It is Norway's second largest city and most important port. Founded in 1070 by King Olaf III, it was Norway's capital in the 12th–13th centuries. In the 14th century, German Hanseatic League merchants acquired control over its trade; their influence in a weakened Norway lasted into the 16th century. Repeatedly destroyed by fire (most notably in 1702 and 1916), Bergen has been resurrected each time. Its economy is based largely on fishing and shipbuilding. It was the birthplace of Edvard Grieg and the violinist Ole Bull.

Bergen-Belsen, or BELSEN, Nazi concentration camp near Bergen and Belsen, villages in what was then Prussian Hannover, Germany. Established in 1943 partly as a prisoner-of-war camp and partly as a Jewish transit camp, it was designed for 10,000 prisoners but eventually held about 60,000, most of whom lacked any food or shelter. It contained no gas chambers, but some 35,000 prisoners died there, including Anne Frank, between January and mid-April 1945. As the first such camp to be liberated by the Western Allies (April 15, 1945), it received instant notoriety. Some 28,000 prisoners died of diseases and other causes in the weeks after their liberation by British troops.

Bergson, Henri (-Louis) (b. Oct. 18, 1859, Paris, France—d. Jan. 4, 1941, Paris), French philosopher. In *Creative Evolution* (1907), he argued that evolution, which he accepted as scientific fact, is not mechanistic but driven by an *élan vital* ("vital impulse"). He was the first to elaborate a process philosophy, rejecting static values and embracing dynamic values such as motion, change, and evolution. His writing style has been widely admired for its grace and lucidity; he won the Nobel Prize for Literature in 1927. Very popular in his time, he remains influential in France.

Henri Bergson, 1928.
Archiv für Kunst und Geschichte, Berlin

beriberi, or VITAMIN B$_1$ DEFICIENCY, Nutritional disorder, with nerve and heart impairment, caused by thiamin deficiency. Its name is from the Sinhalese word for "extreme weakness." Symptoms include fatigue, digestive problems, and limb numbness and weakness. Dry beriberi involves gradual long-nerve degeneration, with muscle atrophy and loss of reflexes. Wet beriberi is more acute, with edema from cardiac failure and poor circulation. Thiamin occurs widely in food but is lost in processing; a well-balanced diet high in unprocessed foods can prevent beriberi. In Western countries, chronic alcoholism is the most common cause.

Bering Sea, Marginal sea, North Pacific Ocean. Enclosed by Alaska, the Aleutian Islands, the Kamchatka Peninsula, and eastern Siberia, it covers some 890,000 sq mi (2,304,000 sq km). It has numerous islands, including Karagin and Nunivak, as well as the St. Lawrence, Aleutian, and Komandor archipelagos. It is crossed diagonally by the International Date Line. The sea is connected to the Arctic Ocean by the Bering Strait, which separates Asia from North America and is believed to have been a land bridge during the Ice Age that enabled migration from Asia to North America. Vitus Bering's exploration of the sea and strait in 1728 and 1741 formed a basis for Russian claims to Alaska.

Berlin, City and state (pop., 2002 est: city, 3,388,000; metro. area, 4,101,000), capital of Germany. Founded in the early 13th century, it was a member of the Hanseatic League in the 14th century. It became the residence of the Hohenzollerns and the capital of Brandenburg. It was successively the capital of Prussia (from 1701), the German Empire (1871–1918), the Weimar Republic (1919–32), and the Third Reich (1933–45). In World War II much of the city was destroyed by Allied bombing. In 1945 it was divided into four occupation zones: U.S., British, French, and Soviet. The three Western powers integrated their sectors into one economic entity in 1948; the Soviets responded with the Berlin blockade. When independent governments were established in eastern and western Germany in 1949, East Berlin was made the capital of East Germany, and West Berlin, though surrounded by East Germany, became part of West Germany. Continuing immigration from East to West Berlin through the 1950s prompted the 1961 erection of the Berlin Wall. The area immediately became the most vivid focal point of the Cold War. The dramatic dismantling of the wall in 1989 marked the international upheaval that accompanied the end of the Soviet Union. Berlin became reunified as Germany's official capital in 1991; the transfer of government from Bonn was completed in 1999. It is the site of the University of Berlin, Charlottenburg Palace, Brandenburg Gate, and Berlin Zoo and is home to the Berlin Opera and Berlin Philharmonic Orchestra.

Berlin, Congress of (June 13–July 13, 1878) Diplomatic meeting of the major European powers at which the Treaty of Berlin replaced the Treaty of San Stefano. Dominated by Otto von Bismarck, the congress solved an international crisis by revising the peace settlement to satisfy the interests of Britain and Austria-Hungary. By humiliating Russia and failing to acknowledge adequately the aspirations of the Balkan peoples, it laid the foundation for future Balkan crises.

Berlin Wall, Barrier surrounding West Berlin that closed off East Germans access to West Berlin from 1961 to 1989 and served as a symbol of the Cold War's division of East and West Germany. The barrier was built in response to the flight of about 2.5 million East Germans to West Germany in the years 1949–61. First erected on the night of Aug. 12–13, 1961, it developed into a system of concrete walls topped with barbed wire and guarded with watchtowers, gun emplacements, and mines. It was opened in the 1989 democratization that swept through eastern Europe and has been largely torn down.

Bermuda, British overseas territory, western Atlantic Ocean. Area: 21 sq mi (54 sq km). Population: (2011 est.) 65,300. Comprising 7 main islands and about 170 additional (named) islets and rocks, it lies about 570 mi (920 km) southeast of Cape Hatteras, N.C., U.S. Capital: Hamilton, on Main Island. Bermuda was named for Juan de Bermúdez, who may have visited the islands in 1503. Colonized by the English in 1612, Bermuda became a crown colony in 1684, and its status changed to an overseas territory in 2002. Its economy is based on tourism and international finance; its gross national product per capita is among the world's highest.

Bermuda Triangle, Triangular section of the North Atlantic Ocean whose boundaries are usually said to be Bermuda, the southern U.S. coast, and the Greater Antilles. The region attracted international attention after numerous planes and ships were said to have mysteriously disappeared there. Reports of unnatural occurrences were popularized, but by the late 20th century much of the myth surrounding the Bermuda Triangle had been dispelled.

Bern, City (pop., 2000 est: city, 128,600; metro. area, 317,300), capital of Switzerland. Lying along a loop of the Aare River, it was founded as a military post in 1191 by Berthold V, duke of Zähringen. It became a free imperial city in 1218. Gradually extending its power, it became an independent state, and in 1353 it entered the Swiss Confederation. It was a scene of disputation in 1528 between Roman Catholics and reformers, which led to its subsequent championing of Protestant doctrines. It became a member of the Helvetic Republic and in 1848 was made the capital of Switzerland. It is headquarters of the international postal, railway, and copyright unions.

Bernadette of Lourdes, Saint, orig. MARIE-BERNARDE SOUBIROUS (b. Jan. 7, 1844, Lourdes, France—d. April 16, 1879, Nevers; canonized Dec. 8, 1933; feast day April 16, but sometimes February 18 in France), French visionary. The daughter of a miller, she had a poverty-stricken childhood and was often ill. In 1858 she had a series of visions of Mary; she defended their authenticity against the doubts of her parents, the clergy, and civil authorities. She joined the Sisters of Charity at Nevers (1866) and remained in seclusion until her death at 35. The grotto at Lourdes became a pilgrimage site; its waters are reputed to have healing powers.

Bernhardt, Sarah, orig. HENRIETTE-ROSINE BERNARD (b. Oct. 22/23, 1844, Paris, France—d. March 26, 1923, Paris), French actress. The illegitimate child of a courtesan, she was encouraged to pursue a theatrical career by one of her mother's lovers, the duke de Morny. After a brief appearance at the Comédie-Française (1862–63), she joined the Odéon theatre (1866–72), where she acted in *Kean* by Alexandre Dumas *père* and *Ruy Blas* by Victor Hugo, charming audiences with her "golden voice." Returning to the Comédie-Française (1872–80), she starred in *Phèdre* to great

Sarah Bernhardt, photograph by Napoleon Sarony, 1880.
Library of Congress, Washington, D.C.

acclaim in Paris and London. She formed her own company in 1880 and toured the world in *The Lady of the Camellias* by Alexandre Dumas *fils*, *Adrienne Lecouvreur* by Eugène Scribe, four plays written for her by Victorien Sardou, and *The Eaglet* by Edmond Rostand. After an injury to her leg forced its amputation (1915), she strapped on a wooden leg and chose roles she could play largely seated. One of the best-known figures in the history of the stage, she was made a member of France's Legion of Honour in 1914.

beryllium, Chemical element, lightest of the alkaline earth metals, chemical symbol Be, atomic number 4. It does not occur uncombined in nature but is found chiefly as the mineral beryl (of which emerald and aquamarine are gemstone varieties). Beryllium metal, particularly in alloys, has many structural and thermal applications; it is used in nuclear reactors. Beryllium has valence 2 in all its compounds, which are generally colourless and taste distinctly sweet. All soluble beryllium compounds are toxic. Beryllium oxide is used in specialized ceramics for nuclear devices, and beryllium chloride is a catalyst for organic reactions.

Bessemer, Sir Henry (b. Jan. 19, 1813, Charlton, Hertfordshire, Eng.—d. March 15, 1898, London), British inventor and engineer. Son of a metallurgist, he set up his own casting business at 17. At that time the only iron-based construction materials were cast iron and wrought iron. So-called steel was made by adding carbon to pure forms of wrought iron; the resulting material was used almost entirely for cutting tools. During the Crimean War Bessemer worked to devise a stronger cast iron for cannon. The result was a process for the inexpensive production of large, slag-free ingots of steel as workable as any wrought iron. He eventually also discovered how to remove excess oxygen from the iron. The Bessemer process (1856) led to the development of the Bessemer converter.

Bessemer, detail of an oil painting by Rudolf Lehmann; in the Iron and Steel Institute, London
Courtesy of The Iron and Steel Institute, London; photograph, The Science Museum, London

Bessemer process, Technique for converting pig iron to steel invented by Henry Bessemer in England in 1856 and brought by him into commercial production in 1860. Air blown through liquid pig iron in a refractory-lined converter oxidizes the carbon and silicon in the iron. Heat released by the oxidation keeps the metal molten. R.F. Mushet contributed the technique for deoxidizing the converted metal that made the process a success. William Kelly conducted experiments with an air-blown converter between 1856 and 1860 in Kentucky and Pennsylvania, but failed to make steel. Alexander L. Holley built the first successful Bessemer steel plant in the U.S. in 1865. High-volume production of low-cost steel in Britain and the U.S. by the Bessemer process soon revolutionized building construction and provided steel to replace iron in railroad rails and many other uses. The Bessemer process was eventually superseded by the open-hearth process.

bestiary, Medieval European work in verse or prose, often illustrated, consisting of a collection of stories, each based on a description of certain qualities of the subject, usually an animal or a plant. The stories were allegories, used for moral and religious instruction and admonition. They ultimately were derived from the Greek *Physiologus*, a text compiled by an unknown author before the mid-2nd century AD. Many traditional attributes of real or mythical creatures derive from bestiaries, such as the phoenix's burning itself to be born again and the parental love of the pelican, which, believed to feed its young by gashing its own breast, became a symbol of Christ.

beta-blocker, in full BETA-ADRENERGIC BLOCKING AGENT, Any of a class of synthetic drugs used to treat a wide range of diseases and conditions of the sympathetic nervous system. Stimulation by epinephrine of beta-adrenergic receptors, which are predominately found in the heart but are also present in vascular and other smooth muscle, results in excitation of the sympathetic nervous system. By preventing that excitation, beta-blockers are useful in controlling anxiety, hypertension, and a variety of heart conditions. They reduce the risk of a second heart attack.

betel, Either of two different plants that are widely used in combination for chewing purposes in southern Asia and the East Indies. The betel nut is the seed of the areca, or betel, palm (*Areca catechu*), family Palmae; the betel leaf is from the betel pepper, or pan plant (*Piper betle*), family Piperaceae. For chewing, a small piece of the areca palm's fruit is wrapped in a leaf of the betel pepper, along with a pellet of lime to cause salivation and release the stimulating alkaloids. Chewing results in a heavy flow of brick-red saliva, which may temporarily dye the mouth, lips, and gums orange-brown. Betel nuts yield an alkaloid that veterinarians use as a worming agent.

*The betel nut, seed of the areca palm (*Areca catechu*)*
Wayne Lukas–Group IV—The National Audubon Society Collection/Photo Researchers

Betelgeuse (from Arabic *bat al-dshauza*, "the giant's shoulder") Brightest star in the constellation Orion, marking the hunter's eastern shoulder. About 430 light-years from Earth, Betelgeuse is easily identifiable by its brightness, its position in brilliant Orion, and its deep reddish colour. It is a red supergiant star, one of the largest known; its diameter is roughly 500 times that of the Sun.

Bethlehem, Arabic BAYT LAHM, Town (pop., 2005 prelim.: 29,000), West Bank, south of Jerusalem. An ancient town of Judaea, it was the early home of King David. A Roman garrison was stationed there during the Second Jewish Revolt (AD 135). Christians regard it as the birthplace of Jesus, and in the early 4th century the Church of the Nativity, located on what is believed to be the site of Jesus' birth, was built there. Bethlehem was included in the British mandate of Palestine (1923–48); in 1950, following the first Arab-Israeli war (1948–49), it was annexed by Jordan. After the Six-Day War (1967), it became part of the West Bank territory under Israeli administration. Under an agreement reached in 1995, Israel ceded rule of the town to a Palestinian Authority. Long an important pilgrim and tourist centre, it is also an agricultural market closely linked to Jerusalem.

Bhagavadgita (Sanskrit: "Song of God") One of the greatest of the Hindu scriptures, constituting part of the *Mahabharata*. It is written in the form of a dialogue between the warrior Prince Arjuna and the charioteer Krishna, an incarnation of Vishnu. It was probably composed in the 1st or 2nd century AD, later than much of the epic. Concerned over the suffering the impending battle will cause, Arjuna hesitates, but Krishna explains that the higher way

is the dispassionate discharge of duty without concern for personal triumph. The *Bhagavadgita* considers the nature of God and ultimate reality and offers three disciplines for transcending the limitations of this world: *jnana* (knowledge or wisdom), karma (dispassionate action), and bhakti (love of God). It has inspired numerous commentaries over the centuries, including those by Ramanuja and Mohandas K. Gandhi.

bhakti, Southern Asian devotional movement, particularly in Hinduism, emphasizing the love of a devotee for his or her personal god. In contrast to Advaita, bhakti assumes a dualistic relationship between devotee and deity. Though Vishnu, Shiva, and Shakti all have cults, bhakti characteristically developed around Vishnu's incarnations as Rama and Krishna. Practices include reciting the god's name, singing hymns, wearing his emblem, and making pilgrimages. The fervour of South Indian hymnists in the 7th–10th centuries spread bhakti and inspired much poetry and art. Poets such as Mirabai conceived of the relationship between the worshiper and the god in familiar human terms (e.g., the lover and beloved), while more abstract poets such as Kabir and his disciple Nanak, the first Sikh Guru and founder of Sikhism, portrayed the divinity as singular and ineffable.

bharata natyam, Principal classical dance style of India, indigenous to Tamil Nadu and prevalent in South India. It expresses Hindu religious themes, and its techniques and terminology are found in the treatise *Natya-shastra*, written by the sage Bharata (3rd century CE). One dancer performs the entire two-hour program, accompanied by drums, drone, and singer. Originally performed only by female temple dancers, the art fell into disrepute as temple dancing became associated with prostitution, but it was revived in its original purity in the late 19th century. It was not brought to the stage until the 1930s.

Bharatpur, or BHURTPORE, City (pop., 2001: 204,587), Rajasthan state, northwestern India. Located west of Agra, it was founded *c.* 1733 and was the capital of the princely state of Bharatpur. It was so strongly fortified that it successfully resisted a British siege in 1805, and it was not taken by them until 1826. The city is renowned for the superb bird sanctuary at nearby Keoladeo National Park.

Bharhut sculpture, Indian sculpture from the mid-2nd century BCE that decorated the great stupa, or relic mound, of Bharhut, in Madhya Pradesh, India. It is now mostly destroyed; the railings and gateways that remain are in Kolkata's (Calcutta's) Indian Museum. The ornamental medallions depicting legends of the Buddha's previous births and events in his life are labeled and so are indispensable for an understanding of Buddhist iconography. The Bharhut style marked the beginning of a tradition of Buddhist narrative relief and decoration of sacred buildings that continued for several centuries.

Standard-bearer on horseback, relief sculpture from the stupa of Bharhut, Madhya Pradesh, India, mid-2nd century BCE; in the Indian Museum, Kolkata.
SCALA/Art Resource, New York

bhiksu, Pali BHIKKU, In Buddhism, a member of the sangha, the ordained order of men established by the Buddha. (Female orders exist in some Mahayana Buddhist traditions). Originally they were mendicant followers of the Buddha who taught Buddhist ways in return for food. Today children may enter monastic life as novices, but candidates for ordination must be 21 years old. There are some 200 rules; sexual relations, taking of life, stealing, or boasting of spiritual attainment will lead to expulsion. A bhiksu shaves his head and face, owns a few essential items, and begs daily for his food. Theravada Buddhism forbids monks to handle money and perform labour. Chan (Zen) Buddhism requires monks to work.

Bhopal, Former princely state, central India. It is crossed by the Vindhya Mountains; the Narmada River is its southern boundary. It was founded in 1723 by an Afghan adventurer. In its struggles with the Marathas, Bhopal was itself friendly to the British and concluded a treaty with them in 1817. It was a major component of the Bhopal Agency and the second largest Muslim principality of the British Empire. At India's independence, Bhopal remained a separate Indian province. When it was incorporated into Madhya Pradesh in 1956, Bhopal city became the state's capital.

Bhopal, City (pop., 2001: 1,437,354), capital of Madhya Pradesh state, India. Situated northwest of Nagpur, it is primarily an industrial city and a major rail junction. It is the site of India's largest mosque and home to several colleges. In 1984 Bhopal became the site of one of the worst industrial accidents in history when tons of toxic gas escaped from a Union Carbide insecticide plant and spread over a densely populated area; the final death toll was estimated to be between 15,000 and 20,000, with some half-million survivors suffering various ailments.

Bhutan, officially KINGDOM OF BHUTAN, Country, south-central Asia. Area: 14,824 sq mi (38,394 sq km). Population: (2011 est.) 701,000. Capital: Thimphu. There are three main ethnic groups: the Buddhist Sharchop (Assamese) in the east; the Tibetan Buddhist Bhutia, about half of the population, in the northern, central, and western areas; and the Hindu Nepalese in the southwest. Languages: Dzongkha (official), other Sino-Tibetan languages, Nepali. Religions: Tibetan Buddhism; also Hinduism. Currency: ngultrum. The northern part of the country lies in the Great Himalayas, with peaks surpassing 24,000 ft (7,300 m) and high valleys lying at 12,000–18,000 ft (3,700–5,500 m). Spurs radiate southward, forming the Lesser Himalayan ranges. Several fertile valleys there, at elevations of 5,000–9,000 ft (1,500–2,700 m), are fairly well populated and cultivated. South of these mountains lies the Duars Plain, controlling access to the strategic mountain passes; much of it is hot and steamy and covered with dense forest. The Bhutanese economy is mainly agricultural; nearly all exports go to India. Bhutan is a constitutional monarchy with a bicameral legislature; the head of state is the monarch, and the head of government is the prime minister. Bhutan's mountains and forests long made it inaccessible to the outside world, and its feudal rulers banned foreigners until well into the 20th century. It nevertheless became the object of foreign invasions; in 1865 it came under British influence, and in 1910 it agreed to be guided by Britain in its foreign affairs. It later became oriented toward British-ruled India, though much of its trade continued to be with Tibet. India took over Britain's role in 1949, and ties between India and Bhutan strengthened. In the late 20th century, Bhutan's rulers, aware of the need to increase international interaction and improve the standard of living, embarked on a program to build roads and hospitals and to create a system of secular education. The kings also slowly divested themselves of authority. The transition from an absolute monarchy to a parliamentary democracy was completed in March 2008, and a new constitution was promulgated in July.

Bhutto, Benazir (b. June 21, 1953, Karachi, Pak.—d. Dec. 27, 2007, Rawalpindi), Pakistani politician, the first woman leader of a Muslim nation in modern history. After receiving an education at Harvard and Oxford, she led the political opposition to Pres. Zia-ul-Haq after the execution of her father, Zulfikar Ali Bhutto, in 1979. She subsequently endured frequent house arrest (1979–

84) and was exiled (1984–86). When Zia died in a plane crash in 1988, she became prime minister of a coalition government. She was unable to do much to combat Pakistan's widespread poverty, governmental corruption, and increasing crime, and her government was dismissed in 1990 on charges of corruption and other malfeasance. A second stint as prime minister (1993–96) ended similarly. In 1999 she was convicted of taking kickbacks from a Swiss company and sentenced in absentia to five years in prison. In October 2007 Bhutto was granted a long-sought amnesty and returned to Pakistan. In December she was killed while campaigning for upcoming elections.

biathlon, Winter sports event combining cross-country skiing with rifle sharpshooting. It originated in Scandinavian hunting. It was first included in the Winter Olympics program in 1960. Competitors cover a course, carrying a single-shot rifle and ammunition and stopping at four points to fire five shots at small targets. Events are either 10 or 20 km long, and there are a variety of race types, including relay, sprint, and pursuit.

Bible, Sacred scriptures of Judaism and Christianity. The Jewish scriptures consist of the Torah (or Pentateuch), the Neviim ("Prophets"), and the Ketuvim ("Writings"), which together constitute what Christians call the Old Testament. The Pentateuch and Joshua relate how Israel became a nation and came to possess the Promised Land. The Prophets describe the establishment and development of the monarchy and relate the prophets' messages. The Writings include poetry, speculation on good and evil, and history. The Roman Catholic and Eastern Orthodox Bible includes additional Jewish writings called the Apocrypha. The New Testament consists of early Christian literature. The Gospels tell of the life, person, and teachings of Jesus. The Acts of the Apostles relates the earliest history of Christianity. The Epistles (Letters) are correspondence of early church leaders (chiefly St. Paul) and address the needs of early congregations. Revelation is the only canonical representative of a large genre of early Christian apocalyptic literature.

biblical translation, Art and practice of translating the Bible. The Old Testament was originally written in Hebrew, with scattered passages of Aramaic. It was first translated in its entirety into Aramaic and then, in the 3rd century AD, into Greek (the Septuagint). Hebrew scholars created the authoritative Masoretic text (6th–10th century) from Aramaic Targums, the original Hebrew scrolls having been lost. The New Testament was originally in Greek or Aramaic. Christians translated both Testaments into Coptic, Ethiopian, Gothic, and Latin. St. Jerome's Latin Vulgate (405) was the standard Christian translation for 1,000 years. New learning in the 15th–16th century generated new translations. Martin Luther translated the entire Bible into German (1522–34). The first complete English translation, credited to John Wycliffe, appeared in 1382, but it was the King James version (1611) that became the standard for more than three centuries. By the late 20th century the entire Bible had been translated into 250 languages and portions of it into more than 1,300.

Bibliothèque Nationale de France, Most important library in France and one of the oldest in the world. The nation's first royal library, the Bibliothèque du Roi ("King's Library"), was established under Charles V (r. 1364–80) but later dispersed; another was established under Louis XI (r. 1461–83). From 1537 the library received a copy of every French publication. It was moved from Fontainebleau to Paris in the late 16th century and opened to the public in 1692. It acquired its current name in 1795, and its collection was expanded through Revolutionary appropriations and Napoleon's acquisitions. In 1995 it moved to a new facility with a controversial design; this facility now houses all its books (more than 12 million), periodicals, and magazines.

bicycle, Lightweight, two-wheeled, steerable machine that is propelled by the rider. The wheels are mounted in a metal frame, and the front wheel is held in a movable fork. The rider sits on a saddle and steers with handlebars attached to the fork, propelling the bicycle with two pedals attached to cranks that turn a chainwheel. An endless chain transmits power from the chainwheel to a sprocket on the back wheel. A heavy, pedalless form built in 1818 was propelled simply by the rider paddling his feet against the ground. In the early 1840s Scottish blacksmith Kirkpatrick Macmillan (1813–78) built bicycles propelled by pedals, cranks, and drive rods; he is widely credited with having invented the bicycle. Important innovations were introduced by Pierre and Ernest Michaux in France in the early 1860s, and by 1865 their company was manufacturing 400 *vélocipèdes* a year. A lighter version produced in England in 1870 (nicknamed the "penny-farthing") featured a large front wheel and small back wheel. By the 1890s the standard bicycle design was established, and, with the smooth ride enabled by the new pneumatic tires, its popularity exploded. The so-called mountain bike became the standard design by the early 1990s. The bicycle is used worldwide as a basic means of transportation.

Biedermeier style, Style of German and Austrian art, furniture, and decoration that developed *c.* 1815 to 1848. Gottlieb ("Papa") Biedermeier was a fictional cartoon character, the comic symbol of middle-class comfort, with an emphasis on family life and the pursuit of hobbies. The subject matter of Biedermeier paintings, which were either genre or historical, was treated sentimentally; Carl Spitzweg (1808–85) is the best-known of the Biedermeier painters. The simplicity and functionality of Biedermeier furniture were derived from the Empire and Directoire styles, but the furniture was characterized by more restrained geometric shapes. The style was revived in the 1960s.

big bang, Model of the origin of the universe, which holds that it emerged from a state of extremely high temperature and density in an explosive expansion 10 billion–15 billion years ago. Its two basic assumptions—that Albert Einstein's general theory of relativity correctly describes the gravitational interaction of all matter and that an observer's view of the universe does not depend on direction of observation or on location—make it possible to calculate physical conditions in the universe back to a very early time called the Planck time (after Max Planck). According to the model proposed by George Gamow in the 1940s, the universe expanded rapidly from a highly compressed early state, with a steady decrease in density and temperature. Within seconds, matter predominated over antimatter and certain nuclei formed. It took another million years before atoms could form and electromagnetic radiation could travel through space unimpeded. The abundances of hydrogen, helium, and lithium and the discovery of cosmic background radiation support the model, which also explains the redshifts of the light from distant galaxies as resulting from the expansion of space.

Bihar, State (pop., 2008 est.: 93,823,000), northeastern India. Bordered by Nepal and West Bengal, Jharkhand, and Uttar Pradesh states, it occupies 38,301 sq mi (99,200 sq km); its capital is Patna. Its area was the site of the ancient kingdoms of Videha and Magadha in the 2nd and 1st millennia BCE. In the 4th century CE the area came under the Gupta empire, whose capital was at Pataliputra (Patna). Bihar was overcome by the Muslims *c.* 1200. In 1765 it was taken by the British and made part of Bengal. The area was the scene of revolts against the British in the mid-19th century and of Mohandas K. Gandhi's nonviolent movement in the early 20th century. Bihar was made a single province of British India in 1936; in 1950 it became a state in independent India. It is one of India's least urbanized yet most densely populated states, and most of its people engage in agriculture. In 2000 the state of Jharkhand was created from Bihar's southern districts.

Bikini, Atoll, western Marshall Islands, central Pacific Ocean. It consists of a ring of 20 small coral islands. Administered by the U.S. from 1947 as part of a UN-sanctioned U.S. Trust Territory of the Pacific Islands, it was used for U.S. nuclear-weapons testing in 1946–58. The 166 inhabitants were removed before the tests began and returned in 1969, but they were evacuated again in 1978 because of high radiation levels. Cleanup there continued, and in the late 1990s Bikini was again deemed safe for habitation. The atoll became part of the Republic of the Marshall Islands in 1979.

Bilbao, Port city (pop., 2001: city, 349,972; metro. area, 947,334), northern Spain. It is located 7 mi (11 km) inland from the Bay of Biscay. The largest city in the Basque Country, it originated as a settlement of mariners and ironworkers and was chartered in 1300. In the 18th century it prospered through trade with Spain's New World colonies. The city was sacked by French troops in the Peninsular War (1808) and besieged during the Carlist Wars. It is a chief port in Spain and a centre of the metallurgical industries, shipbuilding, and banking. Landmarks include the 14th-century Cathedral of Santiago and the 20th-century Guggenheim Museum Bilbao.

bildungsroman (German: "novel of character development"), Class of novel derived from German literature that deals with the formative years of the main character, whose moral and psychological development is depicted. It typically ends on a positive note, with the hero's foolish mistakes and painful disappointments behind him and a life of usefulness ahead. It grew out of folklore tales in which a dunce goes out into the world seeking adventure. One of the earliest novelistic developments of the theme, Johann W. von Goethe's *Wilhelm Meister's Apprenticeship* (1795–96), remains a classic example.

bilingualism, Ability to speak two languages. It may be acquired early by children in regions where most adults speak two languages (e.g., French and dialectal German in Alsace). Children may also become bilingual by learning languages in two different social settings; for example, British children in British India learned an Indian language from their nurses and family servants. A second language can also be acquired in school. *Bilingualism* can also refer to the use of two languages in teaching, especially to foster learning in students trying to learn a new language. Advocates of bilingual education in the U.S. argue that it speeds learning in all subjects for children who speak a foreign language at home and prevents them from being marginalized in English-language schools. Detractors counter that it hinders such children from mastering the language of the larger society and limits their opportunities for employment and higher education.

Bill of Rights (1689) British law, one of the basic instruments of the British constitution. It incorporated the provisions of the Declaration of Rights, which William III and Mary II accepted upon taking the throne. Its main purpose was to declare illegal various practices of James II, such as the royal prerogative of dispensing with the law in certain cases. The result of a long struggle between the Stuart kings and the English people and Parliament, it made the monarchy clearly conditional on the will of Parliament and provided freedom from arbitrary government. It also dealt with the succession to the throne.

Bill of Rights, First 10 amendments to the Constitution of the United States, adopted as a group in 1791. They are a collection of guarantees of individual rights and of limitations on federal and state governments that derived from popular dissatisfaction with the limited guarantees of the Constitution. The first Congress submitted 12 amendments (drafted by James Madison) to the states, 10 of which were ratified. The 1st Amendment guarantees freedom of religion, speech, and the press and grants the right to petition for redress and to assemble peacefully. The 2nd Amendment guarantees the right of the people to keep and bear arms. The 3rd prohibits the quartering of soldiers in private dwellings in peacetime. The 4th protects against unreasonable search and seizure. The 5th establishes grand-jury indictment for serious offenses, protects against double jeopardy in criminal cases, and prohibits compelling testimony by a person against himself. The 6th establishes the rights of the accused to a speedy trial and an impartial jury and guarantees the right to legal counsel and to the obtaining of witnesses in his favour. The 7th preserves the right to trial by jury in serious civil suits and prohibits double jeopardy in civil cases. The 8th prohibits excessive bail and cruel and unusual punishment. The 9th states that enumeration of certain rights in the Constitution does not mean the abrogation of rights not mentioned. The 10th reserves to the states and people any powers not delegated to the federal government.

billiards, Any of various games played on a cloth-topped, cushion-railed rectangular table by driving small, hard balls against one another or into pockets with a long stick called a cue. Carom, or French billiards, is played with three balls, two white and one red, on a table without pockets. The object is to stroke the white cue ball so that it hits the two object balls in succession, scoring a carom (one point). English billiards is also played with three balls but on a pocketed table; it is scored in various ways. Snooker is another popular British billiards game. The principal billiards game in North America is pocket billiards, or pool. The Billiard Congress of America controls U.S. tournament play, including the U.S. Open Pockets Billiard Championship, regarded as the world championship.

binary code, Code used in digital computers, based on a binary number system in which there are only two possible states, off and on, usually symbolized by 0 and 1. Whereas in a decimal system, which employs 10 digits, each digit position represents a power of 10 (100, 1,000, etc.), in a binary system each digit position represents a power of 2 (4, 8, 16, etc.). A binary code signal is a series of electrical pulses that represent numbers, characters, and operations to be performed. A device called a clock sends out regular pulses, and components such as transistors switch on (1) or off (0) to pass or block the pulses. In binary code, each decimal number (0–9) is represented by a set of four binary digits, or bits. The four fundamental arithmetic operations (addition, subtraction, multiplication, and division) can all be reduced to combinations of fundamental Boolean algebraic operations on binary numbers.

binary star, Pair of stars in orbit around a common centre of gravity. Their relative sizes and brightnesses and the distance between them vary widely. Perhaps half of all stars in the Milky Way Galaxy are binaries or members of more complex multiple systems. Some binaries form a class of variable stars. Stars can be identified as binaries in various ways—visually by telescope, through spectroscopic observation, by changes in apparent brightness (when the dimmer star eclipses its companion), or by changes in the proper motion of the visible member (owing to the gravitational pull of the invisible companion).

binomial theorem, In algebra, a formula for expansion of the binomial $(x + y)$ raised to any positive integer power. A simple case is the expansion of $(x + y)^2$, which is $x^2 + 2xy + y^2$. In general, the expression $(x + y)^n$ expands to the sum of $(n + 1)$ terms in which the power of x decreases from n to 0 while the power of y increases from 0 to n in successive terms. The terms can be represented in factorial notation by the expression $[n!/(n - r)!r!)]x^{n-r}y^r$ in which r takes on integer values from 0 to n.

biodegradability, Capacity of a material to decompose by biological action. The term usually refers to the environmental breakdown of waste by microorganisms. Generally, plant and animal products are biodegradable, whereas mineral substances (e.g., metals, glass, plastics) are not. Local conditions, especially the presence or absence of oxygen, affect biodegradability. Disposal of nonbiodegradable waste is a primary source of pollution. Surgical materials made to be absorbed by the body are also called biodegradable.

biodiversity, Quantity of plant and animal species found in a given environment. Sometimes habitat diversity (the variety of places where organisms live) and genetic diversity (the variety of traits expressed within a species) are also considered types of biodiversity. The estimated 3–30 million species on Earth are divided unequally among the world's habitats, with 50–90% of the world's species living in tropical regions. The more diverse a habitat, the better chance it has of surviving a change or threat to it, because it is more likely to be able to make a balancing adjustment. Habitats with little biodiversity (e.g., Arctic tundra) are more vulnerable to change. The 1992 Earth Summit resulted in a treaty for the preservation of biodiversity.

bioengineering, Application of engineering principles and equipment to biology and medicine. It includes the development and fabrication of life-support systems for underwater and space exploration, devices for medical treatment, and instruments for monitoring biological processes. Development has been particularly rapid in the area of artificial organs, which culminated in the implantation of an artificial heart into a human being in 1982. Bioengineers also develop equipment that enables humans to maintain body functions in hostile environments, such as the space suits worn by astronauts during extravehicular maneuvers.

biofeedback, Information supplied instantaneously about an individual's own physiological processes. Data concerning cardiovascular activity (blood pressure and heart rate), temperature, brain waves, or muscle tension is monitored electronically and returned or "fed back" to the individual through a gauge on a meter, a light, or a sound. The goal is for the patient to use that biological data to learn to voluntarily control the body's reactions to stressful external events. A type of behaviour therapy, biofeedback training is sometimes used in combination with psychotherapy to help patients understand and change their habitual reactions to stress. Complaints treated through biofeedback include migraine headaches, gastrointestinal problems, high blood pressure, and epileptic seizures.

biofuel, Mixture of volatile, flammable hydrocarbons derived from plant material or animal waste and used as fuel. Some long-exploited biofuels, such as wood, can be used directly as a raw material that is burned to produce heat. The heat in turn can be used to run generators in a power plant to produce electricity. Sugars and starches from sugarcane, corn, and high-cellulose plants (such as switchgrass) can be converted into ethanol, which is used directly in internal-combustion engines or is mixed with gasoline (gasohol). Oils from plants such as the soybean or oil palm can be chemically processed and blended with petroleum diesel fuel to make biodiesel.

biography, Form of nonfictional literature whose subject is the life of an individual. The earliest biographical writings probably were funeral speeches and inscriptions. The origins of modern biography lie with Plutarch's moralizing lives of prominent Greeks and Romans and Suetonius's gossipy lives of the Caesars. Few biographies of common individuals were written until the 16th century. The major developments of English biography came in the 18th century, with such works as James Boswell's *Life of Johnson*. In modern times impatience with Victorian reticence and the development of psychoanalysis have sometimes led to a more penetrating and comprehensive understanding of biographical subjects.

bioinformatics, Science that links biological data with techniques for information storage, distribution, and analysis to support multiple areas of research. The data of bioinformatics include DNA sequences of genes or full genomes; amino acid sequences of proteins; and three-dimensional structures of proteins, nucleic acids, and protein–nucleic acid complexes. Database projects curate and annotate the data and then distribute it via the World Wide Web. Mining these data leads to scientific discoveries, enables the development of efficient algorithms for measuring sequence similarity in DNA from different sources, and facilitates the prediction of interactions between proteins.

biological rhythm, Periodic biological fluctuation in an organism corresponding to and in response to periodic environmental change, such as day and night or high and low tide. The internal mechanism that maintains this rhythm even without the apparent environmental stimulus is a "biological clock." When the rhythm is interrupted, the clock's adjustment is delayed, accounting for such phenomena as jet lag when traveling across time zones. Rhythms may have 24-hour (circadian rhythm), monthly, or annual cycles.

biological warfare, or GERM WARFARE, Military use of disease-producing or poisonous agents, and the means for defending against such agents. Biological warfare agents include many bacteria, such as those which cause anthrax, brucellosis, and typhus; viruses that cause diseases such as equine encephalitis; fungi such as rice blast, cereal rust, wheat smut, and potato blight; and toxins such as botulinum and ricin that are extracted from living organisms. Biological warfare dates from ancient times when warring groups would try to poison enemy soldiers with rotting or diseased corpses, infect cattle and horses, or spread contagion through civilian populations. Following the horrors of World War I, a 1925 Geneva Protocol prohibited the use of biological agents in warfare; however, this did not prevent Japan from using them in China during World War II. During the Cold War the Soviet Union as well as the U.S. and its allies built huge stockpiles of biological agents. Both sides signed the 1972 Biological Weapons Convention, which prohibits the production, stockpiling, or development of biological weapons and requires the destruction of existing stockpiles, but the Soviets conducted a clandestine program until the 1990s. Biological weapons programs can be concealed easily, and the 1972 convention contains no provisions for inspection and reporting. As a result, many states have been suspected of developing biological warfare agents, and some modern armed forces have prepared defensive measures. These include battlefield sensors, protective garments and masks, sterilizing agents, and vaccines.

biology, Study of living things and their vital processes. An extremely broad subject, biology is divided into branches. The current approach is based on the levels of biological organization involved (e.g., molecules, cells, individuals, populations) and on the specific topic under investigation (e.g., structure and function, growth and development). According to this scheme, biology's main subdivisions include morphology, physiology, taxonomy, embryology, genetics, and ecology, each of which can be further subdivided. Alternatively, biology can be divided into fields especially concerned with one type of living thing—for example, botany (plants), zoology (animals), ornithology (birds), entomology (insects), mycology (fungi), microbiology (microorganisms), and bacteriology (bacteria).

biome, Largest geographic biotic unit, a major community of plants and animals with similar requirements of environmental conditions. It includes various communities and developmental stages of communities and is named for the dominant type of vegetation, such as grassland or coniferous forest. Several similar biomes constitute a biome type; for example, the temperate deciduous forest biome type includes the deciduous forest biomes of Asia, Europe, and North America. The standard European term for biome is "major life zone."

biophysics, Discipline concerned with applications of the principles and methods of the physical sciences to biological problems. Biophysics deals with biological functions that depend on physical agents such as electricity or mechanical force, with the interaction of living organisms with physical agents such as light, sound, or ionizing radiation, and with interactions between living things and their environment as in locomotion, navigation, and communication. Its subjects include bone, nerve impulses, muscle, and vision as well as organic molecules, using such tools as paper chromatography and X-ray crystallography.

biopsy, Procedure in which cells or tissues are removed from a patient and examined. The sample may be obtained from any organ, by any of several methods, including suction through a needle, swabbing, scraping, endoscopy, and cutting out the entire structure or part of it to be tested. Biopsy is a standard step in distinguishing malignant from benign tumours and can provide other information for diagnosis, particularly concerning such organs as the liver or pancreas. Slides of the tissue are prepared and examined by microscope.

biosphere, Relatively thin life-supporting stratum of the earth's surface, extending from a few miles into the atmosphere to the deep-sea vents of the oceans. The biosphere is a global ecosystem that can be broken down into regional or local ecosystems, or biomes. Organisms in the biosphere are classified into trophic levels and communities.

biotechnology, The use of biology to solve problems and make useful products. The growth of the field is linked to the development in the 1970s of genetic engineering. Biotechnology merges biological information with computer technology to advance research in other areas, including nanotechnology and regenerative medicine. Today there are numerous commercial biotechnology firms that manufacture genetically engineered substances for a variety of mostly medical, agricultural, and ecological uses.

bipolar disorder, or MANIC-DEPRESSIVE PSYCHOSIS, Mental illness characterized by the alternation of manic and depressive states. Depression is the more common symptom, and many patients experience only a brief period of overoptimism and mild euphoria during the manic phase. The condition, which seems to be inheritable, probably arises from malregulation of the amines norepinephrine, dopamine, and 5-hydroxytryptamine. It is most commonly treated with lithium carbonate.

bird-of-paradise, or CRANE FLOWER, Ornamental plant (*Strelitzia reginae*) of the family Strelitziaceae. All five species of the genus *Strelitzia* are native to southern Africa. The large, showy *Strelitzia* flower has two erect, pointed petals and five stamens. One main bract, shaped like a boat, is green with red borders. It holds many long-stemmed orange and bright blue flowers, each resembling the crest and beak of a crane, giving the plant its common names.

bird of prey, Any member of the order Falconiformes (eagles, falcons, hawks, and vultures) or Strigiformes (owls). Falconiforms are also called raptors. They are active during the day, whereas owls are nocturnal. Condors and eagles are among the largest and strongest of flying birds. All birds of prey have a hook-tipped beak and sharp curved claws called talons. (Nonpredatory vultures have less-developed talons.) Despite the similarities between owls and raptors, many authorities believe they are not closely related but developed similar features because of their similar predatory lives.

bird-watching, or BIRDING, Observation or identification of wild birds in their natural habitat. Basic equipment includes binoculars, a field guide to aid identification, and a notebook for recording time and place of sightings. The lists of bird observations compiled by members of local bird-watching societies are often useful to scientists in determining dispersal, habitat, and migration patterns of the various species. Bird-watching is primarily a 20th-century phenomenon; before 1900 most students of birds had to shoot them in order to identify them. Its popularity grew through the publication of journals and books, in particular the field guides (beginning in 1934) of Roger Tory Peterson.

birth control, Voluntary limiting of human reproduction, using such means as contraception, sexual abstinence, surgical sterilization, and induced abortion. The term was coined in 1914–15 by Margaret Sanger. Medically, birth control is often advised when childbirth might endanger the mother's health or substantial risk exists of bearing a severely disabled child. Socially and economically, limitation of reproduction frequently reflects a desire to maintain or improve family living standards. Most religious leaders now generally agree that some form of fertility regulation is desirable, though the means are strongly debated.

birth defect, Genetic or trauma-induced abnormality present at birth. A more restrictive term than congenital disorder, it covers abnormalities that arise during the formation of an embryo's organs and tissues and does not include those caused by diseases (e.g., syphilis) that damage structures after they are formed.

birthmark, Unusual mark or blemish on the skin at birth. Most birthmarks are either hemangiomas or moles. They are usually harmless and many fade in childhood; those that do not can sometimes be removed by laser surgery or abrasion.

Biscay, Bay of, or GULF OF GASCONY French GOLFE DE GAS-COGNE Spanish GOLFO DE VIZCAYA, Inlet of the Atlantic Ocean, bounded by southwestern France and northwestern Spain. It has an area of about 86,000 sq mi (223,000 sq km) and a maximum depth of 15,525 ft (4,735 m). It is known for its rough seas. Rivers flowing into the bay include the Loire, Adour, and Garonne. Its ports include (in France) Brest, Nantes, and Bordeaux, and (in Spain) Bilbao, Santander, and Avilés; none can accommodate large vessels. French coastal resorts include La Baule, Biarritz, and Saint-Jean-de-Luz.

Bishkek, or PISHPEK, formerly (1926–91) FRUNZE, City (pop., 2008 est.: 794,300), capital of Kyrgyzstan. It lies on the Chu River just north of the Kyrgyz Mountains and near the Kazakhstan border. In 1825 the Uzbek khanate of Kokand established a fortress on the site, which in 1862 was captured by the Russians. The Russians mistakenly called it Pishpek. When the Kirgiz (Kyrgyz) Autonomous Soviet Socialist Republic was set up in 1926, the city became its capital and was renamed Frunze for a Red Army leader who was born there. It developed as an industrial city, especially in World War II (1939–45) when heavy industries from western Russia were moved there.

bishop, In some Christian churches, the chief pastor and overseer of a diocese, an area containing several congregations. From the 4th century AD until the Reformation, bishops held broad secular and religious powers, including the settling of disputes, ordination of clergy, and confirmation of church members. Some Christian churches (notably the Anglican, Roman Catholic, and Eastern Orthodox churches) continue the bishop's office and the doctrine of Apostolic succession. Others, including some Lutheran and Methodist churches, retain bishops but not the principle of apostolic succession; still others have abolished the office altogether. Popes, cardinals, archbishops, patriarchs, and metropolitans are gradations of bishops. In Roman Catholicism, the pope selects the bishop; in Anglicanism, the dean and chapter of the cathedral of the diocese elect the bishop; in Methodism a synod chooses the bishop.

Bismarck, Otto (Eduard Leopold), prince von (b. April 1, 1815, Schönhausen, Altmark, Prussia—d. July 30, 1898, Friedrichsruh, near Hamburg), Prussian statesman who founded the German Empire in 1871 and served as its chancellor for 19 years. Born into the Prussian landowning elite, Bismarck studied law and was elected to the Prussian Diet in 1849. In 1851 he was appointed Prussian representative to the federal Diet in Frankfurt. After serving as ambassador to Russia (1859–62) and France (1862), he became prime minister and foreign minister of Prussia (1862–71). When he took office, Prussia was widely considered the weakest of the five European powers, but under his leadership Prussia won a war against Denmark in 1864, the Seven Weeks' War (1866), and the Franco-Prussian War (1870–71). Through these wars he achieved his goal of political unification of a Prussian-dominated German Empire. Once the empire was established, he became its chancellor. The "Iron Chancellor" skillfully preserved the peace in Europe through alliances against France. Domestically, he introduced administrative and economic reforms but sought to preserve the status quo, opposing the Social Democratic Party and the Catholic church. When Bismarck left office in 1890, the map of Europe had been changed immeasurably. However, the German Empire, his greatest achievement, survived him by only 20 years because he had failed to create an internally unified people.

Bismarck Archipelago, Island group, western Pacific Ocean. Lying northwest of New Guinea, it forms part of Papua New Guinea. It has a total area of about 18,600 sq mi (48,200 sq km); its largest components include New Britain, New Ireland, the Admiralty Islands, and Lavongai (New Hanover). Annexed by Germany in 1884, it was named for Otto von Bismarck. Occupied by Australia in 1914, it was made a mandated territory of Australia in 1920. The group became part of the UN Trust Territory of New Guinea after World War II and part of Papua New Guinea when it attained independence in 1975.

bismuth, Semimetallic to metallic chemical element, chemical symbol Bi, atomic number 83. Hard, brittle, and lustrous, it has a distinctive gray-white colour with a reddish tinge. It is often found free in nature and also occurs in compounds and in mixed ores. Bismuth alloys are used (because of their low melting points) in making metal castings, special solders, automatic sprinkler heads, fuses, and many fire-detection devices. Bismuth phosphomolybdate is a catalyst in the production of acrylonitrile, an important raw material for fibres and plastics. Salts of bismuth are used in making soothing agents for digestive disorders (especially bismuth subsalicylate), in treating skin infections and injuries, and in lipstick, nail polish, and eye shadow, to which they impart a pearlescent quality.

bitumen, Mixture of tarlike hydrocarbons derived from petroleum. Black or brown, it varies from viscous to solid; the solid form is usually called asphalt. Bitumen occurs in nearly every part of the world and in nearly the whole range of geologic strata. The term may also refer to synthetic hydrocarbon compounds.

bituminous coal, or SOFT COAL, Most abundant form of coal. It is dark brown to black and has a relatively high heat value. Widely abundant and with the broadest range of commercial uses, it has long been used for steam generation in electric power plants and industrial boiler plants. Certain varieties are also used to make coke, a hard substance of almost pure carbon that is important for smelting iron ore. One major problem is that burning large quantities of bituminous coal that has a medium to high sulfur content contributes to air pollution and produces acid rain.

bivalve, Any member of the mollusk class Bivalvia, or Pelecypoda, characterized by having a two-halved (valved) shell. Clams, cockles, mussels, oysters, scallops, and shipworms are bivalves. Most are completely enclosed by the shell, the two valves of which are joined by an elastic ligament, and by two sheets of tissue called the mantle. Bivalves have no head. They feed on phytoplankton by pumping water across the gills and trapping food particles that are then moved to the mouth. Bivalves are found in most parts of the ocean from the intertidal zone to abyssal depths.

Biwa, Lake, Lake, west-central Honshu, Japan. It is Japan's largest lake, measuring 40 mi (64 km) long and up to 12 mi (19 km) wide, with an area of 259 sq mi (670 sq km). Its name refers to the musical instrument that the lake resembles in shape. Its sole outlet, the Yodo River, flows from its southern tip to Ōsaka Bay.

Lake Biwa is noted for its pearl culture industry. Its great scenic beauty, long a subject of Japanese poetry, makes it one of Japan's major tourist attractions.

Bjørnson, Bjørnstjerne (Martinius) (b. Dec. 8, 1832, Kvikne, Nor.—d. April 26, 1910, Paris, France), Norwegian writer, editor, and theatre director. He worked to stimulate national pride by linking Norwegian history and legend to modern ideals. Together with Henrik Ibsen, Alexander Kielland, and Jonas Lie, he is known as one of "the four great ones" of 19th-century Norwegian literature. He won the Nobel Prize for Literature in 1903. His poem "Yes, We Love This Land Forever" is the Norwegian national anthem.

Black Death, Fierce and widespread outbreak of plague, probably bubonic and pneumonic, that ravaged Europe during the 14th century. The epidemic originated in Asia and was transmitted to Europeans in 1347 when a Turkic army besieging a Genoese trading post in the Crimea catapulted plague-infested corpses into the town. It spread from the Mediterranean ports and ravaged all of Europe between 1347 and 1351. Renewed outbreaks occurred in 1361–63, 1369–71, 1374–75, 1390, and 1400. Towns and cities were more heavily hit than the countryside, and whole communities were sometimes destroyed. Much of Europe's economy was devastated. About one-third of the European population, or a total of 25 million people, died in the Black Death.

black-figure pottery, Type of Greek pottery that originated in Corinth c. 700 BC. The figures were painted in black pigment on the natural red clay ground. Finishing details were then incised into the black pigment, revealing the red ground. The great Attic painters (mid 6th century BC), most notably Exekias, developed narrative scene decoration and perfected the style. It continued to be popular until the advent of red-figure pottery (c. 530 BC).

Dionysus and satyrs, amphora painted in the black-figure style by the Amasis Painter, c. 540 BC; in the Antikenmuseum, Basel, Switz.
Courtesy of the Antikenmuseum, Basel, Switz.; photograph, Colorphoto Hans Hinz

Black Forest, German SCHWARZWALD, Mountain region, Baden-Württemberg, southwestern Germany. It extends in a fairly narrow strip about 100 mi (160 km) along the eastern bank of the upper Rhine River, from the Neckar River to the Swiss border. Its highest peak is Feldberg, at 4,897 ft (1,493 m). Its name comes from its dark interior, the higher parts being thickly forested with fir and pine. It is the source of the Neckar and Danube rivers. The setting of many of the Grimm brothers' fairy tales, it is famed for the beauty and charm of its villages and rolling hills. Winter sports are prominent in the area, which also has many mineral springs and watering places, including the spa town of Baden-Baden.

black hole, Cosmic body with gravity so intense that nothing, not even light, can escape. It is suspected to form in the death and collapse of a star that has retained at least three times the Sun's mass. Stars with less mass evolve into white dwarf stars or neutron stars. Details of a black hole's structure are calculated from Albert Einstein's general theory of relativity: a "singularity" of zero volume and infinite density pulls in all matter and energy that comes within an event horizon, defined by the Schwarzschild radius, around it. Black holes cannot be observed directly because they are small and emit no light. However, their enormous gravi-

tational fields affect nearby matter, which is drawn in and emits X rays as it collides at high speed outside the event horizon. Some black holes may have nonstellar origins. Astronomers speculate that supermassive black holes at the centres of quasars and many galaxies are the source of energetic activity that is observed. Stephen W. Hawking theorized the creation of numerous tiny black holes, possibly no more massive than an asteroid, during the big bang. These primordial "mini black holes" lose mass over time and disappear as a result of Hawking radiation. Although black holes remain theoretical, the case for their existence is supported by many observations of phenomena that match their predicted effects.

black humour, Humour marked by the use of morbid, ironic, or grotesquely comic episodes that ridicule human folly. The term came into common use in the 1960s to describe the work of novelists such as Joseph Heller, whose *Catch-22* (1961) is an outstanding example; Kurt Vonnegut, particularly in *Slaughterhouse Five* (1969); and Thomas Pynchon, in *V* (1963) and *Gravity's Rainbow* (1973). A film exemplar is Stanley Kubrick's *Dr. Strangelove* (1963). The term *black comedy* has been applied to some playwrights in the Theatre of the Absurd, especially Eugène Ionesco.

black market, Trading in violation of publicly imposed regulations such as rationing laws, laws against the sale of certain goods, and official rates of exchange among currencies. Black-market activity is common in wartime, when scarce goods and services are often strictly rationed. Black-market foreign-exchange transactions flourish in countries where convertible foreign currency is scarce and foreign exchange is tightly controlled.

Black Sea, Sea between Europe and Asia. Bordered by Ukraine, Russia, Georgia, Turkey, Bulgaria, and Romania, it has a maximum depth of 7,250 ft (2,210 m). The Black Sea proper has an area of 163,000 sq mi (422,000 sq km). It is connected with the Aegean Sea through the Bosporus, the Sea of Marmara, and the Dardanelles, and with the Sea of Azov by Kerch Strait. It receives many rivers, including the Danube, Dniester, Bug, Dnieper, Kuban, Kızıl, and Sakarya. The Crimean Peninsula extends into it from the north. Created when structural upheavals in Asia Minor split off the Caspian basin from the Mediterranean Sea, the Black Sea gradually became isolated; salinity is now less than half that of the world's oceans. Though long popular for its resorts, it has suffered severe pollution in recent decades.

black widow, Any of several black spiders in the genus *Latrodectus* with a venomous bite that is rarely fatal to humans. Black widow species are found worldwide, with three living in North America. In Australia it is called the redback. The females are shiny black, usually with a reddish hourglass-shaped design on the underside of the spherical abdomen and with a body about 1 in. (2.5 cm) long. The black widow preys on insects. The male, about one-fourth the female's size, is often killed and eaten by the female after mating (the source of its name).

Blackbeard, orig. (likely) EDWARD TEACH (b. c. 1680, Bristol?, Eng.—d. Nov. 22, 1718, Ocracoke Island, North Carolina), English pirate. He was probably a privateer in the West Indies until 1716. With his 40-gun warship, he preyed on shipping off the Virginia and Carolina coasts, sharing his prizes with the governor of the North Carolina colony in return for protection. He was eventually killed by a British naval force, and his head, with its great black beard, was affixed to the end of his bowsprit. According to legend, he left a great buried treasure; it has never been found and probably never existed.

Blackfoot, or BLACKFEET, Group of Algonquian-speaking Indian peoples in Alberta, Can., and Montana, U.S., comprising the Piegan (Pikuni), the Blood (Kainah), and the Siksika, or Blackfoot-proper. Together they are referred to as Siksika, or Blackfoot, a name thought to have derived from the discoloration of their moccasins with ashes. They were among the first Algonquians to move westward from timberland to open grassland and, later, among the first to acquire horses and firearms. They were known as the strongest and most aggressive military power on the northwestern plains. At the height of their power, in the first half of the 19th century, they held a vast territory extending from northern Saskatchewan to southwestern Montana. Each group was subdivided into hunting bands led by one or more chiefs. These bands wintered separately but came together in summer to celebrate the sun dance. For three decades, beginning in 1806, the Blackfoot prevented American and Canadian settlements from forming in their territory. They signed their first treaty with the U.S. in 1855, after which they were forced into farming and cattle raising. Blackfoot descendants numbered some 90,000 in the early 21st century.

In a Piegan Lodge, *photograph by Edward S. Curtis, c. 1910.*
Courtesy of the Edward E. Ayer Collection, The Newberry Library, Chicago

blackjack, or TWENTY-ONE, Card game whose object is to be dealt cards having a higher count than those of the dealer, up to but not exceeding 21. The dealer may use a single deck of 52 cards or two or more decks from a holder called a shoe. Aces count as 1 or 11, and face cards as 10. Depending on the rules used, bets may be placed before the deal, after each player has been dealt one card facedown, or after each player has received two cards facedown and the dealer has exposed one of his cards.

Blackshirts, Italian CAMICIE NERE, Armed squads of Italian Fascists under Benito Mussolini who wore black shirts as part of their uniform. The squads, first organized in 1919, targeted socialists, communists, republicans, and others. Hundreds of people were killed as the squads grew in number. In 1922 Blackshirts from all over Italy participated in the March on Rome. In 1923 the private Blackshirts were officially transformed into a national militia. With Mussolini's fall in 1943, the Blackshirts fell into disgrace.

Blackwell, Elizabeth (b. Feb. 3, 1821, Countership, Bristol, Gloucestershire, Eng.—d. May 31, 1910, Hastings, Sussex), British-born U.S. physician. Her family immigrated to the U.S. in 1832. She began her medical education by reading medical books and hiring private instructors. Medical schools rejected her applications until she was accepted at the Geneva Medical (later Hobart) College in 1847. Though ostracized, she graduated at the head of her class in 1849, becoming the first woman doctor in modern times and the first to gain her degree from a U.S. medical school. In 1857, despite much opposition, she established the New York Infirmary, staffed entirely by women, and she later added a full course of medical education for women. She was also a founder of the London School of Medicine for Women. Her sister

Emily (1826–1910) ran the infirmary for many years and served as dean and professor at the associated medical college.

Blanc, Mont, Italian MONTE BIANCO, Mountain massif, Europe. Located in the Alps on the borders of France, Italy, and Switzerland, it is Europe's highest peak, at 15,771 ft (4,807 m). It was first climbed in 1786 by Michel-Gabriel Paccard and Jacques Balmat. Mont Blanc Tunnel, 7.3 mi (11.7 km) long and one of the longest vehicular tunnels in the world, connects France with Italy. The region has become a major tourist and winter sports centre.

blank verse, Unrhymed verse, specifically unrhymed iambic pentameter, the preeminent dramatic and narrative verse form in English. It is also the standard form for dramatic verse in Italian and German. Adapted from Greek and Latin sources, it was introduced in Italy, then in England, where in the 16th century William Shakespeare transformed blank verse into a vehicle for the greatest English dramatic poetry, and its potential for grandeur was confirmed with John Milton's *Paradise Lost* (1667).

Blantyre, City (pop., 2008: 661,444), southern Malawi. It is one of the largest cities in Malawi and is the seat of the country's judiciary. Blantyre was founded in 1876 as a Church of Scotland mission station and named after explorer David Livingstone's Scottish birthplace. It became a British consular post in 1883 and attained municipal status in 1895; it is Malawi's oldest municipality. Its colonial trade laid the foundation for its present importance as Malawi's chief commercial centre. In 1956 Blantyre was united with nearby Limbe.

blast furnace, Vertical shaft furnace that produces liquid metals by the reaction of air introduced under pressure into the bottom of the furnace with a mixture of metallic ore, fuel, and flux fed into the top. Blast furnaces are used to produce pig iron from iron ore for subsequent processing into steel; they are also employed in processing lead, copper, and other metals. The current of pressurized air maintains rapid combustion. Blast furnaces were used in China as early as 200 BC, and appeared in Europe in the 13th century, replacing the bloomery process. Modern blast furnaces are 70–120 ft (20–35 m) high, have 20–45-ft (6–14-m) hearth diameters, use coke fuel, and can produce 1,000–10,000 tons (900–9,000 metric tons) of pig iron daily.

Blaue Reiter, Der (German: "The Blue Rider"), Organization of Expressionist artists formed in Munich in 1911 by Vasily Kandinsky and Franz Marc. The name derived from a volume of essays and illustrations they published. Other members included Paul Klee and August Macke (1887–1914). Influenced by Jugendstil, Cubism, and Futurism but lacking a specific program or philosophy, they exhibited with an international group, including Georges Braque, André Derain, and Pablo Picasso. The group disintegrated at the outbreak of World War I.

blight, Any of various plant diseases whose symptoms include sudden and severe yellowing, browning, spotting, withering, or dying of leaves, flowers, fruit, stems, or the entire plant. Usually the shoots and other young, rapidly growing tissues of a plant are attacked. Most blights are caused by bacteria or fungi; some result from drought. Fungal and bacterial blights are most likely under cool, moist conditions. Most economically important plants are susceptible to one or more blights. Measures taken to fight blight include destroying the infected plant parts; using disease-free seed or stock and resistant varieties; rotating crops; pruning and spacing plants for better air circulation; controlling pests that carry the fungus from plant to plant; avoiding overhead watering and working among wet plants; and, where needed, applying fungicides or antibiotics. Maintaining sanitary conditions is the most important measure for stopping the spread of the infestation.

blindness, Inability to see with one or both eyes. Transient blindness (blackout) can result from vertical acceleration causing high gravitational forces, glomerulonephritis (a kidney disease), or a clot in a blood vessel of the eye. Continuing blindness may arise from injuries or diseases of the eye (e.g., cataract, glaucoma), including the retina, the optic nerve, or the brain's visual centres. Many infectious, noninfectious, and parasitic systemic diseases can cause blindness. Sexually transmitted diseases and rubella in pregnant women can cause blindness in their infants.

blitzkrieg (German: "lightning war") Military tactic used by Germany in World War II, designed to create psychological shock and resultant disorganization in enemy forces through the use of surprise, speed, and superiority in matériel or firepower. The Germans tested the blitzkrieg during the Spanish Civil War in 1938 and against Poland in 1939, and used it in the successful invasions of Belgium, the Netherlands, and France in 1940. The German blitzkrieg coordinated land and air attacks—using tanks, dive-bombers, and motorized artillery—to paralyze the enemy principally by disabling its communications and coordination capacities.

blockade, Act of war whereby one party blocks entry to or departure from an enemy area, often a coast. Blockades are regulated by international law and custom, which require advance warning to neutral states and impartial application. Penalties for breach of blockade are seizure of ship and cargo and their possible condemnation as lawful prizes. Neutral ships may not be destroyed for blockade running.

Bloemfontein, City (pop., 2005 est.: 379,000), judicial capital of the Republic of South Africa. It is also the capital of Free State province. Founded in 1846 as a fort, it became the seat of the British-administered Orange River Sovereignty (1848–54) and later that of Orange Free State, an independent Boer republic formed in 1854. The failure of the Bloemfontein Conference (1899) resulted in the outbreak of the South African War. In the 20th century the city became a geographical transportation hub. Bloemfontein became part of the Mangaung Local Municipality in 2000.

blood, Circulatory fluid in multicellular animals. In many species it also carries hormones and disease-fighting substances. Blood picks up oxygen from the lungs and nutrients from the gastrointestinal tract and carries them to cells throughout the body for metabolism. It picks up carbon dioxide and other wastes from those cells and transports them to the lungs and excretory organs. Blood composition varies among species. Mammalian blood consists of plasma, red and white cells (erythrocytes and leukocytes), and platelets (thrombocytes). Blood disorders include polycythemia (abnormal increase in the number of circulating red blood cells), anemia, leukemia, and hemophilia.

blood analysis, Laboratory examination of the physical and chemical properties and components of a sample of blood. Analysis includes number of red and white blood cells (erythrocytes and leukocytes); red cell volume, sedimentation (settling) rate, and hemoglobin concentration; blood typing; cell shape and structure; hemoglobin and other protein structure; enzyme activity; and chemistry. Special tests detect substances characteristic of specific infections.

blood pressure, Force originating when the heart's pumping pushes the blood against the walls of the blood vessels. Their stretching and contraction help maintain blood flow. Usually measured over an arm or leg artery in humans, blood pressure is expressed as two numbers; normal adult blood pressure is about 120/80 mm of mercury. The higher number (systolic) is measured when the heart's ventricles contract and the lower (diastolic) when they relax.

blood transfusion, Transfer of blood taken from one person into the circulation of another to restore blood volume, increase hemoglobin levels, or combat shock. Once the blood-group antigens and antibodies were discovered, blood typing of donors and recipients rendered transfusion safe. In exchange transfusion, all or most of the blood is removed and replaced with another's blood. Undesirable reactions to transfusion are not uncommon.

blood typing, Classification of blood by inherited antigens associated with erythrocytes (red blood cells). The ABO blood-group system and Rh blood-group system are among those most commonly considered. Without identification of these factors, blood transfusion from an incompatible donor may result in destruction of red cells or coagulation. Blood typing also helps identify disorders such as erythroblastosis fetalis.

Bloody Sunday (1905) Massacre of peaceful demonstrators in Saint Petersburg, marking the beginning of the Russian Revolution of 1905. The priest Georgy Gapon (1870–1906), hoping to present workers' request for reforms directly to Nicholas II, arranged a peaceful march toward the Winter Palace. Police fired on the demonstrators, killing more than 100 and wounding several hundred more. The massacre was followed by strikes in other cities, peasant uprisings, and mutinies in the armed forces. The term "Bloody Sunday" was also used to describe the murder in Dublin, Ireland (Nov. 21, 1920), of 11 Englishmen suspected of being intelligence agents, by the Irish Republican Army; the Black and Tans took revenge and attacked spectators at a football (soccer) match, killing 12 and wounding 60. The term was used again in Londonderry (Derry) when on Jan. 30, 1972, 3 participants in a civil rights march were killed by British soldiers, who allegedly had been fired on by the marchers.

bloomery process, Process for iron smelting. In ancient times, smelting involved creating a bed of red-hot charcoal in a furnace to which iron ore mixed with more charcoal was added. The ore was chemically reduced, but, because primitive furnaces could not reach the melting temperature of iron, the product was a spongy mass of pasty globules of metal intermingled with a semiliquid slag. This hardly usable product, known as a bloom, may have weighed up to 10 lbs (5 kg). Repeated reheating and hot hammering eliminated much of the slag, creating wrought iron, a much better product. By the 15th century, many bloomeries used low shaft furnaces with waterpower to drive the bellows, and the bloom, which might weigh over 200 lbs (100 kg), was extracted through the top of the shaft. The final version of this kind of bloomery hearth survived in Spain until the 19th century. Another design, the high bloomery furnace, had a taller shaft and evolved into the Stückofen, which produced blooms so large they had to be removed through a front opening.

Bloomsbury group, A coterie of English writers, philosophers, and artists. The name was a reference to the Bloomsbury district of London, where between about 1907 and 1930 the group frequently met to discuss aesthetic and philosophical questions. Among the group were E.M. Forster, Lytton Strachey, Clive Bell, the painters Vanessa Bell (1879–1961) and Duncan Grant (1885–1978), John Maynard Keynes, the Fabian writer Leonard Woolf (1880–1969), and Virginia Woolf.

blue whale, Mottled, blue-gray baleen whale (*Balaenoptera musculus*), also called sulfur-bottom whale because of the yellowish diatoms on some individuals. The largest of all animals, the blue whale reaches a maximum length of about 100 ft (30 m) and a maximum weight of 150 tons (136,000 kg). It is found alone or in small groups in all oceans. In summer it feeds on krill in polar waters, and in winter it moves toward the equator to breed. It was once the most important of the commercially hunted baleen whales, and its populations were greatly reduced. Listed as an endangered species, it is now protected.

bluebell, Any plant of the genus *Hyacinthoides*, in the family Hyacinthaceae, native to Eurasia. Bluebell, or wild hyacinth (*H. nonscriptus* or *Endymion nonscriptus*), and Spanish bluebell (*H. hispanicus*), bearing clusters of bell-shaped blue flowers, are cultivated as garden ornamentals; some authorities place them in the

Wild hyacinth (Hyacinthoides nonscriptus).
M.T. Tanton—The National Audubon Society Collection/Photo Researchers

Blueberry.
Grant Heilman/EB Inc.

Western bluebird (Sialia mexicana)
Herbert Clarke

related genus *Scilla* of the same family. Many other plants are commonly known as bluebells, including species of the genera *Campanula*, *Eustoma*, *Polemonium*, and *Clematis*. In the U.S. the name bluebell is usually reserved for *Mertensia virginica*.

blueberry, Any of several shrubs, native to North America, of the genus *Vaccinium* in the heath family. They are prized for their sweet edible fruits, a source of vitamin C and iron. Blueberries grow only in highly acidic and well-drained but moist soils. The highbush blueberry (*V. corymbosum*), economically and ornamentally the most important species, is in the U.S. cultivated primarily in Maine, New Jersey, southwestern Michigan, and eastern North Carolina.

bluebird, Any of three North American bird species (songbird genus *Sialia*) of the chat-thrush group. The eastern bluebird (*S. sialis*), which is 5.5 in. (14 cm) long, and the western bluebird (*S. mexicana*) are red-breasted forms found east and west of the Rockies, respectively. The mountain bluebird (*S. currucoides*), also found in the West, is all blue. Bluebirds arrive from the south in earliest spring. They live in open country and woodlands and nest in holes in trees or in fence posts and bird boxes.

bluegrass, In music, a country-music style that emerged after World War II. It is a direct descendant of the string-band music played by groups such as the Carter Family. Bluegrass is distinguished from its predecessors by its more syncopated rhythm, its high-pitched tenor (lead) vocals, its tight harmonies, its driving rhythms, and a strong influence of jazz and blues. A very prominent place is given to the banjo, always played in the unique three-finger style developed by Earl Scruggs. Mandolin and fiddle are generally featured, and traditional square-dance tunes, religious songs, and ballads furnish much of the repertory. Bluegrass was originated by and got its name from Bill Monroe and his Blue Grass Boys. From the late 1940s on, it continued to grow in popularity; from the 1970s an influx of younger musicians brought some influence from rock music.

blues, Secular musical form incorporating a repeating harmonic structure with melodic emphasis on the flatted or "blue" third and seventh notes of the scale. The specific origins of the blues are not known, but elements of the music of former slaves include the call-and-response pattern and syncopated rhythms of spirituals and work songs. The codification of the structure of the blues occurred in the early 20th century, most commonly as a 12-bar phrase using the chords of the first, fourth, and fifth degrees of the major scale. Its origins as a primarily vocal form induced instrumental per-

formers to imitate the human voice with "bent" notes. Lyric stanzas are usually in three lines, the words of the second generally repeating those of the first. The elaboration of the rural blues from Texas and the Mississippi delta established both lyric and instrumental traditions, often featuring speech-like inflection and guitar accompaniment. The bandleader W.C. Handy's compositions brought blues elements to the popular music of the first decades of the century. The first blues recordings, in the early 1920s, featured singers such as Ma Rainey and Bessie Smith using jazz accompanists; their style would become known as classic blues. The highly personal interpretations and improvisation of the blues, combined with elements of its structure and inflection, served as the foundation for jazz, rhythm and blues, and rock music.

Bluestocking, In mid-18th-century England, any of a group of women who met to discuss literature. Attempting to replace the playing of cards and such social activities with more intellectual pursuits, they held "conversations" to which they invited men of letters and members of the aristocracy with literary interests. The term probably originated when Mrs. Elizabeth Vesey invited the learned Benjamin Stillingfleet to one of her parties; he declined, saying he lacked appropriate dress, until she told him to come "in his blue stockings"—the ordinary worsted stockings he was wearing at the time. The word *bluestocking* came to be applied derisively to a woman who affects literary or learned interests.

B'nai B'rith (Hebrew: "Sons of the Covenant") Oldest and largest Jewish service organization. Founded in New York City in 1843, it now has men's lodges, women's chapters, and youth organizations around the world. Its goals include defending human rights, aiding Jewish college students (mainly through the Hillel Foundation), sponsoring educational programs for adult and youth groups, helping victims of natural disasters, supporting hospitals and philanthropic institutions, and promoting the welfare of Israel. In 1913 it established the Anti-Defamation League to combat anti-Semitism.

Bo Juyi, or PO CHÜ-I (b. 772, Xinzheng, China—d. 846, Luoyang), Chinese poet of the Tang dynasty. He began composing poetry at age 5, and at age 28 he passed the examinations for the Chinese civil service. He rose steadily in official life and became the informal leader of a group of poets who rejected the courtly style of the time, believing that poetry should have a moral and social purpose. His satirical ballads and poems of social protest often took the form of free verse based on old folk ballads. He was revered in both China and Japan, where his poems, notably the "Song of Everlasting Sorrow," became material for other literary works.

boa, Any of about 60 species of stout-bodied snakes (subfamily Boinae, family Boidae) found in both the Old and New Worlds, mostly in warm regions. Species vary in length from about 8 in. (20 cm) to more than 25 ft (7.5 m). Most are terrestrial or semiaquatic; some live in trees. Most species have blotches and diamonds on their brown, green, or yellowish body. Boas bite their prey, then kill by wrapping their body around the prey and crushing it. Several species have heat-sensitive lip pits for detecting warm-blooded prey, and most bear live young. Contrary to folklore, boas are not dangerous to humans.

bobsledding, Sport of sliding down a winding ice-covered run on a large metal sled (bobsled). The sled is equipped with two pairs of runners, a long seat for two or more (usually four) people, a steering wheel or steering ropes, and a hand brake. Bobsledding originated in Switzerland in the 1890s and was included in the first Olympic Winter Games in 1924. Championship competitions are held each year. Bob runs are typically about 4,920 ft (1,500 m) long, with 15–20 banked turns. Four-person sleds attain speeds approaching 100 mph (160 kph).

Boccaccio, Giovanni (b. 1313, Paris, France—d. Dec. 21, 1375, Certaldo, Tuscany), Italian poet and scholar. His life was full of difficulties and occasional bouts of poverty. His early works include *The Love Afflicted* (*c.* 1336), a prose work in five books, and *The Book of Theseus* (*c.* 1340), an ambitious epic of 12 cantos. He is best known for his *Decameron*, a masterpiece of classical Italian prose that had an enormous influence on literature throughout Europe. A group of 100 earthy tales united by a frame story, it was probably composed 1348–53. After this period he turned to humanist scholarship in Latin. With Petrarch, he laid the foundations for Renaissance humanism, and through his writings in Italian he helped raise vernacular literature to the level of the classics of antiquity.

Bode's law, Rule giving the approximate distances of planets from the Sun. First announced in 1766 by the German Johann Daniel Titius (b. 1729—d. 1796), it was popularized, from 1772, by his countryman Johann Elert Bode (b. 1747—d. 1826). It may be given as follows: To each number in the sequence 0, 3, 6, 12, 24, and so on, add 4 and divide the result by 10. The answers closely approximate the distances from the Sun, in astronomical units, of the first seven planets. Bode's law also suggested that a planet should be found between Mars and Jupiter, where the asteroid belt was later discovered. Once thought to have some significance regarding the formation of the solar system, it is now regarded as a numerological curiosity.

bodhi (Sanskrit and Pali: "awakening" or "enlightenment") In Buddhism, the final enlightenment that ends the cycle of death and rebirth and leads to nirvana. This awakening transformed Siddhartha Gautama into the historical Buddha. Bodhi is achieved by ridding oneself of false beliefs and the hindrance of passions through the discipline of the Eightfold Path. Though not supported in canonical texts, commentaries give a threefold classification of bodhi: that of a perfectly enlightened one, or a Buddha; that of an independently enlightened one; and that of an arhat.

bodhi tree, or BO TREE, In Buddhism, the fig tree under which the Buddha sat when he attained enlightenment (bodhi) at Bodh Gaya (near Gaya, India). The tree growing on the site now is believed to be a descendant of the original, planted from a cutting of a tree in Sri Lanka that had been propagated from the original; both trees are sites of pilgrimage for Buddhists. The bo tree or a representation of its leaf has often been used as a symbol of the Buddha.

bodhisattva, Term for the historical Buddha Gautama prior to his enlightenment as well as for other individuals destined to become buddhas. In Mahayana Buddhism the bodhisattva postpones attainment of nirvana in order to alleviate the suffering of others. The ideal supplanted the Theravada Buddhist ideals of the arhat and the self-enlightened buddha, which Mahayana deemed selfish. The number of bodhisattvas is theoretically limitless, and the title has been applied to great scholars, teachers, and Buddhist kings. Celestial bodhisattvas (e.g., Avalokitesvara) are considered manifestations of the eternal Buddha and serve as savior figures and objects of personal devotion, especially in East Asia.

bodybuilding, Developing of the physique through exercise and diet, often for competitive exhibition. Bodybuilding aims at displaying pronounced muscle tone and exaggerated muscle mass and definition for overall aesthetic effect. Weight training is the principal form of exercise used; high-protein foods and vitamin and mineral supplements contribute to the diet. Bodybuilding competition grew largely out of 19th-century European strongman theatrical and circus acts. The first important international competition was the Mr. Universe contest, founded in 1947. It was followed in 1965 by the even more prestigious Mr. Olympia contest. Competition for women began in the 1970s. In 1998 bodybuilding was granted provisional status by the International Olympic Committee. The use of steroids to enhance performance, though generally forbidden, has long been common among bodybuilders.

bog iron ore, Iron ore consisting of hydrated iron oxide minerals such as limonite and goethite formed by precipitation of groundwater flowing into wetlands. Bacterial action contributes to formation of the ore. Economically useful deposits can regrow within 20 years after harvesting. Bog iron was widely used as a source of iron in the past.

Boğazköy, or BOĞAZKALE, Village, north-central Turkey. Located about 90 mi (145 km) east of Ankara, it is on the ruins of the ancient Hittite capital of Hattusas (Hattusha). The site contains archaeological remains, including temples, city gates, and walls, associated with the powerful Hattian dynasty (*c.* 16th–12th century BCE) and was later described by Herodotus. Excavations conducted during the 20th century uncovered hundreds of cuneiform tablets attesting to the ancient city's importance. Hattusas was designated a UNESCO World Heritage site in 1986.

Bogotá, in full CAPITAL DISTRICT OF SANTAFÉ DE BOGOTÁ, City (pop., 2003 est.: 6,850,505), capital of Colombia. It lies on a plateau east of the Andes Mountains. European settlement began in 1538 when Spanish conquistadores overran Bacatá, the main seat of the Chibcha Indians; the name was soon corrupted to Bogotá. It became the capital of the Viceroyalty of New Granada and a centre of Spanish colonial power in South America. It was the scene of revolt against Spanish rule (1810–11), and the revolutionary leader Simón Bolívar took the city in 1819. It became the capital of the confederation of Gran Colombia; when that entity was dissolved in 1830, it remained the capital but of New Granada and later the Republic of Colombia. Today Bogotá is an industrial, commercial, educational, and cultural centre.

Bohemian school, School of visual arts that flourished in and around Prague in the later 14th century. Charles IV attracted artists and scholars to Prague from all over Europe. French and Italian manuscripts inspired a local school of book illumination. Though most of the painters are anonymous, their achievements in panel painting and fresco had an important influence on German Gothic art. A vital Bohemian tradition in architecture provided the impetus for the great German Gothic architecture of the 15th century.

Resurrection, *panel painting by the Master of Wittingau, c. 1380–90; in the National Gallery, Prague.*
Giraudon/Art Resource, New York

Bohr, Niels (Henrik David) (b. Oct. 7, 1885, Copenhagen, Den.—d. Nov. 18, 1962, Copenhagen), Danish physicist. He studied the structure of the atom with J.J. Thomson and Ernest Rutherford at the universities of Cambridge and Manchester. He was among the first to see the importance of an element's atomic number and postulated that any atom could exist only in a discrete set of states characterized by definite values of energy. He became the first to apply the quantum theory to atomic and molecular structure, and his concept of the atomic nucleus was a key step in understanding such processes as nuclear fission. From 1920 to 1962 he directed the newly created Institute for Theoretical Physics in Copenhagen. His work on atomic theory won him a Nobel Prize for Physics in 1922. He was president of the Royal Danish Academy from 1939 until his death. Though he contributed to atomic bomb research in the U.S. during World War II, he later dedicated himself to the cause of arms control. He received the first U.S. Atoms for Peace Award in 1957. Element 107, bohrium, is named in his honour. His son Aage Niels Bohr shared the 1975 Nobel Prize for Physics with Ben Mottelson and James Rainwater for their work on atomic nuclei.

boil, or FURUNCLE, or FURUNCULOSIS, Inflamed pus-filled swelling due to staphylococcus skin infection at a hair follicle. It is painful and feels hard. Boils usually occur in hairy areas exposed to friction and maceration. Scratching an existing skin disorder may introduce staphylococci on the skin into hair follicles and cause a boil to arise. A carbuncle occurs when several adjoining boils merge. Healing requires discharging the pus. Treatment involves antibiotics.

boiling point, Temperature at which a liquid is converted to vapour when heated. At the boiling point, addition of heat results in the transformation of the liquid into its vapour without an increase in temperature. A liquid's boiling point varies according to the liquid's characteristics and the applied pressure. Water at standard atmospheric pressure, or sea level, boils at 212 °F (100 °C), while ethanol boils at about 172 °F (78 °C). At higher altitudes, boiling points are lower and foods can take longer to cook; pressure cookers can be used to increase the pressure so that the boiling point is raised.

bok choy, or CHINESE MUSTARD, *Brassica chinensis*, one of two types of Chinese cabbage. It has glossy dark green leaves and thick, crisp white stalks in a loose head. Its yellow-flowering centre is especially prized.

Bolívar, Simón, known as THE LIBERATOR (b. July 24, 1783, Caracas, New Granada—d. Dec. 17, 1830, near Santa Maria, Colombia), South American soldier and statesman who led the revolutions against Spanish rule in New Granada (now Colombia, Venezuela, and Ecuador), Peru, and Upper Peru (now Bolivia). The son of a Venezuelan aristocrat, Bolívar received a European education. Influenced by European rationalism, he joined Venezuela's independence movement and became a prominent political and military leader. The revolutionaries expelled Venezuela's Spanish governor (1810) and declared the nation's independence in 1811. The young republic was defeated by the Spanish in 1814, and Bolívar went into exile. In 1819 he undertook a daring attack on New Granada, leading some 2,500 men over routes considered impassable. Taking the Spanish by surprise, he defeated them quickly. With the help of Antonio Sucre, he secured the independence of Ecuador in 1822. He completed José de San Martín's revolutionary work in Peru, freeing that country in 1824. On Bolívar's orders, Sucre liberated Upper Peru (1825). As president of both Colombia (1821–30) and Peru (1823–29), Bolívar oversaw the creation in 1826 of a league of Hispanic American states, but the new states soon began warring among themselves. Less successful at ruling countries than at liberating them, Bolívar exiled himself and died on his way to Europe.

Bolivia, officially REPUBLIC OF BOLIVIA, Country, west-central South America. Area: 424,164 sq mi (1,098,581 sq km). Population: (2011 est.) 10,088,000. Capitals: La Paz (administrative), Sucre (judicial). The population consists of three principal groups: Indians, largely Aymara and Quechua; mestizos; and descendants of Europeans. Languages: Spanish, 36 indigenous languages (all official). Religions: Christianity (predominantly Roman Catholic; also Protestant); also vestiges of pre-Columbian religion. Currency: boliviano. Bolivia may be divided into three major regions. The southwestern highlands, or Altiplano, where Lake Titicaca is located, extends through southwestern Bolivia. It is enclosed by the second region, the western and eastern branches of the Andes Mountains. Much of the eastern branch is heavily forested terrain, with many deep river valleys; the western branch is a high plateau bordered by volcanoes, including the country's highest peak, Mount Sajama, which rises to 21,463 ft (6,542 m). The third region is a lowland area that comprises the northern and eastern two-

thirds of the country; its rivers include the Guaporé, Mamoré, Beni, and upper Pilcomayo. Bolivia has a developing mixed economy based on the production of natural gas and agricultural foodstuffs. It is a unitary multiparty republic with two legislative houses; its head of state and government is the president. The Bolivian highlands were the location of the advanced Tiwanaku culture in the 7th–11th centuries and, with its passing, became the home of the Aymara, an Indian group conquered by the Inca in the 15th century. The Inca were overrun by the invading Spanish conquistadores under Francisco Pizarro in the 1530s. By 1600 Spain had established the cities of Charcas (now Sucre), La Paz, Santa Cruz, and what would become Cochabamba and had begun to exploit the silver wealth of Potosí. Bolivia flourished in the 17th century, and for a time Potosí was the largest city in the Americas. By the end of the century, the mineral wealth had been depleted. Talk of independence began as early as 1809, but not until 1825 were Spanish forces finally defeated. Bolivia shrank in size when it lost Atacama province to Chile in 1884 at the end of the War of the Pacific and again when it lost most of Gran Chaco to Paraguay in 1938 as a result of the Chaco War. One of South America's poorest countries, Bolivia was plagued by governmental instability for much of the 20th century. Social and economic tension continued in the early 21st century, fueled by resistance to government efforts to eradicate the growth of coca (from which the narcotic cocaine is derived), by unrest among Bolivia's Indians, and by disagreements over how to exploit the country's vast natural gas reserves.

Böll, Heinrich (Theodor) (b. Dec. 21, 1917, Cologne, Ger.—d. July 16, 1985, Bornheim-Merten, near Cologne, W.Ger.), German writer. As a soldier in World War II he fought on several fronts, a central experience in the development of his antiwar, nonconformist views. His ironic novels on the travails of German life during and after the war captured the changing psychology of the German nation. He became a leading voice of the German left. Among his works are *Acquainted with the Night* (1953), *Billiards at Half-Past Nine* (1959), *The Clown* (1963), *Group Portrait with Lady* (1971), and *The Lost Honor of Katharina Blum* (1974). He won the Nobel Prize for Literature in 1972.

boll weevil, Small beetle (*Anthonomus grandis*) found almost everywhere cotton is cultivated. It is the most serious cotton pest in North America. Adults vary in size according to how much food they received as larvae, but they average about 0.25 in. (6 mm) long, including the long, curved snout. In the spring adults deposit eggs in cotton buds or fruit. After hatching, the larvae live within the cotton boll, destroying the seeds and surrounding fibres. Because the larvae and pupae remain inside the cotton bolls, they cannot be

*Boll weevil (*Anthonomus grandis)
Harry Rogers

killed with insecticides. The boll weevil destroys an estimated three to five million bales of cotton annually.

Bollywood, Indian moviemaking industry that began in Bombay (now Mumbai) in the 1930s and developed into an enormous film empire. Bombay Talkies, launched in 1934 by Himansu Rai, spearheaded the growth of Indian cinema. Throughout the years, several classic genres emerged from Bollywood: the historical epic, notably *Mughal-e-azam* (1960; "The Great Mughal"); the curry western, such as *Sholay* (1975; "The Embers"); the courtesan film, such as *Pakeezah* (1972; "Pure Heart"), which highlights stunning cinematography and sensual dance choreography; and the mythological movie, represented by *Jai Santoshi Maa* (1975; "Hail Santoshi Maa"). Star actors, rather than the films themselves, have accounted for most box-office success. Standard features of Bollywood films include formulaic story lines, expertly choreographed fight scenes, spectacular song-and-dance routines, emotion-charged melodrama, and larger-than-life heroes. At the beginning of the 21st century, Bollywood produced as many as 1,000 feature films annually, and international audiences began to develop among Asians in the U.K. and the U.S.

Bologna, City (pop., 2004 est.: 373,539), capital of Emilia-Romagna region, northern Italy. Located north of Florence, it lies at the northern foot of the Apennines. Originally the Etruscan town of Felsina, it became a Roman military colony *c.* 190 BC. It was subject to the Byzantine exarchate of Ravenna from the 6th century AD. It became a free commune in the 12th century. Incorporated into the Papal States in 1506, it was the scene of the crowning of Charles V in 1530. After a brief period of French occupation, it was restored to the Papal States in 1815, and in 1860 it was united to the Kingdom of Italy. The University of Bologna is among Europe's oldest. The city is a road and rail centre for traffic between northern and southern Italy. It is the site of excellent medieval and Renaissance architecture and is famous for its cuisine. Locally, it was governed by leftists in the second half of the 20th century.

Bologna, University of, Oldest university in Europe, founded in Bologna, Italy, in 1088. It became in the 12th–13th centuries the principal centre for studies in civil and canon law, and it served as a model for the organization of universities throughout Europe. Its faculties of medicine and philosophy were formed *c.* 1200. The faculty of science was developed in the 17th century. In the 18th century women were admitted as students and teachers. The modern university includes faculties of law, political science, economics, letters and philosophy, natural sciences, agriculture, medicine, and engineering.

Bolognese school, Works produced and theories expounded by the Academy of the Progressives, founded in Bologna *c.* 1582 by Lodovico, Agostino, and Annibale Carracci. In reaction against Mannerism, they advocated drawing directly from life. Among their leading students were Domenichino and Guido Reni. Their clear, simple pictures accorded well with the artistic demands of the Counter-Reformation, which wanted works of art to be immediately comprehensible. What began as a regional movement became one of the most influential forces in 17th-century art.

Bolshevik (Russian: "member of the majority") Member of the wing of the Russian Social-Democratic Workers' Party led by Vladimir Ilich Lenin that seized control in the Russian Revolution of 1917. The group arose in 1903 when Lenin's followers insisted that party membership be restricted to professional or full-time revolutionaries. Though they joined with their rivals, the Mensheviks ("members of the minority"), in the Russian Revolution of 1905, the two groups later split, and in 1912 Lenin formed his own party. Its appeal grew among urban workers and soldiers during World War I. .

Bolshoi, Theatre complex in Moscow where concerts, opera, ballet, and dramatic works are presented. The institution (whose name means "Large") dates back to 1776, when Catherine II licensed a company to give all theatrical performances in Moscow; its scope soon expanded to include opera and dance as well as drama. The original complex was built in 1825; it was rebuilt after a fire in 1853. The performing companies have changed over time, but the institution and the rebuilt edifice have survived.

Bolshoi Ballet, Leading ballet company of Russia, noted for elaborate productions of 19th-century classical ballets. The company was formed in 1776 and took the name of its home, Moscow's Bolshoi Theatre, in 1825. Its influential choreographers included Marius Petipa, Carlo Blasis, and Aleksandr Gorsky. Yuri Grigorovich was artistic director from 1964 to 1995. Its many suc-

cessful tours have introduced its outstanding dancers, including Yekaterina Geltzer, Vasily Tikhomirov, Galina Ulanova, and Maya Plisetskaya, to audiences worldwide.

bomber, Military aircraft designed to drop bombs on surface targets. Aerial bombardment can be traced to the Italo-Turkish War (1911), in which an Italian pilot dropped grenades on two Turkish targets. In World War I zeppelins and large two- to four-engined biplanes were used as strategic bombers. In the 1930s small dive bombers were developed; they caused great destruction and panic in the Spanish Civil War and early in World War II. The latter conflict saw further development of heavy strategic bombers, which were used to destroy targets in the enemy's home territory; meanwhile, smaller fighter-bombers supported ground troops on the battlefield. After the war, jet-propelled long-range bombers carrying nuclear bombs were important to Cold War strategy, and they also dropped conventional bombs during the Vietnam War, the Persian Gulf War, and the Afghan conflicts. Efforts to evade increasingly sophisticated electronic early-warning systems have culminated in the development of U.S. stealth bombers, but cheaper and smaller jet fighter-bombers, equipped with electronic sensors and guided "smart" bombs, have proved effective in conflicts ranging from the Balkans to the Middle East.

Bon, Popular annual festival in Japan, usually observed July 13–15, in honor of the spirits of deceased family members and of all the dead. As at the New Year festival, the dead are believed to return to their birthplaces. Memorial stones are cleaned, dances performed, and paper lanterns and fires are lit to welcome the dead and to bid them farewell when their visit ends.

Bon, Indigenous religion of the Tibet Autonomous Region of China. It was originally concerned with magical propitiation of demonic forces, and its practices included blood sacrifices. It later developed a cult of divine kingship (with kings regarded as manifestations of the sky divinity), reformulated in Tibetan Buddhism as the reincarnation of lamas. Bon's order of oracular priests had their counterpart in Buddhist soothsayers, and its gods of air, earth, and underworld in the lesser Tibetan Buddhist deities. Though its religious supremacy ended in the 8th century, Bon survives in many aspects of Tibetan Buddhism and as a living religion on Tibet's northern and eastern frontiers.

bond, In finance, loan contract issued by local, state, and national governments and by private corporations, specifying an obligation to return borrowed funds. The issuer promises to pay interest on the debt when due (usually semiannually) at a stipulated percentage of the face value and to redeem the face value of the bond at maturity in legal tender. Bonds usually indicate a debt of substantial size and are issued in more formal fashion than promissory notes, ordinarily under seal. Government bonds may be backed by taxes, or they may be revenue bonds, backed only by revenue from the specific project (toll roads, airports, etc.) to which they are committed. Bonds are rated based on the issuer's creditworthiness. The ratings, assigned by independent rating agencies, generally run from AAA to D; bonds with ratings from AAA to BBB are regarded as suitable for investment.

bonding, Any of the interactions that account for the association of atoms into molecules, ions, crystals, metals, and other stable species. When atoms' nuclei and electrons interact, they tend to distribute themselves so that the total energy is lowest; if the energy of a group arrangement is lower than the sum of the components' energies, they bond. The physics and mathematics of bonding were developed as part of quantum mechanics. The number of bonds an atom can form—its valence—equals the number of electrons it contributes or receives. Covalent bonds form molecules; atoms bond to specific other atoms by sharing an electron pair between them. If the sharing is even, the molecule is not polar; if it is uneven, the molecule is an electric dipole. Ionic bonds are the extreme of uneven sharing; certain atoms give up electrons, becoming cations. Other atoms take up the electrons and become anions. All the ions are held together in a crystal by electrostatic forces. In crystalline metals a diffuse electron sharing bonds the atoms (metallic bonding). Other types of bonding include hydrogen bonding; bonds in aromatic compounds; coordinate covalent bonds; multicentre bonds, exemplified by boranes (boron hydrides), in which more than two atoms share electron pairs; and the bonds in coordination complexes, still poorly understood.

bone, Rigid connective tissue of vertebrates, consisting of cells embedded in a hard matrix. Bones serve as the body's supporting framework, provide muscle-attachment points for movement, protect the internal organs, house the blood-cell formation system (red bone marrow), and hold about 99% of the calcium vital to many body processes. Bone consists of a matrix of crystals of calcium, chiefly the phosphate and carbonate, embedded among collagen fibres, providing strength and elasticity, and bone cells (less than 5% of its volume). An external layer of compact bone surrounds a central area of spongy bone, except at the marrow cavity. Bone does not grow by cell division; instead, different types of bone cells generate bone matrix, break it down, and maintain it. Bone is remodeled by this process, which strengthens it in areas under greatest stress, permits healing of fractures, and helps regulate calcium levels in body fluid. The process also causes underutilized bone, as in an immobilized limb, to atrophy. Bone disorders include rheumatoid arthritis, osteoarthritis, rickets, osteoporosis, and tumours. Bone can fracture suddenly or over time, as in stress fractures.

bone china, Hard-paste porcelain containing bone ash. It was developed by Josiah Spode (1754–1827) in England c. 1800. The addition of bone ash to china stone and china clay (i.e., hard china) made bone china easier to manufacture; it is stronger, does not chip easily, and has an ivory-white colour that lends itself to decoration. Other factories (Minton, Derby, Worcester, Wedgwood, Rockingham) adopted the formula in the early 19th century. Bone china remains popular for tableware in Britain and the U.S.

Wedgwood bone china plate, Staffordshire, 1815–20; in the Victoria and Albert Museum, London.

Courtesy of the Victoria and Albert Museum, London; photograph, EB Inc.

bone marrow, or MYELOID TISSUE, Soft, gelatinous tissue that fills bone cavities. Red bone marrow contains stem cells, progenitor cells, percursor cells, and functional blood cells. Lymphocytes mature in the lymphoid organs. All other blood-cell formation occurs in red marrow, which also takes part in destruction of old erythrocytes (red blood cells). Yellow bone marrow mainly stores fats. Because the leukocytes (white blood cells) produced in bone marrow are involved in immune defenses, marrow transplants can treat some types of immunodeficiency. Radiation and some anticancer drugs can damage marrow and impair immunity. Bone-marrow examination helps diagnose diseases related to blood and blood-forming organs.

Bonn, City (pop., 2002 est: city, 306,000; metro. area, 878,700), Germany. Located on the Rhine River south of Cologne, it was, until 1990, the capital of West Germany. An old settlement that predated the coming of the Romans, its name was continued in Castra Bonnensia, a 1st-century Roman fortress. By the 9th century it had become the Frankish town of Bonnburg. It grew from the 13th century, becoming capital of the Electorate of Cologne. In 1815 Bonn was awarded to Prussia by the Congress of Vienna, and by the late 19th century it was a fashionable residential town. It was bombed heavily in World War II; its postwar redevelopment was accelerated when in 1949 it was chosen as West Germany's

capital. With Germany's reunification in 1990, the national capital was moved to Berlin. Bonn was the birthplace of Ludwig van Beethoven.

bonobo, Species (*Pan paniscus*) of great ape. It was once considered a subspecies of the chimpanzee, which it closely resembles in size, appearance, and way of life. Its range, the lowland rainforests of central Congo (Kinshasa), is more restricted than that of the chimpanzee, and it has longer, more slender arms, a more slender body, and a less protruding face. Bonobos eat mainly fruits but also leaves, seeds, grass, and small animals. They form communities of 50–120 individuals. A striking feature of their social lives is that they engage in sexual activity with great frequency, often as a means of settling quarrels, and with little regard for gender or age. Populations are shrinking, largely because of hunting and habitat destruction, and bonobos are an endangered species.

bonsai, (Japanese: "tray planting") Living dwarf tree or trees; also, the art of training and growing them in containers. Bonsai specimens are ordinary trees and shrubs, not hereditary dwarfs; they are dwarfed by a system of pruning roots and branches and training branches by tying them with wire. The art originated in China but has been pursued and developed primarily by the Japanese. The direct inspiration for bonsai is found in nature, in trees that grow in harsh, rocky places and are dwarfed and gnarled throughout their existence. Prized characteristics are an aged-looking trunk and branches and weathered-looking exposed upper roots. Bonsai may live for a century or more and are handed down from one generation to another as valued family possessions. Bonsai pots, usually earthenware and of variable shape, are carefully chosen to harmonize in colour and proportion with the tree. A sizable bonsai industry exists as part of the nursery industry in Japan; California is home to a small-scale bonsai industry.

Bonsai pine.

Judith Groffman Faulkner

booby, Any of six or seven species of large tropical seabirds (family Sulidae), named for their presumed lack of intelligence. Two common species are wide-ranging in the Atlantic, Pacific, and Indian oceans; another is found in the Pacific from southern California to northern Peru and on the Galápagos Islands. The booby has a long bill, cigar-shaped body, and long, narrow, angular wings. It flies high above the ocean looking for schools of fish and squid, which it snatches in a vertical dive. Boobies vary in length from 25 to 35 in. (65–85 cm). They nest in colonies but are territorial.

book, Written (or printed) message of considerable length, meant for circulation and recorded on any of various materials that are durable and light enough to be easily portable. The papyrus roll of ancient Egypt is more nearly the direct ancestor of the modern book than is the clay tablet; examples of both date to c. 3000 BC. Somewhat later, the Chinese independently created an extensive scholarship based on books, many made of wood or bamboo strips bound with cords. Lampblack ink was introduced in China c. AD 400 and printing from wooden blocks in the 6th century. The Greeks adopted the papyrus roll and passed it on to the Romans. The parchment or vellum codex superseded the papyrus roll by AD 400. Medieval parchment or vellum leaves were prepared from the skins of animals. By the 15th century, paper manuscripts were common. Printing spread rapidly in the late 15th century. Subsequent technical achievements, such as the development of offset printing, improved many aspects of book culture. In the late 1990s, downloadable electronic books became available over the Internet.

Book of Common Prayer, Liturgical book used by the churches of the Anglican Communion. First authorized for the Church of England in 1549, it went through several versions; the 1662 revision has remained the standard (with minor changes) throughout the Commonwealth of Nations. The Church of England and the Protestant Episcopal Church in the U.S. adopted a liturgy in contemporary language in the 1970s.

Book of the Dead, Ancient Egyptian collection of mortuary texts made up of spells and charms and placed in tombs to aid the deceased in the next world. It was probably compiled and reedited during the 16th century BC. Later compilations included hymns to Re. Scribes produced and sold copies, often colorfully illustrated, for burial use. Of the many extant copies, none contains all of the approximately 200 known chapters.

bookbinding, Joining together of leaves of paper, parchment, or vellum within covers to form a book or codex. Bookbinding developed when the codex replaced the roll. Early bindings were often splendidly decorated, but the typical artistic bookbinding is of decorated leather and was first produced in the monasteries of Egypt's Coptic Church. Rare books, historical documents, and manuscripts may be bound by hand. The cover (case) of the typical book is now affixed to the leaves by machine.

bookkeeping, Recording of the money values of business transactions. Bookkeeping provides the information from which accounts are prepared but is distinct from accounting. Bookkeeping offers information on both the current value, or equity, of an enterprise and on its change in value (due to profit or loss) over a given time period. Managers require such information to examine the results of operations and budget for the future; investors need it to make decisions about buying or selling securities; and credit grantors use it to determine whether to grant a loan. Financial records were kept in Babylon and in ancient Greece and Rome. The double-entry method of bookkeeping began with the development of the Italian commercial republics of the 15th century. The Industrial Revolution stimulated the spread of bookkeeping, and 20th-century taxation and government regulations made it a necessity. Two types of records continue to be used in bookkeeping—journals and ledgers. They can be recorded by hand or entered into a computer. The journal contains daily transactions (sales, purchases, etc.), while the ledger contains the record of individual accounts. Each month an income statement and a balance sheet are posted in the ledger.

Boolean algebra, Symbolic system used for designing logic circuits and networks for digital computers. Its chief utility is in representing the truth value of statements, rather than the numeric quantities handled by ordinary algebra. It lends itself to use in the binary system employed by digital computers, since the only possible truth values, true and false, can be represented by the binary digits 1 and 0. A circuit in computer memory can be open or closed, depending on the value assigned to it, and it is the integrated work of such circuits that give computers their computing ability. The fundamental operations of Boolean logic, often called Boolean operators, are "and," "or," and "not"; combinations of these make up 13 other Boolean operators.

boomerang, Curved throwing stick used chiefly by the aborigines of Australia for hunting and warfare. About 12–30 in. (30–75 cm) in length, the returning boomerang varies in shape from a deep curve to almost straight sides of an angle. The ends are twisted or skewed in opposite directions. It is held at one end, above and behind the thrower's shoulder, and swung forward rapidly. Just before release, the thrower adds spin by flicking the wrist so that the stick will loop around and return to him. Returning boomer-

angs were used only in eastern and western Australia as playthings, in tournament competition, and by hunters to imitate hawks for driving flocks of game birds into nets. The longer, straighter, and heavier nonreturning boomerang can kill animals and even humans.

Bordeaux, City (pop., 2006 est.: city, 232,260; metro. area, 803,117), southwestern France. Lying on the Garonne River above its junction with the Dordogne, Bordeaux has long been noted for its wine production. As Burdigala, it was the chief town of the Bituriges Vivisci, a Celtic people. Under Roman rule it was capital of Aquitania province. As part of the inheritance of Eleanor of Aquitaine, Bordeaux became English in 1154 on her husband's accession to the English throne as Henry II. It enjoyed great prosperity through a thriving trade with the English until it was united with France on the English defeat in the Hundred Years' War (1453). As a Girondin centre, it suffered severely in the French Revolution. In 1870, during the Franco-Prussian War, the French government was transferred to Bordeaux, as it was again in 1914 at the outbreak of World War I. Its university, founded in 1441, educated such figures as Montesquieu. The economy focuses on the service sector.

Borneo, Island, Malay Archipelago. Bounded by the South China Sea, the Sulu and Celebes seas, the Makassar Strait, and the Java Sea, it is the third largest island in the world, measuring about 292,000 sq mi (755,000 sq km). The northern part includes the Malaysian states of Sabah and Sarawak and the sultanate of Brunei; the southern section (Kalimantan) forms part of Indonesia. Borneo is mountainous and largely covered in dense rainforest; its highest point is Mount Kinabalu, at 13,455 ft (4,101 m). Much of it is drained by navigable rivers, including the Rajang, which are the principal lifelines of trade and commerce. It is mentioned in Ptolemy's *Guide to Geography* (*c.* AD 150); Roman trade beads give evidence of an earlier civilization. Brahman and Buddhist images in the Gupta style indicate the influence of Indians who apparently arrived in the 5th century. With the arrival of Islam in the 16th century, various Muslim kingdoms were founded, some of which owed allegiance to Java. Around the same time, the Portuguese, followed by the Spanish, set up trading stations. In the early 17th century the Dutch broke the Portuguese-Spanish monopoly, but they in turn had to deal with newly established British interests. After World War II, Sarawak and North Borneo (later Sabah) became British crown colonies. Strong nationalist sentiment emerged in Dutch Borneo, and sovereignty passed to Indonesia in 1949. The British relinquished Sabah and Sarawak to the Malaysian federation in 1963, while Brunei became independent in 1984.

Borobudur, Buddhist monument in central Java, built *c.* 778–850 under the Shailendra dynasty. Constructed with about 2 million cu ft (57,000 cu m) of gray volcanic stone, it resembles a stepped pyramid. Its base and first five terraces are square; the highest three terraces are circular. Reliefs on its terrace walls represent the ascending stages of enlightenment. The simple and spacious upper circular terraces carry 72 bell-shaped stupas, each containing a statue of the Buddha.

Borobudur, Java, Indonesia.
Robert Harding Picture
Library/Photobank BKK

boron, Semimetallic chemical element, chemical symbol B, atomic number 5. Pure crystalline boron is a black, lustrous, very hard but brittle semiconductor that does not occur naturally. Boron compounds are found widely dispersed as various minerals, including borax and the gemstone tourmaline. The element is used to harden certain steels, among other metallurgical uses, and is also used in semiconductor devices. Its borate compounds, in which it has valence 3, are essential to plant growth and have many uses in soaps, mild antiseptics, and eye ointments. Industrially, they are used as herbicides, fire retardants in fabrics, and catalysts in numerous organic chemical reactions. They are also used in electroplating and glass and ceramic formulations. The exceptional hardness and inertness of certain boron compounds, including boron carbide, aluminum boride, and boron nitride (which has an electronic structure resembling that of diamond), make them useful as abrasives and reinforcing agents, particularly for high-temperature applications.

Bose, Subhas Chandra (b. Jan. 23, 1897, Cuttack, Orissa, India—d. Aug. 18, 1945, Taipei, Taiwan [China]?), Indian revolutionary. Preparing in Britain for a career in the Indian civil service, he resigned his candidacy on hearing of nationalist turmoil back home. Sent by Mohandas K. Gandhi to organize in Bengal, he was deported and imprisoned several times. He favoured industrialization, which put him at odds with Gandhi's economic thought, and, though he was elected president of the Indian National Congress in 1938 and 1939, without Gandhi's support he felt bound to resign. He slipped out of India in 1941 and carried on his struggle against the British from Nazi Germany and later from Southeast Asia. In 1944 he invaded India from Burma (Myanmar) with a small army of Indian nationals and Japanese, but his army was soon forced to retreat. He fled Southeast Asia after the Japanese surrender in 1945 and died of burns suffered in a plane crash.

Bosnia and Herzegovina, Country, Balkan Peninsula, southeastern Europe. It is bounded by Croatia, Serbia, Montenegro, and, along a narrow extension of the country, the Adriatic Sea. Area: 19,772 sq mi (51,209 sq km). Population: (2011 est.) 3,843,000. Capital: Sarajevo. Major ethnic groups are Bosniaks (Bosnian Muslims; more than two-fifths of the population), Serbs (about one-third), and Croats (less than one-fifth). Languages: Bosnian, Serbian, Croatian (all official). Religions: Christianity (Eastern Orthodox [Serbs], Roman Catholic [Croats]), Islam (Bosniaks). Currency: convertible marka. The country's relief is largely mountainous, and elevations of more than 6,000 ft (1,800 m) are common. The land is drained by the Sava, Drina, and Neretva rivers and their tributaries. Though the area possesses a variety of natural resources and an important history of industrial production, it remains one of the poorest regions of the former Yugoslavia. Bosnia and Herzegovina is an emerging republic with two legislative houses. A tripartite presidency is nominally the head of state; a representative of the international community functions as the final authority in this capacity. The head of government is the prime minister (chairman of the Council of Ministers). Habitation long predates the era of Roman rule, during which much of the country was included in the province of Dalmatia. Slav settlement began in the 6th century CE. For the next several centuries, parts of the region were ruled by Croats, Serbs, the Byzantine Empire, and Hungary. In the Middle Ages Bosnia enjoyed periods of independence, and for a brief time in the late 14th century it was the most powerful state in the western Balkans. The Ottoman Empire conquered most of Bosnia in the mid-15th century. It took over the remainder of Bosnia as well as Herzegovina, a land then known as Hum, soon thereafter. During the 16th–18th centuries the area was an important outpost of the Ottoman Turks, who were often at war with Hungary, the empire of the Austrian Habsburgs, and Venice. During this period much of the population converted to Islam. At the Congress of Berlin after the Russo-Turkish War of 1877–78, Bosnia and Herzegovina were assigned to Austria-Hungary, which annexed the combined territories in 1908. Growing Serbian and South Slav nationalism contributed to the 1914 assassination of the Austrian archduke Francis Ferdinand at Sarajevo by a Bosnian Serb, an event that precipitated World War I. After the war the area became part of the Kingdom of Serbs, Croats, and Slovenes, renamed Yugoslavia in 1929. Following World War II, Bosnia and Herzegovina became a republic of communist Yugoslavia. With the collapse of communist regimes in eastern Europe, Bosnia and Herzegovina declared its independence in 1992. The country's Serb population objected, however, and violent conflict ensued among Bosnian Serbs, Bosnian Croats, and Bosniaks. The Dayton peace accords in 1995 established a loosely federated government divided between the Bosniak-Croat Federation of Bosnia and Herzegovina and the Republika Srpska (Bosnian Serb Republic). By the early 21st century much of the infrastructure damaged during the conflict had been reconstructed, but ethnic tensions remained.

boson, Subatomic particle with integral spin that is governed by Bose-Einstein statistics. Bosons include mesons, nuclei of even mass number, and the particles required to embody the fields of quantum field theory. Unlike fermions, there is no limit to the number of bosons that can occupy the same quantum state, a behaviour that gives rise to the superfluidity of helium-4.

Bosporus, Turkish KARADENIZ BOGAZI, Strait separating the European and Asian portions of Turkey. Connecting the Sea of Marmara with the Black Sea, it is 19 mi (31 km) long and 2.3 mi (3.7 km) at its widest. Bosporus literally means "ox ford"; it is traditionally connected with the legendary figure of Io, who in the form of a heifer crossed the Thracian Bosporus in her wanderings. Because of its strategic importance for the defense of Constantinople (modern Istanbul), which straddled its southern end, the Byzantine emperors and later the Ottoman sultans constructed fortifications along its shores. With the growing influence of the European powers in the 19th century, rules were codified governing the transit of vessels through the strait. An international commission assumed control of it after World War I; Turkey resumed control in 1936. Two of the world's longest bridges, completed in 1973 and 1988, span the strait and link the two sections of Istanbul; in 2004 construction began on a rail tunnel beneath it.

Bosporus, Kingdom of the, or CIMMERIAN BOSPORUS, Ancient Greek kingdom, in modern southern Ukraine. It was first settled by Milesians (6th century BC) at Panticapaeum, which later became the capital. Gradually the kingdom grew to include all of the Crimea. It maintained close ties with Athens in the 5th–3rd century BC, reaching the peak of its power in the 4th century BC. It came under the rule of the kings of Pontus after 110 BC. For 300 years it belonged to the Roman Empire, and after AD 342 it was alternately under barbarian and Byzantine control.

Boston, Seaport city (pop., 2010: 617,594), capital of Massachusetts, U.S. Located on Massachusetts Bay, an arm of the Atlantic Ocean, it is the state's largest city. Settled in 1630 by Puritan Englishmen of the Massachusetts Bay Company, Boston became the hub of the self-governing Massachusetts Bay Colony under the leadership of Gov. John Winthrop. At the forefront of the opposition to British trade restrictions on its American colonies, Boston was a locus of events leading to the American Revolution: it was the scene of the Boston Massacre (1770) and Boston Tea Party (1773). It was the centre for the antislavery movement (1830–65). As the Industrial Revolution took hold in the U.S., Boston grew as an important manufacturing and textile centre. Today financial and high-technology industries are basic to the economy of the Boston area. Numerous institutions of higher education are located there, including Boston University.

Bosworth Field, Battle of (Aug. 22, 1485) Final battle in the English Wars of the Roses. It was fought between the forces of King Richard III of York and the contender for the crown, Henry Tudor (later Henry VII) of Lancaster. The battle occurred when Henry returned from exile, landing with an army at Milford Haven and meeting Richard's forces 12 mi (19 km) west of Leicester. The king's men were defeated and put to flight, and Richard was unhorsed and killed in a bog (a scene depicted in William Shakespeare's *Richard III*). The battle established the Tudor dynasty on the English throne.

botfly, Any member of several dipteran families with beelike adults and larvae that are parasitic on mammals. Some species are serious pests of horses, cattle, deer, sheep, rabbits, and squirrels, and one species (the human botfly) attacks humans. Adults of several species lay many eggs (nits) on the host's body, and the emerging larvae penetrate its skin. The larvae reemerge through the skin, then mature into egg-laying adults. In the New World tropics, the botfly's infestation of cattle has led to loss of beef and hides.

Botswana, officially REPUBLIC OF BOTSWANA, formerly BECHUANALAND, Country, southern Africa. Area: 224,607 sq mi (581,730 sq km). Population: (2011 est.) 2,033,000. Capital: Gaborone. Some two-thirds of the population are ethnic Tswana; other main groups include the Khalagari, Ngwato, Tswapong, Birwa, and Kalanga. There are also small groups of Khoekhoe and San, some of whom follow a traditional nomadic way of life. Languages: English (official), Tswana. Religions: Christianity (mostly independent and unaffiliated Christians; also Protestant), traditional beliefs. Currency: pula. Botswana is essentially a sand-filled basin, with a mean elevation of about 3,300 ft (1,000 m). Part of the Kalahari Desert is in the southwest and west, while the Okavango Swamp is in the north. The only sources of permanent surface water are the Chobe River, which marks the Namibian boundary; the Okavango River, in the far northwest; and the Limpopo River, which marks the South African boundary in the southeast. The economy traditionally depends on livestock raising; the development of diamond mining has increased the country's wealth. Botswana is a multiparty republic with one legislative body and an advisory body; the president serves as head of state and government. The region's earliest inhabitants were the Khoekhoe and San. Sites were settled as early as 190 BCE during the southerly migration of Bantu-speaking farmers. Tswana dynasties, which developed in the western Transvaal in the 13th–14th centuries, moved into Botswana in the 18th century and established several powerful states. European missionaries arrived in the early 19th century, but it was the discovery of gold in 1867 that excited European interest. In 1885 the area became the British Bechuanaland Protectorate, remaining so until the 1960s. In 1966 the Republic of Bechuanaland was proclaimed as an independent member of the British Commonwealth, and later that year its name was changed to Botswana. Independent Botswana tried to maintain a delicate balance between its economic dependence on South Africa and its relations with the surrounding black countries; the independence of Namibia in 1990 and South Africa's rejection of apartheid eased tensions.

bottlenose dolphin, or BOTTLE-NOSED DOLPHIN, Widely recognized species (*Tursiops truncatus*) of mammal belonging to the dolphin family, found worldwide in warm and temperate seas. Bottlenose dolphins reach an average length of 8–10 ft (2.5–3 m) and weight of 300–650 lb (135–300 kg). Males are generally larger than females. A familiar performer at marine shows, the species is characterized by a "built-in smile" formed by the curvature of its mouth. It has also become the subject of scientific studies because of its intelligence and its ability to communicate with its kind through sounds and ultrasonic pulses.

botulism, Poisoning by botulinum toxin, one of the most potent toxins known, produced by *Clostridium botulinum* bacteria. It usually results from improperly sterilized canned (mostly home-canned) foods. Heat-resistant spores of these anaerobic bacteria in fresh food may survive canning. The bacteria multiply and secrete toxin, which remains potent if the food is not well heated before it is eaten. Botulism can also result from wound infection. Botulinum toxin blocks nerve-impulse transmission. If botulism is recognized in time, administered antitoxins can neutralize it. The first symptoms of botulism are nausea and vomiting, which usually appear six hours or less after the contaminated food is eaten. Fatigue, blurry vision, and general weakness follow. Respiratory paralysis can cause death if not treated with emergency tracheotomy

and respiratory aid. Most victims recover completely if they survive paralysis. The bacteria's intense toxicity makes it a potentially deadly biological warfare agent.

Boudicca, or BOADICEA (d. AD 60), Ancient British queen. When her husband, a Roman client king of the Iceni, died in AD 60, he left his estate to his daughters and the emperor Nero, hoping for protection. Instead the Romans annexed his kingdom and mistreated his family and tribesmen. Boudicca raised a rebellion in East Anglia, burning Camulodunum (Colchester), Verulamium (St. Albans), and part of Londinium (London) and military posts; according to Tacitus, her forces massacred up to 70,000 Romans and pro-Roman Britons and destroyed the Roman 9th Legion. She is thought to have taken poison or died of shock when the Roman governor rallied his troops and destroyed her huge army.

bougainvillea, Any plant of the genus *Bougainvillea*, comprising about 14 species of shrubs, vines, or small trees (family Nyctaginaceae) native to South America and hardy in warm climates. Many species are spiny. Only the woody vines are widely popular; showy cultivated varieties of several species are often grown indoors. The inconspicuous flowers are surrounded by brightly coloured papery bracts, for which one species, *B. glabra*, is called paperflower. The bracts of various species range from purple to lemon-yellow.

Boulanger, Nadia (-Juliette) (b. Sept. 16, 1887, Paris, France—d. Oct. 22, 1979, Paris), French music teacher and conductor. Having studied composition with Charles-Marie Widor (1844–1937) and Gabriel Fauré, she stopped composing in her twenties (after the death of her sister, Lili, who was also a composer) and devoted the rest of her life to conducting, playing the organ, and teaching at the École Normale (1920–39), Paris Conservatoire (from 1946), and especially the American Conservatory at Fontainebleau (from 1921). She became the most celebrated composition teacher of the 20th century; her many students included Aaron Copland, Roy Harris, Darius Milhaud, Virgil Thomson, Elliott Carter, Leonard Bernstein, and Philip Glass. Her sister, Lili Boulanger (1893–1918), wrote a remarkable amount of vocal and other music and was the first woman composer to win the Prix de Rome (1913).

Bourbon, House of, One of the most important ruling houses of Europe. Its members were descended from Louis I, duc de Bourbon from 1327 to 1342, grandson of the French king Louis IX. Bourbons subsequently ruled in France (1589–1792, 1814–48); in Spain (1700–1868, 1870–73, 1874–1931, and since 1975); and in Naples and Sicily (1735–1861). Among its prominent members were Henry IV, Louis XIII, Louis XIV, Louis XV, Louis XVI, and Philip V.

Bourbon Restoration (1814–30) In France, the period that began when Napoleon abdicated and the Bourbon monarchs were restored to the throne. The First Restoration occurred when Napoleon fell from power and Louis XVIII became king. Louis's reign was interrupted by Napoleon's return to France, but Napoleon was forced to abdicate again, leading to the Second Restoration. The period was marked by a constitutional monarchy of moderate rule (1816–20), followed by a return of the ultras during the reign of Louis's brother, Charles X (1824–30). Reactionary policies revived the opposition liberals and moderates and led to the July Revolution, Charles's abdication, and the end of the Bourbon Restoration.

Bourgeois, Léon (-Victor-Auguste) (b. May 21, 1851, Paris, France—d. Sept. 29, 1925, Château d'Oger, near Épernay), French politician. He entered the civil service in 1876 and was elected to the National Assembly in 1888. He served in several ministerial posts and was briefly premier (1895–96). He was a member of the Senate in 1905–23 and its president from 1920. An advocate of international cooperation, he was appointed to the International Court of Justice in 1903. In 1919 he was France's representative to the League of Nations, emerging as its champion. For this, in 1920 he was awarded the Nobel Prize for Peace.

bouzouki, Long-necked lute used in Greek popular music. Developed from a Turkish instrument early in the 20th century, it has a pear-shaped body and a fretted fingerboard. The modern instrument usually has four courses of strings, which are plucked with a plectrum, typically in a vigorous and agile style.

bovid, Any ruminant of the family Bovidae. Bovids have hollow, unbranched, permanently attached horns; they are grazing or browsing animals found in both the Eastern and Western Hemispheres, most often in grasslands, scrublands, or deserts. Most species live in large herds. Species range in shoulder height from a 10-in. (25-cm) antelope to the 6.5-ft (2-m) bison. Some of the 138 species (including domestic cattle, sheep, goats) are of economic value to humans. Others (including bighorn and some antelope) are hunted for food, sport, horns, or hides.

bowling, Game in which a heavy ball is rolled down a long, narrow lane to knock down a group of 10 wooden objects (called pins). Versions of the game have existed since ancient times. Ninepin bowling was brought to the U.S. in the 17th century by Dutch settlers; it became so popular and so associated with gambling that it was outlawed in several states. The game grew to enormous popularity in the 20th century, both as a recreational activity and (since 1958) as a professional sport. If all the pins are knocked down with the first ball, a strike is recorded (10 points). If pins remain standing but the second ball knocks them down, the player is awarded a spare (10 points). If a strike is thrown in a frame (turn), the number of pins knocked down by the next two balls bowled count in that frame. After a spare, the score of the next ball counts in the spare's frame. Thus, the maximum point total for a single frame is 30. Each game is divided into 10 frames, and each player is allowed to deliver up to two balls per frame (except in the final frame, in which two additional deliveries are permitted following a strike [one additional following a spare]). A perfect score is 300, or 12 strikes in a row. Versions of the game include candlepins, duckpins, and skittles.

bowls, or LAWN BOWLS, or LAWN BOWLING, Bowling game similar to the Italian boccie and the French boules played on a green with wooden balls (called bowls) that are rolled at a target ball (the jack). The object is to roll one's bowls so that they come to rest nearer to the jack than those of an opponent, sometimes achieved by knocking aside an opponent's bowl or jack. One point is awarded for each winning bowl. Depending on the game, players use four, three, or two bowls, and games end at 18 or 21 points.

Boxer Rebellion, Officially supported peasant uprising in 1900 in China that attempted to drive all foreigners from the country. "Boxer" was the English name given to a Chinese secret society that practiced boxing and calisthenic rituals in the belief that it would make its members impervious to bullets. Support for them grew in northern China during the late 19th century, when China's people were suffering from growing economic impoverishment and the country was forced to grant humiliating concessions to Western powers. In June 1900, after Boxers had killed Chinese Christians and Westerners, an international relief force was dispatched to quell the attacks. The empress dowager, Cixi, ordered imperial forces to block its advance; the conflict escalated, hundreds of people were killed, and the matter was not resolved until August, when Beijing was captured and sacked. Hostilities were ended with a protocol (1901) requiring China to pay a large indemnity to 11 countries. Britain and the U.S. later returned much of their reparations, the U.S. using its portion to further Chinese higher education.

boxing, Sport involving attack and defense with the fists. In the modern sport, boxers wear padded gloves and fight bouts of up to 12 three-minute rounds in a roped-off square known as the ring. In ancient Greece fighters used leather thongs on their hands and forearms, while in Rome gladiators used metal-studded leather hand coverings (cesti) and usually fought to the death. Not until implementation of the London Prize Ring rules in 1839 were kicking, gouging, butting, biting, and blows below the belt eliminated from the boxer's standard repertoire. In 1867 the Queensberry rules called for the wearing of gloves, though bare-knuckle boxing continued into the late 1880s. The last of the great bare-knuckle fighters was John L. Sullivan. From Sullivan on, the U.S. became the premier boxing venue, partly because immigrants supplied a constantly renewed pool of boxers. Boxing has been included among the Olympic Games since 1904. Today there are 17 primary weight classes in professional boxing: strawweight, to 105 lbs (48 kg); junior flyweight, to 108 lbs (49 kg); flyweight, to 112 lbs (51 kg); junior bantamweight, to 115 lbs (52 kg); bantamweight, to 118 lbs (53.5 kg); junior featherweight, to 122 lbs (55 kg); featherweight, to 126 lbs (57 kg); junior lightweight, to 130 lbs (59 kg); lightweight, to 135 lbs (61 kg); junior welterweight, 140 lbs (63.5 kg); welterweight, to 147 lbs (67 kg); junior middleweight, 154 lbs (70 kg); middleweight, to 160 lbs (72.5 kg); super middleweight, 168 lbs (76 kg); light heavyweight, to 175 lbs (79 kg); cruiserweight, 190 lbs (86 kg); and heavyweight, over 190 lbs. A bout can be won either by knocking out or felling one's opponent for a count of 10 (a KO) or by delivering the most solid blows and thus amassing the most points. The referee can also stop the fight when one boxer is being badly beaten (a technical knockout, or TKO) or he can disqualify a fighter for rules violations and award the fight to his opponent.

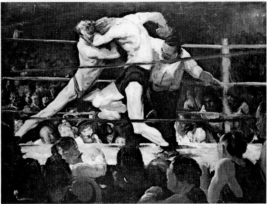

Stag at Sharkey's, *oil on canvas by George Bellows, 1909; in the Cleveland Museum of Art, Ohio, U.S.*
Courtesy of the Cleveland Museum of Art, Ohio, Hinman B. Hurlbut Collection

boyar, Any male member of the upper class of medieval Russian society and state administration. In Kievan Rus (10th–12th centuries) the boyars belonged to the prince's retinue, holding posts in the army and civil administration and advising the prince in matters of state through a boyar council, or duma. In the 13th–14th centuries the boyars constituted a privileged class of rich landowners in northeastern Russia. In the 15th–17th centuries the boyars of Muscovy ruled the country along with the grand prince (later the czar) and legislated through the boyar council. Their importance declined in the 17th century, and the title was abolished by Peter I in the early 18th century.

boycott, Collective and organized ostracism applied in labour, economic, political, or social relations to protest and punish practices considered unfair. The tactic was popularized by Charles Stewart Parnell to protest high rents and land evictions in Ireland in 1880 by the estate manager Charles C. Boycott (b. 1832—d. 1897). Boycotts are principally used by labour organizations to win improved wages and working conditions or by consumers to pressure companies to change their hiring, labour, environmental, or investment practices. U.S. law distinguishes between primary boycotts, which consist of the refusal by employees to purchase the goods or services of their employers, and secondary boycotts, which involve attempts to induce third parties to refuse to patronize the employer. The latter type of boycott is prohibited by federal law. Boycotts were used as a tactic in the U.S. civil rights movement of the 1950s and '60s and also have been applied to influence the conduct of multinational corporations.

Brahma, One of three major gods in late Vedic Hinduism, *c.* 500 BC–*c.* AD 500. He was gradually eclipsed by the other two, Vishnu and Shiva. In classical times the doctrine of Trimurti identified the three as aspects of a supreme deity. Brahma was associated with the creator god Prajapati, whose identity he came to assume. All temples of Shiva or Vishnu contain an image of Brahma, but today there is no sect or cult devoted exclusively to him.

Brahmagupta (b. 598—d. *c.* 665, possibly Bhillamala, Rajasthan, India), Indian mathematician and astronomer. His principal work, the *Brahma-sphuta-siddhanta* ("The Opening of the Universe"), most of which deals with planetary motion, also contains important proofs of various geometrical theorems on quadratic equations, the geometry of right triangles, and the properties of geometric solids.

Brahman, In the Upanishads, the eternal, infinite, and omnipresent spiritual source of the finite and changing universe. The schools of Vedanta differ in interpreting Brahman. The Advaita school defines Brahman as categorically different from any phenomenon, conceiving it as an absolute reality onto which human perceptions of differentiation are projected. The Bhedabheda school maintains that Brahman is not different from the world it produces. The Visistadvaita school holds that phenomenality is a glorious manifestation of Brahman. The Dvaita school maintains that both soul and matter are separate from and dependent on Brahman.

Brahman, or BRAHMIN, Any member of the highest of the four varnas, or social classes, in Hindu India. Their existence as a priestly caste dates to the late Vedic period, and they have long been considered to be of greater ritual purity than members of other castes and alone to be capable of performing certain religious tasks, including preservation of the collections of Vedic hymns. Because of their high prestige and tradition of education, they dominated Indian scholarship for centuries. As the spiritual and intellectual elite, they advised the politically powerful warrior caste, and after Indian independence they supplied many heads of state. They still retain traditional privileges, though these are no longer legally sanctioned. Ritual purity is maintained through taboos, vegetarianism, and abstention from certain occupations.

Brahman, or ZEBU, Any of several varieties of cattle that originated in India and were crossbred in the U.S. with improved beef breeds to produce the hardy beef animal known as the Santa Gertrudis. Similar blending in Latin America resulted in the breed known as Indo-Brazil. The Brahman is characterized by a pronounced hump over the shoulder and neck, horns that usually curve up and back, and drooping ears. Gray is the prevalent colour, with deep shading in the fore and rear quarters of the bull. A red strain has also been developed.

Brahmana, Any of a number of discourses on the Vedas that explain their use in ritual sacrifices and the symbolism of the priests' actions. Dating to 900–600 BC, they constitute the oldest historical sources for Indian ritual. The *Aitareya* and *Kausitaki Brahmana*, compiled by followers of the *Rig Veda*, include discussions of daily sacrifices, the sacrificial fire, new- and full-moon rites, and the rites for installation of kings. The *Pancavimsa, Sadvimsa*, and *Jaiminiya Brahmana* discuss the "going of the cows,"

soma ceremonies, and atonements for mistakes in ritual. The *Satapatha Brahmana* introduces elements of domestic ritual, and the *Gopatha Brahmana* treats the priests' supervision of sacrifices.

Brahmaputra River, River, Central and South Asia. From its

Stupa on the bank of the Brahmaputra River near Song-i, Tibet.
© Naomi Duguid/Asia Access

headsprings in the Tibet Autonomous Region of China (as the Yarlung River), it flows across southern Tibet to break through the Himalayas in great gorges (where it is known as the Dihang). It flows southwest through the Assam Valley and south through Bangladesh (where it is known as the Jamuna). There it merges with the Ganges (Ganga) to form a vast delta. About 1,800 mi (2,900 km) long, the river is an important source for irrigation and transportation. Its upper course was long unknown, and its identity with the Zangbo was established by exploration in 1884–86.

Braille, Universal system of writing and printing for the blind. The Frenchman Louis Braille invented the system in 1824. Characters embossed on paper are read by passing the fingers lightly over the manuscript. The system is based on a matrix of six dots arranged in two columns of three. The 63 combinations possible in this framework stand for letters, numbers, punctuation marks, and common words such as *and* and *the*. A Braille code for English was not adopted until 1932. Modifications also exist for other languages, for mathematical and technical material, and for musical notation. Braille may be handwritten—from right to left—using a stylus to press dots into a piece of paper between hinged metal plates; when the sheet is turned over, the dots face up and are read from left to right. Braille typewriters and electric embossing machines are also used.

brainwashing, Systematic effort to destroy an individual's former loyalties and beliefs and to substitute loyalty to a new ideology or power. It has been used by religious cults as well as by radical political groups. The techniques of brainwashing usually involve isolation from former associates and sources of information; an exacting regimen calling for absolute obedience and humility; strong social pressures and rewards for cooperation; physical and psychological punishments for noncooperation, including social ostracism and criticism, deprivation of food, sleep, and social contacts, bondage, and torture; and constant reinforcement. Its effects are sometimes reversed through deprogramming, which combines confrontation and intensive psychotherapy.

Brandt, Willy, orig. HERBERT ERNST KARL FRAHM (b. Dec. 18,

Willy Brandt.
Authenticated News International

1913, Lübeck, Ger.—d. Oct. 8/9, 1992, Unkel, near Bonn), German statesman. As a young Social Democrat, he fled to Norway to avoid arrest after the rise of the Nazis in the 1930s. There he assumed the name Willy Brandt and worked as a journalist. Returning to Germany after World War II, he was elected to parliament in 1949 and became mayor of West Berlin (1957–66), a post in which he achieved world fame. He led a coalition government as chancellor of the Federal Republic of Germany (1969–74). As chancellor, he improved relations with East Germany, other communist nations in eastern Europe, and the Soviet Union and helped strengthen the European Economic Community. For these efforts he received the Nobel Prize for Peace in 1971. He remained the leader of the Social Democratic Party until 1987.

brandy, Alcoholic beverage distilled from wine or a fermented fruit mash. The name comes from the Dutch *brandewijn*, "distilled wine." Most brandies are aged and contain about 50% alcohol by volume. Some are darkened with caramel. They are usually served alone as after-dinner drinks but are sometimes used in mixed drinks or dessert dishes or as fuel in flamed dishes such as crêpes suzettes and cherries jubilee. They are also used as the base of various liqueurs. The finest brandy is usually thought to be French cognac.

Brasília, City (pop., 2000: 2,043,169), capital of Brazil. It lies between the headwaters of the Tocantins, Paraná, and São Francisco rivers. Though the idea of having the country's capital located in the interior was proposed as early as 1789, Brasília's construction began only in 1956. It was designed by the Brazilian architects Lúcio Costa and Oscar Niemeyer. In 1960 the government began its move from Rio de Janeiro. The city is a governmental rather than an industrial centre, although many Brazilian companies have headquarters there. Brasília National Park is nearby.

Brasov, or BRASHOV, German KRONSTADT, City (pop., 2002: 588,366), Romania. It lies in the foothills of the Transylvanian Alps north of Bucharest. Founded by Teutonic Knights in 1211, it became the centre of a Saxon colony trading in cloth and metalwork throughout much of Walachia and Moldavia. The substantial autonomy of its German inhabitants ended in 1876 with the abolition of their separate national status. Brasov is today a centre for heavy manufacturing.

Bratislava, German PRESSBURG, Hungarian POZSONY, City (pop., 2001 prelim.: 428,672), capital of Slovakia. Settled first by Celts and Romans, it was ultimately inhabited by Slavs in the 8th century. As Pressburg, it developed as a trade centre and became a free royal town in 1291. The first university in what was then Hungary was founded there in 1467. The city served as the Hungarian capital (1541–1784) and was the seat of the Diet until 1848. The Treaty of Pressburg (1805) was signed here by Napoleon and Francis II following the Battle of Austerlitz. After World War I, on the formation of Czechoslovakia, it became capital of the province of Slovakia, and it became the national capital on Slovakia's independence in 1992.

Brattain, Walter H(ouser) (b. Feb. 10, 1902, Amoy, China—d. Oct. 13, 1987, Seattle, Wash., U.S.), U.S. scientist. His American parents brought him to the U.S. soon after his birth. After earning a Ph.D. from the University of Minnesota, he became a researcher at Bell Laboratories in 1929. With John Bardeen and William B. Shockley, he shared the 1956 Nobel Prize for Physics for the development of the transistor and for investigation of the properties of semiconductors.

Brazil, officially FEDERATIVE REPUBLIC OF BRAZIL, Country, east-central South America. Area: 3,287,612 sq mi (8,514,877 sq km). Population: (2011 est.) 192,813,000. Capital: Brasília. Most Brazilians are of European or mixed (Indian-European, European-African) ancestry. Brazil's ethnic groups have intermixed since the earliest days of its colonial history; Indian peoples who have experienced no mixing with immigrants are restricted to the most remote parts of the Amazon River basin. Language: Portuguese (official). Religions: Christianity (predominantly Roman Catholic; also Protestant); also traditional beliefs. Currency: real. Brazil may be divided into many regions, but the Amazon lowlands and the Brazilian Highlands (often called the Central Highlands or Central Plateau) dominate the landscape. The highlands, a plateau with an average elevation of 3,300 ft (1,000 m), are primarily in the southeast, while the Amazon lowlands, with elevations below 800 ft (250 m), are in the north. The Amazon River basin, with its more than 1,000 known tributaries, occupies nearly half of the country's total area. Brazil's other rivers include the São Francisco, Parnaíba, Paraguay, Alto Paraná, and Uruguay. Except for the islands of Marajó and Caviana at the mouth of the Amazon and Maracá to the north, there are no large islands along the roughly 4,600 mi (7,400 km) of Brazil's Atlantic Ocean coast. There are good harbours at Belém, Salvador, Rio de Janeiro, Santos, and Porto Alegre. The country's immense forests are a source of many products, while its savannas support cattle raising. Agriculture is important, and mineral reserves are large. Brazil has a developing market economy based mainly on manufacturing, financial services, and trade. It is a multiparty federal republic with two legislative houses; its head of state and government is the president. Little is known about Brazil's early indigenous inhabitants. Though the area was theoretically allotted to Portugal by the 1494 Treaty of Tordesillas, it was not formally claimed by discovery until Portuguese navigator Pedro Álvares Cabral accidentally touched land in 1500. It was first settled by the Portuguese in the early 1530s on the northeastern coast and at São Vicente (near modern São Paulo); the French and Dutch created small settlements over the next century. A viceroyalty was established in 1640, and Rio de Janeiro became the capital in 1763. In 1808 Brazil became the refuge and seat of the government of John VI of Portugal when Napoleon I invaded Portugal; ultimately the Kingdom of Portugal, Brazil, and Algarve was proclaimed, and John ruled from Brazil (1815–21). On John's return to Portugal, Pedro I proclaimed Brazilian independence. In 1889 his successor, Pedro II, was deposed, and a constitution mandating a federal republic was adopted. Beginning in the 20th century, immigration increased and manufacturing grew, and there were frequent military coups and suspensions of civil liberties. Construction of a new capital at Brasília, intended to spur development of the country's interior, worsened the inflation rate. After 1979 the military government began a gradual return to democratic practices, and in 1989 the first popular presidential election in 29 years was held. A severe economic crisis began in the late 1990s.

Brazil nut, Edible seed of a large South American tree, *Bertholletia excelsa* (family Lecythidaceae), and one of the major commercially traded nuts in the world. The hard-walled fruit, resembling a large coconut, contains 8–24 nuts arranged in it like sections of an orange. Each nut has a very hard shell and is three-sided in shape. Brazil nuts are high in fat and protein and taste somewhat like almond or coconut. The tree grows wild in stands in the Amazon River basin, reaching heights of 150 ft (45 m) or more.

Brazzaville, River port (pop., 2007 est.: 1,355,000), capital of Republic of the Congo. Lying on the north bank of the Congo River across from Kinshasa, it was founded in 1883 by Pierre Savorgnan de Brazza. Developed as a European administrative and residential centre, it was used as a base for later claims of France to lands to the northeast; it became the capital of French Equatorial Africa. The river port forms the terminus of the Congo-ocean transport system, with steamer service to the Congo's upper reaches and a railroad to Pointe-Noire 245 mi (394 km) west.

breadfruit, Fruit of either of two closely related trees belonging to the mulberry family. *Artocarpus communis* (also called *A. incisa* or *A. altilis*) provides a staple food of the South Pacific. Its greenish to brownish-green, round fruits have a white, fibrous pulp. *Treculia africana*, native to tropical Africa, is less important as a food crop. Cultivated in the Malay Archipelago (where it is thought to be indigenous) since remote antiquity, the breadfruit was spread throughout the tropical South Pacific in prehistoric times. It is high in starch and is seldom eaten raw. Unable to tolerate frost, the tree has not been successfully grown in the U.S., even in southernmost Florida. In the South Seas, cloth is made from the inner bark, the wood is used for canoes and furniture, and glue and caulking material are obtained from the milky juice.

Brecht, Bertolt, orig. EUGEN BERTHOLD FRIEDRICH BRECHT (b.

Bertolt Brecht, 1931
Ullstein Bilderdienst

Feb. 10, 1898, Augsburg, Ger.—d. Aug. 14, 1956, East Berlin, E.Ger.), German playwright and poet. He studied medicine at Munich (1917–21) before writing his first plays, including *Baal* (1922). Other plays followed, including *A Man's a Man* (1926), as well as a considerable body of poetry. With the composer Kurt Weill he wrote the satirical musicals *The Threepenny Opera* (1928; film, 1931), which gained him a wide audience, and *The Rise and Fall of the City of Mahagonny* (1930). In these years he became a Marxist and developed his theory of epic theatre. With the rise of the Nazis he went into exile, first in Scandinavia (1933–41), then in the U.S., where he wrote his major essays and the plays *Mother Courage and Her Children* (1941), *The Life of Galileo* (1943), *The Good Woman of Sichuan* (1943), and *The Caucasian Chalk Circle* (1948). Harassed for his politics, in 1949 he returned to East Germany, where he established the Berliner Ensemble theatre troupe and staged his own plays, including *The Resistible Rise of Arturo Ui* (1957). He outlined his theory of drama in *A Little Organum for the Theatre* (1949).

Bremen, City (pop., 2002 est.: city, 540,950; metro. area, 849,800), northwestern Germany. Located on the Weser River, it was established as a diocese in 787 by Charlemagne and was the seat of an archbishopric from 845. In the 10th century it became an economic centre of northern Germany, especially after entering the Hanseatic League in 1358. It joined the German Confederation in 1815 and the reconstituted German Empire in 1871. It suffered extensive damage in World War II; after the war Bremen, with nearby Bremerhaven (pop., 2002 est.: 195,863), became a state of West Germany. Today the state, covering 156 sq mi (404 sq km), forms an integral part of the German economy and serves as headquarters for many industries.

Brest-Litovsk, Treaty of (March 3, 1918) Peace treaty signed at Brest-Litovsk (now in Belarus) by the Central Powers with Soviet Russia, concluding hostilities between those countries in World War I. Russia lost the Ukraine, its Polish and Baltic territories, and Finland by signing the treaty, which was later annulled by the Armistice.

Briand, Aristide (b. March 28, 1862, Nantes, France—d. March 7, 1932, Paris), French statesman. He became secretary-general of the French Socialist Party in 1901 and served in the Chamber of Deputies (1902–32). Between 1909 and 1929 he served 11 times as premier of France, and he held 26 ministerial posts between 1906 and 1932. His achievements included the Pact of Locarno and the Kellogg-Briand Pact. For his efforts for international cooperation, the League of Nations, and world peace, he shared the 1926 Nobel Prize for Peace with Gustav Stresemann.

bridewealth, Payment made by the groom or his kin to the kin of the wife in order to ratify the marriage. The practice is common in most parts of the globe in one form or another, but it is perhaps most prevalent in Africa. It is most often a matter of social and symbolic as well as economic reciprocity, being part of a long series of exchanges between the two intermarrying families. It represents a pledge that the wife will be well treated and serves as compensation for her family's loss. Payment may consist of goods or, less frequently, services, and it may be paid in one sum or regularly over a long period of time. *See* also dowry.

bridge, Structure that spans horizontally to allow pedestrians and vehicles to cross a void. Bridge construction has always presented civil engineering with its greatest challenges. The simplest bridge is the beam (or girder) bridge, consisting of straight, rigid beams of steel or concrete placed across a span. Ancient Roman bridges are famous for their rounded arch form, which permitted spans much longer than those of stone beams and were more durable than wood. A modern version of the arch bridge might have a trussed arch anchored to the abutments and a deck hanging from the arch by vertical cables. Suspension bridges (e.g., Brooklyn Bridge, Golden Gate Bridge) are capable of spanning great distances; their main support members are cables composed of thousands of strands of wire supported by two towers and anchored at each end, and the deck is suspended by vertical cables hung from the main cables. In cable-stayed bridges, cables fan out and down from a central tower to various points on the deck; variations of this design have resulted in bridges of striking design and very long span. Other bridges include the truss bridge, popular (e.g., for railroad bridges) because it uses a relatively small amount of material to carry large loads, and the cantilever bridge, typically made with three spans, with the outer spans anchored down at the shore and the central span resting on the cantilevered arms.

bridge, Card game similar to whist. Bridge is any of several games, including games such as auction bridge and contract bridge, that retain the essential features of whist: Four players participate, two against two in partnership. They play with a 52-card pack, all cards of which are dealt face downward one at a time, clockwise. When play begins, the object is to win tricks, consisting of one card from each player in rotation. The players must, if able, contribute a card of the suit led, and the trick is won by the highest card. All tricks taken in excess of the first six tricks are known as odd tricks. Before play begins, a suit may be designated the trump suit, in which case any card in it beats any card of the other suits. In all types of bridge a certain number of points are needed to win a game, and the winning of two games by the same team allows it to win the rubber.

brig, Two-masted sailing ship with square rigging on both masts. Brigs were both naval and mercantile vessels. As merchantmen, they often followed coastal trading routes, but ocean voyages were not uncommon, and some were even used for whaling and sealing. Naval brigs carried 10–20 guns on a single deck. In the 18th–19th century, they served as couriers for battle fleets and as training vessels for cadets. Brigs of the early U.S. Navy won distinction on the Great Lakes in the War of 1812. Because square rigging required a large crew, merchant brigs became uneconomical, and in the 19th century they began to give way to vessels such as the schooner and the bark.

brigade, Military unit commanded by a brigadier general or a colonel and composed of two or more subordinate units, such as regiments or battalions. Two or more brigades make up a division.

Brighton, Town (pop., 2001: 134,293), southern England. Lying on the English Channel south of London, it was for several centuries a small fishing village, but it gained popularity in the late 18th century when the prince of Wales (later George IV) made the first of his many visits. His powerful patronage stamped the town with the distinguished character still seen in its Regency-style squares. Victorian Brighton grew rapidly with the opening of the railway connecting it to London (1841).

brine shrimp, Any of several small crustaceans (genus *Artemia*) inhabiting brine pools and other highly salty inland waters throughout the world. *A. salina*, which occurs in vast numbers in Great Salt Lake, Utah, is commercially important. Young brine

Brine shrimp (Artemia salina)
Douglas P. Wilson

shrimp hatched there from dried eggs are used widely as food for fish and other small animals in aquariums. Up to 0.6 in. (15 mm) long, the brine shrimp's body has a distinguishable head and a slender abdomen. It normally swims upside down, and it feeds primarily on green algae, which it filters from the water with its legs.

Brisbane, City (pop., 2004 est.: urban agglom. 1,774,890), southeastern Queensland, Australia. Lying on the northern bank of the Brisbane River above its mouth at Moreton Bay, the site was first explored by the English in 1823. It was founded as a penal colony in 1824 and was declared a town in 1834 when it was named in honour of Sir Thomas Brisbane, former governor of New South Wales. Made the capital of Queensland in 1859, it was joined with South Brisbane in the 1920s to form Greater Brisbane. The city, connected by bridges and ferries, is Australia's third largest; it is the hub of rail lines and highways and a busy port. It is the site of the Queensland Cultural Centre and a university.

Bristol, City and unitary authority (pop., 2001: 380,615), southwestern England. Lying at the confluence of the Rivers Avon and Frome, the city received its first charter in 1155. Long a centre of commerce, it was the point of departure in 1497 of John Cabot in his search for a route to Asia. During the 17th–18th centuries it prospered in the triangular trade (rum, molasses, and slaves) between West Africa and the West Indian and American plantation colonies. Though Bristol suffered a decline in trade in the early 19th century, it soon rebounded with the coming of the railway. It suffered severe damage from bombing in World War II but was rebuilt. Today it is an important shipping centre, especially for oil and food products.

Bristol Channel, Inlet of the Atlantic Ocean, southwestern England. It extends about 85 mi (135 km) between southern Wales and southwestern England, ranging from 5 to 43 mi (8–69 km) wide. Lundy Island, once a pirate stronghold, lies in the centre of the channel; it is maintained as a trust preserve. Ships using the English port of Bristol and the Welsh ports of Swansea and Cardiff pass through the channel.

Britain, Name historically applied to the island of Great Britain. Britain is used especially when referring to its pre-Roman and Roman periods and to its early Anglo-Saxon period. It is the Anglicized form of Latin *Britannia.*

Britain, Battle of (June 1940–April 1941) Series of intense raids directed against Britain by the German air force in World War II. The air attacks, intended to prepare the way for a German invasion, were directed against British ports and RAF bases. In September 1940 the attacks turned to London and other cities in a "blitz" of bombings for 57 consecutive nights, which was followed by intermittent raids until April 1941. The RAF was outnumbered but succeeded in blocking the German air force through superior tactics, advanced air defenses, and the penetration of German secret codes.

British Empire, Worldwide system of dependencies—colonies, protectorates, and other territories—that over a span of three centuries came under the British government. Territorial acquisition began in the early 17th century with a group of settlements in North America and West Indian, South Asian, and African trading posts founded by private individuals and trading companies. In the 18th century the British took Gibraltar, established colonies along the Atlantic seacoast of North America and in the Caribbean Sea, and began to add territory in India. With its victory in the French and Indian War (1763), the empire secured Canada and the east-

ern Mississippi Valley and gained supremacy in India. From the late 18th century it began to build power in Malaya and acquired the Cape of Good Hope, Ceylon, and Malta. The British settled Australia in 1788 and subsequently New Zealand. Aden was secured in 1839, and Hong Kong in 1841. Britain went on to control the Suez Canal (1875–1956). In the 19th-century European partition of Africa, Britain acquired Nigeria, Egypt, the territories that would become British East Africa, and part of what would become the Union (later Republic) of South Africa. After World War I, Britain secured mandates to German East Africa, part of the Cameroons, part of Togo, German South-West Africa, Mesopotamia, Palestine, and part of the German Pacific islands. Britain gradually evolved a system of self-government for some colonies after the U.S. gained independence, as set forth in Lord Durham's report of 1839. Dominion status was given to Canada (1867), Australia (1901), New Zealand (1907), the Union of South Africa (1910), and the Irish Free State (1921). Britain declared war on Germany in 1914 on behalf of the entire empire; after World War I the dominions signed the peace treaties themselves and joined the League of Nations as independent states. In 1931 the Statute of Westminster recognized them as independent countries "within the British Empire," referring to the "British Commonwealth of Nations," and from 1949, the Commonwealth of Nations. The British Empire, therefore, developed into the Commonwealth in the mid-20th century, as former British dependencies obtained sovereignty but retained ties to the United Kingdom.

British Library, National library of Great Britain, formed by the British Library Act (1972) and organized July 1, 1973. It consists of the former British Museum library, the National Central Library, the National Lending Library for Science and Technology, and the British National Bibliography. The British Museum library, founded in 1753 based on earlier collections and later increased by the addition of royal libraries, had the right to a free copy of all books published in the United Kingdom. Its collection included a rich series of charters (including those of the Anglo-Saxon kings), codices, psalters, and other papers ranging from the 3rd century BC to modern times. The present-day British Library receives a copy of every publication produced in the United Kingdom and Ireland.

British Museum, Britain's national museum of archaeology and antiquities, established in London in 1753 when the government purchased three large private collections consisting of books, manuscripts, prints, drawings, paintings, medals, coins, seals, cameos, and natural curiosities. In 1881 the natural-history collections were transferred to another building to form the Natural History Museum, and in 1973 the library collections were consolidated to form the British Library. Among the museum's most famous holdings are the Elgin Marbles, the Rosetta Stone, the Portland Vase, and Chinese ceramics. In 1808 the department of prints and drawings opened with over 2,000 drawings. It is now one of the world's largest and most comprehensive collections.

Brno, German BRÜNN, City (pop., 2001 prelim.: 379,185), southeastern Czech Republic. Located southeast of Prague, it lies in an area that shows evidence of prehistoric inhabitance and traces of Celtic and Slavic settlements in the 5th–6th centuries AD. German colonization in the 13th century stimulated its growth; it received city status in 1243. In various wars in the 15th–19th centuries, it was besieged by the Swedes, Prussians, and French. Before World War I it was the capital of the Austrian crown land of Moravia. The inhabitants, predominantly German before World War II, are now mainly Czech. Gregor Mendel worked on his theory of heredity (1865) in the monastery at Brno.

broadband technology, Telecommunications devices, lines, or technologies that allow communication over a wide band of frequencies, and especially over a range of frequencies divided into multiple independent channels for the simultaneous transmission of different signals. Broadband systems allow voice, data, and video to be broadcast over the same medium at the same time. They may also allow multiple data channels to be broadcast simultaneously.

Broadway, Theatre district in New York City. It is named for the avenue that runs through the Times Square area in central Manhattan, where most of the larger theatres are located. Broadway attracted theatre producers and impresarios from the mid-19th century. The number and size of the theatres grew with New York's increasing prosperity, and by the 1890s the brightly lit street was called "the Great White Way." By 1925, the height of theatrical activity in New York, about 80 theatres were located on or near Broadway; by 1980 only about 40 remained. In the 1990s the revitalization of the seedy Times Square neighbourhood attracted larger audiences, though high production costs limited the viability of serious plays in Broadway theatres, which often chose to mount big musicals and other crowd-pleasing commercial ventures.

Brodsky, Joseph, orig. IOSIP ALEKSANDROVICH BRODSKY (b. May 24, 1940, Leningrad, Russia, U.S.S.R.—d. Jan. 28, 1996, New York, N.Y., U.S.), Russian-born U.S. poet. In the Soviet Union his independent spirit and irregular work record led to a five-year sentence to hard labour. Exiled in 1972, he settled in New York. He was poet laureate of the U.S. from 1991 to 1992. His lyric and elegiac poems ponder the universal concerns of life, death, and the meaning of existence. Brodsky's poetry collections include *A Part of Speech* (1980), *History of the Twentieth Century* (1986), and *To Urania* (1988). He was awarded the Nobel Prize for Literature in 1987.

bromine, Nonmetallic chemical element, chemical symbol Br, atomic number 35. One of the halogens, it is a deep red, fuming liquid at ordinary temperatures (freezing point 19 °F [−7.2 °C]; boiling point 138 °F [59 °C]) that contains diatomic molecules (Br_2), and it does not occur free in nature. It is obtained from seawater and brines or salt beds. Extremely irritating and toxic, bromine is a strong oxidizing agent. Its compounds, in which it may have valence 1, 3, 5, or 7, have many uses, including as petroleum additives (ethylene dibromide), in photographic emulsions (silver bromide), as sedatives, and in flour (potassium bromate).

bronchitis, Inflammation in the bronchi of the lungs. Microbes and foreign matter that have entered the airways cause inflammation of the bronchi and stimulate excess secretion of mucus. Symptoms include a productive cough and a sensation of chest congestion. Long-term repetitive injury, as from smoking, may lead to chronic bronchitis, in which severe, irreversible damage leaves the lungs open to infection and fibrosis. Smoking-related chronic bronchitis often occurs in association with emphysema (together called chronic obstructive pulmonary disease). Treatment includes drugs to dilate the bronchi and promote coughing, antibiotics, and lifestyle adaptations (e.g., quitting smoking).

Brontë sisters, Family of English writers. The daughters of an Anglican clergyman, they were brought up in Haworth on the Yorkshire moors. Their mother died early. Charlotte Brontë (April 21, 1816–March 31, 1855) attended the Clergy Daughter's School with her sister Emily and subsequently taught school and served as a governess. She and Emily made an unsuccessful attempt to open a school. Her novel *Jane Eyre* (1847), an immediate success, was a powerful narrative of a woman in conflict with her natural desires and social situation that gave a new truthfulness to Victorian fiction. It was followed by the novels *Shirley* (1849) and *Villette* (1853). In 1854 she married her father's curate, and she died soon after at age 38. Emily (Jane) Brontë (July 30, 1818–Dec. 19, 1848) was perhaps the greatest writer of the three. *Poems by Currer, Ellis and Acton Bell* (1846), published jointly by the sisters (who assumed pseudonyms to avoid the special treatment that they believed reviewers accorded to women), contained 21 of her poems. Many critics believe that her verse alone reveals poetic ge-

nius. Her one novel, *Wuthering Heights* (1847), is a highly imaginative story of passion and hatred set on the Yorkshire moors. Though not a success when published, it later came to be considered one of the finest novels in English. Soon after its publication, her health began to fail, and she died of tuberculosis at 30. Anne Brontë (Jan. 17, 1820–May 28, 1849) contributed 21 poems to *Poems by Currer, Ellis and Acton Bell*; she wrote two novels, *Agnes Grey* (1847) and *The Tenant of Wildfell Hall* (1848). Anne died of tuberculosis at 29.

Bronze Age, Third phase in the development of material culture among the ancient peoples of Europe, Asia, and the Middle East, following the Paleolithic and Neolithic periods and preceding the Iron Age. The term also denotes the first period in which metal was used. The date at which the age began varied by region; in Greece and China it began before 3000 BC, in Britain not until *c.* 1900 BC. The beginning of the period is sometimes called the Chalcolithic (Copper-Stone) Age, referring to the initial use of pure copper (along with its predecessor, stone). By 3000 BC the use of copper was well known in the Middle East, had extended westward into the Mediterranean area, and was beginning to infiltrate Europe. Only in the 2nd millennium BC did true bronze come to be widely used. The age was marked by increased specialization and the invention of the wheel and the ox-drawn plow. From *c.* 1000 BC the ability to heat and forge iron brought the Bronze Age to an end.

brown dwarf, Astronomical object intermediate in mass between a planet and a star. Sometimes described as failed stars, brown dwarfs are believed to form in the same way as stars, from fragments of an interstellar cloud that contract into gravitationally bound objects. However, they do not have enough mass to produce the internal heat that in stars ignites hydrogen and establishes nuclear fusion. Though they generate some heat and light, they also cool rapidly and shrink; they may differ from high-mass planets only in how they form.

Brownian motion, Any of various physical phenomena in which some quantity is constantly undergoing small, random fluctuations. It was named for Robert Brown, who was investigating the fertilization process of flowers in 1827 when he noticed a "rapid oscillatory motion" of microscopic particles within pollen grains suspended in water. He later discovered that similar motions could be seen in smoke or dust particles suspended in air and other fluids. The idea that molecules of a fluid are constantly in motion is a key part of the kinetic theory of gases, developed by James Clerk Maxwell, Ludwig Boltzmann, and Rudolf Clausius (1822–88) to explain heat phenomena.

brucellosis, or MALTA FEVER, or MEDITERRANEAN FEVER, or UNDULANT FEVER, Infectious disease of humans and domestic animals. It is characterized by gradual onset of fever, chills, sweats, weakness, and aches, and it usually ends within six months. It is named after the British physician David Bruce (b. 1855–d. 1931), who first identified (1887) the causative bacteria. Three main species in the genus *Brucella* commonly cause the disease in humans, who contract it from infected animals (goats, sheep, pigs, cattle). Brucellosis is rarely transmitted between humans but spreads rapidly in animals, causing severe economic losses. Drug therapy is not practical for animal brucellosis, but vaccination of young animals is useful. Infected animals must be removed from herds. Antibiotics are effective against acute disease in humans, in whom it can cause liver and heart problems if untreated.

Brugge, or BRUGES, City (pop., 2000 est.: 116,200), northwestern Belgium. First mentioned in 7th-century records, it was the site of a castle built in the 9th century by the first counts of Flanders against Norman invaders. It joined the Hanseatic League and was a major marketplace in the 13th century. As the centre of the Flemish cloth industry, it was the commercial hub of northern Europe. In the 15th century it was home to Jan van Eyck and other painters of the Flemish school. It declined as a port and textile centre but later revived with the construction of canals linking it with the North Sea. Shipbuilding, food processing, chemicals, electronics, and tourism are the main industries.

bruise, or CONTUSION, Visible bluish or purplish mark beneath the surface of unbroken skin, indicating burst blood vessels in deeper tissue layers. Bruises are usually caused by a blow or pressure, but they may occur spontaneously in elderly persons. The yellowish hue that becomes visible as a bruise heals comes from the disintegration and gradual absorption of blood.

Brundtland, Gro Harlem, orig. GRO HARLEM (b. April 20, 1939, Oslo, Nor.), Norwegian politician, first woman prime minister of Norway (1981, 1986–89, 1990–96). Trained as a physician, she worked with various government health services, then served as minister of the environment (1974–79). She served in the Norwegian parliament (1977–97). As leader of the Labour Party group, she served as premier three times. In 1987 she chaired the UN World Commission on Environment and Development, and in 1998 she was elected director-general of the World Health Organization.

Brunei, officially STATE OF BRUNEI DARUSSALAM, Independent sultanate, northern Borneo, western Pacific Ocean. The country is divided into two parts, each surrounded by the Malaysian state of Sarawak; they both have coastlines on the South China Sea and Brunei Bay. Area: 2,226 sq mi (5,765 sq km). Population: (2011 est.) 422,000. Capital: Bandar Seri Begawan. Brunei has a mixture of Southeast Asian ethnic groups: about two-thirds are Malay, one-tenth Chinese, and the remainder indigenous peoples and Indians. Languages: Malay (official), English (widely understood). Religions: Islam (official; predominantly Sunni); also traditional beliefs, Buddhism, Christianity. Currency: Brunei dollar, ringgit. The narrow northern coastal plain gives way to rugged hills in the south. Brunei's western enclave consists of the valleys of the Belait, Tutong, and Brunei rivers and is mainly hilly. The eastern enclave contains the Pandaruan and Temburong river basins and the country's highest point, Pagon Peak (6,070 ft [1,850 m]). Much of Brunei is covered by dense tropical rainforest; very little land is arable. Its economy is dominated by production from major oil and natural gas fields. It has one of the highest per capita incomes in Asia. Brunei is a monarchy (sultanate), with one (legislative) advisory body; the head of state and government is the sultan. Brunei traded with China in the 6th century CE. Through allegiance to the Javanese Majapahit kingdom (13th–15th century), it came under Hindu influence. In the early 15th century, with the decline of the Majapahit kingdom, many converted to Islam, and Brunei became an independent sultanate. When Ferdinand Magellan's ships visited in 1521, the sultan of Brunei controlled almost all of Borneo and its neighbouring islands. In the late 16th century Brunei lost power because of the Portuguese and Dutch activities in the region; they were soon joined by the British. By the 19th century the sultanate of Brunei included Sarawak (including present-day Brunei) and part of North Borneo (now part of Sabah). In 1841 a revolt took place against the sultan, and a British soldier, James Brooke, helped put it down; he was later proclaimed governor. In 1847 the sultanate entered into a treaty with Great Britain, and by 1906 it had yielded all administration to a British resident. Brunei rejected membership in the Federation of Malaysia in 1963, negotiated a new treaty with Britain in 1979, and achieved independence in 1984, with membership in the Commonwealth. Brunei has pursued ways to diversify the economy, notably by encouraging tourism.

Brunhild, or BRUNHILDA, or BRYNHILD, Beautiful Amazon-like heroine of ancient Germanic literature. She is known from Old Norse sources, notably the *Edda* poems and the *Vǫlsunga saga*, and from the German *Nibelungenlied*. She also appears in the operas of Richard Wagner's *Ring* cycle. She vowed to wed only a man of the most outstanding qualities who could surpass her in strength. She was successfully wooed by King Gunther, who de-

feated her in a contest in which the deeds were actually performed by Siegfried in cloak of invisibility. When she later discovered that she had been deceived, she exacted vengeance, and Siegfried was killed. Siegfried's widow in turn sought revenge and brought about the destruction of Gunther's people, the Burgundians. In some Norse sources, Brunhild has supernatural qualities and is described as a Valkyrie.

Brussels, French BRUXELLES, Flemish BRUSSEL, City (pop., 2008 est.: 148,873), capital of Belgium. It is part of the Brussels-Capital Region (pop., 2008 est.: 1,048,491), one of the three federal regions into which Belgium is divided. Brussels lies on the Senne River, a tributary of the Schelde. It began as a trading settlement and ultimately became a holding of the dukes of Brabant. In the first half of the 16th century it became the capital of the Low Countries, then under Habsburg control. In the late 16th century the Low Countries were divided and the southern provinces, where Brussels was located, were successively ruled by Spain, Austria, and France. After the Low Countries were reunited as the United Kingdom of the Netherlands in 1815, Brussels shared the status of capital with The Hague. A centre of rebellion, Brussels became the capital of independent Belgium in 1830. An important financial and commercial city, it is the headquarters of NATO and the seat of the European Union.

Brussels Treaty (1948) Agreement signed by Britain, France, Belgium, the Netherlands, and Luxembourg, creating a collective defense alliance. It led to the formation of NATO and the Western European Union. A goal of the treaty was to show that western European states could cooperate, thus encouraging the U.S. to play a role in the security of western Europe.

buccaneer, Any of the British, French, or Dutch sea adventurers who chiefly haunted the Caribbean and the Pacific seaboard of South America during the latter part of the 17th century, preying on Spanish settlements and shipping. Though inspired by such privateers as Englishman Francis Drake, the buccaneers were not legitimate privateers (the commissions they held were seldom valid), but neither were they the outlawed pirates who flourished in the 18th century. Usually escaped servants, former soldiers, or loggers, they ran their ships democratically, divided plunder equitably, and even provided a form of accident insurance. They influenced the founding of the South Sea Co., and stories of their adventures inspired more serious voyages of exploration as well as the tales of writers Jonathan Swift, Daniel Defoe, and Robert Louis Stevenson.

Bucharest, Romanian BUCUREŞTI, City (pop., 2007 est.: 1,931,838), capital of Romania. Excavations have revealed evidence of prehistoric settlement. The site gained importance when the rulers of Walachia moved there in the 14th century. Vlad III built a fortress there in the 15th century to ward off invading Turks; they eventually took it and made it their Ottoman Walachian capital in 1659. In the 19th century civic unrest helped force the union of Walachia and Moldavia, and Bucharest became the capital of the new Romanian state in 1862. Occupied by the Soviet army after World War II, it came under communist control. During the 1980s it was the scene of political demonstrations against the government of Nicolae Ceauşescu that resulted in his overthrow and execution.

Buchenwald, One of the first and biggest of the German Nazi concentration camps, established in 1937 near Weimar. In World War II it held about 20,000 prisoners, most of whom worked as slave laborers in nearby factories. Though there were no gas chambers, many perished through disease, malnutrition, exhaustion, beatings, and executions. Inmates were used to test the effects of viral infections and vaccines. The commandant's wife was the infamously sadistic Ilsa Koch (1906?–1967), the "Witch of Buchenwald." *See also* Holocaust.

Buck, Pearl, orig. PEARL SYDENSTRICKER (b. June 26, 1892, Hillsboro, W.Va., U.S.—d. March 6, 1973, Danby, Vt.), U.S. author. Buck was reared in China by her missionary parents and later taught in a Chinese university. Her first book to reach a wide audience was *The Good Earth* (1931, Pulitzer Prize), describing the struggles of a Chinese peasant and his slave wife. *Sons* (1932) and *A House Divided* (1935) followed; the trilogy was published as *The House of Earth* (1935). Among her later works are short stories, novels (including five under the pseudonym John Sedges), and an autobiography. She received the Nobel Prize for Literature in 1938.

Buckingham Palace, London residence of the British sovereign. It takes its name from the house built there early in the 18th century for the dukes of Buckingham. Victoria was the first sovereign to live there. John Nash began the reconstruction of Buckingham House as a Neoclassical palace in 1821, but was not allowed to finish. His garden front remains virtually unchanged, but the Mall front was redesigned in 1913 by Sir Aston Webb (1849–1930) as a background for the Queen Victoria Memorial statue.

Budapest, City (pop., 2004 est.: 1,708,000), capital of Hungary. Situated on the Danube River, it acquired its name in 1873 when the towns of Buda and Óbuda on the river's right bank and the town of Pest on its left bank amalgamated. Inhabited from Neolithic times, Buda was the site of a Roman camp in the 2nd century CE. By the 13th century both Buda and Pest had German inhabitants. Buda was fortified by Matthias I Corvinus in the 15th century and became the capital of Hungary. It was taken and held by the Turks (1541–1686), then retaken by Charles V, duke of Lorraine. In 1848–49 both towns experienced nationalistic revolt, and Pest became the capital of Kossuth Lajos's revolutionary government. It became the centre of revolt for Hungarian independence in 1918. After World War II, it came under communist control. It was the base of an unsuccessful uprising in 1956. Antigovernment unrest there in the 1980s led to the declaration of the Hungarian republic in 1989. Budapest is a vital Hungarian transport centre; it is also the site of heavy industry and manufacturing.

Buddha, orig. SIDDHARTHA GAUTAMA (b. *c.* 6th–4th century BCE, Lumbini, near Kapilavastu, Shakya republic, Kosala kingdom—d. Kusinara, Malla republic, Magadha kingdom), Spiritual leader and founder of Buddhism. The term *buddha* (Sanskrit: "awakened one") is a title rather than a name, and Buddhists believe that there are an infinite number of past and future buddhas. The historical Buddha, referred to as the Buddha Gautama or simply as the Buddha, was born a prince of the Shakyas, on the present-day India-Nepal border. He is said to have lived a sheltered life of luxury that was interrupted when he left the palace and encountered an old man, a sick man, and a corpse. Renouncing his princely life, he spent six years seeking out teachers and trying various ascetic practices, including fasting, to gain enlightenment. Unsatisfied with the results, he meditated beneath the bodhi tree, where, after temptations by Mara, he realized the Four Noble Truths and achieved enlightenment. At Sarnath he preached his first sermon to his companions, outlining the Eightfold Path, which offered a middle way between self-indulgence and self-mortification and led to the liberation of nirvana. The five ascetics who heard this sermon became not only his first disciples but also arhats who would enter nirvana upon death. His mission fulfilled, the Buddha died, after eating a meal that may accidentally have contained spoiled pork, and escaped the cycle of rebirth; his body was cremated, and stupas were built over his relics.

Buddhism, Major world religion and philosophy founded in northeastern India between the 6th and 4th centuries BCE. Based on the teachings of Siddhartha Gautama, called the Buddha, Buddhism takes as its goal the escape from suffering and from the cycle of rebirth: the attainment of nirvana. It emphasizes meditation and the observance of certain moral precepts. The Buddha's teachings were transmitted orally by his disciples; during his lifetime he established the Buddhist monastic order (sangha). He adopted some ideas from the Hinduism of his time, notably the doctrine of karma, but also rejected many of its doctrines and all of its gods. In India the emperor Ashoka promoted Buddhism during the 3rd century BCE, but it declined in succeeding centuries and was nearly extinct there by the 13th century. It spread south and flourished in Sri Lanka and Southeast Asia, and it moved through Central Asia and China (including Tibet), Korea, and Japan. In the 19th century Buddhism spread to Europe and the United States, and it became increasingly popular in the West in the second half of the 20th century. Buddhism's main teachings are summarized in the Four Noble Truths, of which the fourth is the Eightfold Path. Buddhism's two major branches, Mahayana and Theravada, have developed distinctive practices and unique collections of canonical texts. In the early 21st century the various traditions of Buddhism together had more than 375 million followers.

Buenos Aires, City (pop., 2001: city, 2,776,138; metro. area, 12,046,799), capital of Argentina. Located on an estuary of the Río de la Plata in east-central Argentina, about 150 mi (240 km) from the Atlantic Ocean, it is nevertheless a major port. First colonized by the Spanish in 1536, it was not permanently settled until 1580. It became the seat of the Viceroyalty of the Río de la Plata in 1776. In 1853 the city and the surrounding area that made up the province of Buenos Aires refused to recognize a new constitution approved by the country's other provinces and began fighting with them intermittently over control of the Argentine government. After being made a federal district and Argentina's capital, it settled its wars with the other provinces (1880) and by World War I (1914–18) had become a thriving port. The country's largest and most influential city, it is an important industrial and transportation centre.

Bug River, or WESTERN BUG RIVER, River, eastern Europe. Rising in western Ukraine, it flows north along the Poland-Ukraine and Poland-Belarus borders to Brest, and turns west into Poland to the Vistula River north of Warsaw, running a total of 516 mi (830 km). It is navigable below Brest. In World War I several battles were fought along its course in 1915. About 200 mi (322 km) of its central course formed part of the Curzon Line, a demarcation line between Poland and Soviet Russia for much of the 20th century.

bugaku, Repertoire of stylized dances of the Japanese imperial court, derived from the traditional dance forms of China, Korea, India, and Southeast Asia. The dances are divided into two basic forms: "dances of the left" (*saho no mai*), accompanied by music derived from China, with dancers wearing red costumes; and "dances of the right" (*uho samai no mai*), accompanied by music introduced from Korea, with dancers wearing costumes of blue or green. The dancers wear elaborate masks of painted wood to portray fictional characters.

Buganda, Precolonial kingdom, East Africa. Located along the northern shore of Lake Victoria in present-day Uganda, the kingdom was founded in the late 14th century by the Ganda people. Ruled by the *kabaka*, or king, by the 19th century Buganda was the most powerful kingdom in the area. In 1900 it became a British protectorate. The Ganda subsequently played a major role in assisting British administration in East Africa. When Uganda became independent in 1962, Buganda was accorded special federal status within the new country. Ensuing tensions with the central government led in 1967 to the kingdom's abolition and the area's integration into Uganda. Buganda was restored in 1993.

bugle, Soprano brass instrument historically used for hunting and military signaling. It developed from an 18th-century semicircular German hunting horn with widely expanding bore. In the 19th century the semicircle was reshaped into an oblong double loop. Natural bugles use only harmonics 2–6 (producing tones of the C triad) in their calls ("Reveille," "Taps," etc.). The keyed bugle, patented in 1810, has six sideholes and keys which give it a complete chromatic scale. In the 1820s valves were added to produce the flügelhorn and, in lower ranges, the baritone, euphonium, and sax-horns.

building construction, Techniques and industry involved in the assembly and erection of structures. Early humans built primarily for shelter, using simple methods. Building materials came from the land, and fabrication was dictated by the limits of the materials and the builder's hands. The erection sequence involved, as now, first placing a foundation (or using the ground). The builder erected the structural system; the structural material (masonry, mud, or logs) served as both skeleton and enclosure. Traditional bearing-wall and post-and-beam systems eventually gave way to framed structures, and builders became adept at sealing and fireproofing with a variety of claddings (exterior coverings) and finishes. Steel-framed buildings are usually enclosed by curtain walls. In modern-day construction, sheathing the skeleton of the building is only the beginning; specialists then begin the bulk of the work inside, installing plumbing, electrical wiring, HVAC (heating, ventilating, and air-conditioning), windows, floor coverings, plasterwork, moldings, ceramic tile, cabinets, and other features.

Bujumbura, formerly USUMBURA, City (pop., 2001: 346,000), capital of Burundi. Lying on the northern end of Lake Tanganyika, it is the country's chief port and largest urban centre. Known as Usumbura in the 1890s when German troops occupied the area and incorporated it into German East Africa, it was included in a Tutsi kingdom. When Burundi achieved independence in 1962, the city's name was changed to Bujumbura. Its industry specializes in textiles and agricultural products; most of Burundi's foreign trade is shipped between the capital and Kigoma, Tanzania.

Bulawayo, City (pop., 2002: 676,787), southwestern Zimbabwe. One of the country's largest cities, it lies 4,400 ft (1,340 m) above sea level. Originally the headquarters of the king of the Ndebele, it was occupied in 1893 by the British. It is Zimbabwe's principal industrial centre and, as headquarters for the country's railroads, its main transshipment point for goods to and from South Africa.

Bulgaria, officially REPUBLIC OF BULGARIA, Country, southeastern Europe. Area: 42,858 sq mi (111,002 sq km). Population: (2011 est.) 7,333,000. Capital: Sofia. Bulgarians make up the great majority of the population; smaller ethnic groups include Turks, Roma (Gypsies), and Macedonians. Languages: Bulgarian (official), regional dialects. Religions: Christianity (predominantly Eastern Orthodox; also other Christians); also Islam. Currency: lev. Three major regions define the landscape. The northernmost is the Danubian Plain, a fertile area occupying one-third of the country. Immediately south lie the Balkan Mountains (Stara Planina). In the southwest and south lie the Rhodope Mountains, with the country's highest point, Musala Peak, rising 9,596 ft (2,925 m). Smaller than the three major regions, Bulgaria's Black Sea coast is a popular eastern European resort area. Major drainage systems include the Black and Aegean seas. Bulgaria had a planned economy modeled on the Soviet system (1946–89). Since 1991 the noncommunist government has privatized some sectors of the economy, including agriculture. Bulgaria is a unitary multiparty republic with one legislative body; its head of state is the president, and its head of government is the prime minister. Evidence of human habitation dates from prehistoric times. Thracians were the first recorded inhabitants, dating from c. 3500 BCE, and their first state dates from about the 5th century BCE. The area was subdued by the Romans, who divided it into the provinces of Moesia and Thrace. In the 7th century CE the Bulgars took the region south of the Danube River. The Byzantine Empire in 681 formally recognized Bulgar control over the area between the Balkans and the Danube, though it would again dominate Bulgaria from the early 11th century to the late 12th century. Late in the 14th century Bul-

garia fell to the Ottoman Turks and again lost its independence. At the end of the Russo-Turkish War (1877–78), Bulgaria rebelled. The ensuing Treaty of San Stefano was unacceptable to the great powers, and the Congress of Berlin (1878) resulted. In 1908 the Bulgarian ruler, Ferdinand, declared Bulgaria's independence. After its involvement in the Balkan Wars (1912–13), Bulgaria lost territory. It sided with the Central Powers in World War I and with Germany in World War II. A communist coalition seized power in 1944, and in 1946 a people's republic was declared. With other eastern European countries in the late 1980s, Bulgaria experienced political unrest; its communist leader resigned in 1989. A new constitution that proclaimed a republic was implemented in 1991. Economic turmoil followed Bulgaria into the 21st century as it sought political stability; it joined NATO in 2004.

Bulge, Battle of the (Dec. 16, 1944–Jan. 16, 1945) In World War II, the last German offensive on the Western Front, an unsuccessful attempt to divide the Allied forces and prevent an invasion of Germany. The "bulge" refers to the wedge that the Germans drove into the Allied lines. In December 1944, Allied forces were caught unprepared by a German counterthrust in the wooded Ardennes region of southern Belgium. The German drive, led by Gerd von Rundstedt's panzer army, was initially successful but was halted by Allied resistance and reinforcements led by George Patton. The Germans withdrew in January 1945, but both sides suffered heavy losses.

Buli style, African wood sculpture made by the Luba people in the village of Buli, Congo (Zaire). The most typical examples are statues of ancestor figures and stools with seats supported on the heads and fingertips of figures. Because the carvings are almost identical and differ from other Luba carvings, they were once thought to be the work of a single artist, known as the Master of Buli, but it was later determined that they were actually produced in a workshop.

bulimia nervosa, Eating disorder, mostly in women, in which excessive concern with weight and body shape leads to binge eating followed by compensatory behaviour such as self-induced vomiting or the excessive use of laxatives or diuretics. The disorder typically begins in adolescence or early adulthood and is associated with depression, anxiety, and low self-esteem. Bulimia can have serious medical complications such as dental decay and dehydration. Treatment may include psychotherapy. Unlike persons with anorexia nervosa, most bulimics remain close to their proper weight.

bull market, In securities and commodities trading, a rising market. A bull is an investor who expects prices to rise and, on this assumption, buys a security or commodity in hopes of reselling it later for a profit. A bullish market is one in which prices are expected to rise.

bullfighting, Spanish CORRIDA DE TOROS, Spectacle, popular in Spain, Portugal, and Latin America, in which matadors ceremonially taunt, and usually kill, bulls in an arena. Spectacles with bulls were common in ancient Crete, Thessaly, and Rome. In the modern era, Roman amphitheatres were rebuilt and embellished for use as bullrings. The largest are in Madrid, Barcelona, and Mexico City. The corrida, which usually involves six individual fights, begins with a procession of matadors and their entourages. At the beginning of each fight an assistant (banderillero) performs a preliminary maneuver to allow the matador to assess the animal's behaviour. The matador then performs his capework, drawing the bull as close to him as possible without being gored. This is followed by the entrance of the picadors, horsemen who jab the bull with lances to weaken its neck and shoulder muscles. The matador then ritually slays the bull using a sword. In the Portuguese version of the ritual, the bull is fought from horseback and is not killed in the arena. In recent times, bullfighting has come under intense criticism from animal-rights activists.

Bundestag, Lower house of the German bicameral legislature. It represents the nation as a whole and is elected by universal suffrage under a system of mixed direct and proportional representation. Members serve four-year terms. The Bundestag in turn elects the chancellor. The term was formerly used to refer to the federal Diet of the German Confederation (1815–66), known as the Reichstag under the Weimar Republic (1919–34). Its building burned down in 1933, and its members were not allowed to meet again for the duration of the Nazi regime (1933–45). The Reichstag was reconstituted as the Bundestag in the governmental reorganization of 1949. Its membership was again reorganized after German unification in 1990.

Bunin, Ivan (Alekseyevich) (b. Oct. 10, 1870, Voronezh, Russia—d. Nov. 8, 1953, Paris, France), Russian poet and novelist. He worked as a journalist and clerk while writing and translating poetry, but he made his name as a short-story writer, with such masterpieces as the title story of *The Gentleman from San Francisco* (1916). His other works include the novella *Mitya's Love* (1925), the collection *Dark Avenues, and Other Stories* (1943), fictional autobiography, memoirs, and books on Leo Tolstoy and Anton Chekhov. He was the first Russian awarded the Nobel Prize for Literature (1933) and is among the best stylists in the language.

bunraku, Japanese traditional puppet theatre, in which nearly life-size dolls act out a chanted dramatic narrative, called *jōruri*, to the accompaniment of a small samisen. Puppet theatre reached its height in the 18th century with the plays of Chikamatsu Monzaemon and declined later because of a lack of good *jōruri* writers.

bureaucracy, Professional corps of officials organized in a pyramidal hierarchy and functioning under impersonal, uniform rules and procedures. Its characteristics were first formulated systematically by Max Weber, who saw in the bureaucratic organization a highly developed division of labour, authority based on administrative rules rather than personal allegiance or social custom, and a "rational" and impersonal institution whose members function more as "offices" than as individuals. For Weber, bureaucracy was a form of legalistic "domination" inevitable under capitalism. Later writers saw in bureaucracy a tendency to concentrate power at the top and become dictatorial, as occurred in the Soviet Union. Robert K. Merton emphasized its red tape and inefficiency due to blind conformity to procedures. More recent theories have stressed the role of managerial cliques, occupational interest groups, or individual power-seekers in creating politicized organizations characterized by internal conflict.

burial, Ritual disposal of human remains. The practice is often intended to facilitate the deceased's entry into the afterworld. Grave burial dates back at least 125,000 years. Types of graves range from trenches to large burial mounds to great stone tombs such as pyramids. Caves have also long been used for the dead—e.g., in ancient Hebrew burials, the sepulchral caves (rock temples) of western India and Sri Lanka, and the Dogon cliff burial sites. Water burial, such as occurred among the Vikings, has also been common. Cremation and the scattering of ashes on water is widely practiced, especially in Asia; in India the remains of the deceased are thrown into the sacred Ganges River. Some peoples (American Indian groups, Parsis, etc.) employ exposure to the elements to dispose of their dead. Among many peoples, the first burial is followed by a second, after an interval that often coincides with the duration of bodily decomposition. This reflects a concept of death as slow passage from the society of the living to that of the dead. Jewish custom requires speedy burial; a prayer known as the Kaddish is recited at the graveside, and a gravestone is normally erected a year after burial. Christian burials are often preceded by a wake, a "watch" held over the deceased's body and sometimes accompanied by festivity. Bodies of Muslims are laid on their right side and facing Mecca.

Burke, Edmund (b. January 12?, 1729, Dublin, Ire.—d. July 9, 1797, Beaconsfield, Buckinghamshire, Eng.), British parliamentarian, orator, and political philosopher. The son of a lawyer, he began legal studies but lost interest, became estranged from his father, and spent some time wandering about England and France. Essays he published in 1757–58 gained the attention of Denis Diderot, Immanuel Kant, and Gotthold Lessing, and he was hired to edit a yearly survey of world affairs (1758–88). He entered politics (1765) as secretary to a Whig leader and soon became involved in the controversy over whether Parliament or the monarch controlled the executive. He argued (1770) that George III's efforts to reassert a more active role for the crown violated the constitution's spirit. Elected to Parliament (1774–80), he contended that its members should exercise judgment rather than merely follow their constituents' desires. Although a strong constitutionalist, he was not a supporter of pure democracy; although a conservative, he eloquently championed the cause of the American colonists, whom he regarded as badly governed, and he supported the abolition of the international slave trade. He tried unsuccessfully to legislate relief for Ireland and to reform the governance of India. He disapproved of the French Revolution for its leaders' precipitous actions and its antiaristocratic bloodshed. He is often regarded as the founder of modern conservatism.

Burkina Faso, formerly UPPER VOLTA, Country, West Africa. A landlocked country, it lies south of the Sahara Desert. Area: 104,543 sq mi (270,764 sq km). Population: (2011 est.) 16,968,000. Capital: Ouagadougou. Ethnic groups include the Mossi, Fulani, Mande, Bobo, Senufo, and Hausa. Languages: French (official), Moore, Dyula, and others. Religions: Islam, traditional beliefs, Christianity. Currency: CFA franc. Burkina Faso consists of an extensive plateau characterized by a savanna, grassy in the north and sparsely forested in the south. The plateau is notched by the valleys of the Black Volta (Mouhoun), Red Volta (Nazinon), and White Volta (Nakambé) rivers, which flow south into Ghana. The economy is largely agricultural. Burkina Faso is a multiparty republic with one legislative body; its head of state is the president and its head of government the prime minister. Probably in the 15th century, the Mossi and Gurma peoples established themselves in eastern and central areas. The Mossi kingdoms of Yatenga and Ouagadougou existed into the early 20th century. A French protectorate was established over the region (1895–97), and its southern boundary was demarcated through an Anglo-French agreement. It was part of the Upper Senegal–Niger colony, then became a separate colony in 1919. It was constituted an overseas territory within the French Union in 1947, became an autonomous republic within the French Community in 1958, and achieved total independence in 1960. Since then it has been ruled primarily by the military and has experienced several coups. The country received its present name in 1984. A new constitution, adopted in 1991, restored multiparty rule; elected government returned in the 1990s. Economic problems plagued the country at the beginning of the 21st century.

burlesque, In literature, comic imitation of a serious literary or artistic form that relies on an extravagant incongruity between a subject and its treatment. It is closely related to parody, though burlesque is generally broader and coarser. Early examples include the comedies of Aristophanes. English burlesque is chiefly drama. John Gay's *The Beggar's Opera* (1728), Henry Fielding's *Tom Thumb* (1730), and Richard Brinsley Sheridan's *The Critic* (1779) are parodies of popular dramatic forms of the period. Victorian burlesque, usually light entertainment with music, was eclipsed by other popular forms by the late 19th century, and burlesque eventually came to incorporate and be identified with striptease acts.

burlesque show, Stage entertainment composed of slapstick sketches, bawdy humour, chorus numbers, and solo dances. Introduced in the U.S. in 1868 by a company of English chorus girls, it developed as a version of the minstrel show, divided into three parts: (1) a series of coarse humorous songs, slapstick sketches, and comic monologues; (2) the olio, or mixture of variety acts (e.g., acrobats, magicians, singers); and (3) chorus numbers and occasionally a takeoff, or burlesque, on politics or a current play. The show ended with an exotic dancer or a boxing match. In the early 20th century, many performers, including Fanny Brice, Al Jolson, and W.C. Fields, began their careers in burlesque. The addition of the striptease in the 1920s made a star of Gypsy Rose Lee, but censorship and competition from motion pictures soon led to burlesque's decline.

Burmese cat, Breed of domestic cat, presumably of Asian origin. Compactly built, it has a small, rounded head and wide-set, round, yellow eyes. The short, finely textured, glossy coat darkens as it matures from milk-chocolate to a rich sable brown and is paler on the underside; the ears, face, legs, and tail may be darker. The tapered tail may be kinked near the tip.

burn, Damage caused to the body by contact with flames, hot substances, some chemicals, radiation (including sunlight), or electricity. Burns are classified by depth of skin damage and by percentage of skin damaged. First-degree burns injure only the epidermis (top layer), with redness, pain, and minimal edema. In a second-degree burn, damage extends into the dermis (inner layer), with redness and blisters. Third-degree burns destroy the entire thickness of the skin. There is no pain, because the skin's pain receptors are destroyed. Burns deeper than the skin can release toxic materials into the bloodstream and may require amputation. Secondary shock follows severe burns, caused by loss of fluid both in the destroyed tissue and in leaks from the damaged area. Treatment depends on severity; first-degree burns need only first aid; third-degree burns require long-term hospitalization. Depending on the type, extent, and site of the burn, it may be left exposed, covered with a bandage, or excised to remove dead tissue in preparation for skin grafts. Complications of burns include respiratory problems, infection, ulcers in the stomach or duodenum, and, especially in brown skin, thick scarring. Seizures and hypertension after burns occur almost entirely in children. Survivors usually require plastic surgery, long-term physical therapy, and psychotherapy.

Bursa, formerly BRUSA, ancient PRUSA, City (pop., 2007: 1,431,172), northwestern Turkey. It was founded in the 3rd century BC, at the foot of the Mysian Mount Olympus near the southeastern shore of the Sea of Marmara, as the seat of the kings of Bithynia. It flourished under the Romans and later under the Byzantine Empire. After Crusaders conquered Constantinople (modern Istanbul) in 1204, it was a seat of Byzantine resistance. The Ottoman Empire took it in the early 14th century and made it their first great capital. Conquered by Timur in the early 15th century, it was later recovered by the Ottomans. Though the Ottoman capital was later moved to Constantinople, Bursa continued to prosper. Under the Republic of Turkey, it is a centre for agriculture and is noted for its carpets and many 15th-century mosques.

bursitis, Inflammation of the lubricating sac (bursa) over a joint or extension of a joint, or between tendons and muscles or bones, caused by infection, injury, arthritis or gout, calcium deposits along a tendon or joint, or repetitive minor irritation. Common types are "housemaid's knee," "soldier's heel," "tennis elbow," and "weaver's bottom." Bursitis in the shoulder is the most common form. Usually occurring in people unaccustomed to physical labour, it may be so painful that the affected part cannot be used. Treatment includes rest, heat, mild exercise, and medication to relieve inflammation and remove calcium deposits.

Burundi, officially REPUBLIC OF BURUNDI, Country, east-central Africa. Area: 10,740 sq mi (27,816 sq km). Population: (2011 est.) 8,575,000. Capital: Bujumbura. The population is divided primarily between the approximately four-fifths who are Hutu and the approximately one-fifth who are Tutsi. The first inhabitants, the Twa Pygmies, make up about 1% of the population. Languages: Rundi (Kirundi), French (both official), Swahili. Religions: Christianity (mostly Roman Catholic; also Protestant, other Christians); also traditional beliefs. Currency: Burundi franc. Burundi occupies a high plateau straddling the divide of the Nile and Congo watersheds. The divide runs north to south, rising to about 8,500 ft (2,600 m). The plateau contains the Ruvubu River basin, the southernmost extension of the Nile basin. In the west the Rusizi River connects Lake Kivu in the north with Lake Tanganyika to the south. Burundi has a developing economy based primarily on agriculture. It is a republic with two legislative houses, and its head of state and government is the president, assisted by vice presidents. Original settlement by the Twa was followed by Hutu settlement, which began about 1000 AD. The Tutsi arrived sometime later; though a minority, they established the kingdom of Burundi in the 16th century. In the 19th century the area came within the German sphere of influence, but the Tutsi remained in power. Following World War I, the Belgians were awarded control of the area. Colonial conditions had intensified Hutu-Tutsi ethnic animosities, and, as independence neared, hostilities flared. Independence was granted in 1962 in the form of a kingdom ruled by the Tutsi. In 1965 the Hutu rebelled but were brutally repressed. The two groups clashed violently throughout the rest of the 20th century, although the number of deaths did not approach the nearly one million people killed in neighbouring Rwanda. In 2001 a power-sharing transitional government was established and paved the way to the promulgation of a new constitution and the installation of a new government in 2005.

Burundi made its Olympic debut at the 1996 Summer Games in Atlanta.

bus, Large motor vehicle designed to carry passengers usually along a fixed route according to a schedule. The first gasoline-powered bus was built in Germany in 1895 and carried eight passengers. The first integral-frame bus was constructed in the early 1920s in the U.S. In the 1930s diesel engines were introduced, providing greater power and fuel efficiency to larger buses. With the development of highway systems, transcontinental bus lines became common in North America. Double-decked buses are used in some European cities; articulated buses pull trailers with flexible joints. Trolley buses, whose electric motors draw power from overhead wires, are now used mostly in European cities.

business cycle, Periodic fluctuation in the rate of economic activity, as measured by levels of employment, prices, and production. Economists have long debated why periods of prosperity are eventually followed by economic crises (stock-market crashes, bankruptcies, unemployment, etc.). Some have identified recurring 8-to-10-year cycles in market economies; longer cycles have also been proposed, notably by Nikolay Kondratev. Apart from random shocks to the economy, such as wars and technological changes, the main influences on the level of economic activity are investment and consumption. An increase in investment, as when a factory is built, leads to consumption because the workers employed to build the factory have wages to spend. Conversely, increases in consumer demand cause new factories to be built to satisfy the demand. Eventually the economy reaches its full capacity, and, with little free capital and no new demand, the process reverses itself and contraction ensues. Natural fluctuations in agricultural markets, psychological factors such as a bandwagon mentality, and changes in the money supply have all been proposed as explanations for initial changes in investment and consumption. After World War II many governments used monetary policy to moderate the business cycle, aiming to prevent the extremes of inflation and depression by stimulating the national economy in slack times and restraining it during expansions.

business law, or COMMERCIAL LAW, or MERCANTILE LAW, Legal rules and principles bearing on business organizations and commercial matters. It regulates various forms of legal business entities, including sole proprietors, partnerships, registered companies with limited liability, agents, and multinational corporations. Nearly all statutory rules governing business organizations are intended to protect creditors or investors. In addition, specific bodies of law regulate commercial transactions, including the sale and carriage of goods (terms and conditions, specific performance, breach of contract, insurance, bills of lading), consumer credit agreements (letters of credit, loans, security, bankruptcy), and relations between employers and employees (wages, conditions of work, health and safety, fringe benefits, and trade unions). It is a broad and continually evolving field.

butterfly, Any of more than 14,000 lepidopteran species found worldwide. Unlike moths, butterflies are active during the day and are usually brightly coloured or strikingly patterned. Distinctive features are club-tipped antennae and a habit of holding the wings vertically over the back when at rest. With few exceptions the larvae and adults eat plants. Butterflies are classified into five or six families. The metalmarks of the family Lycaenidae are found chiefly in the New World tropics; some members of the family Nymphalidae are called snout butterflies. Other species (with their families) include the white and sulphur butterflies (Pieridae), the swallowtail butterfly (Papilionidae), the blue, copper, and hairstreak butterflies (Lycaenidae), and the admiral, monarch, and painted lady (Nymphalidae).

buzzard, Chiefly British term for any of several birds of prey of the hawk genus *Buteo* (family Accipitridae) and, in North America, various New World vultures, especially the turkey vulture. In Australia, a large hawk of the genus *Hamirostra* is called a black-breasted buzzard. The buteos, also called buzzard hawks, can usually be distinguished when soaring by their broad wings and expansive rounded tail. The plumage of most species is dark brown above and white or mottled brown below; the tail and underside of the wings are usually barred. Buteos customarily prey on insects, small mammals, and occasionally birds. They nest in trees or on cliffs. Species range over much of the New World, Eurasia, and Africa. The red-tailed hawk, the most common North American buteo, is about 2 ft (60 cm) long.

Byblos, modern JBAIL, or JUBAYL, Ancient coastal city, eastern Mediterranean Sea. Located north of Beirut, Leb., the site was occupied by at least the Neolithic Period (New Stone Age); extensive settlement developed during the 4th millennium BC. As the chief harbour for the export of cedar to Egypt, it was a great trading centre. Papyrus, an early writing surface produced in Egypt, received its original Greek name, *byblos*, from its export to the Aegean through the city; the English word Bible means essentially "the (papyrus) book." Almost all known early Phoenician inscriptions, most from the 10th century BC, come from Byblos. By that time Tyre had become the preeminent city in Phoenicia, and, though Byblos continued to flourish into Roman times, it never recovered its former supremacy. It was designated a UNESCO World Heritage site in 1984.

Byron, George (Gordon) Byron, 6th Baron, known as LORD BYRON (b. Jan. 22, 1788, London, Eng.—d. April 19, 1824, Missolonghi, Greece), British Romantic poet and satirist. Born with a clubfoot and extremely sensitive about it, he was 10 when he unexpectedly inherited his title and estates. Educated at Cambridge, he gained recognition with *English Bards and Scotch Reviewers* (1809), a satire responding to a critical review of his first published volume, *Hours of Idleness* (1807). At 21 he embarked on a European grand tour. *Childe Harold's Pilgrimage* (1812–18), a poetic travelogue expressing melancholy and disillusionment, brought him fame, while his complex personality, dashing good looks, and many scandalous love affairs, with women and with boys, captured the imagination of Europe. Settling near Geneva, he wrote the verse tale *The Prisoner of Chillon* (1816), a hymn to

liberty and an indictment of tyranny, and *Manfred* (1817), a poetic drama whose hero reflected Byron's own guilt and frustration. His greatest poem, *Don Juan* (1819–24), is an unfinished epic picaresque satire in ottava rima. Among his numerous other works are verse tales and poetic dramas. He died of fever in Greece while aiding the struggle for independence, making him a Greek national hero.

Byzantine architecture, Building style of Constantinople (now Istanbul, formerly ancient Byzantium) after AD 330. Byzantine architects were eclectic, at first drawing heavily on Roman temple features. Their combination of the basilica and symmetrical central-plan (circular or polygonal) religious structures resulted in the characteristic Byzantine Greek-cross-plan church, with a square central mass and four arms of equal length. The most distinctive feature was the domed roof. To allow a dome to rest above a square base, either of two devices was used: the squinch (an arch in each of the corners of a square base that transforms it into an octagon) or the pendentive. Byzantine structures featured soaring spaces and sumptuous decoration: marble columns and inlay, mosaics on the vaults, inlaid-stone pavements, and sometimes gold coffered ceilings. The architecture of Constantinople extended throughout the Christian East and in some places, notably Russia, remained in use after the fall of Constantinople (1453).

Byzantine art, Art associated with the Byzantine Empire. Its characteristic styles were first codified in the 6th century and persisted with remarkable homogeneity until the capture of Constantinople by the Turks in 1453. Concerned almost exclusively with religious expression, it tends to reflect an intensely hierarchical view of the universe. It relies on vigour of line and brilliance of colour; individual features are absent, forms are flattened, and perspective is absent. Walls, vaults, and domes were covered in mosaic and fresco decoration in a total fusion of architectural and pictorial expression. Byzantine sculpture was largely limited to small ivory reliefs. The importance of Byzantine art to European religious art was immense; the style was spread by trade and expansion to the Mediterranean basin, eastern European centres, and especially Russia.

Byzantine Empire, Empire, southeastern and southern Europe and western Asia. It began as the city of Byzantium, which had grown from an ancient Greek colony founded on the European side of the Bosporus. The city was taken in 330 CE by Constantine I, who refounded it as Constantinople. The area at this time was generally termed the Eastern Roman Empire. The fall of Rome in 476 ended the western half of the Roman Empire, and the eastern half continued as the Byzantine Empire, with Constantinople as its capital. The eastern realm differed from the west in many respects: heir to the civilization of the Hellenistic era, it was more commercial and more urban. Its greatest emperor, Justinian (r. 527–565), reconquered some of western Europe, built the Hagia Sophia, and issued the basic codification of Roman law. After his death the empire weakened. Though its rulers continued to style themselves "Roman" long after Justinian's death, "Byzantine" more accurately describes the medieval empire. The long controversy over iconoclasm within the eastern church prepared it for the break with the Roman church. During the controversy, Arabs and Seljuq Turks increased their power in the area. In the late 11th century, Alexius I Comnenus sought help from Venice and the pope; these allies turned the ensuing Crusades into plundering expeditions. In the Fourth Crusade the Venetians took over Constantinople and established a line of Latin emperors. Recaptured by Byzantine exiles in 1261, the empire was now little more than a large city-state. In the 14th century the Ottoman Turks began to encroach. Their extended siege of Constantinople ended in 1453, when the last emperor died fighting on the city walls and the area came under Ottoman control.

C

C, High-level procedural computer programming language with many low-level features, including the ability to handle memory addresses and bits. It is highly portable among platforms and therefore widely used in industry and among computer professionals. C was developed by Dennis M. Ritchie (born 1941) of Bell Laboratories in 1972. The operating system UNIX was written almost exclusively in C, and C has been standardized as part of POSIX (Portable Operating System Interface for UNIX).

cabaret, Restaurant that serves liquor and offers light musical entertainment. The cabaret probably originated in France in the 1880s as a small club that presented amateur acts and satiric skits lampooning bourgeois conventions. The first German *Kabarett* was opened in Berlin *c.* 1900 by Baron Ernst von Wolzogen and accompanied its musical acts with biting political satire. By the 1920s it had become the centre for underground political and literary expression and a showcase for the works of social critics such as Bertolt Brecht and Kurt Weill; this decadent but fertile artistic milieu was later portrayed in the musical *Cabaret* (1966; film, 1972). The English cabaret derived from concerts given in city taverns in the 18th–19th centuries and evolved into the music hall. In the U.S. the cabaret developed into the nightclub, where comedians, singers, or musicians performed. Small jazz and folk clubs and, later, comedy clubs evolved from the original cabaret.

cabinet, Body of senior ministers or, in the U.S., advisers to a chief executive, whose members also serve as the heads of government departments. The cabinet has become an integral part of parliamentary government in many countries, though its form varies. It developed from the British Privy Council, when King Charles II and Queen Anne regularly consulted the council's leading members to reach decisions before meeting with the unwieldy full council. The modern British cabinet consists of departmental ministers, drawn from the members of Parliament and appointed by the prime minister. In the U.S., the cabinet serves as an advisory group to the president without the sanction of law. Members' appointments are subject to Senate approval, and the U.S. Constitution sets cabinet members' order of succession to the presidency. The cabinet includes the secretaries of State, Treasury, Defense, Interior, Agriculture, Commerce, Labor, Health and Human Services, Housing and Urban Development, Transportation, Education, Energy, and Veterans Affairs and the attorney general.

cacao, Tropical New World tree (*Theobroma cacao*) of the chocolate family (Sterculiaceae). Its seeds, after fermentation and roasting, yield cocoa and chocolate. Cocoa butter is extracted from the seed. The tree is grown throughout the wet lowland tropics, often in the shade of taller trees. Its thick trunk supports a canopy of large, leathery, oblong leaves. The small, foul-smelling, pinkish flowers are borne directly on the branches and trunk; they are followed by the fruit, or pods, each yielding 20–40 seeds, or cocoa beans.

CAD/CAM, in full COMPUTER-AIDED DESIGN/COMPUTER-AIDED MANUFACTURING., Integration of design and manufacturing into a system under direct control of digital computers. CAD systems use a computer with terminals featuring video monitors and interactive graphics-input devices to design such things as machine parts, patterns for clothing, or integrated circuits. CAM systems use numerically controlled machine tools and high-performance programmable industrial robots. Drawings developed during the design process are converted directly into instructions for the production machines, thus optimizing consistency between design and finished product, and providing flexibility in altering machine operations. These two processes are sometimes grouped as CAE (computer-aided engineering).

Cádiz, City (pop., 2001: city, 133,363; metro. area, 400,157), southwestern Spain. Located on a peninsula in the Bay of Cádiz northwest of Gibraltar, it is the main seaport of Cádiz province in Andalusia. Founded as Gadir by Phoenicians from Tyre *c.* 1100 BC, it was later ruled by Carthage, Rome (as Gades), and the Visigoths. It was held by the Moors beginning in AD 711. In 1262 Cádiz was captured by Alfonso X of Castile-León. The city enjoyed great prosperity as a centre for Spanish trade with the American colonies in the 16th–18th centuries. It now has naval and mercantile shipbuilding yards.

cadmium, Metallic chemical element, chemical symbol Cd, atomic number 48. It normally occurs along with other metals, especially zinc, in ores. A silvery white metal capable of taking a high polish, cadmium does not corrode under alkaline conditions; one of its major uses is in electroplating other metals and alloys to protect them. Because it absorbs neutrons effectively, it is used in control rods in some nuclear reactors. Its compounds, in which it has valence 2, are very toxic. They are used as pigments, as phosphors in television and computer monitor screens, as pesticides, and in photographic applications and analytical chemistry.

caduceus, Staff carried by Hermes as a symbol of peace. It served as a badge of protection for ancient Greek and Roman heralds and ambassadors. It was originally depicted as a rod or olive branch ending in two shoots and decorated with garlands or ribbons; in later iconography the garlands became two snakes and a pair of wings was attached to the staff to represent Hermes' speed. The caduceus was adopted as a symbol of physicians because of its similarity to the staff of Asclepius.

Caesar, (Gaius) Julius (b. July 12/13, 100 BCE, Rome—d. March 15, 44 BCE, Rome), Celebrated Roman general, statesman, and dictator. A patrician by birth, he held the prominent posts of quaestor and praetor before becoming governor of Farther Spain in 61–60. He formed the First Triumvirate with Pompey and Marcus Licinius Crassus in 60 and was elected consul in 59 and proconsul in Gaul and Illyria in 58. After conducting the Gallic Wars, during which he invaded Britain (55, 54) and crossed the Rhine (55, 53), he was instructed by the Senate to lay down his command, Senate conservatives having grown wary of his increasing power, as had a suspicious Pompey. When the Senate would not command Pompey to give up his command simultaneously, Caesar, against regulations, led his forces across the Rubicon River (49) between Gaul and Italy, precipitating the Roman Civil War. Pompey fled from Italy but was pursued and defeated by Caesar in 48; he then fled to Egypt, where he was murdered. Having followed Pompey to Egypt, Caesar became lover to Cleopatra and supported her militarily. He defeated Pompey's last supporters in 46–45. He was named dictator for life by the Romans. He was offered the crown (44) but refused it, knowing the Romans' dislike for kings. He was in the midst of launching a series of political and social reforms when he was assassinated in the Senate House on the ides of March by conspirators led by Cassius and Brutus. His writings on the Gallic and Civil wars are considered models of classical historiography.

caesaropapism, Political system in which the head of the state is also the head of the church and supreme judge in religious matters. It is often associated with the Byzantine Empire, where emperors presided over church councils and appointed patriarchs. The term has also been applied to other historical eras, including the rule of Tsar Peter I, who made the Russian Orthodox Church a department of the state, and the reign of Henry VIII in England.

caffeine, Heterocyclic compound that, like other alkaloids, has marked physiological effects. It occurs in coffee beans, tea leaves, kola nuts, cacao, maté, and guarana and in the products made from them. Its stimulating effect on the central nervous system, heart, cardiovascular system, and kidneys makes it medically useful in treating respiratory depression caused by overdose of barbiturates, morphine, or heroin. Its positive effects can include improved motor performance, decreased fatigue, increased alertness, and enhanced sensory activity. Excessive caffeine can produce irritability, anxiety, insomnia, and potentially serious symptoms such as heart irregularities and delirium. Much of the caffeine included in many over-the-counter stimulants, cold remedies, and painkillers has been extracted during production of decaffeinated coffee and tea.

Cain and Abel, In the Hebrew scriptures, the sons of Adam and Eve. According to Genesis, Cain, the firstborn, was a farmer, and his brother Abel was a shepherd. Cain was enraged when God preferred his brother's sacrifice of sheep to his own offering of grain, and he murdered Abel. When God asked where Abel was, Cain pretended ignorance, saying, "Am I my brother's keeper?" God punished Cain by sending him into exile but marked him with a sign as a warning to others, promising that he would be avenged if he were killed.

Cairo, Arabic AL-QĀHIRAH, City (pop., 2006: city, 7,786,640; 2007 est.: urban agglom., 16,100,000), capital of Egypt. Located on the banks of the Nile River near the site of a Roman city captured by the Arabs in 641, Al-Fusṭāṭ was first built by the Arabs as a military camp. Cairo's newer section (Al-Qāhirah) was built by the Fāṭimid dynasty (c. 968) and was made the capital in 973; both cities coexisted until Al-Fusṭāṭ was destroyed by fire in 1168, then rebuilt and joined with Cairo by Saladin. From the 13th century, as the capital of the Mamlūk dynasty, it reached its greatest prosperity as a trade and cultural centre. Occupied by French forces under Napoleon I in 1798, it was held by the French for three years. In World War II (1939–45) it was a base of operations for British and U.S. forces and was also the site of two conferences by the Allied powers. The metropolis is a blend of old and new, East and West. It is the centre of one of the largest urban agglomerations in the Middle East and Africa, and the popularity of its movies, music, and literature place it among the chief cultural centres of the Arab world. Among its most noteworthy landmarks are the pyramid complex of Giza, located at the southwestern edge of the city. Cairo is a manufacturing centre. It is also the site of several important universities and colleges, including Al-Azhar University, a centre of scholarship founded in the 10th century.

caisson, In engineering, a type of foundation most commonly used underwater for a bridge, but sometimes used in building construction. It is a large hollow structure that is sunk down through the earth by workers excavating from inside it; ultimately it becomes a permanent part of the pier. There are three types: the open caisson, open at both top and bottom; the box caisson, closed at the bottom; and the pneumatic caisson, with an airtight chamber to accommodate submerged workers. Caisson columns, typically 2 ft (0.6 m) or more in diameter, may be used as an alternative to bearing piles. A round hole is dug or bored to a stable layer of earth and temporarily supported by a steel shell, then filled with concrete poured around a cage of reinforcing bars.

Calah, modern NIMRŪD, Ancient city, Assyria. Lying south of modern Mosul, Iraq, it was founded in the 13th century BC by Shalmaneser I. It remained unimportant until the 9th century BC, when Ashurnasirpal II made it the capital of Assyria. It was the site of a religious building founded in 798 BC by Queen Sammu-remat (Semiramis of Greek legend). Excavations there have yielded thousands of carved ivories from the 9th–8th centuries BC. See photograph above.

calcium, Chemical element, one of the alkaline earth metals, chemical symbol Ca, atomic number 20. The most abundant metallic element in the human body, it is an essential part of bones

Winged bull of alabaster, guardian of a gate of the palace of Ashurnasirpal II at Nimrud; in the Metropolitan Museum of Art, New York City.
Courtesy of the Metropolitan Museum of Art, New York, gift of John D. Rockefeller, Jr., 1932

and teeth and has many physiological functions. It is the fifth most abundant element in Earth's crust but does not occur naturally in the free state. In its compounds calcium has valence 2. It occurs in limestone, chalk, marble, dolomite, eggshells, pearls, coral, and many marine shells as calcium carbonate, or calcite; in apatite as calcium phosphate; in gypsum as calcium sulfate; and in many other minerals. It is used as an alloying agent and in other metallurgical applications; its alloy with lead is used in cable sheathing and grids for batteries. Calcite is used as a lime source, a filler, a neutralizer, and an extender; in pure form it is used in baking powder and as an antacid and calcium supplement. Calcium oxide (lime) and its product after water addition, calcium hydroxide (slaked lime), are important industrially. Other significant compounds are calcium chloride (a drying agent), calcium hypochlorite (a bleach), calcium sulfate (gypsum and plaster of paris), and calcium phosphate (a plant food and stabilizer for plastics).

calculus, Field of mathematics that analyzes aspects of change in processes or systems that can be modeled by functions. Through its two primary tools—the derivative and the integral—it allows precise calculation of rates of change and of the total amount of change in such a system. The derivative and the integral grew out of the idea of a limit, the logical extension of the concept of a function over smaller and smaller intervals. The relationship between differential calculus and integral calculus, known as the fundamental theorem of calculus, was discovered in the late 17th century independently by Isaac Newton and Gottfried Wilhelm Leibniz. Calculus was one of the major scientific breakthroughs of the modern era.

calendar, System for dividing time over extended periods, such as days, months, or years, and arranging these divisions in a definite order. A calendar is essential for the study of chronology, which reckons time by regular divisions, or periods, and uses these to date events. It is also vital for any civilization that needs to measure periods for agricultural, business, domestic, or other reasons. The lunation, or period in which the moon completes a cycle of its phases ($29^{1}/_{2}$ days), is the basis for the month; most ancient calendars were collections of months. Days and seasons, which are a solar phenomena, do not have periods that evenly divide, so ancient calendars employed various means, such as the periodic insertion of an intercalary month, to reconcile the months with the seasons. The Gregorian calendar used almost universally today is a modification of the Julian calendar adopted by Julius Caesar, which used a $365^{1}/_{4}$–day year with 12 months that came to have the number of days we know today.

Calgary, City (pop., 2001: city, 878,866; metro. area, 951,395), southern Alberta, Canada. It was founded in 1875 as a fort on the Bow River for the Northwest Mounted Police. The arrival of the Canadian Pacific Railway in 1883 aided its growth, as did the discovery of nearby oil and gas fields in 1914 and 1947. Its major industries are petroleum refining, meatpacking, and lumbering. The annual Calgary Stampede, founded in 1912, is a world-famous rodeo and celebration of the Old West.

caliph, Arabic KHALĪFAH ("DEPUTY" OR "SUCCESSOR"), Title given to those who succeeded the Prophet Muhammad as real or nominal ruler of the Muslim world, ostensibly with all his powers except that of prophecy. Controversy over the selection of the fourth caliph, ʿAlī, eventually split Islam into the Sunnite and Shīʿite branches. ʿAlī's rival, Muʿāwiyah I, established the Umayyad dynasty of caliphs, which produced 14 caliphs (661–750). The ʿAbbāsid dynasty (750–1258), the most widely observed caliphate, associated with 38 caliphs, moved the capital from Damascus to Baghdad. The Mongol conquest of Baghdad in 1258 effectively ended the dynasty. Other Muslim leaders created caliphates with limited success. The Fāṭimid dynasty proclaimed a new caliphate in 920; ʿAbd al-Raḥmān III announced one in opposition to both the ʿAbbāsids and the Fāṭimids in 928. A scion of the ʿAbbasid line was set up by the Mamlūk dynasty as a sort of puppet caliph after 1258. This caliphate exercised no power whatsoever, and, from 1517 until it was abolished by the Republic of Turkey in 1924, it resided in Istanbul under the control of the Ottoman Empire. Modern Muslim militants consider the abolition of the caliphate a catastrophic event, and its return has been a central pillar of their political program.

calla, Either of two distinct kinds of plants of the arum family. *Calla palustris* is known as the arum lily, water arum, or wild calla. The common name calla is also generally given to several species of *Zantedeschia*, often called calla lilies. The handsome *C. palustris* occurs widely in wet places in cool, northern temperate and subarctic regions. It has heart-shaped leaves, showy white floral leaves, and clusters of brilliant red berries. Its juice is violently poisonous. The most important of the calla lilies, all native to South Africa, is the common florist's calla (*Z. aethiopica*), a stout herb with a fragrant white spathe and arrow-shaped leaves; a popular indoor plant, it is grown commercially for cut flowers.

Callao, City (pop., 2005: 389,579), chief seaport, Peru. It was founded in 1537 by Francisco Pizarro on Callao Bay west of Lima. As the leading shipping point for gold and silver taken by Spanish conquistadores from the Incas, it was frequently assaulted by pirates and by Spain's European rivals. It was destroyed by a tidal wave in 1746 and then rebuilt near its original site. It withstood several sieges by Spanish forces during the wars for independence. The revolutionary leader Simón Bolívar landed there in 1823, and three years later it was the scene of the final Spanish surrender to rebel forces. It suffered heavy earthquake damage in 1940 but has since expanded and modernized.

calligraphy, Art of beautiful, stylized, or elegant handwriting or lettering with pen or brush and ink. It involves the correct formation of characters, the ordering of the various parts, and the harmony of proportions. In the Islamic and Chinese cultures, calligraphy is as highly revered as painting. In Europe in the 14th–16th centuries, two scripts developed that influenced all subsequent handwriting and printing: the roman and italic styles. With the invention of modern printing (1450), calligraphy became increasingly bold and ornamental.

callus, In botany, soft tissue that forms over a wounded or cut plant surface, leading to healing. A callus arises from cells of the cambium. When a callus forms, some of its cells may organize into growing points, some of which in turn give rise to roots while others produce stems and leaves. Thus a callus may be capable of regenerating an entire plant.

calorie, Unit of energy or heat. Various precise definitions are used for different purposes (physical chemistry measurements, engineering steam tables, and thermochemistry), but in all cases the calorie is about 4.2 joules, the amount of heat needed to raise the temperature of 1 g of water by 1 °C (1.8 °F) at normal atmospheric pressure. The calorie used by dietitians and food scientists and found on food labels is actually the kilocalorie (also called Calorie and abbreviated kcal or Cal), or 1,000 calories. It is a measure of the amount of heat energy or metabolic energy contained in the chemical bonds of a food.

calumet, or SACRED PIPE, or PEACE PIPE, One of the central ceremonial objects of many American Indian groups. It was considered a microcosm, its parts and its decorative colours and motifs corresponding to the essential parts of the universe. It was smoked in personal prayer as well as at collective rites. Because of the narcotic effect of the tobacco and the symbolism of the indrawn and ascending smoke, the calumet was employed as a means of communication between the spirit world and humans.

Calvin, John, French JEAN CAUVIN (b. July 10, 1509, Noyon, Picardy, France—d. May 27, 1564, Geneva, Switz.), French Protestant theologian and major figure of the Reformation. He studied religion at the University of Paris and law in Orléans and Bourges. When he returned to Paris in 1531 he studied the Bible and became part of a movement that emphasized salvation by grace rather than by works. Government intolerance prompted him to move to Basel, Switz., where he wrote the first edition of *Institutes of the Christian Religion* (1536). Gaining a reputation among Protestant leaders, he went to Geneva to help establish Protestantism in that city. He was expelled by city fathers in 1538 but returned in 1541, when the town council instituted the church order outlined in his *Ecclesiastical Ordinances*, including enforcement of sexual morality and abolition of Catholic "superstition." He approved the arrest and conviction for heresy of Michael Servetus. By 1555 Calvin had succeeded in establishing a theocracy in Geneva, where he served as pastor and head of the Genevan Academy and wrote the sermons, biblical commentaries, and letters that form the basis of Calvinism.

Calvinism, In Protestantism, the theology developed and advanced by John Calvin. It was further developed by his followers and became the foundation of the Reformed church and Presbyterianism. As shaped by Calvin's successor at Geneva, Theodore Beza (1519–1605), Calvinism emphasizes the doctrine of predestination, holding that God extends grace and grants salvation only to the chosen, or elect. It stresses the literal truth of the Bible, and it views the church as a Christian community in which Christ is head and all members are equal under him. It therefore rejects the episcopal form of church government in favor of an organization in which church officers are elected. Calvinism was the basis of theocracies in Geneva and Puritan New England, and it strongly influenced the Presbyterian church in Scotland.

calypso, Musical style best known as a type of folk song. Calypso originated in Trinidad but is common throughout the Caribbean. The calypso tradition dates to the early 19th century. The subject of a calypso text, usually witty and satiric, is an event of political or social import. The lyric often incorporates Spanish, Creole, and African phrases, employing newly invented expressions such as *bobol* (graft) and *pakoti* (unfaithfulness). The exaggeration of local speech patterns is matched by an offbeat rhythm. Favourite accompanying instruments are the shak-shak (maraca), cuatro (a string instrument), and tamboo-bamboo (bamboo poles of various lengths struck on the ground). Shaped and tuned oil drums, played together in orchestras called steel bands, have also been popular.

Cambodia, officially KINGDOM OF CAMBODIA, Country, Southeast Asia. Area: 69,898 sq mi (181,035 sq km). Population: (2011 est.) 14,702,000. Capital: Phnom Penh. The vast majority of the population belongs to the Khmer ethnic group. Language: Khmer (official). Religions: Buddhism (official); also traditional beliefs. Currency: riel. The landscape is dominated by large central plains; the Dangrek Mountains rise along the northern border. Cambodia lies largely in the basin of the Mekong River; the large lake Tonle Sap is in its western part. Much of the country is tropical forest. It is one of the world's poorest countries. Agriculture employs about three-fourths of the workforce. Cambodia is a constitutional monarchy with two legislative houses; its head of state is the king, and its head of government is the prime minister. In the early centuries CE the area was under Hindu and, to a lesser extent, Buddhist influence. The Khmer state gradually spread in the early 8th century and reached its height under Jayavarman II and his successors in the 9th–12th centuries, when it ruled the Mekong valley and neighbouring states and built Angkor. Buddhism was widely adopted in the 13th century. From the 13th century the state was attacked by Annam and Tai (Siamese) city-states and was subject largely to Tai and Vietnamese hegemony. It became a French protectorate in 1863. It was occupied by the Japanese in World War II and became independent in 1954. Its borders were the scene of fighting in the Vietnam War from 1961, and in 1970 its northeastern and eastern areas were occupied by the North Vietnamese and penetrated by U.S. and South Vietnamese forces. A bombing campaign in Cambodia by U.S. warplanes alienated much of the population, enabling the communist Khmer Rouge under Pol Pot to seize power in 1975. Their regime of terror resulted in the deaths of at least 1.5 million Cambodians. Vietnam invaded in 1978 and drove the Khmer Rouge into the western hinterlands, but Cambodian infighting continued. A peace accord was reached by most Cambodian factions under UN auspices in 1991. Elections were held in 1993, and Norodom Sihanouk was restored to the monarchy. A civilian government slowly emerged under UN tutelage until 1997, when a coup by Hun Sen consolidated his position as prime minister. Hun Sen's party won legislative elections in 1998; also that year, Cambodia became part of ASEAN.

Cambrai, League of (1508–10) Alliance of Pope Julius II, Emperor Maximilian I, King Louis XII, and King Ferdinand V, formed in 1508. Ostensibly directed against the Turks, its actual aim was to attack the Republic of Venice and divide its possessions among the allies. The allies were unable to act together because of their individual ambitions, and the league collapsed in 1510, when the pope joined with Venice, while Ferdinand became neutral.

Cambrian Period, Oldest time division of the Paleozoic Era. During the Cambrian, 542–488.3 million years ago, there were widespread seas and several scattered landmasses. The largest continent was Gondwana. The average climate was probably warmer than today, with less variation between regions. There were no land plants or animals, but there were marine organisms with either shells or skeletons. Because the dominant animals were trilobites, the Cambrian is sometimes referred to as the Age of Trilobites.

Cambridge, City and administrative district (pop., 2001: 108,878), eastern England. It is the county seat of Cambridgeshire. Cambridge lies on the River Cam, a tributary of the Ouse, north of London. Originally a fording site, Cambridge possesses earthworks and Roman remains. Two monastic foundations date from the 11th–12th centuries. Cambridge received its first charter in 1207. It is best known as the site of the University of Cambridge, noted for its educational excellence and outstanding architecture. The city's economy is linked to the university and its research and development services.

Corpus Christi College, University of Cambridge, England.
Shostal Associates

Camelot, In Arthurian legend, the seat of King Arthur's court. It has been variously identified with Caerleon in Wales, Queen Camel in Somerset, Camelford in Cornwall, Winchester in Hampshire, and Cadbury Castle in Somerset. Camelot has come to symbolize a short-lived golden era under a beloved leader.

cameo, Hard or precious stone, glass, ceramic, or shell carved in relief above the surface. It is the opposite of intaglio. Surviving cameos date from the early Sumerian period (*c.* 3100 BC) to the decline of Roman civilization, and from the Renaissance to the Neoclassical period of the 18th century. They were carved with mythological scenes and portraits, and many commemorated specific persons. In the 18th–19th century, cameos adorned diadems, belts, brooches, and bracelets.

"The Rape of Europa," cameo in gold and enamel frame, 16th–17th century; in the Kunsthistorisches Museum, Vienna
Courtesy of the Kunsthistorisches Museum, Vienna

Cameron, David (b. Oct. 9, 1966, London, Eng.), British politician and prime minister (2010–). He was the United Kingdom's youngest prime minister since 1812, and he led Britain's first coalition government since World War II. Cameron, a descendant of King William IV, was born into a family with both wealth and an aristocratic pedigree. After graduating from Oxford, he worked as an adviser to Conservative Party politicians. He spent most of the 1990s in the private sector and entered the House of Commons as a Conservative in 2001. His youth, charisma, and moderate views inspired comparisons to Labour Prime Minister Tony Blair. Cameron quickly advanced through the Conservative ranks, and he was elected party leader in 2005. He presided over a period of increasing Conservative popularity, culminating in the general election of May 2010. Although the Conservatives fell short of outright majority, Cameron was able to form a coalition government with the Liberal Democrats and became prime minister.

Cameroon, officially REPUBLIC OF CAMEROON, Country, West Africa. Area: 183,920 sq mi (476,350 sq km). Population: (2011 est.) 20,073,000. Capital: Yaoundé. The country has numerous ethnic groups, including the Fang, Bamileke and Bamum, Duala, and Fulani. Pygmies (locally known as Baguielli and Babinga) live in the southern forests. Languages: French, English (both official), Fula, Bamileke, Duala. Religions: Christianity (mostly Roman Catholic and Protestant), traditional beliefs, Islam (mainly in the north). Currency: CFA franc. Cameroon has four geographic regions. The southern area consists of coastal plains and a densely forested plateau. The central region rises progressively to the north and includes the Adamawa Plateau. In the north a savanna plain slopes downward toward the Lake Chad basin. To the west and north along the Nigerian border the relief is mountainous and includes Mount Cameroon. Of the main rivers, the Sanaga drains into the Atlantic Ocean, and the Benue flows westward into the Niger River basin in Nigeria. Cameroon has a developing market economy based largely on petroleum and agriculture but with a growing services sector. It is a unitary multiparty republic with one legislative house; its head of state is the president and its head of government the prime minister. Long inhabited before European colonization, Cameroon was populated by Bantu-language speakers coming from equatorial Africa to settle in the south. They were followed by Muslim Fulani from the Niger River basin, who settled in the north. Portuguese explorers visited in the late 15th century, and the Dutch were also active there. In 1884 the Germans took control and extended their protectorate over Cameroon. In World War I joint French-British action forced the Germans to retreat, and after the war the region was divided into French and

British administrative zones. After World War II the two areas became UN trusteeships. In 1960 the French trust territory became an independent republic. In 1961 the southern part of the British trust territory voted for union with the new Republic of Cameroon, and the northern part voted for union with Nigeria. The independent country has faced chronic economic problems, which have produced and exacerbated unrest in the country.

camouflage, Art and practice of concealment and visual deception in war. Its goal is to prevent enemy observation of installations, personnel, equipment, and activities. Camouflage came into wide use in World War I in response to air warfare. Aerial reconnaissance (and later aerial bombardment) required concealment of troops and equipment. By World War II, long-range bombing threatened warring countries in their entirety, and almost everything of military significance was hidden to some degree, using mottled, dull-coloured paint patterns (green, gray, or brown), cloth garnishing, netting, and natural foliage. Dummies and decoys, including fake vehicles and airfields, tricked enemy planes into bombing harmless targets. It remained an important technique after World War II, used with notable success by communist guerrilla units in the Vietnam War.

Camp David Accords (1978) Two agreements reached between Menachem Begin of Israel and Anwar el-Sādāt of Egypt with the help of U.S. President Jimmy Carter at Camp David, Md., U.S. One agreement created a framework for negotiations to arrive at a peace treaty between Egypt and Israel, formally ending some 30 years of being in a state of war. This treaty, normalizing relations, was signed in 1979 and led to the return of the Sinai Peninsula, occupied by Israel in the Six-Day War (1967), to Egypt. The other agreement created a framework for a broader peace in the region that included a plan for Palestinian self-rule in the West Bank and Gaza Strip. The latter provisions were not implemented.

Campylobacter, Genus of gram-negative spiral-shaped bacteria infecting mammals. Many species, especially *C. fetus*, cause miscarriage in sheep and cattle. *C. jejuni* is a common cause of food poisoning. Sources include meats (particularly chicken) and unpasteurized milk. Infection causes acute gastroenteritis, fever, headache, and joint and muscle pain; nerve damage and death may occur in severe cases.

Camus, Albert (b. Nov. 7, 1913, Mondovi, Alg.—d. Jan. 4, 1960, near Sens, France), Algerian-French novelist, essayist, and playwright. Born into a working-class family, Camus graduated from the university in Algiers and then worked with a theatrical company, becoming associated with leftist causes. He spent the war years in Paris, and the French Resistance brought him into the circle of Jean-Paul Sartre and existentialism. He became a leading literary figure with his enigmatic first novel, *The Stranger* (1942), a study of 20th-century alienation, and the philosophical essay "The Myth of Sisyphus" (1942), an analysis of contemporary nihilism and the concept of the absurd. *The Plague* (1947), his allegorical second novel, and "The Rebel" (1951), another long essay, developed related issues. Other major works include the short-story collection *Exile and the Kingdom* (1957) and the posthumous autobiographical novel *The First Man* (1994). His plays include *Le Malentendu* (1944) and *Caligula* (1944). Camus won the Nobel Prize for Literature in 1957. He died in a car accident.

Canaan, Ancient name for an area of shifting boundaries but centred on Palestine. Coastal Canaanite civilization dates to the Paleolithic Period; towns developed in Neolithic times (*c.* 7000–4000 BC). The name appears in writings from the 15th century BC. Invaded by the Hebrews (*c.* 1200 BC), who settled in southern areas, it was later invaded by the Philistines. In the 10th century BC the Israelites, under King David, broke Philistine power, and Canaan became thereafter the Land of Israel, the "Promised Land" of the biblical book of Exodus.

Canada, Country, North America. Area: 3,855,103 sq mi (9,984,670 sq km). Population: (2011 est.) 34,447,000. Capital: Ottawa. People of British and French descent constitute more than half the population; there are significant minorities of Chinese, South Asian, German, Italian, American Indian, and Inuit (Eskimo) origin. Languages: English, French (both official). Religions: Christianity (mostly Roman Catholic; also Protestant, other Christians, Eastern Orthodox); also Islam, Judaism, Hinduism, Buddhism. Currency: Canadian dollar. Canada may be divided into several physiographic regions. A large interior basin centred on Hudson Bay and covering nearly four-fifths of the country is composed of the Canadian Shield, the interior plains, and the Great Lakes–St. Lawrence lowlands. Rimming the basin are highland regions, including the Arctic Archipelago. Mountain ranges include the Rocky, Coast, and Laurentian mountains. Canada's highest peak is Mount Logan (19,551 ft [5,959 m]) in Yukon Territory. Five of Canada's rivers—the St. Lawrence, Mackenzie, Yukon, Fraser, and Nelson—rank among the world's 40 longest. In addition to Lakes Superior and Huron, both shared with the U.S., Canada's Great Bear and Great Slave lakes are among the world's 11 largest lakes in area. The country also includes several major islands, including Baffin, Ellesmere, Victoria, Newfoundland, and Melville, and many small ones. Its border with the U.S., the longest border in the world not patrolled by military forces, extends 5,525 mi (8,890 km). With a developed market economy that is export-directed and closely linked with that of the U.S., Canada is one of the world's most prosperous countries. It is a federal multiparty parliamentary state with two legislative houses; its head of state is the British monarch, whose representative is Canada's governor-general, and the head of government is the prime minister. Originally inhabited by American Indians and Inuit, Canada was visited *c.* 1000 CE by Scandinavian explorers, whose settlement is confirmed by archaeological evidence from Newfoundland. Fishing expeditions off Newfoundland by the English, French, Spanish, and Portuguese began as early as 1500. The French claim to Canada was made in 1534 when Jacques Cartier entered the Gulf of St. Lawrence. A small settlement was made in Nova Scotia (Acadia) in 1604, and by 1608 Samuel de Champlain had reached Quebec. Fur trading was the impetus behind the early colonizing efforts. In response to French activity, the English in 1670 formed the Hudson's Bay Company. The British-French rivalry for the interior of upper North America lasted almost a century. The first French loss occurred in 1713 at the conclusion of Queen Anne's War (War of the Spanish Succession), when Nova Scotia and Newfoundland were ceded to the British. The Seven Years' War (French and Indian War) resulted in France's expulsion from continental North America in 1763. After the American Revolution Canada's population was augmented by loyalists fleeing the United States, and the increasing number arriving in Quebec led the British to divide the colony into Upper and Lower Canada in 1791. The British reunited the two provinces in 1841. Canadian expansionism resulted in the confederation movement of the mid-19th century, and in 1867 the Dominion of Canada, comprising Nova Scotia, New Brunswick, Quebec, and Ontario, came into existence. After confederation, Canada entered a period of westward expansion. The prosperity that accompanied Canada into the 20th century was marred by continuing conflict between the English and French communities. Through the Statute of Westminster (1931), Canada was recognized as an equal partner of Great Britain. With the Canada Act of 1982, the British gave Canada total control over its constitution and severed the remaining legal connections between the two countries. French Canadian unrest continued to be a major concern, with a movement growing for Quebec separatism in the late 20th century. Referendums for more political autonomy for Quebec were rejected in 1992 and 1995, but the issue remained unresolved. In 1999 Canada formed the new territory of Nunavut.

canal, Artificial waterway built for transportation, irrigation, water supply, or drainage. The early Middle Eastern civilizations probably first built canals to supply drinking and irrigation water. The most ambitious navigation canal was a 200-mi (320-km) construction in what is now Iraq. Roman canal systems for military transport extended throughout northern Europe and Britain. The most significant canal innovation was the pound lock, developed by the Dutch c. 1373. The closed chamber, or pound, of a lock is flooded or drained of water so that a vessel within it is raised or lowered in order to pass between bodies of water at different elevations. Canals were extremely important before the coming of the railroad in the mid-19th century. Among the significant waterways in the U.S. were the Erie Canal, several canals linking the Great Lakes, and one connecting the Great Lakes to the Mississippi River. Modern waterway engineering enables larger vessels to travel faster by reducing delays at locks.

Canal Zone, or PANAMA CANAL ZONE, Strip of territory, a historic administrative entity in Panama over which the U.S. formerly exercised jurisdictional rights (1903–79). The zone came into being in 1904 when Panama granted the U.S., in return for annual payments, sole right to operate and control the Panama Canal, including a strip of land 10 mi (16 km) wide along the canal extending from the Atlantic to the Pacific Ocean and bisecting the Isthmus of Panama. The zone was abolished by treaty in 1979, and civil control of the territory was returned to Panama. By the same treaty a commission under joint U.S.-Panamanian ownership was established to operate the canal until the year 2000, when Panama assumed full control.

Canary Islands, Spanish ISLAS CANARIAS, Island group and autonomous community (pop., 2005 est.: 1,968,280) of Spain located in the Atlantic Ocean 67 mi (108 km) off the northwestern coast of Africa. The islands comprise two provinces, Santa Cruz de Tenerife and Las Palmas, with an area of 2,876 sq mi (7,447 sq km). The capital is Santa Cruz de Tenerife. Known in ancient times as the "Fortunate Islands," they were written about by both Plutarch and Pliny the Elder. Believed to be the western limit of the world, they were visited in the Middle Ages by Arabs, Genoese, Majorcans, Portuguese, and French. They were taken by Castile in 1404, and their indigenous inhabitants, the Guanche and Canario, were gradually conquered during the 15th century. The islands became a stop on the usual route for Spanish trading vessels with the New World. Today agriculture is an economic mainstay, as is an expanding tourist trade.

Canberra, City (pop., 2004 est.: metro. area, 377,074), capital of Australia. Located in the Australian Capital Territory, on the Molonglo River, it was chosen in 1909 as the site of the capital.

A statue by Henry Moore sits on the grounds of the National Library of Australia in Canberra.
Robin Smith Photography, New South Wales

An international competition held in 1911 chose the U.S. architect Walter Burley Griffin (b. 1876—d. 1937) to design the city, and construction began in 1913. The transfer of Parliament from Melbourne took place in 1927. The city continues to expand, with residential development taking place in satellite towns. There is light industry and a growing tourist trade, though government functions dominate.

Cancer (Latin: "Crab") In astronomy, the constellation lying between Leo and Gemini; in astrology, the fourth sign of the zodiac, governing approximately the period June 22–July 22. It is represented as a crab (or crayfish), a reference to the crab in Greek mythology that pinched Heracles while he was fighting the Lernaean hydra. Heracles crushed the crab, but his enemy Hera rewarded it by placing it in the sky as a constellation.

cancer, Any of a group of more than 100 distinct diseases that are characterized by the uncontrolled multiplication of abnormal cells. Cancerous cells and tissues have abnormal growth rates, shapes, sizes, and functioning. Cancer may progress in stages from a localized tumour (confined to the site of origin) to direct extension (spread into nearby tissue or lymph nodes) and metastasis (spread to more distant sites via the blood or lymphatic system). This malignant growth pattern distinguishes cancerous tumours from benign ones. Cancer is also classified by grade, the extent to which cell characteristics remain specific to their tissue of origin. Both stage and grade affect the chances of survival. Genetic factors and immune status affect susceptibility. Triggers include hormones, viruses, smoking, diet, and radiation. Cancer can begin in almost any tissue, as well as in the blood and lymph. When it metastasizes, it remains a cancer of its tissue of origin. Early diagnosis and treatment increase the chance of cure. Treatment may include chemotherapy, surgery, and radiation therapy.

Cancún, City (pop., 2000: 397,191) and island resort, southeastern Mexico. The city, on the northeastern coast of the Yucatán Peninsula, is a service town for the resort on Cancún Island (13 mi [21 km] long), which is connected by a causeway to the city. Originally settled by Maya Indians, the area was first described by John Lloyd Stephens and Frederick Catherwood in their *Incidents of Travel in Yucatán* (1843). Cancún remained a fishing village until 1970, when the area was selected as a suitable site for a resort. The plan proved hugely successful; today Cancún is one of Mexico's busiest resorts.

candida, Any of the pathogenic and parasitic fungi that make up the genus *Candida* in the order Saccharomycetales, which contains the ascomycete yeasts. *Candida* primarily occur in the mouth, vagina, and intestinal tract. Though usually benign, candidas can become pathogenic, causing diseases such as candidiasis and thrush.

Candlemas (February 2) In the Christian church, the celebration of the presentation of the infant Jesus and the post-childbirth purification of Mary in the Temple, in accordance with Jewish law. The Greek church calls it Hypapante ("Meeting") in reference to Jesus' meeting there with Simeon, to whom it had been revealed that he would not die before meeting the Messiah. The festival is first documented in Jerusalem in the late 4th century; the custom of observing it with lighted candles (the source of its name) dates to at least the mid 5th century. The popular nonreligious holiday Groundhog Day developed, in part, from the medieval tradition that certain animals interrupted their hibernation on this day.

Canetti, Elias (b. July 25, 1905, Ruse, Bulg.—d. Aug. 14, 1994, Zürich, Switz.), Bulgarian-born British novelist and playwright. Canetti was from a Spanish-speaking Jewish family. His best-known work, the novel *Auto-da-Fé* (1935), deals with the dangers in believing that detached intellectualism can prevail over evil and chaos. He settled in Britain in 1938. Later works that reflect his interest in the psychopathology of power include *Crowds and*

Canetti
Horst Tappe/Camera Press/Globe
Photos

Power (1960); the plays *The Wedding* (1932), *Comedy of Vanity* (1950), and *Life-Terms* (1964); and his series of autobiographies beginning with *The Tongue Set Free* (1977). He was awarded the Nobel Prize for Literature in 1981.

cannabis, Any plant of the genus *Cannabis*. It is widely cultivated throughout the temperate zones for the production of hemp fibre, which is obtained from a tall, canelike variety. A shorter, branchier variety is the source of the drugs marijuana and hashish. Plants cultivated for hemp are distinguished from those used for drugs by their relatively low levels of the psychoactive substance tetrahydrocannabinol (THC). Cannabis plants may also be grown for food or medicinal purposes.

Cannes, City (pop., 2006 est.: 70,610), southeastern France. Located on the Mediterranean Sea southwest of Nice, it is an international resort. Probably settled by Ligurians, it was occupied successively by Phocaeans, Celts, and Romans. In the 10th century the monks of Lérins built fortifications to guard against Muslim sea raiders. Napoleon, on his return from Elba in 1815, camped nearby. A resort since the 19th century, the city is home to the Cannes Film Festival.

cannibalism, The usually ritualistic eating of human flesh by humans. The term derives from the Spanish name (Caríbales or Caníbales) for the Carib people, first encountered by Christopher Columbus. Reliable firsthand accounts of the practice are comparatively rare, causing some to question whether full-blown cannibalism has ever existed. Most agree that the consumption of particular portions or organs was a ritual means by which certain qualities of the person eaten might be obtained or by which powers of witchcraft and sorcery might be exercised. In some cases, a small portion of the dead person was ritually eaten by relatives. Headhunters sometimes consumed bits of the bodies or heads of deceased enemies. The Aztecs apparently practiced cannibalism on a large scale as part of the ritual of human sacrifice.

cannibalism, In zoology, the eating of any animal by another member of the same species. Certain ants regularly consume injured immatures and, when food is scarce, eat healthy immatures; this practice allows the adults to survive the food shortage and live to breed again. Male lions taking over a pride may kill and eat the existing young. After losing her cubs the mother will become impregnated by the new dominant male, thereby ensuring his genetic contribution. Aquarium guppies sometimes regulate their population size by eating most of their young.

canoeing, Use of a canoe or kayak for recreation or competition. Both types of boat are used in water touring, in speed competitions, and in white-water sport, or navigation through rapids (which includes, in the case of kayaks, ocean surf). The Scottish philanthropist John MacGregor (1825–1892) is traditionally credited with establishing the modern outdoor activity of canoeing in the 1860s. Canoeing events became part of the Olympic Games in 1936 (1948 for women). In addition to various singles, pairs, and team still-water events for distance and speed, there are white-water racing competitions and, for kayaks, slalom events involving the use of gates similar to those of slalom skiing.

canon, Musical form and compositional technique. Canons are characterized by having a melody that is imitated at a specified time interval by one or more parts, either at the same pitch or at some other pitch. Imitation may occur in the same note values, in augmentation (longer notes), or in diminution (shorter notes); in retrograde order (beginning at its end), mirror inversion (each ascending melodic interval becoming a descending interval, and vice versa), or retrograde mirror inversion; and so on. Canons range from folk rounds such as "Three Blind Mice" and "Frère Jacques" to the massively complex canons of Johann Sebastian Bach.

canon law, Body of laws established within Roman Catholicism, Eastern Orthodoxy, independent churches of Eastern Christianity, and the Anglican Communion for church governance. Canon law concerns the constitution of the church, relations between it and other bodies, and matters of internal discipline. The monk Gratian, an ecclesiastical lawyer and teacher, published the first definitive collection of Roman Catholic canon law *c.* 1140; the *Decretum Gratiani* drew on older local collections, councils, Roman law, and the Church Fathers. The enlarged *Corpus juris canonici* ("Body of Canon Law") was published in 1500. A commission of cardinals issued the new *Codex juris canonici* ("Code of Canon Law") in 1917, and a revised version was commissioned after the Second Vatican Council and published in 1983. Following the Schism of 1054, the Eastern Orthodox church developed its own canon law under the patriarch of Constantinople. The Anglican, Coptic, and Ethiopian Orthodox churches also formulated their own collections.

canonization, Official act of a Christian church declaring a deceased member worthy of veneration and entering his or her name in the canon (authorized list) of saints. The cult of local martyrs was widespread in the early church, and by the 10th century church authorities were considering the need for formal recognition of saints by Rome, a change that was formalized by Gregory IX in the 13th century. Responsibility for beatification (declaring a person worthy of limited veneration) was assigned to the Roman Curia under Sixtus V (r. 1585–90). A candidate's writings, miracles, and reputation for sanctity are investigated: one official gathers evidence in favor of beatification; another (the "devil's advocate") is charged with seeing that the entire truth is made known about the candidate. Canonization requires proof of two miracles subsequent to beatification. The process in the Eastern Orthodox Church is less formal; popular devotion by the faithful serving as the usual basis for sainthood.

Cantabrian Mountains, Mountain range, northern Spain. The mountains, which extend about 180 mi (300 km), are geologically of similar origin to the Pyrenees, though classified as a separate formation. They include many tall peaks, the highest being Torre de Cerredo (8,787 ft, or 2,678 m), and thus form a more formidable barrier than the Pyrenees. The region is economically important for its coal and iron.

cantata, Work for voice or voices and instruments of the Baroque era. From its beginnings in early 17th-century Italy, both secular and religious cantatas were written. The earliest cantatas were generally for solo voice and minimal instrumental accompaniment. Cantatas soon developed a dramatic character and alternating sections of recitative and aria, paralleling the simultaneous development of opera, and they came to resemble unstaged operatic scenes or acts. In Germany the Lutheran cantata developed more directly out of the expanding choral motet, and almost always involved a chorus. A single chorale (hymn) often served as the basis for an entire cantata, which might have up to 10 diverse numbers, including duets, recitatives, and choral fugues. The most celebrated are the approximately 200 written by Johann Sebastian Bach. After *c.* 1750 the cantata gradually declined.

Canterbury, Historic city and administrative district (pop., 2001: 135,287), southeastern England. Located on the River Great Stour, the site has been occupied since pre-Roman times; the Roman town of Durovernum Cantiacorum was established after Claudius invaded Britain in AD 43. It has been an ecclesiastical metropolis of England since St. Augustine of Canterbury founded a monastery there in 602 and later established a cathedral. The cathedral was the scene of the murder of Archbishop St. Thomas Becket in 1170. After his canonization in 1172, it became a pilgrimage shrine; it is the destination of the pilgrims in Geoffrey Chaucer's *Canterbury Tales.* Canterbury was heavily bombed in World War II, but the cathedral largely escaped damage. The cathedral and other historic buildings were designated a UNESCO World Heritage site in 1988.

cantor, In Judaism and Christianity, an official in charge of music or chants. In Judaism the *ḥazzan* (cantor) leads liturgical prayer and chanting. In medieval Christianity the cantor had charge of a cathedral's music—specifically, of supervising the choir's singing. The term also designated the head of a college of church music.

cantus firmus (Latin: "fixed chant"), Preexistent melody, such as a plainchant excerpt, underlying a polyphonic musical composition (one consisting of several independent voices or parts). In the 11th- and 12th-century organum, the tones of the plainchant melody for such words as "alleluia" and "amen" were held by one voice (the tenor), while another, more active, improvised line was added. Developments introduced by the Notre-Dame school of the late 12th and early 13th centuries included rhythmic patterning of the added voice and the addition of two or three voices. The composition of nonliturgical words for the added voice or voices in the 13th century resulted in the independent motet. Cantus firmus technique remained the basis of most composition of the 14th–15th centuries (though the "chant" was now often a secular melody) and remained important in the 16th-century mass. It was later codified in the pedagogical method called species counterpoint.

Canute the Great, Danish KNUT (d. Nov. 12, 1035), Danish king of England (1016–35), Denmark (1019–35), and Norway (1028–35). He helped his father, Sweyn I, invade England in 1013. Sweyn was accepted as king of England after exiling King Ethelred II but died in 1014; Canute returned and defeated Ethelred's son to win the English throne in 1016. At first he ruled ruthlessly, killing English opponents and appointing Danes in their places, but within a few years he had married Ethelred's widow and was granting earldoms to Englishmen. Canute proved an effective ruler who brought peace and prosperity to England, issued an important law code, and became a strong supporter of the church. With English help he secured the throne of Denmark on his brother's death. His early death and that of his sons led to the restoration of Ethelred's dynasty.

canyon, Very narrow, deep valley cut by a river through resistant rock and having steep, almost vertical sides. Canyons occur most often in arid or semiarid regions. Some canyons (e.g., the Grand Canyon) are spectacular natural features.

Cao Zhan, or TS'AO CHAN (b. 1715?, Jiangning, Jiangsu province, China—d. Feb. 12, 1763, Beijing), Chinese novelist. He is the author of *Dream of the Red Chamber* (1791), generally considered China's greatest novel. A partly autobiographical work written in the vernacular, it describes in lingering detail the decline of a powerful family and an ill-fated love between cousins. Cao finished at least 80 of its 120 chapters; it was completed after his death, probably by Gao E, about whom little is known.

Cape buffalo, Massive, black, horned buffalo (*Syncerus caffer*), formerly found throughout sub-Saharan Africa but now greatly reduced in number by disease and hunting. It is a gregarious animal of open or scrub-covered plains and open forests. When wounded, it is regarded as one of the most dangerous animals. It stands up to 5 ft (1.5 m) tall at the shoulder, and bulls can weigh almost a ton (about 900 kg). Its heavy horns typically curve downward, then up and inward. A smaller subspecies is found in dense West African forests.

Cape Town, Afrikaans KAAPSTAD, City (pop., 2005 est., urban agglom.: 3,103,000), legislative capital of the Republic of South Africa. It is also the capital of Western Cape province. Located on Table Bay, Cape Town has long been an important regional port. The first settlement at Table Bay, it was founded in the 17th century by the Dutch navigator Jan van Riebeeck for the Dutch East India Company, and it soon served as a stopover for ships plying the Europe-to-India route. It was under Dutch rule intermittently until it was taken by the British in 1806. Today it is a commercial and cultural centre.

Cape Verde, officially REPUBLIC OF CAPE VERDE, Island country, east-central Atlantic Ocean. Lying 385 mi (620 km) off the western coast of Senegal, it consists of 10 islands and 5 islets. Area: 1,557 sq mi (4,033 sq km). Population: (2011 est.) 498,000. Capital: Praia. More than two-thirds of its population are of mixed African and European origin (known as *mestiço* or Crioulo); the remainder are African and European. Languages: Portuguese (official), Crioulo (national; a Portuguese creole). Religions: Christianity (predominantly Roman Catholic); also Islam. Currency: Cape Verde escudo. The mountainous western islands are craggy and furrowed by erosion; the flatter islands of the east are largely plains and lowlands. The archipelago is volcanic in origin. Fogo Island has an active volcano; it is also the location of the highest peak, which rises 9,281 ft (2,829 m). The largest islands are Santo Antão, Boa Vista, and São Tiago. Cape Verde has a largely service-based economy, and tourism has been promoted. It is a multiparty republic with one legislative house; its head of state is the president and its head of government the prime minister.

The islands were uninhabited when Diogo Gomes sighted and named Maio and São Tiago in 1460; in 1462 the first settlers landed on São Tiago, founding the city of Ribeira Grande. The city's importance grew with the development of the slave trade, and its wealth attracted attacks so often that it was abandoned in 1712. The prosperity of the Portuguese-controlled islands vanished with the decline of the slave trade in the 19th century, when they were made a coaling and submarine cable station. In 1951 the colony became an overseas province of Portugal. Many islanders preferred outright independence, which was granted in 1975. Once associated politically with Guinea-Bissau, Cape Verde split from it in the wake of a 1980 coup there.

Capetians, or CAPETS, Ruling house of France (987–1328), who laid the foundation of the French state. Descended from Robert the Strong (died 866), they included Hugh Capet (r. 987–96), the first Capetian king; Philip II Augustus (r.1180–1223); and Louis IX (r.1226–70). Capetians also ruled as dukes of Burgundy and Brittany, emperors of Constantinople, counts of Artois and Provence, kings and queens of Naples, and kings of Hungary and Navarre.

capillary, Any of the minute blood vessels that form networks where the arterial and venous circulation meet for exchange of oxygen, nutrients, and wastes with body tissues. Capillaries are just large enough for red blood cells to pass through in single file. Their thin walls are semipermeable, allowing small molecules to pass through in both directions. The smallest lymphatic vessels and minute bile channels in the liver are also called capillaries.

capital, In economics, the stock of resources that are used to produce other goods now and in the future. In classical economics the three factors of production are capital, labour, and land. Capital embodies the man-made resources, which include the buildings, plant, equipment, and inventories created by all three factors. In this sense, capital goods may be contrasted with consumer goods. The creation of capital goods means that consumption is forgone, resulting in saving. The flow of saving becomes a flow of investment. Expenditures on education and training are often referred to as investment in human capital. Financial capital is the term given to the stocks and bonds issued in order to finance the acquisition of capital goods.

capital gains tax, Tax levied on gains realized from the sale or exchange of capital assets. Though capital gains have been taxed in the U.S. since the advent of the federal income tax, certain capital gains are taxed less heavily than regular income, while others are exempted from taxation. This preferential treatment is intended to encourage investment and thereby stimulate economic growth. In theory the tax break encourages investors to risk their capital in new ventures. Critics argue that preferential treatment results in distorted patterns of investment because regular income is converted into capital gains in order to avoid paying income tax.

capital punishment, or DEATH PENALTY, Execution of an offender sentenced to death after conviction by a court of law of a criminal offense. Capital punishment for murder, treason, arson, and rape was widely employed in ancient Greece, and the Romans also used it for a wide range of offenses. It also has been sanctioned at one time or another by most of the world's major religions. In 1794 the U.S. state of Pennsylvania became the first jurisdiction to restrict the death penalty to first-degree murder, and in 1846 Michigan abolished capital punishment for all murders and other common crimes. In 1863 Venezuela became the first country to abolish capital punishment for all crimes. Portugal was the first European country to abolish the death penalty (1867). By the mid-1960s some 25 countries had abolished the death penalty for murder. During the last third of the 20th century, the number of abolitionist countries increased more than threefold. Despite the movement toward abolition, many countries have retained capital punishment, and some have extended its scope. In the U.S., the federal government and roughly three-fourths of the states retain the death penalty, and death sentences are regularly carried out in China, Saudi Arabia, Singapore, and Iran. Supporters of the death penalty claim that life imprisonment is not an effective deterrent to criminal behaviour. Opponents maintain that the death penalty has never been an effective deterrent, that errors sometimes lead to the execution of innocent persons, and that capital punishment is imposed inequitably, mostly on the poor and on racial minorities.

capitalism, or FREE-MARKET ECONOMY, or FREE-ENTERPRISE SYSTEM, Economic system in which most of the means of production are privately owned, and production is guided and income distributed largely through the operation of markets. Capitalism has been dominant in the Western world since the end of mercantilism. It was fostered by the Reformation, which sanctioned hard work and frugality, and by the rise of industry during the Industrial Revolution, especially the English textile industry (16th–18th centuries). Unlike earlier systems, capitalism used the excess of production over consumption to enlarge productive capacity rather than investing it in economically unproductive enterprises such as palaces or cathedrals. The strong national states of the mercantilist era provided the social conditions, such as uniform monetary systems and legal codes, necessary for the rise of capitalism. The ideology of classical capitalism was expressed in Adam Smith's *Wealth of Nations* (1776), and Smith's free-market theories were widely adopted in the 19th century. In the 20th century the Great Depression effectively ended laissez-faire economics in most countries, but the demise of the state-run command economies of eastern Europe and the former Soviet Union and the adoption of some free-market principles in China left capitalism unrivaled (if not untroubled) by the beginning of the 21st century.

Capone, Al(phonse) (b. Jan. 17, 1899, Brooklyn, N.Y., U.S.—d. Jan. 25, 1947, Palm Island, Fla.), U.S. gangster. Quitting school after the sixth grade, he joined the James Street Boys gang, led by Johnny Torrio. In a youthful fight in a brothel-saloon he was slashed across the left cheek, prompting the later nickname "Scarface." In 1919 he joined Torrio in Chicago to help run pros-

titution there. When Torrio retired (1925), Capone became the city's crime czar, running gambling, prostitution, and bootlegging rackets. He expanded his territory by killing his rivals, most famously in the St. Valentine's Day Massacre, in which members of the Bugs Moran gang were machine-gunned in a garage on Feb. 14, 1929. In 1931 Capone was convicted for income-tax evasion and sentenced to 11 years in prison; eventually he served time in the new Alcatraz prison. Granted an early release from prison in 1939, in part because he suffered from an advanced stage of syphilis, he died a powerless recluse at his Florida estate.

Capote, Truman, orig. TRUMAN STRECKFUS PERSONS (b. Sept. 30, 1924, New Orleans, La., U.S.—d. Aug. 25, 1984, Los Angeles, Calif.), U.S. novelist, short-story writer, and playwright. Capote spent much of his youth in small towns in Louisiana and Alabama. His early works, in the Southern Gothic tradition, include the novels *Other Voices, Other Rooms* (1948) and *The Grass Harp* (1951) and the story collection *A Tree of Night* (1949). His later journalistic style was exemplified in the highly successful "nonfiction novel" *In Cold Blood* (1966), an account of a multiple murder. Other works include the novella *Breakfast at Tiffany's* (1958; film, 1961), the musical *House of Flowers* (1954; with Harold Arlen), and the collections *The Dogs Bark* (1973) and *Music for Chameleons* (1980).

Capri, Island, southern Italy. Located at the southern entrance to the Bay of Naples, it has an area of 4 sq mi (10 sq km). Cliffs rise in the west to a height of 1,932 ft (589 m). It was a colony of ancient Greece; later it became a favourite resort of Roman emperors. In the Middle Ages it belonged to the abbey of Montecassino and to the republic of Amalfi before passing to the kingdom of Naples. Its rocky shores abound with caves, notably the famous Blue Grotto. Capri is one of Italy's most popular resorts.

Capricorn, or CAPRICORNUS (Latin: "Goat horn") In astronomy, the constellation lying between Aquarius and Sagittarius; in astrology, the tenth sign of the zodiac, governing approximately the period December 22–January 19. It is represented as a goat with what appears to be a fishtail. One explanation for this odd depiction is that it derives from the Greek myth of Pan. To avoid the monster Typhon, Pan jumped into the water just as he was changing into animal shape. The half of his body above water became a goat, while the submerged half took the shape of a fish. Another relates the form to the Mesopotamian deity Enki.

Caracas, City (pop. 2001: 1,836,000), capital of Venezuela. Its Caribbean Sea port is La Guaira. Lying at an elevation of about 3,000 ft (900 m), Caracas is one of the most developed cities in Latin America. It was founded in 1567 by Diego de Losada. It is the birthplace of Simón Bolívar (1783), under whose leadership it became the first colony to revolt against Spain (*c.* 1810). Caracas has become the country's primary centre of industry, commerce, education, and culture.

caraway, Dried fruit, commonly called the seed, of *Carum carvi*, a biennial herb of the parsley family. Native to Europe and western Asia, it has been cultivated since ancient times. It has a distinctive aroma and a warm, slightly sharp taste. It is used as a seasoning, and the oil is used to flavour alcoholic beverages and as a medicine.

carbine, Light, short-barreled rifle. The first carbines, from the muzzle-loading muskets of the 18th century to the lever-action repeaters of the 19th, were chiefly cavalry weapons or saddle firearms for mounted frontiersmen. During World War II carbine versions of standard bolt-action or semiautomatic infantry rifles were carried by some officers, artillerymen, and other specialists. Carbine versions of modern assault rifles (such as the Russian AK-47 or the U.S. M16 rifle) are intended for close-quarter fighting, partly replacing the submachine gun. Carbine versions of hunting and target rifles are also made.

carbohydrate, Any member of a very abundant and widespread class of natural organic compounds that includes sugars, starch, and cellulose. They are commonly classified as monosaccharides (simple sugars; e.g., glucose, fructose), disaccharides (2-unit sugars; e.g., sucrose, lactose), oligosaccharides (3–10 or so sugars), and polysaccharides (large molecules with up to 10,000 monosaccharide units, including cellulose, starch, and glycogen). Green plants produce carbohydrates by photosynthesis. In most animals, carbohydrates are the quickly accessible reservoir of energy, and oxidation of glucose in tissues supplies energy for metabolism. Many (but by no means all) carbohydrates have the general chemical formula $C_n(H_2O)_n$. The carbon (C) atoms are bonded to hydrogen atoms ($-H$), hydroxyl groups ($-OH$), and carbonyl groups ($-C=O$), whose combinations, order, and geometric arrangement lead to a large number of isomers with the same chemical formula but different properties. The class is further enlarged because each isomer has various derivatives: uronic acids, sugars with an oxidized group; sugar alcohols, sugars with a reduced group; glycosides, compounds of sugars with other molecules containing a hydroxyl group; and amino sugars, sugars with an amino group.

carbon, Nonmetallic chemical element, chemical symbol C, atomic number 6. The usual stable isotope is carbon-12; carbon-13, another stable isotope, makes up 1% of natural carbon. Carbon-14 is the most stable and best known of five radioactive isotopes; its half-life of approximately 5,730 years makes it useful in carbon-14 dating and radiolabeling of research compounds. Carbon occurs in four known allotropes: diamond, graphite, carbon black (amorphous carbon including coal, coke, and charcoal), and hollow cage molecules called fullerenes. Carbon forms more compounds than all other elements combined; several million carbon compounds are known. Each carbon atom forms four bonds (four single bonds, two single and one double bond, two double bonds, or one single and one triple bond) with up to four other atoms. Multitudes of chain, branched, ring, and three-dimensional structures can occur. The study of these carbon compounds and their properties and reactions is organic chemistry. With hydrogen, oxygen, nitrogen, and a few other elements whose small amounts belie their important roles, carbon forms the compounds that make up all living things: proteins, carbohydrates, lipids, and nucleic acids. Biochemistry is the study of how those compounds are synthesized and broken down and how they associate with each other in living organisms. Organisms consume carbon and return it to the environment in the carbon cycle. Carbon dioxide, produced when carbon is burned and from biological processes, makes up about 0.03% of the air, and carbon occurs in Earth's crust as carbonate rocks and the hydrocarbons in coal, petroleum, and natural gas. The oceans contain large amounts of dissolved carbon dioxide and carbonates.

carbon dioxide, Inorganic compound, a colourless gas with a faint, sharp odour and a sour taste when dissolved in water, chemical formula CO_2. Constituting about 0.03% of air by volume, it is produced when carbon-containing materials burn completely, and it is a product of fermentation and animal respiration. Plants use CO_2 in photosynthesis to make carbohydrates. CO_2 in Earth's atmosphere keeps some of the Sun's energy from radiating back into space. In water, CO_2 forms a solution of a weak acid, carbonic acid (H_2CO_3). The reaction of CO_2 and ammonia is the first step in synthesizing urea. An important industrial material, CO_2 is recovered from sources including flue gases, limekilns, and the process that prepares hydrogen for synthesis of ammonia. It is used as a refrigerant, a chemical intermediate, and an inert atmosphere; in fire extinguishers, foam rubber and plastics, carbonated beverages, and aerosol sprays; in water treatment, welding, and cloud seeding; and for promoting plant growth in greenhouses. Under pressure it becomes a liquid, the form most often used in industry. If the liquid is allowed to expand, it cools and partially freezes to the solid form, dry ice.

carbon-14 dating, or RADIOCARBON DATING, Method of determining the age of once-living material, developed by U.S. physicist Willard Libby in 1947. It depends on the decay of the radioactive isotope carbon-14 (radiocarbon) to nitrogen. All living plants and animals continually take in carbon: green plants absorb it in the form of carbon dioxide from the atmosphere, and it is passed to animals through the food chain. Some of this carbon is radioactive carbon-14, which slowly decays to the stable isotope nitrogen-14. When an organism dies it stops taking in carbon, so the amount of carbon-14 in its tissues steadily decreases. Because carbon-14 decays at a constant rate, the time since an organism died can be estimated by measuring the amount of radiocarbon in its remains. The method is a useful technique for dating fossils and archaeological specimens from 500 to 50,000 years old and is widely used by geologists, anthropologists, and archaeologists.

carbon monoxide, Inorganic compound, a highly toxic, colourless, odourless, flammable gas, chemical formula CO. It is produced when carbon (including coal and coke) or carbon-containing fuel (including petroleum hydrocarbons; e.g., gasoline, fuel oil) does not burn completely to carbon dioxide, because of insufficient oxygen. CO is present in the exhaust gases of internal combustion engines and furnaces. It is toxic because it binds to hemoglobin in blood much more strongly than does oxygen and thus interferes with transport of oxygen from lungs to tissues. Symptoms of CO poisoning range from headache, nausea, and syncope to coma, weak pulse, respiratory failure, and death. CO is used industrially as a fuel and in synthesis of numerous organic compounds, including methanol, ethylene, and aldehydes.

Carboniferous Period, Interval of geologic time 359.2–299 million years ago, marked by great changes in world geography. All the landmasses drew closer together as a result of tectonic plate movements. The supercontinent Gondwana occupied much of the Southern Hemisphere. By the end of the period, present-day North America, Greenland, and northern Europe were also linked to Gondwana. Siberia and China (including Southeast Asia) remained individual continents located at high latitudes in the Northern Hemisphere. During this period, swamp forests became widespread, and enormous coal deposits formed. Plants made great advances in adapting to complex forest environments, and vertebrates underwent extensive evolution. Amphibians became widespread and diverse, and reptiles appeared for the first time and rapidly adapted to many habitats.

cardamom, Spice consisting of whole or ground dried fruit, or seeds, of *Elettaria cardamomum*, a perennial herb of the ginger family. The flavour is warm, slightly pungent, and highly aromatic. Cardamom is a popular seasoning. Native to moist forests of southern India, the fruit may be collected from wild plants, but most is cultivated. The whole fruit is a green, three-sided oval capsule containing 15–20 dark, hard, angular seeds.

Cardiff, City and county (pop., 2001: 305,340), capital of Wales. It is located on the Bristol Channel in southeastern Wales. The Romans built a fort there c. AD 75. The town itself was established with the arrival of the Normans in the 11th century. Its population was small into the early 19th century, but by the early 20th century Cardiff had become the largest coal-exporting port in the world. The coal trade ceased in the 1960s, but Cardiff remains the largest city and the principal commercial centre of Wales.

cardinal, Member of the Sacred College of Cardinals. The cardinals' duties include electing the pope, acting as his principal counselors, and aiding in the governance of the Roman Catholic Church. Cardinals serve as officers of the Roman Curia, bishops of major dioceses, and papal envoys. Since 769 only cardinals have been eligible to become pope, and since 1059 the pope has been elected only by cardinals. The first cardinals were the deacons of the seven regions of Rome. Their present-day successors are known as cardinal deacons. Cardinal bishops are the successors of the bishops of the sees just outside Rome and of the patriarchal sees of the Eastern Catholic Church. Cardinal priests are the bishops of important sees around the world and constitute the most numerous order of cardinals. The number of cardinals was limited to 70 for nearly 400 years until 1958, when John XXIII (1958–63) eliminated the restriction. Under Paul VI (1963–78) there were 145 cardinals, and under John Paul II (1978–2005) there were 182. With the increase in the size of the cardinalate came new restrictions imposed by the popes. Paul VI directed that cardinals who do not resign by age 75 relinquish the right to vote for a pope when they reach 80. He also limited the number of voting cardinals to 120, a restriction confirmed during the pontificate of John Paul II. A red biretta and ring are symbolic of the office.

carding, In yarn production, a process of separating individual fibres, causing many of them to lie parallel and removing most of the remaining impurities. Cotton, wool, waste silk, and man-made staple are subjected to carding. Carding produces a thin sheet of uniform thickness that is then condensed to form a thick, continuous, untwisted strand called sliver. When very fine yarns are desired, carding is followed by combing, a process that removes short fibres, leaving a sliver composed entirely of long fibres, all laid parallel and smoother and more lustrous than uncombed types. Carded and combed sliver is then spun.

cardiopulmonary resuscitation (CPR), Emergency procedure to restore breathing and circulation in an unconscious person. A trained rescuer opens the airway and confirms the absence of breathing and pulse. Resuscitation itself consists of alternating mouth-to-mouth breathing and repeated pressure on the chest to circulate the blood.

Carducci, Giosuè (b. July 27, 1835, Val di Castello, near Lucca, Tuscany—d. Feb. 16, 1907, Bologna, Italy), Italian poet. He taught literary history in Bologna for 40 years and in later years served as a senator. He opposed the prevailing Romanticism and advocated a return to classical models of prosody, but his rhetorical tirades provoked resistance to reform. His best volumes of verse, *The New Lyrics* and *The Barbarian Odes* (1887), contain evocations of landscape, memories of childhood, and representations of the glory of ancient Rome. Regarded in his time as Italy's national poet, he won the Nobel Prize for Literature in 1906.

Carib, American Indian people who inhabited the Lesser Antilles and parts of the South American coast at the time of the Spanish conquest. The Island Carib (now extinct) were a warlike, individualistic people who reportedly practiced cannibalism (the term derives from their name). Carib groups on the mainland, some of whom still survive, lived in the Guianas and as far south as the Amazon River; they subsisted by hunting and growing crops and were less aggressive than their island relatives.

Caribbean Sea, Arm of the Atlantic Ocean. It covers about 1,063,000 sq mi (2,753,000 sq km) and washes the northern coast of South America, eastern Central America, and eastern Mexico. It reaches its greatest known depth, about 25,216 ft (7,686 m), in Cayman Trench, between Cuba and Jamaica. Its generally tropical climate varies, depending on mountain elevations, water currents, and trade winds. The economies of its island countries, including Saint Kitts and Nevis, Dominica, Saint Lucia, and Barbados, are greatly dependent on tourism; the region is one of the world's principal winter resort areas.

caricature, Comically distorted drawing or likeness intended to satirize or ridicule its subject. The word, derived from the Italian *caricare* ("to load or charge"), was probably coined by the Carracci family, who defended the practice as a counterpart to idealization. In the 18th century the caricature became connected with journalism and was put to virulent use by political commentators. In the 1880s photo-process engraving made it possible to produce and illustrate daily newpapers cheaply, bringing caricatures to the general public. In the 20th century caricature increasingly moved into the editorial, sports, and theatrical sections of newspapers. Important caricaturists include Jacques Callot, George Cruikshank, Honoré Daumier, Gustave Doré, and Al Hirschfeld.

caries, or TOOTH DECAY, Localized disease that causes decay and cavities in teeth. It begins at the tooth's surface and may penetrate the dentin and the pulp cavity. Microorganisms in the mouth are believed to consume sugars and produce acids that eat away at tooth enamel. The dentin's protein structure is then destroyed by enzymes. Diet, general health, structural tooth defects, and heredity affect the risk of having caries. Prevention involves avoiding excessive sweets, brushing and flossing the teeth, and having regular dental care. Treatment includes restoration of teeth with cavities. Fluoridation of water can reduce the occurrence of caries by as much as 65%.

carillon, Musical instrument consisting of at least 23 cast bronze bells tuned in chromatic order. Usually located in a tower, it is played from a keyboard. Most carillons encompass three to four octaves. The carillon originated in Flanders *c.* 1480, and the art of carillon building reached its height in the Netherlands in the 17th century, when the tuning of the bells became highly refined.

Carillon clavier
Gillett & Johnston (Croydon) Limited

Carlisle, City, administrative district (pop., 2001: 100,734), and seat of the administrative county of Cumbria, northwestern England. It was founded as Luguvallium by the Romans on the River Eden opposite a fortified camp on the line of Hadrian's Wall. Destroyed by Norse invaders *c.* 875, it was restored when claimed from the Scots by William II in 1092. Mary, Queen of Scots, was imprisoned there in 1568. It was besieged during the English Civil Wars, and its Royalist defenders eventually surrendered to Parliamentary forces in 1645. Its cotton textile industry grew in the 18th–19th centuries, and it has remained the centre of northern England's cotton industry.

Carlism, Spanish political movement of traditionalist character that originated in the 1820s. Carlists supported the claims of Ferdinand VII's brother Don Carlos (1788–1855) and his descendants to the throne, rejecting the succession of Ferdinand's daughter Isabella II by invoking the Salic Law (introduced into Spain in 1713), which excluded females from the royal succession. The disputed succession led to several unsuccessful civil rebellions, known as the Carlist Wars (1833–39, 1872–76). Later adherents of Carlism formed the Traditionalist Party (1918), which merged with the Falange in 1937.

carnival, Final celebration before the fasting and austerity of Lent in some Roman Catholic regions. The most famous and probably most exuberant carnival is that of Rio de Janeiro, which is celebrated with masked balls, costumes, and parades; the best-known U.S. celebration is Mardi Gras in New Orleans. The first day of carnival season varies with local traditions, but carnival usually ends on Shrove Tuesday, the day before the start of Lent.

carnivore, Any meat-eating animal, but especially any member of the order Carnivora, consisting of 12 families of primarily predatory mammals: Canidae (e.g., dogs), Ursidae (bears), Procyonidae (raccoons), Mustelidae (weasels), Mephitidae (skunks), Viverridae (civets), Herpestidae (mongooses), Hyaenidae (hyenas), Felidae (cats), Otariidae and Phocidae (seals), and Odobenidae (the walrus). Though most carnivores eat only meat, some rely heavily on vegetation (e.g., the panda). Most have a complex tooth structure and a lower jaw that can move only vertically but can exert great power. The earliest carnivores, which probably evolved from an insectivorous ancestor, appeared during the Paleocene Epoch (about 65–55 million years ago). Carnivores are highly intelligent.

carnivorous plant, Any of about 400 diverse species of plants specially adapted for capturing insects and other tiny animals by ingenious pitfalls and traps and for digesting the nitrogen-rich animal proteins to obtain nutrients. These adaptations are thought to enable such plants to survive under otherwise marginal or hostile environmental conditions. The conspicuous trapping mechanism (a leaf modification) draws the prey's attention to the plant. More than half the species belong to the family Lentibulariaceae, most being bladderworts. The remainder belong to several families composed of the pitcher plants, sundews, and flytraps. Most are found in damp heaths, bogs, swamps, and muddy or sandy shores where water is abundant and where nitrogenous materials are often scarce or unavailable because of acid or other unfavourable soil conditions. The smallest *Drosera* species are often hidden among the moss of a sphagnum bog; most carnivorous plants are small herbaceous perennials. Some become large shrubby vines.

Carnot cycle, In heat engines, the ideal cycle of changes of pressures and temperatures of a working fluid, such as steam or ammonia, conceived by Sadi Carnot. It is the standard of performance of all heat engines operating between a high and a low temperature. In the cycle, the working fluid undergoes four successive changes: (1) the fluid receives heat, expanding at high temperature; (2) it delivers work during the reversible adiabatic expansion (it changes in volume or pressure without losing or gaining heat); (3) it rejects heat (to the heat sink) during compression at low temperature; and (4) it receives work during the reversible adiabatic compression. The efficiency is determined by the difference between the temperatures of the heat source and the heat sink divided by the temperature of the heat source.

carob, Leguminous evergreen tree (*Ceratonia siliqua*) native to the eastern Mediterranean region and cultivated elsewhere. It is sometimes known as locust, or St. John's bread, in the belief that the "locusts" on which John the Baptist fed were carob pods. The tree, about 50 ft (15 m) tall, bears compound, glossy leaves with thick leaflets. Its red flowers are followed by flat, leathery pods that contain 5–15 hard brown seeds embedded in a sweet, edible pulp that tastes similar to chocolate.

Carolingian art, Art produced in Europe during the reign of Charlemagne and his successors until *c.* 900. The outstanding characteristic of the period was a revival of interest in Roman antiquity. Works of Byzantine art and architecture served as mod-

Ivory book cover from the Lorsch Gospels, early 9th century; in the Victoria and Albert Museum, London.
Courtesy of the Victoria and Albert Museum, London, Crown copyright

els. Illuminated manuscripts and relief scenes in ivory and metalwork reflected Classical motifs; mosaics and murals were also produced, but few have survived.

Carolingian dynasty, Family of Frankish aristocrats that ruled nearly all or part of western Europe in 751–987. Pippin I (d. 640), the dynasty's founder, came to power in the office of mayor of the palace under the Merovingian king Chlotar II, with authority over Austrasia. From this post, his descendants, including Charles Martel, continued to usurp authority from the Merovingians, who remained on the throne as figureheads until 751, when Charles's son Pippin III, with papal support, deposed Childeric III and formally took the title of King of the Franks. Under Pippin's son Charlemagne (Carolus Magnus—the source of the dynasty's name), the Carolingian realm was extended into Germany and Italy, where he conquered the Lombards and continued the alliance with Rome. Charlemagne also promoted religious reform and cultural growth and was crowned emperor by Pope Leo III on Dec. 25, 800. On his death, Charlemagne was succeeded by his son Louis the Pious, whose three sons divided the realm in 843. Despite internal strife and foreign invasion, the dynasty survived until 911 in the eastern part of the realm, where German rulers would revive Carolingian political ideals later in the century, and in the western realm until 987.

carp, Hardy, greenish brown fish (*Cyprinus carpio*, family Cyprinidae) native to Asia but introduced into Europe, North America, and elsewhere. Large-scaled, with two barbels (fleshy, whiskerlike feelers) on each side of its upper jaw, the carp lives alone or in small schools in quiet, weedy, mud-bottomed ponds, lakes, and rivers. An omnivore, it often stirs up sediment while rooting about for food, adversely affecting many plants and animals. Carp grow to an average length of about 14 in. (35 cm); some grow to 40 in. (100 cm) and 49 lbs (22 kg). In captivity they may live more than 40 years.

carpal tunnel syndrome (CTS), Painful condition caused by repetitive stress to the wrist over time. The median nerve and the tendons that bend the fingers pass through the carpal tunnel on the inner side of the wrist, between the wrist (carpal) bones on three sides and a ligament on the fourth. Repetitive finger and wrist movements rub the tendons against the walls of the carpal tunnel and may make the tendons swell, squeezing the nerve. Numbness, tingling, and pain in the wrist and hand may progress to loss of muscle control. CTS is most common in assembly-line workers and computer keyboard users. Treatment may include avoidance of the causative activity, ergonomic workplace design, anti-inflammatory drugs, brace or splint use, and surgery.

Carpathian Mountains, Mountain system, eastern Europe. It extends along the Slovakia-Poland border and southward through Ukraine and eastern Romania about 900 mi (1,450 km). Its highest peak, Gerlachovka (in Slovakia), rises 8,711 ft (2,655 m). The Little Carpathians and White Carpathians are its southwestern extensions; the Transylvanian Alps are sometimes called the South Carpathians. The mountains are the source for the Vistula, Dniester, and Tisza rivers. Agriculture, forestry, and tourism are economically important.

Carson, Rachel (Louise) (b. May 27, 1907, Springdale, Pa., U.S.—d. April 14, 1964, Silver Spring, Md.), U.S. biologist and science writer. Carson trained as a marine biologist and had a long career at the U.S. Fish and Wildlife Service. *The Sea Around Us* (1951) won a National Book Award. Her prophetic *Silent Spring* (1962), about the dangers of pesticides in the food chain, is regarded as the seminal work in the history of the environmental movement, which in some respects can be seen to date from its publication.

Cartagena, City (pop., 2003 est.: 902,688), Colombia. Located on the northern coast, it has a good harbour and is Colombia's principal port for oil exports. Founded in 1533, it became one of Spanish America's chief cities. It was strongly fortified and often attacked, notably by British forces under Francis Drake (*c.* 1585–86) and Edward Vernon (*c.* 1741–42). It remained under Spanish control until the province of Cartagena, which included the city, declared independence in 1811. After reverting back to Spanish control in 1815, the city was recaptured by patriot forces in 1821. It declined in the 19th century but regained prominence in the 20th century as an oil-processing centre.

cartel, Organization of a few independent producers for the purpose of improving the profitability of the firms involved. This usually involves some restriction of output, control of price, and allocation of market shares. Members of a cartel generally maintain their separate identities and financial independence while engaging in cooperative policies. Cartels can either be domestic (e.g., the historical example of the German IG Farben) or international (e.g., OPEC). Because cartels restrict competition and result in higher prices for consumers, they are outlawed in some countries. The only industry operating in the U.S. with a blanket exemption from the antitrust laws is major league baseball, but several U.S. firms have been given permission to participate in international cartels.

Carter, Jimmy, orig. JAMES EARL CARTER (b. Oct. 1, 1924, Plains, Ga., U.S.), 39th president of the U.S. (1977–81). He graduated from Annapolis and served in the U.S. Navy until 1953, when he left to manage the family peanut business. He served in the state senate from 1962 to 1966. He ran unsuccessfully for governor in 1966; depressed by this experience, he found solace in evangelical Christianity, becoming a born-again Baptist. In 1970 he ran again and won. As governor (1971–75), he opened Georgia's government offices to African Americans and women and introduced stricter budgeting procedures for state agencies. In 1976, though lacking a national political base or major backing, he won the Democratic nomination and the presidency, defeating the Republican incumbent, Gerald Ford. As president, Carter helped negotiate a peace treaty between Egypt and Israel, signed a treaty with Panama to make the Panama Canal a neutral zone after 1999, and established full diplomatic relations with China. In 1979–80 the Iran hostage crisis became a major political liability. He responded forcefully to the Soviet Union's invasion of Afghanistan in 1979, embargoing the shipment of U.S. grain to the Soviet Union and pressing for a U.S. boycott of the 1980 Summer Olympics in Moscow. The poor state of the economy, which was plagued by high inflation and high unemployment, contributed to Carter's electoral defeat by Ronald Reagan in 1980. He subsequently became involved in numerous international diplomatic negotiations and helped to oversee elections in countries with insecure democratic traditions; he also became the first sitting or former American president to visit Fidel Castro's Cuba. He was awarded the Nobel Prize for Peace in 2002.

Jimmy Carter.
Courtesy: Jimmy Carter Library

Cartesianism, Philosophical tradition derived from the philosophy of René Descartes. A form of rationalism, Cartesianism upholds a metaphysical dualism of two finite substances, mind and matter. The essence of mind is thinking; the essence of matter is extension in three dimensions. God is a third, infinite substance, whose essence is necessary existence. God unites minds with bodies to create a fourth, compound substance, man. Mind-body dualism generates problems concerning the possibility of causal interaction between mind and body and knowledge of the external world, and various lines of Cartesianism developed from different proposed solutions to these problems. A historically important Cartesian theory holds that animals are essentially machines, lacking even the ability to feel pain.

Carthage, Ancient city and state, northern Africa. Located near modern Tunis, Tun., it was built around a citadel called the Byrsa. Founded by colonists from Tyre, probably in the 8th century BC, its people undertook conquests in western Africa, Sicily, and Sardinia in the 6th century BC. Under the descendants of Hamilcar, it came to dominate the western Mediterranean Sea. In the 3rd century BC it fought the first of the three Punic Wars with Rome. Destroyed by a Roman army led by Scipio Africanus the Younger (146 BC), it became the site of a colony founded by Julius Caesar in 44 BC; in 29 BC Augustus made it the administrative centre of the province of Africa. Among the Christian bishops who served there were Tertullian and St. Cyprian. Captured by the Vandals in AD 439 and the Byzantine Empire in the 6th century, it was taken by the Arabs in 705 and was eclipsed by their emphasis on Tunis. The ruins were designated a UNESCO World Heritage site in 1979.

cartilage, Connective tissue in parts of the human skeleton. A network of collagen fibres in a firm, gelatinous base, it contains no blood vessels or nerves. Different types of cartilage are found at the ends of some bones and in nasal and respiratory structures; in the spinal disks; and in the ear and epiglottis (back of the throat). Most of the skeleton of an embryo is made of cartilage, which is later replaced by bone.

cartography, or MAPMAKING, Art and science of representing a geographic area graphically, usually by means of a map or chart. Political, cultural, or other nongeographic features may be superimposed. Ptolemy's eight-volume *Geography* showed a flat, disc-shaped projection of part of the Earth. Medieval European maps followed Ptolemy's guide but placed east at the top of the map. In the 14th century more-accurate maps were developed for use in navigation. The first surviving globe dates from 1492. Discovery of the New World led to new techniques in cartography, notably projection of a curved surface onto a flat surface. In particular, Gerardus Mercator projected landmasses onto a cylinder wrapped around the Earth's Equator. Such cylindrical projections maintain proper directions or bearings, though they cause distortions in distances at high latitudes. Contour maps show relief by connecting points of equal elevation with lines, mean sea level being the reference point. Modern cartography uses aerial photography and satellite radar for a degree of accuracy previously unattainable. Satellites have also made possible the mapping of features of the Moon and of several planets and their moons.

cartoon, Originally, a full-size drawing used for transferring a design to a painting, tapestry, or other large work. Cartoons were used from the 15th century by fresco painters and stained-glass artists. In the 19th century the term acquired its popular meaning of a humorous drawing or parody. Cartoons in that sense are used today to convey political commentary, editorial opinion, and social comedy in newspapers and magazines. The greatest early figure is William Hogarth, in 18th-century Britain. In 19th-century France, Honoré Daumier introduced accompanying text that conveyed his characters' unspoken thoughts. Britain's *Punch* became the foremost 19th-century venue for cartoons; in the 20th century *The New Yorker* set the American standard. A Pulitzer Prize for editorial cartooning was established in 1922.

caryatid, Supporting column sculpted in the form of a draped female figure. Caryatids first appeared in three small buildings (treasuries) at Delphi (550–530 BC). The most celebrated example is the caryatid porch of the Erechtheum (421–406 BC), with six figures, on the Acropolis of Athens. Caryatids are sometimes called *korai* ("maidens"). Their male counterpart is the atlas.

Casablanca, Coastal city (pop., 2004: 2,933,684), western Morocco. It occupies the site of the ancient city of Anfa, destroyed by the Portuguese in 1468. The Portuguese returned in 1515 and built a new town, Casa Branca ("White House"). Abandoned after an earthquake, it was occupied by a Moroccan sultan in 1757. European traders, including the French, began to settle there. In 1907, after French citizens were murdered there, French forces occupied the town. During the subsequent French protectorate, it became Morocco's chief port. Since then, its growth and development have been continuous. In World War II (1939–45) it surrendered to the Allied Powers in 1942, and in 1943 the Casablanca Conference was held there.

Casablanca Conference (Jan. 12–23, 1943) Meeting during World War II at Casablanca, Morocco, between Franklin Roosevelt and Winston Churchill. They planned future global military strategy for the Western allies, reaching agreement on such issues as the invasion of Sicily, operations in the Pacific theatre, and the concentrated bombing of Germany. Most importantly, they issued a demand for an "unconditional surrender" from Germany, Italy, and Japan.

Caspian Sea, Inland salt lake between Europe and Asia, bordering Azerbaijan, Russia, Kazakhstan, and Iran. With a basin 750 mi (1,200 km) long and up to 200 mi (320 km) wide and an area of 149,200 sq mi (386,400 sq km), it is the largest inland body of water in the world. Though it receives many rivers, including the Volga, Ural, and Kura, the sea itself has no outlet. It was important as a commercial route in the premodern era, when it formed part of the Mongol-Baltic trade route for goods from Asia. It is now a major source of petroleum. Its numerous ports include Baku in Azerbaijan and Bandar-e Anzalī and Bandar-e Torkaman in Iran.

Cassatt, Mary (b. May 22, 1844, Allegheny City, Pa., U.S.—d. June 14, 1926, Château de Beaufresne, near Paris, France), U.S. painter and printmaker, active in Paris. She spent her early years traveling in Europe with her wealthy family. After attending the Pennsylvania Academy of the Fine Arts (1860–65) she later studied in Paris, copying Old Masters. In 1874 Cassatt chose Paris as her permanent residence and established her studio there. She shared with the Impressionists an interest in experiment and in the use of bright colours inspired by the out-of-doors. Edgar Degas became her friend, and at his request she exhibited with the Impressionists. She portrayed scenes of everyday life, particularly images of mothers and children, and was skilled at drawing and printmaking. Some of her best works were executed in pastel. Through her social contacts with wealthy private collectors, she promoted Impressionism in the U.S. and exerted a lasting influence on U.S. taste.

cassava, or MANIOC, or YUCA, Tuberous edible perennial plant (*Manihot esculenta*) of the spurge family, from the New World tropics. It is cultivated for its tuberous roots, from which cassava flour, breads, tapioca, a laundry starch, and an alcoholic beverage are derived. It has conspicuous, almost palmate (fan-shaped) leaves and fleshy roots. Different varieties range from low herbs through many-branched shrubs to slender, unbranched trees adapted to diverse habitats.

Cassini-Huygens, Space probe. Launched in 1997, it consisted of the U.S. Cassini spacecraft, which orbited Saturn, and the European Huygens probe, which landed on Titan in 2005. Data from Huygens showed a shoreline with erosion features and a river delta. Cassini discovered lakes of liquid methane on Titan, geysers of water ice on Enceladus, and six new moons and two new rings of Saturn.

caste, Any of the ranked, hereditary, endogamous occupational groups that constitute traditional societies in certain regions of the world, particularly among Hindus in India. There caste is rooted in antiquity and specifies the rules and restrictions governing social intercourse and activity. Each caste has its own customs that restrict the occupations and dietary habits of its members and their social contact with other castes. There are about 3,000 castes, or *jati*s (broadly, "form of existence fixed by birth"), and more than 25,000 subcastes in India. They are traditionally grouped into four major classes, or *varna*s ("colours"). At the top are the Brahmans, followed by the Kshatriyas, Vaishyas, and Shudras. Those with the most defiling jobs (such as those who dispose of body emissions and dead animals) are ranked beneath the Shudras. Considered untouchable, they were simply dubbed as "the fifth" (*panchama*) category. Although a great many spheres of life in modern India are little influenced by caste, most marriages are nevertheless arranged within the caste. This is in part because most people live in rural communities and because the arrangement of marriages is a family activity carried out through existing networks of kinship and caste.

castle, Medieval European stronghold, generally the fortified dwelling of the king or lord of the territory in which it stood. The castle developed rapidly in western Europe from the 9th century. In form it was somewhat sprawling compared to later fortified buildings. The castle's *enceinte* (outer wall) was surrounded by one or more moats, which were crossed by drawbridges that could be raised from the inner side. The gateway itself was heavily protected and often defended by a barbican, or watchtower. One or more baileys, or walled courtyards, surrounded the donjon. The age of the medieval castle came to an end with the increasing use of firearms in the 15th–16th centuries.

castrato, Male soprano or alto voice produced as a result of castration before puberty. The castrato voice was introduced in the Vatican's Sistine Chapel in the 16th century, when women were still banned from church choirs as well as the stage. It reached its greatest prominence in 17th- and 18th-century opera. The illegal and inhumane practice of castration, largely practiced in Italy, could produce a treble voice of extraordinary power, attributable to the lung capacity and physical bulk of the adult male. The unique tone quality and the ability of intensively trained singers to execute virtuosic passagework made castrati the rage among opera audiences and contributed to the spread of Italian opera. Most male singers in 18th-century opera were castrati; the most famous bore the stage names Senesino (Francesco Bernardi; died *c.* 1750), Caffarelli (Gaetano Majorano; 1710–1783), and Farinelli. Castrati sang in the Sistine Chapel choir until 1903.

Castro (Ruz), Fidel (b. Aug. 13, 1926, near Birán, Cuba), Political leader of Cuba (from 1959). Son of a prosperous sugar planter, he became a lawyer and worked on behalf of the poor in Havana. He was a candidate for Cuba's legislature when Gen. Fulgencio Batista overthrew the government in 1952. He organized a rebellion against Batista in 1953, but it failed; captured, he served time in prison and then went to Mexico, where he and others, including Che Guevara, continued to plot Batista's overthrow. Castro led an armed expedition back to Cuba in 1956; most of his men were killed, but a dozen survivors took refuge in the mountains, where they gradually managed to organize guerrillas throughout the island. In 1959 Batista was forced to flee the country. Castro nationalized private commerce and industry and expropriated U.S.-owned land and businesses, vastly expanded health services and eliminated illiteracy, and ruthlessly suppressed opposition, outlawing all political groups but the Communist Party. The U.S. attempted to bring about his overthrow and failed, precipitating the Cuban missile crisis. Castro exercised total control of the government and economy, which was increasingly dependent on subsidies from the Soviet Union. The Soviet Union's collapse (1991) devastated Cuba's economy, and Castro attempted to replace its former revenues through tourism. In 1998 Castro allowed Pope John Paul II to visit Cuba for the first time. Castro strengthened his relationship with Venezuelan Pres. Hugo Chávez in the early 21st century with an initiative through which Cuba provided health care professionals to Venezuela in exchange for discounted oil. In July 2006 Castro passed power on a provisional basis to his brother Raúl while he recovered from surgery. Fidel Castro officially stepped down as president of Cuba in 2008, ending his 49 years in power.

Castro (Ruz), Raúl (b. June 3, 1931, Holguín province, Cuba), head of state of Cuba (since 2008), defense minister, and revolutionary. Best known as the younger brother of Fidel Castro, Raúl embraced socialism as a young adult and belonged to a communist youth group. He participated with Fidel in the 1953 attempt to unseat dictator Fulgencio Batista and spent nearly two years in prison for the assault. In 1956 Raúl helped launch the revolution that resulted in Fidel's becoming premier in 1959 and which began his own tenure as Cuba's defense minister. That same year Raúl married fellow revolutionary Vilma Espín Guillois. Over the ensuing decades, Raúl served in the number two position of the principal government bodies of Cuba. He emerged as a key figure of the Communist Party of Cuba, and he enjoyed the strong support and loyalty of top military officers, known as *raulistas*. Raúl forged links with the Soviet Union and expanded the military's reach into various state-owned enterprises. Throughout the 1990s he supported the economic and agricultural reforms that helped to revive the economy following the collapse of Soviet subsidies. In 2008 he was elected president of Cuba after Fidel announced he was stepping down.

cat, or FELINE, Any member of the family Felidae, the most highly specialized group of mammalian carnivores. Modern-type cats appeared in the fossil record about 10 million years ago. Cats in the genus *Panthera* (leopard, jaguar, tiger, and lion) roar but cannot purr, and their pupils are round. Other cats, including the snow leopard and cougar, can purr but do not roar; the pupil is usually vertical. Cats have sharp, retractable (except in the cheetah) claws, and their teeth are adapted for stabbing, anchoring, and cutting. They almost always land on their feet when they fall from a height. Most species are nocturnal, and their eyes are adapted for seeing in low light. Cats are known for their habit of grooming themselves with their rasplike tongue. Small cats have been domesticated for some 3,500 years. Other cat species include the bobcat, caracal, lynx, ocelot, serval, and wildcat.

catacomb, Subterranean cemetery of galleries with recesses for tombs. The term was probably first applied to the cemetery under St. Sebastian's Basilica that was a temporary resting place for the bodies of Sts. Peter and Paul in the late 3rd century AD, but it came to refer to all the subterranean cemeteries around Rome. In addition to serving as burial sites, catacombs in early Christian Rome were the sites of funeral feasts celebrated in family vaults on the day of burial and on anniversaries. They were used as hiding places during times of persecution; Pope Sixtus II was supposedly captured and killed (AD 258) while hiding in the St. Sebastian's catacomb during Valerian's persecution. Catacombs are also found in Sicily and other parts of Italy, in Egypt, and in Lebanon. See photograph above.

Catalonia, Catalan CATALUNYA, Spanish CATALUÑA, Autonomous community (pop., 2001: 6,343,110) and historic region, northeastern Spain. It encompasses the provinces of Girona, Barcelona, Tarragona, and Lleida and covers an area of 12,399 sq mi (32,113 sq km). Its capital is Barcelona. The Pyrenees separate Catalonia from France; the Mediterranean Sea lies to the east. Its

Arched niche of a tomb with early Christian paintings of scenes from the Old and New Testaments, in the catacomb on Via Latina, Rome
Pont. Comm. di Arch. Sacra/M. Grimoldi

principal rivers, the Ter, Llobrégat, and Ebro, all run into the Mediterranean. Catalonia was one of Rome's first Spanish possessions. Occupied in the 5th century AD by the Goths, it was taken by the Moors in 712 and by Charlemagne in 795. After the unification of Spain (1469), Catalonia lost its centrality in Spanish affairs, and by the 17th century its conflict of interest with Castile-León led to the first of a series of separatist movements. Catalan nationalism became a serious force after 1876. In 1932 a compromise with the central government granted Catalonia autonomy; this was revoked with the 1939 Nationalist victory in the Spanish Civil War, and Francisco Franco's government adopted a repressive policy toward Catalan nationalism. The reestablishment of democratic rule after Franco's death again led to autonomy in 1979. Today it is the richest and most industrialized part of Spain.

catalysis, Modification (usually acceleration) of a chemical reaction rate by addition of a catalyst, which combines with the reactants but is ultimately regenerated so that its amount remains unchanged and the chemical equilibrium of the conditions of the reaction is not altered. Catalysts reduce the activation energy barrier between reactants and products. When more than one reaction is possible, a catalyst that accelerates only one reaction pathway selectively enhances the creation of its product. Catalysis is inhibited if the reactant or the catalyst is removed or altered by any of several types of agents (inhibitors). Catalysis in a single phase (e.g., the catalyst is dispersed in a liquid solution or gaseous mixture with the reactants) is homogeneous; that in more than one phase (e.g., the reactants are liquids and the catalyst a solid) is heterogeneous. Chemisorption, a type of heterogeneous catalysis, often involves bonding between the catalyst's solid surface and the reactant, changing the nature of the chemisorbed molecules. To make the accessible surface area as large as possible, such catalysts are finely powdered or highly porous solids. Catalysis is essential to the modern chemical industry.

catamaran, Twin-hulled sailing and engine-powered boat. Its design was based on a raft of two logs bridged by planks used by peoples in the Indonesian archipelago, Polynesia, and Micronesia. Up to 70 ft (21 m) long, early catamarans were paddled by many men and used for travel, in war, and in recreation. Especially after the sail was added, voyages as long as 2,000 mi (3,700 km) were made. In the 1870s they sailed so successfully against monohulled boats that they were barred from racing. The modern catamaran, which averages about 40 ft (12 m) in length, has been produced since 1950. They are very fast craft, achieving speeds of 20 mph (32 kph).

cataract, Opacity of the eye's crystalline lens. Cataracts causing central visual-field defects are most likely to affect vision. Cataracts may occur in newborns and infants. Diabetes mellitus, prolonged exposure to ultraviolet rays, or trauma can cause them in adults, but they most often occur with age, resulting from gradual loss of transparency of the lens. Treatment is a surgical procedure to replace the lens with an artificial one.

caterpillar, Larva of a butterfly or moth. Caterpillars have a cylindrical body consisting of 13 segments, with three pairs of legs on the thorax and "prolegs" on the abdomen. The head has six eyes on each side, short antennae, and strong jaws. Though not true worms, many caterpillars are called worms (e.g., the inchworm, or looper, and the cutworm). Caterpillar-like larvae are also found in other insect groups (e.g., sawflies and scorpionflies).

Catherine II, Russian YEKATERINA ALEKSEYEVNA, orig. SOPHIE FRIEDERIKE AUGUSTE, PRINCESS VON ANHALT-ZERBST, known as CATHERINE THE GREAT (b. May 2, 1729, Stettin, Prussia—d. Nov. 17, 1796, Tsarskoye Selo, near St. Petersburg, Russia), German-born empress of Russia (1762–96). The daughter of an obscure German prince, she was chosen at age 14 to be the wife of the future Peter III. The marriage was a complete failure. Because her neurotic husband was incapable of ruling, the ambitious Catherine saw the possibility of eliminating him and governing Russia herself. After Peter became emperor in 1762, she conspired with her lover, Grigory G., Count Orlov, to force Peter to abdicate (he was murdered soon after) and have herself proclaimed empress. In her 34-year reign she led Russia into full participation in European political and cultural life. With her ministers she reorganized the administration and law of the Russian Empire and extended Russian territory, adding the Crimea and much of Poland. Though she had once intended to emancipate the serfs, she instead strengthened the system she had once condemned as inhuman. She had great energy and wide interests, and her personal life was notable for her many lovers, including Grigory Potemkin.

Catherine de Médicis, orig. CATERINA DE' MEDICI (b. April 13, 1519, Florence—d. Jan. 5, 1589, Blois, France), Queen consort of Henry II (1547–59), mother of Francis II, Charles IX, and Henry III, and regent of France (1560–74). A member of the Medici family, she married Henry in 1533 and bore him 10 children. She became queen when Henry inherited the crown in 1547, and she greatly mourned his accidental death in 1559. After their son Francis became king, she began a long struggle with members of the Guise family, extremists who sought to dominate the crown. After Francis's premature death in 1560, she became regent for Charles IX until 1563 and dominated the rest of his reign until 1574. She attempted to settle the Wars of Religion between Catholics and Huguenots. She has traditionally been blamed for the Massacre of Saint Bartholomew's Day, but, though she authorized the assassination of Gaspard II de Coligny and his principal followers, it appears that she did not authorize the massacre that followed.

Catherine of Aragon.
Ann Ronan Picture Library/
Heritage-Images

Catherine of Aragon (b. Dec. 16, 1485, Alcalá de Henares, Spain—d. Jan. 7, 1536, Kimbolton, Huntingdon, Eng.), First wife of Henry VIII. The daughter of Ferdinand II and Isabella I, she married Henry in 1509. She gave birth to six children, but only one daughter (later Mary I) survived infancy.

Henry's desire for a legitimate male heir prompted him in 1527 to appeal to Rome for an annulment, but Pope Clement VII refused, triggering the break between Henry and Rome and leading to the English Reformation. In 1533 Henry had his own archbishop of Canterbury, Thomas Cranmer, annul the marriage, and Catherine spent her last years isolated from public life.

Catherine of Siena, Saint, orig. CATERINA BENINCASA (b. March 25, 1347, Siena, Tuscany—d. April 29, 1389, Rome; canonized 1461; feast day April 29), Dominican mystic and patron saint of Italy. She joined the Dominican third order in Siena in 1363 and soon became known for her holiness and severe asceticism. Catherine called for a Crusade against the Muslims as a means of calming domestic conflict in Italy. She also played a major role in returning the papacy from Avignon to Rome. Her writings include four treatises on religious mysticism known as *The Dialogue of St. Catherine.*

Catholic League (1609–35) Military alliance of the Catholic powers of Germany, led by Maximilian I, duke of Bavaria, and designed to stem the growth of Protestantism in Germany. Plans for a league had long been discussed, but the formation of the Protestant Union in 1608 finally caused the Catholics to unite. In alliance with the Habsburg emperors, the League's forces, led by Graf von Tilly, played a key role in the Thirty Years' War. The league was abolished by the Peace of Prague (1635).

catnip, or CATMINT, Aromatic herb (*Nepeta cataria*) of the mint family. Catnip has spikes of small, purple-dotted flowers. It has been used as a seasoning and as a medicinal tea for colds and fever. Because its mintlike flavour and aroma are particularly exciting to domestic cats, it is often used as a stuffing for cat toys.

*Catnip (*Nepeta cataria*).*
Walter Chandoha

Caucasian languages, Group of languages spoken in the Caucasus region that are not members of any language families spoken elsewhere in the world. Caucasian languages, spoken by some nine million people, are divided into three subgroups: the South Caucasian, or Kartvelian family; the Northwest Caucasian, or Abkhaz-Adyghe languages; and the Northeast Caucasian, or Nakh-Dagestanian languages. Kartvelian, with more than 4.5 million speakers, comprises four relatively closely related languages, including Georgian. Northwest Caucasian languages include Abkhaz and a chain of dialects called collectively Circassian. The Northeast Caucasian languages are further divided into two groups, Nakh and Dagestanian. The Nakh languages include Chechen and Ingush, spoken by more than a million people mainly in Chechnya and Ingushetia. Dagestanian is an extraordinarily diversified group of 25–30 languages spoken by some 1.7 million people mainly in northern Azerbaijan and the Republic of Dagestan. Several Dagestanian languages, including Avar, Lak, Dargva, and Lezgi, number their speakers in the hundreds of thousands; others are spoken in only a few villages. In spite of their great diversity, most Caucasian languages have in common large consonant inventories; in some languages the number of consonants distinguished approaches 80. Those Caucasian languages with standard written forms employ the Cyrillic alphabet, with the prominent exception of Georgian. An effort is being made to introduce the Latin alphabet for Chechen in Chechnya.

Caucasus, or CAUCASIA, Mountainous region, between the Black and Caspian seas. Occupying roughly 170,000 sq mi (440,000 sq km), it is divided among Russia, Georgia, Azerbaijan, and Armenia and forms part of the traditional dividing line between Europe and Asia. It is bisected by the Caucasus Mountains; the area north of the Greater Caucasus range is called Ciscaucasia and the region to the south Transcaucasia. Inhabited from ancient times, it was under nominal Persian and Turkish suzerainty until conquered by Russia in the 18th–19th centuries.

Caucasus Mountains, Russian KAVKAZSKY KHREBET, Mountain range between the Black and Caspian seas. It is sometimes considered the southeastern limit of Europe. Of volcanic origin, it forms two distinct chains—the Greater Caucasus in the north and the Lesser Caucasus in the south—that extend about 750 mi (1,200 km) across southern Russia, Georgia, Azerbaijan, and Armenia. Many peaks rise above 15,000 ft (4,600 m); the highest is Mount Elbrus. The range is crossed by several high passes, including the Daryal and Mamison. It possesses considerable waterpower resources, including those in the Kura-Aras Lowland, and valuable petroleum and natural gas reserves. Caucasus Nature Reserve and other areas in the western part of the range were designated a UNESCO World Heritage site in 1999.

cave, Naturally formed underground cavity. A cave often consists of a number of underground chambers, constituting a series of caverns. An assemblage of such caverns interconnected by smaller passageways makes up a cave system. Primary caves, such as lava tubes and coral caves, develop during the time when the host matrix is solidifying or being deposited. Secondary caves, such as marine grottoes, originate after the host matrix has been deposited or consolidated. Most caves are of the latter type, including solution caves formed by the chemical dissolution of a soluble host rock that has been weakened by fracturing and mechanical erosion; Mammoth Cave and Carlsbad Caverns are examples of solution caves.

Cavour, Camillo Benso, count di (b. Aug. 10, 1810, Turin, Piedmont, French Empire—d. June 6, 1861, Turin, Italy), Italian statesman, leading figure of the Risorgimento. Influenced by revolutionary ideas from an early age, he traveled to Paris and London and in 1847 founded the liberal newspaper *Il Risorgimento*, and he helped persuade Charles Albert to grant a liberal constitution. Elected to Parliament in 1848, Cavour held several cabinet posts before becoming prime minister of Piedmont (1852–59, 1860–61). His exploitation of international rivalries and of revolutionary movements brought about the unification of Italy under the house of Savoy, with himself as the first prime minister of the new kingdom (1861).

Cayman Islands, British overseas territory, Caribbean Sea, located about 180 mi (290 km) northwest of Jamaica. The islands include Grand Cayman (the largest), Little Cayman, and Cayman Brac. Area: 102 sq mi (264 sq km). Population: (2011 est.) 56,000. Capital: George Town, on Grand Cayman. English is the official language. Though discovered by Christopher Columbus in 1503, the islands were never occupied by the Spanish. Ceded to the British in 1670, they were subsequently settled by the English arriving from Jamaica. The islands were administered as a dependency of Jamaica until Jamaican independence in 1962. A constitution was enacted in 1972; it was replaced in 2009. The governor of the Cayman Islands is appointed by the British crown. The islands are a popular tourist area and a financial centre.

Cecil (of Chelwood), (Edgar Algernon) Robert Gascoyne-Cecil, 1st Viscount (b. Sept. 14, 1864, London, Eng.—d. Nov. 24, 1958, Tunbridge Wells, Kent), British statesman. The son of the marquess of Salisbury, he served during World War I as minister of blockade and as assistant secretary of state for foreign affairs. He was one of the principal draftsmen of the League of Nations covenant in 1919 and, as president of the League of Nations Union (1923–45), one of the League's most loyal workers until it was superseded by the United Nations. In 1937 he was awarded the Nobel Peace Prize.

Cela (Trulock), Camilo José (b. May 11, 1916, Iria Flavia, Spain—d. Jan. 17, 2002, Madrid), Spanish writer. As a young man Cela served with Francisco Franco's forces in the Spanish Civil War; his literary works, however, represent a renunciation of his former Falangist sympathies. Primarily novels, short narratives, and travel diaries of Spain and Latin America, they are characteristically experimental and innovative in form and content. He is sometimes credited with establishing *tremendismo*, a narrative style tending to emphasize violence and grotesque imagery. He is perhaps best known for his first novel, *The Family of Pascual Duarte* (1942); other works include *The Hive* (1951) and the avant-garde *San Camilo, 1936* (1969). In 1989 he was awarded the Nobel Prize for Literature.

celadon, Chinese, Korean, Siamese, and Japanese stoneware decorated with glazes the colour range of which includes greens of various shades, olive, blue, and gray. The colours are the result of a wash of slip (liquefied clay) containing a high proportion of iron that is applied to the body before glazing. The iron interacts with the glaze during the firing and colours it. Celadons were prized in Eastern cultures long before their comparatively late introduction to the West. A wide demand led to their export to India, Persia, and Egypt in the Tang dynasty (618–907) and to most of Asia in the Song (960–1279) and Ming (1368–1644) dynasties. The ware was popular because of its beauty, because of a superstition that a celadon dish would break or change colour if poisoned food were put into it, and because, to the Chinese, it resembled jade. Yue ware, first made in the Han dynasty (206 BC–AD 220), is the earliest celadon.

Celebes, or SULAWESI, Island (pop., including nearby islands, 2000: 14,946,488), Indonesia. One of the Greater Sunda Islands, it lies in the Malay Archipelago east of Borneo and has an area (including adjacent islands) of 74,005 sq mi (191,671 sq km). The island is mountainous; its tallest peak, Mount Rantekombola, reaches 11,335 ft (3,455 m). Muslims arrived in the 15th century. The Portuguese first visited in 1512 while developing the spice trade of the Moluccas. The first foreign settlement, in 1607 by the Dutch at Macassar (now Makassar), initiated a power rivalry with the native sultans that lasted into the 20th century. Celebes joined Indonesia in 1950, though various rebellions against the central government have been ongoing.

Celebes Sea, Part of the western Pacific Ocean. It is bordered by the Sulu Archipelago, Mindanao, the Sangihe Islands, Celebes, and Borneo. It extends 420 mi (675 km) north-south and 520 mi (837 km) east-west, occupying about 110,000 sq mi (280,000 sq km). It is connected with the Java Sea by the Makassar Strait. More than half of it is below 13,000 ft (4,000 m) deep, and its maximum depth is 20,406 ft (6,220 m). Traders and pirates from Borneo and nearby islands controlled the sea until it came under colonial rule in the late 19th century.

celestial coordinates, Set of numbers used to pinpoint the position in the sky of a celestial object. Coordinate systems used include the horizon system (altitude and azimuth), galactic coordinates, the ecliptic system (measured relative to the orbital plane of Earth), and the equatorial system (right ascension and declination, directly analogous to terrestrial latitude and longitude).

celestial mechanics, Branch of astronomy that deals with the mathematical theory of the motions of celestial bodies. Johannes Kepler's laws of planetary motion (1609–19) and Newton's laws of motion (1687) are fundamental to it. In the 18th century, powerful methods of mathematical analysis were generally successful in accounting for the observed motions of bodies in the solar system. One branch of celestial mechanics deals with the effect of gravitation on rotating bodies, with applications to Earth and other objects in space. A modern derivation, called orbital mechanics or flight mechanics, deals with the motions of spacecraft under the influence of gravity, thrust, atmospheric drag, and other forces; it is used to calculate trajectories for ascent into space, achieving orbit, rendezvous, descent, and lunar and interplanetary flights.

celestial sphere, Apparent surface of the heavens, on which the stars seem to be fixed. For the purpose of establishing celestial coordinate systems to mark the positions of heavenly bodies, it can be thought of as a real sphere at an infinite distance from Earth. Earth's rotational axis, extended to infinity, touches this sphere at the northern and southern celestial poles, around which the heavens seem to turn. The intersection of the plane of Earth's Equator with the sphere marks the celestial equator.

celiac disease, or NONTROPICAL SPRUE, Digestive disorder in which people cannot tolerate gluten, a protein constituent of wheat, barley, malt, and rye flours. In celiac disease, gluten generates an immune response that damages the mucous lining of the small intestine; it is believed that a deficiency of gluten-digesting enzymes may underlie the disease. Poor nutrient absorption causes foul, bulky, fatty stools; malnutrition; stunting of growth; and anemia similar to pernicious anemia. It can run in families. Children begin having intermittent intestinal upset, diarrhea, and wasting at 6–21 months. In adults it usually begins after 30, with appetite loss, depression, irritability, and diarrhea. Symptoms in advanced cases stem from nutritional deficiencies and may require supportive measures. A high-protein diet low in glutens and saturated fats usually relieves symptoms.

celibacy, The deliberate abstinence from sexual activity, usually in connection with a religious role or practice. It has existed in some form in most world religions. It may indicate a person's ritual purity (sexual relations being viewed as polluting) or may be adopted to facilitate spiritual advancement (as sexual activity would take place only within the bonds of matrimony, marriage and family were seen as an entangling distraction). In shamanistic religions, shamans are often celibate. In Hinduism, "holy men" (or women) who have left ordinary secular life to seek final liberation are celibate. Buddhism began as a celibate order, though many sects have since given up celibacy. Chinese taoism has monastics and independent celibate adepts. Islam has no institutional celibacy, but individuals may embrace it for personal spiritual advancement. Judaism has prescribed periods of abstinence, but long-term celibacy has not played a large role. The early Christian church tended to regard celibacy as superior to marriage. Since the 12th century it has been the rule for Roman Catholic clergy, though clerical celibacy was never adopted by Protestantism.

cell, In biology, the basic unit of which all living things are composed; the smallest structural unit of living matter that is able to function independently. A single cell can be a complete organism in itself, as in bacteria and protozoans. Groups of specialized cells are organized into tissues and organs in multicellular organisms such as higher plants and animals. There are two distinct types of cells: prokaryotic cells and eukaryotic cells. Though the structures of prokaryotic and eukaryotic cells differ, their molecular compositions and activities are very similar. The chief molecules in cells are nucleic acids, proteins, and polysaccharides. A cell is bounded by a membrane that enables it to exchange certain materials with its surroundings. In plant cells, a rigid cell wall encloses this membrane.

cello, or VIOLONCELLO, Bowed, stringed instrument, the bass member of the violin family. Its full name means "little violone"— i.e., "little big viol." Its proportions resemble those of the violin. Players hold its body between the legs, its weight supported by a metal spike that touches the floor. It has four strings, tuned an octave below those of the viola. The cello was developed in the early 16th century along with the violin and viola; later innovations increased its power. It gradually displaced the bass viola da gamba in the 18th century, especially as a continuo instrument. It

has been essential to chamber music ensembles for 250 years. The modern orchestra includes 6 to 12 cellos. In the 19th and 20th centuries it was increasingly used as a solo instrument.

cellulose, Complex carbohydrate (polysaccharide) consisting of 1,000–3,000 or more glucose units in a linear chain structure that can pack into fibres of great tensile strength. The basic structural component of plant cell walls, cellulose is the most abundant of all naturally occurring organic compounds (90% of cotton and 50% of wood). Mammals (including humans) cannot digest cellulose, but bacteria in the rumens of cattle and other ruminants and protozoans in the gut of termites produce enzymes that can break it down. Soil fungi can also break down cellulose. Its most important uses are in wood, paper, and fibre products, as an ethanol and methanol source, and specialized applications. Cellulose derivatives are used in plastics, photographic films, rayon fibres, cellophane, coatings, explosives (e.g., nitrocellulose), and foods (e.g., the stabilizer and thickener carboxymethylcellulose).

Celt, Any member of an early Indo-European people who spread over much of Europe from the 2nd millennium to the 1st century BC. They were absorbed into the Roman Empire as Britons, Gauls, Boii, Galatians, and Celtiberians. Early archaeological evidence (c. 700 BC) comes from the Hallstatt site in Austria. People of this Iron Age culture controlled trade routes along the Rhône, Seine, Rhine, and Danube rivers. As they moved west, Hallstatt warriors introduced the use of iron, which helped them dominate other Celtic tribes. By the mid 5th century BC, the La Tène culture emerged along the Rhine and moved into eastern Europe and the British Isles. Celts sacked Rome c. 390 and raided the whole peninsula, then settled south of the Alps (Cisalpine Gaul) and menaced Rome until they were defeated in 225 BC. In the Balkans, they sacked Delphi in 279 but were defeated by the Aetolians. They crossed to Anatolia and looted until they were subdued by Attalus I about 230 BC. Rome controlled Cisalpine Gaul by 192 and in 124 took territory beyond the Alps. In Transalpine Gaul, from the Rhine and the Alps west, the Celts were pressed by Germanic tribes from the west and Romans from the south. By 58 Julius Caesar had begun campaigns to annex all of Gaul. Celtic settlement of Britain and Ireland is deduced from archaeological and linguistic evidence. The Celtic social system comprised a warrior aristocracy and freemen farmers; Druids, with magico-religious duties, ranked higher than warriors. They had a mixed farming economy. Their oral literary composition was highly developed, as was their art; they manufactured gold and silver jewelry, swords and scabbards, and shields inlaid with enamel.

Celtic religion, Beliefs and practices of the ancient Celts of Gaul and the British Isles. Celtic worship centred on the interplay of the divine element with the natural world. Springs, rivers, and hills were thought to be inhabited by guardian spirits, usually female. Some gods were widely worshiped; lesser deities were associated with particular tribes or places. The most honoured god was Lugus, who was skilled in all the arts. Cernunnos was lord of the animals; the goddess of mares and fertility was called Epona (Gaul), Macha (Ireland), or Rhiannon (Britain). Goddesses often came in groups of three. The priests of Celtic religion were the Druids; they maintained an oral tradition and left no writings. Seasonal festivals included Samhain (November 1), which marked summer's end and served as a feast of the dead, and Beltane (May 1). Oak trees, holly, and mistletoe were considered sacred. The Celts believed in life after death as well as transmigration of souls.

Cenozoic Era, Third of the major eras of Earth history, and the interval of time during which the continents assumed their modern configurations and geographic positions. It was also the time when the Earth's flora and fauna evolved toward those of the present. The Cenozoic, from the Greek for "recent life," began c. 65.5 million years ago and is divided into three periods: the Paleogene (65.5–23 million years ago), Neogene (23–2.6 million years ago) and Quaternary (2.6 million years ago to the present).

censorship, Act of changing or suppressing speech or writing that is considered subversive of the common good. In the past, most governments believed it their duty to regulate the morals of their people; only with the rise in the status of the individual and individual rights did censorship come to seem objectionable. Censorship may be preemptive (preventing the publication or broadcast of undesirable information) or punitive (punishing those who publish or broadcast offending material). In Europe, both the Roman Catholic and Protestant churches practiced censorship, as did the absolute monarchies of the 17th and 18th centuries. Authoritarian governments such as those in China, Cuba, Saudi Arabia, and the former Soviet Union have employed pervasive censorship, which is generally opposed by underground movements engaged in the circulation of samizdat literature. In the U.S. in the 20th century, censorship focused largely on works of fiction deemed guilty of obscenity (e.g., James Joyce's *Ulysses* and D.H. Lawrence's *Lady Chatterley's Lover*), though periodic acts of political censorship also occurred (e.g., the effort to purge school textbooks of possible left-wing content in the 1950s). In the late 20th century, some called for censorship of so-called hate speech, language deemed threatening (or sometimes merely offensive) to various subsections of the population. Censorship in the U.S. is usually opposed by the American Civil Liberties Union. In Germany after World War II it became a crime to deny the Holocaust or to publish pro-Nazi publications.

census, Enumeration of people, houses, firms, or other important items in a country or region at a particular time. The first U.S. population census was taken in 1790 to establish a basis for representation in Congress. Censuses were taken in England, France, and Canada in 1801, 1836, and 1871, respectively. China was the last major country to report a census, in 1953. Census information is obtained by using a fixed questionnaire covering such topics as place of residence, sex, age, marital status, occupation, citizenship, language, ethnicity, religious affiliation, and education. From the responses demographers derive data on population distribution, household and family composition, internal migration, labor-force participation, and other topics.

Centaur object, Icy body, similar to an asteroid in size but to a comet in composition, that orbits the Sun mainly between the orbits of Jupiter and Neptune. The first known Centaur object, Chiron, was found in 1977, but its affinity with comets was not recognized until more than a decade later. Subsequently, dozens of Centaur objects have been reported. They are thought to have originated in the Kuiper belt, a vast reservoir of comet nuclei beyond Neptune's orbit.

centipede, Any of about 2,800 species (class Chilopoda) of long, flattened, many-segmented arthropods having one pair of legs on each segment except the hindmost. Centipedes remain under stones, bark, and ground litter by day; at night they prey on other small invertebrates. They move rapidly on 14–177 pairs of legs and have one pair of long, many-jointed antennae and a pair of jawlike, venomous claws just behind the head. The 1-in. (2.5-cm) house centipede of Europe and North America is the only species common in dwellings. The largest centipedes, found in the tropics, may grow as long as 11 in. (28 cm) and can inflict severe bites.

Centipede (genus Scolopendra).
E.S. Ross

Central African Republic, formerly UBANGI-SHARI, Country, central Africa. Area: 240,324 sq mi (622,436 sq km). Population: (2011 est.) 4,950,000. Capital: Bangui. The people form heterogeneous ethnic groups, with the Banda, Baya (Gbaya), Mandjia, and Ngbaka constituting more than two-thirds of the inhabitants.

Languages: French, Sango (both official), several others. Religions: Christianity (mostly other Christians [largely unaffiliated and independent]; also Roman Catholic, Protestant), Islam, traditional beliefs. Currency: CFA franc. The country is landlocked and consists of a large rolling plateau. The northern half is characterized by savanna and is drained by tributaries of the Chari River. The southern half is densely forested. The country has a developing free-enterprise economy of mixed state and private structure, with agriculture as the main component. It is a multiparty republic with one legislative body; its head of state is the president and its head of government the prime minister. For several centuries before the arrival of Europeans, the territory was exploited by slave traders. The French explored and claimed central Africa and in 1889 established a post at Bangui. They subsequently partitioned the territory into several colonies, one of which was Ubangi-Shari (Oubangui-Chari), the future Central African Republic; it later became part of French Equatorial Africa. Ubangi-Shari became a French overseas territory in 1946. It became an autonomous republic within the French Community in 1958 and achieved independence in 1960. In 1965 the military overthrew a civilian government and installed Jean-Bédel Bokassa, who in 1976 renamed the country the Central African Empire. He was overthrown in 1979 and the former name was restored, but the military again seized power in the 1980s. Elections in 1993 led to installation of a civilian government, which attempted to deal with continued political and economic instability that persisted into the 21st century. The government was overthrown in a 2003 coup, which led to the promulgation of a new constitution in 2004. A democratically elected government was installed in 2005.

Central America, Southern portion of North America (pop., 2006 est.: 40,338,000). It extends from the southern border of Mexico to the northwestern border of Colombia and from the Pacific Ocean to the Caribbean Sea. It includes Guatemala, Belize, Honduras, El Salvador, Nicaragua, Costa Rica, and Panama. Some geographers also include five states of Mexico: Quintana Roo, Yucatán, Campeche, Tabasco, and Chiapas. Area: 201,594 sq mi (522,129 sq km). About three-fifths of the region's population is of mixed European and Indian ancestry (called Ladinos in Guatemala and mestizos elsewhere). Language: Spanish (official), except Belize (English, official); also Indian languages. Religion: Christianity (predominantly Roman Catholic; also Evangelical Protestant). The region is largely hilly or mountainous, with humid swamps and lowlands extending along both coasts. Tajumulco Volcano, in western Guatemala, is the highest point, elevation 13,845 ft (4,220 m). The region has some 40 volcanoes, many of them active, and is prone to severe seismic activity. The volcanic zones have fertile soil and are productive agricultural areas. Central America was long inhabited by indigenous peoples, including the Maya, before the Spanish arrived and conquered the region in the early 16th century; they continued to rule for about 300 years. Christopher Columbus skirted the Atlantic coast from Honduras to the Gulf of Darien in 1502; the first European settlement (1510) was on the gulf. Spain organized the region (except Panama) into the Captaincy General of Guatemala (*c.* 1543). The English arrived in the 17th century, settling what became British Honduras (Belize). Independence from Spanish rule came in 1821, and in 1823 the United Provinces of Central America was formed (Guatemala, El Salvador, Honduras, Nicaragua, and Costa Rica). British Honduras, still a colony, did not join the federation, and Panama remained part of Colombia. In 1824 the federation adopted a constitution, but in 1838 Costa Rica, Honduras, and Nicaragua seceded, thus effectively terminating the federation. Treaties of amity were drawn up at a conference of Central American states in Washington, D.C. (1923). The Central American Common Market was established in 1960 to create a customs union and promote economic cooperation. By 2001 Ecuador and El Salvador had adopted the U.S. dollar as their monetary unit. By the mid-2000s El Salvador, Honduras, Guatemala, Nicaragua, and Costa Rica had entered into the Central America–Dominican Republic Free Trade Agreement (CAFTA-DR) with the United States.

central bank, Institution, such as the U.S. Federal Reserve System, charged with regulating the size of a nation's money supply, the availability and cost of credit, and the foreign exchange value of its currency. Central banks act as the fiscal agent of the government, issuing notes to be used as legal tender, supervising the operations of the commercial banking system, and implementing monetary policy. By increasing or decreasing the supply of money and credit, they affect interest rates, thereby influencing the economy. Modern central banks regulate the money supply by buying and selling assets (e.g., through the purchase or sale of government securities). They may also raise or lower the discount rate to discourage or encourage borrowing by commercial banks. By adjusting the reserve requirement (the minimum cash reserves that banks must hold against their deposit liabilities), central banks contract or expand the money supply. Their aim is to maintain conditions that support a high level of employment and production and stable domestic prices. Central banks also take part in cooperative international currency arrangements designed to help stabilize or regulate the foreign exchange rates of participating countries. Central banks have become varied in authority, autonomy, functions, and instruments of action, but there has been consistent increased emphasis on the interdependence of monetary and other national economic policies, especially fiscal policies and debt management policies.

Central Intelligence Agency (CIA), Principal intelligence and counterintelligence agency of the U.S., established in 1947 as a successor to the World War II-era Office of Strategic Services. The law limits its activities to foreign countries; it is prohibited from gathering intelligence on U.S. soil, which is a responsibility of the Federal Bureau of Investigation. Officially a part of the U.S. Defense Department, it is responsible for preparing analyses for the National Security Council. Its budget is kept secret. Though intelligence gathering is its chief occupation, the CIA has also been involved in many covert operations, including the expulsion of Mohammad Mosaddeq from Iran (1953), the attempted Bay of Pigs invasion of Cuba (1961), and support of the Nicaraguan contras in the 1980s.

central limit theorem, In statistics, any of several fundamental theorems in probability. Originally known as the law of errors, in its classic form it states that the sum of a set of independent random variables will approach a normal distribution regardless of the distribution of the individual variables themselves, given certain general conditions. Further, the mean of the normal distribution will coincide with the (arithmetic) mean of the (statistical) means of each random variable.

Central Powers, World War I coalition that was defeated by the Allied Powers. Its primary members were the German empire and Austria-Hungary, the "central" European states that were at war from August 1914 against France, Britain, and Russia. The Ottoman empire entered the war on the side of the Central Powers in October 1914, followed by Bulgaria in October 1915.

Central Treaty Organization (CENTO), originally MIDDLE EAST TREATY ORGANIZATION, or BAGHDAD PACT ORGANIZATION, Mutual-security organization, originally composed of Turkey, Iran, Iraq, Pakistan, and Britain. It was formed in 1955, at the urging of the U.S. and Britain, to counter the threat of Soviet expansion into the Middle East. CENTO was never very effective. Iraq withdrew after its anti-Soviet monarchy was overthrown in 1959. In that same year the U.S. became an associate member, and CENTO's headquarters were moved to Ankara, Tur. After the fall of Mohammad Reza Shah Pahlavi in 1979, Iran withdrew and CENTO was dissolved.

centrifugal force, Fictitious force, peculiar to circular motion, that is equal but opposite to the centripetal force that keeps a particle on a circular path. For example, a stone attached to a string and whirling in a horizontal circular path is accelerated toward the centre of its path by the tension in the string, the only force acting on the string. However, in a reference frame at rest with the stone, another force—the centrifugal force—must be introduced for Newton's laws of motion to apply. Centrifugal force is a useful concept in analyzing behaviour in rotating systems.

centromere, Structure in a chromosome that holds together the two chromatids (the daughter strands of a replicated chromosome). The centromere is the point of attachment of the kinetochore, a structure to which the microtubules of the mitotic spindle become anchored. The spindle is the structure that pulls the chromatids to opposite ends of the cell during the cell division processes of mitosis and meiosis. Once separated, each chromatid becomes a chromosome. Thus, when the cell divides, both daughter cells have complete sets of chromosomes.

century plant, or AMERICAN ALOE, or MAGUEY, Species of agave (*Agave americana*), of Mexico and the southwestern U.S. It takes many years (from five to 100) to mature, flowers only once, and then dies. It is widely cultivated for its large spiny leaves and enormous flower cluster, and may reach 20 ft (6 m) in height. Century plants provide the distinctive ingredient for the alcoholic drinks pulque and mescal.

cephalopod, Any marine mollusk of the class Cephalopoda (e.g., cuttlefish, nautilus, octopus, and squid), which includes the most active and largest living invertebrates. Cephalopods are bilaterally symmetrical and typically have a highly developed centralized nervous system. Their image-forming eyes are similar in structure to vertebrate eyes, and their heads are armed with tentacles that have rows of round suction disks. Most cephalopods can change skin colour to blend in with their surroundings. All can swim, propelling themselves backward by expelling water forcefully. Most are carnivores that feed on fish, crustaceans, and other mollusks.

ceramics, Traditionally, objects created from such naturally occurring raw materials as clay minerals and quartz sand, by shaping the material and then hardening it by firing at high temperatures to make the object stronger, harder, and less permeable to fluids. The principal ceramic products are containers, tableware, bricks, and tiles.

Cerberus, In Greek mythology, the monstrous watchdog of the underworld. He was usually said to have three heads, though Hesiod says he had 50. Heads of snakes grew from his back, and he had a serpent's tail. He devoured anyone who tried to escape Hades's kingdom, and he refused entrance to living humans, though Orpheus gained passage by charming him with music. One of the labours of Heracles was to bring Cerberus up to the land of the living; after succeeding, he returned the creature to Hades.

cerebellum, Part of the brain that integrates sensory input from the inner ear and from proprioceptors in muscle with nerve impulses from the cerebrum, coordinating muscle responses to maintain balance and produce smooth, coordinated movements. Located below the cerebral hemispheres and behind the upper medulla oblongata and pons, each of its two connected hemispheres has a core of white matter within a cortex of gray matter. Disorders usually produce neuromuscular disturbances, in particular ataxia.

cerebral palsy, Paralysis resulting from abnormal development or damage to the brain before or soon after birth. Cases are of four main types: spastic, with spasms contracting the extremities and often also with intellectual disability and epilepsy; athetoid, with slow, changing spasms in the face, neck, and extremities, grimacing, and inarticulate speech (dysarthria); ataxic, with poor coordination, muscle weakness, an unsteady gait, and difficulty performing rapid or fine movements; and mixed, in which symptoms of two or more types are present.

cerebrum, Largest part of the brain. The two cerebral hemispheres consist of an inner core of myelinated nerve fibres, the white matter, and a heavily convoluted outer cortex of gray matter. Nerve fibres in the white matter connect functional areas of the cortex in the same hemispheres, connect functional areas of the cortex in opposite hemispheres, and connect the cerebral cortex to lower centres (e.g., the spinal cord). A front-to-back fissure divides the cerebrum's two hemispheres. Each hemisphere controls the opposite side of the body. The corpus callosum, a thick band of white matter, connects them, allowing integration of sensory data and responses from both sides of the body. Other important cerebral structures include the hypothalamus and the thalamus.

Ceres, Dwarf planet and largest known asteroid in the solar system and the first asteroid discovered, in 1801. Named after the Roman goddess Ceres, it revolves around the Sun in 4.61 Earth years, rotates once in 9.1 hours, and is about 585 mi (940 km) across. Its mass accounts for more than one-third the total mass of the asteroid belt. Ceres was designated a dwarf planet, a category of solar system object defined by the International Astronomical Union in August 2006.

Ceres, In Roman religion, the goddess of the growth of food plants, sometimes worshiped in association with the earth goddess Tellus. Her cult was overlaid by that of Demeter, who was worshiped in Greece and Sicily. According to tradition, her cult was introduced into Rome in 496 BC to check a famine. Her temple on Aventine Hill was known as a centre of plebeian religious and political activities and for its artwork.

Ceres, Classical sculpture; in the Vatican Museum.
Alinari/Art Resource, New York

cerium, Chemical element, a rare earth metal of the lanthanoid series (hence having many properties of the transition elements), chemical symbol Ce, atomic number 58. It is irongray and fairly soft and ductile. Found in many ores, it is about as abundant as copper and three times as abundant as lead. The metal is used in alloys and other metallurgical applications and (because it oxidizes strongly and rapidly) in illumination, ignition, and signaling devices and in propellants. Misch metal, used in lighter flints, is 50% cerium. Cerium compounds (in which it has valence 3 or 4) are used in the mantles of lanterns, in the ceramic, photographic, and textile industries, and in analytical chemistry.

cervicitis, Inflammation of the cervix of the uterus, caused by infection or irritation. It is most common during the years of menstruation. Cervicitis can be acute or chronic and may worsen during pregnancy. It does not cause pain but may lead to polyps. The major symptom is an abundant discharge, which can impair fertility. Treatment may include antibiotics or cauterization or surgery to repair or remove the cervix; this does not affect fertility.

cesarean section, or C-SECTION, Surgical removal of a fetus from the uterus through an abdominal incision at or before full term. It is usually performed when vaginal delivery would endanger the life or health of the mother or the child. Vaginal delivery is often possible in subsequent pregnancies. Cesarean section carries the usual risks of major surgery. Once overused, largely for fear of malpractice suits, its use has been greatly reduced by the natural childbirth movement.

cesium, Chemical element, one of the alkali metals, chemical symbol Cs, atomic number 55. The first element discovered by spectroscopy (1860), it is silvery white, liquid at warm room temperature (melting at 83 °F [28.4 °C]), and very soft when solid. About half as abundant as lead, it occurs in minute quantities as ores. It reacts explosively with cold water and is used to scavenge traces of oxygen and other gases in electron tubes. Other uses are as a catalyst and in photoelectric cells, ion propulsion systems, atomic clocks, and plasma for thermoelectric conversion. Cesium salts have various specialty applications, including in mineral waters.

cetacean, Any of the exclusively aquatic placental mammals constituting the order Cetacea. They are found in oceans worldwide and in some freshwater environments. Modern cetaceans are grouped in two suborders: about 70 species of toothed whales (Odontoceti) and 13 species of toothless baleen whales (Mysticeti). They have a tapered body, no external hind limbs, and a tail ending in a horizontal blade of two lobes, or flukes. Cetaceans must come to the water's surface to breathe through blowholes located on top of their head.

Chaco War (1932–35) Conflict between Bolivia and Paraguay over possession of the Chaco, a wilderness region thought to contain oil reserves. Bolivia, landlocked since the War of the Pacific, also was motivated by the need to gain access to the Atlantic coast through the Río de la Plata system. The war cost about 100,000 lives and so seriously disrupted Bolivia's economy that its deprived masses demanded reform. In a treaty arranged by neighbouring countries and the U.S., Bolivia was given a corridor to the Paraguay River and a port, but Paraguay gained clear title to most of the disputed region.

Chad, officially REPUBLIC OF CHAD, Country, north-central Africa. Area: 495,755 sq mi (1,284,000 sq km). Population: (2011 est.) 12,018,000. Capital: N'Djamena. The Sara are the largest ethnic group, making up about one-fourth of the total population; other groups include the Kebbi, Kanem-Bornu, Tangale, Fulani, and Gorane. Arabs, including a number of peoples, represent a single ethnic group. Languages: French, Arabic (both official), Fula, Sara. Religions: Islam, Christianity, traditional beliefs. Currency: CFA franc. The landlocked country's terrain is a shallow basin that rises gradually from the Lake Chad area in the west. The basin is rimmed by mountains, including the volcanic Tibesti Massif to the north, rising to 11,204 ft (3,415 m) at Mount Koussi. The lowest elevation, 573 ft (175 m), is in the Djourab Depression. Chad's river network is limited to the Chari and Logone rivers and their tributaries, which flow from the southeast into Lake Chad. The economy is agricultural; gold, uranium, and petroleum reserves have not been fully exploited. Chad is a unitary republic with one legislative body; its head of state is the president and its head of government the prime minister. About AD 800 the kingdom of Kanem was founded, and by the early 1200s its borders had expanded to form a new kingdom, Kanem-Bornu, in the north. Its power peaked in the 16th century with its command of the southern terminus of the trans-Sahara trade route to Tripoli. About this time the rival kingdoms of Baguirmi and Ouaddaï (Wadai) evolved in the south. In the years 1883–93 all three kingdoms fell to the Sudanese adventurer Rābiḥ al-Zubayr, who was overthrown in 1900 by a local ruler under French protection. Extending their power, the French in 1910 made Chad a part of French Equatorial Africa, and it was made an overseas territory in 1946. The country achieved independence in 1960 but has had decades of civil war despite frequent intervention by France and Libya, resulting in political instability and a lack of economic development.

Chad, Lake, Lake, west-central Africa. Located at the juncture of the boundaries of Nigeria, Niger, Chad, and Cameroon, the lake covered 9,900 sq mi (25,600 sq km) in the mid-20th century. Its water level has since dropped—owing to severe drought, the desertification of the surrounding Sahel region, and irrigation projects—and, by the beginning of the 21st century, the lake had shrunk to 580 sq mi (1,500 sq km). The lake is fed by the Chari River.

*Turkish coat of chain mail,
16th century*
Courtesy of The John Woodman
Higgins Armory Museum

chain mail, or MAIL, Form of body armour worn by European knights and other medieval warriors. An early form, made by sewing iron rings to fabric or leather, was worn in late Roman times and may have originated in Asia. Medieval armourers interlaced the rings, which were closed by welding or riveting. In the 8th century, mail was a short coat with a separate sleeve for the sword arm. By the Norman Conquest (1066), the coat was long and fully sleeved; a hood, usually fitting under a helmet, covered the head and neck. By the 12th century, mail was fitted to hands, feet, and legs. The addition of plates to increase chest and back protection gradually evolved in the 14th century into complete plate armour, displacing mail.

chain reaction, Process yielding products that initiate further processes of the same kind. Nuclear chain reactions are a series of nuclear fissions initiated by neutrons produced in a preceding fission. A critical mass, large enough to allow more than one fission-produced neutron to be captured, is necessary for the chain reaction to be self-sustaining. Uncontrolled chain reactions, as in an atomic bomb, occur when large numbers of neutrons are present and the reactions multiply very quickly. Nuclear reactors control their reactions through the careful distribution of the fissionable material and insertion of neutron-absorbing materials.

chakra, In Hinduism and Tantra, any of 88,000 focal points in the human body where psychic forces and bodily functions can merge and interact. In Hinduism there are seven and in Tantra four major chakras, each associated with a colour, shape, sense organ, natural element, deity, and mantra. The most important are the heart chakra, the chakra at the base of the spine, and the chakra at the top of the head.

Chalcedon, Council of (451) Fourth ecumenical council of the Christian Church, held in Chalcedon (modern Kadiköy, Tur.). Called by the emperor Marcian, it approved the creeds of Nicaea (325) and Constantinople (381; later known as the Nicene Creed). It also approved the *Tome* of Pope Leo I confirming the two distinct natures in Christ and rejecting the Monophysite heresy. The council then explained these doctrines in its own confession of faith. The council disciplined clergy and declared Jerusalem and Constantinople patriarchates.

chalk, Soft, fine-grained, easily pulverized, white-to-grayish variety of limestone, composed of the shells of minute marine organisms. The purest varieties contain up to 99% calcium carbonate in the form of the mineral calcite. Extensive deposits occur in western Europe south of Sweden and in England, notably in the chalk cliffs of Dover along the English Channel. Other extensive deposits occur in the U.S. from South Dakota to Texas and eastward to Alabama. Chalk is used for making lime and portland cement and as a soil additive. Finely ground and purified chalk is known as whiting and is used as a filler, extender, or pigment in a wide variety of materials, including ceramics, putty, cosmetics, crayons, plastics, rubber, paper, paints, and linoleum. The chalk commonly used in classrooms is a manufactured substance rather than natural chalk.

chamber music, Music composed for small instrumental ensembles and performed without a conductor. Traditionally intended for performance in a room or reception hall, often solely for the performers' own pleasure, chamber music is now often heard in concert halls. It began with the 16th-century instrumental consort and long continued to be associated with aristocratic households. The duo sonata (usually for violin and continuo) and trio sonata appeared in early 17th-century Italy. The string quartet arose in the 1750s and remains the best-known chamber genre and ensemble. The serenade, nocturne, and divertimento were Classical genres for varying instrumental forces, often intended to accompany meals and other activities. Standard ensembles include the string trio (violin, viola, cello), string quintet (two violins, two violas, cello), and piano trio (piano, violin, cello). The chamber orchestra, usually with fewer than 25 musicians, is often used for 18th-century music and usually requires a conductor.

chamber of commerce, or COMMERCIAL ASSOCIATION, Any of various voluntary organizations of business firms, public officials, professional people, and public-spirited citizens whose primary interest is in publicizing, promoting, and developing commercial and industrial opportunities in their local area, and usually also community schools, streets, housing, and public works. The International Chamber of Commerce (founded 1920) acts as the voice of the business community in the international field and runs a court of arbitration for settling commercial disputes. National chambers of commerce exist in most industrialized, free-enterprise countries. The first to use the name was founded in Paris in 1601; the first U.S. chamber of commerce was that of the state of New York, founded in 1768.

Chamberlain, Sir (Joseph) Austen (b. Oct. 16, 1863, Birmingham, Warwickshire, Eng.—d. March 16, 1937, London), British statesman. Son of Joseph Chamberlain and half brother of Neville Chamberlain, he entered the House of Commons in 1892. He held a variety of posts, including chancellor of the Exchequer (1903–05, 1919–21) and secretary of state for India (1915–17). As foreign secretary (1924–29), he helped bring about the Locarno Pact, intended to secure peace in western Europe. For that accomplishment, he shared the 1925 Nobel Prize for Peace with Charles Dawes.

Chamberlain's Men, or LORD CHAMBERLAIN'S MEN, English theatrical company, the most important in Elizabethan and Jacobean England. It was based at the Globe Theatre from 1599 to 1608. In 1603 it was taken under royal patronage as the King's Men. William Shakespeare was connected with the company for most of his career; it also presented works by Ben Jonson, Thomas Dekker, and Francis Beaumont and John Fletcher. It ceased to exist when the theatres were closed at the outbreak of the English Civil Wars in 1642.

chameleon, Any member of a group of primarily tree-dwelling Old World lizards in the family Chamaeleonidae, characterized chiefly by their ability to change body colour. Other traits include toes fused into opposite bundles of two and three, teeth attached to the jaw edge, and a long, slender, extensile tongue. About half of the 150 species are found only in Madagascar; the others occur mostly in sub-Saharan Africa, only a few elsewhere. Most are 7–10 in. (17–25 cm) long, with a body flattened from side to side. The bulged eyes move independently. Each species can undergo a particular range of colour change. Insects are the main diet, but larger species also eat birds.

chamomile, Any of the more than 100 species of Eurasian herbs that make up the genus *Anthemis*, in the aster family (Asteraceae); also, a similar plant in the genus *Chamaemelum* of the same family. Both genera have yellow or white ray flowers and yellow disk flowers. Several *Anthemis* species are cultivated as ornamentals, especially golden marguerite, or yellow chamomile (*A. tinctoria*). The strong-smelling mayweed (*A. cotula*) has been used in medicines and insecticides. Chamomile tea, used as a tonic and an antiseptic as well as in herbal remedies, is made from *C. nobile*, or *A. nobilis*.

Chamomile (Anthemis tomentosa)
Anthony J. Huxley

Chamorro, Violeta (Barrios de) (b. Oct. 18, 1929, Rivas province, Nic.), President of Nicaragua (1990–96). Born into a wealthy family, she married the publisher of *La Prensa*, a newspaper that opposed the Anastasio Somoza dictatorship. After her husband was assassinated in 1978, she took his place as publisher. When the Sandinistas overthrew Somoza, she served briefly on a ruling civilian junta, but her newspaper soon became critical of Daniel Ortega and supportive of U.S. policies, which included extensive support for the anti-Sandinista contras. Advocating an end to military and economic conflicts with the U.S., she was elected president in 1990. Her presidency was troubled by continuing deep political divisions and the significant power still held by the Sandinistas.

champagne, Sparkling wine. Named for the site of its origin, the Champagne region of northeastern France, it is made from only three grapes: pinot and meunier (both black) and chardonnay (white). The juice from these grapes is initially fermented in stainless-steel vats. A mixture of wine, sugar, and yeast is added, and it is then transferred to pressure tanks for a second fermentation that yields carbon dioxide and effervescence. It is chilled, sweetened, bottled, and left to mature. It generally has a crisp, flinty taste that varies in degree of sweetness, depending on the type.

Champlain, Samuel de (b. 1567, Brouage, France—d. Dec. 25, 1635, Quebec, New France), French explorer. He made several expeditions to North America before founding Quebec in 1608 with 32 colonists, most of whom did not survive the first winter. He joined with the northern Indian tribes to defeat Iroquois marauders and promoted the fur trade with the Indians. He discovered Lake Champlain in 1609 and made other explorations of what are now northern New York, the Ottawa River, and the eastern Great Lakes. English privateers besieged Quebec in 1628, when England and France were at war, and he was taken prisoner. In 1632 the colony was restored to France, and in 1633 Champlain made his last voyage to Quebec, where he lived until his death.

Champs-Élysées (French: "Elysian Fields") One of the world's most remarkable avenues, stretching 1.17 mi (1.88 km) from the Arc de Triomphe to the Place de la Concorde, in Paris. It is divided into two parts by the Rond-Point des Champs-Élysées. The lower part, toward the Place de la Concorde, is surrounded by gardens, museums, theaters, and restaurants. The upper part, toward the Arc de Triomphe, was traditionally a luxury commercial district. Twelve imposing avenues radiate to form a star (*étoile*) at the avenue's upper end, with the Arc de Triomphe at its center; it was called Place de l'Étoile from 1753 until 1970, when it was renamed Place Charles de Gaulle.

chancellor, In western Europe, the title of holders of numerous offices of varying importance, ultimately political in nature. The prime ministers of Germany and Austria are called chancellors. In Britain the chancellor of the Exchequer is the cabinet member in charge of finance. In the U.S. the title is used mainly for the chief administrators of universities.

Chandigarh, City (pop., 2001: 808,515) and union territory (pop., 2008 est.: 1,063,000), joint capital of Haryana and Punjab states, northern India. The territory, situated on the border between the two states, has an area of 44 sq mi (114 sq km). Located just south of the Siwalik Range, the site was selected to replace the former capital of Punjab, Lahore, which became part of Pakistan at partition in 1947. The city was laid out in the 1950s by Le Corbusier in collaboration with Indian architects. Today it is especially noted for its educational and cultural institutions.

The Palace of Assembly in Chandigarh, India, designed by Le Corbusier.
Frederick M. Asher

Chandler, Raymond (Thornton) (b. July 23, 1888, Chicago, Ill., U.S.—d. March 26, 1959, La Jolla, Calif.), U.S. writer of detective fiction. Chandler worked as an oil-company executive in California before turning to writing during the Great Depression. Early short stories were followed by screenplays, including *Double Indemnity* (1944), *The Blue Dahlia* (1946), and *Strangers on a Train* (1951). His character Philip Marlowe, a hard-boiled private detective working in the Los Angeles underworld, appears in all seven of his novels, including *The Big Sleep* (1939; film, 1946 and 1978), *Farewell, My Lovely* (1940; film *Murder, My Sweet*, 1944, and *Farewell, My Lovely*, 1975), and *The Long Good-Bye* (1953; film, 1973). Chandler and Dashiell Hammett are regarded as the classic authors of the hard-boiled genre.

Chandra X-ray Observatory, U.S. X-ray space telescope. It was named after astrophysicist Subrahmanyan Chandrasekhar and was launched into orbit in 1999. Its mirror, with an aperture of 1.2 m (4 ft) and a focal length of 10 m (33 ft), produces unprecedented resolution. In addition to a camera, Chandra has a transmission grating, which can create high-resolution spectra in the range of 0.07–10 keV. The telescope's primary focus is black holes, supernova remnants, starburst galaxies, and other exotic objects.

Chandrasekhar, Subrahmanyan (b. Oct. 19, 1910, Lahore, India—d. Aug. 21, 1995, Chicago, Ill., U.S.), Indian-born U.S. astrophysicist. He left the University of Cambridge to join the staff of the University of Chicago in 1938. He determined that, following its red giant phase, a star with a remaining mass greater than 1.4 times that of the Sun (the Chandrasekhar limit) collapses and becomes a neutron star during a supernova explosion. Stellar remnants more massive than about three solar masses collapse even further to become black holes. He shared a 1983 Nobel Prize with William A. Fowler.

Changchun, or CH'ANG-CH'UN, City (pop., 2003 est.: 2,283,800), capital of Jilin province, northeastern China. It was a small village until the end of the 18th century, when peasants from Shandong began to settle in the region. It gained in importance after the completion of the Chinese Eastern Railway. It came under Japanese control following the Sino-Japanese War of 1894–95. At the time the Japanese seized Manchuria in 1931, the capital of the Japanese puppet state of Manchukuo was moved from Mukden (Shenyang) to Changchun. Following World War II, the city suffered severely in the fighting between communist and Nationalist forces but experienced phenomenal growth after 1949. It is now a centre for industrial expansion, as well as the cultural and educational heart of the province.

Changsha, or CH'ANG-SHA, City (pop., 2003 est.: 1,562,200), capital of Hunan province, south-central China. It was important from the time of the Qin dynasty (221–207 BC). In AD 750–1100 Changsha was an important commercial city, and its population increased greatly. Under the Qing dynasty, from 1664, it was the capital of Hunan province, and it was a major rice market. It was besieged during the Taiping Rebellion but never fell. Changsha was the site of Mao Zedong's conversion to communism. It was the scene of major battles in the Sino-Japanese War of 1937–45 and was briefly occupied by the Japanese. Rebuilt since 1949, the city is now a major port and a commercial and industrial centre.

Channel Islands, Island dependencies, United Kingdom. Located in the English Channel 10–30 mi (16–48 km) off the western coast of France, they cover an area of 75 sq mi (194 sq km) and include the islands of Jersey, Guernsey, Alderney, and Sark and several islets. They are domestically independent of the British government. Structures, including menhirs, are evidence of prehistoric occupation. A part of Normandy in the 10th century AD, the islands came under British rule at the time of the Norman Conquest in 1066. The islets of Ecrehous and Les Minquiers were disputed between England and France until 1953, when the International Court of Justice confirmed British sovereignty. The dispute revived in the late 20th century because sovereignty determines the rights to the continental shelf's economic development (especially petroleum). The Channel Islands were the only British territory occupied by Germany in World War II. The islands are famous for their cattle breeds, including the Jersey and Guernsey.

Channel Tunnel, or EUROTUNNEL, Rail tunnel that runs beneath the English Channel between Folkestone, England, and Sangatte (near Calais), France. A rail tunnel was chosen over proposals for a very long suspension bridge, a bridge-and-tunnel link, and a combined rail-and-road link. The 31-mi (50-km) tunnel, which opened in 1994, consists of three separate tunnels, two for rail traffic and a central tunnel for services and security. Trains, which carry motor vehicles as well as passengers, can travel through the tunnel at speeds as high as 100 mph (160 kph).

chanson (French: "song"), French art song. The unaccompanied chanson for a single voice part, composed by the troubadours and later the trouvères, first appeared in the 12th century. Accompanied chansons, with parts for one or more instruments, were written in the 14th–15th centuries by Guillaume de Machaut and others in the strict formes fixes ("fixed forms"). About 1,500 chansons for several voices began to be written by Josquin des Prez and his contemporaries. In recent centuries the term has often been used for any cabaret-style French song.

chanson de geste, Any of several Old French epic poems that form the core of the Charlemagne legends. More than 80 *chansons de geste* have survived in 12th- to 15th-century manuscripts. Dealing chiefly with events of the 8th–9th century, they contain a core of historical truth overlain with legend. Most are anonymous. The *Chanson de Roland* was the formative influence on later *chansons de geste*, which in turn influenced literature throughout Europe.

Chanson de Roland (English: "Song of Roland"), Old French epic poem written c. 1100, the masterpiece and probably the earliest of the *chanson de geste* form. Its probable author was a Norman, Turold (Turoldus), whose name is introduced in its last line. It deals with the Battle of Roncesvalles (778), a skirmish against the Basques that the poem portrays as a heroic battle against the Saracens. Direct and sober in style, it highlights a clash between the recklessly courageous Roland and his prudent friend Oliver, which is also a conflict between divergent conceptions of feudal loyalty.

Chao Phraya River, or MAENAM RIVER, River, Thailand. Flowing south from the highlands on the country's northern border to the head of the Gulf of Thailand near Bangkok, it is some 225 mi (365 km) long and is Thailand's principal river. It is important for the transport of the country's exports. It also forms a highly productive agricultural valley. The name strictly applies only to the river's lower course, which begins at the confluence of the Nan and Ping rivers and is 140 mi (225 km) long.

chaos theory, Mathematical theory that describes chaotic behavior in a complex system. Applications include the study of turbulent flow in fluids, irregularities in biological systems, population dynamics, chemical reactions, plasma physics, meteorology, the motions of groups and clusters of stars, transportation dynamics, and many other fields.

chaparral, Vegetation composed of broad-leaved evergreen shrubs, bushes, and small trees, often forming dense thickets. Chaparral is found in regions with a Mediterranean climate, characterized by hot, dry summers and mild, wet winters. The name is applied mainly to the coastal and inland mountain vegetation of southwestern North America. Chaparral vegetation becomes extremely dry by late summer. The fires that commonly occur during this period are necessary for the germination of many shrub seeds, and they clear away dense ground cover, thus maintaining the shrubby growth form of the vegetation by preventing the spread of trees. New chaparral growth provides good grazing for domestic livestock, and chaparral vegetation also is valuable for watershed protection in areas with steep, easily eroded slopes.

Chaplin, Charlie, in full SIR CHARLES SPENCER CHAPLIN (b. April 16, 1889, London, Eng.—d. Dec. 25, 1977, Corsier-sur-Vevey, Switz.), British-U.S. actor and director. The son of poverty-stricken music-hall entertainers, he became a vaudeville performer at age eight. On tour in New York (1913), he caught the eye of Mack Sennett, who signed him to a film contract. While making his second film, *Kid Auto Races at Venice* (1914), Chaplin developed the costume—baggy pants, derby hat, oversized shoes, and cane—that was to become the hallmark of his famous "little tramp" character. He was soon directing his own films, and he became an instant star in *The Tramp* (1915). After cofounding United Artists in 1919, he produced, directed, and starred in such classics as *The Gold Rush* (1925), *City Lights* (1931), *Modern Times* (1936), *The Great Dictator* (1940), *Monsieur Verdoux* (1947), and *Limelight* (1952). Harassed for his leftist political views, he moved to Switzerland in 1952. In 1972 he returned to the U.S. to accept a special Academy Award.

chariot, Open two- or four-wheeled vehicle of ancient origin. The chariot probably originated in Mesopotamia about 3000 BC; early monuments show heavy vehicles with solid wheels. Chariots were probably first used in royal funeral processions. Two-wheeled horse-drawn versions evolved for speed in battle c. 2000 BC, appearing first in Greece and later in Egypt and the eastern Mediterranean. Chariot racing was popular in Greece at the Olympic Games; in Rome it was the main event in the circus games, where two to four horses drew each lightweight chariot in a competition of four or six vehicles; and in Byzantium such races became the dominant events of civic life.

Charlemagne, or CAROLUS MAGNUS ("CHARLES THE GREAT") (b. April 2, 747?—d. Jan. 28, 814, Aachen, Austrasia), King of the Franks (768–814) and emperor (800–14). The elder son of the Frankish king Pippin III (the Short), he ruled the Frankish kingdom jointly with his brother Carloman until the latter's death in 771. He then became sole king of the Franks and began a series of campaigns to conquer and Christianize neighbouring peoples. He defeated and became king of the Lombards in northern Italy (774). His expedition against the Muslims in Spain failed (778), but he successfully annexed Bavaria (788). Charlemagne fought against the Saxons for many years, finally defeating and Christianizing them in 804. He subdued the Avars of the Danube and gained control of many of the Slav states. With the exception of the British Isles, southern Italy, and part of Spain, he united in one vast state almost all the Christian lands of western Europe. His coronation as emperor at Rome on Christmas Day, 800, after restoring Leo III to the papacy, marks the revival of the empire in Latin Europe and was the forerunner of the Holy Roman Empire. Charlemagne established his capital at Aachen (Aix-la-Chapelle), where he built a magnificent palace. He invited many scholars and poets to assist him in the promotion of the religious and cultural revival known as the Carolingian renaissance. He also codified the laws and increased the use of writing in government and society. He was succeeded on his death by his son Louis the Pious, whom Charlemagne had crowned coemperor in 813.

Charles V, German KARL (b. Feb. 24, 1500, Ghent—d. Sept. 21, 1558, San Jerónimo de Yuste, Spain), Holy Roman emperor (1519–56) and king of Spain (as Charles I, 1516–56). Son of Philip I of Castile and grandson of Ferdinand V and Isabella I and of Emperor Maximilian I, he succeeded to his grandfathers' kingdoms on their deaths in 1516 and 1519, respectively. Important events of his reign include the Diet of Worms and the beginning of the Reformation; his defeat of Francis I, which assured Spanish supremacy in Italy; wars against Turkey under Süleyman I; the formation of the Schmalkaldic League; the Council of Trent; and the Peace of Augsburg. He struggled to hold his vast Spanish and Habsburg empire together against the growing forces of Protestantism, Turkish and French pressure, and even hostility from Pope Adrian VI. In 1555–56 Charles abdicated his claims to the Netherlands and Spain in favour of his son Philip II and the title of emperor to his brother Ferdinand I, and in 1557 he retired to a monastery in Spain.

Charon, In Greek mythology, the son of Erebus (Darkness) and Nyx (Night), whose duty it was to ferry the souls of the dead across the Rivers Styx and Acheron, his payment being the coin placed in the mouth of the corpse before burial. He continues in modern Greek folklore as Charos, or Charontas, the angel of death.

charter, Document granting certain specified rights, powers, privileges, or functions from the sovereign power of a state to a person, corporation, city, or other unit of local organization. In Magna Carta (1215), King John granted certain liberties to the English people. Elsewhere in medieval Europe, monarchs issued charters to towns, guilds, universities, and other institutions, granting the institution certain privileges and sometimes specifying how they should conduct their internal affairs. Later, charters were granted to overseas trading companies (e.g., the British East India Co.), granting them monopolies in certain areas. Britain's colonies in North America were established by charter. Modern charters may be corporate or municipal. A corporate charter, issued by a governmental body, grants individuals the power to form a corporation, or other unit of limited-liability company. A municipal charter is a law that creates a new political subdivision and allows the people within it to organize themselves into a municipal corporation, in effect delegating to the people the powers of local self-government.

Chartism, British working-class movement for parliamentary reform. It was named after the People's Charter, a bill drafted by William Lovett (1800–1877) in 1838 that demanded universal manhood suffrage, equal electoral districts, vote by ballot, annually elected Parliaments, payment of members of Parliament, and abolition of property qualifications for membership. Born amid an economic depression, the movement rose to national importance under the leadership of Feargus O'Connor. Parliament refused to take action on three Chartist petitions presented to it, and the movement declined after 1848.

Chartres, City (pop., 2006 est.: 40,022), northwestern France. Situated on the Eure River southwest of Paris, it was the capital and centre of Druidic worship for the Carnutes, a Celtic tribe. The Normans attacked and burned the city in 858. In the Middle Ages it was held by the counts of Blois and Champagne. The city was

sold to France in 1286 and was occupied by the English from 1417 to 1432. Henry IV was crowned there in 1594. The Germans held it in 1870, and it was severely damaged in World War II. Landmarks include the Gothic Chartres Cathedral.

Chartres Cathedral, Cathedral of Notre-Dame at Chartres, one of the most influential examples of High Gothic architecture. The main part of this great cathedral was built between 1194 and 1220. It replaced a 12th-century church of which only the crypt, the base of the towers, and the western facade remain. Abandonment of the traditional tribune galleries and the use of a unique type of flying buttress allowed for a larger clerestory. Remarkable stained-glass windows and a Renaissance choir screen add to its beauty.

The cathedral at Chartres, Fr.
Everett C. Johnson/DeWys Inc.

chayote, Tendril-bearing perennial vine (*Sechium edule*) of the gourd family, native to the New World tropics, where it is widely cultivated for its edible fruits. Chayote also is grown as an annual plant in temperate climates. The fast-growing vine bears small, white flowers and green or white pear-shaped fruits with furrows. Each fruit contains one seed. The fruits are eaten cooked or raw, and the young root tubers are prepared like potatoes.

*Chayote (*Sechium edule*)*
Eugene Belt/Shostal Associates

Chechnya, Republic, southwestern Russia. Part of the Chechen-Ingush autonomous republic of the former U.S.S.R., it became a republic within Russia in 1992, as did Ingushetia. It is populated mainly by Chechens, a Muslim ethnolinguistic group. Chechnya's demand for independence from Russia in 1992 led to an invasion by Russian troops in 1994. Fighting led to severe devastation of the area, and a series of cease-fires were negotiated and violated. A provisional peace treaty was signed in May 1997. Russian troops withdrew but returned in 1999, and heavy fighting resumed. In 2003 a new constitution was approved that devolved greater powers to the Chechen government but kept the republic in the Russian Federation. In 2009 Russia announced the end of its counterinsurgency operations in Chechnya. The capital, Grozny, is an oil centre with pipelines to the Caspian and Black seas.

checkers, or DRAUGHTS, Board game for two players, each with 12 pieces positioned on the black squares of a 64-square checkerboard. Play consists of advancing a piece diagonally forward to an adjoining square, the goal being to jump and thus capture each of an opponent's pieces until all are removed and victory is declared. When a piece reaches the final (king) row, it is crowned with a piece of the same colour and can begin to move in any direction. Similar games have been played in various cultures and in times extending back to antiquity.

checks and balances, Principle of government under which separate branches are empowered to prevent actions by other branches and are induced to share power. Checks and balances are applied primarily in constitutional governments. They are of fundamental importance in tripartite governments, such as that of the

U.S., that separate powers among legislative, executive, and judicial departments. Checks and balances, which modify the separation of powers, may operate under parliamentary systems through exercise of a parliament's prerogative to adopt a no-confidence vote against a government; the government, or cabinet, in turn, ordinarily may dissolve the parliament. In one-party political systems, informal checks and balances may operate when organs of an authoritarian or totalitarian regime compete for power.

chemical reaction, Any chemical process in which substances are changed into different ones, with different properties, as distinct from changing position or form (phase). Chemical reactions involve the rupture or rearrangement of the bonds holding atoms together, never atomic nuclei. The total mass and number of atoms of all reactants equals those of all products, and energy is almost always consumed or liberated. The speed of reactions varies. Understanding their mechanisms lets chemists alter reaction conditions to optimize the rate or the amount of a given product; the reversibility of the reaction and the presence of competing reactions and intermediate products complicate these studies. Reactions can be syntheses, decompositions, or rearrangements, or they can be additions, eliminations, or substitutions. Examples include oxidation-reduction, polymerization, ionization, combustion (burning), hydrolysis, and acid-base reactions.

chemical symbol, Notation of one or two letters derived from the scientific names of the chemical elements (e.g., S for sulfur, Cl for chlorine, Zn for zinc). Some hark back to Latin names: Au (*aurum*) for gold, Pb (*plumbum*) for lead. Others are named for people or places (e.g. einsteinium, Es, for Einstein). The present symbols express the system set out by the atomic theory of matter. John Dalton first used symbols to designate single atoms of elements, not indefinite amounts, and Jons Jacob Berzelius gave many of the current names. Chemical formulas of compounds are written as combinations of the elements' symbols, with numbers indicating their atomic proportions, using various conventions for ordering and grouping. Thus, sodium chloride is written as NaCl and sulfuric acid as H_2SO_4.

chemical warfare, Use of lethal or incapacitating chemical weapons in war, and the methods of combating such agents. Chemical weapons include choking agents such as the chlorine and phosgene gas employed first by the Germans and later by the Allies in World War I; blood agents such as hydrogen cyanide and cyanogen gas, which block red blood cells from taking up oxygen; blister agents such as sulfur gas and Lewisite, also dispensed as a gas, which burn and blister the skin; and nerve agents such as Tabun, Sarin, Soman, and VX, which block the transmission of nerve impulses to the muscles, heart, and diaphragm. The horrific casualties suffered in World War I led to the 1925 Geneva Protocol, which made it illegal to employ chemical weapons but did not ban their production. Chemical weapons were used a number of times afterward, most notably by Italy in Ethiopia (1935–36), by Japan in China (1938–42), by Egypt in Yemen (1966–67), and by Iran and Iraq against each other (1984–88). During the Cold War the Soviet Union and U.S. built up enormous chemical arsenals; these were dismantled under the terms of the 1993 Chemical Weapons Convention, which prohibits all development, production, acquisition, stockpiling, or transfer of such weapons. Not all countries have signed the convention, and many are suspected of pursuing clandestine chemical programs. Many military forces have adopted various defensive measures, including chemical sensors, protective garments and gas masks, decontaminants, and injectable antidotes, and some have reserved the option of retaliating in kind to any chemical attack. In 1995 a religious cult killed 12 civilians and injured thousands more with Sarin gas in Tokyo; this pointed out the power of chemical agents as weapons of terror as well as the difficulty of protecting civilian populations.

chemistry, Science that deals with the properties, composition, and structure of substances (elements and compounds), the reactions and transformations they undergo, and the energy released or absorbed during those processes. Often called the "central science," chemistry is concerned with atoms as building blocks (rather than with the subatomic domain), with everything in the material world, and with all living things. Branches of chemistry include inorganic, organic, physical, and analytical chemistry; biochemistry; electrochemistry; and geochemistry. Chemical engineering (applied chemistry) uses the theoretical and experimental information obtained in chemistry to build chemical plants and make useful products.

chemotherapy, Treatment of diseases, including cancer, with chemicals. Some cancer drugs interfere with cancer-cell division or enzyme processes. However, they have serious side effects, attacking some healthy cells and reducing resistance to infection. Certain steroids are used to treat breast cancer and prostate cancer, leukemia, and lymphomas. Derivatives of plants such as periwinkle (vincristine, vinblastine) and yew (taxol) have been found effective against Hodgkin disease, leukemia, and breast cancer.

Chen Duxiu, or CH'EN TU-HSIU (b. Oct. 8, 1879, Huaining county, Anhuei province, China—d. May 27, 1942, Jiangjing, near Chongqing), Chinese political and intellectual leader, a founder of the Chinese Communist Party. As a young man, Chen studied in Japan. In China, he started subversive periodicals that were quickly suppressed by the government. In 1915, after the establishment of the Chinese republic, he created the monthly *Qingnian zazhi* ("Youth Magazine"), renamed *Xin qingnian* ("New Youth"), in which he proposed that the youth of China rejuvenate the nation intellectually and culturally; Lu Xun, Hu Shih, and Mao Zedong were all contributors. In 1917 Chen was appointed dean of the School of Letters at Beijing University. In 1919 he was imprisoned briefly for his role in the May Fourth Movement; on his release he became a Marxist. With Li Dazhao, Mao, and others, he founded the Chinese Communist Party in 1920/21. The Communist International had him removed as party leader when the party's alliance with the Nationalist Party fell apart, and he was expelled from the party in 1929. Arrested in 1932, he spent five years in prison.

Chen Shui-bian (b. Feb. 18, 1951, Tainan county, Taiwan), President of the Republic of China (Taiwan) from 2000 to 2008. Chen studied law at National Taiwan University and later became one of the island's leading attorneys. After unsuccessfully defending protesters who opposed the ruling Nationalist Party, he became linked with the opposition movement, and in the mid-1980s he was jailed on charges of libeling a Nationalist official. He subsequently joined the Democratic Progressive Party and became a prominent member of the movement to establish Taiwan's independence. He served in Taiwan's legislature (1989–94) before being elected mayor of Taipei in 1994. Although he did not win reelection in 1998, the loss freed him to run for president in 2000, and he defeated the Nationalist Party's candidate, ending that party's 55-year rule of Taiwan. In 2004 Chen was narrowly reelected, the vote coming one day after he and his running mate, Vice President Annette Lu (Lu Hsiu-lien), were shot and slightly wounded while campaigning in Tainan. Chen's second term was marred by corruption scandals. In 2009 he was convicted of corruption and sentenced to life in prison (this was later reduced to 20 years).

Cheng-Zhu school, or CH'ENG-CHU SCHOOL, Chinese school of Neo-Confucianism. Its leading philosophers were Cheng Yi and Zhu Xi, for whom the school is named. Cheng Yi taught that to understand *li* (basic truths), one should investigate all things in the world through induction, deduction, historical study, or political activity. Zhu Xi maintained that rational investigation was central to moral cultivation. The school dominated Chinese philosophy until the Republican Revolution (1911).

Chengdu, or CH'ENG-TU, City (pop., 2003 est.: 2,664,000), capital of Sichuan province, west-central China. It lies in the fertile Chengdu plain, the site of one of China's most ancient and successful irrigation systems, watered by the Min River. First set up in the late 3rd century BC, the system has survived and has enabled the area to support one of the densest agrarian populations in the world. Chengdu was the capital of various dynasties, and in the 10th century AD it was immensely prosperous; its merchants introduced the use of paper money, which spread throughout China under the Song dynasty. Chengdu was famous for its brocades and satins. The capital of Sichuan since 1368, it has remained a major administrative centre. Today it is a transportation and industrial hub, as well as an educational centre.

Chennai, formerly MADRAS, City (pop., 2001: city, 4,343,645; metro. area, 6,560,242), capital of Tamil Nadu state, southern India. It is located on the Coromandel Coast of the Bay of Bengal. Founded in 1639 by the British East India Company as a fort and trading post, it was known as Fort St. George and was used as a base for the company's expansion in southern India. The city of St. Thomé, established by the Portuguese in the 16th century, was ceded to the British in 1749 and incorporated into it. The English made the city their administrative and commercial capital c. 1800. It is an industrial centre and the site of numerous educational and cultural institutions. It is traditionally considered the burial place of St. Thomas the Apostle.

Cherokee, American Indian people of Iroquoian lineage living mostly in Oklahoma, U.S. Their traditional homeland is eastern Tennessee and the western Carolinas. Cherokee culture resembled that of the Creek and other Southeast Indians. Their name is derived from a Creek word meaning "people of different speech"; many prefer to be known as Keetoowah or Tsalagi. Cherokee is an Iroquoian language, but it differs considerably from other Iroquoian languages. At the time of first European contact, the Cherokee possessed stone implements, and they wove baskets, made pottery, cultivated corn, beans, and squash, and hunted deer, bear, and elk. Wars and treaties in the late 18th century severely reduced Cherokee power and landholdings. After a series of failed raids against U.S. troops and civilian settlements, they ceded land to attain peace and to pay debts. After 1800 the Cherokee were remarkable for their assimilation of European/American culture, forming a government modeled on that of the U.S. and adopting European methods of farming and homemaking. Most became literate following the development of a syllabary by Sequoyah. Beginning c. 1835, when gold was discovered on Cherokee land in Georgia, agitation increased for their removal to the West. The ensuing events culminated in the Trail of Tears, which left some 4,000 Cherokee dead. Cherokee descendants numbered more than 730,000 in the early 21st century.

cherub, In Jewish, Christian, and Islamic literature, a celestial winged being with human, animal, or birdlike characteristics. They are included among the angels, and in the Hebrew scriptures they are described as the throne bearers of God. In Christianity and Islam they are celestial attendants of God and praise him continually. Known as *karūbūn* in Islam, they repeat "Glory to God" ceaselessly, and they dwell in a section of heaven inaccessible to attacks by the Devil. In art they are often depicted as winged infants.

chess, Checkerboard game for two players, each of whom moves 16 pieces according to fixed rules across the board and tries to capture or immobilize (checkmate) the opponent's king. The game may have originated in Asia about the 6th century, though it continued to evolve as it spread into Europe in Byzantine times; its now-standard rules first became generally accepted in Europe in the 16th century. The players, designated white or black, start with their pieces arranged on opposite ends of the board. Kings move one square in any direction—but not into attack (check). Bishops move diagonally, and rooks horizontally or vertically, any number of unobstructed squares. Queens move like either bishops or rooks. Knights move to the nearest nonadjacent square of the opposite colour (an "L" shape) and ignore intervening chessmen.

Pieces capture by moving to an enemy-occupied square. Pawns move forward one square (except one or two on their first move) and are promoted to any non-king piece if they eventually reach the last row. Pawns capture only one diagonal square forward of them. For one turn only, a pawn has the option, known as en passant, of capturing an enemy pawn that has just made a first move of two squares to avoid being captured by moving only one; the capture occurs as though the pawn had moved only one square. When the first row between a king and either rook is clear, and as long as the king and that rook have not moved, a maneuver known as castling can be done in which the king is shifted two squares toward that rook and the rook is placed directly on the other side of the king. Kings cannot castle when in check or through any square in which they would be in check. A draw, known as a stalemate, occurs if a player is not in check but any move he could make would place him in check. A draw also occurs if the same position occurs three times (such as through "perpetual check").

Chester, ancient DEVA, or CASTRA DEVANA, City and administrative district (pop., 2001: 118,207), seat of Cheshire county, England. Located on the River Dee south of Liverpool, it is an active port and railroad centre. The Romans chose it as the headquarters of the 20th Legion; well-preserved Roman walls remain. It was the last place in England to surrender to William the Conqueror, who made it the centre of a palatinate earldom in 1071. It became an important port in the 13th–14th century, trading especially with Ireland. From about the 14th century, it was the scene of the presentation of the mystery plays of the Chester cycle. The gradual silting of the Dee led to the city's decline, but in the 19th century railroad traffic renewed Chester's prosperity.

chestnut, Any of four species of deciduous ornamental and timber trees of the genus *Castanea*, in the beech family. Native to temperate regions of the Northern Hemisphere, they bear burrlike fruits that contain two or three edible nuts. The usually tall trees have furrowed bark and lance-shaped leaves. The American chestnut (*C. dentata*), which once extended over a large area of eastern North America, has been almost eliminated by chestnut blight. The other three species are the European chestnut (*C. sativa*), the Chinese chestnut (*C. mollissima*), and the Japanese chestnut (*C. crenata*). The nuts of these three have local importance as food and are exported in large quantities, and varieties of all three are cultivated as ornamentals. The European chestnut produces useful timber as well; the American chestnut also was an important source of lumber and nuts before the arrival of the blight.

Cheyenne, Plains Indian people of Algonquian language stock, living principally in Montana and Oklahoma, U.S. Originally farmers, hunters, and gatherers who lived in central Minnesota, the Cheyenne moved in the early 19th century to regions around the Platte and Arkansas rivers and split into the Northern Cheyenne and the Southern Cheyenne. In these areas they adopted the lifestyle of the Plains Indians; after acquiring horses, they became more dependent on the buffalo for food and developed a tepee-dwelling nomadic mode of life. They performed the sun dance and placed heavy emphasis on visions in which an animal spirit adopted an individual and bestowed special powers on him or her. They had well-organized military societies and fought constantly with the Kiowa until c. 1840. In the 1870s they participated in various Indian uprisings, joining the Sioux at the Little Bighorn in 1876. Cheyenne descendants numbered more than 20,000 in the early 21st century.

Chhattisgarh, State (pop., 2008 est.: 23,646,000), central India. Bordered by Madhya Pradesh, Uttar Pradesh, Jharkhand, Orissa, Andhra Pradesh, and Maharashtra states, it occupies 52,199 sq mi (135,194 sq km); its capital is Raipur. The Chhattisgarh Plain covers much of the state, with the land becoming hillier to the north and west. The area that is now Chhattisgarh was the eastern portion of Madhya Pradesh state before it was made into a separate state in 2000. It is rich in minerals, but the population is mainly engaged in agriculture.

Chiang Ching-kuo, or JIANG JINGGUO (b. March 18, 1910, Qikou, Zhejiang province, China—d. Jan. 13, 1988, Taipei, Taiwan), Son of Chiang Kai-shek, and his successor as leader of the Nationalist government in Taiwan. He was formally elected by the National Assembly to a six-year presidential term in 1978 and reelected in 1984. He tried to maintain Taiwan's foreign-trade relationships and political independence as other countries began to break off diplomatic relations in order to establish ties with mainland China. Other actions during his presidency included ending martial law, allowing opposition parties, and encouraging native-born Taiwanese to participate in government.

Chiang Kai-shek, or CHIANG CHIEH-SHIH, or JIANG JIESHI (b. Oct. 31, 1887, Zhejiang, China—d. April 5, 1975, Taipei, Taiwan), Head of the Nationalist government in China (1928–49) and later in Taiwan (1949–75). After receiving military training in Tokyo, in 1918 he joined Sun Yat-sen, leader of the Nationalist Party, which was trying to consolidate control over a nation in chaos. In the 1920s Chiang became commander in chief of the revolutionary army, which he sent to crush warlords active in the north. In the 1930s he and Wang Jingwei vied for control of a new central government with its capital at Nanjing. Faced with Japanese aggression in northeastern China (Manchuria) and communist opposition led by Mao Zedong in the hinterland, Chiang decided to crush the communists first. This proved to be a mistake, and Chiang was forced into a temporary alliance with the communists when war broke out with Japan in 1937. After the war China's civil war resumed, culminating in the Nationalists' flight to Taiwan in 1949, where Chiang ruled, supported by U.S. economic and military aid, until his death, when his son, Chiang Ching-kuo, took up the reins of government. His years ruling Taiwan, though dictatorial, oversaw the island's economic development and increasing prosperity even in the face of its precarious geopolitical position. His failure to keep control of mainland China has been attributed to poor morale among his troops, lack of responsiveness to popular sentiment, and lack of a coherent plan for making the deep social and economic changes China required.

Chiang Kai-shek.
Camera Press/Globe Photos

Chiang Mai, City (pop., 2000: 174,438), northwestern Thailand. Located on the Ping River about 80 mi (130 km) east of Myanmar, it was founded in the late 13th century as the capital of the independent Lan Na kingdom. Later subject to Myanmar, it was taken by the Siamese in 1774 but retained a degree of independence from Bangkok until the late 19th century. It is now northern Thailand's religious, economic, and cultural centre. Nearby is the temple complex of Wat Phra That Doi Suthep, whose monastery was built in the 14th century.

chiaroscuro (Italian: "light-dark"), Contrasting effects of light and shade in a work of art. Leonardo da Vinci brought the technique to its full potential, but it is usually associated with such 17th-century artists as Caravaggio and Rembrandt, who used it to outstanding effect. The chiaroscuro woodcut, produced by printing different tones of a colour from separate woodblocks on a single sheet of paper, was first produced in 16th-century Italy.

Chicago, City (pop., 2010: 2,695,598), northeastern Illinois, U.S. Located on Lake Michigan and the Chicago River, Chicago has extensive port facilities. In the 17th century the name was associated with a portage between the Des Plaines and Chicago rivers connecting the St. Lawrence River and the Great Lakes with the Mississippi River. Fort Dearborn was built in the early 1800s on a tract acquired from Native Americans. It expanded rapidly after the completion of the Illinois and Michigan Canal (1848)—which connected Lake Michigan to the Illinois River and thereby to the Mississippi—and also became the nation's chief rail centre. Rebuilt quickly after a hugely destructive fire in 1871, it was the site of the World's Columbian Exposition in 1893. It was the birthplace of the steel-frame skyscraper in the late 19th century, and it boasts designs by eminent architects, including Louis H. Sullivan, Frank Lloyd Wright, and Ludwig Mies van der Rohe. Nuclear scientists produced the first nuclear chain reaction at the University of Chicago in 1942. After World War II the city underwent another building boom, but, as in other large cities, its population subsequently dropped as its suburbs grew. The third largest U.S. city, it is a major industrial, commercial, and transportation centre and is the site of the Chicago Mercantile Exchange and the Chicago Board of Trade. Several museums and the Art Institute of Chicago are located there.

Chicago, University of, Independent university in Chicago, Illinois, U.S. It was founded in 1890 with an endowment from John D. Rockefeller. William Rainey Harper, its first president (1891–1906), did much to establish its reputation, and under Robert M. Hutchins (1929–51) the university came to be recognized for its broad liberal arts curriculum. The world's first department of sociology was established there in 1892 under Robert E. Park. In 1942 it was the site of the first controlled self-sustaining nuclear chain reaction, under the direction of Enrico Fermi. Other notable achievements include the development of carbon-14 dating and the isolation of plutonium. More than 70 scholars associated with the University of Chicago have been awarded Nobel Prizes in their fields. The university comprises an undergraduate college, several professional schools, and centres for advanced research, including the Oriental Institute (Middle Eastern studies), Yerkes Observatory, the Enrico Fermi Institute, and the Center for Policy Study. The university operates the Argonne National Laboratory.

Chicago School, Group of architects and engineers who in the 1890s exploited the twin developments of structural steel framing and the electrified elevator, paving the way for the ubiquitous modern-day skyscraper. Their work earned Chicago a reputation as the "birthplace of modern architecture." Among the school's members were Louis Sullivan, Daniel Burnham, and John Wellborn Root (1850–91).

Chichén Itzá, Ancient ruined Mayan city in Mexico's Yucatán state. Chichén Itzá was founded by the Maya about the 6th century AD in an arid region where water was obtained from natural wells called cenotes. The city was invaded in the 10th century—probably by a Mayan-speaking group under strong Toltec influence—and the invaders constructed another series of buildings, including the famous stepped pyramid known as El Castillo and a ball court. The site, though largely abandoned by the time the Spanish arrived in the 16th century, remained sacred to the Maya people. It was designated a World Heritage site in 1988.

chickenpox, or VARICELLA, Contagious viral disease producing itchy blisters. It usually occurs in epidemics among young children, causes a low fever, and runs a mild course, leaving patients immune. The blisters can scar if scratched. The virus that causes chickenpox (varicella-zoster virus) can reactivate years later, causing shingles. Zoster immune globulin (ZIG) can prevent chickenpox in children with leukemia or immunodeficiency disorders who are exposed to the virus. A vaccine has also been developed.

chickpea, or GARBANZO, Annual legume (*Cicer arietinum*) widely grown for its nutritious seeds. The bushy 2-ft (60-cm) plants bear pinnate leaves and small white or reddish flowers. The yellow-brown peas are borne one or two to a pod. Chickpeas are an important food plant in India, Africa, and Central and South America. They are the main ingredient of hummus, a sauce originating in the Middle East. In southern Europe, chickpeas are a common ingredient in soups, salads, and stews. A kind of meal or flour is also made from chickpeas.

chickweed, Either of two species of small-leaved weeds, in the pink family. Common chickweed, or stitchwort (*Stellaria media*), is native to Europe but widely naturalized. It usually grows to 18 in. (45 cm) but is a low-growing and spreading annual weed in mowed lawns. Mouse-ear chickweed (*Cerastium vulgatum*), also from Europe, is a usually shorter, mat-forming, spreading perennial with many upright stems. It grows in lawns, pastures, and cultivated fields throughout temperate regions. Both species have inconspicuous but delicate white, star-shaped flowers.

chicory, Blue-flowered perennial plant (*Cichorium intybus*) of the aster family (Asteraceae). Native to Europe, it was introduced to the U.S. late in the 19th century. Chicory has a long, fleshy taproot; a rigid, branching, hairy stem; and lobed, toothed leaves, similar in appearance to dandelion leaves, around the base. Both roots and leaves are edible. The roots are used as a flavouring in or substitute for coffee. The plant is also grown as a fodder or herbage crop for cattle.

chiefdom, Type of sociopolitical organization in which political and economic power is exercised by a single person (or group) over many communities. It represents the centralization of power and authority at the expense of local and autonomous groupings. Political authority in chiefdoms, such as those found in western Africa or Polynesia, is inseparable from economic power, including the right by rulers to exact tribute and taxation. A principal economic activity of the heads of chiefdoms is to stimulate the production of economic surpluses, which they then redistribute among their subjects on various occasions.

Chihuahua, Smallest recognized dog breed, named for the Mexican state where it was first noted in the mid-19th century. It probably derived from the Techichi, a small, mute dog kept by the Toltec people as long ago as the 9th century. Typically a feisty-looking, alert dog that is sturdier than its small build would suggest, it stands about 5 in. (13 cm) high and weighs 1–6 lb (0.5–2.7 kg). It has a rounded head, large, erect ears, prominent eyes, and a compact body. The coat varies in colour and may be either smooth and glossy or long and soft.

child abuse, Crime of inflicting physical or emotional injury on a child. The term can denote the use of inordinate physical violence or verbal abuse; the failure to furnish proper shelter, nourishment, medical treatment, or emotional support; incest, rape, or other instances of sexual molestation; and the making of child pornography. Child abuse can cause serious harm to its victims. Estimates of the numbers of children who suffer physical abuse or neglect by parents or guardians range from about 1 percent of all children to about 15 percent, and figures are far higher if emotional abuse and neglect are included. In many cases, the abuser himself suffered abuse as a child. When abuse results in death, evidence of child abuse or battered-child syndrome (e.g., broken bones and lesions, either healed or active) is often used to establish that death was not accidental.

child labour, Employment of boys and girls in occupations deemed unfit for children. Such labour is strictly controlled in many countries as a result of the effective enforcement of laws passed in the 20th century (e.g., the United Nations Declaration of the Rights of the Child in 1959). In developing nations the use of child labour is still common. Restrictive legislation has proved ineffective in impoverished societies with few schools, although some improvements have resulted from global activism, such as boycotts of multinational firms alleged to be exploiting child labour abroad.

child psychology, Study of the psychological processes of children. The field is sometimes subsumed under developmental psychology. Data are gathered through observation, interviews, tests, and experimental methods. Principal topics include language acquisition and development, motor skills, personality development, and social, emotional, and intellectual growth. The field began to emerge in the late 19th century through the work of German psychophysiologist William Preyer, American psychologist G. Stanley Hall, and others. In the 20th century the psychoanalysts Anna Freud and Melanie Klein devoted themselves to child psychology, but its most influential figure was Jean Piaget, who described the various stages of childhood learning and characterized children's perceptions of themselves and the world at each stage.

Children's Crusade (1212) Religious movement in Europe in which thousands, including many children and young people, set out to take the Holy Land from the Muslims by love instead of by force. The events of the Crusade are disputed. According to one version, only partially accurate, the first group of approximately 30,000 was led by a French shepherd boy, Stephen of Cloyes, who had a vision of Jesus and received a letter from him. Stephen led the Crusade to Paris and delivered the letter to King Philip II Augustus, who dispersed the Crusaders. A German boy led the second group across the Alps; a few survived to reach Rome, where Innocent III released them from their vows. Contemporary accounts describing horrible fates of the participants should be treated cautiously because they were written by those hostile to the movement. Though the movement ended without reaching the Holy Land, it excited religious fervour that helped initiate the Fifth Crusade (1217–21).

children's literature, Body of written works produced to entertain or instruct young people. The genre encompasses a wide range of works, including acknowledged classics of world literature, picture books and easy-to-read stories, and fairy tales, lullabies, fables, folk songs, and other, primarily orally transmitted, materials. It emerged as a distinct and independent form only in the second half of the 18th century and blossomed in the 19th century. In the 20th century, with the attainment of near-universal literacy in most developed nations, the diversity in children's books came almost to rival that of adult popular literature.

Chile, officially REPUBLIC OF CHILE, Country, southwestern South America. Area: 291,930 sq mi (756,096 sq km). Population: (2011 est.) 17,270,000. Capital: Santiago. About three-fourths of Chileans are mestizos; most of the rest are of European ancestry or Aracanian (Mapuche) Indians. The indigenous peoples before Spanish colonization included the Diaguita, Picunche, Mapuche, Huilliche, Pehunche, and Cunco Indians. Spanish colonists arrived during the 16th–17th centuries, followed by Basque settlers in the 18th century. A relatively homogeneous population of mestizos has developed. Language: Spanish (official). Religion: Christianity (predominantly Roman Catholic; also Protestant, other Christians). Currency: Chilean peso. Chile is noteworthy for its unique topography: it is a long, narrow country lying between the Andes Mountains and the Pacific Ocean. From north to south it is about 2,700 mi (4,300 km) long and nowhere more than 217 mi (349 km) wide. The north has an arid plateau, the Atacama Desert, and contains several peaks above 16,000 ft (4,900 m), but most of the highest peaks are on the borders with Bolivia and Argentina. The rivers, including the Bío-Bío, are limited in size. There are many lakes, including Lake Llanquihue. The extreme southern coast is marked by many inlets, islands, and archipelagoes; the western half of Tierra del Fuego (including the island on which Cape Horn is located) is in Chilean territory, as are small islets of Juan Fernández and Easter Island. The country is periodically beset by violent earthquakes and tsunamis that originate along major faults of the ocean floor. In 1960 Chile was struck by a magnitude-9.5 earthquake, the largest ever recorded. A magnitude-8.8 earthquake caused extensive damage in 2010. Chile has a partially developed free-market economy based mainly on mining and manufacturing. It is a multiparty republic with two legislative houses; its head of state and government is the president. Originally inhabited by native peoples, including the Mapuche, the area was invaded by the Spanish in 1536. A settlement begun at Santiago in 1541 was governed under the Viceroyalty of Peru but became a separate captaincy general in 1778. Its people revolted against Spanish rule in 1810; independence was finally assured by the victory of Argentine and Chilean forces under José de San Martin at the Battle of Chacabuco in 1817. The area was governed by Chilean Gen. Bernardo O'Higgins until 1823. In the War of the Pacific (1879–83) against Peru and Bolivia, Chile won the rich nitrate fields on the coast of Bolivia, effectively severing that country's access to the coast. Chile remained neutral in World War I (1914–18) and for most of World War II (1939–45), though in 1942 it joined other Latin American countries in declaring war on the Axis. In 1970 Salvador Allende was elected president, becoming the first avowed Marxist to be elected head of state in Latin America. Following economic upheaval, he was overthrown in 1973 in a coup led by Augusto Pinochet, whose military regime harshly suppressed internal opposition. A national referendum in 1988 and elections the following year removed Pinochet from power and returned the country to democratic rule. Chile's economy maintained steady growth through most of the 1990s and in the early 21st century remained one of the strongest in Latin America.

Chimera, In Greek mythology, a fire-breathing female monster. Its foreparts resembled a lion, its middle a goat, and its hindquarters a dragon. It devastated the land around Caria and Lycia until it was killed by Bellerophon. The word is now often used to denote a fantasy or a figment of the imagination.

chimpanzee, Species (*Pan troglodytes*) of great ape that inhabits the rain forests and woodland savannas of equatorial Africa, the closest living relative to humans. Chimps are 3–5.5 ft (1–1.7 m) tall when standing upright, weigh 70–130 lbs (32–60 kg), and have a brown or black coat and a bare face. They do most of their feeding in the trees, swinging from branch to branch; to move any distance they walk, usually on all fours, on the ground. They eat mostly fruits, berries, leaves, and seeds, some termites and ants, and occasionally a young baboon or bush pig. They are capable of problem solving, tool use, and deceit. Chimpanzees are highly social and live in flexible groups (15–100 or more members) known as communities. In the wild they live about 45 years, in captivity more than 50.

*West African, or masked, chimpanzee (*Pan troglodytes verus*).*
Helmut Albrecht/Bruce Coleman Ltd.

China, officially PEOPLE'S REPUBLIC OF CHINA, Country, eastern Asia. Area: 3,696,100 sq mi (9,572,900 sq km). Population: (2011 est.) 1,342,274,000. Capital: Beijing. It is the world's most populous country, the Han (ethnic Chinese) forming more than nine-tenths of the population. Languages: dialects of Han Chinese, Mandarin being the most important. Religions: traditional beliefs, Buddhism, Christianity, Islam, Daoism (all legally sanctioned). Currency: renminbi (of which the unit is the yuan). China has several topographic regions. The southwestern area contains the Plateau of Tibet, which averages more than 13,000 ft (4,000 m) above sea level; its core area, averaging more than 16,000 ft (5,000 m)

in elevation, is called "the Roof of the World" and provides the headwaters for many of Asia's major rivers. Higher yet are the border ranges, the Kunlun Mountains to the north and the Himalayas to the south. China's northwestern region stretches from Afghanistan to the Northeast (Manchurian) Plain. The Tien Shan ("Celestial Mountains") separate China's two major interior basins, the Tarim Basin (containing the Takla Makan Desert) and the Junggar Basin. The Mongolian Plateau contains the southernmost part of the Gobi Desert. The lowlands of the eastern region include the Sichuan Basin, which runs along the Yangtze River (Chang Jiang); the Yangtze divides the eastern region into northern and southern parts. The Tarim is the major river in the northwest. China's numerous other rivers include the Huang He (Yellow River), Xi, Sungari (Songhua), Zhu (Pearl), and Lancang, which becomes the Mekong in Southeast Asia. The country is a single-party people's republic with one legislative house. The head of state is the president, and the head of government is the premier.

The discovery of Peking man in 1927 dates the advent of early hominins (human ancestors) to the Paleolithic Period. Chinese civilization is thought to have spread from the Huang He valley. The first dynasty for which there is definite historical material is the Shang (*c.* 17th century BCE), which had a writing system and a calendar. The Zhou, a subject state of the Shang, overthrew its Shang rulers in the mid-11th century and ruled until the 3rd century BCE. Daoism and Confucianism were founded in this era. A time of conflict, called the Warring States period, lasted from the 5th century until 221 BCE. Subsequently the Qin (or Chin) dynasty (from whose name China is derived) was established, after its rulers had conquered rival states and created a unified empire. The Han dynasty was established in 206 BCE and ruled until 220 CE. A time of turbulence followed, and Chinese reunification was achieved with the founding of the Sui dynasty in 581 and continued with the Tang dynasty (618–907). After the founding of the Song dynasty in 960, the capital was moved to the south because of northern invasions. In 1279 this dynasty was overthrown and Mongol (Yuan) domination began. During that time Marco Polo visited Kublai Khan. The Ming dynasty followed the period of Mongol rule and lasted from 1368 to 1644, cultivating antiforeign feelings to the point that China closed itself off from the rest of the world. The Manchu overran Ming China in 1644 and established the Qing (Manchu) dynasty. Ever-increasing incursions by Western and Japanese interests led in the 19th century to the Opium Wars, the Taiping Rebellion, and the Sino-Japanese War, all of which weakened the Manchu. The dynasty fell in 1911, and a republic was proclaimed in 1912 by Sun Yat-sen. The power struggles of warlords weakened the republic. Under Chiang Kai-shek some national unification was achieved in the 1920s, but Chiang broke with the communists, who had formed their own armies. Japan invaded northern China in 1937; its occupation lasted until 1945. The communists gained support after the Long March (1934–35), in which Mao Zedong emerged as their leader. Upon Japan's surrender at the end of World War II, a fierce civil war began; in 1949 the Nationalists fled to Taiwan, and the communists proclaimed the People's Republic of China. The communists undertook extensive reforms, but pragmatic policies alternated with periods of revolutionary upheaval, most notably in the Great Leap Forward and the Cultural Revolution. The anarchy, terror, and economic paralysis of the latter led, after Mao's death in 1976, to a turn to moderation under Deng Xiaoping, who undertook economic reforms and renewed China's ties to the West. The government established diplomatic relations with the U.S. in 1979. Since the late 1970s the economy has been moving from central planning and state-run industries to a mixture of state-owned and private enterprises in manufacturing and services, in the process growing dramatically and transforming Chinese society. Though China was challenged by the Tiananmen Square incident in 1989, its political environment after 1980 was generally stable and included orderly transitions of power to Deng's successors after his death in 1997. Also in 1997 Hong Kong reverted to Chinese rule, and Macau did the same in 1999. A powerful earthquake caused massive destruction and loss of life in Sichuan province in 2008, but later that year Beijing hosted the Summer Olympic Games.

China Sea, Part of the western Pacific Ocean. Reaching from Japan to the southern end of the Malay Peninsula, it is divided by the island of Taiwan into two sections. The northern section is the East China Sea, or Eastern Sea, which covers an area of some 290,000 sq mi (751,100 sq km), has a maximum depth of 8,912 ft (2,717 m), and is enclosed by eastern China, South Korea, the Japanese island of Kyushu, the Ryukyu Islands, and Taiwan. The southern section is the South China Sea, often called simply the China Sea, which covers an area of 1,423,000 sq mi (3,685,000 sq km), has a maximum depth of about 16,000 ft (5,000 m), and is enclosed by southeastern China, Taiwan, the Philippines, Borneo, and mainland Southeast Asia.

Chinese cabbage, Either of two widely cultivated members of the mustard family, bok choy and *Brassica pekinensis*. The latter vegetable, also called celery cabbage, forms a tight head of crinkled light green leaves. It has long been grown in the U.S. as a salad vegetable. All Chinese cabbages are delicate and crisp, qualities that enable them to combine with a wide variety of foods. Kimchi, the universal Korean pickle, is often made with Chinese cabbage.

Chinese languages, or SINITIC LANGUAGES, Family of languages comprising one of the two branches of Sino-Tibetan. They are spoken by about 95% of the inhabitants of China and by many communities of Chinese immigrants elsewhere. Linguists regard the major dialect groups of Chinese as distinct languages, though because all Chinese write with a common system of ideograms, or characters, and share Classical Chinese as a heritage, traditionally all varieties of Chinese are regarded as dialects. There is a primary division in Chinese languages between the so-called Mandarin dialects—which have a high degree of mutual intelligibility and cover all of the Chinese speech area north of the Yangtze River (Chang Jiang) and west of Hunan and Guangdong provinces—and a number of other dialect groups concentrated in southeastern China. Far more people—more than 885 million—speak a variety of Mandarin Chinese as a first language than any other language in the world. The northern Mandarin dialect of Beijing is the basis for Modern Standard Chinese, a spoken norm that serves as a supradialectal lingua franca. Important dialect groups other than Mandarin are Wu (spoken in Shanghai), Gan, Xiang, Min (spoken in Fujian and Taiwan), Yue (including Cantonese, spoken in Guangzhou [Canton] and Hong Kong), and Kejia (Hakka), spoken by the Hakka. The modern Chinese languages are tone languages, the number of tones varying from four in Modern Standard Chinese to nine in some dialects.

Chinese writing system, System of symbols used to write the Chinese language. Chinese writing is fundamentally logographic: there is an exact correspondence between a single symbol, or character, in the script and a morpheme. Each character, no matter how complex, is fit into a hypothetical rectangle of the same size. The Chinese script is first attested in divinatory inscriptions incised on bone or tortoise shells dating from the Shang dynasty. Early forms of characters were often clearly pictorial or iconic. Shared elements of characters, called radicals, provide a means of classifying Chinese writing. It is thought that an ordinary literate Chinese person can recognize 3,000–4,000 characters. Efforts have been made to reduce the number of characters and to simplify their form, though the fact that they can be read by a speaker of any Chinese dialect and their inextricable link with China's 3,000-year-old culture makes abandonment of the system unlikely. Chinese characters have also been adapted to write Japanese, Korean, and Vietnamese.

chinoiserie, Fanciful European interpretations of Chinese styles in the design of interiors, furniture, pottery, textiles, and gardens.

The expansion of trade with East Asia produced a lively vogue for Chinese fashions in the 17th–18th centuries. The most outstanding chinoiserie interior was the Trianon de Porcelaine (1670–71), built for Louis XIV at Versailles. The style featured lavish gilding and lacquering, the use of blue and white (as in delftware), asymmetrical forms, unorthodox perspective, and Asian motifs. In the 19th century, the fashion gave way to Turkish and other styles considered exotic.

Chios, or KHÍOS, Island, Greece. It lies 5 mi (8 km) west of Turkey, in the Aegean Sea. Of volcanic origin, it is 30 mi (48 km) long and 8–15 mi (13–24 km) wide with an area of 321 sq mi (831 sq km). It was noted in antiquity as Homer's birthplace. It was colonized by Ionians and became subject to Persia in 546 BC. Though later a member of the Delian League, it revolted several times against Athens. It prospered successively under Rome, Venice, Genoa, and the Ottoman Empire; it passed to Greece after the Balkan Wars (1912–13). The city of Chios is the principal municipality.

Chippendale style, Style of furniture derived from designs by Thomas Chippendale. The term specifically refers to English furniture made in a modified Rococo style in the 1750s and '60s, though Chippendale also designed furniture in Gothic and Chinese styles. Some of his designs are adapted from the Louis XV style. Furniture based on his designs was also made in Europe and the American colonies.

Chiron, Comet once thought to be the most distant known asteroid. Discovered in 1977, it travels in an unstable, eccentric orbit between those of Saturn and Uranus. In 1989 astronomers detected a fuzzy cloud (coma) around Chiron. Because such a cloud is a defining feature of comets, Chiron was reclassified as a comet.

chiropractic, System of healing based on the theory that disease results from lack of normal nerve function, often caused by displaced vertebrae putting pressure on nerve roots. Treatment involves manipulations of body structures, primarily the spinal column, and use of other techniques when necessary. It concerns the relationship between musculoskeletal structures and functions of the body and the nervous system. The chiropractic method was propounded in 1895 by Daniel David Palmer (1845–1913). Practitioners are trained at accredited chiropractic colleges.

Chisinau, formerly (1812–1918, 1940–91) KISHINEV, City (pop., 2004: 598,000), capital of Moldova. It lies on a tributary of the Dniester River. Ruled by Moldavia in the 15th century and taken by the Ottoman Turks in the 16th century, it was ceded to Russia in 1812. From 1918 the city was controlled by Romania; it was ceded back to the Soviet Union in 1940 and became the capital of the newly formed Moldavian S.S.R. The city is a commercial centre and the site of a university.

Chittagong, City (pop., 2001 prelim.: city, 2,199,590; metro. area, 3,361,244), chief Indian Ocean port, Bangladesh. It is the country's second most important industrial city, with jute mills, engineering works, and a large oil refinery. Known to Arab sailors by the 10th century AD, it was conquered by Muslims in the 14th century and occupied by the governor of Bengal in the 17th century. Ceded to Britain's East India Company in 1760, it was constituted a municipality in 1864. Damaged in the conflict between India and Pakistan in 1971, its port facilities were rebuilt. It is the site of the University of Chittagong (founded 1966).

chivalry, Knightly class of feudal Europe, and especially the gallantry and honor expected of medieval knights. The ideal of courteous knightly conduct developed in the 12th–13th century. It arose out of feudal obligation and stressed loyalty and obeisance by a knight to his God, his lord, and his lady, thus melding Christian and military virtues. Chivalry was greatly strengthened by the Crusades, a military endeavor on behalf of Christianity, which led to the founding of the earliest orders of chivalry, the Knights of

Malta and the Templars. In addition to loyalty and honor, the chivalric virtues included valor, piety, courtesy, and chastity. Questions of love and honor were combined in the ethos of courtly love. The knight's lady was meant to be unobtainable, ensuring chastity; the feminine ideal thus became melded with the Virgin Mary. In the 14th–15th century, chivalry came to be associated increasingly with aristocratic display and public ceremony, particularly in jousting tournaments, rather than with service in the field.

chive, Small hardy perennial plant (*Allium schoenoprasum*) of the family Alliaceae, related to the onion. Its small, white, elongated bulbs and thin, tubular leaves grow in clumps. Dense, attractive, spherical umbels of bluish or lilac flowers rise above the foliage. The leaves may be cut off at ground level and used for seasoning foods.

*Wild chives (*Allium schoenoprasum*)*
Ingmar Holmasen

chlamydia, Any of the bacterial parasites that make up the genus *Chlamydia*, which cause several diseases in humans, including conjunctivitis and chlamydial pneumonia. One form causes a variety of sexually transmitted diseases. In men, symptoms are similar to those of gonorrhea. In women, chlamydial infection ordinarily produces few, if any, symptoms, and most infected women thus are unaware of their condition. However, untreated infections in women can lead to sterility, a higher risk of premature births, and ectopic pregnancies. Chlamydia frequently causes conjunctivitis or pneumonia in the newborn infant. Treatment is with antibiotics.

chlorella, Any green algae of the genus *Chlorella*, found in fresh or salt water and in soil. They have a cup-shaped chloroplast. Chlorellas are used often in studies of photosynthesis, in mass cultivation experiments, and for purifying sewage wastes. Because they multiply rapidly and are rich in proteins and in B-complex vitamins, they have been studied as a potential food product for humans both on Earth and in outer space. Chlorella farms, closed systems that provide humans with food, water, and oxygen, have been established in the U.S., Japan, the Netherlands, Germany, and Israel.

chlorine, Nonmetallic chemical element, chemical symbol Cl, atomic number 17. It is a toxic, corrosive, greenish yellow gas (as the diatomic molecule Cl_2) that severely irritates the eyes and respiratory system (and was used for that purpose as a chemical-warfare agent in World War I). As the chloride ion and in the hypochlorite ion, it has valence 1; in the chlorite, chlorate, and perchlorate ions, it has higher valences. Chlorine and its compounds are important industrial materials with myriad uses in the manufacture of other chlorinated compounds (e.g., PVC, hydrochloric acid, ethylene dichloride, trichloroethylene, PCBs), in water purification (municipal systems, swimming pools), in textile industries, in flame retardants, in special batteries, and in food processing. Sodium chloride (table salt) is by far the most familiar of its compounds.

chloroform, Clear, colourless, heavy, nonflammable liquid organic compound with a pleasant etherlike odour, chemical formula $CHCl_3$. It was the first substance successfully used as a surgical anesthetic (1847); being somewhat toxic, it has been increasingly displaced by other substances for this purpose. It has some industrial uses, primarily as a solvent.

chlorophyll, Any member of one of the most important classes of pigment molecules involved in photosynthesis. Found in almost all photosynthetic organisms, it consists of a central magnesium atom surrounded by a nitrogen-containing structure called a por-

phyrin ring, to which is attached a long carbon-hydrogen side chain, known as a phytol chain. In structure it is remarkably similar to hemoglobin. Chlorophyll uses energy that it absorbs from light to convert carbon dioxide to carbohydrates. In higher plants it is found in chloroplasts.

chloroplast, Microscopic, ellipsoidal organelle in a green plant cell. It is the site of photosynthesis. It is distinguished by its green colour, caused by the presence of chlorophyll. It contains disk-shaped structures called thylakoids that make possible the formation of ATP, an energy-rich storage compound.

choir, Body of singers with more than one voice to a part. For many centuries, church choirs sang only plainsong. The relative complexity of early polyphony required solo voices rather than choral performance, but by the 15th century polyphony was being performed chorally. The growth of the secular choir (or chorus) coincided with the beginnings of opera. An oratorio choir is part of a different tradition, which stems from the augmented church choirs used to provide choral portions of a given oratorio, whether performed in or out of church.

cholera, Acute bacterial infection with *Vibrio cholerae*, causing massive diarrhea with severe depletion of body fluids and salts. Cholera often occurs in epidemics, spreading in contaminated water or food. The bacteria secrete a toxin that causes the diarrhea, which along with vomiting leads to dehydration, with severe muscle cramps and intense thirst. Stupor and coma may precede death by shock. With fluid and salt replacement, the disease passes in two to seven days, sooner if antibiotics are taken the first day. Prevention requires good sanitation, especially clean drinking water.

cholesterol, Waxy organic compound found in blood and all animal tissues. It is a steroid, with molecular formula $C_{27}H_{46}O$, containing four rings in its structure. Cholesterol is essential to life; it is a primary component of cell membranes and a starting or intermediate material from which the body makes bile acids, other steroid hormones, and vitamin D. It is made in the liver and some other organs, in greater or lesser amounts depending on the amount recently consumed in the diet. It circulates in the blood in compounds called lipoproteins, since it is not water-soluble alone. Excess cholesterol in the blood forms deposits in arteries, which can lead to coronary heart disease. Michael Brown (born 1941) and Joseph Goldstein (born 1940) won a Nobel Prize in 1985 for their work in discovering this process. Since the body makes cholesterol from fats, blood cholesterol cannot be reduced by limiting only the amount of cholesterol in the diet; the amount of fat, especially saturated fat must also be reduced.

Chongqing, or CH'UNG-CH'ING, conventional CHUNGKING, City and municipality with provincial status (pop., 2003 est.: city, 4,239,700; 2002 est.: municipality, 31,070,000), south-central China. The municipality is bordered by Sichuan, Shaanxi, Hubei, Hunan, and Guizhou provinces and has an area of 31,700 sq mi (82,000 sq km). The leading river port and industrial centre of the region, Chongqing ("Double-Blessed") lies at the confluence of the Yangtze (Chang) and Jialing rivers. In the 11th century BC, it was a feudal state under the Xi (Western) Zhou dynasty. Over the next several centuries, its status alternated from being ruled by an empire in northern China to being an independent state. It finally came under Chinese rule in the Ming dynasty, continuing under the Qing dynasty. It was opened to foreign trade in 1890. It played a large role in the revolution of 1911. Once a city of narrow and irregular streets, Chongqing changed greatly as a result of a modernization program introduced during World War II, when it served as the capital of Nationalist China. Since the war it has become an important industrial centre. It is home to Chongqing University (founded 1929).

chorale, Metrical hymn tune associated in common English usage with the Lutheran church in Germany. From early in the Reformation, chorales were to be sung by the congregation during the Protestant liturgy. The words of the Lutheran chorales were often Latin plainsong hymn texts translated into the vernacular. The melodies were often borrowed from secular song and therefore displayed great melodic and structural simplicity. In modern times the chorale is considered to be a musical setting, usually polyphonic (multivoiced), of a traditional religious text.

chord, Grouping of three or more musical tones, especially as sounded simultaneously. The tones C–E–G constitute a "C major chord," or "C major triad." Chords may comprise any number of separate tones, and may be highly dissonant. The term harmony is often used loosely as a synonym.

chorea, Neurological disorder causing irregular, involuntary, purposeless movements. It is believed to be caused by degeneration of the basal ganglia in the cerebral cortex. Sydenham chorea (St. Vitus dance) is usually associated with rheumatic fever. It usually occurs between ages 5 and 15, more often in girls. Typical jerking movements, mostly in the extremities and face, may affect speech and swallowing and range from mild to incapacitating; attacks last several weeks and recur frequently. Senile chorea, a progressive disease resembling Sydenham chorea, usually occurs late in life. Huntington chorea is rare, hereditary, and fatal. It usually begins between ages 35 and 50 and progresses to random, often violent, and eventually totally incapacitating spasms, absent only during sleep. Mental deterioration begins later, and death occurs in 10–20 years. There is no effective therapy. Children of those afflicted have a 50% chance of developing the illness.

choreography, Art of creating and arranging dances. The word is derived from the Greek for "dance" and "write," reflecting its early meaning as a written record of dances. By the 19th century the term was used mainly for the creation of dances, and the written record became known as dance notation. In the 16th century dance masters at the French court arranged their social dances into specific patterns. In the 17th century such dances became more complex and were performed as theatrical ballets by trained professionals. In the late 18th century Jean-Georges Noverre and Gasparo Angiolini introduced choreography that combined expressive mime and dance steps to produce the dramatic ballet. This was further developed in 19th-century Romantic ballets by Marius Petipa, Jules Perrot, and August Bournonville. Radical change in the 20th century began with choreographers of the Ballets Russes, including Michel Fokine and Léonide Massine, and continued with George Balanchine, Martha Graham, Frederick Ashton, Jerome Robbins, Merce Cunningham, and Twyla Tharp.

chorus, In theatre, a group of actors, singers, or dancers who perform as an ensemble to describe and comment on a play's action. Choral performances, which originated in the singing of dithyrambs in honour of Dionysus, dominated Greek drama until the mid-5th century BC, when Aeschylus added a second actor and reduced the chorus from 50 to 12 performers. As the importance of individual actors increased, the chorus gradually disappeared. It was revived in modern plays such as Eugene O'Neill's *Mourning Becomes Electra* (1931) and T.S. Eliot's *Murder in the Cathedral* (1935). Choruses of singers and dancers came to be featured in musical comedies, especially in the 20th century, first as entertainment and later to help develop the plot.

Christchurch, City (pop., 2011 est: 380,900), South Island, New Zealand. Founded in 1850 as a model Church of England settlement, it was the last and most successful colonizing project inspired by Edward Gibbon Wakefield and his New Zealand Co. It is the country's second largest city and an important industrial centre; its port is Lyttelton. Called the "Garden City of the Plains" for its numerous parks and gardens, it is home to the University of Canterbury, Christ's College, and Lincoln University. The city sustained extensive earthquake damage in 2010–11.

Christian caste, In India, social stratification among Christians based on caste membership at the time of an individual's or an ancestor's conversion. Indian Christians are grouped by denomination, geography, and caste. The Syrian Christians along the Malabar coast, descended from 1st-century converts of high birth, retain mid-rank status in Hindu society. Portuguese missionaries of the 16th century converted lower-caste fisherfolk. Missionaries in the 19th century insisted on social reform and tended to draw from the lowest classes. Caste distinctions are breaking down at about the same rate among contemporary Indian Christians and other Indians.

Christian Science, officially CHURCH OF CHRIST, SCIENTIST, Religious denomination founded in the U.S. in 1879 by Mary Baker Eddy. Like other Christian churches, Christian Science subscribes to an omnipotent God and the authority (but not inerrancy) of the Bible and takes the Crucifixion and Resurrection of Jesus as essential to human redemption. It departs from traditional Christianity in considering Jesus divine but not a deity and in regarding creation as wholly spiritual. Sin denies God's sovereignty by claiming that life derives from matter. Spiritual cure of disease is a necessary element of redemption from the flesh and one of the church's most controversial practices. Most members refuse medical help for disease, and members engaged in the full-time healing ministry are called Christian Science practitioners. Elected readers lead Sunday services based on readings from the Bible and Eddy's *Science and Health with Key to the Scriptures*. At the end of the 20th century, the church had about 2,500 congregations in 70 countries; its headquarters is at the Mother Church in Boston.

Christianity, Religion stemming from the teachings of Jesus in the 1st century AD. Its sacred scripture is the Bible, particularly the New Testament. Its principal tenets are that Jesus is the Son of God (the second person of the Holy Trinity), that God's love for the world is the essential component of his being, and that Jesus died to redeem humankind. Christianity was originally a movement of Jews who accepted Jesus as the messiah, but the movement quickly became predominantly Gentile. The early church was shaped by St. Paul and other Christian missionaries and theologians; it was persecuted under the Roman Empire but supported by Constantine I, the first Christian emperor. In medieval and early modern Europe, Christian thinkers such as St. Augustine, Thomas Aquinas, and Martin Luther contributed to the growth of Christian theology, and beginning in the 15th century missionaries spread the faith throughout much of the world. The major divisions of Christianity are Roman Catholicism, Eastern Orthodoxy, and Protestantism. Nearly all Christian churches have an ordained clergy, members of which are typically though not universally male. Members of the clergy lead group worship services and are viewed as intermediaries between the laity and the divine in some churches. Most Christian churches administer two sacraments, baptism and the Eucharist. In the early 21st century there were more than two billion adherents of Christianity throughout the world, found on all continents.

Christina, Swedish KRISTINA (b. Dec. 8, 1626, Stockholm, Swed.—d. April 19, 1689, Rome), Queen of Sweden (1644–54). The successor to her father, Gustav II Adolf, she was a prime mover in concluding the Peace of Westphalia and ending the Thirty Years' War. After 10 years of rule, she stunned Europe by abdicating the throne, claiming that she was ill and that

Christina, engraving by Cornelis Visscher, 1650.
Courtesy of the Svenska Portrattarkivet, Stockholm

the burden of ruling was too heavy for a woman. Her real reasons were her aversion to marriage and her secret conversion to Roman Catholicism, which was proscribed in Sweden. She moved to Rome and subsequently attempted, without success, to gain the crowns of Naples and Poland. One of the wittiest and most learned women of her age, she was a lavish patroness of the arts and an influence on European culture.

Christine de Pisan, or CHRISTINE DE PIZAN (b. 1364, Venice—d. *c.* 1430), French writer. She was the daughter of an astrologer to Charles V and the wife of a court secretary and took up writing to support her children when she was widowed, producing 10 volumes of graceful verse, including ballads, rondeaux, lays, and complaints, many in the courtly-love tradition. Some works, both poetry and prose, champion women, notably *The Book of the City of Ladies* (1405). She also wrote a life of Charles V and *Le Ditié de Jehanne d'Arc* (1429), inspired by Joan of Arc's early victories.

Christmas, Christian festival celebrated on December 25, commemorating the birth of Jesus. December 25 had already been identified by Sextus Julius Africanus in AD 221 as the day on which Christmas would be celebrated, and it was celebrated in Rome by AD 336. During the Middle Ages Christmas became extremely popular, and various liturgical celebrations of the holiday were established. The practice of exchanging gifts had begun by the 15th century. The Yule log, cakes, and fir trees derive from German and Celtic customs. Christmas today is regarded as a family festival with gifts brought by Santa Claus. As an increasingly secular festival, it has come to be celebrated by many non-Christians.

chromaticism, In music, the use of all 12 tones, especially for heightened expressivity. A standard key or mode principally employs 7 tones, leaving 5 tones for discretionary use. Use of all 12 tones in a given piece increased in the 18th and 19th centuries. Strictly controlled chromaticism, as in the ornamentation of Frédéric Chopin, did not threaten the perception of tonality. However, from the mid-19th century on, complaints were heard with ever greater frequency that it was difficult to perceive what a given piece's tonal centre was, the chromaticism in the works of Richard Wagner being the most notorious. The virtual breakdown in tonality in the works of advanced composers led to the free atonality of Arnold Schoenberg and his followers in the early 20th century.

chromium, Metallic chemical element, one of the transition elements, chemical symbol Cr, atomic number 24. A hard, steel-gray metal that takes a high polish, it is used in alloys (e.g., ferrochromium, steel, stainless steel) to increase strength and corrosion resistance. It usually has valence 2, 3, or 6 and always occurs combined with other elements, especially oxygen; chromite is its only commercial source. Various coloured gemstones (e.g., ruby, emerald, serpentine) owe their colour to chromium. Sodium chromate and dichromate are used in leather tanning, in metal surface treatment, and as catalysts. Chromium trioxide is used in chrome plating and as a colorant for ceramics. Chromium oxide, lead chromate, and various other chromium compounds are used as pigments. Chromium dioxide, strongly magnetic, is used in recording tapes and as a catalyst.

chromosome, Microscopic threadlike part of a cell that carries hereditary information in the form of genes. A defining feature of any chromosome is its compactness, which helps organize genetic material for cell division and enables it to fit within structures such as the cell nucleus or the head of a viral particle. Chromosome structure and location differ between viruses, prokaryotic cells, and eukaryotic cells . Every species has a characteristic number of chromosomes; humans have 23 pairs (22 pairs of autosomal, or nonsex, chromosomes and one pair of sex chromosomes). Human chromosomes consist primarily of DNA. During cell division, chromosomes are distributed evenly among daughter cells. In sex-

ually reproducing organisms, the number of chromosomes in somatic (nonsex) cells is diploid, while gametes or sex cells (egg and sperm) produced by meiosis are haploid. Fertilization restores the diploid set of chromosomes in the zygote.

chronic fatigue syndrome (CFS), Sudden debilitating fatigue of unknown cause. It may follow a nonspecific illness with mild fever, tender lymph nodes, sore throat, headaches, weakness, muscle and joint pain, and confusion or difficulty in concentrating. To meet the criteria of CFS, the syndrome must be new, with a definite point of onset, and must persist more than six months. Once dismissed as imaginary, CFS remains controversial. Many authorities question whether it is a distinct disorder, since there is considerable overlap with other conditions such as fibromyalgia and Gulf War syndrome. No diagnostic test for CFS exists. Although a number of theories about the cause of CFS have been advanced, none has been proved. No cure has been found, but most patients improve gradually.

chronic obstructive pulmonary disease, (COPD), Progressive respiratory disease characterized by the combination of signs and symptoms of emphysema and bronchitis. COPD is caused by the inhalation of noxious particles such as those found in tobacco smoke. In rare cases COPD is caused by a genetic defect. The primary symptoms of the disease include breathlessness and a "smoker's cough." There is no cure for COPD. However, symptom severity may be reduced by removal of the noxious trigger. Treatment may include drugs that widen the airways (bronchodilators), pulmonary rehabilitation (supervised exercise), and home oxygen.

chronicle play, or HISTORY PLAY, Play with a theme from history that often holds up the past as a lesson for the present. Chronicle plays developed from medieval morality plays and flourished in times of nationalistic fervour, as in England from the 1580s to the 1630s. They included plays such as *The Victories of Henry the Fifth* and *The True Tragedie of Richard III* and reached maturity with Christopher Marlowe's *Edward II* and William Shakespeare's *Henry VI*.

church, In Christian doctrine, the religious community as a whole, or an organized body of believers adhering to one sect's teachings. The word *church* translates the Greek *ekklesia*, used in the New Testament for the body of faithful and the local congregation. Christians established congregations modeled on the synagogue and a system of governance centred on the bishop. The Nicene Creed characterized the church as one (unified), holy (created by the Holy Spirit), catholic (universal), and apostolic (historically continuous with the Apostles). The schism of Eastern and Western churches (1054) and the Reformation (16th century) ended institutional unity and universality. St. Augustine stated that the real church is known only to God, and Martin Luther held that the true church had members in many Christian bodies and was independent of any organization.

church and state, Relationship between religious and secular authority in society. In most ancient civilizations the separation of religious and political orders was not clearly defined. With the advent of Christianity, the idea of two separate orders emerged, based on Jesus's command to "Render unto Caesar what are Caesar's, and to God the things that are God's" (Mark 12:17). The close association of religion and politics, however, continued even after the triumph of Christianity as emperors such as Constantine exercised authority over both church and state. In the early Middle Ages secular rulers claimed to rule by the grace of God, and later in the Middle Ages popes and emperors competed for universal dominion. During the Investiture Controversy the church clearly defined separate and distinct religious and secular orders, even though it laid the foundation for the so-called papal monarchy. The Reformation greatly undermined papal authority, and the pendulum swung toward the state, with many monarchs claiming to rule church and state by divine right. The concept of secular government, as evinced in the U.S. and postrevolutionary France, was influenced by Enlightenment thinkers. In western Europe today all states protect freedom of worship and maintain a distinction between civil and religious authority. The legal systems of some modern Islamic countries are based on Sharī'ah. In the U.S. the separation of church and state has been tested in the arena of public education by controversies over issues such as school prayer, public funding of parochial schools, and the teaching of creationism.

Churchill, Sir Winston (Leonard Spencer) (b. Nov. 30, 1874, Blenheim Palace, Oxfordshire, Eng.—d. Jan. 24, 1965, London), British statesman and author. Son of Lord Randolph Churchill and the American Jennie Jerome, he had an unhappy childhood and was an unpromising student. After joining the 4th Hussars in 1895, he saw service as both a soldier and a journalist, and his dispatches from India and South Africa attracted wide attention. Fame as a military hero helped him win election to the House of Commons in 1900. He quickly rose to prominence and served in several cabinet posts, including first lord of the Admiralty (1911–15), though in World War I and during the following decade he acquired a reputation for erratic judgment. In the years before World War II, his warnings of the threat posed by Adolf Hitler's Germany were repeatedly ignored. When war broke out, he was appointed to his old post as head of the Admiralty. After Neville Chamberlain resigned, Churchill headed a coalition government as prime minister (1940–45). He committed himself and the nation to an all-out war until victory was achieved, and his great eloquence, energy, and indomitable fortitude made him an inspiration to his countrymen, especially in the Battle of Britain. With Franklin Roosevelt and Joseph Stalin, he shaped Allied strategy through the Atlantic Charter and at the Cairo, Casablanca, and Tehran conferences. Though he was the architect of victory, his government was defeated in the 1945 elections. After the war he alerted the West to the expansionist threat of the Soviet Union. He led the Conservative Party back into power in 1951 and remained prime minister until 1955, when ill health forced his resignation. For his many writings, including *The Second World War* (6 vol., 1948–53) he was awarded the Nobel Prize for Literature in 1953; his later works include his *History of the English-Speaking Peoples* (4 vol., 1956–58). He was knighted in 1953; he later refused the offer of a peerage. He was made an honorary U.S. citizen in 1963. In his late years he attained heroic status as one of the titans of the 20th century.

cicada, Any insect in the order Homoptera that has two pairs of membranous wings, prominent compound eyes, and three simple eyes (ocelli). Most of the 1,500 known species are in the family Cicadidae and are found in tropical deserts, grasslands, and forests. Males produce loud noises by vibrating membranes near the base of the abdomen. Most North American cicadas produce rhythmical ticks, buzzes, or whines, though the "song" of some species is musical. The species are easily distinguishable by song, behaviour, and appearance. Periodic cicadas (species that occur in large numbers in chronologically and geographically isolated broods) appear in regular cycles, including the well-known 17-year cicada (often erroneously called the 17-year locust) and 13-year cicada. The larvae (nymphs) burrow into the

Newly emerged adult cicada (Tibicen pruinosa).
Richard Parker

ground, where they remain for 17 or 13 years, feeding on juices sucked from roots; they then emerge in large numbers to live aboveground as adults for a single week.

Cicero, Marcus Tullius (b. 106 BC, Arpinum, Latium—d. Dec. 7, 43 BC, Formiae), Roman statesman, lawyer, scholar, and writer. Born to a wealthy family, he quickly established a brilliant career in law and plunged into politics, then rife with factionalism and conspiracy. Cicero was elected consul in 63 BC. Of his speeches, perhaps the best known are those he made against Catiline, whose uprising he foiled. He vainly tried to uphold republican principles in the civil wars that destroyed the Roman Republic. After the death of Julius Caesar, he delivered his 14 Philippic orations against Mark Antony. When the triumvirate of Antony, Octavian (later Augustus), and Marcus Lepidus was formed, he was executed. His extant works include 58 orations and more than 900 letters, as well as many poems, philosophical and political treatises, and books of rhetoric. He is remembered as the greatest Roman orator and the innovator of what became known as Ciceronian rhetoric, which remained the foremost rhetorical model for many centuries.

cinchona, Any of about 40 species, mostly trees, that make up the genus *Cinchona* in the madder family. Cinchona is native to the Andes Mountains. Four species have been cultivated in tropical regions for hundreds of years, mostly in Java and, since World War II, in Africa. The bark is processed to obtain various alkaloids. The most significant are quinine, used to treat malaria, and quinidine, used mainly for cardiac rhythmic disorders. High demand for quinine among Europeans living in the tropics led naturalists to smuggle cinchona seeds from South America to plantations in Asia in the mid 1800s and to conduct intensive research leading to new high-yield strains and improved processing methods.

cinéma vérité (French: "truth cinema"), French film movement of the 1960s that strove for candid realism by showing people in everyday situations with authentic dialogue. Influenced by documentary filmmaking and Italian Neorealism, the method produced such outstanding examples as Jean Rouch's *Chronicle of a Summer* (1961) and Chris Marker's *Joli Mai* (1962). A similar movement in the U.S., where it was called "direct cinema," captured the reality of a person or an event by using a handheld camera to record action without narration, as in Frederick Wiseman's *Titicut Follies* (1967) and the Maysles brothers' *Salesman* (1969).

cinematography, Art and technology of motion-picture photography. It involves the composition of a scene, lighting of the set and actors, choice of cameras, camera angle, and integration of special effects to achieve the photographic images desired by the director. Cinematography focuses on relations between the individual shots and groups of shots that make up a scene to produce a film's effect. Well-known cinematographers include Nestor Almendros, Gregg Toland, and Sven Nykvist.

cinnamon, Bushy evergreen tree (*Cinnamomum zeylanicum*) of the laurel family. Native to Sri Lanka, India, and Burma, cinnamon is also cultivated in South America and the West Indies for the spice consisting of its dried inner bark. The light-brown spice has a delicately fragrant aroma and warm, sweet flavor. It was once more valuable than gold. Today cinnamon is used to flavor various foods. In Europe and the U.S. it is especially popular in bakery goods. The oil is distilled from bark fragments for use in food, liqueur, perfume, and drugs.

Ciompi, Revolt of the (1378) Uprising of cloth workers and other craftsmen in Florence that brought a democratic government to power. A struggle between ruling factions triggered the rebellion, which was led by the *ciompi* (wool carders). The rebels demanded a more equitable fiscal policy and the right to establish guilds for those groups not already organized. They took over the government briefly, but worsening economic conditions and the combined efforts of the established guilds soon led to their ouster.

circadian rhythm, Inherent cycle of approximately 24 hours in length that appears to control or initiate various biological processes, including sleep, wakefulness, and digestive and hormonal activity. The natural signal for the circadian pattern is the change from darkness to light. The controlling mechanism for these cyclic processes within the body is thought to be the hypothalamus. Any change in the circadian cycle (such as jet lag and other conditions associated with travel) requires a certain period for readjustment.

Circe, In Greek legend, a sorceress, the daughter of the sun god Helios and the ocean nymph Perse. By means of drugs and incantations she turned humans into lions, wolves, or swine. Odysseus visited her on his return from the Trojan War, and she changed his companions into swine. Odysseus himself was protected by an herb given him by Hermes, and he compelled the sorceress to restore his companions. He and Circe became lovers, but after a yearlong stay he resumed his journey homeward.

circulatory system, System that transports nutrients, respiratory gases, and metabolic products throughout the body. In humans, blood remains within a closed cardiovascular system composed of the heart, blood vessels, and blood. Arteries carry blood away from the heart under high pressure exerted by the heart's pumping action. Arteries divide into smaller arterioles, which branch into a network of tiny capillaries with thin walls across which gases and nutrients diffuse. Capillaries rejoin into larger venules, which unite to form veins, which carry blood back to the heart. The right and left heart chambers send blood into separate pulmonary and systemic circulations. In the first, blood is carried from the heart to the lungs, where it picks up oxygen and releases carbon dioxide; in the second, blood is carried between the heart and the rest of the body, where it carries oxygen, nutrients, metabolic products, and wastes.

circumcision, Cutting away of all or part of the foreskin (prepuce) of the penis. The practice is known in many cultures. It is performed either shortly after birth (e.g., among Muslims and Jews), within a few years of birth, or at puberty. For Jews it represents the fulfillment of the covenant between God and Abraham (Genesis 17:10–14). That Christians were not obliged to be circumcised was first recorded biblically in Acts 15. Evidence regarding the purported medical benefits of circumcision (e.g., reduced risk of cancer) is inconclusive, and the practice persists mainly for cultural reasons.

circus, Entertainment or spectacle featuring animal acts and human feats of daring. The modern circus was founded in England in 1768 by the bareback rider Philip Astley (1742–1814), who built stands around his performance ring and opened Astley's Amphitheatre. One of his riders later established the Royal Circus (1782), the first modern use of the term. The first U.S. circus opened in Philadelphia in 1793. Horse acts were later joined by wild-animal acts. After the invention of the flying trapeze by Jules Léotard (1859), aerial acts were featured. P.T. Barnum expanded the traditional circus by adding two rings to create the three-ring circus (1881) and augmented it with sideshow performers. Circuses traveled throughout the U.S., Europe, and Latin America, performing in a tent (the Big Top) into the 1950s. Today circuses usually perform in permanent buildings, though small troupes still travel with tents in some regions. By the late 20th century, notable circuses also had developed in Africa, India, Spain, Brazil, and Mexico. Perhaps the most innovative trend in circuses at the turn of the 21st century was the establishment of companies such as the Cirque du Soleil; these companies employed no animals, instead emphasizing acts of human skill and daring and integrating elements of contemporary music and dance into the overall performance.

cirrhosis, Degeneration of functioning liver cells and their replacement with fibrous connective tissue, leading to scarring. The most common cause is alcohol abuse with malnutrition. Others include bile duct obstruction, viral infection, toxins, iron or copper accumulation in liver cells, and syphilis. Jaundice, edema, and great abdominal swelling are common in all. Death usually results from internal bleeding or hepatic coma due to blood chemical imbalance.

Cistercian, or WHITE MONK, or BERNARDINE, Member of a Roman Catholic monastic order founded by St. Stephen Harding (1098) at Cîteaux (Latin, Cistercium), Burgundy, by Benedictines dissatisfied with their abbey's laxity. Cistercians were severely ascetic, rejected feudal revenues, and engaged in manual labor. Uniform rules applied to all houses, and all abbots were to meet annually at Cîteaux. St. Bernard de Clairvaux founded 68 abbeys in his lifetime. Discipline declined as the order grew, and Cistercians disappeared from northern Europe after the Reformation. The order underwent reforms in the 16th–17th century; members of the reformed order are popularly known as Trappists after the abbey of La Trapp. Until the 1960s, they slept, ate, and worked in perpetual silence. The original order, which underwent more moderate reforms, also survives.

citizenship, Relationship between an individual and a state in which the individual owes allegiance to the state and in turn is entitled to its protection. In general, full political rights, including the right to vote and to hold public office, are predicated on citizenship. Citizenship entails obligations, usually including allegiance, payment of taxes, and military service. The concept arose in ancient Greece, where citizenship was granted only to property owners. The Romans initially used it as a privilege to be conferred upon or withheld from conquered peoples, but it was granted to all the empire's free inhabitants in AD 212. The concept disappeared in Europe during the feudal era but was revived in the Renaissance. Citizenship may normally be gained by birth within a certain territory, descent from a parent who is a citizen, marriage to a citizen, or naturalization.

citric acid, Colourless, crystalline organic compound ($C_6H_8O_7$), one of the carboxylic acids. It is present in almost all plants (especially citrus fruits) and in many animal tissues and fluids. It is one of a series of compounds involved in the physiological oxidation of fats, proteins, and carbohydrates to carbon dioxide and water. It has a characteristic sharply sour taste and is used in many foods, confections, and soft drinks. It is added to certain foods to improve their stability in metal containers. Industrially, it is used as a water conditioner, cleaning and polishing agent, and chemical intermediate.

citron, Small evergreen tree or shrub (*Citrus medica*). A member of the rue family, citron is cultivated in Mediterranean countries and the West Indies. It has irregular, spreading, spiny branches and large, pale green, broadly oblong leaves. The flowers of the acidic varieties (e.g., the Diamante) are purple on the outside and white on the inside; those of sweet varieties (e.g., the Corsican) are creamy white. The oval or oblong fruit yields firm pulp, either acidic or sweet, that is used only for by-products. The thick peel is cured in brine, candied, and sold as a confection. The fruit of the Etrog variety is used in Jewish religious rites.

citrus, Any of the plants that make up the genus *Citrus*, in the rue family, that yield pulpy fruits covered with fairly thick skins. The genus includes the lemon, lime, sweet and sour oranges, tangerine, grapefruit, citron, and shaddock (*C. maxima*, or *C. grandis*; also called pomelo).

city, Relatively permanent and highly organized centre of population, of greater size or importance than a town or village. The first cities appeared in Neolithic times when the development of agricultural techniques assured surplus crop yields large enough to sustain a permanent population. Ancient Greece saw the creation of the city-state, a form also important in the emergence of the Roman empire as well as the medieval Italian trading centers of Venice, Genoa, and Florence. After the Middle Ages, cities came increasingly under the political control of centralized government and served the interests of the nation-state. The Industrial Revolution further transformed city life, as factory cities blossomed rapidly in England, northwestern Europe, and the northeastern U.S. By the mid-20th century, 30–60% of a country's population might be living in its major urban centers. With the rise of the automobile came the growth of suburbs and urban sprawl, as factories, offices, and residences erected in earlier periods became aged and obsolete. Today many cities suffer from lack of adequate housing, sanitation, recreational space, and transportation facilities, and face problems of inner-city decay or burgeoning shantytowns. Local governments have sought to alleviate these problems through urban planning.

city government, Set of governmental institutions that serve an urban area or urban municipality. All cities derive their existence from a larger political entity, either a state or national government. City government generally includes an executive (a mayor or manager) and a legislature (a council or commission), both of which may be subject to popular election. Their most important functions are the provision of services, including public safety, health care, education, recreation, housing, utilities, transportation, and cultural facilities. Revenues come from local taxes and fees as well as grants and subsidies from its state or national government.

city-state, Political system consisting of an independent city with sovereignty over a fixed surrounding area for which it served as leader of religious, political, economic, and cultural life. The term was coined in the 19th century to describe ancient Greek and Phoenician settlements that differed from tribal or national systems in size, exclusivity, patriotism, and ability to resist incorporation by other communities. They may have developed when earlier tribal systems broke down and splintered groups established themselves as independent nuclei *c.* 1000–800 BC; by the 5th century BC they numbered in the hundreds, with Athens, Sparta, and Thebes among the most important. Incapable of forming any lasting union or federation, they eventually fell victim to the Macedonians, the Carthaginians, and the Roman empire. In the 11th century the city-state revived in Italy; the success of medieval Italy's city-states, including Pisa, Florence, Venice, and Genoa, was due to growing prosperity from trade with the East, and several survived into the 19th century. Germany's medieval city-states included Hamburg, Bremen, and Lübeck. The only city-state extant today is Vatican City.

civil disobedience, or PASSIVE RESISTANCE, Refusal to obey government demands or commands and nonresistance to consequent arrest and punishment. It is used especially as a nonviolent and usually collective means of forcing government concessions and has been a major tactic of nationalist movements in Africa and India, of the U.S. civil rights movement, and of labour and antiwar movements in many countries. Civil disobedience is a symbolic or ritualistic violation of the law, rather than a rejection of the system as a whole. The civil disobedient, finding legitimate avenues of change blocked or nonexistent, sees himself as obligated by a higher, extralegal principle to break some specific law. By submitting to punishment, the civil disobedient hopes to set a moral example that will provoke the majority or the government into effecting meaningful political, social, or economic change. The philosophical roots of civil disobedience lie deep in Western thought. Cicero, Thomas Aquinas, and John Locke, among others, appealed to systems of natural law that take precedence over the laws created by communities or states (positive law). More modern advocates and practitioners of civil disobedience include Henry David Thoreau, Mohandas K. Gandhi, and Martin Luther King, Jr.

civil law, Body of law developed from Roman law and used in continental Europe and most former colonies of European nations, including the province of Quebec and the U.S. state of Louisiana. The most significant codifications of modern civil law were the French (Napoleonic Code) and the German (German Civil Code). The basis of law in civil-law jurisdictions is statute, not custom; civil law is thus to be distinguished from common law. In civil law, judges apply principles embodied in statutes, or law codes, rather than turning to case precedent. French civil law forms the basis of the legal systems of the Netherlands, Belgium, Luxembourg, Italy, Spain, most of France's former possessions overseas, and many Latin American countries. German civil law prevails in Austria, Switzerland, the Scandinavian countries, and certain countries outside Europe, such as Japan, that have westernized their legal systems. The term is also used to distinguish the law that applies to private rights from the law that applies to criminal matters.

civil liberty, Freedom from arbitrary interference in one's pursuits by individuals or by government. The term is usually used in the plural. Civil liberties are protected explicitly in the constitutions of most democratic countries. (In authoritarian countries, civil liberties are often formally guaranteed in a constitution but ignored in practice.) In the U.S., civil liberties are guaranteed by the Bill of Rights and the 13th, 14th, and 15th Amendments to the Constitution of the United States. The Constitution's 13th Amendment prohibits slavery and involuntary servitude; the 14th bars the application of any law that would abridge the "privileges and immunities" of U.S. citizens or deprive any person of "life, liberty, or property…without due process of law" or deny any person equal protection under the law; and the 15th guarantees the right of all U.S. citizens to vote. The related term civil right is often used to refer to one or more of these liberties or indirectly to the obligation of government to protect certain classes of people from violations of one or more of their civil liberties (e.g., the obligation to protect racial minorities from discrimination on the basis of race). In the U.S., civil rights are protected by the Civil Rights Act of 1964 and subsequent legislation.

civil service, Body of government officials employed in civil occupations that are neither political nor judicial. In well-ordered societies, they are usually recruited and promoted on the basis of a merit-and-seniority system, which may include examinations; elsewhere, corruption and patronage are more important factors. They often serve as neutral advisers to elected officials and political appointees. Though not responsible for making policy, they are charged with its execution. The civil service originated in the earliest known Middle Eastern societies; the modern European civil services date to 17th- and 18th-century Prussia and the electors of Brandenburg. In the U.S., senior officials change with each new administration. In Europe, regulations were established in the 19th century to minimize favouritism and to ensure a wide range of knowledge and skills among civil service officers.

Cixi, or TZ'U-HSI, known as THE EMPRESS DOWAGER (b. Nov. 29, 1835, Beijing, China—d. Nov. 15, 1908, Beijing), Imperial consort who controlled the Chinese Qing dynasty for almost half a century. A low-ranking concubine of the Xianfeng emperor (r. 1850–61), Cixi bore his only son, the future Tongzhi emperor, in 1856. After the emperor's death, Cixi joined a triumviral regency that governed in the name of her son, who was only 6 at his accession. During that period the Taiping and Nian rebellions were put down and the government was briefly revitalized. When Cixi's son died in 1875, Cixi violated the laws of succession and had her adoptive nephew enthroned. The regency thus continued, with Cixi becoming sole regent in 1884. In 1889 she nominally relinquished control but returned in 1898 to undo a set of radical reforms and had her nephew imprisoned in his palace. She supported the unsuccessful Boxer Rebellion, which had disastrous consequences for China. In 1902 she began to implement the reforms she had earlier reversed. Before she died, she ordered her nephew poisoned.

clan, Kinship group based on actual or purported descent from a common ancestor, as traced through the male (patriclan) or the female (matriclan) line. Clans are normally exogamous, marriage within the clan being regarded as incest. Clans may segment into subclans or lineages, and genealogical records and myths may be altered to incorporate new members who lack kinship ties with the clan. Clan membership may be useful in ensuring mutual support and defense as well as in the mediation of disputes over property rights and the mode of residence after marriage. Some clans express their unity by means of a common emblem.

Clare of Assisi, Saint (b. July 16, 1194, Assisi, duchy of Spoleto—d. Aug. 11, 1253, Assisi; canonized 1255; feast day August 11), Founder of the order of Poor Clares (Clarissines). Born to a noble family, she became devoted to her fellow Assisian St. Francis. She refused to marry and in 1212 fled to the Porziuncola Chapel, where St. Francis received her vows. She later became abbess of a female religious community that included her sister, St. Agnes, and her mother. Her order, the Second Order of St. Francis, or Poor Clares, adopted the absolute poverty of St. Francis but was strictly cloistered, unlike its counterpart, the Franciscans. Still allied with the Franciscans, the Poor Clares are noted for their poverty and their life of penitential prayer led for the good of church and society.

clarinet, Single-reed woodwind instrument. It is a standard member of both orchestras and bands. It has a cylindrical bore and a flared bell, and it is usually made of African blackwood (*Dalbergia melanoxylon*, more commonly called renadilla). It has a 3¹/₂-octave range; its lower register is rich and its top register is brilliant. It developed from the slightly older two-key chalumeau; the German flute maker Johann Christoff Denner (1655–1707) is said to have invented it at the beginning of the 18th century. The B-flat clarinet is the standard instrument today; the A clarinet often replaces it in sharp keys. Clarinets with the fingering system devised by Theobald Boehm are standard in the U.S., Great Britain, and France; those employing an older fingering style are used in Germany and Russia. Clarinets of other sizes include the C clarinet, much used in the Classical period and often preserved in German orchestration; octave clarinets in A, used in large European bands; and sopranino clarinets in F and later E-flat. The B-flat bass clarinet, with its rich timbre, is the next most frequently employed member of the clarinet family. Contrabass clarinets are made in E-flat or in B-flat.

Clark, Helen (b. Feb. 26, 1950, Hamilton, N.Z.), New Zealand prime minister (1999–2008). She was the first woman in New Zealand to hold the office of prime minister immediately following an election. She received bachelor's (1971) and master's (1974) degrees in political science at the University of Auckland, where she taught from 1973 to 1981. Elected to Parliament in 1981, she held various cabinet portfolios beginning in 1987. She served as deputy prime minister in 1989–90 and was appointed to the Privy Council in 1990, both firsts for a woman in New Zealand. In 1993 she was elected head of the Labour Party, becoming the first woman in New Zealand to head a major party. In 1999, when the Labour Party was able to form a governing coalition, Clark was elected prime minister. She was reelected in both 2002 and 2005, becoming the first New Zealand prime minister to secure three consecutive terms in office. In the 2008 election, however, her party was defeated by the National Party; she subsequently stepped down as Labour leader.

Helen Clark, 2005.
Sean Gallup/Getty Images

class, social, Group of people within a society who possess the same socioeconomic status. The term was first widely used in the early 19th century, following the industrial and political revolutions of the late 18th century. The most influential early theory of class was that of Karl Marx, who focused on how one class controls and directs the process of production while other classes are the direct producers and the providers of services to the dominant class. The relations between the classes were thus seen as antagonistic. Max Weber emphasized the importance of political power and social status or prestige in maintaining class distinctions. Despite controversies over the theory of class, there is general agreement on the characteristics of the classes in modern capitalist societies. In many cases the upper class has been distinguished by the possession of largely inherited wealth, while the working class has consisted mostly of manual labourers and semiskilled or unskilled workers, often in service industries, who earn moderate or low wages and have little access to inherited wealth. The middle class includes the middle and upper levels of clerical workers, those engaged in technical and professional occupations, supervisors and managers, and such self-employed workers as small-scale shopkeepers, businesspeople, and farmers. There is also often an urban substratum of permanently jobless and underemployed workers termed the "underclass."

Classical architecture, Architecture of ancient Greece and Rome, especially from the 5th century BC in Greece to the 3rd century AD in Rome, that emphasized the column and pediment. Greek architecture was based chiefly on the post-and-beam system, with columns carrying the load. Timber construction was superseded by construction in marble and stone. The column, a unit human in scale, was used as a module for all of a temple's proportions. The Doric order, probably the earliest, remained the favorite of the Greek mainland and western colonies. The Ionic order developed in eastern Greece; on the mainland, it was used chiefly for smaller temples and interiors. The greatest Greek architectural achievement was the Athens acropolis. By the late 5th century BC, the orders were applied to such structures as stoas and theaters. The Hellenistic Age produced more elaborate and richly decorated architecture, with often colossal buildings. Many of the great buildings were secular rather than religious, and the Ionic and especially the newer Corinthian orders were widely used. The Romans used the Greek orders and added two new ones (Tuscan and Composite); the Corinthian was by far the most popular. Roman architects used columns not only as functional bearing elements, but also as applied (engaged) decoration. Though rigidly adhering to symmetry, the Romans used a variety of spatial forms. Whereas Greek temples were isolated and almost always faced east-west, Roman temples were oriented with respect to other buildings. Roman columns carried arches as well as entablatures, permitting greater spatial freedom. The discovery of concrete enormously facilitated construction using the arch, vault, and dome, as in the Pantheon. Other public buildings included basilicas, baths, amphitheaters, and triumphal arches. Classical architecture may also refer to architecture of later periods that employs Greek or Roman forms.

classical economics, School of economic thought largely centred in Britain that originated with Adam Smith and reached maturity in the works of David Ricardo and John Stuart Mill. The theories of the classical school were mainly concerned with the dynamics of economic growth. Reacting against mercantilism, classical economics emphasized economic freedom. It stressed ideas such as laissez-faire and free competition. Many of the fundamental principles of classical economics were set forth in Smith's *Wealth of Nations* (1776), in which he argued that a nation's wealth was greatest when its citizens pursued their own self-interest. Neoclassical economists such as Alfred Marshall showed that the forces of supply and demand would ration economic resources to their most effective uses. Smith's ideas were elaborated and refined by Ricardo, who formulated the principle that the price of goods produced and sold under competitive conditions tends to be proportionate to the labour costs incurred in producing them. Mill's *Principles of Political Economy* (1848) gave the ideas greater currency by relating them to contemporary social conditions. Among those who have modified classical economics to reach very different conclusions are Karl Marx and John Maynard Keynes.

Classicism, In the arts, the principles, historical tradition, aesthetic attitudes, or style of the art of ancient Greece and Rome. The term may refer either to work produced in antiquity or to later works inspired by those of antiquity; the term *Neoclassicism* usually refers to art produced later but inspired by antiquity. More broadly, Classicism refers to the adherence to virtues regarded as characteristic of Classicism or as universally and enduringly valid, including formal elegance and correctness, simplicity, dignity, restraint, order, and proportion. Classicism is often opposed to Romanticism. Periods of Classicism in literature, music, and the visual arts have generally coincided.

Classicism and Neoclassicism, Art-historical tradition or aesthetic attitudes based on the art of ancient Greece and Rome. "Classicism" refers to the art produced in antiquity or to later art inspired by that of antiquity; "Neoclassicism" refers to art inspired by that of antiquity and thus is contained within the broader meaning of "Classicism." Classicism is traditionally characterized by harmony, clarity, restraint, universality, and idealism. In the visual arts, Classicism has generally denoted a preference for line over colour, straight lines over curves, and the general over the particular. The Italian Renaissance was the first period of thorough Classicism after antiquity. Neoclassicism became the dominant aesthetic movement in Europe in the late 18th and early 19th centuries, as practiced by Antonio Canova and Jacques-Louis David. It bred a reaction in favour of subjective feeling, longing for the sublime, and a taste for the bizarre that came to be termed Romanticism. Recurring alternations between Classical and non-Classical ideals have often characterized Western aesthetics.

clavichord, Early keyboard instrument, an important forerunner of the piano. It flourished *c.* 1400–1800, especially in Germany. It is usually rectangular, with the keyboard inset. The strings are struck by metal tangents, rather than plucked as on the harpsichord. The tangent becomes the endpoint of the vibrating string; thus the point where it strikes determines the pitch. So-called fretted clavichords permit more than one tangent to strike a single pair of strings (which somewhat limits the notes that can be sounded simultaneously); unfretted clavichords use only one tangent per pair of strings. The player's touch can produce dynamic variation; variation in finger pressure can even produce vibrato. Its tone is silvery and soft, best suited for intimate music.

Clayton-Bulwer Treaty (1850) Compromise agreement designed to harmonize contending British and U.S. interests in Central America. The treaty provided that the two countries jointly control and protect what was to become the Panama Canal. The Clayton-Bulwer treaty was superseded in 1901 by the Hay-Pauncefote Treaty, under which the British government agreed to allow the U.S. to construct and control the canal.

clearinghouse, Institution established by firms engaged in similar activities to enable them to offset transactions with one another in order to limit payment settlements to net balances. Clearinghouses play an important role in settling international payments and the transactions of banks, railroads, and stock and commodity exchanges. Bank clearinghouses are usually voluntary associations of local banks set up to simplify the exchange of checks, drafts, and notes, as well as to settle balances. Increasingly, the automated clearinghouse (ACH) is used to transfer funds electronically. The clearinghouse idea was applied to various forms of trade from an early time. The Amsterdam Exchange Bank, founded in 1609, became Europe's largest clearinghouse and

made the city an international financial centre. The first modern bank clearinghouse was established in London in 1773. The first bank clearinghouse in the U.S. was established in 1853.

clef (French: "key"), Musical notation symbol at the beginning of a staff to indicate the pitch of the notes on the staff. Clefs were originally letters, identifying letter-named pitches, that were affixed to one or more of the staff's lines (thus providing a "key" to their identity). Knowing the identity of a single line permitted the musician to identify all the other lines and spaces above and below. Clefs were first regularly used in the 12th century. The Gothic letter forms of G and F evolved into the modern treble and bass clefs, respectively; the letter C evolved into the rarer alto, tenor, baritone, and soprano clefs.

cleft palate, Fairly common congenital disorder in which a fissure forms in the roof of the mouth. It may affect only the soft palate or extend through the hard palate, so that the nasal cavity opens into the mouth. The septum (dividing wall) between the nostrils is often absent. Cleft lip, a fissure in the lip beneath the nostril, or other abnormalities may accompany it. Cleft palate limits the ability of an infant to suck, which may lead to malnutrition, and causes speech problems in childhood. Surgical repair, usually at about 18 months of age, forms an airtight separation between nose and mouth. Speech training is still needed, and patients may have a high risk of nose, ear, and sinus infections.

Cleopatra, in full CLEOPATRA VII THEA PHILOPATOR (b. 70/69 BCE—d. Aug. 30, 30 BCE, Alexandria), Egyptian queen (of Macedonian descent), last ruler of the Ptolemaic dynasty in Egypt. Daughter of Ptolemy XII (b. 112?—d. 51 BCE), she ruled with her two brother-husbands, Ptolemy XIII (r. 51–47) and Ptolemy XIV (r. 47–44), both of whom she had killed, and with her son, Ptolemy XV, or Caesarion (r. 44–30). She claimed the latter was fathered by Julius Caesar, who had become her lover after entering Egypt in 48 BCE in pursuit of Pompey. She was with Caesar in Rome when he was assassinated (44), after which she returned to Egypt to install her son on the throne. She lured Mark Antony, Caesar's heir apparent, into marriage (36), inviting the wrath of Octavian (later Augustus), whose sister Antony had earlier wed. She schemed against and antagonized Antony's friend Herod the Great, thereby losing his support. At a magnificent celebration in Alexandria after Antony's Parthian campaign (36–34), he bestowed Roman lands on his foreign wife and family. Octavian declared war on Cleopatra and Antony and defeated their joint forces at the Battle of Actium (31). Antony committed suicide and, after a failed attempt to beguile Octavian, so too did Cleopatra, possibly by means of an asp.

Cleopatra, detail of a bas relief, c. 69–30 BC; in the Temple of Hathor, Dandarah, Egypt.
Courtesy of the Oriental Institute, the University of Chicago

Clermont, Council of (1095) Assembly for church reform called by Pope Urban II. When the Byzantine emperor Alexius I Comnenus requested aid against the Muslim Turks, the council became the occasion for launching the First Crusade. Urban thus launched a movement that caught the popular imagination with the idea of retaking Jerusalem.

click, In phonetics, a suction sound made in the mouth. Click sounds occur in various African languages and are often used as interjections in other languages—for example, the sound of disapproval represented in English by *tsk, tsk*. Clicks are a regular part of the consonant system in the Khoisan languages and in Bantu languages such as Xhosa and Zulu that have been strongly influenced by Khoisan.

cliff dwelling, Prehistoric, usually multistoried house of the ancestors of present-day Pueblo Indians, built from *c.* 1000 along the sides or under the overhangs of cliffs. The use of hand-hewn stone building blocks and adobe mortar in these communal dwellings was unexcelled even in later times. Rooms on upper levels could be entered either by doorways from adjoining rooms or by ladders through holes in the ceilings; ground-floor rooms could be entered only through the ceiling. It is thought that the cliff dwellings were built as a defense against invading Navajo and Apache tribes. They were deserted by the inhabitants around the end of the 13th century. Many ruins remain, including notable ones at Canyon de Chelly National Monument, Mesa Verde National Park, and Montezuma Castle National Monument.

climate, Condition of the atmosphere at a particular location over a long period of time (from one month to many millions of years, but generally 30 years). Climate is the sum of atmospheric elements (and their variations): solar radiation, temperature, humidity, clouds and precipitation (type, frequency, and amount), atmospheric pressure, and wind (speed and direction). To the nonspecialist, climate means expected or habitual weather at a particular place and time of year. To the specialist, climate also denotes the degree of variability of weather, and it includes not only the atmosphere but also the hydrosphere, lithosphere, biosphere, and such extraterrestrial factors as the sun.

clinical psychology, Branch of psychology concerned with the diagnosis and treatment of mental disorders. Clinical psychologists evaluate patients through interviews, observation, and psychological tests, and they apply current research findings and methodologies in making diagnoses and assigning treatments. Most clinical psychologists hold an academic degree (Ph.D. or Psy.D.) rather than a medical degree (M.D.); they may provide psychotherapy but cannot prescribe medications. Most practitioners work in hospitals or clinics or in private practice, often in tandem with psychiatrists and social workers, treating mentally or physically disabled patients, prison inmates, drug and alcohol abusers, and geriatric patients, among others.

Clinton, Bill, in full WILLIAM JEFFERSON CLINTON, orig. WILLIAM JEFFERSON BLYTHE III (b. Aug. 19, 1946, Hope, Ark., U.S.), 42nd president of the U.S. (1993–2001). Born shortly after his father's death in a car crash, he later took the last name of his mother's second husband, Roger Clinton. He attended Georgetown University, the University of Oxford (as a Rhodes Scholar), and Yale Law School, then taught law at the University of Arkansas. He served as state attorney general (1977–79) and served several terms as governor (1979–81, 1983–92), during which he reformed Arkansas's educational system and encouraged the growth of industry through favourable tax policies. In 1992 he won the Democratic Party's presidential nomination despite charges of personal impropriety; in the subsequent election he defeated the incumbent, Republican George Bush, and independent candidate H. Ross Perot. As president, Clinton obtained Senate ratification of the NAFTA accord in 1993. Along with his wife, Hillary Rodham Clinton, he devised a plan to overhaul the U.S. health care system, but it was rejected by Congress. He committed U.S. forces to a peacekeeping initiative in Bosnia and Herzegovina. In 1994 the Democrats lost control of Congress for the first time since 1954. Clinton responded by offering a deficit-reduction plan while opposing efforts to slow government spending on social programs. He defeated Robert Dole to win reelection in 1996. In 1997 he helped broker a peace agreement in Northern Ireland. He faced renewed charges of personal impropriety, this time involving his relationship with a White House intern, Monica Lewinsky; he denied the charges before a grand jury but ultimately acknowledged "improper relations" in a televised address. In 1998 Clinton be-

came only the second president in history to be impeached. Charged with perjury and obstruction of justice, he was acquitted by the Senate in 1999. His two terms saw sustained economic growth and successive budget surpluses, the first in three decades.

Clinton, Hillary Rodham, orig. HILLARY DIANE RODHAM (b. Oct. 26, 1947, Chicago, Ill., U.S.), U.S. lawyer, first lady, and politician. She attended Wellesley College and Yale Law School, from which she graduated first in her class. Her early professional interests focused on family law and children's rights. In 1975 she married her Yale classmate Bill Clinton, and she became first lady of Arkansas on his election as governor in 1979. She was twice named one of America's 100 most influential lawyers by the *National Law Journal*. When her husband became president (1993), she wielded power and influence almost unprecedented for a first lady. As head of the Task Force on National Health Care Reform, she proposed the first national health-care program in the U.S. but saw the initiative defeated. In 2000 she was elected to the U.S. Senate from New York, thereby becoming the first wife of a president to win elective office; she was reelected in 2006. Clinton sought the Democratic presidential nomination in 2008 but lost the closely contested race to Barack Obama. In 2009 she became secretary of state in President Obama's administration.

clipper ship, Classic sailing ship of the 19th century, renowned for its beauty, grace, and speed. Apparently originating with the small, swift coastal packet known as the Baltimore clipper, the true clipper evolved first in the U.S. (*c.* 1833) and later in Britain. It was a long, slim, graceful vessel with a projecting bow, a streamlined hull, and an exceptionally large spread of sail on three tall masts. Clippers carried tea from China and goldminers to California. Famous clippers included the American *Flying Cloud* and the British *Cutty Sark*. Though much faster than the early steamships (already in use when the clipper appeared), they were eventually outrun by improved steamship models and largely disappeared from commercial use in the 1870s.

cloisonné, Enameling technique. Delicate strips of gold, brass, silver, copper, or other metal wire are welded to a metal plate in the shape of a design, and the resulting cellular spaces are filled with vitreous enamel paste that is fired, ground smooth, and polished. The earliest surviving examples are six 13th-century BC Mycenaean rings. The technique reached its peak in the West during the Byzantine Empire. Chinese cloisonné was widely produced during the Ming and Qing dynasties; in Japan it was popular in the Edo and Meiji periods.

cloister, Four-sided enclosure surrounded by covered walkways  and usually attached to a monastic or cathedral church; also, the walkways themselves. The earliest cloisters were open arcades, usually with sloping wooden roofs. This form was generally superseded in England by a range of windows lighting a vaulted ambulatory (aisle). In southern climates, the open-arcaded cloister remained standard. An especially fine example is Donato Bramante's two-story open arcade at Santa Maria della Pace, Rome (1500–4).

Open arcaded cloister of Saint-Trophîme, Arles, Fr.
Jean Roubier

clone, Population of genetically identical cells or organisms that originated from a single cell or organism by nonsexual methods. Cloning is fundamental to most living things, since the body cells of plants and animals are clones that come ultimately from a single fertilized egg. More narrowly, the term refers to an individual organism grown from a single body cell of its parent that is genetically identical to the parent. Cloning has been commonplace in horticulture since ancient times; many varieties of plants are cloned simply by obtaining cuttings of their leaves, stems, or roots and replanting them. The body cells of adult humans and other animals are routinely cultured as clones in the laboratory. Entire frogs and mice have been successfully cloned from embryonic cells. British researchers led by Ian Wilmut achieved the first success in cloning an adult mammal in 1996. Having already produced clones from sheep embryos, they were able to produce a lamb (Dolly) using DNA from an adult sheep. The practical applications of cloning are economically promising but philosophically unsettling.

clostridium, Any of the rod-shaped, usually gram-positive bacteria that make up the genus *Clostridium.* They are found in soil, water, and the intestinal tracts of humans and other animals. Some species grow only in the complete absence of oxygen. Dormant cells are highly resistant to heat, drying, toxic chemicals, and detergents. The toxins produced by *C. botulinum,* which causes botulism, are the strongest poisons known. The toxin of *C. tetani* causes tetanus; other species can cause gangrene.

cloud, Any visible mass of water droplets, ice crystals, or a mixture of the two that is suspended in the air, usually at a considerable height. Clouds are usually created and sustained by upward-moving air currents. Meteorologists classify clouds primarily by their appearance. The 10 main cloud families are divided into three groups on the basis of altitude. High clouds, which are found at mean heights of 45,000–16,500 ft (13–5 km), are, from highest to lowest, cirrus, cirrocumulus, and cirrostratus. Middle clouds, at 23,000–6,500 ft (7–2 km), are altocumulus, altostratus, and nimbostratus. Low clouds, at 6,500–0 ft (2–0 km), are stratocumulus, stratus, cumulus, and cumulonimbus. A shallow layer of cloud at or near ground level is called fog.

clove, Small, reddish brown flower bud of the tropical evergreen tree *Syzygium aromaticum* (sometimes called *Eugenia caryophyllata*), of the myrtle family. The tree is believed to be native to the Moluccas of Indonesia. Cloves were important in the earliest spice trade. With a strong aroma and hot and pungent taste, they are used to flavour many foods. Clove oil is sometimes used as a local anesthetic for toothaches. Eugenol, its principal ingredient, is used in germicides, perfumes, and mouthwashes, in the synthesis of vanillin, and as a sweetener or flavour intensifier.

clown, Comic character of mime and pantomime and the circus. The clown developed from the bald-headed, padded buffoons who performed in the farces and mimes of ancient Greece and from the professional comic actors of the Middle Ages. The Italian commedia dell'arte introduced the harlequin, and the clown's whiteface makeup was introduced with the 17th-century French character Pierrot. The distinctive clown costume of oversized shoes, hat, and giant ruff around the neck was established by the popular German clown character Pickelherring. The first circus clown, Joseph Grimaldi, appeared as "Joey" in England (1805) and specialized in pantomime, pratfalls, and slapstick. Famous 20th-century clowns included the Swiss pantomimist Grock (Adrian Wettach), the U.S. circus star Emmett Kelly, and the longtime star of the Moscow circus, Oleg Popov.

Cluny, Monastery founded in 910 by William the Pious, duke of Aquitaine. Established as a pious donation for the cure of the souls of the duke and his wife and family, the monastery at Cluny came to offer a more austere reading of the Benedictine Rule. It was dedicated to the apostles St. Peter and St. Paul, and in practice it came under the protection of the pope. William also established the independence of the monastery from all temporal rulers, religious or secular, and allowed the monks to elect the abbot. These liberties enabled the community to develop its emphasis on the liturgy and prayers for the dead, which inspired a reputation for holiness and attracted numerous benefactors. Cluniac monks were sent to reform monasteries throughout Europe and created a great web of related communities. Cluny's influence on the church in the 11th–12th century has been widely recognized, and its abbots were greatly esteemed. Its predominance was eroded by the rise of the Cistercian order, and in the later Middle Ages the monastery declined. It was suppressed during the French Revolution and closed in 1790. Its Romanesque Basilica of St. Peter and St. Paul (largely demolished in the 19th century) was the world's largest church until the erection of Saint Peter's Basilica.

cluster of galaxies, Gravitationally bound grouping of galaxies, numbering from the hundreds to the tens of thousands. Large clusters of galaxies often exhibit extensive X-ray emission from intergalactic gas heated to tens of millions of degrees. Also, interactions of galaxies with each other and with the intracluster gas may deplete galaxies of their own interstellar gas. The Milky Way Galaxy belongs to the Local Group, which lies on the outskirts of the Virgo Cluster.

Clyde, River, River, southern Scotland. Scotland's most important river, it flows about 100 mi (160 km) from the Southern Uplands to the Atlantic Ocean. The upper Clyde is a clear fishing stream flowing north, but at Biggar it changes course and winds northwest to the Falls of Clyde. Beyond the falls, the widening Vale of Clyde, famous for the breeding of Clydesdale horses, is intensively cultivated. The Clydeside shipyards border the river for 20 mi (32 km) below Glasgow. At Dumbarton it reaches its estuary, the Firth of Clyde, which extends about 65 mi (105 km).

Clydesdale, Breed of heavy draft horse that originated in Lanarkshire, Scotland, near the River Clyde. Though introduced to North America c. 1842, the Clydesdale never became a popular draft horse there. They average 17–18 hands (68–72 in., or 173–183 cm) in height and 2,000 lbs (900 kg) in weight. Their coloration is usually bay, dark brown, or black, with prominent white markings. They are noted for their high leg action while walking or trotting. The breed is characterized by feather (long hair) on the legs, an attractive head, and well-formed legs and feet.

coal, Solid, usually black but sometimes brown, carbon-rich material that occurs in stratified sedimentary deposits. One of the most important fossil fuels, it is found in many parts of the world. Coal is formed by heat and pressure over millions of years on vegetation deposited in ancient shallow swamps. It varies in density, porosity, hardness, and reflectivity. The major types are lignite, subbituminous, bituminous, and anthracite. Coal has long been used as fuel, for power generation, for the production of coke, and as a source of various compounds used in synthesizing dyes, solvents, and drugs. The search for alternative energy sources has periodically revived interest in the conversion of coal into liquid fuels; technologies for coal liquefaction have been known since early in the 20th century.

coal mining, Extraction of coal deposits from the Earth's surface and from underground. Because coal was the basic energy source that fueled the Industrial Revolution, the resulting industrial growth supported the large-scale exploitation of coal deposits. In the late 20th century, open pit mines replaced underground mines as the principal source of coal in the industrial nations. The mining of coal from surface and underground deposits today is a highly productive, mechanized operation.

Coalsack, Dark nebula in the Crux constellation (Southern Cross). It reduces the brightness of stars beyond it by 1–1.5 magnitudes. Easily visible against a starry background, it is probably about 550–600 light-years from Earth and 20–30 light-years in diameter. It figures in legends of peoples of the Southern Hemisphere and has been known to Europeans since *c.* 1500. The Northern Coalsack, in the constellation Cygnus, is similar in nature and appearance but somewhat less obvious.

Coase, Ronald (Harry) (b. Dec. 29, 1910, Willesden, Middlesex, Eng.), British-U.S. economist. He received his doctorate from the London School of Economics and taught principally there and the University of Chicago. In his best-known paper, "The Problem of Social Cost" (1960), he challenged the classical logic of prohibiting behaviour that damages others. He argued that legal scholars should focus on the importance of an efficient marketplace and on negotiation rather than litigation. He was awarded the Nobel Prize in 1991.

coat of arms, or SHIELD OF ARMS, Heraldic device dating to the 12th century in Europe. It was originally a cloth tunic worn over or in place of armour to establish identity in battle. In the full armorial achievement the distinctively patterned shield is ornamented with a crest, helmet, mantling, motto, crown, wreath, and supporters and rests upon a compartment. Arms were later adopted as emblems for schools, churches, guilds, and corporations to reflect their origins or histories.

cobalt, Metallic chemical element, one of the transition elements, chemical symbol Co, atomic number 27. Widely dispersed in small amounts in many minerals and ores, this magnetic, silvery white metal with a faint bluish tinge is used mostly for special alloys (e.g., alnico, tool steel) with exacting applications. At valence 2 or 3 it forms numerous coordination complexes. One is vitamin B_{12} (cyanocobalamin). Cobalt and its compounds are used in electroplating and colouring ceramics and glass and as lamp filaments, catalysts, a trace element in fertilizers, and paint and varnish driers. The pigment cobalt blue has a variable composition, roughly that of cobalt oxide plus alumina. A radioactive isotope of cobalt emits penetrating gamma rays that are used in radiation therapy.

COBOL, in full COMMON BUSINESS-ORIENTED LANGUAGE, High-level computer programming language, one of the first widely used languages and for many years the most popular language in the business community. It developed from the 1959 Conference on Data Systems Languages, a joint initiative between the U.S. government and the private sector. COBOL was created to fulfill two major objectives: portability (ability of programs to be run with minimum modification on computers from different manufacturers) and readability (ease with which a program can be read like ordinary English). It ceased to be widely used in the 1990s.

cobra, Any of several highly venomous elapid snakes that expand their neck ribs to form a hood. They are found in warm regions of Africa, Australia, and Asia. Cobra bites are fatal in about 10% of human cases. Cobras feed primarily on small vertebrates. The Indian cobra (*Naja naja*) kills several thousand people annually, mostly because it enters houses to catch rats. The king cobra (*Ophiophagus hannah*) is the world's largest venomous snake, often more than 12 ft (3.5 m) long. Some African cobras can spit their venom more than 6 ft (1.8 m). Cobras are favourites of snake charmers, who, by their movements rather than their music, tease the deaf snakes into assuming the upreared defense posture.

Black-necked cobra (Naja nigricollis)
E.S. Ross

coca, Tropical shrub (*Erythroxylum coca*) of the family Erythroxylaceae. It is native to the eastern Andes Mountains but cultivated in Africa, northern South America, Southeast Asia, and Taiwan.

Coca (Erythroxylum coca).
W.H. Hodge

Its leaves are the source of cocaine and several other alkaloids. Coca thrives best in hot, damp environments, such as forest clearings; but the leaves most preferred are obtained in drier localities, on the sides of hills. The composition of different specimens of coca leaves is highly variable. Good samples have a strong tealike odor and a pleasant, pungent taste. When chewed, coca leaves produce a sense of warmth in the mouth; because of their potent stimulant and appetite-depressant effects, coca has been used for centuries by South American peasants to ease the effects of punishing physical labor.

cocaine, Heterocyclic compound ($C_{17}H_{21}NO_4$), an alkaloid obtained from coca leaves. It has legal uses in medicine and dentistry as a local anesthetic but far more is used illegally, usually as the hydrochloride. When sniffed in small amounts, cocaine produces feelings of well-being and euphoria, decreased appetite, relief from fatigue, and increased mental alertness. Larger amounts or prolonged use can damage the heart and nasal structures and cause seizures. In altered, more potent, cheaper forms (freebase, crack), cocaine is injected or smoked and is extremely addictive and detrimental to health. Prolonged or compulsive use of any form of purified cocaine can cause severe personality disturbances, inability to sleep, appetite loss, and paranoid psychosis.

coccus, Spherical bacterium. Many species have characteristic arrangements that are useful in identification. Pairs of cocci are called diplococci; rows or chains, streptococci; grapelike clusters, staphylococci; packets of eight or more cells, sarcinae; and groups of four cells in a square arrangement, tetrads. These characteristic groupings occur as a result of variations in the reproduction process.

Cochinchina, French COCHINCHINE, Region, southern Vietnam. Covering 30,000 sq mi (77,700 sq km), the area was a vassal of the Chinese empire and later part of the Khmer kingdom of Cambodia. Its capital, Saigon, was occupied by the French in 1859. It was made a French colony in 1867 and was combined with other French protectorates to form French Indochina in 1887. Incorporated into Vietnam in 1949, it was part of South Vietnam (1954–76) until the country was reunited. It includes the Mekong River delta, one of the greatest rice-producing regions in Asia.

cockatiel, Crested, small, gray Australian parrot (*Nymphicus hollandicus*). It has a yellow head, red ear patches, and a heavy beak used to crack nuts. The cockatiel is in the same family (Cacatuidae) as the larger cockatoo. About 13 in. (32 cm) long, the cockatiel lives in open areas and eats grass seeds. One of the most common pet parrots, it is bred in many colour variations.

Sulfur-crested cockatoo (Cacatua galerita).
Warren Garst/Tom Stack & Associates

cockatoo, Any of 21 species of crested parrots (family Cacatuidae), found in Australia and from New Guinea to the Solomon Islands. Most species are white with touches of red or yellow; some are black. All have a massive beak used to crack nuts, dig up roots, or pry grubs from wood; feeding is aided by a wormlike tongue. Treetop, hole-nesting birds, cockatoos at times form large, noisy flocks that damage crops. The largest cockatoo (the palm, or great black, cockatoo) is about 25–30 in. (65–75 cm) long. Some cockatoos live more than 50 years.

cockroach, or ROACH, Any of more than 3,500 insect species (in suborder Blattaria, order Dictyoptera) that are among the most primitive living, winged insects and among the oldest (more than 320 million years old) fossil insects. Cockroaches have a flattened, oval body; long, threadlike antennae; and a shining, leathery, black or brown covering. They prefer a warm, humid, dark environment and are usually found in tropical or other mild climates, but have become widespread in heated buildings, especially city apartment buildings, in the temperate zone, and infestations can be severe. Only a few species have become pests. Cockroaches eat both animal and plant material. The American cockroach is up to about 2 in. (30–50 mm) long. The German cockroach (less than 0.5 in., or about 12 mm, long) is a common household pest which has been spread throughout the world by ship.

coconut palm, Tree (*Cocos nucifera*) of the palm family, one of the most important crops of the tropics. Its slender, leaning, ringed trunk rises from a swollen base and is topped by a graceful crown of giant, feathery leaves. The large ovoid or ellipsoid mature fruits have a thick, fibrous husk surrounding the familiar single-seeded nut. The nut contains a white and somewhat sweet meat, which is eaten raw; coconut oil is extracted from the meat. The nutritious liquid "milk" at the centre may be drunk directly from the nut. The husk provides coir, a fibre highly resistant to salt water that is used in the manufacture of ropes, mats, baskets, brushes, and brooms. The nutshells are used as containers and often decoratively carved.

cod, Large and economically important marine fish (*Gadus morhua*, family Gadidae) found on both sides of the North Atlantic, usually near the bottom in cold water. It ranges from inshore regions to deep waters. It is valued for its edible flesh, the oil of its liver, and other products. The cod is dark-spotted and ranges from greenish or grayish to brown or blackish; it may also be dull to bright red. It usually weighs up to about 25 lbs (11.5 kg) but can reach a maximum length and weight of more than 6 ft (1.8 m) and 200 lbs (91 kg). It feeds largely on other fishes and various invertebrates.

codeine, Heterocyclic compound, a naturally occurring alkaloid found in opium, used in medicine as a cough suppressant and analgesic drug. It exerts its effects by acting on the central nervous system (brain and spinal cord). Chemically it is methylmorphine, the methyl ether of morphine, an alkaloid of the phenanthrene type; its action is weaker than that of morphine, and it is less likely to lead to drug addiction.

codependency, An extreme dependency by one person on another who is suffering from an addiction. Common characteristics include low self-esteem coupled with a high need for approval. Not a formal psychiatric diagnosis, codependency is a psychological syndrome noted in relatives or partners of alcoholics or substance abusers.

codex, Manuscript book, especially of Scripture, early literature, or ancient mythological or historical annals. The earliest type of manuscript in the form of a modern book (i.e., a collection of pages stitched together along one side), the codex replaced earlier rolls of papyrus and wax tablets. Among its advantages, it could be opened at once to any point in the text, it permitted writing on both sides of the leaf, and it could contain long texts. The oldest extant Greek codex is the Codex Sinaiticus (4th century AD), a biblical manuscript. Codices were developed separately by pre-Columbian Mesoamericans after *c.* AD 1000.

coeducation, Education of males and females in the same school. A modern phenomenon, it was adopted earlier and more widely in the U.S. than in Europe, where tradition proved a greater obstacle to its acceptance. In the 17th century Quaker and other reformers in Scotland, northern England, and New England began urging that girls as well as boys be taught to read the Bible. By the later 18th century girls were being admitted to town schools. By 1900 most U.S. public high schools and some 70% of colleges and universities were coeducational. Pioneering institutions in the U.S. included Oberlin College, Cornell University, and the University of Iowa. In Europe the Universities of Bologna and London and various Scandinavian institutions were the first to open their doors. Other European countries adopted coeducational policies after 1900, and many communist countries instituted strong coeducational programs.

coffee, Tropical evergreen shrub of the genus *Coffea*, in the madder family, or its seeds, called beans; also the beverage made by brewing the roasted and ground beans with water. Two of the 25 or more species, *C. arabica* and *C. canephora*, supply almost all the world's coffee. Arabica coffee is considered to brew a more flavourful and aromatic beverage than Robusta, the main variety of *C. canephora*. Arabicas are grown in Central and South America, the Caribbean, and Indonesia, Robustas mainly in Africa. The shrub bears bouquets of small white flowers with a jasminelike fragrance. The fruit, 0.5–0.75 in. (13–19 mm) long and red when mature, is called a cherry. Coffee contains large amounts of caffeine, the effects of which have always been an important element in the drink's popularity. Coffee drinking began in 15th-century Arabia. It reached Europe by the mid 17th century and immediately became hugely popular. Coffee is now consumed by about one-third of the world's population.

cogeneration, In power systems, use of steam for both power generation and heating. High-temperature, high-pressure steam from a boiler and superheater first passes through a turbine to produce power. It is exhausted at a temperature and pressure suitable for heating purposes, instead of being expanded in the turbine to the lowest possible pressure and then discharged to the condenser, which would waste the remaining energy in the steam. The steam at the higher pressure can provide large amounts of lower-temperature energy for heating buildings or evaporating brine in a chemical plant. Considerable overall energy savings can be obtained by cogeneration.

cogito, ergo sum (Latin: "I think, therefore I am"), Dictum coined in 1637 by René Descartes as a first step in demonstrating the attainability of certain knowledge. It is the only statement to survive the test of his methodic doubt. The statement is indubitable, Descartes argued, because even if an all-powerful demon were to try to deceive him into thinking he exists when he does not, Descartes would have to exist in order to be deceived. Therefore, whenever he thinks, he exists. Furthermore, Descartes maintained, the statement "I am" (*sum*) expresses an immediate intuition, not the conclusion of a process of reasoning, and is thus indubitable.

cognition, Act or process of knowing. Cognition includes every mental process that may be described as an experience of knowing (including perceiving, recognizing, conceiving, and reasoning), as distinguished from an experience of feeling or of willing. Philosophers have long been interested in the relationship between the knowing mind and external reality; psychologists took up the study of cognition in the 20th century.

cognitive dissonance, Mental conflict that occurs when beliefs or assumptions are contradicted by new information. The concept was introduced by the psychologist Leon Festinger (1919–89) in the late 1950s. He and later researchers showed that, when confronted with challenging new information, most people seek to preserve their current understanding of the world by rejecting, explaining away, or avoiding the new information or by convincing themselves that no conflict really exists. Cognitive dissonance is nonetheless considered an explanation for attitude change.

cognitive psychology, Branch of psychology devoted to the study of human cognition, particularly as it affects learning and behaviour. The field grew out of advances in Gestalt, developmental, and comparative psychology and in computer science, particularly information-processing research. Cognitive psychology shares many research interests with cognitive science, and some experts classify it as a branch of the latter. Contemporary cognitive theory has followed one of two broad approaches: the developmental approach, derived from the work of Jean Piaget and concerned with "representational thought" and the construction of mental models ("schemas") of the world, and the information-processing approach, which views the human mind as analogous to a sophisticated computer system.

cognitive science, Interdisciplinary study that attempts to explain the cognitive processes of humans and some higher animals in terms of the manipulation of symbols using computational rules. The field draws particularly on the disciplines of artificial intelligence, psychology, linguistics, neuroscience, and philosophy. Some chief areas of research in cognitive science have been vision, thinking and reasoning, memory, attention, learning, and language processing. Early theories of cognitive function attempted to explain the evident compositionality of human thought (thoughts are built up of smaller units put together in a certain way), as well as its productivity (the process of putting together a thought from smaller units can be repeated indefinitely to produce an infinite number of new thoughts), by assuming the existence of discrete mental representations that can be put together or taken apart according to rules that are sensitive to the representations' syntactic, or structural, properties. This "language of thought" hypothesis was later challenged by an approach, variously referred to as connectionism, parallel-distributed processing, or neural-network modeling, according to which cognitive processes (such as pattern recognition) consist of adjustments in the activation strengths of neuronlike processing units arranged in a network.

cohen, or KOHEN (Hebrew: "priest") Jewish priest descended from Zadok (a descendant of Aaron), priest at the First Temple of Jerusalem. The biblical priesthood was hereditary and male. Before King Josiah's reign (7th century BC), the high priest alone could enter the Holy of Holies on Yom Kippur. Lower-ranking priests accompanied the army in war or administered the Temple. The priestly class was strongest during the period of the Second Temple and was curtailed after its destruction. The rabbinate has replaced the *kohanim* as authorities on the Law, but *kohanim* retain some privileges (except in Reform Judaism).

coherentism, Theory of truth according to which a belief is true just in case, or to the extent that, it coheres with a system of other beliefs. Philosophers have differed over the relevant sense of "cohere," though most agree that it must be stronger than mere consistency. Among rival theories of truth, perhaps the oldest is the correspondence theory, which holds that the truth of a belief consists in its correspondence with independently existing facts. In epistemology, coherentism contrasts with foundationalism, which asserts that ordinary beliefs are justified if they are inferrable from a set of basic beliefs that are justified immediately or directly. Coherentism often has been combined with the idealist doctrine that reality consists of, or is knowable only through, ideas or judgments.

coin collecting, Systematic accumulation and study of coins, tokens, paper money, and objects of similar form and purpose. The long-held view that coin collecting began with the Italian Renaissance has been challenged by growing evidence that the activity is far more venerable. There exist a variety of literary accounts of collecting from ancient Greek and Roman sources, and there is tangible archaeological evidence that coins have been collected at least from the Roman era. Collecting was perhaps less important during the Middle Ages, but during the 15th–16th centuries it again became more popular, mostly among European aristocrats. In the 17th century the nature of collecting shifted slowly toward serious research. As a result, very broad collections were formed,

studied, and catalogued. In the 20th century museums took over the main task of forming large collections of great detail and range. It was also during this time that a popular market for coins began to develop. Previously only the very wealthy purchased ancient coins and the number of sources were few. London became the world's largest numismatic market, serving the interests of public collections and private collectors in many lands. The Internet became an important aspect of coin collecting in the late 1990s, both because it afforded a virtual marketplace that permitted buyers and sellers from anywhere in the world to trade in coins and for the educational effect of the many Web sites devoted to the hobby.

cold, common, Viral infection of the upper and sometimes the lower respiratory tract. Symptoms, which are relatively mild, include sneezing, fatigue, sore throat, and stuffy or runny nose (but not fever); they usually last only a few days. About 200 different strains of virus can produce colds; they are spread by direct or indirect contact. The cold is the most common of all illnesses; the average person gets several every year. Incidence peaks in the fall. Treatment involves rest, adequate fluid intake, and over-the-counter remedies for the symptoms. Antibiotics do not combat the virus but may be given if secondary infections develop.

Cold War, Open yet restricted rivalry and hostility that developed after World War II between the U.S. and the Soviet Union and their respective allies. The U.S. and Britain, alarmed by the Soviet domination of Eastern Europe, feared the expansion of Soviet power and communism in Western Europe and elsewhere. The Soviets were determined to maintain control of Eastern Europe, in part to safeguard against a possible renewed threat from Germany. The Cold War (the term was first used by Bernard Baruch during a congressional debate in 1947) was waged mainly on political, economic, and propaganda fronts and had only limited recourse to weapons. It was at its peak in 1948–53 with the Berlin blockade and airlift, the formation of NATO, the victory of the communists in the Chinese civil war, and the Korean War. Another intense stage occurred in 1958–62 with the Cuban missile crisis, which resulted in a weapons buildup by both sides. A period of détente in the 1970s was followed by renewed hostility. The Cold War ended with the collapse of the Soviet Union in 1991.

Colette, in full SIDONIE-GABRIELLE COLETTE (b. Jan. 28, 1873,

Saint-Sauveur-en-Puisaye, France—d. Aug. 3, 1954, Paris), French writer. Her first four *Claudine* novels (1900–03), the reminiscences of a libertine ingenue, were published by her first husband, an important critic, under his pen name, Willy. After separating from him, she worked as a music-hall performer, a life she fictionalized in *The Vagabond* (1910). Among her mature works are *Chéri* (1920), *My Mother's House* (1922), *The Ripening Seed* (1923), *The Last of Chéri* (1926), *Sido* (1930), and *Gigi* (1944; musical film, 1958), a comedy about a girl reared to be a courtesan. Her novels of the pleasures and pains of love are remarkable for their exact evocation of sounds, smells, tastes, textures, and colours. In her highly eventful life, she freely flouted convention and repeatedly scandalized the French public, but by her late years she had become a national icon.

Colette, 1937.
Charles Leirens/Black Star

colic, Any sudden, violent pain, especially that produced by contraction of the muscular walls of a hollow organ whose opening is partly or completely blocked. In infants, intestinal colic is characterized by drawing up of the legs, restlessness, and constant cry-ing. Colic may accompany enteritis (intestinal inflammation) or an intestinal tumour, as well as certain forms of influenza. Colic caused by spastic bowel contractions is common in lead poisoning. Treatment, aimed at symptom relief, often includes use of a muscle relaxant.

collage (from French *coller*, "to glue") Pictorial technique of applying printed or found materials (e.g., newspaper, fabric, wallpaper) to a flat surface, often in combination with painting. Long popular as a pastime for children and amateurs, it was first given serious attention as an art technique by Pablo Picasso and Georges Braque in 1912–13. Many other 20th-century artists produced collages, including Juan Gris, Henri Matisse, Joseph Cornell, and Max Ernst. In the 1960s collage was employed as a major form of Pop art, exemplified in the work of Robert Rauschenberg.

collective bargaining, Process of negotiation between representatives of workers (usually labour union officials) and management to determine the conditions of employment. The agreement reached may cover not only wages but hiring practices, layoffs, promotions, working conditions and hours, and benefit programs. Collective bargaining developed in England at the end of the 18th century. Although collective bargaining agreements are common in many countries, they are more scarce in developing countries that have large pools of surplus labour. Contract negotiations may occur at the national, regional, or local level, depending on the structure of industry within a country.

collectivism, Any of several types of social organization that ascribe central importance to the groups to which individuals belong (e.g., state, nation, ethnic group, or social class). It may be contrasted with individualism. Jean-Jacques Rousseau was the first modern philosopher to discuss it (1762). Karl Marx was its most forceful proponent in the 19th century. Communism, fascism, and socialism may all be termed collectivist systems.

Cologne, German KÖLN, City (pop., 2002 est.: city, 967,900; metro. area, 1,823,500), western Germany. Located on the Rhine River, it is one of Europe's key inland ports. First settled by Romans in the 1st century BC, its commercial importance grew out of its location on the major European trade routes. In the Middle Ages it also became an ecclesiastical centre and an important hub of art and learning. Despite its almost complete destruction in World War II, the city retains some buildings and monuments of all periods. Its cathedral, the largest Gothic church in northern Europe, is its unofficial symbol. Banking has been an important industry since the Middle Ages. Eau de cologne, first produced commercially in the 18th century, is still made there. The city is also a major media centre, with many publishing houses and production facilities for radio and television. It is famous for its pre-Lenten Carnival.

Colombia, officially REPUBLIC OF COLOMBIA, Country, northwestern South America. Area: 440,831 sq mi (1,141,748 sq km). Population: (2011 est.) 44,726,000. Capital: Bogotá. About half the population are mestizos; most of the rest are of European-African, European, or African ancestry. Language: Spanish (official). Religion: Christianity (predominantly Roman Catholic). Currency: peso. The topography is dominated by the Andes Mountains. To the south and east lie vast lowlands, drained by the Orinoco and Amazon rivers. Colombia's developing economy is based primarily on services, agriculture, and manufacturing, coffee being the principal cash crop. Coca (for the production of cocaine) and opium poppies (for the production of heroin) are grown and trafficked illicitly on a large scale. Rich in minerals, Colombia is the world's largest producer of emeralds and one of South America's largest producers of gold. It is a unitary multiparty republic with two legislative houses; its head of state and government is the president. Its earliest known inhabitants were Chibchan-speaking Indians. The Spanish arrived *c.* 1500 and by 1538 had conquered the area and made it subject to the Viceroyalty of

Peru. After 1740 authority was transferred to the newly created Viceroyalty of New Granada. Parts of Colombia threw off Spanish jurisdiction in 1810, and full independence came after Spain's defeat by revolutionary leader Simón Bolívar in 1819. Civil war in 1840 slowed development. Conflict between the Liberal and Conservative parties led to the War of a Thousand Days (1899–1903). Years of relative peace followed, but hostility erupted again in 1948; the two parties agreed in 1958 to a plan for alternating governments. A new constitution was adopted in 1991, but democratic power remained threatened by civil unrest, which continued into the early 21st century and at the violent centre of which were powerful drug cartels, leftist guerrillas, and right-wing paramilitary groups.

Colombo, City (pop., 2007 est.: 672,743), executive and judicial capital of Sri Lanka. (Sri Jayewardenepura Kotte, a Colombo suburb, is the legislative capital.) Situated on the western coast of the island, it is a major Indian Ocean port with one of the largest artificial harbours in the world. The area was settled in the 8th century by Arab traders. A fort was established by the Portuguese in 1518, and the town was occupied by the Dutch in 1656 and the English in 1796. It became the capital of the island in 1815. Western influence diminished after Sri Lanka gained its independence in 1948. A commercial and industrial centre, Colombo has manufacturing industries that produce machinery and process food products. It is home to the University of Colombo (founded 1921).

colonialism, Western, a political-economic phenomenon whereby various European nations explored, conquered, settled, and exploited large areas of the world. The purposes of colonialism included economic exploitation of the colony's natural resources, creation of new markets for the colonizer, and extension of the colonizer's way of life beyond its national borders. In the years 1500–1900 Europe colonized all of North and South America and Australia, most of Africa, and much of Asia by sending settlers to populate the land or by taking control of governments. The first colonies were established in the Western Hemisphere by the Spanish and Portuguese in the 15th–16th centuries. The Dutch colonized Indonesia in the 16th century, and Britain colonized North America and India in the 17th–18th centuries. Later, British settlers colonized Australia and New Zealand. Colonization of Africa only began in earnest in the 1880s, but by 1900 virtually the entire continent was controlled by Europe. The colonial era ended gradually after World War II; the only territories still governed as colonies today are small islands.

colony, In antiquity, any of the new settlements established in territory conquered by the Greeks (8th–6th century BC), Alexander the Great (4th century BC), and the Romans (4th century BC–AD 2nd century). Greek colonies extended to Italy, Sicily, Spain, the eastern Mediterranean (including Egypt), and the Black Sea. Alexander pushed even farther into Central Asia, South Asia, and Egypt. Roman colonization covered much of the same area and regions south to northern Africa, west to Spain, and north to Britain and Germany. Reasons for colonizing included expansion of trade, acquisition of raw materials, resolution of political unrest or overpopulation, and craving for land and rewards. Colonies retained ties and loyalty to Rome, though rebelliousness was not uncommon. In Roman colonies after 177 BC, colonists retained Roman citizenship and could exercise full political rights. Ancient colonization spread Hellenic and Roman culture to the far reaches of the empires, often assimilating local populations, some of whom acquired Roman citizenship.

Colorado River, River, North America. Rising in the Rocky Mountains of Colorado, U.S., it flows west and south 1,450 mi (2,330 km) to empty into the Gulf of California in northwestern Mexico. It drains a vast sector of the North American continent, about 246,000 sq mi (637,000 sq km). No other river in the world has cut so many deep trenches, of which the Grand Canyon is the largest and most spectacular. It is important for hydroelectric power and irrigation; more than 20 dams, including Hoover Dam, have been built on the Colorado River and its tributaries.

Colosseum, Flavian Amphitheater in Rome, erected *c.* AD 70–82

Colosseum (Flavian Amphitheatre), Rome, c. AD 70–82.
© Goodshoot/Jupiterimages

under the emperors Vespasian and Titus. The name Colosseum was applied some time after the 8th century because of its immense size and capacity, holding some 50,000 people. Unlike earlier amphitheaters, which were nearly all dug into hillsides for extra support, the Colosseum is a freestanding oval colonnaded structure of stone and concrete. It was the scene of combats between gladiators, contests of men with animals, and even mock naval engagements. The Colosseum was damaged by lightning and earthquakes in medieval times and, even more severely, by vandals. A restoration project was undertaken in the 1990s, and in 2000 the Colosseum staged a series of plays that marked the first time in more than 1,500 years that live performances had been held there.

colostomy, Surgical formation of an artificial anus by making an opening from the colon through the abdominal wall. It may be done to decompress an obstructed colon, to allow excretion when part of the colon must be removed, or to permit healing of the colon. Colostomy may be temporary or permanent. A sigmoid colostomy, the most common type of permanent colostomy, requires no appliances (though a light pouch is sometimes worn for reassurance) and allows a normal life except for the route of fecal excretion.

colour, Aspect of any object that may be described in terms of hue, lightness, and saturation. It is associated with the visible wavelengths of electromagnetic radiation, which stimulate the sensor cells of the eye. Red light has the longest wavelengths, while blue has the shortest, with other colours such as orange, yellow, and green between. Hue refers to dominant wavelengths. Lightness refers to the intensity or degree of shading; it corresponds to the subjective sensation of brightness. Saturation pertains to purity, or the amount of white light mixed with a hue. The colours red, green, and blue, known as primary colours, can be combined in varying proportions to produce all other colours. Primary colours combined in equal proportions produce secondary colours. Two colours that combine to form white light are said to be complementary.

colour blindness, Inability to distinguish one or more colours. The human retina contains three types of cone cells that absorb light in different parts of the spectrum. Absence of these types causes colour blindness to red, green, and blue. Colour blindness is a sex-linked recessive trait 20 times more common in men than in women.

Columbia River, River, southwestern Canada and northwestern U.S. Rising in the Canadian Rockies, it flows through Washington state, entering the Pacific Ocean at Astoria, Ore.; it has a total length of 1,240 mi (2,000 km). It was a major transportation artery in the Pacific Northwest until the coming of the railroads. Development of the river began in the 1930s with construction of the Grand Coulee and Bonneville dams, and within 50 years the entire river within the U.S. had been converted into a series of "stair steps" by a total of 11 dams. Its many hydroelectric power plants are basic to the power-generating network of the Pacific Northwest.

Columbus, Christopher, Italian CRISTOFORO COLOMBO, Spanish CRISTÓBAL COLÓN (b. between Aug. 26 and Oct. 31?,

1451, Genoa—d. May 20, 1506, Valladolid, Spain), Genoese navigator and explorer whose transatlantic voyages opened the way for European exploration, exploitation, and colonization of the Americas. He began his career as a young seaman in the Portuguese merchant marine. In 1492 he obtained the sponsorship of the Spanish monarchs Ferdinand II and Isabella I for an attempt to reach Asia by sailing westward over what was presumed to be open sea. On his first voyage he set sail in August 1492 with three ships—the *Santa María*, the *Niña*, and the *Pinta*—and land was sighted in the Bahamas on October 12. He sailed along the northern coast of Hispaniola and returned to Spain in 1493. He made a second voyage (1493–96) with at least 17 ships and founded La Isabela (in what is now the Dominican Republic), the first European town in the New World. This voyage also began Spain's effort to promote Christian evangelization. On his third voyage (1498–1500) he reached South America and the Orinoco River delta. Allegations of his poor administration led to his being returned to Spain in chains. On his fourth voyage (1502–04) he returned to South America and sailed along the coasts of present-day Honduras and Panama. He was unable to attain his goals of nobility and great wealth. His character and achievements have long been debated, but scholars generally agree that he was an intrepid and brilliant navigator.

coma, Complete lack of consciousness, with loss of reaction to stimulus and of spontaneous nervous activity. It is usually associated with cerebral injury of metabolic or physical origin. Simple concussions cause short losses of consciousness. Coma from lack of oxygen may last several weeks and is often fatal. Coma caused by stroke can be sudden, while that caused by metabolic abnormalities (as in diabetes mellitus) or cerebral tumours comes on gradually. Treatment depends on the cause.

Comédie-Française, National theatre of France. The world's longest-established national theatre, it was founded in 1680 by the merger of two theatrical companies in Paris, one of them the troupe that had worked under Molière. The French Revolution divided the company's loyalties, and the revolution's supporters, led by François-Joseph Talma, moved to the theatre's present home in 1791. The company was reconstituted in 1803. Under its rules of organization, established by Napoleon in 1812, its members share responsibilities and profits. Its illustrious actors have included Sarah Bernhardt and Jean-Louis Barrault. The theatre is known for productions of the French classics, though it also performs contemporary plays.

comedy, Genre of dramatic literature that deals with the light and amusing or with the serious and profound in a light, familiar, or satirical manner. Comedy can be traced to revels associated with worship in Greece in the 5th century BC. Aristophanes, Menander, Terence, and Plautus produced comedies in classical literature. It reappeared in the late Middle Ages, when the term was used to mean simply a story with a happy ending (e.g., Dante's *Divine Comedy*), the same meaning it has in novels of the last three centuries (e.g., the fiction of Jane Austen).

comedy of manners, Witty, ironic form of drama that satirizes the manners and fashions of a particular social class or set. Comedies of manners were usually written by sophisticated authors for members of their own social class, and they typically are concerned with social usage and the ability or inability of certain characters to meet social standards, which are often exacting but morally trivial. The plot, usually concerning an illicit love affair or other scandalous matter, is subordinate to the play's brittle atmosphere, witty dialogue, and pungent commentary on human foibles. Its notable exponents include William Congreve, Oliver Goldsmith, Richard Brinsley Sheridan, Oscar Wilde, and Noel Coward.

comet, Any of a class of small icy objects orbiting the Sun and developing diffuse gaseous envelopes and often long glowing tails when near the Sun. They are distinguished from other objects in the solar system by their composition, hazy appearance, and elongated orbits. Most comets originate in the Oort cloud or in the Kuiper belt. Other bodies' gravity can alter their orbits, causing them to pass close to the Sun. Short-period comets return in 200 years or less, others in thousands of years or not at all. A comet typically consists of a small, irregular nucleus, often described as a "dirty snowball," with dust and other materials frozen in water mixed with volatile compounds. When one nears the Sun, the heat vaporizes its surface, releasing gases and dust particles, which form a cloud (coma) around the nucleus. Material in the coma may be pushed away from the Sun by its radiation and the solar wind, forming one or more tails. Meteor showers occur when Earth passes through dust left by the passage of a comet.

comic strip, Series of drawings that read as a narrative, arranged together on the page of a newspaper, magazine, or book. In the 1890s several U.S. newspapers featured weekly drawings that were funny, but without indicated speech. In 1897 Rudolph Dirks's *Katzenjammer Kids*, in the *New York Journal*, featured humorous strips containing words presumably spoken by the characters. Soon speeches in balloons appeared in other cartoons, arranged in a series to form a strip. The comic strip arrived at its maturity in 1907 with Bud Fisher's *Mutt and Jeff*, which appeared daily in the *San Francisco Chronicle*. Important later comic-strip artists include George Herriman, Al Capp, Walt Kelly, and Charles Schulz.

Cominform, in full COMMUNIST INFORMATION BUREAU, Agency of international communism founded under Soviet auspices in 1947. Its original members were the Communist Parties of the Soviet Union, Bulgaria, Czechoslovakia, Hungary, Poland, Romania, Yugoslavia, France, and Italy, but Yugoslavia was expelled in 1948. The Cominform's activities consisted mainly of publishing propaganda to encourage international communist solidarity. It was dissolved by Soviet initiative in 1956 as part of a Soviet program of reconciliation with Yugoslavia.

Comintern, or COMMUNIST INTERNATIONAL, or THIRD INTERNATIONAL, Association of national communist parties founded in 1919. Vladimir Ilich Lenin called the first congress of the Comintern to undermine efforts to revive the Second International. To join, parties were required to model their structure in conformity with the Soviet pattern and to expel moderate socialists and pacifists. Though the Comintern's stated purpose was the promotion of world revolution, it functioned chiefly as an organ of Soviet control over the international communist movement. In 1943, during World War II, Joseph Stalin dissolved the Comintern to allay fears of communist subversion among his allies.

command economy, Economic system in which the means of production are publicly owned and economic activity is controlled by a central authority. Central planners determine the assortment of goods to be produced, allocate raw materials, fix quotas for each enterprise, and set prices. Most communist countries have had command economies; capitalist countries may also adopt such a system during national emergencies (e.g., wartime) in order to mobilize resources quickly.

commando, In British military forces, a unit consisting of marines and soldiers organized for rapid deployment and trained to conduct special operations. The commando originated with the Boers in South Africa, where it was the administrative and tactical unit "commandeered" by law. In World War II the British adopted the term for a new specially trained amphibious raiding force. Modern commandos are units of the Royal Marines with support troops from the British Army; by extension a member of such a unit is also called a commando and is entitled to wear a green beret.

commedia dell'arte, Italian theatrical form that flourished throughout Europe in the 16th–18th centuries. The characters, many portrayed by actors wearing masks—including the witty gentleman's valet Harlequin, the Venetian merchant Pantelone, the honest and simpleminded servant Pierrot, the maidservant Columbina, the unscrupulous servant Scaramouche, and the braggart captain or Capitano—were derived from the exaggeration or parody of regional or stock fictional types. The style emphasized improvisation within a framework of conventionalized masks and stock situations. It was acted by professional companies using vernacular dialects and plenty of comic action; the first known commedia dell'arte troupe was formed in 1545. Outside Italy it had its greatest success in France as the Comédie-Italienne; in England, it was adapted in the harlequinade and the Punch-and-Judy show.

commercial bank, Bank that makes loans to businesses, consumers, and nonbusiness institutions. Early commercial banks were limited to accepting deposits of money or valuables for safekeeping and verifying coinage or exchanging one jurisdiction's coins for another's. By the 17th century most of the essentials of modern banking, including foreign exchange, the payment of interest, and the granting of loans, were in place. It became common for individuals and firms to exchange funds through bankers with a written draft, the precursor to the modern check. Because a commercial bank is required to hold only a fraction of its deposits as cash reserves, it can use some of the money deposited by its customers to extend loans. Commercial banks also offer a range of other services, including savings accounts, safe-deposit boxes, and trust services.

Committee of Public Safety, Political body of the French Revolution that controlled France during the Reign of Terror. It was set up in April 1793 to defend France against its enemies, foreign and domestic. At first it was dominated by Georges Danton and his followers, but they were soon replaced by the radical Jacobins, including Maximilien Robespierre. Harsh measures were taken against alleged enemies of the Revolution, the economy was placed on a wartime basis, and mass conscription was undertaken. Dissension within the committee contributed to the downfall of Robespierre in July 1794, after which it declined in importance.

commodity exchange, Organized market for the purchase and sale of enforceable contracts to deliver a commodity (such as wheat, gold, or cotton) or a financial instrument (such as U.S. treasury bills) at some future date. Such contracts are known as futures and are bought and sold in a competitive auction process on commodity exchanges (also called futures markets). The largest futures and futures-options exchange is the Chicago Board of Trade.

common law, Body of law based on custom and general principles and that, embodied in case law, serves as precedent or is applied to situations not covered by statute. Under the common-law system, when a court decides and reports its decision concerning a particular case, the case becomes part of the body of law and can be used in later cases involving similar matters. This use of precedents is known as stare decisis. Common law has been administered in the courts of England since the Middle Ages; it is also found in the U.S. and in most of the British Commonwealth. It is distinguished from civil law.

Commons, House of, Popularly elected lower house of the bicameral British Parliament. Passage of legislation is its primary function. Because it alone has the power to levy taxes and allocate expenditures, it is Britain's chief legislative authority. It originated in the late 13th century, when landholders and other property owners began sending representatives to Parliament to present grievances and petitions to the king and to accept commitments to the payment of taxes. It was the less powerful house until 1911, when the Reform Bill of that year gave it the power to override the House of Lords. The party with the greatest representation in the Commons forms the government, and the prime minister chooses the cabinet from the party's members. There are 646 members, elected from single-member districts.

Commonwealth, or COMMONWEALTH OF NATIONS, Free association of sovereign states consisting of Britain and many of its former dependencies who have chosen to maintain ties of friendship and cooperation. It was established in 1931 by the Statute of Westminster as the British Commonwealth of Nations. Later its name was changed and it was redefined to include independent nations. Most of the dependent states that gained independence after 1947 chose Commonwealth membership. The British monarch serves as its symbolic head, and meetings of the more than 50 Commonwealth heads of government take place every two years.

Commonwealth of Independent States (CIS), Free association of sovereign states formed in 1991, comprising Russia and a number of other republics that were formerly part of the Soviet Union. Members are Russia, Ukraine, Belarus, Kazakhstan, Kyrgyzstan, Tajikistan, Turkmenistan, Uzbekistan, Armenia, Azerbaijan, and Moldova. Georgia, originally a member, withdrew from the association in 2009. The administrative centre is in Minsk, Belarus. The CIS's functions are to coordinate its members' policies regarding their economies, foreign relations, defense, immigration, environmental protection, and law enforcement.

commune, Group of people living together who hold property in common and live according to a set of principles usually arrived at or endorsed by the group. The utopian socialism of Robert Dale Owen and others led to experimental communities of this sort in the early 19th century in Britain and the U.S., including New Harmony, Brook Farm, and the Oneida Community. Many communes are inspired by religious principles; monastic life is essentially communal. B. F. Skinner's *Walden Two* (1948) inspired many American attempts at communal living, especially in the late 1960s and early 1970s.

commune, In medieval European history, a town that acquired self-governing municipal institutions. Most such towns were defined by an oath binding the citizens or burghers of the town to mutual protection and assistance. The group became an association able to own property, make agreements, exercise jurisdiction over members, and exercise governmental powers. Communes were particularly strong in northern and central Italy, where the lack of a powerful central government allowed them to develop into independent city-states. Those of France and Germany were more often limited to local government.

communism, Political theory advocating community ownership of all property, the benefits of which are to be shared by all according to the needs of each. The theory was principally the work of Karl Marx and Friedrich Engels. Their "Communist Manifesto" (1848) further specified a "dictatorship of the proletariat," a transitional stage Marx called socialism; communism was the final stage in which not only class division but even the organized state—seen by Marx as inevitably an instrument of oppression—would be transcended. That distinction was soon lost, and "communist" began to apply to a specific party rather than a final goal. Vladimir Ilich Lenin maintained that the proletariat needed professional revolutionaries to guide it. Joseph Stalin's version of communism was synonymous to many with totalitarianism. Mao Zedong mobilized peasants rather than an urban proletariat in China's communist revolution. European communism lost most of its following with the collapse of the Soviet Union (1991).

Communist Manifesto, Pamphlet written in 1848 by Karl Marx and Friedrich Engels to serve as the platform of the Communist League. It argued that industrialization had exacerbated the divide between the capitalist ruling class and the proletariat, which had become impoverished, and called on the proletariat to over-

throw the capitalists, abolish private property, and take over the means of production. It predicted an eventual classless society and the gradual elimination of the need for a state. It ends by stating, "The proletarians have nothing to lose but their chains. They have a world to win. Workingmen of all countries, unite."

Como, Lake, ancient LACUS LARIUS, Lake, Lombardy, northern Italy. It lies at an elevation of 653 ft (199 m) in a depression surrounded by limestone and granite mountains. It is 29 mi (47 km) long and up to 2.5 mi (4 km) wide, with an area of 56 sq mi (146 sq km) and a maximum depth of 1,358 ft (414 m). Famous for its natural beauty, its shores have many resorts.

Comoros, officially UNION OF THE COMOROS, Island country, western Indian Ocean. Area: 719 sq mi (1,862 sq km). Population: (2011 est.) 754,000. Capital: Moroni. The people are a mixture of Malay immigrants, Arab traders, and peoples from Madagascar and continental Africa. Languages: Comorian (a Bantu language), Arabic, French (all official). Religion: Islam (official; predominantly Sunni). Currency: Comorian franc. Comoros comprises a group of islands between Madagascar and the eastern African mainland that includes Ngazidja (Grande Comore), Mwali (Mohéli), and Nzwani (Anjouan) but excludes Mayotte. They are generally rocky, with shallow soils and poor harbours, though Mwali, the smallest, has fertile valleys and forested hillsides. Mount Karthala, an active volcano, is the highest point, at 7,746 ft (2,361 m). The climate is tropical. One of the world's poorest nations, Comoros has an economy based on subsistence agriculture. It is a republic with one legislative house. The head of state and government is the president, assisted by vice presidents. Beginning in the 16th century, Comoros was known to European navigators, but the dominant influence on the islands was then and for long afterward Arab. In 1843 France officially took possession of Mayotte and in 1886 placed the other three islands under protection. Subordinated to Madagascar in 1912, the Comoros became an overseas territory of France in 1947. In 1961 they were granted internal autonomy. In 1974 majorities on three of the islands voted for independence, which was declared in 1975. The following decade saw several coup attempts, culminating in the assassination of the president in 1989. French intervention permitted multiparty elections in 1990, but the country remained in a state of chronic instability, including secessionist movements on Nzwani and Mwali. In 1999 the army took control of the government and negotiated a constitution in 2001.

Companions of the Prophet, Arabic SAHABA, or ASHAB, Followers of Muhammad who had personal contact with him, including any Muslim contemporary who saw him. As eyewitnesses, they are the most important sources of Ḥadīth. Sunnite Muslims regard the first four caliphs (among the 10 Companions to whom Muhammad promised paradise) as the most important. Shīʿite Muslims disregard the Companions, whom they consider responsible for the loss of the caliphate by the family of ʿAlī.

comparative advantage, Economic theory first advanced by Robert Torrens and David Ricardo that analyzes international trade in terms of differences in relative opportunity costs. The theory suggests that countries should specialize in the goods they can produce most efficiently rather than trying for self-sufficiency and argues strongly in favour of free international trade.

comparative psychology, Study of similarities and differences in behavioral organization among living beings. The discipline pays particular attention to the psychological nature of humans in comparison with other animals. It began to emerge in the late 19th century and grew rapidly in the 20th century, involving experimental studies on human and animal brain function, learning, and motivation. Well-known studies have included those of Ivan Pavlov on conditioning in laboratory dogs, those of Harry Harlow (1905–81) on the effects of social deprivation in monkeys, and those of various researchers on language abilities in apes.

compiler, Computer software that translates (compiles) source code written in a high-level language (e.g., C++) into a set of machine-language instructions that can be understood by a digital computer's CPU. Compilers are very large programs, with error-checking and other abilities. Some compilers translate high-level language into an intermediate assembly language, which is then translated (assembled) into machine code by an assembly program or assembler. Other compilers generate machine language directly.

compost, Mass of rotted organic matter made from decomposed plant material. It is used in agriculture and gardening generally to improve soil structure rather than as a fertilizer, because it is low in plant nutrients. When properly prepared, it is free of obnoxious odours. Composts commonly contain about 2% nitrogen, 0.5–1% phosphorus, and about 2% potassium. Lime and nitrogen fertilizers and manure may be added to speed decomposition. The nitrogen of compost becomes available slowly and in small amounts. Because of their low nutrient content, composts are applied in large amounts.

comprehension, Act of or capacity for grasping with the intellect. The term is most often used in connection with tests of reading skills and language abilities, though other abilities (e.g., mathematical reasoning) may also be examined. Specialists in administering and interpreting such tests are known as psychometricians or differential psychologists.

Compton Gamma Ray Observatory, Space observatory in service from 1991 to 2000 that was designed to identify the sources of celestial gamma rays. It was named after physicist Arthur Holly Compton. Its mission was to determine whether gamma-ray bursts were in the Milky Way Galaxy or in remote galaxies. The satellite found that the bursts were scattered evenly across the sky, which showed that they came from outside the Milky Way Galaxy and were very powerful objects.

computer, Programmable machine that can store, retrieve, and process data. Today's computers have at least one CPU that performs most calculations and includes a control unit and an arithmetic logic unit. Main memory is an integral part of the computer but is separate from the CPU. Increasingly, personal computers contain specialized graphic processors, with dedicated memory, for handling the computations needed to display complex graphics, such as for three-dimensional simulations and games. Auxiliary data storage is usually provided by an internal hard disk and may be supplemented by other media such as external hard disks, USB flash drives, or optical drives that use CD-ROMs or DVD-ROMs. Peripheral equipment includes input devices (e.g., keyboard, mouse) and output devices (e.g., monitor, printer), as well as the circuitry and cabling that connect all the components. Generations of computers are characterized by their technology. First-generation digital computers, developed during and after World War II, used vacuum tubes and were enormous. The second generation, introduced *c.* 1960, used transistors and were the first successful commercial computers. Third-generation computers (late 1960s and 1970s) were characterized by miniaturization of components and use of integrated circuits. The microprocessor chip, introduced in 1974, defines fourth-generation computers.

computer animation, also known as COMPUTER GENERATED IMAGES (CGI), Form of animated graphics that has replaced "stop-motion" animation of scale-model puppets or drawings. Efforts to lessen the labour and costs of animation have led to simplification and computerization. Computers can be used in every step of sophisticated animation—for example, to automate the movement of the rostrum camera or to supply the in-between drawings for full animation. When a three-dimensional figure is translated into computer terms (digitized), the computer can generate and display a sequence of images that seem to move or rotate the object through space. Hence computer animation can simulate highly complex motion for medical and other scientific researchers, as well as for feature films.

computer science, Study of computers, their design, and their uses for computation, data processing, and systems control, including design and development of computer hardware and software and programming. The field encompasses theory, mathematical activities such as design and analysis of algorithms, performance studies of systems and their components, and estimation of reliability and availability of systems by probabilistic techniques. Because computer systems are often too large and complicated for failure or success of a design to be predicted without testing, experimentation is built into the development cycle.

computer virus, Computer program designed to copy itself into other programs, with the intention of causing mischief or damage. A virus will usually execute when it is loaded into a computer's memory. On execution, it instructs its host program to copy the viral code into any number of other programs and files stored in the computer. The corrupted programs may continue to perform their intended functions while also executing the virus's instructions, thus further propagating it. The infection may transfer itself to other computers through storage devices, computer networks, and on-line systems. A harmless virus may simply cause a cryptic message to appear when the computer is turned on; a more damaging virus can destroy valuable data. Antivirus software may be used to detect and remove viruses from a computer, but the software must be updated frequently for protection against new viruses.

computerized axial tomography (CAT), Diagnostic imaging method using a low-dose beam of X-rays that crosses the body in a single plane at many different angles. Conceived by William Oldendorf and developed independently by Godfrey Hounsfield and Allan M. Cormack, who shared a 1979 Nobel Prize for their inventions, this major advance in imaging technology became generally available in the early 1970s. Detectors record the strength of the exiting X-rays; this information is then processed by computer to produce a detailed two-dimensional cross-sectional image of the body. A series of such images in parallel planes or around an axis can show the location of abnormalities (especially tumours and other masses) more precisely than can conventional X-ray images.

Conakry, Capital (regional pop., 1999 est.: 1,764,000), largest city, and chief Atlantic port of Guinea. Located on Tombo Island and the Kaloum Peninsula, it was founded by the French in 1884. It became the capital successively of the protectorate of Rivières du Sud (1891), the colony of French Guinea (1893), and independent Guinea (1958). Tombo Island, the site of the original settlement, is linked to the peninsula by a causeway. The city was industrialized in the 1950s after iron mining and bauxite production had been developed. It is the seat of the University of Conakry (1962).

concentration camp, Internment centre established by a government to confine political prisoners or members of national or minority groups for reasons of state security, exploitation, or punishment. The prisoners are usually selected by executive decree or military order. Camps are usually built to house many people, typically in highly crowded conditions. Countries that have used such camps include Britain during the South African War, the Soviet Union, the U.S., and Japan, which interned Dutch civilians in the Dutch East Indies during World War II. A variation, called a "reeducation camp," was used in Vietnam after 1975 and in Cambodia under the Khmer Rouge. Most notorious were the death camps of Nazi Germany, including Auschwitz, Bergen-Belsen, Buchenwald, Dachau, and Treblinka.

concept formation, Process of developing abstract rules or mental constructs based on sensory experience. Concept formation figures prominently in cognitive development and was a subject of great importance to Jean Piaget, who argued that learning entails an understanding of a phenomenon's characteristics and how they are logically linked. Noam Chomsky later argued that certain cognitive structures (such as basic grammatical rules) are innate in human beings. Both scholars held that, as a concept emerges, it becomes subject to testing: a child's concept of "bird," for example, will be tested against specific instances of birds. The human capacity for play contributes importantly to this process by allowing for consideration of a wide range of possibilities.

conceptual art, Any of various art forms in which the idea for a work of art is considered more important than the finished product. The theory was explored by Marcel Duchamp from c. 1910, but the term was coined in the late 1950s by Edward Kienholz. In the 1960s and '70s it became a major international movement; its leading exponents were Sol LeWitt (1928–2007) and Joseph Kosuth (b. 1945). Its adherents radically redefined art objects, materials, and techniques, and began questioning the very existence and use of art. Its claim is that the "true" work of art is not a physical object produced by the artist for exhibition or sale, but rather consists of "concepts" or "ideas." Typical conceptual works include photographs, texts, maps, graphs, and image-text combinations that are deliberately rendered visually uninteresting or trivial in order to divert attention to the "ideas" they express. Its manifestations have been extremely diverse; a well-known example is Kosuth's *One and Three Chairs* (1965), which combines a real chair, a photograph of a chair, and a dictionary definition of "chair." Conceptual art was fundamental to much of the art produced in the late 20th century.

Concert of Europe, In the post-Napoleonic era, the consensus among the European monarchies favoring preservation of the territorial and political status quo. The term assumed the responsibility and the right of the great powers to intervene in states threatened by internal rebellion. The powers discussed such intervention at several congresses, including those of Aix-la-Chapelle, Troppau, Laibach, and Verona.

concertina, Portable bellows-operated musical instrument. The first concertina was patented by Sir Charles Wheatstone in London in 1829, and he later produced an instrument with full chromatic capacity. Like the accordion, its sound is produced by free reeds, but it uses buttons rather than keys. The very similar Argentinian bandoneon is square rather than hexagonal.

concerto, Musical composition for solo instrument and orchestra. The solo concerto grew out of the older concerto grosso. Giuseppe Torelli's violin concertos of 1698 are the first known solo concertos. Antonio Vivaldi, the first important concerto composer, wrote more than 350 solo concertos, mostly for violin. Johann Sebastian Bach wrote the first keyboard concertos. From the Classical period on, most concertos have been written for piano, followed in popularity by the violin and then the cello. Wolfgang Amadeus Mozart wrote 27 piano concertos; other notable composers of piano concertos include Ludwig van Beethoven, Felix Mendelssohn, Frédéric Chopin, Franz Liszt, and Johannes Brahms. From the outset the concerto has been almost exclusively a three-movement form, with fast tempos in the first and third movements and a slow central movement. It has generally been intended to display the soloist's virtuosity, particularly in the unaccompanied and often improvised cadenzas near the ends of the first and third movements. Nineteenth-century concertos were often conceived as a kind of dramatic struggle between soloist and orchestra; many later composers preferred that the soloist blend with the orchestra.

concerto grosso, Principal orchestral music of the Baroque era, characterized by contrast between a small group of soloists and a larger orchestra. The small group (concertino) usually consisted of two violins and continuo, the instruments of the older trio so-

nata, though wind instruments were also used. The larger group (ripieno) generally consisted of strings with continuo. Alessandro Stradella (1642–82) wrote the first known concerto grosso c. 1675. Arcangelo Corelli's set of 12 (c. 1680–90), Johann Sebastian Bach's *Brandenburg Concertos* (c. 1720), and George Frideric Handel's Opus 6 concertos (c. 1740) are the most celebrated examples. From 1750 the concerto grosso was eclipsed by the solo concerto.

Conciliar Movement (1409–49) In Roman Catholicism, an effort to strengthen the authority of church councils over that of the papacy. Originally aimed at ending the Western Schism, the Conciliar Movement had its roots in legal and intellectual circles in the 13th century but emerged as a force at the Council of Pisa (1409), which elected a third pope in an unsuccessful attempt to reconcile the parties of the existing pope and antipope. A second council, the Council of Constance (1414–18), ended the schism by voiding all papal offices and electing a new pope. Participants hoped to play an ongoing role in the church, but the popes continued to seek supremacy, and the Council of Basel (1431–49) ended fruitlessly.

conclave, In the Roman Catholic church, the assembly of cardinals gathered to elect a new pope and the system of strict seclusion to which they submit. From 1059 the election became the responsibility of the cardinals. When, after the death of Clement IV (1268), the cardinals dithered for more than two years, the local magistrate locked them in the episcopal palace and fed them only bread and water until they elected Gregory X. The system of meeting in closed conclave was codified in 1904 by Pius X. Voting is by secret ballot; one ballot is held on the first afternoon of the conclave and four on each subsequent day, two in the morning and two in the afternoon, until a new pope is chosen. In 1996 John Paul II declared that, after 30 ballots, the traditional requirement of a two-thirds majority plus one for the election of a pope could be superseded, at the discretion of the cardinals, by election by a simple majority. Ballots are burned in a stove after each vote, and the smoke produced by their burning, which issues from a special pipe through a window, indicates to the crowd assembled in St. Peter's Square whether a new pope has been elected: if there is a new pope, the smoke will be white; if no majority has yet been reached, the smoke will be black. In addition, bells will be rung to confirm the signal. Additives are mixed with the ballots to ensure the proper colour of the smoke.

Concordat of 1801, Agreement between Napoleon and Pope Pius VII that defined the status of the Roman Catholic Church in France and ended the breach caused by the church reforms of the French Revolution. The Roman Catholic faith was acknowledged as the religion of the majority of the French people but was not proclaimed as the established religion of the state. Napoleon gained the right to nominate bishops, but their offices were conferred by the pope. The government agreed to pay the clergy, but confiscated church property was not restored. The Concordat remained in effect until 1905.

A British Airways Concorde taking off from Heathrow Airport near London, on Nov. 7, 2001, en route to New York City.
David Parker—BWP Media/Getty Images

Concorde, First supersonic passenger-carrying commercial airplane. It was built jointly by British and French manufacturers and was in regular service from 1976 to 2003. Its maximum cruising speed was 2,179 km (1,354 mi) per hour, more than twice the speed of sound. A London–New York flight took less than four hours on the Concorde, but financial losses on the plane finally led both the British and French airlines to withdraw it from service.

concubinage, Cohabitation of a man and a woman without the full sanctions of legal marriage. In the Judeo-Christian tradition, the term *concubine* has been generally applied exclusively to women; Western studies of non-Western societies use it to refer to partners who are sanctioned by law but lack the status of full wives.

concussion, Period of nervous-function impairment that results from relatively mild brain injury, often with no bleeding in the cerebral cortex. It causes brief unconsciousness, followed by mental confusion and physical difficulties. These effects usually clear up within hours, but in some cases disturbance of consciousness continues, and there may be residual symptoms. Some level of amnesia often accompanies concussion. Recovery from concussion is almost always complete unless more serious injury, such as skull fracture, accompanies it.

condensation, Formation of a liquid or solid from its vapour. Condensation usually occurs on a surface that is cooler than the adjacent gas. A substance condenses when the pressure exerted by its vapour exceeds the vapour pressure of its liquid or solid phase at the temperature of the surface where the condensation is to occur. The process causes the release of thermal energy. Condensation occurs on a glass of cold water on a warm, humid day when water vapour in the air condenses to form liquid water on the glass's colder surface. Condensation also accounts for the formation of dew, fog, rain, snow, and clouds.

condor, Either of two species of large New World vultures. Two of the largest flying birds, each is about 4 ft (1.2 m) long. Both feed on dead animals. The Andean condor (*Vultur gryphus*), which ranges from the Pacific coast of South America to the high Andes Mountains, has slightly longer wings (10 ft [3 m]) and is black with a white ruff and bare pinkish head and neck. The California condor (*Gymnogyps californianus*) is nearly black, with white wing linings, a bare yellow head, and a red neck. It hovered on the brink of extinction in the 1980s, and every California condor was captured. Careful nurturing has since led to the release of more than 200 condors into the wild.

conducting, Art of leading a group of musical performers. Simple coordination of a group does not always require a conductor (members of a Renaissance choir kept together by one tapping another on the shoulder, for example, and musicians in a recording studio listen to a "click track" on headphones). Before *c.* 1800, the first violinist usually gave the few necessary signals with his bow; the keyboard player might also lead the orchestra, using his hands and head. In the 19th century the larger size of ensembles and growing complexity of music, including its varying tempos and heightened expressiveness, made it necessary for a person to coordinate and interpret the music for the group. The first conductors, including Felix Mendelssohn, Hector Berlioz, and Richard Wagner, were composers themselves. By the end of the 19th century, conducting had become a specialty and the great conductors had become celebrities in their own right.

conductor, Any of various substances that allow the flow of electric current or thermal energy. A conductor is a poor insulator because it has a low resistance to such flow. Electrical conductors are used to conduct electric current, as in the metal wires of an electric circuit. Electrical conductors are usually metallic. Thermal conductors allow thermal energy to flow because they do not absorb radiant heat; they include materials such as metal and glass.

Confederate States of America, or CONFEDERACY, Government of the 11 Southern states that seceded from the Union in 1860–61 until its defeat in the American Civil War in 1865. In the months following Abraham Lincoln's election as president in 1860, seven states of the Deep South (Alabama, Florida, Georgia, Louisiana, Mississippi, South Carolina, and Texas) seceded. After the attack on Fort Sumter in April 1861, Arkansas, North Caro-

lina, Tennessee, and Virginia joined them. The government was directed by Jefferson Davis as president, with Alexander H. Stephens as vice president. Its principal goals were the preservation of states' rights and the institution of slavery. The government's main concern was raising and maintaining an army. It counted on the influence of King Cotton to exert financial and diplomatic pressure on the Union from sympathetic European governments. Battlefield victories for the South in 1861–62 gave the Confederacy the moral strength to continue fighting, but from 1863 dwindling finances and battlefield reverses increasingly led to demoralization. The surrender at Appomattox Court House by Gen. Robert E. Lee precipitated its dissolution.

Confederation of the Rhine (1806–13) Union of all the states of Germany, except Austria and Prussia, under the aegis of Napoleon. Napoleon's primary interest in the confederation, which enabled the French to unify and dominate the country, was as a counterweight to Austria and Prussia. The confederation was abolished after Napoleon's fall from power, but the consolidation it entailed contributed to the movement for German unification.

Confessing Church, German BEKENNENDE KIRCHE, Movement for revival within the German Protestant churches that developed in the 1930s in resistance to Adolf Hitler's attempt to make the churches an instrument of Nazi propaganda and politics. The Confessing Church, whose leaders included Martin Niemöller and Dietrich Bonhoeffer, opposed Hitler's "German Christians" and was forced underground as Nazi pressure intensified. The movement continued in World War II, though it was hampered by the conscription of clergy and laity. In 1948 the church ceased to exist when the reorganized Evangelical Church was formed.

confession, In the Judeo-Christian tradition, acknowledgment of sinfulness, in public or private, regarded as necessary for divine forgiveness. In the Temple period, Yom Kippur included a collective expression of sinfulness, and the day continues in Judaism as one of prayer, fasting, and confession. The early Christian Church followed John the Baptist's practice of confession before baptism, but soon instituted confession and penance for the forgiveness of sins committed after baptism. The fourth Lateran Council (1215) required annual confession. The Roman Catholic and Eastern Orthodox churches consider penance a sacrament, but most Protestant churches do not.

confirmation, Christian rite in which believers reaffirm the faith into which they were baptized as infants or young children. The rite admitting adults to full membership in the community of the faithful did not exist as a distinct ceremony in the early church but probably coincided with baptism, since those who joined did so as adults and were baptized after instruction. As baptism of infants became common, some means of ascertaining their knowledge and commitment as young adults became necessary. A period of instruction was introduced, after which the candidates were examined and confirmed. In Roman Catholicism confirmation became a sacrament, usually performed by a bishop. The rite is also used in the Anglican and Lutheran churches.

Confucianism, Scholarly tradition and way of life propagated by Confucius in the 6th–5th century BC and followed by the Chinese for more than two millennia. Though not organized as a religion, it has deeply influenced East Asian spiritual and political life in a comparable manner. The core idea is *ren* ("humaneness," "benevolence"), signifying excellent character in accord with *li* (ritual norms), *zhong* (loyalty to one's true nature), *shu* (reciprocity), and *xiao* (filial piety). Together these constitute *de* (virtue). Mencius, Xunzi, and others sustained Confucianism, but it was not influential until Dong Zhongshu emerged in the 2nd century BC. Confucianism was then recognized as the Han state cult, and the Five Classics became the core of education. In spite of the influence of Daoism and Buddhism, Confucian ethics have had the strongest influence on the moral fabric of Chinese society. A revival of Confucian thought in the 11th century produced Neo-Confucianism, a major influence in Korea during the Chosŏn dynasty and in Japan during the Tokugawa period.

Confucius, Chinese KONGFUZI, or K'UNG-FU-TZU (b. 551 BC, Ch'ü-fu, state of Lu—d. 479, Lu), Ancient Chinese teacher, philosopher, and political theorist. Born into a poor family, he managed stables and worked as a bookkeeper while educating himself. Mastery of the six arts—ritual, music, archery, charioteering, calligraphy, and arithmetic—and familiarity with history and poetry enabled him to begin a brilliant teaching career in his thirties. Confucius saw education as a process of constant self-improvement and held that its primary function was the training of noblemen (*junzi*). He saw public service as the natural consequence of education and sought to revitalize Chinese social institutions, including the family, school, community, state, and kingdom. He served in government posts, eventually becoming minister of justice in Lu, but his policies attracted little interest. After a 12-year self-imposed exile during which his circle of students expanded, he returned to Lu at age 67 to teach and write. His life and thoughts are recorded in the *Lunyu* (*Analects*).

congestive heart failure, Heart failure resulting in the accumulation of fluid in the lungs and other body tissues. It is related mainly to salt and water retention in the tissues rather than directly to reduced blood flow. Blood pools in the veins (vascular congestion) because the heart does not pump efficiently enough to allow it to return. It may vary from the most minimal symptoms to sudden pulmonary edema or a rapidly lethal shocklike state. Chronic states of varying severity may last years. Symptoms tend to worsen as the body's attempts to compensate for the condition create a vicious circle. The patient has trouble breathing, at first during exertion and later even at rest. Treatment is directed toward increasing the strength of the heart's muscle contraction, reduction of fluid accumulation, and elimination of the underlying cause of the failure.

Congo, Democratic Republic of the, also called CONGO (KINSHASA), formerly (1971–97) REPUBLIC OF ZAIRE, Country, central Africa. Area: 905,568 sq mi (2,345,410 sq km). Population: (2011 est.) 67,758,000. Capital: Kinshasa. Bantu speakers, including the Mongo, the Kongo, and the Luba, form a majority of the country's population; among non-Bantu speakers are Sudanese groups of the north. Languages: French (official); Lingala, Swahili, Kongo, Tshiluba (all national); many others. Religions: Christianity (Roman Catholic, Protestant, other Christians), traditional beliefs, Islam. Currency: Congolese franc. The country, having the third largest land area in Africa, occupies the heart of the Congo River basin and is largely surrounded by high plateaus. At its narrow strip of Atlantic coast, the Congo River empties into the sea. The country straddles the Equator; its climate is humid and tropical. It is among the poorest countries in the world. Its economy is based on mining and agriculture. Exports include diamonds, petroleum, and coffee; mining produces copper, cobalt, and industrial diamonds. The country is a unitary multiparty republic with a bicameral legislature; the head of state is the president, and the head of government is the prime minister. Prior to European colonization, several kingdoms had emerged in the region, including the 16th-century Luba kingdom and the Kuba federation, which reached its peak in the 18th century. European development began late in the 19th century when King Leopold II of Belgium financed Henry Morton Stanley's exploration of the Congo River. The 1884–85 Berlin West Africa Conference recognized the Congo Free State with Leopold as its sovereign. The growing demand for rubber helped finance the exploitation of the Congo, but abuses against local peoples outraged Western nations and forced Leopold to grant the Free State a colonial charter as the Belgian Congo (1908). Independence was granted in 1960. The postindependence period was marked by unrest, culminating in a military coup that brought Gen. Mobutu Sese Seko to power in 1965. He changed the country's name to Zaire in 1971. Mismanagement, corruption,

and increasing violence devastated the infrastructure and the economy. Mobutu was deposed in 1997, and the country's name was restored to Congo. Instability in neighbouring countries, an influx of refugees from Rwanda, and a desire for Congo's mineral wealth led to military involvement by various African countries, which fueled existing civil conflict in Congo. Although unrest continued in the beginning of the 21st century, it was somewhat abated by the promulgation in 2003 of a transitional constitution and by the formation of a transitional unity government that included most rebel groups; a new constitution was promulgated and a formal government elected in 2006.

Congo, Republic of the, known as CONGO (BRAZZAVILLE), formerly MIDDLE CONGO, Republic, west-central Africa. Area: 132,047 sq mi (342,000 sq km). Population: (2011 est.) 3,920,000. Capital: Brazzaville. Roughly half of the population belongs to one of the Kongo tribes. The Teke are less numerous, as are the Mboshi and several other peoples. Languages: French (official), various Bantu languages. Religions: Christianity (mostly Roman Catholic, also independent Christians and Protestants); also traditional beliefs. Currency: CFA franc. A narrow coastal plain edges Congo's 100-mi (160-km) stretch of Atlantic coastline, rising into low mountains and plateaus that slope eastward in a vast plain to the Congo River. The country straddles the Equator; rainforests cover nearly two-thirds of the land, and wildlife is abundant. Congo has a mixed, developing economy. Mining products, crude petroleum, and natural gas account for more than 90% of the country's exports. Congo is a republic with a bicameral legislature; the president serves as head of state and government. In precolonial days the area was home to several thriving kingdoms, including the Kongo, which had its beginnings in the 14th century CE. The slave trade began in the 15th century with the arrival of the Portuguese; it supported the local kingdoms and dominated the area until its suppression in the 19th century. The French arrived in the mid-19th century and established treaties with two of the kingdoms, placing them under French protection prior to their becoming part of the colony of French Congo. In 1910 the colony was renamed French Equatorial Africa, and the area of the Congo became known as Middle (Moyen) Congo. In 1946 Middle Congo became a French overseas territory, and in 1958 it voted to become an autonomous republic within the French Community. Full independence came two years later. The area has suffered from political instability since independence. Congo's first president was ousted in 1963. A Marxist party, the Congolese Labor Party, gained strength; in 1968 another coup, led by Maj. Marien Ngouabi, created the People's Republic of the Congo. Ngouabi was assassinated in 1977. A series of military rulers followed, at first militantly socialist but later oriented toward social democracy. Fighting between local militias in 1997 badly disrupted the economy, and although a 2003 peace agreement largely ended the conflict, sporadic violence continued.

Congo River, or ZAIRE RIVER, River, west-central Africa. Rising in Zambia as the Chambeshi and flowing 2,900 mi (4,700 km) through the Democratic Republic of the Congo to the Atlantic Ocean, it is the second longest river in Africa. It flows through three contrasting regions: the upper Congo, characterized by lakes, waterfalls, and rapids; the middle Congo, with seven cataracts known as Boyoma (Stanley) Falls; and the lower Congo, which divides into two branches forming a vast lake area called the Malebo (Stanley) Pool.

Congregationalism, Movement that arose among English Protestant Christian churches in the late 16th and early 17th century. It developed as one branch of Puritanism and emphasized the right and duty of each congregation to govern itself independent of higher human authority. Its greatest influence and numbers were in the U.S., where Puritans first established it at Plymouth Colony. The Half-Way Covenant (1662) loosened requirements for church membership, and the Great Awakening led U.S. Congregationalism away from its Calvinist roots. Many churches defected to Unitarianism. In general, Congregationalists eschew creeds and emphasize preaching over sacraments, accepting only baptism and the Eucharist. English Congregationalists are now part of the United Reform Church. Most American Congregationalists are now part of the United Church of Christ. Baptist, Disciples of Christ, and Unitarian Universalist churches also practice congregational polity.

conic section, Any two-dimensional curve traced by the intersection of a right circular cone with a plane. If the plane is perpendicular to the cone's axis, the resulting curve is a circle. Intersections at other angles result in ellipses, parabolas, and hyperbolas. The conic sections are studied in Euclidean geometry to analyze their physical properties and in analytic geometry to derive their equations. In either context, they have useful applications to optics, antenna design, structural engineering, and architecture.

conifer, Any member of the order Pinales, woody plants that bear their seeds and pollen on separate, cone-shaped structures. They constitute the largest division of gymnosperms, with more than 550 species. Most are evergreen, upright trees and shrubs. They grow throughout the world (except in Antarctica) and prefer temperate climate zones. Conifers include the pines (*Pinus*), junipers (*Juniperus*), spruces (*Picea*), hemlocks (*Tsuga*), firs (*Abies*), larches (*Larix*), yews (*Taxus*), cypresses (*Cupressus*), bald cypresses (*Taxodium*), Douglas firs (*Pseudotsuga*), arborvitaes (*Thuja*), and related groups. They include the world's smallest and tallest trees. Conifers supply softwood timber used for general construction, mine timbers, fence posts, poles, boxes and crates, and other articles, as well as pulpwood for paper. The wood is also used as fuel and in the manufacture of cellulose products, plywood, and veneers. The trees are the source of resins, volatile oils, turpentine, tars, and pharmaceuticals. Conifer leaves vary in shape but generally have a reduced surface area to minimize water loss. Especially in the pines, firs, and spruces, the leaves are long and stiff and are commonly referred to as needles. Cypresses, cedars, and others have smaller, scalelike leaves. Conifers were the dominant type of vegetation just before the advent of angiosperms.

conjoined twins, or SIAMESE TWINS, Identical twins whose embryos did not separate completely. Conjoined twins are physically joined (typically along the trunk or at the front, side, or back of the head) and often share some organs. Symmetrical conjoined twins usually have no birth anomalies except at the areas of fusion and can sometimes be separated by surgery. In asymmetrical conjoined twins, one is fairly well developed, but the other is severely underdeveloped and dependent on the larger twin for nutrition. The underdeveloped twin may have to be surgically separated to save the larger twin. The term originally referred to Chang and Eng, born in 1811 in Siam, who were joined by a ligament from breastbone to navel. Widely exhibited, they married two sisters and fathered several children.

conjunctivitis, Inflammation of the conjunctiva, the delicate lining of the eyelids and the front of the white of the eye. It may be caused by infection (when it is commonly called "pink eye"), chemical burn, physical injury, or allergy. Often the cornea is also inflamed (keratoconjunctivitis). Infectious causes include several viruses and bacteria, including those that cause trachoma and gonorrhea, both of which can lead to blindness. Conjunctivitis from erythema multiforme, a skin eruption, can also cause blindness.

connectionism, In cognitive science, an approach that proposes to model human information processing in terms of a network of interconnected units operating in parallel. The units are typically classified as input units, hidden units, or output units. Each unit has a default activation level that can vary as a function of the strength of (1) the inputs it receives from other units, (2) the different weights associated with its connections to the other units, and (3) its own bias. Connectionism, unlike traditional computational models in cognitive science, holds that information is distributed throughout entire networks instead of being localized in functionally discrete, semantically interpretable states.

conquistador, Any of a small group of adventurers who took part in the Spanish conquest of South and Central America in the 16th century. Under Hernán Cortés a force of some 500 men with 16 horses conquered Mexico's Aztec empire. A force under Pedro de Alvarado subsequently subdued Guatemala. Francisco Pizarro defeated the Inca in Peru with 180 men and 37 horses; his companion Diego de Almagro led an expedition to Chile. Further expeditions extended Spanish rule over much of South America. Though renowned for their bravery, the conquistadores remain notorious for their avarice and the destruction they wrought on native populations and civilizations. They were soon replaced by administrators and settlers from Spain.

consciousness, Quality or state of being aware. As applied to the lower animals, consciousness refers to the capacity for sensation and, usually, simple volition. In higher animals, this capacity may also include thinking and emotion. In human beings, consciousness is understood to include "meta-awareness," an awareness that one is aware. The term also refers broadly to the upper level of mental life of which the person is aware, as contrasted with unconscious processes. Levels of consciousness (e.g., attention vs. sleep) are correlated with patterns of electrical activity in the brain (brain waves).

conscription, or DRAFT, Compulsory enrollment for service in a country's armed forces. It has existed at least since the Egyptian Old Kingdom in the 27th century BC. It usually takes the form of selective service rather than universal conscription. (The latter generally refers to compulsory military service by all able-bodied men between certain ages, though a few countries—notably Israel—have also drafted women.) In the 19th century Prussia's system of building up a large standing army through conscription became the model for competing European powers. During the American Civil War both the federal government and the Confederacy instituted a draft, but the U.S. did not use it again until entering World War I in 1917. Like the U.S., Britain abandoned conscription at the end of World War I but reverted to it when World War II threatened. During the ensuing Cold War, Britain retained the draft until 1960 and the U.S. until 1973.

consequentialism, In ethics, the doctrine that actions should be judged right or wrong on the basis of their consequences. The simplest form of consequentialism is classical (or hedonistic) utilitarianism, which asserts that an action is right or wrong according to whether it maximizes the net balance of pleasure over pain in the universe. The consequentialism of G.E. Moore, known as "ideal utilitarianism," recognizes beauty and friendship, as well as pleasure, as intrinsic goods that one's actions should aim to maximize. According to the "preference utilitarianism" of R.M. Hare (1919–2002), actions are right if they maximize the satisfaction of preferences or desires, no matter what the preferences may be for. Consequentialists also differ over whether each individual action should be judged on the basis of its consequences or whether instead general rules of conduct should be judged in this way and individual actions judged only by whether they accord with a general rule. The former group are known as "act-utilitarians" and the latter as "rule-utilitarians." *See also* deontological ethics.

conservation law, or LAW OF CONSERVATION, In physics, the principle that certain quantities within an isolated system do not change over time. When a substance in an isolated system changes phase, the total amount of mass does not change. When energy is changed from one form to another in an isolated system, there is no change in the total amount of energy. When a transfer of momentum occurs in an isolated system, the total amount of momentum is conserved. The same is true for electric charge in a system: charge lost by one particle is gained by another. Conservation laws make it possible to predict the macroscopic behaviour of a system without having to consider the microscopic details of a physical process or chemical reaction.

conservatism, Political attitude or ideology denoting a preference for institutions and practices that have evolved historically and are thus manifestations of continuity and stability. It was first expressed in the modern era through the works of Edmund Burke in reaction to the French Revolution, which Burke believed tarnished its ideals through its excesses. Conservatives believe that the implementation of change should be minimal and gradual; they appreciate history and are more realistic than idealistic. Well-known conservative parties include the British Conservative Party, the German Christian Democratic Union, the U.S. Republican Party, and the Japanese Liberal-Democratic Party.

Conservative Judaism, Form of Judaism that mediates between Reform Judaism and Orthodox Judaism. Founded in 19th-century Germany as the Historical School, it arose among German-Jewish theologians who advocated change but found Reform positions extreme. They accepted the Reform emphasis on critical scholarship, but wished to maintain a stricter observance of Jewish law (e.g., dietary laws) and continued belief in the coming of the messiah. In 1886, rabbis of this centrist persuasion founded the Jewish Theological Seminary of America (New York), leading to the development of Conservative Judaism as a religious movement.

conservatory, In architecture, a heavily glazed structure, frequently attached to and directly entered from a dwelling, in which plants are protected and displayed. Unlike the greenhouse, an informal structure situated in the working area of a garden, the conservatory became a popular 19th-century decorative architectural feature proclaiming the status of its owner. The most outstanding example is Joseph Paxton's Crystal Palace.

consonance and dissonance, Perceived qualities of musical chords and intervals. Consonance is often described as relative "stability," and dissonance as "instability." In musical contexts, certain intervals seem to call for motion by one of the tones to "resolve" perceived dissonance. The most consonant intervals are generally recognized as the unison and octave, and the next most consonant interval as the perfect fifth. Consonance tends to reflect the early intervals of the overtone series (which include, in addition to the octave and perfect fifth, the major and minor thirds and the perfect fourth), but many musical factors can affect the perception of consonance and dissonance.

consonant, Any speech sound characterized by an articulation in which a closure or narrowing of the vocal tract completely or partially blocks the flow of air; also, any letter or symbol representing such a sound. Consonants are usually classified according to the place of articulation (e.g., palate, teeth, lips); the manner of articulation, as in stops (complete closure of the oral passage, released with a burst of air), fricatives (forcing of breath through a constricted passage), and trills (vibration of the tip of the tongue or the uvula); and the presence or absence of voicing, nasalization, aspiration, and other features.

Constance, Council of (1414–18) 16th ecumenical council of the Roman Catholic church. It was convened at the request of Emperor Sigismund to deal with three competing popes, examine the writings of Jan Hus and John Wycliffe, and reform the Church. National political rivalries divided the Council of Constance. Two of the three contending popes were deposed; the third abdicated, and in 1417 the council selected a new pope, Martin V. The Council condemned propositions of Hus and Wycliffe, and Hus was burned at the stake by secular authorities.

Constance, Lake, German BODENSEE, ancient LACUS BRIGANTINUS, Lake, bordering Switzerland, Germany, and Austria. Occupying an old glacier basin at an elevation of 1,299 ft (396 m), it has an area of 209 sq mi (541 sq km) and an average depth of 295 ft (90 m). It forms part of the course of the Rhine River, and by the Middle Ages it was a major traffic hub. Spectacular Alpine scenery makes the lakeshore a popular resort area. The remains of Neolithic lake dwellings are found in the area.

Constanţa, Turkish KÖSTENDJE, ancient CONSTANTIANA, or TOMIS, City (pop., 2002: 715,151), chief seaport of Romania. The first known settlement in the area was at the ancient city of Tomis, founded in the 7th century BC by the Greeks. Romans annexed the region in the 1st century BC; Ovid was exiled there in AD 9–17. In the 4th century Tomis was reconstructed by Constantine the Great and renamed Constantiana. It was subject to numerous invasions from the 6th century on, and it declined following the Turkish conquest in the early 15th century. Its modern development as an industrial, trading, and cultural centre dates from its return to Romania in 1878.

Constantine, ancient CIRTA, City (pop., 2004 est.: 544,700), northeastern Algeria. A natural fortress, it is situated on a rocky height some 800 ft (250 m) above the Rhumel River valley. By the 3rd century BC it was one of Numidia's most important towns, and it reached its apex of prosperity under Micipsa in the 2nd century BC. Ruined in subsequent wars, it was restored in AD 313 and renamed for its patron, the Roman emperor Constantine the Great. Overrun by the Arabs in the 7th century, it was ruled by a series of Arab and Berber (Amazigh) dynasties and, intermittently, by the Ottoman Empire until it was captured by the French in 1837. Occupied in 1942 by U.S. troops, it was an important Allied staging area in World War II (1939–45). The city retains its medieval walls, and there are Roman ruins nearby. It is an agricultural market for the surrounding area.

Constantine I, known as CONSTANTINE THE GREAT, officially FLAVIUS VALERIUS CONSTANTINUS (b. Feb. 27, after 280? CE, Naissus, Moesia—d. May 22, 337, Ancyrona, near Nicomedia, Bithynia), First Roman emperor to profess Christianity. The eldest son of Constantius I Chlorus, he spent his youth at the court of Diocletian. Passed over as successor to the throne, he fought to make himself emperor. Victory at the Milvian Bridge outside Rome (312) made him emperor in the West. According to legend, a cross and the words *in hoc signo vinces* ("In this sign, conquer") appeared to him there, and he forthwith adopted Christianity. In 313 he issued, with Licinius, the Edict of Milan, granting tolerance to Christians; he also gave land for churches and granted the church special privileges. He opposed heresies, notably Donatism and Arianism,

Marble colossal head of Constantine the Great, part of the remains of a giant statue from the Basilica of Constantine, in the Roman Forum, c. AD 313.
Hirmer Fotoarchiv, Munich

and he convoked the Council of Nicaea. After defeating and executing Licinius, he gained control of the East and became sole emperor. He moved the capital from Rome to Byzantium, which he renamed Constantinople (324). In 326 he had his wife and eldest son killed for reasons that remain obscure. He angered the Romans by refusing to participate in a pagan rite and never entered Rome again. Under his patronage, Christianity began its growth into a world religion. Constantine is revered as a saint in the Orthodox church.

Constantinople, Council of, Any of several church councils, some of which are recognized as ecumenical, held in the city of Constantinople. The First Council of Constantinople, the second ecumenical council of the Christian church, was summoned by Emperor Theodosius I in 381. It promulgated the Nicene Creed and declared finally the Trinitarian doctrine of the equality of Father, Son, and Holy Spirit. It gave the bishop of Constantinople honour second only to that of the pope. Only Eastern bishops were summoned to the council, but the Greeks claimed that it was ecumenical. It did come to be so regarded, though the Western church did not accept the ranking of Constantinople as second to Rome until the 13th century. The Second Council of Constantinople, held in 553, was called by Justinian I; by endorsing an edict of Justinian's, it lent support to Monophysitism and diminished the earlier Council of Chalcedon. The Third Council of Constantinople, held in 680, condemned the Monothelites, who claimed that Christ had a single will despite his two natures. The Fourth Council of Constantinople, held in 869–870 at the suggestion of Basil I, resulted in the excommunication of St. Photius and increased the animosity between the Eastern and Western churches.

constellation, Any of certain groupings of stars that were imagined by those who named them to form images of objects, mythological figures, or creatures in the sky. They are useful in helping sky gazers and navigators locate certain stars. A constellation's stars are often designated by its name and letters of the Greek alphabet in order of brightness. Of 88 named constellations in Western astronomy, about half retain the names Ptolemy gave the 48 he identified in his *Almagest.*

constitution, Set of doctrines and practices that form the fundamental organizing principle of a political state. It may be written (e.g., the Constitution of the United States) or partly written and uncodified (e.g., Britain's constitution). Its provisions usually specify how the government is to be organized, what rights it shall have, and what rights shall be retained by the people. Modern constitutional ideas developed during the Enlightenment, when philosophers such as Thomas Hobbes, Jean-Jacques Rousseau, and John Locke proposed that constitutional governments should be stable, adaptable, accountable, and open, should represent the governed, and should divide power according to its purpose. The oldest constitution still in force is that of the state of Massachusetts (1780).

Constructivism, Russian movement in art and architecture, initiated in 1914 by the abstract geometric constructions of Vladimir Tatlin. In 1920 Tatlin was joined by Antoine Pevsner and Naum Gabo. Their "Realist Manifesto," which directed their followers to "construct art," gave the movement its name. The group, soon joined by Aleksandr Rodchenko and El Lissitzky, produced abstract works reflecting modern machinery and technology, using plastic, glass, and other industrial materials. Applying the same principles to architecture, they spread the movement's ideals throughout Europe and to the U.S. after Soviet opposition dispersed the group.

constructivism, Theory that interprets mathematical statements as true if and only if there is a proof of them and as false just in case there is a disproof of them. Constructivism opposes the Platonist interpretation, which construes mathematical statements as referring to a domain of timeless mathematical objects existing independently of our knowledge of them. For the constructivist, certain classically valid forms of logical inference (e.g., the law of excluded middle, the law of double negation, the postulation of infinite sets) may no longer be employed unrestrictedly in constructing mathematical proofs. The constructivist therefore recognizes fewer mathematical proofs and theorems than does the Platonist.

Consulate (1799–1804) French government established after the Coup of 18–19 Brumaire. The Constitution of the Year VIII created an executive consisting of three consuls, but the First Consul, Napoleon, wielded all real power, while the other two, Emmanuel Joseph Sieyes and Pierre-Roger Ducos (1747–1816), were figureheads. The principles of representation and legislative supremacy were discarded. The executive branch was given the power to draft new laws, and the legislative branch became little more than a rubber stamp. Elections became an elaborate charade, with voters stripped of real power. Napoleon abolished the Consulate when he declared himself emperor.

consumer price index (CPI), Measure of living costs based on changes in retail prices. Consumer price indexes are widely used to measure changes in the cost of maintaining a given standard of living. The goods and services commonly purchased by the population covered are priced periodically, and their prices are combined in proportion to their relative importance. This set of prices is compared with the initial set of prices collected in the base year to determine the percentage increase or decrease. The population covered may be restricted to wage and salary earners or to city dwellers, and special indexes may be used for special population groups (e.g., retirees). Such indexes do not take into account shifts over time in what the population buys; when modified to take subjective preferences into account, they are called constant-utility indexes. Consumer price indexes are available for more than 100 countries.

consumerism, Movement or policies aimed at regulating the products, services, methods, and standards of manufacturers, sellers, and advertisers in the interests of the buyer. Such regulation may be institutional, statutory, or embodied in a voluntary code accepted by a particular industry, or it may result more indirectly from the influence of consumer organizations. Governments often establish formal regulatory agencies to ensure consumer protection (in the U.S., e.g., the Federal Trade Commission and the Food and Drug Administration). Some of the earliest consumer-protection laws were created to prevent the sale of tainted food and harmful drugs. The U.S. consumer protection movement gained strength in the 1960s and '70s as consumer activists led by Ralph Nader lobbied for laws setting safety standards for automobiles, toys, and numerous household products. Consumer advocates have also won passage of laws obliging advertisers to represent their goods truthfully and preventing sales representatives from using deceptive sales tactics. Consumer advocacy is carried on worldwide by the International Organization of Consumers Unions (IOCU).

consumer's surplus, In economics, the difference between the total amount consumers would be willing to pay to consume the quantity of goods transacted on the market and the amount they actually have to pay for those goods. The former is generally interpreted as the monetary value of consumer satisfaction. The concept was developed in 1844 by the French civil engineer Arsène-Jules-Étienne-Juvénal Dupuit (1804–1866) and popularized by Alfred Marshall. Though economists adopted a nonquantifiable approach to consumer satisfaction in the 20th century, the concept is used extensively in the fields of welfare economics and taxation.

contact lens, Thin artificial lens worn on the surface of the eye to correct refractive defects of vision. Early glass contact lenses, invented in 1887, were uncomfortable and could not be worn long. Plastic-based lenses, made to measurements of corneal curvature taken by optical instruments, were first developed in the mid 20th century. Gas-permeable lenses allow more oxygen to reach the eye, thus increasing comfort and wear time. Contact lenses have advantages over eyeglasses for certain visual defects and may be preferred for the sake of appearance and other reasons.

containment, Strategic U.S. foreign policy of the late 1940s and early 1950s intended to check the expansionist designs of the Soviet Union through economic, military, diplomatic, and political means. It was conceived by George Kennan soon after World War II. An early application of containment was the Truman Doctrine (1947), which provided U.S. aid to Greece and Turkey. .

continent, One of seven large continuous masses of land: Asia, Africa, North America, South America, Antarctica, Europe, and Australia (listed in order of size). Europe and Asia are sometimes considered a single continent, Eurasia. The continents vary greatly in size and in ratio of coastline to total area. More than two-thirds of the world's continental land area lies north of the equator, and all the continents except Antarctica are wedge-shaped, wider in the north than in the south.

continental drift, Large-scale movements of continents over the course of geologic time. The first complete theory of continental drift was proposed in 1912 by Alfred Wegener, who postulated that a single supercontinent, which he called Pangea, fragmented late in the Triassic Period (approximately 250–200 million years ago) and that the parts began to move away from one another. He pointed to the similarity of rock strata in the Americas and Africa as evidence to support his hypothesis. Wegener's ideas received support from the concepts of seafloor spreading and plate tectonics beginning in the 1960s. The modern theory states that the Americas were joined with Europe and Africa until *c.* 190 million years ago, when they split apart along what is now the Mid-Atlantic Ridge. Subsequent tectonic plate movements took the continents to their present positions.

continental shelf, Broad, relatively shallow submarine platform that forms a border to a continent, typically extending from the coast to depths of 330–660 ft (100–200 m). Continental shelves average about 40 mi (65 km) in width. Almost everywhere they are simply a continuation of the continental landmass: narrow, rough, and steep off mountainous coasts but broad and comparatively level offshore from plains. Continental shelves are usually covered with a layer of sand, silts, and silty muds. Their surfaces feature small hills and ridges that alternate with shallow depressions and valley-like troughs. In a few cases, steep-walled V-shaped submarine canyons cut deeply into both the shelf and the slope below.

Continental System, In the Napoleonic Wars, the blockade designed by Napoleon to paralyze Britain through the destruction of British commerce. In the Decrees of Berlin (1806) and Milan (1807), France proclaimed that neutrals and French allies were not to trade with the British. The United Kingdom responded with a counterblockade, which led indirectly to the War of 1812. Because of Britain's naval superiority, the effort to enforce the system proved disastrous for Napoleon.

continuing education, or ADULT EDUCATION, Any form of learning provided for adults. In the U.S. the University of Wisconsin was the first academic institution to offer such programs (1904). Empire College of the State University of New York was the first to be devoted exclusively to adult learning (1969). Continuing education includes such diverse methods as independent study; broadcast, videotape, online, and other forms of distance learning; group discussion and study circles; conferences, seminars, and workshops; and full- or part-time classroom study. Remedial programs, such as high-school equivalency and basic literacy programs, are common. In recent years the variety of subject matter has expanded greatly to include such topics as auto repair, retirement planning, and computer skills.

continuo, or BASSO CONTINUO, In Baroque music, a special subgroup of an instrumental ensemble. It consists of two instruments reading the same part: a bass instrument, such as a cello or bassoon, and a chordal instrument, most often a harpsichord but sometimes an organ or lute. Its appearance in the early 17th century reflected the radically new musical texture of accompanied melody that was especially typical of the new vocal genre of opera.

The continuo (which has a counterpart in the bass and rhythm guitar of a rock band) came to be employed in virtually all ensemble music of the Baroque era.

contra, Member of a counterrevolutionary force that sought to overthrow Nicaragua's left-wing Sandinista government. The original contras had been National Guardsmen during the regime of Anastasio Somoza. The U.S. Central Intelligence Agency played a key role in training and funding the group, whose tactics were decried by the international human-rights community. In 1984 the U.S. Congress banned military aid to the contras; the efforts of the administration of U.S. president Ronald Reagan to circumvent the ban led to the Iran-Contra Affair. A general peace in the region was negotiated by Costa Rican president Oscar Arias Sánchez, and in 1990 Nicaraquan president Violeta Chamorro negotiated the contras' demobilization.

contraception, Birth control by prevention of conception or impregnation. The most common method is sterilization. The most effective temporary methods are nearly 99% effective if used consistently and correctly. Many methods carry health risks; barrier devices and avoidance of intercourse during the most fertile period are safest. Hormonal contraceptives use estrogen and/or progesterone to inhibit ovulation. The "morning-after pill" (high-dose hormones) is effective even after intercourse. The most serious side effect of oral contraceptives is the risk of blood-clotting disorders. Intrauterine devices (IUDs) are placed inside the uterus and appear to cause a mild endometrial inflammation that either inhibits fertilization or prevents a fertilized egg from implanting. Certain types were taken off the market in the 1970s and '80s when it was found that their side effects included a high incidence of pelvic inflammatory disease, ectopic pregnancy, and spontaneous septic abortion. Barrier devices, such as condoms, diaphragms, cervical caps, female condoms (vaginal pouches), and vaginal sponges, prevent sperm from entering the uterus. Condoms also prevent sexually transmitted disease. Used with spermicides, condoms are nearly 100% effective. Fertility awareness techniques have evolved from keeping track of the menstrual cycle (the so-called "rhythm method"; *see* menstruation) to avoid intercourse around the time of ovulation; tracking body temperature and cervical mucus consistency can raise effectiveness to more than 80%. Experimental forms of birth control include an oral contraceptive for men.

contract, Agreement between two or more parties that creates for each party a duty to do something (e.g., to provide goods at a certain price according to a specified schedule) or a duty not to do something (e.g., to divulge an employer's trade secrets or financial status to third parties). A party's failure to honour a contract allows the other party or parties to bring an action for damages in a court of law, though arbitration may also be pursued in an effort to keep the matter confidential. In order to be valid, a contract must be entered into both willingly and freely. A contract that violates this principle, including one made with a legal minor or a person deemed mentally incompetent, may be declared unenforceable. A contract also must have a lawful objective.

control system, Means by which a set of variable quantities is held constant or caused to vary in a prescribed way. Control systems are intimately related to the concept of automation but have an ancient history. Roman engineers maintained water levels in aqueducts by means of floating valves that opened and closed at appropriate levels. James Watt's flyball governor (1769) regulated steam flow to a steam engine to maintain constant engine speed despite a changing load. In World War II, control-system theory was applied to anti-aircraft batteries and fire-control systems. The introduction of analog and digital computers opened the way for much greater complexity in automatic control theory.

convection, Process by which heat is transferred by movement of a heated fluid such as air or water. Most fluids expand when heated. They become less dense and more buoyant, and so rise. The heated molecules eventually cool, become more dense, and sink. This repeated process sets up convection currents that account for the uniform heating of the air in a room or water in a kettle. Air convection can be forced by a fan, and water convection by a pump. Atmospheric convection currents can be set up by local heating effects such as solar radiation or contact with cold surfaces. Such currents are usually vertical and account for atmospheric phenomena such as clouds and thunderstorms.

Cook, James, known as CAPTAIN COOK (b. Oct. 27, 1728, Marton-in-Cleveland, Yorkshire, Eng.—d. Feb. 14, 1779, Kealakekua Bay, Hawaii), British sailor and explorer. He joined the Royal Navy (1755) and in 1763–67 surveyed the St. Lawrence River and the coast of Newfoundland. In 1768 he was appointed commander of the first scientific expedition to the Pacific. Sailing on the HMS *Endeavour*, he found and charted all of New Zealand and explored the eastern coast of Australia. That voyage (1768–71) produced a wealth of scientifically collected material and was also notable for Cook's successful prevention of scurvy among crew members. Promoted to commander, he was sent with two ships to make the first circumnavigation and penetration into the Antarctic. On that expedition (1772–75), which ranks as one of the greatest of all sailing-ship voyages, he successfully completed the first west-east circumnavigation in high latitudes. On a third voyage (1776–79) in search of a Northwest Passage around Canada and Alaska, he was killed by Polynesian natives on Hawaii.

cooperative, Organization owned by and operated for the benefit of those using its services. Cooperatives have been successful in such fields as the processing and marketing of farm products and the purchasing of other kinds of equipment and raw materials, and in the wholesaling, retailing, electric power, credit and banking, and housing industries. The modern consumer cooperative traces its roots to Britain's Rochdale Society of Equitable Pioneers (1844); the movement spread quickly in northern Europe. In the U.S., agricultural marketing cooperatives developed in rural areas in the 19th century; other contemporary examples include consumer and housing cooperatives.

coordinate system, Arrangement of reference lines or curves used to identify the location of points in space. In two dimensions, the most common system is the Cartesian (after René Descartes) system. Points are designated by their distance along a horizontal (x) and vertical (y) axis from a reference point, the origin, designated (0, 0). Cartesian coordinates also can be used for three (or more) dimensions. A polar coordinate system locates a point by its direction relative to a reference direction and its distance from a given point, also the origin. Such a system is used in radar or sonar tracking and is the basis of bearing-and-range navigation systems. In three dimensions, it leads to cylindrical and spherical coordinates.

Copán, Ruined ancient Mayan city, Honduras. It lies near the Guatemalan border on the bank of the Copán River, about 35 mi (56 km) from modern Santa Rosa de Copán. An important centre of Mayan art and astronomy during the Classic Period (c. AD 250–c. 900), it was at its peak early in the 9th century and may have been home to as many as 20,000 people. The site consists of stone temples, two large pyramids, several stairways and plazas, and a ball court. It is particularly noted for the friezes on its buildings. The Maya had completely abandoned the site by c. 1200. It was designated a UNESCO World Heritage Site in 1980.

Stela with portrait sculpture, Copán, Honduras.
Walter Aguiar/EB Inc.

Copenhagen, Danish KØBENHAVN, Capital and largest city (pop., 2001: city, 499,148; metro. area, 1,081,673) of Denmark. It is located on the islands of Zealand (Sjælland) and Amager. A small village existed on the site by the early 10th century. In 1167 Bishop Absalon built a castle there and fortified the town. In 1445 Copenhagen was made the capital and the residence of the royal family. Its palaces include Amalienborg, home to the Danish monarchs, and Christiansborg, now housing Parliament. Tivoli amusement park is a popular attraction. Copenhagen is one of Europe's leading cultural and educational centres; its oldest university was founded in 1479. Historically a trade and shipping hub, it has also become an industrial city. Shipbuilding, machinery production, and canning and brewing are among the chief manufacturing activities.

copepod, Any of the 13,000 known species of crustaceans in the

Copepods (Temora)
Douglas P. Wilson

subclass Copepoda. Copepods are widely distributed and ecologically important, serving as food for many species of fish. Most species are free-living marine forms, found from the sea surface to great depths. Some live in fresh water or in damp vegetation; others are parasites. Most species are 0.02–0.08 in. (0.5–2 mm) long. The largest, a parasite of the fin whale, grows to a length of about 13 in. (32 cm). Unlike most crustaceans, copepods have no carapace. Nonparasitic forms feed on microscopic plants or animals or even on animals as large as themselves. Members of the genus *Cyclops* (order Cyclopoida) are called water fleas.

Copernican system, or COPERNICAN PRINCIPLE, Model of the solar system centred on the Sun, with Earth and other planets revolving around it, formulated by Nicolaus Copernicus in the mid 16th century. Having the Sun in this central position explained the apparent motion of planets relative to the fixed stars and was truer than the Earth-centred Ptolemaic system. Scientifically, the Copernican system led to belief in a much larger universe than before (because, if the Earth revolved around the Sun, the stars would have to be very distant not to appear to alter their position); more broadly, the Copernican principle is invoked to argue against any theory that would give the solar system a special place in the universe. Dethronement of Earth from the centre of the universe caused profound shock: the Copernican system challenged the entire system of ancient authority and required a complete change in the philosophical conception of the universe.

Copernicus, Nicolaus, Polish MIKOŁAJ KOPERNIK (b. Feb. 19, 1473, Toruń, Pol.—d. May 24, 1543, Frauenburg, East Prussia), Polish astronomer. He was educated at Kraków, Bologna, and Padua, where he mastered all the knowledge of the day in mathematics, astronomy, medicine, and theology. Elected a canon of the cathedral of Frauenburg in 1497, he took advantage of his financial security to begin his astronomical observations. His publication in 1543 of *Six Books Concerning the Revolutions of the Heavenly Orbs* marked a landmark of Western thought. Copernicus had first conceived of his revolutionary model decades earlier but delayed publication because, while it explained the retrograde motion of the planets (and resolved their order), it raised new problems that had to be explained, required verification of old observations, and had to be presented in a way that would not provoke the religious authorities. The book did not see print until he was on his deathbed. By attributing to Earth a daily rotation around its own axis and a yearly revolution around a stationary Sun, he developed an idea that had far-reaching implications for the rise of modern science. He asserted, in contrast to Platonic instrumentalism, that astronomy must describe the real, physical system of the world. Only with Johannes Kepler was Copernicus's model fully transformed into a new philosophy about the fundamental structure of the universe.

copper, Metallic chemical element, one of the transition elements, chemical symbol Cu, atomic number 29. Sometimes found in the free state in nature, it is a reddish metal, very ductile and an unusually good conductor of electricity and heat. Most of the world's copper production is used by the electrical industries; the remainder is combined with other metals (e.g., zinc, tin, nickel) to form alloys such as brass, bronze, nickel silver, and Monel. Copper is part of nearly all coinage metals. In compounds copper usually has valence 1 (cuprous) or 2 (cupric). Cuprous compounds include cuprous oxide, a red pigment and a fungicide; cuprous chloride, a catalyst for certain organic reactions; and cuprous sulfide, with a variety of uses. Cupric compounds include cupric oxide, a pigment, decolorizing agent, and catalyst; cupric chloride, a catalyst, wood preservative, mordant, disinfectant, feed additive, and pigment; and cupric sulfate, a pesticide, germicide, feed additive, and soil additive. Copper is a necessary trace element in the human diet and essential to plant growth; in blue-blooded mollusks and crustaceans it plays the same role in hemocyanin as iron does in hemoglobin.

Crystalline copper from Michigan
Courtesy of Ted Boente Collection; photograph, John H. Gerard/EB Inc.

Coptic Orthodox Church, Principal Christian church in Egypt. Until the 19th century it was called simply the Egyptian Church. It agrees doctrinally with Eastern Orthodoxy except that it holds that Jesus has a purely divine nature and never became human, a belief the Council of Chalcedon rejected in AD 451. After the Arab conquest (7th century), service books were written with Coptic and Arabic in parallel texts. Church government is democratic, and the patriarch, who resides in Cairo, is elected. There are congregations outside Egypt, especially in Australia and the U.S., and the church is in communion with the Ethiopian, Armenian, and Syrian Jacobite churches.

copyright, Exclusive right to reproduce, publish, or sell an original work of authorship. It protects from unauthorized copying any published or unpublished work that is fixed in a tangible medium (including a book or manuscript, musical score or recording, script or dramatic production, painting or sculpture, or blueprint or building). It does not protect matters such as an idea, process, or system. Protection in the U.S. now extends for the life of the creator plus 70 years after his or her death. Works made for hire are now protected for a maximum of 95 years from the date of publication or 120 years from the date of the creation of the work. In 1988 the U.S. joined the Bern Convention, an agreement that governs international copyright. The Digital Millennium Copyright Act, adopted in the U.S. in 1998, expanded owners' control over digital forms of their creations and penalized persons who sought to evade technological shields (such as encryption) for copyrighted material.

coral, Any of about 2,300 species of marine cnidarians in the class Anthozoa that are characterized by stonelike, horny, or leathery skeletons (external or internal). The skeletons of these animals are also called coral. Corals are found in warm seas worldwide. The body is of the polyp type. Soft, horny, and blue corals are colonial in habit (i.e., they live in large groups). Stony corals, the most

familiar and widely distributed forms, are both colonial and solitary. Atolls and coral reefs, which are composed of stony coral, grow at an average rate of 0.2–1.1 in. (0.5–2.8 cm) per year.

coral reef, Ridge or hummock formed in shallow ocean areas from the external skeletons of corals. The skeleton consists of calcium carbonate ($CaCO_3$), or limestone. A coral reef may grow into a permanent coral island, or it may take one of four principal forms. Fringing reefs consist of a flat reef area around a nonreef island. Barrier reefs may lie a mile or more offshore, separated from the landmass by a lagoon or channel. Atolls are circular reefs without a central landmass. Patch reefs have irregular tablelike or pinnacle features. Smaller patches occur inside atoll lagoons; larger patches occur as isolated parts of any of the other three reef categories, and they sometimes occur completely separate from other kinds of reefs.

Coral Sea, Part of the South Pacific Ocean. It is located between Queensland, Australia, on the west and Vanuatu and New Caledonia on the east, and bordered on the north by Papua New Guinea and the Solomon Islands. Occupying an area of 1,849,800 sq mi (4,791,000 sq km), it merges with the Tasman Sea and Solomon Sea and is connected to the Arafura Sea via the Torres Strait. It was named for its many coral formations, including the Great Barrier Reef. During World War II it was the scene of a strategic U.S. naval and air victory over the Japanese (1942).

Córdoba, City (pop., 2001: 1,267,521), the second largest in Argentina. It lies on the Primero River along the foothills of the Sierra de Córdoba. Founded in 1573, its location between the coast and the interior settlements favoured its early development. In 1599 Jesuits settled in the city and founded the country's first university (1613). Córdoba's growth was stimulated by the completion of rail connections with the east in 1869 and the San Roque Dam in 1866, which provides irrigation water for orchards and grain fields and hydroelectric power for the city's many factories.

Córdoba, or CORDOVA, ancient CORDUBA, City (pop., 2001: 308,072), capital of Córdoba province, southern Spain. On the banks of the Guadalquivir River, it probably had Carthaginian origins. Occupied by the Romans in 152 BC, it became, under Augustus, the capital of the Roman province of Baetica. It declined under the Visigoths (6th–8th centuries AD), and it was captured by the Muslims in 711. Abd al-Rahman I, of the Umayyad family, made it his capital in 756 and founded the Great Mosque of Córdoba, which still stands. By the 10th century it was the largest city in Europe, filled with palaces and mosques. It fell to the Castilian king Ferdinand III in 1236 and became part of Christian Spain. Modern Córdoba's streets and buildings evoke its Moorish heritage.

core, In earth science, the part of the Earth that starts about 1,800 mi (2,900 km) beneath the surface and extends downward. It consists largely of an iron-rich metallic alloy and is thought to have a two-part structure: an outer fluid region and a solid, extremely dense inner region that measures only about 1,500 mi (2,400 km) across. The alloy composition is mainly iron with small amounts of nickel. This composition is deduced from the chemistry of iron meteorites that presumably came from the breakup of a planetary body that also had an iron core.

Corfu, Greek KÉRKIRA, One of the Ionian Islands, northwestern Greece. With adjacent small islands, it forms the Corfu department (pop., 2001: 111,081) of Greece; the town of Corfu (pop., 2001: 39,048) is the departmental capital. Corfu occupies 229 sq mi (593 sq km). It was settled by the Corinthians about 734 BC. Off its coast the first naval battle in Greek history was fought, between Corfu and Corinth about 664 BC. About 435 BC it sought the aid of Athens against Corinth, precipitating the Peloponnesian War. A Roman possession in 229 BC, it later passed to the Byzantines, then to the Normans. It was ruled by Venice from 1386 to 1797 and was under British administration from 1815 until it was ceded to Greece in 1864. Germans and Italians occupied it during World War II. It is now a popular tourist destination and produces olive oil, figs, oranges, lemons, and wine.

coriander, or CILANTRO, Feathery annual herb (*Coriandrum sativum*) of the parsley family, and its dried fruit, native to the Mediterranean and Middle East. The seeds go by the name coriander; they have a mild, fragrant aroma and aromatic taste and are used to flavour many foods. The delicate young leaves—known in the U.S. by their Spanish name, cilantro—are widely used in Latin American, Indian, and Chinese dishes.

Corinth, Greek KÓRINTHOS, Ancient city of the Peloponnese, Greece. Located on the Gulf of Corinth, the site was occupied before 3000 BC but developed as a commercial centre only in the 8th century BC. In the late 6th century BC, it was outstripped by Athens. Occupied in 338 BC by Philip II, it was destroyed in 146 BC by Rome. In 44 BC Julius Caesar reestablished Corinth as a Roman colony; the New Testament includes the letters addressed to its Christian community by St. Paul. It declined in the later Middle Ages; its ruins are near the modern city of Corinth.

Coriolis force, Apparent force that must be included if Newton's laws of motion are to be used in a rotating system. First described by Gustave-Gaspard Coriolis (1792–1843) in 1835, the force acts to the right of the direction of body motion for counterclockwise rotation and to the left for clockwise rotation. On Earth an object that moves along a north-south path, or longitudinal line, will be apparently deflected to the right in the Northern Hemisphere and to the left in the Southern Hemisphere. The deflection is related to the motion of the object, the motion of the Earth, and latitude. The Coriolis effect is important in meteorology and oceanography as well as ballistics; it also has great significance in astrophysics.

Cork, Seaport city (pop., 2002 prelim.: 123,338), southwestern Ireland. The seat of County Cork, it is situated on Cork Harbour at the mouth of the River Lee. Founded as a monastery in the 7th century, it was often raided and was eventually settled by the Danes. It passed to Henry II of England in 1172. The city was taken by Parliamentarian forces under Oliver Cromwell (1649) and by the duke of Marlborough (1690). It was heavily damaged in 1920 during the Irish uprising against England. Its industries include leatherworking, brewing, and distilling.

cork, Outer bark of the evergreen cork oak (*Quercus suber*), native to the Mediterranean. In its broad sense, cork consists of the irregularly shaped, thin-walled, wax-coated cells that make up the peeling bark of many trees, but commercially only cork-oak bark is called cork. Cork is obtained from the new outer sheath of bark that forms after the original rough outer bark has been removed. This outer sheath can be stripped repeatedly without hurting the tree. Cork is unique because it is made of air-filled, watertight cells that are a remarkably effective insulating medium. The air pockets make

Cork oak (Quercus suber) with sections of cork removed
Eric Carle/Shostal Associates

cork very light in weight. Though specialized plastics and other artificial substances have replaced cork in some of its former uses, it has retained its traditional importance as a stopper for bottles of wine and other alcoholic beverages.

cormorant, Any of the 26–30 species of water birds, constituting the family Phalacrocoracidae, that dive for and feed on fish, mainly those of little value to humans. In the Orient and elsewhere, these glossy black underwater swimmers have been tamed for fishing. Their guano is valued as a fertilizer. Cormorants live on seacoasts, lakes, and some rivers, nesting on cliffs or in bushes or trees. They have a long, hook-tipped bill, patches of bare skin on the face, and a small throat pouch (gular sac). The most widespread species is the common, or great, cormorant (*Phalacrocorax carbo*), which grows up to 40 in. (100 cm) long and breeds from eastern Canada to Iceland, across Eurasia to Australia and New Zealand, and in parts of Africa.

cornet, Valved brass instrument. It evolved in the 1820s from the posthorn. Like the trumpet, it has three valves, but its bore is somewhat more conical. It is a transposing instrument (its music written a tone above the actual sound), usually built in the key of B-flat, though a higher-pitched E-flat instrument is used as well. Its range parallels that of the trumpet. Its agility made it a very popular solo instrument; it often displaced the trumpet in 19th-century orchestras, and it preceded the trumpet in modern dance and jazz bands. Recent developments have made the two instruments very similar, and the cornet's popularity has waned considerably as a result.

Cornwall, Administrative (pop., 2001: 501,267, including the Isles of Scilly) and historic county, southwestern England. Located on a peninsula jutting into the Atlantic Ocean and terminating in Land's End, it is the most remote of English counties; its county seat is Truro. Southern Cornwall is a popular tourist area; much of the coast is now protected by the National Trust. Tin, mined in Cornwall for at least 3,000 years, attracted prehistoric settlers, and there are stone relics in the area. Since 1337 the manors of Cornwall have belonged to the English sovereign's eldest son, who acts as duke of Cornwall.

corona, Outermost region of the Sun's (or any star's) atmosphere, consisting of plasma. The Sun's corona has a temperature of about 3.6 million °F (2 million °C) and a very low density. Extending more than 8 million mi (13 million km) from the photosphere, it has no definite boundaries, continually varying in size and shape as it is affected by the Sun's magnetic field. The solar wind is formed by expansion of coronal gases. Only about half as bright as the full moon, the corona is overwhelmed by the brilliance of the solar surface and normally not visible to the unaided eye, but a total eclipse permits naked-eye observations.

Coronado, Francisco Vázquez de (b. *c.* 1510, Salamanca, Spain—d. Sept. 22, 1554, Mex.), Spanish explorer of the North American Southwest. Appointed governor of Nueva Galicia in west-central Mexico, Coronado was sent north with a large force to locate and capture the legendary Seven Cities of Cíbola, reported to be fabulously wealthy. He was disillusioned to discover instead the Zuni pueblos of New Mexico and a seminomadic Indian tribe in Kansas. Though the treasure he sought eluded him, his explorers were the first Europeans to view the Grand Canyon, and he extended Spanish territory over huge areas of North America. His expedition's failure led to his indictment on his return to Mexico, but he was acquitted.

coronary bypass, Surgical treatment for coronary heart disease to relieve angina pectoris and prevent heart attacks. It became widely used in the 1960s. One or more blood vessels—usually an artery in the chest or a vein from the leg—are transplanted to create new paths for blood to flow from the aorta to the heart muscle, bypassing obstructed sections of the coronary arteries.

coronary heart disease, or ISCHEMIC HEART DISEASE, Progressive reduction of blood supply to the heart muscle due to narrowing or blocking of a coronary artery. Short-term oxygen deprivation can cause angina pectoris. Long-term, severe oxygen depletion causes a heart attack. Coronary bypass or angioplasty is needed if medication and diet do not control the disease.

corporate income tax, Tax imposed by public authorities on the incomes of corporations. Virtually all countries assess taxes on the net profits of corporations; most are flat-rate levies rather than extensively graduated taxes. A corporate income tax was adopted by the U.S. government in 1909; three-fourths of the states also levy corporate income taxes.

corporation, Specific legal form of organization of persons and material resources, chartered by the state, for the purpose of conducting business. As contrasted with the other two major forms of business ownership, the sole proprietorship and the partnership, the corporation has several characteristics that make it a more flexible instrument for large-scale economic activity. Chief among these are limited liability, transferability of shares (rights in the enterprise may be transferred readily from one investor to another without constituting legal reorganization), juridical personality (the corporation itself as a fictive "person" has legal standing and may thus sue and be sued, make contracts, and hold property), and indefinite duration (the life of the corporation may extend beyond the participation of any of its founders). Its owners are the shareholders, who purchase with their investment a share in the proceeds of the enterprise and who are nominally entitled to a measure of control over its financial management. Direct shareholder control became increasingly impossible in the 20th century, however, as the largest corporations came to have tens of thousands of shareholders. The practice of proxy voting by management was legalized and adopted as a remedy, and today salaried managers exercise strong control over the corporation and its assets.

corporatism, Theory and practice of organizing the whole of society into corporate entities subordinate to the state. According to the theory, employers and employees would be organized into industrial and professional corporations serving as organs of political representation and largely controlling the people and activities within their jurisdiction. Its chief spokesman was Adam Müller (b. 1779—d. 1829), court philosopher to the Fürst (prince) von Metternich, who conceived of a "class state" in which the classes operated as guilds, or corporations, each controlling a specific function of social life. This idea found favour in central Europe after the French Revolution, but it was not put into practice until Benito Mussolini came to power in Italy; its implementation there had barely begun by the start of World War II, which resulted in his fall. After World War II, the governments of many democratic western European countries (e.g., Austria, Norway, and Sweden) developed strong corporatist elements in an attempt to mediate and reduce conflict between businesses and trade unions and to enhance economic growth.

corrosion, Wearing away due to chemical reactions, mainly oxidation. It occurs whenever a gas or liquid chemically attacks an exposed surface, often a metal, and is accelerated by warm temperatures and by acids and salts. Normally, corrosion products (e.g., rust, patina) stay on the surface and protect it. Removing these deposits reexposes the surface, and corrosion continues. Some materials resist corrosion naturally; others can be treated to protect them (e.g., by coating, painting, galvanizing, or anodizing).

Corsica, French CORSE, Island (pop., 2006 est.: 279,000) in the Mediterranean Sea and an administrative unit of France. The fourth largest island in the Mediterranean, it has an area of 3,352 sq mi (8,681 sq km). While remains of human occupation date from at least the 3rd millennium BCE, recorded history begins *c.* 560 BCE, when Greeks from Asia Minor founded a town there. Taken by the Romans in the 3rd–2nd centuries BCE, it, together with Sardinia, became a prosperous Roman province. It was conquered later by several peoples, including Byzantines and Arabs, and was granted to Pisa in the 11th century CE. It later was ruled mainly by Genoa through the mid-18th century, and in 1768 it became a province of France. It was the birthplace of Napoleon. Corsica's official administrative status was changed in 1991 from *région* to *collectivité territoriale à statut particulier* ("territorial collectivity with special status"). The island's economic life is based on tourism and agriculture.

Cortés, Hernán, later MARQUÉS DEL VALLE DE OAXACA (b. 1485, Medellín, near Mérida, Extremadura, Castile—d. Dec. 2, 1547, Castilleja de la Cuesta, near Sevilla), Spanish conquistador who won Mexico for Spain. Cortés left Spain for the New World in 1504, joining Diego Velázquez de Cuéllar (b. 1465—d. 1524) in the conquest of Cuba (1511). In 1519, with 508 men and 16 horses, he burned his ships on Mexico's southeastern coast, thus committing himself to conquest. After accumulating thousands of Indian allies who resented Aztec domination, he forged ahead to Tenochtitlán, the Aztec capital (today Mexico City). The emperor Montezuma II, believing Cortés to be the god Quetzalcóatl, welcomed him but was taken prisoner. Hearing that a Spanish force from Cuba was coming to relieve him of command, Cortés left Tenochtitlán under the command of a captain and set out to defeat his Spanish opponents. Returning with the opposition forces now under his command, he discovered that the city had revolted; he led his troops away by night in a costly retreat, but he returned in 1521 to conquer the city and with it the empire. The absolute ruler of a huge territory, he was forced to retire after a disastrous expedition in 1524 to the Honduran jungles. His final years were beset by misfortune.

cortisone, Steroid hormone produced by the adrenal cortex. It participates in the regulation of the conversion of proteins to carbohydrates, and to some extent it regulates salt metabolism. Introduced medically in 1948 for its anti-inflammatory effect to treat arthritis, it has been largely replaced by related compounds that do not produce its undesired side effects, which include edema, increased stomach acidity, and imbalances in sodium, potassium, and nitrogen metabolism.

corvée, Unpaid labor that a European vassal owed a lord or that a citizen in later times owed the state, either in addition to or in lieu of taxes. The corvée was often used when money payment did not provide sufficient labor for public projects, and in wartime it was sometimes used to augment regular troops in auxiliary capacities.

corvette, Fast naval vessel smaller than a frigate. In the 18th–19th century corvettes were three-masted ships with square rigging and carried about 20 guns on the top deck. Often used to send dispatches within a battle fleet, they also escorted merchant ships. Early U.S. corvettes won distinction in the War of 1812. They disappeared as a class after the shift to steam power in the mid-19th century, but in World War II the term was applied to small armed vessels that served as escorts for convoys. Modern corvettes, usually displacing 500–1,000 tons (454–900 metric tons) and armed with missiles, torpedoes, and machine guns, perform antisubmarine, antiaircraft, and coastal-patrol duties in small navies.

Cosmati work, Type of decorative inlay or mosaic used by Roman decorators and architects in the 12th–13th centuries. Small pieces of coloured stone and glass were combined with strips and disks of white marble arranged in geometric patterns. Cosmati work was used for architectural decoration and church furnishings. The term derives from craftsmen of several families named Cosmatus.

Cosmic Background Explorer (COBE), U.S. satellite that from 1989 to 1993 mapped the cosmic background radiation field. In 1964, microwave radiation was discovered that permeated the cosmos uniformly. This radiation provided spectacular support for the big bang theory, which held that the early universe was very hot. In order to test theories of the universe's history, cosmologists needed to know whether the field was truly the same in every direction. COBE's all-sky survey of the radiation showed slight "wrinkles" from density variations. These variations would have stimulated galaxy formation. A spectrometer showed that the background radiation's spectrum precisely matched the theory.

cosmic background radiation, Electromagnetic radiation, mostly in the microwave range, believed to be the highly red-shifted residual effect of the explosion billions of years ago from which, according to the big-bang model, the universe was created. It was discovered by accident in 1964 by Robert W. Wilson and Arno Penzias; its presence supports the predictions of big-bang cosmology.

cosmic ray, High-speed particle (atomic nucleus or electron) that travels through the Milky Way Galaxy. Some cosmic rays originate from the Sun, but most come from outside the solar system. Primary cosmic rays that reach Earth's atmosphere collide with nuclei in it, creating secondaries. Because lower-energy primaries are strongly influenced by the interplanetary magnetic field and Earth's magnetic field, most of those detected near Earth have very high energy, corresponding to speeds about 87% that of light or more. Observations from spacecraft indicate that most cosmic rays come from the Galaxy's disk, but the highest-energy ones are probably extragalactic. Details of their production and acceleration remain unclear, but apparently expanding shock waves from supernovas can accelerate particles. From the early 1930s to the 1950s, cosmic rays were the only source of high-energy particles used in studying the atomic nucleus and its components. Short-lived subatomic particles were discovered through cosmic-ray collisions, leading to the rise of particle physics. Even powerful particle accelerators cannot impart energy anywhere near that of the highest-energy cosmic rays.

cosmology, Field of study that brings together the natural sciences, especially astronomy and physics, in an effort to understand the physical universe as a unified whole. The first great age of scientific cosmology began in Greece in the 6th century BC, when the Pythagoreans introduced the concept of a spherical Earth and, unlike the Babylonians and Egyptians, hypothesized that the heavenly bodies moved according to the harmonious relations of natural laws. Their thought culminated in the Ptolemaic model of the universe (2nd century AD). The Copernican revolution of the 16th century ushered in the second great age. The third began in the early 20th century, with the formulation of special relativity and its development into general relativity by Albert Einstein. The basic assumptions of modern cosmology are that the universe is homogeneous in space (on the average, all places are alike at any time) and that the laws of physics are the same everywhere.

Cossacks, Peoples dwelling in the northern hinterlands of the Black and Caspian seas. The term (from the Turkic *kazak*, "free person") originally referred to semi-independent Tatar groups, which formed in the Dnieper River region. Later it was also applied to peasants who had fled from serfdom in Poland, Lithuania, and Muscovy to the Dnieper and Don regions. The Cossacks had a tradition of independence and received privileges from the Russian government in return for military services. They were used as defenders of the Russian frontier and advance guards for imperial territorial expansion. Attempts in the 17th–18th century to reduce their privileges caused revolts, led by Stenka Razin and Yemelyan Pugachov, and the Cossacks gradually lost their autonomous status.

cost-benefit analysis, In governmental planning and budgeting, the attempt to measure the social benefits of a proposed project in monetary terms and compare them with its costs. The procedure was first proposed in 1844 by Arsène-Jules-Étienne-Juvénal Dupuit (1804–66). It was not seriously applied until the 1936 U.S. Flood Control Act, which required that the benefits of flood-control projects exceed their costs. A cost-benefit ratio is determined by dividing the projected benefits of a program by the projected costs. A wide range of variables, including nonquanti-

tative ones such as quality of life, are often considered because the value of the benefits may be indirect or projected far into the future.

cost of living, Monetary cost of maintaining a particular standard of living, usually measured by calculating the average cost of a number of goods and services. Measurement of the cost of a minimum standard of living is essential in determining relief payments, social-insurance benefits, and minimum wages. The cost of living is customarily measured by a price index such as the consumer price index. Measurements of change in the cost of living are important in wage negotiations. Cost-of-living measurements are also used to compare the cost of maintaining similar living standards in different areas.

Costa Rica, officially REPUBLIC OF COSTA RICA, Country, Central America. Area: 19,730 sq mi (51,100 sq km). Population: (2011 est.) 4,577,000. Capital: San José. Most of the people are of Spanish ancestry or are mestizos. Language: Spanish (official). Religion: Christianity (predominantly Roman Catholic [official]; also Protestant, other Christians). Currency: colón. Costa Rica's Pacific coast rises abruptly into central highlands and a volcanic mountain chain that forms the backbone of the country and descends gradually to the Caribbean coastal plain. The climate ranges from temperate to tropical, and the wide variety of plants and animals includes species found in both North America and South America. The developing market economy is largely based on coffee, pineapple, and banana exports. Sugar is another significant cash crop, and beef is also important. Costa Rica is a unitary multiparty republic with one legislative house; the head of state and government is the president. Christopher Columbus landed in what is now Costa Rica in 1502, in an area inhabited by a number of small independent Indian tribes. These peoples were not easily dominated by European adventurers who followed, and it took some 60 years for the Spaniards to establish a permanent settlement there. Ignored by the Spanish crown because of its lack of mineral wealth, the colony grew slowly. Coffee exports and the construction of a rail line improved its economy in the 19th century. It joined the short-lived Mexican Empire in 1821, was a member of the United Provinces of Central America (1823–38), and adopted a constitution in 1871. In 1890 Costa Ricans held what is considered the first free and honest election in Central America, beginning a tradition of democracy for which Costa Rica is renowned. In 1987 Pres. Óscar Arias Sánchez was awarded the Nobel Prize for Peace for his Central American peace plan. In the early 21st century many Costa Ricans looked to increasingly free trade with the United States as a solution to the country's economic woes.

Côte d'Azur, Region bordering the Mediterranean Sea, southeastern France. Encompassing the French Riviera between Menton and Cannes, it is a major tourist centre noted for its scenery.

Côte d'Ivoire, or IVORY COAST, officially REPUBLIC OF CÔTE D'IVOIRE, Country, western Africa. Area: 123,863 sq mi (320,803 sq km). Population: (2011 est.) 21,504,000. Capital: Yamoussoukro; de facto capital Abidjan. The population consists of various ethnic groups, notably the Akan and Mande. Languages: French (official), Baule, Anyi, Bete, Bambara, Dan. Religions: Islam, Christianity, traditional beliefs. Currency: CFA franc. Côte d'Ivoire can be divided into four major regions: a narrow coastal region, an equatorial rainforest in the west, a cultivated forest zone in the east, and a savanna region in the north. Agriculture employs about half the workforce. The country is a major producer of cocoa and petroleum; other exports include timber and wood products and coffee. It is a republic with one legislative house; its head of state and government is the president, assisted by the prime minister. European powers came to the area to trade in ivory and slaves beginning in the 15th century, and local kingdoms gave way to French influence in the 19th century. The French colony of Côte d'Ivoire was founded in 1893, and full French occupation took place in 1908–18. In 1946 it became a territory in the French Union; in 1947 the northern part of the country separated and became part of Upper Volta (now Burkina Faso). Côte d'Ivoire peacefully achieved autonomy in 1958 and independence in 1960, when Félix Houphouët-Boigny was elected president. The country's first multiparty presidential elections were held in 1990. Political turmoil has persisted since Houphouët-Boigny died in 1993, and a civil war in 2002 left the country divided into northern and southern sections. Attempts at reconciliation were initiated over the following years, including a 2007 power-sharing agreement signed by both sides. A disputed presidential election in 2010 led to a political standoff that was not resolved until 2011.

Cotonou, Port city (pop., 2007 est.: 762,000), de facto capital of Benin. Situated along the Gulf of Guinea, it is the starting point of the Benin-Niger Railway and the site of deepwater port facilities, completed in 1965, that serve both Benin and Togo. Cotonou is the economic hub of Benin and its largest urban centre. Its industries include brewing, textile production, and palm-oil processing. It is home to the National University of Benin (1970).

Council for Mutual Economic Assistance, or COMECON, Organization founded in 1949 to facilitate and coordinate the economic development of Soviet-bloc countries. Its original members were the Soviet Union, Bulgaria, Czechoslovakia, Hungary, Poland, and Romania; other members joined later, including Albania (1949) and the German Democratic Republic (1950). Its accomplishments included the organization of Eastern Europe's railroad grid, the creation of the International Bank for Economic Cooperation, and the construction of the "Friendship" oil pipeline. After the political upheavals in Eastern Europe in the late 1980s, it largely lost its purpose and power. In 1991 it was renamed the Organization for International Economic Cooperation.

counseling, Professional guidance of the individual by use of standard psychological methods such as collecting case-history data, using various techniques of the personal interview, and testing interests and aptitudes. The counselor's goal is generally to orient the individual toward opportunities that can best guarantee fulfillment of his personal needs and aspirations. The counselor usually attempts to clarify the client's own thinking rather than to solve his problems. Professional counselors (such as educational guidance and career counselors) and counseling psychologists (such as marriage and bereavement counselors) are found in a wide variety of institutional settings and in private practice.

Counter-Reformation, or CATHOLIC REFORMATION, In Roman Catholicism, efforts in the 16th and early 17th century to oppose the Protestant Reformation and reform the Catholic Church. Early efforts grew out of criticism of the worldliness and corruption of the papacy and clergy during the Renaissance. Paul III (r. 1534–49) was the first pope to respond, convening the important Council of Trent (1545–63), which reacted to Protestant teachings on faith, grace, and the sacraments, and attempted to reform training for the priesthood. The Roman Inquisition was established in 1542 to control heresy within Catholic territories, and the Jesuits under Ignatius de Loyola undertook educational and missionary work aimed at conversion or reconversion. Emperors Charles V and Philip II took military action against Protestant growth. Later popes of the Counter-Reformation included Pius V, Gregory XIII, and Sixtus V. Sts. Charles Borromeo, Philip Neri, John of the Cross, Teresa of Ávila, Francis de Sales, and Vincent de Paul were among the most influential reforming figures.

counterpoint, Art of combining different melodic lines in a musical composition. The term is often used interchangeably with *polyphony* (music consisting of two or more distinct melodic lines), but *counterpoint* more specifically refers to the compositional technique involved in the handling of these melodic lines. The first recorded use of two melodic lines simultaneously was in 9th-century treatises showing examples of organum (a type of music for multiple voices), though improvised counterpoint—in which the voices probably moved mostly parallel to each other, and thus failed to convey an impression of independence—may date back to some centuries earlier. The desire to ensure pleasant consonances and avoid unpleasant dissonances when improvising called for principles of simultaneous vocal motion (voice leading). Because the relative movement of voices approaching and leaving given intervals was thought to produce effects that were more or less pleasing, rules were created to govern various types of relative motion. The "vertical" aspect of counterpoint—the relationship between the melodic lines—came to be studied as harmony, especially from the 18th century. Though harmony and counterpoint are intimately intertwined, most of the multivoiced music of the Middle Ages and the Renaissance is considered essentially polyphonic or contrapuntal—that is, consisting of a combination of relatively independent and integral melodic lines. In the Baroque era, with the invention of figured bass and the continuo, the balance began to shift toward a harmonic orientation.

countertenor, Adult male alto voice, either natural or falsetto. Some writers use the term only for the natural high tenor, preferring "male alto" for the falsetto voice. Like the castrato tradition, the countertenor developed as a result of the prohibition on women taking part in church choirs. Since the falsetto voice lacks power, it was little used in opera. The countertenor tradition was preserved in the English cathedral choir. Today it is again being widely cultivated internationally, primarily for Renaissance and Baroque music.

country music, or COUNTRY AND WESTERN, Musical style that originated among whites in rural areas of the southern and western U.S. The term *country and western music* was adopted by the music industry in 1949 to replace the derogatory *hillbilly music*. Its roots lie in the music of the European settlers of the Appalachians and other areas. In the early 1920s the genre began to be commercially recorded; Fiddlin' John Carson recorded its first hit. Radio programs such as Nashville's *Grand Ole Opry* and Chicago's *National Barn Dance* fueled its growth, and growing numbers of musicians, such as the Carter Family and Jimmie Rodgers, began performing on radio and in recording studios. With the migration of Southern whites to industrial cities in the 1930s and '40s, country music was exposed to new influences, such as blues and gospel music. Its nostalgic bias, with its lyrics about poverty, heartbreak, and homesickness, held special appeal during a time of great population shifts. In the 1930s "singing cowboy" film stars, such as Gene Autry, altered country lyrics to produce a synthetic "western" music. Other variants include western swing and honky-tonk. In the 1940s there was an effort to return to country's root values, but commercialization proved a stronger influence, and in the 1950s and '60s country music became a huge commercial enterprise. Popular singers often recorded songs in a Nashville style, while many country music recordings employed lush orchestral backgrounds. Country music has become increasingly acceptable to urban audiences, retaining its vitality with diverse performers such as Willie Nelson, Waylon Jennings, Dolly Parton, Randy Travis, Garth Brooks, Emmylou Harris, and Lyle Lovett. Despite the influence of other styles, it has retained an unmistakable character as one of the few truly indigenous American musical styles.

couplet, Two successive lines of verse. A couplet is marked usually by rhythmic correspondence, rhyme, or the inclusion of a self-contained utterance. Couplets may be independent poems, but they usually function as parts of other verse forms, such as the Shakespearean sonnet, which concludes with a couplet. A couplet that cannot stand alone is an open couplet; a couplet whose sense is relatively independent is a closed couplet.

court, Official assembly with judicial authority to hear and determine disputes in particular cases. In early judicial tribunals, judges sat in enclosures (courts in an architectural sense), and lawyers and the general public remained outside a bar (hence the term *bar* in legal contexts). Modern British courts are divided into those trying criminal cases and those trying civil cases; a second distinction is made between inferior courts, or courts of first instance, and superior courts, or courts of appeal. In the U.S. each state has its own system of courts, usually consisting of a superior (appellate) court, trial courts of general jurisdiction, and specialized courts (e.g., probate courts). The U.S. also has a system of federal courts, established to adjudicate distinctively national questions and cases not appropriately tried in state courts. At the apex of the national system is the Supreme Court of the United States. The secondary level consists of the United States Courts of Appeals. United States District Courts form the tertiary level. Crimes committed by military figures may be tried in a court-martial. In the past, ecclesiastical courts had broad jurisdiction.

court-martial, Military court for hearing charges brought against members of the armed forces or others within its jurisdiction; also, the legal proceeding of such a court. Most countries today have military codes of justice administered by military courts, often subject to civilian appellate review. Courts-martial are generally convened as ad hoc courts to try one or more cases referred by some high military authority. The convening officer chooses officers, and sometimes enlisted personnel, from his or her command to sit on the court, determine guilt or innocence, and hand down sentences.

courtly love, Late-medieval code that prescribed the highly conventionalized behaviour and emotions of aristocratic ladies and their lovers. It was the theme of an extensive literature that began with late 11th-century troubadour poetry in France and swiftly pervaded Europe. The courtly lover, who saw himself as enslaved by passion but fired by respect, faithfully served and worshiped his lady-saint. Courtly love was invariably adulterous, largely because upper-class marriage at the time was usually the result of economic interest or the seal of a power alliance. Its literary sources are believed to be found in Arabic literature, transmitted to Europe through Arab-dominated Spain; the growing religious cult of Mary was another influence. Examples of works inspired by the ideal are the *Roman de la rose*, Petrarch's sonnets to Laura, Dante's *Divine Comedy*, and the lyrics of the trouvères and minnesingers.

covalent bond, Force holding atoms in a molecule together as a specific, separate entity (as opposed to, e.g., colloidal aggregates). In covalent bonds, two atoms share one or more pairs of valence electrons to give each atom the stability found in a noble gas. In single bonds (e.g., H$-$H in molecular hydrogen), one electron pair is shared; in double bonds (e.g., O$=$O in molecular oxygen or H$_2$C$=$CH$_2$ in ethylene), two; in triple bonds (e.g., HC$\equiv$CH in acetylene), three. In coordinate covalent bonds, additional electron pairs are shared with another atom, usually forming a functional group, such as sulfate (SO$_4$) or phosphate (PO$_4$). The number of bonds and the atoms participating in each (including any additional paired electrons) give molecules their configuration; the slight negative and positive charges at the opposite ends of a covalent bond are the reason most molecules have some polarity. Carbon in organic compounds can have as many as four single bonds, each pointing to one vertex of a tetrahedron; as a result, certain molecules exist in mirror-image forms. Double bonds are rigid, leading to the possibility of geometric isomers. Some types of bonds, such as the amide linkages that join the amino acids in peptides and proteins (peptide bonds), are apparently single but have some double-bond characteristics because of the electronic structure of the participating atoms. The configurations of enzymes and their substrates, determined by their covalent bonds (particularly the peptide bonds) and hydrogen bonds, are crucial to the reactions they participate in, which are fundamental to all life.

covenant, In the Hebrew scriptures, an agreement or treaty among peoples or nations, but most memorably the promises that

God extended to humankind (e.g., the promise to Noah never again to destroy the earth by flood or the promise to Abraham that his descendants would multiply and inherit the land of Israel). God's revelation of the law to Moses on Mount Sinai created a pact between God and Israel known as the Sinai covenant. In Christianity, Jesus' death established a new covenant between God and humanity. Islam holds that the Last Covenant was between God and the Prophet Muhammad.

Coventry, City and metropolitan borough (pop., 2001: 300,844), central England. The city was the home of Lady Godiva who, with her husband, founded a Benedictine abbey there in 1043. It was probably the centre of the presentation of the Coventry mystery plays in the 15th–16th centuries. During World War II, heavy bombing by the Germans left the town severely damaged. The spire of the 15th-century St. Michael's Cathedral and its ruined nave stand beside the new cathedral built in 1962. Chief industries are motor vehicle manufacturing and telecommunications.

cow, In animal husbandry, the mature female of domesticated cattle. The name is also applied to the mature female of various, usually large, animals (e.g., elephant, whale, or moose), or, more broadly, to any domestic bovine animal regardless of gender or age.

cowbird, Any of six passerine species related to New World blackbirds (family Icteridae) that exhibit brood parasitism. Cowbirds lay their eggs in the nests of other birds, usually one to each host nest. Young cowbirds, which displace nestlings or outcompete them for food, may grow larger than the foster parents. In parts of North America, the brown-headed cowbird (*Molothrus ater*) parasitizes the nests of more than 200 other bird species; others use the nests of only one or two kinds of oriole. Cowbirds forage on the ground, often associating with cattle in order to catch insects stirred up by the cows' hooves. The male of most species is a uniform glossy black, the female grayish brown.

cowboy, Horseman skilled at handling cattle in the U.S. West. From *c.* 1820, cowboys were employed in small numbers on Texas ranches, where they had learned the skills of the *vaquero* (Spanish: "cowboy"). After the Civil War, their numbers rapidly multiplied as cattle raising evolved into a lucrative industry throughout the western territories. Cowboys rounded up and branded the cattle, kept watch over the herd, and drove those ready for market to railroad towns. As the agricultural frontier moved west, the open range was transformed into farms, and by 1890 cowboys had been forced to settle on ranches. The romance of their image lived on in U.S. folklore and through movies and television.

CPU, in full CENTRAL PROCESSING UNIT, Principal component of a digital computer, composed of a control unit, an instruction-decoding unit, and an arithmetic-logic unit. The CPU is linked to main memory, peripheral equipment (including input/output devices), and storage units. The control unit integrates computer operations. It selects instructions from the main memory in proper sequence and sends them to the instruction-decoding unit, which interprets them so as to activate functions of the system at appropriate moments. Input data are transferred via the main memory to the arithmetic-logic unit for processing (i.e., addition, subtraction, multiplication, division, and certain logic operations). Larger computers may have two or more CPUs, in which case they are simply called "processors" because each is no longer a "central" unit.

crab, Any of 4,500 species of short-tailed decapod, found in all oceans, in freshwater, and on land. Its carapace (upper body shield) is usually broad, and its first pair of legs is modified into pincers. Most crabs live in the sea and breathe through gills, which in land crabs are modified to serve as lungs. They walk or crawl, generally with a sideways gait; some are good swimmers. Crabs are omnivorous scavengers, but many are predatory and some are

*Common swimming crab
(Portunus holsatus), showing
its paddle-shaped feet*
Dr. Eckart Pott/Bruce Coleman Ltd.

herbivorous. Two of the largest known crustaceans are the giant crab of Japan (13 ft, or 4 m, from claw tip to claw tip), a spider crab; and the Tasmanian crab (up to 18 in., or 46 cm, long, and weighing more than 20 lbs, or 9 kg). Other species are less than an inch long. Well-known crabs include the hermit crab, edible crab (Britain and Europe), blue crab, Dungeness crab, fiddler crab, and king crab.

Crab Nebula, Bright nebula in the constellation Taurus, about 5,000 light-years from Earth. Roughly 12 light-years in diameter, it is the remnant of a supernova, first observed by Chinese and other astronomers in 1054, that was visible in daylight for 23 days and at night for almost two years. Identified as a nebula *c.* 1731, it was named (for its form) in the mid-19th century. In 1921 it was discovered to be still expanding; the present rate is about 700 mi/second (1,100 km/second). The Crab is one of the few astronomical objects from which electromagnetic radiation has been detected over the entire measurable spectrum. In the late 1960s a pulsar, thought to be the collapsed remnant star of the supernova, was found near its centre.

cramp, Painful, involuntary, sustained contraction of muscle in limbs or some internal organs. Causes may be neurological, reflex, or psychological. Common muscle cramps include swimmer's cramp from overexertion in cold water, heat cramps from loss of salt in sweat, leg cramps, and occupational (e.g., writer's) cramp. Menstrual cramps are uterine muscle contractions before or during menstruation. Cramps occur in diseases including parkinsonism and Huntington chorea. Tetany is severe cramping noticed first in limb muscles.

cranberry, Fruit of any of several small creeping or trailing plants of the genus *Vaccinium* (heath family), related to the blueberry. The small-fruited, or northern, cranberry (*V. oxycoccus*) is found in marshy land in northern North America and Asia and in northern and central Europe. Its crimson berries, about the size of currants and often spotted, have an acid taste. The American cranberry (*V. macrocarpon*), found wild in most of the northeastern U.S. and grown extensively in Massachusetts, New Jersey, and Wisconsin and near the Pacific coast in Washington and Oregon, is more robust than *V. oxycoccus*, with larger, pink to very dark red or mottled red-and-white berries. Cranberries are used in drinks, sauces, jellies, and baked goods.

Cranberry (Vaccinium macrocarpon)
Walter Chandoha

crane, Any of 15 species (family Gruidae) of tall wading birds that resemble herons but are usually larger and have a partly naked head, a heavier bill, more-compact plumage, and an elevated hind toe. In flight, the long neck stretches out in front and the stiltlike legs trail behind. Cranes are found worldwide, living in marshes and on plains, except in South America. Many populations are endangered by hunting and habitat destruction. Cranes eat small animals, grain, and grass shoots. Two well-known species are the whooping crane and the sandhill crane.

craps, Gambling game in which each player in turn throws two dice, attempting to roll a winning combination. The term derives from a Louisiana French word, *crabs*, which means "losing throw." The player with the dice (the shooter) must first put up a stake; the other players bet against the shooter up to the amount of the stake. In some games, bettors may also bet against each other or against the house. A shooter who wins may continue to roll. A 7 or 11 on the first roll wins; a 2, 3, or 12 (craps) loses. Any other number requires the shooter to continue rolling until he or she rolls the same number again for a win or rolls a 7 (craps) and loses.

crater, Circular depression in the surface of a planetary body. Most craters are the result of impacts of meteorites or of volcanic explosions. Meteorite craters are more common on the Moon and Mars and on other planets and natural satellites than on Earth, because most meteorites either burn up in the Earth's atmosphere before reaching its surface or erosion soon obscures the impact site. Craters made by exploding volcanoes (e.g., Crater Lake, Ore.) are more common on the Earth than on the Moon, Mars, or Jupiter's moon Io, where they have also been identified.

creation myth, or COSMOGONY, Symbolic narrative of the creation and organization of the world as understood in a particular tradition. Not all creation myths include a creator, though a supreme creator deity, existing from before creation, is very common. Myths in which the world emerges gradually emphasize the latent power of the earth. In other creation myths, the world is the offspring of primordial parents, derives from a cosmic egg, or is brought up from primordial waters by an animal or devil. Humans may be placed on earth by a god or rise from its depths or from a cultic rock or tree. There are often three stages of creation: that of primordial beings or gods, that of human ancestors who are often semidivine, and that of humans. Creation myths explain or validate basic beliefs, patterns of life, and culture. Rituals dramatize the myth and, particularly in initiations, validate the community's organization and rankings.

creationism, The belief that matter, the various forms of life, and the world were created by God out of nothing. Biblical creationists believe that the story told in Genesis of God's six-day creation of the universe and all living things is literally correct. Scientific creationists believe that a creator made all that exists, though they may not hold that the Genesis story is a literal history of that creation. Creationism became the object of renewed interest among conservative religious groups following the wide dissemination of the theory of biological evolution, first systematically propounded by Charles Darwin in *On the Origin of Species* (1859). In the early 20th century some U.S. states banned the teaching of evolution, leading to the Scopes Trial. In the late 20th century many creationists advocated a view known as intelligent design, which was essentially a scientifically modern version of the argument from design for the existence of God as set forth in the late 18th century by the Anglican clergyman William Paley.

creativity, Ability to produce something new through imaginative skill, whether a new solution to a problem, a new method or device, or a new artistic object or form. The term usually refers to a richness of ideas and originality of thinking. Psychological studies of highly creative people have shown that many have a strong interest in apparent disorder, contradiction, and imbalance, which seem to be perceived as challenges. Such individuals may possess an exceptionally deep, broad, and flexible awareness of themselves. Studies also show that intelligence has little correlation with creativity; thus, a highly intelligent person may not be very creative.

credit, Transaction between two parties in which one (the creditor or lender) supplies money, goods, services, or securities in return for a promised future payment by the other (the debtor or borrower). Such transactions normally include the payment of interest to the lender. Credit may be extended by public or private institutions to finance business activities, agricultural operations, consumer expenditures, or government projects. Large sums of credit are usually extended through specialized financial institutions such as commercial banks or through government lending programs.

credit union, Credit cooperative formed by a group of people with some common bond who, in effect, save their money together and make low-cost loans to each other. The loans are usually short-term consumer loans, mainly for automobiles, household needs, medical debts, and emergencies. Credit unions generally operate under government charter and supervision. They are particularly important in less developed countries, where they may be the only source of credit for their members. The first cooperative societies providing credit were founded in Germany and Italy in the mid-19th century; the first North American credit unions were founded by Alphonse Desjardins in Lévis, Quebec (1900), and Manchester, N.H. (1909). The Credit Union National Association (CUNA), a federation of U.S. credit unions, was established in 1934 and became a worldwide association in 1958.

creed, Officially authorized, usually brief statement of the essential articles of faith of a religious community, often used in public worship or initiation rites. Creeds are most numerous in Western traditions. In Islam the *shahāda* declares that only God is God and Muhammad is his prophet. In Judaism early creeds are preserved in Hebrew scripture, and later creeds include the Thirteen Principles of Faith. In Christianity the Nicene Creed was formulated in AD 381 to exclude Arianism, and the Apostles' Creed was drafted in the 8th century from earlier baptismal creeds. Buddhism, Zoroastrianism, and modern movements of Hinduism also possess creeds; in other religions faith is confessed chiefly through liturgical expressions.

cremation, Disposing of a corpse by burning. In the ancient world cremation took place on an open pyre. It was practiced by the Greeks (who considered it suitable for heroes and war dead) and the Romans (among whom it became a status symbol). The pagan Scandinavians also cremated their dead. In India the custom is very ancient. In some Asian countries only certain people may be cremated (e.g., high lamas in the Tibet Autonomous Region of China). Christianity opposed cremation, and it became rare in Europe after AD 1000 except under extreme circumstances, such as that brought on by the Black Death. The practice reemerged in the late 19th century and was eventually accepted by both Protestants and Roman Catholics.

creole, Any pidgin language that has become established as the native language of a speech community. A creole usually arises when speakers of one language become economically or politically dominant over speakers of another. A simplified or modified form of the dominant group's language (pidgin), used for communication between the two groups, may eventually become the native language of the less-powerful community. Examples include Gullah (derived from English), spoken in the Sea Islands of the southeastern U.S.; Haitian Creole (derived from French), spoken in Haiti; and Papiamentu (derived from Spanish and Portuguese), spoken in Curaçao, Aruba, and Bonaire.

cress, Any of several plants of the mustard family, of interest for their spicy young basal leaves, which are used in salads and as seasonings and garnishes. Watercress is perhaps the most popular of the edible cresses. Common garden cress, or peppergrass (*Lepidium sativum*) is widely grown, especially in its curl-leaved form,

and used as a garnish. Others include weeds (e.g., *Barbarea vulgaris*), wild varieties (e.g., *Cardamine pratensis*), and ornamentals (e.g., *Arabis* species).

Cretaceous Period, Interval of geologic time from *c.* 145.5 to 65.5 million years ago. During the Cretaceous the climate was warmer than today. In the seas, marine invertebrates flourished, and bony fishes evolved. On land, flowering plants arose, and insects, bees in particular, began their thriving partnership with them. Mammals and birds remained inconspicuous throughout the Cretaceous, while the reptiles continued their dominance. The dinosaurs reached the peak of their evolution during this period but rather suddenly became extinct at its end.

Crete, Greek KRÍTI, ancient CRETA, Island (pop., 2008 est.: 606,274) in the eastern Mediterranean Sea and an administrative region of Greece. It stretches for 160 mi (260 km) and varies in width from 7.5 to 37 mi (12 to 60 km), with a total area of 3,218 sq mi (8,336 sq km). Dominated by mountains, it was home to the Minoan civilization from *c.* 3000 BCE and was known for its palaces at Knossos, Phaestus, and Mallia. It reached its peak in the 16th century BCE. A major earthquake *c.* 1450 BCE marked the end of the Minoan era. In 67 BCE Rome annexed Crete, and in 395 CE it passed to Byzantium. In 1204 Crusaders sold the island to Venice, from which it was wrested by the Ottoman Turks in 1669 after one of history's longest sieges. Taken by Greece in 1898, it was autonomous until its union with Greece in 1913. Agriculture is the economic mainstay, and the island is one of Greece's leading producers of olives, olive oil, and grapes; tourism is also important. The museum at Iráklion houses a fine collection of Minoan art.

Creutzfeldt-Jakob disease, or CJD, Rare fatal disease of the central nervous system. It destroys brain tissue, making it spongy and causing progressive loss of mental functioning and motor control. The disease commonly arises in adults between the ages of 40 and 70. Patients usually die within a year. There is no known cure. The disease is caused by a prion that builds up in neurons. Inherited or random mutation accounts for 99% of cases; the rest come from prion exposure during medical procedures and possibly from eating the meat of cattle with mad cow disease.

crevasse, Fissure or crack in a glacier resulting from stress produced by movement. Crevasses range up to 65 ft (20 m) wide, 150 ft (45 m) deep, and several hundred yards long. Crevasses may be bridged by snow and become hidden, and they may close up as the glacier moves.

Crevasse in the Mozama Glacier on Mount Baker, Washington
Bob and Ira Spring

cribbage, Card game, usually for two players, in which each tries to form various counting combinations of cards, the score being kept by moving pegs on a narrow rectangular board. Each player receives six cards. (There is also a five-card variant, as well as four-hand and three-hand variants.) Cribbage was invented by the 17th-century English poet Sir John Suckling. The rules of play, though somewhat involved, are simple enough to make cribbage a popular pastime, particularly in Britain and the northern U.S. The game usually ends at 121 (twice around the board plus one).

cricket (from Middle French *criquet*, "goal stake") Game played by two teams with a ball and bat on a large field centring on two wickets. Each wicket is two sets of three sticks. The teams have 11 players each. A bowler from the defending team throws the ball (with a straight-arm overhand delivery), attempting to hit the wicket, which is one of several ways the batsman may be put out. The team batting fields two batsman at a time, and the batsman being bowled to (the striker) tries to hit the ball away from the wicket. If the batsman hits the ball away from the wicket but has no time to run to the opposite wicket, he need not run; play will resume with another bowl. After a hit, when possible, the striker and the second batsman (the nonstriker) at the other wicket change places. Each time both batsmen can reach the opposite wicket, one run is scored. The batsmen may continue to cross back and forth between the wickets, earning an additional run for each time both reach the opposite side. Matches are divided into innings consisting of one turn at bat for each team; depending on pregame agreement, a match may consist of either one or two innings. Cricket's origins are uncertain, but the first set of rules was written in 1744. During England's colonial era, cricket was exported to countries around the world.

cricket, Any of the approximately 2,400 species of leaping insects (family Gryllidae) known for the musical chirping of the male. Crickets vary in length from around 0.1 to 2 in. (3–50 mm) and have thin antennae, hind legs modified for jumping, and two abdominal sensory appendages (cerci). Their two forewings are stiff and leathery, and the two long, membranous hind wings are used in flying. Male crickets chirp by rubbing a scraper located on one forewing along a row of 50–250 teeth on the opposite forewing. The most common cricket songs are the calling song, which attracts the female; the courtship, or mating, song, which induces the female to copulate; and the fighting chirp, which repels other males.

crime, the intentional commission of an act usually deemed socially harmful or dangerous and specifically defined, prohibited, and punishable under criminal law. Crimes in the common-law tradition were originally defined primarily by judicial decision. Most common-law crimes are now codified. According to a generally accepted principle, *nullum crimen sine lege*, there can be no crime without a law. A crime generally consists of both conduct (the *actus reus*) and a concurrent state of mind (the *mens rea*). Criminal acts include arson, assault and battery, bribery, burglary, child abuse, counterfeiting, embezzlement, extortion, forgery, fraud, hijacking, homicide, kidnapping, perjury, piracy, rape, sedition, smuggling, treason, theft, and usury.

Crimea, Autonomous republic (pop., 2001: 2,033,700), southern Ukraine. It is coextensive with the Crimean Peninsula, which extends into the Black Sea. It covers 10,077 sq mi (26,100 sq km); its capital is Simferopol. Early inhabitants were Cimmerians, though the area later was settled by Greeks in the 6th century BC and was ruled by the kingdom of the Cimmerian Bosporus from the 5th century BC. It became subject to Rome, and part of it later belonged to the Byzantine Empire. Russia annexed Crimea in 1783. It was the scene of the Crimean War (1853–56). In 1921 it became an autonomous republic of the U.S.S.R. During World War II, Nazi armies overran it in 1941; it was retaken by the Soviets in 1944. The area became an oblast of the Ukrainian S.S.R. in 1954. After the dissolution of the Soviet Union in 1991, Crimea obtained partial autonomy from Ukraine.

Crimean War (October 1853–February 1856) War fought mainly in the Crimea between the Russians and an alliance consisting of the Ottoman empire, Britain, France, and Sardinia-Piedmont. It arose from the conflict of great powers in the Middle East and was more directly caused by Russian demands to exercise protection over the Orthodox subjects of the Ottoman sultan. The war was managed and commanded poorly by both sides. Battles were fought at the Alma River, Balaklava, and Inkerman, before the besieged Sevastopol was taken by the allies. Disease accounted for many of the approximately 250,000 men lost by each side. After Austria threatened to join the allies, Russia accepted preliminary peace terms, which were formalized at the Congress of Paris. The war did not settle the relations of the powers in Eastern Europe, but it did alert Alexander II to the need to modernize Russia.

criminal law, Body of law that defines criminal offenses, regulates the apprehension, charging, and trial of suspected offenders, and fixes punishment for convicted persons. Substantive criminal law defines particular crimes, and procedural law establishes rules for the prosecution of crime. In the U.S., substantive criminal law originated for the most part in common law, which was later codified in federal and state statutes. Modern criminal law has been affected considerably by the social sciences, especially in the areas of sentencing, legal research, legislation, and rehabilitation.

criminology, Scientific study of nonlegal aspects of crime, including its causes and prevention. Criminology originated in the 18th century when social reformers began to question the use of punishment for retribution rather than deterrence and reform. In the 19th century, scientific methods began to be applied to the study of crime. Today criminologists commonly use statistics, case histories, official records, and sociological field methods to study criminals and criminal activity, including the rates and kinds of crime within geographic areas. Their findings are used by lawyers, judges, probation officers, law-enforcement and prison officials, legislators, and scholars to better understand criminals and the effects of treatment and prevention.

critical mass, Minimum amount of a given fissionable material necessary to achieve a self-sustaining nuclear chain reaction under specified conditions. Critical mass depends on several factors, including the kind of fissionable material used, its concentration and purity, and the composition and geometry of the surrounding reaction system.

Cro-Magnon, Population of anatomically modern *Homo sapiens* dating from the Upper Paleolithic Period (*c.* 35,000–10,000 BC). First discovered in 1868 at the Cro-Magnon rock shelter in the Dordogne region in southern France, the human skeletons that came to be called Cro-Magnon are now considered representative of humans at that time. Cro-Magnons were relatively more robust and powerful than today's humans, with a somewhat larger brain capacity. The Cro-Magnons are generally associated with the Aurignacian tool industry and artistic tradition. Cro-Magnons seem to have been a settled people, living in caves or primitive huts and lean-tos, moving only when necessary to find new hunting or because of environmental changes. It is difficult to determine how long the Cro-Magnons lasted and what happened to them; presumably they were gradually absorbed into the European populations that came later.

Croatia, officially REPUBLIC OF CROATIA, Country, northwestern Balkans, southeastern Europe. Area: 21,851 sq mi (56,954 sq km). Population: (2011 est.) 4,287,000. Capital: Zagreb. The people are predominantly South Slavs, mainly Croats and a small but significant Serb minority. Language: Croatian (official). Religions: Christianity (predominantly Roman Catholic [Croats]; also Eastern Orthodox [Serbs]); also Islam. Currency: kuna. Croatia includes the traditional regions of Dalmatia and Istria, located along the Adriatic coast, and Croatia-Slavonia, in the northern arm of the country. The central mountain belt contains part of the Dinaric Alps. The northeast is a fertile agricultural area; sugar beets, corn (maize), and wheat are grown, and pigs and cattle are raised. The mountain belt is known for fruit, and the farms of Istria and Dalmatia produce grapes and olives. Important industries include food processing, wine making, and the production and refining of petroleum. Croatia is a multiparty republic with a unicameral legislature. Its head of state is the president, and the head of government is the prime minister. Slavs arrived in the western Balkans in the 6th and 7th centuries. An independent Croatian state developed in the 9th century and was ruled by native kings until 1102, when the crown passed into the hands of the Hungarian dynasty. Some institutions of separate Croatian statehood were maintained, however. The area associated with the name Croatia shifted gradually north and west as its territory was eroded, first with the loss of Dalmatia to Venice by 1420 and then as a result of Ottoman conquests in the 16th century, when the remainder of Croatia came under the rule of the Austrian Habsburgs. Between 1699 and 1815 the Habsburgs gained control of other Croatian lands, but they remained administratively divided. After the reconstitution of the Habsburg empire as Austria-Hungary in 1867, Dalmatia and Istria were ruled by Vienna and Croatia-Slavonia by Hungary. In 1918, after the defeat of Austria-Hungary in World War I, Croatia joined other South Slav territories to form the Kingdom of Serbs, Croats, and Slovenes, which was renamed Yugoslavia in 1929. During World War II the occupying Germans and Italians set up an independent Croatian state, embracing Croatia-Slavonia, part of Dalmatia, and Bosnia and Herzegovina. After the war Croatia was reincorporated as a republic into communist Yugoslavia. Croatia declared its independence in 1991, sparking insurrections by the republic's Serbs and occupation by the Yugoslav army. Croatia retook most of the Serb-occupied regions by 1995 and regained full control of its territory by 2002. The country joined NATO in 2009.

crocodile, Any of about a dozen tropical reptile species (family Crocodilidae) found in Asia, the Australian region, Africa, Madagascar, and the Americas. Crocodiles are long-snouted, lizardlike carnivores. Most feed on fishes, turtles, birds, and small mammals; large individuals may attack domestic livestock or humans. Crocodiles swim and feed in the water, floating at the surface to wait for prey, but bask in the sun and breed on land. They are reputed to be livelier than alligators and more likely to attack humans. They have a narrower snout than alligators and a tooth on each side of the jaw that is visible when the jaw is closed.

Cromwell, Oliver (b. April 25, 1599, Huntingdon, Huntingdonshire, Eng.—d. Sept. 3, 1658, London), English soldier and statesman, lord protector of the republican Commonwealth of England, Scotland, and Ireland (1653–58). He was elected to Parliament in 1628, but Charles I dissolved that Parliament in 1629 and did not call another for 11 years. In 1640 Cromwell was elected to the Short and the Long Parliament. When differences between Charles and Parliament erupted into the English Civil Wars, Cromwell became one of the leading generals on the Parliamentary side, winning many notable victories, including the Battles of Marston Moor and Naseby. He was among those who brought the king to trial and signed his death warrant. After the British Isles were named the Commonwealth, he served as the first chairman of the Council of State. In the next few years he fought against the Royalists in Ireland and Scotland and suppressed a mutiny inspired by the Levelers. When Charles II advanced into England, Cromwell destroyed his army at Worcester (1651), the battle that ended the civil wars. As lord protector, Cromwell raised his country's status once more to that of a leading European power and concluded the Anglo-Dutch War. Though a devout Calvinist, he pursued policies of religious toleration. He refused the title of king offered to him by Parliament in 1657. After his death he was succeeded by his son Richard Cromwell.

Cronus, or CRONOS, or KRONOS, In Greek religion, a male agricultural deity. He was the youngest of the 12 Titans borne by Uranus and Gaea, and his castration of his father separated heaven from earth. With his sister and consort Rhea, he fathered Hestia, Demeter, Hera, Hades, and Poseidon, all of whom he swallowed because he had been warned that he would be overthrown by his own child. Rhea hid his son Zeus and tricked Cronus into swallowing a stone; Zeus later forced Cronus to disgorge the others and then vanquished him in war. He was identified with the Roman god Saturn.

crop rotation, Successive cultivation of different crops in a specified order on the same fields. Some rotations are designed for high immediate returns, with little regard for basic resources. Others are planned for high continuing returns while protecting resources. A typical scheme selects rotation crops from three classifications: cultivated row crops (e.g., corn, potatoes), close-growing grains (e.g., oats, wheat), and sod-forming, or rest, crops (e.g., clover, clover-timothy). In general, cropping systems should include deep-rooting legumes. In addition to the many beneficial effects on soils and crops, well-planned crop rotations make the farm a more effective year-round enterprise by providing more efficient handling of labour, power, and equipment, reduction in weather and market risks, and improved ability to meet livestock requirements.

croquet (French dialect for "crook," "hockey stick") Game in which players using mallets drive wooden balls through a series of wickets, or hoops, set out on a lawn. The object is to be the first to complete the course by passing through all the wickets and hitting a goal peg. Croquet evolved from the 13th-century French game pall-mall. Championship matches are organized by governing bodies in the U.S. and Britain.

cross, Principal symbol of Christianity, recalling the crucifixion of Jesus. There are four basic iconogaphic representations: the *crux quadrata*, or Greek cross, with four equal arms; the *crux immissa*, or Latin cross, with a base stem longer than the other arms; the *crux commissa* (St. Anthony's cross), resembling the Greek letter tau (T); and the *crux decussataa* (St. Andrew's cross), resembling the Roman numeral 10 (X). Tradition holds that the *crux immissa* was used for Christ's crucifixion. Coptic Christians used the ancient Egyptian ankh. Displaying the cross was not common before Constantine I abolished crucifixion in the 4th century. A crucifix shows Christ's figure on a cross and is typical of Roman Catholicism and Eastern Orthodoxy. Making the sign of the cross with the hand may be a profession of faith, prayer, dedication, or benediction.

crossbow, Leading missile weapon of the Middle Ages, consisting of a short bow fixed transversely on a stock, with a groove to guide the missile and a trigger to release it. The missile, known as a bolt, was usually an arrow or dart. First used in antiquity, it was an important advance in warfare. Its destructive power came from its metal bow, which could propel a bolt with enough velocity to pierce chain mail and gave it a range of up to 1,000 ft (300 m). Powerful and versatile, it remained in use even after the introduction of the longbow and firearms and was not discarded until the 15th century. It has been used in modern times to hunt big game.

croup, Acute laryngeal inflammation and spasms in young children, with harsh cough, hoarseness, and difficulty breathing. Causes include infection, allergy, and physical irritation of the larynx. Viral croup, the most common, usually occurs before age 3. It can usually be treated at home with a cool mist vaporizer. Bacterial croup (epiglottitis) generally strikes between ages 3 and 7. Swelling of the epiglottis rapidly causes severe breathing and swallowing difficulty, requiring antibiotics and insertion of a breathing tube.

crow, Any of more than 20 species of black perching birds of the genus *Corvus* (family Corvidae) that are smaller than most ravens and have a thinner bill. They are named for the sound of their call. Common crows are found in North America and Eurasia. They eat grain, berries, insects, carrion, and the eggs of other birds. Crows may damage grain crops, but they also eat many economically harmful insects. At times tens of thousands roost together, but most species

Carrion crow (Corvus corone corone).
Eric Hosking

do not nest in colonies. Crows are considered the most intelligent of all birds (tool use is documented), and pet crows can be taught to imitate speech.

crucible process, Technique for producing cast or tool steel. It was invented in Britain *c.* 1740 by Benjamin Huntsman, who heated small pieces of carbon steel in a closed fireclay crucible placed in a coke fire. This was the first process used in Europe in which the temperature (2,900°F, or 1,600°C) was high enough to melt the steel, producing a homogeneous metal of uniform composition. After 1870 the Siemens regenerative gas furnace replaced the coke-fired furnace. Capable of producing even higher temperatures, the Siemens furnace had a number of combustion holes, each holding several crucibles, and heated as many as 100 crucibles at a time. All high-quality tool steel and high-speed steel was long made by the crucible process. In the 20th century the electric furnace has replaced it in countries with inexpensive electric power.

crucifixion, Method of capital punishment among the Persians, Seleucids, Jews, Carthaginians, and Romans from about the 6th century BC to the 4th century AD. The condemned man was usually whipped and forced to drag the crossbeam to where the upright was standing. His hands were tied or nailed to the crossbeam, which was attached to the upright 9–12 ft (2.5–3.5 m) above the ground, and his feet bound or nailed to the upright. Death was by heart failure or asphyxiation. Political or religious agitators and those without civil rights were crucified. Its overwhelming association today is with Jesus. Crucifixion was abolished by Constantine I in AD 337 after his conversion to Christianity.

cruise missile, Type of low-flying strategic guided missile developed by the U.S. and the Soviet Union in the 1960s and '70s. The V-1 missile was a precursor. Powered by jet engines, cruise missiles may carry either a nuclear or a conventional warhead. They are designed to hug the ground, which makes them hard to detect by radar. They are launched from ships, submarines, airplanes, and the ground.

cruiser, Warship built for high speed and great cruising radius, smaller than a battleship but larger than a destroyer. The term originally meant frigates of the sailing era, used to scout for enemy fleets and raid convoys. After 1880, it was a specific type of armoured warship. By World War II, cruisers served mainly as floating bases for amphibious assaults and as protection for aircraft-carrier task forces. Today U.S. cruisers carry surface-to-air missiles vital to a fleet's air-defense screen. Nuclear propulsion has given some cruisers virtually unlimited range.

Crusades, Military expeditions, beginning in the late 11th century, that were organized by Western Christians in response to centuries of Muslim wars of expansion. Their objectives were to check the spread of Islam, to retake control of the Holy Land, to conquer pagan areas, and to recapture formerly Christian territories. The Crusades were seen by many of their participants as a means of redemption and expiation for sins. Between 1095, when the First Crusade was launched by Pope Urban II at the Council of Clermont, and 1291, when the Latin Christians were finally expelled from their kingdom in Syria, there were numerous expeditions to the Holy Land, to Spain, and even to the Baltic; the Crusades continued for several centuries after 1291, usually as military campaigns intended to halt or slow the advance of Muslim power or to conquer pagan areas. The Crusaders initially enjoyed success, founding a Christian state in Palestine and Syria, but the continued growth of Islamic states ultimately reversed those gains. By the 14th century the Ottoman Turks had established themselves in the Balkans and would penetrate deeper into Europe despite repeated efforts to repulse them. Crusades were also called against heretics (the Albigensian Crusade, 1209–29) and various rivals of the popes, and the Fourth Crusade (1202–04) was diverted against the Byzantine Empire. Crusading declined

rapidly during the 16th century with the advent of the Protestant Reformation and the decline of papal authority. The Crusades constitute a controversial chapter in the history of Christianity, and their excesses have been the subject of centuries of historiography. Historians have also concentrated on the role the Crusades played in the expansion of medieval Europe and its institutions, and the notion of "crusading" has been transformed from a religio-military campaign into a modern metaphor for zealous and demanding struggles to advance the good ("crusades for") and to oppose perceived evil ("crusades against").

crust, Outermost solid part of the Earth, essentially composed of a range of igneous and metamorphic rock types. In continental regions, the crust is made up chiefly of granitic rock, whereas the composition of the ocean floor corresponds mainly to that of basalt and gabbro. On average, the crust extends 22 mi (35 km) downward from the surface to the underlying mantle, from which it is separated by the Mohorovičić discontinuity (the Moho). The crust and top layer of the mantle together form the lithosphere.

crustacean, Any member of the 45,000 arthropod species in the subphylum Crustacea. Distributed worldwide, crustaceans are distinguished by having two pairs of antenna-like appendages in front of the mouth and other paired appendages near the mouth that act like jaws. Most species are marine, including shrimps and barnacles. Some, including crayfishes, live in freshwater habitats; others (e.g., sand fleas, land crabs, and sow bugs) live in moist terrestrial environments. The typical adult body is composed of a series of segments (somites) either fused or linked to each other by flexible areas that form movable joints. The carapace (shell) varies in thickness among species and must be periodically molted to allow growth. Many species of marine crustaceans are scavengers, and many (including copepods and krill) are significant components of the diets of larger organisms.

Cruz, Sor Juana Inés de la (b. Nov. 12, 1651, San Miguel Nepantla, Viceroyalty of New Spain—d. April 17, 1695, Mexico City), Mexican poet, dramatist, scholar, nun, and early feminist. Born out of wedlock to a family of modest means, she was sent to relatives in Mexico City, where her great intelligence became known to the viceroy. She soon became a nun, remaining cloistered for the rest of her life. Sor Juana had one of the largest private libraries in the New World. Her most important works are the poem *First Dream* (1692; translated in *A Sor Juana Anthology*), which recounts the soul's quest for knowledge, and "The Reply to Sister Filotea of the Cross" (1691), her defense of women's right to knowledge.

cryogenics, Study and use of low-temperature phenomena. The cryogenic temperature range is from −238°F (−150°C) to absolute zero. At low temperatures, matter has unusual properties. Substances that are naturally gases can be liquefied at low temperatures, and metals lose electrical resistance as they get colder. Cryogenics dates from 1877, when oxygen was first cooled to the point at which it became a liquid (−297°F, or −183°C); superconductivity was discovered in 1911. Applications of cryogenics include the storage and transport of liquefied gases, food preservation, cryosurgery, rocket fuels, and superconducting electromagnets.

crypt, Subterranean chamber, usually under a church floor. The catacombs of the early Christians were known as *cryptae,* and when churches came to be built over the tombs of saints and martyrs, subterranean chapels were built around the actual tomb. As early as the reign of Constantine I (AD 306–37), the crypt was considered a normal part of a church. Later its size was increased to include the entire space beneath the choir or chancel; the crypt of Canterbury Cathedral is an elaborate underground church with its own apse. Many secular medieval European buildings also had richly decorated crypts.

cryptography, Practice of the enciphering and deciphering of messages in secret code in order to render them unintelligible to all but the intended receiver. Cryptography may also refer to the art of cryptanalysis, by which cryptographic codes are broken. Collectively, the science of secure and secret communications, involving both cryptography and cryptanalysis, is known as cryptology. The principles of cryptography are today applied to the encryption of fax, television, and computer network communications. In particular, the secure exchange of computer data is of great importance to banking, government, and commercial communications.

cryptomonad, Any small organism with two flagella that is considered both a protozoan and an alga. Occurring in both fresh and salt water, cryptomonads contain pigments found only in red algae and blue-green algae (cyanobacteria). They sometimes live harmlessly within other organisms. Some species conduct photosynthesis. Others lack pigment-containing structures and eat organic matter, under certain conditions surviving on minerals alone.

crystal, Any solid material whose atoms are arranged in a definite pattern and whose surface regularity reflects its internal symmetry. Each of a crystal's millions of individual structural units (unit cells) contains all the substance's atoms, molecules, or ions in the same proportions as in its chemical formula. The cells are repeated in all directions to form a geometric pattern, manifested by the number and orientation of external planes (crystal faces). Crystals are classified into seven crystallographic systems based on their symmetry: isometric, trigonal, hexagonal, tetragonal, orthorhombic, monoclinic, and triclinic. Crystals are generally formed when a liquid solidifies, a vapour becomes supersaturated or a liquid solution can no longer retain dissolved material, which is then precipitated. Metals, alloys, minerals, and semiconductors are all crystalline, at least microscopically. (A noncrystalline solid is called amorphous.) Under special conditions, a single crystal can grow to a substantial size; examples include gemstones and some artificial crystals. Few crystals are perfect; defects affect the material's electrical behaviour and may weaken or strengthen it.

Crystal Palace, Giant glass-and-iron exhibition hall in Hyde Park, London, that housed the Great Exhibition of 1851. It was taken down and rebuilt (1852–54) at Sydenham Hill, where it survived until its destruction by fire in 1936. Designed by the greenhouse builder Sir Joseph Paxton (1801–1865), it was a remarkable assembly of prefabricated parts. Its intricate network of slender iron rods sustaining walls of clear glass established an architectural standard for later international exhibitions, likewise housed in glass conservatories.

The Crystal Palace at Sydenham Hill, London. It was designed by Sir Joseph Paxton for the Great Exhibition of 1851 and rebuilt in 1852–54 at Sydenham Hill but was destroyed in 1936.
BBC Hulton Picture Library

Ctesiphon, Ancient city, central Mesopotamia. Located on the Tigris River, southeast of modern Baghdad, Iraq, it was first a Greek army camp opposite the Hellenistic city of Seleucia. It was the capital of Parthia in the 2nd century BC. Destroyed by the Romans in AD 165, it was resettled by the Persian Sāsānian dynasty in the 3rd century. The Arabs conquered the city in 637 but abandoned it by 763 in favour of a new city, Baghdad. The site is famous for the remains of a gigantic vaulted hall, the Ṭāq Kisrā, which has one of the largest single-span brick arches in the world.

Cuba, officially REPUBLIC OF CUBA, Island country, West Indies. Located 90 mi (145 km) south of Florida, it comprises the island of Cuba and surrounding small islands. Area: 42,426 sq mi (109,884 sq km). Population: (2011 est.) 11,240,000. Capital: Havana. The population is largely of African-European or African descent; most of the rest are of European ancestry. Language: Spanish (official). Religions: Christianity (predominantly Roman Catholic; also Protestant), Santería (both formerly discouraged). Currency: Cuban peso. The main island of Cuba is 777 mi (1,250 km) long and 19–119 mi (31–191 km) wide. About one-quarter is mountainous, with Turquino Peak at an elevation of 6,476 ft (1,974 m) the highest peak; the remainder is extensive plains and basins. The climate is semitropical. Cuba was the first communist republic in the Western Hemisphere. It has a centrally planned economy that depends on the export of sugar and, to a much lesser extent, tobacco and nickel. Its cigars are considered the world's best. It is a unitary socialist republic with one legislative house; its head of state and government is the president. Several Indian groups, including the Ciboney and the Arawak, inhabited Cuba at the time of the first Spanish contact. Christopher Columbus claimed the island for Spain in 1492, and the Spanish conquest began in 1511, when the settlement of Baracoa was founded. The native Indians were eradicated over the succeeding centuries, and African slaves, from the 18th century until slavery was abolished in 1886, were imported to work the sugar plantations. Cuba revolted unsuccessfully against Spain in the Ten Years' War (1868–78); a second war of independence began in 1895. In 1898 the U.S. entered the war; Spain relinquished its claim to Cuba, which was occupied by the U.S. for three years before gaining its independence in 1902. The U.S. invested heavily in the Cuban sugar industry in the first half of the 20th century, and this, combined with tourism and gambling, caused the economy to prosper. Inequalities in the distribution of wealth persisted, however, as did political corruption. In 1958–59 the communist revolutionary Fidel Castro overthrew dictator Fulgencio Batista and established a socialist state aligned with the Soviet Union, abolishing capitalism and nationalizing foreign-owned enterprises. Relations with the U.S. deteriorated, reaching a low point with the 1961 Bay of Pigs invasion and the 1962 Cuban missile crisis. In 1980 about 125,000 Cubans, including many officially labeled "undesirables," were shipped to the U.S. With the demise of the Soviet Union in 1991, Cuba lost important financial backing, and its economy suffered greatly. The economy gradually began improving later in the 1990s with the encouragement of tourism and the legalization of small businesses and private employment, though diplomatic relations with the U.S. were not resumed. In the early 21st century, Cuba benefited from a petroleum-trade agreement with Venezuela and eased some of its restrictive economic and social policies. Castro officially stepped down as president in 2008, ending his 49-year rule of Cuba; his younger brother Raúl replaced him as Cuba's leader.

Cuban missile crisis (1962) Major confrontation between the U.S. and the Soviet Union over the presence of Soviet nuclear missiles in Cuba. In October 1962 a U.S. spy plane detected a ballistic missile on a launching site in Cuba. Pres. John F. Kennedy placed a naval blockade around the island, and for several days the U.S. and the Soviet Union hovered on the brink of war. Soviet premier Nikita Khrushchev finally agreed to remove the missiles in return for a secret commitment from the U.S. to withdraw its own missiles from Turkey and to never invade Cuba. The incident increased tensions during the Cold War and fueled the nuclear arms race between the two countries.

Cubism, Movement in the visual arts created by Pablo Picasso and Georges Braque in Paris between 1907 and 1914. They were later joined by Juan Gris, Fernand Léger, Robert Delaunay, and others. The name derives from a review that described Braque's work as images composed of cubes. Picasso's *Demoiselles d'Avignon* (1907) signaled the new style, which was inspired by African sculpture and the later paintings of Paul Cézanne. Cubist work emphasized the flat, two-dimensional, fragmented surface of the picture plane, rejecting perspective, foreshortening, modeling, and chiaroscuro in favour of geometric forms. The work made in this style from 1910 to 1912 is often referred to as Analytical Cubism. Paintings executed during this period show the breaking down, or analysis, of form. Artists favoured right-angle and straight-line construction and colour schemes that were nearly monochromatic. After 1912 the phase known as Synthetic Cubism began. Works from this phase emphasize the combination, or synthesis, of forms in the picture. Colour assumes a strong role in the work; shapes, while remaining fragmented and flat, are larger and more decorative; and collage is often used. Many subsequent 20th-century avant-garde movements were influenced by the experimentation of the Cubists.

cuckoo, Any of some 138 species of tree-dwelling and terrestrial

Cuckoo (Cuculus).
Graeme Chapman/Ardea London

birds of the family Cuculidae. They are found worldwide in temperate and tropical regions but are most diverse in the Old World tropics. New World species are sometimes classified as a separate family (Coccyzidae) and include the roadrunner. Cuckoos range from 6.5 to 36 in. (16 to 90 cm) long. Most are drab gray, but a few are partially or completely brightly coloured or iridescent. Aside from the European cuckoo's familiar two-note call, cuckoos are best known for their habit of brood parasitism; their eggs resemble those of the host species (egg mimicry), and the adult cuckoo removes one or more host eggs to ensure that the substitution is not detected. The newly hatched cuckoo may also eject eggs or nestlings.

cult, Collective veneration or worship (e.g., the cult of the saints—meaning collective veneration of the saints—in Roman Catholicism). In the West, the term has come to be used for groups that are perceived to have deviated from normative religions in belief and practice. They typically have a charismatic leader and attract followers who are in some way disenfranchised from the mainstream of society. Cults as thus defined are often viewed as foreign or dangerous.

Cultural Revolution, officially GREAT PROLETARIAN CULTURAL REVOLUTION (1966–76) Upheaval launched by Mao Zedong to renew the spirit of revolution in China. Mao feared urban social stratification in a society as traditionally elitist as China and also believed that programs instituted to correct for the failed Great Leap Forward showed that his colleagues lacked commitment to the revolution. He organized China's urban youths into groups called the Red Guards, shut down China's schools, and encouraged the Red Guards to attack all traditional values and "bourgeois things." They soon splintered into zealous rival groups, and in 1968 Mao sent millions of them to the rural hinterland, bringing some order to the cities. Within the government, a coalition of Mao's associates fought with more moderate elements, many of whom were purged, were verbally attacked, were physically abused, and subsequently died; leaders Liu Shaoqi and Lin Biao both died under mysterious circumstances. From 1973 to Mao's death in 1976, politics shifted between the hard-line Gang of Four and the moderates headed by Zhou Enlai and Deng Xiaoping. After Mao's death the Cultural Revolution was brought to a close. By that time, nearly three million party members and countless wrongfully purged citizens awaited reinstatement. The Cultural Revolution subsequently was repudiated in China.

culture, Integrated pattern of human knowledge, belief, and behaviour that is both a result of and integral to the human capacity for learning and transmitting knowledge to succeeding generations. Culture thus consists of language, ideas, beliefs, customs, taboos, codes, institutions, tools, techniques, works of art, rituals, ceremonies, and symbols. It has played a crucial role in human evolution, allowing human beings to adapt the environment to their own purposes rather than depend solely on natural selection to achieve adaptive success. Every human society has its own particular culture, or sociocultural system. Variation among cultures is attributable to such factors as differing physical habitats and resources; the range of possibilities inherent in areas such as language, ritual, and social organization; and historical phenomena such as the development of links with other cultures. An individual's attitudes, values, ideals, and beliefs are greatly influenced by the culture (or cultures) in which he or she lives. Culture change takes place as a result of ecological, socioeconomic, political, religious, or other fundamental factors affecting a society.

cuneiform writing, System of writing employed in ancient times to write a number of languages of the Middle East. The original and primary writing material for cuneiform texts was a damp clay tablet, into which the scribe would press a wedge-shaped stroke with a reed stylus. A configuration of such impressions constituted a character, or sign. Proto-cuneiform signs dating from *c.* 3200–3000 BC were drawn rather than impressed and were largely pictographic, though these features were lost as the script evolved. A single cuneiform sign could be a logogram (an arbitrary representation of a word) or a syllabogram (a representation of the sound of a syllable). The first language to be written in cuneiform was Sumerian. Akkadian began to be written in cuneiform *c.* 2350 BC. Later the script was adapted to other South Asian languages. Cuneiform was slowly displaced in the first millennium BC by the rise of Aramaic, written in an alphabet script of Phoenician origin. Knowledge of the value of cuneiform signs was lost until the mid-19th century, when European scholars deciphered the script.

Cupid, classical statue; in the Museo Archeologico Nazionale, Naples
Alinari/Art Resource, New York

Cupid, Ancient Roman god of love in all its varieties, identified with the Greek Eros. Cupid was the son of Mercury and Venus. He was usually represented as a winged infant who carried a bow and quiver of arrows, which he shot at humans to inflict wounds that inspired love or passion. He was also sometimes depicted as a beautiful youth. Though generally considered beneficent, he could be mischievous in matchmaking, often at his mother's behest.

Curaçao, Island (pop., 2009 est.: 141,766) and autonomous state within the Kingdom of the Netherlands, Lesser Antilles, southern Caribbean Sea. It is located north of the coast of Venezuela and about 50 miles (80 km) south-southeast of Aruba. Area: 171 sq mi (444 sq km). Population: (2011 est.) 143,000. Capital: Willemstad. Dutch, Papiamentu, and English are official languages. The principal religion is Roman Catholicism. The currency is the Netherlands Antillean guilder (to be replaced with the Dutch Caribbean guilder by 2012). First visited by Europeans in 1499, it was settled by the Spanish in 1527. Sephardic Jews from Portugal migrated there in the 1500s, originating the oldest continuously inhabited Jewish community in the Western Hemisphere. The Dutch West India Company gained control of the island in 1634. It was awarded to the Netherlands by the 1815 Treaty of Paris. Curaçao was one of the six original Dutch dependencies in the West Indies that were governed collectively from 1845 and reorganized as the Netherlands Antilles in 1954, when they were granted internal self-government. Upon the dissolution of the Netherlands Antilles in 2010, Curaçao achieved a greater degree of independence while remaining a part of the Netherlands. Products include oranges, Curaçao liqueur, and aloes. The chief industry is the refining of oil from Venezuela; tourism is of growing importance. Willemstad, the chief town, has one of the best natural harbours in the West Indies.

curia, In medieval Europe, a court, or a group of persons who attended a ruler at a given time for social, political, or judicial purposes. The ruler and curia made policy decisions (as on war, treaties, finances, church relations), and under a powerful ruler the curia often became active as a court of law. Indeed, curiae became so loaded down with judicial work that they were gradually forced to delegate it to special groups of judges. In England the Curia Regis (King's Court) began at the time of the Norman Conquest (1066) and lasted to about the end of the 13th century. It was the germ from which the higher courts of law, the Privy Council, and the cabinet were to spring.

Curie, Marie, orig. MARIA SKŁODOWSKA (b. Nov. 7, 1867, Warsaw, Pol., Russian Empire—d. July 4, 1934, near Sallanches, France), Polish-born French physical chemist. She studied at the Sorbonne (from 1891). Seeking the presence of radioactivity—recently discovered by Henri Becquerel in uranium—in other matter, she found it in thorium. In 1895 she married fellow physicist Pierre Curie (1859–1906). Together they discovered the elements polonium (which Marie named after her native Poland) and radium, and they distinguished alpha, beta, and gamma radiation. For their work on radioactivity (a term she coined), the Curies shared the 1903 Nobel Prize for Physics with Becquerel. Marie thus became the first woman to receive a Nobel Prize. After Pierre's death, Marie was appointed to his professorship and became the first woman to teach at the Sorbonne. In 1911 she won a Nobel Prize for Chemistry for discovering polonium and isolating pure radium, becoming the first person to win two Nobel Prizes. She died of leukemia caused by her long exposure to radioactivity. In 1995 she became the first woman whose own achievements earned her the honour of having her ashes enshrined in the Pantheon in Paris.

curium, Synthetic radioactive chemical element of the actinide series, chemical symbol Cm, atomic number 96. This transuranium element was discovered in 1944 in plutonium-239 that had been bombarded by helium ions in a cyclotron. Curium is named after physicists Pierre and Marie Curie. It is a silvery metal. Its longest-lasting isotope, curium-247, has a half-life of 15.6 million years. Curium isotopes are used in space probes to provide compact, long-lived sources of electricity through conversion of their heat of radioactive decay.

curling, Game in which two teams of four players each slide a round stone by means of a gooseneck handle on the top over a 138-ft (42-m) stretch of ice toward a target circle. The object is to deliver the stone closest to the centre (called the house). Each player delivers two stones, which average 40 lbs (18.1 kg) apiece, often applying a curl to the stone's trajectory. The player's teammates use a broom to sweep the ice ahead of the oncoming stone in order to facilitate a longer slide or to adjust the arc of the curl. Blocking and knocking out an opponent's stones are important strategies of the sport. Curling originated in Scotland in the early 16th century. World championships have been held since 1959 and are usually dominated by Canadians and Scandinavians. In 1998 curling became a medal sport in the Winter Olympic Games.

The British women's curling team competing in the final match at the 2002 Winter Olympics in Salt Lake City, Utah.
Roberto Schmidt—AFP/Getty Images

currency, In industrialized nations, the portion of the national money supply (consisting of banknotes and government-issued paper money and coins) that does not require endorsement to serve as a medium of exchange. Since the abandonment of the gold standard, governments have not been obligated to repay the holders of currency in any form of precious metal. Consequently, the volume of currency has been determined by the actions of the government or central bank and not by the supply of precious metals. In less-developed societies, or in times of economic scarcity, items such as livestock or tobacco (cigarettes) may serve as currency.

curry (from Tamil *kari*, "sauce") Dish or sauce in Indian cuisine. It is seasoned with a mixture of spices often including turmeric, cumin, coriander, ginger, as well as garlic and chiles. Some of the curry spices are known for their antiseptic and preservative properties. Curries have been a part of South Asian cookery since antiquity. The primarily vegetarian curries of southern India are the most pungent. Those of northern India, where lamb and poultry are eaten, generally avoid hot or pungent ingredients.

Curzon Line, Demarcation line between Poland and Soviet Russia. The British foreign secretary, Lord Curzon, proposed it as a possible armistice line in the Russo-Polish War of 1919–20. His plan was not accepted, and the final peace treaty (1921) provided Poland with almost 52,000 sq mi (135,000 sq km) of land east of the line. With the outbreak of World War II, the Soviet Union revived the line, claiming all the territory east of it. In 1945 a Soviet-Polish treaty officially designated a line almost identical to the Curzon Line as their mutual border.

customs union, Trade agreement by which a group of countries charges a common set of tariffs to the rest of the world while allowing free trade among themselves. It is a partial form of economic integration, intermediate between free-trade zones, which allow mutual free trade but lack a common tariff system, and common markets, which both utilize common tariffs and allow free movement of resources including capital and labour between members. Well-known customs unions include the Zollverein, a 19th-century organization formed by several German states under Prussian leadership, and the European Union, which passed through a customs-union stage on the path to fuller economic integration.

cuttlefish, Any of about 100 species of marine cephalopods in

the order Sepioidea, characterized by a thick, internal calcium-containing shell called the cuttlebone. Species range between 1 and 35 in. (2.5–90 cm) in length and have a somewhat flattened body bordered by a pair of narrow fins. All have eight arms and two longer tentacles used to capture prey. Suction disks are located on the arms and at the tips of the tentacles. Cuttlefish inhabit tropical or temperate coastal waters. They feed mainly on crustaceans, small fishes, and each other. They are used by humans as food, as a source of ink, and for the cuttlebone, a dietary supplement for cage birds.

Cuttlefish (Sepia officinalis)
Douglas P. Wilson

Cuzco, City (pop., 2002 est.: 301,342), south-central Peru. It is located high in the Andes Mountains at an elevation of about 11,150 ft (3,400 m). One of the oldest continuously inhabited cities in the Western Hemisphere, it was founded in the 11th or 12th century and was once the capital of the vast Inca empire. Spanish conquistador Francisco Pizarro captured the city in 1533. It suffered major earthquake damage in 1650 and again in 1950, though many sites have since been restored. Nearby ruins include Sacsahuamán, an ancient Inca fortress, and Machu Picchu, an Inca resort. Cuzco's cathedral (1654) incorporates the foundation and several walls of the Temple of the Sun. Many of the city's other buildings, including the university (1692), also date from the colonial era. The city was designated a UNESCO World Heritage site in 1983.

cyanide, Any chemical compound containing the combining group CN. Ionic and organic cyanide compounds differ in chemical properties, but both are toxic, especially the ionic ones. Cyanide poisoning inhibits cells' oxidative processes; its action is extremely rapid, and an antidote must be given promptly. Cyanides occur naturally in certain seeds (e.g., apple seeds, wild cherry pits). Cyanides, including hydrogen cyanide (HCN, or hydrocyanic acid), are used industrially in the production of acrylic fibres, synthetic rubbers, and plastics as well as in electroplating, case-hardening of iron and steel, fumigation, and concentration of ores.

cyanide process, or MACARTHUR-FORREST PROCESS, Method of extracting silver and gold from their ores by dissolving them in a dilute solution of sodium cyanide or potassium cyanide. The process—invented in 1887 by the Scottish chemists John S. MacArthur, Robert W. Forrest, and William Forrest—includes contacting the finely ground ore with the cyanide solution, separating unwanted solids from the clear solution, and recovering the precious metals from the solution by precipitation with zinc dust.

cybercrime, also known as COMPUTER CRIME, Any use of a computer as an instrument to further illegal ends, such as committing fraud, trafficking in child pornography and intellectual property, stealing identities, or violating privacy. Cybercrime, especially through the Internet, has grown in importance as the computer has become central to commerce, entertainment, and government. The international nature of cybercrimes has led to international cyberlaws.

cybernetics, Science of regulation and control in animals (including humans), organizations, and machines when they are viewed as self-governing whole entities consisting of parts and their organization. It was conceived by Norbert Wiener, who coined the term in 1948. Cybernetics views communication and control in all self-contained complex systems as analogous. It differs from the empirical sciences (physics, biology, etc.) in not being interested in material form but in organization, pattern, and communication in entities. Because of the increasing sophistication of computers and the efforts to make them behave in human-like ways, cybernetics today is closely allied with artificial intelligence and robotics, and it draws heavily on ideas developed in information theory.

cycad, Any of the palmlike woody plants that constitute the order Cycadales, containing two families, Cycadaceae and Zamiaceae. Cycads have crowns of large, feathery compound leaves and cones at the ends of their branches. Some have tall, unbranched, armour-like trunks; others have partially buried stems with swollen trunks. Slow-growing cycads are used as ornamental conservatory plants, but some survive outdoors in temperate regions. The stems of some cycads yield starch that is edible if thoroughly cooked. The young leaves and seeds of others also are edible.

Cyclades, Greek KIKLÁDHES, Group of about 30 islands, southern Aegean Sea. They cover a land area of 976 sq mi (2,528 sq km) and constitute the Cyclades department of Greece, which has its capital at Ermoúpolis. Their name refers to the ancient tradition that they formed a circle around the sacred island of Delos. The chief islands are Andros, Tínos, Náxos, Amorgós, Melos, Páros, Syros, Kéa, Kíthnos, Serifos, Íos, and Thíra. They were the centre of a Bronze Age culture—the Cycladic, noted for its white marble idols—and later belonged to the Mycenaean culture in the 2nd millennium BC. Colonized by Ionians in the 10th–9th century BC, they later were successively held by Persians, Athenians, Ptolemaic Egyptians, and Macedonians. Ruled by Venice after the early 13th century AD, the islands fell to the Turks at different times during the 16th to 18th centuries. They became part of Greece in 1829. The economy is now based on tourism and on the export of wine, hides, pottery, and handicrafts.

cycling, Use of the bicycle in competitive sport or in recreation. The classic professional races are held mainly in Europe; the first was held in Paris in 1868. There are basically two types of race: road races and track races. The first U.S. cycling competition, a six-day race, was held in 1891. Six-day racing was reintroduced to Europe as a two-man team event in the 20th century, but it has largely died out in the U.S. The first Tour de France, the premier race, was held in 1903. Cycling has been part of the Olympics since the first modern games in 1896. Events include a variety of open-road and circuit races for both men and women.

cyclone, Any large system of winds that circulates about a centre of low atmospheric pressure in a counterclockwise direction north of the Equator and in a clockwise direction south of it. Cyclones that occur in the mid- and high latitudes are known as extratropical cyclones; they are frequently preceded by thickening and lowering clouds, followed by precipitation. Cyclones that form in the lower latitudes are known as tropical cyclones; smaller than extratropical cyclones, they tend to be more violent and can cause considerable damage. Wind systems that circulate around a high-pressure centre in directions opposite to that of cyclones are known as anticyclones.

Cyclops, In Greek mythology, any of several one-eyed giants. In the *Odyssey*, the Cyclopes were cannibals who lived in a faraway land (traditionally Sicily). Odysseus was captured by the Cyclops Polyphemus, but he escaped being devoured by blinding the giant. According to Hesiod, there were three Cyclopes (Arges, Brontes, and Steropes) who forged thunderbolts for Zeus. In a later tradition, they were assistants to Hephaestus in this task. Apollo destroyed them after one of their thunderbolts killed Asclepius.

cyclotron, Particle accelerator that accelerates charged atomic or subatomic particles in a constant magnetic field. It consists of two hollow semicircular electrodes, called dees, in a large evacuated cylindrical box. An alternating electric field between the dees continuously accelerates the particles from one dee to the other, while the magnetic field guides them in a circular path. As the speed of the particles increases, so does the radius of their path, and the particles spiral outward. In this manner, a cyclotron can accelerate protons to energies of up to 25 million electron volts.

Cygnus A, Radio-emitting galaxy lying in the constellation Cygnus, about 700 million light-years from Earth. It is the brightest cosmic source of radio waves in the sky and the first radio galaxy to be detected. Because of its peculiar divided appearance, it was once thought to be two galaxies colliding. Astronomers now believe it to be a single galaxy with a large black hole at its core; emanating from this central region are two opposing jets of hot gas that end in radio- and X-ray-emitting lobes called "hot spots."

cymbal, Percussion instrument consisting of a circular metal plate that is struck with a drumstick or two such plates that are struck together. They were used, often ritually, in Assyria, Israel (from c. 1100 BC), Egypt, and other ancient civilizations, spread to East Asia, and reached Europe by the 13th century AD. Western orchestral cymbals derive from those used in the Turkish military bands in vogue in 18th-century Europe. Though Asian cymbals are often flat, Middle Eastern and Western cymbals usually have a central concave dome, or boss, so that only the edges touch when they are clashed. The finest cymbals have long been manufactured in Turkey by means of closely guarded techniques. In popular music, cymbals are not clashed manually; instead, a cymbal suspended on a sticklike stand may be brushed or struck, and horizontal "hi-hat" cymbals are clashed lightly by use of a pedal mechanism.

Cynics, Greek philosophical sect that flourished from the 4th century BC to the 6th century AD. Antisthenes (c. 445–365 BC), a disciple of Socrates, is considered the founder of the movement, but Diogenes of Sinope was its paradigm. Named principally for their meeting place, the Cynosarges, the Cynics considered virtue—including a life of poverty and self-sufficiency and the suppression of desires—to be the sole good, but they were distinguished more for their unconventional manners and way of life than for any system of thought. The Cynics influenced the development of Stoicism.

cypress, Any of 12 species of ornamental and timber evergreen conifers constituting the genus *Cupressus* of the family Cupressaceae, which includes more than 130 species found throughout the world. The leaves are usually paired or in threes and are small and scalelike. A few of the many economically important genera in the cypress family are *Cupressus, Thuja* (arborvitae), *Calocedrus* (incense cedar), and *Juniperus* (juniper). Arborvitae, cypress, and juniper are especially important as timber sources or ornamentals. They also contain useful oils, resins, and tannins.

Italian cypress (Cupressus sempervirens).
W.H. Hodge

Cyprus, officially REPUBLIC OF CYPRUS, Island and country, eastern Mediterranean Sea. Area: 2,276 sq mi (5,896 sq km). Population: (2011 est.) 1,118,000 (whole island). Capital: Nicosia. Cyprus is currently divided into two de facto states. The Republic of Cyprus, the internationally recognized government, occupies the southern two-thirds of the island. Its population is predominantly Greek. Languages: Greek, Turkish (both official). Religion: Christianity (predominantly Eastern Orthodox). Currency: euro. The Turkish Republic of Northern Cyprus (TRNC) occupies the northern third of the island. Its population is overwhelmingly Turkish. Languages: Turkish (official), English. Religion: Islam. Currency: Turkish lira. The third largest island in the Mediterranean, Cyprus lies about 40 mi (65 km) off the southern coast of Turkey. It is largely mountainous, with a fertile heartland and coastal plains. Mount Olympus is its highest peak, 6,401 ft (1,951 m) above sea level. The climate is Mediterranean. Cyprus has a free-enterprise economy based mainly on trade and manufacturing, and it ranks high in the world in merchant shipping. The internationally recognized government is a unitary multiparty republic with a unicameral legislature; its head of state and government is the president. The government of the TRNC, which has not received wide recognition, is a de facto republic with one legislative house; its head of state and government is the president assisted by a council of ministers. Cyprus was inhabited by the early Neolithic Period; by the late Bronze Age it had been visited and settled by Mycenaeans and Achaeans, who introduced Greek culture and language, and it became a trading centre. By 800 BCE Phoenicians had begun to settle there. Ruled over the centuries by the Assyrian, Persian, and Ptolemaic empires, it was annexed by the Roman Republic and Empire in 58 BCE. It was part of the Byzantine Empire in the 4th–12th centuries CE. It was conquered by the English king Richard I (the Lionheart) in 1191. A part of the Venetian trading empire from 1489, it was taken by the Ottoman Empire in 1571. In 1878 the British assumed control, and Cyprus became a British crown colony in 1925. It gained independence in 1960. Conflict between Greek and Turkish Cypriots led to the establishment of a United Nations (UN) peacekeeping mission in 1964. In 1974, fearing a movement to unite Cyprus with Greece, the Republic of Turkey sent troops to occupy the northern third of the island. Turkish Cypriots established a functioning government, which obtained recognition only from Turkey. The UN peacekeeping mission has remained. Negotiations to reunify the island under a single government in 2004 were unsuccessful, but border restrictions were relaxed by both sides. The Republic of Cyprus joined the European Union in 2004 and adopted the euro as its official currency in 2008.

Cyrillic alphabet, Alphabet used for Russian, Serbian, Bulgarian and Macedonian, Belarusian, Ukrainian, and many non-Slavic languages of the former Soviet Union, as well as Khalka Mongolian. The history of the Cyrillic alphabet is complex and much disputed. It is clearly derived from 9th-century Greek uncial capital letters, with the non-Greek letters probably taken from the Glagolitic alphabet, a highly original alphabet in which (along with Cyrillic) Old Church Slavonic was written. A commonly held hypothesis is that followers of Sts. Cyril and Methodius developed Cyrillic in the southern Balkans around the end of the 9th century. The 44 original Cyrillic letters were reduced in number in most later alphabets used for vernacular languages, and some wholly original letters introduced, particularly for non-Slavic languages.

Cyrus II, known as CYRUS THE GREAT (b. c. 585, Media or Persis—d. c. 529, Asia), Conqueror who founded the Achaemenian Empire. The grandson of Cyrus I (fl. late 7th century BC), he came to power by overthrowing his maternal grandfather, the king of the Medes. The empire he developed was thenceforth centered on Persia and included Media, Ionia, Lydia, Mesopotamia, Syria, and Palestine. Cyrus conquered by diplomacy as well as by force. The subject of a rich legend in Persia and Greece (recorded by Xenophon and others), he was called the father of his people. He appears in the Bible as the liberator of the Jews held captive in Babylon. He died battling nomads in Central Asia. His legacy is the founding not only of an empire but of a culture and civilization that continued to expand after his death and lasted for two centuries. He exerted a strong influence on the Greeks and Alexander the Great.

Awarded heroic qualities in legend, he has long been revered by Persians almost as a religious figure. In 1971 Iran celebrated the 2,500th anniversary of his founding of the monarchy.

cyst, Enclosed sac within body tissues. It has a distinct membrane and generally contains liquid. Most cysts are benign, but several kinds may be malignant or precancerous. Benign cysts often press on nearby organs and require removal. Formed by overproduction of epithelium (surface tissue of anatomical structures), cysts may become detached from surrounding structures and move freely. They can contain natural secretions, abnormal breakdown products, or, in infections, bacteria, larval parasites, and microbial products. Some organs, including the kidney, liver, and breast, can become filled with cysts as a result of cystic diseases that may be dangerous or may hide more serious diseases.

cystic fibrosis (CF), or MUCOVISCIDOSIS, Inherited metabolic disorder characterized by production of thick, sticky mucus. It is recessive and the most common inherited disorder (about 1 per 2,000 live births) in those of European ancestry. Concentrated mucous secretions in the lungs plug the bronchi, making breathing difficult, promoting infections, and producing chronic cough, recurrent pneumonia, and progressive loss of lung function, the usual cause of death. The secretions interfere with digestive enzymes and block nutrient absorption. Abnormally salty sweat is the basis for diagnosis of cystic fibrosis. Treatment includes enzyme supplements, a diet high in calories, protein, and fat, vigorous physical therapy, and antibiotics. Persons with cystic fibrosis once seldom survived beyond childhood; now more than half reach adulthood, though males are usually sterile.

cystitis, Inflammation of the urinary bladder. Infections with bacteria, viruses, fungi, or parasites usually spread from nearby sites. Symptoms include burning pain during and right after urination, unusually urgent or frequent urination, and lower back pain. Women, with a shorter urethra than men, are more susceptible to cystitis, most cases resulting from *E. coli* bacteria from the rectum. Acute cystitis, usually bacterial, causes swelling, bleeding, small ulcers and cysts, and sometimes abscesses. Recurrent or persistent infection can lead to chronic cystitis, with bladder-wall thickening. Diagnosis is made by finding bacteria or other organisms in the (normally sterile) urine. It is treated with drugs or surgery.

cytomegalovirus (CMV), Any of several viruses in the herpes family. Active infection produces enlarged cells enclosing foreign matter. Most prevalent in crowded, poor communities, it is transmitted by sexual contact or exposure to infected body fluids. It rarely causes serious illness in otherwise healthy adults; however, it can lead to serious consequences, including blindness, in those with depressed immune systems. In newborns, even without spleen and liver enlargement (10% of cases), CMV is the most common infection and a major cause of congenital deafness; it may also induce retardation and blindness. There is no effective treatment.

Czech Republic, formerly (1918–92, with Slovakia) CZECHO-SLOVAKIA, Country, central Europe. Area: 30,450 sq mi (78,865 sq km). Population: (2011 est.) 10,551,000. Capital: Prague. Czechs make up about nine-tenths of the population; Slovaks and Moravians are the largest minorities. Language: Czech (official). Religion: Christianity (predominantly Roman Catholic, also other Christians, Protestant). Currency: koruna. The landlocked country is dominated by the Bohemian Massif, a ring of mountains rising to 5,256 ft (1,602 m) at Mount Snezka to encircle the Bohemian Plateau. The Morava River valley, known as the Moravian Corridor, separates the Bohemian Massif from the Carpathian Mountains. Woodlands are a characteristic feature of the Czech landscape; most regions have a moderate oceanic climate. The economy, privatized since 1990, is now largely market-oriented. The Czech Republic is a unitary multiparty republic with two legislative houses; its head of state is the president, and the head of government is the prime minister. Until 1918 its history was largely that of Bohemia. In that year the independent republic of Czechoslovakia was born through the union of Bohemia and Moravia with Slovakia. Czechoslovakia came under the domination of the Soviet Union after World War II, and from 1948 to 1989 it was ruled by a communist government. Its growing political liberalization was suppressed by a Soviet invasion in 1968. After 1990, separatist sentiments emerged among the Slovaks, and in 1992 the Czechs and Slovaks agreed to break up their federated state. At midnight on Dec. 31, 1992, Czechoslovakia was peacefully dissolved and replaced by two new countries, the Czech Republic and Slovakia, with the region of Moravia remaining in the former. In 1999 the Czech Republic joined NATO, and in 2004 it became a member of the European Union.

D

D-Day, In U.S. military history, any designated day for the commencement of a major operation. The designation apparently originated in World War I; its meaning is uncertain, though it is probable that the "D" stands for nothing more than "Day." (The designated time for commencement of action on any D-Day was referred to as H-Hour.) The most celebrated D-Day occurred on June 6, 1944, the first day of the Anglo-American invasion of Europe in World War II. *See* Normandy Campaign.

Da Nang, formerly TOURANE, Seaport city (pop., 2003 est.: 590,800), central Vietnam. It was first ceded to France in 1787, and after 1858 it became a French concession beyond the jurisdiction of the protectorate. Da Nang increased in importance after the partition of Vietnam in 1954, and during the Vietnam War it was the site of a U.S. military base. Its port has an excellent deepwater harbour; its manufactures include textiles and machinery.

Dachau, First Nazi concentration camp in Germany, established in 1933. It became the model and training center for all other SS-organized camps. In World War II the main camp was supplemented by about 150 branches in southern Germany and Austria, which were collectively called Dachau. It was the first and most important camp at which laboratories were set up to perform medical experiments on inmates. Such experiments and the harsh living conditions made Dachau one of the most notorious camps, though it was not designed as an extermination camp.

Dada, Nihilistic movement in the arts. It originated in Zürich, Switz., in 1916 and flourished in New York City, Paris, and the German cities of Berlin, Cologne, and Hannover in the early 20th century. The name, French for "hobbyhorse," was selected by a chance procedure and adopted by a group of artists, including Jean Arp, Marcel Duchamp, Man Ray, and Francis Picabia, to symbolize their emphasis on the illogical and absurd. The movement grew out of disgust with bourgeois values and despair over World War I. The archetypal Dada forms of expression were the nonsense poem and the ready-made. Dada had far-reaching effects on the art of the 20th century; the creative techniques of accident and chance were sustained in Surrealism, Abstract Expressionism, conceptual art, and Pop art.

Dadra and Nagar Haveli, Union territory (pop., 2008 est.: 262,000), western India. Located between Gujarat and Maharashtra states and consisting of the entities of Dadra and Nagar Havali, it has a total area of 190 sq mi (491 sq km); its capital is Silvassa. Forests cover part of the area; most of the rest is devoted to cultivation and grazing. Industrial development is limited. It came under Portuguese control in 1783–85. In 1954 indigenous freedom movements forced the Portuguese out, and it became a union territory of India in 1961. The population is predominantly Hindu.

Daedalus, In Greek mythology, a brilliant architect, sculptor, and inventor. He was credited with building for King Minos of Crete the Labyrinth in which the Minotaur was kept. When the king turned against Daedalus and imprisoned him, Daedalus secretly made wings for himself and his son Icarus, intending to escape to Sicily. Despite his father's warnings, Icarus flew too close to the sun; the wax holding the feathers to his wings melted, and he fell into the sea and drowned.

daguerreotype, First successful form of photography. It is named for Louis-Jacques-Mandé Daguerre, who invented the technique in collaboration with Nicéphore Niépce. They found that if a copper plate coated with silver iodide is exposed to light in a camera, then fumed with mercury vapour and fixed (made permanent) by a solution of common salt, a permanent image is formed. The first daguerreotype image was produced in 1837, by which time Niépce had died, so the process was named for Daguerre. Many daguerreotypes, especially portraits, were made in the mid-19th century; the technique was gradually replaced by the wet collodion process, introduced in 1851.

Dahshūr, Ancient pyramid site, northern Egypt. It is located near Memphis on the western bank of the Nile. Two of its pyramids date from the 4th dynasty and were built by Snefru (r. 2575–2551 BC); the smaller is believed to be the first true pyramid. The three remaining pyramids belong to the 12th dynasty (1938–1756 BC). Nearby tombs have yielded a remarkable collection of jewelry and personal accoutrements.

Dakar, City (pop., 2004 est.: city, 1,009,256; urban agglom., 2,098,648), capital of Senegal. One of the chief seaports on the western African coast, it lies midway between the mouths of the Gambia and Sénégal rivers. It was founded by the French in 1857, and its development was spurred by the opening in 1886 of western Africa's first railway, from Saint-Louis to Dakar. In 1902 it became the capital of French West Africa and in 1960 of Senegal. Dakar is one of tropical Africa's leading industrial and service centres. There are museums of ethnography and archaeology there and museums of the sea and of history in nearby Gorée.

Dalai Lama, Head of the dominant Dge-lugs-pa order of Tibetan Buddhism. The first of the line was Dge-'dun-grub-pa (1391–1475), founder of a monastery in central Tibet. His successors were regarded as his reincarnations and, like himself, manifestations of the bodhisattva Avalokitesvara. The second head of the order established the 'Brasspungs monastery near Lhasa as its base, and the third received the title Dalai ("Ocean") from Altan Khan. The fifth, Ngag-dbang-rgya-mtsho (1617–82), established the supremacy of the Dge-lugs-pa over other orders. The 13th Dalai Lama, Thub-bstan-rgya-mtsho (1875–1933), held temporal and spiritual power after the Chinese were expelled in 1912. The 14th and current Dalai Lama, Bstan-'dzin-rgya-mtsho (b. 1935), was enthroned in 1940 but fled to India in 1959 with a large contingent of followers after a failed revolt against the central government, which had gained control of Tibet in 1950–51. He now lives in exile in Dharmsala, India. He was awarded the 1989 Nobel Peace Prize in recognition of his proposals for solving world problems.

Dalí (y Domenech), Salvador (Felipe Jacinto) (b. May 11, 1904, Figueras, Spain—d. Jan. 23, 1989, Figueras), Spanish

"Dali Atomicus," or Dali with everything in suspension, photograph by Philippe Halsman, 1948
© Philippe Halsman

painter, sculptor, printmaker, and designer. He studied in Madrid and Barcelona before moving to Paris, where, in the late 1920s, after reading Sigmund Freud's writings on the erotic significance of subconscious imagery, he joined the Surrealist group of artists. Once Dalí hit on this method, his painting style matured with extraordinary rapidity, and from 1929 to 1937 he produced the paintings that made him the world's best-known Surrealist artist. His paintings depict a dream world in which commonplace objects, painted with meticulous realism, are juxtaposed, deformed, or metamorphosed in bizarre ways. In his most famous painting, *The Persistence of Memory* (1931), limp watches melt in an eerie landscape. With Luis Buñuel he made the Surrealist films *Un Chien andalou* (1928) and *L'Âge d'or* (1930). Expelled from the Surrealist movement when he adopted a more academic style, he later designed stage sets, jewelry, interiors, and book illustrations. His highly accessible art—and the publicity attracted by the eccentricity, exhibitionism, and flamboyant behaviour he cultivated throughout his life—made him extremely wealthy.

Dalian, or TA-LIEN, formerly (1950–81) LÜDA, or LÜ-TA, Japanese and conventional DAIREN, City (pop., 2003 est.: 2,181,600) and deepwater port on the Liaodong Peninsula, Liaoning province, China. Leased to Russia in 1898, it was made a free port and terminus of the Chinese Eastern Railway (1899). The Japanese occupied it (1904) during the Russo-Japanese War, and the lease was transferred to Japan by treaty in 1905. Soviet troops captured the city in 1945, but by a Chinese-Soviet treaty it remained under Chinese sovereignty with preferential rights to the port for the U.S.S.R.; Soviet troops withdrew in 1955. It annexed neighbouring Lüshun in 1950. Industries include fishing, shipbuilding, oil refining, and the manufacture of locomotives, machine tools, textiles, and chemicals.

Dallas, City (pop., 2010: 1,197,816), north-central Texas, U.S. Located on the Trinity River, it was first settled in 1841 and was most likely named for either Joseph Dallas or George Mifflin Dallas. While cotton fed the town's growth, the discovery in 1930 of the great East Texas oil field made the city a major centre of the petroleum industry. It saw spectacular growth after World War II, when several large aircraft-manufacturing firms located in the area. These were followed by electronics and automobile-assembly plants. It is the headquarters of many insurance companies and the Southwest's leading financial centre, as well as a transportation hub. Its many educational institutions include Southern Methodist University (founded 1911). It is known for its cultural activities including opera, ballet, and symphony concerts. The city is also home to the Kalita Humphreys Theater, designed by Frank Lloyd Wright.

Dalmatia, Serbo-Croatian DALMACIJA, Region of Croatia. Comprising a coastal strip and islands along the Adriatic Sea, it is divided from the interior by the Dinaric Alps. Its scenic beauty has made tourism a major economic factor; Dubrovnik and Split are Mediterranean tourist attractions. Occupied by Illyrians from *c.* 1000 BC, it was colonized by Greeks from the 4th century BC and controlled by Rome 2nd–5th century AD. Under Venetian rule in 1420, it passed to Austria after the fall of Napoleon. Most of Dalmatia came under Yugoslavia in 1920. Annexed by Italy during World War II, it passed to Yugoslavia in 1947 as part of the Croatian republic.

dam, Barrier built across a stream, river, or estuary to conserve water for such uses as human consumption, irrigation, flood control, and electric-power generation. The earliest recorded dam is believed to be a masonry structure 49 ft (15 m) high built across the Nile River in Egypt *c.* 2900 BCE. Modern dams are generally built of earth fill, rock fill, masonry, or monolithic concrete. Earth-fill (or embankment) dams, such as Egypt's Aswan High Dam, are usually laid across broad rivers to retain water. The profile of an earth-fill dam is a broad-based triangle. Concrete dams may take various forms. The gravity dam uses its own dead weight to resist

the horizontal force of the water. Concrete-buttress dams reduce material in the wall itself by using support buttresses around the outside base. An arch dam, such as Hoover Dam, is built in a convex arch facing the reservoir and owes its strength essentially to its shape, which is particularly efficient in transferring hydraulic forces to supports.

Damascus, Arabic DIMASHQ, City (pop., 2004: 1,614,500), capital of Syria. Located at an oasis at the base of the Anti-Lebanon Mountains, it has been an important population centre since antiquity. Believed to be among the world's oldest continuously inhabited cities, it has evidence of occupation from the 4th millennium BCE. The first written reference to it is found in Egyptian tablets of the 15th century BCE; biblical sources refer to it as the capital of the Aramaeans, and some Arabic sources have linked it with the *Iram dhāt al-ʿimād*, mentioned in the Qurʾān. The city changed hands repeatedly over the centuries, belonging to Assyria in the 8th century BCE, then Babylon, Persia, Greece, and Rome. It remained under the control of Rome and its successor state, the Byzantine Empire, until it fell to the Arabs in CE 635. Damascus flourished as the capital of the Umayyad dynasty, and the remains of their Great Mosque still stand. Taken by the Ottoman Empire in 1516, it remained under Ottoman rule until 1918; it was occupied by France in 1920 and became part of independent Syria in 1946. Today the city is a flourishing metropolis with many educational and scientific institutions. The old city centre was designated a UNESCO World Heritage site in 1979.

dance, Form of expression that uses bodily movements that are rhythmic, patterned (or sometimes improvised), and usually accompanied by music. One of the oldest art forms, dance is found in every culture and is performed for purposes ranging from ceremonial, liturgical, and magical to the theatrical, social, and simply aesthetic. In Europe, tribal dances often evolved into folk dances, which became stylized in the social dances of the 16th-century European courts. Ballet developed from the court dances and became refined by innovations in choreography and technique. In the 20th century, modern dance introduced a new mode of expressive movement.

dandruff, Skin disorder of the scalp, a mild form of dermatitis. It affects most people at some time, when the scalp, which normally sheds its dead outer skin cells continuously, starts to shed them intermittently, causing a scaly buildup before shedding and noticeable flakes of skin when shedding occurs. Dandruff is not contagious and often goes away spontaneously; special shampoos can control it.

Daniel, One of the Prophets of the Hebrew scriptures, the central figure in the book of Daniel. The book is a composite work, written partly in Hebrew and partly in Aramaic. The first six chapters tell of Daniel and his adventures in Babylon, including the stories of Daniel's delivery from the lion's den, the Jews in the fiery furnace, and the writing on the wall at Belshazzar's feast. The rest of the book offers apocalyptic visions of the end of history and the last judgment. Though it contains references to rulers of the 6th century BC, the book is thought to have been written in the 2nd century BC during the persecutions of the Jews under Antiochus IV Epiphanes. Daniel's upright character made him a model for a persecuted community.

Dante (Alighieri) (b. *c.* May 21–June 20, 1265, Florence—d. Sept. 13/14, 1321, Ravenna), Italian poet. Dante was of noble ancestry, and his life was shaped by the conflict between papal and imperial partisans (the Guelfs and Ghibellines). When an opposing political faction within the Guelfs (Dante's party) gained ascendancy, he was exiled (1302) from Florence, to which he never returned. His life was given direction by his spiritual love for Beatrice Portinari (d. 1290), to whom he dedicated most of his poetry. His great friendship with Guido Cavalcanti shaped his later career as well. *La Vita Nuova* (1293?) celebrates Beatrice in verse. In his difficult years of exile, he wrote the verse collection *The Banquet* (*c.* 1304–07); *De vulgari eloquentia* (1304–07; "Concerning Vernacular Eloquence"), the first theoretical discussion of the Italian literary language; and *On Monarchy* (1313?), a major Latin treatise on medieval political philosophy. He is best known for the monumental epic poem *The Divine Comedy* (written *c.* 1308–21; originally titled simply *Commedia*), a profoundly Christian vision of human temporal and eternal destiny. It is an allegory of universal human destiny in the form of a pilgrim's journey through hell and purgatory, guided by the Roman poet Virgil, and then to Paradise, guided by Beatrice. By writing it in Italian rather than Latin, Dante almost singlehandedly made Italian a literary language, and he stands as one of the towering figures of European literature.

Danube River, German DONAU Slovak DUNAJ Serbo-Croatian and Bulgarian DUNAV Romanian DUNAREA Ukrainian DUNAY, River, central Europe. The second longest European river (after the Volga), it rises in Germany's Black Forest and flows about 1,770 mi (2,850 km) to the Black Sea, passing along or through Germany, Austria, Slovakia, Hungary, Croatia, Serbia, Bulgaria, Romania, Ukraine, and Moldova. Its many tributaries include the Drava, Tisza, and Sava rivers. It has been an important highway between central and eastern Europe from antiquity. The lower Danube is a major avenue for freight transport, and the upper Danube is an important source of hydroelectricity. A regulatory body that consists of its riparian nations was established in 1948 to oversee its use. A major hydroelectric and navigation complex was built in the 1970s at Iron Gate Gorge in Romania. A canal linking Kelheim on the Danube and Bamberg on the Main River, allowing traffic to flow between the North and Black seas, was completed in 1992.

The confluence of the Sava (foreground) and Danube rivers from the Kalemegdan fortress, Belgrade, Serbia.
Jean S. Buldain/Berg & Assoc.

dao, or TAO, In Chinese philosophy, a fundamental concept signifying the correct or divine way. In Confucianism, *dao* signifies a morally correct path of behaviour. In Daoism the concept is more encompassing and includes the visible process of nature, by which all things change, as well as the principle underlying this process. This principle, known as Absolute Dao, can be only imperfectly understood by the practitioner but is the guiding principle in life. Daoists view life and death as stages of Absolute Dao and advocate a way of life that brings one closer to conformity with essential nature.

Daodejing, or TAO-TE CHING, Classic text of Chinese philosophy. Written between the 6th and 3rd centuries BC, it was once called the *Laozi* after its traditional author Laozi, though its true authorship is still unresolved. The *Daodejing* presents a way of life intended to restore harmony and tranquillity to a kingdom racked by disorder. It promotes a course of nonaction, understood as restraint from any unnatural action rather than complete passivity,

thereby allowing the *dao* to resolve things naturally. It was designed as a handbook for rulers, who should rule by inaction, imposing no restrictions or prohibitions on their subjects. The *Daodejing* has had a tremendous influence on all later schools of Chinese philosophy and religion and has been the subject of hundreds of commentaries.

Daoism, or TAOISM, Major Chinese religio-philosophical tradition. Though the concept of dao was employed by all Chinese schools of thought, Daoism arose out of the promotion of dao as the social ideal. Laozi is traditionally regarded as the founder of Daoism and the author of its classic text, the *Daodejing* . Other Daoist classics include the *Zhuangzi* (4th–3rd century BC;) and the *Liezi*. In Daoism, dao is the force or principle about which nothing can be predicated, but that latently contains the forms, entities, and forces of all phenomena. This natural wisdom should not be interfered with; de, or superior virtue, is acquired through action so entirely in accordance with the natural order that its author leaves no trace of himself in his work. The tradition holds that all beings and things are fundamentally one. Daoism's focus on nature and the natural order complements the societal focus of Confucianism, and its synthesis with Buddhism is the basis of Zen.

Dar es Salaam, Largest city (pop., 2002: 2,336,055), capital, and major port of Tanzania. It was founded in 1862 by the sultan of Zanzibar and came under the German East Africa Co. in 1887. It served as the capital of German East Africa (1891–1916), of Tanganyika (1961–64), and subsequently of Tanzania. It is an industrial centre, and its harbour is the major outlet for Tanzania's agricultural and mineral exports. It is the site of the University of Dar es Salaam (1961).

Dardanelles, ancient HELLESPONT, Narrow strait between the peninsula of Gallipoli in Europe and the mainland of Turkey in Asia. Some 38 mi (61 km) long and 0.75–4 mi (1–6 km) wide, it links the Aegean Sea with the Sea of Marmara. Strategically important from antiquity, the Dardanelles was defended by Troy from its position on the Asian side. In 480 BC the Persian Xerxes I crossed the strait to invade Greece; Alexander the Great also crossed it in 334 BC on his expedition against Persia. Held by the Roman Republic and Empire and the Byzantine Empire and later by the Ottoman Empire, it is of great strategic and economic importance as the gateway from the Black Sea to Istanbul and the Mediterranean Sea.

Dardanelles Campaign, or GALLIPOLI CAMPAIGN (1915–16) Unsuccessful British-led operation against Turkey in World War I, intended to invade the Dardanelles strait, conquer the Gallipoli peninsula, and occupy Constantinople (Istanbul). In response to a Russian appeal to relieve pressure against its troops on the Caucasus front, Britain agreed to a naval action against Turkey at the Dardanelles. When bombardment alone failed, British and Australian and New Zealand (ANZAC) troops landed on the Gallipoli peninsula in April 1915, where they met strong resistance from Turkish forces under Mustafa Kemal Atatürk. After six months of standoff, the campaign was halted and Allied troops were skillfully withdrawn under difficult conditions. Allied casualties numbered about 250,000. The failed campaign gave the impression that the Allies were militarily inept, prompting the resignation of Winston Churchill, the chief promoter of the venture, as first lord of the admiralty.

Darfur, Historical region and former province, western Sudan. It was an independent kingdom from *c.* 2500 BCE. Its first traditional rulers, the Daju, probably traded with ancient Egypt; they were succeeded by the Tunjur. Darfur's Christian period (*c.* 900–1200) was ended by the advance of Islam with the empire of Kanem-Bornu. In the 1870s Darfur came under Egyptian rule, and in 1916 it became a province of Sudan. Long-standing ethnic tensions between Arab nomads and sedentary Fur and other agriculturalists erupted in the late 1980s, and sporadic violence ensued.

The conflict escalated in 2003, when rebels among the agriculturalist population began attacking government installations in protest of perceived neglect of non-Arabs and of the country's western region. The government responded with the creation of the Janjaweed (also spelled Jingaweit or Janjawid) militia, which attacked sedentary groups in Darfur. Despite a 2004 cease-fire and the subsequent presence of international peacekeeping troops, by 2007 hundreds of thousands of people had been killed and more than two million displaced.

Darius I, known as DARIUS THE GREAT (b. 550—d. 486 BC), King of Persia (522–486 BC). He was the son of Hystaspes, satrap of Parthia. Much of what is known of him is through his own inscriptions. He took the throne by force, killing Bardiya, a son of Cyrus the Great, calling him an impostor who had usurped power. He continued the conquests of his predecessors, subduing Thrace, Macedonia, some Aegean islands, and land stretching to the Indus valley. He failed in his great expedition against the Scythians (513) but put down the Ionian revolt (499), which had been supported by Eretria and Athens. After that he twice tried to conquer Greece, but a storm destroyed his fleet in 492 and the Athenians defeated him at the Battle of Marathon in 490. He died before a third expedition could be launched. Among the greatest of the Achaemenian dynasty, he was noted for his administrative genius and his building projects, especially those at Persepolis.

Darius I seated before two incense burners, detail of a bas-relief of the north courtyard in the Treasury at Persepolis, late 6th–early 5th century BC; in the Archaeological Museum, Tehrān
Courtesy of the Oriental Institute, the University of Chicago

Darjiling, or DARJEELING, City (pop., 2001: 107,197), West Bengal state, northeastern India. It was purchased in 1835 from the raja of Sikkim and was developed as a sanatorium for British troops. Located at an average elevation of 7,000 ft (2,100 m), it commands views of Mounts Kanchenjunga and Everest. Its economy is based primarily on tea, which is plantation-grown, and tourism.

dark energy, The dominant component (about 70 percent) of the universe. Its nature is not well understood, but it differs from matter in being gravitationally repulsive. Dark energy is detected by its effect on the rate at which the universe expands. Many explanations have been proposed for dark energy; the simplest is that it is an energy density inherent to empty space.

dark matter, Nonluminous matter not directly detectable by astronomers, hypothesized to exist because the mass of the visible matter in the universe cannot account for observed gravitational effects. Dark matter comes in two varieties: baryonic, which is about 5 percent of the universe, and nonbaryonic, which is 22 percent of the universe. The nonbaryonic dark matter is believed to consist of heavy, electromagnetically neutral particles called weakly interacting massive particles (WIMPs).

Darling River, River, southeastern Australia. It is the longest member of the Murray-Darling river system. It rises in several headstreams in the Great Dividing Range and flows generally southwest across New South Wales for 1,702 mi (2,739 km) to join the Murray River at the Victoria border.

Darwin, formerly PALMERSTON, Seaport (pop., 2006: city, 66,291; urban agglom., 105,991), capital of Northern Territory, Australia. Located on Port Darwin, a deep inlet of Clarence Strait in the Timor Sea, it has one of Australia's best harbours. The harbour was named in 1839 for Charles Darwin. The port, settled in 1869, was known as Palmerston until 1911. Located in a largely undeveloped region, Darwin is a supply and shipping centre for northern Australia. A military base in World War II, it was bombed by the Japanese in 1942, then extensively rebuilt. A cyclone in 1974 damaged or destroyed nearly all of the city; rebuilt a second time, it is now one of Australia's most modern cities.

Darwin, Charles (Robert) (b. Feb. 12, 1809, Shrewsbury, Shropshire, Eng.—d. April 19, 1882, Downe, Kent), British naturalist. The grandson of Erasmus Darwin and Josiah Wedgwood, he studied medicine at the University of Edinburgh and biology at Cambridge. He was recommended as a naturalist on HMS *Beagle*, which was bound on a long scientific survey expedition to South America and the South Seas (1831–36). His zoological and geological discoveries on the voyage resulted in numerous important publications and formed the basis of his theories of evolution. Seeing competition between individuals of a single species, he recognized that within a local population the individual bird, for example, with the sharper beak might have a better chance to survive and reproduce and that if such traits were passed on to new generations, they would be predominant in future populations. He saw this natural selection as the mechanism by which advantageous variations were passed on to later generations and less advantageous traits gradually disappeared. He worked on his theory for more than 20 years before publishing it in his famous *On the Origin of Species by Means of Natural Selection* (1859). The book was immediately in great demand, and Darwin's intensely controversial theory was accepted quickly in most scientific circles; most opposition came from religious leaders. Though Darwin's ideas were modified by later developments in genetics and molecular biology, his work remains central to modern evolutionary theory. His many other important works included *Variation in Animals and Plants Under Domestication* (1868) and *The Descent of Man...* (1871). He was buried in Westminster Abbey.

Darwinian medicine, Field of study that applies the principles of evolutionary biology to medicine and public health. It is nearly synonymous with *evolutionary medicine*, though this is a less specific designation. Darwinian medicine is used to provide a scientific foundation for research and clinical practice. Examples of practical applications include the use of evolutionary modeling to understand antibiotic resistance; other applications include deepening scientists' understanding of what disease is and explaining why the metaphor of the human body as a designed machine is inadequate. Darwinian medicine has found use in providing a basis for evolutionarily informed decisions in public health policy.

data compression, Process of reducing the amount of data needed for storage or transmission of a given piece of information (text, graphics, video, sound, etc.), typically by use of encoding techniques. Data compression is characterized as either lossy or lossless depending on whether some data is discarded or not, respectively. Lossless compression scans the data for repetitive sequences or regions and replaces them with a single "token." For example, every occurrence of the word *the* or region with the colour red might be converted to $. ZIP and GIF are the most common lossless formats for text and graphics, respectively. Lossy compression is frequently used for photographs, video, and sound files where the loss of some detail is generally unnoticeable. JPEG and MPEG are the most common lossy formats.

data encryption, Process of disguising information as "ciphertext," or data that will be unintelligible to an unauthorized person. Decryption is the process of converting ciphertext back into its original format, sometimes called plaintext. Computers encrypt data by applying an algorithm to a block of data. A personal key known only to the message's transmitter and intended receiver is used to control the encryption. Well-designed keys are almost impregnable. A key 16 characters long selected at random from 256 ASCII characters could take far longer than the 15-billion-year age of the universe to decode, assuming the perpetrator attempted 100 million different key combinations per second. Symmetric encryption requires the same key for both encryption and decryption. Asymmetric encryption, or public-key cryptography, requires a pair of keys, one for encryption and one for decryption.

data processing, Manipulation of data by a computer. It includes the conversion of raw data to machine-readable form, flow of data through the CPU and memory to output devices, and formatting or transformation of output. Any use of computers to perform defined operations on data can be included under data processing. In the commercial world, data processing refers to the processing of data required to run organizations and businesses.

database, Collection of data or information organized for rapid search and retrieval, especially by a computer. Databases are structured to facilitate storage, retrieval, modification, and deletion of data in conjunction with various data-processing operations. A database consists of a file or set of files that can be broken down into records, each of which consists of one or more fields. Fields are the basic units of data storage. Users retrieve database information primarily through queries. Using keywords and sorting commands, users can rapidly search, rearrange, group, and select the field in many records to retrieve or create reports on particular aggregates of data according to the rules of the database management system being used.

date palm, Tree (*Phoenix dactylifera*) of the palm family, found in the Canary Islands and northern Africa, the Middle East, Pakistan, India, and California. The trunk, strongly marked with the pruned stubs of old leaf bases, ends in a crown of long, graceful, shining, pinnate leaves. The fruit, called the date, is a usually oblong brown berry. Dates have long been an important food in desert regions, and are the source of syrup, alcohol, vinegar, and a strong liquor. All parts of the tree yield products of economic value, being used variously for timber, furniture, basketry, fuel, rope, and packing material. The seeds are sometimes used as stock feed. The tree is grown as an ornamental along the Mediterranean shores of Europe. Its leaves are used for the celebration of Palm Sunday (among Christians) and the Feast of Tabernacles (among Jews). Date sugar, a product of India, is obtained from the sap of a closely related species, *P. sylvestris*.

dating, In geology and archaeology, the process of determining an object's or event's place within a chronological scheme. Scientists may use either relative dating, in which items are sequenced on the basis of stratigraphic clues or a presumed evolution in form or structure, or absolute dating, in which items are assigned a date independent of context. The latter type includes potassium-argon and carbon-14 dating; both are based on the measurement of radioactive decay. The record of changes in polarity of the Earth's magnetic field has provided a timescale for seafloor spreading and long-term marine sedimentation. Dendrochronology has proved useful in archaeology and climatology.

David, Star of, Hebrew MAGEN DAVID ("Shield of David"), Jewish symbol composed of two overlaid equilateral triangles that form a six-pointed star. It appears on synagogues, tombstones, and the flag of Israel. An ancient sign not much used by Jews before the Middle Ages, it was popularized by Kabbalists for protection against evil spirits. The Jewish community of Prague adopted it as an official symbol and its use became widespread in the 17th century. Though it has neither biblical nor Talmudic authority, it became a nearly universal emblem of Judaism in the 19th century. The Nazis' use of it to identify Jews invested it with the symbolism of martyrdom and heroism.

Davis, Bette, in full RUTH ELIZABETH DAVIS (b. April 5, 1908, Lowell, Mass., U.S.—d. Oct. 6, 1989, Neuilly-sur-Seine, France), U.S. film actress. She played small parts onstage before going to Hollywood in 1931. After a series of minor roles, she established her reputation with *Of Human Bondage* (1934) and *Dangerous* (1935, Academy Award). Known for her intense characterizations of strong women, she gave electrifying performances in films such as *The Petrified Forest* (1936), *Jezebel* (1938, Academy Award), *Dark Victory* (1939), *The Little Foxes* (1941), *Now, Voyager* (1942), and *All About Eve* (1950). Her later films include *What Ever Happened to Baby Jane?* (1962) and *The Whales of August* (1987).

Davis Cup, Trophy awarded to the winning team of an international tennis tournament for men. It was donated in 1900 by Dwight F. Davis, himself a player in the first two matches (called ties), for a competition between teams from the U.S. and Britain. Since then, the tournament has developed into a truly international event. More than 100 nations have participated, but winners have been largely confined to the U.S, Australia, France, Britain, and Sweden.

Dawes Plan (1924) Arrangement for Germany's payment of reparations to the Allies after World War I, produced by a committee of experts presided over by Charles Dawes. The total amount of reparations was not determined, but payments were to begin at 1 billion gold marks in the first year and rise to 2.5 billion by 1928. The plan, which also provided for the reorganization of the Reichsbank and for an initial foreign loan of 800 million marks to Germany, was later replaced by the more lenient Young Plan.

Daylight Saving Time, System for uniformly advancing clocks, especially in summer, so as to extend daylight hours during conventional waking time. In the Northern Hemisphere, clocks are usually set ahead one hour in late March or in April and are set back one hour in late September or in October. In the U.S., Daylight Saving Time begins on the second Sunday in March and ends on the first Sunday in November. In most of the countries of western Europe, it starts on the last Sunday in March and ends on the last Sunday in October.

DDT, in full DICHLORODIPHENYLTRICHLOROETHANE, Synthetic insecticide belonging to the family of organic halogens. In 1939 its toxicity to a wide variety of insects was discovered by Paul Hermann Müller, who was awarded a Nobel Prize for his work) and effectively used against many disease vectors. By the 1960s, many species of insects had developed populations resistant to DDT; meanwhile, this highly stable compound was accumulating along the food chain and having toxic effects on various birds and fishes. During the 1960s it and similar chemicals were found to have severely reduced the populations of certain birds, including the bald eagle.

de, or TE (Chinese: "virtue"), In Daoism, the potentiality of *dao* that is present in all things; in Confucianism, the virtue of internal goodness and propriety. In both systems it is regarded as the active principle of *dao*, and it is thus the life or moral principle. In the *Daodejing*, *de* is described as the unconscious functioning of the physical self, which can live harmoniously with nature. Personal *de* is thought to flourish when one abandons ambition and the spirit of contention for a life of naturalness, leading to an awareness of the underlying unity that permeates the universe.

de Gaulle, Charles (-André-Marie-Joseph) (b. Nov. 22, 1890, Lille, France—d. Nov. 9, 1970, Colombey-les-Deux-Églises), French soldier, statesman, and architect of France's Fifth Republic. He joined the army in 1913 and fought with distinction in World War I. He was promoted to the staff of the supreme war council in 1925. In 1940 he was promoted to brigadier general and served briefly as undersecretary of state for defense under Paul Reynaud. After the fall of France to the Germans, he left for England and started the Free French movement. Devoted to France and dedicated to its liberation, he moved to Algiers in 1943 and became president of the French Committee of National Liberation, at first jointly with Henri-Honoré Giraud. After the liberation of Paris, he returned and headed two provisional governments, then resigned in 1946. He opposed the Fourth Republic, and in 1947 he formed the Rally of the French People (RPF), but severed his connections with it in 1953. He retired from public life and wrote his memoirs. When an insurrection in Algeria threatened to bring civil war to France, he returned to power in 1958, as prime minister with powers to reform the constitution. That same year he was elected president of the new Fifth Republic, which ensured a strong presidency. He ended the Algerian War and transformed France's African territories into 12 independent states. He withdrew France from NATO, and his policy of neutrality during the Vietnam War was seen by many as anti-Americanism. He began a policy of détente with Iron Curtain countries and traveled widely to form a bond with French-speaking countries. After the civil unrest of May 1968 by students and workers, he was defeated in a referendum on constitutional amendments and resigned in 1969.

de Klerk, F(rederik) W(illem) (b. March 18, 1936, Johannesburg, S.Af.), President of South Africa (1989–94). He brought the apartheid system to an end and negotiated a transition to majority rule. Replacing P.W. Botha as leader of the National Party and president, de Klerk quickly moved to release all important political prisoners, including Nelson Mandela, and to lift the ban on the African National Congress. He and Mandela jointly received the 1993 Nobel Peace Prize. Following the country's first universal suffrage elections in 1994, Mandela became president and de Klerk was appointed second deputy president. He retired from politics in 1997.

Dead Sea, Arabic AL-BAḤR AL-MAYYIT, Hebrew YAM HA ME-LAḤ, ancient LACUS ASPHALTITES, Landlocked salt lake between Israel and Jordan. The lowest body of water on Earth, it averages about 1,312 ft (400 m) below sea level. It is 50 mi (80 km) long and up to 11 mi (18 km) wide. Its eastern shore is Jordanian, while the southern half of its western shore is Israeli; the northern half of the western shore is within the West Bank, occupied by Israel since the Six-Day War (1967). The Dead Sea lies between Judaea to the west and the Transjordanian plateaus to the east; the Jordan River flows in from the north. It has been associated with biblical history since the time of Abraham.

Dead Sea Scrolls, Caches of ancient, mostly Hebrew, manuscripts found at several sites on the northwestern shore of the Dead Sea (1947–56). The writings date from between the 3rd century BC and the 2nd century AD and total 800–900 manuscripts in 15,000 fragments. Many scholars believe that those deposited in 11 caves near the ruins of Qumrān belonged to a sectarian community whom most scholars believe were Essenes, though other scholars suggest Sadducees or Zealots. The community rejected the rest of the Jewish people and saw the world as sharply divided between good and evil. They cultivated a communal life of ritual purity, called the "Union," led by a messianic "Teacher of Righteousness." The Dead Sea Scrolls as a whole represent a wider spectrum of Jewish belief and may have been the contents of libraries from Jerusalem hidden during the war of AD 66–73. They also cast new light on the emergence of Christianity and the relationship of early Christian and Jewish religious traditions.

deafness, Partial or total inability to hear. In conduction deafness, the passage of sound vibrations through the ear is interrupted. The obstacle may be earwax, a ruptured eardrum, or stapes fixation, which prevents the stapes bone from transmitting sound vibrations to the inner ear. In sensorineural deafness, a defect in the sensory cells of the inner ear (e.g., injury by excessive noise) or in the vestibulocochlear or eighth cranial nerves prevents the transmission of sound impulses to the auditory centre in the brain.

Some deaf people are helped by hearing aids or cochlear implants; others can learn to communicate with sign language and/or lip reading.

Death Valley, Valley, southeastern California, U.S. The lowest, hottest, driest portion of North America, it is about 140 mi (225 km) long and 5–15 mi (8–24 km) wide. The Amargosa River flows into it from the south and contains a small pool, Badwater, near which is the lowest point in the Western Hemisphere at 282 ft (86 m) below sea level. Death Valley was formerly an obstacle to pioneer settlers (hence its name); it later was a centre of borax mining. Declared a national monument in 1933, it was made a national park in 1994; the park covers 5,270 sq mi (13,650 sq km) and extends into Nevada.

Deborah (fl. 12th century BC), Prophet and heroine of the Hebrew scriptures. Her story is told in the book of Judges. With her general, Barak, she is credited with defeating the Canaanite armies led by Sisera. The Israelite victory over the Canaanites, which was aided by a thunderstorm that Israel saw as the coming of God from Mount Sinai, was celebrated in the "Song of Deborah" (Judges 5), possibly the earliest portion of the Bible.

Debrecen, City (pop., 2001: 211,034), eastern Hungary. An important city in eastern Hungary, it has long been a market centre and a religious, political, and cultural arena. Chartered in the 14th century, it became prominent during and after the Turkish occupation. Hungary's short-lived independence from the Habsburgs was proclaimed there in 1849; the city later reverted to Austrian control. During World War II it was briefly the seat of the interim Hungarian government. The Great Reformed Church and Lajos Kossuth University (1912) are located there.

Decadents, Group of poets of the end of the 19th century, including some French Symbolists, notably Stéphane Mallarmé and Paul Verlaine, and the later generation of England's Aesthetic movement, notably Arthur Symons and Oscar Wilde. Many nonpoets, including the novelist Joris-Karl Huysmans and the artist Aubrey Beardsley, are also often associated with the Decadents. The Decadents emphasized art for art's sake, seeing it as autonomous and opposed to nature and to the materialistic preoccupations of industrialized society, and therefore stressed the bizarre, incongruous, and artificial in both their work and their lives.

decathlon, Composite athletic contest that consists of 10 different track-and-field competitions: the 100-, 400-, and 1,500-m runs, the 110-m high hurdles, the javelin and discus throws, shot put, pole vault, high jump, and long jump. Introduced as a three-day event at the 1912 Olympic Games, it later became a two-day event. Competitors are scored according to a table established by the International Amateur Athletic Federation. Decathletes are often regarded as the finest all-around athletes in the world.

Decembrist revolt (December 1825) Unsuccessful uprising by Russian revolutionaries. Following the death of Alexander I, a group of liberal members of the upper classes and military officers staged a rebellion in an effort to prevent the accession of Nicholas I. The poorly organized revolt was easily suppressed. Afterwards 289 Decembrists were tried; five were executed, 31 imprisoned, and the rest banished to Siberia. Their martyrdom inspired later generations of Russian dissidents.

decibel (dB), Unit for measuring the relative intensities of sounds or the relative amounts of acoustic or electric power. Because it requires about a tenfold increase in power for a sound to register twice as loud to the human ear, a logarithmic scale is useful for comparing sound intensity. Thus, the threshold of human hearing (absolute silence) is assigned the value of 0 dB and each increase of 10 dB corresponds to a tenfold increase in intensity and a doubling in loudness. The "threshold of pain" for intensity varies from 120 to 130 dB among different individuals. A related unit is the bel = 10 dB.

deciduous tree, Broad-leaved tree that sheds all its leaves during one season. Deciduous forests are found in three middle-latitude regions with a temperate climate characterized by a winter season and year-round precipitation: eastern North America, western Eurasia, and northeastern Asia. They also extend into more arid regions along stream banks and around bodies of water. Oaks, beeches, birches, chestnuts, aspens, elms, maples, and basswoods (or lindens) are the dominant trees in mid-latitude deciduous forests. Other plants that shed their leaves seasonally may also be called deciduous.

decision theory, In statistics and related subfields of philosophy, the theory and method of formulating and solving general decision problems. Such a problem is specified by a set of possible states of the environment or possible initial conditions; a set of available experiments and a set of possible outcomes for each experiment, giving information about the state of affairs preparatory to making a decision; a set of available acts depending on the experiments made and their consequences; and a set of possible consequences of the acts, in which each possible act assigns to each possible initial state some particular consequence. The problem is dealt with by assessing probabilities of consequences conditional on different choices of experiments and acts and by assigning a utility function to the set of consequences according to some scheme of value or preference of the decision maker. An optimal solution consists of an optimal decision function, which assigns to each possible experiment an optimal act that maximizes the utility, or value, and a choice of an optimal experiment.

Declaration of Independence (July 4, 1776) Document approved by the Continental Congress that announced the separation of 13 North American British colonies from Britain. The armed conflict during the American Revolution gradually convinced the colonists that separation from Britain was essential. Several colonies instructed their delegates to the Continental Congress to vote for independence. On June 7, Richard Henry Lee of Virginia offered a resolution for independence. The congress appointed Thomas Jefferson, John Adams, Benjamin Franklin, Roger Sherman, and Robert R. Livingston to draft a declaration. Jefferson was persuaded to write the draft, which was presented with few changes on June 28. It began with a declaration of individual rights and then listed the acts of tyranny by George III that formed the justification for seeking independence. After debate and changes to accommodate regional interests, including deletion of a condemnation of slavery, it was approved on July 4 as "The Unanimous Declaration of the Thirteen United States of America." It was signed by Congress president John Hancock, printed, and read aloud to a crowd assembled outside, then engrossed (written in script) on parchment and signed by the 56 delegates.

Declaration of the Rights of Man and of the Citizen, Manifesto adopted by France's National Assembly in 1789, which contained the principles that inspired the French Revolution. One of the basic charters of human liberties, it served as the preamble to the Constitution of 1791. Its basic principle was that "all men are born free and equal in rights," specified as the rights of liberty, private property, the inviolability of the person, and resistance to oppression. It also established the principle of equality before the law and the freedoms of religion and speech. The Declaration represented a repudiation of the pre-Revolutionary monarchical regime.

decompression sickness, also called THE BENDS, or CAISSON DISEASE, Harmful effects of rapid change from a higher- to a lower-pressure environment. Small amounts of the gases in air are dissolved in body tissues. When pilots of unpressurized aircraft go to high altitudes or when divers breathing compressed air return to the surface, external pressure on the body decreases and the gases come out of solution. Rising slowly allows the gases to enter the bloodstream and be taken to the lungs and exhaled; with a quicker ascent, the gases (mostly nitrogen) form bubbles in the tissues. In the nervous system, they can cause paralysis, convulsions, motor and sensory problems, and psychological changes; in the joints, severe pain and restricted mobility (the bends); in the respiratory system, coughing and difficulty breathing. Severe cases include shock. Recompression in a hyperbaric chamber followed by gradual decompression cannot always reverse tissue damage.

deconstruction, Method of philosophical and literary analysis, derived mainly from the work of Jacques Derrida, that questions the fundamental conceptual distinctions, or "oppositions," in Western philosophy through a close examination of the language and logic of philosophical and literary texts. Such oppositions are characteristically "binary" and "hierarchical," involving a pair of terms in which one member of the pair is assumed to be primary or fundamental, the other secondary or derivative; examples include nature/culture, speech/writing, and mind/body. To "deconstruct" an opposition is to explore the tensions and contradictions between the hierarchical ordering assumed in the text and other aspects of the text's meaning, especially its figurative or performative aspects. The deconstruction "displaces" the opposition by showing that neither term is primary; the opposition is a product, or "construction," of the text rather than something given independently of it. The speech/writing opposition, according to which speech is "present" to the speaker or author and writing "absent," is a manifestation of what Derrida calls the "logocentrism" of Western culture—i.e., the general assumption that there is a realm of "truth" existing prior to and independent of its representation by linguistic signs. In polemical discussions about intellectual trends of the late 20th century, *deconstruction* was sometimes used pejoratively to suggest nihilism and frivolous skepticism. In popular usage the term has come to mean a critical dismantling of tradition and traditional modes of thought.

decorative arts, Arts concerned with the design and decoration of objects that are utilitarian rather than purely aesthetic, including ceramics, glassware, basketry, jewelry, metalwork, furniture, and textiles. The separation of the decorative arts from the fine arts is a modern distinction.

deduction, In logic, a type of inference or argument that purports to be valid, where a valid argument is one whose conclusion must be true if its premises are true. Deduction is thus distinguished from induction, where there is no such presumption. Valid deductive arguments may have false premises, as demonstrated by the example: "All men are mortal; Cleopatra is a man; therefore, Cleopatra is mortal." Invalid deductive arguments sometimes embody formal fallacies (i.e., errors of reasoning based on the structure of the propositions in the argument); an example is "affirming the consequent": "If A then B; B; therefore, A."

deep-sea vent, Hydrothermal (hot-water) vent formed on the ocean floor when seawater circulates through hot volcanic rocks, often located where new oceanic crust is being formed. Vents also occur on submarine volcanoes. In either case, the hot solution emerging into cold seawater precipitates mineral deposits that are rich in iron, copper, zinc, and other metals. Outflow of these heated waters probably accounts for 20% of the Earth's heat loss. Exotic biological communities are now known to exist around the vents; these ecosystems are totally independent of energy from the Sun, depending not on photosynthesis but rather on chemosynthesis by sulfur-fixing bacteria.

defense mechanism, In psychoanalytic theory, an often unconscious mental process (such as repression) that makes possible compromise solutions to personal problems or conflicts. The compromise generally involves concealing from oneself internal drives or feelings that threaten to lower self-esteem or provoke anxiety. The term was first used by Sigmund Freud in 1894. The major defense mechanisms are repression, the process by which unacceptable desires or impulses are excluded from consciousness; reaction formation, a mental or emotional response that represents the opposite of what one really feels; projection, the attribution of one's own ideas, feelings, or attitudes (especially blame, guilt, or sense of responsibility) to others; regression, reversion to an earlier mental or behavioral level; denial, the refusal to accept the existence of a painful fact; rationalization, the substitution of rational and creditable motives for the true (but threatening) ones; and sublimation, the diversion of an instinctual desire or impulse from its primitive form to a more socially or culturally acceptable form.

deflation, Contraction in the volume of available money or credit that results in a general decline in prices. A less extreme condition is known as disinflation. Attempts are sometimes made to bring on deflation (through raising interest rates and tightening the money supply) in order to combat inflation and slow the economy. Deflation is characteristic of depressions and recessions.

deforestation, Process of clearing forests. Rates of deforestation are particularly high in the tropics, where the poor quality of the soil has led to the practice of routine clear-cutting to make new soil available for agricultural use. Deforestation can lead to erosion, drought, loss of biodiversity through extinction of plant and animal species, and increased atmospheric carbon dioxide. Many nations have undertaken afforestation or reforestation projects to reverse the effects of deforestation, or to increase available timber.

dehydration, Method of food preservation in which moisture (primarily water) is removed. Dehydration inhibits the growth of microorganisms and often reduces the bulk of food. It is an ancient practice, used by prehistoric peoples in sun-drying seeds, by North American Indians in sun-drying meat strips, and by the Japanese in drying fish and rice. It was used to prepare troop rations in World War II, and in recent decades campers and relief agencies have discovered its advantages. Commercial dehydration equipment includes tunnel dryers, kilns, and vacuum dryers. A combination of dehydration and freezing is used in the process of freeze-drying, whereby solid food remains frozen while its liquid escapes as vapour. The dairy industry is one of the largest producers of dehydrated foods, including whole milk, skim milk, and eggs.

dehydration, Loss of water, almost always along with salt, from the body, caused by restricted water intake or excessive water loss. Early symptoms of water deprivation are thirst, decreased saliva, and impaired swallowing. (When more electrolytes than water are lost, osmosis pulls water into cells, and there is no thirst.) Later, tissues shrink, including the skin and eyes. Mild fever rises as plasma volume and cardiac output decrease, and perspiration decreases or stops, greatly reducing heat loss. Urine output falls, and the kidneys cannot filter wastes from the blood. Irreversible shock can occur at this point. The cause of dehydration is treated first; then water and electrolytes must be given in the correct proportions.

Deinonychus, Genus of clawed theropod dinosaurs that flourished in western North America during the Early Cretaceous period (144–99 million years ago). *Deinonychus* walked and ran on two legs, yet its killing devices, large sickle-like talons 5 in. (13 cm) long on the second toe of each foot, required it to stand on one foot while slashing at its prey with the other. Its long, outstretched tail was enclosed in bundles of bony rods that grew out of the tail vertebrae, making it very rigid. About 8–13 ft (2.4–4 m) long and weighing 100–150 lbs (45–68 kg), it had a large brain and was evidently a fast, agile predator.

Deism, Belief in God based on reason rather than revelation or the teaching of any specific religion. A form of natural religion, Deism originated in England in the early 17th century as a rejection of orthodox Christianity. Deists asserted that reason could find evidence of God in nature and that God had created the world and then left it to operate under the natural laws he had devised.

The philosopher Edward Herbert (1583–1648) developed this view in *On Truth* (1624). By the late 18th century Deism was the dominant religious attitude among Europe's educated classes; it was accepted by many upper-class Americans of the same era, including the first three U.S. presidents.

Deledda, Grazia (b. Sept. 27, 1871, Nuoro, Sardinia, Italy—d. Aug. 15, 1936, Rome), Italian novelist. She wrote her first stories, influenced by the *verismo* ("realism") school, at age 17. In her approximately 40 novels, including *After the Divorce* (1902), *Elias Portolu* (1903), and *Ashes* (1904), the ancient ways of her native Sardinia often conflict with modern mores. Her later novel *The Mother* (1920) and the posthumously published autobiographical novel *Cosima* (1937) were widely admired. She received the Nobel Prize for Literature in 1926.

Delft, City (pop., 2001 est.: 96,180), southwestern Netherlands. Founded in 1075 and chartered in 1246, it was a trade centre in the 16th–17th centuries and was famous for its delftware pottery. It was the birthplace of jurist Hugo Grotius (1583) and painter Jan Vermeer (1632). Landmarks include a Gothic church, a Renaissance-style town hall, and a 17th-century armory. Principal manufactures include ceramics.

delftware, or DELFT, Tin-glazed earthenware, with blue-and-white or polychrome decoration, first made in the early 17th century at Delft, Holland. Dutch potters later introduced the art of tin glazing to England along with the name, which now applies to wares manufactured in the Netherlands and England. It is distinguished from faience (made in France, Germany, Spain, and Scandinavia) and majolica (made in Italy).

Delhi, City (pop., 2009 est.: 12,260,000) and national capital territory (pop., 2008 est.: 17,076,000), north-central India. Bordered by the states of Uttar Pradesh and Haryana, it has an area of 573 sq mi (1,483 sq km) and comprises the cities of Delhi (popularly known as Old Delhi) and New Delhi (India's capital) and adjacent rural areas. Delhi was the capital of a Muslim dynasty from 1206 until it was invaded and sacked by Timur in 1398. It again was made the capital by the Mughal Bābur in 1526. Although the Mughal capital was relocated to Agra, Delhi was beautified by Shah Jahān beginning in 1638. Pillaged by Nādir Shah in 1739, it surrendered to the Marathas in 1771 before being taken by the British in 1803. Delhi was a centre of the Indian Mutiny in 1857. In 1911 the British decided to move the capital of British India from Calcutta (now Kolkata) to Delhi, and in 1912 construction began on New Delhi (as the new seat of the central government became known) at a site just south of central Delhi. New Delhi was dedicated in 1931, and it became the capital of independent India in 1947. The area's economic and population centre, however, has remained mainly in Old Delhi. The services sector—including government—is the chief employer. The territory is also the transportation hub for north-central India.

The Parliament building, New Delhi, India.
© William J. Bowe

Delian League, Confederacy of ancient Greek states led by Athens and based on the island of Delos. Founded in 478 BC to combat Persia, its members included Aegean states and islands; Athens supplied commanders and assessed tributes of ships or money. It achieved a major victory in 467–466 when its fleet drove out Persian garrisons on the southern Anatolian coast. After 454 its leaders moved the treasury to Athens for safekeeping, used it to rebuild the city's temples, and treated the league as the Athenian empire. Most league members sided with Athens in the Peloponnesian War, which diverted the league from its Persian campaign. After defeating Athens in battle in 405, Sparta disbanded the league in 404. Fear of Sparta helped revive the league in the early 4th century, but it weakened as Sparta declined and was crushed by Philip II at the Battle of Chaeronea (338).

delinquency, Criminal behaviour carried out by a juvenile. Young males make up the bulk of the delinquent population (about 80% in the U.S.) in all countries in which the behaviour is reported. Theories regarding delinquency's causes focus on the social and economic characteristics of the offender's family, the values communicated by the parents, and the nature of youth and criminal subcultures, including gangs. In general, both "push" and "pull" factors are involved. Most delinquents apparently do not continue criminal behaviour into their adult lives but rather adjust to societal standards. The most common punishment for delinquent offenders is probation, whereby the delinquent is given a suspended sentence and in return must live by a prescribed set of rules under the supervision of a probation officer.

delirium, Condition of disorientation, confused thinking, and rapid alternation between mental states. The patient is restless, cannot concentrate, and undergoes emotional changes (e.g., anxiety, apathy, euphoria), sometimes with hallucinations. Delirium usually results from a disorder affecting the brain such as central nervous system infection, head trauma, or mental disorder. In severe cases of withdrawal from alcohol, delirium tremens results not from the excessive alcohol consumption alone but from exhaustion, malnutrition (particularly lack of thiamine), and dehydration.

delirium tremens (DTs), Delirium seen in severe cases of alcohol withdrawal complicated by exhaustion, lack of food, and dehydration, usually preceded by physical deterioration due to vomiting and restlessness. The whole body trembles, sometimes with seizures, disorientation, and hallucinations. Delirium tremens lasts 3–10 days, with a reported death rate of up to 20% if untreated. Hallucinations may develop independently of delirium tremens and may last days to weeks.

Delphi, Site of the ancient temple and oracle of Apollo in Greece. Located on the slopes of Mount Parnassus, it was the centre of the world in ancient Greek religion. According to legend, the oracle was originally sacred to Gaea, and Apollo acquired it by slaying her child, the serpent Python. From 582 BC Delphi was the site of the Pythian Games. The oracle was consulted not only on private matters but also on affairs of state, such as the founding of new colonies.

delta, Low-lying plain composed of stream-borne sediments deposited by a river at its mouth. Deltas have been important to humankind since prehistoric times. Sands, silts, and clays deposited by floodwaters were extremely productive agriculturally; and major civilizations flourished in the deltaic plains of the Nile and Tigris-Euphrates rivers. In recent years geologists have discovered that much of the world's petroleum resources are found in ancient deltaic rocks. Deltas vary widely in size, structure, composition, and origin, though many are triangular (the shape of the Greek letter delta).

dementia, Chronic, usually progressive deterioration of intellectual functions. Most common in the elderly, it usually begins with short-term-memory loss once thought a normal result of aging but now known to result from Alzheimer disease. Other common causes are Pick disease and vascular disease. Dementia also occurs in Huntington chorea, paresis, and some types of encephalitis. Treatable causes include hypothyroidism, other metabolic diseases, and some malignant tumours. Treatment may arrest dementia's progress but usually does not reverse it.

Demeter, In Greek religion, a consort of Zeus and the goddess of agriculture, especially grain. Though rarely mentioned by Homer and not an Olympian deity, she is probably an ancient goddess. She is best remembered for her role in the story of Perse-

Demeter of Cnidus, sculpture, mid-4th century BC; in the British Museum.
Courtesy of the trustees of the British Museum

phone, in which her lack of attention to the harvest causes a famine. In addition to appearing as a goddess of agriculture, Demeter was sometimes worshiped as a divinity of the Underworld and as a goddess of health, birth, and marriage.

democracy, Form of government in which supreme power is vested in the people and exercised by them directly or indirectly through a system of representation usually involving periodic free elections. In a direct democracy, the public participates in government directly (as in some ancient Greek city-states, some New England town meetings, and some cantons in modern Switzerland). Most democracies today are representative. The concept of representative democracy arose largely from ideas and institutions that developed during the European Middle Ages and the Enlightenment and in the American and French Revolutions. Democracy has come to imply universal suffrage, competition for office, freedom of speech and the press, and the rule of law.

Democritus (b. *c.* 460—d. *c.* 370 BC), Greek philosopher. Though only a few fragments of his work survive, he was apparently the first to describe invisible "atoms" as the basis of all matter. His atoms—indestructible, indivisible, incompressible, uniform, and differing only in size, shape, and motion—anticipated with surprising accuracy those discovered by 20th-century scientists. For his amusement at human foibles, he has been called "the Laughing Philosopher." *See also* atomism.

demography, Statistical study of human populations, especially with reference to size and density, distribution, and vital statistics. Contemporary demographic concerns include the global birth rates, the interplay between population and economic development, the effects of birth control, urban congestion, illegal immigration, and labour force statistics. The basis for most demographic research lies in population censuses and the registration of vital statistics.

demon, or DAEMON, In religions worldwide, any of various evil spirits that mediate between the supernatural and human realms. The term comes from the Greek word *daimon*, a divine or semidivine power that determined a person's fate. Zoroastrianism had a hierarchy of demons, which were in constant battle with Ahura Mazda. In Judaism it was believed that demons inhabited desert wastes, ruins, and graves and inflicted physical and spiritual disorders on humankind. Christianity placed Satan or Beelzebub at the head of the ranks of demons, and Islam designated Iblis or Satan as the leader of a host of evil jinn. Hinduism has many demons, called *asura*s, who oppose the *deva*s (gods). In Buddhism demons are seen as tempters who prevent the achievement of nirvana.

dendrochronology, Method of scientific dating based on the analysis of tree rings. Because the width of annular rings varies with climatic conditions, laboratory analysis of timber core samples allows scientists to reconstruct the conditions that existed when a tree's rings developed. By taking thousands of samples from different sites and different strata within a particular region, researchers can build a comprehensive historical sequence that becomes a part of the scientific record. Such master chronologies are used by archaeologists, climatologists, and others.

Deng Xiaoping, or TENG HSIAO-P'ING (b. Aug. 22, 1904, Guang'an, Sichuan province, China—d. Feb. 19, 1997, Beijing), Chinese communist leader, China's most important figure from the late 1970s until his death. In the 1950s he became a vice-premier of the People's Republic of China and general secretary of the Chinese Communist Party (CCP). He fell from favour during the Cultural Revolution but was rehabilitated in 1973 under the sponsorship of Zhou Enlai. Though seen as a likely successor to Zhou as premier, Deng was again ousted, this time by the Gang of Four, when Zhou died in 1976. However, Mao Zedong died later that year, and in the ensuing political struggle the Gang of Four was arrested; Deng was rehabilitated for a second time. His protégés Zhao Ziyang and Hu Yaobang became premier and CCP general secretary, respectively. Both embraced Deng's wide-reaching reform program, which introduced free-enterprise elements into the economy. Hu died in April 1989, and Zhao was dismissed from the government after the Tiananmen Square incident in June. Deng gradually relinquished his official posts but continued to guide China until his death.

dengue, or BREAKBONE FEVER, or DANDY FEVER, Infectious, disabling mosquito-borne fever. Other symptoms include extreme joint pain and stiffness, intense pain behind the eyes, a return of fever after brief pause, and a characteristic rash. Dengue is caused by a virus carried by mosquitoes of the genus *Aedes*, usually *A. aegypti*, which also carries yellow fever. There are four strains of virus; infection with one type does not confer immunity to the remaining three. Treatment focuses on relieving symptoms. Patients should be isolated during the first three days, when mosquitoes can pick up the disease from them. Prevention relies on mosquito control.

denitrifying bacteria, Soil microorganisms whose action results in the conversion of nitrates in soil to free atmospheric nitrogen, thus exhausting soil fertility and reducing agricultural productivity. Without denitrification, earth's nitrogen supply would eventually accumulate in the oceans, since nitrates are highly soluble and are continuously leached from the soil into nearby bodies of water.

Denmark, officially KINGDOM OF DENMARK, Country, north-central Europe. Area: 16,640 sq mi (43,098 sq km). Its territory includes Greenland and the Faroe Islands, which are self-governing dependencies. Population: (2011 est.) 5,574,000. Capital: Copenhagen. The majority of the population is Danish. Language: Danish (official). Religions: Christianity (predominantly Evangelical Lutheran [official]); also Islam. Currency: Danish krone. Lying between the North and Baltic seas, Denmark occupies the Jutland peninsula and an archipelago to its east. The two largest islands, Zealand (Sjælland) and Funen (Fyn), together make up about one-fourth of the country's total land area. With a 4,500-mi (7,300-km) coastline, Denmark has a generally temperate and often wet climate. It has a mixed economy based on services and manufacturing. It boasts one of the world's oldest and most comprehensive social welfare systems, and its standard of living is among the highest in the world. Denmark is a constitutional monarchy. Its head of state is the Danish monarch, and the head of government is the prime minister. Denmark is inhabited by about 12,000 BCE. During the Viking period the Danes expanded their territory, and by the 11th century the Danish kingdom included parts of what are now Sweden, England, and Norway. Scandinavia was united under Danish rule from 1397 until 1523, when Sweden became independent; a series of debilitating wars with Sweden in the 17th century resulted in the Treaty of Copenhagen (1660), which established the modern Scandinavian frontiers. Denmark gained and lost various other territories, including Norway, in the 19th and 20th centuries; it went through three constitutions between 1849 and 1915 and was occupied by Nazi Germany in 1940–45. A founding member of NATO (1949), Denmark adopted its current constitution in 1953. It became a member of the European Economic Community in 1973 and of the European Union

(EU) in 1993, but it negotiated exemptions from certain EU provisions in response to some Danes' concerns regarding environmental protection and social welfare. In the early 21st century Denmark's handling of immigrants raised great debate.

density, Mass of a unit volume of a material substance. It is calculated by dividing an object's mass by its volume. In the International System of Units, and depending on the units of measurement used, density can be expressed in grams per cubic centimetre (g/cm^3) or kilograms per cubic metre (kg/m^3). The expression "particle density" refers to the number of particles per unit volume, not to the density of a single particle.

dentistry, Profession concerned with the teeth and mouth. It includes repair or removal of decayed teeth, straightening and adjustment of teeth for proper occlusion, and design, manufacture, and fitting of false teeth and other prosthetic devices. X-rays are used to show conditions not visible on examination. Using local anesthesia, caries in teeth are drilled to remove diseased areas and filled with various materials. Decay that reaches a tooth's root risks infection of the nerve and requires root-canal surgery. Teeth that must be extracted are replaced by crowns for single teeth and full or partial dentures or implants for more. Dentists also educate patients on oral hygiene, examine and clean teeth, and apply fluoride compounds for decay resistance.

deontological ethics, Ethical theories that maintain that the moral rightness or wrongness of an action depends on its intrinsic qualities, and not (as in consequentialism) on the nature of its consequences. Deontological ethics holds that at least some acts are morally wrong in themselves (e.g., lying, breaking a promise, punishing the innocent, murder). It often finds expression in slogans such as "Duty for duty's sake." Deontological theories are often formulated in such a way that the rightness of an action consists in its conformity to a moral rule or command, such as "Do not bear false witness." The most important exponent of deontological ethics is Immanuel Kant.

dependency, In international relations, a weak state dominated by or under the jurisdiction of a more powerful state but not formally annexed by it. Examples include American Samoa (U.S.) and Greenland (Denmark). The dominant state may control certain of its affairs, such as defense, foreign relations, and internal security, and allow autonomy in domestic affairs such as education, health, and infrastructural development. In the 1960s and '70s the term referred to an approach to understanding third-world development that emphasized the constraints imposed by the global political and economic order.

depreciation, Accounting charge for the decline in value of an asset spread over its economic life. Depreciation includes deterioration from use, age, and exposure to the elements, as well as decline in value caused by obsolescence, loss of usefulness, and the availability of newer and more efficient means of serving the same purpose. It does not include sudden losses caused by fire, accident, or disaster. Depreciation is often used in assessing the value of property (e.g., buildings, machinery) or other assets of limited life (e.g., a leasehold or copyright) for tax purposes.

depression, Neurotic or psychotic disorder marked by sadness, inactivity, difficulty in thinking and concentration, a significant increase or decrease in appetite and time spent sleeping, feelings of dejection and hopelessness, and sometimes suicidal tendencies. Probably the most common psychiatric complaint, depression has been described by physicians from at least the time of Hippocrates, who called it melancholia. Its course is extremely variable from person to person; it may be fleeting or permanent, mild or severe. Depression is more common in women than in men. The rates of incidence increase with age in men, while the peak for women is between the ages of 35 and 45. Its causes can be both psychosocial (e.g., the loss of a loved one) and biochemical (chiefly, reduced quantities of the monoamines norepinephrine and seroto- nin). Treatment is usually a combination of psychotherapy and drug therapy. A person who experiences alternating states of de- pression and extreme elation is said to suffer from bipolar disor- der.

depression, In economics, a major downswing in the business cycle characterized by sharply reduced industrial production, widespread unemployment, a serious decline or cessation of growth in construction, and great reductions in international trade and capital movements. Unlike recessions, which may be limited to a single country, severe depressions such as the Great Depres- sion encompass many nations.

Derby, One of the classic English horse races (established 1780), run in June over a 1 1/2-mi (2,400 m) course at Epsom Downs, Sur- rey. Many other horse races have been named for the Derby (e.g., the Kentucky Derby), and the term itself has come to signify a race or contest of any type.

derivative, In mathematics, a fundamental concept of differen- tial calculus representing the instantaneous rate of change of a function. The first derivative of a function is a function whose val- ues can be interpreted as slopes of tangent lines to the graph of the original function at a given point. The derivative of a derivative (known as the second derivative) describes the rate of change of the rate of change, and can be thought of physically as accelera- tion. The process of finding a derivative is called differentiation.

derivatives, In finance, contracts whose value is derived from another asset, which can include stocks, bonds, currencies, inter- est rates, commodities, and related indexes. Purchasers of deriv- atives are essentially wagering on the future performance of that asset. Derivatives include such widely accepted products as fu- tures and options. Concern over the risky nature of derivatives grew after some well-publicized corporate losses in 1994 involv- ing Procter & Gamble, Metallgesellschaft AG of Germany, and Orange County, Calif. Anxiety intensified after the collapse in 1995 of the London-based merchant bank Barings PLC (now part of the Dutch ING Group NV). Securities regulators from 16 coun- tries then agreed on measures to improve control of derivatives.

dermatitis, or ECZEMA, Inflammation of the skin, usually itchy, with redness, swelling, and blistering. Causes and patterns vary. Contact dermatitis appears at the site of contact with an irritating substance or allergen. Atopic dermatitis, with patches of dry skin, occurs in infants, children, and young adults with genetic hyper- sensitivities (atopy). Stasis dermatitis affects the ankles and lower legs because of chronic poor blood flow in the veins. Seborrheic dermatitis appears as scaly skin, most often on the scalp (dandruff) and areas rich in sebaceous glands. Neurodermatitis is apparently caused by repeated scratching of an itchy skin area.

Derrida, Jacques (b. July 15, 1930, El Biar, Alg.—d. Oct. 8, 2004, Paris, France), Algerian-born French philosopher. Derrida taught principally at the École Normale Supérieure in Paris (1964– 84). His critique of Western philosophy encompasses literature, linguistics, and psychoanalysis. His thought is based on his dis- approval of the search for an ultimate metaphysical certainty or source of meaning that has characterized most of Western philos- ophy. Instead, he offers deconstruction, which is in part a way of reading philosophic texts intended to make explicit the underly- ing metaphysical suppositions and assumptions through a close analysis of the language that attempts to convey them. His works on deconstructive theory and method include *Speech and Phe- nomena* (1967), *Writing and Difference* (1967), and *Of Gramma- tology* (1967). Among his other works are *Psyche: Invention of the Other* (1987) and *Resistances of Psychoanalysis* (1996).

dervish, In Islam, a member of a Sufi fraternity. These mystics stressed emotional aspects of devotion through ecstatic trances, dancing, and whirling. Dervishes can be either resident in the com-

munity or lay members; wandering or mendicant dervishes are called fakirs and are often regarded as holy men who possess mi- raculous powers. Though viewed as unorthodox and extreme by most Muslims, the movement has endured to the present.

Desai, Anita, orig. ANITA MAZUMDAR (b. June 24, 1937, Mus- soorie, India), Indian novelist and author of children's books. Con- sidered India's premier imagist writer, she excels in evoking char- acter and mood through visual images. Her works include *Fire on the Mountain* (1977), *Clear Light of Day* (1980), *Baumgartner's Bombay* (1988), *Journey to Ithaca* (1995), and the story collection *Diamond Dust* (2000).

desalination, or DESALTING, Removal of dissolved salts from seawater and from the salty waters of inland seas, highly miner- alized groundwaters, and municipal wastewaters. Desalination makes such otherwise unusable waters fit for human consumption, irrigation, industrial applications, and other purposes. Distillation is the most widely used desalination process; freezing and thaw- ing, electrodialysis, and reverse osmosis are also used. All are en- ergy-intensive and therefore expensive. Currently, more than 2 billion gallons (8 million cu m) of fresh water are produced each day by several thousand desalination plants throughout the world, the largest plants being in the Arabian Peninsula.

Descartes, René (b. March 31, 1596, La Haye, Touraine, France—d. Feb. 11, 1650, Stockholm, Swed.), French mathema- tician, scientist, and philosopher, considered the father of modern philosophy. Educated at a Jesuit college, he joined the military in 1618 and traveled widely for the next 10 years. In 1628 he settled in Holland, where he would remain until 1649. Descartes's ambi- tion was to introduce into philosophy the rigour and clarity of mathematics. In his *Meditations on First Philosophy* (1641), he undertook the methodical doubt of all knowledge about which it is possible to be deceived, including knowledge based on author- ity, the senses, and reason, in order to arrive at something about which he can be absolutely certain; using this point as a founda- tion, he then sought to construct new and more secure justifica- tions of his belief in the existence and immortality of the soul, the existence of God, and the reality of an external world. This indu- bitable point is expressed in the dictum *Cogito ergo sum* ("I think, therefore I am"). His metaphysical dualism distinguished radi- cally between mind, the essence of which is thinking, and matter, the essence of which is extension in three dimensions. Though his metaphysics is rationalistic, his physics and physiology are empir- icistic and mechanistic. In mathematics, he founded analytic ge- ometry and reformed algebraic notation.

descent, System of acknowledged social parentage whereby a person may claim kinship ties with another. Descent systems vary widely. The practical importance of descent comes from its use as a means for individuals to assert rights, duties, privileges, or sta- tus. Descent has special influence when rights to succession, in- heritance, or residence follow kinship lines. One method of lim- iting the recognition of kinship is to emphasize the relationship through one parent only. Such unilineal kinship systems are of two main types—patrilineal systems, in which the relationships through the father are emphasized; and matrilineal systems, in which maternal relationships are stressed. These systems differ radically from cognatic systems, in which everyone has similar obligations to, and expectations from, both paternal and maternal kin. The cognatic system is somewhat vague and tends to charac- terize the more industrialized countries, in which individual rights and duties are increasingly defined institutionally or legally.

desert, Large, extremely dry area of land with fairly sparse veg- etation. It is one of the Earth's major types of ecosystems. Areas with a mean annual precipitation of 10 in. (250 mm) or less are generally considered deserts. They include the high-latitude cir- cumpolar areas as well as the more familiar hot, arid regions of the low and mid-latitudes. Desert terrain may consist of rugged mountains, high plateaus, or plains; many occupy broad mountain-rimmed basins. Surface materials include bare bedrock, plains of gravel and boulders, and vast tracts of shifting sand. Wind-blown sands, commonly thought to be typical of deserts, make up only about 2% of North American deserts, 10% of the Sahara, and 30% of the Arabian desert.

Agave shawii growing in a desert in North America.
© Robert and Linda Mitchell

designer drug, Synthetic version of a controlled narcotic substance. Designer drugs usually are synthesized for the first time in an attempt to create a chemical whose molecular structure differs only slightly from that of some well-known controlled substance but whose effects are essentially the same. Because of the difference in molecular structure, the designer drug, unlike the controlled substance, ordinarily will not be specifically listed as illicit by law-enforcement organizations. Many designer drugs are manufactured in clandestine laboratories, often by amateurs; for this reason they are sometimes more dangerous than the drugs they are intended to replace. One of the best-known is MDMA (3,4- methylenedioxymethamphetamine), a variation of methamphetamine, popularly called Ecstasy. Nonnarcotic synthetic chemical compounds designed to interact with specific proteins and enzymes in order to combat disease also have been called designer drugs.

desktop publishing (DTP), Use of a personal computer to perform publishing tasks. DTP allows an individual to combine text, numerical data, and graphic elements in a document that can be output on a printer or a phototypesetter. A typical DTP system includes a personal computer, a high-resolution printer, and input devices such as an optical scanner. Text and graphic elements are commonly created or manipulated with several separate software programs and then combined with a page-makeup program. Powerful DTP programs offer full-featured graphics capabilities.

desmid, Any of a group of one-celled, microscopic green algae characterized by great variation in cell shape. Typically the cell is divided symmetrically into semicells connected at a central point. Desmids are found worldwide, usually in acid bogs or lakes. Since most species have a limited range, the presence of specific desmids is helpful in characterizing water samples.

Desmid (Micrasterias), *highly magnified*
Winton Patnode—Photo Researchers

destroyer, Fast naval vessel used to protect other ships. The term was first applied to vessels built in the 1890s to protect battleships from torpedo boats. By World War I destroyers were often sent ahead of the battle fleet to scout for the enemy, beat back its destroyers with cannon fire, and then launch torpedoes against its battleships and cruisers. When the submarine became the main torpedo-launching vessel, destroyers armed with depth charges protected convoys and battle fleets against submarine attack. In World War II, with the addition of radar and antiaircraft guns, its escort role included air defense. Modern destroyers are run by a crew of about 300 and equipped with surface-to-air missiles, antiship missiles, and one or two big guns. Many carry submarine-hunting helicopters, and some carry cruise missiles.

detective story, Type of popular literature dealing with the step-by-step investigation and solution of a crime, usually murder. The first detective story was Edgar Allan Poe's "The Murders in the Rue Morgue" (1841). The genre soon expanded to novel length. Sherlock Holmes, the first fictional detective to become a household name, first appeared in Arthur Conan Doyle's *A Study in Scarlet* (1887). The 1930s was the golden age of the detective novel, exemplified by the books of Dashiell Hammett. The introduction of mass-produced paperback books in the late 1930s made detective stories readily accessible to a wide public, and well-known fictional detectives were created by G.K. Chesterton, Agatha Christie, Dorothy Sayers, Raymond Chandler, Mickey Spillane, and Georges Simenon. Among present-day mystery writers P.D. James and Dick Francis rank high.

determinant, In linear algebra, a numerical value associated with a matrix having the same number of rows as columns. It is particularly useful in solving systems of (linear) equations and in the study of vectors. For a two-by-two matrix, the determinant is the product of the upper left and lower right terms minus the product of the lower left and upper right terms. Determinants of larger matrices involve more complicated arithmetic combinations of the terms and are usually solved using a calculator or computer.

determinism, In philosophy, the doctrine that all events, including human decisions, are completely determined by previously existing causes. The traditional free will problem arises from the question, Is moral responsibility consistent with the truth of determinism? Among those who believe it is not consistent, some, maintaining the truth of determinism, have concluded that no one is morally responsible for what he does (and therefore that punishment for criminal actions is unjustified); others, maintaining the reality of moral responsibility, have concluded that determinism is false. Those who believe that moral responsibility is consistent with determinism are known as compatibilists. Pierre-Simon Laplace is responsible for the classical formulation of determinism in the 18th century. For Laplace, the present state of the universe is the effect of its previous state and the cause of the state that follows it. If a mind, at any given moment, could know all the laws and all the forces operating in nature and the respective positions and momenta of all its components, it could thereby know with certainty the future and the past of every entity.

deterrence, Military strategy whereby one power uses the threat of reprisal to preclude an attack from an adversary. The term largely refers to the basic strategy of the nuclear powers and the major alliance systems. The premise is that each nuclear power maintains a high level of instant and overwhelming destructive capability against any aggressor. It relies on two basic conditions: the ability to retaliate after a surprise attack must be perceived as credible, and retaliation must be perceived as a possibility, if not a certainty.

deuterium, or HEAVY HYDROGEN, Isotope of hydrogen, chemical symbol ^{2}H or D, atomic number 1 (but atomic weight approximately 2). Harold C. Urey won a Nobel Prize for its discovery and isolation. Its nucleus contains one proton and one neutron. A stable substance found in naturally occurring hydrogen compounds to the extent of about 0.015%, deuterium can be purified by distillation of hydrogen or by electrolysis of water. It enters into all the same chemical reactions as ordinary hydrogen; it forms D_2 and

HD, analogous to molecular hydrogen (H_2), and D_2O (heavy water), analogous to ordinary water (H_2O). Nuclear fusion of deuterium atoms or of deuterium and tritium at high temperatures releases enormous amounts of energy. Such reactions have been used in nuclear weapons and experimental power reactors. Deuterium is useful as a tracer in research into reaction mechanisms and biochemical pathways.

deva (Sanskrit: "divine") In the Vedic religion of India, one of many divine powers, roughly divided into sky, air, and earth divinities. During the Vedic period, the gods were divided into two classes, the devas and the *asura*s. In India the *deva*s gradually came to be more powerful, and the *asura*s came to be thought of as demons. In the monotheistic systems that emerged by the late Vedic period, the *deva*s were subordinate to one supreme being.

devaluation, Reduction in the exchange value of a country's monetary unit in terms of gold, silver, or foreign currency. By decreasing the price of the home country's exports abroad and increasing the price of imports in the home country, devaluation encourages the home country's export sales and discourages expenditures on imports, thus improving its balance of payments.

developmental psychology, Branch of psychology concerned with changes in cognitive, motivational, psychophysiological, and social functioning that occur throughout the human life span. In the late 19th and early 20th centuries, developmental psychologists were concerned primarily with child psychology. In the 1950s they became interested in the relationship between child rearing and adult personality, as well as in examining adolescence in its own right. By the late 20th century they had become interested in all aspects of psychological development and change over the entire life span.

devil, Spirit or power of evil. Though sometimes used to refer to demons, the term more often designates the prince of evil spirits. In the Bible the Devil is known as Satan, Beelzebub, and Lucifer. In Judaism, Satan emerges as subservient to God and as an adversary and accuser of Job and other humans. In postbiblical traditions he emerges as the tempter of humankind and is responsible for all the sins in the Bible. Christian theology holds that his main task is to tempt humans to reject the way of life and redemption in favour of sin and death. In the Qurʾ ān the Devil is frequently associated with Iblīs; he tempts the unfaithful but not the true believer. In Hinduism there is no principal devil, although there are a variety of demons or devilish beings. Buddhists also recognize the existence of many demons, and Mara, the Buddha's opponent and tempter, is sometimes identified as a specific devil.

Devonian Period, Interval of geologic time, 416–359.2 million years ago. It was the fourth period of the Paleozoic Era. During the Devonian a giant continent was situated in the Southern Hemisphere, and other landmasses were located in the equatorial regions. Siberia was separated from Europe by a broad ocean, and North America and Europe were joined. Many types of primitive marine and freshwater fish appeared and proliferated, and the period is sometimes referred to as the "Age of Fishes." Ferns and primitive gymnosperms diversified and created the first forests.

dew, Deposit of water droplets formed at night by the condensation of water vapour from the air onto the surfaces of exposed objects. Dew forms on clear nights, when exposed surfaces lose heat by radiation and are thus usually colder than the air. The cold surface cools the air in its vicinity, and, if the air is humid enough, it may cool below its dew point, the temperature at which water vapour condenses out of the air onto the surface.

Dewey Decimal Classification, or DEWEY DECIMAL SYSTEM, System for organizing the contents of a library based on the division of all knowledge into 10 groups. Each group is assigned 100 numbers. Subdivisions eventually extend into decimal numbers; for example, the history of England is placed at 942, the history of

the Stuart period at 942.06, and the history of the English Commonwealth at 942.063. The system was first formulated in 1873 by Melvil Dewey. Many libraries add a book number created from the Cutter, or Cutter-Sanborn, Tables, which further specify author and genre. The Library of Congress Classification has largely replaced the Dewey system.

Dge-lugs-pa, or GELUKPA, Yellow Hat sect of Tibetan Buddhism, the chief religion in Tibet since the 17th century. It was founded in the 14th century by Tsong-kha-pa (1357–1419). His reforms included strict monastic discipline, celibacy, and improved education for monks. The head of the chief monastery at Lhasa first received the title of Dalai Lama from Altan Khan in 1578. With his aid the Dge-lugs-pa triumphed over the Karma-pa, or Red Hat, sect. The Dge-lugs-pa ruled Tibet until the Chinese Communist takeover (1950); the sect continues to exist, but many of its members, including the Dalai Lama, remain in exile.

Dhaka, or DACCA, City (pop., 2001 prelim.: city, 5,644,235; metro. area, 10,403,597), capital of Bangladesh. It can be traced to the 1st millennium AD, but it did not rise to prominence until the 17th century, when it served as the Mughal capital of Bengal province. It came under British control in 1765 and was the capital of Eastern Bengal and Assam province (1905–12). The capital of East Bengal province in 1947 and of East Pakistan in 1956, it suffered heavy damage during Bangladesh's war of independence in 1971. Together with its port, Dhaka is the country's leading industrial centre. Its historic buildings include temples, churches, and more than 700 mosques, some of which date to the 15th century.

dharma, In Hinduism, the religious and moral law governing individual and group conduct. It is treated in the dharmasutras, the oldest collection of Hindu laws, and in the compilations of law and custom called the dharmashastras. In Buddhism, dharma is the universal truth common to all individuals at all times, and it is regarded as one of the primary sources of Buddhist doctrine and practice. In Jainism, dharma signifies moral virtue as well as the eternal life force.

dhow, One- or two-masted Arab sailing vessel, usually with lateen rigging (slanting, triangular sails), common on the Red Sea and the Indian Ocean. On the larger types, called baggalas and booms, the mainsail is considerably bigger than the mizzensail. Bows are sharp, with a forward and upward thrust, and the sterns of the larger dhows may be windowed and decorated.

diabetes insipidus, Endocrine disorder causing extreme thirst and excessive production of very dilute urine, apparently due to lack of antidiuretic hormone (vasopressin, which regulates the kidney's water conservation and urine production) or failure of the kidney tubules to respond to it. Injections of synthetic vasopressin are effective if the hormone is lacking but not if the response is absent. Disorders of the hypothalamus are one cause of diabetes insipidus.

diabetes mellitus, Disorder of insufficient production of or reduced sensitivity to insulin. Insulin, synthesized in the islets of Langerhans, is necessary to metabolize glucose. In diabetes, blood sugar levels increase (hyperglycemia). Excess sugar is excreted in the urine (glycosuria). Symptoms include increased urine output, thirst, weight loss, and weakness. Type 1, or insulin-dependent diabetes mellitus (IDDM), an autoimmune disease in which no insulin is produced, must be treated by insulin injections. Type 2, or non-insulin-dependent diabetes mellitus (NIDDM), in which tissues do not respond to insulin, is linked to heredity and obesity and may be controlled by diet; it accounts for 90% of all cases, many of which go undiagnosed for years. Untreated diabetes leads to accumulation of ketones in the blood, followed by acidosis (high blood acid content) with nausea and vomiting and then coma. Careful attention to content and timing of meals, with periodic checking of blood sugar, may manage diabetes. If not, injected or oral insulin is necessary. Complications, including heart disease, diabetic retinopathy (a leading cause of blindness), kidney disease, and nerve disorders, especially in the legs and feet, account for most deaths. Degree of blood-sugar control does not always correlate with progression of complications. Gestational diabetes may occur as a complication of pregnancy.

diagnosis, Identification of a disease or disorder. Diagnosis requires a medical history (including family history), a physical examination, and usually tests and diagnostic procedures (e.g., blood analysis, diagnostic imaging). A list of possible causes—the differential diagnosis—is developed and then narrowed down by further tests that eliminate or support specific possibilities.

dialect, Variety of a language spoken by a group of people and having features of vocabulary, grammar, and/or pronunciation that distinguish it from other varieties of the same language. Dialects usually develop as a result of geographic, social, political, or economic barriers between groups of people who speak the same language. When dialects diverge to the point that they are mutually incomprehensible, they become languages in their own right. This was the case with Latin, various dialects of which evolved into the different Romance languages.

dialysis, In chemistry, separation of suspended colloidal particles from dissolved ions or small molecules via their unequal rates of diffusion through pores of semipermeable membranes (e.g., parchment, collodion, cellophane). A slow process, dialysis may be accelerated by heating or by applying an electric field if the particles are charged.

diamond, Mineral composed of pure carbon, the hardest naturally occurring substance known and a valuable gemstone. Diamonds are formed deep in the Earth by tremendous pressures and temperatures over long periods of time. In the crystal structure of diamond, each carbon atom is linked to four other, equidistant, carbon atoms. This tight crystal structure results in properties that are very different from those of graphite, the other common form of pure carbon. Diamonds vary from colourless to black and may be transparent, translucent, or opaque. Most gem diamonds are transparent and colourless or nearly so. Colourless or pale blue stones are most valued, but most gem diamonds are tinged with yellow. Because of their extreme hardness, diamonds have important industrial applications. Most industrial diamonds are gray or brown and are translucent or opaque. In the symbolism of gemstones, the diamond represents steadfast love and is the birthstone for April.

Diamond Sutra, in full DIAMOND-CUTTER PERFECTION OF WISDOM SUTRA, Wisdom text of Mahayana Buddhism. It was composed *c.* AD 300 and translated into Chinese *c.* AD 400. The best known of the wisdom texts contained in the Prajnaparamita, it is written in the form of a dialogue between the Buddha Gautama and a questioning disciple. The work emphasizes the transitory nature of the material world and suggests that spiritual fulfillment can be attained only by transcending ephemeral phenomena and abandoning rationalism.

Diana, Roman goddess of nature, animals, and the hunt. As a fertility deity, she was invoked for aid in conception and childbirth. She was virtually indistinguishable from the Greek goddess Artemis. In her cult in Rome she was considered the protector of the lower classes, especially slaves.

Diana, princess of Wales, orig. LADY DIANA FRANCES SPENCER (b. July 1, 1961, Sandringham, Norfolk, Eng.—d. Aug. 31, 1997, Paris, France), Consort (1981–96) of Charles, prince of Wales. Daughter of Viscount Althorp (later Earl Spencer), she was a kindergarten teacher at the time of her engagement to Charles, whom she married on July 29, 1981, in a globally televised ceremony. They had two sons, Princes William (1982) and Henry (1984). Her beauty and unprecedented popularity as a member of the royal family attracted intense press attention, and she became one of the most photographed women in the world. The marriage gradually broke down; Charles and Diana separated in 1992 and were divorced in 1996. She remained highly visible and continued her activities on behalf of numerous charities. In 1997 she was killed in a car crash in Paris, along with her companion, Emad Mohamed (Dodi) al-Fayed (1955–97), and their driver. Her death brought on a massive public outpouring of grief.

diaphragm, Dome-shaped muscular and membranous structure between the thoracic and abdominal cavities. The principal muscle used in respiration, it is also important in coughing, vomiting, excretion, and other expulsive functions. Spasms of the diaphragm produce hiccups. The aorta passes behind the diaphragm; the inferior vena cava and esophagus pass through it. Protrusion of part of the stomach above the diaphragm is called a hiatal hernia.

diarrhea, Abnormally fast passage of waste material through the large intestine, resulting in frequent defecation with loose feces and sometimes cramps. Causes range widely and can include cholera, dysentery, highly seasoned foods or high alcohol intake, poisons (including food poisoning), drug side effects, and Graves' disease. Mild cases of diarrhea are treated with bismuth subsalicylate (trade name Pepto-Bismol); extreme cases are treated with fluid and electrolyte replacement while the underlying disease passes. Traveler's diarrhea affects up to half of people who travel to developing countries. Its prevention includes taking bismuth subsalicylate tablets, drinking only bottled or canned beverages, and eating only peeled fruits, canned products, and restaurant food that is well-cooked. Severe cases require antibiotics. In cases of severe malnutrition, diarrhea is potentially lethal, and it is responsible for hundreds of thousands of deaths annually in underdeveloped countries.

diary, or JOURNAL, Record of events, transactions, or observations kept daily or at frequent intervals; especially a daily record of personal activities, reflections, or feelings. Written primarily for the writer's use alone, the personal diary usually offers a frankness not found in writing done for publication. The diary form, which began to flower in the late Renaissance, is important as a record of social and political history. The most famous diary in English is that of Samuel Pepys. Other notable journals include those of John Evelyn, Jonathan Swift, Fanny Burney, James Boswell, André Gide, and Virginia Woolf.

Dias, Bartolomeu, or BARTHOLOMEW DIAZ (b. *c.* 1450—d. May 29, 1500, at sea, near Cape of Good Hope), Portuguese navigator and explorer. Given command of an expedition to ascertain the southern limit of Africa, he set sail in 1487. He sailed farther south than previous explorers and became the first European to round the Cape of Good Hope (1488). His voyage opened the sea route to Asia via the Atlantic and Indian oceans. He later commanded a ship in an expedition under Pedro Álvares Cabral, in which he participated in the discovery of Brazil; he was lost at sea when they reached the Cape.

Diaspora Hebrew GALUT ("EXILE") (Greek: "Dispersion"), The dispersion of Jews among the Gentiles after the Babylonian Exile (586 BC), or the aggregate of Jews outside Palestine or present-day Israel. The term also carries religious, philosophical, political, and eschatological connotations, inasmuch as the Jews perceive a special relationship between the land of Israel and themselves. Interpretations of this relationship range from the messianic hope of traditional Judaism for the eventual "ingathering of the exiles" to the view of Reform Judaism that the dispersal of the Jews was providentially arranged by God to foster monotheism throughout the world. Historically, Diaspora Jews outnumbered the Jews in Palestine even before the destruction of Jerusalem in AD 70. Thereafter, the chief centres of Judaism shifted from country to country (e.g., Babylonia, Persia, Spain, France, Germany, Poland, Russia, and the U.S.), and Jewish communities gradually adopted distinctive languages, rituals, and cultures, some submerging themselves in non-Jewish environments more completely than others. While some lived in peace, others became victims of violent anti-Semitism. While the vast majority of Orthodox Jews have supported Zionism, some Orthodox Jews go so far as to oppose the modern State of Israel on the grounds that it is a godless and secular state defying God's will to send his messiah at the time he has preordained.

diatom, Any member of the algal class Bacillariophyceae (division Chromophyta), with about 16,000 species. They are tiny, planktonic, unicellular or colonial algae found floating in all the waters of the earth. The intricate and delicate markings of the silicified cell wall are useful in testing the resolving power of microscope lenses. The beautiful symmetry and design of diatoms justify their title "jewels of the sea." Among the most important and prolific sea organisms, diatoms serve directly or indirectly as food for many animals. Diatomaceous earth, composed of fossil diatoms, is used in filters, insulation, abrasives, paints and varnishes, and as an insecticide.

Diatom (highly magnified)
Eric Grave/Photo Researchers

Dickens, Charles (John Huffam) (b. Feb. 7, 1812, Portsmouth, Hampshire, Eng.—d. June 9, 1870, Gad's Hill, near Chatham, Kent), British novelist, generally considered the greatest of the Victorian period. The defining moment of Dickens's life occurred when he was 12 years old. With his father in debtors' prison, he was withdrawn from school and forced to work in a factory. This deeply affected the sensitive boy. Though he returned to school at 13, his formal education ended at 15. As a young man, he worked as a reporter. His fiction career began with short pieces reprinted as *Sketches by "Boz"* (1836). He exhibited a great ability to spin a story in an entertaining manner and this quality, combined with the serialization of his comic novel *The Pickwick Papers* (1837), made him the most popular English author of his time. The serialization of such works as *Oliver Twist* (1838) and *The Old Curiosity Shop* (1841) followed. After a trip to America, he wrote *A Christmas Carol* (1843) in a few weeks. With *Dombey and Son* (1848), his novels began to express a heightened uneasiness about the evils of Victorian industrial society, which intensified in the semiautobiographical *David Copperfield* (1850), as well as in *Bleak House* (1853), *Little Dorrit* (1857), *Great Expectations* (1861), and others. *A Tale of Two Cities* (1859) appeared in the period when he achieved great popularity for his public readings. Dickens's works are characterized by an encyclopaedic knowledge of London, pathos, a vein of the macabre, a pervasive spirit of benevolence and geniality, inexhaustible powers of character creation, an acute ear for characteristic speech, and a highly individual and inventive prose style.

Dickinson, Emily (Elizabeth) (b. Dec. 10, 1830, Amherst, Mass., U.S.—d. May 15, 1886, Amherst), U.S. poet. Granddaughter of the cofounder of Amherst College and daughter of a respected lawyer and one-term congressman, Dickinson was educated at Amherst (Mass.) Academy and Mount Holyoke Female Seminary. She subsequently spent virtually all her life, increasingly reclusive, in her family home in Amherst. She began writing in the 1850s; by 1860 she was boldly experimenting with language and prosody, striving for vivid, exact words and epigrammatic concision while adhering to the basic quatrains and metres of the Protestant hymn. The subjects of her deceptively simple lyrics, whose depth and intensity contrast with the apparent quiet of her life, include love, death, and nature. Her numerous letters are sometimes equal in artistry to her poems. By 1870 she was dressing only in white and declining to see most visitors. Of her nearly 1,800 poems, only 10 are known to have been published during her lifetime. After posthumous publications (some rather inaccurate), her reputation and readership grew. Her complete works were published in 1955, and she has since become universally regarded as one of the greatest American poets.

dictator, In the Roman republic, a temporary magistrate with extraordinary powers. Nominated in times of crisis by a consul, recommended by the Senate, and confirmed by the Comitia Curiata, the dictator's term was six months or the duration of the crisis, and he had authority over all other magistrates. By 300 BC his powers were limited; no dictators were chosen after 202. The dictatorships of Sulla and Julius Caesar were a new form with almost unlimited powers. Caesar became dictator for life just before his assassination; afterward the office was abolished.

dictionary, Reference work that lists words, usually in alphabetical order, and gives their meanings and often other information such as pronunciations, etymologies, and variant spellings. The earliest dictionaries, such as those created by Greeks of the 1st century CE, emphasized changes that had occurred in the meanings of words over time. The close juxtaposition of languages in Europe led to the appearance, from the early Middle Ages on, of many bilingual and multilingual dictionaries. The movement to produce an English dictionary was partly prompted by a desire for wider literacy, so that common people could read Scripture, and partly by a frustration that no regularity in spelling existed in the language. The first purely English dictionary was Robert Cawdrey's *A Table Alphabetical* (1604), treating some 3,000 words. In 1746–47 Samuel Johnson undertook the most ambitious English dictionary to that time, a list of 43,500 words. Noah Webster's dictionary of Americanisms in the early 19th century sprang from a recognition of the changes and variations within language. The immense *Oxford English Dictionary* was begun in the late 19th century. Today there are various levels of dictionaries, general-purpose dictionaries being most common. Modern lexicographers (dictionary makers) describe current and past language but rarely prescribe its use.

dielectric, Insulating material or a very poor conductor of electric current. Dielectrics have no loosely bound electrons, and so no current flows through them. When they are placed in an electric field, the positive and negative charges within the dielectric are displaced minutely in opposite directions, which reduces the electric field within the dielectric. Examples of dielectrics include glass, plastics, and ceramics.

Dien Bien Phu, Battle of (1953–54) Decisive engagement in the first of the Indochina wars (1946–54) that marked the end of French involvement in Southeast Asia. The French fought the Viet Minh (Lien Viet) for control of a small mountain outpost near Laos. The French occupied the outpost, but the Vietnamese cut all the roads into it, leaving the French to rely on air supplies. Gen. Vo Nguyen Giap then attacked the base with heavy artillery and a force of 40,000 men; the base fell to him despite heavy U.S. aid to the French.

Diet, Japanese national legislature. Under the Meiji Constitution, the Diet had two houses, a House of Peers and a House of Representatives, with equal powers. The Diet's role was largely negative: it could block legislation and veto budgets. It was reconstituted under the U.S.-sponsored constitution of 1947. The (upper) House of Councillors seats 247 members, and the (lower) House of Representatives has 480 members. The prime minister, who leads the majority party in the lower house, must be a member. The House of Representatives can override the House of Councillors on most issues.

Dietrich, Marlene, orig. MARIA MAGDALENE DIETRICH (b. Dec. 27, 1901, Berlin, Ger.—d. May 6, 1992, Paris, France), German-U.S. film actress and singer. After joining Max Reinhardt's

Marlene Dietrich.
Pictorial Parade

theatre company in 1922, she appeared in German films and became an international star as the destructive cabaret singer Lola-Lola in Josef von Sternberg's *The Blue Angel* (1930). Sternberg took her to Hollywood, where they made many films together, including *Morocco* (1930), *Shanghai Express* (1932), and *The Scarlet Empress* (1934), which established her aura of glamorous sophistication and languid sensuality. During World War II she made over 500 appearances before Allied troops. She also starred in films such as *Destry Rides Again* (1939), *A Foreign Affair* (1948), *Witness for the Prosecution* (1957), and *Touch of Evil* (1958). She toured widely as a nightclub performer into the 1960s, singing trademark songs such as "Falling in Love Again."

diffraction, Spreading of waves around obstacles. It occurs with water waves, sound, electromagnetic waves, and small moving particles such as atoms, neutrons, and electrons, which show wavelike properties. When a beam of light falls on the edge of an object, it is bent slightly by the contact and causes a blur at the edge of the shadow of the object. Waves of long wavelength are diffracted more than those of short wavelength.

dill, Fennel-like annual or biennial herb (*Anethum graveolens*) of the parsley family or its dried ripe fruit and leafy tops, which are used to season foods. Native to Mediterranean countries and southeastern Europe, dill is now widely cultivated in Europe, India, and North America. The entire plant is aromatic. Particularly in eastern Europe and Scandinavia, the small stems and immature umbels are used for flavouring foods. Dill has a warm, slightly sharp flavour.

dimethyl sulfoxide (DMSO), Colourless, nearly odourless liquid organic compound. It mixes in all proportions with water, ethanol, and most organic solvents and dissolves a wide variety of compounds (but not aliphatic hydrocarbons). It readily penetrates skin and other tissues and is used to carry drugs and antitoxins through the skin. It has many nonmedical uses—as a solvent, cleaner, pesticide, paint stripper, hydraulic fluid, preservative of cells at low temperatures, and metal complexing agent.

diminishing returns, law of, Economic law stating that if one input used in the manufacture of a product is increased while all other inputs remain fixed, a point will eventually be reached at which the input yields progressively smaller increases in output. For example, a farmer will find that a certain number of farm labourers will yield the maximum output per worker. If that number is exceeded, the output per worker will fall.

dinosaur, Any of the extinct reptiles that were the dominant land animals during most of the Mesozoic Era (251–65 million years ago). The various species appeared at different times, and not all overlapped. The shape of the teeth reveal whether a given dinosaur was a carnivore or an herbivore. Dinosaurs are classified as either ornithischians or saurischians, based on pelvic girdle structure. Most had a long tail, which they held straight out, apparently to maintain balance. Most, if not all, were egg layers. Some were probably warm-blooded. Dinosaur fossils have been found on every continent, including Antarctica. Most types of dinosaurs flourished until late in the Cretaceous Period (65 million years ago), then disappeared within the next million years. Two theories for the cause of this mass extinction following some 140 million years of existence are that volcanism and mountain-building cycles altered the habitat and changed the climate or that one or more aster-

oids hit Earth, resulting in immense dust clouds that blocked sunlight for several years. Birds and crocodiles are thought to be living descendants of the dinosaurs.

Diocletian, Latin GAIUS AURELIUS VALERIUS DIOCLETIANUS, orig. DIOCLES (b. AD 245, Salonae?, Dalmatia—d. 316, Salonae), Roman emperor (284–305). He was serving under the emperor Carinus (r. 283–285) when the co-emperor, Carinus's brother Numerian, was killed. Diocletian's army declared him emperor, but his domain was restricted to Asia Minor and possibly Syria. Carinus attacked Diocletian (285) but was assassinated before achieving victory, allowing Diocletian to become sole emperor. He sought to remove the military from politics and established a tetrarchy (four-ruler system) to spread his influence and combat rebellions throughout the empire. Proclaiming himself and his corulers as gods, he added the trappings of a theocracy to the reign. His fiscal, administrative, and military reorganization laid the foundation for the Byzantine empire in the east and briefly strengthened the fading empire in the west. In 303–304 he issued four edicts decreeing the last great persecution of Christians. He abdicated in 305.

Diocletian, detail of a bust in the Capitoline Museum, Rome.
Alinari/Art Resource, New York

Dionysus, Greek god of vegetation and fruitfulness, known especially as the god of wine and ecstasy. His Roman equivalent was Bacchus. He was known to the ancient Mycenaens, and he became one of the most important of all the Greek gods. A son of Zeus and (according to the standard tradition) Semele, he was brought up by the maenads, or bacchantes. The first creator of wine, he traveled widely teaching the winemaking art, with a following of satyrs, sileni, and nymphs. Festivities called Dionysia or (among the Romans) Bacchanalia were held in his honour; in their earlier years they were wild, ecstatic occasions, and they have often been the subject of artistic representation. Dionysus originally appeared as a bearded man, but later more often as a slim youth. His principal attribute was the thyrsus, a wand bound with vine leaves. The dithyramb, a choral hymn in his honour, is often seen as the basis of Western drama.

Dioscuri, or CASTOR AND POLLUX (from Greek *dioskouroi*, "sons of Zeus") Twin gods of ancient Greece and Rome. They aided shipwrecked sailors and accepted sacrifices for favourable winds. Castor was mortal and Pollux was immortal; when Castor was killed, Pollux disowned his immortality to join his brother. The pair were excellent horsemen and were said to have participated in the hunting of the Calydonian boar, the voyage of the *Argo*, and the rescue of their sister Helen (who had been captured by Theseus). They were believed to have aided the Romans in an important battle early in their history, and a temple in their honour was built in the Roman Forum.

dioxin, Aromatic compound, any of a group of contaminants produced in making herbicides (e.g., Agent Orange), disinfectants, and other agents. Their basic chemical structure consists of two benzene rings connected by a pair of oxygen atoms; when substituents on the rings are chlorine atoms, the molecules are particularly toxic. The best-known, usually called simply dioxin, is 2,3,7,8-tetrachlorodibenzo-*p*-dioxin (2,3,7,8-TCDD). It is extremely stable chemically; it does not dissolve in water but dissolves in oils (and thus accumulates in body fat). The extent of its human toxicity is disputed and the subject of continuing research.

diphtheria, Acute infectious bacterial disease caused by *Corynebacterium diphtheriae.* The bacterium usually enters through the tonsils, nose, or throat and multiplies there, forming a thick membrane that adheres to the tissues and sometimes blocks the trachea, requiring emergency treatment.The bacteria produce a toxin that spreads to cause other symptoms, including fever, chills, sore throat, and lesions in heart muscle and peripheral nerve tissue that may cause death from heart failure and paralysis. Diphtheria is treated with an antitoxin that neutralizes the toxin and produces long-term immunity. Vaccination has greatly reduced its occurrence in Europe and North America.

Diplodocus, Genus of sauropod dinosaur found as fossils in Late Jurassic rocks of North America and related to *Apatosaurus. Diplodocus* and its relatives (diplodocids) were some of the longest land animals that ever lived, some approaching 100 ft (30 m). It had a long neck and extremely small brain and skull. Most diplodocids weighed about 30 tons, and some as much as 80 tons. It was formerly thought that *Diplodocus* may have spent a good deal of time in water, but fossil evidence indicates it moved freely on land, where it apparently fed on soft vegetation. It may be the most commonly displayed dinosaur.

diplomacy, Art of conducting relationships for gain without conflict. It is the chief instrument of foreign policy. Its methods include secret negotiation by accredited envoys (though political leaders also negotiate) and international agreements and laws. Its use predates recorded history. The goal of diplomacy is to further the state's interests as dictated by geography, history, and economics. Safeguarding the state's independence, security, and integrity is of prime importance; preserving the widest possible freedom of action for the state is nearly as important. Beyond that, diplomacy seeks maximum national advantage without using force and preferably without causing resentment.

direct current (DC), Flow of electric charge that does not change direction. Direct current is produced by batteries, fuel cells, rectifiers, and generators with commutators. Direct current was supplanted by alternating current (AC) for common commercial power in the late 1880s because it was then uneconomical to transform it to the high voltages needed for long-distance transmission. Techniques developed in the 1960s overcame this obstacle, and direct current is now transmitted over very long distances, though it must ordinarily be converted to alternating current for final distribution. For some uses, such as electroplating, direct current is essential.

directing, Art of coordinating and controlling all elements in the staging of a play or making of a film. Until the late 19th century, a theatrical director was usually the play's leading actor or the company's actor-manager. Today's stage director combines elements such as actors, decor, costumes, and lighting to shape an imaginative interpretation of the playwright's script. The director must understand the art of acting and provide guidance for the actors. The director also composes the "stage pictures," the shifting arrangements of the actors and other elements on the stage. The film director combines the theatrical director's responsibilities with the technical functions of cinematography, editing, and sound recording.

Directory, French DIRECTOIRE (1795–99) Government set up during the French Revolution by the Constitution of 1795. Legislative power was placed in the Council of Five Hundred and the Council of Ancients, while executive power was placed in a five-member Directory. Though the Directors nominally inherited many of the powers of the Committee of Public Safety, they had no funds to finance their projects or courts to enforce their will. The regime was marked by administrative chaos and corruption and by the uprisings in the Vendée. It was overthrown in Napoleon's Coup of 18–19 Brumaire.

disarmament, Reduction in armaments by one or more nations. Arms reductions may be imposed by a war's victors on the defeated (as happened after Germany's defeat in World War I). Bilateral disarmament agreements may apply to a specific area (such an agreement has kept the Great Lakes weapon-free since 1817). The term is most commonly used for multilateral reduction and limitation agreements, particularly in the context of nuclear weapons.

disco, Style of dance music that arose in the mid-1970s, characterized by hypnotic rhythm, repetitive lyrics, and electronically produced sounds. Disco (short for *discotheque*) evolved largely from New York City underground nightclubs, in which disc jockeys would play dance records for hours without interruption, taking care to synchronize the beats so as to make a seamless change between records. Artists such as Donna Summer, Chic, and the Bee Gees had many hits in the genre, which peaked with the release of the film *Saturday Night Fever* (1977). Disco faded quickly after 1980, but its powerful influence, especially its sequenced electronic beats, still continues to affect much of pop music.

discount rate, or BANK RATE, Interest rate charged by a central bank for loans of reserve funds to commercial banks and other financial intermediaries. The discount rate is one important indicator of the condition of monetary policy in an economy. Because raising or lowering the discount rate alters the rates that commercial banks charge on loans, adjustment of the discount rate is used as a tool to combat recession and inflation.

discus throw, Track-and-field sport of hurling for distance a disk-shaped object known as a discus. The discus is 8.6 in. (219 mm) in diameter and is thicker in the centre than at the perimeter; it must weigh at least 4.4 lbs (2 kg) for men's events, 2.2 lbs (1 kg) for women's. It is thrown by means of a whirling movement made by the athlete within a circle 8.2 ft (2.5 m) in diameter. The sport dates back to the ancient Greek Olympics.

Disney, Walt(er Elias) (b. Dec. 5, 1901, Chicago, Ill., U.S.—d.

Dec. 15, 1966, Los Angeles, Calif.), U.S. animator and entertainment executive. In the 1920s he joined with his brother Roy and his friend Ub Iwerks (1901–71) to establish an animation studio. Together they created Mickey Mouse, the cheerful rodent—customarily drawn by Iwerks, with Disney providing the voice—that starred in the first animated film with sound, *Steamboat Willie* (1928). The brothers formed Walt Disney Productions (later the Disney Co.) in 1929. Mickey Mouse's instant popularity led them to invent other characters such as Donald Duck, Pluto, and Goofy and to make several short cartoon films, including *The Three Little Pigs* (1933). Their first full-length animated film, *Snow White and the Seven Dwarfs* (1937), was followed by classics such as *Pinocchio* (1940), *Fantasia* (1940), and *Cinderella* (1950). A perfectionist, an innovator, and a skilled businessman, Walt Disney maintained tight control over the company in both creative and business aspects. He oversaw the company's expansion into live-action films, television programming, theme parks, and mass merchandising. By his death in 1966, Disney had transformed the family entertainment industry and influenced more than one generation of American children.

Walt Disney, 1950.
Alfred Eisenstaedt—Time Life Pictures/ Getty Images

Disraeli, Benjamin, earl of Beaconsfield (b. Dec. 21, 1804, London, Eng.—d. April 19, 1881, London), British politician and author who was twice prime minister (1868, 1874–80). Of Italian-

Jewish descent, he was baptized a Christian as a child, which enabled his future career, because until 1858, practitioners of Judaism were excluded from Parliament. He first made his mark as a writer with *Vivian Grey* (1826–27); later novels included *Coningsby* (1844) and *Sybil* (1845). He was elected to Parliament as a Conservative in 1837. In 1845 he made a series of brilliant speeches against Sir Robert Peel's decision to repeal the Corn Laws, which helped him to become leader of the Conservatives. He served three stints as chancellor of the Exchequer (1852, 1858–59, 1865–68) and played a prominent role in passing the Reform Bill of 1867. He was prime minister briefly in 1868, then returned in his second ministry (1874–80) to promote social reform. An advocate of a strong foreign policy, he secured a triumph for imperial prestige with his acquisition of Suez Canal shares and won concessions for England at the Congress of Berlin. A trusted friend of Queen Victoria, he introduced a bill conferring on her the title Empress of India. After the Conservatives were defeated in 1880, he kept the party leadership and finished his political novel *Endymion* (1880).

dissociative identity disorder, formerly MULTIPLE PERSONALITY DISORDER, Rare condition indicated by the absence of a clear and comprehensive identity. In most cases two or more independent and distinct personality systems develop in the same individual. Each personality may alternately inhabit the person's conscious awareness to the exclusion of the others, but one is usually dominant. The various personalities typically differ from one another in outlook, temperament, and body language and might assume different first names. The condition is generally viewed as resulting from dissociative mental processes—that is, the splitting off from conscious awareness and control of thoughts, feelings, memories, and other mental components in response to situations that are painful, disturbing, or somehow unacceptable to the person experiencing them. Treatment is aimed at integrating the disparate personalities back into a single and unified personality.

distemper, Viral disease in two forms, canine and feline. Canine distemper is acute and highly contagious, affecting dogs, foxes, wolves, mink, raccoons, and ferrets. Most untreated cases are fatal. Infected animals are best treated with prompt injections of serum globulins; secondary infections are warded off by antibiotics. Immunity can be conferred by vaccination. Feline distemper causes a severe drop in the number of the infected cat's white blood cells. It rarely lasts more than a week, but the mortality rate is high. Vaccines offer effective immunity.

diuretic, Any drug that increases the flow of urine from the body. Diuretics promote removal of excess water, salts, poisons, and metabolic wastes to help relieve edema, kidney failure, or glaucoma. Most types act by decreasing the amount of fluid that is reabsorbed by the kidney's nephrons and passed back into the blood. Diuretics that allow the body to retain potassium are used for patients with hypertension or congestive heart failure.

Divali, or DIWALI, In Hinduism, a five-day religious festival in

Women celebrating the Hindu festival of Divali, Kolkata (Calcutta), 2001.
Deshakalyan Chowdhury—AFP/Getty Images

autumn. It honors Lakshmi, goddess of wealth, or, in Bengal, the goddess Kali. During its celebration, earthenware lamps are lit and placed on the parapets of houses and temples or set adrift on rivers and streams. The fourth day of the festival marks the start of a new year, a time of gift-giving, visiting friends, decorating homes, and wearing new clothes. Divali is celebrated by Jains and Sikhs as well.

diverticulum, Small pouch or sac formed in the wall of a major

organ, usually the esophagus, small intestine, or large intestine (the most frequent site of problems). In the large intestine, feces pushed into a pouch can make it bulge out from the colon wall, a condition known as diverticulosis, which has no symptoms. In the more serious condition called diverticulitis, those sacs become inflamed, causing pain and tenderness, chills, and sometimes fever. Mild cases need only bed rest and antibiotics. In severe cases, perforation or rupture of the colon wall at the diverticulum can cause peritonitis. Rupture may require colostomy. Meckel diverticulum, a congenital malformation of the upper intestine that causes bleeding and inflammation, may require surgical removal.

divertimento, Eighteenth-century chamber music genre consisting of several movements, often of a light and entertaining nature, for strings, winds, or both. Though the name was applied (*c.* 1750–1800) to a confusingly varied range of works, it almost always referred to pieces with a single instrument to a part; this could include string quartets and even keyboard sonatas.

dividend, Individual share of earnings distributed among stockholders of a corporation or company in proportion to their holdings. Usually paid in cash, dividends may also be distributed in the form of additional shares of stock. Preferred stockholders receive a preferential dividend, usually at a fixed rate; common stockholders get a portion of what remains after payment of the dividends on preferred stock.

divination, Practice of discerning the hidden significance of events and foretelling the future. Divination is found in all societies, ancient and modern, though methods vary. In the West, psychics claim innate ability to predict the future, and horoscopes, palm reading, and tarot cards are popular methods of divination. Other methods involve or have involved interpreting dreams, discovering omens in natural events, reading the entrails of animals, casting lots, and consulting oracles. Divination has long been viewed as the province of specially gifted persons, such as prophets, shamans, and magicians.

divine kingship, Religio-political concept that views a ruler as an incarnation, manifestation, mediator, or agent of the sacred. In some nonliterate societies, members view their rulers or chiefs as inheritors of the community's own magical power. The ruler may exercise this power either malevolently or benevolently, but he is usually responsible for influencing the weather and the land's fertility to ensure the harvest necessary for survival. In other societies, particularly those of ancient China, the Middle East, and South America, the ruler was identified with a particular god or as a god himself; in Japan, Peru (among the Inca), Mesopotamia, and the Greco-Roman world, the ruler was regarded as the son of a god. In either case—whether the ruler embodies his own magical power or that of the community—the ruler protects the community from enemies and generally feeds and cares for his people. A third form of divine kingship, one practiced in Europe, is that of the ruler as mediator or executive agent of a god. In this form it is the institution of kingship, more than an individual ruler, that bears the mark of the sacred.

diving, Sport of plunging into water, usually headfirst and often following the execution of one or more acrobatic maneuvers. It emerged as a competitive sport in the late 19th century and became part of the Olympic Games in 1904. Dives are performed from a firm platform 5 or 10 m (16.4 or 32.8 ft) above the water, or from a springboard 1 or 3 m (3.3 or 9.8 ft) above the water. In Olympic contests, only the 10-m platform and 3-m springboard are used. Contestants are required to do certain dives, as well as dives of their own choice, each rated according to its degree of difficulty. Judges score each dive, and the total score is multiplied by the degree of difficulty.

division of labour, Specialization in the production process. Complex jobs can usually be less expensively completed by a large number of people each performing a small number of specialized tasks than by one person attempting to complete the entire job. The idea that specialization reduces costs, and thereby the price the consumer pays, is embedded in the principle of comparative advantage. Division of labour is the basic principle underlying the assembly line in mass production systems.

divorce, Dissolution of a valid marriage, usually freeing the parties to remarry. In societies in which religious authority is strong and the religion holds that marriage is indissoluble (e.g., Roman Catholicism, Hinduism), divorce may be difficult and rare. In the U.S. at the beginning of the 21st century there was about one divorce for every two marriages. The rate of divorce in the U.S. is greater than it is in most other Western countries, though divorce rates climbed in those countries in the last decades of the 20th century. The most common grounds for divorce are absence from the marital home, drug or alcohol addiction, adultery, cruelty, conviction of a crime, desertion, insanity, and nonsupport.

Djibouti, officially REPUBLIC OF DJIBOUTI, formerly (1967–77) FRENCH TERRITORY OF THE AFARS AND ISSAS, Country, eastern Africa, on the Gulf of Aden at the entrance to the Red Sea. Area: 8,950 sq mi (23,200 sq km). Population: (2011 est.) 840,000. Capital: Djibouti. Roughly half of the people are Issas and related Somali clans; Afars are about one-third; the balance includes Yemeni Arabs and Europeans, mostly French. Languages: French, Arabic (both official). Religion: Islam (predominantly Sunni). Currency: Djibouti franc. Djibouti is divided into three principal regions: the coastal plain, the volcanic plateaus in the country's south and centre, and the mountain ranges in the north, reaching 6,654 ft (2,028 m) high at Mount Moussa (Mousa). The land is primarily desert—hot, dry, and desolate; virtually none is arable. Djibouti has a developing market economy that is based almost entirely on trade and commercial services, centring on Djibouti city. The country is a multiparty republic with one legislative house; its head of state and government is the president. Settled by the Arab ancestors of the Afars, it was later populated by Somali Issas. In 825 CE Islam was brought to the area by missionaries. Arabs controlled the trade in this region until the 16th century; it became a French protectorate in the 19th century. It was made a French overseas territory in 1946, assumed the name French Territory of the Afars and Issas in 1967, and gained its independence in 1977. In the late 20th and early 21st centuries, it hosted a sizable population of refugees from conflicts in neighbouring countries.

Djibouti, City (pop., 2006 est.: 325,000), major port, and capital of Djibouti. It is located on the southern shore of the Gulf of Tadjoura in the Gulf of Aden. It was founded by the French in 1888 and made the capital of French Somaliland in 1892. It was linked by rail to Addis Ababa in 1917 and made a free port in 1949. The economic life of both the city and the country depends on the city's function as a transshipment point, especially between Ethiopia and the Red Sea trade. Built on three level areas linked by jetties, the city has a mixture of ancient and modern architecture. Drought and conflict during the 1980s, 1990s, and 2000s brought many refugees to Djibouti from neighbouring countries, swelling its population.

DNA, or DEOXYRIBONUCLEIC ACID, One of two types of nucleic acid (the other is RNA); a complex organic compound found in all living cells and many viruses. It is the chemical substance of genes. Its structure, with two strands wound around each other in a double helix to resemble a twisted ladder, was first described (1953) by Francis Crick and James D. Watson. Each strand is a long chain (polymer) of repeating nucleotides: adenine (A), guanine (G), cytosine (C), and thymine (T). The two strands contain complementary information: A forms hydrogen bonds only with T, C only with G. When DNA is copied in the cell, the strands separate and each serves as a template for assembling a new complementary strand; this is the key to stable heredity. DNA in cells is organized into dense protein-DNA complexes called chromo-

somes. In eukaryotes these are in the nucleus, and DNA also occurs in mitochondria and chloroplasts (if any). Prokaryotes have a single circular chromosome in the cytoplasm. Some prokaryotes and a few eukaryotes have DNA outside the chromosomes in plasmids.

DNA computing, Form of computing in which DNA molecules are used instead of digital logic circuits. The biological cell is regarded as an entity that resembles a sophisticated computer. The four amino acid bases that are constituents of DNA, traditionally represented by the letters A, T, C, and G, are used as operators, as the binary digits 0 and 1 are used in computers. DNA molecules are encoded to a researcher's specifications and then induced to recombine, resulting in trillions of "calculations" simultaneously. The field is in its infancy and its implications are only beginning to be explored.

Dnieper River, Russian DNEPR, ancient BORYSTHENES, River, east-central Europe. One of the longest rivers in Europe, it rises west of Moscow and flows south through Belarus and Ukraine, emptying into the Black Sea after a course of 1,367 mi (2,200 km). Several huge dams on the river are used in generating hydroelectric power. Navigable for nearly its entire length, it is an important shipping artery for eastern Europe.

Dniester River, Russian DNESTR, ancient TYRAS, River, southern central Europe. Rising on the northern side of the Carpathian Mtns., it flows south and east for 840 mi (1,352 km) to the Black Sea near Odessa. It is the second-longest river in Ukraine and the main water artery of Moldova. It is navigable for 750 mi (1,200 km).

Dnipropetrovsk, formerly (1783–1926) EKATERINOSLAV, City (pop., 2001: 3,567,600), south-central Ukraine. Located on the Dnieper River, it was founded in 1783 and named for Catherine the Great; it grew after the railroad arrived in the 1880s. In 1926 the Soviets gave it its current name. A railway junction and a centre of the wheat trade, it has developed into one of the largest industrial cities of Ukraine, with a huge iron and steel industry. It is the site of institutes of higher education, and its cultural amenities include several theatres.

Doberman pinscher, Breed of working dog developed in Apolda, Germany, by Louis Dobermann, a dog-pound keeper, in the late 19th century. This sleek, agile, powerful dog stands 24–28 in. (61–71 cm) high and weighs 60–88 lbs (27–40 kg). It has a short, smooth black, blue, fawn, or red coat, with rust markings on the head, throat, chest, tail base, and feet. Dobermans have a reputation for fearlessness, alertness, loyalty, and intelligence. They have been used in police and military work, as watchdogs, and as guide dogs for the blind.

Doctors Without Borders, French MÉDECINS SANS FRONTIÈRES (MSF), World's largest independent international medical relief agency. It was established by a group of French physicians in 1971. It aids victims of armed conflict, epidemics, and natural and man-made disasters and helps others whose lack of health care is due to geographic remoteness or ethnic or political marginalization. Teams provide primary health care, perform surgery, vaccinate children, rehabilitate hospitals, operate emergency nutrition and sanitation programs, and train local medical staff. Operating independently of governments, the organization depends on volunteer health professionals (more than 2,000 annually) and private donations. It received the 1999 Nobel Peace Prize.

documentary, Fact-based film that depicts actual events and persons. Documentaries can deal with scientific or educational topics, can be a form of journalism or social commentary, or can be a conduit for propaganda or personal expression. The term was first coined by Scottish-born filmmaker John Grierson to describe fact-based features such as Robert Flaherty's *Nanook of the North* (1922). Grierson's *Drifters* (1929) and Pare Lorentz's *The Plow*

That Broke the Plains (1936) influenced documentary filmmaking in the 1930s. During the World War II era documentary filmmaking was a valuable propaganda tool used by all sides. Leni Riefenstahl contributed to the Nazi propaganda efforts in the 1930s; the U.S. made films such as Frank Capra's series *Why We Fight* (1942–45); and Britain released *London Can Take It* (1940). Cinéma vérité documentaries, which gained notoriety in the 1960s, emphasized a more informal and intimate relationship between camera and subject. Television became an important medium for documentary films with goals that were more journalistic (such as CBS's *Harvest of Shame* [1960]) and educational (such as Ken Burns's *Civil War* [1990]).

Dodoma, City (pop., 2002: 149,180), Tanzania. Designated the national capital since 1974, it awaits complete transfer of official functions from Dar es Salaam, the current capital. Located in a sparsely populated agricultural region at an elevation of 3,720 ft (1,135 m), it is a market centre for the surrounding area. Industries produce wood and furniture, beverages, processed food, soap, and oil.

dog, Domesticated mammal (*Canis lupus familiaris*), of the family Canidae (order Carnivora). Domestic dogs seem to have descended from the wolf or a wolflike ancestor. Dogs were among the first animals to be domesticated, and domestication seems to have begun in various parts of the world at roughly the same time. Selective breeding by humans has resulted in myriad domestic breeds that vary widely in size (from the tiny Chihuahua to the huge mastiff), physical form (e.g., the short-legged dachshund and the flat-faced bulldog), coat texture and length (e.g., the sleek Doberman pinscher and the long-haired Afghan hound), and behavioral patterns (e.g., sporting dogs, toy dogs, and working dogs). Most kennel clubs recognize only a portion of the approximately 400 breeds of dog.

doge (Venetian Italian: "duke") Highest official of the republic of Venice in the 8th–18th century. The office originated when the city was nominally subject to the Byzantine empire and became permanent in the 8th century. The doge was chosen from among the ruling families of Venice and held office for life. He held extensive power, as evidenced by the rule of Enrico Dandolo (r. 1192–1205), though from the 12th century the aristocracy placed limits on the doge's authority. Under Francesco Foscari (r.1423–57), Venice undertook the first conquests of the Italian mainland. The last doge was deposed when Napoleon conquered northern Italy in 1797.

dogsled racing, Sport of racing sleds pulled by dogs over snow-covered cross-country courses. It developed from a traditional Eskimo method of transportation. Modern sleds are usually of wood (ash) construction, with leather lashings and steel- or aluminum-covered runners. Sled dogs are usually Eskimo dogs, Siberian huskies, Samoyeds, or Alaskan malamutes; teams typically consist of 4–10 dogs. The course is usually 12–30 mi (19–48 km) long, though some, including the Iditarod, are considerably longer.

Doha, Arabic AL-DAWḤAH, City (pop., 2004: 339,847), capital of Qatar. It is located on the east coast of the Qatar Peninsula and contains about three-fifths of the country's population. Long a centre of pirate activity in the Persian Gulf, Doha was a small village when it became the capital of newly independent Qatar in 1971. The city has been thoroughly modernized. Its Government House (1969) was built on reclaimed waterfront land; its water supply is obtained by distilling seawater. The deepwater port, built in the 1970s, accommodates oceangoing vessels.

doll, Small-scale figure of a human being or animal, used especially as a child's plaything. The doll is perhaps humankind's oldest toy. Some ancient dolls may have served religious or magical functions—as do voodoo dolls in modern times. Dolls were buried in children's graves in Egypt, Greece, and Rome and in early

Painted wooden Egyptian doll, 2000 BC.
Courtesy of the trustees of the British Museum

Christian catacombs. In Europe dolls have been commercially manufactured since about the 16th century. Doll heads were made of wood, terra-cotta, alabaster, and wax, while the bodies were made of carved wood or leather stuffed with sawdust. In about 1820 glazed porcelain (Dresden) doll heads and unglazed bisque (ceramic) heads became popular. These were supplanted in the 20th century by molded plastic. In Japan, dolls are used as traditional festival figures. In India, elaborately dressed dolls were given to child brides by both Hindus and Muslims. Today both antique and modern dolls are often collected.

dolomite, Type of limestone, the carbonate fraction of which is dominated by the mineral dolomite, calcium magnesium carbonate $CaMg(CO_3)_2$. The carbonate mineral dolomite occurs in marbles, talc schists, and other magnesium-rich metamorphic rocks. It occurs in hydrothermal veins, in cavities in carbonate rocks, and less often in various sedimentary rocks as a cement. It is most common as a rock-forming mineral in carbonate rocks.

Dolomites, Italian ALPI DOLOMITICHE, Mountain group, northern Italian Alps. Including a number of impressive peaks, 18 of which rise to more than 10,000 ft (3,050 m), the range and its characteristic rock are named for the 18th-century French geologist Dieudonné Dolomieu, who made the first scientific study of the region. The mountains are formed of light-colored dolomitic limestone, which erosion has carved into grotesque shapes. Popular with tourists and mountain-climbers, the area has a number of resort towns.

dolphin, One of a large group of small, gregarious, streamlined whales or one of two species of oceanic sport and food fishes. Mammalian dolphins are small toothed whales, usually with a well-defined, beaklike snout. (They are sometimes called porpoises, but that name is properly reserved for a blunt-snouted whale family.) The common dolphin (*Delphinus delphis*) and the bottlenose dolphin, both of the family Delphinidae, are found widely in warm temperate seas, though some inhabit tropical rivers. Most of the 32 delphinid species are marine; gray, blackish or brown above and pale below; and about 3–13 ft (1–4 m) long. River dolphins (family Platanistidae; five species) live mainly in fresh water in South America and Asia. One of the two fish species, *Coryphaena hippuras* (family Coryphaenidae), also called mahimahi and dorado, is a popular fish of tropical and temperate waters worldwide. The pompano dolphin (*C. equiselis*) is similar.

Dome of the Rock, or MOSQUE OF OMAR, Oldest existing Islamic monument. It is located on Temple Mount, previously the site of the Temple of Jerusalem. The rock over which it is built is sacred to both Muslims and Jews. In Islam, Muhammad is believed to have ascended into heaven from the site. In Judaism it is the site where Abraham prepared to sacrifice his son Isaac. Built in 685–91 as a place of pilgrimage, the octagonal building has richly decorated walls and a gold-overlaid dome mounted above a circle of piers and columns.

Domesday Book (1086) Original record or summary of William I the Conqueror's survey of England. The most remarkable administrative feat of the Middle Ages, the survey was carried out, against popular resentment, by panels of commissioners who compiled accounts of the estates of the king and his tenants. As summarized in the Domesday Book, it now serves as the starting point for the history of most English towns and villages. Originally called "the description of England," the name Domesday Book (a reference to doomsday, when people face a final accounting of their lives) was later popularly attached to it.

domestic system, or PUTTING-OUT SYSTEM, Production system widespread in 17th-century Europe in which merchant-employers "put out" materials to rural home workers, who then returned finished products to the employers for payment. The domestic system differed from the handicraft system of home production in that the workers neither bought materials nor sold products. It undermined the urban guilds and brought the first widespread industrial employment of women and children. The system was generally superseded by employment in factories but was retained in the 20th century in some industries, notably watchmaking in Switzerland, toy manufacturing in Germany, and many industries in India and China.

domestication, Process of hereditary reorganization of wild animals and plants into forms more accommodating to the interests of people. In its strictest sense, it refers to the initial stage of human mastery of wild animals and plants. The fundamental distinction of domesticated animals and plants from their wild ancestors is that they are created by human labour to meet specific requirements or whims and are adapted to the conditions of continuous care people maintain for them. A variety of animals have been domesticated for food (e.g., cattle, chickens, pigs), clothing (e.g., sheep, silkworms), transportation and labour (e.g., camels, donkeys, horses), and pleasure (e.g., cats, dogs).

dominance, In genetics, the greater influence by one of a pair of genes (alleles) that affect the same inherited trait. If an individual pea plant that has one allele for tallness and one for shortness is the same height as an individual that has two alleles for tallness, the tallness allele is said to be completely dominant. If such an individual is shorter than an individual that has two tallness alleles but still taller than one that has two shortness alleles, the tallness allele is said to be partially or incompletely dominant and the shortness allele is said to be recessive.

Dominica, officially COMMONWEALTH OF DOMINICA, Island country, Lesser Antilles, Caribbean Sea. It is located between the French islands of Guadeloupe and Martinique. Area: 290 sq mi (751 sq km). Population: (2011 est.) 72,500. Capital: Roseau. The majority of the people are of African or mixed African and European descent. Languages: English (official), French patois. Religion: Christianity (predominantly Roman Catholic; also Protestant). Currency: Eastern Caribbean dollar. A mountainous island, Dominica is broken midway by a plain drained by the Layou River. It has a warm tropical climate with heavy rainfall. The main crop is bananas. Dominica is among the poorest of the Caribbean nations. A developing tourist trade was helped by the establishment in 1975 of Morne Trois Pitons National Park, a unique tropical mountain wilderness, but the country was ravaged by hurricanes in 1979 and 1980. With financial help from Britain, it is trying to protect its coastline. It is a republic with one legislative house; its head of state is the president, and its head of government is the prime minister. At the time of Christopher Columbus's arrival in 1493, it was inhabited by the Caribs. Because of its steep coastal cliffs and inaccessible mountains, it remained in the possession of the Caribs until the 18th century; it was then settled by the French and later taken by Britain in 1783. Subsequent hostilities between the settlers and the native inhabitants resulted in the Caribs' near extinction. Incorporated with the Leeward Islands in 1833 and with the Windward Islands in 1940, it became a member of the West Indies Federation in 1958. Dominica became independent in 1978. Offshore banking, a controversial boon to the Dominican economy in the late 20th century, was discontinued early in the 21st century.

Dominican, Member of the Order of Friars Preachers, a Roman Catholic preaching and teaching order founded by St. Dominic. It dates officially from 1216, when Pope Honorius III gave it his approval, though Dominic had begun to build it at least a decade earlier. In contrast with earlier orders, the Dominicans were not organized in autonomous monastic houses, but joined the order at large and could be sent to any house or province on the order's business. The early teaching centers were at Bologna, Paris, Cologne, and Oxford. Dominican preachers spoke out against the Cathari, the Moors, and the Jews and were among the first missionaries under the Spanish and Portuguese explorers. Dominicans were put in charge of the Inquisition when it was founded. Perhaps their most famous member was St. Thomas Aquinas.

Dominican Republic, Country in the West Indies, occupying the eastern two-thirds of the island of Hispaniola, which it shares with Haiti. Area: 18,792 sq mi (48,671 sq km). Population: (2011 est.) 9,440,000. Capital: Santo Domingo. The majority of the people are of mixed European-African ancestry; most of the rest are of European or African descent. Language: Spanish (official). Religion: Christianity (predominantly Roman Catholic; also Protestant). Currency: Dominican peso. The country is generally mountainous, with ranges and hills running from northwest to southeast. The Central Highlands reach 10,417 ft (3,175 m) at Duarte Peak, the highest point in the West Indies. The Cibao Valley in the north is noted for its fertility; the southwestern part of the country is generally dry with large stretches of desert. Traditionally dominated by sugar production, the Dominican Republic's mixed economy became increasingly diversified in the late 20th century, when the country experienced one of the world's highest economic growth rates, though widespread poverty remained despite a growing middle class. It is a multiparty republic with two legislative houses; its head of state and government is the president. The Dominican Republic was originally part of the Spanish colony of Hispaniola. In 1697 the western third of the island, which later became Haiti, was ceded to France; the remainder of the island passed to France in 1795. The eastern two-thirds of the island were returned to Spain in 1809, and the colony declared its independence in 1821. Within a matter of weeks it was overrun by Haitian troops and occupied until 1844. Since then the country has been under the rule of a succession of dictators, except for short interludes of democratic government, and the U.S. has frequently been involved in its affairs. The termination of the dictatorship of Rafael Trujillo in 1961 led to civil war in 1965 and U.S. military intervention. For the rest of the country, politics in the Dominican Republic were dominated by seven-time president Joaquín Balaguer. The country suffered from severe hurricanes in 1979 and 1998.

dominoes, Game of several variations played with a set of flat rectangular blocks (dominoes) whose faces are divided into two equal parts that are blank or bear from one to six dots arranged as on dice faces. The usual set consists of 28 pieces. Dominoes in China may date to the 12th century AD; the Eskimos have also long played a domino-like game. There is no record of dominoes in Europe before the mid-18th century. The principle in nearly all modern dominoes games is to match one end of a piece to another that is identically or reciprocally numbered. The game may be set at 50 or 100 points.

Don River, Tatar DUNA, ancient TANAIS, River, southwestern Russia. Rising south of Moscow in the central Russian uplands, it flows generally south for 1,162 mi (1,870 km) to enter the Gulf of Taganrog in the Sea of Azov. In its middle course it flows into the Tsimlyansk Reservoir, which dominates the Don's lower course. Most of its basin is rich farmland and timberland. A major shipping artery, it is navigable (in the spring) as far as 990 mi (1,584 km) from the Sea of Azov.

Donation of Constantine, Document concerning the supposed grant by the emperor Constantine I (the Great) to Pope Sylvester I (314–335) and later popes of temporal power over Rome and the Western Empire. The gift was said to have been motivated by Constantine's gratitude to Sylvester for miraculously healing his leprosy and converting him to Christianity. Based on legends from the 5th century concerning Sylvester and Constantine, the Donation was probably written at Rome in the mid 8th century and was related to the coronation of Pippin III, the first Carolingian king of the Franks. Proved in the 15th century by Lorenzo Valla to be a forgery, the document was already questioned by the emperor Otto III (r. 996–1002) but was often cited in the 11th–15th centuries to support papal claims in the struggle between church and state.

Donation of Pippin (754) Promise made by the Frankish king Pippin III to win for Pope Stephen II Byzantine imperial lands in Italy conquered by the Lombards. The Donation was made in the context of the papal struggle with the Lombards, the collapse of Byzantine support for the papacy, and Pippin's elevation to the royal throne with papal support. In 756 it was written in a document that became the basis of papal rule over central Italy, which lasted until the 19th century. Pippin won territory from the Lombard king in two military campaigns (754, 756) and gave it to the papacy. The Donation was later confirmed and enlarged by Charlemagne (774).

Donatism, Schismatic Christian movement in North Africa in the 4th century. It arose out of the debate over the status of church leaders who had cooperated with Roman officials during persecutions of Christians. The movement's leader, Donatus (died *c.* AD 355), denied the validity of priestly duties performed by such leaders, insisting that lapsed Christians were not in a state of grace and thus had no authority to administer the sacraments. The struggle over the Donatist heresy came to a head in 311, when Caecilian was consecrated bishop of Carthage by a lapsed bishop. The Donatists declared the election invalid, but Constantine I decided in favor of Caecilian, prompting the Donatists to break with the Roman church in 312. Despite persecution, Donatism survived in North Africa until the advent of Islam (7th century).

Donets Basin, or DONBAS, Large mining and industrial region, southeastern Ukraine and southwestern Russia. Notable for its coal and iron reserves, the exploited area of the coalfield covers nearly 9,000 sq mi (23,300 sq km) south of the Donets River. First mined in the early 19th century, by 1913 the Donets Basin was producing 87% of Russian coal. The coalfields adjoin the rich ironfield of Krivoi Rog, where an ironworks was set up in 1872 in Donetsk; by 1913 it was making 74% of all Russian pig iron. The area today is the largest single producing area of iron and steel in Ukraine and one of the world's major heavy-industrial complexes.

Donets River, River, southwestern Russia and eastern Ukraine. Rising in the Central Russian Upland, it winds south and east through Russia and Ukraine for some 650 mi (1,050 km) to join the Don River below Konstantinovsk. It flows along the northern Donets Basin industrial region, which uses it for heavy shipping and also causes severe pollution problems. A water shortage in the river and industrial area led to the construction in the 1970s of a canal connecting the Dnieper to the Donets. Six weirs make navigation possible upstream to the city of Donetsk.

Donetsk, formerly (1924–61) STALINO, City (pop., 2001: 1,016,000), southeastern Ukraine. In 1872 an ironworks was founded there by a Welshman, John Hughes, to produce iron rails for the growing Russian rail network. Fueled by the rich deposits of the Donets Basin, both coal mining and steelmaking developed rapidly. Extensive destruction in World War II led to postwar modernization, and subsequent growth has been rapid. Modern Donetsk is one of Ukraine's largest metallurgical centres.

Dong Qichang, or TUNG CH'I-CH'ANG (b. 1555, Huating, Kiangsu province, China—d. 1636), Chinese painter, calligrapher, and theoretician of the late Ming period. He is noted especially for his writings on Chinese painting, which he divided into the Northern school, which taught the acquisition of truth, and the Southern school, which emphasized sudden, intuitive understanding. At the centre of the scholarly ideal of the Southern school was the art of calligraphy, which expressed the true nature of the artist without the interposition of pictorial description. Dong Qichang's own paintings stress stark forms, seemingly anomalous spatial renderings, and naive handling of ink and brush. His ideas continue to influence Chinese aesthetic theory.

Doppler effect, Apparent difference between the frequency at which waves—including light, sound, and radio waves—leave a source and that at which they reach an observer. The effect, first described by the Austrian physicist Christian Doppler (1803–1853), is caused by the relative motion of the observer and the wave source. It can be observed by listening to the blowing horn or siren of an approaching vehicle, whose pitch rises as the vehicle approaches the observer and falls as it recedes. It is used in radar and to calculate the speed of stars by observing the change in frequency of their light.

Dorian, Any member of a major division of the ancient Greeks. Coming from the north and northwest, they conquered the Peloponnese *c.* 1100–1000 BC, overran the remnants of the Mycenaean and Minoan civilizations, and ushered in a dark age that lasted almost three centuries, until the rise of the Greek city-states. They had their own dialect and were organized into three tribes. Patterns of settlement determined their alliances in later Greek conflicts. To Greek culture they gave the Doric order of architecture, the tragic choral lyric, and a militarized aristocratic government. They assimilated into Greek societies in some cases, but in Sparta and Crete they held power and resisted cultural advancement.

Dortmund, ancient THROTMANNIA, City (pop., 2002 est.: 589,200), North Rhine–Westphalia, western Germany. First mentioned in AD 885, it became a free imperial city in 1220 and later joined the Hanseatic League. A prosperous trading centre in the 14th century, it declined after the Thirty Years' War and lost its imperial rights in 1803. The development of coal and iron ore mining and the completion of the Dortmund-Ems Canal in 1899 stimulated its regrowth. The city was largely destroyed in World War II but was extensively rebuilt. It is a major transportation and industrial hub of the Ruhr area.

Dostoyevsky, Fyodor (Mikhaylovich) (b. Nov. 11, 1821, Moscow, Russia—d. Feb. 9, 1881, St. Petersburg), Russian novelist. Dostoyevsky gave up an engineering career early in order to write. In 1849 he was arrested for belonging to a radical discussion group; sentenced to be shot, he was reprieved at the last moment and spent four years at hard labour in Siberia, where he developed epilepsy and experienced a deepening of his religious faith. Later he published and wrote for several periodicals while producing his best novels. His novels are concerned especially with faith, suffering, and the meaning of life; they are famous for their psychological depth and insight and their near-prophetic treatment of issues in philosophy and politics. His first, *Poor Folk* (1846), was followed the same year by *The Double. The House of the Dead* (1862) is based on his imprisonment and *The Gambler* (1866) on his own gambling addiction. Best known are the novella *Notes from the Underground* (1864) and the great novels *Crime and Punishment* (1866), *The Idiot* (1869), *The Possessed* (1872), and *The Brothers Karamazov* (1880), which focuses on the problem of evil, the nature of freedom, and the characters' craving for some kind of faith. By the end of his life, he had been acclaimed one of his country's greatest writers, and his works had a profound influence on 20th-century literature.

Douala, City (pop., 2004 est.: 1,532,800), chief port of Cameroon, on the Bight of Biafra. It was the capital of German Kamerun and later of French Cameroun and was taken from the Germans in 1914. Cameroon's largest city, it is one of Central Africa's major industrial centres, and its deepwater port handles most of the country's overseas trade. It is home to a variety of commercial, agricultural, and industrial schools. A museum and handicraft centre encourage the production and preservation of Cameroonian art.

double bass, Lowest-pitched of the modern stringed instruments. It varies in size, up to 80 inches (200 cm) tall. Its shape also varies; its shoulders usually slope more than those of the violin, reflecting its status as a hybrid of the viol and violin families (the name comes from the double-bass viol). It emerged from these families in the late Renaissance, and it has always been less standardized in form than its cousins in the violin family. It normally has four strings; the orchestral instrument often has a lower fifth string (more often, an extension is added to the fourth string), and the jazz instrument has a higher fifth string. Its range is an octave below that of the cello. It is normally bowed in orchestral music and plucked in jazz. In rock bands and some jazz bands, the electric bass is used instead.

double jeopardy, In law, the prosecution of a person for an offense for which he or she already has been prosecuted. In U.S. law, double jeopardy is prohibited by the 5th Amendment to the Constitution of the United States, which states that no person shall "be subject for the same offense to be twice put in jeopardy of life and limb." The clause bars second prosecutions after acquittal or conviction and prohibits multiple convictions for the same offense. Thus a person cannot be guilty of both murder and manslaughter for the same homicide, nor can a person be retried for the same crime after the case has been resolved. A person can, however, be convicted of both murder and robbery if the murder arose from the robbery. The prohibition against double jeopardy is not violated when an individual is charged for behaviour stemming from an offense for which he has been charged in a different jurisdiction or in a different court (e.g., a civil court as opposed to a criminal court).

Douro River, Spanish DUERO, ancient DURIUS, River in Spain and Portugal. The third-longest in the Iberian Peninsula, it rises in the Sierra de Urbión in central Spain, and crosses the Numantian Plateau. It flows generally westward for 556 mi (895 km) across Spain and northern Portugal to the Atlantic Ocean. It has extensive barge traffic in its Portuguese section, and has been harnessed for hydroelectric power.

Dover, ancient DUBRIS PORTUS, Town (pop., 2001: 34,087) and seaport on the Strait of Dover, Dover district, administrative and historic county of Kent, southeastern England. A pre-Roman settlement existed on the site, and in the 4th century AD it was guarded by a Saxon fort. During the 11th century it was chief of the Cinque Ports. Dover Castle, a stronghold of medieval England, was besieged by rebellious barons in 1216. The town was held by Parliamentarians in the English Civil Wars. It was a naval base in World War I and was bombed by Germans in World War II. Landmarks include the castle, a Roman lighthouse, and an ancient fortress church. Dover is famous for the white chalk cliffs rising above it and is a leading passenger port.

Dover, Strait of, French PAS DE CALAIS, ancient FRETUM GALLICUM, Channel separating southeastern England from northwestern France. Connecting the English Channel with the North Sea, it is about 20 mi (32 km) wide at its narrowest point. Lined on the British side with the famous White Cliffs, which are composed of soft chalk, it is one of the world's busiest seaways; its chief ports include Dover and Folkestone in England and Calais and Boulogne in France. It was the scene of several historic naval battles, including the repulse by the English of the Spanish Armada in 1588. Allied troops in the Dunkirk Evacuation crossed to Dover in 1940.

Dow Jones average, Stock price average computed by Dow Jones & Co. Founded in 1882 by Charles H. Dow (1851–1902) and Edward D. Jones (1856–1920), Dow Jones & Co. commenced publication of the *Wall Street Journal* in 1889 and began computing a daily industrials average in 1897. Dow Jones publishes averages based on 20 transportation stocks, 15 utility stocks, and 30 selected industrial stocks, as well as a composite average of all three; the industrial-stocks average is universally followed by U.S. and international investors. The company also publishes several bond averages.

Down syndrome, or TRISOMY 21, Congenital disorder caused by an extra chromosome (trisomy) on the chromosome 21 pair. Those with the syndrome may have broad, flat faces; up-slanted eyes, sometimes with epicanthal folds (whence its former name; mongolism); intellectual disability (usually moderate); heart or kidney malformations; and abnormal fingerprint patterns. Many persons with Down syndrome can live and work independently or in a sheltered environment, but they age prematurely and have a short (55-year) life expectancy. The risk of bearing a child with the disorder increases with the mother's age; it can be detected in the fetus by amniocentesis.

dowry, Money, goods, or estate that a woman brings to her husband in marriage. The dowry has a long history in Europe, South Asia, Africa, and other parts of the world. Some of its basic functions are to protect the wife against ill treatment by her husband, since a dowry can be a conditional gift; to help the husband discharge the responsibilities of marriage, since the dowry makes it possible for the young man to establish a household; to provide the wife with support in case of her husband's death; and to compensate the groom's kin for their payment of bridewealth. In Europe, the dowry served to build the power and wealth of great families and played a role in the politics of grand alliance through marriage. The giving of a dowry more or less disappeared in Europe in the 19th and 20th centuries. The practice grew, however, in South Asia. In some cases, delayed or insufficient dowry made some young wives the victims of murder by their husbands or in-laws, a practice known as "bride burning" or "dowry death."

Dracula, Character created by Bram Stoker in his 1897 novel of the same name. A mesmerizing, ruthless vampire, Dracula captured the public imagination, especially following Bela Lugosi's elegant and chilling portrayal of Count Dracula in Tod Browning's 1931 horror film version. Stoker had named the character for the notoriously cruel Vlad III Tepes (1431–76), a ruler of Walachia, whose epithet was Dracula ("Son of the Dragon"). Vlad was said to have put to death 20,000 men, women, and children by impaling them upright on stakes. The Dracula character became a stock figure in the horror repertoire, portrayed with varying degrees of sympathy and repulsion.

drafting, Precise graphical representation of a structure, machine, or its component parts that communicates the intent of a technical design to the fabricator (or the prospective buyer) of the product. Drawings may present the various aspects of an object's form, show the object projected in space, or explain how it is built. Drafting uses orthographic projection, in which the object is viewed along parallel lines that are perpendicular to the plane of the drawing. Orthographic drawings include top views (plans), flat front and side views (elevations), and cross-sectional views showing profile. Perspective drawing, which presents a realistic illusion of space, uses a horizon line and vanishing points to show how objects and spatial relationships might appear to the eye, including diminution of size and convergence of parallel lines. Drafting was done with precision instruments (T square or parallel rule, triangle, mechanical pens and pencils) until computerization revolutionized production methods in architectural and engineering offices.

drag racing, Form of motor racing in which two contestants race side by side from a standing start over a straight quarter-mile strip of pavement. Winners go on to compete against others in their class until only one is left undefeated. There are three main classes of vehicle: (1) the Top Fuel Eliminator (called a "rail" or "slingshot"), a lightweight, long-chassied vehicle with wide rear tires that is fueled by a special mixture, such as methanol and nitromethane; (2) the "funny car," a high-performance copy of a late-model production car that uses special fuel; and (3) the standard production car, a modified version of a gasoline-powered production car. The Top Fuel class is the fastest, followed by the funny car. Drag racing is most popular in the U.S.

dragon, Legendary monster usually depicted as a huge, bat-winged, fire-breathing lizard or snake with a barbed tail. The dragon symbolized evil in the ancient Middle East, and the Egyptian god Apepi was the great serpent of the world of darkness. The Greeks and Romans sometimes represented dragons as evil creatures and sometimes as beneficent powers acquainted with the secrets of the earth. In Christianity the dragon symbolized sin and paganism, and saints such as St. George were shown triumphing over it. Used as warlike emblems in many cultures, dragons were carved on the prows of Norse ships and depicted on royal ensigns in medieval England. In the Far East the dragon was a beneficent creature, wingless but regarded as a power of the air. In China it symbolized yang in the yin-yang of cosmology, and it served as the emblem of the royal family.

dragonfly, Any member of the insect suborder Anisoptera (order

Odonata), characterized by four large, membranous, many-veined wings, that, when at rest, are held horizontally rather than vertically. Dragonflies are agile and have bulging eyes that often occupy most of the head and a wingspan of about 6 in. (16 cm). The dragonfly is one of the fastest-flying and most predaceous insects; in 30 minutes it can eat its own weight in food. Dragonflies differ from most other insects by having the male copulatory organs at the front part of the abdomen rather than at the back end. Male and female often fly in tandem during sperm transfer.

Dragonfly (Libellula forensis).
E.S. Ross

Drake, Sir Francis (b. *c.* 1540–43, Devonshire, Eng.—d. Jan.

28, 1596, at sea, off Puerto Bello, Pan.), English admiral, the most renowned seaman of the Elizabethan Age. Brought up by his wealthy Hawkins relatives in Plymouth, Drake went to sea at about age 18. He gained a reputation as an outstanding navigator and became wealthy by raiding and plundering Spanish colonies. In 1577 he set sail with five ships, but ultimately only his flagship, the *Golden Hind*, made its way through the Strait of Magellan into the Pacific and up the coast of South and North America. He sailed at least as far north as what is now San Francisco, claiming the area

Sir Francis Drake, oil painting by an unknown artist; in the National Portrait Gallery, London.
Courtesy of The National Portrait Gallery, London

for Elizabeth, and continued westward to the Philippines and around the Cape of Good Hope. Having circumnavigated the globe, he returned to Plymouth, Eng., in 1580 laden with treasure, the first captain ever to sail his own ship around the world. In 1581 he was knighted. Appointed vice admiral (1588), he destroyed ships and supplies destined for the Spanish Armada and delayed the Spanish attack for a year. But he is not known to have played any part in the battle that eventually occurred. In his lifetime, his reputation at home was equivocal, yet his legend grew. On his last voyage he succumbed to fever and was buried at sea.

Drake Passage, Strait, connecting the Atlantic and Pacific oceans between Tierra del Fuego and the South Shetland Islands. Located about 100 mi (160 km) north of the Antarctic Peninsula, it is 600 mi (1,000 km) wide. In this area the climate changes from cool, humid, and subpolar to the frozen conditions of Antarctica. An important trade route in the 19th and early 20th centuries, its stormy seas and icy conditions made the rounding of Cape Horn a difficult journey.

Dravidian languages, Family of 24 languages indigenous to and spoken principally in South Asia by more than 214 million people. Four of the Dravidian languages are among the major literary languages of southern India—Telugu, Tamil, Kannada, and Malayalam. These all have independent scripts and long documented histories. They account for the overwhelming majority of all Dravidian-speakers, and they form the basis of the linguistic states of Andhra Pradesh, Tamil Nadu, Karnataka, and Kerala. All have borrowed liberally from Sanskrit. The only Dravidian language spoken entirely outside of India is Brahui, with more than 2.2 million speakers mainly in Pakistan and Afghanistan. Of the Dravidian languages, Tamil has the greatest geographical extension and the richest and most ancient literature, which is paralleled in India only by that of Sanskrit. The Dravidian family, with no demonstrated relationship to other language families, is assumed to have covered a much more extensive area of South Asia before the spread of Indo-Aryan and was the source of loanwords into early Indo-Aryan dialects.

drawing, Art or technique of producing images on a surface, usually paper, by means of marks in graphite, ink, chalk, charcoal, or crayon. It is often a preliminary stage to work in other media. According to Giorgio Vasari, *disegno* (drawing and design) was the foundation of the three arts of painting, sculpture, and architecture. Beginning in the Italian Renaissance, debate arose regarding the role of drawing, as some saw it as an independent art form and others saw it as a preliminary stage in creating a painting or sculpture. By the 17th century, drawings had definite market value; connoisseurs specialized in collecting them, and forgers began to exploit the demand. In the 20th century, the drawing became fully autonomous as an art form, figuring significantly among the works of virtually every major artist, and the line itself was exploited both for its representational and its purely expressive qualities.

dream, Series of thoughts, images, or emotions occurring during sleep, particularly sleep accompanied by rapid eye movement (REM sleep). Dream reports range from the very ordinary and realistic to the fantastic and surreal. Humans have always attached great importance to dreams, which have been variously viewed as windows to the sacred, the past and the future, or the world of the dead. Dreams have provided creative solutions to intellectual and emotional problems and have offered ideas for artistic pursuits. A type of cognitive synthesis that facilitates conscious insight may occur subconsciously during dreaming. The most famous theory of the significance of dreams is the psychoanalytic model of Sigmund Freud; in Freud's view, desires that are ordinarily repressed (hidden from consciousness) because they represent forbidden impulses are given expression in dreams, though often in disguised (i.e., symbolic) form.

Dresden, City (pop., 2002: 478,600), situated on the Elbe River, eastern Germany. Originally a Slavonic settlement, it was the residence of the margraves of Meissen in the early 13th century. The Dresden china industry originated there but was moved to Meissen in 1710. Napoleon I made Dresden a centre of military operations and won his last great battle there in 1813. Dresden was occupied by Prussia in 1866. In World War II, it was severely damaged by Allied bombing raids in 1945. Several of its historic buildings have been restored or reconstructed. It is known for its art galleries, museums, and other cultural institutions. Industries produce precision and optical instruments.

Dresden Codex, Latin CODEX DRESDENSIS, One of the few pre-Columbian Mayan codices, or collections of hieroglyphic texts, to survive book burnings by Spanish clergy. It contains exceptionally accurate astronomical calculations, including eclipse-prediction tables and the synodic period of Venus. The reputation of the Maya as astronomers is based largely on these figures.

dressage (French: "training"), Equestrian sport involving the execution of precision movements by a trained horse in response to barely perceptible signals from its rider. Particularly important are the animal's pace and bearing in performing walks, trots, canters, and more specialized maneuvers. Training is divided into the elementary *campagne* and the advanced *haute école*. Dressage competitions have been included in the Olympic Games since 1912. Riders compete as individuals and in teams.

Dreyfus, Alfred (b. Oct. 9, 1859, Mulhouse, France—d. July 12, 1935, Paris), French army officer, subject of the Dreyfus Affair (*l'Affaire*). Son of a Jewish textile manufacturer, he studied at the École Polytechnique, then entered the army and rose to the rank of captain (1889). He was assigned to the war ministry when, in 1894, he was accused of selling military secrets to Germany. He was convicted and sentenced to life imprisonment on Devil's Island. The legal proceedings, based on insufficient evidence, were highly irregular, but public opinion and the French press, led by its virulently anti-Semitic section, welcomed the verdict. Doubts began to grow as evidence came out suggesting that C.F. Esterhazy (1847–1923) was the true traitor. The movement for revision of Dreyfus's trial gained momentum when Émile Zola wrote an open letter under the headline "J'Accuse," accusing the army of covering up its errors in making the case. After a new court-martial (1899) again found Dreyfus guilty, he was pardoned by the president of the republic in an effort to resolve the issue. In 1906 a civilian court of appeals cleared Dreyfus and reversed all previous convictions. Formally reinstated and decorated with the Legion of Honour, he later saw active service in World War I. The affair resulted in the separation of church and state in 1905.

Alfred Dreyfus, before 1894.
H. Roger-Viollet

drought, Lack or insufficiency of rain for an extended period that severely disturbs the hydrologic cycle in an area. Droughts involve water shortages, crop damage, streamflow reduction, and depletion of groundwater and soil moisture. They occur when evaporation and transpiration exceed precipitation for a considerable period. Drought is the most serious hazard to agriculture in nearly every part of the world. Efforts have been made to control it by seeding clouds to induce rainfall, but these experiments have had only limited success.

drug, Any chemical agent that affects the function of living things. Some, including antibiotics, stimulants, tranquilizers, antidepressants, analgesics, narcotics, and hormones, have generalized effects. Others, including laxatives, heart stimulants, anticoagulants, diuretics, and antihistamines, act on specific systems. Vaccines are sometimes considered drugs. Drugs may protect against attacking organisms (by killing them, stopping them from reproducing, or blocking their effects on the host), substitute for a missing or defective substance in the body, or interrupt an abnormal process. A drug must bind with receptors in or on cells and cannot work if the receptors are absent or its configuration does not fit theirs. Drugs may be given by mouth, by injection, by inhalation, rectally, or through the skin. The oldest existing catalogue of drugs is a stone tablet from ancient Babylonia (*c.* 1700 BC); the modern drug era began when antibiotics were discovered in 1928. Synthetic versions of natural drugs led to design of drugs based on chemical structure. Drugs must be not only effective but safe; side effects can range from minor to dangerous. Many illegal drugs also have medical uses.

drug resistance, Property of a disease-causing organism that allows it to withstand drug therapy. In any population of infectious agents, some have a mutation that helps them resist the action of a drug. The drug then kills more of the nonresistant microbes, leaving the mutants without competition to multiply into a resistant strain. This situation is more likely if the drug is not taken properly (e.g., a course of antibiotics not completed, anti-HIV drug doses missed) or not prescribed properly (e.g., an antibiotic given for a viral disease). Resistance factors can also be transferred between species that infect the same body. The overprescription of antibiotics in humans and the addition of antibiotics to animal feed have accelerated the evolution of resistant strains of bacteria, making it increasingly difficult to fight off certain disease-causing organisms.

Druid, Member of a learned class of priests, teachers, and judges among the ancient Celtic peoples. The Druids instructed young men, oversaw sacrifices, judged quarrels, and decreed penalties; they were exempt from warfare and paid no tribute. They studied ancient verse, natural philosophy, astronomy and religious lore; their principal doctrine was belief in the immortality of the soul and the transmigration of souls. They sometimes practiced human sacrifice to cure gravely ill people or protect warriors in battle. The Druids were suppressed in Gaul by the Romans in the 1st century AD and in Britain a little later. They lost their priestly functions in Ireland after the coming of Christianity but survived as poets, historians, and judges.

Barrel drum from India with cord-tensioned construction, in the Metropolitan Museum of Art, New York City
Courtesy of the Metropolitan Museum of Art, New York City, gift of Alice E. Getty, 1946

drum, Musical instrument, the sound of which is produced by the vibration of a stretched membrane. Drums are usually either cylindrical or bowl-shaped. The drum is a universal instrument and very ancient; a drum dating to 6000 BC has been found in Moravia. Drums have been important ritually in cultures worldwide. They may have a definite pitch or be unpitched; those of Africa, South and Southeast Asia, and the Middle East are mostly pitched, whereas Western drums are more often unpitched. Drumming has attained its highest degree of development in Africa and India. From the 13th century, the folk dance in Europe was accompanied by a single musician playing simultaneously the pipe or fife and the tabor, a small double-headed snare drum played with one stick. The side drum, or snare drum, has coiled wires or gut strings strung across the lower head, which vibrate against it when the upper head is struck. The powerful bass drum is used especially in marching bands. The pitched timpani are the standard orchestral drums. Until the 17th century, drum parts in Western music were entirely improvised. The drum set used in popular music is played by a single person and normally includes a snare drum, tom-toms, a pedal-operated bass drum, and suspended and hi-hat cymbals.

drupe, Fruit in which the outer layer is a thin skin, the middle layer is thick and usually fleshy (though sometimes tough, as in the almond, or fibrous, as in the coconut), and the inner layer (the pit) is hard and stony. Within the pit is usually one seed. In aggregate fruits such as the raspberry and blackberry (which are not true berries), many small drupes are clumped together. Other representative drupes are the cherry, peach, mango, olive, and walnut.

Drury Lane Theatre, Oldest English theatre still in use. It was built in London by Thomas Killigrew for his acting company as the Theatre Royal (1663). It burned in 1672 and was rebuilt in 1674 with Christopher Wren as architect. It prospered under such actor-managers as Colley Cibber and later under David Garrick and Richard Brinsley Sheridan. An expanded "fireproof" theatre opened in 1794 and burned in 1809. Rebuilt in 1812 with over 2,000 seats, it declined in popularity from the 1840s, but it revived in the 1880s with melodramas and spectacles and was the scene of the acting triumphs of Henry Irving and Ellen Terry. More recently it has played host to many U.S. musicals.

Druze, or DRUSE, Relatively small Middle Eastern religious sect. It originated in Egypt in 1017 and is named for one of its founders, Muḥammad al-Darazī (d. 1019/20). Strictly monotheistic and based in Islam, particularly Ismāʿīlī Islam, Druze beliefs include an eclectic mixture of elements from Gnosticism, Neoplatonism, Judaism, and Iranian religion. The Druze believe in the divinity of al-Ḥākim bi-Amr Allāh (985–1021?), sixth caliph of the Fāṭimid dynasty of Egypt, and expect him to return someday to inaugurate a golden age. The Druze are divided hierachically into two orders—the sages, who are fully initiated in the beliefs of the religion, and the ignorant, who constitute the uninitiated lay majority. They permit no converts, either to or from their religion, and no intermarriage. Their religious system is kept secret from the outside world, and they are permitted to deny their faith if their life is in danger. In the early 21st century they numbered about one million, mostly in Syria and Lebanon.

dry cleaning, System of cleaning textiles with chemical solvents instead of water. The chemicals, often halides or organohalogens (compounds that contain halogen atoms bonded to carbon atoms), dissolve dirt and grease from fabrics. Carbon tetrachloride was once widely used as a dry-cleaning liquid, but its adverse health effects have cut back its use; other organic halogen compounds are now preferred, particularly tetrachloroethylene, which is much more stable and less toxic.

DSL, in full DIGITAL SUBSCRIBER LINE, Broadband digital communications connection that operates over standard copper telephone wires. It requires a DSL modem, which splits transmissions into two frequency bands: the lower frequencies for voice (ordinary telephone calls) and the upper band for digital data, especially for connection to the Internet. Data can be transferred via DSL at much higher rates than with ordinary dial-up modem service; the range of DSL signals, however, is very small. Connections can be made only within a few miles of the nearest transmitting station. DSL and "xDSL" are umbrella terms under which a variety of protocols and technologies fall. ADSL (Asymmetric DSL) is a popular type of DSL in which most of the bandwidth of the connec-

tion is devoted to downloading data from the network to the user, leaving only a small-scale connection for uploading data. In HDSL (High bit-rate DSL) and SDSL (Symmetric DSL) the data stream is symmetric; that is, the upstream and downstream rates are the same. UDSL (Unidirectional DSL), VDSL (Very high data rate DSL), and others still under development are intended to offer even greater rates of data transmission.

Du Fu, or TU FU (b. 712, Xiangyang, China—d. 770, Hunan), Chinese poet, often considered the greatest of all time. After a traditional Confucian education, he failed the important civil service examinations and consequently spent much of his life wandering, repeatedly attempting to gain court positions, with mixed success. His early poetry, which celebrates the natural world and bemoans the passage of time, garnered him renown. He suffered periods of extreme personal hardship, and as he matured his verse began to express profound compassion for humanity. An expert in all the poetic genres of his day, he is renowned for his superb classicism and skill in prosody, though many of the subtleties of his art do not survive translation.

dualism, In philosophy, any pair of irreducible, mutually heterogeneous principles used to analyze the nature and origins of knowledge (epistemological dualism) or to explain all of reality or some broad aspect of it (metaphysical dualism); also, any theory that employs dualisms. Examples of epistemological dualisms are subject and object and sensation and sensibilia; examples of metaphysical dualisms are mind and matter, good and evil, and God and world. Dualism is distinguished from monism and pluralism.

Dubayy, or DUBAI, Constituent emirate (pop., 2005 prelim.: 1,200,309), United Arab Emirates (U.A.E.). It is surrounded by the emirates of Abū Ẓaby and Al-Shariqah (Sharjah), and it has 45 mi (72 km) of coastline on the Persian Gulf. Occupying an area of 1,510 sq mi (3,900 sq km), it is the second most populous and second largest state of the federation. Most of its population live in or near its capital, Dubai city (pop., 2007: 1,225,137). Settled in 1799 by people from Abū Ẓaby, Dubayy became a locally powerful state in the early 19th century, and until the 1930s it was known for its pearl exports. It has since been enriched by petroleum exports. Dubai city is now a centre for most of the banks and insurance companies of the U.A.E.

Dublin, ancient EBLANA, City (pop., 2006 prelim: city, 505,739; Greater Dublin, 1,186,159), capital of Ireland. It sits on the River Liffey. It was settled by Danish Vikings arriving in the area in the 9th century CE; they held it until it was taken by the Irish in the 11th century. Under English control in the 12th century, it was given a charter by Henry II, establishing it as a seat of government. It prospered in the 18th century as a centre of the cloth trade, and its harbour dates from that period. In the 19th and 20th centuries it was the site of occasional but abortive nationalist insurrections, including Robert Emmet's rising in 1803, the 1867 Fenian rebellion, and the 1916 Easter Rising. It is the country's chief port, centre of finance and commerce, and seat of culture. Educational and cultural institutions include the University of Dublin; the National Library and National Museum are housed on the grounds of Leinster House (1748), now the seat of the Oireachtas, the Irish parliament.

Dubrovnik, Port city (pop., 2001: 43,770), Croatia. It is situated on the southern Adriatic coast southwest of Sarajevo. Founded in the 7th century by Roman refugees, it came under Byzantine rule after the fall of Rome. It acknowledged Venetian suzerainty (1205–1358) but remained largely independent and became a mercantile power. It was known as a centre of Slavic literature and art in the 15th–17th centuries. Subjugated by Napoleon I in 1808, it was passed to Austria in 1815 and to Yugoslavia in 1918. It was bombed by the Serbs (1991–92) during Croatia's struggle for independence. The old city, enclosed by medieval city walls, contains 14th-century convents and the 15th-century Rector's Palace.

ductility, Capacity of a material to deform permanently (e.g., stretch, bend, or spread) in response to stress. Most common steels, for example, are quite ductile and hence can accommodate local stress concentrations. Brittle materials, such as glass, cannot accommodate concentrations of stress because they lack ductility, and therefore fracture easily. When a material specimen is stressed, it deforms elastically at first; above a certain deformation, called the elastic limit, deformation becomes permanent.

due process, Legal proceedings carried out fairly and in accord with established rules and principles. Due process standards are sometimes referred to as either substantive or procedural. Substantive due process refers to a requirement that laws and regulations be related to a legitimate government interest (e.g., crime prevention) and not contain provisions that result in the unfair or arbitrary treatment of an individual. The 5th Amendment to the Constitution of the United States states that "no person shall…be deprived of life, liberty, or property, without due process of law." This right was extended to the states by the 14th Amendment (1868). Fundamental to procedural due process are adequate notice before the government can deprive one of life, liberty, or property, and the opportunity to be heard and defend one's rights. The boundaries of due process are not fixed and are the subject of endless judicial interpretation and decision making.

Duisburg, City (pop., 2002 est.: 478,600), North Rhine–Westphalia state, western Germany. It lies at the junction of the Rhine and Ruhr rivers and is connected with the North Sea ports by the Rhine-Herne Canal. Known to the Romans as Castrum Deutonis, it was mentioned in AD 740 as Diuspargum, a seat of the Frankish kings. It passed to Cleves in 1290 and, with Cleves, to Brandenburg in 1614. After suffering heavily in the Thirty Years' War, it revived as the seat of a Protestant university from 1655 to 1818. With increasing industrialization after 1880, it is now one of the world's largest inland ports.

dulcimer, or HAMMERED DULCIMER, Stringed musical instrument in which the strings are beaten with small hammers rather than plucked. Its soundbox is flat and usually trapezoidal; each pair of strings produces a single note, and the pairs slope upward alternately left and right to facilitate rapid playing. The Hungarian *cimbalom* is a large dulcimer with legs and a damper pedal, much used in Roma (Gypsy) orchestras. The Appalachian dulcimer is a narrow zither with a fretted fingerboard and three to five strings, which are stopped with one hand and plucked with a plectrum held in the other.

Duma, Russian GOSUDARSTVENNAYA DUMA ("STATE ASSEMBLY"), Elected legislative body that, with the State Council, constituted the imperial Russian legislature (1906–17). It had only limited power to control spending and initiate legislation, and the four Dumas that convened (1906, 1907, 1907–12, 1912–17) rarely enjoyed the cooperation of the ministers or the emperor, who retained the right to rule by decree when the Duma was not in session. In the Soviet era, soviets were the basic unit of government. After the fall of the Soviet Union (1991), the Russian parliament (composed of the Congress of People's Deputies and the Supreme Soviet) exercised legislative responsibilities until 1993, when conflicts with Pres. Boris Yeltsin reached a crisis. Parliament's revolt was suppressed by military force, and a new constitution established a new parliament composed of a Federation Council (in which all 89 of Russia's republics and regions have equal representation) and a Duma, with 450 members, half elected through proportional representation on a party basis and half through single-member constituencies. The president may override and even dissolve the legislature under certain circumstances.

Dunant, (Jean-) Henri (b. May 8, 1828, Geneva, Switz.—d. Oct. 30, 1910, Heiden), Swiss humanitarian. An eyewitness to the Battle of Solferino, he organized emergency aid services for the Austrian and French wounded. In 1862 he proposed the formation of voluntary relief services in all countries and proposed an international agreement covering the war wounded. In 1864 he founded the Red Cross, and the Geneva Convention came into being. He continued to promote interest in the treatment of prisoners of war, the abolition of slavery, international arbitration, disarmament, and the establishment of a Jewish homeland. In 1901 he shared with Frédéric Passy (1822–1912) the first Nobel Peace Prize.

Duncan, Isadora, orig. ANGELA DUNCAN (b. May 26, 1877, or May 27, 1878, San Francisco, Calif., U.S.—d. Sept. 14, 1927, Nice, Fr.), U.S. interpretive dancer. She rejected the conventions of classical ballet and based her technique on natural rhythms and movement inspired by ancient Greece, dancing barefoot in a tunic without tights. Enjoying little success in the U.S., she moved to Europe in 1898. She toured Europe, giving recitals to great acclaim throughout her life and earning notoriety for her liberated unconventionality, and she founded several dance schools. She was strangled when her long scarf became entangled in the rear wheel of the car in which she was riding. Her emphasis on "free dance" made her a precursor of modern dance, and she became an inspiration to many avant-garde artists.

Dundee, City and royal borough (pop., 2001: 145,663), eastern Scotland. It constitutes the council area of Dundee City in the historic county of Angus. An important seaport, it is situated on the Firth of Tay, an inlet of the North Sea. Earliest mention of the town dates from the late 12th century, and over the next four or five centuries it was repeatedly sacked, with much bloodshed, by the English. Among surviving buildings, the City Churches, a collection of three parish churches housed under one roof, are a focal point in the modern city centre. Dundee was a world centre for jute manufacturing in the 19th century. Textiles are still produced, but since World War II light engineering has become the predominant industry. The University of Dundee was founded in 1881.

dung beetle, Any member of one subfamily (Scarabaeinae) of scarab beetles, which shapes manure into a ball (sometimes as large as an apple) with its scooperlike head and paddle-shaped antennae. They vary from 0.2 to more than 1 in. (5–30 mm) long. In early summer it buries itself and the ball and feeds on it. Later in the season the female deposits eggs in dung balls, on which the larvae will later feed. They are usually round with short wing covers (elytra) that expose the end of the abdomen. They can eat more than their own weight in 24 hours and are considered helpful because they hasten the conversion of manure to substances usable by other organisms.

Dungeness crab, Edible crab (*Cancer magister*) found along the Pacific coast from Alaska to lower California, one of the coast's largest and most important commercial crabs. The male is 7–9 in. (18–23 cm) wide and 4–5 in. (10–13 cm) long. The reddish brown upper surface is lighter toward the back; the legs and undersurface are yellowish. It lives on sandy bottoms below the high-tide mark. Closely related North American species are the rock crab of the Atlantic coast, the Jonah crab in coastal waters from New England to Canada, and the red and Pacific rock crabs, both in Pacific coastal waters. All are edible, but their commercial importance varies.

Dunham, Katherine (b. June 22, 1909, Glen Ellyn, Ill., U.S.—d. May 21, 2006, New York, N.Y.), U.S. dancer, choreographer, and anthropologist noted for her interpretation of tribal and ethnic dances. In 1931 she opened a dance school in Chicago. In 1940 she formed the U.S.'s first all-black dance company, for which she choreographed revues based on her anthropological research in the Caribbean; her early works included *Tropics* and *Le*

Katherine Dunham in Tropical Revue, *1943.*
Courtesy of the Dance Collection, the New York Public Library at Lincoln Center, Astor, Lenox and Tilden Foundations

Jazz Hot. She later received a Ph.D. in anthropology from the University of Chicago. Many well-known black dancers were trained in her studios in Chicago and New York City. In the 1950s she toured in Europe with her company. She also choreographed Broadway stage productions, operas, and movies. Dunham was involved in human rights causes.

Dunkirk Evacuation (1940) In World War II, the evacuation of the British Expeditionary Force and other Allied troops, cut off by the Germans, from the French seaport of Dunkirk (Dunkerque) to England. Naval vessels and hundreds of civilian boats were used in the evacuation, which began on May 26. When it ended on June 4, about 198,000 British and 140,000 French and Belgian troops had been saved. The operation's success was due to fighter cover by the RAF and (unintentionally) to Adolf Hitler's order of May 24 halting the advance of German armored forces into Dunkirk.

Durban, City (pop., 2005 est.: metro. area, 2,643,000) and chief seaport, South Africa. Located on Natal Bay of the Indian Ocean, it was the site of a European trading settlement from 1824 and was named Port Natal by the traders. Land was ceded to them by the Zulu king Shaka, and the Old Fort (now a museum) was built. Durban was founded in 1835 on the site of Port Natal. In the 1840s the Boers clashed with the British over control of Durban. One of the world's major commercial ports, it is the headquarters of South Africa's sugar industry and a centre of diverse manufacturing. Tourism, also important, is based on the city's proximity to game and nature reserves and to beaches.

Durga, In Hinduism, one of the forms of the goddess Devi or Shakti, and the wife of Shiva. She was born fully grown, created out of flames that issued from the mouths of Brahma, Vishnu, Shiva, and other gods and embodying their collective energy (shakti). They created her to slay the buffalo-demon Mahisasura,

Durga, Rajasthani miniature of the Mewar school, mid-17th century; in a private collection.
Pramod Chandra

whom they were unable to overcome. She is usually depicted riding a lion or tiger, each of her multiple arms bearing a weapon.

Durga-puja, Hindu festival held annually in northeastern India in September–October in honor of the goddess Durga. Images of the goddess are made, worshiped for nine days, and then immersed in water. The celebration includes colourful processions and much public and private festivity.

Durham, Saxon DUNHOLME, City (pop., 2001: district, 87,725), administrative and historic county of Durham, northeastern England. It is on a peninsula in the River Wear. This natural defensive site, fortified by William I (the Conqueror) against the Scots, became a seat of the feudal prince-bishops of Durham. Medieval Durham was a place of pilgrimage, holding the remains of St. Cuthbert in its cathedral (begun in 1093). The bishops of Durham helped establish the city as an educational centre. It is the site of the Gulbenkian Museum of Oriental Art and Archaeology, part of the University of Durham.

durian, Tree (*Durio zibethinus*) of the mallow family (Malvaceae) and its fruit, cultivated in Indonesia, the Philippines, Malaysia, and southern Thailand. The tree has oblong, tapering leaves and yellowish green flowers and resembles the elm in shape. The spherical fruit has a hard spiny shell and contains five oval compartments, each filled with an edible, cream-coloured, custardlike pulp, in which are embedded one to five chestnut-sized seeds, which are edible if roasted. The ripe fruits are eaten by many animals. Though the durian has a mild, sweet flavour, it also has a pungent foul odour. It is seldom exported.

Dushanbe, formerly (until 1929) DYUSHAMBE, (1929–61) STALINABAD, City (pop., 2002 est.: 575,900), capital of Tajikistan. It lies on the Varzob River in southwestern Tajikistan. It was built in the Soviet period on the site of three former settlements, the largest of which, Dyushambe, was a part of the khanate of Bukhara; the old city suffered severe damage during the Soviet takeover in 1920. In 1924 it became the capital of the new Tajik Autonomous S.S.R., and rapid industrial and population growth followed. An important transport junction, it accounts for much of the country's industrial output.

Düsseldorf, City (pop., 2002 est.: city, 570,765; metro. area, 1,315,736), capital of North Rhine–Westphalia state, western Germany. Located on the Rhine River, it is the administrative and cultural centre of the industrial Rhine-Ruhr area. Chartered in 1288 by the count of Berg, Düsseldorf passed to the Palatinate-Neuberg line in 1609. Although it suffered considerably in the Thirty Years' War and the War of the Spanish Succession, it later revived. It was transferred to Prussia in 1815 and grew rapidly with the establishment of iron and steel industries in the 1870s. Heavily damaged in World War II, its old buildings were repaired and new ones erected. It is the site of the first German skyscraper, the Wilhelm-Marx-Haus (1924). It is the birthplace of Heinrich Heine.

Dutch Republic, officially REPUBLIC OF THE UNITED NETHERLANDS, Former state (1581–1795), about the size of the modern kingdom of the Netherlands. It consisted of the seven northern Netherlands provinces that formed the Union of Utrecht in 1579 and declared independence from Spain in 1581 (finally achieved in 1648). Political control shifted between the province of Holland and the princes of Orange. In the 17th century the Dutch Republic developed into a world colonial empire far out of proportion to its resources, emerging as a centre of international finance and a cultural capital of Europe. In the 18th century the republic's colonial empire was eclipsed by that of England. In 1795 the Dutch Republic collapsed under the impact of a Dutch democratic revolution and invading French armies.

dwarf star, Any star of average or low luminosity, mass, and size, including white dwarf stars and red dwarf stars. Dwarf stars include most main-sequence stars, including the Sun. Their colour can range from blue to red, corresponding to temperatures varying from over 17,500 °F (10,000 °C) to a few thousand degrees.

dwarfism, Growth retardation resulting in abnormally short adult stature. It is caused by a variety of hereditary and metabolic disorders. Pituitary dwarfism is caused by insufficient growth hormone. Hereditary dwarfisms include achondroplasia, with normal trunk size but short limbs and a large head; hypochondroplasia, similar except for normal head size; and diastrophic dwarfism, with progressive, crippling skeletal deformities. Intelligence is normal in these forms of dwarfism. Some kinds include intellectual disability. Dwarfism may also result from inadequate nutrition in early life.

dysentery, Infectious intestinal disorder. It is characterized by inflammation, abdominal pain and straining, and diarrhea, often containing blood and mucus. Dysentery is spread in food or water contaminated by feces, often by infected individuals with unwashed hands. Bacillary dysentery (shigellosis), caused by *Shigella* bacteria, may be mild or may be sudden, severe, and fatal. Fluid loss causes dehydration. Advanced stages include chronic large-intestine ulceration. It is treated with antibiotics, fluid replacement, and sometimes blood transfusion. Amoebic (or amebic) dysentery, caused by the amoeba *Entamoeba histolytica*, has two forms, one much like bacillary dysentery and the other chronic and intermittent, sometimes with large-intestine ulcerations. It is treated with drugs that kill the amoeba.

dyslexia, Chronic neurological disorder causing inability or great difficulty in learning to read or spell, despite normal intelligence. It inhibits recognition and processing of graphic symbols, particularly those pertaining to language. Symptoms, including very poor reading skills, reversed word and letter sequences, and illegible handwriting, usually become evident in the early school years. With early recognition and specialized approaches to teaching reading, most dyslexics can learn to read. Anomalies have recently been found in reading-related pathways in the brains of dyslexic persons.

dysmenorrhea, Pain or cramps before or during menstruation. In primary dysmenorrhea, caused by endocrine imbalances, severity varies widely. Irritability, fatigue, backache, or nausea may also occur. Long assumed to be psychosomatic, it is now known to be due to excess prostaglandins, which contract the uterus, causing cramps. Pain relievers that block prostaglandin formation can decrease its severity, which may also be eased after childbearing. Secondary dysmenorrhea is caused by other disorders, including genital obstructions, pelvic inflammation, infection, polyps, or tumours. Treatment is directed toward the underlying disorder.

dysplasia, Abnormal formation of a bodily structure or tissue, usually bone, that may occur in any part of the body. Several types are well-defined diseases in humans. In the most common, epiphyseal dysplasia, the ends of children's bones (epiphyses) grow and harden very slowly; dwarfism often results (sometimes only in the legs), and degenerative joint disease usually develops by middle age. Large dogs bred for narrow hips may have hip dysplasia, with abnormalities involving the head of the thighbone and the hip socket.

dysprosium, Chemical element in the lanthanide series and a rare-earth metal, chemical symbol Dy, atomic number 66. It was discovered in 1886 and was named after the Greek word for "hard to obtain." Its high melting point and ability to absorb neutrons make it useful in control rods for nuclear reactors. Its compounds have been used for making laser materials, as components in some electronic equipment, and as phosphor activators.

E

E. coli, in full ESCHERICHIA COLI, Species of bacterium that normally inhabits the stomach and intestines. When *E. coli* is consumed in water, milk, or food or is transmitted through the bite of a fly or other insect, it can cause gastrointestinal illness. Mutations can lead to strains that cause diarrhea by giving off toxins, invading the intestinal lining, or sticking to the intestinal wall. Therapy for gastrointestinal illness consists largely of fluid replacement, though specific drugs are effective in some cases. The illness is usually self-limiting, with no evidence of long-lasting effects. However, one dangerous strain causes bloody diarrhea, kidney failure, and death in extreme cases. Proper cooking of meat and washing of produce can prevent infection from contaminated food sources.

e-commerce, in full ELECTRONIC COMMERCE, business-to-consumer and business-to-business commerce conducted by way of the Internet or other electronic networks. E-commerce originated in a standard for the exchange of documents during the 1948–49 Berlin blockade and airlift. Various industries elaborated upon the system until the first general standard was published in 1975. The electronic data interchange (EDI) standard is unambiguous, independent of any particular machine, and flexible enough to handle most simple electronic transactions. In addition to standard forms for business-to-business transactions, e-commerce encompasses much wider activity—for example, the deployment of secure private networks (intranets) for sharing information within a company, as well as selective extensions of a company's intranet to collaborating business networks (extranets). A new form of cooperation known as a virtual company, actually a network of firms, each performing some of the processes needed to manufacture a product or deliver a service, has flourished.

ear, Organ of hearing and balance. The outer ear directs sound vibrations through the auditory canal to the eardrum, which is stretched across the end of the auditory canal and which transmits sound vibrations to the middle ear. There is a chain of three tiny bones conducts the vibrations to the inner ear. Fluid inside the cochlea of the inner ear stimulates sensory hairs; these in turn initiate the nerve impulses that travel along the auditory nerve to the brain. The inner ear is also an organ of balance: the sensation of dizziness that is felt after spinning is caused when fluid inside the inner ear's semicircular canals continues to move and stimulate sensory hairs after the body has come to rest. The eustachian tube connects the middle ear with the nasal passages; that connection allows the common cold to spread from the nasal passages to the middle ear, especially in infants and small children. The most common cause of hearing loss is otosclerosis, a surgically correctable disease in which one of the bones of the middle ear loses its capacity to vibrate.

Earhart, Amelia (Mary) (b. July 24, 1897, Atchinson, Kan. U.S.—disappeared July 2, 1937, near Howland Island, Pacific Ocean), U.S. aviator, the first woman to fly alone across the Atlantic Ocean. Earhart worked as a military nurse in Canada during World War I and later as a social worker in Boston. In 1928 she became the first woman to cross the Atlantic in a plane, though as a passenger. In 1932 she accomplished the flight alone, becoming the first woman and the second person to do so. In 1935 she became the first person to fly solo from Hawaii to California. In 1937 she set out with a navigator, Fred Noonan, to fly around the world; they had completed over two-thirds of the distance when her plane disappeared without a trace in the central Pacific Ocean. Speculation about her fate has continued to the present.

Earth, Third planet in distance outward from the Sun. Believed to be about 4.56 billion years old, it is some 149,600,000 km (92,960,000 mi) from the Sun. It makes one revolution, or one complete orbit of the Sun, in about 365.25 days. As it revolves, it rotates on its axis once every 23 hours 56 minutes 4 seconds. The fifth largest planet of the solar system, it has an equatorial circumference of 40,076 km (24,902 mi). Its total surface area is roughly 509,600,000 sq km (197,000,000 sq mi), of which about 71% is water. Earth's atmosphere consists of a mixture of gases, chiefly nitrogen and oxygen. Its only natural satellite, the Moon, orbits the planet at a distance of about 384,400 km (238,900 mi). Earth's surface is traditionally subdivided into seven continental masses: Africa, Antarctica, Asia, Australia, Europe, North America, and South America. These continents are surrounded by four major bodies of water: the Arctic, Atlantic, Indian, and Pacific oceans. Broadly speaking, Earth's interior consists of two regions: a core composed largely of molten, iron-rich metallic alloy; and a rocky shell of silicate minerals comprising both the mantle and crust; lithosphere). Fluid motions in the electrically conductive outer core generate a magnetic field around Earth that is responsible for the Van Allen radiation belts. According to the theory of plate tectonics, the crust is divided into a number of large and small plates that float on and travel independently of the mantle. Plate motions are responsible for continental drift and seafloor spreading and for most volcanic and seismic activity on Earth.

Earth Summit, officially UNITED NATIONS CONFERENCE ON ENVIRONMENT AND DEVELOPMENT, Conference held in Rio de Janeiro (June 3–14, 1992) to reconcile worldwide economic development with environmental protection. It was the largest gathering of world leaders in history, with 117 heads of state and representatives of 178 countries. Biodiversity, global warming, sustainable development, and preservation of tropical rain forests were among the topics discussed. Five international agreements were signed amid tensions between the industrialized countries of the North and the poorer developing states of the South, who were reluctant to accept environmental restrictions without increased Northern economic aid. Follow-up meetings were held in 1997 at the UN General Assembly in New York and in 2002 in Johannesburg, S.Af.

earthenware, Pottery that has been fired at low heat and is slightly more porous and coarser than stoneware and porcelain. For practical and decorative purposes, it is usually glazed. The earliest known pottery, a soft earthenware excavated at a Neolithic settlement in Turkey, is thought to be about 9,000 years old. Earthenware is still widely used for cooking, freezing, and serving.

Lead-glazed earthenware water pot, Paris, 15th century, in the National Museum of Ceramics, Sèvres, France.
Courtesy of the Musee National de la Ceramique, Sevres

earthquake, Sudden shaking of the ground caused by a disturbance deeper within the crust of the Earth. Most earthquakes occur when masses of rock straining against one another along fault lines suddenly fracture and slip. The Earth's major earthquakes occur mainly in belts coinciding with the margins of tectonic plates. These include the Circum-Pacific Belt, which affects New Zealand, New Guinea, Japan, the Aleutian Islands, Alaska, and the western coasts of North and South America; the Alpide Belt, which passes through the Mediterranean region eastward through Asia; oceanic ridges in the Arctic, Atlantic, and western Indian oceans; and the rift valleys of East Africa. The "size," or magnitude, of earthquakes is usually expressed in terms of the Richter scale, which assigns levels from 1.0 or lower to 8.0 or higher. The largest quake ever recorded (Richter magnitude 9.5) occurred off the coast of Chile in 1960. The "strength" of an earthquake is rated in intensity scales such as the Mercalli scale, which assigns qualitative measures of damage to terrain and structures that range from "not felt" to "damage nearly total." The most destructive quake of modern times occurred in 1976, when the city of Tangshan, China, was leveled and more than 250,000 people killed.

earthshine, Sunlight reflected from Earth, especially that reflected onto the dark side of the Moon. For a few days before and after each new moon, this doubly reflected light is powerful enough to make the whole Moon visible, producing the effect, in the case of the new moon, of "the new moon holding the old moon in her arms."

Earthshine on the moon.
Courtesy of Yerkes Observatory, Wisconsin

East Anglia, Traditional region of England. It consists of the historic counties of Norfolk and Suffolk and parts of Cambridgeshire and Essex, and its traditional centre is the city of Norwich. The easternmost area in England, it has been settled for thousands of years. Colchester, the oldest recorded town in England, was important in pre-Roman and Roman times. East Anglia was one of the kingdoms of Anglo-Saxon England, and it was ruled by Danes in the 9th century. During the medieval period it was known for its woolen products, but the region's modern economy is predominantly agricultural. Along the coast are many important fishing ports and holiday resorts.

East India Co., or ENGLISH EAST INDIA CO., English chartered company formed for trade with East and Southeast Asia and India, incorporated in 1600. It began as a monopolistic trading body, establishing early trading stations at Surat, Madras (now Chennai), Bombay (Mumbai), and Calcutta (Kolkata). Trade in spices was its original focus; this broadened to include cotton, silk, and other goods. In 1708 it merged with a rival and was renamed the United Co. of Merchants of England Trading to the East Indies. Becoming involved in politics, it acted as the chief agent of British imperialism in India in the 18th–19th century, exercising substantial power over much of the subcontinent. The company's activities in China in the 19th century served as a catalyst for the expansion of British influence there; its financing of the tea trade with illegal opium exports led to the first Opium War (1839–42). From the late 18th century it gradually lost both commercial and political control; its autonomy diminished after two acts of Parliament (1773, 1774) established a regulatory board responsible to Parliament, though the act gave the company supreme authority in its domains. It ceased to exist as a legal entity in 1873.

East India Co., Dutch, Trading company founded by the Dutch in 1602 to protect their trade in the Indian Ocean and to assist in their war of independence from Spain. The Dutch government granted it a trade monopoly in the waters between the Cape of Good Hope and the Straits of Magellan. Under the administration of forceful governors-general, it was able to defeat the British fleet and largely displace the Portuguese in the East Indies. It prospered through most of the 17th century but then began to decline as a trading and sea power; it was dissolved in 1799.

East Timor, officially DEMOCRATIC REPUBLIC OF TIMOR-LESTE, Country occupying the eastern half of the island of Timor, Southeast Asia. Bounded by the Timor Sea and by the western half of Timor, it also includes the enclave of Ambeno (surrounding the town of Pante Makasar on the northwestern coast of Timor) and the islands of Atauro (Kambing) and Jaco. Area: 5,760 sq mi (14,919 sq km). Population: (2011 est.) 1,092,000. Capital: Dili. Languages: Tetum and Portuguese (both official). Religions: Christianity (predominantly Roman Catholic; also Protestant); also Islam, traditional beliefs. Currency: U.S. dollar. The Portuguese first settled on Timor in 1520 and were granted rule over Timor's eastern half in 1860. The Timor political party Fretilin declared East Timor independent in 1975 after Portugal withdrew its troops. It was invaded by Indonesian forces and annexed to Indonesia in 1976. The takeover, which resulted in the deaths of thousands of East Timorese during the next two decades, was disputed by the United Nations. In 1999 an independence referendum won overwhelmingly; though Indonesia officially recognized the referendum, anti-independence militias killed hundreds of people and sent thousands fleeing to the western part of the island before and after the vote. A UN-administered interim authority imposed order and oversaw elections, the promulgation of a constitution, and the return of refugees; East Timor became a sovereign nation in 2002. It is a republic with one legislative body; its president is head of state, and its prime minister is head of government.

Easter, Major festival of the Christian church year, celebrating the resurrection of Jesus on the third day after his crucifixion. In Western churches it falls on a Sunday between March 22 and April 25, depending on the date of the first full moon after the spring equinox. This time span was fixed after the Council of Nicaea (AD 325). In the Eastern Orthodox calendar, which uses a different calculation, it often falls later. A joyful festival and a time of redemption, Easter brings an end to the long period of penance that constitutes Lent. The word is sometimes said to have been derived from Eostre, a Germanic goddess of spring, but other origins of the term more closely associated with Christian traditions have been proposed. Easter has acquired a number of religious and popular customs. The Easter worship service is one of the high points of the Christian calendar, and since the late 2nd century Easter has also been a time for baptism. The painting of eggs and tales of a rabbit who decorates and hides eggs are among the folk customs associated with the holiday.

Easter Island, Spanish ISLA DE PASCUA, native RAPA NUI, Island (pop., 2002: 3,791), eastern Pacific Ocean. Located 2,200 mi (3,600 km) west of Chile, it has an area of 63 sq mi (163 sq km). Initially inhabited *c.* AD 400 by Polynesians from the Marquesas, Easter Island has long been famous for its monolithic stone statues in human form. They are some 10–40 ft (3–12 m) high, the heaviest weighing about 82 tons. They were probably erected *c.* AD 1000–1600. War and disease decimated the island's population over the succeeding centuries, and the statues' origins were forgotten. Annexed by Chile in 1888, the island was designated a UNESCO World Heritage site in 1995.

Easter Rising, or EASTER REBELLION (1916) Republican insurrection in Ireland against the British. It began on Easter Monday, April 24. Led by Patrick Pearse and Tom Clarke, some 1,560 Irish Volunteers and 200 members of the Irish Citizen Army seized the Dublin General Post Office and other strategic points in Dublin. After five days of fighting, British troops put down the rebellion, and 15 of its leaders were tried and executed. Though the uprising itself had been unpopular with most of the Irish, the executions caused revulsion against the British authorities. The Easter Rising signaled the start of the republican revolution in Ireland.

Eastern Hemisphere, Part of the Earth east of the Atlantic Ocean. It includes Europe, Asia, Australia, and Africa. Longitudes 20° W and 160° E are often considered its boundaries.

Eastern Indian bronze, or PALA BRONZE, Metal sculptures produced from the 9th century in the area of modern Bihar and West Bengal in India, extending into Bangladesh. Made of an alloy of eight metals and produced by lost-wax casting, they represent various divinities (e.g., Shiva, Vishnu) and are small and portable. Produced in the great Buddhist monasteries and distributed throughout South Asia, they influenced the art of Burma (Myanmar), Siam (Thailand), and Java.

Eastern Orthodoxy, officially ORTHODOX CATHOLIC CHURCH, One of the three major branches of Christianity. Its adherents live mostly in Greece, Russia, the Balkans, Ukraine, and the Middle East, with a large following in North America and Australia. The titular head of Eastern Orthodoxy is the ecumenical patriarch of Constantinople (Istanbul), but its many territorial churches (including the huge Russian Orthodox church and the Greek Orthodox church) are governed autonomously by head bishops or patriarchs, who must be unmarried or widowed even though lower orders of the clergy may marry. Eastern Orthodoxy also boasts a strong monastic tradition. The separation of the Eastern churches from the Western, or Latin, branch began with the division of the Roman Empire into two parts under Constantine I. A formal break was made in 1054. Doctrinally, Eastern Orthodoxy differs from Roman Catholicism in that it does not accept the primacy of the pope or the clause in the Western creed that states that the Holy Spirit proceeds from both the Father (God) and the Son (Jesus). The Orthodox church accepts the decisions of the seven ecumenical councils as well as several later ones. It maintains that there are seven sacraments and has a worship service that is theologically and spiritually rich. In the early 21st century, Eastern Orthodoxy had more than 200 million adherents worldwide.

Eastern rite church, or EASTERN CATHOLIC CHURCH, Any of several Eastern Christian churches that trace their origins to ethnic or national Eastern churches but are united with the Roman Catholic church. A few of these churches became associated with Rome in the 12th century, but most trace their origins to the failure to unite Eastern and Western churches at the Council of Ferrara-Florence in 1439 or to churches that rejoined Rome in the 16th century or later. Eastern rite churches acknowledge the authority of the pope but are allowed to use their own ancient liturgies and to maintain rites and customs more typical of Eastern Orthodoxy, such as allowing priests to marry and admitting infants to Holy Communion. The Eastern rite includes the Ukrainian Orthodox church, the Maronite Church, and some Armenians, Ruthenians, and Melchites (in Syria). Today Eastern Catholics number more than 12 million.

Eastman, George (b. July 12, 1854, Waterville, N.Y., U.S.—d. March 14, 1932, Rochester, N.Y.), U.S. inventor and manufacturer. Eastman in 1880 perfected a process for making dry plates for photography. In 1889 he introduced transparent film, and in 1892 he reorganized his Rochester company as the Eastman Kodak Co. The introduction of the first Kodak (a coined word that became a trademark) camera helped promote large-scale amateur photography. By 1927 Eastman Kodak had a virtual monopoly of the U.S. photographic industry, and it has remained one of the largest American companies in its field. Eastman's generous bequests to the University of Rochester were acknowledged in the naming of the Eastman School of Music.

Ebola, Virus responsible for a severe and often fatal hemorrhagic fever. Outbreaks in primates, including humans, have been recorded. Initial symptoms are fever, severe headaches and muscle aches, and loss of appetite; blood clots and profuse uncontrollable hemorrhaging appear within days, followed by nausea, vomiting, and diarrhea. Death occurs in 8–17 days; fatality rates range from 50% to 90%. There is no known treatment. It takes its name from the Ebola River in northern Congo (Zaire), where it first emerged in 1976. The virus appears as long filaments, sometimes branched or intertwined. The virus particle contains one molecule of RNA.

How it attacks cells is unknown. It can be transmitted through contact with bodily fluids; unsanitary conditions and lack of adequate medical supplies have been factors in its spread.

ebony, Wood of several species of trees of the genus *Diospyros* (family Ebenaceae), found widely in the tropics. The best is very heavy, almost black, and from heartwood only. Because of its colour, durability, hardness, and ability to take a high polish, ebony is used for cabinetwork and inlaying, piano keys, knife handles, and turned articles. The best Indian and Ceylon ebony is produced by *D. ebenum*, which grows in abundance west of Trincomalee in Sri Lanka. Jamaica, American, or green ebony comes from *Brya ebenus*, a leguminous tree or shrub.

Ebro River, ancient IBERUS, River, northeastern Spain. Rising in the Cantabrian Mountains and flowing 565 mi (910 km) in a southeasterly course to the Mediterranean Sea, between Barcelona and Valencia, the Ebro is the longest river wholly in Spain and the second longest in the Iberian Peninsula. It has the greatest discharge and the largest drainage basin of any Spanish river. It is navigable for only 15 mi (25 km) upstream from its delta.

Ecclesia (Greek, *ekklesia*: "gathering of those summoned") In ancient Greece, the assembly of citizens in a city-state. The Athenian Ecclesia already existed in the 7th century; under Solon it consisted of all male citizens age 18 and older. It controlled policy, including the right to hear appeals in the public court, elect archons, and confer special privileges. After discussion, members voted by a show of hands; a simple majority determined the results. The body could not initiate new business, since motions had to originate in the boule. Ecclesias existed in most Greek city-states through Roman times, though their powers faded under the empire.

Echegaray (y Eizaguirre), José (b. April 19, 1832, Madrid, Spain—d. Sept. 4, 1916, Madrid), Spanish dramatist. A mathematics professor in his early life, he later held government positions, including minister of finance, and helped develop the Banco de España. His first play, *The Checkbook*, was not produced until he was 42 years old; from then on he wrote an average of two plays a year for the rest of his life. These melodramas, now forgotten, were very popular in his day, and he was admired for his fertile imagination and his skillful stage effects. With Frédéric Mistral, he won the 1904 Nobel Prize for Literature.

echinacea, Any member of the coneflower genus *Echinacea*. Commonly called the purple coneflower, echinacea is used as a border plant. The leaves and roots are used in herbal remedies to boost the immune system and in the treatment of colds and flu.

echolocation, Physiological process for locating distant or invisible objects (such as prey) by emitting sound waves that are reflected back to the emitter by the objects. Echolocation is used by an animal to orient itself, avoid obstacles, find food, and interact socially. Most bats employ echolocation, as do most, if not all, toothed whales (but apparently no baleen whales), a few shrews, and two kinds of birds (oilbirds and certain cave swiftlets). Echolocation pulses consist of short bursts of sound at frequencies ranging from about 1,000 Hz in birds to at least 200,000 Hz in whales. Bats use frequencies from about 30,000 to about 120,000 Hz.

eclipse, The passage of all or part of one celestial body into the shadow of another, the eclipsing body. Observers on Earth experience two major types—lunar eclipses and solar eclipses—each of which involves the Sun and the Moon. The type observed depends on whether Earth is the eclipsing body or the body in shadow. In a lunar eclipse the orbit of the Moon carries it through Earth's shadow. Observers see the full Moon dim considerably, but it remains faintly visible. In a solar eclipse the Moon is the eclipsing body, passing between Earth and the Sun while casting a traveling shadow across Earth's lighted surface. Observers along the shadow's path see a total or partial obscuring of the Sun's disk by the Moon's silhouette. The shadow cast by the eclipsing body consists of the central umbra, into which no direct sunlight penetrates (total eclipse), and the encircling penumbra, reached by light from only part of the Sun's disk (partial eclipse). Solar eclipses visible from different parts of Earth occur two to five times a year; one total solar eclipse occurs in most years. When Earth is closest to the Sun and the Moon farthest from Earth, the Moon's silhouette may fall entirely within the Sun's disk, with a ring of the disk visible around it (annular eclipse). Lunar eclipses occur twice in most years. Other kinds of eclipses include those of the Sun by Mercury or Venus (transits), of distant stars by planets or planetary satellites (occultations), and of stars by orbiting companion stars.

ecliptic, Great circle that is the apparent path of the Sun among the constellations in the course of a year; from another viewpoint, the projection on the celestial sphere of the orbit of Earth around the Sun, which intersects the plane of the celestial equator at the vernal and autumnal equinoxes. The constellations of the zodiac are arranged along the ecliptic.

ecology, Study of the relationships between organisms and their environment. Physiological ecology focuses on the relationships between individual organisms and the physical and chemical features of their environment. Behavioral ecologists study the behaviours of individual organisms as they react to their environment. Population ecology is the study of processes that affect the distribution and abundance of animal and plant populations. Community ecology studies how communities of plant and animal populations function and are organized; it frequently concentrates on particular subsets of organisms such as plant communities or insect communities. Ecosystem ecology examines large-scale ecological issues, ones that often are framed in terms of measures such as biomass, energy flow, and nutrient cycling. Applied ecology applies ecological principles to the management of populations of crops and animals. Theoretical ecologists provide simulations of particular practical problems and develop models of general ecological relevance.

econometrics, Statistical and mathematical analysis of economic relationships. Econometrics creates equations to describe phenomena such as the relationship between changes in price and demand. Econometricians estimate production functions and cost functions for firms, supply-and-demand functions for industries, income distribution in an economy, macroeconomic models and models of the monetary sector for policy makers, and business cycles and growth for forecasting. Information derived from these models helps both private businesses and governments make decisions and set monetary and fiscal policy.

economic development, Process whereby simple, low-income national economies are transformed into modern industrial economies. Theories of economic development—the evolution of poor countries dependent on agriculture or resource extraction into prosperous countries with diversified economies—are of critical importance to developing nations. Economic development projects have typically involved large capital investments in infrastructure (roads, irrigation networks, etc.), industry, education, and financial institutions. More recently, the realization that creating capital-intensive industrial sectors provides only limited employment and can disrupt the rest of the economy has led to smaller-scale economic development programs that aim to utilize the specific resources and natural advantages of developing countries and to avoid disruption of their social and economic structures.

economic system, Set of principles and techniques by which a society decides and organizes the ownership and allocation of economic resources. At one extreme, usually called a free-enterprise system, all resources are privately owned. This system, following Adam Smith, is based on the belief that the common good is max-

imized when all members of society are allowed to pursue their rational self-interest. At the other extreme, usually called a pure-communist system, all resources are publicly owned. This system, following Karl Marx and Vladimir Ilich Lenin, is based on the belief that public ownership of the means of production and government control of every aspect of the economy are necessary to minimize inequalities of wealth and achieve other agreed-upon social objectives. No nation exemplifies either extreme. As one moves from capitalism through socialism to communism, a greater share of a nation's productive resources is publicly owned and a greater reliance is placed on economic planning. Fascism, more a political than an economic system, is a hybrid; privately owned resources are combined into syndicates and placed at the disposal of a centrally planned state.

economics, Social science that analyzes and describes the consequences of choices made concerning scarce productive resources. Economics is the study of how individuals and societies choose to employ those resources: what goods and services will be produced, how they will be produced, and how they will be distributed among the members of society. Economics is customarily divided into microeconomics and macroeconomics. Of major concern to macroeconomists are the rate of economic growth, the inflation rate, and the rate of unemployment. Specialized areas of economic investigation attempt to answer questions on a variety of economic activity; they include agricultural economics, economic development, economic history, environmental economics, industrial organization, international trade, labour economics, money supply and banking, public finance, urban economics, and welfare economics. Specialists in mathematical economics and econometrics provide tools used by all economists. The areas of investigation in economics overlap with many other disciplines, notably history, mathematics, political science, and sociology.

Economist, The, Weekly magazine of news and opinion, founded in 1843 and published in London, generally regarded as one of the world's preeminent journals of its kind. It gives thorough and wide-ranging coverage of general news and particularly of international political developments that bear on the world's economy. In accord with the views promoted by its founders and conveyed by legendary *Economist* editor Walter Bagehot, the publication maintains the position that free markets typically provide the best method of running economies and governments. North America accounts for about half of its total readership.

ecosystem, Complex of living organisms, their physical environment, and all their interrelationships in a particular unit of space. An ecosystem's abiotic (nonbiological) constituents include minerals, climate, soil, water, sunlight, and all other nonliving elements; its biotic constituents consist of all its living members. Two major forces link these constituents: the flow of energy and the cycling of nutrients. The fundamental source of energy in almost all ecosystems is radiant energy from the sun; energy and organic matter are passed along an ecosystem's food chain. The study of ecosystems became increasingly sophisticated in the later 20th century; it is now instrumental in assessing and controlling the environmental effects of agricultural development and industrialization.

ecoterrorism, or ECOLOGICAL TERRORISM, or ENVIRONMENTAL TERRORISM, The destruction, or the threat of destruction, of the environment in order to intimidate or coerce governments. The term has also been applied to crimes committed against companies or government agencies in order to prevent or interfere with activities allegedly harmful to the environment. Ecoterrorism includes threats to contaminate water supplies or to destroy or disable energy utilities, for example, and practices such as the deployment of anthrax. Another form of ecoterrorism, often referred to as environmental warfare, consists of the deliberate and illegal destruction, exploitation, or modification of the environment as a strategy of war or in times of armed conflict. Examples include the U.S. military's use of the defoliant Agent Orange during the Vietnam War and the destruction of Kuwaiti oil wells by retreating Iraqi military forces during the 1991 Persian Gulf War. The activities of some environmental activists also have been described as ecoterrorism. These activities include criminal trespass on the property of logging companies and other firms and obstruction of their operations through sabotage as well as the environmentally harmless modification of natural resources in order to make them unsuitable for commercial use (a practice known as "monkeywrenching").

ectopic pregnancy, or EXTRAUTERINE PREGNANCY, Condition in which a fertilized egg is imbedded outside the uterus. Early on, it may resemble a normal pregnancy, with hormonal changes, amenorrhea, and development of a placenta. Later, most patients have pain as the growing embryo stretches the structure it is attached to. Rupture may cause life-threatening bleeding. A tubal pregnancy may result from obstruction of the egg's passage through the fallopian tube. In an ovarian pregnancy, the egg is fertilized before it leaves the ovary. Implantation elsewhere in the abdomen is an abdominal pregnancy.

Ecuador, officially REPUBLIC OF ECUADOR, Country, northwestern South America. Area: 98,985 sq mi (256,370 sq km), including the Galápagos Islands. Population: (2011 est.) 14,650,000. Capital: Quito. About two-fifths of the population are Indian (mostly Quechua), and two-fifths are mestizos; most of the rest are of Spanish ancestry. Languages: Spanish (official), also Quechua and Shuar (both locally official). Religion: Christianity (predominantly Roman Catholic; also Protestant). Currency: U.S. dollar. Pacific coastal lowlands rise to the peaks and highlands of the Andes Mountains, which give way to the Ecuadoran portion of the tropical Amazon River basin in the east. The Andes rise dramatically in two chains that run north to south and are separated by high valleys. The highest peak is Chimborazo, which rises to an elevation of 20,702 ft (6,310 m); nearby Cotopaxi, 19,347 ft (5,897 m) high, is the world's highest active volcano. The country lies in an active earthquake zone and is prone to violent seismic activity. Almost two-fifths of the land is forested, with tropical rainforests in the east. Ecuador straddles the Equator. Its climate varies from tropical in the lowlands to temperate in the highlands. It has a developing economy based primarily on mining, manufacturing, services, and agriculture. Principal exports include crude petroleum, bananas, and shellfish. Ecuador is a unitary multiparty republic with one legislative house; its head of state and government is the president. What is now Ecuador was conquered by the Incas in the second half of the 15th century and came under Spanish control in 1534. Under the Spaniards it was a part of the Viceroyalty of Peru until 1740, when it became a part of the Viceroyalty of New Granada. It gained its independence from Spain in 1822 as part of the republic of Gran Colombia and in 1830 became a sovereign state. A succession of authoritarian governments ruled into the mid-20th century, and the military played a prominent role in politics. Border disputes led to war with Peru in 1941; conflicts with that country continued periodically until there was a final demarcation of the border in 1998. The economy thrived during the 1970s because of large profits from petroleum exports but was depressed in the 1980s because of lower oil prices. In the 1990s social unrest caused political instability and several changes in the presidency. In a controversial move to help stabilize the economy, the government replaced the sucre with the U.S. dollar as the national currency in 2000. In the early 21st century Ecuador continued to struggle with political upheaval, social unrest related to indigenous rights and economic policies, and poor economic performance.

ecumenism, Movement toward unity or cooperation among the Christian churches. The first major step in the direction of ecumenism was the International Missionary Conference of 1910, a gathering of Protestants. Several Protestant denominations inaugurated a Life and Work Conference (on social and practical problems) in 1925 and a Faith and Order Conference (on church doctrine and governance) in 1927. After World War II the World Council of Churches (WCC) was established; the International Missionary Conference joined it in 1961. The Roman Catholic church also has shown strong interest in improving interchurch relations since the Second Vatican Council (1962–65) and, with the patriarch of Constantinople, has lifted the excommunication of 1054. The Eastern Orthodox church was active in the movement since 1920 and joined the WCC at its inception. The more conservative or fundamentalist Protestant denominations have generally refrained from involvement. Another important factor in 20th-century ecumenism was the creation of united churches that reconcile splintered sects, such as the United Church of Christ (1957) and the Evangelical Lutheran Church in America (1988).

Edda, Body of ancient Icelandic literature. Contained in two 13th-century books, it is the fullest and most detailed source for modern knowledge of Germanic mythology. The *Prose Edda* (*Younger Edda*, or *Snorra-Edda*; c. 1222), a handbook on poetics by Snorri Sturluson, explains diction and metre in skaldic and Eddic poetry and recounts tales from Norse mythology. The *Poetic Edda* (*Elder Edda*, or *Sæmundar Edda*; c. 1250–1300) is a collection of mythological and heroic poems of unknown authorship composed c. 800–1100. These austere lays are the oldest surviving antecedents of the *Nibelungenlied* legends.

Eddy, Mary Baker, orig. MARY MORSE BAKER (b. July 16, 1821, Bow, near Concord, N.H., U.S.—d. Dec. 3, 1910, Chestnut Hill, Mass.), U.S. religious leader, founder of Christian Science. A daughter of Congregationalist descendants of old New England families, she married in 1843; her husband died the following year, and she married again in 1853. She suffered from ill health for much of her life. In the early 1860s she was cured of a spinal malady by Phineas P. Quimby (1802–66), who cured ailments without medication. She remained well until shortly after Quimby's

Mary Baker Eddy.
Library of Congress, Washington, D.C.

death; in 1866 she suffered a severe fall and lost hope for recovery, only to be healed by reading the New Testament. She considered that moment her discovery of Christian Science and spent several years evolving her system. In 1875 she published *Science and Health with Key to the Scriptures*, which her followers regarded as divinely inspired. Having divorced in 1873, in 1877 she married one of her followers, Asa G. Eddy (d. 1882). The Church of Christ, Scientist was organized in 1879. Eddy established the Massachusetts Metaphysical College in 1881; she also founded three periodicals, notably *The Christian Science Monitor* (1908).

Edelweiss (Leontopodium alpinum)
Siegfried Eigstler/Shostal Associates

edelweiss, Perennial plant (*Leontopodium alpinum*) of the aster family (Asteraceae), native to alpine areas of Europe and South America. It has 2–10 yellow flower heads in a dense cluster. Below these flower heads, 6–9 lance-shaped, woolly, white leaves are arranged in the form of a star. Most varieties are ornamentals.

edema, Abnormal accumulation of watery fluid in the spaces between connective-tissue cells. Usually a symptom of diseases of the kidneys, heart, veins, or lymphatic system, which affect water balance in the cells, tissues, and blood, edema can be pitting (retaining an imprint when compressed) or nonpitting. Edema may be local (e.g., hives from allergies) or generalized (also called dropsy), sometimes involving body cavities as well as tissues. Treatment must usually focus on the underlying cause.

Edinburgh, City and council area (pop., 2001: 448,624), capital of Scotland. The city and most of the council area, including the busy port of Leith on the Firth of Forth, lie within the historic county of Midlothian. Located in southeastern Scotland, the original burgh, now known as the Old Town, arose in the 11th century, around Edinburgh Castle, the royal residence of Malcolm III Mac-Duncan. In 1329 Robert the Bruce granted Edinburgh a town charter; it became the capital of the Scottish kingdom in 1437. The city was destroyed in 1544 in the border wars with England; its characteristic use of stone architecture began with this rebuilding. During the 18th century Scotland experienced a cultural and intellectual renaissance, and Edinburgh was home to such luminaries as David Hume, Adam Smith, Robert Burns, and Walter Scott. It was the birthplace of *Encyclopædia Britannica* (1768) and the *Edinburgh Review* (1802). The city expanded in the late 18th century with the development of the Georgian-style New Town, separated from the Old Town by a valley. Edinburgh is the centre of Scottish culture and education and is home to the University of Edinburgh, the National Library, the National Gallery, and the Royal Scottish Museum. It is the site of the Scottish Parliament, which first convened in 1999.

Edison, Thomas Alva (b. Feb. 11, 1847, Milan, Ohio, U.S.—d. Oct. 18, 1931, West Orange, N.J.), U.S. inventor. He had very little formal schooling. He set up a laboratory in his father's basement at age 10; at 12 he was earning money selling newspapers and candy on trains. He worked as a telegrapher (1862–68) before deciding to pursue invention and entrepreneurship. Throughout much of his career, he was strongly motivated by efforts to overcome his handicap of partial deafness. For Western Union he developed a machine capable of sending four telegraph messages down one wire, only to sell the invention to Western Union's rival, Jay Gould, for more than $100,000. He created the world's first industrial-research laboratory, in Menlo Park, N.J. There he invented the carbon-button transmitter (1877), still used in telephone speakers and microphones today; the phonograph (1877); and the incandescent lightbulb (1879). To develop the lightbulb, he was advanced $30,000 by such financiers as J.P. Morgan and the Vanderbilts. In 1882 he supervised the installation of the world's first permanent commercial central power system, in lower Manhattan. After the death of his first wife (1884), he built a new laboratory in West Orange, N.J. Its first major endeavour was the commercialization of the phonograph, which Alexander Graham Bell had improved on since Edison's initial invention. At the new laboratory Edison and his team also developed an early movie camera and an instrument for viewing moving pictures; they also developed the alkaline storage battery. Although his later projects were not as successful as his earlier ones, Edison continued to work even in his 80s. Singly or jointly, he held a world-record 1,093 patents, nearly 400 of them for electric light and power. He always invented for necessity, with the object of devising something new that he could manufacture. More than any other, he laid the basis for the technological revolution of the modern electric world.

Edmonton, City (pop., 2001: city, 666,104; metro. area, 937,845), capital of Alberta, Canada. Located on the North Saskatchewan River, in the centre of the province, it began as a series of fur-trading posts built from 1795. With the arrival of the railway and an influx of settlers in the late 19th century, Edmonton began to prosper economically, and in 1905 it became the capital of the new province of Alberta. The 1947 discovery of petroleum in the area greatly stimulated the city's growth; an agricultural and oil-based economy still prevails. It is the distribution centre of northwestern Canada. Its cultural and educational institutions include the University of Alberta (1906).

educational psychology, Branch of psychology concerned with the learning processes and psychological issues associated with the teaching and training of students. The educational psychologist studies the cognitive development of students and the various factors involved in learning, including aptitude and learning measurement, the creative process, and the motivational forces that influence student-teacher dynamics. Two early leaders in the field were G. Stanley Hall and Edward L. Thorndike.

eel, Any of more than 800 fish species (order Anguilliformes) that are slender, elongated, and usually scaleless, with long dorsal and anal fins that are continuous around the tail tip. Eels are found in all seas, from coastal regions to the mid-depths. Freshwater eels are active predaceous fish with small embedded scales. They grow to maturity in fresh water and return to the sea, where they spawn and die. The transparent young drift to the coast and make their way upstream. Freshwater eels, considered valuable food fish, include species ranging from 4 in. (10 cm) to about 11.5 ft (3.5 m) long.

effigy mound, Earthen mound in the form of a bird or animal (e.g, bear, deer, turtle, buffalo), found in the northern central U.S., especially the Ohio River valley. Little is known of the effigy mounds except that most were burial sites. The culture that produced them dates from AD 300 to the mid-17th century.

egg, In biology, the female sex cell, or gamete. In zoology, the Latin term *ovum* is often used to refer to the single cell, whereas the word *egg* may be applied to the entire specialized structure or capsule that consists of the ovum, its various protective membranes, and any accompanying nutritive materials. The egg or ovum, like the male gamete (sperm), bears only a single (haploid; *see* ploidy) set of chromosomes. When female and male gametes unite during fertilization, the double (diploid) set of chromosomes is restored in the resulting zygote. In humans, the ovum matures inside one of the ovary's follicles (hollow group of cells) and is released when the follicle ruptures (ovulation). The ovum passes into the fallopian tube and will degenerate if not fertilized within about 24 hours. In animals, the amount of nutritive material (yolk) deposited in an egg is dependent on the length of time before the developing animal can feed itself or, in the case of mammals, begins to receive nourishment from the maternal circulation. Most animal eggs are enclosed by one or more membranes. Insect eggs are covered by a thick, hard outer membrane, and amphibian eggs are surrounded by a jellylike layer. The term *egg* also refers to the content of the hard-shelled reproductive body produced by a bird or reptile.

ego (Latin: "I"), In psychoanalytic theory, the portion of the psyche experienced as the "self" or "I." It is the part that remembers, evaluates, plans, and in other ways is responsive to and acts in the surrounding physical and social world. According to Sigmund Freud, it coexists with the id (the unconscious, instinctual portion of the psyche) and the superego (the portion representing the conscience, or the internalization of societal norms). The ego is not coextensive with either the personality or the body; rather, it serves to integrate these and other aspects of the person, such as memory, imagination, and behaviour. It mediates between the id and the superego by building up various defense mechanisms.

egoism, In ethics, the principle that we should each act so as to promote our own interests. The great advantage of such a position is that it avoids any possible conflict between morality and self-interest; if it is rational for us to pursue our own interest, the rationality of morality is equally clear. The prescriptive thesis of ethical egoism can be distinguished from the descriptive thesis of psychological egoism. Psychological egoism is a generalization about human motivation, namely, that everyone always acts so as to promote his or her own interests.

egret, Any of several species (mainly in the genus *Egretta*) of wading birds in the same family (Ardeidae) as herons and bit-terns. Egrets live in marshes, lakes, humid forests, and other wetland environments world-wide. They catch and eat small fishes, amphibians, reptiles, mammals, and crustaceans. They nest in trees and bushes or on the ground. Most are white and develop long plumes for the breeding season. The value of plumes as ornamental objects once drove egrets to near-ex-tinction, but changes in fashion and strict conservation mea-sures have allowed their num-bers to increase. The great white egret is about 35 in. (90 cm) long; other common species av-erage 20–24 in. (50–60 cm) long.

Common egret (Egretta alba)
R.F. Head from The National Audubon
Society Collection/Photo Researchers

Egypt, officially ARAB REPUBLIC OF EGYPT,, formerly UNITED ARAB REPUBLIC, Country, Middle East, northeastern Africa. Area: 386,874 sq mi (1,002,000 sq km). Population: (2011 est.) 82,537,000. Capital: Cairo. The people are largely Egyptian Ar-abs. Language: Arabic (official). Religions: Islam (official; pre-dominantly Sunni); also Christianity. Currency: Egyptian pound. Egypt occupies a crossroads between Africa, Europe, and Asia. The majority of its land is in the arid western and eastern deserts, separated by the country's dominant feature, the Nile River. The Nile forms a flat-bottomed valley, generally 5–10 mi (8–16 km) wide, that fans out into the densely populated delta lowlands north of Cairo. The Nile valley (in Upper Egypt) and delta (Lower Egypt), along with scattered oases, support all of Egypt's agricul-ture and have virtually all of its population. Egypt has a develop-ing, mainly socialist, partly free-enterprise economy based prima-rily on industry, including petroleum production, and agriculture. Under the constitution Egypt is a republic with two legislative houses; its head of state is the president, and the head of govern-ment is the prime minister. As of February 2011, however, a mil-itary council assumed control of the country after the president stepped down. Egypt is one of the world's oldest continuous civ-ilizations. Upper and Lower Egypt were united *c.* 3000 BCE, begin-ning a period of cultural achievement and a line of native rulers that lasted nearly 3,000 years. Egypt's ancient history is divided into the Old, the Middle, and the New Kingdom, spanning 31 dy-nasties and lasting to 332 BCE. The pyramids date from the Old Kingdom, the cult of Osiris and the refinement of sculpture from the Middle Kingdom, and the era of empire and the Exodus of the Jews from the New Kingdom. An Assyrian invasion occurred in the 671 BCE, and the Persian Achaemenids established a dynasty in 525 BCE. The invasion by Alexander the Great in 332 BCE inau-gurated the Macedonian Ptolemaic period and the ascendancy of Alexandria as a centre of learning and Hellenistic culture. The Romans held Egypt from 30 BCE to 395 CE; later it was part of the Byzantine Empire. After the Roman emperor Constantine granted tolerance to the Christians in 313, a formal Egyptian (Coptic) church emerged. Egypt came under Arab control in 642 and ulti-mately was transformed into an Arabic-speaking state, with Islam as the dominant religion. Held by the Umayyad and ʿAbbāsid dy-nasties, in 969 it became the centre of the Fāṭimid dynasty. In 1250 the Mamlūk dynasty established a state that lasted until 1517, when Egypt fell to the Ottoman Empire. An economic and cultural

decline ensued. Egypt became a British protectorate in 1914 and received nominal independence in 1922, when a constitutional monarchy was established. A group of army officers led by Gamal Abdel Nasser overthrew the monarchy in 1952. A union with Syria to form the United Arab Republic (1958–61) failed. Following three wars with Israel, Egypt, under Nasser's successor, Anwar el-Sādāt, made peace with the Jewish state, thus alienating many fel-low Arab countries. Sādāt was assassinated by Islamic extremists in 1981 and was succeeded by Ḥosnī Mubārak. Although Egypt took part in the coalition against Iraq during the Persian Gulf War (1990–91), it later began peace overtures with countries in the region. Desire for political, economic, and social reform led to a popular uprising of unprecedented proportions in 2011, which forced Mubārak to step down as president and left Egypt's mili-tary in control of the country.

Egyptian architecture, Houses, palaces, temples, tombs, and other buildings of ancient Egypt. Most Egyptian towns were sit-uated on the floodplain of the Nile and have been lost, but reli-gious structures built on higher ground have survived in many forms. Tomb architecture was often grandiose. The tomb was not simply a place to lay a corpse, but the home of the deceased, pro-vided with goods to ensure continued existence after death. Wood and bricks made of mud were the standard domestic building ma-terials, but, from the Old Kingdom (*c.* 2575–*c.* 2130 BC) on, stone was used for tombs and temples. Egyptian masons used stone to reproduce the forms of wood and brick buildings. Mastabas and step pyramids were used for tomb superstructures, but the most characteristic form of the Old Kingdom was the true pyramid. The finest example is the monumental Great Pyramid of Khufu (Cheops) at Giza. Simple chapel rooms with stelae for burying commoners were located some distance from the royal burial com-pounds. In the New Kingdom (1539–1075 BC), royal tombs were cut into the face of cliffs to discourage looting; elaborate com-plexes of tombs and mortuary temples were built in the Valley of the Kings at Thebes. Two principal types of temple can be distin-guished: cult temples for worship of the gods and funerary, or mor-tuary, temples. Most notable were the great stone cult temples; imposing remains can be seen at Luxor, Karnak, Abydos, and Abu Simbel.

Egyptian art, Ancient sculptures, paintings, and decorative crafts produced in the dynastic periods of the 3rd–1st millennia BCE in the Nile valley of Egypt and Nubia. Egyptian art served those in power as a forceful propaganda instrument that perpetuated the existing framework of society. Much of what has survived is asso-ciated with ancient tombs. The course of art in Egypt paralleled the country's political history and is divided into three periods: Old Kingdom (*c.* 2700–*c.* 2150 BCE), Middle Kingdom (*c.* 2000–*c.* 1670 BCE), and New Kingdom (*c.* 1550–*c.* 1070 BCE). The Old Kingdom's stone tombs and temples were decorated with vigor-ous and brightly painted reliefs illustrating the daily life of the peo-ple. Rules for portraying the human figure were established, spec-ifying proportions, postures, and placement of details, often linked to the subjects' social standing. An artistic decline at the end of the Old Kingdom led to a revival in the more stable political cli-mate of the Middle Kingdom, notable for its expressive portrait sculptures of kings and its excellent relief sculptures and painting. The New Kingdom brought a magnificent flowering of the arts: great granite statues and wall reliefs glorified rulers and gods, painting became an independent art, and the decorative crafts reached new peaks, the treasure of Tutankhamen's tomb typifying the variety of luxury items created.

Egyptian religion, Polytheistic belief system of ancient Egypt from the 4th millennium BCE to the first centuries CE, including both folk traditions and the court religion. Local deities that sprang up along the Nile Valley had both human and animal form and were synthesized into national deities and cults after political unifica-tion *c.* 2925 BCE. The gods were not all-powerful or all-knowing, but were immeasurably greater than humans. Their characters were not neatly defined, and there was much overlap, especially among the leading deities. One important deity was Horus, the god-king who ruled the universe, who represented the earthly Egyptian king. Other major divinities included Re, the sun god; Ptah and Aton, creator gods; and Isis and Osiris. The concept of *maat* ("order") was fundamental: the king maintained *maat* both on a societal and cosmic level. Belief in and preoccupation with the afterlife permeated Egyptian religion, as the surviving tombs and pyramids attest. Burial near the king helped others gain passage to the netherworld, as did spells and passwords from the Book of the Dead.

Ehrlich, Paul (b. March 14, 1854, Strehlen, Silesia, Prussia—d. Aug. 20, 1915, Bad Homburg vor der Höhe, Ger.), German medical scientist. After early work on distribution of foreign substances in the body and on cell nutrition, he found uses for staining agents in diagnosis (including that of tuberculosis) and treatment. He also researched typhoid, fever medications, and eye diseases. In one paper, he showed that different tissues' oxygen consumption reflected the intensity of their cell processes. Ehrlich developed a method of stimulating production of antitoxins by injecting increasing amounts of toxin into animals; his work was crucial to the creation of a diphtheria antitoxin. He and Élie Metchnikoff received the 1908 Nobel Prize for Physiology or Medicine. With Sahachiro Hata, he developed Salvarsan, the first effective syphilis treatment, in 1910.

Eiffel Tower, Parisian landmark built for the Centennial Exposition of 1889. Conceived by the bridge engineer Gustave Eiffel (1832–1923), the 984-ft (300-m) tower of open-lattice wrought iron was a technological masterpiece. Making use of advanced knowledge of the behaviour of metal arch and truss forms under loading, the structure presaged a revolution in civil engineering and architectural design. The tower was the world's tallest building until the Chrysler Building in New York City was topped off in 1929.

Eiffel Tower, Paris.
© Corbis

Eightfold Path, Buddhist doctrine, stated by the Buddha in his first sermon near Benares, India. The path is regarded as the way for individuals to deal with the problems named in the Four Noble Truths. The path consists of right understanding (faith in the Buddhist view of existence), right thought (the resolve to practice the faith), right speech (avoidance of falsehoods, slander, and abuse), right action (abstention from taking life, stealing, and improper sexual behavior), right livelihood (rejection of occupations not in keeping with Buddhist principles), right effort (development of good mental states), right mindfulness (awareness of body, feelings, and thought), and right concentration (meditation). It is also called the Middle Path, because it steers a course between sensuality and asceticism. Following the Path leads to escape from suffering and attainment of nirvana.

Einstein, Albert (b. March 14, 1879, Ulm, Württemberg, Ger.—d. April 18, 1955, Princeton, N.J., U.S.), German-born Swiss-U.S. scientist. Born to a Jewish family in Germany, he grew up in Munich, and in 1894 he moved to Aarau, Switz. He attended a technical school in Zürich (graduating in 1900) and during this period renounced his German citizenship; stateless for some years, he became a Swiss citizen in 1901. Einstein became a junior examiner (or clerk) at the Swiss patent office in 1902 and began producing original theoretical work that laid many of the founda-

tions for 20th-century physics. He received his doctorate from the University of Zürich in 1905, the same year he won international fame with the publication of four articles: one on Brownian motion, which he explained in terms of molecular kinetic energy; one on the photoelectric effect, in which he demonstrated the particle nature of light; and two on his special theory of relativity, the second of which included his formulation of the equivalence of mass and energy ($E = mc^2$). Einstein held several professorships before becoming director of Berlin's Kaiser Wilhelm Institute for Physics in 1913. In 1915 he published his general theory of relativity, which was confirmed experimentally during a solar eclipse in 1919 with observations of the deflection of light passing near the Sun. He received a Nobel Prize in 1921 for his work on the photoelectric effect, his work on relativity still being controversial. For decades he sought to discover the mathematical relationship between electromagnetism and gravitation, which he believed would be a first step toward discovering the common laws governing the behaviour of everything in the universe, but such a unified field theory eluded him. His theories of relativity and gravitation represented a profound advance over Newtonian physics and revolutionized scientific and philosophical inquiry. He resigned his position at the Prussian Academy when Adolf Hitler came to power and moved to Princeton, N.J., where he joined the Institute for Advanced Study. Though a longtime pacifist, he was instrumental in persuading Pres. Franklin Roosevelt in 1939 to initiate the Manhattan Project for the production of an atomic bomb, a technology his own theories greatly furthered, though he did not work on the project himself. Einstein became a U.S. citizen in 1940 but retained his Swiss citizenship. The most eminent scientist in the world in the postwar years, he declined an offer to become the first prime minister of Israel and became a strong advocate for nuclear disarmament.

Einstein's mass-energy relation, Relationship between mass (m) and energy (E) in Albert Einstein's special theory of relativity, expressed $E = mc^2$, where c equals 186,000 mi/second (300,000 km/second), the speed of light. Whereas mass and energy were viewed as distinct in earlier physical theories, in special relativity a body's mass can be converted into energy in accordance with Einstein's formula. Such a release of energy decreases the body's mass.

Eisenhower, Dwight D(avid) (b. Oct. 14, 1890, Denison, Texas, U.S.—d. March 28, 1969, Washington, D.C.), 34th president of the U.S. (1953–61). He graduated from West Point (1915), then served in the Panama Canal Zone (1922–24) and in the Philippines under Douglas MacArthur (1935–39). In World War II Gen. George Marshall appointed him to the army's war-plans division (1941), then chose him to command U.S. forces in Europe (1942). After planning the invasions of North Africa, Sicily, and Italy, he was appointed supreme commander of Allied forces (1943). He planned the Normandy Campaign (1944) and the conduct of the war in Europe until

Dwight D. Eisenhower, 1952.
Fabian Bachrach

the German surrender (1945). He was promoted to five-star general (1944) and was named army chief of staff in 1945. He served as president of Columbia University from 1948 until being appointed supreme commander of NATO in 1951. Both Democrats and Republicans courted Eisenhower as a presidential candidate; in 1952, as the Republican candidate, he defeated Adlai Stevenson with the largest popular vote to that time. He defeated Stevenson again in 1956 in an even larger landslide. His policy of support for Middle Eastern countries facing communist aggression, enunciated in the Eisenhower Doctrine, was a continuation of the containment policy adopted by the Harry Truman administration. He sent federal troops to Little Rock, Ark., to enforce integration of a city high school (1957). When the Soviet Union launched Sputnik I (1957), he was criticized for failing to develop the U.S. space program; he responded by creating NASA (1958). In his last weeks in office the U.S. broke diplomatic relations with Cuba.

Ekron, Canaanite and Philistine city in ancient Palestine. It was one of the five cities of the Philistine Pentapolis and was located in what is now central Israel. Though allocated to Judah after the Israelite conquest, it was a Philistine stronghold in the time of King David; it was later associated with the worship of the deity Baalzebub. Taken by Egypt (*c.* 918 BC), it paid tribute to Assyria in the 7th century BC. The city was known as Akkaron from Hellenistic times.

El Alamein, Battles of (June–July 1942; October 23–November 6, 1942) Two battles between British and Axis forces in Egypt in World War II. Axis forces under Erwin Rommel began a drive eastward along the North African coast in early 1942. Though initially checked by the British, they managed to reach El Alamein on June 30. The first engagement ended in mid-July with Rommel still there, blocked and on the defensive. In October British forces under Bernard Law Montgomery began a devastating attack from El Alamein, routing Rommel's vastly outnumbered forces. By November 6 the British had driven the Germans back into Libya.

El Escorial, Palace-monastery northwest of Madrid, built in 1563–67 for Philip II. It is the burial place of Spanish sovereigns and one of the largest religious establishments in the world. It was conceived by Juan Bautista de Toledo (1530–1597) and completed by Juan de Herrera (*c.* 1530–1597), who is considered responsible for its architectural style. Its plan is a giant rectangle, with a domed church at the center flanked by the palace, monastery, college, library, cloisters, and courts. The massive granite walls, relieved only by a series of unadorned windows and Doric pilasters, with no concession to decorative richness, produced an austerity beyond anything the Italian Renaissance ever envisaged.

El Niño, In oceanography and climatology, the appearance, every few years, of unusually warm surface waters of the Pacific Ocean along the tropical western coast of South America. It affects fishing, agriculture, and local weather from Ecuador to Chile and can cause global climatic anomalies in the equatorial Pacific, Asia, and North America. The name (Spanish for "the Christ Child") was originally used by 19th-century Peruvian fishermen to describe the annual flow of warm equatorial waters southward around Christmastime. The term is now used for an intense ocean warming that stretches from the western Pacific to South America. This "anomalous occurrence" is caused by an unusual weakening of the normally westward-blowing trade winds, which in turn allows warm surface waters to spread eastward.

El Salvador, officially REPUBLIC OF EL SALVADOR, Country, Central America. Area: 8,124 sq mi (21,040 sq km). Population: (2011 est.) 6,072,000. Capital: San Salvador. The majority of the people are mestizos; most of the rest are Indians. Language: Spanish (official). Religion: Christianity (predominantly Roman Catholic; also Protestant, other Christians). Currency: U.S. dollar. The smallest and most densely populated Central American country, it is crossed by two volcanic mountain ranges and has a narrow coastal region and a high central plain in the south. The climate ranges from hot and wet in the lowlands to cooler and wetter in the highlands. Cloud forests predominate at the highest elevations. El Salvador has a developing economy based on services, trade, manufacturing, and agriculture, with coffee, sugarcane, and cotton as the major export crops. Remittances from Salvadorans living in the U.S. are, collectively, among the country's largest sources of income. El Salvador is a republic with one legislative house; its head of state and government is the president. The Spanish arrived in the area in 1524 and subjugated the Pipil Indian kingdom of Cuzcatlán by 1539. The country was divided into two districts, San Salvador and Sonsonate, both attached to Guatemala. When Spanish rule ended in 1821, the Salvadorans opposed incorporation into the Mexican Empire (confronting both Guatemalan and Mexican armies), and, upon its collapse in 1823, Sonsonate and San Salvador combined to form the new state of El Salvador within the United Provinces of Central America. The country attained independence in 1841. From its founding, it experienced a high degree of political turmoil; powerful economic interests controlled the country through most of the 19th and early 20th centuries but were replaced by a military dictatorship that lasted from 1931 to 1979. Elections held in 1982 set up a new government, and, though a new constitution was adopted in 1983, civil war continued throughout the 1980s. Peace accords in 1992 ended the war, but violent crime became a major problem. Despite attempts at economic reform, the country was plagued by inflation and unemployment into the 21st century. In 2006 El Salvador officially entered into the Central American Free Trade Agreement (CAFTA) with the United States.

elasticity, Ability of a deformed material body to return to its original shape and size when the forces causing deformation are removed. Most solids show some elastic behaviour, but there is usually a limit—the material's "elastic limit"—to the force from which recovery is possible. Stresses beyond its elastic limit cause the material to yield, or flow, and the result is permanent deformation or breakage. The limit depends on the material's internal structure; for example, steel, though strong, has a low elastic limit and can be extended only about 1% of its length, whereas rubber can be elastically extended up to about 1,000%. Robert Hooke, one of the first to study elasticity, developed a mathematical relation between tension and extension.

Elba, Island off the western coast of Italy, in the Tyrrhenian Sea. Occupying an area of 86 sq mi (223 sq km), it is the largest island of the Tuscan Archipelago. France obtained Elba from Rome in 1802. When Napoleon abdicated in May 1814, he was exiled to Elba. The island was recognized as an independent principality with Napoleon as its ruler until February 1815, when he returned to France to begin the Hundred Days. Thereafter Elba was restored to Tuscany.

Elbe River, Czech LABE, ancient ALBIS, River, central Europe. One of the continent's major waterways, it rises in the Krkonoše (Giant) Mountains on the border of the Czech Republic and Poland and flows southwest across Bohemia. It then flows northwest across Germany and empties into the North Sea near Cuxhaven. From 1945 to 1990 it formed part of the boundary between East and West Germany. It is 724 mi (1,165 km) long and connected by canals with the Baltic Sea, the Havel River and Berlin, the Ruhr industrial region, and the Rhine River. It is navigable for 1,000-ton barges as far upstream as Prague through the Vltava River. Hamburg, Ger., is 55 mi (88 km) upstream from its mouth.

Elbrus, Mount, Peak, Caucasus Mountains, southwestern Russia. The highest peak in the Caucasus, it is an extinct volcano with twin cones reaching elevations of 18,510 ft (5,642 m) and 18,356 ft (5,595 m). There are many mineral springs along its descending streams, while 53 sq mi (138 sq km) of Elbrus is covered by 22 glaciers. It is a major centre for mountaineering and tourism.

Elburz Mountains, Mountain range, northern Iran. It is 560 mi (900 km) long and extends along the southern shore of the Caspian Sea, from which it is separated by a narrow coastal lowland. It includes Iran's highest peak, Mount Damāvand (Demavend), at 18,605 ft (5,671 m). The forests of the Elburz cover some 12,500 sq mi (32,400 sq km). The Hyrcanian tigers for which they were famous are now rare, but other wild cats, including the leopard and the lynx, are still numerous.

Eleanor of Aquitaine (b. *c.* 1122—d. April 1, 1204, Fontevrault, Anjou, Fr.), Queen consort of Louis VII of France (1137–80) and Henry II of England (1152–89), the most powerful woman of 12th-century Europe. She inherited the duchy of Aquitaine and married the heir to the French throne. Beautiful, capricious, and strong-willed, she accompanied Louis on the Second Crusade (1147–49), and her conduct aroused his jealousy. The marriage was annulled (1152), and she married Henry Plantagenet, soon to be Henry II; the marriage united England, Normandy, and western France under his rule. She bore Henry five sons, including the future kings Richard I the Lionheart and John Lackland, and three daughters who married into other royal houses. Her court at Poitiers became a centre of culture, fostering the poetry of the troubadours. She may have spurred her sons to revolt against Henry (1173); when the rebellion failed she was captured and confined until his death (1189). She was active in government during the reign of Richard I, ruling during his crusade to the Holy Land and ransoming him from Austria. After Richard died (1199) and John became king, she saved Anjou and Aquitaine for John against French threats, then retired to the monastery at Fontevrault.

election, Formal process by which voters make their political choices on public issues or candidates for public office. The use of elections in the modern era dates to the emergence of representative government in Europe and North America since the 17th century. Regular elections serve to hold leaders accountable for their performance and permit an exchange of influence between the governors and the governed. The availability of alternatives is a necessary condition. Votes may be secret or public.

Electra, In Greek legend, the daughter of Agamemnon and Clytemnestra. When Agamemnon was murdered by Clytemnestra and her lover Aegisthus, Electra saved her young brother Orestes from the same fate by sending him away. Orestes later returned, and Electra helped him kill their mother and Aegisthus. She then married her brother's friend Pylades. The story is treated in plays by Aeschylus, Sophocles, and Euripides.

electric automobile, Battery-powered motor vehicle. Originating in the 1880s, electric cars were used for private passenger, truck, and bus transportation in cities, where their low speeds and limited battery range were not drawbacks, and the cars became popular for their quietness and low maintenance costs. Until 1920 they were competitive with gasoline-fueled cars; they became less so after the electric self-starter made gasoline-powered cars more attractive and mass production made them cheaper to produce. In Europe electric vehicles have been used as short-range delivery vans. Renewed interest in electric cars beginning in the 1970s, spurred especially by new consciousness of foreign oil dependency and environmental concern, led to improvements in speed and range. Recent laws, particularly in California, have mandated commercial production. "Hybrid" cars employing both electric and internal combustion engines and providing the best features of both technologies, have recently become commercially available. Experimental vehicles have used solar fuel cells.

electric charge, Quantity of electricity that flows in electric currents or that accumulates on the surfaces of dissimilar nonmetallic substances that are rubbed together briskly. It occurs in discrete natural units, equal to the charge of an electron or proton. It cannot be created or destroyed. Charge can be positive or negative; one positive charge can combine with one negative charge, and the result is a net charge of zero. Two objects that have an excess of the same type of charge repel each other, while two objects with an excess of opposite charge attract each other. The unit of charge is the coulomb, which consists of 6.24×10^{18} natural units of electric charge.

electric current, Movement of electric charge carriers. In a wire, electric current is a flow of electrons that have been dislodged from atoms and is a measure of the quantity of electrical charge passing any point of the wire per unit time. Current in gases and liquids generally consists of a flow of positive ions in one direction together with a flow of negative ions in the opposite direction. Conventionally, the direction of electric current is that of the flow of the positive ions. In alternating current (AC) the motion of the charges is periodically reversed; in direct current (DC) it is not. A common unit of current is the ampere, a flow of one coulomb of charge per second, or 6.24×10^{18} electrons per second.

electric eel, Eel-shaped South American fish (*Electrophorus electricus*) capable of producing an electric shock strong enough to stun a human. The electric eel (not a true eel) is a sluggish inhabitant of slow freshwater, surfacing periodically to gulp air. Long, cylindrical, scaleless, and gray-brown, it sometimes reaches a length of 9 ft (2.75 m) and a weight of 49 lbs (22 kg). The tail region, bordered below by a long anal fin that the fish undulates to move about, contains the electric organs. The shock (up to 650 volts discharged at will) is used mainly to immobilize fish and other prey.

electric field, Region around an electric charge in which an electric force is exerted on another charge. The strength of an electric field E at any point is defined as the electric force F exerted per unit positive electric charge q at that point, or $E = F/q$. An electric field has both magnitude and direction and can be represented by lines of force, or field lines, that start on positive charges and terminate on negative charges. The electric field is stronger where the field lines are close together than where they are farther apart. The value of the electric field has dimensions of force per unit charge and is measured in units of newtons per coulomb.

electric ray, Any of the aquatic rays (families Torpedinidae, Narkidae, and Temeridae) that produce an electrical shock. They are found worldwide in warm and temperate seas, mostly in shallow water but some (genus *Benthobatis*) at depths greater than 3,000 ft (900 m). Slow-moving bottom-dwellers, they feed on fishes and invertebrates. They range in length from less than 1 ft (30 cm) to about 6 ft (1.8 m) and have a short, stout tail. They are soft and smooth-skinned, with a circular or nearly circular body disk formed by the head and pectoral fins. They are harmless unless touched or stepped on. The electric organs, composed of modified muscle tissue, are in the disk near the head. The shock from these organs, which may reach 220 volts and is strong enough to fell a human adult, is used for defense, sensory location, and capturing prey.

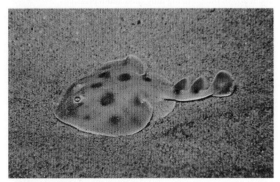

*Electric ray (*Narcine brasiliensis*)*
Douglas Faulkner

electrical engineering, Branch of engineering concerned with the practical applications of electricity in all its forms, including those of electronics. Electrical engineering deals with electric light and power systems and apparatuses; electronics engineering deals with wire and radio communication, the stored-program electronic computer, radar, and automatic control systems. The first practical application of electricity was the telegraph, in 1837. Electrical engineering emerged as a discipline in 1864 when James Clerk Maxwell summarized the basic laws of electricity in mathematical form and predicted that radiation of electromagnetic energy would occur in a form that later became known as radio waves. The need for electrical engineers was not felt until the invention of the telephone (1876) and the incandescent lamp (1878).

electricity, Phenomenon associated with stationary or moving electric charges. The word comes from the Greek *elektron* ("amber"); the Greeks discovered that amber rubbed with fur attracted light objects such as feathers. Such effects due to stationary charges, or static electricity, were the first electrical phenomena to be studied. Not until the early 19th century were static electricity and electric current shown to be aspects of the same phenomenon. The discovery of the electron, which carries a charge designated as negative, showed that the various manifestations of electricity are the result of the accumulation or motion of numbers of electrons. The invention of the incandescent lightbulb (1879) and the construction of the first central power station (1881) by Thomas Alva Edison led to the rapid introduction of electric power into factories and homes.

electrocardiography, Method of tracing the electric current of a heartbeat to provide information on the heart. Electrocardiograms (ECGs) are made by applying electrodes, usually to the arms, legs, and chest wall, attached to an electrocardiograph, which records the tiny heart current. Upward and downward movements on the tracing reflect contractions of the atria and ventricles. Deviations from a standard point to a possible heart disorder and its site, as well as to possible high blood pressure and other diseases.

electroconvulsive therapy, formerly SHOCK THERAPY, Method of treating psychiatric disorders by inducing shock through electric current. Electroconvulsive, or electroshock, therapy involves passing an electric current through the patient's head between two electrodes placed over the temples and thus causing a convulsive seizure; it was used to treat bipolar disorder and other types of depression. Shock was previously induced by administering increasingly large doses of insulin until the patient was thrown into a brief coma; the so-called insulin-shock therapy was used for the treatment of schizophrenia. Both forms of shock therapy were developed in the 1930s. Their use declined after the introduction of tranquilizing drugs and antidepressants.

electrocution, Method of execution in which the condemned person is subjected to a heavy charge of electric current. The prisoner is shackled into a wired chair, and electrodes are fastened to the head and one leg so that the current will flow through the body. One electrical shock may not be enough to kill the person; if a doctor does not confirm the death, several shocks may be applied. The electric chair was first used in 1890. Electrocution also refers to death by other causes of electrical shock (e.g., accidental contact with high-voltage wiring).

electroencephalography, Technique for recording electrical activity in the brain, whose cells emit distinct patterns of rhythmic electrical impulses. Pairs of electrodes on the scalp transmit signals to an electroencephalograph, which records them as peaks and troughs on a tracing called an electroencephalogram (EEG). Different wave patterns on the EEG are associated with normal and abnormal waking and sleeping states. They help diagnose conditions such as tumours, infections, and epilepsy. The electroencephalograph was invented in the 1920s by Hans Berger (1873–1941).

electrolysis, Process in which electric current passed through a substance causes a chemical change, usually the gaining or losing of electrons. It is carried out in an electrolytic cell consisting of separated positive and negative electrodes (anode and cathode, respectively) immersed in an electrolyte solution containing ions or in a molten ionic compound. Reduction occurs at the cathode, where electrons are added that combine with positively charged cations in the solution. Oxidation occurs at the anode, where negatively charged anions give up electrons. Both thus become neutral molecules. For historical reasons, electric current is defined to flow in the opposite direction to the flow of electrons. Thus, current is said to flow from the cathode to the anode, even though electrons flow in the opposite direction. Electrolysis is used extensively in metallurgy to extract or purify metals from ores or compounds and to deposit them from solution (electroplating). Electrolysis of molten sodium chloride yields metallic sodium and chlorine gas; that of a strong solution of sodium chloride in water (brine) yields hydrogen gas, chlorine gas, and sodium hydroxide (in solution); and that of water (with a low concentration of dissolved sodium chloride or other electrolyte) yields hydrogen and oxygen.

electromagnet, Device consisting of a core of magnetic material such as iron, surrounded by a coil through which an electric current is passed to magnetize the core. When the current is stopped, the core is no longer magnetized. Electromagnets are particularly useful wherever controllable magnets are required, as in devices in which the magnetic field is to be varied, reversed, or switched on and off. Suitably designed magnets can lift many times their own weight and are used in steelworks and scrap yards to lift loads of metal. Other devices that utilize electromagnets include particle accelerators, telephone receivers, loudspeakers, and televisions.

electromagnetic field, Property of space caused by the motion of an electric charge. A stationary charge produces an electric field in the surrounding space. If the charge is moving, a magnetic field is also produced. A changing magnetic field also produces an electric field. The interaction of electric and magnetic fields produces an electromagnetic field, which has its own existence in space apart from the charges involved. An electromagnetic field can sometimes be described as a wave that transports electromagnetic radiation.

electromagnetic radiation, Energy propagated through free space or through a material medium in the form of electromagnetic waves. Examples include radio waves, infrared radiation, visible light, ultraviolet radiation, X rays, and gamma rays. Electromagnetic radiation exhibits wavelike properties such as reflection, refraction, diffraction, and interference, but also exhibits particlelike properties in that its energy occurs in discrete packets, or quanta. Though all types of electromagnetic radiation travel at the same speed, they vary in frequency and wavelength, and interact with matter differently. A vacuum is the only perfectly transparent medium; all others absorb some frequencies of electromagnetic radiation.

electromagnetic spectrum, Total range of frequencies or wavelengths of electromagnetic radiation. The spectrum ranges from waves of long wavelength (low frequency) to those of short wavelength (high frequency); it comprises, in order of increasing frequency (or decreasing wavelength): very-low-frequency to ultrahigh-frequency radio waves, microwaves, infrared radiation, visible light, ultraviolet radiation, X-rays, and gamma rays. In a vacuum, all waves of the electromagnetic spectrum travel at the same speed: 299,792,458 m/sec (186,282 mi/sec).

electromyography, Process of graphically recording the electrical activity of muscle, which normally generates an electric current only when contracting or when its nerve is stimulated. Electrical impulses are shown as wavelike tracings on a cathode-ray oscilloscope and recorded as an electromyogram (EMG), usually along with audible signals. The EMG can show whether muscle weakness or wasting is due to nerve impairment (as in amyotrophic lateral sclerosis and poliomyelitis) or muscle impairment or disease (myopathy).

electron, Lightest electrically charged subatomic particle known. It carries a negative charge, the basic charge of electricity. An electron has a small mass, less than 0.1% the mass of an atom. Under normal circumstances, electrons move about the nucleus of an atom in orbitals that form an electron cloud bound in varying strengths to the positively charged nucleus. Electrons closer to the nucleus are held more tightly. The first subatomic particle discovered, the electron was identified in 1897 by J. J. Thomson.

electron microscopy, Technique that allows examination of samples too small to be seen with a light microscope. Electron beams have much smaller wavelengths than visible light and hence higher resolving power. To make them more observable, samples may be coated with metal atoms. Because electrons cannot travel very far in air, the electron beam and the sample must be kept in a vacuum. Two different instruments are used. In the scanning electron microscope, a moving beam of electrons is scanned across a sample; electrons scattered by the object are focused by magnetic "lenses" to produce an image of the object's surface similar to an image on a television screen. The images appear three-dimensional; they may be of small organisms or their parts, of molecules such as DNA, or even of large individual atoms (e.g., uranium, thorium). In the transmission electron microscope, the electron beam passes through a very thin, carefully prepared sample and is focused onto a screen or photographic plate to visualize the interior structure of such specimens as cells and tissues.

electronic music, Any music involving electronic processing (e.g., recording and editing on tape) and whose reproduction involves the use of loudspeakers. In the late 1940s, magnetic tape began to be used, especially in France, to modify natural sounds (playing them backward, at different speeds, etc.), creating the genre known as *musique concrète*. By the early 1950s, composers in Germany and the U.S. were employing assembled conglomerations of oscillators, filters, and other equipment to produce entirely new sounds. The development of voltage-controlled oscillators and filters led, in the 1950s, to the first synthesizers, which effectively standardized the assemblages and made them more flexible. No longer relying on tape editing, electronic music could now be created in real time. Since their advent in the late 1970s, personal computers have been used to control the synthesizers. Digital sampling—composing with music and sounds electronically extracted from other recordings—has largely replaced the use of oscillators as a sound source.

electronics, Branch of physics that deals with the emission, behaviour, and effects of electrons and with electronic devices. The beginnings of electronics can be traced to experiments with electricity. In the 1880s Thomas Alva Edison and others observed the flow of current between elements in an evacuated glass tube. A two-electrode vacuum tube constructed by John A. Fleming (1849–1945) produced a useful output current. The Audion, invented by Lee De Forest (1907), was followed by further improvements. The invention of the transistor at Bell Labs (1947) initiated a progressive miniaturization of electronic components that by the mid-1980s had resulted in high-density microprocessors, which in turn led to tremendous advances in computer technology and computer-based automated systems.

electroplating, Process of coating with metal by means of an electric current. Plating metal may be transferred to conductive surfaces (e.g., metals) or to nonconductive surfaces (e.g., plastics, wood, leather) if a conductive coating has been applied. Usually the current deposits a given amount of metal on the cathode (workpiece) and the anode (source of metal) dissolves to the same ex-

tent, maintaining a fairly uniform solution. Silver plating is used on tableware, electrical contacts, and engine bearings. The most extensive use of gold plating is on jewelry and watch cases. Zinc coatings prevent the corrosion of steel articles, and nickel and chromium plate are used on automobiles and household appliances.

elegy, Meditative lyric poem. The classical elegy was any poem written in elegiac metre (alternating lines of dactylic hexameter and pentameter). Today the term may refer to this metre rather than to content, but in English literature since the 16th century it has meant a lament in any metre. A distinct variety with a formal pattern is the pastoral elegy, such as John Milton's "Lycidas" (1638). Poets of the 18th-century Graveyard School reflected on death and immortality in elegies, most famously Thomas Gray's "An Elegy Written in a Country Church Yard" (1751).

element, chemical, One of the 118 presently known kinds of substances that constitute all matter at and above the level of atoms (the smallest units of any element). All atoms of an element are identical in nuclear charge (number of protons) and number of electrons, but their mass (atomic weight) may differ if they have different numbers of neutrons. Each permanently named element has a one- or two-letter chemical symbol. Elements combine to form a wide variety of compounds. All elements with atomic numbers greater than 83 (bismuth), and some isotopes of lighter elements, are unstable and radioactive. The transuranium elements, with atomic numbers greater than 92, artificially created by bombardment of other elements with neutrons or other particles, were discovered beginning in 1940. The most common elements (by weight) in Earth's crust are oxygen, 46.6%; silicon, 27.7%; aluminum, 8.13%; and iron, 5%. Of the known elements, 11 (hydrogen, nitrogen, oxygen, fluorine, chlorine, and the six noble gases) are gases under ordinary conditions, two (bromine and mercury) are liquids (two more, cesium and gallium, melt at about or just above room temperature), and the rest are solids.

elephant, Any of three ungulate species in the order Proboscidea  (family Elephantidae), characterized by their large size, long trunk, tusks, massive legs, large ears, and huge head. All species are grayish to brown, with sparse, coarse body hair. The trunk is used for breathing, drinking, and reaching for food. Elephants eat grasses, leaves, and fruit. The African savanna, or bush elephant (*Loxodonta africana*), of sub-Saharan Africa, is the largest living land animal, weighing up to 16,500 lbs (7,500 kg) and standing 10–13 ft (3–4 m) tall at the shoulder. The African forest elephant (*L. cyclotis*) is smaller. The Indian elephant (*Elephas maximus*), of South and Southeast Asia, weighs about 12,000 lbs (5,500 kg) and stands about 10 ft (3 m) tall. Elephants live in habitats ranging from thick jungle to savanna, in small family groups led by old cows. Most bulls live in bachelor herds. Elephants migrate seasonally. They may eat more than 500 lbs (225 kg) of vegetation daily. All species are considered endangered by the International Union for Conservation of Nature and Natural Resources (IUCN).

*Asian elephant (*Elephas maximus*).*
E.S. Ross

elephant seal, Either of the two largest pinniped species: the northern elephant seal (*Mirounga angustirostris*), of coastal islands off California and Baja California, or the southern elephant seal (*M. leonina*), of sub-Antarctic regions. Both are gregarious earless seals. The male has an inflatable, trunklike snout. The northern species is yellowish or gray-brown, the southern species blue-gray. Males of both species reach a length of about 21 ft (6.5 m) and a weight of about 7,780 lbs (3,530 kg) and are much larger

*Elephant seal bull (*Mirounga*)*
Anthony Mercieca/Root Resources

than the females. Elephant seals feed on fish and squid or other cephalopods. During the breeding season, bulls fight to establish territories along beaches and to acquire harems of up to 40 cows.

Eleusinian Mysteries, Most famous mystery religion of ancient Greece. It was based on the story of Demeter, whose daughter Persephone was kidnapped by Hades. While searching for her daughter, Demeter stopped at Eleusis, revealed her identity to the royal family, and taught the natives her rites. The Greater Mysteries were celebrated in autumn, beginning with a procession from Athens to the temple at Eleusis. This was followed by a ritual bath in the sea, three days of fasting, and completion of secret rites. Initiates were promised personal salvation and benefits in the afterlife.

Eleusis, Greek ELEVSÍS, Town, with ruins of an ancient city, eastern Greece. Famous as the site of the Eleusinian Mysteries, it is about 14 mi (23 km) west of Athens. It was independent until the 7th century BC, when Athens annexed the city and made the Eleusinian Mysteries a major Athenian religious festival. The Gothic leader Alaric destroyed Eleusis in AD 395. Deserted until the 18th century, it was revived as the modern town of Eleusis (Greek Lepsina), now a suburb of Athens. Some of the ruins have been excavated, including the Hall of Initiation, which dates back some 3,000 years to late Mycenaean times.

elevator, Car that moves in a vertical shaft to carry passengers or freight between the levels of a multistory building. The use of mechanical lifting platforms dates to Roman times. Steam and hydraulic elevators came into use in the 19th century; electric elevators had been introduced by the end of the century. Most modern elevators are electrically propelled through a system of cables and pulleys with the aid of a counterweight, though hydraulic elevators are still used in low buildings. The introduction of an automatic safety device by Elisha Otis (1811–1861) in 1853 made the passenger elevator possible. By opening the way to higher buildings, the elevator played a decisive role in creating the characteristic urban geography of modern cities.

Elgin Marbles, Collection of ancient Greek marble sculptures and architectural fragments in the British Museum. They were removed from the Parthenon in Athens and other buildings by Thomas Bruce, Lord Elgin (1766–1841), ambassador to the Ottoman Empire, and shipped to England between 1802 and 1811. Elgin claimed he was saving the works from destruction by the Turks, who then controlled Greece. He secured permission from the Turks to remove "any pieces of stone" bearing figures or inscriptions. They remained in his private possession, amid mounting criticism, until 1816, when the crown bought them. The controversy over their ownership continued into the 21st century. In

Lapith fighting a Centaur; detail of a metope from the Parthenon at Athens; one of the Elgin Marbles in the British Museum
Hirmer Fotoarchiv, Munich

2008 the New Acropolis Museum in Athens was built in large part to house these fragments of the Parthenon in the hope that they will be returned to Greece.

Eliot, George, orig. MARY ANN EVANS, later MARIAN EVANS (b. Nov. 22, 1819, Chilvers Coton, Warwickshire, Eng.—d. Dec. 22, 1880, London), British novelist. Eliot was raised with a strong evangelical piety but broke with religious orthodoxy in her 20s. She worked as a translator, a critic, and a subeditor of the *Westminster Review* (1851–54). Later she turned to fiction. Adopting a masculine pseudonym to evade prejudice against women novelists, she first brought out *Scenes of Clerical Life* (1858). This was followed by such classic works as *Adam Bede* (1859), *The Mill on the Floss* (1860), *Silas Marner* (1861), *Romola* (1862–63), *Felix Holt, the Radical* (1866), and *Daniel Deronda* (1876). Her masterpiece, *Middlemarch* (1871–72), provides a thorough study of every class of provincial society. The method of psychological analysis she developed would become characteristic of modern fiction. With the journalist, philosopher, and critic George Henry Lewes (1817–78), a married man, she enjoyed a long and happy, though scandalous, liaison; their Sunday-afternoon salons were a brilliant feature of Victorian life.

George Eliot, chalk drawing by F.W. Burton, 1865; in the National Portrait Gallery, London.
Courtesy of the National Portrait Gallery, London

Eliot, T(homas) S(tearns) (b. Sept. 26, 1888, St. Louis, Mo., U.S.—d. Jan. 4, 1965, London, Eng.), U.S.-British poet, playwright, and critic. Eliot studied at Harvard University before moving to England in 1914, where he would work as an editor from the early 1920s until his death. His first important poem, and the first modernist masterpiece in English, was the radically experimental "Love Song of J. Alfred Prufrock" (1915). *The Waste Land* (1922), which expresses with startling power the disillusionment of the postwar years, made his international reputation. His first critical volume, *The Sacred Wood* (1920), introduced concepts much discussed in later critical theory. He married in 1915; his wife was mentally unstable, and they separated in 1933. (He married again, happily, in 1957.) His conversion to Anglicanism in 1927 shaped all his subsequent works. His last great work was *Four Quartets* (1936–42), four poems on spiritual renewal and the connections of the personal and historical past and present. Influential later essays include "The Idea of a Christian Society" (1939) and "Notes Towards the Definition of Culture" (1948). His play *Murder in the Cathedral* (1935) is a verse treatment of St. Thomas Becket's martyrdom; his other plays, including *The Cocktail Party* (1950), are lesser works. From the 1920s on he was the most influential English-language modernist poet. He won the Nobel Prize for Literature in 1948; from then until his death he achieved public admiration unequaled by any other 20th-century poet.

Elisha (fl. 9th century BC), Hebrew prophet. As the successor of Elijah, he was strongly devoted to the Mosaic tradition of Israel and a potent enemy of all foreign gods and cults. He instigated a revolt against the ruling house of Israel, the dynasty of Omri, that resulted in the death of the king and his family. Elisha's story is told in the Hebrew scriptures in the books 1 and 2 Kings.

Elizabeth I (b. Sept. 7, 1533, Greenwich, near London, Eng.—d. March 24, 1603, Richmond, Surrey), Queen of England (1558–1603). Daughter of Henry VIII and his second wife, Anne Boleyn, she displayed precocious seriousness as a child and received the rigorous education normally reserved for male heirs. Her situation was precarious during the reigns of her half brother Edward VI and her half sister Mary I. After Sir Thomas Wyatt's rebellion in 1554, she was imprisoned but later released. Her accession to the throne on Mary's death was greeted with public jubilation. She assembled a core of experienced advisers, including William Cecil and Francis Walsingham, but she zealously retained her power to make final decisions. Important events of her reign included the restoration of England to Protestantism; the execution of Mary, Queen of Scots; and England's defeat of the Spanish Armada. She lived under constant threat of conspiracies by British Catholics. Over time she became known as the Virgin Queen, wedded to her kingdom. Many important suitors came forward, and she showed signs of romantic attachment to the earl of Leicester, but she remained single, perhaps because she was unwilling to compromise her power. She had another suitor, the 2nd earl of Essex, executed in 1601 for treason. Though her later years saw an economic decline and disastrous military efforts to subdue the Irish, her reign had already seen England's emergence as a world power and her presence had helped unify the nation against foreign enemies. Highly intelligent and strong-willed, Elizabeth inspired ardent expressions of loyalty, and her reign saw a brilliant flourishing in the arts, especially literature and music. After her death, she was succeeded by James I.

Elizabeth II, in full ELIZABETH ALEXANDRA MARY (b. April 21, 1926, London, Eng.), Queen of the United Kingdom from 1952. She became heir presumptive when her uncle, Edward VIII, abdicated and her father became king as George VI. In 1947 she married her distant cousin Philip, duke of Edinburgh, with whom she had four children, including Charles, prince of Wales. She became queen on her father's death in 1952. Increasingly aware of the modern role of the monarchy, she favoured simplicity in court life and took an informed interest in government business. In the 1990s the monarchy was troubled by the highly publicized marital difficulties of two of the queen's sons and the death of Diana, princess of Wales. In 2002 the queen's mother and sister died within two months of each other.

Elizabeth II, 1985.
Karsh—Camera Press/Globe Photos

Elizabethan literature, Body of works written during the reign of Elizabeth I (1558–1603). Probably the most illustrious age in the history of English literature, the Elizabethan era saw a flowering of poetry, produced a golden age of drama, and inspired a wide variety of splendid prose. The period encompasses the work of Sir Philip Sidney, Edmund Spenser, Christopher Marlowe, William Shakespeare, and others. Though some patterns and themes persisted, the tone of most forms of literary expression, especially drama, darkened rather suddenly around the start of the 17th century.

Elysium, or ELYSIAN FIELDS, Ancient Greek paradise reserved for heroes to whom the gods had granted immortality. Homer described it as a land of perfect happiness at the end of the earth, on the banks of the Oceanus River. From the time of Pindar (c. 500 BC) on, Elysium was imagined as a dwelling place for those who had lived a righteous life.

Elytis, Odysseus, or ODYSSEAS ELYTĒS,, orig. ODYSSEUS ALEPOUDHELIS (b. Nov. 2, 1911, Iráklion, Crete—d. March 18, 1996, Athens, Greece), Greek poet. The scion of a prosperous family from Lesbos, he began publishing verse influenced by French Sur-

realism in the 1930s. His first two collections reveal his love of the Greek landscape and the Aegean Sea. During World War II he fought against the Italians in Albania and became something of a bard among young Greeks. One of his best-known poems is *The Axion Esti* (1959); later works include *The Sovereign Sun* (1971) and *The Little Mariner* (1986). He won the Nobel Prize for Literature in 1979.

embargo, Legal action by a government or group of governments restricting the departure of vessels or movement of goods from some or all locations to one or more countries. A trade embargo is a prohibition on exports to one or more countries. A strategic embargo restricts only the sale of goods that make a direct and specific contribution to a country's military power; similarly, an oil embargo prohibits only the export of oil. Broad embargoes often allow the export of certain goods (e.g., medicines or foodstuffs) to continue for humanitarian purposes, and most multilateral embargoes include escape clauses that specify a limited set of conditions under which exporters may be exempt from their prohibitions. An embargo is a tool of economic warfare that may be employed for a variety of political purposes, including demonstrating resolve, sending a political signal, retaliating for another country's actions, compelling a country to change its behaviour, deterring it from engaging in undesired activities, and weakening its military capability.

embolism, Obstruction of blood flow by an embolus—a substance (e.g., a blood clot, a fat globule from a crush injury, or a gas bubble) not normally present in the bloodstream. Obstruction of an artery to the brain may cause stroke. Pulmonary embolism (in the pulmonary artery or a branch) causes difficulty breathing, chest pain, and death of a section of lung tissue, with fever and rapid heartbeat. Embolism in a coronary artery can cause heart attack.

embroidery, Art of decorating textiles with needle and thread. Among the basic techniques are cross-stitch, crewel work, and quilting. The Persians and Greeks wore quilted garments as armor. The earliest surviving examples of embroidery are Scythian (c. 5th–3rd century BC). The most notable extant Chinese examples are the imperial silk robes of the Qing dynasty (1644–1911/12). Islamic embroideries (16th–17th century) show stylized geometric patterns based on animal and plant shapes. Northern European embroidery was mostly ecclesiastical until the Renaissance. European skills and conventions prevailed in North America in the 17th–18th century. The Native Americans embroidered skins and bark with dyed porcupine quills; later the beads they acquired in trade took the place of quills. The indigenous peoples of Central America produced a kind of embroidery with feathers. The Bayeux Tapestry is the most famous surviving piece of needlework.

embryo, Early stage of development of an organism in the egg or the uterus, during which its essential form and its organs and tissues develop. In humans, the organism is called an embryo for the first seven or eight weeks after conception, after which it is called a fetus. In mammals, the fertilized egg or zygote undergoes cleavage (cell division without cell growth) to form a hollow ball or blastocyst. During the second week following fertilization, gastrulation (cell differentiation and migration) results in the formation of three tissue types. These three types of tissue develop into different organ systems: the ectoderm develops into the skin and nervous system; the mesoderm develops into connective tissues, the circulatory system, muscles, and bones; and the endoderm develops into the lining of the digestive system, lungs, and urinary system. In humans, by about the fourth week, the head and trunk can be distinguished and the brain, spinal cord, and internal organs begin to develop. By the fifth week, limbs begin to appear and the embryo is about .33 in. (.8 cm) long. By the end of eight weeks, the embryo has grown to about 1 in. (2.5 cm) long and all subsequent change is limited primarily to growth and specialization of existing structures. Any congenital disorders begin in this stage.

embryology, Study of the formation and development of an embryo. Before widespread use of the microscope and the advent of cellular biology in the 19th century, embryology was based on descriptive and comparative studies. From the time of Aristotle it was debated whether the embryo was a preformed, miniature individual or an undifferentiated form that gradually became specialized. The latter theory was proved in 1827 when Karl Ernst Baer discovered the mammalian ovum (egg). The German anatomist Wilhelm Roux (1850–1924), noted for his pioneering studies on frog eggs (from 1885), became the founder of experimental embryology.

emerald, Grass-green variety of beryl that is highly valued as a gemstone. Its physical properties are those of beryl. Its refractive and dispersive powers (i.e., its capacity to deflect light and to break white light into its component colours) are not high, so cut stones display little brilliancy or fire (flashes of colour). The colour that gives this gem its value is due to the presence of small amounts of chromium. The most important production of fine quality gem material is from Colombia; emeralds are also mined in Russia, Australia, South Africa, and Zimbabwe. Synthetic emeralds are identical to natural crystals and may rival them in colour and beauty.

emir, In the Muslim Middle East, a military commander, governor of a province, or high military official. The first leader to call himself emir was the second caliph, Umar ibn al-Khattab. The title was used by all his successors until the abolition of the caliphate in 1924. In the 10th century the commander of the caliph's armies at Baghdad held the title. It was later adopted by the rulers of independent states in central Asia, notably Bukhara and Afghanistan. The United Arab Emirates, despite their name, are all ruled by sheikhs.

emotion, Affective aspect of consciousness. The emotions are generally understood as representing a synthesis of subjective experience, expressive behaviour, and neurochemical activity. Most researchers hold that they are part of the human evolutionary legacy and serve adaptive ends by adding to general awareness and the facilitation of social communication. Some nonhuman animals are also considered to possess emotions, as first described by Charles Darwin in 1872. An influential early theory of emotion was that proposed independently by William James and Carl Georg Lange (1834–1900), who held that emotion was a perception of internal physiological reactions to external stimuli. Walter B. Cannon questioned this view and directed attention to the thalamus as a possible source of emotional content. Later researchers have focused on the brain-stem structure known as the reticular formation, which serves to integrate brain activity and may infuse perceptions or actions with emotional valence. Cognitive psychologists have emphasized the role of comparison, matching, appraisal, memory, and attribution in the forming of emotions. All modern theorists agree that emotions influence what people perceive, learn, and remember, and that they play an important part in personality development. Cross-cultural studies have shown that, whereas many emotions are universal, their specific content and manner of expression vary considerably.

emotivism, In metaethics, the view that moral judgments do not function as statements of fact but rather as expressions of the speaker's or writer's feelings. According to the emotivist, when we say "You acted wrongly in stealing that money," we are not expressing any fact beyond that stated by "You stole that money." It is, however, as if we had stated this fact with a special tone of abhorrence, for in saying that something is wrong, we are expressing our feelings of disapproval toward it. Emotivism was expounded by A. J. Ayer in *Language, Truth and Logic* (1936) and developed by Charles Stevenson in *Ethics and Language* (1945).

emperor, Title of the sovereigns of the ancient Roman empire and, by derivation, various later European rulers, also applied to certain non-European monarchs. Caesar Augustus was the first Roman emperor. Byzantine emperors ruled at Constantinople until 1453. Charlemagne became the first of the Western emperors (later Holy Roman emperors) in 800. After Otto I became emperor in 962, only German kings held the title. In other parts of Europe, monarchs who ruled multiple kingdoms (e.g., Alfonso VI, who ruled Léon and Castile) sometimes took the title emperor. Napoleon's assumption of the title, as a putative successor of Charlemagne, was a direct threat to the Habsburg dynasty. Queen Victoria of Britain took the title empress of India. Non-European peoples whose rulers have been called emperor include the Chinese, Japanese, Mughals, Incas, and Aztecs.

emphysema, or PULMONARY EMPHYSEMA, Abnormal distension of the lungs with air, usually associated with cigarette smoking and chronic bronchitis. Elastic tissue degenerates, severely interfering with exhalation. Capillary walls disappear, leaving lung tissue dry and pale. The walls of the pulmonary alveoli break down, so the lung fills with pools of air. Symptoms include severe breathlessness, weight loss, bluish skin, chest tightness, and wheezing. In bullous emphysema, the alveoli form large air cysts that may rupture, causing lung collapse, or require surgery. Emphysema is irreversible; it normally continues to progress even after the cessation of smoking and may lead to death.

Empire style, Style of furniture and interior decoration that flourished in France during the First Empire (1804–14). It corresponds to the Regency style in England. Responding to the desire of Napoleon for a style inspired by imperial Rome, the architects Charles Percier (1764–1838) and Pierre Fontaine (1762–1853) decorated his state rooms with Classical styles of furniture and ornamental motifs, supplemented by sphinxes and palm leaves to commemorate his Egyptian campaigns. The style influenced the arts (Jacques-Louis David in painting, Antonio Canova in sculpture, the Arc de Triomphe in architecture) and fashion and spread quickly throughout Europe.

empiricism, Either of two closely related philosophical doctrines, one pertaining to concepts and the other to knowledge. The first doctrine is that most, if not all, concepts are ultimately derived from experience; the second is that most, if not all, knowledge derives from experience, in the sense that appeals to experience are necessarily involved in its justification. Neither doctrine implies the other. Several empiricists have allowed that some knowledge is a priori, or independent of experience, but have denied that any concepts are. On the other hand, few if any empiricists have denied the existence of a priori knowledge while maintaining the existence of a priori concepts. John Locke, George Berkeley, and David Hume are classical representatives of empiricism.

emu, Ratite of Australia. After the ostrich, the emu is the second-largest living bird. They stand more than 5 ft (1.5 m) tall and often weigh more than 100 lbs (45 kg). The common emu (*Dromaius novaehollandiae,* family Dromaiidae), the only survivor of several forms exterminated by settlers, has a stout body and long legs. Both sexes are brownish, with a dark-gray head and neck. Emus can run up to 30 mph (50 kph); if cornered, they kick with their large feet. They mate for life and forage in small flocks for fruits and insects but sometimes damage crops.

Emu (Dromaius novaehollandiae)
V. Serventy—Bruce Coleman Inc.

enamelwork, Metal objects decorated with an opaque glaze fused to the surface by intense heat. The resulting surface is hard and durable and can be brilliantly colourful. Objects most suitable for enamelwork are delicate, small (e.g., jewelry, snuffboxes, scent bottles, watches), and made of copper, brass, bronze, or gold. The best-known processes are cloisonné and champlevé. Enamelwork was produced as early as the 13th century BC, reached its peak in the Byzantine Empire, and flourished throughout medieval and Renaissance Europe. In the early 20th century Carl Fabergé produced highly prized objects made of gold, enamel, and jewels.

encephalitis, Inflammation of the brain, most often due to infection, usually with a virus. One class of encephalitis (including multiple sclerosis) attacks the myelin sheath that insulates nerve fibres rather than the neurons themselves. In most cases, symptoms include fever, headache, lethargy, and coma. Convulsions are most common in infants. Characteristic neurological signs include uncoordinated, involuntary movements and localized weakness. The symptoms and a lumbar puncture (to obtain cerebrospinal fluid for analysis) may establish the presence but not the cause. Treatment usually aims to relieve the symptoms and ensure quiet rest. Various symptoms may remain after recovery.

Encke's Comet, Faint comet having the shortest orbital period (about 3.3 years) of any known, first observed in 1786. It was the second comet (after Halley's Comet) to have its period determined (1819), by Johann Franz Encke (1791–1865). Encke also found that the comet's period decreases by about 2^1/$_2$ hours in each revolution and showed that this effect could not be explained by the planets' gravitational influence. Its period continues to decrease, though more slowly, and appears to be related to the effects of outgassing.

encyclopaedia, Reference work that contains information on all branches of knowledge or that treats a particular branch of knowledge comprehensively. It is self-contained and explains subjects in greater detail than a dictionary. It differs from an almanac in that it is not an annual publication that provides information about a particular year, and it differs from pedagogical texts in its attempt to be easy to consult and to be readily understood by the layperson. Though generally written in the form of many separate articles, encyclopaedias vary greatly in format and content. The prototype of modern encyclopaedias is usually acknowledged to be Ephraim Chambers's *Cyclopaedia* (1728). The first modern encyclopaedia was the French *Encyclopédie* (1751–65). The oldest general encyclopaedia in English is the *Encyclopædia Britannica*.

Encyclopædia Britannica, The oldest English-language general encyclopaedia. Its first print edition was published in three volumes in 1768–71 in Edinburgh, Scot. In subsequent editions it grew in size and reputation. The most famous editions include the ninth (1875–89), known as "the scholar's encyclopaedia," and the 11th (1910–11), which, with contributions from more than 1,500 experts of world reputation, was also the first to divide the traditionally lengthy treatises into more-particularized articles. The 15th edition embodied a new structure, dividing the major articles from the shorter ones; released in 1974, with a major revision in 1985, it was discontinued in 2012. From the early 1990s the *Encyclopædia Britannica* also appeared in compact disc versions, and in 1994 Britannica debuted the first Internet-based encyclopaedia. The online version, in its many digital forms, had become the primary focus by the early 21st century. A series of ownership changes led to the encyclopaedia's purchase by American publishers in 1901, and its Chicago-based editorial offices today coordinate the work of contributors from around the world.

endangered species, Any species of plant, animal, or other organism threatened with extinction. International and national agencies work to maintain lists of endangered species, to protect and preserve natural habitats, and to promote programs for recovery and reestablishment of these species. The Species Survival Commission of the International Union for Conservation of Na-

ture and Natural Resources (IUCN) publishes information online about approximately 41,500 endangered species worldwide as the *Red List of Threatened Species*. Separate books for animal and plant species are also published. In the United States, the Fish and Wildlife Service and the National Oceanic and Atmospheric Administration (NOAA) are responsible for the conservation and management of fish and wildlife, including endangered species, and their habitats. Its list now consists of about 1,890 domestic species of endangered or threatened animals and plants.

endocarditis, Inflammation of the heart lining (endocardium), in association with a noninfectious disease (e.g., systemic lupus erythematosus) or caused by infection, usually at the heart valves. Severe bacterial infection causes an acute form with fever, sweating, chills, joint pain and swelling, and embolisms. Subacute endocarditis usually comes from bacteria that do not ordinarily cause disease. Bacterial endocarditis is usually treated with long-term antibiotics. In nonbacterial thrombotic endocarditis, blood clots form along heart valve edges.

endocrinology, Medical discipline dealing with regulation of body functions by hormones and other biochemicals and treatment of endocrine system imbalances. In 1841 Friedrich Gustav Henle first recognized "ductless glands," which secrete products directly into the bloodstream. The field was essentially established in the early 20th century, when Ernest H. Starling, who introduced the term *hormone*, proposed that chemical and nervous regulation of physiological processes were linked. Endocrine therapy is based on replacing deficient hormones with purified extracts. Nuclear technology has led to new treatments; use of radioactive iodine for hyperthyroidism greatly reduced the need for thyroid gland surgery. The detection of minute amounts of hormone with radioimmunoassays permits early diagnosis and treatment of endocrine disorders.

endometriosis, Disorder of the female reproductive system in which endometrium (uterine lining) grows in an abnormal location because some endometrial fragments traverse the fallopian tubes into the abdominal cavity and become embedded on structures there, usually the ovaries, rather than exiting the uterus via the vagina (during menstruation). Symptoms include pain on menstruation, sexual intercourse, defecation, and/or urination; heavy menstrual flow; blood in the urine; and infertility. Diagnosis is best made by laparoscopy. Treatment includes surgery and hormones to suppress ovulation for six to nine months.

endorphin, Any of a group of proteins occurring in the brain and having pain-relieving properties typical of opium and related opiates. Discovered in the 1970s, they include enkephalin, beta-endorphin, and dynorphin. Each is distributed in characteristic patterns throughout the nervous system. Endorphins are released in response to pain or sustained exertion (causing, e.g., the "runner's high"). They are also believed to have a role in appetite control, release of pituitary sex hormones, and shock. There is strong evidence that they are connected with "pleasure centres" in the brain, and they seem to be activated by acupuncture. Knowledge of their behaviour has implications for treating addictions and chronic pain.

energy, Capacity for doing work. Energy exists in various forms—including kinetic, potential, thermal, chemical, electrical, and nuclear—and can be converted from one form to another. For example, fuel-burning heat engines convert chemical energy to thermal energy; batteries convert chemical energy to electrical energy. Though energy may be converted from one form to another, it may not be created or destroyed; that is, total energy in a closed system remains constant. All forms of energy are associated with motion. A rolling ball has kinetic energy, for instance, whereas a ball lifted above the ground has potential energy, as it has the potential to move if released. Heat and work involve the transfer of energy; heat transferred may become thermal energy.

engineering, Professional art of applying science to the optimum conversion of the resources of nature to the uses of humankind. Engineering is based principally on physics, chemistry, and mathematics and their extensions into materials science, solid and fluid mechanics, thermodynamics, transfer and rate processes, and systems analysis. A great body of special knowledge is associated with engineering; preparation for professional practice involves extensive training in the application of that knowledge. Engineers employ two types of natural resources, materials and energy. Materials acquire uses that reflect their properties: their strength, ease of fabrication, lightness, or durability; their ability to insulate or conduct; and their chemical, electrical, or acoustical properties. Important sources of energy include fossil fuels (coal, petroleum, gas), wind, sunlight, falling water, and nuclear fission.

England, Southern part of the island of Great Britain, excluding

Big Ben, London.
© Goodshoot/Jupiterimages

Wales. Area: 50,351 sq mi (130,410 sq km). Population (2001): 49,138,831. It is the largest constituent unit of the United Kingdom of Great Britain and Northern Ireland. England is often erroneously considered synonymous with the island of Great Britain and even with the entire kingdom. Despite the political, economic, and cultural legacy that has perpetuated its name (under which a number of Great Britain's national sports teams still compete), England no longer exists as a governmental or political unit within the United Kingdom. It is a land of low hills and plateaus, with a 2,000-mi (3,200-km) coastline. A substantial upland, the Pennines, divides northern England; the Cheviot Hills define the Scottish border. In the southwest lie the Cotswold Hills and the plateau regions of Exmoor and Dartmoor; in the southeast lie the Downs and in the south the Salisbury Plain. English weather is diverse, with a generally mild but erratic maritime climate. England is divided into eight geographic regions, often referred to as the standard regions of England; they do not serve any administrative function. The South East, centred on London, is an economically dominant area. It contains an extensive range of manufacturing and science-based industries and commercial endeavours. The West Midlands, in west-central England, is a diversified manufacturing region that centres on Birmingham. The region also includes the Shakespeare country, centred on Stratford-upon-Avon. The East Midlands, in east-central England, is also a manufacturing region and contains some of England's best farmland. East Anglia is the easternmost part of England. It is mainly an agricultural region, but high-technology industries have developed there. Manchester and Liverpool are the chief industrial cities of the North West; the region has long been known for textile production, but that has rapidly given way to diversified manufacturing. The Humberside region lies to the east and is noted for textiles and steelmaking, though its economy has become more diversified and there is extensive farmland. The North region extends north to the Scottish border. It includes the celebrated Lake District and is a centre of engineering and pharmaceutical manufacture. The South West region, which includes Cornwall, has a growing tourist industry, and some areas are becoming industrialized. England is especially noted for its long and rich literary tradition, as well as for its architecture, painting, theatres, museums, and universities. It also played an integral role in rock music.

England, Church of, English national church and the mother church of the Anglican Communion. Christianity was brought to England in the 2nd century, and though nearly destroyed by the Anglo-Saxon invasions, it was reestablished after the mission of St. Augustine of Canterbury in 597. Medieval conflicts between church and state culminated in Henry VIII's break with Roman Catholicism in the Reformation. When the pope refused to annul Henry's marriage to Catherine of Aragon, the king issued the Act of Supremacy (1534), which declared the English monarch to be head of the Church of England. Under Henry's successor, Edward VI, more Protestant reforms were instituted. After a five-year Catholic reaction under Mary I, Elizabeth I ascended the throne (1558), and the Church of England was reestablished. The Book of Common Prayer (1549) and the Thirty-nine Articles (1571) became the standards for liturgy and doctrine. The rise of Puritanism in the 17th century led to the English Civil Wars; during the Commonwealth the Church of England was suppressed, but it was reestablished in 1660. The evangelical movement in the 18th century emphasized the church's Protestant heritage, while the Oxford movement in the 19th century emphasized its Roman Catholic heritage. The Church of England has maintained an episcopal form of government, and its leader is the archbishop of Canterbury. In 1992 the church voted to ordain women as priests. In the U.S., the Protestant Episcopal Church is descended from and remains associated with the Church of England.

English Channel, or THE CHANNEL, French LA MANCHE ("THE SLEEVE"), Strait between southern England and northern France. It connects the Atlantic Ocean with the North Sea through the Strait of Dover. The French name, La Manche ("The Sleeve"), is a reference to its shape, which gradually narrows from about 112 mi (180 km) in the west to only 21 mi (34 km) in the east, between Dover, Eng., and Calais, France. Historically both a route for and a barrier to invaders of Britain, it developed into one of the world's busiest sea routes for oil tankers and ore carriers. The Channel Tunnel, completed in 1994, provides a land route between Paris and London.

English Civil Wars (1642–51) Armed conflict in the British Isles between Parliamentarians and supporters of the monarchy (Royalists). Tension between Charles I and the House of Commons had been building for some time, and after his unsuccessful attempt to arrest five members of Parliament, both sides prepared for war. The first phase of the wars (1642–46) was initially characterized by inconclusive encounters, but victories by Parliamentarian forces under Oliver Cromwell at the Battles of Marston Moor and Naseby turned the tide. In 1646 the Royalist forces were disbanded. In 1647 Charles I negotiated with a Scottish group for assistance, starting the second phase of the wars, a series of Royalist rebellions, and a Scottish invasion. All were defeated, and Charles I was executed in 1649. The fighting continued, and Royalist forces under Charles II invaded England in 1651. Parliamentary forces defeated the Royalists at Worcester in 1651 and Charles II fled abroad, effectively ending the civil wars. The wars' political consequence was the establishment of the Commonwealth and Protectorate.

English horn, Orchestral woodwind instrument, a large oboe pitched a 5th below the ordinary oboe. It has a bent metal crook, to hold the double reed, and a bulbous bell. It is a transposing instrument (its music written in a different tone than it actually sounds) in F. It is neither English nor a horn; in its original name, *cor anglais,* *cor* ("horn") referred to its original hornlike curved shape, but the source of *anglais* ("English") is a mystery. It has remained a basically orchestral instrument since its first appearance *c.* 1750.

English language, Language belonging to the Germanic languages branch of the Indo-European language family, widely spoken on six continents. The primary language of the U.S., Britain, Canada, Australia, Ireland, New Zealand, and various Caribbean and Pacific island nations, it is also an official language of India, the Philippines, and many sub-Saharan African countries. It is one of the most widely spoken languages in the world (approximately 1.5 billion speakers), the mother tongue of more than 350 million people, and the most widely taught foreign language. English relies mainly on word order (usually subject-verb-object) to indicate relationships between words. Written in the Latin alphabet, it is most closely related to Frisian, German, and Dutch. Its history began with the migration of the Jutes, Angles, and Saxons from Germany and Denmark to Britain in the 5th and 6th centuries. The Norman Conquest of 1066 brought many French words into English. Greek and Latin words began to enter it in the 15th century, and Modern English is usually dated from 1500. English easily borrows words from other languages and has coined many new words to reflect advances in technology.

engraving, Any of various processes of cutting a design into a plate or block of metal or wood. The cutting is done by a graver, or burin, on a copper, zinc, aluminum, or magnesium plate, and the design is printed with a roller press from ink rubbed into the incised grooves. Wood engraving derives from the woodcut, but the use of the hard, smooth boxwood, cut with the burin commonly used by the copper-plate engraver, produces a finer, more detailed image. By contrast with engraving from metal plates, the printing of wood engravings is done from the surface of the plate or block; the parts that are not to be printed are cut away.

ENIAC, in full ELECTRONIC NUMERICAL INTEGRATOR AND COMPUTER, Early electronic digital computer built in the U.S. in 1945 by J. Presper Eckert and John W. Mauchly. The massive ENIAC, which weighed 30 tons and filled an entire room, used some 18,000 vacuum tubes, 70,000 resistors, and 10,000 capacitors. In December 1945 it solved its first problem, calculations for the hydrogen bomb. After its official unveiling in 1946, it was used to prepare artillery-shell trajectory tables and perform other military and scientific calculations.

Enigma, Device used by the German military to encode strategic messages before and during World War II. The Enigma code was first broken by the Poles in the early 1930s, so that German messages were eventually intercepted and deciphered by Allied code-breakers during the war.

Enkidu, Friend and companion of the Mesopotamian hero Gilgamesh. In the ancient *Epic of Gilgamesh,* Enkidu is a wild man created by the god Anu. After Gilgamesh defeats him, the two become friends (in some versions Enkidu becomes Gilgamesh's servant). He aids Gilgamesh in killing the divine bull sent by the goddess Ishtar to destroy them. The gods then kill Enkidu in revenge, prompting Gilgamesh to search for immortality.

Enlightenment, European intellectual movement of the 17th–18th century in which ideas concerning God, reason, nature, and man were blended into a worldview that inspired revolutionary developments in art, philosophy, and politics. Central to Enlightenment thought were the use and celebration of reason. For Enlightenment thinkers, received authority, whether in science or religion, was to be subject to the investigation of unfettered minds. In the sciences and mathematics, the logics of induction and deduction made possible the creation of a sweeping new cosmology. The search for a rational religion led to Deism; the more radical products of the application of reason to religion were skepticism, atheism, and materialism. The Enlightenment produced modern secularized theories of psychology and ethics by men such as John Locke and Thomas Hobbes, and it also gave rise to radical political theories. Locke, Jeremy Bentham, J.-J. Rousseau, Montesquieu, Voltaire, and Thomas Jefferson all contributed to an evolving critique of the authoritarian state and to sketching the outline of a higher form of social organization based on natural rights. One of the Enlightenment's enduring legacies is the belief that human history is a record of general progress.

Entente Cordiale (French: "Cordial Understanding"), (April 8, 1904) Anglo-French agreement that settled numerous colonial disputes and ended antagonisms between Britain and France. It granted freedom of action to Britain in Egypt and to France in Morocco and resolved several other imperial disputes. The agreement reduced the virtual isolation of each country and was consequently upsetting to Germany, which had benefited from their antagonism. The Entente paved the way for Anglo-French diplomatic cooperation against Germany before World War I and for later military alliances.

entomology, Branch of zoology dealing with the scientific study of insects, including their taxonomy, morphology, physiology, and ecology. Applied aspects of entomology, such as the harmful and beneficial impact of insects on humans, are also studied.

entropy, Measure of a system's energy that is unavailable for work, or of the degree of a system's disorder. When heat is added to a system held at constant temperature, the change in entropy is related to the change in energy, the pressure, the temperature, and the change in volume. Its magnitude varies from zero to the total amount of energy in a system. The concept, first proposed in 1850 by the German physicist Rudolf Clausius (1822–1888), is sometimes presented as the second law of thermodynamics, which states that entropy increases during irreversible processes such as spontaneous mixing of hot and cold gases, uncontrolled expansion of a gas into a vacuum, and combustion of fuel. In popular, nontechnical use, entropy is regarded as a measure of the chaos or randomness of a system.

environmentalism, Advocacy of the preservation or improvement of the natural environment, especially the social and political movement to control environmental pollution. Other specific goals of environmentalism include control of human population growth, conservation of natural resources, restriction of the negative effects of modern technology, and the adoption of environmentally benign forms of political and economic organization. Environmental advocacy at the international level by nongovernmental organizations and some states has resulted in treaties, conventions, and other instruments of environmental law addressing problems such as global warming, the depletion of the ozone layer, and the danger of transboundary pollution from nuclear accidents. Influential U.S. and British environmentalists have included Thomas Robert Malthus, John Muir, Rachel Carson, Barry Commoner, Paul R. Ehrlich, and Edward O. Wilson. In the social sciences, the term refers to any theory that emphasizes the importance of environmental factors in the development of culture and society.

enzyme, Substance that acts as a catalyst in living organisms, regulating the rate at which life's chemical reactions proceed without being altered in the process. Enzymes reduce the activation energy needed to start these reactions; without them, most such reactions would not take place at a useful rate. Because enzymes are not consumed, only tiny amounts of them are needed. Enzymes catalyze all aspects of cell metabolism, including the digestion of food, in which large nutrient molecules (including proteins, carbohydrates, and fats) are broken down into smaller molecules; the conservation and transformation of chemical energy; and the construction of cellular materials and components. Almost all enzymes are proteins; many depend on a nonprotein cofactor, either a loosely associated organic compound (e.g., a vitamin) or a tightly bound metal ion (e.g., iron, zinc) or organic (often metal-containing) group. The enzyme-cofactor combination provides an active configuration, usually including an active site into which the substance (substrate) involved in the reaction can fit. Many enzymes are specific to one substrate. If a competing molecule blocks the active site or changes its shape, the enzyme's activity is inhibited. If the enzyme's configuration is destroyed, its activity is lost. Enzymes are classified by the type of reaction they catalyze: (1) oxidation-reduction, (2) transfer of a chemical group, (3) hydrolysis, (4) removal or addition of a chemical group, (5) isomerization; isomerism), and (6) binding together of substrate units (polymerization). Most enzyme names end in -*ase*. Enzymes are chiral catalysts, producing mostly or only one of the possible stereoisomeric products. The fermentation of wine, leavening of bread, curdling of milk into cheese, and brewing of beer are all enzymatic reactions. The uses of enzymes in medicine include killing disease-causing microorganisms, promoting wound healing, and diagnosing certain diseases.

Eocene Epoch, Major division of the Paleogene Period, from 55.8 million to 33.9 million years ago. It follows the Paleocene Epoch and precedes the Oligocene Epoch. The name, derived from the Greek *eos* ("dawn"), refers to the dawn of recent life; during the Eocene, all the major divisions, or orders, of modern mammals appeared, as well as many essentially modern bird orders. Climates were warm and humid. Temperate and subtropical forests were widespread, but grasslands were limited during this interval.

Eolie Islands, or LIPARI ISLANDS, Volcanic island group, Tyrrhenian Sea, in the west-central Mediterranean Sea. Located off the northern coast of Sicily, the seven major islands and several islets have a total land area of 34 sq mi (88 sq km). The major islands are Alicudi, Eilcudi, Lipari, Panarea, Salina, Stromboli, and Vulcano. Vulcano and Stromboli are active volcanoes. The Greeks believed the islands to be the home of the god Aeolus, king of the winds. They have been inhabited since the Neolithic Period and were held successively by the Greeks, Carthaginians, Romans, Saracens, Normans, Angevins, and Aragonese.

eon, Long span of geologic time. In formal usage, eons are the longest portions of geologic time (eras are the second-longest). Three eons are recognized: the Phanerozoic Eon (dating from the present back to the beginning of the Cambrian Period), the Proterozoic Eon, and the Archean Eon. Less formally, eon often refers to a span of one billion years.

Ephesus, Ancient Ionian Greek city; its ruins lie near the modern village of Selc̆uk in western Turkey. It was situated south of the Cayster River and was the site of the Temple of Artemis. Traditionally founded by the Carians, it was one of the 12 Ionian Cities and was involved in the Persian and Peloponnesian wars. It was taken by Alexander the Great *c.* 333 BC and prospered throughout the Hellenistic period. It passed to Rome in 133 BC and under the emperor Augustus became the capital of the Roman province of Asia. It was an early seat of Christianity, which was visited by St. Paul; the Letter of Paul to the Ephesians was directed to the church there. The Goths destroyed the city and temple in AD 262; neither ever recovered. There are extensively excavated ruins at the modern site.

epic, Long, narrative poem in an elevated style that celebrates heroic achievement and treats themes of historical, national, religious, or legendary significance. Primary (or traditional) epics are shaped from the legends and traditions of a heroic age and are part of oral tradition; secondary (or literary) epics are written down from the beginning, and their poets adapt aspects of traditional epics. The poems of Homer are usually regarded as the first important epics and the main source of epic conventions in western Europe. These conventions include the centrality of a hero, sometimes semidivine; an extensive, perhaps cosmic, setting; heroic battle; extended journeying; and the involvement of supernatural beings.

epic theatre, Dramatic form developed in Germany after World War I by Bertolt Brecht and others, intended to provoke rational thought rather than to create illusion. It presents loosely connected scenes often interrupted by direct addresses to the audience providing analysis, argument, or documentation. Brecht's goal was to use alienating or distancing effects to block the emotional responses of the audience members and force them to think objectively about the play. Actors were instructed to keep a distance between themselves and the characters they portrayed and to emphasize external actions rather than emotions.

epicentre, Point on the surface of the Earth that is directly above the source (or focus) of an earthquake. There the effects of the earthquake usually are most severe.

Epicureanism, Metaphysical and ethical doctrines taught by Epicurus. In metaphysics, the basic concepts of Epicureanism were atomism; mechanical causality limited by the spontaneous "swerve" of atoms, which accounted for the freedom of motion in man and animals; the infinity of the universe; and the existence of gods as beatified and immortal natures completely extraneous to happenings in the world. In ethics, the basic concepts were the identification of the good with pleasure and of the supreme good with the absence of bodily and mental pain; the limitation of all desire and the practice of virtue; withdrawal from public life; and the cultivation of friendship. Because of its dogmatic character and its practical end, Epicureanism did not lend itself easily to development.

epidemiology, Study of disease distribution in populations. It focuses on groups rather than individuals and often takes a historical perspective. Descriptive epidemiology surveys a population to see what segments (e.g., age, sex, ethnic group, occupation) are affected by a disorder, follows changes or variations in its incidence or mortality over time and in different locations, and helps identify syndromes or suggest associations with risk factors. Analytic epidemiology conducts studies to test the conclusions of descriptive surveys or laboratory observations. Epidemiologic data on diseases is used to find those at high risk, identify causes and take preventive measures, and plan new health services.

epigenetics, The study of the chemical modification of specific genes or gene-associated proteins of an organism. Epigenetic modifications define how genetic information is read and used by cells. Epigenetic modifications can be inherited and are influenced by environmental factors, some of which can induce epigenetic signaling that may contribute to biological processes such as aging. Methylation is the principal epigenetic modification of deoxyribonucleic acid (DNA) and of proteins called histones that package DNA into chromatin inside a cell. Epigenetic modifications influence gene expression and enable the differentiation of pluripotent stem cells (cells with the potential to become any of many different kinds of cells) into distinct cell types early in embryological development. The ability to control and alter stem cell differentiation through the manipulation of epigenetic modifications has profound implications for the treatment of conditions such as neurodegenerative disease.

epigram, Short poem treating concisely, pointedly, and often satirically a single thought or event and often ending with a witticism or ingenious turn of thought. By extension, the term applies to a terse, sage, or witty (often paradoxical) saying, usually in the form of a generalization. Writers of Latin epigrams included Catullus and Martial. The form was revived in the Renaissance. Later masters of the epigram have included Ben Jonson; François VI, duke de La Rochefoucauld; Voltaire; Alexander Pope; Samuel Taylor Coleridge; Oscar Wilde; and George Bernard Shaw.

epilepsy, Neurological disorder caused by paroxysmal malfunction of neurons in the brain (seizures). It is characterized by strange movements or sensations in parts of the body, odd behaviours, emotional disturbances, and sometimes convulsions and momentary lapses of consciousness. Seizures may result from abnormal electrical activity in most or all of the brain (generalized), or they may originate in a specific brain area (partial). Causes include brain tumours, infections, genetic or developmental abnormalities, stroke, and head trauma, although no cause can be found in most cases. Treatment is usually with anticonvulsant medications; brain surgery may be beneficial if drugs cannot control seizures.

epinephrine, or ADRENALINE, One of two hormones (the other being norepinephrine) secreted by the adrenal glands, as well as at some nerve endings, where they serve as neurotransmitters. They are similar chemically and have similar actions on the body. They increase the rate and force of heart contractions, increasing blood output and raising blood pressure. Epinephrine also stimulates breakdown of glycogen to glucose in the liver, raising blood glucose levels, and both hormones increase the level of circulating free fatty acids. All these actions ready the body for action in times of stress or danger, times requiring increased alertness or exertion. Epinephrine is used in medical situations including cardiac arrest, asthma, and acute allergic reaction.

Epiphany, Christian festival celebrated on January 6. One of the oldest Christian holy days (along with Christmas and Easter), the festival originated in the Eastern church and was adopted in the Western church by the 4th century. It commemorates the first manifestation of Jesus to the Gentiles, as represented by the Magi. The eve of Epiphany, called Twelfth Night, is thought to mark the arrival of the Wise Men in Bethlehem. Epiphany also celebrates the (much later) baptism of Jesus by John the Baptist and Jesus' first miracle, performed at Cana.

epiphyte, Any plant that grows upon or is attached to another plant or object merely for physical support. Epiphytes are found mostly in the tropics and are also known as air plants because they have no attachment to the ground or other obvious nutrient source. They obtain water and minerals from rain and from debris on the supporting plants. Orchids, ferns, and members of the pineapple family are common tropical epiphytes. Lichens, mosses, liverworts, and algae are epiphytes of temperate regions.

episcopacy, System of church government by bishops. It existed as early as the 2nd century AD, when bishops were chosen to oversee preaching and worship within a specific region, now called a diocese. Today local congregations are shepherded by priests and deacons, but only bishops can ordain priests, perform the rite of confirmation, and consecrate other bishops. Their special duties are closely tied to the idea of Apostolic succession. Some Protestant churches abandoned episcopacy during the Reformation, but it was retained by the Roman Catholic, Eastern Orthodox, Anglican, and Swedish Lutheran churches, among others.

Episcopal Church, USA, also called EPISCOPAL CHURCH IN THE UNITED STATES OF AMERICA, or PROTESTANT EPISCOPAL CHURCH, Descendant of the Church of England in the U.S. Part of the Anglican Communion, it was formally organized in 1789 as the successor of the Church of England in the former British colonies. The church accepts both the Apostles' Creed and the Nicene Creed, as well as a modified version of the Thirty-nine Articles of the Church of England. The highest authority in the church is the General Convention, which is headed by the presiding bishop (elected by the House of Bishops). The Reformed Episcopal Church broke away from the main body in 1873. The church accepted the ordination of women in 1976. In 1988 the church elected its first woman bishop, and in 2003 an openly gay man was consecrated bishop of New Hampshire. These steps generated controversy within the church as well as among other churches of the Anglican Communion.

epistemology, Study of the origin, nature, and limits of human knowledge. Nearly every great philosopher has contributed to the epistemological literature. Some historically important issues in epistemology are: (1) whether knowledge of any kind is possible, and if so what kind; (2) whether some human knowledge is innate (i.e., present, in some sense, at birth) or whether instead all significant knowledge is acquired through experience; (3) whether knowledge is inherently a mental state; (4) whether certainty is a form of knowledge; and (5) whether the primary task of epistemology is to provide justifications for broad categories of knowledge claim or merely to describe what kinds of things are known and how that knowledge is acquired. Issues related to (1) arise in the consideration of skepticism, radical versions of which challenge the possibility of knowledge of matters of fact, knowledge of an external world, and knowledge of the existence and natures of other minds.

epistolary novel, Novel in the form of a series of letters written by one or more characters. It allows the author to present the characters' thoughts without interference, convey events with dramatic immediacy, and present events from several points of view. It was one of the first novelistic forms to be developed. It was foreshadowed by Aphra Behn's poem cycle *Love-Letters Between a Nobleman and His Sister* (1683). The outstanding early example is Samuel Richardson's *Pamela* (1740); distinguished later works include Tobias Smollett's *Humphry Clinker* (1771) and Pierre Laclos's *Les Liaisons dangereuses* (1782). The genre remained popular up to the 19th century. Its reliance on subjective points of view makes it the forerunner of the modern psychological novel.

epitaph, Inscription in verse or prose on a tomb, or, by extension, anything written as if to be inscribed on a tomb. Probably the earliest surviving epitaphs are those written on ancient Egyptian sarcophagi and coffins. Ancient Greek examples are often of literary interest. In Elizabethan times epitaphs began to assume a more literary character. Many of the best known are literary memorials (often deliberately witty) not intended for a tomb.

epoch, Unit of geologic time during which a rock series is deposited. It is a subdivision of a geologic period. Additional distinctions can be made by adding relative time terms, such as *early*, *middle*, and *late*.

Epstein-Barr virus (EBV), Virus of the Herpesviridae family that is the major cause of acute infectious mononucleosis. The virus, named for two of its discoverers, infects only salivary gland cells and one type of white blood cell. Saliva is the only bodily fluid that has been proved to contain infectious EBV particles. In less-developed nations, infection with EBV occurs in almost all children before the age of 5 and is not associated with recognizable symptoms. When EBV infection is delayed until the teen or early adult years, the body commonly responds differently, resulting in mononucleosis. Other, rarer disorders have also been linked with EBV, including certain cancers. There are no specific treatments for any form of EBV infection, and no vaccines have been developed.

equality, Generally, an ideal of uniformity in treatment or status by those in a position to affect either. Acknowledgment of the right to equality often must be coerced from the advantaged by the disadvantaged. Equality of opportunity was the founding creed of U.S. society, but equality among all peoples and between the sexes has proved easier to legislate than to achieve in practice. Social or religious inequality is deeply ingrained in some cultures and thus difficult to overcome. Government efforts to achieve economic equality include enhancing opportunities through tax policy, subsidized training and education, redistributing wealth or resources, and preferential treatment of those historically treated unequally.

Equator, Great circle around the Earth that is everywhere equidistant from the geographic poles and lies in a plane perpendicular to the Earth's axis. This geographic, or terrestrial, Equator divides the Earth into the Northern and Southern Hemispheres and forms the imaginary reference line on the Earth's surface from which latitude is reckoned (i.e., 0° latitude). In astronomy, the celestial equator is the great circle in which the plane of the terrestrial Equator intersects the celestial sphere; it is thus equidistant from the celestial poles. When the Sun lies in its plane, day and night are everywhere of equal length; this happens at the equinoxes.

Equatorial Guinea, officially REPUBLIC OF EQUATORIAL GUINEA formerly SPANISH GUINEA, Country, on the western coast of equatorial Africa and including Bioko Island. Area: 10,831 sq mi (28,051 sq km). Population: (2011 est.) 720,000. Capital: Malabo. The majority of the population are Bantu-speaking Fang people, with a minority of other ethnic groups. The indigenous people of Bioko are the Bubi, descendants of Bantu migrants from the mainland. Languages: Spanish, French (both official), Fang, Bubi, and others. Religions: Christianity (predominantly Roman Catholic, also other Christians); also Islam, traditional beliefs. Currency: CFA franc. Bordered by Cameroon and Gabon, Equatorial Guinea's mainland region is separated by the Bight of Biafra from the island of Bioko to the northwest. The mainland has a coastal plain some 12 mi (20 km) wide, with a long stretch of beach, low cliffs to the south, and hills and plateaus to the east. The Mbini (Benito) River divides the region. Bioko consists of extinct volcanic cones and has several crater lakes and rich lava soils. Dense tropical rainforest prevails throughout the mainland and includes valuable hardwoods. Cacao, timber, and coffee long were the country's primary exports, but since the 1990s petroleum has been the major export. Equatorial Guinea is a republic with one legislative house; the president is the head of state and government, assisted by the prime minister. Equatorial Guinea was ceded by the Portuguese to the Spanish in the late 18th century; it was frequented by slave traders, as well as by British and other merchants. Bioko was administered by British authorities in the early to mid-19th century before the Spanish took over in 1858. The mainland was not effectively occupied by the Spanish until the second half of the 19th century. Independence was declared in 1968, followed by a reign of terror and economic chaos under the dictatorial president Francisco Macías Nguema, who was overthrown by a military coup in 1979 and later executed. Teodoro Obiang Nguema Mbasogo became leader of the country in 1979. New constitutions were adopted in 1982 and 1991, but political power remained concentrated in the office of the president. In the early 21st century the standard of living of most people remained low, despite the country's oil wealth.

equilibrium, Condition in which the net force acting on a particle is zero. A body in equilibrium experiences no acceleration and, unless disturbed by an outside force, will remain in equilibrium indefinitely. A stable equilibrium is one in which small, externally induced displacements from that state produce forces that tend to oppose the displacement and return the body to equilibrium. An unstable equilibrium is one in which the least departures produce forces tending to increase the displacement. A brick lying on the floor is in stable equilibrium, while a ball bearing balanced on a knife-edge is in unstable equilibrium.

equinox, Either of two moments in the year when the Sun is exactly above the Equator and day and night are of equal length all over Earth; also, either of two points in the sky where the ecliptic and the celestial equator intersect. The vernal equinox, when spring begins in the Northern Hemisphere, occurs about March 21, when the Sun moves north across the celestial equator. The autumnal equinox falls about September 23, as the Sun crosses the celestial equator going south.

equinoxes, precession of the, Motion of the points where the Sun crosses the celestial equator, caused by precession of Earth's axis. Hipparchus noticed that the stars' positions were shifted consistently from earlier measures, indicating that Earth, not the stars, was moving. This precession, a wobbling in the orientation of Earth's axis with a cycle of almost 26,000 years, is caused by the gravity of the Sun and the Moon acting on Earth's equatorial bulge. The planets also have a small influence on precession. Projecting Earth's axis onto the celestial sphere locates the northern

and southern celestial poles. Precession makes these points trace out circles on the sky and also makes the celestial equator wobble, changing its points of intersection (equinoxes) with the ecliptic.

era, Very long span of geologic time; in formal usage, a portion of geologic time of the second-greatest magnitude (eons are longer). Three eras are recognized: Paleozoic, Mesozoic, and Cenozoic. Because of the difficulties involved in establishing accurate chronologies, the Precambrian, or earliest, eras are classified independently. An era is composed of one or more geologic periods.

Erech, or URUK, Ancient city, Mesopotamia. Located northwest of Ur on the Euphrates River, it was one of the greatest cities of Sumer and was enclosed by brickwork walls that, according to legend, were built by the mythical hero Gilgamesh. Excavations have traced successive cities that date from the prehistoric Ubaid period (c. 5000 BC) to Parthian times (126 BC–AD 224), when in c. 70 BC an ancient school of learned scribes was still using cuneiform script. Urban life in what is known as the Erech-Jamdat Nasr period (c. 3500–2900 BC) is more fully illustrated at Erech than at any other Mesopotamian city.

Eridu, Ancient Sumerian city on the Persian Gulf. Although it was the chief seaport of Sumer and Babylonia and was located on the Euphrates River near the city of Ur, siltation has since moved the coastline southward and the city's remains are now some distance inland, in modern Iraq. It was revered as the oldest city in Sumer, and its patron god was Enki (Ea). Founded on sand dunes c. 5th millennium BC, its ruins show the sequence of the preliterate Ubaid civilization, with a long succession of superimposed temples portraying the development of an elaborate mud-brick architecture. It was occupied until c. 600 BC.

Eritrea, officially STATE OF ERITREA, Tigrinya HAGERE IERTRA, Country, eastern Africa. It extends about 600 mi (1,000 km) along the Red Sea coast and includes the Dahlak Archipelago. Area: 46,774 sq mi (121,144 sq km). Population: (2011 est.) 5,415,000. Capital: Asmara. There is no official religion or language. The varied population is about half Tigrinya-speaking Christians, with a large minority of Muslims and diverse other peoples. Arabic, English, and Italian are also spoken. Currency: nakfa. The land varies from temperate central highlands to coastal desert plain, with savanna in the western lowlands. The economy is based on livestock herding and subsistence agriculture. Industry, based in Asmara, includes food products, textiles, and leather goods. Eritrea's form of government is a transitional regime with one interim legislative body; the head of state and government is the president. As the site of the main ports of the Aksumite empire, it was linked to the beginnings of the Ethiopian kingdom, but it retained much of its independence until it came under Ottoman rule in the 16th century. In the 17th–19th centuries, control of the territory was disputed among Ethiopia, the Ottomans, the kingdom of Tigray, Egypt, and Italy; it became an Italian colony in 1890. Eritrea was used as the main base for the Italian invasions of Ethiopia (1896, 1935–36) and in 1936 became part of Italian East Africa. It was captured by the British in 1941, federated to Ethiopia in 1952, and made a province of Ethiopia in 1962. Three decades of guerrilla warfare by Eritrean secessionist groups ensued. A provisional Eritrean government was established in 1991 after the overthrow of the Ethiopian government, and independence came in 1993. A new constitution was ratified in 1997 but was never implemented. A border war with Ethiopia that began in 1998 ended in 2000, but boundary disputes persisted into the 21st century.

ermine, or STOAT, Species of the weasel family (*Mustela erminea*). Its white winter coat has historically adorned royal robes and is still used in the fur trade. Ermines are found in North America and northern Eurasia. They are most abundant in thickets, woodland, and semitimbered areas. In summer they are brown, with whitish throat, chest, and belly. Species are 5–12 in. (13–29 cm) long (excluding the 2–5-in., or 5–12-cm, tail) and weigh less than

11 oz (0.3 kg). Voracious carnivores, ermines feed on small mammals, birds, eggs, frogs, and, occasionally, invertebrates.

Eros, Greek god of love. Though Hesiod declared him one of the primeval gods born of Chaos, he was later said to be the son of Aphrodite. His Roman counterpart was Cupid. Eros was depicted as a beautiful winged youth carrying a bow and a quiver of arrows. In later literature and art he became increasingly younger, ending as an infant. His cult centre was at Thespiae, but he also shared a sanctuary with Aphrodite at Athens.

Eros, First asteroid found to travel mainly inside the orbit of Mars and the first to be landed on by a spacecraft. Discovered in 1898 and named for the Greek god of love, Eros is an elongated body about 20.5 mi (33 km) in its greatest dimension. It can approach to within 14 million mi (22 million km) of Earth. In 2000 the Near Earth Asteroid Rendezvous (NEAR Shoemaker) spacecraft orbited Eros, collecting a full year of data, and in 2001 it set down gently on Eros's surface.

erythema, Abnormal skin redness from increased blood flow, caused by dilation and irritation of surface capillaries. It has a variety of manifestations. In erythema multiforme, a symptom complex seen in several diseases, spots appear suddenly, often with a bull's-eye pattern. It may become life-threatening in severe cases; in mild cases symptoms may recur. Hormone treatment may be effective. In erythema nodosum, a hypersensitivity reaction usually associated with strep infection, drugs, or the disease sarcoidosis, painful red nodules appear in the deeper skin layer of the lower legs. They usually disappear over several weeks and do not recur. Another form of erythema is pellagra.

erythroblastosis fetalis, or HEMOLYTIC DISEASE OF THE NEWBORN, Anemia in an infant, caused when a pregnant woman produces antibodies to an antigen in her fetus's red blood cells. An Rh-negative woman with an Rh-positive fetus whose ABO blood group matches hers is likely to have an immune reaction after the first such pregnancy, which sensitizes her when fetal red blood cells enter her bloodstream, usually during labour. If blood typing shows incompatibility, an anti-Rh antibody injection given to the mother after the birth can destroy the fetal red cells, thus preventing trouble in a future pregnancy. If amniocentesis detects products of blood destruction, Rh-negative blood transfusions to the fetus before birth or exchange transfusion after it may save the baby's life. ABO incompatibilities are more common but usually less severe.

escalator, Moving staircase used as transportation between floors or levels in stores, airports, subways, and other mass pedestrian areas. The name was first applied to a moving stairway shown at the Paris Exposition of 1900. Modern escalators are electrically powered, driven by chain and sprocket, and held in place by two tracks. As the treads approach a landing, they pass through a comb device; a switch cuts off power if an object becomes jammed between comb and treads.

escape velocity, Speed sufficient for a body to escape from a gravitational centre of attraction without accelerating further. It decreases with altitude and equals the square root of 2 (about 1.414) times the speed needed to maintain a circular orbit at the same altitude. At the surface of Earth, disregarding atmospheric resistance, escape velocity is about 6.96 mi/second (11.2 km/second). Escape velocity from the surface of the Moon is about one-third of this.

eschatology, Theological doctrine of the "last things," or the end of the world. Mythological eschatologies depict an eternal struggle between order and chaos and celebrate the eternity of order and the repeatability of the origin of the world. The most notable expression of mythological eschatology is in Hinduism, which maintains belief in great cycles of the destruction and creation of the universe. Historical eschatologies are grounded in datable events that are perceived as fundamental to the progress of history. Judaism, Christianity, and Islam all have historical eschatologies. Eschatology in the Hebrew Scriptures sees the catastrophes that beset the people of Israel as due to their disobedience to the laws and will of God and holds that conformity to God's plan will result in renewal and the fulfillment of God's purpose. In Christianity, the end times are thought to have begun with the life and ministry of Jesus, the messiah who will return to establish the Kingdom of God. Millennialism focuses especially on Christ's second coming and the reign of the righteous on earth. In Shī'ite Islam it is believed that the mahdi, or restorer of the faith, will come to inaugurate the last judgment, in which the good will enter heaven and the evil will fall into hell. In Buddhism, eschatological traditions are associated with the Buddha Maitreya and with Pure Land Buddhism, as well as with individual efforts to achieve nirvana.

Eṣfahān, or IṢFAHĀN, City (pop., 2007 est.: 1,628,000), west-central Iran. An ancient Median town, it was known as Aspadana. It was a major city in the 11th–12th century under the Seljūq Turks and during the Ṣafavid dynasty of Iran (16th–18th century). Its golden age began in 1598 when Shah 'Abbās I made it his capital and rebuilt it into one of the 17th century's greatest cities. At its centre he created the immense Maydān-e Shāh, or "Royal Square" (now Maydān-e Emām; "Imam's Square"), a great rectangular garden enclosing the Masjed-e Shāh ("Royal Mosque"; now Masjed-e Emām). In 1722 Afghans took the city, and it went into decline. Recovery began in the 20th century, and it is now a major textile centre; its other industries include steelmaking and petroleum refining. The square was designated a UNESCO World Heritage site in 1979.

Two eyvāns of the Masjed-e Shāh of 'Abbās I the Great at Eṣfahān, Iran, 17th century.
Ray Manley/Shostal Associates

Eskimo, Group of peoples who, with the closely related Aleuts, constitute the native population of the Arctic as well as some of the subarctic regions of Greenland, Alaska (U.S.), Canada, and far eastern Russia (Siberia). Self-designations include such names as Inuit, Inupiat, Yupik, and Alutiiq, each being a more or less local variant meaning "the people." The name Eskimo, first applied by Europeans, may derive from an Innu (Montagnais) word for snowshoes; it is favoured by Arctic peoples in Alaska, while those in Canada and Greenland prefer Inuit. The Eskimo are of Asian origin, like the American Indians, but they are distinguishable from the latter by their climatic adaptations, the presence of the B blood type, and their languages (Eskimo-Aleut), all of which suggest that they are of distinctive origin. Traditional Eskimo culture was totally adapted to an extremely cold, snow- and icebound environment in which vegetable foods were almost nonexistent and caribou, fish, and marine mammals were the major food source. Harpoons and one-person kayaks or larger umiaks were used for hunting on the sea. Clothing was fashioned of caribou furs and sealskins. Snow-block igloos or semisubterranean sod-and-stone houses were used in winter, while in summer animal-skin tents were erected. Dogsleds were the basic means of land transport. Religion centred on shamans and the unseen world of spirits. By the late 20th century, snowmobiles and rifles had replaced dogsleds and harpoons. Many Eskimo abandoned their nomadic hunting pursuits and moved into northern towns and cities. Some formed cooperatives to market their handicrafts and other wares. Early 21st-century population estimates indicated more than 135,000 individuals of Eskimo descent, with approximately 85,000 living in North America, 50,000 in Greenland, and the remainder in Siberia.

Eskimo-Aleut languages, Family of languages spoken in Greenland, Canada, Alaska, U.S., and eastern Siberia by the Eskimo and Aleut peoples. Aleut, distantly related to the Eskimo languages, consists of eastern and western dialects; today both are spoken by fewer than 400 people. The Eskimo languages have two subgroups: Yupik (five languages), spoken on the Chukchi Peninsula in Siberia and in southwestern Alaska; and Inupiaq-Inuktitut, a continuum of dialects spoken across arctic Alaska and Canada to the coasts of Labrador and Greenland. Yupik languages are spoken today by about 13,000 people, while Inupiaq-Inuktitut has more than 100,000 speakers, nearly half of whom speak Greenlandic Inuktitut.

Esperanto, Artificial language created in 1887 by Lazarus Ludwig Zamenhof (1859–1917), a Polish oculist, for use as an international second language. Zamenhof's *Fundamento de Esperanto* (1905) outlines its basic principles. All words, derived from roots commonly found in the European languages, are spelled as pronounced, and grammar is simple and regular. Nouns have no gender and end in *-o*, and there is only one definite article, *la* (e.g., *la amiko*, "the friend"). Adjectives are marked by the ending *-a*. Verbs are regular and have only one form for each tense or mood. The Universal Esperanto Association (founded 1908) has members in 83 countries. Estimates of the number of Esperanto-speakers range from 100,000 to several million.

espionage, Practice of obtaining military, political, commercial, or other secret information by means of spies or illegal monitoring devices. It is sometimes distinguished from the broader category of intelligence gathering by its aggressive nature and its illegality. Counterespionage efforts are directed at detecting and thwarting espionage by others.

essay, Analytic, interpretative, or critical literary composition, usually dealing with its subject from a limited and often personal point of view. Flexible and versatile, the essay was perfected by Michel de Montaigne, who chose the name *essai* to emphasize that his compositions were "attempts" to express his thoughts and experiences. The essay has been the vehicle of literary and social criticism for some, while for others it could serve semipolitical, nationalistic, or polemical purposes and could have a detached, playful, earnest, or bitter tone.

Essen, City (pop., 2002 est.: city, 591,889; metro. area, 5,823,685), North Rhine–Westphalia state, western Germany. Located on the Ruhr River, it is the site of an extensive ironworks and steelworks. It was originally the seat of a convent (founded 852), whose 15th-century cathedral still stands. Essen became a city in the 10th century and was locally sovereign until 1802, when it passed to Prussia. The development of ironworks, steelworks, and coal mines stimulated growth in the 19th century. The city was largely destroyed in World War II, when it was targeted by the Allies as a centre of the German war industry. It has since been rebuilt with large, modern buildings, including concert halls, an economic research institute, and an art institute.

Essene, Member of a Jewish sect active in Palestine from the 2nd century BC to the 1st century AD. The Essenes formed small monastic communities whose members strictly observed the laws of Moses and the Sabbath and held their property in common. They withdrew from society, avoiding temple worship in Jerusalem and supporting themselves by manual labor. They usually excluded women. It is likely that the Dead Sea Scrolls were composed, copied, or collected by the Essenes.

Estonia, officially REPUBLIC OF ESTONIA, Country, northeastern Europe. It consists of a mainland area and some 1,500 islands and islets in the Baltic Sea. Area: 17,462 sq mi (45,227 sq km). Population: (2011 est.) 1,340,000. Capital: Tallinn. Estonians make up about two-thirds of the population. Russians account for almost one-fourth, and there are Ukrainian, Finnish, and Belarusian minorities. Language: Estonian (official). Religion: Christianity (other Christians [mostly unaffiliated], Protestant, Eastern Ortho-

dox). Currency: euro. The land is low and hilly, with numerous lakes, forests, and rivers. It has a cool-temperate and humid climate. The economy is mainly industrial, producing oil shale, machinery, fabricated metal products, and building materials. It is noted for its textiles, and woodworking is a traditional and important industry. Estonia is a unitary multiparty republic with one legislative body; the head of state is the president, and the head of government is the prime minister. It was invaded by Vikings in the 9th century and later by Danes, Swedes, and Russians, but the Estonians were able to withstand the assaults until the Danes took control in 1219. In 1346 the Danes sold their sovereignty over Estonia to the Teutonic Order, which was then in possession of Livonia (southern Estonia and Latvia). In the mid-16th century, Estonia was once again divided: northern Estonia capitulated to Sweden, and Poland gained Livonia, which it surrendered to Sweden in 1629. Russia acquired Livonia and Estonia in 1721. Nearly a century later, serfdom was abolished. From 1881 Estonia underwent intensive Russification. In 1918 Estonia obtained independence from Russia, which lasted until the Soviet Union occupied the country in 1940 and forcibly incorporated it into the U.S.S.R. Germany held the region (1941–44) during World War II, but the Soviet regime was restored in 1944, after which Estonia's economy was collectivized and integrated into that of the Soviet Union. In 1991, along with other parts of the former U.S.S.R., Estonia proclaimed its independence and subsequently held elections. In the 21st century Estonia continued negotiations with Russia to settle their common border, and, along with the other Baltic states, it joined the European Union in 2004.

estrogen, Any of a class of hormones that primarily influence the female reproductive system's development, maturation, and function. The three major estrogens—estradiol, estrone, and estriol—are produced mainly by the ovaries and placenta; the adrenal glands and the testes secrete smaller amounts. Estrogens affect the ovaries, vagina, fallopian tubes, uterus, and mammary glands and play crucial roles in puberty, menstruation, pregnancy, and parturition (labour). They also influence the structural differences between female and male bodies. In experimental animals, loss of estrogens diminishes mating desires and other behavioral patterns.

estuary, Partly enclosed coastal body of water in which river water is mixed with seawater. An estuary is thus defined by salinity rather than geography. Many coastal features designated by other names are in fact estuaries (e.g., Chesapeake Bay). Some of the oldest continuous civilizations have flourished in estuarine environments (e.g., the land between the Tigris and Euphrates rivers, the Nile delta, the Ganges delta, and the lower Huang He valley). Cities such as London (River Thames), New York (Hudson River), and Montreal (St. Lawrence River) developed on estuaries and became important commercial centres.

etching, Method of engraving in which lines or textures are bitten, or etched, into a metal plate, usually copper, with acid. The image produced has a spontaneity of line that comes from drawing on the plate in the same direct way as with pen or pencil on paper. The first etchings date from the early 16th century, but the basic principle had been used earlier for the decoration of armour. Among the pioneers of the medium were Albrecht Altdorfer, Albrecht Dürer, and Parmigianino; the greatest of all etchers was Rembrandt. In the 20th century, etching was especially popular for book illustration.

ethanol, or ETHYL ALCOHOL, or GRAIN ALCOHOL, Organic compound, most important of the alcohols, chemical formula CH_3CH_2OH. Produced by fermentation, it is the intoxicating ingredient in alcoholic beverages. Ethanol for industrial purposes is made by either fermentation or chemical synthesis, then purified by distillation and, to avoid the tax levied on ethyl alcohol for drinking, made unfit to drink by mixing it with compounds such as methanol, benzene, or kerosene. Ethanol has many uses as a solvent, a raw material, an extraction medium, an antifreeze, an antiseptic, and a gasoline additive and substitute. It is toxic, depressing the central nervous system, and addictive to some persons. Moderate amounts depress the inhibitory activities of the brain and so appear to stimulate the mind, but larger amounts seriously impair coordination and judgment; excessive consumption can cause coma and death. Taking ethanol in combination with barbiturates or related drugs is especially dangerous.

Ethernet, Telecommunications networking protocol introduced by Xerox Corp. in 1979. It was developed as an inexpensive way of sending information quickly between office machines connected together in a single room or building, but it rapidly became a standard computer interconnection method. The original data rate of 10 megabits per second has been increased to 100 megabits per second for a new standard known as fast ethernet. The original specification required coaxial cable as the communications medium, but costs have been reduced through the employment of simple paired wires.

ethics, Branch of philosophy that seeks to determine the correct application of moral notions such as good and bad and right and wrong or a theory of the application or nature of such notions. Ethics is traditionally subdivided into normative ethics, metaethics, and applied ethics. Normative ethics seeks to establish norms or standards of conduct; a crucial question in this field is whether actions are to be judged right or wrong based on their consequences or based on their conformity to some moral rule, such as "Do not tell a lie." Theories that adopt the former basis of judgment are called consequentialist; those that adopt the latter are known as deontological. Metaethics is concerned with the nature of ethical judgments and theories. Since the beginning of the 20th century, much work in metaethics has focused on the logical and semantic aspects of moral language. Some major metaethical theories are naturalism, intuitionism, emotivism, and prescriptivism. Applied ethics, as the name implies, consists of the application of normative ethical theories to practical moral problems (e.g., abortion). Among the major fields of applied ethics are bioethics, business ethics, legal ethics, and medical ethics.

Ethiopia, officially FEDERAL DEMOCRATIC REPUBLIC OF ETHIOPIA, formerly ABYSSINIA, Country, eastern Africa. It is situated on the Horn of Africa, the continent's easternmost projection. Area: 410,678 sq mi (1,063,652 sq km). Population: (2011 est.) 82,102,000. Capital: Addis Ababa. The people are about one-third Amhara and one-third Oromo, with the balance mostly Tigray, Afar, Somali, Saho, and Agew. Languages: Amharic, Oromo. Religions: Christianity (predominantly Ethiopian Orthodox; also Protestant), Islam, traditional beliefs. Currency: birr. The landlocked country is mountainous in the north, with lowlands to the east and west. The central Ethiopian Plateau is split by the Great Rift Valley, which divides the eastern and western highlands. The climate is temperate in the highlands, which are mainly savanna, and hot in the arid lowlands. Intensive farming and deforestation have led to severe erosion; this, along with periodic droughts, has produced periodic food shortages. The country's once abundant wildlife has been decimated; many species are endangered. Ethiopia is one of the world's poorest countries. Agriculture is mainly for subsistence, with cereals the main crop. Livestock is also important. Coffee is the main export, followed by hides and skins. A new federal republic was established in 1995; it has two legislative houses, the head of state is the president, and the head of government is the prime minister. Ethiopia, the Biblical land of Kush, was inhabited from earliest antiquity and was once under ancient Egyptian rule. Ge'ez-speaking agriculturalists established the kingdom of Da'amat in the 7th century BCE. After 300 BCE they were superseded by the kingdom of Aksum, whose King Menilek I was, according to legend, the son of King Solomon and the Queen of Sheba. Christianity was introduced in the 4th century CE and became widespread. Ethiopia's prosperous Mediterranean trade was cut off by the Muslim Arabs in the 7th–8th century, and the area's interests were directed southward. Contact with Europe

resumed in the late 15th century with the arrival of the Portuguese. Modern Ethiopia began with the reign of Tewodros II, who began the consolidation of the country. In the wake of European encroachment, the coastal region was made an Italian colony in 1889, but under Emperor Menilek II the Italians were defeated and ousted in 1896. Ethiopia prospered under his rule, and his modernization programs were continued by Emperor Haile Selassie in the 1930s. In 1936 Italy again gained control of the country and held it as part of Italian East Africa until 1941, when it was occupied by the British. Ethiopia incorporated Eritrea in 1952. In 1974 Haile Selassie was deposed, and a Marxist government, plagued by civil wars and famine, controlled the country until 1991. In 1993 Eritrea gained its independence, but there were continued border conflicts with it and neighbouring Somalia.

ethnic cleansing, The creation of an ethnically homogenous geographic area through the elimination of unwanted ethnic groups by deportation, forcible displacement, or genocide. Ethnic cleansing also has involved attempts to remove physical vestiges of the targeted group in the territory through the destruction and desecration of monuments, cemeteries, and houses of worship. Although some critics of the term have claimed that ethnic cleansing is simply a form of genocide, defenders of the usage have noted that, whereas the murder of an ethnic, racial, or religious group is the primary intention of a genocidal policy, the chief goal of ethnic cleansing is the establishment of homogenous lands, which may be achieved by any of a number of methods including genocide. The term was widely employed in the 1990s to describe the brutal treatment of Bosniacs (Bosnian Muslims), ethnic Serbs in the Krajina region of Croatia, and ethnic Albanians in the Serbian province of Kosovo during the conflicts that erupted in the wake of the disintegration of Yugoslavia.

ethnic group, Social group or category of the population that, in a larger society, is set apart and bound together by common ties of language, nationality, or culture. Ethnic diversity, the legacy of political conquests and migrations, is one aspect of the social complexity found in most contemporary societies. The nation-state has traditionally been uneasy with ethnic diversity, and nation-states have often attempted to eliminate or expel ethnic groups. Most nations today practice some form of pluralism, which usually rests on a combination of toleration, interdependence, and separatism. The concept of ethnicity is more important today than ever, as a result of the spread of doctrines of freedom, self-determination, and democracy.

ethnocentrism, Tendency to interpret or evaluate other cultures in terms of one's own. Generally considered a human universal, it is evident in the widespread practice of labeling outsiders as "savages" or "barbarians" simply because their societies differ from those of the dominant culture. Early anthropologists often reflected this tendency, as did Sir John Lubbock, who characterized all nonliterate peoples as being without religion, and Lucien Lévy-Bruhl, who found them to have a "prelogical mentality" because their worldview was unlike that of western Europe. The opposite of ethnocentrism is cultural relativism, the understanding of cultural phenomena within the context in which they occur.

ethnography, Descriptive study of a particular human society. Contemporary ethnography is based almost entirely on fieldwork. The ethnographer lives among the people who are the subject of study for a year or more, learning the local language and participating in everyday life while striving to maintain a degree of objective detachment. He or she usually cultivates close relationships with "informants" who can provide specific information on aspects of cultural life. While detailed written notes are the mainstay of fieldwork, ethnographers may also use tape recorders, cameras, or video recorders. Contemporary ethnographies have both influenced and been influenced by literary theory.

ethnomusicology, Scholarly study of the world's musics from various perspectives. Although it had antecedents in the 18th and early 19th centuries, the field expanded with the development of recording technologies in the late 19th century. The term *ethnomusicology* was introduced about 1950, and the field subsequently became standard in academic institutions. Some ethnomusicologists consider themselves allied with musicology and others with anthropology. Later areas of concern include the study of popular musics as reflections of political, social, and economic movements.

ethology, Study of animal behaviour. It is a combination of laboratory and field science, with strong ties to other disciplines (e.g., neuroanatomy, ecology, evolution). Though many naturalists have studied aspects of animal behaviour through the centuries, the modern science of ethology is considered to have arisen as a discrete discipline with the work in the 1920s of Nikolaas Tinbergen and Konrad Lorenz. Interested in the behavioral process rather than in a particular animal group, ethologists often study one type of behaviour (e.g., aggression) in various unrelated animals.

Etna, Mount, Active volcano, eastern coast of Sicily, Italy. The highest active volcano in Europe, its elevation is more than 10,000 ft (3,200 m); its base has a circumference of about 93 mi (150 km). Mount Etna has repeatedly erupted over the centuries, most violently in 1669, when the lava flow destroyed villages on the lower slope and submerged part of the town of Catania. Activity was almost continuous in the decade following 1971, and in 1983 an eruption that lasted four months prompted authorities to explode dynamite in an attempt to divert lava flows. Mount Etna also experienced violent eruptions in 2001–02, prompting the Italian government to declare a state of emergency.

Etruscan, Any member of an ancient people of Etruria, whose urban civilization reached its height in the 6th century BC. Their origins are obscure. By the 7th century they had incorporated all of Tuscany into their territory, and in the 6th century they pushed north to the Po River valley and became rulers of Rome. The Etruscans gave the city its first public works, including walls and a sewer system. By the end of the 6th century, pressure from other peoples in the region, including Greeks, Romans, and Gauls, weakened Etruria. The Romans expelled their dynasty in 509 BC. The Etruscans had a commercial and agricultural civilization and left a rich cultural heritage, including wall frescoes and realistic tomb portraits. Many features of their culture were adopted by the Romans.

Etruscan art, (*c.* 8th–4th centuries BC) Art of the people of Etruria. The art of the Etruscans falls into three categories: funerary, urban, and sacred. Because of Etruscan attitudes toward the after-

A detail from a fresco dating from the 5th century BC shows Etruscan musicians wearing tunics and sandals.
Scala/Art Resource, New York

life, most of the art that remains is funerary. Characteristic achievements are the wall frescoes—painted in two-dimensional style—and realistic terra-cotta portraits found in tombs. Bronze reliefs and sculptures are also common. Tombs found at Caere, carved underground out of soft volcanic rock, resemble houses. Urban architecture was another specialty; Etruscans were among the first in the Mediterranean to lay out cities with a grid plan, a practice copied by the Romans. In the sacred area, Etruscan temples had a deep front porch with columns and abundant terra-cotta roof sculptures, such as those from the temple at Veii (late 6th century). Etruscan art was influenced by Greek art and in turn influenced the development of realistic portraiture in Italy.

Euboea, Greek ÉVVOIA, Island, Greece, in the Aegean Sea. The second largest of the Greek islands, it is about 110 mi (180 km) long and 4–30 mi (6–48 km) wide. It is mainly mountainous but includes the fertile plain of the Lilas River, which was in antiquity a famous horse-breeding region. Euboea is connected with Boeotia by a bridge built by the Chalcidians. It was dominated by Athens for much of the 5th century BC, while its main cities of Chalcis and Eretria were involved in the Persian and Peloponnesian wars. From 146 BC it was part of the Roman province of Macedon. Euboea was controlled by Venice from 1366, conquered by the Turks in 1470, and passed to Greece in 1830.

eucalyptus, Any of the more than 500 species of mostly very large trees in the genus *Eucalyptus*, in the myrtle family, native to Australia, New Zealand, Tasmania, and nearby islands. Many species are grown widely throughout the temperate regions of the world as shade trees or in forestry plantations. Because they grow rapidly, many species attain great height. The leaf glands of many species, especially *E. salicifolia* and *E. globulus*, contain a volatile, aromatic oil known as eucalyptus oil, used mostly in medicines. Eucalyptus wood is used extensively in Australia as fuel, and the timber is commonly used in buildings and fencing. The bark of many species is used in papermaking and tanning.

Eucharist, or HOLY COMMUNION, or LORD'S SUPPER, Christian rite commemorating the Last Supper of Jesus with his disciples. On the night before his death, according to the Christian scriptures, Jesus consecrated bread and wine and gave them to his disciples, saying "this is my body" and "this is my blood." He also commanded his followers to repeat this rite in his memory, and the Eucharist traditionally involves consecration of bread and wine by the clergy and their consumption by worshipers. Although celebrated spontaneously when the first Christians gathered to share a meal, the Eucharist quickly became a central part of the formal worship service and remained that way despite the many controversies over its nature and meaning. Intended as a means of fostering unity in the church, it has also been a source of division because of differing interpretations of its nature. In Roman Catholicism the Eucharist is a sacrament, and the bread and wine are thought to become the actual body and blood of Jesus through transubstantiation. Anglicans and Lutherans also emphasize the divine presence in the offering and recognize it as a sacrament, while others regard it as a memorial with largely symbolic meaning. Also controversial has been the belief in the Eucharist as a sacrifice, the renewed offering of Christ each time the rite is celebrated at the altar.

Euclid (fl. *c.* 300 BC, Alexandria, Egypt), Greek mathematician of antiquity, known primarily for his highly influential treatise on geometry, the *Elements*. He founded a school in Alexandria during the reign of Ptolemy I. Little is known of his life, but there are many anecdotes. In the most famous, asked by Ptolemy if there is a shorter way to geometry than through his *Elements*, Euclid replies, "There is no royal road to geometry." The *Elements*, based on the works of earlier mathematicians, is a brilliant synthesis of old and new. It has been a major influence on rational thought and a model for many philosophical treatises, and it has set a standard for logical thinking and methods of proof in the sciences. The starting point not just of Euclidean geometry but of an approach to reasoning, it is sometimes said to be the most translated, published, and studied work after the Bible.

Euclidean geometry, Study of points, lines, angles, surfaces, and solids based on Euclid's axioms. Its importance lies less in its results than in the systematic method Euclid used to develop and present them. This axiomatic method has been the model for many systems of rational thought, even outside mathematics, for over 2,000 years. From 10 axioms and postulates, Euclid deduced 465 theorems, or propositions, concerning aspects of plane and solid geometric figures. This work was long held to constitute an accurate description of the physical world and to provide a sufficient basis for understanding it. During the 19th century, rejection of some of Euclid's postulates resulted in two non-Euclidean geometries that proved just as valid and consistent.

eukaryote, Any organism composed of one or more cells, each of which contains a clearly defined nucleus enclosed by a membrane, along with organelles (small, self-contained, cellular parts that perform specific functions). The organelles include mitochondria, chloroplasts, a Golgi apparatus, an endoplasmic reticulum, and lysosomes. All organisms except bacteria and archaea are eukaryotes; bacteria and archaea are prokaryotes.

Euler's formula, Either of two important mathematical theorems of Leonhard Euler. The first is a topological invariance relating the number of faces, vertices, and edges of any polyhedron. It is written $F + V = E + 2$, where F is the number of faces, V the number of vertices, and E the number of edges. A cube, for example, has 6 faces, 8 vertices, and 12 edges, and satisfies this formula. The second formula, used in trigonometry, says $e^{ix} = \cos x + i\sin x$ where e is the base of the natural logarithm and i is the square root of -1. When x is equal to π or 2π, the formula yields two elegant expressions relating π, e, and i: $e^{i\pi} = -1$ and $e^{2i\pi} = 1$.

eunuch, Castrated human male. From remote antiquity on, eunuchs were employed in the Middle East and China as guards and servants in harems or other women's quarters and as chamberlains to kings. The eunuchs' confidential position frequently enabled them to exercise an important influence over their royal masters. Many of the patriarchs of Constantinople during Byzantine times were eunuchs. Eunuch advisers disappeared as a class only with the end of the Ottoman Empire.

euphonium, or TENOR TUBA, Large valved brass instrument, the leading lower-pitched instrument in military bands. It developed from the valved bugle and cornet in Germany *c.* 1840. It has four valves and a wide conical bore resembling the tuba's. Its range is an octave below the trumpet and cornet. It is played either vertically or with the bell facing forward. The very similar baritone has the same range and transposition and is distinguished only by its narrower bore. Both are essential members of bands of all kinds and are often given significant solo roles.

Euphrates River, Turkish FIRAT NEHRI, Arabic NAHR AL FURĀT, River, Middle East. The largest river in Southwest Asia, it rises in Turkey and flows southeast across Syria and through Iraq. Formed by the confluence of the Karasu and the Murat rivers in the high Armenian plateau, the Euphrates descends between major ranges of the Taurus Mountains to the Syrian plateau. It then flows through western and central Iraq to unite with the Tigris and continues, as Shatt al-Arab, to the Persian Gulf. In all, it is 1,740 mi (2,800 km) long. Its valley was heavily irrigated in ancient times, and many great cities, some of whose ruins remain, lined its banks. With the Tigris, it defines an area known historically as Mesopotamia.

euro, Single currency of 17 countries of the European Union (EU), including Germany, France, and Italy. It is also the official currency in several areas outside the EU. The euro was adopted as a unit of exchange in January 1999. Those who advocated the cur-

rency believed it would strengthen Europe as an economic power, increase international trade, simplify monetary transactions, and lead to pricing equality throughout Europe. Euro currency notes and coins were introduced in January 2002 and became the sole national currency in all participating countries by March 1. Britain and Sweden decided not to adopt the euro immediately, and voters in Denmark rejected it.

Eurocommunism, Trend among European communist parties toward independence from Soviet Communist Party doctrine in the 1970s and '80s. The term, coined in the mid-1970s, received wide publicity after the publication of Santiago Carrillo's *Eurocommunism and the State* (1977). The Eurocommunist movement rejected the Soviet doctrine of one monolithic world communist movement and advocated instead that each country's communist party base its policies on the traditions and needs of its own country. With Mikhail Gorbachev's encouragement, all communist parties took independent courses in the late 1980s. Most of the European communist parties declined after the breakup of the Soviet Union.

Europa, In Greek mythology, the daughter either of Phoenix or of Agenor, king of Phoenicia. Her beauty inspired the love of Zeus, who approached her in the form of a white bull and carried her off across the sea to Crete. After bearing Zeus three sons, she married the king of Crete, who adopted her sons. They grew up to become King Minos of Crete, King Rhadamanthus of the Cyclades, and Prince Sarpedon of Lycia. On Crete she was worshiped under the name Hellotis. The continent of Europe is named for her.

Europe, Second smallest continent on Earth. It is bordered by the Arctic Ocean, the Atlantic Ocean, and the Mediterranean, Black, and Caspian seas. The continent's generally accepted eastern boundary runs along the Ural Mountains and the Emba (Zhem) River of Kazakhstan. Its area includes numerous islands, archipelagoes, and peninsulas. Indented by bays, fjords, and seas, continental Europe's irregular coastline is about 24,000 mi (38,000 km) long. Area (approximate, including European Russia): 4,000,000 sq mi (10,400,000 sq km). Population (2007 est.): 700,000,000. The greater part of Europe combines low elevations with low relief; about three-fifths of the land is below 600 ft (180 m) above sea level, and another one-third is between 600 and 3,000 ft (180 and 900 m). The highest points are in the mountain systems crossing the southern part of the continent, including the Pyrenees, Alps, Apennines, Carpathians, and Balkan mountains. A well-watered continent with many rivers, Europe has few sizable lakes. Glaciers cover a significant area, mostly in the north. Roughly one-third of Europe is arable, with much of that land devoted to cereals, principally wheat and barley. About one-third is forested. Europe was the first of the world's regions to develop a modern economy based on commercial agriculture and industry, and it remains one of the world's major industrial regions, with average annual income per capita among the world's highest. The people of Europe constitute about one-tenth of the world's population. Most of the continent's native languages belong to either the Romance, Germanic, or Slavic language groups. Europe's population is mostly Christian.

Modern humans supplanted the scanty Neanderthal population in Europe about 40,000 years ago, and by the beginning of the 2nd millennium BCE the general population groups that would become the historical peoples and countries of Europe were in place. The Greek civilizations were the earliest in Europe, and in the Classical period the Greeks were a conduit for the advanced civilizations of the Middle East, which, along with the unique Greek contribution, laid the foundation for European civilization. By the mid-2nd century BCE the Greeks had come under Roman control, and the vast Roman Empire brought to the conquered parts of Europe the civilization the Greeks had begun. It was through the Romans that Christianity penetrated Europe. The Roman Empire in the West finally collapsed in the 5th century CE, which led to an extensive breakdown of Classical civilization. During the period that followed, known as the Middle Ages, the idea of Europe as a distinct cultural unit emerged. The subsequent Renaissance (15th–16th centuries) began the modern European traditions of science, exploration, and discovery. The Protestant Reformation of the 16th century ended the dominance of the Roman Catholic Church over western and northern Europe, and the Enlightenment period of the 17th and 18th centuries stressed the primacy of reason. In the late 18th century, Enlightenment ideals helped spur the French Revolution, which toppled Europe's most powerful monarchy and spearheaded the movement toward democracy and equality. The late 18th century also marked the beginning of the Industrial Revolution, which led to Europe's military and political dominance over much of the world for the next century. In the early 20th century the European powers were divided by World War I, which led to the effective end of monarchy in Europe and created a host of new countries in central and eastern Europe. World War II marked a waning of world power among the states of western Europe and was followed by the rise of communism in eastern Europe, with the Soviet Union and its satellites sharply divided from the rest of the continent. The Soviet Union collapsed in the late 20th century, leading to the demise of communist regimes throughout Europe. Soviet satellites became independent, and most began to democratize. East and West Germany were reunified. Yugoslavia and its successor states, however, experienced ethnic conflict .

Europe, Council of, Organization of more than 40 European states formed to promote European unity, protect human rights, and facilitate social and economic progress. Established in 1949 by 10 western European states, it has devised international agreements on human rights and established a number of special bodies and expert committees on social, legal, and cultural issues. It is headquartered in Strasbourg, France. (The Council of Europe should not be confused with the European Council, which is a policy-making body of the European Union.)

European Coal and Steel Community (ECSC), Administrative agency designed to integrate the coal and steel industries of France, West Germany, Italy, Belgium, the Netherlands, and Luxembourg. It originated in the plan of Robert Schuman (1950) to establish a common market for coal and steel by those countries willing to submit to an independent authority. Created in 1952, the ECSC came to include all members of the European Union. It initially removed barriers to trade in coal, coke, steel, pig iron, and scrap iron; it later supervised the reduction of its members' excess production. In 1967 its governing bodies were merged into the European Community. When the treaty expired in 2002, the ECSC was dissolved.

European Community (EC), Organization formed in 1967 with the merger of the European Economic Community, European Coal and Steel Community, and European Atomic Energy Community. The merger created a single Commission of the European Community and a single Council of Ministers. Other executive, legislative, and judicial bodies also were collected under the umbrella of the EC. In 1993 the EC became the basis of the European Union, and the European Economic Community was renamed the European Community.

European Defense Community (EDC), Attempt by western European powers, with U.S. support, to counterbalance the overwhelming conventional military ascendancy of the Soviet Union in Europe by creating a supranational European army, including West German forces. A treaty was concluded in 1952, but the French parliament's refusal to ratify the treaty in 1954 brought an end to the project. One consequence of the French action was the decision in 1955 to rearm West Germany and allow its entry into NATO. In 1955 the EDC was replaced by the Western European Union.

European Free Trade Association (EFTA), International organization whose purpose is to remove barriers to trade in indus-

trial goods among its members. The EFTA's current members are Iceland, Liechtenstein, Norway, and Switzerland. It was formed in 1960 by Austria, Denmark, Norway, Portugal, Sweden, Switzerland, and Britain as an alternative to the European Economic Community (EEC). Some of those countries later left the EFTA and joined the EEC. In the 1990s Iceland, Liechtenstein, and Norway joined the European Economic Area, which also included all members of the European Union. Each country in the EFTA maintains its own commercial policy toward countries outside the group.

European Space Agency (ESA), French AGENCE SPATIALE EUROPÉENNE, Space and space-technology research organization headquartered in Paris. It was founded in 1975 from the merger of the European Launcher Development Organisation (ELDO) and the European Space Research Organisation (ESRO), both established in 1964. Members are Austria, Belgium, Britain, Denmark, Finland, France, Germany, Ireland, Italy, the Netherlands, Norway, Portugal, Spain, Sweden, and Switzerland. Canada, through a special cooperative agreement, participates in some projects. The ESA developed the Ariane series of space launch vehicles, and it supports a launch facility in French Guiana. It has launched a system of meteorological satellites (Meteosat) as well as the Giotto space probe, which examined the nucleus of Halley's Comet, and Hipparcos, a satellite that measured the parallaxes, positions, and proper motions of more than 100,000 stars. It is also a participant in the construction of the International Space Station.

European Union (EU), Organization of European countries, formed in 1993 to oversee their economic and political integration. It was created by the Maastricht Treaty and ratified by all members of the European Community (EC), out of which the EU developed. The successful EC had made its members more receptive to greater integration and provided a framework for unified action by member countries in security and foreign policy and for cooperation in police and justice matters. In pursuit of its major goal to create a common monetary system, the EU established the euro, which replaced the national currencies of 12 of the 15 EU members in 2002. Originally confined to western Europe, the EU enlarged to include several central and eastern European countries in the early 21st century. The EU's principal institutions are the European Community, the Council of Ministers (a forum for individual ministries), the European Commission (an administrative bureaucracy), the European Parliament, the European Court of Justice, and the European Central Bank.

euthanasia, or MERCY KILLING, Painless killing of a person who has a painful incurable disease or incapacitating disorder. Most legal systems consider it murder, though in many jurisdictions a physician may lawfully decide not to prolong the patient's life or may give drugs to relieve pain even if they shorten the patient's life. Associations promoting legal euthanasia exist in many countries. The legalization movement has gained ground with advancing medical technology, which has been used to prolong the lives of patients who are enduring extreme suffering or who are comatose or unable to communicate their wishes. Euthanasia was legalized in the Netherlands in 2001 and in Belgium in 2002. In 1997 Oregon became the first state in the U.S. to decriminalize physician-assisted suicide.

evangelicalism, Protestant movement that stresses conversion experiences, the Bible as the only basis for faith, and evangelism at home and abroad. The religious revival that occurred in Europe and America during the 18th century was generally referred to as the evangelical revival. It included Pietism in Europe, Methodism in Britain, and the Great Awakening in America. In London in 1846, the Evangelical Alliance was organized by evangelical Christians from several denominations and countries. In the U.S., the movement grew, in part, because of the popularity of preachers such as Billy Graham, the creation of institutions such as Wheaton College, the publishing of the periodical *Christianity To-*

day, and the founding of professional organizations and associations, such as the National Association of Evangelicals (1942). Developing a sense of international and interdenominational unity, evangelicals formed the World Evangelical Fellowship (WEF) in 1951. More than 110 regional and national organizations and some 110 million people are affiliated with the WEF, now headquartered in Singapore. *See* Christian fundamentalism; Pentecostalism.

evapotranspiration, Loss of water from the soil both by evaporation from the soil surface and by transpiration from the leaves of the plants growing on it. Factors that affect the rate of evapotranspiration include the amount of solar radiation, atmospheric vapor pressure, temperature, wind, and soil moisture. Evapotranspiration accounts for most of the water lost from the soil during the growth of a crop. Estimation of evapotranspiration rates is thus important in planning irrigation schemes.

event horizon, Boundary marking the limits of a black hole. At the event horizon, the escape velocity is equal to the speed of light. Since general relativity states that nothing can travel faster than the speed of light, nothing inside the event horizon can ever cross the boundary and escape beyond it, including light. Thus, nothing that enters a black hole can get out or can be observed from outside the event horizon. Likewise, any radiation generated inside the horizon can never escape beyond it. For a nonrotating black hole, the Schwarzschild radius delimits a spherical event horizon. Rotating black holes have distorted, nonspherical event horizons. Since the event horizon is not a material surface but rather merely a mathematically defined demarcation boundary, nothing prevents matter or radiation from entering a black hole, only from exiting one. Though black holes themselves may not radiate energy, electromagnetic radiation and matter particles may be radiated from just outside the event horizon via Hawking radiation.

Everest, Mount, Tibetan CHOMOLUNGMA, Nepali SAGARMATHA, Peak on the crest of the Himalayas, southern Asia. The highest point on Earth, with a summit at 29,035 ft (8,850 m), it lies on the border between Nepal and the Tibet Autonomous Region of China. Numerous attempts to climb Everest were made from 1921; the summit was finally reached by Edmund Hillary of New Zealand and Tenzing Norgay of Nepal in 1953. In dispute is whether the English explorer George Mallory, whose body was discovered below Everest's peak in 1999, had actually reached the peak earlier, in 1924, and was descending it when he died. The formerly accepted elevation of 29,028 ft (8,848 m), established in the early 1950s, was recalculated in the late 1990s.

Everglades, Subtropical saw-grass marsh region, southern Florida, U.S. Covering more than 4,300 sq mi (11,100 sq km), the area has water moving slowly through it from the lip of Lake Okeechobee to mangrove swamps bordering the Gulf of Mexico and Florida Bay. Everglades National Park, established in 1947, encompasses the southwestern portion of the marsh, covering 2,357 sq mi (6,105 sq km). The largest subtropical wilderness left in the continental U.S., it has a mild climate, which provides an environment for myriad birds, alligators, snakes, and turtles. A large portion of the glades has been reclaimed by drainage canals, altering the habitats of many species.

evergreen, Any plant that retains its leaves through the winter and into the following summer or through several years. Many tropical species of broad-leaved flowering plants are evergreen, but in cold-temperate and Arctic areas the evergreens commonly are cone-bearing shrubs or trees (conifers), such as pines and firs. The leaves of evergreens usually are thicker and more leathery than those of deciduous trees and often are needlelike or scalelike in cone-bearing trees. A leaf (or needle) may remain on an evergreen tree for two years or longer and may fall during any season.

evidence, In law, something (e.g., testimony, documents, or physical objects) presented at a judicial or administrative proceeding for the purpose of establishing the truth or falsity of an allegation of fact. To preserve legal due process and to prevent the jury from being misled, an extensive body of rules has sprung up regarding the handling of evidence. In the U.S., all federal and many state courts adhere to the *Federal Rules of Evidence*, which covers such elements as types of evidence, admissibility, relevance, competency of witnesses, confessions and admissions, expert testimony, and authentication. Most evidence received at trial is in the form of verbal statements of witnesses, who are subject to questioning by attorneys from both sides. Two important categories of evidence are direct evidence, which is offered by a witness whose knowledge of a factual matter is firsthand (as through sight or hearing), and circumstantial evidence.

evil eye, Superstition holding that a glance can cause injury or death to those on whom it falls. The belief was found in ancient Greece and Rome as well as in folk cultures around the world, and it has persisted into modern times. Children and animals are believed to be particularly vulnerable. The evil eye is often thought to stem from envy and malice toward prosperity and beauty, and thus in many cultures unguarded praise of one's possessions or children is thought to invite misfortune. Safeguards include amulets, charms, and sacred texts; in Asia children may have their faces blackened for protection.

evolution, Biological theory that animals and plants have their origin in other preexisting types and that the distinguishable differences are due to modifications in successive generations. It is one of the keystones of modern biological theory. In 1858 Charles Darwin and Alfred Russel Wallace jointly published a paper on evolution. The next year Darwin presented his major treatise *On the Origin of Species by Means of Natural Selection*, which revolutionized all later biological study. The heart of Darwinian evolution is the mechanism of natural selection. Surviving individuals, which vary in some way that enables them to live longer and reproduce, pass on their advantage to succeeding generations. In 1937 Theodosius Dobzhansky applied Mendelian genetics to Darwinian theory, contributing to a new understanding of evolution as the cumulative action of natural selection on small genetic variations in whole populations. Part of the proof of evolution is in the fossil record, which shows a succession of gradually changing forms leading up to those known today. Structural similarities and similarities in embryonic development among living forms also point to common ancestry. Molecular biology (especially the study of genes and proteins) provides the most detailed evidence of evolutionary change. Though the theory of evolution is accepted by nearly the entire scientific community, it has sparked much controversy from Darwin's time to the present; many of the objections have come from religious leaders and thinkers who believe that elements of the theory conflict with literal interpretations of the Bible.

excommunication, Form of censure by which a member of a religious body is excluded from the congregation of believers and from the rites of the church. Excommunication has been used in various religions, notably Christianity, as a punishment for grave offenses such as heresy. In Roman Catholicism an excommunicated person is barred from receiving the sacraments and from burial in consecrated ground. The offender may be absolved by a priest (in some cases, only by a bishop or the pope) and received back into the church after confessing his or her sin and doing penance for it. In Protestant denominations other terms, such as "church discipline," may be attached to essentially the same censure. Although now seldom used, the practice of *ḥerem* in Judaism was a form of excommunication that excluded people from the community for prescribed times or forbade them from hearing the Torah. The term is also applied to the expulsion of Buddhist monks from the sangha.

excretion, Bodily process for disposing of undigested food waste products and nitrogenous by-products of metabolism, regulating water content, maintaining acid-base balance, and controlling osmotic pressure to promote homeostasis. It refers to both urination and defecation and to the processes that take place in the digestive and urinary systems, as the kidney and liver filter wastes, toxins, and drugs from the blood and food reaches the last stage of digestion. Ammonia from protein digestion, the primary excretory product, is converted to urea to be excreted in urine.

exegesis, Scholarly interpretation of religious texts, using linguistic, historical, and other methods. In Judaism and Christianity, it has been used extensively in the study of the Bible. Textual criticism tries to establish the accuracy of biblical texts. Philological criticism deals with grammar, vocabulary, and style in pursuit of faithful translation. Literary criticism classifies texts according to style and attempts to establish authorship, date, and audience. Tradition criticism seeks the sources of biblical materials and traces their development. Redaction criticism examines the way pieces of the tradition have been assembled into a literary composition by editors. Form criticism studies the way narratives are shaped by the cultures that produce them. Historical criticism looks at a text's historical context.

exercise, Training of the body to improve health and fitness. Different types have different purposes, including aerobics for heart and respiratory function and weight loss, weight-bearing exercise for bone strength, weight training for muscle strength, and stretching for flexibility. Specific exercises are used in physical medicine and rehabilitation. Benefits include lower blood pressure, higher HDL cholesterol, improved disease resistance, and better general well-being.

Exeter, ancient ISCA DUMNONIORUM, City and administrative district (pop., 2001: 111,078), administrative and historic county of Devon, England. The county town (seat) of Devon, it is located on the River Exe about 10 mi (16 km) above the English Channel and commands an important river crossing. An early British tribe, the Dumnonii, made Exeter their centre; when it was taken by the Romans, they named it Isca Dumnoniorum. The main town in southwestern England during the Middle Ages, Exeter was subjected to a number of sieges. Alfred the Great twice held it against the Danes (877 and *c.* 894); the Danes finally took the city in 1003 but lost it in 1068 to William I (the Conqueror). Exeter's Norman cathedral, consecrated in 1133, houses the Exeter Book, the largest collection extant of Old English poetry. The city has light manufacturing and is a service centre for an extensive region.

Søren Kierkegaard, drawing by Christian Kierkegaard, c. 1840; in a private collection.
Courtesy of the Royal Danish Ministry of Foreign Affairs

existentialism, Philosophical movement oriented toward two major themes, the analysis of human existence and the centrality of human choice. Existentialism's chief theoretical energies are thus devoted to questions about ontology and decision. It traces its roots to the writings of Søren Kierkegaard and Friedrich Nietzsche. As a philosophy of human existence, existentialism found its best 20th-century exponent in Karl Jaspers; as a philosophy of human decision, its foremost representative was Jean-Paul Sartre. Sartre finds the essence of human existence in freedom—in the duty of self-determination and the freedom of choice—and therefore spends much time describing the human tendency toward "bad faith," reflected in humanity's perverse attempts to deny its own responsibility and flee from the truth of its inescapable freedom.

Exodus, Second book of the Old Testament. The title refers to the departure of the Israelites from Egypt under Moses in the 13th century BC. The book begins with the story of the Israelites' enslavement in Egypt and God's call to Moses to become a prophet. It tells of the plagues sent to persuade the pharaoh to free the Israelites, and it recalls their crossing of the Sea of Reeds (or the Red Sea) and their 40 years of wandering in the Sinai desert. It also recounts how God made a covenant with Israel at Mount Sinai, handing down the Ten Commandments. In Exodus God establishes his reliability as Israel's protector and savior, and lays claim to its loyalty and obedience.

exogamy and endogamy, Practices controlling the relation of the sexes in the selection of marital partners. Exogamous groups require their members to marry outside the group, sometimes even specifying the group into which members must marry. Such groups are usually defined in terms of kinship rather than politics or territory. Exogamy is usually characteristic of unilineal descent groups, in which descent is reckoned either patrilineally or matrilineally. In endogamous groups, marriage outside one's group may be forbidden, or there may merely be a tendency to marry within the group. Endogamy is characteristic of aristocracies and religious and ethnic minorities in industrialized societies but also of the caste system in India and of class-conscious nonliterate societies such as the Masai of East Africa.

exorcism, In Christianity, a ceremony used to drive demons out of a person they have possessed. Jesus healed people tormented by evil spirits, casting them out with a word, and his followers later drove out demons "in his name." By the 3rd century this task was assigned to a specially trained class of lower clergy. Rituals for exorcism of people and places also exist in many other traditions.

expanding universe, Current understanding of the state of the universe. It is based on the finding that all galaxies are moving away from each other. Application of general relativity to cosmology, along with the detection of redshifted light coming from galaxies outside the Milky Way Galaxy, led to the realization in the 1920s that all galaxies are receding. It is unknown whether the universe will expand indefinitely (open universe) or eventually collapse (closed universe) into an extremely dense, congested state, as it began, according to the big-bang model.

expert system, Computer-based system designed to respond like a human expert in a given field. Expert systems are built on knowledge gathered from human experts, analogous to a database but containing rules that may be applied to solving a specific problem. An interface allows the user to specify symptoms and to clarify a problem by responding to questions posed by the system. Software tools exist to help designers build a special-purpose expert system with minimal effort. An outgrowth of work in artificial intelligence, expert systems show promise for an ever-widening range of applications. There are now widely used expert systems in the fields of medicine, personnel screening, and education.

Explorer, Any of the largest (55-member) series of unmanned U.S. spacecraft, launched between 1958 and 1975. Explorer 1, the first satellite sent into orbit by the U.S., discovered the innermost Van Allen radiation belt. Other notable craft in this series include Explorer 38 (1968), which measured galactic radio sources and studied low radio frequencies in space, and Explorer 53 (SAS 3; 1975), which investigated X-ray and gamma-ray sources within and beyond the Milky Way Galaxy. See photograph on following page.

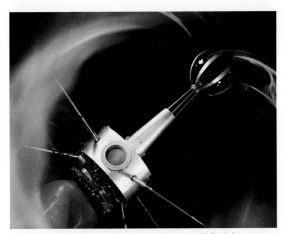

Explorer 10 satellite undergoing testing in a NASA laboratory prior to being launched in 1961.
NASA

explosive, Any substance or device that can produce a volume of rapidly expanding gas in an extremely brief period. Mechanical explosives, which depend on a physical reaction (e.g., overloading a container with compressed air until it bursts), are little used except in mining. Nuclear explosives use either nuclear fission or nuclear fusion. Chemical explosives are of two types: detonating (high) explosives (e.g., TNT, dynamite) have extremely rapid decomposition and development of high pressure; deflagrating (low) explosives (e.g., black powder, smokeless powder) merely burn quickly and produce relatively low pressure. Primary detonating explosives are ignited by a flame, a spark, or an impact; secondary ones require a detonator and sometimes a booster. Modern high explosives use either mixtures of ammonium nitrate and fuel oil or ammonium nitrate-based water gels.

exponential function, In mathematics, a function in which a constant base is raised to a variable power. Exponential functions are used to model changes in population size, in the spread of diseases, and in the growth of investments. They can also accurately predict types of decline typified by radioactive decay. The essence of exponential growth, and a characteristic of all exponential growth functions, is that they double in size over regular intervals. The most important exponential function is e^x, the inverse of the natural logarithmic function.

Expressionism, In the visual arts, artistic style in which the artist depicts not objective reality but the subjective emotions that objects or events arouse. This aim is accomplished through the distortion and exaggeration of shape and the vivid or violent application of colour. Its roots are found in the works of Vincent van Gogh, Edvard Munch, and James Ensor. In 1905 the movement took hold with a group of German artists known as Die Brücke; their works influenced such artists as Georges Rouault, Chaim Soutine, Max Beckmann, Käthe Kollwitz, and Ernst Barlach. The group of artists known as Der Blaue Reiter were also considered Expressionists. Expressionism was the dominant style in Germany after World War I; postwar Expressionists included George Grosz and Otto Dix. Its emotional qualities were adopted by other 20th-century art movements.

extinction (of species), Dying out or termination of a species. It occurs when a species can no longer reproduce at replacement levels. Most past extinctions are thought to have resulted from environmental changes that the doomed species was either unable to adapt to or that caused it to adapt so thoroughly that it became a distinctly new species. The effect of humans on the environment, through hunting, collecting, and habitat destruction, has become the principal factor in plant and animal extinctions.

extradition, Process by which one state, at the request of another, returns a person for trial for a crime punishable by the laws of the requesting state and committed outside the state of refuge. Extradition is regulated within countries by extradition acts and between countries by treaties. Some principles of extradition are common to many countries. Most decline to surrender their own nationals. Countries also generally recognize the right of political asylum. In view of the solidarity of nations in the repression of crime, however, countries are usually willing to cooperate in bringing criminals to justice.

extrasensory perception (ESP), Perception that involves awareness of information about something (such as a person or event) not gained through the senses and not deducible from previous experience. Classic forms of ESP include telepathy, clairvoyance, and precognition. No conclusive demonstrations of the existence of ESP in any individual have been given, but popular belief in the phenomenon remains widespread, and people who claim to possess ESP are sometimes employed by investigative teams searching for missing persons or things.

extrasolar planet, also called EXOPLANET, Planet that orbits a star other than the Sun. The existence of extrasolar planets, many light-years from Earth, was confirmed in 1992 with the detection of three bodies circling a pulsar. The first planet revolving around a more sunlike star, 51 Pegasi, was reported in 1995. Over 200 stars with one or more planets are known. Current detection methods, based on the planets' gravitational effects on the stars they orbit, have revealed only planets much more massive than Earth; some are several times the size of Jupiter. A number of them have highly elliptical orbits, and many are closer to their stars than Mercury is to the Sun. These findings have raised questions regarding astronomers' ideas of how Earth's solar system formed and how typical it is.

eyeglasses, Lenses set in frames to wear in front of the eyes to aid vision or correct vision defects. Their use for farsightedness and nearsightedness has been known since the late Middle Ages. In 1784 Benjamin Franklin invented bifocals, with divided lenses for distant and near vision. Eyeglasses can also correct astigmatism. Most lenses are made of glass or plastic (lighter and more shatterproof than glass but easily scratched). Sunglass lenses are tinted to reduce glare and often treated to reduce ultraviolet light exposure.

Ezekiel (fl. 6th century BC), Priest and prophet of ancient Israel. He was the subject and partial author of the biblical book of Ezekiel. He began to prophesy to the Jews in Palestine *c.* 592 BC, pronouncing God's judgment on a sinful nation. He witnessed the conquest of Jerusalem by Babylon and saw his fellow Israelites taken away into captivity. He offered a promise of Israel's restoration in his famous vision of a valley of dry bones that revive and assemble themselves. He envisaged a theocratic community revolving around a restored Temple in Jerusalem.

F

F-15, or EAGLE, Twin-engine jet fighter built by the Boeing Company. F-15s were delivered to the U.S. Air Force beginning in 1974 and have been sold to U.S. allies in the Middle East. The F-15 is powered by two turbofan engines that can accelerate it to more than twice the speed of sound. The single-seat F-15 is armed with a 20-mm rotary cannon and an array of short-range and medium-range air-to-air missiles. The fighter-bomber version, known as the Strike Eagle, includes a second seat for the weapons officer, who controls the delivery of missiles and bombs. It carried out much of the nighttime precision bombing of Iraqi installations in the Persian Gulf War.

fable, Narration intended to enforce a useful truth, especially one in which animals or inanimate objects speak and act like human beings. Unlike a folktale, it has a moral that is woven into the story and often explicitly formulated at the end. The Western fable tradition began with tales ascribed to Aesop. It flourished in the Middle Ages, reached a high point in 17th-century France in the works of Jean de La Fontaine, and found a new audience in the 19th century with the rise of children's literature. Fables also have ancient roots in the literary and religious traditions of India, China, and Japan.

fairy, In folklore, any of a race of supernatural beings who have magic powers and sometimes meddle in human affairs. Some have been described as of human size, while others are "little people" only a few inches high. The term was first used in medieval Europe. Fairy lore is especially common in Ireland, Cornwall, Wales, and Scotland. Though usually beneficent in modern children's stories, the fairies of the past were powerful and sometimes dangerous beings who could be friendly, mischievous, or cruel, depending on their whim. Fairies were thought to be beautiful, to live much longer than human beings, and to lack souls. They sometimes carried off human infants and left changelings as substitutes. They occasionally took human lovers, but to enter fairyland was perilous for humans, who were obliged to remain forever if they ate or drank there.

fairy tale, Simple narrative typically of folk origin dealing with supernatural beings. Fairy tales may be written or told for the amusement of children or may have a more sophisticated narrative containing supernatural or obviously improbable events, scenes, and personages and often having a whimsical, satirical, or moralistic character. The term embraces popular folktales such as "Cinderella" and "Puss in Boots," as well as art fairy tales of later invention, such as those by Hans Christian Andersen. It is often difficult to distinguish between tales of literary and oral origin, because folktales have received literary treatment from early times, and literary tales can often be traced back to oral tradition.

Faisalabad, formerly (until 1979) LYALLPUR, City (pop., 2005 est.: urban agglom., 2,494,000), Punjab province, eastern Pakistan. Founded in 1890, it became headquarters of the Lower Chenab colony and in 1898 was incorporated as a municipality. It serves as a distribution centre in the central Punjab plain, and its industries produce chemicals and synthetics, textiles, and food products. It is the site of West Pakistan Agricultural University (1961) and of a number of colleges affiliated with the University of the Punjab.

faith healing, Curing of an illness or disability by recourse to divine power, without the use of traditional medicine. A healer such as a clergy member or an inspired layperson may act as intermediary. Certain places, such as the grotto at Lourdes, France, are believed to effect cures among believers. In ancient Greece, temples honoring the god of medicine, Asclepius, were built near springs with healing waters. In Christianity, support for faith healing is based on the miraculous cures wrought by Jesus during his ministry. Christian Science is noted for faith healing, and it is also practiced in a more dramatic way in Pentecostalism through such customs as the laying on of hands.

Falange (Spanish: "Phalanx") Extreme nationalist political group in Spain. Founded in 1933 by José Antonio Primo de Rivera and influenced by Italian fascism, the Falange gained popularity in opposition to the Popular Front government of 1936. Gen. Francisco Franco merged the group with other right-wing factions by decree in 1937 and became the Falange's absolute chief. 150,000 Falangists served in Franco's armed forces in the Spanish Civil War. After their victory, the Falange's fascism was subordinated to the Franco regime's conservative values. On Franco's death in 1975 a law was passed permitting other "political associations," and the Falange was abolished in 1977.

Falasha, Jewish Ethiopians. The Falasha call themselves House of Israel and claim descent from Menilek I, son of King Solomon and the Queen of Sheba. Probably descended from local Agew peoples converted by Jews in southern Arabia, they remained faithful to Judaism after the Ethiopian kingdom was converted to Christianity in the 4th century AD. Persecuted by Christians, they settled in the area around Lake Tana in northern Ethiopia. Though ignorant of the Talmud, members adhered strictly to the Mosaic law and observed some festivals of Judaism. In 1975 the Israeli rabbinate affirmed that Falashas were Jews, and from 1980 to 1992 some 45,000 Falasha emigrated to Israel, leaving probably only a few thousand in Ethiopia.

falconry, Sport of employing falcons or other hawks in hunting game. Falconry has been practiced in the Middle East at least since the 8th century BC. It flourished among the privileged classes in Europe in the Middle Ages. It began to die out after the advent of the shotgun and the enclosure of open lands in the 17th century, but there was a renewed interest in the sport beginning in the 1970s; there are many hawking clubs and falconry associations. The bird most commonly used is the peregrine falcon, though the goshawk and sparrow hawk have also been used. Birds are caught wild or raised from birth. Training involves selective use of a leather hood (called a rufter) and leg thongs (jesses) to keep the animal under control while familiarizing it with its new environment. During the hunt the trained bird is released to bring down its prey; it then returns to the hawker or is collected at the kill site.

Falkland Islands, Spanish ISLAS MALVINAS, British overseas territory (pop., 2001: 2,491), in the southwestern South Atlantic Ocean. Located about 300 mi (480 km) northeast of the southern tip of South America, the Falklands are made up of two main islands, East Falkland and West Falkland, and about 200 smaller islands. The islands are spread out over some 4,700 sq mi (12,200 sq km). The capital is Stanley, on East Falkland. The population is English-speaking and of British descent. The economy is based on sheep raising. The French founded the islands' first settlement, on East Falkland in 1764, and the British settled West Falkland in 1765. In 1770 the Spanish purchased the French settlement and expelled the British, but the latter's settlement was restored in 1771. In 1820 Argentina proclaimed its sovereignty over the Falklands, but the British took them back in 1833. Argentina invaded in 1982, and the British reclaimed the islands after a brief conflict.

Falkland Islands War, or MALVINAS WAR (1982) Brief but undeclared war between Argentina and Great Britain over control of the Falkland Islands (Islas Malvinas) and associated island dependencies. Both countries long had claimed sovereignty over the Falklands and had been in protracted negotiations over them. On April 2, 1982, Argentina's military government, impatient with the negotiations, occupied the islands with some 10,000 troops. British prime minister Margaret Thatcher responded by sending a naval task force to the region, and within three months British forces had defeated the Argentines and reoccupied the islands. Britain lost about 250 men, and Argentina about 700. Argentina's defeat discredited its military government and helped lead to the restoration of civilian rule in 1983.

fallacy, formal and informal, In philosophy, reasoning that fails to establish its conclusion because of deficiencies in form or wording. Formal fallacies are types of deductive argument that instantiate an invalid inference pattern; an example is "affirming the consequent: If A then B; B; therefore, A." Informal fallacies are types of inductive argument the premises of which fail to establish the conclusion because of their content. There are many kinds of informal fallacy; examples include *argumentum ad hominem* ("argument against the man"), which consists of attacking the arguer instead of his argument; the fallacy of false cause, which consists of arguing from the premise that one event precedes another to the conclusion that the first event is the cause of the second; the fallacy of composition, which consists of arguing from the premise that a part of a thing has a certain property to the conclusion that the thing itself has that property; and the fallacy of equivocation, which consists of arguing from a premise in which a term is used in one sense to a conclusion in which the term is used in another sense.

fallout, Descent of radioactive materials from the atmosphere to the earth. Radioactivity in the atmosphere may arise from natural causes such as cosmic rays as well as from nuclear explosions and atomic reactor operations. The explosion of nuclear weapons leads to three types of fallout: local, tropospheric, and stratospheric. The first, intense but relatively short-lived, occurs as larger radioactive particles are deposited near the site of the explosion. Tropospheric fallout occurs when the finer particles enter the troposphere, and it spreads over a larger area in the month after the explosion. Stratospheric fallout, made of fine particles in the stratosphere, may continue years after the explosion, and the distribution is nearly worldwide. Many different radioisotopes are formed during a nuclear explosion, but only long-lived isotopes (e.g., cesium-137, strontium-90) are deposited as stratospheric fallout.

Falun Gong, or FALUN DAFA, Controversial spiritual movement combining healthful exercises with meditation for the purpose of "moving to higher levels." Its teachings draw from Buddhism, Confucianism, Daoism, and the Western New Age movement. It was founded in China in 1992 by Li Hongzhi, a former grain-bureau clerk from Jilin province. He originally registered it as a form of the natural-healing discipline *qigong*, but he later withdrew it from China's Qigong Research Association to stress its spiritual (rather than health-related) emphasis. Its members nevertheless claim great health benefits from its practice. It claims a worldwide following of 100 million, with 70 million in China; Chinese authorities claim it has as few as 2 or 3 million members. The movement has been regarded as a threat by the Chinese government, which started arresting its followers in mid-1999. Many Falun Gong members were later tried and given long prison sentences. Li emigrated to the U.S. in 1998.

family, Basic social unit consisting of persons united by ties of marriage (affinity), "blood" (consanguinity), or adoption and usually representing a single household. The essence of the family group is the parent-child relationship, whose outlines vary widely among cultures. One prominent familial form is the nuclear family, consisting of the marital pair living with their offspring in a separate dwelling. While some scholars believe this to be the oldest form, others point to the inconclusive prehistorical record and the widespread existence of other forms such as the polygynous family (a husband, two or more wives, and their offspring) and the extended family (including at least parents, married children, and their offspring). The family as an institution provides for the rearing and socialization of children, the care of the aged, sick, or disabled, the legitimation of procreation, and the regulation of sexual conduct in addition to supplying basic physical, economic, and emotional security for its members.

family, In pedology, a group of soils that have similar profiles and include one or more subdivisions called series. The primary characteristics that define each of the nearly 6,600 identified soil families are the physical and chemical properties—especially texture, mineral composition, temperature, and depth—that are important for the growth of plants.

famine, Extreme and protracted shortage of food, resulting in widespread hunger and a substantial increase in the death rate. General famines affect all classes or groups in the region of food shortage; class famines affect some classes or groups much more severely than others; regional famines affect only a particular region of a country. Causes may be natural or human. Natural causes include drought, flooding, unfavourable weather conditions, plant disease, and insect infestation. Human causes include war, overpopulation, faulty distribution systems, and high food prices. Several severe famines occurred in the 20th century, including those in China (1928–29, at least 3 million dead; 1959–61, 15–30 million), the U.S.S.R. (1921, more than 5 million; 1932–33, 6–8 million), India (1943–44, 1.5 million), Cambodia (1975–79, 1 million), and North Korea (1995–99, 2.5 million), and continued into the 21st century, as in sub-Saharan Africa.

Fang, Bantu-speaking peoples of southern Cameroon, mainland Equatorial Guinea, and northern Gabon. The Fang number about 3.6 million. Under colonial rule they engaged in ivory trading and after World War I in cacao farming. By 1939 much of the population was Christian, but since 1945 syncretistic sects have grown rapidly. The Fang are politically influential, especially in Gabon.

fantasia, Musical composition free in form and inspiration, often for an instrumental soloist. Most fantasias try to convey the impression of improvisation. The first were Italian works for lute (*c.* 1530). Keyboard fantasias became common in the late 16th century; both organ and harpsichord fantasias flourished in the 17th and 18th centuries in Britain, Germany, and France. Fugal, imitative texture, sometimes highly learned in character, was common from the beginning, often alternating with running passagework and highly chromatic chordal passages in free rhythms. Ensemble fantasias were widely composed as well.

farce, Light, dramatic composition that uses highly improbable situations, stereotyped characters, violent horseplay, and broad humour. Farce is generally regarded as intellectually and aesthetically inferior to comedy in its crude characterizations and implausible plots, but it has remained popular throughout the West from ancient times to the present.

Faroe Islands, or FAEROE ISLANDS, Group of islands in the Atlantic Ocean that form a self-governing overseas administrative division of Denmark. Area: 540 sq mi (1,399 sq km). Population: (2011 est.) 48,600. Lying north of the British Isles, the islands are politically situated within the kingdom of Denmark. There are 17 inhabited islands and many islets and reefs. The largest island, Strømø, holds the capital of Tórshavn. The islands are high and rugged, with coasts that are deeply indented with fjords. The economy is based on fishing and sheep raising. First settled by Irish monks (*c.* 700), the islands were colonized by the Vikings (*c.* 800) and were ruled by Norway from the 11th century until 1380, when they passed to Denmark. They unsuccessfully sought independence in 1946 but received self-government in 1948. In the early 21st century they continued discussions with Denmark on full independence.

fascism, Philosophy of government that stresses the primacy and glory of the state, unquestioning obedience to its leader, subordination of the individual will to the state's authority, and harsh suppression of dissent. Martial virtues are celebrated, while liberal and democratic values are disparaged. Fascism arose during the 1920s and '30s partly out of fear of the rising power of the working classes; it differed from contemporary communism (as practiced under Joseph Stalin) by its protection of business and landowning elites and its preservation of class systems. The leaders of the fascist governments of Italy (1922–43), Germany (1933–45), and Spain (1939–75)—Benito Mussolini, Adolf Hitler, and Francisco Franco—were portrayed to their publics as embodiments of the strength and resolve necessary to rescue their nations from political and economic chaos. Japanese fascists (1936–45) fostered belief in the uniqueness of the Japanese spirit and taught subordination to the state and personal sacrifice.

fashion, Any mode of dressing or adornment that is popular during a particular time or in a particular place (i.e., the current style). It can change from one period to the next, from generation to generation. It serves as a reflection of social and economic status, a function that explains the popularity of many styles throughout costume history; in the West, courts have been a major source of fashion. In the 19th and 20th centuries, fashion increasingly became an profitable, international industry as a result of the rise of world-renowned fashion houses and fashion magazines.

fasting, Abstaining from food, usually for religious or ethical reasons. In ancient religions it was used to prepare worshipers or priests to approach deities, to pursue a vision, to demonstrate penance for sins, or to assuage an angered deity. All the major world religions include fasting among their practices. Judaism has several fast days, notably Yom Kippur. For Christians Lent is set aside as a 40-day period of penitence before Easter, including the traditional fast days of Ash Wednesday and Good Friday. In Islam the month of Ramadan is observed as a period of total abstention from food from dawn to dusk. Fasting to make a political protest is often referred to as a hunger strike; hunger strikes have been employed by, among others, 19th-century female suffragists, Mohandas K. Gandhi, and late-20th-century Irish nationalists. Moderate fasting is also sometimes practiced for its claimed health benefits.

fat, Any organic compound of plant or animal origin that is not volatile, does not dissolve in water, and is oily or greasy. Chemically, fats are identical to animal and vegetable oils, consisting mainly of triglycerides (esters of glycerol with fatty acids). Fats that are liquid at room temperature are called oils. Differences in melting temperature and physical state depend on the saturation of the fatty acids and the length of their carbon chains. The glycerides may have only a few different component fatty acids or as many as 100 (in butterfat). Almost all natural fats and oils incorporate only fatty acids that are constructed from two-carbon units and thus contain only even numbers of carbon atoms. Natural fats such as corn oil have small amounts of compounds besides triglycerides, including phospholipids, plant steroids, tocopherols (vitamin E), vitamin A, waxes, carotenoids, and many others, including decomposition products of these constituents. Sources of fats in foods include ripe seeds and some fruits (e.g., corn, peanuts, olives, avocados) and animal products (e.g., meat, eggs, milk). Fats contain more than twice as much energy (calories) per unit of weight as proteins and carbohydrates. Digestion of fats in foods, often partial, is carried out by enzymes called lipases. The breakdown products are absorbed from the intestine into the blood, which carries microscopic fat droplets reconstituted from digested fats (or synthesized in cells) to sites of storage or use. Fats are readily broken down—primarily into glycerol and fatty acids—by hydrolysis, a first step for many of their industrial uses.

Fatah, inverted acronym of ḤARAKAT AL-TAḤRĪR AL-WAṬANĪ AL-FILASṬĪNĪ ("PALESTINE NATIONAL LIBERATION MOVEMENT"), Palestinian guerrilla organization and political party, whose name means "conquest" in Arabic. Founded by Yāsir ʿArafāt and Khalīl al-Wazīr in the late 1950s, the movement relied on guerrilla warfare and occasional acts of terrorism in an attempt to wrest Palestine from Israeli control. It eventually became the largest faction within the Palestine Liberation Organization and attacked Israeli interests worldwide. Originally based in Damascus, it was forced to relocate several times before a political agreement was reached with Israel in 1993. A number of factions within Fatah rejected the goal of peace with Israel and split from the main organization. In 1994 the Palestinian Authority was established, and Fatah dominated the governing body for more than a decade. In the 2006 elections for the Palestinian Legislative Council, the group was unexpectedly defeated by the rival organization Ḥamās.

Fates, In Greek and Roman mythology, the three goddesses who determined human destiny. The Fates were usually depicted as old women: Clotho, the Spinner; Lachesis, the Allotter; and Atropos, the Inflexible. Clotho spun the thread of human life, Lachesis dispensed it, and Atropos cut the thread. They determined the length of each person's life as well as its share of suffering. Their Roman names were Nona, Decuma, and Morta.

Fátima, Village in central Portugal, site of a shrine dedicated to the Virgin Mary. From May to October 1917, three peasant children reported a vision of a woman who identified herself as the Lady of the Rosary. On October 13, a crowd of about 70,000 witnessed an amazing solar phenomenon just after the children had seen their vision. The first national pilgrimage to the site occurred in 1927. Construction of a basilica started in 1928; now flanked by retreat houses and hospitals, it faces a square where many miraculous cures have been reported.

Fāṭimah, or FATIMA (b. *c.* 605, Mecca, Arabia—d. 633, Medina), Daughter of Muhammad and the object of veneration in Shīʿite Islam. In 622 she emigrated with her father from Mecca to Medina, where she married his cousin ʿAlī. Their sons, Ḥasan and al-Ḥusayn ibn ʿAlī, are considered by Shīʿites to be the rightful inheritors of the tradition of Muhammad. Fāṭimah's marriage was unhappy, but she and her husband were reconciled by the Prophet, and she cared for her father in his last illness (632). She clashed with his successor, Abū Bakr, over property and died a year later. Later tradition added to the majesty of her life, and the Fāṭimid dynasty derived its name from hers.

Fāṭimid dynasty (909–1171) Ismāʿīli Shīʿite dynasty of North Africa and the Middle East. Its members traced their descent from Fāṭimah, a daughter of the Prophet Muhammad. As Shīʿite Muslims, they opposed the Sunnite caliphate of the ʿAbbāsid dynasty, which they were determined to supplant. From Yemen they expanded into North Africa and Sicily, and in 909 their imam emerged to proclaim the new dynasty. The first four Fāṭimid caliphs ruled from Tunisia, but the conquest of Egypt in 969 occasioned the building of a new capital, Cairo. At its height, the dynasty controlled Mecca and Medina, Syria, Palestine, and Africa's Red Sea coast. Seeking to overthrow the ʿAbbāsids, the Fāṭimids maintained a network of missionaries and agents in ʿAbbāsid territories. In 1057–59 the Fāṭimid caliph was briefly proclaimed in Baghdad, the ʿAbbāsid capital, but Fāṭimid fortunes declined thereafter. Attacks by Crusaders, Turks, and Byzantines and factionalism in the armed forces weakened the caliphate; disputes over succession to the title of caliph led to the dynasty's final end, however, as many of the Asian missionaries broke away, and the central government came to rely on non-Ismāʿīlī troops. The last caliph died in 1171, and the dynasty was succeeded by the Sunnite Ayyūbid dynasty.

fatty acid, Organic compound that is an important component of lipids in plants, animals, and microorganisms. Fatty acids are carboxylic acids with a long hydrocarbon chain, usually straight, as the fourth substituent group on the carboxyl ($-COOH$) group that makes the molecule an acid. If the carbon-to-carbon bonds in that chain are all single, the fatty acid is saturated; artificial saturation is called hydrogenation. A fatty acid with one double bond is monounsaturated; one with more is polyunsaturated. These are more reactive chemically. Most unsaturated fats are liquid at room temperature, so food manufacturers hydrogenate them to make them solid. A high level of saturated fatty acids in the diet raises blood cholesterol levels. A few fatty acids have branched chains. Others (e.g., prostaglandins) contain ring structures. Fatty acids in nature are always combined, usually with glycerol as triglycerides in fats. Oleic acid (unsaturated, with 18 carbon atoms) is almost half of human fat and is abundant in such oils as olive, palm, and peanut. Most animals, including mammals, cannot synthesize some unsaturated "essential" fatty acids; humans need linoleic, linolenic, and arachidonic acids in their diet.

Faulkner, William (Cuthbert), orig. WILLIAM CUTHBERT FALKNER (b. Sept. 25, 1897, New Albany, Miss., U.S.—d. July 6, 1962, Byhalia, Miss.), U.S. writer. Faulkner dropped out of high school and only briefly attended college. He spent most of his life in Oxford, Miss. He is best known for his cycle of works set in fictional Yoknapatawpha County, which becomes an emblem of the American South and its tragic history. His first major novel, *The Sound and the Fury* (1929), was marked by radical technical experimentation, including stream of consciousness. His American reputation, which lagged behind his European reputation, was boosted by *As I Lay Dying* (1930), *Light in August* (1932), *Absalom, Absalom!* (1936), and *Go Down, Moses* (1942), which contains the story "The Bear." *The Portable Faulkner* (1946) finally brought his work into wide circulation, and he won the Nobel Prize for Literature in 1949. His *Collected Stories* (1950) won the National Book Award. Both in the U.S. and abroad, especially in Latin America, he was among the most influential writers of the 20th century.

fault, In geology, a fracture in the rocks of the Earth's crust, where compressional or tensional forces cause the rocks on the opposite sides of the fracture to be displaced relative to each other. Faults range in length from a few inches to hundreds of miles, and displacement may also range from less than an inch to hundreds of miles along the fracture surface (the fault plane). Most, if not all, earthquakes are caused by rapid movement along faults. Faults are common throughout the world. A well-known example is the San Andreas Fault near the western coast of the U.S. The total movement along this fault during the last few million years appears to have been several miles.

Faust, Legendary German necromancer or astrologer who sold

his soul to the devil for knowledge and power. There was a historical Faust (perhaps two; both died *c.* 1540), who traveled widely performing magic, referred to the devil as his crony, and had a wide reputation for evil. The *Faustbuch* (1587), a collection of tales purportedly by Faust, told of such reputed wizards as Merlin and Albertus Magnus. It was widely translated; an English version inspired Christopher Marlowe's *Tragicall History of D. Faustus* (1604), which emphasized Faust's eternal damnation. Magic manuals bearing Faust's name did a brisk business; the

Faust, detail from the title page of the 1616 edition of The Tragical History of Dr. Faustus *by Christopher Marlowe.*

classic *Magia naturalis et innaturalis* was known to Johann W. von Goethe, who, like Gotthold Lessing, saw Faust's pursuit of knowledge as noble; in Goethe's great *Faust* the hero is redeemed. Inspired by Goethe, many artists took up the story, including Hector Berlioz (in the dramatic cantata *The Damnation of Faust*) and Charles Gounod (in the opera *Faust*).

Fauvism, Style of painting that flourished in France *c.* 1898–1908, characterized by the use of intensely vivid colour and tur-

bulent emotionalism. The dominant figure of the group was Henri Matisse; others were André Derain, Maurice de Vlaminck, Raoul Dufy, Georges Braque, and Georges Rouault. The name derives from the judgment of a critic who visited their first exhibit in Paris (1905) and referred to the artists disparagingly as "les fauves" ("wild beasts"). They were influenced by the masters of Post-Impressionism, Vincent van Gogh and Paul Gauguin. Fauvism was a transitional phase for most of the artists, who by 1908, having renewed their interest in Paul Cézanne's vision of order and structure, abandoned Fauvism for Cubism. Matisse alone continued on the course he had pioneered.

Faxian, or FA-HSIEN, orig. SEHI (fl. 399–414), Chinese Buddhist monk who initiated relations with India. Eager to learn of his religion at its source, he traveled to India in 402 and spent a decade visiting the major Buddhist shrines and seats of learning, especially sites in eastern India, including Kapilavastu, Bodh Gaya, and Pataliputra. He deepened his knowledge by conversing with monks and gathered sacred texts that had not yet been translated into Chinese. He returned to China by sea in 412, after spending two years in Sri Lanka. His *Record of Buddhist Kingdoms* contains valuable information about Indian Buddhism in this era.

fayd, In Islamic philosophy, the emanation of created things from God. The term is not used in the Qurʾān, but Muslim philosophers such as al-Fārābī and Avicenna borrowed the notion from Neoplatonism. They conceived of creation as a gradual process arising from God's superabundance. Creation begins at the most perfect level, God, and descends through the world of the spirit to the least perfect level, the world of matter. The *fayd* theory was refuted by al-Ghazālī in the 11th century.

feather, Component structure of the outer covering and flight surfaces of all modern birds. Unique to birds, feathers apparently evolved from the scales of birds' reptilian ancestors. Like hair, feathers are made of keratin, a fibrous protein. They are variously specialized for insulation, flight, formation of body contours, display, and sensory reception. Contour feathers form most of the surface of the bird, streamlining it for flight and often waterproofing it. The basal portion may be downy and thus act as insulation. The major contour feathers of the wing (remiges) and tail (rectrices) function in flight. Contour feathers grow in tracts (pterylae) separated by bare areas (apteria) and develop from follicles in the skin. Down feathers have loose-webbed barbs, all rising from the tip of a very short shaft. Their function is insulation, and they may be found in both pterylae and apteria in adult birds. They also constitute the first feather coat of most young birds. Filoplumes are hairlike feathers with a few soft barbs near the tip. They are associated with contour feathers and may be sensory or decorative in function. Bristlelike, vaneless feathers occur around the mouth, eyes, and nostrils of birds. Some bristles function as eyelashes on ground-dwelling birds; bristles over the nostrils may serve as filters.

federalism, Political system that binds a group of states into a larger, noncentralized, superior state while allowing them to maintain their own political identities. Certain characteristics and principles are common to all successful federal systems: a written constitution or basic law stipulating the distribution of powers; diffusion of power among the constituent elements, which are substantially self-sustaining; and territorial divisions to ensure neutrality and equality in the representation of various groups and interests. Changes require the consent of those affected. Successful federal systems also have a sense of common nationality and direct lines of communication between the citizens and all the governments that serve them. Examples of modern federal systems include the U.S., Brazil, Germany, and Nigeria.

felony and misdemeanour, In Anglo-American law, two categories of criminal offense. A crime is classed as one or the other according to its seriousness. In U.S. law, a felony is typically defined as a crime punishable by a term of imprisonment of not less than one year. Misdemeanours are often defined as offenses punishable only by fines or by short terms of imprisonment in local jails. Crimes in Britain are classified into indictable offenses (which may be tried by a jury) and summary offenses (which may be tried by a judge without juries). Codes in Europe also distinguish offenses of greater dangerousness from lesser crimes.

female genital cutting, or FEMALE CIRCUMCISION, or FEMALE GENITAL MUTILATION, or CLITORIDECTOMY, Surgical procedure ranging from drawing blood, to removing the clitoris alone, to infibulation or Pharaonic circumcision—removing the external genitals, joining the sides and leaving a small opening. The practice dates to ancient times; usually performed on young girls and in a ritual context, it is purported by its practitioners to guard a girl's virginity and reduce her sexual desires. Because it is usually undertaken in unhygienic conditions, cutting may lead to severe bleeding, infection, debilitating pain, and death; long-term consequences can include an inability to urinate or expel menstrual blood, pain during sexual intercourse, and prolonged childbirth. In some cultures women are reinfibulated after childbirth, while others discourage this practice.

feminism, Social movement that seeks equal rights for women. Widespread concern for women's rights dates from the Enlightenment; one of the first important expressions of the movement was Mary Wollstonecraft's *A Vindication of the Rights of Woman* (1792). The 1848 Seneca Falls Convention, convened by Elizabeth Cady Stanton, Lucretia Mott, and others, called for full legal equality with men, including full educational opportunity and equal compensation; thereafter the woman suffrage movement began to gather momentum. It faced particularly stiff resistance in the United Kingdom and the United States, where women gained the right to vote in 1918 and 1920, respectively. By mid-century a second wave of feminism emerged to address the limited nature of women's participation in the workplace and prevailing notions that tended to confine women to the home. A third wave of feminism arose in the late 20th century and was notable for challenging middle-class white feminists and for broadening feminism's goals to encompass equal rights for all people regardless of race, creed, economic or educational status, physical appearance or ability, or sexual preference.

fencing, Sport involving attack and defense with a light sword, specifically a foil, épée, or sabre. There is evidence of swordplay from ancient times through the Middle Ages. In the 14th century swordplay became important in both war and the European gentleman's daily life, and by the 15th century guilds of fencing masters had formed. Strokes that were originally jealously guarded secrets of the individual guilds eventually became orthodox fencing moves. By the later 17th century various rules and conventions had been imposed. In modern competition—except for sabre matches—hits are made with the point only; in matches using foils and sabres, touches to only certain points of the opponents body are counted, whereas in épée no such restrictions apply. Each valid hit scores one or more points. Men's fencing was included in the first modern Olympic Games in 1896, women's in the 1924 games. Electrical scoring was introduced in 1936 to eliminate the frequent inaccuracy of human judgment.

Feng shui, Traditional Chinese method of arranging the human and social world in auspicious alignment with the forces of the cosmos, including qi and yin-yang. It was devised during the Han dynasty (206 BC–AD 220). Specialists, called diviners, use compasslike instruments to determine the exact cosmic forces affecting a site, appropriate sites being chosen particularly in relation to bodies of water and mountains. Feng shui, especially as it affects interior design, has recently become popular in Britain and the U.S.

fennel, Perennial or biennial aromatic herb (*Foeniculum vulgare*) of the parsley family, native to southern Europe and Asia Minor and widely cultivated. The greenish brown to yellowish brown oblong oval seeds smell and taste similar to anise. The seeds and extracted oil are used for scenting soaps and perfumes and for flavouring candies, liqueurs, medicines, and foods, particularly pastries, sweet pickles, and fish. The thickened base of Florence fennel (*F. vulgare dulce*) is eaten as a vegetable.

Fenrir, In Norse mythology, a monstrous wolf. He was the son of the god Loki and a giantess. The gods bound Fenrir to a rock with a magical chain, where he is destined to remain until doomsday, or Ragnarok, when he will break his chains and fall upon the gods. In one version of the myth, he will devour the sun and swallow the chief god, Odin, only to be slain by Vidar, Odin's son. Fenrir figures prominently in Norwegian and Icelandic poetry of the 10th–11th century.

Fermat's last theorem, Statement that there are no natural numbers x, y, and z such that $x^n + y^n = z^n$, in which n is a natural number greater than 2. About this, Pierre de Fermat wrote in 1637 in his copy of Diophantus's *Arithmetica*, "I have discovered a truly remarkable proof but this margin is too small to contain it." Although the theorem was subsequently shown to be true for many specific values of n, leading to important mathematical advances in the process, the difficulty of the problem soon convinced mathematicians that Fermat never had a valid proof. In 1995 the British mathematician Andrew Wiles (b. 1953) and his former student Richard Taylor (b. 1962) published a complete proof, finally solving one of the most famous of all mathematical problems.

fermentation, Process that allows respiration to occur in the absence of oxygen. Biologically, it allows cells to obtain energy from molecules (e.g., glucose) anaerobically. Glycolysis, the breakdown of glucose, is a form of fermentation. Alcoholic fermentation occurs when yeast cells convert carbohydrate sources to ethanol and carbon dioxide. Fermentation reactions are common in muscle cells, yeasts, some bacteria, and plants.

Fermi, Enrico (b. Sept. 29, 1901, Rome, Italy—d. Nov. 28, 1954, Chicago, Ill., U.S.), Italian-born U.S. physicist. As a professor at the University of Rome, he began the work, later fully developed by P.A.M. Dirac, that led to Fermi-Dirac statistics. He developed a theory of beta decay that applies to other reactions through the weak force, which was not improved until 1957, when the weak force was found not to conserve parity. He discovered neutron-induced radioactivity, for which he was awarded a 1938 Nobel Prize. After receiving the award in Sweden, he never returned to fascist Italy but instead moved directly to the U.S., where he joined the faculty of Columbia University and soon became one of the chief architects of practical nuclear physics. A member of the Manhattan Project, he was an important figure in the development of the atomic bomb; in 1942 he directed the first controlled nuclear chain reaction. He received the Congressional Medal of Merit in 1946. In 1954 he became the first recipient of the U.S. government's Enrico Fermi Award. Element number 100, fermium, was named in his honour.

fern, Any of about 10,000–12,000 species (division Pteridophyta) of nonflowering vascular plants that have true roots, stems, and complex leaves and reproduce by spores. Though ferns were once classified with the primitive horsetails and club mosses, botanists have since made a clear distinction between the scalelike, one-veined leaves of those plants and the more complexly veined fronds of the ferns, which are more closely related to the leaves of seed plants. Ferns come in a wide variety of sizes and shapes. Many are small, fragile plants; others are treelike. The life cycle is characterized by an alternation of generations between the mature, fronded form (the sporophyte) familiar in greenhouses and gardens and the form that strongly resembles a moss or liverwort (the gametophyte). Ferns are popular houseplants.

ferrimagnetism, Type of permanent magnetism that occurs in solids, in which the magnetic fields associated with individual atoms spontaneously align themselves, some parallel (as in ferromagnetism), and others antiparallel, or paired off in opposite directions (as in antiferromagnetism). The materials are less magnetic than ferromagnets, as the antiparallel atoms dilute the magnetic effect of the parallel arrangement. Ferrimagnetism occurs mainly in magnetic oxides known as ferrites. Above a temperature called the Curie point, the spontaneous alignment is disrupted and ferrimagnetism is destroyed, but it is restored upon cooling below the Curie point.

ferromagnetism, Physical phenomenon in which certain electrically uncharged materials strongly attract others. It is associated with iron, cobalt, nickel, and some alloys or compounds containing these elements. It is caused by the alignment patterns of the material's atoms, each of which acts as a simple electromagnet, due to the motion and spin of the electrons. The tiny magnets spontaneously align themselves in the same direction, so their magnetic fields reinforce each other. Ferromagnetic materials are magnetized easily. Above a temperature called the Curie point, they cease to be magnetic, but they become ferromagnetic again upon cooling below the Curie point.

Fertile Crescent, Region, Middle East. The term describes a crescent-shaped area of arable land, probably more agriculturally productive in antiquity than it is today. Historically the area stretched from the southeastern coast of the Mediterranean Sea around the Syrian Desert north of the Arabian Peninsula to the Persian Gulf; in general, it often includes the Nile River valley as well. Sedentary agricultural settlements in the Fertile Crescent can be dated to *c.* 8000 BC. It was the scene of the struggles and migrations of some of the earliest known peoples, including Sumerians, Assyrians, Akkadians, various Semitic groups, Babylonians, and Phoenicians.

fertilization, Reproductive process in which a male sex cell (sperm) unites with a female sex cell (egg). During the process, the chromosomes of the egg and sperm will merge to form a zygote, which will divide to form an embryo. In humans, sperm travel from the vagina through the uterus to a fallopian tube, where they surround an egg released from an ovary usually two or three days earlier. Once one sperm has fused with the egg cell membrane, the outer layer becomes impenetrable to other sperm.

fertilizer, Natural or artificial substance containing the chemical elements that improve growth and productiveness of plants. Fertilizers enhance the natural fertility of the soil or replace the chemical elements taken from the soil by previous crops. The use of manure and composts as fertilizers is probably almost as old as agriculture. Modern chemical fertilizers include one or more of the three elements most important in plant nutrition: nitrogen, phosphorus, and potassium. Of secondary importance are the elements sulfur, magnesium, and calcium.

Fès, or FEZ, Arabic FĀS, City (pop., 2004: 946,815), northern Morocco. The oldest of Morocco's four imperial cities, it was founded on opposite banks of the Wadi Fès by Idrīs I about 789 and Idrīs II about 809. The two parts were united by the Almoravid dynasty in the 11th century to become a major Islamic city. Fès reached its zenith under the Marinid dynasty as a centre of learning and commerce in the mid-14th century and has kept its religious primacy through the ages. The site of the oldest mosque in northern Africa, it is also the seat of an Islamic university founded in 859. A centre for trade and traditional crafts, it was until the late 19th century the only place where the fez hat was made.

fetal alcohol syndrome (FAS), Various congenital disorders in a newborn caused by the mother drinking alcohol during pregnancy. The main symptoms are retarded growth, abnormalities of the central nervous system, and certain face and head abnormalities. The child may be mentally retarded. Behavioral problems (e.g., poor concentration, impulsiveness) are sometimes the only obvious symptoms. The syndrome is common in babies born to chronic alcoholics, but health care organizations now commonly recommend that women cease drinking alcohol entirely while pregnant. Other disorders have been linked to alcohol in breast milk.

fetish, Object believed to have magical power to protect or aid its owner, and by extension, an object regarded with superstitious or extravagant trust or reverence. In the 18th century it was applied to West African amulets; it has also been used for various items in American Indian religion. In psychology, a fetish is an object that substitutes for a person as the focus of sexual desire.

fetus, Unborn young of any vertebrate, particularly mammals, after it has acquired its basic form. In humans, this stage begins about eight weeks after conception. The fetal stage, marked by increased growth and full development of the organ systems, climaxes in birth. By the end of the third month, the arms and legs of the human fetus begin to move and reflexive movements (such as sucking) begin. Four months after conception, the fetus is about 5.3 in. (135 mm) long and weighs about 6 oz (170 g). During the fifth month, downy hairs (lanugo) cover the body and the skin becomes less transparent. At seven months, a protective greasy substance (vernix caseosa) covers the reddish, wrinkled skin. Fat is deposited under the skin during the eighth month, when the fetus typically weighs about 5 lbs (2.2 kg). A full-term fetus is about 266 days old.

feudalism, Term that emerged in the 17th century that has been used to describe economic, legal, political, social, and economic relationships in the European Middle Ages. Derived from the Latin word *feudum* (fief) but unknown to people of the Middle Ages, the term "feudalism" has been used most broadly to refer to medieval society as a whole, and in this way may be understood as a socio-economic system that is often called manorialism. It has been used most narrowly to describe relations between lords and vassals that involve the exchange of land for military service. Feudalism in this sense is thought to have emerged in a time of political disorder in the 11th century as a means to restore order, and it was later a key element in the establishment of strong monarchies. "Feudalism" also has been applied, often inappropriately, to non-Western societies where institutions similar to those of medieval Europe are thought to have existed. The many ways "feudalism" has been used have drained it of specific meaning, however, and caused some scholars to reject it as a useful concept for understanding medieval society.

fever, or PYREXIA, Abnormally high body temperature or a disease characterized by it. It most often occurs with infection. Normal core body temperature, measured orally, does not exceed 99°F (37.2°C). Up to 105°F (40.6°C), fever causes weakness and is best treated with aspirin, acetaminophen, or other antipyretic drugs. At 108°F (42.2°C) or more, it can lead to convulsions and death. In treatment, it is important to know the underlying cause. Fever appears to be a defense against infectious disease, stimulating leukocytes and increasing antibody production and perhaps killing or inhibiting bacteria and viruses that live within a narrow temperature range.

Fezzan, Arabic FAZZĀN, ancient PHAZANIA, Historic region, southwestern Libya. A part of the Sahara, most of its inhabitants dwell in oases in the interior. Central and southern Fezzan are noted for the cultivation of date palms, which cover several hundred thousand acres scattered in numerous oases. It was conquered by the Romans in the 1st century BC and by the Arabs in the 7th century AD. The Ottomans made it part of their empire in 1842. Fezzan was amalgamated with Tripolitania and Cyrenaica by the Italians in 1912, and it later became a province of the United Kingdom of Libya (1951–63). Thereafter it was part of Libya.

Fibonacci numbers, In mathematics, a sequence of numbers with surprisingly useful applications in botany and other natural sciences. Beginning with two 1's, each new term is generated as the sum of the previous two: 1, 1, 2, 3, 5, 8, 13, ... The 13th-century mathematician Leonardo of Pisa (*c.* 1170–after 1240), also known as Fibonacci, discovered the sequence but did not explore its uses, which have turned out to be wide and various. For example, the number of petals in most types of flowers and numbers involved in branching and seed-formation patterns come from the Fibonacci sequence. The ratio of any two successive terms approaches the value of the golden ratio as the terms become large.

fibre optics, Thin transparent fibres of glass or plastic that transmit light through their length by internal reflections, used for transmitting data, voice, and images. Fibre-optic technology has virtually replaced copper wire in long-distance telephone lines and is used to link computers in local area networks, with digitized light pulses replacing the electric current formerly used for the signal. Telecommunication using fibre optics is usually conducted with infrared light. Fibre optics uses light in the visible wavelengths to transmit images directly, in various technical devices such as those developed for endoscopy.

fibromyalgia, Chronic syndrome that is characterized by musculoskeletal pain, often at multiple sites. The cause is unknown. A significant number of persons with fibromyalgia also have mental disorders, especially depression. Many also have overlapping symptoms of other so-called functional somatic syndromes—especially chronic fatigue syndrome—such as fatigue, stiffness, irritable bowel syndrome, and sleep disturbances. It is common in young and middle-aged women. No treatment has been proved fully effective, although medications, physical therapy, or counseling may reduce disability and help the patient cope.

fief, In European feudalism, a vassal's source of income, granted to him by his lord in exchange for his services. The fief usually consisted of land and the labor of peasants who were bound to cultivate it. The income it provided supported the vassal, who fought for his lord as a knight. Dignities, offices, and money rents were also given in fief.

field hockey, or HOCKEY, Game played with curve-ended sticks between two teams of 11 players. It is played on a field 100 yd (91.4 m) by 60 yd (55 m) in size. The object is to use the sticks to direct a ball into the opponent's goal. Field hockey originated in English schools in the late 19th century, and the British Army introduced it into India and the Far East. By 1928 it had become India's national game. Men's field hockey has been included in the Olympic Games since 1908, women's since 1980. The game was introduced into the U.S. in 1901 and became particularly popular at women's schools, colleges, and clubs. Several international championship tournaments are held during the year, including the World Cup.

fig, Any plant of the genus *Ficus*, in the mulberry family, especially *Ficus carica*, the common fig. Yielding the well-known figs of commerce, *F. carica* is native to an area from Asiatic Turkey to northern India, but natural seedlings grow in most Mediterranean countries, where figs are used extensively, both fresh and dried. It is a bush or small tree with broad, rough, deciduous leaves. Hundreds of different varieties are grown in various parts of the world. The fig was one of the first fruit trees to come under cultivation. Its fruit contains significant amounts of calcium, potassium, phosphorus, and iron.

fighter aircraft, Aircraft designed primarily to secure control of essential airspace by destroying enemy aircraft in combat. Designed for high speed and maneuverability, they are armed with weapons capable of striking other aircraft in flight. Developed early in World War I, they engaged in aerial combat with other fighters, shot down enemy bombers, and conducted various tactical missions. Most were biplanes with wooden frames and cloth skins, equipped with light machine guns synchronized to fire through the propeller. World War II saw the development of all-metal monoplanes that exceeded speeds of 450 mph (725 kph). Famous fighters of the period included the Focke-Wulf 190, the P-47 and P-51, and the Zero. Jet aircraft were produced at the end of the war, and jet fighters such as the U.S. Sabre and the Soviet MiG saw extensive service in the Korean War and later conflicts.

figure skating, Sport in which ice skaters, singly or in pairs, perform various jumps, spins, and footwork. The figure skate blade has a special serrated toe pick, or toe rake, at the front. Figure-skating events, held in the 1908 and 1920 Olympic Games, have constituted part of the Winter Olympics since they were inaugurated in 1924. Until 1991, competition included a compulsory section in which prescribed figures were traced. Competition for individuals includes two free-skating programs: a short program with mandatory requirements and a long program designed to show the skater's skill and grace. Jumps fall into two main groups: the edge jumps (such as the axel, the salchow, and the loop), which take off from one foot; and the toe jumps (such as the toe loop, the flip, and the lutz), which are edge jumps assisted by a vault off the toe pick of the other foot. Additional pair moves, involving a man and a woman skating together, include lifts and throw jumps. Figure-skating programs are judged on both technical merit and artistic impression.

Michelle Kwan (U.S.) performing at the world figure-skating championships, Vancouver, B.C., Can., 2001.
Jeff Haynes—AFP/Getty Images

Fiji, officially REPUBLIC OF FIJI, Country and archipelago, South Pacific Ocean. It lies east of Vanuatu and southwest of Samoa. Area: 7,055 sq mi (18,272 sq km). Population: (2011 est.) 852,000. Capital: Suva. The majority of Fijians are of mixed Melanesian-Polynesian ancestry, with a large South Asian minority. Languages: English (official), Fijian. Religions: Christianity (mostly Protestant, also other Christians, Roman Catholic), Hinduism, Islam. Currency: Fiji dollar. Fiji lies 1,300 mi (2,100 km) north of New Zealand and comprises some 540 islets and 300 islands, of which about 100 are inhabited. The main islands are Viti Levu and Vanua Levu. Fiji also includes the dependency of Rotuma, an island located about 400 mi (640 km) to the northwest. The two large islands are mountainous and volcanic in origin, rising abruptly from densely populated coasts to forested central mountains. The smaller islands are also volcanic, and all are ringed by rocky shoals and coral reefs. The coastal deltas of the principal rivers contain most of the fertile arable land. The climate is tropical oceanic. Fiji has a market economy based largely on agriculture (particularly sugar production), tourism, and light industries; gold and silver are mined. Fiji is a republic with two legislative houses; its head of state is the president, while the head of government is the prime minister. The first settlers arrived from Melanesia some 3,500 years ago. The first European sighting was by the Dutch in the 17th century; the islands were sighted in 1774 by Capt. James Cook and in 1789 by Capt. William Bligh, who returned in 1792 to explore them. Traders and the first missionaries arrived in 1835, and European settlers began arriving in the 1860s. In 1874 Fiji was proclaimed a crown colony. It became independent as a member of the Commonwealth in 1970 and was declared a republic in 1987 following a military coup. Elections in 1992 restored civilian rule. A new constitution was approved in 1997. Coups in 2000 and 2006 created continuing political instability in the early 21st century.

film noir (French: "dark film"), Film genre that offers dark or fatalistic interpretations of reality. The term is applied to U.S. films of the late 1940s and early '50s that often portrayed a seamy or criminal underworld and cynical characters. The films were noted for their use of stark, expressionistic lighting and stylized camera work, often employed in urban settings. The genre includes films such as John Huston's *The Maltese Falcon* (1941), Jacques Tourneur's *Out of the Past* (1947), Alfred Hitchcock's *Spellbound* (1945), and Billy Wilder's *Double Indemnity* (1944) and *Sunset Boulevard* (1950). The trend was on the wane by the mid-1950s, but the influence of these films is evident in many subsequent ones, including classics such as Roman Polanski's *Chinatown* (1974) and Ridley Scott's *Blade Runner* (1982). More recent examples include *L.A. Confidential* (1997) and *The Man Who Wasn't There* (2001).

fin whale, or FINBACK WHALE, or RAZORBACK WHALE, or COMMON RORQUAL, Swift, slender-bodied baleen whale (*Balaenoptera physalus*) named for the ridge on its back. It is 59–89 ft (18–27 m) long, with a triangular dorsal fin, short baleen, and several dozen grooves along its throat and chest. It is gray, with white on the underparts and on the right side of the lower jaw. It is found in oceans worldwide, in groups of a few to several hundred. It lives in polar waters in summer, feeding on crustaceans and small fishes, and moves to warmer waters in winter to breed. Once commercially valuable, it has been substantially reduced in numbers by overhunting and is now listed as an endangered species.

finance, Process of raising funds or capital for any kind of expenditure. Consumers, business firms, and governments often do not have the funds they need to make purchases or conduct their operations, while savers and investors have funds that could earn interest or dividends if put to productive use. Finance is the process of channeling funds from savers to users in the form of credit, loans, or invested capital through agencies including commercial banks, savings and loan associations, and such nonbank organizations as credit unions and investment companies. Finance can be divided into three broad areas: business finance, personal finance, and public finance. All three involve generating budgets and managing funds for the optimum results.

finery process, Early method of converting cast iron to wrought iron, superseding the bloomery process after blast furnaces became widespread. Pieces of cast iron were placed on a finery hearth, on which charcoal was being burned with a plentiful supply of air, so that carbon in the iron was removed by oxidation, leaving semisolid malleable iron behind. From the 15th century on, this two-stage process gradually replaced direct making of malleable iron. It was in turn replaced by the puddling process.

fingerprinting, Act of taking an impression of a person's fingerprint. Because each person's fingerprints are unique, fingerprinting is used as a method of identification, especially in police investigations. The standard method of fingerprint classification was developed by Sir Francis Galton and Sir Edward Henry; their system was officially introduced at Scotland Yard in 1901. The U.S. Federal Bureau of Investigation maintains a fingerprint file on more than 250 million people; fingerprints retrieved from a crime scene may be compared with those on file to identify suspects. DNA analysis, which examines regions of DNA unique to each person, is sometimes called DNA fingerprinting.

Finland, officially REPUBLIC OF FINLAND, Country, northern Europe. Area: 130,666 sq mi (338,424 sq km). Population: (2011 est.) 5,387,000. Capital: Helsinki. The majority of the people are Finns; there is a small Sami (Lapp) population in Lapland. Languages: Finnish and Swedish are both "national" languages; the Sami speak a Finno-Ugric language. Religion: Christianity (predominantly Protestant; also Eastern Orthodox). Currency: euro. Finland is one of the world's most northern and geographically remote countries, about one-third of it lying north of the Arctic Circle. Heavily forested, it contains thousands of lakes, numerous rivers, and extensive areas of marshland. Except for a small highland region in the extreme northwest, Finland's relief doesn't vary greatly. The south has relatively mild weather; the north has severe and prolonged winters and short summers. Finland has a developed free-market economy combined with state ownership of a few key industries. It is among the wealthiest countries in Europe and in the world. Lumbering is a major industry, and manufacturing is highly developed; service industries are also notable. Finland is a multiparty republic with one legislative house; its head of state is the president, and the head of government is the prime minister. Archaeological discoveries have led some to suggest that human habitation in Finland dates back at least 100,000 years. Ancestors of the Sami apparently were present in Finland by about 7000 BCE. The ancestors of the present-day Finns came from the southern shore of the Gulf of Finland in the 1st millennium BCE. The area was gradually Christianized from the 11th century CE. From the 12th century Sweden and Russia contested for supremacy in Finland, until in 1323 Sweden ruled most of the country. Russia was ceded part of Finnish territory in 1721; in 1808 Alexander I of Russia invaded Finland, which in 1809 was formally ceded to Russia. The subsequent period saw the growth of Finnish nationalism. Russia's losses in World War I and the Russian Revolution of 1917 set the stage for Finland's independence in 1917. Finland was defeated by the Soviet Union in the Russo-Finnish War (1939–40) but renewed its fight with the Soviets (the "War of Continuation") after Germany attacked the U.S.S.R. in 1941. In 1944, facing defeat again, Finland made peace with the Soviets, ceding territory and paying reparations. Finland's economy recovered after World War II. It joined the European Union in 1995.

Finnbogadóttir, Vigdís (b. April 15, 1930, Reykjavík, Ice.), Teacher and president of Iceland (1980–96). After graduating from Reykjavík College in 1949, Finnbogadóttir attended the University of Grenoble and the Sorbonne in France and the University of Uppsala in Sweden. She also studied in Denmark and at the University of Iceland, where she later taught. From 1972 to 1980, while serving as director of the Reykjavík Theatre Company, Finnbogadóttir presented French lessons and cultural programming on Iceland State Television. In 1980 she was drafted as a candidate for the presidency of Iceland and was narrowly elected, defeating three male opponents, thereby becoming the first woman in the world to be elected head of state in a national election. She was reelected three times (1984, 1988, and 1992) before retiring from office in 1996.

Finno-Ugric languages, Branch of the Uralic language family spoken by about 25 million people in northeastern Europe, northern Asia, and (through immigration) North America. More than 20 million are accounted for by two languages, Finnish and Hungarian. The Ugric subbranch comprises Hungarian and Ob-Ugrian. The latter consists of two language complexes of western Siberia, Khanty and Mansi, spoken by fewer than 15,000 people. The Finnic branch comprises the Sami (Saami, Lappish) languages, the Baltic Finnic languages, Mordvin, Mari, and the Permic languages. Sami is spoken by some 20,000 people in northern Scandinavia and adjacent Russia. Baltic Finnic comprises Finnish, Estonian (with 1.1 million speakers worldwide), and a string of declining languages in Latvia and Russia. Mordvin is spoken by 1.1 million people in scattered enclaves of central European Russia. Mari is also spoken in central Russia and in scattered areas east toward the Ural Mountains; its two major varieties have about 600,000 speakers. The Permic languages, spread over a broad swath of northeastern European Russia, comprise Udmurt (spoken by some 500,000 people) and Komi (spoken by fewer than 400,000 people but with two literary forms). Finno-Ugric languages written in Russia use variants of the Cyrillic alphabet, while those outside Russia use the Latin alphabet.

fire, Rapid burning of combustible material, producing heat and usually accompanied by flame. For eons, lightning was the only source of fire. The earliest controlled use of fire seems to date to c. 1,420,000 years ago, but not until c. 7000 BC did Neolithic humans acquire reliable firemaking techniques, including friction from hardwood drills and sparks struck from flint against pyrites. Fire was used initially for warmth, light, and cooking; later it was used in fire drives in hunting and warfare, and for clearing forests of underbrush to facilitate hunting. The first agriculturalists used fire to clear fields and produce ash for fertilizer; such "slash-and-burn" cultivation is still used widely today. Fire also came to be used for firing pottery and for smelting bronze (c. 3000 BC) and later iron (c. 1000 BC). Much of the modern history of technology and science can be characterized as a continual increase in the amount of energy available through fire and brought under human control.

fire ant, Any of a genus (*Solenopsis*) of insects in the ant family, several species of which are common in southern North America. They are red or yellowish and can inflict a severe sting. The semipermanent nest consists of a loose mound with open craters for ventilation. The workers are notorious for damaging planted grain and attacking poultry.

fire walking, Religious ceremony that involves walking across hot coals, red-hot stones, or burning wood. It has been practiced in many parts of the world, including ancient Greece, India, Japan, China, Tahiti, New Zealand, Bulgaria, and Spain. The most common form of fire walking involves striding across a layer of embers spread thinly over the bottom of a shallow trench. More rarely, devotees may walk through a blazing log fire. The reasons for fire walking include purification and as an ordeal to prove innocence. Devotees believe that only those who lack faith will be burned, and many fire walkers do escape without injury.

firefly, or LIGHTNING BUG, Any of the nocturnal luminous beetles of the family Lampyridae, consisting of about 1,900 species that inhabit tropical and temperate regions (including the common glowworm). Adult fireflies are 0.2–1 in. (5–25 mm) long and have light-producing organs on the underside of the abdomen. The soft, flattened, dark-brown or black body is often marked with orange or yellow. Some adult fireflies do not eat; others feed on pollen and nectar. Most fireflies produce short, rhythmic flashes in a pattern that is characteristic of the species and an important mating signal.

fireplace, Opening made in the base of a chimney to hold an open fire. The opening is framed, usually ornamentally, by a mantel (or mantelpiece). A medieval development that replaced the open central hearth for heating and cooking, the fireplace was sometimes large enough to accommodate a sitting space called an inglenook. Early fireplaces were made of stone; later, brick came into use. In 1624 Louis Savot developed a fireplace in which air was drawn through passages under the hearth and discharged into the room through a grill, a design adapted in the 20th century.

fireproofing, Use of fire-resistant materials in a building to prevent structural collapse and allow safe egress of occupants in case of fire. The fire-resistive ratings of various materials and constructions are established by laboratory tests and usually specified in terms of hours a material or assembly can be expected to withstand exposure to fire. Building codes require application of cementitious material or insulation to structural steel frames, fire-resistant construction (e.g., using concrete block) of enclosures around ex-

its, flame-spread ratings of finish materials such as carpeting and wall coverings, and use of such inherently fire-resistant materials as reinforced concrete and heavy timber.

firewall, Computer security system that controls the flow of data from one computer or network to another. Firewalls are mainly intended to protect the resources of a private network from being directly accessed by a user from an external network, especially via the Internet. Users inside the private network may also be prevented from directly accessing external computers. To accomplish this, all communications are routed through a "proxy server" that determines whether a message or file will be allowed to enter or exit the private network.

fiscal policy, Measures employed by governments to stabilize the economy, specifically by adjusting the levels and allocations of taxes and government expenditures. When the economy is sluggish, the government may cut taxes, leaving taxpayers with extra cash to spend and thereby increasing levels of consumption. An increase in public-works spending may likewise pump cash into the economy, having an expansionary effect. Conversely, a decrease in government spending or an increase in taxes tends to cause the economy to contract. Fiscal policy is often used in tandem with monetary policy. Until the 1930s, fiscal policy aimed at maintaining a balanced budget; since then it has been used "countercyclically," as recommended by John Maynard Keynes, to offset the cycle of expansion and contraction in the economy. Fiscal policy is more effective at stimulating a flagging economy than at cooling an inflationary one, partly because spending cuts and tax increases are unpopular and partly because of the work of economic stabilizers.

fish, Any of more than 30,000 species of predominantly cold-blooded vertebrates found worldwide in fresh and salt water. Living species range from the primitive lampreys and hagfishes through the cartilaginous sharks, skates, and rays to the abundant and diverse bony fishes. Species range in length from 0.4 in. (10 mm) to more than 60 ft (20 m). The body is generally tapered at both ends. Most species that inhabit surface or midwater regions are streamlined or are flattened side to side; most bottom dwellers are flattened top to bottom. Tropical species are often brightly coloured. Most species have paired fins and skin covered with either bony or toothlike scales. Fishes generally respire through gills. Most bony fishes have a swim bladder, a gas-filled organ used to adjust swimming depth. Most species lay eggs, which may be fertilized externally or internally. Fishes first appeared more than 450 million years ago.

fishing, or SPORT FISHING, Sport of catching fish—freshwater or saltwater—typically with rod, line, and hook. Fishing is as old as the human ability to use tools to capture prey. The first significant modern innovations, including use of a reel, a rod with line guides, and a hook with an offset point, came in the late 17th and early 18th centuries. Horsehair was used as line until the mid 19th century, when it was replaced by textile materials; these in turn were replaced by nylon in the 1930s. Wood and bamboo rods yielded to rods of fibreglass and other synthetic materials. Forms of sport fishing practiced today include fly fishing (freshwater), in which a fly-like hook is repeatedly cast upon the water surface to attract biting fish; bait fishing (fresh- and saltwater), in which live or artificial bait is set or drawn below the surface; and big-game fishing (saltwater), in which heavy-duty tackle is used to land large marine species (including tuna, marlin, and swordfish) from a motorized boat.

Fitzgerald, Ella (b. April 25, 1917, Newport News, Va., U.S.—d. June 15, 1996, Beverly Hills, Calif.), U.S. singer. She won an amateur contest at Harlem's Apollo Theatre in 1934 and became the star of drummer Chick Webb's big band the following year. Her association with manager and impresario Norman Granz in the late 1940s led to performances with Jazz at the Philharmonic and a famous series of "Songbook" recordings, each featuring the work of a single popular-song composer. Fitzgerald was one of the greatest scat singers in jazz; her clear, girlish voice and virtuosity made her one of the best-selling vocal recording artists in history.

Five, The, or THE MIGHTY FIVE, Group of Russian composers who, in the 1860s, banded together in an attempt to create a truly national school of Russian music. The Five were César Cui (1835–1918), Aleksandr Borodin, Mily Balakirev, Modest Mussorgsky, and Nikolay Rimsky-Korsakov. A somewhat larger group around this core was referred to as "the Mighty Handful."

Five Classics, Chinese WUJING, Five ancient Chinese books associated with Confucius. For more than 2,000 years they were invoked as authorities on Chinese society, government, literature, and religion. Chinese students usually studied the shorter Four Books before attempting the Five Classics, which consist of the *Yijing* ("Classic of Changes"), the *Shujing* ("Classic of History"), the *Classic of Poetry,* the *Collection of Rituals,* and the *Chunqiu* ("Spring and Autumn Annals"). The Five Classics were taught from 136 BC (when Confucianism became the state ideology of China) until the early 20th century. Proficiency in the texts was required for any scholar applying for a post in the vast government bureaucracy. After 1950 only select texts were taught in public schools. *See* Chinese examination system.

fjord, or FIORD, Long, narrow arm of the sea, often extending well inland, that results from marine inundation of a glaciated valley. Many fjords are remarkably deep; it is assumed that the huge glaciers that formed in these valleys were so heavy that they eroded the bottoms of the valleys far below sea level. After the glaciers melted, the waters of the sea invaded the valleys.

flag, Combination of symbols represented on a piece of cloth, serving as a medium of social, typically political, communication. It is usually rectangular and attached by one edge to a staff or is hoisted on a pole with halyards. Flags appear to be as old as civilized human society, though their origin is not well understood. The Chinese may have been the first to develop cloth flags, and it is believed that they were introduced to Europe by returning Crusaders. Most national flags in use today were designed in the 19th and 20th centuries.

flagellants, Medieval religious sects that included public beatings with whips as part of their discipline and devotional practice. Flagellant sects arose in northern Italy, and had become large and widespread by *c.* 1260. Groups marched through European towns, whipping each other to atone for their sins and calling on the populace to repent. They gained many new members in the mid-14th century while the Black Death was ravaging Europe. Though periodically suppressed by the authorities, flagellant sects enjoyed sporadic resurgences into the 16th century.

flagellum, Hairlike structure that acts mainly as an organelle of movement in the cells of many living organisms. Characteristic of the protozoan group Mastigophora, flagella also occur on the sex cells of algae, fungi, mosses, and slime molds. Flagellar motion causes water currents necessary for respiration and circulation in sponges and cnidarians. Most motile bacteria move by means of flagella. The structures and patterns of movement of flagella in prokaryotes differ from those in eukaryotes.

Flamboyant style, Phase of late Gothic architecture in 15th-century France and Spain. It evolved out of the Rayonnant style's increasing emphasis on decoration. Its most conspicuous feature is the dominance in stone window tracery of a flamelike S-shaped curve. Wall surface was reduced to the minimum to allow an almost continuous window expanse. Structural logic was obscured by covering buildings with elaborate tracery. Attractive French examples include Notre-Dame d'Épine near Châlons-sur-Marne, Saint-Maclou in Rouen (*c.* 1500–14), and the northern spire of Chartres Cathedral. Spanish Flamboyant architects developed their own intricate forms of vaulting with curvilinear patterns; the Capilla del Condestable in Burgos Cathedral (1482–94) and Segovia Cathedral (begun 1525) provide examples. Flamboyant Gothic, which became increasingly ornate, gave way in France to Renaissance forms in the 16th century.

flamenco, Form of song, dance, and instrumental (mostly guitar) music commonly associated with the Andalusian Roma (Gypsies) of southern Spain. (There, the Roma people are known as Gitanos.) The roots of flamenco, though somewhat mysterious, seem to lie in the Roma migration from Rajasthan (in northwest India) to Spain between the 9th and 14th centuries. Its essence is *cante,* or song, often accompanied by guitar music and improvised dance. The *cante jondo* ("profound song" or "deep song"), thought to be the oldest form, is characterized by profound emotion and deals with themes of death, anguish, despair, or religious doubt. After the mid-19th century, flamenco song was usually accompanied by guitar music and a *palo seco* (Spanish: "dry stick," a stick that was beat on the floor to keep time) and a dancer performing a series of choreographed dance steps and improvised styles. *Baile,* or dance, has been the dominant element of flamenco since that time, though it is never performed without accompaniment. Essential to traditional flamenco is the *duende,* an intensely focused, trancelike state of transcendent emotion. It is usually enhanced by rhythmic hand clapping and encouraging interjections (*jaleo*) from fellow performers.

flamethrower, Military assault weapon that projects a stream of blazing oil or gasoline against enemy positions. It consists of one or more fuel tanks, a cylinder of compressed gas to supply the propelling force, and a flexible hose with a trigger-nozzle that ignites and sprays the fuel. Portable flamethrowers are carried on the backs of ground troops; larger units may be installed on tank turrets. Modern flamethrowers, first used in combat in World War I, were used by all major powers in World War II and later wars. They are often used in areas of dense underbrush and against fortified positions at close range.

flamingo, Any of six species of tall wading birds constituting the family Phoenicopteridae. The plumage is mainly pink, and the face is bare. Flamingos have webbed feet, a slender body, a long thin neck, large wings, and a short tail. They are about 3–5 ft (90–150 cm) tall. Flamingos flock by the hundreds—sometimes by the millions—in flight formations and wading groups. They walk the shallows, stirring up organic matter, especially tiny mollusks and crustaceans, which they strain from the muddy water with their sievelike bills. The various species are found in tropical and subtropical North America along the coasts of the Atlantic Ocean and Gulf of Mexico and in South America, Africa, southern Europe, Asia, Madagascar, and India.

Flanders, Flemish VLAANDEREN, Medieval principality extending along the coast of the Low Countries. Its lands are now included in the French *département* of Nord, the Belgian provinces of East Flanders and West Flanders, and the Dutch province of Zeeland. Ruled by Baldwin I in 862, Flanders began to grow as a commercial centre, fostered by its strategic location between the Mediterranean Sea and the Scandinavian and Baltic countries. It passed to Burgundy in 1384 and then to the Austrian Habsburgs in 1477. It remained part of the Netherlands under Spanish rule in the 17th century. It was the scene of fighting during both World War I and World War II. Limited autonomy was granted to Belgian Flanders in the 1980s, and it became one of the three regions in the new federation of Belgium in 1993.

flea, Any member of 2,000 species and subspecies of small, wingless, bloodsucking (parasitic) insects (order Siphonaptera), found from the Arctic Circle to the Arabian deserts. Specialized anatomical structures allow the flea to attach itself to the skin of mammals or birds and consume their blood. Though domestic cats and dogs are well-known hosts, rodents are the mammals most com-

Flea (Ctenocephalides)
William E. Ferguson

monly afflicted by fleas. The adult flea is 0.04–0.4 in. (1–10 mm) long and lives from a few weeks to more than a year. Powerful leg muscles allow it to jump distances up to 200 times its body length. Flea infestations have had enormous consequences; fleas were the principal transmission agents of the bubonic plague in the medieval epidemics.

Fleming, Sir Alexander (b. Aug. 6, 1881, Lochfield, Ayr, Scot.—d. March 11, 1955, London, Eng.), Scottish bacteriologist. While serving in the Royal Army Medical Corps in World War I, he conducted research on antibacterial substances that would be nontoxic to humans. In 1928 he inadvertently discovered penicillin when he noticed that a mold contaminating a bacterial culture was inhibiting the bacteria's growth. He shared a 1945 Nobel Prize with Ernst Boris Chain and Howard Walter Florey, who both carried Fleming's basic discovery further in isolating, purifying, testing, and producing penicillin in quantity.

Fleming, Ian (Lancaster) (b. May 28, 1908, London, Eng.—d. Aug. 12, 1964, Canterbury, Kent), British suspense novelist. He worked as a Moscow journalist, banker, stockbroker, naval intelligence officer, and newspaper manager before publishing *Casino Royale* (1953), the first of 12 novels featuring James Bond, the stylish, high-living secret service agent 007, one of the most successful characters of 20th-century fiction. Packed with violent action, espionage, and sex, all 12 books—including *From Russia, with Love* (1957), *Dr. No* (1958), *Goldfinger* (1959), and *Thunderball* (1961)—became popular movies.

Flemish art, Art of the 15th to early 17th century in Flanders. The precursors of the Flemish school were located in Dijon, the first capital of the dukes of Burgundy, who established a powerful Flemish-Burgundian political alliance that lasted from 1363 to 1482. Philip III (the Good) moved the Burgundian capital to Bruges and in 1425 hired Jan van Eyck as his painter. The next generation of artists built on van Eyck's heritage and, toward the end of the 15th century, began looking to Italy for pictorial inspiration. Rogier van der Weyden, Petrus Christus, Dirck Bouts, Hugo van der Goes, Hans Memling, and Gerard David brought innovation, but little of their work compared with van Eyck's artistic vision. In the 16th century Pieter Bruegel the Elder, under the influence of Hiëronymus Bosch, depicted peasant life with an eye for the grotesque. The great master of the 17th century, Peter Paul Rubens, demonstrated unrivaled skill in oil painting; his style epitomized the Flemish Baroque period.

flerovium, Synthetic radioactive chemical element, chemical symbol Fl, atomic number 114. This transuranium element was first produced in 1999 from the collision of calcium-48 and plutonium-244 and plutonium-242 in a cyclotron. Shortly after creation, the flerovium nucleus decayed into copernicium. The four isotopes of flerovium have half-lives of 0.16–0.97 second. These long half-lives were seen as the "shores" of the "island of stability," atoms that are much more stable than other transuranium elements. Theoretical calculations point to an as-yet-unproduced isotope of flerovium as being the "peak" of that island. It is named after Russian physicist Georgy Flerov.

flintlock, Ignition system for firearms developed in the early 16th century. It superseded the matchlock and the wheel lock and remained in use until the mid-19th century. The most successful version, the true flintlock, was invented in France in the 17th century. When the trigger was pulled, a spring action caused the frizzen (striker) to strike the flint, showering sparks onto the gunpowder in the priming pan; the ignited powder, in turn, fired the main charge in the bore, propelling the ball.

flood, High-water stage in which water overflows its natural or artificial banks onto normally dry land, such as a river inundating its floodplain. Uncontrollable floods likely to cause considerable damage commonly result from excessive rainfall in a brief period, but they may also result from ice jams during the spring rise in rivers, and from tsunamis. Common measures of flood control include improving channels, constructing protective levees and storage reservoirs, and implementing programs of soil and forest conservation to retard and absorb runoff from storms.

floor, Rigid building assembly that divides space horizontally into stories. It forms the bottom of a room. It may consist of joist-supported wood planks or panels, decking or panels supported by wood or steel beams, a slab of stone or concrete on the ground, or a reinforced-concrete slab carried by concrete beams and columns. The floor assembly must support its own dead load plus the live load of occupants, activities, and furnishings. The horizontal supports beneath its top surface—and the vertical supports into which they frame—must be sufficiently large and spaced closely enough to prevent sagging of the assembly.

Florence, Italian FIRENZE, City (pop., 2001 prelim.: 352,227), capital of Tuscany, central Italy. Built on both sides of the Arno River, the city has been during its long history a republic, a seat of the duchy of Tuscany, and a capital (1865–71) of Italy. Founded as a Roman military colony in the 1st century BCE, it was controlled in turn by the Goths, Byzantines, and Lombards. A leading city of Tuscany by the late 12th century, it was ruled after 1434 by the powerful Medici family. It became a republic under religious reformer Girolamo Savonarola, after whose downfall the Medici were restored as dukes of Florence (1531). Florence's vernacular became the Italian language, and from the 14th to the 16th century Florence was among the greatest cities of Europe, preeminent in commerce, finance, learning, and the arts. Many notables flourished there, including Leonardo da Vinci, Michelangelo, Filippo Brunelleschi, Dante, Niccolò Machiavelli, and Galileo. The buildings, including the Baptistery of St. John, the Gothic Duomo, and the Uffizi Gallery, are works of art themselves abounding in yet more works of art. Among the palaces and parks are the Pitti Palace and its Boboli Gardens. The university was founded in 1321. The economy is based primarily on tourism, though it also has developed newer sectors such as information technology and high-fashion clothing. The region around the city has a modern and dynamic economy based on small industrial production and quality exports.

floriculture, Branch of ornamental horticulture concerned with growing and marketing flowers and ornamental plants, as well as with flower arrangement. Because flowers and potted plants are largely produced in plant-growing structures in temperate climates, floriculture is largely thought of as a greenhouse industry; however, many flowers are cultivated outdoors. Both the production of bedding plants and the production of cuttings to be grown in greenhouses or for indoor use (foliage plants) are usually considered part of floriculture.

flower, Reproductive portion of any flowering plant (angiosperm). Popularly, the term applies especially when part or all of the reproductive structure is distinctive in colour and form. Flowers present a multitude of combinations of colour, size, form, and anatomical arrangement. In some plants, individual flowers are very small and are borne in a distinctive cluster (inflorescence). Each flower consists of a floral axis that bears the essential organs of reproduction (stamens and pistils) and usually accessory organs (sepals and petals); the latter may serve both to attract pollinating insects and to protect the essential organs. Flower parts are arrayed usually in whorls, but sometimes spirally. Four distinct whorls are common: the outer calyx (sepals), the corolla (petals), the androecium (stamens), and, in the centre, the gynoecium (pistils). The sepals are usually greenish and often resemble reduced leaves; the petals are usually colourful and showy. Pollen is produced in the stamens. A pollen-receptive stigma rests atop each pistil. The pistil, made up of one or more carpels, encloses an ovary that contains the ovules, or potential seeds. After fertilization, the ovary enlarges to form the fruit. Flowers have been symbols of beauty in most civilizations of the world, and flower giving is still among the most popular of social amenities.

fluid, Any liquid or gas that cannot sustain a shearing force when at rest and that undergoes a continuous change in shape when subjected to such a stress. Compressed fluids exert an outward pressure that is perpendicular to the walls of their containers. A perfect fluid lacks viscosity, but real fluids do not.

fluorescence, Emission of electromagnetic radiation, usually visible light, caused by excitation of atoms in a material, which then reemit almost immediately (within about 10^{-8} seconds). The initial excitation is usually caused by absorption of energy from incident radiation or particles, such as X-rays or electrons. Because reemission occurs so quickly, the fluorescence ceases as soon as the exciting source is removed, unlike phosphorescence, which persists as an afterglow. A fluorescent lightbulb is coated on the inside with a powder and contains a gas; electricity causes the gas to emit ultraviolet radiation, which then stimulates the tube coating to emit light. The pixels of a television or computer screen fluoresce when electrons from an electron gun strike them. Fluorescence is often used to analyze molecules, and the addition of a fluorescing agent with emissions in the blue region of the spectrum to detergents causes fabrics to appear whiter in sunlight. X-ray fluorescence is used to analyze minerals.

fluorine, Nonmetallic chemical element, chemical symbol F, atomic number 9. The lightest halogen, it is the most reactive element, forming compounds with all others except helium, neon, and argon (the lighter noble gases). Its only valence is 1, in F_2 (the diatomic molecule) and fluorides. A toxic, pale yellow gas with a pungent odour, it can be produced only by electrolysis under special conditions. Its chief source is fluorite; it also occurs in cryolite, fluorapatite, seawater, bones, and teeth. Hydrogen fluoride (HF) is a raw material for many other fluorides. Its water solution, hydrofluoric acid, is used to clean metals and to polish, etch, or frost glass. Other fluorides are useful catalysts and raw materials. Sodium fluoride (NaF) is added to water and tin fluoride (SnF_2) to dental-care products to reduce dental caries. Fluorocarbons are hydrocarbons in which some hydrogen atoms have been replaced by fluorine atoms; examples include Freons and Teflon.

flute, Woodwind instrument in which the sound is produced by blowing against a sharp edge. In its broad sense, a flute may be end-blown, like the recorder, or may have a globular shape, like the ocarina. In its narrow sense, discussed below, flute refers to the transverse flute of Western music. The transverse flute, a tubular instrument held sideways to the right, appeared in Greece and Etruria by the 2nd century BC. By the 16th century a family of boxwood flutes, with fingerholes but no keys, was in use in Europe. Keys began to be added in the late 17th century. Theobald Boehm's 19th-century innovations resulted in the modern flute, which permits thorough expressive control and great agility. The cylindrical tube may be made of wood or, more often, a precious metal or alloy. Its range is from about middle C to the C three octaves higher. The flute family includes the piccolo (pitched an octave higher), the alto flute, and the rare bass flute.

Fly River, River, south-central New Guinea. One of the island's largest rivers, it flows almost wholly through Papua New Guinea, except for a short stretch of its middle course, which forms the border between Papua New Guinea and Indonesia. Rising in the Victor Emanuel Range in the central highlands, it flows south for about 700 mi (1,100 km) to the Gulf of Papua on the Coral Sea; much of it is navigable.

flying buttress, Masonry structure typically consisting of an inclined bar carried on a half arch that extends ("flies") from the upper part of a wall to a pier some distance away and carries the thrust of a roof or vault. A pinnacle (vertical ornament of pyramidal or conical shape) often crowns the pier, adding weight and enhancing stability. The flying buttress evolved in the Gothic era from earlier simpler, hidden supports. The design increased the supporting power of the buttress and allowed for the creation of the high-ceilinged churches typical of Gothic architecture.

flying fish, Any of about 40 species of oceanic fishes (family Exocoetidae). They are found worldwide in warm waters and are noted for their ability to "fly." All species are less than 18 in. (45 cm) long and have winglike, rigid fins and an unevenly forked tail. Two-winged species have only the pectoral fins enlarged; four-winged species have both the pectoral and the pelvic fins enlarged. Rather than flying, they actually glide after jumping from the water. They can make several consecutive glides; the strongest fliers can travel as much as 600 ft (180 m) in a single glide, and compound glides may cover 1,300 ft (400 m). The behaviour is primarily a means of escaping predators.

flying squirrel, Any member of two distinct groups of rodents that are able to make gliding leaps by means of parachute-like membranes connecting their forelegs and hind legs on each side. North American and Eurasian flying squirrels, in the squirrel family (Sciuridae), are slender, long-limbed forest dwellers with soft fur and large eyes. They are 3–24 in. (8–60 cm) long, excluding the often-flattened tail, and feed on nuts, fruit, other plant material, and insects. They seldom descend to the ground. They can glide 200 ft (about 60 m) or more from one tree to another. The scaly-tailed flying squirrels of Africa (family Anomaluridae) have rows of scales on the underside of their tufted tail that help them climb and cling to trees. They are similar in appearance and feeding preferences to the sciurids and are about 4–16 in. (10–40 cm) long without the tail.

Fo, Dario (b. March 24, 1926, Leggiuno-Sangiano, Italy), Italian playwright. He and his wife, Franca Rame, founded a theatre company that developed a leftist theatre of politics and later established an acting troupe with funding from the Italian Communist Party. In 1970 they set up a touring collective to perform in factories and other public sites. Fo's popular one-man show *Mistero Buffo* (1973) was censured by the Vatican. He wrote more than 70 plays, including the satire *Accidental Death of an Anarchist* (1974) and *The Pope and the Witch* (1989). He was awarded the Nobel Prize in 1997.

fog, Cloud of small water droplets near ground level that is dense enough to reduce horizontal visibility to less than about 3,000 ft (1,000 m). Fog may also refer to clouds of smoke particles (smog), ice particles, or mixtures of these components. When visibility is more than 3,000 ft, the phenomenon is termed mist or haze, depending on whether it is caused by water drops or by solid particles. Fog is formed by the condensation of water vapour on condensation nuclei that are always present in natural air. The most stable fogs occur when the surface is colder than the air above. Fogs can also occur when cold air moves over a warm, wet surface and becomes saturated by the evaporation of moisture from the surface. Convection currents carry the fog upward as it forms, and it appears to rise as steam or smoke from the wet surface.

folk art, Art produced in a traditional fashion by peasants, seamen, country artisans, or tradespeople with no formal training, or by members of a social or ethnic group that has preserved its traditional culture. It is predominantly functional, typically produced by hand for use by the maker or by a small group or community.

Paintings are usually incorporated as decorative features on clock faces, chests, chairs, and interior and exterior walls. Sculptural objects in wood, stone, and metal include toys, spoons, candlesticks, and religious items. Folk architecture may include public and residential buildings, such as eastern European wooden churches and U.S. frontier log cabins. Other examples of visual folk arts are woodcuts, scrimshaw, pottery, textiles, and traditional clothing.

folk dance, Dance that has developed without a choreographer and that reflects the traditional life of the common people of a country or region. The term was coined in the 18th century and is sometimes used to distinguish between dances of the people and those of the aristocracy. Courtly and formal dances of the 16th–20th centuries often developed from folk dances; these include the gavotte, gigue, mazurka, minuet, polka, samba, tango, and waltz.

folk music, Music held to be typical of a nation or ethnic group, known to all segments of its society, and preserved usually by oral tradition. Knowledge of the history and development of folk music is largely conjectural. Musical notation of folk songs and descriptions of folk music culture are occasionally encountered in historical records, but these tend to reflect primarily the literate classes' indifference or even hostility. As Christianity expanded in medieval Europe, attempts were made to suppress folk music because of its association with heathen rites and customs, and uncultivated singing styles were denigrated. During the Renaissance, new humanistic attitudes encouraged acceptance of folk music as a genre of rustic antique song, and composers made extensive use of the music; folk tunes were often used as raw material for motets and masses, and Protestant hymns borrowed from folk music. In the 17th century folk music gradually receded from the consciousness of the literate classes, but in the late 18th century it again became important to art music. In the 19th century, folk songs came to be considered a "national treasure," on a par with cultivated poetry and song. National and regional collections were published, and the music became a means of promoting nationalistic ideologies. Since the 1890s, folk music has been collected and preserved by mechanical recordings. Publications and recordings have promoted wide interest, making possible the revival of folk music where traditional folk life and folklore are moribund. After World War II, archives of field recordings were developed throughout the world. While research has usually dealt with "authentic" (i.e., older) material not heavily influenced by urban popular music and the mass media, the influence of singer-songwriters such as Woody Guthrie, Pete Seeger, Joan Baez, and Bob Dylan expanded the genre to include original music that largely retains the form and simplicity of traditional compositions.

folklore, Oral literature and popular tradition preserved among a people. It may take the form of fairy tales, ballads, epics, proverbs, and riddles. Studies of folklore began in the early 19th century and first focused on rural folk and others believed to be untouched by modern ways. Several aims can be identified. One was to trace archaic customs and beliefs. In Germany Jacob and Wilhelm Grimm published their classic collection of fairy tales in 1812. James George Frazer's *The Golden Bough* (1890) reflects the use of folklore as a tool to reconstruct ancient beliefs and rituals. Another motive for the study of folklore was nationalism, which reinforced ethnic identity and figured in struggles for political independence. The catalog of motifs of folktales and myths developed by Antti Aarne and Stith Thompson encouraged comparisons of variants of the same tale or other item from different regions and times. In the mid-20th century, new trends emerged. Any group that expressed its inner cohesion by maintaining shared traditions qualified as a "folk," whether the linking factor be occupation, language, place of residence, age, religion, or ethnic origin. Emphasis also shifted from the past to the present, from the search for origins to the investigation of present meaning and function. Change and adaptation within tradition were no longer necessarily regarded as corruptive.

Fontainebleau, Château in northern France, southeast of the town of Fontainebleau. One of the largest structures built by the kings of France, it was originally a medieval hunting lodge, but was rebuilt (from 1528) under Francis I. Its numerous renovations show the transition from early Renaissance to Mannerist (Late Renaissance) styles. The château is a succession of five courts of different shapes. Of particular interest is the Gallery of Francis I (*c.* 1533–45), a long, narrow room decorated with stucco relief sculpture and painting by Rosso Fiorentino.

Fontainebleau, school of, French and foreign artists associated with the court at Fontainebleau in the 16th century. In 1528 Francis I began to rebuild the palace and hired Rosso Fiorentino and Francesco Primaticcio to produce the mural decoration, stuccowork, and sculptural reliefs; also among the Italian artists was Benvenuto Cellini. Many engravings were made of the work being done, and much of the most decorative painting and sculpture can still be seen there. The Italian masters successfully adapted their own styles to the French taste and were assisted by French and Flemish artists; together they produced a distinctive style of Mannerism. The innovation of stucco ornament in combination with mural painting had great influence on French art of the time.

Diana the Huntress, *oil on canvas by an anonymous artist of the school of Fontainebleau, c. 1550; in the Louvre, Paris.*
Giraudon/Art Resource, New York

food chain, Sequence of transfer of matter and energy from organism to organism in the form of food. These interconnected feeding relationships intertwine locally into a food web because most organisms consume or are consumed by more than one other type of organism. Plants and other photosynthetic organisms (such as phytoplankton), which convert solar energy to food, are the primary food source. In a predator chain, a plant-eating animal is eaten by a larger animal. In a parasite chain, a smaller organism consumes part of a larger host and may itself be parasitized by even smaller organisms. In a saprophytic chain, microorganisms live on dead organic matter. Because energy, in the form of heat, is lost at each step, or trophic level, chains do not normally encompass more than four or five trophic levels.

foot, End part of the leg, consisting of the heel, arch, and toes, on which a person stands. Its major function is locomotion. The human foot cannot grasp and is adapted for running and striding (a step unique to humans that can cover great distances with minimal energy expenditure). Its arched structure helps it support the body's weight.

foot, metrical, Basic unit of verse metre. Any of various fixed combinations or groups of stressed and unstressed (or long and short) syllables comprise a foot. The prevailing kind and number of feet determines the metre of a poem. The most common feet in English verse are the iamb, an unstressed followed by a stressed syllable; the trochee, a stressed followed by an unstressed syllable; the anapest, two unstressed syllables followed by a stressed syllable; and the dactyl, a stressed syllable followed by two unstressed syllables.

foot-and-mouth disease (FMD), or HOOF-AND-MOUTH DISEASE, Highly contagious viral disease of cloven-footed mammals (including cattle), spread by ingestion and inhalation. The afflicted animal develops fever and painful blisters on the tongue, lips, other tissues of the mouth, muzzle or snout, teats, and feet. FMD is endemic in many places. Because of its rapid spread and impact on animal productivity, it is considered the most economically devastating livestock disease in the world. It is not a human health hazard. No effective treatment exists; vaccines control epidemics but have not eliminated them. Since the virus can persist, quarantine, slaughter, cremation or burial of carcasses, and decontamination must be rigorous. Strict surveillance has kept North America largely FMD-free since 1929. In early 2001 a major outbreak occurred in the United Kingdom, followed shortly by outbreaks in the Netherlands and France.

football, or ASSOCIATION FOOTBALL, or SOCCER, Game in which two 11-member teams try to propel a ball into the opposing team's goal, using any part of the body except the hands and arms. Only the goalkeeper, when positioned within the penalty area in front of the goal, may use hands and arms. The game's first uniform set of rules was put in place in 1863, when England's Football Association was created. Professional leagues began appearing in the late 1880s, first in England and then in other countries. The Fédération Internationale de Football Association (FIFA) was founded in 1904, and has hosted the World Cup every four years since 1930. Football has been included in the Olympic Games since 1908. Now played on all continents in over 200 countries, with over 250 million players, it is the world's most popular ball game.

football, gridiron, Game played, predominantly in the U.S. and Canada, on a rectangular field having two goalposts at each end. In the U.S. it is played between two teams of 11 players each. The object is to get an oblong ball, in possession of one side at a time, over a goal line or between goalposts by running, passing, or kicking. A team must advance the ball 10 yards in four attempts (called downs) in order to continue to have the ball for another four downs. A kick through the goalposts (field goal) counts as three points. A run or completed pass over the goal line (touchdown) counts as six points. Following a touchdown, a team may attempt to kick the ball through the goalposts for one additional point or to run or pass the ball over the goal line for two additional points. Gridiron football (so-called because of the markings on the field), derived from rugby and soccer, emerged in the late 19th century as a collegiate sport; the early rules were mostly written by representatives from Yale, Harvard, and Princeton universities. Each year the college football season concludes with a host of bowl games held on and around New Year's Day. Professional football began in the 1890s but did not become a major sport until after World War II. The National Football League was formed in 1922. The NFL is now divided into an American and a National conference; the conference winners compete for the Super Bowl championship. A Football Hall of Fame is located in Canton, Ohio, U.S. Canadian football differs from U.S. football principally by having 12 players on a team rather than 11, employing a larger field, and allowing only three downs to move the ball 10 yards. These variations allow for a more wide-open style of game, with an emphasis on passing.

Forbidden City, Imperial Palace complex in Beijing, containing hundreds of buildings and some 9,000 rooms. It served the emperors of China from 1421 to 1911. No commoner or foreigner was allowed to enter it without special permission. The moated palaces, with their golden tiled roofs and red pillars, are surrounded by high walls with a tower on each corner. The palaces consist of the outer throne halls and an inner courtyard, each palace forming an architectural whole. North of the front gate, a great courtyard lies beyond five marble bridges. Farther north, raised on a marble terrace, is the massive, double-tiered Hall of Supreme Harmony, once the throne hall, one of the largest wooden structures in China. The palaces and buildings are now public museums.

force, Agency that alters the direction, speed, or shape that a body would exhibit in the absence of any external influence. It is a vector quantity, having both magnitude and direction. Force is commonly explained in terms of Newton's laws of motion. All known natural forces can be traced to the fundamental interactions. Force is measured in newtons (N); a force of 1 N will accelerate a mass of 1 kg at a rate of 1 m/sec/sec.

Ford, Henry (b. July 30, 1863, Wayne county, Mich., U.S.—d. April 7, 1947, Dearborn, Mich.), U.S. industrialist and pioneer automobile manufacturer. Ford worked his way up from a machinist's apprentice (at age 15) to the post of chief engineer at the Edison Company in Detroit. He built his first experimental car in 1896. In 1903, with several partners, he formed the Ford Motor Company. In 1908 he designed the Model T; demand became so great that Ford developed new mass-production methods, including the first moving assembly line in 1913. He developed the Model A in 1928 to replace the Model T, and in 1932 he introduced the V-8 engine. He observed an eight-hour workday and paid his workers far above the average, holding that well-paid labourers become the consumers that industrialists require, but strenuously opposed labour unions. As the first to make car ownership affordable to large numbers of Americans, he exerted a vast and permanent influence on American life.

foreign aid, Transfer of capital, goods, or services from one country to another. Foreign aid may be given in the form of capital transfers or technical assistance and training for either civilian or military purposes. Its use in the modern era began in the 18th century, when Prussia subsidized some of its allies. After World War II, foreign aid developed into a more sophisticated instrument of foreign policy. International organizations, such as the United Nations Relief and Rehabilitation Administration, were created to provide aid to war-ravaged countries and newly freed colonies. Foreign aid is often given with conditions attached, such as the requirement that all or part of it be used to buy goods from the donor country.

foreign exchange, Purchase or sale of one national currency in exchange for another nation's currency, usually conducted in a market setting. Foreign exchange makes possible international transactions such as imports and exports and the movement of capital between countries. The value of one foreign currency in relation to another is defined by the exchange rate.

Foreign Legion, French, French LÉGION ÉTRANGÈRE, French military corps consisting originally of foreign volunteers in the pay of France but now including many Frenchmen. It was founded in 1831 as a highly disciplined professional army to help control French colonies in Africa. Since its founding, it has been in almost continuous combat; its forces have fought or been stationed in such places as Europe, Mexico, Syria, and Southeast Asia. The new volunteer swears to serve not France but the legion; after three years of service with good conduct, foreign-born soldiers are eligible for French citizenship. Since the legion keeps a volunteer's past secret, it has been romanticized as a haven for those seeking new identities, including criminals, but legionnaires typically are professional soldiers. Originally headquartered in Algeria, the legion moved its headquarters to France after Algerian independence.

Foreign Ministers, Council of, Organization of the foreign ministers of the U.S., Britain, France, and the Soviet Union—the World War II Allied Powers. In meetings between 1945 and 1972, they attempted to reach postwar political agreements. They produced treaties of peace with Italy, Hungary, Romania, Finland, and Bulgaria and resolved the Trieste problem in 1946. They convened the Geneva Conference on the Korean War in 1954, and in 1955 agreed on an Austrian treaty. They recessed after failing to agree on German unification in 1959; in 1972 they paved the way for both East and West Germany to enter the UN.

foreign policy, General objectives that guide the activities and relationships of one state in its interactions with other states. The development of foreign policy is influenced by domestic considerations, the policies or behaviour of other states, or plans to advance specific geopolitical designs. Leopold von Ranke emphasized the primacy of geography and external threats in shaping foreign policy, but later writers emphasized domestic factors. Diplomacy is the tool of foreign policy, and war, alliances, and international trade may all be manifestations of it.

forensic medicine, Science of applying medical knowledge to legal questions, recognized as a specialty since the early 19th century. Its primary tool has always been the autopsy, to identify the dead (e.g., plane-crash victims) or determine cause of death, which can significantly affect trials dealing with insurance and inheritance. Forensic psychiatry determines the mental health of an individual about to stand trial. Forensic genetics allows paternity to be determined and can identify blood or other tissue samples as coming from a particular person. Forensic toxicology, concerned with such topics as intentional poisonings and drug use, is increasingly important in cases of industrial and environmental poisoning.

forensic psychology, Application of psychology to legal issues, often for the purpose of offering expert testimony in a courtroom. In civil and criminal cases, forensic psychologists may evaluate individuals to determine questions such as competency to stand trial, relationship of a mental disorder to an accident or crime, and potential for future dangerous behaviour. In addition to conducting interviews and administering psychological tests, they usually gather a forensic history, which includes information such as hospital records, police reports, and statements of witnesses. They are also expected to have a grasp of relevant legal questions. In a child-custody case, a forensic psychologist may be asked to evaluate home environments, parents, and the character of the child in order to recommend a custody decision in the child's best interests.

forging, In metallurgy, the process of shaping metal and increasing its strength by hammering or pressing. In most forging an upper die is forced against a heated workpiece positioned on a stationary lower die. To increase the force of the blow, power is sometimes applied to augment gravity. The number of blows struck is carefully gauged by the operator to give maximum effect with minimum wear on the die. Forging presses employ hydraulic or mechanical pressure instead of blows; most can exert only a few hundred tons of pressure, but giant presses, used for forging parts of jet aircraft, are capable of up to 50,000 tons of pressure.

form, In the philosophy of Plato and Aristotle the active, determining principle of a thing. The term was traditionally used to translate Plato's *eidos*, by which he meant the permanent reality that makes a thing what it is, in contrast to the particulars that are finite and subject to change. Each form is the pattern of a particular category of thing in the world; thus, there are forms of human, stone, shape, colour, beauty, and justice. Whereas the physical world, perceived with the senses, is in constant flux and knowledge derived from it restricted and variable, the realm of forms, apprehensible only by the mind, is eternal and changeless. Particular things derive what reality they have by "participating" in, or imperfectly copying, the forms. Aristotle rejected the abstract Platonic notion of form and argued that every sensible object consists of both matter and form, neither of which can exist without the other. For Aristotle, the matter of a thing consists of those of its elements which, when the thing has come into being, may be said to have "become" it; the form of a thing is the arrangement or organization through which such elements have become the thing in question. Thus a certain lump of bronze is the matter that, given a certain form, becomes a statue or, given another, becomes a sword. The Aristotelian concept of form was adapted and developed by St. Thomas Aquinas and other scholastic philosophers. The En-lightenment philosopher Immanuel Kant used the notion of form to describe the mentally imposed conditions of sensible experience, namely space and time.

formal system, In logic, a formal language together with a deductive apparatus by which some well-formed formulas can be derived from others. Each formal system has a formal language composed of primitive symbols that figure in certain rules of formation (statements concerning the expressions allowable in the system) and a set of theorems developed by inference from a set of axioms. In an axiomatic system, the primitive symbols are undefined and all other symbols are defined in terms of them. In Euclidean geometry, for example, such concepts as "point," "line," and "lies on" are usually posited as primitive terms. From the primitive symbols, certain formulas are defined as well formed, some of which are listed as axioms; and rules are stated for inferring one formula as a conclusion from one or more other formulas taken as premises. A theorem within such a system is a formula capable of proof through a finite sequence of well-formed formulas, each of which either is an axiom or is validly inferred from earlier formulas.

formaldehyde, or METHANAL, Simplest aldehyde, chemical formula HCHO. Formaldehyde (37%) in water solution, called formalin, is used as a preservative, an embalming agent, and a disinfectant. Large amounts of formaldehyde are used in the manufacture of various familiar plastics. Bakelite (the first completely synthetic plastic) is the trademark for formaldehyde and phenol polymer, and Formica is the trademark for formaldehyde and urea polymer. The reaction of formaldehyde with proteins (called amino formylation) leads to its use in the tanning industry and for treating various vegetable proteins to render them fibrous.

fortification, Structure erected to strengthen a military position against attack. The defense of cities and trade centers, usually by high walls, has been important for centuries. The citadel was the fortress of the ancient world, appearing in cities of Egypt, Greece, and the Roman empire. By Classical Greek times, fortress architecture began incorporating ramparts (walled embankments) and towers. Roman fortresses of the 2nd century tended to be square or rectangular, and were usually of dressed (cut) stone. The medieval castle remained almost impregnable until gunpowder came into use.

FORTRAN, Procedural computer programming language developed for numerical analysis by John W. Backus and others at IBM in 1957. The name derives from FORmula TRANslation. For many years it was the most widely used high-level language for scientific and engineering computations. Though other languages, such as various versions of C, are now popular for such uses, FORTRAN is still the language of choice for numerical analysis. It has been revised several times and now includes capabilities for handling structured data, dynamic ("on-the-fly") data allocation, recursions (procedures that call themselves), and other features.

forum, In ancient Roman cities, a centrally located open area surrounded by public buildings and colonnades and serving as a multipurpose public gathering place. The forum was an adaptation of the Greek agora and acropolis. In Rome the *forum Romanum* referred to the flat and formerly marshy space between the Palatine and Capitoline hills. In the Roman republic, this was the site of public meetings, law courts, and gladiatorial games and was lined with shops and open-air markets. Under the Roman empire, when the forum evolved into a center for religious and secular ceremonies and spectacles, it held many of Rome's most imposing temples, basilicas, and monuments. New forums were built, some devoted to judicial or administrative affairs and some to trade. The aesthetic harmony of Trajan's Forum (2nd century AD), with its complex of buildings and courtyards and its tiers of shops, influenced many subsequent town planners.

fossil, Remnant, impression, or trace of an animal or plant of a past geologic age that has been preserved in the Earth's crust. The data recorded in fossils, known as the fossil record, constitute the primary source of information about the history of life on the Earth. Only a small fraction of ancient organisms are preserved as fossils, and usually only organisms that have a solid skeleton or shell. A shell or bone that is buried quickly after deposition may retain organic tissue, though it becomes petrified (converted to a stony substance) over time. Unaltered hard parts, such as the shells of clams, are relatively common in sedimentary rocks. The soft parts of animals or plants are rarely preserved. The embedding of insects in amber and the preservation of mammoths in ice are rare but striking examples of the fossil preservation of soft tissues. Traces of organisms may also occur as tracks, trails, or even borings.

fossil fuel, Any of a class of materials of biologic origin occurring within the Earth's crust that can be used as a source of energy. Fossil fuels include coal, petroleum, and natural gas. They all contain carbon and were formed as a result of geologic processes acting on the remains of (mostly) plants and animals that lived and died hundreds of millions of years ago. All fossil fuels can be burned to provide heat, which may be used directly, as in home heating, or to produce steam to drive a generator for the production of electricity. Fossil fuels supply nearly 90% of all the energy used by industrially developed nations.

Foucault pendulum, Large pendulum that is free to swing in any direction. As it swings back and forth, the earth rotates beneath it, so its perpendicular plane of swing rotates in relation to the earth's surface. Devised by J.-B.-L. Foucault in 1851, it provided the first laboratory demonstration that the earth spins on its axis. A Foucault pendulum always rotates clockwise in the Northern Hemisphere and counterclockwise in the Southern Hemisphere (a consequence of the Coriolis force). The rate of rotation depends on the latitude, becoming slower as the pendulum is placed closer to the equator; at the equator, a Foucault pendulum does not rotate.

foundation, Nongovernmental, nonprofit organization with assets provided by donors and managed by its own officials and with income expended for socially useful purposes. Foundations can be traced back to ancient Greece. The late 19th century first saw the establishment of large foundations with broad purposes and great freedom of action, usually originating in the fortunes of wealthy industrialists. Today foundations are classified as community (having support from many donors and located in a specific community), corporation-sponsored, and independent. Notable examples include the Smithsonian Institution (1846), the Carnegie Corp. of New York (1911), the Rockefeller Foundation (1913), and the Ford Foundation (1936), one of the largest in the world. Nongovernmental organizations are known colloquially as "NGOs."

foundationalism, In epistemology, the view that some beliefs can justifiably be held directly (e.g., on the basis of sense perception or rational intuition) and not by inference from other justified beliefs. Other types of beliefs (e.g., beliefs about material objects or about theoretical entities of science) are not regarded as basic or foundational in this way but are held to require inferential support. Foundationalists have typically recognized self-evident truths and reports of sense-data as basic, in the sense that they do not need support from other beliefs. Such beliefs thus provide the foundations on which the edifice of knowledge can properly be built.

founding, Process of pouring molten metal into a mold. When the metal solidifies, the result is a casting, a metal object conforming to that shape. Multitudinous metal objects are molded at some point during their manufacture. Modern foundries capable of large-scale production are characterized by a high degree of mechanization, automation, and robotics; microprocessors accurately control the automated systems. Advances in chemical binders have resulted in stronger molds and cores and in more accurate castings. Accuracy and purity are increased in vacuum conditions, and further advances are expected from zero-gravity casting in space.

Four Books, Chinese SISHU, Ancient Confucian texts used as the basis of study for civil service examinations in China (1313–1905). They served as an introduction to Confucianism and were traditionally studied before the more difficult Five Classics. The publication of the four texts as a unit in 1190 with commentaries by Zhu Xi helped revitalize Confucianism in China. The texts are *Daxue, Zhongyong, Lunyu* (the *Analects*, which reputedly contains direct quotations from Confucius and is deemed the most reliable source of his teachings), and *Mencius*.

Four Noble Truths, Statement of the basic doctrines of Buddhism. They were formulated by the Buddha Gautama in his first sermon. The truths are (1) existence is suffering; (2) desire, or thirst, is its cause; (3) the cessation of suffering is possible; and (4) the way to accomplish this is to follow the Eightfold Path. Though differently interpreted, these four truths are recognized by virtually all Buddhist schools.

Fourier series, In mathematics, an infinite series used to solve special types of differential equations. It consists of an infinite sum of sines and cosines, and because it is periodic (i.e., its values repeat over fixed intervals), it is a useful tool in analyzing periodic functions. Though investigated by Leonhard Euler, among others, the idea was named for Joseph Fourier, who fully explored its consequences, including important applications in engineering, particularly in heat conduction.

foxglove, Any of about 20 species of herbaceous plants of the  genus *Digitalis*, in the family Plantaginacea, especially *D. purpurea*, the common, or purple, foxglove. Native to Europe, the Mediterranean region, and the Canary Islands, foxgloves typically produce ovate to oblong leaves toward the lower part of the stem, which is capped by a tall, one-sided cluster of pendulous, bell-shaped, purple, yellow, or white flowers, often marked with spots within. *D. purpurea* is cultivated as the source of the heart-stimulating drug digitalis.

Foxglove (Digitalis)
Derek Fell

foxhunting, Chase of a fox by horsemen with a pack of hounds. In England, home of the sport, it dates from at least the 15th century, when it probably developed out of stag and hare hunting. Modern foxhunting became popular among the upper classes in the 19th century. A hunt is led by the master; the dogs (usually 15–20 matched pairs) are controlled by the huntsman and two or three assistants. The hunt may take place on any grounds (woodlands, heath, or fields) where a fox is suspected to be. The riders, outfitted in distinctive scarlet coats, meet at a host's house, and the hounds are sent off to search out the fox; when it is found, the hunt begins. The fox is chased until it either escapes or is cornered and killed. Although foxhunting reached its peak in popularity before World War I, it continued to be practiced afterward, most notably in the United Kingdom. However, growing opposition to the sport, largely based on charges of animal cruelty and elitism, led to its ban in Scotland (2002) and in England and Wales (2005).

fractal geometry, In mathematics, the study of complex shapes with the property of self-similarity, known as fractals. Rather like holograms that store the entire image in each part of the image, any part of a fractal can be repeatedly magnified, with each magnification resembling all or part of the original fractal. This phenomenon can be seen in objects like snowflakes and tree bark. The term fractal was coined by Benoit B. Mandelbrot in 1975. This new system of geometry has had a significant impact on such diverse fields as physical chemistry, physiology, and fluid mechanics; fractals can describe irregularly shaped objects or spatially nonuniform phenomena that cannot be described by Euclidean geometry. Fractal simulations have been used to plot the distributions of galactic clusters and to generate lifelike images of complicated, irregular natural objects, including rugged terrains and foliage used in films.

fracture, Break in a bone, caused by stress. It causes pain, tenderness, and inability to use the part with the fracture. The site appears deformed, swollen, and discoloured, and the bone moves in abnormal ways. It must be protected from weight bearing and movement between the broken ends while it heals, producing puttylike new tissue that hardens to join the broken pieces together. Complications include failure to heal, healing in the wrong position, and loss of function despite good healing. Fractures in joints present a particularly serious problem, often requiring surgery.

France, officially FRENCH REPUBLIC, Country, northwestern Europe. It includes the island of Corsica. Area: 210,026 sq mi (543,965 sq km). Population: (2011 est.) 63,278,000. Capital: Paris. The people are mainly French. Language: French (official). Religions: Christianity (predominantly Roman Catholic; also Protestant); also Islam, Judaism. Currency: euro. France has extensive plains, rivers, and a number of mountain ranges, including the Pyrenees and the Alps. The climate is generally moderate. More than half of the land is suitable for agriculture, and forests, largely unexploited, cover about one-fourth of the area. France has a developed mixed economy with a preponderance of small firms. It is a republic with two legislative houses; its head of state is the president, and the head of government is the prime minister. France is one of the major economic powers of the world and was a founding member of the European Community. Culturally, France has enjoyed a significant role in the world from the early Middle Ages onward. Archaeological excavations in France indicate continuous settlement from Paleolithic times. By the 5th century BCE the Gauls migrated south from the Rhine River valley to the Mediterranean coast of modern France, and in 600 BCE Ionian Greeks established several settlements, including one at Marseille. Julius Caesar completed the Roman conquest of Gaul in 50 BCE. During the 6th century CE the Salian Franks ruled; by the 8th century power had passed to the Carolingians, so named for the influential reign of Charlemagne. The Hundred Years' War (1337–1453) resulted in the return to France of land that had been held by England; by the end of the 15th century, France approximated its modern boundaries. The 16th century was marked by the Wars of Religion between Protestants (Huguenots) and Roman Catholics. Henry IV's Edict of Nantes (1598) granted substantial religious toleration, but this was revoked in 1685 by Louis XIV, who helped to raise monarchical absolutism to new heights. In 1789 the French Revolution proclaimed the rights of the individual and destroyed the ancien régime. Under the rule of Napoleon (1799–1814/15), France fought to expand its dominion. It then became a monarchy again until the founding of the Second Republic (1848–52), after which Napoleon III ruled as emperor before the creation of the Third Republic in 1871. World War I (1914–18) ravaged the northern part of France. After Nazi Germany's invasion of France during World War II, the collaborationist Vichy regime governed. Liberated by Allied and Free French forces in 1944, France restored parliamentary democracy under the Fourth Republic. A costly war in Indochina and rising nationalism in French colonies during the 1950s overwhelmed the Fourth Republic. In January 1959 Charles de Gaulle became the first president of the Fifth Republic. He presided over the dissolution of most of France's overseas colonies. In 1981 France elected its first social-

ist president, François Mitterrand. At various times from 1986 through the beginning of the 21st century, France balanced a form of divided government known as "cohabitation," with a president and prime minister of different political parties.

France, Anatole, orig. JACQUES-ANATOLE-FRANÇOIS THIBAULT (b. April 16, 1844, Paris, France—d. Oct. 12, 1924, Saint-Cyr-sur-Loire), French novelist and critic. France's characteristically ironic and urbane skepticism appeared in his early novels, including *Le Crime de Sylvestre Bonnard* (1881) and *At the Sign of the Reine Pédauque* (1893). Later he introduced both bitter satire and humanitarian concerns into many works, such as the tetralogy L'Histoire Contemporaine (1897–1901), whose final volume, *Monsieur Bergeret in Paris* (1901), reflects his support for Alfred Dreyfus. The comedy *Crainquebille* (1903) proclaims the hostility toward the bourgeois order that led him to embrace socialism, and he was ultimately drawn to communism. He won the Nobel Prize for Literature in 1921.

Francis I, German FRANZ (b. Dec. 8, 1708, Nancy, Duchy of Lorraine—d. Aug. 18, 1765, Innsbruck, Austria), Holy Roman emperor (1745–65). The son of the duke of Lorraine, he succeeded to the duchy in 1729 (as Francis Stephen). In 1736 he married Maria Theresa, heiress to Emperor Charles VI, who agreed to the marriage on the condition that Francis cede Lorraine to Stanislaw I of Poland, in compensation for which Francis was granted Tuscany (1737). He served with Maria Theresa as coregent (1740–45) and was elected emperor during the War of the Austrian Succession. He was overshadowed by his wife during his rule but was remembered for his cultural interests.

Franciscan, Member of a Christian religious order dedicated to the apostolic life of poverty and preaching founded in 1209 by St. Francis of Assisi. The Franciscans actually consist of three orders. The First Order comprises priests and lay brothers who have sworn to a life of prayer, preaching, and penance. The Second Order (founded 1212) consists of cloistered nuns known as the Poor Clares. The Third Order consists of religious members and laypersons who observe Franciscan principles in teaching, charity, and social service. The Rule of St. Francis stipulated that Franciscan friars could own no property of any kind, either individually or communally. The friars wandered and preached among the people, helping the poor and sick. Their impact was immense; within 10 years they numbered 5,000. A milder version of the rule was approved in 1223, and after the death of St. Francis in 1226 the order was divided by conflicts over the vow of poverty. A moderate interpretation of the rule was established while St. Bonaventure was minister general of the order (1257–74), and the friars spread throughout Europe, their missionaries penetrating as far as Syria and Africa. Though continuing controversy over the definition of poverty led to the intervention of the Pope John XXII, who persecuted the advocates of strict poverty, and to divisions of the order that lasted into the 19th century, the Franciscans flourished. They remain the largest Roman Catholic religious order.

Franco, Francisco, in full FRANCISCO PAULINO HERMENEGILDO TEÓDULO FRANCO BAHAMONDE (b. Dec. 4, 1892, El Ferrol, Spain—d. Nov. 20, 1975, Madrid), Spanish general and head of the government of Spain (1939–75). A career army officer, he was noted as a skillful leader and became army chief of staff in 1935. He joined the insurgents in the Spanish Civil War and was named El Caudillo ("The Leader") of the Nationalist forces (1936). In 1937 he reorganized the fascist Falange party into a more pluralistic group and made it the regime's official political movement. Though in sympathy with the Axis Powers in World War II, Spain remained formally neutral, but after the war Franco was ostracized as the "last surviving fascist dictator." Relations with other nations regularized with the onset of the Cold War, as Franco became a leading anticommunist statesman. In the 1950s and '60s, his domestic policies moderated, and Spain made great economic progress. He provided for his succession by an official referendum in 1947 that made the Spanish state a monarchy, ratifying his powers as regent for life. In 1969 he designated Prince Juan Carlos as his successor.

Franco-Prussian War, or FRANCO-GERMAN WAR (1870–71) War in which a coalition of German states led by Prussia defeated France, ending French hegemony in continental Europe and creating a unified Germany. The immediate cause was the candidacy of Prince Leopold of Hohenzollern-Sigmaringen for the Spanish throne, which raised the possibility of a combination of Prussia and Spain against France. Following diplomatic maneuvers to block Leopold's candidacy, the Prussian chancellor Otto von Bismarck published the Ems Telegram to provoke the French government into declaring war, which it did. The other German states sided with Prussia, and German troops under Gen. Helmuth von Moltke, superior in numbers and organization, scored repeated victories. After Napoleon III surrendered at the Battle of Sedan, French resistance was carried on by a new government, which deposed the emperor and established the Third Republic. Paris surrendered, but while treaty negotiations were going on, an insurrection by radicals in Paris created a short-lived government, the Paris Commune. After its suppression, a harsh peace treaty was implemented: Germany annexed Alsace and half of Lorraine, and France was occupied until a large indemnity was paid. The German empire was established when William I of Prussia was proclaimed German emperor in 1871. The peace was an unstable one, however, marked by France's determination to recover Alsace-Lorraine and Germany's mounting imperialism, led by Prussian militarism. Their mutual animosity was a driving force that led to World War I.

Franco-Russian Alliance, or DUAL ALLIANCE (1894) Political and military pact between France and Russia that was one of the basic European alignments of the pre–World War I era. In the event of war, France wanted support against Germany, and Russia against Austria-Hungary. The alliance was formalized through an exchange of letters in order to preserve secrecy, and it was to be in force as long as the opposing Triple Alliance. The alliance was renewed and strengthened in 1899 and 1912.

Frank, Member of a Germanic-speaking people who invaded the western Roman Empire in the 5th century. The Franks lived east of the Rhine River in the 3rd century and came under Roman influence. They gained control of northern Gaul by 494 and southern Gaul by 507, and the conversion of their leader Clovis I to Catholic Christianity won them the support of the clergy and the Gallo-Roman population in Gaul. The Franks established one of the most powerful kingdoms of the early Middle Ages, ruling lands in present-day France (to which they gave their name), Belgium, and western Germany. The Merovingian dynasty to which Clovis belonged was succeeded by the Carolingian dynasty, whose most notable ruler, Charlemagne, created a great empire across Christian Europe. The division of the realm in the 9th century and the subsequent dissolution of a unified Frankish empire foreshadowed the formation of the modern countries of western Europe.

Frank, Anne(lies Marie) (b. June 12, 1929, Frankfurt am Main, Ger.—d. March 1945, Bergen-Belsen concentration camp, near Hannover), German diarist. Frank was a young Jewish girl who kept a record of the two years her family spent in hiding in Amsterdam to escape Nazi persecution. After their discovery by the Gestapo in 1944, the family was transported to concentration camps; Anne died of typhus at Bergen-Belsen. Friends searching the hiding place found her diary, which her father published as The Diary of a Young Girl (1947). Precocious in style and insight, it traces her emotional growth amid adversity and is a classic of war literature.

Frankfurt (am Main), City (pop., 2002 est.: city, 641,076; metro. area, 1,896,741), western Germany. Located on the Main River, it was the site of a Roman military settlement in the 1st century AD. It served as a royal residence of the Carolingians from the 9th century through the Middle Ages. A free imperial city (1372–1806), it lost its status under Napoleon but regained it in 1815. It was the capital of Germany from 1816 until it was annexed by Prussia in 1866. Its Old Town, once the largest surviving medieval city in Germany, was mostly destroyed in World War II; some landmarks survive, including its red sandstone cathedral, dedicated in 1239. International trade fairs have been held in Frankfurt since 1240; in the modern era, book, automobile, and computer fairs are popular annual events. The city's manufactures include machinery and printing materials, as well as the high-quality sausages known as frankfurters. Frankfurt is the birthplace of Johann Wolfgang von Goethe.

Frankfurt school, Group of thinkers associated with the Institut für Sozialforschung (Institute for Social Research), founded in Frankfurt in 1923 by Felix J. Weil, Carl Grünberg, Max Horkheimer, and Friedrich Pollock. Other important members of the school are Theodor Adorno, Walter Benjamin, Herbert Marcuse, and Jürgen Habermas. After the Nazi seizure of power in 1933, Horkheimer moved the institute to Columbia University in New York City, where it functioned until 1941; it was reestablished in Frankfurt in 1950. Though the institute was originally conceived as a centre for neo-Marxian social research, there is no doctrine common to all members of the Frankfurt school. Intellectually, the school is most indebted to the writings of G.W.F. Hegel and the Young Hegelians, Immanuel Kant, Karl Marx, Wilhelm Dilthey, Friedrich Nietzsche, and Sigmund Freud.

frankincense, Fragrant gum resin obtained from trees of the genus Boswellia (family Burseraceae), particularly several varieties found in Somalia, Yemen, and Oman. This important incense resin was used in ancient times in religious rites and in embalming. It constituted part of the Jewish incense of the sanctuary and is frequently mentioned in the Pentateuch; it was one of the gifts of the magi to the infant Jesus. It is used today in incense and fumigants and as a fixative in perfumes.

Franklin, Aretha (Louise) (b. March 25, 1942, Memphis, Tenn., U.S.), U.S. popular singer. Franklin's family moved from Memphis to Detroit when she was two. Her father, C.L. Franklin, was a well-known revivalist preacher; his church and home were visited by musical luminaries such as Clara Ward, Mahalia Jackson, B.B. King, and Dinah Washington. Franklin made her first recording at age 12. At first she performed only gospel music, but at age 18 she switched from sacred to secular music. After struggling for a number of years to achieve crossover success, in 1967 her powerful and fervent voice took the country by storm as she began to release a string of songs including "I Never Loved a Man," "Respect," "Chain of Fools," "Think," and "Natural Woman." Her rousing mixture of gospel and rhythm and blues defined the golden age of soul music of the 1960s. In 1987 she became the first woman inducted into the Rock and Roll Hall of Fame.

Franklin, Benjamin (b. Jan. 17, 1706, Boston, Mass.—d. April 17, 1790, Philadelphia, Pa., U.S.), American printer and publisher, author, scientist and inventor, and diplomat. He was apprenticed at age 12 to his brother, a local printer. He taught himself to write effectively, and in 1723 he moved to Philadelphia, where he founded the Pennsylvania Gazette (1729–48) and wrote Poor Richard's almanac (1732–57), often remembered for its proverbs and aphorisms emphasizing prudence, industry, and honesty. He became prosperous and promoted public services in Philadelphia, including a library, a fire department, a hospital, an insurance company, and an academy that became the University of Pennsylvania. His inventions include the Franklin stove and bifocal spectacles, and his experiments helped pioneer the understanding of electricity. He served as a member of the colonial legislature (1736–51). He was a delegate to the Albany Congress (1754), where he put forth a plan for colonial union. He represented the colony in England in a dispute over land and taxes (1757–62); he returned there in 1764. The issue of taxation gradually caused him to abandon his longtime support for continued American colonial membership in the British Empire. Believing that taxation ought to be the prerogative of the representative legislatures, he opposed the Stamp Act. He served as a delegate to the second Continental Congress and as a member of the committee to draft the Declaration of Independence. In 1776 he went to France to seek aid for the American Revolution. Lionized by the French, he negotiated a treaty that provided loans and military support for the U.S. He also played a crucial role in bringing about the final peace treaty with Britain in 1783. As a member of the 1787 Constitutional Convention, he was instrumental in achieving adoption of the Constitution of the U.S. He is regarded as one of the most extraordinary and brilliant public servants in U.S. history.

Franklin, Rosalind (Elsie) (b. July 25, 1920, London, Eng.—d. April 16, 1958, London), British biologist. After graduating from the University of Cambridge, she conducted important experimental work for the coal and coke industries. She later produced the X-ray diffraction pictures that allowed James D. Watson and Francis Crick to deduce that the three-dimensional form of DNA was a double helix. In studies of the tobacco mosaic virus, she helped show that its RNA is located in its protein rather than in its central cavity and that this RNA is a single-stranded helix rather than the double helix found in the DNA of bacterial viruses and higher organisms. Her death from cancer at age 37 probably cost her a share of the 1962 Nobel Prize awarded to Watson, Crick, and Maurice Wilkins.

Franz Josef Land, Russian ZEMLYA FRANTSA-IOSIFA, Archipelago, northeastern Barents Sea. Consisting of about 190 islands, it is the northernmost territory of Russia and the most northerly land of the Eastern Hemisphere. With a land area of about 6,229 sq mi (16,134 sq km), the islands comprise a series of lowland plateaus, 85% of which is ice-covered. The Arctic climate supports polar bears and the Arctic fox, with numerous bird species. The Soviet Union annexed the islands in 1926 and maintained permanent weather stations there.

Fraunhofer lines, In astronomical spectroscopy, dark lines in a star's spectrum caused by selective absorption of its radiation at specific wavelengths by the various chemical elements in its atmosphere. First observed in 1802, they are named for the German physicist Joseph von Fraunhofer (1787–1826), who from *c.* 1814 plotted over 500 of them and designated the brightest with the first few letters of the alphabet. About 25,000 Fraunhofer lines are known to exist in the Sun's spectrum, between the wavelengths of 2,950 and 10,000 angstroms.

Fredegund (d. 597, Paris), Queen consort of the Frankish king Chilperic I. Originally a servant, she became Chilperic's mistress after he killed his wife (*c.* 568). The murder set off a 40-year feud with the family of his half brother Sigebert I, whose assassination Fredegund ordered in 575. Known for her ruthlessness and appetite for intrigue, she also made attempts on the lives of his widow and son. After Chilperic was murdered (584), possibly at her order, she took his riches and fled to Paris, where she lived until her death. Her son, Chlotar II, triumphed over Fredegund's rival and took control of the Frankish kingdom in 613.

Frederick II, German FRIEDRICH, known as FREDERICK THE GREAT (b. Jan. 24, 1712, Berlin—d. Aug. 17, 1786, Potsdam, near Berlin), King of Prussia (1740–86). The son of Frederick William I, he suffered an unhappy early life, subject to his father's capricious bullying. After trying to escape in 1730, he submitted to his father but continued to pursue intellectual and artistic interests. On his father's death (1740), Frederick became king and asserted his leadership. He seized parts of Silesia during the War of the Austrian Succession, strengthening Prussia considerably. He invaded Saxony in 1756 and marched on into Bohemia. Frederick was al-

most defeated in the Seven Years' War (1756–63), until his admirer Peter III signed a Russo-Prussian peace treaty that lasted until 1780. The First Partition of Poland in 1772 led to enormous territorial gains for Prussia. Austro-Prussian rivalry led to the War of the Bavarian Succession (1778–79), a diplomatic victory for Frederick, but continued fear of Habsburg ambitions led him to form a league of German states against Joseph II. Under Frederick's leadership Prussia became one of the great states of Europe, with vastly expanded territories and impressive military strength. In addition to modernizing the army, Frederick also espoused the ideas of enlightened despotism and instituted numerous economic, civil, and social reforms.

free fall, In mechanics, the state of a body that moves freely in any manner in the presence of gravity. The planets are in free fall in the gravitational field of the Sun. A body in free fall follows an orbit such that the sum of gravitational and inertial forces equals zero.

Free French, French movement to continue warfare against Germany after France's 1940 defeat in World War II. Led by Charles de Gaulle in exile in London, the Free French Forces gained power in 1942 with the growing underground Resistance movement in France and the defection of many Vichy France troops stationed in North Africa. After a power struggle with Henri Honore Giraud, commander in chief of French forces in North Africa, de Gaulle succeeded by 1944 in controlling the entire French war effort. The 300,000 Free French forces took part in the Allied invasions of southern France and Normandy and were the first Allied troops to liberate Paris.

free trade, Policy in which a government does not discriminate against imports or interfere with exports. A free-trade policy does not necessarily imply that the government abandons all control and taxation of imports and exports, but rather that it refrains from actions specifically designed to hinder international trade, such as tariff barriers, currency restrictions, and import quotas. The theoretical case for free trade is based on Adam Smith's argument that the division of labour among countries leads to specialization, greater efficiency, and higher aggregate production. The way to foster such a division of labour, Smith believed, is to allow nations to make and sell whatever products can compete successfully in an international market.

free verse, Poetry organized according to the cadences of speech and image patterns rather than according to a regular metrical scheme. Its rhythms are based on patterned elements such as sounds, words, phrases, sentences, and paragraphs, rather than on the traditional units of metrical feet. Free verse thus eliminates much of the artificiality and some of the aesthetic distance of poetic expression. It became current in English poetics in the early 20th century.

free will problem, Problem arising from the apparent inconsistency between causal determinism in nature and the human power or capacity to choose among alternatives or act freely in certain situations, thus independently of natural, social, or divine compulsions. Its significance derives from the fact that free will is generally considered a necessary presupposition of moral responsibility, while determinism has (at least until the advent of quantum mechanics) been regarded a necessary presupposition of natural science. Arguments for free will are based on the subjective experience of freedom, on sentiments of guilt, on revealed religion, and on the supposition of responsibility for personal actions that underlies the concepts of law, reward, punishment, and incentive. In theology, the existence of free will must be reconciled with God's foreknowledge, with divine omniscience and goodness (in allowing humans to choose badly), and with divine grace, which allegedly is necessary for any meritorious act.

freedom of speech, Right, as stated in the 1st and 14th Amendments to the Constitution of the United States, to express information, ideas, and opinions free of government restrictions based on content. A modern legal test of the legitimacy of proposed restrictions on freedom of speech was stated in the opinion by Oliver Wendell Holmes, Jr. in *Schenk* v. *U.S.* (1919): a restriction is legitimate only if the speech in question poses a "clear and present danger"—i.e., a risk or threat to safety or to other public interests that is serious and imminent. Many cases involving freedom of speech and of the press also have concerned defamation, obscenity, and prior restraint.

Freemasonry, Teachings and practices of the fraternal order of Free and Accepted Masons, the largest worldwide secret society. Originating with the guilds of medieval stonemasons, the organization became an honorary society in the 17th and 18th century, adopting the rites and trappings of ancient religious orders and chivalric brotherhoods. The first association of lodges, the Grand Lodge, was founded in England in 1717, and Freemasonry soon spread to other countries in the British Empire. Freemasons took an active role in the American Revolution and later in U.S. politics, and in the 19th century popular fears of their influence led to the Anti-Masonic movement. Membership is extended only to adult males willing to express belief in a Supreme Being and the immortality of the soul. In Latin countries, the lodges have often attracted freethinkers and anticlerical types; in Anglo-Saxon nations, membership has mostly been drawn from white Protestants. Freemasonry has also given rise to social organizations such as the Ancient Arabic Order of the Noble Mystic Shrine, or Shriners.

Freetown, Capital (pop., 2006 est.: metro. area, 818,700) and largest city of Sierra Leone. Located at the mouth of the Sierra Leone River, it has the best harbour in western Africa. It was founded in 1787 by an English abolitionist, Granville Sharp, as a haven for freed African slaves from England. Later more freed slaves from Nova Scotia and runaway slaves from Jamaica settled there. Their descendants, known as Creoles, are now outnumbered by Mende and Temne immigrants from the interior. In 1821 Freetown became the seat of government for Britain's West African possessions. Incorporated as a municipality in 1893, it became Sierra Leone's capital in 1961. It is the nation's commercial, educational, and transportation centre. The city sustained extensive damage during the civil war that wracked the country in the 1990s and has seen an increase in population due to the war.

freezing point, Temperature at which a liquid becomes a solid. When the pressure surrounding the liquid is increased, the freezing point is raised. The addition of some solids can lower the freezing point of a liquid, a principle used when salt is applied to melt ice on frozen surfaces. For pure substances, the freezing point is the same as the melting point. In mixtures and certain organic compounds, the early solid formation changes the composition of the remaining liquid, usually steadily lowering its freezing point, a principle that is applied in mixture separation. The freezing point of pure water at standard atmospheric pressure is 32°F (0°C). To change a liquid at its freezing point to a solid at the same temperature, the heat of fusion must be removed.

French and Indian War, North American phase of a war between France and Britain to control colonial territory (1754–63). The war's more complex European phase was the Seven Years' War. Earlier phases of the quest for overseas mastery were King William's War (1689–97), Queen Anne's War (1702–13), and King George's War (1744–48). The North American dispute was whether the upper Ohio River valley was a part of the British empire or part of the French Empire; the bigger question was which national culture would dominate the heart of North America. British settlers were the majority in the coveted area, but French exploration, trade, and Indian alliances predominated. In 1754 the French ousted a British force, including a colonial militia under Col. George Washington, at Fort Necessity, Pa. Until 1757 the French continued to dominate, but in 1758 Britain increased aid to its troops and won victories at Louisbourg, Fort Frontenac, and Fort Duquesne (Pittsburgh). The final British victory at the Battle of Quebec (1759) led to the fall of New France (1760). In the Treaty of Paris (1763) France ceded its North American territory to Britain.

French Guiana, French GUYANE FRANÇAISE, Overseas department of France, northeastern coast of South America. Area: 32,253 sq mi (83,534 sq km). Population: (2011 est.) 243,000. Capital: Cayenne. It is bounded by Brazil to the south and east, by Suriname to the west, and by the Atlantic Ocean to the northeast. Most of French Guiana is low-lying, with mountains in the south and a swampy coastal plain. The Maroni River forms the border with Suriname. French Guiana's population is mostly Creole. The principal languages are French (official) and creole; nine-tenths of the people are Roman Catholic. Originally settled by the Spanish, French, and Dutch, the territory of French Guiana was awarded to France in 1667, and the inhabitants were made French citizens after 1877. By 1852 the French began using the territory for penal settlement; the penal colony at Devils Island was notorious. French Guiana became a department of France in 1946; the penal colonies were closed by 1953.

French horn, Orchestral and military brass instrument, a valved circular horn with a wide bell. It is normally a transposing instrument (its music written in a different tone than its actual sound) in F. It has a wide bore and three (sometimes four) rotary valves; its conical mouthpiece produces a mellower tone than the cup-shaped mouthpieces of other brass instruments. Horns long relied on separable crooks—circular lengths of tubing that could be attached and removed rapidly—for music modulating to new keys. Since *c.* 1900 the standard horn has been a "double" instrument, with built-in crooks in F and B-flat that can be selected rapidly by means of a thumb valve. The modern symphony orchestra usually includes four horns. Though difficult to play and prone to producing conspicuous errors, its tone is widely admired.

French Indochina, Former name (until 1950) for the eastern part of mainland Southeast Asia. The region now comprises the countries of Cambodia, Laos, and Vietnam. After establishing its rule by 1893, France governed it through the Indochinese Union. During World War II it was occupied by Japan, but the French continued to administer it until the Japanese ousted them in 1945. After the Japanese surrender, the Viet Minh under Ho Chi Minh proclaimed the Democratic Republic of Vietnam. Laos and Cambodia were reoccupied by the French, who founded the Indochinese Federation. The First Indochina war soon erupted, and the French ratified treaties (1949–50) that recognized Vietnam, Laos, and Cambodia as independent states within the French Union. The area achieved full independence from France after the Geneva Conference of 1954.

French language, Romance language spoken as a first language by about 72 million people in France, Belgium, Switzerland, Canada (mainly Quebec), and many other countries and regions formerly governed by France. French is an official language of more than 25 countries. Its earliest written materials date from the 9th century. Numerous regional dialects were eventually pushed aside by Francien, the dialect of Paris, adopted as the standard language in the mid-16th century. This largely replaced the dialects of northern and central France, known as the *langue d'oïl* (from *oïl*, the northern word for "yes"), and greatly reduced the use of the Occitan language of southern France, known as *langue d'oc* (from *oc*, Occitan for "yes"). Regional dialects survive mostly in uneducated rural speech. French grammar has been greatly simplified from Latin. Nouns do not have cases, and masculine and feminine gender are marked not in the noun but in its article or adjective. The verb is conjugated for three persons and for singular and plural; though spelled differently, several of these forms are pronounced identically.

French Polynesia, formerly FRENCH OCEANIA, French overseas collectivity, south-central Pacific Ocean. Area: 1,544 sq mi (4,000 sq km): Population: (2011 est.) 272,000. Capital: Papeete, on Tahiti. French Polynesia comprises 130 islands in five archipelagoes: the Society Islands, the Tuamotu Archipelago, the Gambier Islands, the Marquesas Islands, and the Austral Islands. Tahiti, in the Society group, is the largest island. More than two-thirds of the population of French Polynesia lives on Tahiti. Most of the islands came under French control in the 1840s, and in the 1880s the French colony of Oceania was established. It became an overseas territory of France after World War II and was granted partial autonomy in 1977.

French Revolution, Movement that shook France between 1787 and 1799, reaching its first climax in 1789, and ended the ancien régime. Causes included the loss of peasant support for the feudal system, broad acceptance of the reformist writings of the philosophes, an expanding bourgeoisie that was excluded from political power, a fiscal crisis worsened by participation in the American Revolution, and crop failures in 1788. The efforts of the regime in 1787 to increase taxes levied on the privileged classes initiated a crisis. In response, Louis XVI convened the Estates-General, made up of clergy, nobility, and the Third Estate (commoners), in 1789. Trying to pass reforms, it swore the Tennis Court Oath not to disperse until France had a new constitution. The king grudgingly concurred in the formation of the National Assembly, but rumours of an "aristocratic conspiracy" led to the Great Fear of July 1789, and Parisians seized the Bastille on July 14. The assembly drafted a new constitution that introduced the Declaration of the Rights of Man and of the Citizen, proclaiming liberty, equality, and fraternity. The Constitution of 1791 also established a short-lived constitutional monarchy. The assembly nationalized church lands to pay off the public debt and reorganized the church. The king tried to flee the country but was apprehended at Varennes. France, newly nationalistic, declared war on Austria and Prussia in 1792, beginning the French Revolutionary Wars. Revolutionaries imprisoned the royal family and massacred nobles and clergy at the Tuileries in 1792. A new assembly, the National Convention—divided between Girondins and the extremist Montagnards—abolished the monarchy and established the First Republic in September 1792. Louis XVI was judged by the National Convention and executed for treason on Jan. 21, 1793. The Montagnards seized power and adopted radical economic and social policies that provoked violent reactions, including the Wars of the Vendée and citizen revolts. Opposition was broken by the Reign of Terror. Military victories in 1794 brought a change in the public mood, and Maximilien Robespierre was overthrown in the Convention on 9 Thermidor, year II (in 1794 in the French republican calendar), and executed the next day. Royalists tried to seize power in Paris but were crushed by Napoleon on 13 Vendémaire, year IV (in 1795). A new constitution placed executive power in a Directory of five members. The war and schisms in the Directory led to disputes that were settled by coups d'état, chiefly those of 18 Fructidor, Year V (in 1797), and 18–19 Brumaire, Year VIII (in 1799), in which Napoleon abolished the Directory and declared himself leader of France.

Freon, Trademark for any of several organic compounds containing fluorine (fluorocarbons) and sometimes chlorine (chlorofluorocarbons, or CFCs). Nonflammable, nontoxic, and noncorrosive, they have low boiling points, which makes them useful as refrigerants. By the mid-1970s they were in wide use in refrigeration and air conditioning systems, as blowing agents for plastic foams, as fire-extinguishing agents, and in aerosol sprays. Evidence has accumulated that decomposition of CFCs in the stratosphere destroys ozone there, so most of their uses have been banned. International agreements signed by most of the industrialized countries have called for the phasing out of CFC use.

frequency, Number of waves that pass a fixed point per unit time; also, the number of cycles or vibrations undergone in unit time by a body in periodic motion. Frequency f is the reciprocal of the time T taken to complete one cycle (the period), or $1/T$. The frequency with which earth rotates is once per 24 hours. Frequency is usually expressed in units called hertz (Hz). One hertz is equal to one cycle per second; one kilohertz (kHz) is 1,000 Hz, and one megahertz (MHz) is 1,000,000 Hz. The musical pitch A above middle C (the A string of a violin) has been widely standardized as 440 Hz.

frequency distribution, In statistics, a graph or data set organized to show the frequency of occurrence of each possible outcome of a repeatable event observed many times. Simple examples are election returns and test scores listed by percentile. A frequency distribution can be graphed as a histogram or pie chart. For large data sets, the stepped graph of a histogram is often approximated by the smooth curve of a distribution function (called a density function when normalized so that the area under the curve is 1). The famed bell curve or normal distribution is the graph of one such function. Frequency distributions are particularly useful in summarizing large data sets and assigning probabilities.

Freud, Sigmund (b. May 6, 1856, Freiberg, Moravia, Austrian Empire—d. Sept. 23, 1939, London, Eng.), Austrian neuropsychologist, founder of psychoanalysis, and one of the major intellectual figures in the 20th century. Trained in Vienna as a neurologist, Freud went to Paris in 1885 to study with Jean-Martin Charcot, whose work on hysteria led Freud to conclude that mental disorders might be caused purely by psychological rather than organic factors. Returning to Vienna (1886), Freud collaborated with the physician Josef Breuer (1842–1925) in further studies on hysteria, resulting in the development of some key psychoanalytic concepts and techniques, including free association, the unconscious, resistance (later defense mechanisms), and neurosis. In 1899 he published *The Interpretation of Dreams*, in which he analyzed the complex symbolic processes underlying dream formation: he proposed that dreams are the disguised expression of unconscious wishes. In his controversial *Three Essays on the Theory of Sexuality* (1905), he delineated the complicated stages of psychosexual development (oral, anal, and phallic) and the formation of the Oedipus complex. During World War I, he wrote papers that clarified his understanding of the relations between the unconscious and conscious portions of the mind and the workings of the id, ego, and superego. Freud eventually applied his psychoanalytic insights to such diverse phenomena as jokes and slips of the tongue, ethnographic data, religion and mythology, and modern civilization. Works of note include *Totem and Taboo* (1913), *Beyond the Pleasure Principle* (1920), *The Future of an Illusion* (1927), and *Civilization and Its Discontents* (1930). Freud fled to England when the Nazis annexed Austria in 1938; he died shortly thereafter. Despite the relentless and often compelling challenges mounted against virtually all of his ideas, both in his lifetime and after, Freud has remained one of the most influential figures in contemporary thought.

Freyja, Most important Norse goddess, one of a group of fertility deities called Vanir. Her father was the sea god Njörd, and her brother and male counterpart was Freyr. She was the goddess of battle and death as well as love and fertility. Half the heroes slain in battle went to her domain, Folkvangr, the other half to Odin's Valhalla. She taught a powerful magic to the Aesir, probably involving sexuality.

friction, Force that resists sliding or rolling of one solid object over another. Some friction is beneficial, such as the traction used to walk without slipping. Most friction, though, is undesirable opposition to motion, such as between moving parts of machines. For example, about 20% of the work done by an automobile engine is needed to overcome friction between moving parts. Friction is a result of attractive forces between the contact regions of two bodies, and the amount of friction is almost independent of the area of contact. Kinetic friction arises between surfaces in relative motion, static friction acts between surfaces at rest with respect to each other, and rolling friction occurs when an object rolls over a surface.

Friedman, Milton (b. July 31, 1912, Brooklyn, N.Y., U.S.—d. Nov. 16, 2006, San Francisco, Calif.), U.S. economist. Friedman studied at Rutgers and Columbia before joining the faculty of the University of Chicago in 1946. There he became the leading U.S. advocate of monetarism. He oversaw the economic transition in Chile after the overthrow of Salvador Allende. In the 1980s his ideas were taken up by Pres. Ronald Reagan and Britain's Margaret Thatcher. His many books include *A Theory of the Consumption Function* (1957) and *Capitalism and Freedom* (1962), both with his wife, Rose Friedman, and *A Monetary History of the United States, 1867–1960* (1963) and *Monetary Trends of the United States and the United Kingdom* (1981), with economist Anna Schwartz. He received the Nobel Prize in 1976.

Friends, Society of, known as QUAKERS, Protestant denomination that arose in England in the mid-17th century. The movement began with radical English Puritans called Seekers, who rejected the Anglican church and other existing Protestant sects. They took their faith from itinerant preachers such as George Fox, who emphasized "inward light," or inward apprehension of God, as the source of religious authority. Quaker meetings are characterized by patient silence in which members wait for inspiration to speak. The movement grew rapidly after 1650 (when a judge gave them their name because "we bid them tremble at the word of God"), but its members were often persecuted or imprisoned for rejecting the state church and refusing to pay tithes or swear oaths. Some emigrated to America, where they were persecuted in Massachusetts Bay Colony but found toleration in Rhode Island and in the Quaker colony of Pennsylvania, which was chartered by Charles II under the sponsorship of William Penn in 1681. Other marks that became characteristic of Quakerism were plain speech and dress, pacifism, and opposition to slavery. The group also emphasizes philanthropy, especially aid to refugees and famine victims; the American Friends Service Committee and (British) Friends Service Council shared the 1947 Nobel Peace Prize.

frieze, Any long, narrow, horizontal panel or ornamental band used for decorative purposes around the walls of a room or exterior walls of a building. In Greco-Roman architecture it is a horizontal band, often decorated with relief sculpture, between the architrave and cornice of a building. The most famous decorative frieze is on the outer wall of the Parthenon in Athens, a 525-ft (160-m) representation of the ritual procession of the Panathenaic festival.

frigate, Either of two different types of warships, of the 17th–19th centuries and of World War II and after. The sailing ship known as a frigate was a three-masted, fully rigged vessel, often carrying 30–40 guns in all. Smaller and faster than ships of the line, frigates served as scouts or as escorts protecting merchant convoys; they also cruised the seas as merchant raiders themselves. With the transition to steam, the term gradually gave way to cruiser. In World War II, Britain revived the term *frigate* to describe escort ships equipped with sonar and depth charges and used to guard convoys from submarines. In the postwar decades frigates also adopted an antiaircraft role, adding radar and surface-to-air missiles. Modern frigates may displace more than 3,000 tons (2,700 metric tons), sail at a speed of 30 knots, and carry a crew of 200.

Frigg, or FRIIA, Norse goddess, the wife of Odin and mother of Balder. She was considered the patron of marriage and fertility. Some Icelandic stories depict her as a devoted mother, while others stress her loose morals. Frigg was also known to other Germanic peoples, and her name survives in the word Friday ("Friia's day").

Frisch, Ragnar (Anton Kittil) (b. March 1895, Oslo, Nor.—d. Jan. 31, 1973, Oslo), Norwegian economist. He received his Ph.D. from the University of Oslo and taught there from 1931 to 1965. He was a pioneer of econometrics and one of the founders of the Econometric Society. He is famous for the development of large-scale econometric modeling linked to economic planning and national income accounting. In 1969 he shared the first Nobel Prize in Economics with Jan Tinbergen.

Frisian Islands, Chain of islands, North Sea. They extend 3 to 20 mi (5 to 32 km) off the northern European mainland, along the Dutch and German coasts and the southern part of Denmark's Jutland peninsula. Although they form a single physical feature, it is customary to subdivide them into the West Frisian Islands (held by the Netherlands), East Frisian Islands (Germany), and North Frisian Islands (Germany and Denmark). After the North Sea established a southwestern outlet to the Atlantic about 7,000–5,000 BCE, its southeasterly shore probably coincided with the present curve of the Frisians. Periodic subsidence, storms, and flooding have since produced this long chain of islands separated from the mainland by a narrow belt of shallow waters and tidal mud flats. The Dutch and German governments have spent large sums to protect the islands' seaward coasts and reclaim the land for farming. The beaches and resorts attract many tourists.

frog, Any of various tailless amphibians in the order Anura. The

Costa Rican flying tree frog (Agalychnis spurrelli).
Heather Angel

name may be limited to any member of the family Ranidae (true frogs); more broadly, it often distinguishes smooth-skinned, leaping anurans from squat, warty, hopping ones (toads). Frogs generally have protruding eyes, strong, webbed hind feet adapted for leaping and swimming, and smooth, moist skin. Most are predominantly aquatic, but some live on land. They range in length (snout to anus) from 0.4 to 12 in. (9.8 mm–30 cm). Though frogs have poisonous skin glands, they rely on camouflage for protection from predators. Most eat insects and other small arthropods or worms, but several also eat other frogs, rodents, and reptiles. They usually breed in freshwater, where they lay eggs that hatch into tadpoles. Since 1989 researchers have become increasingly alarmed by striking declines in frog populations worldwide, suspected to be linked to climatic factors or a fungal disease.

Fronde, the (1648–53) Series of civil wars in France during the minority of Louis XIV. The Fronde (named for the "sling" of a children's game played in the streets of Paris in defiance of authorities) was in part an attempt to check the growing power of royal government, but its failure paved the way for the absolutism of Louis XIV's reign. The first phase, the Fronde of the Parlement (1648–49), was an attempt to place constitutional limits on the queen regent, Anne of Austria, and her chief minister, Jules Mazarin. Uprisings forced the government to concede to the Parlement's demands. The more serious second phase, the Fronde of the Princes (1650–53), sprang from aristocratic opposition to Mazarin. The military leader the Great Condé was arrested, causing his friends to rebel (in the so-called first war of the princes). His supporters joined the Parisian party (the Old Fronde) in successfully calling for Condé's release and Mazarin's resignation. Condé lost his position when Anne joined with the Old Fronde against him, precipitating the second war of the princes (1651–53). After losses in battle, he fled. The king entered Paris in triumph in 1652, followed by Mazarin in 1653. The Fronde was the last serious challenge to the monarchy until the French Revolution.

front, In meteorology, the interface or transition zone between two air masses of different density and temperature. Frontal zones are frequently accompanied by low barometric pressure, marked changes in wind direction and relative humidity, and considerable cloudiness and precipitation.

frost, Atmospheric moisture that crystallizes directly on the ground and on exposed objects. The term also refers to the occurrence of subfreezing temperatures that affect plants and crops. Frost crystals, sometimes called hoarfrost in the aggregate, form when water vapour in the atmosphere passes into the ice-crystal phase without going through the intermediate liquid phase. Frost forms under conditions that would form dew if the temperature were above freezing. In agriculture, frost refers to the freezing of the water in plant cells, which causes the cells to burst and thereby destroys the plant.

frostbite, Freezing of living tissue, when it loses enough heat in below-freezing weather for ice to form. High winds, wet skin, tight clothes, and alcohol use increase the risk of frostbite. Cell damage, tissue dehydration, and oxygen depletion caused by freezing and thawing can lead to blood-cell disruption, clotting in capillaries, and gangrene. The toes, fingers, ears, and nose are usually affected first, becoming cold, hard, white, or bloodless. The lack of pain is dangerous. Core temperature should be brought to near normal before rapid thawing in warm (under 115 °F [46 °C]) water. Toxoid booster injections are recommended. The outlook is best when freezing is short-term, thawing is by rapid rewarming, and large blisters extending to the end of the part develop early. Tissue that is refrozen after thawing must almost always be amputated. Affected parts become more susceptible to recurrence. Frostbite is best prevented by wearing dry, layered, loose clothing and remaining alert.

fructose, or LEVULOSE, or FRUIT SUGAR, Organic compound, one of the simple sugars (monosaccharides), chemical formula $C_6H_{12}O_6$. It occurs in fruits, honey, syrups (especially corn syrup), and certain vegetables, usually along with its isomer glucose. Fructose and glucose are the components of the disaccharide sucrose (table sugar); hydrolysis of sucrose yields invert sugar, a 50:50 mixture of fructose and glucose. The sweetest of the common sugars, fructose is used in foods and medicines.

fruit, In its strict botanical sense, the fleshy or dry ripened ovary (enlarged portion of the pistil) of a flowering plant, enclosing the seed or seeds. Apricots, bananas, and grapes, as well as bean pods, corn grains, tomatoes, cucumbers, and (in their shells) acorns and almonds, are all technically fruits. Popularly, the term is restricted to the ripened ovaries that are sweet and either succulent or pulpy. The principal botanical purpose of the fruit is to protect and spread the seed. There are two broad categories of fruit: fleshy and dry. Fleshy fruits include berries, such as tomatoes, oranges, and cherries, which consist entirely of succulent tissue; aggregate fruits, including blackberries and strawberries, which form from a single flower with many pistils, each of which develops into fruitlets; and multiple fruits, such as pineapples and mulberries, which develop from the mature ovaries of an entire inflorescence. Dry fruits include the legumes, cereal grains, capsules, and nuts. Fruits are important sources of dietary fiber and vitamins (especially vitamin C). They can be eaten fresh; processed into juices, jams, and jellies; or preserved by dehydration, canning, fermentation, and pickling.

fruit bat, Any of numerous tropical Old World bats in the family Pteropodidae as well as several species of herbivorous New World bats. Old World fruit bats are widely distributed from Africa to South Asia and Australasia. Most species rely on vision rather than on echolocation to avoid obstacles. Some species are solitary, some gregarious; most roost in the open in trees, though some inhabit caves, rocks, or buildings. Some are red or yellow, and some are striped or spotted. They eat fruit or flowers (including pollen and nectar). The smallest species in the family, the long-tongued fruit bats, reach a head and body length of about 2.5 in. (6–7 cm) and a wingspan of about 10 in. (25 cm). The same family contains the largest of all bats, the flying foxes, which attain lengths up to 16 in. (40 cm) and a wingspan of 5 ft (1.5 m). New World fruit bats are generally smaller and make use of echolocation. They are found in the tropics, with many species belonging to the genera *Artibeus* and *Sturnira*.

fruit fly, Any dipteran species of two families: large fruit flies (Trypetidae) and small fruit flies, or vinegar flies (Drosophilidae). The larvae feed on fruit or other vegetation. The adults' wings are banded or spotted with brown. Many species attack cultivated fruits, sometimes causing enough damage to create significant economic loss. Some species are leaf miners; others burrow in plant stems. Well-known fruit-fly pests include the Mediterranean fruit fly and the apple maggot of the U.S., the Mexican and Oriental fruit flies, and the olive fruit fly of the Mediterranean region.

Fruit fly (Trypetidae)
E.S. Ross

FTP, in full FILE TRANSFER PROTOCOL, Internet protocol that allows a computer to send files to or receive files from another computer. Like many Internet resources, FTP works by means of a client-server architecture; the user runs client software to connect to a server on the Internet. On the FTP server, a program called a daemon allows the user to download and upload files. Before the World Wide Web was introduced, FTP was one of the most popular methods of exchanging information over the Internet and many Web sites still use it to disseminate their larger files.

fugue, Musical composition characterized by systematic imitation of one or more themes in counterpoint. Fugues vary greatly in their actual form. The principal theme (subject) is imitated—i.e., repeated successively in similar form at different pitch levels by different parts or voices—in the so-called exposition. The countersubject is the continuation of the subject that accompanies the subject theme's subsequent entries in the other voices. Episodes using modified themes often separate the subject's entries. The fugue emerged gradually from the imitative polyphony of the 13th century. Johann Sebastian Bach's keyboard fugues are the most famous of all. The works of Bach and George Frideric Handel inspired the later fugues of Wolfgang Amadeus Mozart, Ludwig van Beethoven, and others, many of whom commonly included fugues in the final movements of symphonies, string quartets, and sonatas.

Fuji, Mount, or FUJIYAMA, Japanese FUJI-SAN, Mountain, central Japan. The highest mountain in Japan, it rises to 12,388 ft (3,776 m) near the Pacific coast in central Honshu. Mount Fuji, with its graceful volcanic cone (dormant since 1707), has become famous internationally. It is considered a sacred symbol of Japan, and thousands of Japanese climb to the shrine on its peak every summer. The mountain is the major feature of Fuji-Hakone-Izu National Park, created in 1936.

Fujian, or FU-CHIEN, conventional FUKIEN, Province (pop., 2002 est.: 34,660,000), southeastern China. Located on the southeastern coast, it is bounded by the East China Sea and Taiwan Strait and Guangdong, Jiangxi, and Zhejiang provinces. It has an area of 47,500 sq mi (123,100 sq km), and its capital is Fuzhou. The province's boundaries were established during the Nan (Southern) Song dynasty (1127–1279), when it became an important shipbuilding and commercial centre for overseas and coastal trade. It declined when the Ming dynasty (1368–1644) banned maritime commerce. Its coastal cities were occupied by the Japanese in 1939–45 during World War II, and the 3rd Field Army took control of the province in 1949. In addition to being an important agricultural region, it is an area of special economic zones established in 1979 to attract foreign investment to China.

Fujiwara style, Japanese sculptural style of the late Heian period (897–1185). The style of the principal icons accorded with the emotional appeal of Pure Land Buddhism, introduced to counter the older esoteric sects. The sculpted figures, though still full and fleshy, were more elegant and heavily polychromed, with elaborate cut-gold (*kirikane*) patterns in the drapery. The facial type was aristocratic. Delicacy of expression was achieved by a joined-wood technique invented by Jōchō. Interest in decorative effects can be seen in the applied jewelry, which in earlier periods had been painted or modeled on the sculpture's surface.

Fukuoka, City (pop., 2006 est.: 1,414,417) and port, northwestern Kyushu, Japan. It incorporates the former city of Hakata and is located on the southern coast of Hakata Bay. An ancient port, it was the scene of attempted invasions by Kublai Khan in the 13th century. It is now a regional commercial, industrial, administrative, and cultural centre. It contains an active fishing port and is the site of Kyushu University (1911). Hakata *ningyo*, elaborately costumed ceramic figurines found in most Japanese homes, are made there.

Fulani, Primarily Muslim people, numbering about 18 million, found in many parts of West Africa, from Lake Chad west to the Atlantic coast. Their language is Fula, an Atlantic language of the Niger-Congo family. Originally they were herders, but interaction with other groups produced marked cultural changes. In the 1790s the Fulani priest Usman dan Fodio led a holy war (jihad) that created a large empire. Its decay in the 19th century aided the establishment of British rule over northern Nigeria. Many Fulani of northern Nigeria have adopted the Hausa language and culture and established themselves as an urban aristocracy.

fullerene, Any of a class of all-carbon molecules whose atoms are arranged in closed hollow shells. Allotropes of carbon first identified in 1985, they have varying (but even) numbers of atoms bonded into structures having 12 pentagonal and 2 or more hexagonal faces. Fullerenes comprising dozens to hundreds of carbon atoms have been prepared. The best known and most stable fullerene, buckminsterfullerene (C_{60}, nicknamed buckyball), has 60 carbon atoms arranged in a pattern like that on a standard soccer ball. It is named for R. Buckminster Fuller, whose geodesic dome designs its structure resembles. Chemists have made fullerene derivatives (e.g., with attached hydrogen or halogen atoms or organic groups; *see* functional group) and have prepared doped fullerenes (e.g., with alkali metal atoms such as potassium; *see* dopant) that show superconductivity at relatively high temperatures. One or more metal or noble-gas atoms can be trapped in the molecule's hollow interior, resulting in unique complexes called endohedral fullerenes.

fulling, Process that increases the thickness and compactness of woven or knitted wool by subjecting it to moisture, heat, friction, and pressure until shrinkage of 10–25% is achieved. Shrinkage occurs in both the warp and weft, producing a smooth, tightly finished fabric that is light, warm, and relatively weatherproof. A common example is loden cloth, first produced in Austria in the 16th century.

Fulton, Robert (b. Nov. 14, 1765, Lancaster county, Pa., U.S.—d. Feb. 24, 1815, New York, N.Y.), U.S. inventor and engineer. Born to Irish immigrant parents, he studied painting with Benjamin West in London but soon turned to engineering. After designing a system of inland waterways, he tried unsuccessfully to interest the French and British governments in his prototypes of submarines and torpedoes. In 1801 he was commissioned by Robert R. Livingston to build a steamboat, and in 1807 Fulton's *Clermont* made the 150-mi (240-km) journey up the Hudson River from New York City to Albany in 32 hours, cutting 64 hours off the usual sailing time. It became the first commercially successful steamboat in the U.S. He later designed several other steamboats, including the world's first steam warship (1812). He was a member of the commission that recommended building the Erie Canal.

Funafuti, Coral atoll (pop., 2002: 4,492), Tuvalu, west-central Pacific Ocean. It is the location of the capital of Tuvalu, Vaiaku, on Fongafale islet. Funafuti comprises some 30 islets and has a total land area of 0.9 sq mi (2.4 sq km). It encircles a lagoon that affords good anchorage. A U.S. military base was established there in 1943; the U.S. dropped its claim to the atoll in 1983. Fongafale village has a hotel, a hospital, and an airstrip.

functional analysis, Branch of mathematical analysis dealing with functionals, or functions of functions. It emerged as a distinct field in the 20th century, when it was realized that diverse mathematical processes, from arithmetic to calculus procedures, exhibit very similar properties. A functional, like a function, is a relationship between objects, but the objects may be numbers, vectors, or functions. Groupings of such objects are called spaces. Differentiation is an example of a functional because it defines a relationship between a function and another function (its derivative). Integration is also a functional. Functional analysis focuses on classes of functions, such as those that can be differentiated or integrated.

Functionalism, In architecture, the doctrine that a building's form should be determined by practical considerations of use, material, and structure and not by a preconceived picture in the designer's mind. Though not an exclusively modern conception, it is closely associated with the Modernist architecture of the second quarter of the 20th century. The fight for an "honest" form of expression by architects such as Louis Sullivan and Le Corbusier came about as a result of changes in building techniques, needs for new types of buildings, and discontent with historical revivalism, which had been paramount in the 19th and early 20th centuries.

functionalism, In psychology, a broad school of thought that originated in the U.S. in the late 19th century and emphasized the total organism in its endeavours to adjust to the environment. Reacting against the school of structuralism led by Edward Bradford Titchener, functionalists such as William James, George Herbert Mead, and John Dewey stressed the importance of empirical, rational thought over an experimental trial-and-error philosophy. The movement concerned itself primarily with the practical applications of research and was critical of early forms of behaviourism.

fundamentalism, Christian, Conservative Protestant movement that arose out of 19th-century millennialism in the U.S. It emphasized as fundamental the literal truth of the Bible, the imminent physical Second Coming of Jesus, the virgin birth, resurrection, and atonement. It spread in the 1880s and '90s among Protestants dismayed by labour unrest, Catholic immigration, and biblical criticism. Scholars at Princeton Theological Seminary provided intellectual arguments, published as 12 pamphlets (1910–15). Displeasure over the teaching of evolution, which many believed could not be reconciled with the Bible, and over biblical criticism gave fundamentalism momentum in the 1920s. In the 1930s and '40s, many fundamentalist Bible institutes and colleges were established, and fundamentalist groups within some Baptist and Presbyterian denominations broke away to form new churches. In the later 20th century, fundamentalists made use of television as a medium for evangelizing and became vocal in politics as the "Christian right." *See also* evangelicalism; Pentecostalism.

fundamentalism, Islamic, Conservative religious movement that seeks a return to Islamic values and Islamic law in the face of Western modernism, which is seen as corrupt and atheistic. Though popularly associated in the West with Middle Eastern terrorists, only a few Islamic fundamentalists are terrorists, and not all Arab terrorists are fundamentalists. The Iranian revolution of 1979 established an Islamic fundamentalist state, and the Taliban has established its version of the same in much of Afghanistan. Islamic fundamentalist movements have varying degrees of support in North Africa, Pakistan, Bangladesh, and Muslim S.East Asia, but Islamic fundamentalism represents a minority viewpoint in the context of world Islam.

fungus, Any of about 80,000 known species of organisms be-

Bracket fungus (Polyporus) growing on wood.
H.S. Knighton

longing to the kingdom Fungi, including yeasts, rusts, smuts, molds, mushrooms, and mildews. Though formerly classified as plants, fungi lack chlorophyll and the organized plant structures of stems, roots, and leaves. The thallus, or body, of a typical fungus consists of a mycelium through which cytoplasm flows. The mycelium generally reproduces by forming spores, either directly or in special fruiting bodies that make up the visible part of a fungus. The soil provides an ideal habitat for many species, although fungi can also live in the air and water and on plants and animals. Fungi are found in all regions of the world that have sufficient moisture to enable them to grow. Lacking chlorophyll, fungi are unable to carry out photosynthesis and must obtain nutrients by secreting enzymes onto the surface on which they are growing. These enzymes digest organic matter, forming solutions of nutrients that can be absorbed through the mycelium. Decomposition of organic matter by fungi results in the release of carbon, oxygen, nitrogen, and phosphorus into the soil or the atmosphere. Essential to many food and industrial processes, fungi are used in the production of enzymes, organic acids, vitamins, and antibiotics. Fungi can also destroy crops, cause diseases in humans (e.g., candidiasis and ringworm), and ruin clothing and food with mildew and rot. Parasitic fungi invade living organisms, often causing disease and death, whereas other fungi establish symbiotic relationships with algae (forming lichens), plants (forming mycorrhizae), and certain insects.

fur seal, Any of nine species of eared seals valued for their fur, especially the chestnut-coloured underfur. Fur seals live in groups and feed on fish and other animals. They were driven nearly to extinction by fur hunters, and most species are now protected by law. The northern fur seal (*Callorhinus ursinus*) is a migratory inhabitant of northern seas. The male is deep brown, has a grayish mane, grows to about 10 ft (3 m) long, and weighs about 650 lb (300 kg). The dark gray female is much smaller. The eight species of southern fur seals (genus *Arctocephalus*) occur in the Southern Hemisphere and on Guadalupe Island, Mex. They are brown or black and average 4–6 ft (1.2–1.8 m) long.

Furies, Group of Greco-Roman goddesses of vengeance. The Furies lived in the underworld and ascended to earth to pursue the wicked. They were known to the Greeks as the Erinyes, but those who feared to speak their name often called them by euphemisms such as Eumenides ("Kind Ones"). According to Hesiod, they were daughters of Gaea, the earth goddess. Aeschylus made them the terrifying chorus of his tragedy *Eumenides*, and Euripides was the first to speak of them as three in number.

futures, Commercial contracts calling for the purchase or sale of specified quantities of a good at specified future dates. The good in question may be grain, livestock, precious metals, or financial instruments such as treasury bills. Up until the time the contract calls for the delivery of the good, the contract is subject to speculation. Futures contracts originated in the trade in agricultural commodities; for example, American grain farmers were able to sell their harvest in advance on the Chicago Board of Trade, a commodity exchange.

Futurism, Early 20th-century art movement, centred in Italy, that celebrated the dynamism, speed, and power of the machine and the vitality and restlessness of modern life. The term was coined by Filippo Marinetti, who in 1909 published a manifesto glorifying the new technology of the automobile and the beauty of its speed and power. In 1910 Umberto Boccioni and others published a manifesto on painting. They adopted the Cubist technique of depicting several views of an object simultaneously with fragmented planes and outlines and used rhythmic spatial repetitions of the object's outlines in transit to render movement. Their preferred subjects were speeding cars and trains, racing cyclists, and urban crowds; their palette was more vibrant than the Cubists'. With Boccioni, the most prominent Futurist artists were his teacher, Giacomo Balla (1871–1958), and Gino Severini (1883–1966). Boccioni's death in 1916 and World War I brought an end to the movement, which had a strong influence in postrevolutionary Russia and on Dada.

Futurism, Literary, artistic, and political movement. Futurism, which began in Italy about 1909, was marked especially by violent rejection of tradition and an effort to give formal expression to the dynamic energy and movement of mechanical processes. Its most significant results were in the visual arts and poetry. Futurism was first announced in a manifesto by Filippo Marinetti. The principal Italian Futurist artists were Giacomo Balla (1871–1958), Umberto Boccioni, Carlo Carrà (1881–1966), and Gino Severini (1883–1966). Russian Futurism, founded soon afterward by Vladimir Mayakovsky and Velimir Khlebnikov (1885–1922), went beyond the Italian model in its revolutionary political and social outlook. The movement's influence had ceased to be felt by 1930.

Fuzhou, or FU-CHOU, conventional FOOCHOW, City (pop., 2003 est.: 1,387,266), capital of Fujian province, China. Located on the bank of the Min River, it was the capital of the kingdom of Yue in the 2nd century BC. Fuzhou, important militarily in the 1st century AD, came later under the Tang dynasty. During the Song dynasty (960–1279), it was a centre for overseas trade and also an important cultural centre. It reached its height of prosperity when it was opened as a treaty port after the first Opium War (1839–42). It is now a centre for industrial chemicals. In the city and nearby hills are notable examples of traditional Chinese architecture, including pagodas and temples.

fuzzy logic, Logic based on the concept of fuzzy sets, in which membership is expressed in varying probabilities or degrees of truth—that is, as a continuum of values ranging from 0 (does not occur) to 1 (definitely occurs). As additional data are gathered, many fuzzy-logic systems are able to adjust the probability values assigned to different parameters. Because some such systems appear able to learn from their mistakes, they are often considered a crude form of artificial intelligence. The term and concept date from a 1965 paper by Lotfi A. Zadeh (born 1921). Fuzzy-logic systems achieved commercial application in the early 1990s. Advanced clothes-washing machines, for example, use fuzzy-logic systems to detect and adapt to patterns of water movement during a wash cycle, increasing efficiency and reducing water consumption. Other products using fuzzy logic include camcorders, microwave ovens, and dishwashers. Other applications include expert systems, self-regulating industrial controls, and computerized speech- and handwriting-recognition programs.

G

Gabar, Derogatory name applied to Iranian Zoroastrians. The word may derive from the Arabic *kāfir* ("infidel"). After the Muslim conquest of Persia in the 7th century BC, the Zoroastrians became an outcast minority, saddled with many social and economic disabilities. Since the 19th century they have received support from the Parsis of India. Persecuted after the Islamic fundamentalist revolution of 1978–79, they currently number a few thousand.

gable, Triangular section formed by a roof with two slopes, extending from the eaves to the ridge where the two slopes meet. It may be miniaturized over a dormer window or entranceway. If the gable end projects above the roof level to form a parapet, the edge is often trimmed to form an ornamental silhouette (e.g., curved or stepped), as in Dutch town houses of the 16th and 17th centuries. In Asia, gables often feature projecting roof tiles and grotesque sculptures of animals at the ridge and eaves.

Gabon, officially GABONESE REPUBLIC, Country, central Africa. Area: 103,347 sq mi (267,667 sq km). Population: (2011 est.) 1,534,000. Capital: Libreville. Gabon has more than 40 ethnic groups: the Fang, more than one-fourth of the total population, live north of the Ogooué River; the largest grou§ps south of the river are the Sira (including the Punu) and Nzebi. Languages: French (official), several Bantu languages (notably Fang). Religions: Christianity (mostly Roman Catholic; also Protestant, other Christians); also Islam, traditional beliefs. Currency: CFA franc. Gabon straddles the Equator on the western coast of Africa. It has a narrow coastal plain and becomes hilly in the south and north. The basin of its chief river, the Ogooué, covers most of the country; about three-fourths is equatorial rainforest, which supports numerous plant and animal species. Gabon has reserves of manganese that are among the largest in the world; it also has huge deposits of petroleum and natural gas. Gabon has a developing mixed economy based largely on the exploitation of these mineral and timber resources. It is a unitary multiparty republic with the president as head of state and the prime minister as head of government; the parliament consists of two houses. Artifacts dating from late Paleolithic and early Neolithic times have been found in Gabon, but it is not known when the Bantu speakers who established Gabon's ethnic composition arrived. Pygmies were probably the original inhabitants. The Portuguese began arriving in the late 15th century and were followed by French, Dutch, and English traders. The Fang started migrating there in the late 18th century. The slave trade dominated commerce in the 18th and much of the 19th century. The French then took control, and Gabon was administered (1843–86) with French West Africa. In 1886 the colony of French Congo was established to include both Gabon and the Congo; in 1910 Gabon became a separate colony within French Equatorial Africa. An overseas territory of France from 1946, it became an autonomous republic within the French Community in 1958 and declared its independence in 1960. Rule by a sole political party was established in the 1960s, but discontent with it led to riots in Libreville in 1989. Legalization of opposition parties enabled new elections in 1990. The country continued to face economic difficulties despite large revenues from petroleum exports.

Gaborone, formerly (until 1969) GABERONES, City (pop., 2001 prelim.: 185,891), capital of Botswana. It is located in southeastern Botswana near the border with South Africa. The seat of government was transferred there from Mafikeng, S.Af., in 1965, one year before Botswana became independent of Britain. Gaborone is on the Cape-Zimbabwe railway and is the site of government offices, parliament buildings, health facilities, a thermal power station, and an airport. It is the seat of the University of Botswana (1976) and also has a national museum and art gallery (1968).

Gabriel, In the Bible and the Qur'ān, one of the archangels. In the Bible he was the heavenly messenger sent to explain Daniel's visions; he also revealed to Zechariah the coming birth of John the Baptist and appeared to Mary in the Annunciation to tell her she was to be the mother of Jesus. In Christian tradition it is believed that he will blow the trumpet on Judgment Day. In the Qur'ān he is known as Jibrīl, and Muslims believe that he brought God's revelations to Muhammad.

Gaea, Greek goddess of the earth. She was both mother and wife to Uranus, or Heaven, from whom she was separated by her son Cronus, a Titan. According to Hesiod, she was the mother of all 12 Titans, as well as of the Furies and the Cyclopes. She may have originated as a mother goddess worshiped in pre-Hellenic Greece before the introduction of the cult of Zeus.

Gaea, terra-cotta statuette from Tanagra, Greece; in the Musée Borély, Marseille.
Giraudon/Art Resource, New York

Gaelic football, Irish sport, an offshoot of the violent medieval game *mêlée*. In the modern game, sides are limited to 15 players. Players may not throw the ball but may dribble it with hand or foot and may punch or punt it toward their opponents' goal. Goals count as either one or three points, depending on whether the ball passes above (one) or below (three) a crossbar attached to the goalposts. It is played mostly in Ireland and the U.S.

gagaku, Traditional court and religious music of Japan. It first appeared in Japan as an import from Korea in the 5th century AD and had become established at court by the 8th century. Though little notation from before the 12th century survives, a mostly later body of music continues to be performed at Shintō ceremonies. Gagaku employs transverse flute (*ryuteki*), double-reed pipe (*hichiriki*), mouth organ (*shō*), gong (*shōko*), drums, and stringed instruments including the *biwa* and koto. It may accompany dance (*bugaku*) or be played independently (*kangen*); it is further classified either as *tōgaku*, the so-called music of the left (which included Chinese and Indian materials), or as *komagaku*, the music of the right (including Korean examples). (The terms *left* and *right* were derived from the Confucian-based administration system of the capital during the Heian period.)

Gagarin, Yury (Alekseyevich) (b. March 9, 1934, near Gzhatsk, Russian S.F.S.R.—d. March 27, 1968, near Moscow), Soviet cosmonaut. Son of a carpenter on a collective farm, he graduated from the Soviet air force's cadet school in 1957. In April 1961, aboard Vostok 1, he became the first human to travel into space. The spacecraft orbited Earth once in 1 hour 29 minutes. Gagarin's flight brought him worldwide fame, and he was much honoured in the Soviet Union. He never went into space again, but he trained other cosmonauts. He was killed at age 34 when his jet crashed during a training flight.

Gahanbar, In Zoroastrianism, any of six festivals occurring at irregular intervals during the year and marking the change of seasons in Iran. Globally they are aligned with the six stages in the creation of the world: the heavens, water, the earth, vegetation, animals, and humanity. Each festival lasts five days. The Parsis celebrate the Gahanbar festivals in two stages, beginning with liturgical rites and sacrificial offerings and concluding with a solemn feast.

galactic coordinate, In astronomy, a galactic latitude or longitude, useful for describing the relative positions and motions of components of the Milky Way Galaxy. Galactic latitude is measured in degrees north or south of the plane of the Milky Way. Galactic longitude is measured in degrees east of the galactic centre in the constellation Sagittarius.

galactic halo, In astronomy, a nearly spherical volume of thinly scattered stars, globular clusters, and tenuous gas observed surrounding spiral galaxies. It may extend far beyond the disk and contain most of the galaxy's mass. The halo of the Milky Way Galaxy is thought to have a radius greater than 100,000 light-years and to be predominantly composed of dark matter.

Galahad, In Arthurian legend, the pure knight who achieved a vision of God through the Holy Grail. The illegitimate son of Lancelot and the princess Elaine, he alone was worthy to sit in the Siege Perilous at the Round Table, reserved for the one destined to succeed in the quest for the Grail. Unlike his father, who was given to earthly and adulterous love, Galahad was chaste and filled with spiritual fervour. By finding the Grail, he healed the Fisher King and brought fertility back to the land. He appears in many Arthurian romances, notably in Sir Thomas Malory's *Le Morte Darthur.*

Galápagos Islands, Spanish ARCHIPIÉLAGO DE COLÓN, Island group, eastern Pacific Ocean. A province (pop., 2001: 18,640) of Ecuador, the Galápagos are a group of 19 islands lying on the Equator 600 mi (1,000 km) west of the mainland. Their total land area of 3,093 sq mi (8,010 sq km) is scattered over 23,000 sq mi (59,500 sq km) of ocean. Visited by the Spanish in 1535, they were unclaimed when Ecuador took official possession of them in 1832. They became internationally famous after being visited in 1835 by British naturalist Charles Darwin; their unusual fauna, including the giant tortoise (Spanish *galápago*), contributed to his ideas on natural selection. Ecuador made the Galápagos a wildlife sanctuary in 1935 and a national park in 1959; in 1978 they were designated a UNESCO World Heritage site.

Galați, German GALATZ, City (pop., 2002: 298,584), southeastern Romania. Located at the confluence of the Danube and Siret rivers, it was occupied by the Turks from the early 16th century until 1829; its growth was encouraged by its status as a free port (1837–83). During World War II, retreating German troops devastated the town and reduced the population, substantially Jewish, to less than half. Extensively rebuilt, it is one of Romania's chief ports and the site of the country's largest shipyard.

galaxy, Any of the billions of systems of stars and interstellar matter that make up the universe. Galaxies vary considerably in size, composition, structure, and activity, but nearly all are arranged in groups, or clusters, containing from a few galaxies to as many as 10,000. Each is composed of millions to trillions of stars; in many, as in the Milky Way Galaxy, nebulae can be detected. A large fraction of the bright galaxies in the sky are spiral galaxies, with a main disk in which spiral arms wind out from the centre. The arms contain the greatest concentration of a spiral galaxy's interstellar gas and dust, where stars can form. Surrounding the centre (nucleus) is a large, usually nearly spherical nuclear bulge. Outside this and the disk is a sparse, more or less spherical galactic halo. In elliptical galaxies, which vary greatly in size, stars are distributed symmetrically in a spherical or spheroidal shape. Dwarf ellipticals (with only a few million stars) are by far the most common kind of galaxy, though none is conspicuous in the sky. Irregular galaxies, such as the Magellanic Clouds, are relatively rare. Radio galaxies are very strong sources of radio waves. Seyfert galaxies, with extremely bright nuclei, often emit radio waves and may be related to quasars.

Galilean satellite, Any of the four large satellites of Jupiter discovered by Galileo in 1610. In order of distance from Jupiter: Io (the most volcanically active body in the solar system), Europa (suspected to contain a liquid ocean under its frozen surface), Ganymede (the largest satellite in the solar system), and Callisto. Both Ganymede and Callisto are larger than Pluto and Mercury.

Galilee, Hebrew HA-GALIL, Northernmost region of biblical and modern Israel. It contains two of the four holy cities of Judaism, Tiberias and Zefat. It was the boyhood home of Jesus Christ and the setting for much of his ministry. It became the centre of Jewish scholarship after the destruction of Jerusalem (AD 70). In the modern era, the first wave of Jewish immigrants settled there (1882). The first kibbutz, Deganya, was established in 1909 on the shore of Lake Tiberias, through which flows the Jordan River.

Galileo (Galilei) (b. Feb. 15, 1564, Pisa—d. Jan. 8, 1642, Arcetri, near Florence), Italian mathematician, astronomer, and physicist. Son of a musician, he studied medicine before turning his attention to mathematics. His invention of the hydrostatic balance (c. 1586) made him famous. In 1589 he published a treatise on the centre of gravity in solids, which won him the post of mathematics lecturer at the University of Pisa. There he disproved the Aristotelian contention that bodies of different weights fall at different speeds; he also proposed the law of uniform acceleration for falling bodies and showed that the path of a thrown object is a parabola. The first to use a telescope to study the skies, he discovered (1609–10) that the surface of the Moon is irregular, that the Milky Way is composed of stars, and that Jupiter has moons. His findings led to his appointment as philosopher and mathematician to the grand duke of Tuscany. During a visit to Rome (1611), he spoke persuasively for the Copernican system, which put him at odds with Aristotelian professors and led to Copernicanism's being declared false and erroneous (1616) by the church. Obtaining permission to write about the Copernican system so long as he discussed it noncommittally, he wrote his *Dialogue Concerning the Two Chief World Systems* (1632). Though considered a masterpiece, it enraged the Jesuits, and Galileo was tried before the Inquisition, found guilty of heresy, and forced to recant. He spent the rest of his life under house arrest, continuing to write and conduct research even after going blind in 1637.

Galileo, NASA mission to study Jupiter and its Galilean satellites with an orbiting spacecraft and an atmospheric probe, launched in 1989. Though the failure of its high-gain antenna resulted in its data being transmitted back to Earth very slowly, the mission returned a wealth of valuable information. En route to Jupiter, the craft took the first detailed images of two asteroids. On its arrival in 1995, its atmospheric probe descended by parachute into Jupiter's upper cloud layers, detecting large thunderstorms. In a series of flybys of the Galilean moons, the orbiter observed volcanoes on Io hotter than any on Earth and found evidence of a liquid ocean below Europa's icy surface, a magnetic field around Ganymede, and a possible subsurface ocean on Callisto.

gall, Abnormal, localized outgrowth or swelling of plant tissue caused by infection from bacteria, fungi, viruses, or nematodes, or by irritation by insects and mites. The common plant disease crown gall, characterized by the proliferation of galls on the roots and lower stems, is caused by the bacterium *Agrobacterium tumefaciens.*

gallbladder, Muscular membranous sac under the liver that stores and concentrates bile. Pear-shaped and expandable, it holds about 1.7 fluid oz (50 ml). Its inner surface absorbs water and inorganic salts from bile, which becomes 5–18 times more concentrated than when it leaves the liver. The gallbladder contracts to discharge bile through the bile duct into the duodenum. Disorders include gallstones and inflammation (cholecystitis). Surgical removal of the gallbladder (cholecystectomy) has no serious side effects.

gallery, In architecture, a long, covered space open on one side, such as a portico or a colonnade. It may be recessed into a wall or elevated on columns or corbels, and it often serves as a passageway. Within an interior, a gallery may be a platform or upper floor projecting from a wall (e.g., in a legislative house) with seating for spectators. In a church nave, the long, narrow platforms supported by colonnades are called tribune galleries. In a theatre, the gallery is the highest balcony and generally has the cheapest seats. Galleries appeared in Renaissance houses as long, narrow rooms used both as promenades and to exhibit art. The modern art gallery is their descendant.

galley, Large seagoing vessel propelled primarily by oars. The Egyptians, Cretans, and other ancient peoples used sail-equipped galleys for war and commerce. The Phoenicians apparently introduced the bireme (*c.* 700 BC), which had two banks of oars staggered on either side. The Greeks first built the trireme *c.* 500 BC. War galleys would cruise in columns and would engage the enemy as a line abreast. A galley would close with the enemy at the bow, which was equipped with a ram, grappling irons, and missile-hurling devices. Invention of the lateen (fore-and-aft) sail and the stern rudder rendered the galley obsolete for commerce, but its greater maneuverability maintained its military importance into the 16th century.

Gallic Wars (58–50 BC) Campaigns in which Julius Caesar conquered Gaul. Clad in his blood-red cloak as a "distinguishing mark of battle," he led his troops to victories throughout the province, relying on superior strategy, tactics, discipline, and military engineering. In 58 he drove back the Helvetii from Rome's northwestern frontier, then subdued the Belgic group of Gallic peoples in the north (57), reconquered the Veneti (56), crossed the Rhine River to raid Germany (55), and crossed the English Channel to raid Britain (55, 54). His major triumph was the defeat of Vercingetorix in 52. He described the campaigns in *De bello Gallico*.

Gallicanism, French eccelesiastical and government policies designed to restrict the papacy's power. It affirmed the independence of the French king in the temporal realm, the superiority of an ecumenical council over the pope, and the union of king and clergy to limit the intervention of the pope within France. Gallicanism was opposed to Ultramontanism, which championed papal authority. The doctrine was important in the medieval struggle between church and state. In 1438, after several conflicts between kings and popes, Charles VII issued the Pragmatic Sanction of Bourges, affirming that a pope was subject to a general council and that his jurisdiction was conditioned by the royal will.

gallstone, Mass of crystallized substances that forms in the gallbladder. The most common type occurs when the liver secretes bile with too much cholesterol to stay in solution. Liver damage, chronic gallbladder disease, or biliary-tract cancer may predispose one to stone formation. In the gallbladder, stones may cause inflammation or produce no symptoms. A stone obstructing the bile duct causes severe pain (biliary colic). Gallstones usually must be removed with the gallbladder or broken up with ultrasound. In some cases a stone can be treated by giving the patient bile salts, which help redissolve cholesterol. If the gallbladder must be removed, laparoscopy is the method of choice.

Galsworthy, John (b. Aug. 14, 1867, Kingston Hill, Surrey, Eng.—d. Jan. 31, 1933, Grove Lodge, Hampstead), English novelist and playwright. Galsworthy gave up a law career to become a writer, and many of his works have legal themes. He published several works before *The Man of Property* (1906), the first novel of The Forsyte Saga (completed 1922). The family chronicle by which he is chiefly remembered, it consists of three novels linked by two interludes. He continued the story of the Forsytes in three further novels collected in *A Modern Comedy* (1929). His plays, written in a naturalistic style, usually examine a controversial ethical or social problem; they include *The Silver Box* (1906), *Strife* (1909), *Justice* (1910), and *Loyalties* (1922). He won the Nobel Prize for Literature in 1932.

Gama, Vasco da, 1st count da Vidigueira (b. *c.* 1460, Sines, Port.—d. Dec. 24, 1524, Cochin, India), Portuguese navigator. On his first voyage to India (1497–99), he traveled around the Cape of Good Hope with four ships, visiting trading cities in Mozambique and Kenya en route. Portugal's King Manuel I acted quickly to open trade routes with India, but a massacre of Portuguese in India caused him to dispatch a fleet of 20 ships in 1502, led by da Gama, to establish Portuguese supremacy in the region. Da Gama, then an admiral, forced allegiance along the way from local rulers and attacked Arab shipping. After various battles, he secured obedience to Portuguese rule and returned home. In 1524 he was appointed Portuguese viceroy in India but died shortly after arriving in Goa. His voyages to India opened the sea route from western Europe to the East.

Gambia, The, officially REPUBLIC OF THE GAMBIA, Country, western Africa. Constituting an enclave in Senegal, it lies along the Gambia River, stretching inland 295 mi (475 km) from the Atlantic Ocean. Area: 4,491 sq mi (11,632 sq km). Population: (2011 est.) 1,776,000. Capital: Banjul. About two-fifths of the population are Malinke, followed by Fulani (about one-fifth), Wolof (about one-eighth), and other groups. Language: English (official). Religions: Islam; also Christianity. Currency: dalasi. The Gambia has a wet-and-dry tropical climate and is generally hilly, with savanna in the uplands and swamps in low-lying areas. It has a developing market economy based largely on the production and export of peanuts, though only about one-fourth of the land is arable. The river serves as a major transportation artery. Tourism is an important source of revenue. The Gambia is a multiparty republic with one legislative body; its head of state and government is the president. Beginning about the 13th century CE, the Wolof, Malinke, and Fulani peoples settled in different parts of what is now The Gambia and established villages and then kingdoms in the region. European exploration began when the Portuguese sighted the Gambia River in 1455. In the 17th century, when Britain and France both settled in the area, the British Fort James, on an island about 20 mi (32 km) from the river's mouth, was an important collection point for the slave trade. In 1783 the Treaty of Versailles reserved the Gambia River for Britain. After the British abolished slavery in 1807, they built a fort at the mouth of the river to block the continuing slave trade. In 1889 The Gambia's boundaries were agreed upon by Britain and France; the British declared a protectorate over the area in 1894. Independence was proclaimed in 1965, and The Gambia became a republic within the Commonwealth in 1970. It formed a limited confederation with Senegal in 1982, which was dissolved in 1989. During the 1990s the country faced political problems, but its biggest concern was its poor economy, which continued into the 21st century.

Gambia River, River, western Africa. Rising in Guinea and flowing northwest through Senegal and west through The Gambia to the Atlantic Ocean, it is 700 mi (1,120 km) long. It is the only western African river that is easily accessible to oceangoing shipping. From its source in the highlands of the Fouta Djallon, it follows a winding course to its mouth, which is a ria, or drowned estuary. The flats of the middle and upper river support rice and peanuts and are more heavily settled than the area around the river's lower course.

game theory, Branch of applied mathematics devised to analyze certain situations in which there is an interplay between parties that may have similar, opposed, or mixed interests. Game theory was originally developed by John von Neumann and Oscar Morgenstern in their book *The Theory of Games and Economic Behavior* (1944). In a typical game, or competition with fixed rules, "players" try to outsmart one another by anticipating the others' decisions, or moves. A solution to a game prescribes the optimal strategy or strategies for each player and predicts the average, or expected, outcome. Until a highly contrived counterexample was devised in 1967, it was thought that every contest had at least one solution.

gamelan, Indigenous orchestra of Java and Bali and, more generally, of Indonesia and Malaysia. A gamelan usually consists largely of gongs, xylophones, and metallophones (rows of tuned metal bars struck with a mallet). Gamelan polyphony is complex and many-voiced. The melody is taken by the voice, flute, or *rebab* (a bowed stringed instrument); under it, most of the other instruments provide rhythmic paraphrases of the melody, producing a shimmering, variegated texture. The gamelan has influenced many Western composers, including Claude Debussy, Olivier Messiaen, John Cage, Steve Reich, and Philip Glass.

gametophyte, In certain plants, the sexual phase (or an individual representing the phase) in the alternation of generations. The alternate, nonsexual phase is the sporophyte. In the gametophyte phase, male and female organs (gametangia) develop and produce eggs and sperm (gametes), which unite in fertilization (syngamy). The fertilized egg (zygote) develops into the sporophyte, which produces numerous single-celled spores, which in turn develop directly into new gametes.

gamma ray, Penetrating very short-wavelength electromagnetic radiation, similar to an X-ray but of higher energy, that is emitted spontaneously by some radioactive substances. Gamma radiation also originates in the decay of certain subatomic particles and in particle-antiparticle annihilation. Gamma rays can initiate nuclear fission, can be absorbed by ejection of an electron, and can be scattered by free electrons.

gamma-ray astronomy, Study of astronomical objects and phenomena that emit gamma rays. Gamma-ray telescopes are designed to observe high-energy astrophysical systems, including stellar coronas, white dwarf stars, neutron stars, black holes, supernova remnants, clusters of galaxies, and diffuse gamma-ray background radiation found along the plane of the Milky Way Galaxy. Because Earth's atmosphere blocks most gamma rays, observations are generally conducted by high-altitude balloons or spacecraft. In the 1960s defense satellites designed to detect X-rays and gamma rays from clandestine nuclear testing serendipitously discovered enigmatic gamma-ray bursts coming from deep space. In the 1970s Earth-orbiting observatories found a number of gamma-ray point sources, including an exceptionally strong one, dubbed Geminga, that was later identified as a nearby pulsar. The Compton Gamma Ray Observatory, launched in 1991, mapped thousands of celestial gamma-ray sources; it also showed that the mysterious bursts are distributed across the sky, implying that their sources are at the distant reaches of the universe rather than in the Milky Way.

Ganda, or BAGANDA, People of southern Uganda. They speak Luganda, a Bantu language of the Benue-Congo group. Numbering 3.7 million, the Ganda are Uganda's largest ethnic group. Traditionally hoe cultivators, they also grow cotton and coffee for export and keep livestock. In the 19th century the Ganda developed the centralized state known as Buganda.

Gandhara art, Style of Buddhist art that developed in what is now northwestern Pakistan and eastern Afghanistan from the 1st to the 7th century AD. It was contemporaneous with Mathura art. The Gandhara region had earlier been a site of much Buddhist missionary activity, and the Kushan rulers maintained contact with Rome; the Gandhara school incorporated motifs and techniques from Classical Roman art (e.g., vine scrolls, cherubs with gar-

The Buddha preaching, relief from Gandhara, schist, c. 2nd century AD; in the Prince of Wales Museum of Western India, Bombay.
P. Chandra

lands, tritons, centaurs), but the iconography was based on the interpretation of Buddhist legends. Sculptural materials included green phyllite, gray-blue mica, and stucco; sculptures were originally painted and gilded.

Gandhi, Indira (Priyadarshini), orig. INDIRA PRIYADARSHINI NEHRU (b. Nov. 19, 1917, Allahabad, India—d. Oct. 31, 1984, New Delhi), Prime minister of India (1966–77, 1980–84). The only child of Jawaharlal Nehru, she studied in India and at the University of Oxford. In 1942 she married Feroze Gandhi (d. 1960), a fellow member of the Indian National Congress. In 1959 she was given the largely honorary position of party president, and in 1966 she achieved actual power when she was made leader of the Congress Party and, consequently, prime minister. She instituted major reforms, including a strict population-control program. In 1971 she mobilized Indian forces against Pakistan in the cause of East Bengal's secession. She oversaw the incorporation of Sikkim in 1974. Convicted in 1975 of violating election laws, she declared a state of emergency, jailing opponents and passing many laws limiting personal freedoms. She was de-

Indira Gandhi
AP

feated in the following election but returned to power in 1980. In 1984 she ordered the army to move into the Golden Temple complex of the Sikhs at Amritsar, with the intent of crushing the Sikh militants hiding inside the temple; some 450 Sikhs died in the fighting. She was later shot and killed by her own Sikh bodyguards in revenge.

Gandhi, Mohandas K(aramchand), known as MAHATMA GANDHI (b. Oct. 2, 1869, Porbandar, India—d. Jan. 30, 1948, Delhi), Preeminent leader of Indian nationalism and prophet of nonviolence in the 20th century. Gandhi grew up in a home steeped in religion, and he took for granted religious tolerance and the doctrine of ahimsa (noninjury to all living beings). He studied law in England but seemed too diffident to become a successful lawyer. He took a job with an Indian firm in South Africa. There he became an effective advocate for Indian rights. In 1906 he first put into action satyagraha, his technique of nonviolent resistance. His success in South Africa gave him an international reputation, and in 1915 he returned to India and within a few years became the leader of a nationwide struggle for Indian home rule. By 1920 Gandhi commanded influence hitherto unattained by any political leader in India. He refashioned the Indian National Congress into an effective political instrument of Indian nationalism and undertook major campaigns of nonviolent resistance in 1920–22, 1930–34 (including his momentous march to the sea to collect salt to protest a government monopoly), and 1940–42. In the 1930s he also campaigned to end discrimination against India's lower-caste "untouchables" (now called Dalits; officially designated as Scheduled Castes) and concentrated on educating rural India and promoting cottage industry. India achieved dominion status in 1947, but the partition of the subcontinent into India and Pakistan was a great disappointment to Gandhi, who had long worked for Hindu-Muslim unity. In September 1947 he ended rioting in Calcutta (Kolkata) by fasting. Known as the Mahatma ("Great-Souled"), Gandhi had won the affection and loyalty of millions. In January 1948 he was shot and killed by a young Hindu fanatic.

Gandhi, Rajiv (Ratna) (b. Aug. 20, 1944, Bombay [Mumbai], India—d. May 21, 1991, Sriperumbudur, near Madras [Chennai]), Indian politician, prime minister of India (1984–89). Son of Indira Gandhi, he studied engineering at the University of Cambridge and became a commercial airline pilot in 1968. He entered politics after the death of his brother, Sanjay, in 1980. Sworn in as prime minister the day his mother was assassinated (Oct. 31, 1984), he led the Congress (I) Party to a landslide victory in elections that year. His administration took vigorous measures to reform the government bureaucracy and liberalize the country's economy, but his attempts to discourage separatist movements failed, and his government became embroiled in financial scandals. He resigned in 1989 but remained leader of the Congress (I) Party. He was assassinated in 1991 while running for reelection.

Ganesha, or GANESA, Elephant-headed Hindu god, the son of Shiva and Parvati. He is also revered in Jainism, and he is important in the art and mythology of Buddhist Asia. As the remover of obstacles, Ganesha is invoked when beginning worship or starting any new venture. He was popular with Indian nationalists, who saw British colonialism as one obstacle to be removed. The patron of letters and learning, he is the legendary scribe who wrote down the *Mahabharata*. His popularity continued to grow through the 20th century. His festival is especially popular in the Indian state of Maharashtra.

Ganesha dancing, relief from Farrukhabad, Uttar Pradesh, India, 10th century AD; in the State Museum, Lucknow, India.
Pramod Chandra

Ganges delta, or GANGES-BRAHMAPUTRA DELTA, Region in West Bengal state, India, and Bangladesh. An area of about 220 mi (355 km) wide along the Bay of Bengal, it is covered by the network of streams forming the mouths of the Ganges (Ganga) and Brahmaputra rivers. In Bangladesh the Brahmaputra is joined by the Tista River and, from there to its junction with the Ganges, is known as the Jamuna River. The main streams, the Ganges and the Jamuna, unite to form the Padma River. The river farthest west that enters the Bay of Bengal is the Hugli River. Many smaller streams of the delta form a swamp region for about 160 miles (260 km) along the coast, known as the Sundarbans. The delta was struck in 1970 by one of history's most devastating cyclones.

Ganges River, Hindi GANGA, River, northern India and Bangladesh. Held sacred by followers of Hinduism, it is formed from five headstreams rising in Uttaranchal state. On its 1,560-mi (2,510-km) course, it flows southeast through the Indian states of Uttar Pradesh, Bihar, and West Bengal. In central Bangladesh it is joined by the Brahmaputra and Meghna rivers. Their combined waters (called the Padma River) empty into the Bay of Bengal and form a delta 220 mi (354 km) wide, which is shared by India and Bangladesh. Its plain is one of the most fertile and densely populated regions in the world. Millions of Hindus bathe in the river annually at special holy places (*tirthas*). Many cast the ashes of their dead into its waters, and cremation temples are found along its banks in numerous places.

gangrene, Localized soft-tissue death (necrosis) from prolonged blood-supply blockage. It can occur in atherosclerosis, diabetes mellitus, or decubitus ulcer, and after severe burns or frostbite. In dry gangrene, gradual blood-supply decrease turns the part discoloured and cold, then dark and dry. Treatment requires improving blood flow. Moist gangrene comes from a sudden blood-supply cutoff. Bacterial infection causes swelling, discoloration, and then a foul smell. Along with antibiotics, tissue removal may be needed to prevent spread, which can be fatal. A more virulent form, gas gangrene, is named for gas bubbles under the skin produced by a highly lethal toxin from clostridium bacteria. The wound oozes brownish, smelly pus. Infection spreads rapidly, causing death. All dead and diseased tissue must be removed and antibiotics given; an antitoxin can also be used.

Gangtok, Town (pop., 2001: 29,354), capital of Sikkim state, northeastern India. At an elevation of 5,600 ft (1,700 m), it overlooks the Ranipool River. It was the governmental seat of the kingdom of Sikkim until the monarchy was abolished (1975) and India annexed Sikkim (1976). It was an important point on the trans-Himalayan trade route until the border with China was closed in 1962. The former royal palace and chapel are located there; the noted Buddhist monastery of Rumtek is nearby.

Gansu, or KAN-SU, conventional KANSU, Province (pop., 2002 est.: 25,930,000), north-central China. It is bordered by Mongolia, the autonomous regions of Xinjiang, Inner Mongolia, and Ningxia, and the provinces of Shaanxi, Sichuan, and Qinghai. It has an area of 141,500 sq mi (366,500 sq km). Its capital is Lanzhou. For centuries a passage between the upper Huang He (Yellow River) region and western China, it became part of Chinese territory in the 3rd century BCE. It was renowned as the entranceway into China used by Marco Polo. Eastern Gansu is the main site of earthquakes in China; in 1920 an earthquake there destroyed many towns and caused 246,000 deaths. Wheat is the province's chief crop, and wheat flour rather than rice is the basis of the local diet.

Ganymede, In Greek legend, the son of King Tros (or Laomedon) of Troy. Because of his unusual beauty, he was carried off by Zeus disguised as an eagle, and he became cupbearer to the gods. Other versions of the legend trace his abduction to other gods or to King Minos of Crete. The story has long been held to have homosexual implications, and the word catamite is derived from his Latin name, Catamitus.

Ganymede and Zeus in the form of an eagle, antique marble statue; in the Vatican Museum
Anderson—Alinari/Art Resource, New York

Gao Xingjian (b. Jan. 4, 1940, Ganzhou, Jiangxi province, China), Chinese émigré novelist and playwright. His novel *Soul Mountain* (1989) resulted from a pilgrimage in the form of a 10-month walking tour along the Yangtze River. Gao's works were banned in China after the publication of his play *Fugitives* (1989), which reflected the 1989 events in Tiananmen Square. In 1987 he settled in France and later became a French citizen. He was awarded the Nobel Prize for Literature in 2000.

Garbo, Greta, orig. GRETA LOUISA GUSTAFSSON (b. Sept. 18, 1905, Stockholm, Swed.—d. April 15, 1990, New York, N.Y.,

Greta Garbo in Camille *(1936).*
Culver Pictures

U.S.), Swedish-U.S. film star. She was working as a salesclerk when she was chosen to appear in publicity films for the store where she worked. Her modest success encouraged her to study at the Royal Dramatic Theatre's training school, where the film director Mauritz Stiller discovered her. He cast her in *The Story of Gösta Berling* (1924) and became her mentor and coach. Stiller and Garbo were hired by MGM in 1925, and Garbo's beauty and enigmatic personality made her a star in her first U.S. film, *The Torrent* (1926). Aloof, mysterious, yet passionate, she mesmerized audiences in films such as *Love* (1927), *Anna Christie* (1930), *Grand Hotel* (1932), *Anna Karenina* (1935), *Camille* (1936), and *Ninotchka* (1939). Her reclusive life after her sudden retirement at age 36 added to her mystique.

García Márquez, Gabriel (José) (b. March 6, 1928, Aracataca, Colom.), Latin American writer. He worked many years as a journalist in Latin American and European cities and later also as a screenwriter and publicist, before settling in Mexico. His best-known work, the novel *One Hundred Years of Solitude* (1967), recounts the history of the fictional village of Macondo, the setting of much of his work; enormously admired and influential, it became the principal vehicle for the style known as magic realism. Later novels include *The Autumn of the Patriarch* (1975), *Love in the Time of Cholera* (1985), *The General in His Labyrinth* (1989), and *Memories of My Melancholy Whores* (2004). His collections of short stories and novellas include *No One Writes to the Colonel* (1968) and *Leaf Storm* (1955). In 2002 he published *Vivir para contarla*, an autobiographical account of his early years. He received the Nobel Prize for Literature in 1982.

Gabriel García Márquez, 1982.
© Lutfi Ozkok

Garda, Lake, ancient LACUS BENACUS, Lake, northern Italy. Largest of the Italian lakes, it is 34 mi (54 km) long and 2 to 11 mi (3 to 18 km) wide, with a shoreline of 77.5 mi (125 km). It borders Lombardy, Veneto, and Trentino–Alto Adige. Separated from the Adige River valley by the narrow ridge of Mount Baldo, it is fed by the Sarca River at its northern end, while the Mincio flows out toward the Po River to the south. The lake is encircled by the Gardesana scenic route, opened in 1931. Well sheltered by the Alps to the north, Lake Garda has a temperate Mediterranean climate. It is a popular resort area.

gardenia, Any of the more than 140 species of ornamental shrubs and trees in the genus *Gardenia*, in the madder family, native to tropical and subtropical Africa and Asia. Gardenias have white or yellow tubular flowers, evergreen leaves, and large berrylike fruits containing a sticky orange pulp. Cape jasmine (*G. jasminoides*), native to China, is the fragrant species sold by florists.

gargoyle, Carved spout that drains water from a rooftop gutter. The Gothic gargoyle was usually a grotesque bird or animal sitting on the back of a cornice and projecting forward for several feet in order to throw the water far from the building. The term is often loosely applied to any grotesque or fantastic beast, such as the *chimères* (chimeras) that decorate the parapets of Notre-Dame de Paris.

Garibaldi, Giuseppe (b. July 4, 1807, Nice, French Empire—d. June 2, 1882, Caprera, Italy), Italian patriot and soldier of the Risorgimento. He came under the influence of Giuseppe Mazzini in 1834, took part in a failed mutiny intended to provoke a republican revolution in Piedmont, and escaped to France. He lived in exile in South America (1836–48) and learned guerrilla warfare tactics during liberation attempts in Brazil and Uruguay. He returned to Italy in 1848 with his small band of "Red Shirts" and fought in Milan in the war of independence against Austria. Af-

Giuseppe Garibaldi, 1866.
Deutsche Fotothek, Dresden

ter Pope Pius IX fled Rome (1848), Garibaldi for a while defended the city from the French when they attempted to reinstate papal rule. His bold retreat through central Italy made him a well-known figure. He lived in exile again until 1854, and in 1859 he led an army in another war against Austria. In 1860, with no government backing, he raised an army of about 1,000 men and attacked Sicily; by the end of his campaign, he commanded 30,000 men, with whom he seized Naples. He handed all of southern Italy over to Victor Emmanuel II and hailed him as the first king of a united Italy. With secret support from Victor Emmanuel, he led unsuccessful campaigns into the Papal States in 1862 and 1867.

garlic, Bulbous perennial plant (*Allium sativum*) of the family Alliaceae, native to central Asia and growing wild in Italy and southern France. The bulbs are used as a flavouring. A classic ingredient in many national cuisines, garlic has a powerful onion-like aroma and pungent taste. Since ancient and medieval times it has been prized for its medicinal properties; it was formerly carried as a charm against vampires and other evils. Garlic bulbs are used sliced or crushed to flavour sauces, stews, and salad dressings. The membranous skin of the garlic bulb encloses up to 20 edible bulblets called cloves.

garnet, Any of a group of common silicate minerals with identical crystal structure but highly variable chemical composition. Garnets are most often found in metamorphic rocks but also occur in certain types of igneous rocks, and, usually in minor amounts, in some sedimentary rocks. They may be colourless, black, or many shades of red and green. Garnets are hard, and they fracture with sharp edges. They are used as abrasives for fine sanding and polishing of wood, leather, glass, metals, and plastics, as sandblasting agents, and in nonskid surface coatings. Garnet is the birthstone for January. Garnets have been mined in New York, Maine, and Idaho in the U.S., the world's leading producer; notable quantities have also been found in Australia, China, India, and elsewhere.

gas, One of the three fundamental states of matter, in which matter has no definite shape, is very fluid, and has a density about 0.1% that of liquids. Gas is very compressible but tends to expand indefinitely, and it fills any container. A small change in temperature or pressure produces a substantial change in its volume; these relationships are expressed as equations in the gas laws. The kinetic theory of gases, developed in the 19th century, describes gases as assemblages of tiny particles (atoms or molecules) in constant motion and contributed much to an understanding of their behaviour. The term *gas* can also mean gasoline, natural gas, or the anesthetic nitrous oxide.

gasoline, British PETROL, Mixture of volatile, flammable hydrocarbons derived from petroleum, used as fuel for internal-combustion engines and as a solvent for oils and fats. Gasoline became the preferred automobile fuel because it releases a great deal of energy when burned, it mixed readily with air in a carburetor, and it initially was cheap due to a large supply. Costs have now increased greatly except where subsidized. Gasoline was first produced by distillation. Later processes increased the yield from crude oil by splitting large molecules into smaller ones. Still other methods, such as conversion of straight-chain hydrocarbons into their branched-chain isomers, followed. The resulting gasoline is a complex mixture of hundreds of hydrocarbons. A gasoline's octane number indicates its ability to resist knocking (premature combustion) and can be altered by changing the proportions of certain components. The compound tetraethyl lead, once used to reduce knocking, has been banned as toxic. Other additives include detergents, antifreezes, and antioxidants. Since the mid-20th century gasoline fumes have been recognized as a major component of urban air pollution. Efforts to reduce dependence on gasoline, which is a nonrenewable resource, include use of gasohol, a 9:1 mix of gasoline and ethanol, and the development of electric automobiles.

gastritis, Inflammation in the stomach. Acute gastritis, usually caused by ingesting something irritating or by infection, starts suddenly, with severe pain, vomiting, thirst, and diarrhea, and subsides rapidly. Treatment involves a short fast and then a bland diet, sedatives, and antispasmodics. Chemical gastritis, from ingestion of corrosive chemicals, requires emptying and washing out the stomach. Chronic gastritis has vague symptoms, including abdominal discomfort or pain, poor appetite, gas, and irregular bowel movements. Causes include prolonged use of aspirin or other irritating drugs, infection with *Helicobacter pylori*, and pernicious anemia. Treatment for chronic gastritis depends on the cause.

gastroenteritis, Acute infectious syndrome of the stomach lining and intestines. Symptoms include diarrhea, vomiting, and abdominal cramps. Severity varies from transient diarrhea to life-threatening dehydration, children and the very old being more at risk for the latter. Many microorganisms produce it, either by secreting toxins or by invading the gut walls. Forms of gastroenteritis include food poisoning, cholera, and traveler's diarrhea. Depending on cause and severity, treatment includes antibiotics or simply supportive care.

gastroesophageal reflux disease (GERD), Disorder characterized by frequent passage of gastric contents from the stomach back into the esophagus. Symptoms of GERD may include heartburn, coughing, frequent clearing of the throat, and difficulty in swallowing. It can be caused by relaxation of the muscle that connects the esophagus and the stomach, delayed emptying of the esophagus or stomach, hiatal hernia, obesity, or pregnancy. Treatment is with antacids or acid-inhibiting medications and lifestyle changes such as not eating before bedtime, avoiding acidic or fatty foods or beverages, cessation of smoking, and weight loss. Surgery may be necessary in severe cases.

Gates, Bill, in full WILLIAM HENRY GATES III (b. Oct. 28, 1955, Seattle, Wash., U.S.), U.S. computer programmer and businessman. As a teenager, he helped computerize his high school's payroll system and founded a company that sold traffic-counting systems to local governments. At 19 he dropped out of Harvard University and cofounded Microsoft Corp. with Paul G. Allen (b. 1954). Microsoft began its domination of the fledgling microcomputer industry when Gates licensed the operating system MS-DOS to IBM in 1980 for use in IBM's first personal computer. As Mi-

crosoft's largest shareholder, Gates became a billionaire in 1986, and within a decade he was the world's richest private individual. Beginning in 1995, he refocused Microsoft on the development of software solutions for the Internet, and he also moved the company into the computer hardware and gaming markets with the Xbox video machine. In 1999 he and his wife created the largest charitable foundation in the U.S. In 2008 Gates relinquished day-to-day oversight of Microsoft in order to devote more time to charity work. He remained, however, the company's chairman.

gaucho, Any of the nomadic and colourful horsemen of the Argentine and Uruguayan Pampas, who remain folk heroes famed for hardiness and lawlessness. Gauchos flourished from the mid 18th to the mid 19th century. At first they rounded up the herds of horses and cattle that roamed freely on the vast grasslands east of the Andes. In the early 19th century they fought in the armies that defeated the Spanish colonial regime and then for the caudillos who jockeyed for power after independence. Argentine writers have celebrated the gauchos, and gaucho literature is an important part of the Latin American cultural tradition.

Gawain, Knight of King Arthur's Round Table. A nephew of Arthur, he appears in early Arthurian legend as a model of perfection. In later romances, his character is marred by arrogance and by an inability to perceive the significance of the grail. In the 14th-century Middle English poem *Sir Gawain and the Green Knight*, he accepted a challenge from a mysterious Green Knight, who offered to let Gawain chop off his head if he could return the blow one year later. When the blow was struck, the Knight picked up his head and left the court, and Gawain set out in search of him. After passing through a series of temptations, Gawain met the Green Knight's blows and suffered only a small wound, his neck protected by a magical green sash.

gay rights movement, or HOMOSEXUAL RIGHTS MOVEMENT, Civil-rights movement that advocates equal rights for gay men, lesbians, bisexuals, and transsexuals. Supporters of gay rights seek to eliminate sodomy laws barring homosexual acts between consenting adults and call for an end to discrimination against gay men and lesbians in employment, credit, lending, housing, marriage, adoption, public accommodations, and other areas of life. The first group to campaign publicly was founded in Berlin in 1897 by Magnus Hirschfeld (1868–1935) and had 25 local chapters in Europe by 1922; suppressed by the Nazis, it did not survive World War II. The first U.S. support group, the Mattachine Society, was founded in Los Angeles *c.* 1950; the Daughters of Bilitis, for lesbians, was founded in San Francisco in 1955. The Dutch Association for the Integration of Homosexuality COC, founded as the COC (Cultuur en Ontspannings Centrum ["Culture and Recreation Center"]) in 1946 and headquartered in Amsterdam, is a prominent European group and the oldest existing gay rights organization. Many date the expansion of the modern gay rights movement to the Stonewall rebellion in New York City in 1969, when a raid by police on a gay bar called the Stonewall Inn provoked a riot by bar patrons. "Stonewall" came to be commemorated annually by the observance of Gay and Lesbian Pride Week in cities around the world. The International Lesbian and Gay Association (founded 1978), headquartered in Brussels, lobbies for human rights and opposes discrimination against homosexuals. Although the movement is strongest in western Europe and North America, gay rights organizations exist in many countries throughout the world. Among the major issues pressed by gay rights advocates in the 1990s and into the 21st century were the passage of hate crime laws and the establishment of legal rights for homosexuals to marry, adopt children, and serve openly in the military.

Gaza Strip, Arabic QIṬĀ' GHAZZAH, Hebrew REẒU'AT 'AZZA, Territory, southeastern Mediterranean Sea coast. Area: 140 sq mi (365 sq km). Population: (2011 est.) 1,574,000. The region lies northeast of the Sinai Peninsula and is also the location of the city of Gaza, which has been a prosperous trading centre for much of its history and was first mentioned in the 15th century BCE. Often besieged by invaders, including Israelites, Assyrians, Babylonians, and Persians, it declined in importance after the Crusades. It was ruled by the Ottoman Empire from the 16th century. After World War I (1914–18) the city and the strip became part of the British mandate of Palestine. Following the first Arab-Israeli war (1948–49), the territory was occupied by Egypt, and the city became that country's headquarters in Palestine. The occupied area was later reduced to an area 25 mi (40 km) long, which became known as the Gaza Strip, still under Egyptian control. In the Six-Day War (1967) it was captured by Israel. The area's chief economic problem was the extreme poverty of the large number of Palestinian Arab refugees living there. In 1987, rioting among Gaza's Palestinians marked the beginning of the first *intifāḍah*. Continued unrest led in 1993 to an agreement between Israel and the Palestine Liberation Organization granting limited self-rule to the Palestinian population of the Gaza Strip and West Bank. A breakdown in further negotiations in 2000 led to another outbreak of violence. In an attempt to stem the fighting, Israel withdrew all its soldiers and settlers from the Gaza Strip in 2005, and control of the territory was transferred to the Palestinians.

gazelle, Any of numerous species of graceful antelope (genus *Gazella*) found on open plains and arid lands from Mongolia to the Atlantic coast of North Africa and throughout eastern and central tropical Africa. Gazelles are 2–3 ft (60–90 cm) high at the shoulder. They range in herds that usually contain 5 to 10 individuals but may include several hundred. They are generally brown with white underparts and rump, and many have a horizontal dark band along each side. A light stripe runs down each side of the face. The horns have numerous raised rings and are variously shaped, but all are slightly upturned at the ends. Some species are considered endangered.

*Thomson's gazelle (*Gazella thomsoni*).*
E.R. Degginger/EB Inc.

Gaziantep, City (pop., 2000: 853,513), south-central Turkey. Located north of Aleppo, it was strategically situated near ancient trade routes and has been inhabited since the early 4th millennium BC. Known as Hamtap, it was an important stronghold guarding the Syrian-Byzantine border routes. It was captured by Turks in 1183 and later changed hands among various invaders until its absorption into the Ottoman Empire in the early 16th century. Called Aintab (or Ayıntap) under the Ottomans, it was occupied by the British and French after World War I (1914–18). By then it was a centre of Turkish nationalist resistance to European occupation, and, upon its return to Turkey in 1922, it was renamed in honour of its heroic stand (Turkish *gazi*, "champion").

Gdańsk, German DANZIG, City (pop., 2000 est.: 456,574), capital of Pomorskie province, northern Poland. Located at the mouth of the Vistula River on the Baltic Sea, it was first mentioned in the late 10th century as a Polish town. The capital of the dukes of Pomerania in the 13th century, it was taken by the knights of the Teutonic Order in 1308. In 1466 Casimir IV regained the territory for Poland, and Gdańsk expanded greatly. From 1793 it was controlled mainly by Prussia; following World War I, it was a free city governed by Poland. In 1938 Adolf Hitler demanded that Gdańsk be given back to Germany; Poland's refusal was the excuse for his attack on Poland in 1939, which precipitated World War II. The city, greatly damaged during the war, was returned to Poland in 1945. It is now fully restored, with renewed port facilities. The independent labour union Solidarity was founded there in 1980.

Geb, In ancient Egyptian religion, the god of the earth and the physical support of the world. Geb and his sister Nut belonged to the second generation of deities at Heliopolis. In Egyptian art he was often depicted as lying at the feet of the air god, Shu, with Nut, the sky goddess, arched above them. He was the third divine ruler among the gods, and the pharaohs claimed descent from him.

gecko, Any of about 1,000 species of harmless but noisy lizards in the family Gekkonidae. Geckos are small, usually nocturnal reptiles that have soft skin, a short, stout body, a large head, and weak limbs often equipped with suction-padded digits. The pads contain tiny hairlike projections that cling to surfaces, allowing geckos to climb absolutely smooth and vertical surfaces and even to run across ceilings. Most are 1–6 in. (3–15 cm) long, including the tail, and they are usually drably coloured, with gray, brown, or white predominating. They live in warm areas worldwide in habitats ranging from deserts to rainforests. They are sometimes kept as pets in houses or apartments and are beneficial to humans by eating undesirable insects.

Geiger counter, or GEIGER-MÜLLER COUNTER, Device used for detecting and counting individual particles of radiation. Invented by the German physicist Hans Geiger (1882–1945) and later refined with help from Walther Müller, the device is a gas-filled metal tube with a wire through its axis and a high voltage applied to the wire. As particles enter the tube, they create a large avalanche of ionization in the gas, which then discharges, creating a brief electric pulse. The tube produces the same large output pulse for virtually every charged particle that passes through the gas and so is useful for detecting individual particles. It can therefore indicate lower levels of radiation than is possible with other types of detectors.

Geisel, Theodor Seuss, known as DR. SEUSS (b. March 2, 1904, Springfield, Mass., U.S.—d. Sept. 24, 1991, La Jolla, Calif.), U.S. writer and illustrator.He studied at Dartmouth College and did doctoral work at the University of Oxford. He began working in 1927 as a freelance cartoonist, illustrator, and writer. Under his pseudonym, Geisel began creating immensely popular children's books peopled with outlandish invented creatures and brimming with nonsense words. *And to Think That I Saw It on Mulberry Street* (1937), his first Dr. Seuss book, was followed by such huge successes as *Horton Hatches the Egg* (1940), *The Cat in the Hat* (1957), *How the Grinch Stole Christmas* (1957), *Yertle the Turtle* (1958), and *Green Eggs and Ham* (1960). Such perennial bestsellers, and his posthumous *Oh, the Places You'll Go!* (1993), made him the best-selling children's author in the world.

Gemini (Latin: "Twins") In astronomy, the constellation lying between Cancer and Taurus; in astrology, the third sign of the zodiac, governing approximately the period May 21–June 21. It is represented by a set of twins. The twins are most often identified as the mythological Castor and Pollux (Dioscuri), but have also been equated with other famous pairs such as Romulus and Remus.

Gemini, Series of 12 two-person spacecraft launched into Earth orbit by the U.S. between 1964 and 1967, following the one-person Mercury program and before the three-person Apollo program. Designed to test astronauts' ability to maneuver spacecraft manually, the Gemini series helped develop techniques for orbital rendezvous and docking, procedures that were required later in the Apollo Moon-landing missions. It also gave NASA engineers a chance to improve spacecraft environmental control and electrical power systems.

gemstone, Any of various minerals prized for beauty, durability, and rarity. A few noncrystalline materials of organic origin (e.g., pearl, red coral, and amber) also are classified as gemstones. Of the more than 3,500 identified natural minerals, fewer than 100 are used as gemstones and only 16 have achieved importance: beryl, chrysoberyl, corundum, diamond, feldspar, garnet, jade, lazurite, olivine, opal, quartz, spinel, topaz, tourmaline, turquoise, and zircon. Some of these (e.g., beryl and corundum) provide more than one type of gem. In virtually all cases, the minerals have to be cut and polished for use in jewelry.

gender, In language, a grammatical category contrasting distinctions of sex or animateness. Gender marking may be natural, with linguistic markers of gender corresponding to real-world gender, or purely grammatical, with markers of gender in part semantically based and in part semantically arbitrary. In languages with grammatical gender, nouns are partitioned into sets. Membership of a noun in a set may be expressed by its form and/or by the forms of other parts of speech controlled by the noun. Closely related to gender systems in language are class systems, as in Bantu languages, in which the number of sets into which nouns are partitioned is much larger, with distinct categories for things such as plants, animals, and tools, though, as with nouns in Romance and Germanic languages, assignment of most nouns to classes is semantically arbitrary.

gene, Unit of heredity that occupies a fixed position on a chromosome. Genes achieve their effects by directing protein synthesis. They are composed of DNA, except in some viruses that contain RNA instead. The sequence of nitrogenous bases along a strand of DNA determines the genetic code. When the product of a particular gene is needed, the portion of the DNA molecule that contains that gene splits, and a complementary strand of RNA, called messenger RNA (mRNA), forms and then passes to ribosomes, where proteins are synthesized. A second type of RNA, transfer RNA (tRNA), matches up the mRNA with specific amino acids, which combine in series to form polypeptide chains, the building blocks of proteins. Experiments have shown that many of the genes within a cell are inactive much or even all of the time, but they can be switched on and off. Mutations occur when the number or order of bases in a gene is disrupted.

genealogy, Study of family origins and history. It is found in most parts of the world and is international in scope. Originally concerned with tracing royal, aristocratic, or clerical lines, genealogy has broadened its scope over the centuries, and many ordinary people now pursue it as a hobby. In preliterate cultures genealogical information was transmitted orally, usually as a list of names; later generations recorded this information. Divine origins were often ascribed to kings and heroes. Modern genealogists use artifacts, including ancient records, coins, deeds, tapestries, paintings, and monuments, to help them in their work.

General Agreement on Tariffs and Trade (GATT), Set of multilateral trade agreements aimed at the abolition of quotas and the reduction of tariff duties among the signing nations. Originally signed by 23 countries at Geneva in 1947, GATT became the most effective instrument in the massive expansion of world trade in the later 20th century. By 1995, when GATT was replaced by the World Trade Organization (WTO), 125 nations had signed its agreements, which governed 90% of world trade. GATT's most important principle was trade without discrimination, in which member nations opened their markets equally to one another. Once a country and its largest trading partners agreed to reduce a tariff, that tariff cut was automatically extended to all GATT members. GATT also established uniform customs regulations and sought to eliminate import quotas. It sponsored many treaties that reduced tariffs, the last of which, signed in Uruguay in 1994, established the WTO.

Genesis, First book of the Bible. Its name, taken from its first verse, means "beginning." Genesis provides the creation story for Judaism and Christianity and begins the history of the Israelite people. In addition to God's creation of the universe, it includes the story of Adam and Eve, Cain and Abel, Noah and the Flood, the Tower of Babel, and God's covenant with the three patriarchs,

Abraham, Isaac, and Jacob, concluding with the story of Jacob's son Joseph. It is traditionally ascribed to Moses, but modern scholarship has identified at least three literary strains in it, dating from 950 BC to the 5th century BC, though incorporating material from much earlier. It is one of the five books that make up the Pentateuch.

genetic drift, Change in the pool of genes of a small population that takes place strictly by chance. Genetic drift can result in genetic traits being lost from a population or becoming widespread in a population without respect to the survival or reproductive value of the gene pairs (alleles) involved. A random statistical effect, genetic drift can occur only in small, isolated populations in which the gene pool is small enough that chance events can change its makeup substantially. In larger populations, any specific allele is carried by so many individuals that it is almost certain to be transmitted by some of them unless it is biologically unfavourable.

genetic engineering, Artificial manipulation, modification, and recombination of DNA or other nucleic-acid molecules in order to modify an organism or population of organisms. The term initially meant any of a wide range of techniques for modifying or manipulating organisms through heredity and reproduction. Now the term denotes the narrower field of recombinant-DNA technology, or gene cloning, in which DNA molecules from two or more sources are combined, either within cells or in test tubes, and then inserted into host organisms in which they are able to reproduce. This technique is used to produce new genetic combinations that are of value to science, medicine, agriculture, or industry. Through recombinant-DNA techniques, bacteria have been created that are capable of synthesizing human insulin, human interferon, human growth hormone, a hepatitis-B vaccine, and other medically useful substances. Recombinant-DNA techniques, combined with the development of a technique for producing antibodies in great quantity, have made an impact on medical diagnosis and cancer research. Plants have been genetically adjusted to perform nitrogen fixation and to produce their own pesticides. Bacteria capable of biodegrading oil have been produced for use in oil-spill cleanups. Genetic engineering also introduces the fear of adverse genetic manipulations and their consequences (e.g., antibiotic-resistant bacteria or new strains of disease).

genetically modified organism (GMO), An organism whose genome has been altered in order to favour the expression of desired physiological traits or the output of desired biological products. Genetically modified foods were first approved for human consumption in the United States in 1995. The techniques used to produce genetically modified organisms include cloning and recombinant DNA technology. The primary applications of GMOs are in the areas of agriculture and biomedical research. GMOs offer numerous benefits to society, including increased crop yields and the development of novel therapeutic agents to prevent and treat a wide range of human diseases. Concerns surrounding the use of GMOs include risks posed to human health and the generation of insecticide-resistant "superbugs."

genetics, Study of heredity in general and of genes in particular. Modern genetics began in the 19th century with the work of Gregor Mendel, who formulated the basic concepts of heredity. In 1909 the word *gene* was coined by Wilhelm Johannsen, thus giving genetics its name. In the same year, Thomas Hunt Morgan provided evidence that genes occur on chromosomes and that adjacent genes on the same chromosome form linkage groups. This led to the important discovery that genes affect molecular action at the cell level, as evidenced by human hereditary diseases such as inborn errors of metabolism. Molecular genetics began in earnest in the 1940s when Oswald Avery showed that DNA is the chromosome component that carries genetic information. The molecular structure of DNA was deduced by James D. Watson, Francis Crick, and Maurice Wilkins. These and other developments led to the deciphering of the genetic code of the DNA molecule, which in turn made possible the recombination techniques of genetic engineering, discovered in the 1970s. An understanding of genetics is necessary for the diagnosis, prevention, and treatment of hereditary diseases, the selective breeding of plants and animals, and the development of industrial processes that use microorganisms.

Geneva, French GENÈVE, German GENF, Italian GINEVRA, City (pop., 2001 est.: urban agglom., 464,000), capital of Geneva canton, southwestern Switzerland. At the tip of Lake Geneva on the Rhône River, it was by the 6th century BC a centre of the Celtic Allobroges and was later conquered by the Romans. In the 16th century John Calvin transformed Geneva into a theocratic state and the intellectual centre of Protestant Europe. In the 18th century, as the birthplace of Jean-Jacques Rousseau and the sanctuary of Voltaire, it attracted the elite of the Enlightenment. It joined the Swiss Confederation in 1814. It was the site of the Geneva Convention in 1864, and the League of Nations was founded there in 1919. An international hub of commerce and finance, it is the headquarters of the International Red Cross (1864) and the European branch of the United Nations.

Geneva, Lake, French LAC LÉMAN, German GENFERSEE, Lake, on the border of southwestern Switzerland and southeastern France. About 134 sq mi (347 sq km) of the lake's area is Swiss and 90 sq mi (234 sq km) French. Lying at an elevation of 1,220 ft (372 m), it is 45 mi (72 km) long with an average width of 5 mi (8 km). It is formed by the Rhône River, which enters at the eastern end and leaves at the western end through the city of Geneva. The water level is subject to fluctuations known as seiches, in which the lake's water mass rhythmically swings from shore to shore.

Geneva Conventions, Series of four international agreements (1864, 1906, 1929, 1949) signed in Geneva, Switz., that established the humanitarian principles by which the signatory countries are to treat an enemy's military and civilian nationals in wartime. The first convention was initiated by Jean-Henri Dunant; it established that medical facilities were not to be war targets, that hospitals should treat all wounded impartially, that civilians aiding the wounded should be protected, and that the Red Cross symbol should serve to identify those covered by the agreement. The second convention amended and extended the first. The third stated that prisoners of war should be treated humanely and that prison camps should be open to inspection by neutral countries. The 1949 conventions made further provisions for civilians falling into a belligerent's hands. Guerrilla combatants were extended protection in two 1977 amendments, which the U.S. did not sign. Violations of the Geneva Conventions were among the crimes included in the jurisdictions of the international criminal tribunals for the former Yugoslavia (1993) and Rwanda (1994) and the International Criminal Court (2002).

Genghis Khan, or CHINGGIS KHAN, orig. TEMÜJIN (b. 1162, near Lake Baikal, Mongolia—d. Aug. 18, 1227), Mongolian warrior-ruler who consolidated nomadic tribes into a unified Mongolia and whose troops fought from China's Pacific coast to Europe's Adriatic Sea, creating the basis for one of the greatest continental empires of all time. The leader of a destitute clan, Temüjin fought various rival clans and formed a Mongol confederacy, which in 1206 acknowledged him as Genghis Khan ("Universal Ruler"). By that year the united Mongols were ready to move out beyond the steppe. He adapted his method of warfare, moving from depending solely on cavalry to using sieges, catapults, ladders, and other equipment and techniques suitable for the capture and destruction of cities. In less than 10 years he took over most of Juchen-controlled China; he then destroyed the Muslim Khwārezm-Shah dynasty while his generals raided Iran and Russia. He is infamous for slaughtering the entire populations of cities and destroying fields and irrigation systems but admired for his military brilliance and ability to learn. He died on a military campaign, and the empire was divided among his sons and grandsons.

genius, Person of extraordinary intellectual power. The genius displays originality, creativity, and the ability to think and work in areas not previously explored. Though geniuses have usually left their unique mark in a particular field, studies have shown that the general intelligence of geniuses is also exceptionally high. Genius appears to be a function of both hereditary and environmental factors.

genius, In ancient Roman religion, the attendant spirit of a person or place. It originally represented the housefather, who gave continuity to a family or clan over generations; its female counterpart was the housemother, called the *juno*. In later times, the *genius* was seen as an individual's guardian spirit or higher self, and it was worshiped by that individual, especially on his birthday. There were also *genii* of places and of groups such as legions, states, and guilds.

genocide, Deliberate and systematic destruction of a racial, religious, political, or ethnic group. The term was coined by Raphael Lemkin, a Polish-born jurist who served as an adviser to the U.S. Department of War during World War II, to describe the premeditated effort to destroy a population. In 1946 the UN General Assembly declared genocide a punishable crime. By this declaration, genocide by definition may be committed by an individual, group, or government, against one's own people or another, in peacetime or in wartime. This last point distinguishes genocide from "crimes against humanity," whose legal definition specifies wartime. Suspects may be tried by a court in the country where the act was committed or by an international court. An example of genocide more recent than the Holocaust is the slaughter of Tutsi people by the Hutu in Rwanda in the 1990s.

genre painting, Painting of scenes from everyday life, of ordinary people at work or play, depicted in a realistic manner. In the 18th century, the term was used derogatorily to describe painters specializing in one type of picture, such as flowers, animals, or middle-class life. By the mid-19th century it was being used more approvingly, and it is still popularly used to describe works by 17th-century Dutch and Flemish painters such as Jan Steen, Gerard Terborch, Adriaen van Ostade, and Johannes Vermeer, and later masters such as J.-B.-S. Chardin in France, Pietro Longhi in Italy, and George Caleb Bingham in the U.S.

genus, Biological classification. It ranks below family and above species, consisting of structurally or phylogenetically related species or a single species exhibiting unusual differences. For example, the species of roses collectively form the genus *Rosa* and those of horses, donkeys, and zebras form the genus *Equus*. The genus name, capitalized and usually italicized, is the first word of a scientific name in the system of binomial nomenclature.

geographic information system (GIS), Computerized system that relates and displays data collected from a geographic entity in the form of a map. The ability of GIS to overlay existing data with new information and display it in colour on a computer screen is used primarily to conduct analyses and make decisions related to geology, ecology, land use, demographics, transportation, and other domains, most of which relate to the human use of the physical environment. Through the process of geocoding, geographic data from a database is converted into images in the form of maps.

geography, Science of the Earth's surface, which describes and analyzes the spatial variations in physical, biological, and human phenomena that occur on the surface of the globe and treats their interrelationships and their significant regional patterns. Once associated entirely with mapping and the exploration of the Earth, the field today is wide-ranging, and geographers use a variety of methods and techniques drawn from numerous disciplines. Subfields of geography include physical, human, and regional geography, which may range in scale from worldwide to a continent, a country, or a city.

geologic time, Interval of time occupied by the Earth's geologic history, extending from *c.* 3.9 billion years ago (corresponding to the age of the oldest known rocks) to the present day. It is, in effect, the part of the Earth's history that is recorded in rock strata. The geologic time scale is classified in nested intervals distinguished by characteristic geologic and biologic features. From longest to shortest duration, the intervals are eon, era, period, and epoch.

geology, Scientific study of the Earth, including its composition, structure, physical properties, and history. Geology is commonly divided into subdisciplines concerned with the chemical makeup of the Earth, including the study of minerals (mineralogy) and rocks (petrology); the structure of the Earth (structural geology) and volcanic phenomena (volcanology); landforms and the processes that produce them (geomorphology and glaciology); geologic history, including the study of fossils (paleontology), the development of sedimentary strata (stratigraphy), and the evolution of planetary bodies and their satellites (astrogeology); and economic geology and its various branches, such as mining geology and petroleum geology. Some major fields closely allied to geology are geodesy, geophysics, and geochemistry.

geomagnetic field, Magnetic field associated with the Earth. It is essentially dipolar (i.e., it has two poles, the northern and southern magnetic poles) on the Earth's surface. Away from the surface, the field becomes distorted. Most geomagnetists explain the field by means of dynamo theories, whereby a source of energy in the Earth's core causes a self-sustaining magnetic field. In the dynamo theories, fluid motion in the Earth's core involves the movement of conducting material within an existing magnetic field, thus creating a current and a self-enforcing field.

Geometric style, Style of vase painting that flourished in Athens *c.* 1000–700 BC. Vases decorated in this style feature horizontal bands filled with geometric patterns such as zigzags, triangles, and swastikas in dark paint on a light ground. The rhythmic effect is similar to that of basketry. The abstract motifs developed into stylized animal and human forms in such narrative scenes as funerals, dances, and boxing matches. Small bronze and clay figurines, elaborately decorated fibulas, and limestone seals were also produced. The patterns remained popular and influenced much later Greek art.

geopolitics, The study of geographic influences on power relationships in international politics. Geopolitical theorists have sought to demonstrate the importance in the determination of foreign policies of considerations such as the acquisition of natural boundaries, access to important sea routes, and the control of strategically important land areas. The term was first employed in the early 20th century by the Swedish political scientist Rudolph Kjellén (1864–1922). Geopolitical factors have become less significant in the foreign policies of states because of improvements in communications and transportation.

Georgia, Country, Transcaucasia, western Asia. Located within the Caucasus Mountains, on the southeastern shores of the Black Sea, it includes the autonomous republics of Abkhazia and Ajaria (Adjara). Area:26,911 sq mi (69,700 sq km). Population: (2011 est.) 4,474,000 (excluding Abkhazia and South Ossetia). Capital: Tbilisi. Two-thirds of the people are Georgian (Kartveli); minorities include Armenians, Russians, and Azerbaijanians. Language: Georgian (official). Religions: Christianity (Eastern Orthodox, Armenian Apostolic); also Islam. Currency: Georgian lari. Most of Georgia is mountainous, and many peaks rise above 15,000 ft (4,600 m). The Caucasus protect it against cold air from the north, and the climate is mainly subtropical. Fertile lowlands lie near the shores of the Black Sea. Georgia has a well-developed industrial base noted for its hydroelectric power, coal mining and steel making, machinery production, and textiles. Agricultural land is in short supply, and farming is difficult. Crops include tea, citrus fruits, grapes (for wine), sugar beets, and tobacco. Georgia is a unitary multiparty republic with one legislative body; the head of state and government is the president, assisted by the prime minister. Ancient Georgia was the site of the kingdoms of Iberia and Colchis, whose fabled wealth was known to the ancient Greeks. The area was part of the Roman Republic by 65 BCE and became Christian in 337 CE. For the next three centuries, it was involved in the conflicts between the Byzantine and Persian empires; after 654 it was controlled by Arab caliphs, who established an emirate in Tbilisi. It was ruled by the Bagratids from the 8th to the 12th century, and the zenith of Georgia's power was reached in the reign of Queen Tamara, whose realm stretched from Azerbaijan to Circassia, forming a pan-Caucasian empire. Invasions by Mongols and Turks in the 13th–14th century disintegrated the kingdom, and the fall of Constantinople to the Ottoman Empire in 1453 isolated it from Western Christendom. There were repeated invasions over the next three centuries by the Armenians, Ottomans, and Persians. Georgia sought Russian protection in 1783 and in 1801 was annexed by the Russian Empire. After the Russian Revolution of 1917, the area was briefly independent; in 1921 a Soviet regime was installed, and in 1936 Georgia became the Georgian S.S.R., a full member of the Soviet Union. In 1990 a noncommunist coalition came to power in the first free elections ever held in Soviet Georgia, and in 1991 Georgia declared independence. In the 1990s, while President Eduard Shevardnadze tried to steer a middle course, internal dissension sparked conflicts in Abkhazia.

Georgian poetry, Body of lyrical poetry produced in Britain in the early 20th century. Desiring to make new poetry more accessible to the public, Rupert Brooke and Sir Edward Marsh produced five anthology volumes—containing works by Robert Graves, Walter de la Mare, Siegfried Sassoon (1886–1967), and others—called *Georgian Poetry* (1912–22). "Georgian" was meant to suggest the opening of a new poetic age with the accession in 1910 of George V; however, much of the Georgians' work was conventional, and the name came to refer to backward-looking literature rooted in its time.

Georgian style, Architecture, interior design, and decorative arts of Britain during the reigns (1714–1830) of the first four Georges. It encompassed Palladianism, turned to an austere Neoclassicism, moved on to Gothic Revival, and ended with the Regency style. The era is said to mark the summit of house design in Britain. Its legacy can be seen in the city squares of uniform, symmetrical brick London townhouses, their facades employing Classical pilasters, pedimented doors and windows, and graceful moldings. Their interiors, often furnished with Chippendale and Sheraton pieces, were characterized by harmonious proportions, quiet colors, and Roman-derived stucco ornamentation.

geothermal energy, Power obtained by using heat from the Earth's interior. Most geothermal resources are in regions of active volcanism. Hot springs, geysers, pools of boiling mud, and fumaroles are the most easily exploited sources. The ancient Romans used hot springs to heat baths and homes, and similar uses are still found in Iceland, Turkey, and Japan. Geothermal energy's greatest potential lies in the generation of electricity. It was first used to produce electric power in Italy in 1904. Today geothermal power plants are in operation in New Zealand, Japan, Iceland, Mexico, the U.S., and elsewhere.

germ theory, Theory that certain diseases are caused by invasion of the body by microorganisms. Louis Pasteur, Joseph Lister, and Robert Koch are given much of the credit for its acceptance in the later 19th century. Pasteur showed that organisms in the air cause fermentation and spoil food; Lister was first to use an antiseptic to exclude germs in the air to prevent infection; and Koch first linked a specific organism with a disease (anthrax). The full implications of germ theory for medical practice were not immediately apparent after it was proven; surgeons operated without masks or head coverings as late as the 1890s.

German historical school of economics, Branch of economic thought, developed chiefly in Germany in the later 19th century, in which the economic situation of a nation is understood as the result of its total historical experience. Objecting to the deductively reasoned "laws" of classical economics, exponents of the historical approach examined the development of the entire social order, of which economic motives and decisions were only one component. They viewed government intervention in the economy as a positive and necessary force. Early founders, including Wilhelm Roscher and Bruno Hildebrand, developed the idea of the historical method and sought to identify general stages of economic development through which all countries must pass. Members of the later school, notably Gustav von Schmoller (1813–1917), carried out more detailed historical research and attempted to discover cultural trends through historical inquiry.

German language, Official language of Germany and Austria and one of the official languages of Switzerland, used by more than 100 million speakers. It belongs to the West Germanic group of the Germanic languages. German has four noun cases and masculine, feminine, and neuter genders. Its many dialects belong to either the High German (*Hochdeutsch*) or Low German (*Plattdeutsch*) groups. Modern High German, spoken in the central and southern highlands of Germany, Austria, and Switzerland, is now standard written German, used in administration, higher education, literature, and the mass media in both High and Low German speech areas.

German-Soviet Nonaggression Pact, or NAZI-SOVIET NONAGGRESSION PACT (Aug. 23, 1939) Agreement stipulating mutual nonaggression between the Soviet Union and Germany. The Soviet Union, whose proposed collective security agreement with Britain and France was rebuffed, approached Germany, and in the pact the two states pledged publicly not to attack each other. Its secret provisions divided Poland between them and gave the Soviet Union control of Latvia, Lithuania, Estonia, and Finland. The Soviets hoped to buy time to build up their forces to face German expansionism; Germany wished to proceed with its invasion of Poland and the countries to its west without having to worry about the Red Army. News of the pact shocked and horrified the world. Nine days after its signing, Germany began World War II by invading Poland. The agreement was voided when Germany attacked the Soviet Union in 1941. Until 1989 the Soviet Union denied the existence of the secret protocols because they were considered evidence of its involuntary annexation of the Baltic states.

Germanic languages, Branch of the Indo-European language family, comprising languages descended from Proto-Germanic. These are divided into West Germanic, including English, German, Frisian, Dutch, Afrikaans, and Yiddish; North Germanic, including Danish, Swedish, Icelandic, Norwegian, and Faeroese (the language of the Faroe Islands); and East Germanic, now extinct, comprising Gothic and the languages of the Vandals, Burgundians, and a few other tribes. The Gothic Bible of AD 350 is the earliest extensive Germanic text. The West Germanic languages developed around the North Sea and in overseas areas colonized by their speakers. The North Germanic, or Scandinavian, languages, were carried as far west as Greenland and as far east as Russia in the Viking expansion of the early Middle Ages. The continental Scandinavian languages were strongly influenced by Low German in the late Middle Ages, but Icelandic and Faeroese have preserved many characteristics of Old Scandinavian grammar.

Germanic law, Law of the various Germanic peoples from ancient times to the Middle Ages. It was essentially unwritten tribal custom, which evolved from popular practice and moved with the tribe. With the spread of Christianity, ecclesiastical law, derived from Roman law, gained importance, especially in matters of marriage and succession. A mercantile law, developed by the 12th century to meet the needs of traders, further eroded the power of local law.

Germanic religion, Beliefs, rituals, and mythology of the pre-Christian Germanic peoples, in a geographic area extending from the Black Sea across central Europe and Scandinavia to Iceland and Greenland. The religion died out in central Europe with the conversion to Christianity (4th century) but continued in Scandinavia until the 10th century. The Old Norse literature of medieval Iceland, notably the *Poetic Edda* (c. 1270) and the *Prose Edda* (c. 1222), recounts the lore of the Germanic gods. The earth was held to have been created out of a cosmic void called Ginnungagap; in another account the first gods formed it from the body of a primeval giant, Aurgelmir. There were two sets of gods in the Germanic pantheon, the warlike Aesir and the agricultural Vanir. Germanic religion also encompassed belief in female guardian spirits, elves, and dwarfs. Rites were conducted in the open or in groves and forests; animal and human sacrifice was practiced. Ragnarok is the Germanic doomsday.

Germany, officially FEDERAL REPUBLIC OF GERMANY, Country, north-central Europe. Area: 137,879 sq mi (357,104 sq km). Population: (2011 est.) 81,604,000. Capital: Berlin. The majority of the people are German. Language: German (official). Religions: Christianity (Protestant, Roman Catholic, other Christians); also Islam. Currency: euro. The land is generally flat in the north and hilly in the northeast and central region, rising to the Bavarian Alps in the south. The Rhine River basin dominates the central and western part of the country; other important rivers include the Elbe, Danube, and Oder. Germany has a developed free-market economy largely based on services and manufacturing. It is one of the richest countries in the world. Exports include motor vehicles and iron and steel products. Germany is a federal multiparty republic with two legislative houses; the head of state is the president, and the head of government is the chancellor. Germanic tribes entered Germany c. 2nd century BCE, displacing the Celts. The Romans failed to conquer the region, which became a political entity only with the division of the Carolingian empire in the 9th century CE. The monarchy's control was weak, and power increasingly devolved upon the nobility, organized in feudal states. The monarchy was restored under Saxon rule in the 10th century, and the Holy Roman Empire, centring on Germany and northern Italy, was revived. Continuing conflict between the Holy Roman emperors and the Roman Catholic popes undermined the empire, and its dissolution was accelerated by Martin Luther's revolt (1517), which divided Germany, and ultimately Europe, into Protestant and Catholic camps, culminating in the Thirty Years' War (1618–48). Germany's population and borders were greatly reduced, and its numerous feudal princes gained virtually full sovereignty. In 1862 Otto von Bismarck came to power in Prussia and in 1871 united the Germans, founding the German Empire. It was dissolved in 1918 after its defeat in World War I, and the Weimar Republic was declared. Germany was stripped of much of its territory and all of its colonies. In 1933 Adolf Hitler became chancellor and established a totalitarian state, the Third Reich, dominated by the Nazi Party. Hitler invaded Poland in 1939, plunging the world into World War II, and he was responsible for the Holocaust, the systematic killing of some six million Jews and millions of others. Following its defeat in 1945, Germany was divided by the Allies into four zones of occupation. Disagreement with the Soviet Union over their reunification led to the creation in 1949 of the Federal Republic of Germany (West Germany) and the German Democratic Republic (East Germany). Berlin, the former capital, remained divided. West Germany became a prosperous parliamentary democracy, East Germany a one-party state under Soviet control. In 1952 Germany became a founding member of the European Coal and Steel Community, the forerunner of the European Union. The East German communist government was overthrown peacefully in 1989, and Germany was reunited in 1990. After the initial euphoria over unity, the political and economic integration of the former East Germany into the federal republic resulted in heavy financial burdens for the wealthier former West Germans. However, the country continued to move toward deeper political and economic integration with western Europe through its membership in the European Union.

Germany, East, officially GERMAN DEMOCRATIC REPUBLIC, Former republic (1945–90), north-central Europe. It is now the eastern portion of the Federal Republic of Germany. In 1945 occupied Germany was divided into U.S., British, French, and Soviet zones. In 1949 the U.S., British, and French zones were combined as West Germany, while the Soviet zone became a communist state as East Germany. Declared a sovereign country in 1955, it became a founding member of the Warsaw Pact. The Berlin Wall was constructed at the border of the divided city of Berlin in 1961 to stem the flight of East German citizens to the West. The communist government was dismantled in 1989–90, and the country adopted the constitution and name of Germany when the states were united in October 1990.

Germany, West, officially FEDERAL REPUBLIC OF GERMANY, Former republic (1949–90), west-central Europe. It consisted of the western two-thirds of what is now the Federal Republic of Germany. It was formed in 1949 when the U.S., British, and French zones of occupation in Germany were united, while the Soviet zone became East Germany. It became a sovereign country and a member of NATO in 1955, though its occupiers retained military bases. It united with Saarland in 1957, and it joined the UN in 1973. It was reunited with East Germany in October 1990.

germination, Sprouting of a seed, spore, or other reproductive body, usually after a period of dormancy. Absorption of water, passage of time, chilling, warming, oxygen availability, and light exposure may all operate in initiating the germination process. The carefully controlled mass germination of cereal seeds supplies enzymes for the making of alcoholic beverages and for other industries; spores of the commercially cultivated mushroom *Agaricus brunescens* are also mass germinated.

Gershwin, George, orig. JACOB GERSHVIN (b. Sept. 26, 1898, Brooklyn, N.Y., U.S.—d. July 11, 1937, Hollywood, Calif.), U.S. composer. Born to Russian-Jewish immigrants, he heard jazz performed live from about age six. In his teens he worked as a song plugger (playing piano in Tin Pan Alley to demonstrate sheet music for potential customers), and in 1916 he published his first song. In 1919 his "Swanee" was performed by Al Jolson and achieved extraordinary success. Gershwin's first complete score was for the show *La, La Lucille* (1919). The bandleader Paul Whiteman commissioned from him the hugely successful orchestral work *Rhapsody in Blue* (1924). It was revolutionary for its incorporation of the jazz idiom (blue notes, syncopated rhythms, onomatopoeic instrumental effects) into a symphonic context. Gershwin's first major Broadway success, *Lady, Be Good!* (1924), was a collaboration with his brother, lyricist Ira Gershwin. They soon established themselves as one of the great teams in Broadway history; their shows included *Oh, Kay!* (1926), *Strike Up the Band* (1927), *Funny Face* (1927), *Girl Crazy* (1930), and the satire *Of Thee I Sing* (1931), the first musical to win a Pulitzer Prize. He also scored several successful films. His most ambitious work was the "folk opera" *Porgy*

George Gershwin, working on the score for Porgy and Bess, 1935.

Pictorial Parade

and Bess (1935), a collaboration with Ira and novelist DuBose Heyward. Gershwin's classical compositions include a piano concerto (1925) and the tone poem *An American in Paris* (1928). His early death was the result of a brain tumour.

Gesta Romanorum (Latin: "Deeds of the Romans"), Latin collection of anecdotes and tales, probably compiled in early 14th-century England. Very popular in its time, it became a source for much later literature, including works by Geoffrey Chaucer and William Shakespeare. It contains stories from Classical history and legend and from various Asian and European sources, many about magicians and monsters, ladies in distress, and escapes from perilous situations, all unified by their moral purpose and realistic detail. Its author is unknown. Its didactic nature and the allegorical explanations attached to the stories in the early versions suggest that it was intended as a manual for preachers. It is likely that it was compiled in England.

Gestalt psychology, Twentieth-century school of psychology that provided the foundation for the modern study of perception. The German term Gestalt, referring to how a thing has been "put together" (*gestellt*), is often translated as "pattern" or "configuration" in psychology. Its precepts, formulated as a reaction against the atomistic orientation of previous theories, emphasized that the whole of anything is different from the sum of its parts: organisms tend to perceive entire patterns or configurations rather than bits and pieces. The school emerged in Austria and Germany at the end of the 19th century and gained impetus through the works of Max Wertheimer, Wolfgang Köhler, and Kurt Koffka (1886–1941); its principles were later expanded by Kurt Lewin. A form of psychotherapy only loosely related to Gestalt principles and influenced by existentialism and phenomenology was developed by Frederick S. (Fritz) Perls (1893–1970) in the 1940s. Gestalt therapy directs the client toward appreciating the form, meaning, and value of his perceptions and actions.

Gestapo, in full GEHEIME STAATSPOLIZEI (German: "Secret State Police") Political police of Nazi Germany. It was created by Hermann Goring in 1933 from the political and espionage units of the Prussian police and by Heinrich Himmler from the police of the remaining German states. Himmler was given command in 1934. The Gestapo operated without civil restraints, and its actions were not subject to judicial appeal. Thousands of Jews, leftists, intellectuals, trade unionists, political clergy, and homosexuals disappeared into concentration camps after being arrested by the Gestapo. In World War II the Gestapo suppressed partisan activities in the occupied territories, and a section of the Gestapo under Adolf Eichmann organized the deportation of Jews to the extermination camps in Poland.

get, Jewish divorce document written in Aramaic and obtained from a rabbinic court. In Orthodox and Conservative Judaism it is the only valid way to end a marriage, though outside Israel a civil divorce is required first. In Reform Judaism a civil divorce suffices. To obtain a get, mutual consent of husband and wife is usually required, except in special cases such as apostasy, impotence, insanity, or refusal to cohabit.

Gethsemane, Garden outside Jerusalem associated with the last hours of Jesus. According to Christian tradition, it is where Jesus prayed after the Last Supper and before his arrest and Crucifixion. The name Gethsemane originates from a Hebrew term meaning "oil press," suggesting that the garden was a grove of olive trees. Though its exact location cannot be determined, Armenian, Greek, Latin, and Russian churches have accepted an olive grove on the western slope of the Mount of Olives as the site.

geyser (Icelandic *geysir*, "to gush forth") Any hot spring that discharges jets of steam and hot water intermittently. Geysers are generally associated with recent volcanic activity. They are produced by the heating of underground waters by contact with, or close proximity to, magma (molten rock). Geyser discharges as high as 1,600 ft (500 m) have been recorded, but about 150 ft (45 m) is much more common (e.g., Old Faithful in Yellowstone National Park). Occasionally a geyser will adopt a fairly regular and predictable pattern of intermittent activity and discharge for a few minutes every hour or so. Yellowstone has more than half of the world's total number of geysers.

Ghana, officially REPUBLIC OF GHANA, formerly GOLD COAST, Country, West Africa. Area: 92,098 sq mi (238,533 sq km). Population: (2011 est.) 24,661,000. Capital: Accra. Ghana is home to Akan, Mossi, Ewe, and Ga-Adangme peoples. Languages: English (official), Akan, Ewe, Hausa. Religions: Christianity (Protestant, other Christians, Roman Catholic), traditional beliefs, Islam. Currency: cedi. The land is generally flat, dominated by the Volta River basin. The north is characterized by grassland plains; the south is heavily forested. The southern coastal plain is the historical Gold Coast. The varied wildlife includes lions, leopards, and elephants. Ghana has a developing mixed economy based largely on agriculture and mining. Cacao is the mainstay of the economy; mineral exports include gold and diamonds. Ghana is a unitary multiparty republic with one legislative house; its head of state and government is the president. The modern state is named for the ancient Ghana empire that flourished until the 13th century CE in the western Sudan, about 500 mi (800 km) northwest of the modern state. The Akan peoples then founded their first states in modern Ghana. Gold-seeking Mande traders arrived by the 14th century and Hausa merchants by the 16th. During the 15th century the Mande founded the states of Dagomba and Mamprussi in the northern half of the region. The Asante (Ashanti), an Akan people, originated in the central forest region and formed a strongly centralized empire that was at its height in the 18th–19th century. European exploration of the region began early in the 15th century, when the Portuguese landed on the Gold Coast; they later established a settlement at Elmina as headquarters for the slave trade. By the mid-18th century the Gold Coast was dominated by numerous forts controlled by Dutch, British, and Danish merchants. Britain made the Gold Coast a crown colony in 1874, and British protectorates over the Asante and the northern territories were established in 1901. In 1957 the Gold Coast became the independent state of Ghana. Since independence several political coups have occurred, but the coup of 1981 produced a government that lasted into the 1990s and made a smooth transition into another administration at the beginning of the 21st century.

Ghana empire, First of the great medieval trading empires of western Africa (7th–13th century). Located in what is now southeastern Mauritania and part of Mali, it acted as intermediary between Arab and Berber salt traders to the north and gold and ivory producers to the south. Gold was secured through barter from those living at the empire's southern limit and exchanged in the capital for commodities, especially salt. As the empire grew richer it extended its reach, incorporating gold-producing southern lands and cities to the north. The king exacted tribute from the princes of subject tribes. Ghana began to decline with the rise of the Muslim Almoravids; the Almoravid leader Abu Bakr seized the Ghanaian capital of Kumbi in 1076. The empire's subject peoples began to break away, and in 1240 the empire's remains were incorporated into the Sundiata empire of Mali.

Ghats, Eastern and Western, Two mountain ranges forming the edges of the Deccan plateau in southern India. The Eastern Ghats extend about 700 mi (1,100 km) along the southeastern and eastern coast north to the mouth of the Mahanadi River; their average elevation is about 2,000 ft (600 m). The Western Ghats run some 800 mi (1,300 km) along the southwestern and western coast north to the mouth of the Tapti River; their average elevations range from 3,000 ft (900 m) to 5,000 ft (1,500 m). Because they receive heavy rainfall during the monsoon season, the Western Ghats comprise peninsular India's principal watershed.

ghazel, or GHAZAL, or GAZEL, In Islamic literature, a lyric poem, generally short and graceful in form and typically dealing with love. The genre developed in late 7th-century Arabia. Ghazels begin with a rhymed couplet whose rhyme is repeated in all subsequent even lines, while the odd lines are unrhymed. The two main types of ghazel are native to the Hejaz (what is now western Saudi Arabia) and Iraq. It reached its greatest refinement in the works of Hafez. American poets such as Adrienne Rich have used variations of the form.

Ghent, Flemish GENT, French GAND, City (pop., 2000 est.: 224,180), capital of East Flanders province, northwestern Belgium. One of the chief towns of the medieval county of Flanders, Ghent was one of the largest towns in northern Europe by the 13th century. Its prosperity was based on its manufacture of luxury cloths, which were famous throughout Europe. It began to decline in the late 16th century, when its cloth was unable to compete with England's. Its economy revived with the introduction of cotton-spinning machinery (in particular, a power loom smuggled out of England), and it subsequently became the centre of the Belgian textile industry. Ghent has many fine museums, notably the Museum of Fine Arts, which contains a treasury of paintings by Flemish masters who lived and worked in Ghent during the 16th and 17th centuries. Belgium's second largest port, it is also a horticultural centre.

ghetto, Formerly, a street or quarter of a city set apart as a legally enforced residential area for Jews. Forced segregation of Jews spread throughout Europe in the 14th–15th centuries. Ghettos were customarily enclosed with walls and gates and kept locked at night and during Christian festivals. Since outward expansion was usually impossible, most ghettos grew upward; congestion, fire hazards, and unsanitary conditions often resulted. Ghettos were abolished in western Europe in the 19th century; those revived by the Nazi Party were overcrowded holding places preliminary to extermination. More recently, the term *ghetto* has been applied to impoverished urban areas exclusively settled by a minority group or groups and perpetuated by economic and social pressures rather than legal and physical measures.

ghost, Soul or specter of a deceased person. Belief in ghosts has been common since ancient times and is reflected in folklore around the world. It is based on the notion that the spirit is separable from the body and can continue its existence after the death of the body. Ghosts are believed to inhabit the netherworld and to be capable of returning to the world of the living, appearing as living beings or in a nebulous likeness of the deceased. They are thought to be especially likely to haunt places or people connected with some strong emotion of their past life, such as fear, remorse, or the terror of a violent death. The traditional visual manifestations of haunting include ghostly apparitions, the movement of objects, or the appearance of strange lights; auditory signs include disembodied laughter and screams, knocking, or footsteps.

giant star, Star with a relatively large radius for its mass and temperature; this yields a large radiating area, so such stars are bright. Subclasses include supergiant stars, red giants (with low temperatures, but very bright), and subgiants (with slightly reduced radii and brightness). Some giants are hundreds of thousands of times brighter than the Sun. Giants and supergiants may have masses 10–30 times that of the Sun and volumes millions of times greater and are thus low-density stars.

Giardia lamblia, or G. INTESTINALIS, Single-celled protozoan parasite. Pear- or beet-shaped, the cells have two nuclei and eight flagella and attach with a sucking organ to human intestinal mucous membranes. They cause the disease giardiasis. Generally spread when traces of human feces containing the parasite are ingested, giardiasis is most common among children in close contact with other children, but it also occurs among adults. Diarrhea, pain, and distension of the stomach may occur. It is common wherever there is contamination of domestic or surface water in lakes, rivers, and reservoirs, and it is a major cause of diarrhea worldwide. Beaver feces are often responsible for giardiasis among campers who take water from lakes and rivers.

gibbon, Any of about six species (genus *Hylobates*) of lesser apes (family Hylobatidae), found in Indo-Malayan forests. Gibbons use their long arms to swing from branch to branch. They walk erect on the ground, live in small groups, and feed on shoots and fruits, as well as on some insects, birds' eggs, and young birds. They have long hair and are about 16–26 in. (40–65 cm) long. Their coats vary from tan or silvery to brown or black. They have large canine teeth, and their voices are noted for their volume, musical quality, and carrying power.

Gibbons (family Hylobatidae).
Edmund Appel/Photo Researchers, Inc.

Gibraltar, British overseas territory, on the Mediterranean coast of southern Spain. Area: 2.25 sq mi (5.8 sq km). Population (2007 est.): 29,257. It occupies a narrow peninsula 3 mi (5 km) long and 0.75 mi (1.2 km) wide that is known as the Rock. It appears from the east as a series of sheer, inaccessible cliffs, which makes it strategically important. The territory is the site of a British air and naval base that guards the Strait of Gibraltar. The Moors held Gibraltar from 711 to 1462, and in 1501 it was annexed by Spain. Captured by the British in 1704, it became a British crown colony in 1830. Gibraltar was an important port in World Wars I and II. The sovereignty of the territory has remained a source of constant friction between the United Kingdom and Spain, though residents voted in 1967 to remain part of Britain. Spain lifted its border blockade in the mid-1980s. Formal talks that began between the governments of Britain, Spain, and Gibraltar in 2004 helped to further ease tensions. Gibraltar is known for Barbary macaques, which occupy many of Gibraltar's caves and are Europe's only free-living monkeys.

The Rock of Gibraltar
Hans Huber

Gibraltar, Strait of, ancient FRETUM HERCULEUM, Channel, connecting the Mediterranean Sea with the Atlantic Ocean. Lying between southernmost Spain and northwesternmost Africa, it is 36 mi (58 km) long and narrows to 8 mi (13 km) between Point Marroquí (Spain) and Point Cires (Morocco). At the strait's eastern extreme, 14 mi (23 km) apart, stand the Pillars of Heracles, which

have been identified as the Rock of Gibraltar at Gibraltar and one of two peaks in North Africa: Mount Hacho (held by Spain), near the Spanish exclave of Ceuta, or Jebel Moussa (Musa), in Morocco. The strait has long been of great strategic and economic importance.

Gide, André (-Paul-Guillaume) (b. Nov. 22, 1869, Paris, France—d. Feb. 19, 1951, Paris), French writer. The son of a law professor, Gide began writing at an early age. His early prose poem *Fruits of the Earth* (1897) reflects his increasing awareness of his homosexuality. The novellas *The Immoralist* (1902) and *Strait Is the Gate* (1909) showed his mastery of classical construction, and *Lafcadio's Adventures* displayed his gift for mordant satire. In 1908 he cofounded *La Nouvelle Revue Française*, the literary review that would unite progressive French writers for 30 years. The autobiographical *If It Die...* (1924) is among the great works of confessional literature. *Corydon* (1924), a defense of homosexuality, was violently attacked. *The Counterfeiters* (1926) is his most complex novel. He become a champion of society's victims and outcasts and was for a time attracted to communism; with the outbreak of World War II he gained a greater appreciation for tradition. He received the Nobel Prize for Literature in 1947.

André Gide, oil painting by P.A. Laurens, 1924; in the National Museum of Modern Art, Paris.
© 1970 A.D.A.G.P.; photograph, Giraudon/Art Resource, New York

GIF, in full GRAPHICS INTERCHANGE FORMAT, Standard computer file format for graphic images. GIF files use data compression to reduce the file size. The original version of the format was developed by CompuServe in 1987. The current version supports animated GIFs (a graphics image that moves). GIF and JPEG are the most commonly used graphics formats on the Internet.

Gila monster, One of the only two species (both in the family Helodermatidae) of venomous lizards, named for the Gila River basin and found in the southwestern U.S. and northern Mexico. The Gila monster (*Heloderma suspectum*) grows to about 20 in. (50 cm) long, is stout-bodied with black and pink blotches or bands, and has beadlike scales. During warm weather, it feeds at night on small mammals, birds, and eggs and stores fat in the tail and abdomen for the winter. It is sluggish but has a strong bite. The venom (a neurotoxin) is conducted along grooves in the teeth from glands in the lower jaw. Bites are rarely fatal to humans. The other venomous species is the Mexican beaded lizard (*H. horridum*).

Gilgamesh, Hero of the ancient Akkadian-language *Epic of Gilgamesh.* The great literary work of ancient Mesopotamia, the epic is known from 12 incomplete tablets discovered at Nineveh in the library of Ashurbanipal. Gaps in the narrative have been filled in with fragments found elsewhere. The character Gilgamesh is probably based on the Gilgamesh who ruled Uruk in the 3rd millennium BC. The epic presents Gilgamesh as a great warrior and builder, who rejects the marriage proposal of the goddess Ishtar. With the aid of his friend and companion Enkidu, he kills the divine bull that Ishtar sends to destroy him. Enkidu's death prompts Gilgamesh to seek Utnapishtim, survivor of the legendary flood, to learn how to escape death. He obtains a youth-renewing plant only to have it stolen. The epic ends with the return of the spirit of Enkidu, who gives a dismal report on the underworld.

ginkgo, Tree (*Ginkgo biloba*, family Ginkgoaceae) that is the only living representative of the gymnosperm order Ginkgoales. Native to China, it is often termed a living fossil because it is unclear whether uncultivated groups can be found in the wild. It has been planted since ancient times in Chinese and Japanese temple gardens and is now valued in many parts of the world as an attractive, fungus- and insect-resistant ornamental tree. It tolerates cold weather and, unlike most gymnosperms, can survive the adverse atmospheric conditions of urban areas. Pyramidal in shape, it has a columnar, sparingly branched trunk.

*Ginkgo (*Ginkgo biloba*)*
Grant Heilman/EB Inc.

The light-coloured wood, soft and weak, has little economic value. The fan-shaped, leathery leaves, most divided into two lobes by a central notch, resemble the leaflets of the maidenhair fern. The silvery nut, when roasted, is considered a delicacy. Studies have suggested that *Ginkgo biloba* supplements can enhance memory function in the elderly and delay the onset of Alzheimer disease.

ginseng, Either of two herbs of the family Araliaceae or their roots, which have long been used as a drug in East Asia and as the ingredient for a stimulating tea. *Panax quinquefolium*, the North American ginseng, is native from Quebec and Manitoba southward to the coasts of the Gulf of Mexico. Asian ginseng (*P. schinseng*) is native to northeastern China and Korea and is cultivated in Korea and Japan. Ginseng has a sweetly aromatic flavour. Its root has long been regarded by the Chinese as a panacea for illness; its purported effects include improved mental performance, ability to learn, and memory and sensory awareness.

Giotto (di Bondone) (b. 1266–67/1276, Vespignano, near Florence—d. Jan. 8, 1337, Florence), First of the great Italian painters, active in Florence. He decorated chapels and churches in Assisi, Rome, Padua, Florence, and Naples with frescoes and panel paintings. Because little of his life and few of his works are documented, attributions and a stylistic chronology of his paintings remain problematic and often highly speculative. His works in Rome include the heavily restored mosaic of *Christ Walking on*

Lamentation, fresco by Giotto, c. 1305–06; in the Arena Chapel, Padua, Italy.
SCALA/Art Resource, New York

the Water over the entrance to St. Peter's Basilica, and an altarpiece from St. Peter's, now in the Vatican Museum. In Padua, his fresco of the Last Judgment decorates the western wall of the Arena Chapel, and the rest of the chapel is covered with his narrative frescoes featuring scenes from the lives of the Virgin Mary and Christ. Later in his career he executed frescoes in four chapels in the church of Santa Croce in Florence, two of which survive. In 1334 he was appointed surveyor of Florence Cathedral; his design for the campanile was altered after his death. The most important extant panel painting attributed to him is *The Madonna in Glory* (*c.* 1305–10). He achieved great fame in his lifetime, and he is considered the father of European painting for breaking with the impersonal stylizations of Byzantine art and introducing new ideals of naturalism and humanity, three-dimensional space, and three-dimensional form. The course of Italian painting was dominated by his students and followers. His work points to the innovations of the Renaissance style that developed a century later.

giraffe, species of ruminant (*Giraffa camelopardalis*) that is the

*Masai giraffe (*Giraffa camelopardalis tippelskirchi*).*
© Animals Animals

tallest of all mammals. It reaches an overall height of 18 ft (5.5 m) or more. The legs and neck are extremely long. The giraffe has a short body, a tufted tail, a short mane, and short, skin-covered horns. The back slopes downward to the hindquarters. The coat is pale buff, with reddish brown spots. It feeds primarily on acacia leaves. It lives in herds on savannas and in open bush country and is native to most of sub-Saharan Africa. Giraffes are still numerous in eastern Africa, where they are protected, but hunting has reduced their populations elsewhere. The only other member of the family Giraffidae is the okapi.

Girondin, or GIRONDIST, Label applied to a loose grouping of republican politicians, some of them originally from the *département* of Gironde, who played a leading role in the Legislative Assembly from October 1791 to September 1792 during the French Revolution. Their opponents often called them Brissotins, after their most prominent spokesman, Jacques-Pierre Brissot. While in dominance, they supported foreign war as a means to unite the people behind the Revolution. In 1792 the National Convention was divided between them and the more radical Montagnards; in 1793 they were driven from the National Convention and the Montagnards seized power. Many Girondins were guillotined in the Reign of Terror.

Gjellerup, Karl Adolph (b. June 2, 1857, Roholte, Den.—d. Oct. 11, 1919, Klotzsche, Ger.), Danish poet and novelist. The son of a parson, he studied theology, but after coming under the influence of Darwinism and the ideas of Georg Brandes, he considered himself an atheist, which he proclaimed in *An Idealist* (1878) and *The Teutons' Apprentice* (1882). In his later years he became interested in Buddhism and other Asian religions, and he wrote about reincarnation in *The Pilgrim Kamanita* (1906). He shared the 1917 Nobel Prize for Literature with Henrik Pontoppidan.

glacier, Large mass of perennial ice that forms on land through the recrystallization of snow and that moves forward under its own weight. The term *ice sheet* is commonly applied to a glacier that occupies an extensive tract of relatively level land and that flows from the centre outward. Glaciers occur where snowfall in winter exceeds melting in summer, conditions that prevail only in high mountain areas and polar regions. Glaciers occupy about 11% of the Earth's land surface but hold roughly three-fourths of its fresh water; 99% of glacier ice lies in Antarctica and Greenland.

gladiator (Latin: swordsman), Professional combatant in ancient Rome who engaged in fights to the death as sport. Gladiators originally performed at Etruscan funerals, the intent being to give the dead man armed attendants in the next world. At Rome gladiator matches were wildly popular from 264 BC. By the time of Julius Caesar, 300 pairs would fight at a single show; by the time of Trajan, 5,000 combatants of various classes would fight. In the late Roman republic the audience called for death with thumbs downward (or thumbs toward their breasts) and for mercy with handkerchiefs (or thumbs downward, according to some sources). The victor earned palm branches or money, and after a few victories a gladiator could be freed. Most were slaves or criminals, but a talented or handsome one could become a favourite of society; since they often served as bodyguards, they occasionally became politically important. Domitian delighted in using dwarfs and women as gladiators. With the coming of Christianity the games began to fall into disfavour, but they may have continued into the 6th century.

Gladstone, William E(wart) (b. Dec. 29, 1809, Liverpool, Eng.—d. May 19, 1898, Hawarden, Flintshire, Wales), British politician and prime minister (1868–74, 1880–85, 1886, 1892–94). He entered Parliament in 1833 as a Tory, but after holding various government posts, including chancellor of the Exchequer (1852–55, 1859–66), he slowly converted to liberalism and became Liberal Party leader in 1866. In his first term as prime minister (1868–74), he oversaw national education reform, voting reform, and the disestablishment of the Irish Protestant church (1869). In 1875–76 he denounced the indifference of Benjamin Disraeli's government to the Bulgarian Horrors. In his second term, he secured passage of the Reform Bill of 1884. His cabinet authorized the occupation of Egypt (1882), but his failure to rescue Gen. Charles George Gordon in Khartoum (1885) cost Gladstone much popularity and his government's defeat. In 1886, throwing his weight behind support for Irish Home Rule, he was able to regain control of Parliament, but when his Home Rule Bill was rejected he resigned. He devoted the next six years to trying to convince the electorate to grant Home Rule to Ireland. Liberals won a majority again in 1892, and in his fourth cabinet he piloted through another Home Rule Bill, but it was soundly rejected by the House of Lords. He was buried in Westminster Abbey.

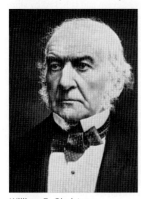

William E. Gladstone.
Culver Pictures

gland, Collection of cells or tissue that removes specific substances from the blood, alters or concentrates them, and then either releases them for further use by the body or eliminates them. Typically, the functional cells of a gland rest on a membrane and are surrounded by a meshwork of blood vessels. Endocrine, or ductless, glands (e.g., pituitary, thyroid, adrenal) discharge hormones into the bloodstream directly rather than through ducts. Exocrine glands (e.g., digestive, mammary, salivary, sweat) discharge their products through ducts.

Glasgow, City and council area (pop., 2004 est.: city, 577,670; 2001: urban agglom., 1,168,270), western Scotland. Located on the River Clyde 20 mi (32 km) from its mouth on the Atlantic coast, Glasgow forms an independent council area that lies entirely within the historic county of Lanarkshire. The largest city in

Scotland, Glasgow began to develop with the arrival (*c.* AD 550) of St. Kentigern (St. Mungo), who established a religious community. The present cathedral (13th century) was built on the site of the chapel. Glasgow was made a royal burgh in 1450 and prospered in the 18th century, when American produce (tobacco, sugar, and rum) made fortunes for Glasgow merchants. Its economy wavered as the tobacco trade was cut off by the American Revolution and the cotton industry by the American Civil War. With the Industrial Revolution came coal mining, iron founding, and, especially, shipbuilding. Manufactures now include textiles, food and beverages, and chemicals. A notable education centre, Glasgow has many cultural amenities, including the Scottish Opera, the Scottish Ballet, the Royal Scottish National Orchestra, and Kelvingrove Art Gallery and Museum. The Glasgow Science Centre includes the 459-ft- (140-m-) high Glasgow Tower, the tallest free-standing structure in Scotland and the only structure of its height in the world that revolves 360° from its base.

glasnost (Russian: "openness") Soviet policy of open discussion of political and social issues. It was instituted by Mikhail Gorbachev in the late 1980s and began the democratization of the Soviet Union. Glasnost also permitted criticism of government officials and allowed the media freer dissemination of news and information.

glass, Solid material, typically a mix of inorganic compounds, usually transparent or translucent, hard, brittle, and impervious to the natural elements ("vitreous properties"). It is made by cooling molten ingredients fast enough so no visible crystals form. A poor conductor of heat and electricity, glass takes on colours when certain metal oxides are included in the mix. Most glass breaks easily. Obsidian is a naturally occurring glass. Everyday glass (soda-lime or soda-lime-silica) is made of silica (silicon dioxide), soda (sodium carbonate), and limestone (calcium carbonate), with magnesia (magnesium oxide) for sheet glass or alumina (aluminum oxide) for bottle glass. Fused silica is an excellent glass but expensive because of pure silica's very high melting point. Borosilicate glass (e.g., Pyrex) is used for cookware and laboratory glassware because it expands very little when heated. Lead crystal is used for fine tableware. It has a heavy feel because of its lead oxide content and a sparkle due to its high refraction index. Even more specialized glasses include optical, photosensitive, metallic, and fibre-optic. Since glass has no sharp melting point, most types can be shaped while hot and plastic by many techniques, mostly blowing or molding.

glaucoma, Disease marked by increased pressure in the eye. A result of blockage of the flow of fluid (aqueous humour) at the outer edge of the iris, this pressure is transmitted to the optic nerve head and the retina. Chronic glaucoma can be treated with drugs that contract the pupil. Acute glaucoma may be intermittent. Permanent relief requires surgery to provide an outlet for the fluid. Either type causes vision impairment or blindness if untreated.

glider, Nonpowered heavier-than-air craft capable of sustained flight. Early experimenters in glider flight included George Cayley, who built the first man-carrying glider in 1853, and Otto Lilienthal (1848–1896), who introduced tail stabilizers on his first practical man-carrying craft in 1891. Improvements by Octave Chanute (1832–1910) in 1896 and by Wilbur and Orville Wright in 1902 perfected the control needed for developing the Wrights' powered airplane in 1903. The slender-winged glider was launched by being towed behind an airplane or a car. Gliders were used in World War II to carry troops. Today they are mainly used for recreation; the sailplane type is built for soaring on the lift from thermals.

Global Positioning System (GPS), Precise satellite-based navigation and location system originally developed for U.S. military use. GPS is a fleet of more than 24 communications satellites that transmit signals globally around the clock. With a GPS receiver, one can quickly and accurately determine the latitude, the longitude, and in most cases the altitude of a point on or above Earth's surface. A single GPS receiver can find its own position in seconds from GPS satellite signals to an accuracy of one metre; accuracy within one centimetre can be achieved with sophisticated military-specification receivers. This capability has reduced the cost of acquiring spatial data for making maps while increasing cartographic accuracy. Other applications include measuring the movement of polar ice sheets or even finding the best automobile route between given points.

global warming, Increase in the global average surface temperature resulting from enhancement of the greenhouse effect, primarily by air pollution. In 2007 the UN Intergovernmental Panel on Climate Change forecasted that by 2100 global average surface temperatures would increase 3.2–7.2 °F (1.8–4.0 °C), depending on a range of scenarios for greenhouse gas emissions, and stated that it was now 90 percent certain that most of the warming observed over the previous half century could be attributed to greenhouse gas emissions produced by human activities (i.e., industrial processes and transportation). Many scientists predict that such an increase in temperature would cause polar ice caps and mountain glaciers to melt rapidly, significantly raising the levels of coastal waters, and would produce new patterns and extremes of drought and rainfall, seriously disrupting food production in certain regions. Other scientists maintain that such predictions are overstated. The 1992 Earth Summit and the 1997 Kyoto Protocol to the United Nations Framework Convention on Climate Change attempted to address the issue of global warming, but in both cases the efforts were hindered by conflicting national economic agendas and disputes between developed and developing nations over the cost and consequences of reducing emissions of greenhouse gases.

globalization, Process by which the experience of everyday life, marked by the diffusion of commodities and ideas, is becoming standardized around the world. Factors that have contributed to globalization include increasingly sophisticated communications and transportation technologies and services, mass migration and the movement of peoples, a level of economic activity that has outgrown national markets through industrial combinations and commercial groupings that cross national frontiers, and international agreements that reduce the cost of doing business in foreign countries. Globalization offers huge potential profits to companies and nations but has been complicated by widely differing expectations, standards of living, cultures and values, and legal systems as well as unexpected global cause-and-effect linkages.

Globe Theatre, London theatre in which the plays of William Shakespeare were performed after 1599. It was built by two brothers, Cuthbert and Richard Burbage; half the shares were kept by the Burbages, and the rest were assigned equally to Shakespeare and other members of the Chamberlain's Men. The wooden theatre, built in the shape of an O with no roof over the central area, was destroyed by fire in 1613, rebuilt in 1614, and finally pulled down in 1644. Reconstructed (beginning 1987) near the site of the original theatre, the new Globe Theatre inaugurated its first regular season in 1996.

glockenspiel, Percussion instrument consisting of a set of tuned steel bars, arranged like a piano keyboard, which are struck with hammers. An alternative form of the instrument is played by means of an actual keyboard. Its normal range is 2¹/₂ octaves. The bell lyre, held vertically, is the portable form of glockenspiel used in marching bands.

Glorious Revolution, or BLOODLESS REVOLUTION, or REVOLUTION OF 1688, In English history, the events of 1688–89 that resulted in the deposition of James II and the accession of his daughter Mary II and her husband William III. James's overt Roman Catholicism, his suspension of the legal rights of dissenters,

and the prospect of a Catholic heir to the throne brought discontent to a head, which caused opposition leaders to invite the Protestant William of Orange to bring an army to redress the nation's grievances. The support remaining for James dwindled, and he fled to France. The Convention Parliament asked William and Mary to rule jointly and set out the Bill of Rights.

glossolalia, or SPEAKING IN TONGUES, Utterances approximating words and speech that are nonetheless generally unintelligible, usually produced during states of intense religious excitement. Speakers and witnesses may interpret the phenomenon as possession by a supernatural entity, conversation with divine beings, or the channeling of a divine proclamation. Glossolalia occurred in ancient Greek religion and is mentioned in the Christian New Testament. According to The Acts of the Apostles, it first occurred among followers of Jesus at Pentecost and reappeared wherever conversion to Christianity occurred. Today it is mainly associated with Pentecostalism and with charismatic Protestant movements but is also found in many other religious traditions.

Gloucester, ancient GLEVUM, City and administrative district (pop., 2001: 109,888), administrative and historic county of Gloucestershire, southwestern England. The county seat of Gloucestershire, it lies on the River Severn and is linked by ship canal to docks in the Severn estuary. It was founded as the Roman colony of Glevum in AD 96–98. An abbey was founded there in 681; the town later became the capital of the Anglo-Saxon kingdom of Mercia. Important economically even before the Norman Conquest (1066), it was incorporated in 1483 and continued to flourish as a trading centre. It has varied industries, including the manufacture of railway rolling stock and aircraft, and light and heavy engineering works.

glowworm, Any crawling, luminous insect that emits light either continuously or in prolonged glows rather than in the brief flashes characteristic of most fireflies. Glowworms include larvae and adult (often wingless) females of fireflies and certain other beetle species and larvae of certain gnat species. They are widely distributed. The great diversity in the size, number, location, and structure of the bioluminescent organs suggests that the light-producing ability of the various species evolved independently.

glucose, or DEXTROSE, or GRAPE SUGAR, or CORN SUGAR, Organic compound, a simple sugar (monosaccharide), chemical formula $C_6H_{12}O_6$. The product of photosynthesis in plants, it is found in fruits and honey. As the major circulating free sugar in blood, it is the source of energy in cell function and a major participant in metabolism. Control of its level and metabolism is of great importance. Glucose and fructose make up sucrose. Glucose units in long chains make up polysaccharides (e.g., cellulose, glycogen, starch). Glucose is used in foods, medicine, brewing, and wine making and as the source of various other organic chemicals.

glycogen, Principal storage carbohydrate of animals, occurring primarily in the liver and resting muscles. It is also found in various bacteria, fungi, and yeasts. Glycogen is a branched polysaccharide, a long chain of glucose units, into which it is broken down when energy is needed.

glycogen storage disease, or GLYCOGENOSIS, Any of numerous types of hereditary enzyme deficiency resulting in altered metabolism of glycogen. The problems are classified in two groups, those affecting the liver and those involving striated muscle, both primary glycogen storage sites. Symptoms in the liver group range from symptomatic hypoglycemia with ketosis to asymptomatic liver enlargement (hepatomegaly). In the muscle group, they range from weakness and cramps to fatal heart enlargement.

glycolysis, or GLYCOLYTIC PATHWAY, or EMBDEN-MEYERHOF-PARNAS PATHWAY, Sequence of 10 chemical reactions taking place in most cells that breaks down glucose, releasing energy that is then captured and stored in ATP. One molecule of glucose (plus coenzymes and inorganic phosphate) makes two molecules of pyruvate (or pyruvic acid) and two molecules of ATP. The pyruvate enters into the tricarboxylic acid cycle if enough oxygen is present or is fermented into lactic acid or ethanol if not. Thus, glycolysis produces both ATP for cellular energy requirements and building blocks for synthesis of other cellular products.

gnat, Any member of several species of small dipterans, most of which bite or annoy humans. Midges are also sometimes called gnats. In North America the name is also applied to the blackfly, fruit fly, and other small flies that hover about the eyes of humans and other animals.

Gnosticism, Religious and philosophical movement popular in the Roman world in the 2nd–3rd century AD. The term, based on the Greek *gnōsis* ("secret knowledge"), was coined in the 17th century, when it was applied liberally to ancient Christian heretical sects, especially those described by their orthodox contemporaries as radically dualistic and world-denying, and those who sought salvation through esoteric revelation and mystical spirituality. In the late 19th and the early 20th century, that view of Gnosticism was replaced with several groupings, and the discovery of the Nag Hammadi texts in 1945 greatly enhanced the understanding of Gnosticism. The relationship with ancient Christianity remains uncertain, but the *Gospel of Thomas* and the *Gospel of Mary* (which portrays Mary Magdalene as a leading apostle) are generally seen as being grounded in Gnosticism. They emphasized the teachings of Jesus, rather than his death and resurrection, as the key to salvation. The teachings of Valentinus were the basis of the *Gospel of Truth,* a fusion of Christian and Gnostic beliefs. Other texts previously considered Gnostic are now assigned to distinct religious traditions, especially Hermeticism, Mandaeanism, and Manichaeism. The texts of the Sethians have the best claim to the designation "Gnostic"; they describe one supreme, good God and the creation, by a junior heavenly being (Sophia), of an arrogant creature who then claims to be God. That creature withholds from humanity moral knowledge and eternal life, but Sophia plants the divine spirit within people to save them. Male and female saviours (including Jesus) were sent from the world above to instruct humanity in the knowledge of the true God and humanity's own divine nature. In general, Gnostics taught cosmological dualism, strict asceticism, repudiation of material creation as evil, docetism, and the existence of the divine spark in humans.

Goa, State (pop., 2008 est.: 1,628,000), southwestern India. Located on the western coast, it is bordered by Maharashtra and Karnataka states and has a 65-mi (105-km) coastline on the Arabian Sea. It has an area of 1,429 sq mi (3,702 sq km), which includes the offshore island of Goa. The capital is Panaji. It was ruled by Hindu dynasties and Muslim sultanates until the late 15th century and came under Portuguese control in 1510. Their settlement of Old Goa became the capital of Portuguese India. After India attained independence in 1947, it demanded that Portugal cede Goa. Indian troops finally occupied Goa in 1961; it was subsequently incorporated into India as part of the territory of Goa, Daman, and Diu. It became a state in 1987. Goa is predominantly agricultural; its distinctive architecture and fine beaches also make it a popular tourist destination.

Gobi, also called GOBI DESERT, Desert, Central Asia. One of the great desert and semidesert regions of the world, the Gobi stretches across Central Asia over large areas of Mongolia and China. It occupies an arc of land 1,000 mi (1,609 km) long and 300–600 mi (500–1,000 km) wide, with an estimated area of 500,000 sq mi (1,300,000 sq km). Contrary to the image often associated with a desert, much of the Gobi is not sandy but covered with bare rock.

God, Deity or Supreme Being. Each of the major monotheistic world religions worships a Supreme Being, who is the sole god of the universe, the maker of all things, omniscient and all-powerful.

God is also good. In ancient Israel God was named Yahweh. The God of the Hebrew Bible also became the God of Christianity, but generic words, such as *theos* in Greek or *Deus* in Latin, were often used to refer to him. In Islam the term is Allah.

god and goddess, Generic terms for the many deities of ancient and modern polytheistic religions. There may be deities of earthly and celestial phenomena as well as deities related to human values, pastimes, and institutions, including love, marriage, hunting, war, and the arts. They may be capable of being killed but are often immortal and always more powerful than humans, though they are often described in human terms, with all the flaws, thoughts, and emotions of humans.

Gödel's theorem, Principle of the foundations of mathematics. One of the most important discoveries of 20th-century mathematics, it states the impossibility of defining a complete system of axioms that is also consistent (does not give rise to contradictions). Any formal system (e.g., a computer program or a set of mathematical rules and axioms) powerful enough to generate meaningful statements can generate statements that are true but that cannot be proven or derived within the system. As a consequence, mathematics cannot be placed on an entirely rigorous basis. Named for Kurt Godel, who published his proof in 1931, it immediately had consequences for philosophy (particularly logic) and other areas. Its ramifications continue to be debated.

Goethe, Johann Wolfgang von (b. Aug. 28, 1749, Frankfurt am Main—d. March 22, 1832, Weimar, Saxe-Weimar), German poet, novelist, playwright, statesman, and scientist. In 1773 Goethe provided the Sturm und Drang movement with its first major drama, *Götz von Berlichingen,* and in 1774 with its first novel, *The Sorrows of Young Werther,* an extraordinarily popular work in its time, in which he created the prototype of the Romantic hero. In 1775 he arrived at Weimar, where he accepted an appointment to the ducal court; he would remain there for the rest of his life, and his presence helped to establish Weimar as a literary and intellectual centre. His poetry includes lyrics in praise of natural beauty and ballads that echo folk themes. His contact with ancient Classical culture during an Italian sojourn (1786–88) deeply influenced his later work. From 1794 Friedrich Schiller became his most important and influential friend. *Wilhelm Meister's Apprenticeship* (1795–96) is often called the first bildungsroman; it was followed many years later by *The Wanderings of Wilhelm Meister* (1821; 2nd ed. 1829). Many works were inspired by a series of passionate loves for women. His chief masterpiece, the drama *Faust* (*Part One,* 1808; *Part Two,* 1832), represents Faust tragically, as a singularly modern figure who is condemned to remain unsatisfied by life. Goethe also wrote extensively on botany, colour theory, and other scientific topics. In his late years he was celebrated as a sage and visited by world luminaries. The greatest figure of German Romanticism, he is regarded as a giant of world literature.

Gogh, Vincent (Willem) van (b. March 30, 1853, Zundert, Neth.—d. July 29, 1890, Auvers-sur-Oise, near Paris, France), Dutch painter. At 16 he was apprenticed to art dealers in The Hague, and he worked in their London and Paris branches (1873–76). After brief attempts at missionary work and theology, he studied drawing at the Brussels Academy; late in 1881 he settled at The Hague to work with a Dutch landscape painter, Anton Mauve. During his early years he painted three types of subjects—still life, landscape, and figure—all interrelated by their reference to the daily life of peasants (e.g., *The Potato Eaters,* 1885). After briefly studying at the Antwerp Academy, in 1886 he left to join his brother Theo, an art dealer, in Paris. There he met Henri de Toulouse-Lautrec, Paul Gauguin, and others involved in Impressionism and Post-Impressionism. By the summer of 1887 he was painting in pure colours and using broken brushwork that was at times pointillistic, and by the beginning of 1888 his Post-Impressionist style had crystallized. He left Paris in February 1888 for Arles, in southeastern France. The pictures he created over the following

12 months—depicting blossoming fruit trees, views of the town and surroundings, self-portraits, portraits of Roulin the postman and other friends, interiors and exteriors of the house, sunflowers, and landscapes—marked his first great period. Gauguin arrived in October 1888, and for two months he and van Gogh worked together; but, while each influenced the other to some extent, their relations rapidly deteriorated. On Christmas Eve 1888, physically and emotionally exhausted, van Gogh snapped under the strain; after arguing with Gauguin, he cut off the lower half of his own left ear. At the end of April 1889, van Gogh entered an asylum but continued to paint; during his 12-month stay he completed 150 paintings and drawings. A move to Auvers-sur-Oise in 1890 was followed by another burst of activity, but he soon suffered a relapse and died that July of a self-inflicted gunshot wound. His 10-year artistic career produced more than 800 paintings and 700 drawings, of which he sold only one in his lifetime. His work had a powerful influence on the development of modern painting, and he is considered the greatest Dutch painter since Rembrandt.

goitre, Enlargement of the thyroid gland, causing a prominent swelling in the front of the neck. The thyroid normally weighs 0.5 to 0.9 oz (15 to 25 g); however, goitrous thyroid glands can grow to more than 2 lbs (1,000 g). A large goitre may interfere with breathing and swallowing and cause a choking feeling. Endemic goitre, the most common, is due to iodine deficiency, which causes a reduction in thyroid hormone synthesis (hypothyroidism). As a result, there is a compensatory increase in secretion of the anterior pituitary hormone thyrotropin. Thyrotropin not only stimulates thyroid hormone production but also causes an increase in size and number of cells in the thyroid. Advanced cases are treated with thyroid hormone or with surgical removal of the thyroid if it obstructs breathing. There are numerous other causes of goitre, including defects in thyroid hormone synthesis and inflammation of the thyroid. An enlarged thyroid may have normally functioning tissue or may produce too much hormone (hyperthyroidism).

Golan Heights, Arabic AL-JAWLĀN, Hilly area, southwestern Syria. It overlooks the upper Jordan River valley; its maximum elevation is 7,297 ft (2,224 m). It was occupied by the Israeli army during the Six-Day War of 1967. After the Arab-Israeli war of 1973, a UN buffer zone was established between Syrians and Israelis in the heights. In 1981 Israel unilaterally annexed the part of the Golan that it held. Talks between the two countries on the status of the heights began in 2000.

gold, Metallic chemical element, one of the transition elements, chemical symbol Au, atomic number 79. It is a dense, lustrous, yellow, malleable precious metal, so durable that it is virtually indestructible, often found uncombined in nature. Jewelry and other decorative objects have been crafted from gold for thousands of years. It has been used for coins, to back paper currencies, and as a reserve asset. Gold is widely distributed in all igneous rocks, usually pure but in low concentrations; its recovery from ores and deposits has been a major preoccupation since ancient times. The world's gold supply has seen three great leaps, with Christopher Columbus's arrival in the Americas in 1492, with discoveries in California and Australia (1850–75), and discoveries in Alaska, Yukon, and South Africa (1890–1915). Pure gold is too soft for prolonged handling; it is usually used in alloys with silver, copper, and other metals. In addition to being used in jewelry and as currency, gold is used in electrical contacts and circuits, as a reflective layer in space applications and on building windows, and in filling and replacing teeth. Dental alloys are about 75% gold, 10% silver. In jewelry, its purity is expressed in 24ths, or karats: 24-karat is pure, 12-karat is 50% gold, etc. Its compounds, in which it has valence 1 or 3, are used mainly in plating and other decorative processes; a soluble chloride compound has been used to treat rheumatoid arthritis.

gold rush, Rapid influx of fortune seekers to the site of newly discovered gold deposits. In North America, the first major gold strike occurred in California in 1848, when James Marshall, a carpenter building a sawmill for John Sutter, found gold. Within a year about 80,000 "forty-niners" (as the fortune seekers of 1849 were called) had flocked to the California gold fields, and 250,000 had arrived by 1853. Some mining camps grew into permanent settlements, and the demand for food, housing, and supplies propelled the new state's economy. As gold became more difficult to extract, companies and mechanical mining methods replaced individual prospectors. Smaller gold rushes occurred throughout the second half of the 19th century in Colorado, Nevada, Idaho, Montana, South Dakota, Arizona, and Alaska, resulting in the rapid settlement of many areas; where gold veins proved small, the settlements later became ghost towns. Major gold rushes also occurred in Australia (1851), South Africa (1886), and Canada (1896).

gold standard, Monetary system in which the standard unit of currency is a fixed quantity of gold or is freely convertible into gold at a fixed price. The gold standard was first adopted in Britain in 1821. Germany, France, and the U.S. instituted it in the 1870s, prompted by North American gold strikes that increased the supply of gold. The gold standard ended with the outbreak of World War I in 1914; it was reestablished in 1928, but because of the relative scarcity of gold, most nations adopted a gold-exchange standard, supplementing their gold reserves with currencies (U.S. dollars and British pounds) convertible into gold at a stable rate of exchange. Though the gold-exchange standard collapsed during the Great Depression, the U.S. set a minimum dollar price for gold, an action that allowed for the restoration of an international gold standard after World War II. In 1971 dwindling gold reserves and an unfavourable balance of payments led the U.S. to suspend the free convertibility of dollars into gold, and the gold standard was abandoned.

Golden Bull of 1356, Constitution for the Holy Roman Empire promulgated by Charles IV. Stamped with a golden seal, the document gave seven electors the power to choose the ruler of Germany by a simple majority. It also specified the electors and established succession by primogeniture. Intended to eliminate papal influence in German political affairs, it did away with the pope's previous right to examine rivals and approve results, and also increased the power of the princes.

Golden Gate Bridge, Suspension bridge spanning the Golden Gate, San Francisco. From its completion in 1937 until the completion of New York's Verrazano-Narrows Bridge in 1964, it had the longest main span in the world, 4,200 ft (1,280 m). It remains incomparable in its magnificence. Its construction, supervised by Joseph B. Strauss (1870–1938), involved many difficulties: rapidly running tides, frequent storms and fogs, and the problem of blasting rock under deep water to plant earthquake-resistant foundations.

Golden Gate Bridge, San Francisco.

George Hall/Woodfin Camp and Associates

golden ratio, Numerical proportion considered to be an aesthetic ideal in classical design. It refers to the ratio of the base to the height of a rectangle or to the division of a line segment into two in such a way that the ratio of the shorter part to the longer is equal to that of the longer to the whole. It works out to about 1.61803:1. A rectangle constructed from golden sections (segments in this ratio) is called a golden rectangle.

Golden Temple, Punjabi DARBAR SAHIB, or HARIMANDIR, Chief house of worship for the Sikhs of India and their most important pilgrimage site, located in the city of Amritsar in Punjab state. Founded by Guru Ramdas (1574–81) and completed by Guru Arjan Dev in 1604, the temple has entrances on four sides, signifying a welcome to all creeds and castes. Though destroyed in the 1760s by Afghan invaders, it was rebuilt, and in the early 19th century it acquired its marble walls and gold-plated copper domes. The surrounding buildings include a meeting hall, reference library, and museum, as well as the shrine known as the Akal Takhat. In 1984 the complex was seriously damaged during a confrontation between Sikh separatists and government troops; it was subsequently restored.

goldfish, Ornamental aquarium and pond fish (*Carassius auratus*) of the carp family, native to East Asia but introduced into many other areas. The goldfish was domesticated by the Chinese at least as early as the Song dynasty (960–1279). It is naturally greenish brown or gray, but its colour varies. Selective breeding has produced more than 125 breeds, including the veiltail, with a three-lobed, flowing tail, and the common, pet-shop comet. They feed on plants and small animals and, in captivity, on small crustaceans and other foods. They have become naturalized in many parts of the eastern U.S.

Goldfish (Carassius auratus)
W.S. Pitt/Eric Hosking

Golding, Sir William (Gerald) (b. Sept. 19, 1911, St. Columb Minor, near Newquay, Cornwall, Eng.—d. June 19, 1993, Perranarworthal, near Falmouth, Cornwall), British novelist. Educated at the University of Oxford, Golding worked as a schoolmaster until 1960. His first and best-known novel was *Lord of the Flies* (1954; film, 1963, 1990), about a group of boys isolated on an island who revert to savagery. Later works, several of which are likewise parables of the human condition that show the thinness of the veneer of civilization, include *The Inheritors* (1955), *Pincher Martin* (1956), *The Spire* (1964), *Rites of Passage* (1980, Booker Prize), and *Close Quarters* (1987). He won the Nobel Prize for Literature in 1983.

golf, Game in which a player using special clubs attempts to sink a small ball with as few strokes as possible into each of the 9 or 18 successive holes on an outdoor course. Each hole has associated with it a par, or score standard, usually from par 3 to par 5. The origins of the game are difficult to ascertain, although evidence now suggests that early forms of golf were played in the Netherlands first and then in Scotland. Golf developed in Scotland—the courses were originally fields of grass that sheep had clipped short in their characteristic grazing style. Golf balls were originally made of wood; wood was replaced in the 17th century by boiled feathers stuffed in a leather cover, in the 19th century by gutta-percha, and in the 20th century by hard rubber. Clubs, limited in number to 14, are known by the traditional names of "irons" (primarily for mid-range to short shots) and "woods" (primarily for longer shots); today irons are more likely made of stainless steel, and woods are actually made of metal such as steel or titanium.

Golgi, Camillo (b. July 7, 1843/44, Corteno, Italy—d. Jan. 21, 1926, Pavia), Italian physician and cytologist. He devised a way to stain nerve tissue and with it discovered a neuron, now called the Golgi cell, that has many short, branching extensions (dendrites) and connects other neurons. This led to identification of the neuron as the basic structural unit of the nervous system. He also discovered the Golgi tendon organ (the point at which sensory nerve fibres branch out within a tendon) and the Golgi apparatus

Camillo Golgi, 1906.
Courtesy of the Wellcome Trustees

(a cell organelle that packages large molecules for transport). He shared a 1906 Nobel Prize with Santiago Ramón y Cajal (b. 1852—d. 1934).

gonorrhea, Sexually transmitted disease. It is characterized by genitourinary inflammation, caused by the bacterium *Neisseria gonorrhoeae* (gonococcus). Symptoms in men include burning on urination, discharge of pus, and, with deeper infection, frequent urination, sometimes with blood. Women may have mild vaginal discharge and burning, but there is usually no sign until a sex partner is infected or complications—sometimes serious—arise from its spread beyond the cervix. If spontaneous recovery does not occur, it may cause sterility in both sexes but is rarely fatal. Gonorrhea is common worldwide. Penicillin, generally a successful treatment, reduced its incidence, but resistant strains are increasingly found. Many cases are not reported. Penicillin may also mask coexisting syphilis (since the dose to cure gonorrhea does not cure syphilis).

Good Friday, Friday before Easter, commemorating the crucifixion of Jesus. As early as the 2nd century it was kept by Christians as a day of penance and fasting. The Eastern Orthodox and Roman Catholic churches have special liturgies for the day, which include readings and prayers commemorating Christ's sufferings on the cross. Protestant churches also hold special services on Good Friday.

Good Hope, Cape of, Rocky promontory, southwestern coast, Western Cape province, South Africa. It was sighted by the Portuguese navigator Bartolemeu Dias in 1488 on his return voyage to Portugal after finding the southern limits of the African continent. Known for the stormy weather and rough seas encountered there, the cape lies at the convergence of warm currents from the Indian Ocean and cool currents from Antarctic waters. A part of the Cape of Good Hope Nature Reserve established in 1939, the cape was the site of the first Dutch settlement at Table Bay in 1652.

Good Neighbor Policy, Popular name for the policy toward Latin America pursued in the 1930s by U.S. Pres. Franklin D. Roosevelt. In a marked departure from its traditional interventionism, which was abhorrent to Latin Americans, the U.S. repudiated its assumed right to intervene unilaterally in Latin American affairs, abrogated most provisions of the Platt Amendment (1901), which had restricted the national sovereignty of Cuba, and withdrew its Marines from Haiti. U.S. anticommunist policies after World War II led to renewed distrust between the U.S. and Latin America and brought an end to the noninterventionism of the Good Neighbor Policy.

Goodall, Jane (b. April 3, 1934, London, Eng.), British ethologist. Soon after finishing high school, she fulfilled her childhood ambition of traveling to Africa, where she assisted Louis Leakey, who suggested she study chimpanzees. She received a Ph.D. from Cambridge University for her work and remained at the research centre she founded in Gombe, Tanz., until 1975. In 1977 she cofounded the Jane Goodall Institute for Wildlife Research, Education, and Conservation in the U.S. Her observations established, among other things, that chimpanzees are omnivorous rather than vegetarian, can make and use tools, and have complex and highly developed social behaviours. Noteworthy among her writings are *In the Shadow of Man* (1971) and *The Chimpanzees of Gombe* (1986). She was made a Dame of the British Empire in 2003.

Gorbachev, Mikhail (Sergeyevich) (b. March 2, 1931, Privolye, Stavropol region, Russia, U.S.S.R.), Soviet official and last president of the Soviet Union (1990–91). After earning a law degree from Moscow State University (1955), he rose through the ranks to become a full Politburo member (1980) and general secretary of the Communist Party of the Soviet Union (1985–91). His extraordinary reform policies of glasnost and perestroika were resisted by party bureaucrats; to reduce their power, Gorbachev changed the Soviet constitution in 1988 to allow multicandidate elections and removed the monopoly power of the party in 1990. He cultivated warmer re-

Mikhail Gorbachev, 1985.
Colton—Picture Search/Black Star

lations with the U.S., and in 1989–90 he supported the democratically elected governments that replaced the communist regimes of eastern Europe. In 1990 he was awarded the Nobel Peace Prize. Russia's economic and political problems led to a 1991 coup attempt by hard-liners. In alliance with president Boris Yeltsin, Gorbachev quit the Communist Party, disbanded its Central Committee, and shifted political powers to the Soviet Union's constituent republics. Events outpaced him, and the various republics formed the Commonwealth of Independent States under Yeltsin's leadership. On Dec. 25, 1991, Gorbachev resigned the presidency of the Soviet Union, which ceased to exist that same day.

Gordimer, Nadine (b. Nov. 20, 1923, Springs, Transvaal, S.Af.), South African writer. The daughter of Jewish immigrants, she published her first book, the story collection *The Soft Voice of the Serpent*, in 1952. Her later works include *The Conservationist* (1974, Booker Prize), *Burger's Daughter* (1979), *July's People* (1981), *A Sport of Nature* (1987), *My Son's Story* (1990), *None to Accompany Me* (1994), and *The House Gun* (1998). Written in a clear, controlled, unsentimental style, her works often concern exile and alienation. She was a strong opponent of her country's apartheid policy, and concerns about black-white relations are frequently expressed in her fiction. She received the Nobel Prize for Literature in 1991.

gorilla, Largest of the great apes. A stocky, powerful forest dweller native to equatorial Africa, the gorilla (*Gorilla gorilla*) has black skin and hair, large nostrils, and prominent brow ridges. Adults have long, powerful arms; short, stocky legs; an extremely thick, strong chest; and a protruding abdomen. Adult males have a prominent crest on top of the skull and a "saddle" of gray or silver hairs on the lower part of the back. Males, about twice as heavy as females, may reach a height of about 5.5 ft (1.7 m) and a weight of 300–600 lbs (135–275 kg). Gorillas are mainly terrestrial, walking about on all four limbs. They live in stable family groups of six to 20 animals that are led by one or two silverbacked males. They eat leaves, stalks, and shoots. They are unaggressive and even shy unless provoked. They are calmer and more persistent than chimpanzees; though not as adaptable, gorillas are highly intelligent and capable of problem solving. The go-

Male gorilla (Gorilla gorilla).
Kenneth W. Fink/Root Resources

rilla is hunted for its body parts and meat, and its habitat is disappearing. It is an endangered species throughout its range; the mountain subspecies is critically endangered.

goryō, In Japanese mythology, vengeful spirits of the dead. They were originally thought to be spirits of nobles who had been killed unjustly and who avenged themselves by bringing about natural disasters, disease, and wars. Identified by divination, they were appeased by being granted status as gods. Later the belief arose that anyone could become a *goryō* by willing it at the moment of death or by meeting an untimely death. Various forms of exorcism and magical practices, such as the Buddhist recitation of *nembutsu* (invoking the name of the Buddha Amida), have been used to ward them off.

Gospel, Any of the four New Testament books narrating the life and death of Jesus. The Gospels of Matthew, Mark, Luke, and John are placed at the beginning of the New Testament and make up about half its total text. Since the 18th century, the first three have been called the Synoptic Gospels, because they give similar accounts of the ministry of Jesus. The term is also applied to apocryphal works of the 2nd century (e.g., The Gospel of Thomas).

Göteborg, or GOTHENBURG, City (pop., 2001 est.: 471,267), southwestern Sweden. The country's chief seaport and second largest city, it lies along the Göta River estuary, about 5 mi (8 km) above the Kattegat. Founded in 1603, the city was destroyed in the Kalmar War with Denmark (1611–13) but was refounded in 1619. Many of the early inhabitants were Dutch, who built urban canals and laid out the city centre. A prosperous period began with the completion of the Göta Canal (1832) and the start of a transoceanic shipping service. It retains some historic architecture, and a moat still encircles the old part of the city. The port's principal exports are automobiles (Volvo), ball bearings, and paper.

Goth, Member of a Germanic people whose two branches, the Ostrogoths and the Visigoths, harassed the Roman Empire for centuries. Legend holds that the Goths originated in southern Scandinavia, crossed to the southern shore of the Baltic Sea, and then migrated to the Black Sea in the 2nd century. They raided the Roman provinces in Asia Minor and the Balkan peninsula in the 3rd century and drove the Romans out of the province of Dacia during the reign of Aurelian. In the 4th and 5th centuries, the Visigoths smashed a Roman army, sacked the city of Rome, and created a kingdom in Spain that would last until the Muslim conquests of the 8th century. The Ostrogoths established an important kingdom in Italy in the late 5th century that was destroyed by Justinian in the 6th century. The adjective "Gothic" was applied disparagingly and inappropriately to medieval architecture by much later writers.

Gothic architecture, Architectural style in Europe that lasted from the mid 12th century to the 16th century, particularly a style of masonry building characterized by cavernous spaces with the expanse of walls broken up by overlaid tracery. In the 12th–13th centuries, feats of engineering permitted increasingly gigantic buildings. The rib vault, flying buttress, and pointed (Gothic) arch were used as solutions to the problem of building a very tall structure while preserving as much natural light as possible. Stained-glass window panels rendered startling sun-dappled interior effects. One of the earliest buildings to combine these elements into a coherent style was the abbey of Saint-Denis, Paris (c. 1135–44). The High Gothic years (c. 1250–1300), heralded by Chartres Cathedral, were dominated by France, especially with the development of the Rayonnant style. Britain, Germany, and Spain produced variations of this style, while Italian Gothic stood apart in its use of brick and marble rather than stone. Late Gothic (15th-century) architecture reached its height in Germany's vaulted hall churches. Other late Gothic styles include the British Perpendicular style and the French and Spanish Flamboyant style.

Gothic art, Architecture, sculpture, and painting that flourished in Western and central Europe in the Middle Ages. It evolved from Romanesque art and lasted from the mid-12th century to the end of the 15th century. Its loftiest form of expression is architecture, as in the great cathedrals of northern Europe. Sculpture was closely tied to architecture and often used to decorate the exteriors of cathedrals and other religious buildings. Painting evolved from stiff, two-dimensional forms to more natural ones. Religious and secular subjects were depicted in illuminated manuscripts. Panel and wall painting evolved into the Renaissance style in Italy in the 15th century, but retained its Gothic features until the early 16th century elsewhere in Europe.

gothic novel, European Romantic, pseudo-medieval fiction with a prevailing atmosphere of mystery and terror. Such novels were often set in castles or monasteries equipped with subterranean passages, dark battlements, and hidden panels, and they had plots involving ghosts, madness, outrage, superstition, and revenge. Horace Walpole's *Castle of Otranto* (1765) initiated the vogue, which peaked in the 1790s. Ann Radcliffe's *The Mysteries of Udolpho* (1794) and *The Italian* (1797) are among the finest examples. Matthew Gregory Lewis's *The Monk* (1796) introduced more horrific elements into the English gothic. Gothic traits appear in Mary Shelley's *Frankenstein* (1818) and Bram Stoker's *Dracula* (1897) and in the works of many major writers, and they persist today in thousands of paperback romances.

Gothic Revival, Architectural movement (*c.* 1730–*c.* 1930) most commonly associated with Romanticism. The first nostalgic imitation of Gothic architecture appeared in the 18th century, when scores of houses with castle-style battlements were built in England, but only toward the mid-19th century did a true Gothic Revival develop. The mere imitation of Gothic forms and details then became its least important aspect, as architects focused on creating original works based on underlying Gothic principles. French architects, particularly E.-E. Viollet-le-Duc, were the first to think about applying the Gothic skeleton structure to a modern age. Though the movement began losing force toward the end of the century, Gothic-style churches and collegiate buildings continued to be constructed in Britain and the U.S. well into the 20th century.

gout, Hereditary metabolic disorder in which excess uric-acid salts, normally excreted in urine, are deposited as needle-sharp crystals in joints, causing attacks of severe inflammation. The most common site is the base of the big toe. One of the oldest diseases in medical literature, gout is far more common in men. Attacks usually do not begin until middle age. They cause heat, redness, and extreme tenderness and pain and often subside in a week or two. Colchicine is used to treat acute attacks. Drugs such as allopurinol inhibit uric-acid synthesis.

government, Political system by which a body of people is administered and regulated. Different levels of government typically have different responsibilities. The level closest to those governed is local government. Regional governments comprise a grouping of individual communities. National governments nominally control all the territory within internationally recognized borders and have responsibilities not shared by their subnational counterparts. Most governments exercise executive, legislative, and judicial powers and split or combine them in various ways. Some also control the religious affairs of their people; others avoid any involvement with religion. Political forms at the national level determine the powers exercised at the subnational levels; these have included autocracy, democracy, fascism, monarchy, oligarchy, plutocracy (government by the wealthy), theocracy, and totalitarianism.

grace, In Christian theology, the unmerited gift of divine favour, which brings about the salvation of a sinner. The concept of grace has given rise to theological debate over the nature of human depravity and the extent to which individuals may contribute to their own salvation through free will. Though in principle the ideas of merit and grace are mutually exclusive, the question of whether grace may be given as a reward for good works or for faith alone was important in the Protestant Reformation. There has also been controversy over the means of grace: Roman Catholics, Eastern Orthodox, and some Protestants believe that it is conferred through the sacraments, while some other Protestants (e.g., Baptists) hold that participation in grace results from personal faith alone.

graft, In horticulture, the act of placing a portion of one plant (called a bud or scion) into or on a stem, root, or branch of another (called the stock) in such a way that a union forms and the partners continue to grow. Grafting is used for various purposes: to repair injured trees, produce dwarf trees and shrubs, strengthen plants' resistance to certain diseases, retain varietal characteristics, adapt varieties to adverse soil or climatic conditions, ensure pollination, produce multifruited or multiflowered plants, and propagate certain species (such as hybrid roses) that can be propagated in no other way. In theory, any two plants that are closely related botanically and that have a continuous cambium can be grafted. Grafts between species of the same genus are often successful and between genera occasionally so, but grafts between families are nearly always failures.

Graham, Martha (b. May 11, 1894, Allegheny county, Pa., U.S.—d. April 1, 1991, New York, N.Y.), U.S. dancer, teacher, choreographer, and foremost exponent of modern dance. She studied from 1916 with Ted Shawn at the Denishawn School of Dancing and Related Arts, then left in 1923 for New York, where she founded her own school in 1927 and a performing company in 1929. She choreographed more than 160 works, creating unique "dance plays" and using a variety of themes to express emotion and conflict. Many are based on American themes, including *Appalachian Spring* (1944); other works include *Primitive Mysteries* (1931), *El Penitente* (1940), *Letter to the World* (1940), *Cave of the Heart* (1946), *Clytemnestra* (1958), *Phaedra* (1962), and *Frescoes* (1978). She collaborated for many years with Louis Horst, her musical director, and with Isamu Noguchi, who designed many of her sets. She retired from dancing in 1970 but continued to teach and choreograph. Her technique became the first significant alternative to classical ballet, and her influence extended worldwide through her choreography and her students.

grail, or HOLY GRAIL, In Arthurian legend, a sacred cup that was the object of a mystical quest by knights of the Round Table. The grail legend may have been inspired by classical and Celtic stories of magic cauldrons and horns of plenty. It was first given Christian significance as a mysterious, holy object by Chrétien de Troyes in the 12th-century romance *Perceval, or the Count of the Holy Grail*. The grail was sometimes said to be the same cup used by Jesus at the Last Supper and later by Joseph of Arimathea to catch the blood flowing from the wounds of Jesus on the cross. The most notable figure connected with the grail was Sir Galahad, who, according to Sir Thomas Malory's *Le Morte Darthur*, found the grail and achieved mystical union with God.

gramadevata, Folk deities widely worshiped in rural India. Often female figures, they may have originated as agricultural deities, and they are offered animal sacrifices to ward off disease, crop failures, and other natural disasters. Many are purely local, spirits of a place (e.g., a crossroads) or of a person who has died an untimely death. They are worshiped in the form of stones or earthenware icons fixed in simple shrines or set up under a village tree.

grammar, Rules of a language governing its phonology, morphology, syntax, and semantics; also, a written summary of such rules. The first Europeans to write grammar texts were the Greeks, notably the Alexandrians of the lst century BC. The Romans applied the Greek grammatical system to Latin. The works of the

Latin grammarians Donatus (4th century AD) and Priscian (6th century) were widely used to teach grammar in medieval Europe. By 1700, grammars of 61 vernacular languages had been printed. These were mainly used for teaching and were intended to reform or standardize language. In the 19th–20th centuries linguists began studying languages to trace their evolution rather than to prescribe correct usage. Descriptive linguists studied spoken language by collecting and analyzing sample sentences. Transformational grammarians examined the underlying structure of language. The older approach to grammar as a body of rules needed to speak and write correctly is still the basis of primary and secondary language education.

Grampian Mountains, or GRAMPIAN HILLS, Mountain system, Scotland. Extending across central Scotland, it forms a natural boundary between the Scottish Highlands and Lowlands. Its highest peak, Ben Nevis, is the highest mountain in Britain.

Gran Chaco, Spanish CHACO, or EL CHACO, Lowland alluvial plain, south-central South America. An arid lowland, it is bounded by the Andes Mountains to the west and the Paraguay and Paraná rivers to the east; its northern and southern margins, generally considered to be a marshy area in Bolivia and the Salado River in Argentina, respectively, are less well defined. Its area is about 280,000 sq mi (725,000 sq km). The region's heartland, in the fork of the Paraguay and Pilcomayo rivers, was fought over by Bolivia and Paraguay in the Chaco War (1932–35). By a 1938 treaty a larger eastern part went to Paraguay and a smaller western part to Bolivia. Chaco's wildlife is abundant, and there are at least 60 known species of snakes. Cattle grazing is a major economic activity. The area remains isolated and is only sparsely populated.

Granada, City (pop., 2001: 240,661), capital of Granada province, Andalusia autonomous community, southern Spain. Located at the northwestern slope of the Sierra Nevada, it was the site of the Iberian settlement Elibyrge in the 5th century BC and of the Roman Illiberis. As the seat of the Moorish kingdom of Granada, it was the final stronghold of the Moors in Spain, falling to Roman Catholic monarchs Ferdinand II and Isabella I in 1492. Nearby is the Alhambra, as well as the Alcazaba fortress that guarded it. The city has fine Renaissance, Baroque, and Neoclassical architecture and is a major tourist centre. It has been the see of an archbishop since 1493; the University of Granada was founded in 1526.

Grand Alliance, War of the (1689–97) Third major war of Louis XIV of France, in which his expansionist plans were blocked by an alliance led by Britain, the United Provinces of the Netherlands, and the Austrian Habsburgs. The deeper issue underlying the war was the rivalry between the Bourbon and Habsburg dynasties. Louis launched a campaign in the 1680s to position the Bourbons for future succession to the Spanish throne. To oppose him, the Habsburg emperor Leopold I joined other European nations in the League of Augsburg. The league proved ineffective, but in 1690 Britain, Brandenburg, Saxony, Bavaria, and Spain, alarmed at Louis's successes, joined with Leopold to form the Grand Alliance. As war broke out in Europe and in overseas colonies, including America, Louis found his military inadequately prepared, and France suffered heavy naval losses. In 1695 Louis started secret peace negotiations, which culminated in the Treaty of Rijswijk (1697). The underlying conflict between the Habsburg and Bourbon rulers and English-French conflicts remained unresolved and resurfaced four years later in the War of the Spanish Succession.

Grand Canal, Series of waterways in northern China that link Hangzhou with Beijing. Some 1,085 mi (1,747 km) in length, it is the world's longest man-made waterway. It was build to enable successive Chinese regimes to transport surplus grain from the agriculturally rich Yangtze (Chang) and Huai river valleys to feed the capital cities and large standing armies in the north. The oldest

portion, in the south, may date from the 4th century BC. Expanded over the centuries, it continues to be used today for shipping and irrigation.

Grand Canyon, Extensive canyon system cut by the Colorado River, northwestern Arizona, U.S. Noted for its rock formations and coloration, it is about 0.1–18 mi (0.2–29 km) wide and extends from northern Arizona to Grand Wash Cliffs, near the Nevada border, a distance of about 277 mi (446 km). The deepest section, 56 mi (90 km) long, is within Grand Canyon National Park, which covers the river's length from Lake Powell to Lake Mead. The surrounding plateau is 6,000–9,000 ft (1,800–2,750 m) above sea level, and the canyon is in places more than 1 mi (1.6 km) deep. The national park, now containing 1,904 sq mi (4,931 sq km), was created in 1919. The former Grand Canyon National Monument, established in 1932, was added, with other lands, in 1975. In 1979 the Grand Canyon was designated a UNESCO World Heritage site.

grand jury, Jury that examines accusations against persons suspected of committing a crime and, if the evidence warrants it, issues formal charges on which the accused are later tried. It does not decide guilt or innocence, only whether there is "probable cause" to believe that a person committed a crime. Public officials (prosecutors and police) provide information and summon witnesses for the jury. The proceedings are usually secret. Some U.S. states have abolished the grand jury and authorize indictments by prosecutors.

Grand National, British steeplechase horse-racing event held annually in Liverpool, Eng. Established in 1839, it attracts more attention throughout the world than any other such event, because of its extreme difficulties and dangers. The course is covered twice for a distance of 4.48 mi (7.2 km), including 31 jumps, some of them spectacularly hazardous.

Grand Prix racing, Automobile racing in which formula cars are run on closed highways or courses that simulate road conditions. Formula cars are open-wheel, open-cockpit, rear-engine vehicles and are generally smaller than those used in speedway races such as the Indianapolis 500. Grand Prix racing began in 1906 and today comprises more than 15 major international events. Its popularity grew particularly from the 1950s, when world championships were established.

grand unified theory, or GRAND UNIFICATION THEORY (GUT) Theory that attempts to unify the electroweak force with the strong force. The unification of all four fundamental interactions is sometimes called unified field theory. Such theories generally predict that a proton decays into lighter particles. So far, no successful GUTs have been devised.

granite, Coarse- or medium-grained intrusive rock that is rich in quartz and alkali feldspar. One of the most common rocks of the Earth's crust, it is formed by the cooling of magma. Granite was once used extensively as paving blocks and building stone, but today its principal uses are as roadway curbing, veneer for building faces, and tombstones. Granite characteristically forms irregular masses of extremely variable size, ranging from less than 5 mi (8 km) in maximum dimension to larger masses (batholiths) that are often hundreds of square miles in area.

Grant, Ulysses S., orig. HIRAM ULYSSES GRANT (b. April 27, 1822, Point Pleasant, Ohio, U.S.—d. July 23, 1885, Mount McGregor, N.Y.), U.S. general and 18th president of the U.S. (1869–77). He served in the Mexican War (1846–48) under Zachary Taylor. After two years' service on the Pacific coast (1852–54), during which he attempted to supplement his army pay with ultimately unsuccessful business ventures, he resigned his commission. His decision might have been influenced by his fondness for alcohol, which he reportedly drank often during this period. He worked unsuccessfully at farming in Missouri and at his family's leather

Ulysses S. Grant.
Library of Congress, Washington, D.C.

business in Illinois. When the American Civil War began (1861), he was appointed brigadier general; his 1862 attack on Fort Donelson, Tenn., produced the first major Union victory. He drove off a Confederate attack at Shiloh but was criticized for heavy Union losses. He devised the campaign to take the stronghold of Vicksburg, Miss., in 1863, cutting the Confederacy in half from east to west. Following his victory at the Battle of Chattanooga in 1864, he was appointed commander of the Union army. While Gen. William T. Sherman made his famous march across Georgia, Grant attacked forces under Gen. Robert E. Lee in Virginia, bringing the war to an end in 1865. Grant's administrative ability and innovative strategies were largely responsible for the Union victory. In 1868 his successful Republican presidential campaign made him, at 46, the youngest man yet elected president. His two terms were marred by administrative inaction and political scandal involving members of his cabinet, including the Crédit Mobilier scandal and the Whiskey Ring conspiracy. He was more successful in foreign affairs, where he was aided by his secretary of state, Hamilton Fish. He supported amnesty for Confederate leaders and protection for the civil rights of former slaves. His veto of a bill to increase the amount of legal tender (1874) diminished the currency crisis during the next 25 years. In 1881 he moved to New York City; when a partner defrauded an investment firm co-owned by his son, the family was impoverished. His memoirs were published by his friend Mark Twain.

grape, Any of the 60 plant species that make up the genus *Vitis* (family Vitaceae), native to the northern temperate zone, including varieties that may be eaten as table fruit, dried to produce raisins, or crushed to make grape juice or wine. *V. vinifera* is the species most commonly used in wine making. The grape is usually a woody vine, climbing by means of tendrils. In arid regions it may form an almost erect shrub. Botanically, the fruit is a berry. Grapes contain such minerals as calcium and phosphorus and are a source of vitamin A. All grapes contain sugar (glucose and fructose) in varying quantities depending on the variety.

Grape (Vitis).
Grant Heilman/EB Inc.

graph theory, Mathematical theory of networks. A graph consists of vertices (also called points or nodes) and edges (lines) connecting certain pairs of vertices. An edge that connects a node to itself is called a loop. In 1735 Leonhard Euler published an analysis of an old puzzle concerning the possibility of crossing every one of seven bridges (no bridge twice) that span a river surrounding two central landmasses. Euler's proof that no such path exists and his generalization of the problem to all possible networks are now recognized as the origin of both graph theory and topology. Since the mid-20th century, graph theory has become a standard tool for analyzing and designing communications networks, power transmission systems, transportation networks, and computer architectures.

graphical user interface (GUI), Computer display format that allows the user to select commands, call up files, start programs, and do other routine tasks by using a mouse to point to pictorial symbols (icons) or lists of menu choices on the screen as opposed to having to type in text commands. The first GUI to be used in a personal computer appeared in Apple's Lisa, introduced in 1983; its GUI became the basis of Apple's extremely successful Macintosh (1984). The Macintosh's GUI style was widely adapted by other manufacturers of personal computers and PC software. In 1985 Microsoft Corp. introduced Windows, a GUI (which later grew into an operating system) that gave MS-DOS–based computers many of the same capabilities as the Macintosh. In addition to being used for operating-system interfaces, GUIs are used in other types of software, including browsers and application programs.

graphite, or PLUMBAGO, or BLACK LEAD, Mineral allotrope of carbon. It is dark gray to black, opaque, and very soft. Its layered structure, with rings of six atoms arranged in widely spaced parallel sheets, gives it its slippery quality. It occurs in nature and is used (mixed with clay) as the "lead" in pencils. It is also used in lubricants, crucibles, polishes, arc lamps, batteries, brushes for electric motors, and nuclear reactor cores.

grass, Any of many low, green, nonwoody plants that make up the families Poaceae (formerly Gramineae), Cyperaceae (sedges), and Juncaceae (rushes). Only the approximately 10,000 species in the family Poaceae are true grasses. They are the most economically important of all flowering plants because of their nutritious grains and soil-forming function, and they are the most widespread and most numerous of plants. The cereal grasses include wheat, corn, rice, rye, oats, barley, and millet. Grasses provide forage for grazing animals, shelter for wildlife, and construction materials, furniture, utensils, and food for humans. Some species are grown as garden ornamentals, cultivated as turf for lawns and recreational areas, or used as cover plants for erosion control. Most have hollow, segmented, round stems, bladelike leaves, and extensively branching fibrous root systems.

grasshopper, Any of the leaping insects of the family Acrididae

Short-horned grasshopper (Acrididae)
Earl L. Kubis/Root Resources

(short-horned grasshoppers) or Tettigoniidae (long-horned grasshoppers), both in the order Orthoptera. Grasshoppers are most common in tropical forests, semiarid regions, and grasslands. Colours range from green to olive or brown, sometimes with yellow or red markings. Grasshoppers eat plant material and may damage crops. Some species are more than 4 in. (11 cm) long. The male can produce a buzzing sound either by rubbing its front wings together or by rubbing toothlike ridges on the hind legs against a raised vein on each front wing. Grasshoppers are a favourite food of many birds, frogs, and snakes.

Graves disease, or TOXIC DIFFUSE GOITRE, or EXOPHTHALMIC GOITRE, Most common type of hyperthyroidism (oversecretion of thyroid hormone), usually with goitre and exophthalmos (eyeball protrusion). Increased thyroid hormone levels result in increased cardiac output, rapid heartbeat, and possibly heart failure. Stress may trigger a severe worsening (thyroid storm), which can lead to circulatory collapse and death. Graves disease is considered an autoimmune disease. It can sometimes be controlled by drugs; severe cases require partial or total removal of the thyroid gland. Graves disease is named after Robert James Graves, one of the first physicians to fully describe the disease.

gravitational radiation, The transmission of variations in the gravitational field as waves. According to general relativity, the curvature of space-time is determined by the distribution of masses, and the motion of masses is determined by the curvature. In consequence, variations of the gravitational field should be transmitted from place to place as waves, just as variations of an electromagnetic field travel as waves. Gravitational radiation has only been indirectly observed.

gravity, Universal force of attraction that acts between all bodies that have mass. Though it is the weakest of the four known forces, it shapes the structure and evolution of stars, galaxies, and the entire universe. The laws of gravity describe the trajectories of bodies in the solar system and the motion of objects on Earth, where all bodies experience a downward gravitational force exerted by Earth's mass, the force experienced as weight. Isaac Newton was the first to develop a quantitative theory of gravity, holding that the force of attraction between two bodies is proportional to the product of their masses and inversely proportional to the square of the distance between them. Albert Einstein proposed a whole new concept of gravity, involving the four-dimensional continuum of space-time, which is curved by the presence of matter. In his general theory of relativity, he showed that a body undergoing uniform acceleration is indistinguishable from one that is stationary in a gravitational field.

gravity, centre of, Imaginary point where the total weight of a material body may be thought to be concentrated. Since weight and mass are proportional, the same point may also be called the centre of mass, but the centre of mass does not require a gravitational field. A body's centre of gravity may coincide with its geometric centre, especially if the body is symmetric and composed of homogeneous material. In asymmetric, unhomogeneous, or hollow objects, the centre of gravity may be at some distance from the geometric centre or even at a point in space external to the object, such as between the legs of a chair.

Graz, City (pop., 2001: 226,424), capital of Steiermark (Styria) state, southeastern Austria. The country's second largest city, it lies on the Mur River at the foot of the Styrian Alps. It grew from a fortress settlement and received town rights *c.* AD 1240. It became the centre of Steiermark during the Middle Ages and was the residence of the Leopoldine Habsburgs after 1379. Its fortifications, built in the 15th and 16th centuries, successfully withstood numerous sieges by Hungarians and Turks; the fortifications were converted into parks in the 19th century. Astronomer Johannes Kepler taught at its university, founded in 1585. A rail and industrial centre, Graz has an active trade in agricultural products; tourism is also important.

Great Australian Bight, Bay of the Indian Ocean, southern Australian coast. Its generally accepted boundaries are from Cape Pasley, Western Australia, to Cape Carnot, South Australia—a distance of 720 mi (1,160 km). The head of the bight abuts on the arid Nullarbor Plain and is bounded by cliffs 200–400 ft (60–120 m) high. Near Eucla on the bight's shores is the Nuytsland Reserve. Lying in the track of the winter western winds, the bight has a reputation for storms and rough seas.

Great Barrier Reef, Extensive complex of coral reefs, shoals, and islets in the Pacific Ocean, off the northeastern coast of Australia. The largest deposit of coral in the world, it extends for more than 1,250 mi (2,000 km) along the coast of Queensland and has an area of some 135,000 sq mi (350,000 sq km). The reef has been formed over millions of years from the skeletons of a mass of living marine organisms. In addition to at least 300 species of hard coral, marine life includes anemones, worms, gastropods, lobsters, crayfish, prawns, crabs, and a variety of fishes. Encrusting red algae form the purplish red algal rim that is one of the reef's characteristic features. A major tourist attraction, nearly all of it is within Great Barrier Reef National Park; the reef was designated a UNESCO World Heritage site in 1981.

Great Britain, or BRITAIN, Island, western Europe. It is the largest island in Europe, comprising England, Scotland, and Wales and covering 88,787 sq mi (229,957 sq km). With Northern Ireland, it constitutes the United Kingdom of Great Britain and Northern Ireland. Less formally, the names Great Britain and Britain are used to refer to the entire United Kingdom.

Great Depression, Longest and most severe economic depression ever experienced by the Western world. It began in the U.S. soon after the New York Stock Market Crash of 1929 and lasted until about 1939. By late 1932 stock values had dropped to about 20% of their previous value, and by 1933 11,000 of the U.S.'s 25,000 banks had failed for a combination of reasons, including declining property values, bank runs by panicked customers, and defaults on loans. These and other conditions—worsened by monetary policy mistakes, adherence to the gold standard (until 1933), and the introduction of voluntary wage-and-price controls through the National Recovery Administration—led to much-reduced levels of demand and hence of production, resulting in high unemployment (by 1932, 25–30%). Since the U.S. was the major creditor and financier of postwar Europe, the U.S. financial breakdown precipitated or exacerbated economic failures around the world, especially in Britain and Germany. Isolationism spread as nations sought to protect domestic production by imposing tariffs and quotas, ultimately reducing the value of international trade by more than half by 1932. The Great Depression contributed to political upheaval. It led to the election of U.S. Pres. Franklin Roosevelt, who upon taking office declared a national "bank holiday" during which all banks were closed until being deemed solvent by government inspectors. He also introduced major changes in the structure of the U.S. economy through his New Deal programs of economic relief and reform. The Great Depression also advanced Adolf Hitler's rise to power in Germany in 1933 and fomented political extremism in other countries. Before the Great Depression, governments relied on impersonal market forces to achieve economic correction. Afterward, government action came to assume a principal role in ensuring economic stability.

Great Fire of London (September 2–5, 1666) Worst fire in London's history. It destroyed a large part of the city, including most of the civic buildings, St. Paul's Cathedral, 87 parish churches, and about 13,000 houses. It began accidentally at the house of the king's baker in Pudding Lane near London Bridge, and a violent east wind encouraged the flames. On the fourth day houses were blown up by gunpowder to master the fire. The Thames River swarmed with vessels filled with people trying to save their goods, and some fled to the hills of Hampstead and Highgate, but most of the houseless Londoners settled in Moorfields.

great horned owl, Horned owl species (*Bubo virginianus*) that ranges from Arctic tree limits south to the Strait of Magellan. A powerful, mottled-brown predator, it is often more than 2 ft (60 cm) long, with a wingspan often approaching 80 in. (200 cm). It usually eats small rodents and birds, but has been known to carry off larger prey. Adapted to desert and forest, the species migrates only when food is scarce.

Great Lakes, Chain of lakes, east-central North America. Comprising Lakes Superior, Michigan, Huron, Erie, and Ontario, it forms a natural boundary between the U.S. and Canada. The Great Lakes cover an area of about 94,850 sq mi (245,660 sq km) and constitute the largest freshwater surface in the world. Connected to form a single waterway that discharges down the St. Lawrence River into the Atlantic Ocean, with the St. Lawrence Seaway they form a shipping lane more than 2,000 mi (3,200 km) long that carries oceangoing traffic as far west as Duluth, Minn. Large quantities of iron ore, coal, grain, and manufactured goods are moved between lake ports and shipped overseas. While commercial fishing was once a major industry on the lakes, pollution and other factors led to its collapse; recovery has been slow and partial. The lakes are used for many recreational activities, including boating and sailing.

Great Mosque of Eṣfahān, Persian MASJED-E JĀMIʿ, Complex of buildings, chiefly of the Seljūq period, in Eṣfahān, Iran. The mosque (completed c. 1130) has a central courtyard framed by four huge *eyvān*s, or vaulted niches. It is renowned for its fine brickwork, vaulting, and two domed sanctuaries. The brick dome of the main sanctuary (c. 1070–75) is supported by heavy piers. The smaller domed chamber (1088) is known for its beauty of proportion; its dome, resting on a series of arches, is a structural masterpiece. The dome and the four-*eyvān* plan became standard for Seljūq mosques.

Great Mother of the Gods, or CYBELE, Deity of the ancient Mediterranean world. Her cult originated in Phrygia in Asia Minor and spread to the Greek world, where she was identified with Rhea. It reached Rome by the 3rd century BC and became a major cult during the empire. Known by a variety of local names, Cybele was venerated as the universal mother of gods, humans, and animals. Her lover was the fertility god Attis. Her priests, the Galli, castrated themselves when they entered her service, and on her festival day they spattered their blood on her altar and her sacred pine tree.

Cybele, terra-cotta statuette, from Camirus, Rhodes, early 5th century BC; in the British Museum, London.

Great Plague of London (1664–66) Epidemic of plague that ravaged London, killing more than 75,000 of a total population estimated at 460,000. As early as 1625, 40,000 Londoners had died of the plague, but this was the worst and the last of the epidemics. Most of the devastation was in the city's outskirts, in areas where the poor were densely crowded. The disease spread throughout the country, but from 1667 only sporadic cases appeared until 1679. The plague's decline was attributed to various causes, including the Great Fire of London. Daniel Defoe's *Journal of the Plague Year* (1722) provides a valuable picture of the time.

Great Plains, Continental slope of central North America. It stretches from the Rio Grande at the U.S.-Mexico border in the south to the Mackenzie River delta along the Arctic Ocean in the north and from the Interior Lowlands and the Canadian Shield in the east to the Rocky Mountains in the west. The plains embrace parts of 10 U.S. states and 3 Canadian provinces, covering an area of about 1,125,000 sq mi (2,900,000 sq km). A high plateau of semiarid grassland, these prairie regions in the U.S. and Canada produce the major proportion of wheat grown in each country and are important cattle- and sheep-herding areas. Parts of the plains have reserves of coal and lignite, petroleum, and natural gas.

Great Red Spot, Storm system on the planet Jupiter. It is a high-pressure centre that moves in longitude but remains centred at about latitude 22° south. Oval in shape, it measures about 12,000 km (7,500 mi) north to south, roughly the diameter of Earth, and 20,000 km (12,400 mi) east to west. It has been observed continuously since 1878. Its colour varies from brick-red to brownish; it tends to change colour over a period of years. See photograph above.

Jupiter's Great Red Spot (top right) and the surrounding region. Below the spot is one of the large white ovals associated with the feature.

Great Rift Valley, or RIFT VALLEY, or EAST AFRICAN RIFT SYSTEM, Rift system, extending from Jordan in the Middle East south to Mozambique in southern Africa. It is some 4,000 mi (6,400 km) long and averages 30–40 mi (48–64 km) wide. The rift has been forming for some 30 million years, as Africa and the Arabian Peninsula separate, and has produced such massifs as Kilimanjaro and Mount Kenya. The system's main branch, the Eastern Rift Valley, is occupied in the north by the Jordan River, the Dead Sea, and the Gulf of Aqaba. It continues south along the Red Sea to several lakes in Kenya. Less obvious in Tanzania, with its eastern rim eroded, it continues south to the Indian Ocean near Beira, Mozam. The western branch of the system, the Western Rift Valley, extends north from the northern end of Lake Malawi in an arc that includes lakes Rukwa, Tanganyika, Kivu, Edward, and Albert.

Great Saint Bernard Pass, ancient MONS JOVIS, Pass in the Alps. One of the highest of the Alpine frontier passes, at 8,100 ft (2,469 m) it lies on the Italian-Swiss border east of the Mont Blanc group and connects Martigny-Ville, Switz., with Aosta, Italy. Historically the most important trans-Alpine route, it was often used by pilgrims to Rome and later by medieval armies. In 1800 it was crossed by Napoleon and his 40,000 troops on their way to northern Italy. A famous hospice on the pass, founded by St. Bernard of Menthon in the 11th century, is still kept by Augustinian monks who, with their St. Bernard dogs, provide services to travelers. The old road, open only five months a year, has been partly superseded by a tunnel beneath the pass, which allows year-round travel.

Great Salt Lake, Lake, northern Utah, U.S. It is the largest inland body of salt water in the Western Hemisphere and one of the most saline in the world. It fluctuates greatly in size, depending on rates of evaporation and the flow of the rivers into it. Its surface area has varied from about 2,400 sq mi (6,200 sq km) at its highest levels in 1873 and the mid 1980s to about 950 sq mi (2,460 sq km) at its low level in 1963. At times of median water level, it is generally less than 15 ft (4.5 m) deep. Surrounded by stretches of sand, salt land, and marsh, the lake remains isolated, though in recent years it has become important as a source of minerals, as a beach and water-sports attraction, and as a wildlife preserve.

Great Victoria Desert, Arid region, Western Australia and South Australia. Lying between Gibson Desert on the north and Nullarbor Plain on the south, it extends east from Kalgoorlie almost to the Stuart Range. Much of its eastern end is occupied by the Central and North West Aboriginal reserves. A vast expanse of sand hills, it is crossed by the Laverton–Warburton Mission Track, which links the mission station in the Warburton Range with Laverton, 350 mi (560 km) southwest. There are several national parks and reserves in the area, including the Great Victoria Desert Nature Reserve and the Nullarbor National Park.

Great Wall of China, Chinese WANLI CHANGCHENG, Defensive wall, northern China. One of the largest building-construction projects ever carried out, it runs (with all its branches) about 4,500 mi (7,300 km) east to west from the Bo Hai (Gulf of Chihli) to a point deep in Central Asia. Large parts of the fortification date from the 7th to the 4th century BCE. In the 3rd century BCE the emperor Shihuangdi connected existing defensive walls into a single system fortified by watchtowers. These served both to guard the rampart and to communicate with the capital, Xianyang (near modern Xi'an) by signal—smoke by day and fire by night. Originally constructed partly of masonry and earth, it was faced with brick in its eastern portion. It was rebuilt in later times, especially in the 15th and 16th centuries. The basic wall is about 23–26 ft (7–8 m) high; at intervals towers rise above it to varying heights. It was designated a UNESCO World Heritage site in 1987.

great white shark, or WHITE SHARK, Large, aggressive shark (*Carcharodon carcharias*, family Lamnidae), considered the species most dangerous to humans. It is found in tropical and temperate regions of all oceans and is noted for its voracious appetite. Its diet includes fishes, sea turtles, birds, sea lions, small whales, carcasses, and ships' garbage. The great white is heavy-bodied and has a crescent-shaped tail and large, saw-edged, triangular teeth. It can reach a length of more than 20 ft (6 m) and is generally gray, bluish, or brownish, with the colour shading suddenly into a whitish belly. Though it is widely feared, only a few hundred humans are known to have ever been killed by the great white shark.

Great Zimbabwe, Extensive stone ruins in southeastern Zimbabwe. Located southeast of Masvingo, Zimbabwe, it is the largest of many such ruins in southern Africa. The primary ruins of this former city extend more than 60 acres (24 hectares) and include a hilltop fortress and walls of stone monoliths. The centre of a great inland empire ruled by the Karanga (Shona) people who traded on the shores of the Indian Ocean, Great Zimbabwe flourished between the 11th and 15th centuries. Portuguese explorers probably encountered the ruins in the 16th century, but it was not until the late 19th century that the existence of the ruins was confirmed, generating much archaeological research. Great Zimbabwe was named a UNESCO World Heritage site in 1986.

Greco, El, orig. DOMÉNIKOS THEOTOKÓPOULOS (b. 1541, Candia, Crete—d. April 7, 1614, Toledo, Spain), Cretan-born Spanish painter, the first great master of Spanish painting. Documentation on his early life is limited, but it is known that he was in Venice c. 1566–70 and may have studied in Titian's workshop. In 1572 he was a member of the guild of St. Luke in Rome. His first commission in Spain (1577) was for altarpieces for the church of Santo Domingo el Antiguo in Toledo (1577–79); the paintings for the high altar show the influence of Titian and Michelangelo. In these works he developed his signature style: he chose a method of space elimination that is common to middle and late 16th-century Italian painters known as Mannerists. The elogonated figures in these works were also characteristic of his oeuvre. El Greco's Mannerist method of composition is nowhere more clearly expressed than in his masterpiece, *The Burial of the Count de Orgaz* (1586–88), where all of the action takes place in the frontal plane. From 1590 until his death his output was prodigious. His major commissions included the complete altar composition for the Hospital de la Caridad at Illescas (1603–05), for which he also worked as architect and sculptor. He excelled as a portraitist. His workshop produced many replicas of his works, but his style was so individual that his only followers were his son and a few forgotten imitators.

Greece, officially HELLENIC REPUBLIC, Country, Balkan Peninsula, southeastern Europe. Area: 50,949 sq mi (131,957 sq km). Population: (2011 est.) 11,372,000. Capital: Athens. The people are predominantly Greek. Language: Greek (official). Religion: Christianity (predominantly Eastern Orthodox [official]). Currency: euro. The land, with its 2,000-odd islands and extensive coastline, is intimately linked with the sea. About one-fifth of this mountainous country consists of lowland, much of this as coastal plains along the Aegean or as mountain valleys and small plains near river mouths. The interior is dominated by the Pindus (Modern Greek: Píndos) Mountains, which extend from Albania on Greece's northwestern border into the Peloponnese (Pelopónnisos). Mount Olympus (Ólympos) is the country's highest peak. Among the Greek islands are the Aegean and Ionian groups and Crete (Kríti). The climate is Mediterranean. Greece has an advanced developing economy characterized mainly by private enterprise and based on agriculture, manufacturing, and tourism. It

is a unitary multiparty republic with one legislative house; the head of state is the president, and the head of government is the prime minister. The earliest urban society in Greece was the palace-centred Minoan civilization, which reached its height on Crete c. 2000 BCE. It was succeeded by the mainland Mycenaean civilization, which arose c. 1600 BCE following a wave of Indo-European invasions. About 1200 BCE a second wave of invasions destroyed the Bronze Age cultures, and a Dark Age followed, known mostly through the epics of Homer. At the end of this time, Classical Greece began to emerge (c. 750 BCE) as a collection of independent city-states, including Sparta in the Peloponnese and Athens in Attica. The civilization reached its zenith after repelling the Persians at the beginning of the 5th century BCE and began to decline after the civil strife of the Peloponnesian War at the century's end. In 338 BCE the Greek city-states were taken over by Philip II of Macedon, and Greek culture was spread by Philip's son Alexander the Great throughout his empire. The Romans, themselves heavily influenced by Greek culture, conquered the city-states in the 2nd century BCE. After the fall of Rome, Greece remained part of the Byzantine Empire until the mid-15th century, when it became part of the expanding Ottoman Empire; it gained its independence in 1832. It was occupied by Nazi Germany during World War II. Civil war followed and lasted until 1949, when communist forces were defeated. In 1952 Greece joined NATO. A military junta ruled the country from 1967 to 1974, when democracy was restored and a referendum declared an end to the Greek monarchy. In 1981 Greece joined the European Community, the first eastern European country to do so. Upheavals in the Balkans in the 1990s strained Greece's relations with some neighbouring states. Greece revised its constitution in 2001.

Greek alphabet, Writing system developed in Greece c. 1000 BC, the direct or indirect ancestor of all modern European alphabets. Derived from the North Semitic alphabet via that of the Phoenicians, it modified an all-consonant alphabet to represent vowels. Letters for sounds not found in Greek became the Greek letters *alpha*, *epsilon*, *iota*, *omicron*, and *upsilon*, representing the vowels *a*, *e*, *i*, *o*, and *u*. This greatly increased the accuracy and legibility of the new system. While the Chalcidian version of the Greek alphabet probably gave rise to the Etruscan alphabet and thus indirectly to the Latin alphabet, in 403 BC Athens officially adopted the Ionic version. This became the classical Greek alphabet, which had 24 letters, all of them capitals—ideal for monuments; various scripts better suited to handwriting were later derived from it.

Greek fire, Any of several flammable mixtures used in ancient and medieval warfare, particularly a petroleum-based mixture invented by the Byzantine Greeks in the 7th century. Flammable materials such as pitch and sulfur had been used in war since ancient times, but true Greek fire was especially deadly. Thrown in pots or discharged from tubes, it apparently caught fire spontaneously, and water could not put it out. Greek fire launched from tubes mounted on ship prows wrought havoc on the Arab fleet attacking Constantinople in 673. Its effectiveness was a prime reason for the long survival of the Byzantine Empire. The recipe was so secret that its precise composition remains unknown.

Greek language, Indo-European language spoken mostly in Greece. Its history can be divided into four phases: Ancient Greek, Koine, Byzantine Greek, and Modern Greek. Ancient Greek is subdivided into Mycenaean Greek (14th–13th centuries BC) and Archaic and Classical Greek (8th–4th centuries BC). The language of the latter periods had numerous dialects (e.g., Ionic, Attic). The second phase, Koine (Hellenistic Greek), arose during the reign of Alexander the Great in the 4th century BC. A common language with simplified grammar, it spread throughout the Hellenized world. Purists who rejected Koine as a corruption of Attic Greek successfully advocated adoption of the Classical language for all writing. Thus, the written form, Byzantine Greek (5th–15th centuries AD), stayed rooted in the Attic tradition while the spoken language continued to develop. Modern Greek, dating from the 15th century, has many local dialects. Standard Modern Greek, Greece's official written and spoken language, is largely based on a form called Demotic (used in popular speech) but includes elements of Katharevusa, the written language formerly used in government and public life.

Greek law, Legal systems of the ancient Greeks. Each city-state administered its own laws, many of which were laid down in written statutes. The harsh law code of Draco and the more humane one of Solon are two of the most famous. Unlike Roman law, Greek law produced little analytical jurisprudence, though the philosophers examined abstract concepts of justice. Those who sat in judgment based their verdicts less on notions of equity than on the statutes' literal meaning. Both private and criminal procedures began with the summoning of the defendant to the magistrate and the filing of a written complaint. A type of arbitration was available in civil suits. Enforcement of a judgment was generally left to the plaintiff.

Greek mythology, Oral and literary traditions of the ancient Greeks concerning their gods and heroes and the nature and history of the cosmos. The Greek myths and legends are known today primarily from Greek literature, including such classic works as Homer's *Iliad* and *Odyssey*, Hesiod's *Works and Days* and *Theogony*, Ovid's *Metamorphoses*, and the dramas of Aeschylus, Sophocles, and Euripides. The myths deal with the creation of the gods and the world, the struggle among the gods for supremacy and the triumph of Zeus, the love affairs and quarrels of the gods, and the effects of their adventures and powers on the mortal world, including their link with natural phenomena such as thunderstorms or the seasons and their connection with cultic sites or rituals. Among the great stories of Greek mythology and legend are those of the Trojan War, the voyage of Odysseus, Jason's search for the Golden Fleece, the exploits of Heracles, the adventures of Theseus, and the tragedy of Oedipus.

Greek Orthodox Church, Independent Eastern Orthodox church of Greece. The term is sometimes used erroneously for Eastern Orthodoxy in general. It remained under the patriarch of Constantinople until 1833, when it became independent. It is governed by 67 metropolitan bishops, presided over by an archbishop.

Greek pottery, Pottery made in ancient Greece. Its painted decoration has become the primary source of information about the development of Greek pictorial art. It was made in a variety of sizes and shapes, according to its intended use; large vessels were used for storage and transportation of liquids (wine, olive oil, water), smaller pots for perfumes and unguents. The earliest style, known as the Geometric style (*c.* 1000–700 BC), features geometric patterns and, eventually, narrative scenes with stylized figures. From the late 8th to the early 7th century BC, a growing Eastern influence resulted in the "Orientalizing" of motifs (e.g., sphinx, griffin), notably in pieces made in Corinth (*c.* 700 BC), where the painters developed black-figure pottery. Athenians adopted the black-figure style and from 600 BC on became the dominant manufacturers of Greek pottery. They invented red-figure pottery *c.* 530 BC. By the 4th century BC the figured decoration of pottery had declined, and by the end of the century it had died out in Athens.

Greek religion, Beliefs, rituals, and mythology of the ancient Greeks. Though the worship of the sky god Zeus began as early as the 2nd millennium BC, Greek religion in the established sense began *c.* 750 BC and lasted for over a thousand years, extending its influence throughout the Mediterranean world and beyond. The Greeks had numerous gods who controlled various natural or social forces (e.g., Poseidon the sea, Demeter the harvest, Hera marriage). Different deities were worshiped in different localities, but Homer's epics helped create a unified religion, in which the major gods were believed to live on Mount Olympus under the rule of Zeus. The Greeks also worshiped various gods of the countryside:

Pan, nymphs, naiads, dryads, Nereids, and satyrs, along with the Furies and the Fates. Heroes from the past, such as Heracles and Asclepius, were also venerated. Animal sacrifices were of great importance, usually made at a temple on the altar of the god. Other cultic activities included prayers, libations, processions, athletic contests, and divination, particularly through oracles and birds. Great religious festivals included the City Dionysia at Athens and the festival of Zeus in the western Peloponnese that included the Olympic Games. Death was seen as a hateful state; the dead lived in the realm of Hades, and only heroes enjoyed Elysium. Great wrongdoers suffered in Tartarus. Mystery religions emerged to satisfy the desire for personal guidance, salvation, and immortality. Greek religion faded with the rise of Christianity and lost its last great advocate with the death of Julian in AD 363.

Greek Revival, Architectural style based on 5th-century-BC Greek temples that spread throughout Europe and the U.S. in the early 19th century. The revival was symptomatic of the public's preoccupation with Greek culture at the time. Architects often tacked majestic facades with Grecian columns onto existing buildings; banks and institutions became imitation Doric temples; and homes in the Greek Revival style often had large porticoes made up of heavy pilasters and reinterpreted pediments. The British Museum (1847), utilizing the Greek Ionic order on a massive scale, is the most powerful English example of the style. In the U.S., where the style was adopted on a large scale, many strange distortions found acceptance.

green revolution, Great increase in production of food grains (especially wheat and rice) that resulted in large part from the introduction into developing countries of new, high-yielding varieties, beginning in the mid-20th century. Its early dramatic successes were in Mexico and the Indian subcontinent. The new varieties require large amounts of chemical fertilizers and pesticides to produce their high yields, raising concerns about cost and potentially harmful environmental effects. Poor farmers, unable to afford the fertilizers and pesticides, have often reaped even lower yields with these grains than with the older strains, which were better adapted to local conditions and had some resistance to pests and diseases.

greenhouse effect, Warming of the Earth's surface and lower atmosphere caused by water vapour, carbon dioxide, and other trace gases in the atmosphere. Visible light from the Sun heats the Earth's surface. Part of this energy is radiated back into the atmosphere in the form of infrared radiation, much of which is absorbed by molecules of carbon dioxide and water vapour in the atmosphere and reradiated toward the surface as more heat. (Despite the name, the greenhouse effect is different from the warming in a greenhouse, where panes of glass allow the passage of visible light but hold heat inside the building by trapping warmed air.) The absorption of infrared radiation causes the Earth's surface and lower atmosphere to warm more than they otherwise would, making the Earth's surface habitable. An increase in atmospheric carbon dioxide caused by widespread combustion of fossil fuels may intensify the greenhouse effect and cause long-term climatic changes. Likewise, an increase in atmospheric concentrations of other trace greenhouse gases such as chlorofluorocarbons, nitrous oxide, and methane resulting from human activities may also intensify the greenhouse effect. From the beginning of the Industrial Revolution through the end of the 20th century, the amount of carbon dioxide in the atmosphere increased 30% and the amount of methane more than doubled. It is also estimated that the U.S. is responsible for about one-fifth of all human-produced greenhouse-gas emissions.

Greenland, Island and self-governing overseas administrative division of Denmark, in the North Atlantic Ocean. It is the world's largest island. Area: 836,330 sq mi (2,166,086 sq km). Population: (2011 est.) 56,700. Capital: Nuuk. Two-thirds of it lies within the Arctic Circle. It is dominated by the massive Greenland Ice Sheet.

Fishing is central to the economy; there are also commercial mineral deposits, including a large gold deposit, as well as offshore oil exploration. About four-fifths of the population are native Greenlanders, principally of Inuit descent, residing in coastal areas. The Inuit probably crossed to northwestern Greenland from mainland North America, along the islands of the Canadian Arctic, from about 2500 BCE to about 1100 CE. The Norwegian Erik the Red visited Greenland in 982; his son Leif Eriksson introduced Christianity in the 11th century. The original Norse settlements became extinct in the 15th century, but Greenland was recolonized by Denmark in 1721. Greenland became part of the Kingdom of Denmark in 1953. Home rule was established in 1979. At the beginning of the 21st century, the movement for full independence began to gain support, as did the belief among many scientists that global warming was responsible for the accelerated melting of the ice sheet.

Greenpeace, International environmental organization. Founded in Canada in 1971 to oppose U.S. nuclear testing in Alaska, it later expanded its goals to include saving endangered species, stopping environmental abuses, and increasing public awareness of environmental problems. It has specialized in "direct, nonviolent action" in protests often designed to garner wide publicity. Its members have frequently steered small inflatable craft between the harpoon guns of whalers and their prey. In 1985 the *Rainbow Warrior*, a Greenpeace ship being used to obstruct French nuclear testing in the South Pacific, was sunk by French agents, resulting in the death of a photographer. Greenpeace has offices in some 40 countries.

Greenwich, Outer borough (pop., 2001: 214,403), Greater London, on the southern bank of the River Thames. The meridian that passes through the borough serves as the basis for standard time as well as for reckonings of longitude throughout the world. Greenwich Park was enclosed by the duke of Gloucester in 1433; it was the site of the Royal Observatory (founded 1675). Other historic buildings include the Queen's House, now part of the National Maritime Museum, and the Royal Naval College (1873–1998). These and other historic places were designated a UNESCO World Heritage site in 1997. The Millennium Dome, constructed in the 1990s, was used for millennial celebrations to usher in the year 2000.

Greenwich Mean Time (GMT), Former name for mean solar time of the longitude (0°) of the former Royal Observatory at Greenwich, England, or Greenwich meridian. GMT was used to avoid potentially confusing references to local time systems (zones). In accord with tradition, 0000 GMT (denoting the start of a solar day) occurred at noon. In 1925 the numbering system for GMT was changed so that the day (like the civil day) began at midnight. Some confusion resulted, and in 1928 the International Astronomical Union changed the designation of the standard time of the zero meridian to Universal Time, which remains in general use. The term GMT is still used for some purposes (including navigation) in English-speaking countries.

Gregorian calendar, Solar dating system now in general use. It was proclaimed in 1582 by Pope Gregory XIII as a reform of the Julian calendar. By the Julian reckoning, the solar year comprised 365¼ days. The addition of a "leap day" every four years was intended to maintain correspondence between the calendar and the seasons; however, a slight inaccuracy in the measurement of the solar year caused the calendar dates of the seasons to regress almost one day per century. By Pope Gregory's time, the Julian calendar was 10 days out of sync with the seasons; in 1582, to bring the vernal equinox (and thus Easter) back to its proper date, 10 days were dropped (October 5 became October 15). Most of Catholic Europe soon adopted the new calendar; Great Britain and its colonies (1752) and Russia (1918) followed much later. The Gregorian calendar differs from the Julian only in that no century year is a leap year unless it is exactly divisible by 400 (e.g., 1600,

2000). A further refinement, the designation of years evenly divisible by 4,000 as common (not leap) years, will keep the calendar accurate to within one day in 20,000 years.

Gregorian chant, Liturgical music of the Roman Catholic church consisting of unaccompanied melody sung in unison to Latin words. It is named for Pope Gregory I, who may have contributed to its collection and codification and who was traditionally represented as having received all the melodies directly from the Holy Spirit. Of the five bodies of medieval Latin liturgical music, it is the dominant repertoire, and the name is often used broadly to include them all. Gregorian chant apparently derived principally from Jewish cantillation, with other elements entering from the Eastern Church and elsewhere. Chant has traditionally been performed at the mass and the canonical hours (the eight prayer services traditionally held daily in monasteries). Its texts come primarily from the biblical psalms, metrical hymns, and texts specific to the mass and the hours. The melodies are classified as belonging to one or another of the eight church modes. Chant rhythm is not strictly metrical, and its notation does not indicate rhythm. Since the Second Vatican Council, the performance of chant has diminished greatly.

Gregory I, Saint, known as GREGORY THE GREAT (b. *c.* 540, Rome—d. March 12, 604, Rome), Pope (590–604) and doctor of the church. A Roman patrician, by age 32 he had attained the office of urban prefect. He then felt called to the religious life. He built several monasteries and served as a papal representative before being elected pope in 590, to which he only reluctantly assented. He became the architect of the medieval papacy, seeking, among other things, to curb corruption by centralizing the papal administration. In 598 he won temporary peace with the Lombards, and he allowed the Byzantine usurper Phocas to make permanent peace with them in 602. Eager to convert pagan peoples, Gregory sent Augustine of Canterbury on a mission to England (596). Under Gregory, Gothic Arian Spain *see* Arianism) became reconciled with Rome. He laid the basis for the Papal States. He was a strong opponent of slavery, and he extended tolerance to Jews. He wrote the *Pastoral Rule*, a guide for church government, and other works. His extensive recodification of the liturgy and chant led to his name being given to Gregorian chant. He is remembered as one of the greatest of all the medieval popes.

Gregory VII, Saint, orig. HILDEBRAND (b. 1020, near Soana, Papal States—d. May 25, 1085, Salerno, Principality of Salerno; canonized 1606; feast day May 25), Pope (1073–85). Educated in a monastery in Rome where his uncle was abbot, he rose to become a cardinal and archdeacon of Rome and was finally chosen pope in 1073. One of the great medieval reformers, Gregory attacked simony and clerical marriage and insisted that his papal legates had authority over local bishops. He is remembered chiefly for his conflict with Emperor Henry IV in the Investiture Controversy. Gregory's excommunication of the emperor gave rise to a bitter quarrel that ended when Henry begged for forgiveness in a memorable scene at Canossa, Italy, in 1077. A renewed quarrel led Gregory to excommunicate the emperor again in 1080, and Henry's forces took Rome in 1084. Gregory was rescued by Robert Guiscard, but the devastation of Rome forced the pope to withdraw to Salerno, where he died.

Grenada, Island country, Lesser Antilles, Caribbean Sea. Area: 133 sq mi (344 sq km). Population: (2011 est.) 108,000. Capital: St. George's. Most Grenadans are of African or mixed (primarily African-European) ancestry; many of the rest are of South Asian descent. Language: English (official). Religions: Christianity (mostly Roman Catholic; also Protestant); also Rastafarianism. Currency: East Caribbean dollar. Grenada is the most southerly of the Lesser Antilles, lying about 100 mi (160 km) north of Venezuela; its territory includes the southern Grenadines. Volcanic in origin, it is dominated by a thickly forested mountain ridge rising to 2,757 ft (840 m) at Mount St. Catherine. The southern coast is indented with beaches and natural harbours. The tropical maritime climate supports rich vegetation. Often called the Isle of Spice, Grenada is known for its nutmeg, cinnamon, and vanilla as well as for cocoa. It has a developing market economy dependent on agricultural exports and tourism. The head of state is the British sovereign, represented by the governor-general; the head of government is the prime minister. The warlike Carib Indians dominated Grenada when Christopher Columbus sighted the island in 1498 and named it Concepción; the Caribs ruled it for the next 150 years. In the early 1670s it became subject to the French crown and remained so until 1762, when British forces captured it. In 1833 the island's black slaves were freed. Grenada was the headquarters of the government of the British Windward Islands (1885–1958) and a member of the West Indies Federation (1958–62). It became a self-governing state in association with Britain in 1967 and gained its independence in 1974. In 1979 a left-wing government took control in a bloodless coup. Relations with its U.S.-oriented Latin American neighbours became strained as Grenada leaned toward Cuba and the Soviet bloc. In order to counter this trend, the U.S. invaded the island in 1983; democratic self-government was reestablished in 1984. Grenada's relations with Cuba, once suspended, were restored in 1997.

grenade, Small explosive, chemical, or gas bomb used at short range. Invented in the 15th century, it became so important that 17th-century European armies had specially trained grenade throwers, or grenadiers. After *c.* 1750 grenades were largely abandoned because the increasing range and accuracy of firearms had lessened opportunities for close combat. They returned to widespread use in the 20th century, when their effectiveness in World War I trench warfare made them a standard part of the combat infantryman's equipment, which they have remained. Most common is the explosive grenade, with a core of TNT or another high explosive encased in an iron jacket and a fuse that detonates it either on impact or after a brief (usually four-second) delay. Chemical and gas grenades generally burn rather than explode.

Gresham's law, Observation that "bad money drives out good." It is named for Sir Thomas Gresham (1519–1579), financial agent of Queen Elizabeth I, who was one of the first to elucidate it (he had been preceded by Copernicus). The meaning expressed is that, if two coins have the same face value but are made from metals of unequal value, the cheaper will tend to drive the other out of circulation; the more valuable coin will be hoarded or used for foreign exchange instead of for domestic transactions.

Grimm, Brothers, German folklorists and philologists. Jacob Ludwig Carl Grimm (b. Jan. 4, 1785, Hanau, Hesse-Kassel [Germany]—d. Sept. 20, 1863, Berlin) and Wilhelm Carl Grimm (b. Feb. 24, 1786, Hanau, Hesse-Kassel [Germany]—d. Dec. 16, 1859, Berlin) spent most of their lives in literary research as librarians and professors at the Universities of Göttingen and Berlin. They are most famous for *Kinder- und Hausmärchen* (1812–15), known in English as *Grimm's Fairy Tales*, a collection of 200 tales taken mostly from oral sources, which helped establish the science of folklore. Together and separately, they also produced many other scholarly studies and editions. Wilhelm's chief solo work was *The German Heroic Tale* (1829); Jacob's *German Mythology* (1835) was a highly influential study of pre-Christian German faith and super-

Jacob (right) and Wilhelm Grimm, oil portrait by Elisabeth Jerichau-Baumann, 1855; in the National-Galerie, Berlin

Staatliche Museen zu Berlin—Preussischer Kulturbesitz

stition. Jacob's extensive *Deutsche Grammatik* (1819–37), on the grammars of all Germanic languages, elaborates the important linguistic principle now known as Grimm's law. In the 1840s the brothers worked on the *Deutsches Wörterbuch*, a vast historical dictionary of the German language that required several generations to complete.

gross domestic product (GDP), Total market value of the goods and services produced by a nation's economy during a specific period of time. GDP is customarily reported on an annual basis. It is defined to include all final goods and services—that is, those that are produced by the economic resources located in that nation regardless of their ownership and are not resold in any form. GDP differs from gross national product (GNP), which is defined to include all final goods and services produced by resources owned by that nation's residents, whether located in the nation or elsewhere.

Grotius, Hugo, orig. HUIGH DE GROOT (b. April 10, 1583, Delft, Neth.—d. Aug. 28, 1645, Rostock, Mecklinburg-Schwerin), Dutch jurist, humanist, and poet. He enrolled at Leiden University at age 11 and as a teenager accompanied Johan van Oldenbarnevelt on a mission to France, where he remained to study law and publish a book on politics (1598). Appointed the official historiographer of Holland, he wrote the history of the Dutch revolt against Spain. Increasingly involved in politics, he wrote a defense of Dutch trading rights for the Dutch East India Company and called for free access to the ocean for all nations. He became attorney general of Holland in 1607. Imprisoned in 1618 when his patron Oldenbarnevelt was executed by Prince Maurice, he escaped to Paris in 1621 (by hiding in a trunk of books) and returned 10 years later, having achieved great international prestige. His legal works advance the idea that nations are bound by natural law; his masterpiece, *On the Law of War and Peace* (1625), one of the first great contributions to modern international law, prescribes rules for the conduct of war. He also published many translations and works of classical scholarship.

Hugo Grotius, detail of a portrait by Michiel Janszoon van Mierevelt; in the Rijksmuseum, Amsterdam.

Courtesy of the Rijksmuseum, Amsterdam

groundwater, or SUBSURFACE WATER, Water that occurs below the surface of the Earth, where it occupies spaces in soils or geologic strata. Most groundwater comes from precipitation, which gradually percolates into the Earth. Typically, 10–20% of precipitation eventually enters aquifers. Most groundwater is free of pathogenic organisms, and purification for domestic or industrial use is not necessary. Furthermore, groundwater supplies are not seriously affected by short droughts and are available in many areas that do not have dependable surface water supplies.

group theory, In modern algebra, a system consisting of a set of elements and an operation for combining the elements, which together satisfy certain axioms. These require that the group be closed under the operation (the combination of any two elements produces another element of the group), that it obey the associative law, that it contain an identity element (which, combined with any other element, leaves the latter unchanged), and that each element have an inverse (which combines with an element to produce the identity element). If the group also satisfies the commutative law, it is called a commutative, or abelian, group. The set of integers under addition, where the identity element is 0 and the inverse is the negative of a positive number or vice versa, is an abelian group.

group therapy, Form of psychotherapy in which several patients or clients discuss their personal problems, usually in the presence of a therapist or counselor. In one approach to group therapy, the chief aim is to raise members' awareness and morale and combat feelings of isolation by cultivating a sense of belonging to the group; a notable example is Alcoholics Anonymous. The other principal approach strives to foster free discussion and uninhibited self-revelation; members are helped to self-understanding and more successful behaviour through mutual examination of their reactions to people in their lives, including one another.

growth hormone (GH), or SOMATOTROPIN, Peptide hormone secreted by the anterior lobe of the pituitary gland. It promotes growth of bone and other body tissues by stimulating protein synthesis and fat breakdown (for energy). Excessive production causes gigantism, acromegaly, or other malformations; deficient production results in dwarfism, dramatically relieved if GH is given before puberty. Genetic engineering techniques now permit large-scale production of adequate amounts of GH for that purpose.

Guadalajara, City (pop., 2000: city, 1,646,183; metro. area, 3,677,531), capital of Jalisco state, west-central Mexico. Mexico's second largest city, it lies near the Río Grande de Santiago at an elevation of about 5,100 ft (1,550 m). Founded by the Spanish in 1531, it was relocated several times under pressure from Indians. In 1810 it was occupied briefly by the independence leader Miguel Hidalgo. Since 1940 it has become a major industrial producer while retaining a rich agricultural trade. The governor's palace, begun in 1743, is a noted example of Spanish Mexican architecture. Guadalajara is the site of two universities.

Guadalcanal, Island, Solomon Islands, west-central South Pacific Ocean. The largest of the Solomon Islands, Guadalcanal has an area of 2,069 sq mi (5,358 sq km); the national capital, Honiara, lies on the northern coast. The economy is based mainly on fishing and agriculture, with some gold mining. The island was visited by the Spanish in the 16th century and by the British in the late 18th century; it was annexed in 1893 as part of the British Solomon Islands Protectorate. During World War II it was the scene of prolonged fighting between U.S. and Japanese forces (1942–43), which resulted in the Allied capture of a Japanese air base there. Several naval battles were also fought in the region. Ethnic tensions between Guadalcanal islanders and migrants from the nearby island of Malaita worsened after World War II. After the islands achieved independence from Great Britain in 1978, ethnically based disputes simmered on the island, sparking violence and rioting in the late 20th and early 21st centuries.

Guadalupe Hidalgo, Treaty of (Feb. 2, 1848) Treaty between the U.S. and Mexico that ended the Mexican War, named for the Mexico City neighbourhood where it was signed. It drew the U.S.-Mexico boundary at the Rio Grande and the Gila River. For $15 million the U.S. received more than 525,000 sq mi (1.36 million sq km) of land and agreed to settle the more than $3 million in claims made by U.S. citizens against Mexico. By leaving Mexicans unsure of their country's future and reopening the question of the expansion of slavery in the vast territory ceded to the U.S., the treaty was a factor in the civil wars that followed in both countries.

Guadeloupe, Overseas department and overseas region of France, eastern West Indies. Area: 629 sq mi (1,630 sq km). Population: (2011 est.) 407,000. Capital: Basse-Terre city. It consists of the twin islands of Basse-Terre and Grande-Terre, separated by the Salée River, a narrow channel. Until 2007 Guadeloupe also included the dependencies of Saint-Barthélemy and Saint-Martin

(the northern two-thirds of the island of Saint Martin), located 150 mi (240 km) to the northwest. Basse-Terre city was founded in 1643. The largest urban area, chief port, and economic hub is Pointe-à-Pitre on Grande-Terre. Forests and tree crops such as coffee abound on the mountains of Basse-Terre, while sugarcane is cultivated on the generally low-lying Grande-Terre. The Carib Indians held off the Spanish and French for a number of years before the islands became part of France in 1674. The British occupied Guadeloupe for short periods in the 18th–19th century; the islands became officially French in 1816. In 1946 they were made a department of France. The people of Saint-Barthélemy and Saint-Martin voted to secede from Guadeloupe in 2003, and in 2007 those territories became overseas collectivities of France. Tourism is a major part of Guadeloupe's economy.

Guam, Island, largest and southernmost of the Mariana Islands, Micronesia, North Pacific Ocean. Guam is an unincorporated U.S. territory. Area: 217 sq mi (561 sq km). Population: (2011 est.) 160,000. Capital: Hagåtña (Agana). Guam is divided into a northern plateau and a southern chain of volcanic hills. The indigenous population is Chamorro, Malayo-Indonesian with a considerable admixture of Spanish, Filipino, and Mexican ancestry. Chamorro and English are both official languages. Possibly visited by Ferdinand Magellan in 1521, Guam was formally claimed by Spain in 1565 and remained Spanish until it was ceded to the U.S. in 1898 after the Spanish-American War. During World War II the Japanese occupied the island (1941–44). It subsequently became a major U.S. air and naval base. In 1950 it was made a U.S. territory and placed under the Department of the Interior. The military bases and tourism are the island's economic mainstays.

Guan Hanqing, or KUAN HAN-CH'ING (b. 1241?, Dadu, China—d. 1320?, China), Chinese dramatist. He belonged to a writers' guild that provided plays for performing groups. His plays often dealt with everyday events and sympathetically portrayed women of low social standing. He wrote over 60 plays, 14 of which survive, including *Injustice to Dou E*, *Butterfly Dream*, and *Saving a Prostitute*. Guan is often considered the greatest playwright of the Chinese classical theatre.

Guangdong, or KUANG-TUNG, conventional KWANGTUNG, Southernmost mainland province (pop., 2002 est.: 78,590,000) of China. It is bounded by the South China Sea to the south, and along its coast are Hong Kong and Macau; also bordering it are Fujian, Jiangxi, and Hunan provinces and Guangxi autonomous region. It has an area of 76,100 sq mi (197,100 sq km). The capital is Guangzhou (Canton). It was first incorporated into the Chinese empire in 222 BCE. Overseas trade through Guangzhou swelled the population of the province in the 16th–17th century. It was the site of illicit opium importation by the British, which led to the first Opium War (1839–42). Kowloon was ceded to Britain in 1860 and Macau to Portugal in 1887; both were restored to China in the late 1990s. Guangdong was a base for the Nationalists under Sun Yat-sen from 1912. Japanese forces occupied the province in 1938–45. Its centuries of foreign contact have given it a degree of self-sufficiency that sets it apart from the rest of China; more recently it has developed several special economic zones.

Guangxi, or KUANG-HSI, conventional KWANGSI, in full ZHUANG AUTONOMOUS REGION OF GUANGXI, Autonomous region (pop., 2002 est.: 48,220,000), southern China. Lying on the Gulf of Tonkin, it is bordered by Vietnam and by Guangdong, Hunan, Guizhou, and Yunnan provinces. It has an area of 85,100 sq mi (220,400 sq km) and is largely hilly, with river valleys where rice is grown. The capital is Nanning. Its recorded history dates from 45 BCE, and it was given its present name during the Song dynasty (960–1279 CE). With Guangdong, it became the base of the Nationalists under Sun Yat-sen in the early 20th century. Local leaders later formed the Guangxi Clique in opposition to Chiang Kai-shek, who crushed their revolt in 1929. Guangxi was declared a province of the People's Republic of China in 1949, and in 1958 it became an autonomous region. Noted for its agricultural production, it is also an important source for forest products.

Guangzhou, or KUANG-CHOU, conventional CANTON, City (pop., 2003 est.: 4,653,131), capital of Guangdong province, China. Located on the Zhu (Pearl) River about 90 mi (145 km) from the sea, it is southern China's chief port. Incorporated into China's Qin empire (221–207 BCE), it later became an important city under the Ming dynasty. The first Chinese seaport opened to foreigners, it was regularly visited by Arab and Hindu traders and, in the 16th century, by the Portuguese. The English arrived in the 17th century, followed by the French and Dutch. Guangzhou's resistance to the English opium trade led to war (1839–42), and it was occupied by the British and French in 1856–61. In the late 19th century it was the seat of revolutionary political ideas promoted by the Nationalist Party. It was bombed and then occupied by the Japanese in 1938–45. Its industrial growth subsequently expanded, and, with China's renewed ties to the West from the late 1970s, it became one of several economic investment areas for foreigners. One of China's largest cities, its expanding economy added to the region's growth.

guano, Accumulated excrement and remains of birds, bats, and seals, valued as fertilizer. Bird guano comes mainly from islands off the coasts of Peru, Baja California, and Africa that are heavily populated by cormorants, pelicans, and gannets. Bat guano is found in caves throughout the world, and seal guano has accumulated to great depths on islands off northwestern Peru; both are lower in fertilizer value than bird guano.

Guatemala, officially REPUBLIC OF GUATEMALA, Country, Central America. Area: 42,130 sq mi (109,117 sq km). Population: (2011 est.) 14,729,000. Capital: Guatemala City. Mestizos make up more than three-fifths of the population; most of the rest are Indian, predominantly Maya. Language: Spanish (official). Religion: Christianity (predominantly Roman Catholic; also Protestant). Currency: quetzal, dollar. Guatemala has extensive lowlands in the Petén portion of the Yucatán Peninsula and along the littoral of the Caribbean Sea in the north. Mountains occupy much of the country and cut across its midsection. The northern tropical rainforests of the Petén produce fine woods and rubber. Guatemala has a developing market economy based largely on agriculture; coffee is one of its leading exports, along with sugar and bananas. It is a republic with one legislative body; its head of state and government is the president. From simple farming villages dating from 2500 BCE, the Maya of Guatemala and the Yucatán developed a sophisticated civilization. Its heart was the northern Petén, where the oldest Mayan stelae and the ceremonial centre of Tikal are found. Mayan civilization declined after 900 CE, and the Spanish began subjugating the descendants of the Maya in 1523. Independence from Spain was declared by the Central American colonies in Guatemala City in 1821, and Guatemala was incorporated into the Mexican Empire until its collapse in 1823. In 1839 Guatemala became independent under the first of a series of dictators who held power almost continuously for the next century. In 1945 a liberal-democratic coalition came to power and instituted sweeping reforms. Attempts to expropriate land belonging to U.S. business interests prompted the U.S. government in 1954 to sponsor an invasion by exiled Guatemalans. In the following years Guatemala's social revolution came to an end, and most of the reforms were reversed. Chronic political instability and violence henceforth marked Guatemalan politics; most of some 200,000 deaths that resulted from subsequent political violence were blamed on government forces. Thousands more died in 1976 when a powerful earthquake devastated the country. In 1991 Guatemala abandoned its long-standing claims of sovereignty over Belize, and the two countries established diplomatic relations. It continued to experience violence as guerrillas sought to seize power. A peace treaty was signed in 1996, but labour discontent, widespread crime and poverty, and violations of human rights continued into the 21st century.

Guatemala City, City (pop., 2007 est.: 1,024,000), capital of Guatemala. It is the largest city in Central America and lies in the central highlands at an elevation of about 4,900 ft (1,490 m). Founded in 1776, it replaced earthquake-damaged Antigua Guatemala as the capital of the captaincy general of Guatemala. After independence from Spain, it served as capital of the province of Central America under the Mexican Empire of Agustín de Iturbide and later of the Republic of Guatemala. It is the country's political, social, cultural, and economic centre and the site of San Carlos University of Guatemala (1676); its museums include the National Archaeological Museum, which houses a collection of rare Mayan artifacts. The modern city was largely rebuilt after a series of earthquakes in 1917–18; it was severely damaged again in 1976.

guava, Any of many trees and shrubs of the genus *Psidium* (myrtle family), native to the New World tropics. The two important species are common guava (*P. guajava*) and cattley, or strawberry, guava (*P. littorale* or *P. cattleianum*). The sweet pulp of the common guava fruit has a musky, sometimes pungent odour. The pulp of the strawberry guava fruit has a strawberry-like flavour. Guavas are processed into jams, jellies, and preserves. Fresh guavas are rich in vitamins A, B, and C; they are eaten raw or sliced and are served as desserts.

Guayaquil, in full SANTIAGO DE GUAYAQUIL, Largest city (pop., 2001 prelim.: 1,952,029) and chief port, Ecuador. It is situated on the Guayas River 45 mi (72 km) from the Pacific Ocean. Founded by the Spanish in 1537, it was frequently attacked by buccaneers. In 1822 it was the scene of a historic conference between revolutionary leaders Simón Bolívar and José de San Martín, after which Bolívar emerged as sole leader of the South American liberation movement. As the focus of Ecuador's international trade and domestic commerce, it has become a major Pacific port. It is the site of three universities.

Guelphs and Ghibellines, Opposing factions in German and Italian politics during the Middle Ages. The terms Guelph and Ghibelline (from Waiblingen, the castle of the Welfs' Hohenstaufen opponents) first acquired significance in Italy during the reign of the Hohenstaufen emperor Frederick I Barbarossa, who tried to assert imperial authority over northern Italy and was opposed by Pope Alexander III. The split between the Guelphs, who sided with the papacy, and the Ghibellines, who were sympathetic to the Holy Roman emperors, contributed to chronic strife in the cities of northern Italy in the 13th–14th century, reflected in Dante's *Divine Comedy.*

Guernsey, British crown dependency and the second largest of the Channel Islands, south of England's coast. Area: 30 sq mi (78 sq km). Population: (2011 est.) 65,300. Capital: St. Peter Port (pop., 2001: 16,448). The island of Guernsey is situated in the English Channel just west of Normandy, France. With Alderney and Sark, Herm, Jethou, and other islets, it forms the Bailiwick of Guernsey. The island was known as Sarnia to the Romans. It was home to Victor Hugo (1855–70). The Guernsey breed of cattle originated there.

Guevara, Che, orig. ERNESTO GUEVARA DE LA SERNA (b. June 14, 1928, Rosario, Arg.—d. October 1967, Bolivia), Theoretician and tactician of guerrilla warfare and prominent figure in Fidel Castro's revolution in Cuba (1956–59). Born to a middle-class family, he completed medical studies in 1953 and subsequently traveled widely in Latin America, eventually settling in Guatemala. The overthrow of Guatemala's Pres. Jacobo Arbenz persuaded him that the U.S. would always oppose leftist governments and that only violent revolution would end the poverty of the Latin American masses. He left Guatemala for Mexico, where he met Castro and joined his cause. After the Cuban revolution he held several key posts as one of Castro's most trusted aides; handsome and charismatic, he served as one of the revolution's most effec-

Che Guevara.
Lee Lockwood/Black Star

tive voices. He left Cuba in 1965 to organize guerrilla fighters in Congo and later Bolivia. Captured and shot by the Bolivian army, he immediately achieved international fame and the status of a martyred hero among leftists worldwide.

Guianas, the, Region, northern South America. The region is bounded on the north by the Atlantic Ocean and Caribbean Sea, on the east and south by Brazil, and on the west by Venezuela, and covers an area of about 181,000 sq mi (468,800 sq km). It consists of Guyana (formerly British Guiana), Suriname (formerly Dutch Guiana), and French Guiana; most of it is covered by dense forests containing valuable timber. Settlements are largely confined to the coast and river valleys. The earliest known inhabitants were the Surinam Indians. Its coast was sighted by Christopher Columbus in 1498, and the area was explored by the Spanish in the early 16th century. The Dutch founded settlements *c.* 1580 and the French and English in the early 17th century.

guided missile, Projectile provided with means for altering its direction after it leaves its launching device. Almost all modern missiles are propelled by rocket or jet engines and have guidance mechanisms, usually including sensors, to help the missile find its target. Heat-seeking missiles, for example, carry infrared sensors that allow them to home in on the exhaust of jet engines.

guild, Association of craftsmen or merchants formed for mutual aid and for the advancement of their professional interests. Guilds flourished in Europe between the 11th and 16th century and were of two types: merchant guilds, including all the merchants of a particular town or city; and craft guilds, including all the craftsmen in a particular branch of industry (e.g., weavers, painters, goldsmiths). Their functions included establishing trade monopolies, setting standards for quality of goods, maintaining stable prices, and gaining leverage in local governments in order to further the interests of the guild. Craft guilds also established hierarchies of craftsmen based on level of training (e.g., masters, journeymen, and apprentices).

guillotine, Instrument for inflicting capital punishment by decapitation. A minimal wooden structure, it supported a heavy blade that, when released, slid down in vertical guides to sever the victim's head. It was introduced in France in 1792 in the French Revolution, though similar devices had been used in Scotland, England, and other European countries, often for executing criminals of noble birth. The name derived from a French physician and member of the National Assembly, Joseph-Ignace Guillotin (1738–1814), who was instrumental in passing a law requiring all sentences of death to be carried out "by means of a machine," so that execution by decapitation would no longer be confined to nobles and executions would be as painless as possible. The last execution by guillotine in France took place in 1977.

Guinea, officially REPUBLIC OF GUINEA, formerly FRENCH GUINEA, Country, western Africa. Area: 94,926 sq mi (245,857 sq km). Population: (2011 est.) 10,222,000. Capital: Conakry. The Fulani people are in the majority, followed by the Malinke, the Susu, and many other groups. Language: French (official), indigenous languages. Religions: Islam; also Christianity. Currency: Guinean franc. Facing the Atlantic Ocean to the west, Guinea has four geographic regions. Lower Guinea comprises the coast and coastal plain, which are interspersed with lagoons and mangrove swamps. To the east the Fouta Djallon highlands rise sharply from the coastal plain to elevations above 3,000 ft (900 m); western Africa's three major rivers—the Niger, Sénégal, and Gambia—

originate there. Upper Guinea comprises the Niger Plains. The Forest Region, an isolated highland in the southeast, rises to 5,748 ft (1,752 m) at Mount Nimba, the country's highest peak. Most of the country has a humid tropical climate, and there are extensive tracts of tropical rainforest. Export crops include rice, bananas, and coffee. Guinea is a major world producer of bauxite. Its developing mixed economy is based on agriculture, mining, and trade. Guinea was a multiparty republic with one legislative house; the head of state and government was the president, assisted by the prime minister. The constitution was suspended in December 2008 after a military junta took control of the country, and a transitional government was established. In successive migrations *c.* 900 CE, the Susu swept down from the desert and pushed the original inhabitants, the Baga, to the Atlantic coast. Small kingdoms of the Susu rose in importance in the 13th century and later extended their rule to the coast. In the mid-15th century the Portuguese visited the coast and developed a slave trade. In the 16th century the Fulani established domination over the Fouta Djallon region; they ruled into the 19th century. In the early 19th century the French arrived and in 1849 proclaimed the coastal region a French protectorate. In 1895 French Guinea became part of the federation of French West Africa. In 1946 it was made an overseas territory of France, and in 1958 it achieved independence. Following a military coup in 1984, Guinea began implementing Westernized government systems. A new constitution was adopted in 1991, and the first multiparty elections were held in 1993. During the 1990s Guinea accommodated several hundred thousand war refugees from neighbouring Liberia and Sierra Leone, and conflicts between these countries and Guinea have continued to flare up over the refugee population into the early 21st century.

Guinea-Bissau, officially REPUBLIC OF GUINEA-BISSAU, formerly (until 1974) PORTUGUESE GUINEA, Country, western Africa. Its territory includes the Bijagós Archipelago, off the Atlantic coast to the southwest. Area: 13,948 sq mi (36,125 sq km). Population: (2011 est.) 1,606,000. Capital: Bissau. The four major ethnic groups are the Balante, Fulani, Malinke, and Mandyako. Languages: Portuguese (official), Crioulo, Balante, Fula, Malinke, Mandyako. Religions: traditional beliefs, Islam, Christianity. Currency: CFA franc. Most of the country consists of low, marshy terrain and flat plateau. The climate is generally hot and tropical. Much of the wildlife is aquatic; crocodiles, snakes, and birds such as pelicans and flamingos abound. Guinea-Bissau has a developing, primarily agricultural economy; cashews are by far the most important cash crop. Guinea-Bissau has a transitional government, established in the month following an April 2012 military coup. Prior to the coup, Guinea-Bissau was a republic with one legislative house; its head of state and government was the president, assisted by the prime minister. More than 1,000 years ago the coast of Guinea-Bissau was occupied by agriculturists using iron implements. They grew irrigated and dry rice and were also the major suppliers of marine salt to the western Sudan. At about the same time, the area came under the influence of the Mali empire and became a tributary kingdom known as Kaabu. After 1546 Kaabu was virtually autonomous; vestiges of it lasted until 1867. The earliest overseas contacts came in the 15th century with the Portuguese, who imported slaves from the Guinea area to the offshore Cape Verde Islands. Portuguese control of Guinea-Bissau was marginal despite their claims to sovereignty there. The end of the slave trade forced the Portuguese inland in search of new profits. Their subjugation of the interior was slow and sometimes violent; it was not effectively achieved until 1915, though sporadic resistance continued until 1936. Guerrilla warfare in the 1960s led to the country's independence in 1974, but political turmoil continued, and the government was overthrown by a military coup in 1980. A new constitution was adopted in 1984, and the first multiparty elections were held in 1994. A destructive civil war in 1998 was followed by a military coup in 1999, but the coup was followed by elections. A bloodless coup in 2003 was also followed by elections. A coup in 2012 interrupted a presidential election.

Guise, house of, Noble French Roman Catholic family that played a major role in French politics during the Reformation. Claude de Lorraine (1496–1550) was created the 1st duke de Guise in 1527 for his service to Francis I in the defense of France. Claude's sons François, 2nd duke de Guise, and Charles, cardinal de Lorraine (1524–1574), gained great power during the reign of Francis II. Supported by Spain and the papacy, their persecution of the Huguenots led to the unsuccessful Amboise Conspiracy (1560), an attempted assassination of the leaders of the Guise party and transfer of power to the house of Bourbon. The Guise-led massacre of a Huguenot congregation at Vassy precipitated the Wars of Religion, in which Henri I, 3rd duke de Guise, was a prominent leader. Charles de Lorraine, 4th duke de Guise (1571–1640), lived through the rapid decline of the family's power. Henri II, 5th duke de Guise, tried unsuccessfully to revive the family's power; the direct line expired with the death of his grand-nephew in 1675.

guitar, Plucked stringed instrument. It normally has six strings, a fretted fingerboard, and a soundbox with a pronounced waist. It probably originated in Spain in the early 16th century. By 1800 it was being strung with six single strings; 19th-century innovations gave it its modern form. Modern classical guitar technique owes much to Francisco Tárrega (1852–1909), and Andrés Segovia gave the instrument prominence in the concert hall. However, it has always been primarily an amateur's instrument, and it remains an important folk instrument in many countries. The 12-string guitar is strung in six double courses. The Hawaiian, or steel, guitar is held horizontally and the strings are stopped by the pressure of a metal bar, producing a sweet glissando tone. The electric guitar represented a major development. Electric pickups were attached to the acoustic guitar in the 1920s. In the 1940s Les Paul invented the solid-body guitar; lacking a soundbox, it transmits only the string vibrations. With its long-sustained notes, affinity for strong amplification, and capacity for producing wailing melodic lines as well as harshly percussive rhythms, it soon became the principal instrument of Western popular music.

Guiyang, or KUEI-YANG, City (pop., 2003 est.: 1,372,600), capital of Guizhou province, southern China. It is situated south of Chongqing. The Sui (581–618) and Tang (618–907) dynasties established military outposts there, but the city developed only after the Mongol invasion of southwestern China in 1279. Chinese settlement followed, and, under the Ming (1368–1644) and Qing (1644–1911) dynasties, Guiyang became the seat of a prefecture. The Sino-Japanese War (1937–45) spurred its growth into a major provincial city and industrial centre.

Guizhou, or KUEI-CHOU, conventional KWEICHOW, Province (pop., 2002 est.: 38,370,000), southwestern China. It is bordered by Yunnan, Sichuan, and Hunan provinces, Chongqing municipality, and Guangxi autonomous region. It has an area of 67,200 sq mi (174,000 sq km). Its capital is Guiyang. Guizhou has rough topography, poor communications, and consequent isolation. About three-fourths of the people are Han Chinese; there are also aboriginal peoples, including the Miao. Guizhou came under Chinese influence during the Ming dynasty (1368–1644), when it was made a province. During the Qing dynasty (1644–1911), struggles between the minorities, especially the Miao, were common. Serious revolts occurred in the 19th century and in 1941–44, as a result of exploitation by local warlords. The communists took the area in 1949. Its mineral resources are rich and support some mining.

Gujarat, State (pop., 2008 est.: 56,408,000) and historic region, western India. Lying on the Arabian Sea and with a coastline of 992 mi (1,596 km) that includes the union territory enclaves of Daman and Diu, it is bordered by Pakistan; the states of Rajasthan, Madhya Pradesh, and Maharashtra; and Dadra and Nagar Haveli union territory. It has an area of 75,685 sq mi (196,024 sq km), and the capital is Gandhinagar. During the 4th and 5th centuries CE, it was ruled by the Gupta dynasty; it derived its name from the Gurjaras, who ruled the area in the 8th and 9th centuries. After a period of economic and cultural achievement, it fell successively under Arab Muslim, Mughal, and Maratha rule. In 1818 it came under British control, and after 1857 it was a province of British India. Following Indian independence in 1947, most of Gujarat was included in the state of Bombay, which was divided into Gujarat and Maharashtra in 1960. Gujarat is a leading industrialized state of India and a petroleum producer. It is also famous for its arts and crafts.

Gulag, System of Soviet labour camps and prisons that from the 1920s to the mid-1950s housed millions of political prisoners and criminals. The term (an abbreviation of the Russian words for Chief Administration of Corrective Labour Camps) was largely unknown in the West until the 1973 publication of Aleksandr Solzhenitsyn's *Gulag Archipelago*. The Gulag consisted of hundreds of camps, under the control of the secret police, where prisoners felled timber, worked in the mines, or laboured on construction projects. At least 10% died each year from harsh working conditions, inadequate food, and summary executions. The Gulag reached its height in the years of collectivization of Soviet agriculture (1929–32), during Joseph Stalin's purges (1936–38), and immediately after World War II, shrinking only after Stalin's death in 1953. An estimated 15–30 million Russians died in the camps.

Gulf Stream, Warm ocean current, part of a general clockwise-rotating system of currents in the North Atlantic. A major contribution of the Gulf Stream is its warming effect on the climates of adjacent land areas. In winter, the air over the ocean west of Norway is more than 40°F (22°C) warmer than the average for that latitude, one of the greatest temperature anomalies in the world. Winters in southwestern England are extraordinarily mild for this northern latitude because of the Gulf Stream. Regions of the Gulf Stream, such as the Grand Banks, have been among the most productive commercial fishing grounds in the world.

Gulf War syndrome, Cluster of illnesses in veterans of the Persian Gulf War (1990–91). These illnesses are characterized by variable and nonspecific symptoms such as fatigue, muscle and joint pains, headaches, memory loss, and posttraumatic stress reactions. It is believed to be caused by exposure to chemicals called anticholinesterases, which are found in nerve toxins, insecticides, and prophylactic anti-nerve toxin drugs. The disorder does not appear to be fatal but can be associated with considerable distress and disability.

gum, In botany, an adhesive substance of vegetable origin, mostly obtained as exudate from the bark of trees or shrubs belonging to the pea family. Gum arabic (from a species of acacia) is used in lithography. Gum tragacanth (from several shrub species in the genus *Astragalus*) is used as a coating and binding agent in pill manufacture, as an emulsifier in processed foods, and as a thickener in sauces. Some plant gums are used in the manufacture of cosmetics.

gum, or GINGIVA, Mucous-membrane-covered connective tissue attached to and surrounding the necks of the teeth and the alveolar bone of the jaw. The edges of the gums around the teeth are free and extend into the spaces between the teeth. Fibres of the ligament that holds the teeth in their sockets enter the gum and hold it tightly against the teeth. Pink, speckled, and tough, healthy gums have limited sensitivity to pain, temperature, and pressure. Changes in colour, loss of speckling, or abnormal sensitivity are early signs of gingivitis, in which pockets form between the gum and teeth and become infected, with inflammation, bleeding, and, in severe cases, loss of teeth.

Gum Nebula, Largest known emission nebula in terms of how much of the sky it occupies as seen from Earth, extending over about 35° in the southern constellations Puppis and Vela. A complex of diffuse, glowing gas too faint to see with the unaided eye, it was discovered in the 1950s. It lies roughly 1,000 light-years from Earth and may be the remnant of an ancient supernova.

gun, Weapon consisting essentially of a metal tube from which a missile or projectile is shot by the force of exploding gunpowder or some other propellant. The term is often limited today to the so-called big guns, cannon larger than a howitzer or mortar. It may also be used to refer to military small arms such as the rifle, machine gun, and pistol, as well as to nonmilitary firearms such as the shotgun. Though the Chinese used gunpowder in warfare from the 9th century, guns were not developed until the Europeans acquired gunpowder in the 13th century. The earliest guns (c. 1327) resembled old-fashioned soda bottles; they apparently were fired by applying a red-hot wire to a touchhole drilled through the top. Separating the barrel and the powder chamber resulted in breechloaders, which continued to be used in naval swivel guns and fortress wallpieces well into the 17th century. Small arms, as distinguished from hand cannon, did not exist until the development of the matchlock in the 15th century.

Guo Moruo, or KUO MO-JO, orig. GUO KAIZHEN (b. Nov. 1892, Shawan, Luoshan county, Sichuan province, China—d. June 12, 1978, Beijing), Chinese scholar and writer. In his youth he abandoned medical studies to devote himself to foreign literature, producing a popular translation of Johann Wolfgang von Goethe's *Sorrows of Young Werther* (1922). He wrote prolifically in every genre, including poetry, fiction, plays, nine autobiographical volumes, translations of Western works, and historical and philosophical treatises, including a monumental study of ancient inscriptions. Initially a liberal democrat, he became a Marxist in the 1920s, and his work was banned by the Guomindang. Following the 1949 revolution, he was named to the highest official literary positions and later to the presidency of the Chinese Academy of Sciences.

Gupta dynasty (4th–6th centuries) Rulers of an empire in northern and parts of central and western India. The dynasty was founded by Chandra (Candra) Gupta I (r. 320–c. 330). The Gupta era was once regarded as India's Classical period, but new archaeological evidence has given the Mauryan empire that designation. Nevertheless, the Gupta period is noted for the flourishing of Sanskrit literature, its sophisticated metal coins, its advanced mathematics (which made use of decimal notation and the numeral zero and at that time was more advanced than anywhere else), and its astronomical advances.

Guru, Title of the first 10 leaders of Sikhism. The first was Nanak, who before his death (1539) began the tradition that allowed the Guru to name his successor. He was followed by Angad (1539–1552), Amar Das, Ramdas (1574–1581), Arjan, Hargobind, Hari Rai, Hari Krishen (1661–1664), Tegh Bahadur (1664–1675), and Gobind Singh. In time the Guru became as much a military as a spiritual leader. Gobind Singh discontinued the office in 1708 and vested its authority in the Sikh sacred scripture, the Adi Granth.

guru, In Hinduism, a personal spiritual teacher. In ancient India, knowledge of the Vedas was transmitted through oral teaching from guru to pupil. The rise of the bhakti movement further increased the importance of gurus, who were often looked on as living embodiments of spiritual truth and were identified with the deity. They prescribed spiritual disciplines to their devotees, who followed their dictates in a tradition of willing service and obedience. Men or women may be gurus, though generally only men have established lineages.

Gustav II Adolf, Latin GUSTAVUS ADOLPHUS (b. Dec. 9, 1594, Stockholm, Swed.—d. Nov. 6, 1632, Lützen, Saxony), King of Sweden (1611–32) who made Sweden a major European power. The son of Charles IX, Gustav inherited his father's dynastic quarrels with Sigismund III Vasa and until 1629 faced a legitimist inva-

sion from Poland. He ended the war with Denmark in 1613, but Sweden was forced to pay a crushing war indemnity. He ended the war with Russia (1617) and annexed Ingria and Kexholm. Internal tensions were largely resolved by his trusted chancellor, Axel Gustafsson Oxenstierna. Gustav's sweeping domestic reforms included establishing an efficient central administration and improving education. Resuming the war with Sigismund in 1621, Gustav obtained much of Polish Livonia (Latvia and Estonia). He saw his Polish campaigns as part of the struggle of Protestantism against the Counter-Reformation. He entered the Thirty Years' War in 1630 as a defensive maneuver, to secure the Swedish state and church from danger. An outstanding military tactician, he led an army of unusual quality, and his position was strengthened by alliances with France, Brandenburg, and Saxony. Success in the Battle of Breitenfeld let him sweep through central Germany and claim large territorial cessions, particularly Pomerania (1631). At Lützen in 1632, the Swedes defeated Albrecht W.E. von Wallenstein's army, but Gustav was killed in battle.

Gutenberg, Johannes (Gensfleisch zur Laden zum) (b. c. 1395, Mainz—d. probably Feb. 3, 1468, Mainz), German inventor of a method of printing from movable type. Born to a patrician family in Mainz, he apparently worked at such crafts as goldsmithing and gem cutting in Mainz and Strasbourg and was experimenting with printing by 1438. He obtained backing in 1450 from the financier Johann Fust (c. 1400–66); Fust's impatience and other factors led to Gutenberg's loss of his establishment to Fust in 1455. Gutenberg's masterpiece, and the first book ever printed from movable type, is the "Forty-Two-Line" Bible, completed no later than 1455. A magnificent Psalter was published in 1457, after the loss of his press. The only other works still attributed to him are minor. His invention's unique elements included a mold, with which type could be cast precisely and in large quantities; a type-metal alloy; a new press, derived from those used in winemaking, papermaking, and bookbinding; and an oil-based printing ink. None of these features existed in Chinese or Korean printing, in the existing European technique of stamping letters on various surfaces, or in woodblock printing. Gutenberg's invention, seminal to the course of Western civilization, remained the source of the basic elements of typesetting for 500 years.

Guy-Blaché, Alice, orig. ALICE GUY (b. July 1, 1873, Paris, France—d. March 24, 1968, Mahwah, N.J., U.S.), French-born U.S. pioneer of French and American film industries. The first woman director, she is also generally acknowledged to be the first director to film a narrative story. She directed her first film, *The Cabbage Fairy*, in 1896 to demonstrate the entertainment possibilities of the motion-picture camera manufactured by her employer, Léon Gaumont. She became the Gaumont film company's head of production, directing nearly all early Gaumont films. About 1901 Guy began to work on longer, more elaborate projects, notably *Esmeralda* (1905), based on Victor Hugo's *The Hunchback of Notre Dame*, and *The Life of Christ* (1906). From 1906 to 1907 she directed about 100 films, using experimental sound technology. She married cameraman Herbert Blaché in 1907 and followed him to the U.S., where in 1910 she founded the successful Solax Company. As president of Solax she directed about 45 films and supervised nearly 300 other productions. Only a handful of the hundreds of films she made survive.

Guyana, officially CO-OPERATIVE REPUBLIC OF GUYANA, formerly (until 1966) BRITISH GUIANA, Country, northeastern South America. Area: 83,012 sq mi (214,999 sq km). Population: (2011 est.) 756,000. Capital: Georgetown. More than two-fifths of the people are of South Asian descent; most of the rest are of African, Indian, or mixed ancestry. Language: English (official). Religions: Christianity (Protestant, Roman Catholic), Hinduism, Islam. Currency: Guyanese dollar. Guyana has a narrow Atlantic coastal plain that extends up to 10 mi (16 km) inland and includes reclaimed land protected by seawalls and canals. Inland, a high rainforest covers three-fourths of the country. The Acaraí Mountains in the south provide headwaters for the Essequibo River. Guyana has a developing market economy with both public and private ownership. Major exports include sugar, rice, and bauxite. It is a unitary multiparty republic with one legislative house; its head of state and government is the president. Indians inhabited Guyana prior to European settlement, but little is known of them except that their name for the land, *guiana* ("land of water"), gave the country its name. It was colonized by the Dutch in the 17th century. The British occupied the territory during the French Revolutionary Wars and afterward purchased the colonies of Demerara, Berbice, and Essequibo, which were united in 1831 as British Guiana. The slave trade was abolished in 1807, but emancipation of the 100,000 slaves in the colonies was not complete until 1838. From the 1840s, South Asian and Chinese indentured servants were brought to work the plantations; by 1917 almost 240,000 South Asians had migrated to British Guiana. It was made a crown colony in 1928 and granted home rule in 1953. Political parties began to emerge, developing along ethnic lines as the People's Progressive Party (largely South Asian) and the People's National Congress (PNC; largely Afro-Guyanese [Guyanese of African descent]). The PNC formed a coalition government and led the country into independence as Guyana in 1966. Since 1970 Guyana has been a member of the Commonwealth (an international group made up of the United Kingdom and a number of its former dependencies). In 1980 Guyana adopted a new constitution. In the last decades of the 20th century, Guyana moved away from the socialist approach first taken following independence. At the beginning of the 21st century, it was still struggling to achieve economic and political stability.

gymnasium, In Germany, a state-maintained secondary school that prepares pupils for higher academic education. This type of nine-year school originated in Strasbourg in 1537. Though the usual graduation age is 19 or 20, pupils may terminate their studies at age 16 and enter a vocational school. Secondary or postprimary education is also provided by middle schools (*Mittelschulen*), teachers' colleges, and commercial schools.

gymnastics, Competitive sport in which individuals perform optional and prescribed acrobatic exercises, mostly on special apparatus, in order to demonstrate strength, balance, and body control. Part of the ancient Olympic Games, gymnastics was virtually reinvented in the modern era by the German Friedrich Jahn (1778–1852). The sport became part of the revived Olympics in 1896; women's gymnastics was instituted in 1936. Men's events include the horizontal bar, parallel bars, pommel horse, vaulting, rings, and floor exercises. Women's events include the balance beam, uneven parallel bars, vaulting, floor exercises, and rhythmic sportive gymnastics.

gymnosperm, Any woody plant that reproduces by means of a seed (or ovule) in direct contact with the environment, as opposed to an angiosperm, or flowering plant, whose seeds are enclosed by mature ovaries, or fruits. The four surviving gymnosperm divisions are Pinophyta (order Pinales, the most widespread), Cycadophyta (order Cycadales), Ginkgophyta (order Ginkgoales), and Gnetophyta (order Gnetales). More than half are trees; most of the rest are shrubs. Gymnosperms occur on all continents except Antarctica and especially in the temperate latitudes. Those widely found in the Northern Hemisphere are junipers, firs, larches, spruces, and pines; in the Southern Hemisphere, podocarps (*Podocarpus*). The wood of gymnosperms is often called softwood to differentiate it from the hardwood of angiosperms. Many timber and pulp trees are also planted as ornamentals. Gymnosperms also are a minor source of food; of essential oils used in soaps, air fresheners, disinfectants, pharmaceuticals, cosmetics, and perfumes; of tannin, used for curing leather; and of turpentines. Gymnosperms were a major component in the vegetation that was compressed over millions of years into coal. Most are evergreen. They produce male and female reproductive cells in separate male and female strobili.

gynecomastia, Breast enlargement in a male. It usually involves only the nipple and nearby tissue of one breast. More rarely, the whole breast grows to a size normal in a female. True gynecomastia is related to an increase in estrogens. Testicular or pituitary-gland tumours commonly cause gynecomastia. Similar conditions (pseudogynecomastia) are caused by excessive body fat, inflammatory disorders, granular lesions, or growth of tumours. Treatment involves hormone therapy, correction of the estrogen disorder, or tumour removal.

gyroscope, A mechanical or optical device used to maintain orientation during motion. A mechanical gyroscope consists of a rapidly spinning wheel set in a framework that permits it to tilt freely in any direction or to rotate about any axis. The momentum of such a wheel causes it to retain its attitude when the framework is tilted. An optical gyroscope, laser or fibre, measures the interference pattern generated by two light beams, traveling in opposite directions within a mirrored ring or fibre loop, in order to detect very small changes in motion. Gyroscopes are used in compasses, in automatic pilots on ships and aircraft, in the steering mechanisms of torpedoes, in antiroll equipment on large ships, and in inertial guidance systems.

H

Haarlem, City (pop., 2001 est.: 148,377), western Netherlands. It lies along the Spaarne River, west of Amsterdam. By the 12th century it had become a fortified town and the residence of the counts of Holland. It was chartered in 1245 and incorporated in the United Netherlands in 1577. Its prosperity peaked in the 17th century, when it was a refuge for Huguenots and also an artistic centre. It is an industrial city and the centre for a tulip-growing region. Sites of interest include the 13th-century town hall and the 14th-century Great Church.

habeas corpus (Latin: "you should have the body"), In common law, any of several writs issued to bring a party before a court. The most important such writ (*habeas corpus ad subjiciendum*) is used to correct violations of personal liberty by directing judicial inquiry into the legality of a detention. Common grounds for relief include a conviction based on illegally obtained evidence, a denial of effective assistance of counsel, or a conviction by a jury that was improperly selected or impaneled. The writ may be used in civil matters to challenge a person's custody of a child or the institutionalization of a person declared incompetent.

habitat, Place where an organism or a community of organisms lives, including all living and nonliving factors or conditions of the surrounding environment. A host organism inhabited by parasites is as much a habitat as a place on land such as a grove of trees or an aquatic locality such as a small pond. "Microhabitat" refers to the conditions and organisms in the immediate vicinity of a plant or animal.

Hachiman, One of the most popular of Japan's Shintō deities. Referred to as the god of war, he is believed to be the deification of Ōjin, the 15th emperor. He is the patron of the Minamoto clan and of warriors in general. His first shrine was built in 725, and today half the Shintō shrines are dedicated to him. In the 8th century Hachiman was accepted as a Buddhist divinity; he is the guardian deity of the great Buddhist temple at Tōdai.

Hades, Greek god of the underworld. He was also known as Pluto; his Roman equivalent was Dis. Hades was the son of the Titans Rhea and Cronus and the brother of Zeus and Poseidon. His queen was Persephone, the daughter of Demeter, whom he kidnapped from earth and carried off to the underworld. Stern and pitiless, unmoved by prayer or sacrifice, he presided over the trial and punishment of the wicked after death. His name was also sometimes used to designate the dwelling place of the dead, and it later became a synonym for Hell.

Ḥadīth, In Islam, the tradition or collection of traditions attributed to the Prophet Muhammad that include his sayings, acts, and approval or disapproval of things. Ḥadīth is revered by Muslims as a major source of religious law and moral guidance. It consists of two parts: the oral law itself and the *isnād*, or chain of authorities who passed it down to posterity. The various collections of Ḥadīth provide the major source for studying the development of Islam in its first few centuries.

Hadrian, Latin CAESAR TRAIANUS HADRIANUS AUGUSTUS, orig. PUBLIUS AELIUS HADRIANUS (b. Jan. 24, AD 76, Italica, Baetica?—d. July 10, 138, Baiae, near Naples), Roman emperor (117–38), Trajan's nephew and successor. After years of intrigue, he was adopted and named successor just before Trajan's death. He executed his senatorial opponents, abandoned Trajan's conquests in Armenia and Mesopotamia, and coped with unrest in Mauretania and Parthia. He traveled widely, and many of his accomplishments

Hadrian, bust in the National Archaeological Museum, Naples.
Anderson—Alinari/Art Resource, New York

were related to his visits abroad. He began construction of Hadrian's Wall, and he visited and disciplined troops in Algeria and elsewhere. An admirer of Greek civilization, he completed the temple of Zeus in Athens and created a federation of Greek cities. He launched a building program at Delphi and was initiated into the Eleusinian mysteries. After his young companion Antinoüs drowned in the Nile (130), he grieved openly; he erected statues of the boy throughout the realm, and cults sprang up widely. He named Antoninus Pius his successor, to be followed by Marcus Aurelius.

Haemophilus, Genus of tiny rod-shaped bacteria. All are strict parasites occurring in the respiratory tracts of warm-blooded animals, including humans, and in certain cold-blooded animals. Some require oxygen, others do not. *H. influenzae* causes severe bacterial diseases in young children, including meningitis, otitis, and pneumonia. Another species of *Haemophilus* causes a sexually transmitted disease in humans known as chancroid, or soft chancre. Yet another causes secondary infection in persons with influenza.

Haggadah, or HAGGADA, In Judaism, the text that guides the performance of ritual acts and prayers at the Seder dinner celebrating Passover. The Haggadah retells the story of Exodus, offering commentaries that provide a religious philosophy of Jewish history and supplying answers to the traditional questions asked by children at the beginning of the Seder. More broadly, the term Haggadah can refer to the part of rabbinical literature not concerned with the law (e.g., stories, parables, legends, history, and astronomy).

Hagia Sophia (Greek: "Holy Wisdom") Church in Istanbul, later a mosque and now a museum. It is the masterpiece of Byzantine architecture. Designed under Justinian I by Anthemius of Tralles and Isidorus of Miletus, the original building was completed in less than six years (AD 532–37). It combined a longitudinal basilica and a centralized building in a wholly original manner, with a huge main dome (rebuilt 563) supported on pendentives and semidomes on either side. In plan it is almost square. There are three aisles separated by columns with galleries above and great marble piers rising up to support the dome. The walls above the galleries, as well as the base of the dome, are pierced by windows, whose light obscures the supports, giving the impression that the canopy floats on air.

hagiography, Literature describing the lives of the saints. Christian hagiography includes stories of saintly monks, bishops, princes, and virgins, with accounts of their martyrdom and of the miracles connected with their relics, tombs, icons, or statues. Written as early as the 2nd century and popular during the Middle Ages, hagiographies focus on lives of individual saints or on stories of a class of saints (e.g., martyrs).

Hague, The, Dutch 'S-GRAVENHAGE, or DEN HAAG, City (pop., 2010 est.: 488,553), seat of government of the Netherlands. Located 4 mi (6 km) from the North Sea, it is the administrative capital of the Netherlands, home to its court and government, though Amsterdam is the official capital. The counts of Holland built a castle at The Hague in 1248. The complex now forms the Binnenhof in the old quarter of the city, which became the seat of the Dutch government in 1585. The city grew rapidly in the 19th and

20th centuries. A centre of government, international law, and corporate administration, most of its businesses are engaged in trade, banking, and insurance. The International Court of Justice is housed in the Peace Palace (1913). The city is filled with notable architecture, much of which survived despite the heavy damage inflicted on the city during the German occupation in World War II.

Hague Conventions, Series of international agreements signed at The Hague (1899, 1907). The first conference was requested by Russia to discuss rules to limit warfare and attempt arms limitations. Twenty-six countries attended and approved several proposed conventions, including prohibition of the use of asphyxiating gases (not renewed in 1907) and creation of a Permanent Court of Arbitration. The 1907 meeting, called by Theodore Roosevelt, was attended by 44 countries and also had arms limitation as a goal, which again went unmet. An agreement to reconvene in eight years confirmed the principle that international conferences were the best way to handle international problems. Though World War I prevented the next meeting from taking place, the conferences influenced creation of the League of Nations and the United Nations.

Haifa, Hebrew HEFA, City (pop., 2005 est.: 269,300) and chief port, northwestern Israel. Located on the Bay of Haifa, overlooking the Mediterranean Sea, it is first mentioned in the Talmud (c. 1st–4th century AD). Conquered in 1100 by Christian Crusaders, it was taken by Napoleon I in 1799 and by Egyptian Gen. Ibrāhīm Pasha in 1839. It was occupied by British forces in 1918, and it became part of Britain's mandate in Palestine. It came under Israeli control in 1948, during the first Arab-Israeli war. Situated on the northern slopes of Mount Carmel, with the exception of its port section on the bay, it is a tourist resort and a commercial centre. Haifa is the world headquarters of the Bahā'ī faith.

haiku, Unrhymed Japanese poetic form. It consists of 17 syllables arranged in three lines of 5, 7, and 5 syllables, respectively. The form expresses much and suggests more in the fewest possible words. It gained distinction in the 17th century, when Bashō elevated it to a highly refined art. Haiku remains Japan's most popular poetic form and is widely imitated in English and other languages.

hail, Precipitation of balls or pieces of ice with a diameter of 0.2 in. (5 mm) to more than 6 in. (about 15 cm). In contrast, ice pellets (sleet; sometimes called small hail) have a diameter less than 0.2 in. Hail can be extremely destructive to buildings and crops; if it is large enough, it may be dangerous to animals. Hailstones 6 in. in diameter and larger have fallen during storms in the U.S. Midwest. Hailstorms are most common in the midlatitudes and usually last about 15 minutes. They ordinarily occur in mid-to-late afternoon and may accompany thunderstorms.

Hail Mary, Latin AVE MARIA, Principal Roman Catholic prayer addressed to the Virgin Mary. It begins with the greetings spoken to Mary by the Archangel Gabriel and by her cousin Elizabeth in the Gospel of Luke: "Hail Mary, full of grace, the Lord is with thee. Blessed art thou among women and blessed is the fruit of thy womb, Jesus." A closing petition, "Holy Mary, Mother of God, pray for us sinners, now and at the hour of our death," came into general use by the end of the 14th century. Churchgoers who attend confession are often asked to repeat the prayer as penance for sins.

Haile Selassie, orig. TAFARI MAKONNEN (b. July 23, 1892, near Harer, Eth.—d. Aug. 27, 1975, Addis Ababa), Emperor of Ethiopia (1930–74). Tafari was a son of Ras (Prince) Makonnen, a chief adviser to Emperor Menilek II. After Menilek's daughter, Zauditu, became empress (1917), Ras Tafari (who had married Menilek's great-granddaughter) was named regent and heir apparent to the throne. When Zauditu died in 1930, Tafari took the name of Haile

Haile Selassie, 1967.
AP

Selassie ("Might of the Trinity") to mark his imperial status. As emperor he sought to modernize his country and steer it into the mainstream of African politics. He brought Ethiopia into the League of Nations and the UN and made Addis Ababa the centre for the Organization of African Unity (now the African Union). Through most of his reign he remained popular among the majority Christian population. He was deposed in 1974 in a military coup by Mengistu Haile Mariam and kept under house arrest. He was apparently killed by his captors. Haile Selassie was regarded as the messiah of the African race by the Rastafarian movement.

Hainan, or HAI-NAN, Province (pop., 2007 est.: 8,360,000) and island of China. With an area of 13,200 sq mi (34,300 sq km), the province also includes the Xisha and Nansha islands. It is located in the South China Sea, separated from Guangdong province by a narrow strait. For centuries part of Guangdong, Hainan became a separate province in 1988, the southernmost province of China and the smallest. Its capital is Haikou. It was under Chinese rule from the 2nd century BCE but was not closely controlled until the Tang dynasty (618–907 CE). Chinese began settling the island in the 16th–17th centuries, gradually forcing the indigenous peoples into the interior. Hainan was occupied by the Japanese in 1939–45, after which it reverted back to China. The island, designated a special economic zone after becoming a province, has since then experienced considerable economic growth.

Haiphong, Seaport city (pop., 2004 est.: 591,100), northern Vietnam. Situated in the Red River delta, about 10 mi (16 km) from the Gulf of Tonkin, it is the country's third largest city and serves as the port of the capital, Hanoi, about 50 mi (80 km) to the west. Established in 1874, it developed commercially as a port and as the terminus of a railway. It became a leading industrial centre, and after 1954 many new plants were built there with aid given by Soviet-bloc countries and by China. It sustained heavy damage from U.S. bombing during the Vietnam War but was subsequently rebuilt.

hair, Threadlike outgrowths of the skin. Babies shed a layer of downy, slender hairs (lanugo) before or just after birth. The fine, short, unpigmented hairs (vellus) then grow. Starting at puberty, terminal hair, longer, coarser, and more pigmented, develops in the armpits, crotch, sometimes on parts of the trunk and limbs, and, in males, on the face. Scalp hair, eyebrows, and eyelashes are different types. The number of scalp hairs, which grow about 0.5 in. (13 mm) per month, averages 100,000–150,000. The hair shaft (above the skin) is dead tissue, composed of keratin. Only a few growing cells at the base of the root are alive. Hair is formed by cell division at the base of the follicle (a tiny pocket in the skin), part of a cycle of growing, resting, and falling out. Vellus lasts about four months, scalp hairs three to five years.

Haiti, officially REPUBLIC OF HAITI, Country in the West Indies, occupying the western third of the island of Hispaniola, which it shares with the Dominican Republic to the east. Area: 10,695 sq mi (27,700 sq km). Population: (2011 est.) 9,720,000. Capital: Port-au-Prince. Almost the entire population is of African or African-European descent. Languages: Haitian Creole, French (both official). Religions: Christianity (mainly Roman Catholic; also Protestant); also Vodou. Currency: gourde. Most of the land is mountainous, about two-thirds above 1,600 ft (490 m) in elevation. The mountain ranges alternate with fertile but overpopulated lowlands. Haiti's tropical climate is modified by the mountains and subject to periodic droughts and hurricanes. Its longest river is the Artibonite. The poorest country in the Americas, Haiti has a developing market economy based in large part on agriculture and light industries; coffee is the main cash crop. It is a multiparty republic with two legislative houses; the chief of state is the president, and the head of government is the prime minister. Haiti gained its independence in 1804, after former slaves led by Toussaint-Louverture in the 1790s and by Jean-Jacques Dessalines in 1803 rebelled against French rule. The new republic encompassed the entire island of Hispaniola, but the eastern portion of the island was restored to Spain in 1809. It was reunited under Haitian Pres. Jean-Pierre Boyer (1818–43); after his overthrow the eastern portion revolted and formed the Dominican Republic. Haiti's government was marked by instability, with frequent coups and assassinations. It was occupied by the U.S. in 1915–34. In 1957 the dictator Francòis ("Papa Doc") Duvalier came to power. Despite economic decline and civil unrest, Duvalier ruled until his death in 1971. He was succeeded by his son, Jean-Claude ("Baby Doc") Duvalier, who was forced into exile in 1986. Haiti's first free presidential elections, held in 1990, were won by Jean-Bertrand Aristide. He was deposed by a military coup in 1991, after which tens of thousands of Haitians attempted to flee to the U.S. in small boats. When the military government stepped down in 1994, Aristide returned from exile and resumed the presidency. His associate René Préval replaced him in 1995, and in 2000 Aristide reclaimed the presidency, only to be driven from office and out of the country in 2004 as economic and political instability continued to plague Haiti. An international stabilization mission was established under the leadership of first the U.S. armed forces and then the United Nations. Under its oversight, an interim government led the country until 2006, when Préval again won election as president. In January 2010 a powerful earthquake struck the country, causing widespread destruction in Port-au-Prince and the surrounding region. Estimates of the death toll from the quake ranged upward to 200,000 or more.

hajj, In Islam, the pilgrimage to Mecca required of all Muslims at least once in their lifetime, provided they are physically and financially able. It is one of the Five Pillars of Islam. By tradition the pilgrimage is undertaken between the 7th and 12th days of the last month of the Islamic year. At Mecca, the pilgrims are obliged to perform several rituals, including walking seven times around the Ka'bah shrine. They must also visit holy places outside Mecca and sacrifice an animal in honor of Abraham's near-sacrifice of Isaac. In conclusion, they return to Mecca and perform a farewell circling of the shrine.

Halakhah, or HALAKHA, In Judaism, all laws and ordinances evolved since biblical times to regulate worship and the daily lives of the Jewish people. In contrast to the laws written in the Torah, the Halakhah represents an oral tradition. These laws were passed from generation to generation before being written down in the 1st–3rd century AD in the compilation called the Mishna, which became the foundation of the Talmud.

halberd, Weapon consisting of an ax blade and a sharp spike mounted on the end of a long staff. Usually about 5–6 ft (1.5–2 m) long, it was an important weapon in middle Europe in the 15th and early 16th centuries. It enabled a foot soldier to contend with an armoured man on horseback; the spiked head kept the rider at a distance, and the ax blade could strike a heavy cleaving blow. Firearms and the declining use of armour made the halberd obsolete.

Hale-Bopp, Comet, Comet discovered in 1995 by the amateur astronomers Alan Hale and Thomas Bopp at a distance from the Sun of about seven astronomical units, beyond Jupiter's orbit and farther than any comet detected before by amateurs. Astronomers estimated its nucleus to be at least 20 mi (30 km) in diameter. At

its closest approach to the Sun in April 1997, it was one of the intrinsically brightest comets in several centuries, though not the brightest as seen from Earth. The approach of the comet triggered the mass suicide near San Diego, Calif., U.S., in March 1997 of 39 members of a religious cult known as Heaven's Gate, whose leader maintained that they would be reincarnated in a spacecraft following in the comet's wake.

half-life, Interval of time required for one-half of the atomic nuclei of a radioactive sample to decay (change spontaneously into other nuclear species by emitting particles and energy), or the time required for the number of disintegrations per second of a radioactive material to decrease by one-half. Half-lives are characteristic properties of the various unstable atomic nuclei and the particular way in which they decay. Alpha decay and beta decay are generally slower processes than gamma decay.

halftone process, In printing, a technique of breaking up an image into a series of dots to permit reproduction of the full tone range of a photograph or artwork. It is traditionally done by placing a glass screen printed with a tight grid of lines over the plate being exposed. The grid breaks up the image into hundreds of tiny dots, each of which is read by the camera as either black or white—or, in the case of colour art, as either a single printing colour or white. The resulting image, called a halftone, is then rephotographed for printing. Screens are made with a varying number of lines per inch, depending on the application; for newspapers the range is about 80–120, whereas glossy magazines usually require 133–175 lines per inch.

Halifax, City (pop., 2001: 119,292), capital of Nova Scotia, Canada. Located on Halifax Harbour, an inlet of the Atlantic Ocean, it was settled by the British in 1749 as a counterbalance to French holdings at Cape Breton. It served as a British army and navy base until its defenses were taken over by the Canadian government in 1906. The city suffered from a munitions-ship explosion in 1917 that killed nearly 2,000 people. During World Wars I and II, Halifax was Canada's most important naval base. The city is Nova Scotia's leading commercial and industrial centre, and its port is one of the busiest in Canada. Its educational institutions include Dalhousie University (1818); historic buildings include St. Paul's Church (1750), Canada's oldest Protestant church. In 1996 Halifax amalgamated with several surrounding communities to form Halifax Regional Municipality (pop., 2001: 359,183).

The Old Town Clock on Citadel Hill, Halifax, Nova Scotia
John de Visser

Halley's Comet, or COMET HALLEY, First comet whose return was predicted, proving that at least some comets are members of the solar system. Edmond Halley showed in 1705 that comets seen in 1531, 1607, and 1682 were really one comet, and he predicted its return in 1758. Later calculations identified it with the large, bright comet seen during the Norman Conquest (and depicted in the Bayeux Tapestry) and with other comet sightings at intervals of about 76 years, the first in 240 BC. The only easily seen comet that returns in a single lifetime, it approached Earth twice in the 20th century (1910, 1985–86). Its nucleus is roughly 9 mi (15 km) across.

hallmark, Symbol stamped on an item of silver or gold to indicate that it conforms to legal standards of purity. Hallmarking in Britain dates from 1300; no gold or silver could be sold until tested for purity and struck with the king's mark. A maker's mark was introduced in 1363; at first a symbol, such as a fish or key, it came to include or be replaced by initials. A "hallmark" was a mark made at Goldsmith's Hall, London. In the U.S., no hallmarks were initially required. In the late 18th and early 19th century, local regulations were established in New York, Boston, Baltimore, and elsewhere; makers' marks appeared and the words "coin" and "sterling" were stamped on silver objects. In 1906 the use of the words came under federal regulation. Hallmarks on gold, similar to those on silver, are also subject to federal regulation.

Halloween, Holiday observed on October 31, the eve of All Saints' Day. Its pagan origins can be traced to the Celtic festival of Samhain, celebrated in ancient England and Ireland to mark the beginning of the Celtic new year. The souls of the dead were supposed to revisit their homes on Samhain eve, and witches, goblins, black cats, and ghosts were said to roam abroad. The night was also thought to be the most favorable time for divinations concerning marriage, luck, health, and death. The pagan observances influenced the Christian festival of All Hallows' Eve, celebrated on the same date. The holiday was gradually secularized and was introduced into the U.S. by the late 19th century. Still associated with evil spirits and the supernatural, it is celebrated by children in costume who gather candy by ringing doorbells and calling out "trick or treat," "trick" referring to the pranks and vandalism that are also part of the Halloween tradition.

Hallstatt, Site in upper Austria where objects characteristic of

the Early Iron Age (from *c.* 1100 BC) were first identified. More than 2,000 graves were near a salt mine that preserved implements, parts of clothing, and bodies of miners. The remains are divided into four phases (A, B, C, D), differing according to burial practices, presence of low grave mound or tumulus, relative quantity of bronze and iron, and style of pottery, weapons, jewelry, and clothing. Decoration in general is geometric and symmetrical, with a tendency toward the extravagant.

Bronze bucket found at early Iron Age cemetery at Hallstatt, Austria, about 6th century BC.
Courtesy of the trustees of the British Museum

hallucinogen, Substance that produces psychological effects normally associated only with dreams, schizophrenia, or religious visions. It produces changes in perception (ranging from distortions in what is sensed to perceptions of objects where there are none), thought, and feeling. Those that have aroused the most controversy include Ecstasy, LSD, mescaline, psilocybin (from certain mushrooms), and bufotenine (from the skin of toads); some would add marijuana. The mode of action is still not clear; serotonin, epinephrine, or other neurotransmitters may be affected.

halogen, Any of six nonmetallic elements—fluorine, chlorine, bromine, iodine, astatine, and element 117—with similar chemical properties. They occur in the second rightmost column of the periodic table. All are highly reactive oxidizing agents with valence 1 (for fluorine, the only valence). They combine readily with most metals and nonmetals to form a variety of compounds, and they never occur uncombined in nature. Astatine, a radioactive element, occurs naturally in minute amounts as an intermediate decay product; it has no stable nonradioactive isotopes. Only a few atoms of element 117 have been artificially produced, and it is not found in nature. Halogen salts

formed with metal atoms (halides) are very stable; sodium chloride is the most familiar. The halogen lamp takes its name from the halogens included in the gas within its tungsten-filament bulb, added to prolong filament life and increase brightness.

Ḥamās acronym of ḤARAKAT AL-MUQĀWAMAH AL-ISLĀMIYYAH, English ISLAMIC RESISTANCE MOVEMENT (Arabic: "Zeal"), Militant Palestinian Islamic movement. The group is dedicated to the destruction of Israel and the creation of a Palestinian Islamic state. It was founded in 1987 by Sheikh Aḥmad Yāsīn, and its leadership comes from the Palestinian branch of the Muslim Brotherhood. Ḥamās's aims are more militant: it takes the position that Palestine cannot be surrendered to non-Muslims. It opposed the 1993 peace agreement between the Palestine Liberation Organization and Israel. Beginning in 2000, the group intensified its violent acts against Israelis, including numerous suicide bombings. In 2006 Ḥamās participated in the elections for the Palestinian Legislative Council and won a surprise victory over Fatah.

Hamburg, City (pop., 2002 est.: city, 1,726,363; metro. area, 2,515,468), constituting a state, northern Germany. Covering 292 sq mi (755 sq km), it is located on the Elbe River and is Germany's largest port. It grew around the 9th-century castle of Hammaburg. Treaties with Lübeck in the mid-13th century led to the formation of the Hanseatic League, of which it was a leader. Incorporated into the French Empire (1810–14), it became a member of the German Confederation as a free city in 1815. In World War II Allied firebombing killed some 55,000 people and devastated the city. It was rapidly rebuilt after the war. The birthplace of Felix Mendelssohn and Johannes Brahms and home to the Hamburg Opera, it enjoys a distinguished musical history. It is Germany's foremost industrial city and northern Germany's chief economic centre.

Hammarskjöld, Dag (Hjalmar Agne Carl) (b. July 29, 1905, Jönköping, Swed.—d. Sept. 18, 1961, near Ndola, Northern Rhodesia), Second secretary-general of the UN (1953–61). His father was prime minister of Sweden and chairman of the Nobel Prize Foundation. Hammarskjöld studied law and economics in Uppsala and Stockholm, then taught at Stockholm (1933–36). He served in the finance ministry, as president of the board of the Bank of Sweden, and in the foreign ministry, where he became chair of the Swedish delegation to the UN (1952). He was appointed secretary-general in 1953 and was reappointed in 1957. His first three years were quiet, but he subsequently dealt with the Suez Crisis, conflict in Lebanon and Jordan, and civil strife following the creation of the Republic of the Congo (1960). He died in a plane crash on a peace mission to Africa. He was posthumously awarded the Nobel Prize for Peace in 1961. As secretary-general, Hammarskjöld is generally thought to have combined great moral force with subtlety in meeting international challenges.

hammer throw, Athletic event in which a hammer is thrown for distance. The hammer consists of a 16-lb (7.26-kg) metal ball attached to a spring steel wire handle that measures not more than 4 ft (1.2 m) in length. The thrower makes three full, quick turns of the body before flinging the hammer. The sport developed centuries ago in the British Isles; it has been a regular part of track-and-field competitions there since 1866 and an Olympic sport since 1900.

hammerhead shark, Any of the swift, powerful sharks in the family Sphyrnidae, having a broad, flattened, hammer- or spade-shaped head, with the eyes and nostrils at the ends of the sidewise projections. Widely distributed in all oceans, in warm and temperate waters, they feed on fish, stingrays, skates, and other sharks. Some species are fished for leather and oil. Three species seem to be particularly dangerous to humans: the great hammerhead (the largest hammerhead, growing to 15 ft, or 4.5 m, or more), the scalloped hammerhead, and the smooth hammerhead. All three are grayish and found throughout the tropics.

Hammurabi (fl. 18th century BC), Sixth and best-known ruler of the 1st (Amorite) dynasty of Babylon. His kingdom was one of several prominent realms in Babylonia. His desire to control the Euphrates River led him to conquer the cities of Uruk (Erech) and Isin in 1787 BC, but he gave up on further military campaigns in that area, turning instead to the northwest and the east in 1784. Twenty years of peace followed, and then 14 years of almost continuous warfare that resulted in a unified Mesopotamia. He used control of waterways (damming them to deny his enemies water or to create a flood by releasing them) to defeat his enemies. He also engaged in building and restoring temples, city walls, public buildings, and canals. His laws, collected in the Code of Hammurabi, demonstrated his desire to be a just ruler.

Hammurabi, limestone relief; in the British Museum

Hammurabi, Code of, Most complete and perfect extant collection of Babylonian laws, developed during the reign (*c* 1792–50 BC) of Hammurabi. It consists of 282 of his legal decisions, collected toward the end of his reign and inscribed on a diorite stela set up in the temple of Marduk. The text is in the Akkadian language. Despite a few references to family solidarity, trial by ordeal, and the *lex talionis* (an eye for an eye, a tooth for a tooth), it represents an advance over tribal custom in that it recognizes no blood feud, private retribution, or marriage by capture. The principal portion of the code is preserved in the Louvre Museum in Paris.

Hamsun, Knut, orig. KNUT PEDERSEN (b. Aug. 4, 1859, Lom, Nor.—d. Feb. 19, 1952, near Grimstad), Norwegian novelist, dramatist, and poet. Of peasant origin, he had almost no formal education. His semiautobiographical first novel, *Hunger* (1890), about a starving young writer, revealed his impulsive, lyrical style. It was followed by such works as *Mysteries* (1892), *Pan* (1894), and *Victoria* (1898), with which he established himself as a leader of the Neoromantic revolt against social realism. *Growth of the Soil* (1917) and his many other novels express a message of fierce individualism and back-to-nature philosophy. He won the Nobel Prize for Literature in 1920. His antipathy to modern Western culture led to his support of Nazi Germany during its wartime occupation of Norway; he was imprisoned and tried after the war, and his reputation was seriously damaged.

Han River, River, east-central China. A principal tributary of the Yangtze River (Chang Jiang), it has a total length of about 950 mi (1,530 km). It rises in the mountains in southwestern Shaanxi province; known by various names in its upper course, it becomes the Han at Hanzhong and flows through a fertile basin some 60 mi (100 km) long and 12 mi (19 km) wide, then cuts through a series of deep gorges and emerges into the central Yangtze basin in Hubei province. Its lower course forms a dense network of water transport covering the southern part of the North China Plain.

Han Yu, or HAN YÜ (b. 768, Henan province, China—d. 824, Chang'an), Chinese poet and prose writer, the first proponent of Neo-Confucianism. An orphan, he joined the Chinese bureaucracy and served in several high government posts. He attacked Daoism and Buddhism, which were then at the height of their influence, and sought to restore Confucianism to its former status. He revived

Han Yu, portrait by an unknown artist; in the National Palace Museum, Taipei, Taiwan.

interest in the writings of Mencius and other neglected Confucian classics. His own works were written in a simple prose style unlike the elaborate manner popular at the time, and he became known as the "Prince of Letters."

handball, Any of a variety games in which a small rubber ball is struck against a wall with the hand or fist. It can be played in a three- or four-walled court or against a single wall by two or four players (in singles or doubles games, respectively). The object is to make the ball rebound off the wall so that it cannot be returned by the opponent. The game runs to 21 points. Handball games were played in ancient Rome and later (as pelota) in Spain and France. Modern handball developed in Ireland, where it is still popular. It was played widely among late-19th-century Irish immigrants in New York City, whence it eventually spread around North America.

Hanfeizi, or HAN-FEI-TZU (d. 233 BC, China), Greatest of China's legalist philosophers. Much about his life is unknown; it ended when he was sent on a diplomatic mission to the court of the first Qin emperor, who had admired his writings; he was imprisoned and forced to drink poison. His works are collected in the *Hanfeizi*, presumably compiled after his death. In 55 sections of varying lengths, it presents a synthesis of legal theories up to his time. To Hanfeizi it was axiomatic that political institutions must change with changing historical circumstances and must be adapted to the prevailing pattern of human behaviour, which is determined not by moral sentiments but by economic conditions. Rulers should not try to make people good but only to restrain them from doing evil.

hang gliding, Sport of flying in unpowered aircraft that are light enough to be carried by the pilot. Takeoff is usually achieved by launching into the air from a cliff or hill. Hang gliders were developed by the pioneers of practical flight. In Germany, starting in 1891, Otto Lilienthal made several thousand flights before a fatal gliding accident in 1896. In the U.S. collaboration between Augustus Herring and Octave Chanute resulted in successful flights of a biplane hang glider in 1896. Modern hang gliding emerged toward the end of the 1960s. In the early 1960s enthusiasts in California were gliding down coastal dunes on homebuilt delta-shaped wings they had adapted from kite designs developed by Francis and Gertrude Rogallo. The Rogallos' kites had attracted attention because of NASA's interest in using them for spacecraft retrieval. By the early 1970s the sport had spread throughout the U.S. and into Europe. World championships in hang gliding have been held and records kept since 1975.

Hangzhou, or HANG-CHOU, conventional HANGCHOW, City (pop., 2003 est.: 2,059,800), capital of Zhejiang province, China. It lies at the head of Zhejiang Bay and is the southern terminus of the Grand Canal. Its buildings and gardens are renowned, and some of China's most famous monasteries are located nearby. As Lin'an, it was the capital of the Nan (Southern) Song dynasty AD 1127–1279. A prosperous centre of commerce with an estimated population then of 1–1.5 million, it was visited in the late 13th century by the Italian traveler Marco Polo, who called it Kinsai. Its importance as a port decreased as the bay silted up, but it remained a commercial centre and was opened to foreign trade in 1896. In addition to its cultural importance, it is also the centre for an industrial area.

Hannibal (b. 247 BC, North Africa—d. c.183–181 BC, Libyssa, Bithynia), Carthaginian general, one of the great military leaders of antiquity. Taken to Spain by his father, the Carthaginian general Hamilcar Barca (d. 229/228 BC), he was sworn to eternal enmity with Rome. After the death of his father and brother-in-law, he took charge of Carthage's army in Spain (221). He secured Spain, then crossed the Ebro River into Roman territory and entered Gaul. He marched over the Alps into Italy; encumbered by elephants and horses, he was beset by Gallic tribes, harsh winter weather, and defection of his Spanish troops. He defeated Gaius Flaminius but was severely harassed by Quintus Fabius Maximus Cunctator. In 216 he won the Battle of Cannae. In 203 he left for northern Africa to help Carthage fend off Scipio Africanus the Elder's forces. He lost decisively to Scipio's ally, Masinissa, at the Battle of Zama but escaped. He headed the Carthaginian government (c. 202–195); forced to flee, he sought refuge with Antiochus III, whose fleet he commanded against Rome, with disastrous results. After the Battle of Magnesia (190) the Romans demanded he be handed over; he eluded them until, seeing no escape, he took poison.

Hannover, English HANOVER, City (pop., 2002 est.: city, 516,415; metro. area, 996,586), capital of Lower Saxony state, northwestern Germany. Located on the Leine River, it is first mentioned in documents in AD 1100. It joined the Hanseatic League in 1386. From 1495 it belonged to the Welf dynasty (later the house of Hanover). It was the capital of the kingdom of Hanover (1815–66) and then was annexed by Prussia. Hannover became the capital of Lower Saxony in 1946. It suffered destruction in World War II but was rebuilt, and it is now an educational, financial, and commercial centre with highly diversified industries.

Hanoi, City (pop., 2009: 2,644,536), capital of Vietnam. Located in northern Vietnam on the western bank of the Red River, it became the capital of Vietnam's Ly dynasty in 1010. It was the main capital of Vietnam until 1802, when the Nguyen dynasty transferred the capital south to Hue. Under French rule Hanoi again became an important administrative centre, and in 1902 it was made the capital of French Indochina. It became the capital of North Vietnam after the French defeat in 1954. During the Vietnam War many of its monuments and palaces were destroyed by U.S. bombing. As the capital of a united Vietnam since 1976, it has steadily been rebuilt and its industrial base has grown. The city observed its 1,000th anniversary in October 2010.

Hanover, house of, British royal house of German origin. It was descended from George Louis, elector of Hanover, who succeeded to the British crown as George I in 1714. The dynasty also provided the monarchs George II, George III, George IV, William IV, and Victoria. By the Act of Settlement (1701) the crown was to go to Anne (of the house of Stuart) and then, if she lacked issue, to Sophia (1665–1714), electress of Hanover (granddaughter of James I) and her descendants. The house of Hanover was succeeded in 1901 by the house of Saxe-Coburg-Gotha, renamed in 1917 the house of Windsor.

Hanseatic League, or HANSA (from German *Hanse,* "association") Organization founded in the late medieval period by northern German towns and merchant communities to protect their trading interests. The league dominated commercial activity in northern Europe from the 13th to the 15th century. It protected transport of goods by quelling pirates and brigands and fostered safe navigation by building lighthouses. Most important, it sought to organize and control trade by winning commercial privileges and monopolies and by establishing trading bases overseas. In extreme cases its members resorted to warfare, as when they raised an armed force that defeated the Danes in 1368 and confirmed the

league's supremacy in the Baltic Sea. Over 150 towns were at some point associated with the league, including Bremen, Hamburg, and Lübeck.

hantavirus, Genus of viruses of the family Bunyaviridae that cause pneumonia and hemorrhagic fevers. Carried by rodents, they spread to humans directly or by inhalation but apparently are not transmitted from one person to another. An outbreak in the 1990s in the southwestern U.S. caused a mysterious, often fatal, flulike illness with rapid respiratory failure in previously healthy adults. The culprit was a hantavirus type carried by mice and not previously associated with human illness in the U.S.

Hanukkah, In Judaism, a holiday celebrating the rededication of the Second Temple of Jerusalem in 164 BC, after its desecration three years earlier by order of Antiochus IV Epiphanes. The Maccabees recaptured Jerusalem and reconsecrated the Temple after leading a successful revolt against Syrian rule. The lighting of the menorah recalls the story that a one-day supply of oil burned miraculously in the Temple for eight days until new oil could be obtained. Sometimes called the Feast of Dedication or Feast of Lights, it is celebrated for eight days in December, during which the ceremonial candles are lit and children play games and receive gifts. Originally a minor holiday, it has become more lavishly celebrated as a result of its proximity to Christmas.

Hanuman, Monkey god of Hindu mythology, a central figure in the *Ramayana*. He was a guardian spirit, the offspring of a nymph and the wind god. His great heroic exploit was recovering Rama's wife, Sita, from captivity by the demon Ravana. Hanuman also flew to the Himalayas and carried back a mountain of medicinal herbs to cure Rama's grievously wounded brother Laksmana. Worshiped in the form of a monkey, he is an important deity because of his strength and his faithfulness to Rama.

harai, Purification ceremonies in the Shinto religion, used to cleanse an individual before he may approach a deity. Salt, water, and fire are the chief agents of purification, and the rites range from bathing in the cold sea to washing the hands before entering a temple. Priests undergo more rigorous harai rites intended to regulate the body, heart, environment, and soul. Great purification ceremonies are held twice a year in Japan, on June 30 and December 31.

Harare, formerly SALISBURY, City (pop., 2007 est.: 1,572,000), capital of Zimbabwe. Located in northeastern Zimbabwe, it was founded as Salisbury by the British in 1890. It was the capital of, successively, the colony of Southern Rhodesia, the Federation of Rhodesia and Nyasaland (1953–63), and Rhodesia (1965–79). Under the new government of independent Zimbabwe (1980), it was renamed Harare. It is a cultural and educational centre and the site of the University of Zimbabwe (1957). The centre of Zimbabwe's industry and commerce, it is the distribution point for the area's agricultural produce. There are important gold mines nearby.

Harbin, Chinese HA'ERBIN, or HA-ERH-PIN, City (pop., 2003 est.: 2,735,095), capital and largest city of Heilongjiang province, northeastern China. Located on the Sungari (Songhua) River in the centre of Northeast China (Manchuria), it grew with the arrival of the Chinese Eastern Railway, built by the Russians in the late 19th century. A Russian military base during the Russo-Japanese War, it was a haven for Russian refugees after the Russian Revolution of 1917 and had the largest Russian population of any city outside the Soviet Union. Chinese communist forces took the city in 1946 and from it were able to bring all of northeastern China under their control. It then became the region's chief industrial base and a shipping centre for agricultural products.

hardness, Resistance of a mineral to scratching, described relative to a standard scale of 10 minerals known as the Mohs hardness scale. Hardness is an important diagnostic property in mineral identification. There is a general link between hardness and chemical composition (via crystal structure); thus, most hydrous minerals, halides, carbonates, sulfates, and phosphates are relatively soft; most sulfides are relatively soft (two exceptions being marcasite and pyrite); and most anhydrous oxides and silicates are hard.

Hare Krishna movement, officially INTERNATIONAL SOCIETY FOR KRISHNA CONSCIOUSNESS (ISKCON), 20th-century Hindu religious movement. It was founded in the U.S. by A.C. Bhaktivedanta Swami (1896–1977) in 1965. The organization claims a lineage of spiritual masters dating back to Caitanya (1485–1534?), whom it regards as an incarnation of Krishna. Hare Krishna became popular in the U.S. and Europe among young people of the 1960s and '70s counterculture, who often appeared in public places dressed in saffron robes, chanting, dancing, and asking for contributions. Members of the group are vegetarians. They renounce alcohol and drugs and chant several hours every day. Peace and joy are to be gained by surrendering to Krishna. Since the founder's death in 1977, the communes in which many members live have been governed by an international commission. The movement has endured several schisms since its founding and was among the first groups to be attacked by anticult organizations.

harem, Arabic ḤARĪM, In Muslim society, that part of a house set apart for the women of the family or the part from which males not of the family are excluded. Through extension it has come to refer generally to the mandatory seclusion of women from the outside world. Institutions similar to the harem existed in the pre-Islamic civilizations of the Middle East; in the courts of pre-Islamic Assyria, Persia, and Egypt, they were often the loci of political intrigues involving rival court factions. Large harems for wives (and often for concubines) were common in wealthy Middle Eastern households until the 20th century. From the 15th to the 20th century, the great harem, termed the seraglio, of the sultans of the Ottoman Empire housed several hundred women. In Iran—and in parts of Central and South Asia influenced by Persian culture—the institution of seclusion has traditionally been known as purdah. In the present-day Islamic world, seclusion of women is practiced only within conservative communities; concubinage has been generally outlawed. Similar systems have existed in other parts of Asia.

Harlem Renaissance, A blossoming (*c.* 1918–37) of African American culture, particularly in the creative arts, centred in Harlem in New York City. As a literary movement, it laid the groundwork for all later African American literature and had a significant impact on black literature and consciousness worldwide. Its leading literary figures included James Weldon Johnson, Claude McKay, Countee Cullen, Langston Hughes, Zora Neale Hurston, Jessie Redmon Fauset, Jean Toomer, Arna Bontemps, Rudolph Fisher, Alain Locke (1886–1954), and Wallace Thurman (1902–34). Their work both fed and took inspiration from the creative and commercial growth of jazz and a concurrent burgeoning of work by black visual artists such as Aaron Douglas. Central to the movement were efforts to explore all aspects of the African American experience and to reconceptualize "the Negro" independent of white stereotypes.

Harlequin, Principal stock character of the Italian commedia dell'arte. In the 16th century he was a wily, unscrupulous comic servant, but by the early 17th century he was a faithful valet involved in amorous exploits. His costume of peasant clothes covered with coloured patches developed into a tight-fitting costume decorated with bright triangles and diamond shapes. He carried a *batte*, or slapstick, and wore a black half-mask. In mid-18th-century England Harlequin was portrayed by John Rich in dance pantomimes. He was also the principal character of the slapstick form known as a harlequinade in England and elsewhere.

harmonica, or MOUTH ORGAN, Small rectangular wind instrument consisting of free metal reeds set in slots in a small wooden frame and blown through two parallel rows of wind channels. Successive notes of the diatonic (seven-note) scale are obtained by alternately blowing and sucking; the tongue covers channels not required. In chromatic (12-note scale) models, a finger-operated stop selects either of two sets of reeds tuned a semitone apart. The harmonica was invented in 1821 by Friedrich Buschmann (1805–64) of Berlin, who borrowed the basic principle from the Chinese *sheng*. It is widely used in blues as well as folk music and country music.

harmonium, or REED ORGAN, Free-reed keyboard instrument in which wind from a foot-operated bellows causes metal reeds to vibrate. Pitch is determined by the size of the reed; there are no pipes. Separate sets of reed produce different tone colours, the sound quality being determined by the size and shape of the tone chamber surrounding each reed. The harmonium developed in the early to mid-19th century in Europe and America, and it was a very popular church and home instrument into the 1930s.

Harmonium by Jacob Alexandre, Paris, 19th century
Behr Photography

harmony, In music, the sound of two or more notes heard simultaneously. In a narrower sense harmony refers to the extensively developed system of chords and the rules that govern relations between them in Western music. Harmony has always existed as the "vertical" (the relationship between simultaneous melodic lines) aspect of older music that is primarily contrapuntal; the rules of counterpoint are intended to control consonance and dissonance, which are fundamental aspects of harmony. However, the sense of harmony as dominating the individual contrapuntal lines followed from the invention of the continuo *c.* 1600; the bass line became the generating force upon which harmonies were built. This approach was formalized in the 18th century in a treatise by Jean-Philippe Rameau, who argued that all harmony is based on the "root" or fundamental note of a chord. Tonality is principally a harmonic concept and is based not only on a seven-note scale of a given key but on a set of harmonic relations and progressions based on triads (three-note chords) drawn from the scale.

harness racing, Horse-racing sport. In harness racing, Standardbred horses are harnessed to lightweight, two-wheeled, bodiless (seat-only) vehicles known as sulkies. The sport's origins date to ancient chariot races. Today two types of horses are used, trotters and pacers. The former employ a gait in which the legs move in diagonal pairs, the latter a gait in which the legs move in lateral pairs. Since the establishment of pari-mutuel racing under lights in the 1940s, the sport has grown tremendously in popularity.

harp, Plucked stringed instrument in which the resonator, or belly, is perpendicular to the plane of the strings. Harps are roughly triangular. In early harps and many folk harps, the strings are strung between the resonating "body" and the "neck." Early harps and many folk harps lack the forepillar or column—forming the third side of the triangle—that characterizes frame harps; the column permits high string tension and higher-pitched tuning. Small, primitive harps date back to at least 3000 BC in the ancient Mediterranean and Middle East. In Europe they became particularly important in Celtic societies. The large modern orchestral harp emerged in the 18th century. It has 47 strings and a range of almost seven octaves. It plays the entire chromatic (12-note) scale by means of seven pedals, each of which can alter the pitch of a note (in all octaves) by two semitones through tightening or relaxing the strings by turning a forklike projection against it; it is thus known as the double-action harp. Its massive resonator permits considerable volume of tone.

harp seal, Migratory earless seal (*Pagophilus groenlandicus,* sometimes *Phoca groenlandica*) of the North Atlantic and Arctic oceans. The adult male is light grayish or yellowish, with brown or black on the head and a similarly coloured U-shaped marking on the back and sides. The female is less clearly marked. Adults are about 6 ft (1.8 m) long and typically weigh between 265 and 300 lbs (120 and 135 kg). Harp seals feed on fish and crustaceans and spend much of the year at sea. They breed near Newfoundland, Can., and in the Greenland and White seas. Until two weeks old, the pups bear a fluffy white coat highly valued by the fur trade; public indignation over hunting methods (including clubbing) has led to increased regulation and supervision of sealing activities in the Newfoundland area.

harpsichord, Keyboard instrument in which the strings are set in vibration by a plucking mechanism. The latter consists of plectra made of quill (or sometimes leather) mounted on vertical wooden jacks that are activated by the keys. A cloth damper touches the string when the player releases the key. It often has two parallel keyboards (or manuals) and generally has two or more sets of strings, each of which produces different tone qualities; these permit the simultaneous sounding of pitches an octave higher or lower than the note struck. The notes' loudness is not affected by the power with which the keys are struck, and there is no way to sustain a note after the key is released. Primitive harpsichords existed by the mid-15th century. In the 17th–18th centuries the harpsichord became a very important solo, accompanimental, and ensemble instrument. From *c.* 1750 the pianoforte, with its greater dynamic capacity, began to displace it, and by 1820 the harpsichord had largely vanished. It was revived in the late 19th century by scholars, performers, and instrument builders.

Harpsichord with soundboard by Hans Ruckers, Amsterdam, 1612

From the National Trust Property, Fenton House, Hampstead, London; by gracious permission of Her Majesty Queen Elizabeth, the Queen Mother

Hārūn al-Rashīd (b. March 763 or February 766, Rayy, Iran—d. March 24, 809, Tūs, Iran), Fifth caliph of the ʿAbbāsid dynasty. Neither a great ruler nor a prepossessing character, Hārūn ruled (786–809) at a time when Islamic society reached its zenith in terms of wealth, learning, and power. He is best remembered, however, as a central character in *The Thousand and One Nights*, where he is portrayed as the epitome of the learned and just ruler. In his early years he was strongly influenced by his mother and by his tutor Yaḥyā of the Barmakid line of viziers. He succeeded his brother after the latter's untimely death and ruled over a realm that was torn increasingly by strife, as regional leaders sought autonomy. On his death, his sons al-Maʾmun and al-Amīn fell into open civil war.

Harvard University, Oldest institution of higher learning in the U.S. and widely considered one of the most prestigious. Founded in 1636 in Cambridge, Mass., it was named Harvard College for a Puritan minister, John Harvard (1607–38), who bequeathed to the school his books and half of his estate. It became a university with the establishment of the medical school in 1782. Schools of divinity and law were established in the early 19th century. Charles Eliot, during his long tenure as president (1869–1909), made Harvard an institution with national influence. Harvard has educated seven U.S. presidents, many Supreme Court justices, cabinet officers, and congressional leaders, dozens of major literary and intellectual figures, and numerous Nobel laureates. Its undergraduate school, Harvard College, contains about one-third of the total student body. Radcliffe College (1879) was a coordinate undergraduate women's college. From 1960 women graduated from both Harvard and Radcliffe, and in 1999 Radcliffe was absorbed by Harvard, the name surviving in the Radcliffe Institute for Advanced Study. Harvard University also has graduate or professional schools of business, education, government, dentistry, architecture and landscape design, and public health. Among its affiliated research institutes are the Museum of Comparative Zoology, the Peabody Museum of Archaeology and Ethnology, and the Fogg Art Museum. Its Widener Library is one of the largest and most important libraries in the world.

Haryana, State (pop., 2008 est.: 23,778,000), northwestern India. It is bordered by the states of Rajasthan, Punjab, Himachal Pradesh, and Uttar Pradesh, by the union territory and city of Chandigarh, and by the Delhi national capital territory and occupies an area of 17,070 sq mi (44,212 sq km). The city of Chandigarh is the joint administrative capital of Haryana and Punjab. The region is the legendary birthplace of Hinduism, and its festivals attract many pilgrims. Most of Haryana lies on the flat Indo-Gangetic Plain, an area that has experienced waves of migration since the time of Alexander the Great. It came under the control of the British East India Company in 1803, became a part of Punjab in 1858, and became a separate state in 1966. Its economy is mainly agricultural.

Harz Mountains, Mountain range, central Germany. Lying between the Weser and Elbe rivers, it is 60 mi (100 km) long and about 20 mi (32 km) wide. The northwestern and highest portion is known as the Oberharz, and the more extensive southeastern part is the Unterharz; the Brocken group, dividing the two, is considered part of the Oberharz. The highest peak is Mount Brocken. The Harz owes its early settlement and intensive development from the 10th to the 16th century to mining and metallurgy (silver, lead, iron, copper, and zinc). Its most important industry is tourism.

hashish, Hallucinogenic drug preparation derived from resin from the flowers of cannabis plants. Marijuana, a product of the same plant, is far less potent. Hashish is smoked or eaten. The active ingredient, tetrahydrocannabinol (THC), makes up 10–15% of hashish.

Hasidism, Pietistic and mystical movement in Judaism that originated in 18th-century Poland. It was a reaction against rigid legalism and Talmudic learning in favour of a joyful form of worship that served as a spiritual outlet for the common people. Hasidism began with the preaching of the man later known as the Baʿal Shem Ṭov. Teaching that God was immanent in all things and that piety was more important than scholarship, he won followers known as Hasidim ("loyalists"). Dov Baer founded the first Hasidic community *c.* 1710, and countless small communities soon sprang up in Poland, Russia, Lithuania, and Palestine, each led by a zaddik. Communal services were marked by dancing, shouting, and singing, through which participants reached a state of spiritual ecstasy. Though excommunicated from Orthodox Judaism in 1772, the Hasidim continued to flourish. By the 19th century Hasidism had become an ultraconservative movement that was accepted by the Orthodox as legitimate. Huge numbers of Hasidim fell victim to the Holocaust, but their survivors established vital movements in Israel and the U.S. The Lubavitcher sect, based in Brooklyn, N.Y., numbers about 200,000.

Haskala, or HASKALAH, Intellectual movement in European Judaism in the 18th–19th century, which sought to supplement traditional Talmudic studies with education in secular subjects, European languages, and Hebrew. Partly inspired by the Enlightenment, the Haskala was sometimes called the Jewish Enlightenment. It originated with prosperous and socially mobile Jews, who hoped to use reforms to enable the Jews to escape ghetto life and enter the mainstream of European society and culture. This meant adding secular subjects to the school curriculum, adopting the language of the larger society in place of Yiddish, abandoning traditional garb, and reforming synagogue services. One of its leaders was Moses Mendelssohn, who began a revival of Hebrew writing. Haskala's emphasis on the study of Jewish history and ancient Hebrew as a means of reviving Jewish national consciousness influenced Zionism, and its call to modernize religious practices led to the emergence of Reform Judaism.

Hasmonean dynasty, Dynasty of ancient Judaea, descendants of the Maccabee family. The name derives from their ancestor Hasmoneus, but the first of the ruling dynasty was Simon Maccabeus, who became leader of the Maccabean revolt against the Seleucid king c. 143 BC and, in victory, was made high priest, ruler, and ethnarch of Judaea. The last Hasmonean was deposed and executed in 37 BC by the Romans under Mark Antony.

Hastings, Battle of (Oct. 14, 1066) Battle that ended in the defeat of Harold II of England by William, duke of Normandy, and established the Normans as rulers of England. On his deathbed Edward the Confessor had granted the English throne to Harold, earl of Wessex, despite an earlier promise to make William his heir. William crossed to England from Normandy with a skilled army of 4,000–7,000 men, landing at Pevensey in Sussex and moving eastward along the coast to Hastings. Harold met the Norman invaders with an army of 7,000 men, many of whom were exhausted from the forced march south to meet William following Harold's victory at the battle of Stamford Bridge three weeks earlier. The English were defeated after a day-long battle in which Harold was killed. After the battle, the Norman duke moved his army to London and was crowned William I on December 25.

hate crime, In law, a crime directed at a person or persons on the basis of characteristics such as race, religion, ethnicity, or sexual orientation. The concept emerged in the U.S. in the late 1970s, and since then laws have been passed in many U.S. states mandating additional penalties for violent crimes motivated by bias or bigotry against particular groups. Several other Western countries, including Australia, Britain, and Canada, have adopted laws designed to curb violent crime against racial and religious minorities. For example, German law forbids public incitement and instigation of racial hatred, including the distribution of Nazi propaganda.

Hatshepsut, limestone sculpture, c. 1485 BC; in the Metropolitan Museum of Art, New York City.

Courtesy of the Metropolitan Museum of Art, New York, Rogers Fund and Contributions from Edward S. Harkness, 1929

Hathor, In ancient Egyptian religion, the goddess of the sky, of women, and of fertility and love. Her principal animal form was a cow, and she was strongly associated with motherhood. Her worship was linked at Heliopolis with that of Re, whose wife or daughter she was said to be. In Upper Egypt she was worshiped with Horus, and in the necropolis at Thebes she was held to be the patroness of the dead.

Hatshepsut, Queen of Egypt (c. 1472–58 BC). Daughter of Thutmose I and wife of Thutmose II, she first acted as regent for her stepson, Thutmose III, but soon ordered herself crowned as pharaoh. She attained unprecedented power, adopting the titles and regalia of a pharaoh, complete with a false beard. She devoted much of the profit from expanded trade and tribute to an extensive building program, most notably to a splendid temple at Dayr al-Baḥrī. Thutmose III, who had become head of the army, succeeded her; whether she died naturally or was deposed and killed is uncertain.

Hauptmann, Gerhart (Johann Robert) (b. Nov. 15, 1862,

Gerhart Hauptmann, etching by Hermann Struck, 1904; in the Schiller-Nationalmuseum, Marbach, Ger.

Courtesy of the Schiller-Nationalmuseum, Marbach, Ger.

Bad Salzbrunn, Silesia, Prussia—d. June 6, 1946, Agnetendorf, Ger.), German playwright and poet. He studied sculpture before turning to literature in his early 20s. His first play, the starkly realistic social drama *Before Dawn* (1889), made him famous and signaled the end of highly stylized German drama. His naturalistic plays on themes of social reality and proletarian tragedy, including *The Weavers* (1892), *The Beaver Coat* (1893), and *Drayman Henschel* (1898), made him the most prominent German playwright of his era. He was awarded the Nobel Prize in 1912. In his novels, stories, epic poems, and later plays, he abandoned naturalism for mystical religiosity and mythical symbolism.

Hausa, People of northwestern Nigeria and southern Niger. Their language, also called Hausa, is an Afroasiatic language of the Chadic group. The Hausa, numbering some 32 million, are the largest ethnic group in the area. In the mid 14th century a confederation of Hausa states was formed, influenced by the spread of Islam from the Mali empire. Hausa society traditionally was, and to some extent continues to be, organized on a feudal basis. The head of an emirate is surrounded by titled officeholders who hold villages as fiefs, from which their agents collect taxes. The economy has traditionally rested on agriculture, though craftwork and trade are also important. Hausa society is markedly hierarchical; the ranking, both of offices and social classes, is expressed in an elaborate etiquette.

Havana, Spanish LA HABANA, City, capital, and province (pop., 2001 est.: 2,181,500) of Cuba. The city lies on the island's northern coast. The largest city in the Caribbean, it is Cuba's chief port, and it has one of the best harbours in the Western Hemisphere. It was founded by the Spanish in 1515 and moved to its present location in 1519. The de facto capital of Cuba by 1553, it was Spain's chief naval station in the New World. Its harbour was the scene of the destruction of the U.S. battleship *Maine* in 1898, the immediate cause of the Spanish-American War. Before 1959, when Fidel Castro came to power, Havana was a haven for U.S. tourists, offering gambling and showy nightlife. In addition to being Cuba's commercial and industrial centre, it contains many buildings of Spanish colonial style, including the 17th-century Cathedral of Havana, the Museum of the City of Havana, and Morro Castle. Old Havana and its fortifications are a UNESCO World Heritage site.

Hawaii, Hawaiian HAWAI'I, formerly SANDWICH ISLANDS, State, U.S., comprising a group of islands in the central Pacific Ocean. Area: 6,468 sq mi (16,752 sq km). Population: (2010) 1,360,301. Capital: Honolulu. Hawaii lies 2,397 mi (3,857 km) west of San Francisco. The state's major islands are, from west to east, Niihau, Kauai, Oahu, Molokai, Lanai, Kahoolawe, Maui, and Hawaii; there are 124 islets. The state's active volcanoes include Mauna Loa and Kilauea. The majority of the state's residents live on Oahu. The original Hawaiians were of Polynesian origin and came from the Marquesas Islands c. 300 CE. Capt. James Cook visited the islands in 1778 and called them the Sandwich Islands. At the beginning of the 19th century, Kamehameha I united the group under his rule. American whalers began to stop there; they were followed in 1820 by New England missionaries, and Western influences changed the islands. While Kamehameha III in 1851 placed Hawaii under U.S. protection, a coup fomented by U.S. sugar interests resulted in the monarchy's overthrow and the establishment of a Republic of Hawaii (1893). In 1898 the new republic and the U.S. agreed on annexation, and in 1900 Hawaii became a U.S. territory. The bombing of Pearl Harbor by the Japanese in 1941 led to U.S. involvement in World War II, and Hawaii became a major naval station. Hawaii became the 50th U.S. state on Aug. 21, 1959. Its largest industry is tourism. It is also a world astronomy centre, with telescopes atop Mauna Kea.

Hawaii, Volcanic island, part of the state of Hawaii, U.S. It lies south of Maui and constitutes Hawaii county, with Hilo (pop., 2000: 40,759) the island's main town. Known as the Big Island, it is the largest in area at 4,028 sq mi (10,433 sq km) and southeasternmost of the Hawaiian Island group. It is the youngest geologically and was formed by five volcanoes connected by lava ridges. Kilauea, the world's most active volcano, is located there in Hawaii Volcanoes National Park. The island has other volcanic peaks, including Mauna Kea. Sugar, tourism, cattle, orchids, and coffee are the basis of the economy.

Hawaiian, Any of the aboriginal people of Hawaii. They are the descendants of Polynesians who migrated to Hawaii in two waves: the first from the Marquesas Islands probably *c.* AD 400; the second from Tahiti in the 9th or 10th century. Without metals, pottery, or beasts of burden, Hawaiians made implements of stone, wood, shell, teeth, and bone. They had a highly developed oral culture and possessed percussion, string, and wind instruments. Their basic unit of land, the *ahupuaa,* usually extended from the shore to the mountaintop, providing the occupants with the means to grow and gather all they needed. Hawaiians had four principal gods and many lesser deities. Their laws, which included intricate taboos, bore heavily upon the people, especially women. After the arrival of Christian missionaries in 1820, some of the more repressive laws and taboos were abolished, but the native population was devastated by Western diseases. Numbering about 300,000 in 1778, full-blooded Hawaiians today number fewer than 10,000.

hawk, Any of many small to medium-sized, diurnal birds of prey, particularly those in the genus *Accipiter.* The term is often applied to other birds in the Accipitridae family (including buzzards, harriers, and kites) and sometimes to certain falcons. Hawks usually eat small mammals, reptiles, and insects but occasionally kill birds. There is often no difference in plumage between sexes. Hawks are found on the six major continents. Most nest in trees, but some nest on the ground or on cliffs. True hawks (accipiters) can usually be distinguished in flight by their long tails and short, rounded wings. They are exemplified by the 12-in (30-cm) sharp-shinned hawk (*A. striatus*), gray above with fine rusty barring below, found throughout much of the New World.

*Red-tailed hawk (*Buteo jamaicensis).
Alan Carey

Hawking radiation, Radiation theoretically emitted from just outside the event horizon of a black hole. Stephen W. Hawking proposed in 1974 that subatomic particle pairs (photons, neutrinos, and some massive particles) arising naturally near the event horizon may result in one particle's escaping the vicinity of the black hole while the other particle, of negative energy, disappears into it. The flow of particles of negative energy into the black hole reduces its mass until it disappears completely in a final burst of radiation.

hay fever, Seasonal sneezing, nasal congestion, and tearing and itching of the eyes caused by allergy to the pollen of certain plants. These plants are chiefly those pollinated by the wind (e.g., ragweed in North America, timothy grass in Britain). Antihistamines and corticosteroids may provide temporary relief, but the most effective long-range treatment is desensitization. Unless properly treated, about one-third of patients with hay fever develop asthma.

Hayek, Friedrich (August) von (b. May 8, 1899, Vienna, Austria—d. March 23, 1992, Freiburg, Ger.), Austrian-born British economist. He moved to London in 1931 and held positions at the University of London and the London School of Economics, becoming a British citizen in 1938. Later posts included a professorship at the University of Chicago (1950–62). Throughout his life Hayek criticized socialism, often contrasting it with a system of free markets. In his works he opposed the theories of John Maynard Keynes and argued that government intervention in the free market is destructive of individual values and could not prevent such economic ailments as inflation, unemployment, and recession. His books include *The Road to Serfdom* (1944), *The Constitution of Liberty* (1960), and *The Political Order of a Free People* (1979). His views have been highly influential among conservatives, including Margaret Thatcher. In 1974 he shared the Nobel Prize with Gunnar Myrdal.

headache, Pain in the upper portion of the head. Episodic tension headaches are the most common, usually causing mild to moderate pain on both sides. They result from sustained contraction of face and neck muscles, often due to fatigue, stress, or frustration. Headaches are treated with aspirin, acetaminophen, or other NSAIDs. Chronic daily headaches are similar but more frequent. They usually have a psychological cause and respond to certain antidepressants. They may also come from overuse of pain relievers. Migraine and cluster headaches are vascular headaches. Headaches may also be caused by distension of arteries at the base of the brain, from fever, hangover, or an attack of high blood pressure. Headache can be a symptom of meningitis, hemorrhagic stroke, or tumour.

health, Extent of continuing physical, emotional, mental, and social ability to cope with one's environment. Good health is harder to define than bad health (which can be equated with presence of disease) because it must convey a more positive concept than mere absence of disease, and there is a variable area between health and disease. A person may be in good physical condition but have a cold or be mentally ill. Someone may appear healthy but have a serious condition (e.g., cancer) that is detectable only by physical examination or diagnostic tests or not even by these.

health insurance, System for the advance financing of medical expenses through contributions or taxes paid into a common fund to pay for all or part of health services specified in an insurance policy or law. The key elements are advance payment of premiums or taxes, pooling of funds, and eligibility for benefits on the basis of contributions or employment without an income or assets test. Health insurance may apply to a limited or comprehensive range of medical services and may provide for full or partial payment of the costs of specific services. Benefits may consist of the right to certain medical services or reimbursement of the insured for specified medical costs. Private health insurance is organized and administered by an insurance company or other private agency; public health insurance is run by the government. Both forms of health insurance are to be distinguished from socialized medicine and government medical-care programs, in which doctors are employed directly or indirectly by the goverment, which also owns the health-care facilities (e.g., Britain's National Health Service).

Heaney, Seamus (Justin) (b. April 13, 1939, near Castledàwson, County Londonderry, N.Ire.), Irish poet. After studying at Queen's University in Belfast, he became a teacher and lecturer. Appalled by the violence in his native Northern Ireland, he moved to the republic of Ireland in 1972. From the 1980s he taught at Harvard, Oxford, and Cambridge. His works, rooted in Northern Irish rural life, evoke historical events and draw on Irish myth, but they also reflect the land's recent troubled decades. His collections include *Death of a Naturalist* (1966), *Door into the Dark* (1969), *North* (1975), *The Haw Lantern* (1987), *Seeing Things* (1991), *The Spirit Level* (1996), and *District and Circle* (2006). *Preoccupations* (1980) and *Finders Keepers* (2002) include essays on poetry and poets. He also made a noteworthy translation of *Beowulf*. He received the Nobel Prize for Literature in 1995.

hearing, or AUDITION, or SOUND RECEPTION, Physiological process of perceiving sound. Hearing entails the transformation of sound vibrations into nerve impulses, which travel to the brain and are interpreted as sounds. Members of two animal groups, arthropods and vertebrates, are capable of sound reception. Hearing enables an animal to sense danger, locate food, find mates, and, in more complex creatures, engage in communication. All vertebrates have two ears, often with an inner chamber housing auditory hair cells (papillae) and an outer eardrum that receives and transmits sound vibrations. Localization of sound depends on the recognition of minute differences in intensity and in the time of arrival of the sound at the two ears. Sound reception in mammals is generally well developed and often highly specialized, as in bats and dolphins, which use echolocation, and whales and elephants, which can hear mating calls from tens or even hundreds of miles away. Dogs and other canines can similarly detect faraway sounds. The human ear can detect frequencies of 20–20,000 hertz (Hz); it is most sensitive to those between 1,000 and 3,000 Hz. Impulses travel along the central auditory pathway from the cochlear nerve to the medulla to the cerebral cortex. Hearing may be impaired by disease, injury, or old age; some disorders, including deafness, may be congenital.

heart, Organ that pumps blood, circulating it to all parts of the body. The human heart is a four-chambered double pump with its right and left sides fully separated by a septum and subdivided on both sides into an atrium above and a ventricle below. The right atrium receives venous blood from the superior and inferior venae cavae and propels it into the pulmonary circulation. The left atrium takes in blood from the pulmonary veins and sends it into the systemic circulation. Electrical signals from a natural pacemaker cause the heart muscle to contract. Valves in the heart keep blood flowing in one direction. Their snapping shut after each contraction causes the sounds heard as the heartbeat.

heart attack, or MYOCARDIAL INFARCTION, Death of a section of heart muscle when its blood supply is cut off, usually by a blood clot in a coronary artery narrowed by atherosclerosis. Hypertension, diabetes mellitus, high cholesterol, cigarette smoking, and coronary heart disease increase the risk. Symptoms include severe chest pain, often radiating to the left arm, and shortness of breath. Up to 20% of victims die before reaching the hospital. Diagnosis is done by electrocardiography and by analysis for enzymes in the blood. Treatment aims to limit the area of tissue death (infarct) and prevent and treat complications. Thrombolytic (clot-dissolving) drugs may be administered. Beta-blockers alleviate pain and slow the heart rate. Angioplasty or coronary bypass restores blood flow to heart muscle. Follow-up may include drugs, exercise programs, and counseling on diet and lifestyle changes.

heart failure, Inability of one or both sides of the heart to pump enough blood for the body. Causes include pulmonary heart disease, hypertension, and coronary atherosclerosis. A person with left-sided heart failure experiences shortness of breath after exertion, difficulty in breathing while lying down and night breathlessness, and abnormally high pressure in the pulmonary veins. A person with right-sided failure experiences abnormally high pressure in the systemic veins, liver enlargement, and accumulation of fluid in the legs. A person with failure of both ventricles has an enlarged heart and a three-beat heartbeat. Treatment includes bed rest, medications such as digitalis, control of excess salt and water retention, and elimination of the underlying cause.

heart transplant, Procedure to remove a diseased heart and replace it with a healthy one from a legally dead donor. The first was performed in 1967 by Christiaan Barnard. The diseased heart is removed (except for some atrial tissue to preserve nerve connections to the natural pacemaker). The new heart is put in place and connected to the recipient's blood vessels. Patients and donors are matched for tissue type, but the patient's immune system must still be suppressed to prevent rejection. A successful transplant can enable the recipient to have an active life for many years.

heat, Energy transferred from one body to another as the result of a difference in temperature. Heat flows from a hotter body to a colder body when the two bodies are brought together. This transfer of energy usually results in an increase in the temperature of the colder body and a decrease in that of the hotter body. A substance may absorb heat without an increase in temperature as it changes from one phase to another—that is, when it melts or boils. The distinction between heat (a form of energy) and temperature (a measure of the amount of energy) was clarified in the 19th century by such scientists as J.-B. Fourier, Gustav Kirchhoff, and Ludwig Boltzmann.

heat-treating, Changing the properties of materials such as metals or glass by processes involving heating. It is used to harden, soften, or modify other properties of materials that have different crystal structures at low and high temperatures. The type of transformation depends on the temperature that the material is heated to, how fast it is heated, how long it is kept heated, what temperature it is first cooled to, and how fast it is cooled. For example, quenching hardens steel by heating it to high temperatures and then quickly immersing it in room temperature oil, water, or salt brine to "freeze" the new crystal structure; in cryogenic treatments the cooling bath ranges from −180 to −70 °C (−300 to −100 °F), and it is often used in treating high-carbon and high-alloy steels. The two main approaches to softening a metal (to restore its ductility) are annealing, in which its temperature is slowly raised, held for some time, and slowly cooled, and tempering, in which it is slowly heated in an oil bath and held for some hours.

heather, or SCOTCH HEATHER, Low evergreen shrub (*Calluna vulgaris*) of the heath family, widespread in western Europe and Asia, North America, and Greenland. It is the chief vegetation on many wastelands of northern and western Europe. *C. vulgaris* is distinguished from true heaths, which are sometimes loosely called heather, by the lobes of its calyx, which conceal the petals; in true heaths the petals cover the calyx. Scotch heather has purple stems, close-leaved green shoots, and feathery spikes of bell-shaped flowers. It has various economic uses: large stems are made into brooms, shorter ones are tied into bundles that serve as brushes, and long trailing shoots are woven into baskets.

heatstroke, Debility caused by exposure to heat and humidity, usually for many hours, called sunstroke when caused by direct sunlight. Body temperature is 106–110°F (41–43°C) or higher. Perspiration almost stops, leading to the rapid temperature rise, collapse, and coma. Cooling with ice-water baths or packs, with massage to promote circulation, is urgent to save the victim's life. Even after body temperature drops, circulatory disorder and brain damage may cause death.

heaven, Dwelling place of God or the gods and the abode of the blessed dead. The term also refers to the celestial sphere, the place of the sun, moon, planets, and stars and the source of light, which symbolizes good. For later Judaism and Christianity, heaven is the destination of the faithful after a general resurrection of the dead, in contrast to hell, the place of punishment for the wicked. Islam has a similar belief. In Chinese religion, heaven is equated with the divine will, which guides the operation of all physical and moral laws. In some Mahayana Buddhist sects, heaven is a paradise for those who have received the saving grace of Amitabha.

"The Angel Shows John the Heavenly Jerusalem," from the Apocalypse of St. John, c. *1020; in the Staatsbibliothek Bamberg, Germany (MS. 140).*
Courtesy of the Staatsbibliothek Bamberg, Germany

Heb-Sed festival, One of the oldest festivals of ancient Egypt, celebrated by the king after 30 years of rule and repeated every three years thereafter. The event was probably a ritual reenactment of the unification of Egypt, traditionally accomplished by Menes c. 3000 BCE. After beginning the celebration by offering a sacrifice to the gods, the king was crowned with the white crown of Upper Egypt, followed by the red crown of Lower Egypt. He then ran a ritual course four times, before being carried in procession to the chapels of the gods of Upper and Lower Egypt.

Hebei, or HO-PEH, conventional HOPEH, formerly CHIHLI, Province (pop., 2002 est.: 67,350,000), northern China. It is bordered by the Bo Hai (Gulf of Chihli), the provinces of Liaoning, Shandong, Henan, and Shanxi, and the Inner Mongolia autonomous region; Beijing and Tianjin municipalities are enclaves within it. It has an area of 78,200 sq mi (202,700 sq km). Its capital is Shijiazhuang. Historically a chief barrier to northern invasion, it contains part of the Great Wall of China. From 1644 to 1911/12 it was ruled by the Qing dynasty. It was occupied by the Japanese in 1937 and taken by the Chinese communists in 1949. The provincial capital was at Baoding until 1958, when it was transferred to Tianjin, and in 1966 it returned to Baoding. In 1968 the provincial capital was moved to Shijiazhuang. Culturally and economically, Hebei is the most advanced province in northern China. The North China Plain, covering southern Hebei, has been inhabited by humans for several millennia. The fossil remains of *Homo erectus pekinensis* were discovered there.

Hebraic law, Law codes of ancient Israel found in the Jewish Scripture (Old Testament). Three separate codes are usually distinguished: the Book of the Covenant, the Deuteronomic Code, and the Priestly Code. The Book of the Covenant is found in Exodus 20–23 and is similar to the much earlier Code of Hammurabi in Babylon. The Deuteronomic Code in Deuteronomy 12–26 is a revision of earlier Israelite laws and was used in the effort to purify the worship of Yahweh (God) from Canaanite and other influences. The Priestly Code, found in parts of Exodus, all of Leviticus, and much of Numbers, covers mostly ceremonial practices.

Hebrew alphabet, Script used to write the Hebrew language and a number of other languages used as vernaculars by Jews, including Ladino and Yiddish. The modern 22-letter alphabet in use today differs only slightly from the script adapted by Jewish scribes in the early centuries BC from the square script used to write Imperial Aramaic. Prior to this adaptation, Hebrew was written in a linear script borrowed ultimately from the Phoenicians and first attested in the 9th century BC; though the linear script passed out of favour among Jews, Samaritans, adherents of an ancient offshoot of Judaism, continued to use it into modern times. Hebrew is written from right to left, and the letter shapes—at least originally—represented only consonants. Later certain of the consonants were utilized to denote vowels in certain positions, and by c. AD 600 a system of diacritics, or "points," were used to show all vowels in the text of the Bible.

Hebrew language, Semitic language that is both a sacred language of Judaism and a modern vernacular in Israel. Like Aramaic, to which it is closely related, Hebrew has a documented history of nearly 3,000 years. The earliest fully attested stage of the language is Biblical Hebrew: the earlier parts ("Standard Biblical Hebrew") date before 500 BC and include even older poetic passages; the later parts ("Late Biblical Hebrew") were composed c. 500–200 BC. Post-Biblical Hebrew, variously termed Rabbinic or Mishnaic Hebrew, is characterized by an early period when Hebrew was still probably to some degree a vernacular and a later period, after c. AD 200, when Aramaic became the everyday speech of Jews in the Middle East. The 6th and 7th centuries marked a transition to Medieval Hebrew. The resurrection of Hebrew as a vernacular is closely linked with the 18th-century Haskala movement and 20th-century Zionism. Contemporary Israeli Hebrew is spoken by about five million people in Israel and abroad.

Hebrides, or WESTERN ISLES, ancient EBUDAE, Group of islands, western Scotland, in the North Atlantic Ocean. They are separated into two groups, the Outer Hebrides and the Inner Hebrides, divided by the Little Minch Strait. The Outer Hebrides are administered as the Eilean Siar (Western Isles) council area (pop., 2001: 26,502). The northern Inner Hebrides lie within the Highland council area, and the southern Inner Hebrides are part of Argyll and Bute council area. Composed of more than 40 islands, only a few of which are inhabited, the Hebrides were originally settled by Celts. Norse raids, which led to Norse rule, began after the 8th century and lasted until 1266, when the islands were ceded to Scotland. Their economy centres on farming, fishing, and weaving, the latter noted especially for Harris tweed.

Hebron, Arabic AL-KHALĪL, City (pop., 2005 est.: 160,500) in the West Bank, southwest of Jerusalem. It is a sacred city of Judaism and Islam as the home and burial place (at the Cave of Machpelah) of the patriarch Abraham. King David made Hebron his capital briefly in the 10th century BC. Except for a period of Crusader control in the 12th century, various Muslim dynasties ruled the city from AD 635 until after World War I (1914–18). It was part of the British mandate of Palestine from the early 1920s until the first Arab-Israeli war in 1948, when it came under the control of Transjordan (later Jordan). Along with the rest of the West Bank, it was annexed by Jordan in 1950 but was captured by Israel during the Six-Day War (1967). It remained under full Israeli administration until 1997, when Israel and the Palestine Liberation Organization agreed on a partial Israeli pullout from Hebron and other West Bank cities.

Hector, In Greek legend, the eldest son of Priam and Hecuba, the husband of Andromache, and the chief warrior of the Trojan army. In Homer's *Iliad* he is notable not only for his military prowess but also for his nobility of character. He was a favorite of Apollo, who helped him slay Achilles' friend Patroclus in combat; in reprisal, Achilles killed Hector in battle and dragged his naked body around the walls of Troy.

Hecuba, In Greek legend, the wife of the Trojan king Priam and mother of Hector. At the end of the Trojan War she was taken prisoner. According to Euripides, her youngest son, Polydorus, had been placed in the care of Polymestor, king of Thrace. When she arrived in Thrace, she learned that Polydorus had been murdered. In revenge, she blinded Polymestor and killed his two sons. In other versions of the legend, she was later turned into a dog, and her grave beside the Hellespont became a landmark for ships.

hedgehog, Any of 14 species of insectivores in the family Erinaceidae. They eat primarily insects and other arthropods but will also eat plant material. The nine species of spiny hedgehogs have short, barbless spines on the back, a round body, small head, pointed face, and little or no tail. Species range from 4 to 17 in. (10 to 44 cm) long. Spiny hedgehogs are native to Great Britain, northern Africa, and Asia; one species was introduced into New Zealand. The five species of gymnure, or hairy hedgehog, are Asian. They have coarse guard hairs but no spines and are extremely malodorous. The common gymnure may be 18 in. (46 cm) long and have a 12-in. (30-cm) tail.

Hegel, Georg Wilhelm Friedrich (b. Aug. 27, 1770, Stuttgart, Württemberg—d. Nov. 14, 1831, Berlin), German philosopher. After working as a tutor, he was headmaster of the gymnasium at Nürnberg (1808–16); he then taught principally at the University of Berlin (1818–31). His work, following on that of Immanuel Kant, Johann Gottlieb Fichte, and F.W. Schelling, marks the pinnacle of post-Kantian German idealism. Inspired by Christian insights and possessing a fantastic fund of concrete knowledge, Hegel found a place for everything—logical, natural, human, and divine—in a dialectical scheme that repeatedly swung from thesis to antithesis and back again to a higher and richer synthesis. His panoramic system engaged philosophy in the consideration of all the problems of history and culture, none of which could any longer be deemed foreign to its competence. At the same time, it deprived all the implicated elements and problems of their autonomy, reducing them to symbolic manifestations of the one process, that of the Absolute Spirit's quest for and conquest of its own self. His influence has been as fertile in the critical reactions he precipitated as in his positive impact. His principal works are *Phenomenology of Mind* (1807), *Encyclopedia of the Philosophical Sciences* (1817), and *Philosophy of Right* (1821). He is regarded as the last of the great philosophical system builders.

Hegelianism, Diversified philosophical movement that developed out of G. W. F. Hegel's system of thought. Four stages can be distinguished. The first consists of the Hegelian school in Germany in the period 1827–50. The school divided into three currents. The right, or "Old Hegelians," sought to uphold Hegelianism's compatibility with evangelical orthodoxy and conservative political policies. The left, or "Young Hegelians," interpreted Hegel's identification of the rational with the real in a revolutionary sense. The center preferred to fall back on interpretations of the Hegelian system in its genesis and significance. In the second phase (1850–1904), usually called Neo-Hegelian, the works of the center played a preponderant role. After Wilhelm Dilthey discovered unpublished papers from Hegel's youth in the early 20th century, there arose in Germany yet another movement; this third phase, the Hegel renaissance, stressed the reconstruction of the genesis of Hegel's thought. In the fourth stage, after World War II, the revival of Marxist studies in Europe finally thrust into the foreground the value of the Hegelian heritage for Marxism.

Heidegger, Martin (b. Sept. 26, 1889, Messkirch, Schwarzwald, Ger.—d. May 26, 1976, Messkirch, W.Ger.), German philosopher. He taught at the universities of Marburg (1923–27) and Freiburg (1927–44). In 1927 he published his magnum opus, *Being and Time*. It strongly influenced Jean-Paul Sartre and other existentialists, and, despite Heidegger's protestations, he was classed as the leading atheistic existentialist. His declared purpose in the work was to raise anew the question of the meaning of being. His preliminary analysis of human existence (*Dasein,* or "being-there") employed the method of phenomenology. In the early 1930s his thought underwent a *Kehre* ("turning around"), which some have seen as an abandonment of the problem of *Being and Time*. Heidegger joined the Nazi Party in 1933 and supported Hitler's policies as rector of Freiburg (1933–34) and less actively through the end of the war. His complicity with the Nazis, which he never publicly disavowed, has prompted debates about whether

Martin Heidegger.
Camera Press/Globe Photos

his philosophy is inherently "totalitarian." Heidegger's work strongly influenced hermeneutics and poststructuralism.

Heidelberg, City (pop., 2002 est.: 141,509), southwestern Germany, situated on the Neckar River. First mentioned in historical record in 1196, it was the capital of the Rhenish Palatinate and the residence of the electoral counts palatine until 1720. It was a centre of German Calvinism in the 16th century. Heidelberg was devastated during the Thirty Years' War (1622) and by the French in 1689 and 1693. It is the site of the 13th-century Heidelberg Castle, a major tourist attraction, and of the University of Heidelberg (1386), the oldest university in Germany.

Heidenstam, (Carl Gustaf) Verner von (b. July 6, 1859, Olshammar, Swed.—d. May 20, 1940, Övralid), Swedish poet and novelist. His first book of poems, *Pilgrimage and Wander Years* (1888), drew on his years living in southern Europe and the Middle East and was an immediate success. With his essay "Renaissance" (1889), he became a leader of the opposition in Sweden to naturalism, calling for a rebirth of the literature of fantasy, beauty, and nationalism. Many of the poems he wrote in this vein are translated in *Sweden's Laureate* (1919). He also wrote historical fiction, including *The Charles Men* (1897–98) and *The Tree of the Folkungs* (1905–07). He was awarded the Nobel Prize for Literature in 1916.

Heilongjiang, or HEI-LUNG-CHIANG, conventional HEILUNG-KIANG, Province (pop., 2002 est.: 38,130,000), northeastern China. With an area of 179,000 sq mi (463,600 sq km), it is China's northernmost province; its capital is Harbin. It borders Russia (mostly along the Amur River), Jilin province, and Inner Mongolia. It was part of an area formerly known as Manchuria. Little developed before the 19th century, it was under Russian dominance until 1917, when China took control. It was taken by Japan in 1931 but retaken in 1945 by Soviet forces, who returned it to Chinese (communist) control. After the 1960 Sino-Soviet rift, its border was the scene of frequent clashes. The area is now one of expanding industrialization.

Heimlich maneuver, Emergency procedure for dislodging a foreign body from a choking victim's throat, devised by the U.S. surgeon Henry J. Heimlich. It is used only when the airway is totally obstructed, as shown by inability to speak or breathe. The rescuer reaches around the victim from behind, grasps one fist in the other just below the victim's rib cage, and makes several upward thrusts into the victim's belly. This expels the foreign object with air from the victim's own lungs. An unconscious victim is laid faceup and the thrusts are given by a kneeling or squatting rescuer.

Hejaz, Arabic AL-ḤIJĀZ, Region of western Saudi Arabia. It occupies an extensive area along the Red Sea coast of the Arabian Peninsula, from Jordan to the ʿAsīr region. Its northern portion was inhabited by the 6th century BC. In the 7th century AD two of its cities, Mecca and Medina, were the birthplace of Islam; they remain Islam's holiest cities. In 1258 the region came under the control of the Mamlūk dynasty, and in 1517 control passed to the Ottomans. In 1916 Sharif Ḥusayn ibn ʿAlī revolted and proclaimed himself king of the Hejaz. Ibn Saʿūd, the ruler of Nejd, assumed the title in 1926, and in 1932 he united Hejaz, Nejd, and other districts to form the Kingdom of Saudi Arabia.

Hel, In Norse mythology, the realm of the dead and, later, the goddess of the dead. She was the daughter of Loki. Her kingdom, Niflheim, or the World of Darkness, was divided into several sections. Murderers, perjurers, and adulterers suffered torment in a castle filled with serpents' venom, while the dragon Nidhogg sucked their blood. Those who fell in battle went to Valhalla and thus avoided Hel.

Helen, In Greek mythology, the most beautiful woman in Greece, who was the indirect cause of the Trojan War. She was a daughter of Zeus, either by Leda or by Nemesis. Her brothers were the Dioscuri, and her sister was Clytemnestra, wife of Agamemnon. Helen was the wife of Menelaus. When Paris, son of Priam, was asked to decide which goddess was the most beautiful, he chose Aphrodite, who rewarded him with the most beautiful woman in the world. Seducing Helen with the goddess's help, Paris carried her off to Troy, and the Greeks sent a military force to pursue them. At the war's end, with Paris dead, Helen returned to Sparta with Menelaus.

Helicon, Mount, Mountain, east-central Greece, part of the Helicon range, a continuation of the higher Parnassus range. Located near the Gulf of Corinth, it is 5,738 ft (1,749 m) high. It was celebrated by the ancient Greeks as the home of the Muses; on it were the fountains of Aganippe and Hippocrene, the supposed sources of poetic inspiration.

helicopter, Aircraft with one or more power-driven horizontal rotors that enable it to take off and land vertically, move in any direction, or remain stationary in the air. Since a rotor is essentially a rotating airfoil, a helicopter is often described as a rotary-wing aircraft, in contrast to a conventional fixed-wing airplane. One of the earliest ideas for flying, it appeared in China and Renaissance Europe as a toy and in Leonardo da Vinci's designs. The Frenchman Paul Cornu made the first manned flight in 1907. Igor Sikorsky produced the first successful prototype in 1939, which was followed by rapid development in the U.S. and Europe. It is widely used for civilian transport, rescue work, and various commercial purposes. It has been used by military forces since the Korean War (1950–53) for transporting material, moving assault troops, and directly attacking other forces.

Heliopolis, biblical ON, Ancient holy city, Egypt. The city, which is now mainly ruins lying northeast of Cairo, was the seat of worship of the Egyptian sun god Ra. Its great temple of Ra was second in size only to that of Amon at Thebes, and its priesthood wielded great influence. In the New Kingdom, the temple became the repository of royal records. The city's surviving monument is the obelisk of Sesostris I, the oldest in existence. Two obelisks erected there by Thutmose III and known as Cleopatra's Needles now stand on the Thames River embankment in London and in Central Park, New York City.

Helios, Sun god of ancient Greece. He drove his chariot from east to west across the sky each day and sailed across the ocean each night in a huge cup. He was especially worshiped on Rhodes, where he was considered the chief god as early as the 5th century BC. In Greece he was later displaced by Apollo. The Romans worshiped him as Sol.

helium, Chemical element, chemical symbol He, atomic number 2. A noble gas, it is colourless, odourless, tasteless, completely unreactive, and nontoxic. First found by spectroscopy of the Sun's atmosphere in 1868, it is the second most abundant and second-lightest element in the universe (after hydrogen). Helium makes up a tiny proportion of the atmosphere but as much as 7% of natural gas. It is the product of radioactive decay and is used in helium dating. It is used as an inert gas in welding, rocket propulsion, balloon flight, hyperbaric chambers, deep-sea diving, gas chromatography, luminous signs, and cryogenics. Liquid helium, which exists only below −452 °F (−268.9 °C, about 4° C above absolute zero), is a "quantum fluid", with unique properties, including superfluidity, superconductivity, and near-zero viscosity.

hell, Abode of evildoers after death, or the state of existence of souls damned to punishment after death. Most ancient religions included the concept of a place that divided the good from the evil or the living from the dead (e.g., the gloomy subterranean realm of Hades in Greek religion, or the cold and dark underworld of Niflheim or Hel in Norse mythology). The view that hell is the final dwelling place of the damned after a last judgment is held by Zoroastrianism, Judaism, Christianity, and Islam. The Jewish concept of Gehenna as an infernal region of punishment for the wicked was the basis for the Christian vision of hell as the fiery domain of Satan and his evil angels and a place of punishment for those who die without repenting of their sins. In Hinduism hell is only one stage in the career of the soul as it passes through the phases of reincarnation. The schools of Buddhism have varying conceptions of hell, usually entailing some kind of punishment or purgatory. In Jainism, hell is a purgatory in which sinners are tormented by demons until the evil of their lives has been exhausted.

Hellenistic Age, In the eastern Mediterranean and the Middle East, the period between the death of Alexander the Great (323 BC) and the conquest of Egypt by Rome (30 BC). Alexander and his successors established Greek monarchies that controlled the area from Greece to Afghanistan. The Macedonian Antigonid kingdom, the Middle Eastern Seleucid kingdom, and the Egyptian Ptolemaic kingdom spread Greek culture, mixed Greek and non-Greek populations, and fused Greek and Oriental elements. They produced effective bureaucracies and a common, creative culture based at Alexandria. A great flowering of the arts, literature, and science occurred particularly in the period 280–160. The decline of the Hellenic states occurred as Rome gained strength and won wars against Macedonia and against Mithradates VI Eupator, turning the kingdoms and their allies into Roman provinces. Egypt was the last to fall, after having been drawn into the civil war between Mark Antony and Octavian (Augustus).

Helsinki, Swedish HELSINGFORS, City (pop., 2002 est.: city, 559,718; metro. area, 964,953), capital of Finland. Located in southern Finland on a peninsula with natural harbours, it is the country's leading seaport. Often called the "white city of the north" because many of its buildings are made of a local light-coloured granite, it was founded by Sweden in 1550 and moved to its present site in 1640. With Finland it came under Russian rule in 1808. Under Russian Tsar Alexander I, Helsinki became the capital of the grand duchy of Finland in 1812, and it remained as the capital of the country. In 1917 Finland declared independence from Russia, and a brief but bloody civil war ensued in the capital. In subsequent decades it developed into an important trade centre. It was damaged by Russian bombing during World War II but was rebuilt. It was the site of a 1975 international diplomatic conference. Helsinki has theatres, an opera and ballet company, and several symphony orchestras, and it hosted the 1952 Olympic Summer Games.

Helsinki Accords, International agreement signed in 1975, designed to reduce tension between the Soviet and Western blocs. It was an attempt to secure common acceptance of the post-World War II status quo in Europe, including the division of Germany. The accords, signed by all the countries of Europe (except Albania) as well as the U.S. and Canada, were nonbinding and lacked treaty status. They were sought by the Soviet Union to gain implicit recognition of its postwar hegemony in eastern Europe. In return, the U.S. and its western European allies pressed for respect for human rights and cooperation in economic, scientific, and other humanitarian areas. Follow-up meetings in Belgrade (1977–78), Madrid (1980–83), and Ottawa (1985) were marked by strong criticism of Soviet human-rights abuses and by Soviet counter-accusations. A 1990 conference in Paris formally ended the Cold War and recognized German reunification.

Helvetic Republic, Republic founded in March 1798, constituting the greater part of Switzerland, after it had been conquered by France in the French Revolutionary Wars. The government was patterned after that of the Directory in France. Delegates called on Napoleon to mediate in factional disputes, and in 1803 he substituted a new Swiss Confederation for the republic, forcing it into close association with France.

hemangioma, Congenital benign tumour made of blood vessels in the skin. Capillary hemangioma (nevus flammeus, port-wine stain), an abnormal mass of capillaries on the head, neck, or face, is pink to dark bluish-red and even with the skin. Size and shape vary. It becomes less noticeable or disappears with age. Immature hemangioma (hemangioma simplex, strawberry mark), a reddish nub of dilated small blood vessels, enlarges in the first six months and may become ulcerated but usually recedes after the first year. Cavernous hemangioma, a rare, red-blue, raised mass of larger blood vessels, can occur in skin or in mucous membranes, the brain, or the viscera. Fully developed at birth, it is rarely malignant. Hemangiomas can often be removed by cosmetic surgery.

hematology, Branch of medicine concerned with the nature, function, and diseases of the blood. It covers the cellular and serum composition of blood, the coagulation process, blood-cell formation, hemoglobin synthesis, and disorders of all these. Marcello Malpighi, in the 17th century, was the first to examine red blood cells (erythrocytes). In the 18th century, the British physiologist William Hewson (1739–74) examined the lymphatic system and blood clotting. In the 19th century, the bone marrow was recognized as the site of blood-cell formation, and diseases of the blood such as anemia and leukemia were identified. In the early 20th century, the ABO blood-group system was discovered and the role of nutrition in blood formation was studied. Post-World War II studies have delved further into the nature of blood diseases and improved treatments and have examined hemoglobin synthesis and the role of platelets in blood coagulation.

hematuria, Blood in the urine. It usually indicates injury or disease of the kidney or another structure of the urinary system or possibly, in males, the reproductive system. It may result from infection, inflammation, tumours, kidney stones, or other disorders. How the blood looks and when it appears in the urine stream reflect whether it originates in the urethra, the bladder, or the kidney.

Hemingway, Ernest (Miller) (b. July 21, 1899, Cicero [now in Oak Park], Ill., U.S.—d. July 2, 1961, Ketchum, Idaho), U.S. writer. He began work as a journalist after high school. He was wounded while serving as an ambulance driver in World War I. One of a well-known group of expatriate writers in Paris, he soon embarked on a life of travel, skiing, fishing, and hunting that would be reflected in his work. His story collection *In Our Time* (1925) was followed by the novel *The Sun Also Rises* (1926). Later novels include *A Farewell to Arms* (1929) and *To Have and Have Not* (1937). His lifelong love for Spain (including a fascination with bullfighting) led to his working as a correspondent during the Spanish Civil War, which resulted in the novel *For Whom the Bell Tolls* (1940). Other short-story collections include *Men Without*

Ernest Hemingway, photograph by Yousuf Karsh, 1959.
Courtesy of Mary Hemingway; photograph, © Karsh from Rapho/Photo Researchers

Women (1927), *Winner Take Nothing* (1933), and *The Fifth Column* (1938). He lived primarily in Cuba from *c.* 1940, the locale of his novella *The Old Man and the Sea* (1952, Pulitzer Prize). He was awarded the Nobel Prize for Literature in 1954. He left Cuba shortly after its 1959 revolution; a year later, depressed and ill, he shot himself. The succinct and concentrated prose style of his early works strongly influenced many British and American writers for decades.

hemlock, Any of 14 species of coniferous evergreen trees that make up the genus *Tsuga*, in the pine family, native to North America and central and eastern Asia. Some are important timber trees, and many are popular ornamentals. Other plants commonly called hemlock include ground hemlock, poison hemlock, and water hemlock (parsley family). A true hemlock is a tall, pyramidal tree with purplish or reddish-brown bark, slender horizontal or drooping branches, and short, blunt leaves that grow from woody cushionlike structures on the twigs.

hemoglobin, Protein in the blood of many animals (in vertebrates it is in red blood cells) that transports oxygen from the lungs to the tissues. It is bright red when combined with oxygen and purple-blue in the deoxygenated state. Each molecule is made up of a globin (a type of protein) and four heme groups. Heme, a complex heterocyclic compound, is an organic molecule derived from porphyrin with an iron atom at the centre. Variant hemoglobins can be used to trace past human migrations and to study genetic relationships among populations.

hemophilia, Hereditary bleeding disorder caused by deficiency of a coagulation factor. Lack of factor VIII causes classic hemophilia; other types are caused by deficiency of factor IX or XI. The first two are transmitted by sex-linked heredity; the third has dominant inheritance and occurs in females as well as males. Spontaneous bleeding may occur. Even trivial injury can cause life-threatening blood loss. Drugs can be given to stop bleeding. Heavy blood loss requires blood transfusions.

hemorrhagic fever, Disease with high fever and hemorrhage of internal organs and into the skin. It is caused by several kinds of virus (of which Ebola, dengue, and yellow fever are the best known), some carried by ticks, mosquitoes, or animals. Initial symptoms may include head, muscle, joint, and abdominal pain; nausea and vomiting; sweating and thirst; and coldlike symptoms. It comes on suddenly and can cause severe kidney damage. Patients who are severely ill may also experience shock and neurologic effects.

hemorrhoid, or PILE, Mass formed by distension of the network of veins supplying the anal canal. It may develop from infection or increased abdominal pressure (as in pregnancy or heavy lifting). Mild hemorrhoids may require only ointments, laxatives, and baths. If clotting, bleeding, or pain occurs, surgical removal may be needed. Internal hemorrhoids, with little nerve supply, can be destroyed in several ways without anesthesia. External hemorrhoids, under the skin, are cut out under local anesthesia.

Cannabis sativa.
John Kohout/Root Resources

hemp, Stout, aromatic, erect annual herbaceous plant of the genus *Cannabis* (family Cannabaceae) that is grown for its fibre or its seeds, which contain about 30 percent oil and may be eaten. Hemp originated in Central Asia and is now cultivated widely in the temperate zones. A tall, canelike variety is raised for the fibre, which is strong and durable and is used for cordage and for artificial sponges and coarse fabrics, such as sacking (burlap) and canvas. It is distinguished from cannabis plants grown for the drug marijuana by its lower content of tetrahydrocannabinol (THC) content.

Henan, or HO-NAN, conventional HONAN, Province (pop., 2002 est.: 96,130,000), north-central China. It is bounded by Shanxi, Hebei, Shandong, Anhui, Hubei, and Shaanxi. It has an area of 64,500 sq mi (167,000 sq km), and its capital is Zhengzhou. An early civilization there gave rise to the Shang dynasty (18th–12th centuries BCE). Kaifeng was the capital of several dynasties in the 10th century CE before becoming the capital of the Bei (Northern) Song dynasty (960–1127); Zhengzhou then became the provincial capital. Henan's principal crop is wheat. Henan has large deposits of coal, petroleum, and natural gas, which fuel the economies of its major cities. It is also a railroad transportation hub.

henna, Tropical shrub or small tree (*Lawsonia inermis*) of the loosestrife family, native to northern Africa, Asia, and Australia, and the reddish-brown dye obtained from its leaves. The plant bears small opposite leaves and small, fragrant, white to red flowers. In addition to being grown for its dye, it is used as an ornamental.

Henry VIII (b. June 28, 1491, Greenwich, near London, Eng.—d. Jan. 28, 1547, London), King of England (1509–47). Son of Henry VII, Henry married his brother's widow, Catherine of Aragon (the mother of Mary I), soon after his accession in 1509. His first chief minister, Thomas Cardinal Wolsey, exercised nearly complete control over policy in 1515–27. In 1527 Henry pursued a divorce from Catherine to marry Anne Boleyn, but Pope Clement VII denied him an annulment. Wolsey, unable to help Henry, was ousted. The new minister, Thomas Cromwell, in 1532 initiated a revolution when he decided that the English church should separate from Rome, allowing Henry to marry Anne in 1533. A new archbishop, Thomas Cranmer, declared the first marriage annulled. A daughter, Elizabeth I, was born to Anne soon after. Becoming head of the Church of England represented Henry's major achievement, but it had wide-ranging consequences. Henry, once profoundly devoted to the papacy and rewarded with the title Defender of the Faith, was excommunicated, and he was obliged to settle the nature of the newly independent church. In the 1530s his power was greatly enlarged, especially by transferring to the crown the wealth of the monasteries and by new clerical taxes, but his earlier reputation as a man of learning became buried under his enduring fame as a man of blood. Many, including St. Thomas More, were killed because they refused to accept the new order. The king grew tired of Anne, and in 1536 she was executed for adultery. He immediately married Jane Seymour, who bore him a son, Edward VI, but died in childbirth. Three years later, at Cromwell's instigation, he married Anne of Cleves, but he hated her and demanded a quick divorce; he had Cromwell beheaded in 1540. By now Henry was becom-

Henry VIII, oil on panel by the studio of Hans Holbein the Younger, after 1537; in the Walker Art Gallery, Liverpool, England.
The Bridgeman Art Library/National Museums and Galleries on Merseyside (Walker Art Gallery, Liverpool)

ing paranoid, as well as enormously fat and unhealthy. In 1540 he married Catherine Howard, but he had her beheaded for adultery in 1542. In 1542 he waged a financially ruinous war against Scotland. In 1543 he married Catherine Parr, who survived him. He was succeeded on his death by his son, Edward.

Henry the Navigator, Portuguese HENRIQUE O NAVEGADOR, orig. HENRIQUE, INFANTE (PRINCE) DE PORTUGAL, DUQUE (DUKE) DE VISEU, SENHOR (LORD) DA COVILHA (b. March 4, 1394, Porto, Port.—d. Nov. 13, 1460, Vila do Infante, near Sagres), Portuguese prince and patron of explorers. He helped his father, John I, capture the Moroccan city of Ceuta in 1415 and served as governor of Ceuta and later of the Portuguese province of Algarve. He established his own court at Sagres and sponsored voyages of discovery in the Madeira Islands and along the western coast of Africa. As grand master of the Order of Christ, he gained funds for backing voyages aimed at the conversion of pagans. His patronage led to the development of the Portuguese caravel and improved navigational instruments and the advancement of cartography.

heparin, Naturally occurring mixture of organic compounds used as a short-term anticoagulant to prevent thrombosis during and after surgery and for initial treatment of various heart, lung, and circulatory disorders in which there is increased risk of blood clotting. Comprising complex carbohydrate molecules called mucopolysaccharides, it normally is present in the human body in liver and lung tissues. It was discovered in 1922 and originally used to prevent clotting in blood taken for laboratory tests.

hepatitis, Inflammation of the liver. There are seven known types of viral hepatitis (A–G). Types A, spread mainly through food contaminated with feces, and B, transmitted sexually or by injection, cause jaundice and flulike symptoms. The hepatitis C virus spreads mostly by shared needles in intravenous drug use and can cause liver cirrhosis and cancer after a long latent period. Until recently there was no test to detect it in blood, and many people were exposed through blood transfusions. Hepatitis D becomes active only in the presence of type B; it causes severe chronic liver disease. Type E, like Type A, is transmitted by contaminated food or water; its symptoms are more severe than Type A's and can result in death. The hepatitis F virus (HFV), which was first reported in 1994, is spread like Type A and E. The hepatitis G virus (HGV), isolated in 1996, is believed to be responsible for many sexually transmitted and bloodborne cases of hepatitis. Vaccines exist for types A and B (the second also prevents type D). Drug treatment for B and C is not always effective. The other types may not need drug treatment. Chronic active hepatitis causes spidery and striated skin markings, acne, and abnormal hair growth. It results in liver tissue death (necrosis) progressing to cirrhosis. Alcoholic hepatitis, from long-term overconsumption of alcohol, can be reversed and cirrhosis prevented by early treatment including quitting or sharply reducing drinking. Other drugs can also cause noninfectious hepatitis. An autoimmune hepatitis affects mainly young women and is treated with corticosteroids to relieve symptoms.

Katharine Hepburn.
Brown Brothers

Hepburn, Katharine (Houghton) (b. May 12, 1907, Hartford, Conn., U.S.—d. June 29, 2003, Old Saybrook, Conn.), U.S. actress. She made her Broadway debut in 1928 and became a star with her first film, *A Bill of Divorcement* (1932). Her following grew with *Morning Glory* (1933, Academy Award), *Little Women* (1933), and *Bringing Up Baby* (1938), to which she brought a spirited individuality and strength of character. She starred in the Broadway hit *The Philadelphia Story* (1939; film, 1940). Among her other notable films were *The African Queen* (1951), *Summertime* (1955), and *Suddenly Last Summer* (1959). She made eight films with her longtime lover Spencer Tracy, including *Woman of the Year* (1942), *Pat and Mike* (1952), and *Guess Who's Coming to Dinner* (1967, Academy Award), and won two more Oscars for *The Lion in Winter* (1968) and *On Golden Pond* (1981).

Hephaestus, or HEPHAISTOS, Greek god of fire. He was originally a deity of Asia Minor and nearby islands (especially Lemnos); his Roman counterpart was Vulcan. Born lame, or crippled at an early age, he was cast out of heaven by his parents, Zeus and Hera. His wife was Aphrodite, goddess of love. He was the patron of smiths and craftsman and was often depicted working at his forge. Volcanoes were believed to be the fires of his workshops.

heptathlon, Women's athletics competition. Contestants take part in seven different track-and-field events: 100-m hurdles, shot put, high jump, long jump, javelin throw, and 200- and 800-m runs. The two-day event replaced the women's pentathlon in the Olympic Games after 1981.

Hera, Greek queen of the gods and sister-wife of Zeus. Her Roman counterpart was Juno. She was worshiped as queen of heaven and patron of marriage and women. She also held the title Eileithyia, the goddess of birth. She was the patron deity of Samos and Argos, which held celebrations and processions in her honor. Her sacred animal was the cow. In literature she was depicted as a jealous wife who vindictively pursued the women Zeus seduced.

Heracles, Latin HERCULES, Legendary hero of ancient Greece and Rome. Known for his great strength, he was the son of Zeus and Alcmene, the granddaughter of Perseus. Zeus's jealous wife Hera sent two serpents to kill Heracles in his cradle, but the infant strangled them. He grew up to marry a princess, then killed her in a fit of rage sent by Hera and was forced to become the servant of Eurystheus, ruler of Greece. Eurystheus obliged Heracles to perform the famous 12 labors, including cleansing the Augean stables, fetching the golden apples of the Hesperides, and descending into Hades to bring back the three-headed dog Cerberus. He married Deianeira, who later sent him a shirt smeared with poison, which she mistakenly believed was a love potion. In agony, Heracles burned himself to death on a pyre, and his spirit ascended to heaven. He became an immortal and married Hebe.

Heracles breaking the horns of the hind of Arcadia, flanked by Athena and Artemis, detail of a Greek vase painting, c. 540 BCE; in the British Museum.

heraldry, Art and science of devising, displaying, and granting armorial insignia and of tracing and recording genealogies. The use of heraldic symbols as a means of identification spread throughout the European nobility in the 13th century. The principal vehicle for displaying the heraldic devices is the shield; in the full armorial achievement, the shield is augmented by the helmet, crest, mantling, crown, wreath, motto, compartment (base), and supporters. Arms are hereditary; all male descendants of the first person to whom they were granted bear the arms. As insignia of honour, they are protected by law in the European monarchies, Ireland, Switzerland, South Africa, and Zimbabwe.

herbivore, Animal adapted to subsist solely on plant tissues. Herbivores range from insects (e.g., aphids) to large mammals (e.g., elephants), but the term is most often applied to ungulates. Adaptations for a herbivorous diet include the four-chambered stomach of ruminants, the ever-growing incisor teeth of rodents, and the specialized grinding molars of cattle, sheep, and goats. Certain herbivores eat only one type of food (e.g., the koala), but most have at least moderate variety in their diet.

Herculaneum, Ancient city, Campania, Italy. Located at the northwestern foot of Vesuvius, it was destroyed, together with Pompeii and Stabiae, by the eruption of 79 CE. It was buried under a mass of tufa about 50 to 60 ft (15 to 18 m) deep, which made excavation difficult but preserved many fragile items. Excavation began in the 18th century and uncovered numerous artifacts, including paintings and furniture. Later work uncovered the palaestra (sports ground) and a vast central swimming pool.

heredity, Transmission of traits from parents to offspring through genes, the functional units of heritable material that are found within all living cells. From his studies in the mid-19th century, Gregor Mendel derived certain basic concepts of heredity, which eventually became the foundation for the modern science of genetics. Each member of the parental generation transmits only half its genes to the offspring, and different offspring of the same parents receive different combinations of genes. Many characteristics are polygenic (i.e., influenced by more than one gene). Many genes exist in numerous variations (alleles) throughout a population. The polygenic and multiple allelic nature of many traits gives a vast potential for variability among hereditary characteristics. While the genotype (an individual's total hereditary makeup) determines the broad limits of features an individual may develop, the actual features that do develop (the phenotype) are dependent on complex interactions between genes and their environment.

heresy, Doctrine rejected as false by religious authorities. In Christianity, the orthodox theology of the church is thought to be based on divine revelation, and heretics are viewed as perversely rejecting the guidance of the church. Numerous Christian heresies appeared from the 2nd century onwards. Early heresies included Arianism, the Monophysite heresy, Pelagianism, and Donatism. Some heresies, such as Montanism, expressed faith in a new prophet who added to the body of Christian revelation. Some types of Gnosticism were heretical branches of Christianity. The major means of combating heretics in the early church was excommunication. In the 12th–13th century, the Inquisition was established to combat heresy, and heretics who refused to recant were often executed. In the 16th century the Protestant Reformation brought an end to the doctrinal unity of Western Christendom, and the concept of heresy became less important in the various Christian churches, though it continues to exist. The concept of heresy also exists in Judaism, Buddhism, Hinduism, and Islam.

hermaphroditism, Condition of having both male and female reproductive organs. It is normal in most flowering plants and in some invertebrate animals. True human hermaphrodites are extremely rare. Tissue of the ovary and testes may occur separately or be combined, external genitals may show traits of both sexes, and XY and XX sex chromosome pairs are present. If the condition is detected at birth, the child's sex can be chosen, usually on the basis of which sex organs dominate; those of the other sex are removed surgically. Individuals raised as members of one sex who develop characteristics of the other at puberty may be treated with surgery, and sex hormones may help them continue to live according to the sexual identity to which they are accustomed.

hermeneutics, Study of the general principles of biblical interpretation. Its primary purpose is to discover the truths and values of the Bible, which is seen as a receptacle of divine revelation. Four major types of hermeneutics have emerged: literal (asserting that the text is to be interpreted according to the "plain meaning"), moral, allegorical (interpreting narratives as having a level of reference beyond the explicit), and anagogical or mystical. More recently the word has come to refer to all "deep" reading of literary and philosophical texts.

Hermes, Greek god, son of Zeus and Maia. The earliest centre of his cult was probably Arcadia, where he was worshiped as a god of fertility. He was also associated with the protection of cattle and sheep. In Homer's *Odyssey* he appears as the messenger of the gods and the conductor of the dead to Hades. As a messenger he also became the god of roads and doorways and the protector of travelers. He was also the god of dreams. His Roman counterpart was Mercury.

Hermes leading a satyr chorus, vase by Douris, 5th century BC; in the British Museum
Courtesy of the trustees of the British Museum

Hermetic writings, Occult texts on philosophical or theological subjects ascribed to Hermes Trismegistos ("Hermes the Thrice-Greatest"), identical to the Egyptian god Thoth, who was credited with inventing writing. The collection, written in Greek and Latin, was probably put together in the 1st–3rd century AD. Written in the form of dialogues, it synthesizes Near Eastern religion, Platonism, Stoicism, and other philosophies. It also reflects ideas and beliefs widely held in the early Roman empire on astrology, alchemy, and magic. The goal of the writings was the deification of humanity through knowledge of the transcendent God.

Hermeticism, or HERMETISM, Italian ERMETISMO, Modernist poetic movement originating in Italy in the early 20th century. Works produced within the movement are characterized by unorthodox structure, illogical sequences, and highly subjective language. Its formalistic devices were partly derived from Futurism, but the cryptic brevity, obscurity, and involution of the Hermetics was forced on them by fascist censors. Giuseppe Ungaretti, Salvatore Quasimodo, and Eugenio Montale were the principal exponents of the movement, which was named for Hermes Trismegistos, a reputed author of occult symbolic works.

hermit, or EREMITE, Individual who shuns society to live in solitude, often for religious reasons. The first Christian hermits appeared in Egypt in the 3rd century AD, escaping persecution by withdrawing to the desert and leading a life of prayer and penance. The first hermit was probably Paul of Thebes *c.* AD 250. Other famous hermits included St. Anthony of Egypt, who established an early form of Christian monasticism in the 4th century, and the pillar hermit Simeon Stylites. The communal life of monasteries eventually tempered the austerities of the hermit's life. In Western Christianity the eremitic life died out, but it has persisted in Eastern Christianity.

hermit crab, Any crab (families Paguridae and Coenobitidae) that uses empty shells or other hollow objects as a shelter for partial containment and protection of the body. They are found worldwide in sandy- or muddy-bottomed waters and occasionally on land and in trees. They have two pairs of antennae and four pairs of legs; the first pair of legs is modified to form pincers, shaped to cover the shell entrance when the animal is inside. As the crab grows, it periodically leaves its shell and finds a larger one to occupy. The reddish brown large hermit crab (*Pagurus pollicaris*; 4–5 in., or 10–12 cm, long) and the small hermit crab (*P. longicarpus*) are found in North American Atlantic coastal waters.

Hermit crab (Pagurus samuelis).
Russ Kinne—Photo Researchers

Hermitage, Largest museum in Russia and one of the most important in the world. Located in St. Petersburg, it derives its name from the "Hermitage" pavilion adjoining the Winter Palace, built in 1764–67 for Catherine II (the Great) as a private gallery for her treasured collections. On her death in 1796, the imperial collections were estimated to total 4,000 pictures. After the Winter Palace was destroyed by fire in 1837, the Hermitage was reconstructed and opened to the public by Nicholas I in 1852. After the Bolshevik Revolution, the collections were transferred to public ownership. The museum is now housed in five interconnected buildings, including the Winter Palace and the Small, Old, and New Hermitages. Along with thousands of art objects from Central Asia, India, China, Egypt, the pre-Columbian Americas, Greece, and Rome, the Hermitage houses outstanding collections of Western painting. Russian history is represented by archaeological material from prehistoric times onward.

Hermon, Mount, Arabic JABAL AL-SHAYKH, Snowcapped mountain on the Lebanese-Syrian border. Located west of Damascus and rising to 9,232 ft (2,814 m), it is the highest point on the eastern coast of the Mediterranean Sea and is sometimes considered the southernmost extension of the Anti-Lebanon Mountains. A sacred landmark since the Bronze Age, it represented the northwestern limit of Israelite conquest under Moses and Joshua. Since the Six-Day War (1967), about 40 sq mi (100 sq km) of its southern and western slopes have been part of the Israeli-administered Golan Heights.

hernia, Protrusion of any organ or tissue from its normal cavity. The term usually refers to an abdominal hernia, which may be a congenital disorder or acquired after birth. Tissue may protrude through the abdominal muscle at the groin (inguinal), upper thigh (femoral), or navel (umbilical); its circulation can become cut off, leading to inflammation, infection, and gangrene. If the tissue cannot be pushed back into place and kept there by a truss, surgery may be necessary. Other common hernias are hiatal hernia (protrusion of part or all of the stomach above the diaphragm) and herniated disk (protrusion of tissue from a disk in the vertebral column through its outer layer).

hero, Mythological or legendary figure, often of divine descent, who is endowed with great strength or ability, like the heroes celebrated in early epics such as *Gilgamesh*, *The Iliad*, *Beowulf*, or the *Chanson de Roland*. Usually illustrious warriors or adventurers, heroes are often represented as fulfilling a quest (e.g., Aeneas, in Virgil's *Aeneid*, founding the Roman state, or Beowulf ridding his people of the monstrous Grendel and his mother). Heroes often possess special qualities such as unusual beauty, precocity, and skills in many crafts. Often inclined to boasting and foolhardiness, they defy pain and death to live fully, creating a moment's glory that survives in the memory of their descendants.

heroin, Heterocyclic compound, a highly addictive alkaloid derivative of morphine (chemically, it is diacetylmorphine) that makes up a large portion of illicit narcotics traffic. Easily made from morphine, it was developed and first used as an analgesic, but its undesirable effects outweighed its value, and it is illegal in most countries. Injection brings an ecstatic, warm, glowing sensation, followed by relaxation and contentment. Within half a day withdrawal symptoms set in, with a craving for more. Development of tolerance, requiring ever greater amounts for the same effects, leads to drug addiction. Illegal street heroin is usually only 2–5% pure; unwitting injection of relatively pure heroin is a major cause of overdose, resulting in depressed respiration, coma, and death.

heron, Any of about 60 species of long-legged wading birds in the same family (Ardeidae) as egrets and bitterns. They are found worldwide but are most common in the tropics. They wade in the shallow waters of pools, marshes, and swamps, catching frogs, fishes, and other aquatic animals. They nest on rough stick platforms in bushes or trees near water. Herons commonly stand with their neck bent in an southern shape and fly with their legs trailing and their head held back. They have broad wings and a long, straight, sharp-pointed bill. They are subdivided into typical herons (including the 50-in., or 130-cm, great blue heron of North America), night herons, and tiger herons.

herpes simplex, Infection caused by herpes simplex virus. Type I typically produces a cluster of small blisters (cold sores, or fever blisters), usually on the lips or face; it can also infect the eyes. Type II, transmitted mostly through sexual contact, causes genital blisters, which rupture, becoming very painful. Oral sex can give either type the chance to infect the usual site of the other. In both types, the virus remains after symptoms end and can reactivate, causing blisters to reappear. Babies born to mothers with active herpes can become infected during birth; this can be prevented by cesarean section. There is no cure, but drugs can reduce severity and risk of transmission.

herring, Either the Atlantic or the Pacific subspecies of *Clupea harengus* (once considered two separate species), slab-sided, northern fishes that are small-headed and streamlined, with silvery iridescent sides and a deep-blue, metallic-hued back. The name also refers to some other members of the family Clupeidae. Adults range in length from 8 to 15 in. (20–38 cm). One of the most abundant species of fish, herring travel in enormous schools. They eat planktonic crustaceans and fish larvae. In Europe they are processed and sold as kippered herring; in eastern Canada and the northeastern U.S., most of the herring used are young fishes canned as sardines. Herring taken in the Pacific are used mainly to make fish oil and meal.

Hertz, Heinrich (Rudolf) (b. Feb. 22, 1857, Hamburg, Ger.—d. Jan. 1, 1894, Bonn), German physicist. While a professor at Karlsruhe Polytechnic (1885–89), he produced electromagnetic waves in the laboratory and measured their length and velocity. He showed that the nature of their vibration and their susceptibility to reflection and refraction were the same as those of light waves, and he proved that light and heat are electromagnetic radiations. He was the first to broadcast and receive radio waves. In 1889 he was appointed professor at the University of Bonn, where he continued his research on the discharge of electricity in rarefied gases. The hertz (Hz), a unit of frequency in cycles per second, is named for him.

Herzl, Theodor (b. May 2, 1860, Budapest, Hungary—d. July 3, 1904, Edlach, Austria), Hungarian Zionist leader. Growing up Jewish in Hungary, he believed that assimilation was the best strategy to deal with the anti-Semitism he encountered. He became a Zionist while covering the Alfred Dreyfus affair as a journalist in Paris. In 1897 he organized a world congress of Zionism, which was attended by about 200 delegates, and he became the first president of the World Zionist Organization, established by the congress. Herzl's indefatigable organizing, propagandizing, and diplomacy had much to do with making Zionism a political movement of worldwide significance. Though he died more than 40 years before the establishment of the state of Israel, his remains were moved to Jerusalem in 1949 and entombed on a hill now known as Mount Herzl.

Hesse, Hermann (b. July 2, 1877, Calw, Ger.—d. Aug. 9, 1962, Montagnola, Switz.), German

novelist and poet. He left the seminary because of his inability to adapt to the life there. His first novel was *Peter Camenzind* (1904); it was followed by *Beneath the Wheel* (1906), *Gertrud* (1910), and *Rosshalde* (1914). An opponent of militarism, he settled permanently in Switzerland at the outbreak of World War I (1914–18). His later works deal with the individual's search for spiritual fulfillment, often through mysticism. *Demian* (1919), influenced by his experience with psychoanalysis, made him famous. *Siddhartha* (1922), about the early life of Buddha,

Hermann Hesse, 1957.
Wide World Photos

reflects his interest in Eastern spiritualism. *Steppenwolf* (1927), which examines the conflict between bourgeois acceptance and spiritual self-realization, was highly influential in its time and brought him cult status among the young of more than one generation. *Narcissus and Goldmund* (1930) and *The Glass Bead Game* (1943; also published as *Magister Ludi*) concern duality and the conflict between the contemplative and the active life. He won the Nobel Prize for Literature in 1946. His mysticism and his interest in self-realization kept him popular long after his death.

Hezbollah or ḤIZBULLĀH, or ḤIZB ALLĀH (Arabic: "Party of God"), Lebanese Shīʿite Islamist organization. Founded in southern Lebanon in 1982 as a response to Israel's invasion there, its original goals were to drive Israeli troops out of Lebanon and form a Shīʿite Islamic republic similar to that created by the Iranian revolution of 1979. Its political stance, in the main, has been anti-Western, and its members have been implicated in many of the terrorist activities that were perpetrated in Lebanon during the 1980s, including kidnappings, car bombings, and airline hijackings, a number of which were directed at U.S. citizens. It has purportedly received strong material support from Syria and Iran and throughout the 1990s engaged in an intensive guerrilla campaign against Israeli forces in southern Lebanon. At the same time, Hezbollah actively aided the long disfranchised Shīʿite community in Lebanon, providing social services not offered by the government. In the 1990s the party's candidates won seats in Lebanon's parliamentary elections, and the group's leaders have since sought to soften its earlier image. Despite a unilateral withdrawal of Israeli troops from Lebanon in 2000, the party continued sporadic attacks across the Lebanese-Israeli border, and in 2006 it fought a 34-day war with Israel.

hibernation, State of greatly slowed metabolism and low body temperature in winter in certain animals. True hibernators include many cold-blooded animals and a few mammals (e.g., bats, hedgehogs) that go into a near-dead state with a near-freezing body temperature and very slow breathing and heart rate. Mammals such as bears that sleep in dens with only slightly lowered body temperature wake easily and are not considered true hibernators. Most hibernators build up a reserve of body fat or store food ahead of time. They may wake and eat several times during the winter.

Cold-blooded animals must hibernate where the weather drops below freezing. Hibernation's warm-weather equivalent is estivation.

hibiscus, Any of numerous species of shrubs, trees, and herbaceous plants that make up the genus *Hibiscus*, in the mallow family, native to warm temperate and tropical regions. Several are cultivated as ornamentals for their showy flowers. The tropical Chinese hibiscus, or China rose (*H. rosa-sinensis*), has large, somewhat bell-shaped reddish blossoms. The East African hibiscus (*H. schizopetalus*), a drooping shrub, is often grown in hanging baskets indoors. Other members of the genus include okra, rose of Sharon, and many flowering plants known by the common name mallow.

China rose (Hibiscus rosa-sinensis)
Sven Samelius

hiccup, Spasmodic contraction of the diaphragm that causes a sudden breath in, cut off when the vocal cords snap together, creating the characteristic sound. Causes include overdistended stomach, gastric irritation, and nerve spasms. The many folk remedies for hiccups interrupt the rhythm of the spasms. The most common and effective treatment is to hold the breath as long as possible. Hiccups usually stop within minutes, though they may last days, weeks, or longer. Prolonged severe hiccups are treated with nerve blocks or by surgically cutting the nerve that supplies the diaphragm.

Hicks, Sir John R(ichard) (b. April 8, 1904, Leamington Spa, Warwickshire, Eng.—d. May 20, 1989, Blockley, Gloucestershire), British economist. He taught at several institutions, notably the University of Oxford, and he was knighted in 1964. His classic work *Value and Capital* (1939) helped resolve basic conflicts between business-cycle theory and the equilibrium theory, which holds that economic forces tend to balance one another rather than simply reflect cyclical trends. He shared the 1972 Nobel Prize with Kenneth Arrow.

hieroglyph, Character in any of several systems of writing that is pictorial in nature, though not necessarily in the way it is read. The term was originally used for the oldest system of writing Ancient Egyptian. Egyptian hieroglyphs could be read iconically (the representation of a house enclosure stood for the word *pr*, "house"), phonetically (the "house" sign could have the phonetic value *pr*), or associatively (a sign representing one thing could stand for a homophone meaning something else). Unlike contemporary cuneiform writing, phonetic hieroglyphs denoted consonants, not syllables, so there was no regular way to write vowels; by convention, Egyptologists insert the vowel *e* between consonants in order to pronounce Egyptian words. The standardized orthography of the Middle Kingdom (2050–1750 BC) employed about 750 hieroglyphs. In the early centuries AD, use of hieroglyphs declined—the last dated text is from AD 394—and the meaning of the signs was lost until their decipherment in the early 19th century. The term *hieroglyph* has been applied to similar systems of writing, notably a script used to write the ancient Anatolian language Luvian and a script used by the Maya.

high-definition television (HDTV), Any system producing significantly greater picture resolution than that of the ordinary 525-line (625-line in Europe) television screen. Conventional television transmits signals in analog form. Digital HDTV systems, by contrast, transmit pictures and sounds in the form of digital data. These numerical data are broadcast using the same high radio frequencies that carry analog waves, and computer processors in the digital television set then decode the data. Digital HDTV can provide sharper, clearer pictures and sound with very little interference or other imperfections. Of perhaps greater importance, digital television sets will potentially be able to send, store, and manipulate images as well as receive them, thereby merging the functions of the television set and the computer.

high jump, Track-and-field event of jumping for height. The equipment includes a semicircular runway allowing an approach run of at least 49 ft (15 m), the raised bar and its vertical supports, and a cushioned landing area. Jumpers must leave the ground from one foot. Three failed jumps at a height result in disqualification. Early jumping styles, including the near-erect scissors jump and the facedown Western roll-and-straddle, were largely superseded from 1968 by the faceup "Fosbury flop," named for its leading proponent, the U.S. jumper Dick Fosbury.

Highland Games, Athletic games originating in the Scottish Highlands and now held there and in various parts of the world, usually under the auspices of a local Caledonian society. Events include flat and hurdle races, long and high jumps, hammer and weight throws, and the caber toss, the hurling end-over-end of a tapered fir pole about 17 ft (5 m) long and 90 lbs (40 kg) in weight. Competitions in bagpipe playing and Highland dancing also form an important part of the meetings.

Hijrah English HEGIRA (Arabic: "Migration"), Journey of Muhammad from Mecca to Medina in 622 to escape persecution and found a community of believers. The date represents the beginning of Islam. The second caliph, ʿUmar ibn al-Khaṭṭāb, began the practice of using the event as the starting point for the Muslim calendar; years are now denoted by the initials AH (Latin Anno Hegirae, "in the year of the Hegira"). The disciples who traveled with Muhammad to Medina were called the Companions of the Prophet.

Hildegard von Bingen (b. 1098, Böckelheim, West Franconia—d. Sept. 17, 1179, Rupertsberg, near Bingen), German abbess and visionary mystic. She became prioress at the Benedictine cloister of Disibodenberg in 1136. Having experienced visions since childhood, she was eventually permitted to write *Scivias* (1141–52), in which she recorded 26 prophetic, symbolic, and apocalyptic visions; it was followed by two more such collections. She founded a convent at Rupertsberg *c.* 1147, where she continued to prophesy; she became known as the "Sibyl of the Rhine," and her advice was sought by the most powerful and eminent figures of Europe. Her other works include a morality play, a book of saints' lives, treatises on medicine and natural history, and extensive correspondence. Her *Symphonia armonie celestium revelationum* consists of 77 lyrical poems, all with monophonic melodies; she is apparently the first woman composer in the Western tradition whose music is known. Though long regarded as a saint, she has never been formally canonized.

Sir Edmund Hillary, 1956.
UPI/Bettmann Archive

Hillary, Sir Edmund (Percival) (b. July 20, 1919, Auckland, N.Z.—d. Jan. 11, 2008, Auckland), New Zealand mountain climber and explorer. Hillary was a professional beekeeper but enjoyed climbing in the New Zealand Alps. In 1951 he joined a New Zealand party to the central Himalayas and then went on to help in a reconnaissance of the southern flank of Everest. In 1953, as a member of the British Everest expedition, he and Tenzing Norgay reached the summit on May 29, becoming the first known climbers to do so. The achievement brought Hillary worldwide fame and he was knighted that same year. In 1958 he participated in the first crossing of Antarctica by vehicle. From the 1960s he helped build schools and hospitals for the Sherpa people.

Himachal Pradesh, State (pop., 2008 est.: 6,550,000), northern India. Located in the western Himalayas, it is bordered by the Tibet Autonomous Region of China and the states of Uttarakhand, Haryana, Punjab, and Jammu and Kashmir and covers an area of 21,495 sq mi (55,673 sq km); its capital is Shimla. The area's history dates to the Vedic period, when the Aryans entered the region and gradually assimilated the indigenous peoples. It was exposed to successive invasions through the centuries, ending with British domination in the 19th century. Between 1948 and the achievement of statehood in 1971, it underwent various changes in size and administrative status. It is one of the least-urbanized states in India, and most of the people are subsistence farmers.

Himalayas, or HIMALAYA, Mountain system, southern Asia. It forms a barrier between the Plateau of Tibet to the north and the plains of the Indian subcontinent to the south. It constitutes the greatest mountain system on Earth and includes more than 110 peaks rising to elevations above 24,000 ft (7,300 m), including Mount Everest. The system extends some 1,550 mi (2,500 km) from east to west and covers about 230,000 sq mi (595,000 sq km). It is traditionally divided into four parallel ranges: from north to south, the Tethys (or Tibetan) Himalayas, the Great Himalayas (including the major peaks), the Lesser Himalayas (including peaks of 12,000–15,000 ft [3,700–4,500 m]), and the Outer Himalayas (including the lowest peaks). Between the eastern and western extremities of the broad Himalayan arc lie several Indian states and the kingdoms of Nepal and Bhutan. It acts as a great climatic divide, causing heavy rain and snow on the southern side but aridity north of the range, and represents at many points a virtually impassable barrier, even by air. The mountains' glaciers and snows are the source of 19 major rivers, including the Indus, Ganges (Ganga), and Brahmaputra.

Ḥimṣ, or HOMS, ancient EMESA, City (pop., 2004 est.: 800,400), central Syria. It is located near the Orontes River. As Emesa, it contained a large temple to the sun god El Gebal and was the birthplace of the priest-king Elagabalus, who became Roman emperor in AD 218. The emperor Aurelian defeated Queen Zenobia of Palmyra there in 272. It was taken in 636 by the Muslims, who renamed it Ḥimṣ. In 1516 it passed into Ottoman hands, where it remained (except for a brief period of Egyptian control in the 1830s) until the creation of Syria after World War I (1914–18). Ḥimṣ is a thriving agricultural market centre and has oil and sugar refineries. It is the central link between the interior cities and the Mediterranean Sea coast.

Hinayana, Name given to the more conservative schools of Buddhism. A Sanskrit word meaning "Lesser Vehicle" (because it is concerned with the individual's salvation), it was first applied pejoratively to the established Buddhist schools by followers of the more liberal Mahayana ("Greater Vehicle," because it is concerned with universal salvation) tradition. The ancient Hinayana schools continued to prosper after the rise of the Mahayana in the 1st century AD, but Theravada Buddhism was the only Hinayana school that maintained a strong position after the collapse of Indian Buddhism in the 13th century.

Hindenburg disaster, Explosion of the dirigible *Hindenburg*, the largest rigid airship ever constructed. Launched in 1936 in Germany, it started the first commercial air service across the North Atlantic and made 10 successful round trips. On May 6, 1937, as it was landing in Lakehurst, N.J., U.S., its hydrogen gas burst into flames, destroying the airship and killing 36 of the 97 persons aboard. The disaster, recorded on film and phonograph disk, effectively ended the use of rigid airships in commercial transportation.

Hindi language, Indo-Aryan language of India, spoken or understood by more than 30% of the country's population. Modern Standard Hindi is a lingua franca (as well as native language) of millions of people in North India and the official language of the Indian Union. It is effectively a continuation of Hindustani, which developed from Khari Boli, the speech of certain classes and districts in Delhi affiliated with the Mughal court in the 16th–18th centuries. A heavily Persianized variant of Khari Boli used by Muslim authors formed the basis for Urdu. Hindustani was codified by the British at Fort William College in Calcutta (now Kolkata). There Hindu intellectuals promoted a Sanskritized form of Hindustani written in the Devanagari script in the late 18th and early 19th centuries; it became the progenitor of modern literary Hindi as used by Hindu authors. During the Indian independence movement, Hindustani was regarded as a national unifying factor, but after the partition in 1947 this attitude changed, and the name has practically dropped from use in favour of either Hindi or Urdu. Linguists, particularly George Abraham Grierson, have also used the term *Hindi* to refer collectively to all the dialects and regional literary languages of the northern Indian plain. Hindi has drastically simplified the complex grammar of Old Indo-Aryan while preserving certain phonetic features.

Hindu-Arabic numerals, Set of 10 symbols—1, 2, 3, 4, 5, 6, 7, 8, 9, 0—that represent numbers in the decimal number system. They originated in India in the 6th or 7th century and were introduced to Europe through Arab mathematicians around the 12th century. They represented a profound break with previous methods of counting, such as the abacus, and paved the way for the development of algebra.

Hindu Kush, Latin CAUCASUS INDICUS, Mountain system, south-central Asia. Some 500 mi (800 km) long, it runs from the Pamirs in the east near the Pakistan-China border through Pakistan to western Afghanistan. The system forms a drainage divide between the Amu Darya (ancient Oxus River) valley to the northwest and the Indus River valley to the southeast. Its passes have historically been of great military significance, providing access to the northern plains of the Indian subcontinent. It includes about two dozen summits above 23,000 ft (7,000 m), including the highest, Tirich Mir, at 25,230 ft (7,690 m).

Wildflowers blooming in the Hindu Kush in the Chitral district of northern Pakistan.
© Brian A. Vikander

Hinduism, Oldest of the world's major religions. It evolved from the Vedic religion of ancient India. The major branches of Hinduism are Vaishnavism and Shaivism, each of which includes many different sects. Though the various sects each rely on their own set of scriptures, they all revere the ancient Vedas, which were likely composed about the mid-2nd millennium BCE. The philosophical Vedic texts called the Upanishads explored the search for knowledge that would allow humankind to escape the cycle of reincarnation. Fundamental to Hinduism is the belief in a cosmic principle of ultimate reality called *brahman* and its identity with the individual soul, or *atman*. All creatures go through a cycle of rebirth, or samsara, which can be broken only by spiritual self-realization, after which liberation, or *moksha*, is attained. The principle of karma determines a being's status within the cycle of rebirth. The Hindu deities having the widest following are Vishnu and Shiva, who are worshipped in various avatars, or incarnations. The goddess Durga also has a wide following. The major sources of classical stories about the gods are the *Mahabharata* (which includes the *Bhagavadgita*, one of the most important religious texts of Hinduism), the *Ramayana*, and the Puranas. Historically, the hierarchical social structure of the caste system was also important in Hinduism. In the 20th century Hinduism blended with Indian nationalism to become a powerful political force in Indian politics. In the early 21st century there were more than 850 million Hindus worldwide.

Hindustan, Historically, name applied to northern India, in contrast to the Deccan, or southern India. It is also sometimes used for all of India. It included the region bounded to the north by the Himalayas and to the south by the Vindhya Mountains and Narmada River, comprising the Ganges (Ganga) River valley from the Punjab to Assam. The name was also applied to a small area comprising the upper basin of the Ganges.

Hippocrates (b. *c.* 460 BC, island of Cos, Greece—d. *c.* 375,

Larissa, Thessaly), Greek physician regarded as the father of medicine. During his lifetime, he was admired as a physician and teacher. Plato and Aristotle mention him in several of their own works, and Aristotle's student Meno recounts his ideas about the causes of disease. The Hippocratic Collection (*Corpus Hippocraticum*) was assembled for the Library of Alexandria in Egypt. About 60 medical writings have survived that bear Hippocrates' name, most of which were not written by him. The collection deals with anatomy, clinical subjects, diseases of women and children, prognosis, treatment, surgery, and medical ethics. The Hippocratic Oath (suspected not to have been written by Hippocrates), also part of the Hippocratic Collection, dictates the obligations of the physician to students of medicine and the duties of pupil to teacher. In the oath, the physician pledges to prescribe only beneficial treatments, to refrain from causing harm or hurt, and to live an exemplary life.

Hippocrates, Roman bust copied from a Greek original, c. 3rd century BCE; in the collection of the Antichità di Ostia, Italy.
Courtesy of the Soprintendenza alle Antichità di Ostia, Italy

hippopotamus, Huge amphibious African mammal (*Hippopotamus amphibius*). Once found throughout sub-Saharan Africa, it is now restricted to parts of eastern and southeastern Africa. It has a barrel-shaped body, an enormous mouth, short legs, and four toes on each foot. It commonly reaches a length of 11.5 ft (3.5 m), a height of 5 ft (1.5 m) at the shoulder, and a weight of 7,000 lb (3,200 kg). The skin is very thick, nearly hairless, and grayish brown above, lighter and pinkish below. The ears and nostrils protrude above water when the rest of the body is submerged. Hippopotamuses live near rivers, lakes, swamps, or other permanent bodies of water, usually in groups of 7 to 15. During the day they sleep and rest in or near the water. At night they go on land to feed on grasses, which they crop with their hard-edged lips. In water they can swim fast, walk along the bottom, and remain submerged (with ears and nostrils closed) for five minutes or more. The rare pygmy hippopotamus (*Hexaprotodon liberiensis*) is the only other species of the family Hippopotamidae. Living along streams and in wet forests and swamps of West Africa, it is about the size of a domestic pig.

Hirohito, or SHŌWA EMPEROR (b. April 29, 1901, Tokyo, Japan—d. Jan. 7, 1989, Tokyo), Longest-reigning of Japan's monarchs (1926–89). His rule coincided with Japan's 20th-century militarism and its aggression against China and Southeast Asia and in the Pacific Ocean during World War II. Though the Meiji Constitution invested the emperor with supreme authority, in practice he merely ratified the policies formulated by his ministers and advisers. Historians have debated whether Hirohito could have diverted Japan from its militaristic path and what responsibility he should bear for the actions of the government and military during the war. In August 1945 he broke the precedent of imperial silence when he made a national radio broadcast to announce Japan's surrender, and in 1946 he made a second broadcast to repudiate the traditional quasi-divine status of Japan's emperors.

Hiroshima, City (pop., 2002 est.: 1,113,786), southwestern

Honshu, Japan. Founded as a castle town in the 16th century, it was from 1868 a military centre. In 1945 it became the first city ever to be struck by an atomic bomb, dropped by the U.S. in the last days of World War II. Rebuilding began in 1950, and Hiroshima is now the largest industrial city in the region. It has become a spiritual centre of the peace movement to ban nuclear weapons; Peace Memorial Park is dedicated to those killed by the bomb, and Atomic Bomb Dome is the ruin of the only building to survive the blast.

Cenotaph in Peace Memorial Park, Hiroshima, Japan; Atomic Bomb Dome is visible through the arch.
Bob Glaze—Artstreet

histamine, Organic compound found in nearly all animal tissues, in microorganisms, and in some plants. Its release stimulates many smooth muscles to contract, such as those in the gastrointestinal tract, uterus, and the bronchi. It causes fine blood vessels to dilate and become more permeable, causing the runny nose, watery eyes, and tissue swelling of hay fever and some other allergies. Histamine appears to have a physiological role in the body's defenses against a hostile environment, since it may be released when the body is subjected to trauma, infection, or some drugs. Under extreme circumstances, the effects of histamine lead to exaggerated responses with distressing results, as may occur in some allergic conditions. Stinging nettles and certain insect venoms contain histamine. In humans, histamine is formed by removal of a carboxyl group from histidine. Its effects are counteracted by antihistamines.

histology, Branch of biology concerned with the composition and structure of plant and animal tissues in relation to their specialized functions. Its aim is to determine how tissues are organized at all structural levels, from cells and intercellular substances to organs. Histologists examine extremely thin slices of human tissue under microscopes, using dye to increase the contrast between cellular components.

historiography, Writing of history, especially that based on the critical examination of sources and the synthesis of chosen particulars from those sources into a narrative that will stand the test of critical methods. Two major tendencies in history writing are evident from the beginnings of the Western tradition: the concept of historiography as the accumulation of records and the concept of history as storytelling, filled with explanations of cause and effect. In the 5th century BCE the Greek historians Herodotus and, later, Thucydides emphasized firsthand inquiry in their efforts to impose a narrative on contemporary events. The dominance of Christian historiography by the 4th century introduced the idea of world history as a result of divine intervention in human affairs, an idea that prevailed throughout the Middle Ages in the work of such historians as Bede. Humanism and the gradual secularization of critical thought influenced early modern European historiography. The 19th and 20th centuries saw the development of modern methods of historical investigation based on the use of primary source materials. Modern historians, aiming for a fuller picture of the past, have tried to reconstruct a record of ordinary human activities and practices; the French Annales school has been influential in this respect.

history, philosophy of, Branch of philosophy concerned with questions about the meaningfulness of history and the nature of historical explanation. Philosophy of history in the traditional sense is conceived to be a first-order inquiry, its subject matter being the historical process as a whole and its broad aim being to provide an overall elucidation of its course. As a second-order inquiry, philosophy of history focuses on the methods by which practicing historians treat the human past. The former, often referred to as speculative philosophy of history, has had a long and varied career; the latter, known as critical or analytical philosophy of history, rose to prominence only in the 20th century.

Hitler, Adolf (b. April 20, 1889, Braunau am Inn, Austria—d. April 30, 1945, Berlin, Ger.), Dictator of Nazi Germany (1933–45). As a soldier in the German army in World War I, he was wounded and gassed. In 1920 he became head of propaganda for the renamed National Socialists (Nazi Party) and in 1921 party leader. He set out to create a mass movement, using unrelenting propaganda. The party's rapid growth climaxed in the Beer Hall Putsch (1923), for which he served nine months in prison; there he started to write his virulent autobiography, *Mein Kampf.* Believing that "races" were unequal and that this was part of the natural order, he exalted the "Aryan race" while propounding anti-Semitism, anticommunism, and extreme German nationalism. The economic slump of 1929 facilitated Hitler's rise to power. In the Reichstag elections of 1930 the Nazis became the country's second largest party and in 1932 the largest. Hitler ran for president in 1932 and lost but entered into intrigues to gain power, and in 1933 Paul von Hindenburg invited him to be chancellor. Adopting the title of Führer ("Leader"), Hitler gained dictatorial powers through the Enabling Act and suppressed opposition with assistance from Heinrich Himmler and Joseph Goebbels. Hitler also began to enact anti-Jewish measures, which culminated in the Holocaust. His aggressive foreign policy led to the signing of the Munich Agreement with France, Britain, and Italy, which permitted German annexation of Czechoslovakia's Sudetenland. He became allied with Benito Mussolini in the Rome-Berlin Axis. The German-Soviet Nonaggression Pact (1939) enabled him to invade Poland, precipitating World War II. As defeat grew imminent in 1945, he married Eva Braun in an underground bunker in Berlin, and the next day they committed suicide.

Hitler Youth, German HITLER-JUGEND, Organization set up by Adolf Hitler in 1933 for educating and training male youths aged 13–18 in Nazi principles. Under the leadership of Baldur von Schirach (1907–1974), by 1935 it included almost 60% of all German boys, and by 1936 it became a state agency that all young "Aryan" Germans were expected to join. The youths lived a Spartan life of dedication, fellowship, and Nazi conformity, with little parental guidance. A parallel organization, the League of German Girls, trained girls for domestic duties and motherhood.

Hittite, Any member of an Indo-European people whose empire (Old Kingdom *c.* 1650–1500 BCE, New Kingdom *c.* 1350–1180 BCE) was centred in Anatolia and northern Syria. Old Kingdom records detail Hittite territorial expansion; New Kingdom documents contain accounts of the Battle of Kadesh, one of the greatest conflicts of the ancient world, which was fought against Egypt. Hittite kings had absolute power and were viewed as deputies of the gods, at death becoming gods themselves. Hittite society was feudal and agrarian; iron-working technology was developed. The

kingdom fell abruptly, possibly because of large-scale migrations of Sea Peoples and Phrygians into parts of the empire.

HIV, in full HUMAN IMMUNODEFICIENCY VIRUS, Retrovirus associated with AIDS. HIV attacks and gradually destroys the immune system, leaving the host unprotected against infection. It cannot be spread through casual contact but instead is contracted mainly through exposure to blood and blood products (e.g., by sharing hypodermic needles or by accidental needle sticks), semen and female genital secretions, or breast milk. A pregnant woman can pass the virus to her fetus across the placenta. The virus first multiplies in lymph nodes near the site of infection. Once it spreads through the body, usually about 10 years later, symptoms appear, marking the onset of AIDS. Multidrug "cocktails" can delay onset, but missing doses can lead to drug resistance. Like other viruses, HIV needs a host cell to multiply. It attacks helper T cells and can infect other cells. A rapid mutation rate helps it foil both the immune system and treatment attempts. No vaccine or cure exists. Abstinence from sex, use of condoms or other means to prevent sexual transmission of the disease, and avoidance of needle sharing have reduced infection rates in some areas.

hives, or URTICARIA, Allergic skin reaction in which slightly raised, flat-topped, very itchy swellings appear suddenly. The acute form, probably most often caused by food allergies, subsides in 6–24 hours, but the chronic form, believed to be due to emotional and mental stress, lasts much longer. Acute hives may also be triggered by drugs, especially penicillin, inhaled allergens or toxins, or diseases. Treatment involves identifying and avoiding the allergen; epinephrine and antihistamines may help the acute skin symptoms.

Hmong, Mountain-dwelling peoples of China, Vietnam, Laos, and Thailand who speak Hmong-Mien languages. There are also émigré communities in the U.S., France, and elsewhere. Agriculture is the chief means of subsistence for the Hmong; most grow corn (maize) and rice as subsistence crops and flowers, fruit, and vegetables as cash crops. Many venerate spirits, demons, and ancestral ghosts. Households are typically multigenerational. In China, where they are one of several ethnically distinct minorities within the official minority called Miao, many Hmong follow the Chinese practice of arranged marriage. Worldwide they number approximately 5 million individuals.

Hmong-Mien languages, or MIAO-YAO LANGUAGES, Language family of southern China, northern Vietnam, Laos, and Thailand with more than 10 million speakers. Hmongic (Miao) languages include Hmu, Hmong, Qo Xiong, Bunu, and Ho Ne; Mienic (Yao) languages include Mien, Mun, Biao Min, and others. In the 19th and early 20th centuries, many Hmong and Mien speakers emigrated from China to Southeast Asia. Hmong-Mien languages share some characteristics with other languages of the area, most notably Chinese. However, scholars have not reached consensus on the genetic relationships between Hmong-Mien and other languages; some believe that Hmong-Mien is part of the Sino-Tibetan linguistic family, while others believe that there is no genetic relationship between Hmong-Mien and any other living language.

Ho Chi Minh, orig. NGUYEN SINH CUNG (b. May 19, 1890, Hoang Tru, Viet.—d. Sept. 2, 1969, Hanoi), President (1945–69) of the Democratic Republic of Vietnam (North Vietnam). Son of a poor scholar, he was brought up in a rural village. In 1911 he found work on a French steamer and traveled the world, then spent six years in France, where he became a socialist. In 1923 he went to the Soviet Union; the next year he went to China, where he started organizing exiled Vietnamese. He founded the Indochina Communist Party in 1930 and its successor, the Viet Minh, in 1941. In 1945 Japan overran Indochina, overthrowing its French colonial rulers; when the Japanese surrendered to the Allies six months later, Ho and his Viet Minh forces seized the opportunity, occupied Hanoi, and proclaimed Vietnamese independence. France refused to relinquish its former colony, and the First Indochina War broke out in 1946. Ho's forces defeated the French in 1954 at Dien Bien Phu, after which the country was partitioned into North and South Vietnam. Ho, who ruled in the north, was soon embroiled with the U.S.-backed regime of Ngo Dinh Diem in the south in what became known as the Vietnam War; North Vietnamese forces prevailed over the south six years after Ho's death.

Ho Chi Minh City, formerly SAIGON, City (pop., 2004 est.: city, 3,452,100; 2005 est.: urban agglom., 5,065,000), southern Vietnam. It lies along the Saigon River north of the Mekong River delta. The Vietnamese first entered the region, then part of the kingdom of Cambodia, in the 17th century. In 1862 the area, including the town, was ceded to France. After World War II Vietnam declared its independence, but French troops seized control and the First Indochina War began. The Geneva conference in 1954 divided the country, and Saigon became the capital of South Vietnam. In the Vietnam War, it was the headquarters for U.S. military operations; it was captured by North Vietnamese troops in 1975 and renamed for Ho Chi Minh. Rebuilding since the war has promoted its commercial importance.

Hobart, City (pop., 2006: city, 47,701; urban agglom., 200,524), chief port, and capital, Tasmania, Australia. Located on the Derwent River estuary at the base of Mount Wellington, Hobart is Tasmania's largest and Australia's most southerly city. Established in 1803, it moved to its present site in 1804 and became a major port for ships whaling in the southern oceans. Its lack of natural resources limited its development. It now has a deepwater port, rail lines, and an airport, making it a centre of communications, trade, and tourism. The city is the site of Anglican and Roman Catholic cathedrals and the first Jewish synagogue in Australia (built 1843–45).

Hobbes, Thomas (b. April 5, 1588, Westport, Wiltshire, Eng.—d. Dec. 4, 1679, Hardwick Hall, Derbyshire), English philosopher and political theorist. The son of a vicar who abandoned his family, Hobbes was raised by his uncle. After graduating from the University of Oxford he became a tutor and traveled with his pupil in Europe, where he engaged Galileo in philosophical discussions on the nature of motion. He later turned to political theory, but his support for absolutism put him at odds with the rising antiroyalist sentiment of the time. He fled to Paris in 1640, where he tutored the future King Charles II of England. In Paris he wrote his best-known work, *Leviathan* (1651), in which he attempted to justify the absolute power of the sovereign on the basis of a hypothetical social contract in which individuals seek to protect themselves from one another by agreeing to obey the sovereign in all matters. Hobbes returned to Britain in 1651 after the death of Charles I. In 1666 Parliament threatened to investigate him as an atheist. His works are considered important statements of the nascent ideas of liberalism as well as of the longstanding assumptions of absolutism characteristic of the times.

Thomas Hobbes, detail of an oil painting by John Michael Wright; in the National Portrait Gallery, London.
Courtesy of the National Portrait Gallery, London

Hodgkin lymphoma, or HODGKIN DISEASE, or LYMPHORETIC-ULOMA, Most common malignant lymphoma. It starts with local painless swelling of lymph nodes and sometimes of the spleen, liver, or other organs, followed by weight loss and weakness. Diagnosis can be confirmed only by biopsy, usually from a lymph node. The cause remains unknown. Treatment with chemotherapy, radiation, or both depends on the stage of the disease. More than 90% of patients diagnosed early can be cured, as can many with advanced disease.

hog, Heavy, fat-producing domesticated pig developed in the U.S. in the late 19th and early 20th century. As the growing use of cheaper vegetable oils decreased the importance of lard as a source of fat, meatpackers sought hogs yielding more lean meat and less fat, and breeders (mostly European) began crossbreeding programs to obtain lean meat and vigorous animals. Today the term hog is often used for any pig weighing more than 120 lbs (54 kg).

Hohenstaufen dynasty, German dynasty that ruled the Holy Roman Empire (1138–1208, 1212–54). It was founded by Count Frederick (died 1105), who built Staufen Castle and was appointed duke of Swabia as Frederick I (1079). Hohenstaufen emperors included Frederick I Barbarossa (r. 1155–90), Henry VI (r.1191–97), and Frederick II (r.1220–50). The dynasty continued the struggle with the papacy begun under their predecessors.

Hohenzollern dynasty, Dynasty prominent in European history, chiefly as the ruling house of Brandenburg-Prussia (1415–1918) and of imperial Germany (1871–1918). The first recorded ancestor, Burchard I, was count of Zollern in the 11th century. Two main branches were formed: the Franconian line (including burgraves of Nürnberg, electors of Brandenburg, kings of Prussia, and German emperors) and the Swabian line (including counts of Zollern, princes of Hohenzollern-Sigmaringen, and princes and then kings of Romania). The Franconian branch became Lutheran at the Reformation but turned to Calvinism in 1613 and acquired considerable territory in the 15th–17th centuries. Both Prussian and German sovereignties were lost at the end of World War I (1914–18). The Swabian line remained Catholic at the Reformation and ruled in Romania until 1947. The Hohenzollern monarchs included Frederick William I, Frederick II (the Great), Frederick William II, and Frederick William III of Prussia; William I and William II of Germany; and Carol I and Carol II of Romania.

Hohhot, or HU-HO-HAO-T'E, or HUHEHOT, Mongol KUK-UKHOTO, City (pop., 2003 est.: 826,354), capital of Inner Mongolia autonomous region, northern China. The original Mongol city was an important religious centre for Tibetan Buddhism and later a Muslim trading community. After World War II (1939–45) it developed into an industrial centre with sugar refining, woolens, and an iron and steel industry. Its university (1957) was the first in Inner Mongolia. The city is a regional cultural centre.

Hokkaido, formerly YEZO, Island (pop., 2006 est.: 5,605,531) and province, northern Japan. Northernmost of the four main islands of Japan, it is bordered by the Sea of Japan (East Sea), the Sea of Okhotsk, and the Pacific Ocean and has an area of 30,109 sq mi (77,982 sq km). Its administrative headquarters is Sapporo. Within its borders are several high peaks, including Mount Asahi (7,513 ft [2,290 m]), and Japan's longest river, the Ishikari. Long the domain of the aboriginal Ainu, Hokkaido attracted serious Japanese settlement beginning in 1869. It has a varied economy, supported by iron and steel, and the largest coal deposits in Japan. The Seikan Tunnel (1988) under the Tsugaru Strait links it with Honshu.

Holi, Hindu spring festival. It is held on the full-moon day of Phalguna (February–March) and celebrated with reckless abandon. All distinctions of caste, age, sex, and status are disregarded. Participants throw coloured powders on each other, and street celebrations are noisy and riotous. The festival is especially associated with the worship of Krishna, and it is considered an imitation of his play with the wives and daughters of the cowherds.

holistic medicine, Doctrine of prevention and treatment that emphasizes looking at the whole person—body, mind, emotions, and environment—rather than a single function or organ. It promotes use of a wide range of health practices and therapies, including acupuncture, homeopathy, and nutrition, stressing "self-care" with traditional commonsense essentials. In the extreme, it may accord equal validity to a wide range of health-care approaches, some incompatible and not all scientific. It does not ignore mainstream Western medical practices but does not see them as the only effective therapies.

holly, Any of approximately 400 species of red- or black-berried

ornamental shrubs and trees that make up the genus *Ilex* (family Aquifoliaceae), including the popular Christmas hollies. English holly (*I. aquifolium*) bears shiny, spiny, dark, evergreen leaves; American holly (*I. opaca*) has oblong, prickly leaves; both have usually red fruits. There are spineless and yellow-fruited forms of both species.

*American holly (*Ilex opaca*).*
© Noble Proctor—The National Audubon Society Collection/Photo Researchers

Hollywood, District of the city of Los Angeles, Calif., U.S. Its name is synonymous with the American movie industry. In 1887 it was laid out as a subdivision by Harvey Wilcox, a prohibitionist who envisioned a community based on his religious principles. It was consolidated with Los Angeles in 1910 and became the centre of the movie industry by 1915. By the 1960s it also was the source of much American network television programming.

Holocaust, Hebrew SHOʾAH, Systematic state-sponsored killing of Jews and others by Nazi Germany and its collaborators during World War II. Fueled by anti-Semitism, the Nazi persecution of Jews began soon after Adolf Hitler became chancellor of Germany in 1933 with a boycott of Jewish businesses and the dismissal of Jewish civil servants. Under the Nürnberg Laws (1935), Jews lost their citizenship. About 7,500 Jewish businesses were gutted and some 1,000 synagogues burned or damaged in the Kristallnacht pogrom in 1938, and thereafter Jews were imprisoned in concentration camps or forced into ghettos. German victories early in World War II (1939–45) brought most European Jews under the control of the Nazis and their satellites. As German armies moved into Poland, the Balkans, and the Soviet Union, special mobile killing units, the *Einsatzgruppen*, rounded up and killed Jews, Roma (Gypsies), communists, political leaders, and intellectuals. Other groups targeted by the Nazis included homosexuals and the mentally retarded, physically disabled, and emotionally disturbed. At the Wannsee Conference (1942), a "final solution" was formulated for the extermination of European Jewry, and thereafter Jews from all over Nazi-occupied Europe were systematically evacuated to concentration and extermination camps, where they were either killed or forced into slave labour. Underground resistance movements arose in several countries, and Jewish risings took place against overwhelming odds in the ghettos of Poland. Individuals such as Raoul Wallenberg saved thousands by their efforts; whether the Allied governments and the Vatican could have done more to aid Jews has long been a matter of controversy. By the end of the war, an estimated six million Jews and millions of others had been killed by Nazi Germany and its collaborators.

Holocene Epoch, formerly RECENT EPOCH, Latest interval of the Earth's geologic history, dating from about 11,700 years ago to the present. The younger of the two epochs that constitute the Quaternary Period, the Holocene follows the last glacial stage of the Pleistocene Epoch. It is characterized by relatively warm climatic conditions. During this epoch, humans refined the skills that led to the present level of civilization.

holography, Method of recording or reproducing a three-dimensional image, or hologram, by means of a pattern of interference produced using a laser beam. To create a hologram, a beam of coherent light (a laser) is split; half the beam falls on a recording medium (such as a photographic plate) unaltered, and the other half is first reflected off the object to be imaged. The two beams together produce an interference pattern of stripes and whorls on the plate. The developed plate is the hologram. When light is shone on the hologram, a three-dimensional image of the original object is produced by the recorded interference pattern. Some holograms require laser light to reproduce the image; others may be viewed in ordinary white light. Holography was invented in 1947 by the Hungarian-British physicist Dennis Gabor (1900–1979), who won a 1971 Nobel Prize for his invention.

Holy Alliance, Loose organization of most of the European sovereigns, formed in 1815 by Alexander I of Russia, Francis I of Austria, and Frederick William III of Prussia, after the final defeat of Napoleon. Its avowed purpose was to promote the influence of Christian principles in the affairs of nations, but it accomplished little and became a symbol of conservatism and repression in central and eastern Europe.

Holy League (1576–98) Association of Roman Catholics during the French Wars of Religion. It was first organized under the leadership of the 3rd duke de Guise, to oppose concessions granted to the Protestant Huguenots by Henry III. In 1584, when the Huguenot leader Henry of Navarra (later Henry IV) became heir to the throne, the Holy League set up an alternative candidate, with Spain's assistance. To put an end to the league, which challenged his authority, Henry III had the duke de Guise assassinated (1588), an act that, rather than destroying the League, led to Henry's own assassination in 1589. The league opposed the accession of Henry IV, but its power waned when he became a Roman Catholic in 1593.

Holy Roman Empire, German HEILIGES RÖMISCHES REICH, Realm of varying extent in medieval and modern western and central Europe. Traditionally believed to have been established by Charlemagne, who was crowned emperor by Pope Leo III in 800, the empire lasted until the renunciation of the imperial title by Francis II in 1806. The reign of the German Otto I (the Great; r. 962–973), who revived the imperial title after Carolingian decline, is also sometimes regarded as the beginning of the empire. The name Holy Roman Empire (not adopted until the reign of Frederick I Barbarossa) reflected Charlemagne's claim that his empire was the successor to the Roman Empire and that this temporal power was augmented by his status as God's principal vicar in the temporal realm (parallel to the pope's in the spiritual realm). The empire's core consisted of Germany, Austria, Bohemia, and Moravia. Switzerland, the Netherlands, and northern Italy sometimes formed part of it; France, Poland, Hungary, and Denmark were initially included; and Britain and Spain were nominal components. From the mid-11th century the emperors engaged in a great struggle with the papacy for dominance, and, particularly under the powerful Hohenstaufen dynasty (1138–1208, 1212–54), they fought with the popes over control of Italy. Rudolf I became the first Habsburg emperor in 1273, and from 1438 the Habsburg dynasty held the throne for centuries. Until 1356 the emperor was chosen by the German princes; thereafter he was formally elected by the electors. Outside their personal hereditary domains, emperors shared power with the imperial diet. During the Reformation the German princes largely defected to the Protestant camp, opposing the Catholic emperor. At the end of the Thirty Years' War, the Peace of Westphalia (1648) recognized the individual sovereignty of the empire's states; the empire thereafter became a loose federation of states and the title of emperor principally honorific. In the 18th century, issues of imperial succession resulted in the War of the Austrian Succession and the Seven Years' War. The greatly weakened empire was brought to an end by the victories of Napoleon.

Holy Spirit, or HOLY GHOST, or PARACLETE, In Christianity, the third person of the Holy Trinity. Though references to the spirit of Yahweh (God) abound in the Old Testament, Christian teaching about the Holy Spirit is derived mainly from the Gospels. The Holy Spirit descended on Jesus at his baptism, and outpourings of the Spirit are mentioned in the Acts of the Apostles, in which healing, prophecy, exorcism, and speaking in tongues are associated with its activity. The Holy Spirit also came to the disciples during Pentecost. The definition of the Holy Spirit as a divine person equal in substance to the Father and the Son was made at the Council of Constantinople (AD 381).

Holy Synod, Ecclesiastical governing body created by Tsar Peter I in 1721 to head the Russian Orthodox Church, replacing the patriarchate of Moscow. Peter created the Synod, made up of representatives of the hierarchy obedient to his will, to subject the church to the state, and appointed a secular official, the chief procurator, to supervise its activities. The Synod persecuted all dissenters and censored publications, and Peter disposed of church property and revenues for state purposes at his own discretion. In 1917 a church council reestablished the patriarchate, but the new Soviet government soon nationalized all church-held lands.

Home Rule, Irish, Movement to secure internal autonomy for Ireland within the British Empire. The slogan "Home Rule" was popularized in 1870 when the Home Government Association (later the Home Rule League) called for an Irish parliament. It was led from 1877 by Charles Stewart Parnell, whose obstructionist tactics in the British Parliament publicized his country's grievances. The Home Rule bills introduced by Prime Minister William E. Gladstone in 1886 and 1893 were defeated. A third bill became law in 1914 despite the militant opposition of the Ulster unionists; but its enactment was accompanied by an act that suspended its coming into effect until the end of World War I, by which time the Sinn Féin (republican) party had displaced the Home Rule party as the elected representatives of Irish nationalists. A system akin to Home Rule was established in the six counties of Ulster (Northern Ireland) in 1921. In 1922 the remaining 26 counties in the south achieved dominion status as the Irish Free State (Ireland from 1937), and the link with the British Commonwealth was severed in 1949.

homeopathy, System of therapeutics founded in 1796 by Samuel Hahnemann on the principle that "like cures like." That is, substances that in healthy persons would produce the symptoms from which the patient suffers are used to treat the patient. Hahnemann further stated that the potency of a curative agent increases as the substance is diluted. When it was introduced, homeopathy was a mild, welcome alternative to heavy-handed therapies such as bleeding, but it has since been criticized for focusing on symptoms rather than causes. With the rise of alternative medicine, it has seen a resurgence.

Homer (fl. 9th or 8th century BCE, Ionia?), Greek poet, one of the greatest and most influential writers of all time. Though almost nothing is known of his life, tradition holds that he was blind. The ancient Greeks attributed to him the great epic poems *The Iliad* and *The Odyssey*. Modern scholars generally agree that he composed (but probably did not literally write) *The Iliad*, most likely relying on oral traditions, and at least inspired the composition of *The Odyssey*. *The Iliad*, set during the Trojan War, tells the story of the wrath of Achilles; *The Odyssey* tells the story of Odysseus as he travels home from the war. The two epics provided the basis of Greek education and culture in the Classical age, and they have remained among the most significant poems of the European tradition.

hominid, Any member of the zoological family Hominidae (order Primates), which consists of the great apes (orangutans, gorillas, chimpanzees, and bonobos) as well as human beings. Formerly, only humans (with their extinct forebears) were categorized as hominids, and the great apes were categorized as pongids—that is, members of the primate family Pongidae. However, morphological and molecular studies now indicate that humans are closely related to chimpanzees, while gorillas are more distant and orangutans more distant still. As a result, it has become more common among zoologists to consider humans and great apes to be hominids.

Homo erectus (Latin: "upright man"), Extinct species of early hominin, perhaps a direct ancestor of human beings (*Homo sapiens*). *Homo erectus* flourished from c. 1,700,000 to 200,000 years ago, ranging widely from Africa (where the species probably originated) to Asia to parts of Europe. Most of the anatomical differences between *H. erectus* and *H. sapiens* concern the skull and teeth, *H. erectus* showing a low, thick braincase (800–1,100 cc) with jutting browridges and a wide nose, palate, and jaw together with large teeth that are nevertheless hominin and not apelike. The limb bones are similar to those of *H. sapiens*, indicating that *H. erectus* was of medium stature and walked upright. The species is associated with the Acheulean tool tradition and was the first hominin to master fire and inhabit caves.

Homo habilis (Latin: "handy man"), Extinct species of early hominin that is generally regarded as the earliest member of the human genus, *Homo*. *Homo habilis* inhabited parts of sub-Saharan Africa about 2–1.5 million years ago. Remains were first discovered in 1959 and 1960 at Olduvai Gorge in northern Tanzania; additional remains have since been found in the Lake Turkana region of northern Kenya and, arguably, at Sterkfontein in South Africa. The cranial capacity of *H. habilis* ranged from 500 to 800 cc. Limb bones suggest that the species walked upright efficiently, and the fossil of a hand suggests that *H. habilis* was capable of precise manipulation of objects. Crude tools found along with *H. habilis* remains provide further evidence that this species could shape stone.

Homo sapiens (Latin: "wise man"), Species to which all modern human beings belong. The oldest known fossil remains date to c. 120,000 years ago—or much earlier (c. 400,000 years ago) if evidence of certain archaic varieties is included. *Homo sapiens* is distinguished from earlier hominin species by characteristics and habits such as bipedal stance and gait, brain capacity averaging about 1,350 cc, high forehead, small teeth and jaw, defined chin, construction and use of tools, and ability to use symbols. Most scholars believe that modern humans developed in Africa c. 150,000 years ago and spread to the Middle East c. 100,000 years ago and to other parts of Eurasia c. 40,000–50,000 years ago (this is known as the "single-origin" model). Others contend that modern humans developed from various regional populations of archaic *H. sapiens* or even other species of *Homo* in Eurasia beginning c. 250,000 years ago (the "multiregional" model). In the first model the genetic differences that exist between the peoples of the world would not be very old; in the second model they would be significantly older. In any case, by c. 11,000 BC modern *H. sapiens* had peopled virtually the entire globe.

homosexuality, Sexual interest in and attraction to members of one's own sex. Female homosexuality is frequently referred to as lesbianism; the word *gay* is often used as an alternative for both "homosexual" and "lesbian," though it may refer specifically to male homosexuality. At different times and in different cultures, homosexual behaviour has variously been encouraged, approved of, tolerated, punished, and banned. Homosexuality was not uncommon in ancient Greece and Rome, particularly between adult and adolescent males. Jewish, Christian, and Muslim cultures have generally viewed it as sinful, although many religious leaders have said it is the act, and not the inclination, that their faiths proscribe. Attitudes toward homosexuality are generally in flux, partly because of increased political activism. Until the early 1970s many medical organizations, such as the American Psychiatric Association, classified homosexuality as a mental illness, but that designation was widely dropped in subsequent years. Long-standing beliefs about homosexuals (including the stereotype that gay men are weak and effeminate and lesbians aggressive and masculine) have also largely faded; some countries, cultures, and religious groups, however, continue to view homosexuality as deviant. Homosexual orientation, like sexuality in general, apparently results from a combination of hereditary factors and social or environmental influences, and it tends to coexist with heterosexual feelings in varying degrees in different individuals.

homozygote and heterozygote, Two genetic possibilities for a fertilized egg. If the two sex cells (gametes) that fuse during fertilization carry the same form of a gene for a specific trait, the organism is said to be a homozygote for that trait. If the gametes carry differing forms of the gene, the result is a heterozygote. Because genes may be either dominant or recessive, the genetic composition (genotype) of an organism cannot always be determined by the organism's physical appearance (phenotype).

Honduras, officially REPUBLIC OF HONDURAS, Country, Central America. Area: 43,433 sq mi (112,492 sq km). Population: (2011 est.) 7,755,000. Capital: Tegucigalpa. The great majority of the population are mestizos. Language: Spanish (official). Religion: Christianity (predominantly Roman Catholic; also Protestant). Currency: Honduran lempira. The second largest country in Central America, Honduras has an almost 400-mi (645-km) coastline on the Caribbean Sea to the north and a 45-mi (72-km) coast centred on the Gulf of Fonseca on the Pacific Ocean side of the isthmus. More than three-fourths of Honduras is mountainous and wooded. The eastern lowlands include part of the Mosquito Coast. Most of the people live in isolated communities in the mountainous interior, where the climate is hot and rainy. The economy is primarily agricultural; bananas, coffee, and sugar are the main export crops, and corn is the chief domestic staple. Honduras is a multiparty republic with one legislative house, and the head of state and government is the president. The Maya civilization flourished in the region in the 1st millennium CE. There are architectural and sculptural remains of a ceremonial centre at Copán, which was in use from *c.* 465 to *c.* 800. Christopher Columbus reached Honduras in 1502, and Spanish settlement followed. A major war between the Spaniards and the Indians broke out in 1537; the conflict ended in the decimation of the Indian population through disease and enslavement. After 1570 Honduras was part of the captaincy general of Guatemala, until Central American independence in 1821. It was then part of the United Provinces of Central America but withdrew in 1838 and declared its independence. In the 20th century, under military rule, there was nearly constant civil war. A civilian government was elected in 1981. The military remained influential, however, as the activity of leftist guerrillas increased. Flooding caused by a hurricane in 1998 devastated the country, killing thousands of people and leaving hundreds of thousands homeless. In 2001 Honduras was hit by a severe drought. Recovery and rebuilding efforts followed for the next several years. In 2009 Pres. Manuel Zelaya was ousted in a coup—the first military coup in Central America since the end of the Cold War. A military-supported interim regime held power only until January 2010, when an elected president took office.

Hong Kong, Chinese XIANGGANG, or HSIANG-KANG, Special administrative region of China. Area: 426 sq mi (1,104 sq km). Population: (2011 est.) 7,125,000. Located on China's southern coast, it consists of the island of Hong Kong and adjacent islets in the South China Sea (ceded by China to the British in 1842), the Kowloon Peninsula (ceded in 1860), and the New Territories (leased by the British from China from 1898 to 1997). The entire territory was returned to China in 1997. The New Territories, lying north of the Kowloon Peninsula and constituting an enclave in China's Guangdong province, are more than nine-tenths of the total area. The administrative centre of Victoria on Hong Kong island's northwestern coast is also the centre of economic activities. Hong Kong has an excellent natural harbour and is one of the world's major trade and financial centres. It has many educational institutions, including the University of Hong Kong (1911).

Hongwu emperor, or HUNG-WU EMPEROR, orig. ZHU YUAN-ZHANG (b. Oct. 21, 1328, Haozhou, China—d. June 24, 1398), Founder of China's Ming dynasty. A poor peasant orphaned at 16, he entered a monastery to avoid starvation. Later, as a rebel leader, he came in contact with educated gentry from whom he received an education and political guidance. He was advised to present himself not as a popular rebel but as a national leader against the foreign Mongols whose Yuan dynasty was on the point of collapse. Defeating rival national leaders, Zhu proclaimed himself emperor in 1368, establishing his capital at Nanjing and adopting Hongwu as his reign title. He drove the last Yuan emperor from China that year and reunified the country by 1382. His rule was despotic: he eliminated the posts of prime minister and central chancellor and had the next level of administration report directly to him. He prohibited eunuchs from participating in government and appointed civilian officials to control military affairs.

Honshu, Island (pop., 2004 est.: 103,152,000), Japan. The largest of the four main islands of Japan, its coastline extends 6,266 mi (10,084 km); it has an area of 88,012 sq mi (227,950 sq km). It is regarded as the Japanese mainland, and much of the country's early history took place in its southwestern region. Honshu's Pacific coast is the country's main economic centre, lined with the metropolitan areas of Tokyo-Yokohama, Nagoya, and Ōsaka-Kōbe. Honshu contains Japan's tallest mountain, Mount Fuji, and its largest lake, Lake Biwa.

hop, In botany, either of two species of the genus *Humulus*, non-woody annual or perennial vines in the hemp family, native to temperate North America, Eurasia, and South America. The hops used in the brewery industry are the dried female flower clusters (cones) of the common hop (*H. lupulus*), a long-lived perennial with rough twining stems. Hops impart a mellow bitterness and delicate aroma to brewed beverages and aid in their preservation. The Japanese hop (*H. japonicus*) is a quick-growing annual species used as a screening vine.

Hop vine (Humulus lupulus) with female flowers (cones), which are used in brewing.
Grant Heilman/EB Inc.

hormone, Organic compound (often a steroid or peptide) that is produced in one part of a multicellular organism and travels to another part to exert its action. Hormones regulate physiological activities including growth, reproduction, and homeostasis in vertebrates; molting and maintenance of the larval state in insects; and growth, bud dormancy, and leaf shedding in plants. Most vertebrate hormones originate in specialized tissues and are carried to their targets through the circulation. Among the many mammalian hormones are ACTH, sex hormones, thyroxine, insulin, and epinephrine. Insect hormones include ecdysone, thoracotropic hormone, and juvenile hormone. Plant hormones include ethylene, abscisin, auxins, gibberellins, and cytokinins.

Hormuz, Strait of, formerly STRAIT OF ORMUZ, Channel linking the Persian Gulf with the Gulf of Oman and the Arabian Sea. It is 35–60 mi (55–95 km) wide and separates Iran from the Arabian Peninsula. It contains the islands of Qeshm, Hormoz, and Hengām and is strategically and economically important as a route for oil tankers collecting from various ports on the Persian Gulf.

Horn, Cape, Southern extremity of South America. Located on Horn Island in the southern Tierra del Fuego archipelago, it projects south into Drake Passage. It was named Hoorn for the birthplace of Dutch navigator Willem Schouten, who rounded it in 1616. Navigation of the rough waters around the cape is hazardous, and the climate is windy and cold year-round.

Horn of Africa, Region of eastern Africa. The easternmost African extension of land between the Indian Ocean and the Gulf of Aden, it is occupied by Ethiopia, Eritrea, Somalia, and Djibouti, whose cultures have been linked throughout their long history.

hornbill, Any of 54 species of Old World tropical birds (family Bucerotidae) noted for the bony helmet on the bill of some species. Hornbills range from 16 to 63 in. (40 to 160 cm) long and typically have a large head, prominent bill, thin neck, broad wings, long tail, and brown or black plumage, usually with bold white markings. They nest in cavities, usually in large trees. The male of most species walls up the female in the nest, closing the hole with mud, except for a small opening through which he passes food. The female breaks out after the eggs hatch, but the young may be walled up again.

*Red-billed hornbill (*Tockus erythrorhynchus)
Mark Boulton—The National Audubon Society Collection/Photo Researchers

horned owl, Any owl of the genus *Bubo* (family Strigidae), with hornlike tufts of feathers, especially the great horned owl. Other horned owls, all birds of prey, are found in Europe, Asia, and northern Africa (the eagle owl, or Eurasian eagle owl) and in Africa, India, Myanmar (Burma), and the Indonesian archipelago. They typically prey on rodents.

horoscope, Astrological chart showing the positions of the sun, moon, and planets in relation to the signs of the zodiac at a specific time. It is used to analyze the character of individuals born at that time, providing information about the current state of their life and predicting their future. Basic to a horoscope is the belief that each heavenly body has its own character, which is modified according to its relation to other celestial bodies at a given moment. To cast a horoscope, the heavens are divided into 12 zones called houses; these influence such aspects of human life as health, wealth, marriage, friendships, or death.

*Great horned owl (*Bubo virginianus).
E.R. Degginger

horror story, Story intended to elicit a strong feeling of fear. Such tales are of ancient origin and form a substantial part of folk literature. They may feature supernatural elements such as ghosts, witches, or vampires or address more realistic psychological fears. In Western literature, the literary cultivation of fear and curiosity for its own sake emerged in the 18th century with the gothic novel. Classic practitioners of the horror and gothic genres include Horace Walpole, Mary Shelley, E.T.A. Hoffmann, Edgar Allan Poe, Sheridan Le Fanu (1814–73), Wilkie Collins, Bram Stoker, Ambrose Bierce, and Stephen King.

horse, Equine species (*Equus caballus*) long used by humans as a means of transport and as a draft animal. Its earliest ancestor was the dawn horse. The only living horse not descended from the domestic horse is Przewalski's horse. The horse was apparently first domesticated by nomadic peoples of Central Asia in the 3rd millennium BC. For many centuries horses were primarily used in warfare. The saddle was introduced in China in the first centuries AD. Horses were reintroduced to the New World, after wild horses had become extinct there some 10,000 years earlier, by the Spanish in the 16th century. A mature male is called a stallion or, if used for breeding, a stud; mature females are called mares. A castrated stallion is called a gelding. Young horses (foals) are also known as colts (males) and fillies (females). A horse's height is measured in 4-in. (10.2-cm) units, or hands, from the highest point of the back (withers) to the ground. Breeds are classified by size and build: draft (heavy) horses (e.g., Belgian, Percheron) are heavy-limbed and up to 20 hands high; ponies (e.g., Shetland, Iceland) are less than 14.2 hands high; and light horses (e.g., Arabian, Thoroughbred) are intermediate, rarely taller than 17 hands.

horse racing, Sport of running horses at speed. Typically, Thoroughbreds are raced with a rider astride and Standardbreds with the horse pulling a conveyance with a driver. Though racing has an ancient lineage, the first regularly organized national races were established in England under Charles II (r. 1660–85), and the first in North America were held on Long Island in 1665. These early races were match events between two or three horses and were run in heats; a horse had to complete at least two heats to be judged the winner. By the mid-18th century, larger fields of runners and single-race "dash" events were the norm. Handicap racing emerged in the mid-18th century as well, as gambling came to be a standard part of horse racing. Pari-mutuel betting was instituted in the 20th century. Thoroughbred racing, conducted on a flat, elliptical, mile-long track, attracts the largest purses, followed by harness racing and quarter-horse racing. The most important U.S. Thoroughbred races are the Kentucky Derby, Preakness Stakes, and Belmont Stakes.

horsefly, Any member of the dipteran genus *Tabanus* or, more generally, of the family Tabanidae. These stout flies range from as small as a housefly to as large as a bumblebee. Sometimes called greenheaded monsters, horseflies have metallic or iridescent eyes. Adults are fast, strong fliers usually found around streams, marshes, and wooded areas. They may carry animal diseases, including anthrax, tularemia, and trypanosomiasis. The bites of the bloodsucking females can be painful, and a swarm may suck more than 3 oz (about 90 ml) of blood a day from an animal. Males feed on nectar, honeydew, and plant sap. Horseflies of the genus *Chrysops*, usually called deerflies, are smaller and have dark markings on the wings.

horsepower, Common unit of power, the rate at which work is done. In the English system, one horsepower equals 33,000 foot-pounds of work per minute—that is, the power necessary to lift a total of 33,000 lbs a distance of one foot in one minute. This value was adopted by James Watt in the late 18th century after experiments with strong dray horses and is actually about 50% more than the rate an average horse can sustain for a working day. The electrical equivalent of one horsepower is 746 watts in the International System of Units; the heat equivalent is 2,545 BTU per hour. The metric horsepower equals 4,500 kg-m per minute (32,549 foot-pounds per minute), or 0.9863 horsepower.

horseshoe crab, Any of four extant species of marine arthropods (order Xiphosura, subphylum Chelicerata), found on the eastern coasts of Asia (three species) and North America (one species). Despite the name, horseshoe crabs are not crabs; they are

Horseshoe crab (Limulus polyphemus).
Runk/Schoenberger—Grant Heilman/EB Inc.

more closely related to scorpions. Fossil relatives date back 505 million years. They are most abundant in estuarine waters. The North American species, *Limulus polyphemus*, can grow to more than 2 ft (60 cm) long. The body consists of three parts hinged together: a broad, horseshoe-shaped cephalothorax; a much smaller, segmented abdomen; and a long, sharp tailspine, or telson. They spawn on sandy beaches in spring and summer. Adults feed on marine worms; larvae feed on small organisms.

Horus, Ancient Egyptian god with the head of a falcon, whose eyes were the sun and moon. The kings of Egypt were called living incarnations of Horus. During the 1st dynasty Horus was known principally as an opponent of Seth, but after about 2350 BCE he became associated with the Osiris cult and was identified as the son of Osiris. He destroyed Seth, the killer of Osiris, and became ruler of all Egypt. His left eye (the moon) was damaged by Seth but was healed by Thoth. In the Ptolemaic period, the victory of Horus over Seth became a symbol of Egypt triumphing over its occupiers.

Hōryū Temple, Japanese HŌRYŪ-JI, Buddhist complex near Nara, Japan, comprising the oldest known wood buildings in the world. The temple was founded by Prince Shōtoku in 607 during the Asuka period, destroyed by fire in 670, and reconstructed c. 680–708. It retains the *chū-mon* (middle gate) of the roofed cloister enclosing the rectangular temple precinct, a five-storied pagoda, and a *kondō* (main hall).

hospice, Home or hospital for relieving physical and emotional suffering of dying persons. In patients expected to live only months or weeks, hospice care offers an alternative to aggressive life-prolonging measures, which often only increase discomfort and isolation. Hospices provide a sympathetic environment in which prevention (not just control) of physical pain has top priority, along with patients' emotional and spiritual needs. Care may be provided in a health facility, on an outpatient basis, or at home.

hospital, Institution for diagnosing and treating the sick or injured, housing them during treatment, examining patients, and managing childbirth. Outpatients, who can leave after treatment, come in for emergency care or are referred for services not available in a private doctor's office. Hospitals may be public (government-owned) or private (profit-making or not-for-profit); in most countries except the U.S., most are public. They may also be general, accepting all types of medical or surgical cases, or special (e.g., children's hospitals, mental hospitals), limiting service to a single type of patient or illness. However, general hospitals usually also have specialized departments, and special hospitals tend to become affiliated with general hospitals.

hosta, Any of about 40 species of hardy herbaceous perennials, also called plantain lily, of the genus *Hosta*, in the agave family (Agavaceae), native to eastern Asia. They prefer light shade but will grow under a variety of conditions. They are frequently grown for their conspicuous foliage, which may be light to dark green, yellow, blue, or variegated. The ribbed leaves grow in a cluster at the base, and stalks bearing clusters of tubular white or bluish-purple flowers emerge from the leaves.

hot spring, or THERMAL SPRING, Spring that issues water at temperatures substantially higher than the air temperature of the surrounding region. Most hot springs result from the interaction of groundwater with magma or with solid but still-hot igneous rocks.

Some, however, are not related to volcanic activity. In such cases, deep circulation of water is thought to carry the water to the lower parts of the Earth's crust, where the temperature of the rocks is high.

hotel, Building that provides lodging, meals, and other services to the traveling public on a commercial basis. Inns have existed since ancient times (e.g., along the Roman road system during the Roman Empire) to serve merchants and other travelers. Medieval European monasteries operated inns to guarantee haven for travelers in dangerous regions. The spread of travel by stagecoach in the 18th century stimulated the development of inns, as did the Industrial Revolution. The modern hotel was largely the result of the railroads; when traveling for pleasure became widely popular, large hotels were often built near railroad stations. In 1889 the Savoy Hotel in London set a new standard, with its own electricity and a host of special services; the Statler Hotel in Buffalo, N.Y. (1908), another landmark, catered to the growing class of business travelers. After World War II, new hotels tended to be larger and were often built near airports. Hotel chains became common, making purchasing, sales, and reservations more efficient. Hotels fall into three categories: transient hotels; resort hotels, intended primarily for vacationers; and residential hotels, essentially apartment buildings offering room and meal service.

Houphouët-Boigny, Félix (b. Oct. 18, 1905?, Yamoussoukro, French West Africa—d. Dec. 7, 1993, Yamoussoukro, Côte d'Ivoire), President of Côte d'Ivoire from independence until his death (1960–93). He worked as a rural doctor and planter before entering politics in the 1940s. In the late 1950s he was a member of France's National Assembly and cabinet and simultaneously president of the territorial assembly and mayor of Abidjan. As president he pursued liberal free-enterprise politics and developed a strong cash-crop economy, cooperating closely with the French. Under his rule Côte d'Ivoire became one of the most prosperous nations in sub-Saharan Africa. His later years were marred by an economic downturn, civil unrest, and criticism of the enormous Roman Catholic basilica that he had built at Yamoussoukro, his birthplace.

Houston, City (pop., 2010: 2,099,451), southern Texas, U.S. An inland port, it is linked by the Houston Ship Channel to the Gulf of Mexico and to the Gulf Intracoastal Waterway at Galveston. Founded in 1836, it was named for Sam Houston; it was the capital of the Republic of Texas (1837–39). The state's largest city and leading port, it is a centre for oil, petrochemical, and aerospace research and development. The area is also important for rice, cotton, and cattle. It has several institutions for higher learning, including Rice University and Baylor College of Medicine. Houston is home to a symphony orchestra and ballet, an opera, and various theatre companies.

howler monkey, Any of several species of slow-moving tropical American monkeys (genus *Alouatta*) noted for their roaring cries, which carry over a distance of 2–3 mi (3–5 km). Five widely distributed species are the largest New World monkeys, generally reaching lengths of 16–28 in. (40–70 cm), excluding the 20–30-in. (50–75-cm) tail. Howlers are stoutly built and bearded, with a hunched appearance and a thickly furred, prehensile tail. Their hair is long and thick and, depending on the species, black, brown, or red. Howlers live in groups in territories mapped out by howling matches with neighbouring clans. They feed primarily on leaves.

Hu Jintao, or HU CHIN-T'AO (b. Dec. 25, 1942, Taizhou, Jiangsu province, China), General secretary of the Chinese Communist Party (CCP; from 2002) and president of China (from 2003). After studying engineering at Tsinghua University in Beijing, Hu laboured as a construction worker in Gansu province, where he met Song Ping, a party elder who became Hu's mentor and later introduced him to the CCP general secretary, Hu Yaobang. By the mid-

1980s Hu Jintao had risen to general secretary of the Chinese Communist Youth League (CCYL), and in 1985 he was appointed party secretary for Guizhou province, where he helped implement educational and economic reforms. Named a member of the CCP Central Committee in 1987, he was sent to Tibet the following year as a provincial party secretary. In 1992 he was appointed a member of the Secretariat of the CCP Central Committee, and in 1998 he was elected vice president of China. Hu succeeded President Jiang Zemin as general secretary of the CCP in 2002 and was elected president the following year. In 2004 he became head of the Central Military Commission after Jiang resigned the post.

Hu Shih, or HU SHI (b. Dec. 17, 1891, Shanghai, China—d. Feb. 24, 1962, Taiwan), Chinese Nationalist scholar and diplomat who helped establish the vernacular as the official written language. Hu studied under John Dewey at Columbia University and was profoundly influenced by Dewey's philosophy and pragmatic methodology. Back in China, he began writing in vernacular Chinese, the use of which spread rapidly. Because he eschewed dogmas such as Marxism and anarchism as solutions for China's problems, he found himself opposed by the communists but also distrusted by the Nationalists. In 1937, when war broke out with Japan, he and the Nationalists were reconciled, and Hu became ambassador to the U.S. He finished his life as president of Taiwan's Academia Sinica.

Hua Hengfang, also known as HUA RUOTING (b. 1833, Wuxi, Jiangsu province, China—d. 1902, China), Chinese mathematician and translator of Western mathematical works. Apparently inspired by Li Shanlan, Hua was an early enthusiastic proponent of Western-style mathematics. Hua's personal struggles to understand mathematical materials resulted in exceptionally lucid translations—particularly his fluent and accessible presentations of works on algebra and calculus. His translations were widely read and adopted by many of the new Western-style schools founded in China in the 19th century by the government and Christian missionaries.

Huang He, or HUANG HO English YELLOW RIVER, River, northern, central, and eastern China. The second longest river in China and one of the world's longest, it flows 3,395 mi (5,464 km) from the Plateau of Tibet generally east to the Yellow Sea (Huang Hai). In its lower reaches it has often overflowed its banks, flooding vast areas of rich farmland. Its outlet has shifted over the years to enter the Yellow Sea at points as far apart as 500 mi (800 km). Irrigation and flood-control works have been maintained for centuries, and dams, begun in the mid-1950s, exploit the river's hydroelectric potential.

Hubble, Edwin P(owell) (b. Nov. 20, 1889, Marshfield, Mo., U.S.—d. Sept. 28, 1953, San Marino, Calif.), U.S. astronomer. He earned a degree in mathematics and astronomy at the University of Chicago, then made a brief foray into law before returning to astronomy. After earning his Ph.D., he began working at Mount Wilson Observatory. In 1922–24 he discovered that certain nebulae contained Cepheid variable stars; he determined that these were several hundred thousand light-years away (outside the Milky Way Galaxy) and that the nebulae they were in were actually other galaxies. In studying those galaxies, he made his second remarkable discovery (1927): that the galaxies were receding from the Milky Way at rates that increased with distance. This implied that the universe, long considered unchanging, was expanding; even more remarkable, the ratio of the galaxies' speed to their distance was a constant. Hubble's original calculation of the constant was incorrect; it made the Milky Way larger than all other galaxies and the entire universe younger than the surmised age of Earth. Later astronomers determined that galaxies were systematically more distant, resolving the discrepancy.

Hubble Space Telescope (HST), Most sophisticated optical observatory ever placed into orbit around Earth. Because it is above Earth's obscuring atmosphere, it can obtain images much brighter, clearer, and more detailed than ground-based telescopes can. Named for Edwin Hubble, it was built under NASA supervision and deployed on a 1990 space-shuttle mission. The reflector telescope's mirror optics gather light from celestial objects and direct it to an array of cameras and spectrographs. A defect in the primary mirror initially caused it to produce fuzzy images; in 1993 another shuttle mission corrected this and other problems. Subsequent missions to the HST have been for maintenance, repairs, and instrument upgrades.

Hubble's constant, Constant used to relate the velocities of remote galaxies to their distances from Earth. Denoted H_0 and named in honour of Edwin Hubble, it expresses the rate of expansion of the universe. Its actual value has been debated for decades; improved measurements have narrowed the range in which it falls to about 13.3–14.5 miles/second (21.5–23.4 km/second) per million light-years. The reciprocal of H_0, which is between 13 billion and 14 billion years, gives the time since the galaxies began to separate from each other—i.e., the approximate age of the universe. Hubble used the redshifts of distant galaxies measured by Vesto Slipher (1875–1969) and his own distance estimates of those galaxies to establish the cosmological velocity-distance law (Hubble law): velocity = H_0 × distance, according to which the greater a galaxy's distance, the faster it is receding. Derived from theoretical considerations and confirmed by observations, the Hubble law has made secure the concept of an expanding universe.

Hubei, or HU-PEI, conventional HUPEH, Province (pop., 2002 est.: 59,880,000), east-central China. It lies north of the Yangtze River (Chang Jiang) and is bordered by Shaanxi, Henan, Anhui, Jiangxi, and Hunan provinces and by Chongqing municipality. It has an area of 72,400 sq mi (187,500 sq km), and its capital is Wuhan. Once part of the kingdom of Chu (3rd century BCE), it became part of the Qin dynasty's empire after being subjugated by Shihuangdi. Until the reign of Kangxi, Hubei and Hunan formed one province; they were divided in the mid-17th century. The area was the scene of battles after the 1850 Taiping Rebellion. The revolution of 1911–12 began in Hubei. The province was heavily bombed during the Sino-Japanese War of 1937–45. Restoration began after the communist Chinese takeover. In addition to agricultural production, Hubei has important heavy industrial production.

Hubertusburg, Peace of (1763) Treaty between Prussia and Austria ending the Seven Years' War in Germany. Signed five days after the Treaty of Paris, it guaranteed that Frederick II the Great maintained his possession of Silesia and confirmed Prussia's stature as a major European power.

Hudson, Henry (b. c. 1565, England—d. after June 22, 1611, in or near Hudson Bay?), English navigator and explorer. Sailing for the Muscovy Company of London in search of the Northeast Passage to the Far East, he was blocked by ice fields. In 1609 he set out in the *Half Moon* to find a similar passage for the Dutch East India Company, but, when stopped by storms, he instead sought the Northwest Passage, which he had recently heard about from other explorers, and cruised along the Atlantic coast and up the Hudson River. In 1610 he set out again for America, this time on behalf of the Muscovy Company and the English East India Company, and discovered Hudson Bay. Finding no outlet to the Pacific and in the close confinement of an Arctic winter, Hudson's crew fell to quarreling, and on the homeward voyage they mutinied and set Hudson adrift in a small boat, never to be found. His discoveries formed the basis for Dutch colonization of the Hudson River and for English claims to much of Canada.

Hudson Bay, Inland sea, indenting east-central Canada. With an area of 480,000 sq mi (1,243,000 sq km), it is bounded by Nunavut, Manitoba, Ontario, and Quebec. It is connected with the Atlantic Ocean via the Hudson Strait and with the Arctic Ocean via the Foxe Channel. Named for Henry Hudson, who navigated its eastern coast in 1610, the bay and the surrounding area, known as Rupert's Land, were controlled by the Hudson's Bay Company (1821–69). Hudson Bay is shallow, with an average depth of 330 ft (100 m); the coast is mainly a marshy lowland. The islands it contains are administratively part of Nunavut. For conservation purposes, the Canadian government has designated the whole Hudson Bay basin a "mare clausum" (closed sea).

Hudson River, River, New York, U.S. Originating in the Adirondack Mountains and flowing for about 315 mi (507 km) to New York City, it was named for Henry Hudson, who explored it in 1609. Dutch settlement of the Hudson valley began in 1629. The river became a strategic waterway during the American Revolution and was the scene of many battles. Linked by canals with the Great Lakes and with the Delaware River and lower St. Lawrence River valleys, the Hudson is now a major commercial route; its southern end forms the New York–New Jersey boundary.

Hue, City (pop., 2004 est.: 277,100), central Vietnam. The seat of the Chinese military authority in the kingdom of Nam Viet about 200 BC, it passed to the Chams about AD 200. In 1306 it was ceded to Dai Viet (Vietnam). It is the site of the imperial citadel, from which the Nguyen family reigned from the mid-16th to the mid-20th century. It was occupied by the Japanese (1940–45). It became the seat of a committee of noncommunist Vietnamese in April 1947 but lost this role in 1949 when the newly declared state of Vietnam chose Saigon as its capital. Hue was largely destroyed during the 1968 Tet Offensive of the Vietnam War; it has since been rebuilt.

Hughes, (James Mercer) Langston (b. Feb. 1, 1902, Joplin, Mo., U.S.—d. May 22, 1967, New York, N.Y.), U.S. poet and writer. He published the poem "The Negro Speaks of Rivers" when he was 19, briefly attended Columbia University, and worked on an Africa-bound freighter. His literary career was launched when Hughes, working as a busboy, presented his poems to Vachel Lindsay as he dined. Hughes's poetry collections include *The Weary Blues* (1926) and *Montage of a Dream Deferred* (1951). His later *The Panther and the Lash* (1967) reflects black anger and militancy. Among his other works are short stories (including "The

Langston Hughes, photograph by Jack Delano, 1942.
Library of Congress, Washington, D.C.

Ways of White Folks," 1934), autobiographies, many works for the stage, anthologies, and translations of poetry by Federico García Lorca and Gabriela Mistral. His well-known comic character Jesse B. Semple, called Simple, appeared in his newspaper columns.

Hugli River, or HOOGHLY RIVER, River, West Bengal state, northeastern India. The most westerly and commercially the most important stream of the Ganges-Brahmaputra delta, it provides access to Kolkata (Calcutta) from the Bay of Bengal. Formed by the junction of the Bhagirathi and Jalangi rivers, it flows south about 160 mi (260 km) through a heavily industrialized area home to more than half of West Bengal's population. Above Kolkata the river is silted up, but it is navigable to the city by ocean liners. It enters the Bay of Bengal through an estuary 3–20 mi (5–32 km) wide, which is spanned by two bridges.

Huguenots, French Protestants of the 16th–17th century, many of whom suffered severe persecution for their faith. The first French Huguenot community was founded in 1546, and the confession of faith drawn up by the first synod in 1559 was influenced by the ideas of John Calvin. Their numbers increased rapidly and they became a political force, led by Gaspard II de Coligny. Conflicts with the Roman Catholic government and others, including the House of Guise, led to the Wars of Religion (1562–98). A Huguenot political party was formed in 1573 to fight for religious and civil liberties. The powerful anti-Huguenot Holy League was formed in 1576. Henry IV ended the civil wars by abjuring Protestantism in 1593 and converting to Catholicism, but in 1598 he promulgated the Edict of Nantes, granting rights to Protestants. Civil wars occurred again in the 1620s, the Huguenots lost their political power, and they continued to be harassed and forcibly converted. In 1685 Louis XIV revoked the Edict of Nantes; over the next several years, more than 400,000 French Protestants left France.

Huitzilopochtli, Aztec sun and war god. He was usually portrayed as a hummingbird or as a warrior with a helmet of feathers and a turquoise snake staff. His animal disguise was the eagle. His mother was an earth goddess, his brothers stars in the sky, and his sister a moon goddess. Some myths presented him as the divine leader of the tribe during the long migration that brought the Aztecs to the Valley of Mexico. The 15th month of the ceremonial year was dedicated to him, and human sacrifices were made in his honour, in keeping with the belief that he needed human blood and hearts as daily nourishment.

human evolution, Evolution of modern human beings from now-extinct nonhuman and humanlike forms. Genetic evidence points to an evolutionary divergence between the lineages of humans and the great apes on the African continent 8–5 million years ago (mya). The earliest fossils considered to be remains of hominins (members of the human lineage) date to at least 4 mya in Africa; they include the genus *Australopithecus* and other forms. The next major evolutionary stage, *Homo habilis*, inhabited sub-Saharan Africa about 2–1.5 mya. *Homo habilis* appears to have been supplanted by a taller and more humanlike species, *Homo erectus*, which lived from *c.* 1,700,000 to 200,000 years ago, gradually migrating into Asia and parts of Europe. Between *c.* 600,000 and 200,000 years ago, *Homo heidelbergensis*, sometimes called archaic *Homo sapiens*, lived in Africa, Europe, and perhaps parts of Asia. Having features resembling those of both *H. erectus* and modern humans, *H. heidelbergensis* may have been an ancestor of modern humans and also of the Neanderthals (*H. neanderthalensis*), who inhabited Europe and western Asia from *c.* 200,000 to 28,000 years ago. Fully modern humans (*H. sapiens*) seem to have emerged in Africa only *c.* 150,000 years ago, perhaps having descended directly from *H. erectus* or from an intermediate species such as *H. heidelbergensis*.

human eye, Sense organ that receives visual images and transmits them to the brain. The human eye is roughly spherical. Light passes through its transparent front and stimulates receptor cells on the retina (cones for colour vision, rods for black-and-white vision in faint light), which in turn send impulses through the optic nerve to the brain. Vision disorders include near- and farsightedness and astigmatism (correctable with eyeglasses or contact lenses), colour blindness, and night blindness. Other eye disorders (including detached retina and glaucoma) can cause visual-field defects or blindness.

Human Genome Project, U.S. research effort initiated in 1990 by the U.S. Department of Energy and the National Institutes of Health to analyze the DNA of human beings. The project, intended to be completed in 15 years, proposed to identify the chromosomal location of every human gene, to determine each gene's precise chemical structure in order to show its function in health and disease, and to determine the precise sequence of nucleotides of the entire set of genes (the genome). Another project was to address the ethical, legal, and social implications of the information obtained. The information gathered will be the basic reference for research in human biology and will provide fundamental insights into the genetic basis of human disease. The new technologies developed in the course of the project will be applicable in numerous biomedical fields. In 2000 the government and the private corporation Celera Genomics jointly announced that the project had been virtually completed, five years ahead of schedule.

human nature, Fundamental dispositions and traits of humans. Theories about the nature of humankind form a part of every culture. In the West, debate has traditionally centred on whether humans are selfish and competitive or social and altruistic (Karl Marx, Émile Durkheim). Recent research in genetics, evolutionary biology, and cultural anthropology suggests that humans may be both, and that there is a complex interaction between genetically inherited factors ("nature") and developmental and social factors ("nurture"). Basic drives shared with other primates include food, sex, security, play, and social status. Gender differences include greater investment in reproduction and child-rearing among females, hence less risk-taking; and concomitantly less investment and greater risk-taking among males.

human rights, Rights that belong to an individual as a consequence of being human. The term came into wide use after World War II, replacing the earlier phrase "natural rights," which had been associated with the Greco-Roman concept of natural law since the end of the Middle Ages. As understood today, human rights refer to a wide variety of values and capabilities reflecting the diversity of human circumstances and history. They are conceived of as universal, applying to all human beings everywhere, and as fundamental, referring to essential or basic human needs. Human rights have been classified historically in terms of the notion of three "generations" of human rights. The first generation of civil and political rights, associated with the Enlightenment and the English, American, and French revolutions, includes the rights to life and liberty and the rights to freedom of speech and worship. The second generation of economic, social, and cultural rights, associated with revolts against the predations of unregulated capitalism from the mid-19th century, includes the right to work and the right to an education. Finally, the third generation of solidarity rights, associated with the political and economic aspirations of developing and newly decolonized countries after World War II, includes the collective rights to political self-determination and economic development. Since the adoption of the Universal Declaration of Human Rights in 1948, many treaties and agreements for the protection of human rights have been concluded through the auspices of the United Nations, and several regional systems of human rights law have been established. In the late 20th century ad hoc international criminal tribunals were convened to prosecute serious human rights violations and other crimes in the former Yugoslavia and Rwanda. The International Criminal Court, which came into existence in 2002, is empowered to prosecute crimes against humanity, crimes of genocide, and war crimes.

human sacrifice, Offering of the life of a human being to a god. In some ancient cultures, the killing of a human being, or the substitution of an animal for a person, was an attempt to commune with the god and to participate in the divine life. It also sometimes served as an attempt to placate the god and expiate the sins of the people. It was especially common among agricultural people (e.g., in the ancient Near East), who sought to guarantee the fertility of the soil. The Aztecs sacrificed thousands of victims (often slaves or prisoners of war) annually to the sun, and the Incas made human sacrifices on the accession of a ruler. In ancient Egypt and elsewhere in Africa, human sacrifice was connected with ancestor worship, and slaves and servants were killed or buried alive along with dead kings in order to provide service in the afterlife. A similar tradition existed in China. The Celts and Germanic peoples are among the European peoples who practiced human sacrifice.

humanism, Any belief, method, or philosophy that has a central emphasis on the human realm. The term is most commonly applied to the cultural movement in Renaissance Europe characterized by a revival of Classical letters, an individualistic and critical spirit, and a shift of emphasis from religious to secular concerns. This movement dates to the 13th century and the work of the Florentine scholar-statesman Brunetto Latini. Its diffusion was facilitated by the publication of Classical ideas, both in the vernacular and in Latin.

humanities, Branches of knowledge that investigate human beings, their culture, and their self-expression. Distinguished from the physical and biological sciences and, sometimes, from the social sciences, the humanities include the study of languages and literatures, the arts, history, and philosophy. The modern conception of the humanities has roots in the classical Greek *paideia*, a course in general education dating from the 5th century BC that prepared young men for citizenship. It also draws on Cicero's *humanitas*, a program of training for orators set forth in 55 BC. The Renaissance humanists contrasted *studia humanitatis* ("studies of humanity") with studies of the divine; by the 19th century the distinction was instead drawn between the humanities and the sciences.

Hume, David (b. May 7, 1711, Edinburgh, Scot.—d. Aug. 25, 1776, Edinburgh), Scottish philosopher, historian, and economist. He conceived of philosophy as the inductive, experimental science of human nature. His first major work, *A Treatise of Human Nature* (1739–40), explains the origin of ideas, including the ideas of space, time, and causality, in sense experience; presents an elaborate account of the affective, or emotional, aspects of the mind and assigns a subordinate role to reason in this order ("Reason is, and ought only to be, the slave of the passions"); and describes moral goodness in terms of "feelings" of approval or disapproval that a person has when he considers human behaviour in the light of the agreeable or disagreeable consequences either to himself or to others. The *Treatise* was poorly received, and late in life Hume repudiated it as juvenile. He revised Book I of the *Treatise* as *An Enquiry Concerning Human Understanding* (1758); a revision of Book III was published as *An Enquiry Concerning the Principles of Morals* (1751). His *Dialogues Concerning Natural Religion* (1779), containing a refutation of the argument from design and a critique of the notion of miracles, was withheld from publication during his lifetime at the urging of friends. From his account of the origin of ideas Hume concluded that we have no knowledge of a "self" as the enduring subject of experience; nor do we have knowledge of any "necessary connection" between causally related events. Immanuel Kant, who developed his critical philosophy in direct reaction to Hume, said that Hume had awakened him from his "dogmatic slumbers." In Britain, Hume's moral theory influenced Jeremy Bentham to adopt utilitarianism. With John Locke and George Berkeley, Hume is regarded as one of the great philosophers of empiricism.

Hume, John (b. Jan. 18, 1937, Londonderry, N.Ire.), Leader of the Social Democratic and Labour Party (SDLP) in Northern Ireland from 1979 to 2001 and coercipient with David Trimble of the Nobel Prize for Peace in 1998. A schoolteacher, Hume became a Roman Catholic leader in the Northern Ireland civil rights movement in the 1960s. He was elected to the parliaments of Northern Ireland (1969), Europe (1979), and Britain (1983). A moderate, he condemned the use of violence by the Irish Republican Army (IRA). In the late 1980s he attempted to persuade the IRA to abandon the armed struggle against Britain and enter democratic politics. He risked his personal safety to engage in sometimes secret dialogues with leaders of Sinn Féin, the IRA's political wing, and he played a leading role in negotiating the Good Friday Agreement (Belfast Agreement), the multiparty peace accord between unionists and nationalists reached in April 1998. Elected to the new Northern Ireland Assembly in June, he resigned his seat two years later because of ill health.

humidity, Amount of water vapour in the air. One of the most variable characteristics of the atmosphere, humidity is an important factor in climate and weather: it regulates air temperature by absorbing thermal radiation both from the Sun and the Earth; it is directly proportional to the latent energy available for the generation of storms; and it is the ultimate source of all forms of condensation and precipitation. Humidity varies because the water-holding capacity of air is determined by temperature. When a volume of air at a given temperature holds the maximum amount of water vapour possible, the air is said to be saturated. Relative humidity is the water-vapour content of the air relative to its content at saturation. Saturated air has a relative humidity of 100%; near the Earth the relative humidity rarely falls below 30%.

hummingbird, Any of about 320 species of New World birds

*Allen's hummingbird
(Selasphorus sasin)*
Arvil L. Parker

(family Trochilidae), many of which have glittering colours and elaborately specialized feathers. They are most abundant in South America, though about 12 species are found in the U.S. and Canada. Hummingbirds range in length from slightly more than 2 in. (5 cm) to 8 in. (20 cm), weigh 0.07–0.7 oz (2–20 g), and have a long, slender bill. The bee hummingbird of Cuba is the smallest living bird. Hummingbirds can fly forward, straight up and down, sideways, and backward and can hover in front of flowers to obtain nectar and insects. Smaller species can beat their wings as fast as 80 beats per second.

humpback whale, Long-finned baleen whale (*Megaptera novaeangliae*). They live along all major ocean coasts, sometimes swimming close inshore or even into harbours and up rivers. Humpbacks grow to 40–52 ft (12–16 m) long. They are black above, with some white below, and have large knobs on the head and jaws. The humpback migrates between polar waters in summer and tropical or subtropical breeding grounds in winter. It feeds on shrimplike crustaceans, small fish, and plankton. It is probably the most vocal of all whales (with "songs" of 5–35 minutes) and one of the most acrobatic (capable of turning a somersault). Much reduced in number by overhunting, humpbacks have been protected worldwide since the 1960s, and some populations seem to be increasing.

humus, Nonliving, finely divided organic matter in soil, derived from microbial decomposition of plant and animal substances. Ranging in colour from brown to black, it consists primarily of carbon but also contains nitrogen and smaller amounts of phosphorus and sulfur. As it decomposes, its components are changed into forms usable by plants. Humus is classified according to how well it is incorporated into the mineral soil, the types of organisms involved in its decomposition, and the vegetation from which it is derived. It is valued by farmers and gardeners because it provides nutrients essential for plant growth, increases the soil's water absorption, and improves soil workability.

Hun, Any member of a nomadic pastoralist people who invaded southeastern Europe *c.* AD 370. Appearing from central Asia after the mid-4th century, they first overran the Alani, who occupied the plains between the Volga and Don rivers, and then overthrew the Ostrogoths living between the Don and Dniester rivers. About 376 they defeated the Visigoths living in what is now approximately Romania and reached the Danubian frontier of the Roman Empire. As warriors, they inspired almost unparalleled fear throughout Europe; they were accurate mounted archers, and their rapid, ferocious charges brought them overwhelming victories. They ex-

tended their power over many of the Germanic peoples of central Europe and allied themselves with the Romans. By 432 the leadership of the various groups of Huns had been centralized under a single king, Rua (Rugila). After his death (434), he was succeeded by his two nephews, Bleda and Attila. By a peace treaty with the Eastern Roman Empire, the Romans agreed to double the subsidies they had been paying the Huns; when they apparently failed to pay the stipulated sums, Attila launched a heavy assault on the Roman Danubian frontier (441), and other attacks spread the Huns' control into Greece and Italy. At Attila's death (453), his many sons divided up his empire and began a series of costly struggles with their subjects. The Huns were finally routed in 455 by an alliance of Gepidae, Ostrogoths, Heruli, and others in a great battle in Pannonia. The Eastern Roman government then closed the frontier to the Huns, who gradually disintegrated as a social and political unit.

Hunan, or HU-NAN, Province (pop., 2002 est.: 66,290,000), south-central China. It lies south of the Yangtze River (Chang Jiang) and is bordered by Guizhou, Hubei, Jiangxi, and Guangdong provinces, Chongqing municipality, and Guangxi autonomous region. It has an area of 81,300 sq mi (210,500 sq km), and its capital is Changsha. Part of the 3rd-century-BCE kingdom of Chu, it passed to the Qin dynasty and became part of the Chinese empire during the Han dynasty (206 BCE–220 CE). Hubei and Hunan were one province until split in the mid-17th century. Hunan was invaded in the mid-1850s by Taiping rebels, and in 1927 Mao Zedong led an armed uprising there. It was also the scene of bitter fighting during the Sino-Japanese War (1937–45). Much of the terrain is mountainous; Mount Heng, one of China's sacred mountains, is located there. The economy is basically agricultural. Hunan is one of China's major rice-producing regions.

Hundred Days, French CENT JOURS (1815) In French history, the period between Napoleon's arrival in Paris after escaping from exile on Elba and the return of Louis XVIII to Paris. Napoleon landed on French soil on March 1 and reached Paris on March 20. Austria, Britain, Prussia, and Russia swiftly concluded an alliance against Napoleon and forced a series of military engagements that led up to the Battle of Waterloo. On June 22 Napoleon abdicated a second time and was removed to St. Helena; Louis returned to Paris on July 8.

Hundred Years' War (1337–1453) Intermittent armed conflict between England and France over territorial rights and the issue of succession to the French throne. It began when Edward III invaded Flanders in 1337 in order to assert his claim to the French crown. Edward won a major victory at the Battle of Crécy (1346); after his son Edward the Black Prince managed to capture John II at the Battle of Poitiers (1356), the French were obliged to surrender extensive lands under the treaties of Brétigny and Calais (1360). When John II died in captivity, his son Charles V refused to respect the treaties and reopened the conflict, putting the English on the defensive. After Charles V's death in 1380 both countries were preoccupied with internal power struggles, and the war lapsed into uncertain peace. In 1415, however, Henry V decided to take advantage of civil war in France to press English claims to the French throne. By 1422, the English and their Burgundian allies controlled Aquitaine and all France north of the Loire, including Paris. A turning point came in 1429, when Joan of Arc raised the English siege of Orléans. The French king Charles VII conquered Normandy and then retook Aquitaine in 1453, leaving the English in possession only of Calais. The war laid waste to much of France and caused enormous suffering; it virtually destroyed the feudal nobility and thereby brought about a new social order. By ending England's status as a power on the continent, it led the English to expand their reach and power at sea.

Hungarian language, Finno-Ugric language of Hungary, with substantial minority populations in Slovakia, Transylvania in Romania, and northern Serbia. Hungarian has about 14.5 million speakers worldwide—more than any other Uralic language—including 400,000–500,000 in North America. The earliest known text in Hungarian dates from the late 12th century; a continuous literary tradition begins in the 15th century. Contact with Turkic, Iranian, and Slavic languages, and, more recently, High German dialects and Latin, has given Hungarian many loanwords.

Hungary, officially REPUBLIC OF HUNGARY, Country, central Europe. Area: 35,919 sq mi (93,030 sq km). Population: (2011 est.) 9,972,000. Capital: Budapest. The people are an amalgam of Magyars and various Slavic, Turkish, and Germanic peoples. Language: Hungarian (Magyar; official). Religion: Christianity (mostly Roman Catholic; also Protestant). Currency: forint. The Great Alfold (Great Hungarian Plain), with fertile agriculture land, occupies nearly half of the country. Hungary's two most important rivers are the Danube and the Tisza. Lake Balaton, in the Transdanubian highlands, is the largest lake in central Europe. Forests cover nearly one-fifth of the land. Hungary is one of the more prosperous countries of eastern Europe and a major world producer of bauxite. A conversion from a socialist to a free-market economy was begun in the late 1980s. Hungary is a unitary multiparty republic with one legislative house; the head of state is the president, and the head of government is the prime minister. The western part of the country was incorporated into the Roman Empire in 14 BCE. The Magyars, a nomadic people, settled in the Great Alfold in the late 9th century. Stephen I, crowned in 1000, Christianized the country and organized it into a strong and independent state. Invasions by the Mongols in the 13th century and by the Ottoman Empire in the 15th century devastated the country, and by 1568 the territory of modern Hungary was divided into three parts: Royal Hungary had fallen to the Habsburgs; Transylvania had gained autonomy in 1566 under the Ottoman Turks; and the central plain remained under Ottoman control until the late 17th century, when the Austrian Habsburgs took over. Hungary declared its independence from Austria in 1849, and in 1867 the Dual Monarchy of Austria-Hungary was established. Its defeat in World War I (1914–18) resulted in the dismemberment of Hungary, leaving it only those areas in which Magyars predominated. In an attempt to regain some of this lost territory, Hungary cooperated with the Germans against the Soviet Union during World War II (1939–45). After the war a pro-Soviet provisional government was established, and in 1949 the Hungarian People's Republic was formed. Opposition to this Stalinist regime broke out in 1956 but was suppressed. Nevertheless, from 1956 to 1988 communist Hungary grew to become the most tolerant of the Soviet-bloc nations of Europe. It gained its independence in 1989 and soon attracted the largest amount of direct foreign investment in eastern and central Europe. It joined NATO in 1999 and the European Union in 2004.

hunting, Pursuit of game animals, principally as sport. To early humans hunting was a necessity, and it remained so in many societies until recently. The development of agriculture made hunting less necessary as a sole life support, but game was still pursued in order to protect crops, flocks, or herds, as well as for food. Weapons now commonly used in hunting include the rifle, shotgun, and the bow and arrow, and methods include stalking, still-hunting (lying in wait), tracking, driving, and calling. Dogs are sometimes employed to track, flush, or capture prey. In Europe much of the land once hunted upon was owned by the aristocracy, and gamekeepers were employed to regulate the amount of game that could be hunted in a given area. By the 1800s the land hunted upon was not or had never been privately owned, and there began to develop a "tragedy of the commons," in that no one hunter had any motive to limit the number of animals killed; certain species were hunted to, or very close to, extinction. To counter this development, ethical codes were established that give the quarry a fair chance to escape; attempts were made to minimize the suffering of wounded game; and game laws, licensing, and limited hunting seasons were established to protect game stocks. For instance, a modern license

may authorize a hunter to kill only two deer during the brief season for deer, and he or she must present a kill to a game warden who will then document and tag the animal. There are often penalties and fines for being found with an animal that is not so marked.

hunting and gathering culture, also called FORAGING CULTURE, Any human culture or society that depends on a combination of hunting, fishing, and gathering wild foods for subsistence. Until c. 11,000–12,000 years ago, all peoples were foragers. Many foraging peoples continued to practice their traditional way of life into the 20th century; by mid-century all such peoples had developed extensive contacts with settled groups. In traditional hunting and gathering societies, social groups were small, usually made up of either individual family units or a number of related families collected together in a band. Typically women and children collected relatively stationary foods such as plants, eggs, shellfish, and insects, while men hunted large game. The diet was well-balanced and ample, and food was shared. Hunting and gathering societies had considerable free time to spend on social and religious activities.

Huntington chorea, Relatively rare, hereditary neurological disease that is characterized by irregular and involuntary movements of the muscles. Huntington chorea is caused by a genetic mutation that causes degeneration of neurons in a part of the brain that controls movement. Symptoms usually appear between ages 35 and 50. They begin with occasional jerking or writhing movements, which are absent during sleep, and progress to random, uncontrollable, and often violent twitchings and jerks. Symptoms of mental deterioration begin later and include memory loss, dementia, bipolar disorder, or schizophrenia. There is no effective therapy or cure, and the disease invariably proves fatal. A child of a person with Huntington chorea has a 50% chance of developing the disease.

hurdling, Track-and-field event, a footrace over a series of obstacles called hurdles. Runners must remain in assigned lanes throughout a race, and, though they may knock hurdles down while running over them, they may do so only with a leg or foot, not a hand. Modern hurdlers use a sprinting style between hurdles, display an exaggerated forward lean while clearing the hurdle, and then bring the trailing leg through at nearly a right angle to the body, which enables them to continue forward without breaking stride after clearing the hurdle. Hurdling distances are 110 m and 400 m for men and 100 m and 400 m for women.

hurling, Irish sport resembling both field hockey and lacrosse. It is played between two 15-player teams. The game is mentioned in Irish manuscripts dating back to the 13th century BC. The stick used—a tapered, slightly curved device with a cupped blade at the end—is called a hurley. A point is scored by hitting the ball over the crossbar of the opposing team's goalposts, and three points are scored by driving it under the crossbar. It is considered the national pastime of Ireland.

Husain, M(aqbool) F(ida), Husain also spelled HUSSAIN (b. Sept. 17, 1915, Pandharpur, Maharashtra state, India—d. June 9, 2011, London, Eng.), Indian artist. His narrative paintings, executed in a modified Cubist style, could be caustic and funny as well as serious and sombre. His themes—usually treated in series—included topics as diverse as Mohandas K. Gandhi, Mother Teresa, the *Ramayana,* the *Mahabharata,* the British raj, and motifs of Indian urban and rural life. One of the most celebrated and internationally recognized Indian artists of the 20th century, he also received recognition as a printmaker, photographer, and fimmaker.

Ḥusayn ibn ʿAlī (b. c. 1854, Constantinople, Ottoman Empire—d. 1931, Amman, Transjordan), Sharif of the Hāshimite line, Ottoman-appointed emir of Mecca (1908–16), and self-proclaimed king of the Arabs (1916–24). His claim to be the new caliph (1924) led to a short and unsuccessful war against Ibn Sa'ūd. Husayn was exiled to Cyprus. One of his sons, 'Abdullāh, became king of Transjordan (present-day Jordan); another became king of Syria and later Iraq as Fayṣal I.

hussar, Member of a European light-cavalry unit used for scouting, modeled on the 15th-century Hungarian light-horse corps. The brilliantly coloured Hungarian hussar's uniform was imitated in other European armies; it consisted of a busby (high cylindrical cloth cap), a jacket with heavy braiding, and a dolman (loose coat worn hanging from the left shoulder). Several hussar regiments of the British army were converted from light dragoons in the 19th century; they survive today as armoured units.

Hussite, Member of a group of 15th-century Bohemian religious reformers, followers of Jan Hus. After Hus's death in 1415, the Hussites broke with Rome. In addition to giving communion in both bread and wine, they supported freedom of preaching, poverty of the clergy, civil punishment of notorious sinners, and expropriation of church property. Many were nobles and knights, and a papal crusade against them failed in 1431. During peace negotiations in 1433 the Hussites split into two factions, the moderate Utraquists and the radical Taborites. The Utraquists joined the Catholics and defeated the Taborites at the battle of Lipany in 1434; they survived schisms until 1620, when they were absorbed by the Catholics. Another segment of Hussites, Unitas Fratrum, set up an independent organization in 1467 and lasted until the Counter-Reformation. In 1722 a group of Hussites fled Moravia and settled on the estate of Count Nikolaus Ludwig von Zinzendorf (1700–1760) in Saxony, establishing the community of Herrnhut and founding the Moravian church.

Hutterite, Member of the Hutterite Brethren, an Anabaptist sect that takes its name from its Austrian founder, Jakob Hutter, who was burned as a heretic in 1536. His followers modeled themselves on the early church in Jerusalem by holding their goods in common. Persecuted in Moravia and the Tirol, they moved eastward to Hungary and the Ukraine. In the 1870s many emigrated to the U.S. and settled in South Dakota. The society still exists in the western U.S. and Canada, where it has colonies of 60–150 members, who operate collective farms. Hutterites are pacifists who take no part in politics and remain separate from outside society.

Hutu, Bantu-speaking people of Rwanda and Burundi, with a large refugee population in Congo (Kinshasa). Numbering about 9.5 million, the Hutu comprise the vast majority in both Rwanda and Burundi but were traditionally subject to the Tutsi, who under German and Belgian colonial regimes succeeded in cultivating a lord-vassal relationship. The two cultures are deeply intertwined; both speak Rwanda and Rundi and adhere to similar religious beliefs (traditional and Christian). The Tutsi remained dominant in Rwanda until 1961, when the Hutu expelled most of them and took over the government. After an unsuccessful Hutu coup attempt in Burundi in 1965, that country's Hutu remained subordinate under a Tutsi-dominated military government. Violent clashes occurred in Burundi in 1972, 1988, and 1993 and in Rwanda in 1990 and 1994–96, the later including a Hutu-initiated genocidal campaign in which more than a million people were killed and 1–2 million fled to refugee camps in Zaire (now Congo) and Tanzania.

hyacinth, Any of the approximately 30 species of bulbous, ornamental herbaceous plants that make up the genus *Hyacinthus* (family Hyacinthaceae), native primarily to the Mediterranean region and tropical Africa. The common garden hyacinths are derived from *H. orientalis.* Most species have narrow, untoothed leaves at the base of the plant and fragrant flowers (usually blue, but sometimes pink, white, or other colours in cultivated varieties) borne in a cluster at the top of the leafless stems.

Hyades, Open cluster of several hundred stars in the constellation Taurus. The bright star Aldebaran appears to be a member of the cluster but is much closer to Earth than the Hyades, which is about 130 light-years away. Five genuine members of the group are visible to the unaided eye.

hybrid, Offspring of parents that differ in genetically determined traits. The parents may be of two different species, genera, or (rarely) families. The terms "mongrel" and "crossbreed" refer usually to animals or plants resulting from a cross between two races, breeds, strains, or varieties of the same species. Because of basic biological incompatibilities, sterile hybrids (those that cannot produce living young) such as the mule (a hybrid between a jackass and a mare) commonly result from crosses between species. Some species hybrids, however, are fertile and can be sources for the formation of new species. Many economically or aesthetically important cultivated plants (e.g., bananas, coffee, peanuts, dahlias, roses, bread wheats, alfalfa, etc.) originated through natural or artificially induced hybridization. Hybridization is important biologically because it increases necessary genetic variation within a species.

Hyderabad, City (pop., 2001: 3,637,483), capital of Andhra Pradesh state, southern India. Founded by the sultans of Golconda in the 16th century, the town was plundered and destroyed following the Mughal occupation in 1685. In 1724 it became the capital of the independent kingdom of Hyderabad. A walled city, it has many buildings in a blend of Hindu and Muslim styles. Adjacent Secunderabad grew as a British cantonment, connected to Hyderabad by an embankment 1 mi (1.6 km) long. It is the site of Osmania University (1918) and the University of Hyderabad (1974).

Hyderabad, or HAYDARABAD, City (pop., 2005 est.: urban agglom., 1,392,000), Sind province, Pakistan. Located east of the Indus River, it was founded in 1768 by Ghulam Shah Kalhora. It remained the capital of Sind until 1843, when it surrendered to the British and the capital was transferred to Karachi. It is now a transportation, commercial, and industrial centre. Notable antiquities include the tombs and palaces of former rulers; characteristic of the city are *badgirs* ("wind-catchers") fixed to housetops to catch sea breezes during the hot season.

hydra, Any of 20–30 species of freshwater cnidarians (genus *Hydra*). The polyp-type body is a thin, usually translucent tube that measures up to slightly more than 1 in. (25 mm) long. Food is ingested and wastes are ejected from the open, tentacled end. Individuals are usually hermaphroditic. Reproduction by budding is also common. Species differ in colour, tentacle length and number, and gonad position and size. All hydras feed on other small invertebrates (e.g., crustaceans).

hydraulics, Branch of science concerned with the practical applications of fluids, primarily liquids, in motion. It is related to fluid mechanics, which in large part provides its theoretical foundation. Hydraulics deals with such matters as the flow of liquids in pipes, rivers, and channels and their confinement by dams and tanks. Some of its principles apply also to gases, usually when variations in density are relatively small. The scope of hydraulics extends to such mechanical devices as actuators and control systems.

hydrocarbon, Any of a class of organic compounds composed only of carbon and hydrogen. The carbon atoms form the framework, and the hydrogen atoms attach to them. Hydrocarbons, the principal constituents of petroleum and natural gas, serve as fuels, lubricants, and raw materials for production of plastics, fibres, rubbers, solvents, explosives, and industrial chemicals. All burn to carbon dioxide and water with enough oxygen or to carbon monoxide without it. The two major categories are aliphatic, with the carbon atoms in straight or branched chains or in nonaromatic rings, and aromatic. Aliphatic compounds may be saturated (paraffins) or, if any carbon atoms are joined by double or triple bonds, unsaturated (e.g., olefins, alkenes, alkynes). All but the simplest hydrocarbons have isomers. Ethylene, methane, acetylene, benzene, toluene, and naphthalene are hydrocarbons.

hydrocephalus, Accumulation of cerebrospinal fluid (CSF) in the ventricles (cavities) of the brain. Hydrocephalus is caused by overproduction of CSF, congenital blockage that prevents drainage, or complications of head injuries or infections. Normally, CSF circulates through the brain and spinal cord and drains into the circulation. In infants and young children, hydrocephalus causes the brain and skull to enlarge because the fontanels have not yet closed. Without surgery to divert the excess fluid into the blood or abdomen, accumulating fluid eventually compresses the brain, causing convulsions, intellectual disability, and death.

hydrochloric acid, or MURIATIC ACID, Solution in water of hydrogen chloride (HCl), a gaseous inorganic compound. It is a strong acid, virtually completely dissociated into hydronium cations (H_3O^+) and chloride anions (Cl^-), and is corrosive and irritating. The acid reacts with most metals, to produce hydrogen and the metal's chloride, and with oxides, hydroxides, and many salts. It is used extensively in industrial processing of metals and concentrating of some ores; in boiler scale removal, food processing, metal cleaning, and pickling; and as a chemical intermediate, laboratory reagent, and alcohol denaturant. Hydrochloric acid is present in the stomach's gastric juice and is involved in the devlopment of peptic ulcers.

hydroelectric power, Electricity produced from generators driven by water turbines that convert the energy in falling or fast-flowing water to mechanical energy. Water at a higher elevation flows downward through large pipes or tunnels (penstocks). The falling water rotates turbines, which drive the generators, which convert the turbines' mechanical energy into electricity. The advantages of hydroelectric power over such other sources as fossil fuels and nuclear fission are that it is continually renewable and produces no pollution. Norway, Sweden, Canada, and Switzerland rely heavily on hydroelectricity because they have industrialized areas close to mountainous regions with heavy rainfall. The U.S., Russia, China, India, and Brazil get a much smaller proportion of their electric power from hydroelectric generation.

hydrogen, Lightest chemical element, chemical symbol H, atomic number 1. A colourless, odourless, tasteless, flammable gas, it occurs as the diatomic molecule H_2. Its atom consists of one proton (the nucleus) and one electron; the isotopes deuterium and tritium have an additional one and two nuclear neutrons, respectively. Though only the ninth most abundant element on Earth, it represents about 75% of all matter in the universe. Hydrogen was formerly used to fill airships; nonflammable helium has replaced it. It is used to synthesize ammonia, ethanol, aniline, and methanol; to treat petroleum fuels; as a reducing agent and to supply a reducing atmosphere; to make hydrogen chloride and hydrogen bromide; and in hydrogenation (e.g., of fats). Liquid hydrogen (boiling point -423 °F [-252.8 °C]) is used in scientific and commercial applications to produce extremely low temperatures and as a rocket propellant and a fuel for fuel cells. Combustion of hydrogen with oxygen gives water as the sole product. The properties of most acids, especially in water solutions, arise from the hydrogen ion (H^+, also referred to as the hydronium ion, H_3O^+, the form in which H^+ is found in a water environment).

hydrogen bomb, or H-BOMB, or THERMONUCLEAR BOMB, Weapon whose enormous explosive power is generated by the nuclear fusion of hydrogen isotopes. The high temperatures required for the fusion reaction are produced by detonating an atomic bomb (which draws its energy from nuclear fission). The bomb's explosion produces a blast that can destroy structures within a radius of several miles, an intense white light that can cause blindness, and heat fierce enough to set off firestorms. It also creates radioactive

fallout that can poison living creatures and contaminate air, water, and soil. Hydrogen bombs, which may be thousands of times more powerful than atomic bombs, can be made small enough to fit in the warhead of a ballistic missile or even in an artillery shell. Edward Teller and other U.S. scientists developed the first H-bomb and tested it at Enewetak atoll (Nov. 1, 1952). The Soviet Union first tested an H-bomb in 1953, followed by Britain (1957), China (1967), and France (1968). Most modern nuclear weapons employ both fusion and fission.

hydrogen bonding, Interaction involving a hydrogen atom located between a pair of other atoms having a high affinity for electrons; such a bond is weaker than an ionic bond or covalent bond but stronger than van der Waals forces. Hydrogen bonds can exist between atoms in different molecules or in parts of the same molecule. One atom of the pair (the donor), generally a fluorine, nitrogen, or oxygen atom, is covalently bonded to a hydrogen atom ($-FH$, $-NH$, or $-OH$), whose electrons it shares unequally; its high electron affinity causes the hydrogen to take on a slight positive charge. The other atom of the pair, also typically F, N, or O, has an unshared electron pair, which gives it a slight negative charge. Mainly through electrostatic attraction, the donor atom effectively shares its hydrogen with the acceptor atom, forming a bond. Because of its extensive hydrogen bonding, water (H_2O) is liquid over a far greater range of temperatures that would be expected for a molecule of its size. Water is also a good solvent for ionic compounds and many others because it readily forms hydrogen bonds with the solute. Hydrogen bonding between amino acids in a linear protein molecule determines the way it folds up into its functional configuration. Hydrogen bonds between nitrogenous bases in nucleotides on the two strands of DNA (guanine pairs with cytosine, adenine with thymine) give rise to the double-helix structure that is crucial to the transmission of genetic information.

hydrometallurgy, Extraction of metal from ore by dissolving the metal (as one of its salts) and then recovering it from the solution. The operations usually involved are leaching (dissolving in water), commonly with additional agents; separating the waste and purifying the leach solution; and precipitating the metal or one of its pure compounds from the leach solution by chemical or electrolytic means. Though hydrometallurgy originated in the 16th century, its principal development took place in the 20th century. The development of ion exchange, solvent extraction, and other processes now permits more than 70 metallic elements to be produced by hydrometallurgy, including most gold, much silver, and large tonnages of copper and zinc.

hydroponics, Cultivation of plants in nutrient-enriched water, with or without the mechanical support of an inert medium such as sand or gravel. Fertilizer solution is pumped through the system periodically. As the plants grow, concentration of the solution and frequency of pumping are increased. A wide variety of vegetables and florist crops can be grown satisfactorily in gravel. Automatic watering and fertilizing saves on labour, but installation costs are high and fertilizer solution must be tested frequently. Yields are about the same as for soil-grown crops.

hydrostatics, Branch of physics that deals with the characteristics of fluids at rest, particularly with the pressure in a fluid or exerted by a fluid (gas or liquid) on an immersed body. In applications, the principles of hydrostatics are used for problems relating to pressure in deep water (pressure increases with depth) and high in the atmosphere (pressure lessens with altitude).

hyena, Any of three species of coarse-furred, doglike carnivores (family Hyaenidae) found in Asia and Africa. Actually more closely related to cats than to dogs, they have four toes on each foot, long forelegs, nonretractile claws, and enormously strong jaws and teeth. They live alone or in packs and may be active by night or day. Hyenas are noted for scavenging but will also attack live prey. The spotted, or laughing, hyena, whose calls alternately resemble wailing and maniacal laughter, ranges through much of sub-Saharan Africa. Yellowish or grayish with dark spots, it is about 6.5 ft (1.8 m) long, including the 12-in. (30-cm) tail, and weighs up to 175 lbs (80 kg). It has been known to attack people and even carry off young children.

hymn, Song used in Christian worship, usually sung by the congregation and written in stanzas with rhyme and metre. The term comes from the Greek *hymnos* ("song of praise"), but songs in honour of God or the gods exist in all civilizations. Christian hymnody grew out of the singing of psalms in the Temple of Jerusalem. The earliest known Christian hymn dates from *c.* AD 200. Hymns were prominent in the Byzantine liturgy from early times, and in the Western church they were sung by congregations until the Middle Ages, when choirs took over hymn singing. Congregational singing was reestablished during the Reformation. Martin Luther and his followers were great hymn writers, while the Calvinists preferred setting psalms to music. The compositions of Isaac Watts and John Wesley were notable in English hymnody. The Counter-Reformation led to the composition of many Roman Catholic hymns, and the Roman Catholic church restored congregational singing of hymns after the Second Vatican Council in the 1960s.

hypertension, or HIGH BLOOD PRESSURE, Condition in which blood pressure is abnormally high. Over time, it damages the kidneys, brain, eyes, and heart. Hypertension accelerates atherosclerosis, increasing the risk of heart attack, stroke, and kidney failure. More common in the elderly and blacks, it usually has no symptoms but can be detected by a routine blood-pressure test. Secondary hypertension, caused by another disorder (most often kidney disease or hormone imbalance), accounts for 10% of cases. The other 90% have no specific cause (essential hypertension). A low-salt diet, weight loss, smoking cessation, limited alcohol intake, and exercise can prevent or treat hypertension or reduce medication if drug therapy proves necessary. Malignant hypertension, a severe, rapidly progressing form, requires emergency treatment with drugs to dilate the blood vessels.

hypertext, or HYPERLINK, Linking of related information by electronic connections in order to allow a user easy access between them. Conceptualized by Vannevar Bush (1945) and invented by Douglas Engelbart in the 1960s, hypertext is a feature of some computer programs that allows the user to select a word and receive additional information, such as a definition or related material. In Internet browsers, hypertext links (hotlinks) are usually denoted by highlighting a word or phrase with a different font or colour. Hypertext links create a branching or network structure that permits direct, unmediated jumps to related information. Hypertext has been used most successfully as an essential feature of the World Wide Web. Hyperlinks may also involve objects other than text (e.g., selecting a small picture may provide a link to a larger version of the same picture).

hypnosis, State that resembles sleep but is induced by a person (the hypnotist) whose suggestions are readily accepted by the subject. The hypnotized individual seems to respond in an uncritical, automatic fashion, ignoring aspects of the environment (e.g., sights, sounds) not pointed out by the hypnotist. Even the subject's memory and awareness of self may be altered by suggestion, and the effects of the suggestions may be extended (posthypnotically) into the subject's subsequent waking activity. The history of hyp-

notism is as old as that of sorcery and magic. It was popularized in the 18th century by Franz Anton Mesmer (as "mesmerism") and was studied in the 19th century by the Scottish surgeon James Braid (1795–1860). Sigmund Freud relied on it in exploring the unconscious, and it eventually came to be recognized in medicine and psychology as useful in helping to calm or anesthetize patients, modify unwanted behaviours, and uncover repressed memories. There remains no generally acceptable explanation for hypnosis, though one prominent theory focuses on the possibility of discrete dissociative states affecting portions of consciousness.

hypoglycemia, Below-normal levels of blood glucose, quickly reversed by administration of oral or intravenous glucose. Even brief episodes can produce severe brain dysfunction. Fasting hypoglycemia can be life-threatening; it occurs most often in patients with diabetes mellitus who mistime insulin therapy or miss meals. It also results from insulin-producing tumours, starvation, or metabolic disorders. Reactive hypoglycemia occurs when the body produces too much insulin in response to sugar intake. Symptoms range from irritability to confusion and seizures, leading to coma and death in severe cases.

hypotension, or LOW BLOOD PRESSURE, Condition in which blood pressure is abnormally low. It may result from reduced blood volume (e.g., from heavy bleeding or plasma loss after severe burns) or increased blood-vessel capacity (e.g., in syncope). Orthostatic hypotension—drop in blood pressure on standing—results from failure of the reflexes that contract muscles and constrict blood vessels in the legs to offset gravity as one rises. Hypotension is also a factor in poliomyelitis, shock, and barbiturate poisoning.

hypothermia, Abnormally low body temperature, with slowing of physiological activity. It is artificially induced (usually with ice baths) for certain surgical procedures and cancer treatments. Accidental hypothermia can result from falling into cold water or overexposure in cold weather. Underlying conditions such as cerebrovascular disease or intoxication increase the risk from exposure. Hypothermia is serious when body temperature is below 95 °F (35 °C) and an emergency below 90 °F (32.2 °C), at which point shivering stops. Pulse, respiration, and blood pressure are depressed. Even when the victim appears dead, revival may be possible with very gradual passive rewarming (e.g., with blankets).

hypoxia, Condition in which tissues are starved of oxygen. The extreme is anoxia (absence of oxygen). There are four types: hypoxemic, from low blood oxygen content (e.g., in altitude sickness); anemic, from low blood oxygen-carrying capacity (e.g., in carbon monoxide poisoning); distributive, from low blood flow (e.g., generally in shock or locally in atherosclerosis); and histotoxic, from poisoning (e.g., with cyanide) that keeps cells from using oxygen. If not reversed quickly, hypoxia can lead to necrosis (tissue death), as in heart attack.

hysterectomy, Surgical removal of the uterus, either completely (total hysterectomy) or leaving the cervix (subtotal hysterectomy). It is performed in the presence of cancer or a benign fibroid tumour if the fibroid is large or rapidly growing, causes excessive bleeding or discomfort, or seems to be breaking down. Hysterectomy may also be performed after cesarean section in cases of complications such as uncontrolled bleeding, gross infection, or pelvic cancer.

I

Ibadan, City (pop., 2002 est.: 3,080,000), southwestern Nigeria. Situated northeast of Lagos, it is the nation's second largest city. First settled by the Egba, the modern city probably grew from a camp set up by Yoruba armies from Ife, Ijebu, and Oyo; it was taken by the British in 1893. An important commercial centre, it contains six parks, the most important of which is Agodi Garden. It is the seat of the University of Ibadan (1948) as well as a polytechnic and other specialized institutions. Two major stadiums and television studios are also located there.

Iberian, Any member of a prehistoric people of southern and eastern Spain. They were largely untouched by the migrations of Celtic peoples to northern and central Spain beginning in the 8th century BC. Culturally they were influenced by Greek and Phoenician trading colonies. On the eastern coast, tribes seem to have formed independent city-states; in the south, they formed monarchies. Their economy was based on agriculture, mining, and metallurgy. Their non-Indo-European language continued into Roman times.

Iberian Peninsula, or IBERIA, Peninsula, southwestern Europe, occupied by Spain and Portugal. Its name derives from its ancient inhabitants whom the Greeks called Iberians, probably after the Ebro (Iberus) River, the peninsula's second longest river. The Pyrenees form a land barrier in the northeast from the rest of Europe, and in the south at Gibraltar the peninsula is separated from North Africa by a narrow strait. Its western and northern coasts are bordered by the Atlantic Ocean, and its eastern coast by the Mediterranean Sea. It includes Cape da Roca, in Portugal, the most westerly point of continental Europe.

ibex, Any of several species of surefooted, sturdy wild goats found in the mountains of Europe, Asia, and North Africa. Ibex are typically about 3 ft (90 cm) tall at the shoulder and have brownish gray fur that is darker on the underparts. The male has a beard and large, semicircular horns.

ibis, Any of about 26 species of medium-sized wading birds (subfamily Threskiornithinae) of the same family as the spoonbills. Ibises are found in all warm regions except on South Pacific islands. They wade in shallow lagoons, lakes, bays, and marshes, using their slender down-curved bills to feed on small fishes and soft mollusks. Species range from 22 to 30 in. (55 to 75 cm) long. Ibises fly with neck and legs extended, alternately flapping and sailing. They usually breed in vast colonies.

Iblīs, In Islam, the personal name of the Devil. Iblīs, one of God's angels, refused to venerate Adam at creation. He and his followers were thrown down from heaven and await punishment at the Last Judgment. Until then he is allowed to tempt everyone but true believers to do evil. Referred to as Shayṭān (Satan) in this context, it was he who purportedly tempted Adam and Eve in the Garden of Eden and caused the Fall. Iblīs has long been a figure of speculation among Muslim scholars because of his ambiguous identification in the Qur'ān as either an angel or a *jinnī*.

Ibn Khaldūn, orig. ABŪ ZAYD ʿABD AL-RAḤMĀN IBN KHALDŪN (b. May 27, 1332, Tunis, Tun.—d. March 17, 1406, Cairo, Egypt), Noted Arab historian. He was employed in court posts by various rulers in Tunis, Fès, and Granada. After retiring from politics in 1375, he wrote his masterpiece, the *Muqaddimah* ("Introduction"), in which he examined the nature of society and social change and developed one of the earliest rational philosophies of history. He also wrote a definitive history of Muslim North Africa,

Kitāb al-ʿIbār. In 1382 he went to Cairo, where he was appointed professor of law and religious judge. In 1400 he was trapped in Damascus during that city's siege by Timur, spending seven weeks in the Central Asian conqueror's camp before securing his own release and that of a number of colleagues. He is regarded as the greatest premodern Arab historian.

Ibn Saʿūd, in full ʿABD AL-ʿAZĪZ IBN ʿABD AL-RAḤMĀN IBN

Ibn Saʿūd
Camera Press/Globe Photos

FAYṢAL ĀL SAʿŪD (b. *c.* 1880, Riyadh, Arabian Peninsula—d. Nov. 9, 1953, Al-Ṭāʾif, Saud. Ar.), Founder of modern-day Saudi Arabia. Though the Saʿūd dynasty had ruled much of Arabia from 1780 to 1880, in Ibn Saʿūd's infancy the family was forced out by its rivals, the Rashīds. At age 21 Ibn Saʿūd led a daring raid against the Rashīds and recaptured the family capital, Riyadh. He was driven out two years later but reconstituted his forces and fought on, using puritanical Wahhābī Islam to rally nomadic tribesmen to his cause, thereby forming the Ikhwān. In 1920–22 he defeated the Rashīds and doubled his own territory. In 1924 he conquered the Hejaz. In 1932 he formally created the Kingdom of Saudi Arabia, which he ruled as an absolute monarch. He signed his first oil deal in 1933 but remained virtually penniless until the 1950s, when oil revenues began pouring in. His sons succeeded him.

Ibn Ṭūlūn Mosque, Huge, majestic red-brick mosque in Cairo. It was built (876–879) by Aḥmad ibn Ṭūlūn (835–884), the Muslim governor of Egypt and Syria. The mosque's crenellated walls have merlons that are shaped and perforated in a decorative pattern, and its three courts are lined with arcades of broad arches and heavy pillars. The arches are decorated with elaborately carved stucco. The main space is divided by pillars into five long aisles originally ornamented with panels of carved wood. Classed as a historic monument in 1890, the mosque has since been completely restored.

ibuprofen, Analgesic, one of the NSAIDs, especially effective against minor pain, fever, and inflammation. It works by inhibiting prostaglandin synthesis. It may irritate the gastrointestinal tract and should not be taken by anyone who has an allergy to aspirin or takes anticoagulants. Brand names include Advil, Motrin, and Nuprin.

ICANN, in full INTERNET CORPORATION FOR ASSIGNED NAMES AND NUMBERS, Nonprofit private organization incorporated in 1998 and tasked with taking over from the U.S. government various administrative duties associated with running the Internet. ICANN's functions include overseeing the top-level domains (TLDs; e.g., .com, .net, .org, .edu), registering and maintaining the directory of domain names (e.g., www.britannica.com) used in the Internet Protocol (IP), and resolving trademark disputes over domain names.

ICBM, in full INTERCONTINENTAL BALLISTIC MISSILE, Land-based, nuclear-armed ballistic missile with a range of more than 3,500 mi (5,600 km). Only the U.S., Russia, and China field land-based missiles of this range. The first ICBMs were deployed by the Soviet Union in 1958, with the U.S. following the next year and China some 20 years later. The principal U.S. ICBM is the silo-launched Minuteman missile. Submarine-launched ballistic missiles (SLBMs) with ranges comparable to ICBMs include the Trident missile, deployed by the U.S. and Britain, and several systems deployed by Russia, China, and France.

ice, Solid form of liquid water and water vapour. Below 32 °F (0 °C), liquid water forms a hard solid and water vapour forms frost on surfaces and snowflakes in clouds. Unlike most liquids, water expands on freezing, so ice is less dense than liquid water and therefore floats. It consists of compact aggregates of many crystals (with hexagonal symmetry), although ice formed from the bulk liquid does not normally have crystal faces. Molecules in the crystal are held together by hydrogen bonds. With a very high dielectric constant, ice conducts electricity much better than most nonmetallic crystals. At very high pressures, at least five other crystal forms of ice occur.

ice age, or GLACIAL AGE, Any geologic period during which thick ice sheets cover vast areas of land. Such periods of large-scale glaciation may last several million years and drastically reshape surface features of entire continents. A number of major ice ages have occurred throughout Earth's history; the most recent were during the Pleistocene Epoch (2.6 million–11,700 years ago).

ice dancing, Sport in which ice-skating pairs perform to music routines similar to ballroom dances. Ice dancers are judged on the difficulty and originality of their dance steps, their interpretation of the music, and their timing and unison. Unlike figure skating, ice dancing does not allow movements of strength or technical skill (particularly overhead lifts, jumps, and spins of more than one-and-a-half rotations). It has been an Olympic event since 1976.

ice hockey, Game played on an ice rink by two teams of six players on skates. The object is to drive a puck (a small, hard rubber disk) into the opponents' goal with a hockey stick, thus scoring one point. A game consists of three 20-minute periods. The first true ice-hockey game was played in 1875 between two student teams at Montreal's McGill University. The National Hockey League, consisting of U.S. and Canadian professional teams, was organized in 1917. Hockey was introduced at the Olympic Games in 1920. It is a very aggressive game, and the puck is often taken from a player by means of a hit to the body, called a check. Some contact, such as checking from behind and slashing with the stick, is illegal and draws a penalty.

iceberg, Floating mass of ice that has broken from the seaward end of a glacier or a polar ice sheet. Icebergs are typically found in open seas, especially around Greenland and Antarctica. They form mostly during each hemisphere's spring and summer, when warmer weather increases the rate of calving (separation) of icebergs at the boundaries of the Greenland and Antarctic ice sheets and smaller outlying glaciers. In the Northern Hemisphere, about 10,000 icebergs are produced each year from the Greenland glaciers, and an average of 473 flow into the North Atlantic shipping lanes, where they are a hazard to navigation, especially because only about 10% of an iceberg is exposed above the surface of the sea.

Iceland, officially REPUBLIC OF ICELAND, Island country, northern Atlantic Ocean, between Norway and Greenland. Area: 39,769 sq mi (103,000 sq km). Population: (2011 est.) 319,000. Capital: Reykjavík. The people are overwhelmingly Nordic. Language: Icelandic (official). Religion: Christianity (Evangelical Lutheran [official]). Currency: króna. One of the most active volcanic regions in the world, Iceland contains about 200 volcanoes and accounts for one-third of Earth's total lava flow. One-tenth of the area is covered by cooled lava beds and glaciers, including Vatnajökull. Iceland's rugged coastline is more than 3,000 mi (4,800 km) long. The economy is based heavily on fishing and fish products but also includes hydropower production, livestock, and aluminum processing. Iceland is a unitary multiparty republic with one legislative house; its head of state is the president, and the head of government is the prime minister. Iceland was settled by Norwegian seafarers in the 9th century and was Christianized by 1000. Its legislature, the Althingi, founded in 930, is one of the oldest

legislative assemblies in the world. Iceland united with Norway in 1262 and with Denmark in 1380. It became an independent state of Denmark in 1918, but it severed those ties to become an independent republic in 1944. Vigdís Finnbogadóttir, the first woman in the world to be elected a head of state, served four terms as the republic's president (1980–96).

Icelanders' sagas, or FAMILY SAGAS, Class of heroic prose narratives written in the 13th century about the great families who lived in Iceland from 930 to 1030. They represent the zenith of classical Icelandic saga writing and are far in advance of any contemporary medieval literature in their realism, controlled style, character delineation, and overwhelming tragic dignity. Their artistic unity, length, and complexity suggest that they were written by individual authors rather than composed orally. Justice, not courage, is often the primary virtue, as in the greatest of the family sagas, *Njáls saga.*

Iceman, Body of a man found sealed in a glacier in the Tirolean Ötztal Alps in 1991 and dated to 3300 BC. It has revealed significant details of everyday life during the Neolithic Period. The Iceman (also called Similaun Man or Ötzi, after the glacier and valley) is tattooed on parts of his body and has trimmed hair; it had previously been thought that tattooing and hair cutting began much later in Europe. He wore neatly stitched deerskin clothing, a woven grass cape, and leather shoes stuffed with grass for insulation. He carried two fungi on leather thongs, probably for medicinal purposes, and a birchbark box containing food supplies. His other equipment included a copper ax, a flint dagger, a yew bow, and a deerskin quiver holding expertly finished arrows. Although it was initially believed that he had died of freezing, X-ray examination in 2001 showed that an arrowhead was lodged in his left shoulder, suggesting that he had likely bled to death after being shot.

icon, In Eastern Orthodoxy, the representation of sacred persons or events in murals, mosaics, or paintings on wood. After the Iconoclastic Controversy of the 8th–9th century, which disputed the religious function and meaning of icons, the Eastern churches formulated an official doctrine that approved their use, stating that since God had assumed material form in the person of Jesus, he and other sacred personages could be represented in works of art. Usually depicting Jesus or Mary but also sometimes saints, icons are relied on as objects of veneration and as tools for instruction.

"Annunciation," reverse of a double-sided painted panel icon from Constantinople, early 14th century; in the Skopolije Museum, Skopje, Macedonia
Hirmer Fotoarchiv, Munich

iconoclasm, Destruction of religious images. In Christianity and Islam, iconoclasm was based on the Mosaic prohibition against making graven images, which were associated with idolatry. The making of portraits of Christ and the saints was opposed in the early Christian church, but icons had become popular in Christian worship by the end of the 6th century, and defenders of icon worship emphasized the symbolic nature of the images. Opposition to icons by the Byzantine emperor Leo III in 726 led to the Iconoclastic Controversy, which continued in the Eastern church for more than a century before icons were again accepted. Statues and portraits of saints and religious figures were also common in the Western church, though some Protestant sects eventually rejected them. Islam still bans all icons, and iconoclasm has played a role in the conflicts between Muslims and Hindus in India.

iconostasis, In Eastern Christian churches of Byzantine tradition, a solid screen of stone, wood, or metal separating the sanctuary from the nave. It has a royal door in the center and two smaller doors on either side. Covered with panel icons, it always includes the icon of the Incarnation (mother with child) on the left and the second coming of Christ on the right; icons of the four Evangelists, the Annunciation, and the Last Supper cover the royal doors themselves.

id, In Freudian psychoanalytic theory, one of the three aspects of the human personality, along with the ego and superego. The id is the source of instinctual impulses such as sex and aggression as well as primitive needs that exist at birth. It is entirely nonrational and functions according to the pleasure-pain principle, seeking immediate fulfillment of its impulses whenever possible. Its working processes are completely unconscious in the adult, but it supplies the energy for conscious mental life, and it plays an especially important role in modes of expression that have a nonrational element, such as the making of art. The primary methods for unmasking its content, according to Sigmund Freud, are dream analysis and free association.

Ida, Mount, Name of two separate mountains, one in Turkey and the other on the island of Crete. The Turkish mountain is located in western Anatolia, near the site of ancient Troy, and once held a Classical shrine where Paris is said to have judged the beauty of three Greek goddesses. From its highest point, about 5,800 ft (1,800 m), the gods are said to have witnessed the Trojan War. The second mountain, in west-central Crete, is the island's highest point, reaching 8,058 ft (2,456 m). It also held a Classical shrine, which included the cave where Zeus, the chief deity of the Greek pantheon, was said to have been reared.

idealism, In metaphysics, the view that stresses the central role of the ideal or the spiritual in the constitution of the world and in mankind's interpretation of experience. Idealism may hold that the world or reality exists essentially as spirit or consciousness, that abstractions and laws are more fundamental in reality than sensory things, or, at least, that whatever exists is known to mankind in dimensions that are chiefly mental—that is, through and as ideas. Metaphysical idealism asserts the ideality of reality; epistemological idealism holds that in the knowledge process the mind can grasp only its own contents. Metaphysical idealism is thus directly opposed to materialism, and epistemological idealism is opposed to realism. Absolute idealism includes the following principles: (1) the everyday world of things and persons is not the world as it really is but merely as it appears in terms of uncriticized categories; (2) the best reflection of the world is in terms of a self-conscious mind; (3) thought is the relation of each particular experience with the infinite whole of which it is an expression; and (4) truth consists in relationships of coherence between thoughts, rather than in a correspondence between thoughts and external realities.

identity theory, In the philosophy of mind, the doctrine that mental events are identical to physico-chemical events in the brain. So-called "type" identity theory asserts that each type of mental event, such as pain, is identical to some type of event in the brain, such as the firing of c-fibres. In response to objections based on the assumed "multiple realizability" of mental states, "token" identity theory makes the weaker claim that each token of a mental event, such as a particular pain, is identical to some token of a brain event of some type.

ideology, Form of social or political philosophy in which practical elements are as prominent as theoretical ones. The term was coined in 1796 by the French writer Antoine-Louis-Claude,

Comte Destutt de Tracy (b. 1754—d. 1836), as a label for his "science of ideas." Certain characteristics of his thought proved generally true of ideologies, including a more or less comprehensive theory of society, a political program, anticipation of a struggle to implement that program (thus requiring committed followers), and intellectual leadership. Destutt de Tracy's ideas were adopted by the French Revolutionary government in building its version of a democratic, rational, and scientific society. Napoleon first gave the term a negative connotation with his scorn for what he called *idéologues*. Ideology is often contrasted unfavourably with pragmatism. The significance of ideology follows from the fact that power is rarely exercised without some ideas or beliefs that justify support.

igloo, Temporary dome-shaped winter home or hunting-ground dwelling of Canadian and Greenland Inuit (Eskimos), made from blocks of snow. The builder chooses a deep snowdrift of fine-grained, compact snow and cuts it into blocks. After a row of blocks has been laid in a circle, their top surfaces are shaved off in a sloping angle to form the first rung of a spiral. Additional blocks are added to the spiral to draw it inward until a dome is completed, leaving a ventilation hole at the top.

igneous rock, Any of various crystalline or glassy noncrystalline rocks formed by the cooling and solidification of molten earth material (magma). Igneous rocks comprise one of the three principal classes of rocks, the others being metamorphic and sedimentary rocks. Though they vary widely in composition, most igneous rocks consist of quartz, feldspars, pyroxenes, amphiboles, micas, olivines, nepheline, leucite, and apatite. They may be classified as intrusive or extrusive rocks.

ignition system, In a gasoline engine, the means used for producing an electric spark to ignite the fuel-air mixture in the cylinders to produce the motive force. The ignition system consists of a storage battery recharged by a generator, an induction coil, a device to produce timed high-voltage discharges from the induction coil, a distributor, and a set of spark plugs. The battery provides an electric current of low voltage, usually 12 volts, that is converted by the system to some 40,000 volts. The distributor routes the successive bursts of high-voltage current to each spark plug in the proper firing order.

iguana, Any of about 13 of the larger members of the lizard family Iguanidae. Best known is the common iguana (*Iguana iguana*), which ranges from Mexico southward to Brazil. It reaches a maximum length of 6 ft (1.8 m). It lives in trees, especially trees overhanging water, into which it will plunge if disturbed. It is greenish, with brown bands that form regular rings on the tail. It primarily eats tender leaves and fruits but will also eat small birds and crustaceans. Species of the southwestern U.S. and Mexico include the chuckwalla (*Sauromalus obesus*) and desert iguana (*Dipsosaurus dorsalis*).

Iguazú Falls, or IGUAÇU FALLS, formerly VICTORIA FALLS, A series of cataracts on the Iguazú River near the border between Argentina and Brazil. The horseshoe-shaped falls were discovered by Álvar Núñez Cabeza de Vaca in 1541. They vary between 200 and 269 ft (60 and 82 m) in height and extend for 1.7 miles (2.7 km)—nearly three times wider than North America's Niagara Falls—and are divided into 275 waterfalls or cataracts. The scenic beauty and wildlife of the falls are protected by two separate national parks: Iguaçu National Park (1939) in Brazil and Iguazú National Park (1934) in Argentina. Both parks were designated UNESCO World Heritage sites in 1984 and 1986, respectively. See photograph on following page.

IJssel River, River, in the Netherlands. An important distributary of the Rhine River, it leaves the Lower Rhine (Neder Rijn)

Iguazú Falls on the Iguazú River at the Argentina-Brazil border.
© R. Manley/Superstock

just southeast of Arnhem and flows northeastward for 70 mi (110 km) to enter the IJsselmeer. Zutphen, Deventer, and Zwolle are important cities along its course.

IJsselmeer, English LAKE IJSSEL, Shallow freshwater lake, northern and central Netherlands. Fed by the IJssel River, it was formed from the southern part of the former Zuiderzee by a dam, which separates it from both the Waddenzee and the North Sea. It previously had a total area of 1,328 sq mi (3,440 sq km), though this has been reduced by reclamation projects that have increased the land area of the Netherlands by more than 600 sq mi (1,600 sq km). Regulated by sluices, the formerly brackish water has been replaced by fresh water from the IJssel River, and eel fisheries have been established.

ijtihād, In Islamic law, the analysis of problems not covered precisely in the Qur'ān, the Ḥadīth, or the scholarly consensus called the *ijmā'*. In the early Muslim scholarly community, every jurist had the right to exercise such original thinking, but the growth of legal schools prompted Sunnite Muslim authorities to declare that the principal legal issues had been settled by the 10th century. Shī'ite Muslims have always recognized *ijtihād*, and jurists considered learned enough for this kind of analysis have great authority. In the 20th century an attempt was made to restore *ijtihād* among Sunnites to help Islam adapt to the modern world.

ikebana, Japanese art of flower arranging. It was introduced in Japan in the 6th century by Chinese Buddhist missionaries, who had formalized the ritual of offering flowers to the Buddha. The first school of flower arranging in Japan was founded in the early 7th century. The art is based on harmony of simple linear construction and appreciation of the subtle beauty of flowers and natural material (branches, stems). Several major schools, with differing histories and theories of artistic style, exist to this day. In its highest form, ikebana is spiritual and philosophical in nature, but in modern Japan it is more often practiced as a sign of refinement by marriageable young women or older matrons.

Ikhwān (Arabic: "Brethren"), Religious and military brotherhood that helped Ibn Sa'ūd unite the Arabian Peninsula. First organized in 1912, its members were settled in colonies around oases in an effort to break down tribal loyalties and force the Bedouin to abandon their nomadic way of life. They also embraced the arch-traditionalist Islamic principles of Muḥammad ibn 'Abd al-Wahhāb. From 1919 they won many victories in Arabia and Iraq, with conquests including Mecca and Medina. By 1926 the Ikhwān were becoming uncontrollable, attacking Ibn Sa'ūd for innovations such as telephones and automobiles. They staged a bloody revolt, which was not put down until 1930, and then only with British help. Members who had remained loyal were eventually absorbed into the National Guard of Saudi Arabia.

ileum, Final and longest segment of the small intestine. It is the site of absorption of vitamin B_{12} and reabsorption of about 90% of conjugated bile salts. It extends about 13 ft (4 m), from the jejunum (middle section of the small intestine) to the ileocecal valve, where it joins the large intestine. Disorders produce vitamin B_{12} deficiency and extensive diarrhea (since bile salts in the large intestine interfere with water absorption).

'ilm al-ḥadīth, Form of analysis established by 9th-century Muslim traditionalists to verify the merits of the Ḥadīth. Of the many accounts of Muhammad's statements and actions that constituted the Ḥadīth, some were thought to be forgeries or of doubtful reliability. Scholars judged their merit by scrutinizing the *isnād*s that detailed the chain of authority through which the story had been handed down.

Imagism, Movement in U.S. and English poetry characterized by the use of concrete language and figures of speech, modern subject matter, metrical freedom, and avoidance of romantic or mystical themes. It grew out of the Symbolist movement and was initially led by Ezra Pound, who, inspired by the criticism of T. E. Hulme (1883–1917), formulated its credo *c.* 1912; Hilda Doolittle was also among the founders. Around 1914 Amy Lowell largely took over leadership of the group. Imagism influenced the works of Conrad Aiken, T. S. Eliot, Marianne Moore, D. H. Lawrence, Wallace Stevens, and others.

imam, Head of the Muslim community. In Sunnite Islam the imam was identical with the caliph, designating the political successor of Muhammad. The Sunnites held the imam to be a man capable of error but deserving obedience provided he maintained the ordinances of Islam. In Shī'ite Islam the imam became a figure of absolute religious authority, possessed of unique insights into the Qur'ān and divinely appointed and preserved from sin. With the historical disappearance of the last imam, there arose a belief in the hidden imam, who is identified with the mahdi. The term *imam* is also given to Muslims who lead prayers in mosques and has been used as an honorary title.

Imeni Ismail Samani Peak, formerly COMMUNISM PEAK, or STALIN PEAK, Peak, western Pamirs, northeastern Tajikistan. Located in the Akademii Nauk Range, it rises to 24,590 ft (7,495 m) and is the highest point in Tajikistan and in the range. It was first climbed by a Russian team in 1933.

Imhotep, Greek IMOUTHES (fl. 27th century BC, Memphis, Egypt), Egyptian sage and astrologer, later worshiped as the god of medicine. In Greece he was identified with Asclepius. Imhotep was chief minister to the Egyptian king Djoser and is remembered as a skilled physician as well as the architect of the step-pyramid at Saqqara in Memphis. Deified around the time of the Persian conquest in 525 BC, he was said to be the son of Ptah and the war goddess Sekhmet. The cult of Imhotep reached its zenith in Greco-Roman times, when sick people slept in his temples with the hope that the god would reveal remedies to them in dreams.

Immaculate Conception, In Roman Catholicism, the dogma that Mary was not tainted by original sin. Early exponents included St. Justin Martyr and St. Irenaeus; St. Bonaventure and St. Thomas Aquinas were among those who opposed it. In 1439 the Council of Basel stated that the belief was in accordance with Catholic faith, and in 1709 Pope Clement XI made the feast of the Immaculate Conception a holy day of obligation. In 1854 Pius IX issued a papal bull making it official church dogma.

immune system, Cells, cell products, organs, and structures of the body involved in the detection and destruction of foreign invaders, such as bacteria, viruses, and cancer cells. Immunity is based on the system's ability to launch a defense against such invaders. For the system to function properly, it must be able to distinguish between the material of its own body (self) and material that originates outside of it (nonself). Failure to make this distinction can result in autoimmune diseases. An exaggerated or inappropriate response by the immune system to nonharmful substances (e.g., pollen, animal dander) can result in allergies. The system's principal cells include lymphocytes that recognize antigens and related accessory cells (such as phagocytic macrophages, which engulf and destroy foreign material). Lymphocytes arise in the bone marrow from stem cells, with T lymphocytes (T cells) migrating to the thymus to mature and B lymphocytes (B cells) maturing in the bone marrow. Mature lymphocytes enter the bloodstream, and many become lodged, along with accessory cells, in various body tissues, including the spleen, lymph nodes, tonsils, and intestinal lining. Organs or tissues containing such concentrations are termed *lymphoid*. Within these organs and tissues the lymphocytes are confined within a delicate network of connective tissue that channels them so they come into contact with antigens. T cells and B cells can mature and multiply further in lymphoid tissue when suitably stimulated. Fluid (lymph) draining from lymphoid tissues is conveyed to the blood through lymphatic vessels. Lymph nodes distributed along these vessels filter the lymph, exposing macrophages and lymphocytes contained within to any antigen present. The spleen plays a similar role, sampling the blood for the presence of antigens. The capability of lymphocytes to pass between lymphoid tissue, the blood, and lymph is an important element in the system's functioning.

immunity, In law, exemption or freedom from liability. Under international treaty, a diplomatic representative is exempt from local laws, both civil and criminal. In many countries, judges, legislators, and government officials, including the heads of state, enjoy limited or absolute immunity at home to protect them from personal liability for wrongful acts or omissions that arise from the performance of their duties. A public prosecutor may grant immunity from prosecution to a witness who is suspected of criminal activity in return for testimony against other suspected criminals.

immunodeficiency, Defect in immunity that impairs the body's ability to resist infection. The immune system may fail to function for many reasons. Immune disorders caused by a genetic defect are usually evident early in life. Others can be acquired at any age through infections (e.g., AIDS) or immunosuppression. Aspects of the immune response that may be affected include lymphocytes, other leukocytes, antibodies, and complement. Severe combined immunodeficiency (SCID), which arises from several different genetic defects, disrupts all of these. Depending on the cause, treatment for immunodeficiency may be administration of immunoglobulins, bone-marrow transplant, or therapy for the underlying disease.

immunosuppression, Suppression of immunity with drugs, usually to prevent rejection of an organ transplant. Its aim is to allow the recipient to accept the organ permanently with no unpleasant side effects. In some cases the dosage can be reduced or even stopped without causing rejection. Other uses are in the treatment of certain autoimmune diseases and for prevention of erythroblastosis fetalis. Its main drawback is the increased risk of infection for the duration of treatment and of lymphoma in the case of long-term immunosuppression.

impact test, Test of the ability of a material to withstand impact, used by engineers to predict its behaviour under actual conditions. Many materials fail suddenly under impact, at flaws, cracks, or notches. The most common impact tests use a swinging pendulum to strike a notched bar; heights before and after impact are used to compute the energy required to fracture the bar. In the Charpy test, the test piece is held horizontally between two vertical bars, much like the lintel over a door. In the Izod test, the specimen stands erect, like a fence post.

impatiens, Any of about 900 species of herbaceous plants in the genus *Impatiens* (balsam family), so named because the seedpod bursts when slightly touched. Garden balsam (*I. balsamina*), na-

tive to the tropics of Asia, is a favourite showy annual in U.S. gardens; its flowers are irregular, single or clustered, and of almost every colour but blue. Familiar related weeds in eastern North America are spotted jewelweed (*I. biflora* or *I. capensis*) and pale touch-me-not (*I. pallida*). Most impatiens have weak, hollow stems and require high moisture. Close relatives are geraniums and nasturtiums.

impeachment, Criminal proceeding instituted against a public official by a legislative body. In the U.S. the president, vice president, and other federal officers, including judges, may be impeached by the U.S. House of Representatives. The House draws up articles of impeachment that itemize the charges and their factual bases. Once approved by a majority of House members, the articles are submitted to the Senate, which holds a trial. At its conclusion, each member votes for or against conviction on each article; conviction requires a two-thirds majority. A convicted official can be removed from office. The Constitution of the United States specifies that an officer is to be impeached for "high crimes and misdemeanors"; experts agree that impeachment is permitted for noncriminal misconduct (e.g., violation of the Constitution). Two U.S. presidents, Andrew Johnson and Bill Clinton, were impeached; both were acquitted. In 1974, articles of impeachment were drawn up against Pres. Richard Nixon, who resigned before formal proceedings could begin. In Britain, where the House of Commons prosecutes and the House of Lords judges impeachment proceedings, impeachment was formerly a means by which Parliament could get rid of unpopular ministers, usually court favourites protected by the monarch. The procedure fell into disuse in the early 19th century, when cabinet ministers became responsible to Parliament rather than to the sovereign.

imperialism, State policy, practice, or advocacy of extending power and dominion, especially by direct territorial acquisition or by gaining political and economic control of other areas. Because imperialism always involves the use of power, often in the form of military force, it is widely considered morally objectionable, and the term accordingly has been used by states to denounce and discredit the foreign policies of their opponents. Imperialism in ancient times is clear in the unending succession of empires in China, western Asia, and the Mediterranean. Between the 15th century and the middle of the 18th, England, France, the Netherlands, Portugal, and Spain built empires in the Americas, India, and the East Indies. Russia, Italy, Germany, the United States, and Japan became imperial powers in the period from the middle of the 19th century to World War I. The imperial designs of Japan, fascist Italy, and Nazi Germany in the 1930s culminated in the outbreak of World War II. After the war the Soviet Union consolidated its military and political control of the states of eastern Europe. From the early 20th century the U.S. was accused of imperialism for intervening in the affairs of developing countries in order to protect the interests of U.S.-owned international corporations. Economists and political theorists have debated whether imperialism benefits the states that practice it and whether such benefits or other reasons ever justify a state in pursuing imperialist polices. Some theorists, such as Niccolò Machiavelli, have argued that imperialism is the justified result of the natural struggle for survival among peoples. Others have asserted that it is necessary in order to ensure national security. A third justification for imperialism, offered only infrequently after World War II, is that it is a means of liberating peoples from tyrannical rule or bringing them the blessings of a superior way of life.

impetigo, Bacterial inflammatory skin disease, the most common skin infection in children. Initial blisters rupture, drying to a crust. Caused by staphylococcus or streptococcus, it is very contagious in newborns, becoming less so with age. Poor hygiene, crowding, and humid, hot weather may promote its spread. A broad-spectrum antibiotic applied to the blisters can treat simple impetigo; more extensive cases, especially in infants, may require a systemic antibiotic.

impotence, Inability to achieve or maintain erection of the penis; hence, inability to participate fully in sexual intercourse. Erectile impotence (failure to achieve erection) may have either physical causes (e.g., alcoholism, endocrine disease) or psychological ones (e.g., anxiety, hostility toward the partner). Ejaculatory impotence (inability to reach orgasm, sometimes with an erection maintained for a long time) nearly always has an emotional cause.

Impressionism, Movement in art that developed in France in the late 19th century. In painting it included works produced *c.* 1867–86 by a group of artists who shared approaches, techniques, and discontent with academic teaching, originally including Claude Monet, Pierre-Auguste Renoir, Camille Pissarro, Alfred Sisley, and Berthe Morisot. Later Édouard Manet, whose earlier style had strongly influenced several of them, Mary Cassatt, Edgar Degas, Paul Cézanne and others joined them. The identifying feature of their work was an attempt to record a scene accurately and objectively, capturing the transient effects of light on colour and texture. To this end they abandoned the traditional muted browns, grays, and greens in favour of a lighter, more brilliant palette; stopped using grays and blacks for shadows; built up forms out of discrete flecks and dabs of colour; and often painted out of doors, rather than in the studio. They abandoned traditional formal compositions in favour of a more casual and less contrived disposition of objects within the picture frame, and their subject matter included landscapes, trees, houses, and even urban street scenes and railroad stations. After the French Academy's Salon consistently rejected most of their works, they held their own exhibition in 1874; seven others followed. A critic described them derisively as "impressionists," and they adopted the name as an accurate description of their intent. Before dissolving in the late 1880s, the group had revolutionized Western painting.

imprinting, Form of learning wherein a very young animal fixes its attention on the first object with which it has visual, auditory, or tactile experience and thereafter follows that object. In nature, the object is almost always a parent; in experiments, other animals and inanimate objects have been used. Imprinting has been studied extensively only in birds, but a comparable form of learning apparently takes place among many mammals and some fishes and insects. Ducklings and chicks, which can imprint in a few hours, lose receptivity to imprinting stimuli within 30 hours of hatching.

improvisation, Creation of music in real time. Improvisation usually involves some preparation beforehand, particularly when there is more than one performer. Despite the central place of notated music in the Western tradition, improvisation has often played a role, from the earliest organum through the use of continuo (partially improvised accompaniment played on a bass line) in the 17th and 18th centuries. It has taken forms such as creation of a melody over a bass line for dancing, elaborate ornamentation added to a repeated section in an aria, keyboard variations on popular songs, concerto cadenzas, and free solo fantasias. Perhaps at its lowest ebb in the 19th century, improvisation returned to concert music in "experimental" compositions and in "authentic" performances of older music. Its most important contemporary Western form is jazz. It is also a defining feature of the raga.

in vitro fertilization (IVF), or TEST-TUBE CONCEPTION, Procedure, used to overcome infertility, in which eggs are removed from a woman, fertilized with sperm outside the body, and inserted into the uterus of the same or another woman. The first child thus conceived was born in 1978. IVF includes extraction of eggs, collection of sperm, fertilization in culture, and introduction into the uterus at the eight-cell stage. In a successful procedure, the embryo is implanted in the uterine wall, and pregnancy begins. The most common problem is failed implantation. IVF has been a source of moral, ethical, and religious controversy since its development.

Inari, In Japanese mythology, the patron god of rice cultivation and prosperity. He was worshiped especially by merchants and tradesmen, and he also served as patron deity of swordsmiths, brothels, and entertainers. Inari was variously depicted as a bearded old man riding a fox or as a woman with long hair, carrying sheaves of rice. The fox is sometimes identified as his messenger. The god's most popular shrine is the Fushimi Inari Shrine near Kyōto.

Inari, wood figurine, Tokugawa period (1603–1867); in the Musée Guimet, Paris
Courtesy of the Musée Guimet, Paris

Inca, Group of South American Indians who ruled an empire that extended along the Pacific coast and Andes Mountains from what is now northern Ecuador to central Chile. According to tradition (the Inca left no written records), the founder of the Incan dynasty led the tribe to Cuzco, which became their capital. Under the fourth emperor, they began to expand, and under the eighth they began a program of permanent conquest by establishing garrisons among the conquered peoples. Under Topa Inca Yupanqui and his successor, the empire reached its southernmost and northernmost extent. By the early 16th century the Inca controlled an empire of some 12 million subjects. They constructed a vast network of roads; their architecture was highly developed, and the remains of their irrigation systems, palaces, temples, and fortifications are still in evidence throughout the Andes. Incan society was highly stratified and featured an aristocratic bureaucracy. Their pantheon, worshiped in a highly organized state religion, included a sun god, a creator god, and a rain god. The Incan empire was overthrown in 1532 by the Spanish conquistadores, who made great use of the Incan road system during their conquests. The Inca's descendants are the Quechua-speaking peasants of the Andes. In Peru nearly half the population is of Incan descent. They are primarily farmers and herders living in close-knit communities. Their Roman Catholicism is infused with belief in pagan spirits and divinities.

incandescent lamp, Any of various devices that produce light by heating a suitable material to a high temperature. In an electric incandescent lamp, or lightbulb, a filament is enclosed in a glass shell that is either evacuated or filled with an inert gas. The filament gives off light when heated by an electric current. The first practical electric incandescent lamps were independently produced in the late 1870s by Joseph Swan and Thomas Alva Edison. Edison has received the major credit because of his development of the power lines and other equipment needed for a lighting system. Inefficient in comparison with fluorescent lamps and electric discharge lamps, incandescent lighting is today reserved mainly for domestic use.

Incarnation, Central Christian doctrine that God became man in the form of Jesus, the son of God and the second person of the Holy Trinity. In Jesus the divine and human nature are joined but neither is changed or diminished. This difficult doctrine gave rise to a variety of heresies, some denying Jesus's divine nature, others his human nature. For orthodox believers the conflict was settled at the Councils of Nicaea (AD 325) and Chalcedon (AD 451).

incest, Sexual relations between persons who, because of the nature of their kinship ties, are prohibited by law or custom from intermarrying. The incest taboo is generally universal, although it is imposed differently in different societies. Usually, the closer the genetic relationship between two people, the stronger and more highly charged is the taboo prohibiting or discouraging sexual relations. Some sociobiologists consider that inbred populations have diminished reproductive success and become gene pools for hereditary disorders. Some cultural anthropologists argue instead that the incest prohibition, with the corresponding rules of exogamy, acts to require males to seek sexual and marital partners outside the group, thereby establishing useful alliances. Other theories emphasize the need to control sexual jealousies within the family or to prepare children to function with restraint in adult society. No single explanation seems satisfactory, causing some to question whether incest should be treated as a unitary subject. Most cases of incest that come before criminal courts concern sexual intercourse between fathers and relatively young daughters.

In'chŏn, or INCHEON, formerly JINSEN, or CHEMULPO, Seaport city (pop., 2002 est.: 2,596,102), South Korea, near Seoul. A fishing port since the 14th century, it was a Korean treaty port in 1883 and developed as an international commercial port before the Japanese occupation (1910–45). During the Korean War it was the site of a successful UN troop landing in 1950. It now has metropolitan city (provincial) status. Its industries produce iron and steel, glass, chemicals, and lumber.

incidental music, Music composed to accompany a play. The practice dates back to ritualistic Greek drama, and it is thus connected to the use of music in other kinds of ritual. Sometimes limited to the role of introduction or interlude (setting a mood or a historical period, for example), it may also accompany spoken dialogue. Film and television music is sometimes considered incidental music.

income tax, Levy imposed by public authority on the incomes of persons or corporations within its jurisdiction. In nations with an advanced system of private enterprise, income taxes represent the chief source of government revenue. Income tax levied on individuals or family units is known as personal income tax. In 1799 Britain enacted a general income tax to finance the Napoleonic Wars. In the U.S. an income tax was first tried during the Civil War; the Supreme Court held it to be constitutional in 1881 but declared another income tax unconstitutional in 1894. In 1913 the 16th Amendment to the Constitution made the personal income tax permanent. The fairness of personal income taxation is based on the premise that one's income is the best single index of one's ability to contribute to the support of the government; most personal income taxes are conceived on the theory that when people's financial circumstances differ, their tax liabilities should also differ. Thus U.S. income taxes are progressive taxes, falling more heavily on those who earn more money, and individual income tax deductions are allowed for items such as interest paid on home mortgage debt, unusual medical expenses, philanthropic contributions, and state and local income and property taxes. Enforcement has been facilitated by withholding the tax from wages and salaries.

incontinence, Inability to control the excretion of urine or feces. Starting and stopping urination relies on normal function in pelvic and abdominal muscles, diaphragm, and control nerves. Babies' nervous systems are too immature for urinary control. Later incontinence may reflect disorders (e.g., neural tube defect causing "neurogenic bladder"), paralysis of urinary system muscles, long-term bladder distension, or certain urogenital malformations. Weak pelvic muscles can allow small urine losses on coughing or sneezing ("stress incontinence"). Uncontrolled defecation can result from spinal or bodily injuries, old age, extreme fear, or severe diarrhea.

incunabulum, Book printed before 1501. The date, though convenient, is arbitrary and unconnected to any development in the printing art. The term was probably first applied to early printing in general *c.* 1650. The total number of editions produced by 15th-century European presses is generally estimated at above 35,000, excluding ephemeral literature (e.g., single sheets, ballads, and devotional tracts) that is now lost or exists only in fragments in places such as binding linings.

India, officially REPUBLIC OF INDIA, Country, South Asia. It

Boats on the Ganges River at Varanasi, Uttar Pradesh state, India.
© Wolszczak/Fotolia

fronts the Bay of Bengal on the southeast and the Arabian Sea on the southwest. Area: 1,222,559 sq mi (3,166,414 sq km). Population: (2011 est.) 1,216,728,000. Capital: New Delhi. The peoples of India comprise widely varying mixtures of ethnic strains drawn from peoples settled in the subcontinent before the dawn of history or from invaders. Languages: Hindi, English (both official), and other Indo-European languages, including Bengali, Kashmiri, Marathi, and Urdu; Dravidian languages; hundreds from several other language families. Religions: Hinduism; also Islam, Christianity, Sikhism, Buddhism, Jainism. Currency: rupee. India has three major geographic regions: the Himalayas, along its northern border; the Indo-Gangetic Plain, formed by the alluvial deposits of three great river systems, including the Ganges (Ganga); and the southern region, noted for the Deccan plateau. Agricultural products include rice, wheat, cotton, sugarcane, coconut, spices, jute, tobacco, tea, coffee, and rubber. The manufacturing sector is highly diversified and includes both heavy and high-technology industries. India is a multiparty federal republic with two legislative houses; its head of state is the president, and the head of government is the prime minister. India has been inhabited for thousands of years. Agriculture in India dates to the 7th millennium BCE, and an urban civilization, that of the Indus valley, was established by 2600 BCE. Buddhism and Jainism arose in the 6th century BCE in reaction to the caste-based society created by the Vedic religion and its successor, Hinduism. The first Muslim contact with the subcontinent was in the 8th century CE. Muslim invasions began after *c.* 1000, establishing the long-lived Delhi sultanate in 1206 and the Mughal dynasty in 1526. Vasco da Gama's voyage to India in 1498 initiated several centuries of commercial rivalry between the Portuguese, Dutch, English, and French. British conquests in the 18th and 19th centuries led to the rule of the British East India Co., and direct administration by the British Empire began in 1858. After Mohandas K. Gandhi helped end British rule in 1947, Jawaharlal Nehru became India's first prime minister, and Nehru, his daughter Indira Gandhi, and his grandson Rajiv Gandhi retained that office for all but a few years during more than three succeeding decades. The subcontinent was partitioned into two countries—India, with a Hindu majority, and Pakistan, with a Muslim majority—in 1947. A later clash with Pakistan resulted in the creation of Bangladesh in 1971. In the 1980s and '90s Sikhs sought to establish an independent state in Punjab, and ethnic and religious conflicts took place in other parts of the country as well. In 2004 Manmohan Singh, a Sikh, became the country's first non-Hindu prime minister. The Kashmir region in the northwest has been a source of constant tension.

Indian law, Legal practices and institutions of India. Indian law draws on a number of sources, beginning with the customs of the ancient Vedas and later accretions of Hindu law, which largely concern social matters such as marriage and succession. After the Arab invasions of the 8th century, Islamic law was introduced in some areas, particularly in the north. English common law became the residual law in jurisdictions under British colonial control, while the Portuguese and French used their own laws in their colonies. Since independence (1947), India has aimed at developing a unified civil code and updating its criminal code.

Indian Mutiny, or SEPOY MUTINY (1857–58) Widespread rebellion against British rule in India begun by Indian troops (sepoys) in the service of the English East India Company. The mutiny began when sepoys refused to use new rifle cartridges (which were thought to be lubricated with grease containing a mixture of pigs' and cows' lard and thus religiously impure). They were shackled and imprisoned, but their outraged comrades shot their British officers and marched on Delhi. The ensuing fighting was ferocious on both sides and ended in defeat for the mutineers. Its immediate result was that the East India Company was abolished in favour of direct rule of India by the British government; in addition, the British government began a policy of consultation with Indians. British-imposed social measures that had antagonized Hindu society (e.g., a proposed bill that would remove legal obstacles to the re-marriage of Hindu women) were also halted.

Indian National Congress, or CONGRESS PARTY, Broadly based political party of India, founded in 1885. The Congress Party was a moderate reform party until 1917, when it was taken over by its "extremist" Home Rule wing. In the 1920s and '30s, under Mohandas K. Gandhi, it promoted noncooperation to protest the feebleness of the constitutional reforms of 1919. During World War II, the party announced that India would not support the war until granted complete independence. In 1947 an Indian independence bill became law, and in 1950 the constitution took effect. Jawaharlal Nehru dominated the party from 1951 to 1964. The Indian National Congress formed most of India's governments from 1947 to 1996, but at the end of the 20th century, its support plummeted. After several years out of power, it returned to government in 2004.

Indian Ocean, Body of salt water stretching between Africa in the west, Australia in the east, Asia in the north, and Antarctica in the south. With an area of 28,360,000 sq mi (73,440,000 sq km), it covers approximately one-seventh of the Earth's surface, and it is the smallest of the world's three major oceans. Its greatest depth (24,442 ft [7,450 m]) is in the Java Trench. Its chief marginal seas include the Red Sea, Arabian Sea, Persian Gulf, Andaman Sea, Bay of Bengal, and Great Australian Bight. Its major islands and island groups include Madagascar, Sri Lanka, and the Mascarenes.

Indian philosophy, Any of the numerous philosophical systems developed on the Indian subcontinent, including both orthodox (*astika*) systems, namely the Nyaya, Vaisheshika, Samkhya, Yoga, Mimamsa, and Vedanta schools of philosophy; and unorthodox (*nastika*) systems, such as Buddhism and Jainism. The history of Indian philosophy may be divided into three periods: the prelogical (to the beginning of the Common Era), the logical (1st–11th century), and the ultralogical (11th–18th century). What Dasgupta calls the prelogical stage covers the pre-Mauryan and the Mauryan periods (*c.* 321–185 BCE) in Indian history. The logical period begins roughly with the Kusanas (1st–2nd century CE) and was developed most fully in the Gupta era (3rd–5th century) and in the age of imperial Kanauj (7th century). In the 19th century newly founded universities introduced Indian intellectuals to Western thought, particularly British empiricism and utilitarianism. Indian philosophy in the early 20th century was influenced by German idealism. Later Indian philosophers made significant contributions to analytic philosophy.

Indic writing systems, Set of several dozen scripts used now or in the past to write many South and Southeast Asian languages. Aside from the Kharoshthi (Kharosthi) script, used *c.* 4th century BC–3rd century AD, all extant writing of the region descends from the Brahmi script, first attested in the Middle Indo-Aryan rock inscriptions of Ashoka (3rd century BC). In the first six centuries after Ashoka, Brahmi appears to have diversified into northern and southern variants. The northern types gave rise to the so-called Gupta scripts (4th–5th centuries), which are ultimately the progenitors of the Devanagari script (now used to write Sanskrit,

Hindi, Marathi, and Nepali), the Bengali and Oriya scripts, and Gurmukhi, the script of the Sikh scriptures, used also for modern Punjabi in India. The southern types gave rise to the Sinhalese, Telugu, and Kannada scripts on the one hand, and to the Pallava script on the other. The latter formed the basis of numerous other scripts, including those of the Tamil and Malayalam languages, a host of Southeast Asian scripts (e.g., those used to write Mon, Burmese, Khmer, Thai, and Lao), and a number of Austronesian languages.

indictment, In criminal law, a formal written accusation of a crime affirmed by a grand jury and handed up to the court for trial of the accused. In the U.S., the indictment is one of three principal methods of charging offenses, the others being the information (a written accusation resembling an indictment, prepared and presented to the court by a prosecuting official) and, for petty offenses, a complaint by the aggrieved party or by a police officer. An indictment may contain several counts.

individualism, Political and social philosophy that emphasizes individual freedom. Modern individualism emerged in Britain with the ideas of Adam Smith and Jeremy Bentham, and the concept was described by Alexis de Tocqueville as fundamental to the American temper. Individualism encompasses a value system, a theory of human nature, and a belief in certain political, economic, social, and religious arrangements. According to the individualist, all values are human-centred, the individual is of supreme importance, and all individuals are morally equal. Individualism places great value on self-reliance, on privacy, and on mutual respect. Negatively, it embraces opposition to authority and to all manner of controls over the individual, especially when exercised by the state. As a theory of human nature, individualism holds that the interests of the normal adult are best served by allowing him maximum freedom and responsibility for choosing his objectives and the means for obtaining them. The institutional embodiment of individualism follows from these principles. All individualists believe that government should keep its interference in the lives of individuals at a minimum, confining itself largely to maintaining law and order, preventing individuals from interfering with others, and enforcing agreements (contracts) voluntarily arrived at. Individualism also implies a property system according to which each person or family enjoys the maximum of opportunity to acquire property and to manage and dispose of it as he or they see fit. Although economic individualism and political individualism in the form of democracy advanced together for a while, in the course of the 19th century they eventually proved incompatible, as newly enfranchised voters came to demand governmental intervention in the economic process. Individualistic ideas lost ground in the later 19th and early 20th century with the rise of large-scale social organization and the emergence of political theories opposed to individualism, particularly communism and fascism. They reemerged in the latter half of the 20th century with the defeat of fascism and the fall of communist regimes in the Soviet Union and eastern Europe.

Indo-Aryan languages, or INDIC LANGUAGES, Major subgroup of the Indo-Iranian branch of the Indo-European language family. Indo-Aryan languages are spoken by more than 800 million people, principally in India, Nepal, Pakistan, Bangladesh, and Sri Lanka. The Old Indo-Aryan period is represented by Sanskrit. Middle Indo-Aryan (*c.* 600 BCE–1000 CE) consists principally of the Prakrit dialects, including Pali. Modern Indo-Aryan speech is largely a single dialect continuum spread over an undivided geographical space, so demarcations between languages and dialects are somewhat artificial. Complicating the situation are competing distinctions between languages with an old literary tradition, local language identification by native speakers (as in censuses), supraregional languages such as Modern Standard Hindi and Urdu, and labels introduced by linguists, particularly those of George Abraham Grierson. In the centre of the Indo-Aryan speech area (the "Hindi zone"), covering northern India and extending south as far as Madhya Pradesh, the most common language of administration and education is Modern Standard Hindi. Important regional languages in the northern Indian plain are Haryanvi, Kauravi, Braj, Awadhi, Chhattisgarhi, Bhojpuri, Magahi, and Maithili. Regional languages in Rajasthan include Marwari, Dhundhari, Harauti, and Malvi. In the Himalayan foothills of Himachal Pradesh are Grierson's Pahari languages. Surrounding the Hindi zone, the most significant languages are, moving clockwise, Nepali (East Pahari), Assamese, Bengali, Oriya, Marathi, Gujarati, Sindhi, the speech of southern, northwestern, and northern Punjab province in Pakistan (called West Punjabi or Lahnda by Grierson), Punjabi, and Dogri. In Jammu and Kashmir and the far north of Pakistan are the Dardic languages; the most important are Kashmiri, Kohistani, Shina, and Khowar. The Nuristani languages of northwestern Afghanistan are sometimes considered a separate branch of Indo-Iranian. Sinhalese (spoken in Sri Lanka), Divehi (spoken in the Maldive Islands), and Romany are also Indo-Aryan languages.

Indo-European languages, Family of languages with the greatest number of speakers, spoken in most of Europe and areas of European settlement and in much of southwestern and southern Asia. They are descended from a single unrecorded language believed to have been spoken more than 5,000 years ago in the steppe regions north of the Black Sea and to have split into a number of dialects by 3000 BC. Carried by migrating tribes to Europe and Asia, these developed over time into separate languages. The main branches are Anatolian, Indo-Iranian (including Indo-Aryan and Iranian), Greek, Italic, Germanic, Armenian, Celtic, Albanian, the extinct Tocharian languages, Baltic, and Slavic. The study of Indo-European began in 1786 with Sir William Jones's proposal that Greek, Latin, Sanskrit, and Celtic were all derived from a "common source." In the 19th century linguists added other languages to the Indo-European family, and scholars such as Rasmus Rask established a system of sound correspondences. Proto-Indo-European has since been partially reconstructed via identification of roots common to its descendants and analysis of shared grammatical patterns.

Indochina, or INDOCHINESE PENINSULA, Region of mainland Southeast Asia. The term, now largely superseded by the name Southeast Asia, was used mainly by Westerners to describe the intermingling of Indian and Chinese cultural influences in the region. Indochinese Peninsula typically referred to Cambodia, Laos, and Vietnam, though it was sometimes expanded to include Myanmar (Burma), Thailand, and the mainland portion of Malaysia.

Indochina wars, 20th-century conflicts in Vietnam, Laos, and Cambodia. The first conflict (1946–54; often called the French Indochina War) involved France, which had ruled Vietnam as its colony (French Indochina), and the newly independent Democratic Republic of Vietnam under Ho Chi Minh; the war ended in Vietnamese victory in 1954. Vietnam was then divided into the communist-dominated north and the U.S.-supported south; war soon broke out between the two. North Vietnam won the war (the Vietnam War) despite heavy U.S. involvement, and the country was reunited in 1976. Cambodia experienced its own civil war between communists and noncommunists during that period, which was won by the communist Khmer Rouge in 1975. After several years of horrifying atrocities under Pol Pot, the Vietnamese invaded in 1979 and installed a puppet government. Fighting between the Khmer Rouge and the Vietnamese continued throughout the 1980s; Vietnam withdrew its troops by 1989. In 1993 UN-mediated elections established an interim government, and Cambodia's monarchy was reestablished. In Laos, North Vietnam's victory over South Vietnam brought the communist Pathet Lao into complete control in Laos.

Indonesia, officially REPUBLIC OF INDONESIA, formerly NETHERLANDS EAST INDIES, Archipelago country, located off the coast of mainland Southeast Asia. It comprises some 17,500 islands, of which more than 7,000 are uninhabited. Area: 737,815 sq mi (1,910,931 sq km). Population: (2011 est.) 241,343,000. Capital: Jakarta (on Java). Indonesia has more than 300 ethnic groups, which in the western islands fall into three broad divisions: the inland wet-rice cultivators (primarily of Java and neighbouring islands); the coastal trading, farming, and fishing peoples, including the Malays of Sumatra; and the inland societies of shifting cultivators, such as the Dayak communities of Borneo. In the east the distinction is between coastal and interior peoples. Languages: Indonesian (Bahasa Indonesia; official), several hundred languages from different ethnic groups. Religions: Islam; also Christianity, Hinduism, traditional beliefs. Currency: rupiah. The Indonesian archipelago stretches 3,200 miles (5,100 km) from west to east. Major islands include Sumatra, Java (with more than half of Indonesia's population), Bali, Lombok, Sumbawa, about three-fourths of Borneo (Kalimantan), Celebes (Sulawesi), the Moluccas, and the western portions of Timor and New Guinea. The islands are characterized by rugged volcanic mountains and tropical rainforests. Geologically unstable, Indonesia has frequent earthquakes and hundreds of active volcanoes, including Krakatoa (Krakatau). Roughly one-fifth of its land is arable, and rice is the staple crop. Petroleum, natural gas, timber products, garments, and rubber are major exports. Indonesia is a multiparty republic with two legislative houses; its head of state and government is the president.

Austronesian-speaking peoples began migrating to Indonesia about the 3rd millennium BCE. Commercial relations were established with Africa about the 1st century CE, and Hindu and Buddhist cultural influences from India began to take hold. Indian traders also brought Islam to the islands, and by the 13th century it had spread throughout the islands—except Bali, which retained its Hindu religion and culture. Indonesia now has the largest Muslim population of any country. European influence began in the 16th century, and the Dutch gradually established control of Indonesia from the late 17th century until 1942, when the Japanese invaded. Sukarno declared Indonesia's independence in 1945, which the Dutch granted, with nominal union to The Netherlands, in 1949; Indonesia dissolved this union in 1954. The suppression of an alleged coup attempt in 1965 resulted in the deaths of hundreds of thousands of people the government claimed to be communists, and by 1968 Gen. Suharto had taken power. His government forcibly incorporated East Timor into Indonesia in 1975–76, with much loss of life. In the 1990s the country was beset by political, economic, and environmental problems, and Suharto was deposed in 1998. Muslim leader Abdurrahman Wahid was elected president in 1999 but was replaced in 2001 by his vice president, Megawati Sukarnoputri, the eldest daughter of Sukarno. In 2004 she was succeeded by Susilo Bambang Yudhoyono. In 1999 the people of East Timor voted for independence from Indonesia, which was granted; after a period under UN supervision, it achieved full sovereignty in 2002. In 2004 a large tsunami generated by an earthquake off the western coast of Sumatra caused widespread death and destruction.

Indra, In the ancient Vedic religion of India, chief of the gods and patron of warriors. Armed with lightning and thunderbolts and strengthened by drinking the elixir soma, he vanquished demonic enemies and killed the dragon that kept the monsoon rains from breaking. In later Hinduism Indra was demoted to a rain god and regent of the heavens. He was father to Arjuna, hero of the *Mahabharata*. Indra also appears in Buddhist and Jain mythologies.

induction, In logic, a type of nonvalid inference or argument in which the premises provide some reason for believing that the conclusion is true. Typical forms of inductive argument include reasoning from a part to a whole, from the particular to the general, and from a sample to an entire population. Induction is traditionally contrasted with deduction. Many of the problems of inductive logic, including what is known as the problem of induction, have been treated in studies of the methodology of the natural sciences.

indulgence, In Roman Catholicism, the remission of temporal punishment for a sin after the sin has been forgiven through the sacrament of penance. The theology of indulgences is based on the concept that, even though the sin and its eternal punishment are forgiven through penance, divine justice demands that the sinner pay for the crime either in this life or in purgatory. The first indulgences were intended to shorten times of penance by substituting periods of fasting, private prayers, almsgiving, and monetary payments that were to be used for religious purposes. Pope Urban II granted the first plenary, or absolute, indulgence to participants in the First Crusade, and subsequent popes offered indulgences on the occasion of the later Crusades. After the 12th century they were more widely used, and abuses became common as indulgences were put up for sale to earn money for the church or to enrich unscrupulous clerics. Jan Hus opposed them, and Martin Luther's Ninety-five Theses (1517) were in part a protest against indulgences. In 1562 the Council of Trent put an end to the abuses but not to the doctrine itself.

Indus civilization (*c.* 2500–*c.* 1700 BC) Earliest known urban culture of the Indian subcontinent and the most extensive of the world's three earliest civilizations. It stretched from near the present-day Iran-Pakistan border on the Arabian Sea in the west to near Delhi in the east, and 500 mi (800 km) to the south and 1,000 mi (1,600 km) to the northeast. It is known to have included two large cities, Harappa and Mohenjo Daro (in what is now Pakistan), whose large size suggests centralization in two large states or one state with two capitals. Alternatively, Harappa may have succeeded Mohenjo Daro. It was a literate civilization; the language has been tentatively identified as Dravidian. Wheat and barley were grown, many animals (including cats, dogs, and cattle) were domesticated, and cotton was cultivated. The best-known artifacts are seals depicting real and imaginary animals. How and when the civilization came to an end is unclear; Mohenjo Daro was attacked and destroyed in the mid-2nd millennium BC, but in the south there was continuity between the Indus civilization and the Copper Age civilizations of central and western India.

Indus River, Trans-Himalayan river of southern Asia. It is one of the world's longest rivers, with a length of 1,800 mi (2,900 km). Its annual average flow of 272 billion cu yd (207 billion cu m) is twice that of the Nile. It rises in southwestern Tibet and flows northwest through valleys of the Himalayas. After crossing into the Kashmir region, it continues northwestward through the Indian- and Pakistani-administered areas and then turns south into Pakistan. Swelled by tributaries from the Punjab region, including the Jhelum, Chenab, Ravi, Beas, and Sutlej rivers, it widens and flows more slowly. It has supplied water for irrigation on the plains of the Indus valley since early times.

The upper Indus River flows through the rugged terrain of northern Pakistan.
Jaroslav Poncar/Bruce Coleman, Ltd.

industrial design, Design of products made by large-scale industry for mass distribution. Among the considerations for such products are structure, operation, appearance, and conformance to production, distribution, and selling procedures; appearance is the principal consideration in industrial design. The International Council of Societies of Industrial Design was founded in London in 1957 and within 25 years had members in more than 40 countries. Two significant trends have persisted: streamlining, a design principle pioneered by Raymond Loewy and others in the 1930s; and planned obsolescence, design changes that tempt owners to replace goods with new purchases more frequently than would normally be necessary.

industrial engineering, Application of engineering principles and techniques of scientific management to the maintenance of high levels of productivity at optimum cost in industrial enterprises. Frederick W. Taylor pioneered in the scientific measurement of work, and Frank (1868–1924) and Lillian (1878–1972) Gilbreth refined it with time-and-motion studies. As a result, production processes were simplified, enabling workers to increase production. The industrial engineer selects tools and materials for production that are most efficient and least costly to the company. The engineer may also determine the sequence of production and the design of plant facilities or factories.

industrial medicine, or OCCUPATIONAL MEDICINE, Branch of medicine dealing with workers' health and the prevention and treatment of diseases and injuries in the workplace. Workplace hazards include exposure to dangerous materials including asbestos and coal dust, radiation exposure, and machinery capable of causing injuries ranging from minor to life-threatening. Industrial medical programs mandate protective devices around machines' moving parts, proper ventilation of work areas, use of less toxic materials, containment of production processes, and protective equipment and clothing. Good industrial medical programs improve labour-management relations, increase workers' overall health and productivity, and reduce insurance costs.

industrial-organizational psychology, or I-O PSYCHOLOGY, Application of the concepts and methods of experimental, clinical, and social psychology to the workplace. I-O psychologists are concerned with such matters as personnel evaluation and placement, job analysis, worker-management relations (including morale and job satisfaction), workforce training and development (including leadership training), and productivity improvement. They may work closely with business managers, industrial engineers, and human-resources professionals.

Industrial Revolution, Process of change from an agrarian, handicraft economy to one dominated by industry and machine manufacture. It began in England in the 18th century. Technological changes included the use of iron and steel, new energy sources, the invention of new machines that increased production (including the steam engine and the spinning jenny), the development of the factory system, and important developments in transportation and communication (including the railroad and the telegraph). The Industrial Revolution was largely confined to Britain from 1760 to 1830 and then spread to Belgium and France. Other nations lagged behind, but, once Germany, the U.S., and Japan achieved industrial power, they outstripped Britain's initial successes. Eastern European countries lagged into the 20th century, and not until the mid-20th century did the Industrial Revolution spread to such countries as China and India. Industrialization effected changes in economic, political, and social organization. These included a wider distribution of wealth and increased international trade; political changes resulting from the shift in economic power; sweeping social changes that included the rise of working-class movements, the development of managerial hierarchies to oversee the division of labour, and the emergence of new patterns of authority; and struggles against externalities such as industrial pollution and urban crowding.

industrialization, Process of converting to a socioeconomic order in which industry is dominant. The changes that took place in Britain during the Industrial Revolution of the late 18th and 19th century led the way for the early industrializing nations of western Europe and North America. Industrialization entailed both technology and profound social developments. The freeing of labourers from feudal and customary obligations created a free market in labour, with a pivotal role for the entrepreneur. Cities attracted large numbers of people, massing workers in new industrial towns and factories. Later industrializers attempted to manipulate some of the elements: the Soviet Union eliminated the entrepreneur; Japan stimulated and sustained the entrepreneur's role; Denmark and New Zealand industrialized primarily by commercializing and mechanizing agriculture.

inertia, Inherent property of a body that makes it oppose any force that would cause a change in its motion. A body at rest and a body in motion both oppose forces that might cause acceleration. The inertia of a body can be measured by its mass, which governs its resistance to the action of a force, or by its moment of inertia about a specified axis, which measures its resistance to the action of a torque about the same axis.

inertial guidance system, An electronic system that continuously monitors the position, velocity, and acceleration of a vehicle, usually a submarine, missile, or airplane, and thus provides navigational data or control. The basic components of an inertial guidance system are gyroscopes, accelerometers, and a computer.

infancy, In humans, the period of life between birth and the acquisition of language usually one to two years later. The average newborn infant weighs 7.5 lbs (3.4 kg) and is about 20 in (51 cm) long. At birth, infants display a set of inherited reflexes involving such acts as sucking, blinking, and grasping. They are sensitive to light-dark visual contrasts and movements and show a noticeable preference for gazing at the human face; they also begin to recognize the human voice. By 4 months of age most babies are able to sit up, and most begin crawling in 7–10 months; by 12 months most are able to start walking. Virtually all infants begin to comprehend some words several months before they themselves speak their first meaningful words.

infanticide, Killing of the newborn. Infanticide has often been interpreted as a primitive method of birth control and a means of ridding a group of its weak or undesirable children; but most societies actively welcome children and put them to death (or allow them to die) only under exceptional circumstances—e.g., when there is little or no likelihood of being able to provide support. As late as the 18th century in European countries unwanted infants were disposed of by abandonment and exposure. Firstborn sacrifice, or the offering of one's most precious possession to the deities, is known from the Bible and from the histories of Egypt, Greece, Rome, and India.

infection, Invasion of the body by any of various agents—including bacteria, fungi, protozoans, viruses, and worms—and its reaction to them or their toxins. Infections are called subclinical until they perceptibly affect health, when they become infectious diseases. Infection can be local (e.g., an abscess), confined to one body system (e.g., pneumonia in the lungs), or generalized (e.g., septicemia). Infectious agents can enter the body by inhalation, ingestion, sexual transmission, passage to a fetus during pregnancy or birth, wound contamination, animal bites, or insect bites. The body responds with an attack on the invader by leukocytes, production of antibodies or antitoxins, and often a rise in temperature. The antibodies may result in short-term or lifelong immunity. Despite significant progress in preventing and treating infectious diseases, they remain a major cause of illness and death, particularly in regions of poor sanitation, poor nutrition, and crowding.

infertility, Inability of a couple to conceive and reproduce. It is defined as failure to conceive after one year of regular intercourse without contraception. Inability to conceive when desired can result from a defect at any of the stages required for fertility. About one in every eight couples is infertile. Most cases involve the female partner, 30–40% involve the male, and 10% are caused by unknown factors. In women, causes include ovulation or hormone problems, fallopian-tube disorders, and a chemical balance that is hostile to sperm; in men, causes include impotence, low sperm count, and sperm abnormalities. Either partner can have a blockage of the pathways the sperm must travel, often treatable by sur-

gery. Emotional factors may contribute; return of normal fertility may require only counseling. Fertility drugs can stimulate the release of eggs (often more than one, leading to multiple births). Low sperm count may be overcome by limiting intercourse to the time of ovulation, the most fertile period. If these methods are unsuccessful, couples may try artificial insemination, in vitro fertilization, or surrogate motherhood, or they may choose adoption instead.

infinite series, In mathematics, the sum of infinitely many numbers, whose relationship can typically be expressed as a formula or a function. An infinite series that results in a finite sum is said to converge. One that does not, diverges. Mathematical analysis is largely taken up with studying the conditions under which a given function will result in a convergent infinite series. Such series (e.g., the Fourier series) are particularly useful in solving differential equations.

inflation, In cosmology, a hypothesized period of exponential expansion of the universe, shortly after the big bang, which may account for some of the universe's observed properties, such as the distribution of energy and matter. Grand unified theories of the forces of nature suggest that inflation could have occurred during the first 10^{-32} second after the universe began, when the strong force was decoupling from the weak and electromagnetic forces. During this time, the universe would have expanded by more than 100 orders of magnitude. Interpreted in the context of general relativity, inflation occurred while the universe existed in a state of nonzero energy density (false vacuum).

inflation, In economics, increases in the level of prices. Inflation is generally thought of as an inordinate rise in the general level of prices. Four theories are commonly used to explain inflation. The first and oldest, the quantity theory, promoted in the 18th century by David Hume, assumes that prices will rise as the supply of money increases. Milton Friedman refined the quantity theory in the mid-20th century, arguing that the prescription for stable prices is to increase the money supply at a rate equal to that at which the economy is expanding. A second approach is John Maynard Keynes's theory of income determination, which assumes that inflation occurs when the demand for goods and services is greater than the supply. It calls for the government to control inflation by adjusting levels of spending and taxation and by raising or lowering interest rates. A third approach is the cost-push theory. It traces inflation to a phenomenon known as the price-wage spiral, in which workers' demands for wage increases lead employers to increase prices to reflect their higher costs, thereby sowing the seeds of a further round of wage demands. A fourth approach is the structural theory, which emphasizes structural maladjustments in the economy, as when in developing countries imports tend to increase faster than exports, pushing down the international value of the developing country's currency and causing prices to rise internally.

inflorescence, Cluster of flowers on one or a series of branches, which together make a large showy blossom. Categories depend on the arrangement of flowers on an elongated main axis (peduncle) or on sub-branches from the main axis, and on the timing and position of flowering. In determinate inflorescences, the youngest flowers are at the bottom or outside (e.g., onion flowers). In indeterminate inflorescences, the youngest flowers are at the top or in the center (e.g., snapdragon, lily of the valley, and *Astilbe* flowers). Other indeterminate inflorescences are the dangling male and female catkins of oak trees, the spike of barley, and the flat head (capitulum) of the dandelion.

influenza, or FLU, or GRIPPE, Acute viral infection of the upper or lower respiratory tract. Influenza viruses A (the most common), B, and C produce similar symptoms, but infection with or vaccination against one does not give immunity against the others. Chills, fatigue, and muscle aches begin abruptly. The temperature soon reaches 38–40 °C (101–104 °F). Head, muscle, abdominal, and joint aches may be accompanied by sore throat. Recovery starts in three to four days, and respiratory symptoms become more prominent. Bed rest, high fluid intake, and aspirin or other antifever drugs are standard treatment. Influenza A tends to occur in wavelike annual pandemics. Mortality is usually low, but in rare outbreaks it reaches immense proportions. Most deaths result from pneumonia or bronchitis.

information processing, Acquisition, recording, organization, retrieval, display, and dissemination of information. Today the term usually refers to computer-based operations. Information processing consists of locating and capturing information, using software to manipulate it into a desired form, and outputting the data. An Internet search engine is an example of an information-processing tool, as is any sophisticated information-retrieval system.

information science, Discipline that deals with the processes of storing and transferring information. It attempts to bring together concepts and methods from such varied disciplines as library science, computer science and engineering, linguistics, and psychology to develop techniques and devices to aid in the handling of information. In its early stages in the 1960s, information science was concerned primarily with applying the then-new computer technology to the processing and managing of documents. The applied computer technologies and theoretical studies of information science have since permeated many other disciplines. Computer science and engineering still tend to absorb its theory- and technology-oriented subjects, and management science tends to absorb information-systems subjects.

infrared astronomy, Study of astronomical objects by observing the infrared radiation they emit. Its techniques enable examination of many celestial objects that give off energy at wavelengths in the infrared region of the electromagnetic spectrum but that cannot otherwise be seen from Earth because they do not emit much visible light or because that light is blocked by dust clouds, which infrared radiation can penetrate. Infrared astronomy originated in the early 19th century with the work of William Herschel, who discovered infrared radiation while studying sunlight. The first systematic infrared observations of other stars were made in the 1920s; modern techniques, such as the use of interference filters for ground-based telescopes, were introduced in the early 1960s. Because atmospheric water vapour absorbs many infrared wavelengths, observations are carried out with telescopes sited on high mountaintops and from airborne and space-based observatories. Infrared astronomy allows studies of the dust-obscured core of the Milky Way Galaxy and the hearts of star-forming regions and has led to many discoveries including brown dwarf candidates and disks of matter around certain stars.

infrared radiation, Portion of the electromagnetic spectrum that extends from the microwave range to the red end of the visible light range. Its wavelengths vary from about 0.7 to 1,000 micrometres. Most of the radiation emitted by a moderately heated surface is infrared, and it forms a continuous spectrum. Molecular excitation produces extensive infrared radiation but in a discrete spectrum of lines or bands. Infrared wavelengths are useful for night-vision equipment, heat-seeking missiles, molecular spectroscopy, and infrared astronomy, among other things. The trapping of infrared radiation by atmospheric gases is also the basis of the greenhouse effect.

Ingres, Jean-Auguste-Dominique (b. Aug. 29, 1780, Montauban, France—d. Jan. 14, 1867, Paris), French painter. He studied with Jacques-Louis David in Paris before attending the École des Beaux-Arts (1799–1801), where he won a Prix de Rome scholarship. Critics condemned one of his first public works, the awe-inspiring portrait *Napoleon on His Imperial Throne* (1806), as stiff and archaic, but its style was one he developed intentionally. In

Valpinçon Bather, *oil painting by Jean-Auguste-Dominique Ingres, 1808; in the Louvre, Paris.*

Giraudon/Art Resource, New York

Italy (1806–24) he prospered with portraits and history paintings. His small-scale portrait drawings are meticulously rendered. Back in Paris he received critical acclaim at last and won admission to the academy with *The Vow of Louis XIII* (1824). He succeeded David as the leader of French Neoclassical painting, a style that was the antithesis of the lush Romanticism of contemporary artists such as Eugène Delacroix, Ingres's chief rival. In 1825 he opened a teaching studio, which became one of the largest in Paris. By the mid 1840s he was France's most sought-after society portraitist. Some of his most notable later works are female nudes, which are often notable for their elongated distortion. None of his many students attained distinction, but his influence is seen in the work of Edgar Degas, Pierre-Auguste Renoir, and Pablo Picasso.

inheritance, Devolution of property on an heir or heirs upon the death of its owner. In civil law jurisdictions it is called succession. The concept depends on a common acceptance of the notion of private ownership of goods and property. Under some systems land is considered communal property and rights to it are redistributed, rather than bequeathed, on the death of a community member. In many countries a minimum portion of the decedent's estate must be assigned to the surviving spouse and often to the progeny as well. Intestacy laws, which govern the inheritance of estates whose distribution is not directed by a will, universally view kinship between the decedent and the beneficiary as a primary consideration. Inheritance usually entails payment of an inheritance tax.

injunction, In civil proceedings, a court order compelling a party to do or to refrain from doing a specified act. It is an equitable remedy for harm for which no adequate remedy exists in law. Thus it is used to prevent a future harmful action (e.g., disclosing confidential information, instituting a national labour strike, or violating a group's civil rights) rather than to compensate for an injury that has already occurred. It also provides relief from harm for which an award of money damages is not a satisfactory solution. A defendant who violates an injunction may be cited for contempt.

Inner Mongolia, Chinese NEI MONGOL, or NEI-MENG-KU, Autonomous region (pop., 2002 est.: 23,790,000), China. Stretching some 1,800 mi (2,900 km) across north-northeastern China, it has an area of 454,600 sq mi (1,177,500 sq km). Its capital is Hohhot. Mongols and Chinese make up the bulk of the population, most of which is concentrated in the agricultural belt near the Huang He (Yellow River). Inner Mongolia is an inland plateau lying at an elevation of about 3,300 ft (1,000 m); it is fringed by mountains and valleys. Its northern portion lies within the Gobi Desert, and its southern border is partly marked by the Great Wall. Inner Mongolia was separated from Mongolia (Outer Mongolia) in 1912 and was established as an autonomous region in 1947. Its harsh climate restricts intensive agriculture; some industrial development has occurred there.

Innocent III, orig. LOTHAR OF SEGNI (b. 1160/61, Gavignano Castle, Campagna di Roma, Papal States—d. July 16, 1216, Perugia), Pope (1198–1216). Innocent, who was trained in both theology and law, brought the medieval papacy to the height of its prestige and power. He crowned Otto IV as Holy Roman emperor, but Otto's determination to unite Germany and Sicily angered him, and in 1212 he gave his support to the Hohenstaufen candidate, Frederick II. After Innocent excommunicated King John of England for refusing to recognize Stephen Langton as archbishop of Canterbury, John was obliged to submit and to declare England a fief of the Holy See (1213). Innocent launched the Fourth Crusade, which captured Constantinople, and the Albigensian Crusade, which attempted to suppress heresy in southern France. He approved the Mendicant orders founded by St. Dominic and St. Francis of Assisi, and he convoked the fourth Lateran Council, which promulgated the doctrine of transubstantiation and endorsed annual confession for all Christians.

Innsbruck, City (pop., 2001: 113,392), on the Inn River in western Austria, southwest of Salzburg. A small market town in the 12th century, it was located beside a bridge (*Brücke*) over the Inn. It was chartered in 1239, passed to the Habsburgs in 1363, and in 1420 became the capital of Tirol. Napoleon gave the city to Bavaria in 1806, and in 1809 it was the site of an uprising of Tirolian patriots against the Bavarians and the French. The old town has narrow streets lined with medieval houses and arcades. A winter sports centre, Innsbruck was the site of the Winter Olympic Games in 1964 and 1976.

input-output analysis, Economic analysis developed by Wassily Leontief, in which the interdependence of an economy's various productive sectors is observed by viewing the product of each industry both as a commodity for consumption and as a factor in the production of itself and other goods. For example, input-output analysis will break down a nation's total production of trucks, showing that some trucks are used in the production of more trucks, some in farming, some in the production of houses, and so on. An input-output analysis is usually summarized in a gridlike table showing what various industries buy from and sell to one another.

Inquisition, In the Middle Ages, a judicial procedure that was used to combat heresy; in early modern times, a formal Roman Catholic judicial institution. *Inquisito*, a Latin term meaning investigation or inquest, was a legal procedure that involved the assemblage of evidence and the prosecution of a criminal trial. Use of the procedure against the heresies of the Cathari and Waldenses was approved by Pope Gregory IX in 1231. Suspected heretics were arrested, interrogated, and tried; the use of torture was approved by Innocent IV in 1252. Penalties ranged from prayer and fasting to imprisonment; convicted heretics who refused to recant could be executed by lay authorities. Medieval inquisitors functioned widely in northern Italy and southern France. The Spanish Inquisition was authorized by Sixtus IV in 1478; the pope later tried to limit its powers but was opposed by the Spanish crown. The auto-da-fé, the public ceremony at which sentences were pronounced, was an elaborate celebration, and the grand inquisitor Tomás de Torquemada was responsible for burning about 2,000 heretics at the stake. The Spanish Inquisition was also introduced into Mexico, Peru, Sicily (1517), and the Netherlands (1522), and it was not entirely suppressed in Spain until the early 19th century.

insanity, In criminal law, a disease, defect, or condition of the mind that renders one unable to understand the nature of a criminal act or the fact that it is wrong. Tests of insanity are not intended as medical diagnoses but rather only as determinations of whether a person may be held criminally responsible for his or her actions. The most enduring definition of insanity in Anglo-American law was that proposed by Alexander Cockburn (1843). Many U.S. states and several courts have adopted a standard under which the accused must lack "substantial capacity either to appreciate the criminality of his conduct or to conform his conduct to the require-

ments of the law." Some states have abolished the insanity plea altogether, while other states allow a finding of "guilty but mentally ill."

insect, Any member of the class Insecta, the largest arthropod class, including nearly 1 million known species (about three-fourths of all animals) and an estimated 5–10 million undescribed species. Insect bodies have three segments: head, thorax (which bears three pairs of legs and usually two pairs of wings), and many-segmented abdomen. Many species undergo complete metamorphosis. There are two subclasses: Apterygota (primitive, wingless forms, including silverfish and bristletails) and Pterygota (more advanced, winged or secondarily wingless forms). The approximately 27 orders of Pterygota are generally classified by wing form: e.g., Coleoptera (beetles), Diptera (dipterans), Heteroptera (bugs). Insects are found in almost all terrestrial and freshwater and some marine habitats.

insectivore, Any member of the mammalian order (Insectivora) that includes the hedgehogs, moles, and sometimes shrews (some of which are considered primates by some authorities), or, more generally, any animal that eats mainly insects. The mammalian insectivores are generally small, active, and nocturnal. They are found in most parts of the world except Antarctica, Australia, and South America. Most species are solitary (except during the breeding season) and short-lived.

Inside Passage, or INLAND PASSAGE, Natural sheltered sea route along the U.S.-Canadian coast from Seattle, Wash., to Skagway, Alaska. Extending northwest for more than 1,000 mi (1,600 km), it comprises channels and straits between the mainland and islands (including Vancouver Island) that protect it from Pacific storms. It is the favoured route for coastal shipping to Alaska. Ports in British Columbia include Victoria, Vancouver, and Prince Rupert; those in Alaska include Ketchikan, Wrangell, and Juneau.

insider trading, Illegal use of insider information for profit in financial trading. Since 1934, the Securities and Exchange Commission has prohibited trading while in possession of material nonpublic information.

insomnia, Inability to sleep adequately. The causes may include poor sleeping conditions, circulatory or brain disorders, breathing disorders (e.g., sleep apnea), mental distress (e.g., tension or depression), or physical discomfort. Mild insomnia may be treated by improving sleeping conditions or through traditional remedies such as warm baths, milk, or systematic relaxation. Apnea and its associated insomnia may be treated surgically or mechanically with breathing apparatus. Severe or chronic insomnia may necessitate the temporary use of barbiturates or tranquilizers, but such drugs are often addictive and may be decreasingly effective as the body builds up tolerance. Other methods of treatment include psychotherapy and hypnosis.

instinct, Involuntary response by an animal, resulting in a predictable and relatively fixed behaviour pattern. Instinctive behaviour is an inherited mechanism that serves to promote the survival of an animal or species. It is most apparent in fighting and sexual activity. The simplest form is the reflex. All animals have instinct, but, in general, the higher the animal form, the more flexible the behaviour. Among mammals, learned behaviour often prevails over instinctive behaviour.

instrumentalism, or EXPERIMENTALISM, Philosophy advanced by John Dewey holding that what is most important in a thing or idea is its value as an instrument of action and that the truth of an idea lies in its usefulness. Dewey favored these terms over the term pragmatism to label the philosophy on which his views of education rested. His school claimed that cognition has evolved not for speculative or metaphysical purposes but for the practical purpose of successful adjustment. Ideas are conceived as instruments for transforming the uneasiness arising from facing a problem into the satisfaction of solving it.

insulator, Substance that blocks or retards the flow of electric current or heat. An insulator is a poor conductor because it has a high resistance to such flow. Electrical insulators are commonly used to hold conductors in place, separating them from one another and from surrounding structures to form a barrier between energized parts of an electric circuit and confine the flow of current to wires or other conducting paths. Electrical insulators include rubber, plastic, porcelain, and mica. Thermal insulators. which break up the heat-flow path by absorbing radiant heat, include fiberglass, cork, and rock wool.

insulin, Polypeptide hormone that regulates blood glucose levels. Secreted by the islets of Langerhans in the pancreas when blood glucose rises, as after a meal, it helps transfer the glucose into the body's cells to be oxidized for energy or converted and stored as fatty acids or glycogen. When blood glucose falls, insulin secretion stops and the liver releases more glucose into the blood. Insulin has various related functions in the liver, muscles, and other tissues, controlling the balance of glucose with related compounds. Insulin-related disorders include diabetes mellitus and hypoglycemia. Frederick Banting and J.J.R. Macleod won a Nobel Prize in 1923 for discovering insulin, and Frederick Sanger won one in 1958 for determining its amino acid sequence.

insurance, Contract that, by redistributing risk among a large number of people, reduces losses from accidents incurred by an individual. In return for a specified payment (premium), the insurer undertakes to pay the insured or a beneficiary a specified amount of money in the event that the insured suffers loss through the occurrence of an event covered by the insurance contract (policy). By pooling both the financial contributions and the risks of a large number of policyholders, the insurer is able to absorb losses much more easily than is the uninsured individual. Insurers may offer insurance to any individual able to pay, or they may contract with members of a group (e.g., employees of a firm) to offer special rates for group insurance. Marine insurance, covering ships and voyages, is the oldest form of insurance; it originated in ancient times with loans to shipowners that were repayable only on safe completion of a voyage, and it was formalized in medieval Europe. Fire insurance arose in the 17th century, and other forms of property insurance became common with the spread of industrialization in the 19th century. It is now possible to insure almost any kind of property, including homes, businesses, motor vehicles, and goods in transit.

integrated circuit (IC), or MICROCIRCUIT, or CHIP, or MICRO-CHIP, Assembly of microscopic electronic components (transistors, diodes, capacitors, and resistors) and their interconnections fabricated as a single unit on a wafer of semiconducting material, especially silicon. Early ICs of the late 1950s consisted of about 10 components on a chip 0.12 in. (3 mm) square. Very large-scale integration (VLSI) vastly increased circuit density, giving rise to the microprocessor. The first commercially successful IC chip (Intel, 1974) had 4,800 transistors; Intel's Pentium (1993) had 3.2 million, and more than a billion are now achievable.

integration, In calculus, the process of finding a function whose derivative is a given function. The term, sometimes used interchangeably with "antidifferentiation," is indicated symbolically with the integral sign ∫. (The differential dx usually follows to indicate x as the variable.) The basic rules of integration are: (1) $\int(f + g)dx = \int fdx + \int gdx$ (where f and g are functions of the variable x), (2) $\int kfdx = k\int fdx$ (k is a constant), and (3)

$$\int x^n dx = \left(\frac{1}{n+1}\right)x^{n+1} + C$$

(C is a constant). Note that any constant value may be added onto an indefinite integral without changing its derivative. Thus, the indefinite integral of $2x$ is $x^2 + C$, where C can be any real number. A definite integral is an indefinite integral evaluated over an interval. The result is not affected by the choice for the value of C.

intellectual disability, or MENTAL RETARDATION, Subaverage intellectual ability that is present from birth or infancy and is manifested by abnormal development, learning difficulties, and problems in social adjustment. A standardized intelligence test is a common method of identification. Individuals with IQ scores of 53–70 are usually classified as having mild intellectual disability and are able to learn academic and prevocational skills with some special education. Those with scores of 36–52 are classified as having moderate intellectual disability and are able to learn functional academic skills and undertake semiskilled work under supervised conditions. Those in the severe (21–35) and profound (below 21) ranges require progressively more supervision or full-time custodial care. Intellectual disability can be caused by genetic disorders (such as Down syndrome), infectious diseases (such as meningitis), metabolic disorders, poisoning from lead, radiation, or other toxic agents, injuries to the head, and malnutrition.

intellectual property, Property that derives from the work of an individual's mind or intellect. Early copyright law aimed to protect the economic interests of book publishers rather than the intellectual rights of authors. Modern copyright law protects the labour of elaborating an idea, but not the idea itself. The concept of discovery also plays a role in intellectual property rights: a patent is awarded to one who can demonstrate that he or she has invented something not previously known. The World Trade Organization requires members to establish and enforce minimum levels of copyright, patent, and trademark protection within their jurisdictions. The World Intellectual Property Organization, which began operations in 1970, promotes the worldwide protection of both industrial property (inventions, trademarks, and designs) and copyrighted materials (literary, musical, photographic, and other artistic works).

intelligence, In education, the ability to learn or understand or to deal with new or challenging situations. In psychology the term may more specifically denote the ability to apply knowledge to manipulate one's environment or to think abstractly as measured by objective criteria (such as the IQ test). Intelligence is usually thought of as deriving from a combination of inherited characteristics and environmental (developmental and social) factors. The subject remains hotly debated, and many have tried to show that either biology (especially genes) or environment (especially conditions reflecting socioeconomic class) are more or less exclusively responsible for producing differences in intelligence. Particularly contested have been studies purporting to show links between ethnic heritage and intelligence, most of which have not been accepted in the scientific community. General intelligence is often said to comprise various specific abilities (verbal ability, ability to apply logic in solving problems, etc.), but critics contend that such compartments fail to reflect the nature of cognition and that other models, perhaps based on information processing, are needed. High intelligence (as measured by tests) is sometimes shown to correlate with social achievement, but most experts believe other factors are important and that intelligence is no guarantor of success (and its lack is no guarantor of failure).

intelligence, In government and military operations, evaluated information concerning the strength, activities, and probable courses of action of international actors that are usually, though not always, enemies or opponents. The term also refers to the collection, analysis, and distribution of such information and to the secret intervention in the political or economic affairs of other countries, an activity commonly known as "covert action." Intelligence is an important component of national power and a fundamental element in decision making regarding national security, defense, and foreign policies. It is conducted on three levels: strategic, tactical, and counterintelligence. Despite the public image of intelligence operatives as cloak-and-dagger secret agents, much intelligence work involves an undramatic search of "open" sources, such as radio broadcasts and various publications. Among covert sources of intelligence are imagery intelligence, which includes aerial and space reconnaissance, signals intelligence, which includes electronic eavesdropping and code breaking, and human intelligence, which involves the secret agent working at the classic spy trade. Leading national intelligence organizations are the Central Intelligence Agency (CIA) in the U.S.; the Federal Security Service in Russia; MI5 and MI6 in Britain; and the Mossad in Israel.

intentionality, Property of being directed toward an object. Intentionality is exhibited in various mental phenomena. Thus, if a person experiences an emotion toward an object, he has an intentional attitude toward it. Other examples of intentional attitudes toward an object are, looking for, believing in, and thinking about. Intentional attitudes also include propositional attitudes. One characteristic of intentionality is "inexistence": A person may be intentionally related to an object that does not exist. Thus, what a person looks for (and intentionally seeks) may not exist, and an event he believes to occur may not occur at all. Another characteristic is referential opacity: A sentence truly ascribing an intentional state to a person may become false when some alternative description of the object of that state is substituted for it. Suppose that his pen is the millionth pen produced this year, so that "his pen" and "the millionth pen produced this year" have the same reference. It may be true to say that he is in the intentional state of searching for his pen but false to say that he is in the intentional state of searching for the millionth pen produced this year; similarly, he may believe that this is his pen and yet not believe this is the millionth pen produced this year.

interactionism, In philosophy of mind, a species of mind-body dualism that holds that mind and body, though separate and distinct substances, causally interact. Interactionists assert that a mental event (as when a person forms the intention to put his hand in a fire) can be the cause of a physical action. Conversely, the physical event (his hand coming into contact with the fire) can be the cause of a mental event (his feeling an intense pain). The classical formulation of interactionism is due to René Descartes, who could not satisfactorily explain how the interaction takes place, apart from the speculation that it occurs in the pineal gland. This problem led some philosophers to deny that mind and body really interact and to explain appearances to the contrary by appealing to divine intervention to create mental or physical effects for physical or mental causes or to a divinely ordained "preestablished harmony" between the courses of mental and physical events. Benedict de Spinoza argued for a monistic theory on which mind and body were both attributes of a single underlying substance.

interchangeable parts, Identical components that can substitute one for another, particularly important in manufacturing. Mass production, which transformed the organization of work, came about by the development of the machine-tool industry by a series of 19th-century innovators. With precision equipment, large numbers of identical parts could be produced at low cost and with a small workforce.

interference, In physics, the net effect of combining two or more wave trains moving on intersecting or coincident paths. Constructive interference occurs if two components have the same frequency and phase; the wave amplitudes are reinforced. Destructive interference occurs when the two waves are out of phase by one-half period; if the waves are of equal amplitude, they cancel each other. Two waves moving in the same direction but having slightly different frequencies interfere constructively at regular intervals, resulting in a pulsating frequency called a beat. Two

waves traveling in opposite directions but having equal frequencies interfere constructively in some places and destructively in others, resulting in a standing wave.

interferon, Any of several related proteins produced by all vertebrates and possibly some invertebrates. They play an important role in resistance to infection. The body's most rapidly produced and important defense against viruses, they can also combat bacteria and parasites, inhibit cell division, and promote or impede cell differentiation. Interferon's effect is indirect—it reacts with susceptible cells, which then resist virus multiplication—in contrast to antibodies, which act by combining directly with a specific virus. Various types of interferons are distinguished by their characteristics as proteins and by which cells produce them. Some are now produced by genetic engineering. Initial hopes that interferon would be a wonder drug for a wide variety of diseases were deflated by its serious side effects, but a few rare conditions respond to it.

interior design, Design of interior spaces, closely related to architecture and sometimes including interior decoration. The designer's goal is to produce a coordinated and harmonious whole in which the architecture, site, function, and visual aspects of the interior are unified, pleasing to mind and body, and appropriate to the activities to be pursued there. Design criteria include harmony of colour, texture, lighting, scale, and proportion. Furnishings must be in proportion to the space they occupy and to the needs and lifestyles of the residents. The design of such nonresidential spaces as offices, hospitals, stores, and schools places clear organization of functions ahead of purely aesthetic concerns.

interleukin, Any of a class of naturally occurring proteins important in regulation of lymphocyte function. Several known types are recognized as crucial constituents of the body's immune system. Antigens and microbes stimulate production of interleukins, which induce production of various types of lymphocytes in a complex series of reactions that ensure a plentiful supply of T cells that fight specific infectious agents.

internal-combustion engine, Any engine in which a fuel-air mixture is burned in the engine proper so that the hot gaseous products of combustion act directly on the surfaces of its moving parts, such as those of pistons or turbine rotor blades. Internal-combustion engines include gasoline engines, diesel engines, gas turbine engines, pure jet engines, and rocket engines and motors, and are one class of heat engines. They are commonly divided into continuous-combustion engines and intermittent-combustion engines. In the first type (e.g., jet engines) fuel and air flow steadily into the engine, where a stable flame is maintained for continuous combustion. In the second (e.g., gasoline–reciprocating-piston engines), discrete quantities of fuel and air are periodically ignited.

International Atomic Energy Agency (IAEA), International organization officially founded in 1957 to promote the peaceful use of nuclear energy. Based in Vienna, its activities include research on the applicability of nuclear energy to medicine, agriculture, water resources, and industry; provision of technical assistance; development of radiation safeguards; and public relations programs. Following the Persian Gulf War, IAEA inspectors were called on to certify that Iraq was not manufacturing nuclear weapons. The IAEA and its director general, Mohamed ElBaradei, were awarded the Nobel Prize for Peace in 2005.

International Brigades, Groups of foreign volunteers who fought on the Republican side against the Nationalist forces in the Spanish Civil War (1936–39). So-called because their members initially came from some 50 countries, the International Brigades were recruited, organized, and directed by the Comintern, with headquarters in Paris. The U.S. contingent called itself the Abraham Lincoln Batallion. Many of the mostly young recruits were communists before they became involved in the conflict; more

"The Internationals—United with the Spaniards We Fight the Invader," poster by Parrilla, published by the International Brigades, 1936–37.
Courtesy of the Abraham Lincoln Brigade Archives, Brandeis University Library

joined the party during the course of the war. The total number of volunteers reached about 60,000. The brigades were formally withdrawn from Spain late in 1938.

International Court of Justice (ICJ), or WORLD COURT, Principal judicial body of the United Nations, located at The Hague. Its predecessor organization was the Permanent Court of International Justice, the judicial body of the League of Nations. Its first session was held in 1946. Its jurisdiction is limited to disputes between states willing to accept its authority on matters of international law. Its decisions are binding, but it has no enforcement power; appeals must be made to the UN Security Council. Its 15-member body of judges, each of whom serves a nine-year term, is elected by countries party to the court's founding statute. No two judges may come from the same country.

International Criminal Court (ICC), Permanent judicial body established by the Rome Statute of the International Criminal Court (1998) to prosecute individuals accused of genocide, war crimes, and crimes against humanity. The court commenced operations on July 1, 2002, after the requisite number of countries (60) ratified the Rome Statute (some 140 countries signed the agreement). The ICC was established as a court of last resort to prosecute the most heinous offenses in cases where national courts fail to act. It is headquartered in The Hague. By 2002 China, Russia, and the U.S. had declined to participate in the ICC, and the U.S. had campaigned actively to have its citizens exempted from the court's jurisdiction.

International Date Line, Imaginary line from the North Pole to the South Pole that arbitrarily separates each calendar day from the next. It corresponds along most of its length to the 180th meridian of longitude but deviates to the east through the Bering Strait to avoid dividing Siberia and then deviates to the west to include the Aleutian Islands with Alaska. South of the Equator, another eastward deviation allows certain island groups to have the same day as New Zealand. The date line is a consequence of the worldwide use of timekeeping systems arranged so that local noon corresponds approximately to the time at which the Sun crosses the local meridian of longitude.

international law, Body of legal rules, norms, and standards that apply between sovereign states and other entities that are legally recognized as international actors. The term was coined by the English philosopher Jeremy Bentham. Important elements of international law include sovereignty, recognition (which allows a country to honour the claims of another), consent (which allows for modifications in international agreements to fit the customs of a country), freedom of the high seas, self-defense (which ensures that measures may be taken against illegal acts committed against a sovereign country), freedom of commerce, and protection of nationals abroad. International courts, such as the International Court of Justice, resolve disputes on these and other matters, including war crimes.

International Monetary Fund (IMF), Specialized agency of the United Nations system. It was conceived at the Bretton Woods Conference (1944) and officially founded in 1945 as a voluntary cooperative institution to help ensure the smooth international buying and selling of currency. More than 180 countries are members of the IMF. Its principal functions are stabilizing currency-exchange rates, financing the short-term balance-of-payments deficits of member countries, and providing advice and technical assistance to borrowing countries. Members contribute operating funds and receive voting rights according to their volume of international trade, national income, and international reserve holdings; the U.S. holds in excess of one-sixth of the voting rights, more than twice the percentage of any other member. The IMF has no coercive power over members, but it can refuse to lend money to members that do not agree to adhere to its policies; as a last resort it can ask members to withdraw from the organization. Critics of the IMF contend that the austerity and privatization measures it requires of borrowing countries reduce economic growth, deepen and prolong financial crises, and create severe hardships for the world's poorest people.

international organization, Institution drawing membership from at least three states, having activities in several states, and whose members are held together by a formal agreement. Only a few existed before 1850; several thousand were active in the early 21st century. Some are intergovernmental (e.g., the United Nations), and some are nongovernmental (e.g., Amnesty International). Some have multiple worldwide or regional purposes (e.g., the European Union), and some have single purposes (e.g., the World Intellectual Property Organization). One effect of their proliferation is a stronger sense of interdependence among states, which in turn has stimulated recognition of the need for cooperation to address international and global problems.

International Phonetic Alphabet (IPA), Set of symbols intended as a universal system for transcribing speech sounds. The promulgation and updating of the IPA has been a principal aim of the International Phonetic Association (Association Phonétique Internationale), founded in Paris in 1886. The first IPA chart was published in 1888. IPA symbols are based on an extended version of the Latin alphabet, with modifications of some letters and the use of additional symbols, some of which had been used in earlier phonetic alphabets. Diacritics are used primarily to show various kinds of secondary articulation.

international relations, Study of the relations of states with each other and with international organizations and certain subnational entities (e.g., bureaucracies and political parties). It is related to a number of other academic disciplines, including political science, geography, history, economics, law, sociology, psychology, and philosophy. The field emerged at the beginning of the 20th century largely in the West and particularly in the U.S. as that country grew in power and influence. The study of international relations has always been heavily influenced by normative considerations, such as the goal of reducing armed conflict and increasing international cooperation. At the beginning of the 21st century, research focused on issues such as terrorism, religious and ethnic conflict, the emergence of substate and nonstate entities, the spread of weapons of mass destruction and efforts to counter nuclear proliferation, and the development of international institutions.

International Space Station (ISS), Space station assembled from modules in Earth orbit largely by the U.S. and Russia, with assistance and components from a multinational consortium. The project, which began as a U.S. effort, was long delayed by funding and technical problems. Originally called Freedom in the 1980s, it was redesigned in the 1990s to reduce costs and expand international involvement, at which time it was renamed. In-orbit construction started in late 1998 with the launches of a Russian control module and a U.S.-built connecting node, which were linked in orbit by space shuttle astronauts. In mid 2000 a habitat and control-centre module was added, and later in the year the ISS received its first resident crew, comprising two Russians and an American. Other elements were subsequently joined to the station, with the overall plan calling for a complex of laboratories and habitats crossed by a long truss supporting four large solar power arrays. Station construction involved at least 16 countries, including Canada, Japan, Brazil, and 11 members of the European Space Agency. Much of the early work aboard the ISS would focus on long-term life-sciences and material-sciences research in the weightless environment. It was expected to serve as the basis for human operations in Earth orbit for at least the first quarter of the 21st century.

International Style, Architectural style that developed in Europe and the U.S. in the 1920s and '30s and dominated Western architecture in the mid 20th century. The term was first used in 1932 by Henry-Russell Hitchcock and Philip Johnson in their essay "The International Style: Architecture Since 1922." The style's most common characteristics are rectilinear forms, open interior spaces, large expanses of glass, steel, and reinforced-concrete construction, and light, taut plane surfaces devoid of applied ornamentation. Walter Gropius, Ludwig Mies van der Rohe, and Le Corbusier are among the architects most clearly associated with the style.

Savoye House, Poissy, Fr., an International Style residence by Le Corbusier, 1929–30
Pierre Belzeaux—Rapho/Photo Researchers

International System of Units, or SYSTÈME INTERNATIONAL D'UNITÉS, or SI SYSTEM, International decimal system of weights and measures derived from and extending the metric system of units. Adopted by the 11th General Conference on Weights and Measures in 1960, it was developed to eliminate overlapping but different systems of units of measures fostered by rapid advances in science and technology in the 19th–20th centuries. Its fundamental units include the metre (m) for length, the kilogram (kg) for mass, and the second (sec) for time. Derived units include those for force (newton, N), energy (joule, J), and power (watt, W).

international unit, Any of several precision standards used in measuring physical quantities, such as mass, length, and time, and also lighting systems, radiation processes, and pharmacology. The luminous intensity or candlepower of a light is expressed in candelas. The second is based on the frequency of radiation emitted by cesium-133 atoms. In radioactive decay, the international unit is the number of disintegrations per second in a sample. In pharmacology, the international unit is the quantity of a substance (vitamin, hormone, or toxin) that produces a specified effect when tested according to an internationally accepted procedure.

Internet, Publicly accessible computer network connecting many smaller networks from around the world. It grew out of a U.S. Defense Department program called ARPANET (Advanced Research Projects Agency Network), established in 1969 with connections between computers at the University of California at Los Angeles, Stanford Research Institute, the University of California-Santa Barbara, and the University of Utah. ARPANET's purpose was to conduct research into computer networking in order to provide a secure and survivable communications system in case of war. As the network quickly expanded, academics and researchers in other fields began to use it as well. In 1971 the first program for sending e-mail over a distributed network was developed; by 1973, the year international connections to ARPANET were made (from Britain and Norway), e-mail represented most of the traffic on ARPANET. The 1970s also saw the development of mailing lists, newsgroups and bulletin-board systems, and the TCP/IP communications protocols, which were adopted as standard protocols for ARPANET in 1982–83, leading to the widespread use of the term Internet. In 1984 the domain name addressing system was introduced. In 1986 the National Science Foundation established the NSFNET, a distributed network of networks capable of handling far greater traffic, and within a year more than 10,000 hosts were connected to the Internet. In 1988 real-time conversation over the network became possible with the development of Internet Relay Chat protocols. In 1990 ARPANET ceased to exist, leaving behind the NSFNET, and the first commercial dial-up access to the Internet became available. In 1991 the World Wide Web was released to the public (via FTP). The Mosaic browser was released in 1993, and its popularity led to the proliferation of World Wide Web sites and users. In 1995 the NSF-NET reverted to the role of a research network, leaving Internet traffic to be routed through network providers rather than NSF supercomputers. That year the Web became the most popular part of the Internet, surpassing the FTP protocols in traffic volume. By 1997 there were more than 10 million hosts on the Internet and more than 1 million registered domain names. Internet access can now be gained via radio signals, cable-television lines, satellites, and fibre-optic connections, though most traffic still uses a part of the public telecommunications (telephone) network. The Internet is widely regarded as a development of vast significance that will affect nearly every aspect of human culture and commerce in ways still only dimly discernible.

Interpol, officially INTERNATIONAL CRIMINAL POLICE ORGANIZATION, International organization whose purpose is to fight international crime. Interpol promotes the widest possible mutual assistance between the criminal police authorities of affiliated countries and seeks to establish and develop all institutions likely to contribute effectively to the prevention and suppression of ordinary crime. The organization traces its history to 1914, when a congress of international criminal police, attended by delegates from 14 countries, was held in Monaco. Interpol was formally founded in Austria in 1923 with 20 member countries; after World War II its headquarters moved to Paris and, in 1989, to Lyon, France. By the early 21st century, its membership exceeded 180 countries. Interpol pursues criminals who operate in more than one country (e.g., smugglers), those who stay in one country but whose crimes affect other countries (e.g., counterfeiters of foreign currency), and those who commit a crime in one country and flee to another.

interpolation, In mathematics, estimation of a value between two known data points. A simple example is calculating the mean of two population counts made 10 years apart to estimate the population in the fifth year. Estimating outside the data points (e.g., predicting the population five years after the second population count) is called extrapolation. If more than two data points are available, a curve may fit the data better than a line. The simplest curve that fits is a polynomial curve. Exactly one polynomial of any given degree—an interpolating polynomial—passes through any number of data points.

interstellar medium, Content of the region between the stars, including vast, diffuse clouds of gases and minute solid particles. Such tenuous matter in the Milky Way Galaxy accounts for about 5% of its total mass. By no means a complete vacuum, the interstellar medium contains mainly hydrogen gas, with a smaller amount of helium and sizable quantities of dust particles of uncertain composition. Primary cosmic rays also travel through interstellar space, and magnetic fields extend across much of it. Most interstellar matter occurs in cloudlike concentrations, which can condense to form stars. Stars, in turn, continually lose mass through stellar winds. Supernovas and planetary nebulae also feed mass back to the interstellar medium, where it mixes with matter that has not yet formed stars.

interval, In music, the inclusive distance between one tone and another, whether sounded successively (melodic interval) or simultaneously (harmonic interval). In Western music, intervals are generally named according to the number of scale-steps within a given key that they embrace; thus, the ascent from C to G (C–D–E–F–G) is called a fifth because the interval embraces five scale degrees. There are four perfect intervals: prime, or unison; octave; fourth; and fifth. The other intervals (seconds, thirds, sixths, sevenths) have major and minor forms that differ in size by a half step (semitone). Both perfect and major intervals may be augmented, or enlarged by a half tone. Perfect and minor intervals may be diminished, or narrowed by a half tone.

intifāḍah (Arabic: "shaking off"), Palestinian revolt (1987–93, 2000–) against the Israeli occupation in the Gaza Strip and West Bank. Initially a spontaneous reaction to 20 years of occupation and worsening economic conditions, it was soon taken over by the Palestine Liberation Organization (PLO). Its tactics included strikes, boycotts, and confrontations with Israeli troops. The International Red Cross estimated that some 800 Palestinians, more than 200 under the age of 16, had been killed by Israeli security forces by 1990. Several dozen Israelis were killed during the same period. *Intifāḍah* pressure is credited with helping make possible the 1993 Israeli-PLO agreement on Palestinian self-rule. A breakdown in further negotiations in late 2000 led to another outburst of violence, which quickly became known as the Aqṣā *intifāḍah*, named for the Aqṣā Mosque in Jerusalem, where the fighting began.

intonation, In phonetics, the melodic pattern of an utterance. Intonation is primarily a matter of variation in the pitch level of the voice, but in languages such as English, stress and rhythm are also involved. Intonation conveys differences of expressive meaning (e.g., surprise, doubtfulness). In many languages, including English, intonation serves a grammatical function, distinguishing one type of phrase or sentence from another. Thus, "it's gone" is an assertion when spoken with a drop in pitch at the end, but a question when spoken with a rise in pitch at the end.

introvert and extravert, Basic personality types, according to the theories of Carl Gustav Jung. The introvert, who directs thoughts and feelings inward, is often shy, contemplative, and reserved. The extravert, who directs attention toward other people and the outside world, is usually outgoing, responsive, and aggressive. This typology is now regarded as simplistic because almost no one can be described as wholly introverted or extraverted.

intrusive rock, Igneous rock formed from magma forced into older rocks at depths within the Earth's crust, which then slowly solidifies below the Earth's surface, though it may later be exposed by erosion. Igneous intrusions form a variety of rock types.

intuitionism, In metaethics, a form of cognitivism that holds that moral statements can be known to be true or false immediately through a kind of rational intuition. In the 17th and 18th centuries, intuitionism was defended by Ralph Cudworth, Henry More (1614–87), Samuel Clarke (1675–1729), and Richard Price (1723–91); in the 20th century its supporters included H.A. Prichard (1871–1947), G.E. Moore, and David Ross. Intuitionists have differed over the kinds of moral truths that are amenable to direct apprehension. For example, whereas Moore thought that it is self-

evident that certain things are morally valuable, Ross thought that we know immediately that it is our duty to do acts of a certain type.

inventory, In business, any item of property held in stock by a firm, including finished goods held for sale, goods in the process of production, raw materials, and items that will be consumed in the process of producing salable goods. Inventories appear on a company's balance sheet as assets. Inventory turnover, which indicates the rate at which goods are converted into cash, is a key factor in appraising a firm's financial condition. For financial statements, inventories may be priced either at cost or at market value.

Inverness, Royal burgh (pop., 2001: 44,084), Highland council area, in the historic county of Inverness-shire, northwestern Scotland. Located on the River Ness and the Caledonian Canal, it has long been the centre of the Scottish Highlands. In the 6th century it was the capital of the Pictish king Brude. By the 12th century it had become a burgh near the castle of Malcolm III Canmore. Inverness is now an educational and tourist centre. Its manufacturing has expanded in conjunction with the growth of offshore oil production.

The 19th-century castle on the River Ness, Inverness, Scotland.
J. Allan Cash Photolibrary/EB Inc.

invertebrate, Any animal that lacks a vertebral column, or backbone. They include the protozoans, annelids, cnidarians, echinoderms, flatworms, nematodes, mollusks, and arthropods. More than 90% of living animals are invertebrates. Worldwide in distribution, they range in size from minute protozoans to giant squids. Apart from the absence of a vertebral column, invertebrates have little in common. They are generally soft-bodied and have an external skeleton for muscle attachment and protection.

Investiture Controversy, Struggle between the papacy and the secular rulers of Europe over the latter's presentation of the symbols of office to churchmen. Pope Gregory VII condemned lay investiture in 1078 as an unjustified assertion of secular authority over the church; the issue was pivotal in his dispute with King Henry IV and in the larger struggle over Henry's refusal to obey papal commands. Henry successfully drove Gregory from Rome and installed an antipope, but it would be Gregory's rejection of lay investiture that would ultimately prevail. Henry I of England renounced lay investiture (1106) in return for the guarantee that homage would be paid to the king before consecration, and the Concordat of Worms (1122) forged a similar compromise between Henry V and Calixtus II.

investment, Process of exchanging income for an asset that is expected to produce earnings at a later time. An investor refrains from consumption in the present in hopes of a greater return in the future. Investment may be influenced by rates of interest, with the rate of investment rising as interest rates fall, but other factors more difficult to measure may also be important—for example, the business community's expectations about future demand and profit, technical changes in production methods, and expected relative costs of labour and capital. Investment cannot occur without saving, which provides funding. Because investment increases an economy's capacity to produce, it is a factor contributing to economic growth.

investment bank, Firm that originates, underwrites, and distributes new security issues of corporations and government agencies. The Banking Act of 1933 required the separation of investment banking and commercial banking functions. Investment banks operate by purchasing all the new securities issued by a corporation at one price and selling fractions of the new issue to the investing public at prices high enough to yield a profit. The investment bank is responsible for setting the public offering price, which it bases on probable demand and assessments of the economic climate. A syndicate of investment banking firms underwrites and distributes most security issues in order to divide the risk of the new issue. An initial public offering (IPO) refers to the issuance of the first public shares of a formerly nonpublic company.

investment casting, Precision casting for forming metal shapes with minutely precise details. Casting bronze or precious metals typically involves several steps, including forming a mold around the sculptured form; detaching the mold (in two or more sections); coating its inside with wax; forming a second mold, of heat-resisting clay, around the wax shell, and filling the interior with a clay core; baking the assembly (hardening the clay and melting the wax, which escapes through openings in the outer mold); pouring molten bronze into the space vacated by the wax; and breaking the mold to expose the cast form. In modern foundries, plastics, or occasionally frozen mercury, are used instead of wax.

iodine, Nonmetallic chemical element, chemical symbol I, atomic number 53. The heaviest nonradioactive halogen, it is a nearly black crystalline solid (diatomic molecule I_2) that sublimes to a deep violet, irritating vapour. It is never found in nature uncombined. Its sources (mostly in brines and seaweeds) and compounds are usually iodides; iodates (small amounts in saltpeter) and periodates also occur. Dietary iodine is essential for thyroid gland function; in areas of the world where food contains insufficient iodine, an iodine compound such as potassium iodide (KI) is added to table salt (sodium chloride) to prevent iodine deficiency. Elemental iodine is used in medicine, in synthesizing some organic chemicals, in manufacturing dyes, in analytical chemistry to measure fat saturation and to detect starch, and in photography. The radioactive isotope iodine-131, with an eight-day half-life, is very useful in medicine and other applications.

ion, Atom or group of atoms with one or more positive or negative electric charges. Positively charged ions are cations, negatively charged ones anions. Ions are formed when electrons are added to or removed from neutral molecules or other ions, as sodium (Na) and chlorine (Cl) atoms react to form Na^+ and Cl^-; when ions combine with other particles, as hydrogen cations (H^+) and ammonia (NH_3) combine to form ammonium cations (NH_4^+); or when a covalent bond between two atoms is ruptured in such a way that the resulting particles are charged, as water (H_2O) dissociates into hydrogen and hydroxide ions (H^+ and OH^-). Many crystalline substances are composed of ions held in regular geometric patterns by the attraction of oppositely charged particles for each other. Ions migrate to the electrode of opposite charge in an electric field and are the conductors of current in electrolytic cells. Compounds that form ions are called electrolytes. Ions are also formed in gases when heated to very high temperatures or when an electrical discharge passes through them.

Ionesco, Eugène, orig. EUGEN IONESCU (b. Nov. 26, 1909, Slatina, Rom.—d. March 28, 1994, Paris, France), Romanian-born French playwright. He studied in Bucharest and Paris, where he lived from 1945. His first one-act "antiplay," *The Bald Soprano* (1950), inspired a revolution in dramatic techniques and helped inaugurate the Theatre of the Absurd. He followed it with other one-act plays in which illogical events create an atmosphere both comic and grotesque, including *The Lesson* (1951), *The Chairs* (1952), and *The New Tenant* (1955). His most popular full-length play, *Rhinoceros* (1959), concerns a provincial French town in which all the citizens are metamorphosing into rhinoceroses. Other plays include *Exit the King* (1962) and *A Stroll in the Air* (1963). He was elected to the Académie Française in 1970.

Eugène Ionesco, 1959.
Mark Gerson

Ionia, Ancient region, western coast of Asia Minor (modern Turkey) bordering the Aegean Sea. It consisted of a coastal strip that extended from the mouth of the Hermus River to the Halicarnassus Peninsula, a distance of 100 mi (160 km). In the 8th century BC there were 12 major Greek cities in the region, including Phocaea, Erythrae, Colophon, and Miletus on the mainland, and the islands Chios and Samos. It was very prosperous, and until 500 BC Ionic philosophy and architecture and the Ionic dialect were highly influential in Greece. In the mid-6th century BC it fell to Lydia and then to the Persians. After a brief period of independence beginning in 334 BC, it became part of the Seleucid kingdom. In 133 BC it passed to the Romans and became part of the Roman province of Asia. It was devastated during the Turkish conquest of Asia Minor.

Ionian, Any ancient Greek inhabitant of Ionia, from the time of the collapse of Mycenae. Ionian cities colonized southern Italy and opened up the Black Sea from *c.* 700 BC. Their contributions to Greek culture included the epics of Homer and the earliest elegiac and iambic poetry. They began the study of geography, philosophy, and historiography in the 6th century. After Alexander the Great their literary language was the basis of Koine, or "common speech," the language of practically all Greek writing to the present day.

Ionian Islands, ancient HEPTANESOS, Group of seven Greek islands (pop., 2001: 214,274) in the Ionian Sea. They include Corfu, Cephalonia, Zacynthus, Leucas, Ithaca, Cythera, and Paxos and have a combined land area of 891 sq mi (2,307 sq km). Controlled by Venice in the 15th and 16th centuries, they were taken by Russian and Turkish forces in 1799. In 1815 the Treaty of Paris placed them under the control of Britain; the British ceded them to Greece in 1864.

Ionian Sea, Part of the Mediterranean Sea lying between Greece, Sicily, and Italy. Though once considered part of the Adriatic Sea, to which it connects by the Strait of Otranto, it is now considered a separate body. The Mediterranean reaches its greatest depth (16,000 ft or 4,900 m) in the Ionian south of Greece. Along its eastern shore are the Ionian Islands.

ionic bond, Electrostatic attraction between oppositely charged ions in a chemical compound. Such a bond forms when one or more electrons are transferred from one neutral atom (typically a metal, which becomes a cation) to another (typically a nonmetallic element or group, which becomes an anion). The two types of ion are held together by electrostatic forces in a solid that does not comprise neutral molecules as such; rather, each ion has neighbours of the opposite charge in an ordered overall crystalline structure. When, for example, crystals of common salt (sodium chloride, NaCl) are dissolved in water, they dissociate into two kinds of ions in equal numbers, sodium cations (Na^+) and chloride anions (Cl^-).

ionization, Process by which electrically neutral atoms or molecules are converted to electrically charged atoms or molecules (ions) by the removal or addition of negatively charged electrons. It is one of the principal ways in which radiation transfers energy to matter, and hence of detecting radiation. In general, ionization occurs whenever sufficiently energetic charged particles or radiant energy travels through gases, liquids, or solids. A certain minimal level of ionization is present in the earth's atmosphere because of continuous absorption of cosmic rays from space and ultraviolet radiation from the sun.

ionosphere, Region of the Earth's atmosphere in which the number of ions, or electrically charged particles, is large enough to affect the propagation of radio waves. The ionosphere begins at an altitude of about 30 mi (50 km) but is most distinct above about 50 mi (80 km). The ionization is caused mainly by solar radiation at X-ray and ultraviolet wavelengths. The ionosphere is responsible for the long-distance propagation, by reflection, of radio signals in the shortwave and broadcast bands.

ipecac, or IPECACUANHA, Dried rhizome and roots of either of two tropical New World plants (*Cephaelis acuminata* and *C. ipecacuanha*) of the madder family. It has been used since ancient times especially as a source of a drug to treat poisoning by inducing nausea and vomiting. The name also refers to the drug itself.

IQ, in full INTELLIGENCE QUOTIENT, Number intended to represent a measure of relative intelligence as determined by the subject's responses to a series of test problems. The IQ was originally computed as the ratio of a person's mental age to his or her chronological (physical) age, multiplied by 100, but use of the concept of mental age has been largely discontinued, and IQ is now generally assessed on the basis of the statistical distribution of scores. The most widely used intelligence tests are the Stanford-Binet test (1916), for children, and the Wechsler test (1939), originally for adults but now also for children. A score above 130 is considered to reflect "giftedness," while a score below 70 is considered to reflect mental impairment or intellectual disability. Intelligence tests have provoked great controversy, particularly about what kinds of mental ability constitute intelligence and whether IQ adequately represents these abilities, and about cultural and class bias in test construction and standardization procedures.

Iran, officially ISLAMIC REPUBLIC OF IRAN, formerly PERSIA, Country, Middle East, southwestern Asia. Area: 636,374 sq mi (1,648,200 sq km). Population: (2011 est.) 75,276,000. Capital: Tehrān. Persians constitute the largest ethnic group; other ethnic groups include Azerbaijanians, Kurds, Lurs, Bakhtyārī, and Baloch. Languages: Persian (Farsī; official), numerous others. Religions: Islam (official; predominantly Shīʿite); also Zoroastrianism. Currency: rial. Iran occupies a high plateau, rising higher than 1,500 feet (460 metres) above sea level, and is surrounded largely by mountains. More than half of its surface area consists of salt deserts and other wasteland. About one-tenth of its land is arable, and another one-fourth is suitable for grazing. Iran's rich petroleum reserves account for about one-tenth of world reserves and are the basis of its economy. It is a unitary Islamic republic with one legislative house and several oversight bodies dominated by clergy. The head of state and government is the president, but supreme authority rests with the *rahbar* (leader), a ranking cleric. Human habitation in Iran dates to some 100,000 years ago, but recorded history began with the Elamites *c.* 3000 BCE. The Medes flourished from *c.* 728 but were overthrown in 550 by the Persians, who were in turn conquered by Alexander the Great in the 4th century BCE. The Parthians created an empire that lasted from 247 BCE to 226 CE, when control passed to the Sāsānian dynasty. Various Muslim dynasties ruled from the 7th century. In 1501 the Ṣafavid dynasty was established and lasted until 1736. The Qājār dynasty ruled from 1796, but in the 19th century the country was economically controlled by the Russian and British empires. Reza Khan seized power in a coup (1921). His son Mohammad Reza Shah Pahlavi alienated religious leaders with a program of modernization and Westernization and was overthrown in 1979; Shīʿite cleric Ruhollah Khomeini then set up an Islamic republic, and Western influence was suppressed. The destructive Iran-Iraq War of the 1980s ended in a stalemate. Since the 1990s the government has gradually moved to a more liberal conduct of state affairs.

Iran-Iraq War (1980–88) Protracted and indecisive conflict prompted by Iraq's invasion of its eastern neighbour. Following the 1979 Iranian Revolution, the Iraqi leadership sought to exploit Iran's military and political chaos in order to resolve border disputes, gain control of Iran's oil-rich western (largely Arab) province, and achieve hegemony in the Persian Gulf. Iraq was successful early (1980–82) but began to lose ground and sought to negotiate peace. Iran refused, and the war turned into a bloody stalemate that included the first use of chemical warfare since World War I (1914–18). After additional Iraqi advances, Iran agreed to a cease-fire in 1988. However, the resumption of normal diplomatic relations and the withdrawal of troops did not take place until the signing of a formal peace agreement on Aug. 16, 1990.

Iranian languages, Major subgroup of the Indo-Iranian branch of the Indo-European language family. Iranian languages are probably spoken by more than 80 million people in southwestern and southern Asia. Only two Old Iranian languages are known, Avestan and Old Persian. A greater number of Middle Iranian languages (*c.* 300 BC–AD 950) are known; these are divided into a western and an eastern group. Modern Iranian languages fall into four groups. The southwestern group includes Modern Persian (Farsi), Dari (in northern Afghanistan), Tajiki (in Tajikistan and other Central Asian republics); Luri and Bakhtiari (in southwestern Iran); and Tat. The northwestern group includes Kurdish (spoken in Kurdistan) and Baluchi (in southwestern Pakistan, southeastern Iran, and southern Afghanistan). The southeastern group includes Pashto (in Afghanistan and northwestern Pakistan) and the 10 or so Pamir languages (in eastern Tajikistan and adjacent parts of Afghanistan and China). The northeastern group includes Ossetic, spoken by the Ossetes in the central Caucasus Mountains, and Yaghnobi, formerly spoken in a single valley of the Pamirs. Nearly all the Modern Iranian languages have been written—if at all—in adaptations of the Arabic alphabet.

Iranian religions, Ancient religions of the peoples of the Iranian plateau. The Medes and Persians were dominated by a powerful priestly tribe, the magi. The magi were responsible for chanting accounts of the origin and descent of the gods, and they were probably the source of the dualism that later characterized Zoroastrianism, the best known of the Iranian religions. The chief god of the pre-Zoroastrian pantheon was Ahura Mazda, the creator of the universe and the one who maintains the cosmic and social order. Mithra was the second most important deity and the protector of covenants. Other major deities included Anahita, the war goddess; Rashnu, the god of justice; and astral deities such as Tishtrya, identified with the star Sirius. The ancient Iranians did not build temples or make images of their gods, preferring to worship in the open. The central ritual was the *yazna*, which consisted of a festive meal at which the worshipers made animal sacrifices and invited the deity to attend as a guest. Fire was regarded as a sacred element. The sacred drink *hauma*, which contained a mind-altering drug, was used to inspire worshipers with insight into truth and to stimulate warriors going into battle.

Iraq, officially REPUBLIC OF IRAQ. Country, Middle East, southwestern Asia, northwest of the Persian Gulf. Area: 167,618 sq mi (434,128 sq km). Population: (2011 est.) 32,665,000. Capital: Baghdad. The population consists mainly of an Arab majority and a Kurdish minority. Languages: Arabic, Kurdish (both official). Religions: Islam (official; mostly Shīʿite); also Christianity. Currency: dinar. The country can be divided into four major regions: the Tigris-Euphrates alluvial plains in central and southeastern Iraq; Al-Jazīrah, an upland region in the north between the Tigris and Euphrates rivers; deserts in the west and south, covering about two-fifths of the country; and highlands in the northeast. Iraq has the world's second largest proven reserves of petroleum, and it has substantial reserves of natural gas. Agriculture is also a major component of the economy. Iraq is a multiparty republic with one legislative house; its head of state is the president, and its head of government is the prime minister. Called Mesopotamia in Classical times, the region gave rise to the world's earliest civilizations, including those of Sumer, Akkad, and Babylon. Conquered by Alexander the Great in 331 BCE, the area later became a battleground between Romans and Parthians, then between Sāsānians and Byzantines. Arab Muslims conquered it in the 7th century CE, and various Muslim dynasties ruled until the Mongols took over in 1258. The Ottoman Empire took control in the 16th century and ruled until the British occupied the country during World War I (1914–18). The British created the kingdom of Iraq in 1921 and occupied Iraq again during World War II (1939–45). The monarchy was restored following the war, but a revolution caused its downfall in 1958. Following a series of military coups, the socialist Baʿth Party, eventually led by Ṣaddām Ḥussein, took control and established totalitarian rule in 1968. The Iran-Iraq War in the 1980s and the Persian Gulf War in 1990–91 caused extensive death and destruction. The economy languished under a UN economic embargo imposed on Iraq in the 1990s. The embargo began to erode by the early 21st century, and in 2003, during the Iraq War, the Baʿth Party was driven from power.

Iraq War, or SECOND PERSIAN GULF WAR (2003–11) War in Iraq that consisted of two phases: a brief conflict in 2003 between Iraq and a combined force of troops largely from the U.S. and Great Britain; and a subsequent U.S.-led occupation of Iraq and protracted Iraqi armed insurgency against it. The trade embargo and weapons-inspection process that the UN imposed on Iraq following the Persian Gulf War (1990–91) had partly fallen into abeyance by 2001. U.S. Pres. George W. Bush argued that the September 11 attacks on the U.S. in that same year highlighted the threat to U.S. security posed by hostile countries such as Iraq. In November 2002 the UN issued Security Council Resolution 1441 demanding that Iraq readmit weapons inspectors and comply with all previous resolutions. Although inspectors did return to Iraq, Bush and Blair declared in early 2003 (despite objections by many world leaders) that Iraq was continuing to hinder UN inspections and that it still retained proscribed weapons. On March 20 the U.S. and Britain (with smaller troop contingents from other countries) launched a series of air attacks on Iraq, and a ground invasion followed. Iraqi forces were rapidly defeated, and on April 9 U.S. forces took control of the capital, Baghdad. British forces completed their occupation of the southern city of Al-Baṣrah the same day, and by May 1 the major combat operations of the invasion had been completed. However, the U.S. and other occupying forces were soon embroiled in escalating guerrilla warfare in Iraq that hindered Iraq's recovery and killed thousands of soldiers and tens of thousands of civilians. The war, long opposed by many throughout the world, also became increasingly unpopular in the U.S. Sectarian fighting and insurgent attacks on U.S. and Iraqi forces peaked in 2006 and 2007. In early 2007 the U.S. implemented a strategy that came to be known as the "surge"—temporarily increasing the number of troops in Iraq by more than 20,000 in a bid to stabilize the country. By the end of the year, violence had decreased substantially, although the role of the surge in im-

proving security remained a source of debate. In 2008 the U.S. began to gradually reduce the number of its troops in Iraq, completing its withdrawal in December 2011.

Ireland, Country, western Europe, occupying the greater part of the island of Ireland west of Great Britain. Area: 27,133 sq mi (70,273 sq km). Population: (2011 est.) 4,606,000. Capital: Dublin. Although Ireland has been invaded and colonized by Celts, Norsemen, Normans, English, and Scots, ethnic distinctions are nonexistent. Languages: Irish, English (both official). Religion: Christianity (predominantly Roman Catholic; also Protestant). Currency: euro. Ireland's topography consists largely of broad lowlands drained by rivers that include the Shannon; its coasts are fringed with mountains. About three-fifths of the population is urban; agriculture employs only a small percentage of the workforce. High technology, tourism, and other service industries are pivotal to the Irish economy, while mining, manufacturing, and construction also remain important. Ireland is a unitary multiparty republic with two legislative houses; its head of state is the president, and the head of government is the prime minister. Human settlement in Ireland began *c.* 6000 BC, and Celtic migration dates from *c.* 300 BC. St. Patrick is credited with having Christianized the country in the 5th century. Norse domination began in 795 and ended in 1014, when the Norse were defeated by Brian Boru. Gaelic Ireland's independence ended in 1175 when Roderic O'Connor, Ireland's high king, accepted English King Henry II as his overlord. Beginning in the 16th century, Irish Catholic landowners fled religious persecution by the English and were replaced by English and Scottish Protestant migrants. The United Kingdom of Great Britain and Ireland was established in 1801. The Irish Potato Famine of the 1840s led as many as two million people to emigrate, and about one million people died from starvation or from typhus or other famine-related diseases. The British government's grudging and ineffective relief measures built momentum for Irish Home Rule. The Easter Rising (1916) was followed by the Anglo-Irish War (1919–21), during which the Irish Republican Army used guerrilla tactics to force the British government to negotiate. The signing of the Anglo-Irish Treaty on Dec. 6, 1921, when ratified by the Dáil the following month, granted southern Ireland dominion status as the Irish Free State. Internecine struggle between supporters and opponents of the treaty culminated in the Irish Civil War (1922–23). In 1937 the Free State adopted the name Éire (Ireland) and became a sovereign independent country. It remained neutral during World War II. In 1948 the Dáil passed the Republic of Ireland Act, which took effect in April 1949, declaring Ireland a republic and removing it from the British Commonwealth of Nations. Britain recognized the new status of Ireland but declared that unity with the six counties of Northern Ireland could not occur without consent of the parliament of Northern Ireland. In 1973 Ireland joined the European Economic Community (later the European Community); it is now a member of the European Union. In the last decades of the 20th century, the issue of the political status of Northern Ireland prompted hostilities between Catholics and Protestants in the north and deep concern in the south, where there were a number of serious terrorist incidents. The Irish government played a pivotal role in negotiating and winning public support in 1998 for the Good Friday Agreement (Belfast Agreement), under which Ireland agreed to remove from its constitution its claim to the territory of the entire island (enacted in 1999). Ireland continued to play an important consultative role in Northern Ireland, such as helping to negotiate an agreement between the Democratic Union Party and Sinn Féin coalition government in 2010, under which policing and justice powers were to be devolved to Northern Ireland's government

iridium, Metallic chemical element, one of the transition elements, chemical symbol Ir, atomic number 77. A very rare, precious, silvery white, hard, brittle metal that resists most acids, it is one of the densest substances known on Earth. It probably does not occur uncombined in nature but is found in natural alloys with other noble (i.e., chemically inactive or inert) metals. The pure metal is too hard to work with to have any significant uses; alloys with platinum are used in jewelry, pen points, surgical pins and pivots, electrical contacts and sparking points, and extrusion dies. The international prototype kilogram, the primary standard for weight, is made of an alloy comprising 90% platinum and 10% iridium. The discovery of abnormally high amounts of iridium in rocks dating to the boundary between the Cretaceous and Paleogene periods led to a much-debated hypothesis that an iridium-containing asteroid striking Earth led to a catastrophic chain of events including the extinction of dinosaurs and many other forms of life.

iris family, Family Iridaceae, composed of about 1,700 species of perennial herbaceous plants, as well as a few shrubs, in some 80 genera. It is known for ornamentals such as irises (genus *Iris*), gladioli, crocuses, and freesias. Irises have swordlike, smooth leaves and bear showy flowers in a great variety of colours and sizes on a smooth stem. Most abundant and diverse in Africa, they are found nearly worldwide across temperate, subtropical, and tropical zones. The underground stems may be rhizomes (e.g., New World *Iris* species), bulbs (e.g., southwestern European *Iris* species), or corms (e.g., *Gladiolus*).

Irish Potato Famine (1845–49) Famine that occurred in Ireland when the potato crop failed in successive years. By the early 1840s almost half the Irish population, particularly the rural poor, was depending almost entirely on the potato for nourishment. Reliance on only one or two high-yielding varieties made the crop vulnerable to disease, including late blight, caused by the water mold *Phytophthora infestans*, which ruined the crop. The British government provided minimal relief to the starving Irish, limited to loans and soup kitchens. The famine was a watershed in Ireland's demographic history: about one million people died from starvation or famine-related diseases, and perhaps as many as two million emigrated. Population continued to decline thereafter, and by independence in 1921 the Irish population was barely half of the 8.4 million it had been before the famine.

Irish Republican Army (IRA), Republican paramilitary organization, founded in 1919, seeking the establishment of a republic, the end of British rule in Northern Ireland, and the reunification of Ireland. The IRA used armed force to achieve the same objectives as Sinn Féin, though the two operated independently. After the establishment of the Irish Free State (1922) as a dominion in the British Commonwealth, the IRA refused to accept its legitimacy, and violence continued despite the IRA cease-fire that ended the civil war of 1922–23. The IRA was declared illegal in 1931, and the Irish legislature provided for internment without trial for its members. After the declaration of the Republic of Ireland and its departure from the Commonwealth in 1949, IRA activity focused on Northern Ireland. It gained popular support there in the 1960s, when Roman Catholics in Northern Ireland began a civil rights campaign against discrimination by the dominant Protestant majority. In 1969 the IRA split into the Marxist Official wing, which eschewed violence, and the Provisionals (Provos), who used terror tactics against Ulster Protestants and the British military—tactics that included the 1979 assassination of Lord Mountbatten and the killing of some 1,800 people by the early 1990s. In 1994 the IRA declared a cease-fire, and its political representatives were included in multiparty talks beginning in 1997. Negotiations produced the 1998 Good Friday Agreement (Belfast Agreement), in which the IRA agreed to decommission (disarm). In the ensuing years the IRA destroyed some of its weapons but resisted decommissioning its entire armoury, hampering implementation of the peace agreement. In July 2005, however, the IRA announced that it was ending its armed campaign and instead would pursue only peaceful means to achieve its objectives.

Irish Sea, Arm of the North Atlantic Ocean that separates Ireland from Great Britain. Connected with the Atlantic by North Channel and by St. George's Channel, it is about 130 mi (210 km) long and 150 mi (240 km) wide. Its total area is about 40,000 sq mi (100,000 sq km). Its greatest depth measures about 576 ft (175 m). The Isle of Man and Anglesey are its two principal islands.

Irkutsk, City (pop., 2006 est.: 578,073), east-central Russia. Located on the Angara River, it was founded as a wintering camp in 1652. It soon became a commercial centre for the fur trade and a base on the Russian trade route to China and Mongolia. Its importance grew after the opening of the Trans-Siberian Railroad in 1898. An industrial and cultural centre, it is the seat of Irkutsk State University and the Siberian branch of the Academy of Sciences.

iron, Metallic chemical element, one of the transition elements, chemical symbol Fe, atomic number 26. Iron is the most used and cheapest metal, the second most abundant metal and fourth most abundant element in Earth's crust. It occurs rarely as a free metal, occasionally in natural alloys (especially in meteorites), and in hundreds of minerals and ores, including hematite, magnetite, limonite, and siderite. The human body contains about one-sixth of an ounce (4.5 g) of iron, mostly in hemoglobin and its precursors; iron in the diet is essential to health. Iron is ferromagnetic at ordinary temperatures and is the only metal that can be tempered. Its uses in steels of various types, as well as in cast and wrought iron (collectively, "ferrous metals"), are numerous. Alteration of its properties by impurities, especially carbon, is the basis of steelmaking. Iron in compounds usually has valence 2 (ferrous) or 3 (ferric). Ferrous and ferric oxides (FeO and Fe_2O_3, respectively) are used as pigments and the latter as jewelers' rouge. Rust is ferric oxide containing water; ferric oxide is widely used as a magnetic recording material in computer data-storage devices and magnetic tapes. Ferrous and ferric sulfates and chlorides are all of industrial importance as mordants, reducing agents, flocculating agents, or raw materials and in inks and fertilizers.

Iron Age, Final technological and cultural stage in the Stone–Bronze–Iron-Age sequence (or Three-Age System) in which iron largely replaced bronze in implements and weapons. The start of the Iron Age varied geographically, beginning in the Middle East and southeastern Europe *c.* 1200 BC but in China not until *c.* 600 BC. Though the large-scale production of iron implements brought new patterns of more permanent settlement, use of iron for weapons put arms in the hands of the masses for the first time and set off a series of large-scale movements and conquests that did not end for 2,000 years and that changed the face of Europe and Asia.

Iron Curtain, Political, military, and ideological barrier erected by the Soviet Union after World War II to seal off itself and its dependent eastern European allies from open contact with the West and other noncommunist areas. Winston Churchill employed the term in a speech in Fulton, Mo., U.S., about the division of Europe in 1946. The restrictions and the rigidity of the Iron Curtain eased slightly after Joseph Stalin's death in 1953, though the construction of the Berlin Wall in 1961 restored them. The Iron Curtain largely ceased to exist in 1989–90 with the communists' abandonment of one-party rule in eastern Europe.

iron-deficiency anemia, Most common type of anemia, which may develop in times of high iron loss and depletion of iron stores (e.g., rapid growth, pregnancy, menstruation) or in settings of low dietary iron intake or inefficient iron uptake (e.g., starvation, intestinal parasites, gastrectomy). Much of the world's population is iron-deficient to some degree. Symptoms include low energy level and sometimes paleness, shortness of breath, cold extremities, sore tongue, or dry skin. In advanced cases, red blood cells are small, pale, and low in hemoglobin, blood iron levels are reduced, and body iron stores are depleted. Treatment with iron usually brings quick improvement.

ironclad, Type of warship developed in Europe and the U.S. in the mid-19th century, characterized by the iron armour that protected the hull. In the Crimean War (1853–56) the French and British successfully attacked Russian fortifications with "floating batteries," ironclad barges mounting heavy guns. In 1859 the French completed the first iron warship, the *Gloire*; its iron plates, 4.5 in. (11 cm) thick, were backed by heavy timber. Britain and the U.S. soon followed. Union forces launched armored gunboats on the Mississippi at the start of the American Civil War, and a flotilla captured Fort Henry (1862). The first battle between ironclads was the Battle of the *Monitor* and *Merrimack* (1862). Later refinements led to the battleship.

French ironclad Gloire, *engraving by Smythe after a painting by A.W. Weedon*
Courtesy of the trustees of the British Museum; photograph, J.R. Freeman & Co. Ltd.

irony, Language device in which the real intent is concealed or contradicted by the literal meaning of words or a situation. Verbal irony, either spoken or written, arises from an awareness of contrast between what is and what ought to be. Dramatic irony, an incongruity in a theatrical work between what is expected and what occurs, depends on the structure of a play rather than its use of words, and it is often created by the audience's awareness of a fate in store for the characters that they themselves do not suspect.

Irrawaddy River, River, Myanmar (Burma). It flows 1,350 mi (2,170 km) across the centre of the country and empties into the Andaman Sea. The country's most important commercial waterway, it is formed by the confluence of the Nmai and the Mali rivers, and in the central dry zone it is joined by its major tributary, the Chindwin River. Chief ports are Mandalay, Chauk, Prome (Pyay), and Henzada.

irrigation, Artificial supply of water to land, to maintain or increase yields of food crops, a critical element of modern agriculture. Irrigation can compensate for the naturally variable rate and volume of rain. Water is pumped from natural ponds, lakes, streams, and wells; basin systems and dams hold back larger streams and annual floods. Below the dam, gates to concrete-lined canals are opened, conveying the water over the land through gravity flow. More elaborate, expensive canals flow from huge constructed reservoirs, which hold a year-round water supply. Today portable irrigation systems of lightweight aluminum pipe are in wide use. Drip irrigation, a newer method, uses narrow tubing to supply water directly to the base of each plant. Agricultural irrigation, water towers, and machines invented to lift and distribute water are ancient innovations. Early Egyptians were irrigating with Nile River water by 5000 BC, and such other ancient civilizations as Babylon and China seem to have developed largely as a result of irrigation-based agriculture.

irritable bowel syndrome, or IBS, Chronic disorder characterized by abdominal pain, intestinal gas, and diarrhea, constipation, or both. Other symptoms may include abdominal pain that is re-

lieved after defecation or a sensation of incomplete rectal evacuation. IBS is caused by a motility disturbance of the intestines that may result from increased intestinal sensitivity to distension. Stress or the consumption of fatty foods, milk products, certain fruits or vegetables (e.g., broccoli and cabbage), alcohol, or caffeine may cause similar symptoms. Treatment includes relaxation, exercise, and avoidance of aggravating foods. Antidiarrheal medications or fibre supplements may help lessen symptoms. Although IBS may cause discomfort and emotional distress, the disorder does not result in any permanent intestinal damage.

Irving, Washington (b. April 3, 1783, New York, N.Y., U.S.—d. Nov. 28, 1859, Tarrytown, N.Y.), U.S. author, called the "first American man of letters." He began his career as a lawyer but soon became a leader of the group that published *Salmagundi* (1807–08), a periodical containing whimsical essays and poems. After his comic satire *A History of New York...by Diedrich Knickerbocker* (1809), he wrote little until his very successful *The Sketch Book* (1819–20), containing his best-known stories, "The Legend of Sleepy Hollow" and "Rip Van Winkle." It was followed by a sequel, *Bracebridge Hall* (1822). He held diplomatic positions in Madrid, Spain, and writings such as *The Alhambra* (1832) reflect his interest in Spain's past.

Washington Irving, oil painting by J.W. Jarvis, 1809; in the Historic Hudson Valley collection.
Courtesy of Historic Hudson Valley

Isabella I, known as ISABELLA THE CATHOLIC, Spanish ISABEL LA CATÓLICA (b. April 22, 1451, Madrigal de las Altas Torres, Castile—d. Nov. 26, 1504, Medina del Campo, Spain), Queen of Castile (1474–1504) and of Aragon (1479–1504). Daughter of John II of Castile and León, she married Ferdinand V in 1469. Her reign began with civil war over her succession (1474–79), but in 1479 the kingdoms of Castile and Aragon came together in the persons of their rulers, though they remained separately governed. In a long campaign (1482–92), Isabella and Ferdinand succeeded in conquering Granada, the last Muslim stronghold in Spain. In 1492 Isabella approved support of Christopher Columbus's journey to the New World. That

Isabella I, portrait by an unknown artist; in the Real Academia de la Historia, Madrid, Spain.
Archivo Mas, Barcelona

same year she was involved in the expulsion of the Jews under the Inquisition. Along with her spiritual advisers, she reformed the Spanish churches.

Isaiah (fl. 8th century BC, Jerusalem), Prophet of ancient Israel after whom the biblical book of Isaiah is named. He is believed to have written only some of the book's first 39 chapters; the rest are by one or more unknown authors. Isaiah's call to prophesy came c. 742 BC, when Assyria was beginning the westward expansion that later overran Israel. A contemporary of Amos, Isaiah denounced economic and social injustice among the Israelites and urged them to obey the Law or risk cancellation of God's covenant. He correctly predicted the destruction of Samaria, or northern Israel, in 722 BC, and he declared the Assyrians to be the instrument of God's wrath. The Christian Gospels lean more heavily on the book of Isaiah than on any other prophetic text, and its "swords-into-plowshares" passage has universal appeal.

Ise Shrine, in full GRAND SHRINE OF ISE, Japanese ISE-DAIJINGŪ, Foremost Shintō shrine in Japan, at Ise, in southern Honshu. The Inner Shrine (traditionally founded 4 BC) is dedicated to the sun goddess Amaterasu. The Outer Shrine (5th century), 4 mi (6 km) away, is dedicated to Toyuke Ōkami, god of food, clothing, and housing. At both shrines the main building is a thatched hut built in the ancient Japanese style of unpainted Japanese cypress (*hinoki*). A distinctive feature of Shintō architecture is the *chigi*, a scissor-shaped finial at the front and rear of the roof. Since the 7th century the buildings have been reconstructed every 20 or 21 years.

Entrance to the Outer Shrine of the Grand Shrine of Ise, Japan.
FPG

Ishtar, In Mesopotamian religion, the goddess of war and sexual love. Known as Ishtar in Akkadia, she was called Astarte by western Semitic peoples and was identified with Inanna in Sumeria. In early Sumeria she was the goddess of the storehouse as well as of rain and thunderstorms. Once a fertility goddess, she evolved into a deity of contradictory qualities, of joy and sorrow, fair play and enmity. In Akkadia she was associated with the planet Venus and was the patroness of prostitutes and alehouses. Her popularity became universal in the ancient Middle East, and she was called Queen of the Universe.

Ishtar, with her cult-animal the lion, and a worshipper, modern impression from a cylinder seal, c. 2300 BC; in the Oriental Institute, University of Chicago
Courtesy of the Oriental Institute, University of Chicago

Ishtar Gate, Enormous burnt-brick double entryway built in the ancient city of Babylon *c.* 575 BC. The gate was more than 38 ft (12 m) high and was decorated with glazed brick reliefs. Through the gatehouse ran the stone- and brick-paved Processional Way. Some 120 brick lions lined the street and some 575 dragons and bulls, in 13 rows, adorned the gate.

Isis, One of the major goddesses of ancient Egypt, the wife of Osiris. When Osiris was killed by Seth, she gathered up the pieces of his body, mourned for him, and brought him back to life. She hid their son Horus from Seth until Horus was fully grown and could avenge his father. Worshiped as a goddess of protection, she had great magical powers and was invoked to heal the sick or protect the dead. By Greco-Roman times she was dominant among Egyptian goddesses, and her cult reached much of the Roman world as a mystery religion.

Islam, Major world religion founded by Muhammad in Arabia in the early 7th century CE. The Arabic word *islam* means "surrender"—specifically, surrender to the will of the one God, called Allah in Arabic. Islam is a strictly monotheistic religion, and its adherents, called Muslims, regard the Prophet Muhammad as the last and most perfect of God's messengers, who include Adam, Abraham, Moses, Jesus, and others. The sacred scripture of Islam is the Qur'ān, which contains God's revelations to Muhammad. The sayings and deeds of the Prophet recounted in the sunna are also an important source of belief and practice in Islam. The religious obligations of all Muslims are summed up in the Five Pillars of Islam, which include belief in God and his Prophet and obligations of prayer, charity, pilgrimage, and fasting. The fundamental concept in Islam is the Sharī'ah, or Law, which embraces the total way of life commanded by God. Observant Muslims pray five times a day and join in community worship on Fridays at the mosque, where worship is led by an imam. Every believer is required to make a pilgrimage to Mecca, the holiest city, at least once in a lifetime, barring poverty or physical incapacity. The month of Ramadan is set aside for fasting. Alcohol and pork are always forbidden, as are gambling, usury, fraud, slander, and the making of images. In addition to celebrating the breaking of the fast of Ramadan, Muslims celebrate Muhammad's birthday and his ascension into heaven. The 'Īd al-Aḍḥā festival inaugurates the season of pilgrimage to Mecca. Muslims are enjoined to defend Islam against unbelievers through jihad. Divisions occurred early in Islam, brought about by disputes over the succession to the caliphate. About 90% of Muslims belong to the Sunni branch. The Shī'ites broke away in the 7th century and later gave rise to other sects, including the Ismā'īlīs. Another significant element in Islam is the mysticism known as Sufism. Since the 19th century the concept of the Islamic community has inspired Muslim peoples to cast off Western colonial rule, and in the late 20th century fundamentalist movements threatened or toppled a number of secular Middle Eastern governments. In the early 21st century, there were more than 1.2 billion Muslims in the world.

Islam, Pillars of, Five duties incumbent on every Muslim. The first is the profession of faith in the one God and in Muhammad as his Prophet. The others are prayer five times a day, the giving of alms to the poor, fasting during the month of Ramadan, and the hajj, or pilgrimage to Mecca.

Islamabad, Capital (pop., 2007 est.: 780,000) of Pakistan, located northeast of Rawalpindi. Established in 1959 to replace Karachi as the capital, it was designed to blend modern and traditional Islamic architecture. The city itself is small, with an area of 25 sq mi (65 sq km), but the planned capital area has an expanse of 350 sq mi (906 sq km) of natural terraces and meadows surrounding the city. It is the seat of the University of Islamabad (founded 1965).

Islamic arts, The architecture, literature, and visual arts of the populations that adopted Islam from the 7th century. Islamic visual arts are decorative, colourful, and generally nonrepresentational; the characteristic Islamic decoration is the arabesque. From 750 CE to the mid-11th century, ceramics, glass, metalwork, textiles, illuminated manuscripts, and woodwork flourished; lustred glass became the greatest Islamic contribution to ceramics. Manuscript illumination became an important and greatly respected art, and miniature painting flourished in Iran after the Mongol invasions (1220–60). Calligraphy, an essential aspect of written Arabic, developed in manuscripts and architectural decoration. Islamic ar-

Arabesque decoration on the dome of the Mādar-e Shāh madrasah, built by Ḥusayn I, early 18th century, at Eṣfahān, Iran.
Ray Manley/Shostal Associates

chitecture finds its highest expression in the mosque and related religious buildings. Early Islamic religious architecture drew upon Christian architectural features such as domes, columnar arches, and mosaics, but also included large courtyards for congregational prayer. Religious architecture came into its own in the period of the caliphates with the creation of the hypostyle mosque in Iraq and Egypt. Islamic literature is written in four main languages: Arabic, Persian, Turkish, and Urdu. Arabic is of overwhelming importance as the language of the revelation of Islam and of the Qurʾān. The Persians used the genres, forms, and rules of Arabic poetry in their own language but elaborated on them. They also developed a new genre, the *masñawī*, composed of a series of rhyming couplets, which they employed for epic poetry. Persian literature in turn influenced both Urdu and Turkish literature, especially with regard to vocabulary and metres. In the realm of popular literature, the best-known work is *The Arabian Nights' Entertainment*, a rich collection of fairy tales from different parts of the Muslim world.

Islamic caste, Any one of several units of social stratification among Muslims in India and Pakistan. Their development can be traced to the caste system of Hinduism and the tendency of Muslim converts from Hinduism to maintain their social differences. The highest status is reserved for Muslim Arab immigrants, called *ashrāf*. This level is itself divided into subgroups. The highest subgroup claims descent from Muhammad through his daughter, Fatima. The non-*ashrāf* Muslim castes consist of three levels: converts from high Hindu castes, artisan castes, and the untouchables.

island, Any area of land smaller than a continent and entirely surrounded by water. Islands may occur in oceans, seas, lakes, or rivers. A group of islands is called an archipelago. Continental islands are simply unsubmerged parts of a continental mass that are entirely surrounded by water; Greenland, the world's largest island, is of the continental type. Oceanic islands are produced by volcanic activity, when lava accumulates to enormous thickness until it finally protrudes above the ocean surface. The piles of lava that form Hawaii rise as high as 32,000 ft (9,700 m) above the ocean floor.

Ismāʿīlī, Member of a sect of the Shīʿite branch of Islam. It came into existence after the death of the sixth imam, Jaʿfar ibn Muhammad, in 765. His son Ismāʿīl was accepted as successor only by a minority, who became known as Ismāʿīlītes. Their doctrine, formulated in the late 8th and early 9th century, made a distinction between ordinary Muslim believers and the elect, who shared a secret wisdom. The Qarāmiṭah subsect was popular in Iraq, Yemen, and Bahrain in the 9th–11th centuries, and the Fāṭimid subsect conquered Egypt in 969 and established the Fāṭimid dynasty. A subgroup of the Fāṭimids was the Nizārīs, who gained control of fortresses in Iran and Syria in the late 11th century and were known as Assassins. The major Nizārī line survived into modern times under the leadership of the Aga Khan, moving from Iran to India in 1840. The Druze separated from the Ismāʿīlīs early in the 11th century and formed a closed society of their own.

isnād, In Islam, a list of authorities who have transmitted accounts of the teachings or actions of Muhammad, one of the Companions of the Prophet, or of a later authority. Each of these accounts, known as Ḥadīth, includes an *isnād* that gives the chain of authorities by which it has been handed down, using the form, "It has been related to me by A on the authority of B on the authority of C on the authority of D that Muhammad said…." *See also* ʿilm al-ḥadīth.

isolationism, National policy of avoiding political or economic entanglements with other countries. Isolationism has been a recurrent theme in U.S. history. It was given expression in the Farewell Address of Pres. George Washington and in the early 19th-century Monroe Doctrine. The term is most often applied to the political atmosphere in the U.S. in the 1930s. The failure of Pres. Woodrow Wilson's internationalism, liberal opposition to war as an instrument of policy, and the rigours of the Great Depression were among the reasons for Americans' reluctance to concern themselves with the growth of fascism in Europe. The Johnson Act (1934) and the Neutrality acts (1935) effectively prevented economic or military aid to any country involved in the European disputes that were to escalate into World War II. U.S. isolationism encouraged the British in their policy of appeasement and contributed to French paralysis in the face of the growing threat posed by Nazi Germany.

isomer, One of two or more substances with identical molecular formulas but different configurations, differing only in the arrangement of their component atoms. It usually refers to stereoisomers (rather than constitutional isomers or tautomers), of which there are two types. Optical isomers, or enantiomers, occur in mirror-image pairs. Geometric isomers are often the result of rigidity in the molecular structure; in organic compounds, this is usually due to a double bond or a ring structure. In the case of a double bond between two carbon atoms, if each has two other groups bonded to it and all are rigidly in the same plane, the corresponding groups can be on the same side (*cis*) of the C=C bond or across the C=C bond (*trans*) from each other. An analogous distinction can be made for ring structures that are all in a plane, between isomers whose substituent groups are on the same side and isomers whose substituent groups are on both sides of the plane. Diastereomers that are not enantiomers also fall into this category. Most *cis-trans* isomers are organic compounds.

isotope, One of two or more species of atoms of a chemical element having nuclei with the same number of protons but different numbers of neutrons. They have the same atomic number and hence nearly identical chemical behaviour but different atomic masses. Most elements found in nature are mixtures of several isotopes; tin, for example, has 10 isotopes. In most cases, only stable isotopes of elements are found in nature. The radioactive forms break down spontaneously into different elements. Isotopes of all elements heavier than bismuth are radioactive; some occur naturally because they have long half-lives.

Israel, officially STATE OF ISRAEL, Country, Middle East, at the eastern end of the Mediterranean Sea. Area: 8,357 sq mi (21,643 sq km). Population (2009 est.): 7,128,000 (includes population of Golan Heights and east Jerusalem; excludes population of the West Bank). Capital (proclaimed): Jerusalem (the city's status as capital has not received wide international recognition). Jews constitute some four-fifths of the population and Arabs about one-fifth. Languages: Hebrew, Arabic (both official). Religions: Judaism; also Islam, Christianity. Currency: new Israeli sheqel (NIS). Israel can be divided into four major regions: the Mediterranean coastal plain in the west; a hill region extending from the northern border into central Israel; the Great Rift Valley, containing the Jordan River, in the east; and the arid Negev, occupying nearly the entire southern half of the country. Its major drainage system is the interior basin formed by the Jordan River; Lake Tiberias (Sea of Galilee) provides water to much of the country's agricultural land. Israel has a mixed economy based largely on services and manufacturing; exports include machinery and electronics, diamonds, chemicals, citrus fruits, vegetables, and textiles. Its population is nine-tenths urban and is concentrated largely in the Mediterranean coastal plain and around Jerusalem. It is a multiparty republic with one legislative house, the Knesset; its head of state is the president, and the head of government is the prime minister. The record of human habitation in Israel dates to the Paleolithic Period. Efforts by Jews to establish a national state there began in the late 19th century. Britain supported Zionism and in 1923 assumed political responsibility for what was then called Palestine. Migration of Jews to Palestine, which increased during the period of Nazi persecution, led to deteriorating relations with Arabs. In 1947 the UN voted to partition the region into separate Jewish and Arab states. The State of Israel was proclaimed in 1948, and Egypt, Transjordan (later Jordan), Syria, Lebanon, and Iraq immediately declared war on it. Israel won that war as well as the 1967 Six-Day War, in which it occupied the West Bank, Gaza Strip, Golan Heights, and east Jerusalem. Another war with its Arab neighbours followed in 1973, but the Camp David Accords led to a peace treaty between Israel and Egypt in 1979. Israel invaded Lebanon in 1982 to expel the Palestine Liberation Organization (PLO) from that country, and in late 1987 an uprising broke out among Palestinians of the occupied territories of the West Bank and Gaza Strip. Peace negotiations between Israel and the Arab states and Palestinians began in 1991. Israel and the PLO agreed in 1993 to a five-year plan to extend self-government to the Palestinians of the occupied territories. Israel signed a peace treaty with Jordan in 1994. Israeli soldiers and a Lebanese militia, Hezbollah, clashed throughout the 1990s. Israeli troops withdrew from Lebanon in 2000, and negotiations between Israel and the Palestinians broke down amid violence that claimed hundreds of lives. In an effort to stem the fighting, Israel in 2005 withdrew its soldiers and settlers from parts of the West Bank and from all of the Gaza Strip, which came under Palestinian control.

Israel, tribes of, In the Bible, the 12 clans of the ancient Hebrew people, which were named for the sons of Jacob (Reuben, Simeon, Levi, Judah, Issachar, Zebulun, Joseph, Benjamin, Gad, Asher, Dan, and Naphtali) and his wives, Leah and Rachel, and concubines, Bilhah and Zilpah. The tribe of Levi did not receive land in the settlement of Canaan but instead was given the priestly office. To maintain the traditional number of 12 tribes, the line of Joseph was divided into the tribes of Ephraim and Manasseh. In Israel's later history, the tribes of Judah and Benjamin formed a southern kingdom called Judah with its capital at Jerusalem, while the 10 northern tribes formed the kingdom of Israel. After being conquered by Assyria in 721 BC, the northern tribes were exiled from the kingdom and were assimilated by other peoples. Disappearing from history, they became known as the 10 lost tribes of Israel and remained part of Jewish folklore and eschatological beliefs. The tribes of Judah and Benjamin survived until Nebuchadrezzar's conquest of Judah in 586 BC, when many from the kingdom were exiled to Babylon.

Israelite, In early Jewish history, a member of the 12 tribes of Israel. After the establishment (930 BC) of two Jewish kingdoms (Israel and Judah) in Palestine, only the ten northern tribes constituting the kingdom of Israel were known as Israelites. When Israel was conquered by the Assyrians (721 BC), its population was absorbed by other peoples, and the term Israelite came to refer to those who were still distinctively Jewish—the descendants of the kingdom of Judah. In liturgical usage, an Israelite is a Jew who is neither a cohen nor a Levite.

Istanbul, formerly CONSTANTINOPLE, ancient BYZANTIUM, City and seaport (pop., 2000: 8,803,468), Turkey. Situated on a peninsula at the entrance to the Black Sea, Turkey's largest city lies on either side of the Bosporus and thus is located in both Europe and Asia. Byzantium was founded as a Greek colony in the 8th century BC. Passing to the Persian Achaemenian dynasty in 512 BC and then to Alexander the Great, it became a free city under the Romans in the 1st century AD. The emperor Constantine I made the city the seat of the Eastern Roman Empire in 330, later naming it Constantinople. It remained the capital of the subsequent Byzantine Empire after the fall of Rome in the late 5th century. In the 6th–13th centuries it was frequently besieged by Persians, Arabs, Bulgars, and Russians. It was captured by the Fourth Crusade (1203) and turned over to Latin Christian rule. It was returned to Byzantine rule in 1261. In 1453 it was captured by the Ottoman Empire and made the Ottoman capital. When the Republic of Turkey was founded in 1923, the capital was moved to Ankara, and Constantinople was officially renamed Istanbul in 1930. Many of the city's historic sites are located in the medieval walled city (Stamboul). Among its architectural treasures are the Hagia Sophia, the Mosque of Süleyman, and the Blue Mosque. Its educational institutions include the University of Istanbul (founded 1453), Turkey's oldest university.

The Blue Mosque (Sultan Ahmed Mosque) with its distinctive ensemble of six minarets, Istanbul.
© Robert Frerck—CLICK/Chicago

Istria, Peninsula, extending into the northeastern Adriatic Sea. It has an area of 1,220 sq mi (3,160 sq km). Its northern portion is part of Slovenia, while the central and southern parts belong to Croatia. A tiny strip of coast in the northwest is the site of Trieste and belongs to Italy. Istria's ancient Illyrian inhabitants were overthrown by Romans in 177 BC, and Slavic peoples settled there from the 7th century AD. It passed through the hands of various Mediterranean powers until Austria gained control in 1797 and developed Trieste as a port. Istria was seized by Italy in 1919; Yugoslavia occupied most of the peninsula in 1947. Yugoslavian Istria became part of Croatia and Slovenia at those states' independence in 1991.

Italian language, Romance language spoken in Italy (including Sicily and Sardinia) and in parts of Switzerland and France (including Corsica). Its 66 million speakers worldwide include many immigrants and their descendants in the Americas. Written Italian dates from the 10th century. Standard Italian is based on the dialect of Florence. Most Italians also speak regional dialects. These include Upper Italian (Gallo-Italian); Venetan in northeastern Italy; Tuscan; the dialects of Marche, Umbria, and Rome; those of Abruzzi, Puglia, Naples, Campania, and Lucania; and those of Calabria, Otranto, and Sicily.

Italy, officially ITALIAN REPUBLIC, Country, south-central Europe. It comprises the boot-shaped peninsula extending far into the Mediterranean Sea as well as Sicily, Sardinia, and a number of smaller islands. Area: 116,346 sq mi (301,336 sq km). Population: (2011 est.) 60,769,000. Capital: Rome. The people are overwhelmingly Italian. Language: Italian (official). Religion: Christianity (predominantly Roman Catholic). Currency: euro. More than three-fourths of Italy is mountainous or highland country. The Alps stretch from east to west along Italy's northern boundary, and the Apennines stretch southward the length of the peninsula. Most of the country's lowlands lie in the valley of its major river, the Po. Three tectonic plates converge in southern Italy and Sicily, creating intense geologic activity; southern Italy's four active volcanoes include Mount Vesuvius and Mount Etna. The economy is based largely on services and manufacturing; exports include machinery and transport equipment, chemicals, textiles, clothing and shoes, and food products (olive oil, wine, fruit, and tomatoes). Italy is a republic with two legislative houses. The head of state is the president, and the head of government is the prime minister. Italy has been inhabited since Paleolithic times. The Etruscan civilization arose in the 9th century BCE and was overthrown by the Romans in the 4th–3rd centuries BCE. Barbarian invasions of the 4th–5th centuries CE destroyed the Western Roman Empire. Italy's political fragmentation lasted for centuries but did not diminish its impact on European culture, notably during the Renaissance. From the 15th to the 18th century, Italian lands were ruled by France, the Holy Roman Empire, Spain, and Austria. When Napoleonic rule ended in 1815, Italy was again a grouping of independent states. The Risorgimento successfully united most of Italy, including Sicily and Sardinia by 1861, and the unification of peninsular Italy was completed by 1870. Italy joined the Allies during World War I, but social unrest in the 1920s brought to power the Fascist movement of Benito Mussolini, and Italy allied itself with Nazi Germany in World War II. Defeated by the Allies in 1943, Italy proclaimed itself a republic in 1946. It was a charter member of NATO (1949) and of the European Economic Community (now the European Union). It completed the process of setting up regional legislatures with limited autonomy in 1970s. After World War II it experienced rapid changes of government but remained socially stable.

Ithnā ʿAshariyyah, or IMĀMĪS, English TWELVERS, The largest school of Shīʿite Islam, believing in a succession of 12 imams beginning with ʿAlī ibn Abū Ṭālib, the fourth caliph and the son-in-law of Muhammad. The last of the 12 imams recognized by the school was Muḥammad al-Mahdī al-Ḥujjah, who disappeared in 873 and is thought by believers to be alive and in occultation, ready to return at the Last Judgment. The Ithnā ʿAshariyyah believe that imams are the preservers of the faith and the only interpreters of the esoteric meanings of law and theology. The imams are thought to influence the world's future, and pilgrimages to the tombs of the imams secure special rewards. This school became the state religion of Iran under the Ṣafavid dynasty (1501–1736). The Ithnā ʿAshariyyah also constitute a majority in Iraq and Bahrain, with sizable minorities in other Muslim countries. *Compare* Ismāʿīlī.

Itō Hirobumi (b. Oct. 14, 1841, Suō province, Japan—d. Oct. 26, 1909, Harbin, China), Japanese statesman, prime minister, and writer of the Meiji Constitution. He played a minor role in the Meiji Restoration, through which he came in contact with Kido Takayoshi and Ōkubo Toshimichi. When Ōkubo was assassinated in 1878, Ito succeeded him as home minister. He persuaded the government to adopt a constitution and then traveled abroad to research constitutions. In 1889 the emperor promulgated the resultant document. Later, as prime minister, Itō negotiated an end to extraterritoriality with Britain; other Western nations followed suit, signaling that the West was beginning to treat Japan as an equal. Frustrated with the ability of the political parties to impede passage of government programs in the Diet, in 1900 Itō founded his own party, the Rikken Seiyūkai. This foray cost him control of the genro (elder statesmen) but made cooperation between high-ranking bureaucrats and party politicians acceptable. In 1906 Ito became resident general in Korea; he was assassinated in 1909 by a Korean nationalist.

ivory carving, Carving of ivory into decorative or utilitarian objects. It has flourished since prehistoric times. Most Stone Age carvings have been found in southern France, in the forms of small

"An Elopement" (sometimes called "Lancelot and Guinevere"), ivory mirror case, French Gothic, 14th century

Courtesy of the Museum of Liverpool, England

nude female figures and animals. A masterpiece of early Egyptian carving is an ivory statuette of Khufu, builder of the Great Pyramid. In China ivory carvings have been found in the tombs of the Shang dynasty (18th–12th century BC). The major artistic use of ivory in Japan was for netsukes, toggles used as fasteners on men's clothing. The early Inuit (Eskimos) produced such utilitarian objects as harpoon shafts and bucket handles out of ivory and often etched them with geometric or curving patterns.

Iwo Jima, Island, the middle of the three Volcano Islands, Japan. Situated in the western Pacific, it is about 5 mi (8 km) long, 800 yards to 2.5 mi (730 m–4 km) wide, and has an area of 8 sq mi (20 sq km). It was under Japanese control until 1945, when it was the scene of one of the severest campaigns of World War II. After extensive bombing by U.S. planes (December 1944–February 1945), it was invaded by U.S. marines and was finally completely taken by mid-March; it became a strategic base for U.S. planes en route to Japan. In 1968 it was returned to Japan.

Izanagi and Izanami, Brother and sister gods in the Japanese creation myth. They created the first land mass, and their sexual union produced many islands and deities. In giving birth to the fire god, Izanami was burned to death and went to the land of darkness. Izanagi tried to rescue her, but she had eaten the food of the place and could not leave; in disgust he left her rotting corpse and divorced her. As he bathed to purify himself afterwards, other deities were born from him, including the sun goddess Amaterasu, the moon god Tsukiyomi, and the storm god Susanoo. His bath is the basis for Shinto purification rites.

İzmir, formerly SMYRNA, City (pop., 2007: 2,606,294), western Turkey. On the Aegean seacoast, it is one of Turkey's largest ports and its third largest city. It was founded as early as 3000 BC and was settled by the Greeks before 1000 BC. It was captured by the Lydians about 600 BC and ceased to exist until it was refounded by Alexander the Great in the 4th century BC. It became one of the principal cities of Anatolia. After being conquered in turn by the Crusaders and by Timur (Tamerlane), it was annexed to the Ottoman Empire about 1425. It became part of the Republic of Turkey in 1923. It has grown rapidly since 1945 and has a large industrial economy and a growing tourist trade.

ʿIzrāʾīl, In Islam, the angel of death. One of the four archangels (with Jibrāʾīl, Mīkāʾīl, and Isrāfīl), he is of cosmic size, with 4,000 wings and a body formed from innumerable eyes and tongues. He was the only angel brave enough to go down to earth and face Iblīs in order to bring God the materials to create man. For this service he was made the angel of death and given a register of all mankind, which lists the blessed and the damned.

Izumo shrine, Oldest Shintō shrine in Japan (the present building is said to date from 1346), located northwest of Izumo on the island of Honshu. The temple complex covers 40 acres (16 hectares) and contains a valuable art collection. Enclosed by hills on three sides, it is approached through an avenue of pines. Most of its present buildings were constructed in the 19th century.

J

jacaranda, Any plant of the genus *Jacaranda* (family Bignon-iaceae), especially the two orna-

Jacaranda acutifolia
Walter Dawn

mental trees *J. mimosifolia* and *J. cuspidifolia*. Jacarandas are grown widely in warm parts of the world and in greenhouses for their showy blue or violet flowers and attractive, oppositely paired, compound leaves. The genus includes about 50 species native to Central and South America and the West Indies. The name is also applied to several tree species of the genera *Machaerium* and *Dalbergia* in the pea family, the sources of commercial rosewood.

Jackson, Andrew (b. March 15, 1767, Waxhaws region, S.C.—d. June 8, 1845, the Hermitage, near Nashville, Tenn., U.S.), Seventh president of the U.S. (1829–37). He fought briefly in the American Revolution near his frontier home, where his family was killed in the conflict. In 1788 he was appointed prosecuting attorney for western North Carolina. When the region became the state of Tennessee, he was elected to the U.S. House of Representatives (1796–97) and the Senate (1797–98). He served on the state supreme court (1798–1804) and in 1802 was elected major general of the Tennessee militia. When the War of 1812 began, he offered the U.S. the services of his 50,000-man volunteer militia. Sent to the Mississippi Territory to fight the Creek Indians, who were allied with the British, he defeated them after a short campaign (1813–14) at the Battle of Horseshoe Bend. After capturing Pensacola, Fla., from the British-allied Spanish, he marched overland to engage the British in Louisiana. A decisive victory at the Battle of New Orleans made him a national hero; he was dubbed "Old Hickory" by the press. After the U.S. acquired Florida, Jackson was named governor of the territory (1821). One of four candidates in the 1824 presidential election, he won an electoral-vote plurality, but the House of Representative instead selected John Quincy Adams as president. Jackson's victory over Adams in the 1828 presidential election is commonly regarded as a turning point in U.S. history. Jackson was the first president from west of the Appalachian Mountains, the first to be born in poverty, and the first to be elected through a direct appeal to the mass of voters rather than through the support of a recognized political organization. The era of his presidency has come to be known as "Jacksonian Democracy." Upon taking office he replaced many federal officials with his political supporters, a practice that became known as the spoils system. His administration acquiesced in the illegal seizure of Cherokee land in Georgia and then forcibly expelled the Indians who refused to leave. When South Carolina claimed a right to nullify a federally imposed tariff, Jackson asked for and received Congressional authority to use the military to enforce federal laws in the state. His reelection in 1832 was partially the result of his controversial veto of a bill to recharter the Bank of the United States, which was unpopular with many of his supporters. The intensity of the political struggles during his tenure led to the strengthening of the Democratic Party and to the further development of the two-party system.

Jacob, François (b. June 17, 1920, Nancy, France), French biologist. After receiving his doctorate, he went to work at the Pasteur Institute in Paris. Beginning in 1958, he worked with Jacques Monod studying the regulation of bacterial enzyme synthesis. They discovered regulator genes, so called because they control the activities of other genes. Jacob and Monod also proposed the existence of an RNA messenger, a partial copy of DNA that carries genetic information to other parts of the cell. The two men shared a 1965 Nobel Prize with André Lwoff.

Jacobean literature, Body of works written during the reign of James I of England (1603–25). The successor to Elizabethan literature, Jacobean literature was often dark in mood, questioning the stability of the social order; some of William Shakespeare's greatest tragedies may date from the beginning of the period, and other dramatists, including John Webster, were often preoccupied with the problem of evil. The era's comedy included the acid satire of Ben Jonson and the varied works of Francis Beaumont and John Fletcher. Jacobean poetry included the graceful verse of Jonson and the Cavalier poets but also the intellectual complexity of the Metaphysical poetry of John Donne and others. In prose, writers such as Francis Bacon and Robert Burton showed a new toughness and flexibility of style. The era's monumental prose achievement was the King James Version of the Bible (1611).

Jacquard loom, Loom incorporating a special device to control individual warp yarns. It enabled production of fabrics with intricate woven patterns such as tapestry, brocade, and damask, and has also been adapted to the production of patterned knitted fabrics. Developed in France by J.-M. Jacquard in 1804–05, it used interchangeable punched cards that controlled the weaving of the cloth so that any desired pattern could be obtained automatically. It aroused bitter hostility among weavers, who feared that its labour-saving capabilities would deprive them of jobs; the weavers of Lyon not only burned the machines but attacked Jacquard as well. Eventually the loom's advantages led to its general acceptance, and by 1812 there were 11,000 in use in France. Use of the loom spread to England in the 1820s and from there virtually worldwide.

jade, Either of two tough, compact, typically green gemstones

Dragon among clouds, carved jade medallion or button, Qing dynasty, probably late 18th century (reign of Qianlong); in the Victoria and Albert Museum, London

Courtesy of the board of trustees of the Victoria and Albert Museum, London, Wells Legacy

that take a high polish. Both have been carved into jewelry, ornaments, small sculptures, and utilitarian objects from earliest recorded times. The more highly prized of the two jadestones is jadeite; the other is nephrite. Both types may be white or colourless, but colours such as red, green, and gray may occur.

Jaʿfar ibn Muḥammad (b. 699/700, Medina, Arabia—d. 765, Medina), Sixth imam of the Shīʿite branch of Islam and the last to be recognized by all the Shīʿite sects. He was the great-grandson of ʿAlī. As a possible claimant to the caliphate, Jaʿfar was viewed as a threat to both the Umayyad and ʿAbbāsid dynasties. He traveled to Baghdad in 762 to prove to the caliph that he was not seeking power, then returned to his native Medina, where his pupils included Abū Ḥanīfah. After his death the Shīʿites began to splinter. One sect, the Ismāʿīliyyah, became followers of his son, Ismail. Another, the Ithnā ʿAshariyyah, traced a succession from Jaʿfar to the Twelfth Imam awaited at the Last Judgment.

Jagiellon dynasty, Family of monarchs of Poland-Lithuania, Bohemia, and Hungary that became one of the most powerful in east-central Europe in the 15th–16th centuries. It was founded by Jogaila, grand duke of Lithuania, who became Władysław II Jagiełło of Poland after marriage to Queen Jadwiga (1373?–99) in

1386. Władysław III Warneńczyk (1424–44) extended the dynasty by also assuming the throne of Hungary (1440). He was succeeded by Casimir IV, who placed his son on the thrones of Bohemia (1471) and Hungary. During the reigns of Casimir's sons John Albert (1459–1501) and Alexander (1461–1506), the Jagiellon rulers lost much of their power in Poland to the nobility. When Sigismund I succeeded Alexander in 1506, he strengthened the government and saw the Teutonic Order convert its lands into the secular duchy of Prussia (1525), a Polish fief. In 1526 the death of Louis II ended Jagiellon rule in Bohemia and Hungary. In 1561 Sigismund II Augustus incorporated Livonia into Poland, but when he died, leaving no heirs, the Jagiellon dynasty ended (1572).

jaguar, Largest New World cat. Once found in wooded regions from the U.S.-Mexican border south to Patagonia, the jaguar (*Panthera onca*) survives, in reduced numbers, only in remote areas of Central and South America; the largest known population is in the Amazon rain forest. The male is 5.5–9 ft (1.7–2.7 m) long, including the 23–35-in. (60–90-cm) tail, and weighs 220–350 lbs (100–160 kg). The coat is typically orange-tan with black spots arranged in rosettes having a black spot in the centre. A solitary predator, the jaguar usually hunts rodents, deer, birds, and fish; it will also take cattle, horses, and dogs.

jai alai (Basque: "merry festival"), Court game resembling handball. Of Basque origin, it developed from pelota and was given its present name when it was imported to Cuba in 1900. It is played between two or four players with a ball and a hurling device consisting of a long, curved wicker basket strapped to the wrist. The use of this hurling device, called a cesta, allows the ball to reach speeds up to 240 km/hr (150 mph). The court, 53.3 m (58.3 yards) long, is three-walled. The object of the game is to bounce the ball off the front wall with such speed and spin that the opponent is unable to return it. Pari-mutuel betting on jai alai is permitted in the U.S.

Jainism, Religion of India established between the 7th and 5th centuries BCE. It was founded by Vardhamana, who was called Mahavira, as a reaction against the Vedic religion, which required animal sacrifices. Jainism's core belief is ahimsa, or noninjury to all living things. Jainism has no belief in a creator god, though there are a number of lesser deities for various aspects of life. Jains believe their religion is eternal and hold that it was revealed in stages by a number of Conquerors, of whom Mahavira was the 24th. Living as an ascetic, Mahavira preached the need for rigorous penance and self-denial as the means of perfecting human nature, escaping the cycle of rebirth, and attaining moksha, or liberation. Jains view karma as an invisible material substance that interferes with liberation and can be dissolved only through asceticism. By the end of the 1st century CE the Jains had split into two sects, each of which later developed its own canon of sacred writings: the Digambaras, who held that an adherent should own nothing, not even clothes, and that women must be reborn as men before they can attain moksha; and the more moderate Svetambaras, who retained a few possessions such as a robe, an alms bowl, a whisk broom, and a *mukhavastrika* (a piece of cloth held over the mouth to protect against the ingestion and killing of small insects). In keeping with their principle of reverence for life, Jains are known for their charitable works, including building shelters for animals. Jainism preaches universal tolerance and does not seek to make converts. In the early 21st century Jainism had some 5 million followers.

Jaipur, Capital (pop., 2001: 2,322,575) of Rajasthan state, northwestern India. A walled town surrounded by hills (except to the south), it was founded in 1727 by Maharaja Sawai Jai Singh to replace Amber as the capital of the princely state of Jaipur. The city, known for its beauty, is unique in its straight-line planning; its buildings are mostly rose-coloured, and Jaipur is sometimes called the "pink city." It is a popular tourist destination; historic

Hawa Mahal (Hall of Winds), Jaipur, Rajasthan, India.
Frederick M. Asher

structures include the city palace, the Hawa Mahal ("Hall of Winds"), Ram Bagh palace, and Nahargarh (Tiger Fort).

Jakarta, formerly (1949–72) DJAKARTA, Capital (pop., 2000: city, 8,347,083; 2003 est.: urban agglom., 12,300,000) and largest city of Indonesia. Located on the northwestern coast of Java, it was founded in 1527 after the sultan of Bantam defeated the Portuguese on the site. The Dutch razed the city in 1619, rebuilding and renaming it Batavia and establishing it as the headquarters of the Dutch East India Company. In 1949 the city was renamed and made Indonesia's capital. It grew rapidly, soon becoming one of the world's most populous cities. A major trade, industrial, and financial centre, it is also the seat of several universities.

Jamaica, Island country, West Indies, located south of Cuba. The third largest island in the Caribbean, it is 146 mi (235 km) long and 35 mi (56 km) wide. Area: 4,244 sq mi (10,991 sq km). Population: (2011 est.) 2,709,000. Capital: Kingston. The population consists mostly of descendents of African slaves. Languages: English (official), Jamaican Creole. Religions: Christianity (mainly Protestant; also Roman Catholic); also Rastafarianism. Currency: Jamaican dollar. Jamaica has three major regions: the coastal lowlands, which encircle the island and are heavily cultivated; a limestone plateau, which covers half of the island; and the interior highlands, with forested mountain ranges, including the Blue Mountains. Agriculture employs about one-fifth of the workforce, and the major agricultural export is raw sugar, with molasses and rum as by-products. Industry focuses on the production of bauxite and alumina and on the garment industry. Tourism is very important. Jamaica is a constitutional monarchy with two legislative houses. Its head of state is the British monarch, represented by the governor-general, and its head of government is the prime minister. The island was settled by Arawak Indians *c.* 600 CE. It was sighted by Christopher Columbus in 1494; Spain colonized it in the early 16th century but neglected it because it lacked gold reserves. Britain gained control in 1655, and by the end of the 18th century Jamaica had become a prized colonial possession because of the volume of sugar produced by slave labourers. Slavery was abolished in the late 1830s, and the plantation system collapsed. Jamaica gained full internal self-government in 1959 and became an independent country within the British Commonwealth in 1962. In the late 20th century the government, led by Michael Manley, nationalized many businesses.

Jammu and Kashmir, State (pop., 2008 est.: 12,366,000), northern India. With an area of 39,146 sq mi (101,387 sq km), it occupies the southern portion of the Kashmir region of the northwestern Indian subcontinent and is bordered by Pakistan and China, by the portions of Kashmir administered by those two countries, and by the Indian states of Himachal Pradesh and Punjab. The land is predominantly mountainous and includes segments of the Karakoram and Himalaya ranges. Part of Kashmir's Ladakh region is included in the state. There are two major lowland areas: the plains of the Jammu region and the fertile and heavily populated Vale of Kashmir. The majority of the state's people are Muslims, although Hindus predominate in the southeastern Jammu area, and eastern Ladakh is largely Buddhist. Formerly a princely state, Jammu and Kashmir became an Indian state in 1947, even as India and Pakistan were fighting for control of the entire Kashmir region.

Jansenism, Roman Catholic reform movement inspired by the writings of Cornelius Jansen. Influenced by the works of St. Augustine and especially by Augustine's attacks on Pelagianism and the doctrine of free will, Jansen adopted Augustine's doctrines of predestination and the necessity of God's grace, a stance considered uncomfortably close to Calvinism by Roman Catholic authorities, who banned his book the *Augustinus* in 1642. After Jansen's death in 1638, his followers made their base at the abbey in Port-Royal, France. Blaise Pascal, the most famous Jansenist, defended their teachings in his *Provincial Letters* (1656–57). In 1709 Louis XIV ordered the Port Royal abbey demolished. Followers of Jansen started a Jansenist church in 1723, which endured into the late 20th century.

Janus, Roman god of doorways and archways, after whom the month of January is named. Often depicted as a double-faced head, he was a deity of beginnings. The worship of Janus dated back to the earliest years of Rome, and the city had many freestanding ceremonial gateways called *jani*, used for symbolically auspicious entrances or exits. The most famous was the Janus Geminus, whose double doors were left open in time of war and closed when Rome was at peace. The festival of Janus, the Agonium, took place on January 9.

The god Janus, beardless, Roman coin; in the Bibliothèque Nationale, Paris
Larousse

Japan, Island country, East Asia, western Pacific Ocean. Its four main islands are Hokkaido, Honshu, Shikoku, and Kyushu. It is separated from the Asian mainland by the Sea of Japan (East Sea). Area: 145,927 sq mi (377,950 sq km). Population: (2011 est.) 127,937,000. Capital: Tokyo. The Japanese overwhelmingly are a single Asian ethnic group. Language: Japanese (official). Religions: Shintō, Buddhism; also Christianity. Currency: yen. Situated in one of Earth's most geologically active zones, Japan experiences volcanic eruptions and earthquakes. Mountain ranges cover some four-fifths of its land surface; its highest mountain is Mount Fuji. The economy, one of the world's biggest, is based largely on manufacturing and services; exports include electronic and electrical equipment, motor vehicles, chemicals, and iron and steel products. The government's involvement in banking results in unique cooperation between the public and private sectors. Japan is one of the world's principal seagoing nations, with an important marine fishing sector. It is a constitutional monarchy with two legislative houses; its symbol of state is the emperor, and the head of government is the prime minister. Human habitation in Japan is thought to date to at least 30,000 years ago. The Yamato court established the first unified Japanese state in the 4th–5th century CE; during that period, Buddhism arrived in Japan by way of Korea. For centuries Japan borrowed heavily from Chinese culture, but it began to sever its links with the mainland by the 9th century. The Fujiwara family was dominant through the 11th century. In 1192 Minamoto Yoritomo established Japan's first *bakufu*, or shogunate. The Muromachi period (1338–1573) was marked by warfare between powerful families. Unification was achieved in the late 16th and early 17th centuries under the leadership of Oda Nobunaga, Toyotomi Hideyoshi, and Tokugawa Ieyasu. During the Edo (Tokugawa) period (1603–1867), the government imposed a policy of isolation. Under the leadership of the emperor Meiji (1867–1912), it adopted a constitution (1889) and began a program of modernization and Westernization. Japanese imperialism led to war with China (1894–95) and Russia (1904–05) as well as to the annexation of Korea (1910) and northeastern China (1931). During World War

II, Japan attacked U.S. forces in Hawaii and the Philippines (December 1941) and occupied European colonial possessions in Southeast Asia. In 1945 the U.S. dropped atomic bombs on Hiroshima and Nagasaki, and Japan surrendered to the Allies. A new democratic constitution was drafted (1947) during the U.S. postwar occupation. Japan also began rebuilding its ruined industrial base, using new technology. A tremendous economic recovery followed, and Japan became one of the world's wealthiest countries. It was able to maintain a favourable balance of trade despite a long-term economic recession. In March 2011 a severe underwater earthquake off northeastern Japan generated devastating tsunami waves that caused massive destruction and loss of life in coastal areas there.

Japan, Sea of, or EAST SEA, Branch of the western Pacific Ocean, bounded by Japan, by Sakhalin Island, and by Russia and Korea on the Asian mainland. It has a surface area of about 377,600 sq mi (978,000 sq km), a mean depth of 5,748 ft (1,752 m), and a maximum depth of 12,276 ft (3,742 m). Its relatively warm waters contribute greatly to the mild climate of Japan. The growing trade among East Asian countries has increased its use as a commercial waterway.

Japanese beetle, Scarab beetle (*Popillia japonica*) that is a major pest of plants. Introduced accidentally from Japan into the U.S. in 1916, Japanese beetles are known to feed on more than 200 species of plant. Their larvae feed underground on roots; adults feed on flowers, fruit, and foliage. They range from Maine to South Carolina, and infestations have occurred in other parts of North America. The adult, about 0.4 in. (10 mm) long, is bright metallic green with coppery-brown wing covers. Control efforts include the use of poisonous sprays and a disease-inducing bacterium and introduction of the beetle's natural enemies (certain parasitic wasp and fly species).

Japanese language, Language spoken by about 125 million people on the islands of Japan, including the Ryukyus. The only other language of the Japanese archipelago is Ainu, now spoken by only a handful of people on Hokkaido, though once much more widespread. Japanese is not closely related to any other language, though a distant genetic kinship to Korean is now thought probable by some scholars, and an even more remote relationship to the Altaic languages is possible. Japanese is first attested in the 8th century AD, when Middle Chinese characters were utilized solely for their phonetic value to write native Japanese words. Japanese retains a huge stock of loanwords from Middle Chinese, long adapted to native phonetics.

Japanese writing system, System of modified Chinese characters used for writing the Japanese language. The Japanese developed a mixed system, partly logographic (based on the Chinese writing system) and partly syllabic. In the 9th or 10th century two sets of syllabic signs evolved: *hiragana*, simplified cursive versions of Chinese characters; and *katakana*, based on elements of Chinese characters. Modern Japanese is written with the two syllabaries and Chinese characters.

Winter jasmine (Jasminum nudiflorum)
Valerie Finnis

jasmine, Any of about 225–450 tropical and subtropical species of fragrant, flowering, woody, climbing shrubs that make up the genus *Jasminum* of the olive family, native to all continents except North America. The jasmine used in perfumery and aromatherapy comes from the fragrant white flowers of common, or poet's, jasmine (*J. officinale*), native to

Iran. The dried flowers of Arabian jasmine (*J. sambac*) make jasmine tea. Many fragrant-flowered plants from other families are also commonly called jasmine.

jaundice, Excess bile pigments (bilirubin) in the bloodstream and tissues, causing a yellow to orange—even greenish—colour in the skin, the whites of the eyes, and the mucous membranes. Bilirubin may be overproduced or inadequately removed by the liver or leak into the bloodstream after removal; jaundice may also be due to impaired bile flow. Causes include anemia, pneumonia, and liver disorders (e.g., infection or cirrhosis). While bilirubin excess usually does no harm, retention jaundice signals severe liver malfunction.

Java, or DJAWA, or JAWA, Island (pop., 2005 prelim.: 127,679,800), Indonesia. Lying southeast of Sumatra, it is Indonesia's fourth largest island, and it contains more than half of the country's population. Its area, including offshore islands, is 49,255 sq mi (127,570 sq km). The capital of Java and of Indonesia is Jakarta. The island's highest point is Mount Semeru, an active volcano reaching an elevation of 12,060 ft (3,676 m). It is inhabited by three major ethnic groups: the Javanese (who constitute the bulk of the population), the Sundanese, and the Madurese. The fossilized remains of *Homo erectus*, or "Java man," indicate that the island was occupied some 800,000 years ago. Indian traders began arriving in the 1st century CE, bringing Hindu influences. The Majapahit dynasty was founded in eastern Java in 1293; it fell early in the 16th century when Muslim kingdoms arose. In 1619 the Dutch East India Company took control of Batavia (Jakarta) and extended its influence. Ruled by the Dutch until the 1940s when it was occupied by Japan, it became part of newly independent Indonesia in 1950.

Java, Modular object-oriented programming language developed by Sun Microsystems in 1995 specifically for the Internet. Java is based on the idea that the same software should run on many different kinds of computers, consumer gadgets, and other devices; its code is translated according to the needs of the machine on which it is running. The most visible examples of Java software are the interactive programs called "applets" that animate sites on the World Wide Web, where Java is a standard creative tool. Java provides an interface to HTML.

Java man, Common name of fossilized *Homo erectus* remains found in 1891 at Trinil, Java. The remains, a skullcap and thighbone, represent the first known fossils of *H. erectus* (though originally assigned to *Pithecanthropus erectus*) and, together with numerous other finds along the Solo River, suggest that *H. erectus* was present in eastern Asia some 1,000,000 years ago and persisted there for at least 500,000 years and possibly as long as 800,000 years. Java man predates the finds at Zhoukoudian (Peking Man) in China and is considered somewhat more primitive.

Java Sea, Part of the western Pacific Ocean between Java and Borneo islands. Measuring 900 mi (1,450 km) long by 260 mi (420 km) wide, it occupies a total area of 167,000 sq mi (433,000 sq km). A shallow sea, it has a mean depth of 151 ft (46 m). It was the scene of a World War II naval battle (1942) that resulted in an Allied defeat and Japan's invasion of Java.

javelin throw, Track-and-field sport of throwing a wooden or metal spear for distance. It is hurled after a short run and must land point-first. The men's javelin is 8.5 ft (260 cm) long, the women's 7.2 ft (220 cm). Included in the ancient Greek Olympic Games as part of the pentathlon, the javelin throw has been part of the modern Olympic program since its inception in 1896. A women's event was added in 1932.

Jaya Peak, Indonesian PUNCAK JAYA, formerly MOUNT SUKARNO, Peak, Papua province, Indonesia. The 16,500-ft (5,030-m) peak, located on New Guinea, is the highest in the South Pacific and the tallest island peak in the world.

Jazīrah, Al-, or EL-GEZIRA, Region, southeast Sudan. Southeast of the confluence of the Blue Nile and the White Nile rivers, it is the site of one of the largest irrigation projects in the world. Begun by the British in 1925, the project distributes the waters of the Blue Nile through a 2,700-mi (4,300-km) network of canals and ditches. It has made the region the most productive agricultural area of Sudan.

jazz, Musical form, often improvisational, developed by African Americans and influenced by both European harmonic structure and African rhythms. Though its specific origins are not known, the music developed principally as an amalgam in the late 19th- and early 20th-century musical culture of New Orleans. Elements of the blues and ragtime in particular combined to form harmonic and rhythmic structures upon which to improvise. Social functions of music played a role in this convergence: whether for dancing or marching, celebration or ceremony, music was tailored to suit the occasion. Instrumental technique combined Western tonal values with emulation of the human voice. Emerging from the collective routines of New Orleans jazz, trumpeter Louis Armstrong became the first great soloist in jazz; the music thereafter became primarily a vehicle for profoundly personal expression through improvisation and composition. Elaboration of the role of the soloist in both small and large ensembles occurred during the swing era (*c.* 1930–45), the music of pianist and bandleader Duke Ellington in particular demonstrating the combination of composed and improvised elements. In the mid-1940s saxophonist Charlie Parker pioneered the technical complexities of bebop as an outgrowth of the refinement of swing: his extremes of tempo and harmonic sophistication challenged both performer and listener. The trumpeter Miles Davis led groups that established the relaxed aesthetic and lyrical phrasing that came to be known as cool jazz in the 1950s, later incorporating modal and electronic elements. Saxophonist John Coltrane's music explored many of the directions jazz would take in the 1960s, including the extension of bebop's chord progressions and experimental free improvisation.

jeep, Outstanding light vehicle of World War II, developed by the U.S. Army Quartermaster Corps. It weighed 1.25 tons, had a four-cylinder engine, and could climb 60° grades and operate on rough terrain thanks to its four-wheel drive and high clearance. The origin of it name is uncertain; one theory traces it to the military designation "vehicle, GP" (i.e., general-purpose). Since the war the jeep has been adapted for civilian use, though it has been replaced in the U.S. military by the High Mobility Multipurpose Wheeled Vehicle (HMMWV), or Humvee.

Jefferson, Thomas (b. April 13, 1743, Shadwell, Va.—d. July 4, 1826, Monticello, Va., U.S.), Third president of the U.S. (1801–09). He was a planter and became a lawyer in 1767. While a member of the House of Burgesses (1769–75), he initiated the Virginia Committee of Correspondence (1773) with Richard Henry Lee and Patrick Henry. In 1774 he wrote the influential *A Summary View of the Rights of British America*, stating that the British Parliament had no authority to legislate for the colonies. A delegate to the Second Continental Congress, he was appointed to the committee to draft the Declaration of Independence and became its primary author. He was elected governor of Virginia (1779–81) but was unable to organize effective opposition when British forces invaded the colony (1780–81). Criticized for his conduct, he retired, vowing to remain a private citizen. Again a member of the Continental Congress (1783–85), he drafted the first of the Northwest Ordinances for dividing and settling the Northwest Territory. In 1785 he succeeded Benjamin Franklin as U.S. minister to France. Appointed the first secretary of state (1790–93) by George Washington, he soon became embroiled in a bitter conflict with Alexander Hamilton over the country's foreign policy and their opposing interpretations of the Constitution. Their divisions gave rise to political factions and eventually to political parties. Jefferson served as vice president (1797–1801) under John Adams but opposed Adams's signing of the Alien and Sedition Acts (1798);

the Virginia and Kentucky Resolutions, adopted by the legislatures of those states in 1798 and 1799 as a protest against the Acts, were written by Jefferson and James Madison. In the presidential election of 1800 Jefferson and Aaron Burr received the same number of votes in the electoral college; the decision was thrown to the U.S. House of Representatives, which chose Jefferson on the 36th ballot. As president, Jefferson attempted to reduce the powers of the embryonic federal government and to eliminate the national debt; he also dispensed with a great deal of the ceremony and formality that had attended the office of president to that time. In 1803 he oversaw the Louisiana Purchase, which doubled the land area of the country, and he authorized the Lewis and Clark Expedition. In an effort to force Britain and France to cease their molestation of U.S. merchant ships during the Napoleonic Wars, he signed the Embargo Act. In 1809 he retired to his plantation, Monticello, where he pursued his interests in science, philosophy, and architecture. He served as president of the American Philosophical Society (1797–1815), and in 1819 he founded and designed the University of Virginia. In 1812, after a long estrangement, he and Adams were reconciled and began a lengthy correspondence that illuminated their opposing political philosophies. They died within hours of each other on July 4, 1826, the 50th anniversary of the signing of the Declaration of Independence. Though a lifelong slaveholder, Jefferson was an anomaly among the Virginia planter class for his support of gradual emancipation. In January 2000 the Thomas Jefferson Memorial Foundation accepted the conclusion, supported by DNA evidence, that Jefferson had fathered at least one child with Sally Hemings, one of his house slaves.

Jehovah's Witness, Member of an international religious movement founded in Pittsburgh, Pa., by Charles T. Russell in 1872. The movement was originally known as the International Bible Students Association, but its name was changed by Russell's successor, Joseph Franklin Rutherford (1869–1942). The Witnesses are a millennialist group whose beliefs are based primarily on the apocalyptic sections of the Bible, notably Daniel and the Book of Revelation. They refuse to perform military service or salute the flag, actions which have brought them into direct conflict with governments around the world. They are famous for their door-to-door evangelizing and for refusing blood transfusions; they believe there is scriptural justification for all their actions and beliefs. Their goal is the establishment of God's kingdom on earth, and they hold that Jesus—who is believed to be God's first creation rather than one person in a trinity—is God's agent in this plan. Their national headquarters is in Brooklyn, N.Y.; their major publications, the *Watchtower* and *Awake!*, are published in about 80 languages.

jellyfish, Any of about 200 described species of free-swimming marine cnidarians (in the classes Scyphozoa and Cubozoa), many of which have a bell-shaped body. The term is also frequently applied to other similar cnidarians (e.g., Portuguese man-of-war) and some unrelated forms (e.g., ctenophores and salps). In scyphozoan jellyfish, the free-swimming medusa form is the dominant stage, with the sessile polyp form found only during larval development. Jellyfish live in all oceans and include the familiar disk-shaped animals that are often found drifting along the shoreline. Most species are 1–16 in. (2–40 cm) in diameter; some are 6 ft (1.8 m) in diameter, with tentacles more than 100 feet (30 m) long. Though some jellyfish simply filter-feed, most feed on small animals (e.g., crustaceans) that they catch in their tentacles, whose stinging cells immobilize the prey; contact can be irritating and sometimes dangerous to humans. The cubozoan jellyfish comprise 50 species of box jellies (the rather spherical body is squared off at the edges), which are usually 1–2 in. (2–4 cm) in diameter.

Jensen, Johannes V(ilhelm) (b. Jan. 20, 1873, Farsø, Den.—d. Nov. 25, 1950, Copenhagen), Danish novelist, poet, and essayist. He initially studied medicine but later turned to writing. He first made an impression as a writer of tales, including the more

than 100 published under the recurring title *Myths*. His early writings also include a historical trilogy, *The Fall of the King* (1900–01), about Christian II of Denmark. His best-known work is *The Long Journey* (1908–22), a series of six novels that chronicles humanity's rise from primitive times to the time of Christopher Columbus's arrival in the Americas. He received the Nobel Prize for Literature in 1944.

Jericho, Arabic ARĪḤĀ, Town (pop., 2005 prelim.: 19,800), West Bank territory. Inhabited since *c.* 9000 BCE, it is famous in biblical tradition as the first town attacked by the Israelites under Joshua after they crossed the Jordan River. It was abandoned or destroyed several times and rebuilt in the same area. Captured by the British in 1918, it became part of the British mandate of Palestine. Incorporated into Jordan, it became the site of two huge camps of Arab refugees following the first Arab-Israeli war (1948). During the Six-Day War (1967), the town was occupied by Israel, and much of the refugee population was dispersed. In 1994 it was turned over to the Palestinian Authority under an Israeli-Palestinian self-rule agreement.

Jersey, British crown dependency, largest and southernmost of the Channel Islands, in the English Channel. Area: 46 sq mi (118 sq km). Population: (2011 est.) 94,100. Capital: St. Helier (pop., 2001: 28,310). Separated from Normandy in 1204, it kept its Norman law and local customs but was administered for the English king by a warden. It was given legislative authority in 1771. It is now governed by a popularly elected assembly, which is presided over by a royally appointed bailiff. There is also a lieutenant governor, who represents the British monarch. Jersey fabric and Jersey cattle take their names from the island.

Jerusalem, Hebrew YERUSHALAYIM, Arabic AL-QUDS, City (pop., 2006 est.: 729,100), ancient city of the Middle East that since 1967 has been wholly under the rule of the State of Israel. Located in the heart of historic Palestine, it is nestled between the West Bank and Israel. The Old City is a typical walled Middle Eastern enclosure; the modern city is an urban agglomeration of high-rises and housing complexes. It is holy to Judaism as the site of the Temple of Jerusalem, to Christianity because of its association with Jesus, and to Islam because of its connection with the Mi'rāj (the Prophet Muhammad's ascension to heaven). Jewish shrines include the Western Wall. Islamic holy places include the Dome of the Rock. In 1000 BCE David made it the capital of Israel. Razed by the Babylonians in the 6th century BCE, it thereafter enjoyed only brief periods of independence. The Romans devastated it in the 1st and 2nd centuries CE, banishing the Jewish population. From 638 it was ruled by various Muslim dynasties, except for short periods during the Crusades when it was controlled by Christians. Rule by the Ottoman Empire ended in 1917, and the city became the capital of the British mandate of Palestine. It was thereafter the subject of competing Zionist and Palestinian national aspirations. Israel claimed the city as its capital after the Arab-Israeli War in 1948 and took the entire city during the Six-Day War of 1967. Its status as Israel's capital has remained a point of contention: official recognition by the international community has largely been withheld pending final settlement of regional territorial rights.

Jerusalem, Council of, Conference of the Christian Apostles at Jerusalem *c.* AD 50, which decreed that Gentile Christians did not have to observe the Mosaic law of the Jews. It was occasioned by the controversy over whether circumcision was necessary for Gentile converts to Christianity. Led by Sts. Peter the Apostle and James, the council decided the issue in favor of St. Paul and the Gentile Christians, thus helping to separate early Christianity from Judaism.

Jesuit, Member of the Roman Catholic order of religious men called the Society of Jesus. First organized by St. Ignatius of Loyola in 1534 at the University of Paris, the order was approved by

Pope Paul III in 1540. It discontinued many practices of medieval religious life, such as obligatory penances and fasts and a common uniform, and instead focused on military-style mobility and adaptability. Its organization was characterized by centralized authority, probation lasting many years before final vows, and special obedience to the pope. The Jesuits served as a preaching, teaching, and missionary society, actively promoting the Counter-Reformation, and by the time of Ignatius's death in 1556 their efforts were already worldwide. The success of their enterprise and their championship of the pope earned them much hostility from both religious and political foes. Under pressure from France, Spain, and Portugal, Pope Clement XIV abolished the order in 1773, but it was restored by Pius VII in 1814. The Jesuits have since become the largest male religious order.

Jesus, In Christianity, the son of God and the second person of the Holy Trinity. Christian doctrine holds that by his crucifixion and resurrection he paid for the sins of all mankind. His life and ministry are recounted in the four Gospels of the New Testament. He was born a Jew in Bethlehem before the death of Herod the Great in 4 BC, and he died while Pontius Pilate was Roman governor of Judaea (AD 28–30). His mother, Mary, was married to Joseph, a carpenter of Nazareth. Of his childhood after the birth narratives in Matthew and Luke, nothing is known, except for one visit to Jerusalem with his parents. He began his ministry about age 30, becoming a preacher, teacher, and healer. He gathered disciples in the region of Galilee, including the 12 Apostles, and preached the imminent arrival of the kingdom of God. His moral teachings, outlined in the Sermon on the Mount, and his reported miracles won him a growing number of followers, who believed that he was the promised messiah. On Passover he entered Jerusalem on a donkey, where he shared the Last Supper with his disciples and was betrayed to the Roman authorities by Judas Iscariot. Arrested and tried, he was condemned to death as a political agitator and was crucified and buried. Three days later visitors to his tomb found it empty. According to the Gospels, he appeared several times to his disciples before ascending into heaven.

jet engine, Any of a class of internal-combustion engines that propel aircraft by means of the rearward discharge of a jet of fluid, usually hot exhaust gases generated by burning fuel with air drawn in from the atmosphere. Jets rely on the third of Newton's laws of motion (action and reaction are equal and opposite). The first jet-powered airplane was introduced in 1939 in Germany. The jet engine, consisting of a gas-turbine system, significantly simplified propulsion and enabled substantial increases in aircraft speed, size, and operating altitudes. Modern types of jet engines include turbojets, turbofans, turboprops, turboshafts, and ramjets.

jet lag, Desynchronization of biological rhythms after moving from one time zone to another. Symptoms include fatigue, loss of concentration, sleep disturbances, malaise, sluggishness, disorientation, gastrointestinal upset, and loss of appetite. Jet lag reflects an interruption of normal light and dark cycles, which influence secretion of the hormone melatonin. Melatonin plays an important role in regulating the circadian rhythm of sleep and wakefulness; because melatonin secretion occurs in response to light-dark cycles, carefully timed exposure to small amounts of light can have a dramatic effect in alleviating jet lag. In addition, melatonin supplements can be used to accelerate the resynchronization of the body clock to a new time zone. Duration and severity of jet lag depend on how much distance is covered in how little time. Travel by jet, after which the phenomenon may persist for some days, first brought the condition to notice, accounting for the name.

jet stream, Any of several long, narrow, high-speed air currents that flow eastward in a generally horizontal zone in the stratosphere or upper troposphere. Jet streams are characterized by wind motions that generate strong vertical shearing action, considered largely responsible for the clear-air turbulence experienced by aircraft. They also have an effect on weather patterns. Jet streams circle the Earth in meandering paths, shifting position as well as speed with the seasons. In the winter they are nearer the Equator and their speeds are higher than in the summer. There are often two, sometimes three, jet-stream systems in each hemisphere.

Jew, Any person whose religion is Judaism. In a wider sense the term refers to any member of a worldwide ethnic and cultural group descended from the ancient Hebrews who traditionally practiced the Jewish religion. The Hebrew term *Yehudi*, translated as *Judaeus* in Latin and *Jew* in English, originally referred to a member of the tribe of Judah. In Jewish tradition, any child born of a Jewish mother is considered a Jew; in Reform Judaism a child is considered a Jew if either parent is Jewish.

Jharkhand, State (pop., 2008 est.: 30,010,000), northeastern India. It is bordered by Bihar, West Bengal, Orissa, Chhattisgarh, and Uttar Pradesh states and occupies 28,833 sq mi (74,677 sq km); its capital is Ranchi. The state lies mainly on the Chota Nagpur plateau, a series of plateaus, hills, and valleys. Many aboriginal peoples live there. The area now constituting Jharkhand was a part of Bihar state after Indian independence in 1947 until it was made into a separate state in 2000. It is rich in minerals (notably copper), although much of the population is engaged in agriculture.

Jia Xian (fl. *c.* 1050, China), Mathematician and astronomer active at the beginning of the greatest period of traditional Chinese mathematics. He held a relatively low military office during the reign (1022/23–1063/64) of Emperor Renzong of the Song dynasty. He was a pupil of mathematician and astronomer Chu Yan, who contributed to the revision of the Chongtian calendar in 1023, and he served in the Imperial Astronomical Bureau. Jia's name was mainly quoted in connection with his method of extracting roots (solutions) of polynomials of degree higher than three and with the related Jia Xian triangle, which contains the binomial coefficients for equations up to the sixth degree. This diagram is similar to Blaise Pascal's triangle, which was discovered independently later in the West.

Jiang Qing, or CHIANG CH'ING, orig. LI JINHAI (b. 1914?, Zhucheng, Shandong, China—d. May 14, 1991, Beijing), Third wife of Mao Zedong and member of the radical Gang of Four. Jiang married Mao in the 1930s but entered politics only in the 1960s. As first deputy head of the Cultural Revolution, Jiang acquired far-reaching powers over China's cultural life and oversaw the total suppression of a wide variety of traditional cultural activities. Arrested after Mao's death and accused of fomenting the widespread civil unrest that characterized the Cultural Revolution, she refused to confess guilt and received a suspended death sentence that was commuted to life imprisonment. Her death was reported as a suicide.

Jiang Zemin (b. Aug. 17, 1926, Yangzhou, Jiangsu, China), General secretary of the Chinese Communist Party (CCP; 1989–2002) and president of China (1993–2003). He started his career in Shanghai as an engineer, received training abroad, and gradually rose through the ranks of the CCP. He was named mayor of Shanghai in 1985 and chairman of China's Central Military Commission in 1989. He replaced Zhao Ziyang as general secretary in June 1989 following the Tiananmen Square incident. Jiang combined a pragmatic, reform-minded economic policy with an insistence that the party maintain strong control over the government. After serving the maximum two five-year terms as president, Jiang was succeeded by Hu Jintao. He remained in charge of the Central Military Commission until stepping down in favour of Hu in 2004.

Jiangsu, or CHIANG-SU, conventional KIANGSU, Province (pop., 2002 est.: 73,810,000), eastern China. It lies on the Yellow Sea and is also bordered by Shandong, Anhui, and Zhejiang provinces and Shanghai municipality. With an area of 39,600 sq mi (102,600 sq km), it is one of the smallest and most densely populated provinces of China, and it is also one of the wealthiest. Its capital is Nanjing (Nanking). It occupies a wide alluvial plain that is divided into two sections by the estuary of the Yangtze River (Chang Jiang). Once a part of the ancient state of Wu, the region was part of the Nanjing province under the Ming dynasty (1368–1644). It became a separate province in 1667 and served as the headquarters (1853–64) for the Taiping Rebellion. It was an important base for China's Nationalist Party, which made Nanjing the nation's capital from 1928 to 1937 and again from 1946 to 1949. The province was occupied by Japan during the Sino-Japanese War (1937–45) and came under communist control in 1949. It produces steel, electronics, and agricultural products.

Jiangxi, or CHIANG-HSI, conventional KIANGSI, Province (pop., 2002 est.: 42,220,000), south-central China. It is bordered by Hubei, Anhui, Zhejiang, Fujian, Guangdong, and Hunan provinces. It has an area of 63,600 sq mi (164,800 sq km), and its capital is Nanchang. Located in the drainage basin of the Gan River, it is one of China's richest agricultural provinces, and it is also renowned for its porcelain industry, which dates from the 11th century. The opening of the Grand Canal under the Tang dynasty (618–907) set it on the main trade route between northern and southern China. During the Yuan dynasty (1206–1368), it included part of Guangdong; its current boundaries were established in the Ming dynasty. It was taken in 1926 by Chiang Kai-shek and was fought over by the Nationalists and the communists. Much of the province was occupied by the Japanese from 1938 to 1945 and came under communist control in 1949. Agricultural production, as well as a thriving timber industry, contributes to the economy.

Jibrīl, or JABRAIL, In Islam, the archangel who acts as intermediary between God and humankind and who bore divine revelations to Muhammad and previous prophets. His biblical counterpart is Gabriel. Jibrīl aided Muhammad in times of crisis and guided him during his ascent into heaven. Muslim belief holds that Jibrīl appeared to Adam after his expulsion from Paradise to show him how to write, raise wheat, and work iron and also that Jibrīl aided Moses in delivering the Israelites from Egypt.

Jiddah, or JEDDAH, City (pop., 2004: 2,801,481), western Saudi Arabia. Located on the Red Sea, it is a major port and the country's diplomatic capital. It takes its name (which means "ancestress" or "grandmother") from the reputed tomb of Eve, which was located there until it was destroyed by the Saudi government in 1928. Jiddah has long been a point of entry for Muslim pilgrims journeying to the holy cities of Mecca and Medina. It belonged to the Ottoman Empire until 1916, when it surrendered to British forces during World War I (1914–18). It was captured by the tribal leader Ibn Saʿūd in 1925 and was incorporated into Saudi Arabia in 1927.

jihad, In Islam, the central doctrine that calls on believers to combat the enemies of their religion. According to the Qurʾān and the Ḥadīth, jihad is a duty that may be fulfilled in four ways: by the heart, the tongue, the hand, or the sword. The first way (known in Sufism as the "greater jihad") involves struggling against evil desires. The ways of the tongue and hand call for verbal defense and right actions. The jihad of the sword involves waging war against enemies of Islam. Believers contend that those who die in combat become martyrs and are guaranteed a place in paradise. In the 20th and 21st centuries the concept of jihad has sometimes been used as an ideological weapon in the effort to combat Western influences and secular governments and to establish an ideal Islamic society.

Jiménez, Juan Ramón (b. Dec. 24, 1881, Moguer, Spain—d. May 29, 1958, San Juan, P.R.), Spanish poet. His early poetry reflects the influence of Rubén Darío; this highly emotional style gave way to a more austere tone c. 1917. He achieved popularity in America with *Platero and I* (1917), a prose story of a man and his donkey. During the Spanish Civil War (1936–39), he allied himself with Republican forces; after their defeat he moved to Puerto Rico, where he spent most of the rest of his life. His poetic output was immense. He was awarded the Nobel Prize for Literature in 1956.

Jimmu, Legendary first emperor of Japan and founder of the imperial dynasty. He is credited with establishing his state in 660 BC on the plains of Yamato. (An actual state on the Yamato plains dates from the 3rd century AD.) Jimmu was believed to be a descendant of Ninigi, who was in turn the grandson of the sun goddess Amaterasu.

Jinan, or CHI-NAN, conventional TSINAN, City (pop., 2003 est.: 2,346,000), capital of Shandong province, eastern China. It dates to the Zhou dynasty (1046–256 BC) and earlier and has been an administrative centre since the 8th century BC. Nearby Mount Tai was one of China's greatest holy mountains; many Buddhist cave temples were built in the hills south of the city in the 4th–7th century AD. It was made the capital of Shandong under the Ming dynasty (1368–1644). Opened to foreign commerce in 1904, it developed further after becoming a railroad junction in 1912. It is now a major administrative and industrial centre and Shandong's chief cultural centre, with agricultural, medical, and engineering colleges and a large university (1926).

jinja, In the Shintō religion, a place where a god is enshrined or to which it is summoned. Originally rural sites of great natural beauty, *jinja* now include urban shrines. They vary in size from small roadside places of prayer to large building complexes such as the Grand Ise Shrine. There are more than 97,000 such shrines in Japan.

Jinnah, Mohammed Ali (b. Dec. 25, 1876, Karachi, India—d. Sept. 11, 1948, Karachi, Pak.), Indian Muslim politician, founder and first governor-general of Pakistan (1947–48). He was educated in Bombay (now Mumbai) and London, where he became a lawyer at age 19. After returning to India, he practiced law and was elected to India's Imperial Legislative Council in 1910. Committed to home rule for India and to maintaining Hindu-Muslim unity, he joined the Muslim League in 1913 and worked to ensure its collaboration with the Indian National Congress. He was opposed to Mohandas K. Gandhi's noncooperation movement and withdrew from the Congress. In the late 1920s and early '30s, he was seen as too moderate by some Muslims but too Muslim by the Congress Party. From 1937, when the Congress Party refused to form coalition governments with the Muslim League in the provinces, Jinnah began to work for the partitioning of India and on creating a Muslim state. Pakistan emerged as an independent country in 1947, and Jinnah became its first head of state. He died in 1948, revered as the father of the nation.

jinni, or GENIE, plural JINN, In Arabic mythology, any of the supernatural spirits less powerful than angels or devils. Evil spirits of air or fire, they could take animal or human form and could dwell in inanimate objects or under the earth. They had the bodily needs of human beings and could be killed but were otherwise free of physical restraints. Jinn delighted in punishing humans for any harm done to them, but people who knew the proper magical procedure could exploit them to their own advantage. The jinn were popular subjects for folklore, notably in the tale of Aladdin in *The Thousand and One Nights*.

Jīzah, Al-, or GIZA, City (pop., 2006: 2,891,275), Upper Egypt. Located on the western bank of the Nile River, it is a suburb of Cairo. A noted entertainment district, it is also the centre of Egypt's motion-picture industry. Rising just west of the city are the Great Sphinx and the Pyramids of Giza, built during Egypt's 4th dynasty (c. 2575–c. 2465 BCE).

jizya, or JIZYAH, Poll tax that early Islamic rulers demanded from their non-Muslim subjects. This tax applied especially to followers of Judaism, Christianity, and Zoroastrianism, who were tolerated in the practice of their religion because they were "peoples of the book." Originally intended to be used for charitable purposes, the revenues from the jizya were paid into the private treasuries of rulers, and the Ottoman sultans used the proceeds to pay military expenses. Many converted to Islam in order to escape the tax.

Joan of Arc, Saint, French JEANNE D'ARC (b. *c.* 1412 CE, Domrémy, Bar, France—d. May 30, 1431, Rouen; canonized May 16, 1920; feast day May 30), French military heroine. She was a peasant girl who from an early age believed she heard the voices of Saints Michael, Catherine, and Margaret. When she was about 16, her voices began urging her to aid France's dauphin (crown prince) and save France from the English attempt at conquest in the Hundred Years' War. Dressed in men's clothes, she visited the dauphin and convinced him, his advisers, and the church authorities to support her. With her inspiring conviction, she rallied the French troops and raised the English siege of Orléans in 1429. She soon defeated the English again at Patay. The dauphin was crowned king at Reims as Charles VII, with Joan beside him. Her siege of Paris was unsuccessful, and in 1430 she was captured by the Burgundians and sold to the English. Abandoned by Charles, she was turned over to the ecclesiastical court at Rouen, controlled by French clerics who supported the English, and tried for witchcraft and heresy (1431). She fiercely defended herself but finally recanted and was sentenced to life imprisonment. When she again asserted that she had been divinely inspired, she was burned at the stake.

jogging, Aerobic exercise involving running at an easy pace. *Jogging* (1967) by Bill Bowerman and W.E. Harris boosted jogging's popularity for fitness, weight loss, and stress relief. Many medical authorities endorse jogging, but others warn of risks to feet, shins, knees, and backs. Jogging only every other day, warming up properly, and using well-designed shoes and proper technique can reduce risks.

Johannesburg, City (pop., 2001: metro. area, 3,225,810), northeastern South Africa. The capital of Gauteng province and one of the country's largest cities, it bestrides a highland region called the Witwatersrand. It was founded in 1886 after the discovery of gold nearby and was occupied by the British during the South African War in 1900. It was a legally segregated city until 1991; nonwhites were restricted to living in outlying areas called townships, including Soweto. Greater Johannesburg extends more than 600 sq mi (1,600 sq km) and includes more than 500 suburbs and townships. It is a leading industrial and financial centre. Its cultural and educational institutions include the Johannesburg Art Gallery, the Civic Theatre, the University of the Witwatersrand, and the University of Johannesburg.

John, known as JOHN LACKLAND (b. Dec. 24, 1167, Oxford, Eng.—d. Oct. 18/19, 1216, Newark, Nottinghamshire), King of England (1199–1216). The youngest son of Henry II, he joined his brother Richard (later Richard I) in a rebellion against Henry (1189). John became lord of Ireland and, when Richard was imprisoned in Germany on his way back from the Third Crusade, he tried to seize control of England (1193). On Richard's return, John was banished (1194), but the two were later reconciled. Crowned king in 1199, John lost Normandy (1204) and most of his other French lands in a war with Philip II (Philip Augustus). After Innocent III excommunicated him for refusing to recognize Stephen Langton as archbishop of Canterbury, John was obliged to declare England a fief of the Holy See (1213). He launched a military campaign against France in 1214 but made no lasting gains. His heavy taxes and aggressive assertion of feudal privileges led to the outbreak of civil war (1215). The barons forced him to sign the Magna Carta, but the civil war continued until his death.

John XXIII, orig. ANGELO GIUSEPPE RONCALLI (b. Nov. 25, 1881, Sotto il Monte, Italy—d. June 3, 1963, Rome; beatified

John XXIII, 1963
Keystone/FPG

Sept. 3, 2000; feast day October 11), Pope (1958–63). He studied theology in Rome, was ordained a priest in 1904, and held a variety of church offices. In 1944 he was named papal nuncio to newly liberated France, where he successfully revived sympathy for the Vatican. Made a cardinal in 1953, he was elected pope after the death of Pius XII (1939–58). Because of his advanced age, he was expected to be little more than a caretaker in the office, but instead he became the major reforming pope of the century. Eager to lead the church into the modern era, he called the Second Vatican Council in 1962, inviting Eastern Orthodox and Protestant observers to join Catholic delegates. He also sought to repair relations with the Jews. The council went on to make major reforms in Catholic liturgy and administration, though John died before its conclusion. An energetic advocate of world peace, he was one of the most popular popes in history. In 2000 he was beatified by John Paul II (1978–2005).

John Paul II, Blessed, orig. KAROL WOJTYŁA (b. May 18, 1920, Wadowice, Pol.—d. April 2, 2005, Vatican City; beatified May 1, 2011; feast day October 22), Pope (1978–2005), the bishop of Rome and head of the Roman Catholic Church, the first non-Italian pope in 455 years and the first ever from a Slavic country. He studied for the priesthood at an underground seminary in Kraków during World War II and was ordained in 1946. He earned a doctorate in philosophy in Rome (1948) and returned home to serve in a parish, earning a second doctorate (also 1948), in sacred theology, from the Jagiellonian University. He became archbishop of Kraków in 1964 and cardinal in 1967.

John Paul II, 1979.
Lochon-Francolon-Simon/Gamma Liaison

Elected pope after the 33-day pontificate of John Paul I (b. 1912—d. 1978), he became known for his energy, charisma, and intellect as well as for his conservative theological views and fervent anticommunism. In 1981 John Paul was shot in St. Peter's Square by a Turkish gunman, but he recovered, resumed his work, and forgave his would-be assassin. His trips abroad attracted some of the largest crowds ever assembled. His nonviolent activism spurred movements that contributed to the peaceful dissolution of the Soviet Union in 1991. He championed economic and political justice in developing nations. In naming 44 cardinals from five continents (February 2001), John Paul reached out to cultures around the world. He also canonized more saints, from more parts of the world, than had any other pope. His ecumenical efforts, including meetings with Jewish, Muslim, and Eastern Orthodox religious leaders, were widely praised, but he often drew criticism for his traditionalist views on issues of gender and sexuality. Although afflicted with Parkinson disease since the early 1990s, John Paul remained active and made a historic trip to Jerusalem in March 2000, during which he sought to improve relations between the Roman Catholic Church and Jews. He was beatified on May 1, 2011.

Johnson, Andrew (b. Dec. 29, 1808, Raleigh, N.C., U.S.—d. July 31, 1875, near Carter Station, Tenn.), 17th president of the U.S. (1865–69). Born in poverty, he never attended school, and he taught himself to read and write. After a short apprenticeship as a tailor, he moved with his family to Greeneville, Tenn., where he opened his own tailor shop. Before he was 21 he organized a workingman's party. Elected to the state legislature (1835–43), he became a spokesman for small farmers. He then served in the U.S. House of Representatives (1843–53) and as governor of Tennessee (1853–57). Elected to the U.S. Senate (1857–62), he opposed antislavery agitation, but, in 1860, after the election of Pres. Abraham Lincoln, he vehemently rejected Southern secession, a position he maintained even after Tennessee seceded in 1861. During the American Civil War he was the only Southern senator who refused to join the Confederacy. In 1862 he was appointed military governor of Tennessee, then under Union control. In 1864 he was selected to run for vice president with President Lincoln; he assumed the presidency after Lincoln's assassination. During Reconstruction he favoured a moderate policy of readmitting former Confederate states to the Union with few provisions for reform or civil rights for freedmen. In 1867, Johnson's vetoes of legislation to establish a Freedmen's Bureau and other civil rights measures angered moderate as well as Radical Republicans; in response, they united to pass the Tenure of Office Act (1867), which forbade the president from removing civil officers without senatorial consent. In 1868, in defiance of the act, Johnson dismissed secretary of war Edwin M. Stanton, an ally of the Radicals. The House then voted to impeach the president—the first such occurrence in U.S. history. In the subsequent Senate trial, the charges proved weak, and the necessary two-thirds vote needed for conviction failed by one vote. Johnson remained in office until 1869, but he had lost the ability to lead. He returned to Tennessee, where he won reelection to the Senate shortly before he died.

Andrew Johnson.
Library of Congress, Washington, D.C.

Johnson, Eyvind (b. July 29, 1900, Svartbjörnsbyn, near Boden, Swed.—d. Aug. 25, 1976, Stockholm), Swedish novelist. He endured a grim boyhood of hard labour. His early novels evince feelings of frustration; *Bobinack* (1932) is an exposé of the machinations of modern capitalism, and *Rain at Daybreak* (1933) is an attack on modern office drudgery. *Return to Ithaca* (1946) and *The Days of His Grace* (1960) have been widely translated. Johnson's working-class novels experimented with new forms and techniques; they also introduced new themes to Swedish literature. He shared the 1974 Nobel Prize for Literature with Harry Martinson.

Johnson, Lyndon B(aines) (b. Aug. 27, 1908, Gillespie county, Texas, U.S.—d. Jan. 22, 1973, San Antonio, Texas), 36th president of the U.S. (1963–69). He taught school in Houston, Texas, before going to Washington, D.C., in 1932 as a congressional aide. In Washington he was befriended by Sam Rayburn, speaker of the House of Representatives, and his political career blossomed. He won a seat in the U.S. House (1937–49) as a supporter of the New Deal, which was under conservative attack. His loyalty impressed Pres. Franklin D. Roosevelt, who made Johnson his protégé. He won election to the U.S. Senate in 1949 in a vicious campaign that involved fraud on both sides. As Democratic whip (1951–55) and majority leader (1955–61), he developed a talent for consensus building through methods both tactful and ruthless. He was largely responsible for passage of the civil rights bills of 1957 and 1960, the first in the 20th century. In 1960 he was elected vice president under John F. Kennedy; he became president after Kennedy's assassination in 1963. In his first few months in office he won passage of the Civil Rights Act of 1964, the most comprehensive and far-reaching legislation of its kind in American history. Later that year he announced his Great Society program of social-welfare and civil rights legislation. His attention to domestic matters, however, was diverted by the country's escalating involvement in the Vietnam War, which provoked large student demonstrations and other protests, beginning in the late 1960s. Meanwhile, discontent and alienation among the young and racial minorities increased as the promises of the Great Society failed to materialize. By 1967 Johnson's popularity had declined steeply, and in early 1968 he announced that he would not seek reelection. He retired to his Texas ranch.

joint, Structure connecting two or more bones. Most joints, including synovial (fluid-containing) joints and those between vertebrae, which incorporate a disk, can move. Immovable joints include the sutures of the skull. Ligaments connect the bones of a joint, but muscles keep them in place. Joint disorders include various forms of arthritis, injuries (e.g., sprains, fractures, and dislocations), congenital disorders, and vitamin deficiencies.

Joliot-Curie, (Jean-) Frédéric, orig. JEAN-FRÉDÉRIC JOLIOT (b. March 19, 1900, Paris, France—d. Aug. 14, 1958, Arcouest), French physical chemist. In 1926 he married Irène Curie (1900–58), daughter of Pierre and Marie Curie; he would eventually append her name to his. In 1932 he first observed production of an electron-positron pair. Frédéric and Irène are remembered for their discovery of new radioactive isotopes prepared artificially, for which they were jointly awarded a 1935 Nobel Prize. Frédéric served in the Resistance during World War II and became a member of the Communist Party; in the postwar years he served as the highest government official in the realm of atomic energy but was dismissed for his political beliefs. From 1946 to 1956 Irène directed the Radium Institute, where she had first worked in 1918; Frédéric succeeded her in the post. Both died of conditions caused by their long exposure to radioactivity.

Jordan, officially HASHEMITE KINGDOM OF JORDAN, Country, Middle East, southwestern Asia, lying east of the Jordan River. Jordan has 16 mi (26 km) of coastline on the Gulf of Aqaba. Area: 34,277 sq mi (88,778 sq km). Population: (2011 est.) 6,180,000. Capital: Amman. The vast majority of the population are Arabs, about one-third of whom are Palestinian Arabs who fled to Jordan from neighbouring Israel and the West Bank as a result of the Arab-Israeli wars. Language: Arabic (official). Religion: Islam (official; predominantly Sunni). Currency: Jordanian dinar. Four-fifths of the country is desert; less than one-tenth of the land is arable. The highest point of elevation, Mount Ramm (5,755 ft [1,754 m]), rises in the uplands region on the east bank of the Jordan River. The Jordan Valley region contains the Dead Sea. Jordan's economy is based largely on manufacturing and services (including tourism); exports include clothing, phosphate, potash, pharmaceuticals, fruits and vegetables, and fertilizers. Jordan is a constitutional monarchy with two legislative houses; the head of state and government is the king, assisted by the prime minister. Jordan shares much of its history with Israel, since both occupy parts of the area known historically as Palestine. Much of present-day Jordan was once part of the kingdom of Israel under David and Solomon (*c.* 1000 BCE). It fell to the Seleucids in 330 BCE and to Muslim Arabs in the 7th century CE. The Crusaders extended the kingdom of Jerusalem east of the Jordan River in 1099. The region became part of the Ottoman Empire during the 16th century. In 1920 the area comprising Jordan (then known as Transjordan) was established within the British mandate of Palestine. Britain recognized Transjordan's partial independence in 1923, although the British mandate did not end until 1948. In 1950, after the end of hostilities with the new State of Israel, Jordan annexed the West Bank and east Jerusalem, administering the territory until Israel gained control of it in the Six-Day War of 1967. In 1970–71 Jordan was wracked by fighting between the government and guerrillas of the Palestine Liberation Organization (PLO), a struggle that ended with the PLO being expelled from Jordan. In 1988 King Ḥussein renounced all Jordanian claims to the West Bank in favour of the PLO. In 1994 Jordan and Israel signed a full peace agreement. Ḥussein died in 1999 and was succeeded by his son Abdullāh II.

Jordan, Michael (Jeffrey) (b. Feb. 17, 1963, Brooklyn, N.Y., U.S.), U.S. basketball player. As a freshman in 1982, he helped the University of North Carolina win the collegiate national championship. Drafted by the Chicago Bulls in 1984, he won 10 scoring titles and 5 Most Valuable Player awards while leading the Bulls to six championships (1991–93, 1996–98). He was also part of the 1984 and 1992 U.S. Olympic basketball teams that won gold medals. He retired briefly in 1993, hoping to play professional baseball, but returned to the Bulls in 1995. He retired again in 1999, but, after a stint as an owner and general manager of the Washington Wizards, Jordan returned to play for that team in 2001. Known as "Air Jordan" for his exceptional leaping ability, he combined acrobatic play with a fierce competitive spirit and was considered among the game's greatest players. His success on the court and in the business world made him one of the most popular and recognized athletes of all time.

Jordan River, River, Middle East. It rises on the Syria-Lebanon border, flows through Lake Tiberias (Sea of Galilee), and then receives its main tributary, the Yarmūk River. It drains into the Dead Sea at 1,312 ft (400 m) below sea level after a total course of 223 mi (360 km). In Christianity it is known as the place where John the Baptist baptized Jesus.

Joseph, Saint (fl. 1st century AD, Nazareth, Galilee region of Palestine; principle feast day March 19; Feast of St. Joseph the Worker May 1), In the New Testament, the husband of Mary and the earthly father of Jesus. Descended from the house of David, he was a carpenter in Nazareth. Betrothed to Mary when he found her already pregnant, an angel appeared to him in a vision and told him the expected child was the son of God. He and Mary journeyed to Bethlehem to be counted in the Roman census, and while they were there the child was born. The last mention of Joseph occurs in the Gospel of Luke, when he and Mary take the 12-year-old Jesus to Jerusalem.

Josephson effect, Flow of electric current between two pieces of superconducting material separated by a thin layer of insulating material. This flow was predicted by the British physicist Brian Josephson in 1962, based on the BCS theory. According to Josephson, pairs of electrons can move from one superconductor to the other across the insulating layer (tunneling). The locus of this action is called a Josephson junction. The Josephson current flows only if no battery is connected across the two conductors. A major application of this discovery is in superfast switching devices used in computers, which can be 100 times faster than ordinary semiconducting circuits.

journalism, Collection, preparation, and distribution of news and related commentary and feature materials through media such as pamphlets, newsletters, newspapers, magazines, radio, film, television, and books. The term was originally applied to the reportage of current events in printed form, specifically newspapers, but in the late 20th century it came to include electronic media as well. It is sometimes used to refer to writing characterized by a direct presentation of facts or description of events without an attempt at interpretation. Colleges and universities confer degrees in journalism and sponsor research in related fields such as media studies and journalism ethics.

JPEG, in full JOINT PHOTOGRAPHIC EXPERTS GROUP, Standard computer file format for storing graphic images in a compressed form for general use. JPEG images are compressed using a math-ematical algorithm. A variety of encoding processes can be used, depending on whether the user's goal is the highest quality of image (lossless) or smallest file size (lossy). The JPEG and GIF formats are the most commonly used graphics formats on the Internet for lossy and lossless data compression, respectively.

Juárez, or CIUDAD JUÁREZ, City (pop., 2000: 1,187,275), northern Chihuahua state, Mexico. Located on the Rio Grande opposite El Paso, Texas, it was formerly known as El Paso del Norte and was renamed in 1888 for Mexico's national hero, Benito Juárez, who headquartered there in 1865. Today it is an important border city and functions as the marketing centre for a cotton-growing area. The city has grown greatly since the 1970s because of the increase in the number of export-oriented assembly plants (maquiladoras) located there. It contains the Guadalupe mission (1662).

Juárez, Benito (Pablo) (b. March 21, 1806, San Pablo Guelatao, Oaxaca, Mex.—d. July 18, 1872, Mexico City), National hero and president (1861–72) of Mexico. A Zapotec Indian, Juárez initially studied for the priesthood but later took a law degree and became a legislator, a judge, and a cabinet minister. He led La Reforma, a liberal political and social revolution in Mexico, and, when liberal forces gained control of the national government in 1855, he was able to implement his ideas. In 1857 he was elected head of the Supreme Court, which, under a new constitution, placed him first in the order of presidential succession.

Benito Juárez.
Library of Congress, Washington, D.C.

In 1858 a coup by conservative forces sent Mexico's president into exile, but Juárez succeeded him and headed a liberal government that opposed the regime installed by the conservatives. After three years of civil war, the liberals prevailed. Juárez was elected president in 1861 and twice reelected. Early in his first term, the French under Napoleon III invaded and occupied Mexico, putting Maximilian of Austria in power in 1864. When Napoleon later withdrew his troops, Juárez defeated Maximilian's armies and had him executed in 1867. Juárez's final years were marred by a loss of popular support and by personal tragedy. He died in office.

Jubba River, River, Somalia. Originating in southern Ethiopia, it flows south 545 mi (875 km) to the Indian Ocean just north of Kismaayo, one of Somalia's three main ports. It is the only river in the region that is reliably navigable.

Judaea, or JUDEA, Southern division of ancient Palestine successively under Persian, Greek, and Roman rule. It was bounded on the north by Samaria and on the west by the Mediterranean Sea. It succeeded the Hebrew kingdom of Judah, which was destroyed by the Babylonians. The revived kingdom of Judaea was established by the Maccabees, who resisted the suppression of Judaism under foreign rule. Family disputes led to Roman intervention in 63 BC. Under Roman control, Herod (the Great) was made king of Judaea in 37 BC. After Herod's death the country was ruled alternately by his descendants and by Roman procurators. As a result of the Jewish revolt in AD 66, the city of Jerusalem was destroyed (AD 70). The name Judaea is used by Israelis to describe approximately the same area in the modern West Bank territory.

Judaism, Religious beliefs and practices of the Jews. One of the three great monotheistic world religions, Judaism began as the faith of the ancient Hebrews, and its sacred text is the Hebrew Bible, particularly the Torah. Fundamental to Judaism is the belief that the people of Israel are God's chosen people, who must serve as a light for other nations. God made a covenant first with Abraham and then renewed it with Isaac, Jacob, and Moses. The worship of Yahweh (God) was centred in Jerusalem from the time of David. The destruction of the First Temple of Jerusalem by the Babylonians (586 BCE) and the subsequent exile of the Jews led to hopes for national restoration under the leadership of a messiah. The Jews were later allowed to return by the Persians, but an unsuccessful rebellion against Roman rule led to the destruction of the Second Temple in 70 CE and the Jews' dispersal throughout the world in the Jewish Diaspora. Rabbinic Judaism emerged to replace the beliefs and practices associated with the Temple at Jerusalem, as the Jews carried on their culture and religion through a tradition of scholarship and strict observance. The great body of oral law and commentaries were committed to writing in the Talmud and Mishna. The religion was maintained despite severe persecutions by many nations.

Two branches of Judaism emerged in the Middle Ages: the Sephardic, centred in Spain and culturally linked with the Babylonian Jews; and the Ashkenazic, centred in France and Germany and linked with the Jewish culture of Palestine and Rome. Elements of mysticism also appeared, notably the esoteric writings of the Kabbala and, in the 18th century, the movement known as Hasidism. The 18th century was also the time of the Jewish Enlightenment (Haskala). Conservative and Reform Judaism emerged in 19th-century Germany as an effort to modify the strictness of Orthodox Judaism. By the end of the 19th century Zionism had appeared as an outgrowth of reform. European Judaism suffered terribly during the Holocaust, when millions were put to death by the Nazis, and the rising flow of Jewish emigrants to Palestine led to the declaration of the State of Israel in 1948. In the early 21st century there were nearly 15 million Jews worldwide.

Judas Iscariot (d. *c.* AD 30), Disciple who betrayed Jesus. He was one of the original 12 disciples. Judas made a deal with the Jewish authorities to betray Jesus into their custody; in return for 30 pieces of silver, he brought the armed guard to the Garden of Gethsemane and identified Jesus with a kiss. He later regretted his deed and committed suicide; according to Matthew 27, he returned the money to the priests before hanging himself. His surname may mean "man of Kerioth," or it may link him to the Sicarii, a band of radical Jewish terrorists.

Judgment, Day of, In Christianity, the final judgment of God on all people at the end of history. It will occur at the second coming of Christ, when the dead are resurrected. It is especially important in millennialist denominations. In Islam, the Day of Judgment is described in the Quran and the Hadith. Religions that include reincarnation (e.g., Hinduism) lack a Day of Judgment; the determination of how an individual is to be reborn being a particular judgment on the merit of the life just lived.

judicial review, Examination by a country's courts of the actions of the legislative, executive, and administrative branches of government to ensure that those actions conform to the provisions of the constitution. Actions that do not conform are unconstitutional and therefore null and void. The practice is usually considered to have begun with the ruling by the Supreme Court of the United States in *Marbury* v. *Madison* (1803). Several constitutions drafted in Europe and Asia after World War II incorporated judicial review. Especially subject to scrutiny in the U.S. have been actions bearing on civil rights (or civil liberty), due process of law, equal protection under the law, freedom of religion, freedom of speech, and rights of privacy.

judiciary, Branch of government in which judicial power is vested. The principal work of any judiciary is the adjudication of disputes or controversies. Regulations govern what parties are allowed before a judicial assembly, or court, what evidence will be admitted, what trial procedure will be followed, and what types of judgments may be rendered. Typically present in court are the presiding judge, the parties to the matter (sometimes called litigants), the lawyers representing the parties, and other individuals including witnesses, clerks, bailiffs, and jurors when the proceeding involves a jury. Though the courts' stated function is to administer justice according to rules enacted by the legislative branch, courts also unavoidably make law. In deciding, for example, how legislative provisions are to be applied to specific cases, the courts in effect make law by laying down rules for future cases; this is known as the doctrine of precedent. In some jurisdictions, courts have the power of judicial review, enabling them to declare unconstitutional legislation or acts of the executive.

judo, Martial art that emphasizes the use of quick movement and leverage to throw an opponent. Its techniques are generally intended to turn an opponent's force to one's own advantage rather than to oppose it directly. The opponent must be thrown cleanly, pinned, or mastered through the application of pressure to arm joints or the neck. Judo is now practiced primarily as sport. It became an Olympic sport in 1964; women's judo was added in 1992. The sport evolved out of jujitsu in late-19th-century Japan.

Jugendstil, Artistic style that arose near the end of the 19th century in Germany and Austria. Its name was derived from the Munich magazine *Die Jugend* ("Youth"), founded in 1896, which featured Art Nouveau designs. Its early phase, primarily floral in character, was rooted in English Art Nouveau and Japanese prints; a more abstract phase emerged after 1900. Primarily a style in architecture and the decorative arts, it also included the great Austrian painter Gustav Klimt.

Julian Alps, Range of the eastern Alps. It extends southeast from the Carnic Alps in northeastern Italy to the city of Ljubljana, Slvn. The highest peak is Triglav (9,396 ft [2,864 m]), also the highest point in Slovenia.

Julian of Norwich, or JULIANA OF NORWICH (b. 1342, probably Norwich, Norfolk, Eng.—d. after 1416), English mystic. After being healed of a serious illness (1373), she wrote two accounts of her visions; her *Revelations of Divine Love* is remarkable for its clarity, beauty, and profundity. She spent her later life as a recluse in Norwich.

Julius II, orig. GIULIANO DELLA ROVERE (b. Dec. 5, 1443, Albisola, republic of Genoa—d. Feb. 21, 1513, Rome), Pope (1503–13). The nephew of Sixtus IV, he fled Rome in 1494 to escape assassination by Alexander VI. Elected pope in 1503, Julius set out to restore the Papal States, subjugating Perugia and Bologna (1508) and defeating Venice (1509) with the aid of the League of Cambrai. His first effort to expel the French from northern Italy failed, but a popular revolt drove them out in 1512, and Parma and Piacenza were added to the Papal States. The greatest art patron of all the popes, Julius was a close friend of Michelangelo, from whom he commissioned the sculpture of Moses and the paintings in the Sistine Chapel. He also commissioned Raphael's Vatican frescoes.

July Days (1917) Period in the Russian Revolution of 1917 during which Petrograd workers and soldiers staged armed demonstrations against the provisional government that resulted in a temporary decline of Bolshevik influence and in the formation of a new provisional government headed by Aleksandr Kerensky. To undermine Bolshevik popularity, the government produced evidence that Vladimir Ilich Lenin had ties with the German government. The public reacted against the Bolsheviks, Lenin fled to Finland, and Leon Trotsky and other leaders were jailed. The reorganized government was overthrown by the Bolsheviks in October.

July Plot, or RASTENBURG ASSASSINATION PLOT, Abortive attempt on July 20, 1944, by German military leaders to assassinate Adolf Hitler, seize control of the government, and seek more favourable peace terms from the Allies. According to plan, Col.

Claus von Stauffenberg (1907–44) left a bomb in a briefcase in a conference room at the field headquarters at Rastenburg, East Prussia, where Hitler was meeting with top military aides. But the briefcase was pushed behind a table support, and Hitler survived the blast with minor injuries. Meanwhile, the other conspirators in Berlin failed to act. The chief conspirators, including Stauffenberg, Gen. Ludwig Beck, Gen. Erwin Rommel, and other top officers, were promptly shot or forced to commit suicide. In subsequent days, Hitler's police rounded up about 200 conspirators, who were shot, hanged, or viciously strangled.

July Revolution (1830) Insurrection that brought Louis-Philippe to the throne of France. It was precipitated on July 26 by Charles X's publication of restrictive ordinances contrary to the spirit of the Charter of 1814. Demonstrations were followed by three days of fighting (July 27–29), Charles's abdication, and the proclamation of Louis-Philippe as king. The bourgeoisie secured a political and social ascendancy that was to characterize the subsequent July Monarchy.

June Days (June 23–26, 1848) In French history, a brief and bloody civil uprising in Paris in the early days of the Second Republic. The new government instituted numerous radical reforms, but the new assembly, composed mainly of moderate and conservative candidates, was determined to cut costs and end risky experiments such as public works programs to provide for the unemployed. Thousands of Parisian workers—suddenly cut off from the state payroll—were joined by radical sympathizers and took to the streets in spontaneous protest. The assembly gave Gen. Louis-Eugène Cavaignac authority to suppress the uprising, and he brought up artillery against the protesters' barricades. At least 1,500 rebels were killed, 12,000 were arrested, and many were exiled to Algeria.

junk, Classic Chinese sailing vessel of ancient unknown origin, still in wide use. High-sterned, with a projecting bow, the junk carries up to five masts on which are set square sails consisting of panels of linen or matting flattened by bamboo strips. Each sail can be spread or closed at a pull, like a venetian blind. The massive rudder takes the place of a keel. Chinese junks were sailing to Indonesian and Indian waters by the early Middle Ages.

Juno, In Roman religion, the chief goddess and female counterpart of Jupiter. She was identified with the Greek goddess Hera. With Jupiter and Minerva she was a member of the Capitoline triad of deities traditionally introduced into Rome by the Etruscans. She was connected with all aspects of the lives of women, particularly marriage. Individualized, she became a female guardian spirit; as every man had his genius, so every woman had her juno. Her temple in Rome eventually housed the Roman mint, and she was invoked as the savior of the state. Her sacred bird was the peacock.

Juno, classical sculpture; in the Museo Archeologico Nazionale, Naples
Alinari/Art Resource, New York

Jupiter, Fifth planet from the Sun, the largest nonstellar object in the solar system. It has 318 times the mass and more than 1,400 times the volume of Earth. Its enormous mass gives it nearly 2.5 times the gravity of Earth (measured at the top of Ju-

piter's atmosphere), and it exerts strong effects on other members of the solar system. It is responsible for the Kirkwood gaps in the asteroid belt and changes in the orbits of comets; it may act as a "sweeper," pulling in bodies that might otherwise collide with other planets. Jupiter has more than 60 moons and a diffuse ring system discovered in 1979 by the Voyager spacecraft. The planet is a gas giant, composed mainly of hydrogen and helium in proportions near those of the Sun, which it orbits every 11.9 years at an average distance of 483 million mi (778 million km). Its rapid rotation (9 hr 55.5 min) acts on electric currents to give it the largest magnetic field of any of the planets and causes intense storms, including one that has lasted hundreds of years (the Great Red Spot). Little is known of its interior, but it is presumed to have a deep layer of metallic hydrogen and a dense core. Its central temperature is estimated to be 45,000 °F (25,000 °C); it radiates twice as much heat as it receives from the Sun, probably largely heat left over from its formation.

Jupiter, or JOVE, Chief god of ancient Rome and Italy. Like his Greek counterpart, Zeus, he was worshiped as a sky god. With Juno and Minerva he was a member of the triad of deities traditionally believed to have been introduced into Rome by the Etruscans. Jupiter was associated with treaties, alliances, and oaths; he was the protecting deity of the republic and later of the reigning emperor. His oldest temple was on the Capitoline Hill in Rome. He was worshiped on the summits of hills throughout Italy, and all places struck by lightning became his property. His sacred tree was the oak.

Jura Mountains, Mountain range, central Europe. It extends 225 mi (360 km) along the boundary of France and Switzerland. Its highest peak is Mount Neige, some 5,650 ft (1,700 m) high, located in France. Its western slopes are the source of the Doubs and Ain rivers in France.

Jurassic Period, Interval of geologic time, 199.6–145.5 million years ago, that is one of the three major divisions of the Mesozoic Era. It was preceded by the Triassic Period and followed by the Cretaceous. During the Jurassic, Pangea began to break up into the present-day continents. Marine invertebrates flourished, and large reptiles dominated many marine habitats. On land, ferns, mosses, cycads, and conifers thrived, some developing flowerlike structures in place of cones. The dinosaurs rose to supremacy on land, and by the end of the Jurassic the largest species had evolved. Archaeopteryx, the first primitive bird, appeared before the end of the period. Early mammals, tiny shrewlike creatures that appeared near the close of the preceding Triassic, managed to survive and evolve.

jurisprudence, Science or philosophy of law. Jurisprudence may be divided into three branches: analytical, sociological, and theoretical. The analytical branch articulates axioms, defines terms, and prescribes the methods that best enable one to view the legal order as an internally consistent, logical system. The sociological branch examines the actual effects of the law within society and the influence of social phenomena on the substantive and procedural aspects of law. The theoretical branch evaluates and criticizes law in terms of the ideals or goals postulated for it.

jury, In law, a body of individuals selected and sworn to inquire into a question of fact and to render a verdict according to the evidence. Juries may deal with questions of law in addition to questions of fact, though federal juries in the U.S. are usually limited to dealing with questions of fact. The modern jury can vary in size depending on the proceeding but usually has either 6 or 12 members. By U.S. law, federal grand juries and petit juries must be "selected at random from a fair cross-section of the community in the district or division wherein the court convenes." State jury selection varies somewhat. The Supreme Court of the United States has stated in a series of decisions that a jury is to be composed of "peers and equals" and that systematic exclusion from a jury of a particular class of people (e.g., on the basis of sex, skin colour, or ancestry) violates the equal-protection clause of the 14th Amendment to the Constitution of the United States and the defendant's right to a jury trial. A defendant is not, however, entitled to a jury of any particular composition.

just-in-time manufacturing (JIT), Production-control system, developed by Toyota Motor Corp. and imported to the West, that has revolutionized manufacturing methods in some industries. By relying on daily deliveries of most supplies, it eliminates waste due to overproduction and lowers warehousing costs. Supplies are closely monitored and quickly altered to meet changing demands, and small and accurate resupply deliveries must be made just as they are needed. Because there are no spares, the components must be free of defects. Plants wholly dedicated to the JIT concept require a logistics staff to schedule production, balancing product demand with plant capacity and availability of inputs. JIT has worked most effectively for large automobile manufacturers, which may have several thousand suppliers feeding parts into 100 factories that assemble components for 20 assembly lines.

just war theory, Set of conditions under which a resort to war is morally legitimate (*jus ad bellum*); also, rules for the moral conduct of war (*jus in bello*). Among the proposed conditions for the just resort to war are that the cause be just (e.g., self-defense against an attack or the threat of imminent attack), that the authority undertaking the war be competent, that all peaceful alternatives be exhausted, and that there be a reasonable hope of success. Two of the most important conditions for the just conduct of war are that the force used be "proportional" to the just cause the war is supposed to serve (in the sense that the evil created by the war must not outweigh the good represented by the just cause) and that military personnel be discriminated from innocents (noncombatant civilians), who may not be killed. The concept of just war was developed in the early Christian church; it was discussed by St. Augustine in the 4th century and was still accepted by Hugo Grotius in the 17th century. Interest in the concept thereafter declined, though it was revived in the 20th century in connection with the development of nuclear weapons (the use of which, according to some, would violate the conditions of proportionality and discrimination) and the advent of "humanitarian intervention" to put an end to acts of genocide and other crimes committed within the borders of a single state.

justice, In philosophy, the concept of a proper proportion between a person's deserts (what is merited) and the good and bad things that befall or are allotted to him or her. Aristotle's discussion of the virtue of justice has been the starting point for almost all Western accounts. For him, the key element of justice is treating like cases alike, an idea that has set later thinkers the task of working out which similarities (need, desert, talent) are relevant. Aristotle distinguishes between justice in the distribution of wealth or other goods (distributive justice) and justice in reparation, as, for example, in punishing someone for a wrong he has done (retributive justice). The notion of justice is also essential in that of the just state, a central concept in political philosophy.

justification, In Christian theology, the passage of an individual from sin to a state of grace. Some theologians use the term to refer to the act of God in extending grace to the sinner, while others use it to define the change in the condition of a sinner who has received grace. St. Paul used the term to explain how people

moved from sin to grace through the death and resurrection of Jesus and not through any human effort. St. Augustine saw it as an act of God that makes sinners righteous, while Martin Luther stressed justification through faith alone.

Justinian I, orig. PETRUS SABBATIUS (b. 483, Tauresium, Dardania—d. Nov. 14, 565, Constantinople), Byzantine emperor (527–565). Determined to regain former Roman provinces lost to barbarian invaders, Justinian conquered the Vandals in northern Africa in 534 and enjoyed an initial victory over the Ostrogoths in Italy in 540. War with the Goths, however, lasted another two decades and brought great devastation before Justinian gained control of the whole of Italy in 562. He was unable to prevent Bulgars, Slavs, Huns, and Avars from carrying out raids along the empire's northern frontier. He also carried on an intermittent war with Persia until 561. He reorganized the imperial government and commissioned the reform and codification of the great body of Roman law known as the Code of Justinian. His efforts to root out corruption triggered a revolt in Constantinople in 532 that nearly toppled his government; his wife, Theodora, helped him put down the revolt. Like all Roman emperors, Justinian was an active builder, and his many public works projects included the reconstruction of cities and the construction of the church of Hagia Sophia, one of the finest and most famous buildings in the world.

Justinian I, detail of a mosaic, 6th century; in the Basilica of San Vitale, Ravenna
Alinari—Giraudon/Art Resource, New York

Justinian, Code of, Collections of laws and legal interpretations developed under the sponsorship of the Byzantine emperor Justinian I from 529 to 565. Strictly speaking, they did not constitute a new legal code. Rather, Justinian's committees of jurists provided basically two reference works that contained collections of past laws and extracts of the opinions of the great Roman jurists. Also included were an elementary outline of the law and a collection of Justinian's new laws.

jute, Either of two herbaceous annuals (*Corchorus capsularis* and *C. olitorius*, in the linden family), or their fibre. The plants grow 10–12 ft (3–4 m) high and have long, serrated, tapered, light green leaves and small yellow flowers. Jute has been grown and processed in the Bengal area of India and Bangladesh since ancient times. Its biggest use is in burlap sacks and bags, which are used to ship and store many agricultural products. High-quality jute cloths are used as backing for tufted carpets and hooked rugs. Coarser jute fibres are made into twines, rough cordage, and doormats.

Jutland, Danish JYLLAND, Peninsula, northern Europe. Forming the Danish mainland and the German state of Schleswig-Holstein, it is bounded to the west and north by the North Sea. Politically, its name applies only to the mainland of Denmark. It has an area of 11,496 sq mi (29,775 sq km) and is divided into several administrative regions. In World War I, the Battle of Jutland was fought off its coast.

K

K2, or QOGIR FENG, or MOUNT GODWIN-AUSTEN, Mountain in the Karakoram Range. The world's second highest peak, it reaches 28,251 ft (8,611 m); it lies partly in China and partly in the Pakistani-administered portion of the Kashmir region. It was discovered and measured in 1856 by Col. T.G. Montgomerie and was given the symbol K2 because it was the second peak measured in the Karakoram Range. In 1954 the Italians Achille Compagnoni and Lino Lacedelli became the first climbers to reach its summit.

Ka'bah, Most sacred Muslim shrine, located near the centre of the Great Mosque in Mecca. All Muslims face toward it in their daily prayers. The cube-shaped structure, made of gray stone and marble, has its corners roughly oriented to the points of the compass; the interior contains only pillars and silver and gold lamps. Pilgrims to Mecca walk around the Ka'bah seven times and on its eastern side touch the Black Stone of Mecca, which may date from the pre-Islamic religion of the Arabs. Tradition holds that the Ka'bah was built by Abraham and Ishmael. In 630 Muhammad purged the place of its pagan idols and rededicated it to Islam.

Kabbala, or CABBALA, Jewish mysticism as it developed in the 12th century and after. Essentially an oral tradition, it laid claim to secret wisdom of the unwritten Torah communicated by God to Adam and Moses. It provided Jews with a direct approach to God, a notion regarded as heretical and pantheistic by Orthodox Judaism. A major text was the 12th-century *Book of Brightness*, which introduced the doctrine of transmigration of souls to Judaism and provided Kabbala with extensive mythical symbolism. In 13th-century Spain the tradition included the *Book of the Image*, which asserted that each cycle of history had its own Torah, and the *Book of Splendour*, which dealt with the mystery of creation. In the 16th century the centre of Kabbala was Safed, Galilee, where it was based on the esoteric teachings of the greatest of all Kabbalists, Isaac ben Solomon Luria. The doctrines of Lurianic Kabbala, which called for Jews to achieve a cosmic restoration (Hebrew: *tiqqun*) through an intense mystical life and an unceasing struggle against evil, were influential in the development of modern Hasidism.

kabuki, Popular Japanese entertainment that combines music, dance, and mime in highly stylized performances. The word is written using three Japanese characters—*ka* ("song"), *bu* ("dance"), and *ki* ("skill"). Kabuki dates from the end of the 16th century, when it developed from the nobility's nō theatre and became the theatre of townspeople. In its early years it had a licentious reputation, its actors often being prostitutes; women and young boys were consequently forbidden to perform, and kabuki is today performed by an adult all-male cast. Its texts, unlike nō texts, are easily understood by its audience. The lyrical but fast-moving and acrobatic plays, noted for their spectacular staging, elaborate costumes, and striking makeup in place of masks, are vehicles in which the actors demonstrate a wide range of skills. Kabuki employs two musical ensembles, one onstage and the other offstage. It shares much of its repertoire with bunraku, a traditional puppet theatre.

Kabul, City (pop., 2006 est.: 2,536,300), capital of Afghanistan. Located on the Kābul River in a valley strategically located between mountain passes, it has existed for some 3,500 years. It became the capital of the Mughal dynasty in the 16th century, and it remained under Mughal rule until 1738, when it was captured by the Iranian conqueror Nādir Shah. Kabul has been the capital of Afghanistan since 1776. When the Soviet Union invaded Afghanistan in 1979, it established a military command in Kabul. After the Soviet withdrawal in 1989, factional fighting among Afghan guerrillas continued intermittently and the city suffered widespread destruction. In 1996 the Taliban captured Kabul and imposed an austere form of Islamic rule. The city began to recover from years of violence only when the Taliban government was overthrown in 2001.

kachina, also spelled KATSINA, Ancestral being of the Pueblo Indians. As each tribe has its own kachinas, there are more than 500 of these spirit-beings. They are believed to reside with a tribe for half of each year and can be seen by the community if its men properly perform a ritual while wearing kachina regalia. The being depicted through the regalia is thought to be actually present with the performer, temporarily transforming him. Kachinas are also represented by small wooden dolls that are carved and decorated by the men of the tribe and used to teach children the identities of each kachina and its associated symbolism.

Hopi kachina of Laqán, the squirrel spirit, c. 1950; in the National Museum of the American Indian, New York, N.Y.
Courtesy of the Museum of the American Indian, Heye Foundation, New York City

Kahlo (y Calderón de Rivera), (Magdalena Carmen) Frida (b. July 6, 1907, Coyoacán, Mex.—d. July 13, 1954, Coyoacán), Mexican painter. The daughter of a German Jewish photographer, she had polio as a child and at 18 suffered a serious bus accident. She subsequently underwent some 35 operations; during her recovery, she taught herself to paint. She is noted for her intense self-portraits, many reflecting her physical ordeal. Like many artists working in post-revolutionary Mexico, Kahlo was influenced by Mexican folk art; this is apparent in her use of fantastical elements and bold use of colour, and in her depictions of herself wearing traditional Mexican, rather than European-style, dress. Her marriage to painter Diego Rivera (from 1929) was tumultuous but artistically rewarding. The Surrealists André Breton and Marcel Duchamp helped arrange exhibits of her work in the U.S. and Europe, and though she denied the connection, the dreamlike quality of her work has often led historians to identify her as a Surrealist. She died at 47. Her house in Coyoacán is now the Frida Kahlo Museum.

"Diego and I," oil on masonite, self-portrait (with forehead portrait of Diego Rivera) by Frida Kahlo, 1949; in the gallery of Mary-Anne Martin/Fine Art, New York City
Courtesy Mary-Anne Martin/Fine Art, New York City

Kaifeng, or K'AI-FENG, City (pop., 2003 est.: 594,887), northern Henan province, China. In the 4th century BC it became the capital of the state of Wei, and the first of its canals was built. It was destroyed by the Qin dynasty in the late 3rd century BC, and until the 5th century AD it was only a market town. It became an important commercial centre in the 7th century, enriched by traffic along the Grand Canal, and it was the capital of the Five Dynasties and the Song dynasty. Kaifeng was the site of China's only well-documented Jewish community (12th–16th centuries).

Kairouan, or AL-QAYRAWĀN, City (pop., 2004: 117,903), northeastern Tunisia. An Islamic religious centre, it was founded in 670 CE by the Arab general ʿUqbah ibn Nāfiʿ (Sīdī ʿUqbah) and became the first Arab city in the Maghrib. It was chosen as the Maghrib's capital by the Aghlabid dynasty c. 800. It served as an administrative, commercial, religious, and intellectual centre under the Fāṭimid and Zīrid dynasties. The rise of Tunis, the new capital, as well as Kairouan's devastation by Bedouins in the 11th century, led to its decline. The Great Mosque, one of the city's numerous mosques, was originally built by Sīdī ʿUqbah in the 7th century. The old city of Kairouan was designated a UNESCO World Heritage site in 1988.

Kalahari, Desert region, southern Africa. It covers an area of 360,000 sq mi (930,000 sq km) and lies mostly in Botswana but also occupies portions of Namibia and South Africa. It was crossed by the British explorers David Livingstone and William C. Oswell in 1849. Although the region has no permanent surface water apart from the Boteti River, it supports trees, low scrub, and grasses as well as abundant wildlife. It includes the Kalahari Gemsbok National Park and the Gemsbok National Park.

kalām, Islamic speculative theology. It arose during the Umayyad dynasty over varying interpretations of the Qurʾān and over questions the Qurʾān provoked, including those on predestination, free will, and the nature of God. The most prominent early school was the 8th-century Muʿtazilah, which asserted the supremacy of reason, championed free will, and rejected an anthropomorphic characterization of God. The 10th-century school of Ashʿariyyah moved *kalām* back toward traditional faith, accepting, for example, the eternal, uncreated nature of the Qurʾān and its literal truth. The school also represented the successful adaptation of Hellenistic philosophical reasoning to Muslim orthodox theology.

kaleidoscope, Optical device consisting of mirrors that reflect images of bits of coloured glass or other objects in a symmetrical geometric design through a viewer. The design may be changed endlessly by rotating the section containing the loose fragments. A simple kaleidoscope consists of two thin, wedge-shaped mirror strips touching along a common edge. The mirrors are enclosed in a tube with a viewing eyehole at one end. At the other end is a thin, flat box that can be rotated; it is made from two glass disks, the outer one ground to act as a diffusing screen. In this box are pieces of coloured glass, beads, etc. When the box is turned, the objects inside tumble into an arbitrary grouping, and when the diffusing screen is illuminated, the sixfold or eightfold multiplication creates a striking symmetrical pattern. The kaleidoscope was invented by Sir David Brewster c. 1816.

Kali, sandstone relief from Bheraghat, near Jabalpur, Madhya Pradesh state, India, 10th century AD.
Pramod Chandra

Kali, Destructive and devouring Hindu goddess. She is a terrifying aspect of Devi, who in other forms appears as peaceful and benevolent. Kali is commonly associated with death, violence, sexuality, and, paradoxically, with motherly love. Noted for killing the demon Raktavija, she is usually depicted as a hideous, black-faced hag smeared with blood. In her four hands she holds, variously, a sword, a shield, the severed head of a giant, or a noose for strangling. Nearly naked, she wears a garland of skulls and a girdle of severed hands. She is often shown standing or dancing on her husband, Shiva. Until the 19th century the thugs of India worshiped Kali and offered their victims to her. In the late 20th century she became a symbol of feminine empowerment in some circles.

Kaliningrad, formerly KÖNIGSBERG, City (pop., 2006 est.: 423,651), western Russia. Situated on the Pregolya River, it was founded in 1255 as Königsberg and was the capital of the dukes of Prussia and later the capital of East Prussia. In 1724 it absorbed the nearby cities of Löbenicht and Kneiphof. Virtually destroyed by Soviet forces during World War II, it came under the sovereignty of the U.S.S.R. and was rebuilt in 1946 as Kaliningrad. It is the seat of the University of Kaliningrad and the birthplace of Immanuel Kant.

Kamchatka Peninsula, Peninsula, eastern Russia. It lies between the Sea of Okhotsk on the west and the Pacific Ocean and Bering Sea on the east. It is 750 mi (1,200 km) long and 300 mi (480 km) across at its widest point, and it has an area of 140,000 sq mi (370,000 sq km). Mountain ranges extend along it; of its 127 volcanoes, 22 are active, including Klyuchevskaya Volcano (15,584 ft [4,750 m]), the highest peak in Siberia. Much of the volcanic region was designated a UNESCO World Heritage site in 1996 (extended 2001).

kamikaze, Any of the Japanese pilots in World War II who made deliberate suicidal crashes into enemy targets, usually ships. The word means "divine wind," a reference to a typhoon that dispersed a Mongol invasion fleet threatening Japan from the west in 1281. The practice was most prevalent in the final year of the war. Most kamikaze planes were ordinary fighter aircraft or light bombers, usually loaded with bombs or extra gasoline tanks before their suicidal dive. Such attacks sank 34 ships and damaged hundreds of others; at Okinawa they inflicted the greatest losses ever suffered by the U.S. Navy in a single battle, killing almost 5,000 men.

Kampala, City (pop., 2008 est.: 1,480,200), capital of Uganda. The country's largest city, it is located in southern Uganda, north of Lake Victoria. It was selected in 1890 by Capt. Frederick Lugard as the headquarters of the British East Africa Company. Lugard's fort on Old Kampala Hill remained the Ugandan colonial administrative headquarters until 1905. In 1962 Kampala became the capital of independent Uganda. It is the site of the headquarters of most of Uganda's large firms and of Makerere University (1922) and the Uganda Museum.

Kanchenjunga, Peak in the Himalayas. The world's third highest mountain, it reaches 28,169 ft (8,586 m). It is located on the border between Nepal and Sikkim state, India, northwest of Darjiling. Rinzin Namgyal, a 19th-century explorer, made the first map of the peak. In 1955 a British expedition led by Charles Evans made the first successful climb.

Kandinsky, Vasily (Vasilievich) (b. Dec. 4, 1866, Moscow, Russia—d. Dec. 13, 1944, Neuilly-sur-Seine, France), Russian painter, a pioneer of pure abstraction in modern painting. Trained in the law and offered a law professorship, he chose painting instead and set out for Germany. After art studies in Munich, by 1909 he began his lifelong pursuit: a kind of painting in which colours, lines, and shapes, freed from the distracting business of depicting recognizable objects, might evolve into a visual "language" capable of expressing general ideas and evoking deep emotions. In his book *Concerning the Spiritual in Art* (1912) he set forth these ideas, comparing the expressiveness of forms and colour to qualities in music. In 1911 he and Franz Marc founded an informally organized group of like-minded artists called Der Blaue Reiter ("The Blue Rider"). From 1921 to 1933 he taught at the influential Bauhaus in Weimar; during this period Kandinsky continued to evolve in the general direction of geometric abstraction, but with a dynamism and a taste for detail. When the Nazis closed the Bauhaus, he immigrated to Paris. During this final period his painting became a synthesis of the organic manner of the Munich period and the geometric manner of the Bauhaus period. The visual language that he had been aiming at since at least 1910 turned into collections of signs that look like almost-decipherable messages written in pictographs and hieroglyphs. His influence on 20th-century art and abstract art in general was profound.

Kanem-Bornu, Former African empire around Lake Chad. It was ruled by the Sef dynasty in the 9th–19th century. Its territory at various times included what is now southern Chad, northern Cameroon, northeastern Nigeria, eastern Niger, and southern Libya. Probably founded in the mid-9th century, it became an Islamic state at the end of the 11th century. Its location made it a trading hub between North Africa, the Nile Valley, and the sub-Saharan region. From the 16th century Kanem-Bornu, sometimes called simply Bornu, was extended and consolidated. The Sef dynasty died out in 1846.

kangaroo, Most specifically, any of six large Australasian marsupials of the family Macropodidae. The term is also used to refer to any of the family's 54 species. Most kangaroos graze on the Australian plains, but tree kangaroos are arboreal; they climb trees and leap from branch to branch. Kangaroos generally have long, powerful hind legs and feet and a long tail, thickened at the base. The hind legs enable their spectacular leaps and are also useful for self-defense; the tail is used for balance. The head is small, the ears large and rounded, and the fur soft and woolly. Females have one young (called a joey) annually; it is suckled in its mother's pouch for six months and often returns to be carried in the pouch later as well. The gray kangaroo, the best-known and second-largest species, can leap more than 30 ft (9 m). The red kangaroo is the largest species; the male may stand 6 ft (1.8 m) tall and weigh 200 lbs (90 kg). Millions are killed annually for their meat and hides and because they compete with livestock for forage.

Western gray kangaroo (Macropus fuliginosus).
Warren Garst/Tom Stack and Associates

kangaroo rat, Any of about 25 species (genus *Dipodomys*, family Heteromyidae) of rodents that leap about on their hind legs; found in dry regions of North America. They have large heads, large eyes, short forelimbs, long hind limbs, and furlined external cheek pouches that open alongside the mouth. They are 4–6.5 in. (10–16 cm) long without the long tail, which usually ends in a furry tuft. They are pale buff to brown above and white below, with a white stripe on each hip. They forage by night for seeds, leaves, and other vegetation, carrying food in their cheek pouches to store in their burrows, but seldom drink water.

Kangaroo rat (Dipodomys).
Anthony Mercieca/Root Resources

Kangxi emperor, or K'ANG-HSI EMPEROR (b. May 4, 1654, Beijing, China—d. Dec. 20, 1722, Beijing), Second emperor of the Qing dynasty. His personal name was Xuanye. One of China's most capable rulers, Kangxi (r. 1661–1722) laid the foundation for a long period of political stability and prosperity. Under his reign, the Treaty of Nerchinsk was signed with Russia, parts of Outer Mongolia were added to China's territory, and control was extended over Tibet. Domestically, Kangxi's reign was a time of large-scale public works, such as repairing the Grand Canal to permit transportation of rice to feed the northern population, and dredging and banking the Huang He (Yellow River) to prevent destructive flooding. Kangxi reduced taxes many times and opened four ports to foreign ships for trade. Though an ardent proponent of Neo-Confucianism, he also welcomed Jesuit missionaries, whose accomplishments led him to permit the propagation of Roman Catholicism in China. He commissioned many books, including the Kangxi dictionary and a history of the Ming dynasty.

Kannada language, formerly KANARESE LANGUAGE, Dravidian language, the official language of the Indian state of Karnataka. It is spoken by more than 33 million people in Karnataka; an additional 11 million Indians may speak it as a second language. The earliest inscriptional records in Kannada are from the 6th century. Kannada script is closely akin to Telugu script in origin. Like other major Dravidian languages, Kannada has a number of regional and social dialects and marked distinctions between formal and informal usage.

Kano, City (pop., 2005 est.: 2,993,000), northern Nigeria. Its traditional founder was Kano, a blacksmith of the Gaya people who in ancient times went to Dalla Hill in search of iron. It became the capital of the Hausa state of Kano in the early 12th century. It was the capital of an emirate in the 19th century before being captured by the British in 1903. Modern Kano is a major commercial and industrial centre. The old city is enclosed by a massive city wall dating from the 15th century; the central mosque there is Nigeria's largest.

Kanpur, or CAWNPORE, City (pop., 2001: 2,551,337), Uttar Pradesh, northern India. The British acquired it in 1801 and made it one of their frontier stations. In 1857, during the Indian Mutiny, it was the site of the massacre of British troops and civilians by native forces. One of the largest cities in India, it is a hub of road and rail transportation and a major commercial and industrial centre. Its educational institutions include a university and the Indian Institute of Technology.

Kantianism, System of critical philosophy created by Immanuel Kant and the philosophies that have arisen from the study of his writings. Kantianism comprises diverse philosophies that share Kant's concern to explore the nature and limits of human knowledge in the hope of raising philosophy to the level of a science. Each submovement of Kantianism has tended to focus on its own selection and reading of Kant's many concerns. In the 1790s there emerged in Germany the so-called semi-Kantians, who altered features of Kant's system they viewed as inadequate, unclear, or even wrong; its members included Friedrich Schiller, Friedrich Bouterwek (1766–1828), and Jakob Friedrich Fries (1773–1843). The period from 1790 to 1835 was the age of the post-Kantian idealists. A major revival of interest in Kantian philosophy began *c.* 1860.

Kantorovich, Leonid (Vitalyevich) (b. Jan. 19, 1912, St. Petersburg, Russia—d. April 7, 1986, U.S.S.R.), Soviet mathematician and economist. A professor at Leningrad State University (1934–60), he developed the linear programming model as a tool of economic planning. He used mathematical techniques to show how decentralization of decision making in a planned economy ultimately depends on a system in which prices are based on the relative scarcity of resources. His nondogmatic critical analyses of Soviet economic policy often clashed with the views of his orthodox Marxist colleagues. His most notable work is *The Best*

Use of Economic Resources (1959). In 1975 he and Tjalling Koopmans (1910–85) shared the Nobel Prize for their work on optimal allocation of scarce resources.

Kao-hsiung, Port city (pop., 2005 est.: 1,512,677), southwestern Taiwan. It is Taiwan's leading port and a major industrial centre. Settled late in the Ming dynasty, it became a treaty port in 1863 and a customs station in 1864. It grew in importance during the Japanese occupation (1895–1945) and served as the southern terminus of the main north-south railway line. The city was named Takao by the Japanese and was made a municipality in 1920. It came under Chinese rule in 1945.

Kapoor, Raj (b. Dec. 14, 1924, Peshawar, India—d. June 2, 1988, New Delhi), Indian film actor and director. In the 1930s Kapoor worked as a clapper boy for Bombay Talkies and as an actor for Prithvi Theatres, two companies owned by his father. Kapoor's first major screen role was in *Aag* (1948; "Fire"), which he also produced and directed. In 1950 he formed his own Bombay (now Mumbai) film studio, RK, and the next year he achieved romantic stardom in *Awara* (1951; "The Vagabond"). He wrote, produced, directed, and starred in many successful films. Although he portrayed romantic leads in his early movies, his best-known characters were based on Charlie Chaplin's tramp. His use of sexual imagery often challenged traditionally strict Indian film standards, and many of his film songs became musical hits.

Kaposi sarcoma, Usually lethal cancer appearing as red-purple or blue-brown spots on the skin and other organs. It has been linked to one of the herpes viruses, and there is considerable debate about how it should be classified. When described in 1872 by Moritz Kaposi, it was extremely rare, confined to specific Mediterranean and African populations. Since *c.* 1980 it has become common in AIDS patients. More homosexual male HIV patients have developed it than heterosexual intravenous-drug-using HIV patients. Remissions have occurred, but there is no known cure.

Karachi, City (pop., 2007 est.: 12,130,000), Pakistan. Located in southern Pakistan on the Arabian Sea northwest of the mouth of the Indus River, it was a small fishing village when traders arrived in the early 18th century. It was captured by the British in 1839 and was a major port of the British Empire by 1914. The provincial capital of Sindh from 1936, it was also the first capital of independent Pakistan (1947–59). Karachi is Pakistan's largest city, principal seaport, and a major industrial and commercial centre. It is the seat of the University of Karachi and the terminus of Pakistan's railway system.

Karaism, or QARAISM, Jewish religious movement that denied the authenticity of the oral law and defended the Hebrew Bible as the only basis of doctrine and practice. It originated in 8th-century Persia, where its members were called Ananites after Anan ben David, who worked out a code of life independent of the Talmud. Members later adopted the name Karaites from the Hebrew *qara* ("to read"), emphasizing their reliance on a personal reading of the Bible. The movement spread through Egypt and Syria, winning only small numbers of followers and enduring many schisms. It still has about 10,000 members in Israel.

Karakoram Range, Mountain system, south-central Asia. Extending 300 mi (480 km) from eastern Afghanistan to the Kashmir region, it is one of the highest mountain systems in the world; its loftiest peak is K2, at 28,251 ft (8,611 m) the world's second highest peak. Surrounded by other steep mountain ranges, the Karakorams are virtually inaccessible, although the completion of the Karakoram Highway in 1978 improved transportation in the region. Because of the harsh environment, the area is thinly populated.

Karakorum, Ancient capital, Mongol empire. Its ruins lie on the upper Orhon River in north-central Mongolia. It was settled *c.* 750. Genghis Khan established his headquarters there in 1220. In 1235 his son and successor, Ögödei, enclosed the city with walls and built a palace. Chinese forces invaded Mongolia and destroyed Karakorum in 1388. It was later partially rebuilt but was abandoned by the 16th century. The ruins are included in a regional UNESCO World Heritage site designated in 2004.

karate, Martial art in which an attacker is disabled by crippling kicks and punches. Emphasis is on concentration of as much of the body's power as possible at the point and instant of impact. Striking surfaces include the hand (particularly the knuckles and the hand's outer edge), ball of the foot, heel, forearm, knee, and elbow. In sporting matches (usually lasting about three minutes) and in sparring, blows and kicks are stopped short of contact. Performances are scored by a panel of judges. Karate evolved in East Asia over a period of centuries, becoming systematized in Okinawa in the 17th century, probably by people forbidden to carry weapons. It was imported into Japan in the 1920s and spread from there to other countries.

Karlfeldt, Erik Axel (b. July 20, 1864, Folkärna, Swed.—d. April 8, 1931, Stockholm), Swedish poet. His strong ties to the peasant culture of his rural homeland remained a dominant influence on his writing all his life. His essentially regional, tradition-bound poems, some published in English in *Arcadia Borealis* (1938), were very popular. He was elected to the Swedish Academy in 1904 and made its permanent secretary in 1912. He refused the Nobel Prize for Literature in 1918 but was awarded it posthumously in 1931.

karma, In Indian philosophy, the influence of an individual's past actions on his future lives or reincarnations. It is based on the conviction that the present life is only one in a chain of lives. The accumulated moral energy of a person's life determines his or her character, class status, and disposition in the next life. The process is automatic, and no interference by the gods is possible. In the course of a chain of lives, people can perfect themselves and reach the level of Brahma, or they can degrade themselves to the extent that they return to life as animals. The concept of karma, basic to Hinduism, was also incorporated into Buddhism and Jainism.

Karnak, Village, Upper Egypt. Its name has been given to the northern part of the ruins of Thebes on the Nile River's eastern bank (the southern part is called Luxor). Among its many religious buildings stood the largest of all Egyptian temples, the Temple of Amon. Itself a complex of temples, added to and altered many times, it reflects the fluctuating fortunes of the Egyptian empire. There are no fewer than 10 pylons, separated by courts and halls. The most striking feature is the vast hypostyle hall commissioned by Ramses I (r. 1292–90 BC), with an area of some 54,000 sq ft (5,000 sq m). Twelve enormous columns, some 80 ft (24 m) high, raised the roofing slabs of the central aisle to produce a clerestory. Karnak is part of a UNESCO World Heritage site (designated 1979) centred on Thebes.

Karnataka, formerly MYSORE, State (pop., 2008 est.: 57,399,000), southwestern India. Lying on the Arabian Sea, it is bordered by the states of Goa, Maharashtra, Andhra Pradesh, Tamil Nadu, and Kerala. It has an area of 74,051 sq mi (191,791 sq km). Its capital is Bangalore. Much of its territory is situated on the Karnataka Plateau, in the southern plateau region of the Indian subcontinent and in the hill region of the Western Ghats. The area was ruled by a series of Hindu dynasties before coming under British control in 1831. Mysore returned to native rule in 1881 as a princely state. Its name was changed to Karnataka ("Lofty Land") in 1973. The majority of the population is engaged in agriculture. Rice and sugarcane are cultivated on the coastal plain, and coffee and tea are grown in the hill region. Dravidian languages, especially Kannada, are spoken by most of the population.

Kashmir, Region of the northwestern Indian subcontinent. It is bounded to the northeast and east by China, to the south by India, to the west by Pakistan, and to the northwest by Afghanistan. The land is predominantly mountainous and includes K2 and other peaks of the Karakoram Range. India and Pakistan have disputed over the region since India's partition in 1947. Pakistan occupies the northern and western portions, and India administers the largest area, in the south and southeast, organized as the state of Jammu and Kashmir. In addition, China has administered portions of the northeastern section since 1962.

kashruth, In Judaism, the rules forbidding the eating of certain foods and requiring that other foods be prepared in a specific way. These rules determine which foods can be called kosher. Most information regarding kashruth is found in the Hebrew Bible in the books of Leviticus, Deuteronomy, Genesis, and Exodus. Jews observing kashruth may eat only fish with scales and fins and animals that chew the cud and have cloven feet; shellfish and pork are thus forbidden. Animals and birds must be slaughtered according to ritual and with prayer. Meat and dairy products must be strictly separated; they may not be eaten at the same meal or from the same set of dishes. No restrictions apply to the use of fruits and vegetables. During Passover, bread and other baked goods must be made without leaven.

Kathmandu, or KATMANDU, City (pop., 2001: 671,846), capital of Nepal. Situated near the confluence of the Baghmati and Vishnumati rivers at an elevation of 4,344 ft (1,324 m), it was founded in 723. Its name refers to a temple (*kath*, "wood"; *mandir*, "temple") said to have been built from the wood of a single tree in 1596. The seat of the ruling Shah family of the Gurkha people since 1768, it is Nepal's most important business and commercial centre and the site of Tribhuvan University.

Katsina, City (pop., 2006: local government area, 318,459), northern Nigeria. It was probably founded about 1100 and was the capital of the kingdom of Katsina, one of the earliest Hausa states, and an ancient centre of learning. The city's Fulani emirs retain traditional and advisory roles. It is a market for local agricultural products as well as a centre for traditional crafts and industry.

katydid, Any of numerous species in several subfamilies of the  long-horned grasshopper family (Tettigoniidae). Generally green with long wings, katydids live on trees, bushes, or grasses, and many species resemble leaves. They are powerful jumpers; many species do not fly but merely flutter their wings during leaps. They feed chiefly on plant matter, though some also eat other insects. The true katydids of eastern North America are considered great singers; each species has its own repetitive song, which is produced only at night.

Fork-tailed bush katydid (Scudderia furcata).
E.S. Ross

Kaunas, Russian KOVNO, City (pop., 2001: 378,943), southern Lithuania. Founded as a fortress in 1030, it passed to Russia in 1795 after the third partition of Poland. It was the capital of independent Lithuania (1920–40), then it was annexed by the Soviet Union. Many historic buildings survive in the Old Town. In addition to being an important industrial centre, it is an educational and cultural centre, with polytechnic, medical, and agricultural institutes.

kava, or KAVA KAVA, Nonalcoholic, yellow-green, somewhat bitter beverage made from the root of the pepper plant (mainly *Piper methysticum*) in most South Pacific islands. It is traditionally consumed in the kava ceremony, which includes the ritual making and drinking of kava and a ceremonial feast. It is taken to relieve stress and anxiety and as a mood elevator.

Kawabata Yasunari (b. June 11, 1899, Ōsaka, Japan—d. April 16, 1972, Zushi), Japanese novelist. His writing echoes ancient Japanese forms in prose influenced by post-World War I French literary currents such as Dadaism and Expressionism. His best-known novel is *Snow Country* (1948), the story of a forlorn geisha. His other major works (published together in 1952) are *A Thousand Cranes* and *The Sound of the Mountain*. The loneliness and preoccupation with death in many of his mature works may derive from his losing all his near relatives while he was young. He was awarded the Nobel Prize for Literature in 1968. He committed suicide shortly after his friend Mishima Yukio.

Kawasaki, City (pop., 2006 est.: 1,342,262) and port, east-central Honshu, Japan. It lies on Tokyo Bay, between Tokyo and Yokohama. Almost completely destroyed in World War II, it has since been rebuilt. It is a major industrial centre for machinery and chemicals manufacturing and has large shipbuilding facilities. It is the site of a 12th-century Buddhist temple.

kayak, Type of canoe covered by a deck except for a cockpit in which the paddler sits. It has a pointed bow and stern and no keel; the paddler faces forward, grasping a double-bladed paddle and dipping the blades alternately on either side. Usually built for one occupant, it can be designed for two or three. Kayaks were traditionally used for fishing and hunting by Eskimos, who stretched seal or other animal skins over a driftwood or whalebone frame and rubbed the skins with animal fat for waterproofing. The paddler wore an overlapping shield to allow the kayak to be righted without taking on water if it rolled over. Now often made of molded plastic or fiberglass, kayaks are widely used for recreation.

Kazakhstan, or KAZAKSTAN, officially REPUBLIC OF KAZAKHSTAN, Country, Central Asia. Area: 1,052,090 sq mi (2,724,900 sq km). Population: (2011 est.) 16,560,000. Capital: Astana. Kazakhs, a Turkic-speaking people who are the region's original inhabitants, make up more than half of the population; Russians constitute nearly one-third, as do small minorities of Ukrainians, Uzbeks, Germans, and others. Languages: Kazakh, Russian. Religions: Islam (mostly Sunni), Christianity. Currency: tenge. From the steppe and desert lands of western and central Kazakhstan, the terrain rises to high mountains in the southeast along the border with Kyrgyzstan and China. Its highest point is Mount Khan-Tengri, 22,949 ft (6,995 m) high. The country is intensively developed agriculturally, but much of the land area is used for pasture, with sheep and goats as the main livestock. Manufacturing includes cast iron and rolled steel; mining and oil drilling are also important. Kazakhstan is a unitary republic with a parliament consisting of two chambers; its head of state and government is the president, assisted by the prime minister. The area came under Mongol rule in the 13th century. The Kazakhs consolidated a nomadic empire in the 15th–16th century. Under Russian rule by the mid-19th century, it became part of the Kirgiz Autonomous Republic formed by the Soviets in 1920, and in 1925 its name was changed to the Kazakh Autonomous S.S.R. Kazakhstan obtained its independence from the Soviet Union in 1991. After several years of economic troubles, it began a period of sustained growth.

Kazan, City (pop., 2006 est.: 1,112,673), capital of the Tatarstan republic, western Russia. Located at the confluence of the Volga and Kazanka rivers, it was founded in the 13th century by Mongols of the Golden Horde; it became the capital of an independent khanate in the 15th century. In 1552 Ivan IV (the Terrible) captured Kazan and subjugated the khanate. The city was burned in a revolt (1773–74), but after its reconstruction it grew in importance as a trading centre, and by the beginning of the 20th century it had become one of the chief manufacturing cities of Russia.

Keats, John (b. Oct. 31, 1795, London, Eng.—d. Feb. 23, 1821, Rome, Papal States), English Romantic poet. The son of a livery-stable manager, he had a limited formal education. He worked as

Keats, detail of an oil painting by Joseph Severn, 1821; in the National Portrait Gallery, London
Courtesy of the National Portrait Gallery, London

a surgeon's apprentice and assistant for several years before devoting himself entirely to poetry at age 21. His first mature work was the sonnet "On First Looking into Chapman's Homer" (1816). His long *Endymion* appeared in the same year (1818) as the first symptoms of the tuberculosis that would kill him at age 25. During a few intense months of 1819 he produced many of his greatest works: several great odes (including "Ode on a Grecian Urn," "Ode to a Nightingale," and "To Autumn"), two unfinished versions of the story of the titan Hyperion, and "La Belle Dame Sans Merci." Most were published in the landmark collection *Lamia, Isabella, The Eve of St. Agnes, and Other Poems* (1820). Marked by vivid imagery, great sensuous appeal, and a yearning for the lost glories of the Classical world, his finest works are among the greatest of the English tradition. His letters are among the best by any English poet.

Kegon, Buddhist philosophy introduced into Japan from China in the 8th century. The name Kegon (meaning "flower ornament") is a translation of the Sanskrit *avatamsaka*, after the school's chief text, the *Avatamsaka-sutra*, which deals with the buddha Vairocana. The school was founded in China as Huayan in the late 6th century and reached Japan *c.* 740. Kegon taught that all living things are interdependent and that the universe is self-creating, with Vairocana at its centre. Though the Kegon school is no longer an active faith teaching a separate doctrine, it continues to administer the famous Tōdai Temple monastery at Nara.

Keller, Helen (Adams) (b. June 27, 1880, Tuscumbia, Ala., U.S.—d. June 1, 1968, Westport, Conn.), U.S. author and educator who was blind and deaf. Keller was deprived by illness of sight and hearing at the age of 19 months, and her speech development soon ceased as well. Five years later she began to be instructed by Anne Sullivan (1866–1936), who taught her the names of objects by pressing the manual alphabet into her palm. Eventually Keller learned to read and write in Braille. She wrote several books, including *The Story of My Life* (1902). Her childhood was dramatized in William Gibson's play *The Miracle Worker* (1959; film, 1962).

Helen Keller at age 66.
Courtesy of the American Foundation for the Blind

Kellogg-Briand Pact, or PACT OF PARIS (1928) International agreement not to use war as an instrument of national policy. It was conceived by Aristide Briand, who hoped to engage the U.S. in a system of protective alliances to guard against aggression from a resurgent Germany. The U.S. secretary of state, Frank Kellogg, proposed a general multilateral treaty, and the French agreed. Most states signed the treaty, but its lack of enforceability and exceptions to its pacifist pledges rendered it useless.

kelp, Any of about 30 genera of large seaweeds that make up the order Laminariales (brown algae), found in colder seas. *Laminaria*, abundant along the Pacific coasts and the British Isles, is a source of commercial iodine. Its stipe (stemlike structure) is 3–10 ft (1–3 m) long. The largest known kelp, *Macrocystis*, grows up to 215 ft (65 m) long. Its body, which has a large rootlike holdfast, a hollow stipe, and branching blades with hollow gas bladders, resembles that of higher plants. It is rich in minerals and algin, a complex carbohydrate used as an emulsifier to prevent crystal formation in ice cream. Species of kelp are widely eaten in East Asia.

Kennedy, John F(itzgerald) (b. May 29, 1917, Brookline, Mass., U.S.—d. Nov. 22, 1963, Dallas, Texas), 35th president of the U.S. (1961–63). The son of Joseph P. Kennedy, he graduated from Harvard University in 1940 and joined the navy the following year. He commanded a patrol torpedo (PT) boat in World War II and was gravely injured in an attack by a Japanese destroyer; he was later decorated for heroism. Elected to the U.S. House of Representatives in 1946 and the U.S. Senate in 1952, he supported social-welfare legislation and became increasingly committed to civil rights; in foreign affairs, he supported the Cold War policies of the Truman administration. In 1960 he won the Democratic nomination for president, beating out Lyndon B. Johnson, who became his running mate. In his acceptance speech Kennedy declared, "We stand on the edge of a New Frontier"; thereafter the phrase "New Frontier" was associated with his programs. After a vigorous campaign managed by his brother Robert F. Kennedy and aided financially by his father, he narrowly defeated the Republican candidate, Richard Nixon. He was the youngest person and the first Roman Catholic elected president. In his inaugural address he called on Americans to "ask not what your country can do for you, ask what you can do for your country." His legislative program, including massive income-tax cuts and a sweeping civil-rights measure, received little support in the Congress, though he did win approval of the Peace Corps and the Alliance for Progress. In 1961 he committed the U.S. to land a man on the Moon by the end of the decade. In foreign affairs he approved a plan drawn up during the Eisenhower administration to land an invasion force of Cuban exiles on their homeland, but the Bay of Pigs invasion (1961) was a fiasco. Determined to combat the spread of communism in Asia, he sent military advisers and other assistance to South Vietnam. During the Cuban missile crisis (1962) he imposed a naval blockade on Cuba and demanded that the Soviet Union remove its nuclear missiles from the island. In 1963 he successfully concluded the Nuclear Test-Ban Treaty with Britain and the Soviet Union. In November 1963, while riding in a motorcade in Dallas, he was assassinated by a sniper, allegedly Lee Harvey Oswald. The killing is considered the most notorious political murder of the 20th century. Kennedy's youth, energy, and charming family brought him world adulation and sparked the idealism of a generation, for whom the Kennedy White House became known as "Camelot." Revelations about his powerful family and his personal life, especially concerning his extramarital affairs, tainted his image in later years.

John F. Kennedy, 1961.
AP

Kentucky Derby, One of the classic U.S. Thoroughbred horse races. It was established in 1875 and run annually on the first Saturday in May at Churchill Downs track in Louisville, Ky. With the Preakness and the Belmont Stakes, it makes up U.S. racing's coveted Triple Crown. The field is limited to three-year-olds. The track distance is 1.25 mi (2,000 m).

Kenya, officially REPUBLIC OF KENYA, Country, eastern Africa. Area: 224,961 sq mi (582,646 sq km). Population: (2011 est.) 40,770,000. Capital: Nairobi. With a small group of European settlers' descendants, there are dozens of ethnic groups, including the Kikuyu, Luhya, Luo, Kamba, Kalenjin, and Maasai. Languages: Swahili, English (both official), Kikuyu, Luhya, Luo, others. Religions: Christianity (Roman Catholic, Protestant, other Christians); also traditional beliefs, Islam. Currency: Kenya shilling. Kenya can be divided into five regions: the Lake Victoria basin in the southwest; the vast plateau of eastern Kenya; the 250-mi- (400-km-) long coastal belt along the Indian Ocean; the highlands of the Mau Escarpment on the western side of the Great Rift Valley in western Kenya; and the highlands and mountains of the Aberdare Range on the eastern side of the Rift Valley, including Mount Kenya. It is noted for such wildlife as lions, leopards, elephants, buffalo, rhinoceroses, zebras, hippopotamuses, and crocodiles. About one-tenth of the land is arable, and more than one-third is used for grazing cattle, goats, and sheep. Agriculture employs much of the workforce, and tea and coffee are the leading exports. Kenya is a unitary multiparty republic with one legislative house; its head of state and government is the president, assisted by the prime minister. The coastal region was dominated by Arabs until it was seized by the Portuguese in the 16th century. The Maasai people held sway in the north and moved into central Kenya in the 18th century, while the Kikuyu expanded from their home region in south-central Kenya. The interior was explored by European missionaries in the 19th century. After the British took control, Kenya was established as a British protectorate (1895) and a crown colony (1920). The Mau Mau rebellion of the 1950s was directed against European colonialism. In 1963 the country became fully independent, and a year later a republican government under Jomo Kenyatta was elected. In 1992 Kenyan President Daniel arap Moi allowed the country's first multiparty elections in three decades; however, the government continued to be marked by corruption and mismanagement. Opposition leader Mwai Kibaki was elected president in 2002 and pledged to fight corruption, but it continued to affect the country's economic and political credibility.

Kenya, Mount, Swahili KIRINYAGA, Extinct volcano, central Kenya. Lying just south of the Equator and rising to 17,058 ft (5,199 m), it is the highest mountain in Kenya. The first European to discover the mountain was Johann Ludwig Krapf in 1849. Mount Kenya National Park, occupying an area of 277 sq mi (718 sq km), contains a variety of large animals, including elephants and buffalo. The town of Nanyuki lies at the mountain's northwestern foot and is the chief base for ascents.

Kenyatta, Jomo (b. *c.* 1894, Ichaweri, British East Africa—d. Aug. 22, 1978, Mombasa, Kenya), First prime minister (1963–64) and then president (1964–78) of independent Kenya. Of Kikuyu descent, Kenyatta left the East African highlands *c.* 1920 to become a civil servant and political activist in Nairobi. He organized a union of the British colonial territories of Kenya, Uganda, and Tanganyika. In 1945 he helped organize the sixth Pan-African Congress, attended by such figures as W.E.B. Du Bois and Kwame Nkrumah. In 1953 he was sentenced to a seven-year prison term for directing the Mau Mau rebellion, though he denied the charges. In 1962 he negotiated the constitutional

Kenyatta
John Moss/Black Star

terms leading to Kenya's independence. As its leader he headed a strong central government, rejected calls to nationalize property, and made Kenya one of the most stable and economically dynamic African states. Critics complained of the dominance of his Kenya African National Union (KANU) party and the creation of a political and economic elite. Many of his policies were continued under his successor, Daniel arap Moi.

Kepler, Johannes (b. Dec. 27, 1571, Weil der Stadt, Württemberg—d. Nov. 15, 1630, Regensburg), German astronomer. Born into a poor family, he received a scholarship to the University of Tübingen. He received an M.A. in 1594, after which he became a mathematics teacher in Austria. He developed a mystical theory that the cosmos was constructed of the five regular polyhedrons, enclosed in a sphere, with a planet between each pair. He sent his paper on the subject to Tycho Brahe, who invited Kepler to join his research staff. In attempting to understand atmospheric refraction of light, he became the first to explain accurately how light behaves within the eye, how eyeglasses improve vision, and what happens to light in a telescope. In 1609 he published his finding that the orbit of Mars was an ellipse and not the perfect circle hitherto presumed to be the orbit of every celestial body. This fact became the basis of the first of Kepler's three laws of planetary motion. He also determined that planets move faster as they near the Sun (second law), and in 1619 he showed that a simple mathematical formula related the planets' orbital periods to their distance from the Sun (third law). In 1620 he defended his mother from charges of witchcraft, thereby preserving his own reputation as well.

Kerala, State (pop., 2008 est.: 34,232,000), southwestern India.

Boat traffic on the coastal waterways of Kerala.
Gerald Cubitt

It lies on the Arabian Sea, is bordered by Karnataka and Tamil Nadu states, and surrounds the coastal enclave of Mahe (part of Puducherry union territory). It has an area of 15,005 sq mi (38,863 sq km), and its capital is Thiruvananthapuram (Trivandrum). During the 3rd century BCE it was an independent Dravidian kingdom known as Keralaputra. The Kulashekhara dynasty ruled the region in the 9th–12th centuries, when the regional Malayalam language took hold; it is still the dominant language. Portuguese intervention from 1498 was followed by Dutch rule in the 17th century. The Dutch were ousted in the mid-18th century by the princely state of Venad (Travancore), which itself came under British rule as part of the Madras Presidency in the early 19th century. It acquired its present name and shape in 1956. Kerala is one of India's most densely populated states.

kerosene, or KEROSINE, Organic compound, a clear, oily, highly flammable liquid with a strong odour, distilled from petroleum (10–25% of total volume). It is a mixture of about 10 different types of fairly simple hydrocarbons, depending on its source. It is less volatile than gasoline, boiling at 285–610 °F (140–320 °C). It is burned in lamps, heaters, and furnaces and is used as a fuel or fuel component for diesel and tractor engines, jet engines, and rockets and as a solvent for greases and insecticides.

Kevlar, Trademarked name of poly-para-phenylene terephthalamide, a nylonlike polymer first produced by Du Pont in 1971. Kevlar can be made into strong, tough, stiff, high-melting fibres, five times stronger per weight than steel; it is used in radial tires, heat- or flame-resistant fabrics, bulletproof clothing, and fibre-reinforced composite materials for aircraft panels, boat hulls, golf-club shafts, and lightweight bicycles.

key, In music, system of pitches and harmonies generated from a scale of seven tones, one of which is predominantly important. Keys are a basic element of tonality and represent an outgrowth of modal music. When a given piece is said to be "in C," C is its "tonic," or central tone. Most Western music from about 1700 until about 1900 is characterized by use of the 12 major and 12 minor keys of the tonal system.

Keynes, John Maynard, Baron Keynes of Tilton (b. June

5, 1883, Cambridge, Cambridgeshire, Eng.—d. April 21, 1946, Firle, Sussex), British economist, known for his revolutionary theories on the causes of prolonged unemployment. The son of the distinguished economist John Neville Keynes (1852–1949), he served in the British treasury during World War I and attended the Versailles Peace Conference. He resigned in protest over the Treaty of Versailles, denouncing its provisions in *The Economic Consequences of the Peace* (1919), and he returned to teaching at the University of Cambridge. The international economic crisis of the 1920s and

John Maynard Keynes, detail of a watercolour by Gwen Raverat, about 1908; in the National Portrait Gallery, London

Courtesy of the National Portrait Gallery, London

'30s prompted him to write *The General Theory of Employment, Interest and Money* (1935–36), the most influential economic treatise of the 20th century. It refuted laissez-faire economic theories, arguing that the treatment for economic depression was either to enlarge private investment or to create public substitutes for private investment. Keynes argued that in mild economic downturns, monetary policy in the form of easier credit and lower interest rates might stimulate investment. More severe crises called for deliberate public deficits, either in the shape of public works or subsidies to the poor and unemployed. Keynes's theories were put into practice by many Western democracies, notably by the U.S. in the New Deal. Interested in the design of new international financial institutions at the end of World War II, Keynes was active at the Bretton Woods Conference in 1944.

KGB, Russian KOMITET GOSUDARSTVENNOY BEZOPASNOSTI ("Committee for State Security") Soviet agency responsible for intelligence, counterintelligence, and internal security. It was the descendant of earlier agencies. The Cheka was established in 1917 to investigate counterrevolution and sabotage. Its successor, the GPU (later OGPU), was the new Soviet Union's first secret-police agency (1923); it also administered corrective labor camps and oversaw the forcible collectivization of Russia's farms. By 1931 it had its own army and its spies and informers were ubiquitous. In 1934 it was absorbed into the NKVD, which carried out extensive purges. In 1941 the state-security and espionage functions were combined in the MGB. In 1954 the KGB was created. At its peak, it was the world's largest secret-police and espionage organization. It lost power under Mikhail Gorbachev, especially after leading a failed coup d'état (1991). It was renamed after the dissolution of the Soviet Union, and its internal-security functions were segregated from its espionage and counterespionage operations.

khan, Historically, the ruler or monarch of a Mongol tribe. Early on a distinction was made between the title of khan and that of *khākān*, or "great khan." Later the term *khan* was adopted by the Seljuq and Khwārezm-Shāh dynasties as a title for the highest nobility. Gradually it became an affix to the name of any Muslim property owner. Today it is often used as a surname.

Khārijite, Member of the earliest Islamic sect, which emerged in the mid-7th century during conflicts over the succession of the caliphate. The Khārijites ("separatists") took sides against ʿAlī, the Prophet's son-in-law (whose followers later made up the Shīʿite branch of Islam), and led a series of uprisings, assassinating ʿAlī and harassing his rival Muʿāwiyah. They later caused further disruptions for the Umayyad caliphs. Their constant attacks on Muslim governments were based on their belief that the caliph should be chosen by the entire Muslim community. They called for a literal interpretation of the Qurʾān and were harsh and puritanical in the exercise of their religion. The movement's ʿIbādiyyah subsect survived into the 20th century in North Africa, Oman, and Zanzibar.

Kharkiv, City (pop., 2001: 1,470,000), northeastern Ukraine. Founded in 1655 as a military stronghold to protect Russia's southern borderlands, it became a seat of provincial government in 1732. It served as the capital of the Ukrainian Soviet Socialist Republic (1921–34). The second largest city in Ukraine, it is a heavy industry centre, manufacturing agricultural machinery and electrical equipment.

Khartoum, City (pop., 2000 est.: 3,949,000), capital of Sudan. Located just south of the confluence of the Blue and White Nile rivers, it was originally an Egyptian army camp (1821). The Mahdists besieged and destroyed the town in 1885, killing Charles George Gordon, the British governor-general. Reoccupied by the British in 1898, it served as the seat of the Anglo-Egyptian government until 1956, when it became the capital of the independent republic of Sudan. A major trade and communications centre, it is the seat of several universities.

Khmer, or CAMBODIAN, or KAMPUCHEAN, Any member of the ethnolinguistic group that constitutes most of the population of Cambodia. Smaller numbers of Khmer also live in southeastern Thailand and the Mekong River delta of southern Vietnam. Traditional Khmer are a predominantly agricultural people, subsisting on rice and fish and living in villages. Their crafts include weaving, pottery making, and metalworking. They follow Theravada Buddhism, which coexists with pre-Buddhist animistic beliefs. Indian culture has historically been a strong influence on Khmer culture.

Khmer language, or CAMBODIAN LANGUAGE, Mon-Khmer language spoken by more than seven million people in Cambodia (where it is the national language), southern Vietnam, and parts of Thailand. Khmer is written in a distinctive script, which, like the writing systems of Burmese, Thai, and Lao, is descended from the South Asian Pallava script; the earliest inscription in Old Khmer is from the 7th century. During the Angkor period (9th–15th centuries), Khmer lent many words to Thai, Lao, and other languages of the region. Khmer itself has borrowed many learned words from Sanskrit and Pali.

Khmer Rouge (French: "Red Khmer"), Radical communist movement that ruled Cambodia from 1975 to 1979. The Khmer Rouge, under the leadership of Pol Pot, opposed the government of the popular Norodom Sihanouk. They gained support after Sihanouk was toppled by Lon Nol (1970) and after U.S. forces bombed the countryside in the early 1970s. In 1975 the Khmer Rouge ousted Lon Nol. Their extraordinarily brutal regime led to the deaths (from starvation, hardship, and execution) of one to two million people. Overthrown in 1979 by the Vietnamese, they retreated to remote areas and continued their struggle for power in Cambodia. The last Khmer Rouge guerrillas surrendered in 1998.

Khoisan languages, Group of more than 20 languages presently spoken by perhaps several hundred thousand Khoekhoe and San peoples of southern Africa. A number of Khoisan languages are now either extinct or spoken by very few people. Their most distinctive linguistic characteristic is the original and extensive use of click consonants. The genetic unity of the Khoisan languages remains disputed.

Khomeini, Ruhollah, orig. RUHOLLAH MUSAVI (b. May 17, 1900?, Khomeyn, Iran—d. June 3, 1989, Tehrān), Shīʿite cleric and leader of Iran (1979–89). He received a traditional religious education and settled in Qom *c.* 1922, where he became a Shīʿite scholar of some repute and an outspoken opponent first of Iran's ruler, Reza Shah Pahlavi (r. 1926–41), and then of his son, Mohammad Reza Shah Pahlavi (r. 1941–79). Popularly recognized as a grand ayatollah in the early 1960s, he was imprisoned and then exiled (1964) for his criticism of the government. He settled first in Iraq—where he taught at the shrine city of Al-Najaf for some years—and then, in 1978, near Paris, where he continued to speak out against the shah. During that time he also refined his theory of *velāyat-e faqīh* ("government of the jurist"), in which the Shīʿite clergy—traditionally politically quiescent in Iran—would govern the state. Iranian unrest increased until the shah fled in 1979; Khomeini returned shortly thereafter and was eventually named Iran's political and religious leader (*rahbar*). He ruled over a system in which the clergy dominated the government, and his foreign policies were both anti-Western and anticommunist. During the first year of his leadership, Iranian militants seized the U.S. embassy in Tehrān—greatly exacerbating tensions with the U.S.—and the devastating Iran-Iraq War (1980–88) began.

Khorāsān, or KHURĀSĀN, Historical region situated in what is now northeastern Iran, southern Turkmenistan, and northern Afghanistan. The region was first named by the Sāsānian dynasty, in whose language it means "Land of the Sun." It was overrun by Muslim armies *c.* 650. It was conquered *c.* 1220 by Genghis Khan and *c.* 1380 by Timur. Its population is composed of many ethnic groups as a result of numerous migrations and invasions over the centuries. The languages spoken are Turkish, Persian, and Kurdish.

Khrushchev, Nikita (Sergeyevich) (b. April 17, 1894, Kalinovka, Ukraine, Russian Empire—d. Sept. 11, 1971, Moscow, Russia, U.S.S.R.), Soviet leader. The son of a miner, he joined the Communist Party in 1918. In 1934 he was elected to its Central Committee, and in 1935 he became first secretary of the Moscow party organization. He participated in Joseph Stalin's purges of party leaders. In 1938 he became head of the Ukrainian party and in 1939 was made a member of the Politburo. After Stalin's death in 1953, he emerged from a bitter power struggle as the party's first secretary, and Nikolay Bulganin became premier. In 1955, on his first trip outside the Soviet Union, Khrushchev showed

Nikita Khrushchev, 1960.
Werner Wolf/Black Star

his flexibility and the brash, extraverted style of diplomacy that would become his trademark. At the party's Twentieth Congress in 1956, he delivered a secret speech denouncing Stalin for his "intolerance, his brutality, his abuse of power." Thousands of political prisoners were released. Poland and Hungary used de-Stalinization to reform their regimes; Khrushchev allowed the Poles relative freedom, but he crushed the Hungarian Revolution by force (1956) when Imre Nagy attempted to withdraw from the Warsaw Pact. Opposition within the party crystallized in 1957, but Khrushchev secured the dismissal of his enemies and in 1958 assumed the premiership himself. Asserting a doctrine of peaceful coexistence with capitalist nations, he toured the U.S. in 1959, but

a planned Paris summit with Pres. Dwight D. Eisenhower in 1960 was canceled after the U-2 Affair. In 1962 he attempted to place Soviet missiles in Cuba; in the ensuing Cuban missile crisis, he retreated. Ideological differences and the signing of the Nuclear Test-Ban Treaty (1963) led to a split with the Chinese. Agricultural failures that necessitated importation of wheat from the West, the China quarrel, and his often arbitrary administrative methods led to his forced retirement in 1964.

Khyber Pass, Pass in the Spīn Ghār (Safīd Kūh) Range on the border between Afghanistan and Pakistan. About 33 mi (53 km) long, it has historically been the gateway for invasions of the Indian subcontinent from the northwest; it was traversed by Persians, Greeks, Mughals, and Afghans from the north and by the British from the south. The Pashtun Afridi people of the Khyber area long resisted foreign control, but during the Second Anglo-Afghan War in 1879, the Khyber tribes came under British rule. It is now controlled by Pakistan.

kibbutz, Israeli communal settlement in which all wealth is held in common and profits are reinvested in the settlement. The first kibbutz was founded in Palestine in 1909; most have since been agricultural. Adults live in private quarters; children are generally housed and cared for as a group. Meals are prepared and eaten communally. Members have regular meetings to discuss business and to take votes on matters requiring decisions. Jobs may be assigned by rotation, by choice, or by skill. The kibbutz movement declined dramatically in the late 20th century. But kibbutzim continued to play in important role in the tourism industry in Israel, attracting students and other short-term residents, mostly Jews from overseas seeking a link with the past.

kidney, One of a pair of organs that maintain water balance and expel metabolic wastes. Human kidneys are bean-shaped organs about 4 in. (10 cm) long, in the small of the back. They filter the entire 5-quart (about 4.5-liter) water content of the blood every 45 minutes. Glucose, minerals, and needed water are returned to the blood by reabsorption. The remaining fluid and wastes pass into collecting ducts, flowing to the ureter and bladder as urine. Each kidney has over 1 million functional units (nephrons) involved in the process of filtration and reabsorption. The kidneys also secrete renin, an enzyme involved in blood pressure regulation. Disorders include kidney failure, kidney stones, and nephritis.

kidney failure, or RENAL FAILURE, Partial or complete loss of kidney function. Acute failure causes reduced urine output and blood chemical imbalance, including uremia. Most patients recover within six weeks. Damage to various kidney structures can result from chemical exposure, major blood loss, crush injury, hypertension, severe burns, severe kidney infections, diabetes mellitus, renal artery or urinary tract blockage, and liver diseases. Complications include heart failure, pulmonary edema, and high potassium levels. Chronic failure usually results from long-term kidney diseases. The blood becomes too acidic, bones can lose calcium, and nerves can degenerate. The kidneys can sustain life until they lose about 90% of their function. If one is removed, the other increases in size and function to compensate. Failure of both usually requires dialysis or kidney transplant.

kidney stone, or RENAL CALCULUS, Mass of minerals and organic matter that may form in a kidney. Urine contains many salts in solution, and low fluid volume or high mineral concentration can cause these salts to precipitate and grow, forming stones. Large stones can block urine flow, be a focus for infection, or cause renal colic (painful spasms). They can obstruct the urinary system at various points. Treatment deals with any underlying problem (e.g., infection or obstruction), tries to dissolve stones with drugs or ultrasound (lithotripsy), or removes large ones surgically.

Kiev, Ukrainian KYIV, City (pop., 2008: 2,745,006), capital of Ukraine. Located along the Dnieper River, it was founded in the

6th or 7th century, and by the late 9th century its princes had expanded their territory to establish the state of Kievan Rus. In 1240 it was destroyed by the Mongols of the Golden Horde. After being rebuilt, it came under Lithuanian, Polish, and Cossack rule. It was incorporated into Russia in 1793, and in 1934 Kiev became the capital of the Ukrainian Soviet Socialist Republic. It became Ukraine's national capital after the country achieved its independence in 1991. An important industrial city, it is also an educational and cultural centre; it is the seat of a national university and the National Academy of Sciences of Ukraine.

Kievan Rus, First eastern Slavic state. It was founded by the Viking Oleg, ruler of Novgorod from *c.* 879, who seized Smolensk and Kiev (882), which became the capital of Kievan Rus. Extending his rule, Oleg united local Slavic and Finnish tribes, defeated the Khazars, and, in 911, arranged trade agreements with Constantinople. Kievan Rus peaked in the 10th and 11th centuries under Vladimir I and Yaroslav, becoming eastern Europe's chief political and cultural centre. At Yaroslav's death in 1054, his sons divided the empire into warring factions. The 13th-century Mongol conquest decisively ended its power.

Kigali, City (pop., 2002: 603,049), capital of Rwanda. Located in the middle of the country, it was a trading centre during the German colonial administration (after 1895) and a regional centre during the Belgian colonial period (1919–62). It became the capital of independent Rwanda in 1962. The fast-growing city was adversely affected by the country's political turmoil in the 1990s.

Kikuyu, or GIKUYU, Bantu-speaking people who live in the highland area of south-central Kenya, near Mount Kenya. Numbering some six million, they are the largest ethnic group in Kenya. They traditionally lived in separate domestic family homesteads, but during the Mau Mau rebellion the British colonial government moved them into villages for security purposes, and this arrangement became permanent. Their traditional economy rested on intensive hoe cultivation of millet and other crops; the main modern cash crops are coffee, corn, and fruits and vegetables. Many Kikuyu serve in government posts.

Kilauea, Crater, eastern side of Mauna Loa, Hawaii Volcanoes National Park, U.S. The world's largest active volcanic crater, it is about 3 mi (5 km) long, 2 mi (3.2 km) wide, and 500 ft (150 m) deep, lying at an altitude of 4,090 ft (1,250 m). In its floor is the vent known as Halemaumau Pit, legendary home of the fire goddess Pele. Its frequent eruptions are usually contained within the vent as a boiling lake of lava, but occasionally the lava escapes; since 1983 a series of eruptions produced lava that reached the sea 30 mi (48 km) away.

Kilimanjaro, Volcanic mountain, northeastern Tanzania. Situated in Kilimanjaro National Park (established 1973), it includes the peaks of three extinct volcanoes: Kibo, Mawensi, and Shira. Its highest peak is Kibo, which rises to 19,340 ft (5,895 m) and is the highest point in Africa. The first Europeans to see Kilimanjaro were German missionaries (1848). Kibo was first scaled in 1889 and Mawensi (16,896 ft [5,150 m]) in 1912.

Crater rim of Kilimanjaro at dawn.
Gerald Cubitt

killer whale, or ORCA, A species (*Orcinus orca*) of toothed whale found in all seas from the Arctic to the Antarctic. Largest of the dolphins, the male may be 30 ft (9 m) long and weigh over 10,000 lbs (4,500 kg). The killer whale is black, with white on the underparts, above each eye, and

Killer whale (Orcinus orca).
Miami Seaquarium

on each flank. The snout is blunt, and the strong jaws have 40–50 large, sharp, conical teeth. Killer whales live in groups of a few to about 50 individuals. They feed on fishes, cephalopods, penguins, and marine mammals; though they are fierce predators of seals and even other whales, there is no recorded instance of a killer whale attacking a human. They are often kept in captivity and trained as performers in marine shows.

kiln, Oven for firing, drying, baking, hardening, or burning a substance, particularly clay products but originally also grain and meal. Modern kilns are used in ceramics to fire clay and porcelain objects, in metallurgy for roasting iron ores, for burning lime and dolomite, and in making portland cement.

Kim Dae Jung (b. Jan. 6, 1924?, Mokp'o, Haeui Island, Korea [now in South Cholla province, South Korea]—d. Aug. 18, 2009, Seoul), South Korean politician and the first opposition leader to become president. He first entered politics in 1954, opposing the policies of Syngman Rhee, but did not win a seat in government until 1961. After being arrested several times in the 1970s, Kim was sentenced to death on charges of sedition and conspiracy; that sentence was commuted to 20 years in prison. In 1985, after a brief exile in the U.S., he resumed his role as a leader of the political opposition. In 1997 he was elected president of South Korea, serving from 1998 to 2003. In 2000 he received the Nobel Prize for Peace.

Kim Il-sung (b. April 15, 1912, Man'gyŏndae, Korea—d. July 8, 1994, P'yŏngyang), Communist leader of North Korea from 1948 until his death. When Korea was effectively divided between a Soviet-occupied northern half and a U.S.-supported southern half at the end of World War II, Kim Il-sung helped establish a communist provisional government and became its first premier. The North invaded South Korea in an attempt to reunify the country, but the subsequent Korean War ended without reunification. After the war, Kim introduced a philosophy of self-reliance (*juche*) under which North Korea tried to develop its economy with little help from foreign countries. His omnipresent personality cult enabled him to rule unchallenged for 46 years in one of the world's most-isolated societies.

kindergarten, School or class intended for children age four to six as a prominent part of preschool education. The kindergarten originated in the early 19th century as an outgrowth of the ideas and practices of Robert Owen in Britain, Johann Heinrich Pestalozzi in Switzerland and his pupil Friedrich Froebel (who coined the term) in Germany, and Maria Montessori in Italy. Kindergartens generally stress the social and emotional growth of the child, encouraging self-understanding through play activities and creative expression.

kinetic energy, Form of energy that an object has by reason of its motion. The kind of motion may be translation (motion along a path from one place to another), rotation about an axis, vibration, or any combination of motions. The total kinetic energy of a body or system is equal to the sum of the kinetic energies resulting from each type of motion. The kinetic energy of an object depends on its mass and velocity. For instance, the amount of kinetic energy KE of an object in translational motion is equal to one-half the product of its mass m and the square of its velocity v, or $KE = \frac{1}{2}mv^2$, provided the speed is low relative to the speed of light. At higher speeds, relativity changes the relationship.

king, Male sovereign over a nation or territory, of higher rank than any other ruler except an emperor. A king's female counterpart is a queen. Some kings have been elected, as in medieval Germany, but most inherit the position. The community may concentrate all spiritual and political power in the sovereign, or power may be shared constitutionally with other government institutions. Some kings are heads of state but not heads of government. In the past, some were regarded as semidivine representatives of God on Earth; others were viewed as gods in their own right or supernatural beings who became gods after death. Since the 17th century the power held by monarchs, particularly those in western Europe, has been widely regarded as deriving from the people.

King, Martin Luther, Jr. (b. Jan. 15, 1929, Atlanta, Ga., U.S.—d. April 4, 1968, Memphis, Tenn.), U.S. civil-rights leader. The son and grandson of Baptist preachers, King became an adherent of nonviolence while in college. Ordained a Baptist minister himself in 1954, he became pastor of a church in Montgomery, Ala.; the following year he received a doctorate from Boston University. He was selected to head the Montgomery Improvement Association, whose boycott efforts eventually ended the city's policies of racial segregation on public transportation. In 1957 he formed the Southern Christian Leadership Conference and began lecturing nationwide, urging active nonviolence to achieve civil rights for African Americans. In 1960 he returned to Atlanta to become copastor with his father of Ebenezer Baptist Church. He was arrested and jailed for protesting segregation at a lunch counter; the case drew national attention, and presidential candidate John F. Kennedy interceded to obtain his release. In 1963 King helped organize the March on Washington, an assembly of more than 200,000 protestors at which he made his famous "I have a dream" speech. The march influenced the passage of the Civil Rights Act of 1964, and King was awarded the 1964 Nobel Prize for Peace. In 1965 he was criticized from within the civil-rights movement for yielding to state troopers at a march in Selma, Ala., and for failing in the effort to change Chicago's housing segregation policies. Thereafter he broadened his advocacy, addressing the plight of the poor of all races and opposing the Vietnam War. In 1968 he went to Memphis, Tenn., to support a strike by sanitation workers; there on April 4, he was assassinated by James Earl Ray. A U.S. national holiday is celebrated in King's honour on the third Monday in January.

Martin Luther King, Jr.
Julian Wasser

king crab, or ALASKAN KING CRAB, or JAPANESE CRAB, Marine decapod (*Paralithodes camtschatica*), an edible crab. It is found in the shallow waters off Japan and along the Alaska coast; it also inhabits the Bering Sea. One of the largest crabs, it often weighs 10 lbs (4.5 kg) or more. Its size and tasty flesh make it a valued food, and large numbers are fished commercially each year.

Common king snake
(Lampropeltis getula).
Jack Dermid

king snake, Any of seven species of snake (genus *Lampropeltis*, family Colubridae) found in numerous habitats from southeastern Canada to Ecuador. They kill by constriction; named for their practice of eating other snakes, they also take small mammals, amphibians, birds, and birds' eggs. They are mainly terrestrial and relatively slow-moving. Strikingly marked and smooth-scaled, they have a small head and are usually less than 4 ft (1.2 m) long, though some specimens may approach 7 ft (2 m). The common king snake, found throughout the U.S. and in northern Mexico, is usually black or dark brown, variously blotched, ringed, or speckled with yellow or white.

kingdom of God, or KINGDOM OF HEAVEN, In Christianity, the spiritual realm over which God reigns as king, or the eventual fulfillment of God's will on earth. Although rare in pre-Christian Jewish literature, the idea of God as king was fundamental to Judaism, and Jewish ideas on the kingdom of God most likely shaped New Testament usage. The term is often used in the New Testament, and it was a central theme in the preaching of John the Baptist and Jesus. Theologians differ as to whether Jesus implied that the kingdom had arrived in his person or whether it was expected as a future event. Christian orthodoxy now holds that the kingdom has been partially realized by the presence of the church in the world and that it will be fully realized after the Last Judgment.

Kings, Valley of the, Narrow gorge, Upper Egypt, near the ancient city of Thebes. It is the burial site of nearly all of the kings (pharaohs) of the 18th–20th dynasties (1539–1075 BC), from Thutmose I to Ramses X. The valley contains 62 tombs, virtually all of which were robbed in antiquity. Only the tomb of Tutankhamen escaped pillage; after its excavation in the 1920s, its treasures were placed in the Egyptian Museum in Cairo. The longest tomb belongs to Queen Hatshepsut, whose burial chamber is nearly 700 ft (215 m) from the entrance. The largest tomb, built for the sons of Ramses II, contains scores of burial chambers. The valley is part of a UNESCO World Heritage site (designated 1979) centred on Thebes.

Kingston, City (pop., 2004 est.: urban agglom., 594,500), capital and chief port of Jamaica. Located on the southeastern coast of the island, it was founded in 1692 after Port Royal was destroyed by an earthquake. It soon became the commercial centre of Jamaica and was made the political capital in 1872. Historic buildings include a 17th-century church, a moated fortress, and the 18th-century Headquarters House. It is the seat of the University of the West Indies.

Kinshasa, formerly LÉOPOLDVILLE, Capital and largest city (pop., 2005 est.: 5,717,000), Democratic Republic of the Congo. Situated on the southern bank of the Congo River, it was founded as Léopoldville in 1881 by Henry Morton Stanley. It became the capital of the Belgian Congo in the 1920s. After World War II it emerged as the largest city in sub-Saharan Africa and became the capital of the independent republic in 1960. It was given its present name in 1966. A major river port and a commercial centre, it is the seat of the University of Kinshasa (1954).

kinship, System of social organization between people who are or are held to be biologically related or who are given the status of relatives by marriage, adoption, or other ritual. Kinship is the broad term for all the relationships that people are born into or create later in life that are considered binding in the eyes of society. Every person belongs to a family of orientation (e.g., mother, father, brothers, and sisters), and many adults also belong to a family of procreation (which includes a spouse or spouses and children). Familial bonds of descent and marriage may be traced through a genealogy, a written or oral statement of the names of individuals and their kin relations to one another. Inheritance and succession (the transmission of power and position in society) usually follow kinship lines.

Kipling, (Joseph) Rudyard (b. Dec. 30, 1865, Bombay, India—d. Jan. 18, 1936, London, Eng.), Indian-born British novelist, short-story writer, and poet. The son of a museum curator, he was reared in England but returned to India as a journalist. He soon became famous for volumes of stories, beginning with *Plain Tales*

Rudyard Kipling.
Elliott and Fry Collection/Bassano
Studios

from the Hills (1888; including "The Man Who Would Be King"), and later for the poetry collection *Barrack-Room Ballads* (1892; including "Gunga Din" and "Mandalay"). His poems, often strongly rhythmic, are frequently narrative ballads. During a residence in the U.S., he published a novel, *The Light That Failed* (1890); the two *Jungle Book*s (1894, 1895), stories of the wild boy Mowgli in the Indian jungle that have become children's classics; the adventure story *Captains Courageous* (1897); and *Kim* (1901), one of the great novels of India. He wrote six other volumes of short stories and several other verse collections. His children's books include the famous *Just So Stories* (1902) and the fairy-tale collection *Puck of Pook's Hill* (1906). He was awarded the Nobel Prize for Literature in 1907. His extraordinary popularity in his own time declined as his reputation suffered after World War I because of his widespread image as a jingoistic imperialist.

Kiribati, officially REPUBLIC OF KIRIBATI, Island country, central Pacific Ocean. It consists of 33 islands. The three major island groups are the Gilbert, Phoenix, and Line islands (excluding the three Line Islands that are U.S. territories); Kiribati also includes Banaba Island, the former capital of the Gilbert and Ellice Islands colony. Area: 313 sq mi (811 sq km). Population: (2011 est.) 101,000. Capitals: Bairiki (executive); Ambo (legislative), and Betio (judicial), on South Tarawa. The indigenous people are mostly Micronesians. Languages: English (official), Gilbertese. Religions: Christianity (mostly Roman Catholic; also Protestant); also Bahā'ī. Currency: Australian dollar. With the exception of Banaba (which is a coral island and higher in elevation), all the islands of Kiribati are low-lying coral atolls built on a submerged volcanic chain and encircled by reefs. Only about 20 of the islands are inhabited; nearly all of the population of Kiribati live in the Gilbert Islands. The economy is based on subsistence farming and fishing. Kiribati is a republic with one legislative house; its head of state and government is the president. The islands were settled by Austronesian-speaking people before the 1st century CE. Fijians and Tongans arrived *c.* the 14th century. In 1765 the British commodore John Byron discovered the island of Nikunau; the first permanent European settlers arrived in 1837. In 1916 the Gilbert and Ellice Islands and Banaba became a crown colony of Britain; the Phoenix Islands joined the colony in 1937. Most of the Line Islands joined the colony in 1972, but in 1976 the Ellice Islands were separated and in 1978 formed the country of Tuvalu. The colony became self-governing in 1977, and in 1979 it became the Republic of Kiribati.

Kisangani, formerly (until 1966) STANLEYVILLE, City (pop., 2004 est.: 682,599), northeastern Democratic Republic of the Congo. The nation's major inland port after Kinshasa, it is located on the Congo River, below Boyoma Falls. The city was founded in 1883 by Europeans and was known first as Falls Station and then as Stanleyville (for Henry Morton Stanley). It has been the major centre of the northern Congo since the late 1800s. It is the seat of the University of Kisangani (1963) and other institutions of higher education.

Kissinger, Henry A(lfred) (b. May 27, 1923, Fürth, Ger.), German-born U.S. political scientist and foreign-policy adviser (1969–76). He immigrated with his family to the U.S. in 1938. He taught at Harvard University, where he directed the Defense Stud-

ies Program (1959–69). He was appointed assistant for national security affairs by Pres. Richard Nixon in 1968 and served as head of the National Security Council from 1969 to 1975; he was secretary of state from 1973 to 1977. He developed the policy of détente toward the Soviet Union, which led to the Strategic Arms Limitation Talks agreements. He also initiated the first official U.S. contact with China. Although he at first advocated a hard-line policy on Vietnam, he later negotiated the cease-fire agreement that ended the Vietnam War, for which he shared the Nobel Prize for Peace in 1973 with Le Duc Tho (who refused it). After leaving government service, he became an international consultant, lecturer, and writer.

Kitakyūshū, City (pop., 2006 est.: 990,585), northern Kyushu, Japan. It was created in 1963 by the amalgamation of several cities. Part of its long coastline is included in the Inland Sea National Park. It is one of Japan's leading manufacturing centres. Undersea tunnels and a bridge link the city with Shimonoseki, Honshu.

kite, Light frame covered with paper or cloth, often provided with a balancing tail, and designed to be flown in the air at the end of a long string; it is held aloft by wind. Its name comes from the kite, a member of the hawk family. Kites have been in use in Asia from time immemorial, and religious significance is still connected to some ceremonial kite-flying there. In a famous experiment in 1752, Benjamin Franklin hung a metal key from a kite line during a storm to attract electricity. Kites were used to carry weather-recording devices aloft before the advent of balloons and airplanes. Types of kite commonly in use today include the hexagonal (or three-sticker), the malay (modified diamond), and the box kite, invented in the 1890s. Newer wing-like kites, with pairs of controlling strings for superior maneuverability, are also flown.

kiwi, Any of three species (genus *Apteryx*) of chicken-sized, grayish brown ratite birds, found in New Zealand. Their Maori name refers to the male's shrill call. Kiwis have vestigial wings hidden within the plumage; nostrils at the tip (rather than the base) of the long flexible bill; soft, hairlike feathers; and stout, muscular legs. Each of the four toes has a large claw. Kiwis live in forests, where they sleep by day and forage for worms, insects and their larvae, and berries at night. They run swiftly and use their claws in defense when cornered.

kiwi fruit, Edible fruit of the vine *Actinidia chinensis* (family Actinidiaceae), native to mainland China and the island of Taiwan and grown commercially in New Zealand and California. It became popular in the nouvelle cuisine of the 1970s. It has a slightly acid taste and is high in vitamin C. Kiwi can be eaten raw or cooked, and the juice is sometimes used as a meat tenderizer.

Kızıl River, ancient HALYS RIVER, River, central and north-central Turkey. The longest river wholly within Turkey and the largest in Anatolia, it rises in north-central Turkey and flows southwestward. It turns north and empties into the Black Sea after a total course of 734 mi (1,182 km). Unsuitable for navigation, it is a source of irrigation and hydroelectricity for the region.

klezmer music (Yiddish: "vessel of song"), Traditional music played by professional musicians (*klezmorim*) in the Jewish ghettos of eastern Europe, especially for weddings and other ceremonies. The klezmer tradition has its roots in medieval Europe. By the 19th century its style was well-developed, influenced not only by the liturgical music of the synagogue (which allows only unaccompanied singing), but also that of the local non-Jewish cultures. It is primarily lively dance music. Klezmer ensembles have varied considerably; in the U.S., where a klezmer revival began in the 1980s, a typical band consists of four to six musicians playing some combination of violin, clarinet, trumpet, trombone, tuba, accordion, double bass, and percussion.

Klinefelter syndrome, Chromosomal disorder that occurs in one out of 500 males. With an extra X chromosome in each cell

(XXY), patients look male, with firm, small testes, but they produce no sperm and may have enlarged breasts and buttocks and very long legs. Testosterone is low and pituitary reproductive hormones high. Intelligence is usually normal, but social adjustment can be difficult. Rarer variants cause additional abnormalities, including intellectual disability. In the XX male syndrome, Y chromosome material has been transferred to another chromosome, causing changes typical of Klinefelter syndrome. All variants are treated with androgens.

Knesset (Hebrew: "Assembly") Unicameral national legislature of Israel. The first Knesset opened in 1949. Its name and the number of its seats (120) are based on the Jewish assembly of biblical times; its traditions and organization are based on the Zionist Congress, the political system of the Jewish community in pre-Israel Palestine, and more loosely the British House of Commons. Its members are elected by proportional representation for four-year terms; candidates are chosen by their parties.

knight, French CHEVALIER, German RITTER, In the European Middle Ages, a formally professed cavalryman, generally a vassal holding land as a fief from the lord he served. At about 7 a boy bound for knighthood became a page, then at 12 a damoiseau ("lordling"), varlet, or valet, and then a shieldbearer or esquire. When judged ready, he was dubbed knight by his lord in a solemn ceremony. The Christian ideal of knightly behaviour required devotion to the church, loyalty to military and feudal superiors, and preservation of personal honour. By the 16th century knighthood had become honorific rather than feudal or military.

Knights of Malta, or HOSPITALLERS, in full (since 1961) SOVEREIGN MILITARY HOSPITALLER ORDER OF ST. JOHN OF JERUSALEM, OF RHODES AND OF MALTA, Religious order founded at Jerusalem in the 11th century to care for sick pilgrims. Recognized by the pope in 1113, the order built hostels along the routes to the Holy Land. The Hospitallers acquired wealth and lands and began to combine the task of tending the sick with waging war on Islam, eventually becoming a major military force in the Crusades. After the fall of the crusader states, they moved their headquarters to Cyprus and later to Rhodes (1309). They ruled Rhodes until it fell to the Turks in 1523; thereupon they moved to Malta, where they ruled until their defeat by Napoleon I in 1798. In 1834 they moved to their present headquarters in Rome.

Knossos, Ancient royal city, Crete. It was King Minos's capital and the centre of the Minoan civilization. Settled by migrants from Asia Minor in the 7th millennium BC, it gave rise to a sophisticated Bronze Age culture. Two great palaces were built in the Middle Minoan period, the second *c.* 1720 BC after an earthquake leveled the city. About 1580 BC Minoan culture began to extend to mainland Greece, where it greatly influenced the Mycenaean culture. After its palace was destroyed by fire *c.* 1400 BC, it was reduced to town status, and Aegean political focus shifted to Mycenae. Knossos was the site of the legendary labyrinth of Daedalus.

knot, In cording, the interlacement of parts of one or more ropes, cords, or other pliable materials, commonly used to bind objects together. Knots have existed from the time humans first used vines and cordlike fibers to bind stone heads to wood in primitive axes, and were also used in the making of nets and traps. Knot making became sophisticated when it began to be used in the ropes, or rigging, that controlled the sails of early sailing vessels, and thus became the province of sailors. Knots are still depended on by campers and hikers, mountaineers, fishermen, and weavers, among others.

koala, Tree-dwelling marsupial (*Phascolarctos cinereus*) of coastal eastern Australia. About 24–33 in. (61–85 cm) long and tailless, the koala has a stout, pale gray or yellowish body; broad face; big, round, leathery nose; small, yellow eyes; and fluffy ears. Its feet have strong claws and some opposable digits. The koala feeds only on eucalyptus leaves. The single offspring remains in

*Koala (*Phascolarctos cinereus*).*
Anthony Mercieca—The National Audubon Society Collection/Photo Researchers

the rearward-opening pouch for up to seven months. Koala populations have dwindled seriously, formerly because they were killed for their fur and now because of loss of habitat and the spread of disease.

koan, In Zen Buddhism, a brief paradoxical statement or question used as a discipline in meditation. The effort to solve a koan is designed to exhaust the analytic intellect and the will, leaving the mind open for response on an intuitive level. There are about 1,700 traditional koans, which are based on anecdotes from ancient Zen masters. They include the well-known example "When both hands are clapped a sound is produced; listen to the sound of one hand clapping."

Kōbe, City (pop., 2006 est.: 1,528,687), west-central Honshu, Japan. It is situated on Ōsaka Bay and occupies a narrow shelf of land between mountains and the sea. With neighbouring cities Ōsaka and Kyōto, it is the centre of a major industrial zone. Until the Meiji Restoration it was only a fishing village, but it grew rapidly in the late 19th century. It was severely bombed during World War II and was entirely rebuilt after 1945. It suffered a major earthquake in 1995. Kōbe is an important Japanese port and a centre of shipbuilding and steel production; it is the seat of Kōbe University.

Koch, (Heinrich Hermann) Robert (b. Dec. 11, 1843, Clausthal, Hannover—d. May 27, 1910, Baden-Baden, Ger.), German physician. As the first to isolate the anthrax bacillus, observe its life cycle, and develop a preventive inoculation for it, he was the first to prove a causal relationship between a bacillus and a disease. He perfected pure-culture techniques, based on Louis Pasteur's concept. He isolated the tuberculosis organism and established its role in the disease (1882). In 1883 he discovered the causal organism for cholera and how it is transmitted and also developed a vaccination for rinderpest. Koch's postulates remain fundamental to pathology: the organism should always be found in sick animals and never in healthy ones; it must be grown in pure culture; the cultured organism must make a healthy animal sick; and it must be reisolated from the newly sick animal and recultured and still be the same. Awarded a Nobel Prize in 1905, he is considered a founder of bacteriology.

koine, Newly formed compromise language that usually arises from a leveling of features distinguishing dialects of a common base language, or of features distinguishing several closely related languages. The new language is hence deregionalized and does not reflect social or political dominance of any one group of speakers. The classical example of a koine (as well as the source of the term) is Hellenistic Greek, which developed from Attic Greek through replacement of the most distinctively Attic features by features of Ionic or other dialects. A koine may serve as a lingua franca and often forms the basis of a new standard language.

kola nut, or COLA NUT, Caffeine-containing nut of two evergreen trees (*Cola acuminata* and *C. nitida*) of the cocoa family (Sterculiaceae), native to tropical Africa and cultivated extensively in the New World tropics. The trees grow to 60 ft (18.3 m) in height and have oblong leathery leaves, yellow flowers, and star-shaped fruit. The nut has been used in medicines and in soft drinks, though American "colas" today instead use synthetic flavorings that

Kola nut (Cola nitida)
W.H. Hodge

mimic its taste. Kola nuts are also used where grown as a medium of exchange or are chewed to diminish sensations of hunger and fatigue, to aid digestion, and to combat intoxication, hangover, and diarrhea.

Kolkata, formerly CALCUTTA, City (pop., 2001: city, 4,580,-546; metro. area, 13,205,697), northeastern India. Capital of West Bengal state, former capital (1772–1911) of British India, and India's second largest metropolitan area, it is located on the Hugli (Hooghly) River, about 96 mi (154 km) from the river's mouth. The English East India Company established a trading centre at the site in 1690, which grew and became the seat of the British province called the Bengal Presidency. It was captured by the nawab (local ruler) of Bengal, who in 1756 imprisoned a number of British there (in a prison known as the Black Hole of Calcutta); the city was retaken by the British under Robert Clive. It was an extremely busy 19th-century commercial centre, but it began to decline with the removal of the colonial capital to Delhi in 1911. The decline continued when Bengal was partitioned between India and Pakistan in 1947 and when Bangladesh was created in 1971. The flood of refugees from those political upheavals boosted the city's population but also significantly added to its widespread poverty. Despite its problems, Kolkata remains the dominant urban area of eastern India and a major educational and cultural centre.

Kollwitz, Käthe, orig. KÄTHE SCHMIDT (b. July 8, 1867, Königsberg, East Prussia—d. April 22, 1945, near Dresden, Ger.), German graphic artist and sculptor. She studied painting in Berlin and Munich but devoted herself primarily to etchings, drawings, lithographs, and woodcuts. She gained firsthand knowledge of the miserable conditions of the urban poor when her physician husband opened a clinic in Berlin. She became the last great practitioner of German Expressionism and an outstanding artist of social protest. Two early series of prints, *Weavers' Revolt* (1895–98) and *Peasants' War* (1902–08), portray the plight of the oppressed with the powerfully simplified, boldly accentuated forms that became her trademark. After her son died in World War I, she created a cycle of prints dedicated to the theme of a mother's love. She was the first woman elected to the Prussian Academy of Arts, where she was head of the Master Studio for Graphic Arts (1928–33). The Nazis banned her works from exhibition. The bombing of her home and studio in World War II destroyed much of her work.

Self-Portrait with Hand on Forehead, *etching by Käthe Kollwitz, 1910; in the National Gallery of Art, Washington, D.C.*
National Gallery of Art, Washington, D.C., Rosenwald Collection (B-7792)

Komodo dragon, Largest living lizard (*Varanus komodoensis*), a member of the monitor lizard family Varanidae. They live on Komodo Island and a few neighbouring islands in Indonesia. Driven almost to extinction, they are now protected. Komodos grow to 10 ft (3 m) long, weigh up to 300 lb (135 kg), and may live up to 100 years. They dig a burrow as deep as 30 ft (9 m). Carrion is their main diet, but adults may eat smaller Komodos. They can run swiftly and occasionally attack and kill humans.

Konya, ancient ICONIUM, City (pop., 2007: 967,055), central Turkey. First settled in the 3rd millennium BC, it is one of the oldest urban centres in the world. Iconium was influenced by Greek culture from the 3rd century BC but had come under Roman rule by 25 BC. It was taken by the Seljūq dynasty about 1072. Renamed Konya, it was a major cultural centre in the 13th century and was home to the Sufi brotherhood known as "whirling dervishes." Later ruled by the Mongols, it was annexed to the Ottoman Empire about 1467. It declined during Ottoman rule but revived after the Istanbul-Baghdad railway opened in 1896. An important industrial centre, it is also a trade centre for the agricultural area surrounding it.

kookaburra, or LAUGHING JACKASS, Eastern Australian species (*Dacelo gigas*) of forest kingfisher (subfamily Daceloninae). Its call, which sounds like fiendish laughter, can be heard very early in the morning and just after sunset. A gray-brown, woodland-dwelling bird, it reaches a length of 17 in. (43 cm), with a 3.2–4-in. (8–10-cm) beak. In its native habitat it eats invertebrates and small vertebrates, including venomous snakes. In western Australia and New Zealand, where it has been introduced, it has been known to attack chickens and ducklings.

Kookaburra (Dacelo gigas)
Bucky Reeves—The National Audubon Society Collection/Photo Researchers

Kordofan, or KURDUFAN, Region, south-central Sudan. Lying west of the White Nile River, it was originally inhabited by Nubian-speaking peoples. Controlled by the Christian Tungur dynasty (900–1200 CE), it was later taken by Arabs, and in the 17th century a sultanate was established. Egyptian rule began in the 1820s. The slave trade played an important part in the region's economy until its eradication in 1878 by Charles George Gordon. Egyptian rule was ended by a revolt in 1882 led by al-Mahdī. Kordofan became a province of the Sudan in 1899.

Korea, Korean CHOSŎN, or TAEHAN, Former kingdom, a peninsula (Korean peninsula) on the eastern coast of Asia. In 1948 it was partitioned into two republics, North Korea and South Korea. The Korean peninsula was probably settled in prehistoric times by Tungusic-speaking peoples who migrated in waves from Manchuria and Siberia. According to tradition, the ancient kingdom of Chosŏn (Old Chosŏn) was established in the northern part of the peninsula during the Bronze Age. Conquered by China in 108 BCE, it later developed into the Three Kingdoms of Silla, Koguryŏ, and Paekche. Silla conquered the other two in the 7th century CE and ruled until 936, when the Koryŏ kingdom became prominent. In the 13th century Koryŏ suffered a series of invasions by the Mongols but retained its political and cultural identity. Land reforms and the rise of a new bureaucracy led to the establishment of the kingdom of Chosŏn in 1392. With its capital at Seoul, it was ruled by the Chosŏn (Yi) dynasty until 1910. Invaded repeatedly by neighbouring countries, Chosŏn attempted to shut out foreign contacts but was forced after 1873 to open ports to Japan. Rivalry over Korea and Manchuria brought on the Russo-Japanese War (1904–05), after which Korea became a Japanese protectorate. Formally annexed to Japan in 1910, it was freed from Japanese control in 1945 at the end of World War II. After the war it was divided into two zones of occupation, Soviet in the north and U.S. in the south.

Korea, North, officially DEMOCRATIC PEOPLE'S REPUBLIC OF KOREA, Country, East Asia, occupying the northern half of the Korean peninsula. Area: 47,399 sq mi (122,762 sq km). Population: (2011 est.) 24,336,000. Capital: P'yŏngyang. Ethnically, the population is almost completely Korean. Language: Korean (official). Religions: Ch'ŏndogyo, traditional beliefs, Christianity,

Buddhism. Foreign missionaries were expelled during World War II. Currency: won. North Korea's land area largely consists of mountain ranges and uplands; its highest peak is Mount Paektu (9,022 ft [2,750 m]). North Korea has a centrally planned economy based on heavy industry (iron and steel, machinery, chemicals, and textiles) and agriculture. Cooperative farms raise crops such as rice, corn, barley, and vegetables. The country is rich in mineral resources, including coal, iron ore, and magnesite. It is a republic with one legislature; the head of state and government is the supreme leader and chairman of the National Defense Commission. After the Japanese were defeated in World War II, the Soviet Union occupied Korea north of latitude 38° N; there the Democratic People's Republic of Korea was established as a communist state in 1948. Seeking to unify the peninsula by force, it launched an invasion of South Korea in 1950, initiating the Korean War. UN troops intervened on the side of South Korea, and Chinese soldiers reinforced the North Korean army in the war, which ended with an armistice in 1953. Led by Kim Il-Sung, North Korea became one of the most harshly regimented societies in the world, with a state-owned economy that failed to produce adequate supplies of food and consumer goods for its citizens. Under his son and successor, Kim Jong Il, the country endured periods of severe food shortages from the late 1990s that caused widespread famine. Hopes that North Korea was seeking to end its long isolation—notably through meetings between Kim and the leaders of South Korea (2000) and Japan (2002)—were tempered by concerns over its nuclear weapons program. In the following years efforts to improve relations between North and South Korea stalled and at times deteriorated markedly. Kim died in 2011 and was succeeded by his son Kim Jong-Eun.

Korea, South, officially REPUBLIC OF KOREA, Country, East Asia, occupying the southern half of the Korean peninsula. It is west of Japan and includes Cheju Island, located about 60 mi (97 km) south of the peninsula. Area: 38,486 sq mi (99,678 sq km). Population: (2011 est.) 48,755,000. Capital: Seoul. The population is almost entirely ethnically Korean. Language: Korean (official). Religions: Christianity (Protestant, other Christians, Roman Catholic), traditional beliefs, Buddhism, new religions, Confucianism. Currency: won. Most of South Korea's land area consists of mountains and uplands; its highest peak is Mount Halla (6,398 ft [1,950 m]) on Cheju Island. The densely populated lowlands are heavily cultivated for wet rice. The Naktong, Kŭm, and Han are the principal rivers. The economy is based largely on services, manufacturing (including petrochemicals, electronic goods, and steel), and high-technology industries. South Korea is a republic with one legislative house; its head of state and government is the president, assisted by the prime minister. The Republic of Korea was established in 1948 in the portion of the Korean peninsula south of latitude 38° N, which had been occupied by the U.S. after World War II. In 1950 North Korean troops invaded South Korea, precipitating the Korean War. UN forces intervened on the side of South Korea, while Chinese troops backed North Korea; the war ended with an armistice in 1953. The devastated country was rebuilt with U.S. aid, and South Korea prospered in the postwar era, transforming itself from an agrarian economy to one that was industrial and highly export-oriented. It experienced an economic downturn beginning in the mid-1990s that affected many countries in the area. Efforts at reconciliation between North and South Korea, including the first-ever summit between their leaders (2000) and reunions of families from both countries, were accompanied by periods of continuing tension.

Korean language, Official language of North Korea and South Korea, spoken by more than 75 million people, including substantial communities of ethnic Koreans living elsewhere. Korean is not closely related to any other language, though a distant genetic kinship to Japanese is now thought probable by some scholars, and an even more remote relationship to the Altaic languages is possible. Korean was written with Chinese characters to stand in various ways for Korean meanings and sounds as early as the 12th century, though substantial documentation is not evident until the invention of a unique phonetic script for it in 1443. This script, now called Hangul, represents syllables by arranging simple symbols for each phoneme into a square form like that of a Chinese character. Grammatically, Korean has a basic subject-object-verb word order and places modifiers before the elements they modify.

Korean War (1950–53) Conflict arising after the post-World War II division of Korea, at latitude 38° N, into North Korea and South Korea. At the end of World War II, Soviet forces accepted the surrender of Japanese forces north of that line, as U.S. forces accepted Japanese surrender south of it. Negotiations failed to reunify the two halves, the northern half being a Soviet client state and the southern half being backed by the U.S. In 1950 North Korea invaded South Korea, and U.S. Pres. Harry Truman ordered troops to assist South Korea. The UN Security Council, minus the absent Soviet delegate, passed a resolution calling for the assistance of all UN members in halting the North Koreans. At first North Korean troops drove the South Korean and U.S. forces down to the southern tip of the Korean peninsula, but a brilliant amphibious landing at Inch'ŏn, conceived by Gen. Douglas MacArthur, turned the tide in favour of the UN troops, who advanced near the border of North Korea and China. The Chinese then entered the war and drove the UN forces back south; the front line stabilized at the 38th parallel. MacArthur insisted on voicing his objections to U.S. war aims in a public manner and was relieved of his command by Truman. U.S. Pres. Dwight D. Eisenhower participated in the conclusion of an armistice that accepted the front line as the de facto boundary between the two Koreas. The war resulted in the deaths of approximately 2,000,000 Koreans, 600,000 Chinese, 37,000 Americans, and 3,000 Turks, Britons, and other nationals in the UN forces.

Kosciusko, Mount, Peak, southeastern New South Wales, Australia. Located in the Snowy Mountains of the Australian Alps, Mount Kosciusko is the highest mountain in mainland Australia, reaching 7,310 ft (2,228 m). It is located in Kosciusko National Park, which has an area of 2,498 sq mi (6,469 sq km); it is near Mounts Townsend, Twynam, North Ramshead, and Carruthers, whose melting snows feed the rivers and reservoirs that make up the Snowy Mountains Hydroelectric Scheme. The mountain was named in 1840 in honour of Tadeusz Kosciuszko.

Košice, City (pop., 2003 est.: 235,281), eastern Slovakia. Settled in the 9th century and chartered in 1241, it served as a trading settlement during the late Middle Ages. It developed rapidly after becoming part of Czechoslovakia in 1920. Occupied in 1938 by Hungary, it was liberated in 1945 and became the first seat of the postwar Czechoslovakian government. A part of independent Slovakia since 1993, it is the political, economic, and cultural centre of southeastern Slovakia.

Kosovo, Albanian KOSOVA, Self-declared independent country in the central Balkans, formerly a province of Serbia. Area: 4,212 sq mi (10,908 sq km). Population: (2011 est.) 1,826,000. Capital: Pristina. Ethnic Albanians make up about nine-tenths of the population, and Serbs account for the bulk of the remainder. Languages: Albanian, Serbian (both official). Religions: Islam (Albanians); also Christianity (Eastern Orthodox [Serbs], Roman Catholic [Albanians]). Currency: euro. Kosovo's borders are largely mountainous, surrounding high plains and hills in the interior. Kosovo has long been one of the least-developed areas of the Balkans. Major components of the economy include public services, small businesses, agriculture, construction, food and beverage production, metal processing, and mining. Kosovo is a multiparty transitional republic with one legislative body; its head of state is the president, and its head of government is the prime minister. Kosovo was an autonomous province within Yugoslavia until 1989, when Serbia took control of Kosovo's administration, prompting protests from the region's Albanian population. An Albanian secessionist rebellion escalated into the Kosovo conflict (1998–99), which culminated in NATO air strikes and the withdrawal of Yugoslav and Serbian forces. The region was administered by the United Nations (UN) beginning in 1999. Kosovo declared independence from Serbia in 2008. That December the UN transferred most of its powers of oversight to the European Union. In 2010 the International Court of Justice ruled that Kosovo's declaration of independence did not violate international law.

Kosovo conflict (1998–99) Ethnic war in Kosovo, Yugoslavia. In 1989 the Serbian president, Slobodan Milošević, abrogated the constitutional autonomy of Kosovo. He and the minority of Serbs in Kosovo had long bristled at the fact that Muslim Albanians were in demographic control of an area considered sacred to Serbs (Kosovo was the seat of the Serbian Orthodox church, the inspiration for Serbian epic poetry, and the site of the Turkish defeat of the Serbs in 1389 and Serbian victory over the Turks in 1912). In response, the Albanian Kosovars began a campaign of nonviolent resistance. Growing tensions led in 1998 to armed clashes between Serbs and the Kosovo Liberation Army (KLA), which had begun killing Serbian police and politicians. The Contact Group (U.S., Britain, Germany, France, Italy, and Russia) demanded a cease-fire, the unconditional withdrawal of Serbian forces, the return of refugees, and unlimited access for international monitors. Although Milošević agreed to meet most of the demands, he failed to implement them. The KLA regrouped and rearmed during the cease-fire and renewed its offensive. The Serbs responded with a ruthless counteroffensive, inducing the UN Security Council to condemn the Serbs' excessive use of force, including ethnic cleansing (killing and expulsion), and to impose an arms embargo, but the violence continued. After diplomatic negotiations at Rambouillet, France, broke down, Serbia renewed its assault, and NATO responded with an 11-week bombing campaign that extended to Belgrade and significantly damaged Serbia's infrastructure. The bombing was halted after NATO and Yugoslavia signed an accord in June 1999 outlining Serbian troop withdrawal and the return of nearly 1,000,000 ethnic Albanian refugees as well as 500,000 displaced within the province; there were sporadic reprisals against Serbs who remained in Kosovo.

Kossuth, Lajos (b. Sept. 19, 1802, Monok, Hung.—d. March 20, 1894, Turin, Italy), Hungarian patriot. A lawyer from a noble family, he was sent to the national Diet (1832), where he developed his radical political and social philosophy. Imprisoned on political charges (1837–40), he later wrote for a reform journal and gained a devoted following. Reelected to the Diet (1847–49), he led the "national opposition," and after the February Revolution (1848) he persuaded the delegates to vote for independence from Austria. Appointed provisional governor, he became virtual dictator of Hungary. In 1849 Russian armies intervened on behalf of Austria, forcing Kossuth to resign. He fled to Turkey, where he was interned for two years. After his release he lectured in the U.S. and England, and later, from his home in Turin, he watched Hungary reconcile itself with the Austrian monarchy. After the Compromise of 1867, he retired from political life.

Lajos Kossuth, lithograph, 1856.

koto, Japanese musical instrument, a long zither with movable bridges and usually 13 strings. It is placed on the ground or a low table, and the strings are plucked by plectra on the fingers of the right hand while the left hand alters the pitch or ornaments the sound of individual strings by pressing or manipulating them on the other side of each bridge. The koto is played solo, in chamber ensembles—especially with the *shakuhachi* (a bamboo flute) and the samisen (a fretless lute)—and in gagaku music. The koto is Japan's national instrument.

Kowloon, or JIULONG, Peninsula on the southeastern Chinese mainland, part of the Hong Kong special administrative region. It lies just north of Hong Kong Island and is surrounded on three sides by Victoria Harbour; the New Territories adjoin it to the north. An industrial, commercial, and tourist centre, it includes the urban area of Kowloon and New Kowloon (pop., 2005 est.: 2,070,000). Much of its territory consists of reclaimed land.

kraft process, Chemical method for producing wood pulp using caustic soda and sodium sulfide as the liquor in which the pulpwood is cooked to loosen the fibres. The process (from German *kraft,* "strong") produces particularly strong and durable paper; another advantage is its capability of digesting pine chips; resins dissolve in the alkaline liquor and are recovered as tall oil, a valuable by-product. Recovery of sodium compounds is important in the economy of the process. In modern kraft mills, operations are completely contained; waste streams are recycled and reused, eliminating water pollution.

Krakatoa, or KRAKATAU, Island volcano in the centre of the Sunda Strait, between Java and Sumatra, Indonesia. Its eruption in 1883 was one of the most catastrophic in history. Its explosions were heard in Australia, Ceylon (Sri Lanka), and the Philippines, and large quantities of ash fell over an area of some 300,000 sq mi (800,000 sq km). It caused a tidal wave 120 ft (36 m) high that killed 36,000 people in Java and Sumatra. It erupted again in 1927 and has remained active.

Kraków, or CRACOW, City (pop., 2005 est.: 757,430), southern Poland. Located on both sides of the upper Vistula River, it was the capital of a principality in 1138. After surviving a Mongol invasion in 1241, it was made the capital of a reunited Poland in 1320. Its importance diminished after the capital was moved to Warsaw in 1611. During the Partitions of Poland it came under Austrian rule. Returned to Poland in 1918, it was held by Germany during World War II. Rebuilt since the war, it is an industrial centre with a giant steelworks on the city's outskirts. Kraków is also a cultural centre. Its university was founded in 1364.

Krasnoyarsk, City (pop., 2002: 911,700), east-central Russia. Located on the upper Yenisey River, it was founded by Cossacks in 1628. In the late 17th century, it was often attacked by the Tatars and Kirghiz. The Trans-Siberian Railroad brought a period of rapid growth in the 1890s. A commercial and industrial centre, it is the site of one of the world's largest hydroelectric stations, built in the 1960s.

kremlin, Central fortress in medieval Russian cities, usually located at a strategic point along a river and separated from the surrounding parts of the city by a wall with ramparts, moat, towers, and battlements. Several capitals of principalities were built around old kremlins, which generally contained cathedrals, palaces, governmental offices, and munitions stores. The Moscow Kremlin (established 1156) served as the centre of Russian government until 1712 and again after 1918. Its crenellated brick walls and 20 towers were built in the 15th century by Italian architects. The palaces, cathedrals, and government buildings within the walls encompass a variety of styles, including Byzantine, Russian Baroque, and Classical.

Krikalyov, Sergey Konstantinovich (b. Aug. 27, 1958, Leningrad, Russia, U.S.S.R.), Russian cosmonaut. He became a cosmonaut in 1985 and flew his first space mission in 1988–89, during which he spent 151 days on the Mir space station. In 1991–92, during which he spent 311 days on Mir, he was in space when the Soviet Union broke apart. Krikalyov became the first cosmonaut to serve aboard a U.S. spacecraft when he flew as a mission specialist on the space shuttle in 1994. On his next three spaceflights, he visited the International Space Station. Krikalyov accumulated the record for most time in space: 803 days.

krill, Any member of the crustacean suborder Euphausiacea, comprising shrimplike animals that live in the open sea. The name also refers to the genus *Euphausia* within the suborder and sometimes to a single species, *E. superba*. The described species, numbering more than 80, range in size from about 0.25 to 2 in. (8–60 mm). Most have bioluminescent organs on the lower side, making them visible at night. They are an important source of food for various fishes, birds, and whales, particularly blue and fin whales. Krill may occur in vast swarms at the ocean surface, where they feed at night, and at depths greater than about 6,000 ft (2,000 m). Because of their vast numbers and nutritive qualities (they are an especially rich source of vitamin A), krill have been regarded as a potential source of food for humans.

Krishna, One of the most widely venerated Hindu gods, worshiped as the eighth incarnation of Vishnu and as the supreme deity. Many Krishna legends are drawn from the *Mahabharata* and the *Purana*s. His earliest appearance is in the *Mahabharata* as the divine charioteer of Arjuna, whom Krishna convinces that the war Arjuna is about to fight is just. In later works Krishna was a slayer of demons, a secret lover of all devotees, and a devoted son and father. He also lifted the sacred hill of Govardhana on one finger to protect his devotees from Indra's wrath. In art Krishna is often depicted with blue-black skin, wearing a loincloth and a crown of peacock feathers. As a divine lover, he is shown playing the flute, surrounded by adoring females.

Kristallnacht, or CRYSTAL NIGHT, or NIGHT OF BROKEN GLASS, Night of violence against Jews, carried out by members of the German Nazi Party on Nov. 9–10, 1938, so called because of the broken glass left in its aftermath. The violence, instigated by Joseph Goebbels, left 91 Jews dead and hundreds seriously injured. About 7,500 Jewish businesses were gutted and some 1,000 synagogues burned or damaged. The Gestapo arrested 30,000 Jewish males, offering to release them only if they emigrated and surrendered their wealth. The incident marked a major escalation in the Nazi program of Jewish persecution, foreshadowing the Holocaust.

Kropotkin, Peter (Alekseyevich) (b. Dec. 21, 1842, Moscow, Russia—d. Feb. 8, 1921, Dmitrov, near Moscow), Russian revolutionary and geographer, foremost theorist of anarchism. The son of a prince, he renounced his aristocratic heritage in 1871. Although he achieved renown in such fields as geography, zoology, sociology, and history, he shunned material success for the life of a revolutionist. He was imprisoned on political charges (1874–76) but escaped and fled to western Europe. He was imprisoned in France on trumped-up charges of sedition (1883–86), and in 1886 he settled in England, where he remained until the Russian Revolution of 1917 allowed him to return home. While in exile, he wrote several influential books, including *Memoirs of a Revolutionist* (1899) and *Mutual Aid* (1902), in which he attempted to put anarchism on a scientific basis and argued that cooperation rather than conflict is the chief factor in the evolution of species. On his return to Russia, he was

Peter Alekseyevich Kropotkin.
Brown Brothers

bitterly disappointed that the Bolsheviks had made their revolution by authoritarian rather than libertarian methods, and he retired from politics.

krypton, Chemical element, chemical symbol Kr, atomic number 36. One of the noble gases, it is colourless, odourless, tasteless, and almost totally inert, combining only with fluorine under very rigourous conditions. Krypton occurs in trace amounts in the atmosphere and in rocks and is obtained by fractional distillation of liquefied air. It is used in luminescent tubes, flash lamps, incandescent light bulbs, lasers, and tracer studies.

Kshatriya, or KSATRIYA, In Hindu India, the second-highest of the four varnas, or social classes, traditionally the military or ruling class. In ancient times before the caste system was completely defined, they were considered first in rank, placed higher than the Brahmans, or priestly class. The legend that they were degraded by an incarnation of Vishnu as a punishment for their tyranny may reflect a historical struggle for supremacy between priests and rulers. In modern times the Kshatriya varna includes members from a variety of castes, united by their status in government or the military or their land ownership.

Kuala Lumpur, City (pop., 2000 prelim.: 1,297,526), capital of Malaysia. Founded as a tin-mining camp in 1857, it was made capital of the Federated Malay States in 1895, of the independent Federation of Malaya in 1957, and of Malaysia in 1963. It was designated a municipality in 1972. The most important Malay city on the Malay Peninsula, it is a commercial centre and the site of the Petronas Twin Towers, the world's tallest buildings when they were completed in 1998. Its educational institutions include the University of Malaya and a branch of the National University of Malaysia. In 1999 government offices began moving to the new administrative centre at Putrajaya just south of Kuala Lumpur.

Kublai Khan (b. 1215—d. 1294), Grandson of Genghis Khan

Kublai Khan; in the National Palace Museum, Taipei
Courtesy of the National Palace Museum, Taipei, Taiwan, Republic of China

who conquered China and established the Yuan, or Mongol, dynasty. When Kublai was in his 30s, his brother, the emperor Möngke, gave him the task of conquering and administering Song-dynasty China. Recognizing the superiority of Chinese thought, he gathered around himself Confucian advisers who convinced him of the importance of clemency toward the conquered. In subduing China and establishing himself there, he alienated other Mongol princes; his claim to the title of khan was also disputed. Though he could no longer control the steppe aristocracy effectively, he succeeded in reunifying China, subduing first the north and then the south by 1279. To restore China's prestige, Kublai engaged in wars on its periphery with Myanmar, Java, Japan, and the nations of eastern Southeast Asia, suffering some disastrous defeats. At home, he set up a four-tiered society, with the Mongols and other Central Asian peoples forming the top two tiers, the inhabitants of northern China ranking next, and those of southern China on the bottom. Posts of importance were allotted to foreigners, including Marco Polo. Kublai repaired the Grand Canal and public granaries and made Buddhism the state religion. Although his reign was one of great prosperity, his politics were pursued less successfully by his followers.

Kuiper belt, or EDGEWORTH-KUIPER BELT, Disk-shaped belt of billions of small icy bodies orbiting the Sun beyond the orbit of Neptune, mostly at distances 30–50 times Earth's distance from the Sun. Gerard Peter Kuiper (1905–73) proposed the existence of this large flattened distribution of objects in 1951 in connection with his theory of the origin of the solar system. Kenneth Edgeworth (1880–1972) independently had made similar proposals in 1943 and 1949. Whether the belt extends thinly as far as the Oort cloud is not known. Gravitational disturbances by Neptune of objects in the belt are thought to be the origin of most short-period comets. The first Kuiper belt object was discovered in 1992; the orbit, icy composition, and diminutive size of Pluto qualify this body, formerly considered a planet, as a giant Kuiper belt object.

kulak (Russian: "fist") Wealthy or prosperous landed peasant in Russia. Before the Russian Revolution of 1917, kulaks were major figures in peasant villages, often lending money and playing central roles in social and administrative affairs. In the War Communism period (1918–21), the Soviet government undermined the kulaks' position by organizing poor peasants to administer the villages and requisition grain from richer peasants. The kulaks regained their position under the New Economic Policy, but in 1929 the government began a drive for rapid collectivization of agriculture and "liquidation of the kulaks as a class" (dekulakization). By 1934 most kulaks had been deported to remote regions or arrested and their land and property confiscated.

Kumasi, formerly COOMASSIE, City (pop., 2000: metro. area, 1,170,270), south-central Ghana. A 17th-century Asante king chose the site for his capital and conducted land negotiations under a kum tree, which gave the town its name. Located on north-south trade routes, it became a major commercial centre. The British gained control of the city in 1874. It is called the "Garden City of West Africa" and remains the seat of Asante kings. Its central market is one of the largest in western Africa. Kwame Nkrumah University of Science and Technology (1951) is located there.

kumquat, Any of several evergreen shrubs or small trees of the genus *Fortunella* (rue, or citrus, family), or their fruit. Native to eastern Asia, kumquats are cultivated throughout the subtropics. The mainly thornless branches bear dark green, glossy leaves and white, orangelike flowers. The small, bright orange-yellow, round or oval fruit has mildly acid, juicy pulp and a sweet, edible, pulpy skin. Kumquats may be eaten fresh, preserved, or candied, or made into jams and jellies. In the U.S., hybrids have been produced with other citrus fruits.

kundalini, In some tantric forms of Yoga, the cosmic energy believed to be within everyone. It is pictured as a coiled serpent lying at the base of the spine. Through a series of exercises involving posture, meditation, and breathing, a practitioner can force this energy up through the body to the top of the head. This brings about a sensation of bliss, as the ordinary self is dissolved into its eternal essence, atman.

kung fu, Pinyin GONGFU, Chinese martial art that is simultaneously a spiritual and a physical discipline. It has been practiced at least since the Zhou dynasty (1111–255 BC). Its prescribed stances and actions are based on keen observations of human skeletal and muscular anatomy and physiology, and many of its movements are imitations of the fighting styles of animals. Its combative techniques resemble those used in karate and tae kwon do. Self-discipline is emphasized. Kung fu performed as exercise resembles t'ai chi ch'uan.

Kunlun Mountains, or K'UN-LUN MOUNTAINS, Mountain system, east-central Asia. It extends for 1,250 mi (2,000 km) through the western regions of China. From the Pamirs of Tajikistan, it runs east along the border between Xinjiang and Tibet autonomous regions to the Sino-Tibetan ranges in Qinghai province. It divides the northern limit of the Plateau of Tibet from the interior plains of Central Asia. Its highest peak, Mount Muztag, measures 25,338 ft (7,723 m).

Kunming, or K'UN-MING, City (pop., 2003 est.: 1,597,800), capital of Yunnan province, southern China. Situated on the northern shore of Lake Dian, it has long been a commercial centre at the junction of major trade routes. Originally known as Tuodong in the 8th–9th century AD and a part of the independent state of Nanzhao, it came under Chinese control with the Mongol invasion of 1253. The city became the provincial capital of Yunnan in 1276 and was visited by Marco Polo. It became a municipality in 1928 and was transformed into a modern city in 1937 during the Sino-Japanese War (1937–45), when Chinese evacuees from the north introduced industrial plants and universities to Kunming.

Kura River, Azerbaijani KÜR, Georgian MTKVARI, River in Turkey, Georgia, and Azerbaijan. The largest river in Transcaucasia, it rises in eastern Turkey and flows north. After entering Georgia, it turns east and flows southeast to enter the Caspian Sea. It is 848 mi (1,364 km) long and used in places for irrigation.

Kurd, Member of an ethnic and linguistic group native to parts of what are now Iran, Iraq, Turkey, Armenia, and Syria. Kurds speak one of two dialects of Kurdish, a West Iranian language related to Modern Persian. Traditionally nomadic, most were forced into farming by the redrawing of state borders after World War I (1914–18). Most Kurds are Sunni Muslims; Sufism is widely practiced. Plans for a Kurdish state, promised by the Treaty of Sèvres (1920), which dissolved the Ottoman Empire, were never realized. Kurds in Turkey, Iran, and Iraq have been variously persecuted and pressured to assimilate; Iraqi attacks were particularly severe during the Iran-Iraq War (1980–88) and following the Persian Gulf War (1990–91).

Kurdistan, Broad designation given to a mountainous region that includes parts of Turkey, Iran, Iraq, Armenia, and Syria, inhabited predominantly by Kurds. Settlement is chiefly concentrated in the towns of Diyarbakır, Bitlis, and Van in Turkey, Mosul and Karkūk in Iraq, and Kermānshāh in Iran. Since early times the region has been the home of the Kurds, a people whose ethnic origins are uncertain. The Treaty of Sèvres, signed in 1920, provided for the recognition of a Kurdish state, but the agreement was never ratified.

Kuril Islands, Archipelago, eastern Russia. It extends for some 750 mi (1,200 km) from the southern tip of Russia's Kamchatka Peninsula to the northeastern coast of Japan's Hokkaido island. The 56 islands occupy 6,000 sq mi (15,600 sq km) and together with Sakhalin Island form an administrative region (pop., 2006 est.: 526,235) of Russia. The Kurils were originally settled by the Russians in the 17th–18th century. Japan seized the southern islands and in 1875 obtained the entire chain. After World War II they were ceded to the Soviet Union, and the Japanese population was repatriated and replaced by Soviets. Japan still claims historical rights to the southernmost islands.

Kush, or CUSH, Ancient kingdom, Nubia region of the Nile River valley. In the 2nd millennium BC it was subject to Egypt. In the 8th century BC Kushite King Piye invaded and conquered Egypt. It was ruled from 719 BC by Piye's brother Shabaka, who also invaded Egypt and set up the 25th dynasty; he subsequently made Memphis his capital. In the mid-7th century BC the Kushite kingdom's capital was transferred to Meroë, where the Kushites ruled for another 1,000 years.

Kushan art, or KUSANA ART, Art produced during the Kushan dynasty (late 1st–3rd century AD), in an area that now includes parts of Central Asia, northern India, Pakistan, and Afghanistan. There are two major stylistic divisions among artifacts of the period: the imperial art of Iranian derivation, and the Buddhist art of mixed Greco-Roman and Indian sources. The former is exemplified by stiff, frontal portraits (including those on coins) emphasizing the individual's power and wealth. The second, more realistic, style is typified by the schools of Gandhara and Mathura art.

Kuwait, officially STATE OF KUWAIT, Country, Middle East, southwestern Asia. It is on the Arabian Peninsula at the northwest corner of the Persian Gulf. Area: 6,880 sq mi (17,818 sq km). Population: (2011 est.) 3,650,000. Capital: Kuwait city. Its population is overwhelmingly Arab. Languages: Arabic (official), Persian, English. Religion: Islam (official). Currency: Kuwaiti dinar. Except for Al-Jahrā᾿ oasis, at the western end of Kuwait Bay, and a few fertile patches in the southeastern and coastal areas, it is largely desert; annual precipitation totals 1–7 in. (25–180 mm). Kuwait has almost no arable land, but there is a small amount of pastureland for livestock. Its extensive petroleum and natural gas deposits are the basis of its economy. Its estimated reserves of petroleum represent roughly one-tenth of global reserves, ranking Kuwait third, behind Iraq and Saudi Arabia. It is a constitutional monarchy with one legislative body; the head of state and government is the emir, assisted by the prime minister. Traces of civilization on Faylakah, an island in Kuwait Bay, date to the 3rd millennium BCE. These flourished until *c.* 1200 BCE, when they disappeared from the historical record. Greek colonists settled the island in the 4th century BCE. The nomadic ῾Anizah tribe of central Arabia founded Kuwait city in 1710, and ῾Abd al-Raḥīm of the Ṣabāḥ dynasty became sheikh in 1756; the family continues to rule Kuwait. In 1899, to thwart German and Ottoman influences, Kuwait agreed to give Britain control of its foreign affairs. Following the outbreak of war with the Ottoman Empire in World War I (1914–18), Britain established a protectorate there. In 1961, after Kuwait had gained full independence from Britain, Iraq laid claim to Kuwait. British troops were sent to defend Kuwait; the Arab League recognized its independence, and Iraq dropped its claim. Iraq reasserted these claims in the aftermath of the Iraq-Iraq War and invaded and occupied Kuwait in 1990. A U.S.-led military coalition drove the Iraqi army out of Kuwait the next year. Iraqi forces set fire to most of Kuwait's oil wells, but these were extinguished, and petroleum production soon returned to prewar levels.

Kuwait, or KUWAIT CITY, City (pop., 2005: city, 32,403; urban agglom., 1,810,000), capital of Kuwait. It is located at the head of the Persian Gulf. It was founded in the 18th century and was a trading city relying on sea and caravan traffic. Until 1957 it was enclosed by a mud wall separating it from the desert and was only 5 sq mi (13 sq km) in area. The development of the country's oil industry after World War II (1939–45) transformed the city into a modern metropolis. Almost all of the country's population is concentrated near the capital. The city was damaged during the Iraqi occupation and the Persian Gulf War (1990–91) but soon recovered.

Kuznets, Simon (Smith) (b. April 30, 1901, Kharkov, Ukraine, Russian Empire—d. July 8, 1985, Cambridge, Mass., U.S.), Russian-U.S. economist and statistician. He immigrated to the U.S. in 1922 and joined the National Bureau of Economic Research in 1927; he later taught at the University of Pennsylvania (1930–54), Johns Hopkins University (1954–60), and Harvard University (1960–71). His work emphasized the complexity of underlying data in the construction of economic models, stressing the need for information on population structure, technology, labour quality, government structure, trade, and markets. He also described the existence of cyclical variations in growth rates (now called "Kuznets cycles") and their links with underlying factors such as population. In 1971 he received the Nobel Prize.

Kwangju, City (pop., 2003 est.: 1,401,525), southwestern South Korea, capital of South Chŏlla province. It occupies an area of 193 sq mi (501 sq km) and constitutes a metropolitan city (province) by itself. It has been a centre of trade and local administration since the Three Kingdoms (57 BC); its modern industrial development began with a railway connection to Seoul in 1914. Kwangju was the site of an armed uprising between civilians and the government in 1980. It is the seat of Chosŏn University (founded 1946).

kwashiorkor, Condition caused by severe protein deficiency. It is common in tropical and subtropical regions in young children weaned on a diet chiefly of starchy foods such as grains, cassava, plantain, and sweet potato. It causes potbelly, edema, weakness, irritability, dry skin with rash, reddish-orange hair discoloration, diarrhea, anemia, and fat deposits in the liver. Mental development may be stunted. Adults who had the disease in childhood may be at risk of diseases such as cirrhosis. Treatment is protein supplementation, often in the form of dried skim milk. For long-term prevention, development of high-protein plant mixtures based on local food preferences and availability is encouraged. Nondietary causes include inadequate absorption of nutrients by the intestines, chronic alcoholism, kidney disease, and trauma (e.g., infection, burns) causing abnormal protein loss.

Kyōto, City (pop., 2003 est.: 1,386,372), west-central Honshu, Japan. It is situated northeast of Ōsaka, and together with Kōbe it is part of a major urban-industrial region. The centre of Japanese culture and Japanese Buddhism, Kyōto ("Capital City") was the capital of Japan and the site of the imperial family residence for more than 1,000 years (794–1868). The modern city has venues that present Nōh theatre and Kabuki. It is a manufacturing centre, and many small workshops produce textiles and porcelain; tourism is also important. Buddhist temples, Shintō shrines, and other historic buildings are found throughout the city and surrounding area; 17 of these were collectively designated a UNESCO World Heritage site in 1994. Its educational institutions include Kyōto University (founded 1897) and Dōshisha University (1875).

Kyrgyzstan, officially KYRGYZ REPUBLIC, Country, Central Asia. In the southeast the Kok Shaal-Tau Range, part of the Tien Shan, forms the border with China. Area: 77,199 sq mi (199,945 sq km). Population: (2011 est.) 5,168,000. Capital: Bishkek. The Kyrgyz make up about two-thirds of the population; most of the remainder consists of Uzbeks and Russians. Languages: Kyrgyz, Russian (both official). Religions: Islam (mostly Sunni); also Christianity. Currency: som. Kyrgyzstan is a largely mountainous country. At its eastern edge rises Victory (Pobedy) Peak, which at 24,406 ft (7,439 m) is the country's highest point of elevation. The country's valleys and plains, occupying only one-seventh of the total area, are home to most of its people. The economy is based largely on agriculture, including livestock raising and the cultivation of cereals, potatoes, cotton, and sugar beets. Gold mining and industries such as food processing and the production of machinery are also important. It is a unitary multiparty republic with one legislative house; its head of state and government is the president, assisted by the prime minister. The Kyrgyz, a nomadic people of Central Asia, settled in the Tien Shan region in ancient times. They were conquered by Genghis Khan's son Jöchi in 1207. The area became part of the Qing dynasty of China in the mid-18th century. It came under Russian control in the 19th century, and its long rebellion against Russia (and later the Soviet Union) that began in 1916 resulted in a long period of brutal repression. Kirgiziya became an autonomous province of the Soviet Union in 1924 and was made the Kirgiz S.S.R. in 1936. Kyrgyzstan gained independence in 1991. It subsequently struggled with creating a democratic process and with establishing a stable economy.

Kyushu, Island (pop., 2004 est.: 14,780,000), southernmost of Japan's four main islands. Located off the eastern coast of Asia, it is separated from Honshu to the north by the Shimonoseki Strait and from Shikoku to the east by the Bungo Strait. The island, with an area of 14,183 sq mi (36,733 sq km), is mountainous; several famous peaks rise some 5,000–6,000 ft (1,500–2,000 m) high, including Mount Aso. Its chief cities include Fukuoka and Kitakyūshū. It was the first part of the Japanese empire opened to foreigners in the 19th century.

L

La Niña, Cyclic counterpart to El Niño, consisting of a cooling of surface waters of the Pacific Ocean along the western coast of South America. While its local effects on weather and climate are generally the opposite of those associated with El Niño, its global effects can be more complex. La Niña events often follow El Niños, which occur at irregular intervals of about 5–10 years.

La Paz, City (pop., 2001: city, 789,558; 2003 metro. area est., 1,477,000), administrative capital of Bolivia. Located in west-central Bolivia, it is the world's highest capital, built over 12,000 ft (3,650 m) above sea level. The city centre lies in a canyon formed by the La Paz River. Founded in 1548 by the Spanish on the site of an Inca village, it was originally called Nuestra Señora de La Paz ("Our Lady of Peace"). Following the Battle of Ayacucho (1824), the decisive battle in the colony's wars of independence, the city was renamed La Paz de Ayacucho, though informally it continues to be called La Paz. Since 1898 it has been the administrative capital of Bolivia, though Sucre remains the judicial capital. It is Bolivia's principal industrial centre and also the site of the University of San Andrés (1830), the National Museum of Art, and the National Museum of Archaeology.

La Plata, City (pop., 2001: 563,943), eastern Argentina. After Buenos Aires became the national capital, La Plata was chosen (1882) as the new seat of Buenos Aires province and was modeled on the U.S. capital of Washington, D.C. It was renamed for Argentine first lady Eva Perón in 1952, but after the overthrow of Pres. Juan Peron in 1955 it resumed its original name. Located near the Río de la Plata estuary, it is a seaport with a large artificial harbour. Its industries include meatpacking and oil refining.

La Scala, Opera house in Milan, Italy. Built in 1776 by Empress Maria Theresa of Austria (which country then ruled Milan), it replaced an earlier theatre that had burned. With the works of 19th-century composer Gioacchino Rossini, Italian opera regained international attention, and La Scala, as the site of many of Rossini's premieres, had by the 1830s become the opera landmark it has remained ever since. Associated with the main theatre are a smaller theatre, La Piccola Scala; a ballet company and ballet school; and a singing school.

Laayoune, or EL AAIÚN, City (pop., 2004: 183,691), Western Sahara, northwestern Africa. The capital (1940–76) of the former Spanish Sahara and (since 1976) of the Laâyoune province of Morocco (though Morocco's claim is not internationally recognized), Laayoune lies in the northern part of Western Sahara, 8 miles (13 km) inland from the Atlantic Ocean. It was developed by Spain in 1938 as the administrative and military centre of the Europeans living in Spanish Sahara. It is Western Sahara's largest urban centre, and it has been a major site of Moroccan infrastructural investment, including the construction of housing and a large desalination plant.

labour, In economics, the general body of wage earners. In classical economics, labour is one of the three factors of production, along with capital and land. Labour can also be used to describe work performed, including any valuable service rendered by a human agent in the production of wealth, other than accumulating and providing capital. Labour is performed for the sake of its product or, in modern economic life, for the sake of a share of the aggregate product of the community's industry. The price per unit of time, or wage rate, commanded by a particular kind of labour in the market depends on a number of variables, such as the technical efficiency of the worker, the demand for that person's partic-

ular skills, and the supply of similarly skilled workers. Other variables include training, experience, intelligence, social status, prospects for advancement, and relative difficulty of the work. All these factors make it impossible for economists to assign a standard value to labour. Instead, economists often quantify labour hours according to the quantity and value of the goods or services produced.

labour law, Body of law that applies to matters such as employment, wages, conditions of work, labour unions, and labour-management relations. Laws intended to protect workers, including children, from abusive employment practices were not enacted in significant numbers until the late 19th century in Europe and slightly later in the U.S. In Asia and Africa, labour legislation did not emerge until the 1940s and '50s. Employment laws cover matters such as hiring, training, advancement, and unemployment compensation. Wage laws cover the forms and methods of payment, pay rates, social security, pensions, and other matters. Legislation on working conditions regulates hours, rest periods, vacations, child labour, equality in the workplace, and health and safety. Laws on trade unions and labour-management relations address the status of unions, the rights and obligations of workers' and employers' organizations, collective bargaining agreements, and rules for settling strikes and other disputes.

Labrador, Large peninsula, northeastern Canada. Divided between the provinces of Quebec and Newfoundland and Labrador, it occupies an area of about 625,000 sq mi (1,620,000 sq km). Its highest mountains are over 5,000 ft (1,520 m), and its coast is lined with islands. It forms the easternmost portion of the plateau known as the Canadian Shield. Politically, Labrador refers to the Newfoundland and Labrador portion of the peninsula; the Quebec portion is Ungava Peninsula. Political control of the region was disputed by the two provinces until the Quebec-Newfoundland border was established in 1927.

Labrador Current, Surface oceanic current flowing southward along the western side of the Labrador Sea. Originating at the Davis Strait, the current is a combination of the West Greenland Current, the Baffin Island Current, and inflow from Hudson Bay. It maintains temperatures of less than 32°F (0°C) and has a low salinity. The current is limited to the continental shelf and reaches depths only slightly greater than 2,000 ft (600 m). It carries several thousand icebergs southward each year.

labyrinth, or MAZE, System of intricate passageways and blind alleys. Labyrinth was the name given by the ancient Greeks and Romans to buildings, entirely or partly underground, containing a number of chambers and passages that made egress difficult. From the European Renaissance on, labyrinths or mazes consisting of intricate paths separated by high hedges were a feature of formal gardens.

lace, Ornamental openwork fabric formed by the looping, interlacing, braiding, or twisting of threads, originally primarily of linen. Almost all high-quality artistic lace is made by one of two techniques: needle lace involves a difficult technique that originated in Italy; bobbin lace is a more widespread craft that originated in Flanders. The art of lace is a European achievement. Fully developed lace did not appear before the Renaissance. By 1600 lace had become a fabric of luxury and an important article of commerce. The Industrial Revolution in the 19th century led to the use of machines to produce less-expensive lace made of cotton, and lace gradually disappeared from both men's and women's fashions. By 1920 the industry was dying. Fine handmade lace is still made in Belgium, Slovenia, and elsewhere, but chiefly as souvenirs.

lacquerwork, Any of a variety of decorative objects or surfaces, usually of wood, to which a coloured, highly polished, and opaque type of varnish called lacquer has been applied. True lacquerwork is Chinese or Japanese in origin. The technique was copied in Europe, where it was known as "japanning," but European lacquerwork lacks the hardness and brilliance of Asian lacquer. True lacquer is the purified and dehydrated sap of the *Rhus vernicifera* tree, native to China and cultivated in Japan. Lacquer becomes extremely hard but not brittle on exposure to air and takes a high polish. Many thin layers are applied, allowed to dry, and smoothed before the surface is ready for decoration by carving, engraving, or inlay.

lacrosse (French: "the crosier") Outdoor goal-scoring sport played with sticks called crosses. A crosse has a long handle and a triangular head with a mesh pouch for catching, carrying, and throwing a hard rubber ball. The object of the game is to sling the ball into an opponent's goal (for one point). French settlers in Canada adapted the modern game from an ancient American Indian activity (baggataway) that was at once sport, combat training, and mystical ceremony. It became an organized sport in the late 19th century. Modern teams have 10 players. The game is divided into four periods of 15 minutes each. Lacrosse is especially popular as a collegiate sport and is played by both men and women.

lactation, Production of milk by female mammals after giving birth. The milk is discharged by the mammary glands in the breasts. Hormones triggered by delivery of the placenta and by nursing stimulate milk production. Colostrum (milk that the mother produces in the first few days after giving birth) has more proteins, minerals, and antibodies and fewer calories and fats than the mature milk that develops later. Mature milk supplies nutrients, hormones, and substances that provide the infant with immunity against infectious agents. Most physicians recommend that babies be fed mother's milk exclusively for the first six months and that nursing continue through the first year. As the child is weaned, lactation tapers off; while nursing continues, fertility is reduced. Problems with lactation may involve hormones, suckling pattern, physical difficulties, or emotional factors. Mothers taking certain drugs or with some diseases (e.g., AIDS) should not nurse, because of risks to the baby.

lactic acid, Carboxylic acid found in certain plant juices, in blood and muscle, and in soil. In blood it occurs in the form of its salts (lactates) when glycogen is broken down in muscle; it can be reconverted to glycogen in the liver. Stiffness and soreness after prolonged heavy exercise are due to accumulated lactic acid in the muscles. The end product of bacterial fermentation, lactic acid is the most common acidic constituent of fermented milk products (e.g., sour milk and cream, cheese, buttermilk, yogurt). It is used in other foods as a flavouring or preservative and industrially in tanning leather and dyeing wool and as a raw material or catalyst in many chemical processes.

lactose, Slightly sweet sugar (disaccharide) composed of two monosaccharides, glucose and galactose, linked together. Lactose-intolerant adults, and more rarely infants, cannot digest lactose because they lack the enzyme (lactase) that splits it into simpler sugars and suffer diarrhea and bloating when they eat foods containing it. Lactose, which makes up 2–8% of the milk of mammals, is the only common sugar of animal origin. Commercial lactose is obtained from whey, a liquid by-product of cheese. It is used in foods, in pharmaceuticals, and in nutrient broths used to produce penicillin, yeast, and riboflavin, and other products.

ladino, Central American whose primary language is Spanish and who wears modern dress. Genetically ladinos may be of Indian, African, or mixed descent. An Indian may become a ladino by abandoning the Indian dress and customs. Many rural ladinos practice subsistence agriculture much like that of their Indian neighbours, but they tend to emphasize cash crops and modern farming techniques, which the Indians shun. In small towns ladi-

nos commonly engage in commerce as well as farming. In the cities they engage in all occupations, from day labourer to university professor.

Ladoga, Lake, Lake, northwestern Russia. The largest lake in Europe, it covers an area of 6,700 sq mi (17,600 sq km). It is 136 mi (219 km) long and has an average width of 51 mi (82 km); its greatest depth is 754 ft (230 m). It contains 660 islands of more than 2.5 acres (1 hectare) in area. Its outlet is the Neva River, in the southwestern corner. Formerly divided between the U.S.S.R. and Finland, it now lies entirely within Russia. During the Siege of Leningrad (1941–44) in World War II, the lake was the lifeline that connected the city with the rest of the Soviet Union.

Laetoli footprints, Several trails of bipedal footprints, presumed to be those of *Australopithecus afarensis*, preserved in volcanic ash at Laetoli in northern Tanzania and dated to approximately 3.5 million years ago. They were discovered in 1978 by a team led by the Leakey family. The footprints indicate that the mechanism of weight and force transference through the early hominin foot was virtually identical to that of modern humans and suggest that two of the individuals, one larger and one smaller, walked together in stride and were close enough to have been touching.

Lafayette, Marie-Joseph-Paul-Yves-Roch-Gilbert du Motier, marquis de (b. Sept. 6, 1757, Chavaniac, France—d. May 20, 1834, Paris), French military leader. Born to an ancient noble family of great wealth, he was a courtier at the court of Louis XVI but sought glory as a soldier. In 1777 he went to America, was appointed a major general, became a close friend of George Washington, and fought with distinction at the Battle of the Brandywine. He returned to France in 1779, persuaded Louis to send a 6,000-man force to aid the colonists, and returned to America in 1780 to command an army in Virginia and help win the Siege of Yorktown. Hailed as "the Hero of Two Worlds," he returned to France in 1782, became a leader of liberal aristocrats, and was elected to the Estates General in 1789. He presented the Declaration of the Rights of Man and of the Citizen to the National Assembly. Elected commander of the national guard of Paris, he sought to protect the king, favouring a constitutional monarchy. When his guards fired on a crowd of petitioners in the Champ de Mars (1791), he lost popularity and resigned his position. He commanded the army against Austria (1792), then defected to the Austrians, who held him captive until 1797. Returning to France, Lafayette became a gentleman farmer. In the Bourbon Restoration, he served in the Chamber of Deputies (1814–24) and commanded the national guard in the July Revolution (1830).

Lagerkvist, Pär (Fabian) (b. May 23, 1891, Växjö, Swed.—d. July 11, 1974, Stockholm), Swedish novelist, poet, and dramatist. He was involved early in life with socialism and soon began to support literary and artistic radicalism. Though his early works are characterized by extreme pessimism, he declared his faith in humanity with his great prose monologue *The Triumph over Life* (1927). In the 1930s and '40s his writings protested fascism and brutality. The novel *The Dwarf* (1944) was his first bestseller and his first undisputed critical success. He won world recognition with the novel *Barabbas* (1950). He was awarded the Nobel Prize for Literature in 1951.

Lagerlöf, Selma (Ottiliana Lovisa) (b. Nov. 20, 1858, Mårbacka, Swed.—d. March 16, 1940, Mårbacka), Swedish novelist. She was working as a schoolmistress when she wrote her first novel, *Gösta Berlings saga* (1891), a chronicle of life in her native Värmland. Later works include *Jerusalem* (1901–02), which established her as Sweden's foremost novelist, and *The Wonderful Adventures of Nils* and its sequel (1906–07), a geography reader for children in fantasy form. A naturally gifted storyteller, she rooted her work in legend and saga. In 1909 she became the first woman and the first Swedish writer to win the Nobel Prize for Literature.

lagoon, Area of relatively shallow, quiet water with access to the sea but separated from it by sandbars, barrier islands, or coral reefs. Coastal lagoons have low to moderate tides and constitute about 13% of the world's coastline. Their water is colder than the sea in winter and warmer in summer. In warm regions, evaporation may more than balance any freshwater input and may result in hypersaline water and even the buildup of thick salt deposits. Coral-reef lagoons occur on marginal reefs such as the Great Barrier Reef, but the most spectacular examples, some more than 30 mi (50 km) across, are associated with Pacific atolls.

Lagos, City (pop., 2002: 8,030,000) and chief port, Nigeria. It is Nigeria's largest city, built on four main islands—Lagos, Iddo, Ikoyi, and Victoria—that are connected to each other and to the mainland by bridges. Its population is centered on Lagos Island, on the Bight of Benin. Part of the kingdom of Benin in the 16th century, it was inhabited largely by the Yoruba. Beginning in 1808, as Britain attempted to end the slave trade, Lagos came into increasingly greater contact with the British. It was ceded to Britain in 1861, became a crown colony, and was governed from Sierra Leone (1866–74) and as part of the Gold Coast colony (1874–86). Joined with the protectorate of Southern Nigeria in 1906, it was made the capital of the colony of Nigeria in 1914. It was the capital (1960–91) of independent Nigeria until Abuja became the new capital. It is a major trade and industrial centre.

Lahore, City (pop., 2007 est.: 6,577,000), capital of Punjab province, northeastern Pakistan. The second largest city of Pakistan, it lies in the upper Indus plain on the Ravi River. It was the capital of the Ghaznavid dynasty in the 12th century and was captured by the Mughal Bābur's troops in 1524; it was later under Akbar and Jahāngīr. Ruled by Sikhs in the early 19th century, it passed to the British in 1849. After Indian independence, Lahore became part of Pakistan in 1947. It is the site of the mosque of Wazir Khan (1634); a mosque built by Aurangzeb; and the Shalimar gardens, laid out in 1641. It is the seat of Pakistan's oldest educational institution, the University of the Punjab (founded 1882).

laissez-faire (French: "allow to do"), Policy dictating a minimum of governmental interference in the economic affairs of individuals and society. It was promoted by the physiocrats and strongly supported by Adam Smith and John Stuart Mill. Widely accepted in the 19th century, laissez-faire assumed that the individual who pursues his own desires contributes most successfully to society as a whole. The function of the state is to maintain order and avoid interfering with individual initiative. The popularity of the laissez-faire doctrine waned in the late 19th century, when it proved inadequate to deal with the social and economic problems caused by industrialization.

lake, Relatively large body of slow-moving or standing water that occupies an inland basin. Lakes are most abundant in high northern latitudes and in mountain regions, particularly those that were covered by glaciers in recent geologic times. The primary sources of lake water are melting ice and snow, springs, rivers, runoff from the land surface, and direct precipitation. In the upper part of lakes there is a good supply of light, heat, oxygen, and nutrients, well distributed by currents and turbulence. As a result, a large number of diverse aquatic organisms can be found there. The most abundant forms are plankton (chiefly diatoms), algae, and flagellates. In the lower levels and in the sediments, the main forms of life are bacteria.

Lake District, Mountainous region, administrative county of Cumbria, northwestern England. Roughly coextensive with Lake District National Park, the country's largest, it occupies an area of 866 sq mi (2,243 sq km). It contains numerous lakes, including Windermere (England's largest), Grasmere, and Coniston Water, as well as England's highest mountains, the loftiest being Scafell Pike, which rises to 3,210 ft (978 m). The district was home to several English poets, including William Wordsworth, Robert Southey, and Samuel Taylor Coleridge, who celebrated its landscape. It became a national park in 1951.

Lake Turkana remains, Collection of hominin fossils found along the shores of Lake Turkana (Lake Rudolf) in northwestern Kenya. The Koobi Fora site, excavated by the Leakey family and others, has proved to be the richest trove of hominin remains anywhere in the world, yielding fossils that represent perhaps 230 individuals, including members of *Homo habilis, Homo erectus,* and *Australopithecus.* On the western shore was found a remarkably well-preserved skeleton of an 11-year-old boy ("Turkana Boy") later classified as *H. ergaster* or *H. erectus* and dated to *c.* 1.8 million years ago. This surprisingly human specimen suggests that *H. ergaster* may have been the direct ancestor of the hominins that left Africa for Eurasia *c.* 1 million years ago.

Lakshadweep, Union territory (pop., 2008 est.: 69,000) of India. Located in the Arabian Sea off India's southwestern coast, it includes about three dozen islands (10 of which are inhabited), with a total land area of 12 sq mi (32 sq km). The capital is Kavaratti. Once ruled by the Hindu Kulashekhara dynasty, it became a predominantly Muslim domain in the 12th century. Britain gained sovereignty over it at the end of the 18th century and assumed direct administration in 1908. It passed to India in 1947 and became a union territory in 1956. Coconut palms are the agricultural mainstay, and fishing and tourism are also important.

Lakshmi, or LAKSMI, Hindu and Jain goddess of wealth and good fortune. The consort of Vishnu, she is said to have taken different forms with him in each of his incarnations. She is a principal object of worship during Divali, when her presence is sought in homes, temples, and businesses for the whole of the year to come.

lama, In Tibetan Buddhism, a spiritual leader. Some lamas are considered to be reincarnations of their predecessors; others have won respect for their high level of spiritual development. The most honored of the reincarnate lamas is the Dalai Lama; second in spiritual authority is the Panchen Lama. The process of discovering the new incarnation of a lama, especially the Dalai Lama, is elaborate and exacting. Oracular messages, unusual signs during the lama's death or during a birth thereafter, and examinations of candidates identify a successor. The child thus identified as the lama's incarnation is given extensive monastic training from an early age.

lamprey, Any of about 22 species of primitive, jawless fishes (with hagfishes in class Agnatha). Lampreys live in coastal and freshwater in temperate regions worldwide except Africa. Eel-like, scaleless animals, they are 6–40 in. (15–100 cm) long. Lam-

Lamprey (Lampetra) *on rainbow trout.*
Oxford Scientific Films/Bruce Coleman Ltd.

preys have well-developed eyes, a single nostril on top of the head, a cartilaginous skeleton, and a sucking mouth with horny teeth surrounding the round opening. They spend years as burrowing larvae; adults of most species move into the sea. They attach to fish with their mouth and feed on their host's blood and tissues. Some species will remain in freshwater, notably the sea lamprey, which entered the Great Lakes and nearly eliminated lake trout and other commercially important fishes there.

Lancelot, or LAUNCELOT, One of the greatest knights in Arthurian legend, the lover of Guinevere and the father of Galahad. He first appeared in a 12th-century romance by Chrétien de Troyes, and he is a major character in Sir Thomas Malory's *Morte Darthur*. His full name, Sir Lancelot du Lac, refers to his upbringing by the Lady of the Lake, the enchantress who carried him off in infancy and trained him to be a model of chivalry before sending him to Arthur's court. There he became the favorite of King Arthur and the lover of Queen Guinevere. His adultery with Guinevere caused him to fail in the quest for the grail and set in motion the events that led to the destruction of Camelot. He was displaced as the model knight by Galahad, his son by the grailkeeper's daughter Elaine.

land mine, Explosive charge buried just below the surface of the earth, used in military operations against troops and vehicles. It may be fired by the weight of vehicles or troops on it, the passage of time, or remote control. Though improvised land mines (buried artillery shells) were used in World War I, they only became important in warfare during World War II and have been widely used since. Most early mines had metal cases; later models were sometimes made of other materials to prevent magnetic detection. They are typically used to disrupt or prevent the massed attack of tanks or infantry, but in post–World War II conflicts they have also been used to render land useless to enemy civilian populations. A treaty banning land mines—not signed by the U.S., Russia, and China—went into effect in 1997.

Land's End, Westernmost peninsula, Cornwall, England. Its tip is the southwesternmost point of England and lies about 870 mi (1,400 km) from John o' Groats, traditionally considered the northernmost point of Britain. Off its coast lie dangerous reefs, one group of which, a mile from the mainland, is marked by the Longships lighthouse.

Landsat, officially EARTH RESOURCES TECHNOLOGY SATELLITES, Any of a series of unmanned U.S. scientific satellites. The first three were launched in 1972, 1975, and 1978. They were designed mainly to collect information about Earth's natural resources. They were also equipped to monitor atmospheric and oceanic conditions and to detect variations in pollution levels and other ecological changes. Three more Landsat satellites were launched successfully, in 1982, 1984, and 1999; radio communication with Landsat 6 was lost immediately after its launch in 1993.

language, System of conventional spoken or written symbols used by people in a shared culture to communicate with each other. A language both reflects and affects a culture's way of thinking, and changes in a culture influence the development of its language. Related languages become more differentiated when their speakers are isolated from each other. When speech communities come into contact (e.g., through trade or conquest), their languages influence each other. Most existing languages are grouped with other languages descended "genetically" from a common ancestral language. The broadest grouping of languages is the language family. For example, all the Romance languages are derived from Latin, which in turn belongs to the Italic branch of the Indo-European language family, descended from the ancient parent language, Proto-Indo-European. Other major families include, in Asia, Sino-Tibetan, Austronesian, Dravidian, Altaic, and Austroasiatic; in Africa, Niger-Congo, Afro-Asiatic, and Nilo-Saharan;

and in the Americas, Uto-Aztecan, Maya, Otomanguean, and Tupian. Relationships between languages are traced by comparing grammar and syntax and especially by looking for cognates (related words) in different languages. Language has a complex structure that can be analyzed and systematically presented. All languages begin as speech, and many go on to develop writing systems. All can employ different sentence structures to convey mood. They use their resources differently for this but seem to be equally flexible structurally. The principal resources are word order, word form, syntactic structure, and, in speech, intonation. Different languages keep indicators of number, person, gender, tense, mood, and other categories separate from the root word or attach them to it. The innate human capacity to learn language fades with age, and languages learned after about age 10 are usually not spoken as well as those learned earlier.

lanthanoid, Any of the series of 15 consecutive chemical elements in the periodic table from lanthanum to lutetium (atomic numbers 57–71). With scandium and yttrium, they make up the rare earth metals. Their atoms have similar configurations and similar physical and chemical behaviour; the most common valences are 3 and 4.

lanthanum, Metallic chemical element, one of the transition elements, chemical symbol La, atomic number 57. It was discovered in 1839, and its name derives from the Greek for "to lie hidden." Lanthanum is a ductile and malleable silvery white metal, soft enough to be cut with a knife. Highly purified lanthanum oxide is an ingredient in the manufacture of low-dispersion, high-refraction glasses for lens components.

Laos, officially LAO PEOPLE'S DEMOCRATIC REPUBLIC, Country, Southeast Asia. Area: 91,429 sq mi (236,800 sq km). Population: (2011 est.) 6,392,000. Capital: Vientiane. Major ethnic groups include the Lao-Lum (valley Lao), who make up about half of the population; the Lao-Tai, a highland tribal people; the Lao-Theung (Mon-Khmer), descendants of the region's earliest inhabitants; and the Lao-Soung group, including the Hmong and Man. Languages: Lao (official), English, Vietnamese, French. Religions: Buddhism, traditional beliefs. Currency: kip. Laos is largely mountainous, especially in the north; its highest point is Mount Bia (9,245 ft [2,818 m]). Tropical forests cover more than half of the country's total land area; only a tiny portion of its total area is suitable for agriculture. The floodplains of the Mekong River provide the country's only lowlands and its major wet-rice fields. Laos has a centrally planned economy based primarily on agriculture (including rice, sweet potatoes, sugarcane, cassava, and opium poppies) and international aid. It is a unitary single-party people's republic with one legislative house; its head of state is the president, and its head of government is the prime minister. The Lao people migrated into Laos from southern China after the 8th century CE, displacing indigenous peoples. In the 14th century Fa Ngum founded the first Laotian state, Lan Xang. Except for a period of rule by Myanmar (Burma; 1574–1637), the Lan Xang kingdom ruled Laos until 1713, when it split into three kingdoms—Vien Chan, Champassak, and Luang Prabang. During the 18th century the rulers of the three Laotian kingdoms became vassals of Siam (Thailand). France gained control of the region in 1893, and Laos became a French protectorate. In 1945 Japan seized control and declared Laos independent. The area reverted to French rule after World War II. By the end of the First Indochina War, the leftist Pathet Lao movement controlled two provinces of the country. The Geneva Conference of 1954 unified and granted independence to Laos. Pathet Lao forces fought the Laotian government and took control in 1975, establishing the Lao People's Democratic Republic; about one-tenth of the population fled into neighbouring Thailand. Laos held its first election in 1989 and promulgated a new constitution in 1991. Although its economy was adversely affected by the regional economic recession beginning in the mid-1990s, it realized a longtime goal in 1997 when it joined ASEAN.

Laozi, or LAO-TZU (fl. 6th century BC, China), First philosopher of Chinese Daoism. He is traditionally named as the author of the *Daodejing,* though modern scholars hold that the work had more than one author. Legends about his life abound, but little or no certain information survives. The historical Laozi, if he existed, may have been a scholar and caretaker of sacred books at the royal court of the Zhou dynasty. According to legend, he was carried 72 years in his mother's womb, and he met Confucius as a young man. He is venerated as a philosopher by the Confucianists, as a saint or god by the common people of China, and as a divinity and the representative of the *dao* by Daoists.

laparoscopy, or PERITONEOSCOPY, Procedure for inspecting the abdominal cavity using a laparoscope; also surgery requiring use of a laparoscope. Laparoscopes use fibre-optic lights and small video cameras to show tissues and organs on a monitor. Laparoscopic surgical procedures include gallbladder, appendix, and tumour removal; tubal ligation; and hysterectomy. After carbon dioxide is pumped in to expand the space for the instruments, small incisions are made and the laparoscope and instruments inserted. Less invasive than traditional (open) surgery, laparoscopy reduces postoperative pain, recovery time, and length of hospital stay.

Lapland, Region, northern Europe. Located within the Arctic Circle, it stretches across northern Norway, Sweden, and Finland and into Russia's Kola Peninsula. Occupying an area of 150,000 sq mi (389,000 sq km), it is bounded by the Norwegian Sea, the Barents Sea, and the White Sea. Since it straddles several national borders, it does not exist as any unified administrative entity. It is named for the Sami (Lapp) people, who have inhabited the region for several thousand years. Those still practicing reindeer herding have liberty of movement across national boundaries. Industries include mining and fishing.

Lares, In Roman religion, guardian deities. Originally gods of cultivated fields, Lares were later worshiped in association with the Penates, the gods of the household. The household Lar, considered the centre of the family cult, was often represented as a youthful figure holding a drinking horn and cup. Two Lares might be portrayed standing on either side of Vesta or some other deity. A prayer was said to the Lar or Lares every morning, and offerings were made at family festivals. Public Lares presided over local districts marked by a crossroads; state Lares (*praestites*), guardians of Rome, were worshiped in a temple on the Via Sacra.

larva, Active, feeding stage in the development of many animals, occurring after birth or hatching and before the adult form is reached. Larvae are structurally different from adults and often are adapted to a different environment. Some species have free-living larvae but sessile (affixed) adults, the moving larvae thus helping to spread the species; others have aquatic larvae but terrestrial adults. Most larvae are tiny; many are dispersed by entering a host's body, where the adult form of the parasite emerges. Many invertebrates (e.g., cnidarians) have simple larvae. Flukes have several larval stages, and annelids, mollusks, and crustaceans have various larval forms. Insect larvae are called caterpillars, grubs, maggots, or worms; the larval stage of many insects may last much longer than the adult stage (e.g., some cicadas live 17 years as larvae and a week as adults). Echinoderms also have larval forms. The larvae of frogs and toads are called tadpoles.

laryngitis, Inflammation of the larynx, causing hoarseness. Simple laryngitis usually occurs with infections such as the common cold. Other causes include inhalation of irritants. The larynx's lining becomes swollen and secretes mucus. In chronic laryngitis, caused by excessive smoking, drinking, or vocal-cord use, the larynx is dry and has polyps. Other types are caused by diphtheria spreading from the upper throat, tuberculosis bacteria spreading from the lungs, and advanced syphilis. The last can produce severe scarring and permanent hoarseness.

Las Palmas, or LAS PALMAS DE GRAN CANARIA, Seaport city (pop., 2001: 354,863), northeastern Grand Canary Island, Spain. The largest city and chief port of the Canary Islands, it was founded in 1478 and served as a base for the Spanish conquest of Tenerife and La Palma islands. It grew after the port was constructed in 1883. It is a year-round resort; historic sites include a 15th-century cathedral and the house of Christopher Columbus.

Las Vegas, City (pop., 2010: 583,756), southeastern Nevada, U.S. It is famous for its luxury hotels, casinos, and nightclubs, located in the area known as "the Strip." Mormons from Utah settled the site in 1855 and abandoned it in 1857. It became a railroad town in 1905 and was incorporated in 1911. Gambling was legalized in 1931, and Las Vegas expanded rapidly after 1940. Its connections to crime syndicates began in 1946, when Bugsy Siegel opened the Flamingo Hotel. By the turn of the 21st century it was one of the country's fastest-growing metropolitan areas, attracting a year-round population as well as tourists.

Lascaux Grotto, Cave near Montignac, Fr., that contains perhaps the most outstanding known display of prehistoric art. Discovered in 1940, it consists of a main cavern and several steep galleries, all magnificently decorated with engraved, drawn, and painted animals, some of them portrayed in a "twisted perspective." Among the most notable images are four great aurochs bulls, a curious unicorn-type animal that may represent a mythical creature, and a rare narrative composition involving a bird-man figure and a speared bison. About 1,500 bone engravings have also been found at the site, which has been dated to the late Aurignacian period (*c.* 15,000 BC). Because of heavy tourist traffic, the cave was closed to the public in 1963, but a full-scale facsimile, Lascaux II, was opened in 1983.

laser, Device that produces an intense beam of coherent light (light composed of waves having a constant difference in phase). Its name, an acronym derived from "light amplification by stimulated emission of radiation," describes how its beam is produced. The first laser, constructed in 1960 by Theodore Maiman (born 1927) based on earlier work by Charles H. Townes, used a rod of ruby. Light of a suitable wavelength from a flashlight excited the ruby atoms to higher energy levels. The excited atoms decayed swiftly to slightly lower energies (through phonon reactions) and then fell more slowly to the ground state, emitting light at a specific wavelength. The light tended to bounce back and forth between the polished ends of the rod, stimulating further emission. The laser has found valuable applications in microsurgery, compact-disc players, communications, and holography, as well as for drilling holes in hard materials, alignment in tunnel drilling, long-distance measurement, and mapping fine details.

Lateran Council, Any of five ecumenical councils of the Roman Catholic church held in the Lateran Palace in Rome. The First Lateran Council (1123), held during the papacy of Calixtus II, reiterated decrees of earlier ecumenical councils (condemning simony, forbidding clergymen to marry, etc.). The Second Lateran Council (1139) was called by Innocent II to end the schism created by the election of a rival pope. The Third Lateran Council (1179), held during the papacy of Alexander III, established a two-thirds majority of the College of Cardinals as a requirement for papal election and condemned the heresies of the Cathari. Innocent III called the Fourth Lateran Council (1215) in an effort to reform the church; its decrees obliged Catholics to make a yearly confession, sanctioned the doctrine of transubstantiation, and made preparations for a new Crusade. The Fifth Lateran Council (1512–17), convoked by Julius II, affirmed the immortality of the soul and restored peace among warring Christian rulers.

Latin alphabet, or ROMAN ALPHABET, Most widely used alphabet, the standard script of most languages that originated in Europe. It developed before 600 BC from the Etruscan alphabet (in turn derived from the North Semitic alphabet by way of the Phoenician and Greek alphabets). The earliest known Latin inscriptions date from the 7th–6th cent. BC. The classical Latin alphabet had 23 letters, 21 derived from the Etruscan. In medieval times the letter J became differentiated from I, and U and W became differentiated from V, producing the 26-letter alphabet of modern English. In ancient Roman times there were two types of Latin script, capital letters and cursive. Uncial script, mixing both types, developed in the 3rd century AD.

Latin America, Countries of South America and North America (including Central America and the islands of the Caribbean Sea) south of the U.S.; the term is often restricted to countries where either Spanish or Portuguese is spoken. The colonial era in Latin America began in the 15th–16th centuries when explorers such as Christopher Columbus and Amerigo Vespucci made voyages of discovery to the New World. The conquistadores who followed, including Hernán Cortés and Francisco Pizarro, brought Spanish rule to much of the region. In 1532 the first Portuguese settlement was made in Brazil. The Roman Catholic church soon established many missions in Latin America. Roman Catholicism is still the chief religion in most Latin American countries, though the number of Protestants and Evangelicals has grown. Spanish and Portuguese colonists arrived in increasing numbers; they enslaved the native Indian population, which was soon decimated by ill treatment and disease, and then imported African slaves to replace them. A series of movements for independence, led by José de San Martín, Simón Bolívar, and others, swept Latin America in the early 19th century. Federal republics were promulgated across the region, but many of the new countries collapsed into political chaos and were taken over by dictators or military juntas, a situation that persisted into the 20th century. In the 1990s a trend toward democratic rule reemerged; in socialist-run countries many state-owned industries were privatized, and efforts toward regional economic integration were accelerated.

Latin language, Indo-European language of the Italic group; ancestor of the modern Romance languages. Originally spoken by small groups of people living along the lower Tiber River, Latin spread with the growth of Roman political power, first throughout Italy and then through most of western and southern Europe and the central and western Mediterranean coastal regions of Africa. The earliest known Latin inscriptions date from the 7th century BC; Latin literature dates from the 3rd century BC. A gap soon appeared between literary (classical) Latin and the popular spoken language, Vulgar Latin. The Romance languages developed from dialects of the latter. During the Middle Ages and much of the Renaissance, Latin was the language most widely employed in the West for scholarly and literary purposes. Until the latter part of the 20th century, its use was required in the liturgy of the Roman Catholic church.

latitude and longitude, Coordinate system by which the position or location of any place on the Earth's surface can be determined and described. Latitude is a measurement of location north or south of the Equator. Lines of latitude are known as parallels, or parallels of latitude. Longitude is a measurement of location east or west of the prime meridian, which passes through Greenwich, Eng. The combination of meridians of longitude and parallels of latitude establishes a grid by which exact positions can be determined: for example, a point described as 40° N, 30° W is located 40° of arc north of the Equator and 30° of arc west of the Greenwich meridian.

Latvia, officially REPUBLIC OF LATVIA, Country, northeastern Europe, along the shores of the Baltic Sea and the Gulf of Riga. Area: 24,938 sq mi (64,589 sq km). Population: (2011 est.) 2,217,000. Capital: Riga. Three-fifths of the population are Latvians, or Letts, who speak Latvian, one of two surviving Baltic languages. Russians make up about one-third of the population. Languages: Latvian (official), Russian. Religion: Christianity (Protestant, Roman Catholic, Eastern Orthodox). Currency: lats.

The landscape is an undulating plain, with fairly flat lowlands alternating with hills. Latvia is a fully industrialized country. Heavy industry (notably the production of metals, ships, and railcars) once was more important than it is today; now leading manufactures include beverages, furniture, foodstuffs, and textiles. Latvia is a unitary multiparty republic with one legislative body; its head of state is the president, and the government is led by the prime minister. It was settled by the Balts in ancient times. During the 10th and 11th centuries there were incursions into Latvia from the west (Swedes) and east (Slavs), and later it was dominated by German-speaking Saxons, who Christianized Latvia in the 12th–13th century. The Order of the Brothers of the Sword conquered Latvia by the 1230s. From the mid-16th to the early 18th century the region was split between Poland and Sweden, but by the end of the 18th century all of Latvia had been annexed by Russia. Latvia declared its independence after the Russian Revolution of 1917. In 1939 it was forced to grant military bases to the Soviet Union, and in 1940 the Soviet Red Army invaded. Next held by Nazi Germany (1941–44), the country was recaptured by the Soviets and incorporated into the Soviet Union. With the breakup of the Soviet Union, Latvia gained its independence in 1991. Subsequently it sought to privatize the economy and build ties with western Europe (becoming a member of both the European Union and the North Atlantic Treaty Organization in 2004), as well as to improve uneasy relations with Russia.

Laurasia, Hypothetical former supercontinent in the Southern Hemisphere, which included modern North America, Europe, and Asia (except peninsular India). The concept that the continents were at one time joined was first set forth in detail by Alfred Wegener in 1912. He envisioned a single great landmass, Pangea, which supposedly began to separate early in the Jurassic Period (approximately 200 million to 146 million years ago). Subsequent research distinguished between a northern landmass, Laurasia, and Gondwana. Laurasia is thought to have fragmented into the present continents largely during the end of the Cretaceous Period and the beginning of the Paleogene Period.

Lausanne, Treaty of (1923) Final treaty concluding World War I, between Turkey (successor to the Ottoman Empire) and the Allies. Signed in Lausanne, Switz., it replaced the Treaty of Sèvres (1920). It recognized the boundaries of the modern state of Turkey, as well as British possession of Cyprus and Italian possession of the Dodecanese, and the Turkish straits between the Aegean and Black seas were declared open to all shipping.

lava, Molten rock originating as magma in the Earth's mantle that pours out onto the Earth's surface through volcanic vents at temperatures of about 1,300–2,200 °F (700–1,200 °C). Mafic lavas, such as basalt, form flows known by the Hawaiian names *pahoehoe* and *aa*. *Pahoehoe* is smooth and gently undulating; the lava moves through natural pipes known as lava tubes. *Aa* is very rough, covered with a layer of loose, irregular fragments called clinker, and flows in open channels. Lava that starts out as *pahoehoe* may turn into *aa* as it cools. Lavas of intermediate composition form a block lava flow, which also has a top consisting largely of loose rubble, but the fragments are fairly regular in shape, mostly polygons with relatively smooth sides.

*Spanish lavender (*Lavandula stoechas*).*
W.H. Hodge

lavender, Any of about 30 species of evergreen shrubs that make up the genus *Lavandula* in the mint family, the leaves and flowers of which contain scented oil glands. The spikes of flowers are purple, less commonly pink or white. Native to the Mediterranean, lavender is cultivated widely. Several species yield essential oil for fine perfumes and cosmetics. The narrow, fragrant leaves and flowers are dried for use in sachets and potpourris. Lavender is widely used in aromatherapy for its clean, fresh scent.

law, Discipline and profession concerned with the customs, practices, and rules of conduct that are recognized as binding by the community. Enforcement of the body of rules is through a controlling authority, such as a group of elders, a regent, a court, or a judiciary. Comparative law is the study of the differences, similarities, and interrelationships of different systems of law. Important areas in the study and practice of law include administrative law, antitrust law, business law, constitutional law, criminal law, environmental law, family law, health law, immigration law, intellectual property law, international law, labour law, maritime law, procedural law, property law, public interest law, tax law, trusts and estates, and torts.

laws, conflict of, Opposition or contradiction in the applicable laws of different states or jurisdictions regarding the rights of the parties in a case. Rules have been created to help determine which set of laws is applicable in a given case, which judicial system is most appropriate for trying the case, and the extent to which other jurisdictions are expected to honour or enforce the outcome of the trial.

Laxness, Halldór, orig. HALLDÓR KILJAN GUDJÓNSSON (b. April 23, 1902, Reykjavík, Ice.—d. Feb. 8, 1998, near Reykjavík), Icelandic novelist. He converted to Roman Catholicism while traveling in Europe as a young man but later dissociated himself from Christianity and turned to socialism, an ideology reflected in his novels from the 1930s and '40s. Works exploring the social issues of Iceland include *Salka Valka* (1936), which deals with the plight of working people in a fishing village; *Independent People* (1935), the story of an impoverished farmer's struggle for economic independence; and the nationalist trilogy *Iceland's Bell* (1943–46). His later works were more lyrical and introspective. He received the Nobel Prize for Literature in 1955.

Le Havre, Seaport city (pop., 2006 est.: 182,580), northern France. It lies along the English Channel and the Seine River estuary, northwest of Paris. The second port of France after Marseille, it serves as a base for exports; it is also an important industrial centre. It was only a fishing village until 1517, when Francis I had a harbour built there. Enlarged and fortified in the 17th century under cardinal de Richelieu and Louis XIV, it was adapted to accommodate bigger vessels in the late 18th century. Most of the city was destroyed during World War II. Later rebuilt, the city's 17th-century church of Notre-Dame is one of the few surviving old buildings.

lead, Metallic chemical element, chemical symbol Pb, atomic number 82. Lead is a soft, silvery white or grayish, malleable, ductile, dense metal that conducts electricity poorly. Its stable isotopes are all end products of radioactive decay of uranium and other heavy elements. Known since ancient times, lead is so durable and resistant to corrosion that Roman lead pipes are still usable. Lead is used in roofing, as cable coverings, in pipes, conduits, and structures. Other uses are in storage batteries, ammunition, and low-melting-point alloys (e.g., solder, pewter) and as shielding against sound, vibrations, and radiation. Lead is rarely found free in nature; its major ore is the sulfide galena (PbS). Because it and its compounds are poisons, lead-based paints and gasoline additives have been phased out in many countries. Lead in compounds has valence 2 and 4; an oxide (litharge, PbO) is the most widely used. Lead compounds are added to lead crystal, glazes, and ceramics and are used as pigments, drying agents for paints and varnishes, insecticides and herbicides, and fireproofing agents and in matches, explosives, and pyrotechnics. Almost half of all lead is recovered from recycled scrap. The "lead" in pencils is graphite.

lead poisoning, or PLUMBISM, Poisoning by accumulation of lead in the body. Large doses cause gastroenteritis in adults and brain disorders in children. Anemia, constipation and abdominal spasm, confusion, a progressive paralysis, and sometimes brain cancer result from chronic exposure. Children are particularly susceptible to nerve and brain damage; sensitive tests show that even low levels of lead can harm children and are linked to behavioral problems. Sources in the home include lead-based paint, lead drinking-water pipes, and lead-glazed tableware. Babies, who put things in their mouths, are at highest risk. Working where lead is used and exposure to some insecticides are other risk factors. The U.S. phaseout of lead in gasoline was completed in 1996; similar bans are being implemented worldwide. Treatment involves giving antidotes that bind the lead in the tissues.

leaf, Any flattened, green outgrowth from the stem of a vascular plant. Leaves manufacture oxygen and glucose, which nourishes and sustains both plants and animals. Leaves and stem tissue grow from the same apical bud. A typical leaf has a broad, expanded blade (lamina), attached to the stem by a stalklike petiole. The leaf may be simple (a single blade), compound (separate leaflets), or reduced to a spine or scale. The edge (margin) may be smooth or jagged. Veins transport materials to and from the leaf tissues, radiating from the petiole through the blade. They are arranged in a netlike pattern in dicot leaves and are parallel in monocot leaves. The leaf's outer layer (epidermis) protects the interior (mesophyll), whose soft-walled, unspecialized green cells (parenchyma) produce carbohydrate food by photosynthesis. In autumn the green chlorophyll pigments of deciduous leaves break down, revealing other pigment colors (yellow to red), and the leaves drop off the tree. Leaf scars that form during wound healing after the leaves drop are useful for identifying winter twigs. In conifers, evergreen needles, which are a type of leaf, persist for two or three years.

League of Nations, Organization for international cooperation established by the Allied Powers at the end of World War I. A league covenant, embodying the principles of collective security and providing for an assembly, a council, and a secretariat, was formulated at the Paris Peace Conference (1919) and contained in the Treaty of Versailles. The covenant also set up a system of colonial mandates. Headquartered at Geneva, the League was weakened by the failure of the U.S., which had not ratified the Treaty of Versailles, to join the organization. Discredited by its failure to prevent Japanese expansion into China, Italy's conquest of Ethiopia, and Germany's seizure of Austria, the League ceased its activities during World War II. It was replaced in 1946 by the United Nations.

Leaning Tower of Pisa, White marble campanile in Pisa, Italy, famous for the uneven settling of its foundation, which caused it to lean 5.5 degrees (about 15 ft [4.5 m]) from the perpendicular. Begun in 1173 as the third and final structure of the city's cathedral complex, it was designed to stand 185 ft (56 m) high. Work was suspended several times as engineers sought solutions; the tower, still leaning, was completed in the 14th century. Subsiding at the rate of 0.03 in (1.2 mm) a year, the structure was in danger of collapse, and in 1990 it was closed as engineers undertook a strengthening project that decreased the lean by 17 in (44 cm) to about 13.5 ft (4.1 m). The work was completed in May 2001.

learning, Process of acquiring modifications in existing knowledge, skills, habits, or tendencies through experience, practice, or exercise. Learning includes associative processes, discrimination of sense-data, psychomotor and perceptual learning, imitation, concept formation, problem solving, and insight learning. Animal learning has been studied by ethologists and comparative psychologists, the latter often drawing explicit parallels to human learning. The first experiments concerning associative learning were conducted by Ivan Pavlov in Russia and Edward L. Thorndike in the U.S. Critics of the early stimulus-response (S-R) theories, such as Edward C. Tolman, claimed they were overly reductive and ignored a subject's inner activities. Gestalt-psychology researchers drew attention to the importance of pattern and form in perception and learning, while structural linguists argued that language learning was grounded in a genetically inherited "grammar." Developmental psychologists such as Jean Piaget highlighted stages of growth in learning. More recently, cognitive scientists have explored learning as a form of information processing, while some brain researchers, such as Gerald Maurice Edelman, have proposed that thinking and learning involve an ongoing process of cerebral pathway building. Related topics of research include attention, comprehension, motivation, and transfer of training.

learning disabilities, Chronic difficulties in learning to read, write, spell, or calculate, which are believed to have a neurological origin. Though their causes and nature are still not fully understood, it is widely agreed that the presence of a learning disability does not indicate subnormal intelligence. Rather it is thought that the learning-disabled have a neurologically based difficulty in processing language or figures, which must be compensated for with special learning strategies or with extra effort and tutoring. Examples of learning disabilities include difficulty in reading (dyslexia), writing (dysgraphia), and mathematics (dyscalculia). Learning disabilities may be diagnosed through testing, and children may be enrolled in programs offering special help; left unrecognized, learning disabilities may result not only in poor classroom performance but also in low self-esteem and disruptive behaviour.

Lebanon, officially LEBANESE REPUBLIC, Country, Middle East, southwestern Asia, on the eastern shore of the Mediterranean Sea. Area: 4,036 sq mi (10,452 sq km). Population: (2011 est.) 4,143,000. Capital: Beirut. The Lebanese are ethnically a mixture of Phoenician, Greek, Armenian, and Arab elements. Languages: Arabic (official), French, English, Armenian, Kurdish. Religions: Islam, Christianity, Druze. Currency: Lebanese pound. Uplands include the Lebanon Mountains in the central region and the Anti-Lebanon and Hermon ranges along the eastern border; a low coastal plain stretches along the Mediterranean. The Līṭānī River flows southward through the fertile Al-Biqāʿ (Bekaa) valley region. Originally, much of the country was forested—the cedars of Lebanon were famous in antiquity—but woodlands now cover only a tiny fraction of the country. Lebanon is not agriculturally self-sufficient and must rely on food imports. Its traditional role as the financial centre of the Middle East has been undermined since the outbreak of the Lebanese civil war (1975–90). It is a unitary multiparty republic with one legislative house; its head of state is the president, and the head of government is the prime minister. Much of present-day Lebanon corresponds to ancient Phoenicia, which was settled *c.* 3000 BCE. From the 7th century CE onward, Christians fleeing Syrian persecution settled in northern Lebanon and founded the Maronite Church. Arab tribal peoples settled in southern Lebanon, and by the 11th century religious refugees from Egypt had founded the Druze faith. Part of the medieval Crusader states, Lebanon was later ruled by the Mamlūk dynasty. In 1516 the Ottoman Empire seized control; the Ottomans, who first ruled by proxy, ended the local rule of the Druze Shihāb princes in 1842. Deteriorating relations between religious groups resulted in the massacre of Maronites by Druze in 1860. France intervened, forcing the Ottomans to form an autonomous province for an area known as Mount Lebanon under a Christian governor. Following World War I (1914–18), the whole of Lebanon was administered by the French military as part of a French mandate; the country was fully independent by 1946. After the Arab-Israeli war of 1948–49, tens of thousands of Palestinian refugees settled in southern Lebanon. In 1970 the Palestine Liberation Organization (PLO) moved its headquarters to Lebanon and began raids into northern Israel. Political, religious, and socioeconomic divisions and a growing Palestinian "state within a state" fueled the descent

into a civil war that divided the country into numerous political and religious factions. At various points during the civil war external actors, primarily Syria and Israel, involved themselves in the conflict. In 1976 Syria intervened on behalf of the Christians, and in 1982 Israeli forces invaded in an effort to drive Palestinian forces out of southern Lebanon. Israeli troops withdrew from all but a narrow buffer zone in the south by 1985; thereafter, guerrillas from the Lebanese Shīʿite militia Hezbollah clashed with Israeli troops regularly. Israeli troops withdrew from Lebanon in 2000, and Syrian forces disengaged from the country in 2005. In mid-2006 Hezbollah and Israel engaged in a 34-day war, primarily fought in Lebanon, in which more than 1,000 people were killed. Israeli troops subsequently withdrew from most of Lebanon in October 2006.

Lebanon Mountains, Arabic JABAL LUBNĀN, ancient LIBANUS, Mountain range, Lebanon. Running parallel to the Mediterranean Sea coast, it is about 150 mi (240 km) long. The northern section is the highest part of the range and includes the loftiest peak, Qurnat al-Sawdāʾ, at 10,131 ft (3,088 m) in elevation. On its western slopes are the remaining groves of the famous cedars of Lebanon. The snowy peaks may have given Lebanon its name in antiquity; *laban* is Aramaic for "white."

Lee, Robert E(dward) (b. Jan. 19, 1807, Stratford, Westmoreland county, Va., U.S.—d. Oct. 12, 1870, Lexington, Va.), U.S. and Confederate military leader. He was the son of Henry Lee. After graduating from West Point, he served in the engineering corps and in the Mexican War under Winfield Scott. He transferred to the cavalry in 1855 and commanded frontier forces in Texas (1856–57). In 1859 he led U.S. troops against the slave insurrection attempted by John Brown at Harpers Ferry. In 1861 he was offered command of a new army being formed to force the seceded Southern states back into the

Robert E. Lee, 1865.
Library of Congress, Washington, D.C.

Union. Though opposed to secession, he refused. After his home state of Virginia seceded, he became commander of Virginia's forces in the American Civil War and adviser to Jefferson Davis, president of the Confederacy. Taking command of the Army of Northern Virginia (1862) after Joseph Johnston was wounded, Lee repulsed the Union forces in the Seven Days' Battles. He won victories at Bull Run, Fredericksburg, and Chancellorsville. His attempts to draw Union forces out of Virginia by invading the North resulted in failures at Antietam and Gettysburg. In 1864–65 he conducted defensive campaigns against Union forces under Ulysses S. Grant that caused heavy Union casualties. Lee ended his retreat behind fortifications built at Petersburg and Richmond. By April 1865 dwindling forces and supplies forced Lee, now general of all Confederate armies, to surrender at Appomattox Court House. After several months of recuperation, he accepted the post of president of Washington College (later Washington and Lee University), where he served until his death.

leech, Any annelid worm of the class Hirudinea (about 300 known species), with a small sucker containing the mouth at the front end and a large sucker at the back end. Species range from tiny to about 8 in. (20 cm) long. Leeches live primarily in freshwater or on land. Some species are predators, some eat organic debris, and others are parasitic. Aquatic leeches may feed on the blood of fishes, amphibians, birds, and mammals, or they may eat snails, insect larvae, and worms. True land leeches feed only on the blood of mammals. Substances in the leech's saliva anesthetize the wound area, dilate the blood vessels, and prevent the blood from clotting. For centuries, some species have been used to drain off blood. Hirudin, extracted from the European medicinal leech, is used medically as an anticoagulant.

Leeds, City and metropolitan borough (pop., 2001: 715,404), metropolitan county of West Yorkshire, historic county of Yorkshire, England. It lies along the River Aire, northeast of Manchester. It originated as an Anglo-Saxon township and was incorporated as a city in 1626, becoming an early centre of the woolen industry. The completion in 1816 of the Leeds and Liverpool Canal stimulated its growth, and the factory production of ready-made clothing expanded rapidly at the end of the 19th century. It is the seat of the University of Leeds.

leek, Hardy, vigorous, biennial plant (*Allium ampeloprasum* variety *porrum*, sometimes called *A. porrum*) of the family Alliaceae, native to the eastern Mediterranean and the Middle East. It has a mild, sweet, onionlike flavour. In Europe it is widely used in soups and stews and is cooked whole as a vegetable. It became the national emblem of Wales following an ancient victory by an army of Welshmen who wore leeks as a distinguishing sign. The long, narrow leaves and nearly cylindrical bulb of the first season are replaced in the second season by a tall, solid stalk bearing leaves and a large umbel with many flowers.

Leek (Allium ampeloprasum, variety porrum).
G.R. Roberts

legend, Traditional story or group of stories told about a particular person or place. Formerly the term referred to a tale about a saint. Legends resemble folktales in content; they may include supernatural beings, elements of mythology, or explanations of natural phenomena, but they are associated with a particular locality or person. They are handed down from the past and are popularly regarded as historical though they are not entirely verifiable.

legion, Military organization, originally the largest permanent unit in the Roman army. It was the basis of the military system by which imperial Rome conquered and ruled its empire. The early Roman Republic found the Greek phalanx too unwieldy for fragmented fighting in the hills and valleys of central Italy. To replace it the Romans evolved a new tactical system based on small and flexible infantry units called maniples. These were grouped in larger units called cohorts, which ranged from 360 to 600 men, depending on the era. Ten cohorts made up a legion, which moved into battle with four cohorts in the first line and three each in the second and third lines.

Legion of Honour, officially NATIONAL ORDER OF THE LEGION OF HONOUR, Highest-ranking order and decoration of the French republic. It was created by Napoleon in 1802 as a general military and civil order of merit. Membership is open to men and women, French citizens and foreigners, irrespective of rank, birth, or religion. Admission into the Legion requires 20 years of civil achievement in peacetime or extraordinary military bravery and service in times of war.

Legionnaire disease, Type of pneumonia, first identified in American Legion conventioneers in 1976, 29 of whom died. The cause was identified as a previously unknown bacterium, *Legionella pneumophila*, later revealed as causing earlier mysterious outbreaks at widely separated places. Usually, malaise and headache are followed by high fever and often chills, dry cough, short-

ness of breath, and pain, occasionally with mental confusion. Contaminated water (e.g., in water-distribution systems, humidifiers, and whirlpool spas) is usually suspected as the source. The disease is treated with antibiotics.

legislature, Lawmaking branch of a government. Before the advent of legislatures, the law was dictated by monarchs. Early European legislatures include the English Parliament and the Icelandic Althing (founded *c.* 930). Legislatures may be unicameral or bicameral. Their powers may include passing laws, establishing the government's budget, confirming executive appointments, ratifying treaties, investigating the executive branch, impeaching and removing from office members of the executive and judiciary, and redressing constituents' grievances. Members may be appointed or directly or indirectly elected; they may represent an entire population, particular groups, or territorial subdistricts. In presidential systems, the executive and legislative branches are clearly separated; in parliamentary systems, members of the executive branch are chosen from the legislative membership.

legume, Any of about 200,000 species in about 700 genera of flowering plants that make up the order Fabales, consisting of the single family Fabaceae, or Leguminosae (the pea family). The term also refers to their characteristic fruit, also called a pod. Legumes are widespread on all habitable continents. Leaves of many members appear feathery, and flowers are almost universally showy. In economic importance, this order is surpassed only by the grass and sedge order (Cyperales). In the production of food, the legume family is the most important of any family. The pods are part of the diet of nearly all humans and supply most dietary protein in regions of high population density. In addition, legumes perform the invaluable act of nitrogen fixation. Because they contain many of the essential amino acids, legume seeds can balance the deficiencies of cereal protein. Legumes also provide edible oils, gums, fibres, and raw material for plastics; some are ornamentals. Included in this family are acacia, alfalfa, beans, broom, carob, clover, cowpea, lupine, mimosa, peas, peanuts, soybeans, tamarind, and vetch.

Leif Eriksson, or LEIF ERIKSSON THE LUCKY, Norwegian LEIV ERIKSSON DEN HEPNE (fl. 11th century), Icelandic explorer, possibly the first European to reach North America. The second son of Erik the Red, he was on his way back from Norway to Greenland, where he had been sent by Olaf I Tryggvason to Christianize the natives (*c.* 1000), when he sailed off course and landed probably at Nova Scotia, which he called Vinland. This standard account comes from the Icelandic *Eiriks saga.* Another account, the *Groenlendinga saga,* says he learned of Vinland from a man who had been there 14 years earlier and that Leif reached North America after 1000.

leishmaniasis, Human protozoal infection spread by the bite of a bloodsucking sand fly. It occurs worldwide but is especially prevalent in tropical areas. It is caused by various species of the flagellate protozoan *Leishmania,* which infect rodents and canines. Visceral leishmaniasis, or kala-azar, occurs throughout the world but is especially prevalent in the Mediterranean area, Africa, Asia, and Latin America; it affects the liver, spleen, and bone marrow and is usually fatal if not treated. Cutaneous leishmaniasis is endemic in areas around the Mediterranean, in central and northern Africa, and in southern and western Asia; it is also found in Central and South America and parts of the southern U.S. It is characterized by lesions on the skin of the legs, feet, hands, and face, most of which heal spontaneously after many months.

leitmotiv, In music, a melodic idea associated with a character or an important dramatic element. It is associated particularly with the operas of Richard Wagner, most of which rely on a dense web of associative leitmotifs. Most composers after Wagner (and some of his immediate predecessors) continued to use this musico-dramatic principle, but few as rigorously as he did.

lemming, Any of several species of small rodents belonging to the family Cricetidae and found primarily in northern temperate and polar regions of North America and Eurasia. Lemmings have short legs, small ears, and long, soft fur. They are 4–7 in. (10–18 cm) long, including the stumpy tail, and are grayish or reddish brown above, paler below. They feed on roots, shoots, and grasses and live in burrows or rock crevices. They are noted for regular population fluctuations, and for their periodic migrations in spring and fall. Those of the Norway lemming (*Lemmus lemmus*) are the most dramatic, because many of the migrants drown in the sea. However, lemmings are hesitant to enter water and, contrary to legend, do not plunge into the sea in a deliberate death march.

lemur, In general, any of the prosimian primates (including galagos), all of which have a naked, moist tip to their muzzle; comb-like, forward-directed lower front teeth; and clawlike nails on the second toes of the feet. More strictly, the name refers to the typical lemurs (the nine species in the family Lemuridae), found only on Madagascar and the Comoro Islands, which have large eyes; a foxlike face; a slender, monkeylike body; and long hind limbs. All lemurs are docile and gregarious. Species range from 5 in. (13 cm) to about 2 ft (60 cm) long. The bushy tail may be longer than the body, and the woolly fur is reddish, gray, brown, or black. Most are active at night and spend most of their time in trees, eating fruits, leaves, buds, insects, and small birds and birds' eggs. A number of species are listed as endangered.

Lena River, River, east-central Russia, one of the longest rivers in the world. From its source in a Siberian mountain lake west of Lake Baikal, it flows 2,734 mi (4,400 km) north across Russia to enter the Arctic Ocean. Its basin covers an area of 961,000 sq mi (2,490,000 sq km), and it has many tributaries, including the Vitim and Olekma rivers. The land along its upper course and tributaries is rich in minerals, including gold and coal. Explorers first reached its delta on the Laptev Sea in the early 1630s.

Lenin, Vladimir (Ilich), orig. VLADIMIR ILICH ULYANOV (b. April 22, 1870, Simbirsk, Russia—d. Jan. 21, 1924, Gorki, near Moscow), Founder of the Russian Communist Party, leader of the Russian Revolution of 1917, and architect and builder of the Soviet state. Born to a middle-class family, he was strongly influenced by his eldest brother, Aleksandr, who was hanged in 1887 for conspiring to assassinate the tsar. He studied law and became a Marxist in 1889 while practicing law. He was arrested as a subversive in 1895 and exiled to Siberia, where he married Nadezhda Krupskaya. They lived in western Europe after 1900. At the 1903 meeting in London of the Russian Social-Democratic Workers' Party, he emerged as the leader of the Bolshevik faction. In several revolutionary newspapers that he founded and edited, he put forth his theory of the party as the vanguard of the proletariat, a centralized body organized around a core of professional revolutionaries; his ideas, later known as Leninism, would be joined with Karl Marx's theories to form Marxism-Leninism, which became the communist worldview. With the outbreak of the Russian Revolution of 1905, he returned to Russia, but he resumed his exile in 1907 and continued his energetic agitation for the next 10 years. He saw World War I as an opportunity to turn a war of nations into a war of classes, and he returned to Russia with the Russian Revolution of 1917 to lead the Bolshevik coup that overthrew the provisional government of Aleksandr Kerensky. As revolutionary leader of the Soviet state, he signed the Treaty of Brest-Litovsk with Germany (1918) and repulsed counterrevolutionary threats in the Russian Civil War. He founded the Comintern in 1919. His policy of War Communism prevailed until 1921, and to forestall economic disaster he launched the New Economic Policy. In ill health from 1922, he died of a stroke in 1924.

Leningrad, Siege of (Sept. 8, 1941–Jan. 27, 1944) Prolonged siege of the city of Leningrad (now St. Petersburg) by German forces in World War II. German forces invaded the Soviet Union in June 1941 and approached Leningrad from the west and south while Germany's Finnish allies came from the north. By November 1941 the city was almost completely encircled and its supply lines to the Soviet interior cut off. In 1942 alone, in excess of 650,000 of Leningrad's citizens died from starvation, disease, and shelling from distant German artillery. Sparse food and fuel supplies reached the city by barge in the summer and by sled in winter across Lake Ladoga. The supplies kept the city's arms factories operating and its two million inhabitants barely alive, while another one million children and sick and elderly people were evacuated. Soviet offensives in 1943 partially broke the German encirclement and were followed in January 1944 by a successful Soviet attack that drove the Germans westward from the city's outskirts, ending the siege.

lens, Piece of glass or other transparent substance that is used to form an image of an object by converging or diverging rays of light from the object. Because of the curvature of its surface, different rays of light are refracted through different angles. A convex lens causes rays to converge on a single point, the focal point. A concave lens causes rays to diverge as though they are coming from a focal point. Both types cause the rays to form a visual image of the object. The image may be real—inverted and photographable or visible on a screen—or it may be virtual—erect and visible only by looking through the lens.

Lent, In the Christian church, a period of penitential preparation for Easter, observed since apostolic times. Western churches once provided for a 40-day fast (excluding Sundays), in imitation of Jesus' fasting in the wilderness; one meal a day was allowed in the evening, and meat, fish, eggs, and butter were forbidden. These rules have gradually been relaxed, and only Ash Wednesday—the first day of Lent in Western Christianity, when the penitent traditionally have their foreheads marked with ashes—and Good Friday are now kept as Lenten fast days. Rules of fasting are stricter in the Eastern churches.

Leo I, Saint, known as LEO THE GREAT (b. 4th century, Tuscany?—d. Nov. 10, 461, Rome; Western feast day November 10, Eastern feast day February 18), Pope (440–461). He was a champion of orthodoxy and a Doctor of the Church. When the monk Eutyches of Constantinople asserted that Jesus Christ had only a single divine nature, Leo wrote the *Tome,* which established the coexistence of Christ's human and divine natures. Leo's teachings were embraced by the Council of Chalcedon (451), which also accepted his teaching as the "voice of Peter." Leo dealt capably with the invasions of barbaric tribes, persuading the Huns not to attack Rome (452) and the Vandals not to sack the city (455). Leo was also an exponent of the precept of papal primacy, and his personal example and letters and sermons contributed greatly to the growth of papal authority.

Leo X, orig. GIOVANNI DE' MEDICI (b. Dec. 11, 1475, Florence—d. Dec. 1, 1521, Rome), Pope (1513–21), one of the most extravagant of the Renaissance pontiffs. The second son of Lorenzo de' Medici, he was educated at his father's court in Florence and at the University of Pisa. He was named a cardinal in 1492, and in 1494 he was exiled from Florence by the revolt of Girolamo Savonarola. He returned in 1500 and soon consolidated Medici control of the city. As pope, he became a patron of the arts and accelerated construction of St. Peter's Basilica. He strengthened the papacy's political power in Europe, but his lavish spending depleted his treasury. He discouraged reforms at the fifth Lateran Council, and he responded inadequately to the Reformation, excommunicating Martin Luther in 1521 and failing to address the need for change, a lapse that signaled the end of the unified Western church.

Leonardo da Vinci (b. April 15, 1452, Anchiano, Republic of Florence—d. May 2, 1519, Cloux, France), Italian Renaissance painter, sculptor, draftsman, architect, engineer, and scientist. The son of a landowner and a peasant, he received training in painting, sculpture, and mechanical arts as an apprentice to Andrea del Verrocchio. In 1482, having made a name for himself in Florence, he entered the service of the duke of Milan as "painter and engineer." In Milan his artistic and creative genius unfolded. About 1490 he began his project of writing treatises on the "science of painting," architecture, mechanics, and anatomy. His theories were based on the belief that the painter, with his powers of perception and ability to pictorialize his observations, was uniquely qualified to probe nature's secrets. His numerous surviving manuscripts are noted for being written in a backward script that requires a mirror to be read. In 1502–03, as military architect and engineer for Cesare Borgia, he helped lay the groundwork for modern cartography. After five years of painting and scientific study back in Florence (1503–08), he returned to Milan, where his scientific work flourished. In 1516, after an interlude under Medici patronage in Rome, he entered the service of Francis I of France; he never returned to Italy. Though only some 17 completed paintings survive, they are universally seen as masterpieces. The power of *The Last Supper* (1495–98) comes in part from its masterly composition. In the *Mona Lisa* (*c.* 1503–06) the features and symbolic overtones of the subject achieve a complete synthesis. The unique fame that Leonardo enjoyed in his lifetime and that, filtered by historical criticism, has remained undimmed to the present day rests largely on his unlimited desire for knowledge, a trait that guided all his thinking and behaviour.

leopard, or PANTHER, Big cat (*Panthera pardus*) of the bush and forest, found throughout sub-Saharan Africa, in North Africa, and in Asia. The average leopard weighs 110–200 lbs (50–90 kg) and is about 6 ft (210 cm) long, excluding the 35-in. (90-cm) tail, and 24–28 in. (60–70 cm) high at the shoulder. The background colour is typically yellowish above and white below. The dark spots arranged in rosettes over much of the body lack a central spot, unlike those of the jaguar. The leopard is solitary and mainly nocturnal. An agile climber, it frequently stores the remains of its kills in tree branches. It generally preys on antelope and deer. It also hunts dogs and, in Africa, baboons. It sometimes takes livestock and may attack humans. The leopard is considered an endangered species by the U.S. but not by the IUCN (International Union for Conservation of Nature).

*Leopard (*Panthera pardus*)*
Leonard Lee Rue III

lepidopteran, Any of the more than 155,000 species of butterflies, moths, and skippers that constitute the order Lepidoptera (from Greek: "scaly wing"). The name refers to the dusting of minute scales that covers the wings and bodies of these insects. A slender proboscis is used for sucking. Nearly all lepidopterans are

plant eaters, and species are found on every continent except Antarctica. Females may lay from a few to a thousand or more eggs at a time. All lepidopterans undergo complete metamorphosis. Many types move from one region to another, sometimes crossing thousands of miles of ocean, but the only species that truly migrates—the same individuals making a two-way flight—is the monarch butterfly.

leprechaun, In Irish folklore, a fairy in the form of a tiny old man wearing a cocked hat and leather apron. Solitary by nature, leprechauns lived in remote places and worked as shoemakers. Each was believed to possess a hidden crock of gold. If captured and threatened, a leprechaun might reveal the gold's hiding place, provided his captor never took his eyes off him. Usually the captor was tricked into glancing away, and the leprechaun vanished. The word derives from the Old Irish *luchorpan* ("little body").

leprosy, or HANSEN DISEASE, Chronic disease of the skin, peripheral nerves, and mucous membranes of the nose, throat, and eyes, caused by the bacterium *Mycobacterium leprae*. In tuberculoid leprosy, cells of the immune system crowd into infected areas of the skin, forming hard nodules, or tubercles, that spread along nerve fibres. This type of reaction commonly leads to claw hand, gross deformity of the foot, and paralysis of muscles of the face, eye, and neck. In the lepromatous type, bacilli multiply freely in deep layers of the skin and spread widely through lymphatic channels and along nerve fibres, causing thickening and corrugation of the skin, raising soft nodules on the ears, nose, and cheeks, and sometimes destroying the septum of the nose and the palate. Leprosy has a long history. Until the 20th century, infected people were ostracized from society or at best segregated and cared for in isolated leper colonies. Today the disease is entirely curable through multidrug therapy, though tissue damage caused before drug treatment cannot be reversed. Some 600,000 new cases arise every year, mostly in Asia, Africa, Central and South America, and the Pacific Islands. About 60 percent of new cases occur in India.

lepton, Any member of a class of fermions that respond only to electromagnetic, weak, and gravitational forces and do not take part in strong interactions. Leptons have a half-integral spin and obey the Pauli exclusion principle. They can either carry one unit of electric charge or be neutral. The charged leptons are the electrons, muons, and taus. Each has a negative charge and a distinct mass. Each charged lepton has an associated neutral partner, or neutrino, which has no electric charge and very little if any mass.

lesbianism, also called SAPPHISM, or FEMALE HOMOSEXUALITY, the quality or state of intense emotional and usually erotic attraction of a woman to another woman. First used in the late 16th century, the word "lesbian" referred to the Greek island of Lesbos. The connotation of female homosexuality was added in the late 19th century, when an association was made with the poetry of Lesbian poet Sappho (*c.* 610–*c.* 580 BC). At the turn of the 21st century, issues of concern to lesbians in Europe and North America included legal recognition for same-sex unions, child-rearing rights, women's health-care, taxes, inheritance, and the sharing of medical benefits with a partner.

Lesbos, or MYTILENE, or MITILÍNI, Third largest island (pop., 2001: 90,642) in the Aegean Sea. It occupies an area of 630 sq mi (1,630 sq km), and with two other islands it forms a Greek department. Its main town is Mytilene. Lesbos was the birthplace of the poet Sappho and is the source of the term *lesbian*. Inhabited since *c.* 3000 BC, it was settled in *c.* 1050 BC by the Aetolians. After being under Persian rule (527–479 BC), it joined the Delian League. In the Peloponnesian War, it fell to Sparta (405 BC), but then it was recovered for Athens (389 BC). It later flourished under Byzantium. It was ruled by the Ottoman Empire (1462–1911) before being annexed by Greece. Fishing is important economically, as is the export of olives.

Lesotho, officially KINGDOM OF LESOTHO, formerly BASUTO-LAND, Country, southern Africa, an enclave lying within the Republic of South Africa. Area: 11,720 sq mi (30,355 sq km). Population: (2011 est.) 1,925,000. Capital: Maseru. Almost all of the population are Sotho, a Bantu-speaking people. Languages: Sotho, English (both official), Zulu. Religions: Christianity (official; Roman Catholic, other Christians, Protestant); also traditional beliefs. Currency: loti. About two-thirds of the total area is mountainous; the highest point is Mount Ntlenyana (11,424 ft [3,482 m]). The Maloti Mountains in the central northwest are the source of two of South Africa's largest rivers, the Tugela and the Orange, and home to the Lesotho Highlands Water Project, a large-scale development that diverts water and generates power. Mineral resources are scant. Agriculture employs nearly two-fifths of the workforce; the chief farm products are corn, sorghum, and wheat. Livestock provides exports (cattle, wool, mohair). Industries focus mainly on light manufacturing (textiles and apparel, furniture, jewelry). Lesotho is a constitutional monarchy with two legislative houses; its head of state is the king, and the head of government is the prime minister. Bantu-speaking farmers began to settle the area in the 16th century, and a number of chiefdoms arose. The most powerful of them organized the Basotho in 1824 and obtained British protection in 1843 as tension between the Basotho and the South African Boers increased. It became a British territory in 1868 and was annexed to the Cape Colony in 1871. The colony's effort to disarm the Basotho resulted in revolt in 1880, and four years later it separated from the colony and became a British High Commission Territory. It became independent in 1966. A new constitution, effective in 1993, ended seven years of military rule. At the beginning of the 21st century, Lesotho suffered from a deteriorating economy and one of the world's highest rates of HIV/AIDS infection.

lettuce, Cultivated annual salad plant (*Lactuca sativa*) that produces clusters of crisp, water-filled leaves. The best-known varieties are head, or cabbage, lettuce (variety *capitata*); leaf, or curled, lettuce (variety *crispa*); cos, or romaine, lettuce (variety *longifolia*); and asparagus lettuce (variety *asparagina*). Head lettuce is further divided into butter heads and crisp heads (e.g., iceberg lettuce). In the U.S, large-scale farms grow mainly crisp-head varieties, shipping them nationwide. Small-scale, local farmers raise leaf and butter-head varieties. Lettuce is an early annual crop that grows best in cool weather and with ample water. Though usually consumed in salads, it may also be cooked.

*Lettuce (*Lactuca sativa*, variety* capitata*)*
Derek Fell

leukemia, Cancer of blood-forming tissues with high levels of leukocytes. Radiation exposure and hereditary susceptibility are factors in some cases. In acute leukemias, anemia, fever, bleeding, and lymph-node swelling develop rapidly. Acute lymphocytic leukemia, found mostly in children, was once over 90% fatal in six months. Drug therapy can now cure more than half these children. Acute myelogenous (granulocytic) leukemia, found mostly in adults, has frequent remissions and recurrences, and few patients survive long. Chronic myelogenous leukemia most often begins in the 40s; weight loss, low fever, weakness, and other symptoms may not develop immediately. Chemotherapy helps the symptoms but may not prolong life. Chronic lymphocytic leukemia, mostly in the elderly, may be inactive for years. Survival rates are better than in myelogenous leukemia; most deaths are caused by infection or hemorrhage.

leukocyte, or WHITE BLOOD CELL, or WHITE CORPUSCLE, Any of several types of blood cells that help defend the body from infec-tion. The different mature forms—granulocytes, including neutro-phils (heterophils), basophils, and eosinophils; monocytes, including macrophages; and lymphocytes—have different functions, including ingesting bacteria, protozoans, or infected or dead body cells; producing antibodies; and regulating the action of other leukocytes. They act mostly in the tissues and are in the bloodstream only for transport. Blood normally contains 5,000–10,000 leukocytes per cu mm.

Levant, Historical name for the countries along the shores of the eastern Mediterranean Sea. It was applied to the coastlands of Anatolia and Syria, sometimes extending from Greece to Egypt. The term was often associated with Venetian trading ventures. It was also used as a synonym for the Middle or Near East. In the 16th–17th centuries the term High Levant referred to the Far East (East Asia). The name Levant States was given to the French mandate of Syria and Lebanon after World War I (1914–18).

levirate and sororate, Customs or laws regulating marriage following the death of a spouse, or in some cases during the lifetime of the spouse. The levirate decrees a dead man's brother to be the widow's preferred marriage partner. In ancient Hebrew society, this practice served to perpetuate the line of a man who died childless. Often, the brother who marries his sister-in-law is a proxy for the deceased and no new marriage is contracted, since all progeny are acknowledged as the seed of the dead man. The sororate decrees the marriage of a man to his deceased wife's sister or, under so-called sororal polygyny, to the wife's younger sisters as they come of age. The latter was practiced by some American Indian tribes in the 19th century and continues among the Australian Aborigines.

Leviticus Rabbah (*c.* AD 450) Compilation of 37 compositions on topics suggested by the Old Testament Book of Leviticus. Their message is that the laws of history focus on the holy life of Israel (the Jewish people). If the Jews obey the laws of society aimed at Israel's sanctification, then the foreordained history will unfold as Israel hopes. Israel, for its part, can affect its own destiny. Thus salvation at the end of history depends on sanctification in the here and now.

levodopa, or L-DOPA, Organic compound (L-3,4-dihydroxyphenylalanine) from which the body makes dopamine, a neurotransmitter deficient in persons with parkinsonism. When given orally in large daily doses, levodopa can lessen the effects of the disease. However, it becomes less effective over time and causes abnormal involuntary movements (dyskinesia).

Lewis, Meriwether (b. Aug. 18, 1774, near Charlottesville, Va.—d. Oct. 11, 1809, near Nashville, Tenn., U.S.), U.S. explorer. After serving in the militia during the Whiskey Rebellion (1794) in western Pennsylvania, he transferred into the regular army. In 1801 he became private secretary to Pres. Thomas Jefferson, who selected him to lead the first overland expedition to the Pacific Northwest, including the area of the Louisiana Purchase. At Lewis's request, William Clark was appointed to share the command. The success of the Lewis and Clark Expedition (1804–06) was greatly due to Lewis's preparation and skill. At its conclusion, he and Clark each received 1,600 acres of land as a reward. Lewis was named governor of Louisiana Territory in 1808. He died under mysterious circumstances in an inn on the Natchez Trace while en route to Washington; whether his death resulted from murder or suicide is still a subject of controversy.

Lewis and Clark Expedition (1804–06) First overland expedition to the U.S. Pacific coast and back, led by Meriwether Lewis and William Clark. Initiated by Pres. Thomas Jefferson, the expedition set out to find an overland route to the Pacific, documenting its exploration through the new Louisiana Purchase. About 40 men, skilled in various trades, left St. Louis in 1804. They traveled up the Missouri River into present-day North Dakota, where they built Fort Mandan (later Bismarck) and wintered among the Mandan Sioux. They left the next spring, hiring Toussaint Charbonneau and his Indian wife, Sacagawea, who served as guide and interpreter. They traveled through Montana and by horse over the Continental Divide to the headwaters of the Clearwater River. They built canoes to carry them to the Snake River and then to the mouth of the Columbia River, where they built Fort Clatsop (later Astoria, Ore.) and spent the winter. On the journey back the group divided, then reunited to canoe down the Missouri to St. Louis, arriving to great acclaim in September 1806. All but one member of the expedition survived. The journals kept by Lewis and others documented Indian tribes, wildlife, and geography and did much to dispel the myth of an easy water route to the Pacific.

Lhasa, Capital (pop., 2003 est.: 129,490), Tibet Autonomous Region, China. Located at an elevation of 11,975 ft (3,650 m) in the Tibetan Himalayas near the Lhasa River, it has served as the religious centre of Tibet since at least the 9th century AD. Lhasa became Tibet's capital in 1642 and remained so after the Chinese communists asserted control of the region in 1951; it was designated capital of the Tibet Autonomous Region in 1965. The 7th-century temple of Gtsug-lag-khang is considered the holiest in Tibet. Other landmarks include the temple of Klu-khang; the Potala Palace, the Dalai Lama's former winter residence; and monasteries. Lhasa is sometimes known as the "Forbidden City" because of its inaccessibility and the traditional hostility of its religious leaders toward outsiders.

Lhotse, Peak in the Himalayas. Located on the Nepal-China boundary and reaching 27,890 ft (8,501 m), it is one of the world's highest mountains. It is sometimes considered part of Mount Everest's massif because it is joined to that peak by a 25,000-ft (7,600-m) ridge. The Swiss climbers Fritz Luchsinger and Ernest Reiss made the first ascent of the mountain in 1956. Lhotse is Tibetan for "south peak." E[1] was its original survey symbol, denoting Everest-1, given it by the Survey of India in 1931.

Li Ao (b. 772, China—d. 841), Chinese scholar and high official of the Tang dynasty, who helped reinvigorate Confucianism at a time when it was severely challenged by Buddhism and Daoism. Little is known of Li's life, though he is believed to have known Han Yu. He was much influenced by Buddhism, and he helped integrate many Buddhist ideas into Confucianism. He anticipated the ideas of Neo-Confucianism by asserting that human nature and human destiny were central to Confucianism, and he helped establish Mencius as a figure almost equal to Confucius in the eyes of Neo-Confucians.

Li Bai, or LI BO, or LI PAI, or LI PO, or TAIBAI (b. 701, Jiangyou, Sichuan province, China—d. 762, Dangtu, Anhui province), Chinese poet. A student of Daoism, he spent long periods wandering and served as an unofficial court poet. His lyrics are celebrated for their exquisite imagery, rich language, allusions, and cadence. A romantic, he was a famous wine drinker and wrote of the joys of drinking, as well as about friendship, solitude, nature, and the passage of time. Popular legend says that he drowned when, sitting drunk in a boat, he tried to seize the moon's reflection in the water. He rivals Du Fu for the title of China's greatest poet.

Li Chunfeng (b. 602, Qizhou, Yong county, China—d. 670, Chang'an), Chinese mathematician and astronomer. He was given a position in the Imperial Astronomical Bureau in 627 following his critique of the Wuyin calendar. He became the deputy director of the Imperial Astronomical Bureau about 641. He participated in the compilation of the official histories of the Jin (265–420) and Sui (581–618) dynasties, writing the chapters containing historical outlines of Chinese astronomy, astrology, metrology, and a mathematical theory of music. In 648 he became the director of the Imperial Astronomical Bureau, and he coedited a collection of

mathematical treatises used as manuals in the Mathematical College of the State University. Later he prepared the Linde calendar, which was promulgated in 665 and used until 728.

Li Hongzhang, or LI HUNG-CHANG (b. Feb. 15, 1823, Hefei, Anhui province, China—d. Nov. 7, 1901, Beijing), Chinese statesman who represented China in the series of humiliating negotiations at the end of the Sino-French War (1883–85), Sino-Japanese War (1894–95), and Boxer Rebellion (1900). Much earlier in his career, Li had helped with the suppression of the Taiping Rebellion (1850–64) and had put down the Nian Rebellion (c. 1852–68). At that time, he came in contact with Westerners (notably England's Charles George Gordon) and Western weapons and became convinced that China needed Western-style firepower if it wanted to protect its sovereignty. In 1870, when Li was appointed governor-general of the capital province, Zhili, he was able to build arsenals, found a military academy, establish two modern naval bases, purchase warships, and undertake other "self-strengthening" measures. Through modernization he hoped to preserve traditional China, but within traditional China Li's innovations could not develop fully, and he was fatally hampered by the system he was trying to protect.

Li Tang, or LI T'ANG (b. c. 1050—d. c. 1130), Chinese painter. He earned the highest rank in the academy of painting of Emperor Huizong, and after the North fell to the Mongols he went to the South and entered the academy of Emperor Song Gaozong. His landscapes serve as a vital link between the earlier, and essentially Northern, variety of monumental landscape, and the more lyrical Southern style of the Ma-Xia school (based on the work of Ma Yuan and Xia Gui). Li perfected the brushstroke texture known as the "ax stroke," which gives a tactile sense to painted rocks and suggests the precise and comprehensive reality that Southern Song artists sought to give their landscapes.

Li Ye, literary name JINGZHAI (b. 1192, Luangcheng, Hebei province, China—d. 1279, Yuanshi), Chinese mathematician and scholar-official who contributed to the solution of polynomial equations in one variable. When the Mongols invaded his home district in 1233, Li wandered homeless in Shanxi, Shandong, and Henan provinces. During this period he composed his main work, *Ceyuan haijing* (1248; "Sea Mirror of Circle Measurements"), which contains 170 problems based on one geometric diagram of a circular city wall circumscribed by a right-angled triangle. Although the problems are highly contrived, they enabled Li to list some 692 algebraic formulas for triangular areas and segment lengths. In 1264 Li was appointed to the Hanlin Academy by Kublai Khan. Li strongly criticized the political and intellectual climate of his time, though, and soon used ill health as a pretext to retire and live as a hermit.

Li Zhizao (b. 1565, Hangzhou, China—d. Nov. 1, 1630, Beijing), Chinese mathematician, astronomer, and geographer whose translations of European scientific books greatly contributed to the spread of Western science in China. In 1601 he met the Italian Jesuit Matteo Ricci, who baptized him in 1610. By engraving and printing numerous copies of Ricci's world map, Li altered many Chinese views of world geography. Li and Ricci translated Christopher Clavius's arithmetic primer *Epitome arithmeticae practicae* (1585; "Selected Arithmetic Methods") as *Tongwen suanzhi* (1614). This book systematically introduced European-style mathematical notation, while Li included complementary elements from traditional Chinese mathematics. He also brought together and published a series of books composed by the Jesuits with Chinese help, *Tianxue chuhan* (1629; "First Collection of Writings on Heavenly Learning"), that included 20 Western scientific and religious titles.

Liao River, River, Liaoning province and Inner Mongolia autonomous region, China. The East Liao rises in the mountains of Jilin province and the West Liao in southeastern Inner Mongolia. They merge and flow southwest as the Liao to empty into the Gulf of Liaodong, after a course of 836 mi (1,345 km). The river's drainage basin occupies 83,000 sq mi (215,000 sq km). It is navigable by small boats for about 400 mi (645 km) from its mouth.

Liaodong Peninsula, or LIAO-TUNG PENINSULA, Peninsula, extending from the southern coastline of Liaoning province, northeastern China. It partly separates the Bo Hai (Gulf of Chihli) on the west from Korea Bay on the east. It forms part of a mountain belt that continues in the Changbai Mountains; on the peninsula the range is known as the Qian Mountains. Near the southern tip of the peninsula lies the port of Dalian.

Liaoning, formerly (1903–28) FENGTIAN, or FENG-T'IEN, Province (pop., 2002 est.: 42,030,000), northeastern China. It lies on the Yellow Sea and is bordered by North Korea, Jilin and Hebei provinces, and Inner Mongolia. With an area of 58,300 sq mi (151,000 sq km), it is the southernmost of the three provinces that form northeastern China. Its capital is Shenyang. It has four main topographical regions: the central plains, the Liaodong Peninsula, the western highlands, and the eastern mountain zone. In 1932–45 it was part of the Japanese puppet state of Manchukuo. Shenyang was taken by the Chinese communists in 1948. Liaoning is China's most industrialized province, producing steel, cement, crude oil, and electrical power.

liberalism, Political and economic doctrine that emphasizes the rights and freedoms of the individual and the need to limit the powers of government. Liberalism originated as a defensive reaction to the horrors of the European wars of religion of the 16th century. Its basic ideas were given formal expression in works by Thomas Hobbes and John Locke, both of whom argued that the power of the sovereign is ultimately justified by the consent of the governed, given in a hypothetical social contract rather than by divine right. In the economic realm, liberals in the 19th century urged the end of state interference in the economic life of society. Following Adam Smith, they argued that economic systems based on free markets are more efficient and generate more prosperity than those that are partly state-controlled. In response to the great inequalities of wealth and other social problems created by the Industrial Revolution in Europe and North America, liberals in the late 19th and early 20th centuries advocated limited state intervention in the market and the creation of state-funded social services, such as free public education and health insurance. In the U.S. the New Deal program undertaken by Pres. Franklin D. Roosevelt typified modern liberalism in its vast expansion of the scope of governmental activities and its increased regulation of business. After World War II a further expansion of social welfare programs occurred in Britain, Scandinavia, and the U.S. Economic stagnation beginning in the late 1970s led to a revival of classical liberal positions favouring free markets, especially among political conservatives in Britain and the U.S. Contemporary liberalism remains committed to social reform, including reducing inequality and expanding individual rights.

liberalism, theological, School of religious thought characterized by concern with inner motivation as opposed to external controls. It was set in motion in the 17th century by René Descartes, who expressed faith in human reason, and it was influenced by such philosophers as Benedict de Spinoza, G. W. Leibniz, and John Locke. Its second stage, which coincided with the Romantic movement of the late 18th and 19th century, was marked by an appreciation of individual creativity, expressed in the writings of philosophers such as Jean-Jacques Rousseau and Immanuel Kant as well as of the theologian Friedrich Schleiermacher. The third stage, from the mid-19th century through the 1920s, emphasized the idea of progress. Stimulated by the Industrial Revolution and by Charles Darwin's *Origin of Species* (1859), thinkers such as T. H. Huxley and Herbert Spencer in England and William James and

John Dewey in the U.S. focused on the psychological study of religious experience, the sociological study of religious institutions, and philosophical inquiry into religious values.

liberation theology, Roman Catholic movement that originated in the late 20th century in Latin America and seeks to express religious faith by helping the poor and working for political and social change. It began in 1968, when bishops attending the Latin American Bishops' Conference in Medellín, Colom., affirmed the rights of the poor and asserted that industrialized nations were enriching themselves at the expense of the Third World. The movement's central text, *A Theology of Liberation* (1971), was written by the Peruvian priest Gustavo Gutiérrez (b. 1928). Liberation theologians have sometimes been criticized as purveyors of Marxism, and the Vatican has sought to curb their influence by appointing more conservative prelates.

Liberia, officially REPUBLIC OF LIBERIA, Republic, western Africa. Area: 37,420 sq mi (96,917 sq km). Population: (2011 est.) 3,953,000. Capital: Monrovia. Liberia's ethnic groups include the Americo-Liberians, descendants of the black freedmen who emigrated from the U.S. in the 19th century; and 16 indigenous peoples of the Mande, Kwa, and Mel linguistic groups. Languages: English (official), indigenous languages. Religions: traditional beliefs, Christianity, Islam. Currency: Liberian dollar. Liberia has coastal lowlands extending 350 mi (560 km) along the Atlantic; farther inland are hills and low mountains. Roughly one-fifth of Liberia consists of tropical rainforest. Agriculture is the main component of the economy, but only a portion of the arable land is cultivated. The country also has rich iron ore reserves, which are a major source of exports. The principal cash crops are rubber, coffee, and cacao; the staple crops are rice and cassava. Constitutionally, Liberia is a multiparty republic with two legislative houses, and its head of state and government is the president. Africa's oldest republic, Liberia was established on land acquired for freed U.S. slaves by the American Colonization Society, which founded a colony at Cape Mesurado in 1821. In 1822 Jehudi Ashmun, a Methodist minister, became the director of the settlement and Liberia's real founder. In 1824 the territory was named Liberia, and its main settlement was named Monrovia. Joseph Jenkins Roberts proclaimed Liberian independence in 1847 and expanded its boundaries. Border disputes with the French and British lasted until 1892, when its boundaries were officially established. In 1980 a coup led by Gen. Samuel K. Doe marked the end of the Americo-Liberians' long political dominance over the indigenous Africans. A rebellion in 1989 escalated into a destructive civil war in the 1990s. A peace agreement was reached in 1996, but fighting broke out again in 1999 and lasted until 2003. The National Transitional Government, supported by United Nations peacekeeping troops, was established later that year and ruled until a new administration was democratically elected and installed. Presidential elections were held in late 2005, and Ellen Johnson Sirleaf was declared the winner; she became the first woman to be elected head of state in Africa.

libertarianism, Political philosophy that stresses personal liberty. Libertarians believe that individuals should have complete freedom of action, provided their actions do not infringe on the freedom of others. Libertarianism's distrust of government is rooted in 19th-century anarchism. Typical libertarians oppose not only the income tax and other government impositions but also programs seen by many as beneficial, such as social security and the postal service. In the U.S. their views often crosscut traditional party boundaries (e.g., libertarians oppose gun control, as do most Republicans, but support the legalization of prohibited drugs, as do some liberal Democrats). Among the thinkers embraced by libertarians are Henry David Thoreau and Ayn Rand.

Libra (Latin: "Scales") In astronomy, the constellation lying between Scorpio and Virgo; in astrology, the seventh sign of the zodiac, governing approximately the period September 22–October 23. Its symbol is either a woman holding a balance scale or the scale alone. The woman is sometimes identified with Astraea, the Roman goddess of justice.

library, Collection of information resources, in print or in other forms, that is organized and made accessible for reading or study. The word derives from the Latin *liber* ("book"). The origin of libraries lies in the keeping of written records, a practice that dates at least to the 3rd millennium BCE in Babylonia. The first libraries as repositories of books were those of the Greek temples and those established in conjunction with the Greek schools of philosophy in the 4th century BCE. Today's libraries frequently contain periodicals, microfilms, tapes, videos, compact discs, and other materials in addition to books. The growth of online communications networks has enabled library users to search electronically linked databases worldwide..

Library of Congress, U.S. library, the largest and one of the greatest of what may be considered national libraries. Founded in Washington, D.C., in 1800, it was housed in the Capitol until the building was burned by British troops in 1814; it moved to permanent quarters in 1897. In addition to serving as a reference source for members of Congress and other government officers, it is outstanding among the learned institutions of the world, with magnificent collections of books, manuscripts, music, prints, and maps. It contains some 18 million books, 2.5 million recordings, 12 million photographs, 4.5 million maps, and more than 54 million manuscripts.

Libreville, City (pop., 2007 est.: 576,000), capital of Gabon, located on the northern shore of the Gabon Estuary. Pongoue people first settled the region after the 16th century, followed by the Fang in the 19th century. The French built a fort on the estuary's northern bank in 1843, and in 1849 a settlement of freed slaves and a group of Pongoue villages were given the name Libreville. In 1850 France abandoned its fort and resettled on the plateau, now the commercial and administrative centre of the city. It is well industrialized and is Gabon's educational centre. Libreville was the capital of French Equatorial Africa from 1888 to 1904.

Libya, officially GREAT SOCIALIST PEOPLE'S LIBYAN ARAB JAMĀHĪRIYYAH, Country, North Africa. Area: 647,184 sq mi (1,676,198 sq km). Population: (2011 est.) 6,423,000. Capital: Tripoli. Imazighen, once the major ethnic group, have been largely assimilated into the predominant Arab culture; sub-Saharan Africans are among the other ethnic groups. Languages: Arabic (official); Italian and English are understood in the major cities. Religions: Islam (official; predominantly Sunni); also Christianity. Currency: Libyan dinar. The majority of Libya is covered by the Sahara. Tripolitania, in the northwest, is Libya's most important agricultural region and its most populated area. The production and export of petroleum are the basis of Libya's economy; other resources include natural gas, manganese, and gypsum. Livestock raising, including sheep and goats, is important in the north. Libya has been governed by a transitional council since August 2011, after a civil war drove Muammar Qaddafi, Libya's de facto leader for more than four decades, from power. The early history is that of Fezzan, Cyrenaica, and Tripolitania, which the Ottoman Empire combined under one regency in Tripoli in the 16th century. In 1911 Italy claimed control of Libya, and by the outbreak of World War II (1939–45) 150,000 Italians had immigrated there. It was the scene of much fighting in the war. It became an independent state in 1951 and a member of the Arab League in 1953. The discovery of petroleum in the late 1950s brought wealth to Libya. In 1969 a group of army officers led by Qaddafi deposed King Idris I and made the country an Islamic republic. Under Qaddafi, Libya supported the Palestinian Liberation Organization (PLO) and allegedly provided aid for international militant groups. Intermittent warfare with Chad that had begun in the 1970s ended with Libya's defeat in 1987. UN sanctions imposed on Libya in the 1990s for its purported connection to terrorism were lifted in 2003. In

2011 protests against the regime's repressive policies quickly spiraled into civil war. After six months of fighting, Qaddafi was forced from power. He evaded capture for several weeks before being killed by rebel forces in Surt.

lichen, Any of about 15,000 species of small, colourful, scaly plants that consist of a symbiotic association of algae (usually green) and fungi. These extremely hardy, slow growers often are pioneer species in sparse environments such as mountaintops and the far North. Fungal cells, anchored to the substrate with hairlike growths (rhizines), form the base. In the body (thallus), numerous algal cells are distributed among fewer fungal cells. Through photosynthesis the algal cells provide simple sugars and vitamins for both partners in this symbiotic association. The fungal cells protect the algal cells from environmental extremes. Lichens may form a thin, crustlike, tightly bound covering over their substrate (e.g., cracks in rocks), or they may be small and leafy, with loose attachments to the substrate. Their colours range from brown to bright orange or yellow. In far northern Europe and Asia, lichens provide two-thirds of caribou and reindeer food. They have been the source of medicines and dyes.

licorice, Perennial herb (*Glycyrrhiza glabra*) of the pea family

and the flavouring, confection, and medicine made from its roots. Native to southern Europe, the plant is cultivated around the Mediterranean and in parts of the U.S. It grows to 3 ft (1 m) and bears graceful compound leaves, blue-violet flower clusters, and flat, flexible seedpods 3–4 in. (7–10 cm) long. It is 42 times sweeter than table sugar, and its flavour, similar to anise, can mask unpleasant medicinal tastes.

Spanish licorice (Glycyrrhiza glabra).
A to Z Botanical Collection/EB Inc.

Liechtenstein, official name PRINCIPALITY OF LIECHTENSTEIN, Principality, western Europe. It is located between Switzerland and Austria. Area: 62 sq mi (160 sq km). Population: (2011 est.) 36,300. Capital: Vaduz. The Liechtensteiners are descended from the Alemanni tribe that came into the region after 500 CE. Languages: German (official), Alemanni dialect, Walser dialect. Religions: Christianity (predominantly Roman Catholic; also Protestant); also Islam. Currency: Swiss franc. The eastern two-thirds of Liechtenstein's small territory is composed of the foothills of the Rhätikon Massif, part of the central Alps. The western section of the country is occupied by the Rhine River floodplain. Liechtenstein has no natural resources of commercial value, and virtually all raw materials, including wood, have to be imported. Manufacturing includes metalworking, pharmaceuticals, optical lenses, electronics, and food processing. A tourist centre, Liechtenstein is also a centre of banking because of its stable political situation and its absolute bank secrecy. It is a constitutional monarchy with one legislative house; its head of state is the prince, and the head of government is the prime minister. The Rhine plain was occupied for centuries by two independent lordships of the Holy Roman Empire, Vaduz and Schellenberg. The principality of Liechtenstein, consisting of these two lordships, was founded in 1719 and remained part of the Holy Roman Empire. It was included in the German Confederation (1815–66). In 1866 it became independent, recognizing Vaduz and Schellenberg as unique regions forming separate electoral districts. In 1921 it adopted Swiss currency, and in 1923 it joined the Swiss customs union. A coalition that ruled Liechtenstein for almost 60 years dissolved in 1997. A referendum in 2003 approved wider powers for the prince.

lied, German song, particularly an art song for voice and piano of the late 18th or the 19th century. The Romantic movement fostered serious popular poetry by poets such as Johann Wolfgang von Goethe. Composers often set such poetry to folk-influenced music, but the lied could also be highly sophisticated and even experimental. At first generally performed at private social gatherings, it eventually moved into the concert-hall repertoire. The most influential and prolific lied composer was Franz Schubert, who wrote more than 600; Robert Schumann, Felix Mendelssohn, Johannes Brahms, Hugo Wolf, Gustav Mahler, and Richard Strauss are most prominent in the lied's subsequent history.

Liège, Flemish LUIK, City (pop., 2009 est.: 193,816), eastern Belgium. Located at the confluence of the Meuse and Ourthe rivers, it was inhabited in prehistoric times and was known to the Romans as Leodium. It became a town when St. Hubert transferred his see there in 721, and it was noted as a centre of learning in the Middle Ages. Annexed to France in 1795, it was later assigned with the rest of Belgium to the Netherlands in 1815. A centre of the successful revolt for Belgian independence in 1830, it is now an industrial research centre and a major port.

Liezi, or LIEH-TZU, Chinese Daoist classic. Though Liezi is traditionally named as its author, in its present form it probably dates from the 3rd or 4th century AD. Like earlier Daoist classics, it emphasizes the mysterious *dao* (way). The "Yang Zhu" chapter acknowledges the futility of challenging the *dao* and asserts that all one can look forward to in life is sex, music, physical beauty, and material abundance. This fatalistic belief in a life of radical self-interest was a new development in Daoism.

life, Matter characterized by the ability to metabolize nutrients (process materials for energy and tissue building), grow, reproduce, and respond and adapt to environmental stimuli. Fossil evidence suggests that Earth's first living organisms, bacteria and cyanobacteria, arose about 3.5 billion years ago. All known lifeforms possess either DNA or RNA. Viruses, which possess DNA and RNA, cannot reproduce without a host cell and do not metabolize nutrients, and it is uncertain whether they should be classified as living or nonliving. Scientists disagree on the likelihood of extraterrestrial life.

Liffey, River, River, Ireland. Rising southwest of Dublin, it flows northwest, then runs west in the Kildare lowland. It crosses east through Dublin, where it is channeled into canals, and empties into Dublin Bay, an arm of the Irish Sea, after a course of 50 mi (80 km). The river is personified as Anna Livia Plurabelle in James Joyce's *Finnegans Wake.*

ligament, Tough fibrous band of connective tissue that supports internal organs and holds bones together properly in joints. It is composed of dense bundles of fibres and spindle-shaped cells (fibroblasts and fibrocytes), with little ground substance. White ligament is rich in sturdy, inelastic collagen fibres; yellow ligament is rich in tough elastic fibres, which allow more movement.

light, That portion of the electromagnetic spectrum visible to the human eye. It ranges from the red end to the violet end of the spectrum, with wavelengths from 700 to 400 nanometres and frequencies from 4.3×10^{14} to 7.5×10^{14} Hz. Like all electromagnetic radiation, it travels through empty space at a speed of about 186,000 mi/sec (300,000 km/sec). In the mid-19th century, light was described by James Clerk Maxwell in terms of electromagnetic waves, but 20th-century physicists showed that it exhibits properties of particles as well; its carrier particle is the photon. Light is the basis for the sense of sight and for the perception of colour.

light-emitting diode (LED), Semiconductor diode that produces visible or infrared light when subjected to an electric current, as a result of electroluminescence. Visible-light LEDs are used in many electronic devices as indicator lamps (e.g., an on/off indicator) and, when arranged in a matrix, to spell out letters or numbers on alphanumeric displays. Infrared LEDs are used in optoelectronics (e.g., in auto-focus cameras and television remote controls) and as light sources in some long-range fibre-optic communications systems. LEDs are formed by the so-called III-V compound semiconductors related to gallium arsenide. They consume little power and are long-lasting and inexpensive.

light-year, Distance traveled by light moving in a vacuum in one year, at its accepted speed of 186,282 mi/second (299,792 km/second). It equals about 5.9 trillion mi (9.5 trillion km), 63,240 astronomical units, or 0.307 parsec.

lighthouse, Structure, usually with a tower, built onshore or on the seabed to signal danger or provide aid to seafarers. The first known lighthouse was the Pharos of Alexandria. The modern lighthouse dates only from the early 18th century. The towers were initially made of wood and often washed away in severe storms. The first lighthouse made of interlocking masonry blocks was built on the treacherous Eddystone Rocks reef, off Plymouth, Eng. (1759). Interlocking masonry blocks remained the principal material of lighthouse construction until they were replaced by concrete and steel in the 20th century. Modern construction methods have facilitated the building of offshore lighthouses. The most common illuminant is the electric filament lamp. Refinements in lenses (e.g., the Fresnel lens) and reflectors made it possible to substantially increase the light's intensity. Radio and satellite-based navigation systems have greatly reduced the need for large lighthouses in sighting land.

lighting, Use of an artificial source of light for illumination. It is a key element of architecture and interior design. Residential lighting uses mainly either incandescent lamps or fluorescent lamps and often depends heavily on movable fixtures plugged into outlets; built-in lighting is typically found in kitchens, bathrooms, and corridors and in the form of hanging pendants in dining rooms and sometimes recessed fixtures in living rooms. Lighting in nonresidential buildings is predominantly fluorescent. High-pressure sodium-vapor lamps have higher efficiency and are used in industrial applications. Halogen lamps have residential, industrial, and photographic applications. Depending on their fixtures, lamps (bulbs) produce a variety of lighting conditions. Incandescent lamps placed in translucent glass globes create diffuse effects; in recessed ceiling-mounted fixtures with reflectors, they can light walls or floors evenly. Fluorescent fixtures are typically recessed and rectangular, with prismatic lenses, but other types including indirect cove lights and luminous ceilings, in which lamps are placed above suspended translucent panels. Mercury-vapor and high-pressure sodium-vapor lamps are placed in simple reflectors in industrial spaces, in pole-mounted streetlight fixtures, and in indirect up-lighting fixtures for commercial applications.

lightning, Visible discharge of electricity when part of the atmosphere acquires enough electrical charge to overcome the resistance of the air. During a thunderstorm, lightning flashes can occur within clouds, between clouds, between clouds and air, or from clouds to the ground. Lightning is usually associated with cumulonimbus clouds (thunderclouds) but also occurs in nimbostratus clouds, in snowstorms and dust storms, and sometimes in the dust and gases emitted by a volcano. A typical lightning flash involves a potential difference between cloud and ground of several hundred million volts. Temperatures in the lightning channel are on the order of 30,000 K (50,000 °F). A cloud-to-ground flash comprises at least two strokes: a pale leader stroke that strikes the ground and a highly luminous return stroke. The leader stroke reaches the ground in about 20 milliseconds; the return stroke reaches the cloud in about 70 microseconds. The thunder associated with lightning is caused by rapid heating of air along the length of the lightning channel. The heated air expands at supersonic speeds. The shock wave decays within a metre or two into a sound wave, which, modified by the intervening air and topography, produces a series of rumbles and claps.

lignite, Yellow to dark brown, rarely black, coal that has been formed from peat under moderate pressure; it is one of the first products of coalification and is intermediate between peat and subbituminous coal. Dry lignite contains about 60–70% carbon. Almost half of the world's total coal reserves contain lignite and subbituminous coal, but lignite has not been exploited to any great extent because lignite is inferior to higher-rank coals (e.g., bituminous coal) in heating value, ease of handling, and storage stability. In some areas, however, the scarcity of fuel has led to extensive developments.

lilac, Any of about 25 species of fragrant, northern, spring-flowering garden shrubs and small trees that make up the genus *Syringa* in the olive family, native to eastern Europe and temperate Asia. Lilacs have deep green leaves and large, oval clusters of compound blooms coloured deep purple, lavender, blue, red, pink, white, or creamy yellow; they are often highly fragrant. The common lilac (*S. vulgaris*) reaches 20 ft (6 m) in height and produces many suckers (shoots from the stem or root). The name syringa was formerly used for the mock orange of the saxifrage family; and the butterfly bush is commonly called summer lilac.

Liliuokalani, orig. LYDIA KAMAKAEHA (b. Sept. 2, 1838, Honolulu, Hawaii—d. Nov. 11, 1917, Honolulu), Hawaiian queen, the last Hawaiian monarch to govern the islands (1891–93). She succeeded her brother, David Kalakaua, to the throne and tried to restore the traditional monarchy. She opposed the reciprocity treaty that gave commercial concessions to the U.S. In 1893 she was declared deposed by Sanford B. Dole and the Missionary Party, which favoured U.S. annexation. An uprising in her name was suppressed and the rebels jailed. To win pardons for her supporters, she formally abdicated in 1895. A talented musician, she composed the song "Aloha Oe."

Queen Liliuokalani.

Lille, City (pop., 2006 est.: city, 226,014; metro. area, 1,016,205), northern France, situated on the Deûle River. Fortified in the 11th century, it changed hands several times during the Middle Ages. Louis XIV besieged and captured the city in 1667. It was taken by the duke of Marlborough in 1708 and ceded to France in 1713. It was occupied by the Germans during both World War I and World War II. It is traditionally France's textile centre; other industries include machinery manufacturing and chemical plants. Its museum has a rich art collection.

Lilongwe, Capital and one of the largest cities (pop., 2008: 669,021) in Malawi. Lilongwe is located on an inland plain 50 mi (80 km) west of the southern end of Lake Malawi. An agricultural market centre for the fertile Central Region Plateau, it replaced Zomba as the national capital in 1975. The old part of the city functions as a service and commercial centre, while the newer district of Capital Hill houses government buildings and embassies, except for the country's judiciary, which is housed in the city of Blantyre.

lily family, Family Liliaceae (order Liliales), which contains about 635 species of flowering herbs and shrubs in 16 genera. The genus *Lilium* includes the true lilies. Native primarily to temperate and subtropical regions, these monocots usually have six-segmented flowers, three-chambered capsular fruits, and leaves with parallel veins. Among the oldest cultivated plants, true lilies are erect perennials with leafy stems, scaly bulbs, usually narrow leaves, and solitary or clustered flowers, some quite fragrant, in a variety of colours. Most species store nutrients underground in a bulb, corm, or tuber. Important garden ornamentals in the family include Solomon's seal, tulip, and fritillary. In addition, some tulip species and some members of the genus *Lilium* may be eaten.

Lima, City (pop. 2007: metro. area, 8,472,935), capital of Peru. It is located inland from the Pacific Ocean port of Callao and near the Andes Mountains. Its nickname, El Pulpo ("The Octopus"), refers to its sprawling metropolitan area. It was founded by Francisco Pizarro in 1535 on the feast of the Epiphany, prompting the name Ciudad de los Reyes ("City of Kings"), but the name never took. Lima later became the capital of the Viceroyalty of Peru. The city was destroyed by an earthquake in 1746 but was rebuilt. It grew rapidly during the 20th century and now accounts for nearly one-third of Peru's total population. It is the country's economic and cultural centre. Historic sites include the cathedral (begun in the 16th century) and the National University of San Marcos (1551).

limerick, Popular form of short, humorous verse, often nonsensical and frequently ribald. It consists of five lines, rhyming *aabba*, and the dominant metre is anapestic, with two feet in the third and fourth lines and three feet in the others. The origin of the term is obscure, but a group of poets in County Limerick, Ire., wrote limericks in Irish in the 18th century. The first collections in English date from *c.* 1820. Among the most famous are those in Edward Lear's *Book of Nonsense* (1846).

limestone, Sedimentary rock composed mainly of calcium carbonate ($CaCO_3$), usually in the form of calcite and, less commonly, aragonite. It may contain considerable amounts of magnesium carbonate (dolomite) as well. Most limestones have a granular texture; in many cases, the grains are tiny fragments of fossil animal shells. Much knowledge of the Earth's history has been derived from the study of fossils embedded in limestone and other carbonate rocks. Limestone is used as a soil conditioner, in the manufacture of glass, and in agriculture. Ornamental varieties are used for flooring, exterior and interior facings of buildings, and monuments.

limit, Mathematical concept based on the idea of closeness, used mainly in studying the behaviour of functions close to values at which they are undefined. For example, the function $1/x$ is not defined at $x = 0$. For positive values of x, as x is chosen closer and closer to 0, the value of $1/x$ begins to grow rapidly, approaching infinity as a limit. This interplay of action and reaction as the independent variable moves closer to a given value is the essence of the idea of a limit. Limits provide the means of defining the derivative and integral of a function.

limitations, statute of, Legislative act restricting the time within which legal proceedings may be brought, usually to a fixed period after the occurrence of the events that gave rise to the cause of action. Such statutes are enacted to protect persons against claims made after evidence has been lost, memories have faded, or witnesses have disappeared. The periods prescribed for different actions in different jurisdictions vary considerably.

Limoges ware, Porcelain, largely service ware, produced in Limoges, France, from the 18th century. Faience of undistinguished quality was produced there from 1736, but the manufacture of hard-paste, or true, porcelain dates only from 1771. In 1784 the factory was acquired as an adjunct of the royal factory at Sèvres, and the decorations of the two wares became similar. After 1858 Limoges became a mass exporter of porcelain to the U.S. under the name Haviland.

Limpopo River, River, South Africa. Rising as the Crocodile (Krokodil) River in the Witwatersrand, South Africa, it flows northeast along the border of South Africa and southeast across Mozambique to empty into the Indian Ocean. Along its middle course it divides South Africa from Botswana and Zimbabwe. It is 1,100 mi (1,800 km) long but is navigable only 130 mi (208 km) from the coast. The first European to visit it was Vasco da Gama, who named its mouth the Espíritu Santo River in 1498.

Lin Biao, or LIN PIAO (b. Dec. 5, 1907, Huanggang, Hubei province, China—d. Sept. 13, 1971?, Mongolia?), Chinese military leader and government official who played a prominent role in the Cultural Revolution. He joined the Socialist Youth League in 1925 and Chiang Kai-shek's Northern Expedition in 1926. When Chiang turned on the communists in 1927, Lin fled to join Mao. During the Long March Lin became legendary for never losing a battle, and he prevailed against the Japanese in the 1930s and the Nationalists in the 1940s. In the early 1960s his reformation and indoctrination of the army in accordance with Mao's teachings became a model for the rest of society, and during the Cultural Revolution he was designated Mao's successor. Subsequent events are unclear, but in September 1971 the Chinese government reported that Lin died in a plane crash in Mongolia in an attempt to flee China; his death has remained a mystery.

Lin Yutang, or LIN YÜ-T'ANG (b. Oct. 10, 1895, Longxi, Fujian province, China—d. March 26, 1976, Hong Kong), Chinese writer. The son of a Presbyterian minister, he studied in the U.S. and Europe. In 1932 he established a highly successful Western-style satirical magazine of a type totally new to China; soon he introduced two other publications. A prolific writer of works in Chinese and English, he produced his first English-language book, *My Country and My People*, in 1935. From 1936 he lived chiefly in the U.S. His other works include *The Wisdom of China and India* (1942), books on Chinese history and philosophy, and highly acclaimed English translations of Chinese literary masterpieces.

Lincoln, Abraham (b. Feb. 12, 1809, near Hodgenville, Ky., U.S.—d. April 15, 1865, Washington, D.C.), 16th president of the U.S. (1861–65). Born in a Kentucky log cabin, he moved to Indiana in 1816 and to Illinois in 1830. After working as a storekeeper, a rail-splitter, a postmaster, and a surveyor, he enlisted as a volunteer in the Black Hawk War (1832) and was elected captain of his company. He taught himself law and in 1836 passed the bar examination. In 1837 he moved his practice from New Salem to Springfield, Ill. He became a successful circuit-riding lawyer, noted for his shrewdness, common sense, and honesty (earning the nickname "Honest Abe"). From 1834 to 1840 he served in the Illinois state legislature, and in 1847 he was elected as a Whig to the U.S. House of Representatives. In 1856 he joined the Republican Party, which nominated him as its candidate in the 1858 Senate election. In a series of seven debates with Stephen A. Douglas (the Lincoln-Douglas Debates), he argued against the extension of slavery into the territories. Though morally opposed to slavery, he was not an abolitionist; indeed, he attempted to rebut Douglas's charge that he was a dangerous radical, by reassuring audiences that he did not favour political equality for blacks. Despite his loss in the election, the debates brought him national attention. In the 1860 presidential election, he ran against Douglas again and won by a large margin in the electoral college, though he received only two-fifths of the popular vote. The South opposed his position on slavery in the territories, and before his inauguration seven Southern states had seceeded from the Union. The ensuing American Civil War completely consumed Lincoln's administration. He excelled as a wartime leader, creating a high command for directing all the country's energies and resources toward the war effort and combining statecraft and overall command of the armies with what some have called military genius. However, his abrogation of some civil liberties, especially the writ of habeas corpus, and the closing of several newspapers by his generals disturbed both Democrats and Republicans, including some members of his own cabinet. To unite the North and influence foreign opinion, he issued the Emancipation Proclamation (1863); his Gettysburg Address (1863) further ennobled the war's purpose. The continuing war affected some Northerners' resolve and his reelection was not assured, but strategic battle victories turned the tide, and he easily defeated George B. McClellan in 1864. His platform included passage of the 13th Amendment outlawing slavery (ratified 1865). At his second inaugural, with victory in sight, he spoke of moderation in reconstructing the South and building a harmonious Union. On April 14, five days after the war ended, he was shot and mortally wounded by John Wilkes Booth.

Lindbergh, Charles A(ugustus) (b. Feb. 4, 1902, Detroit, Mich., U.S.—d. Aug. 26, 1974, Maui, Hawaii), Aviator who made the first nonstop solo flight across the Atlantic Ocean. He left college to enroll in army flying schools and became an airmail pilot in 1926. He obtained backing from St. Louis businessmen to compete for a prize for flying from New York to Paris, and in 1927 in the monoplane *Spirit of St. Louis* he made the flight in 33.5 hours, becoming an instant hero in the U.S. and Europe. In 1929 he married the writer Anne Morrow (1906–2001), who would later serve as his copilot and navigator. In 1932 their child was kidnapped and murdered, a crime that received worldwide attention. They moved to England to escape the publicity, returning to the U.S. in 1940 to criticism over his speeches calling for U.S. neutrality in World War II. During the war Lindbergh was an adviser to Ford Motor Company and United Aircraft Corporation. After the war he was a consultant to Pan American Airways and the the U.S. Department of Defense and served on many aeronautical boards and committees. In 1953 he wrote the Pulitzer Prize-winning *The Spirit of St. Louis*.

Charles A. Lindbergh in front of his airplane Spirit of St. Louis, *1927.*
Library of Congress, Washington, D.C.

Linear A and Linear B, Linear forms of writing used by Aegean civilizations during the 2nd millennium BC. Examples of Linear A, a syllabary (a writing system in which one character represents a whole syllable) written from left to right, date from 1850 BC to 1400 BC. The language written in Linear A remains unknown. Linear B, adapted from Linear A, was borrowed from the Minoan civilization by the Mycenaean Greeks, probably c. 1600 BC, and used to write the Mycenaean Greek dialect. Examples of Linear B script have been found on clay tablets and vases from c. 1400–1200 BC. These texts represent the oldest known form of Greek. Linear B was deciphered as Greek in 1952 by Michael Ventris and John Chadwick.

linear accelerator, or LINAC, Type of particle accelerator that imparts a series of relatively small increases in energy to subatomic particles as they pass through a sequence of alternating electric fields set up in a linear structure. The small accelerations add together to give the particles a greater energy than could be achieved by the voltage used in one section alone. One of the world's longest linacs is the 2-mi (3.2-km) machine at the Stanford Linear Accelerator Center, which can accelerate electrons to energies of 50 billion electron volts. Much smaller linacs, both proton and electron types, have important practical applications in medicine and industry.

linear algebra, Branch of algebra concerned with methods of solving systems of linear equations; more generally, the mathematics of linear transformations and vector spaces. "Linear" refers to the form of the equations involved—in two dimensions, $ax +$

by = c. Geometrically, this represents a line. If the variables are replaced by vectors, functions, or derivatives, the equation becomes a linear transformation. A system of equations of this type is a system of linear transformations. Because it shows when such a system has a solution and how to find it, linear algebra is essential to the theory of mathematical analysis and differential equations. Its applications extend beyond the physical sciences into, for example, biology and economics.

linga, or LINGAM, In Hinduism, the symbol of the god Shiva and of generative power. Fashioned from wood, gems, metal, or stone, lingas are the main objects of worship in temples to Shiva and family shrines throughout India. Historically, the linga was a representation of the phallus, as sculptures from the 1st–2nd century AD, the earliest dates of linga worship, make clear, and most modern Hindus think of it in these terms. The stylization of the linga as a smooth cylindrical mass asserts an aniconic meaning. A sexual dimension remains in the most common form in which the linga appears today. The yoni, symbol of the female sex organ, often forms the base of the linga, a reminder that the male and female principles together represent the totality of existence. The linga is worshiped with offerings of flowers, water, fruit, leaves, and rice; the purity of the materials and the cleanliness of the worshiper are particularly stressed.

Sandstone linga, *c. 900; in the British Museum.*

Lingayat, Member of a Hindu sect that worships Shiva as the only deity. It has a wide following in southern India. Its followers take their name ("linga-wearers") from the small lingas that both men and women wear on a cord around the neck. The Lingayats' belief in a single deity and their concept of bhakti (devotion) as an intuitive and loving knowledge of God show the influence of Ramanuja. They reject Brahma and the authority of the Vedas; their opposition to child marriage and the ill-treatment of widows anticipated the social reform movements of the 19th century.

lingua franca, Language used for communication between two or more groups that have different native languages. It may be a standard language—for example, English and French are often used for international diplomacy, and Swahili is used by speakers of the many different local languages of eastern Africa. A lingua franca may also be a pidgin, like Melanesian Pidgin, widely used in the southern Pacific. The term lingua franca (Latin: "Frankish language") was first applied to a pidgin based on French and Italian developed in the Mediterranean.

linguistics, Study of the nature and structure of language. It traditionally encompasses semantics, syntax, and phonology. Synchronic linguistic studies aim to describe a language as it exists at a given time; diachronic studies trace a language's historical development. Greek philosophers in the 5th century BC who debated the origins of human language were the first in the West to be concerned with linguistic theory. The first complete Greek grammar, written by Dionysus Thrax in the 1st century BC, was a model for Roman grammarians, whose work led to the medieval and Renaissance vernacular grammars.

With the rise of historical linguistics in the 19th century, linguistics became a science. In the late 19th and early 20th centuries Ferdinand de Saussure established the structuralist school of linguistics, which analyzed actual speech to learn about the underlying structure of language. In the 1950s Noam Chomsky challenged the structuralist program, arguing that linguistics should study native speakers' unconscious knowledge of their language (competence), not the language they actually produce (performance). His general approach, known as transformational generative grammar, was extensively revised in subsequent decades as the extended standard theory, the principles-and-parameters (government-binding) approach, and the minimalist program. Other grammatical theories developed from the 1960s were generalized phrase structure grammar, lexical-functional grammar, relational grammar, and cognitive grammar. Chomsky's emphasis on linguistic competence greatly stimulated the development of the related disciplines of psycholinguistics and neurolinguistics. Other related fields are anthropological linguistics, computational linguistics, mathematical linguistics, sociolinguistics, and the philosophy of language.

Linotype, Trademark name for a typesetting machine by which characters are cast in type metal as a complete line, rather than as individual characters (as on the Monotype typesetting machine). It was patented in 1884 by Ottmar Mergenthaler. It has now been almost entirely supplanted by photocomposition. In Linotype, a keyboard is manipulated to compose each line of text. The slugs produced by the machine are rectangular solids of type metal (an alloy of lead, antimony, and tin) with raised characters that are a mirror image of the desired printed line. After hot-metal casting, the slug of type, air-cooled briefly, is placed in a "stick" for insertion in the proper position into the press form being made up.

Linux, Nonproprietary operating system (OS) for digital computers. In 1991 Linus Torvalds of Finland began asking for volunteer programmers over the Internet to collaborate on the development of a UNIX-like OS for personal computers; the "1.0" release of Linux was in 1994. A true multiuser, multitasking system, Linux contained features (e.g., virtual memory, shared libraries, memory management, and TCP/IP networking) formerly only found on mainframe computers. Thousands of volunteers, as well as several companies that sell prepackaged Linux products, have been able to contribute to the OS because its source code is freely available. A reliable, fast-performing system with good security features, Linux is popular for corporate computer network and Web servers.

lion, Large, powerfully built cat (*Panthera leo*), the proverbial "king of beasts." It is now found mainly in parts of sub-Saharan Africa, though about two hundred constitute an Asiatic race living under strict protection in India. Lions inhabit grassy plains and open savanna. The male is 6–7 ft (1.8–2.1 m) long, excluding the 3-ft (1-m) tail, stands about 4 ft (1.2 m) high at the shoulder, and weighs 370–500 lbs (170–230 kg). The female, or lioness, is considerably smaller. The male's coat is usually buff yellow or orange-brown; lionesses are more consistently tawny or sandy. The male's outstanding characteristic is his mane. Lions are unique among cats in that they live in a group, or pride, often consisting of about 15 individuals. Lionesses are the chief hunters. They prey

Male lion (Panthera leo).
R.I.M. Campbell/Bruce Coleman Ltd.

on animals of all sizes, including hippopotamuses, but prefer wildebeests, antelopes, and zebras. After eating, a lion may rest for a week.

lipid, Any of a diverse group of organic compounds that are grouped together because they do not interact appreciably with water. One of the three large classes of substances in foods and living cells, lipids contain more than twice as much energy (calories) per unit of weight as the other two (proteins and carbohydrates). They include the fats and edible oils (e.g., butter, olive oil, corn oil), which are primarily triglycerides; phospholipids (e.g., lecithin), which are important in cell structure and metabolism; waxes of animal or plant origin; and sphingolipids, complex substances found in various tissues of the brain and nervous system. Since insolubility is the defining characteristic, cholesterol and related steroids, carotenoids, prostaglandins, and various other compounds are also classifiable as lipids.

liquid, One of the three principal states of matter, intermediate between a gas and a solid. A liquid has neither the orderliness of a solid nor the randomness of a gas. Liquids have the ability to flow under the action of very small shear stresses. Liquids in contact with their own vapour or air have a surface tension that causes the interface to assume the configuration of minimum area (i.e., spherical). Surfaces between liquids and solids have interfacial tensions that determine whether the liquid will wet the other material. With the exception of liquid metals, molten salts, and solutions of salts, the electrical conductivities of liquids are small.

liquid crystal, Substance that flows like a liquid but maintains some of the ordered structure characteristic of a crystal. Some organic substances do not melt directly when heated but instead turn from a crystalline solid to a liquid crystalline state. When heated further, a true liquid is formed. Liquid crystals have unique properties. The structures are easily affected by changes in mechanical stress, electromagnetic fields, temperature, and chemical environment.

liquid crystal display (LCD), Optoelectronic device used in displays for watches, calculators, notebook computers, and other electronic devices. Current passed through specific portions of the liquid crystal solution causes the crystals to align, blocking the passage of light. Doing so in a controlled and organized manner produces visual images on the display screen. The advantage of LCDs is that they are much lighter and consume less power than other display technologies (e.g., cathode-ray tubes). These characteristics make them an ideal choice for flat-panel displays, as in portable laptop and notebook computers.

Lisbon, Portuguese LISBOA, City (pop., 2001: 564,657), capital of Portugal. The country's chief seaport and largest city, it lies on the Tagus River near the river's entrance into the Atlantic Ocean. It was under Roman rule from 205 BCE; Julius Caesar made it a municipium called Felicitas Julia. It was ruled by a series of barbarian tribes from the 5th century and was captured by Moors in the 8th century. The Crusaders under Afonso I gained control of it in 1147, and it became the national capital in 1256. It flourished as a leading European trading city in the 14th–16th centuries. One of the greatest earthquakes ever recorded struck Lisbon in 1755, killing 70,000. Urban renewal following the earthquake was unrivaled in scope. In 1998 Lisbon hosted the World's Fair (Expo '98). The city is a major commercial, administrative, educational, and manufacturing centre. It was the birthplace of poet Luís de Camões.

litchi, or LICHEE, or LYCHEE, Fruit of the tree *Litchi chinensis* (family Sapindaceae), believed to be native to southern China and adjacent regions but now also cultivated elsewhere. It has been a favourite fruit of the Cantonese since ancient times and is a popular dessert in U.S. Chinese restaurants. The fresh pulp tastes musky; when dried, it is acidic and very sweet. The handsome tree develops a compact crown of foliage, with compound leaves that are bright green year-round. Clusters of small, inconspicuous flowers form small, oval red fruits.

literacy, Ability to read and write. The term may also refer to familiarity with literature and to a basic level of education obtained through the written word. In ancient civilizations such as those of the Sumerians and Babylonians, literacy was the province of an elite group of scholars and priests. Though more prevalent in classical Greece and Rome, it was often limited to members of the upper classes. The spread of literacy in Europe in the Middle Ages was evidenced by the use of writing for functions once conducted orally, such as the indenture of servants and the notation of evidence at trials. The rise of literacy in Europe was closely tied to great social transformations, notably the Protestant Reformation, which brought individual study of the Bible, and the development of modern science. The spread of literacy during the Reformation and the Renaissance was greatly facilitated by the development of printing from movable type and by the adoption of vernacular languages in place of Latin. Compulsory schooling, established in Britain, Europe, and the U.S. in the 19th century, has led to high rates of literacy in the modern industrialized world.

literary criticism, Discipline concerned with philosophical, descriptive, and evaluative inquiries about literature, including what literature is, what it does, and what it is worth. The Western critical tradition began with Plato's *Republic* (4th century BCE). A generation later, Aristotle, in his *Poetics*, developed a set of principles of composition that had a lasting influence. European criticism since the Renaissance has primarily focused on the moral worth of literature and the nature of its relationship to reality. At the end of the 16th century, Sir Philip Sidney argued that it is the special property of literature to offer an imagined world that is in some respects superior to the real one. A century later John Dryden proposed the less idealistic view that literature must primarily offer an accurate representation of the world for "the delight and instruction of mankind," an assumption that underlies the great critical works of Alexander Pope and Samuel Johnson. A departure from these ideas appeared in the criticism of the Romantic period, epitomized by William Wordsworth's assertion that the object of poetry is "truth…carried alive into the heart by passion." The later 19th century saw two divergent developments: an aesthetic theory of "art for art's sake," and the view (expressed by Matthew Arnold) that literature must assume the moral and philosophical functions previously filled by religion. The volume of literary criticism increased greatly in the 20th century, and its later years saw a radical reappraisal of traditional critical modes and the development of a multiplicity of critical factions.

lithium, Chemical element, lightest alkali metal, chemical symbol Li, atomic number 3. It is soft, white, lustrous, and very reactive, forming compounds in which it has valence 1. The metal is used in certain alloys, as a coolant in nuclear reactors, and (because of its reactivity) as a reagent, scavenger, and rocket fuel. Lithium hydride is used as a source of hydrogen; lithium hydroxide is used as an additive in storage batteries and to absorb carbon dioxide. Halides of lithium are used as moisture absorbents, and lithium soaps are used as thickeners in lubricating greases. Lithium carbonate is an important drug for treating depression and bipolar disorder.

lithography, Printing process that makes use of the immiscibility of grease and water. Aloys Senefelder of Prague (1771–1834) exploited the properties of a stone with a calcium carbonate base and a fine, porous surface, and perfected his printing process in

1798. In Senefelder's process, the stone, with a design drawn on it with crayon or greasy ink, was wetted with water; after various etching and protecting steps, it was brushed with oily ink; it retained the ink only on the design. This inked surface was then printed—either directly on paper, by a special press (as in most fine-art printmaking), or onto a rubber cylinder and thence onto paper (as in commercial printing). The method of preparing stones for hand printing, still the lithographic method preferred by artists, has hardly changed. Commercial lithographic printing on a modern rotary offset printing press can produce high-quality, finely detailed impressions at high speed, reproducing any material that can be photographed in the platemaking process. It now accounts for more than 40% of all printing, packaging, and publishing, more than twice the percentage produced by any other single printing process.

lithosphere, Rigid, rocky outer layer of the Earth, consisting of the crust and the solid outermost layer of the upper mantle. It extends to a depth of about 60 mi (100 km). It is broken into about a dozen separate, rigid blocks, or plates. Slow convection currents deep within the mantle, generated by radioactive heating of the interior, are believed to cause the lateral movements of the plates (and the continents that rest on top of them) at a rate of several inches per year.

Lithuania, officially REPUBLIC OF LITHUANIA, Country, the largest of the three Baltic States, northeastern Europe. Area: 25,212 sq mi (65,300 sq km). Population: (2011 est.) 3,218,000. Capital: Vilnius. Lithuanians make up about four-fifths of the population; there are smaller numbers of Russians, Poles, and Belarusians. Languages: Lithuanian (official), Russian, Polish, Belarusian. Religion: Christianity (predominantly Roman Catholic; also Eastern Orthodox). Currency: litas. The country consists of low-lying plains alternating with hilly uplands, watered by rivers that meander westward to the Baltic Sea. Manufacturing, including metalworking, woodworking, and textile production, is especially important in the east and south. Agriculture focuses on livestock breeding, especially dairy farming and pigs, and the cultivation of cereals, flax, sugar beets, potatoes, and fodder crops. Lithuania is a unitary multiparty republic with one legislative house; its head of state is the president, and the head of government is the prime minister. Lithuanian tribes united in the mid-13th century to oppose the Teutonic Knights. Gediminas, one of the grand dukes, expanded Lithuania into an empire that dominated much of eastern Europe in the 14th–16th centuries. In 1386 the Lithuanian grand duke became the king of Poland, and the two countries remained closely associated for the next 400 years. Lithuania was acquired by Russia in the Third Partition of Poland in 1795 and joined in the Polish revolt in 1863. Occupied by Germany during World War I, it declared its independence in 1918. In 1940 the Soviet Red Army gained control of Lithuania, which was soon incorporated into the Soviet Union. Germany occupied Lithuania again from 1941, but the Red Army regained control in 1944. With the breakup of the U.S.S.R., Lithuania declared its independence in 1990 and gained full independence in 1991. In the 1990s and early 21st century it sought economic stability, and in 2004 it became a member of the European Union.

Little Entente, Mutual defense arrangement formed in 1920–21 between Czechoslovakia, Yugoslavia, and Romania, with French support. It was directed against German and Hungarian domination in the Danube River basin and toward protection of its members' territorial integrity. It was successful in the 1920s, but after Adolf Hitler's rise to power (1933) its members adopted increasingly independent foreign policies. The entente collapsed after Germany annexed the Czech Sudetenland (1938).

Little St. Bernard Pass, Mountain pass, Savoy Alps. Situated southwest of the Italian border in southeastern France, it connects Bourg-St.-Maurice, France, with La Thuile, Italy. Hannibal probably led the Carthaginian army over the pass on his way toward

Rome in 218 BC. It was the principal route across the Alps into Gallia Comata, a province of Gaul, until Montgenèvre Pass was opened in 77 BC. Beside the pass is a hospice founded in the 11th century by St. Bernard of Menthon.

liturgical drama, Play acted in or near the church in the Middle Ages. The form probably dated from the 10th century, when the "Quem quaeritis" ("Whom do you seek") section of the Easter mass was performed as a small scene in the service. The plays gradually increased in length, with themes derived from biblical stories (particularly those of Easter and Christmas), and they flourished in the 12th–13th centuries. Their Latin dialogue was frequently chanted to simple melodies. They continued to be written into the 16th century, but the connection with the church eventually ended as the plays came under secular sponsorship and were acted in the vernacular.

Liturgical movement, 19th- and 20th-century effort to encourage the active participation of the laity in the liturgy of the Christian churches by creating simpler rites more attuned to early Christian traditions and more relevant to modern life. The movement began in the Roman Catholic church in the mid-19th century and spread to other Christian churches in Europe and the U.S. The Second Vatican Council (1962–65) called for translation of Latin liturgies into the vernaculars of individual countries and the reform of all sacramental rites. The Lutheran Church revised the *Lutheran Book of Worship* in 1978, and the Episcopal Church adopted a revised *Book of Common Prayer* in 1979.

Liu Shaoqi, or LIU SHAO-CH'I (b. Nov. 24, 1898, Ningxiang district, Hunan province, China—d. Nov. 12, 1969, Kaifeng, Henan province), Chairman of the People's Republic of China (1959–68) and chief theoretician of the Chinese Communist Party (CCP). An activist communist background from the 1920s helped Liu's rise within the CCP in the 1930s and '40s, while his excellent education and studies in the Soviet Union made him an effective spokesman for the new government in China. When Mao resigned as chairman after the failure of his Great Leap Forward, Liu assumed the title. His policies for revitalizing agriculture by permitting peasants to cultivate private plots and giving them monetary incentives were ones to which Mao later strongly objected. In 1968 Liu was purged from power for being a "capitalist roader," and Lin Biao was appointed Mao's successor.

liver, Largest gland in the body, with several lobes. It secretes bile; metabolizes proteins, carbohydrates, and fats; stores glycogen, vitamins, and other substances; synthesizes coagulation factors; removes wastes and toxic matter from the blood; regulates blood volume; and destroys old red blood cells. The portal vein carries blood from the gastrointestinal tract, gallbladder, pancreas, and spleen to the liver to be processed. A duct system carries bile from the liver to the duodenum and the gallbladder. Liver tissue consists of a mass of cells tunneled with bile ducts and blood vessels. About 60% are hepatic cells, which have more metabolic functions than any other cells. A second type, Kupffer cells, play a role in blood-cell formation, antibody production, and ingestion of foreign particles and cell debris. The liver manufactures plasma proteins, including albumin and clotting factors, and synthesizes enzymes that modify substances such as nutrients and toxins, filtered from the blood. Liver disorders include jaundice, hepatitis, cirrhosis, tumours, vascular obstruction, abscess, and glycogen-storage diseases.

Liverpool, City (pop., 2001: 439,473), northwestern England, on the estuary of the River Mersey. It forms the nucleus of the metropolitan county of Merseyside in the historic county of Lancashire. King John granted its charter in 1207. Its growth was slow until the 18th century, when it expanded rapidly as a result of trade with the Americas and the West Indies, becoming Britain's most important port after London. The Liverpool and Manchester Railway (opened 1830) was the first in England to link two major cities. Heavily damaged in World War II, Liverpool declined in importance as a port and an industrial centre in the postwar era. The birthplace of the Beatles, it is also the seat of the University of Liverpool (1903). Liverpool's docklands and several areas of the historic centre of the city were collectively designated a UNESCO World Heritage site in 2004.

living will, Document in which an individual specifies medical measures to be taken or withheld in the event that one becomes disabled. Advances in medical technology now allow the body to be kept alive in circumstances that would normally result in death (e.g., inability to eat, breathe, or maintain the heartbeat), but many people do not want to be kept alive if there is no chance of recovery. Because it is impossible to express one's wishes when in a vegetative state, a living will allows them to be stated in advance. Such a document usually specifies conditions under which a do-not-resuscitate (DNR) order is to take effect and authorizes another person to make decisions on the patient's behalf.

Livonia, Region, eastern coast of Baltic Sea, north of Lithuania. Originally inhabited by the Livs, a Finno-Ugric people, it eventually expanded to include nearly all of modern Latvia and Estonia. In the 13th century it was conquered and Christianized by the Order of the Brothers of the Sword and organized into the Livonian confederation. A Russian invasion set off the Livonian War (1558–82), in which Russia, Poland, and Sweden seized portions of it. Sweden eventually gained control of most of it but ceded the region to Russia in 1721. In 1918 the northern portion became part of independent Estonia and the southern portion joined independent Latvia.

lizard, Any of about 5,500 species of reptiles constituting the suborder Sauria. They are most diverse and abundant in the tropics but are found from the Arctic Circle (one species) to southern Africa, South America, and Australia. Like snakes, lizards have scales, paired male copulatory organs, and a flexible skull. Typical lizards have a moderately cylindrical body, four well-developed legs (although some lizards are legless), a tail slightly longer than the head and body combined, and movable lower eyelids. They range in size from 1-in. (3-cm; geckos) to the 10-ft (3-m; Komodo dragon). Ornamentation includes crests on the head, back, or tail; spines; brightly coloured throat fans; and throat frills. Most species feed on insects and rodents, but some, such as the iguana, eat plants.

Ljubljana, City (pop., 2002 prelim.: 257,338), capital of Slovenia. Located on the Ljubljanica River, it is surrounded by the northern Dinaric Alps. The site of the Roman city of Emona in the 1st century BC, it was destroyed in the 5th century AD and rebuilt by the Slavs as Luvigana. It passed to Carniola in the 12th century and came under Habsburg rule in 1277. Taken by the French in 1809, it was the administrative seat of the Illyrian Provinces until 1813 and the capital of the kingdom of Illyria from 1816 to 1849. It was the centre of Slovene nationalism under Austrian rule, and in 1918 it became part of the Kingdom of Serbs, Croats, and Slovenes (later Yugoslavia). It remained the Slovene capital after Slovenia's independence in 1992. A railroad and commercial centre, it is the site of the University of Ljubljana (founded 1595).

Lloyd George of Dwyfor, David Lloyd George, Earl (b.

Jan. 17, 1863, Manchester, Eng.—d. March 26, 1945, Ty-newydd, near Llanystumdwy, Caernarvonshire, Wales), British prime minister (1916–22). He entered Parliament in 1890 as a Liberal and retained his seat for 55 years. He served as president of the Board of Trade (1905–08), then as chancellor of the Exchequer (1908–15). Rejection of his controversial "People's Budget" (to raise taxes for social programs) in 1909 by the House of Lords led to a constitutional crisis and passage of the Parliament Act of 1911. He devised the National Insurance Act of 1911, which laid the foundation of the British welfare state. As minister of munitions (1915–16), he used unorthodox methods to ensure that war supplies were forthcoming during World War I. He replaced H.H. Asquith as prime minister in 1916, with Conservative support in his coalition government. His small war cabinet ensured speedy decisions. Distrustful of the competence of the British high command, he was constantly at odds with Gen. Douglas Haig. In the 1918 elections his decision to continue a coalition government further split the Liberal Party. He was one of the three great statesmen responsible for the Treaty of Versailles at the Paris Peace Conference. He began the negotiations that culminated in the Anglo-Irish treaty of 1921. He resigned in 1922 and headed an ailing Liberal Party (1926–31).

Lloyd Webber, Andrew, later BARON LLOYD-WEBBER (b. March 22, 1948, London, Eng.), British composer. He studied at Oxford and at the Royal College of Music. His first collaboration with lyricist Tim Rice (b. 1944), *Joseph and the Amazing Technicolor Dreamcoat* (1968), was followed by the rock opera *Jesus Christ Superstar* (1971), which blended classical forms with rock music. Their last major collaboration was *Evita* (1978). Lloyd Webber's eclectic rock-based works helped revitalize musical theatre. In both London and New York City, his musical *Cats* (1981), based on poems by T.S. Eliot, became the longest-running musical in history. He later collaborated on *Starlight Express* (1984), *The Phantom of the Opera* (1986), and *Sunset Boulevard* (1993), among other stage works; in 2006 *The Phantom of the Opera* surpassed *Cats* to become the longest-running show on Broadway. He was knighted in 1992 and ennobled in 1997.

lobbying, Any attempt by a group or individual to influence the decisions of government. The term originated in 19th-century efforts to influence the votes of legislators, generally in the lobby outside a legislative chamber. The effort may be a direct appeal to a decision maker in either the executive or legislative branches, or it may be indirect (e.g., through attempts to influence public opinion). It may include oral or written efforts of persuasion, campaign contributions, public-relations campaigns, research supplied to legislative committees, and formal testimony before such committees. A lobbyist may be a member of a special-interest group, a professional willing to represent any group, or a private individual. In the U.S., the Federal Regulation of Lobbying Act (1946) requires that lobbyists and the groups they represent register and report contributions and expenditures.

lobotomy, Surgical procedure in which nerve pathways in a lobe or lobes of the brain are severed from those in other areas. Introduced in 1935 by António Egas Moniz and Almeida Lima, it came to be used to help grossly disturbed patients. Favoured for patients who did not respond to shock therapy, it did reduce agitation but often caused increased apathy and passivity, inability to concentrate, and decreased emotional response. It was widely performed until *c.* 1956, when drugs that were more effective in calming patients became available. Lobotomies are no longer performed; however, psychosurgery, the surgical removal of specific regions of the brain, is occasionally used to treat patients whose symptoms have resisted all other treatments.

lobster, Any of numerous species of marine shrimplike decapods that are bottom-dwellers and mostly nocturnal. Lobsters scavenge for dead animals but also eat live fish, small mollusks and other bottom-dwelling invertebrates, and seaweed. One or more pairs of legs are often modified into pincers, usually larger on one side than the other. True lobsters have a distinct snout on the upper body shell. The American lobster (*Homarus americanus*) and scampi are the most commercially im-

*American lobster (*Homarus americanus*)*
John H. Gerard

portant, being highly prized as food. The American lobster, found from Labrador to North Carolina, weighs about 1 lb (0.5 kg) and is about 10 in. (25 cm) long when caught in shallow water. Most deepwater specimens weigh about 5.5 lbs (2.5 kg); some may weigh 40 lbs (20 kg).

Locke, John (b. Aug. 29, 1632, Wrington, Somerset, Eng.—d. Oct. 28, 1704, Oates, Essex), English philosopher. Educated at Oxford, principally in medicine and science, he later became physician and adviser to the future 3rd earl of Shaftesbury (1667–72). He moved to France, but after Shaftesbury's fall in 1683 he fled to the Netherlands, where he supported the future William III. Locke returned to England after the Glorious Revolution (1688) to become commissioner of appeals, a post he held until his death. In his major philosophical work, *Essay Concerning Human Understanding* (1690), he argued that knowledge begins in sensation or introspection rather than in innate ideas, as the philosophers of rationalism held. From sensation and reflection the mind receives "ideas," which are the material of knowledge. Some ideas represent actual qualities of objects (such as size, shape, or weight) and others perceived qualities, which do not exist in objects except as they affect observers (such as colour, taste, or smell); Locke called the former qualities "primary" and the latter "secondary." Ideas that are given directly in sensation or reflection are simple, and simple ideas may be "compounded" to form complex ideas. Locke did not succeed in giving a clear account of the origin of the idea of substance (it is "a something-I-know-not-what") or the idea of the "self," though his account of personal identity in terms of memory was influential. In the philosophy of language, he identified the meanings of words with ideas rather than things. In *Two Treatises of Government* (1690), he defended a doctrine of natural rights and a conception of political authority as limited and conditional on the ruler's fulfillment of his obligation to serve the public good. A classic formulation of the principles of political liberalism, this work influenced the American and French revolutions and the Constitution of the U.S. He is considered the founding figure of British empiricism.

lockout, Tactic used by employers in labour disputes, in which employees are locked out of the workplace or otherwise denied employment. In the 1880s and '90s, factory owners in the U.S. often used lockouts against the Knights of Labor, which was struggling to organize industries such as meatpacking and cigar making. The lockout has been used less frequently in modern times, usually as part of a pact among members of employers' associations to frustrate labour unions by closing work facilities in response to strikes.

locomotive, Self-propelled vehicle used for hauling railroad cars on tracks. Early experimental steam locomotives were built in Wales and England by Richard Trevithick from 1803. The first practical steam locomotive, the *Rocket*, was developed in 1829 by George Stephenson, in whose "steam blast" system the steam from a multitube boiler drove pistons connected to a pair of flanged driving wheels. The first U.S. steam locomotive was built by John Stevens in 1825, and the first commercially usable locomotive, the *Tom Thumb*, by Peter Cooper in Baltimore in 1830. Later improvements enabled a locomotive to move up to 200 freight cars at 75 mph (120 kph). Steam from wood or coal fuel was the main source of power until the mid-20th century, though electric power had been used from the early 20th century, especially in Europe. After World War II diesel power replaced steam because of its higher efficiency and lower cost, though diesel-electric and gas turbine-electric combinations were also used.

locust, Any of several species of grasshoppers (family Acrididae) that undergo population explosions and migrate long distances in destructive swarms. In North America the names *locust* and *grasshopper* are interchangeable and used for any acridid; cicadas are sometimes called locusts. In Europe *locust* refers to large species and *grasshopper* to small ones. Locusts are found worldwide.

Sporadic locust swarms may be explained by the theory that swarming species have a solitary phase (the normal state) and a gregarious phase. Nymphs that mature in the presence of many other locusts develop into the gregarious type; thus migratory swarms form as a result of overcrowding. Swarms may be almost unimaginably large, towering 5,000 ft (1,500 m) high; in 1889 a Red Sea swarm was estimated to cover 2,000 sq mi (5,000 sq km). Locust plagues can be extremely destructive of crops.

Łódz, City (pop., 2001 prelim.: 793,217), central Poland. Located southwest of Warsaw, it was a village in the 14th century and gained municipal rights in 1798. The Russian-ruled Congress Kingdom of Poland established it as a centre of the textile industry in 1820, and by the late 19th century it was Poland's leader in the production of cotton textiles. It was occupied by the Germans during World Wars I and II. It is now a cultural centre and Poland's second largest city.

logarithm, In mathematics, the power to which a base must be raised to yield a given number (e.g., the logarithm to the base 3 of 9, or $\log_3 9$, is 2, because $3^2 = 9$). A common logarithm is a logarithm to the base 10. Thus, the common logarithm of 100 (log 100) is 2, because $10^2 = 100$. Logarithms to the base e, in which $e = 2.71828...$, called natural logarithms (ln), are especially useful in calculus. Logarithms were invented to simplify cumbersome calculations, since exponents can be added or subtracted to multiply or divide their bases. These processes have been further simplified by the incorporation of logarithmic functions into digital calculators and computers.

logic, Study of inference and argument. Inferences are rule-governed steps from one or more propositions, known as premises, to another proposition, called the conclusion. A deductive inference is one that is intended to be valid, where a valid inference is one in which the conclusion must be true if the premises are true. All other inferences are called inductive. In a narrow sense, logic is the study of deductive inferences. In a still narrower sense, it is the study of inferences that depend on concepts that are expressed by the "logical constants," including: (1) propositional connectives such as "not," (symbolized as ¬), "and" (symbolized as ∧), "or" (symbolized as ∨), and "if-then" (symbolized as ⊃), (2) the existential and universal quantifiers, "(∃x)" and "(∀x)," often rendered in English as "There is an x such that ..." and "For any (all) x, ...," respectively, (3) the concept of identity (expressed by "="), and (4) some notion of predication. The study of the logical constants in (1) alone is known as the propositional calculus; the study of (1) through (4) is called first-order predicate calculus with identity. The logical form of a proposition is the entity obtained by replacing all nonlogical concepts in the proposition by variables. The study of the relations between such uninterpreted formulas is called formal logic.

logical positivism, Early school of analytic philosophy, inspired by David Hume, the mathematical logic of Bertrand Russell and Alfred North Whitehead, and Ludwig Wittgenstein's *Tractatus* (1921). The school, formally instituted at the University of Vienna in a seminar of Moritz Schlick (1882–1936) in 1922, continued there as the Vienna Circle until 1938. It proposed several revolutionary theses: (1) All meaningful discourse consists either of (a) the formal sentences of logic and mathematics or (b) the factual propositions of the special sciences; (2) Any assertion that claims to be factual has meaning only if it is possible to say how it might be verified; (3) Metaphysical assertions, including the pronouncements of religion, belong to neither of the two classes of (1) and are therefore meaningless. Some logical positivists, notably A.J. Ayer, held that assertions in ethics (e.g., "It is wrong to steal") do not function logically as statements of fact but only as expressions of the speaker's feelings of approval or disapproval toward some action.

logistics, In military science, all the activities of armed-force units in support of combat units, including transport, supply, communications, and medical aid. The term, first used by Henri Jomini, Alfred Thayer Mahan, and others, was adopted by the U.S. military in World War I and gained currency in other nations in World War II. Its importance grew in the 20th century with the increasing complexity of modern warfare. The ability to mobilize large populations has escalated military demands for supplies and provisions, and sophisticated technology has added to the cost and intricacy of weapons, communications systems, and medical care, creating the need for a vast network of support systems. In World War II, for instance, only about 3 in 10 U.S. soldiers served in a combat role.

logos (Greek: "word," "reason," "plan") In Greek philosophy and theology, the divine reason that orders the cosmos and gives it form and meaning. The concept is found in the writings of Heracleitus (6th century BC) and in Persian, Indian, and Egyptian philosophical and theological systems as well. It is particularly significant in Christian theology, where it is used to describe the role of Jesus as the principle of God active in the creation and ordering of the cosmos and in the revelation of the divine plan of salvation. This is most clearly stated in the Gospel of John the Apostle, which identifies Christ as the Word (Logos) made flesh.

Lohengrin, Hero-knight of medieval Germanic legends. He was called the knight of the swan because he arrived in a boat drawn by a swan to help a noble lady in distress. He married her but forbade her to ask his origin; when she forgot this promise, he left her, never to return. The first version of his legend appeared *c.* 1210 in Wolfram von Eschenbach's *Parzival*, in which the swan knight was the son and heir of Parzival (Perceval). The anonymous 15th-century epic *Lorengel* provided the basis for Richard Wagner's opera *Lohengrin* (1850).

Loire River, River, southeastern France. The longest river in France, it flows north and west for 634 mi (1,020 km) to the Bay of Biscay, which it enters through a wide estuary below Saint-Nazaire. Embankments were built as early as the 12th century, and in subsequent centuries it was used extensively for the transport of goods. A canal system built in the 17th and 18th centuries is inadequate for modern vessels.

Loki, In Norse mythology, a trickster who was able to change his shape and sex. His father was the giant Fárbauti, but he was included among the Aesir, a tribe of the gods. A companion of the great gods Odin and Thor, Loki helped them with his clever plans but sometimes embarrassed them. He also appeared as the enemy of the gods, entering their banquets uninvited and demanding drink. After causing the death of the god Balder, he was punished by being bound to a rock. Loki created a female, Angerboda, with whom he produced three evil progeny: Hel, the goddess of death; Jörmungand, the evil serpent surrounding the world; and Fenrir, the wolf.

Lomond, Loch, Lake, Scotland. Located at the southern edge of the Highlands, it is the country's largest lake 24 mi (39 km) long and 0.75 to 5 mi (1.2 to 8 km) wide, with an area of 27 sq mi (70 sq km). It drains by the short River Leven into the Firth of Clyde at Dumbarton. Its eastern shore near Ben Lomond is the region made famous by the outlaw Rob Roy.

London, officially GREATER LONDON, Capital and largest city (pop., 2006 est.: 7,517,700) of the United Kingdom, situated in southeastern England on the River Thames. It is the political, industrial, cultural, and financial centre of the country. Formally known as the metropolitan county of Greater London (established 1965), it has an area of 659 sq mi (1,706 sq km) and consists of two regions: Inner London comprises 14 of London's 33 boroughs (including the original City of London), and Outer London encompasses the other 19 boroughs. Greater London is an administrative entity, with an elected mayor and assembly. Founded by the Romans as Londinium in the 1st century CE, it passed to the Saxons in the 5th–6th century. The Danes invaded England and London in 865. Following the Norman Conquest (1066), William I (the Conqueror) established the central stronghold of the fortress known as the Tower of London. Norman kings selected Westminster as their seat of government. The church known as Westminster Abbey had been built earlier by Edward the Confessor. The largest city in Europe north of the Alps by 1085, it was struck by the Black Death in 1348–49. Trade grew significantly in the mid-16th century, fueled by the establishment of Britain's overseas empire. In 1664–65 the plague killed about 70,000 Londoners, and in 1666 the Great Fire of London consumed five-sixths of the City of London; it was afterward rebuilt. London was the centre of world trade from the late 18th century to 1914. It opened the world's first electric underground railway in 1890. Severely damaged by German bombs in the Battle of Britain during World War II, it was again rebuilt and grew rapidly in the postwar period. Among its sites of interest are Buckingham Palace, the Tate galleries, the National Gallery, the British Museum, and the Victoria and Albert Museum.

London, City (pop., 2001: metro. area, 432,451), southeastern Ontario. It lies on the Thames River, near several of the Great Lakes. Its name and site were chosen in 1792 for the location of a capital of Upper Canada, but the plans failed to materialize. First settled in 1826, it was incorporated as a city in 1855. It became an important transportation and industrial centre as a result of its interlake location. It is the seat of the University of Western Ontario.

London, Treaty of (April 1915) Secret treaty between neutral Italy and the Allied forces of France, Britain, and Russia to bring Italy into World War I. The Allies wanted Italy's participation because of its border with Austria. Italy was promised Trieste, southern Tyrol, northern Dalmatia, and other territories in return for a pledge to enter the war within a month. Despite the opposition of most Italians, who favoured neutrality, Italy joined the war against Austria-Hungary in May.

London Bridge, Any of several successive structures spanning the River Thames. The Old London Bridge of nursery-rhyme fame was built by Peter of Colechurch between 1176 and 1209, replacing an earlier timber bridge. Because of obstructions encountered in building the cofferdams, the arch spans varied from 15 to 34 ft (4.6–10.4 m); the uneven construction resulted in frequent need for repair, but the bridge survived more than 600 years. Its roadway was loaded with a jumble of houses and shops, many projecting out over the river. It was demolished and replaced in the 1820s by New London Bridge, designed and built by John Rennie, Sr. (1761–1821), and his son John Rennie, Jr. (1794–1874). In the 1960s it was again replaced; the old masonry facing was dismantled and reerected at Lake Havasu City, Ariz., as a tourist attraction.

London Naval Conference (Jan. 21–April 22, 1930) Conference held in London to discuss naval disarmament and review the treaties of the Washington Conference. Representatives of Britain, the U.S., France, Italy, and Japan agreed to regulate submarine warfare and to place limits on new construction of cruisers, destroyers, submarines, and other warships. A treaty limiting battleship size was not signed, and the treaties renewed in 1935 were canceled on the outbreak of World War II.

London Stock Exchange, London marketplace for securities. It was formed in 1773 by a group of stockbrokers who had been doing business informally in local coffeehouses. In 1801 its members raised money for construction of a building in Bartholomew Lane; they established rules for the exchange the following year. In 1973 the London Stock Exchange merged with several regional

British stock exchanges. In 1991 the exchange replaced its governing council with a board of directors, and it became a public limited company.

long jump, or BROAD JUMP, Track-and-field sport consisting of a horizontal jump for distance. It was formerly performed from both standing and running starts, as separate events, but the standing long jump is no longer included in major competitions. The running long jump was an event in the Olympic Games of 708 BC and in the modern Games from 1896. In 1948 the women's long jump became an Olympic event.

Long March (1934–35) Trek of 6,000 mi (10,000 km) by Chinese Communists, resulting in the relocation of their revolutionary base from southeastern China to northwestern China and the emergence of Mao Zedong as their undisputed leader. Having withstood four of Chiang Kai-shek's campaigns against their base area, the Communists were nearly defeated by his fifth attack. The remaining 85,000 troops broke through Nationalist lines and fled first westward under Zhu De and then north under Mao. By the time Mao arrived at Shaanxi, he was followed by only about 8,000 survivors, most of the rest having been killed by fighting, disease, and starvation (among the casualties were Mao's two children and a brother). At their new base the Communists were able to build up their strength at a safe remove from the Nationalists in preparation for their eventual victory in 1949.

Long Parliament, Session of the English Parliament summoned in November 1640 by Charles I, so named to distinguish it from the Short Parliament of April–May 1640. Charles called the session to raise the money needed for his war against the Scots. Resistant to Charles's demands, the Parliament caused the king's advisers to resign and passed an act forbidding its own dissolution without its members' consent. Tension between the king and Parliament increased until the English Civil War broke out in 1642. After the king's defeat (1646), the army, led by Thomas Pride, exercised political power and in 1648 expelled all but 60 members of the Long Parliament. The remaining group, called the Rump, brought Charles to trial and execution (1649); it was forcibly ejected in 1653. In 1659, after the end of Oliver Cromwell's protectorate, the Parliament was reestablished; those who were excluded in 1648 were restored to membership. The Parliament dissolved itself in 1660.

longbow, Leading missile weapon of the English from the 14th century into the 16th century. Probably of Welsh origin, it was usually 6 ft (2 m) tall and shot arrows more than a yard long. The best were made of yew, might require a force of 100 lbs (45 kg) to draw, and had an effective range of 200 yards (180 m). English archers used longbows in the Hundred Years' War, and the weapon played an important role in the battles of Crécy, Poitiers, and Agincourt.

Longmen caves, or LUNG-MEN CAVES, Series of Chinese cave temples carved into the rock of a high riverbank south of Luoyang, in Henan province. Construction began late in the Northern Wei dynasty (386–534/535 CE) and continued sporadically through the 6th century and the Tang dynasty. Delicately crafted to create ethereal effects in stone, the temples contain images of the Buddha clothed as a Chinese scholar. Work at Longmen culminated in 672–675 with the construction of a monumental shrine known as Fengxian Si, which includes a seated Buddha more than 56 ft (17 m) high.

longship, or VIKING SHIP, Sail-and-oar vessel widely used in northern Europe for more than 1,500 years. It was a 45–75-ft (14–23-m) galley with up to 10 oars on a side, a square sail, and a 50–60-man capacity. Double-ended and built with overlapped planks, it was exceptionally sturdy in high seas. Examples have been found from as early as 300 BC. It carried the Vikings on their piratical raids of the 9th century and bore Leif Eriksson to America in 1000. Dutch, French, English, and German merchants and warriors also used it.

Lords, House of, Upper house of Britain's bicameral Parliament. From the 13th and 14th centuries it was the house of the aristocracy. Until 1999 its membership included clergy, hereditary peers, life peers (peers appointed by the prime minister since 1958), and the judges of the Supreme Court of Judicature (Britain's final court of appeal). Though it predates the House of Commons and dominated it for centuries, its power has gradually diminished. Its power to affect revenue bills was constrained by the Parliament Act of 1911, and in 1949 its power to delay by more than a year the enactment of any bill passed by the Commons was revoked. In 1999 the hereditary peers lost their right to sit in the House of Lords, though an interim reform retains their voice in a more limited fashion. The body's chief value has been to provide additional consideration to bills that may be not be well formulated.

Lord's Prayer, Prayer taught by Jesus to his disciples and used by all Christians as the basic prayer in common worship. It appears in two forms in the New Testament: a shorter version in Luke 11:2–4, and a longer version, part of the Sermon on the Mount, in Matthew 6:9–13. In both contexts it is offered as a model of how to pray. It is sometimes called the Pater Noster (Latin: "Our Father") for its first two words.

Loren, Sophia, orig. SOFIA VILLANI SCICOLONE (b. Sept. 20, 1934, Rome, Italy), Italian film actress. After a poverty-stricken childhood in war-torn Naples, she became a model and movie extra in Rome. Coached by the producer Carlo Ponti (later her husband), she acted in Italian movies from 1950, including *The Gold of Naples* (1954). Her later films, in which she became noted for her statuesque beauty and earthy femininity, include *The Black Orchid* (1959), *El Cid* (1961), *Two Women* (1961, Academy Award), *Boccaccio '70* (1962), *Yesterday, Today, and Tomorrow* (1964), *Marriage Italian Style* (1964), and *A Special Day* (1977).

Sophia Loren in Boccaccio '70 *(1962).*
Brown Brothers

Lorenz, Konrad (Zacharias) (b. Nov. 7, 1903, Vienna, Austria—d. Feb. 27, 1989, Altenburg), Zoologist and founder (with Nikolaas Tinbergen) of modern ethology. While still a schoolboy he nursed sick animals from the nearby zoo. In 1935 he first elucidated and demonstrated the phenomenon of imprinting in ducklings and goslings. He later examined the roots of human aggression (in the best-selling *On Aggression*, 1963) and the nature of human thought. His other popular works include *King Solomon's Ring* (1949) and *Man Meets Dog* (1950). He shared a 1973 Nobel Prize with Tinbergen and Karl von Frisch.

Los Angeles, City (pop., 2000: 3,694,820), southern California, U.S. The second largest city in the U.S., it is situated between the San Gabriel Mountains and the Pacific Ocean. Bisected by the Santa Monica Mountains, which separate the neighbourhoods of Hollywood, Beverly Hills, and Pacific Palisades from the San Fernando Valley, it is near the San Andreas Fault, and earthquakes are frequent. It began in 1771 as a Spanish mission; in 1781 settlers claimed the land as El Pueblo de los Angeles ("the Town of the Queen of the Angels"). Taken by U.S. forces in the Mexican War, it prospered in the wake of the 1849 gold rush. Incorporated in 1850, the city grew rapidly after the arrival of the railroads in 1876 and 1885. In 1913 an aqueduct was built to supply it with water from the slopes of the Sierra Nevada. It was struck by a major earthquake in 1994. Sites of interest include early Spanish missions, the Getty Museum, the Los Angeles County Museum of Art, and the Museum of Contemporary Art. Educational institutions include the University of Southern California, Occidental College, and the University of California at Los Angeles.

Lost Generation, Group of U.S. writers who came of age during World War I and established their reputations in the 1920s; more broadly, the entire post–World War I American generation. The term was coined by Gertrude Stein in a remark to Ernest Hemingway. The writers considered themselves "lost" because their inherited values could not operate in the postwar world and they felt spiritually alienated from a country they considered hopelessly provincial and emotionally barren. The term embraces Hemingway, F. Scott Fitzgerald, John Dos Passos, E.E. Cummings, Archibald MacLeish, and Hart Crane, among others.

lost-wax casting, Traditional method of producing molds for metal sculpture and other castings. It requires a positive, a core made of refractory material and an outer layer of wax. The positive can be produced either by direct modeling in wax over a prepared core (direct lost-wax casting), or by casting in a piece mold or flexible mold taken from a master cast. The wax positive is invested with a mold made of refractory materials and heated to melt the wax, leaving a narrow cavity between the core and the investment. Molten metal is poured into this cavity. When the metal has solidified, the investment and core are broken away.

lotus, Any of several different plants whose flowers have been given symbolic meaning by many cultures. The lotus of the Greeks is *Ziziphus lotus* (family Rhamnaceae), a shrub native to southern Europe; wine made from its fruit was thought to produce contentment and forgetfulness. The Egyptian lotus is a white water lily (*Nymphaea lotus*). The sacred lotus of the Hindus is an aquatic plant (*Nelumbo nucifera*) with white or delicate pink flowers; the lotus of eastern North America is *Nelumbo pentapetala*, a similar plant with yellow blossoms. *Lotus* is also a genus of the pea family, containing about 100 species found in temperate regions of Europe, Asia, Africa, and North America; the 20 or more species in North America are grazed by animals. The lotus is a common ornament in architecture, and since ancient times it has symbolized fertility, purity, sexuality, birth, and rebirth of the dead.

Lotus Sutra, Text central to the Japanese Tendai (Chinese Tiantai) and Nichiren sects of Mahayana Buddhism. It represents the Buddha as divine and eternal, having attained perfect enlightenment eons ago. All beings are invited to become fully enlightened Buddhas through the grace of innumerable bodhisattvas. Composed largely in verse, the sutra contains many charms and mantras. First translated into Chinese in the 3rd century AD, it was extremely popular in China and Japan, where the simple act of chanting it was thought to bring salvation.

Louis, Joe, in full JOSEPH LOUIS BARROW (b. May 13, 1914, Lafayette, Ala., U.S.—d. April 12, 1981, Las Vegas, Nev.), U.S. boxer. Louis was born into a sharecropper's family and only began boxing after the family moved to Detroit. He won the U.S. Amateur Athletic Union title in 1934 and turned professional that year. During his career he defeated six previous or subsequent heavyweight champions: Primo Carnera, Max Baer, Jack Sharkey, James J. Braddock, Max Schmeling, and Jersey Joe Walcott. Nicknamed "the Brown Bomber," Louis gained the world heavyweight championship by defeating Braddock in 1937 and held the title until 1949. Two of Louis's most famous bouts, those with the German boxer Max Schmeling, were invested with nationalist and racial implications, as Schmeling was seen, unfairly, as the embodiment of Aryanism and the Nazi party. Louis lost to Schmeling in 1936 but defeated him in one round in 1938, causing much

jubilation among Americans, and especially African Americans. He successfully defended his title 25 times (21 by knockout) before retiring in 1949. His service in the U.S. Army during World War II no doubt prevented him from defending his title many more times. He made unsuccessful comeback attempts against Ezzard Charles in 1950 and Rocky Marciano in 1951.

Louis XIII style, Style of the visual arts produced in France during the reign of Louis XIII, including the regency of his mother, Marie de Médicis, who introduced much of the art of her native Italy. The Mannerism of Italy and Flanders was so influential that a true French style did not develop until the mid-17th century, when the influence of Caravaggio was assimilated by Georges de La Tour and the Le Nain brothers, and the influence of the Carracci brothers was extended by Simon Vouet, who trained the academic painters of the next generation. The sculpture of the period was undistinguished. The most prolific area of the arts was architecture. Here, too, the Italian influence is seen, as in the Palais de Justice at Rennes and the Luxembourg Palace in Paris, both designed by Salomon de Brosse, and the chapel of the Sorbonne in Paris, designed by Jacques Lemercier. The furniture of the period is typically massive and solidly built and commonly decorated with cherubs, ornate scrollwork, fruit-and-flower swags, and grotesque masks.

Louis XIV, known as THE SUN KING (b. Sept. 5, 1638, Saint-Germain-en-Laye, France—d. Sept. 1, 1715, Versailles), King of France (1643–1715), ruler during one of France's most brilliant periods and the symbol of absolute monarchy of the Neoclassical age. He succeeded his father, Louis XIII, at age four, under the regency of his mother, Anne of Austria. In 1648 the nobles and the Paris Parlement, who hated the prime minister, Cardinal Mazarin, rose against the crown and started the Fronde. In 1653, victorious over the rebels, Mazarin gained absolute power, though the king was of age. In 1660 Louis married Marie-Thérèse of Austria (1638–83), daughter of Philip IV of Spain. When Mazarin died in 1661, Louis astonished his ministers by informing them that he intended to assume responsibility for ruling the kingdom. A believer in dictatorship by divine right, he viewed himself as God's representative on earth. He was assisted by his able ministers, Jean-Baptiste Colbert and the marquis de Louvois. Louis weakened the nobles' power by making them dependent on the crown. A patron of the arts, he protected writers and devoted himself to building splendid palaces, including the extravagant Versailles, where he kept most of the nobility under his watchful eye. In 1667 he invaded the Spanish Netherlands in the War of Devolution (1667–68) and again in 1672 in the Third Dutch War. The Sun King was at his zenith; he had extended France's northern and eastern borders and was adored at his court. In 1680 a scandal involving his mistress, the marchioness de Montespan (1641–1707), made him fearful for his reputation, and he openly renounced pleasure. The queen died in 1683, and he secretly married the pious marchioness de Maintenon. After trying to convert French Protestants by force, he revoked the Edict of Nantes in 1685. Fear of his expansionism led to alliances against France during the War of the Grand Alliance (1688–97) and the War of the Spanish Succession (1701–14). Louis died at age 77 at the end of the longest reign in European history.

Louis XIV style, Style of the visual arts produced in France during the reign of Louis XIV. In 1648 Charles Le Brun founded the Royal Academy of Painting and Sculpture, which rigidly dictated styles for the rest of the reign. The most influential painter was Nicolas Poussin, who forged the way for French Classicism. Sculpture reached a new zenith with the works of François Girardon and Pierre Puget. A national style in the decorative arts evolved through the Gobelin factory. Furniture was veneered, inlaid, heavily gilded, and commonly decorated with shells, satyrs, garlands, mythological heroes, and dolphins; the style is particularly associated with André-Charles Boulle. In architecture, Jean-Baptiste Colbert rigidly controlled the renovation of the Palace of Versailles, with landscaping by André Le Nôtre.

Louis XV style, Rococo style of French decorative arts during the reign of Louis XV, when artists produced exquisite decor for the homes of royalty and nobility. Emphasis was laid on the ensemble, so that paintings and sculptures became part of the decorative arts. The full range of richness in decorative techniques was represented—superb carving, ornamentation of all types of metal, inlay work in exotic woods, metal, mother-of-pearl, and ivory, and exquisite lacquered chinoiserie that rivaled products from East Asia. Fantasy joined nature and Asian themes in providing decorative motifs. Notable artists and designers include Jean-Honoré Fragonard, François Boucher, and Jean-Baptiste Oudry.

Louis XVI style, Style of the visual arts produced in France from *c.* 1760 to the French Revolution. The predominant style in painting, architecture, sculpture, and the decorative arts was Neoclassicism—a reaction against the excesses of the Rococo style and a response to Jean-Jacques Rousseau's call for "natural" virtue, as well as a response to the excavations at Pompeii and Herculaneum. The most prominent painter was Jacques-Louis David, whose severe compositions recalled the style of Nicolas Poussin. The foremost sculptor of the day was Jean-Antoine Houdon. The style in furniture was classical, yet workmanship was more complex than in any earlier period. Jean-Henri Riesener and other German craftsmen were among the most prominent cabinetmakers.

louse, human, Any of three types of sucking louse that infest humans. The body louse (mainly *Pediculus humanus humanus*, also called human louse or cootie) and head louse (*P.h. capitis*) are spread by person-to-person contact and through shared clothing, bedding, combs, and other personal items. Body lice carry the organisms that cause relapsing fever, trench fever, and typhus. Head lice may cause impetigo. Both are readily spread under conditions of overcrowding, especially among children. The crab louse, or pubic louse (*Phthirus pubis*), infests primarily the pubic region and occasionally other hairy regions. Its first pair of legs is smaller than the other two pairs, making it look like a crab. Crab lice are transmitted primarily through sexual intercourse. Lice infestations can be quickly cured with shampoos, soaps, and lotions containing benzene hexachloride, along with the thorough washing of bedding and clothing.

*Male human louse (*Pediculus humanus*), magnified about 15¹/₂ ×.*
William E. Ferguson

Louvre Museum, National museum and art gallery of France, in Paris. It was built as a royal residence, begun under Francis I in 1546 on the site of a 12th-century fortress. It ceased to be used as a palace when the court moved to Versailles in 1682, and plans were made in the 18th century to turn it into a public museum. In 1793 the revolutionary government opened the Grand Gallery; Napoleon built the northern wing; and two major western wings were completed and opened by Napoleon III. The completed Louvre included a vast complex of buildings forming two main quadrilaterals and enclosing two large courtyards. A controversial steel-and-glass pyramid entrance designed by I.M. Pei opened in 1989. The painting collection is one of the richest in the world, representing all periods of European art up to Impressionism; its collection of French 15th–19th-century paintings is unsurpassed.

lovebird, Any of nine species of small parrots (genus *Agapornis,* subfamily Psittacinae) of Africa and Madagascar. Popular as pets for their pretty colours and the seemingly affectionate closeness of pairs, lovebirds are 4–6 in. (10–16 cm) long, chunky, and short-tailed. Most have a red bill and a prominent eye ring. The two sexes look alike. Large flocks forage in woods and scrublands for seeds and may damage crops. Hardy and long-lived, they are combative toward other birds and have a loud, squawky voice. Though not easy to tame, they can be taught to perform tricks and mimic human speech to a limited extent.

*Lovebirds (*Agapornis personata*).*
Toni Angermayer

Lovelace, Ada King, countess of, orig. AUGUSTA ADA BYRON, LADY BYRON (b. Dec. 10, 1815, London, Eng.—d. Nov. 29, 1852, London), English mathematician. Her father was the poet Lord Byron. In 1835 she married William King, 8th Baron King; when he was created an earl in 1838, she became countess of Lovelace. Having studied with the famous mathematician-logician Augustus De Morgan, she was introduced to Charles Babbage's Difference Engine (calculator) and studied plans for his Analytical Engine (computer) as early as 1833. In 1843 she translated and annotated an article about the Analytical Engine by Italian mathematician Luigi Federico Menabrea. In correspondence with Babbage, she also described how the Analytical Engine could be "programmed" to calculate certain numbers; this work has been called the first computer program, and in consequence she has been called the first computer programmer. Ada, a computer programming language, is named for her.

Low Countries, Coastal region, northwestern Europe, consisting of Belgium, the Netherlands, and Luxembourg. Known as the Low Countries because much of the land along the North Sea is below or at sea level, they are often called the Benelux countries, from the initial letters of their names.

LSD, in full LYSERGIC ACID DIETHYLAMIDE, Highly potent hallucinogenic drug. An organic compound, LSD can be derived from the alkaloids ergotamine and ergonovine, found in the ergot fungus, but most LSD is produced synthetically. It can block the action of the neurotransmitter serotonin and produces marked deviations from normal perceptions and behaviour lasting 8–10 hours or longer. Mood shifts, time and space distortions, and impulsive behaviour may progress to paranoia and aggression. Flashbacks to LSD-induced hallucinations can occur years later. LSD is not an approved drug, and no clinically valuable uses have been found for it.

Lu Xun, or LU HSÜN, orig. ZHOU SHUREN (b. Sept. 25, 1881, Shaoxing, Zhejiang province, China—d. Oct. 19, 1936, Shanghai), Chinese writer. He became associated with the nascent Chinese literary movement in 1918 (part of the larger May Fourth Movement), when he published his short story "Diary of a Madman," a condemnation of traditional Confucian culture and the first Western-style story written wholly in Chinese. Though best known for his fiction, he was also a master of the prose essay, a vehicle he used especially late in life. He never joined the Communist Party himself, but he recruited many of his countrymen to communism and came to be considered a revolutionary hero.

Luanda, or LOANDA, City (pop., 2004 est.: 2,783,000), capital of Angola. Situated on the Atlantic coast, it is Angola's largest city and its second busiest seaport. Founded in 1576 by Paulo Dias de

Novais, it became the administrative centre for the colony of Angola in 1627. It was a major outlet for slave traffic to Brazil until the 19th century. It is a commercial and industrial area, with oil-refining capacity. It is the seat of the University of Luanda; the old fortress of São Miguel lies beyond the port. It was damaged during the persistent Angolan civil war that ended in 2002.

Lübeck, City (population 2002 est.: 213,486), northern Germany. Founded on the site of a Slavic settlement in 1143, it developed as a trading post. It became a free city in 1226 and the seat of the Hanseatic League in 1358. It declined after the 16th century, and its trade was ruined during the Napoleonic Wars. It revived after the Elbe-Lübeck canal was built in 1900. Its status as a self-governing entity ended in 1937, when the Nazis made it part of the Prussian province of Schleswig-Holstein. It is one of Germany's largest Baltic ports. Historic sites include a 12th-century cathedral and several Gothic churches.

Lublin, City (pop., 2000 est.: 355,803), eastern Poland, situated on the Bystrzyca River. Founded as a stronghold in the late 9th century, the settlement received town rights in 1317. In 1795 it passed to Austria and in 1815 to Russia. In 1918 the first independent temporary Polish government was proclaimed in Lublin. In World War II the Nazi concentration camp Majdanek was established in one of its suburbs. After the war Lublin served briefly as the seat of the national government. It is now an industrial and cultural centre for southeastern Poland.

Lubumbashi, formerly (until 1966) ELISABETHVILLE, City (pop., 2005 est.: 1,102,000), Democratic Republic of the Congo. It was established by Belgian colonists in 1910 near the border with Zambia and grew to become the centre of one of the world's largest copper mining and smelting operations. It was the centre of Katanga province's secession movement in the early 1960s.

Lucas, Robert E., Jr. (b. Sept. 15, 1937, Yakima, Wash., U.S.), U.S. economist. He studied at the University of Chicago and began teaching there in 1975. He questioned the influence of John Maynard Keynes in macroeconomics and the efficacy of government intervention in domestic affairs. He criticized the Phillips curve for failing to provide for the dampened expectations of companies and workers in an inflationary economy. His theory of rational expectations, which suggests that individuals may alter the expected results of national fiscal policy by making private economic decisions based on anticipated results, won him the 1995 Nobel Prize.

Lucerne, German LUZERN, City (pop., 2000: 59,496), central Switzerland. Located southwest of Zürich, on Lake Lucerne and its Reuss River outlet, it developed around an 8th-century monastery. It joined the Swiss Confederation in 1332. A stronghold of Catholicism during the Reformation, it later took part in the Sonderbund war. It is a tourist centre, with its medieval walls, towers, and covered bridges. Among its many monuments is the famous *Lion of Lucerne,* carved in rock, which commemorates the Swiss Guards slain while defending the Tuileries Palace in Paris in 1792.

Lucifer, In classical mythology, the morning star (the planet Venus at dawn), personified as a male figure. Lucifer (Latin: "Light-Bearer") carried a torch and served as herald of the dawn. In Christian times, Lucifer came to be regarded as the name of Satan before his fall; it was thus used by John Milton in *Paradise Lost.*

Lucknow, City (pop., 2001: 2,185,927), capital of Uttar Pradesh state, northern India. It is located on the Gomati River southeast of Delhi. It was captured by the Mughal ruler Bābur in 1528 and under his grandson Akbar became part of Oudh province. In 1775 it became the capital of Oudh. Lucknow is now an important rail centre with paper factories and other industrial development. Notable sites include the Great Imambara (tomb) of one of the nabobs of Oudh, the Residency where the British were besieged during the Indian Mutiny of 1857, and the University of Lucknow.

Lucy, Nickname for a remarkably complete (40% intact) hominin skeleton found by Donald Johanson at Hadar, Eth., in 1974 and dated to 3.2 million years ago. The specimen is usually classified as *Australopithecus afarensis* and suggests—by having long arms, short legs, an apelike chest and jaw, and a small brain but a relatively humanlike pelvis—that bipedal locomotion preceded the development of a larger (more humanlike) brain in hominin evolution. Lucy stood about 3 ft 7 in. (109 cm) tall and weighed about 60 lbs (27 kg).

Luddite, Member of organized groups of early 19th-century English craftsmen who surreptitiously destroyed the textile machinery that was replacing them. The movement began in Nottingham in 1811 and spread to other areas in 1812. The Luddites, or "Ludds," were named after a probably mythical leader, Ned Ludd. They operated at night and often enjoyed local support. Harsh repressive measures by the government included a mass trial at York in 1813 that resulted in many hangings and banishments. The term Luddite was later used to describe anyone opposed to technological change.

Lugano, Lake, or LAGO CERESIO, Lake in Switzerland and Italy, located between Maggiore and Como lakes. Straddling the border of the two countries, it has an area of 19 sq mi (49 sq km) and a maximum depth of 945 ft (288 m). Between Melide and Bissone, the lake is so shallow that a stone dam across it carries the St. Gotthard railway. The resort town of Lugano, on its shores in Switzerland, is Italian in appearance.

Lake Lugano, near Lugano, Switz.
R.G. Everts—Rapho/Photo Researchers

lugeing, Sled racing using a small sled that is ridden in a supine position. The sled, called a luge, is steered with the feet and subtle shoulder movements. Dating back to the 15th century, lugeing is a traditional winter sport in Austria and is also practiced in other countries. The course used is similar to that employed in bobsledding, and speeds above 90 mph (145 km/hr) are not uncommon. Lugeing became a Winter Olympics sport in 1964.

luminescence, Emission of light by an excited material through a process not caused solely by a rise in temperature. The excitation is usually achieved with ultraviolet radiation, X-rays, electrons, alpha particles, electric fields, or chemical energy. The colour, or wavelength, of the light emitted is determined by the material, while the intensity depends on both the material and the input energy. Examples of luminescence include light emissions from neon lamps, luminescent watch dials, television and computer screens, fluorescent lamps, and fireflies.

Luna, Any of a series of unmanned Soviet lunar probes, launched between 1959 and 1976, responsible for various lunar "firsts." Luna 2 (1959) was the first spacecraft to strike the Moon; Luna 3 (1959) was the first to circle the Moon and took the first photographs of its far side. Luna 9 (1966) made the first successful lunar soft landing. Luna 16 (1970) was the first unmanned spacecraft to carry lunar soil samples back to Earth. Luna 17 (1970) soft-landed a robot vehicle for exploration; it also contained television equipment and sent live pictures of several miles of the Moon's surface.

lung, Either of two light, spongy, elastic organs in the chest, used for breathing. Each is enclosed in a membrane (pleura). Contraction of the diaphragm and the muscles between the ribs draw air into the lungs through the trachea, which splits into two primary bronchi, one per lung. Each bronchus branches into secondary bronchi (one per lobe of lung), tertiary bronchi (one per segment of lung), and many bronchioles leading to the pulmonary alveoli. There oxygen in the inspired gas is exchanged for carbon dioxide from the blood in the surrounding capillaries. Adequate tissue oxygen supply depends on sufficient distribution of air (ventilation) and blood (perfusion) in the lungs. Lung injuries or diseases (e.g., emphysema, embolism, pneumonia) can affect either or both.

Lunyu, English ANALECTS, One of four Confucian texts that, when published together in 1190 by Zhu Xi, made up the Four Books. Scholars consider *Lunyu* the most reliable source of the doctrine of Confucius. It covers almost all the basic ethical concepts of Confucianism—for example, ren (benevolence), *junzi* (the superior man), Tian (Heaven), *zhong yong* (doctrine of the mean), *li* (proper conduct), and *zheng ming* (rectification of names). It also contains many direct quotations from Confucius and personal glimpses of the sage as recorded by his disciples.

Lupercalia, Ancient Roman festival held each February 15. Its origins are uncertain, but the likely derivation of its name from *lupus* (Latin: "wolf") may signal a connection with a primitive deity who protected herds from wolves or with the legendary she-wolf who nursed Romulus and Remus. Each Lupercalia began with the sacrifice of goats and a dog; two of its priests (Luperci) were then led to the altar and their foreheads were anointed with blood. After all had feasted, the Luperci cut thongs from the skins of the sacrificed animals and ran around the Palatine hill, striking at any woman who came near them; a blow from the thong was supposed to bestow fertility.

lupus erythematosus, Either of two inflammatory autoimmune diseases, both more common in women. In the discoid type, a skin disease, red patches with grayish brown scales appear on the upper cheeks and nose (often in a butterfly pattern), scalp, lips, and/or inner cheeks. Sunlight worsens it. Antimalarial drugs may help. The second type, systemic (disseminated) lupus erythematosus (SLE), may affect any organ or structure, especially the skin (with marks like those of the discoid type), kidneys, heart, nervous system, serous (moisture-forming) membranes (e.g., in synovial joints or lining the abdomen), and lymph nodes, with acute episodes and remissions. Symptoms vary widely. Kidney and central-nervous-system involvement can be life-threatening. Treatment includes pain relief, control of inflammation, and trying to limit damage to vital organs.

Lusaka, City (pop., 2005 est.: urban agglom., 1,260,000), capital of Zambia. In the 1890s the area was taken by the British South Africa Company during the formation of Northern Rhodesia; it became the capital in 1935. After the federation of Northern and Southern Rhodesia in 1953, it was a centre of the civil disobedience movement that led to the creation of the independent state of Zambia in 1960, with Lusaka as its capital. Possessing some light industry, it is also a commercial centre for the surrounding agricultural region. The University of Zambia (founded 1965) is located nearby.

Lusitania, British ocean liner sunk by a German submarine off the coast of Ireland on May 7, 1915. The British Admiralty had warned the *Lusitania* to avoid the area and to use the evasive tactic of zigzagging, but the crew ignored these recommendations. Though unarmed, the ship was carrying munitions for the Allies, and the Germans had circulated warnings that the ship would be sunk. The loss of life—1,198 people drowned, including 128 U.S. citizens—outraged public opinion. The U.S. protested Germany's action, and Germany limited its submarine campaign against Britain. When Germany renewed unrestricted submarine warfare, the U.S. entered World War I in April 1917.

lute, Plucked stringed instrument popular in 16th–17th-century Europe. It originated from the Arab *'ūd*, which reached Europe in the 13th century. Like the *'ūd*, the lute has a deep pear-shaped body with an ornamental sound-hole, a fretted neck with a bent-back pegbox, and strings hitched to a bridge glued to the instrument's belly. In later years it acquired several unstopped bass strings. It became the preferred instrument for cultivated amateur musicians and acquired an extensive literature of song accompaniments and solo and consort music.

Angel playing a lute, from "Presentation in the Temple," painted altarpiece by Vittore Carpaccio, 1510; in the Accademia, Venice
SCALA/Art Resource, New York

Luther, Martin (b. Nov. 10, 1483, Eisleben, Saxony—d. Feb. 18, 1546, Eisleben), German priest who sparked the Reformation. Luther studied philosophy and law before entering an Augustinian monastery in 1505. He was ordained two years later and continued his theological studies at the University of Wittenberg, where he became a professor of biblical studies. On a trip to Rome in 1510 he was shocked by the corruption of the clergy and was later troubled by doubts centring on fear of divine retributive justice. His spiritual crisis was resolved when he hit on the idea of justification by faith, the doctrine that salvation is granted as a gift through God's grace. He urged reform of the Roman Catholic Church, protesting the sale of indulgences and other abuses, and in 1517 he distributed to the archbishop of Mainz and several friends his Ninety-five Theses (according to legend, Luther nailed the theses to the door of the castle church in Wittenberg); the theses questioned Roman Catholic teaching and called for reform. In 1521 he was excommunicated by Pope Leo X and declared an outlaw at the Diet of Worms. Under the protection of the elector of Saxony, Luther took refuge in Wartburg. There he translated the Bible into German; his superbly vigorous translation has long been regarded as the greatest landmark in the history of the German language. He later returned to Wittenberg, and in 1525 he married the former nun Katherine of Bora, with whom he raised five children. Though his preaching was the principal spark that set off the Peasants' War (1524–25), his vehement denunciation of the peasants contributed to their defeat. His break with Rome led to the founding of the Lutheran Church; the Lutheran confession of faith or, Augsburg Confession, was produced with Luther's sanction by Philipp Melanchthon in 1530. Luther's writings included hymns, a liturgy, and many theological works.

Lutheranism, Protestant movement founded on the principles of Martin Luther. Lutheranism arose at the start of the Reformation, after Luther posted his Ninety-five Theses in Wittenberg. It spread through much of Germany and into Scandinavia, where it was established by law. It was brought to the New World by the colonists of New Netherland and New Sweden and spread through the U.S. Middle Atlantic states in the 18th century and the Midwest in the 19th century. Its doctrines are contained in the catechisms of Luther and in the Augsburg Confession. Lutheran doctrine emphasizes salvation by faith alone and the primacy of the Bible as the church's authority. The Lutheran ministry is one of service—not special status—and is described as the priesthood of all believers. Lutherans accept two sacraments (baptism and the Eucharist) and believe in predestination to salvation. The Lutheran World Federation is based in Geneva.

Lutuli, Albert (John Mvumbi) (b. 1898, Rhodesia—d. July 21, 1967, Stanger, S.Af.), Zulu chief and president of the African National Congress (1952–60). Trained at a mission school, Lutuli taught and served a small community as chief before being elected ANC president. He was frequently imprisoned for his anti-apartheid activities. He set forth his views in *Let My People Go* (1962). In 1960 he became the first African to be awarded the Nobel Prize for Peace.

Luxembourg, officially GRAND DUCHY OF LUXEMBOURG, Country, western Europe. Area: 999 sq mi (2,586 sq km). Population: (2011 est.) 517,000. Capital: Luxembourg. Most of the population is ethnically French or German, though there is a proportion of foreign residents, chiefly Portuguese, Italians, French, Belgians, and Germans. Languages: Luxembourgish, French, German. Religion: Christianity (predominantly Roman Catholic). Currency: euro. The country has a maximum length of 51 mi (82 km) and a maximum width of 35 mi (56 km). It is divided into two regions: the Oesling, an extension of the Ardennes Mountains in the northern third of the country consisting of a high plateau dissected by river valleys; and the Bon Pays, or Gutland, a rolling plateau that occupies the rest of the land. Luxembourg's economy is largely based on heavy industry and international trade and banking, and its per capita income is among the highest in the world. It is a constitutional monarchy with one legislative body; its head of state is the grand duke, and the head of government is the prime minister. At the time of Roman conquest (53 BCE), the area was inhabited by two Belgic tribes, the Treveri and the Mediomatrici. After 400 CE Germanic tribes invaded the region. It later came into Charlemagne's empire. Made a duchy in 1354, it was ceded to the house of Burgundy in 1443 and to the Habsburgs in 1477. In the mid-16th century it became part of the Spanish Netherlands. The Congress of Vienna in 1815 made it a grand duchy and awarded it to the Netherlands. After an uprising in 1830, its western portion became part of Belgium, while the remainder was held by the Netherlands. In 1867 the European powers guaranteed the neutrality and independence of Luxembourg. In the late 19th century it built a great steel industry by exploiting its extensive iron ore deposits. It was invaded and occupied by Germany in both World Wars. Following World War II, it abandoned its neutrality by joining NATO in 1949. It joined the Benelux Economic Union in 1944 and the European Coal and Steel Community, a forerunner of the European Economic Community, in 1952. Luxembourg ratified the Maastricht Treaty on European Union in 1992 and adopted the euro as its official monetary unit in 1999.

Luxembourg, City (pop., 2011 est.: 94,034), capital of Luxembourg. A rocky promontory along the Alzette River was the site of a Roman fortress and later of a Frankish castle, around which the medieval town developed. Siegfried, count of Ardennes, purchased this castle and made the duchy of Luxembourg independent in 963. The strongest in Europe after Gibraltar, the castle was garrisoned by the Prussians as a bulwark of the German Confederation (1815–66); it was dismantled by treaty in 1867. Long an important road and railway focus, the city is also an important industrial and financial centre. It is the seat of the European Court of Justice and several administrative offices of the European Union.

Luxemburg, Rosa (b. March 5, 1871, Zamość, Pol., Russian Empire—d. Jan. 15, 1919, Berlin, Ger.), Polish-born German political radical, intellectual, and author. As a Jew in Russian-con-

Rosa Luxemburg.
Interfoto/Friedrich Rauch, Munich

trolled Poland, she was drawn early into underground political activism. In 1889 she fled to Zürich, Switz., where she obtained her doctorate. Having become involved in the international socialist movement, in 1892 she cofounded what would become the Polish Communist Party. The Russian Revolution of 1905 convinced her that the world revolution would originate in Russia. She advocated the mass strike as the proletariat's most important tool. Imprisoned in Warsaw for agitation, she then moved to Berlin to teach and write (1907–14). Early in World War I she cofounded the Spartacus League, and in 1918 she oversaw its transformation into the German Communist Party; she was murdered during the Spartacus Revolt less than a month later. She believed in a democratic path to socialism after a world revolution to overthrow capitalism and opposed what she recognized as Vladimir Ilich Lenin's emerging dictatorship.

Luxor, Arabic AL-UQSUR, City (pop., 2006: 202,232), Upper Egypt. Its name has been given to the southern part of the ruins of Thebes (the northern part is called Karnak). It is centred on the Great Temple of Amon, which was built on the eastern bank of the Nile River by King Amenhotep III in the 14th century BC. Tutankhamen and Horemheb completed the temple, and Ramses II added to it. Ruins include pillars and courts of the original temple as well as the remains of Coptic churches and a mosque. The modern city serves as a tourist centre and as a market for the surrounding agricultural district. Luxor is part of a UNESCO World Heritage site (designated in 1979) centred on Thebes.

Lviv, or LVOV, City (pop., 2001: 733,000), western Ukraine. Founded *c.* 1256 by Prince Daniel of Galicia, it came under Polish rule in 1349. Lviv became one of the great medieval trading towns and changed hands many times. It was taken by the Cossacks in 1648 and by the Swedes in 1704. Given to Austria in 1772, it became the capital of the Austrian province of Galicia. It passed to Poland in 1919, after an unsuccessful attempt by Ukrainians to set up a republic (1918). It was seized by the Soviet Union in 1939 and, after German occupation, annexed by the Soviets in 1945. It is now a centre for Ukrainian culture and the seat of a university (founded 1661).

Lyme disease, Tick-borne bacterial disease. It was identified in 1975 and named for Old Lyme, Conn. It is caused by a spirochete, *Borrelia burgdorferi*, transmitted by ticks, which pick it up in the blood of infected animals, mostly deer. Humans can be bitten by ticks in tall grass or fallen leaves. Lyme disease has three stages: a target-shaped rash, often with flulike symptoms; migrating arthritic pain and neurological symptoms (disturbances to memory, vision, or locomotion); and crippling arthritis with symptoms like those of multiple sclerosis and sometimes with facial paralysis, meningitis, or memory loss. Most cases do not progress beyond the first stage, but those that do reach the third stage within two years. Prevention involves avoiding tick bites. Diagnosis can be difficult, especially if the initial rash is not noticed. Early antibiotic treatment can prevent progression. Advanced cases need more powerful antibiotics, and symptoms may recur.

lymph, Pale fluid that bathes tissues, maintaining fluid balance and removing bacteria. It enters the blood system at a vein under the collarbone that it reaches via channels and ducts, being driven through them mainly by surrounding muscle activity. The lymphatic organs (spleen and thymus) and lymph nodes filter out bacteria and other particles the lymph takes up from body tissues. Lymph contains lymphocytes and macrophages, the primary cells of the immune system.

lymph node, Small, rounded mass of lymphoid tissue contained in connective tissue. They occur all along lymphatic vessels, with clusters in certain areas (e.g., neck, groin, armpits). They filter bacteria and other foreign materials out of lymph and expose them to lymphocytes and macrophages that can engulf them; these cells multiply in response to accumulation of such materials, which is why lymph nodes swell during infections. The nodes also produce lymphocytes and antibodies, to be carried by lymph throughout the lymphatic system. In Hodgkin disease and other lymphomas, malignant lymph cells proliferate, causing lymph node enlargement. Other cancers often invade lymphatic vessels, which can carry cells from the tumour to lymph nodes, where they are trapped and grow into secondary tumours. Lymph nodes are therefore removed in cancer surgery to detect or prevent tumour spread.

lymphatic system, System of lymph nodes, vessels, and nodules and lymphoid tissue, including the thymus, spleen, tonsils, and bone marrow, through which lymph circulates and is filtered. Its primary function is to return proteins, waste products, and fluids to the blood; molecules too big to enter the capillaries pass through the more permeable walls of lymphatic vessels. Valves keep lymph flowing in one direction, more slowly than blood and at a lower pressure. The lymphatic system also has a role in the immune system. Nodes filter bacteria and foreign matter from lymph. Smaller nodules, which often produce lymphocytes, form in areas more exposed to such materials. They can merge and become permanent, as in the tonsils. Blockage of a lymph vessel may cause fluid to collect in the tissues, producing lymphedema (tissue swelling). Other lymphatic system disorders include lymphocytic leukemias and lymphoma.

lymphocyte, Type of leukocyte fundamental to the immune system, regulating and participating in acquired immunity. Each has receptor molecules on its surface that bind to a specific antigen. The two primary types, B cells and T cells, originate from stem cells in bone marrow and travel to lymphoid tissues. When a B cell binds to an antigen, it multiplies to form a clone of identical cells. Some of these, acted on by helper T cells, differentiate into plasma cells that produce antibodies against the antigen. Others (memory cells) multiply, providing long-term immunity to the antigen.

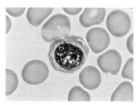

Human lymphocyte (phase-contrast microphotograph).
Manfred Kage/Peter Arnold

lymphoid tissue, Cells, tissues, and organs composing the immune system, including the bone marrow, thymus, spleen, and lymph nodes. The most highly organized components are the thymus and lymph nodes, and the least organized are the cells that wander in the loose connective-tissue spaces under membranes lining most body systems, where they can establish lymph nodules (local lymphocyte production centre) in response to antigens. The most common lymphoid tissue cell is the lymphocyte. Others are macrophages, which engulf foreign materials and probably

alter them to initiate the immune response, and reticular cells, which produce and maintain thin networks of fibres as a framework for most lymphoid organs.

lymphoma, Any of a group of malignant diseases that usually start in the lymph nodes or lymphoid tissues. The two major types, Hodgkin lymphoma and non-Hodgkin lymphoma, each have several subtypes. Diagnosis of either type requires biopsy, usually from the lymph nodes. Non-Hodgkin lymphomas may be diffuse (widespread) or nodular (concentrated in nodules); nodular lymphomas generally develop more slowly.

lynching, Execution of a presumed offender by a mob without trial, under the pretense of administering justice. It sometimes involves torturing the victim and mutilating the body. Lynching has often occurred under unsettled social conditions. The term derives from the name of Charles Lynch, a Virginian who headed an irregular court to persecute loyalists during the American Revolution. In the United States, lynching was widely used in the post-Reconstruction South against blacks, often to intimidate other blacks from exercising their civil rights.

lynx, Any of three species of short-tailed forest cat (genus *Lynx*) found in Europe, Asia, and northern North America. The North American lynx (*Lynx canadensis*) is regarded as distinct from the Eurasian and Spanish (Iberian) species. The lynx has long legs, large paws, tufted ears, hairy soles, and a broad, short head. Its coat, which forms a bushy ruff on the neck, is tawny to cream-coloured and mottled with brown and black. Its dense, soft winter fur has been used for trimming garments. Lynx are approximately 30–40 in. (80–100 cm) long, without the 4–8-in. (10–20-cm) tail, and stand about 24 in. (60 cm) high at the shoulder. They weigh 20–45 lb (10–20 kg). Nocturnal and silent except during mating season, lynx live alone or in small groups. They climb and swim well and feed on birds, small mammals, and occasionally deer. Some regional populations of lynx are considered endangered.

Lyon, English LYONS, City (pop., 2006 est.: city, 472,305; metro. area, 1,417,463), east-central France. Located at the confluence of the Rhône and Saône rivers, it was founded as the Roman military colony Lugdunum in 43 BC and became a principal city of Gaul. It was incorporated in 1032 into the Holy Roman Empire and in 1312 into the kingdom of France. It flourished economically in the 15th century, and by the 17th century it was the silk-manufacturing centre of Europe. It was a centre of the French Resistance movement during World War II. A major river port, it has a diversified economy, including textile, metallurgical, and printing industries. Its many ancient buildings include a Roman theatre, a 12th-century Gothic cathedral, and a 15th-century palace.

lyre, Stringed musical instrument consisting of a resonating body with two arms and a crossbar to which the strings extending from the resonator are attached. Lyrelike instruments existed in Sumer before 2000 BC. Greek lyres were of two types, the kithara and the lyra. The latter had a rounded body and a curved back—often a tortoiseshell—and a skin belly. It was the instrument of the amateur; professionals used the more elaborate kithara. In ancient Greece the lyre was an attribute of Apollo and symbolized wisdom and moderation. In medieval Europe new varieties of lyre emerged that, like the kithara, were box lyres, although their precise relation to the lyres of Classical antiquity is not known. The lyres of modern East Africa probably reflect ancient diffusion of the instrument via Egypt.

M

Maastricht Treaty, officially TREATY ON EUROPEAN UNION, Agreement that established the European Union (EU) as successor to the European Community. It bestowed EU citizenship on every national of its member states, provided for the introduction of a central banking system and a common currency, and committed the member states to work toward a common foreign and security policy. Signed in 1992, it was ratified and took effect in 1993.

Maat, In ancient Egyptian religion, the personification of truth, justice, and the cosmic order. Maat was the daughter of Re, the sun god, and she stood at the head of his bark as it traveled through the sky and the underworld. She was also associated with Thoth, the god of wisdom. The judgment of the dead was believed to be determined by the weighing of the heart of the deceased on a scale she balanced. In its abstract sense, *maat* was the divine order established at creation and reaffirmed at the accession of each new king of Egypt.

Mabinogion, Collection of 11 medieval Welsh tales based on mythology, folklore, and heroic legends. The tales have multiple authors and are versions of stories told and retold through the centuries. Among the finest are four stories known as "The Four Branches of the Mabinogi," written in the late 11th century. Some show Celtic, Norman, and French influence; "Peredur Son of Efrawg," for example, parallels Chrétien de Troyes's *Perceval*. Four other tales show little continental influence: "Kulhwch and Olwen," "Lludd and Llefelys," "The Dream of Macsen," and "The Dream of Rhonabwy."

macadamia, Any of about 10 species of ornamental evergreen trees, in the family Proteaceae, and their edible, richly flavoured dessert nuts. Macadamias originated in the coastal rainforests and scrubs of northeastern Australia. Those grown commercially in Hawaii and Australia are principally of two species, the smooth-shelled *Macadamia integrifolia* and the rough-shelled *M. tetraphylla*. Macadamias are grown in quantity also in parts of Africa and South and Central America. Hard to propagate and slow to bear fruit, the trees grow only in rich, well-drained soil in areas receiving 50 in. (130 cm) of rain annually. Fragrant pink or white flower clusters on trees with large, shiny, leathery leaves produce bunches of 1–20 fruits. The nuts contain much fat but are a good source of minerals and vitamin B.

Macadamia (Macadamia ternifolia)
Walter Dawn

macaque, Any of about 12 primarily Asian species of omnivorous, diurnal monkeys (genus *Macaca*) with cheek pouches for carrying food. Some species have long tails, some have short tails, and some have none. Males are 16–28 in. (41–70 cm) long (excluding the tail) and weigh 12–40 lb (5.5–18 kg). Troops live in mountains and lowlands and along shores. The rhesus monkey (*M. mulatta*) has been important to medical and psychological research. Malays train pig-tailed macaques (*M. nemestrina*) to pick coconuts.

Macau, or MACAO, Chinese AOMEN, Special administrative region, southern China. Area: 11.8 sq mi (30.6 sq km). Population: (2011 est.) 561,000. Located on the South China Sea coast about 40 mi (64 km) west of Hong Kong, it consists of a small peninsula, which projects from Guangdong province, and two small islands. Macau city is the administrative centre. Portuguese traders first arrived in Macau in 1513, and it soon became the chief market centre for trade between China and Japan. Portugal declared it an overseas province in 1844 and an overseas territory in 1951. In 1999 Portugal returned it to Chinese rule. Tourism and gambling are the mainstays of its economy.

macaw, Any of about 18 species of large tropical New World parrots (subfamily Psittacinae) with very long tails and big sickle-shaped beaks. Macaws eat fruits and nuts. They are easily tamed and often kept as pets; some learn to mimic human speech, but most only screech. A few have lived 65 years. Best known is the scarlet macaw (*Ara macao*), found from Mexico to Brazil, a 36-in. (90-cm) bright-red bird with blue and yellow wings, blue and red tail, and white face.

MacBride, Seán (b. Jan. 26, 1904, Paris, France—d. Jan. 15, 1988, Dublin, Ire.), Irish statesman. He was born to Irish patriots: his mother was William Butler Yeats's beloved Maud Gonne (1866–1953), and his father was Maj. John MacBride, executed for his part in the 1916 Easter Rising. Briefly chief of staff of the Irish Republican Army (1936–37), he founded Clann na Poblachta ("Party of the Republic") in 1946 and served in the Irish legislature (1947–58) and as minister of external affairs (1948–51). He was the first chairman of Amnesty International (1961–75). He also served as UN assistant secretary-general for South West Africa and Namibia (1973–77). In 1974 he was awarded the Nobel Prize for Peace for his efforts on behalf of human rights.

Macedonia, officially REPUBLIC OF MACEDONIA, Country, Balkan Peninsula, southeastern Europe. Area: 9,928 sq mi (25,713 sq km). Population: (2011 est.) 2,060,000. Capital: Skopje. Nearly two-thirds of the population are Macedonians, and about one-fourth are Albanians. Languages: Macedonian, Albanian. Religions: Christianity (predominantly Eastern Orthodox; also Roman Catholic), Islam. Currency: denar. Located on a high plateau studded with mountains, Macedonia is one of the poorest countries in Europe. Agriculture remains central to the economy, with tobacco, fruit, vegetables, and wine notable. Dairy farming is also significant. The manufacturing base includes ferronickel, sheet steel, automotive parts, electrical equipment, and clothing. Macedonia is a unitary multiparty republic with one legislative house; its head of state is the president, and the head of government is the prime minister. The Macedonian region has been inhabited since before 7000 BCE. Under Roman rule, part of the region was incorporated into the province of Moesia in 29 CE. It was settled by Slavic tribes by the mid-6th century and was Christianized during the 9th century. Seized by the Bulgarians in 1185, it was ruled by the Ottoman Empire from 1371 to 1912. The north and centre of the region were annexed by Serbia in 1913 and became part of the Kingdom of Serbs, Croats, and Slovenes (later Yugoslavia) in 1918. When Yugoslavia was partitioned by the Axis powers in 1941, Yugoslav Macedonia was occupied principally by Bulgaria. In 1946 Macedonia became one of the six constitutive republics of federal Yugoslavia. After Croatia and Slovenia seceded from Yugoslavia, fear of Serbian dominance prompted Macedonia to declare its independence in 1991. Because Greece, which also has a region traditionally known as Macedonia, has consistently opposed the international recognition of the Republic of Macedonia by its constitutional name, Macedonia was only able to join the United Nations in 1993 under the name The Former Yugoslav Republic of Macedonia. Greece has also prevented it from joining NATO and the European Union because of the "name dispute," which is the subject of ongoing negotiations under UN auspices. In 2001 ethnic strife endangered national stability when pro-Albanian rebel forces in the north, near the Kosovo border, led guerrilla attacks on government forces. Since then, however, relationships between Albanians and Macedonians have gradually improved.

Macedonian Wars, Three wars fought by Philip V of Macedonia and his successor, Perseus, against Rome (215–205 BC, 200–197, 171–167). The first war, fought by Rome in the context of the Second Punic War, ended favourably for the Macedonians. Rome was victorious in the next two wars. The Macedonian forces were assisted by Carthage and the Seleucids, Rome by the Aetolian League and Pergamum. After Rome's victory at the Battle of Pydna (168), Macedonian territory was divided into four republics. Another conflict, fought in 149–148, may be considered a fourth Macedonian War; it resulted in a decisive Roman victory, and in its aftermath Macedonia became the empire's first province.

Machiavelli, Niccolò (b. May 3, 1469, Florence—d. June 21, 1527, Florence), Italian statesman, historian, and political theorist. He rose to power after the overthrow of Girolamo Savonarola in 1498. Working as a diplomat for 14 years, he came in contact with the most powerful figures in Europe. He was dismissed when the Medici family returned to power in 1512, and during the next year he was arrested and tortured for conspiracy. Though soon released, he was not permitted to return to public office. His famous treatise *The Prince* (1513, published 1532) is a handbook for rulers; though dedicated to Lorenzo de' Medici, ruler of Florence from 1513, it failed to win Machiavelli his favour. Machiavelli viewed *The Prince* as an objective description of political reality. Because he viewed human nature as venal, grasping, and thoroughly self-serving, he suggested that ruthless cunning is appropriate to the conduct of government. Though admired for its incisive brilliance, the book also has been widely condemned as cynical and amoral, and "Machiavellian" has come to mean deceitful, unscrupulous, and manipulative. His other works include a set of discourses on Livy (completed *c.* 1518), the comedy *The Mandrake* (completed *c.* 1518), *The Art of War* (published 1521), and the *Florentine Histories* (completed *c.* 1525).

Niccolò Machiavelli, detail of an oil painting by Santi di Tito; in the Palazzo Vecchio, Florence.
Alinari/Art Resource, New York

machine gun, Automatic weapon capable of rapid, sustained fire, usually 500–1,000 rounds per minute. Developed in the late 19th century by such inventors as Hiram Maxim, it profoundly altered modern warfare. The World War I battlefield was dominated by the belt-fed machine gun, which remained little changed into World War II. Modern machine guns are classified into three groups: the squad automatic weapon, chambered for small-calibre assault-rifle ammunition and operated by one soldier; the general-purpose machine gun, firing full-power rifle ammunition and operated by two; and the heavy machine gun, firing rounds of 12.7 mm (.5 in) or higher and often mounted on an armoured vehicle.

machine language, or MACHINE CODE, Elemental language of computers, consisting of a string of 0s and 1s. Because machine language is the lowest-level computer language and the only language that computers directly understand, a program written in a more sophisticated language (e.g., C, Pascal) must be converted to machine language prior to execution. This is done via a compiler or assembler. The resulting binary file (also called an executable file) can then be executed by the CPU.

Mach's principle, Hypothesis that the inertial forces acting on a body in accelerated motion are determined by the quantity and distribution of matter in the universe. Albert Einstein found its suggested connection between geometry and matter helpful in formulating his theory of general relativity; unaware that George Berkeley had proposed similar views in the 18th century, he attributed the idea to Ernst Mach. He abandoned the principle when he realized that inertia is assumed in the geodesic equation of motion and need not depend on the existence of matter elsewhere in the universe.

Machu Picchu, Ancient fortress city of the Incas in the Andes Mountains, south-central Peru. Perched near Cuzco in a narrow saddle between two sharp peaks, at an elevation of 7,710 ft (2,350 m), it escaped detection by the Spaniards, and its existence was made known only in 1911 by U.S. explorer Hiram Bingham. One of the few pre-Columbian urban centres found nearly intact, it is about 5 sq mi (13 sq km) in area and includes a temple and a citadel. The period of occupancy is uncertain. Made a UNESCO World Heritage site in 1983, it is a popular tourist attraction.

Machu Picchu.
Mayes/FPG

Macleod, J(ohn) J(ames) R(ickard) (b. Sept. 6, 1876, Cluny, near Dunkeld, Perth, Scot.—d. March 16, 1935, Aberdeen), Scottish physiologist. He taught in U.S., Canadian, and Scottish universities, becoming noted for his work on carbohydrate metabolism. With Frederick Banting and Charles Best he discovered insulin, an achievement for which he and Banting shared a Nobel Prize in 1923.

macroeconomics, Study of the entire economy in terms of the total amount of goods and services produced, total income earned, level of employment of productive resources, and general behaviour of prices. Until the 1930s, most economic analysis focused on specific firms and industries. The aftermath of the Great Depression and the development of national income and production statistics brought new interest to the field of macroeconomics. The goals of macroeconomic policy include economic growth, price stability, and full employment.

macular degeneration, Degeneration of the macula (central part of the retina), with corresponding visual-field defect. It is the leading cause of blindness in old age. Probably due to reduced blood circulation, it is now known to have a genetic component. It is twice as common in smokers as in nonsmokers, and it is also correlated with lifelong sun exposure. Peripheral vision usually remains, but loss of central visual acuity makes reading or fine work difficult or impossible, even with special magnifying eyeglasses. Some forms of macular degeneration can be halted (but not reversed) by laser surgery.

Macumba, Afro-Brazilian religion characterized by the syncretism of traditional African religions, Brazilian spiritualism, and Roman Catholicism. Of the several Macumba sects in Brazil, the most important are Candomblé and Umbanda. African elements include an outdoor ceremonial site, the sacrifice of animals (e.g., cocks), spirit offerings (e.g., candles and flowers), and dances. Macumba rites are led by mediums, who fall prostrate in trances and communicate with holy spirits. Roman Catholic elements include the cross and the worship of saints, who are given African names.

mad cow disease, or BOVINE SPONGIFORM ENCEPHALOPATHY (BSE), Fatal neurodegenerative disease of cattle. Symptoms include behavioral changes (e.g., agitation), gradual loss of coordination and locomotive function, and, in advanced stages, weight loss, fine muscular contractions, and abnormal gait. Brain tissue becomes pitted with holes and spongy. Death usually follows within a year. The disease is similar to the neurodegenerative disease of sheep called scrapie. No treatment is known. A BSE epidemic in Britain that began in the mid-1980s is believed to have been caused by the use of cattle feed containing supplements made from ruminant carcasses and trimmings. Hundreds of thousands of infected cattle were slaughtered and the use of animal-derived protein supplements ended. The cause of both BSE and scrapie is attributed to an infectious aberrant protein called a prion. The unusual occurrence of Creutzfeldt-Jakob disease, another prion-related illness, in young people beginning in the mid-1990s may be linked to eating meat from cattle with BSE.

Madagascar, officially REPUBLIC OF MADAGASCAR, Country, occupying the island of Madagascar, in the western Indian Ocean off the southeast coast of Africa. The island is the world's fourth largest, about 975 mi (1,570 km) long and 355 mi (570 km) wide. It is separated from the African coast by the Mozambique Channel. Area: 226,658 sq mi (587,041 sq km). Population: (2011 est.) 21,307,000. Capital: Antananarivo. Almost all of the population belongs to about 20 Malayo-Indonesian groups. Languages: Malagasy, French, English. Religions: Christianity (Protestant, Roman Catholic), traditional beliefs, Islam. Currency: ariary. Madagascar's high central plateau rises to 9,436 ft (2,876 m) at the volcanic Tsaratanana massif; the island was once heavily forested, and forests still cover one-fifth of the land area. Agriculture dominates the economy; staple crops include rice, sugarcane, and cassava. Cash crops include cloves and vanilla. Aquaculture is also economically important. Madagascar is ruled by a transitional regime; its head of state and government is the president, assisted by the prime minister. Indonesians migrated to Madagascar c. 700 CE. The first European to visit the island was Portuguese navigator Diogo Dias in 1500. Trade in arms and slaves allowed the Malagasy kingdoms to develop at the beginning of the 17th century. In the 18th century the Merina kingdom became dominant; with British assistance, it gained control of a large part of Madagascar in the early 19th century. In 1868 Merina signed a treaty granting France commercial access to the northwestern coast, and in 1895 French troops took the island. Madagascar became a French overseas territory in 1946. In 1958 France agreed to let the territory decide its own fate; as the Malagasy Republic, it gained independence in 1960 and severed ties with France in the 1970s, taking the name Democratic Republic of Madagascar in 1975 (the word "Democratic" was dropped in 1992). Following a brief period of military rule, in 1975 Didier Ratsiraka became president, and he ruled for most of the next 25 years. In the wake of the serious political crisis sparked by the 2001 presidential election, Marc Ravalomanana emerged as president and Ratsiraka left the country. In 2009 Ravalomanana resigned under pressure from Andry Rajoelina and the military, and Rajoelina assumed the presidency of a transitional regime.

Madeira Islands, Island group (pop., 2001 prelim.: 242,603) and autonomous region of Portugal, in the North Atlantic Ocean. Madeira, the largest of the Madeira Islands, is the site of the region's capital, Funchal. Madeira Island is 34 mi (55 km) long and 14 mi (22 km) wide and has deep ravines and rugged mountains. Possibly known to ancient Phoenicians, it was rediscovered by the Portuguese navigator João Gonçalves Zarco, who founded Funchal in 1421. It allegedly had the world's first sugarcane plantation. Its Madeira wine has been an important export since the 17th century. Tourism is also important.

Madhya Pradesh, State (pop., 2008 est.: 69,279,000), central India. It is bordered by the states of Rajasthan, Uttar Pradesh, Chhattisgarh, Maharashtra, and Gujarat. Occupying an area of 119,016 sq mi (308,252 sq km), it is India's second largest state. Its capital is Bhopal. It is the source of some of the most important rivers of India, including the Narmada, the Tapti (Tapi), the Mahanadi, and the Wainganga. It was part of the Mauryan empire of the 4th–3rd centuries BCE and was ruled by numerous other dynasties. Under Muslim control from the 11th century CE, it was annexed by the Mughal Empire in the 16th century. It was under Maratha rule by 1760 and passed to the British early in the 19th century. The state was formed after India gained its independence in 1947; its boundaries were altered in 1956. In 2000 the eastern portion of the state was made into the state of Chhattisgarh. Though Madhya Pradesh is rich in mineral resources, its economic mainstay is agriculture.

Madhyamika, School in the Mahayana Buddhist tradition. Its name means "middle" and derives from its middle position between the realism of the Sarvastivada school and the idealism of the Yogacara school. The most renowned Madhyamika thinker was Nagarjuna.

Madison, James (b. March 16, 1751, Port Conway, Va.—d. June 28, 1836, Montpelier, Va., U.S.), Fourth president of the U.S. (1809–17). After graduating from the College of New Jersey (now Princeton University), he served in the Virginia state legislature (1776–80, 1784–86). At the Constitutional Convention (1787), his Virginia, or large-state, Plan furnished the Constitution's basic framework and guiding principles, earning him the title "father of the Constitution." To promote its ratification, he collaborated with Alexander Hamilton and John Jay on the Federalist papers, a series of articles on the Constitution and republican government published in newspapers in 1787–88 (Madison wrote 29 of the 85 articles). In the U.S. House of Representatives (1789–97), he sponsored the Bill of Rights. He split with Hamilton over the existence of an implied congressional power to create a national bank; Madison denied such a power, though later, as president, he requested a national bank from Congress. In protest of the Alien and Sedition Acts, he drafted one of the Virginia and Kentucky Resolutions in 1798 (Thomas Jefferson drafted the other). From 1801 to 1809 he was Jefferson's secretary of state. Elected president in 1808, he immediately faced the problem of British interference with neutral U.S. merchant vessels, which Jefferson's Embargo Act (1807) had failed to discourage. Believing that Britain was bent on permanent suppression of American commerce, Madison proclaimed nonintercourse with Britain in 1810 and signed a declaration of war in 1812. During the ensuing War of 1812 (1812–14), Madison and his family were forced to flee Washington, D.C., as advancing British troops burned the executive mansion and other public buildings. During Madison's second term (1813–17) the second Bank of the United States was chartered and the first U.S. protective tariff was imposed. He retired to his Virginia estate, Montpelier, with his wife, Dolley (1768–1849), whose political acumen he had long prized. He participated in Jefferson's creation of the University of Virginia, later serving as its rector (1826–36), and produced numerous articles and letters on political topics.

Madonna, In Christian art, a depiction of the Virgin Mary. Though often shown with the infant Jesus, the Madonna (Italian: "My lady") may also be represented alone. Byzantine art was the first to develop a set of Madonna types—the Madonna and child enthroned, the Ma-

The Grand-Duke's Madonna, *oil painting by Raphael, 1505; in the Pitti Palace, Florence.*
Scala/Art Resource, New York

donna as intercessor, the Madonna nursing the child, and so on. Western art adapted and added to the Byzantine types during the Middle Ages, producing images of the Virgin that sought to inspire piety through beauty and tenderness. In the Renaissance and Baroque periods, the most popular image of the Madonna foreshadowed the crucifixion, showing the Virgin looking gravely away from the playful child.

madrasah (Arabic: "school") Islamic theological seminary and law school attached to a mosque. The residential madrasah was a newer building form than the mosque, flourishing in most Muslim cities by the end of the 12th century. The Syrian madrasahs in Damascus tended to follow a standardized plan: An elaborate facade led into a domed hallway and then into a courtyard where instruction took place, with at least one *eyvan* (vaulted hall) opening onto it. The madrasah at the Qalaun Mosque in Cairo (1283–85) has a unique cruciform *eyvan* on the richly carved *qibla* (wall facing Mecca) side and a smaller *eyvan* opposite. Residential cells for scholars occupy the other two sides.

Madrid, City (pop., 2001: city, 2,938,723; metro. area, 5,086,635), capital of Spain and of Madrid autonomous community. Located on the central plateau of the Iberian Peninsula, 2,100 ft (635 m) above sea level, it is one of Europe's highest capitals. The original town grew up around the Moorish alcazar (castle), overlooking the Manzanares River. King Alfonso VI captured the town from the Muslims in 1083. Philip II moved the Spanish court to Madrid in 1561, and in 1607 Philip III made it the official capital. It was occupied by French troops during the Napoleonic Wars but returned to Spanish control in 1812. During the Spanish Civil War (1936–39), Madrid was held by those loyal to the Republic. Spain's principal transportation centre for the interior provinces, it is an important commercial, industrial, and cultural centre. Major institutions include the Prado Museum and the University of Madrid. On March 11, 2004, Madrid suffered a series of terrorist attacks when Islamist militants detonated bombs on commuter trains, killing 191 people and injuring some 1,800 others.

madrigal, Form of vocal chamber music, usually polyphonic and unaccompanied, of the 16th–17th centuries. It originated and developed in Italy, under the influence of the French chanson and the Italian *frottola*. Usually written for three to six voices, madrigals came to be sung widely as a social activity by cultivated amateurs, male and female. The texts were almost always about love; most prominent among the poets whose works were set to music are Petrarch, Torquato Tasso, and Battista Guarini. In Italy, Orlande de Lassus, Luca Marenzio, Don Carlo Gesualdo, and Claudio Monteverdi were among the greatest of the madrigalists; Thomas Morley, Thomas Weelkes, and John Wilbye created a distinguished body of English madrigals.

Maeterlinck, Maurice (Polydore-Marie-Bernard), later COMTE MAETERLINCK (b. Aug. 29, 1862, Ghent, Belg.—d. May 6, 1949, Nice, France), Belgian playwright and poet. He studied law in Ghent but soon turned to writing poems and plays. His *Pelléas et Mélisande* (1892), considered the masterpiece of Symbolist drama, was the basis of Claude Debussy's opera (1902). In his Symbolist plays, Maeterlinck used poetic speech, gesture, lighting, setting, and ritual to create images that reflect his protagonists' moods and dilemmas. His other writings include a collection of Symbolist poems (*Hothouses*, 1899) and plays such as *Monna Vanna* (1902), *The Blue Bird* (1908), and *The Burgomaster of Stilmonde* (1918). He was also noted for his popular treatments of scientific subjects, including *The Life of the Bee* (1901) and *The Intelligence of Flowers* (1907). Maeterlinck was awarded the Nobel Prize for Literature in 1911.

Maffei I and II, Two galaxies relatively close to the Milky Way Galaxy, first detected in the late 1960s by the Italian astronomer Paolo Maffei. Maffei I is a large elliptical galaxy, while Maffei II is a spiral galaxy. Though they are large and nearby, they are hidden in the Milky Way's zone of avoidance. At a distance of about 10 million light-years, they appear to be major members of one of the nearest galaxy groups outside the Local Group.

Mafia, Society of criminals of primarily Italian or Sicilian origin. The Mafia arose in Sicily in the late Middle Ages, possibly as a secret organization to overthrow the rule of foreign conquerors. It drew its members from the small private armies, or *mafie*, hired by landlords to protect their estates. By 1900 the Mafia "families" of western Sicily controlled their local economies. In the 1920s Benito Mussolini jailed most of the members, but they were released by the Allies after World War II and resumed their activities. In the 1970s their control of the heroin trade led to fierce rivalry among the clans, followed in the 1980s by renewed governmental efforts to imprison the Mafia leadership. In the U.S., Sicilian immigrants included former Mafia members who set up similar criminal operations. Their operations expanded from bootlegging in the 1920s to gambling, narcotics, and prostitution, and the Mafia, or Cosa Nostra, became the largest U.S. syndicated crime organization. About 24 Mafia groups or "families" controlled operations in the U.S.; the heads (or "dons") of the largest families formed a commission whose main function was judicial and could override a don's authority. At the beginning of the 21st century the Mafia's power was greatly diminished through convictions of top officials, defections, and murderous internal disputes.

Magdeburg, City (pop., 2002 est.: 229,755), capital of Saxony-Anhalt state, east-central Germany. Located on the Elbe River, it was a trading settlement as early as the 9th century, and by the 13th century it was a leading member of the Hanseatic League. It embraced the Reformation in 1524 and was governed by Protestant titular archbishops. In 1631, during the Thirty Years' War, it was burned and sacked. Captured by the French during the Napoleonic Wars, it soon passed to the Prussians, and in 1815 it became the capital of the province of Saxony. It was heavily bombed during World War II. One of Germany's most important inland ports, it is a railroad junction. The composer Georg Philipp Telemann was born there.

The cathedral at Magdeburg, Germany.
W. Krammisch/Bruce Coleman Inc.

Magellan, Ferdinand, Portuguese FERNÃO DE MAGALHÃES, Spanish FERNANDO DE MAGALLANES (b. *c.* 1480, Sabrosa, or Porto?, Port.—d. April 27, 1521, Mactan, Phil.), Portuguese navigator and explorer. Magellan was born to the nobility. From 1505 he served in expeditions to the East Indies and Africa. Having twice asked King Manuel I for higher pay and been refused, he went to Spain in 1517 and offered his services to King Charles I (later Emperor Charles V), proposing to sail west to the Moluccas (Spice Islands) to prove that they lay in Spanish rather than Portuguese territory. In 1519 he left Sevilla with five ships and about 270 men. He sailed around South America, quelling a mutiny on the way and discovering the Strait of Magellan. With three ships left, Magellan crossed the "Sea of the South," later called the Pacific Ocean because of their calm crossing. He was killed by inhabitants of Mactan Island in the Philippines, but two of his ships reached the Moluccas, and one, the *Victoria*, commanded by Juan Sebastián del Cano (1476?–1526), continued west to Spain, accomplishing the first circumnavigation of the world in 1522.

Magellan, Strait of, Spanish ESTRECHO DE MAGALLANES, Strait, linking the Atlantic Ocean and Pacific Ocean, between the southern tip of South America and Tierra del Fuego. It extends westward from the Atlantic between Cape Vírgenes and Cape Espíritu Santo and curves northwest at Froward Cape to reach the Pacific. Lying mostly within Chilean territorial waters, it is about 350 mi (560 km) long and 2–20 mi (3–32 km) wide. Named for Spanish navigator Ferdinand Magellan, the first European to pass there (1520), it remained an important shipping route until the Panama Canal opened in 1914.

Magellanic Cloud, Either of two irregular companion galaxies of the Milky Way Galaxy named for Ferdinand Magellan, whose crew discovered them during the first voyage around the world. They share a gaseous envelope and lie about 22° apart in the sky near the south celestial pole. They are visible to the unaided eye in the Southern Hemisphere but cannot be seen from most northern latitudes. The Large Magellanic Cloud is about 160,000 light-years from Earth, and the Small Magellanic Cloud is 190,000 light-years away. They are excellent laboratories for the study of the formation and evolution of stars.

Maggiore, Lake, ancient LACUS VERBANUS, Lake, northern Italy and southern Switzerland, bordered on the north by the Swiss Alps. Occupying an area of 82 sq mi (212 sq km), it is Italy's second largest lake. It is 34 mi (54 km) long, with a maximum width of 7 mi (11 km) and a maximum depth of 1,220 ft (372 m). Traversed from north to south by the Ticino River, it is also fed by the Tresa River from Lake Lugano on the east. It is a popular resort area.

Maghrib, or MAGHREB, Region of North Africa bordering the Mediterranean Sea. It comprises the coastal plains of Morocco, Algeria, Tunisia, and, often, Libya. In earlier times the term sometimes included parts of Muslim Spain. During Roman times the region was called Africa Minor, but, following the Muslim conquests of the 7th–8th centuries, it came to be known as the Maghrib ("West") inasmuch as it comprised the most westerly reaches of the Muslim world. The region has since developed its own unique culture within the larger Islamic world. Berbers and Arabs are the two main ethnic groups. Arabic is the predominant language. Berber and French are also widely spoken.

Magi, In Christian tradition, wise men from the East who came to pay homage to the infant Jesus. According to Matthew 2:1–12, they followed a miraculous guiding star to Bethlehem and brought gifts of "gold and frankincense and myrrh." Herod asked them to report the location of Jesus' birth on their return journey, but an angel warned them of his evil intentions. In later Christian tradition they were said to be kings and were given the names Melchior, Balthasar, and Gaspar. Their visit was seen as evidence that the Gentiles as well as the Jews would worship Jesus, and it is celebrated in the feast of Ephiphany. See photograph above.

magic, Use of means (such as charms or spells) believed to have supernatural power over natural forces. It constitutes the core of many religious systems and plays a central social role in many nonliterate cultures. Magic is often distinguished from religion as being more impersonal and mechanical and emphasizing technique. Its techniques are usually regarded as means to specific ends (an enemy's defeat, rainfall, etc.), although another view ascribes a more symbolic, expressive character to such activity. Thus, a rainmaking ritual may both elicit rainfall and stress the

The Adoration of the Magi, *oil painting by Albrecht Dürer, 1504; in the Uffizi, Florence.*
SCALA/Art Resource, New York

symbolic importance of rain and the agricultural activities associated with it. Both the magician and the magical rite are typically surrounded by taboos, purification procedures, and other activities that draw the participants into the magical sphere. Strains of magic in Western tradition, formerly associated with heretics, alchemists, witches, and sorcerers, persist in modern times in the activities of satanists and others. The art of entertaining by performing apparently magical feats (sometimes called conjuring) relies on the use of sleight of hand and other means.

magic realism, or MAGICAL REALISM, Latin-American literary phenomenon characterized by the matter-of-fact incorporation of fantastic or mythical elements into otherwise realistic fiction. The term was first applied to literature in the 1940s by the Cuban novelist Alejo Carpentier (1904–1980), who recognized the tendency of his region's contemporary storytellers as well as contemporary novelists to illuminate the mundane by means of the fabulous. Prominent practitioners include Gabriel Garcia Marquez, Jorge Amado, Jorge Luis Borges, Miguel Angel Asturias, Julio Cortazar, and Isabel Allende (born 1942). The term has been applied to literature and art outside of Latin America as well.

magma, Molten or partially molten rock from which igneous rocks form, usually consisting of silicate liquid. Magma migrates either at depth or to the Earth's surface, where it is ejected as lava. The interactions of several physical properties, including chemical composition, viscosity, content of dissolved gases, and temperature, determine the characteristics of magma. Numerous events that can occur during crystallization influence the resulting rock: separation of early crystals from liquid prevents reaction between them; magma can cool too rapidly for reaction to occur; and loss of volatiles may remove some components from the magma.

Magna Carta (Latin: "Great Charter") Document guaranteeing English political liberties, drafted at Runnymede, a meadow by the Thames, and signed by King John in 1215 under pressure from his rebellious barons. Resentful of the king's high taxes and aware of his waning power, the barons were encouraged by the archbishop of Canterbury, Stephen Langton, to demand a solemn grant of their rights. Among the charter's provisions were clauses providing for a free church, reforming law and justice, and controlling the behavior of royal officials. It was reissued with alterations in 1216, 1217, and 1225. Though it reflects the feudal order rather than democracy, the Magna Carta is traditionally regarded as the foundation of British constitutionalism.

magnesium, Chemical element, one of the alkaline earth metals, chemical symbol Mg, atomic number 12. The silvery white metal does not occur free in nature, but compounds such as the sulfate (Epsom salts), oxide (magnesia), and carbonate (magnesite) have long been known. The metal, which burns in air with a bright white light, is used in photographic flash devices, bombs, flares, and pyrotechnics; it is also a component of lightweight alloys for aircraft, spacecraft, cars, machinery, and tools. The compounds, in which it has valence 2, are used as insulators and refractories and in fertilizers, cement, rubber, plastics, foods, and pharmaceuticals (antacids, purgatives, laxatives). Magnesium is an essential element in human nutrition; it is the cofactor in enzymes of carbohydrate metabolism and in chlorophyll.

magnetic field, Region around a magnet, electric current, or changing electric field in which magnetic forces are observable. The field around a permanent magnet or wire carrying a steady direct current is stationary, while that around an alternating current or changing direct current is continuously changing. Magnetic fields are commonly represented by continuous lines of force, or magnetic flux, that emerge from north-seeking magnetic poles and enter south-seeking poles. The density of the lines indicates the magnitude of the field, the lines being crowded together where the magnetic field is strong. The SI unit for magnetic flux is the weber.

magnetic force, Attraction or repulsion that arises between electrically charged particles that are in motion. While only electric forces exist among stationary electric charges, both electric and magnetic forces exist among moving electric charges. The magnetic force between two moving charges is the force exerted on one charge by a magnetic field created by the other. This force is zero if the second charge is traveling in the direction of the magnetic field due to the first and is greatest if it travels at right angles to the magnetic field. Magnetic force is responsible for the action of electric motors and the attraction between magnets and iron.

magnetic resonance imaging (MRI), Computer production of images from magnetic resonance. The structural and biochemical information it provides is helpful in the diagnosis of abnormalities without the possibly harmful effects of X rays or gamma rays. It is invaluable in detecting and delineating tumours and in providing images of the brain, the heart, and other soft-tissue organs. MRI may produce anxiety because the patient must often lie quietly inside a narrow tube. Another disadvantage is that it requires a longer scanning time than other computer-assisted forms of scanning, which makes it more sensitive to motion and of less value in scanning the chest or abdomen. However, MRI images provide better contrast between normal and diseased tissue than those produced by other computer-assisted imagery.

magnetism, Phenomenon associated with magnetic fields, the effects of such fields, and the motion of electric charges. Some types of magnetism are diamagnetism, paramagnetism, ferromagnetism, and ferrimagnetism. Magnetic fields exert forces on moving electric charges. The effects of such forces are evident in the deflection of an electron beam in a cathode-ray tube and the motor force on a current-carrying conductor. Other applications of magnetism range from the simple magnetic door catch to medical imaging devices and electromagnets used in high-energy particle accelerators.

magnetosphere, Region around a planet (such as Earth) or a natural satellite that possesses a magnetic field where magnetic phenomena and the high atmospheric conductivity caused by ionization strongly influence the behaviour of charged particles. A planet or moon's magnetic field, like its gravitational field, becomes weaker with distance from the body. The solar wind sweeps a body's magnetosphere out away from the Sun in a "tail" trailing well beyond it.

magnitude, In astronomy, the measure of the brightness of a star or other celestial body. The brighter the object, the lower the number assigned as a magnitude. In ancient times six magnitude classes were used, the first containing the brightest stars. In the present system a difference of one magnitude is defined as a ratio of brightness of 2.512 times. Thus, a difference of five magnitudes corresponds to a brightness ratio of 100 to 1. Apparent magnitude is an object's brightness as seen from Earth (e.g., -26.7 for the Sun, about -11 for the Moon). Absolute magnitude is an object's brightness as it would be seen at a distance of 10 parsecs (32.6 light-years; e.g., 4.8 for the Sun).

magnolia, Any of about 240 species of trees and shrubs in the genus *Magnolia*, native to North and South America, the Himalayas, and East Asia. They are valued for their fragrant flowers and handsome leaves. *Magnolia* is one of two genera in the family Magnoliaceae, which contains 227 species. Magnolias are among the most primitive of flowering plants; their primitive features include long floral axes, spiral arrangement of flower parts, and simple water-conducting cells.

magus, Member of an ancient Persian clan specializing in cultic activities. The magi were a priestly caste during the Seleucid, Parthian, and Sasanian dynasties, and parts of the Avesta are probably derived from them. Their priesthood is believed to have served several religions, including Zoroastrianism. From the 1st century AD onward, the word magus in its Syriac form (*magusai*) was applied to magicians and soothsayers, chiefly from Babylonia. As long as the Persian empire lasted there was a distinction between the Persian magi, credited with profound religious knowledge, and the Babylonian magi, often considered outright imposters.

Magyar, Any member of the dominant ethnic group in Hungary. Speakers of a Finno-Ugric language, they migrated from their early home in the region of present-day Bashkortostan in eastern European Russia across the southern Russian and Ukrainian steppes into the northern Balkans in the 9th century. After collisions with neighbouring peoples, the Magyars crossed the Carpathians and settled in the middle basin of the Danube River in the late 9th century, subjugating Slavs and other peoples there. Skilled and fierce horsemen, they raided deep into the heart of Europe in the 10th century and were greatly feared until their defeat by Otto I at the Battle of Lechfeld in 955. They adopted Christianity in the 11th century under King Stephen I, the founder of Hungary, who made the kingdom part of the European community.

Mah-jongg, Game of Chinese origin usually played by four persons with 144 domino-like tiles that are drawn and discarded until one player secures a winning hand. The object of play is similar to that of the rummy card games. It is probably of 19th-century origin. The name was coined by J. P. Babcock, who introduced the game to the West after World War I. The mah-jongg set includes a pair of dice, a quantity of tokens or chips used for scorekeeping, and a rack for keeping tiles upright and keeping their faces hidden from other players.

Mahabharata, One of the two major Sanskrit epics of India, valued for its literary merit and its religious inspiration. It tells of the struggle for supremacy between two groups of cousins, the Kauravas and the Pandavas. Many myths and legends are woven into the poem, along with didactic material on topics such as the proper conduct of a warrior and the way to attain emancipation from rebirth. Together with the second major epic, the *Ramayana,* it is an important source of information about the evolution of Hinduism. Contained within the *Mahabharata* is the *Bhagavadgita,* Hinduism's single most important religious text. The sage Vyasa (fl. *c.* 5th century BC) is traditionally named as the *Mahabharata*'s author, but he probably compiled existing material. The poem reached its present form *c.* AD 400.

Maharashtra, State (pop., 2008 est.: 106,894,000), west-central India. It lies on the Arabian Sea and is bordered by the states of Gujarat, Madhya Pradesh, Chhattisgarh, Andhra Pradesh, Karnataka, and Goa and the union territory of Dadra and Nagar Haveli; its capital is Mumbai (Bombay). Occupying an area of 118,800 sq mi (307,690 sq km), it covers much of the Deccan plateau, containing the valleys of the Krishna, Bhima, and Godavari rivers. The population is a mixture of ethnic groups; Marathi is the state language. The region was divided into Hindu kingdoms in the 8th–13th centuries; they were followed by a series of Muslim dynasties. A Maratha kingdom ruled by 1674, and by the 18th century a Maratha empire had been established. The British gained control early in the 19th century. When India won independence in 1947, the area was known as Bombay state; it was divided on linguistic lines in 1960, creating Gujarat in the north and Maharashtra in the south. Its economy is based on agriculture and manufacturing; industries include oil refining and cotton textiles.

Ghats along the Godavari River in Nashik, Maharashtra, India.
© Ann & Bury Peerless Slide Resources & Picture Library

Mahasanghika, Early Buddhist school in India that anticipated the Mahayana tradition. Its emergence in the 4th century BC, about 100 years after the Buddha's death, represented the first major schism in the Buddhist community. Though accounts of the second Buddhist council attribute the split to a dispute over rules, later texts emphasize differences between the Mahasanghikas and the Theravadins regarding the nature of the Buddha and sainthood. The Mahasanghikas believed in a plurality of buddhas and held that the Buddha in his earthly existence was only an apparition.

Mahayana, One of the three major Buddhist traditions. It arose in the 1st century AD and is widely followed today in China (including Tibet), Korea, and Japan. Mahayanists distinguish themselves from the more conservative Theravada Buddhists of Sri Lanka, Myanmar (Burma), Thailand, Laos, and Cambodia. Whereas the Theravadins view the historical Buddha as a (merely) human teacher of the truth, Mahayanists see him as an earthly manifestation of a celestial Buddha. Mahayanists revere bodhisattvas, key figures in universal salvation. Compassion, the chief virtue of the bodhisattva, is valued as highly as wisdom, the virtue emphasized by the ancient Buddhists. Within Mahayana Buddhism, some branches emphasize esoteric practices (e.g., Shingon, Tibetan Buddhism).

mahdi (Arabic: "divinely guided one"), In Islamic eschatology, a messianic deliverer who will bring justice to the earth, restore true religion, and usher in a short golden age before the end of the world. Though the mahdi is not mentioned in the Qurʾān and is questioned by Sunnite theologians, he is important in Shīʿite doctrine. The doctrine of the mahdi gained currency during the religious and political upheavals of early Islam (7th–8th century) and received new emphasis in periods of crisis (e.g., after most of Spain was reconquered by Christians in 1212, and during Napoleon's invasion of Egypt). The title has been claimed by Islamic revolutionaries, notably in North Africa.

Mahesh Yogi, Maharishi, orig. MAHESH PRASAD VARMA (b. 1917?, Jabalpur, India—d. Feb. 5, 2008, Vlodrop, Neth.), Indian religious leader, founder of Transcendental Meditation (TM). He took a degree in physics before going to the Himalayas to study the Advaita school of Vedanta religious thought with the yogi Guru Dev for 13 years. He arrived in the U.S. in 1959, preaching the virtues of TM; in the 1960s the Beatles were perhaps his most celebrated followers. The Maharishi (the title means "Great Sage") returned to India in the late 1970s and moved to the Netherlands in 1990. His organization, which includes real estate holdings, schools, and clinics, was worth more than $3 billion in the late 1990s.

Mahfouz, Naguib (b. Dec. 11, 1911, Cairo, Egypt—d. Aug. 30, 2006, Cairo), Egyptian writer. He worked in the cultural section of the Egyptian civil service from 1934 to 1971. His major work, the *Cairo Trilogy* (1956–57)—including the novels *Palace Walk*, *Palace of Desire*, and *Sugar Street*—represents a penetrating overview of 20th-century Egyptian society. Subsequent works offer critical views of the Egyptian monarchy, colonialism, and contemporary Egypt. Other well-known novels include *Midaq Alley* (1947), *Children of Gebelawi* (1959), and *Miramar* (1967). He also wrote short-story collections, some 30 screenplays, and several stage plays. In 1988 he became the first Arabic writer to win the Nobel Prize for Literature.

Mahler, Gustav (b. July 7, 1860, Kalištĕ, Bohemia, Austrian Empire—d. May 18, 1911, Vienna, Austria), Austrian-Jewish composer and conductor. He attended the Vienna Conservatory, where he studied piano and composition. He wrote his first significant work, the cantata *Das Klagende Lied* (1880), as he was eking out an existence by giving lessons. In 1880 he became a conductor, and though his dictatorial manner was disliked and critics found his interpretations extreme, by 1886 he had achieved success in Prague. He also began the first of his 10 symphonies (1888–1910), his main compositional legacy. In 1897 he was named director of the Vienna Opera; his stormy reign there was acknowledged as an artistic success. He moved to the Metropolitan Opera in 1908 and the New York Philharmonic in 1909–10. Ill with heart disease and mourning his daughter's death, he wrote the masterly orchestral song cycle *Das Lied von der Erde* (1908–09) and his ninth symphony. His orchestral songs *Des Knaben Wunderhorn* (1892–98) and *Kindertotenlieder* (1904; *Songs on the Deaths of Children*) are frequently performed. His emotionally charged and subtly orchestrated music drew together many different strands of Romanticism. Although his music was largely ignored for 50 years after his death, he was later regarded as an important forerunner of 20th-century techniques of composition.

mahogany family, Family Meliaceae (order Sapindales), composed of 575 species in 51 genera of trees and (rarely) shrubs native to tropical and subtropical regions. Trees of the genus *Swietenia* and *Entandrophragma*, commonly called mahogany, and of the genus *Cedrela* (especially the cigar-box cedar, *C. odorata*) are economically important timber trees. The China tree (*Melia azedarach*), also called chinaberry, bead tree, and Persian lilac, is an ornamental Asian tree with fragrant, lilac-coloured flowers and attractive but poisonous round yellow fruits, often cultivated in tropical and warm temperate areas. Most members of the family have large compound leaves and branched flower clusters. A few have edible fruits.

Main River, River, central Germany. Rising in northern Bavaria, and flowing west, it passes through Frankfurt before emptying into the Rhine River; it is 326 mi (524 km) long. It forms part of the Main-Danube Canal, which links the Rhine and Danube rivers to create a 2,200-mi (3,500-km) waterway from the North Sea to the Black Sea.

Maitreya (Miroku) in meditation, gilt bronze figure, Japanese, Asuka period, 7th century; in the Cleveland Museum of Art
The Cleveland Museum of Art, John L. Severance Fund, 50.86

Maitreya, In Buddhist tradition, the future Buddha who will descend to earth to preach again the dharma (law) when the teachings of the Buddha Gautama have completely decayed. Until then, Maitreya is believed to be a bodhisattva residing in the Tusita heaven. Mentioned in scriptures from the 3rd century AD, he is the earliest bodhisattva around whom a cult developed and is still the only one generally honored by the Theravada tradition. His images, found throughout the Buddhist world, convey an air of expectancy and promise.

majolica, Italian MAIOLICA, Tin-glazed earthenware introduced from Moorish Spain by way of the island of Majorca and produced in Italy from the 14th century. Majolica is usually restricted to five colours: cobalt blue, antimony yellow, iron red, copper green, and manganese purple; the purple and blue were used, at various periods, mainly for outline. White tin enamel was used also, for highlights or alone on the white tin glaze. The most common shape of the pottery was a display dish, decorated in the *istoriato* style, a 16th-century Italian narrative style that uses the pottery body solely as support for a purely pictorial effect.

Majorca, Spanish MALLORCA, ancient BALEARIS MAJOR, Island, Balearic Islands (Baleares) autonomous community, Spain. The largest of the Balearic Islands, it lies in the western Mediterranean Sea and occupies an area of 1,405 sq mi (3,640 sq km). Palma, the capital of the autonomous community, is located on the island. The kingdom of Majorca was established by James I of Aragon in the 13th century and was united with Aragon in the 14th century. During the Spanish Civil War (1936–39), it was a base for Italian aid to the Nationalists. Now a popular tourist centre, it was a favourite destination of Frédéric Chopin, who wrote some of his finest mazurkas and preludes there.

Makassar, formerly UJUNGPANDANG, City (pop., 2000: 1,100,019), Celebes (Sulawesi), Indonesia. Already a thriving port when the Portuguese arrived in the 16th century, it came under control of the Dutch, who built a trading station there in 1607 and finally deposed the sultan in 1667. It was made a free port in the mid-19th century and the capital of the Dutch-sponsored state of Indonesia Timur (East Indonesia) in 1946. By 1950 it was part of the Republic of Indonesia. It is the home of Hasanuddin University (founded 1956).

Makassar Strait, Narrow passage of the west-central Pacific Ocean, Indonesia. Located between Borneo and Celebes (Sulawesi), it connects the Celebes Sea to the Java Sea. It is 500 mi (800 km) long and 80–230 mi (130–370 km) wide. It contains numerous islands, the largest of which are Laut and Sebuku. In 1942, during World War II, it was the scene of naval and air battles as the Allies tried to prevent the Japanese from occupying Borneo.

makeup, In the performing arts, material used by actors for cosmetic purposes and to help create the characters they play. Not needed in Greek and Roman theatre because of the use of masks, makeup was used in the religious plays of medieval Europe, in which the angels' faces were painted red and those of God and Christ white or gold. In Elizabethan England, crude makeup methods included powdering the face with chalk (to play ghosts and murderers) or blackening it with burnt cork (to play Moors). As stage lighting improved in the 19th century, theatrical makeup became more artistic; stick greasepaint, invented by Ludwig Leichner in the 1860s, enabled actors to create more subtle characterizations. Stage makeup proved too heavy for motion pictures; in 1910 Max Factor created semiliquid greasepaint makeup suitable for early filmmaking, and in 1928 he created panchromatic makeup to keep pace with the development of incandescent lighting and more sensitive film. Makeup was later further modified for colour filmmaking and for television.

Malabar Coast, Region, southwestern coast of India, stretching from the Western Ghats to the Arabian Sea. It now includes most of Kerala state and the coastal region of Karnataka state. It has sometimes been used to refer to the entire western coast of peninsular India. A large part of it was within the ancient kingdom of Keralaputra. The Portuguese established trading posts there; they were followed by the Dutch in the 17th century and the French in the 18th century. The British gained control of the region in the late 18th century.

Malabo, formerly (until 1973) SANTA ISABEL, City (pop., 2007 est.: 96,000), capital of Equatorial Guinea. Located on the northern edge of the island of Bioko, it is the republic's commercial and financial centre. The main activity of its harbour is the export of cocoa, timber, and coffee. Its population fluctuated in the 1960s and '70s: the European population declined after 1969 riots there, and the African population declined when Nigerian contract workers returned to Nigeria in the mid 1970s.

Malacca, Strait of, Channel connecting the Indian Ocean and the South China Sea. It lies between Sumatra and the Malay Peninsula. It is 500 mi (800 km) long and is funnel-shaped; only 40 mi (65 km) wide in the south, it broadens in the north to 155 mi (249 km). Numerous islets hinder passage at its southern entrance. The shortest sea route between India and China, it is one of the most heavily traveled shipping channels in the world.

malaria, A serious relapsing infection caused by protozoa of the genus *Plasmodium*, transmitted by the bite of the *Anopheles* mosquito. Known since before the 5th century BC, it occurs in tropical and subtropical regions near swamps. The roles of the mosquito and the parasite were proved in the early 20th century. Annual cases worldwide are estimated at 250 million and deaths at 2 million. Malaria from different *Plasmodium* species differs in severity, mortality, and geographic distribution. The parasites have an extremely complex life cycle; in one stage they develop synchronously inside red blood cells. Their mass fissions at 48- or 72-hour intervals cause attacks lasting 4–10 hours. Shaking and chills are followed by fever of up to 105 °F (40.6 °C), with severe headache and then profuse sweating as temperature returns to normal. Patients often have anemia, spleen enlargement, and general weakness. Complications can be fatal. Malaria is diagnosed by detecting the parasites in blood. Quinine was long used to alleviate the fevers. Synthetic drugs, such as chloroquine, destroy the parasites in blood cells, but many strains are now resistant. Carriers of a gene for a hemoglobinopathy have natural resistance. Malaria prevention requires preventing mosquito bites: eliminating mosquito breeding places and using insecticides or natural predators, window screens, netting, and insect repellent.

Malawi, officially REPUBLIC OF MALAWI, formerly NYASALAND, Country, southeastern Africa. Area: 45,747 sq mi (118,484 sq km). Population: (2011 est.) 15,381,000. Capital: Lilongwe (judiciary meets in Blantyre). Almost the entire population consists of Bantu-speaking Africans. Languages: English, Chewa, Lomwe. Religions: Christianity (Protestant, Roman Catholic), Islam, traditional beliefs. Currency: Malawian kwacha. Malawi's terrain is characterized by dramatic highlands and extensive lakes, with forests occupying about one-fourth of the total land area. The Great Rift Valley runs north-south and contains Lake Nyasa (Lake Malawi). Agriculture employs more than four-fifths of the workforce; staple crops include corn (maize), peanuts (groundnuts), beans, and peas, and cash crops include tobacco, tea, sugarcane, and cotton. Coal mining and limestone quarrying also contribute to the economy. Major industrial products are food products, beverages, chemicals, and textiles. Malawi is a multiparty republic with one legislative house; its head of state and government is the president. Inhabited since 8000 BCE, the region was settled by Bantu-speaking peoples between the 1st and 4th centuries CE. They established separate states, and *c.* 1480 they founded the Maravi confederacy, which encompassed most of central and southern Malawi. In northern Malawi the Ngonde people established a kingdom *c.* 1600, and in the 18th century the Chikulamayembe state was founded. The slave trade flourished during the 18th–19th century; Islam and Christianity arrived in the region *c.* 1860. Britain established colonial authority in 1891, creating the Nyasaland Districts Protectorate. It became the British Central Africa Protectorate in 1893 and Nyasaland in 1907. The colonies of Northern and Southern Rhodesia and Nyasaland formed a federation (1951–53), which was dissolved in 1963. The next year Malawi achieved independence as a member of the British Commonwealth. In 1966 it became a republic, with Hastings Kamuzu Banda as president. In 1971 he was designated president for life, and he ruled for three decades before being defeated in multiparty presidential elections in 1994. A new constitution was adopted in 1995.

Malawi, Lake, or LAKE NYASA, Lake, southern Africa, bounded on the west and south by Malawi, on the east by Mozambique, and on the north by Tanzania. It is the southernmost and third largest of the Great Rift Valley lakes. It is about 360 mi (580 km) long with an average width of 25 mi (40 km); it covers an area of 11,430 sq mi (29,604 sq km). It contains Likoma Island, site of an Anglican cathedral completed in 1911. On the heavily populated Malawi shore there are several government stations. The lake is fed by 14 rivers, and its sole outlet is the Shire River. There are about 200 recorded species of fish in the lake.

Malay, Any member of an ethnic group that probably originated in Borneo and expanded into Sumatra and the Malay Peninsula. They constitute more than half the population of Peninsular Malaysia. They are mainly a rural people, growing rice for food and rubber as a cash crop. Heavily influenced by India, they were Hinduized before converting to Islam in the 15th century. Their culture has also been influenced by the cultures of the Thai, Javanese, and Sumatrans. Malay society has traditionally been somewhat feudal; class distinctions are still marked, and marriages have traditionally been arranged by parents and governed by Islamic law.

Malay Archipelago, Largest group of islands in the world, located off the southeastern coast of Asia between the Indian and Pacific oceans. It consists of the more than 13,000 islands of Indonesia and some 7,000 islands of the Philippines. Formerly called the East Indies, the archipelago extends along the Equator for more than 3,800 mi (6,100 km). Principal islands include the Greater Sunda Islands (Sumatra, Java, Borneo, and Celebes), the Lesser Sundas, the Moluccas, New Guinea, Luzon, Mindanao, and the Visayan Islands.

Malay language, Austronesian language with some 33 million first-language speakers in the Malay Peninsula, Sumatra, Borneo, and other parts of Indonesia and Malaysia. Because Malay was spoken on both sides of the Strait of Malacca, a crucial trade route between India and China, Malay-speaking groups were drawn into international commerce centuries before European penetration of the region, and Malay became a lingua franca in Indonesian ports, giving rise to a range of pidgins and creoles known as Bazaar Malay (Melayu Pasar). In 20th-century Indonesia, a standardized form of Malay was adopted as the national language, Indonesian; written in Latin letters, it is now spoken or understood by about 70% of the population. Similar standardizations of Malay comprise the national languages of Malaysia and Brunei. The oldest known Malay texts are 7th-century inscriptions from southern Sumatra in an Indic script; a continuous Malay literary tradition did not begin until the Islamization of the Malay Peninsula in the 14th century.

Malay Peninsula, Peninsula, Southeast Asia. Comprising the mainland portion of Malaysia and southwestern Thailand, it occupies an area of 70,000 sq mi (181,300 sq km), has a width of 200 mi (322 km), and extends south for 700 mi (1,127 km) to Cape Balai, the southernmost point of the Asian continent; the island country of Singapore lies just south across the Johore Strait. Its central mountain range, rising to 7,175 ft (2,187 m) at Mount Tahan, divides the peninsula lengthwise and is the source of many rivers. Both its western and eastern coasts are exposed to monsoons. It has large tracts of tropical rainforest and is a major producer of rubber and tin.

Malayalam language, Dravidian language spoken by more than 36 million people mainly in the Indian state of Kerala. Malayalam is closely related to Tamil, from which it is estimated to have separated about the 10th century AD. The earliest literary composition in the language is from the 13th century. Like other major Dravidian languages, Malayalam has a number of regional dialects, social dialects that reflect differences in caste and religion, and marked distinctions in formal and informal usage. Literacy among Malayalam speakers is believed to be higher than literacy among speakers of any other Indian language.

Malaysia, Country, Southeast Asia. It is composed of two regions—Peninsular, or West, Malaysia and East Malaysia—separated by 400 mi (640 km) of the South China Sea. West Malaysia occupies the southern half of the Malay Peninsula (Malaya) and is bordered to the north by Thailand. East Malaysia lies on the northwestern part of the island of Borneo and consists of the states of Sarawak and Sabah. Area: 127,724 sq mi (330,804 sq km). Population: (2011 est.) 28,161,000. Capital: Kuala Lumpur; administrative centre: Putrajaya. Because of Malaysia's location on the heavily traveled Strait of Malacca, the population is a highly diverse mix, in which ethnic Malays and Chinese form the largest groups, and the most prominent of the smaller ethnic groups include the various indigenous peoples and South Asians. Languages: Malay (official), Chinese, and assorted Austronesian and Indo-European languages. Religions: Islam (official), Buddhism, Christianity, Hinduism, some local religions. Currency: ringgit. Peninsular Malaysia is largely mountainous; East Malaysia has coastal plains rising to hills and then to a mountainous core. Much of Malaysia is covered by rainforest. Tree crops, notably rubber and palm oil, are the most important cash crops; rice is the chief staple crop. Petroleum drilling and production and tin mining are important, as is the manufacture of electronic products, rubber goods, cement, and iron and steel products. Malaysia is a federal constitutional monarchy with two legislative houses; the head of state is the paramount ruler, and the head of government is the prime minister. Peninsular Malaysia has been inhabited for at least 6,000 years. Small kingdoms existed in the 2nd–3rd century CE when adventurers from India first arrived. Sumatran exiles founded the city-state of Malacca c. 1400, and it flourished as a trading and Islamic religious centre until its capture by the Portuguese in 1511. Malacca passed to the Dutch in 1641. The British founded a settlement on Singapore Island in 1819, and by 1867 they had established the Straits Settlements, including Malacca, Singapore, and Penang. During the late 19th century, Chinese began to migrate to Peninsular Malaysia (at the time called Malaya). Japan invaded Malaya in 1941 and captured Singapore in 1942. After Japan's defeat in 1945, opposition to British rule led to the creation of the United Malays National Organization (UMNO) in 1946, and in 1948 the peninsula was federated with Penang. Malaya gained independence from Britain in 1957. Malaya, Singapore, and the former British colonies of Sarawak and Sabah on the island of Borneo joined to form the Federation of Malaysia in 1963; Singapore, however, withdrew from the federation in 1965. Malaysia's economy expanded greatly from the late 1970s, though it experienced the regional economic slump of the mid- to late 1990s; the economy subsequently recovered.

Maldives, officially REPUBLIC OF MALDIVES, Archipelago country, north-central Indian Ocean southwest of Sri Lanka. It is a chain of about 1,200 small coral islands and sandbanks (some 200 of which are inhabited), grouped in clusters, or atolls. The islands extend more than 510 mi (820 km) north-south and 80 mi (130 km) east-west. Area: 115 sq mi (298 sq km). Population: (2011 est.) 325,000. Capital: Male (Male'). The population is ethnically mixed; ancestors include Tamil and Sinhalese peoples as well as Arabs, Chinese, and others from surrounding Asian areas. Languages: Dhivehi (or Maldivian; official), Arabic. Religion: Islam (official; predominantly Sunni). Currency: rufiyaa. All the islands are low-lying, none rising more than 6 ft (1.8 m) above sea level. The atolls have sandy beaches, lagoons, and a luxuriant growth of coconut palms, together with breadfruit trees and tropical bushes. One of the world's poorest countries, the Maldives has a developing economy based on fishing, tourism, boatbuilding, and boat repairing. It is a republic with one legislative house; its head of state and government is the president. The archipelago was settled in the 5th century BCE by Buddhists probably from Sri Lanka and southern India; according to tradition, Islam was adopted in 1153. The Portuguese held sway in Male in 1558–73. The islands were a sultanate under the Dutch rulers of Ceylon (Sri Lanka) during the 17th century. After the British gained control of Ceylon in 1796, the area became a British protectorate, a status formalized in 1887. The islands won full independence from Britain in 1965, and in 1968 a republic was founded and the sultanate abolished. The Maldives joined the British Commonwealth in 1982. Its economy has gradually improved, aided by the growth of tourism. In 2004 the archipelago was damaged by a large tsunami. A new constitution adopted in 2008 established Islam as the state religion, created greater governmental checks and balances, and allowed women to run for president.

Male, Chief atoll (pop., 2006: 92,555) and capital of the Maldives. Located in the centre of the Maldives, it comprises two groups of islets: North Male and South Male. It has central courts, a government hospital, an international airport, and public and private schools and is a trade and tourist centre.

Mali, officially REPUBLIC OF MALI, Country, western Africa. Area: 482,077 sq mi (1,248,574 sq km). Population: (2011 est.) 15,525,000. Capital: Bamako. The Bambara constitute about one-third of the total population. Other ethnic groups include the Fulani and the Imazighen (Berbers). Languages: French (official), Dogon, Bambara, Songhai, Soninke, Senufo, Arabic. Religions: Islam; also traditional beliefs, Christianity. Currency: CFA franc. Mali's terrain is largely flat, and in the north its plains stretch into the Sahara. The upper Niger River basin is in the south; about two-fifths of the total length of the Niger River flows through Mali. Only a tiny fraction of Mali's total land area is considered arable. Mali's most important exploited mineral is gold; other mineral reserves, which are largely unexploited, include iron ore, bauxite, and copper. Agriculture constitutes the major economic activity. Staple crops include millet, sorghum, corn, and rice; cash crops include cotton and peanuts. Mali is a multiparty republic with one legislative house; its head of state is the president, and the head of government is the prime minister. Inhabited since prehistoric times, the region was on a trans-Saharan caravan route. The Malinke empire of Mali was founded in the 13th century on the upper and middle Niger. In the 15th century the Songhai empire in the Timbuktu-Gao region gained control. Morocco invaded the area in 1591, and Timbuktu gradually declined in importance. In the mid- to late-19th century the French conquered the area, which became part of French West Africa. In 1946 the area, known as the French Sudan, became an overseas territory of the French Union. In 1958 it was proclaimed the Sudanese Republic, and it joined with Senegal (1959–60) to form the Mali Federation. Senegal seceded, and in 1960 the independent Republic of Mali was formed. The government was overthrown by military coups in 1968 and 1991. A civilian government was restored in 1992, and thereafter democratic multiparty elections were held every five years. Mali experienced continuing economic problems and had to deal with Tuareg insurgencies in the northern part of the country. Military dissatisfaction with the government's response to the latter issue led to a coup in March 2012 and a brief period of military rule before a civilian government was restored the following month. During the period of military rule, however, Tuareg rebels gained control over the northern portion of the country and declared it to be the independent state of Azawad.

Mali empire, Trading empire that flourished in West Africa in the 13th–16th centuries. It developed from the state of Kangaba on the upper Niger River and was probably founded before AD 1000. The Malinke inhabitants of Kangaba acted as middlemen in the gold trade in ancient Ghana. Growing in the 13th century under the leadership of Sundiata, it continued to expand in the 14th century and absorbed Gao and Timbuktu. Its boundaries extended to the Hausa people in the east and to Fulani and Tukulor peoples in the west. It eventually outgrew its political and military strength, and many of its subject areas revolted. By c. 1550 it had ceased to be an important political entity.

Malmö, Port city (pop., 2000 est.: city, 259,579; metro. area, 522,857), southern Sweden, located across the Sound from Copenhagen. Originally known as Malmhaug, it was chartered in the late 13th century. Following its union with Sweden in 1658, it suffered an economic decline, partly because of the loss of trade. The building of the harbour in 1775 and the arrival of the railroad after 1800 stimulated economic development. Sweden's third largest city, it is an important commercial centre. Its economy is based on export products, shipbuilding, and textile manufactures. Its historic buildings include a 16th-century fortress, the town hall, and the 14th-century St. Peter's Church.

malnutrition, Condition resulting from inadequate diet or from inability to absorb or metabolize nutrients. Food intake may be insufficient to supply calories or protein or deficient in one or more essential vitamins or minerals. The latter case can lead to specific nutritional deficiency diseases (including beriberi, pellagra, rickets, and scurvy). Metabolic defects, especially of the digestive system, liver, kidneys, or red blood cells, prevent proper digestion, absorption, and metabolism of nutrients.

Malta, officially REPUBLIC OF MALTA, Island country, south of Sicily in the Mediterranean Sea. It consists of the three inhabited islands Malta (the largest), Gozo, and Comino and the two uninhabited islets Comminotto and Filfla. Area: 122 sq mi (316 sq km). Population: (2011 est.) 419,000. Capital: Valletta. Malta's population, nearly all native-born, has a mixture of Italian, Arab, British, and Phoenician heritage. Languages: Maltese, English (both official). Religion: Roman Catholic (official). Currency: euro. About one-third of its total land area is arable, and Malta is self-sufficient in most food production. Tourism is its major industry. It is a unitary multiparty republic with one legislative house; its head of state is the president, and its head of government is the prime minister. Evidence indicates that Malta was inhabited as early as 5000 BCE. Although there is limited evidence of a Phoenician presence, it seems clearer that the Carthaginians had arrived in Malta by the 6th century BCE, and the island came under Roman control in 218 BCE. In 60 CE St. Paul the Apostle was shipwrecked on the island and converted the inhabitants to Christianity. It was under Byzantine rule until the Arabs seized control in 870. In 1091 the Normans defeated the Arabs, and Malta was ruled by a succession of feudal lords until the early 16th century. In 1530 it came under the control of the Hospitallers; Napoleon seized control in 1798, and the British took it in 1800. The 1802 Treaty of Amiens returned the islands to the Hospitallers; however, the Maltese protested and acknowledged British sovereignty, which was ratified in the 1814 Treaty of Paris. Malta became self-governing in 1921 but reverted to a colonial regime in 1936. Malta was heavily bombed by Germany and Italy during World War II, and in 1942 it received Britain's George Cross for "heroism and devotion," the first time that this medal was not conferred to an individual. In 1964 Malta gained independence within the Commonwealth, and it became a republic in 1974. When its alliance with Britain ended in 1979, Malta proclaimed its neutral status. In 2004 it joined the European Union, and it adopted the euro as its official currency in 2008.

Maltese language, Principal language of Malta, developed from a dialect of Arabic closely related to those of Algeria and

Tunisia. It has been strongly influenced by the Romance languages, especially Italian. Maltese is the only form of Arabic written in the Latin alphabet.

Malthus, Thomas Robert (b. Feb. 13/14, 1766, Rookery, near Dorking, Surrey, Eng.—d. Dec. 29, 1834, St. Catherine, near Bath, Somerset), British economist and demographer. Born into a prosperous family, he studied at the University of Cambridge and was elected a fellow of Jesus College in 1793. In 1798 he published *An Essay on the Principle of Population*, in which he argued that population will always tend to outrun the food supply—that the increase of population will take place, if unchecked, in a geometrical progression, while the means of subsistence will increase only in an arithmetical progression. He believed population would expand to the limit of subsistence and would be held there by famine, war, and ill health. He enlarged on his ideas in later editions of his work (to 1826). He argued that relief measures for the poor should be strictly limited since they tended to encourage the growth of excess population. His theories, though largely disproven, had great influence on contemporary social policy and on such economists as David Ricardo.

Mamlūk dynasty, or MAMLUKE DYNASTY (1250–1517) Rulers of Syria and Egypt. The term *mamlūk* is an Arabic word for slave. Slave soldiers had been used in the Islamic world since the 9th century, and they often exploited the military power vested in them to seize control from the legitimate political authorities. In 1250 a group of *mamlūk* generals seized the throne of the Ayyūbid dynasty on the death of the sultan Al-Malik al-Ṣāliḥ Ayyūb (r. 1240–49). The resulting dynasty legitimized its rule by reconstituting the caliphate of the ʿAbbāsid dynasty (destroyed by the Mongols in 1258) and by acting as patrons to the rulers of Mecca and Medina. Under Mamlūk rule the remaining crusaders were expelled from the eastern Mediterranean coast, and the Mongols were driven back from Palestine and Syria. Culturally, historical writing and architecture flourished during their rule. A shift in their ethnic makeup from Turkish to Circassian corresponded with their slow decline; their failure to adopt field artillery as weapons (except in siege warfare) contributed to their defeat by the Ottoman Empire in 1517. They afterward remained intact as a social class, however, and continued to exercise a high degree of political autonomy, though they were only one of several forces influencing Egyptian political life. Their power was finally broken by the Albanian-Egyptian officer Muḥammad ʿAlī in a massacre that occurred in 1811.

mammal, Any member of the class (Mammalia) of warm-blooded vertebrates having four limbs (except for some aquatic species) and distinguished from other chordate classes by the female's milk-secreting glands and the presence of hair at some stage of development. Other unique characteristics include a jaw hinged directly to the skull, hearing through bones in the middle ear, a muscular diaphragm separating the pectoral and abdominal cavities, and nonnucleated mature red blood cells. Mammals range in size from tiny bats and shrews to the enormous blue whale. Monotremes (platypus and echidna) lay eggs; all other mammals bear live young. Marsupial newborns complete their development outside the womb, sometimes in a pouchlike structure. Placental mammals are born at a relatively advanced stage of development. The earliest mammals date from the late Triassic Period (which ended 206 million years ago); their immediate ancestors were the reptilian therapsids. For 70 million years mammals have been the dominant animals in terrestrial ecosystems, a consequence of two principal factors: the great behavioral adaptability provided by the ability of mammalian young to learn from their elders (a consequence of their dependence on their mothers for nourishment) and the physical adaptability to a wide range of climates and conditions provided by their warm-bloodedness.

Man, Isle of, Island, in the Irish Sea off the northwestern coast of England. Area: 221 sq mi (572 sq km). Population: (2011 est.) 84,700. Capital: Douglas (pop., 2001: 25,347). It is a crown dependency of Britain, with its own legislature. The popularly elected House of Keys constitutes one of the most ancient legislative assemblies in the world. The island is about 30 mi (48 km) long and 10 mi (16 km) wide. The Manx breed of tailless cats is believed to have originated there. It was home to Irish missionaries beginning in the 5th century CE and was held by the Norse (9th–13th centuries), Scots (13th–14th centuries), and English settlers (from the 14th century). It was made a crown possession in 1828.

mana, Among Polynesian and Melanesian peoples, a supernatural force or power that may be ascribed to persons, spirits, or inanimate objects. Mana may be either good or evil, beneficial or dangerous, but it is not impersonal; it is never spoken of except in connection with powerful beings or things. The term was first used in the 19th century in the West in connection with religion, but mana is now regarded as a symbolic way of expressing the special qualities attributed to persons of status in a hierarchical society, of providing sanction for their actions, and of explaining their failures.

Managua, City (pop., 2005: 937,489), capital of Nicaragua. Located on the southern shore of Lake Managua, it was of minor importance during Spanish colonial times. It was selected as the nation's capital in 1857 when a choice between León and Granada could not be settled. It was devastated by earthquake and fire in 1931 and by another major earthquake in 1972. It was the scene of fighting in 1978–79 during the civil war. The largest city and commercial centre of Nicaragua, it has several institutions of higher education, including the University of Managua, now part of the National University of Nicaragua. Sites of interest include Darío Park, with its monument to poet Rubén Darío.

Managua, Lake, or XOLOTLAN, Lake, western Nicaragua. It occupies an area of 400 sq mi (1,035 sq km), extending 36 mi (58 km) long and 16 mi (25 km) wide. Located north of the city of Managua, it is fed by numerous streams rising in the central highlands and is drained by the Tipitapa River, which flows into Lake Nicaragua. Momotombo Volcano (4,199 ft [1,280 m]) is on the northwestern shore.

Manama, Arabic AL-MANĀMAH, City (pop., 2001: 143,035), capital of Bahrain. Situated at the northeastern tip of Bahrain island, it is Bahrain's largest city, with about one-fifth of the emirate's population. It is one of the most important ports on the Persian Gulf. A commercial and financial centre enriched by Bahrain's oil wealth, it is linked by causeway with the nearby island city of Muḥarraq. First mentioned in Muslim chronicles *c.* 1345, it was taken by the Portuguese in 1521 and by the Persians in 1602. It has been held, with brief interruptions, by the Khalīfah dynasty since 1783. Manama was the seat of the British political resident for the Persian Gulf (1946–71), after which it became the capital of independent Bahrain.

manatee, Any of three species (family Trichechidae) of slow-moving, shallow-water herbivorous mammals. Manatees have a tapered body ending in a rounded flipper, no hind flippers, and foreflippers near the head. The Caribbean manatee (*Trichechus manatus*) lives along coasts of the southeastern U.S. and northern South America; the Amazonian manatee (*T. inunguis*) and the West African manatee (*T. senegalensis*) inhabit rivers and estuaries. Adults are 8–15 ft (2.5–4.5 m) long and weigh up to 1,500 lbs (700 kg). Manatees live singly or in small herds and are protected by law in most areas. The manatee or its relative, the dugong, may have given rise to the folklore of mermaids.

Manaus, City (pop., 2003 est.: 1,517,500), northwestern Brazil. Located in the heart of the Amazon rainforest, it lies along the northern bank of the Negro River above its junction with the Amazon River. The first European settlement was a small fort built in 1669. The village, called Villa da Barra, became the capital of the

Río Negro captaincy general in 1809. It prospered from 1890 to 1920 as the hub for the region's only supply of rubber, after which it declined. Though 900 mi (1,450 km) from the sea, it again became a major inland port and commercial centre, reviving economically in the mid-20th century. It has botanical gardens and an opera house, and the National Research Institute of Amazonia (INPA) and the Federal University of Amazonas are located there.

Manchester, City and metropolitan borough (pop., 2004 est.: 437,000), in the metropolitan county of Greater Manchester, northwestern England. Lying northwest of London and east of Liverpool, it was the site of a Roman fort (78–86 CE) but was abandoned after the 4th century. By 919 the town of Manchester had sprung up nearby. In the 16th century it was important in the wool trade, and with the onset of the Industrial Revolution in the 18th century it became an important manufacturing city known for its textile production. The world's first modern railroad, the Liverpool and Manchester, opened in 1830. The city was beset by urban and industrial problems in the second half of the 20th century. Thereafter it was redeveloped, ushering in a cultural renaissance. Its many educational institutions include the University of Manchester.

Manchu, People, many of Juchen ancestry, who acquired a Manchu identity in the 17th century before conquering Ming China and forming the Qing dynasty (1644–1911/12). Though official policy aimed to maintain the Manchu as a distinct people, this did not prevent considerable intermarriage and adoption of Chinese customs in areas of maximum contact with Chinese. China today recognizes the Manchu as a distinct ethnic group; its more than 10 million members live mainly in northeastern China.

Manchuria, or NORTHEAST, Chinese DONGBEI, or TUNG-PEI, Historical region, northeastern China. It consists of the modern provinces of Liaoning, Jilin, and Heilongjiang; the northeastern portion of Inner Mongolia autonomous region is sometimes also included. Throughout the early Chinese dynasties, China had only limited control over Manchuria. In 1211 Genghis Khan invaded and occupied Manchuria. Chinese rebellions overthrew the Yuan dynasty of the Mongols in 1368, and the Ming dynasty was established. The Qing (Manchu) dynasty originated there (early 17th century) and eventually spread over China. Russia and Japan fought each other for a foothold in the region during the Russo-Japanese War (1904–05); after its defeat, Russia ceded southern Manchuria to Japan. The Japanese occupied all of Manchuria in 1931 and created the puppet state of Manchukuo in 1932. The Soviets captured Manchuria in 1945, and Chinese communist guerrillas soon came to power. In 1953 Beijing divided the region into its three current provinces. It is now one of China's most important industrial areas.

Mandaeanism, Ancient Middle Eastern Gnostic sect surviving in Iraq and southwestern Iran. Like other dualistic systems, it stresses salvation of the soul through esoteric knowledge, or gnosis, of its divine origin. (Its name derives from *mandayya,* "having knowledge.") In its cosmology, evil Archons obstruct the soul's ascent through the heavenly spheres to reunion with the supreme deity. Unlike many Gnostic systems, Mandaeanism supports marriage and forbids sexual license. It is also characterized by elaborate cultic rituals, particularly for baptism. Mandaeans view Jesus as a false messiah but revere John the Baptist, whose life is chronicled in their sacred writings.

mandala, In Tantric Hinduism and Buddhism, a diagram representing the universe, used in sacred rites and as an instrument of meditation. The mandala serves as a collection point for universal forces. By mentally "entering" the mandala and moving toward its centre, one is guided through the cosmic processes of disintegration and reintegration. Mandalas may be painted on paper or cloth, drawn on the ground, or fashioned of bronze or stone. Two types of mandalas represent different aspects of the universe: the

garbha-dhatu ("womb world"), in which the movement is from one to the many, and the *vajra-dhatu* ("diamond world"), from the many into one.

Mandalay, City (pop., 2004 est.: 1,176,900), central Myanmar (Burma). Situated on the Irrawaddy River, it is the country's second largest city, after Yangôn. It was built in 1857–59 by King Mindon to replace Amarapura as his capital. The last capital of the Myanmar kingdom, it fell to Britain in 1885. It was nearly destroyed during the Japanese occupation in World War II. An important Buddhist religious centre, it is the site of the famous Mahamuni pagoda and of 730 pagodas that house marble tablets inscribed with Buddhist scriptures.

Mandela, Nelson (b. July 18, 1918, Umtata, Cape of Good Hope, S.Af.), South African black nationalist leader and statesman. The son of a Xhosa chief, Mandela studied law at the University of Witwatersrand and in 1944 joined the African National Congress (ANC). After the Sharpeville massacre (1960), he abandoned his nonviolent stance and helped found the "Spear of the Nation," the ANC's military wing. Arrested in 1962, he was sentenced to life imprisonment. He retained wide support among South Africa's black population and became an international cause célèbre. Released by Pres. F.W. de Klerk in 1990, he replaced Oliver Tambo as president of the ANC in 1991. In 1993 Mandela and de Klerk were awarded the Nobel Peace Prize for their efforts to end apartheid and bring about the transition to nonracial democracy. In 1994 he was elected president in the country's first universal suffrage elections; by the time he stepped down in 1999, Mandela was the most universally respected figure of postcolonial Africa.

Nelson Mandela, 1990.
© Christopher Morris/Black Star

mandolin, Small stringed instrument related to the lute. It evolved in the 17th century in Italy, but its present form was strongly influenced by the 19th-century maker Pasquale Vinaccia (1806–82) of Naples. It has a pear-shaped body with a deeply vaulted back, a short fretted fingerboard, and four pairs of steel strings. (The American folk mandolin is a shallow, flat-backed version.) It is played with a plectrum; each pair of strings is strummed rapidly back and forth to produce a characteristic tremolo.

Manet, Édouard (b. Jan. 23, 1832, Paris, France—d. April 30, 1883, Paris), French painter and printmaker. His father, a prosperous civil servant, wanted him to pursue a naval career, but he was a poor student interested only in drawing. After having a few paintings accepted by the Salon, in 1863 the jury of the Salon rejected his *Déjeuner sur l'herbe,* and so Manet instead exhibited it at the Salon des Refusés (established to exhibit the many works rejected by the official Salon). This large canvas aroused loud disapproval from critics, who were offended by the presence of a naked woman in the company of two young men clothed in contemporary dress. At the Salon of 1865, his painting *Olympia,* created two years earlier, also caused a scandal: the painting's reclining female nude gazes brazenly at the viewer and is depicted in a harsh, brilliant light that obliterates traditional modeling and turns her into an almost two-dimensional figure. In the mid 1870s he became friendly with Claude Monet and the other Impressionists; while Manet would not participate in their independent exhibitions, for a time he experimented with some of their techniques. In 1882 he created the painting *A Bar at the Folies-Bergère* (1882), a daring, controversial composition that was radical in its obliteration of the boundary between the viewer and what is viewed. The critical resistance to Manet's work did not abate until near the end of his career; it was not until the 20th century that his reputation was secured by art historians and critics. His daring, unflinching approach to his painting and to the art world assured both him and his work a pivotal place in the history of modern art.

A Bar at the Folies-Bergère, *oil on canvas by Édouard Manet, 1882; in the Courtauld Institute Galleries, London.*
Courtauld Institute Galleries, London (Courtauld Collection)

manganese, Metallic chemical element, one of the transition elements, chemical symbol Mn, atomic number 25. It is a silvery white, hard, brittle metal, widely distributed in Earth's crust in combination with other elements. Nodules rich in manganese occur in huge quantities on the seafloor, but no economical way to mine them has been devised. More than 95% of the manganese produced is used in iron and steel alloys and much of the rest in nonferrous aluminum and magnesium alloys to improve their corrosion resistance and mechanical properties. Manganese compounds, in which it has various valences, are used in fertilizers and textile printing and as reagents and raw materials. Potassium permanganate is used for disinfecting, deodorizing, and bleaching and as a reagent in analysis. Manganese is essential to plants for growth and to higher animals to promote the action of many enzymes.

mango, Evergreen tree and fruit (*Mangifera indica*) of the sumac, or cashew, family, one of the most important and widely cultivated fruits of the tropical world. The yellow to orange fruit is juicy, distinctively spicy, and a rich source of vitamins A, C, and D. Mango fruit varies in shape, colour, and size from ovoid to long, from vividly red and yellow to dull green, and from plum- to melon-size. It is used in Theravada Buddhist ceremonies. The long-lived tree reaches 50–60 ft (15–18 m) and has long, lance-shaped leaves and clusters of small, pinkish, fragrant flowers.

mangrove, Any of certain shrubs and trees that belong primarily to the families Rhizophoraceae, Acanthaceae, Lythraceae, Combretaceae, and Arecaceae (palm) and that grow in dense thickets or forests along tidal estuaries, in salt marshes, and on muddy coasts. The term also applies to the thickets and forests of such plants. Mangroves characteristically have prop roots (exposed, supporting roots). In addition, in many species respiratory, or knee, roots project above the mud and have small openings through which air enters, passing through the soft, spongy tissue to the roots beneath the mud. Mangrove fruits put out an embryonic root before they fall from the tree; the root may fix itself in the mud before the fruit separates from the parent. Likewise, branches and trunks put out adventitious roots which, once they are secure in the mud, send up new shoots. The common mangrove

(*Rhizophora mangle*) grows to about 30 ft (9 m) tall and bears short, thick, leathery leaves on short stems and has pale yellow flowers. Its fruit is sweet and wholesome.

Manhattan, Borough (pop., 2000: 1,537,195) of New York City, southeastern New York, U.S. It includes all of Manhattan island and three smaller islands in the East River. Bounded by the Hudson River, Harlem River, East River, and Upper New York Bay, it is said to have been purchased by Peter Minuit in 1626 from the Manhattan Indians with trinkets valued at 60 guilders. Incorporated as New Amsterdam in 1653, it was obtained by Britain in 1664 and renamed New York City. In 1898 Manhattan was chartered as one of five boroughs making up Greater New York. It is one of the world's great commercial, financial, and cultural centres. Among its many points of interest are Central Park, the Empire State Building, the site of the former World Trade Center, the United Nations headquarters, Wall Street, the Metropolitan Museum of Art, the Museum of Modern Art, Lincoln Center for the Performing Arts, Carnegie Hall, Columbia University, the Juilliard School, and New York University.

Manhattan Project (1942–45) U.S. government research project that produced the first atomic bomb. In 1939 U.S. scientists urged Pres. Franklin D. Roosevelt to establish a program to study the potential military use of fission, and $6,000 was appropriated. By 1942 the project was code-named Manhattan, after the site of Columbia University, where much of the early research was done. Research also was carried out at the University of California and the University of Chicago. In 1943 a laboratory to construct the bomb was established at Los Alamos, N.M., and staffed by scientists headed by J. Robert Oppenheimer. Production also was carried out at Oak Ridge, Tenn., and Hanford, Wash. The first bomb was exploded in a test at Alamogordo air base in southern New Mexico. By its end the project had cost some $2 billion and had involved 125,000 people.

Manichaeism, Dualistic religion founded by Mani in Persia in the 3rd century AD. Inspired by a vision of an angel, Mani viewed himself as the last in a line of prophets that included Adam, Buddha, Zoroaster, and Jesus. His writings, now mostly lost, formed the Manichaean scriptures. Manichaeism held that the world was a fusion of spirit and matter, the original principles of good and evil, and that the fallen soul was trapped in the evil, material world and could reach the transcendent world only by way of the spirit. Zealous missionaries spread its doctrine through the Roman empire and the East. Vigorously attacked by both the Christian church and the Roman state, it disappeared almost entirely from Western Europe by the end of the 5th century but survived in Asia until the 14th century.

Manifest Destiny, Concept of U.S. territorial expansion westward to the Pacific Ocean. The phrase was coined in 1845 by the editor John L. O'Sullivan, who described the U.S. annexation of Texas and, by extension, the occupation of the rest of the continent as a divine right of the American people. The term was used to justify the U.S. annexation of Oregon, New Mexico, and California and later U.S. involvement in Alaska, Hawaii, and the Philippines.

Manila, City (pop., 2000: city, 1,581,082; metro. area, 9,932,560), capital of the Philippines. Located on Luzon island on the eastern shore of Manila Bay, it is the chief port and the economic, political, and cultural centre of the Philippines. The walled Muslim settlement originally built on the site was destroyed by Spanish conquistadors, who founded the fortress city of Intramuros in 1571. It was briefly held by the British (1762–63) during the Seven Years' War. During the Spanish-American War, U.S. forces gained control of Manila in 1898. Occupied by the Japanese in 1942, it was widely damaged during the fight for its recapture by U.S. forces in 1945. In 1946 it became the capital of the newly independent Republic of the Philippines, and was rebuilt.

Quezon City became the capital in 1948, but Manila regained that position in 1976. In addition to its diversified industries, including shipbuilding and food processing, it is the seat of several universities.

Manipur, State (pop., 2008 est.: 2,627,000), northeastern India. Occupying an area of 8,621 sq mi (22,327 sq km), it is bordered by Myanmar (Burma) and the states of Nagaland, Assam, and Mizoram. The capital is Imphal. Manipur's two main physical features are the Manipur River valley and the western mountainous region. In 1762 and 1824 Manipur requested British assistance in repelling invasions from Myanmar. The British administered the area in the 1890s, but in 1907 a local government took over; a tribal uprising in 1917 led to a new government administered from Assam. In 1947 Manipur acceded to the Indian union; it was ruled as a union territory until it became a state in 1972. Agriculture and forestry are economic mainstays.

Boatman on a canal south of Logtak Lake, near Imphal, Manipur, India.
Gerald Cubitt

Mann, Thomas (b. June 6, 1875, Lübeck, Ger.—d. Aug. 12, 1955, near Zürich, Switz.), German novelist and essayist, considered the greatest German novelist of the 20th century. After a brief period of office work, Mann devoted himself to writing, as had his elder brother Heinrich (1871–1950). *Buddenbrooks* (1901), his first novel, was an elegy for old bourgeois virtues. In the novella *Death in Venice* (1912), a sombre masterpiece, he took up the tragic dilemma of the artist in a collapsing society. Though ardently patriotic at the start of World War I, after 1919 he slowly revised his views of the authoritarian German state. His great novel *The Magic Mountain* (1924) clarified his growing espousal of Enlightenment principles as one strand of a complex and multifaceted whole. An outspoken opponent of Nazism, he fled to Switzerland on Adolf Hitler's accession; he settled in the U.S. in 1938 but returned to Switzerland in 1952. His tetralogy *Joseph and His Brothers* (1933–43) concerns the biblical Joseph. *Doctor Faustus* (1947), his most directly political novel, analyzes the darker aspects of the German soul. The often hilarious *Felix Krull, Confidence Man* (1954) remained unfinished. He is noted for his finely wrought style enriched by humour, irony, and parody and for his subtle, many-layered narratives of vast intellectual scope. His essays examined such figures as Leo Tolstoy, Sigmund Freud, Johann Wolfgang von Goethe, Friedrich Nietzsche, Anton Chekhov, and Friedrich Schiller. He received the Nobel Prize for Literature in 1929.

Mannerism, Artistic style that predominated in Italy from the end of the High Renaissance in the 1520s to the beginnings of the Baroque period *c.* 1590. Mannerism originated in Florence and Rome but ultimately spread as far as central and northern Europe. A reaction to the harmonious Classicism and idealized naturalism of High Renaissance art, Mannerism was concerned with solving intricate artistic problems, such as portraying nudes in complex poses. The figures in Mannerist works frequently have graceful but queerly elongated limbs, small heads, and stylized facial features, while their poses seem difficult or contrived. The deep, linear perspectival space of High Renaissance painting is flattened and obscured so that the figures appear as a decorative arrangement of forms in front of a flat background of indeterminate dimensions. Mannerists sought a continuous refinement of form and concept, pushing exaggeration and contrast to great limits. After being superseded by the Baroque style, it was seen as decadent and degenerate. By the 20th century it was appreciated anew for its

technical bravura and elegance. Major artists who practiced the style include Parmigianino, Federico Zuccaro, and Il Bronzino.

Mannheim, City (pop., 2002: city, 308,385; metro. area, 1,568,679), southwestern Germany. One of Europe's largest inland ports, it is situated on the Rhine River at the mouth of the Neckar River. It was a village in the 8th century, fortified by Elector Frederick IV, and chartered in 1607. The town was twice destroyed in wars during the 17th century and was rebuilt when the Palatine electors moved their residence there in 1720. Destroyed again in 1795, the city was rebuilt and became a centre of the revolutionary movement in 1848. Mannheim is an industrial centre, manufacturing chemicals, textiles, and fertilizers.

manorialism, or SEIGNORIALISM, Political, economic, and social system by which the peasants of medieval Europe were tied to their land and their lord through serfdom. The basic unit was the manor, a self-sufficient landed estate, or fief, under the control of a lord. Free tenants paid rent or provided military service in exchange for the use of the land. Peasants farmed small plots of land and owed rent and labor to their lord, and most were not free to leave the estate. The manorial system was flourishing in Western Europe by the 8th century and had begun to decline by the 13th century, while in Eastern Europe it achieved its greatest strength after the 15th century.

manta ray, or DEVIL RAY, or DEVILFISH, Any of several genera of warm-water marine rays, constituting the family Mobulidae, that are wider than they are long. Extensions of the pectoral fins project from the front of the head, looking like devils' horns; these sweep plankton and small fishes into their mouths. The long, whiplike tail may have one or more stinging spines. Mantas swim near the surface by flapping their pectoral fins. The largest species, the powerful but inoffensive Atlantic manta, or giant devil, ray (*Manta birostris*), may grow to over 23 ft (7 m) wide; contrary to old tales, it does not envelop and eat divers.

mantis, or PRAYING MANTIS, Any of more than 1,500 species of the insect suborder Mantodea (order Orthoptera). The long-bodied, slow-moving mantis (or mantid) eats only living insects, using its large forelimbs to capture and hold its struggling prey. The female is likely to eat the male after mating. The European *Mantis religiosa* and the Chinese mantis (*Tenodera aridifolia sinensis*) have been introduced to North America. The latter grows to 3–8 in. (8–20 cm) long. The name mantis ("diviner") reflects an ancient Greek belief in its supernatural powers.

mantle, That part of the Earth that lies beneath the crust and above the central core. On average, the mantle begins about 22 mi (35 km) below the surface and ends at a depth of about 1,800 mi (2,900 km). Predominant in the rock material are olivines, pyroxenes, and the silicate perovskite, a dense form of enstatite.

mantra, In Hinduism and Buddhism, a sacred utterance (syllable, word, or verse) believed to possess mystical or spiritual power. Mantras may be spoken aloud or uttered in thought, and they may be either repeated or sounded only once. Most have no apparent verbal meaning, but they are thought to have profound significance and to serve as distillations of spiritual wisdom. Repetition of a mantra can induce a trancelike state and can lead the participant to a higher level of spiritual awareness. Widely used mantras include om in Hinduism and *om mani padme hum* in Tibetan Buddhism.

Manu, In the mythology of India, the first man and the legendary author of the *Manu-smrti*. Manu appears in the Vedas as the performer of the first sacrifice. He is also known as the first king, and most rulers of medieval India claimed him as an ancestor. In the story of the great flood, Manu combines the characteristics of Noah and Adam. He built a boat after being warned of the flood by a fish. His boat came to rest on a mountaintop, and as the flood receded Manu poured out an oblation of milk and butter. A year later a woman calling herself the "daughter of Manu" was born from the waters, and these two became the parents of a new human race to replenish the earth.

Manu-smrti, officially MANAVA-DHARMA-SHASTRA, Most authoritative of the books of the Hindu law code (*Dharma-shastra*). It is attributed to the legendary first man and lawgiver, Manu. In its present form it dates from the 1st century BC. It prescribes the dharma of each Hindu, stating the obligations attached to his or her social class and stage of life. Making no distinction between religious and secular law, it deals with cosmogony, sacraments, and other religious topics as well as with marriage, hospitality, dietary restrictions, the conduct of women, and the law of kings.

Manual of Discipline, or RULE OF THE COMMUNITY, Major document produced by the Essene community of Jews. The manual, written on scrolls found in 1947 in caves at Qumrān, explains the sect's religious and moral ideals and describes its admission ceremony, mystical doctrines, and organizational and disciplinary statutes.

Mao Dun, or MAO TUN, orig. SHEN DEHONG, or SHEN YANBING (b. July 4, 1896, Tongxiang, Zhejiang province, China—d. March 27, 1981, Beijing), Chinese literary critic, author, and editor. A founder of the League of Left-Wing Writers (1930), he served as minister of culture after the communist government was established (1949–64). Many Western critics consider his trilogy of novellas *Shi* (1930; "Eclipse") to be his masterpiece. English translations of his works include *Spring Silkworms and Other Stories* (1956) and the novel *Rainbow* (1992). He is generally considered China's greatest novelist of realism.

Mao Zedong, or MAO TSE-TUNG (b. Dec. 26, 1893, Shaoshan, Hunan province, China—d. Sept. 9, 1976, Beijing), Chinese Marxist theorist, soldier, and statesman who led China's communist revolution and served as chairman of the People's Republic of China (1949–59) and chairman of the Chinese Communist Party (CCP; 1931–76). The son of a peasant, Mao joined the revolutionary army that overthrew the Qing dynasty but, after six months as a soldier, left to acquire more education. At Beijing University he met Li Dazhao and Chen Duxiu, founders of the CCP, and in 1921 he committed himself to Marxism. At that time, Marxist thought held that revolution lay in the hands of urban workers, but in 1925 Mao concluded that in China it was the peasantry, not the urban proletariat, that had to be mobilized. He became chairman of a Chinese Soviet Republic formed in rural Jiangxi province; its Red Army withstood repeated attacks from Chiang Kaishek's Nationalist army but at last undertook the Long March to a more secure position in northwestern China. There Mao became the undisputed head of the CCP. Guerrilla warfare tactics, appeals to the local population's nationalist sentiments, and Mao's agrarian policies gained the party military advantages against their Nationalist and Japanese enemies and broad support among the peasantry. Mao's agrarian Marxism differed from the Soviet model, but, when the communists succeeded in taking power in China in 1949, the Soviet Union agreed to provide the new state with technical assistance. However, Mao's Great Leap Forward and his criticism of "new bourgeois elements" in the Soviet Union and China alienated the Soviet Union irrevocably; Soviet aid was withdrawn in 1960. Mao followed the failed Great Leap Forward with the Cultural Revolution, also considered to have been a disastrous mistake. After Mao's death, Deng Xiaoping began introducing social and economic reforms.

Maoism, Variation of Marxism and Leninism developed by Mao Zedong. It diverged from its antecedents in its agrarian focus: Mao substituted the dormant power of the peasantry (discounted by traditional Marxists) for the urban proletariat that China largely lacked. The Maoist faith in revolutionary enthusiasm and the positive value of the peasants' lack of sophistication as opposed to technological or intellectual elites fueled the Great Leap Forward of the 1950s and the Cultural Revolution of the 1960s and '70s. The disastrous consequences of both upheavals led Mao's successors to abandon Maoism as counterproductive to economic growth and social order. Maoism was embraced by insurgent guerrilla groups worldwide; under the Khmer Rouge it became Cambodia's national ideology.

Maori, Any member of a Polynesian people of New Zealand. Maori traditional history describes their origins in terms of waves of migration from a mythical land between the 12th and 14th centuries, but archaeologists have dated habitations in New Zealand back to at least AD 800. Their first European contact was with Abel Janszoon Tasman (1642), who did battle with a group of Maori. Later Europeans were initially welcomed, but the arrival of muskets, disease, Western agricultural methods, and missionaries corroded Maori culture and social structure, and conflicts arose. The British assumed formal control of New Zealand in 1840; war over land broke out repeatedly over the next three decades. By 1872 all fighting had ended and great tracts of Maori land had been confiscated. Today about 9% of New Zealanders are classified as Maori; nearly all have some European ancestry. Though largely integrated into modern urban life, many Maori keep alive traditional cultural practices and struggle to retain control of their ancestral lands.

map, Graphic representation, drawn to scale and usually on a flat surface, of features—usually geographic, geologic, or geopolitical—of an area of the Earth or of any celestial body. Globes are maps represented on the surface of a sphere. Cartography is the art and science of making maps and charts. Major types of maps include topographic maps, showing features of the Earth's land surface; nautical charts, representing coastal and marine areas; hydrographic charts, which detail ocean depths and currents; and aeronautical charts, which detail surface features and air routes.

Maputo, formerly (until 1976) LOURENÇO MARQUES, Port city (pop., 2007: 1,099,102), capital of Mozambique. It lies on the northern bank of Espírito Santo Estuary of Delagoa Bay, an inlet of the Indian Ocean. It derived its former name from the Portuguese trader who first explored the region in 1544. The town developed around a Portuguese fortress completed in 1787. Created a city town in 1887, it superseded Moçambique as the capital of Portuguese East Africa in 1907. Since the nation's independence in 1975, the collapse of tourism and reduced access to foreign trade have damaged the city's economy.

Mar del Plata, Coastal city (pop., 2001: 541,733), east-central Argentina. It was the site of a Spanish mission (1746–51). In 1856 Portuguese explorer Jose Coelho Mierelles founded the fishing village La Peregrina. Mar del Plata was established in 1874 and promoted as a seaside resort; it became a city in 1907. It is famous for its luxurious casino. In addition to tourism, its economy is based on construction, textiles, and commercial fishing and canning. It is the seat of the National University of Mar del Plata.

Mara, Buddhist Lord of the Senses, who repeatedly tempted the Buddha Gautama. When Gautama seated himself under the bodhi tree to await enlightenment, the evil Mara appeared in the guise of a messenger claiming that a rival had usurped the family throne. After sending a storm of rain, rocks, ashes, and darkness to frighten away the gods who had gathered, he challenged Gautama's right to sit beneath the tree and sent forth his three daughters, Trsna, Rati, and Raga (thirst, desire, and delight), to seduce Gautama, but to no avail. After the Buddha had achieved enlightenment, Mara pressed him to abandon any attempt to preach, but the gods successfully persuaded him to preach the law.

Maracaibo, City (pop., 2000 est.: 1,764,038), northwestern Venezuela. Located on the channel connecting Lake Maracaibo with the Gulf of Venezuela, it is Venezuela's second largest city. Founded in 1571 as Nueva Zamora, it became a centre for inland trade after Gibraltar, at the head of the lake, was destroyed in 1669. It changed hands several times during Venezuela's struggle for independence from Spain. Within a decade of the discovery of oil in 1917, it became the oil metropolis of Venezuela and South America.

Maracaibo, Lake, Inlet of the Caribbean Sea, northwestern Venezuela. The largest natural lake in South America, it occupies an area of 5,130 sq mi (13,280 sq km), extending southward for 130 mi (210 km) from the Gulf of Venezuela and reaching a width of 75 mi (121 km). Many rivers flow into the lake, notably the Catatumbo River. It is in one of the world's richest oil-producing regions, which supplies about two-thirds of Venezuela's total petroleum output. Its oil fields are located along the eastern shore, extending 20 mi (32 km) into the lake.

marathon, Long-distance footrace run on an open course of 26 miles 385 yards (42.2 km). First held at the revived Olympic Games in 1896, it commemorates the legendary feat of a Greek soldier who is said to have run from Marathon to Athens in 490 BC, a distance of about 25 mi (40 km), to report the Greek victory at the Battle of Marathon, after which he dropped dead. Marathons today are usually open events for both men and women, often run by thousands of participants, including the venerable Boston Marathon (established 1897). The women's marathon became an Olympic event in 1984.

Marathon, Battle of (490 BC) Decisive battle on the plain of Marathon outside Athens in the Persian Wars. Darius I led his enormous army against a much smaller Athenian force led by Miltiades. The Athenians attacked with great speed, while the Persian cavalry was absent, devastating the Persian line and resulting in Darius's departure from Greece. The victory was overwhelming: 6,400 Persians but only 192 Athenians died. It is said that a messenger ran about 25 mi (40 km) back to Athens, where he announced the victory before dying of exhaustion. In another version, an Athenian runner was sent to Sparta before the battle to ask for help, running 150 mi (240 km) in two days; Sparta refused, so Athens fought with help only from Plataea.

marble, Granular limestone or dolomite that has recrystallized under the influence of heat, pressure, and aqueous solutions. The main mineral in marble is calcite. Commercially, "marble" includes all decorative calcium-rich rocks that can be polished, as well as some serpentines. Marbles are used principally for buildings and monuments, interior decoration, statuary, tabletops, and novelties. Colour and appearance are their most important qualities. Statuary marble, the most valuable variety, must be pure white and of uniform grain size.

march, Musical form having an even metre with strongly accented beats, originally intended to facilitate military marching. Development of the European march may have been stimulated by the Ottoman invasions of the 14th–16th centuries. Marches were not notated until the late 16th century; until then, time was generally kept by percussion alone, often with improvised fife embellishment. With the extensive development of brass instruments, especially in the 19th century, marches became widely popular and were often elaborately orchestrated. Composers such as Wolfgang Amadeus Mozart, Ludwig van Beethoven, and Gustav Mahler wrote marches, often incorporating them into their operas, sonatas, or symphonies. The later popularity of John Philip Sousa's band marches was unmatched.

Marconi, Guglielmo (b. April 25, 1874, Bologna, Italy—d. July 20, 1937, Rome), Italian physicist and inventor. He began experimenting with radio waves in 1894. In 1896 he went to England, where he developed a successful system of radio telegraphy. His work on the development of shortwave wireless communication constitutes the basis of nearly all modern radio broadcasting. His improved aerials greatly extended the range of

Guglielmo Marconi, c. 1908.
Library of Congress, Washington, D.C.

radio signaling. In 1899 he established communication across the English Channel. In 1900 he established the American Marconi Co. In 1901 he sent signals across the Atlantic for the first time. He acquired numerous patents, though probably his most famous one, No. 7777, for an apparatus that enabled several stations to operate on different wavelengths without interference, was later overturned. Marconi shared the 1909 Nobel Prize for Physics with K. Ferdinand Braun (1850–1918). He was made a marquis and was nominated to the Italian Senate (1929), and he was elected president of the Royal Italian Academy (1930).

Mardi Gras (French: "Fat Tuesday") Carnival celebrated on or culminating on Shrove Tuesday, the day before Ash Wednesday, the start of Lent. Traditionally, households consumed all the remaining foods that would be forbidden during Lent (e.g., eggs) on that day. It is a one-day event in France, but in the U.S. it lasts several days in New Orleans, where it is marked by parades, street celebrations, and extravagant costumes.

Marduk, or BEL, In Mesopotamian religion, the chief god of the city of Babylon and the national god of Babylonia. He began as a god of thunderstorms, and according to legend he became lord of all the gods after conquering the monster of primeval chaos, Tiamat. Marduk's star was the planet Jupiter, and his sacred animals were horses, dogs, and a dragon with a forked tongue, representations of which adorned Babylon's walls.

mare, Any flat, low, dark plain on the Moon. Maria are huge impact basins containing lava flows marked by ridges, depressions (graben), and faults; though *mare* means "sea" in Latin, they lack water. The best-known is probably Mare Tranquillitatis ("Sea of Tranquillity"), the site of the Apollo 11 manned Moon landing. Most of the approximately 20 major maria are on the side of the Moon that always faces Earth; they are its largest surface features and can be seen from Earth with the unaided eye. The dark features of the "man in the moon" are maria.

Maria Theresa, German MARIA THERESIA (b. May 13, 1717, Vienna, Austria—d. Nov. 29, 1780, Vienna), Archduchess of Austria and queen of Hungary and Bohemia (1740–80). She was the eldest daughter of Emperor Charles VI, who promulgated the Pragmatic Sanction to allow her to succeed to the Habsburg domains. Opposition to her succession led in 1740 to the War of the Austrian Succession. After Emperor Charles VII died (1745), she obtained the imperial crown for her husband, who became Francis I. She helped initiate financial and educational reforms, promoted commerce and the development of agriculture, and reorganized the army, all of which strengthened Austria's resources. Continued conflict with Prussia led to the Seven Years' War and later to the War of the Bavarian Succession. After her husband's death (1765), her son became emperor as Joseph II. She criticized many of his actions but agreed to the partition of Poland (1772). A key figure in the power politics of 18th-century Europe, Maria Theresa brought unity to the Habsburg monarchy and was considered one of its most capable rulers. Her 16 children also included Marie-Antoinette and Leopold II.

mariachi, Traditional Mexican street ensemble. The performer, the musical style, and the musical ensemble are called mariachi. Mariachi music emerged in the late 1700s or early 1800s. In the

19th century, mariachi bands consisted solely of stringed instruments, including the guitar, the *guitarrón* (a large fretless six-string bass guitar), and the *vihuela* (a guitarlike stringed instrument); since the 1920s the ensembles have generally included violins and trumpets—now more or less essential elements—and often other wind instruments as well. Initially mariachi music was strictly instrumental, but it has come to include vocal elements.

Mariana Islands, formerly LADRONE (or LADRONES) ISLANDS, Island group, western Pacific Ocean. Located east of the Philippines, it comprises 15 islands and is administratively divided into Guam and the Northern Mariana Islands. The population is descended from the pre-Spanish Chamorro people and Spanish, Mexican, German, Philippine, and Japanese settlers. Spanish cultural traditions are strong. After Ferdinand Magellan became the first European to reach them in 1521, they were visited frequently but were not colonized until 1668, at which time Jesuit missionaries changed their name to honor Mariana of Austria, regent of Spain.

Mariana Trench, also called MARIANAS TRENCH, Submarine trench in the floor of the western North Pacific Ocean. It is the deepest known depression on Earth, with a maximum depth measured at between about 35,800 and 36,200 ft (10,910 and 11,035 m). The trench extends in an arc from east of the Northern Mariana Islands to southwest of Guam, a distance of more than 1,580 mi (2,540 km), and has a mean width of 43 mi (69 km).

Marie-Antoinette (-Josèphe-Jeanne d'Autriche-Lorraine)

(b. Nov. 2, 1755, Vienna—d. Oct. 16, 1793, Paris, France), Queen consort of Louis XVI of France. The daughter of Emperor Francis I and Maria Theresa, she was married in 1770 to the French dauphin. After he became king (1774), she was criticized for her extravagance and frivolous circle of court favourites. She was unjustly implicated in the Affair of the Diamond Necklace (1786), which discredited the monarchy. After the French Revolution began, she influenced Louis to resist attempts by the National Assembly to restrict the royal prerogative. She became the target of agitators, who attributed to her the celebrated remark, after being told the people had no bread, "Let them eat cake!" She tried to save the crown by negotiating secretly with monarchist factions and with her brother, Emperor Leopold II. News of her intrigues further enraged the French and led to the overthrow of the monarchy (1792). After a year in prison, she was tried and guillotined in 1793.

Marie-Antoinette, detail of a portrait by Élisabeth Vigée-Lebrun; in the Château de Versailles.
Cliché Musées Nationaux, Paris

marijuana, Crude drug made from the dried and crushed leaves or flowers of plants of the genus *Cannabis*. The active ingredient is tetrahydrocannabinol (THC). Also called cannabis, pot, grass, and weed, marijuana has long been used as a sedative or an analgesic (pain reliever). It was in use in China by the 3rd millennium BCE and had reached Europe by 500 CE. Today it is used worldwide, though it has generally been illegal at least since the International Opium Convention of 1925. Its psychological and physical effects, including mild euphoria and alterations in vision and judgment, vary with strength and amount consumed, the setting, and the user's experience. Chronic use may lead to tolerance and may produce withdrawal symptoms in some users; in most cases the drug is psychologically habit-forming. Marijuana has been shown to be medically therapeutic for patients suffering from pain associated with certain chronic diseases or disorders. In 2001 Canada became the first country to legalize the use of medical marijuana by people with terminal illnesses and chronic conditions. Supporters of legalization claim that it is a more benign drug than alcohol, while opponents contend that it is addictive and leads to use of more serious drugs. A resin from cannabis is the source of hashish.

marimba, Xylophone with resonators under each bar. The original African instrument uses tuned calabash resonators. In Mexico and Central America, where it was brought by African slaves, the wooden bars may be affixed to a frame supported by legs or hung at the player's waist. The orchestral marimba uses long metal tubes as resonators.

marine, Member of a military force trained for service at sea and in land operations related to naval campaigns. They existed as far back as the 5th century BC, when the Greek fleets were manned by *epibatai*, or heavily armed sea soldiers. In the Middle Ages ordinary soldiers were often assigned to shipboard duty; not until the naval wars of the 17th century was the distinct role of marines rediscovered almost simultaneously by the British and the Dutch, who raised the first two modern marine corps, the Royal Marine (1664) and the Koninklijke Nederlandse Corps Mariniers (1665).

marine biology, Science that deals with the animals and plants of the sea and estuaries and with airborne and terrestrial organisms that depend directly on bodies of saltwater for food and other necessities. Marine biologists study the relations between ocean phenomena and the distribution and adaptations of organisms. Of particular interest are adaptations to the chemical and physical properties of seawater, the movements and currents of the ocean, the availability of light at various depths, and the composition of the sea floor. Other important areas of study are marine food chains, the distribution of economically important fish and crustaceans, and the effects of pollution. In the later 19th century, the emphasis was on collecting and cataloging marine organisms, for which special nets, dredges, and trawls were developed. In the 20th century, improved diving equipment, submersible craft, and underwater cameras and television have made direct observation possible.

Mariner, Any of a series of unmanned U.S. space probes sent near Venus, Mars, and Mercury. Mariners 2 (1962) and 5 (1967) passed Venus within 22,000 mi (35,000 km) and 2,500 mi (4,000 km), respectively, and made measurements of temperature and atmospheric density. Mariners 4 (1965), 6 and 7 (1969), and 9 (1971–72) obtained striking photographs of the surface of Mars and analyzed its atmosphere and magnetic field. Mariner 10 is the only spacecraft ever to have visited Mercury (1974–75).

Marīnid dynasty, Berber dynasty that followed the Almohad dynasty in North Africa in the 13th–15th centuries. The Marīnids were a tribe of the Zanātah group, which was allied to the Umayyads in Córdoba. In 1248 a Marīnid leader, Abū Yaḥyā, captured Fès and made it the Marīnid capital. The capture of Marrakech (1269) made the Marīnids the masters of Morocco. They waged inconclusive war in Spain and Africa that gradually depleted their resources, reducing the realm to anarchy in the 15th century. Saʿdī sharifs captured Fès in 1554.

Mariology, Study of doctrines concerning Mary, the mother of Jesus, or the content of those doctrines. The New Testament contains little information about Mary, though the tradition that she remained a virgin despite giving birth to Jesus was accepted in the early church. Various feast days in her honour were established in both the Eastern and Western liturgical traditions, and she became an especially important figure in Roman Catholicism. Pius IX proclaimed the doctrine of the Immaculate Conception in 1854. Mary is seen as the spiritual mother and heavenly intercessor of every Catholic and as a partner with Jesus in the redemption of human beings. In 1950 Pius XII proclaimed the doctrine that at her death Mary was bodily assumed into heaven.

maritime law, or ADMIRALTY LAW, or ADMIRALTY, Body of legal rules that governs ships and shipping. One early compilation of maritime regulations is the 6th-century Digest of Justinian. Roman maritime law and the 13th-century Consolat de Mar ("Consulate of the Sea") both brought temporary uniformity of maritime law to the Mediterranean, but nationalism led many countries to develop their own maritime codes. Maritime law deals mainly with the eventualities of loss of a ship (e.g., through collision) or cargo, with insurance and liability relating to those eventualities, and with collision compensation and salvage rights. There has been an increasing tendency to make maritime laws uniform; the chief organization overseeing maritime law is the International Maritime Committee, composed of the maritime law associations of several countries.

marjoram, or SWEET MARJORAM, Perennial herb (*Majorana hortensis*) of the mint family, or its fresh or dried leaves and flowering tops. Native to the Mediterranean and western Asia, marjoram is cultivated as an annual where winter temperatures kill the plant. It is used to flavor many foods. Various other aromatic herbs or undershrubs of the genera *Origanum* and *Majorana* of the mint family are also called marjoram.

market, Means by which buyers and sellers are brought into contact with each other and goods and services are exchanged. The term originally referred to a place where products were bought and sold; today a market is any arena, however abstract or far-reaching, in which buyers and sellers make transactions. The commodity exchanges in London and New York, for example, are international markets in which dealers communicate by telephone and computer links as well as through direct contact. Markets trade not only in tangible commodities such as grain and livestock but also in financial instruments such as securities and currencies. Classical economists developed the theory of perfect competition, in which they imagined free markets as places where large numbers of buyers and sellers communicated easily with each other and traded in commodities that were readily transferable; prices in such markets were determined only by supply and demand. Since the 1930s, economists have focused more often on the theory of imperfect competition, in which supply and demand are not the only factors that influence the operations of the market. In imperfect competition the number of sellers or buyers is limited, rival products are differentiated (by design, quality, brand name, etc.), and various obstacles hinder new producers' entry into the market.

marketing, Activities that direct the flow of goods and services from producers to consumers. In advanced industrial economies, marketing considerations play a major role in determining corporate policy. Once primarily concerned with increasing sales through advertising and other promotional techniques, corporate marketing departments now focus on credit policies, product development, customer support, distribution, and corporate communications. Marketers may look for outlets through which to sell the company's products, including retail stores, direct-mail marketing, and wholesaling. They may make psychological and demographic studies of a potential market, experiment with various marketing strategies, and conduct informal interviews with target audiences. Marketing is used both to increase sales of an existing product and to introduce new products.

marlin, Any of four species (genus *Makaira*, family Istiophoridae) of deep-blue to blue-green marine fish with a long body, a long dorsal fin, a rounded spear extending from the snout (which it uses to club the fish it feeds on), and usually pale vertical stripes. They are highly prized for sport and food. Species range in weight from about 100 lbs (45 kg) to more than 1,500 lbs (700 kg). The Indo-Pacific black marlin (*M. nigicans*) has a distinctive, stiff pectoral fin set at an angle.

Marmara, Sea of, Inland sea lying between the Asian and European parts of Turkey. It is connected with the Black Sea through the Bosporus, and with the Aegean Sea through the Dardanelles. It is 175 mi (280 km) long and nearly 50 mi (80 km) wide, and it occupies an area of 4,382 sq mi (11,350 sq km). The sea has two distinct island groups. The Kızıl Islands in the northeast are primarily resort areas. The Marmara Islands in the southwest are rich in granite, slate, and marble, which have been quarried since antiquity.

marmoset, Any species of arboreal, diurnal, long-tailed South American monkey (family Callitrichidae) classified in two groups: eight species with short tusks (lower canine teeth), called marmosets, and 25 with long tusks, called tamarins. Marmosets move in a quick, jerky manner and eat insects and sometimes fruit and small animals. Members of the common marmoset genus *Callithrix* are 6–10 in. (15–25 cm) long, excluding the 10–16-in. (25–40-cm) tail. The dense, silky fur is white, reddish, or blackish; the ears are generally tufted. Marmosets have been kept as pets since the early 17th century.

marmot, Any of about 14 species (genus *Marmota*) of stout-bodied, diurnal, terrestrial squirrels found in North America, Europe, and Asia. Marmots are 12–24 in. (30–60 cm) long, excluding the short tail, and weigh 7–17 lbs (3–7.5 kg). Most species live in burrows or among boulders. They frequently sit upright and emit a whistling alarm call. Marmots live almost entirely on green plants, storing fat for hibernation. The black-and-white hoary marmot (*M. caligata*), of Siberia and northwestern North America, which hibernates for up to nine months, is hunted for food and fur. The yellow-bellied marmot (*M. flaviventris*) inhabits the western U.S. and British Columbia.

Olympic marmot (Marmota olympus).
E.R. Degginger

Marne, First Battle of the (Sept. 6–12, 1914) Military offensive by French and British troops in World War I. After the invading German forces had moved to within 30 mi (50 km) of Paris at the Marne River, Joseph-Jacques-Césaire Joffre counterattacked and halted the German advance. French reinforcements were driven to the front by 600 Paris taxis, the first automotive transport of troops. French and British troops forced the Germans to retreat north of the Aisne River, where they dug in to conduct the trench warfare of the next three years. The Allied success thwarted Germany's plan for a quick victory on the Western Front.

Marne, Second Battle of the (July 15–18, 1918) Last large German attack in World War I. As part of its final offensive to split the French forces, German troops under Erich Ludendorff crossed the Marne River but were met by strong French resistance under Ferdinand Foch. Allied counterattacks, especially at the Marne salient, forced the Germans to retreat to their former position along the Aisne and Vesle rivers.

Marne River, River, northeastern France. It flows northwest into the Seine River near Paris. It is navigable for 220 mi (350 km) of its total length of 326 mi (525 km) and has extensive canals. Its valley was the scene of crucial battles in World War I.

Maronite Church, Eastern-rite community centered in Lebanon. It traces its origin to St. Maron, a Syrian hermit of the 4th–5th century AD, and St. John Maron, under whom the invading Byzantine forces were defeated in 684. For several centuries the Maronites were considered heretics, followers of Sergius, patriarch of Constantinople, who taught that Jesus had only a divine will and not a human will. No permanent affiliation with Rome took place until the 16th century. A hardy mountain people, the Maronites preserved their freedom in Lebanon during the Muslim caliphate. In 1860 the Ottoman government incited a massacre of the Maronites by the Druze, an event that led to the establishment of Maronite autonomy within the Ottoman empire. The Maronites obtained self-rule under French protection in the early 20th century. Since the establishment of a fully independent Lebanon in 1943, they have constituted a major religious group in the country. Their spiritual leader (after the pope) is the patriarch of Antioch, and the church retains the ancient West Syrian liturgy.

Marrakech, or MARRAKESH, City (pop., 2004: 823,154), west-central Morocco. One of the four imperial cities, it lies in the centre of the Haouz plain. It was founded in the mid-11th century by Yūsuf ibn Tāshufīn as the capital of the Almoravid dynasty. It fell to the Almohad dynasty in 1147, passed to the Marīnid dynasty in 1269, and was the capital under the Sa'did dynasty in the 16th century. In the premodern era, it was one of Islam's great cities. In 1912 it was captured by the French, who dominated the city until 1956. Now a popular tourist destination, it has many historical buildings and a well-known souk within its ancient city centre (designated a UNESCO World Heritage site in 1985).

Marrano, Spanish Jew who converted to Christianity to escape persecution but continued to practice Judaism secretly. During fierce persecutions in the late 14th century, many Jews died rather than renounce their faith, but at least 100,000 converted to Christianity in order to survive. In time the Marranos came to form a compact society within Spain, growing rich and gaining political power. They were viewed with suspicion, and the name Marrano was originally a term of abuse. Resentment against them led to riots and massacres in 1473. In 1480 the Inquisition intensified the persecution, and thousands of Marranos lost their lives. In 1492 a royal edict ordered the expulsion of all Jews who refused to renounce their faith. Many Marranos settled in North Africa and Western Europe. By the 18th century, emigration and assimilation had led to the disappearance of the Marranos in Spain.

marriage, Legally and socially sanctioned union, usually between a man and a woman, that is regulated by laws, rules, customs, beliefs, and attitudes that prescribe the rights and duties of the partners and accords status to their offspring (if any). The universality of marriage is attributed to the many basic social and personal functions it performs, such as procreation, regulation of sexual behaviour, care of children and their education and socialization, regulation of lines of descent, division of labour between the sexes, economic production and consumption, and satisfaction of personal needs for social status, affection, and companionship. Until modern times marriage was rarely a matter of free choice, and it was rarely motivated by romantic love. In most eras and most societies, permissible marriage partners have been carefully regulated. In societies in which the extended family remains the basic unit, marriages are usually arranged by the family. The assumption is that love between the partners comes after marriage, and much thought is given to the socioeconomic advantages accruing to the larger family from the match. Some form of dowry or bridewealth is almost universal in societies that use arranged marriages. The rituals and ceremonies surrounding marriage are associated primarily with religion and fertility and validate the importance of marriage for the continuation of a family, clan, tribe, or society. In recent years the definition of marriage as a union between members of opposite sexes has been challenged, and in 2000 the Netherlands became the first country to legalize same-sex marriages.

Mars, Ancient Roman god of war and protector of Rome, second only to Jupiter in importance. His festivals occurred in the spring (March) and fall (October). Until the time of Augustus, Mars had only two temples in Rome. His sacred spears were kept in a sanctuary; on the outbreak of war, the consul had to shake the spears, saying "Mars vigila!" ("Mars, awake!") Under Augustus, Mars became not only the guardian of Rome in its military affairs but the emperor's personal guardian. He was identified with the Greek god Ares.

Mars, Fourth planet from the Sun, named after the Roman god of war. Its mean distance from the Sun is 228 million km (142 million mi). Its day is 24 hours 37 minutes and its year about 687 Earth days. It has two small moons, Phobos and Deimos. Mars's equatorial diameter is 3,396 km (2,110 mi), about half that of Earth. Its mass is about one-tenth of Earth's and its surface gravity about one-third as strong. No magnetic field has been detected on Mars, suggesting, as does its low density, the absence of a substantial metallic core. Like Earth, it has seasons and an atmosphere, but its average daytime surface temperature is only −10 °F (−20 °C). Mars's thin atmosphere is mainly carbon dioxide, with some nitrogen and argon and traces of water vapour. Spacecraft images show a cratered surface, with volcanoes, lava plains, flood channels, and canyons, many large by Earth standards; Olympus Mons, for example, is the largest known volcano in the solar system. Wind is an important element on Mars, sculpting features such as dunes and occasionally causing global dust storms. In the distant past Mars appears to have had a denser, warmer atmosphere and much more water than at present. Images from the Mars Global Surveyor spacecraft suggest that some liquid water may have flowed near the planet's surface in relatively recent times. No life has been detected on the planet.

Mars Pathfinder, First spacecraft to land on Mars since the Viking 1976 missions. Launched in 1996 by NASA, Pathfinder descended to the Martian surface in July 1997 using parachutes, rockets, and air bags. It then deployed instruments, including Sojourner, a small, six-wheeled robotic rover, which explored as far as 1,600 ft (500 m) from the lander and sent pictures back for over a month. The mission's main objective was to show that low-cost Mars landings and exploration are feasible.

Marseille, or MARSEILLES, City (pop., 2006 est.: city, 839,043; metro. area, 1,418,481), southeastern France. One of the Mediterranean's major seaports and the second largest city in France, it is located on the Gulf of Lion, west of the French Riviera. It was settled by Greeks during the 7th century BCE and was annexed by the Romans, who called it Massilia, in 49 BCE. It declined along with the Roman Empire but revived as a commercial port during the Crusades era; it passed to the French crown in 1481. The plague of 1720 killed half of its population. In the 19th century the development of France's colonial empire added to the city's importance. Following World War II, rapid industrial growth took place around the port complex at Fos-sur-Mer and in suburbs such as Marignane and Vitrolles.

marsh, Freshwater or marine wetland ecosystem characterized by poorly drained mineral soils and by plant life dominated by grasses. Fewer plant species grow in marshes than on well-watered but not waterlogged land; grasses, sedges, and reeds or rushes are most common. Commercially, rice is by far the most important freshwater marsh plant: it supplies a major portion of the world's grain. Salt marshes are formed on intertidal land by seawater flooding and draining, and salt-marsh grasses will not grow on permanently flooded flats.

marsh mallow, Perennial herbaceous plant (*Althaea officinalis*) of the mallow family, native to eastern Europe and northern Africa and naturalized in North America. Found usually in marshy areas near the sea, the marsh mallow has strongly veined, heart-shaped or oval leaves and pinkish flowers borne on stalks about 6 ft (1.8 m) tall. The root was formerly processed to make marshmallows.

Marshall, George C(atlett) (b. Dec. 31, 1880, Uniontown, Pa., U.S.—d. Oct. 16, 1959, Washington, D.C.), U.S. Army officer and statesman. After graduating from the Virginia Military Institute, he served in the Philippines (1902–03) and in World War I. He was later an aide to Gen. John Pershing (1919–24) and assistant commandant of the army's infantry school (1927–33), where he taught many future commanders. As chief of staff of the U.S. Army (1939–45), he directed army operations throughout World War II. After his retirement in 1945, Pres. Harry Truman sent him to China to mediate the civil war there. As secretary of state (1947–49), Marshall proposed the European aid program known as the Marshall Plan and initiated discussions that led to the formation of NATO. He resigned because of ill health but was called back by Truman to become secretary of defense (1950–51) and to prepare the armed forces for the Korean War. In 1953 he was awarded the Nobel Prize for Peace.

Marshall Islands, officially REPUBLIC OF THE MARSHALL IS-LANDS, Island country, central Pacific Ocean. It is composed of two parallel chains of low-lying coral atolls: the Ratak, or Sunrise, to the east and the Ralik, or Sunset, to the west. The chains lie 125 mi (200 km) apart and extend some 800 mi (1,290 km) northwest to southeast. The islands and islets number more than 1,200. Area: 70 sq mi (181 sq km). Population: (2011 est.) 55,000. Capital: Majuro. The indigenous people are Micronesian. Languages: Marshallese, English. Religion: Christianity (Protestant, Roman Catholic, other Christians). Currency: U.S. dollar. The largest atoll is Kwajalein, consisting of about 90 islets, with a total land area of 6 sq mi (16 sq km). Much of Kwajalein is used as a missile-testing range by the U.S. military, which provides a major source of revenue to the Marshall Islands. Subsistence farming, fishing, and the raising of pigs and poultry are the principal economic activities. The Marshall Islands is a republic with one legislative house (the Nitijela, or Parliament); its head of state and government is the president. The islands were sighted in 1529 by the Spanish navigator Álvaro Saavedra (or de Saavedra). Germany purchased the islands from Spain in 1885 and declared them a protectorate the following year. Japan seized them in 1914 and after 1919 administered them as a League of Nations mandate. During World War II the U.S. seized Kwajalein and Enewetak, and the Marshall Islands were made part of the UN Trust Territory of the Pacific Islands under U.S. jurisdiction in 1947. Bikini and Enewetak atolls served as testing grounds for U.S. nuclear weapons from 1946 to 1958. The Marshall Islands became an internally self-governing republic in 1979. It signed a compact of free association with the U.S. in 1982 and became fully self-governing in 1986. The compact was amended in 2004.

marsupial, Any mammal of the infraclass Marsupialia, characterized by premature birth and continued development outside the womb. The young remain attached to the mother's teats for a period corresponding to the late stages of fetal development of a placental mammal. More than 170 species (e.g., bandicoots, kangaroos, koalas, wombats) are found in Australia, New Guinea, and nearby islands. About 65 species of opossum occur in the Americas and seven species of ratlike marsupials in South America. Many species have a pouch (marsupium), a fold of skin covering the nipples on the mother's lower belly, where the young continue their development.

martial art, Any of several arts of combat and self-defense that are widely practiced as sport. There are armed and unarmed varieties, most based on traditional fighting methods used in East Asia. In modern times, derivatives of armed martial arts include kendo (fencing with wooden swords) and *kyudo* (archery). Unarmed varieties include aikido, judo, karate, kung fu, and tae kwon do. Because of the influence of Taoism and Zen Buddhism, there is a strong emphasis in all the martial arts on the practitioner's mental and spiritual state. A hierarchy of expertise, ranging from the novice ("white belt") to the master ("black belt"), is usually recognized.

martial law, Temporary rule of a designated area by military authorities in time of emergency when the civil authorities are deemed unable to function. Under martial law, civil rights are usually suspended, and the activities of civil courts are restricted or supplanted entirely by military tribunals. Such "acts done by necessity" are limited only by international law and the conventions of civilized warfare. Though temporary in theory, a state of martial law may in fact continue indefinitely.

Martin du Gard, Roger (b. March 23, 1881, Neuilly-sur-Seine, France—d. Aug. 22, 1958, Bellême), French novelist and dramatist. Originally trained as a paleographer and archivist, he brought to his literary works a spirit of objectivity and a scrupulous regard for detail. He first attracted attention with the novel *Jean Barois* (1913), the story of an intellectual torn between the Roman Catholic faith of his childhood and the scientific materialism of his maturity. He is best known for the eight-novel cycle *Les Thibault* (1922–40), the record of a family's development that chronicles the social and moral issues facing the French bourgeoisie in the pre-World War I era. He received the 1937 Nobel Prize for Literature.

Martinique, Island of the Windward Islands, West Indies, and overseas department of France. Area: 436 sq mi (1,128 sq km). Population: (2011 est.) 401,000. Capital: Fort-de-France. It is 50 mi (80 km) long and 22 mi (35 km) wide and is largely mountainous; its highest point, Mount Pelée, is an active volcano. Tourism is the basis of its economy. Carib Indians, who had ousted earlier Arawak inhabitants, resided on the island when Christopher Columbus visited it in 1502. In 1635 a Frenchman established a colony there, and in 1674 it passed to the French crown. The British captured and held the island from 1762 to 1763 and occupied it again during the Napoleonic Wars, but each time it was returned to France. Made a department of France in 1946, it remained under French administration despite a communist-led independence movement in the 1970s. In the last decades of the 20th century, Martinique and other French overseas possessions achieved greater autonomy but stopped short of independence.

Martinson, Harry (Edmund) (b. May 6, 1904, Jämshög, Swed.—d. Feb. 11, 1978, Stockholm), Swedish novelist and poet. He spent his childhood in foster homes and his young adulthood as a merchant seaman, labourer, and vagrant. He described his early experiences in two autobiographical novels, *Flowering Nettle* (1935) and *The Way Out* (1936), and in travel sketches. Among his best-known works are the poetry collection *Trade Wind* (1945), the novel *The Road* (1948), and the epic poem *Aniara* (1956). In 1949 he became the first self-taught working-class writer ever elected to the Swedish Academy. He shared the 1974 Nobel Prize for Literature with Eyvind Johnson.

martyr, Person who voluntarily suffers death rather than deny his or her religion. Readiness for martyrdom was a collective ideal in ancient Judaism, notably in the era of the Maccabees, and its importance has continued into modern times. Roman Catholicism sees the suffering of martyrs as a test of their faith. Many saints of the early church underwent martyrdom during the persecutions of the Roman emperors. Martyrs need not perform miracles to be canonized. In Islam, martyrs are thought to comprise two groups of the faithful: those killed in jihad and those killed unjustly. In Buddhism, a bodhisattva is regarded as a martyr because he voluntarily postpones enlightenment to alleviate the suffering of others.

Marx, Karl (Heinrich) (b. May 5, 1818, Trier, Rhine province, Prussia [Ger.]—d. March 14, 1883, London, Eng.), German political philosopher, economic theorist, and revolutionary. He studied humanities at the University of Bonn (1835) and law and philosophy at the University of Berlin (1836–41), where he was exposed to the works of G.W.F. Hegel. Working as a writer in Cologne and Paris (1842–45), he became active in leftist politics.

In Paris he met Friedrich Engels, who would become his lifelong collaborator. Expelled from France in 1845, he moved to Brussels, where his political orientation matured and he and Engels made names for themselves through their writings. Marx was invited to join a secret left-wing group in London, for which he and Engels wrote the *Communist Manifesto* (1848). In that same year, Marx organized the first Rhineland Democratic Congress in Germany and opposed the king of Prussia when he dissolved the Prussian Assembly. Exiled, he moved to London in 1849, where he spent the rest of his life. He worked part-time as a European correspondent for the *New York Tribune* (1851–62) while writing his major critique of capitalism, *Das Kapital* (3 vol., 1867–94). He was a leading figure in the First International from 1864 until the defection of Mikhail Bakunin in 1872.

Marxism, Ideology and socioeconomic theory developed by Karl Marx and Friedrich Engels. The fundamental ideology of communism, it holds that all people are entitled to enjoy the fruits of their labour but are prevented from doing so in a capitalist economic system, which divides society into two classes: nonowning workers and nonworking owners. Marx called the resulting situation "alienation," and he said that when the workers repossessed the fruits of their labour, alienation would be overcome and class divisions would cease. The Marxist theory of history posits class struggle as history's driving force, and it sees capitalism as the most recent and most critical historical stage—most critical because at this stage the proletariat will at last arise united. The failure of the European Revolutions of 1848 and an increasing need to elaborate on Marxist theory, whose orientation is more analytical than practical, led to adaptations such as Leninism and Maoism. In the late 20th century the collapse of the Soviet Union and its Eastern bloc allies seemed to mark the end of Soviet Marxism as a practical political or economic model. Meanwhile, China adopted many elements of a free-market economy in what it called a development rather than a repudiation of Marxist theory. In the West, Marxism continues to be appreciated as a critique of market capitalism and a theory of historical change.

Mary, or ST. MARY, or VIRGIN MARY (fl. beginning of the Christian Era), Mother of Jesus. According to the Gospels, she was betrothed to St. Joseph when the archangel Gabriel appeared to her to announce the coming birth of Jesus. Other incidents in the Gospels in which she appears include the visit to Elizabeth, mother of John the Baptist; the birth of Jesus and his presentation in the Temple; the coming of the Magi and the flight to Egypt; the marriage at Cana in Galilee; the attempt to see Jesus while he was teaching; and watching at the cross. Eastern Orthodoxy, Roman Catholicism, and most Protestant denominations hold Jesus to have been divinely conceived and Mary to have remained a virgin. The Roman Catholic church also holds to the doctrine of her Immaculate Conception and her bodily assumption into heaven. Catholics pray to Mary as an intercessor.

Mary, Queen of Scots, orig. MARY STUART (b. Dec. 8, 1542, Linlithgow Palace, West Lothian, Scot.—d. Feb. 8, 1587, Fotheringhay Castle, Northamptonshire, Eng.), Queen of Scotland (1542–67). She became queen when her father, James V (1512–42), died six days after her birth. She was sent by her mother, Mary of Guise, to be raised at the court of the French king Henry II and was married in 1558 to his son Francis II. After Francis's brief rule as king (1559–60) ended with his premature death, Mary returned to Scotland (1561), where she was distrusted because of her Catholic upbringing. In 1565 the red-haired queen married her ambitious cousin Henry Stewart, Lord Darnley, and became a victim of intrigues among the Scottish nobles. Darnley conspired with them to murder her confidant David Riccio. After the birth of her son James (later James I of England) in 1566, Mary was estranged from Darnley, who was murdered in 1567. Ignoring objections by the jealous Scottish nobility, she married James Hepburn, earl of Bothwell (1535?–78), a suspect in Darnley's murder. The rebellious nobles deserted her army at Carberry Hill and forced her to abdicate in favour of her son (1567). After failed attempts to win back the throne, she sought refuge in England with her cousin Elizabeth I, who arranged to keep her in captivity. Several uprisings by English Catholics in Mary's favour convinced Elizabeth to have Mary tried and condemned; she was beheaded at Fotheringhay Castle in 1587.

Mary Magdalene, Saint (fl. 1st century, Palestine; feast day July 22), Follower of Jesus and the first person to see the resurrected Christ. According to Luke 8:2 and Mark 16:9, Jesus cleansed her of seven demons. She accompanied him in Galilee, and she witnessed his Crucifixion and burial. On Easter morning she went with two other women to anoint the corpse, but the tomb was empty. Christ later appeared to her and instructed her to tell the Apostles that he was ascending to God. Popular tradition has long associated her with the repentant prostitute who anointed Christ's feet.

Masada, Ancient mountain fortress, southeastern Israel. It occupies the entire top of a mesa that is 1,424 ft (434 m) tall and has an area of about 18 acres (7 hectares). It is best known for the fortifications built by Herod the Great in the 1st century BC; it was captured by the Zealots, a Jewish sect, in their revolt against Rome in AD 66. After the fall of Jerusalem, Masada, the last remnant of Jewish rule in Palestine, refused to surrender. In 73, after a lengthy siege, it was finally taken by the Romans, who found that nearly all of the some 1,000 Zealots there had committed suicide rather than be captured. In the 20th century the fortress became a symbol of Jewish national heroism; now one of Israel's most visited tourist attractions, it was designated a UNESCO World Heritage site in 2001.

Masaryk, Tomáš (Garrigue) (b. March 7, 1850, near Gölding, Moravia, Austrian Empire—d. Sept. 14, 1937, Lány, Czech.), First president of Czechoslovakia (1918–35). After receiving a doctorate from the University of Vienna, he taught philosophy at the Czech University of Prague (1882) and wrote on the Czech Reformation; his most important works were a study of Marxism (1898) and *Russia and Europe* (1913). In the Austrian Reichsrat (1891–93, 1907–14), he supported democratic policies and criticized Austria-Hungary's alliance with Germany. In 1915 he went to western Europe, where he organized the Czech national council, which in 1918 gained recognition as the de facto government of the future Czechoslovakia. He negotiated its liberation as one of the Fourteen Points in the projected post-World War I peace settlement. Elected president of the new country (1918–35), he was occupied with settling conflicts between the Czech and Slovak parties.

maser, Device that produces and amplifies electromagnetic radiation in the microwave range of the spectrum. The first maser was built in 1951 by Charles H. Townes. Its name is an acronym for "microwave amplification by stimulated emission of radiation." The wavelength produced by a maser is so constant and reproducible that it can be used to control a clock that will gain or lose no more than a second over hundreds of years. Masers have been used to amplify faint signals returned from radar and communications satellites, and have made it possible to measure faint radio waves emitted by Venus, giving an indication of the planet's temperature. The maser was the principal precursor of the laser.

Maseru, City (pop., 2006: urban centre, 227,880; urban agglom., 436,399), capital of Lesotho. It lies on the Caledon River near the border with Free State province, Republic of South Africa. In 1869 the chief of the Basotho (Sotho) nation, Moshoeshoe I, founded the town near his mountain stronghold of Thaba Bosiu. Diamond mining is important economically. The country's only urban centre, Maseru is the site of government buildings as well as a technical school and Lesotho Agricultural College. Roma, to the southeast, is the seat of the National University of Lesotho (1945).

Mashhad, or MESHED, City (pop., 2007 est.: 2,469,000), northeastern Iran. It is situated in the valley of the Kashaf River, at an elevation of 3,231 ft (985 m). It was damaged in a Mongol attack in 1220 and was sacked by Turkmen and Uzbeks in the 16th and 17th centuries. Nādir Shah (r. 1736–47) made Mashhad his capital. The city is the burial place of Hārūn al-Rashīd and a site of pilgrimage for Shīʿite Muslims visiting the tomb of the eighth Shīʿite imam, ʿAlī al-Riḍāʾ.

Masjed-e Shah, Celebrated 17th-century mosque in Eṣfahān, Iran. The mosque, part of the rebuilding effort of the Ṣafavid shah ʿAbbās I, was located at the centre of Eṣfahān, along a great central mall called the *maydān*. Along with neighbouring structures of the period, it is notable for its logically precise vaulting and use of coloured tiles.

mask, Object worn either to disguise or protect the face or to project the image of another personality or being. Masks have been used in art and religion since the Stone Age. In most societies that regularly use masks in ceremonies, their form is dictated by tradition, and they are thought to have supernatural power. Death masks, associated with the return of the spirit to the body, were used in ancient Egypt, Asia, the Inca civilization, and later in Europe and were sometimes kept as portraits of the dead. Masks worn on holidays such as Halloween and Mardi Gras signal release from inhibition and good-natured license. Masks have been widely used in the theatre, beginning with ancient Greek drama and continuing through medieval mystery plays and the Italian commedia dell'arte, as well as in other theatre traditions (e.g., Japanese Noh theatre).

masque, Short dramatic entertainment performed by masked actors. It originated in the folk ceremony known as mummery and evolved into elaborate court spectacles in the 16th–17th centuries. A masque presented an allegorical theme using speeches, dances, and songs, in a performance often embellished with rich costumes and spectacular scenery. The genre reached its height in 17th-century England when the court poet, Ben Jonson, collaborating with Inigo Jones on many notable masques (1605–34), gave it literary force. The masque later developed into opera.

mass, Quantitative measure of inertia, or the resistance of a body to a change in motion. The greater the mass, the smaller is the change produced by an applied force. Unlike weight, the mass of an object remains constant regardless of its location. Thus, as a satellite moves away from the gravitational pull of the Earth, its weight decreases but its mass remains the same. In ordinary, classical chemical reactions, mass can be neither created nor destroyed. The sum of the masses of the reactants is always equal to the sum of the masses of the products. For example, the mass of wood and oxygen that disappears in combustion is equal to the mass of water vapour, carbon dioxide, smoke, and ash that appears. However, Albert Einstein's special theory of relativity shows that mass and energy are equivalent, so mass can be converted into energy and vice versa. Mass is converted into energy in nuclear fusion and nuclear fission. In these instances, conservation of mass is seen as a special case of a more general conservation of mass-energy.

mass, Celebration of the Eucharist in the Roman Catholic church. It is considered a sacramental reenactment of the death and resurrection of Jesus as well as a true sacrifice in which the body and blood of Jesus (the bread and wine) are offered to God. It is also seen as a sacred meal that unifies and nourishes the community of believers. The mass includes readings from Scripture, a sermon, an offertory, a eucharistic prayer, and communion. The rite was greatly changed after the Second Vatican Council, notably in the adoption of vernacular languages in place of Latin.

mass production, Application of the principles of specialization, division of labour, and standardization of parts to the manufacturing of goods on a large scale. Modern mass-production methods have led to such improvements in the cost, quality, quantity, and variety of goods available that the largest global population in history is now sustained at the highest general standard of living ever. The requirements for mass production of a particular product include the existence of a market large enough to justify a large investment; a product design that can use standardized parts and processes; a physical layout that minimizes materials handling; division of labour into simple, short, repetitive steps; continuous flow of work; and tools designed specifically for the tasks to be performed.

mass spectrometry, or MASS SPECTROSCOPY, Analytic technique by which chemical substances are identified by sorting gaseous ions by mass using electric and magnetic fields. A mass spectrometer uses electrical means to detect the sorted ions, while a mass spectrograph uses photographic or other nonelectrical means; either device is a mass spectroscope. The process is widely used to measure masses and relative abundances of different isotopes, to analyze products of a separation by liquid or gas chromatography, to test vacuum integrity in high-vacuum equipment, and to measure the geological age of minerals.

Massachusetts Institute of Technology (MIT), U.S. private university in Cambridge, famous for its scientific and technological training and research. Founded in 1861, MIT has schools of architecture and planning, engineering, humanities and social sciences, management (the Sloan School), and science and a college of health sciences and technology. Though it is best known for its programs in engineering and the physical sciences, other areas such as economics, political science, urban studies, linguistics, and philosophy are also strong. Among its facilities are a nuclear reactor, a computation centre, geophysical and astrophysical observatories, a linear accelerator, a space research centre, supersonic wind tunnels, an artificial-intelligence laboratory, a centre for cognitive science, and an international-studies centre.

Massif Central, Plateau region, south-central France. It is bordered by the lowlands of Aquitaine, the Loire basin, the Rhône-Saône valley, and the Mediterranean coastlands of Languedoc. Comprising about one-sixth of France, it occupies an area of 35,006 sq mi (90,665 sq km). It consists mainly of plateaus with elevations of 2,000 to 3,000 ft (600 to 900 m). Its highest peak is Puy de Sancy, which reaches 6,184 ft (1,885 m). It is the source of many rivers, including the Loire, Allier, Cher, and Creuse.

mastectomy, Surgical removal of a breast, usually because of breast cancer. If the cancer has spread, radical mastectomy may remove surrounding tissue and/or nearby structures, including chest muscles and lymph nodes. Modified radical mastectomy leaves at least the main chest muscle, has an equally high survival rate, and makes reconstruction easier. Simple mastectomy is removal of the breast only. Lumpectomy is removal of the tumour only.

mastitis, Inflammation of the breast. Acute mastitis, usually caused by bacteria, begins almost exclusively in the first three weeks of nursing and can be cured with antibiotics without stopping nursing. The breasts may become swollen, red, hard, and tender; without treatment abscesses may occur. Mastitis can be localized or widespread, and the breast's lymphatic system may be involved. Girls may have brief hormone-induced breast inflammation soon after birth and during puberty. Chronic mastitis usually occurs in systemic diseases (e.g., tuberculosis, syphilis). One rare type is seen mostly in older women with a history of difficult nursing. Some mastitis cases resemble certain cancers.

mastoiditis, Inflammation of the mastoid process, a bony projection just behind the ear, almost always due to otitis media. It may spread into small cavities in the bone, blocking their drainage. Very severe cases infect the whole middle ear cleft. It causes pain behind the ear and on the side of the head. Temperature and pulse rate may rise. Tissues over the bone may swell until an abscess develops, indicating destruction of the bone's outer layer. Complications of inward spread include abscess inside the skull, thrombosis, and inner-ear infection; meningitis is a serious danger. Now rare with treatment of otitis media, mastoiditis usually responds to early antibiotic treatment; if not, surgical drainage with removal of all diseased bone is necessary.

Mata Hari, orig. MARGARETHA GEERTRUIDA ZELLE (b. Aug. 7, 1876, Leeuwarden, Neth.—d. Oct. 15, 1917, Vincennes, near Paris, France), Dutch courtesan and alleged spy in World War I. In 1895 she married Campbell MacLeod, a Scottish officer, and lived in Java and Sumatra (1897–1902), after which they returned to Europe and separated. In 1905 she began to dance in Paris, calling herself Mata Hari (a Malay expression for the sun). Beautiful and exotic and willing to dance virtually nude, she soon had numerous lovers, including military officers. Details of her spying activities are unclear, but she apparently spied for Germany from 1916. She was arrested by the French in 1917, tried by a military court, and shot by firing squad.

Mata Hari.
Harlinque/H. Roger-Viollet

matchlock, Device for igniting gunpowder, invented in the 15th century. The first mechanical ignition system, it represented a major advance in small-arms manufacture. It consisted of an S-shaped arm, called a serpentine, that held a match, and a trigger device that lowered the serpentine so the lighted match would fire the priming powder in the pan at the side of the barrel. The flash in the pan penetrated a small port in the breech and lit the main charge. Though slow and somewhat clumsy, the matchlock was useful because it protected all the working elements inside the lock and freed the user's hand. Early matchlock guns included the musket.

materialism, In metaphysics, the doctrine that all of reality is essentially of the nature of matter. In the philosophy of mind, one form of materialism, sometimes called central-state materialism, asserts that states of the mind are identical to states of the human brain. In order to account for the possible existence of mental states in creatures that do not share the human nervous system (e.g., octopuses and Martians), proponents of functionalism identified particular mental states with the functional or causal roles those states play with respect to other physical and mental states of the organism; this allows for the "multiple realizability" of the same mental state in different physical states. (Strictly speaking, functionalism is compatible with both materialism and non-materialism, though most functionalists are materialists.) As a form of materialism, functionalism is "nonreductive," because it holds that mental states cannot be completely explained in terms that refer only to what is physical. Though not identical with physical states, mental states are said to "supervene" on them, in the sense that there can be no change in the former without some change in the latter. "Eliminative" materialism rejects any aspect of the mental that cannot be explained wholly in physical terms; in particular, it denies the existence of the familiar categories of mental state presupposed in folk psychology.

materials science, Study of the properties of solid materials and how those properties are determined by the material's composition and structure, both macroscopic and microscopic. Materials science grew out of solid-state physics, metallurgy, ceramics, and chemistry, since the numerous properties of materials cannot be understood within the context of any single discipline. With a basic understanding of the origins of properties, materials can be selected or designed for an enormous variety of applications, from structural steels to computer microchips. Materials science is therefore important to many engineering fields, including electronics, aerospace, telecommunications, information processing, nuclear power, and energy conversion.

mathematical physics, Branch of mathematical analysis that emphasizes tools and techniques of particular use to physicists and engineers. It focuses on vector spaces, matrix algebra, differential equations (especially for boundary value problems), integral equations, integral transforms, infinite series, and complex variables. Its approach can be tailored to applications in electromagnetism, classical mechanics, and quantum mechanics.

mathematics, Science of structure, order, and relation that has evolved from counting, measuring, and describing the shapes of objects. It deals with logical reasoning and quantitative calculation. Since the 17th century it has been an indispensable adjunct to the physical sciences and technology, to the extent that it is considered the underlying language of science. Among the principal branches of mathematics are algebra, analysis, arithmetic, combinatorics, Euclidean and non-Euclidean geometries, game theory, number theory, numerical analysis, optimization, probability, set theory, statistics, topology, and trigonometry.

mathematics, foundations of, Scientific inquiry into the nature of mathematical theories and the scope of mathematical methods. It began with Euclid's *Elements* as an inquiry into the logical and philosophical basis of mathematics—in essence, whether the axioms of any system (be it Euclidean geometry or calculus) can ensure its completeness and consistency. In the modern era, this debate for a time divided into three schools of thought: logicism, formalism, and intuitionism. Logicists supposed that abstract mathematical objects can be entirely developed starting from basic ideas of sets and rational, or logical, thought; a variant of logicism, known as mathematical Platonism, views these objects as existing external to and independent of an observer. Formalists believed mathematics to be the manipulation of configurations of symbols according to prescribed rules, a "game" independent of any physical interpretation of the symbols. Intuitionists rejected certain concepts of logic and the notion that the axiomatic method would suffice to explain all of mathematics, instead seeing mathematics as an intellectual activity dealing with mental constructions independent of language and any external reality. In the 20th century, Gödel's theorem ended any hope of finding an axiomatic basis of mathematics that was both complete and free from contradictions.

Matilda of Canossa, Italian MATILDE, known as MATILDA THE GREAT COUNTESS (b. 1046, Lucca, Tuscany—d. July 24, 1115, Bondeno, Romagna), Countess of Tuscany. A close friend of Pope Gregory VII, she backed him in his struggle against King Henry IV, and it was at her castle at Canossa that the king performed his barefoot penance before Gregory (1077). After Henry's second excommunication, she was intermittently at war with him until his death (1106), sometimes donning armour to lead her own troops, and she helped finance the pope's military operations and encouraged Henry's son Conrad to rebel against his father (1093). Her unwavering support for the popes of Rome was honoured by her reburial in St. Peter's Basilica in 1634.

matriarchy, Social system in which familial and political authority is wielded by women. Under the influence of Charles Darwin's theories of evolution and, particularly, the work of the Swiss anthropologist Johann Jakob Bachofen (b. 1815, Basel, Switz.—d. 1887, Basel), some 19th-century scholars believed that matriarchy followed a stage of general promiscuity and preceded male ascendancy (patriarchy) in human society's evolutionary sequence. Like other elements of the evolutionist view of culture, the notion of matriarchy as a universal stage of development is now generally discredited, and the modern consensus is that a strictly matriarchal society has never existed. Nevertheless, in those societies in which matrilineal descent occurs, access to socially powerful positions is mediated through the maternal line of kin.

matrix, Set of numbers arranged in rows and columns to form a rectangular array. Matrix elements may also be differential operators, vectors, or functions. Matrices have wide applications in engineering, physics, economics, and statistics, as well as in various branches of mathematics. They are usually first encountered in the study of systems of equations represented by matrix equations of the form $Ax = B$, which may be solved by finding the inverse of matrix A or by using an algebraic method based on its determinant.

matsuri, Civil or religious festival in Japan, especially a Shintō shrine festival. It traditionally has two parts: a solemn ritual of worship and a joyous celebration. The participants first purify themselves by periods of abstinence and by bathing. The inner doors of the shrine are then opened, a drum or bells are sounded, and the deity or sacred power (*kami*) is called to descend. The ritual continues with offerings, prayers, and ceremonial music and dancing. The celebration usually includes a feast, dancing, theatrical performances, divination, and athletic contests. A portable shrine housing the *kami* is often taken out and carried in procession.

matter, Material substance that constitutes the observable universe and, together with energy, forms the basis of all objective phenomena. Atoms are the basic building blocks of matter. Every physical entity can be described, physically and mathematically, in terms of interrelated quantities of mass, inertia, and gravitation. Matter in bulk occurs in several states; the most familiar are the gaseous, liquid, and solid states (plasmas, glasses, and various others are less clearly defined), each with characteristic properties. According to Albert Einstein's special theory of relativity, matter and energy are equivalent and interconvertible.

Matterhorn, French MONT CERVIN, Italian MONTE CERVINO, Mountain in the Alps, on the border between Italy and Switzerland. Rising to 14,692 ft (4,478 m), it appears from the Swiss side to be an isolated peak, but it is actually the end of a ridge. The Italian slope is more difficult to climb than the Swiss slope. It was first scaled on July 14, 1865, by British explorer Edward Whymper, who ascended the Swiss side. Three days later Giovanni A. Carrel led an Italian group in the first ascent from the Italian side.

The Matterhorn overlooking an Alpine valley.
© Corbis

Matthew, Saint (fl. 1st century AD, Palestine; Western feast day September 21, Eastern feast day November 16), One of the Twelve Apostles, traditional author of the first Gospel. According to the Gospels, he was a tax collector known as Levi when Jesus called him to be a disciple. Other information about him is scarce. The Gospel of Matthew is directed at a Jewish-Christian audience in a Jewish environment and may have been written originally in Hebrew, but it is now doubted that the apostle Matthew was its author. Tradition holds that Matthew conducted his ministry in Judaea, after which he served as a missionary to Ethiopia and Persia. Legend differs as to whether he died a martyr's death.

Mau Mau, Militant Kikuyu-led nationalist movement of the 1950s in Kenya. The Mau Mau (the name's origin is uncertain) advocated violent resistance to British domination in Kenya. In response to actions by Mau Mau rebels, the British Kenya government banned the movement in 1950 and launched a series of military operations between 1952 and 1956. Some 11,000 Kikuyu, 100 Europeans, and 2,000 African loyalists were killed in the fighting; another 20,000 Kikuyu were put into detention camps. Despite their losses, Kikuyu resistance spearheaded the independence movement, and Jomo Kenyatta, jailed as a Mau Mau leader in 1953, became prime minister of independent Kenya in 1963. In 2003 the ban on the Mau Mau was lifted.

Mauriac, François (b. Oct. 11, 1885, Bordeaux, France—d. Sept. 1, 1970, Paris), French writer. Mauriac grew up in a pious and strict Catholic family, and he subsequently placed at the heart of all his works the soul grappling with the problems of sin, grace, and salvation. He is best known for his austere, psychological novels, including *Young Man in Chains* (1913); *The Kiss to the Leper* (1922); *Thérèse* (1927); *Vipers' Tangle* (1932), often considered his masterpiece; and *A Woman of the Pharisees* (1941). He wrote polemical works against totalitarianism and fascism in the 1930s and worked with the Resistance during World War II. In 1952 he was awarded the Nobel Prize for Literature.

Mauritania, officially ISLAMIC REPUBLIC OF MAURITANIA, Country, northwestern Africa. It is bordered by the Atlantic Ocean. Area: 398,000 sq mi (1,030,700 sq km). Population: (2011 est.) 3,282,000. Capital: Nouakchott. The Moors (of mixed Arab-Amazigh [Berber] and Sudanic descent) constitute the great majority of the population. Languages: Arabic (official), Fula, Soninke, Wolof (all national). Religion: Islam (official; predominantly Sunni). Currency: ouguiya. Most of Mauritania is made up of low-lying desert that forms the extreme western part of the Sahara. Only a tiny fraction of its land is arable, but almost two-fifths is suitable for grazing, and the herding of goats, sheep, and camels occupies a significant portion of the largely nomadic population. Oil, ocean fishing, and iron ore production are major sources of revenue. Mauritania is a republic with two legislative houses; its head of state and government is the president, assisted by the prime minister. Inhabited in ancient times by Ṣanhājah Imazighen, in the 11th–12th century it was the centre of the Amazigh Almoravid dynasty, which imposed Islam on many of the neighbouring peoples. Arab tribes arrived in the 15th century and formed several powerful confederations: Trarza and Brakna, which dominated the Sénégal River region; Kunta in the east; and Rigaibāt in the north. The Portuguese arrived in the 15th century. France gained control of the coastal region in 1817, and in 1904 a formal French protectorate was extended over the territory. In 1920 it was added to French West Africa as a territory. In 1960 Mauritania achieved independence and left the French Community. The country's first president, Moktar Ould Daddah, was ousted in a coup in 1978, and a military government was established. In 1991 a new constitution was adopted, and a civilian government was installed in 1992. The country has faced continued economic hardship and political unrest, including coups in 2005 and 2008.

Mauritius, officially REPUBLIC OF MAURITIUS, Island country, lying east of Madagascar in the western Indian Ocean. One of the Mascarene Islands, it extends 38 mi (61 km) north-south and 29 mi (47 km) east-west. Its outlying territories are Rodrigues Island to the east, the Cargados Carajos Shoals to the northeast, and the Agalega Islands to the north. Area: 788 sq mi (2,040 sq km). Population: (2011 est.) 1,288,000. Capital: Port Louis. About two-thirds of the population are of South Asian descent, and most of the rest are of mixed European, South Asian, and African ancestry. Languages: English (official), Creole (lingua franca), various ethnic languages. Religions: Hinduism, Christianity, Islam. Currency: Mauritian rupee. Volcanic in origin and almost surrounded by coastal reefs, Mauritius rises to 2,717 ft (828 m) at Piton de la Petite Rivière Noire. The chief water source is Lake Vacoas. About half of the land is arable; sugarcane is the major crop, though the government has sponsored agricultural diversification. The country depends heavily on food imports, mainly rice. The population density is one of the highest in the world. Mauritius is a republic with one legislative house; the head of state is the president, and the head of government is the prime minister. The island was visited, but not settled, by the Portuguese in the early 16th century. The Dutch took possession (1598–1710), called it Mauritius for the governor Maurice of Nassau, and attempted to settle it (1638–58, 1664–1710) before abandoning it to pirates. The French East India Company occupied it in 1721, renamed it Île de France, and governed it until the French crown took over its administration in 1767. Sugar planting was the main economic activity, and the colony prospered. The British captured the island in 1810 and were granted formal control of it under the Treaty of Paris in 1814; the name Mauritius was reinstated and slavery was later abolished. In the late 19th century, competition from beet sugar caused an economic decline, compounded by the opening of the Suez Canal in 1869. After World War II Mauritius adopted political and economic reforms, and in 1968 it became an independent state within the Commonwealth. In 1992 it became a republic. It has successfully diversified its economy, notably into clothing manufacturing, information technology, and business and financial services.

Mauryan empire (*c.* 321–*c.* 185 BC) In ancient India, a state centred at Pataliputra (later Patna) near the junction of the Son and Ganges (Ganga) rivers. After the death of Alexander the Great, Chandragupta Maurya (Candra Gupta), the dynastic founder, carved out an empire that encompassed most of the subcontinent except for the Tamil south. Ashoka (r. *c.* 269–232 BC), the famous Buddhist emperor, left stone edicts that include some of the oldest deciphered original texts of India. The empire declined after Ashoka's death, but in its heyday it was an efficient and highly organized autocracy.

mawlid, or MILAD, In Islam, the birthday of a holy figure, especially Muhammad. His birthday is fixed by tradition as the 12th day of the month of Rabīʿ I (actually the day of his death). First celebrated by the Muslim faithful in the 13th century, Muhammad's birthday was preceded by a month of merrymaking, which ended with animal sacrifices and a torchlight procession. The day of the *mawlid* included a public sermon and a feast. Though *mawlid* festivities are considered idolatrous by some Islamic fundamentalists, they continue to be widely celebrated throughout the Muslim world and have been extended to popular saints and the founders of Sufi brotherhoods.

May Day, In Europe, the day (May 1) for traditional springtime celebrations. It probably originated in pre-Christian agricultural rituals. Celebrations included a May king and queen, a Maypole, and people carrying trees, green branches, or garlands. May Day was designated an international labour day by the International Socialist Congress of 1899, and it remains the standard Labour Day worldwide, with a few exceptions, including Canada and the U.S. A major holiday in the Soviet Union and other communist countries, it was the occasion for important political demonstrations.

May Fourth Movement, Chinese intellectual revolution and sociopolitical reform movement (1917–21). In 1915 young intellectuals inspired by Chen Duxiu began agitating for the reform and strengthening of Chinese society through acceptance of Western science, democracy, and schools of thought, one objective being to make China strong enough to resist Western imperialism. On May 4, 1919, reformist zeal found focus in a protest by Beijing's students against the Versailles Peace Conference's decision to transfer former German concessions in China to Japan. After more than a month of demonstrations, strikes, and boycotts of Japanese goods, the government gave way and refused to sign the peace treaty with Germany. The movement spurred the successful reorganization of the Nationalist Party and gave birth to the Chinese Communist Party.

Maya, Group of Mesoamerican Indians who between AD 250 and 900 developed one of the Western Hemisphere's greatest civilizations. By AD 200 they had developed cities containing palaces, temples, plazas, and ball courts. They used stone tools to quarry the immense quantities of stone needed for those structures; their sculpture and relief carving were also highly developed. Mayan hieroglyphic writing survives in books and inscriptions. Mayan mathematics featured positional notation and the use of the zero; Mayan astronomy used an accurately determined solar year and precise tables of the positions of Venus and the Moon. Calendrical accuracy was important for the elaborate rituals and ceremonies of the Mayan religion, which was based on a pantheon of gods. Ritual bloodletting, torture, and human sacrifice were employed in an attempt to propitiate the gods, ensure fertility, and stave off cosmic chaos. At the height of its Classic period, Mayan civilization included more than 40 cities of 5,000–50,000 people. After 900 the civilization declined rapidly for unknown reasons. Descendants of the Maya are now subsistence farmers in southern Mexico and Guatemala.

maya, In Hinduism, a powerful force that creates the cosmic illusion that the phenomenal world is real. The word maya originally referred to the wizardry with which a god can make human beings believe in what turns out to be an illusion, and its philosophical sense is an extension of this meaning. The concept is especially important in the Advaita school of the orthodox system of Vedanta, which sees maya as the cosmic force that presents the infinite Brahman as the finite phenomenal world.

Maya Codices, Books in Mayan hieroglyphic writing that survived the Spanish conquest. They are made of fig-bark paper folded like an accordion, with covers of jaguar skin. Though most Mayan books were destroyed as pagan by Spanish priests, four are known to have survived: the Dresden Codex, probably dating from the 11th or 12th century, a copy of earlier texts of the 5th–9th century; the Madrid Codex, dating from the 15th century; the Paris Codex, slightly older than the Madrid Codex; and the Grolier Codex, discovered in 1971 and dated to the 13th century. They deal with astronomical calculations, divination, and ritual.

Maya languages, or MAYAN LANGUAGES, Family of about 30 American Indian languages and language complexes, spoken by more than three million people, mainly in southern Mexico and Guatemala. While some have few remaining speakers, Yucatec in Mexico and K'iche (Quiché), Kaqchikel (Cakchiquel), Mam, and Q'eqchi' (Kekchí) in Guatemala count speakers in the hundreds of thousands. Maya languages were recorded in an indigenous script, as well as in colonial documents in a Spanish-based orthography, including the *Popol Vuh* and the Yucatec prophetic texts known as the *Books of Chilam Balam*.

Mayan hieroglyphic writing, System of writing used by people of the Maya civilization until the 17th century AD. The script is known to have existed since at least 200 BC. Of the various scripts developed in pre-Columbian Mesoamerica, Mayan writing is by far the most elaborate and abundantly attested: about 800 signs have been inventoried in more than 5,000 instances. Signs—some representational, some quite abstract—are either logographic, representing words, or syllabic, representing consonant-vowel sequences. Typically, up to five signs are fitted into tight square or rectangular clusters, which are further arranged into rows or grids. The language of Classic Period writing (*c.* AD 250–900) is generally thought to be Cholan, ancestral to several modern Maya languages; later inscriptions are in Yucatec. By the early 21st century, scholars had an accurate grasp of 60–70% of Mayan inscriptions, with some texts almost completely readable and some still quite opaque. Most inscriptions record significant events and dates in the lives of Mayan rulers.

Mayflower Compact (1620) Document signed by 41 male passengers on the *Mayflower* before landing at Plymouth (Massachusetts). Concerned that some members might leave to form their own colonies, William Bradford and others drafted the compact to bind the group into a political body and pledge members to abide by any laws that would be established. The document adapted a church covenant to a civil situation and was the basis of the colony's government.

Mayotte, Island and French overseas department, in the Indian Ocean off the coast of East Africa. The southeasternmost island of the Comoros archipelago, it is located northwest of Madagascar. Area: 144.5 sq mi (374.2 sq km). Population: (2011 est.) 210,000. Capital: Mamoudzou. Most of its people are of Malagasy origin. Originally inhabited by descendants of Bantu and Malayo-Indonesian peoples, it was converted to Islam by Arab invaders in the 15th century. Taken by Malagasy people from Madagascar at the end of the 18th century, it came under French control in 1843. Together with the other Comoros islands and Madagascar, it became part of a single French overseas territory in the early 20th century. It has been administered separately since 1975, when the three northernmost islands of the Comoros declared independence. Mayotte's status was changed to departmental collectivity in 2001. A local referendum in 2009 approved the change of Mayotte's status to an overseas department, effective in 2011.

Mazatlán, Port city (pop., 2000: 327,989), southwestern Sinaloa state, north-central Mexico. It occupies a peninsula overlooking Olas Altas Bay on the Gulf of California. It is Mexico's largest Pacific Ocean port, and its island-studded harbour is known for its fine sandy beaches. Lying diagonally across the gulf from the tip of Baja California, it provides a communications link between Baja and the mainland. Mazatlán, called the "Pearl of the Pacific," is a fishing centre and a popular tourist resort.

Mazzini, Giuseppe (b. June 22, 1805, Genoa—d. March 10, 1872, Pisa, Italy), Italian patriot and a major figure in the making of modern Italy. A lawyer, he joined the secret independence group Carbonari. After he was imprisoned for its activities, he moved to Marseille (1831), where he founded the patriotic movement Young Italy. He later expanded his plan for a world republican federation and in Switzerland founded Young Europe. In London (1837) he continued his revolutionary activities by correspondence with agents worldwide. He founded the People's International League (1847) and received support from English liberals. In 1848 he returned to Italy to help govern the short-lived Republic of Rome, but returned to England after the pope reestablished control in Rome. Mazzini founded the Friends of Italy (1851) and backed unsuccessful uprisings in Milan, Mantua, and Genoa. An uncompromising republican, he disapproved of the new united Kingdom of Italy (1861).

Mbabane, Capital and largest town (pop., 2007 est.: 78,000) of Swaziland. Located in western Swaziland, it developed near the cattle kraal of the Swazi king Mbandzeni in the late 19th century. The actual town was founded in 1902, when the British assumed control of Swaziland and set up an administrative headquarters there. A Mozambican railway link near Mbabane was established in 1964, primarily to export iron ore extracted in the region; production of the ore had virtually ceased by the late 1970s.

mbira, or THUMB PIANO, African musical instrument consisting of a set of tuned metal or bamboo tongues attached to a board or resonator. The tongues are depressed and released with the thumbs and fingers to produce melodies and song accompaniments. The mbira dates to at least the 16th century in Africa, and it was imported to Latin America by slaves.

McCartney, Sir (James) Paul (b. June 18, 1942, Liverpool, Eng.), British singer and songwriter. Born to a working-class family, he learned piano but switched to guitar after hearing American rock-and-roll recordings. In the mid-1950s he met John Lennon, with whom he formed the Quarrymen, which evolved into the Beatles. He and Lennon cowrote scores of songs, including some of the most popular songs of the 20th century. He released his first solo album in 1970. With his wife, the photographer Linda Eastman (1941–98), he formed the group Wings; their hit albums include *Band on the Run* (1973) and *Wings at the Speed of Sound* (1976). After the band dissolved, McCartney had a string of hits in the 1980s. In Rio de Janeiro in 1990, he set a world record by performing before a paying audience of more than 184,000. He was knighted in 1997.

McClintock, Barbara (b. June 16, 1902, Hartford, Conn., U.S.—d. Sept. 2, 1992, Huntington, N.Y.), U.S. geneticist. She received her doctorate from Cornell University. In the 1940s and '50s, her experiments with variations in the coloration of kernels of corn revealed that genetic information is not stationary. She isolated two control elements in genetic material and found not only that they moved but that the change in position affected the behaviour of neighbouring genes, and she suggested that these elements were responsible for the diversity in cells during an organism's development. Her pioneering research, whose importance was not recognized for many years, eventually resulted in her being awarded a 1983 Nobel Prize.

McKinley, Mount, Athabascan DENALI, Highest mountain in North America. Located near the centre of the Alaska Range in south-central Alaska, U.S., and in Denali National Park, it rises to 20,320 ft (6,194 m). The northern peak was first scaled in 1910, and in 1913 Hudson Stuck and Harry Karstens ascended the southern peak, the true summit. It was named Densmores Peak in 1889 after a prospector but was renamed in 1896 in honour of Pres. William McKinley.

McMurdo Sound, Bay, western extension of the Ross Sea, Antarctica. Lying at the edge of the Ross Ice Shelf, the channel is 92 mi (148 km) long and up to 46 mi (74 km) wide; it has been a major centre for Antarctic explorations. First discovered in 1841 by Scottish explorer James C. Ross, it served as one of the main access routes to the Antarctic continent. Ross Island, on the shores of the sound, was the site of headquarters for British explorers Robert Falcon Scott and Ernest Shackleton.

Mead, Margaret (b. Dec. 16, 1901, Philadelphia, Pa., U.S.—d. Nov. 15, 1978, New York, N.Y.), U.S. anthropologist. She studied under Franz Boas and Ruth Benedict at Columbia University and did fieldwork in Samoa before completing her Ph.D. (1929). The first and most famous of her 23 books, *Coming of Age in Samoa* (1928), presents evidence in support of cultural determinism with respect to the formation of personality or temperament. Her other books include *Sex and Temperament in Three Primitive Societies* (1935), *Male and Female* (1949), and *Culture and Commitment* (1970). Her theories caused later 20th-century anthropologists to question both the accuracy of her observations and the soundness of her conclusions. In her later years she became a prominent voice on such wide-ranging issues as women's rights and nuclear proliferation, and her great fame owed as much to the force of her personality and her outspokenness as to the quality of her scientific work. She served in curatorial positions at the American Museum of Natural History for over 50 years.

mean, median, and mode, In mathematics, the three principal ways of designating the average value of a list of numbers. The arithmetic mean is found by adding the numbers and dividing the sum by the number of numbers in the list. This is what is most often meant by an average. The median is the middle value in a list ordered from smallest to largest. The mode is the most frequently occurring value on the list. There are other types of means. A geometric mean is found by multiplying all values in a list and then taking the root of that product equal to the number of values (e.g., the square root if there are two numbers). The geometric mean is typically used in cases of exponential growth or decline. In statistics, the mean of a random variable is its expected value—i. e., the theoretical long-run arithmetic mean of the outcomes of repeated trials, such as a large number of tosses of a die.

mean-value theorems, In mathematics, two theorems, one associated with differential calculus and one with integral calculus. The first proposes that any differentiable function defined on an interval has a mean value, at which a tangent line is parallel to the line connecting the endpoints of the function's graph on that interval. For example, if a car covers a mile from a dead stop in one minute, it must have been traveling exactly a mile a minute at some point along that mile. In integral calculus, the mean value of a function on an interval is, in essence, the arithmetic mean of its values over the interval. Because the number of values is infinite, a true arithmetic mean is not possible. The theorem shows how to find the mean value using a definite integral.

meaning, In philosophy and linguistics, the sense of a linguistic expression, sometimes understood in contrast to its referent. For example, the expressions "the morning star" and "the evening star" have different meanings, though their referent (Venus) is the same. Some expressions have meanings but no referents ("the present king of France") or referents but no meanings ("that"). The literal or conventional meaning of an expression may differ from what a speaker of that expression means by uttering it on a particular occasion; this is the case with similes, statements uttered ironically, and statements that convey various "conversational implicatures," as in the following examples: "She entered the house and shot him" implicates that she shot him in the house after she entered it, though this is not part of the sentence's literal meaning; "John has three sons" implicates that John has no more than three sons, though again the sentence does not literally say this. Other non-literal aspects of meaning include the potential for carrying out various "speech acts"; e.g., uttered in the appropriate circumstances, the sentence "I christen thee the *Joseph Stalin*," constitutes the act of naming a ship, and the sentence "I am cold" constitutes a request to close the window.

measles, or RUBEOLA, Highly contagious viral childhood disease. It initially resembles a severe cold with red eyes and fever; a blotchy rash and higher fever later develop. After recovery, patients have lifelong immunity. Adult patients tend to have more severe cases. Antibiotics now prevent death from secondary infections. Measles itself, for which there is no drug, requires only bed rest, eye protection, and steam for bronchial irritation. A vaccine developed in the 1960s proved not to give permanent immunity and is too heat-sensitive for use in tropical areas. The worldwide incidence of measles continues to rise. Research is currently directed toward development of a more stable vaccine.

Mecca, Arabic AL-MAKKAH, City (pop., 2004: 1,294,106), western Saudi Arabia. The holiest city of Islam, it was the birthplace of the Prophet Muhammad. It was his home until 622 CE, when he was forced to flee to Medina; he returned and captured the city in 630. It came under the control of the Egyptian Mamlūk dynasty in 1269 and of the Ottoman Empire in 1517. King Ibn Saʿūd occupied it in 1925, and it became part of the Kingdom of Saudi Arabia. It is a religious centre to which Muslims must attempt a pilgrimage once during a lifetime; only Muslims may enter Mecca, and services related to pilgrimages are the main economic activity. The Great Mosque contains the Kaʿbah.

mechanical engineering, Branch of engineering concerned with the design, manufacture, installation, and operation of engines, machines, and manufacturing processes. Mechanical engineering involves application of the principles of dynamics, control, thermodynamics and heat transfer, fluid mechanics, strength of materials, materials science, electronics, and mathematics. It is concerned with machine tools, motor vehicles, textile machinery, packaging machines, printing machinery, metalworking machines, welding, air conditioning, refrigerators, agricultural machinery, and many other machines and processes essential to an industrial economy.

mechanics, Science of the action of forces on material bodies. It forms a central part of all physical science and engineering. Beginning with Newton's laws of motion in the 17th century, the theory has since been modified and expanded by the theories of quantum mechanics and relativity. Newton's theory of mechanics, known as classical mechanics, accurately represented the effects of forces under all conditions known in his time. It can be divided into statics, the study of equilibrium, and dynamics, the study of motion caused by forces. Though classical mechanics fails on the scale of atoms and molecules, it remains the framework for much of modern science and technology.

Medea, In Greek mythology, the daughter of King Aeëtes of Colchis. After helping Jason, leader of the Argonauts, to obtain the Golden Fleece from her father, the two were married and she returned with him to Iolcos, where she killed the king who had deprived Jason of his inheritance. Forced into exile, the couple settled in Corinth. In Euripides' tragedy *Medea*, Jason later deserts her for the daughter of King Creon, and Medea takes revenge by killing Creon, his daughter, and her own two children by Jason before fleeing to Athens.

Medellín, City (pop., 2003: 1,955,753), northwestern Colombia. It is one of the country's largest cities and is heavily industrialized. Founded in 1675 as a mining town, it grew rapidly after the completion of the Panama Canal and the arrival of the railroad in 1914. It is now noted for its textile mills, clothing factories, and steel mills. It is one of Colombia's largest trading centres for coffee. It also became a centre for the illegal international distribution of narcotics (mainly cocaine) in the late 20th century.

mediation, In law, a nonbinding intervention between parties to promote resolution of a grievance, reconciliation, settlement, or compromise. It is used especially in labour disputes. In many industrialized countries, the government provides mediation services in order to protect the public interest. In the U.S., the National Mediation Board functions in this capacity. Mediation is also commonly used in international conflicts.

Medici, Lorenzo de', known as LORENZO THE MAGNIFICENT (b. Jan. 1, 1449, Florence—d. April 9, 1492, Careggi, near Florence), Florentine statesman and patron of arts and letters. The grandson of Cosimo de'Medici, he was the most brilliant of the Medici family. He ruled Florence with his younger brother, Giuliano, from 1469. Giuliano was assassinated in 1478 by the Pazzi, a leading Florentine banking family, which was in league with Pope Sixtus IV (who did not support the assassination) and the king of Naples. Lorenzo's direct appeal to the king allowed him to regain power in Florence, and he was sole ruler of the city until his death. His 13-year-old son Giovanni was created a cardinal by Pope Innocent VIII and later became pope as Leo X. Lorenzo used the Medici riches to pa-

Lorenzo de' Medici, terra-cotta bust by Andrea del Verrocchio, c. 1485; in the National Gallery of Art, Washington, D.C.

Courtesy of the National Gallery of Art, Washington, D.C., Samuel H. Kress Collection, 1943

tronize many artists, including Sandro Botticelli, Leonardo da Vinci, and Michelangelo, and he remains perhaps the most famous patron of all time. His policies bankrupted the Medici bank, but the political power of the Medici remained strong in Florence and Tuscany.

medicine, The practice concerned with the maintenance of health and the prevention, diagnosis, and treatment of disease. Medicine may be practiced in doctors' offices, health maintenance organization facilities, hospitals, and clinics. In addition to family practice, internal medicine, and specialties for specific body systems, it includes research, public health, epidemiology, and pharmacology. Each country sets its own requirements for medical degrees (M.D.'s) and licenses. Medical boards and councils set standards and oversee medical education. Boards of certification have stringent requirements for physicians seeking to practice a specialty, and they stress continuing education. Advances in therapy and diagnosis have raised complex legal and moral issues in areas such as abortion, euthanasia, and patients' rights. Recent changes include treating patients as partners in their own care and taking cultural factors into consideration.

medicine man, Priestly healer or shaman, especially among the American Indians. The medicine man (often a woman in some societies) commonly carries a kit of objects such as feathers, stones, or hallucinogenic plants that have magical associations. The work of healing often involves the extraction—by sucking, pulling, or other means—of offending substances from the patient's body. Singing, recitation of myths, and other ceremonies often accompany the healing rite.

Medina, Arabic AL-MADĪNAH, ancient YATHRIB, City (pop., 2004: 918,889), western Saudi Arabia, north of Mecca. It developed from an oasis settled by Jews *c.* 135 CE. In 622 the Prophet Muhammad fled from Mecca to Medina. It served as capital of the Islamic state until 661. It was held by the Ottoman Empire from 1517 to 1804, when it was seized by the Wahhābiyyah. An Ottoman-Egyptian force retook it in 1812. Ottoman rule ceased during World War I (1914–18), and in 1925 it fell to the forces of Ibn Saʿūd. The second holiest city of Islam, it is often visited by Muslims in conjunction with the hajj, the pilgrimage to Mecca. Among its many mosques is the Prophet's Mosque, containing the tomb of Muhammad.

meditation, Private religious devotion or mental exercise, in which techniques of concentration and contemplation are used to reach a heightened level of spiritual awareness. The practice has existed in all religions since ancient times. In Hinduism it has been systematized in the school of Yoga. One aspect of Yoga, *dhyana* (Sanskrit: "concentrated meditation"), gave rise to a school of its own among the Buddhists, becoming the basis of Zen. In many religions, meditation involves verbal or mental repetition of a single syllable, word, or text (e.g., a mantra). Visual images (e.g., a mandala) or mechanical devices such as prayer wheels or rosaries can be useful in focusing concentration. In the 20th century, movements such as Transcendental Meditation emerged to teach meditation techniques outside a religious context.

Mediterranean fruit fly, or MED FLY, Fruit fly (*Ceratitis capitata*) proven to be particularly destructive to citrus crops, at great economic cost. The Med fly lays up to 500 eggs in citrus fruits (except lemons and sour limes), and the larvae tunnel into the fruit, making it unfit for human consumption. Because of this pest, quarantine laws regulating fruit importation have been enacted worldwide.

Mediterranean Sea, Inland sea enclosed by Europe, Africa, and Asia. Its west-east extent is approximately 2,500 mi (4,000 km), while its average north-south extent is about 500 mi (800 km). The Mediterranean Sea occupies an area of about 970,000 sq mi (2,510,000 sq km). It has a maximum depth of about 16,000 ft (4,900 m). In the west the Strait of Gibraltar connects the Mediterranean with the Atlantic Ocean. In the northeast the Sea of Marmara, the Dardanelles, and the Bosporus link it with the Black Sea. The Suez Canal connects the Mediterranean with the Red Sea in the southeast. A submarine ridge between Sicily and Africa divides the sea into eastern and western parts, which are subdivided into the Adriatic, Aegean, Tyrrhenian, Ionian, and Ligurian seas. Its largest islands are Majorca, Corsica, Sardinia, Sicily, Crete, Cyprus, and Rhodes. The Rhône, Po, and Nile rivers form its only large deltas.

Medusa, In Greek mythology, the most famous of the monsters known as Gorgons. Anyone who looked directly at Medusa turned to stone. She was the only Gorgon who was mortal. The hero Perseus, looking only at her reflection in a shield given to him by Athena, killed her by cutting off her head. Perseus later gave the severed head to Athena, who placed it in her shield; according to another account, he buried it in the marketplace of Argos.

Medvedev, Dmitry (b. Sept. 14, 1965, Leningrad, U.S.S.R. [now St. Petersburg, Russia]), Russian president (2008–12) and prime minister (2012–). Medvedev taught law at St. Petersburg State University (1990–99). During this time he also worked in the St. Petersburg mayor's office, where he met future president Vladimir Putin. In 2000 Medvedev headed Putin's presidential election campaign. He became Putin's chief of staff in 2003, and two years later he was appointed first deputy prime minister. Throughout his service under Putin, Medvedev distinguished himself as an able administrator with an eye toward reform, although his admiration of Western popular culture created some controversy. In December 2007 Putin named Medvedev his heir apparent. The central message of Medvedev's subsequent presidential campaign was "Freedom is better than no freedom." After a landslide electoral victory, Medvedev took office on May 7, 2008, and immediately nominated Putin as his prime minister. Throughout Medvedev's term, he and Putin worked virtually in tandem as joint heads of government, and the crowning achievement of his administration was the accession of Russia to the World Trade Organization in December 2011. Medvedev did not seek reelection, paving the way for Putin to successfully pursue a third term as president in 2012. Nominated by Putin, Medvedev was confirmed as prime minister by the legislature on May 8, 2012.

meerkat, or SURICATE, Colonial species (*Suricata suricatta*) of

the mongoose family (Herpestidae). It is a burrowing carnivore found in southwestern Africa that differs from mongooses in having four (rather than five) toes on each foot. Meerkats are noted for their constant vigilance for predators. This sentinel behaviour involves one member of the group finding an elevated position, standing on its hind legs, and alerting the group of danger when it is seen. The meerkat grows to a total length of 17–24 in. (43–60 cm). Insects and other small animals constitute most of its diet, but bulbous roots are also eaten for the water they contain. It is diurnal and easily tamed as a pet. The yellow mongoose (*Cynictis penicillata*) is sometimes called the red meerkat.

*Meerkat, or suricate (*Suricata suricatta).*
© Gordon Langsbury/Bruce Coleman Ltd.

megalith, Huge, often undressed stone used in various types of Neolithic and Early Bronze Age monuments. The most ancient form of megalithic construction is probably the dolmen, a type of burial chamber consisting of several upright supports and a flat roofing slab. Another form is the menhir, a simple upright stone usually placed with others to form a circle, as at Stonehenge and Avebury in England, or a straight alignment, as at Carnac in France. The meaning of megalithic monuments remains largely unknown, but all share certain architectural and technical features suggesting that their creators sought to impose a conspicuously human design on the landscape and imbue it with cultural symbols.

megalopolis, A major conurbation. Generally the term describes any densely populated social and economic entity encompassing two or more cities and the increasingly urbanized space between them. It particularly came to describe the urbanized region of the northeastern U.S. that arose in the second half of the 20th century. Stretching between the metropolitan areas of Boston on the northeast to Washington, D.C., on the southwest, it included the metropolitan areas of New York City, Philadelphia, and Baltimore, Md. The name, meaning "great city," was coined by French geographer Jean Gottmann.

Meghalaya, State (pop., 2008 est.: 2,536,000), northeastern India. Occupying an area of 8,660 sq mi (22,429 sq km), it is bordered by Bangladesh and Assam state. Its few urban centres include Shillong, its capital. The Khasi, the tribal hill people of Meghalaya, speak a Mon-Khmer language. The area came under nominal British rule in the 19th century. It was included in Assam and was made a separate state in 1972. Although it has vast mineral resources, its economy centres on agriculture.

Mehmed II, byname MEHMED THE CONQUEROR (b. March 30, 1432, Adrianople, Thrace, Ottoman Empire—d. May 3, 1481, near Constantinople), Ottoman sultan (1444–46, 1451–81). His father, Murad II, abdicated in his favour when Mehmed was 12 but reclaimed the throne two years later in the aftermath of a Christian Crusade. Mehmed regained the throne when his father died (1451) and began to plan the conquest of Constantinople (Istanbul), the feat for which he is most renowned. In 1453 he captured the city and undertook returning it to its previous level of grandeur. In the next 25 years he conquered large sections of the Balkans. Under his reign, criminal and civil laws were codified in one body of law; he collected a library of Greek and Latin works and had eight colleges built.

Mei Juecheng (b. May 19, 1681, Xuan Cheng, Anhui province, China—d. Nov. 20, 1763, China), Chinese court official, mathematician, and astronomer. He learned mathematics from his grandfather Mei Wending. In 1713 he joined the Mengyangzhai (imperial bureau created to synthesize Western and Chinese scientific knowledge) as one of the chief editors of *Lüli yuanyuan* (c. 1723; "Source of Mathematical Harmonics and Astronomy"). Purely a work of Chinese authorship, the *Lüli yuanyuan* reapportioned credit to Chinese scholars for many discoveries that earlier Jesuit-Chinese compendiums had credited to Europeans. Studying Western algebra enabled Mei to decipher Chinese mathematical treatises from the Song (920–1279) and Yuan (1206–1368) dynasties whose methods had been lost; this led him to expound a theory of the Chinese origin of Western knowledge. While now acknowledged as grossly overstated, Mei's views helped to revive interest in traditional Chinese mathematics and remained highly influential for many decades.

Meiji emperor, orig. MUTSUHITO (b. Nov. 3, 1852, Kyōto, Japan—d. July 30, 1912, Tokyo), Emperor of Japan during whose reign (1867–1912) the Tokugawa shogunate was overthrown, Japan was transformed into a world power, and the imperial throne came to the forefront of the political scene after centuries of being overshadowed by shogunal rule. He believed in the need to modernize Japan along Western lines. Under the Meiji emperor the domains (*han*) and old class system were abolished, a new school

system was introduced, and the Meiji Constitution was promulgated. Also during his reign Taiwan was annexed after the Sino-Japanese War (1894–95), Korea was annexed (1910), and Japan defeated Russia in the Russo-Japanese War (1904–05).

meiosis, or REDUCTION DIVISION, Division of a gamete-producing cell in which the nucleus splits twice, resulting in four sex cells (gametes, or eggs and sperm), each possessing half the number of chromosomes of the original cell. Meiosis is characteristic of organisms that reproduce sexually and have a diploid set of nuclear chromosomes. Before meiosis, chromosomes replicate and consist of joined sister strands (chromatids). Meiosis begins as homologous paternal and maternal chromosomes line up along the midline of the cell. The chromosomes exchange genetic material by the process of crossing-over, in which chromatid strands from homologous pairs entangle and exchange segments to produce chromatids containing genetic material from both parents. The pairs then separate and are pulled to opposite ends of the cell, which then pinches in half to form two daughter cells, each containing a haploid set (half the usual number) of double-stranded chromosomes. In the second round of meiotic division, the double-stranded chromosomes of each daughter cell are pulled apart, resulting in four haploid gametes. When two gametes unite during fertilization, each contributes its haploid set of chromosomes to the new individual, restoring the diploid number.

Meir, Golda, orig. GOLDIE MABOVITCH, later GOLDIE MYERSON

Golda Meir
Dennis Brack/Black Star

(b. May 3, 1898, Kiev, Russian Empire—d. Dec. 8, 1978, Jerusalem), Ukrainian-born Israeli stateswoman, fourth prime minister of Israel (1969–74). Her family immigrated to Milwaukee, Wis., U.S., in 1906, where she became a leader of the Milwaukee Labor Zionist Party. In 1921 she and her husband immigrated to Palestine, where she emerged as a forceful negotiator with British authorities during World War II (1939–45). A signer of Israel's declaration of independence in 1948, she served in the Knesset (parliament; 1949–74) and held the posts of minister of labour (1949–56) and foreign minister (1956–66). As prime minister, she sought diplomatic solutions to ease the region's tensions. The failure of her government to anticipate an Arab attack during the Yom Kippur War of 1973 led her to resign six months later.

Meissen porcelain, German hard-paste, or true, porcelain pro-

Meissen hard-paste porcelain bird, c. 1750; in the Victoria and Albert Museum, London
Courtesy of the Victoria and Albert Museum, London; photograph, EB Inc.

duced at the Meissen factory, near Dresden in Saxony (now Germany), from 1710 until the present day. It was the first successfully produced true porcelain in Europe and dominated the style of European porcelain until c. 1756. The high point of the Meissen factory was reached after 1731 with the modeling of Johann Joachim Kandler. The onion pattern, introduced c. 1739, was widely copied. Meissen porcelain is marked with crossed blue swords.

meistersinger (German: "master singer"), Any of certain German musicians and poets, chiefly of the artisan and trading classes, in the 14th to 16th centuries. These amateur guilds spread throughout Germany until most towns had one. Their main activity was monthly singing contests. Because of their educational aims of fostering morality and religious belief, they came to be instrumental in promulgating the Protestant message during the Reformation, though their music is not regarded as highly distinguished. The most famous meistersinger, Hans Sachs (1494–1576), devoted his art exclusively to the Lutheran cause after 1530.

Meknès, City (pop., 2004: 536,232), north-central Morocco. It was one of Morocco's four imperial cities, founded in the 10th century by a Berber tribe. Originally a group of villages among olive groves, it became the Moroccan capital in 1673 under Maulāy Ismā'īl, who built palaces and mosques that earned for Meknès the name "Versailles of Morocco." After his death it declined, and in 1911 it was occupied by the French. It is now a commercial centre for agricultural products, fine embroidery, and carpets.

Mekong River, Chinese LANCANG JIANG, or LAN-TS'ANG CHIANG, Longest river of Southeast Asia. Rising in southern Qinghai province, China, it flows south through eastern Tibet and across the highlands of Yunnan province. It then forms part of the border between Myanmar (Burma) and Laos, as well as between Laos and Thailand. It runs through Laos and Cambodia before entering the South China Sea in a delta south of Ho Chi Minh City in Vietnam after a course of 2,700 mi (4,350 km). Vientiane, Laos, and Phnom Penh, Camb., stand on its banks. Since 1957 the Mekong Committee, an international effort, has initiated projects to harness the river for hydroelectricity and irrigation.

melanin, Any of several organic compounds, dark biological pigments that give coloration (shades of yellow to brown) to skin, hair, feathers, scales, eyes, and some internal tissues, notably the substantia nigra in the brain. In humans, melanins help protect the skin against the damaging effects of ultraviolet radiation, but melanoma may arise from cells that produce it. The amount in the skin depends on both genetic and environmental factors. Melanin is produced from the amino acid tyrosine; albinos lack the enzyme that catalyzes that reaction.

melanoma, Dark-coloured malignant tumour of skin cells that produce the protective skin-darkening pigment melanin. Melanomas are prone to metastasize and are associated with the highest death rate of any skin cancer. Removal, together with a collar of surrounding healthy skin, cures melanoma if done early. A common cause of melanoma is skin damage from sunlight. It is very rare in persons with dark skin.

Melbourne, City (pop., 2006: 3,592,590), capital of Victoria, southeastern Australia. It is situated at the head of Port Phillip Bay and the mouth of the Yarra River. The area was discovered by Europeans in 1802 and incorporated into the colony of New South Wales. The first permanent settlement was founded in 1835 by settlers from Tasmania, and in 1837 it was named for the British prime minister, Lord Melbourne. The city was made the capital of Victoria in 1851, and it grew rapidly with the gold rush of the early 1850s. It served as the first capital of the Australian commonwealth (1901–27), until Canberra became the new capital. Second in size to Sydney, it is an industrial, commercial, and financial centre and the seat of several universities, including the University of Melbourne.

melodrama, Sentimental drama marked by extravagant theatricality, subordination of character development to plot, and focus on sensational incidents. It usually has an improbable plot that features such stock characters as the noble hero, the long-suffering heroine, and the hard-hearted villain, and it ends with virtue triumphing over vice. Written by such playwrights as Guilbert de Pixérécourt and Dion Boucicault, melodramas were popular in Europe and the U.S. during the 19th century. They often featured spectacular events such as shipwrecks, battles, fires, earthquakes, and horse races. Melodrama died out as a theatrical form in the early 20th century but remained popular in silent film. It can still be seen in contemporary film genres such as the action movie.

melting point, Temperature at which the solid and liquid states of a pure substance can exist in equilibrium. As heat is applied to a solid, its temperature increases until it reaches the melting point. At this temperature, additional heat converts the solid into a liquid without a change in temperature. The melting point of solid water (ice) is $32°F$ ($0°C$). Though the melting point of a solid is generally considered to be the same as the freezing point of the corresponding liquid, they may differ because a liquid may freeze into different crystal systems and impurities can lower the freezing point.

membrane, In biology, the thin layer that forms the outer boundary of a living cell or of an internal cell compartment. The outer boundary is the plasma membrane, and the compartments enclosed by internal membranes are called organelles. Biological membranes have a dual function: separation of vital but incompatible metabolic processes conducted in the organelles; and passage of nutrients, wastes, and metabolic products between organelles and between the cell and the outside environment. Membranes consist largely of a double layer of lipids in which are embedded large proteins, many of which transport ions and water-soluble molecules across the membrane.

memoir, History or record composed from personal observation and experience. Closely related to autobiography, a memoir differs chiefly in the degree of emphasis on external events. Unlike writers of autobiography, who are concerned primarily with themselves as subject matter, writers of memoir usually have played roles in, or have closely observed, historical events, and their main purpose is describing or interpreting those events.

memory, Power or process of recalling or reproducing what has been learned or experienced. Research indicates that the ability to retain information is fairly uniform among normal individuals; what differs is the degree to which persons learn or take account of something to begin with and the kind and amount of detail that is retained. Attention, motivation, and especially association facilitate this process. Visual images are generally better remembered than are other forms of sense-data. Memory prodigies, or people with "photographic" or "eidetic" memories, often draw heavily on visual associations, including mnemonics. Many psychologists distinguish between short- and long-term memory. The former (variously said to last 10 seconds to 3 minutes) is less subject to interference and distortion than the latter. Long-term memory is sometimes divided into episodic (i.e., event-centred) and semantic (i.e., knowledge-centred) memory. Various models of memory have been proposed, from the Enlightenment notion of impressions made on brain tissues (restyled as "memory molecules" or coded "engrams" in the 20th century) to B.F. Skinner's "black box" to more recent ideas concerning information processing or the formation of neuronal groups. Disorders of or involving memory include Alzheimer disease, amnesia, Korsakoff syndrome, post-traumatic stress disorder, and senile dementia.

Memphis, Capital of ancient Egypt during the Old Kingdom (c. 2575–c. 2130 BCE), located on the western bank of the Nile River south of modern Cairo. Founded c. 2925 BCE by Menes, it was by the 3rd dynasty a flourishing community. Despite the rivalry of Heracleopolis and Thebes, it remained important, particularly in the worship of Ptah. Beginning in the 8th century BCE, it fell successively to Nubia, Assyria, Persia, and Macedonia under Alexander the Great. Its importance as a religious centre was undermined by the rise of Christianity and Islam. It was abandoned after the Muslim conquest of Egypt in 640 CE. Its ruins include the great temple of Ptah, royal palaces, and an extensive necropolis. Nearby are the pyramids of Saqqara and those at Giza.

Mencius, Chinese MENGZI, or MENG-TZU, orig. MENG K'O (b. *c.* 372—d. *c.* 289 BC), Chinese philosopher. The book *Mencius* contains statements on innate human goodness, a topic warmly debated by followers of Confucius up to modern times. That the four principles (*si duan*)—the feelings of commiseration, shame, courtesy, and right and wrong—are all inborn in humans was a self-evident truth to Mencius; the four principles, when properly cultivated, will develop into the four cardinal virtues of *ren* (benevolence), righteousness, decorum, and wisdom. His development of orthodox Confucianism earned him the title "second sage."

Mencius, detail, ink and colour on silk; in the National Palace Museum, Taipei
Courtesy of the National Palace Museum, Taipei, Taiwan, Republic of China

Mencius, or MENGZI, or MENG-TZU, Chinese Confucian text concerning government, written by Mencius. The book maintains that the welfare of the common people comes before every other consideration. When a ruler no longer practices benevolence and righteousness, the mandate of heaven (his right to rule) is withdrawn and he should be removed. *Mencius* did not become a classic until the 12th century, when it was published by Zhu Xi together with *Daxue*, *Zhongyong*, and *Lunyu* (*Analects*) as the Four Books.

Mendel, Gregor (Johann) (b. July 22, 1822, Heinzendorf, Austria—d. Jan. 6, 1884, Brünn, Austria-Hungary), Austrian botanist and plant experimenter who laid the mathematical foundation of the science of genetics. He became an Augustinian monk in 1843 and later studied at the University of Vienna. In 1854, working in his monastery's garden, he began planning the experiments that led to his formulation of the basic principle of heredity. He used the edible pea for his studies, crossing varieties that had maintained constant differences in distinct traits such as height (tall or short) and seed colour (green or yellow). He theorized that the occurrence of the visible alternative traits, in the constant hybrids and in their progeny, was due to the occurrence of paired elementary units of heredity, now known as genes. What was new in Mendel's interpretation of his data was his recognition that genes obey simple statistical laws. His system proved to be of general application and is one of the basic principles of biology. His work was rediscovered in 1900 by three botanists, Carl Erich Correns, Erich Tschermak von Seysenegg, and Hugo de Vries, who independently obtained similar results and found that both the experimental data and the general theory had been published 34 years previously.

Menderes River, Name of two rivers in Turkey. The first (Turkish: Büyük Menderes) runs through southwestern Turkey. It empties into the Aegean Sea after a course of 363 mi (584 km). Its Classical name, Maeander (whence the English *meander*), is derived from the winding course of its lower reaches. The second, Menderes Çay (Turkish: Küçük Menderes Çayı), was known in antiquity as the Scamander; it rises in northwestern Turkey and flows 60 mi (97 km) west across the plain of ancient Troy, emptying into the Dardanelles.

Menelaus, In Greek mythology, the king of Sparta and the younger son of Atreus. When his wife, Helen, was abducted by Paris, he asked the other Greek kings to join him in an expedition against Troy, thus beginning the Trojan War. He served under his brother Agamemnon. At the war's end he recovered Helen and brought her back to Sparta instead of killing her as he had intended.

Having forgotten to appease the gods of defeated Troy, he endured a hard voyage home, and many of his ships were lost.

meninges, Three fibrous membranes that surround the brain and spinal cord to protect the central nervous system. The pia mater, a very thin membrane, adheres to the surface of the brain and spinal cord. The subarachnoid space, containing cerebrospinal fluid, separates the pia mater from a second membrane, the arachnoid. Around the brain, fine filaments connect these two membranes, which are believed to be impermeable to fluid. The third membrane, the dura mater, is strong, thick, and dense. It envelops the arachnoid, covers the inside of the skull, and surrounds and supports the large venous channels carrying blood from the brain. Several septa divide it and support different parts of the brain. In the spine, the dura mater and the arachnoid mater are separated by the subdural space; the arachnoid and pia mater are separated by the subarachnoid space. The extradural space (between the dura mater and the wall of the vertebral canal) is the site of epidural anesthesia.

meningitis, Inflammation of the meninges. Bacteria (including meningococcus, among others), often from infection elsewhere, produce the most dangerous forms. Symptoms develop rapidly: vomiting, then severe bursting headache, then stiff neck. Young children may have convulsions. The patient may die within hours. Pus in cerebrospinal fluid can block brain passages and spinal spaces, leading to life-threatening hydrocephalus. Speedy diagnosis (by lumbar puncture) and treatment (with antibiotics) can prevent brain damage and death. Viral meningitis usually has a short course and requires no therapy.

Mennonite, Member of a Protestant church named for Menno Simonsz. They trace their origins to the Swiss Brethren (established 1525), nonconformists who rejected infant baptism and stressed the separation of church and state. Persecution scattered them across Europe; they found political freedom first in the Netherlands and northern Poland, and from there moved to Ukraine and Russia. They first emigrated to North America in 1663. Many Russian Mennonites emigrated to the U.S. Midwest and to Canada in the 1870s when they lost their exemption from Russian military service. Today Mennonites are found in many parts of the world, especially in North and South America. Their creed stresses the authority of the Scriptures, the example of the early church, and baptism as a confession of faith. They value simplicity of life, and many refuse to swear oaths or serve in the military. The various Mennonite groups include the strictly observant Amish and Hutterites as well as the more moderate Mennonite church.

menopause, Final cessation of menstruation, ending female fertility. It usually begins between ages 45 and 55. A gradual decline in function of the ovaries reduces estrogen production. Ovulation becomes irregular and gradually ceases. The length of the menstrual cycle and periods may vary; flow may lessen or increase. Adjustment of the endocrine system to estrogen reduction causes hot flashes, often at night, with a warm sensation, flushing, and sweating; other symptoms, such as irritability and headaches, may be related more to reactions to aging. Removal or destruction of the ovaries to treat disease causes artificial menopause, with similar but more sudden effects. Changes in hormone balance usually cause no physical or mental disturbances. However, the protective effect of estrogen against osteoporosis and atherosclerosis is lost, and risks of fracture and coronary heart disease increase.

The term *male menopause* is sometimes used to describe an equivalent aging-related decline in testicular function that results in testosterone deficiency in men. This process is alternatively referred to as late-onset hypogonadism or andropause.

menorah, Multibranched candelabra used by Jews during the festival of Hanukkah. It holds nine candles (or has nine receptacles for oil). Eight of the candles stand for the eight days of Hanukkah—one is lit the first day, two the second, and so on. The ninth

Roman soldiers carrying the menorah from the Temple of Jerusalem, AD 70; detail of a relief on the Arch of Titus, Rome, AD 81.

Alinari/Art Resource, New York

candle, or *shammash* ("servant") light—usually set in the centre and raised above the others—is used to light the others. The menorah is an imitation of the seven-branched golden candelabra of the Tabernacle, which signified the seven days of creation. The menorah is also an ancient symbol of Jewish identity and the official symbol of the modern state of Israel.

Menshevik, Member of the non-Leninist wing of the Russian Social-Democratic Workers' Party. The group evolved in 1903 when L. Martov called for a mass party modeled after western European groups, as opposed to Vladimir Ilich Lenin's plan to restrict the party to professional revolutionaries. When Lenin's followers obtained a majority on the party central committee, they called themselves Bolsheviks ("those of the majority"), and Martov and his group became the Mensheviks ("those of the minority"). The Mensheviks played active roles in the Russian Revolution of 1905 and in the St. Petersburg soviet, but they became divided over World War I and later by the Russian Revolution of 1917. They attempted to form a legal opposition party but in 1922 were permanently suppressed.

menstruation, Periodic discharge from the vagina of blood, secretions, and shed mucous lining of the uterus (endometrium). The endometrium prepares to receive a fertilized egg by thickening and producing secretions. If the egg released by the ovary is not fertilized, the endometrium breaks down and is expelled by contractions of the uterus. The first menstruation (menarche) occurs after other changes of puberty, usually at 11–13 years of age, apparently triggered by the passing of a weight threshold. Bleeding may be irregular or heavy at first. In adult women, menstrual periods begin at an average interval of 28 days and last about five days; some variation among women and in the same woman is normal. Uterine contractions are felt as cramps. The amount of blood lost is usually less than 1.7 oz (50 ml). Menstruation ends with menopause. Menstrual disorders include dysmenorrhea (painful menstruation) and amenorrhea (no bleeding), heavy or light bleeding, and uterine bleeding.

mental disorder, Any illness with a psychological origin, manifested either in symptoms of emotional distress or in abnormal behaviour. Most mental disorders can be broadly classified as either psychoses or neuroses. Psychoses (e.g., schizophrenia and bipolar disorder) are major mental illnesses characterized by severe symptoms such as delusions, hallucinations, and an inability to evaluate reality in an objective manner. Neuroses are less severe and more treatable illnesses, including depression, anxiety, and paranoia as well as obsessive-compulsive disorders and post-traumatic stress disorders. Some mental disorders, such as Alzheimer disease, are clearly caused by organic disease of the brain, but the causes of most others are either unknown or not yet verified. Schizophrenia appears to be partly caused by inherited genetic factors. Some mood disorders, such as mania and depression, may be caused by imbalances of certain neurotransmitters in the brain; they are treatable by drugs that act to correct these imbalances. Neuroses often appear to be caused by psychological factors such as emotional deprivation, frustration, or abuse during childhood, and they may be treated through psychotherapy. Certain neuroses, particularly the anxiety disorders known as phobias, may represent maladaptive responses built up into the human equivalent of conditioned reflexes.

menthol, Crystalline organic compound of the isoprenoid family. It has a strong, minty, cooling odour and taste. It is obtained from the oil of the Japanese mint or made synthetically and is used in cigarettes, cosmetics, chest rubs, cough drops, toothpastes, and flavourings. Of its two optical isomers, only l-menthol has the desirable cooling effect.

mercantilism, Economic theory and policy influential in Europe from the 16th to the 18th century that called for government regulation of a nation's economy in order to increase its power at the expense of rival nations. Though the theory existed earlier, the term was not coined until the 18th century; it was given currency by Adam Smith in his *Wealth of Nations* (1776). Mercantilism's emphasis on the importance of gold and silver holdings as a sign of a nation's wealth and power led to policies designed to obtain precious metals through trade by ensuring "favourable" trade balances, meaning an excess of exports over imports, especially if a nation did not possess mines or have access to them. In a favourable trade balance, payments for the goods or services had to be made with gold or silver. Colonial possessions were to serve as markets for exports and as suppliers of raw materials to the mother country, a policy that created conflict between the European colonial powers and their colonies, in particular fanning resentment of Britain in the North American colonies and helping bring about the American Revolution. Mercantilism favoured a large population to supply labourers, purchasers of goods, and soldiers. Thrift and saving were emphasized as virtues because they made possible the creation of capital. Mercantilism provided a favourable climate for the early development of capitalism but was later severely criticized, especially by advocates of laissez-faire, who argued that all trade was beneficial and that strict government controls were counterproductive.

mercerization, Chemical treatment applied to cotton fibres or fabrics to make them permanently able to accept dyes and various chemical finishes more easily. The method, patented in 1850 by the English calico printer John Mercer, also gives cotton cloth increased tensile strength and greater absorptive properties. Higher-quality cotton goods are usually mercerized. The treatment consists of dipping the yarn or fibre in a solution of sodium hydroxide and then treating the material with water or acid to neutralize the sodium hydroxide.

merchant marine, Commercial ships of a nation, whether privately or publicly owned, and the personnel who operate such ships, as distinct from the personnel of naval vessels. Merchant ships are used to transport people, raw materials, and manufactured goods. Merchant fleets can be important economic assets for nations with limited natural resources or a small industrial base. By carrying the commerce of other nations on the seas, a merchant fleet contributes to its home nation's foreign-exchange earnings, promotes trade, and provides employment. The U.S. Merchant Marine Academy (founded 1943) is in Kings Point, N.Y.

Mercury, In Roman religion, the god of merchants, commonly identified with the Greek messenger of the gods, Hermes. His temple on Rome's Aventine Hill was dedicated in 495 BC. The goddess Maia was identified as his mother, and the two were honoured in a festival on May 15. Mercury is sometimes depicted holding a purse, symbolic of his business functions. More often he is given the attributes of Hermes and portrayed wearing winged sandals or a winged cap and carrying a caduceus.

Mercury, Innermost planet of the solar system. Its average distance from the Sun is about 36 million mi (58 million km), but its highly elliptical orbit carries it 7.5 million mi (12 million km) nearer to and farther from the Sun. It is the smallest major planet, having a diameter of about 3,030 mi (4,880 km) and a mass about one-eighteenth of Earth's. With the shortest period of revolution (only 88 Earth days) and the highest average orbital speed (30 mi/sec [48 km/sec]) of any planet, it is aptly named after the Roman fleet-footed messenger god. It spins very slowly, making one complete rotation relative to the stars every 59 Earth days, while its solar day (from one sunrise to the next) is 176 Earth days, owing to its revolution around the Sun. Its surface is heavily cratered. Its most impressive feature is perhaps the 960-mi (1,550-km) Caloris Basin, formed by a huge meteorite impact. Mercury also has steep cliffs that extend for hundreds of miles. The discovery of a magnetic field in its vicinity suggests it has a large iron core, which would account for a mean density almost as high as Earth's. Its atmosphere is negligible; its surface gravity, about one-third that of Earth's, holds an exceedingly tenuous layer of gases. Temperatures at its surface change dramatically, ranging from a high that can exceed 800 °F (425 °C) on the sunward side to a low of about −290 °F (−180 °C) at the end of its night.

Mercury, First series of U.S. manned spaceflights (1961–63), which began about three weeks after Yury A. Gagarin became the first human in space. In May 1961 Alan B. Shepard rode the first Mercury space capsule, Freedom 7, on a 15-minute, 302-mi (486-km) suborbital flight, attaining a maximum altitude of 116 mi (186 km). The first U.S. manned flight in orbit was that of the Friendship 7, carrying John H. Glenn, Jr., in February 1962; it completed three orbits. The last Mercury flight, Faith 7, launched in May 1963, was the longest, making 22 orbits in about 34 hours.

mercury, or QUICKSILVER, Metallic chemical element, chemical symbol Hg, atomic number 80. Mercury is the only elemental metal that is liquid at ordinary temperatures, with a freezing point of −38 °F (−39 °C) and a boiling point of 674 °F (356.9 °C). Silvery white, dense, toxic, and a good conductor of electricity, mercury is occasionally found free in nature but usually occurs as the red sulfide ore, cinnabar (HgS). It has many uses—in dental and industrial amalgams, as a catalyst, in electrical and measuring apparatus and instruments (e.g., thermometers), as the cathode in electrolytic cells, in mercury-vapour lamps, and as a coolant and neutron absorber in nuclear power plants. Many of mercury's compounds, in which it has valence 1 or 2, are pigments, pesticides, and medicinals. It is a dangerous pollutant because it concentrates in animal tissues in increasing amounts up the food chain.

mercury poisoning, Harmful effects of mercury compounds. Manufacture of paints, various household items, and pesticides uses mercury; the finished product and the waste products released into air and water may contain mercury. The aquatic food chain can concentrate organic mercury compounds in fish and seafood, which, if eaten by humans, can affect the central nervous system, impairing muscle, vision, and cerebral function, leading to paralysis and sometimes death. Acute mercury poisoning causes severe digestive-tract inflammation. Mercury accumulates in the kidneys, causing uremia and death. Chronic poisoning, from occupational inhalation or skin absorption, causes metallic taste, oral inflammation, blue gum line, extremity pain and tremor, weight loss, and mental changes (depression and withdrawal). Drugs containing mercury can cause sensitivity reactions, sometimes fatal. In young children, acrodynia (pink disease) is probably caused by an organic mercury compound in house paints.

Merlin, Magician and wise man in Arthurian legend. In Geoffrey of Monmouth's *History of the Kings of England*, Merlin was an adviser to King Arthur, with magical powers that recalled his Celtic origins. Later narratives made him a prophet of the grail and gave him credit for the idea of the Round Table. In Sir Thomas Malory's *Morte Darthur* he brought Arthur to the throne and served as his mentor throughout his reign. His downfall was linked to his infatuation for an enchantress, who imprisoned him after learning the magic arts from him.

Merovingian art, Visual arts produced under the Merovingian dynasty of the 5th–8th centuries AD. They consisted mainly of small-scale metalwork, little of which has survived, and several

important manuscripts. The style blends Roman Classical style with native Germanic-Frankish traditions, which favoured abstraction and geometric patterning. The human figure was rarely attempted; artists were concerned primarily with surface design. Though modest, Merovingian art was influential long after the end of the dynasty.

Merovingian dynasty (476–750) Frankish dynasty considered the first French royal house. It was named for Merovech (fl. *c.* 450), whose son Childeric I (d. 482?) ruled a tribe of Salian Franks from his capital at Tournai. His son, Clovis I, united nearly all of Gaul in the late 5th century except Burgundy and present-day Provence. On his death the realm was divided among his sons, but by 558 it was united under his last surviving son, Chlotar I. The pattern of dividing and then reuniting the realm continued for generations. After the reign of Dagobert I (623–639), the authority of the Merovingian kings declined, and real power gradually came to rest in the hands of the mayors of the palace. In 751 the last Merovingian king, Childeric III, was deposed by Pippin III (the Short), the first of the Carolingian dynasty. *See also* Brunhild; Fredegund.

mesa (Spanish: "table") Flat-topped tableland with one or more steep sides, common in the Colorado Plateau regions of the U.S.; a butte is similar but smaller. Both are formed by erosion; during denudation, or downcutting and stripping, areas of harder rock in a plateau act as flat protective caps for portions of underlying land situated between such places as stream valleys, where erosion is especially active. This results in a table mountain (mesa) or fortress hill.

mescaline, Hallucinogen, the active principle in the flowering heads of the peyote cactus. An alkaloid related to epinephrine and norepinephrine and first isolated in 1896, mescaline is usually extracted from the peyote and purified, but can also be synthesized. When it is taken as a drug, its hallucinogenic effects begin in two to three hours and may last over 12 hours; the hallucinations vary greatly among individuals and from one time to the next, but they are usually visual rather than auditory. Side effects include nausea and vomiting.

Mesoamerican civilization, Complex of aboriginal cultures that developed in parts of Mexico and Central America before the Spanish conquest in the 16th century. This civilization and the Andean civilization in South America constituted a New World counterpart to those of ancient Egypt, Mesopotamia, and China. Humans have been present in Mesoamerica from as early as 21,000 BC; a shift from hunting and gathering to agriculture, which began *c.* 7000 BC as the climate warmed with the end of the Ice Age, was completed by *c.* 1500 BC. The earliest great Mesoamerican civilization, the Olmec, dates to *c.* 1150 BC. The Middle Formative period (900–300 BC) was a time of increased cultural regionalism and the rise of the Zapotec people. Civilizations of the Late Formative and Classic periods (lasting until *c.* AD 900) include the Maya and the civilization centred at Teotihuacán; later societies include the Toltec and the Aztec.

Mesoamerican religions, Religions of the pre-Columbian cultures of Mexico and Central America, notably the Olmec, Maya, Toltec, and Aztec. All religions of Mesoamerica were polytheistic. The gods had to be constantly propitiated with offerings and sacrifices. The religions also shared a belief in a multilevel universe that had gone through five creations and four destructions by the time of the Spanish conquest. Mesoamerican religions heavily emphasized the astral bodies, particularly the sun, the moon, and Venus, and the observations of their movements by astronomer-priests were extraordinarily detailed and accurate. The Aztecs approached the supernatural through a complex calendar of ceremonies that included songs, dances, acts of self-mortification, and human sacrifices performed by a professional priesthood, in the belief that the welfare of the universe depended on offerings of blood and hearts as nourishment for the sun. The Mayan religion likewise called for human sacrifices, though on a smaller scale. Information on the astronomical calculations, divination, and ritual of the Mayan priests has been gathered from the Maya Codices.

Mesolithic Period, or MIDDLE STONE AGE, Ancient technological and cultural stage (*c.* 8000–2700 BC) between the Paleolithic and Neolithic periods in northwestern Europe. Mesolithic hunters, using a tool kit of chipped and polished stone together with bone, antler, and wooden tools, achieved a greater efficiency than their predecessors and were able to exploit a wider range of animal and vegetable food sources. Immigrant Neolithic farmers probably absorbed many indigenous Mesolithic hunters and fishers. There is no direct counterpart to the Mesolithic outside Europe, and the term is no longer used to reflect a hypothetical worldwide sequence of sociocultural evolution.

Mesopotamia, Region between the Tigris and Euphrates rivers in the Middle East, constituting the greater part of modern Iraq. The region's location and fertility gave rise to settlements some 10,000 years ago, and it became the cradle of some of the world's earliest civilizations and the birthplace of writing. It was first settled by the Sumerians, who were succeeded by the Akkadians and later by the Babylonians. Successive peoples came to dominate the region until the rise of the Persian Achaemenian dynasty in the 6th century BCE. The Achaemenids were overthrown by Alexander the Great in the early 4th century BCE, and Mesopotamia was ruled by the Seleucid dynasty from *c.* 312 BCE until the mid-2nd century BCE, when it became part of the Parthian empire. In the 7th century CE the region was conquered by Muslim Arabs. The region's importance declined after the Mongol invasion in 1258. Rule by the Ottoman Empire over most of the region began in the 16th century. The area became a British mandate in 1920; the following year Iraq was established there.

Mesopotamian religions, Religious beliefs and practices of the Sumerians and Akkadians, and later of their successors, the Babylonians and Assyrians, who inhabited ancient Mesopotamia. The deities of Sumer were usually associated with aspects of nature, such as fertility of the fields and livestock. The gods of Assyria and Babylonia, rather than displacing those of Sumer and Akkad, were gradually assimilated into the older system. Among the most important of the many Mesopotamian gods were Anu, the god of heaven; Enki, the god of water; and Enlil, the "Lord of the Air," or the wind god. Deities were often associated with particular cities. Astral deities such as Shamash and Sin were also worshipped. The Mesopotamians were skilled astrologers who studied the movements of the heavenly bodies. Priests also determined the will of the gods through the observation of omens, especially by reading the entrails of sacrificed animals. The king functioned as the chief priest, presiding at the new-year festival held in spring, when the kingship was renewed and the triumph of the deity over the powers of chaos was celebrated.

Mesozoic Era, Second of the Earth's three major geologic eras and the interval during which the continental landmasses as known today were separated from the supercontinents Laurasia and Gondwana by continental drift. It lasted from *c.* 251 to *c.* 65.5 million years ago and includes the Triassic, Jurassic, and Cretaceous periods. The Mesozoic saw the evolution of widely diversified and advanced flora and fauna, quite different from those that had developed earlier during the Paleozoic Era or that would develop later during the Cenozoic Era.

mesquite, Any of the spiny, deep-rooted shrubs or small trees that make up the genus *Prosopis* of the pea family. Mesquites form extensive thickets in areas from South America to the southwestern U.S. Two races occur: one of tall trees (50 ft [15 m]), the other low and far-reaching, called running mesquite. Water-seeking roots grow as deep as 70 ft (20 m). Stems bear compound olive-

green to white hairy leaves, then dense, cream-coloured catkins of flowers, followed by clusters of long, narrow, pale yellow beans. In warmer parts of the U.S., mesquites are considered pests and are eradicated. Cattle eat the beans, which contain a sweet pulp. The wood, formerly used in railroad ties, now has value only for unusual furniture and trinkets and as aromatic firewood.

messiah, In Judaism, the expected king of the line of David who will deliver the Jews from foreign bondage and restore Israel's golden age. The term used for the messiah in the Greek New Testament, *christos*, was applied to Jesus, who is accepted by Christians as the promised redeemer. Messiah figures also appear in various other religions and cultures; Shiite Muslims, for example, look for a restorer of the faith known as the mahdi, and Maitreya is a redeeming figure in Buddhism.

Messier catalog, List of about 109 star clusters, nebulae, and galaxies compiled by the French astronomer Charles Messier (1730–1817), who discovered many of them. Still a valuable guide to amateur astronomers, it was superseded by the New General Catalogue (NGC); both NGC and M reference numbers remain in common use.

Messina, Strait of, ancient FRETUM SICULUM, Channel between southern Italy and northeastern Sicily. It is 2 to 10 mi (3 to 16 km) wide. The city of Messina lies on its bank in Sicily, opposite Reggio di Calabria. Ferry service across the strait links Messina with the Italian mainland.

mestizo, Any person of mixed blood. In Spanish America the term denotes a person of combined Indian and European extraction. In some countries, such as Ecuador, it has acquired social and cultural connotations: a pure-blooded Indian who has adopted European dress and customs is called a mestizo (or *cholo*). In Mexico the term's meaning has varied so greatly that it has been abandoned in census reports. In the Philippines it denotes a person of mixed foreign (e.g., Chinese) and native ancestry.

metal, Any of a class of substances with, to some degree, the following properties: good heat and electricity conduction, malleability, ductility, high light reflectivity, and capacity to form positive ions in solution and hydroxides rather than acids when their oxides meet water. About three-quarters of the elements are metals; these are usually fairly hard and strong crystalline solids with high chemical reactivity that readily form alloys with each other. Metallic properties increase from lighter to heavier elements in each vertical group of the periodic table and from right to left in each row. The most abundant metals are aluminum, iron, calcium, sodium, potassium, and magnesium. The vast majority are found as ores rather than free. The cohesiveness of metals in a crystalline structure is attributed to metallic bonding: The atoms are packed close together, with their very mobile outermost electrons all shared throughout the structure. Metals fall into the following classifications (not mutually exclusive and most not rigidly defined): alkali metals, alkaline earth metals, transition elements, noble (precious) metals, platinum metals, lanthanoid (rare earth) metals, actinoid metals, light metals, and heavy metals. Many have essential roles in nutrition or other biochemical functions, often in trace amounts, and many are toxic as both elements and compounds.

metal fatigue, Weakened condition of metal parts of machines, vehicles, or structures caused by repeated stresses or loadings, ultimately resulting in fracture under a stress much weaker than that necessary to cause fracture in a single application. Fatigue-resistant metals have been developed and their performance improved by surface treatments, and fatigue stresses have been significantly reduced in aircraft and other applications by designing to avoid stress concentrations.

metallography, Study of the structure of metals and alloys, particularly using microscopic and X-ray diffraction techniques. Visual and optical microscopic observation of metal surfaces and fractures can reveal valuable information about the crystalline, chemical, and mechanical makeup of the material. In electron microscopes a beam of electrons instead of a beam of light is directed onto the specimen. The development of transmission electron microscopes has made it possible to examine internal details of very thin metal foils. X-ray diffraction techniques are used to study phenomena related to the grouping of the atoms themselves.

metalwork, Useful and decorative objects fashioned of various metals. The oldest technique is hammering. After *c.* 2500 BCE, casting was also developed; in casting, molten metal is poured into a mold and allowed to cool. Various decorative techniques are used. Gold and silver have been worked since ancient times. Gold and silver objects were in such demand in the 12th century that goldsmiths and silversmiths organized guilds. High-quality gold and silver objects were produced in pre-Columbian America. Copper was worked in ancient Egypt and was widely used for household utensils in 17th–18th-century Europe. Both bronze and brass were widely used in ancient Greece. Pewter plates and tankards were made in the Middle Ages and remained popular until they were superseded by cheaper earthenware and porcelain in the 18th century. Wrought iron has been used for decorative hinges, gates, and railings since the 16th century. Lead has traditionally been used for roof coverings.

metamorphic rock, Any of a class of rocks that result from the alteration of preexisting rocks in response to changing geological conditions, including variations in temperature, pressure, and mechanical stress. The preexisting rocks may be igneous, sedimentary, or other metamorphic rocks. The structure and mineralogy reflect the particular type of metamorphism that produced the rock and the composition of the parent rock. Metamorphic rocks are commonly classified by type of facies, predictable mineral assemblages associated with certain temperature and pressure conditions (e.g., granulite facies).

metamorphosis, In biology, any striking developmental change of an animal's form or structure, accompanied by physiological, biochemical, and behavioral changes. The best-known examples occur among insects, which may exhibit complete or incomplete metamorphosis. The complete metamorphosis of butterflies, moths, and some other insects involves four stages: egg, larva (caterpillar), pupa (chrysalis or cocoon), and adult. The change from tadpole to frog is an example of metamorphosis among amphibians; some echinoderms, crustaceans, mollusks, and tunicates also undergo metamorphosis.

metaphor, Figure of speech in which a word or phrase denoting one kind of object or action is used in place of another to suggest a likeness or analogy between them (as in "the ship plows the seas" or "a volley of oaths"). A metaphor is an implied comparison (as in "a marble brow"), in contrast to the explicit comparison of the simile ("a brow white as marble"). Metaphor is common at all levels of language and is fundamental in poetry, in which its varied functions range from merely noting a likeness to serving as a central concept and controlling image.

Metaphysical poetry, Highly intellectualized poetry written chiefly in 17th-century England. Less concerned with expressing feeling than with analyzing it, Metaphysical poetry is marked by bold and ingenious conceits (e.g., metaphors drawing sometimes forced parallels between apparently dissimilar ideas or things), complex and subtle thought, frequent use of paradox, and a dramatic directness of language, the rhythm of which derives from living speech. John Donne was the leading Metaphysical poet; others include George Herbert, Henry Vaughan, Andrew Marvell, and Abraham Cowley.

metaphysics, Branch of philosophy that studies the ultimate structure and constitution of reality—i.e., of that which is real,

insofar as it is real. The term, which means literally "what comes after physics," was used to refer to the treatise by Aristotle on what he himself called "first philosophy." In the history of Western philosophy, metaphysics has been understood in various ways: as an inquiry into what basic categories of things there are (e.g., the mental and the physical); as the study of reality, as opposed to appearance; as the study of the world as a whole; and as a theory of first principles. Some basic problems in the history of metaphysics are the problem of universals—i.e., the problem of the nature of universals and their relation to so-called particulars; the existence of God; the mind-body problem; and the problem of the nature of material, or external, objects. Major types of metaphysical theory include Platonism, Aristotelianism, Thomism, Cartesianism, idealism, realism, and materialism.

meteor, or SHOOTING STAR, or FALLING STAR, Streak of light in the sky that results when a particle or small chunk of stony or metallic matter from space enters Earth's atmosphere and is vapourized by friction. The term is sometimes applied to the falling object itself, properly called a meteoroid. Most meteoroids, traveling at five times the speed of sound or more, burn up in the upper atmosphere, but a large one may survive its fiery plunge and reach the surface as a solid body (meteorite).

meteor shower, Entry into Earth's atmosphere of multiple meteoroids, traveling in parallel paths, usually spread over several hours or days. Most meteor showers come from matter released during passage of a comet through the inner solar system, and they recur annually as Earth crosses the comet's orbital path. Meteor showers are usually named for a constellation (e.g., Leonid for Leo) or star in their direction of origin. Most showers are visible as a few dozen meteors per hour, but occasionally Earth crosses an especially dense concentration of meteoroids, as in the great Leonid meteor shower of 1833, in which hundreds of thousands of meteors were seen in one night all over North America.

meteorite, Any interplanetary particle or chunk of stony or metallic matter (meteoroid) that survives passage through Earth's atmosphere and strikes the ground or that reaches the surface of another planet or moon. On Earth the speed of entry—at least 7 miles/sec (11 km/sec)—generates enough friction with the air to vaporize part or all of the meteoroid and produce a streak of light (meteor). Though vast numbers of meteoroids enter Earth's atmosphere each year, only a few hundred reach the ground.

meteorology, Scientific study of atmospheric phenomena, particularly of the troposphere and lower stratosphere. Meteorology entails the systematic study of weather and its causes, and provides the basis for weather forecasting.

methadone, Organic compound, a potent synthetic narcotic drug, the most effective form of treatment for addiction to heroin and other narcotics. It has been widely used in heroin-addiction programs in the U.S. since the 1960s. Though addictive itself, it is easier to stop using than heroin. It also causes no euphoric effects and does not lead to development of tolerance, so increasing doses are not required. A person taking a daily maintenance dose does not experience either heroin withdrawal symptoms or a heroin rush from any attempt to resume heroin, so heroin's psychological hold on the user can be broken.

methane, or MARSH GAS, Organic compound, chemical formula CH_4, colourless, odourless gas that occurs in natural gas (called firedamp in coal mines) and from bacterial decomposition of vegetation in the absence of oxygen (including in the rumens of cattle and other ruminants and in the gut of termites). The simplest member of the paraffin hydrocarbons, methane burns readily, forming carbon dioxide and water if supplied with enough oxygen for complete combustion or carbon monoxide if the oxygen is insufficient. Mixtures of 5–14% methane in air are explosive and have caused many mine disasters. The chief source of methane is natural gas, but it can also be produced from coal. Abundant, cheap, and clean, methane is used widely as a fuel in homes, commercial establishments, and factories; as a safety measure, it is mixed with trace amounts of an odorant to allow its detection. It is also a raw material for many industrial materials, including fertilizers, explosives, chloroform, carbon tetrachloride, and carbon black, and is the principal source of methanol.

methanol, or METHYL ALCOHOL, or WOOD ALCOHOL, Simplest of the alcohols, chemical formula CH_3OH. Once produced by destructive distillation of wood, it is now usually made from the methane in natural gas. Methanol is an important industrial material; its derivatives are used in great quantities for making a vast number of compounds, among them many important synthetic dyes, resins, drugs, and perfumes. It is also used in automotive antifreezes, in rocket fuels, and as a solvent. It is flammable and explosive. A clean-burning fuel, it may substitute (at least in part) for gasoline. It is also used for denaturation of ethanol. A violent poison, it causes blindness and eventually death when drunk.

Methodism, Protestant religious movement originated by John Wesley in 18th-century England. Wesley, an Anglican clergyman, underwent an epiphany in 1738 in which he felt an assurance of personal salvation, and he soon began open-air preaching. Methodism began as a movement to revitalize the Church of England and did not formally break with the church until 1795. The Methodists' well-organized system of church government combined a strong central authority with effective local organization and the employment of lay preachers. Especially successful among the working class in industrial areas, the movement expanded rapidly in the 19th century. The Methodist Episcopal Church was founded in the U.S. in 1784, and Methodist circuit riders won many followers on the frontier. British and U.S. missionaries have since spread Methodism throughout the world. Methodist doctrine emphasizes the power of the Holy Spirit, the need for a personal relationship with God, simplicity of worship, and concern for the underprivileged.

metre, In poetry, the rhythmic pattern of a poetic line. Various principles have been devised to organize poetic lines into rhythmic units. Quantitative verse, the metre of Classical Greek and Latin poetry, measures the length of time required to pronounce syllables, regardless of their stress; combinations of long and short syllables form the basic rhythmic units. Syllabic verse is most common in languages that are not strongly accented, such as French or Japanese; it is based on a fixed number of syllables within a line. Accentual verse occurs in strongly stressed languages, such as the Germanic; only stressed syllables within a line are counted. Accentual-syllabic is the usual form in English poetry; it combines syllable counting and stress counting. The most common English metre, iambic pentameter, is a line of 10 syllables, or 5 iambic feet; each foot contains an unstressed syllable followed by a stressed syllable. Free verse does not follow regular metrical patterns.

metre, Basic unit of length in the metric system and the International System of Units. In 1983 the General Conference on Weights and Measures decided that the accepted value for the speed of light would be exactly 299,792,458 metres per second, so the metre is now defined as the distance traveled by light in a vacuum in 1/299,792,458 second. One metre is equal to about 39.37 in. in the U.S. Customary System.

metric system, International decimal system of weights and measures, based on the metre (m) for length and the kilogram (kg) for mass, originally adopted in France in 1795. All other metric units were derived from the metre, including the gram (g) for weight (1 cc of water at its maximum density) and the litre (l, or L) for capacity (0.001 cu m). In the 20th century, the metric system became the basis for the International System of Units, which is now used officially almost worldwide.

metrology, Science of measurement. Measuring a quantity means establishing its ratio to another fixed quantity of the same kind, known as the unit of that kind of quantity. A unit is an abstract idea, defined either by reference to a randomly chosen material standard or to a natural phenomenon. For example, the metre, the standard of length in the metric system, was formerly defined (1889–1960) by the separation of two lines on a particular metal bar, but it is now defined as the distance traveled by light in a vacuum in 1/299,792,458 second.

Metropolitan Museum of Art, Most comprehensive collection of art in the U.S. and one of the foremost in the world. It was incorporated in New York City in 1870, and the present building in Central Park on Fifth Avenue was opened in 1880. The Metropolitan was built with the private fortunes of businessmen; today it is owned by the city but supported mainly by private endowment. Its outstanding Egyptian, Mesopotamian, East Asian, Middle Eastern, Greek and Roman, European, pre-Columbian, and U.S. collections include—in addition to paintings, sculpture, and graphic arts—architecture, glass, ceramics, textiles, metalwork, furniture, arms and armour, and musical instruments. It also incorporates a Costume Institute and the Thomas J. Watson Library, one of the world's greatest art and archaeology reference collections. Much of the medieval collection is housed at The Cloisters in Manhattan's Fort Tryon Park; its building (1938) incorporates parts of medieval monasteries and churches.

Metternich (-Winneburg-Beilstein), Klemens (Wenzel Nepomuk Lothar), prince von (b. May 15, 1773, Coblenz, archbishopric of Trier—d. June 11, 1859, Vienna, Austria), Austrian statesman. He served in the diplomatic service as Austrian minister in Saxony (1801–03), Berlin (1803–05), and Paris (1806–09). In 1809 Francis I of Austria appointed him minister of foreign affairs, a position he would retain until 1848. He helped promote the marriage of Napoleon and Francis's daughter Marie-Louise. By skillful diplomacy and deceit, he kept Austria neutral in the war between France and Russia (1812) and secured its position of power before finally allying with Prussia and Russia (1813). In gratitude for his diplomatic achievements, the emperor created Metternich a hereditary prince. As the organizer of the Congress of Vienna (1814–15), he was largely responsible for the policy of balance of power in Europe to ensure the stability of European governments. After 1815 he remained firmly opposed to liberal ideas and revolutionary movements. He was forced to resign by the revolution of 1848. He is remembered for his role in restoring Austria as a leading European power.

Metternich, black and white chalk drawing by Anton Graff, c. 1803–05; in the Kupferstichkabinett, Dresden, Ger.
Courtesy of the Staatliche Kunstsammlungen, Dresden, Ger.

Metz, City (pop., 2006 est.: 124,435), northeastern France. It derives its name from the Mediomatrici, a Gallic tribe who made the city their capital. Fortified by the Romans, it became a bishopric in the 4th century AD. It passed to Frankish rule in the 5th century and became the capital of Lorraine in 843. It prospered as a free town within the Holy Roman Empire. Taken by the French in

1552, it was formally ceded to France in 1648. It fell to German rule in 1871 but was returned to France after World War I. It is the birthplace of Paul Verlaine.

Porte des Allemands ("Gate of the Germans"), Metz, France.
P. Salou/Shostal Associates

Meuse River, Dutch MAAS, River, western Europe. It rises in northeastern France and flows north into Belgium, where it forms part of the border between Belgium and the Netherlands. It divides at Venlo, Neth., one branch flowing into the Hollandsch Canal (an outlet of the North Sea) and another joining the Waal River to become the Merwede River, which eventually empties into the North Sea. The Meuse is 590 mi (950 km) long, and it is an important waterway in western Europe. Its valley was the scene of heavy fighting in World War I. The crossing of the Meuse was critical to Germany's invasion of France in 1940 in World War II.

Mexican Revolution (1910–20) Lengthy struggle that began with the overthrow of Porfirio Díaz, whose elitist and oligarchic policies had caused widespread dissatisfaction. Francisco Madero, Pancho Villa, Pascual Orozco, and Emiliano Zapata amassed supporters, and in 1911 Madero was declared president, but his slow-paced reforms alienated both former allies and foes. He was deposed by Gen. Victoriano Huerta, whose own drunken and despotic dictatorship quickly fell to Villa, Venustiano Carranza, and Álvaro Obregón. Carranza declared himself president in 1914 over Villa's objections and, after further bloodshed, prevailed. He oversaw the writing of the liberal constitution of 1917 but did little to implement its key provisions; in 1920 he was killed while fleeing a rebellion. With the election of the reform-minded Obregón, the revolutionary period ended, though sporadic clashes continued until Lázaro Cárdenas took office in 1934.

Mexican War, or MEXICAN-AMERICAN WAR (1846–48) War between the U.S. and Mexico. It grew from a border dispute after the U.S. annexed Texas in 1845; Mexico claimed that the southern border of Texas was the Nueces River, while the U.S. claimed it was the Rio Grande. A secret mission by John Slidell to negotiate the dispute and purchase New Mexico and California for up to $30 million was aborted when Mexico refused to receive him. In response to the snub, Pres. James Polk sent troops under Zachary Taylor to occupy the disputed land between the two rivers. In April 1846 Mexican troops crossed the Rio Grande and attacked Taylor's troops; Congress approved a declaration of war in May. Ordered to invade Mexico, Taylor captured Monterrey and defeated a large Mexican force under Antonio Santa Anna at the Battle of Buena Vista in February 1847. Polk then ordered Gen. Winfield Scott to move his army by sea to Veracruz, capture the city, and march inland to Mexico City. Scott followed the plan, meeting resistance at Cerro Gordo and Contreras, and entered Mexico City in September. Under the Treaty of Guadalupe Hidalgo, Mexico ceded to the U.S. nearly all of present New Mexico, Utah, Nevada, Arizona, California, Texas, and Colorado for $15,000,000 and U.S. assumption of its citizens' claims against Mexico. Casualties included about 13,000 American deaths, all but 1,700 of which were caused by disease. The war, which made a national hero of Taylor, reopened the slavery-extension issue supposedly settled by the Missouri Compromise.

Mexico, officially UNITED MEXICAN STATES, Country, southern North America. The Rio Grande forms part of its northeastern border with the U.S. Area: 758,450 sq mi (1,964,375 sq km). Population: (2011 est.) 114,492,000. Capital: Mexico City. More than three-fifths of Mexico's people are mestizos, about one-fifth are American Indians, and the bulk of the rest are of European ancestry. Languages: Spanish (official); more than 50 Indian languages are spoken. Religion: Christianity (predominantly Roman Catholic; also Protestant). Currency: Mexican peso. Mexico has two major peninsulas, the Yucatán in the southeast and Baja California in the northwest. The high Mexican Plateau forms the core of the country and is enclosed by mountain ranges: the Sierra Madre Occidental, the Sierra Madre Oriental, and the Cordillera Neo-Volcánica. The last has the country's highest peak, the volcano Citlaltépetl, which reaches 18,406 ft (5,610 m). Mexico has a mixed economy based on agriculture, manufacturing, and the extraction of petroleum and natural gas. About one-eighth of the land is arable; major crops include corn, wheat, rice, beans, coffee, cotton, fruits, and vegetables. Mexico is the world's largest producer of silver, bismuth, and celestite. It has significant reserves of oil and natural gas. Manufactures include processed foods, chemicals, transport vehicles, and electrical machinery. It is a federal republic with two legislative houses; its head of state and government is the president. Some scholars date human arrival in Mexico to as early as 30,000 to 40,000 years ago, but most believe it was somewhat later. The area produced a string of great early civilizations, including the Olmec, Toltec, and Maya. The Aztec empire, another important civilization located in Mexico, was conquered in 1521 by Spanish explorer Hernán Cortés, who established Mexico City on the site of the Aztec capital, Tenochtitlán. Francisco de Montejo conquered the remnants of Maya civilization in 1526, and Mexico became part of the Viceroyalty of New Spain. In 1821 rebels negotiated independence from Spain, and in 1823 a new congress declared Mexico a republic. In 1845 the U.S. voted to annex Texas, initiating the Mexican War. Under the Treaty of Guadalupe Hidalgo in 1848, Mexico ceded a vast territory in what is now the western and southwestern U.S. The Mexican government endured several rebellions and civil wars in the late 19th and early 20th centuries. During World War II (1939–45) it declared war on the Axis powers, and in the postwar era it was a founding member of the United Nations (1945) and the Organization of American States (1948). In 1993 it ratified the North American Free Trade Agreement. The election of Vicente Fox to the presidency (2000) ended 71 years of rule by the Institutional Revolutionary Party. After the government involved the military in its efforts against the country's powerful illegal drug cartels in 2006, violence mounted through the decade and into the next, with tens of thousands killed.

Mexico, Gulf of, Gulf, southeastern coast of North America, connected to the Atlantic Ocean by the Straits of Florida and to the Caribbean Sea by the Yucatán Channel. Covering an area of 600,000 sq mi (1,550,000 sq km), it is bounded by the U.S., Mexico, and Cuba. It has a maximum depth, in the Mexico Basin, of 17,070 ft (5,203 m). The Gulf Stream enters it from the Caribbean Sea and flows out to the Atlantic. The Mississippi and the Rio Grande are the major rivers draining into the gulf. Its major ports are Veracruz in Mexico, and Galveston, New Orleans, Pensacola, and Tampa in the U.S.

Mexico City, Spanish CIUDAD DE MÉXICO, City (pop., 2000: city, 8,605,239; 2003 metro. area est., 18,660,000), capital of Mexico. Located at an elevation of 7,350 ft (2,240 m), it is officially coterminous with the Federal District, which occupies 571 sq mi (1,477 sq km). Mexico City is one of the world's largest cities and one of the world's fastest-growing metropolitan areas. It generates about one-third of Mexico's industrial production. It lies on an ancient lake bed, the site of the Aztec capital, Tenochtitlán, which was taken by the Spanish explorer Hernán Cortés in 1521. It was the seat of the Viceroyalty of New Spain throughout the colonial period. Captured by Mexican revolutionaries under Gen. Agustín de Iturbide in 1821, it was seized by the U.S. in 1847 during the Mexican War and by the French (1863–67) under Maximilian. It was greatly improved during the rule of Porfirio Díaz (1876–80, 1884–1911). In 1985 it was struck by a severe earthquake that killed at least 7,000 people. The old city centre, the Zócalo, has many historic buildings, including the Metropolitan Cathedral (built on the site of an Aztec temple) and the National Palace (built on the ruins of the palace of Montezuma II). Its educational institutions include the National Autonomous University of Mexico (founded 1551), the College of Mexico, and the Ibero-American University. The city was designated a UNESCO World Heritage Site in 1987.

mezzotint (from Italian *mezza tinta*, "halftone") Engraving produced by pricking the surface of a metal plate with innumerable small holes that will hold ink. When the engraving is printed, the ink produces large areas of tone with soft, subtle gradations. Engraved or etched lines are often introduced to give the design greater definition. Mezzotint was invented in Holland by German-born Ludwig von Siegen in the 17th century but thereafter was practiced primarily in England. Its adaptability to making colour prints made it ideal for the reproduction of paintings. After the invention of photography, it was rarely used. In recent years the technique has been revived, especially by U.S. and Japanese printmakers.

MGM, in full METRO-GOLDWYN-MAYER, INC., U.S. corporation and film studio. It was formed when the film distributor Marcus Loew, who bought Metro Pictures in 1920, merged it with the Goldwyn production company in 1924 and with Louis B. Mayer Pictures in 1925. Louis B. Mayer was executive head of the studio for 25 years, assisted by production manager Irving Thalberg. It reached its peak in the 1930s and '40s, when it had most of Hollywood's famous stars under contract. It produced such hits as *Grand Hotel* (1932), *The Philadelphia Story* (1940), *Gaslight* (1944), *Ben-Hur* (1959), *Doctor Zhivago* (1965), and *2001: A Space Odyssey* (1968). It was especially celebrated for its lavish musicals, including *The Wizard of Oz* (1939), *On the Town* (1949), *An American in Paris* (1951), *Singin' in the Rain* (1952), and *Gigi* (1958). MGM began to decline in the 1950s and sold off many of its assets in the 1970s. It diversified into hotels and casinos and later merged with United Artists Corp. as MGM/UA Entertainment. In 1986 it was bought by Ted Turner, who resold the production and distribution units. Various transfers of ownership led to its purchase in 1992 by Crédit Lyonnais, which restored the name MGM Inc. It was subsequently bought by Tracinda Corp.

Miami, City (pop., 2000: 362,470), southeastern Florida, U.S., situated on Biscayne Bay at the mouth of the Miami River. The southernmost large city in the continental U.S., it has a beach 7 mi (11 km) long. A Spanish mission was founded near the site in 1567, but permanent settlement did not begin until 1835, when U.S. forces built Fort Dallas for the removal of Seminole Indians to the West. The arrival of the railway in 1896 spurred development, and Miami was incorporated the same year. The city has been damaged by occasional hurricanes, notably in 1926 and 1935. Nearly 300,000 Cuban refugees have arrived since 1959, establishing "Little Havana" within the city. It is a major resort and retirement centre, and its port handles the world's largest number of cruise-ship passengers. It is also a banking centre. Educational institutions include the University of Miami and Florida International University.

Michael, In the Bible and the Qur'ān, one of the archangels. The captain of the heavenly hosts, he was invoked by early Christian armies against the heathen. In Christian tradition he is thought to escort the soul into the presence of God at the time of death. In art he is depicted as a warrior, sword in hand, in triumph over a dragon. His feast day, known in England as Michaelmas, is September 29.

Michelangelo (di Lodovico Buonarroti) (b. March 6, 1475, Caprese, Republic of Florence—d. Feb. 18, 1564, Rome, Papal States), Italian sculptor, painter, architect, and poet. He served a brief apprenticeship with Domenico Ghirlandaio in Florence before beginning the first of several sculptures for Lorenzo de'Medici. After Lorenzo's death in 1492, he left for Bologna and then for Rome. There his *Bacchus* (1496–97) established his fame and led to a commission for the *Pietà* (now in St. Peter's Basilica), the masterpiece of his early years, in which he demonstrated his unique ability to extract two distinct figures from one marble block. His *David* (1501–04), commissioned for the cathedral of Florence, is still considered the prime example of the Renaissance ideal of perfect humanity. On the side, he produced several Madonnas for private patrons and his only universally accepted easel painting, *The Holy Family* (known as the *Doni Tondo*). Attracted to ambitious sculptural projects, which he did not always complete, he reluctantly agreed to paint the ceiling of the Sistine Chapel (1508–12). The first scenes, depicting the story of Noah, are relatively stable and on a small scale, but his confidence grew as he proceeded, and the later scenes evince boldness and complexity. His figures for the tombs in Florence's Medici Chapel (1519–33), which he designed, are among his most accomplished creations. He devoted his last 30 years largely to the *Last Judgment* fresco in the Sistine Chapel, to writing poetry (he left more than 300 sonnets and madrigals), and to architecture. He was commissioned to complete St. Peter's Basilica, begun in 1506 and little advanced since 1514. Though it was not quite finished at Michelangelo's death, its exterior owes more to him than to any other architect. He is regarded today as among the most exalted of artists.

microbiology, Scientific study of microorganisms, a diverse group of simple life-forms including protozoans, algae, molds, bacteria, and viruses. Microbiology is concerned with the structure, function, and classification of these organisms and with ways of controlling and using their activities. Its foundations were established in the later 19th century, with the work of Louis Pasteur and Robert Koch. Since then many disease-causing microorganisms have been identified, and means of controlling their harmful effects have been developed. In addition, means of channeling the activities of various microorganisms to benefit medicine, industry, and agriculture have been discovered. Molds, for example, produce antibiotics, notably penicillin.

microeconomics, Study of the economic behaviour of individual consumers, firms, and industries and the distribution of total production and income among them. It considers individuals both as suppliers of land, labour, and capital and as the ultimate consumers of the final product, and it examines firms both as suppliers of products and as consumers of labour and capital. Microeconomics seeks to analyze the market or other mechanisms that establish relative prices among goods and services and allocate society's resources among their many possible uses.

microelectromechanical system (MEMS), Miniature devices formed by combining mechanical parts and electronic circuits, typically on a semiconductor chip, with dimensions from tens to a few hundred micrometres (millionths of a metre). Common applications for MEMS include sensors, actuators, and process-control units.

Micronesia, Island group, western Pacific Ocean. A subdivision of Oceania, it comprises Kiribati, Guam, Nauru, the Northern Marianas, the Federated States of Micronesia, the Marshall Islands, and Palau. Located mostly north of the Equator, Micronesia includes the westernmost of the Pacific Islands.

Micronesia, Federated States of, Island country, western Pacific Ocean. It comprises the four states Yap, Chuuk (Truk), Pohnpei (Ponape), and Kosrae, all in the Caroline Islands. Area: 270.6 sq mi (700.9 sq km). Population: (2011 est.) 102,000. Capital: Palikir, on Pohnpei, the largest island. The people are mostly Micronesian. Languages: Malayo-Polynesian languages, English. Religion: Christianity (mostly Roman Catholic; also Protestant). Currency: U.S. dollar. The islands and atolls extend about 1,750 mi (2,800 km) east-west and about 600 mi (965 km) north-south. U.S. government grants constitute the main source of revenue; subsistence farming and fishing are the principal economic activities. Micronesia is a republic in free association with the U.S.; it has one legislative house, and its head of state and government is the president. The islands were probably settled by people from the area of what are now Vanuatu and Fiji some 3,500 years ago. They were colonized by Spain in 1886 and came under Japanese rule after World War I. They were captured by Allied forces during World War II, and in 1947 they became part of the UN Trust Territory of the Pacific Islands, administered by the U.S. The islands became an internally self-governing federation in 1979. In 1982 the federation signed a compact of free association with the U.S., which is responsible for Micronesia's defense; the compact was renewed in 2003.

microprocessor, Miniature electronic device that contains the arithmetic, logic, and control circuitry needed to function as a digital computer's CPU. Microprocessors are integrated circuits that can interpret and execute program instructions as well as handle arithmetic operations. Their development in the late 1970s enabled computer engineers to develop microcomputers. Microprocessors led to "intelligent" terminals, such as bank ATMs and point-of-sale devices, and to automatic control of much industrial instrumentation and hospital equipment, programmable microwave ovens, and electronic games. Many automobiles use microprocessor-controlled ignition and fuel systems.

microwave, Portion of the electromagnetic spectrum that is situated between radio waves and infrared radiation. Microwaves have wavelengths ranging from 30 cm to 1 mm, corresponding to frequencies from about 1 gigahertz (10^9 Hz) to 1 terahertz (10^{12} Hz). They are the principal carriers of television, telephone, and data transmissions between stations on Earth and between the Earth and satellites. Radar beams are short pulses of microwaves used to locate ships and planes, track weather systems, and determine the speeds of moving objects. Microwaves are absorbed by water and fat in foodstuffs and produce heat from the inside. Materials such as glass and ceramics do not absorb microwaves, and metals reflect them.

Midas, In Greek and Roman legend, a king of Phrygia. Midas captured the satyr Silenus but treated him kindly, and as a reward was granted a wish by Dionysus. He asked that everything he touched turn to gold; but after turning his daughter to gold when she embraced him, he asked to be released from his wish. In another legend Midas was invited to judge a music contest between Apollo and the satyr Marsyas. When Midas decided against Apollo, Apollo punished him by giving him donkey's ears.

Middle Ages, Period in European history traditionally dated from the fall of the Roman Empire to the dawn of the Renaissance. In the 5th century the Western Roman Empire endured declines in population, economic vitality, and the size and prominence of cities. It also was greatly affected by a dramatic migration of peoples that began in the 3rd century. In the 5th century these peoples, often called barbarians, carved new kingdoms out of the decrepit Western Empire. Over the next several centuries these kingdoms oversaw the gradual amalgamation of barbarian, Chris-

tian, and Roman cultural and political traditions. The longest-lasting of these kingdoms, that of the Franks, laid the foundation for later European states. It also produced Charlemagne, the greatest ruler of the Middle Ages, whose reign was a model for centuries to come. The collapse of Charlemagne's empire and a fresh wave of invasions led to a restructuring of medieval society. The 11th–13th centuries mark the high point of medieval civilization. The church underwent reform that strengthened the place of the pope in church and society but led to clashes between the pope and emperor. Population growth, the flourishing of towns and farms, the emergence of merchant classes, and the development of governmental bureaucracies were part of cultural and economic revival during this period. Meanwhile, thousands of knights followed the call of the church to join the Crusades. Medieval civilization reached its apex in the 13th century with the emergence of Gothic architecture, the appearance of new religious orders, and the expansion of learning and the university. The church dominated intellectual life, producing the Scholasticism of St. Thomas Aquinas. The decline of the Middle Ages resulted from the breakdown of medieval national governments, the great papal schism, the critique of medieval theology and philosophy, and economic and population collapse brought on by famine and disease.

Middle East, or MIDEAST, or NEAR EAST, Geographic region where Europe, Africa, and Asia meet. It is an unofficial and imprecise term that now generally encompasses the lands around the southern and eastern shores of the Mediterranean Sea—notably Egypt, Jordan, Israel, Lebanon, and Syria—as well as Iran, Iraq, and the countries of the Arabian Peninsula. Afghanistan, Libya, Turkey, and The Sudan are sometimes also included. The term was formerly used by Western geographers and historians to describe the region from the Persian Gulf to Southeast Asia; Near East is sometimes used to describe the same area.

Middle English, Vernacular spoken and written in England *c.* 1100–1500, the descendant of Old English and the ancestor of Modern English. It can be divided into three periods: Early, Central, and Late. The Central period was marked by the borrowing of many Anglo-Norman words and the rise of the London dialect, used by such poets as John Gower and Geoffrey Chaucer in a 14th-century flowering of English literature. The dialects of Middle English are usually divided into four groups: Southern, East Midland, West Midland, and Northern.

Midgard, In Norse mythology, the dwelling place of humankind. According to legend, it was made from the body of the first created being, the giant Aurgelmir (Ymir). The gods killed him and rolled his body into the central void of the universe, forming the land from his flesh, the oceans from his blood, the mountains from his bones, and so on. Aurgelmir's skull, held up by four dwarfs, became the dome of the heavens. The sun, moon, and stars were made of scattered sparks caught in the skull.

MIDI, in full MUSICAL INSTRUMENT DIGITAL INTERFACE, Protocol for transmission of musical data between digital components, such as synthesizers and a computer's sound card. MIDI uses 8-bit asynchronous serial transmission with a data rate of 31.25 kilobytes per second. The transmitted data do not directly represent musical sound but specify various aspects (pitch, loudness, starting and stopping points in time). The data are then applied to waveforms stored digitally on a computer chip to create a specific sound.

Midrash, In Judaism, a large collection of writings that examine the Hebrew Bible in the light of oral tradition. Midrashic activity reached its height in the 2nd century AD with the schools of Ishmael ben Elisha and Akiba ben Joseph. The Midrashim are divided into two groups: Halakhah, which clarify legal issues; and Haggadah, nonlegal writings intended simply to enlighten. The Midrashim are extensively quoted in the Talmud.

Midway, Battle of (June 3–6, 1942) Major World War II naval battle between the U.S. and Japan. Japanese naval forces under Yamamoto Isoroku sought to seize Midway Island by engaging the numerically inferior U.S. Pacific fleet. U.S. intelligence had broken the Japanese naval code, and the U.S. prepared for the assault by mobilizing about 115 land-based aircraft as well as three aircraft carriers. On June 3 its bombers began striking Japan's carrier force. Japan was unable to match the U.S. air power and, after heavy losses, abandoned efforts to land on Midway. The battle brought the Pacific naval forces of Japan and the U.S. to approximate parity and marked the turning point of the war between the two countries.

midwifery, Care of women during pregnancy and childbirth. It is known to date to ancient biblical, Greek, and Roman times. It declined in the Middle Ages, when the first medical schools in Europe came into existence. However, it advanced considerably from the 17th to the 19th century. Later, with advances in obstetrics and gynecology, most women in developed countries gave birth in hospitals, and the high mortality for mothers and infants in childbirth decreased. In the 1960s the natural childbirth movement, feminism, and other factors renewed interest in the personal care given by midwives. Licensed and certified midwives receive formal training either as a midwife or as a nurse and then a midwife. Licensed midwives often also provide pre- and postnatal care and reproductive health advice. Lay midwives usually have no formal training and are unlicensed.

Mies van der Rohe, Ludwig, orig. MARIA LUDWIG MICHAEL MIES (b. March 27, 1886, Aachen, Ger.—d. Aug. 17, 1969, Chicago, Ill., U.S.), German-born U.S. architect and designer. Mies learned masonry from his father and later worked in the office of Peter Behrens. His first great work was the German Pavilion for the 1929 International Exposition in Barcelona, Spain, a travertine platform with chromed steel columns and spaces defined by planes of extravagant onyx, marble, and frosted glass. The steel-and-leather Barcelona chair he designed for the space went on to become a 20th-century classic. He was director of the Bauhaus in 1930–33, first in Dessau and then, during its final months, in Berlin. After moving to the U.S. in 1937, he became director of the School of Architecture at Chicago's Armour Institute (now the Illinois Institute of Technology), where he designed the school's new campus (1939–41). The International Style, with Mies its undisputed leader, reached its zenith during the next 20 years. His other projects included Chicago's Lake Shore Drive Apartments (1949–51), and the Seagram Building (1956–58, with Philip Johnson) in New York City. These buildings, steel skeletons sheathed in glass curtain-wall facades, exemplify Mies's dictum that "less is more." His later works include Berlin's New National Gallery (1963–68). Modernist steel-and-glass office buildings influenced by his work were built all over the world over the course of the 20th century.

migraine, Recurrent headache, usually on one side of the head. Severe throbbing pain is sometimes accompanied by nausea and vomiting. Some migraine patients have warning symptoms before the headache, including visual disturbance, weakness, numbness, or dizziness. Migraine attacks can be triggered by a variety of factors, including stress, changes in weather or sleep patterns, and menstruation. Drugs may be taken as an attack begins (to abort it) or daily by patients with very frequent attacks (to prevent them or reduce their severity).

migrant labour, Semiskilled or unskilled workers who move from one region to another, offering their services on a temporary, usually seasonal, basis. In North America, migrant labour is generally employed in agriculture and moves seasonally from south to north following the harvest. In Europe and the Middle East, migrant labour usually involves urban rather than agricultural employment and calls for longer periods of residence. The migrant labour market is often disorganized and exploitative. Many workers are supervised by middlemen such as labour contractors and

crew leaders, who recruit and transport them and dispense their pay. Labourers commonly endure long hours, low wages, poor working conditions, and substandard housing. In some countries, child labour is widespread among migrant labourers, and even in the U.S. those children who do not work often do not go to school, since schools are usually open only to local residents. Workers willing to accept employment on these terms are usually driven by even worse conditions in their home countries. Labour organizing is made difficult by mobility and by low rates of literacy and political participation, though some migrant labourers in the U.S. have been unionized.

migration, human, Permanent change of residence by an individual or group, excluding such movements as nomadism and migrant labour. Migrations may be classed as internal or international and as voluntary or forced. Voluntary migration is usually undertaken in search of a better life; forced migrations include expulsions during war and the transportation of slaves or prisoners. The earliest humans migrated from Africa to all the continents except Antarctica within about 50,000 years. Other mass migrations include the forced migration of 20 million people as slaves from Africa to North America in the 16th–19th centuries and the Great Atlantic Migration of 37 million people from Europe to North America between 1820 and 1980. War-related forced migrations and refugee flows continue to be very large, as are voluntary migrations from developing nations to industrialized ones. Internal migrations have tended to be from rural areas to urban centers.

Milan, Italian MILANO, City (pop., 2007 est.: 1,303,437), capital of Lombardy region, northern Italy. The area was settled by the Gauls *c.* 600 BCE. Known as Mediolanum, it was conquered by the Romans in 222 BCE. Attacked in 452 CE by Attila and in 539 by the Goths, it fell to Charlemagne in 774. Milan's power grew in the 11th century, but it was destroyed by the Holy Roman Empire in 1162. Rebuilt as part of the Lombard League in 1167, Milan achieved independence in 1183. In 1450 Francesco Sforza founded a new dynasty there; after 1499 it was ruled alternately by the French and the Sforza family until 1535, when the Habsburgs obtained it. Napoleon took power in 1796, and in 1805 it became the capital of his Kingdom of Italy. Milan was incorporated into unified Italy in 1860. It was heavily damaged during World War II but was rebuilt. It is Italy's most important economic centre, noted for its fashion industry as well as finance, retail and wholesale trade, media and publishing, and other services. Its historic sites include the medieval Duomo, Europe's third largest cathedral; the Palazzo di Brera (1651); the monastery that houses Leonardo da Vinci's *Last Supper*; and La Scala opera house.

mildew, Conspicuous mass of threadlike hyphae and fruiting structures produced by various fungi (kingdom Fungi; *see* fungus). Mildew grows on cloth, fibres, leather goods, and plants, using these substances as food for growth and reproduction. Downy mildew and powdery mildew are plant diseases that affect hundreds of species.

mile, Any of various units of distance, including the statute mile of 5,280 ft (1.61 km). It originated from the Roman *mille passus,* or "thousand paces," which measured 5,000 Roman ft (4,840 English ft [1.475 km]). A nautical mile is the length on the Earth's surface of one minute of arc or, by international definition, 1,852 m (6,076.12 ft [1.1508 statute mi]); it remains in universal use in both marine and air transportation. A knot is one nautical mile per hour.

military law, Law prescribed by statute for governing the armed forces and their civilian employees. It in no way relieves military personnel of their obligations to their country's civil code or to the codes of international law. Mutiny, insubordination, desertion, misconduct, and other offenses injurious to military discipline constitute violations of military law; offenders may be subject to court-martial. Lesser offenses may be penalized summarily by a commanding officer (e.g., through the withdrawal of privileges or the cancellation of liberty).

militia, Military organization of citizens with limited military training who are available for emergency service, usually for local defense. In many countries the militia is of ancient origin. The Anglo-Saxons required every able-bodied free male to serve. In colonial America it was the only defense against hostile Indians when regular British forces were not available. In the American Revolution the militia, called the Minutemen, provided the bulk of the American forces. Militias played a similar role in the War of 1812 and the American Civil War. State-controlled volunteer militias in the U.S. became the National Guard. British militia units, begun in the 16th century for home defense and answerable to the county sheriff or lord lieutenant, were absorbed into the regular army in the 20th century. Today various paramilitary organizations, from U.S. white supremacists to revolutionaries in the developing world, use the term *militia* to accentuate their populist origins.

Milky Way Galaxy, Large spiral galaxy (roughly 150,000 light-years in diameter) that contains Earth's solar system. It includes the multitude of stars whose light is seen as the Milky Way, the irregular luminous band that encircles the sky, defining the plane of the galactic disk. The Milky Way system contains hundreds of billions of stars and large amounts of interstellar gas and dust. Because the dust obscures astronomers' views of many of its stars, large areas could not be studied before the development of infrared astronomy and radio astronomy. Its precise constituents, shape, and true size and mass are still not known. It contains large amounts of dark matter and a massive black hole at its core. The Sun lies in one of the Galaxy's spiral arms, about 27,000 light-years from the centre.

Mill, John Stuart (b. May 20, 1806, London, Eng.—d. May 8, 1873, Avignon, France), British philosopher and economist, the leading expositor of utilitarianism. He was educated exclusively and exhaustively by his father, James Mill. By age 8 he had read in the original Greek Aesop's *Fables*, Xenophon's *Anabasis*, and all of Herodotus, and he had begun a study of Euclid's geometry; at age 12 he began a thorough study of scholastic logic. In 1823 he cofounded the Utilitarian Society with Jeremy Bentham, though he would later significantly modify the utilitarianism he inherited from Bentham and his father to meet the criticisms it encountered. In 1826 he and Bentham cofounded London University (now University College). From 1828 to 1856 he was an assistant examiner in India House, where from 1836 he was in charge of the East India Company's relations with the Indian states. In the 1840s he published his great systematic works in logic and political economy, chiefly *A System of Logic* (2 vol., 1843) and *Principles of Political Economy* (2 vol., 1848). As head of the examiner's office in India House from 1856 to 1858 he wrote a defense of the company's government of India when the transfer of its powers was proposed. In 1859 he published *On Liberty*, a trenchant defense of individual freedom. His *Utilitarianism* (1863) is a closely reasoned attempt to answer objections to his ethical theory and to address misconceptions about it; he was especially insistent that "utility" include the pleasures of the imagination and the gratification of the higher emotions and that his system include a place for settled rules of conduct. In 1869 he published *The Subjection of Women* (written 1861), now the classical theoretical statement of the case for woman suffrage. Prominent as a publicist in the reforming age of the 19th century, he remains of lasting interest as a logician and ethical theorist.

millennialism, or MILLENARIANISM, Belief in the millennium of Christian prophecy (Revelation 20), the 1,000 years when Christ is to reign on earth, or any religious movement that foresees a coming age of peace and prosperity. There are two expressions of millennialism. Premillennialism holds that the Second Coming of Christ will occur before the millennium and will initiate the final battle between good and evil, which will be followed by the establishment of the 1,000-year kingdom on earth or in heaven. Postmillennialism maintains that Jesus will return after the creation of the millennial kingdom of peace and righteousness, which prepares the way for the Second Coming. Throughout the Christian era, periods of social change or crisis have tended to lead to a resurgence in millennialism. The legend of the last emperor and the writings of Joachim of Fiore are important examples of medieval millennialism, and, during the Reformation, Anabaptists, Bohemian Brethren, and other groups held millennial beliefs. It is now associated especially with such Protestant denominations as the Adventists, Jehovah's Witnesses, and Mormons. In a broader sense, many non-Christian traditions, including Pure Land Buddhism and the Ghost Dance religion, are understood as millennialist.

millipede, Any of about 10,000 species of the arthropod class Diplopoda, found worldwide. Most species live in and eat decaying plant matter. Some injure living plants, and a few are predators and scavengers. Millipedes are 1–11 in. (2.5–28 cm) long and have from 11 to more than 100 diplosomites, double segments formed from the fusion of two segments. The head is legless; the next three segments have one pair of legs each; and the remaining segments have two pairs each. In defense, millipedes do not bite; most species tuck headfirst into a tight coil, and many secrete a pungent, toxic liquid or gas.

Miłosz, Czesław (b. June 30, 1911, Šateiniai, Lith., Russian Empire—d. Aug. 14, 2004, Kraków, Pol.), Polish-U.S. author, translator, and critic. Miłosz was a socialist by the time he published his first book of verse at age 21. During the Nazi occupation of Poland, he was active in the resistance. After serving briefly as a diplomat for communist Poland, he immigrated to the U.S., where he taught for decades at the University of California at Berkeley; he became a naturalized U.S. citizen in 1970. His poetry, including such collections as *Bells in Winter* (1978), is noted for its classical style and preoccupation with philosophical and political issues. His well-known essay collection *The Captive Mind* (1953) condemned the accommodation of many Polish intellectuals to communism. U.S. critic Helen Vendler wrote that Miłosz's *Treatise on Poetry* (1957) seemed to her "the most comprehensive and moving poem" of the latter half of the 20th century. He was awarded the Nobel Prize for Literature in 1980.

Milton, John (b. Dec. 9, 1608, London, Eng.—d. Nov. 8?, 1674, London?), English poet and pamphleteer. Milton attended the University of Cambridge (1625–32), where he wrote poems in Latin, Italian, and English; these include the companion poems "L'Allegro" and "Il Penseroso," both written *c.* 1631. In 1632–39 he engaged in private study—writing the masque *Comus* (first performed 1634) and the elegy "Lycidas" (1638)—and toured Europe, spending most of his time in Italy. Concerned with the republican cause in England, he spent much of 1641–60 pamphleteering for civil and religious liberty and serving in Oliver Cromwell's government. His best-known prose is in the pamphlets *Areopagitica*, on freedom of the press, and *Of Education* (both 1644). He also wrote tracts on divorce and against the monarchy and the Church of England. He lost his sight *c.* 1651 and thereafter dictated his works. After the Restoration he was arrested as a prominent defender of the Commonwealth but was soon released. *Paradise Lost* (1667, 1674), considered the greatest epic poem in English, uses blank verse and reworks Classical epic conventions to recount the Fall of Man; Milton's characterization of Satan has been widely admired. *Paradise Regained* (1671) is a shorter epic in which Christ overcomes Satan the tempter, and *Samson Agonistes* (1671) is a dramatic poem in which the Old Testament figure conquers self-pity and despair to become God's champion. *History of Britain* was incomplete when published in 1670, and an unfinished work on theology was discovered in 1823. Milton is generally considered the greatest English poet after William Shakespeare.

mime and pantomime, Dramatic performance in which a

Marcel Marceau, French mime, as Bip, a character of his own invention, playing the violin.
Ronald A. Wilford Associates, Inc.

story is told solely by expressive body movement. Mime appeared in Greece in the 5th century BC as a comic entertainment that stressed mimetic action but included song and spoken dialogue. A separate Roman form developed from *c.* 100 BC and centred on crude and licentious subjects. Roman pantomime differed from Roman mime by its loftier themes and its use of masks, which called for expression through posture and hand gestures. Mime was also important in Asian drama from ancient times, and it is an element in major Chinese and Japanese dramatic forms (e.g., nō theatre). The Roman tradition of pantomime was modified in the 16th-century commedia dell'arte, which in turn influenced the 18th-century French and English comic interludes that developed into 19th-century pantomime, a children's entertainment emphasizing spectacle. Modern Western mime developed into a purely silent art in which meanings are conveyed through gesture, movement, and expression. Famous mimes include Jean-Gaspard Deburau, Étienne Decroux (who developed a systematic language of gesture), and Marcel Marceau. Charlie Chaplin was an accomplished mime, as were Sid Caesar and the circus clown Emmett Kelly.

mimicry, Similarity between organisms that confers a survival advantage on one. In Batesian mimicry, an organism lacking defenses mimics a species that does have defenses. In Müllerian mimicry, all species in a group are similar even though all individually have defenses. In aggressive mimicry, a predatory species mimics a benign species so that it can approach its prey without alarming it, or a parasitic species mimics its host. Some plant species mimic the colour patterns and scents of animals for the purposes of pollination and dispersal. Mimicry differs from camouflage in that camouflage hides the organism, whereas mimicry benefits the organism only if the organism is detected.

mimosa, Any member of the more than 450 species that make up the genus *Mimosa* in the pea family (Fabaceae), native to tropical and subtropical areas throughout both hemispheres. Most are herbaceous plants or undershrubs; some are woody climbers; a few are small trees. They are often prickly. Mimosas are widely cultivated for the beauty of their foliage and for their interesting response to light and mechanical stimuli: the leaves of some species droop in response to darkness and close up their leaflets when touched. The name comes from this "mimicking" of animal sensibility. The roots of some species are poisonous; others contain skin irritants. Many acacias are commonly but incorrectly called mimosas.

Minamoto Yoritomo (b. 1147, Japan—d. Feb. 9, 1199, Kamakura), Founder of the Kamakura shogunate, or *bakufu*. A member of the Minamoto warrior clan, Yoritomo was banished in his youth as a consequence of his father's revolt against the reigning Taira family. In exile Yoritomo found support for his cause in Hōjō Toki-

masa, and in 1185 he defeated the Taira. In 1192 the cloistered emperor granted him the title of shogun, which made him the supreme authority over all military forces in the country. He established his own governors (*shugo*) and stewards (*jitō*) throughout Japan, thereby creating a governmental infrastructure in competition with, and gradually superseding, that of the imperial court. He was thus able to rule without actually overthrowing the emperor, a pattern that was to be emulated by future shogunates.

mind-body problem, Metaphysical problem of the relationship between mind and body. The modern problem stems from the thought of René Descartes, who is responsible for the classical formulation of dualism. Descartes's interactionism had many critics even in his own day. Thomas Hobbes denied the existence of mental substance. Materialism of a sort was also supported by Descartes's correspondent Pierre Gassendi (1592–1655). Benedict de Spinoza posited a single substance of which the mental and the material are attributes; his theory is known as psycho-physical parallelism. More recent views include the double-aspect theory, identity theory, eliminative materialism (which denies the reality of the familiar categories of mental state posited in so-called folk psychology), and theories of supervenience.

mineral, Any naturally occurring homogeneous solid that has a definite (but not fixed) chemical composition and a distinctive internal crystal structure. Minerals are usually formed by inorganic processes. Synthetic equivalents of various minerals, such as emeralds and diamonds, are manufactured for commercial purposes. Although most minerals are chemical compounds, a small number (e.g., sulfur, copper, gold) are elements. Minerals combine with each other to form rocks. For example, granite consists of the minerals feldspar, quartz, mica, and amphibole in varying amounts. Rocks are generally, therefore, an intergrowth of various minerals.

mineral processing, or ORE DRESSING, Mechanical treatment of crude ores to separate the valuable minerals. Mineral processing was at first applied only to ores of precious metals but later came to be used to recover other metals and nonmetallic minerals. It is also used during coal preparation to enrich the value of raw coal. The primary operations are comminution and concentration. Comminution is carried out by large jaw crushers and by smaller cylindrical grinding mills. Common methods of concentration are gravity separation and flotation separation. Gravity methods include jigging (ground ore is fed into a pulsating body of water so that the heavier mineral fractions settle out, leaving lighter wastes at the top) or washing the ore down inclined planes, spirals, or shaking tables so that mineral and waste fractions settle in different areas.

Minerva, In Roman religion, the goddess of handicrafts, the professions, the arts, and, later, war. She was commonly identified with the Greek Athena. Some scholars believe that worship of Minerva began when Athena's cult was introduced at Rome from Etruria. Minerva was one of the Capitoline triad, along with Jupiter and Juno, and her shrine in Rome was a meeting place for craftsmen's guilds. The worship of Minerva attained its greatest vogue under the emperor Domitian, who claimed her special protection.

minesweeper, Naval vessel used to clear submarine mines from an expanse of water. In naval warfare, they are used to clear mines from sea-lanes to protect merchant shipping as well as to clear paths for warships to engage in battle or amphibious warfare. The earliest examples used sweeping wires with sawlike projections to cut the cables anchoring submarine mines and allow them to rise to the surface, where they would be destroyed by gunfire. The wide use of magnetic mines (set off by the magnetic field of steel ships) in the Korean War led to wood-hulled minesweepers.

miniature painting, Small, detailed painting, usually a portrait, executed in watercolour on vellum (parchment), prepared card, copper, or ivory that can be held in the hand or worn as a piece of jewelry. The name derives from the *minium*, or red lead, used to emphasize initial letters in medieval illuminated manuscripts. Combining the traditions of illumination and the Renaissance medal, it flourished from the early 16th to the mid-19th century. The earliest datable examples were painted in France by Jean Clouet the Younger at the court of Francis I; in England H. Holbein the Younger produced masterpieces in miniature under Henry VIII and inspired a long tradition of the practice, known as "limning." Nicholas Hilliard served as miniature painter to Elizabeth I for more than 30 years. In the 17th–18th centuries, painting in enamel on metal became popular in France. In Italy Rosalba Carriera introduced the use of ivory (*c.* 1700) as a luminous surface for transparent pigments, stimulating a great revival of the medium in the late 18th century. By the mid-19th century miniature paintings were regarded as luxury items and rendered obsolete by the new medium of photography.

Minimalism, Twentieth-century movements in art and music characterized by extreme simplicity of form and rejection of emotional content. In the visual arts, Minimalism originated in New York City in the 1950s as a form of abstract art and became a major trend in the 1960s and '70s. The Minimalists believed that a work of art should be entirely self-referential; personal elements were stripped away to reveal the objective, purely visual elements. Leading Minimalist sculptors include Carl Andre and Donald Judd; Minimalist painters include Ellsworth Kelly and Agnes Martin. In music, Minimalism arose in the 1960s. It employs a steady pulsing beat, incessant repetition of tones and chords with only gradual changes in their components, a slow rate of harmonic change, and little or no counterpoint. Its principal antecedents are the musics of India and Southeast Asia. Its most important early practitioners include La Monte Young (b. 1935), Terry Riley (b. 1935), whose *In C* (1964) is perhaps its most seminal work, Steve Reich, Philip Glass, and John Adams.

minimum wage, Wage rate established by collective bargaining or by government regulation, specifying the lowest rate at which workers may be employed. A legal minimum wage is one mandated by government for all workers in an economy, with few exceptions. Privately negotiated minimum wages determined by collective bargaining apply to a specific group of workers in the economy, usually in specific trades or industries. The modern minimum wage, combined with compulsory arbitration of labour disputes, first appeared in Australia and New Zealand in the 1890s. In 1909 Britain established trade boards to set minimum wage rates in certain trades and industries. The first minimum wage in the U.S. (which applied only to women) was enacted by Massachusetts in 1912. Minimum wage laws or agreements now exist in most nations.

mining, Excavation of materials from the Earth's crust, including those of organic origin, such as coal and petroleum. Modern mining is costly and complicated. First, a mineral vein that can likely produce enough of the desired substance to justify the cost of extraction must be located. Then the size of the vein or deposit is determined, and mining engineers decide the best way to mine it. Most of the world's yearly mineral production is extracted by surface mining, which includes open-pit mining, strip mining, and quarrying. For ore bodies that lie a considerable distance below the surface, underground mining must be considered. In both techniques, excavating and extracting mineral substances involve costly combinations of drilling, blasting, hoisting, and hauling, as well as measures for health and safety and reduction of environmental impact.

Minoan, Any member of a non-Indo-European people who flourished (*c.* 3000–*c.* 1100 BC) on the island of Crete during the Bronze Age. The sea was the basis of their economy and power.

Their sophisticated culture, based at Knossos, was named for the legendary King Minos. It represented the first high civilization in the Aegean area. The Minoans exerted great influence on the Mycenaean culture of the Greek islands and mainland. Minoan culture reached its peak *c.* 1600 BC and was noted for its cities and palaces, extended trade contacts, and use of writing. Its art included elaborate seals, pottery, and, notably, the vibrant frescoes decorating palace walls, which depicted both religious and secular scenes, including goddesses reflective of a matriarchal religion. Palace ruins show evidence of paved streets and piped water. Familiar Minoan art motifs are the snake (symbol of the goddess) and the bull and leaping dancer, also of mystical significance.

Minos, In Greek legend, a king of Crete, the son of Zeus and Europa. He gained the throne with the aid of Poseidon and also became ruler of the Aegean islands. His wife Pasiphaë fell in love with a bull and gave birth to the Minotaur, which was imprisoned in the Labyrinth. Minos waged war against Athens and exacted a tribute of youths and maidens to feed the Minotaur until Theseus killed the monster with the aid of Minos's daughter Ariadne. Minos was killed in Sicily when boiling water was poured over him as he was taking a bath. Many scholars now consider that Minos was a royal or dynastic title for the priestly rulers of Bronze Age, or Minoan, civilization in Knossos (Minoan means "of Minos").

Minotaur, In Greek mythology, a monster of Crete with the body of a man and the head of a bull. It was the offspring of Pasiphaë, wife of King Minos, and a snow-white bull sent by Poseidon and intended for sacrifice. When Minos kept it instead, the god punished him by making his wife fall in love with the bull. The Minotaur (whose name means "Minos bull") was imprisoned in the Labyrinth built by Daedalus. After defeating Athens in a war, Minos forced the Athenians to send human tribute to be devoured by the Minotaur. The third year the tribute was sent, Theseus volunteered to go, and with the help of Ariadne he killed the monster.

Minsk, Capital (pop., 2001 est.: 1,699,000) and largest city of Belarus. Settled before 1067, it became the seat of a principality in 1101. It passed to Lithuania in the 14th century and later to Poland. Annexed by Russia in the second partition of Poland in 1793, it became a provincial centre. Minsk was occupied by French troops in 1812. It grew in importance as an industrial centre after the arrival of the railways in 1870. During World War I it was occupied first by the Germans and then by the Poles. It was almost entirely destroyed in World War II, especially during the Soviet advance in 1944. Once the capital of the Belorussian S.S.R., it remained the capital when Belarus gained independence in 1991. It is the country's administrative and industrial centre.

mint, In botany, any strong-scented herb of the genus *Mentha*, composed of about 25 species of perennial herbs and certain related genera of the mint family (Lamiaceae, or Labiatae), which contains about 7,000 species of flowering plants in about 236 genera. Mints are important to humans as herb plants useful for their flavour, fragrance, and medicinal properties. True mints have square stems and oppositely arranged aromatic leaves. Small flowers, usually pale purple, pink, or white, are arranged in clusters, either forming separate whorls or crowded together in a terminal spike. All *Mentha* species contain volatile oil in resinous dots in the leaves and stems. Included in this genus are peppermint, spearmint, marjoram, rosemary, and thyme; other members of the mint family include lavender, hyssop, and catnip.

minuet, Dignified couple dance derived from a French folk dance, dominant in European court ballrooms in the 17th–18th century. Using small, slow steps to music in 3/4 time, dancers often performed choreographed figures combined with stylized bows and curtsies. The most popular dance of the 18th-century aristocracy, it fell from favour after the French Revolution in 1789. It was of great importance in art music; commonly incorporated into the suite *c.* 1650–1775, it was the only dance form retained in the symphony, sonata, string quartet, and other multimovement art-music genres up to *c.* 1800.

Minuteman missile, U.S. ICBM first deployed in 1962. Its three generations—the Minuteman I (1962–73), the Minuteman II (1966–95), and the Minuteman III (from 1970)—have constituted most of the land-based nuclear arsenal of the U.S. since the 1960s. They were the first U.S. ICBMs to be based in underground silos, use solid fuel, and be fitted with multiple independently targeted reentry vehicles. Under the terms of the Strategic Arms Reduction Talks, the Minuteman II force was dismantled and the Minuteman III scheduled for downgrading to a single warhead.

Miocene Epoch, Major division of the Neogene Period, from 23 million to 5.3 million years ago. The extensive fossil record of terrestrial life during the Miocene provides a fairly complete picture of the development of vertebrates, especially mammals. Miocene mammals were essentially modern, and half of the known modern families are present in the Miocene record. The horse evolved, mainly in North America, and advanced primates, including apes, were present in southern Europe. Some interchange of faunas occurred in the Northern Hemisphere between the Old World and the New. Free communication was possible between Africa and Eurasia, but South America and Australia remained isolated.

Mir, Russian space station. It consists of a core module launched in 1986 and five additional modules launched separately over the next decade and attached to the core unit to create a large, versatile space laboratory. The third generation of Russian space stations, Mir featured six docking ports for modules and other spacecraft, expanded living quarters, more power, and modernized research equipment. It supported human habitation between 1986 and 2000, including an uninterrupted stretch of occupancy of almost 10 years, and it hosted a series of U.S. astronauts in 1995–98 as part of a Mir-space shuttle cooperative endeavour. In 1995, Valery Polyakov (b. 1942) set a world endurance record of nearly 438 days in space aboard Mir. In March 2001 the abandoned station was brought down in a controlled reentry, with the surviving pieces falling into the Pacific Ocean.

miracle, Extraordinary event attributed to a supernatural power. Belief in miracles exists in all cultures and nearly all religions. The Upanishads assert that the experience of religious insight and transformation is the only "miracle" worth considering, but popular Hinduism attributes miraculous powers to the ascetic yogis. Confucianism had little room for miracles. Daoism, however, mingled with Chinese folk religion to produce a rich crop of miracles. Though Buddha Gautama deprecated his own miraculous powers as devoid of spiritual significance, accounts of his miraculous birth and life were later woven into his legend and into those of later Buddhist saints. Miracles are taken for granted throughout the Hebrew scriptures and were fairly common in the Greco-Roman world. The New Testament records miracles of healing and other wonders performed by Jesus. Miracles also attest to the holiness of Christian saints. Muhammad renounced miracles as a matter of principle (the Qur'ān was the great miracle), but his life was later invested with miraculous details. Muslim popular religion, particularly under the influence of Sufism, abounds in miracles and wonder-working saints.

mirage, In optics, the deceptive appearance of a distant object caused by the bending of light rays (refraction) in layers of air of varying density. Under certain conditions, such as over a stretch of pavement or desert air heated by intense sunshine, the air cools rapidly with elevation and therefore increases in density and refractive power. Sunlight reflected down from the upper portion of an object will be directed through the cool air in the normal way; although the light would not be seen ordinarily because of the angle, it curves upward after it enters the rarefied hot air near the

ground, thus being refracted to the observer's eye as though it had originated below the heated surface. When the sky is the object of the mirage, the land is mistaken for a lake or sheet of water.

miʿraj, In Islamic tradition, the ascension of Muhammad into heaven. One night, according to the tradition, Muhammad was visited by two archangels, who opened his body and purified his heart of all doubt, error, and paganism. He was carried to heaven, where he ascended the seven levels to reach the throne of God. Along the way he and the archangel Jibrīl met the prophets Adam, Yaḥyā (John the Apostle), ʿĪsā (Jesus), Yūsuf (Joseph), Idrīs, Hārūn (Aaron), Mūsā (Moses), and Ibrāhīm (Abraham) and visited hell and paradise. He learned that he was more highly regarded by God than all the other prophets. The *miʿraj* is popularly celebrated with readings of the legend on the 27th day of Rajab, called the *Laylat ʿal-Mirāj* ("Night of the Ascension").

MIRV, in full MULTIPLE INDEPENDENTLY TARGETED REENTRY VEHICLE, Any of several nuclear warheads carried on the front end of a ballistic missile. The technique allows separately targeted nuclear warheads to be released from the missile on different trajectories, thus attacking several targets from only one launcher. MIRVed ballistic missiles were first deployed by the U.S. and then the Soviet Union in the 1970s, followed by Britain and France in the 1980s and possibly China in the 1990s. Because multiple warheads represent a significant increase in firepower, they have often been an issue in arms control negotiations. The Strategic Arms Reduction Talks commit both the U.S. and Russia to limit the number of MIRVs on some missiles.

miscarriage, or SPONTANEOUS ABORTION, Spontaneous expulsion of an embryo or fetus from the uterus before it can live outside the mother. More than 60% are caused by an inherited defect in the fetus, which might result in a fatal abnormality. Other causes may include acute infectious disease, especially if it reduces the fetus's oxygen supply; abnormalities of the uterus that have physical or hormonal origins; and death of the fetus from umbilical-cord knotting. The main sign of impending miscarriage is vaginal bleeding.

Mishima Yukio, orig. HIRAOKA KIMITAKE (b. Jan. 14, 1925, Tokyo, Japan—d. Nov. 25, 1970, Tokyo), Japanese writer. Having failed to qualify physically for military service in World War II, Mishima worked in a Tokyo factory and after the war studied law. He won acclaim with his first novel, *Confessions of a Mask* (1949). Many of his characters are obsessed with unattainable ideals and erotic desires, as in *The Temple of the Golden Pavilion* (1956). His epic *The Sea of Fertility*, 4 vol. (1965–70), is perhaps his most lasting achievement. He strongly opposed Japan's close ties to the West in the postwar era (notably the new constitution that forbade rearmament) and yearned to preserve Japan's martial spirit and reverence for the emperor. In a symbolic gesture of these beliefs, he died by committing seppuku (ritual disembowelment) after seizing a military headquarters. He is often considered one of Japan's most important 20th-century novelists.

Mishna, or MISHNAH, Oldest authoritative collection of Jewish oral law, supplementing the written laws in the Hebrew Scriptures. It was compiled by a series of scholars over two centuries and was given final form in the 3rd century AD by Judah ha-Nasi. Annotations by later scholars in Palestine and Babylonia resulted in the Gemara; the Mishna and Gemara are usually said to make up the Talmud. The Mishna has six major sections, on daily prayer and agriculture, Sabbath and other religious ritual, married life, civil and criminal law, the Temple of Jerusalem, and ritual purification.

mission, Organized effort to spread the Christian faith. St. Paul evangelized much of Asia Minor and Greece, and the new religion spread rapidly along the trade routes of the Roman Empire. The advance of Christianity slowed with the disintegration of the Roman Empire after AD 500 and the growth of Arab power in the 7th—

8th century, but Irish and Anglo-Saxon missionaries continued to spread the faith in western and northern Europe, while missionaries of the Greek church in Constantinople worked in eastern Europe and Russia. Missions to Islamic areas and Asia began in the medieval period, and when Spain, Portugal, and France established overseas empires in the 16th century, the Roman Catholic church sent missionaries to the Americas and the Philippines. A renewed wave of Roman Catholic missionary work in the 19th century focused on Africa and Asia. Protestant churches were slower to undertake foreign missions, but in the 19th and early 20th century there was a great upsurge in Protestant missionary activity. Missionary work continues today, though it is often discouraged by the governments of former European colonies that have won independence.

Mission style, or SPANISH MISSION STYLE, Style of the missions established by Spanish Franciscans in Florida, Texas, Arizona, New Mexico, and especially California (1769–1823). Their portals were often handsomely ornate, but the overall impression is one of simple geometric volumes of white stucco complemented by sharply incised windows and simplified interior details. Mission style also commonly refers to a style largely created in the early 20th century by Gustav Stickley, who marketed a line of plain, heavy oak furnishings inspired by those of the Spanish missions, as well as a series of house designs to suit modest incomes.

Mississippi River, River, central U.S. It rises at Lake Itasca in Minnesota and flows south, meeting its major tributaries, the Missouri and Ohio rivers, about halfway along its journey to the Gulf of Mexico. It enters the gulf southeast of New Orleans, after a course of 2,350 mi (3,780 km). It is the largest river in North America, and with its tributaries it drains an area of 1.2 million sq mi (3.1 million sq km). Spanish explorer Hernando de Soto was the first European to discover the river, in 1541. French explorers Louis Jolliet and Jacques Marquette traveled down it in 1673 as far as the Arkansas River. French explorer La Salle reached the delta in 1682 and claimed the entire Mississippi region for France, as Louisiana. France kept control over the upper river, but the lower portion passed to Spain in 1769. It was designated the western boundary of the U.S. in 1783. France sold it to the U.S. in 1803 as part of the Louisiana Purchase. During the American Civil War, Union forces captured Vicksburg, Miss., in 1863, breaking the Confederate hold on the river. As the central river artery of the U.S., it is one of the busiest commercial waterways in the world.

Missouri River, River, central U.S. The longest tributary of the Mississippi River, it rises in the Rocky Mountains of southwestern Montana. It flows east to central North Dakota and south across South Dakota, forming sections of the South Dakota–Nebraska boundary, the Nebraska-Iowa boundary, the Nebraska-Missouri boundary, and the Kansas-Missouri boundary. It then meanders east across central Missouri to join the Mississippi River north of St. Louis, after a total course of 2,315 mi (3,726 km). It has been nicknamed "Big Muddy" because of the amount of silt that it carries. The first Europeans to visit its mouth were French explorers Jacques Marquette and Louis Jolliet in 1673. The first exploration of the river from its mouth to its headwaters was made in 1804–05 by the Lewis and Clark Expedition. Since the mid 20th century, programs have been instituted along its banks to check its turbulent flooding and to harness it for irrigation.

Mistral, Frédéric (b. Sept. 8, 1830, Maillane, France—d. March 25, 1914, Maillane), French poet. A leader of the 19th-century revival of Provençal, Mistral cofounded the Félibrige, an influential association for maintaining the customs and language of Provence and later the whole of southern France. He devoted 20 years to creating a scholarly dictionary of Provençal. His literary output includes lyrics; short stories; *Memoirs of Mistral* (1906), his best-known work; and long narrative poems, including *Mirèio*

Frédéric Mistral, etching, 1864

Gabriela Mistral, 1941.

(1859) and *The Song of the Rhône* (1897), his two greatest works. He shared the 1904 Nobel Prize for Literature with José Echegaray.

Mistral, Gabriela, orig. LUCILA GODOY ALCAYAGA (b. April 7, 1889, Vicuña, Chile—d. Jan. 10, 1957, Hempstead, N.Y., U.S.), Chilean poet. Mistral combined writing with a career as a cultural minister and diplomat and as a professor in the U.S. Her reputation as a poet was established in 1914 when she won a prize for three "Sonnets of Death." Her passionate lyrics, with love of children and of the downtrodden as principal themes, are collected in such volumes as *Desolation* (1922), *Destruction* (1938), and *The Wine Press* (1954). In 1945 she became the first Latin American to win the Nobel Prize for Literature.

Mithra, In Indo-Iranian myth, the god of light. He was born bearing a torch and armed with a knife, beside a sacred stream and under a sacred tree, a child of the earth itself. He soon rode, and later killed, the life-giving cosmic bull, whose blood fertilizes all vegetation. This deed became the prototype for a bull-slaying fertility ritual. As god of light, Mithra was associated with the Greek Helios and the Roman Sol Invictus. The first written reference to Mithra dates to 1400 BC.

mitosis, Cell division, or reproduction, in which a cell gives rise to two genetically identical daughter cells. Strictly applied, the term describes the duplication and distribution of chromosomes. Prior to mitosis, each chromosome is replicated, producing two strands (chromatids) attached at a centromere. During mitosis, the membrane around the cell's nucleus dissolves and the chromatids of each chromosome are separated and pulled to each end of the cell. As the nuclear membrane re-forms around each set of chromosomes, the cytoplasm of the parent cell begins to divide to form two daughter cells. Following mitosis, the cell membrane pinches in to separate the daughter cells. Mitosis is essential to life because it provides new cells for growth and for replacement of worn-out cells. It may take minutes or hours, depending on the kind of cells and species of organisms. It is influenced by time of day, temperature, and chemicals.

Mizoram, State (pop., 2008 est.: 980,000), northeastern India. Occupying an area of 8,140 sq mi (21,081 sq km), it is bounded by Myanmar (Burma) and Bangladesh and the states of Tripura, Assam, and Manipur. It is largely mountainous; its capital is Aizawl. The various ethnic groups of Mizoram are known collectively as the Mizo, and they speak a variety of Tibeto-Burman languages and dialects. They were in revolt against India for decades, and the establishment of Mizoram as a union territory in 1972 failed to appease them. The conflict was settled in 1987 with the promotion of Mizoram to statehood. The economy is based on agriculture.

Moabites, Semitic people who lived in the highlands east of the Dead Sea (now in west-central Jordan). The Moabites' culture dates from the late 14th century BC to 582 BC, when they were conquered by the Babylonians. According to the Old Testament, they were descended from Moab, a son of Lot. Though their language, religion, and culture were closely related to those of the Israelites, the Moabites were not part of the Israelite community. David's great-grandmother Ruth was a Moabite. The Moabite Stone, a stela discovered in 1868, is the only written document of any length that survives from Moab; it tells of King Omri of Israel's reconquest of Moabite lands, which the Moabites ascribed to the anger of their god, Chemosh.

mobile, Abstract sculpture that has moving parts, driven either by motors or by the natural force of air currents. Its revolving parts create a new visual experience of constantly changing volumes and forms. The term was initially suggested by Marcel Duchamp for a 1932 Paris exhibition of such works by Alexander Calder, who became the mobile's greatest exponent.

Moche, Dominant civilization on the northern coast of present-day Peru in the 1st–8th centuries AD. The name comes from the great site of Moche in the Moche River valley, which was apparently the capital of the Moche peoples. Their settlements extended along northern Peru's hot, arid coast from the Lambayeque River valley south to the Nepeña River valley. They irrigated extensively, and their agriculture supported many urban centres, which featured stepped pyramids. They were skilled metalworkers and produced sophisticated craft goods, including fine mold-made pottery. The cause of their demise is unknown.

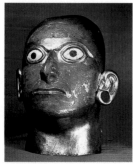

Mask of copper and gold alloy with eyes of shell, found in the Huaca de la Luna, Moche River valley, about 400 BC–AD 600; in the Linden-Museum, Stuttgart, Ger.
Ferdinand Anton

mockingbird, Any of several New World birds of a family (Mimidae) known for their mimicry of birdsong. The common, or northern, mockingbird (*Mimus polyglottos*) can imitate the songs of 20 or more species within 10 minutes. About 10 in. (27 cm) long, it is gray, with darker, white-marked wings and tail. It ranges from the northern U.S. to Brazil; it has been introduced into Hawaii and thrives in suburban areas. It sings from perches, even at night, and vigorously defends its territory. Other *Mimus* species range from Central America to Patagonia, and the blue mockingbird (genus *Melanotis*) inhabits much of Mexico. Various subspecies of the Galápagos mockingbird (genus *Nesomimus*) inhabit the different islands.

modal logic, Formal systems incorporating modalities such as necessity, possibility, impossibility, contingency, strict implication, and certain other closely related concepts. The most straightforward way of constructing a modal logic is to add to some standard nonmodal logical system a new primitive operator intended to represent one of the modalities, to define other modal operators in terms of it, and to add axioms and/or transformation rules involving those modal operators. For example, one may add the symbol L, which means "It is necessary that," to classical propositional calculus; thus, Lp is read as "It is necessary that p." The possibility operator M ("It is possible that") may be defined in terms of L as Mp = ¬L¬p (where ¬ means "not"). In addition to the axioms and rules of inference of classical propositional logic, such a system might have two axioms and one rule of inference of its own. Some characteristic axioms of modal logic are: (A1) Lp ⊃ p and (A2) L(p ⊃ q) ⊃ (Lp ⊃ Lq). The new rule of inference in

this system is the Rule of Necessitation: If p is a theorem of the system, then so is Lp. Stronger systems of modal logic can be obtained by adding additional axioms. Some add the axiom Lp ⊃ LLp; others add the axiom Mp ⊃ LMp.

mode, In music, any of a variety of concepts used to classify scales and melodies. In Western music, the term is particularly used for the medieval church modes. Keys in tonal music are normally said to be in either major or minor mode, depending particularly on the third degree of the scale. The concept of mode may involve much more than simply a classification of scales, extending to embrace an entire vocabulary of melodic formulas and perhaps other aspects of music that traditionally occur in tandem with a given set of formulas. The term *mode* has also been used for purely rhythmic patterns such as those of the Ars Antiqua, which were based on ancient Greek poetic metres.

modem, Electronic device that converts digital data into analog (modulated-wave) signals suitable for transmission over analog telecommunications circuits (e.g., traditional phone lines) and demodulates received analog signals to recover the digital data transmitted. The "modulator/demodulator" thus makes it possible for existing communications channels to support a variety of digital communications, including e-mail, Internet access, and fax transmissions. An ordinary modem, operating over traditional phone lines, has a data transmission speed limit of about 56 kilobits per second. ISDN lines allow communications at over twice that rate, and cable modems and DSL lines have transmission rates of over a million bits per second.

modern dance, Theatrical dance that developed in the U.S. and Europe in the 20th century as a reaction to traditional ballet. Precursors included Loie Fuller and Isadora Duncan. Formal teaching of modern dance began with the establishment of the Denishawn schools by Ruth St. Denis and Ted Shawn in 1915. Many of their students, principally Doris Humphrey and Martha Graham, further contributed to modern dance's definition as a technique based on principles of fall and recovery (Humphrey) and of contraction and release (Graham). Movement often stressed the expression of emotional intensity and contemporary subjects rather than focusing on the formal, classical, and often narrative aspects of ballet. Later developments included a revolt in the 1950s against Graham's expressionism, led by Merce Cunningham, whose choreography included ballet technique and the element of chance.

Modernism, In the arts, a radical break with the past and concurrent search for new forms of expression. Modernism fostered a period of experimentation in the arts from the late 19th to the mid-20th century, particularly in the years following World War I. In an era characterized by industrialization, rapid social change, advances in science and the social sciences (e.g., Darwinism, Freudian theory), Modernists felt a growing alienation incompatible with Victorian morality, optimism, and convention. The Modernist impulse is fueled in various literatures by industrialization and urbanization, by the search for an authentic response to a much-changed world. Among English-language writers, the best-known Modernists are T.S. Eliot, James Joyce, Gertrude Stein, and Virginia Woolf. Composers, including Arnold Schoenberg, Igor Stravinsky, and Anton Webern, sought new solutions within new forms and used as-yet-untried approaches to tonality. In dance a rebellion against both balletic and interpretive traditions had its roots in the work of Émile Jaques-Delcroze, Rudolf Laban, and Loie Fuller. Each of them examined a specific aspect of dance—such as the elements of the human form in motion or the impact of theatrical context—and helped bring about the era of modern dance. In the visual arts the roots of Modernism are often traced back to painter Édouard Manet, who beginning in the 1860s broke away from inherited notions of perspective, modeling, and subject matter. The avant-garde movements that followed—including Impressionism, Post-Impressionism, Cubism, Futurism, Expressionism, Constructivism, De Stijl, and Abstract Expressionism— are generally defined as Modernist. Over the span of these movements, artists increasingly focused on the intrinsic qualities of their media—e.g., line, form, and colour—and moved away from inherited notions of art. By the beginning of the 20th century, architects also had increasingly abandoned past styles and conventions in favour of a form of architecture based on essential functional concerns. In the period after World War I these tendencies became codified as the International style, which utilized simple, geometric shapes and unadorned facades and which abandoned any use of historical reference; the buildings of Ludwig Mies van der Rohe and Le Corbusier embodied this style. After World War II the style manifested itself in clean-lined, unadorned glass skyscrapers and mass housing projects.

Modigliani, Franco (b. June 18, 1918, Rome, Italy—d. Sept. 25, 2003, Cambridge, Mass., U.S.), Italian-born U.S. economist. He fled fascist Italy for the U.S. in 1939 and earned a doctorate from the New School for Social Research in 1944. He taught at several universities, including the Massachusetts Institute of Technology (1962–88; thereafter professor emeritus). His work on personal savings prompted him to formulate the life-cycle theory, which asserts that individuals build up savings during their younger working lives for use during their own old age and not as an inheritance for their descendants. In order to analyze financial markets, he invented a technique for calculating the value of a company's expected future earnings that became a basic tool in corporate decision making and finance. He received the Nobel Prize in 1985.

modulation, In music, the transition from one mode or key to another. There are three principal methods of modulation in classical harmony: diatonic, in which a pivot chord is common to both keys; chromatic, in which the notes of the pivot chord are altered by a semitone; and enharmonic, in which the notes of the pivot chord, while retaining their original tones, simply assume different names. Modulation may be transitory, as in the course of thematic development, or structural, contributing to the harmonic definition of the form.

Mohawk, North American Indian people, the easternmost group of the Iroquois Confederacy, living in Canada and the U.S. Their language is a member of the Iroquoian language family. Their name for themselves is Kahniakehake, which means "people of the flint," and within the confederacy they were considered to be the "keepers of the eastern door." Traditionally the Mohawk lived near what is now Schenectady, N.Y. They were semisedentary; women raised crops of corn (maize), and men hunted during the fall and winter and fished during the summer. Related families lived together in longhouses. Most Mohawk sided with the British in both the French and Indian War and the American Revolution, in the latter under Joseph Brant. By the mid-20th century the Mohawk had garnered a strong reputation as structural ironworkers; many have been involved in the building of major bridges and skyscrapers. Early 21st-century population estimates indicated some 47,000 individuals of Mohawk descent.

Moi, Daniel (Toroitich) arap (b. 1924, Sacho, Kenya Colony), Five-term president of Kenya (1978–2002). Trained as a teacher, Moi served in the cabinet and as vice president (1967–78) under Pres. Jomo Kenyatta before succeeding him as president. Head of the dominant Kenya African National Union (KANU) party, he governed autocratically, finally permitting multiparty elections in 1991, when international pressure forced his hand. His subsequent electoral victories (1992, 1997) led to civil unrest and charges of stealing the elections. During his time in office some sectors of the economy grew, but critics have attributed this to the strong political patronage system. Under Kenya's constitution, Moi was not allowed to stand in the 2002 presidential election and was succeeded by the winner, opposition candidate Mwai Kibaki.

moksha, or MOKSA, In Hinduism and Jainism, the ultimate spiritual goal, the soul's release from the bonds of transmigration. The soul, once entered upon a bodily existence, remains trapped in a chain of successive rebirths until it has attains the perfection or enlightenment that allows it release. The methods by which release is sought and attained differ from one philosophical school to the next, but most schools consider moksha to be the highest purpose of life.

mold, In biology, a conspicuous mass of mycelium and fruiting

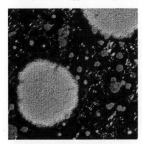

Mold on surface of jelly
Ingmar Holmasen

structures produced by various fungi (kingdom Fungi; *see* fungus). Molds of the genera *Aspergillus*, *Penicillium*, and *Rhizopus* are associated with food spoilage and plant diseases, but some have beneficial uses, such as in the manufacture of antibiotics (e.g., penicillin) and certain cheeses. *Neurospora*, or orange bread mold, has been invaluable in the study of genetics. Water molds (phylum Oomycota, kingdom Chromista) live in fresh or brackish water or wet soils, absorbing dead or decaying organic matter.

Moldavia, Former principality, southeast-central Europe. Located on the lower Danube River, it was founded in the 14th century by the Vlachs and achieved independence in 1349. In the mid-16th century it became part of the Ottoman Empire. In the 18th century it came under increasing Russian influence. It lost its northwestern territory, Bukovina, to Austria in 1774 and its eastern portion, Bessarabia, to Russia in 1812. In 1859 Moldavia and Walachia formed the state of Romania. In 1918 portions of historical Moldavia east of the Prut River threw off Russian rule and joined Romania. In 1940 Romania was compelled to cede to the Soviet Union its territories between the Prut and Dniester rivers; these became part of the Moldavian Soviet Socialist Republic. This Soviet republic became the independent country of Moldova in 1991.

Moldova, officially REPUBLIC OF MOLDOVA, Country, northeastern Balkan Peninsula, southeastern Europe. It is bordered by Ukraine and Romania. Area: 13,067 sq mi (33,843 sq km). Population: (2011 est.) 3,927,000. Capital: Chişinău. Nearly half the population is Moldovan; there also are large numbers of Russians and Ukrainians, especially in Transdniestria (Transnistria; Pridnestrovie), the self-proclaimed republic located on the east bank of the Dniester River. Languages: Moldovan (official), Russian, Ukrainian. Religions: Christianity (mostly Eastern Orthodox, also other Christians), Islam. Currency: Moldovan leu. Most of Moldova is a fertile region lying between the Dniester and Prut rivers; the northern and central regions of the country are forested. The economy is based on agriculture; the major farm products are grapes, winter wheat, corn, and dairy products. Industry is centred on food processing. Moldova is a unitary parliamentary republic with one legislative body; its head of state is the president, and the head of government is the prime minister. The area of present-day Moldova consists of that part of the historic principality of Moldavia lying east of the Prut River (part of Romania before 1940) and, adjoining it on the south, the region of Bessarabia along the Black Sea coast. The two regions were incorporated as the Moldavian Soviet Socialist Republic in 1940. In 1991 Moldavia declared independence from the Soviet Union. It adopted the Moldovan spelling of Moldova, having earlier legitimized use of the Latin rather than the Cyrillic alphabet. Moldova was admitted to the UN in 1992. In 2000 it abandoned its semipresidential form of government to become a parliamentary republic.

mole, or MOL, Standard unit for measuring everyday quantities of such minute entities as atoms or molecules. For any substance, the number of atoms or molecules in a mole is Avogadro's number (6.02×10^{23}) of particles. Defined exactly, it is the amount of pure substance containing the same number of chemical units that there are in exactly 12 g of carbon-12. For each substance, a mole is its atomic weight, molecular weight, or formula weight in grams. The number of moles of a solute in a litre of solution is its molarity (M); the number of moles of solute in 1,000 g of solvent is its molality (m). The two measures differ slightly and have different uses.

mole, Any burrowing, often blind insectivore in the family Talpidae (including 42 species of true moles) or Chrysochloridae (18 species of golden moles). Most species have short legs and tail, a pointed head, velvety grayish fur, no external ears, and a strong odour. They range from 3.5 to 8 in. (9 to 20 cm) long. The forelimbs are rotated outward like oars and have broad or pointed claws on the toes. Moles are active day and night, digging surface tunnels in search of earthworms, grubs, and other invertebrates and excavating deep (10 ft [3 m]), vented burrows (molehills) for occupancy. The star-nosed mole (*Condylura cristata*) of northeastern North America has 22 pink, tentacle-like touch organs radiating from its muzzle.

mole, Pigmented flat or fleshy skin mark, made up mostly of cells that produce melanin, which gives moles their light to dark brown or black colour and, in the dermis, a bluish cast. Thicker moles also contain nerve elements and connective tissue. Moles often begin in childhood, usually as flat spots between the dermis and epidermis. Those that remain there are more likely to become malignant. Most move into the dermis and become slightly raised. In children, moles may undergo changes resembling cancer but are benign. Malignant melanoma can begin in moles but almost never before puberty. During pregnancy, moles may enlarge and new ones may appear. Moles sometimes disappear with age. The term *nevus* refers to a congenital skin mark, whereas a mole may develop after birth. Epidermal nevi are usually the same colour as the surrounding skin.

molecular weight, also called MOLECULAR MASS, Mass of a molecule of a substance, based on 12 as the atomic weight of carbon-12. It is calculated in practice by summing the atomic weights of the atoms making up the substance's molecular formula. The molecular weight of a hydrogen molecule (chemical formula H_2) is 2 (after rounding off); for many complex organic molecules (e.g., proteins, polymers) it may be in the millions.

molecule, Smallest identifiable unit into which a pure substance can be divided and retain its composition and chemical properties. Division into still smaller parts, eventually atoms, involves destroying the bonding that holds the molecule together. For noble gases, the molecule is a single atom; all other substances have two (diatomic) or more (polyatomic) atoms in a molecule. The atoms are the same in elements, such as hydrogen (H_2), and different in compounds, such as glucose ($C_6H_{12}O_6$). Atoms always combine into molecules in fixed proportions. Molecules of different substances can have the same constituent atoms, either in different proportions, as in carbon monoxide (CO) and carbon dioxide (CO_2), or bonded in different ways. The covalent bonds in molecules give them their shapes and most of their properties. (The concept of molecules has no significance in solids with ionic bonds.) Analysis with modern techniques and computers can determine and display the size, shape, and configuration of molecules, the positions of their nuclei and electron clouds, the lengths and angles of their bonds, and other details. Electron microscopy can even produce images of individual molecules and atoms.

mollusk, or MOLLUSC, Any of some 75,000 species of soft-bodied invertebrate animals (phylum Mollusca), many of which are wholly or partly enclosed in a calcium carbonate shell secreted by the mantle, a soft covering formed from the body wall. Between the mantle and the body is the mantle cavity. Mollusks occur in most habitats from the deep sea to high mountains. Living mollusks are usually grouped into eight classes: Gastropoda, Bivalvia or Pelecypoda, Cephalopoda, Scaphopoda (tusk shells), Aplacophora (Solenogasters), Caudofoveata (sometimes included in the Aplacophora order), Polyplacophora (chitons), and Monoplacophora. Mollusks are economically important as food, and their shells are widely used in jewelry and decorative items.

Moloch, Ancient Middle Eastern deity to whom children were sacrificed. The laws given to Moses by God expressly forbade the Israelites to sacrifice children to Moloch, as the Egyptians and Canaanites did. A shrine to Moloch outside the walls of Jerusalem was destroyed during the reign of Josiah the reformer.

Moluccas, Indonesian MALUKU, Island group (pop., 2005 est.: 2,059,200), eastern Indonesia, lying between Celebes (Sulawesi) and New Guinea. The Moluccas comprise three large islands (Halmahera, Ceram, and Buru) and many smaller ones. Their combined area is about 30,066 sq mi (77,870 sq km). They constitute the Indonesian provinces of Maluku and North Maluku; the provincial capitals are, respectively, Ambon and Ternate. The population is ethnically diverse, including Malays and Papuans and people of Dutch, Portuguese, and Javanese descent. Known as the "Spice Islands," the Moluccas were part of the Asian spice trade before being discovered by the Portuguese in 1511, and they were fought over by the Spanish, English, and Dutch, eventually coming under the Dutch. Occupied by the Japanese during World War II, the islands were afterward incorporated into the state of East Indonesia and then into the Republic of Indonesia in 1949.

molybdenum, Metallic chemical element, one of the transition elements, chemical symbol Mo, atomic number 42. It is a silvery gray, relatively rare metal with a high melting point (4,730 °F [2,610 °C]) that does not occur uncombined in nature. Since molybdenum and its alloys have useful strength at temperatures that melt most other metals and alloys, they are used in high-temperature steels. Applications include reaction vessels; aircraft, missile, and automobile parts; and electrodes, heating elements, and filament supports. Some molybdenum compounds (in which it has various valences) are used as pigments and catalysts. Molybdenum disulfide is a solid lubricant, used alone or added to greases and oils.

Mombasa, City (pop., 2006 est.: 823,500), Kenya, located on the island of Mombasa off the southern coast of Kenya. The island has an area of 5.5 sq mi (14.25 sq km) and is linked to the mainland by causeway, bridge, and ferry; the city includes a mainland area of 100 sq mi (259 sq km). Founded by Arab traders in the 11th century, it was visited in 1498 by the Portuguese navigator Vasco da Gama. With its strategic position for the Indian Ocean trade, it was continually fought over, passing among the Arabs, Persians, Portuguese, and Turks until 1840, when Zanzibar gained control. It came under British administration in 1895 and was the capital of the East Africa Protectorate until 1907. It is Kenya's chief port and second largest city; it is also a major agricultural market.

momentum, Product of the mass of a particle and its velocity. Newton's second law of motion states that the rate of change of momentum is proportional to the force acting on the particle. Albert Einstein showed that the mass of a particle increases as its velocity approaches the speed of light. At the speeds treated in classical mechanics, the effect of speed on the mass can be neglected, and changes in momentum are the result of changes in velocity alone. If a constant force acts on a particle for a given time, the product of the force and the time interval, the impulse, is equal to the change in momentum. For any array of several objects, the total momentum is the sum of the individual momenta.

Mon-Khmer languages, Family of about 130 Austroasiatic languages, spoken by more than 80 million people in South and Southeast Asia. Vietnamese has far more speakers than all other Austroasiatic languages combined. Other languages with many speakers are Muong, with about a million speakers in northern Vietnam; Khmer; Kuay (Kuy), with perhaps 800,000 speakers; and Mon, spoken by more than 800,000 people in southern Myanmar and parts of Thailand. Of all the Mon-Khmer languages, only Mon, Khmer, and Vietnamese have written traditions dating earlier than the 19th century. Old Mon, which is attested from the 7th century, was written in a script of South Asian origin that was later adapted by the Burmese. Typical phonetic features of Mon-Khmer languages are a large vowel inventory and lack of tone distinctions.

Monaco, officially PRINCIPALITY OF MONACO, Independent principality, southern Europe, on the Mediterranean Sea near the France-Italy border. Area: 0.78 sq mi (2.02 sq km). Population: (2011 est.) 36,000. Nearly half of Monaco's population are French citizens; minorities include Italians and Britons; less than one-fifth of the population are of Monegasque descent. Language: French (official). Religions: Christianity (predominantly Roman Catholic [official]); also Judaism. Currency: euro. Monaco is a constitutional monarchy with one legislative body; the head of state is the prince, and the head of government is the minister of state, assisted by the Council of Government. Inhabited since prehistoric times, the area was known to the Phoenicians, Greeks, Carthaginians, and Romans. In 1191 the Genoese took possession of it. In 1297 the reign of the Grimaldi family began. The Grimaldis allied themselves with France except for the period from 1524 to 1641, when they were under the protection of Spain. France annexed Monaco in 1793, and it remained under French control until the fall of Napoleon, when the Grimaldis returned. In 1815 it was put under the protection of Sardinia. A treaty in 1861 called for the sale of the towns of Menton and Roquebrune to France and the establishment of Monaco's independence. Monaco, situated along the Côte d'Azur, is one of Europe's most luxurious resorts, known for its Monte-Carlo gambling centre, international sports-car races, and beaches. In 1997 the 700-year rule of the Grimaldis, then under Prince Rainier, was celebrated.

monarch butterfly, Species (*Danaus plexippus*, family Danaidae) of milkweed butterfly, occurring worldwide but mainly in the Americas. It is the only lepidopteran species to make a true migration (a two-way flight by the same individual). In North America, thousands of monarchs gather in autumn, migrate southward, sometimes more than 1,800 mi (2,900 km), and return north in spring. The distinctive coloration of the adult's wings (reddish brown, with black veins, a black border, and two rows of spots) warns predators of its bad taste. Several other species derive protection by mimicking its coloration.

monarchy, Undivided sovereignty or rule by a single person, who is the permanent head of state. The term is now used to refer to countries with hereditary sovereigns. The monarch was the ideal head of the new nation-states of the 16th and 17th centuries; his powers were nearly unlimited, though in Britain Parliament was able to restrict the sovereign's freedom of action, particularly through the Magna Carta (1215) and the Bill of Rights (1689). The old idea that the monarch represented (within the limits of his dominions) the rule of God over all things culminated in the 17th century in the doctrine of the divine right of kings, exemplified by Louis XIV. Monarchical absolutism adapted to the Enlightenment by evolving into "benevolent despotism," as typified by the rule of Catherine II of Russia. The French Revolution dealt absolute monarchy a crushing blow, and World War I effectively destroyed what remained of it, the rulers of Russia, Germany, and Austria-Hungary being held responsible for the war and postwar misery. The institution developed into the constitutional monarchy in western Europe, though absolute (or near-absolute) monarchies continue to exist in the Middle East.

monasticism, Institutionalized religious movement whose members are bound by vows to an ascetic life of prayer, meditation, or good works. Members of monastic orders are usually celibate, and they live apart from society either in a community of monks or nuns or as religious recluses. The earliest Christian monastic communities were founded in the deserts of Egypt, most notably by the hermit St. Anthony of Egypt (251–356). It was given its more familiar cenobitic form by St. Pachomius (*c.* 290–346). St. Basil the Great composed a very influential rule for the Eastern church, and John Cassian (360–465) helped spread monasticism to western Europe. The Benedictine order, founded by St. Benedict of Nursia in the 6th century, called for moderation of ascetic practices and established worship services at regular hours. Throughout the Middle Ages, monasticism played a vital role not only in spreading Christianity but also in preserving and adding to literature and learning. It underwent periodic reforms, notably by the Cluniacs in the 10th century and the Cistercians in the 12th century, and saw the founding of mendicant orders such as the Dominicans and Franciscans. Monasticism has also been important in Eastern religions. In early Hindu times (*c.* 600–200 BCE) there were hermits who lived in groups (ashrams), though they did not lead a strictly organized communal life. Jainism may be the first religion to have had an organized monastic life, which was characterized by extreme asceticism. Buddhist monks observe a moderate rule that avoids extremes of self-indulgence and self-mortification.

Monet, Claude (b. Nov. 14, 1840, Paris, France—d. Dec. 5,

1926, Giverny), French landscape painter. Monet spent his early years in Le Havre, where his first teacher, Eugène Boudin, taught him to paint in the open air. Moving to Paris, he formed lifelong friendships with other young painters, including Pierre-Auguste Renoir, Alfred Sisley, and Paul Cézanne. Beginning in the mid 1860s, Monet pursued a new style; rather than trying to reproduce faithfully the scene before him in detail, he recorded on the spot the impression that relaxed, momentary vision might receive. In 1874 he helped organize an independent exhibition, apart from the official Salon, of work he and his friends produced in this style. One of Monet's works at the exhibition, *Impression: Sunrise* (1872), inspired the journalist Louis Leroy to give the group its name. Throughout the 1870s, Monet and the other Impressionists explored this style and exhibited together. By 1881 the original group had begun to disintegrate; only Monet continued with the same fervour to carry on the scrutiny of nature. In his mature works Monet developed his method of producing a series of several studies of the same motif (e.g., haystacks, 1891, and Rouen Cathedral, 1894), changing canvases as the light or his interest shifted. In 1893, in the garden at his home in Giverny, Monet created the water-lily pond that inspired his most famous works, the lyrical *Nymphéas* (water-lilies) paintings. Wildly popular retrospective exhibitions of his work toured the world during the last decades of the 20th century and established his unparalleled public appeal, sustaining his reputation as one of the most significant and popular figures in the modern Western painting tradition.

Women in the Garden, *oil on canvas by Claude Monet, 1866–67; in the Louvre, Paris.*
Giraudon/Art Resource, New York

monetarism, School of economic thought that maintains that the money supply is the chief determinant of economic activity. Milton Friedman and his followers promoted monetarism as an alternative to Keynesian economics; their economic theories became influential in the 1970s and early 1980s. Monetarism holds that a change in the money supply directly affects and determines production, employment, and price levels, though its influence is evident only over a long and often variable period of time. Fundamental to the monetarist approach is the rejection of fiscal policy in favour of "monetary rule." Friedman and others asserted that fiscal measures such as tax-policy changes or increased government spending have little significant effect on the fluctuations of the business cycle. They argued that government intervention in the economy should be kept to a minimum and asserted that economic conditions would change before specific policy measures designed to address them could take effect. Steady, moderate growth of the money supply, in their view, offered the best hope of assuring a constant rate of economic growth with low inflation. U.S. economic performance in the 1980s cast doubts on monetarism, and the proliferation of new types of bank deposits made it difficult to calculate the money supply.

monetary policy, Measures employed by governments to influence economic activity, specifically by manipulating the money supply and interest rates. Monetary and fiscal policy are two ways in which governments attempt to achieve or maintain high levels of employment, price stability, and economic growth. Monetary policy is directed by a nation's central bank. In the U.S., monetary policy is the responsibility of the Federal Reserve System, which uses three main instruments: open-market operations, the discount rate, and reserve requirements. In the post-World War II era, economists reached a consensus that, in the long run, inflation results when the money supply grows at too rapid a rate.

money, Commodity accepted by general consent as a medium of economic exchange. It is the medium in which prices and values are expressed, and it circulates from person to person and country to country, thus facilitating trade. Throughout history various commodities have been used as money, including seashells, beads, and cattle, but since the 17th century the most common forms have been metal coins, paper notes, and bookkeeping entries. In standard economic theory, money is held to have four functions: to serve as a medium of exchange universally accepted in return for goods and services; to act as a measure of value, making possible the operation of the price system and the calculation of cost, profit, and loss; to serve as a standard of deferred payments, the unit in which loans are made and future transactions are fixed; and to provide a means of storing wealth not immediately required for use. Metals, especially gold and silver, have been used for money for at least 4,000 years; standardized coins have been minted for perhaps 2,600 years. In the late 18th and early 19th century, banks began to issue notes redeemable in gold or silver, which became the principal money of industrial economies. Temporarily during World War I and permanently from the 1930s, most nations abandoned the gold standard. To most individuals today, money consists of coins, notes, and bank deposits. In terms of the economy, however, the total money supply is several times as large as the sum total of individual money holdings so defined, since most of the deposits placed in banks are loaned out, thus multiplying the money supply several times over.

money, quantity theory of, Economic theory relating changes in the price level to changes in the quantity of money. It has often been used to analyze the factors underlying inflation and deflation. The quantity theory was developed in the 17th and 18th centuries by philosophers such as John Locke and David Hume and was intended as a weapon against mercantilism. Drawing a distinction between money and wealth, advocates of the quantity theory argued that if the accumulation of money by a nation merely raised prices, the mercantilist emphasis on a favourable balance of trade would only increase the supply of money without increasing wealth. The theory contributed to the ascendancy of free trade over

protectionism. In the 19th–20th centuries it played a part in the analysis of business cycles and in the theory of rates of foreign exchange.

money market, Set of institutions, conventions, and practices whose aim is to facilitate the lending and borrowing of money on a short-term basis. The money market is, therefore, different from the capital market, which is concerned with medium- and long-term credit. The transactions that occur on the money market involve not only banknotes but assets that can be turned into cash at short notice, such as short-term government securities and bills of exchange. Though the details and mechanisms of the money market vary greatly from country to country, in all cases its basic function is to enable those with surplus short-term funds to lend and those with the need for short-term credit to borrow. This function is accomplished through middlemen who provide their services for a profit. In most countries the government plays a major role in the money market, acting both as a lender and as a borrower and often using its position to influence the money supply and interest rates according to its monetary policy. The U.S. money market covers financial instruments ranging from bills of exchange and government securities to funds from clearinghouses and certificates of deposit. In addition, the Federal Reserve System provides considerable short-term credit directly to the banking system. The international money market facilitates the borrowing, lending, and exchange of currencies between countries.

money order, Certificate requiring the issuer to pay a certain sum of money on demand to a specific person or organization. Money orders provide a fast, safe, and convenient means of transferring small sums of money. They are issued by governments (usually through postal authorities), banks, and other qualified institutions to buyers who pay the issuer the face amount of the money order plus a service charge. Because they are exchangeable for cash on demand, they are a generally accepted means of payment. The American Express Co. began issuing money orders in 1882; the company also created the first traveler's checks nine years later.

money supply, Liquid assets held by individuals and banks. The money supply includes coins, currency, and demand deposits (checking accounts). Some economists consider time and savings deposits to be part of the money supply because such deposits can be managed by governmental action and are nearly as liquid as currency and demand deposits. Other economists believe that deposits in mutual savings banks, savings and loan associations, and credit unions should be counted as part of the money supply. Central banks regulate the money supply to stabilize their national economies.

Möngke (b. 1208, Mongolia—d. 1259, Sichuan province, China), Mongol leader. Grandson of Genghis Khan and brother of Kublai Khan, he was elected great khan in 1251. Under Möngke, the Mongols conquered Iran, Iraq, and Syria as well as the Thai kingdom of Nan-chao and the area of present-day Vietnam. He died before the Mongols could complete the conquest of China, which happened under the reign of Kublai.

Mongol, Member of an Asian people originally from the Mongolian Plateau who share a common language and a nomadic tradition of herding sheep, cattle, goats, and horses. In the 10th–12th centuries the Khitan, Juchen (Chin dynasty), and Tatars ruled in Mongolia, but Mongol power was greatest in the 13th century, when Genghis Khan, his sons (notably Ögödei), and his grandsons Batu and Kublai Khan created one of the world's largest empires. It declined greatly in the 14th century, when China was lost to the Ming dynasty and the Golden Horde was defeated by Muscovy. Ming incursions effectively ended Mongol unity, and by the 15th–16th centuries only a loose federation existed. Today the plateau is divided between independent Mongolia and Chinese-controlled Inner Mongolia. Other Mongols live in Siberia. Tibetan Buddhism is the principal Mongol religion.

Mongolia, or OUTER MONGOLIA, Country, north-central Asia, between Russia and China. Area: 603,909 sq mi (1,564,116 sq km). Population: (2011 est.) 2,765,000. Capital: Ulaanbaatar (Ulan Bator). Some four-fifths of the population are Mongols; minorities consist of Kazakhs, Russians, and Chinese. Languages: Khalkha Mongolian, Turkic languages, Russian, Chinese. Religions: traditional beliefs, Buddhism, Islam. Currency: tugrik (Tug). Mongolia has an average elevation of about 5,200 ft (1,580 m) above sea level. Three mountain ranges stretch across the north and west: the Altai, the Hangayn (Khangai), and the Hentiyn (Khentei). The south and east are occupied by the Gobi Desert. Livestock raising, especially sheepherding, accounts for nearly three-fourths of the total value of agricultural production; wheat is the major crop. Mongolia's rich mineral resources include coal, iron ore, and copper. Mongolia is a unitary multiparty republic with one legislative house; its head of state is the president, and the head of government is the prime minister. In Neolithic times it was inhabited by small groups of hunters and nomads. During the 3rd century BCE it became the centre of the Xiongnu tribal league. Turkic-speaking peoples held sway in the 4th–10th centuries CE. In the early 13th century Genghis Khan united the Mongol tribes and conquered Central Asia. His successor, Ögödei, conquered the Jin dynasty of China in 1234. Kublai Khan established the Yuan (Mongol) dynasty in China in 1279. The Mongols were confined to their original homeland on the steppes after the 14th century. Ligdan Khan (ruled 1604–34) attempted to unite Mongol tribes against the Manchu, but after his death the Mongols became part of the Chinese Qing dynasty. After the fall of the Qing in 1912, Mongol princes, supported by Russia, declared Mongolia's independence from China, and in 1921 the Soviet Red Army helped drive off Chinese and Russian forces. The Mongolian People's Republic was established in 1924. The country adopted a new constitution in 1992 and shortened its name to Mongolia.

Mongolian languages, Family of about eight Altaic languages spoken by five to seven million people in central Eurasia. All Mongolian languages are relatively closely related; those languages whose speakers left the core area in Mongolia the earliest tend to be the most divergent. The most remote language is Mogholi (Moghul, Mongol), now spoken by fewer than 200 people in western Afghanistan. Less divergent are the languages of several ethnic groups in northwestern China, eastern Qinghai, and adjacent parts of Gansu and Inner Mongolia, altogether spoken by fewer than 500,000 people. The core languages are Mongolian proper, the dominant dialect in the Republic of Mongolia and the basis of Modern Standard Mongolian, and a group of peripheral dialects. The core group of Mongolian speakers traditionally have used Classical Mongolian as their literary language; it is written in a vertical alphabetic script borrowed from the Uighurs. Modern Mongolian was written in this script until 1946, when the People's Republic of Mongolia introduced a script using a modified Cyrillic alphabet. With political democratization in the 1990s, the old script has been revived. In Inner Mongolia it has been in continuous use.

mongoose, Any of the 37 species of carnivores constituting the family Herpestidae, found in Africa, Asia, and southern Europe. Rudyard Kipling's famous "Rikki-tikki-tavi" was an Indian, or gray, mongoose (*Herpestes edwardsii*); the meerkat is also a member of the mongoose family. Species range from 7 to 35 in. (17 to 90 cm) long, excluding the furry 6–12-in. (15–30-cm) tail. Mongooses have short legs, a pointed nose, and small ears. Most species are active during the day. The gray to brown fur may have light flecks or dark markings. Mongooses live in burrows, alone, in pairs, or in large groups, and they eat small mammals, birds, rep-

tiles, eggs, and fruit. A few species are semiaquatic. Though not immune to venom, some species attack and kill poisonous snakes by cracking the skull with a powerful bite.

monism, In metaphysics, the doctrine that the world is essentially one substance or contains only one kind of substance. Monism is opposed both to dualism and to pluralism. Examples of monism include materialism, pantheism, and metaphysical idealism.

monkey, Any member of two tropical anthropoid primate groups: Old World monkeys and New World monkeys. Almost all species are tropical or subtropical, and almost all are diurnal. Most species are arboreal, using all four limbs to leap from tree to tree. They can sit upright and stand erect. Most species run along branches rather than swinging arm over arm like the apes. Monkeys are highly social omnivores, organized in clans as large as several hundred individuals headed by an old male. Sexually mature males of all species are always potent, and all nonpregnant females have a monthly menstrual cycle. Most species bear a single young, which is reared by the mother for years.

monkeypox, Viral disease of both animals and humans that causes symptoms similar to those of smallpox, though less severe. The monkeypox virus is usually found in primates and rodents in Central and West Africa but has spread to other parts of the world through the export of infected small mammals. It can be transmitted to humans through an animal bite and from person to person through prolonged close contact. Symptoms of the disease include fever, headache, general malaise and fatigue, and swollen lymph nodes. A rash of raised bumps appears on the infected person's face and body. Treatment is limited to alleviating symptoms. Outbreaks are contained by isolating patients and controlling the trade of animals.

Monnet, Jean (b. Nov. 9, 1888, Cognac, France—d. March 16, 1979, Houjarray), French economist and diplomat. He managed his family's brandy business before becoming a partner of an investment bank (1925). In World War II he chaired a Franco-British economic committee and proposed a Franco-British union. In 1947 he created and directed the successful Monnet Plan to rebuild and modernize France's economy. In 1950, with Robert Schuman, he proposed the plan for the European Coal and Steel Community, predecessor of the European Economic Community and the European Union, and served as its first president (1952–55). He was also the founder and president of the action committee for the United States of Europe (1955–75).

monody, Accompanied solo song style of the early 17th century. It represented a reaction against the contrapuntal style (based on the combination of simultaneous melodic lines) of the 16th-century madrigal and motet. Ostensibly in an attempt to emulate ancient Greek music, composers placed renewed emphasis on proper articulation as well as expressive interpretation of texts, and they thus replaced counterpoint with simply accompanied recitative. This resulted in a decisive distinction between melody and accompaniment, which coincides with the early appearance of basso continuo. A collection of songs published by Giulio Caccini in 1602 exemplifies early monody.

mononucleosis, infectious, or GLANDULAR FEVER, Common infection, caused by Epstein-Barr virus. It occurs most often at ages 10–35. Infected young children usually have little or no illness but become immune. Popularly called "the kissing disease," it is spread mostly by oral contact with exchange of saliva. It usually lasts 7–14 days. The most common symptoms are malaise, sore throat, fever, and lymph-node enlargement. Liver involvement is usual but rarely severe. The spleen often enlarges and in rare cases ruptures fatally. Less frequent features include rash, pneumonia, encephalitis (sometimes fatal), meningitis, and peripheral neuritis. Relapse and second attacks are rare. Diagnosis may require blood analysis. There is no specific therapy.

monophony, Music consisting of a single unaccompanied melodic line. The concept often also includes melody that is accompanied by a drone or by drumming. Gregorian chant and Byzantine chant constitute the oldest written examples of monophonic repertory.

Monophysite heresy (5th–6th century AD) Doctrine that emphasized the single nature (the term means literally "of one nature") of Christ, as a wholly divine being rather than part-divine and part-human. Monophysitism began to appear in the 5th century; though condemned as a heresy at the Council of Chalcedon (451), it was tolerated by such Byzantine leaders as Justin II, Theodora, and Zeno, resulting in a full-fledged schism between East and West. Several Monophysite churches, including the Coptic Orthodox Church, were founded in the 6th century.

monopolistic competition, Market situation in which many independent buyers and sellers may exist but competition is limited by specific market conditions. The theory was developed almost simultaneously by Edward Hastings Chamberlin in his *Theory of Monopolistic Competition* (1933) and Joan V. Robinson in her *Economics of Imperfect Competition* (1933). It assumes product differentiation, a situation in which each seller's goods have some unique properties, thereby giving the seller some monopoly power.

monorail, Electric railway that runs on a single rail either above or under the railway cars. The first systems were introduced in the early 20th century; the earliest probably opened in 1901 in Wuppertal, Germany. Short-run monorails have since been built in such cities as Tokyo and Seattle. Because of higher costs and slower speeds than conventional rail systems, the monorail has not gained wide support. High-speed monorail vehicles that use magnetic levitation have been undergoing research for many years.

monotheism, Belief in the existence of one god. It is distinguished from polytheism. The earliest known instance of monotheism dates to the reign of Akhenaton of Egypt in the 14th century BC. Monotheism is characteristic of Judaism, Christianity, and Islam, all of which view God as the creator of the world, who oversees and intervenes in human events, and as a beneficent and holy being, the source of the highest good. The monotheism that characterizes Judaism began in ancient Israel with the adoption of Yahweh as the single object of worship and the rejection of the gods of other tribes and nations without, initially, denying their existence. Islam is quite clear in confessing one, eternal, unbegotten, unequaled God, while Christianity holds that a single God is reflected in the three persons of the Holy Trinity.

Monroe, James (b. April 28, 1758, Westmoreland county, Va.—d. July 4, 1831, New York, N.Y., U.S.), Fifth president of the U.S. (1817–25). After serving in the American Revolution, he studied law under Thomas Jefferson, then governor of Virginia. From 1783 to 1786 he served in the Congress under the Articles of Confederation. In 1790 he was elected to the U.S. Senate, where he opposed the adminstration of George Washington. He nevertheless became

James Monroe, oil sketch by E.O. Sully, 1836, after a contemporary portrait by Thomas Sully; in Independence National Historical Park, Philadelphia.
Courtesy of the Independence National Historical Park Collection, Philadelphia

Washington's minister to France in 1794, though he was recalled two years later for misleading the French about U.S. politics. From 1799 to 1802 he served as governor of Virginia. In 1803 Pres. Jefferson sent him to France to help negotiate the Louisiana Purchase; he was then appointed minister to Britain (1803–07). He returned to Virginia and was again elected governor in 1810, though he resigned the office after 11 months to serve as U.S. secretary of state (1811–17) and secretary of war (1814–15). He served two terms as president, presiding in a period that became known as the Era of Good Feelings. He oversaw the Seminole War of 1817–18 and the acquisition of the Floridas (1819–21), and he signed the Missouri Compromise (1820). With Secretary of State John Quincy Adams, he developed the principles of U.S. foreign policy later called the Monroe Doctrine.

Monroe, Marilyn, orig. NORMA JEANE MORTENSON (b. June 1, 1926, Los Angeles, Calif., U.S.—d. Aug. 5, 1962, Los Angeles), U.S. film actress. She endured a loveless childhood and a brief teenage marriage. After working as a photographer's model, she made her screen debut in 1948 and won bit parts in *The Asphalt Jungle* (1950) and *All About Eve* (1950). She achieved stardom as a blonde sex symbol in the comedies *Gentlemen Prefer Blondes* (1953), *How to Marry a Millionaire* (1953), and *The Seven Year Itch* (1955). After studying at the Actors Studio, she starred in more-ambitious films, in-

Marilyn Monroe.
Brown Brothers

cluding *Bus Stop* (1956), *Some Like It Hot* (1959), and *The Misfits* (1961). Her private life, which included marriages to Joe DiMaggio and Arthur Miller, was widely publicized. She died at age 36 of an apparently self-administered barbiturate overdose. Her vulnerability and sensuousness combined with her death raised her to the status of an American cultural icon.

Monroe Doctrine, U.S. foreign-policy statement first enunciated by Pres. James Monroe on Dec. 2, 1823, declaring the Western Hemisphere off-limits to European colonization. Concerned that the European powers would attempt to restore Spain's former colonies, he declared, inter alia, that any attempt by a European power to control any nation in the Western Hemisphere would be viewed as a hostile act against the U.S. It was reiterated in 1845 and 1848 by Pres. James K. Polk to discourage Spain and Britain from establishing footholds in Oregon, California, or on Mexico's Yucatán Peninsula. In 1865 the U.S. massed troops on the Rio Grande to back up demands that France withdraw from Mexico. In 1904 Pres. Theodore Roosevelt added the Roosevelt Corollary, stating that in the event of flagrant wrongdoing by a Latin American state, the U.S. had the right to intervene in its internal affairs. As the U.S. became a world power, the Monroe Doctrine came to define the Western Hemisphere as a U.S. sphere of influence.

Monrovia, Port city (pop., 2003 est.: 550,200), capital of Liberia, located on the Atlantic coast. It was founded in 1822 by the American Colonization Society as a settlement for freed U.S. slaves and named for Pres. James Monroe. Bushrod Island contains the artificial harbour and free port of Monrovia, the only such port in West Africa. It is Liberia's largest city and its administrative and commercial centre. Many of the city's buildings were damaged during the civil war that began in 1990, and its increased population includes many formerly rural people displaced by the war. It is the seat of the University of Liberia.

monsoon, Major wind system that seasonally reverses its direction (e.g., one that blows for six months from the northeast and six months from the southwest). The most prominent examples occur in Africa and southern Asia. The primary cause of monsoons is the difference between annual temperature trends over land and sea. Seasonal changes in temperature are large over land but small over oceans. A monsoon blows from cold toward warm regions: from sea toward land in summer and from land toward sea in winter. Most summer monsoons produce copious amounts of rain; winter monsoons tend to cause drought.

montage (French: "mounting"), Pictorial technique in which cut-out illustrations, or fragments of them, are arranged together and mounted on a support, producing a composite picture made from several different pictures. It differs from collage in using only ready-made images chosen for their subject or message. The technique is widely used in advertising. Photomontage uses photographs only. In motion pictures, montage is the sequential assembling of separate pieces of thematically related film by the director, film editor, and visual and sound technicians, who cut and fit each part with the others to produce visual juxtapositions and complex audio patterns.

Montale, Eugenio (b. Oct. 12, 1896, Genoa, Italy—d. Sept. 12, 1981, Milan), Italian poet, prose writer, editor, and translator. Montale began his literary activities after World War I, cofounding a journal, writing for other journals, and serving as a library director in Florence. His first book of poems, *Cuttlefish Bones* (1925), expressed the bitter pessimism of the postwar period. He was identified with Hermeticism in the 1930s and '40s, and his works became progressively introverted and obscure. With *The Storm and Other Poems* (1956) his writing showed the increasing skill, warmth, and directness characteristic of his late period. His stories and sketches were collected in *The Butterfly of Dinard* (1956). He received the Nobel Prize for Literature in 1975.

Monte Albán, Ridgetop site of the ruins of the ancient centre of Zapotec culture, located near Oaxaca, Mex. Construction at the site began around the 8th century BC. Monte Albán reached its height AD 250–700. The site contains great plazas, truncated pyramids, a *tlachtli* court for an ancient ballgame, underground passageways, and about 170 tombs, the most elaborate yet uncovered in the New World. The great plaza atop the highest hill is flanked by four platforms; two temples stand on the platform to the south. In its final phase, Monte Albán was inhabited by the Mixtec.

Monte-Carlo, Resort (pop., 2000: 15,507), one of the four sections (*quartiers*) of Monaco. It is situated northeast of Nice on the French Riviera. In 1856 Charles III of Monaco granted a charter allowing a joint-stock company to build a casino, which opened in 1861. The district around it, called Monte-Carlo, became a luxurious playground for the world's wealthy. The government took over the casino's operating company in 1967.

Montenegro, European country located in the west-central Balkans. Area: 5,333 sq mi (13,812 sq km). Population: (2011 est.) 620,000. Capital: Cetinje. The administrative centre is Podgorica. The country's name ("Black Mountain") refers to its ancient stronghold near the Adriatic Sea, Mount Lovćen, which rises to 5,738 ft (1,749 m). Montenegro's landscape ranges from arid hills to forests and fertile valleys. The majority of its population are Montenegrins who follow the Eastern Orthodox Church; there are sizable Bosniak and Albanian minorities. Among the country's industries are metallurgy, mining, and the manufacture of consumer goods; agricultural pursuits include raising grains and animal husbandry. Tourism is an economic mainstay. Montenegro is a multiparty republic with one legislative house; the head of state is the president, and the head of government is the prime minister. Under the Roman Empire the region was part of the province of Illyricum. Settled by Slavs in the 7th century, it was incorporated into the Serbian empire in the late 12th century. It retained its independence following the defeat of the Serbs by the Ottoman Empire in 1389 at the Battle of Kosovo. Often at war with the Ottomans and Albanians, it began an alliance with Russia early in the 18th century. In the Balkan Wars of 1912–13, it cooperated against the Ottoman Empire. It supported Serbia during and after World War I. It was then absorbed into Serbia; the union became part of the Kingdom of Serbs, Croats, and Slovenes (from 1929, Yugoslavia). During World War II Montenegro was occupied by the Italians and was the scene of heavy fighting. In 1946 the federal constitution of the new Yugoslavia made Montenegro one of Yugoslavia's six nominally autonomous federated units. In 1992, one year after the breakup of Yugoslavia, Montenegro and Serbia combined as the new Federal Republic of Yugoslavia. In 2003, following agitation for independence in Montenegro, the Serbian, Montenegrin, and Yugoslav parliaments ratified a new constitutional agreement that maintained the federation, under the name Serbia and Montenegro. In 2006 Montenegro achieved complete separation from Serbia.

Monterrey, City (pop., 2000: 1,110,997), capital of Nuevo León state, northern Mexico. It lies at an elevation of about 1,750 ft (530 m). It was founded in 1579, but its growth was slow until the late 19th century. In 1846 it was taken by U.S. Gen. Zachary Taylor in the Mexican War. In 1882 rail connections were established with Laredo, Texas, U.S., and in 1930 construction began on the Inter-American Highway, leading to the development of large-scale smelting and heavy-industry enterprises. It has several institutions of higher education.

Montesquieu, Charles-Louis de Secondat, baron de (La Brède et de) (b. Jan. 18, 1689, Château La Brède, near Bordeaux, France—d. Feb. 10, 1755, Paris), French philosophe and satirist. Born into a noble family, he held public office in Bordeaux from 1714. His satirical *Persian Letters* (1721) was hugely successful. From 1726 he traveled widely to study social and political institutions. His magnum opus, the enormous *The Spirit of the Laws* (1750), contained an original classification of governments by their manner of conducting policy, an argument for the separation of the legislative, judicial, and executive powers, and a celebrated but less influential theory of the political influence of climate. The work profoundly influenced European and American political thought and was relied on by the framers of the U.S. Constitution. His other works include *Causes of the Greatness and Decadence of the Romans* (1734).

Montessori, Maria (b. Aug. 31, 1870, Chiaravalle, near Ancona, Italy—d. May 6, 1952, Noordwijk aan Zee, Neth.), Italian educator. Montessori took a degree in medicine (1894) and worked in a clinic for retarded children before going on to teach at the University of Rome. In 1907 she opened her first children's school, and for the next 40 years she traveled throughout Europe, India, and the U.S., lecturing, writing, and setting up Montessori schools. Today there are hundreds of such schools in the U.S. and Canada alone; their principal focus is on preschool education, but some provide elementary education to grade 6. The Montessori system is based on belief in children's creative potential, their drive to learn, and their right to be treated as individuals. It relies on the use of "didactic apparatuses" to cultivate hand-eye coordination, self-directedness, and sensitivity to premathematical and preliterary instruction.

Montevideo, Port city (pop., 2004: 1,383,416), capital of Uruguay. Situated on the northern shore of the Río de la Plata estuary, it was founded by the Spanish in 1726 to stem the Portuguese advance into the area from Brazil. From 1807 to 1830 it was alternately occupied by British, Spanish, Argentine, Portuguese, and Brazilian forces. It became the capital of newly independent Uruguay in 1830. A major seaport of South America, it is the commercial, political, and cultural centre of Uruguay. It is the site of Uruguay's only institutions of higher education, which include the Universidad de la República and the Universidad del Trabajo del Uruguay.

Montreal, City (pop., 2001: metro. area, 3,426,350), southeastern Canada. It occupies about one-third of Montreal Island, near the confluence of the Ottawa and St. Lawrence rivers. The metropolitan area encompasses Montreal and other islands, as well as both shores of the St. Lawrence. It is built on the slopes of Mount Royal, from which the city's name is derived. English and French are spoken throughout the city, which is the chief centre of French Canadian industry and culture. The site was occupied by the Huron Indian settlement of Hochelaga when visited by French explorer Jacques Cartier in 1535. The first European settlement was founded by the French in 1642 and was given the name Ville-Marie de Montréal. Rapid colonization based on the fur trade began in the first half of the 18th century, and the city soon grew beyond its walls. It surrendered to British forces in 1760 and, with all of New France, became part of the British North American empire in 1763. Montreal served as the capital of Canada from 1844 to 1849. It is one of Canada's chief ports for both oceangoing and inland shipping. It is Canada's second largest city and a major cultural centre, with a complex of theatre and concert halls and several museums. It is the seat of McGill and Concordia universities (both English-language) and the Universities of Montreal and Quebec at Montreal (both French-language).

Montreux Convention (1936) Agreement concerning the Dardanelles strait. In response to Turkey's request to refortify the area, the signers of the Treaty of Lausanne and others met in Montreux, Switz., and agreed to return the zone to Turkish military control. The convention allowed Turkey to close the straits to all warships when it was at war and to permit merchant ships free passage.

mood, or MODE, In grammar, a category that reflects the speaker's view of an event's reality, likelihood, or urgency. Often marked by special verb forms (inflections), moods include the indicative, for factual or neutral situations (e.g., "You did your work"); the imperative, to convey commands or requests ("Do your work"); and the subjunctive. The subjunctive's functions vary widely. It may express doubt, possibility, necessity, desire, or future time. In English it often indicates a condition contrary to fact (e.g., "If he were to work here, he would have to learn to be punctual").

Moon, Sole natural satellite of Earth, which it orbits at a mean distance of about 384,400 km (238,900 mi). It is less than one-third the size of Earth (radius about 1,738 km [1,080 mi] at its equator), about 1/81 as massive, and about two-thirds as dense. Its surface gravity is about one-sixth that of Earth, and its gravitational pull is largely responsible for Earth's tides. The Moon shines by reflected sunlight, but its albedo is only 7%. It rotates on its axis in 27.3 days, in exactly the time it takes to orbit Earth, and it therefore always presents the same face to Earth. However, that face is lit by the Sun at different angles as the Moon revolves around Earth, causing it to display different phases over the month, from new to full. Most astronomers believe the Moon formed from a cloud of fragments ejected into Earth orbit when a Mars-sized body struck the proto-Earth early in the solar system's history. Its surface has been studied by telescope since Galileo first observed it in 1609 and firsthand by a total of 12 U.S. astronauts during the six successful lunar landing missions of the Apollo program. The dominant process affecting the surface has been impacts, both from micrometeorite bombardment, which grinds rock fragments into fine dust, and from meteorite strikes, which produced the craters profusely scattered over its surface mostly early in its history, over four billion years ago. The maria are huge, ancient lava flows. In the late 1990s unmanned spacecraft found possible signs of water ice near the Moon's poles.

Moore, Henry (b. July 30, 1898, Castleford, Eng.—d. Aug. 31, 1986, Much Hadham), English sculptor and graphic artist. The son of a coal miner, he was enabled to study at the Royal College of Art by a rehabilitation grant after being wounded in World War I. His early works were strongly influenced by the Mayan sculpture he saw in a Paris museum. From *c.* 1931 on he experimented with abstract art, combining abstract shapes with the human figure and at times leaving the human figure behind altogether. When materials grew scarce during World War II, he concentrated on drawings of Londoners sheltering from bombs in Underground stations. Commissions for a *Madonna and Child* and a family group turned his style from abstraction to the more humanistic approach that became the basis of his international reputation. He returned to experimentation in the 1950s with angular, pierced standing figures in bronze. Much of his work is monumental, and he is particularly well known for a series of reclining nudes. Among his major commissions were sculptures for UNESCO's Paris headquarters (1957–58), Lincoln Center (1963–65), and the National Gallery of Art (1978).

moraine, Accumulation of rock debris (till) carried or deposited by a glacier. The material may range in size from blocks or boulders to sand and clay, is unstratified when dropped by the glacier, and shows no sorting or bedding. Several kinds of moraines are recognized, depending on how they are deposited by the glacier; these include lateral moraines along the margins of the glacier and terminal moraines at its leading edge.

Medial moraine of Gornergletscher (Gorner Glacier) in the Pennine Alps near Zermatt, Switz.
Jerome Wyckoff

Moravia, Region, central Europe. Bounded by Bohemia, Silesia, Slovakia, and northeastern Austria and crossed by the Morava River, it was inhabited from the 4th century BC. It was dominated by the Avars in the 6th and 7th centuries AD and later settled by Slavic tribes, and in the 9th century it became the state of Great Moravia and included Bohemia as well as parts of modern Poland and Hungary. It was destroyed by the Magyars in 906. In 1526 it came under Habsburg rule. After the Revolution of 1848 Moravia became an Austrian crown land with its capital at Brno. In 1918 it was incorporated into the new state of Czechoslovakia. Germany annexed parts of it in 1938; after World War II they were restored to Czechoslovakia. It was included in the Czech Socialist Republic created in 1968 and in the Czech Republic in 1993.

Moravian Church, Protestant denomination founded in the 18th century. It traces its origins to the Unity of Brethren, a 15th-century Hussite movement in Bohemia and Moravia. The original Brethren movement was eroded by persecution, but it was renewed in 1722 at Herrnhut, a theocratic community established in Saxony. In America the Moravians founded Bethlehem, Pa. (1740), and several other settlements, and carried out missionary work among the Indians. The Moravians ordain bishops but are governed by synods of elected representatives; they are guided by the Bible as their only rule of faith and worship.

More, Saint Thomas (b. Feb. 7, 1478, London, Eng.—d. July 6, 1535, London; canonized May 19, 1935; feast day June 22), English statesman and humanist. He studied at Oxford and was successful as a lawyer from 1501. He served as an undersheriff of London (1510–18) and endeared himself to Londoners as a fair judge and consultant. He wrote the notable *History of King Richard III* (1513–18) and the renowned *Utopia* (1516), which was an immediate success with humanists, including Desiderius Erasmus. In 1517 More was named to the king's council, and he became Henry VIII's secretary and confidant. In 1523 he was elected speaker of the House of Commons. He wrote *A Dialogue Concerning Heresies* (1529) to refute heretical writings. After the fall of Cardinal Wolsey (1529), More succeeded him as lord chancellor, but he resigned in 1532 when he could not affirm Henry's divorce from Catherine. He also refused to accept the Act of Supremacy. In 1534 More was charged with high treason and imprisoned in the Tower of London, where he wrote his *Dialogue of Comfort Against Tribulation*. In 1535 he was tried and sentenced to death by hanging, which the king commuted to beheading.

Morgan le Fay ("Morgan the Fairy") Enchantress in Arthurian legend. Skilled in the arts of healing and changing shape, she ruled Avalon, the island where King Arthur retreated to be healed of his wounds after his last battle. She had learned her magic powers from books and from Merlin. In other stories she is Arthur's sister and enemy, and seduces him to produce a son who later kills Arthur.

Mormon, Member of the Church of Jesus Christ of Latter-day Saints or of a sect closely related to it (e.g., the Community of Christ). The Mormon religion was founded by Joseph Smith, who claimed to have received an angelic vision telling him of the location of golden plates containing God's revelation; this he published in 1830 as the *Book of Mormon*. Smith and his followers accepted the Bible as well as the Mormon sacred scriptures but diverged significantly from orthodox Christianity, especially in their assertion that God exists in three distinct entities as Father, Son, and Holy Spirit. Mormons also believe that faithful members of the church will inherit eternal life as gods. Other unique doctrines include the belief in preexisting souls waiting to be born and in salvation of the dead through retroactive baptism. The church became notorious for its practice of polygamy, though it was officially sanctioned only between 1852 and 1890. Smith and his followers migrated from Palmyra, N.Y., to Ohio, Missouri, and finally Illinois, where Smith was killed by a mob in 1844. In 1846–47, under Brigham Young, the Mormons made a 1,100-mi (1,800-km) trek to Utah, where they founded Salt Lake City. In the early 21st century, the church had a worldwide membership of nearly 10 million, swelled yearly by the missionary work that church members, both men and women, are encouraged to perform.

Mormon, Book of, Holy scripture of the Mormons, supplemental to the Bible. First published in 1830, it is held by all branches of Mormonism to be a divinely inspired work translated by the founder of their religion, Joseph Smith. It relates the history of a tribe of Hebrews who migrated from Jerusalem to America *c.* 600 BC. They eventually split into two groups: the Lamanites, who were ancestors of the American Indians; and the Nephites, who were instructed by Jesus before being destroyed by the Lamanites. The prophet Mormon recorded their history on gold tablets, which were buried and remained hidden for centuries. Moroni, Mormon's son, appeared to Smith in angelic form and revealed their location.

Moroccan crises (1905–06, 1911) Two European incidents centring on Germany's attempt to block France's control of Morocco and to restrict French power. While visiting Tangier in 1905, the German emperor William II issued a statement of support for Moroccan independence, which caused international panic. The crisis was resolved at the Algeciras Conference (1906), which recognized France's special political interests in Morocco. The second crisis occurred in 1911 when a German gunboat arrived in Agadir, ostensibly to protect German economic interests during a local uprising. The French objected and made preparations for

war, as did Britain, but a settlement was negotiated that gave France rights to a protectorship over Morocco. In return, Germany acquired part of the French Congo.

Morocco, officially KINGDOM OF MOROCCO, Country, North Africa. Area: 170,773 sq mi (442,300 sq km). Population: (2011 est.) 31,968,000. Capital: Rabat. The Imazighen are the country's largest ethnolinguistic group; there are French, Spanish, and Bedouin minorities. Languages: Arabic (official), Tamazight, French. Religion: Islam (official; mostly Sunni). Currency: dirham. Morocco is a mountainous country with an average elevation of 2,600 ft (800 m) above sea level. A mountain chain known as the Rif runs along the northern coast; the Atlas Mountains rise in the country's centre and include Mount Toubkal (13,665 ft [4,165 m]), Morocco's highest peak. The area is a zone of severe seismic activity, and earthquakes are frequent. Fertile lowlands support agriculture; major crops include barley, wheat, and sugar beets. Morocco is one of the world's largest suppliers of phosphate. Its industrial centre is Casablanca, the largest city. It is a constitutional monarchy with two legislative houses; its head of state and head of government is the king, assisted by the prime minister. The Imazighen entered Morocco near the end of the 2nd millennium BCE. Phoenicians established trading posts along the Mediterranean coast during the 12th century BCE, and Carthage had settlements along the Atlantic coast in the 5th century BCE. After the fall of Carthage, the region's leaders became loyal allies of Rome, and in 42 CE it was annexed by the Romans as part of the province of Mauretania. It was invaded by Muslims in the 7th century. The Almoravid dynasty conquered it and the Muslim areas of Spain in the mid-11th century; the Almohad dynasty overthrew the Almoravids in the 12th century and in turn were conquered by the Marīnid dynasty in the 13th century. After the fall of the Marīnids in the mid-15th century, the Saʿdī dynasty ruled for a century, beginning *c.* 1550. Attacks by Barbary Coast pirates compelled Europeans to enter the area; the French fought Morocco over the boundary with Algeria, Europeans obtained trading rights in 1856, and the Spanish seized part of Moroccan territory in 1859. Morocco was a French and Spanish protectorate from 1912 until its independence in 1956. In the 1970s it reasserted claim to the Spanish Sahara, and in 1976 Spanish troops withdrew from the region, leaving behind the Algerian-supported Saharan guerrillas of the Polisario movement. Relations with Mauritania and Algeria deteriorated, and fighting over the region continued. Attempts at mediation have been made by the international community.

Moroni, Town (pop., 2003: 41,557), capital of the Comoros Islands, located on Grande Comore (Njazidja) island in the Indian Ocean. Founded by Arabic-speaking settlers, it is the largest settlement of the Comoros and has served as the capital since 1958. The port of Moroni consists of a small quay in a natural cove. The town retains an Arabic character and has several mosques, including Chiounda, a pilgrimage centre.

morpheme, In linguistics, the smallest grammatical unit of speech. It may be an entire word (*cat*) or an element of a word (*re-* and *-ed* in *reappeared*). In so-called isolating languages, like Vietnamese, each word contains a single morpheme; in languages such as English, words often contain multiple morphemes. The study of morphemes is included in morphology.

morphine, Heterocyclic compound, narcotic analgesic alkaloid originally isolated from opium. It is among the most powerful naturally occurring compounds in its ability to reduce pain and distress; its calming effect protects the system against exhaustion in traumatic shock, internal hemorrhage, congestive heart failure, and other debilitating conditions. Morphine is usually given by injection but may be taken by mouth. Its most serious drawback is its addictiveness; many doctors are reluctant to use amounts adequate to relieve severe pain, even though short-term use in such cases rarely leads to drug addiction. This remains controversial even in terminal cases, when addiction is arguably irrelevant; another issue in such cases is that large doses depress respiration and may thus hasten death.

morphology, In biology, the study of the size, shape, and structure of organisms in relation to some principle or generalization. Whereas anatomy describes the structure of organisms, morphology explains the shapes and arrangement of parts of organisms in terms of such general principles as evolutionary relations, function, and development.

morphology, In linguistics, the internal construction system of words and its study. Languages vary widely in the number of morphemes a word can have. English has many words with multiple morphemes (e.g., *replacement* is composed of *re-*, *place*, and *-ment*). Many American Indian languages have a highly complex morphology; other languages, such as Chinese, have a simple one. Morphology includes the grammatical processes of inflection, marking categories like person, tense, and case (e.g., the *-s* in *jumps* marks the third-person singular in the present tense), and derivation, the formation of new words from existing words (e.g., *acceptable* from *accept*).

Morrison, Toni, orig. CHLOE ANTHONY WOFFORD (b. Feb. 18, 1931, Lorain, Ohio, U.S.), U.S. writer. She studied at Howard and Cornell universities, taught at various universities, and worked as an editor before publishing *The Bluest Eye* (1970), a novel dealing with some of the shocking realities of the lives of poor blacks, and *Sula* (1973). The brilliant *Song of Solomon* (1977) brought her national attention. Her later novels include *Tar Baby* (1981), *Beloved* (1987, Pulitzer Prize), *Jazz* (1992), *Paradise* (1998), *A Mercy* (2008), and *Home* (2012). The African American experience, particularly that of women, is the principal theme of her fiction. Her use of fantasy, her sinuous poetic style, and her interweaving of mythic elements give her stories texture and great power. She was awarded the Nobel Prize for Literature in 1993.

Morse code, System for representing letters, numerals, and punctuation marks by a sequence of dots, dashes, and spaces. It is transmitted as electrical pulses of varied lengths or analogous mechanical or visual signals, such as flashing lights. The original system was invented by Samuel F.B. Morse in 1838 for his telegraph; the International Morse Code, a simpler and more precise variant with codes for letters with diacritic marks, was devised in 1851. With minor changes, this code has remained in use for certain types of radiotelegraphy, including amateur radio.

mortar, Short-range artillery piece with a short barrel and low muzzle velocity that fires an explosive projectile in a high-arched trajectory. Large mortars were used against fortifications and in siege operations from medieval times through World War I. Since 1915, small portable models have been standard infantry weapons, especially for mountain or trench warfare. Medium mortars, with a caliber of about 3–4 in. (70–90 mm), a range of up to about 2.5 mi (4 km), and a bomb weight of up to 11 lbs (5 kg), are now widely used.

mosaic, Surface decoration of small coloured components—such as stone, glass, tile, or shell—closely set into an adhesive ground. Mosaic pieces, or tesserae, are usually small squares, triangles, or other regular shapes. Mosaics cannot create the variations of light and shadow that paintings can, but glass tesserae can achieve a greater brilliance, especially those to which gold and silver foil have been applied. This technique was responsible for the great shimmering mosaics of the Byzantine period. The earliest known mosaics date from the 8th century BCE and were made of pebbles, a technique refined by the Greeks in the 5th century. The Romans used mosaics widely, particularly for floors. Pre-Columbian Americans favoured mosaics of garnet, turquoise, and mother-of-pearl, which usually encrusted shields, masks, and cult statues.

Moscow, Russian MOSKVA, Capital and largest city (pop., 2006 est.: 10,425,075) of Russia. It is located on both sides of the Moskva River in western Russia, about 400 mi (640 km) southeast of St. Petersburg and about 600 mi (970 km) east of Poland. Inhabited since Neolithic times, the site was first mentioned as a village in 1147 and became the capital of the principality of Moscow (Muscovy) in the late 13th century. It expanded in the 15th and 16th centuries under its grand dukes Ivan III and Ivan IV and became the capital of a united Russia (1547–1712). In 1812 it was occupied by the French under Napoleon and was almost entirely destroyed by fire. In 1918 it became the capital of the Union of Soviet Socialist Republics and expanded greatly. It suffered much damage from German bombing in World War II. In 1993 it was the scene of armed conflict between opposing government factions after the dissolution of parliament by Boris Yeltsin. The spiritual home of the Russian Orthodox church for more than 600 years, it is a political, industrial, transportation, and cultural centre. Its most notable structure is the Kremlin, a medieval fortress on the Moskva with Red Square along its eastern wall. The Lenin Mausoleum is nearby, and the Cathedral of St. Basil the Blessed is at the southern end of the square. Moscow is also home to the Bolshoi Theatre, Moscow State University, and many other institutions of higher education.

Moselle River, or MOSEL RIVER, River, western Europe, about 340 mi (545 km) long. Rising in northeastern France, it flows north, forming part of the border between Germany and Luxembourg, then northeast into the Rhine River at Koblenz, Ger. In this part of the valley are the vineyards that produce the famous Moselle wines. The river, which is navigable for most of its course, passes Nancy, Metz, and Thionville in France and Trier in Germany. Among its chief tributaries are the Orne and the Saar.

Moses (fl. 14th–13th century BCE), Prophet of Judaism. According to the Book of Exodus, he was born in Egypt to Hebrew parents, who set him afloat on the Nile in a reed basket to save him from an edict calling for the death of all newborn Hebrew males. Found by the pharaoh's daughter, he was reared in the Egyptian court. After killing a brutal Egyptian taskmaster, he fled to Midian, where Yahweh (God) revealed himself in a burning bush and called Moses to deliver the Israelites from Egypt. With the help of his brother Aaron, Moses pleaded with the pharaoh for the Israelites' release. The pharaoh let them go after Yahweh had visited a series of plagues on Egypt, but then sent his army after them. Yahweh parted the waters of the Red Sea to allow the Israelites to pass, then drowned the pursuing Egyptians. Yahweh made a covenant with the Israelites at Mount Sinai and delivered the Ten Commandments to Moses, who continued to lead his people through 40 years of wandering in the wilderness until they reached the edge of Canaan. He died before he could enter the Promised Land. Authorship of the first five books of the Bible is traditionally ascribed to him.

mosque, Islamic public place of prayer. The *masjid jāmi'*, or "congregational mosque," is the centre of community worship and the site of Friday prayer services. Though the mosque—originally a sacred plot of ground—has been influenced by local architectural styles, the building has remained essentially an open space, usually roofed, with a minaret sometimes attached. Statues and pictures are not permitted as decoration. The *minbar*, a seat at the top of steps placed at the right of the mihrab, is used by the preacher (*khaṭīb*) as a pulpit. Occasionally there is also a *maqṣūrah*, a box or wooden screen originally used to shield a worshiping ruler from assassins. The minaret, originally any elevated place but now usually a tower, is used by the muezzin (crier) to proclaim the call to worship five times each day. During prayer, Muslims orient themselves toward the *qiblah* wall, which is invariably oriented toward the Ka'bah in Mecca. The mosque has traditionally been the centre of social, political, and educational life in Islamic societies.

mosquito, Any of 2,500 dipteran species in the family Culicidae.

Mosquito (Theobaldia anulata)
N.A. Callow/EB Inc.

The females of most species require a blood meal to mature their eggs. Through bloodsucking, females of various species (genera *Aedes*, *Anopheles*, and *Culex*) transmit human diseases, including dengue fever, encephalitis, filariasis, malaria, yellow fever, and elephantiasis. The adult has a long proboscis, a slender, elongated body, and long, fragile legs. The males (and sometimes the females) feed on plant juices. The female's characteristic sound is made by the vibration of thin membranes on the thorax. The females lay their eggs on the surface of a body of usually stagnant water, and the eggs hatch into aquatic larvae (wrigglers). In the far north larvae pass the winter frozen into ice. The wrigglers are eaten by fishes and aquatic insects, the adults by birds and dragonflies. Control measures have included elimination of breeding sites, application of surface films of oil to clog the larvae's breathing tubes, and use of larvicides.

moss, Any of at least 12,000 species of small, spore-bearing land plants in the bryophyte division, found worldwide except in salt water. Mosses are simple and ancient plants that have survived nearly unchanged since the Permian Period (290–248 million years ago). Commonly found in moist, shady locations (e.g., forest floors), mosses may range in size from microscopic to more than 40 in. (1 m) long. They prevent erosion and release nutrients from the substrates on which they grow. The life cycle shows clear alternation of generations between the sexual gametophyte, with stemlike and leaflike structures that produce eggs and swimming sperm, and the sporophyte, a raised stalk that ends in a spore case (sporangium). Mosses also reproduce asexually by branching. The economically important genus *Sphagnum* forms peat. Many so-called mosses are not bryophytes, including Irish moss (a red form of algae); beard moss, Iceland moss, oak moss, and reindeer moss (all lichens); Spanish moss (a name used variously for a lichen or an air plant of the pineapple family); and club moss (an evergreen herb of the family Lycopodiaceae).

Mossad, Hebrew MOSSAD MERKAZI LE-MODIIN U-LETAFKIDIM MEYUHADIM ("CENTRAL INSTITUTE FOR INTELLIGENCE AND SECURITY"), Most important of Israel's major intelligence agencies. The Mossad carries out foreign espionage and covert political and paramilitary operations. Its director reports directly to the prime minister. It has enjoyed considerable success in operations against the country's Arab neighbours and Palestinian organizations, and it has an excellent reputation internationally for its effectiveness. Its secret agents are credited with the apprehension of Adolf Eichmann in Argentina, the execution of the killers of Israeli athletes at the 1972 Olympics, and the rescue of Israeli hostages in the Entebbe incident. In the late 20th and early 21st centuries, the Mossad was criticized for its treatment of detainees, many of whom were allegedly tortured and killed while in custody, and for its efforts to assassinate some Palestinian political leaders.

most-favoured-nation treatment, Guarantee of same trading opportunities (i.e., tariff concessions) already granted to the most favoured nation (MFN). It is a method of establishing equal trading opportunities among states by making originally bilateral agreements multilateral. Attempts to guarantee equal trading opportunities were incorporated into commercial treaties as far back as the early 17th century. The Anglo-French treaty signed in 1860 became the model for many later trade agreements, establishing a set of interlocking tariff concessions later extended worldwide by most-favoured-nation treatment. MFN treatment has always applied primarily to the duties charged on imports, but specific provisions have extended the principle to other areas of economic contact, including property rights, patents, and copyrights.

Mosul, Arabic AL-MAWṢIL, City (pop., 2011 est.: 1,475,000), northwestern Iraq. Located across the Tigris River from the ruins of ancient Nineveh, which it succeeded, Mosul prospered until 1258, when it was ravaged by the Mongols. It was a centre of the Ottoman Empire (c. 1534–1918). After World War I (1914–18) it was occupied by the British and in 1926 was ceded to Iraq. The country's second largest city and a chief commercial centre in the northwest, it has manufacturing (cement, textiles) and an oil refinery and nearby oil fields. It has many ancient buildings, some dating from the 13th century, including the Great Mosque and the Red Mosque.

motel, Hotel designed for persons traveling by automobile, with convenient parking space provided (the name blends the words "motor hotel"). Originally usually consisting of a series of separate or attached roadside cabins, motels serve commercial and business travelers and persons attending conventions and business meetings as well as vacationers and tourists. By 1950 the automobile was the principal mode of travel in the U.S., and motels were built near large highways, just as hotels had been built near railroad stations.

motet, Latin choral composition, generally in one movement. Its origins are in the 13th century, when words (French *mots*) began to be added to originally wordless polyphonic lines in settings of plainchant. It grew directly out of the clausula, a polyphonic decoration of a portion of organum, but it soon split off to become a separate composition, while retaining a meaningless fragment of chant text and melody in the tenor part. The upper texts often became a confusing mixture of sacred and secular—and even anticlerical—poems, indicating its intended performance in courtly as well as ecclesiastical settings. The motet was the most important musical genre of the 13th century and an essential vehicle for the development of polyphony. In the Renaissance, sacred motets, now employing a single text, were written by composers such as Josquin des Prez, Orlande de Lassus, and William Byrd, though it remains unclear how often they were performed in church settings. In the 17th–18th centuries, motets were written by Jean-Baptiste Lully, Marc-Antoine Charpentier, Heinrich Schütz, and Johann Sebastian Bach. After c. 1750 the genre declined, and its distinguishing characteristics became diffuse.

moth, Any of more than 150,000 lepidopteran species, found in all but polar habitats. Moths are chiefly nocturnal and have a stouter body, duller colouring, and proportionately smaller wings than butterflies. They have distinctive feathery antennae and, when at rest, fold their wings, wrap them around the body, or hold them extended at their sides. Wingspans range from about 4 mm (0.16 in.) to nearly 30 cm (about 1 ft). The life cycle has four stages: egg, larva (caterpillar, or worm), pupa (chrysalis), and adult (imago). Both larvae and adults of most species are plant eaters, and many seriously damage forests, agricultural crops, and fabrics.

Mother Goose, Fictitious old woman, reputedly the source of the body of traditional children's songs and verses known as nursery rhymes. Often pictured as a beak-nosed, sharp-chinned old woman riding on the back of a flying gander, she was first associated with nursery rhymes in *Mother Goose's Melody* (1781), published by the successors of John Newbery. The name apparently derived from the title of Charles Perrault's collection of fairy tales *Ma Mère l'oye* (1697; "My Mother Goose"). The persistent rumour that Mother Goose was an actual Boston woman is false.

motion picture, or MOVIE, Series of still photographs on film, projected in rapid succession onto a screen. Motion pictures are filmed with a movie camera, which makes rapid exposures of people or objects in motion, and shown with a movie projector, which reproduces sound synchronized with the images. The principal inventors of motion-picture machines were Thomas Alva Edison in the U.S. and the Lumière brothers in France. Film production was centred in France in the early 20th century, but by 1920 the U.S. had become dominant. As directors and stars moved to Hollywood, movie studios expanded, reaching their zenith in the 1930s and '40s, when they also typically owned extensive theatre chains. Moviemaking was marked by a new internationalism in the 1950s and '60s, which also saw the rise of the independent filmmaker. The sophistication of special effects increased greatly from the 1970s. The U.S. film industry, with its immense technical resources, has continued to dominate the world market to the present day.

motion sickness, Sickness caused by contradiction between external data from the eyes and internal cues from the balance centre in the inner ear. For example, in seasickness the inner ear senses the ship's motion, but the eyes see the still cabin. This stimulates stress hormones and accelerates stomach muscle contraction, leading to dizziness, pallor, cold sweat, and nausea and vomiting. Minimizing changes of speed and direction may help, as may reclining, not turning the head, closing the eyes, or focusing on distant objects. Drugs can prevent or relieve motion sickness but may have side effects. Pressing an acupuncture point on the wrist helps some people.

motorcycle, Bicycle or tricycle propelled by an internal combustion engine. The first motor tricycle was built in 1884 in England, and the first gasoline-engine motorcycle was built by Gottlieb Daimler in 1885. Motorcycles were widely used after 1910, especially by the armed forces in World War I. After 1950 a larger, heavier motorcycle was used for touring and sport competitions. The moped, a light, low-speed motor bicycle that can also be pedaled, was developed mainly in Europe, and the sturdier Italian-made motor scooter also became popular for its economy.

motorcycle racing, Sport of running motorcycles on tracks, closed circuits, or natural terrain. The main types are (1) road racing, conducted on a course made up wholly or partly of public roads; (2) trials, conducted both on and off the highway; (3) speedway racing, conducted on a short, flat, oval dirt track; (4) drag racing, conducted on a straight quarter-mile strip of pavement; (5) hill climbs, conducted on a large dirt mound; and (6) motocross. The first international road race took place in Douran, France, in 1905. The most famous race is the Tourist Trophy, established on Britain's Isle of Man in 1907. Motorcycle racing in North America began in 1903; since 1937 the Daytona 200-mi (320-km) race has been the leading U.S. race.

mountain, Landform that rises well above its surroundings, generally exhibiting steep slopes, a relatively confined summit area, and considerable local relief (inequalities of elevation). Mountains are considered larger than hills, but the term has no standardized geologic meaning. Mountains are formed by the folding, faulting, or upwarping of the Earth's surface due to the movement of plates or by the emplacement of volcanic rock onto the surface. For example, the Himalayan Mountains where India meets the Eurasian Plate were formed by a collision between plates that caused extreme compressional folding and the uplifting of large areas. The mountain ranges around the Pacific basin are attributed to the sinking of one plate beneath another.

mountaineering, or MOUNTAIN CLIMBING, Sport of attaining, or attempting to attain, high points in mountainous regions, mainly for the joy of the climb. The pleasures of mountaineering lie not only in the conquest of the peak but also in the physical and spiritual satisfactions brought about through intense personal effort, ever-increasing proficiency, and contact with natural grandeur. The greater rewards do not come without considerable risk and danger. The first great peak ascended in modern times was Mont Blanc, in 1786. Other Alpine peaks followed, capped by the ascent of the Matterhorn in 1865. By the 1910s, most peaks of the Andes, the Rockies, and other Western Hemisphere ranges had been climbed, including Mount McKinley (1913). Beginning in the

1930s a series of successful ascents of mountains in the Himalayas occurred; the summits of many of the Himalayan mountains were not reached until the 1950s, however. Of these climbs, the best known is the 1953 ascent of Mount Everest by Edmund Hillary and Tenzing Norgay. In the 1960s mountaineering became an increasingly technical sport, emphasizing the use of specialized anchoring, tethering, and grappling gear in the ascent of vertical rock or ice faces.

mouse, Any of many species (family Muridae) of small, scampering rodents. They are distinguished from rats principally by their smaller size. Mice are basically Asian in origin, but species have been introduced worldwide. Species in other rodent families (e.g., deer mouse, pocket mouse) are called mice without scientific basis. Mice eat grains, roots, fruit, grass, and insects. They can become pests but are mostly beneficial; they are the main prey of most fur-bearers and of predators that might otherwise take more valuable prey. The white laboratory mouse is a form of house mouse.

House mouse (Mus musculus).
Ingmar Holmasen

mouth, or ORAL CAVITY, or BUCCAL CAVITY, Orifice through which food and air enter the body. It opens to the outside at the lips and empties into the throat at the rear and is bounded by the lips, cheeks, hard and soft palates, and glottis. Its chief structures are the teeth, tongue, and palate. It is the site of chewing and speech formation. The mouth is lined by mucous membranes containing small glands that, along with the salivary glands, keep it moist and clear of food and other debris.

Mozambique, officially REPUBLIC OF MOZAMBIQUE, formerly PORTUGUESE EAST AFRICA, Country, southeast coast of Africa. Area: 308,642 sq mi (799,380 sq km). Population: (2011 est.) 22,949,000. Capital: Maputo. The great majority of the people are Bantu-speaking Africans. Ethnolinguistic groups include the Makua, Tsonga, Malawi, Shona, and Yao peoples. Languages: Portuguese (official), Bantu languages, Swahili. Religions: traditional beliefs, Christianity, Islam. Currency: metical. Mozambique may be divided into two broad regions: the lowlands in the south and the highlands in the north, separated by the Zambezi River. It has a centrally planned, developing economy based on agriculture, international trade, and light industry. Some industries were nationalized after 1975. Mozambique is a multiparty republic with one legislature; its head of state and government is the president. Inhabited in prehistoric times, it was settled by Bantu peoples *c.* the 3rd century CE. Arab traders occupied the coastal region from the 14th century, and the Portuguese controlled the area from the early 16th century. The slave trade later became an important part of the economy and, although outlawed in the mid-18th century, continued illegally. In the late 19th century, private trading companies began to administer parts of the inland areas. It became an overseas province of Portugal in 1951. An independence movement became active in the 1960s, and, after years of war, Mozambique was granted independence in 1975. A single-party state under Frelimo (the Mozambique Liberation Front), it was wracked by civil war in the 1970s and '80s. In 1990 a new constitution ended its Marxist collectivism and introduced privatization, a market economy, and multiparty government. A peace treaty was signed with the rebels in 1992, ending the civil war. The country's first multiparty elections were held two years later.

Mozart, Wolfgang Amadeus, orig. JOHANNES CHRYSOSTO-MUS WOLFGANGUS THEOPHILUS MOZART (b. Jan. 27, 1756, Salzburg, Archbishopric of Salzburg—d. Dec. 5, 1791, Vienna), Austrian composer. Son of the violinist and composer Leopold Mozart (1719–87), he was born the year of the publication of Leopold's best-selling treatise on violin playing. He and his older sister, Maria Anna (1751–1829), were prodigies; at age five he began to compose and gave his first public performance. From 1763 Leopold toured throughout Europe with his children, showing off the "miracle that God allowed to be born in Salzburg." The first round of touring (1763–69) took them as far as France and England, where Wolfgang met Johann Christian Bach and wrote his first symphonies (1764). Tours of Italy followed (1769–73); there he first saw the string quartets of Joseph Haydn and wrote his own first Italian opera. In 1775–77 he composed his violin concertos and his first piano sonatas. His mother died in 1778. He returned to Salzburg as cathedral organist and in 1781 wrote his opera seria *Idomeneo*. Chafing under the archbishop's rule, he was released from his position in 1781; he moved in with his friends the Weber family and began his independent career in Vienna. He married Constanze Weber, gave piano lessons, and wrote *The Abduction from the Seraglio* (1782) and many of his great piano concertos. The later 1780s were the height of his success, with the string quartets dedicated to Haydn (who called Mozart the greatest living composer), the three great operas on Lorenzo Da Ponte's librettos—*The Marriage of Figaro* (1786), *Don Giovanni* (1787), and *Così fan tutte* (1790)—and his superb late symphonies. In his last year he composed the opera *The Magic Flute* and his great *Requiem* (left unfinished). Despite his success, he always lacked money (possibly because of gambling debts and a fondness for fine clothes) and had to borrow heavily from friends. His death at age 35 may have resulted from a number of illnesses; among those that have been suggested are miliary fever, rheumatic fever, and Schönlein-Henoch syndrome. No other composer left such an extraordinary legacy in so short a lifetime.

MP3, abbreviation of MPEG-1, AUDIO LAYER 3, Standard technology and format for the compression of audio signals into very small computer files. For example, sound data from a compact disc (CD) can be compressed to one-twelfth the original size without sacrificing sound quality. Because of small file size and ease of production from CD sources, the MP3 format is very popular for transmitting music files over the Internet. Although recording companies have sued many Web sites for facilitating the exchange of such copyrighted material, many now provide sample songs in MP3 format to promote CD sales, and some musicians bypass recording companies and issue their songs over the Internet in MP3 format only.

mudra, In Buddhism and Hinduism, a symbolic gesture of the hands and fingers used in ceremonies, dance, sculpture, and painting. Hundreds of mudras are used in ceremony and dance, often in combination with movements of the wrists, elbows, and shoulders. In ceremonies, especially in Buddhism, a mudra acts as a kind of seal, affirming a mystical or magical vow or utterance, such as a prayer to ward off evil. A mudra often accompanies the utterance of a mantra.

mufti, Islamic legal authority charged with issuing an opinion (fatwa) in answer to an inquiry by a judge or a private individual. Such a judgment requires extensive knowledge of the Qurʾān and the Ḥadīth as well as of legal precedents. During the Ottoman Empire the mufti of Istanbul was Islam's chief legal authority, presiding over the whole judicial and theological hierarchy. The development of modern legal codes in Islamic countries has significantly reduced the authority of mufti, and they now deal only with questions of personal status such as inheritance, marriage, and divorce.

Mughal architecture, Building style that flourished in India under the Mughal emperors from the mid 16th to the late 17th century. The Mughal period marked a striking revival of Islamic architecture in northern India, where Persian, Indian, and various provincial styles were fused to produce works of great refinement.

White marble and red sandstone were favoured materials. Most of the early Mughal buildings used arches only sparingly, relying on post-and-beam construction. The use of the double dome, a recessed archway inside a rectangular *fronton* (arena), and parklike surroundings are typical of the Shah Jahan period (1628–58), when Mughal design reached its zenith. Symmetry and balance between the parts of a building were stressed, as was delicate ornamental detail. Important Mughal undertakings include the Taj Mahal and the palace-fortress at Delhi (begun 1638).

Mughal dynasty, or MOGUL DYNASTY, Muslim dynasty that ruled most of northern India from the early 16th to the mid-18th century. The dynasty's rulers, descended from Timur and Genghis Khan, included unusually talented rulers over the course of seven generations, and the dynasty was further distinguished by its emperors' efforts to integrate Hindus and Muslims into a united Indian state. Prominent among the Mughal rulers were the founder, Bābur (r. 1526–30); his grandson Akbar (r. 1556–1605); and Shah Jahān. Under Aurangzeb (r. 1658–1707) the empire reached its greatest extent, but his intolerance sowed the seeds for its decline. It broke up under pressure from factional rivalries, dynastic warfare, and the invasion of northern India in 1739 by Nādir Shah.

Mughal painting, Style of painting, confined mainly to book illustrations and miniatures, that evolved in India during the Mughal dynasty (16th–19th centuries). In the initial phases the technique often involved a team of artists: one determined the composition, a second did the actual colouring, and a specialist in portraiture worked on individual faces. Probably the earliest example of Mughal painting is the illustrated folktale *Tutinameh* ("Tales of a Parrot"). Essentially a court art, it flourished under the emperors' patronage and declined when they lost interest.

Bird perched on rocks, Mughal painting, c. 1610; in the State Museum, Hyderābād, Andhra Pradesh, India
P. Chandra

Muhammad, or MOHAMMED (b. *c.* 570, Mecca, Arabia—d. June 8, 632, Medina), Arab prophet who established the religion of Islam. The son of a merchant of the ruling tribe, he was orphaned at age six. He married a rich widow, Khadījah, with whom he had six children, including Fāṭimah, a daughter. According to tradition, in 610 he was visited by the angel Gabriel, who informed Muhammad that he was the messenger of God. His revelations and teachings, recorded in the Qurʾān, are the basis of Islam. He began to preach publicly *c.* 613, urging the rich to give to the poor and calling for the destruction of idols. He gained disciples but also acquired enemies, whose plan to murder Muhammad forced him to flee Mecca for Medina in 622. This flight, known as the Hijrah, marks the beginning of the Islamic era. Muhammad's followers defeated a Meccan force in 624; they suffered reverses in 625 but repelled a Meccan siege of Medina in 627. He won control of Mecca by 629 and of all Arabia by 630. He made his last journey to Mecca in 632, establishing the rites of the hajj, or pilgrimage to Mecca. He died later that year and was buried at Medina. His life, teachings, and miracles have been the subjects of Muslim devotion and reflection ever since.

Muḥammad ʿAlī (b. 1769, Kavala, Macedonia, Ottoman Empire—d. Aug. 2, 1849, Alexandria, Egypt), Viceroy of Egypt (1805–48) for the Ottoman Empire and founder of the dynasty that ruled Egypt until 1953. He reorganized Egyptian society in the aftermath of the Napoleonic occupation, eliminating the remnants of the Mamlūks, restricting native merchants and artisans, and stamping out peasant rebellions. He nationalized most land, introduced the cultivation of cash crops, and attempted to develop modern industry, but his efforts were undermined by a lack of trained workers, the deleterious effects of excessive taxation, and a common disaffection with peasant conscription. He succeeded in securing for his family the hereditary right to rule Egypt and The Sudan (1841), which opened the way to eventual independence from Ottoman domination.

mujahideen, Arabic MUJĀHIDŪN ("THOSE ENGAGED IN JIHAD"), In its broadest sense, those Muslims who proclaim themselves warriors for the faith. Its Arabic singular, *mujāhid*, was not an uncommon personal name from the early Islamic period onward. However, the term did not gain popular currency as a collective or plural noun referring to "holy warriors" until the 18th century in India, where it became associated with Muslim revivalism. In the 20th century the term was used most commonly in Iran and Afghanistan. In Iran the Mojāhedin-e Khalq ("Mujahideen of the People"), a group combining Islamic and Marxist ideologies, engaged in a long-term guerrilla war against the leadership of the Islamic republic. The name was most closely associated, however, with members of a number of guerrilla groups operating in Afghanistan that opposed invading Soviet forces and eventually toppled the Afghan communist government during the Afghan War (1979–92). Rival factions thereafter fell out among themselves precipitating the rise of one faction, the Taliban. Like the term *jihad*—to which it is lexicographically connected—the name has been used rather freely, both in the press and by Islamic militants themselves, and often has been used to refer to any Muslim groups engaged in hostilities with non-Muslims or even with secularized Muslim regimes.

mullah, Muslim title applied to a scholar or religious leader, especially in the Middle East and the Indian subcontinent. It means "lord" and has also been used in North Africa as an honorific attached to the name of a king, sultan, or member of the nobility. The title is now given to a variety of religious leaders, including teachers in religious schools, scholars of canon law, leaders of prayer in the mosques (imams), and reciters of the Qur'ān (*qurrā'*). The word can also refer to the entire class that upholds the traditional interpretation of Islam.

multiple birth, Birth of more than one child from one pregnancy. Twins are most common, born in 1 of about every 80 pregnancies. Identical twins develop from a single fertilized egg, which splits into two genetically identical embryos (though physical traits may be modified during their development); they occur randomly but are more likely in older mothers. Incomplete or late division results in conjoined twins. Fraternal twins develop from two eggs fertilized by two sperm and are no more genetically alike than are other siblings. Most common among persons of African ancestry and least common among those of Asian ancestry, fraternal twins seem to run in families. Repeated twinning produces triplets, quadruplets, and so on; these multiples may be identical, fraternal, or a combination. The use of fertility drugs has increased the number of high-order multiple births. Medical and psychological "twin studies" compare fraternal and identical twins to learn about genetic influences on various characteristics and diseases.

multiple sclerosis, Disease of the brain and spinal cord in which gradual, patchy destruction of the myelin sheath of nerve fibres causes interruption or disordered transmission of nerve impulses. Its early symptoms may include limb weakness or trembling, visual problems, sensory disturbances, unsteady walking, and defective bladder control, which come and go irregularly. Attacks grow more severe, and some symptoms become permanent, sometimes with eventual complete paralysis. Average survival from onset is about 25 years, but a rare acute form progresses over months. The cause remains uncertain and treatment unsatisfactory. Corti-

costeroids may ease symptoms. MS may be due to a delayed immune response that attacks the myelin sheaths; suggested causes include various common viruses. Dietary causes have also been suggested.

multiprocessing, Mode of computer operation in which two or more processors are connected and are active at the same time. In such a system, each processor is executing a different program or set of instructions, thus increasing computation speed over a system that has only one processor (which means only one program can be executed at a time). Because the processors must sometimes access the same resource (as when two processors must write to the same disk), a system program called the task manager has to coordinate the processors' activities.

multitasking, Mode of computer operation in which the computer works on multiple tasks at the same time. A task is a computer program (or part of a program) that can be run as a separate entity. On a single-processor system, the CPU can perform preemptive (also called time slicing or time sharing) multitasking, where it executes part of one program, then switches to another program, and then returns to the first one. On multiprocessing systems, each processor can handle a separate task.

Mumbai, formerly BOMBAY, City (pop., 2001: city, 11,978,450; metro. area, 16,434,386), capital of Maharashtra state, western India. Located partly on Mumbai Island, it is flanked by Mumbai Harbour and the Arabian Sea. It is India's principal port on that sea and one of the largest and most densely populated cities in the world. The town was acquired by the Portuguese in 1534. It was ceded to the English as part of the dowry of Catherine of Braganza, who married Charles II in 1661. Granted to the East India Company in 1668, it became the company's headquarters until 1708. After the opening of the Suez Canal in 1869, Mumbai grew to be the largest distributing entrepôt in India. It remains India's economic hub and the heart of financial and commercial activity, its cultural and education centre, and headquarters of its film industry.

Entrance to Mumbai Harbour, marked by the Gateway of India (foreground), Mumbai, India.
© Cris Haigh—Stone/Getty Images

mummy, Body embalmed or preserved for burial in the manner of the ancient Egyptians. The process varied from age to age in Egypt, but it always involved removing the internal organs, treating the body with resin, and wrapping it in linen bandages. (In later Egyptian times, the organs were replaced after treatment.) Among the many other peoples who practiced mummification were those of the Torres Strait, near Papua New Guinea, and the Incas.

mumps, or EPIDEMIC PAROTITIS, Acute contagious viral disease with inflammatory swelling of the salivary glands. Epidemics often occur, mostly among 5- to 15-year-olds. Cold symptoms with low fever are followed by swelling and stiffening in front of the ear, often on both sides. This rapidly spreads toward the neck and under the jaw. Pain is seldom severe, with little redness, but chewing and swallowing are difficult. During recovery in patients past puberty, other glands may be affected, but usually not seriously. The testes may atrophy, but sterility is very rare. While inflammation of the brain and meninges is fairly common, chances of recovery are good. Mumps needs no special treatment, and patients usually develop immunity. Vaccination can prevent it.

Mundell, Robert A(lexander) (b. Oct. 24, 1932, Kingston, Ont., Can.), Canadian-born economist who received the Nobel Prize in Economic Sciences in 1999 for his work on monetary dynamics and optimum currency areas. Mundell earned degrees from the University of British Columbia (B.A., 1953), the University of Washington (M.A., 1954), and the Massachusetts Institute of Technology (Ph.D., 1956). He taught economics at the University of Chicago (1956–57) and Columbia University (1974–). Through research for the International Monetary Fund, Mundell analyzed the effect of exchange rates on monetary policies. In 1961 he theorized that an economic region characterized by free movement of labour and trade could support a single currency. His theories contributed to the creation of the euro, the single currency adopted by the European Union on Jan. 1, 1999.

Munich, German MÜNCHEN, City (pop., 2007 est.: city, 1,311,573; 2005 est.: metro. area, 1,940,477), capital of Bavaria, Germany. Located along the Isar River, it was founded in 1158 at the site of an ancient monastery. It became the capital of Bavaria under the ruling Wittelsbach family. The city developed as a centre of music and theatre through the 19th century. After World War I it became a centre of right-wing political ferment; it was the site of the 1923 Beer Hall Putsch, Adolf Hitler's attempted rising against the Bavarian government, and subsequent Nazi Party activities. It was the site for the signing of the 1938 Munich Agreement. In World War II it suffered heavily from Allied bombing. Some medieval structures survived, including the cathedral and town hall. Today Munich is a trade, cultural, educational, and industrial centre known for its many museums and for manufacturing and beer and ale brewing.

Munich agreement (1938) Settlement reached by Germany, France, Britain, and Italy permitting German annexation of Czechoslovakia's Sudetenland. Adolf Hitler's threats to occupy the German-populated part of Czechoslovakia stemmed from his avowed broader goal of reuniting Europe's German-populated areas. Though Czechoslovakia had defense treaties with France and the Soviet Union, both countries agreed that areas in the Sudetenland with majority German populations should be returned. Hitler demanded that all Czechoslovaks in those areas depart; when Czechoslovakia refused, Britain's Neville Chamberlain negotiated an agreement permitting Germany to occupy the areas but promising that all future differences would be resolved through consultation. The agreement, which became synonymous with appeasement, was abrogated when Hitler annexed the rest of Czechoslovakia the next year.

mural, Painting applied to and made integral with the surface of a wall or ceiling. Its roots can be found in the universal desire that led prehistoric peoples to create cave paintings—the desire to decorate their surroundings and express their ideas and beliefs. The Romans produced large numbers of murals in Pompeii and Ostia, but mural painting (not synonymous with fresco) reached its highest degree of creative achievement in Europe with the work of such Renaissance masters as Masaccio, Fra Angelico, Leonardo da Vinci, Michelangelo, and Raphael. In the 20th century, the mural was embraced by artists of the Cubist and Fauve movements in Paris, revolutionary painters in Mexico (e.g., Diego Rivera, José Clemente Orozco, David Alfaro Siqueiros), and Depression-era artists under the sponsorship of the U.S. government (e.g., Ben Shahn, Thomas Hart Benton).

Murasaki Shikibu (b. *c.* 978, Kyōto, Japan), Japanese writer. Her real name is unknown, and the primary source of knowledge about her life is a diary she kept (1007–10). Her *Tale of Genji* (completed *c.* 1010) is a long and complex tale, concerned mostly with the loves of Prince Genji and the women in his life. Supremely sensitive to human emotions and the beauties of nature, it provides delightful glimpses of life at the court of the empress Jōtō mon'in, whom Murasaki served. It is generally considered the greatest work of Japanese literature and perhaps the world's first novel.

Murcia, City (pop., 2001: 370,745), capital of the autonomous community of Murcia, southeastern Spain. The site was settled before the Roman occupation of Spain in the 3rd century BC. It became the Muslim city of Mursīyah in AD 825, when it was made a provincial capital by the emir of Córdoba. It was the birthplace of Ibn al-'Arabī (1165). The Segura River divides the city into older and newer parts. The 14th-century cathedral was restored in the 18th century. It is a communications and agricultural-trade centre for surrounding areas. Its silk industry dates from Moorish times.

Murmansk, Seaport (pop., 2006 est.: 320,962), northwestern Russia. Situated on the eastern shore of Kola Bay near the Barents Sea, it is the world's largest city north of the Arctic Circle. Its ice-free harbour makes it Russia's only port with unrestricted access to the Atlantic. Founded in 1915 as a supply port in World War I, it was a base for the British, French, and U.S. forces against the Bolsheviks in 1918; it also served as a major supply base during World War II. In addition to a Russian naval base, it has a large fishing fleet and fish-processing industry.

Murray River, Principal river of Australia. Rising near Mount Kosciusko, in southeastern New South Wales, it flows across southeastern Australia from the Snowy Mountains to the Great Australian Bight of the Indian Ocean; it is 1,609 mi (2,589 km) long. It forms the boundary between Victoria and New South Wales and then turns south and flows into Encounter Bay through Lake Alexandrina. River shipping was important in the 19th century, but navigation practically ceased with growing competition from railways and the demand for irrigation water. The river valley is of great economic importance, fostering the production of grains, fruit, and wine as well as cattle and sheep raising.

Muscat, or MASQAT, City (pop., 2003: city, 24,769; urban agglom., 638,000), capital of Oman, located on the Gulf of Oman. Situated on a cove surrounded by volcanic mountains, it came under Persian control in the 6th century BC, and Islam was introduced into the region in the 7th century AD. The Portuguese gained control in 1508 and made Muscat a trading post and naval base until they were expelled in 1650. Held again by the Persians (1650–1741), it later became part of the sultanate of Oman. Two 16th-century Portuguese forts overlook the city; the sultan's Indian-style palace is built at the edge of the sea.

muscle, Contractile tissue that produces motion for functions, including body movements, digestion, focusing, circulation, and body warmth. It can be classified as striated, cardiac, and smooth or as phasic and tonic (responding quickly or gradually to stimulation, respectively). Striated muscle, whose fibres appear striped under a microscope, is responsible for voluntary movement. Most of these muscles are phasic. They are attached to the skeleton and move the body by contracting in response to signals from the central nervous system; contraction is achieved by the sliding of thin filaments (of actin) between thick ones (of myosin); stretch receptors in the tissue provide feedback, allowing smooth motion and fine motor control. The branched fibres of cardiac muscle give it a netlike structure; contraction originates in the heart's muscle tissue itself with a signal from the natural pacemaker; vagus and sympathetic nerves control heart rate. Smooth muscle, the muscle of internal organs and blood vessels, is generally involuntary and tonic; its cells can operate either collectively or individually (in response to separate nerve endings) and have different shapes. Disorders of voluntary muscle cause weakening, atrophy, pain, and twitching. Some systemic diseases (e.g., dermatomyositis, polymyositis) can cause muscle inflammation.

muscle tumour, Abnormal tissue growth in or originating from muscle tissue. There are three major types. Leiomyomas are tumours of smooth muscles, seen most often in the uterus but also in the digestive, urinary, and female genital systems. Part of the tumour may become malignant, but it usually does not spread or recur. Rhabdomyomas occur most often in cardiac muscle. Some forms spread, and it may remain contained in tissue or become diffuse and hard to remove. Rhabdomyomas involving both smooth and striated muscle are often malignant and may grow very large. The several types of rhabdomyosarcoma are rare; they arise in skeletal muscle, usually in the leg or arm, and are extremely malignant.

muscular dystrophy, Inherited disease that causes progressive weakness in the skeletal (and occasionally heart) muscle. Muscle tissue degenerates and regenerates randomly and is replaced by scar tissue and fat. There is no specific treatment. Physical therapy, braces, and corrective surgery may help. Duchenne muscular dystrophy, the most common, strikes only males. Symptoms, including frequent falls and difficulty in standing up, start in boys 3–7 years old; muscle wasting progresses from the legs to the arms and then the diaphragm. Pulmonary infection or respiratory failure usually causes death before age 20. The gene can now be detected in female carriers and male fetuses. Becker dystrophy, also sex-linked, is less severe and begins later. Patients remain able to walk and usually survive into their 30s and 40s. Myotonic muscular dystrophy affects adults of both sexes, with myotonia and degeneration two to three years later, along with cataracts, baldness, and gonadal atrophy. Limb-girdle dystrophy affects the pelvic or shoulder muscles in both sexes. Facioscapulohumeral (face, shoulder-blade, and upper-arm) dystrophy starts in childhood or adolescence and affects both sexes; after initial symptoms of difficulty raising the arms, the legs and pelvic muscles can be affected; the main facial effect is difficulty in closing the eyes. Life expectancy is normal.

Muse, In Greco-Roman religion and myth, any of a group of sister goddesses, daughters of Zeus and Mnemosyne (Memory). A festival was held in their honour every four years near Mount Helicon, the centre of their cult in Greece. They probably began as the patron goddesses of poets, though later their range was extended to include all the liberal arts and sciences. Nine Muses are usually named: Calliope (heroic or epic poetry), Clio (history), Erato (lyric or love poetry), Euterpe (music or flutes), Melpomene (tragedy), Polyhymnia (sacred poetry or mime), Terpsichore (dancing and choral song), Thalia (comedy), and Urania (astronomy).

Museum of Modern Art (MoMA), Museum in New York City, the world's most comprehensive collection of U.S. and European art from the late 19th century to the present. It was founded in 1929 by a group of private collectors. The original building on 53rd St. opened in 1939; a later addition and sculpture garden were designed by Philip Johnson (1953). A condominium tower and western wing, doubling the exhibition space, were completed in 1984. Its collections of Cubist, Surrealist, and Abstract Expressionist paintings are extensive; other holdings include sculpture, graphic arts, industrial design, architecture, photography, and film. Through its permanent collections, exhibitions, and many publications, it exerts a strong influence on public taste and artistic production.

mushroom, Fleshy spore-bearing structure of certain fungi, typically of the phylum Basidiomycota. It arises from the mycelium, which may live hundreds of years or a few months, depending on its food supply. Some species grow cellular strands (hyphae) in all directions, forming a circular mat with a "fairy ring" of fruiting bodies around the outside. Popularly, "mushroom" refers to the edible sporophores, while "toadstool" refers to inedible or poisonous sporophores, but there is no scientific distinction between the two names. Umbrella-shaped sporophores with spore-shedding gills on the undersurface are found chiefly in the agaric family (Agaricaceae). Mushrooms that are cap-shaped and bear spores in an easily detachable layer on the underside of the cap belong to the family Boletaceae. Together the agarics and boletes include most of the forms known as mushrooms. The morels (phylum Ascomycota) are popularly included with the true mushrooms because of their shape and fleshy structure. Since some poisonous mushrooms closely resemble edible ones, mushrooms intended for eating must be accurately identified. Mushroom poisoning can cause nausea, diarrhea, vomiting, cramps, hallucinations, coma, and sometimes death.

mushroom poisoning, or TOADSTOOL POISONING, Sometimes fatal effect of eating any of the 70–80 species of poisonous mushrooms, or toadstools. Many contain toxic alkaloids. The most deadly, *Amanita phalloides* ("death cup"), causes violent abdominal pain, vomiting, and bloody diarrhea. Severe liver, kidney, and central-nervous-system damage lead to coma. Over half the victims die. Treatment with thioctic acid, glucose, and penicillin or by filtering the blood with charcoal may be effective. *A. muscaria* causes vomiting, diarrhea, excessive perspiration, and confusion, with recovery within 24 hours. *Gyromitra esculenta* toxin is usually destroyed by cooking, but in susceptible people it affects the central nervous system and breaks down blood cells, causing jaundice. Some poisonous mushrooms resemble harmless ones, so extreme caution is needed in wild-mushroom gathering.

music, Art concerned with combining vocal or instrumental sounds for beauty of form or emotional expression, usually according to cultural standards of rhythm, melody, and, in most Western music, harmony. Music most often implies sounds with distinct pitches that are arranged into melodies and organized into patterns of rhythm and metre. The melody will usually be in a certain key or mode, and in Western music it will often suggest harmony that may be made explicit as accompanying chords or counterpoint. Music is an art that, in one guise or another, permeates every human society. It is used for such varied social purposes as ritual, worship, coordination of movement, communication, and entertainment.

music hall and variety theatre, Popular entertainment that featured successive acts by singers, comedians, dancers, and actors. The form derived from the taproom concerts given in city taverns in England in the 18th–19th centuries. To meet the demand for entertainment for the working class, tavern owners often annexed nearby buildings as music halls, where drinking and smoking were permitted. The originator of the English music hall as such was Charles Morton, who built Morton's Canterbury Hall (1852) and Oxford Hall (1861) in London. Leading performers included Lillie Langtry, Harry Lauder (1870–1950), and Gracie Fields. Music halls evolved into larger, more respectable variety theatres, such as London's Hippodrome and the Coliseum. Variety acts combined music, comedy acts, and one-act plays and featured celebrities such as Sarah Bernhardt and Herbert Tree.

musical, or MUSICAL COMEDY, Theatrical production that is characteristically sentimental and amusing in nature, having a simple but distinctive plot and offering music, dancing, and dialogue. Its roots can be traced to 18th- and 19th-century genres such as ballad opera, singspiel, and opéra comique. *The Black Crook* (1866), often called the first musical comedy, attracted patrons of opera and serious drama as well as those of burlesque shows. European composers such as Sigmund Romberg brought to the U.S. a form of operetta that was the generic source for musical comedy. George M. Cohan ushered in the genre's heyday, and in the 1920s and '30s it entered its richest period with the works of Jerome Kern, George Gershwin and Ira Gershwin, Cole Porter, Richard Rodgers, and Oscar Hammerstein. Kern and Hammerstein's *Show Boat* (1927) was perhaps the first musical to employ music thoroughly integrated with the narrative. The genre flourished in the 1950s with works by composers such as Leonard Bernstein, but it began to decline in the late 1960s, by which time musicals had begun to diverge in many different directions, incorporating elements such as rock music, operatic styling, extravagant lighting and staging, social comment, nostalgia, and pure spectacle. Later notable musical composers included Stephen Sondheim and Andrew Lloyd Webber.

musical notation, Written, printed, or other visual representation of music. There are two basic approaches to notating music. Tablature (such as guitar chord diagrams) depicts the actions a performer is to take (in particular, showing where to put the fingers to produce a given sound). Symbolic notation describes the sounds themselves and includes methods that vary from assigning pitches different letters of the alphabet to representing a given combination of notes by a graphic sign. The Western notation system combines rhythmic notation (the appearance of a note indicates its duration) with pitch notation (the line or space on a staff where a note is placed indicates its pitch). Thus, a single symbol shows both pitch and duration, and a string of these symbols notates both melody and rhythm.

musicology, Scholarly and scientific study of music. In the late 18th and early 19th centuries, such study was done by amateurs such as Ludwig von Köchel. As interest in earlier music grew, greater professionalism was required, including the ability to decipher and assess musical manuscripts and historical documents. Musicology's first great monument was the first edition of Johann Sebastian Bach's complete works (1851–99). The scope of musicology may be summarized as covering the study of the history and phenomena of music, including (1) form and notation, (2) biography, (3) the development of musical instruments, (4) music theory (harmony, melody, modes, etc.), and (5) aesthetics, acoustics, and physiology of the voice, ear, and hand. In recent decades music theory has again become a separate specialization.

musk ox, Arctic ruminant (bovid species *Ovibos moschatus*) with a musky odour, large head, and small ears. The neck, legs, and tail are short. Males stand 5 ft (1.5 m) tall and may weigh almost 900 lb (400 kg). Both sexes have horns. The broad-based horns of males, up to 2 ft (60 cm) long, start at the middle of the head, dip downward along the sides, and then curve upward. The shaggy, dark brown coat reaches nearly to the feet. Eskimos make a fine cashmerelike cloth from the thick wool undercoat, which is shed in summer. Musk oxen travel in herds of 20–30, eating grass, lichen, willow, and other low-growing plants.

musket, Muzzle-loading shoulder firearm developed in 16th-century Spain. Designed as a larger version of the harquebus, muskets were fired with matchlocks until flintlocks were developed in the 17th century; flintlocks were replaced by percussion locks in the early 19th century. Early muskets were often handled by two persons and fired from a portable rest. Typically 5.5 ft (1.7 m) long and weighing about 20 lbs (9 kg), they fired a ball about 175 yards (160 m) with little accuracy. Later types were smaller, lighter, and accurate enough to hit a person at 80–100 yards (75–90 m). The musket was replaced in the mid-19th century by the breech-loading rifle.

Muslim Brotherhood, Arabic AL-IKHWĀN AL-MUSLIMŪN, Religio-political organization founded in Egypt in 1928 by Ḥasan al-Bannā (1906–49) that promoted the Qur'ān and Ḥadīth as the proper basis for society. It quickly gained many followers throughout North Africa and the Middle East and influenced the development of Muslim groups in other regions. It became politicized after 1938, rejecting Westernization, modernization, and secularization. Suppressed in Egypt after a 1954 assassination attempt on Gamal Abdel Nasser, it operated clandestinely in the 1960s and '70s. Beginning in the late 1980s, it experienced an upsurge; though its candidates were often listed under other parties, Brotherhood candidates competed in legislative elections in Egypt and Jordan.

mussel, Any of numerous bivalve species of either the marine family Mytilidae, found worldwide, or the freshwater superfamily Unionacea, called naiads, found mostly in the U.S. and Southeast Asia. Marine mussels are usually wedge-shaped or pear-shaped and 2–6 in. (5–15 cm) long. They may be smooth or ribbed and often have a hairy covering. The shells of many species are dark blue or greenish brown on the outside and pearly on the inside. Mussels attach themselves to solid objects or to one another, often forming dense clusters. Some burrow into soft mud or wood. They are eaten by birds and starfishes, and some species are raised commercially for food.

Atlantic ribbed mussels (Modiolus demissus)
Walter Dawn

Mussolini, Benito (Amilcare Andrea), known as IL DUCE (b. July 29, 1883, Predappio, Italy—d. April 28, 1945, near Dongo), Italian dictator (1922–43). An unruly but intelligent youth, he became an ardent socialist and served as editor of the party newspaper, *Avanti!* (1912–14). When he reversed his opposition to World War I, he was ousted by the party. He founded the pro-war *Il Popolo d'Italia*, served with the Italian army (1915–17), then returned to his editorship. Advocating government by dictatorship, he formed a political group in 1919 that marked the beginning of fascism. A dynamic and captivating orator at rallies, he organized the March on Rome (1922) to prevent a socialist-led general strike. After the government fell, he was appointed prime minister, the youngest in Italian history. He obtained a law to establish the fascists as the majority party and became known as *Il Duce* ("The Leader"). He restored order to the country and introduced social reforms and public works improvements that won widespread popular support. His dreams of empire led to the invasion of Abyssinia (later Ethiopia) in 1935. Supported in his fascist schemes by Adolf Hitler but wary of German power, Mussolini agreed to the Rome-Berlin Axis and declared war on the Allies in 1940. Italian military defeats in Greece and North Africa led to growing disillusionment with Mussolini. After the Allied invasion of Sicily (1943), the Fascist Grand Council dismissed him from office. He was arrested and imprisoned but rescued by German commandos, then became head of the Hitler-installed puppet government at Salò in northern Italy. As German defenses in Italy collapsed in 1945, Mussolini tried to escape to Austria but was captured and executed by Italian partisans.

Benito Mussolini.
H. Roger-Viollet

mustard family, Family Brassicaceae (also called Cruciferae), composed of 338 genera of mostly herbaceous plants with peppery-flavored leaves. The pungent seeds of some species lead the spice trade in volume traded. Mustard flowers take the form of a Greek cross, with four petals, usually white, yellow, or lavender, and an equal number of sepals. The seeds are produced in podlike fruits. Members of the mustard family include many plants of economic importance that have been extensively altered and domesticated by humans. The most important genus is *Brassica*; turnips, radishes, rutabagas, and many ornamental plants are also members of the family. As a spice, mustard is sold in seed, powder, or paste form.

mutation, Alteration in the genetic material of a cell that is transmitted to the cell's offspring. Mutations may be spontaneous or induced by outside factors (mutagens). They take place in the genes, occurring when one base is substituted for another in the sequence of bases that determines the genetic code, or when one or more bases are inserted or deleted from a gene. Many mutations are harmless, often masked by the presence of a dominant normal gene. Some have serious consequences; for example, a particular mutation inherited from both parents results in sickle-cell anemia. Only mutations that occur in the sex cells (eggs or sperm) can be transmitted to the individual's offspring. Alterations caused by these mutations are usually harmful. In the rare instances in which a mutation produces a beneficial change, the percentage of organisms with this gene will tend to increase until the mutated gene becomes the norm in the population. In this way, beneficial mutations serve as the raw material of evolution.

Mu'tazilah, In Islam, one of two early religious groups. The term applies primarily to members of a theological school that flourished in Al-Baṣrah and Baghdad in the 8th–10th century. These Mu'tazilah were the first Muslims to employ systematically the categories and methods of Hellenistic philosophy to derive their dogma. The tenets of their faith included belief in the oneness of God (*tawḥīd*), advocation of human free will (the ability to choose between good and evil), and the fundamental belief in God's fairness (i.e., God will punish only those deserving of punishment). Their doctrine of a created Qur'ān (the eternal nature of which was advocated by their opponents) held sway in the caliphal court briefly in the early 9th century and was the first instance in the Muslim world in which political authorities attempted to enforce any form of doctrinal rigour; the Mu'tazilah theological program soon lost political sway, however, and had faded by the 13th century. Though it was ultimately abandoned by Sunnite Muslims (the group's methods came to be accepted by some Shī'ite groups), its true importance lay in the fact that it forced other theological groups to embrace a more rigorous dialectical method.

Myanmar, or BURMA, officially REPUBLIC OF THE UNION OF MYANMAR, Country, Southeast Asia, on the Bay of Bengal and the Andaman Sea. Area: 261,228 sq mi (676,577 sq km). Population: (2011 est.) 54,000,000. Capitals: official, Nay Pyi Taw (Naypyidaw), proclaimed 2006; historical, Yangon (Rangoon), 1948–2006. Inhabitants are chiefly Burman; others include Chin, Shan, and Karen. Languages: Myanmar (Burmese; official), many indigenous languages. Religions: Buddhism, traditional beliefs, Christianity, Islam, Hinduism. Currency: Myanmar kyat. Myanmar may be divided into five main regions: the northern mountains, the western ranges, the coastal plains, the central lowlands, and the Shan Plateau in the east. Major rivers are the Irrawaddy and the Salween. The tropical climate is greatly influenced by the monsoons of southern Asia. Only about one-sixth of this largely mountainous land is arable. It has a centrally planned, developing economy that is largely nationalized and based on agriculture and trade. Rice is the most important crop and principal export; teak is also important. Myanmar was ruled by a military regime (1988–2011), but a new constitution took effect in January 2011 that designated the president as head of state and government. The area was long inhabited, with the Mon and Pyu states dominant from the 1st century BCE to the 9th century CE. It was united in the 11th century under a Burmese dynasty that was overthrown by the Mongols in the 13th century. The Portuguese, Dutch, and English traded there in the 16th–17th century. The modern Myanmar (Burmese) state was founded in the 18th century by Alaungpaya. Conflict with the British over Assam resulted in a series of wars, and Myanmar fell to the British in 1885. Under British control, it became Burma, a province of India. It was occupied by Japan in World War II and became independent in 1948. The military took power in a coup in 1962 and nationalized major economic sectors. Civilian unrest in the 1980s led to antigovernment rioting that was suppressed by force. In 1990 opposition parties won in national elections, but the army remained in control, changing the name of the country to Myanmar. Trying to negotiate for a freer government amid the unrest, Aung San Suu Kyi was awarded the Nobel Peace Prize in 1991. The military relinquished authority to a civilian government in 2011.

myasthenia gravis, Chronic autoimmune disease causing muscle weakness. Autoantibodies block the response of muscle cells to acetylcholine. Muscles weaken with repeated use but regain their strength after rest. The pattern varies, but usually muscles used in eye movements, facial expressions, chewing, swallowing, and respiration are affected first, then neck, trunk, and limb muscles. Severe cases impede breathing. Anticholinesterase drugs stimulate nerve-impulse transmission, and corticosteroids may help. Removal of the thymus has improved severe cases. Remission lasting several years may occur.

Mycenaean, Any member of a group of warlike Indo-European peoples who entered Greece from the north starting *c.* 1900 BC and established a Bronze Age culture on the mainland and nearby islands. Their culture was dependent on that of the Minoans of Crete, who for a time politically dominated them. They threw off Minoan control *c.* 1400 and were dominant in the Aegean until they themselves were overwhelmed by the next wave of invaders *c.* 1150. Mycenae continued to exist as a city-state into the period of Greek dominance, but by the 2nd century AD it was in ruins. Mycenaean myths and legends lived on through oral transmission into later stages of Greek civilization and form the basis of Homeric epic and Greek tragedy. Their language is believed to be the most ancient form of Greek.

mycobacterium, Any of the rod-shaped bacteria that make up the genus *Mycobacterium*. The two most important species cause tuberculosis and leprosy in humans; another species causes tuberculosis in both cattle and humans. Some mycobacteria live on decaying organic matter; others are parasites. Most are found in soil and water in a free-living form or in diseased tissue of animals. Various antibiotics have had some success against mycobacterium infections.

mycoplasma, Any of the bacteria that make up the genus *Mycoplasma*. They are among the smallest of bacterial organisms. The cell varies from a spherical or pear shape to that of a slender branched filament. *Mycoplasma* species are gram-negative and do not require oxygen. They are colonial microorganisms that lack cell walls. They are parasites of joints and the mucous membranes lining the respiratory, genital, or digestive tracts of cud-chewing animals, carnivores, rodents, and humans. Toxic by-products excreted by the bacteria accumulate in the host's tissues, causing damage. One species causes a widespread but rarely fatal pneumonia in humans.

mynah, or MYNA, Any of several Asian songbird species of the starling family (Sturnidae). The hill mynah (*Gracula religiosa*) of southern Asia, called the grackle in India, is about 10 in. (25 cm) long and glossy black with white wing patches, yellow wattles, and orange bill and legs. In the wild, it chuckles and shrieks; caged, it learns to imitate human speech far better than its chief rival, the gray parrot. The common, or Indian, mynah (*Acridotheres tristis*) was introduced into Australia, New Zealand, and Hawaii. The crested mynah (*A. cristatellus*), native to China and Indonesia, was introduced into British Columbia, Canada, but has not spread.

Myrdal, (Karl) Gunnar (b. Dec. 6, 1898, Gustafs, Dalarna, Swed.—d. May 17, 1987, Stockholm), Swedish economist and sociologist. He received his Ph.D. from Stockholm University and taught there from 1933 until 1967. His early work emphasized pure theory, but he later focused on applied economics and social problems. He explored the social and economic problems of African Americans in the U.S. (1938–40) and in 1944 published the classic study *An American Dilemma*, in which he presented his theory that poverty breeds poverty. In regard to development economics, he argued that rich and poor countries, rather than converging economically, might well diverge, the poor countries becoming poorer as the rich countries enjoyed economies of scale and the poor ones were forced to rely on primary products. In 1974 he shared the Nobel Prize with Friedrich von Hayek. His wife, Alva Myrdal (1902–86), was a sociologist, diplomat, UN administrator, and antiwar activist; she shared the 1982 Nobel Peace Prize with Alfonso García Robles.

mystery religion, Any of various secret cults of the Greco-Roman world. Derived from primitive tribal ceremonies, mystery religions reached their peak of popularity in Greece in the first three centuries CE. Their members met secretly to share meals and take part in dances and ceremonies, especially initiation rites. The cult of Demeter produced the most famous of the mystery religions, the Eleusinian Mysteries, as well as the Andania mysteries. Dionysus was worshipped in festivals that included wine, choral singing, sexual activity, and mime. The Orphic cult, by contrast, based on sacred writings attributed to Orpheus, required chastity and abstinence from meat and wine. Mystery cults also attached to Attis, Isis, and Jupiter Dolichenus, among others.

mysticism, The theory and practice of religious ecstasies. Traditionally conceived as the spiritual quest for union with the Absolute, the Infinite, or God and the perception of its essential oneness, mysticism is now understood to encompass many other varieties of ecstatic experience and perception, including that of nothingness or of the disappearance of the soul. Forms of mysticism are found in all major religions. Ancient and medieval Christian mystics included St. Augustine, St. Bernard of Clairvaux, St. Teresa of Ávila, and Meister Eckhart and his 14th-century successors. Whereas Hinduism and, in Islam, Sufism generally aim at unity with or absorption by the divine, Buddhism and the esoteric Jewish mysticism known as Kabbala are directed toward nothingness; Buddhism in addition emphasizes meditation as a means of moving toward enlightenment. Other mystical traditions are found within Daoism and shamanism.

myth, Traditional story of ostensibly historical events that serves to unfold part of the worldview of a people or explain a practice, belief, or natural phenomenon. Myths relate the events, conditions, and deeds of gods or superhuman beings that are outside ordinary human life and yet basic to it. These events are set in a time altogether different from historical time, often at the beginning of creation or at an early stage of prehistory. A culture's myths are usually closely related to its religious beliefs and rituals. The modern study of myth arose with early 19th-century Romanticism. Wilhelm Mannhardt, James George Frazer, and others later employed a more comparative approach. Sigmund Freud viewed myth as an expression of repressed ideas, a view later expanded by Carl Gustav Jung in his theory of the "collective unconscious" and the mythical archetypes that arise out of it. Bronisław Malinowski emphasized how myth fulfills common social functions, providing a model or "charter" for human behaviour. Claude Lévi-Strauss discerned underlying structures in the formal relations and patterns of myths throughout the world. Mircea Eliade and Rudolf Otto held that myth is to be understood solely as a religious phenomenon. Features of myth are shared by other kinds of literature. Origin tales explain the source or causes of various aspects of nature or human society and life. Fairy tales deal with extraordinary beings and events but lack the authority of myth. Sagas and epics claim authority and truth but reflect specific historical settings.

myxedema, Physiological reaction to low levels of thyroid hormone in adults, either due to thyroid-gland removal, lack of function, or atrophy, or secondary to a pituitary-gland disorder. Gradual changes include enlarged tongue, thick, puffy skin, drowsiness, cardiac enlargement, and slow metabolism. Low thyroid hormone affects levels of other hormones, and may result in low blood sodium and disorders of the reproductive system (including reduced fertility), adrenal glands, and circulatory system. Treatment is with thyroid hormone.

myxovirus, Any of a group of viruses that are agents of influenza and can cause the common cold, mumps, and measles in humans, canine distemper, rinderpest in cattle, and Newcastle disease in fowl. The virus particle is encased in a fatty membrane, variable in shape from spheroidal to threadlike, and studded with spikelike protein projections; it contains RNA. These viruses react with a protein on the surface of red blood cells; many of them cause red blood cells to clump together.

N

NAACP, in full NATIONAL ASSOCIATION FOR THE ADVANCEMENT OF COLORED PEOPLE, Oldest and largest U.S. civil rights organization. It was founded in 1909 to secure political, educational, social, and economic equality for African Americans; W.E.B. Du Bois and Ida B. Wells were among its 60 founders. Headquartered in Baltimore, Md., the NAACP has undertaken litigation, political activity, and public education programs. In 1939 it organized the independent Legal Defense and Education Fund as its legal arm, which sued for school desegregation in *Brown* v. *Board of Education* (1954). During World War II it pressed for desegregation of the armed forces, which was achieved in 1948. In 1967 its general counsel, Thurgood Marshall, became the U.S. Supreme Court's first African American justice.

NAFTA, in full NORTH AMERICAN FREE TRADE AGREEMENT, Trade pact signed by Canada, the U.S., and Mexico in 1992, which took effect in 1994. Inspired by the success of the European Community in reducing trade barriers among its members, NAFTA created the world's largest free-trade area. It basically extended to Mexico the provisions of a 1988 Canada-U.S. free-trade agreement, calling for elimination of all trade barriers over a 15-year period, granting U.S. and Canadian companies access to certain Mexican markets, and incorporating agreements on labour and the environment.

naga, In Hindu and Buddhist mythology, a semidivine being, half human and half serpent. *Naga*s can assume either wholly human or wholly serpentine form. They live in an underground kingdom filled with beautiful palaces that are adorned with gems. Brahma is said to have relegated the *naga*s to the nether regions and to have commanded them to bite only the truly evil or those destined to die prematurely. *Naga*s are also associated with waters—rivers, lakes, seas, and wells—and are regarded as guardians of treasure. In Buddhism it is believed that the snake king sheltered the Buddha from rain for seven days while he was meditating.

Naga Hills, Hill region, northeastern India and northwestern Myanmar (Burma). A northern extension of the Arakan Mountains system, the hills reach a height of 12,552 ft (3,826 m) at Mount Saramati on the frontier. The densely forested hills receive heavy monsoon rains. The area is inhabited by tribes of Naga peoples living in small villages.

Nagaland, State (pop., 2008 est.: 2,187,000), northeastern India. It borders Myanmar (Burma) and the states of Manipur, Assam, and Arunachal Pradesh and has an area of 6,401 sq mi (16,579 sq km). Its capital is Kohima. Except for a small area of plain, the entire state is covered with ranges of hills that are northward extensions of the Arakan Mountains system. Myanmar ruled the region from 1819 to 1826, when the British began annexing its hill areas. The Naga people accepted statehood within an independent India in 1963. There are more than 20 major Naga tribes and subtribes, with different dialects and customs. About two-thirds are Christian, and most others are Hindu or Muslim. Agriculture is the mainstay of the economy. Crops include rice, millet, sugarcane, potatoes, and tobacco.

Nagasaki, City (pop., 2003 est.: 418,523), western Kyushu, Japan. It is a seaport and commercial city at the mouth of the Urakami River, where it empties into Nagasaki Harbour. It was the only Japanese port open to foreign trade in 1639–1859. After the Portuguese and English traders were expelled in 1639, only the Dutch, Chinese, and Koreans were allowed into the harbour. In the 19th century it was the winter port of the Russian Asiatic fleet

(until 1903). It became a major shipbuilding centre in the early 20th century. In 1945 the second atomic bomb attack was carried out there by the U.S. during World War II; some 40,000 were killed immediately, up to 40,000 more died soon after, and many more were injured. The bomb also destroyed about 40% of the city's buildings. Nagasaki has been rebuilt and is a spiritual centre for movements to ban nuclear weapons.

Nagoya, City (pop., 2006 est.: 2,223,148), central Honshu, Japan. Located east of Kyōto, at the head of Ise Bay, it is one of Japan's leading industrial cities. Manufactures include textiles, watches, bicycles, sewing machines, machine tools, chemicals, and ceramics. The city dates from 1610, when a large castle was erected by the Owari branch of the Tokugawa shogunate; the castle was destroyed during World War II and rebuilt in 1959. The city's educational and cultural institutions include Nagoya University and the Tokugawa Art Museum. The Atsuta Shrine in Nagoya and nearby Ise Shrine are the oldest and most highly esteemed Shintō shrines in Japan.

Nagpur, City (pop., 2001: 2,052,066), northeastern Maharashtra state, India. It is situated along the Nag River, almost at the geographic centre of India. Founded in the 18th century by a Gond prince, it became the capital of members of the Maratha confederacy. In the 19th century it was under British control. The city's products include textiles, iron goods, pharmaceuticals, transport equipment, cotton, and oranges. It is dominated by the centrally located former British fort. It is an educational and cultural centre.

Nahuatl language, Uto-Aztecan language of Mexico, which continues to be spoken by more than a million modern Mexicans in various markedly divergent dialects. Nahuatl was the language of perhaps the majority of the inhabitants of pre-Conquest central Mexico, including Tenochtitlán (now Mexico City), the capital of the Aztec empire. Soon after the Conquest in the 1520s, Nahuatl began to be written in a Spanish-based orthography, and an abundance of documents survive from the colonial period, including annals, municipal records, poetry, formal addresses, and *The History of the Things of New Spain*, a remarkable compendium of Nahua culture compiled by Indian informants under the direction of the Franciscan friar Bernardino de Sahagún (1499–1590).

Naipaul, Sir V(idiadhar) S(urajprasad) (b. Aug. 17, 1932, Trinidad), Trinidadian novelist. Descended from Hindu Indians who immigrated to Trinidad as indentured servants, Naipaul left Trinidad in 1950 to attend Oxford University and settled in England. He won critical recognition with *A House for Mr. Biswas* (1961), about an immigrant's attempt to assert his identity and independence. Other novels that explore, in an often harshly critical tone, the disintegration and alienation typical of postcolonial nations include *In a Free State* (1971, Booker Prize), *Guerrillas* (1975), and *A Bend in the River* (1979). He also wrote *The Enigma of Arrival* (1987), *Half a Life* (2001), and nonfictional studies of India. Naipaul was awarded the Nobel Prize for Literature in 2001.

Nairobi, City (pop., 2006 est.: 2,864,700), capital of Kenya. It is located in south-central Kenya at an elevation of about 5,500 ft (1,680 m). Founded *c.* 1899 as a colonial railroad site, it became the capital of British East Africa in 1905. As a government and trade centre, it attracted many settlers from rural Kenya, making it one of the largest cities in Africa. When Kenya gained independence in 1963, it remained the capital, with its area greatly expanded by the new constitution. It is Kenya's principal commercial and industrial city, producing beverages, processed food, cigarettes, and furniture. The city exports many products via the port of Mombasa. Noted institutions and landmarks include the University of Nairobi and the National Museum of Kenya. Tourism is an important industry, with Nairobi National Park attracting many visitors.

Nalanda, Buddhist monastic centre, often spoken of as a university, in northern Bihar state, India. Though it is traditionally dated to the time of the Buddha (6th–5th centuries BC), archaeological excavations date its foundations to the 5th century AD. It housed a population of several thousand teachers and students. Topics studied included logic, grammar, astronomy, and medicine. The Chinese pilgrims Xuanzang and Yijing provided vivid accounts of Nalanda in the late 7th century. Nalanda continued to flourish through the 12th century and became a centre of religious sculpture. It was probably sacked during Muslim raids *c.* 1200 and never recovered.

Namib, Desert region, extending 1,200 mi (1,900 km) from Namibe, Angola, along the entire coast of Namibia to the Olifants River in South Africa. It is an almost rainless area, 50–80 mi (80–130 km) wide over most of its length, traversed by rail lines linking Walvis Bay with the Republic of South Africa. It is basically a smooth platform of bedrock of various types and ages. In the southern half the platform is covered with sand. The eastern part, the Inner Namib, supports large numbers of antelope. The shore area has a dense population of marine birds, including flamingos, pelicans, and penguins.

Namibia, officially REPUBLIC OF NAMIBIA, Country, southwest coast of Africa. Area: 318,193 sq mi (824,116 sq km). Population: (2011 est.) 2,324,000. Capital: Windhoek. About one-third of the people are Ovambo. Others include Nama, Kavango, Herero, and San. Languages: English (official), various Bantu languages (notably Ovambo), Afrikaans, San. Religions: Christianity (Protestant, Roman Catholic, other Christians); also traditional beliefs. Currency: Namibian dollar. Namibia may be divided into three broad regions: the Namib Desert, the Central Plateau, and the Kalahari Desert. The economy is based largely on agriculture and on the production and export of diamonds. Namibia is a republic with two legislative houses; its head of state and government is the president. Long inhabited by indigenous peoples, it was explored by the Portuguese in the late 15th century. In 1884 it was annexed by Germany as German South West Africa. It was captured in World War I by South Africa (and subsequently called South West Africa until 1968), which received it as a mandate from the League of Nations in 1919 and refused to give it up after World War II. A UN resolution in 1966 ending the mandate was challenged by South Africa in the 1970s and '80s. Through long negotiations involving many factions and interests, Namibia achieved independence in 1990. The country has been severely affected by the AIDS epidemic; a large proportion of the population has become infected with HIV.

Nanak (b. April 15, 1469, Rai Bhoi di Talvandi, near Lahore, India—d. 1539, Kartarpur, Punjab), Indian founder of Sikhism. Born into a Hindu merchant caste, he worked as a storekeeper until a spiritual experience incited him to leave his job and family and begin a 20-year phase of travel. He eventually settled in Kartarpur, a village in Punjab, to which he attracted many disciples, and he became the first Guru of the Sikhs. His doctrine stressed the unity and uniqueness of God and offered salvation through disciplined meditation on the divine name. It stipulated that meditation must be inward and rejected all external aids such as idols, temples, mosques, scriptures, and set prayers. After his death the stories told of his life were collected in anthologies called the *Janam-sakhi*s.

Nanchang, or NAN-CH'ANG, City (pop., 2003 est.: 1,419,813), capital of Jiangxi province, southeastern China. An old walled city on the right bank of the Gan River, it was founded in 201 BC. In AD 959 it became the capital of the Southern Tang dynasty. At the end of the Mongol period it was a battleground between the founder of the Ming dynasty and local warlords. In the early 16th century a rebellion was launched against the Ming regime. Nanchang suffered severely during the Taiping Rebellion (1850–64). In 1927 it

was the site of revolutionary activities of the Chinese Communist Party. Since 1949 it has become industrialized; its products include textiles, milled rice, and automotive parts.

Nanga Parbat, Peak, western Himalayas. It is located in the Pakistani-administered portion of the Kashmir region. In 1895 the British climber Albert F. Mummery led the first expedition to the 26,660-ft (8,126-m) summit, but he died in the attempt. Severe weather and frequent avalanches caused the deaths of at least 30 other climbers before the Austrian Hermann Buhl reached the top in 1953.

Nanjing, or NAN-CHING, conventional NANKING, City (pop., 2003 est.: 2,966,000), capital of Jiangsu province, east-central China. Located on the southeastern bank of the Yangtze River (Chang Jiang) northwest of Shanghai, the site has been inhabited for thousands of years. The present city was founded in 1368 by the Ming dynasty, which had its capital there (1368–1421). It was taken by the British in the Opium Wars of 1842 and was largely destroyed in 1864 after having served (since 1853) as the capital of the Taiping revolutionaries. Nanjing was opened as a treaty port in 1899 and was the Nationalist capital from 1928 to 1937; it was then taken by the Japanese, and it was the site of the Nanjing Massacre in the Sino-Japanese War of 1937–45. It was taken by communist forces in 1949 and became the provincial capital in 1952. Nanjing is a port city and a major industrial and communications centre with a number of universities and colleges. Nearby monuments include mausoleums of Sun Yat-sen and a Ming emperor.

Nanjing, Treaty of (Aug. 29, 1842) Treaty that ended the first Opium War, the first of the unequal treaties between China and foreign imperialist powers. China paid the British an indemnity, ceded the territory of Hong Kong, and agreed to establish a "fair and reasonable" tariff. British merchants, who had previously been allowed to trade only at Guangzhou (Canton), were now permitted to trade at five "treaty ports" and with whomever they pleased. The treaty was supplemented in 1843 by the British Supplementary Treaty of the Bogue, which allowed British citizens to be tried in British courts and granted Britain any rights in China that China might grant to other countries.

Nanning, or NAN-NING, formerly (1913–45) YUNG-NING, City (pop., 2003 est.: 1,031,672), capital of Guangxi province, southern China. Located on the banks of the Yung River, it was the site of a county seat first established in AD 318. A frontier prefecture under the Song dynasty, it was later ruled successively by the Ming and Qing dynasties and was opened to foreign trade in 1907. It was occupied by the Japanese during the Sino-Japanese War (1937–45), although it was briefly a U.S. air base. It was a supply base for communist forces during the anti-French war in Southeast Asia and the Vietnam War. Formerly known mainly as a commercial and administrative centre, it now has diversified manufacturing as well.

nanoparticle, Ultrafine unit with dimensions measured in nanometres (nm; billionths of a metre). Nanoparticles possess unique physical properties such as very large surface areas and can be classified as hard or soft. They exist naturally in the environment and are produced as a result of human activities. Manufactured nanoparticles can have various compositions and thus may have practical applications in a variety of areas, ranging from environmental remediation to engineering and medicine. Examples of naturally occurring nanoparticles include terpenes released from trees and materials emitted in smoke from volcanic eruptions and fires. Quantum dots and nanoscale zero-valent iron are examples of manufactured nanoparticles.

nanotechnology, Manipulation of atoms, molecules, and materials to form structures on the scale of nanometres (billionths of a metre). These nanostructures typically exhibit new properties or behaviours due to quantum mechanics. In 1959 Richard Feynman first pointed out some potential quantum benefits of miniaturization. A major advancement was the invention of molecular-beam epitaxy by Alfred Cho and John Arthur at Bell Laboratories in 1968 and its development in the 1970s, which enabled the controlled deposition of single atomic layers. Scientists have made some progress at building devices, including computer components, at nanoscales. Faster progress has occurred in the incorporation of nanomaterials in other products, such as stain-resistant coatings for clothes and invisible sunscreens.

Nansen, Fridtjof (b. Oct. 10, 1861, Store-Frøen, near Kristiania, Nor.—d. May 13, 1930, Lysaker, near Oslo), Norwegian explorer and statesman. In 1888 he led the first expedition to cross the ice fields of Greenland. On a later expedition, in 1895, in an attempt to reach the North Pole, he reached the farthest northern latitude then attained. He engaged in scientific research (1896–1917) and led oceanographic expeditions in the North Atlantic in 1900 and 1910–14. He undertook diplomatic missions as Norway's first minister to Britain (1906–08) and as head of Norway's delegation to the new League of Nations (1920). He directed the repatriation from Russia of over 400,000 prisoners of war for the League and organized famine relief in Russia for the Red Cross. In 1922 he was awarded the Nobel Prize for Peace; he used the prize money for international relief work. In 1931 the Nansen International Office for Refugees was established in Geneva.

Nantes, Edict of (April 13, 1598) Law promulgated by Henry IV of France to grant religious liberty and full civil rights to the Protestant Huguenots. It stipulated that Protestant pastors were to be paid by the state, and public worship was permitted in most of the kingdom, though not in Paris. It also restored Catholicism in all areas where Catholic practice had been interrupted by the Wars of Religion. The edict was resented by the Catholic clergy; Cardinal de Richelieu annulled its political clauses in 1629, and the full edict was revoked by Louis XIV in 1685.

napalm, Organic compound, the aluminum soap or salt of a mixture of fatty acids, used to thicken gasoline for use as an incendiary in flamethrowers and firebombs. The thickened mixture, itself also called napalm, burns more slowly and can be propelled more accurately and over greater distances than gasoline. When it comes in contact with surfaces, including the human body, it sticks tenaciously and continues to burn. It was developed and first used by the U.S. in World War II. Its use in the Vietnam War became highly controversial.

Naples, Italian NAPOLI, ancient NEAPOLIS, City (pop., 2001 prelim.: 993,386), capital of Campania, southern Italy. Located on the northern side of the Bay of Naples, southeast of Rome, it was founded c. 600 BCE by refugees from an ancient Greek colony and was conquered by the Romans in the 4th century BCE. It became part of the realms of the Byzantines and Saracens. In the 11th century it was conquered by the Norman ruler of Sicily, and through the 19th century it was the capital of the Kingdom of the Two Sicilies and the Kingdom of Naples. It was entered by Giuseppe Garibaldi's expedition in 1860. Heavily damaged in World War II by Allied and German bombing, it was later rebuilt, but it suffered severe earthquake damage in 1980. It is a commercial and cultural centre and a major port with diversified industries. Among the city's attractions are medieval castles, churches, and a university.

Napoleon, French NAPOLÉON BONAPARTE, orig. Italian NAPOLEONE BUONAPARTE (b. Aug. 15, 1769, Ajaccio, Corsica—d. May 5, 1821, St. Helena Island), French general and emperor (1804–15). Born to parents of Italian ancestry, he was educated in France and became an army officer in 1785. He fought in the French Revolutionary Wars and was promoted to brigadier general in 1793. After victories against the Austrians in northern Italy, he negotiated the Treaty of Campo Formio (1797). He attempted to conquer Egypt (1798–99) but was defeated by the British under Horatio Nelson in the Battle of the Nile. The Coup of 18–19 Brumaire

brought him to power in 1799, and he installed a military dictatorship, with himself as First Consul. He introduced numerous reforms in government, including the Napoleonic Code, and reconstructed the French education system. He negotiated the Concordat of 1801 with the pope. After victory against the Austrians at the Battle of Marengo (1800), he embarked on the Napoleonic Wars. The formation of coalitions of European countries against him led Napoleon to declare France a hereditary empire and to crown himself emperor in 1804. He won his greatest military victory at the Battle of Austerlitz against Austria and Russia in 1805. He defeated Prussia at the Battles of Jena and Auerstedt (1806) and Russia at the Battle of Friedland (1807). He then imposed the Treaty of Tilsit on Russia, ending the fourth coalition of countries against France. Despite his loss to Britain at the Battle of Trafalgar, he sought to weaken British commerce and established the Continental System of port blockades. He consolidated his European empire until 1810 but became embroiled in the Peninsular War (1808–14). He led the French army into Austria and defeated the Austrians at the Battle of Wagram (1809), signing the Treaty of Vienna. To enforce the Treaty of Tilsit, he led an army of about 600,000 into Russia in 1812, winning the Battle of Borodino, but was forced to retreat from Moscow with disastrous losses. His army greatly weakened, he was met by a strong coalition of allied powers, who defeated him at the Battle of Leipzig (1813). After Paris was taken by the allied coalition, Napoleon was forced to abdicate in 1814 and was exiled to the island of Elba. In 1815 he mustered a force and returned to France to reestablish himself as emperor for the Hundred Days, but he was decisively defeated at the Battle of Waterloo. He was sent into exile on the remote island of St. Helena, where he died six years later. One of the most celebrated figures in history, Napoleon revolutionized military organization and training and brought about reforms that permanently influenced civil institutions in France and throughout Europe.

Napoleonic Wars (1799–1815) Series of wars that ranged France against shifting alliances of European powers. Originally an attempt to maintain French strength established by the French Revolutionary Wars, they became efforts by Napoleon to affirm his supremacy in the balance of European power. A victory over Austria at the Battle of Marengo (1800) left France the dominant power on the continent. Only Britain remained strong, and its victory at the Battle of Trafalgar (1805) ended Napoleon's threat to invade England. Napoleon won major victories in the Battles of Ulm and Austerlitz (1805), Jena and Auerstedt (1806), and Friedland (1807) against an alliance of Russia, Austria, and Prussia. The resulting Treaties of Tilsit (1807) and the Treaty of Schönbrunn (1809) left most of Europe from the English Channel to the Russian border either part of the French Empire, controlled by France, or allied to it by treaty. Napoleon's successes resulted from a strategy of moving his army rapidly, attacking quickly, and defeating each of the disconnected enemy units. His enemies' responding strategy was to avoid engagement while withdrawing, forcing Napoleon's supply lines to be overextended; the strategy was successfully used against him by the duke of Wellington in the Peninsular War and by Mikhail, Prince Barclay de Tolly, in Russia. In 1813 the Quadruple Alliance formed to oppose Napoleon and amassed armies that outnumbered his. Defeated at the Battle of Leipzig, he was forced to withdraw west of the Rhine River, and after the invasion of France (1814) he abdicated. He rallied a new army to return in the Hundred Days (1815), but a revived Quadruple Alliance opposed him. His final defeat at the Battle of Waterloo was caused by his inability to surprise and to prevent the two armies, led by Wellington and Gebhard von Blücher, from joining forces to defeat him. With his second abdication and exile, the era of the Napoleonic Wars ended.

Narayanan, Kocheril Raman (b. Oct. 27, 1920, Uzhavoor, India—d. Nov. 9, 2005, New Delhi), President of India (1997–2002). He was the first member of the country's lowest social caste—the group traditionally considered to be untouchable—to occupy the office. Raised in poverty, he attended the University of Travancore on a scholarship and graduated from the London School of Economics with top academic honours. In 1949 he became a diplomat, despite opposition from upper-caste officials, and was ambassador to several countries, including China and the U.S. After serving as a cabinet minister in parliament, he was named vice president in 1992 and president in 1997.

narcissism, Mental disorder characterized by extreme self-absorption, an exaggerated sense of self-importance, and a need for attention and admiration from others. First identified by Havelock Ellis in 1898, the disorder is named for the mythological Narcissus, who fell in love with his own reflection. In addition to an inflated self-image and addiction to fantasy, narcissism is characterized by an unusual coolness and composure, which is shaken only when the narcissistic confidence is threatened, and by the tendency to take others for granted or to exploit them. According to Sigmund Freud, narcissism is a normal stage in children's development, but it is considered a disorder when it occurs after puberty.

narcolepsy, Sleep disorder with sudden, uncontrollable spells of daytime sleep and disturbances of nighttime sleep. It usually begins in youth or early adulthood and is presumably due to dysfunction of certain brain structures. Narcoleptics can fall asleep anywhere and anytime—for instance, while talking, eating, or driving. Sleep usually lasts a moment, rarely over an hour, and the narcoleptic is easily awakened. Sleep paralysis, normal when falling asleep or waking, occurs during full consciousness in narcolepsy, with brief but complete inability to move.

narcotic, Drug that produces analgesia, narcosis (stupor or sleep), and drug addiction. In most people narcotics also produce euphoria. Those that occur naturally in the opium poppy, notably morphine, have been used since ancient Greek times. The main therapeutic use of narcotics is for pain relief. Most countries limit the production, sale, and use of narcotics because of their addictive properties and detrimental effects and the incidence of drug abuse. With the development in the 19th century of the hypodermic needle and of heroin, five to 10 times as potent as morphine, the use and abuse of narcotics increased dramatically. A narcotic overdose can cause central nervous system depression, respiratory failure, and death.

Narmada River, or NERBUDDA RIVER, River, central India. Rising in Madhya Pradesh state, it is 801 mi (1,289 km) long. It flows west into the Gulf of Khambhat (Cambay) and forms the traditional boundary between Hindustan and the Deccan. Called Namade by the Greek geographer Ptolemy in the 2nd century AD, it has always been an important route between the Arabian Sea and the Ganges (Ganga) River valley. It is a pilgrimage route for Hindus, who regard it their most sacred river after the Ganges.

NASA, in full NATIONAL AERONAUTICS AND SPACE ADMINISTRATION, Independent U.S. government agency established in 1958 for research and development of vehicles and activities for aeronautics and space exploration. Its goals include improving human understanding of the universe, the solar system, and Earth and establishing a permanent human presence in space. NASA, previously the National Advisory Committee for Aeronautics (NACA), was created largely in response to the Soviet Union's launch of Sputnik in 1957. Its organization was well under way in 1961, when Pres. John F. Kennedy proposed that the U.S. put a man on the Moon by the end of the 1960s. Later unmanned programs (e.g., Viking, Mariner, Voyager, Galileo) explored other planets and interplanetary space, and orbiting observatories (e.g., the Hubble Space Telescope) have studied the cosmos. NASA also developed and launched various satellites with Earth applications, such as Landsat and communications and weather satellites. It planned and developed the space shuttle and led the development and construction of the International Space Station.

Nassau, City (pop., 2002: 179,300), capital of The Bahamas. Located on the northeastern coast of New Providence island, it was settled by the English in the 17th century and became a rendezvous for pirates in the 18th century. Forts were built there to ward off attacks by encroaching Spaniards. During the American Civil War, it became a base for Confederate blockade runners. It is now a popular resort; its economy is based on tourism.

Nasser, Gamal Abdel, also spelled JAMĀL ʿABD AL-NĀSIR (b.

Gamal Abdel Nasser, photograph by Yousuf Karsh.
© Karsh from Rapho/Photo Researchers

Jan. 15, 1918, Alexandria, Egypt—d. Sept. 28, 1970, Cairo), Egyptian army officer who was prime minister (1954–56) and president (1956–70) of Egypt. In his youth, he took part in anti-British demonstrations. As an army officer, he led a coup that deposed the royal family (1952) and installed Gen. Muḥammad Naguib as head of state. In 1954 he deposed Naguib and made himself prime minister. The Muslim Brotherhood tried to assassinate him but failed. In 1956 he promulgated a constitution that made Egypt a one-party socialist state with himself as president. In the same year, he nationalized the Suez Canal and secured Soviet assistance to build the Aswan High Dam after the U.S. and Britain canceled their offer of aid. Soon thereafter, Egypt weathered an attack by British, French, and Israeli forces. A charismatic figure, he aspired to lead the Arab world and succeeded briefly in forming the United Arab Republic with Syria (1958–61). He led the Arab world in the disastrous Six-Day War against Israel but had tentatively accepted a U.S. peace plan for Egypt and Israel when he died of a heart attack. He was succeeded by Anwar el-Sādāt.

Nasser, Lake, or LAKE NUBIA, Lake, southern Egypt and northern Sudan. About 300 mi (480 km) long, it was formed in the 1960s by the construction of the Aswan High Dam in order to control the annual floods of the Nile River, whose waters now feed the lake. Its waters, when discharged downstream, have brought some 1,250 sq mi (3,240 sq km) of additional land under irrigation. Its formation flooded a number of archaeological sites, including those found at Abu Simbel. In Sudan it is known as Lake Nubia.

Nataraja, The Hindu god Shiva in his form as the cosmic dancer. The most common images show him with four arms and flying locks, dancing on a dwarf (a symbol of human ignorance) and encircled by a ring of flames. The Nataraja sculpture shows Shiva as the source of all movement within the cosmos, represented by the loop of flames. The dance's purpose is to release humans from illusion; the place where the god performs the dance is believed to lie both at the centre of the universe and within the human heart.

Nataraja, dancing Shiva, Indian bronze image, 12th–13th century AD; in the Museum of Asiatic Art, Amsterdam.
Courtesy of the Rijksmuseum, Amsterdam

nation, People whose common identity creates a psychological bond and a political community. Their political identity usually comprises such characteristics as a common language, culture, ethnicity, and history. More than one nation may comprise a state, but the terms nation, state, and country are often used interchangeably. A nation-state is a state populated primarily by the people of one nationality.

Nation of Islam, or BLACK MUSLIMS, African American religious movement that mingles elements of Islam and black nationalism. It was founded in 1931 by Wallace D. Fard, who established its first mosque in Detroit, Mich. Fard retired into obscurity and his assistant Elijah Muhammad, who founded a second temple in Chicago, took over in 1934. He asserted the moral and cultural superiority of Africans over whites and urged African Americans to renounce Christianity as a tool of the oppressors. His teachings also included the traditional Islamic tenets of monotheism, submission to God, and strong family life. The Nation of Islam grew quickly after World War II, and in the early 1960s it achieved national prominence through the work of Malcolm X. Leadership disputes led Malcolm to form a separate organization and finally to his assassination in 1965. In the 1970s Elijah Muhammad was succeeded by his son, Wallace D. Muhammad (1933–2008), who renamed the organization the American Muslim Mission. In 1985 he dissolved the Mission, urging its members to become orthodox Muslims. A splinter group headed by Louis Farrakhan retains the movement's original name and principles. In the early 21st century there were approximately 10,000 members of the Nation of Islam.

National Assembly, French ASSEMBLÉE NATIONALE, French parliamentary body. The name was used first during the French Revolution to designate the revolutionary assembly formed by representatives of the Third Estate (1789) and then as a short form for the National Constituent Assembly (1789–91). It was used again when the National Assembly of 1871–75 drafted a new constitution. In the Third Republic (1875–1940), the name designated the two houses of parliament, the Senate and the Chamber of Deputies. In the Fourth Republic (1946–58) and Fifth Republic (from 1958), the name was applied only to the lower house (the former Chamber of Deputies). The National Assembly consists of 577 deputies, elected in single-seat constituencies for five-year terms.

National Convention, French CONVENTION NATIONALE, Governing assembly (1792–95) of the French Revolution. Comprising 749 deputies elected after the overthrow of the monarchy (1792), it sought to provide a new constitution for France. The struggle between the radical Montagnards and the moderate Girondins dominated the Convention until the Girondins were purged in 1793. The democratic constitution already approved by the Convention was not put into effect while the Montagnards controlled the assembly (1793–94). After the Thermidorian Reaction (1794), the balance of power in the Convention was held by members of the Plain. The Girondins were recalled, and the Constitution of 1795 was approved for the Directory regime that replaced the Convention.

national debt, or PUBLIC DEBT, Total indebtedness of a government, especially as evidenced by securities issued to investors. The national debt grows whenever the government operates at a budget deficit—that is, when government spending exceeds government revenues in a year. To finance its debt, the government can issue securities such as bonds or treasury bills. The level of national debt varies from country to country, from less than 10% of the gross domestic product (GDP) to more than double it. Public borrowing is thought to have an inflationary effect on the economy and thus is often used during recessions to stimulate consumption, investment, and employment.

National Gallery of Art, Museum in Washington, D.C., part of the Smithsonian Institution. It was founded in 1937 when Andrew W. Mellon donated his collection of European paintings to the U.S. He also donated funds to construct the gallery's Neoclassical building, opened in 1941. Now known as the West Building, it is connected by plaza and underground concourse to the East Building, designed by I.M. Pei (completed 1978). The museum houses an extensive collection of U.S. and European paintings, sculpture, decorative arts, and graphic arts from the 12th to 21st centuries; especially well represented are works by Italian Renaissance, 17th-century Dutch, and 18th- and 19th-century French artists.

national park, Area set aside by a national government for the preservation of its natural environment. Most national parks are kept in their natural state. Those in the U.S. and Canada emphasize land and wildlife preservation, those in Britain focus mainly on the land, and those in African nations focus primarily on animals. The world's first national park, Yellowstone, was established in the U.S. by Pres. Ulysses S. Grant in 1872. Canada's first national park, Banff, was established in 1885. Japan and Mexico established their first national parks in the 1930s; Britain's national parks date to 1949. The U.S. National Park Service, established in 1916, now also manages national monuments, preserves, recreation areas, and seashores, as well as lakeshores, historic sites, parkways, scenic trails, and battlefields.

National Security Council (NSC), U.S. agency that advises the president on domestic, foreign, and military policies related to national security. With the Central Intelligence Agency, it was established by the 1947 National Security Act. It provides the White House with a foreign-policy-making instrument independent of the State Department. It has four members—the president, vice president, and secretaries of state and defense—and its staff is headed by the national security adviser.

National Socialism, or NAZISM, Totalitarian movement led by Adolf Hitler as head of Germany's Nazi Party (1920–45). Its roots lay in the tradition of Prussian militarism and discipline and German Romanticism, which celebrated a mythic past and proclaimed the rights of the exceptional individual over all rules and laws. Its ideology was shaped by Hitler's beliefs in German racial superiority and the dangers of communism. It rejected liberalism, democracy, the rule of law, and human rights, stressing instead the subordination of the individual to the state and the necessity of strict obedience to leaders. It emphasized the inequality of individuals and "races" and the right of the strong to rule the weak. Politically, National Socialism favoured rearmament, reunification of the German areas of Europe, expansion into non-German areas, and the purging of "undesirables," especially Jews.

nationalism, Loyalty and devotion to one's nation or country, especially as above loyalty to other groups or to individual interests. Before the era of the nation-state, the primary allegiance of most people was to their immediate locality or religious group. The rise of large, centralized states weakened local authority, and society's increasing secularization weakened loyalty to religious groups, though shared religion—along with common ethnicity, political heritage, and history—is one of the factors that draws people together in nationalist movements. Early nationalist movements in 18th- and early 19th-century Europe were liberal and internationalist, but they gradually became more conservative and parochial. Nationalism is considered a major contributing cause of World War I, World War II, and many other wars of the modern era. In Africa and Asia in the 20th century, nationalist movements often arose in opposition to colonialism. After the fall of the Soviet Union, powerful nationalist sentiments in eastern Europe and the former Soviet republics contributed to ethnic conflicts, such as those in the territories of the former Yugoslavia.

NATO, in full NORTH ATLANTIC TREATY ORGANIZATION, International military alliance created to defend western Europe against a possible Soviet invasion. A 1948 collective-defense alliance between Britain, France, the Netherlands, Belgium, and Luxembourg was recognized as inadequate to deter Soviet aggression, and in 1949 the U.S. and Canada agreed to join their European allies in an enlarged alliance. A centralized administrative structure was set up, and three major commands were established, focused on Europe, the Atlantic, and the English Channel (disbanded in 1994). The admission of West Germany in 1955 led to the Soviet Union's creation of the opposing Warsaw Treaty Organization, or Warsaw Pact. France withdrew from military participation in 1966. Since NATO ground forces were smaller than those of the Warsaw Pact, the balance of power was maintained by superior weaponry, including intermediate-range nuclear weapons. After the Warsaw Pact's dissolution and the end of the Cold War in 1991, NATO withdrew its nuclear weapons and attempted to transform its mission. It involved itself in the Balkan conflicts of the 1990s. Article 5 of the North Atlantic Treaty stated that an attack on one signatory would be regarded as an attack on the rest. This article was first invoked in 2001 in response to the terrorist September 11 attacks against the U.S. Additional countries joined NATO in 1999, 2004, and 2009 to bring the number of full members to 28. In 2009 France announced its plan to rejoin NATO's integrated military command.

natural gas, Colourless, highly flammable gaseous hydrocarbon consisting primarily of methane and ethane. It may also contain heavier hydrocarbons, carbon dioxide, hydrogen, hydrogen sulfide, nitrogen, helium, and argon. It commonly occurs in association with crude oil. Natural gas is extracted from wells drilled into the Earth. Some natural gas can be used as it comes from the well, without any refining, but most requires processing. It is transported either in its natural gaseous state by pipeline or, after liquefaction by cooling, by tankers. Liquefied natural gas occupies only about 1/600 of the volume of the gas. It has grown steadily as a source of energy since the 1930s.

natural law, In jurisprudence and political philosophy, a system of right or justice common to all humankind and derived from nature rather than from the rules of society, or positive law. The concept can be traced to Aristotle, who held that what was "just by nature" was not always the same as what was "just by law." In one form or another, the existence of natural law was asserted by the Stoics, Cicero, the Roman jurists, St. Paul, St. Augustine, Gratian, St. Thomas Aquinas, John Duns Scotus, William of Ockham, and Francisco Suárez. In the modern period, Hugo Grotius insisted on the validity of natural law even on the assumption that God does not exist, and Thomas Hobbes defined a law of nature as "a precept of general rule found out by reason, by which a man is forbidden to do that which is destructive of his life." Hobbes attempted to construct an edifice of law by rational deduction from a hypothetical "state of nature" and a social contract of consent between rulers and subjects. John Locke departed from Hobbes in describing the state of nature as an early society in which free and equal men observe the natural law. Jean-Jacques Rousseau postulated a savage who was virtuous in isolation and actuated by two principles "prior to reason": self-preservation and compassion. The authors of the U.S. Declaration of Independence refer only briefly to "the Laws of Nature" before citing equality and other "unalienable" rights as "self-evident." The French Declaration of the Rights of Man and of the Citizen asserts liberty, property, security, and resistance to oppression as "imprescriptible natural rights." Interest in the concept of natural law declined dramatically in the 19th century, partly as a result of skeptical attacks by Jeremy Bentham and other proponents of utilitarianism; it was revived in the mid-20th century in light of the crimes committed by the Nazi regime during World War II. Skepticism of natural law and natural rights remained strong, however, and later writers almost invariably talked of human rights rather than natural rights.

natural selection, Process that results in adaptation of an organism to its environment by means of selectively reproducing changes in its genotype. Variations that increase an organism's chances of survival and procreation are preserved and multiplied from generation to generation at the expense of less advantageous variations. As proposed by Charles Darwin, natural selection is the mechanism by which evolution occurs. It may arise from differences in survival, fertility, rate of development, mating success, or any other aspect of the life cycle. Mutation, gene flow, and genetic drift, all of which are random processes, also alter gene abundance. Natural selection moderates the effects of these processes because it multiplies the incidence of beneficial mutations over generations and eliminates harmful ones, since the organisms that carry them leave few or no descendants.

naturalism, Aesthetic movement of the late 19th to early 20th century. The movement was inspired by the principles and methods of natural science, especially Darwinism, which were adapted to literature and art. In literature, naturalism extended the tradition of realism, aiming at an even more faithful, pseudoscientific representation of reality, presented without moral judgment. Characters in naturalistic literature typically illustrate the deterministic role of heredity and environment on human life. The movement originated in France, where its leading exponent was Émile Zola. In America it is associated with the work of writers such as Stephen Crane and Theodore Dreiser. Visual artists associated with naturalism chose themes from life, capturing subjects unposed and not idealized, thus giving their works an unstudied air. Following the lead of the Realist painter Gustave Courbet, painters chose themes from contemporary life, and many deserted the studio for the open air, finding subjects among peasants and tradespeople, capturing them as they found them. As a result, finished canvases had the freshness and immediacy of sketches. Zola, the spokesman for literary naturalism, was also the first to champion Édouard Manet and the Impressionists. While naturalism was short-lived as a historical movement, it contributed to art an enrichment of realism, new areas of subject matter, and a largeness and formlessness that was closer to life than to art. Its multiplicity of impressions conveyed the sense of a world in constant flux.

naturalism, In philosophy, the theory that affirms that all beings and events in the universe are natural and therefore can be fully known by the methods of scientific investigation. Though naturalism has often been equated with materialism, it is much broader in scope. Strictly speaking, naturalism has no ontological bias toward any particular set of categories of reality: dualism and monism, atheism and theism, idealism and materialism are all compatible with it. Naturalism was most influential in the 1930s and '40s, chiefly in the U.S. among philosophers such as F.J.E. Woodbridge (1867–1940), Morris R. Cohen (1880–1947), John Dewey, Ernest Nagel (1901–85), Sidney Hook (1902–89), and W.V.O. Quine.

naturalization, Process of granting nationality or citizenship to an alien. It may be granted after voluntary application or through legislation, marriage to a citizen, or parental action. Involuntary naturalization occurs when one's home territory is annexed by a foreign state. Qualifications for naturalization may include a minimum residency period, a minimum age, law-abiding character, good health, self-sufficiency, satisfactory knowledge of the new country, and willingness to give up one's former nationality.

Nauru, officially REPUBLIC OF NAURU, Island country, southeastern Micronesia, western South Pacific Ocean. Area: 8.2 sq mi (21.2 sq km). Population: (2011 est.) 9,300. There is no official capital, but government offices are located in Yaren district. About two-thirds of the population are indigenous Nauruans. Languages: Nauruan, English. Religion: Christianity (mostly Protestant; also Roman Catholic). Currency: Australian dollar. Nauru is a coral island with a central plateau 100–200 ft (30–60 m) high. A thin strip of fertile land encircling the island is the major zone of human settlement. It lacks harbours; ships must anchor to buoys beyond a reef. Nauru once had the world's largest concentration of phosphate, and its economy was based on phosphate mining and processing; however, the deposits have been depleted, and the economy has been converting to fishing and other ventures. Nauru is a republic with one legislative house; its head of state and government is the president. It was inhabited by Pacific Islanders when the first British explorers arrived in 1798 and named it Pleasant Island because of their friendly welcome. Annexed by Germany in 1888, it was occupied by Australia at the start of World War I, and in 1919 it was placed under a joint mandate of Britain, Australia, and New Zealand. During World War II it was occupied by the Japanese. Made a UN trust territory under Australian administration in 1947, Nauru gained complete independence in 1968 and became a full member of the Commonwealth and the UN in 1999.

nausea, Discomfort in the pit of the stomach associated with disgust for food and a feeling that vomiting will follow, as it often does. Nausea results from irritation of nerve endings in the stomach or duodenum, which stimulate brain centres that control nausea and vomiting. Nausea can be a symptom of minor or serious disorders. Common causes include indigestion (from eating too fast or from stress around mealtime), food poisoning, motion sickness, and pregnancy (morning sickness). Nausea may also arise from any cause of abnormal lack of appetite (e.g., shock, pain, influenza, badly fitting dentures, liver or kidney disease). Simple nausea often is relieved by vomiting.

Navajo, or NAVAHO, North American Indian people living mostly in northwestern New Mexico, Arizona, and southeastern Utah, U.S. The Navajo speak an Athabaskan language related to that of the Apache. The Navajo and Apache migrated from Canada to the Southwest *c.* AD 900–1200, after which the Navajo came under the influence of the Pueblo Indians. Painted pottery and the famous Navajo rugs, as well as sandpainting, are products of this influence. The craft of silversmithing probably came from Mexico in the mid-19th century. The traditional economy was based on farming and later herding of sheep, goats, and cattle. The basic social unit was the band. Religion focused on the emergence of the first people from worlds beneath the Earth's surface. In 1863 the U.S. government ordered Col. Kit Carson to put an end to Navajo and Apache raiding; his offensives resulted in the incarceration of about 8,000 Navajo and the destruction of crops and herds. Today many Navajo live on or near the Navajo Reservation (24,000 sq mi [64,000 sq km] in New Mexico, Arizona, and Utah); thousands earn their living as transient workers. Their language has been tenaciously preserved; they used it to great effect during World War II by transmitting coded messages in Navajo. The Navajo are the most populous Native American group in the U.S., with some 300,000 individuals of Navajo descent in the early 21st century.

navigation, Science of directing a craft by determining its position, course, and distance traveled. Early mariners followed landmarks visible on shore and studied prevailing winds for clues to direction. The Phoenicians and Polynesians sailed out of sight of land and used the stars to set their course. The compass (first used by the Chinese *c.* 1100) was the first navigational aid that gave a constant reference point, though its accuracy was limited, especially in heavy seas. Modern compasses are stabilized by gyroscopes and housed in binnacles that compensate for the craft's motion. Ship speed was first calculated by dropping overboard a log attached to a reel of line knotted at regular intervals; the number of knots exposed while the log drifted and a sandglass emptied gave the vessel's speed in knots (nautical mph). Charts are another essential navigational tool. Fixing a position requires charts detailing known locations, together with instruments that calculate a vessel's bearing relative to them. The earliest instrument for determining latitude was the quadrant, which measured the altitude of the polestar or the noonday sun. Other early instruments included the sextant and the astrolabe. Longitude (used for navigation with increasing success in the 17th–18th century) was fixed using chronometers and tables showing positions of celestial bodies throughout the year. In the 20th century, radio beacons and satellite networks allowed aircraft and ships to determine their position. Dead reckoning uses an accurate history of a vessel's headings and speeds drawn from gyroscopes and from computerized measurements of the craft's acceleration.

Navratilova, Martina (b. Oct. 18, 1956, Prague, Czech.), Czech-born U.S. tennis player. She became the undisputed top-seeded player in the world in 1979 after winning the Wimbledon women's singles and doubles. In 1982 she won 90 of 93 matches, and in 1983 she won 86 of 87 matches. By 1992 she had accumulated more championships (158) than any other player, male or female, in tennis history, and she retired from singles play in 1994 with 167 titles. Over the next two years Navratilova appeared in only a handful of doubles events, and from 1997 to 1999 she did not play. In 2000 she returned to professional play, competing in several doubles events. In 2003 she won the mixed doubles at Wimbledon, tying Billie Jean King for most Wimbledon titles (20). With the victory, Navratilova, age 46, became the oldest player to win at Wimbledon. After winning the mixed doubles at the U.S. Open in 2006, she retired from competitive play. Her career totals include 59 grand slam titles: 18 singles, 31 doubles, and 10 mixed doubles.

navy, Warships and craft of every kind maintained by a nation for fighting on, under, or over the sea. A large modern navy includes aircraft carriers, cruisers, destroyers, frigates, submarines, minesweepers and minelayers, gunboats, and various types of support, supply, and repair ships, as well as naval bases and ports. Naval ships are the chief means by which a nation extends sea power. Their two chief functions are to achieve sea control and sea denial. Control of the sea enables a nation and its allies to carry on maritime commerce, amphibious assaults, and other seaborne operations that may be essential in wartime. Denial of the sea deprives enemy merchant vessels and warships of safe navigation.

Náxos, Largest island (pop., 2001: 18,188) of the Cyclades, Greece. It is about 22 mi (35 km) long and 16 mi (26 km) wide, with an area of 165 sq mi (427 sq km). The capital and chief port, Náxos, on the western coast, is on the site of the island's ancient and medieval capitals. In ancient times, it was famous for its wines and the worship of Dionysus. In mythology, it is where Theseus abandoned Ariadne. In the 7th–6th centuries BC a deep-grained white marble was exported for statuary. It was captured by the Persians in 490 BC and by Athens in 471 BC. A Venetian duchy ruled from 1207 to 1566; it was later ruled by the Turks. In 1830 it joined the Greek kingdom. Ruins of a Mycenaean settlement have been found there. Náxos produces white wine, citrus, and emery.

Nazareth, Hebrew NAẒERAT, Arabic AL-NĀṢIRAH, City (pop., 2010 est.: 73,000), northern Israel, southeast of Haifa. It is Israel's largest Arab city. In the New Testament, it is the childhood home of Jesus. It contains many Christian churches and is a pilgrimage centre. Captured by Christians several times during the Crusades, it was taken by the Ottoman Empire in 1517. It was part of British-mandate Palestine from 1918 and became part of Israel in 1948. Christian Arabs form about one-third of the population.

N'Djamena, formerly FORT-LAMY, City (pop., 2005: urban agglom., 888,000), capital of Chad. It lies adjacent to Cameroon on the eastern bank of the Chari River, where it joins the Logone River. Founded in 1900 as Fort-Lamy, it remained a small settlement until after Chad's independence in 1960. In 1973 its name was changed to N'Djamena. It was occupied by Libyan forces in 1980–81 during the civil war that began in the 1960s. It is an important marketplace for cotton, cattle, and fish. It is the site of the nation's only university, the University of Chad (founded 1971).

Neanderthal, Species of the human genus (*Homo*) that inhabited much of Europe, the Mediterranean lands, and Central Asia *c.* 200,000–24,000 years ago. The name derives from the discovery in 1856 of remains in a cave above Germany's Neander Valley.

Most scholars designate the species as *Homo neanderthalensis* and do not consider Neanderthals direct ancestors of modern humans (*Homo sapiens*); however, both species share a common ancestor that lived as recently as 130,000 years ago. Some scholars report evidence of limited interbreeding between Neanderthals and early modern humans of European and Asian stock. Neanderthals were short, stout, and powerful. Their braincases were long, low, and wide, and their cranial capacity equaled or surpassed that of modern humans. Their limbs were heavy, but they seem to have walked fully erect and had hands as capable as those of modern humans. They were cave dwellers who used fire, wielded stone tools and wooden spears to hunt animals, buried their dead, and cared for their sick or injured. They may have used language and may have practiced a primitive form of religion.

Nebuchadrezzar II, or NEBUCHADNEZZAR (b. *c.* 630—d. *c.* 561BC), Second and greatest king of the Chaldean dynasty of Babylonia. He began his military career as an administrator (*c.* 610 BC) and ascended the throne on his father's death, just after winning Syria from the Egyptians (605 BC). He attacked Judah, capturing Jerusalem in 597 and recapturing it in 587/586, and deporting prominent citizens to Babylon. He devoted time and energy to restoring Babylon, by paving roads, rebuilding temples, and digging canals. At least in folk tradition, he is credited with building the Hanging Gardens of Babylon.

nebula, Any of various tenuous clouds of gas and dust in interstellar space. Nebulae constitute only a small percentage of a galaxy's mass. Dark nebulae (e.g., the Coalsack) are very dense, cold molecular clouds that appear as large, obscure, irregularly shaped areas in the sky. Bright nebulae (e.g., the Crab Nebula, planetary nebula) appear as faintly luminous, glowing surfaces; they emit their own light or reflect that of stars near them. The term *nebula* also formerly referred to galaxies outside the Milky Way Galaxy.

nectarine, Smooth-skinned peach (*Prunus persica* 'nectarina'),

Nectarine (Prunus persica var. nectarina)
J.C. Allen and Son

grown throughout warmer temperate regions. They result when some peaches self-pollinate or are crossed so that they express a genetic factor for smooth skin. Nectarines are commonly eaten fresh or cooked in desserts and jams; they are a good source of vitamins A and C.

needlepoint, Type of embroidery in which the stitches are counted and worked with a needle over the threads, or mesh, of a canvas foundation. It was known as canvas work until the early 19th century. If the canvas has 16 or more mesh holes per linear inch, the embroidery is called petit point; most needlepoint was petit point in the 16th–18th century. Needlepoint as it is known today originated in the 17th century, when the fashion for furniture upholstered with embroidered fabrics prompted the development of a more durable material to serve as the embroidery's foundation. Wool is generally used for needlepoint, silk yarn less often. Needlepoint kits, containing canvas stamped with a design and all the materials needed for the project, were sold as early as the mid-18th century.

Nefertiti (fl. 14th century BC), Queen of Egypt and wife of Akhenaton (r. 1353–36 BC). She is known from her portrait bust found at Tell el-Amarna, the king's new capital. She may have been an Asian princess from Mitanni. She appears with Akhenaton in reliefs at Tell el-Amarna and followed his new cult of the sun god Aton. Of her six daughters, two became queens of Egypt. In the 12th year of Akhenaton's reign, Nefertiti either retired after losing favour or died. See photograph above.

Nefertiti, painted limestone bust, c. 1350 BCE; in the Egyptian Museum, Berlin.
Bildarchiv Preussischer Kulturbesitz, Ägyptisches Museum, Staatliche Museen zu Berlin/Preussischer Kulturbesitz, Berlin; photograph, Jurgen Liepe

Negev, or HA-NEGEV, Desert region, southern part of Israel. Bounded by the Sinai Peninsula and the Jordan Rift Valley, it has an area of about 4,700 sq mi (12,200 sq km). It was a pastoral region in biblical times and an important source of grain for the Roman Empire. After the Arab conquest of Palestine (7th century AD), it was left desolate, and for more than 1,200 years it had only a small population of Bedouin. Modern agricultural development began with three kibbutzim in 1943; others were founded after World War II (1939–45), when irrigation projects were initiated. Assigned to Israel in the partition of Palestine in 1948, it was the scene of clashes between Israeli and Egyptian forces in 1948–49. It is the site of many preplanned Israeli settlements, including the port city of Elat, Israel's outlet to the Red Sea. Beersheba is an important administrative centre. The region produces grain, fruit, and vegetables; mineral resources include potash, bromine, and copper.

Negritude, Literary movement of the 1930s, '40s, and '50s. It began among French-speaking African and Caribbean writers living in Paris as a protest against French colonial rule and the policy of assimilation. Its leading figures—Léopold Senghor of Senegal, Aimé Césaire of Martinique, and Léon Damas (1912–78) of French Guiana—began to examine Western values critically and to reassess African culture. The group believed that the value and dignity of African traditions and peoples must be asserted, that Africans must look to their own heritage for values and traditions, and that writers should use African subject matter and poetic traditions. The movement faded in the early 1960s after its objectives had been achieved in most African countries.

Nehru, Jawaharlal (b. Nov. 14, 1889, Allahabad, India—d. May 27, 1964, New Delhi), First prime minister of independent India (1947–64). Son of the independence advocate Motilal Nehru (1861–1931), Nehru was educated at home and in Britain and became a lawyer in 1912. More interested in politics than law, he was impressed by Mohandas K. Gandhi's approach to Indian independence. His close association with the Indian National Congress began in 1919; in 1929 he became its president, presiding over the historic Lahore session that proclaimed complete independence (rather than dominion status) as India's political goal. He was imprisoned nine times between 1921 and 1945 for his political activity. When India was granted limited self-government in 1935, the Congress Party under Nehru

Jawaharlal Nehru, photograph by Yousuf Karsh, 1956.
Karsh—Rapho/Photo Researchers

refused to form coalition governments with the Muslim League in some provinces; the hardening of relations between Hindus and Muslims that followed ultimately led to the partition of India and the creation of Pakistan. Shortly before Gandhi's assassination in 1948, Nehru became the first prime minister of independent India. He attempted a foreign policy of nonalignment during the Cold War, drawing harsh criticism if he appeared to favour either camp. During his tenure, India clashed with Pakistan over the Kashmir region and with China over the Brahmaputra River valley. He wrested Goa from the Portuguese. Domestically, he promoted democracy, socialism, secularism, and unity, adapting modern values to Indian conditions. His daughter, Indira Gandhi, became prime minister two years after his death.

nematode, or ROUNDWORM, Any of more than 15,000 named

and many more unnamed species of worms in the class Nematoda (phylum Aschelminthes). Nematodes include plant and animal parasites and free-living forms found in soil, freshwater, saltwater, and even vinegar and beer malts. They are bilaterally symmetrical and usually tapered at both ends. Some species have separate sexes; others are hermaphroditic. They range from microscopic to about 23 ft (7 m) long. Nematode parasites can occur in almost any body organ but are most common in the digestive, circulatory, or respiratory system. Hookworms, pinworms, and eelworms are nematodes.

Nematode (Ascaris lumbricoides)
Javier Palaus Soler/Ostman Agency

Neo-Confucianism, In China, a rationalistic revival of Confucianism in the 11th century that influenced Chinese thought for 800 years. The movement sought to reestablish the supremacy of the Confucian heritage over the increasingly popular Buddhism and Daoism. Its two principal schools of thought were the Lixue (School of Principle), whose chief philosopher was Zhu Xi, and the Xinxue (School of Mind), represented by Lu Xiangshan and Wang Yangming. Neo-Confucianism was introduced into Japan by Zen Buddhists and became the guiding philosophy of the Tokugawa period (1603–1867), providing a heavenly sanction for the existing social order. Its emphasis on classical literature led to renewed interest in the Japanese classics and a revival of Shintō studies.

Neo-Paganism, Any of several movements that attempt to revive the polytheistic religions of Europe and the Middle East. Largely a product of the 1960s, contemporary Neo-Paganism has flourished particularly in the U.S., Britain, and Scandinavia. Its adherents often have deep ecological concerns and an attachment to nature; many worship an earth-mother goddess and center their rituals on the change of the seasons. Since the late 1970s, Neo-Paganism has also attracted feminists open to female personifications of the deity. Major Neo-Pagan groups include the Church of All Worlds, Feraferia, Pagan Way, the Reformed Druids of North America, the Church of the Eternal Source, and the Viking Brotherhood.

Neoclassical architecture, Revival of Classical architecture during the 18th and early 19th centuries. The movement concerned itself with the logic of entire Classical volumes, unlike Classical revivalism, which tended to reuse Classical parts. Neoclassical architecture is characterized by grandeur of scale; simplicity of geometric forms; Greek, especially Doric, or Roman detail; dramatic use of columns; and a preference for blank walls. The new taste for antique simplicity represented a general reaction to the excesses of the Rococo style. Neoclassicism thrived in the U.S. and Europe, with examples occurring in almost every

major city. Russia's Catherine II transformed St. Petersburg into an unparalleled collection of Neoclassical buildings as advanced as any contemporary French and English work. By 1800 nearly all new British architecture reflected the Neoclassical spirit. France's boldest innovator was Claude-Nicolas Ledoux, who had a central role in the evolution of Neoclassical architecture. In the U.S. Neoclassicism continued to flourish throughout the 19th century, as many architects looked to make the analogy between the young country and imperial Rome when designing major government buildings. The style also spread to colonial Latin America.

neofascism, Political philosophy and movement that arose in Europe in the decades following World War II. Like earlier fascist movements, neofascism advocated extreme nationalism, opposed liberal individualism, attacked Marxist and other left-wing ideologies, indulged in racist and xenophobic scapegoating, and promoted populist right-wing economic programs. Unlike the fascists, however, neofascists placed more blame for their countries' problems on non-European immigrants than on leftists and Jews, displayed little interest in taking lebensraum (German: "living space") through the military conquest of other states, and made concerted efforts to portray themselves as democratic and "mainstream." The National Front in France, led by Jean-Marie Le Pen, and the Liberal-Democratic Party in Russia, led by Vladimir Zhirinovsky, are often cited as neofascist.

Neolithic Period, or NEW STONE AGE, Final stage of technological development or cultural evolution among prehistoric humans. It is characterized by the use of stone tools shaped by polishing or grinding, the domestication of plants or animals, the establishment of permanent villages, and the practice of such crafts as pottery and weaving. The Neolithic followed the Paleolithic Period (and in northwestern Europe the Mesolithic) and preceded the Bronze Age. Its beginning is associated with the villages that emerged in South Asia *c.* 9000 BC and flourished in the Tigris and Euphrates river valleys from *c.* 7000 BC. Farming spread northward throughout Eurasia, reaching Britain and Scandinavia only after 3000 BC. Neolithic technologies also spread to the Indus River valley of India by 5000 BC and to the Huang Ho valley of China by *c.* 3500 BC. The term is not applied to the New World, though Neolithic modes of life were achieved independently there by *c.* 2500 BC.

Nepal, Country, southern Asia. Area: 56,827 sq mi (147,181 sq km). Population: (2011 est.) 26,629,000. Capital: Kathmandu. Most of the people are Nepalese of Indo-European ancestry; there is a significant minority of Tibeto-Nepalese peoples. Languages: Nepali (official), English, various others. Religions: Hinduism; also Buddhism, Islam. Currency: Nepalese rupee. Nepal contains some of the most rugged mountainous terrain in the world. The Great Himalayas, including Mount Everest, are in its central and northern parts. As a result of its years of geographic and self-imposed isolation, it is one of the world's least-developed countries. Its market economy is mostly based on agriculture, including livestock raising; tourism is also important. The region developed under early Buddhist influence, with dynastic rule dating to about the 4th century CE. Nepal was formed into a single kingdom in 1769 and fought border wars in the 18th–19th century. Its independence was recognized by Britain in 1923. Nepal operated as a constitutional monarchy from 1959 into the early 21st century. A new constitution in 1990 restricted royal authority and accepted a democratically elected parliamentary government. Nepal signed trade agreements with India in 1997. The country was stunned in 2001 when the crown prince killed most members of the royal family, including himself. After a historic vote by a constituent assembly in 2008, the monarchy was abolished, and Nepal became a multiparty republic with an interim legislature. The president is head of state, and the prime minister is head of government.

nephritis, Inflammation of the kidneys. There are numerous kinds, involving different kidney tissues. The most common type is Bright disease. Symptoms vary with the type of nephritis; severe cases can result in kidney failure. Causes include infection, allergy or autoimmune disease, blockage in the urinary system, and hereditary diseases. Treatment addresses the cause where possible.

Neptune, Eighth planet from the Sun, discovered in 1846 and named for the Roman god of the sea. It has an average distance from the Sun of 2.8 billion mi (4.5 billion km), taking nearly 164 years to complete one orbit and rotating every 16.11 hours. Neptune has more than 17 times Earth's mass, 58 times its volume, and 12% stronger gravity at the top of its atmosphere. It has an equatorial diameter of 30,775 mi (49,528 km). Neptune consists largely of hydrogen and helium. It has no solid surface; its interior is believed to consist of a fluid mixture of rock, ices, and gas. Its atmosphere contains substantial amounts of methane gas, whose absorption of red light causes Neptune's deep blue-green colour. The Voyager 2 space probe in 1989 discovered winds of over 1,570 mi/hour (700 m/second), the fastest known for any of the Sun's planets, and dark spots that appear to be storms similar to Jupiter's Great Red Spot. Neptune receives little solar radiation, but it radiates substantially more energy than it receives, which indicates an internal heat source. Neptune's weak magnetic field traps charged particles in a belt around the planet. Neptune has a system of rings, made up largely of dust-size particles, and at least 13 moons; the largest is Triton, almost as big as Earth's Moon.

Neptune, In Roman religion, the god of water. Neptune was originally the god of fresh water, but by 399 BC he was identified with the Greek god Poseidon and thus became a deity of the sea. His female counterpart, Salacia, probably began as a goddess of spring water but was later equated with the Greek goddess Amphitrite. Neptune's festival (Neptunalia) took place in the heat of summer (July 23), when fresh water was scarcest. In art Neptune is often given Poseidon's attributes, the trident and dolphin.

Neruda, Pablo, orig. NEFTALÍ RICARDO REYES BASOALTO (b. July 12, 1904, Parral, Chile—d. Sept. 23, 1973, Santiago), Chilean poet and diplomat. He began writing poetry at age 10, and at 20 he published his most widely read work, *Twenty Love Poems and a Song of Despair* (1924), inspired by an unhappy love affair. In 1927 he was named an honorary consul, and he later represented Chile in several Asian and Latin American countries; late in life he was ambassador to France. While in Asia he began *Residence on Earth* (1933, 1935, 1947), a verse cycle remarkable for its examination of social decay and personal isolation. In 1945 he was elected senator and joined the Communist Party; he later spent years in exile when the government turned toward the right. *Canto General* (1950), his great epic poem about the American continents, was deeply influenced by Walt Whitman and is the culminating expression of his political beliefs. *Elemental Odes* (1954) celebrates common, everyday objects. He was awarded the Nobel Prize for Literature in 1971.

Pablo Neruda.
Camera Press/Globe Photos

nerve gas, Weapon of chemical warfare that affects the transmission of nerve impulses through the nervous system. The organophosphorus nerve agents Tabun, Sarin, and Soman were developed by Germany during World War II but not used. They and a newer agent, VX, were produced in huge quantities by the U.S. and Soviet Union during the Cold War; their stockpiling and use during war are now banned by the Chemical Weapons Convention of 1993. A single droplet of VX or Sarin, if inhaled or in contact with the skin, can be absorbed into the bloodstream and paralyze the nervous system, leading to respiratory failure and immediate death. Sarin was used in 1995 in a lethal attack in the Tokyo subways by members of AUM Shinrikyo.

nervous system, System of specialized cells (neurons, or nerve cells) that conduct stimuli from a sensory receptor through a neuron network to the site (e.g., a gland or muscle) where the response occurs. In humans, it consists of the central and peripheral nervous systems, the former consisting of the brain and spinal cord and the latter of the nerves, which carry impulses to and from the central nervous system. The cranial nerves handle head and neck sensory and motor activities, except the vagus nerve, which conducts signals to visceral organs. Each spinal nerve is attached to the spinal cord by a sensory and a motor root. These exit between the vertebrae and merge to form a large mixed nerve, which branches to supply a defined area of the body. Disorders include amyotrophic lateral sclerosis, chorea, epilepsy, myasthenia gravis, neural tube defect, parkinsonism, and poliomyelitis. Effects of disorders range from transient tics and minor personality changes to major personality disruptions, seizures, paralysis, and death.

Ness, Loch, Lake, Highland council area, Scotland. It is 788 ft (240 m) deep and about 23 mi (36 km) long and has the largest volume of fresh water in Britain. It forms part of the Caledonian Canal system developed by Thomas Telford. On its shores are remains of two fortresses. Surface oscillations, or seiches, caused by differential heating, are common. Reports of an aquatic monster inhabiting Loch Ness date back centuries but remain unproved.

Nestorian, Member of a Christian sect that originated in Asia Minor and Syria in the 5th century AD, inspired by the views of Nestorius. Nestorians stressed the independence of Christ's divine and human natures. Nestorian scholars played a prominent role in the formation of Arab culture after the Arab conquest of Persia; Nestorianism also spread to India, China, Egypt, and Central Asia, where certain tribes were almost entirely converted. Today the Nestorians are represented by the Church of the East, or Persian church, usually referred to in the West as the Assyrian or Nestorian church. Most of its members, who number more than 200,000, live in Iraq, Syria, and Iran.

Netherlands, officially KINGDOM OF THE NETHERLANDS, byname HOLLAND, Country, northwestern Europe. Area: 16,040 sq mi (41,543 sq km). Population: (2011 est.) 16,683,000. Capital: Amsterdam. Seat of government: The Hague. Most of the people are Dutch. Languages: Dutch (official), English. Religions: Christianity (Roman Catholic, Protestant); also Islam. Currency: euro. The Netherlands' southern and eastern region consists mostly of plains and a few high ridges; its western and northern region is lower and includes polders on the site of the Zuiderzee and the common delta of the Rhine, Meuse, and Schelde rivers. Coastal areas are almost completely below sea level and are protected by dunes and artificial dikes. Although densely populated, the country has a low birth rate. Its developed market economy is based largely on financial services, light and heavy industries, and trade. It is a constitutional monarchy with a parliament comprising two chambers; its head of state is the monarch, and the head of government is the prime minister. Celtic and Germanic tribes inhabited the region at the time of the Roman conquest. Under the Romans trade and industry flourished, but by the mid-3rd century CE Roman power had waned, eroded by resurgent Germanic tribes and the encroachment of the sea. A Germanic invasion (406–407) ended Roman control. The Merovingian dynasty followed the Romans but was supplanted in the 7th century by the Carolingian dynasty, which converted the area to Christianity. After Charlemagne's death in 814, the area was increasingly the target of Viking attacks. It became part of the medieval kingdom of Lotharingia, which avoided incorporation into the Holy Roman Empire by investing its bishops and abbots with secular powers, leading to the establishment of an imperial church. Beginning in the 12th century, much land was reclaimed from the sea as dike building occurred on a large scale; Flanders developed as a textiles centre. The dukes of Burgundy gained control in the late 14th century. By the early 16th century the Low Countries came to be ruled by the Spanish Habsburgs. The Dutch had taken the lead in fishing and shipbuilding, which laid the foundation for Holland's remarkable 17th-century prosperity. Culturally, this was the period of Jan van Eyck, Thomas à Kempis, and Desiderius Erasmus. Calvinism and Anabaptist doctrines attracted many followers. In 1581 the seven northern provinces, led by Calvinists, declared their independence from Spain, and in 1648, following the Thirty Years' War, Spain recognized Dutch independence. The 17th century was the golden age of Dutch civilization. Benedict de Spinoza and René Descartes enjoyed the intellectual freedom, and Rembrandt and Johannes Vermeer painted their masterpieces. The Dutch East India Co. secured Asian colonies, and the country's standard of living soared. In the 18th century Dutch maritime power declined; the region was conquered by the French during the French revolutionary wars and became the Kingdom of Holland under Napoleon (1806). The Netherlands remained neutral in World War I and declared neutrality in World War II but was occupied by Germany. After the war it lost the Netherlands Indies (Indonesia from 1949) and Netherlands New Guinea (in 1962; now the Indonesian provinces of Papua and West Papua). It joined NATO in 1949 and was a founding member of the European Economic Community (later renamed the European Community and now embedded in the European Union). At the outset of the 21st century the Netherlands benefitted from a strong, highly regulated mixed economy but struggled with the social and economic challenges of immigration.

Netherlands Antilles, formerly CURAÇAO, Former (1954–2010) nonmetropolitan island territory of the Netherlands, in the Caribbean Sea. Area: 308 sq mi (800 sq km). Population: (2010 est.) 204,000. Capital: Willemstad, on Curaçao. It consisted of two widely separated groups of islands in the Caribbean Sea: Sint Eustatius, the southern section of St. Martin, and Saba made up the northern group, at the northern end of the Leeward Islands; and Curaçao, Bonaire, and, until 1986, Aruba constituted the southern group, about 500 mi (800 km) to the southwest, off the coast of Venezuela. Originally inhabited by Arawak and Carib Indians, the islands were encountered by Spanish explorers in the late 15th century and were claimed for Spain. In the 17th century the Dutch gained control, and in 1845 the islands were brought under collective administration, with its seat of government in Curaçao. In 1954 they were reorganized as the Federation of the Netherlands Antilles and became an integral part of the Netherlands with full autonomy in domestic affairs. Aruba seceded from the federation in 1986. In 2006 the island and the Dutch government agreed to dismantle the Netherlands Antilles, which took place in 2010. Sint Maarten and Curaçao became autonomous states within the Netherlands. Bonaire, Saba, and Sint Eustatius became special municipalities of the Netherlands.

Neuilly, Treaty of (November 27, 1919) Peace treaty between Bulgaria and the Allied Powers after World War I, signed at Neuilly-sur-Seine, France. Bulgaria was forced to reduce its army to 20,000 men, cede lands to Yugoslavia and Greece that involved the transfer of 300,000 people, and pay reparations to the Allies.

neural network, Type of parallel computation in which computing elements are modeled on the network of neurons that constitute animal nervous systems. This model, intended to simulate the way the brain processes information, enables the computer to "learn" to a certain degree. A neural network typically consists of a number of interconnected processors, or nodes. Each handles a designated sphere of knowledge, and has several inputs and one output to the network. Based on the inputs it gets, a node can "learn" about the relationships between sets of data, sometimes using the principles of fuzzy logic. For example, a backgammon program can store and grade results from moves in a game; in the next game, it can play a move based on its stored result and can regrade the stored result if the move is unsuccessful. Neural networks have been used in pattern recognition, speech analysis, oil exploration, weather prediction, and the modeling of thinking and consciousness.

neural tube defect, Congenital defect of the brain or spinal cord from abnormal growth of their precursor, the neural tube, usually with spine or skull defects. The tube may fail to close properly, have parts missing, or have a blockage. In spina bifida, vertebrae are open over the back of the spinal cord, usually at the base. This may not affect function if no further defects (local absence of skin or meninges, protrusion of tissue, defect opening into the spinal cord) exist. The more serious forms can cause paralysis and impair bladder and bowel function. In encephalocele, a meningeal sac containing brain tissue protrudes from the skull. The effects depend on the amount of tissue involved. Adequate folic-acid intake by women of childbearing age reduces the risk of neural tube defects. Early surgery can prevent or minimize disability.

neuralgia, Pain of unknown cause in the area covered by a peripheral sensory nerve. In trigeminal neuralgia (tic douloureux), brief attacks of severe shooting pain along a branch of the trigeminal nerve (in front of the ear) usually begin after middle age, more often in women. Initially weeks or months apart, they become more frequent and easily triggered by touching the affected area, talking, eating, or cold. Analgesics help, but permanent cure requires surgery. Glossopharyngeal neuralgia causes recurring severe pain, most often in men over 40. Excruciating pains begin in the throat and radiate to the ears or down the neck, with or without a trigger (e.g., sneezing, yawning, chewing). Usually separated by long intervals, attacks subside before analgesics take effect. Surgery may help in extreme cases.

neuritis, Inflammation of one or several nerves. The cause may be mechanical, vascular, allergic, toxic, metabolic, or viral. Symptoms—tingling, burning, or stabbing pains with sensory nerves and anything from muscle weakness to paralysis with motor nerves—are usually confined to the part of the body served by the inflamed nerve. In Bell palsy, facial nerve inflammation causes a characteristic facial muscle distortion. Analgesics can relieve the pain. Once the underlying cause is treated, recovery is usually rapid but may be incomplete in severe cases, with residual motor and sensory disturbances.

neuron, or NERVE CELL, Any of the cells of the nervous system. Sensory neurons relay information from sense organs, motor neurons carry impulses to muscles and glands, and interneurons transmit impulses between sensory and motor neurons. A typical neuron consists of dendrites (fibres that receive stimuli and conduct them inward), a cell body (a nucleated body that receives input from dendrites), and an axon (a fibre that conducts the nerve impulse from the cell body outward to the axon terminals). Both axons and dendrites may be referred to as nerve fibres. Impulses are relayed by neurotransmitter chemicals released by the axon terminals across the synapses (junctions between neurons or between a neuron and an effector cell, such as a muscle cell) or, in some cases, pass directly from one neuron to the next. Large axons are insulated by a myelin sheath formed by fatty cells called Schwann cells. Bundles of fibres from neurons held together by connective tissue form nerves.

neuropathy, Disorder of the peripheral nervous system. It may be genetic or acquired, progress quickly or slowly, involve motor, sensory, and/or autonomic nerves, and affect only certain nerves or all of them. It can cause pain or loss of sensation, weakness, paralysis, loss of reflexes, muscle atrophy, or, in autonomic neuropathies, disturbances of blood pressure, heart rate, or bladder and bowel control; impotence; and inability to focus the eyes. Some types damage the neuron itself, others the myelin sheath that insulates it. Examples include carpal tunnel syndrome, amyotrophic lateral sclerosis, poliomyelitis, and shingles. Causes include diseases (e.g., diabetes mellitus, leprosy, syphilis), injury, toxins, and vitamin deficiency (e.g., beriberi).

neuroplasticity, Capacity of neurons and neural networks in the brain to change their connections and behaviour in response to new information, sensory stimulation, development, damage, or dysfunction. Rapid change or reorganization of the brain's cellular or neural networks can take place in many different forms and under many different circumstances. Neuroplasticity occurs when neurons in the brain sprout and form synapses. As the brain processes sensory information, frequently used synapses are strengthened while unused synapses weaken. Eventually, unused synapses are eliminated completely in a process known as synaptic pruning, which leaves behind efficient networks of neural connections. Neuroplasticity occurs during development in childhood, following physical injury such as loss of a limb or sense organ, and during reinforcement of sensory information such as in learning. Neuroplasticity forms the basis of research into brain-computer interface technology, in which computers are designed to interact with the brain to restore sensation in people with an impaired sense such as the loss of vision. Research on neuroplasticity is also aimed at improving scientists' understanding of how to reactivate or deactivate damaged areas of the brain in people affected by stroke, emotional disorders, chronic pain, psychopathy, or social phobia; such research may lead to improved treatments for these conditions.

neuropsychology, Science concerned with the integration of psychological observations on behaviour with neurological observations on the central nervous system (CNS), including the brain. The field emerged through the work of Paul Broca and Carl Wernicke (1848–1905), both of whom identified sites on the cerebral cortex involved in the production or comprehension of language. Great strides have since been made in describing neuroanatomical systems and their relation to higher mental processes. The related field of neuropsychiatry addresses itself to disorders such as aphasia, Korsakoff syndrome, Tourette syndrome, and other CNS abnormalities.

neurosis, Mental and emotional disorder that affects only part of the personality, is accompanied by a less distorted perception of reality than in a psychosis, and is characterized by various physiological and mental disturbances (such as visceral symptoms and impaired concentration). The neuroses include anxiety attacks, certain forms of depression, hypochondriasis, hysterical reactions, obsessive-compulsive disorders, phobias, various sexual dysfunctions, and some tics. They have traditionally been thought to be based on emotional conflict in which a blocked impulse seeks expression in a disguised response or symptom. Behavioral psychologists regard them as learned, inappropriate responses to stress, which can be unlearned.

neurotransmitter, Chemical released by neurons to stimulate neighbouring neurons, allowing impulses to be passed from one cell to the next throughout the nervous system. A nerve impulse arriving at the axon terminal of one neuron stimulates release of a neurotransmitter, which crosses the microscopic gap in milliseconds to the adjoining neuron's dendrite. Many chemicals are believed to act as neurotransmitters. The few that have been identified include acetylcholine, dopamine, and serotonin. Some neurotransmitters activate neurons; others inhibit them. Some mind-altering drugs act by changing synaptic activity.

neutrino, Fundamental particle with no electric charge, little mass, and a spin value of $1/2$. Neutrinos belong to the lepton family of subatomic particles. There are three types of neutrino, each associated with a charged lepton: the electron, the muon, and the tau. Neutrinos are the most penetrating of subatomic particles because they react with matter only by the weak force. They do not cause ionization, because they are not electrically charged. All types of neutrino have masses much smaller than their charged partners.

neutron, One of the constituent particles of every atomic nucleus except ordinary hydrogen. Discovered in 1932 by James Chadwick (1891–1974), it has no electric charge and has nearly 1,840 times the mass of the electron. Free neutrons undergo beta decay with a half-life of about 10 minutes. Thus, they are not readily found in nature, except in cosmic rays. They are a penetrating form of radiation. When bombarded with neutrons, various elements undergo nuclear fission and release more free neutrons. If enough free neutrons are produced, a chain reaction can be sustained. This process led to the development of nuclear power as well as the atomic bomb. Neutron beams produced in cyclotrons and nuclear reactors are important probes of matter, revealing details of structure in both organic and inorganic susbtances.

neutron bomb, or ENHANCED RADIATION WARHEAD, Small thermonuclear weapon that produces minimal blast and heat but releases large amounts of lethal radiation. The blast and heat are confined to a radius of only a few hundred yards; within a somewhat larger area, the bomb throws off a massive wave of neutron and gamma radiation, which is extremely destructive to living tissue. Such a bomb could be used with deadly efficiency against tank and infantry formations on the battlefield without endangering towns or cities only a few miles away. It can be carried in a missile or delivered by a howitzer or even an attack aircraft.

neutron star, Any of a class of extremely dense, compact stars thought to be composed mainly of neutrons with a thin outer atmosphere of primarily iron atoms and electrons and protons. Though typically about 12 mi (20 km) in diameter, they have a mass roughly twice the Sun's and thus extremely high densities (about 100 trillion times that of water). Neutron stars have very strong magnetic fields. A solid surface differentiates them from black holes. Below the surface, the pressure is much too high for individual atoms to exist; protons and electrons are compacted together into neutrons. The discovery of pulsars in 1967 provided the first evidence of the existence of neutron stars, predicted in the early 1930s and believed by most investigators to be formed in supernova explosions.

New Age movement, Movement that spread through occult communities in the 1970s and '80s. It looked forward to a "New Age" of love and peace and offered a foretaste of the coming era through personal transformation and healing. The movement's strongest supporters were followers of esotericism, a religious perspective based on the acquisition of mystical knowledge. At its height, the movement attracted millions of Americans, who practiced astrology, yoga, and channeling and used crystals as healing tools. Adherents sought to bring about global transformation, and in 1987 many participated in the Harmonic Convergence, an attempt to accomplish that goal.

New Caledonia, French unique collectivity, southwestern South Pacific Ocean. It consists of the islands of New Caledonia and Walpole, the Isle of Pines, and several other island groups. Area: 7,172 sq mi (18,575 sq km). Population: (2011 est.) 255,000. Capital: Nouméa. Two small islands—Matthew and Hunter, to the east of New Caledonia—are claimed by both France (for New Caledonia) and Vanuatu. The main island, New Caledonia, has rich deposits of nickel that are among the largest in the world. Archaeological excavations indicate an Austronesian presence in the area *c.* 2000–1000 BCE. The islands were visited by Capt. James Cook in 1774 and by various navigators and traders in the 18th–19th century. They were occupied by France in 1853 and were a penal colony from 1864 to 1897. New Caledonians joined the Free French cause of Charles de Gaulle in 1940; the islands were the site of Allied bases during the Pacific war. They became a French overseas territory in 1946. In 1987 residents voted by referendum to remain part of France.

New Church, or SWEDENBORGIANS, Church whose members follow the teachings of Emanuel Swedenborg. Swedenborg did not himself found a church, but he believed that his writings would be the basis of a "new church," which he associated with the "new Jerusalem" mentioned in the Book of Revelation. In 1788, soon after his death, a group of his followers established a church in London. The first Swedenborgian society in the U.S. was organized in Baltimore in 1792. Baptism and the Lord's Supper are the two sacraments of the church, and New Church Day (June 19) is added to the established Christian festivals. There are three New Church groups: the General Conference of the New Church, the General Convention of the New Jerusalem in the U.S.A., and the General Church of the New Jerusalem.

New Deal, U.S. domestic program of Pres. Franklin Roosevelt to bring economic relief (1933–39). The term was taken from Roosevelt's speech accepting the 1932 presidential nomination, in which he promised "a new deal for the American people." New Deal legislation was enacted mainly in the first three months of 1933 (Roosevelt's "hundred days") and established such agencies as the Civil Works Administration and the Civilian Conservation Corps to alleviate unemployment, the National Recovery Administration to revive industrial production, the Federal Deposit Insurance Corp. and the Securities and Exchange Commission to regulate financial institutions, the Agricultural Adjustment Administration to support farm production, and the Tennessee Valley Authority to provide public power and flood control. A second period of legislation (1935–36), often called the second New Deal, established the National Labor Relations Board, the Works Progress Administration, and the social security system. Some legislation was declared unconstitutional by the U.S. Supreme Court, and some programs did not accomplish their aims, but many reforms were continued by later administrations and permanently changed the role of government.

New Delhi, City (pop., 2001: 302,363), capital of India, located on the western bank of the Yamuna River, south of Delhi city (Old Delhi) in the Delhi national capital territory. Construction of the city began in 1912, and it was formally dedicated in 1931. In contrast to the narrow and winding streets characteristic of Old Delhi, New Delhi has a straight diagonal street pattern that features large green spaces and broad vistas. The main east-west axis is Central Vista Park, a thoroughfare lined with government buildings, museums, and research centres.

New Guinea, Indonesian IRIAN, Island, eastern Malay Archipelago, western Pacific Ocean, north of Australia. Divided roughly in half between Indonesia (west) and Papua New Guinea (east), New Guinea is the second largest island in the world (after Greenland). It is about 1,500 mi (2,400 km) long and 400 mi (650 km) wide at its widest point, with an area of about 309,000 sq mi (800,000 sq km). The terrain ranges from lowland rainforest to fertile highlands and a rugged mountainous spine; its climate is tropical. Copper and gold are its chief mineral resources. The majority of the people of New Guinea are subsistence farmers.

New Orleans, City (pop., 2010: 343,829), southeastern Louisiana, U.S. Situated between the Mississippi River and Lake Pontchartrain, it is the state's largest city and a major deepwater port. Founded in 1718 by French colonist Jean-Baptiste Le Moyne de Bienville, it was ceded to Spain in 1763. In 1800 it was ceded back to France and three years later sold to the U.S. by Napoleon. Incorporated in 1805, it was the state capital from 1812 to 1849. During the American Civil War the city was captured and occupied by Union forces (1862). A notable tourist centre, its attractions include Mardi Gras and the French Quarter, a popular tourist area noted for its nightclubs and Creole architecture and cuisine. It is

also a medical, industrial, and educational centre. It was devastated by Hurricane Katrina in August 2005, when the levees protecting the city were breached and nearly all the city was flooded.

new religious movement (NRM), Any religion originating in recent centuries having characteristic traits including eclecticism and syncretism, a leader who claims extraordinary powers, and a "countercultural" aspect. Regarded as outside the mainstream of society, NRMs in the West are extremely diverse but include millennialist movements (e.g., the Jehovah's Witnesses), Westernized Hindu or Buddhist movements (e.g., the Hare Krishna movement), so-called "scientific" groups (e.g., Scientology), and nature religions. In the East they include China's 19th-century Taiping movement and present-day Falun Gong movement, Japan's Tenrikyo and PL Kyodan, and Korea's Ch'ondogyo and Unification Church. Some NRMs fade away or meet tragic ends; others, such as the Mormon church, eventually become accepted as mainstream.

New South Wales, State, southeastern Australia. Area: 309,130 sq mi (800,642 sq km). Population: (2006) 6,549,177; (2010 est.) 7,232,589. Capital: Sydney. It is bounded by Queensland, the Pacific Ocean, Victoria, and South Australia. The dominant geographic feature is the Great Dividing Range. Inhabited from prehistoric times, New South Wales was claimed for Britain by Capt. James Cook in 1770. The colony included the entire continent except for Western Australia. The interior was explored throughout the 19th century, and colonies were set up there, separate from New South Wales. In 1901 it became part of the Commonwealth of Australia. The state ceded the area of the Australian Capital Territory in 1911. New South Wales is the centre of commercial farming, industry, and culture in Australia.

New Testament, Second of the two major divisions of the Christian Bible. Christians see the New Testament as the fulfillment of the promise of the Old Testament. It recounts the life and ministry of Jesus and interprets their meaning for the early church, focusing especially on the new covenant created between God and the followers of Jesus. There are 27 books in the New Testament: four Gospels, or stories of the life and teachings of Christ; the Acts of the Apostles, a historical narrative of the first years of the Christian church; 21 epistles, or letters of advice and instruction to early Christians; and the Book of Revelation, a description of the coming apocalypse. Most were written in the later 1st century AD, though none can be dated precisely. Only two authors are known for certain: St. Paul, credited with 13 epistles; and St. Luke, writer of the third gospel and the Book of Acts. Attributions of other authors range from highly likely (for the other three gospels) to completely unknown (for the Epistle to the Hebrews). These documents circulated among the early churches and were used as preaching and teaching sources. The earliest known list of the current New Testament canon dates from AD 367 in a work by St. Athanasius. A church council of 382 gave final approval to the list.

New Wave, French NOUVELLE VAGUE, Group of individualistic French film directors of the late 1950s, including Claude Chabrol, François Truffaut, Jean-Luc Godard, Louis Malle, Eric Rohmer, Alain Resnais, and others. Most of the New Wave directors were associated with the important film magazine *Cahiers du Cinéma*, in which they developed the highly influential auteur theory, calling for films to express the director's personal vision. Their films were characterized by a brilliance of technique that sometimes overshadowed the subject matter. Among the most important New Wave films were Godard's *Breathless* (1959), Truffaut's *The 400 Blows* (1959), and Resnais's *Hiroshima mon amour* (1959).

New Year's Day, First day of the new year, celebrated with religious, cultural, and social observances around the world. It is usually marked by rites and ceremonies that symbolize casting off the old year and rejoicing in the new. Most of the world recognizes January 1 as the start of a new year because the Gregorian calendar, from its papal origin in 1582, has become the international reference for treaties, corporate contracts, and other legal documents. Nevertheless, numerous religious and national calendars have been retained. For example, in the Persian calendar (used in Iran and Afghanistan) New Year's Day falls on the spring equinox (March 20 or 21 in the Gregorian calendar). The more widely employed Islamic (Hijrī) calendar is based on 12 lunar months of 29 or 30 days; thus, the Islamic New Year's Day gradually regresses through the longer Gregorian calendar. The Hindu new year starts on the day following the first new moon on or after the spring equinox. The Chinese new year begins at sunset on the new moon in the sign of Aquarius (late January or early February). The Hebrew calendar is based on 12 lunar months (13 in certain years) of 29 or 30 days; the Jewish New Year's Day, or Rosh Hashanah, can fall anytime from September 6 to October 5 in the Gregorian calendar.

New York City, City (pop., 2010: 8,175,133), southeastern New York, at the mouth of the Hudson River. The largest city in the U.S. and an important seaport, it consists of five boroughs: the Bronx, Brooklyn, Manhattan, Queens, and Staten Island. The site of a Dutch trading post on Manhattan Island, it was colonized as New Amsterdam by Dutch director general Peter Minuit, who bought it from the Indians in 1626. The colony surrendered to the British in 1664 and was renamed New York. It was the capital of the state (1784–97) and of the U.S. (1789–90). The economy grew after the opening of the Erie Canal in 1825, and the city expanded rapidly after the American Civil War, developing transportation and communications systems. In 1898 the five boroughs were merged into a single city. Long a magnet for immigrants to the U.S., it is a centre of world trade and finance, media, art, entertainment, and fashion. Because of its prominence and its central role in world commerce, the city was a target for acts of terrorism. In the September 11 attacks of 2001, hijackers intentionally flew airliners into the twin towers of the World Trade Center, destroying them and destroying or damaging several adjacent buildings and killing some 2,800 people.

New York Stock Exchange (NYSE), Leading marketplace for securities. The exchange began as an informal meeting of 24 men in 1792 on what is now Wall Street in New York City. It was formally constituted as the New York Stock and Exchange Board in 1817, and its present name was adopted in 1863. Since 1868 membership has been obtained by purchasing a seat from an existing member; membership has been limited to 1,366 since 1953. The exchange provided capital for the industrialization of the U.S. in the 19th century. After the panic of 1837 it began to demand that companies disclose information about their finances to the public as a condition of offering stock. The stock-market crash of 1929 led to regulation by the Securities and Exchange Commission. To be listed on the NYSE, a company must meet minimum requirements, including quantitative criteria such as earnings, market value, number of shares outstanding, and trading volume and qualitative criteria such as voting rights from common stockholders, the publication of periodic financial statements, and a majority of independent members in the company's board of directors. In 2008 the NYSE's parent company, NYSE Euronext, agreed to acquire the American Stock Exchange.

New Zealand, Island country, South Pacific Ocean. Area: 104,515 sq mi (270,692 sq km). Population: (2011 est.) 4,407,000. Capital: Wellington. Most of the people are of European origin; about one-tenth are Maori, and some are Pacific Islanders and Chinese. Languages: English, Maori (both official). Religions: Christianity (Protestant, Roman Catholic); also Buddhism, Hinduism. Currency: New Zealand dollar. New Zealand consists of the North Island and the South Island, which are separated by Cook Strait, and several smaller islands. Both main islands are bisected by mountain ranges. New Zealand has a developing market economy based largely on agriculture (dominated by sheep raising), small-scale industries, and services. It is a constitutional monarchy with

one legislative house; its head of state is the British monarch, represented by the governor-general, and the head of government is the prime minister. Polynesian occupation dates to *c.* 1000 CE. First sighted by Dutch explorer Abel Janszoon Tasman in 1642, the main islands were charted by Capt. James Cook in 1769. Named a British crown colony in 1840, the area was the scene of warfare between colonists and native Maori through the 1860s. The capital was moved from Auckland to Wellington in 1865, and in 1907 the colony became the Dominion of New Zealand. It administered Western Samoa (now Samoa) from 1919 to 1962 and participated in both World Wars. When Britain joined the European Economic Community in the early 1970s, its influence led New Zealand to expand its export markets and diversify its economy. New Zealand also became more independent in its foreign relations and took a strong stand against nuclear proliferation. The literacy rate is nearly 100%. The cultural milieu is predominantly European, although there has been a revival of traditional Maori culture and art, and Maori social and economic activism have been central to political developments in New Zealand since the late 20th century.

newspaper, Publication usually issued daily, weekly, or at other regular times that provides news, views, features, and other information of public interest and often carries advertising. Forerunners of the modern newspaper appeared as early as ancient Rome. More or less regular papers printed from movable type appeared in Germany, Italy, and the Netherlands in the early 17th century. The first English daily was *The Daily Courant* (1702–35). Though preceded by official papers, James Franklin's *New-England Courant* (1721) was the first independent newspaper in Britain's North American colonies. By 1800 the principles of a free press and a basic formula for both serious and popular papers were taking root in much of Europe and the U.S. In the 19th century the number of U.S. papers and their circulations rose dramatically, owing to wider literacy, broadening appeal, lower prices, and technological advances in typesetting, printing, communications, and transport. By late in the century, newspapers had achieved great power. Competition for readers often led to sensationalism and, in the 20th century, gave rise to the so-called tabloids. Since 1900 newspaper publishing worldwide has expanded greatly; in large countries it has experienced consolidation and mergers. Nearly all the world's major newspapers began publishing online editions in the early 21st century.

newton, Absolute unit of force, abbreviated N, in the metre-kilogram-second (MKS) system of physical units. It is defined as the force necessary to provide a mass of 1 kg with an acceleration of 1 m per second per second. One newton is equal to a force of 100,000 dynes in the centimetre-gram-second (CGS) system, or a force of about 0.2248 lb in the foot-pound-second (English or U.S.) system. It is named for Isaac Newton, whose second law of motion describes the changes a force can produce in the motion of a body.

Newton, Sir Isaac (b. Jan. 4, 1643, Woolsthorpe, Lincolnshire, Eng.—d. March 31, 1727, London), English physicist and mathematician. The son of a yeoman, he was raised by his grandmother. He was educated at Cambridge University (1661–65), where he discovered the work of René Descartes. His experiments passing sunlight through a prism led to the discovery of the heterogeneous, corpuscular nature of white light and laid the foundation of physical optics. He built the first reflecting telescope in 1668 and became a professor of mathematics at Cambridge in 1669. He worked out the fundamentals of calculus, though this work went unpublished for more than 30 years. His most famous publication, *Principia Mathematica* (1687), grew out of correspondence with Edmond Halley. Describing his works on the laws of motion, orbital dynamics, tidal theory, and the theory of universal gravitation, it is regarded as the seminal work of modern science. He was elected president of the Royal Society of London in 1703 and became the first scientist ever to be knighted in 1705. During his career he engaged in heated arguments with several of his colleagues, including Robert Hooke (over authorship of the inverse square relation of gravitation) and G.W. Leibniz (over the authorship of calculus). The battle with Leibniz dominated the last 25 years of his life; it is now well established that Newton developed calculus first, but that Leibniz was the first to publish on the subject. Newton is regarded as one of the greatest scientists of all time.

Newton's law of gravitation, Statement that any particle of matter in the universe attracts any other with a force (F) that is proportional to the product of their masses (m_1 and m_2) and inversely proportional to the square of the distance (R) between them. In symbols: $F = G(m_1m_2)/R^2$, where G is the gravitational constant. Isaac Newton put forth the law in 1687 and used it to explain the observed motions of the planets and their moons, which had been reduced to mathematical form by Johannes Kepler early in the 17th century.

Neyshābūr, or NĪSHĀPŪR, Town (pop., 2006: 208,860), northeastern Iran. Its name derives from its founder, the Sāsānian king Shāpūr I. One of the four great cities of the region of Khorāsān, it was the residence of the 5th-century Sāsānian king Yazdegerd II. It declined by the mid-7th century but flourished again under the Ṭāhirid (821–873) and Sāmānid (819–999) dynasties. It was the residence of the Seljūq sultan Toghrïl Beg in the 11th century but again declined in the 12th century. The tombs of the renowned poet and scholar Omar Khayyam and the mystic poet Farīd al-Dīn ʿAṭṭār are nearby.

niacin, or NICOTINIC ACID, or VITAMIN B$_3$, Water-soluble vitamin of the vitamin B complex, essential to growth and health in animals, including humans. It is found in the body only in combined form as a coenzyme, nicotinamide adenine dinucleotide (NAD), which is involved in the metabolism of carbohydrates and the oxidation of sugar derivatives and other substances. One of the most stable vitamins, it survives most cooking and most preserving processes. It is widely found in dietary sources, especially lean meat. Deficiency causes pellagra. It is used as a drug to reduce high cholesterol levels in the blood.

Niagara Falls, Great falls of the Niagara River, on the U.S.-Canadian border. They are divided by Goat Island into the Horseshoe (or Canadian) Falls and the American Falls. At the foot of the American Falls is the Cave of the Winds, a large rocky chamber formed by erosion. The river below the falls flows between high cliffs, forming Whirlpool Rapids. Bridges spanning the river include Rainbow Bridge between the U.S. and Canadian cities of Niagara Falls. French missionary Louis Hennepin visited in 1678. Tourism is a major industry, and the falls are a hydroelectric centre.

Niamey, City (pop., 2001: city, 707,951; 2005 est.: urban agglom., 850,000), capital of Niger, along the Niger River. Originally an agricultural village of Maouri, Zerma, and Fulani peoples, it became the capital of Niger colony in 1926 and grew rapidly after World War II. At the intersection of trade routes, it has residents from other parts of Niger, as well as Yoruba and Hausa traders, merchants, officials, and craftsmen from Nigeria, Benin, and Togo. It is a commercial centre and home to Université Abdou Moumouni (1971).

Nibelungenlied (German: "Song of the Nibelungs"), Middle High German epic poem written *c.* 1200 by an unknown poet from the Danube region in what is now Austria. It is preserved in three main 13th-century manuscripts. Elements of great antiquity are discernible in the poem, traceable to Old Norse literature, stories in the *Poetic Edda*, and Scandinavian sagas. The principal characters are Prince Siegfried, Queen Brunhild, Princess Kriemhild, her brother King Gunther, and his henchman Hagen; the story focuses on deceit, revenge, and slaughter. Many variations and adaptations of the poem appeared in later centuries, including Richard Wagner's opera cycle *Der Ring des Nibelungen* (1853–74).

Nicaea, Council of (AD 325) First ecumenical council of the Christian Church, held at Nicaea (now Iznik, Turkey). Called by Emperor Constantine I, the council condemned Arianism and drew up the Nicene Creed. It failed to set a uniform date for Easter.

Nicaragua, officially REPUBLIC OF NICARAGUA, Country, Central America. Area: 50,337 sq mi (130,373 sq km). Population: (2011 est.) 5,870,000. Capital: Managua. Most of the people are mestizos. Languages: Spanish (official), indigenous languages, English. Religion: Christianity (predominantly Roman Catholic; also Protestant). Currency: córdoba. Nicaragua's western half consists of thickly forested mountain ranges and fertile valleys. Parallel to the Pacific coast is a belt of 40 dormant and active volcanoes. The eastern coastline along the Caribbean Sea is known as the Mosquito Coast. Earthquakes are common and sometimes severe. Nicaragua has a developing market economy based largely on agriculture, light industries, and trade. It is a republic with one legislative house; its head of state and government is the president. The area has been inhabited for thousands of years, most notably by the Maya. Christopher Columbus arrived in 1502, and Spanish explorers discovered Lake Nicaragua soon thereafter. Nicaragua was governed by Spain until the early 1820s. It became a part of Mexico (1822–23) and then part of the United Provinces of Central America until 1838, when full independence was achieved. The U.S. intervened in political affairs by maintaining troops there (1912–33). Ruled by the dictatorial Somoza family (1937–79), Nicaragua was taken over by the Sandinista party after a popular revolt. The Sandinistas were then opposed by armed insurgents, the U.S.-backed Contras, from 1981. The Sandinista government nationalized several sectors of the economy but lost national elections in 1990. The new government reprivatized many public enterprises. Sandinista leader Daniel Ortega returned to power after winning the presidential election of 2006.

Nice, ancient NICAEA, City (pop., 2004 est.: 339,000) southeastern France. It is located on the Côte d'Azur of the Mediterranean Sea, near the Italian border. Founded by Greeks *c.* 350 BC, it was conquered by Romans in the 1st century AD and became a trading station. It was held by the counts of Provence in the 10th century. In 1388 it passed to the counts of Savoy. The city was ceded to France in 1860. Sheltered by beautiful hills, Nice has a pleasant climate and is the leading resort of the French Riviera.

Nicene Creed, Ecumenical Christian statement of faith accepted by the Roman Catholic, Eastern Orthodox, Anglican, and major Protestant churches. Originally written in Greek, it was long thought to have been drafted at the Council of Nicaea (325), but is now believed to have been issued by the Council of Constantinople (381), based on a baptismal creed already in existence.

Nichiren Buddhism, One of the largest schools of Japanese Buddhism, founded by Nichiren. It believes that the essence of the Buddha's teachings are contained in the Lotus Sutra and that the beliefs of other Buddhist schools are erroneous. In Nichiren Buddhism, the chanting of the title of the Lotus Sutra can lead to salvation. After Nichiren's death the school split into various subsects, notably Nichiren-shu, which controls the temple founded by Nichiren at Mount Minobu, and Nichiren-sho-shu, which is headquartered in a temple at the foot of Mount Fuji. Nichiren-sho-shu has adherents in the U.S.; in Japan its lay organization is the Soka-gakkai.

nickel, Metallic chemical element, one of the transition elements, chemical symbol Ni, atomic number 28. Nickel is silvery white, tough, harder than iron, ferromagnetic, and highly resistant to rusting and corrosion. It occasionally occurs free and is fairly common but not often concentrated in igneous rocks. As pure metal, it is used to coat other metals and as a catalyst. In alloys, it is used in coins, Monel metal, nickel silver, nickel-chrome and stainless steels, permanant magnets, and cutlery. Its compounds, in which it most often has valence 2, have a variety of industrial uses, as catalysts and mordants and in electroplating.

Nicosia, Greek LEFKOSIA, Turkish LEFKOŞA, City (pop., 2004 est.: Greek sector, 219,200; 1996: Turkish sector, 39,973), capital of Cyprus. Lying on the Pedieos River, it is bordered by mountains to the north and south. It was a kingdom in the 7th century BC and has been the capital of the island since the 10th century AD. It came successively under the control of the Byzantines, Venetians, and Ottomans; the British held it from 1878 until 1960. During the 20th century the city grew beyond the existing circular Venetian walls. The population in the surrounding area is engaged mainly in agriculture. A UN buffer zone has separated the city's Greek and Turkish sectors since 1974.

nicotine, Principal alkaloid of tobacco, occurring throughout the plant but mostly in the leaves. It is a heterocyclic compound containing a pyridine ring; its chemical formula is $C_{10}H_{14}N_2$. Nicotine is the chief addictive ingredient in cigarettes and cigars and in snuff. It has a unique biphasic effect: inhaled in short puffs, it is a stimulant, but it can be a tranquilizer when inhaled slowly and deeply. In larger doses nicotine is a highly toxic poison, used as an insecticide, fumigant, and vermifuge.

Niger, officially REPUBLIC OF NIGER, Country, western Africa, on the southern edge of the Sahara. Area: 489,191 sq mi (1,267,000 sq km). Population: (2011 est.) 16,469,000. Capital: Niamey. More than half the people are Hausa; there are also Songhai-Zerma and Kanuri. Languages: French (official), Hausa, Arabic. Religions: Islam (predominantly Sunni); also traditional beliefs. Currency: CFA franc. A landlocked country, Niger is characterized by savanna in the south and desert in the centre and north; most of the population lives in the south. The Niger River dominates in the southwest and the Aïr Massif (a mountainous region) in the north-central part of the country. Niger has a developing economy based largely on agriculture and mining. Under the constitution it is a republic with one legislative body, with the president as the head of state and the prime minister as the head of government. There is evidence of Neolithic culture in the region, and there were several precolonial kingdoms. First explored by Europeans in the late 18th century, it became part of French West Africa in 1904. It became an overseas territory of France in 1946 and gained independence in 1960. The first multiparty elections were held in 1993. Ibrahim Baré Maïnassara led a military coup in 1996, but after his assassination in 1999 the country returned to democratic government. There was another military coup in 2010, but the military junta transferred power to a democratically elected president in 2011.

Niger-Congo languages, Family of some 1,400 languages of Africa. All of these are considered to be distinct languages and not simply dialects. The named dialects of these languages number many thousands more, not to mention the variant names for those languages and dialects. Niger-Congo languages are spoken by about 85% of the population of Africa, from Dakar, Senegal, in the west to Mombasa, Kenya, and in the east and south to Cape Town, S.Af. The name Niger-Congo was introduced in 1955 by Joseph H. Greenberg. As understood today, Niger-Congo has nine branches: Mande, Kordofanian, Atlantic (formerly West Atlantic), Kru, Gur, Kwa, Ijoid, Adamawa-Ubangi (formerly Adamawa-Eastern), and Benue-Congo.

Niger River, or JOLIBA, or KWORRA, Principal river of western Africa. The third longest on the continent, it rises in Guinea near the Sierra Leone border and flows into Nigeria and the Gulf of Guinea. It is 2,600 mi (4,183 sq km) long, and its middle course is navigable for about 1,000 mi (1,600 km). Peoples living along the Niger include the Bambara, the Malinke, and the Songhai. It was explored by Mungo Park beginning in 1796.

Nigeria, officially FEDERAL REPUBLIC OF NIGERIA, Country, western Africa. Area: 356,669 sq mi (923,768 sq km). Population: (2011 est.) 162,471,000. Capital: Abuja. There are more than 250 ethnic groups, including Hausa, Fulani, Yoruba, and Igbo. Languages: English (official), Hausa. Religions: Christianity (Protestant, other Christians, Roman Catholic), Islam, traditional beliefs. Currency: naira. Nigeria consists of plateaus and the lowlands between them, which are major river basins fed especially by the Niger River. It has a developing mixed economy based largely on petroleum production and agriculture; manufacturing is growing in importance. Services, trade, and transportation employ more than two-fifths of the workforce. Nigeria is a federal republic with two legislative bodies; its head of state and government is the president. Inhabited for thousands of years, the region was the centre of the Nok culture from 500 BCE to 200 CE and of several precolonial empires, including Kanem-Bornu, Benin, and Oyo. The Hausa and Fulani also had states. Visited in the 15th century by Europeans, it became a centre for the slave trade. The area began to come under British control in 1861 and was made a British colony in 1914. Nigeria gained independence in 1960 and became a republic in 1963. Ethnic strife soon led to military coups, and military groups ruled the country from 1966 to 1979 and from 1983 to 1999. Civil war between the federal government and the former Eastern region, Biafra (1967–70), ended in Biafra's surrender after the death by starvation of perhaps a million Biafrans. In 1991 the capital was moved from Lagos to Abuja. The government's execution of Ken Saro-Wiwa in 1995 led to international sanctions, and civilian rule was finally reestablished in 1999 with the election of a president. Ethnic strife—formerly held in check by periods of military rule—erupted in the early 21st century, as did protests over oil production in the Niger delta. Friction also increased between Muslims and Christians after some of the northern and central states adopted Islamic law (the Sharīʿah).

nightingale, Any of several small Old World thrushes (family Turdidae) renowned for their song. The name refers in particular to the Eurasian nightingale (*Erithacus megarhynchos*), a brown bird, 6.5 in. (16 cm) long, with a rufous tail. It sings day and night from perches in shrubbery. Its strong and varied song, with prominent crescendo effects, has been regarded for centuries throughout Europe and Asia as the most beautiful of all birdsongs. The thrush nightingale, or sprosser (*E. luscinia*), is a closely related, more northerly species with slightly darker plumage. The term is also applied to other birds with rich songs (e.g., the wood thrush).

Eurasian nightingale (Erithacus megarhynchos) H. Reinhard/Bruce Coleman Inc.

Nightingale, Florence (b. May 12, 1820, Florence, Italy—d. Aug. 13, 1910, London, Eng.), Italian-born British nurse, founder of trained nursing as a profession. As a volunteer nurse, she was put in charge of nursing the military in Turkey during the Crimean War. Her first concern was sanitation: patients' quarters were infested with rats and fleas, and the water allowance was one pint per head per day for all purposes. She used her own finances to purchase supplies. She also spent many hours in the wards; her night rounds giving personal care to the wounded established her image as the "Lady with the Lamp." Her efforts to improve soldiers' welfare led to the Army Medical School and a Sanitary Department in India. She started the first scientifically based nursing school, was instrumental in setting up training for midwives and nurses in workhouse infirmaries, and helped reform workhouses. She was the first woman awarded the Order of Merit (1907).

nihilism, Any of various philosophical positions that deny that there are objective foundations for human value systems. In 19th-century Russia the term was applied to a philosophy of skepticism that opposed all forms of aestheticism and advocated utilitarianism and scientific rationalism; it was popularized through the figure of Bazarov in Ivan Turgenev's *Fathers and Sons* (1862). Rejecting the social sciences, classical philosophical systems, and the established social order, nihilism rejected the authority of the state, the church, and the family. It gradually became associated with political terror and degenerated into a philosophy of violence.

Nike, Greek goddess of victory. She was the daughter of the giant Pallas and the river Styx. Nike was originally an attribute of both Athena and Zeus, represented as a small figure carried in their hand. She gradually came to be recognized as a mediator between gods and mortals, and was frequently shown carrying a palm branch, wreath, or staff as the messenger of victory. When depicted on her own, she was often a winged figure hovering over the victor in a competition. At Rome she was worshiped as Victoria.

Nile River, Arabic BAḤR AL-NĪL, River, eastern and northeastern Africa. The longest river in the world, it is about 4,132 mi (6,650 km) long from its remotest headstream (which flows into Lake Victoria) to the Mediterranean Sea. After leaving the lake, it flows generally north through Uganda, South Sudan, Sudan, and Egypt. Its major tributaries—including the Ghazāl River, the Blue Nile, and the Atbara River—join it before it enters Lake Nasser near the Egypt-Sudan border. Below the Aswan High Dam, which impounds the lake, it continues northward to its delta near Cairo, where it empties into the Mediterranean. The first use of the Nile for irrigation in Egypt began when seeds were sown in the mud left after its annual floodwaters had subsided. It has supported continuous human settlement for at least 5,000 years, and networks of canals and waterworks have been built since the 19th century. The Aswan High Dam, built in 1959–70, provides flood protection, hydroelectric power, and a dependable water supply for both crops and humans. The Nile is also a vital waterway for the transport of people and goods.

Nilo-Saharan languages, Group of perhaps 115 African languages spoken by more than 27 million people from Mali to Ethiopia and from southernmost Egypt to Tanzania. The concept of Nilo-Saharan as a single stock combining a number of earlier groupings was introduced in 1963 by Joseph H. Greenberg; most Africanists accepted it as a working hypothesis, though shifts have taken place. In terms of numbers of speakers, the most significant divisions of Nilo-Saharan languages include Central Sudanic, Fur, Nilotic, Nubian, Saharan, Songhai, and Surmic. Songhai is spoken by more than 2 million people in Mali and Niger, and Kanuri (a Saharan language) is spoken by about 4.5 million in northeastern Nigeria and adjacent Chad and Niger. Central Sudanic comprises languages of southern Chad, western South Sudan, and northeastern Democratic Republic of the Congo. Nubian languages (including the only Nilo-Saharan language with an ancient written tradition) are spoken along the Nile in northern Sudan and southern Egypt. The Nilotic languages are spoken by some 14 million people, including the Dinka, Nuer, Luo, Turkana, Kalenjin, and Maasai.

Ninety-five Theses, Propositions for debate on the question of indulgences, written by Martin Luther and, according to legend, posted on the door of the castle church in Wittenberg, Ger., on Oct. 31, 1517. This event is now seen as the beginning of the Protestant Reformation. The theses were written in response to the selling of indulgences to pay for the rebuilding of St. Peter's Basilica in Rome. They represented an implicit criticism of papal policy and stressed the spiritual, inward character of the Christian faith. Widely circulated, they aroused much controversy. In 1518 Luther published a Latin manuscript with explanations of the theses.

Ningxia, or NINGSIA, in full HUI AUTONOMOUS REGION OF NINGXIA, Autonomous region (pop., 2002 est.: 5,720,000), northern

China. It is bounded by Shaanxi and Gansu provinces and Inner Mongolia autonomous region and has an area of 25,600 sq mi (66,400 sq km). China's Great Wall runs along its northeastern boundary. The capital is Yinchuan. It is nearly coextensive with the ancient kingdom of the Tangut people, whose capital was captured by Genghis Khan in the early 13th century. The region is mostly desert and is sparsely settled, but the vast plain of the Huang He (Yellow River) in the north has been irrigated for centuries; over the years an extensive system of canals has been built.

Niobe, In Greek mythology, the prototype of the bereaved mother. The daughter of Tantalus, she married King Amphion of Thebes and bore him six sons and six daughters. She made the mistake of boasting of her fertility to the Titaness Leto, who had only two children, Apollo and Artemis. As punishment for her pride, Apollo killed all of Niobe's sons and Artemis all her daughters. Niobe was so overwhelmed with grief that the gods turned her into a rock on Mount Sipylus (near modern Izmir, Turkey), which weeps endlessly as the snow above it melts.

Nippur, Ancient Mesopotamian city southeast of Babylon. Located in what is now southeastern Iraq, it was originally on the Euphrates River, whose course later changed. By 2500 BC it was the centre of worship of the Sumerian storm god Enlil. Parthian construction later buried Enlil's sanctuary, and the city fell into decay in the 3rd century AD. It was abandoned in the 12th or 13th century. Excavations have revealed temples, a ziggurat, and thousands of clay tablets that are a primary source of information on ancient Sumerian civilization. Also uncovered were an Akkadian tomb and a large temple devoted to the Mesopotamian goddess of healing.

Female figure, made of gypsum, with a gold mask that stood at a temple altar in Nippur, c. 2700 BC; in the Iraq Museum, Baghdad
Courtesy of the Iraq Museum, Baghdad; photograph, David Lees

nirvana (Sanskrit: "Extinction") In Indian religious thought, the transcendent state of freedom achieved by the extinction of desire and of individual consciousness. Nirvana is the supreme goal of the disciplines of meditation, particularly in Buddhism. Release from desire (and consequent suffering) and the continuous round of rebirths constitutes enlightenment, or the experience of nirvana. Theravada Buddhism conceives of nirvana as tranquillity and peace; Mahayana Buddhism equates it with *sunyata* (emptiness), *dharma-kaya* (the essence of the Buddha), and *dharma-datu* (ultimate reality).

nitrogen, Gaseous chemical element, chemical symbol N, atomic number 7. A colourless, odourless, tasteless gas, it makes up 78% of Earth's atmosphere and is a constituent of all living matter. As the nearly unreactive diatomic molecule N_2, it is useful as an inert atmosphere or to dilute other gases. Nitrogen is commercially produced by distillation of liquefied air. Nitrogen fixation, achieved naturally by soil microbes and industrially by the Haber-Bosch process, converts it to water-soluble compounds (including ammonia and nitrates). Industrially, ammonia is the starting material for most other nitrogen compounds (especially nitrates and nitrites), whose main uses are in agricultural fertilizers and explosives. In compounds, nitrogen usually has valence 3 or 5. It forms several oxides including nitrous oxide (N_2O; laughing gas), nitric oxide (NO), nitrogen dioxide (NO_2), and other forms (such as N_2O_3 and N_2O_5). Some of the nitrogen oxides, often referred to generically as NO_x, are notorious as contributors to urban air pollution. Other compounds include the nitrides, exceptionally hard materials made from nitrogen and a metal; cyanides; azides, used in detonators and percussion caps; and thousands of organic compounds containing nitrogen in functional groups or in a linear or ring structure.

nitrogen fixation, Any natural or industrial process that causes free nitrogen in the air to combine chemically with other elements to form more reactive nitrogen compounds such as ammonia, nitrates, or nitrites. Soil microorganisms (e.g., *Rhizobium* bacteria living in root nodules of legumes) are responsible for more than 90% of all nitrogen fixation. Though nitrogen is part of all proteins and essential in both plant and animal metabolism, plants and animals cannot use elemental nitrogen such as the nitrogen gas (N_2) that forms 80% of the atmosphere. Symbiotic nitrogen-fixing bacteria invade the root hairs of host plants, where they multiply and stimulate the formation of root nodules, enlargements of plant cells and bacteria in close association. Within the nodules the bacteria convert free nitrogen to nitrates, which the host plant uses for its development. Nitrogen fixation by bacteria associated with legumes is of prime importance in agriculture. Before the use of synthetic fertilizers in the industrial countries, usable nitrogen was supplied as manure and by crop rotation that included a legume crop.

nitroglycerin, or GLYCERYL TRINITRATE, Organic compound, powerful explosive and ingredient of most forms of dynamite. It is a colourless, oily, somewhat toxic liquid with a sweet, burning taste. Its safe use as a blasting explosive became possible after Alfred Nobel developed dynamite in the 1860s with an inert porous material (moderator) such as charcoal or diatomaceous earth. Nitroglycerin is also used in a mixture in rocket propellants. In medicine, it is used to dilate blood vessels, especially to ease angina pectoris.

nitrous oxide, or LAUGHING GAS, Inorganic compound, one of the oxides of nitrogen. A colourless gas with a pleasantly sweetish odour and taste, it has an analgesic effect when inhaled; it is used as an anesthetic (often called just "gas") in dentistry and surgery. This effect is preceded by mild hysteria, sometimes with laughter, hence the name *laughing gas*. It is also used as a propellant in food aerosols and as a leak detector.

Nixon, Richard M(ilhous) (b. Jan. 9, 1913, Yorba Linda, Calif., U.S.—d. April 22, 1994, New York, N.Y.), 37th president of the U.S. (1969–74). He studied law at Duke University and practiced in California (1937–42). After serving in World War II, he was elected to the U.S. House of Representatives (1946). As a member of the House Un-American Activities Committee, he received national attention for his hostile questioning of Alger Hiss. In 1950 he was elected to the Senate following a bitter campaign in which he unfairly portrayed his opponent as a communist sympathizer; the epithet "Tricky Dick" dates from this period. He won the vice presidency in 1952 as the running mate of Republican Dwight D. Eisenhower. During the campaign he delivered a nationally televised address, the "Checkers" speech (named for the dog he admitted receiving as a political gift), to rebut charges of financial misconduct. He and Eisenhower were reelected easily in 1956. As the Republican presidential candidate in 1960, he lost narrowly to John F. Kennedy. After failing to win the 1962 California gubernatorial race, he announced his retirement from politics and criticized the press, declaring that it would not "have Dick Nixon to kick around anymore." He moved to New York to practice law. He reentered politics by running for president in 1968, narrowly defeating Hubert H. Humphrey with his "southern strategy" of seeking votes from southern and western conservatives in both parties. As president, he began to withdraw U.S. military forces from South Vietnam while resuming the bombing of North Vietnam. His expansion of the Vietnam War to Cambodia and Laos in 1970 provoked widespread protests in the U.S. He established direct relations with China and made a state visit there in 1972, the first by a U.S. president. On a visit to the Soviet Union

later that year, he signed agreements resulting from the Strategic Arms Limitation Talks between the U.S. and the Soviet Union held between 1969 and 1972, known as SALT I. In domestic affairs, Nixon responded to persistent inflation and increasing unemployment by devaluing the dollar and imposing unprecedented peacetime controls on wages and prices. His administration increased funding for many federal civil rights agencies and proposed legislation that created the Occupational Safety and Health Administration (OSHA) and the Environmental Protection Agency (EPA). In 1972 he won reelection with a landslide victory over George McGovern. Assisted by Henry A. Kissinger, he concluded a peace agreement with North Vietnam (1973), though the war did not come to an end until 1975. His administration helped to undermine the coalition government of Chile's Marxist Pres. Salvador Allende, leading to Allende's overthrow in a military coup in 1973. Nixon's second term was overshadowed by the Watergate scandal, which stemmed from illegal activities by Nixon and others related to the burglary and wiretapping of the headquarters of the Democratic Party. After lengthy congressional investigations and facing near-certain impeachment, Nixon resigned the presidency on Aug. 8, 1974, the first president to do so. Though never convicted of wrongdoing, he was pardoned by his successor, Gerald Ford. In retirement, he wrote his memoirs and several books on foreign policy, which modestly rehabilitated his reputation and earned him a role as an elder statesman and foreign-policy expert.

Nizhny Novgorod, formerly (1932–90) GORKY, City (pop., 2002: 1,311,200), western Russia. It is located on the southern bank of the Volga River at its confluence with the Oka River. It was founded in 1221 and was annexed to Moscow in 1392. It was strategically important in the Russian conquest of the Volga through the mid-16th century. In 1932 it was renamed for Maksim Gorky, who was born there. Under the Soviet regime it was a place of internal exile for Andrey Sakharov. The city has several 16th- and 17th-century buildings and is one of Russia's major industrial centres.

Nkrumah, Kwame (b. September 1909, Nkroful, Gold

Nkrumah, 1962
Marc and Evelyne Bernheim/Woodfin Camp and Associates

Coast—d. April 27, 1972, Bucharest, Rom.), Nationalist leader and president of Ghana (1960–66). Nkrumah worked as a teacher before going to the U.S. to study literature and socialism (1935–45). In 1949 he formed the Convention People's Party, which advocated nonviolent protests, strikes, and noncooperation with the British authorities. Elected prime minister of the Gold Coast (1952–60) and then president of independent Ghana, Nkrumah advanced a policy of Africanization and built new roads, schools, and health facilities. After 1960 he devoted much of his time to the Pan-African movement, at the expense of Ghana's economy. Following an attempted coup in 1962, he increased authoritarian controls, withdrew from public life, increased contacts with communist countries, and wrote works on political philosophy. With the country facing economic ruin, he was deposed in 1966 while visiting Beijing.

Nobel, Alfred (Bernhard) (b. Oct. 21, 1833, Stockholm, Swed.—d. Dec. 10, 1896, San Remo, Italy), Swedish chemist, engineer, and industrialist. His attempts to find a safe way to handle nitroglycerin resulted in the invention of dynamite and the blasting cap. He built a network of factories to manufacture dynamite and corporations to produce and market his explosives. He went on to develop more powerful explosives and to construct and perfect detonators for explosives that did not explode on simple firing (e.g., when lit with a match). Nobel registered more than 350 patents, many unrelated to explosives (e.g., artificial silk and leather). A complex personality, both dynamic and reclusive, he was a pacifist but was labeled the "merchant of death" for inventing explosives used in war. Perhaps to counter this label, he left most of his immense fortune, from worldwide explosives and oil interests, to establish the Nobel Prizes, which would become the most highly regarded of all international awards.

Nobel Prize, Any of the prizes awarded annually by four institutions (three Swedish and one Norwegian) from a fund established under the will of Alfred B. Nobel. The will specified that awards should be given "to those who, during the preceding year, shall have conferred the greatest benefit on mankind." Since 1901, prizes have been awarded for physics, chemistry, physiology or medicine, literature, and peace; since 1969, a sixth prize, established by the Bank of Sweden, has been awarded in economic sciences. The Nobel Prizes are regarded as the most prestigious prizes in the world.

nocturne, Nineteenth-century character piece for piano. The name was first used *c.* 1812 by the Scottish composer John Field (1782–1837) for works employing a lyrical melody over an accompaniment of broken chords. Frédéric Chopin's romantic nocturnes, similar in style, are the most celebrated.

Noel-Baker (of the City of Derby), Philip John Noel-Baker, Baron, orig. PHILIP JOHN BAKER (b. Nov. 1, 1889, London, Eng.—d. Oct. 8, 1982, London), British statesman and advocate of disarmament. He worked for the League of Nations secretariat (1919–22) and taught international relations at the University of London (1924–29). He served in the House of Commons (1929–31, 1936–70) and in ministerial posts (1945–61). He helped draft the UN charter, and he campaigned widely for peace through multilateral disarmament. An Olympic runner in 1912, 1920, and 1924, he later served as president of UNESCO's International Council on Sport and Physical Recreation (1960–82). In 1959 he was awarded the Nobel Prize for Peace.

Noh theatre, or NO THEATRE, Classic Japanese theatrical form. One of the world's oldest extant theatrical forms, Noh theatre has a heroic theme, a chorus, and highly stylized action, costuming, and scenery. Its all-male performers are storytellers who use their visual appearances and movements to suggest their tale rather than enact it. Noh (from Japanese *nō*, meaning "talent" or "skill") developed from ancient forms of dance-drama and became a distinctive form in the 14th century. The five types of Noh plays are the *kami* ("god") play, which involves a sacred story of a Shintō shrine; the *shura mono* ("fighting play"), which centres on warriors; the *katsura mono* ("wig play"), which has a female protagonist; the *gendai mono* ("present-day play") or *kyōjo mono* ("madwoman play"), which is varied in content; and the *kiri* or *kichiku* ("final" or "demon") play, which features devils and strange beasts. Kan'ami (1333–84) and his son Zeami (1363–1443) wrote many of the most beautiful Noh texts; more than 200 remain in the modern Noh repertoire.

noise, Undesired sound that is intrinsically objectionable or that interferes with other sounds being listened to. In electronics and information theory, noise refers to those random, unpredictable, and undesirable signals, or changes in signals, that mask the desired information content. In radio, this noise is called static; in television, it is called snow. White noise is a complex signal or sound covering the entire range of component frequencies, or tones, all of which possess equal intensity.

Nok culture, Ancient Iron Age African culture. It existed on the Benue Plateau of Nigeria between about 500 BC and AD 200 and was first discovered in 1928 in the village of Nok. Artifacts having similar features were found over an area that stretched about 300 miles (480 km) east to west and 200 miles (320 km) north to south. The most characteristic of these are hollow, coil-built clay figurines of animals and stylized human beings, usually heads. Other artifacts include iron and stone tools and stone ornaments.

nomadism, Way of life of peoples who do not live continually in the same place but move cyclically or periodically. It is based on temporary centres whose stability depends on the available food supply and the technology for exploiting it. A hunting and gathering society is a type of nomadic group. Pastoral nomads, who depend on domestic livestock, migrate in an established territory to find pasture for their animals. Tinker or trader nomads, such as the Roma (Gypsies; *see* Rom) and the Irish and Scottish Travellers, are associated with a larger society but maintain their mobile way of life. Nomadism declined in the 20th century as urban centres expanded and governments sought to regulate or eliminate it.

non-Euclidean geometry, Any theory of the nature of geometric space differing from the traditional view held since Euclid's time. These geometries arose in the 19th century when several mathematicians working independently explored the possibility of rejecting Euclid's parallel postulate. Different assumptions about how many lines through a point not on a given line could be parallel to that line resulted in hyperbolic geometry and elliptic geometry. Mathematicians were forced to abandon the idea of a single correct geometry; it became their task not to discover mathematical systems but to create them by selecting consistent axioms and studying the theorems that could be derived from them. The development of these alternative geometries had a profound impact on the notion of space and paved the way for the theory of relativity.

nonaligned movement, In international politics, the group of states sharing the peacetime policy of avoiding political or economic affiliations with major power blocs. At its beginning the nonaligned movement consisted primarily of Asian and African states that were once colonies of the Western powers and were wary of being drawn into a new form of dependence by the West or by the communist bloc. Founded by Jawaharlal Nehru, Gamal Abdel Nasser, and others, the movement held its first official meeting in 1961 in Bandung, Indon.; 25 countries attended. Meetings have since been held on a three-year schedule. While the Soviet Union existed, the movement tended to seek development assistance from both the U.S. and the Soviet Union but to refrain from forming political or military alliances with either country. Since the dissolution of the Soviet Union in 1991, the nonaligned movement has been chiefly concerned with debt forgiveness and with development of fairer trade relationships with the West. By the early 21st century the movement had more than 110 members.

Nonconformist, Any English Protestant who does not conform to the doctrines or practices of the established Church of England. The term was first used after the Restoration of the monarchy in 1660 to describe congregations that had separated from the national church. Such congregations, also called Separatists or Dissenters, often rejected Anglican rites and doctrines as being too close to Catholicism. In the late 19th century, Nonconformists of various denominations joined together to form the Free Church Federal Council. In England and Wales the term is generally applied to all Protestant denominations outside Anglicanism, including Baptists, Congregationalists, Unitarians, Presbyterians, Methodists, Quakers, and Churches of Christ.

nongovernmental organization (NGO), Organization that is not part of any government. A key distinction is between not-for-profit groups and for-profit corporations; the vast majority of NGOs are not-for-profit. In some countries, particularly socialist ones, some NGOs are government-organized. The purposes of NGOs cover the entire range of human interests and may be domestic or international in scope. Many NGOs are key sources of information for governments on issues such as human rights abuses and environmental degradation. Some NGOs fulfill quasi-governmental functions for ethnic groups that lack a state of their own. NGOs may be financed by private donations, international organizations, governments, or a combination of these. In Britain, quasi-autonomous nongovernmental organizations, or "quangos," are organizations that have nonelected boards and receive public funds which they also disburse.

nonsense verse, Humorous or whimsical verse that features absurd characters and actions and often contains evocative but meaningless words coined for the verse. It is unlike the ritualistic gibberish of children's counting-out rhymes in that it makes such words sound purposeful. It differs from other comic verse in its resistance to any rational or allegorical interpretation. Most nonsense verse has been written for children and is modern, dating from the beginning of the 19th century. Examples include Edward Lear's *Book of Nonsense* (1846), Lewis Carroll's "Jabberwocky" (1871), and Hilaire Belloc's *Bad Child's Book of Beasts* (1896).

Nordic skiing, Skiing techniques and events of Scandinavian origin that include cross-country skiing and ski jumping. Nordic events were included in the first Winter Olympics in 1924.

norepinephrine, or NORADRENALINE, One of two catecholamine hormones (epinephrine is the other) secreted by the adrenal glands, as well as at nerve endings, as a neurotransmitter. It resembles adrenaline chemically and in its actions on the body, which mimic sympathetic nervous system stimulation. It constricts most blood vessels and is given for certain types of shock. Norepinephrine is formed from tyrosine and converted to epinephrine. It was discovered by Ulf von Euler-Chelpin (1905–83) in the mid-1940s.

normal distribution, In statistics, a frequency distribution in the shape of the classic bell curve. It accurately represents most variations in such attributes as height and weight. Any random variable with a normal distribution has a mean and a standard deviation that indicates how much the data as a whole deviate from the mean. The standard deviation is smaller for data clustered closely around the mean value and larger for more dispersed data sets.

Norman, Any of the Vikings, or Norsemen, who settled in northern France (or the Frankish kingdom) and their descendants. As pagan pirates from Denmark, Norway, and Iceland, they raided the European coast in the 8th century. They settled in the lower Seine valley by *c.* 900. In 911 they were granted territory around what is now Rouen by King Charles III and then extended their territory westward. They founded the duchy of Normandy, governed by a line of rulers who called themselves counts or dukes of Normandy. Though the Normans converted to Christianity and adopted the French language, they continued to display their Viking ancestors' recklessness and appetite for conquest. In the 11th century they seized England in the Norman Conquest and colonized southern Italy and Sicily. The Normans also participated in the reconquest of Spain and in the Crusades, and the Normans of Italy and Sicily were rivals of the Byzantine emperors.

Norman Conquest (1066) Military conquest of England by William, duke of Normandy (later William I), mainly through his victory over Harold II at the Battle of Hastings. Edward the Confessor had designated William as his successor in 1051. When Harold, duke of Wessex, was crowned king of England in 1066 instead, William assembled an invasion force of 5,000 knights. After defeating Harold's army near Hastings on October 14 and advancing to London, he was crowned king in Westminster Abbey on Christmas Day, 1066. Native revolts continued until 1071, notably in Northumbria. The Norman Conquest brought great social and political changes to England, linking the country more closely with western Europe and replacing the old English aristocracy

with a Norman aristocracy. The English language was subjected to a long period of influence by Anglo-French, which remained in literary and courtly use until the reign of Edward III and in legal reporting until the 17th century.

Normandy Campaign, Allied invasion of northern Europe in World War II that began on June 6, 1944, with the largest amphibious landing in history in Normandy, France. Also called Operation Overlord, the landing transported 156,000 U.S., British, and Canadian troops across the English Channel in over 5,000 ships and 10,000 planes. Commanded by Gen. Dwight D. Eisenhower, the Allied forces landed at five beaches on the Normandy coast and soon established lodgement areas, despite stiff German resistance and heavy losses at the code-named Omaha Beach and Juno Beach. Allied air supremacy prevented rapid German reinforcements, and discord between Adolf Hitler and his generals stalled crucial counterattacks. Though delayed by heavy fighting near Cherbourg and around Caen, the Allied ground troops broke out of the beachheads in mid-July and began a rapid advance across northern France. The Normandy Campaign is traditionally considered to have concluded with the liberation of Paris on Aug. 25, 1944.

North America, Continent, Western Hemisphere. The third-largest continent on earth, it lies mostly above the Arctic Circle and the Tropic of Cancer. It is almost completely surrounded by bodies of water, including the Pacific Ocean, the Bering Strait, the Arctic Ocean, the Atlantic Ocean, and the Caribbean Sea and Gulf of Mexico. Area: 9,361,791 sq mi (24,247,039 sq km). Population (2001 est.): 454,225,000. Shaped like an inverted triangle, North America was apparently the first continent to achieve its current approximate size and shape. Its geologic structure is built around a stable platform of Precambrian rock called the Canadian Shield. To the southeast are the Appalachian Mountains and to the west are the younger and much taller Cordilleras. These mountains extend the length of the continent and occupy about one-third of the total land area. The Rocky Mountains constitute the eastern Cordillera. The highest point is Mount McKinley. The Mississippi River basin, including its major tributaries, the Missouri and Ohio, occupies more than one-eighth of the continent's total area. Generally temperate climatic conditions prevail. Arable land accounts for about one-eighth of the land area and forests for about one-third. English, the primary language of the U.S., predominates, followed by Spanish; French is spoken in parts of Canada. Most of the continent's population of European descent is found in the U.S. and Canada. Intermarriage between whites and Indians was common in Mexico, and mestizos constitute about three-fifths of the Mexican population. North America has a mixture of developed, partly developed, and developing economies, adequate reserves of most metallic resources, and the world's largest reserves of cadmium, copper, lead, molybdenum, silver, and zinc. It is the world's leading food producer, largely because of mechanized and scientific farming in the U.S. and Canada. Among the continent's democratically governed states are Canada, Mexico, Costa Rica, and the U.S. The nations of North America have sought hemispheric unity as members of the Organization of American States, which also includes South American countries. They also sought stronger economic ties, and in 1992 Canada, the U.S., and Mexico signed the North American Free Trade Agreement (NAFTA), which called for the elimination of most tariffs and other trade barriers between the three countries. The first inhabitants were American Indians, who migrated from Asia about 20,000 years ago. The greatest pre-Columbian civilizations were in Mesoamerica and included the Olmec, Maya, Toltec, and Aztec, who were conquered by the Spanish. The continent long remained sparsely settled and undeveloped. Beginning in the 17th century it underwent a profound transformation with the coming of Europeans and the Africans they introduced as slaves. The style of life became Latin American south of the Rio Grande and Anglo-American to the north, with enclaves of French culture in Canada and Louisiana.

Slavery, practiced in the 16th–19th centuries, added a significant minority culture of African origin, especially in the U.S. and the Caribbean. The huge industrial economy of the U.S., its abundant resources, and its military strength give the continent considerable global influence.

North Island, Island (pop., 2006: 3,120,303), New Zealand. The smaller of the country's two principal islands, it is separated from South Island by the Cook Strait. It has an area of 44,702 sq mi (115,777 sq km). A large and growing majority of the population of New Zealand lives on North Island, concentrated in the cities of Wellington and Auckland.

North Pole, Northern end of the Earth's geographic axis, located at latitude 90° N. It is the northern point from which all meridians of longitude start. Lying in the Arctic Ocean and covered with drifting pack ice, it has six months of constant sunlight and six months of total darkness each year. Robert E. Peary claimed to have reached the pole by dogsled in 1909, but that is now in dispute; Roald Amundsen and Richard E. Byrd claimed to have reached it by air in 1926. The geographic pole does not coincide with the magnetic North Pole, which in the early 21st century lay at about 82°45′ N, 114°25′ W, or with the geomagnetic North Pole, which is at about 79°45′ N, 71°45′ W.

North Sea, Arm of the Atlantic Ocean. Extending south from the Norwegian Sea between Norway and the British Isles, it connects the Skagerrak (channel between Norway and Denmark) with the English Channel. It covers an area of about 220,000 sq mi (570,000 sq km), with depths generally ranging from 120 to 300 ft (37 to 91 m). There are, however, shallower areas in the southwest with depths of less than 100 ft (30 m), as well as some deep trenches in the north and the west with depths exceeding 1,000 ft (300 m). Some parts of the sea feature excellent fishing, while others have extensive oil and natural gas deposits.

Northeast Passage, Maritime route along the northern coast of Europe and Asia. It lies between the Atlantic and Pacific oceans mainly off northern Siberia. Early explorers included Willem Barents, Olivier Brunel, and Henry Hudson. In 1778 Capt. James Cook saw both sides of the Bering Strait and demonstrated that Asia and North America are two separate continents. The passage was first traversed by Adolf Erik Nordenskiöld in 1878–79. Since the late 1960s it has been kept open in summer by icebreakers.

Northern Dvina River, Russian SEVERNAYA DVINA, River, northern Russia. Formed by the junction of the Sukhona and Yug rivers, it is one of the largest and most important waterways of the northern European part of Russia. It flows northwest for 462 mi (744 km) and enters the Dvina inlet of the White Sea below the city of Arkhangelsk. Navigable for most of its length, it was used by early fur hunters and colonists, and monasteries and towns were established at important confluences. It retains its economic importance and is linked with the Volga-Baltic Waterway via the Sukhona River.

Northern Ireland, Part of the United Kingdom of Great Britain and Northern Ireland occupying the northeastern portion of the island of Ireland. Area: 5,461 sq mi (14,144 sq km). Population (2001): 1,685,267. Capital: Belfast. It is bounded by the republic of Ireland, the Irish Sea, the North Channel, and the Atlantic Ocean. Northern Ireland is often referred to as the province of Ulster. The people are descended from indigenous Irish and immigrants from England and Scotland. Language: English (official). Religions: Protestantism (the majority) and Roman Catholicism (a minority). Currency: pound sterling. Northern Ireland's industries include engineering, shipbuilding (which has been in severe decline), automobile manufacturing, textiles, food and beverage processing, and clothing. The service industry employs about three-fourths of the workforce, and manufacturing employs less than one-fifth of workers. Agriculture is important, with most farm in-

come derived from livestock. Northern Ireland shares most of its history with the republic of Ireland, though Protestant English and Scots immigrating in the 16th–17th centuries tended to settle in Ulster. In 1801 the Act of Union created the United Kingdom, which united Great Britain and Ireland. In response to mounting Irish sentiment in favour of Home Rule, the Government of Ireland Act was adopted in 1920, providing for two partially self-governing units in Ireland: the northern six counties constituting Northern Ireland and the southern counties now making up the republic of Ireland. In 1968 civil rights protests by Roman Catholics sparked violent conflicts with Protestants and led to the occupation of the province by British troops in the early 1970s. The Irish Republican Army (IRA) mounted a prolonged campaign of violence in an effort to force the withdrawal of British troops as a prelude to Northern Ireland's unification with Ireland. In 1972 Northern Ireland's constitution and parliament were suspended, bringing the province under direct rule by the British. Violence continued for three decades before dropping off in the mid-1990s. In 1998 talks between the British government and the IRA resulted in a peace agreement that provided for extensive Home Rule in the province. In 1999 power was devolved to an elected assembly, though the body was hampered by factional disagreements. Sporadic sectarian strife continued in the early 21st century, as the IRA gradually carried out decommissioning (disarming).

Northern Mariana Islands, Self-governing commonwealth in political union with the U.S., in the western Pacific Ocean. Composed of 22 islands north of Guam, the Northern Marianas extend 450 mi (720 km). Area: 176.5 sq mi (457.1 sq km). Population: (2011 est.) 46,100. Capital: Chalan Kanoa, on Saipan. Saipan, Tinian, and Rota are the principal inhabited islands. Others include Alamagan and Agrihan; Pagan was evacuated for a time after a 1981 volcanic eruption. The indigenous people are Micronesian; other inhabitants are Chamorro and Filipino. The islands were discovered by Ferdinand Magellan in 1521. They were colonized by Spain in 1668. Sold by Spain to Germany in 1899, they were occupied by Japan in 1914 and became a Japanese mandate from the League of Nations after 1919. They were the scene of fierce fighting in World War II; Tinian was the base for U.S. planes that dropped atomic bombs on Hiroshima and Nagasaki. The Northern Marianas were granted to the U.S. as a UN trust territory in 1947 and became self-governing in 1978 (when the residents became U.S. citizens). The UN trusteeship ended in 1986.

Northern Territory, Territory, northern Australia. Area: 520,902 sq mi (1,349,129 sq km). Population: (2006) 192,898; (2010 est.) 229,711. Capital: Darwin. The only sizable town besides the capital is Alice Springs. Most of the people are of European descent; about one-fifth are Australian Aboriginals. It consists mainly of tableland, with the Simpson Desert in the southeast and the Arnhem Land plateau in the north. It was inhabited by Aboriginals for thousands of years; they held Uluru/Ayers Rock as central to their culture. The coast was explored by the Dutch in the 17th century and surveyed in the early 19th century by Matthew Flinders. It was first included as part of New South Wales and was annexed to South Australia in 1863. It reverted to being under direct control of the Commonwealth of Australia in 1911. The northern parts were bombed by the Japanese in World War II and occupied by Allied troops. It was granted self-government within the Commonwealth in 1978. It remains sparsely inhabited; its economy rests on cattle farming, mining, government services, and a growing tourism industry.

Northern Wei sculpture, Chinese sculpture, dominated by simple images of the Buddha, dating from the era of the Northern Wei dynasty (AD 386–534/535). The art represents the first major influence of Buddhism on China, and may be divided into two major periods. The first style (c. 452–494), an amalgam of foreign influences traceable to the Buddhist art of India, is characterized by heavy stylization of blocky volumes. The second style (c. 494–

535) clothes the Buddha in the costume of the Chinese scholar and emphasizes a sinuous cascade of drapery falling over an increasingly flattened figure.

Northwest Passage, Sea passage between the Atlantic and Pacific oceans along the northern coast of North America. The search for a commercial sea route around the American land barrier dates from the end of the 15th century and attracted explorers such as Jacques Cartier, Francis Drake, Martin Frobisher, and Capt. James Cook. The passage was finally navigated successfully in 1903–05 by Roald Amundsen. As a modern trade route it has been only marginally useful, because of the difficulties in navigating around the polar ice cap and the giant icebergs in the Atlantic between Greenland and Baffin Island and in the Pacific in the Bering Strait. The U.S. and Canadian governments have tried to encourage international commerce in the passage, noting how much it would shorten many international shipping distances. However, the cost of strengthening ships against ice and potentially high insurance rates for vessels used in Arctic service have been factors inhibiting the development of the Northwest Passage as a trade route.

Norway, officially KINGDOM OF NORWAY, Country, western Scandinavian Peninsula, northern Europe. Area (including Svalbard and Jan Mayen): 148,718 sq mi (385,179 sq km). Population: (2011 est.) 4,953,000. Capital: Oslo. Most of the people are Norwegian, though there are several ethnic minorities, including some 30,000 to 40,000 Sami (Lapps). Languages: Norwegian, Sami (official). Religion: Christianity (predominantly Evangelical Lutheran [official]). Currency: Norwegian krone. Norway is among Europe's largest countries. It is a mountainous land with extensive plateau regions in its southwestern and central parts. Traditionally a fishing and lumbering country, it greatly increased its mining and manufacturing activities since World War II. It has a developed economy largely based on services, petroleum and natural gas production, and light and heavy industries. Literacy is virtually 100%. Norway is a constitutional monarchy with one legislative house; its head of state is the king, and the head of government is the prime minister. Several principalities were united into the kingdom of Norway in the 11th century. It had the same king as Denmark from 1380 to 1814, when it was ceded to Sweden. The union with Sweden was dissolved in 1905, and Norway's economy grew rapidly. It remained neutral during World War I, although its shipping industry played a vital role in the conflict. It declared its neutrality in World War II but was invaded and occupied by German troops. Norway maintains a comprehensive welfare system and is a member of NATO. Its citizens rejected membership in the European Union in 1994.

Norwegian Sea, Open sea, Northern Hemisphere. It is bordered by Greenland, Iceland, Spitsbergen, and Norway. A submarine ridge linking Greenland, Iceland, the Faroe Islands, and northern Scotland separates the Norwegian Sea from the Atlantic Ocean. The sea is crossed by the Arctic Circle, but the warm Norway Current that flows northeast off the Norway coast produces generally ice-free conditions. Colder currents mixing with this warm water create excellent fishing grounds.

nose, Prominent structure between and below the eyes. With the complex nasal cavity behind it, it functions for breathing and smelling. Behind the front section (vestibule), which includes the nostrils, it is divided vertically by three convoluted ridges (conchae) into air passages. In the highest one, the olfactory region, a small segment of mucous membrane lining contains neurons covered by a moisture layer, in which microscopic particles in inhaled air dissolve and stimulate the neurons. The rest of the cavity warms and moistens inhaled air and filters particles and bacteria out of it. Sinus cavities in the bone on both sides of the nose drain into the air passages. During swallowing, the soft palate closes off the back of the nose against food.

Notre-Dame de Paris (1163–*c.* 1350) Gothic cathedral on the Île de la Cité in Paris. Probably the most famous Gothic cathedral, Notre-Dame is a superb example of the Rayonnant style. Two massive Early Gothic towers (1210–50) crown the western facade, which is divided into three stories and has doors adorned with Early Gothic carvings and surmounted by a row of figures of Old Testament kings. The single-arch flying buttresses at the eastern end are notable for their boldness and grace. Its three great rose windows, which retain their 13th-century glass, are of awe-inspiring beauty.

Notre-Dame de Paris.
© Corbis

Nouakchott, City (pop., 2000: 558,195; 2005 est.: 743,500), capital of Mauritania. It is on a plateau near the Atlantic coast of western African, north-northeast of Dakar, Senegal. It was a small village until Mauritania was granted full independence from France in 1960. Then the city was developed as the capital of the new nation. It was a major refugee centre during the Saharan droughts of the 1970s and grew rapidly. A port facility was built nearby for the export of petroleum and copper.

nova, Any of a class of stars whose luminosity temporarily increases by several thousand up to a million times normal. Most appear to be close binary stars, one of which is a white dwarf star drawing in matter from the other until it becomes unstable, causing an outburst in which the outer layer of material is shed. A nova reaches maximum luminosity within hours after its outburst and may shine intensely for several days or even a few weeks; it then slowly returns to its former level. The process can repeat at intervals ranging from a few dozen to hundreds of thousands of years. Stars that become novas are usually too faint to see with the unaided eye until their sudden increase in luminosity, sometimes great enough to make them readily visible in the night sky. To observers, such objects may appear to be new stars; hence their name (Latin for "new").

novel, Fictional prose narrative of considerable length and some complexity that deals imaginatively with human experience through a connected sequence of events involving a group of persons in a specific setting. The genre encompasses a wide range of types and styles, including picaresque, epistolary, gothic, romantic, realist, and historical novels. Though forerunners of the novel appeared in a number of places, including Classical Rome and 11th-century Japan, the European novel is usually said to have begun with Miguel de Cervantes's *Don Quixote.* The novel was established as a literary form in England in the 18th century through the work of Daniel Defoe, Samuel Richardson, and Henry Fielding. The typical elements of a conventional novel are plot, character, setting, narrative method and point of view, scope, and myth or symbolism. These elements have been subject to experimentation since the earliest appearance of the novel.

Novgorod, City (pop., 2002: 217,200), northwestern Russia. Located on the Volkhov River north of Lake Ilmen, it is one of the oldest Russian cities. First mentioned in the chronicles of AD 859, it came under Rurik *c.* 862. It was of great importance in the 11th to 15th centuries, when it was the capital of the principality of Novgorod. It prospered by trade with Central Asia, Byzantium, and the Hanseatic League. The centre of the Novgorod school of painting, it was ruled by Alexander Nevsky in the 13th century. It became a rival of Moscow, was destroyed by Ivan IV in 1570, and declined with the rise of St. Petersburg. It was held by the Germans in World War II and suffered heavy damage. Many historic buildings were later restored, and these were designated a UNESCO World Heritage site in 1992. The city is a centre of tourism.

Novgorod school, Important school of Russian medieval icon and mural painting that flour-

ished around Novgorod in the 12th–16th centuries. Novgorod, Russia's cultural centre in the 13th–14th centuries, when most of the rest of the country was occupied by the Mongols, preserved the Byzantine traditions that formed the basis of Russian art but introduced lighter and brighter colours, flatter forms, softening of facial types, and increasing use of a graceful, rhythmic line to define form. Until the early 14th century, artistic activity was dominated by mural painting. A new artistic impetus was provided by the introduction of the iconostasis. When icons were displayed together on the iconostasis rather than scattered about the walls of the church, they demanded a coherent overall impression, which was achieved by strong, rhythmic lines and colour harmonies. Figures took on the elongated shape that became standard in Russian art. In the 16th century artistic leadership passed to the Moscow school.

"Miracle of St. George over the Dragon," icon by an anonymous artist of the Novgorod school, egg tempera on panel, beginning of the 15th century; in the State Tretyakov Gallery, Moscow, I.A. Ostroukhov Collection
Novosti Press Agency

Novosibirsk, formerly (1895–1925) NOVONIKOLAYEVSKY, City (pop., 2006 est.: 1,397,015), south-central Russia, in Asia. The capital of Novosibirsk province, it is the chief city of western Siberia and lies on the Ob River where the latter is crossed by the Trans-Siberian Railroad. The city began in 1893 and was named for Tsar Nicholas II in 1895. During World War II many factories from the western part of the U.S.S.R. were moved there. It is renowned for industry and scientific research. As Siberia's cultural and educational centre, it developed the satellite town Akademgorodok with research institutes and a university.

nuclear energy, or ATOMIC ENERGY, Energy released from atomic nuclei in significant amounts. In 1919 Ernest Rutherford discovered that alpha rays could split the nucleus of an atom. This led ultimately to the discovery of the neutron and the release of huge amounts of energy by the process of nuclear fission. Nuclear energy is also released as a result of nuclear fusion. The release of nuclear energy can be controlled or uncontrolled. Nuclear reactors carefully control the release of energy, whereas the energy release of a nuclear weapon or resulting from a core meltdown in a nuclear reactor is uncontrolled.

nuclear fission, Division of a heavy atomic nucleus into two fragments of roughly equal mass, accompanied by the release of a large amount of energy, the binding energy of the subatomic par-

ticles. The energy released in the fission of one uranium nucleus is about 50 million times greater than that released when a carbon atom combines with oxygen atoms in the burning of coal. The energy appears as kinetic energy of the fragments, which converts to thermal energy as the fragments collide in matter and slow down. Fission also releases two or three free neutrons. The free neutrons can bombard other nuclei, leading to a series of fissions called a chain reaction. The energy released from nuclear fission is used to generate electricity, to propel ships and submarines, and is a source of the vast destructive power of nuclear weapons.

nuclear fusion, Process by which nuclear reactions between light elements form heavier ones, releasing huge amounts of energy. In 1939 Hans Bethe suggested that the energy output of the sun and other stars is a result of fusion reactions among hydrogen nuclei. In the early 1950s American scientists produced the hydrogen bomb by inducing fusion reactions in a mixture of the hydrogen isotopes deuterium and tritium, forming a heavier helium nucleus. Though fusion is common in the sun and other stars, it is difficult to produce artificially and is very difficult to control. If controlled nuclear fusion is achieved, it might provide an inexpensive energy source because the primary fuel, deuterium, can be extracted from ordinary water, and eight gallons of water could provide the energy equivalent to 2,500 gallons of gasoline.

nuclear magnetic resonance (NMR), Selective absorption of very high-frequency radio waves by certain atomic nuclei subjected to a strong stationary magnetic field. Nuclei that have at least one unpaired proton or neutron act like tiny magnets. When a strong magnetic field acts on such nuclei, it sets them into precession. When the natural frequency of the precessing nuclear magnets corresponds to the frequency of a weak external radio wave striking the material, energy is absorbed by the nuclei at a frequency called the resonant frequency. NMR is used to study the molecular structure of various solids and liquids. Magnetic resonance imaging, or MRI, is a version of NMR used in medicine to view soft tissues of the human body in a hazard-free, noninvasive way.

Nuclear Non-proliferation Treaty (NPT), officially TREATY ON THE NON-PROLIFERATION OF NUCLEAR WEAPONS, International agreement intended to prevent the spread of nuclear technology. It was signed by the U.S., Britain, the Soviet Union, and 59 other countries in 1968. The three major signatories agreed not to assist states lacking nuclear weapons to obtain or produce them; the nonnuclear signatories agreed not to attempt to obtain nuclear weapons in exchange for assistance in developing nuclear power for peaceful purposes. France and China, both nuclear powers, declined to ratify the treaty until 1992, and some nuclear powers, including Israel and Pakistan, have never signed it. In 1995, when the treaty was due to expire, it was extended indefinitely by a consensus vote of 174 countries at the United Nations.

nuclear physics, Branch of physics dealing with the structure of the atomic nucleus and radiation from unstable nuclei. A principal research tool of nuclear physics is a high-energy beam of particles, such as protons or electrons, directed as projectiles against nuclear targets. By analyzing the directions and energies of the recoiling particles and any resulting nuclear fragments, nuclear physicists can obtain details of nuclear structure, the strong force that binds nuclear components together, and the release of energy from the nucleus.

Nuclear Test-Ban Treaty, officially TREATY BANNING NUCLEAR WEAPONS TESTS IN THE ATMOSPHERE, IN OUTER SPACE AND UNDER WATER, Treaty that prohibits all tests of nuclear weapons except those conducted underground. U.S.-Soviet test-ban talks began after concerns arose in the 1940s and '50s about the dangers of radioactive fallout from above-ground nuclear tests. These talks made little progress until the Cuban missile crisis of 1962. In the following year, Britain, the U.S., and the Soviet Union signed the treaty, and more than 100 other governments soon followed. France and China were notable nonsignatories. In 1996 the treaty was replaced by the Comprehensive Test-Ban Treaty, which will not take effect until it is signed by all 44 countries with nuclear power plants. India refuses to do so on the ground that the treaty lacks disarmament provisions and permits nonexplosive testing.

nuclear weapon, or ATOMIC WEAPON, or THERMONUCLEAR WEAPON, Bomb or other warhead that derives its force from nuclear fission, nuclear fusion, or both and is delivered by an aircraft, missile, or other system. Fission weapons, commonly known as atomic bombs, release energy by splitting the nuclei of uranium or plutonium atoms; fusion weapons, known as hydrogen bombs or thermonuclear bombs, fuse nuclei of the hydrogen isotopes tritium or deuterium. Most nuclear weapons actually combine both processes. Nuclear weapons are the most potent explosive devices ever invented. Their destructive effects include not only a blast equivalent to thousands of tons of TNT but also blinding light, searing heat, and lethal radioactive fallout. The number of nuclear weapons reached a peak of some 32,000 for the United States in 1966 and some 33,000 for the Soviet Union in 1988. Since the end of the Cold War, both countries have decommissioned or dismantled thousands of warheads. Other declared nuclear powers are the United Kingdom, France, China, India, Pakistan, and North Korea. Israel is widely assumed to possess nuclear weapons. Some countries, such as South Africa, Brazil, Argentina, and Iraq, have acknowledged pursuing nuclear weapons in the past but have abandoned their programs.

nucleic acid, Any of the naturally occurring chemical compounds that are capable of being broken down to yield phosphoric acid, sugars, and a mixture of organic bases (purines and pyrimidines). Nucleic acids direct the course of protein synthesis, thereby regulating all cell activities. The two main types, DNA and RNA, are composed of similar materials but differ in structure and function. Both are long chains of repeating nucleotides. The sequence of purines and pyrimidines (bases)—adenine (A), guanine (G), cytosine (C), and either thymine (T; in DNA) or uracil (U; in RNA)—in the nucleotides, in groups of three (triplets, or codons), constitutes the genetic code.

nucleus, Specialized structure occurring in most cells (except bacteria) and separated from the rest of the cell by the nuclear membrane. This membrane seems to be continuous with the cell's endoplasmic reticulum and has pores that permit the passage of large molecules. The nucleus controls and regulates the cell's activities (e.g., growth and metabolism) and carries the genes. Nucleoli are small bodies often seen within the nucleus that play an important part in the synthesis of RNA and protein. A cell normally contains only one nucleus.

nucleus, Central, positively charged core of an atom. It consists of positively charged protons and neutral neutrons, known collectively as nucleons, held together by the strong force. The number of nucleons can range from 1 to about 270, depending on the element. Isotopes are atoms of the same element that have the same number of protons but different numbers of neutrons. Some nuclei, especially heavier ones, are unstable, or radioactive, emitting energy in the form of alpha rays, beta rays, or gamma rays. The nucleus makes up nearly all the mass but only a minute fraction of the volume of the atom.

Nuku'alofa, Town (pop., 2006 prelim.: city, 23,438; urban agglom., 34,058), capital, and chief port of Tonga. Located on the northern shore of Tongatapu Island in the southern Pacific Ocean, it has a deep-draft harbour that is protected by reefs. Commercial activities centre on the export of copra and bananas. Landmarks include the 19th-century royal palace, a chapel, and royal tombs.

number theory, Branch of mathematics concerned with properties of and relations among integers. It is a popular subject among amateur mathematicians and students because of the wealth of seemingly simple problems that can be posed. Answers are much harder to come up with. It has been said that any unsolved mathematical problem of any interest more than a century old belongs to number theory. One of the best examples, recently solved, is Fermat's last theorem.

numerical analysis, Branch of applied mathematics that studies methods for solving complicated equations using arithmetic operations, often so complex that they require a computer, to approximate the processes of analysis (i.e., calculus). The arithmetic model for such an approximation is called an algorithm, the set of procedures the computer executes is called a program, and the commands that carry out the procedures are called code. An example is an algorithm for deriving π by calculating the perimeter of a regular polygon as its number of sides becomes very large. Numerical analysis is concerned not just with the numerical result of such a process but with determining whether the error at any stage is within acceptable bounds.

numerical control (NC), Control of a system or device by direct input of data in the form of numbers, letters, symbols, words, or a combination of these forms. It is a principal element of computer-integrated manufacturing, particularly for controlling the operation of machine tools. NC is also essential to the operation of modern industrial robots. The two basic types of NC systems are point-to-point, in which a device is programmed to perform a series of motions with fixed starting and stopping points, and continuous-path, in which a point-to-point programmed device has sufficient memory to be "aware" of its former actions and their results and to act in accordance with this information.

numerology, Use of numbers to interpret a person's character or divine the future. It is based on the assertion by Pythagoras that all things can be expressed in numerical terms because they are ultimately reducible to numbers. Using a method analogous to that of the Greek and Hebrew alphabets (in which each letter also represented a number), modern numerology attaches a series of digits to an inquirer's name and uses these, along with the date of birth, to reveal the person's true nature and prospects.

Nun, or NU, Oldest of the Egyptian gods and father of Re, the sun god. Nun represented the dark, turbulent waters out of which the cosmos was churned. Since it was believed that the primeval ocean continued to surround the ordered cosmos, the creation myth was reenacted each day as the sun rose from the waters. Nun was also thought to exist as the source of the annual flooding of the Nile.

Nürnberg, also known as NUREMBERG, City (pop., 2002 est.: city, 491,307; metro. area, 1,018,211), Bavaria, southern Germany, on the Pegnitz River. It grew up around a castle in the 11th century, and in 1219 it received its first charter. It became one of the greatest of the German free imperial cities, reaching the height of its power in the 16th century. In 1806 it became part of the kingdom of Bavaria. In the 1930s it was a centre of the Nazi Party; the site of the Nazis' annual Nürnberg Rallies, in 1935 it gave its name to the anti-Semitic Nürnberg Laws. It was severely damaged in World War II. After the war it was the scene of the Nürnberg trials. The city was rebuilt and is now a commercial and manufacturing centre. Nürnberg's historic sites include the 11th-century royal palace. Its Academy of Arts (founded 1662) is the oldest in Germany. The city was the birthplace of Albrecht Dürer.

Nürnberg Laws (1935) Two measures designed by Adolf Hitler and approved by a Nazi Party convention at Nürnberg, Ger., on Sept. 15, 1935. The laws deprived Jews of German citizenship and forbade marriage or sexual relations between Jews and "citizens of German or cognate blood." Supplementary decrees defined a Jew as a person with at least one Jewish grandparent and declared that Jews could not vote or hold public office.

Nürnberg trials (1945–46) Trials of former Nazi Party leaders held in Nürnberg, Ger. At the end of World War II, the International Military Tribunal was established by the U.S., Britain, France, and the Soviet Union to indict and try former Nazis as war criminals. The tribunal defined the offenses as crimes against peace (planning and waging of war in violation of treaties), crimes against humanity (extermination, deportation, and genocide), and war crimes. After 216 court sessions, 3 of the original 22 defendants were acquitted, 4 (including Karl Dönitz and Albert Speer) were sentenced to prison for terms of 10 to 20 years, 3 (including Rudolf Hess) were sentenced to life imprisonment, and 12 (including Wilhelm Keitel, Joachim von Ribbentrop, Alfred Rosenberg, Arthur Seyss-Inquart, and Julius Streicher) were sentenced to death by hanging. Hermann Göring committed suicide before he could be executed, and Martin Bormann was convicted in absentia.

nursery rhyme, Verse customarily told or sung to small children. Though the oral tradition of nursery rhymes is ancient, the largest number date from the 16th, 17th, and (most frequently) 18th centuries. Apparently most rhymes were originally composed for adults, many as popular ballads and songs. The earliest known published collection is *Tommy Thumb's* (*Pretty*) *Song Book* (1744), including "Little Tom Tucker," "Sing a Song of Sixpence," and "Who Killed Cock Robin?" The most influential collection was *Mother Goose's Melody* (1781), including "Jack and Jill," "Ding Dong Bell," and "Hush-a-bye Baby on the Tree Top."

nursing, Health-care profession providing physical and emotional care to the sick and disabled and promoting health in all individuals through activities including research, health education, and patient consultation. Nursing gained recognition in the 19th century with the activities of Florence Nightingale. Many nurses have specialties (e.g., psychiatry, critical care). Nurse-practitioners, clinical nurse specialists, nurse-anesthetists, and nurse-midwives undertake tasks traditionally performed by physicians. Nursing degrees go as high as the doctorate, and staff positions include administration. In addition to health-care settings, nurses practice in schools, the military, industry, and private homes. Community (public health) nurses educate the public on topics such as nutrition and disease prevention.

nursing home, Facility for care (usually long-term) of patients who are not sick enough to need hospital care but are not able to remain at home. Historically, most residents were elderly or ill or had chronic irreversible and disabling disorders, and medical and nursing care was minimal. Today nursing homes have a more active role in health care, helping patients prepare to live at home or with a family member when possible. They help conserve expensive hospital facilities for the acutely ill and improve the prospects of the chronically disabled. However, quality of care varies widely, and the potential for abuse exists.

Nut, In Egyptian religion, a goddess of the sky. She represented the vault of the heavens and was often depicted as a woman arched over the earth god Geb. Nut was believed to swallow the sun in the evening and to give birth to it again in the morning. She was sometimes portrayed as a cow, the form she took to carry the sun god, Re, on her back to the sky. On five days preceding the New Year, Nut gave birth successively to the deities Osiris, Horus, Seth, Isis, and Nephthys.

nut, Dry, hard, one-seeded fruit consisting of a kernel, usually oily, surrounded by a hard or brittle shell that does not split open at maturity. Nuts include chestnuts, filberts, and walnuts; but other so-called nuts are botanically seeds (Brazil nut, pistachio), legumes (peanut), or drupes (almond and coconut). Most edible nuts

are well known as dessert nuts. Some nuts are sources of oil or fat. Not all nuts are edible; some are used for ornament.

nutmeg, Spice made from the seed of a tropical tree (*Myristica fragrans*), native to the Moluc-

Nutmeg *(Myristica fragrans)*
G.R. Roberts

cas of Indonesia. It has a distinctive pungent fragrance and is used in cooking and sachets and as incense. The tree yields fruit eight years after sowing, reaches its prime in 25 years, and bears fruit for 60 years or longer. The name nutmeg is also applied in different countries to other fruits or seeds, including the Brazilian nutmeg (*Cryptocarya moschata*), the Peruvian nutmeg (*Laurelia aromatica*), and the California nutmeg (*Torreya californica*).

Nuuk, or GODTHÅB, City (pop., 2000 est.: 13,838), capital of Greenland. Located on the southwestern coast near the mouth of Godthåb Gulf, it is Greenland's main port. The modern city dates from 1721, when a Norwegian missionary founded a colony near the site of Vesterbygden, a 10th-century Norse settlement. It is the seat of the parliament and supreme court and has foreign consulates, a teachers' college, and research stations. Government administration, hunting, fishing, and farming are the main occupations. Most transportation is by boat or helicopter.

Nyerere, Julius (Kambarage) (b. March 1922, Butiama, Tanganyika—d. Oct. 14, 1999,

Nyerere, 1981
Hanos/Liaison Agency

London, Eng.), First prime minister of independent Tanganyika (1961), first president of Tanzania (1964–85), and the major force behind the Organization of African Unity (OAU; now African Union). He taught in Catholic schools before studying history and economics in Britain. As leader of the Tanganyika African National Union (TANU), he advocated peaceful change, social equality, and ethnic harmony. In elections in 1958–60 TANU won many seats in the legislature. As president he collectivized village farmlands, carried out mass literacy campaigns, and instituted universal education. He sought to make Tanzania economically self-sufficient, an effort that ultimately failed. In 1979 he authorized the invasion of Uganda to overthrow Idi Amin. Within the OAU he advocated the overthrow of white-suprematist governments in South Africa, Rhodesia, and South West Africa. After retiring from politics in 1990, Nyerere devoted the rest of his life to farming and diplomacy.

nylon, Any synthetic plastic material composed of polyamides of high molecular weight and usually, but not always, manufactured as a fibre. Nylons were developed by Du Pont in the 1930s. The successful production of a useful fibre by chemical synthesis from compounds readily available from air, water, and coal or petroleum stimulated expansion of research on polymers, leading to a rapidly growing family of synthetics. Nylon can be made to form fibres, filaments, bristles, or sheets to be manufactured into yarn, textiles, and cordage, and it can also be formed into molded products. It has high resistance to wear, heat, and chemicals. Most applications are in the form of filaments in such articles as hosiery, parachutes, and outerwear.

O

oasis, Fertile tract of land that occurs in a desert wherever a permanent supply of fresh water is available. Oases vary in size from about 2.5 acres (1 hectare) around small springs to vast areas of naturally watered or irrigated land. Underground water sources account for most oases; their springs and wells are supplied from sandstone aquifers whose intake areas may be more than 500 mi (800 km) away. Two-thirds of the population of the Sahara live in oases, where the date palm is the main source of food; the palm also provides shade for growing citrus fruits, figs, peaches, apricots, vegetables, and cereal grains.

Obama, Barack, in full BARACK HUSSEIN OBAMA, JR. (b. Aug. 4, 1961, Honolulu, Hawaii, U.S.), 44th president of the U.S. (2009–). Obama graduated from Columbia University (1983) and Harvard Law School (1991), where he was the first African American to serve as president of the *Harvard Law Review*. He moved to Chicago, where he served as a community organizer and lectured in constitutional law at the University of Chicago before he was elected (1996) to the Illinois Senate as a member of the Democratic Party. In 2004 he was elected to the U.S. Senate and quickly became a major national political figure. In 2008 Obama won an upset victory over former U.S. first lady Hillary Clinton to become the Democratic presidential nominee. He easily defeated Republican candidate John McCain and became the first African American president. In 2009 he was awarded the Nobel Peace Prize "for his extraordinary efforts to strengthen international diplomacy and cooperation between peoples."

obelisk, Tapered four-sided pillar, originally erected in pairs at the entrance to ancient Egyptian temples. The Egyptian obelisk was carved from a single piece of stone, usually granite, and embellished with hieroglyphics. It was wider at its square or rectangular base than at its pyramidal top, and could be over 100 ft (30 m) high. During the Roman empire, many obelisks were transported from Egypt to Italy. A well-known modern obelisk is the Washington Monument.

obesity, Excessive body fat. It is usually caused by sedentary habits and a diet high in fat, alcohol, or total calories. Calories consumed but not used are stored as fat. Rare causes include glandular defects and excess steroids. Obesity raises the risk of heart disease and diabetes mellitus. Treatment, by reducing calorie intake and increasing exercise, is best undertaken with a doctor's advice.

obia, or OBEAH, In West African folklore, a gigantic animal that steals into villages by night to kidnap girls on behalf of witches. In some Caribbean cultures the word is used to refer to overpowering and extremely evil forms of witchcraft and sorcery. Bewitched objects, buried with the intent of causing harm, are sometimes called obia. A person who uses the power of obia is called an obiama or obiaman.

object-oriented programming (OOP), Computer programming that emphasizes the structure of data and their encapsulation with the procedures that operate upon it. It is a departure from traditional or procedural programming. OOP languages incorporate objects that are self-contained collections of computational procedures and data structures. Programs can be written by assembling sets of these predefined objects in far less time than is possible using conventional procedural languages. OOP has become extremely popular because of its high programming productivity. C++ and Objective-C (early 1980s) are object-oriented versions of C that have gained much popularity.

oblation, In Christianity, the offering up by the faithful of any gift for use usually by the clergy, the church, or the sick or poor. The bread and wine offered for consecration in the Eucharist are oblations. In the Middle Ages children dedicated to a monastery and left there to be brought up were called oblates. Later, oblates were laity who lived at or in close connection with a monastery but who did not take religious vows. Members of certain Roman Catholic communities take the title oblate (e.g., the Oblates Regular of St. Benedict).

oboe, Double-reed woodwind instrument. The oboe developed out of the more powerful shawm in the early 17th century. Intended (unlike the shawm) for indoor use with stringed instruments, its tone was softer and less brilliant. With its sweet but piercing sound, it was by the end of the 17th century the principal wind instrument of the orchestra and military band and, after the violin, the leading solo instrument of the time. The early oboe had only 2 keys, but in France by 1839 the number of keys had gradually increased to 10. With the decline in popularity of the military band, the oboe likewise declined somewhat in popularity. Today the orchestra generally includes two oboes. The oboe d'amore, an alto oboe with a pear-shaped bell, was especially popular in the 18th century; the modern alto oboe is the English horn.

obscenity, Act, utterance, writing, or illustration that is deemed deeply offensive according to contemporary community standards of morality and decency. Though most societies have placed restrictions on the content of literary and graphic works, it was not until relatively modern times that sexuality became a major focus of societal concern. One of the first systematic efforts to suppress books deemed to be immoral or heretical was undertaken by the Roman Catholic church in the 16th century. Modern obscenity laws can be viewed as direct responses to the social and technological changes (e.g., the creation of the printing press and the development of the Internet) that have permitted the wide and easy distribution of sexually explicit materials. The Supreme Court of the United States has ruled that materials are obscene if they appeal predominantly to a prurient interest in sexual conduct, depict or describe sexual conduct in a patently offensive way, and lack serious literary, artistic, political, or scientific value. Material deemed obscene under this definition is not protected in the U.S. by the free-speech guarantee of the 1st Amendment.

observatory, Structure containing telescopes and other instruments for observing celestial objects and phenomena. Observatories can be classified by the part of the electromagnetic spectrum they can receive. Most are optical, observing in and near the region of the visible spectrum. Some are equipped to detect radio waves; others (space observatories) are Earth satellites and other spacecraft that carry special telescopes and detectors to study celestial sources of high-energy radiation (e.g., gamma rays, ultraviolet radiation, X-rays) from above the atmosphere. Stonehenge may have been an early predecessor of the optical observatory. Perhaps the first observatory that used instruments to accurately measure the positions of celestial objects was built *c.* 150 BC by Hipparchus. The first notable premodern European observatory was that at Uraniborg, built for Tycho Brahe in 1576. Observatory House, in Slough, Eng., built and operated by William Herschel, was one of the technical wonders of the 18th century. Today the world's largest groupings of optical telescopes are atop Mauna Kea, in Hawaii, and Cerro Tololo, in Chile. Other major observatories include Arecibo Observatory; Mount Wilson Observatory; Palomar Observatory; and Royal Greenwich Observatory.

obsessive-compulsive disorder, Mental disorder in which an individual experiences obsessions or compulsions, either singly or together. An obsession is a persistent disturbing preoccupation with an unreasonable idea or feeling (such as of being contaminated through shaking hands with someone). A compulsion is an irresistible impulse to perform an irrational act (such as repeatedly washing the hands). The two phenomena are usually, but not always, linked in the obsessive-compulsive person. Onset of the illness has been linked to malregulation of the neurotransmitter serotonin as well as to the ill effects of high stress.

obstetrics and gynecology, Medical and surgical specialty concerned with the management of pregnancy and childbirth and with the health of the female reproductive system. Obstetrics, first practiced by midwives, developed as a medical discipline in the 17th–19th centuries, adopting the use of forceps in delivery, anesthetics, and antiseptic methods. The last two made cesarean section possible. Obstetricians confirm pregnancy, diagnose ectopic pregnancy, conduct prenatal care, perform amniocentesis, deliver babies, and perform abortions. In the late 20th century a backlash against the excessive medicalization of birth led to a revival of midwifery and encouragement of natural childbirth. Gynecologists do routine pelvic exams, take samples for Pap smears, advise on and prescribe birth control, and treat reproductive system disorders (e.g., endometriosis, hormonal imbalances, problems with menstruation and menopause). They perform surgery to prevent conception (tubal ligation), repair pelvic injuries, and remove cysts and tumours from the uterus, cervix, and ovaries. Both specialties are involved in diagnosis and treatment of infertility.

occultism, Theories, practices, and rituals based on esoteric knowledge of the world of spirits and unknown forces. The wide range of occult beliefs and practices includes astrology, alchemy, divination, magic, and witchcraft and sorcery. Devotees of occultism seek to explore spiritual mysteries through what they regard as higher powers of the mind. The Western tradition of occultism has its roots in Hellenistic magic and alchemy (especially the Hermetic writings ascribed to Thoth) and in the Jewish mysticism associated with the Kabbala.

ocean, Large, continuous body of salt water. Ocean covers nearly 71% of the Earth's surface and is divided into major oceans and smaller seas. The three principal oceans, the Pacific, Atlantic, and Indian, are largely delimited by land and submarine topographic boundaries. All are connected to what is sometimes called the Southern Ocean, the waters encircling Antarctica. Important marginal seas, primarily in the Northern Hemisphere, are partially enclosed by landmasses or island arcs. The largest are the Arctic Ocean and adjacent seas, Caribbean and adjacent waters, Mediterranean, Bering Sea, Sea of Okhotsk, Yellow Sea, China Sea, and Sea of Japan.

ocean liner, Large merchant ship that visits designated ports on a regular schedule, carrying whatever cargo and passengers are available on the date of sailing. The first liners were operated in the North Atlantic, notably by Samuel Cunard of Britain, beginning in 1840. Their heyday lasted from the late 19th to the mid-20th century. Many were extraordinarily luxurious. Among the most famous were Cunarders such as the *Mauretania* and the *Queen Mary*; the German *Vaterland* (later renamed *Leviathan*), for many years the largest ship afloat; the ill-fated *Titanic*; and the *United States*. Their reign ended in the 1960s with the rise of jet travel, but liners ranging from cruise ships to refrigerated cargo ships continued to sail.

Oceania, Collective name for the islands scattered throughout most of the Pacific Ocean. The term especially refers to islands of the central and southern Pacific, including those of Micronesia, Melanesia, and Polynesia; New Zealand is often included and sometimes Australia. In its most restricted sense, excluding Australia but including Papua New Guinea, Oceania includes more than 10,000 islands and has a land area of about 317,000 sq mi (821,000 sq km).

Oceanic religions, Non-Christian religions practiced in Oceania. Traditional Melanesian religions, which are giving way under the pressures of Christianity and capitalism, hold that ancestral ghosts and other spirits are participants in daily life. Their presence and effects are manifested in dreams, in divination, and in human successes and failures. Magic is widely practiced, and sorcery is seen as the major cause of death and illness. The traditional religions of Micronesia, which have largely died out, recognized several high gods and many other spirits, including the spirits of ancestors and the dead. Magic played an important role. In Polynesia, each of the gods, whether high or local, had its own ritual requirements, and schools of priests were often required to carry them out. All things were believed to possess mana, which had to be protected by complicated rules and taboos. The Polynesians often offered human sacrifices on important occasions, such as the formal investiture of a priest or chief. With the introduction of modern goods, the peoples of all these islands became susceptible to cargo cults.

ocelot, Species (*Leopardus pardalis*) of cat found in forests, grasslands, and brush-covered regions from Texas to northern Argentina. The ocelot is 36–52 in. (90–130 cm) long, excluding the 12–16-in. (30–40-cm) tail. It stands about 18 in. (45 cm) and weighs 24–35 lbs (11–16 kg). The upper body varies from whitish to tawny yellow to gray. The head, neck, and body are marked by specific patterns of black stripes and spots: spots on the head, two stripes on each cheek, oblong spots arranged in chainlike bands on the body, and bars or blotches on the tail. The ocelot hunts at night for small mammals, birds, reptiles, and fish. It is listed as an endangered species in the U.S.

*Ocelot (*Leopardus pardalis*).*
Warren Garst/Tom Stack and Associates

Ockham's razor, Methodological principle of parsimony in scientific explanation. Traditionally attributed to William of Ockham, the principle prescribes that entities are not to be multiplied beyond necessity. In practice, this means that if a phenomenon can be explained without assuming the existence of an entity, then philosophers and scientists should not assume the entity's existence. The history of science provides many examples of the principle's application (e.g., the rejection by scientists of the hypothesis of a luminiferous ether in response to Albert Einstein's Special Theory of Relativity).

OCR, in full OPTICAL CHARACTER RECOGNITION, Scanning and comparison technique intended to identify printed text or numerical data. It avoids the need to retype already printed material for data entry. OCR software attempts to identify characters by comparing shapes to those stored in the software library. The software tries to identify words using character proximity and will try to reconstruct the original page layout. High accuracy can be obtained by using sharp, clear scans of high-quality originals, but it decreases as the quality of the original declines.

October Manifesto, Document issued by Tsar Nicholas II in October 1905. In response to the unrest caused by the Russian Revolution of 1905 and on the advice of his minister Sergey Witte, Nicholas promised to guarantee civil liberties and establish a popularly elected Duma. The manifesto satisfied the moderate revolutionaries, and further unrest was crushed. In 1906 the Fundamental Laws were established to serve as a constitution and to create the Duma. The Duma was in fact given only a limited voice in the government, and the civil rights actually granted were far less substantial than those promised by the manifesto.

octopus, In general, any eight-armed cephalopod of the order Octopoda; specifically, members of a large, widely distributed group (genus *Octopus*) of shallow-water species. Species range from about 2 in. (5 cm) to 18 ft (5.5 m) long with an arm span up to 30 ft (9 m). The head is usually only slightly demarcated from the saccular body. Each arm is contractile and bears fleshy suckers. Two sharp beaks and a filelike organ in the mouth drill crustacean shells and rasp away flesh. Most octopuses crawl along the bottom; when alarmed, they may jet-propel themselves backward, and they sometimes eject an inky substance to cloud the water and protect themselves from predators. They can change colour rapidly, a reflection of their environment or mood. The common octopus (*O. vulgaris*) is thought to be the most intelligent of all invertebrates.

Octopus granulatus, *a South African species.*

Anthony Bannister—The Natural History Photographic Agency/EB Inc.

ode, Ceremonious lyric poem on an occasion of dignity in which personal emotion and universal themes are united. The form is usually marked by exalted feeling and style, varying line length, and complex stanza forms. The term *ode* derives from a Greek word alluding to a choric song, usually accompanied by a dance. Forms of odes include the Pindaric ode, written to celebrate public events such as the Olympic games, and the form associated with Horace, whose intimate, reflective odes have two- or four-line stanzas and polished metres. Both were revived during the Renaissance and influenced Western lyric poetry into the 20th century. The ode (*qaṣīdah*) also flourished in pre-Islamic Arabic poetry.

Odessa, City (pop., 2001: 1,029,000), southwestern Ukraine. A Tatar fortress was established in Odessa in the 14th century. The city was ceded to Russia in 1791 and became its second most important port after Saint Petersburg, with grain as its principal export. It was a centre of revolutionary activity in 1905, and it suffered heavy damage in World War II. Odessa is a major seaport and industrial centre, with shipbuilding, engineering, and oil refineries. It is also a cultural centre, with a university, museums, and theatres.

Odin, or WOTAN, One of the principal Norse gods. A war god from earliest times, Odin appeared in Scandinavian heroic literature as the protector of heroes. Fallen warriors were believed to join him in Valhalla. Odin was the great magician among the gods and was associated with runic writing. His eight-legged horse, Sleipnir, could gallop through the air and over the sea. Odin was usually depicted as a tall old man with a flowing beard and only one eye (the other he gave in exchange for wisdom); he wore a cloak and a wide-brimmed hat and carried a spear. The wolf and the raven were dedicated to him.

Odysseus, Roman ULYSSES, Hero of Homer's *Odyssey*. According to Homer, Odysseus was the king of Ithaca. His shrewdness, resourcefulness, and endurance enabled him to capture Troy (through the device of the Trojan horse) and endure nine years of wandering and adventures before reaching his home in Ithaca, where his wife, Penelope, and son, Telemachus, awaited him. Classical opinion was divided on whether he was an unscrupulous politician or a wise and honourable statesman. Odysseus has been one of the most frequently portrayed figures in literature, treated by numerous Greek and Roman poets and by later writers such as William Shakespeare (*Troilus and Cressida*), Níkos Kazantzákis (*The Odyssey: A Modern Sequel*), and (metaphorically) by James Joyce (*Ulysses*) and Derek Walcott (*Omeros*).

Ōe Kenzaburō (b. Jan. 31, 1935, Ehime prefecture, Shikoku, Japan), Japanese novelist. Ōe first attracted attention on the literary scene while still a student at the University of Tokyo. His works, written in a rough prose style that at times nearly violates the natural rhythms of Japanese, reflect his life and epitomize the rebellion of the post-World War II generation. They include *A Personal Matter* (1964), which uses the birth of an abnormal baby to investigate the problem of culturally disinherited youth; *Hiroshima Notes* (1965); and *The Silent Cry* (1967). He received the Nobel Prize for Literature in 1994.

Oedipus, In Greek mythology, a king of Thebes who unwittingly killed his father and married his mother. In the most familiar version of the story, Laius, king of Thebes, was warned by an oracle that his son would slay him. When his wife, Jocasta, bore a son, he exposed the baby on a mountainside, but the infant Oedipus was saved by a shepherd and adopted by the king of Corinth. In early manhood, as Oedipus traveled toward Thebes, he met Laius, who provoked a quarrel; in the ensuing fracas, Oedipus killed him. He then rid Thebes of the destructive Sphinx by answering its riddle; as a reward he was given the throne of Thebes and the hand of the widowed queen—his mother. They had four children, including Antigone. When at last they learned the truth, Jocasta committed suicide and Oedipus blinded himself and went into exile. Oedipus has served as the hero of many tragedies, most notably Sophocles' *Oedipus Rex* and *Oedipus at Colonus*.

offset printing, or OFFSET LITHOGRAPHY, or LITHO-OFFSET, In commercial printing, a widely used technique in which the inked image on a printing plate is imprinted on a rubber cylinder and then transferred (offset) to paper or other material. The rubber cylinder gives great flexibility, permitting printing on wood, cloth, metal, leather, and rough paper. In offset printing the matter to be printed is neither raised above the surface of the printing plate (as in letterpress printing) nor sunk below it (as in intaglio, or gravure, printing). Offset printing, a development of lithography, is based on the principle that water and grease do not mix, so that a greasy ink can be deposited on grease-treated printing areas of the plate, while nonprinting areas, which hold water, reject the ink. The offset plate is usually of zinc or aluminum or a combination of metals, with the surface treated to render it porous and then coated with a photosensitive material. Exposure to an image hardens the coating on printing areas; the coating on nonprinting areas is washed away, leaving wetted metal that will reject ink.

O'Higgins, Bernardo (b. probably Aug. 20, 1776/78, Chillán, Chile, Viceroyalty of La Plata—d. October 1842, Peru), South American revolutionary leader and first Chilean head of state (1817–23). The illegitimate son of a Spanish officer of Irish origin, he was educated in Peru, Spain, and England, where his Chilean nationalism was awakened. When Napoleon invaded Spain (1808) and Spanish control of Chile relaxed, he became a member of Chile's new congress. He led the defensive forces when Chile was invaded by royalists from Peru in 1814; defeated, he fled to Argentina. He returned in 1817 with José de San Martín and defeated the Spanish. Elected supreme director of Chile, he established a working governmental organization, but his reforms antagonized conservatives and he resigned.

oil, Any greasy substance liquid at room temperature and insoluble in water. It may be a fixed (nonvolatile) oil, an essential oil, or a mineral oil. Fixed oils and fats (derived from animals and plants) have the same chemical composition—both are esters of glycerol and fatty acids. These oils have a variety of industrial and food uses. Linseed, tung, and other drying oils are highly unsaturated; these and large quantities of soybean, sunflower, and safflower oils (also constituents of foods) are used in paints and varnishes. When exposed to air they absorb oxygen and polymerize, forming a tough coating. Some specialty oils and oil derivatives are also used in leather dressing and textile manufacture.

oil shale, Any fine-grained sedimentary rock that contains solid organic matter (kerogen) and yields significant quantities of oil when heated. This shale oil is a potentially valuable fossil fuel, but the present methods of mining and refining it are expensive, damage the land, pollute the water, and produce carcinogenic wastes. Thus, oil shale will probably not be exploited on a wide scale until other petroleum resources have been nearly depleted. Estonia, China, and Brazil have facilities for producing relatively limited quantities, and the U.S. government operates an experimental plant in Colorado.

okapi, Ruminant species (*Okapia johnstoni*) in the giraffe family that lives alone in Congo rain forests, eating leaves and fruit. Its neck and legs are proportionately shorter than the giraffe's, and females, which are larger than males, stand about 5 ft (1.5 m) at the shoulder. The sleek coat is deep brown on the front of the body; the upper legs are black-and-white-striped, and the lower legs are white, with black rings above the hooves. The male's short horns are covered with skin except at the tips.

Okapi (Okapia johnstoni).
Kenneth W. Fink/Root Resources

Okhotsk, Sea of, Arm of the northwestern Pacific Ocean. Bounded by the Siberian coast, the Kamchatka Peninsula and the Kuril Islands, Hokkaido, and Sakhalin Island, it covers 611,000 sq mi (1,580,000 sq km). It connects the ports of the Russian Far East. Ice floes impede navigation in winter, and dense fog is a hindrance during the summer.

Okinawa, Island of Japan, located in the Ryukyu archipelago, in the East China Sea. The largest island in the Ryukyu chain, it is about 70 mi (112 km) long and 7 mi (11 km) wide, with an area of 466 sq mi (1,206 sq km). It was the site of severe fighting between the U.S. and Japan in World War II. In April 1945 U.S. troops made an amphibious landing there, which was heavily defended by the Japanese. In a three-month-long campaign, both sides sustained heavy casualties before U.S. forces gained control of the island. In 1972 the United States returned jurisdiction over Okinawa to Japan, though the U.S. military continued to maintain installations there.

Oktoberfest, Annual festival in Munich, Germany, lasting two weeks and ending on the first Sunday of October. It began in 1810 as a horse race celebrating the wedding of the crown prince of Bavaria, later King Louis I (1786–1868). The race was soon combined with the state agricultural fair, and food and drink were offered. In the late 20th century the Munich breweries celebrated Oktoberfest by setting up large temporary beer halls, each seating 3,000–5,000 people, and hiring bands to entertain the crowds as they ate and drank. Total beer consumption during the festival exceeds a million gallons.

Old Believers, Russian dissenters who refused to accept liturgical reforms imposed on the Russian Orthodox Church by Nikon in 1652–58. Numbering in the millions in the 17th century, the Old Believers endured persecution for years, and several of their leaders were executed. They split into a variety of sects, of which the two main groups were the Popovtsy (priestly sects) and Bezpopovtsy (priestless sects). In 1971 the council of the Russian Orthodox Church rescinded all the anathemas of the 17th century and recognized the full validity of the old rites.

Old English, or ANGLO-SAXON, Language spoken and written in England before AD 1100. It belongs to the Anglo-Frisian group of Germanic languages. Four dialects are known: Northumbrian (in northern England and southeastern Scotland), Mercian (central England), Kentish (southeastern England), and West Saxon (southern and southwestern England). Mercian and Northumbrian are often called the Anglian dialects. Most extant Old English writings are in the West Saxon dialect. The great epic poem of Old English is *Beowulf*; the first period of extensive literary activity occurred in the 9th century. Old English had three genders (masculine, feminine, neuter) for nouns and adjectives; nouns, pronouns, and adjectives were also inflected for case. Old English had a greater proportion of strong (irregular) verbs than does Modern English, and its vocabulary was more heavily Germanic.

Old Norse language, Classical Germanic language used *c.* 1150–1350, the literary language of the Icelandic sagas, skaldic poetry, and Eddas. The terms Old Norse and Old Icelandic are sometimes used interchangeably because Icelandic records of this period are more plentiful and of greater literary value than those in the other Scandinavian languages, but Old Norse also embraces the ancestors of modern Norwegian, Danish, Swedish, and Faroese.

Old Testament, Sacred scriptures of Judaism and, with the New Testament, of Christianity. Written almost entirely in the Hebrew language between 1200 and 100 BC, the Old Testament (also called the Hebrew Bible or Tanakh) is an account of God's dealings with the Hebrews as his chosen people. In the Hebrew Bible, the first six books tell how the Israelites became a people and settled in the Promised Land, the following seven books describe the development of Israel's monarchy and the messages of the prophets, and the last 11 books contain poetry, theology, and some additional historical works. Christians divided some of the original Hebrew books into two or more parts, specifically, Samuel, Kings, and Chronicles (two parts each), Ezra-Nehemiah (two separate books), and the Minor Prophets (12 separate books). The content of the Old Testament varies according to religious tradition, the Jewish, Roman Catholic, and Protestant canons all differing from each other as to which books they include.

Olduvai Gorge, Archaeological site on the eastern Serengeti Plain, northern Tanzania. It is a steep-sided ravine about 30 mi (48 km) long and 295 ft (90 m) deep. Deposits exposed in the sides of the gorge cover a time span from *c.* 2,100,000 to 15,000 years ago and have yielded the remains of more than 50 hominins as well as the most complete sequence of stone tool industries. The site first came to public notice in 1959 when Louis and Mary Leakey uncovered the first specimens of *Paranthropus*, a hominin related to *Australopithecus*. Remains of *Homo habilis*, *Homo erectus*, and *Homo sapiens* have since been found. These discoveries have strengthened the argument that the human lineage originated in Africa.

oleander, Any of the ornamental evergreen shrubs of the genus *Nerium* (dogbane family), which have poisonous milky juice. Numerous varieties of flower colour in the common oleander, or rosebay (*N. oleander*), have been introduced from greenhouse culture and are grown outdoors in warmer climates. All parts of the plant are very toxic if eaten, and contact with them may cause skin irritation.

Oligocene Epoch, Major division of the Paleogene Period, from *c.* 33.9 million to 23 million years ago. It follows the Eocene Epoch and precedes the Miocene Epoch. The term (from the Greek for "few recent forms") refers to the small number of modern animals that originated during this epoch. Oligocene climates appear to have been temperate, and many regions were nearly tropical. Grasslands expanded, and forested regions dwindled. The vertebrates of the northern continents had an essentially modern aspect that is a result less of the appearance of new forms than of the extinction of archaic vertebrates at the close of the Eocene.

oligopoly, Market situation in which producers are so few that the actions of each of them have an impact on price and on competitors. Each producer must consider the effect of a price change on the others. A cut in price by one may lead to an equal reduction by the others, with the result that each firm will retain about the same share of the market as before but with a lower profit margin. Competition in oligopolistic industries thus tends to manifest itself in nonprice forms such as advertising and product differentiation. Oligopolies in the U.S. include the steel, aluminum, and automobile industries.

olive, Subtropical, broad-leaved tree (*Olea europaea*) or its edible fruit. The olive was being grown on the island of Crete *c.* 3500 BC, and Semitic peoples apparently were cultivating it as early as 3000 BC. Its cultivation was important to the ancient Greeks and Romans and spread to all the countries bordering the Mediterranean. Today olives are grown primarily for olive oil, valued both for its distinctive taste and fragrance and for its dietary benefits. Fresh olives must be treated to neutralize their extreme bitterness before they can be eaten. The olive family (Oleaceae) comprises about 900 species in 24 genera of woody plants. Native to forested regions, members of the family grow worldwide except in the Arctic; they are evergreen in tropical and warm temperate climes and deciduous in colder zones. The family includes ash trees, which yield hardwood timber, and horticultural favourites such as the lilac, jasmine, privet, and forsythia. Many members of the family are cultivated for their beautiful and fragrant flowers.

Olmec, First elaborate pre-Columbian culture of Mesoamerica. The Olmec lived on the lowland coast of the Gulf of Mexico in what is now southern Mexico. They developed a wide trading network, their cultural influence spreading north to the Valley of Mexico and south to Central America; later native religions and iconography throughout Mesoamerica have Olmec roots. Their oldest known building site, San Lorenzo, which dates to *c.* 1150 BC, is remarkable for its colossal stone sculptures of human heads. The dominant motif in Olmec art is the figure of a god that is a hybrid of a jaguar and a human infant. A later Olmec ceremonial centre, La Venta, is marked by great mounds, a narrow plaza, and several other ceremonial enclosures. In the 21st century, inscribed carvings suggestive of later Mayan glyphs also were found at La Venta. Olmec buildings, monuments, and art style all indicate a complex and nonegalitarian society.

Olympia, Ancient sanctuary and site of the Olympic Games, northwestern Peloponnese, southern Greece. Located 10 mi (16 km) inland from the Ionian Sea, it was on the northern bank of the Alpheus River. A centre of Greek religious worship, it held the primarily athletic contests in honour of Zeus every four years, beginning in 776 BCE. In the temple of Zeus, built *c.* 460 BCE, was the statue of Zeus by Phidias, one of the Seven Wonders of the World. Excavations have uncovered many ruins, including temples and the stadium.

Olympic Games, Sports festival. In ancient Greece it was a Panhellenic festival held every fourth year and made up of contests of sports, music, and literature. Since 1896 the name has been used for a modified revival of the ancient Games, consisting of international athletic contests held at four-year intervals. The original Games included footraces, the discus and javelin throws, the long jump, boxing, wrestling, the pentathlon, and chariot races. After the subjugation of Greece by Rome, the Games declined; they were finally abolished about AD 400. They were revived in the late 19th century through efforts led in part by Pierre, baron de Coubertin; the first modern Games were held in Athens. The first Winter Games were held in 1924. The direction of the modern Olympic movement and the regulation of the Games are vested in the International Olympic Committee, headquartered at Lausanne, Switz. Until the 1970s the Games adhered to a strict code of amateurism, but since that time professional players have also been allowed to participate. Programs for the Summer Games include competition in archery, baseball, basketball, boxing, canoeing, cycling, diving, equestrian sports, fencing, field hockey, foot-

ball (soccer), gymnastics, handball, judo, the modern pentathlon, rowing, sailing, shooting, softball, swimming, table tennis, tennis, track and field (athletics), the triathlon, volleyball, water polo, weightlifting, and wrestling. The program for the Winter Games includes the biathlon, bobsledding, ice hockey, lugeing, skeleton sledding, snowboarding, and numerous ice skating and skiing events. Events are periodically added and dropped.

Olympus, Mount, Mountain peak, northeastern Greece. At 9,570 ft (2,917 m), it is the highest mountain in Greece. It is part of the Olympus range, lying on the border between Macedonia and Thessaly, near the Gulf of Salonika. The summit is snowcapped and often has cloud cover. In ancient Greece, it was regarded as the abode of the gods and the site of the throne of Zeus.

Olympus Mons, Large volcano on Mars, the largest known volcano in the solar system. It consists of a central structure that ascends about 13 mi (21 km) above Mars's mean radius and is 335 mi (540 km) wide at the base; it is surrounded by an outward-facing cliff rising as much as 6 mi (10 km) above the surrounding area. At the summit is a crater 53 mi (85 km) in diameter. For comparison, Earth's largest volcano, Mauna Loa, is 75 mi (120 km) wide at the base and rises 5.6 mi (9 km) above the ocean floor.

om, In Hinduism and other Indian religions, a sacred syllable considered the greatest of all mantras. The syllable *om* is composed of the three sounds *a-u-m* (in the Sanskrit language, the vowels *a* and *u* join to become *o*), which represent three important triads: earth, atmosphere, and heaven; the major Hindu gods, Brahma, Vishnu, and Shiva; and the sacred Vedic scriptures, Rig, Yajur, and Sama. Thus om mystically embodies the essence of the universe. It is uttered at the beginning and end of Hindu prayers, chants, and meditation and is also freely used in Buddhist and Jain rituals.

Oman, officially SULTANATE OF OMAN, formerly MUSCAT AND OMAN, Country, Middle East, southwestern Asia. It is on the southeast coast of the Arabian Peninsula. Area: 119,500 sq mi (309,500 sq km). Population: (2011 est.) 2,810,000. Capital: Muscat. The Omanis are predominantly Arab and tribal in organization. There are also many migrant workers from South Asia and eastern Africa who reside there. Languages: Arabic (official), others. Religions: Islam (official); also Hinduism, Christianity. Currency: Omani rial. Oman is a hot, arid country with high humidity along the coast. The Ḥajar Mountains parallel the shore of the Gulf of Oman, reaching an elevation of more than 10,000 ft (3,000 m). A broad expanse of sandy desert covers much of the country. Oman has a developing mixed economy, and the production and export of petroleum is its largest sector. It is a hereditary monarchy, with two advisory bodies; its head of state and government is the sultan. Human habitation dates to about the 3rd millennium BCE. The Omani tribal system dates to Arab migration during the 2nd century CE. It was ruled by imams (Muslim religious leaders) of the Ibāḍī sect from the early Islamic period (mid-8th century) until the 12th century, when local rule was established. The Portuguese controlled the coastal areas *c.* 1507–1650, when they were expelled. The Āl Bū Saʿīd, a dynasty founded in the mid-18th century, still rules Oman. The kingdom expanded into eastern Africa in the 18th–19th century, where its capital was at Zanzibar. Oil was discovered in 1964. In 1970 the sultan was deposed by his son, who began a policy of modernization, and under him Oman joined the Arab League and the United Nations. In the Persian Gulf War, Oman cooperated with the forces allied against Iraq. It subsequently continued to expand its foreign relations.

Oman, Gulf of, Northwestern arm of the Arabian Sea, between the eastern part of the Arabian Peninsula and Iran. It is about 200 mi (320 km) wide and 350 mi (560 km) long and connects with the Persian Gulf through the Strait of Hormuz. It is the only entrance to the Persian Gulf from the Arabian Sea and Indian Ocean and is important as a shipping route for the oil-producing area around the Persian Gulf.

Omdurman, City (pop., 2005 est.: urban agglom., 4,518,000), east-central Sudan. It is situated on the left bank of the Nile River just below the confluence of the Blue and White Niles. It was an insignificant village until the victory of al-Mahdī over the British in 1885. It grew rapidly after al-Mahdī and his successor, ʿAbd Allāh, made it their capital. It was captured by Anglo-Egyptian forces in 1898 but continued to develop into the cultural, religious, and commercial centre of Sudan. Sites of interest include ʿAbd Allāh's house (now a museum) and the tomb of al-Mahdī.

The tomb of al-Mahdī in Omdurman, Sudan.
Charles Beery/Shostal Associates

Omega Centauri, Brightest globular cluster, located in the constellation Centaurus. It has a magnitude of 3.7 and is visible to the unaided eye as a faint luminous patch. One of the nearer globular clusters (about 17,000 light-years away), it is estimated to contain hundreds of thousands of stars, including several hundred variable stars. John Herschel was the first to recognize it as a star cluster and not a nebula.

omen, Observed phenomenon that is interpreted as signifying good or bad fortune. The many and varied omens that the ancients noted included lightning, cloud movements, the flights of birds, and the paths of sacred animals. Each type of omen was gauged according to specific meaningful characteristics, such as the kinds of bird in flight or the direction of flight in relation to the observer.

omnivore, Animal that eats both plant and animal matter. Most omnivorous species do not have highly specialized food-processing structures or food-gathering behaviour. Many animals generally considered carnivores are actually omnivorous; for example, the red fox eats fruits and berries as well as mammals and birds.

Omsk, City (pop., 2002: 1,133,900), west-central Russia. It is located in southwestern Siberia at the confluence of the Irtysh and Om rivers. Founded in 1716 as a military stronghold, Omsk became a city in 1804. It remained the headquarters of the Siberian Cossacks until the late 19th century. In 1918–19 it was the seat of the anti-Bolshevik government of Adm. Aleksandr Kolchak. Its growth was spurred by the building of the Trans-Siberian Railroad in the 1890s and the onset of World War II. Pipelines from the Volga-Urals and western Siberian oil fields supply the refinery, and the petrochemical industry is also is important.

oncogene, Gene that can cause cancer. It is a sequence of DNA that has been altered or mutated from its original form, the proto-oncogene. Proto-oncogenes promote the specialization and division of normal cells. A change in their genetic sequence can result in uncontrolled cell growth, ultimately causing the formation of a cancerous tumour. In humans, proto-oncogenes can be transformed into oncogenes in three ways: point mutation (alteration of a single nucleotide base pair), translocation (in which a segment of the chromosome breaks off and attaches to another chromosome), or amplification (increase in the number of copies of the proto-oncogene). Oncogenes were first discovered in certain retroviruses and were later identified as cancer-causing agents in many animals.

O'Neill, Eugene (Gladstone) (b. Oct. 16, 1888, New York, N.Y., U.S.—d. Nov. 27, 1953, Boston, Mass.), U.S. playwright. The son of a touring actor, he spent an itinerant youth as a seaman, heavy drinker, and derelict, then began writing plays while recovering from tuberculosis (1912). His one-act *Bound East for Cardiff* (1916) was produced by the experimental Provincetown Players, which also staged his other early plays (1916–20). *Beyond the Horizon* was produced on Broadway in 1920, earning him his first Pulitzer Prize. Enormously prolific, he often wrote about tortured family relationships and the conflict between idealism and materialism. Soon recognized as a major dramatist, he became widely translated and produced. His many plays of the 1920s include *The Emperor Jones* (1921), *The Hairy Ape* (1922), *Anna Christie* (1922; Pulitzer Prize), *Desire Under the Elms* (1925), *The Great God Brown* (1926), and *Strange Interlude* (1928; Pulitzer Prize). Among his later plays are *Mourning Becomes Electra* (1931), *Ah! Wilderness* (1933; his only comedy), *The Iceman Cometh* (1946), and the autobiographical *Long Day's Journey into Night* (produced 1956; Pulitzer Prize), considered his masterpiece. O'Neill was awarded the Nobel Prize for Literature in 1936, the first U.S. playwright so honoured.

onion, Herbaceous biennial plant (*Allium cepa*) of the family Alliaceae, probably native to southwestern Asia but now grown worldwide, and its edible bulb. Among the hardiest and oldest garden vegetable plants, onions bear a cluster of small, greenish white flowers on one or more leafless stalks. The leaf bases swell to form the underground mature edible onion. Onions are pungent; because they contain a sulfur-rich volatile oil, peeling or slicing them can bring tears to a person's eyes. Onions vary in size, shape, colour, and pungency. Though low in standard nutrients, they are valued for their flavour. Onions have been claimed to cure colds, earaches, and laryngitis and have been used to treat animal bites, powder burns, and warts; like their close relative garlic, they are being studied for other suspected beneficial qualities.

Onion (Allium cepa)
Walter Chandoha

ontology, Theory of being as such. It was originally called "first philosophy" by Aristotle. In the 18th century Christian Wolff contrasted ontology, or general metaphysics, with special metaphysical theories of souls, bodies, or God, claiming that ontology could be a deductive discipline revealing the essences of things. This view was later strongly criticized by David Hume and Immanuel Kant. Ontology was revived in the early 20th century by practitioners of phenomenology and existentialism, notably Edmund Husserl and his student Martin Heidegger. In the English-speaking world, interest in ontology was renewed in the mid-20th century by W.V.O. Quine; by the end of the century it had become a central discipline of analytic philosophy.

Oort cloud, Vast spherical cloud of small, icy bodies orbiting the Sun at distances ranging from about 0.3 light-year to one light-year or more that is probably the source of most long-period comets. In 1950 the Dutch astronomer Jan Hendrik Oort (1900–92) noted that no comets have orbits that would indicate an interstellar origin. He proposed that the Sun is surrounded by billions of these objects, which are only occasionally detectable when they enter the inner solar system. The Oort cloud is believed to be composed of primordial bodies dating from the formation of the solar system. Whether the Oort cloud merges, in its inner region, into the disk-shaped Kuiper belt is not known.

Op art, or OPTICAL ART, Branch of mid-20th-century geometric abstract art that deals with optical illusion. Op art painters devised complex optical spaces by manipulating repetitive forms such as parallel lines, checkerboard patterns, and concentric circles or by creating chromatic tension from the juxtaposition of complementary colours, thereby creating the illusion of movement. Principal artists of the Op movement in the late 1950s and the '60s include Victor Vasarely, Bridget Riley (b. 1931), and Larry Poons (b. 1937).

opal, A hydrated, noncrystalline silica mineral used extensively as a gemstone. Its chemical composition is similar to that of quartz but generally with a variable water content. Pure opal is colourless, but impurities generally give it various dull colours ranging from yellow and red to black. Black opal is especially rare and valuable. White opal and fire opal, characterized by yellow, orange, or red colour, are much more common. Various forms of common opal are widely used as abrasives, insulation material, and ceramic ingredients. Opal is most abundant in volcanic rocks, especially in areas of hot-spring activity. The finest gem opals have been found in Australia; other areas that yield gem material include Japan, Mexico, Honduras, India, New Zealand, and the U.S.

Black opal from Australia; in the collection of the Department of Earth Sciences, Washington University, St. Louis, Mo.
John H. Gerard/EB Inc.

OPEC, in full ORGANIZATION OF THE PETROLEUM EXPORTING COUNTRIES, Multinational organization established in 1960 to coordinate the petroleum production and export policies of its members. Iran, Iraq, Kuwait, Saudi Arabia, and Venezuela were the original members; they were joined by Qatar (1961), Indonesia and Libya (1962), Abu Dhabi (1967; membership transferred to the United Arab Emirates, 1974), Algeria (1967), Nigeria (1971), and Angola (2007). Ecuador (1973) and Gabon (1975) are no longer OPEC members. Policy decisions are taken by consensus at its Vienna headquarters. In 1973 OPEC began a series of oil price increases in retaliation for Western support of Israel in the 1973 Arab-Israeli war, and OPEC members' income greatly increased as a result. Internal dissent, the development of alternative energy sources in the West, and Western exploitation of oil sources in non-OPEC countries subsequently combined to reduce the organization's influence. OPEC countries supply about two-fifths of the world's oil consumption and possess about two-thirds of the world's proven oil reserves.

open-hearth process, or SIEMENS-MARTIN PROCESS, Steel-making technique that for most of the 20th century accounted for most steel made in the world. William Siemens made steel from pig iron in a reverberatory furnace of his design in 1867. The same year the French manufacturer Pierre-Émile Martin (1824–1915) used the idea to produce steel by melting wrought iron with steel scrap. Siemens used the waste heat given off by the furnace: he directed the fumes from the furnace through a brick checkerwork, heating it to a high temperature, and then used the same path to introduce air into the furnace; the preheated air significantly increased the flame temperature. The open-hearth process furnace (which replaced the Bessemer process) has itself been replaced in most industrialized countries by the basic oxygen process and the electric furnace.

open market operation, Any of the purchases and sales of government securities and commercial paper by a central bank in an effort to regulate the money supply and credit conditions. Open market operations can also be used to stabilize the prices of government securities. When the central bank buys securities on the open market, it increases the reserves of commercial banks, making it possible for them to expand their loans and investments. It

also increases the price of government securities, equivalent to reducing their interest rates, and decreases interest rates generally, thus encouraging investment. If the central bank sells securities, the effects are reversed. Open market operations are usually performed with short-term government securities such as treasury bills.

opera, Entirely musical drama consisting of vocal pieces with instrumental accompaniment, typically punctuated with orchestral overtures and interludes. Opera emerged at the end of the 16th century in Florence, fueled by the convergence of several cultural currents, including an established tradition of musical theatre, a desire to experiment with Classical ways, and the traditional attribution of magical power to music within the greater cosmic order. Performances at court known as *intermedi* laid the foundation for opera in that they employed costumes, scenery, music, and dancing. Using the *intermedi* tradition as a springboard, informal academies of intellectuals—such as Giovanni Bardi's Camerata—promoted a new form of theatre that strove to emulate the dramatic ideals of the ancients. The result was opera. Most of the music of the first opera, *La Dafne* (1598) by Jacopo Peri, has been lost; the earliest surviving opera is Peri's *Euridice* (1600). Those works were the first to include opera's hallmark stylistic feature, recitative, a highly inflected form of solo vocalization somewhere between speech and song. Opera spread rapidly to other Italian cities. In Mantua, Claudio Monteverdi composed *Orfeo* (1607), the oldest opera to hold a place in the contemporary repertoire. The earliest public (rather than court) opera theatres opened in Venice in 1637; competition stimulated greater musical variety, more complicated plots, and elaborate arias (solo songs). Beyond Italy, Jean-Baptiste Lully had by the end of the 17th century merged elements of the local theatre tradition with court ballet to establish a uniquely French operatic style. Jean-Philippe Rameau carried French opera through the first half of the 18th century, while George Frideric Handel cultivated Italian-style opera in England. By the mid-18th century solo singing had become so ornate as to obscure the textual and narrative elements of opera. German composer Christoph Willibald Gluck spearheaded a reform movement to restore simplicity and balance to opera's vocal, instrumental, and dramatic components. Gluck's reforms influenced many of his successors, including Austrian composer Wolfgang Amadeus Mozart in the later 18th century. Gioachino Rossini, Gaetano Donizetti, and Vincenzo Bellini dominated opera in Italy during the first half of the 19th century. Rossini and Donizetti were recognized for blending serious and comic elements in a single opera, while Bellini expertly exploited the melancholic qualities of both the orchestra and the human voice. The large-scale "grand opera" tradition arose within the international community of early 19th-century Paris. Champions of the new style included Luigi Cherubini, Gaspare Spontini, Giacomo Meyerbeer, and Hector Berlioz. Meanwhile, the German Romantic tradition spawned a style of opera with a notably dark, mysterious, mythological quality, as exemplified by the monumental works of Richard Wagner. Giuseppe Verdi refined and remained loyal to the conventions of Italian opera, and his works ultimately became a pillar of the Western operatic tradition. In the early 20th century Richard Strauss, working in the German tradition, and Giacomo Puccini, the last exponent of the Italian style, were the most popular opera composers. By that time, however, other composers, including Austrians Arnold Schoenberg and Alban Berg, had already shifted opera in an experimental direction. No major style developed in the later 20th century, but the genre endured, with Italian composer Gian Carlo Menotti, Americans Philip Glass and John Adams, and British composers Thea Musgrave and Benjamin Britten among those who propelled the tradition into the 21st century.

operating system (OS), Software that controls the operation of a computer, directs the input and output of data, keeps track of files, and controls the processing of computer programs. Its roles include managing the functioning of the computer hardware, running the applications programs, serving as an interface between the computer and the user, and allocating computer resources to various functions. When several jobs reside in the computer simultaneously and share resources (multitasking), the OS allocates fixed amounts of CPU time and memory in turn or allows one job to read data while another writes to a printer and still another performs computations. Through a process called time-sharing, a large computer can handle interaction with hundreds of users simultaneously, giving each the perception of being the sole user. Modern computer operating systems are becoming increasingly machine-independent, capable of running on any hardware platform; a widely used platform-independent operating system in use today on mainframe computers is UNIX. Most personal computers run on Microsoft's Windows operating system, which grew out of and eventually replaced MS-DOS.

operations research, Application of scientific methods to management and administration of military, government, commercial, and industrial systems. It began during World War II in Britain when teams of scientists worked with the Royal Air Force to improve radar detection of enemy aircraft, leading to coordinated efforts to improve the entire system of early warning, defense, and supply. It is characterized by a systems orientation, or systems engineering, in which interdisciplinary research teams adapt scientific methods to large-scale problems that must be modeled, since laboratory testing is impossible. Examples include resource allocation and replacement, inventory control, and scheduling of large-scale construction projects.

operetta, Musical drama similar to opera, usually with a romantically sentimental plot, employing songs, dances, and orchestral interludes interspersed with spoken dialogue. The modern tradition began with Jacques Offenbach, who wrote some 90 operettas and inspired a Viennese tradition that began with the works of Franz von Suppé and Johann Strauss. In Britain most of the 14 comic operettas (1871–96) of W.S. Gilbert and Arthur Sullivan have been enduringly popular. In the U.S. the works of such composers as Victor Herbert, Reginald De Koven, John Philip Sousa, and Sigmund Romberg were widely popular in the early 20th century.

operon, Genetic regulatory system of single-celled organisms (prokaryotes) and their viruses, in which genes coding for functionally related proteins are clustered along the DNA, enabling their expression to be coordinated in response to the cell's needs. By providing a means to produce proteins only when and where they are required, the operon allows the cell to conserve energy. A typical operon consists of a group of structural genes that code for enzymes involved in a metabolic pathway, such as the biosynthesis of an amino acid. A single unit of messenger RNA is transcribed from the operon and is then translated into separate proteins. Operons are controlled by various regulatory elements that respond to environmental cues. The operon system was first proposed by François Jacob and Jacques Monod in the early 1960s.

ophthalmology, Medical specialty dealing with the eyes, dating to 1805. Frans C. Donders's 1864 advances in optics allowed eyeglasses to be fitted to vision problems. The ophthalmoscope made it possible to look inside the eye and relate eye defects to internal conditions. More recent advances include eye exams, early treatment of congenital defects, and eye banks to store corneas for transplants. Ophthalmologists test visual function and examine the eye for faulty development, disease, injury, degeneration, aging, or refractive errors. They prescribe treatment for eye disease and lenses for refraction and perform surgery when needed.

opium, Organic compound, a narcotic drug known since ancient Greek times, obtained from exuded juice of immature fruit capsules of the opium poppy. Opium has legitimate medical uses, as the source of the alkaloids codeine and morphine and their deriv-

atives. It is also used illicitly, either raw or purified as alkaloids and their derivatives (including heroin). Opium alkaloids of one type (e.g., morphine, codeine) act on the nervous system, mimicking the effects of endorphins; they are analgesic, narcotic, and potentially addicting. Those of a second type, including papaverine and noscapine, relieve smooth muscle spasms and are not analgesic, narcotic, or addicting. Habitual opium use produces physical and mental deterioration and shortens life. Overdose can cause death by depressing respiration.

opium poppy, Flowering plant (*Papaver somniferum*) of the family Papaveraceae, native to Turkey. Opium, morphine, codeine, and heroin are all derived from the milky fluid found in its unripe seed capsule. A common garden annual in the U.S., the opium poppy bears blue-purple or white flowers 5 in. (13 cm) wide on plants about 3–16 ft (1–5 m) tall, with lobed or toothed silver-green foliage. It is also grown for its tiny nonnarcotic ripe seeds, which are kidney-shaped and grayish blue to dark blue; the seeds are used in bakery products and for seasoning, oil, and birdseed.

Opium Wars, Two trading wars of the mid-19th century in China. The first (1839–42) was between China and Britain, and the second (1856–60; also called the Arrow War or Anglo-French War) was between China and a British-French alliance. Trade developed between China and Western countries from the late 16th century. The Chinese, accustomed to tributary relationships with others, required that Westerners pay for Chinese goods with silver currency. To offset a growing negative flow of silver at home, the British created a market for opium in China and began importing it there illegally. As demand for opium grew, China tried to stop the practice, and hostilities broke out. Britain quickly triumphed, and the resultant Treaty of Nanjing (1842)—the first of a series of unequal treaties between China and Western countries and, eventually, Japan—was a blow to China. The outbreak of the second war resulted in the Treaty of Tianjin (1858), which required further Chinese concessions. When China refused to sign subsequent treaties, Beijing was captured and the emperor's summer palace burned. The overall result of these conflicts was to weaken the Chinese imperial system, greatly expand Western influence in China, and pave the way for such uprisings as the Taiping and Boxer rebellions.

opportunity cost, In economic terms, the opportunities forgone in the choice of one expenditure over others. For a consumer with a fixed income, the opportunity cost of buying a new dishwasher might be the value of a vacation trip never taken or several suits of clothes unbought. The concept of opportunity cost allows economists to examine the relative monetary values of various goods and services.

optics, Science concerned with the production and propagation of light, the changes it undergoes and produces, and closely related phenomena. Physical optics deals with the nature and properties of light; geometric optics deals with the formation of images by mirrors, lenses, and other devices that use light. Optical data processing involves manipulation of the information content of an image formed by coherent (one-wavelength) optical systems. The study of optics has led to the development of devices such as eyeglasses and contact lenses, telescopes, microscopes, cameras, binoculars, lasers, and optical fibres.

optometry, Profession concerned with examining the eyes for defects or faults of refraction. Optometrists prescribe optical aids (e.g., eyeglasses, contact lenses), supervise eye exercise programs to treat vision problems, and examine the eyes for disorders such as glaucoma and cataracts. They are generally not licensed to prescribe drugs or trained to perform surgery.

Opus Dei (Latin: "work of God"), Roman Catholic lay and clerical organization whose actions and beliefs have been both criticized and praised. Its members seek personal Christian perfection, strive to implement Christian ideals in their chosen occupations, and promote Christian values to society as a whole. Opus Dei, in full Prelature of the Holy Cross and Opus Dei, was founded in 1928 in Spain by Josemaría Escrivá de Balaguer y Albá (canonzied in 2002). It is theologically conservative and accepts the teaching authority of the church without question. It was granted special status as the first and only personal prelature in the church by Pope John Paul II in 1982 and has established numerous vocational schools and universities. It is also highly controversial, accused of secrecy, using cult-like recruiting practices, and having grand political ambitions. There are separate organizations for men and women, which, since 1982, have been headed by a prelate elected by its members. At the beginning of the 20th century priests constituted only a tiny percentage of the organization, numbering roughly 1,600 of the nearly 84,000 members living in 80 countries.

oracle, Source of a divine communication delivered in response to a petitioner's request. Ancient Greece and Rome had many oracles. The most famous was that of Apollo at Delphi, where the medium was a woman over 50 called the Pythia. After bathing in the Castalian spring, she apparently would descend into a basement cell, mount a sacred tripod, and chew the leaves of the laurel, sacred to Apollo. Her utterances, which were often highly ambiguous, were interpreted by priests. Other oracles, including those at Claros (Apollo), Amphicleia (Dionysus), Olympia (Zeus), and Epidaurus (Asclepius), were consulted through various other methods; for example, the oldest of the oracles, that of Zeus at Dodona, spoke through the whispering of the leaves of a sacred oak. At some shrines, the inquirer would sleep in the holy precinct and receive an answer in a dream.

oral tradition, Cultural information passed on from one generation to the next by storytellers. The forms of oral tradition include poetry (often chanted or sung), folktales, and proverbs as well as magical spells, religious instruction, and recollections of the past. Music and rhyme commonly serve as both entertainment and aids to memory. Epic poems concerning the destiny of a society or summarizing its myths often begin as oral tradition and are later written down. In oral cultures, oral tradition is the only means of communicating knowledge. The prevalence of radio, television, and newspapers in Western culture has led to the decline of oral tradition, though it survives among old people and some minority groups as well as among children, whose games, counting rhymes, and songs are transmitted orally from generation to generation.

Oran, City (pop., 2004 est.: 772,900), northwestern Algeria. Situated on the Mediterranean Sea, it is about midway between Tangier, Morocco, and Algiers. With the adjacent Mers el-Kebir, it is the country's second largest port. Founded in the 10th century by Andalusians as a base for trade with the northern African hinterland, it was held by the Spanish from 1509 to 1708, when it fell to the Ottomans. It was devastated by an earthquake in 1790, and in 1792 the Ottomans settled a Jewish community there. In 1831 it was occupied by the French, who established a modern port and naval base. In World War II (1939–45) it came under the control of the Allied Powers. Most of its European inhabitants left after Algerian independence in 1962. It is divided into a waterfront and the old and new city sections built on terraces above it.

Orange, house of, Princely dynasty and royal family of the Netherlands. The title began with William I (the Silent), prince of Orange-Nassau, who was stadtholder (viceroy) of the Netherlands, as were his descendants until 1795. In 1815 William VI became William I, king of the Netherlands. Through his descendants, the male line of the royal dynasty continued until 1890, when Wilhelmina, daughter of William III, became queen. In 1908 she decreed that her descendants should be styled princes and princesses of Orange-Nassau.

orangutan, or ORANG, Species (*Pongo pygmaeus*, family Hominidae) of arboreal great ape, found only in the lowland swamp forests of Borneo and Sumatra but originally in the tropical forests of South Asia as well. The orangutan (Malaysian for "person of the forest") has a short thick body, long arms, short legs, and shaggy reddish hair. Males are about 4.5 ft (137 cm) tall and weigh about 185 lb (85 kg); females are smaller. Orangutans are placid, deliberate, ingenious, and persistent. Males have flat, fatty cheekpads and a baglike, pendulous swelling at the throat. Orangutans use all four limbs to walk and climb. They eat mostly figs and other fruits and some leaves, bark, and insects. They sleep in trees on a platform built of interwoven branches. Adults are solitary and live far apart, coming together only for a brief courtship. The mother carries and nurses the single young for almost three years. Though generally silent, the adult male has a loud, roaring "long call." The orangutan is an endangered species.

Male orangutan (Pongo pygmaeus) with cheek pads.
Russ Kinne/Photo Researchers

oratorio, Large-scale musical composition on a sacred subject for solo voices, chorus, and orchestra. The term derives from the oratories, community prayer halls set up by St. Philip Neri in the mid 16th century in a Counter-Reformation attempt to provide locales for religious edification outside the church itself, and the oratorio remained a nonliturgical (and non-Latin) form for moral musical entertainment. The first oratorio, really a religious opera, was written in 1600 by Emilio del Cavaliere, and the oratorio's development closely followed that of opera. Giacomo Carissimi produced an important body of Italian oratorios, and Marc-Antoine Charpentier transferred the oratorio to France in the later 17th century. In Germany the works of Heinrich Schütz anticipate the oratorio-like Passions of Johann Sebastian Bach. The most celebrated oratorio composer was George Frideric Handel; his great English works include the incomparable *Messiah* (1742). Handel inspired Franz Joseph Haydn's great *Creation* (1798) and exerted great influence on the 19th-century oratorio, whose composers include Hector Berlioz, Felix Mendelssohn, and Franz Liszt. Though the oratorio thereafter declined, 20th-century oratorio composers included Edward Elgar, Igor Stravinsky, Arthur Honegger, and Krzysztof Penderecki.

orchestra, Instrumental ensemble of varying size and composition. Today the term *orchestra* usually refers to the traditional large Western ensemble of bowed stringed instruments with brass, woodwind, and percussion instruments, with several players to each string part. The development of the orchestra coincides with the early history of opera. A major antecedent of the modern orchestra was that of the mid-17th-century French court, especially as employed by Jean-Baptiste Lully; it was dominated by 24 bowed strings but also often included woodwind instruments. Trumpets, horns, and timpani were often added in the early 18th century and were standard by the time of Franz Joseph Haydn. During the 19th century there was a considerable expansion, particularly in the number and variety of wind and percussion instruments; some works called for well over 100 musicians. The symphony orchestra changed little in the 20th century.

orchestration, Art of choosing which instruments to use for a given piece of music. The sections of the orchestra historically were separate ensembles: the stringed instruments for indoors, the woodwind instruments for outdoors, the horns for hunting, and trumpets and drums for battle or royal ceremony. Once entirely dependent on what was available or customary, composers began to explore the musical potential of instrumental combinations with the advent of the modern orchestra in the mid- to late 18th century. The first great orchestration text was written by Hector Berlioz in 1844.

orchid, Any of the more than 22,000 species in nearly 1,000 genera of nonwoody perennial plants that make up the family Orchidaceae. Bearing attractive flowers, orchids grow in most of the nonpolar world, especially in tropical regions, in soil or on other plants. Hybrids with showy flowers for the commercial trade come from the genera *Cattleya*, *Cymbidium*, *Vanda*, and *Laelia*. Flowers vary widely in size, colour, and shape, but all are bilaterally symmetrical and have three sepals. Most orchids photosynthesize, but some live on dead organic material or absorb food from a fungus living in their roots. Vanilla is extracted from the seedpod of the genus *Vanilla*. Many folk medicines, local beverages, and foods are prepared from parts of orchid plants.

*Orchid (*Polystachya bella*).*
Sven Samelius

orchitis, Inflammation and swelling of the testes, caused by infection (most often mumps) or chemical or physical injury. The testicles' rich blood and lymphatic supply block most infections in the absence of severe injury. Usual symptoms are high fever, sudden pain in the testicle, nausea and vomiting, and swelling, tightness, and tenderness of the gland. Fluids with pus or blood may accumulate in the scrotum, which is generally red and thickened. Treatment may include antibiotics, bed rest, support of the testes, compresses, and surgery or drainage.

ordinary differential equation, Equation containing derivatives of a function of a single variable. Its order is the order of the highest derivative it contains (e.g., a first-order differential equation involves only the first derivative of the function). Because the derivative is a rate of change, such an equation states how a function changes but does not specify the function itself. Given sufficient initial conditions, however, such as a specific function value, the function can be found by various methods, most based on integration.

Ordovician Period, Interval of geologic time, 488.3–443.7 million years ago, the second oldest period of the Paleozoic Era. It follows the Cambrian and precedes the Silurian Period. During the Ordovician, many of the landmasses were aligned in the tropics. Life was dominated by marine invertebrates, but some forms of land plants may have appeared during the early part of the period. Spores suggesting a tropical terrestrial environment have been found in rocks of that age. At the close of the Ordovician, rapid cooling and glaciation combined with a substantial fall in sea level produced a significant mass extinction event, second only to the Permian extinction in severity.

Øresund, Almost tideless strait between Sjælland island, Denmark, and Skåne, Sweden, connecting the Kattegat Strait with the Baltic Sea. It is one of the busiest sea lanes in the world, though ice sometimes impedes navigation in severe winters. Three large islands within it divide the waters into channels. The strait's principal ports are Copenhagen and Helsingør in Denmark and Malmö and Hälsingborg in Sweden.

organ, Keyboard instrument in which pressurized air produces notes by means of a series of tuned pipes. The simplest organs consist of a single rank of pipes, each corresponding to a single key. They are arranged over a wind chest connected to the keys by a

The Bruckner Organ, 18th century; in the church of the Abbey of Sankt Florian, Austria
Toni Schneiders

set of valves and fed with a supply of air by electrically or mechanically activated bellows. By pulling out knobs, called stops, the player engages new ranks of pipes. Two distinct types of pipes are used: flue pipes (both open and stopped) produce sound by directing air against the edge of an opening in the pipe, whereas reed pipes sound by means of a thin metal tongue inside the pipe that vibrates against a fixed projection next to it. A large organ may have five or more banked keyboards, or manuals, each of which controls a distinctive group of pipes. Most organs also have pedalboards played with the feet. A large organ's pipes may vary in length from about 1 in. to 32 ft (2.5 cm to 10 m), resulting in a huge nine-octave range. The earliest organ (*c.* 250 BC) was the Greek *hydraulis*, in which the wind was regulated by water pressure. The bellows-fed organ appeared about the 7th century AD. The organ became firmly associated with the church by the 10th century. As organs became widespread, different regions pursued different modes of construction and sought different tonal ideals. The Baroque German organ is ideally suited to polyphony, while the French taste for variety of timbres eventuated in Aristide Cavaillé-Coll's vast "orchestral" organs.

organic farming, or ORGANIC GARDENING, System of crop cultivation that uses biological methods of fertilization and pest control as substitutes for chemical fertilizers and pesticides, which are regarded by supporters of organic methods as harmful to health and the environment and unnecessary for successful cultivation. It was initiated as a conscious rejection of modern agri-chemical techniques in the 1930s by the British agronomist Sir Albert Howard. Miscellaneous organic materials, including animal manure, compost, grass turf, straw, and other crop residues, are applied to fields to improve both soil structure and moisture-holding capacity and to nourish soil life, which in turn nourishes plants. (Chemical fertilizers, by contrast, feed plants directly.) Biological pest control is achieved through preventive methods, including diversified farming, crop rotation, the planting of pest-deterrent species, and the use of integrated pest management techniques. Bioengineered strains are avoided. Since organic farming is time-consuming, organically grown produce tends to be expensive. Organic produce formerly accounted for a minuscule portion of total American farm output, but it has seen a huge proportional increase in sales in recent years.

Organization of American States (OAS), International organization formed in 1948 to replace the Pan-American Union. It promotes economic, military, and cultural cooperation among its members, which include almost all the independent states of the Western Hemisphere. (Cuba's membership was suspended in 1962.) The OAS's main goals are to maintain peace in the Western Hemisphere and to prevent intervention in the region by any outside state. Since the end of the Cold War in the early 1990s, the OAS has more actively encouraged democratic government in member states, in part by organizing missions to observe and monitor elections.

organized crime, Crime committed on a national or international scale by a criminal association; also, the associations themselves. Such associations engage in offenses such as cargo theft, fraud, robbery, kidnapping for ransom, and the demanding of "protection" payments. Their principal source of income derives from the supply of illegal goods and services for which there is continuous public demand, such as drugs, prostitution, "loan-sharking" (i.e., the lending of money at extremely high interest rates), and gambling. They are characterized by a hierarchy of ranks with assigned responsibilities; the coordination of activities among subgroups; the division of geographic territory among different associations; a commitment to total secrecy; efforts to corrupt law-enforcement authorities; and the use of extreme violence, including murder, against rival associations, informers, and other enemies. International rings of smugglers, jewel thieves, and drug traffickers have existed throughout Europe and Asia, and Sicily and Japan have centuries-old criminal organizations. In the U.S., organized crime flourished in the 20th century, especially during the Prohibition era. In the late 20th and early 21st centuries, it became immensely powerful in Russia, taking advantage of a weak and impoverished government and widespread official corruption.

organum, Early polyphonic setting of plainchant, the earliest form of counterpoint. The oldest written organum (*c.* 900), which evidently reflects a prevailing improvisational practice, consists of two lines moving simultaneously, note against note, the added line often paralleling the chant line a fourth or a fifth below. Later the added line acquired greater melodic individuality and independence. Organum consisting of more than one note against each chant note (florid or melismatic organum) appeared by the early 12th century. Three- and four-voice organum were first composed by the Notre-Dame school. Organum died out with the advent of the 13th-century motet.

original sin, In Christian doctrine, the condition or state of sin into which each human being is born, or its origin in Adam's disobedience to God when he ate the fruit of the tree of knowledge of good and evil. His guilt was transmitted to his descendants. Though Genesis describes Adam's sufferings as the consequence of his disobedience, it does not make Adam's sin hereditary. The main scriptural basis of the doctrine is found in the writings of St. Paul; St. Augustine helped make humanity's sinful nature a central element in orthodox Christian theology. Medieval theologians continued to explore the issue, and Thomas Aquinas offered a more optimistic view of human nature in his teachings on original sin than had Augustine. Martin Luther and John Calvin accepted a more Augustinian understanding, and modern evolutionary theory and biblical source criticism raised new challenges for the definition of original sin.

Orinoco River, Major river, South America. It rises on the western slopes of the Parima Mountains along the border between Venezuela and Brazil. It flows in a giant arc through Venezuela for about 1,700 mi (2,740 km) and enters the Atlantic Ocean near the island of Trinidad. It forms part of the border between Colombia and Venezuela. With its tributaries, it is the northernmost of South America's four major river systems. The aquatic fauna include the piranhas and the Orinoco crocodile. The river basin is largely inhabited by indigenous Indian groups.

Orion, In Greek mythology, a powerful hunter. He was sometimes said to be the son of Poseidon. He drove the wild beasts out of the island of Chios and fell in love with Merope, daughter of the island's king. Disapproving of Orion, the king had him blinded, but his vision was restored by the rays of the rising sun. He later went to Crete to live and hunt with Artemis. Some legends hold that he was killed by Artemis or Apollo out of jealousy; another tells that he was fatally bitten by a scorpion. After his death the gods placed him in the sky as a constellation.

Orion Nebula, Bright nebula, faintly visible to the unaided eye in the sword of the hunter's figure in the constellation Orion. About 1,500 light-years from Earth, it contains hundreds of very hot young stars clustered about a group of four massive stars known as the Trapezium. Radiation primarily from these four stars excites the nebula to glow. Discovered in the early 17th century, it was the first nebula to be photographed (1880).

Orissa, State (pop., 2008 est.: 39,899,000), eastern India. It lies on the Bay of Bengal and is bordered by Andhra Pradesh, Chhattisgarh, Jharkhand, and West Bengal states. It occupies an area of 60,119 sq mi (155,707 sq km), and its capital is Bhubaneshwar; Cuttack is the largest city. Human habitation dates to at least 2100 BCE. Part of the ancient kingdom of Kalinga, it was a stronghold of Hinduism before its conquest by the Afghan rulers of Bengal in 1568, when it became part of the Mughal Empire. It was ruled by Britain from 1803 until India's independence in 1947 and became a state in 1950. Situated in a tropical savanna that is subject to heavy rainfall during the southwest monsoon, it has a largely rural population, which is engaged mainly in agriculture. Crops include rice, oilseed, jute, and sugarcane. Orissa has a rich artistic heritage and contains some of the best examples of Indian art and architecture.

Orkney Islands, Island group (pop., 2001: 19,245), Scotland. Lying north of the Scottish mainland, it comprises more than 70 islands and islets and constitutes the Orkney council area. The Orkney Islands, only 20 of which are inhabited, were the Orcades of ancient Classical literature. There is much evidence of prehistoric inhabitants. Norse raiders arrived in the late 8th century AD and colonized the islands in the 9th century. Thereafter they were ruled by Norway and Denmark until Scotland annexed them in 1472. It is a prosperous agricultural area. Kirkwall is the administrative seat.

ornamentation, In music, the addition of notes for expressive and aesthetic purposes. For example, a long note may be ornamented by repetition or by alternation with a neighboring note ("trill"); a skip to a nonadjacent note can be filled in with the intervening notes; or the resolution of a dissonance, because of its inevitability, can be delayed.

ornithology, Branch of zoology dealing with the study of birds. Early writings on birds were largely anecdotal (including folklore) or practical (e.g., treatises on falconry and game-bird management). From the mid-18th century on, ornithology progressed from the description and classification of new species discovered in scientific expeditions to the examination of internal anatomy to the study of bird ecology and ethology. Ornithology is one of the few scientific fields in which nonprofessionals make substantial contributions; the field observations of birders provide valuable information on behaviour, ecology, distribution, and migration. Other information is gained by means of radar, radio transmitters, portable audio equipment, and bird banding, which provides information on longevity and movements.

Orpheus, Greek legendary hero who sang and played the lyre so beautifully that animals, trees, and rocks danced around him. When his wife, Eurydice, was killed by a snake, he went to the underworld in search of her, and his music and grief so moved Hades that he agreed to let Orpheus take Eurydice back to the land of the living on the condition that neither of them look back as they left. On seeing the Sun, Orpheus turned to share his delight with Eurydice, and she disappeared. Orpheus was later torn to pieces by maenads, and his head, still singing, floated to Lesbos, where an oracle of Orpheus was established. By the 5th century BC, a Hellenistic mystery religion (the Orphic mysteries), based on Orpheus's songs and teachings, had arisen. His story became the subject of some of the earliest operas.

Orthodox Judaism, Religion of Jews who adhere strictly to traditional beliefs and practices; the official form of Judaism in Israel. Orthodox Jews hold that both the written law (Torah) and the oral law (codified in the Mishna and interpreted in the Talmud) are immutably fixed and remain the sole norm of religious observance. Orthodox Judaism has held fast to such practices as daily worship, dietary laws, intensive study of the Torah, and separation of men and women in the synagogue. It also enjoins strict observance of the Sabbath and does not permit instrumental music during communal services. A leading center of Orthodoxy in the U.S. is New York's Yeshiva Univ.

Orwell, George, orig. ERIC ARTHUR BLAIR (b. 1903, Motihari, Bengal, India—d. Jan. 21, 1950, London, Eng.), British novelist, essayist, and critic. Instead of accepting a scholarship to a university, Orwell went to Burma to serve in the Indian Imperial Police (1922–27), an experience that changed him into a literary and political rebel. On returning to Europe, he lived in self-imposed poverty, gaining material for *Down and Out in Paris and London* (1933), and became a socialist. He went to Spain to report on the Spanish Civil War and stayed to join the Republican militia. His war experiences, which gave him a lifelong dread of communism (he would later provide British intelligence services with lists of his fellow British communists), are recounted in *Homage to Catalonia* (1938). His novels typically portray a sensitive, conscientious, emotionally isolated individual at odds with an oppressive or dishonest social environment. His most famous works are the anti-Soviet satirical fable *Animal Farm* (1945) and *Nineteen Eighty-four* (1949), a dystopic vision of totalitarianism whose influence was widely felt in the postwar decades. His literary essays are also admired.

George Orwell.
BBC Copyright

Ōsaka, ancient NANIWA, City (pop., 2006 est.: 2,635,420) and seaport, west-central Honshu, Japan, on the northeastern shore of Ōsaka Bay. A long-established city and port, Naniwa was made a castle town by Toyotomi Hideyoshi in the 16th century. It was the leading commercial city of Japan during the Edo (Tokugawa) period and the leading industrial city from the late 19th century. It was badly damaged by U.S. bombing during World War II. Once noted for its large textile industry, it is now a leading financial centre with heavy industries, including machinery, iron and steel, and chemicals. With Kōbe and Kyōto, it is part of Japan's second largest urban and industrial agglomeration. It is also a cultural and educational centre, with several universities and theatres.

Osiris, Ancient Egyptian god of the underworld. Osiris was slain by the god Seth, who tore apart the corpse and flung the pieces all over Egypt. According to some accounts, the goddess Isis, consort of Osiris, and her sister Nephthys found the pieces and gave new life to Osiris, who became the ruler of the underworld. Isis and Osiris then conceived Horus. In the Egyptian concept of divine kingship, the king at death became Osiris and the new king was identified with Horus. Osiris also represented the power that brought life out of the earth. Festivals reenacting his fate were celebrated annually in towns throughout Egypt.

Oslo, formerly (1624–1925) CHRISTIANIA, City and municipality (pop., 2002 est.: municipality, 512,589), capital of Norway. It lies at the northern end of Oslo Fjord and constitutes a separate county. It was founded by King Harald III Sigurdsson c. 1050. Haakon V built the Akershus fortress c. 1300. After it was destroyed by fire in 1624, King Christian II of Denmark-Norway built a new town farther west and called it Christiania. It grew in the 19th century, partly by absorbing neighbouring towns, and replaced Bergen as Norway's largest and most influential city. It was renamed Oslo in 1925 and developed rapidly after World War II. It is the country's principal commercial, industrial, and transportation centre, and its harbour is the largest and busiest in Norway.

osmosis, Spontaneous passage or diffusion of water or other solvent through a semipermeable membrane. If a solution is separated from a pure solvent by a membrane that is permeable to the solvent but not to the solute, the solution will tend to become more dilute by absorbing solvent through the membrane. The pressure caused by the migration of solvent through the membrane is called osmotic pressure.

osteoarthritis, or OSTEOARTHROSIS, or DEGENERATIVE JOINT DISEASE, Most common joint disorder, afflicting over 80% of those who reach age 70. It does not involve excessive inflammation and may have no symptoms, especially at first. Cartilage softens and wears away, and bone grows in its place, distorting the joint's surface and causing pain, stiffness, and limited movement, usually in weight-bearing joints (vertebrae, knees, hips). Treatment may include analgesics, rest, weight loss, corticosteroids, and/or physical therapy and rehabilitation or an exercise program. Hip or knee replacement or surgical removal of unhealthy tissue may be needed.

osteopathy, Health-care profession founded by the U.S. physician Andrew Taylor Still (1828–1917) as a reform movement against the rather primitive 19th-century drugs and surgical techniques. It emphasizes the relationship between musculoskeletal structure and organ function. Osteopathic physicians learn to recognize and correct structural problems through manipulative and other therapies. Osteopathic hospitals provide general or specialized health care, including maternity and emergency care.

osteoporosis, Generalized loss of bone density, causing skeletal weakness. Around age 40, the rate of bone resorption in humans starts to exceed the rate of bone formation. Women experience accelerated bone loss after menopause, when the estrogen level decreases. When the amount of bone falls below a certain threshold, fractures occur with little or no trauma. Prevention begins with adequate calcium intake in youth, when bone mass is built, and then throughout life. Weight-bearing exercise and vitamin D are important at all ages. Medications can inhibit bone resorption or prevent bone loss in patients who are at risk for developing osteoporosis.

ostrich, Two-toed, long-necked ratite (*Struthio camelus,* family Struthionidae) found in Africa, the largest living bird. An adult male ostrich may be nearly 9 ft (2.75 m) tall and weigh more than 330 lb (150 kg). Males are black, with white wing and tail plumes; females are brown. Ostriches live in flocks of 5–50, usually among grazing animals, and eat plants and an occasional small animal. Roaring, hissing males fight for three to five hens, which lay 15–60 eggs in a communal nest scraped in the ground. The male sits at night; the females take turns by day. One-month-old chicks can run with adults, at 40 mph (65 km/hr). To escape detection, an ostrich may lie on the ground with its neck outstretched, a habit that may have given rise to the notion that ostriches bury their heads in the sand.

otitis, Inflammation of the ear. Otitis externa is dermatitis, usually bacterial, of the auditory canal and sometimes the external ear. It can cause a foul discharge, pain, fever, and sporadic deafness. Otitis media is due to allergy or viral or bacterial infection of the middle ear. The bacterial form may be acute (causing earache, fever, and pus and requiring antibiotics) or chronic. It can invade the bone (mastoiditis), requiring surgery. Otitis in the inner ear (labyrinthitis) often arises from respiratory infection, syphilis, or otitis media. Symptoms include vertigo, vomiting, and hearing loss. Recovery is usually quick unless there is pus formation, which can destroy the inner-ear structures, causing permanent deafness in that ear.

Ottawa, City (pop., 2001: 774,072), capital of Canada. It is located in southeastern Ontario, on the Ottawa, Gatineau, and Rideau rivers. The area was inhabited by American Indians when it was visited by Samuel de Champlain in 1613, and the nearby rivers served traders and explorers over the next two centuries. Its settlement developed after the construction of the Rideau Canal in 1826. Originally named Bytown, it was incorporated as the city of Ottawa in 1855. To resolve political disputes between Toronto and Quebec City and between Montreal and Kingston, it was selected as Canada's capital by Queen Victoria in 1857. In 2001 the city's population grew significantly after it was amalgamated with several local municipalities. The federal government is the major employer; many commercial and financial associations are also located there. It is the site of several educational and cultural institutions, including the National Arts Centre and the National Gallery of Canada.

Ottoman Empire, Former empire centred in Anatolia. It was named for Osman I (1259–1326), a Turkish Muslim prince in Bithynia who conquered neighbouring regions once held by the Seljūq dynasty and founded his own ruling line *c.* 1300. Ottoman troops first invaded Europe in 1345, sweeping through the Balkans. Though defeated by Timur in 1402, by 1453 the Ottomans, under Mehmed II (the Conquerer), had destroyed the Byzantine Empire and captured its capital, Constantinople (now Istanbul), which henceforth served as the Ottoman capital. Under Selim I (r. 1512–20) and his son Süleyman I (the Magnificent; r. 1520–66), the Ottoman Empire reached its greatest peak. Süleyman took control of parts of Persia, most of Arabia, and large sections of Hungary and the Balkans. By the early 16th century the Ottomans had also defeated the Mamlūk dynasty in Syria and Egypt; and their navy under Barbarossa soon seized control of much of the Barbary Coast. Beginning with Selim, the Ottoman sultans also held the title of caliph, the spiritual head of Islam. Ottoman power began to decline in the late 16th century. Ottoman forces repeatedly besieged Vienna. After their final effort at taking the Austrian capital failed (1683), that and subsequent losses led them to relinquish Hungary in 1699. Corruption and decadence gradually undermined the government. In the late 17th and 18th centuries the Russo-Turkish Wars and wars with Austria and Poland further weakened the empire, which in the 19th century came to be called the "sick man of Europe." Most of its remaining European territory was lost in the Balkan Wars (1912–13). It sided with Germany in World War I (1914–18); postwar treaties dissolved the empire, and in 1922 the sultanate was abolished by Mustafa Kemal Atatürk, who proclaimed the Republic of Turkey the following year.

Ouagadougou, City (pop., 2006: 1,181,702), capital of Burkina Faso, western Africa. It was the capital of the historic Mossi kingdom of Wagadugu, which was founded in the 15th century. The Mossi king still lives in the city, though his powers have been eclipsed by the French colonial and postindependence administrations. A manufacturing centre, it is the country's largest city and is connected by rail to Abidjan, Côte d'Ivoire. A biennial film festival, the largest in Africa, is held in the city.

ovary, In zoology, the female reproductive organ that produces eggs and sex hormones (estrogen and progesterone). Human females have two ovaries, almond-shaped organs about 1.5 in. (4 cm) long. They contain hollow balls of cells (follicles) that hold immature eggs. About 150,000–500,000 follicles usually are present at birth; by young adulthood, only about 34,000 remain. The number continues to decrease until menopause, when the few remaining follicles decay and the ovaries shrink and produce far less estrogen. Only 300–400 follicles mature and release an egg, which develops into an embryo if fertilized or, if not, passes from the body with menstruation. In botany, an ovary is the enlarged base of a flower's female organ (pistil). It contains ovules, which develop into seeds when fertilized, and matures into a fruit.

overpopulation, Situation in which the number of individuals of a given species exceeds the number that its environment can sustain. Possible consequences are environmental deterioration,

impaired quality of life, and a population crash (sudden reduction in numbers caused by high mortality and failure to produce viable offspring).

overture, Musical introduction to a larger, often dramatic, work. Originating with Claudio Monteverdi's *Orfeo* (1607), overtures served as openings for operas. The large-scale two- or three-part "French overture" invented by Jean-Baptiste Lully (1658) for his operas and ballets was widely imitated for a century. The sinfonia, the standard Italian overture form in the late 17th and 18th centuries, was a principal precursor of the three-part sonata form and thus provided the model for the earliest symphonies, which consisted of three movements. In the 19th century, overtures independent of any larger work usually illustrated a literary or historical theme. Overtures to operettas and musicals have traditionally been medleys of their themes.

Owens, Jesse, orig. JAMES CLEVELAND OWENS (b. Sept. 12, 1913, Oakville, Ala., U.S.—d. March 31, 1980, Phoenix, Ariz.), U.S. track-and-field athlete. At Ohio State University in 1935, he broke or equaled four world track records in one day, setting a new long-jump record that would stand for 25 years. In the 1936 Olympics in Berlin he won four gold medals, tying the Olympic record in the 100-m run, breaking the Olympic record in the 200-m run, running the final segment for the world-record-breaking U.S. 400-m relay team, and breaking the listed world record for the long jump. This performance by an African American dramatically foiled Adolf Hitler's intention to use the games to show Aryan racial superiority. For a time, Owens held alone or shared the world records for all sprint distances recognized by the International Amateur Athletic Federation.

Jesse Owens, 1936.
AP

owl, Any bird of prey in the mostly nocturnal order Strigiformes, including typical owls (family Strigidae) and barn, bay, and grass owls (Tytonidae). Their virtually silent flight and protective (usually brown) coloration aid in capturing insects, birds, and small mammals. Owls have round, forward-looking eyes, a sharply hooked beak, and acute hearing and vision. They are 5–28 in. (13–70 cm) long. The feathers of some species form a disk framing the face or ear tufts that help locate prey by reflecting sound to the ears. Owls can turn their heads 180°; some species can turn as much as 270°. They nest in buildings, in trees, or on the ground. Typical owls occur worldwide except in Antarctica.

Oxford, ancient OXONIA, City and administrative district (pop., 2001: 134,248), county seat of Oxfordshire, England. Situated on the River Thames, the town is best known for the University of Oxford. First occupied in Saxon times as a fording point, it became a burg, built to defend the northern frontier of Wessex from Danish attack; it was first mentioned in the Anglo-Saxon Chronicle in AD 912. Little remains of the town's Norman period of occupation. Oxford is generally known as the "City of Spires" because of its skyline of Gothic towers and steeples. Most of these 15th–17th-century buildings belong to the university. The city was the Royalist headquarters in the English Civil Wars. Its modern economy is varied and includes, in addition to educational services, printing and publishing industries and automobile manufacturing.

Oxford, University of, Autonomous university at Oxford, Oxfordshire, England. It was founded in the 12th century and modeled on the University of Paris, with initial faculties of theology, law, medicine, and the liberal arts. Of the earliest colleges, University College was founded in 1249, Balliol *c.* 1263, and Merton in 1264. Early scholars of note include Roger Bacon, John Duns Scotus, William of Ockham, and John Wycliffe. In the Renaissance, Desiderius Erasmus and St. Thomas More helped enhance its already considerable reputation. By then faculties of physical science, political science, and other fields had been added. The first women's college, Lady Margaret Hall, was established in 1878. There are 32 other colleges and collegial institutions. Oxford houses the Bodleian Library and the Ashmolean Museum of Art and Archaeology. Oxford University Press (1478) is the world's oldest, largest, and most famous university publisher. Oxford has been associated with many of the greatest names in British history.

Oxford English Dictionary, The (OED), Definitive historical dictionary of the English language. It was conceived by London's Philological Society in 1857, and sustained editorial work began in 1879 under James Murray. Published in 10 volumes between 1884 and 1928, it first appeared under its current name in 1933. Its definitions are arranged mostly in order of historical occurrence and illustrated with dated quotations from English-language literature and records. Its second edition was published in 20 volumes in 1989.

Oxford movement, or TRACTARIAN MOVEMENT (1833–45) Movement within the Church of England that aimed to emphasize the church's Catholic inheritance as a source of legitimacy and deeper spirituality. Its main intent was to defend the Church of England as a divine institution against the threats of liberal theology, rationalism, and government interference. Though some in the movement (notably John Henry Newman and Henry E. Manning) ended up converting to Catholicism, most did not. Their concern for a higher standard of worship influenced not only the Church of England but also other British Protestant sects. The movement was also instrumental in the establishment of Anglican monasteries and convents.

oxidation-reduction, or REDOX, Any chemical reaction in which the oxidation number of a participating chemical species changes. Addition of hydrogen or electrons or removal of oxygen is reduction, and removal of hydrogen or electrons or addition of oxygen is oxidation. The processes always occur simultaneously: one substance is oxidized by the other, which it reduces. The conditions of the substances before and after are called oxidation states, to which numbers are given and with which calculations can be made. (Valence is a similar but not identical concept.) The chemical equation that describes the electron transfer can be written as two separate half reactions that can in theory be carried out in separate compartments of an electrolytic cell, with electrons flowing through a wire connecting the two. Strong oxidizing agents include fluorine, ozone, and oxygen itself; strong reducing agents include alkali metals such as sodium and lithium.

oxygen, Gaseous chemical element, chemical symbol O, atomic number 8. It constitutes 21% (by volume) of air and more than 46% (by weight) of Earth's crust, where it is the most plentiful element. It is a colourless, odourless, tasteless gas, occurring as the diatomic molecule O_2. In respiration, it is taken up by animals and some bacteria (and by plants in the dark), which give off carbon dioxide (CO_2). In photosynthesis, green plants assimilate carbon dioxide in the presence of sunlight and give off oxygen. The small amount of oxygen that dissolves in water is essential for the respiration of fish and other aquatic life. Oxygen takes part in combustion and in corrosion but does not itself burn. It has valence 2 in compounds; the most important is water. It forms oxides and is part of many other molecules and functional groups, including nitrate, sulfate, phosphate, and carbonate; alcohols, aldehydes, carboxylic acids, and ketones; and peroxides. Obtained for industrial use by distillation of liquefied air, oxygen is used in steelmak-

ing and other metallurgical processes and in the chemical industry. Medical uses include respiratory therapy, incubators, and inhaled anesthetics. Oxygen is part of all gas mixtures for manned spacecraft, scuba divers, workers in closed environments, and hyperbaric chambers. It is also used in rocket engines as an oxidizer (in liquefied form) and in water and waste treatment processes.

Oxyrhynchus, Archaeological site, Egypt, on the western bank of the Nile River. Many ancient papyri dating from 250 BC to AD 700 were discovered there in the late 19th and early 20th centuries. The papyri, written mainly in Greek and Latin, contain both religious texts and masterpieces of Greek classical literature. Some of these texts, once considered lost, were by Pindar and Callimachus. The modern village of Al-Bahnasā is located on the site.

oyster, Any bivalve of two families, Ostreidae (true oysters) or

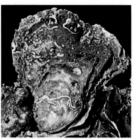

European flat oyster (Ostrea edulis)
G. Tomsich/Photo Researchers

Aviculidae (pearl oysters), found in temperate and warm coastal waters worldwide. Both valves (halves) have a rough, often dirty-gray outer surface and a smooth white inner lining (nacre). The lower valve, which affixes to a surface, is nearly flat. The smaller upper valve is convex and has rougher edges. The oyster filters its food, minute organic particles, from the water. Cultivated as food, oysters are regarded as a delicacy. Pearls are the accumulation of nacre around a piece of foreign matter.

ozone, Pale blue gas (O_3) that is irritating, explosive, and toxic. Like ordinary oxygen gas (O_2), it contains oxygen atoms, but the bonding of three atoms per molecule gives it distinctive properties. It is formed in electrical discharges and accounts for the distinctive odour of the air after thunderstorms or near electrical equipment. Usually manufactured on the spot by passing an electric discharge through oxygen or air, it is used in water purification, deodorization, bleaching, and various chemical reactions that require a strong oxidizing agent. Small amounts that occur naturally in the stratospheric ozone layer absorb ultraviolet (UV) radiation that otherwise could severely damage living organisms. Near Earth's surface, ozone contributes to air pollution, ozone produced by auto emissions in the presence of sunlight being a deleterious component of smog, and also accelerates the deterioration of rubber.

ozone layer, or OZONOSPHERE, Region in the upper atmosphere, about 9–22 mi (15–35 km) high, with significant concentrations of ozone, formed by the effect of solar ultraviolet (UV) radiation on oxygen and also present in trace quantities elsewhere in Earth's atmosphere. Ozone strongly absorbs solar UV radiation, causing the atmospheric temperature to climb to about 30 °F (−1 °C) at the top of the layer and preventing much of this radiation from reaching Earth's surface, where it would injure many living things. Chlorofluorocarbons (CFCs) and some other air pollutants that diffuse into the ozone layer destroy ozone. In the mid-1980s scientists discovered that a "hole"—an area where the ozone is diminished to less than 40 percent of its normal density—develops periodically in the ozone layer above Antarctica. This severe regional depletion, explained as a natural seasonal depletion, appears to have been exacerbated by the effects of CFCs and may have led to an increase in skin cancer caused by UV exposure. The Montreal Protocol first imposed restrictions on the manufacture and use of CFCs and other ozone-destroying pollutants in 1987; those restrictions were strengthened and expanded by subsequent amendments to that agreement.

P

pacemaker, Source of rhythmic electrical impulses that trigger heart contractions. In the heart's electrical system, impulses generated at a natural pacemaker are conducted to the atria and ventricles. Heart surgery or certain diseases can interrupt conduction (heart block), requiring use of a temporary or permanent artificial pacemaker. A small electrode attached to an electric generator outside the body is threaded through a vein into the heart. The generator, inserted beneath the skin, produces regular pulses of electric charge to maintain the heartbeat. Permanent pacemakers can also be implanted on the heart's surface.

Pacific, War of the (1879–83) Conflict involving Chile, Bolivia, and Peru over disputed territory on the mineral-rich Pacific coast. National boundaries in the region were not definitively established prior to the conflict, and in the 1870s Chile controlled nitrate fields claimed by Peru and Bolivia. When demand for nitrates rose, war broke out over the territory. Chile defeated both countries and took control of valuable mining areas in each; Bolivia lost its entire Pacific coast. A 1904 treaty gave Bolivian commerce freedom of transit through Chilean territory, but Bolivia continued to try to escape its landlocked status. Peru foundered economically for decades after the war. A final accord between Peru and Chile was only reached in 1929 through U.S. mediation.

Pacific Islands, Trust Territory of the, Former United Nations trusteeship, administered by the U.S. from 1947 to 1986. It consisted of more than 2,000 islands scattered over about 3,000,000 sq mi (7,770,000 sq km) of the tropical western Pacific Ocean, north of the Equator. It covered the region known as Micronesia and comprised three major island groups: the Marianas, the Carolines, and the Marshalls. The seat of government was Saipan in the Northern Mariana Islands. In 1986 the U.S. declared the trust territory agreements no longer in effect. The Federated States of Micronesia and the Republic of the Marshall Islands became sovereign states, and the Northern Mariana Islands became a commonwealth of the U.S. The Republic of Palau became a sovereign state in 1994.

Pacific Ocean, Body of salt water extending from the Antarctic region in the south to the Arctic circle in the north and lying between the continents of Asia and Australia on the west and North and South America on the east. It occupies about one-third of the surface of the earth and is by far the largest of the world's oceans. Its area, excluding adjacent seas, is approximately 63,800,000 sq mi (165,250,000 sq km), twice that of the Atlantic Ocean and more than the whole land area of the globe. Its mean depth is 14,040 ft (4,280 m). The western Pacific is noted for its many peripheral seas.

pacifism, The doctrine that war and violence as a means of settling disputes is morally wrong. The first genuinely pacifist movement was Buddhism, whose founder demanded from his followers absolute abstention from any act of violence against their fellow creatures. The ancient Greek conception of pacifism applied to individual conduct rather than to the actions of peoples or kingdoms. The Romans conceived of *pax*, or peace, as a covenant between states or kingdoms that creates a "just" situation based on mutual recognition. This judicial approach was applicable only to the "civilized world," however. Though the spoken words of Jesus as recorded in the New Testament could be interpreted as a kind of pacifism (and in fact were so interpreted by many of his early followers), from the early 3rd century through the Middle Ages the Christian church itself held that armies were necessary to combat nonbelievers or demons. In the 17th and 18th centuries, much pacifist thinking was based on the idea that transferring power from sovereigns to the people would result in peace, because, it was claimed, wars were a product of sovereigns' ambitions and pride. In the 19th and 20th centuries, pacifism inspired widespread interest in general disarmament and in the creation of international organizations for the peaceful resolution of disputes, such as the League of Nations and the United Nations. Pacifism as a national policy, rather than as a standard of individual conduct, has yet to satisfactorily address the problem of an aggressor that does not possess similar moral scruples. Individual pacifism may lead one to become a conscientious objector. Historically important pacifists include Leo Tolstoy, Mohandas K. Gandhi, and Martin Luther King, Jr.

pagan, Traditional designation of a practitioner of classical polytheisms. The early Christians often used the term to refer to non-Christians who worshiped multiple deities. Christian missionaries frequently sought to stamp out pagan practices by building churches on the sites of pagan shrines or by associating Christian holidays with pagan rituals (e.g., linking Christmas with the celebration of the winter solstice). The term *pagan* was also used to refer to non-Christian philosophers, and in the 20th century it was used to identify members of certain new religious movements. *See* Neo-paganism.

pageant, Large-scale, spectacular theatrical production or procession. In the Middle Ages, a pageant was the wagon on which religious plays such as mystery plays were performed. Because the plays were associated with ceremony and spectacle, the term came to refer to any extravagant dramatic event or colourful celebration. Pageants often serve to express the shared identity of a community or religious group. Secular pageants include coronations and royal weddings; other modern examples are seen in Mardi Gras and other carnival processions.

Paget disease of bone, or OSTEITIS DEFORMANS, Chronic bone disease of middle age. Named for James Paget, it is characterized by excessive bone destruction alternating with disordered bone construction (with dense, brittle bones and deformity that can compress internal structures). The long bones, vertebrae, pelvis, and skull are most often affected, more often in men. The risk of cancer, usually osteosarcoma, is high. Increased blood supply to the area of bone destruction may lead to heart or circulatory problems. Both calcitonin (which regulates bone growth) and bisphosphonates (which block excessive bone breakdown) are drugs of treatment.

A square pagoda of the Daigo Temple, Kyōto, Japan.
Manley Features/Shostal Associates

pagoda, Towerlike multistoried structure of stone, brick, or wood, usually associated with a Buddhist temple complex and enshrining sacred relics. The pagoda evolved from the Indian stupa. The pagoda's crowning ornament is pyramidal or conical in Myanmar (Burma), Thailand, Cambodia, and Laos and bottle-shaped in the Tibet Autonomous Region of China. In other parts of China and in Korea and Japan, a pagoda is a tall tower repeating a basic story unit in diminishing proportions. The stories may be circular, square, or polygonal. The pagoda form is intended mainly as a monument and has very little usable interior space.

Pahari painting, or HILL PAINTING, Style of miniature painting and book illustration that developed in the independent states of the Himalayan foothills in India *c.* 1690–1790. Combining the bold intensity of the Basohli school with the delicacy and lyricism of the Kangra school, Pahari painting is closely related to Rajasthani painting. It shares with the Rajput art of the northern Indian plains a preference for depicting legends of the cowherd god Krishna.

Pahlavi, Mohammad Reza Shah (b. Oct. 26, 1919, Tehrān, Iran—d. July 27, 1980, Cairo, Egypt), Shah of Iran (1941–79), noted for his pro-Western orientation and autocratic rule. After an education in Switzerland, he replaced his father, Reza Shah Pahlavi, as ruler when the latter was forced into exile by the British. His rule was marked by a power struggle with his premier, Mohammad Mosaddeq, who briefly succeeded in deposing him in 1953; covert intervention by British and U.S. intelligence services returned him to the throne the next year. His program of rapid modernization and oil-field development initially brought him popular support, but his autocratic style and suppression of dissent, along with corruption and the unequal distribution of Iran's new oil wealth, increased opposition led by exiled cleric Ayatollah Ruhollah Khomeini. In 1979 Pahlavi was forced into exile.

Pahlavi, Reza Shah (b. March 16, 1878, Alasht, Qājār Iran—d. July 26, 1944, Johannesburg, S.Af.), Shah of Iran (1926–41). An army officer, he rose through the ranks and in 1921 led a coup that overthrew the Qājār dynasty. He sought to bring order and end Iran's political chaos and its domination by Britain and Soviet Russia following World War I (1914–18). He constructed roads, schools, and hospitals, opened a university, and built the Trans-Iranian Railway. He emancipated women, nationalized several economic sectors, and reduced the clergy's power. He often used repressive methods, which eventually cost him his popularity. During World War II (1939–45), fearing that Pahlavi might side with Germany, the U.S. and Britain occupied Iran. The Allies forced him to abdicate (1941) in favour of his son, Mohammad Reza Shah Pahlavi.

pain, Physical suffering associated with a bodily disorder (such as a disease or injury) and accompanied by mental or emotional distress. Pain, in its simplest form, is a warning mechanism that helps protect an organism by influencing it to withdraw from harmful stimuli (such as a pinprick). In its more complex form, such as in the case of a chronic condition accompanied by depression or anxiety, it can be difficult to isolate and treat. Pain receptors, found in the skin and other tissues, are nerve fibres that react to mechanical, thermal, and chemical stimuli. Pain impulses enter the spinal cord and are transmitted to the brain stem and thalamus. The perception of pain is highly variable among individuals; it is influenced by previous experiences, cultural attitudes (including gender stereotypes), and genetic makeup. Medication, rest, and emotional support are the standard treatments. The most potent pain-relieving drugs are opium and morphine, followed by less-addictive substances and non-narcotic analgesics such as aspirin and ibuprofen.

Paine, Thomas (b. Jan. 29, 1737, Thetford, Norfolk, Eng.—d. June 8, 1809, New York, N.Y., U.S.), English-American writer and political pampleteer. After a series of professional failures in England, he met Benjamin Franklin, who advised him to immigrate to America. He arrived in Philadelphia in 1774 and helped edit the *Pennsylvania Magazine*. In January 1776 he wrote *Common Sense*, a 50-page pamphlet eloquently advocating independence; more than 500,000 copies were quickly sold, and it greatly strengthened the colonists' resolve. As a volunteer aide to Gen. Nathanael Greene during the American Revolution he wrote his 16 "Crisis" papers (1776–83), each signed "Common Sense"; the first, beginning "These are the times that try men's souls," was read to the troops at Valley Forge on George Washington's order. In 1787 Paine traveled to England and became involved in debate

Thomas Paine, detail of a portrait by John Wesley Jarvis; in the Thomas Paine Memorial House, New Rochelle, N.Y.
Courtesy of the Thomas Paine National Historical Association

over the French Revolution; his *The Rights of Man* (1791–92) defended the revolution and espoused republicanism. Viewed as an attack on the monarchy, it was banned, and Paine was declared an outlaw in England. He then went to France, where he was elected to the National Convention (1792–93). After he criticized the Reign of Terror, he was imprisoned by Maximilien Robespierre (1793–94). His *The Age of Reason* (1794, 1796), the first part of which was published while he was still in prison, earned him a reputation as an atheist, though it in fact espouses Deism. He returned to the U.S. in 1802; criticized for his Deist writings and little remembered for his service to the Revolution, he died in poverty.

painting, Art consisting of representational, imaginative, or abstract designs produced by application of coloured paints to a two-dimensional, prepared, flat surface. The elements of design (i.e., line, colour, tone, texture) are used in various ways to produce sensations of volume, space, movement, and light. The range of media (e.g., tempera, fresco, oil, watercolour, ink, gouache, encaustic, casein) and the choice of a particular form (e.g., mural, easel, panel, miniature, illuminated manuscript, scroll, screen, fan) combine to realize a unique visual image. Painting as an art form dates back to prehistoric cave paintings. The early cultural traditions of tribes, religions, guilds, royal courts, and states controlled the craft, form, imagery, and subject matter of painting and determined its function (e.g., ritualistic, devotional, decorative). Painters were considered skilled artisans rather than creative artists until eventually, in East Asia and Renaissance Europe, the fine artist emerged with the social status of a scholar and courtier. Fine artists signed their work and decided its design and often its subject and imagery. Over time painters have increasingly gained the freedom to invent their own visual language and to experiment with new forms and unconventional materials and techniques. In the early 20th century painters began to experiment with nonrepresentational art in which formal qualities such as line, colour, and form were explored rather than subject matter. Throughout the century styles vacillated between representational and nonrepresentational painting. In the late 20th century some critics forecast the "death of painting" in the face of new media such as video and intallation art, yet talented new artists repeatedly brought painting back to the centre of artistic production.

Pakistan, officially ISLAMIC REPUBLIC OF PAKISTAN, Country, southern Asia. Area: 307,374 sq mi (796,096 sq km). Population: (2011 est.) 187,343,000. Capital: Islamabad. The population is a complex mix of indigenous peoples who have been affected by successive waves of migrations of Aryans, Persians, Greeks, Pashtuns, Mughals, and Arabs. Languages: Urdu (national), English, Punjabi, Pashto, Sindhi, Balochi. Religions: Islam (official; predominantly Sunni); also Christianity, Hinduism. Currency: Pakistani rupee. Pakistan may be divided into four regions: the northern mountains, the Balochistan Plateau, the Indus Plain, and the desert areas. The Himalayan and Trans-Himalayan ranges form the great mountain areas of the northernmost part of the country; some of the highest peaks are K2 and Nanga Parbat. The country has a developing mixed economy based largely on agriculture, light industries, and services. Remittances from Pakistanis working abroad are a major source of foreign exchange. Pakistan is a federal republic with two legislative houses; its head of state is the president, and its head of government is the prime minister. The area has been inhabited since the 3rd millennium BCE. From the 3rd century BCE to the 2nd century CE, it was part of the Mauryan and Kushan kingdoms. The first Muslim conquests were in the 8th century CE. The British East India Co. subdued the reigning Mughal dynasty in 1757. During the period of British colonial rule, what is now (Muslim) Pakistan was part of (Hindu) India. The new state of Pakistan came into existence in 1947 by act of the British Parliament. The Kashmir region remained a disputed territory between Pakistan and India, with tensions resulting in military clashes and full-scale war in 1965. Civil war between East and West Pakistan in 1971 resulted in independence for Bangladesh (formerly East Pakistan) in 1972. Many Afghan refugees migrated to Pakistan during the Soviet-Afghan war in the 1980s and remained there during the Taliban and post-Taliban periods. Pakistan elected Benazir Bhutto, the first woman to head a modern Islamic state, in 1988. She and her party were ousted in 1990, but she returned to power in 1993–97. Conditions became volatile during that period. Border flare-ups with India continued, and Pakistan conducted tests of nuclear weapons. Political conditions worsened, and the army carried out a coup in 1999.

palate, Roof of the mouth, separating the oral and nasal cavities. The front two-thirds, the hard palate, is a plate of bone covered by mucous membrane. It gives the tongue a surface against which to make speech sounds and shape food during chewing and keeps pressures in the mouth from closing off the nasal passage. The flexible soft palate behind it is made of muscle and connective tissue and ends in the uvula, a fleshy projection. It rises to block the nasal cavity and upper pharynx off from the mouth and lower pharynx for swallowing or to create a vacuum for drinking. Cleft palate, a congenital disorder involving a gap in the palate, can be corrected surgically.

Palau, officially REPUBLIC OF PALAU, Island country, western Pacific Ocean. Area: 188 sq mi (488 sq km). Population: (2011 est.) 20,600. Capital: Melekeok. The population is of mixed Malay, Melanesian, Filipino, and Polynesian ancestry. Languages: Palauan, English (both official). Religion: Christianity (mostly Roman Catholic; also Protestant, other Christians). Currency: U.S. dollar. The islands of the Palau group are fertile, with mangrove swamps along the coasts, backed by savanna and palms rising to rainforests in the hills. The major source of employment is government service. Subsistence farming and fishing are the main occupations in the rural areas. Palau is a republic with two legislative houses; its head of state and government is the president. The islands had been under nominal Spanish ownership when they were sold to Germany in 1899. They were seized by Japan in 1914 and taken by Allied forces in 1944 during World War II. Palau became part of the U.S. Trust Territory of the Pacific Islands in 1947 and became a sovereign state in 1994; the U.S. provides economic assistance and maintains a military presence in the islands.

Palembang, City (pop., 2000: 1,451,419) and river port, Indonesia. It is located on both banks of the Musi River. It was the capital of a Buddhist kingdom from the 7th to the 14th century AD and was subsequently overthrown by the Hindu Majapahit empire. The Dutch East India Company established a trading post there and in 1659 built a fort. Palembang was occupied by the Japanese during World War II and was the capital of South Sumatra until that state was included in the Republic of Indonesia in 1950. The port is accessible to ocean traffic and conducts considerable trade with ports on the Malay Peninsula and in Thailand and China.

Palenque, Ruined ancient Mayan city of the Late Classic Period (c. AD 600–900) in what is now Chiapas state, Mexico. It is considered the most beautiful of Mayan sites. The Palenque builders designed temple pyramids and palaces with mansard-style roofs and walls embellished with delicate stucco reliefs of rulers, gods, and ceremonies. The principal structure is the palace, a labyrinth of galleries with interior courts and a four-story square tower. The

great Temple of the Inscriptions is noted for its hieroglyphics and a vast funerary crypt, filled with jade, that was discovered in 1952. The city's ruins were designated a UNESCO World Heritage site in 1987.

Paleocene Epoch, or PALAEOCENE EPOCH, Earliest division of the Paleogene Period, from 65.5 million to 55.8 million years ago. It precedes the Eocene Epoch and follows the Cretaceous Period. The Paleocene was characterized by a generally warming climate, with little or no frost; seasonal variation probably consisted of alternating dry and wet seasons. By the Paleocene the dinosaurs and other reptilian groups that were dominant during the Cretaceous had disappeared, and the epoch saw the rapid proliferation and evolution of mammals.

Paleolithic Period, or OLD STONE AGE, Ancient technological or cultural stage characterized by the use of rudimentary chipped stone tools. During the Lower Paleolithic (c. 2,500,000–200,000 years ago), simple pebble tools and crude stone choppers were made by the earliest humans. About 700,000 years ago, the first rough hand ax appeared; it was later refined and used with other tools in the Acheulean industry. A flake-tool tradition emerged in the Middle Paleolithic, as exemplified by implements of the Mousterian industry. The Upper Paleolithic (40,000–10,000 BC) saw the emergence of more complex, specialized, and diverse regional stone-tool industries, such as the Aurignacian, Solutrean, and Magdalenian. The two principal forms of Paleolithic art are small sculptures—such as the so-called Venus figurines and various carved or shaped animal and other figures—and monumental paintings, incised designs, and reliefs on the walls of caves such as Altamira (in Spain) and Lascaux Grotto (in France). The end of the Paleolithic is marked by the emergence of the settled agricultural villages of the Neolithic Period.

paleontology, or PALAEONTOLOGY, Scientific study of life of the geologic past, involving analysis of plant and animal fossils preserved in rocks. It is concerned with all aspects of the biology of ancient life forms: their shape and structure, evolutionary patterns, taxonomic relationships with each other and with modern species, geographic distribution, and interrelationships with the environment. Paleontology has played a key role in reconstructing the Earth's history and has provided evidence to support the theory of evolution. Data from paleontologic studies have also aided petroleum geologists in locating deposits of oil and natural gas, which are frequently associated with the remains of certain ancient life forms.

Paleozoic Era, or PALAEOZOIC ERA, Major interval of geologic time, c. 542–251 million years ago. From the Greek for "ancient life," it is the first era of the Phanerozoic Eon and is followed by the Mesozoic Era. It is divided into six periods: (from oldest to youngest) the Cambrian, Ordovician, Silurian, Devonian, Carboniferous, and Permian. During the early Paleozoic, much of North America was covered by a warm, shallow sea with many coral reefs. Fossils from this time include marine invertebrates and primitive fish; the plants were predominantly algae, with some mosses and ferns. During the late Paleozoic, huge, swampy forest regions covered much of the northern continents. Plant and animal life flourished. Amphibians left the oceans to live on land, reptiles evolved as fully terrestrial life-forms, and insect life began. Ferns grew to tree size, and precursors of the conifers appeared.

Palermo, ancient PANORMUS, City (pop., 2001: 686,722), seaport, and capital of Sicily. Located on the Bay of Palermo, the city was founded by Phoenician traders in the 8th century BC; it was later a Carthaginian settlement. It was taken by the Romans in 254 BC. Conquered by the Arab troops of the Aghlabid dynasty in 831, it flourished as a centre of trade with North Africa. Palermo was thus quite prosperous when it fell to the Norman adventurers Roger I and Robert Guiscard in 1072. The ensuing era of Norman rule (1072–1194) was Palermo's golden age, particularly after the founding of the Norman kingdom of Sicily in 1130 by Roger II. In 1194 Germany's Hohenstaufen ruler, Frederick II, took over. Palermo was conquered by the French under Charles of Anjou in 1266, but Angevin oppression was ended in 1282 by a popular uprising called the Sicilian Vespers. After 1412 the crown of Sicily was united with that of Aragon and subsequently with that of Spain. Palermo declined during this long period of Spanish rule. The city was taken by Italian patriot Giuseppe de Garibaldi in 1860 and made part of the kingdom of Italy. Heavily bombed during World War II, it was captured by Allied forces in 1943. Notable buildings from the Norman and later periods include the cathedral that contains the tombs of Roger II and Frederick II. Palermo is Sicily's chief port, and ship repair is an important industry.

Palestine, biblical CANAAN, Region, at the eastern end of the Mediterranean Sea. It extends east to the Jordan River, north to the border between Israel and Lebanon, west to the Mediterranean, and south to the Negev desert, reaching the Gulf of Aqaba. The political status and geographic area designated by the term have changed considerably over the course of three millennia. The eastern boundary has been particularly fluid, often understood as lying east of the Jordan and extending at times to the edge of the Arabian Desert. A land of sharp contrasts, Palestine includes the Dead Sea, which is the lowest natural point of elevation on Earth, and mountain peaks higher than 2,000 ft (610 m) above sea level. In the 20th and 21st centuries it has been the object of conflicting claims by Jewish and Arab national movements. The region is sacred to Judaism, Christianity, and Islam. Settled since early prehistoric times, mainly by Semitic groups, it was occupied in biblical times by the kingdoms of Israel, Judah, and Judaea. It was subsequently held by virtually every power of the Middle East, including the Assyrians, Persians, Romans, Byzantines, Crusaders, and Ottomans. It was governed by Britain after the end of World War I (1914–18)—from 1922, under a League of Nations mandate—until 1948, when the State of Israel was proclaimed. Armies from Egypt, Transjordan, Syria, and Iraq attacked the next day. They were defeated by the Israeli army.

Palestine Liberation Organization (PLO), Arabic MUNAẒẒAMAT AL-TAḤRĪR AL-FILASṬĪNIYYAH, Umbrella political organization representing the Palestinian people in their drive for a Palestinian state. It was formed in 1964 to centralize the leadership of various groups. After the Six-Day War of 1967, the PLO promoted a distinctively Palestinian agenda. In 1969 Yāsir 'Arafāt, leader of Fatah, the PLO's largest faction, became its chairman. From the late 1960s the PLO engaged in guerrilla attacks on Israel from bases in Jordan, from which it was expelled in 1971. PLO headquarters moved to Lebanon. In 1974 'Arafāt advocated limiting PLO activity to direct attacks against Israel, and the Arab community recognized the PLO as the sole legitimate representative of all Palestinians. It was admitted to the Arab League in 1976. In 1982 Israel invaded Lebanon and expelled PLO forces based there. In 1988 the PLO leadership, then based in Tunis, declared a Palestinian state and the following year elected 'Arafāt as president. It also recognized Israel's right to exist, though several militant factions dissented. In 1993 Israel recognized the PLO by signing an agreement with it granting Palestinian self-rule in parts of the West Bank and Gaza Strip. The PLO became an integral part of the Palestinian National Authority.

Pali language, Middle Indo-Aryan language of the 5th century BC in which the most essential documents of Theravada Buddhism are written. Linguistically, Pali is a homogenization of the northern Middle Indo-Aryan dialects in which the Buddha's teachings were orally recorded and transmitted. According to the tradition of Sri Lankan chronicles, the Theravada canon was first written down in the 1st century BC, though its oral transmission continued long afterward. No single script was ever developed for Pali;

scribes used scripts of their own languages to copy canonical texts and commentaries, and most extant palm-leaf manuscripts of Pali are of relatively recent date.

palm, Any of about 2,800 species of flowering, subtropical trees, shrubs, and vines that make up the family Arecaceae (or Palmae). Many are economically important. Palms furnish food, shelter, clothing, timber, fuel, building materials, fibres, starch, oils, waxes, and wines for local populations in the tropics. Many species have very limited ranges; some grow only on single islands. The fast growth and many by-products of palms make exploitation of the rainforest appealing to agribusiness. The usually tall, unbranched, columnar trunk is crowned by a tuft of large, pleated, fan- or feather-shaped leaves, with often prickly petioles (leafstalks), the bases of which remain after leaves drop, often covering the trunk. Trunk height and diameter, leaf length, and seed size vary greatly. Small flowers are produced in large clusters. Among the most important palms are the sugar palm (*Arenga pinnata*, or *A. saccharifera*), coconut palm, date palm, and cabbage palmetto.

Royal palm (Roystonea regia).
E.R. Degginger/EB Inc.

Palm Sunday, or PASSION SUNDAY, In Christianity, the first day of Holy Week and the Sunday before Easter, commemorating Jesus' triumphal entry into Jerusalem. It usually includes a procession of members of the congregation carrying palms, representing the palm branches the crowd scattered in front of Jesus as he rode into the city. The liturgy also includes readings recounting the suffering and death of Jesus. Palm Sunday was celebrated in Jerusalem as early as the 4th century and in the West by the 8th century.

Palma, in full PALMA DE MALLORCA, City (pop., 2006 est.: 284,000), capital of the Balearic Islands and *communidad autónoma* (autonomous community), Spain. Palma lies on the southwestern coast of Majorca island on Palma Bay in the western Mediterranean Sea. Romans conquered Majorca in 123 BC, and it was later ruled by Byzantines and by the Arabs before being taken by James I of Aragon in 1229. The city's old sections have many notable homes built in the 16th and 18th centuries. Historic buildings include the Gothic cathedral and Bellver Castle. The economy is varied and includes tourism and light manufacturing.

palmistry, Reading of an individual's character and divination of the future by interpreting lines on the palm of the hand. Palmistry may have originated in ancient India, and it was probably from their original Indian home that the traditional fortune-telling of the Gypsies was derived. It was also practiced in China, Tibet, Persia, Mesopotamia, Egypt, and ancient Greece. In medieval Europe it was used to discover witches, who were thought to have pigmentation spots as signs of a pact with the devil. Though palmistry is still practiced, there is no known scientific basis for it.

Pamirs, High mountain region, Central Asia. Located mostly in Tajikistan, it also borders parts of Afghanistan, Pakistan, China, and Kyrgyzstan. It includes many peaks that are higher than 20,000 ft (6,100 m) in elevation, as well as many glaciers. Its highest point, Imeni Ismail Samani (Communism) Peak, rises in the northwestern part of the range to an elevation of 24,590 ft (7,495 m). The region is sparsely populated, and almost all the inhabitants are Tajiks. It is a central mountain knot from which extend several great ranges, including the Karakorams and Hindu Kush.

Pampas, the, Vast grassy plains in South America, primarily in Argentina. They extend west from the Atlantic coast to the Andean foothills. The Argentine Pampas covers 295,000 sq mi (764,000 sq km) and slopes gradually downward from northwest to southeast. The western portion is dry and largely barren; the humid eastern portion is the nation's economic heart. Herds of wild cattle and horses, introduced by the Spaniards and rounded up by Argentina's famed gauchos, roamed the Pampas until the later 19th century, when the land was fenced into huge *estancias* (ranches). The region is prominent in Argentina's gaucho literature and musical folklore. Since the late 20th century, parts of the Pampas have become noted grape-growing regions, particularly the region around Mendoza, which produces more than half the wines of South America.

Pan, Greek fertility deity with a half-human, half-animal form. The Romans associated him with Faunus. Pan was usually said to be the son of Hermes. He was often represented as a vigorous and lustful figure with the horns, legs, and ears of a goat; in later art his human parts were more emphasized. Some Christian depictions of the Devil bear a striking resemblance to Pan. Pan haunted the high hills, where he was chiefly concerned with flocks and herds. Like a shepherd, Pan was a piper, and he rested at noon. He could inspire irrational terror in humans, and the word *panic* comes from his name.

Pan-American Highway, International highway system connecting North and South America. Conceived in 1923 as a single route, the road grew to include a number of designated highways in participating countries, including the Inter-American Highway from Nuevo Laredo, Mex., to Panama City, Pan. The whole system, extending from Alaska and Canada to Chile, Argentina, and Brazil, totals nearly 30,000 mi (48,000 km). Only some 240 miles (400 km) in the Panama-Colombia border area remain uncompleted.

Pan-Germanism, Movement to politically unify all German-speaking people. The desire for German unification began in the early 19th century and was advanced by Ernst Arndt and other early nationalists. The Pan-German League was organized in 1894 by Ernst Hasse (1846–1908) to heighten German nationalist awareness, especially among German-speaking people outside Germany. The movement, which pressed for German expansion in Europe, gained support after World War I under the Weimar Republic and was actively promoted by Adolf Hitler and the Nazi Party. After Germany's defeat in 1945 and the expulsion of Germans from formerly German areas of eastern Europe, the movement declined.

Pan-Slavism, Movement to unite Slav peoples of eastern and central Europe. It began in the early 19th century when Slav intellectuals studied their common cultures. Political goals for Slavic unity increased in 1848, when a Slav congress organized by František Palacký met in Prague to press for equal rights under Austrian rule. In the 1860s the movement became popular in Russia, to which Pan-Slavs looked for protection from Turkish and Austro-Hungarian rule; this led Russia and Serbia into wars against the Ottoman Empire in 1876–77. In the 20th century, nationalist rivalries among the Slav peoples prevented their effective collaboration.

Panama, officially REPUBLIC OF PANAMA, Country, Central America. It is bounded by the Caribbean Sea to the north and the Pacific Ocean to the south. Area: 28,640 sq mi (74,177 sq km). Population: (2011 est.) 3,643,000. Capital: Panama City. Most of the people are of mixed heritage (primarily mestizos [Indian-European] and African-European). Languages: Spanish (official), English, indigenous languages. Religion: Christianity (predominantly Roman Catholic; also other Christians). Currency: balboa. Panama consists of three distinct areas: the lowlands ("hot lands"; nearly nine-tenths of the country), the temperate lands, and the

highlands ("cold lands"). It has a market economy based on services, mostly transportation, communications, and storage connected with the Panama Canal as well as international banking and tourism. It is a multiparty republic with one legislative house; its head of state and government is the president. The land was inhabited by Indians when the Spanish arrived in 1501. The first successful Spanish settlement was founded by Vasco Núñez de Balboa in 1511. Panama was part of the Viceroyalty of New Granada until it declared its independence from Spain in 1821 to join Colombia. In 1903 it revolted against Colombia and was recognized by the U.S., to which it ceded the Canal Zone. The completed canal was opened in 1914; control of the canal passed to a joint U.S.-Panamanian commission in 1979. In 1968 Gen. Omar Torrijos Herrera had overthrown the elected president and imposed a dictatorship. After his death, Gen. Manuel Noriega took control of the military, increased his power over Panamanian politics, and became dictator. An invasion by U.S. troops in 1989 overthrew him, and Panama returned to democratic government. In 1999 the canal came under the full control of Panama. In 2006 Panamanians approved a plan to expand the canal, and work on it began the following year.

Panama Canal, Lock-type canal, Panama. Extending across the Isthmus of Panama, it connects the Atlantic and Pacific oceans. It is about 50 mi (82 km) long from deepwater to deepwater, with an average depth of 43 ft (13 m). The width varies between 500 to 1,000 ft (150 to 300 m). In 1881 a French company began constructing the canal, but the enterprise collapsed in 1889. Under a 1903 treaty Panama granted the U.S. the Panama Canal Zone and the rights to build and operate a canal. Work began in 1904; facing enormous obstacles, George Washington Goethals directed the construction from 1907, and the canal opened on Aug. 15, 1914. The canal enabled ships traveling between the two oceans to avoid the lengthy circumnavigation of South America and was a boon to world commerce. After disputes over sovereignty, a 1977 treaty provided for Panama to take control of the canal by 2000; it did so in 1999. Except for small craft, no vessel can pass through the canal under its own power. Ships are towed by electric locomotives, and it generally takes 15–20 hours to complete the passage (including waiting time). Sets of double locks enable ships to pass in opposite directions simultaneously.

Panama City, City (pop., 2000: 415,964), capital of Panama. Near the Pacific Ocean entrance of the Panama Canal, on the Bay of Panama, the site was originally an Indian fishing village. The old city was founded in 1519 but was completely destroyed by British buccaneer Henry Morgan in 1671. It was rebuilt in 1674 just west of the old site. In 1751 the area became part of the Viceroyalty of New Granada and later part of Colombia. It was the centre of the Panamanian revolt against Colombia in 1903, when it became the capital of Panama. After the canal opened in 1914, the city developed rapidly, becoming the commercial and transportation centre of the country. The economy depends largely on revenue from canal traffic and associated services.

Panchatantra (Sanskrit: "Five Treatises" or "Five Chapters"), Collection of Indian beast fables written in Sanskrit that has had extensive circulation throughout the world. The original work, now lost, may have been written down between 100 BC and AD 500. A textbook for instructing three sons of a king, it contained aphorisms that glorify shrewdness and cleverness over altruism. As early as the 11th century one version reached Europe, where it was known as *The Fables of Bidpai* (for the narrator, an Indian sage).

Panchen Lama, Any of the line of reincarnated lamas who head the Tashilhunpo Monastery in Tibet, traditionally second only to the Dalai Lama in spiritual authority in the dominant sect of Tibetan Buddhism. A Panchen Lama installed by the Chinese Nationalist government in 1949 later became an official under the Chinese communists. He remained in Tibet after the 14th Dalai Lama fled into exile in 1959 but was imprisoned in 1964 after criticizing the government. He was released in the late 1970s and died in 1989. The Dalai Lama and government subsequently chose different successors.

pancreas, Compound gland functioning as both an exocrine (secreting through a duct) and an endocrine (ductless) gland. It continuously secretes pancreatic juice (containing water, bicarbonate, and enzymes needed to digest carbohydrates, fat, and protein) through the pancreatic duct to the duodenum. Scattered among the enzyme-producing cells are the islets of Langerhans, which secrete insulin and glucagon directly into the bloodstream. Disorders include inflammation (pancreatitis), infections, tumours, and cysts. If more than 80–90% of the pancreas must be removed, the patient will need to take insulin and pancreatic extracts.

pancreatitis, Inflammation of the pancreas, associated with alcohol, trauma, or pancreatic-duct obstruction. Activated enzymes escaping into pancreatic tissues cause irritation and inflammation. If it does not subside, bleeding, tissue death and scarring, pus formation, and infection may occur. Symptoms include severe pain (worst when lying on the back), low fever, nausea, and hypertension. Acute cases are treated by controlling pain, preventing or relieving shock, inhibiting pancreatic-juice secretion (including eliminating oral intake of food), avoiding infection, and replacing lost fluids and salts. Chronic pancreatitis can destroy enough of the pancreas to cause pancreatic-juice deficiency and diabetes mellitus. Treatment may include a low-fat diet, avoiding overeating and alcohol, pancreatic extracts, and insulin.

panda, or GIANT PANDA, Species (*Ailuropoda melanoleuca*, family Ursidae) of white-and-black forest-dwelling carnivore, found in central China, that subsists almost exclusively on bamboo. Because they cannot digest cellulose, wild pandas (of which there are about 1,600) spend as much as 16 hours a day eating up to 40 lb (18 kg) of bamboo leaves, stems, and shoots to obtain needed nutrients. More than 120 individuals live in captivity, mostly in China. Large males may attain 6 ft (1.8 m) in length and weigh more than 220 lb (100 kg); females are usually smaller. Giant pandas live alone except when breeding. They have a slow reproductive cycle and are difficult to breed in captivity.

Pandora, In Greek mythology, the first woman. After Prometheus stole fire from heaven and bestowed it on mortals, Zeus decided to counteract this blessing and commissioned Hephaestus to fashion a woman out of earth, upon whom the gods bestowed their choicest gifts. After marrying Prometheus's brother, Pandora opened a jar containing all kinds of misery and evil, which escaped and flew out over the earth. In one version, Hope alone remained inside, the lid having been shut before she could escape.

Pangea, or PANGAEA, Hypothetical protocontinent proposed by Alfred Wegener in 1912 as part of his theory of continental drift. Pangea (from Greek: *pangaia*, "all earth") supposedly covered about half the Earth and was completely surrounded by a world ocean called Panthalassa. Early in the Jurassic Period (approximately 200 million to 146 million years ago), Pangea began to break apart. Its segments, Laurasia (composed of all the present-day northern continents) and Gondwana (the present-day southern continents) gradually receded, resulting in the formation of the Atlantic and Indian oceans.

panic, In economics, a severe financial disturbance, such as widespread bank failures, feverish stock speculation followed by a market crash, or a climate of fear caused by economic crisis or anticipation of such a crisis. The term is applied only to the initial, violent stage of financial upheaval rather than the whole decline in the business cycle. Until the 19th century, economic fluctuations were largely connected with shortages of goods, market expansion, and speculation (as in the South Sea Bubble). Panics in the industrialized societies of the 19th–20th centuries have re-

flected the increasing complexity of advanced economies. The Panic of 1857 in the U.S. had its seeds in the railroads' defaulting on their bonds and in the decline in the value of railroad securities; its effects were complex, including not only the closing of many banks but also severe unemployment in the U.S. and a money-market panic in Europe. The Panic of 1873, which began with financial crises in Vienna and New York, marked the start of a long-term contraction in the world economy. The most infamous panic began with the U.S. stock-market crash of 1929.

Pankhurst, Emmeline, orig. EMMELINE GOULDEN (b. July 14, 1858, Manchester, Eng.—d. June 14, 1928, London), British feminist. In 1879 she married Richard Pankhurst (1834–98), author of Britain's first women's-suffrage bill and the Married Women's Property Acts (1870, 1882). In 1889 she founded the Women's Franchise League, which in 1894 secured for married women the right to vote in local elections. In 1903, after holding municipal offices in Manchester, she founded the Women's Social and Political Union (WSPU). From 1912 she advocated extreme militancy, mainly in the form of arson, and was arrested 12 times in one year. Weeks before her death in 1928, Britain passed a bill to give voting rights to all women. Her daughter Christabel H. Pankhurst (1880–1958)—later Dame Christabel—organized the militant tactics of the WSPU and directed actions that included hunger strikes and huge outdoor rallies. She later became a religious evangelist and moved to the U.S.

Emmeline Pankhurst in prison clothes, 1908
BBC Hulton Picture Library

panpipe, or SYRINX, Wind instrument consisting of pipes of different lengths made of cane (less often wood, clay, or metal) arranged in a row. It is blown across the top, each pipe producing a different note. The panpipe dates from *c.* 2000 BC and is found worldwide, especially in eastern Africa, South America, and Melanesia.

p'ansori (Korean: "story singing"), A form of sung folk narrative. The form seems to have originated during the reign of Sukchong (1675–1720). Once a narrative performance that incorporated shamanistic chants, *p'ansori* became a vehicle for treating popular customs and everyday life. Six of the original 12 titles were revised by the master *p'ansori* writer Sin Chaehyo, of which five are still performed.

pantheism, Doctrine that the universe is God and, conversely, that there is no god apart from the substance, forces, and laws manifested in the universe. Pantheism characterizes many Buddhist and Hindu doctrines and can be seen in such Hindu works as the Vedas and the Bhagavadgita. Numerous Greek philosophers contributed to the foundations of Western pantheism. In the Middle Ages and the Renaissance, the tradition was continued in Neoplatonism and Judeo-Christian mysticism. In the 17th century Benedict de Spinoza formulated the most thoroughly pantheistic philosophical system, arguing that God and Nature are merely two names for one reality.

Pantheon, Building in Rome begun 27 BC, probably as an ordinary rectangular Classical temple, and completely rebuilt by Hadrian (*c.* AD 118–128). It is remarkable for its size and design; the exact method of construction has never been determined. A circular building of concrete faced with brick, it has a great concrete dome, 142 ft (43 m) in diameter, and a front porch of Corinthian columns with a triangular pediment. The vast space is lit solely by the 27-ft (8-m) oculus at the dome's centre. The interior is lined with coloured marble, and the walls are marked by seven deep recesses screened by pairs of columns.

panzer division (German *panzer*, "armoured") Self-contained military unit of the German army, built around the capabilities of armoured vehicles. In World War II, it consisted of a tank brigade with four battalions; a motorized infantry brigade with four rifle battalions; an artillery regiment; and reconnaissance, antitank, and military-engineering battalions and service units. Germany had six panzer divisions in 1939 and 20 by 1941. It remains the principal offensive element of the German army.

Pap smear, or PAPANICOLAOU SMEAR, Sample of cells from the vagina and cervix of the uterus for laboratory staining and examination to detect genital herpes and early-stage cancer, especially of the cervix. Developed by the Greek-born U.S. physician George Nicolas Papanicolaou (1883–1962), this technique also can be applied to cells obtained from other surfaces.

papacy, System of central government of the Roman Catholic Church. Bishops led the early church, the bishop of Rome being accorded special respect by the end of the 1st century AD in part because of the belief that St. Peter was the first bishop of that city. St. Cyprian challenged that position of honour in the 3rd century, and in the 4th–5th century the power of the see of Constantinople rose to challenge that of Rome; the rivalry would culminate in the Schism of 1054 between the Eastern and Western churches. After the collapse of the Roman Empire, the papacy found protection under the wing of Charlemagne and his successors; in the 9th–10th century the German emperors controlled it. In 1059 Pope Nicholas II responded by vesting the right to name a new pope exclusively with the College of Cardinals. To establish the papacy's supremacy in Christian society, Gregory VII excommunicated Henry IV of Germany for disobedience to papal commands and decreed that civil rulers could not invest churchmen with temporal power. In the next centuries the papacy developed into one of the most important and influential institutions in Europe; Urban II, Innocent III, and Gregory IX were among the most significant popes of the period. The worldliness and corruption of the papal court that emerged at the same time and the "Babylonian Captivity" of the papacy at Avignon led to the Great Schism and eventually to the Reformation. The Council of Trent inaugurated the Counter-Reformation. In the 19th century the papacy lost its remaining temporal powers when the Papal States were incorporated into the new Kingdom of Italy. It maintained a conservative religious position, proclaiming infallibility in doctrinal matters and espousing the idea that the pope is the absolute ruler of the church. The Second Vatican Council gave the bishops, clergy, and laity more voice.

papal infallibility, In Roman Catholicism, the doctrine that the pope, acting as supreme teacher and under certain conditions, as when he speaks *ex cathedra* ("from the chair"), cannot err when he teaches in matters of faith or morals. It is based on the belief that the church, entrusted with the teaching mission of Jesus, will be guided by the Holy Spirit in remaining faithful to that teaching. The First Vatican Council (1869–70) stated the conditions under which a pope may be said to have spoken infallibly: he must intend to demand irrevocable assent from the entire church in some aspect of faith or morals. The doctrine remains a major obstacle to ccumenical endeavours and is the subject of controversy even among Roman Catholic theologians.

Papal States, Italian STATI PONTIFICI, Territories of central Italy over which the pope had sovereignty from 756 to 1870. The extent of the territory and the degree of papal control varied over the centuries. As early as the 4th century, the popes had acquired considerable property around Rome (called the Patrimony of St. Peter). From the 5th century, with the breakdown of Roman imperial au-

thority in the West, the popes' influence in central Italy increased as the people of the area relied on them for protection against the barbarian invasions. When the Lombards threatened to take over the whole peninsula in the 750s, Pope Stephen II (or III) appealed for aid to the Frankish ruler Pippin III (the Short). On intervening, Pippin "restored" the lands of central Italy to the Roman see, ignoring the claim of the Byzantine (Eastern Roman) Empire to sovereignty there. This Donation of Pippin (754) provided the basis for the papal claim to temporal power. More land was gained when the papacy acquired the duchy of Benevento in 1077, and Popes Innocent III and Julius II further expanded the papal domain. The rise of communes and rule by local families weakened papal authority in the towns, and by the 16th century the papal territory was one of a number of petty Italian states. They were an obstacle to Italian unity until 1870, when Rome was taken by Italian forces and became the capital of Italy. In 1929 the Lateran Treaty settled the pope's relation to the Italian state and set up an independent city-state.

papaya, Large palmlike plant (*Carica papaya*; family Caricaceae), cultivated throughout the tropics and warm subtropics, and its succulent juicy fruit. A popular breakfast fruit in many countries, it is also used in salads, pies, sherbets, juices, and confections. The juice of the unripe fruit contain an enzyme that is useful in various remedies for indigestion and in meat tenderizers.

papillomavirus, Any of a group of viruses that cause warts and other harmless tumours in humans. More than 100 distinct types are known. Different types are responsible for warts of the hands, plantar warts (of the feet), and throat warts. Genital warts are caused by other types, which are spread by sexual intercourse. Some types of papillomaviruses that cause genital infections have been linked with various cancerous tumours, especially cervical cancers; their presence can be detected through a Pap smear.

Papua, formerly IRIAN JAYA, Province (pop., 2010 prelim.: 2,833,381), Indonesia. It includes most of the western half of the island of New Guinea and the offshore islands of the Schouten island group. The Maoke Mountains rise to 16,503 ft (5,030 m) at Jaya Peak. The first Europeans to sight Papua were the Portuguese in 1511, and the region was claimed by the Dutch in 1828. The entire western half of New Guinea was transferred to Indonesia in 1963 and was made a province in 1969, with its capital at Jayapura. Rebels led a separatist movement there in the late 1990s, and the province achieved greater autonomy in 2001. In 2006 the Indonesian government designated the western portion of Papua as West Papua (Papua Barat) province.

Papua New Guinea, officially INDEPENDENT STATE OF PAPUA NEW GUINEA, Island country, southwestern Pacific Ocean. Area: 178,704 sq mi (462,840 sq km). Population: (2011 est.) 6,188,000. Capital: Port Moresby. Most of the people are Papuan (four-fifths) and Melanesian; ethnic minorities are Polynesian, Chinese, and European. Languages: English, Tok Pisin, Hiri Motu (all official); indigenous languages. Religions: Christianity (Protestant, Roman Catholic); also traditional beliefs. Currency: kina. The island of New Guinea constitutes about seven-eighths of the total land area of Papua New Guinea; the country also includes Bougainville Island and the Bismarck Archipelago. The New Guinea terrain ranges from swampy lowland plains in the south and north to high central mountains (the highlands) in the northwest and southeast. Much of the land is covered with tropical rainforest. Some of the outlying islands are volcanic. The country has a developing mixed economy based largely on subsistence agriculture and the export of minerals. It is a constitutional monarchy with one legislative house; its head of state is the British monarch, represented by the governor-general, and the head of government is the prime minister. The area has been inhabited since prehistoric times, and farming has been practiced since *c.* 7000 BCE. The Portuguese sighted the coast in 1511, and the first European landing was about 1526–27. The first European colony was founded in 1793 by the

British. In 1828 the Dutch claimed the western half as part of the Dutch East Indies. In 1884 Britain annexed the southeastern part and Germany took over the northeastern sector. In 1906 the British part (renamed Papua) passed to Australia, which also governed the German sector after World War I. After World War II, Australia governed both sectors as the Territory of Papua and New Guinea. Dutch New Guinea was annexed to Indonesia in 1969. Papua New Guinea achieved independence in 1975 and joined the British Commonwealth. By the mid-1990s the government of Papua New Guinea was seeking to resolve a long-standing conflict with Bougainville independence fighters, and in 2001 the two sides agreed on a peace treaty; Bougainville became an autonomous region in 2005.

Papuan languages, Group of about 800 languages spoken by indigenous peoples of New Guinea and parts of some neighbouring islands, including Alor, Bougainville, Halmahera, New Britain, New Ireland, and Timor. Spoken by some three to four million people, Papuan languages belong to several dozen families, the higher genetic relationships of which are still uncertain. This diversity, conjoined with the numerous Austronesian languages spoken on smaller parts of New Guinea and on adjacent islands, makes the region the most linguistically heterogeneous area of the world. The vast majority of Papuan languages have fewer than 100,000 speakers; Enga, spoken in the highlands of Papua New Guinea, is the most common of the Papuan languages and has some 200,000 speakers.

papyrus, Writing material of ancient times and the plant from which it comes, *Cyperus papyrus* (sedge family), also called paper plant. This grasslike aquatic plant has woody, bluntly triangular stems and grows to about 15 ft (4.6 m) high in quietly flowing water up to 3 ft (90 cm) deep. The ancient Egyptians used the stem of the plant to make sails, cloth, mats, cords, and principally paper. Paper made from papyrus was the chief writing material in ancient Egypt, Greece, and Rome. In the 8th–9th century AD, other plant fibres replaced papyrus in the manufacture of paper. The plant is now often used as a pool ornamental in warm areas or in conservatories.

parachute, Umbrella-like device for slowing the descent of a body falling through the atmosphere. Separate panels sewn together form a canopy attached by suspension lines to a harness worn by the user. Originally designed to provide a safe escape from a disabled aircraft, parachutes are also used for dropping supplies and for slowing returning space capsules. The parachute was conceived by the 14th century, but practical demonstrations began only in the 1780s in France, leading in 1797 to a 3,200-ft (1,000-m) exhibition jump from a balloon by André-Jacques Garnerin (1769–1823); in 1802 he made a jump of 8,000 ft (2,400 m). Early parachute material was canvas, which was later replaced by silk and then nylon.

paradox, Apparently self-contradictory statement whose underlying meaning is revealed only by careful scrutiny. Its purpose is to arrest attention and provoke fresh thought, as in the statement "Less is more." In poetry, paradox functions as a device encompassing the tensions of error and truth simultaneously, not necessarily by startling juxtapositions but by subtle and continuous qualifications of the ordinary meanings of words. When a paradox is compressed into two words, as in "living death," it is called an oxymoron.

paradoxes of Zeno, Arguments by which Zeno of Elea upheld the doctrine of Parmenides that real Being is unique and unchanging. Zeno's arguments were aimed at discrediting the beliefs in plurality and motion that were inconsistent with Parmenides' doctrine. His best-known arguments are those against the reality of motion. One argument begins from the fact that a body in motion can reach a given point only after having traversed half the distance. But before traversing half, it must traverse half of this half, and so on ad infinitum; consequently, the goal can never be reached.

Paraguay, officially REPUBLIC OF PARAGUAY, Country, south-central South America. Area: 157,048 sq mi (406,752 sq km). Population: (2011 est.) 6,459,000. Capital: Asunción. Most Paraguayans are mestizos; there are much smaller groups of American Indians and people of African, European, and Asian ancestry. Languages: Spanish and Guaraní (both official). Religion: Christianity (predominantly Roman Catholic; also Protestant). Currency: guaraní. Paraguay is a landlocked country of plains and swampland. The Paraguay River, flowing from north to south, divides the country into two geographic regions: the eastern region, which is an extension of the Brazilian Plateau, and the western region, which forms the northern part of the Gran Chaco plains. Paraguay has a developing market economy that is based largely on agriculture, trade, and light industries. It is a multiparty republic with two legislative houses; its head of state and government is the president. Seminomadic tribes speaking Guaraní were in the area long before it was settled by Spain in the 16th–17th century. Paraguay was part of the Viceroyalty of the Río de la Plata until it became independent in 1811. It suffered from dictatorial governments in the 19th century and was devastated by the War of the Triple Alliance (1864, 1865–70), which it fought against Brazil, Argentina, and Uruguay. The Chaco War (1932–35), with Bolivia over territorial rights in the Gran Chaco, was settled primarily in Paraguay's favour by the peace treaty of 1938. Military governments, including that of Alfredo Stroessner, predominated from the mid-20th century until a civilian president, Juan Carlos Wasmosy, was elected in 1993. The country suffered from political unrest and a financial crisis beginning in the late 1990s and continuing into the 21st century.

Paraguay River, River, South America. The fifth largest river in South America, it is 1,584 mi (2,550 km) long and the principal tributary of the Paraná River. Rising in the Mato Grosso region of Brazil about 980 ft (300 m) above sea level, it crosses Paraguay to its confluence with the Paraná near the Argentine border. The Gran Chaco plain extends west from the river.

parakeet, Any of 115 species in 30 genera (subfamily Psittacinae) of small, slender seed-eating parrots with a long, tapering tail. Parakeets are found worldwide in warm regions. They typically form large flocks. Most species lay four to eight eggs in a tree hole. The most popular caged parakeet is the budgerigar (*Melopsittacus undulatus*), mistakenly called lovebird; about 8 in. (19 cm) long, it may be any colour but usually has cheek spots and close barring on the upper parts.

*Budgerigar (*Melopsittacus undulatus*), a popular parakeet.*
Bruce Coleman Ltd.

parallax, Difference in the direction of a celestial object as seen by observers from two widely separated points, a measurement used to find a body's distance. The two positions of the observers and that of the object form a triangle; its apex angle (at the object) is twice the parallax, which becomes smaller with increasing distance. Observations for calculating the Sun's parallax can be made simultaneously from two different places on Earth's surface; that value reaches a maximum of 8.794 seconds of arc for observers at points separated by Earth's diameter. Observing the difference in an object's position as seen from Earth at points six months apart in its orbit (stellar, or annual, parallax) allows measurements of distances (e.g., of stars) too large to be made from two places on Earth's surface. The nearest star system, Alpha Centauri, has a stellar parallax of 0.76 second of arc. Highly precise parallaxes, and thus the positions, of more than 100,000 stars in the Sun's vicinity were determined from data collected by the European Space Agency's Hipparcos satellite (launched 1989).

paralysis, or PALSY, Loss or impairment of voluntary use of one or more muscles. It may be flaccid (with loss of muscle tone) or spastic (stiff). Hemiplegia (one-sided paralysis) is usually caused by stroke or brain tumour on the opposite side. Diplegia (two-sided paralysis, as in cerebral palsy) results from generalized brain disease. Spinal-cord damage (from bone or joint disease, fracture, or tumour affecting the vertebrae; inflammatory and degenerative diseases; or pernicious anemia) paralyzes the body at and below the level of the damage (paraplegia if the legs and lower body only; quadriplegia if arms and legs). Poliomyelitis and polyneuritis (neuritis of multiple nerves) result in paralysis with muscle wasting. Bell palsy (a type of neuritis) paralyzes the muscles of one side of the face. Muscular dystrophy causes paralysis by attacking muscle. Metabolic causes include myasthenia gravis. Paralysis may also have psychiatric causes.

paramagnetism, Kind of magnetism that occurs in materials weakly attracted by a strong magnet. Compounds containing iron, palladium, platinum, and the rare-earth elements exhibit strong paramagnetism because they have atoms with some incomplete inner electron shells. Their unpaired electrons make the atoms behave like tiny permanent magnets that align with and strengthen an applied magnetic field. As the temperature rises, strong paramagnetism decreases because of the greater random motion of the atoms. Weak paramagnetism, found in many solid metallic elements, is independent of temperature.

Paramaribo, City (pop., 2004: 242,946), seaport, and capital of Suriname. Located on the Suriname River near the Atlantic Ocean, it was originally an Indian village before becoming a French settlement (*c.* 1640). In 1651 it became a British colony but was ceded to the Dutch in 1667. It is built on a shingle reef that stands 16 ft (5 m) above the river at low tide. Much of the distinctive Dutch colonial architecture and a canal system remain. Since 1945 the city has grown considerably because of tourism and industries.

paramecium, Any of the free-living, single-celled protozoans that make up the genus *Paramecium*. Most are about the size of the period at the end of this sentence. They vary in shape and are surrounded by a rigid protein layer (pellicle) covered with hundreds of cilia that beat rhythmically to propel them and to direct bacteria and other food particles into their oral groove. Food particles are collected into food vacuoles, where digestion takes place. Two (occasionally three) contractile vacuoles close to the surface near the ends of the cell expand and contract as they discharge metabolic wastes and excess fluid. Paramecia have two kinds of nuclei: a large macronucleus (the centre of all metabolic activities) and at least one small micronucleus (which stores the genetic material necessary for sexual reproduction).

Paraná River, River, South America. It is the continent's second longest river (after the Amazon River) and rises on the plateau of southeast-central Brazil. It flows generally south 3,032 mi (4,880 km) to join the Uruguay River and form the Río de la Plata estuary on the Atlantic Ocean. Its drainage basin includes most of southeastern Brazil, Paraguay, eastern Bolivia, and northern Argentina. From its origin at the confluence of the Grande and Paranaíba rivers to its junction with the Paraguay River, it is known as the Alto (Upper) Paraná. Completion of the Itaipú Dam between Paraguay and Brazil in the 1980s submerged the massive Guaíra Falls and created a large reservoir.

paranoia, Mental disorder characterized by delusions of persecution or grandeur, usually without hallucinations. Paranoia was formerly classified as a distinct psychosis but is now generally treated as one of several varieties of schizophrenia or, in milder cases, of personality disorder. The paranoid person generally suffers from exaggerated self-reference, a tendency to construe independent events and acts as pertaining to him- or herself.

parapsychology, Discipline concerned with investigating events that cannot be accounted for by natural law and knowledge that cannot have been obtained through the usual sensory abilities. Parapsychology studies the cognitive phenomena often called extrasensory perception, in which a person acquires knowledge of other people's thoughts or of future events through channels apparently beyond the five senses. It also examines physical phenomena such as the levitation of objects and the bending of metal through psychokinesis. Though belief in such phenomena may be traced to earliest times, parapsychology as a subject of serious research originated in the late 19th century, partly in reaction to the growth of the spiritualist movement. The Society of Psychical Research was established in London in 1882, and similar societies were later founded in the U.S. and in many European countries. In the 20th century research into parapsychology was also conducted at some universities, notably at Duke University under J. B. Rhine.

parasitism, Relationship between two species in which one benefits at the expense of the other. Ectoparasites live on the body surface of the host; endoparasites live in their hosts' organs, tissues, or cells and often rely on a third organism (the carrier, or vector) to transmit them to the host. The cuckoo and cowbird practice brood parasitism, laying eggs in other birds' nests to be raised by the foster parents. In social parasitism, one type of animal parasitizes animals of the same type (e.g., one ant species on different ant species). Hyperparasitism occurs when parasites are parasitized (e.g., protozoans hyperparasitize a flea on a dog).

pardon, In law, release from guilt or remission of punishment. The power to pardon is generally exercised by the state's chief executive officer. A pardon may be full or conditional. A conditional pardon imposes a lesser punishment or some other obligation. Some states still bar pardoned offenders from holding public office or obtaining professional licenses.

Paris, City (pop., 2005 est.: 2,153,600; metro. area, 9,854,000), river port, capital of France. It is now located on both banks of the Seine River. The original settlement from which Paris evolved, Lutetia, was in existence by the late 3rd century BCE on an island in the Seine. Lutetia was captured and fortified by the Romans in 52 BCE. During the 1st century CE the city spread to the left bank of the Seine. By the early 4th century it was known as Paris. It withstood several Viking sieges (885–887) and became the capital of France in 987, when Hugh Capet, the count of Paris, became king. The city was improved during the reign of Philip II, who formally recognized the University of Paris *c.* 1200. In the 14th–15th centuries its development was hindered by the Black Death and the Hundred Years' War. In the 17th–18th centuries it was improved and beautified. Leading events of the French Revolution took place in Paris (1789–99). Napoleon III commissioned Georges-Eugène Haussmann to modernize the city's infrastructure and add several new bridges over the Seine. The city was the site of the Paris Peace Conference, which ended World War I. During World War II Paris was occupied by German troops. It is now the financial, commercial, transportation, artistic, and intellectual centre of France. The city's many attractions include the Eiffel Tower, Notre-Dame de Paris, the Louvre, the Panthéon, Pompidou Centre, and the Paris Opéra, as well as boulevards, public parks, and gardens.

Paris, Congress of (1856) Conference in Paris to produce the treaty that ended the Crimean War. The treaty was signed between Russia on one side and France, Britain, Sardinia-Piedmont, and Turkey on the other. It guaranteed the independence and territorial integrity of Turkey. Russia was forced to surrender Bessarabia to Moldavia, warships of all nations were barred from the

Black Sea, and the Danube River was opened to shipping of all countries. The congress also adopted the first codified law of the sea, which banned privateering and defined a legal naval blockade.

Paris, Treaty of (1763) Treaty concluding the Seven Years' War (including the French and Indian War). It was signed by Britain and Hanover on one side and France and Spain on the other. France renounced to Britain the mainland of North America east of the Mississippi, its conquests in India since 1749, and four West Indian islands. Britain restored to France four other West Indian islands and the West African colony of Gorée (Senegal). In return for recovering Havana and Manila, Spain ceded Florida to Britain and received Louisiana from the French.

Paris, Treaty of (1814) Treaty signed in Paris that ended the Napoleonic Wars between France and the Allies (Austria, Britain, Prussia, Russia, Spain, Sweden, and Portugal). The terms were generous to France, since Napoleon had abdicated and the Bourbon dynasty was restored. France was allowed to retain its boundaries of 1792 and ceded only several islands to Britain. Other terms were left to be discussed later.

Paris, Treaty of (1815) Second treaty between France and the Allies, following Napoleon's Hundred Days and final defeat. It was harsher than the first Treaty of Paris (1814). France was required to return to its borders of 1790 and was stripped of the Saar and Savoy regions; it was also obliged to pay an indemnity of 700 million francs and to support a 150,000-man army of occupation for three to five years.

Paris Commune, or COMMUNE OF PARIS (March 18–May 28, 1871) Insurrection of Paris against the French government. After France's defeat in the Franco-Prussian War and the collapse of the Second Empire, the republican Parisians feared that the conservative majority in the National Assembly would restore the monarchy. On March 18 the National Guard in Paris resisted orders to disarm, and after municipal elections were won by the revolutionaries, they formed the Commune government. Factions included the so-called Jacobins, who wanted the Paris Commune to control the revolution (as its namesake had in the French Revolution); the Proudhonists, socialist followers of Pierre-Joseph Proudhon who supported a federation of communes; and the Blanquistes, socialist followers of Auguste Blanqui who demanded violent action. Government forces quickly suppressed communes elsewhere in France, then entered Paris on May 21. In a week of fierce fighting, they crushed the Communards, who had set up barricades in the streets and burned public buildings, including the Tuileries Palace. About 20,000 insurrectionists and 750 government troops were killed. In the aftermath, the government took harsh repressive action; 38,000 suspects were arrested and more than 7,000 were deported.

Paris Peace Conference (1919–20) Meeting that inaugurated the international settlement after World War I. It opened on Jan. 12, 1919, with representatives from more than 30 countries. The principal delegates were France's Georges Clemenceau, Britain's David Lloyd George, the U.S.'s Woodrow Wilson, and Italy's Vittorio Emanuele Orlando, who with their foreign ministers formed a Supreme Council. Commissions were appointed to study specific financial and territorial questions, including reparations. The major products of the conference were the League of Nations; the Treaty of Versailles, presented to Germany; the Treaty of Saint-Germain, presented to Austria; and the Treaty of Neuilly, presented to Bulgaria. The inauguration of the League of Nations on Jan. 16, 1920, brought the conference to a close. Treaties were subsequently concluded with Hungary (Treaty of Trianon, 1920) and Turkey (Treaties of Sèvres, 1920, and Lausanne, 1923).

parity, In economics, equality in price, rate of exchange, purchasing power, or wages. In international exchange, parity exists when the exchange rate between two currencies makes the purchasing power of both currencies equal. Adjustments to maintain parity can occur in the marketplace as prices change in response to supply and demand, or through the intervention of national governments or international agencies such as the International Monetary Fund. In U.S. agricultural economics, the term parity is used for a system of regulating the prices of farm commodities, usually by government price supports and production quotas, to guarantee farmers the purchasing power they had in a past base period. Parity is also used in personnel administration to establish equitable wage rates for various classes of employees.

Parker, Charlie, orig. CHARLES CHRISTOPHER PARKER, JR. (b. Aug. 29, 1920, Kansas City, Kan., U.S.—d. March 12, 1955, New York, N.Y.), U.S. saxophonist and composer. He played with Jay McShann's big band (1940–42) and those of Earl Hines (1942–44) and Billy Eckstine (1944) before leading his own small groups in New York City. (A nickname acquired in the early 1940s, Yardbird, was shortened to Bird and used throughout his career.) Parker frequently worked with Dizzy Gillespie in the mid-1940s, making a series of small-group recordings that heralded the arrival of bebop as a mature outgrowth of the improvisation of the late swing era. His direct, cutting tone and unprecedented dexterity on the alto saxophone made rapid tempos and fast flurries of notes trademarks of bebop, and his complex and yet subtle harmonic understanding brought an altogether new sound to the music. Easily the most influential jazz musician of his generation, Parker suffered chronic drug addiction, and his early death contributed to making him a tragic legend.

Charlie Parker, 1949.
AP

parkinsonism, Neurological disorder causing progressive loss of control of movement. It was first described in 1817 by British physician James Parkinson (1755–1824). The cause of primary parkinsonism, or Parkinson disease, is unknown. The mean age of onset is about 57, but juvenile parkinsonism is also known. Neurons in the brain that normally produce dopamine deteriorate. When 60–80% are destroyed, signals suppressing unintended movement are disrupted and symptoms appear, including tremor at rest, muscle rigidity, trouble in starting movements, and loss of balance. Known causes include sleeping sickness; certain poisons; repeated blows to the head, as in boxing; and the drug MPTP. Environmental toxins or genetic susceptibility may account for some cases. Drug therapy requires careful scheduling and combinations to delay development of tolerance and side effects. Surgical pallidotomy (destruction of the globus pallidus, a brain structure involved in motor control) and transplantation of fetal dopamine-producing tissue remain experimental.

Parks, Rosa, orig. ROSA LOUISE MCCAULEY (b. Feb. 4, 1913, Tuskegee, Ala., U.S.—d. Oct. 24, 2005, Detroit, Mich.), U.S. civil rights activist. She worked as a seamstress in Montgomery, Ala., where she joined the NAACP in 1943. In 1955 she was arrested after refusing to give her seat on a public bus to a white man. The resultant boycott of the city's bus system, organized by Martin Luther King, Jr., and others, brought the civil rights movement to new prominence. In 1957 Parks moved to Detroit, where she was a staff assistant (1965–88) to U.S. Rep. John Conyers. She was awarded the Congressional Gold Medal in 1999.

Parliament, Legislative assembly of Britain and of other governments modeled after it. The British Parliament consists of the monarch, the House of Lords, and the House of Commons, and traces its roots to the union (*c.* 1300) of the Great Council and the King's Court, two bodies that treated with and advised the king. In the 14th century, Parliament was split into two houses, with the lords spiritual and temporal (i.e., not only the nobility but also high officials of the church) debating in one and the knights and burgesses in the other. In the 14th century Parliament also began to present petitions ("bills") to the king, which with his assent would become law. Robert Walpole was the first party leader to head the government as prime minister (1721–42).

parliamentary procedure, or RULES OF ORDER, Generally accepted rules, precedents, and practices used in the governance of deliberative assemblies. They are intended to maintain decorum, ascertain the will of the majority, preserve the rights of the minority, and facilitate the orderly transaction of business. Rules of parliamentary procedure originated in Britain in the 16th and 17th centuries and were subsequently adopted by legislatures around the world. *Robert's Rules of Order*, codified in 1876 by U.S. Gen. Henry M. Robert (1837–1923) and regularly refined and enlarged, is the standard set of rules used by legislatures in the U.S.

parody, In literature, a work in which the style of an author is closely imitated for comic effect or in ridicule. Differing from both burlesque (by the depth of its technical penetration) and travesty (which treats dignified subjects in a trivial manner), parody mercilessly exposes the tricks of manner and thought of its victim and therefore cannot be written without a thorough appreciation of the work it ridicules. Examples date from as early as ancient Greece and occur in nearly all literatures and all periods.

parole, Supervised conditional liberty from prison granted prior to the expiration of a prisoner's sentence. Modern use of parole stems from a change in penal philosophy to emphasize rehabilitation rather than retribution. In some jurisdictions, those convicted of certain crimes (e.g., rape or murder) are not eligible for parole. Conditions of parole vary, but in all cases their violation may constitute grounds for reincarceration. Parole supervision ranges from little more than a periodic police check to intensive supervision by trained personnel.

parrot, Any of the 333 species of birds in the family Psittacidae.

Rainbow lorikeet
(Trichoglossus haematodus).
Bruce Coleman Ltd.

About 220 species of true parrots (subfamily Psittacinae) are found worldwide in warm regions. Many are brilliantly coloured. They have a blunt tongue and eat seeds, buds, and some fruit and insects. Their vocal apparatus permits many species to mimic human speech with great accuracy. The African gray parrot (*Psittacus erithacus*), intelligent and a particularly good talker, is about 13 in. (33 cm) long and is gray except for a red tail and white face; it lives up to 80 years. The 31 species of Amazon parrots (genus *Amazona*), also good mimics, are 10–16 in. (25–40 cm) long and predominantly green. Four other subfamilies are found chiefly around New Zealand and Australia, as are the cockatoos and cockatiel (family Cacatuidae); these are often considered parrots as well because they are classified with Psittacidae in the order Psittaciformes.

parsec, Unit of measure used by astronomers to express distances to stars and galaxies. It is the distance at which the radius of Earth's orbit would subtend an angle of one second of arc, so an object one parsec away would have a parallax of one second. An object's distance in parsecs is the reciprocal of its parallax in seconds of arc. For example, Alpha Centauri, with a parallax of 0.76 second, is 1.33 parsecs from the Sun and Earth. One parsec equals 3.26 light-years, or 19.2 trillion mi (30.9 trillion km).

Parshvanatha (fl. 8th century BC), In Jainism, the 23rd Tirthankara, or saint, of the present age. He founded a religious order and formulated four vows binding on its members (not to kill, steal, lie, or own property; a vow of celibacy was added later by Mahavira). According to legend, Parshvanatha once saved a family of serpents trapped in a log in an ascetic's fire. One of the snakes, later reborn as Dharana, the lord of the underworld kingdom of nagas (snakes), sheltered Parshvanatha from a storm sent by an enemy demon. In sculpture and painting Parshvanatha is depicted with a canopy of snake hoods over his head.

Parthenon, Chief temple of Athena on the Acropolis at Athens. Built 447–432 BC by Ictinus and Callicrates under Pericles, it is considered the culmination of the Doric order. Though the white marble temple has suffered damage over the centuries, including the loss of most of its sculpture, its basic structure remains intact. The colonnade supports an entablature consisting of a plain architrave, a frieze of alternating triglyphs (grooved blocks) and metopes (plain blocks with relief sculpture) and, at the two ends, a triangular pediment. The colonnade consists of eight columns on the ends and 17 on the sides, enclosing a cella; the interior originally held a great gold-and-ivory statue by Phidias. Such architectural devices as entasis of the columns and an upward curvature of the base are used to correct optical illusions. Its sculpture rivaled its architecture. The pediment sculptures represent the birth of Athena and her battle with Poseidon; a continuous frieze shows the annual Panathenaic procession of citizens honoring Athena. The entire work is a marvel of harmony and clarity.

partial derivative, In differential calculus, the derivative of a function of several variables with respect to change in just one of its variables. Partial derivatives are useful in analyzing surfaces for maximum and minimum points and give rise to partial differential equations. As with ordinary derivatives, a first partial derivative represents a rate of change or a slope of a tangent line. For a three-dimensional surface, two first partial derivatives represent the slope in each of two perpendicular directions. Second, third, and higher partial derivatives give more information about how the function changes at any point.

particle accelerator, Device that accelerates a beam of fast-moving, electrically charged atoms (ions) or subatomic particles. Accelerators are used to study the structure of atomic nuclei and the nature of subatomic particles and their fundamental interactions. At speeds close to that of light, particles collide with and disrupt atomic nuclei and subatomic particles, allowing physicists to study nuclear components and to make new kinds of subatomic particles. The cyclotron accelerates positively charged particles, while the betatron accelerates negatively charged electrons. Synchrotrons and linear accelerators are used either with positively charged particles or electrons. Accelerators are also used for radioisotope production, cancer therapy, biological sterilization, and one form of radiocarbon dating.

partnership, Association of two or more persons or entities that conduct a business for profit as co-owners. Except in the case of the limited liability partnership, which shares with the corporation the characteristic of being treated as a single entity whose members have limited personal liability, a partnership is traditionally viewed as an association of individuals rather than an entity with a separate and independent existence. A partnership cannot exist beyond the lives of the partners. The partners are taxed as individuals and are personally liable for torts and contractual obligations. Each is viewed as the agent of the others, and traditionally all are jointly and severally liable for the tortious acts of any partner.

Parvati, Wife of the Hindu god Shiva. Parvati is the benevolent aspect of Shakti, the Hindu supreme goddess. According to the traditional account of her marriage, she won Shiva's notice only after severe ascetic discipline. The couple had two children, the elephant-headed Ganesha and the six-headed Skanda. In sculpture Parvati is always depicted as a mature and beautiful woman. The sacred Tantras are framed as a discussion between Parvati and Shiva.

Parvati, bronze image, early Cola period, 10th century AD; in the Freer Gallery of Art, Washington, D.C.
Courtesy of the Smithsonian Institution, Freer Gallery of Art, Washington, D.C.

pas de deux (French: "step for two"), Dance for two performers. A characteristic part of classical ballet, it includes an adagio, or slow dance, by the ballerina and her partner; solo variations by the male dancer and then the ballerina; and a coda, or conclusion, with both partners dancing together to display their virtuosity. Celebrated pas de deux occur in *Sleeping Beauty*, *Swan Lake*, and *Giselle*.

Pascal, Computer programming language named for Blaise Pascal and based partly on ALGOL. It was developed by Niklaus Wirth of Zurich's Federal Institute of Technology in the late 1960s as an educational tool for systematic teaching of programming, with fast, reliable compilers. It was made available to the public in 1974 and was used by many universities for the next 15 years. Pascal strongly influenced languages developed later, such as Ada. Complex data structures and algorithms can be described concisely by Pascal, and its programs are easy to read and debug.

pascal, Unit of pressure, abbreviated Pa, in the International System of Units. Named for Blaise Pascal, the unit is a pressure of one newton per square meter (1 N/m^2). It is inconveniently small for many purposes, and the kilopascal (kPa), $1,000 \text{ N/m}^2$, is more commonly used in engineering work (1 lb per sq in. equals 6.895 kPa).

Pascal's law, or PASCAL'S PRINCIPLE, In fluid mechanics, the statement that in a fluid at rest in a closed container, a pressure change in one part is transmitted without loss to every portion of the fluid and to the walls of the container. The principle was first stated by Blaise Pascal, who also discovered that the pressure at a point in a fluid at rest is the same in all directions, and that the pressure would be the same on all planes passing through a specific point.

Pashtun, Any member of a Pashto-speaking people of southeastern Afghanistan and northwestern Pakistan. The Pashtun, who number about 7.5 million in Afghanistan and 14 million in Pakistan, constitute the majority of the population of Afghanistan. Their origins are unclear: Pashtun tradition asserts that they are descended from Afghana, grandson of King Saul of Israel, but most scholars believe that they arose from an intermingling of ancient Aryans from the north or west with subsequent invaders. Each Pashtun tribe is divided into clans, subclans, and patriarchal families. Disputes among the Pashtun over property, women, and personal injury often result in blood feuds between families and whole clans. Most tribal people are sedentary farmers; some are migratory herders and caravaners. Large numbers of the Pashtun have always been attracted to military service.

passage, rite of, Any of numerous ceremonial events, existing in all societies, that mark the passage of an individual from one social or religious status to another. The term was coined by the French anthropologist Arnold van Gennep (1873–1957) in 1909. Many of the most important rites are connected with the biological stages of life—birth, maturity, reproduction, and death. Other rites celebrate changes that are wholly cultural, such as initiation into special societies. In modern societies, graduation from school is a rite of passage. Scholars often interpret rites of passage as mechanisms by which society confronts and incorporates change without disrupting the equilibrium necessary to social order.

Passion play, Religious drama of medieval origin dealing with the suffering, death, and resurrection of Jesus. Early Passion plays were written in Latin and consisted of Gospel readings alternating with poetic descriptions of the events of Christ's Passion (i.e., his sufferings between the Last Supper and his death). Use of the vernacular for these poetic passages led to the development of independent vernacular plays. By the 16th century many of the plays had been overtaken by secular influences and had become mere popular entertainments. Some survived into the 21st century, most notably the one performed by local villagers every 10 years at Oberammergau, Ger.

passionflower family, Family Passifloraceae, composed of about 705 species of herbaceous or woody vines, shrubs, and trees in 16 genera. Members of this family grow mostly in warm regions. Many species produce edible fruits. Members of the largest genus, *Passiflora*, are highly prized for their showy, unusual flowers. A pedestal-like structure in the centre of the flower carries the reproductive parts of both sexes. The passionflower blossom is often used to symbolize events in the last hours (Passion) of Jesus, which accounts for the name of the group.

Passover, In Judaism, the holiday commemorating the liberation of the Hebrews from slavery in Egypt. Before sending a plague to destroy the firstborn of the Egyptians, God instructed Moses to tell the Israelites to place a special mark above their doors as a signal for the angel of death to pass over (i.e., spare the residents). The festival of Passover begins on the 15th and ends on the 22nd (in Israel, the 21st) day of the month of Nisan (March or April). During Passover only unleavened bread may be eaten, symbolizing the Hebrews' suffering in bondage and the haste with which they left Egypt. On the first night of Passover, a Seder is held, and the Haggadah is read aloud.

pastel, Drawing medium consisting of fragile, finger-size crayons called pastels, made of powdered pigments combined with a minimum of nongreasy binder (usually gum tragacanth or, from the mid-20th century, methyl cellulose). Because pigment applied with pastel does not change in colour value, the final effect can be seen immediately. Pastel remains on the surface of the paper and thus can be easily obliterated unless protected by glass or a fixative spray of glue size or gum solution. When pastel is applied in short strokes or linearly, it is usually classed as drawing; when it is rubbed, smeared, and blended to achieve painterly effects, it is often regarded as a painting medium.

Pasternak, Boris (Leonidovich) (b. Feb. 10, 1890, Moscow, Russia—d. May 30, 1960, Peredelkino, near Moscow), Russian poet and prose writer. He studied music and philosophy and after the Russian Revolution of 1917 worked in the library of the Soviet commissariat of education. His early poetry, though avant-garde, was successful, but in the 1930s a gap widened between his work and officially approved literary modes, and he supported himself by doing translations. The novel *Doctor Zhivago* (1957; film, 1965), an epic of wandering, spiritual isolation, and love amid the harshness of the revolution and its aftermath, was a best-seller in the West but until 1987 circulated only in secrecy in the Soviet Union. Pasternak was awarded the Nobel Prize for Literature in 1958, but he was forced to decline it because of Soviet opposition to his work.

Pasteur, Louis (b. Dec. 27, 1822, Dole, France—d. Sept. 28, 1895, Saint-Cloud, near Paris), French chemist and microbiologist. Early in his career, after studies at the École Normale Supérieure, he researched the effects of polarized light on chemical compounds. In 1857 he became director of scientific studies at the École. His studies of fermentation of alcohol and milk (souring) showed that yeast could reproduce without free oxygen (the Pasteur effect); he deduced that fermentation and food spoilage were due to the activity of microorganisms and could be prevented by excluding or destroying them. His work overturned the concept of spontaneous generation (life arising from nonliving matter) and led to heat pasteurization, allowing vinegar, wine, and beer to be produced and transported without spoiling. He saved the French silk industry by his work on silkworm diseases. In 1881 he perfected a way to isolate and weaken germs, and he went on to develop vaccines against anthrax in sheep and cholera in chickens, following Edward Jenner's example. He turned his attention to researching rabies, and in 1885 his inoculating with a weakened virus saved the life of a boy bitten by a rabid dog. In 1888 he founded the Pasteur Institute for rabies research, prevention, and treatment.

Pasteurella, Genus (named after Louis Pasteur) of rod-shaped bacteria that cause several serious infections in domestic animals and milder infections in humans. Members are gram-negative, do not move, and do not require oxygen. The widespread infections they cause, referred to by the general term *pasteurelloses*, are transmitted by direct contact and, in some cases, by ticks and fleas. Control by vaccine is variable, as is treatment with penicillin and other antibiotics.

pasteurization, Partial sterilization of a substance, especially milk or other beverages, by using heat to destroy microorganisms while leaving its chemical makeup unaltered. The process is named for Louis Pasteur, its originator. Pasteurization of milk requires temperatures of about 145 °F (63 °C) for about 30 minutes, or higher temperatures for shorter periods. The treatment destroys any disease-causing organisms (principally *Mycobacterium tuberculosis*) as well as organisms that cause spoilage.

pastoral, Literary work dealing in a usually artificial manner with shepherds or rural life, typically contrasting the innocence and serenity of the simple life with the misery and corruption of city or court life. The characters are often the vehicles for the author's moral, social, or literary views. The poet and his friends are often presented as shepherds and shepherdesses; two or more shepherds sometimes contend in "singing matches." The conventions of pastoral poetry were largely established by Theocritus, whose bucolics are its earliest examples. Virgil's *Eclogues* were influential as well, as was Edmund Spenser's *Shepheardes Calender* in the Renaissance. The idea of pastoral as meaning a simpler world that somehow mirrors a more complex one also appears in novelists as different as Fyodor Dostoyevsky, Lewis Carroll, and William Faulkner.

Patagonia, Semiarid scrub plateau, southern Argentina. It is the largest desert region in the Americas, with an area of about 260,000 sq mi (673,000 sq km). Its approximate boundaries are the Colorado River in the north, the Atlantic Ocean in the east, the Strait of Magellan in the south, and the Andes Mountains in the west. A region of vast and virtually treeless plains, it has a variety of wildlife, including llamas, pumas, and eagles. Natural resources include petroleum, iron ore, copper, uranium, and manganese.

patent, Government grant to an inventor of the exclusive right to make, use, or sell an invention, usually for a specified term. It may be granted for a process or method that is new, useful, and not obvious, or for a new use of a known process, machine, or composition of matter or material, including asexually reproduced plants and genetically engineered organisms. It may also be granted for any new, original, and ornamental design for an article of manufacture. The first recorded patent for an industrial invention was granted in 1421 in Florence to the architect and engineer Filippo Brunelleschi. Until recently there were wide variations in the patent systems implemented by different countries. The duration of patents recognized generally ranged from 16 to 20 years. In some countries (e.g., France), some patents were given shorter terms because the inventions had an overall general usefulness. In communist countries (e.g., the Soviet Union), patents per se were not recognized; instead, certificates were issued to inventors to ensure that they received some form of compensation for their work. The agreement establishing the World Trade Organization in the 1990s specifies a minimum set of exclusive rights that all patentees must be accorded and mandates a minimum patent term of 20 years from the date an application is filed. Patents are considered personal property and may be sold, assigned, or otherwise transferred.

patio process, or MEXICAN PROCESS, Method of isolating silver from its ore, apparently dating from pre-Columbian times. The ore was crushed and ground by mule power in arrastras, reducing it to a fine mud. This was then spread over a courtyard or patio, sprinkled with mercury, salt, and copper sulfate, and mixed by driving mules over it. Chemical reactions caused the silver to dissolve in the mercury. When the amalgamation was complete, the material was agitated with water in large tubs and the mud run off. The amalgam at the bottom was collected and heated to drive off the mercury. Used for much of the world's silver production for 350 years, the process was replaced by the cyanide process early in the 20th century.

patriarch, Title applied to Old Testament leaders such as Methuselah, Abraham, Isaac, and Jacob. It was once given also to some Roman Catholic bishops who wielded great authority. It is still used in Eastern Orthodoxy, which now has nine patriarchates: Constantinople, Alexandria, Antioch, Jerusalem, Moscow, Georgia, Serbia, Romania, and Bulgaria.

patrician, In ancient Rome, any member of a group of citizen families who, in contrast to the plebeians, formed a privileged nobility. They attempted to hold on to magistracies, priesthoods, and legal and religious knowledge, and the great civil struggle of the Roman republic was the effort of the plebeians to achieve equality and break the patrician monopoly. Gradually the patricians lost their monopoly—except in a few areas, such as selected priesthoods and the office of interrex—and in the late republic (1st century BC) the distinction lost political importance. After 27 BC, patrician rank was necessary for ascent to the imperial throne. After Constantine's reign (AD 337), the term became an honorary title with no particular power.

patristic literature, Body of literature that comprises those works (excluding the New Testament) written by Christians before the 8th century. It refers to the works of the Church Fathers. Most patristic literature is in Greek or Latin, but much survives in Syriac and other Middle Eastern languages. The works of the Apostolic Fathers contain the earliest patristic literature. By the mid-2nd century, Christians wrote to justify their faith to the Roman government and to refute Gnosticism. In the 4th and 5th centuries, Augustine of Hippo and others laid the foundation for much of medieval and modern Christian thought. Significant patristic authors include Justin Martyr, Origen, Tertullian, Eusebius of Caesarea, Athanasius, Basil the Great, St. Gregory of Nyssa, Gregory of Nazianzus, John Chrysostom, Ambrose, Ephraem Syrus (306?–373), St. Jerome, Theodore of Mopsuestia, St. Cyril of Alexandria (*c.* 375–444), St. Maximus the Confessor (*c.* 580–662), and Pope Gregory I.

pattern recognition, In computer science, the imposition of identity on input data, such as speech, images, or a stream of text, by the recognition and delineation of patterns it contains and their relationships. Stages in pattern recognition may involve measurement of the object to identify distinguishing attributes, extraction of features for the defining attributes, and comparison with known patterns to determine a match or mismatch. Pattern recognition has extensive application in astronomy, medicine, robotics, and remote sensing by satellites.

Paul, Russian PAVEL PETROVICH (b. Oct. 1, 1754, St. Petersburg, Russia—d. March 23, 1801, St. Petersburg), Tsar of Russia (1796–1801). He was the son of Peter III and Catherine II, whom he succeeded as emperor in 1796. He reversed many of Catherine's policies, strengthened the autocracy, and established the law of succession within the male line of the Romanov dynasty. He provoked the hostility of the nobles and the army with his tyrannical rule and capricious foreign policy, which drew Russia into war with France. In a plot by the nobles to depose him and place his son Alexander (later Alexander I) on the throne, Paul was assassinated.

Paul, Saint, orig. SAUL (b. AD 10?, Tarsus in Cilicia—d. 67?, Rome), Early Christian missionary and theologian, known as the Apostle to the Gentiles. Born a Jew in Tarsus, Asia Minor, he was trained as a rabbi but earned his living as a tentmaker. A zealous Pharisee, he persecuted the first Christians until a vision of Jesus, experienced while on the road to Damascus, converted him to Christianity. Three years later he met St. Peter and Jesus' brother James and was henceforth recognized as the 13th Apostle. From his base in Antioch, he traveled widely, preaching to the Gentiles. By asserting that non-Jewish disciples of Christ did not have to observe Jewish law, he helped to establish Christianity as a separate religion rather than a Jewish sect. On a journey to Jerusalem, he aroused such hostility among the Jews that a mob gathered, and he was arrested and imprisoned for two years. The circumstances of his death are unknown. Paul's ministry and religious views are known largely from his letters, or epistles, collected in the New Testament, which are the first Christian theological writing and the source of much Christian doctrine. It was due to Paul more than anyone else that Christianity became a world religion.

pavane, Stately court dance introduced from southern Europe into England in the 16th century. The dance, consisting of forward and backward steps to music in duple time, was originally used to open ceremonial balls; later its steps became livelier and it came to be paired with the quick galliard in triple time.

Pavane, "The Dance in the Garden" illumination from the Roman de la rose, Toulouse, early 16th century; in the British Library (Harley MS 4425, fol. 14v)
Reproduced by permission of the British Library

Pavlova, Anna (Pavlovna) (b. Feb. 12, 1881, St. Petersburg, Russia—d. Jan. 23, 1931, The Hague, Neth.), Russian ballet dancer. She studied at the Imperial Ballet School from 1891 and joined the Mariinsky Theatre company in 1899, becoming prima ballerina in 1906. In 1913 she left Russia to tour with her own company, which showcased her outstanding performances in classical ballets such

Anna Pavlova.
Culver Pictures

as *Giselle*; the most famous numbers were a succession of short solos such as *The Dying Swan*, choreographed for her by Michel Fokine. Her tours took ballet to audiences in many countries for the first time and did much to popularize ballet worldwide.

pawnbroking, Business of advancing loans to customers who have pledged household goods or personal belongings as security. The pawnbroker's trade is one of the oldest known, having existed 2,000–3,000 years ago in China, as well as in ancient Greece and Rome. Pawnbroking was common in medieval Europe despite laws against usury. Private pawnbrokers were usually those exempt from the laws, notably the Jews. In 1462 the Franciscans set up the *montes pietatis*, which granted interest-free loans to the poor, though they were later forced to charge interest to prevent premature exhaustion of their funds. Public pawnshops existed briefly in the Middle Ages but were reestablished in the 18th century to free debtors from the high interest rates of private pawnshops. Most European countries now maintain public pawnshops; in the U.S. only private pawnshops exist. Social-welfare programs and increased access to easy credit has led to a decline in pawnbroking's importance.

Paz, Octavio (b. March 31, 1914, Mexico City, Mex.—d. April 19, 1998, Mexico City), Mexican poet, writer, and diplomat. Educated at the University of Mexico, Paz published his first book of poetry, *Savage Moon*, in 1933. He later founded and edited several important literary reviews. Influenced in turn by Marxism, Surrealism, existentialism, Buddhism, and Hinduism, his poetry uses rich imagery in dealing with metaphysical questions, and his most prominent theme is the human ability to overcome existential solitude through erotic love and artistic creativity. His prose works include *The Labyrinth of Solitude* (1950), an influential essay on Mexican history and culture. He was Mexico's ambassador to India (1962–68). He was awarded the Nobel Prize for Literature in 1990.

PCB, in full POLYCHLORINATED BIPHENYL, Any of a class of highly stable organic compounds prepared by the reaction of chlorine with biphenyl, a two-ring compound. The commercial product, a mix of several PCB isomers, is a colourless, viscous liquid that is almost insoluble in water, does not degrade under high temperatures, and is a good electrical insulator. PCBs became widely used as lubricants, heat-transfer fluids, and fire-resistant dielectric fluids in transformers and capacitors in the 1930s and '40s. In the mid 1970s they were found to cause liver dysfunction in humans and came under suspicion as carcinogens; their manufacture and use were consequently restricted in the U.S. and many other countries, though illegal dumping by manufacturers continued. They persist in the environment and have entered the food chain, causing great harm especially to invertebrates and fish.

Peace Corps, U.S. government agency of volunteers, formed in 1961 by Pres. John F. Kennedy. Its purpose is to assist other countries in their development efforts by providing skilled workers in the fields of education, agriculture, health, trade, technology, and community development. Volunteers are expected to serve for two years as good neighbours in the host country, to speak its language, and to live on a level comparable to that of their local counterparts. By its 50th anniversary in 2011, more than 200,000 Peace Corps volunteers had served in 139 countries.

peacock, Any of three species (family Phasianidae) of resplendent birds of open lowland forests. Blue, or Indian (*Pavo cristatus*), and green, or Javanese (*P. muticus*), peacock males are 35–50 in. (90–130 cm) long and have a 60-in. (150-cm) train of metallic green tail feathers tipped with an iridescent eyespot ringed with blue and bronze. The train is erected, fanned out, and vibrated during courtship. Females (peahens) are duller and have no train. The male forms a harem of two to five hens, which lay their eggs in a depression in the ground. The blue and green male Congo peacock (*Afropavo congensis*) has a short rounded tail; the reddish and brown hen has a topknot.

Pearl Harbor, Inlet, southern coast of Oahu island, Hawaii, U.S. It lies 6 mi (10 km) west of Honolulu, forming a landlocked harbour connected with the Pacific Ocean. In 1887 Hawaii granted the U.S. the exclusive use of the harbour as a coaling and repair station, and in 1908 a naval station was established. In 1941 the harbour was attacked without warning by the Japanese air force, causing great loss of life and precipitating U.S. entry into World War II. It is now the headquarters of the U.S. Pacific Fleet.

peasant, Any member of a class that tills the soil as small landowners or agricultural labourers. The peasant economy generally has a simple technology and a division of labour by age and sex. The basic unit of production is the family or household. Peasant families traditionally consume what they produce, though a portion of their output may be sold in the market or paid to a landlord. Productivity per worker and yields per unit of land are usually low. Peasants as a class tend to disappear as a society industrializes, though peasantlike social structures may persist under new economic regimens.

Peasants' Revolt, or WAT TYLER'S REBELLION (1381) First great popular rebellion in English history. It was triggered by the poll tax of 1381, which angered labourers and artisans already resentful of the limits on wages fixed by the Statute of Labourers (1351). Centred in southeastern England and East Anglia, the revolt was led by Wat Tyler (d. 1381), who marched into London with a band of Kentish rebels. They captured the Tower of London and beheaded officials responsible for the poll tax. Richard II promised reforms, but Tyler was killed in his presence by the mayor of London. The last of the rebels were subdued in East Anglia two weeks later.

peat, Organic fuel consisting of a light, spongy material formed in temperate, humid environments by the accumulation and partial decomposition of vegetable remains under conditions of poor drainage. Peat deposition is the first step in the formation of coal. Dried peat burns readily, with a smoky flame and a characteristic odour. It is used for domestic heating and can be used to fire boilers. It is only a minor contributor to the world energy supply, but large deposits occur in Canada, China, Indonesia, Russia, Scandinavia, and the U.S. Major users include Finland, Ireland, Russia, and Sweden.

peat moss, or SPHAGNUM MOSS, Any of more than 150–300 species of plants that make up the bryophyte genus *Sphagnum*, which grow in dense clumps around ponds, in swamps and bogs, on moist, acid cliffs, and on lakeshores from tropical to subpolar regions. These pale-green to deep-red plants can hold 20 times their weight in water. As they die and are compressed, they form organic peat, which is harvested and dried as fuel, as seedbed cover, and as shipping packaging for plants and live aquatic animals. Gardeners stir peat into soil to increase soil moisture, porosity, and acidity and to reduce erosion.

Pechora River, River, northeastern Russia. It rises in the northern Ural Mountains and flows south, then west and north to enter the Barents Sea after a course of 1,124 mi (1,809 km). It is frozen from early November to early May. Its basin contains large deposits of coal, petroleum, and natural gas.

pedigree, Record of ancestry or purity of breed. Pedigrees of domesticated animals are maintained by governmental or private record associations or breed organizations in many countries. In human genetics, pedigree diagrams are used to trace the inheritance of a specific trait, abnormality, or disease. Standard symbols are used to represent males, females, mating (marriage), and offspring. The offspring symbols appear from left to right in the order of birth and are connected to the marriage line by a vertical line. Possession of the character under study is shown by a solid or blackened symbol, and absence is shown by an open or clear symbol.

Pegasus, In Greek mythology, a winged horse. It sprang from the blood of Medusa as she was beheaded by Perseus. Bellerophon captured Pegasus and rode him in several of his exploits, including his fight with the Chimera, but when he tried to ride the winged horse to heaven he was unseated and killed, and Pegasus was placed in the sky as a constellation. The flight of Pegasus is often regarded as a symbol of poetic inspiration.

Pei, I(eoh) M(ing) (b. April 26, 1917, Guangzhou, China), Chinese-born U.S. architect. He immigrated to the U.S. in 1935 and studied at the Massachusetts Institute of Technology and Harvard University. After working for the architectural firm of Webb & Knapp, he formed his own partnership in 1955. Early in his career he created the Mesa Laboratory building for the National Center for Atmospheric Research, Boulder, Colo. (1968), which mimics the broken silhouettes of the surrounding peaks. His innovative East Building of the National Gallery of Art, Washington, D.C. (1978), was hailed as one of his finest achievements. Other works include Boston's John Hancock Tower (1973), Beijing's Fragrant Hill Hotel (1982), a controversial glass pyramid for a courtyard at the Louvre Museum, Paris (1989), and the Suzhou Museum (2006) in China. Pei's designs represent an elaboration on the rectangular forms and irregular silhouettes of the International Style but with a uniquely skillful arrangement of geometric shapes and a dramatic use of varied materials, spaces, and surfaces; in his Miho Museum (1997) in Shiga, Japan, for example, he achieved a harmony between the building, much of it underground, and its mountain environment. In 1983 Pei received the Pritzker Architecture Prize.

Pelagianism, Christian heresy of the 5th century that emphasized free will and the goodness of human nature. Pelagius (354?–after 418), a British monk who settled in Africa in 410, was eager to raise moral standards among Christians. Rejecting the arguments of those who attributed their sins to human weakness, he argued that God made humans free to choose between good and evil and that sin is an entirely voluntary act. His disciple Celestius denied the church's doctrine of original sin and the necessity of infant baptism. Pelagius and Celestius were excommunicated in 418, but their views continued to find defenders until the Council of Ephesus condemned Pelagianism in 431.

Pelé, orig. EDSON ARANTES DO NASCIMENTO (b. Oct. 23, 1940, Três Corações, Braz.), Brazilian football (soccer) player, in his time perhaps the most celebrated athlete in the world. He joined the Santos Football Club in 1956 and helped lead that team to a world club championship in 1962. He was part of three Brazilian national teams that won World Cup championships (1958, 1962, 1970). In 1969, during his 909th match,

Pelé.
AFP/Pictorial Parade

he scored his 1,000th goal. He combined kicking power and accuracy with a remarkable ability to anticipate other players' moves. In 1975 he joined the New York Cosmos of the North American Soccer League (NASL); he retired after leading the team to the league championship in 1977. He was the 1978 recipient of the International Peace Award, and in 1980 he was named Athlete of the Century.

Brown pelican (Pelecanus occidentalis).
Norman Tomalin/Bruce Coleman Inc.

pelican, Any of about eight species constituting the genus *Pelecanus* (family Pelecanidae), white or brown birds distinguished by a large, elastic throat pouch. Some species are 70 in. (180 cm) long, have a wingspan of 10 ft (3 m), and weigh up to 30 lbs (13 kg). Most species drive fish into shallow water and, using the pouch as a dip net, scoop them up and immediately swallow them. Pelicans inhabit freshwaters and seacoasts in many parts of the world; they breed in colonies on islands, laying one to four eggs in a stick nest. Chicks thrust their bills down the parent's gullet to obtain regurgitated food.

pellagra, Nutritional disorder caused largely by a deficiency of niacin, marked by skin lesions and digestive and neurological disturbances. Dermatitis usually appears first, with abnormal sensitivity to sunlight. It may look like a severe sunburn, later becoming reddish brown, rough, and scaly. Diarrhea usually alternates with constipation, along with mouth and tongue inflammation and cracking and dry scaling of the lips. Later, mental abnormalities may include nervousness, depression, and delirium. Mild cases of niacin deficiency respond to a well-balanced diet alone. Pellagra still occurs where diets consist mostly of corn, which is low in both niacin and tryptophan (converted to niacin in the body), with little or no protein-rich food. It can also be a side effect of chronic alcoholism.

Peloponnese, Peninsula, forming the southern part of mainland Greece. A large, mountainous body of land jutting south into the Mediterranean Sea, the peninsula has an area of 8,278 sq mi (21,439 sq km) and is joined to the rest of mainland Greece by the Isthmus of Corinth. The Mycenaean civilization flourished there in the 2nd millennium BC at Mycenae and Pylos. Its chief cities during the classical period were Corinth and Sparta. Under the Romans it was part of the province of Achaea from 146 BC to c. 4th century AD. It was part of the Byzantine Empire until it was taken by the Franks; they held it in the 13th–15th centuries, when it was often known as Morea. The modern city of Patras (pop., 2001: 163,446), in the north, is a commercial centre.

Peloponnesian League, or SPARTAN ALLIANCE, Military coalition of Greek city-states led by Sparta, formed in the 6th century BC. League decisions about war, peace, or alliance were determined by congresses summoned by the Spartans. The league was a major force in Greek affairs, forming the core of resistance to the Persian invasions in 490 and 480 and fighting Athens in the Peloponnesian War. Its power declined after its defeat at Leuctra in 371, and the league disbanded in 366/365.

Peloponnesian War (431–404 BC) War fought between Athens and Sparta, the leading city-states of ancient Greece, along with their allies, which included nearly every other Greek city-state. Its principal cause was a fear of Athenian imperialism. The Athenian alliance relied on its strong navy, the Spartan alliance on its strong army. The war fell into two periods, separated by a six-year truce.

Fighting broke out in 431, with Pericles commanding the Athenians. In the first 10 years, Archidamus led the Spartans to defeats. Plague struck Athens in 429, killing Pericles and much of the army. In 428 Cleon almost convinced Athens to massacre the rebellious citizens of Mytilene on Lesbos, but Athens rescinded the order. In 421 both states agreed to accept the Peace of Nicias. This lasted six years, until Athens launched its disastrous Sicilian expedition. By 413 Athens's forces were demolished. In 411 an oligarchy briefly took power. When democratic leaders were restored by the navy later that year, they refused Spartan peace offers, and the war continued until 405, when the Athenian navy was destroyed at the Battle of Aegospotami with Persian help. Under blockade, Athens surrendered in 404. Its empire was dismantled, and the Spartans installed the Thirty Tyrants.

pelota (Spanish: "little ball") Any of several games in which players take turns, using a glove or implement, hitting a rubber ball either directly at one another or off a wall. The latter version is related to handball and jai alai, which are played by two or four players on one-, two-, or three-walled courts using gloves, rackets, or bats. In Spain and elsewhere, pelota is a professional sport on which spectators wager.

pelvic inflammatory disease (PID), Acute inflammation of the pelvic cavity in women, caused by bacterial infection (usually gonorrhea or chlamydia) of the reproductive system. Usually a sexually transmitted disease, it occurs mainly in sexually active women under age 25, more often in those using intrauterine devices (IUDs). PID can resemble gonorrhea, with abdominal and lower pelvic pain, chills, nausea, fever, and thick, foul-smelling vaginal discharge. Fallopian tube scarring can cause infertility and ectopic pregnancy. Treatment requires antibiotics, bed rest, pain medication, and sexual abstinence until the infection disappears. Sexual partners must also be treated to prevent reinfection.

Penang, Malay PINANG, Island (pop., 2005 est.: 1,468,800), Malaysia. It lies in the Strait of Malacca off the northwestern coast of West (Peninsular) Malaysia, part of the state of Pulau Pinang. The capital and chief port is George Town (pop., 2000: 180,573), in the northeast. British colonization began in 1786. In 1826 Penang (known until 1867 as Prince of Wales Island) combined with Malacca and Singapore to form the Straits Settlements. From the mid-19th century it was a market for tin and rubber. In 1948 it became part of the Federation of Malaya, later Malaysia. In the late 20th century it became one of Malaysia's prime tourist centres, with resort hotels mainly on the northern coast at Batu Feringgi.

Penates, Roman household gods. They were worshiped privately as protectors of the household and also publicly as protectors of the Roman state. They were sometimes associated with other deities of the house, such as Vesta, and their name was often used interchangeably with that of the Lares. Each house had a shrine with their images, which were worshiped at the family meal and on special occasions. Offerings were portions of the regular meal or of special cakes, wine, honey, and incense. The number and precise identities of the Penates were a puzzle even to the ancients.

pendulum, Body suspended from a fixed point so that it can swing back and forth under the influence of gravity. A simple pendulum consists of a bob (weight) suspended at the end of a string. The periodic motion of a pendulum is constant, but can be made longer or shorter by increasing or decreasing the length of the string. A change in the mass of the bob alone does not affect the period. Because of their constancy, pendulums were long used to regulate the movement of clocks. Other, special kinds of pendulums are used to measure the value of g, the acceleration due to gravity, and to show that the earth rotates on its axis.

penguin, Any of 17 species (order Sphenisciformes) of flightless seabirds that breed mainly on islands in subantarctic waters and on cool coasts of Africa, Australia, New Zealand, and South

America. A few species inhabit temperate regions, and the Galápagos penguin (*Spheniscus mendiculus*) lives in the equatorial tropics off South America. Species differ mainly in size and head pattern; all have a dark back and a white belly. The smallest species, the little blue penguin (*Eudyptula minor*), is about 14 in. (35 cm) tall; the largest, the emperor penguin (*Aptenodytes forsteri*), is almost 4 ft (120 cm) tall. At sea for weeks at a time, flocks feed on fish, squid, and crustaceans.

penicillin, Antibiotic derived from the *Penicillium* mold. It was discovered in 1928 by Alexander Fleming; by 1940, Howard Walter Florey, Ernst Boris Chain, and others had produced commercial quantities that proved vital to the treatment of war casualties, making penicillin the first successful antibiotic for human bacterial infections. Many natural and semisynthetic (ampicillin, amoxicillin) variants have since been produced. All work by inhibiting the enzymes responsible for bacterial cell wall synthesis (and therefore do not work against microorganisms without cell walls or with certain variant cell walls; e.g., the tuberculosis bacillus). Among the bacteria susceptible to penicillin are those causing strep throat, spinal meningitis, gas gangrene, and syphilis. Overuse has led to drug resistance in some strains. Penicillin's chief side effect is allergy, which can be life-threatening.

Peninsular War (1808–14) Part of the Napoleonic Wars, fought on the Iberian Peninsula. After French forces occupied Portugal (1807) and Napoleon installed his brother Joseph Bonaparte as king of Spain (1808), a rebellion in Madrid began what was called in Spain "the War of Independence," and insurrections soon erupted in other cities. By 1810 the French overcame the Spanish rebels in Madrid and elsewhere in Spain. Meanwhile, the British under the future duke of Wellington landed in Portugal (1808), where they fought the French in inconclusive campaigns until 1812. After Napoleon withdrew French forces to bolster his invasion of Russia, Wellington began his gradual advance into Spain. The British victory at the Battle of Vitoria (1813) and their march into southwestern France forced the French to withdraw from Spain and to reinstall Ferdinand VII as king (1814).

Pennines, Upland mass, northern England. The Pennines extend south from Northumberland to Derbyshire; the highest point is Cross Fell, at 2,930 ft (893 m). Water action has developed underground caverns in the uplands' limestone, which is extensively quarried. Sheep farming is also important. Archaeological remains in the area include the ancient Roman Hadrian's Wall.

penology, Branch of criminology dealing with prison management and the treatment of offenders. Penological studies have sought to clarify the ethical bases of punishment, along with the motives and purposes of society in inflicting it; differences throughout history and between nations in penal laws and procedures; and the social consequences of the policies in force at a given time. Influential historical works have included Cesare Beccaria's *On Crimes and Punishments* (1764), Jeremy Bentham's "Panopticon" scheme (*c.* 1800), Cesare Lombroso's *Crime* (1876), and Michel Foucault's *Discipline and Punish* (1975).

pension, Series of periodic money payments made to a person who retires from employment because of age, disability, or the completion of an agreed span of service. The payments generally continue for the rest of the recipient's natural life, and they are sometimes extended to a widow or other survivor. Military pensions have existed for many centuries; private pension plans originated in Europe in the 19th century. There are two basic types of pension plans: defined contribution and defined benefit. A defined contribution plan invests a defined amount each pay period. The individual may have some discretion as to how the money is invested. The benefit, the amount of the pension, depends on the success of those investments. A defined benefit plan pays a known amount according to some formula, but the amount invested in the fund may vary. Pensions may be funded by making payments into a pension trust fund or by the purchase of annuities from insurance companies. In plans known as multiemployer plans, various employers contribute to one central trust fund administered by a joint board of trustees.

pentathlon, Athletic contest entailing five distinct types of competitions. In the ancient Olympic Games, the pentathlon included a sprint, the long jump, discus throw, javelin throw, and a wrestling match. A modified version (with a medium-distance race substituted for the wrestling match) was included in the revived Olympic Games (1912–24). The modern, or military, pentathlon, included in the Olympics from 1912 and made a team event in 1952, includes an equestrian steeplechase, fencing, pistol shooting, a freestyle swim, and a cross-country run. Women's pentathlon competition (shot put, high jump, hurdling race, sprint, and long jump) was replaced in 1981 by the heptathlon.

Pentecost (from Greek *pentecoste*, "fiftieth day") Christian festival commemorating the descent of the Holy Spirit on the disciples of Jesus, occurring on the Jewish Pentecost, after Jesus' death, resurrection, and ascension. The disciples began to speak in the many languages of the people assembled there, a sign that the disciples should spread the Christian message throughout the world. Jewish Pentecost was a thanksgiving feast for the first fruits of the wheat harvest and was associated with remembrance of God's gift of the Law to Moses on Mount Sinai. Christian Pentecost is celebrated on the Sunday concluding the 50-day period following Easter. It is also the name of the Jewish celebration of Shavuot ("Festival of Weeks").

Pentecostalism, Protestant religious movement that originated in the U.S. in the 19th–20th century. It is characterized by a belief that all Christians should seek a postconversion religious experience called baptism with the Holy Spirit. The experience corresponds to the descent of the Holy Spirit on the twelve Apostles (Pentecost) and is evidenced by speaking in tongues, prophesying, and healing. Pentecostalism grew out of the 19th-century Holiness movement and shares its emphasis on biblical literalism, conversion, and moral rigor. The charismatic movement in Roman Catholic and mainstream Protestant denominations represents the same spirit. Today there are many Pentecostalist denominations in the U.S. and around the world, including the Assemblies of God. Penetcostalism has been especially successful in the Caribbean, Latin America, and Africa.

pepper, or GARDEN PEPPER, Any of many plants in the genus *Capsicum* of the nightshade family, notably *C. annuum*, *C. frutescens*, and *C. boccatum*, native to Central and South America and cultivated extensively throughout tropical Asia and the equatorial New World for their edible, pungent fruits. Red, green, and yellow mild bell or sweet peppers, rich in vitamins A and C, are used in seasoning and as a vegetable food. The pungency of hot peppers, including tabasco, chili, and cayenne peppers, comes from the compound capsaicin in the internal partitions of the fruit. The spice black pepper comes from an unrelated plant.

Red peppers (Capsicum annuum) from which paprika is made
G.R. Roberts

peppermint, Strongly aromatic perennial herb (*Mentha piperita*, mint family), source of a widely used flavouring. Native to Europe and Asia, it has been naturalized in North America. The stalked, smooth, dark green leaves and blunt, oblong clusters of pinkish lavender flowers are dried for use as a flavouring agent. Oil of peppermint is widely used to flavour confectionery, chewing gum, toothpastes, and medicines. The oil also contains menthol, long used medicinally as a soothing balm.

peptide, Organic compound composed of a series of amino acids linked by peptide bonds between a carbon atom of one and a nitrogen atom of the next. Peptide chains longer than a few dozen amino acids are called proteins. Biosynthesis of peptides from a succession of amino acids carried by transfer RNA molecules takes place on ribosomes and is catalyzed and controlled by enzymes. Many hormones, antibiotics, and other compounds that participate in life processes are peptides.

Perceval, Hero of Arthurian legend. His childlike innocence protected him from worldly temptation. In Chrétien de Troyes's 12th-century *Le Conte du Graal,* Perceval visits the castle of the wounded Fisher King and sees the Grail, but he fails to ask about it and therefore fails to heal the Fisher King. He subsequently sets out in search of the Grail and grows spiritually. In later Grail legend he was displaced by Galahad as the hero of the Grail quest but continued to play an important role. His story was told in Wolfram von Eschenbach's 13th-century *Parzifal,* which provided the basis for Richard Wagner's opera *Parsifal* (1882).

peregrine falcon, or DUCK HAWK, Falcon species (*Falco peregrinus*) found worldwide but rare today because of bioaccumulation of pesticides. Peregrines are 13–19 in. (33–48 cm) long and gray above, with black-barred whitish underparts. They fly high and dive at tremendous speed (up to 175 mph, or 280 kph—the greatest speeds attained by any bird), striking with clenched talons and killing by impact. They usually nest in a scrape on a high cliff ledge near water, where bird prey is plentiful. Breeding programs have reintroduced the species into the wild and introduced it into urban areas, where it finds a clifflike habitat among skyscrapers and preys chiefly on the rock dove. Despite the programs' success, the species remains vulnerable.

Peregrine falcon (Falco peregrinus).
Kenneth W. Fink/Root Resources

perennial, Any plant that persists for several years, usually with new herbaceous growth from a part that survives from season to season. Trees and shrubs are perennial, as are some herbaceous flowers and vegetative ground covers. Perennials have only a limited flowering period, but, with maintenance throughout the growing season, they provide a leafy presence and shape to the garden landscape. Popular flowering perennials include bellflowers, chrysanthemums, columbines, larkspurs, hollyhocks, phlox, pinks, poppies, and primroses.

Peres, Shimon, orig. SHIMON PERSKI (b. Aug. 16, 1923, Wołożyn, Pol.), Polish-born Israeli statesman. He immigrated to Palestine with his family in 1934 and joined the Haganah organization in 1947. After Israel achieved independence, he held a number of positions in the defense establishment (1948–65). In 1968 he helped establish the Israel Labour Party. The indecisive 1984 election led to a power-sharing arrangement with Likud candidate Yitzhak Shamir, the two men alternating as prime minister. During Peres's tenure (1984–86), Israel withdrew from most of Lebanon. He was foreign minister under Yitzhak Rabin (1992–95); Peres, Rabin, and Palestinian leader Yāsir ʿArafāt shared the 1994

Nobel Prize for Peace. Peres became prime minister again upon Rabin's assassination in 1995 but was narrowly defeated in his bid for reelection by Likud leader Benjamin Netanyahu in 1996. Although Peres declined to seek reelection as leader of the Labour Party in 1997, he later served as foreign minister (2001–02), deputy prime minister (2001–02), and vice prime minister (2005) in the national unity government led by Likud's Ariel Sharon. In 2003 Peres resumed the chair of the Labour Party but was unexpectedly defeated in the party's leadership election in 2005. He subsequently left the Labour Party to join the centrist party Kadima. In 2007 Peres was elected president of Israel, a largely ceremonial post.

perestroika (Russian: "restructuring"), Program instituted in the Soviet Union by Mikhail Gorbachev in the mid-1980s to restructure Soviet political and economic policy. Gorbachev proposed reducing the direct involvement of the Communist Party leadership in the country's governance and increasing the local governments' authority. Seeking to bring the Soviet Union up to economic par with capitalist countries such as Germany, Japan, and the U.S., he decentralized economic controls and encouraged enterprises to become self-financing. The economic bureaucracy, fearing loss of its power and privileges, obstructed much of his program.

performance art, Art form that arose in Europe and the U.S. in the 1960s. The term describes an art that is live but operates outside the traditional conventions of theatre or music. Early examples represented a challenge to orthodox art forms and cultural norms by creating an ephemeral art experience that could not be captured or purchased. By the 1970s performance art was used as a general term to describe a multitude of activities, including happenings, body art, actions, events, and non-matrix theatre. Prominent performance artists have included Joseph Beuys, John Cage, Dennis Oppenheim, Yoko Ono, Nam June Paik, Meredith Monk, and Laurie Anderson.

Pericles (b. *c.* 495, Athens—d. 429 BC, Athens), Athenian general and statesman largely responsible for the full development of Athenian democracy and the Athenian empire. Related to the influential Alcmaeonid family, he was elected to power sometime after 461, and he quickly helped adopt essential democratic reforms. He asserted Athenian control over the Delian League and used the league's treasury to rebuild the Acropolis, which had been sacked by the Persians. His influential consort Aspasia bore him a son, who was legitimated when his legitimate sons died. In 447–446 Athens lost Megara, giving Sparta direct access to Attica. Though Athens and Sparta agreed on a Thirty Years' Peace (446–445), Pericles had strengthened the Long Walls from Athens to the port at Piraeus for protection. When war broke out in 431, he relied on the navy to keep the city supplied. Attica's population was brought inside the Long Walls, leaving the countryside open to Spartan pillaging. When plague broke out, killing one-fourth of the population, he was deposed and fined. He was reelected, but he too died of the plague. His great funeral oration (*c.* 430) remains one of the greatest defenses of democracy, and his era is remembered as the Golden Age of Athens.

Pericles, detail of a marble herm; in the Vatican Museum
Anderson—Alinari/Art Resource, New York

period, In geology, the basic unit of the geologic time scale. During these spans of time, specific systems of rocks were formed. Originally, the method for defining the sequence of periods was relative; it was based on stratigraphy and paleontology. Carbon-14 dating and similar methods are now used to determine absolute ages for various periods.

periodic table, Organized array of all the chemical elements in approximately increasing order of their atomic weight. The elements show a periodic recurrence of certain properties, a characteristic that was first discovered in 1869 by Dmitry I. Mendeleyev. Those in the same column (group) of the table as usually arranged have similar properties. In the 20th century, when the structure of atoms was understood, the table was seen to precisely reflect increasing order of atomic number. Members of the same group in the table have the same number of electrons in the outermost shells of their atoms and form bonds of the same type, usually with the same valence; the noble gases, with full outer shells, generally do not form bonds. The periodic table has thus greatly deepened understanding of bonding and chemical behaviour. It also allowed the prediction of new elements, many of which were later discovered or synthesized.

periodontitis, Inflammation of soft tissues around the teeth. Poor dental hygiene leads to deposition of bacterial plaque on the teeth below the gum line, irritating and eroding nearby tissues. If it is not treated, the gum margin recedes, exposing the roots of the teeth. The process eventually involves the bone anchoring the teeth, which loosen and may fall out. Removal of all plaque deposits and affected soft tissues can arrest but not reverse bone deterioration.

peritonitis, Inflammation of the peritoneum, with pus accumulating between the parietal and the visceral peritoneum, abdominal pain and distension, vomiting, and fever. It may be acute or chronic, local or generalized. Acute peritonitis usually results from inflammation elsewhere (e.g., by spread of bacterial infection). Primary peritonitis often comes from a perforated gastrointestinal tract, as with rupture in appendicitis. Control of the source problem may be followed by remission, adhesions, or abscesses (much rarer since the development of antibiotics).

permafrost, Perennially frozen earth, with a temperature below $32\,°F$ ($0\,°C$) continuously for two years or more. Permafrost is estimated to underlie 20% of the Earth's land surface and reaches depths of 5,000 ft (1,500 m) in northern Siberia. It occurs in 85% of Alaska, more than half of Russia and Canada, and probably all of Antarctica. Permafrost has a significant effect on plant and animal life, and it presents special problems in engineering projects. All land use in permafrost environments must take into account the terrain's special sensitivity; if the delicate natural balance is not maintained, extensive degradation and ecological damage may result.

Permian Period, Interval of geologic time, 299–251 million years ago. The last of the six periods of the Paleozoic Era, it follows the Carboniferous Period. During the Permian, the continents joined to form a single supercontinent, Pangea. Hot, dry conditions prevailed almost everywhere, and deserts were widespread. Life evolved as a continuation of established lines. Marine invertebrates evolved into several lineages. Marine and freshwater fishes and amphibians thrived. Reptiles evolved into three distinct groups: the cotylosaurs, the pelycosaurs, and the therapsids. Land plants evolved from ferns and seed ferns to conifers and adapted to drier and well-drained land conditions. Toward the close of the Permian Period, the largest mass extinction in Earth's history took place.

permutations and combinations, Number of ways a subset of objects can be selected from a given set of objects. In a permutation, order is important; in a combination, it is not. Thus, there are six permutations of the letters A, B, C selected two at a time (AB, AC, BC, BA, CA, CB) yet only three combinations (AB, AC, BC). The number of permutations of r objects chosen from a set of n objects, expressed in factorial notation, is $n! \div (n - r)!$ The number of combinations is $n! \div [r!(n - r)!]$. The $(r + 1)$st coefficient in the binomial expansion of $(x + y)^n$ coincides with the combination of n objects chosen r at a time. Probability theory evolved from the study of gambling, including figuring out combinations of playing cards or permutations of win-place-show possibilities in a horse race, and such counting methods played an important role in its development in the 17th century.

pernicious anemia, Slow-developing disease in which vitamin B_{12} deficiency impairs red-blood-cell production. It can result from a diet lacking in vitamin B_{12} or when intrinsic factor, a substance needed for intestinal absorption of B_{12}, either is not produced by stomach cells or cannot bind to the vitamin. It causes weakness, waxy pallor, shiny tongue, and stomach, intestinal, and neurological problems. Its slow development can allow anemia to become very severe by the time of diagnosis. Monthly B_{12} injections into muscle soon reverses the anemia, but the injections must be continued for life.

Perón, Eva (Duarte de), known as EVITA, orig. MARÍA EVA DUARTE (b. May 7, 1919, Los Toldos, Arg.—d. July 26, 1952, Buenos Aires), Second wife of Argentine president Juan Perón and a powerful though unofficial political leader. Born into poverty, she was an actress when she married Perón. She was instrumental in the success of his first presidential campaign and won the adulation of the masses. Evita acted as de facto minister of health and labour, awarding generous wage increases to workers. With "voluntary" contributions from businesses, labour unions, and the elite, she established thousands of hospitals, schools, and orphanages. After her death from cancer at age 33, her grief-stricken working-class followers sought to have her canonized.

Perón, Juan (Domingo) (b. Oct. 8, 1895, Buenos Aires province, Arg.—d. July 1, 1974, Buenos Aires), President of Argentina (1946–55, 1973–74). After attending military school, he served in the 1930s in Italy, where he observed the successes of the Fascists. In 1943 he helped overthrow Argentina's ineffective civilian government. As secretary of labour and social welfare, he built a loyal following among industrial workers, who helped elect him president in 1946. Perón's political views drew on both the far left and the far right: while he showered workers with much-needed benefits, he restricted civil liberties severely. The charisma of his second wife, Eva Perón, greatly increased the regime's standing with the populace. He was reelected in 1951, but a disastrous economic decline and increasing disaffection among many elements of Argentine society led to his overthrow in 1955 by democratically inspired military officers. He lived in exile in Spain for two decades but continued to influence Argentine affairs. When the Peronist party was made legal, he was reelected president in absentia; he died less than a year after returning to Argentina and assuming the presidency.

Perseus (b. c. 213/212—d. c. 165 BC, Alba Fucens, near Rome), Last king of Macedonia (r. 179–168). Son of Philip V, he fought against Rome (199) and Aetolia (189). He persuaded the king to execute his brother Demetrius. As king he extended his influence in neighbouring states and tried to gain the trust of the Greek world, but he alarmed Greece by visiting Delphi with an army. Eumenes II of Pergamum informed Rome of Perseus's allegedly aggressive designs, provoking the Third Macedonian War (171–168). The struggle ended in a final defeat of the Macedonians by the Romans, ending the monarchy, and Perseus spent the rest of his life in captivity.

Perseus, In Greek mythology, the slayer of the Gorgon Medusa. He was the son of Zeus and Danaë. His grandfather had him thrown into the sea in a chest with his mother as an infant because of a prophecy that Perseus would kill him. Perseus and his mother survived, and as a young man Perseus set out to gain the head of Medusa. On his way home he rescued the Ethiopian princess Andromeda from a sea monster, and she became his wife. When he took his mother back to her native Argos, he threw a discus that accidentally killed his grandfather, thus fulfilling the prophecy.

Persia, Historical name for a region roughly coterminous with modern Iran. The term was used for centuries, chiefly in the West, and originally described a region of southern Iran formerly known as Persis or Parsa. Parsa was the name of an Indo-European nomadic people who migrated into the area *c.* 1000 BC; the use of the name was gradually extended by the ancient Greeks and other Western peoples to apply to the whole Iranian plateau. The people of Iran have always called their country Iran, and in 1935 the government requested that the name Iran be used instead of Persia.

Persian Gulf, Arm of the Arabian Sea. It is about 615 mi (990 km) long and rarely exceeds a depth of 300 ft (90 m). It is connected with the Gulf of Oman and the Arabian Sea through the Strait of Hormuz. It contains the island kingdom of Bahrain and is bordered by Iran, the United Arab Emirates, Oman, Saudi Arabia, Qatar, Kuwait, and Iraq. It has long been a maritime trade route between the Middle East and South Asia; its modern economy is dominated by petroleum production.

Persian Gulf War, or GULF WAR (1990–91) International conflict triggered by Iraq's invasion of Kuwait in August 1990. Though justified by Iraqi leader Ṣaddām Ḥussein on grounds that Kuwait was historically part of Iraq, the invasion was presumed to be motivated by Iraq's desire to acquire Kuwait's rich oil fields and expand its power in the region. The United States, fearing Iraq's broader strategic intentions and acting under UN auspices, eventually formed a broad coalition, which included a number of Arab countries, and began massing troops in northern Saudi Arabia. When Iraq ignored a UN Security Council deadline for it to withdraw from Kuwait, the coalition began a large-scale air offensive (Jan. 16–17, 1991). Ṣaddām responded by launching ballistic missiles against neighbouring coalition states as well as Israel. A ground offensive by the coalition (February 24–28) quickly achieved victory. Estimates of Iraqi military deaths range up to 100,000; coalition forces lost about 300 troops. The war also caused extensive damage to the region's environment. The Iraqi regime subsequently faced widespread popular uprisings, which it brutally suppressed. A UN trade embargo remained in effect after the end of the conflict, pending Iraq's compliance with the terms of the armistice. The foremost term was that Iraq destroy its nuclear, biological, and chemical weapons programs. The embargo continued into the 21st century and ceased only after the Iraq War started in 2003.

Persian language, or FARSI LANGUAGE, Iranian language spoken by more than 25 million people in Iran as a first language, and by millions more as a second. Modern Persian is a koine developed from southwestern dialects in the 7th–9th centuries, after the introduction of Islam brought a massive infusion of loanwords from Arabic. Its standardization and literary cultivation took place in northeastern Persia and Central Asia in the 11th–12th centuries. Polities outside Persia itself (e.g., Mughal India, Ottoman Turkey) have at times been major literary centres. Its status in those countries led to a very strong Persian influence on Urdu and Ottoman Turkish. Other Turkic and Indo-Aryan languages, Caucasian languages, and Iranian languages have also borrowed heavily from Persian. It is written in a slightly modified form of the Arabic alphabet.

Persian Wars, or GRECO-PERSIAN WARS (492–449 BC) Series of wars between Greek states and Persia, particularly two invasions of Greece by Persia (490, 480–479). When Darius I came to power in Persia in 522, the Ionian Greek city-states in Anatolia were under Persian control. They rose up unsuccessfully in the Ionian

revolt (499–494). The support lent by Athens provoked Darius to invade Greece (492). His fleet was destroyed in a storm. In 490 he assembled a huge army on a plain near Athens; his devastating defeat at the Battle of Marathon sent him back to Persia. In 480 the Persians under Xerxes I again invaded Greece, seeking to avenge the defeat. This time all Greece fought together, with Sparta in charge of the army and Athens of the navy. A band of Spartans under Leonidas was overcome at the Battle of Thermopylae, allowing the Persian army to reach Athens, which they sacked (480). When the Persian navy was soundly defeated at the Battle of Salamis, Xerxes withdrew it to Persia. His army was defeated at the Battle of Plataea in 479 and driven from Greece, and the navy met a similar fate at Mycale on the Anatolian coast. Sporadic fighting went on for 30 more years, during which Athens formed the Delian League to free the Ionians. The Peace of Callias (449) ended the hostilities.

personal computer (PC), Microcomputer designed for use by one person at a time. A typical PC assemblage comprises a CPU; internal memory consisting of RAM and ROM; data storage devices (including a hard disc, a floppy disc, or CD-ROM); and input/output devices (including a display screen, keyboard, mouse, and printer). The PC industry began in 1977 when Apple Computer, Inc. (now Apple Inc.), introduced the Apple II. Radio Shack and Commodore Business Machines also introduced PCs that year. IBM entered the PC market in 1981. The IBM PC, with increased memory capacity and backed by IBM's large sales organization, quickly became the industry standard. Apple's Macintosh (1984) was particularly useful for desktop publishing. Microsoft Corp. introduced MS Windows (1985), a graphical user interface that gave PCs many of the capabilities of the Macintosh, initially as an overlay of MS-DOS. Windows went on to replace MS-DOS as the dominant operating system for personal computers. Uses of PCs multiplied as the machines became more powerful and application software proliferated. Today, PCs are used for word processing, Internet access, and many other daily tasks.

personality, Totality of an individual's behavioral and emotional characteristics. Personality embraces a person's moods, attitudes, opinions, motivations, and style of thinking, perceiving, speaking, and acting. It is part of what makes each individual distinct. Theories of personality have existed in most cultures and throughout most of recorded history. The ancient Greeks used their ideas about physiology to account for differences and similarities in temperament. In the 18th century Immanuel Kant, Charles-Louis Montesquieu, and Giambattista Vico proposed ways of understanding individual and group differences; in the early 20th century Ernst Kretschmer and the psychoanalysts Sigmund Freud, Alfred Adler, and Carl Jung offered competing personality theories. Freud's model rested on the power of psychosexual drives as mediated by the structural components of the id, ego, and superego and the interplay of conscious and unconscious motives. Particularly important was the array of defense mechanisms an individual employed. Jung, like Freud, emphasized unconscious motives but de-emphasized sexuality and advanced a typal theory that classified people as introverts and extraverts; he further claimed that an individual personality was a persona (i.e., social facade) drawn from the "collective unconscious," a pool of inherited memories. Later theories by Erik H. Erikson, Gordon W. Allport, and Carl R. Rogers were also influential. Contemporary personality studies tend to be empirical (based on the administration of projective tests or personality inventories) and less theoretically sweeping and tend to emphasize personal identity and development. Personality traits are usually seen as the product of both genetic predisposition and experience.

personality disorder, Mental disorder that is marked by deeply ingrained and lasting patterns of inflexible, maladaptive, or antisocial behaviour to the degree that an individual's social or occupational functioning is impaired. Rather than being illnesses, personality disorders are enduring and pervasive features of the personality that deviate markedly from the cultural norm. They include the dependent, histrionic, narcissistic, obsessive-compulsive, antisocial, avoidant, borderline (unstable), paranoid, and schizoid types. The causes appear to be both hereditary and environmental. The most effective treatment combines behavioral and psychotherapeutic therapies.

perspective, Depiction of three-dimensional objects and spatial relationships on a two-dimensional plane. In Western art, illusions of volume and space are generally created by use of the linear perspective system, based on the observation that objects appear to shrink and parallel lines to converge at an infinitely distant vanishing point as they recede in space from the viewer. The vanishing point may have been known to the Greeks and Romans but had been lost until Filippo Brunelleschi rediscovered the principles of linear or "mathematical" perspective early in the 15th century. Linear perspective dominated Western painting until the late 19th century, when Paul Cézanne flattened the conventional picture plane. The Cubists and other 20th-century painters abandoned depiction of three-dimensional space altogether.

Perth, City (pop., 2004 est.: 43,590), central Scotland. Located on the River Tay, northwest of Edinburgh, Perth was a Roman settlement; it became a royal burgh in 1210. It was the capital of Scotland until about 1452. At the Church of St. John the Baptist in 1559, John Knox denounced idolatry; the result was the plunder of Perth's monasteries and altars. It was a Jacobite city during the Scottish uprisings of 1715 and 1745. The economy is based on whisky blending and distilling and on manufacturing. It is also an agricultural market centre.

Perth, City (pop., 2006: 1,445,078), capital of Western Australia state, Australia. Located on the Swan River 10 mi (16 km) from its mouth, Perth was settled in 1829. It developed rapidly after the discovery of goldfields around Kalgoonie in the early 1890s and the opening of Fremantle Harbour in 1897. It is now a major industrial centre with a rapidly expanding economy. It hosted the 1987 America's Cup yacht race and is the seat of the University of Western Australia, Murdoch University, and Curtin University of Technology.

Peru, officially REPUBLIC OF PERU, Country, western South America. Area: 496,225 sq mi (1,285,216 sq km). Population: (2011 est.) 29,249,000. Capital: Lima. Almost half of the people are Quechua; nearly one-third are mestizos; and most of the remainder are Aymara and people of European ancestry. Languages: Spanish, Quechua, Aymara (all official). Religion: Christianity (predominantly Roman Catholic; also Protestant). Currency: nuevo sol. Peru is the third largest country in South America and may be divided into three geographic regions from west to east: the Costa (coast), which consists of a long, narrow belt of desert lowlands; the Sierra (highlands), which is the Peruvian portion of the Andes Mountains; and Amazonia, the vast forested eastern foothills and plains, consisting mainly of the tropical rainforests of the Amazon River basin. Peru has a developing mixed economy based largely on services, manufacturing, agriculture, and mining. Most industries, including the petroleum industry, were nationalized in the late 1960s and early '70s, but many were privatized again in the 1990s. Peru is a unitary multiparty republic with one legislative house; its head of state and government is the president. Peru was the centre of the Inca empire, whose capital, Cuzco, was established in the 11th or 12th century. In 1533 the region was conquered by Spanish adventurer Francisco Pizarro, and it thereafter was dominated by Spain for almost 300 years as the Viceroyalty of Peru. It declared its independence in 1821, and freedom was achieved in 1824. Peru was defeated by Chile in the War of the Pacific (1879–83). In 1941 a boundary dispute with Ecuador erupted into war, which gave Peru control over a larger part of the Amazon basin; further disputes ensued until the border was demarcated again in 1998. The government was overthrown by a military junta in 1968; civilian rule was restored in 1980. The government of Alberto Fujimori dissolved the legislature in 1992 and promulgated a new constitution the following year. The government later successfully combated the Shining Path and Túpac Amaru rebel movements. Fujimori won a second term in 1995, but charges of fraud accompanied his election to a third term in 2000; his government crumbled later that year. Fujimori was succeeded by Alejandro Toledo (2001–06), Peru's first democratically elected president of Quechuan ethnicity.

Peshawar, City (pop., 2005 est.: urban agglom., 1,240,000), capital of North-West Frontier province, Pakistan. It is located west of the Bara River near the Khyber Pass. Once the capital of the ancient Buddhist kingdom of Gandhara, it was a centre of the caravan trade with Afghanistan and Central Asia. It was controlled by a succession of ruling groups until it was captured by the Muslims in 988. By the 16th century Peshawar was ruled by the Afghans. It was under British control (1849–1947) and served as an important military base. The city is still militarily important; its ancient bazaar remains a meeting place for foreign merchants and traders.

Peter I, Russian PYOTR ALEKSEYEVICH, known as PETER THE GREAT (b. June 9, 1672, Moscow, Russia—d. Feb. 8, 1725, St. Petersburg), Tsar of Russia (1682–1725). Son of Tsar Alexis, he reigned jointly with his half brother Ivan V (1682–96) and alone from 1696. Interested in progressive influences from western Europe, he visited several countries there (1697–98). After returning to Russia, he introduced Western technology, modernized the government and military system, and transferred the capital to the new city of St. Petersburg (1703). He further increased the power of the monarchy at the expense of the nobles and the Orthodox church. Some of his reforms were implemented brutally, with considerable loss of life. Suspecting that his son Alexis was conspiring against him, he had Alexis tortured to death in 1718. He pursued foreign policies to give Russia access to the Baltic and Black seas, engaging in war with the Ottoman Empire (1695–96) and with Sweden in the Second Northern War (1700–21). His campaign against Persia (1722–23) secured for Russia the southern and western shores of the Caspian Sea. In 1721 he was proclaimed emperor; his wife succeeded him as the empress Catherine I. For raising Russia to a recognized place among the great European powers, Peter is widely considered one of the outstanding rulers and reformers in Russian history, but he has also been decried by nationalists for discarding much of what was unique in Russian culture, and his legacy has been seen as a model for Joseph Stalin's brutal transformation of Russian life.

Peter the Apostle, Saint, orig. SIMON (d. *c.* AD 64, Rome), Disciple of Jesus, recognized as the leader of the Twelve Apostles. Jesus called him Cephas (Aramaic for "Rock"; rendered in Greek as "Petros") and said "Upon this rock I will build my church" (Matthew 16:18). When Jesus was arrested, according to the biblical account, Peter denied him three times, as Jesus had foretold. Accounts of Peter's life and ministry rely on the four Gospels, the Acts of the Apostles, the epistles of Peter, and the epistles of St. Paul. Peter worked with Paul in Antioch and later carried on missionary work in Asia Minor. According to tradition, he eventually went to Rome, where he suffered martyrdom by being crucified upside down. Saint Peter's Basilica is said to have been built on the site of his grave in Rome. In Roman Catholicism he is regarded as the first in the unbroken succession of popes. Jesus' promise to give him the "keys of the kingdom" led to the popular perception of Peter as the gatekeeper of heaven. The Roman Catholic church celebrates five feast days in honour of Peter, and in each the name of Paul is associated.

petition, Written instrument directed to an individual, government official, legislative body, or court in order to seek redress of grievances or to request a favour. In some jurisdictions, petitions brought by a sufficient number of people (represented by their signatures) are used to place a candidate on a ballot, to submit an issue to the electorate, or to exert pressure on legislators to vote in a certain way. In the U.S., the right to petition is guaranteed by the 1st Amendment to the Constitution.

Petition of Right (1628) Petition sent by Parliament to King Charles I complaining of a series of breaches of law. The petition sought recognition of four principles: no taxation without the consent of Parliament, no imprisonment without cause, no quartering of soldiers on subjects, and no martial law in peacetime. To continue receiving subsidies for his policies, Charles was compelled to accept the petition, but he later ignored its principles.

Petrarch, Italian FRANCESCO PETRARCA (b. July 20, 1304, Arezzo, Tuscany—d. July 18/19, 1374, Arquà, near Padua, Carrara), Italian scholar, poet, and humanist. After 1326 he abandoned the study of law for his true interests, literature and the religious life. He took minor ecclesiastical orders and moved to Avignon, where in 1327 he first saw Laura, the idealized subject of his chaste love and of his celebrated Italian love lyrics; mainly sonnets and odes written over some 20 years, most were included in his *Canzoniere* or *Rime* (1360). The greatest scholar of his age, especially of Classical Latin, he traveled widely, visiting learned men, searching out manuscripts, and undertaking diplomatic missions. He strongly advocated the continuity between Classical culture and the Christian message; in combining the two ideals he is considered the founder and a great representative of humanism. His Latin works, reflecting his religious and philosophical interests, include *On Illustrious Men* (begun *c.* 1337), the epic poem *Africa* (begun *c.* 1338), the autobiographical treatise *Petrarch's Secret* (written 1342–58), *De vita solitaria* (1345–47; "The Life of Solitude"), and *Epistolae metricae* (begun *c.* 1345; "Metrical Letters"). After 1367 he lived in and near Padua. His influence on European literature was enormous and lasting, and his deep consciousness of the Classical past as a source of literary and philosophical meaning for the present was of great importance in paving the way for the Renaissance.

petrochemical, Strictly, any of a large class of chemicals (as distinct from fuels) derived from petroleum and natural gas. The category has been broadened to include a much larger range of organic compounds and a few inorganic compounds (including carbon black, sulfur, and ammonia). Some materials cannot be classifed unequivocally because they have alternative sources (benzene from coal, ethanol from fermentation). Like crude oil and natural gas, most petrochemicals consist mainly of carbon and hydrogen and are called hydrocarbons. Petrochemicals used as raw materials (feedstocks) include ethylene, propylene, butadiene, benzene, toluene, xylene, and naphthalene. Among the myriad petrochemical products are plastics (e.g., polyethylene, polypropylene, polystyrene), soaps and detergents, solvents, drugs, fertilizers, pesticides, explosives, synthetic fibres and rubberss, paints, epoxies, flooring and insulating materials, luggage, and recording disks and tapes.

petroleum, or CRUDE OIL, Complex mixture of hydrocarbons derived from the geologic transformation and decomposition of plants and animals that lived hundreds of millions of years ago. As a technical term, *petroleum* encompasses the liquid (crude oil), gaseous (natural gas), and viscous or solid (bitumen, asphalt) forms of hydrocarbons that occur in the Earth, but the meaning is often restricted to the liquid oil form. Crude oil and natural gas are the most important primary fossil fuels. Asphalt has been used since ancient times to caulk ships and pave roads. In the mid 1800s petroleum began to replace whale oil in lamps, and the first well specifically to extract it was drilled in 1859. The development of the automobile gave petroleum a new role as the source of gasoline. Petroleum and its products have since been used as fuels for heating, for land, air, and sea transport, and for electric power generation and as petrochemical sources and lubricants. Crude oil and natural gas, produced mostly in Saudi Arabia, the U.S., and Russia, now account for about 60% of world energy consumption; the

U.S. is by far the largest consumer. At present rates of consumption, the known supply will be exhausted by the mid 21st century. Petroleum is recovered from drilled wells, transported by pipeline or tanker ship to refineries, and there converted to fuels and petrochemicals.

petunia, Any of many species of flowering plants in the genus *Petunia*, in the nightshade family, which originated in South America. The innumerable varieties of showy, trumpet-shaped flowers are immensely popular. There are two types: the compact, erect sort seen in summer garden beds, and the sprawling, long-stemmed sort seen in hanging baskets and window boxes. From early summer until frost, petunias bloom profusely with single or double blossoms; crisped, fringed, or ruffled flowers; and spectacular hues from pure white to deep crimson or purple, speckled or veined in contrasting colours. Leaves are soft, flabby, and covered with fine, sticky hairs. Technically perennials, petunias are most often grown as annuals.

peyote, Either of two species of the genus *Lophophora* in the cac-

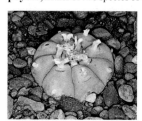

Peyote (*Lophophora williamsii*)
Dennis E. Anderson

tus family, native to North America, almost exclusively to Mexico. The body of the peyote cactus is spineless, soft, usually blue-green, and only 3 in. (8 cm) wide and 2 in. (5 cm) tall. The more common species, mescal (*L. williamsii*), has pink to white flowers. *L. diffusa*, more primitive, has white to yellow flowers and a yellow-green body. Well known for its hallucinogenic effects (primarily due to the alkaloid mescaline), peyote figures prominently in old and recent religious rituals of certain American Indian peoples. The sale, use, or possession of dried mescal buttons (flowering heads) or live plants is prohibited by law in many places.

pH, Quantitative measure of the strength of the acidity or alkalinity of a solution. It is defined as the negative common logarithm of the concentration of hydrogen ions $[H^+]$ in moles/litre: $pH = -\log_{10}[H^+]$. The letters of its name are derived from the absolute value of the power (p) of the hydrogen ion concentration (H). The product of the concentrations in water of H^+ and OH^- (the hydroxide ion) is always about 10^{-14}. The strongest acid solution has more than 1 mole/litre of H^+ (and about 10^{-14} of OH^-), for a pH of less than 0. The strongest basic solution has about 10^{-14} mole/litre of H^+ (and about 1 of OH^-), for a pH of 14. A neutral solution has about 10^{-7} mole/litre of both H^+ and OH^-, for a pH of 7. The pH value, measured by a pH meter, titration, or indicator (e.g., litmus) strips, helps inform chemists of the nature, composition, or extent of reaction of substances, biologists of the composition and environment of organisms or their parts or fluids, physicians of the functioning of bodily systems, and agronomists of the suitability of soils for crops and any treatments needed. The pH is now defined in electrochemical terms.

Phaethon, In Greek mythology, the son of Helios, the sun god, and a nymph. Taunted as illegitimate, Phaethon asked for permission to drive the chariot of the sun through the heavens for a single day in order to prove that Helios was his father. He proved unable to control the horses, and, after making a gash in the heavens that became the Milky Way, he rode too close to earth and began to scorch it. To prevent further damage, Zeus hurled a thunderbolt, killing him.

Phanerozoic Eon, Span of geologic time from 542 million years ago, the end of the Proterozoic Eon, to the present. The Phanerozoic, the eon of visible life, is divided into three major eras: the Paleozoic, Mesozoic, and Cenozoic. Although life originated in

Precambrian time, it was in the Phanerozoic that many forms arose and evolved. The Earth gradually assumed its present configuration and physical features through such processes as plate tectonics, mountain building, and glaciation.

pharaoh, Epithet applied to Egyptian kings from *c.* 1500 to 343 BC. The term later evolved into a generic term for all ancient Egyptian kings. Pharaohs were regarded as gods, retaining their divine status even after death. A pharaoh's will was supreme, and he governed by royal decree, with the assistance of viziers. The common people nevertheless judged a pharaoh by his deeds; many were criticized, plotted against, and even deposed and killed.

Pharisee, Member of a Jewish religious party in Palestine that emerged *c.* 160 BC in opposition to the Sadducees. The Pharisees held that the Jewish oral tradition was as valid as the Torah. They struggled to democratize the Jewish religion, arguing that the worship of God was not confined to the Temple of Jerusalem and fostering the synagogue as an institution of worship. Their belief that reason must be applied in the interpretation of the Torah and its application to contemporary problems is now basic to Jewish theology.

pharmacy, Science dealing with collection, preparation, and standardization of drugs. Pharmacists, who must earn a qualifying degree, prepare and dispense prescribed medications. They formerly mixed and measured drug products from raw materials according to doctors' prescriptions, and they are still responsible for formulating, storing, and providing correct dosages of medicines, now usually produced by pharmaceutical companies as premeasured tablets or capsules. They also advise patients on the use of both prescription and over-the-counter drugs. Laws regulating the pharmaceutical industry are based on the national pharmacopoeia, which outlines the purity and dosages of numerous medicinal products.

pharyngitis, Inflammation and infection (usually bacterial or viral) of the pharynx. Symptoms include pain (sore throat, worse on swallowing), redness, swollen lymph nodes, and fever. Throat culture may be the only way to distinguish infection with streptococcus bacteria (strep throat), which can cause rheumatic fever if not treated in time with antibiotics, from viral infections, which do not respond to antibiotics and require only symptom relief.

pharynx, Inside of the throat, from the oral and nasal cavities to the trachea and esophagus. It has three connected sections: the nasopharynx, at the back of the nasal cavity; the oropharynx, in the back of the oral cavity down to the epiglottis (a flap of tissue that closes off the larynx during swallowing); and the laryngopharynx, from the epiglottis to the esophagus. The oropharynx contains the palatine tonsils. The eustachian tubes connect the middle ears to the pharynx, allowing air pressure on the eardrum to be equalized. Disorders include pharyngitis, tonsillitis, and cancer.

phase, In thermodynamics, a chemically and physically uniform quantity of matter that can be separated mechanically from a non-homogeneous mixture. It may consist of a single substance or of a mixture of substances. The three basic phases of matter are solid, liquid, and gas; other phases that are considered to exist include crystalline, colloidal, glass, amorphous, and plasma. The different phases of a pure substance are related to each other in terms of temperature and pressure. For example, if the temperature of a solid is raised enough, or the pressure is reduced enough, it will become a liquid.

phase, In wave motion, the fraction of the time required to complete a full cycle that a point completes after last passing through the reference position. Two periodic motions are said to be in phase when corresponding points of each reach maximum or minimum displacements at the same time. If the crests of two waves pass the same point at the same time, they are in phase for that position. If the crest of one and the trough of the other pass the same

point at the same time, the phase angles differ by 180° and the waves are said to be of opposite phase. Phase differences are important in alternating electric current technology.

phenomenology, Philosophical discipline originated by Edmund Husserl. Husserl developed the phenomenological method to make possible "a descriptive account of the essential structures of the directly given." Phenomenology emphasizes the immediacy of experience, the attempt to isolate it and set it off from all assumptions of existence or causal influence and lay bare its essential structure. Phenomenology restricts the philosopher's attention to the pure data of consciousness, uncontaminated by metaphysical theories or scientific assumptions. Husserl's concept of the life-world—as the individual's personal world as directly experienced—expressed this same idea of immediacy. With the appearance of the *Annual for Philosophical and Phenomenological Research* (1913–30), under Husserl's editorship, his personal philosophizing flowered into an international movement. Its most notable adherents were Max Scheler and Martin Heidegger.

phenotype, All the observable characteristics of an organism, such as shape, size, colour, and behaviour, that result from the interaction of its genotype (total genetic makeup) with the environment. The phenotype may change throughout the life of an individual because of environmental changes and the changes associated with aging. Different environments can influence the development of inherited traits (e.g., size is affected by available food supply) and can alter expression by similar genotypes (e.g., twins brought up in dissimilar families may mature differently). Furthermore, not all inherited possibilities in the genotype are expressed in the phenotype, because some are the result of inactive, recessive, or inhibited genes.

phenylketonuria (PKU), or PHENYLPYRUVIC OLIGOPHRENIA, Inability to normally metabolize phenylalanine, the accumulation of which interferes with normal childhood development. Central nervous system effects include intellectual disability and seizures, with behavioral signs seen at four to six months of age. Abnormal metabolism also leads to low melanin levels, with light hair, eye, and skin colour. Tests detect this recessive genetic disorder in two-thirds of the 1 in 10,000 newborns born with high levels of phenylalanine. Keeping phenylalanine out of the diet (by total avoidance of meat, dairy, and high-protein foods and aspartame) until adolescence permits normal development. Protein is supplied in a phenylalanine-free formula. Pregnant women with PKU must resume the diet to prevent severe damage to the unborn child.

pheromone, Any chemical compound secreted by an organism in minute amounts to elicit a particular reaction from other organisms of the same species. Pheromones are widespread among insects and vertebrates (except birds) and are present in some fungi, slime molds, and algae. The chemicals may be secreted by special glands or incorporated into other substances (e.g., urine), shed freely, or deposited in selected locations. Pheromones are used to bring creatures together (e.g., in termite, bee, and ant colonies), lead them to food (e.g., in scent trails laid by ants), signal danger (e.g., when released by wounded fish to alert others), attract a mate and elicit sexual behaviour (numerous examples, possibly including humans), and influence sexual development (in many mammals and certain insects). Alarm pheromones often last a shorter time and travel a shorter distance than other types. In vertebrates, chemical stimuli often influence parent-young responses. Sex-attractant pheromones are used in certain products to lure and trap unwanted or harmful insects.

Philadelphia, City (pop., 2010: 1,526,006) and port, southeastern Pennsylvania, U.S., at the confluence of the Delaware and Schuylkill rivers. The site was occupied by the Delaware Indians before William Penn founded the city in 1682. It was the capital of Pennsylvania 1683–1799 and the capital of the U.S. between 1790 and 1800. It played a prominent role in opposing British policies and was the site of the first and second Continental Congresses, the signing of the Declaration of Independence, and the Constitutional Convention. The population grew in the 18th century, with many immigrants from Scotland, Ireland, and Germany. It was the largest and most important city of the U.S. in the 19th century and a centre of the antislavery movement. In 1876 it was the site of the U.S. Centennial Exposition. It is also the site of the U.S.'s oldest art museum (the Pennsylvania Academy of the Fine Arts, founded in 1805) and the first U.S. hospital (the Pennsylvania Hospital, founded in 1751). It is the largest city in the state and a centre of commerce, finance, industry, and culture. Its numerous educational institutions include the University of Pennsylvania.

philately, Collection and study of postage stamps. The first postage stamps were issued in England in 1840, and in the U.S. in 1842. Stamp collectors usually specialize, collecting stamps of one country, one period of time, or one subject (e.g., birds, flowers, art). Value depends on rarity and condition. An issue of stamps that includes a printer's error may have increased value.

Inverted airplane airmail stamp, U.S., 1918
Lee Boltin

Philippines, officially REPUBLIC OF THE PHILIPPINES, Island country, western Pacific Ocean, on an archipelago off the southeast coast of Asia. Area: 115,831 sq mi (300,000 sq km). Population: (2011 est.) 95,849,000. Capital: Manila; other government offices and ministries are located in Quezon City and other Manila suburbs. Filipinos are predominantly of Malay descent, frequently with Chinese and sometimes American or Spanish ancestry. Languages: Filipino (Pilipino) and English (both official); the other main groups are Cebuano, Ilocano, Hiligaynon, and Bicol. Religions: Christianity (predominantly Roman Catholic; also Protestant, other Christians); also Islam. Currency: Philippine piso (peso). The Philippines consist of about 7,100 islands and islets. The two principal islands are Luzon in the north and Mindanao in the south. The Visayan group is in the central Philippines, Mindoro is directly south of Luzon, and Palawan is isolated in the west. The topography is varied; inactive volcanoes and mountain ranges are the main features of most of the larger islands. The country has a predominantly market economy based largely on agriculture, light industries, and services. The Philippines is a unitary republic with two legislative houses; its head of state and government is the president. First visited by Ferdinand Magellan in 1521, the islands were colonized by the Spanish, who retained control until the Philippines were ceded to the U.S. in 1898 following the Spanish-American War. The Commonwealth of the Philippines was established in 1935 to prepare the country for political and economic independence, which was delayed by World War II and the invasion of Japanese troops. The islands were liberated by U.S. forces in 1944–45, and the Republic of the Philippines was proclaimed in 1946, with a government patterned on that of the U.S. In 1965 Ferdinand Marcos was elected president. He declared martial law in 1972, which lasted until 1981. After 20 years of dictatorial rule, Marcos was driven from power in 1986. Corazon Aquino became president and instituted a period of democratic rule that continued with the elections of subsequent presidents. The government has tried to come to terms with Muslim independence fighters in the southern islands by establishing the Muslim Mindanao autonomous region in southwestern Mindanao and nearby islands.

Philistine, Member of a group of Aegean origin that settled on the southern coast of Palestine. The Philistines first settled the region during the 12th century BC, about the time the Israelites arrived. They lived in five cities (the Pentapolis) that together made up Philistia, from which the Greeks derived the name Palestine. They first fought the Israelites in the 11th century BC. In the 10th century BC they were defeated by the Israelite king David. They were later ruled by Assyria, Egypt, Babylonia, Persia, Greece, and Rome. The group appears prominently in the Old Testament—from which much of the information about them is derived—though they left no written records of their own. It is from these many and coloured biblical references that the term assumes its modern significance in the English language.

philodendron, Any of about 450 species of climbing herbaceous plants that make up the genus *Philodendron* in the arum family, native to the New World tropics. Some are popular indoor foliage plants in colder areas and landscape plants in warmer climates. The leaves are often large and smooth-edged to variously lobed and cut. The inflorescence is seldom produced indoors. Many forms are available in cultivation, foremost among them the common heart-leaf (*Philodendron scandens oxycardium*). Large varieties include the spade-leaf philodendron (*P. domesticum* or *P. hastatum*), with triangular leaves up to 2 ft (60 cm) long, and the selloum philodendron (*P. selloum*), with deeply cut leaves up to 3 ft (1 m) long.

philosophy, Critical examination of the rational grounds of our most fundamental beliefs and logical analysis of the basic concepts employed in the expression of such beliefs. Philosophy may also be defined as reflection on the varieties of human experience, or as the rational, methodical, and systematic consideration of the topics that are of greatest concern to humanity. Philosophical inquiry is a central element in the intellectual history of many civilizations. Difficulty in achieving a consensus about the definition of the discipline partly reflects the fact that philosophers have frequently come to it from different fields and have preferred to reflect on different areas of experience. All the world's great religions have produced significant allied philosophical schools. Western philosophers such as Thomas Aquinas, George Berkeley, and Søren Kierkegaard regarded philosophy as a means of defending religion and dispelling the antireligious errors of materialism and rationalism. Pythagoras, René Descartes, and Bertrand Russell, among others, were primarily mathematicians whose views of reality and knowledge were influenced by mathematics. Figures such as Thomas Hobbes, Jean-Jacques Rousseau, and John Stuart Mill were mainly concerned with political philosophy, whereas Socrates and Plato were occupied chiefly by questions in ethics. The Pre-Socratics, Francis Bacon, and Alfred North Whitehead, among many others, started from an interest in the physical composition of the natural world. Other philosophical fields include aesthetics, epistemology, logic, metaphysics, philosophy of mind, and philosophical anthropology.

phlebitis, Inflammation of the wall of a vein. Causes include nearby infection, trauma, surgery, and childbirth. The area over the vein is painful, swollen, red, and hot. A tender, cordlike mass may be felt under the skin. It usually occurs in surface veins in the lower leg and can be treated with pain relievers and bed rest, with mild exercise after inflammation subsides. Phlebitis can last for years; in such cases, irritation of the vein's inner lining leads to blood-clot formation, a condition known as thrombophlebitis. In deeper veins, this requires anticoagulants to prevent embolisms.

Phnom Penh, City (pop., 2005 est.: 1,313,900), capital of Cambodia, at the junction of the Sab River (a tributary of the Tonle Sap) with the Mekong River. Founded in 1434 as the capital of the Khmer kingdom, it was abandoned several times before being reestablished in 1865. It was a cultural centre, with many institutions of higher learning. When the Khmer Rouge came to power in Cambodia in 1975, they forced the city's population into the countryside to work in the fields. The city was repopulated beginning in 1979, and its educational institutions began a difficult period of recovery from the virtual extermination of Cambodia's educated class. Although the city is 180 mi (290 km) from the sea, it is a major port of the Mekong River valley; it is linked to the South China Sea via a channel of the Mekong delta in Vietnam.

phobia, Extreme and irrational fear of a particular object, class of objects, or situation. A phobia is classified as a type of anxiety disorder (a neurosis), since anxiety is its chief symptom. Phobias are generally believed to result when fear produced by an original threatening situation (such as a near-drowning in childhood) is transferred to other similar situations (such as encounters with bodies of water), the original fear often being repressed or forgotten. Behaviour therapy can be helpful in overcoming phobias, the phobic person being gradually exposed to the anxiety-provoking object or situation in a way that demonstrates that no threat really exists.

Phoenicia, Ancient region, Middle East. Corresponding to modern Lebanon, with adjoining parts of Syria and Israel, its chief cities were Sidon, Tyre, and Berot (modern Beirut). The Phoenicians were notable merchants, traders, and colonizers of the Mediterranean region in the 1st millennium BC. The area was conquered successively by the Assyrians, Babylonians, Persians, and Macedonians under Alexander the Great. In 64 BC it was incorporated into the Roman province of Syria.

Phoenician, One of a people of ancient Phoenicia. They were merchants, traders, and colonizers who probably arrived from the Persian Gulf c. 3000 BC. By the 2nd millennium BC they had colonies in the Levant, North Africa, Anatolia, and Cyprus. They traded wood, cloth, dyes, embroideries, wine, and decorative objects; ivory and wood carving became their specialties, and the work of Phoenician goldsmiths and metalsmiths was well known. Their alphabet became the basis of the Greek alphabet.

phoenix, In ancient Egypt and in classical antiquity, a fabulous bird associated with the worship of the sun. The Egyptian phoenix was said to be as large as an eagle, with brilliant scarlet and gold plumage and a melodious cry. Only one phoenix existed at a time, and it lived no less than 500 years. As its end approached, it built a nest of aromatic boughs and spices, set it on fire, and was consumed in the flames. From the pyre was born a new phoenix, which sealed its predecessor's ashes in an egg of myrrh and flew to Heliopolis to deposit them on the altar of the sun god. The phoenix thus symbolized immortality.

phoneme, Smallest unit of speech distinguishing one word (or word element) from another (e.g., the sound *p* in *tap*, which differentiates that word from *tab* and *tag*). The term is usually restricted to vowels and consonants, but some linguists include differences of pitch, stress, and rhythm. A phoneme may have variants, called allophones, that differ phonetically without affecting meaning. Phonemes may be recorded with special symbols, such as those of the International Phonetic Alphabet. In transcription, linguists conventionally place symbols for phonemes between slash marks: /p/.

phonetics, Study of speech sounds. It deals with their articulation (articulatory phonetics), their acoustic properties (acoustic phonetics), and how they combine to make syllables, words, and sentences (linguistic phonetics). The first phoneticians were Indian scholars (c. 300 BC) who tried to preserve the pronunciation of Sanskrit holy texts. The Classical Greeks are credited as the first to base a writing system on a phonetic alphabet. Modern phonetics began with Alexander Melville Bell (1819–1905), whose *Visible Speech* (1867) introduced a system of precise notation for writing down speech sounds. In the 20th century linguists focused on developing a classification system that can permit comparison of all human speech sounds. Another concern of modern phonetics is the mental processes of speech perception.

phonics, Method of reading instruction that breaks language down into its simplest components. Children learn the sounds of individual letters first, then the sounds of letters in combination and in simple words. Simple reading exercises with a controlled vocabulary reinforce the process. Phonics-based instruction was challenged by proponents of "whole-language" instruction, a process in which children are introduced to whole words at a time, are taught using real literature rather than reading exercises, and are encouraged to keep journals in which "creative" spelling is permitted. A strong backlash against whole-language teaching polarized these two approaches to reading instruction. Many schools have since come to use a combination of the two techniques.

phonology, Study of sound patterns within languages. Diachronic (historical) phonology traces and analyzes changes in speech sounds and sound systems over time (e.g., the process by which *sea* and *see*, once pronounced with different vowel sounds, have come to be pronounced alike). Synchronic (descriptive) phonology investigates sound patterns at a single stage in a language's development, to identify which ones can occur and in what position (in English, for example, *nt* and *rk* appear within or at the end of words but not at the beginning).

phosphorus, Nonmetallic chemical element, chemical symbol P, atomic number 15. The ordinary allotrope, called white phosphorus, is a poisonous, colourless, semitransparent, soft, waxy solid that glows in the dark and combusts spontaneously in air, producing dense white fumes of the oxide P_4O_{10}; it is used as a rodenticide and a military smokescreen. Heat or sunlight converts it to the red phosphorus allotrope, a violet-red powder that does not phosphoresce or ignite spontaneously. Much less reactive and soluble than white phosphorus, it is used in manufacturing other phosphorus compounds and in semiconductors, fertilizers, safety matches, and fireworks. Black phosphorus, made by heating the white form under pressure, is flaky like graphite. Phosphorus seldom occurs uncombined in nature. As the phosphate ion, it is abundant and widely distributed, in apatite, phosphorite, and many other minerals. Phosphorus has valence 3 or 5 in compounds, which have many uses in industry. Phosphine (PH_3) is a chemical raw material and a doping agent (deliberately added impurity) for solid-state electronics components. Organic phosphorus compounds are used as plasticizers, gasoline additives, insecticides (e.g., parathion), and nerve gases. In living organisms the role of phosphorus is essential; it is a component of DNA and RNA, ATP, and bone.

photoengraving, Any of several processes for producing printing plates by photographic means. In general, a plate coated with a photosensitive substance is exposed to an image, usually on film; the plate is then treated in various ways, depending on the printing process to be used. Photoengraving is particularly useful for reproducing photographs via the halftone process.

photography, Method of recording permanent images by the action of light projected by a lens in a camera onto a film or other light-sensitive material. It was developed in the 19th century through the artistic aspirations of two Frenchmen, Nicéphore Niepce and Louis-Jacques-Mandé Daguerre, whose combined discoveries led to the invention of the first commercially successful process, the daguerreotype (1837). In addition, two Englishmen, Thomas Wedgwood and William Henry Fox Talbot, patented the negative-positive calotype process (1839) that became the forerunner of modern photographic technique. Photography was initially used for portraiture and landscapes. In the 1850s and '60s, Mathew B. Brady and Roger Fenton pioneered war photography and photojournalism. From its inception, two views of photography predominated: one approach held that the camera and its resulting images truthfully document the real world, while the other considered the camera simply to be a tool, much like a paintbrush, with which to create artistic statements. The latter notion, known as Pictorialism, held sway from the late 1860s through the first decade of the 20th century, as photographers manipulated their negatives and prints to create hazy, elaborately staged images that resembled paintings. By the 1920s and '30s, a new, more realistic style of photography gained prominence, as photographers such as Paul Strand, Edward Weston, and Ansel Adams began to pursue sharply focused, detailed images. The Great Depression and two world wars inspired many photographers, including Walker Evans and Dorothea Lange, to pursue documentary, often socially conscious photography. Inspired by such work, many photojournalists, including Alfred Eisenstaedt and Margaret Bourke-White, also emerged during this period. In the second half of the 20th century, the urban social scene became a subject of much interest to photographers, as did celebrity portraiture and fashion photography. At the turn of the 21st century, photographers took advantage of digital capabilities by experimenting with enormous formats and new manipulative techniques. As technological advances improve photographic equipment, materials, and techniques, the scope of photography continues to expand enormously.

photometry, Precision measurement of the brightness, colour, and spectrum of stars and other celestial objects to obtain data on their structure, temperature, and composition. About 130 BC Hipparchus used a system that divided the stars into six magnitudes, from brightest to faintest. Beginning in the 17th century, use of the telescope led to the discovery of many fainter stars, and the scale was extended. The use of photographic and, since the 1940s, photoelectric equipment has vastly extended the sensitivity and wavelength range of astronomical photometry. The main (UBVRI) classification system uses wave bands in the ultraviolet, blue, visual, red, and infrared ranges. More elaborate systems can distinguish giant and dwarf stars, detect metals in stars, and determine surface gravity.

photon, or LIGHT QUANTUM, Minute energy packet of electromagnetic radiation. In 1900 Max Planck found that heat radiation is emitted and absorbed in distinct units, which he called quanta. In 1905 Albert Einstein explained the photoelectric effect, proposing the existence of discrete energy packets in light. The term photon came into use for these packets in 1926. The energies of photons range from high-energy gamma rays and X rays to low-energy infrared and radio waves, though all travel at the same speed, the speed of light. Photons have no electric charge or rest mass and are the carriers of the electromagnetic field.

photosphere, Visible surface of the Sun, about 250 mi (400 km) thick. It emits most of the Sun's light that reaches Earth directly. Temperatures range from about 18,000 °F (10,000 °C) at the bottom to 8,000 °F (4,000 °C) at the top; its density is about 1/1,000 that of air at the surface of Earth. Sunspots are photospheric phenomena. The photosphere has a granular structure. Each grain (cell), a mass of hot gas several hundred miles in diameter, rises from inside the Sun, radiates energy, and sinks back within minutes to be replaced by others in a constantly changing pattern.

photosynthesis, Process by which green plants and certain other organisms transform light into chemical energy. In green plants, light energy is captured by chlorophyll in the chloroplasts of the leaves and used to convert water, carbon dioxide, and minerals into oxygen and energy-rich organic compounds (simple and complex sugars) that are the basis of both plant and animal life. Photosynthesis consists of a number of photochemical and enzymatic reactions. It occurs in two stages. During the light-dependent stage (light reaction), chlorophyll absorbs light energy, which excites some electrons in the pigment molecules to higher energy levels; these leave the chlorophyll and pass along a series of molecules, generating formation of NADPH (an enzyme) and high-energy ATP molecules. Oxygen, released as a by-product, passes into the atmosphere through pores in the leaves. NADPH and ATP drive the second stage, the dark reaction (or Calvin cycle, discovered by Melvin Calvin), which does not require light. During this stage glucose is generated using atmospheric carbon dioxide. Photosynthesis is crucial for maintaining life on Earth; if it ceased, there would soon be little food or other organic matter on the planet, and most types of organisms would disappear.

phrenology, Study of the shape of the skull as an indication of mental abilities and character traits. Franz Joseph Gall stated the principle that each of the innate mental faculties is based in a specific brain region ("organ"), whose size reflects the faculty's prominence in a person and is reflected by the skull's surface. He examined the skulls of persons with particular traits (including "criminal" traits) for a feature he could identify with it. His followers Johann Kaspar Spurzheim (1776–1832) and George Combe (1788–1858) divided the scalp into areas they labeled with traits such as combativeness, cautiousness, and form perception. Though popular well into the 20th century, phrenology has been wholly discredited.

phylogeny, History of the evolution of a species or group, especially lines of descent and relationships among broad groups. The fundamental proposition is that plants or animals of different species descended from common ancestors. Because the evidence for such relationships is almost always incomplete, most judgments of phylogenicity are based on indirect evidence and cautious speculation. Modern taxonomy, the science of classifying organisms, is based on phylogeny. Early taxonomic systems had no theoretical basis; organisms were grouped according to apparent similarity. Biologists who propose a phylogeny obtain evidence from the fields of paleontology, comparative anatomy, comparative embryology, biochemistry, and molecular biology. The data and conclusions of phylogeny indicate that today's living creatures are the product of a historical process of evolution and that degrees of resemblance within and between groups correspond to degrees of relationship by descent from common ancestors.

physics, Science that deals with the structure of matter and the interactions between the fundamental constituents of the observable universe. Long called natural philosophy, physics (from Greek *physikos*) is concerned with all aspects of nature, covering the behaviour of objects under the action of given forces and the nature and origin of gravitational, electromagnetic, and nuclear force fields. The goal of physics is to formulate comprehensive principles that bring together and explain all discernible phenomena.

physiocrat, Member of a school of economics, founded in 18th-century France, that held that government should not interfere with the operation of natural economic laws. Generally regarded as the first scientific school of economics, the physiocratic school (the name refers to the "rule of nature") was founded by François Quesnay, who demonstrated the economic relation between a workshop and a farm and asserted that the farm alone added to a nation's wealth. Land and agriculture were therefore believed to be the source of all wealth. The physiocrats envisaged a society in which written law would be in harmony with natural law. They pictured a predominantly agricultural society, attacking mercantilism for its emphasis on manufacturing and foreign trade and its mass of economic regulations. Quesnay's disciples included Victor Riqueti, count de Mirabeau, and Pierre Samuel du Pont de Nemours (1739–1817). The school was in decline by 1768, and after the dismissal of a sympathetic comptroller general in 1776 the leading physiocrats were exiled. Though many of their theories, notably their theory of wealth, were later demolished, their introduction of scientific method to economics had a permanent effect on the discipline.

physiology, Study of the functioning of living organisms or their constituent tissues or cells. Physiology was usually considered separately from anatomy until the development of high-powered microscopes made it clear that structure and function were inseparable at the cellular and molecular levels. An understanding of biochemistry is fundamental to physiology. Physiological processes are dynamic; cells change their function in response to changes in the composition of their local environment, and the organism responds to alterations in both its internal and its external environment. Many physiological reactions are aimed at preserving a constant physical and chemical internal environment (homeostasis).

phytoflagellate, Any of several protozoans that have flagella in addition to sharing many characteristics with typical algae, especially the pigment chlorophyll and various other pigments. Some species, though similar in form, lack chlorophyll. Phytoflagellates may obtain nutrients by photosynthesis, by absorption through the body surface, or by ingestion of food particles. Cryptomonads are among the more important phytoflagellates.

Piaf, Edith, orig. EDITH GIOVANNA GASSION (b. Dec. 19, 1915, Paris, France—d. Oct. 11, 1963, Paris), French popular singer and actress. Her mother, a café singer, abandoned her at birth; Piaf became blind at age three as a result of meningitis but recovered her sight four years later. Her father, a circus acrobat, took her along on tours and encouraged her to sing. She sang for years in the streets of Paris until discovered by a cabaret owner who gave her her first nightclub job and suggested she change her name to Piaf, Parisian slang for "sparrow." She was soon singing her *chansons* (ballads) in the large music halls of Paris. During World War II she entertained French prisoners of war and aided several in their escapes. She spent the postwar years touring, gaining worldwide fame with her intense performances of songs such as "Non, je ne regrette rien" ("No, I regret nothing"). Her throaty, expressive voice, combined with her fragile appearance and a dramatic tight spotlight on her face and hands, made her concerts memorable.

piano, or PIANOFORTE, Keyboard instrument with wire strings that sound when struck by hammers operated by a keyboard. It was invented in Florence by Bartolomeo Cristofori before 1720, with the particular aim of permitting note-to-note dynamic variation (lacking in the harpsichord). It differs from the older clavichord in that its hammers (rather than tangents) are thrown at the strings and bounce back, permitting the struck string to vibrate loudly. A cast-iron frame is needed to withstand the strings' tremendous tension. Pianos have taken various shapes. The original harpsichord (or wing) shape has survived in the modern grand piano; the less-expensive square (actually rectangular) piano, standard in the early 19th century, was replaced by the upright piano, in which the strings are vertical. For at least 150 years the piano was the most important instrument in Western music.

piazza, Open square or marketplace, surrounded by buildings, in an Italian town or city. It was equivalent to the plaza of Spanish-speaking countries. The term became more widely used in the 16th–18th century, denoting any large open space with buildings around it. In 17th–18th-century Britain, long covered walks or galleries with roofs supported by columns were called piazzas; in the U.S. in the 19th century, piazza was another name for a veranda formed by projecting eaves.

picaresque novel, Early form of the novel, usually a first-person narrative, relating the episodic adventures of a rogue or low-born adventurer (Spanish, *pícaro*). The hero drifts from place to place and from one social milieu to another in an effort to survive. The genre originated in Spain and had its prototype in Mateo Alemán's *Guzmán de Alfarache* (1599). It appeared in various European literatures until the mid-18th century, when the growth of the realistic novel led to its decline. Because of the opportunities for satire they present, picaresque elements enriched many later novels, such as Nikolay Gogol's *Dead Souls* (1842), Mark Twain's *Huckleberry Finn* (1884), and Thomas Mann's *Confessions of Felix Krull* (1954).

Picasso, Pablo (Ruiz y) (b. Oct. 25, 1881, Málaga, Spain—d. April 8, 1973, Mougins, France), Spanish-born French painter, sculptor, printmaker, ceramicist, and stage designer. Trained by his father, a professor of drawing, he exhibited his first works at

13. After moving permanently to Paris in 1904, he replaced the predominantly blue tones of his so-called Blue Period (1901–04) with those of pottery and flesh in his Rose Period (1904–06). His first masterpiece, *Les Demoiselles d'Avignon* (1907), was controversial for its violent treatment of the female body and the mask-like faces derived from his study of African art. From 1909 to 1912 Picasso worked closely with Georges Braque—the only time Picasso ever worked with another painter in this way—and they developed what came to be known as Cubism. The artists presented a new kind of reality that broke away from Renaissance tradition, especially from the use of perspective and illusion. Neither Braque nor Picasso desired to move into the realm of total abstraction in their Cubist works, although they implicitly accepted inconsistencies such as different points of view, different axes, and different light sources in the same picture. By 1912 they had taken Cubism further by gluing paper and other materials onto their canvases. Between 1917 and 1924 Picasso designed stage sets for five ballets for Sergey Diaghilev's Ballets Russes. In the 1920s and '30s, the Surrealists spurred him to explore new subject matter, particularly the image of the Minotaur. The Spanish Civil War inspired perhaps his greatest work, the enormous *Guernica* (1937), whose violent imagery condemned the useless destruction of life. After World War II he joined the Communist Party and devoted his time to sculpture, ceramics, and lithography as well as painting. In his late years he created variations on the works of earlier artists, the most famous being a series of 58 pictures based on *Las Meninas* of Diego Velázquez. For nearly 80 of his 91 years Picasso devoted himself to an artistic production that contributed significantly to and paralleled the whole development of modern art in the 20th century.

picketing, Act by workers of standing in front of or near a workplace to call attention to their grievances, discourage patronage, and, during strikes, to discourage strikebreakers. Picketing is also used in non-work-related protests. The U.S. Norris-LaGuardia Act (1932) made it easier for workers to picket by restricting the use of court injunctions against strikes, but the Taft-Hartley Act (1947) outlawed mass picketing.

Pict, Any member of an ancient people of what is now eastern and northeastern Scotland. The name (from Latin *picti,* "painted") referred to their body painting or tattooing. They were probably descended from pre-Celtic peoples. They attacked Hadrian's Wall in 297 and warred constantly with the Romans. They united their two kingdoms by the 7th century and converted to Christianity, and in 843 Kenneth I, king of the Scots, included them in the kingdom of Alba, later Scotland.

pictography, Expression of words and ideas through drawings (pictographs), considered a forerunner of true writing. Pictographs are drawn in a standardized way, omitting unnecessary details. A pictograph that stands for a specific idea or meaning is an ideogram; one that stands for an individual word is a logogram.

pidgin, Language with a very limited vocabulary and a simplified grammar. Pidgins usually arise to permit communication between groups with no language in common; if a pidgin becomes established as the native language of a group, it is known as a creole. Pidgins such as Chinese Pidgin English and Melanesian Pidgin English arose through contact between English-speaking traders and inhabitants of East Asia and the Pacific islands. Other pidgins appeared with the slave trade in Africa and with the importation of West African slaves to Caribbean plantations. Most of the small vocabulary of a pidgin language (Melanesian Pidgin has only 2,000 words, Chinese Pidgin English only 700) is usually drawn from a single language (Melanesian Pidgin, for example, has an English word stock of more than 90%).

Pietà (Italian: "Pity"), Depiction of the Virgin Mary supporting the body of the dead Christ. The theme grew out of that of the Lamentation, the moment between the Descent from the Cross and the

Pietà, *marble sculpture by Michelangelo, 1499; in St. Peter's Basilica, Rome.*
SCALA/Art Resource, New York

Entombment. It first appeared in Germany in the early 14th century. It enjoyed greater popularity in northern Europe than in Italy through the 15th century, yet the supreme representation is Michelangelo's sculpture from 1499 in St. Peter's Basilica. The Pietà was widely represented in both painting and sculpture. Michelangelo's conception of Mary bearing Jesus' body on her knees was standard until the 16th century, when artists began to place Jesus at Mary's feet. Though most religious art declined after the 17th century, the Pietà retained its popularity through the 19th century.

Pietism, Reform movement in German Lutheranism that arose in the 17th century. Philipp Jakob Spener (1635–1705), a Lutheran pastor, originated the movement when he organized an "assembly of piety," a regular meeting of Christians for devotional reading and spiritual exchange. Spener advocated greater involvement of the laity in worship, more extensive study of scripture, and ministerial training that emphasized piety and learning rather than disputation. Under Spener's successor, August Hermann Francke (1663–1727), the University of Halle became a centre of the movement. Pietism influenced the Moravian and Methodist churches.

piezoelectricity, Appearance of an electric field in certain nonconducting crystals as a result of the application of mechanical pressure. Pressure polarizes some crystals, such as quartz, by slightly separating the centers of positive and negative charge. The resultant electric field is detectable as a voltage. The converse effect also occurs: an applied electric field produces mechanical deformation in the crystal. Using this effect, a high-frequency alternating electric current can be converted to an ultrasonic wave of the same frequency, while a mechanical vibration, such as sound, can be converted into a corresponding electrical signal. Piezoelectricity is utilized in microphones, phonograph pickups, and telephone communications systems.

pigeon, Plump, small-billed, monogamous birds of the family Columbidae, found almost worldwide and recognizable by their head-bobbing strut. Unlike other birds, pigeons suck liquids and provide the young with regurgitated "pigeon's milk." The 175 species of true pigeons include the Old and New World *Columba* species and the Old World *Streptopelia* species; all eat seeds and fruit. Common street pigeons, or rock doves, are descendants of the Eurasian rock dove (*Columba livia*). From antiquity pigeons were trained to carry messages over long distances. About 115 species of fruit pigeons occur in Africa, southern Asia, Australia, and the Pacific islands. The three species of crowned pigeons (genus *Goura*), of New Guinea, are nearly the size of a turkey.

pike, Ancient and medieval infantry weapon consisting of a long, metal-pointed spear with a heavy wooden shaft 10–20 ft (3–6 m) in length. Its use by Swiss foot soldiers in the 14th century contributed to the decline of the feudal knights. A variation is used by the picador in bullfighting.

pilgrimage, Journey to a shrine or other sacred place undertaken to gain divine aid, as an act of thanksgiving or penance, or to demonstrate devotion. Medieval Christian pilgrims stayed at hospices set up specifically for pilgrims, and on their return trip they wore on their hats the badge of the shrine visited. The chief attractions for pilgrims in the Middle Ages were the Holy Land, Santiago de Compostela in Spain, and Rome, but there were hundreds of local pilgrimage sites, including the tomb of St. Francis of Assisi and that of St. Thomas Becket in Canterbury. More recent pilgrimage sites include the shrine of Our Lady of Guadalupe in Mexico (1531), Lourdes in France (1858), and Fátima in Portugal (1917). The tradition of pilgrimage is also important in Buddhism, with sites including Bodh Gaya, where the Buddha received enlightenment, and Varanasi, where he delivered his first sermon. In Islam all members of the faith are enjoined to perform the hajj, the pilgrimage to Mecca, at least once in their lifetime.

Pilgrims, First settlers of Plymouth (Massachusetts), the first permanent colony in New England (1620). The members of the English Separatist Church, a radical faction of Puritanism, composed a third of the 102 colonists who sailed aboard the *Mayflower* to North America, and they became the dominant group in the colony. The settlers were later collectively referred to as the Forefathers; the term Pilgrim Fathers was applied to them by Daniel Webster at the bicentennial celebration (1820).

Pillars of Heracles, Two promontories at the eastern end of the Strait of Gibraltar. They include the Rock of Gibraltar (at Gibraltar) in Europe and one of two peaks in northern Africa: Mount Hacho (held by Spain), near the Spanish exclave of Ceuta, or Jebel Moussa (Musa), in Morocco. The pillars are fabled to have been set there by Heracles (Hercules) as a memorial to his labour of seizing the cattle of the three-bodied giant Geryon.

pimiento, or PIMENTO, Any of various mild peppers of the genus *Capsicum* that have distinctive flavour but lack pungency, including the European paprikas. A common flavouring in Hungarian dishes, paprika is made by grinding dried peppers. The term *pimento* sometimes refers to allspice because early Spanish explorers of the West Indies and Central America mistook the highly aromatic berries of the tropical allspice tree for a type of pepper and called it *pimenta*.

pine, Any of 10 genera of coniferous trees (rarely shrubs) of the

Cluster of pollen-bearing male cones of Austrian (black) pine (Pinus nigra).
Grant Heilman Photography

family Pinaceae, native to northern temperate regions, especially about 90 species of ornamental and timber evergreen conifers of the genus *Pinus*. Needlelike leaves and cones are solitary or in bunches. Shallow root systems make pines susceptible to wind and surface disturbance. The family includes fir, Douglas fir, hemlock, spruce, larch, and cedar. Many species are sources of softwood timber, paper pulp, oils, and resins. Some are cultivated as ornamentals.

pineal gland, or PINEAL BODY, Endocrine gland in the brain that produces melatonin. It is large in children and begins to shrink at puberty. The gland may play a significant role in sexual maturation, circadian rhythm and sleep induction, and seasonal affective disorder and depression. In animals it is known to play a major role

Pineapple (Ananas comosus)
Courtesy of Dole Food Company, Inc.

in sexual development, hibernation, and seasonal breeding.

pineapple, Fruit-bearing plant (*Ananas comosus*) of the family Bromeliaceae, native to the New World tropics and subtropics but introduced elsewhere. Pineapple is served fresh where available and in canned form worldwide. It is a key ingredient in Polynesian cuisine. Like agave and some yuccas, the plant has a rosette of 30–40 stiff, succulent leaves on a thick, fleshy stem. A determinate inflorescence forms 15–20 months after planting. After fertilization, the many lavender flowers fuse and become fleshy to form the 2–4 lb (1–2 kg) fruit. Ripening takes 5–6 months.

Pioneer, First series of unmanned U.S. deep-space probes. Pioneers 0–4 were all intended to be lunar missions, but only Pioneer 4 succeeded in escaping Earth's gravity (1964). Pioneer 1 was the first spacecraft launched by NASA (1958). Pioneers 6–9 were successfully launched into solar orbits (1965–68) to study the solar wind, solar magnetic field, and cosmic rays. Pioneer 10, launched in 1972, was the first space probe to traverse the asteroid belt and the first to fly by Jupiter (1973), where it discovered Jupiter's huge magnetic tail. It then became the first man-made object to exit the solar system. Pioneer 11's data and photographs (1979) enabled scientists to identify two previously undiscovered moons and an additional ring around Saturn and radiation belts in its magnetosphere. Two Pioneer Venus spacecraft, the Orbiter and the Multiprobe (Pioneer 12 and 13, respectively), reached Venus in 1978. The Orbiter observed the planet's clouds and atmosphere and mapped its surface by radar; the Multiprobe released four instrument packages into the atmosphere at different locations.

pipa, or P'I-P'A, Short-necked Chinese lute. It has a pear-shaped body and a fretted fingerboard, and the silk strings are plucked with the fingernails. It is prominent in the opera orchestra and as an ensemble, solo, and accompanying instrument. The Japanese *biwa* is a similar instrument.

Piraeus, City (pop., 2001: 175,697), port of Athens, Greece. The port and its "long walls," fortified barriers connecting it with Athens, were completed in the mid-5th century BC. The walls were destroyed by Sparta at the end of the Peloponnesian War. Rebuilt under the Athenian leader Conon in 393 BC, Piraeus was burned in 86 BC by the Roman commander Lucius Cornelius Sulla. The city regained importance after AD 1834, when Athens became capital of the newly independent Greece. The largest port in Greece, it is the centre for all sea communication with the Greek islands.

Pirandello, Luigi (b. June 28, 1867, Agrigento, Sicily, Italy—d. Dec. 10, 1936, Rome), Italian playwright and novelist. He earned a doctorate in philology at the University of Bonn but turned to writing poetry, short stories, and several novels, including the successful *The Late Mattia Pascal* (1904). His first major play, *Right You Are (if You Think You Are)* (1917), explored the relativity of truth, a lifelong subject for Pirandello. *Six Characters in Search of an Author* (1921) contrasted art and life; it was followed by the tragedy *Henry IV* (1922). His other plays include *Each in His Own Way* (1924) and *Tonight We Improvise* (1930). He established the Teatro d'Arte in Rome and toured the world with his company (1925–27). Recognized as a major figure in 20th-century theatre, he was awarded the Nobel Prize for Literature in 1934.

Luigi Pirandello.
Courtesy of the Italian Institute, London

piranha, or CARIBE, Any of several species of deep-bodied, carnivorous fishes in the genus *Serrasalmus* (family Characidae), abundant in rivers of eastern and central South America and noted for voracity. The red-bellied piranha (*S. nattereri*) grows to 2 ft (60 cm) long, but most species are smaller. Some species are silvery with an orange belly and throat; others are almost completely black. All have sharp, saw-edged teeth that close in a scissorlike bite. Traveling in groups, they usually prey on other fishes, but red-bellied piranhas occasionally converge on larger animals. Though generally scavengers, they are attracted to the scent of blood and can quickly reduce even a large animal to a skeleton.

Pisces (Latin: "Fishes") In astronomy, the constellation lying between Aries and Aquarius; in astrology, the twelfth sign of the zodiac, governing approximately the period February 19–March 20. Its symbol is two fish tied together. These are a reference to the Greek myth of Aphrodite and Eros, who jumped into a river to escape the monster Typhon and were changed into fish. In another version of the myth, two fish carried them to safety.

pistachio, Any of nine species of aromatic trees and shrubs, some ornamental, that make up the genus *Pistacia* of the sumac (or cashew) family, native to Eurasia, with one species in southwestern North America and another in the Canary Islands. Commercial pistachio nuts are seeds from the fruit of *P. vera*. They have a pleasing, mild, resinous flavour and are used extensively as food and for yellowish green colouring in confections. The tree bears leaves with thick, wide, leathery, featherlike leaflets and small fruit in clusters.

pistol, Small firearm designed to be operated with one hand. The name may derive from the city of Pistoia, Italy, where handguns were made as early as the 15th century. It was originally a cavalry weapon. However, because the firepower of pistols must be kept low in order to reduce them to manageable weight, and because only skilled soldiers can shoot them accurately beyond 10 yards, they have never been satisfactory military weapons. In legal use, pistols are most frequently carried by police and other security personnel and serve mainly as a defensive weapon of last resort. Their compact size, low cost, and ease of operation make them a common weapon in violent crime, so that pistols are a common object of laws regulating the ownership of firearms. The two classes of pistol are revolvers and automatics. Automatics have a mechanism, actuated by the energy of recoil, that feeds cartridges from a magazine in the grip.

piston and cylinder, In mechanical engineering, a sliding cylinder with a closed head (the piston) that moves up and down (or back and forth) in a slightly larger cylindrical chamber (the cylinder) by or against pressure of a fluid, as in an engine or pump. The cylinder of a steam engine is closed by plates at both ends, with provision for the piston rod, which is rigidly attached to the piston, to pass through one of the end cover plates. The cylinder of an internal-combustion engine is closed at one end by a plate called the head and open at the other end to permit free oscillation of the connecting rod, which joins the piston to the crankshaft.

pit viper, Any species of viper (subfamily Crotalinae) that has, in addition to two movable fangs, a heat-sensitive pit organ between each eye and nostril which together help it accurately aim its strike at its warm-blooded prey. Pit vipers are found from deserts to rain forests, primarily in the New World. They may be terrestrial, arboreal, or aquatic. Some species lay eggs; others produce live young.

pitch, In music, position of a single sound in the complete range of sound; this quality varies with the number of vibrations per second (hertz, Hz) of the sounding body and is perceived as highness or lowness. A higher pitch has a higher number of vibrations. In Western music, standard pitches have long been used to facilitate tuning. A confusing variety of pitches prevailed until the 19th century, when the continual rise in pitch made some international agreement a matter of practical necessity. In 1939 the A above middle C was standardized as 440 Hz.

pitot tube, Instrument for measuring the velocity (speed) of a flowing fluid. Invented by Henri Pitot (1695–1771), it consists of a tube with a short, right-angled bend, which is placed vertically in a moving fluid with the mouth of the bent part directed upstream; the pressure, measured with an attached device, depends on the fluid flow and can be used to calculate the velocity. Pitot tubes are used to measure airspeed in wind tunnels and aboard aircraft in flight; they are also used to measure the flow of liquids.

Pitt, William, the Elder, later 1ST EARL OF CHATHAM (b. Nov. 15, 1708, London, Eng.—d. May 11, 1778, Hayes, Kent), British statesman and orator, twice virtual prime minister (1756–61, 1766–68). He entered Parliament in 1735 and provoked controversy with his maiden speech, which criticized the ministry of Robert Walpole. With the outbreak of the Seven Years' War, he was named secretary of state and became virtual prime minister. His leadership brought many British victories that greatly extended the British Empire. His wide popular appeal led to the nickname "the Great Commoner," though he was disliked by many in government for his high-handedness. He resigned in 1761 when the cabinet refused to declare war on Spain. Although ill with gout, he became a champion of liberty and spoke in favour of American colonial resistance to the Stamp Act. He formed another government in 1766, in which he served as lord privy seal, but he resigned in 1768 because of ill health. Widely mourned on his death in 1778, he was buried in Westminster Abbey.

Pittsburgh Platform, Manifesto of Reform Judaism, drawn up in 1885 by a conference of rabbis chaired by Isaac Mayer Wise in Pittsburgh, Pa. It declared that Judaism taught the highest conception of God, but it recognized the efforts of other religions to grasp the truth. The Bible was understood as the primary instrument of moral and religious instruction even though it reflected the primitive ideas of the time of its composition. It rejected the Mosaic and rabbinic laws regulating diet and dress, accepting only those laws that elevate the spirit. The Pittsburgh Platform looked forward to the messianic kingdom and accepted the immortality of the soul but not resurrection of the body. It advocated social justice and universal moral reform and maintained that Judaism was an evolving religion. It remained the official philosophy of the U.S. Reform movement until 1937, when the Columbus Platform moved Reform Judaism back to a more traditional position.

pituitary gland, or HYPOPHYSIS, Endocrine gland lying on the underside of the brain that plays a major role in regulating the endocrine system. The anterior pituitary lobe secretes six hormones that play specific roles in stimulating production of cortisol and androgens by the adrenal cortex (corticotropin), growth of eggs and sperm (follicle-stimulating hormone), production of progesterone and testosterone (luteinizing hormone), linear growth in children and bone maintenance in adults (growth hormone), milk production (prolactin), and production of thyroid hormone (thyrotropin). The posterior lobe stores and releases two hormones, oxytocin and vasopressin, from nerve cells in specialized regions of the hypothalamus that control pituitary function. These hormones stimulate uterine contraction and milk secretion (oxytocin) and blood pressure and fluid balance (vasopressin).

Pius IX, orig. GIOVANNI MARIA MASTAI-FERRETTI (b. May 13, 1792, Senigallia, Papal States—d. Feb. 7, 1878, Rome; beatified Sept. 3, 2000; feast day Feb. 7), Pope (1846–78). He became an archbishop in 1827, a cardinal in 1840, and pope on the death of Gregory XVI (1831–46). He set out to make liberal reforms, but the revolutionary fervour of 1848 frightened him into extreme conservatism. He proclaimed the dogma of the Immaculate Conception (1854) and convened the First Vatican Council (1869–70), which promulgated

Pius IX.
Felici/M. Grimoldi

the doctrine of papal infallibility. After losing temporal power to Victor Emmanuel II upon Italian unification, he regarded himself as a "prisoner in the Vatican" and refused any contact with the Italian government. Pius's pontificate was the longest in history. He was beatified in 2000 by Pope John Paul II (1978–2005).

placenta, Organ in most mammals that develops in the uterus along with a fetus to mediate metabolic exchange. The umbilical cord attaches it to the fetus at the navel. Nutrients and oxygen in the mother's blood pass across the placenta to the fetus, and metabolic wastes and carbon dioxide from the fetus cross in the other direction; the two blood supplies do not mix. Other substances (e.g., alcohol or drugs) in the mother's blood can also cross the placenta, with effects including congenital disorders and drug addiction in the newborn; some microorganisms can cross it to infect the fetus, but so do the mother's antibodies. The placenta, weighing a pound or more at the end of pregnancy, is expelled at parturition. Some animals eat it as a source of nutrients; in some species this stimulates lactation.

plague, Infectious fever caused by the bacterium *Yersinia pestis*, carried by the rat flea. It usually spreads to humans only when the flea runs out of rodent hosts. It takes three forms. Bubonic, the mildest, has characteristic swollen lymph nodes (buboes) and is spread only by the flea. It accounts for three-fourths of plague cases. Pneumonic plague has extensive lung involvement and is spread in droplets from the lungs; it is often fatal in three or four days without treatment. In septicemic plague, bacteria overwhelm the bloodstream and often cause death within 24 hours, before other symptoms have a chance to develop. In the 14th century, plague ravaged Europe and Asia and was called the Black Death. Plague does not respond to penicillin, but other antibiotics are effective. Sanitary measures against fleas and rodents, quarantine, and extreme caution in handling infectious materials help to suppress epidemics. A vaccine can prevent plague.

plain, Any relatively level area of the Earth's surface that exhibits gentle slopes and small local relief (differences in elevation). Occupying slightly more than one-third of the terrestrial surface, plains are found on all continents except Antarctica. Some are tree-covered, and others are grassy. Still others support scrub brush and bunch grass, and a few are nearly waterless deserts. With certain exceptions, plains have become the sites of major centres of population, industry, commerce, and transportation.

Planck, Max (Karl Ernst Ludwig) (b. April 23, 1858, Kiel, Schleswig—d. Oct. 4, 1947, Göttingen, W.Ger.), German physicist. He studied at the Universities of Munich and Kiel, then became professor of theoretical physics at the University of Berlin (1889–1928). His work on the second law of thermodynamics and blackbody radiation led him to formulate the revolutionary quantum theory of radiation, for which he received a Nobel Prize in 1918. He also discovered the quantum of action, now known as Planck's constant, h. He championed Albert Einstein's special theory of relativity, but he opposed the indeterministic, statistical worldview introduced by Niels Bohr, Max Born, and Werner Heisenberg after the advent of quantum mechanics. As the influential president of the Kaiser Wilhelm Society (later the Max Planck Society) until his resignation in 1937, he appealed to Adolf Hitler to reverse his devastating racial policies. His son was later implicated in the July Plot against Hitler and was executed.

planet, Any large natural body that orbits the Sun or another star and that is not radiating energy from internal nuclear fusion; dwarf planets, comets, asteroids, meteoroids, and natural satellites are excluded. The word *planet* comes from the Greek for "wanderer," because the planets' positions change relative to those of the stars. The eight (formerly nine) recognized planets that orbit the Sun are, in order of increasing distance, Mercury, Venus, Earth, Mars, Jupiter, Saturn, Uranus, and Neptune. The first four are called terrestrial planets and the next four giant, or Jovian, planets. The terrestrial planets (of which Earth is the largest) are rocky with comparatively thin or negligible atmospheres. The Sun's heat is thought to have prevented the abundant volatile substances in the solar nebula from condensing in them as they formed. The giant planets formed farther out, where the gases were cool enough to condense, so the planets grew very massive and accumulated huge atmospheres of light gases, mainly hydrogen and helium. None of the giant planets has an accessible surface; their gaseous atmospheres gradually merge with their liquid interiors. Pluto, although it was recognized as a planet for decades, is distinct from either group, being much smaller than any of the eight planets and resembling a giant comet nucleus. In 2006 the International Astronomical Union demoted Pluto to the category of dwarf planet, which reflected astronomers' conclusion that it is a very large member of the Kuiper belt. Additional bodies rivaling or exceeding Pluto in size (e.g., Eris) exist in the outer region of the solar system. The term *minor planet* is sometimes used to refer to any of the asteroids that lie mostly between the terrestrial and the giant planets. In astrology great importance is placed on the planets' positions in the 12 constellations of the zodiac.

planetarium, Institution devoted to popular education in astronomy and related fields, especially space science, whose main teaching tool is a hemispheric screen onto which images of celestial objects as seen from Earth are projected from an instrument also known as a planetarium, or planetarium projector. Major planetariums have extensive exhibit space, museum collections, sizable staffs, projection domes 80 ft (25 m) or more across, and seating capacities of over 600.

planetary nebula, Any of a class of bright nebulae that may somewhat resemble planets when viewed through a small telescope but are, in fact, expanding shells of luminous gas around dying stars. A planetary nebula is the outer envelope shed by a red giant star not massive enough to become a supernova. Instead, the star's intensely hot core becomes exposed and ionizes the surrounding shell of gas, which is expanding at tens of miles per second.

planetesimal, One of a class of bodies that are theorized to have formed the planets after condensing from diffuse matter early in the history of the solar system. According to the nebular hypothesis, part of an interstellar cloud of dust and gas underwent gravitational contraction to form a solar nebula comprising a disk of matter with a central hub. As the disk contracted further, clumps of matter left behind in its midplane coalesced successively into bodies the size of pebbles and boulders and then into planetesimals up to several hundred miles across. These then combined under the force of gravity to form protoplanets, precursors of most of the current planets.

Plantagenet, House of, or HOUSE OF ANJOU, Royal house of England (1154–1485) that provided 14 kings, including six from the cadet houses of Lancaster and York. The line descended from Geoffrey, count of Anjou (died 1151), and the empress Matilda, daughter of the English king Henry I. Some historians apply the name House of Anjou, or Angevin dynasty, to only Henry II, Richard I, and John, and label their successors, including Edward I, Edward II, and Edward III, as Plantagenets. The name may have originated as a nickname (Plante-geneste) for Count Geoffrey, who planted broom shrubs (Latin *Genista*) to improve his hunting covers. The Wars of the Roses saw the defeat of the last Plantagenet king, Richard III, in 1485. The legitimate line ended with Edward of Warwick (died 1499).

plantain, Tall plant (*Musa paradisiaca*) of the banana family that is closely related to the common banana (*M. sapientum*). Believed to have originated in Southeast Asia, the plantain grows 10–33 ft (3–10 m) tall and has a conical false "trunk" formed by the leaf sheaths of its spirally arranged, long, thin leaves. The green-coloured fruit is larger than that of the banana and contains more starch. Because the starch is maximal before the fruit ripens, the fruit is not eaten raw but is boiled or fried, often with coconut juice or sugar as flavouring. It may also be dried for later use in cooking or ground for use as meal, which can be further refined to a flour. The plantain is a staple food and beer-making crop for East African peoples and is also eaten in the Caribbean and Latin America.

plasma, Liquid part of blood (including dissolved chemicals but not the cells and platelets). This straw-coloured fluid serves as the blood's transport medium, helps maintain blood pressure, distributes body heat, and maintains the pH balance in the bloodstream and body. More than 90% consists of water, about 7% proteins, and the rest other substances, including waste products of metabolism. Important plasma proteins include albumin, coagulation factors, and globulins, including gamma globulin and a hormone that stimulates erythrocyte formation. Serum is the liquid part of the blood that remains after clotting.

plasma, Electrically conducting medium in which there are roughly equal numbers of positively and negatively charged particles, produced when the atoms in a gas become ionized. Plasma is sometimes called the fourth state of matter (the first three being solid, liquid, and gas). A plasma is unique in the way it interacts with itself, with electric and magnetic fields, and with its environment. It can be thought of as a collection of ions, electrons, neutral atoms and molecules, and photons in which some atoms are being ionized at the same time as electrons are recombining with other ions to form neutral particles, while photons are continuously being produced and absorbed. It is estimated that more than 99% of the matter in the universe exists in the plasma state.

plasmid, Genetic element not contained within a chromosome. It occurs in many bacterial strains. Plasmids are circular DNA molecules that replicate independently of the bacterial chromosome. They are not essential for the bacterium but may give it a selective advantage. Some plasmids determine the production of proteins that can kill other bacteria; others make bacteria resistant to antibiotics. Plasmids are extremely valuable tools in the fields of molecular biology and genetics, specifically in the area of genetic engineering.

plastic surgery, Surgery to correct disfigurement, restore function, or improve appearance. It may involve reshaping or moving tissues to fill a depression, cover a wound, or improve appearance. Cosmetic surgery solely to improve appearance is not the main focus of plastic surgery. It is utilized after disfigurement by burns or tumour removal or for reconstructive work, and it may involve hiding incisions in skin folds or using buried sutures to hold wounds closed. Reconstructive plastic surgery corrects severe functional impairments, fixes physical abnormalities, and compensates for tissue lost to trauma or surgery. Microsurgery and computerized diagnostic imaging techniques have revolutionized the field.

plastics, Polymers that can be molded or shaped, usually by heat and pressure. Most are lightweight, transparent, tough organic compounds that do not conduct electricity well. They fall into two classes: Thermoplastics (e.g., polyethylene, polystyrene) can be melted and formed again and again; thermosetting plastics, or thermosets (e.g., polyurethane, epoxy), once formed, are destroyed rather than melted by heating. Few plastics contain only the polymer resin; many also contain plasticizers (to change the melting point and make them softer), colorants, reinforcements, and fillers (to improve mechanical properties such as stiffness), and stabilizers and antioxidants (to protect against aging, light, or biological agents). Traditional plastics are not biodegradable; recycling of plastics, especially thermoplastics, has become an important industry, and the development of low-cost biodegradable plastics and plastic substitutes is a significant pursuit of industrial research. Major commercial uses of plastics include cars, buildings, packaging, textiles, paints, adhesives, pipes, electrical and electronic components, prostheses, toys, brushes, and furniture. Common plastics include polyethylene terephthalate, or PET (beverage bottles), PVC (pipes and hoses), foamed polystyrene, or Styrofoam (insulated food containers), and Lucite (shatterproof windows).

plate tectonics, Theory that the Earth's lithosphere (the crust and upper portion of the mantle) is divided into about 12 large plates and several small ones that float on and travel independently over the asthenosphere. The theory revolutionized the geological sciences in the 1960s by combining the earlier idea of continental drift and the new concept of seafloor spreading into a coherent whole. Each plate consists of rigid rock created by upwelling magma at oceanic ridges, where plates diverge. Where two plates converge, a subduction zone forms, in which one plate is forced under another and into the Earth's mantle. The majority of the earthquakes and volcanoes on the Earth's surface occur along the margins of tectonic plates. The interior of a plate moves as a rigid body, with only minor flexing, few earthquakes, and relatively little volcanic activity.

plateau, Extensive area of flat upland, usually bounded by an escarpment on all sides but sometimes enclosed by mountains. Plateaus are extensive, and together with enclosed basins they cover about 45% of the Earth's land surface. The essential criteria for a plateau are low relative relief and some altitude. Low relief distinguishes plateaus from mountains, although their origin may be similar. Plateaus, being high, often create their own local climate; the topography of plateaus and their surroundings often produce arid and semiarid conditions.

platelet, or THROMBOCYTE, Small, colourless, irregular blood cell crucial in coagulation. Produced in bone marrow and stored in the spleen, platelets accumulate to block a cut in a blood vessel and provide a surface for fibrin strands to adhere to, contract to pull the strands together, and take part in the conversion sequence of coagulation factors. They also store and transport several chemicals.

Plateresque, Main architectural style in Spain and its New World colonies in the late 15th and 16th centuries. The name (which comes from a comparison to the detailed work of silversmiths) came to be generally applied to late Gothic and early Renaissance Spanish architecture, which was characterized by minutely detailed relief ornament derived from Moorish, Gothic, and Italian Renaissance sources and applied without regard for structure. Favourite motifs for this ornament included twisted columns, heraldic escutcheons, and sinuous scrolls; clusters of ornament often contrasted with broad expanses of flat wall surface. Over time, the style evolved so that ornamentation became purer and more unified with the overall structure. Outstanding examples of the style include Diego de Siloé's Granada Cathedral (1528–43), Diego de Riaño's work on the Seville Cathedral (c. 1530), and Rodrigo Gil de Hontañón's facade of the University of Alcalá de Henares (1541–53).

platinum, Metallic chemical element, one of the transition elements, chemical symbol Pt, atomic number 78. A very heavy, silvery white precious metal, it is soft and ductile, with a high melting point (3,216 °F [1,769 °C]) and good resistance to corrosion and chemical attack. Small amounts of iridium are commonly added for a harder, stronger alloy that retains platinum's advantages. Platinum is found usually as alloys of 80–90% purity in placer deposits or more rarely combined with arsenic or sulfur. It is indispensable in high-temperature laboratory work for electrodes, dishes, and electrical contacts that resist chemical attack even when very hot. Platinum is used in dental alloys and surgical pins; alloys typically containing 90–95% platinum are used in expensive jewelry. The international primary standard for the kilogram is made of 90% platinum, 10% iridium. Platinum has va-

lence 2 or 4 in its compounds, which include many coordination complexes. It and some compounds are useful catalysts, particularly for hydrogenation and in catalytic converters for reducing automobile emissions.

Plato (b. 428/427, Athens, Greece—d. 348/347 BC, Athens), Greek philosopher, who with his teacher Socrates and his student Aristotle laid the philosophical foundations of Western culture. His family was highly distinguished; his father claimed descent from the last king of Athens, and his mother was related to Critias and Charmides, extremist leaders of the oligarchic terror of 404. Plato (whose acquired name refers to his broad forehead, and thus his range of knowledge) must have known Socrates from boyhood. After Socrates was put to death in 399, Plato fled Athens for Megara, then spent the next 12 years in travel. Upon his return, he founded the Academy, an institute of scientific and philosophical research, where Aristotle was one of his students. Building on but also departing from Socrates' thought, he developed a profound and wide-ranging philosophical system, subsequently known as Platonism. His thought has logical, epistemological, and metaphysical aspects, but much of its underlying motivation is ethical. It is presented in his many dialogues, in most of which Socrates plays a leading role.

Platonic solid, also known as REGULAR POLYHEDRON, Geometric solid all of whose faces are identical regular polygons and all of whose angles are equal. There are only five such polyhedrons. The cube is constructed from the square, the dodecahedron from the regular pentagon, and the tetrahedron, octahedron, and icosahedron (with 20 faces) from the equilateral triangle. They are known as the Platonic solids because of Plato's attempt to relate each to one of the five elements that he believed formed the world.

Platonism, Any philosophy that embodies some major idea of Plato's, especially in taking abstract forms as metaphysically more basic than material things. Though there was in antiquity a tradition about Plato's "unwritten doctrines," Platonism then and later was based primarily on a reading of the dialogues. It is characterized by an intense concern for the quality of human life—always ethical, often religious, and sometimes political, based on a belief in unchanging and eternal realities (the Platonic forms), independent of the changing things of the physical world perceived by the senses. This belief in absolute values rooted in an eternal world distinguishes Platonism from the philosophies of Plato's immediate predecessors and successors and from later philosophies inspired by them.

platypus, or DUCKBILL, Monotreme amphibious mammal (*Ornithorhynchus anatinus*) of lakes and streams in eastern Australia and Tasmania. About 23 in. (60 cm) long, the squat-bodied platypus has a ducklike snout, short legs, webbed feet, and a beaverlike tail. Each day it eats nearly its own weight in crustaceans, fishes, frogs, mollusks, tadpoles, and earthworms; lacking teeth, it crushes its food with ridges in the bill. The female lays one to three eggs in a nest in a long twisting passage above the waterline. The young are weaned about four months after hatching. The male's heel bears a spur connected to a poison-secreting gland. Large fishes and perhaps snakes prey on platypuses. Formerly trapped for their dense, soft fur, they are now protected by law.

player piano, Piano that mechanically plays music encoded as perforations on a paper roll. An early version, patented in 1897 by the American engineer E.S. Votey, was a cabinet placed in front of an ordinary piano, with wooden "fingers" projecting over the keyboard. A paper roll with perforations corresponding to the notes passed over a tracker bar to activate the release of air by pneumatic devices that set the fingers in motion; the user could control tempo and loudness by levers and pedals. Soon this mechanism was built into the piano itself. The later "reproducing piano" could reproduce the nuances of tempo and dynamics in great performances, the roll having been produced by the performance itself. After the

1920s the phonograph led to the instrument's quick decline. Modern versions, such as the Yamaha Disklavier, are operated by digital memory on a computer disk.

playing cards, Small rectangular cards used for playing games and sometimes for divination and conjuring. Modern cards are divided into four suits: spades, hearts, diamonds, and clubs. A complete pack, or deck, of cards includes 13 cards in each suit (10 numbered cards and 3 court cards—king, queen, and jack, or knave); 2 extra cards, called jokers (many times portraying a medieval jester), are often included as well. The origin of playing cards is obscure—China and India being the two most likely sources—as is the meaning of their symbols. The earliest reference to cards in Europe occurs in Italy in 1299. The 52-card French deck is now standard throughout the world, but decks with fewer cards evolved in Germany and Spain. Other suit emblems were also used (e.g., bells in Germany, cups in Spain and Italy).

plea bargaining, Negotiation of an agreement between the prosecution and the defense whereby the defendant pleads guilty to a lesser offense or (in the case of multiple offenses) to one or more of the offenses charged, in exchange for more lenient sentencing, recommendations, a specific sentence, or a dismissal of other charges. Supporters claim plea bargaining speeds court proceedings and guarantees a conviction; opponents believe it prevents justice from being served.

plebeian (Latin, *plebs*) Member of the general citizenry, as opposed to the patrician class, in the ancient Roman republic. Plebeians were originally excluded from the Senate and from all public offices except military tribune, and they were forbidden to marry patricians. Seeking to acquire equal rights, they carried on a campaign called Conflict of the Orders, developing a separate political organization and seceding in protest from the state at least five times. The campaign ceased when a plebeian dictator (appointed 287 BC) made measures passed in the plebeian assembly binding on the whole community.

plebiscite, Vote by the people of an entire country or district to decide an issue. Voters are asked to accept or reject a given proposal rather than choose between alternative proposals. By means of plebiscites, intermediaries such as political parties can be bypassed. Because plebiscites offer a way to claim a popular mandate without permitting an opposition party, totalitarian regimes have used them to legitimize their power.

Pleiades, Open cluster of stars in the constellation Taurus, about 400 light-years from Earth. It contains a large amount of bright nebulous material and several hundred stars, of which six or seven can be seen by the unaided eye and have figured prominently in the myths and literature of many cultures. In the Northern Hemisphere, the rising of the Pleiades near dawn in spring has from ancient times marked the opening, and their morning setting in autumn the end, of seafaring and farming seasons.

Pleistocene Epoch, Earlier and longer of the two epochs that constitute the Quaternary Period. The Pleistocene began c. 2.6 million years ago and ended c. 11,700 years ago. It was preceded by the Pliocene Epoch of the Neogene Period and followed by the Holocene Epoch. At the height of the Pleistocene glacial ages, more than 30% of the land area of the Earth was covered by glacial ice; during the interglacial stages, probably only about 10% was covered. The animals of the Pleistocene began to resemble those of today, and new groups of land mammals, including humans, appeared. At the end of the epoch, mass extinctions occurred: in North America more than 30 genera of large mammals became extinct within a span of roughly 2,000 years. Of the many causes that have been proposed for these extinctions, the two most likely are changing environment with changing climate and disruption of the ecological pattern by early humans.

Pliocene Epoch, Second epoch of the Neogene Period, from c. 5.3 million to c. 2.6 million years ago. It follows the Miocene Epoch, and it precedes the Pleistocene Epoch of the Quaternary Period. Pliocene environments were generally cooler and drier than those of the preceding Neogene and Paleogene epochs. In general, Pliocene mammals grew larger than those of earlier epochs. The more-advanced primates continued to evolve, and it is possible that the australopithecines, the first creatures that can be termed human, developed late in the Pliocene.

plumbing, System of pipes and fixtures installed in a building for the distribution of potable water and the removal of waterborne wastes. Plumbing is usually distinguished from water and sewage systems, which serve a group of buildings or a city. Improvement in plumbing systems was very slow, with virtually no progress made from the time of the Roman system of aqueducts and lead pipes until the 19th century. Eventually the development of separate, underground water and sewage systems eliminated open sewage ditches. Present-day water pipes are usually made of steel, copper, brass, plastic, or other nontoxic material. A building's waste-disposal system has two parts: the drainage system and the venting system. The drainage portion comprises pipes leading from various fixture drains to the central main, which is connected to the sewage system. The venting system consists of pipes leading from an air inlet (usually on the roof) to various points within the drainage system; by providing the circulation of air within the system, it protects the trap seals of fixtures from siphonage and back pressure.

pluralism, In political science, the view that in liberal democracies power is (or should be) dispersed among a variety of economic and ideological pressure groups and is not (or should not be) held by a single elite or group of elites. Pluralism assumes that diversity is beneficial to society and that the disparate functional or cultural groups of which society is composed—including religious groups, trade unions, professional organizations, and ethnic minorities—should be autonomous. Pluralism was stressed most vigorously during the early 20th century by a group of English writers that included Frederic W. Maitland and Harold J. Laski; it was defended in the later 20th century by the American scholars Robert Dahl and David B. Truman.

pluralism, In metaphysics, the doctrine opposed to monism. Whereas monists such as Parmenides, Benedict de Spinoza, and G.W.F. Hegel maintain that reality consists of only one ultimate substance, pluralists assert that reality consists of manifold entities of many different types and that the diversity of things is more striking and important than their unity. In *A Pluralistic Universe* (1909), William James held that it is characteristic of empirically minded thinkers to note the changeability of things, the multiplicity of their being and their relations with one another, and the unfinished character of the world.

Pluto, Solar system body, regarded as the ninth planet from the Sun until struck from the list of planets and reclassified as a dwarf planet in August 2006. It was discovered in 1930 by Clyde W. Tombaugh (1906–97) and named after the Greek god of the underworld. Its average distance from the Sun is about 3.7 billion mi (5.9 billion km)—it is located within the Kuiper belt—but its eccentric orbit brings it closer to the Sun than Neptune for 22 years during its 248-year orbit. Its axis is tipped 120°, so it rotates nearly on its side and "backward" once every 6.39 days, locked synchronously with the orbit of its largest moon, Charon, discovered in 1978. Pluto also has three other small moons. Pluto has a diameter of about 1,455 mi (2,340 km), less than 1% of Earth's mass, and only about 6% of Earth's surface gravity. Its estimated average surface temperature is near −390 °F (−235 °C). Its thin atmosphere contains nitrogen, methane, and perhaps other heavier gases. Pluto is thought to be made of frozen gases with a significant fraction of rocky material. Its size, composition, and orbital location in the Kuiper belt sparked a long debate over its classification as a major planet, which culminated in a decision by the International Astronomical Union to drop it from the planetary ranks.

plutonium, Radioactive metallic chemical element, chemical symbol Pu, atomic number 94. A member of the actinoid series of transition elements, it is the most important transuranium element because of its use in certain types of nuclear reactors and in nuclear weapons. It is found in nature only in traces produced by natural neutron irradiation in uranium ores. It is produced artificially by neutron irradiation of uranium-238. Plutonium is a silvery metal that tarnishes in air; it is warm because of energy released in alpha decay. Its isotopes, all radioactive, are highly toxic radiological poisons because they give off alpha particles and are specifically absorbed by bone marrow.

Plymouth, City (pop., 2001: 243,795) in Devon, southwestern England. Located on Plymouth Sound southwest of London, the city was named Sudstone in Domesday Book (1086); its harbour is called Sutton Harbour. It was the port from which the English fleet sailed against the Spanish Armada in 1588. In 1690 its dockyard was built on the western bank of the River Tamar. During World War II Plymouth suffered bomb damage from air raids. The rebuilt city has some of the finest commercial, shopping, and civic centres in Britain and new bridges over the Rivers Plym and Tamar.

***p-n* junction,** Electric contact in transistors and related devices between two different types of material called *p*-type and *n*-type semiconductors. These materials are pure semiconductor materials, such as silicon, to which impurities have been added. Materials of *p*-type contain "holes" (vacancies formerly occupied by electrons) that behave like positively charged particles, whereas *n*-type materials contain free electrons. Electric current flows more easily across a *p-n* junction in one direction than in the other. If the positive pole of a battery is connected to the *p*-side of the junction, and the negative pole to the *n*-side, charge flows across the junction. If the battery is connected in the opposite direction, very little charge can flow. The *p-n* junction forms the basis for computer chips, solar cells, and other electronic devices.

pneumatic device, Any of various tools and instruments that generate and use compressed air. Examples include rock drills, pavement breakers, riveters, forging presses, paint sprayers, blast cleaners, and atomizers. Compressed-air power is flexible, economical, and safe. In general, pneumatic systems have relatively few moving parts, contributing to high reliability and low maintenance costs.

pneumococcus, Spheroidal bacterium (*Streptococcus pneumoniae*) that causes human diseases including pneumonia, sinusitis, ear infection, and meningitis. Usually occurring in the upper respiratory tract, this gram-positive coccus is often found in a chain configuration and surrounded by a polysaccharide capsule. Pneumococci are separated into types depending on the specific capsular polysaccharide formed. Their disease-causing ability resides in the capsule, which delays or prevents their destruction by cells in the bloodstream that normally engulf foreign material.

pneumonia, Inflammation and solidification of lung tissue caused by infection, foreign particle inhalation, or irradiation but usually by bacteria. *Mycoplasma pneumoniae* is the most common cause in healthy individuals. The bronchi and alveoli may be inflamed. Coughing becomes severe and may bring up flecks of blood. It can be serious but is rarely fatal. *Streptococcus pneumoniae* is more common and generally more severe but usually affects only those with low resistance, especially in hospitals. A highly lethal form caused by *Klebsiella pneumoniae* is almost always confined to hospitalized patients with low immunity. Other bacterial pneumonias include *Pneumocystis carinii* pneumonia (rare except in AIDS) and Legionnaire disease. Most respond to

antibiotic treatment. Viruses set the stage for bacterial pneumonia by weakening the individual's immune system more often than they cause pneumonia directly. Fungal pneumonia usually occurs in hospitalized persons with low resistance, but contaminated dusts can cause it in healthy individuals. It can develop rapidly and may be fatal. X-ray treatment of structures in the chest may cause temporary lung inflammation.

Po River, ancient PADUS, River, northern Italy. The country's longest river, it is about 405 mi (652 km) long. It rises in the Cottian Alps on the western frontier and flows northeast to Turin, then east across Piedmont and Lombardy into the Adriatic Sea. Its delta is one of the most complex of any European river, with at least 14 mouths. It is navigable from its mouth to Pavia. Industrial cities in its valley include Milan, Padua, and Verona. It has suffered devastating autumn floods, including those in 589, 1438, 1951, and 1966.

Podgorica, formerly (1946–92) TITOGRAD, City (pop., 2003: 169,132), capital of Montenegro. As a feudal state capital in the early Middle Ages, it was known as Ribnica; it was called Podgorica from 1326. It fell to the Turks in 1474 but was restored to Montenegro in 1878. It was occupied in 1916 by Austria, in 1941 by Italy, and in 1943 by Germany. In 1946 it became Titograd in honour of Marshal Tito, but its former name was restored in 1992 after the collapse of communist rule. It is the site of a university (founded 1974).

podiatry, or CHIROPODY, Medical specialty dealing with the foot. Podiatrists diagnose and treat foot diseases, disabilities, and deformities by means of physical medicine and rehabilitation, special shoes and other mechanical devices, drugs, and minor surgery.

Poe, Edgar Allan (b. Jan. 19, 1809, Boston, Mass., U.S.—d. Oct. 7, 1849, Baltimore, Md.), U.S. poet, critic, and short-story writer. Poe was raised by foster parents in Richmond, Va., following his mother's death in 1811. He briefly attended the University of Virginia and then returned to Boston, where in 1827 he published a pamphlet of youthful, Byronic poems. By 1835 he was in Richmond as editor of the *Southern Literary Messenger*, the first of several periodicals he was to edit or write for. There he married a 13-year-old cousin, who died in 1847. At various times he lived in Baltimore, New York, and Philadelphia. Alcohol, the bane of his irregular and eccentric life, caused his death at age 40. His works are famous for his cultivation of mystery and the macabre and include "The Fall of the House of Usher," "The Masque of the Red Death," "The Black Cat," "The Tell-Tale Heart," and "The Pit and the Pendulum." "The Murders in the Rue Morgue" and "The Purloined Letter" initiated the modern detective story. His poems (less highly regarded now than formerly) are musical and sensuous, as in "The Bells," a showcase of sound effects; they include touching lyrics inspired by women (e.g., "Annabel Lee") and the uncanny (e.g., "The Raven").

poetry, Writing that formulates a concentrated imaginative awareness of experience in language chosen and arranged to create a specific emotional response through its meaning, sound, and rhythm. It may be distinguished from prose by its compression, frequent use of conventions of metre and rhyme, use of the line as a formal unit, heightened vocabulary, and freedom of syntax. Its emotional content is expressed through a variety of techniques, from direct description to symbolism, including the use of metaphor and simile.

pogrom (Russian: "devastation" or "riot"), Mob attack, condoned by authorities, against persons and property of a religious, racial, or national minority. The term is usually applied to attacks on Jews in Russia in the late 19th and early 20th centuries. After the assassination of Tsar Alexander II (1881), false rumours associating Jews with the murder aroused Russian mobs in more than 200 cities and towns to attack Jews and destroy their property.

Mob attacks diminished in the 1890s, but they again became common in 1903–06. Although the government did not organize pogroms, its anti-Semitic policy (1881–1917) and reluctance to stop the attacks led many anti-Semites to believe that their violence was legitimate. Pogroms also occurred in Poland and in Germany during Adolf Hitler's regime.

poinsettia, Popular flowering plant (*Euphorbia pulcherrima*), best-known member of the diverse spurge family. Native to Mexico and Central America, it grows in moist, wet, wooded ravines and on rocky hillsides. What appear to be flower petals are actually coloured leaflike bracts that surround a central cluster of tiny yellow flowers. Cultivated varieties are available with white, pink, mottled, and striped bracts, but the solid red varieties are in greatest demand during the Christmas season. Milky latex in the stems and leaves can be irritating to sensitized persons or animals, but the claim that poinsettias are deadly poisonous is greatly exaggerated.

*Poinsettia (*Euphorbia pulcherrima*).*
Grant Heilman/EB Inc.

Pointe-Noire, City (pop., 2005 est.: 663,400) and port, southwestern Republic of the Congo. It was the capital (1950–58) of the Middle Congo region of French Equatorial Africa. With independence in 1958, it was replaced by Brazzaville as the national capital, but it remained important for trade. Its port facilities were completed in 1939 and expanded during World War II. It is the country's second largest city and a principal port and commercial centre, especially for the oil industry.

pointillism, In painting, the practice of applying small strokes or dots of contrasting colour to a surface so that from a distance they blend together. The term (and its synonym, divisionism) was first used to describe the paintings of Georges Seurat.

poison, Any substance (natural or synthetic) that, at a certain dosage, damages living tissues and injures or kills. Poisons spontaneously produced by living organisms are often called toxins, venoms if produced by animals. Poisons may be ingested, inhaled, injected, or absorbed through the skin. They do not always have an all-or-none effect; degrees of poisoning may occur, and at a given dose some substances are far more toxic than others (e.g., a pinch of potassium cyanide can kill, whereas a single dose of ordinary table salt must be massive to kill). Poisoning may be acute (a single dose does significant damage) or chronic (repeated or continuous doses produce an eventual effect, as with chemical carcinogens). The effects produced by poisons may be local (hives, blisters, inflammation) or systemic (hemorrhage, convulsions, vomiting, diarrhea, clouding of the senses, paralysis, respiratory or cardiac arrest). Agricultural pesticides are often poisonous to humans. Some industrial chemicals can be very toxic or carcinogenic. Most therapeutic drugs and health-care products can be poisons if taken inappropriately or in excess. Most forms of radiation can be toxic.

poker, Any of several card games in which a player bets that the value of his or her hand is greater than that of the hands held by others. Each subsequent player must either equal or raise the bet or drop out. The pot is eventually won by either the player showing the best hand when it comes to a showdown or the only player left when everyone else has dropped out, or "folded." In this case the winner need not show his hand and could conceivably have won the pot with a lower hand than any other at the table. It is for this reason that poker is described as a game of bluff. Three principal forms of the game have developed: straight poker, in which all cards of the standard five-card hand are dealt facedown; stud poker, in which some but not all of a player's cards are dealt faceup; and community-card poker, in which some cards are exposed and used by all the players to form their best hand. In draw poker, the main variant of straight poker, cards may be discarded and additional cards drawn. The traditional ranking of hands is (1) straight flush (five cards of the same suit in sequence, the highest sequence—ace, king, queen, jack, ten—being called a royal flush), (2) four of a kind, (3) full house (three of a kind, plus a pair), (4) flush (five of a single suit), (5) straight (five in sequence), (6) three of a kind, (7) two pair, (8) one pair.

Pol Pot, orig. SALOTH SAR (b. May 19, 1925/28, Kompong Thom province, Cambodia—d. April 15, 1998, near Anlong Veng), Prime minister of Cambodia. He joined the anti-French resistance under Ho Chi Minh in the 1940s and became a member of the Cambodian Communist Party in 1946. After studying radio technology in Paris, he returned to Cambodia in 1953 and taught French until he fell under police suspicion in 1963. For the next 12 years he built up the Communist Party. U.S. anticommunist activity in Cambodia in the early 1970s, including helping to depose Norodom Sihanouk and a bombing campaign in the countryside, drove many to join him. In 1975 his Khmer Rouge forces captured Phnom Penh, which he ordered entirely evacuated. Even the sick were wheeled out in hospital beds, and in the first weeks it is estimated that tens of thousands died. The ruthlessness with which he pursued his intention to return to "year zero" and create an ethnically pure, agrarian, communist state resulted in the deaths of one to two million people. Overthrown by the Vietnamese in 1979, he led an anti-Vietnamese guerrilla war until he was repudiated by the Khmer Rouge and sentenced to life imprisonment (1997); he died the next year.

Poland, officially REPUBLIC OF POLAND, Country, central Europe. Area: 120,726 sq mi (312,679 sq km). Population: (2011 est.) 38,216,000. Capital: Warsaw. Most of the people are Polish; there are minorities of Ukrainians, Germans, and Belarusians. Language: Polish (official). Religion: Christianity (predominantly Roman Catholic; also Eastern Orthodox). Currency: zloty. Poland consists almost entirely of lowlands in the northern and central regions; the southern border is largely formed by the Sudeten and the Carpathian Mountains. The Vistula and Oder, the principal river systems, both drain into the Baltic Sea. Industries include mining, manufacturing, and public utilities. Poland is a unitary multiparty republic with two legislative houses; its head of state is the president, and its head of government is the prime minister. Established as a kingdom in 922 under Mieszko I, Poland was united with Lithuania in 1386 under the Jagiellon dynasty (1386–1572) to become the dominant power in east-central Europe, enjoying a prosperous golden age. In 1466 it wrested western and eastern Prussia from the Teutonic Order, and its lands eventually stretched to the Black Sea. Wars with Sweden and Russia beginning in the late 17th century led to the loss of considerable territory. In 1697 the electors of Saxony became kings of Poland, virtually ending Polish independence. In the late 18th century Poland was divided between Prussia, Russia, and Austria and ceased to exist. After 1815 the former Polish lands came under Russian domination, and from 1863 Poland was a Russian province, subjected to intensive Russification. After World War I an independent Poland was established by the Allies. The invasion of Poland in 1939 by the U.S.S.R. and Germany precipitated World War II, during which the Nazis sought to purge Poland's culture and its large Jewish population in the Holocaust. Reoccupied by Soviet forces in 1945, Poland was controlled by a Soviet-dominated government from 1947. In the 1980s the Solidarity labour movement led by Lech Wałęsa achieved major political reforms, and free elections were held in 1989. An economic austerity program instituted in 1990 sped the transition to a market economy. Poland became a member of NATO in 1999 and the European Union in 2004.

Poland, partitions of (1772, 1793, 1795) Territorial divisions of Poland by Russia, Prussia, and Austria that progressively reduced its territory until it ceased to exist as a state. In the First Partition (1772), a Poland weakened by civil war and Russian intervention agreed to a treaty signed by Russia, Prussia, and Austria that deprived it of half its population and almost one-third of its land area. In the Second Partition (1793), Poland was forced to cede additional lands to Prussia and Russia. To quell a nationalist uprising led by Tadeusz Kościuszko, Russia and Prussia invaded Poland and divided the remnants of the state among themselves and Austria in the Third Partition (1795). Only with the establishment of the Polish Republic in 1918 were the results of the partitions reversed.

polar bear, White semiaquatic bear (*Ursus maritimus*) found throughout Arctic regions, generally on drifting oceanic ice floes. A swift, wide-ranging traveler and a good swimmer, it stalks and captures its prey. It primarily eats seal but also fish, seaweed, grass, birds, and caribou. The male weighs 900–1,600 lbs (410–720 kg) and is about 5.3 ft (1.6 m) tall at the shoulder and 7–8 ft (2.2–2.5 m) long. It has a short tail. The hairy soles of its broad feet protect it from the cold and help it move across the ice. Though shy, it is dangerous when confronted.

Polaris, or NORTH STAR, Earth's present northern polestar (the star visible from the Northern Hemisphere toward which Earth's axis points), at the end of the "handle" of the Little Dipper in the constellation Ursa Minor. Polaris is actually a triple star, composed of a binary star and a Cepheid variable. Precession of Earth's axis made the star Thuban, in the constellation Draco, the North Star in ancient Egyptian times; it will cause the North Pole to point toward Vega, in the constellation Lyra, 12,000 years from now.

pole vault, Track-and-field event consisting of a vault for height over a crossbar with the aid of a long pole. It became a competitive sport in the mid-19th century and was included in the first modern Olympic Games. In competition, each vaulter is given three chances to clear a specific height. The bar is raised progressively until a winner emerges.

police, Body of agents organized to maintain civil order and public safety, enforce the law, and investigate crime. Characteristics common to most police forces include a quasi-military organization, a uniformed patrol and traffic-control force, plainclothes divisions for criminal investigations, and a set of enforcement priorities that reflects the community's way of life. Administration may be centralized at the national level downward, or decentralized, with local police forces largely autonomous. Recruits usually receive specialized training and take an exam. The modern metropolitan police force began with Sir Robert Peel in Britain *c.* 1829. Secret police are often separate, clandestine organizations established by national governments to maintain political and social orthodoxy, which typically operate with little or no restraint.

poliomyelitis, or POLIO, or INFANTILE PARALYSIS, Acute infectious viral disease that can cause flaccid paralysis of muscles. Severe epidemics killed or paralyzed many people, mostly children and young adults, until the 1960s, when Jonas Salk's injectable killed vaccine and Albert B. Sabin's oral attenuated live vaccine controlled polio in the developed world. Flulike symptoms with diarrhea may progress to back and limb pain, muscle tenderness, and stiff neck. Destruction of spinal cord motor cells causes paralysis, ranging from transient weakness to complete, permanent paralysis, in fewer than 20% of patients. Patients may lose the ability to use their limbs, to breathe, or to swallow and speak. They may need physical medicine and rehabilitation, mechanical breathing assistance, or tracheal suction to remove secretions. A "postpolio syndrome" occurs decades later in some cases, with weakness of muscles that had recovered.

polis, In ancient Greece, an independent city and its surrounding region under a unified government. A polis might originate from the natural divisions of mountains and sea and from local tribal and cult divisions. Usually the town was walled and contained a citadel on raised ground (acropolis) and a marketplace (agora). Government was centred in the town; usually there was an assembly of citizens, a council, and magistrates. Ideally, all citizens participated in the government and in the cults, as well as in defense and economy. Women, minors, metics, and slaves were not citizens. Hellenism spread many of the institutions into the Middle East.

Polisario Front, officially POPULAR FRONT FOR THE LIBERATION OF SAGUIA EL HAMRA AND RÍO DE ORO, Saharawi political and military group. Initially an insurgent against Spanish control of Western Sahara, it turned to agitation against Morocco and Mauritania when the Spanish withdrew in 1976 and those two countries partitioned the country. Mauritania made peace with the group in 1979, whereupon Morocco annexed the whole territory. The Polisario Front continued its resistance, mostly from bases in Algeria. In 1991 it agreed to a cease-fire and a referendum, which has been repeatedly postponed by Morocco, to determine the state's fate.

Polish Corridor, Strip of land that gave Poland access to the Baltic Sea. Transferred to the newly constituted state of Poland as part of the Treaty of Versailles (1919), the corridor, 20 to 70 mi (30 to 110 km) wide, separated eastern Prussia from the main part of Germany. The Germans resented the transfer, though the region had been historically Polish before the partitions of Poland and was inhabited by a Polish majority. When Poland refused to accede to Adolf Hitler's demands for extraterritorial highways across the corridor and cession of the free port city of Danzig (Gdańsk), Germany seized the pretext to invade Poland (1939), beginning World War II.

Polish Succession, War of the (1733–38) European conflict waged ostensibly to determine the successor to Augustus II. Austria and Russia supported his son Augustus III, while most Poles, France, and Spain supported Stanisław I, a former Polish king (1704–09) and father-in-law of France's Louis XV. Stanisław was elected king in 1733, but a Russian threat forced him to flee, and Augustus was elected in his place. France, with Sardinia and Spain, declared war on Austria (1733), seeking to reclaim territory in Italy held by Austria. An inconclusive campaign ended in the preliminary Peace of Vienna (1735), which redistributed the disputed Italian territory and recognized Augustus as king. A final treaty was signed in 1738.

Politburo, Supreme policy-making body of the Communist Party of the Soviet Union, the model for the politburos in other countries. The first Politburo, created in 1917 to provide leadership during the Bolshevik uprising, was dissolved when the coup was accomplished. The party congress of 1919 instructed the Central Committee to elect a new Politburo, which soon overshadowed the Central Committee in power. In 1952 it was replaced by a larger Presidium of the Central Committee; after Joseph Stalin's death, stress was placed on "collective leadership" to correct for his abuses. The name Politburo was revived in 1966. Its members included the general secretary of the Communist Party, the minister of defense, the head of the KGB, and the heads of the most important republics or urban party branches. It was dissolved with the breakup of the Soviet Union in 1991.

political economy, Academic discipline that explores the relationship between individuals and society and between markets and the state, using methods drawn from economics, political science, and sociology. The term is derived from the Greek terms *polis* (city or state) and *oikonomos* (one who manages a household). Political economy is thus concerned with how countries are managed, taking into account both political and economic factors. The field today encompasses several areas of inquiry, including the politics of economic relations, domestic political and economic issues, the comparative study of political and economic systems, and the study of international political economy.

political party, Group of persons organized to acquire and exercise political power. Formal political parties originated in their modern form in Europe and the U.S. in the 19th century. Whereas mass-based parties appeal for support to the whole electorate, cadre parties aim at attracting only an active elite; most parties have features of both types. All parties develop a political program that defines their ideology and sets out the agenda they would pursue should they win elective office or gain power through extra-parliamentary means. Most countries have single-party, two-party, or multiparty systems. In the U.S., party candidates are usually selected through primary elections at the state level.

political philosophy, Branch of philosophy that analyzes the state and related concepts such as political obligation, law, social justice, and constitution. The first major work of political philosophy in the Western tradition was Plato's *Republic*. Aristotle's *Politics* is a detailed empirical study of political institutions. The Roman tradition is best exemplified by Cicero and Polybius. St. Augustine's *City of God* began the tradition of Christian political thinking, which was developed by Thomas Aquinas. Niccolò Machiavelli studied the nature and limits of political power. Thomas Hobbes's *Leviathan* (1651) raised the problem of political obligation in its modern form. Hobbes was followed by John Locke, and Jean-Jacques Rousseau in the exposition of a social-contract theory. G.W.F. Hegel's understanding of historical development in terms of thesis, antithesis, and synthesis stimulated Karl Marx's dialectical materialism. John Stuart Mill developed Jeremy Bentham's utilitarian theory of law and political institutions, so as to reconcile them with individual liberty. In the 20th century John Dewey sought to counteract the dehumanizing aspects of modern capitalist society through a freer form of education. Until the end of the Cold War, the field of political philosophy was characterized by a division between Marxists and more traditional liberal thinkers, as well as by disagreements between left- and right-leaning liberals, such as John Rawls and Robert Nozick (1938–2002), respectively. From the 1970s, feminist political philosophy drew attention to the apparent gendered nature of many concepts and problems in Western political philosophy, especially autonomy, rights, liberty, and the public-private distinction.

political science, Academic discipline concerned with the empirical study of government and politics. Political scientists have investigated the nature of states, the functions performed by governments, voter behaviour, political parties, political culture, political economy, and public opinion, among other topics. Though it has roots in the political philosophies of Plato and Aristotle, political science in the modern sense did not begin until the 19th century, when many of the social sciences were established. Its empirical and generally scientific orientation is traceable to the work of Henri de Saint-Simon and Auguste Comte. The first institution dedicated to its study, the Free School of Political Science, was founded in Paris in 1871.

pollen, Mass of microscopic spores in a seed plant that appears usually as a fine dust. Each pollen grain is tiny, varies in shape and structure, is formed in the stamens in seed plants, and is transported by various means to the pistil, where fertilization occurs. The outer layer of a pollen grain is very resistant to disintegration; treatment with intense heat, strong acids, or strong bases has little effect on it. Because the grains often are very distinctive, some plant species may be identified by their pollen grains alone. Common components of both recent and ancient geologic sediments,

pollen grains have provided much information on the origin and geologic history of plant life on land. Pollen is produced in such quantities that it is a significant part of the airborne components of earth's atmosphere. The protein-containing substance in many pollen grains (e.g., ragweed and many grasses) causes the allergic reaction commonly known as hay fever.

pollination, Transfer of pollen grains in seed plants from the stamens, where they form, to the pistil. Pollination is required for fertilization and the production of seeds. On the surface of the pistil the pollen grains germinate and form pollen tubes that grow downward toward the ovules. During fertilization, a sperm cell in a pollen tube fuses with the egg cell of an ovule, giving rise to the plant embryo. The ovule then grows into a seed. Since the pollen-bearing parts of the stamens are rarely in direct contact with the pistil, plants commonly rely on external agents for pollen transport. Insects (especially bees) and wind are the most important pollinators; other agents include birds and a few mammals (notably certain bats). Water transport of pollen is rare. An egg may be fertilized by self-pollination (when the sperm comes from pollen produced by the same flower or by another flower on the same plant) or by cross-pollination (when the sperm comes from the pollen of a different plant).

Pollock, (Paul) Jackson (b. Jan. 28, 1912, Cody, Wyo., U.S.—d. Aug. 11, 1956, East Hampton, N.Y.), U.S. painter. He grew up in California and Arizona. In the early 1930s he studied in New York City under Thomas Hart Benton, and later he was employed on the WPA Federal Art Project. In 1945 he married the artist Lee Krasner. Two years later, after several years of semiabstract work stimulated by psychotherapy, Pollock began to lay his canvas on the floor and pour or drip paint onto it in stages. This process permitted him to record the force and scope of his gestures in trajectories of enamel or aluminum paint that "veiled" the figurative elements found in his earlier work. The results were huge areas covered with complex and dynamic linear patterns that fuse image and form and engulf the vision of the spectator in their scale and intricacy. Pollock believed that art derived from the unconscious and judged his work and that of others on its inherent authenticity of personal expression. He became known as a leading practitioner of Abstract Expressionism, particularly the form known as action painting. Championed by critic Clement Greenberg and others, he became a celebrity. When he died in a car crash at 44, he was one of the few American painters to be recognized during his lifetime and afterward as the peer of 20th-century European masters of modern art.

Jackson Pollock painting in his studio on Long Island, New York, 1950.
© Hans Namuth

polo, Game played by teams of players on horseback. Players use mallets with long flexible handles to drive a wooden ball through goalposts. It was first played in Persia in the 6th century BC; from there it spread to Arabia, Tibet (*polo* is Balti for "ball"), South Asia, and the Far East. The first British polo clubs were formed in India in the mid-19th century; the game came to the U.S. a few decades later. Polo has long been primarily played by the wealthy, because of the expense of acquiring and maintaining a stable of polo "ponies" (actually full-sized adult horses, bred for docility, speed, endurance, and intelligence). The standard team is made up of four players whose positions are numbered 1–4. A game consists of six 7.5-minute periods called chukkers or chukkas. The field is 300 yards (274.3 m) long by 160 yards (146.3 m) wide; an indoor version of the game is played on a smaller field.

Polo, Marco (b. *c.* 1254, Venice [Italy]—d. Jan. 8, 1324, Venice), Venetian merchant and traveler who journeyed from Europe to Asia (1271–95). Born into a Venetian merchant family, he joined his father and uncle on a journey to China, traveling along the Silk Road and reaching the court of Kublai Khan *c.* 1274. The Polos remained in China for about 17 years, and the Mongol emperor sent Marco on several fact-finding missions to distant lands. Marco may also have governed the city of Yangzhou (1282–87). The Polos returned to Venice in 1295, after sailing from eastern China to Persia and then journeying overland through Turkey. Captured by the Genoese soon after his return, Marco was imprisoned along with a writer, Rustichello, who helped him to write the tale of his travels. The book, *Il milione*, was an instant success, though most medieval readers considered it an extravagant romance rather than a true story.

Marco Polo, title page of the first printed edition of The Travels of Marco Polo, *1477.*
Courtesy of the Columbia University Libraries, New York

Polyakov, Valery Vladimirovich (b. April 27, 1942, Tula, Russia, U.S.S.R.), Russian cosmonaut. He studied medicine in Moscow and in 1971 worked at the Institute of Biomedical Problems, the U.S.S.R's leading space medicine institution. The next year, he was selected as a cosmonaut. He made two long-duration flights to the Mir space station (1988–89; 1994–95). The second was the longest continuous stay in space, 438 days, from Jan. 8, 1994, to March 22, 1995.

polyester, Organic compound, any of a class of polymers formed by ester linkages between monomers. They are usually prepared from equivalent amounts of glycols and dibasic carboxylic acids, which undergo condensation polymerization to produce the polyester and water. Polyesters are strong, colourfast, and resistant to corrosion and chemical attack but tend to build up a static electric charge. In addition to the familiar fibres and films (e.g., Dacron, Mylar), polyesters are used to make reinforced plastics, automotive parts, boat hulls, foams, laminates, tapes, piping, bottles, disposable filters, encapsulations, and coatings.

polyethylene (PE), Any of the polymers of ethylene, the largest class of plastics. Its simple basic structure, of ethylene monomers, can be linear (high-density and ultrahigh-molecular-weight polyethylene; HDPE and UHMWPE, respectively) or branched to a greater or lesser degree (low-density and linear low-density polyethylene; LDPE and LLDPE, respectively). The branched polyethylenes have similar structural characteristics (e.g., low crystalline content), properties (high flexibility), and uses (packaging film, plastic bags, mulch, insulation, squeeze bottles, toys, and housewares). HDPE has a dense, highly crystalline structure of high strength and moderate stiffness; uses include beverage bottles, liquid detergent jugs, crates, barrels, and luggage. UHMWPE is made with molecular weights 6–12 times that of HDPE; it can be spun and stretched into stiff, highly crystalline fibres with a tensile strength many times that of steel; uses include bulletproof vests.

polygamy, Marriage to more than one spouse at a time. Although the term may also refer to polyandry (marriage to more than one

man), it is often used as a synonym for polygyny (marriage to more than one woman), which appears to have once been common in most of the world and is still found widely in some cultures. Polygyny seems to offer the husband increased prestige, economic stability, and sexual companionship in cultures where pregnancy and lactation dictate abstinence, while offering the wives a shared labour burden and an institutionalized role where a surplus of unmarried women might otherwise exist. The polygynous family is often fraught with bickering and sexual jealousy; to preserve harmony, one wife may be accorded seniority, and each wife and her children may have separate living quarters. Polyandry is relatively rare; in parts of the Himalayas, where brothers may marry a single woman, the practice serves to limit the number of descendants and keep limited land within the household.

polymerization, Any process in which monomers combine chemically to produce a polymer. The monomer molecules—which in the polymer usually number from at least 100 to many thousands—may or may not all be the same. In nature, enzymes carry out polymerization under ordinary conditions to form proteins, nucleic acids, and carbohydrate polymers; in industry, the reaction is usually done with a catalyst, often under high pressure or heat. In addition polymerization, monomers are added successively to the reactive ends of a growing polymer molecule, similar to adding links to a chain; during the reactions, no by-products are formed. In condensation polymerization, growth of the polymer advances stepwise—monomers having reactive functional groups combine into larger molecules with their own functional groups; each reaction splits off a small molecule, often water, as a by-product.

polymorphism, Discontinuous genetic variation that results in the occurrence of several different forms or types of individuals among the members of a single species. The most obvious example of polymorphism is the separation of most higher organisms into male and female sexes. Another example is the different blood types in humans. A polymorphism that persists over many generations is usually maintained because no one form has an overall advantage or disadvantage over the others in terms of natural selection. Some polymorphisms have no visible manifestations. The castes that occur in social insects are a special form of polymorphism that results from differences in nutrition rather than from genetic variation.

Polynesia, Island group, scattered across a huge triangular area of the east-central Pacific Ocean. A subdivision of Oceania, Polynesia includes New Zealand, Hawaii, Samoa, the Line Islands, French Polynesia, the Cook Islands, the Phoenix Islands, Tuvalu, Tonga, Tokelau, Wallis and Futuna, Pitcairn Island, and Easter Island. Fiji is sometimes included because of its Polynesian population. The islands are mostly small coral atolls; some are of volcanic origin. Most of the inhabitants are Polynesians, some of whom might be related to the Malay. Their languages belong to a subfamily of the Austronesian languages. Contact with European culture began in the late 1700s with the arrival of Spanish explorers, which radically altered life in Polynesia. Colonizers, imposing Western belief systems and cultural ways, effectively wiped out local traditions and customs. Present-day Samoa and Tonga retain more of the traditional culture than the other islands.

polyoma virus, Minute infectious agent normally present in extremely small amounts in wild mice without causing obvious ill effects. It may induce cancerous tumours if grown in tissue culture and injected in large quantities into newborn mice or young hamsters, guinea pigs, and rabbits. It belongs to the Papovaviridae family of viruses.

polyp, Growth projecting from the wall of a cavity lined with a mucous membrane. Shape varies widely; it may have a stalk or many lobes. Polyps most often occur in the nose, urinary bladder, and digestive tract, especially in the rectum and colon. Symptoms, if any, depend on location and size; they may result from pressure or from blockage of a passage. Polyps occasionally bleed. Because a small percentage are precursors to cancers or actually contain cancers, it is advisable to have them removed and examined microscopically and to undergo routine colonoscopy after age 50.

polytheism, Belief in many gods. Though Judaism, Christianity, and Islam are monotheistic, most other religions throughout history have been polytheistic. The numerous gods may be dominated by a supreme god or by a small group of powerful gods. The gods originated as abstractions of the forces of nature such as the sky or the sea and of human and social functions such as love, war, marriage, or the arts. In many religions the sky god is powerful and all-knowing (e.g., Dievs), and the earth goddess is maternal and associated with fertility. Gods of death and the underworld (e.g., Osiris and Hel) are also important. In addition to many gods, polytheistic religions generally also include malevolent or benevolent spiritual forces or powers.

polyurethane, Any of a class of very versatile polymers that are made into flexible and rigid foams, fibres, elastomers (elastic polymers), surface coatings, and adhesives. They are produced by reacting a diisocyanate (a compound with two functional groups of the type —NCO) with a diol (a compound with two hydroxyl, or —OH, groups). Foamed polyurethanes, used for insulation and mattress and upholstery filler, are made with organic compounds containing carboxyl groups, causing a reaction that liberates carbon dioxide bubbles throughout the product. Spandex fibres are highly elastic and have replaced natural and synthetic rubber fibres for many textile purposes. Polyurethane elastomers are made into auto parts, rollers, flexible molds, medical equipment, and shoe soles. Polyurethane surface coatings are applied as sealants to wood, concrete, and machine parts and as linings for tanks and pipes; moisture-curing polyurethane resin is used as a general-purpose waterproof glue.

pomegranate, Fruit of *Punica granatum*, a bush or small tree of Asia, which with a little-known species from the island of Socotra constitutes the family Punicaceae. Native to Iran and long cultivated around the Mediterranean and in India, it also grows in the warmer parts of the New World. The orange-sized and obscurely six-sided fruit has smooth, leathery, brownish yellow to red skin. Several chambers contain many thin, transparent vesicles of reddish, juicy pulp, each containing an angular, elongated seed. The fruit is eaten fresh, and the juice is the source of the grenadine syrup used in flavourings and liqueurs. The plant grows 16–23 ft (5–7 m) tall and has elliptical, bright green leaves and handsome orange-red flowers. Throughout the Orient, the pomegranate has since earliest times occupied a position of importance alongside the grape and the fig. It is mentioned in the Bible, by the Prophet Muhammad, and in Greek mythology.

Pompeii, Ancient city, southern Italy, southeast of Naples. Founded in the 6th century BC (or earlier) by Oscan-speaking descendants of the Neolithic inhabitants of Campania, Pompeii came under Greek and Etruscan influence and then was occupied by the Samnites, an Italic tribe, in the late 5th century BC. The city was allied with Rome and colonized by 80 BC. It was damaged by an earthquake in AD 63 and was completely destroyed by the eruption of Mount Vesuvius in 79. Volcanic debris buried the town and protected the ruins for years. Archaeological excavations, begun in 1748, have uncovered much of the city, including forums, temples, baths, theatres, and hundreds of private homes.

Ponce de León, Juan (b. 1460, Tierra de Campos Palencia, Leon—d. 1521, Havana, Cuba), Spanish explorer. He may have accompanied Christopher Columbus's expedition in 1493 and later fought in the West Indies (1502), becoming governor of eastern Hispaniola. He colonized Puerto Rico (1508–09) and founded a settlement near modern San Juan. Rumours of a fountain of youth in the Bahamas inspired him to lead an expedition in 1513,

but he landed instead on the northern coast of Florida near modern St. Augustine. He sailed along Florida's southern and western coasts, then returned to Spain to secure the title of military governor (1514). He sailed again to colonize Florida in 1521 but was wounded in an Indian attack and died in Cuba.

Pontoppidan, Henrik (b. July 24, 1857, Fredericia, Den.—d. Aug. 21, 1943, Ordrup, near Copenhagen), Danish realist writer of novels and short stories. He studied engineering and worked as a teacher before taking up writing. His works, typically written in a cold, aloof, epic style, present a comprehensive picture of his country and his epoch. His earlier works are informed with a desire for social progress; his later ones despair of its realization. His major novels include the semiautobiographical *Lucky Peter* (1898–1904) and the five-volume cycle *The Realm of the Dead* (1912–16). He shared the 1917 Nobel Prize for Literature with Karl Gjellerup.

poodle, German water retriever. Poodles have a long muzzle, hanging ears, and docked tail. The dense, solid-coloured, wiry topcoat covers a woolly undercoat. Poodles' hair was traditionally clipped to permit them to swim efficiently when retrieving; today they are usually clipped in ornamental patterns. A dog with unclipped hair, which forms ropelike cords, is called a corded poodle. The standard poodle is more than 15 in. (38 cm) tall and weighs up to 70 lb (32 kg); the miniature stands 10–15 in. (25.5–38 cm); the toy is under 10 in. (25.5 cm) and weighs about 7 lb (3 kg). The poodle is the national dog of France, where it was once trained to scent and dig up truffles. Poodles are regarded as the most intelligent of all domestic dog breeds.

Standard poodle
Sally Anne Thompson/EB Inc.

pool, or POCKET BILLIARDS, Billiards game played on an oblong table having six pockets with 15 object balls and a white cue ball. At the beginning of play, the balls are arranged (racked) in a pyramid formation with its apex on a spot near the foot of the table. The first player breaks the formation by driving the cue ball into it; to continue play, he or she must hit a ball into a pocket. In the popular "8-ball" game, the first player (or team) to sink either the seven solid-coloured balls (numbered 1–7) or the seven banded (striped) balls (9–15), finishing with the black 8-ball, wins. In "9-ball," only the balls numbered 1–9 are used, and they must be sunk sequentially; the player who sinks the 9-ball wins. Pool probably reached its present form in England and France by *c.* 1800; today it is most popular in North America.

Pop art, Art in which commonplace objects (such as comic strips, soup cans, road signs, and hamburgers) were used as subject matter. The Pop art movement was largely a British and American cultural phenomenon of the late 1950s and '60s. Works by such Pop artists as the Americans Roy Lichtenstein, Andy Warhol, Claes Oldenburg, Tom Wesselman, James Rosenquist, and Robert Indiana and the Britons David Hockney and Peter Blake, among others, were characterized by their portrayal of any and all aspects of popular culture that had a powerful impact on contemporary life; their iconography—taken from television, comic books, movie magazines, and all forms of advertising—was presented emphatically and objectively and by means of the precise commercial techniques used by the media from which the iconography itself was borrowed. Some of the more striking forms that Pop art took were Lichtenstein's stylized reproductions of comic strips and Warhol's meticulously literal paintings and silk-screen prints of soup-can labels and Marilyn Monroe. Pop art represented an attempt to return to a more objective, universally acceptable form of art after the dominance in both the United States and Europe of the highly personal Abstract Expressionist movement. Its effects—including its decisive destruction of the boundary between "high" and "low" art—have continued to be powerfully felt throughout the visual arts to the present day.

pope, Ecclesiastical title of the bishop of Rome, head of the Roman Catholic church. In the early church, especially in the 3rd–5th century, it was a title of affectionate respect for any bishop. It is still used for the Eastern Orthodox patriarch of Alexandria and for Orthodox priests, but around the 9th century it came to be reserved in the West exclusively for the bishop of Rome. Catholic doctrine regards the pope as the successor of St. Peter the Apostle and accords him supreme jurisdiction over the church in matters of faith and morals, as well as in church discipline and government. Papal infallibility in matters of doctrine was asserted by the First Vatican Council in 1870.

Popular Front for the Liberation of Oman (PFLO), orig.

DHOFAR LIBERATION FRONT, Resistance group founded in 1963 by Arab nationalists and religious conservatives to depose Sultan Sa'īd ibn Taymūr (r. 1932–70). In 1968 its leadership was taken over by Marxists. In 1970 the sultan was deposed by his son, Qābūs ibn Sa'īd, who softened the resistance with a combination of military pressure and economic development.

popular music, Any music intended to be received and appreciated by ordinary people in a literate, technologically advanced society dominated by urban culture. Unlike traditional folk music, popular music is written by known individuals, usually professionals, and does not evolve through the process of oral transmission. Historically, popular music was any non-folk form that acquired mass popularity—from the songs of the medieval minstrels and troubadours to those elements of fine art music originally intended for a small, elite audience but that became widely popular. After the Industrial Revolution, true folk music began to disappear, and the popular music of the Victorian era and the early 20th century was that of the music hall and vaudeville, with its upper reaches dominated by waltz music and operettas. In the U.S., minstrel shows performed the compositions of songwriters such as Stephen Foster. In the 1890s Tin Pan Alley emerged as the first popular song-publishing industry, and over the next half century its lyricism was combined with European operetta in a new kind of play known as the musical. Beginning with ragtime in the 1890s, African Americans had begun combining complex African rhythms with European harmonic structures, a synthesis that would eventually create jazz. The music audience greatly expanded, partly because of technology. By 1930, phonograph records had replaced sheet music as the chief source of music in the home. The microphone enabled more intimate vocal techniques to be commercially adapted. The ability of radio broadcasting to reach rural communities aided the dissemination of new styles, notably country music. U.S. popular music achieved international dominance in the decades after World War II. By the 1950s, the migration of African Americans to cities in the North had resulted in the cross-fertilization of elements of blues with the uptempo rhythms of jazz to create rhythm and blues. Rock and roll, with figures such as Elvis Presley, soon developed as an amalgam of rhythm and blues with country music and other influences. In the 1960s, British rock groups, including the Beatles, became internationally influential. Rock quickly attracted the allegiance of Western teenagers, who replaced young adults as the chief audience for popular music. From the late 1960s black pop achieved greater sophistication and a wide audience. The history of pop through the 1990s was basically that of rock and its variants, including disco, heavy metal, punk rock, and rap, which spread throughout the world and became the standard musical idiom for young people in many countries.

Populations I and II, Two broad classes of stars and stellar groupings, whose members differ primarily in age, chemical composition, and location in galaxies. They were distinguished and named by Walter Baade (1893–1960). Population I consists of younger stars, clusters, and associations. These occur in and near the arms of the Milky Way Galaxy and other spiral galaxies and have been detected in irregular galaxies (such as the Magellanic Clouds). Population I objects are thought to have originated from interstellar gas that underwent various processes, including supernova explosions, which enriched their constituent matter with heavier elements. Population II consists of older (generally 1 billion–15 billion years old) stars and clusters, presumably formed from interstellar gas clouds that emerged very early in a galaxy's history. Consisting almost entirely of hydrogen and helium, they are found in the galactic halos of spiral galaxies, in globular clusters, and, in large numbers, in elliptical galaxies. Astronomers sometimes refer to a Population III as the very first generation of stars to emerge after the big bang.

populism, Political program or movement that champions the common person, usually by favourable contrast with an elite. Populism usually combines elements of the left and right, opposing large business and financial interests but also frequently being hostile to established socialist and labour parties. In the U.S. the term was applied to the program of the Populist movement of the 1890s.

porcelain, Vitrified pottery with a white, fine-grained body that is usually translucent. It was first made in China during the Tang dynasty (618–907) and in its advanced form during the Yuan dynasty (1279–1368). The three main types are true (or hard-paste) porcelain, artificial (or soft-paste) porcelain, and bone china. Attempts by medieval European potters to imitate true porcelain led to the discovery of soft-paste porcelain, which can be cut with a file. The secret of true porcelain was discovered c. 1707 in Saxony. Standard English bone china was produced c. 1800 when Josiah Spode II (1754–1827) added calcined bones to the hard-paste porcelain formula. Hard-paste porcelain, though strong, chips more readily than bone china.

porcupine, Heavy-bodied, solitary, slow-moving, nocturnal rodent with quills (modified hairs) along the back, tail, and, on certain crested species, the neck and shoulders. The quills are easily detached when touched. The New World species (four genera in family Erethizontidae) are arboreal and have barbed quills; the Old World species (four genera in family Hystricidae) are terrestrial and have unbarbed quills. The North American porcupine (*Erethizon dorsatum*), about 31 in. (80 cm) long with a tail about 12 in. (30 cm) long and quills about 3 in. (8 cm) long, drives its powerful tail against an assailant. For food, it favours the tender tissue beneath tree bark. Crested porcupines, the typical Old World porcupines, run backward, quills erect, into the enemy. They eat roots, fruit, and other vegetation. The African crested porcupine, the largest terrestrial rodent in Europe and Africa, may weigh 60 lb (27 kg) and have quills 14 in. (35 cm) long.

pornography, Depiction of erotic behaviour intended to cause sexual excitement. The word originally signified any work of art or literature depicting the life of prostitutes. Though pornography is clearly ancient in origin, its early history is obscure because it was customarily not thought worthy of transmission or preservation. Nevertheless, in the artwork of many historic societies, including ancient India, ancient Greece, and Rome, erotic imagery was commonplace and often appeared in religious contexts. *The Art of Love*, by Ovid, is a treatise on seduction and sensual arousal. The invention of printing led to the production of ambitious works of pornographic writing intended to entertain as well as to arouse. In 18th-century Europe, pornography became a vehicle for social and political protest through its depiction of the misdeeds of royalty and other aristocrats, as well as those of clerics, a traditional target. The development of photography and motion pictures in the 19th and 20th centuries contributed greatly to the proliferation of pornography, as did the advent of the Internet in the late 20th century. During the 20th century, restrictions on pornography were relaxed throughout much of Europe and North America, though regulations remained strict in Asia, the Middle East, and Africa. Child pornography is almost universally prohibited.

porpoise, Any toothed whale in the family Phocoenidae (or, by some authorities, part of the dolphin family Delphinidae). The four species (genus *Phocoena*) of the common, or harbour, porpoise are primarily fish eaters that travel in pairs or large groups. They are gray or black above and white below. The shy *P. phocoena,* found throughout the Northern Hemisphere, rarely leaps. The other species of *Phocoena* are found along Californian and South American coasts. The active, gregarious Dall porpoise (*Phocoenoides dalli*) of the North Pacific and the True porpoise (*P. truei*) of Japan often swim with ships, usually in groups of 2 to 20. Both eat cephalopods and fishes and are black with a large white patch on each side. The black finless porpoise (*Neomeris phocoenoides*), a small, slow animal, inhabits the Pacific and Indian oceans. At most 7 ft (2 m) long, porpoises are shorter and chubbier than dolphins and have a blunt snout. Like the dolphins, they are known for their high intelligence.

Port-au-Prince, City (metro. area pop., 1997: 1,556,000), seaport, and capital of Haiti, West Indies, on the southeastern shore of the Golfe de la Gonâve. Founded by the French in 1749, it was destroyed by earthquakes in 1751 and 1770 and has frequently suffered from fires and civil strife. In 1807 the port was opened to foreign commerce. It is the country's principal port and commercial centre, producing sugar, flour, cottonseed oil, and textiles.

Port Louis, City (pop., 2003 est.: 147,688), capital, and main port of Mauritius. It was founded *c.* 1736 by the French as a port for ships rounding the Cape of Good Hope to and from Asia and Europe. With the completion of the Suez Canal in 1869, the city's importance declined. It is the principal commercial centre of the island of Mauritius; its primary exports are textiles and sugar. Manufacturing and service industries, including tourism, are also based in the city. Aapravasi Ghat, an immigration depot used from 1849 to 1923 and designated a UNESCO World Heritage site in 2006, is located there.

Port Moresby, City (pop., 2000: 254,158), capital of Papua New Guinea, on the southeastern coast of the Gulf of Papua. Its large, sheltered harbour was explored by British Capt. John Moresby in 1873. The British annexed the area in 1883–84. The town became a main Allied base in World War II. The National Capital District, established in 1974, includes all of Port Moresby; it became the capital when Papua New Guinea became independent in 1975. A commercial centre, the city is also the site of a university.

Port of Spain, City (pop., 2000: 49,031), seaport, and capital of Trinidad and Tobago. Formerly the capital of the West Indies Federation, it is located in the northwestern part of the island of Trinidad on the Gulf of Paria. It is an air transport centre for the Caribbean and has a diversified economy, producing rum, beer, and lumber. It is also a principal port and shipping centre; exports include oil, sugar, citrus, and asphalt.

Port Said, Seaport city (pop., 2006: 570,603), northeastern Egypt. It is on the Mediterranean Sea at the northern end of the Suez Canal. It was founded in 1859 on a narrow sandy strip separating the Mediterranean from Lake Manzilah and became the world's most important coaling station. It was the landing point of French and British troops during the Suez Crisis (1956) that followed Egypt's nationalization of the Suez Canal. In the Six-Day War of 1967, Israeli forces occupied the eastern bank of the canal, which was closed until 1975. The city was revitalized after 1975, and its industries include textiles, clothing, cosmetics, and glass.

Porter, Cole (Albert) (b. June 9, 1891, Peru, Ind., U.S.—d. Oct. 15, 1964, Santa Monica, Calif.), U.S. composer and lyricist.

Porter was born to an affluent family and studied violin and piano as a child and composed an operetta at age 10. As a student at Yale University he composed about 300 songs, including "Bulldog"; he went on to study law and then music at Harvard. He made his Broadway debut with the musical comedy *See America First* (1916). In 1917 he went to France and became an itinerant playboy; though rather openly homosexual, he married a wealthy divorcée. He wrote songs for the Broadway success *Paris* (1928), and this led to a series of his own hit musicals, including *Anything Goes* (1934), *Red, Hot and Blue* (1934), *Kiss Me, Kate* (1948), *Can-Can* (1953), and *Silk Stockings* (1955). Porter also worked on a number of films, such as *High Society* (1956). His witty, sophisticated songs, for which he wrote both words and music, include "Night and Day," "I Get a Kick Out of You," "Begin the Beguine," and "I've Got You Under My Skin." Porter's large output might have been even more vast had not a riding accident in 1937 necessitated 30 operations and eventually the amputation of a leg.

Portland Vase, Roman vase (1st century AD) of dark-blue glass

decorated with white figures, the finest surviving Roman example of cameo glass. It came into the possession of the duke of Portland in the 18th century. The vase has been extensively copied, particularly in the Victorian period. The most accurate copies were made in jasperware with white figures in relief (by Josiah Wedgwood, 1790) and in glass (1876). In 1845, while in the British Museum (where it still resides), the original vase was smashed, necessitating painstaking restoration.

Portland Vase, Roman cameo glass, 1st century CE; in the British Museum.
Courtesy of the trustees of the British Museum

Porto-Novo, City (pop. 2004 est.: 234,300), seaport, and capital of Benin, on the Gulf of Guinea, western Africa. Situated on a coastal lagoon in the southeastern part of the country, it was probably founded in the late 16th century as the centre of the kingdom of Porto-Novo. The Portuguese established a trading post in the 17th century, and it became a centre of the Atlantic slave trade. It became a short-lived French protectorate in 1863 and attained that status again in 1882. The ruins of old African palaces remain, and there are many colonial-style buildings, including the old Portuguese cathedral. Porto-Novo was established as the official capital of the country by the constitution, but only the legislature is found there; the president, most government ministers, and the judiciary reside in Cotonou.

Portugal, officially PORTUGUESE REPUBLIC, Country, on the west coast of the Iberian Peninsula, southwestern Europe. Area: 35,558 sq mi (92,094 sq km). Population: (2011 est.) 10,555,000. Capital: Lisbon. Most of the people are Portuguese. Language: Portuguese (official). Religion: Christianity (predominantly Roman Catholic). Currency: euro. Administratively, the Atlantic islands of the Azores and Madeira are part of Portugal. Portugal is divided roughly in half by the Tagus River; the highlands rise mostly north of the Tagus and stretch northeast into Spain. Portugal has an industrialized economy in which both public and private sectors participate. Major industries were nationalized after a military coup in 1974, but many were returned to the private sector beginning in the late 1980s. Although motor vehicle manufacture is significant, light industries predominate; important products include textiles and clothing, paper and wood products, and chemicals. Portugal is a republic with a unicameral legislature; the head of state is the president, and the head of government is the prime minister. In the 1st millennium BCE, Celtic peoples settled the Iberian Peninsula. They were conquered *c.* 140 BCE by the Romans, who ruled until the 5th century CE, when the area was invaded by Germanic tribes. A Muslim invasion in 711 left only the northern part of Portugal in Christian hands. In 1179 it became the kingdom of Portugal and expanded as it reconquered the Muslim-held sectors. The boundaries of modern continental Portugal were completed under King Afonso III (reigned 1248–79). From 1580 to 1640 Portugal was united with Spain. In the 15th and 16th centuries the monarchy encouraged exploration that took Portuguese navigators to Africa, India, Indonesia, China, the Middle East, and South America. Although Portugal established several colonies, they achieved independence over the years. António de Oliveira Salazar ruled Portugal as a dictator from 1932 to 1968. The country's dictatorship was overthrown in the April 25, 1974, Revolution of the Carnations. A new constitution was adopted in 1976, and civilian rule resumed. Portugal was a charter member of NATO and is a member of the European Union (EU). In 1999 the government adopted the euro as the country's official monetary unit and returned Macau, its last overseas territory, to Chinese rule.

Portuguese man-of-war, Any of various floating, warm-water marine cnidarians (genus *Physalia*, class Hydrozoa) found worldwide but mostly in the Gulf Stream and the Indian and Pacific oceans. The medusa-form body consists of a translucent, jellylike, gas-filled float, which may be 3–12 in. (9–30 cm) long. Polyps beneath the float bear hanging tentacles up to 165 ft (50 m) long. Nematocysts on some polyps paralyze fish and other prey. Other polyps then attach to, spread over, and digest the victim. A third type of polyp is involved in reproduction. The painful sting of *Physalia* can cause fever, shock, or disruption of heart and lung function.

Poseidon, Greek god of water and the sea, son of Cronus and Rhea. His brothers were Zeus and Hades. When the three brothers deposed their father, the kingdom of the sea fell by lot to Poseidon. Unpredictable and sometimes violent, he was also god of earthquakes, and he was closely associated with horses. Most of his offspring were giants and savage creatures. By Medusa he was the father of the winged horse Pegasus. The Isthmian Games were held in his honor. In art he was often shown holding a trident and accompanied by a dolphin and tuna. The Romans identified him with Neptune.

Poseidon, marble statue from Melos, 2nd century BCE; in the National Archaeological Museum, Athens.
Alinari/Art Resource, New York

positivism, Any philosophical system that confines itself to the data of experience, excludes a priori or metaphysical speculations, and emphasizes the achievements of science. Positivism is closely connected with empiricism, pragmatism, and logical positivism. More narrowly, the term designates the philosophy of Auguste Comte, who held that human thought had passed inevitably through a theological stage into a metaphysical stage and was passing into a positive, or scientific, stage. Believing that the religious impulse would survive the decay of revealed religion, he projected a worship of mankind, with churches, calendar, and hierarchy.

positron emission tomography (PET), Imaging technique used in diagnosis and biomedical research. A chemical compound labeled with a radioactive isotope that emits positrons is injected into the body, and detectors measure their activity in the tissues as they combine with electrons and are annihilated. Computers analyze, integrate, and reconstruct the data to produce images of the organs scanned. PET is particularly useful for studying brain and heart functions.

Post-Impressionism, Movement in Western painting that represented both an extension of Impressionism and a rejection of its limitations. The term was coined by Roger Fry for the works of Paul Cézanne, Georges Seurat, Vincent van Gogh, Paul Gauguin, Henri de Toulouse-Lautrec, and others. Most of these painters first pursued Impressionism, a style based, in its strictest sense, on the objective recording of nature in terms of the fugitive effects of colour and light. The Post-Impressionists rejected this aim in favour of more ambitious expression, admitting their debt, however, to the pure, brilliant colours of Impressionism, its freedom from traditional subject matter, and its technique of defining form with short brushstrokes of broken colour. Each painter in the movement pursued unique, personal subject matter and, while sharing stylistic goals with the other Post-Impressionists, had a personal form of expression. For example, Cézanne abandoned the Impressionists' virtuoso depiction of evanescent light effects in order to pursue his preoccupation with the underlying structures of natural forms and the problem of unifying surface patterns with spatial depth. Both Gauguin and van Gogh rejected the indifferent objectivity of Impressionism in favour of a more personal, spiritual expression. The Post-Impressionists often exhibited together but, unlike the Impressionists, who were a close-knit and convivial group, they painted mainly alone. In general, Post-Impressionism led away from a naturalistic approach and toward the two major movements of early 20th-century art that followed it: Cubism and Fauvism.

post-traumatic stress disorder (PTSD), Psychological reaction occurring after a highly stressful event and typically characterized by flashbacks, recurrent nightmares, and avoidance of reminders of the event; depression and anxiety are often present. Traumatic events that can lead to PTSD include automobile accidents, rape or assault, military combat, torture, and such natural disasters as floods, fires, or earthquakes. Long-term effects can include marital and family problems, difficulties at work, and abuse of alcohol and other drugs. Antidepressant medication and psychotherapy, including group therapy, are used in treating the disorder.

postal system, System that allows persons to send letters, parcels, or packages to addressees in the same country or abroad. Postal systems are usually government-run and paid for by a combination of user charges and government subsidies. There are early references to postal services in Egypt *c.* 2000 BC and in Zhou-dynasty China *c.* 1000 BC. The Roman Empire developed various centralized methods of relaying messages. In the Middle Ages there were no centralized postal services. Private postal systems developed with the rise of nation-states during the Renaissance; subsequently, postal services became government monopolies. Charges based on weight rather than distance and the use of prepaid stamps were first proposed in 1837. The General Postal Union (1875; later Universal Postal Union) improved international mail delivery by allowing member countries to retain the postage they collected on outgoing international mail and requiring them to treat incoming international mail as they did domestic mail. Airmail and automated mail handling were developed in the 20th century.

postmodernism, Any of several artistic movements since about the 1960s that have challenged the philosophy and practices of modern arts or literature. In literature this has amounted to a reaction against an ordered view of the world and therefore against fixed ideas about the form and meaning of texts. In its reaction against Modernist ideals such as autotelic art and the original masterpiece, postmodern writing and art emphasize devices such as pastiche and parody and the stylized technique of the antinovel and magic realism. Postmodernism has also led to a proliferation of critical theories, most notably deconstruction and its offshoots, and the breaking down of the distinction between "high" and "low" culture.

poststructuralism, Movement in literary criticism and philosophy begun in France in the late 1960s. Drawing upon the linguistic theories of Ferdinand de Saussure, the anthropology of Claude Lévi-Strauss, and the deconstructionist theories of Jacques Derrida, it held that language is not a transparent medium that connects one directly with a "truth" or "reality" outside it but rather a structure or code, whose parts derive their meaning from their contrast with one another and not from any connection with an outside world. Writers associated with the movement include Roland Barthes, Jacques Lacan, Julia Kristeva, and Michel Foucault.

Potala Palace, Religious and administrative complex, near Lhasa, Tibet, China. It covers 5 sq mi (13 sq km) atop a hill 425 ft (130 m) above the Lhasa River valley. Potrang Karpo (the White Palace, completed 1648) once served as the seat of the Tibetan government and the main residence of the Dalai Lama; from the mid-18th century it was used as a winter palace. Potrang Marpo (the Red Palace, 1694) houses several chapels, sacred statues, and the tombs of eight Dalai Lamas; it remains a major pilgrimage site for Tibetan Buddhists. The complex, which has a total of 1,000 rooms, was declared a world heritage site in 1994.

potassium, Chemical element, one of the alkali metals, chemical symbol K, atomic number 19. It is a soft, silvery white metal, not found free in nature and rarely used as the metal (except as a chemical reagent) because of its extreme reactivity. Potassium is essential for life and is present in all soils. Potassium ions (K^+) and sodium ions act at cell membranes in electrochemical impulse transmission and in transport. Potassium in compounds has valence 1. The chloride is used as a fertilizer and a raw material for producing other compounds, and the hydroxide for making liquid soaps and detergents and in preparing various salts. The iodide is added to table salt to protect against iodine deficiency. The nitrate is also called saltpetre, and the carbonate is called potash.

Potsdam Conference (July 17–Aug. 2, 1945) Allied conference held in the Berlin suburb of Potsdam after Germany's surrender in World War II. Harry Truman, Joseph Stalin, and Winston Churchill (later replaced by Clement R. Attlee) met to discuss European peace settlements, the administration of defeated Germany, the demarcation of the boundaries of Poland, the occupation of Austria, the definition of the Soviet Union's role in eastern Europe, the determination of reparations, and the further prosecution of the war against Japan. The four occupation zones of Germany conceived at the Yalta Conference were set up, each to be administered by the commander-in-chief of the Soviet, British, U.S., or French army of occupation. Poland's boundary became the Oder and Neisse rivers in the west, and the country received part of former East Prussia. Stalin refused to let the Western powers interfere with his control of eastern Europe.

Potter, (Helen) Beatrix (b. July 28, 1866, South Kensington, Middlesex, Eng.—d. Dec. 22, 1943, Sawrey, Lancashire), English author and illustrator of children's books. In her childhood Potter spent holidays in Scotland and the English Lake District, which inspired her love of animals and stimulated her imaginative and technically superb watercolour drawings. The illustrated animal stories she sent to a sick child when she was 27 were published as *The Tale of Peter Rabbit* (1902), which became one of the best-selling children's books of all time. More than 20 sequels followed, featuring such original characters as Jeremy Fisher, Squirrel Nutkin, Jemima Puddle-Duck, and Mrs. Tiggy-Winkle.

pottery, One of the oldest and most widespread of the decorative arts, consisting chiefly of functional objects (such as vessels, plates, and bowls) made of clay and hardened with heat. Earthenware is the oldest and simplest form; stoneware is fired at a high temperature to cause it to vitrify and harden; and porcelain is a fine, generally translucent form of pottery. The Chinese began their sophisticated production of pottery in the Neolithic Period and produced porcelain as early as the 7th century CE. Chinese porcelain, or "china," was widely exported to Europe and had a profound influence on European manufacturers and on taste. Classical Greek and Islamic cultures are also known for their artistic and technical innovations in pottery.

power, In science and engineering, the time rate of doing work or delivering energy. Power (P) can be expressed as the amount of work done (W), or energy transferred, divided by the time interval (t): $P = W/t$. A given amount of work can be done by a low-powered motor in a long time or by a high-powered motor in a short time. Units of power are those of work (or energy) per unit time, such as foot-pounds per minute, joules per second (called watts), or ergs per second. Power can also be expressed as the product of the force (F) applied to move an object and the speed (v) of the object in the direction of the force: $P = Fv$.

poxvirus, Any of a group of viruses responsible for a wide range of pox diseases in humans and other animals. Poxvirus was the cause of smallpox. (Human chickenpox is caused by varicella-zoster virus.) The virus particle is somewhat brick-shaped, and its surface is studded with hollow spikes. It contains DNA. Unlike other DNA viruses, poxviruses appear to develop entirely within the cytoplasm of affected cells. The virus of rabbitpox has been used with mixed success in Australia to control the wild rabbit population.

Poznań, German POSEN, City (pop., 2000 est.: 574,896), west-central Poland. Located on the Warta River, Poznań is one of the oldest cities in Poland, dating from the 9th century AD. It reached the height of prosperity as a trade centre from the 15th to the 17th century but declined after the Second Northern War. In 1793 Poznań was annexed to Prussia, intensifying a Germanization that had begun in the 13th century. In 1918 it reverted to Poland. During World War II it was occupied by the Germans and suffered extensive damage. Rebuilt after the war, it has become the administrative, industrial, and cultural centre of western Poland. It is also an academic centre with scientific and literary institutes. Its varied industries include textile mills, metallurgical works, and chemical plants.

Prado Museum, Spain's national art museum, housing the world's greatest collection of Spanish painting as well as other European works. Founded in Madrid in 1818 by Ferdinand VII, it was opened to the public in 1819 as the Royal Museum of Painting. Its holdings were formed over three centuries from the various royal collections of the Habsburg and Bourbon monarchs in Spain. In 1868 it became the National Museum of the Prado after the exile of Isabella II. In 1872 it acquired many notable paintings formerly owned by Spanish convents and monasteries. It owns the outstanding collections of the works of El Greco, Diego Velázquez, and Francisco de Goya and numerous works by other Spanish masters such as José de Ribera and Francisco Zurbarán. Among its other holdings are collections of Greco-Roman statuary and many Flemish and Italian masterpieces.

pragmatics, In linguistics and philosophy, the study of the use of natural language in communication; more generally, the study of the relations between languages and their users. It is sometimes defined in contrast with linguistic semantics, which can be described as the study of the rule systems that determine the literal meanings of linguistic expressions. Pragmatics is then the study of how both literal and nonliteral aspects of communicated linguistic meaning are determined by principles that refer to the physical or social context (broadly construed) in which language is used. Among these aspects are conversational and conventional "implicatures" (e.g., "John has three sons" conversationally implicates that John has no more than three sons; "He was poor but honest" conventionally implicates an unspecified contrast between poverty and honesty). Other aspects include metaphor and other tropes and speech acts.

pragmatism, Philosophical movement first given systematic expression by Charles Sanders Peirce and William James and later taken up and transformed by John Dewey. Pragmatists emphasize the practical function of knowledge as an instrument for adapting to reality and controlling it. Pragmatism agrees with empiricism in its emphasis on the priority of experience over a priori reasoning. Whereas truth had traditionally been explained in terms of correspondence with reality or in terms of coherence, pragmatism holds that truth is to be found in the process of verification. Pragmatists interpret ideas as instruments and plans of action rather than as images of reality; more specifically, they are suggestions and anticipations of possible conduct, hypotheses or forecasts of what will result from a given action, or ways of organizing behaviour.

Prague, City (pop., 2001 est.: 1,178,576), capital of the Czech Republic. Situated on both sides of the Vltava River, the site was settled as early as the 9th century CE. By the 14th century it was one of Europe's leading cultural and trade centres. It was the focal point of opposition to the Habsburgs in the early 17th century. The treaty ending the Austro-Prussian War was signed there in 1866. It became the capital of an independent Czechoslovakia in 1918. Prague was occupied by Germany during World War II and by the U.S.S.R. and other Warsaw Pact military forces in 1968. In 1989 it was the centre of a movement that led to the peaceful overthrow of the communist government. Prague is the country's major economic and cultural centre, famous for its music, literature, and architecture.

Prague Spring (1968) Brief period of liberalization in Czechoslovakia under Alexander Dubček. In April 1968 he instituted agricultural and industrial reforms, a revised constitution to guarantee civil rights, autonomy for Slovakia, and democratization of the government and the Communist Party. By June, many Czechs were calling for more rapid progress toward real democracy. Although Dubček believed he could control the situation, the Soviet Union and the Warsaw Pact countries, alarmed by the threat of a social-democratic Czechoslovakia, invaded the country in August, deposed Dubček, and gradually restored control by reinstalling hard-line communists as leaders.

Praia, City (pop., 2000: 94,757), port, and capital of Cape Verde. It is located on the southern shore of São Tiago (Santiago) Island, in the Atlantic Ocean, about 400 mi (640 km) off the western African bulge. It ships agricultural products, including bananas, coffee, and sugarcane, and it is a submarine cable station.

prairie, Level or rolling grassland, especially that found in central North America. Decreasing amounts of rainfall, from 40 in. (100 cm) at the forested eastern edge to less than 12 in. (30 cm) at the desertlike western edge, affect the species composition of the prairie grassland. The vegetation is composed primarily of perennial grasses, with many species of flowering plants of the pea and composite families. The three main types of prairie are the tallgrass prairie; midgrass, or mixed-grass, prairie; and shortgrass prairie, or shortgrass plains. Coastal prairie, Pacific or California prairie, Palouse prairie, and desert plains grassland are covered primarily with combinations of mixed-grass and shortgrass species.

Prairie school, Group of architects, including Frank Lloyd Wright, who created low-lying "prairie houses" in the U.S. Midwest *c.* 1900–17. Prairie houses were generally built of brick, wood, and plaster, with stucco walls and bands of casement windows. The Prairie architects emphasized horizontal lines by using

low roofs with wide, projecting eaves. They discarded elaborate floor plans and detailing for flowing internal spaces organized around a central fireplace or hearth. The resulting low, spreading structures are characterized by light, crossing volumes and spaces; they reach out to nature, not to other buildings. Other architects working in the style included George Grant Elmslie (1871–1952) and Barry Byrne (1883–1967).

Prajapati, Creator figure in the Vedic period of India. In early Vedic literature, the name was applied to various primal figures. Later it signified one deity, the "lord of all creatures," who was said to have produced the universe and all its beings after preparing himself through ascetic practices. Other stories allude to his own creation from the primal waters. His female emanation was Vac, the personification of the sacred word; Usas, the dawn, was identified as his female partner or his daughter. In the post-Vedic age, Prajapati came to be identified with Brahma.

Prajnaparamita, Body of sutras and their commentaries in Mahayana Buddhism. The main texts, written 100 BCE–150 CE, represent *prajna* (wisdom) as the supreme perfection and the primary avenue to nirvana. The content of this wisdom is the realization that all phenomena are illusory. The name Prajnaparamita also refers to the personification of the literature or of wisdom, often depicted as a woman with her hands in the teaching gesture or holding a lotus and sacred book.

Prajnaparamita, 13th-century stone sculpture from Singosari, East Java; in the Museum Pusat, Jakarta, Indonesia

Courtesy of the Rijksmuseum voor Volkenkunde, Leiden, Neth.

prayer, Silent or spoken petition made to God or a god. Prayer has been practiced in all religions throughout history. Its characteristic postures (bowing the head, kneeling, prostration) and position of the hands (raised, outstretched, clasped) signify an attitude of submission and devotion. Prayer may involve confessions of sin, requests, thanks, praise, offerings of sacrifice, or promises of future acts of devotion. In addition to spontaneous private prayer, most religions have fixed formulas of prayer (e.g., the Lord's Prayer), often recited in group worship. The four prophetic religions (Judaism, Christianity, Islam, and Zoroastrianism) prescribe a daily set form of individual prayer, such as the Shema, to be recited twice a day by every male Jew, and the Islamic salat, performed five times a day.

prayer wheel, In Tibetan Buddhism, a mechanical device used as an equivalent to the recitation of a mantra. The prayer wheel consists of a hollow metal cylinder, often beautifully embossed, mounted on a rod and containing a consecrated paper bearing a mantra. Each turn of the wheel by hand is considered equivalent to orally reciting the prayer. Variants to the handheld prayer wheel are large cylinders that can be set in motion by hand or attached to windmills or waterwheels and thus kept in continuous motion.

Pre-Raphaelites, Group of young British painters, led by Dante Gabriel Rossetti, William Holman Hunt, and John Everett Millais, who banded together in 1848 in reaction against what they considered the unimaginative and artificial historical painting of the 18th and early 19th centuries, seeking to express a new moral seriousness and sincerity in their works. Their name, the Pre-Raphaelite Brotherhood, honoured the simple depiction of nature in Italian art before Raphael; the symbolism, imagery, and mannered style of their paintings often suggest a faux-medieval world.

Later members included Edward Burne-Jones and George Frederic Watts (1817–1904). The group also functioned as a school of writers who often used medieval settings, sometimes with shocking effect, as in William Morris's *The Defence of Guenevere* (1858), which deals with issues of love and sex. Though active less than 10 years, the group had a profound influence on the arts.

pre-Socratics, Earliest Greek philosophers (those who preceded Socrates) whose attention to questions about the origin and nature of the physical world has led to their being called cosmologists or naturalists. Among the most significant were the Milesians Thales, Anaximander, and Anaximenes, Xenophanes of Colophon, Parmenides, Heracleitus of Ephesus, Empedocles, Anaxagoras, Democritus, Zeno of Elea, and Pythagoras.

Precambrian time, Interval of geologic time from *c.* 4 billion years ago, the age of the oldest known rocks, to 542 million years ago, the beginning of the Cambrian Period. This interval represents more than 80% of the geologic record and thus provides important evidence of how the continents evolved. The Precambrian is divided into the Archean and Proterozoic eons, with the boundary between them at 2.5 billion years ago. It was originally defined as the era that predated the emergence of life in the Cambrian Period. It is now known, however, that life on Earth had begun by the early Archean Eon. Soft-bodied organisms without skeletons began to appear toward the end of the Precambrian during the Ediacaran Age.

predestination, In Christianity, the doctrine that God has long ago determined who will be saved and who will be damned. Three types of predestination doctrine have developed. One doctrine holds that God singled out the saved because he foresaw their future merits. A second doctrine (often identified with John Calvin) states that from eternity God has determined the saved and the damned, regardless of their merit or lack thereof. A third doctrine, set forth by Thomas Aquinas and Martin Luther, ascribes salvation to the unmerited grace of God but links the lack of grace to sin. In Islam, issues of predestination and free will were argued extensively. The Mutazila held that God would be unjust if he predestined all human actions; the Ashariya advocated a strict predestination that became the mainstream Islamic view.

preeclampsia and eclampsia, Hypertensive conditions unique to pregnancy. Preeclampsia is marked by hypertension, protein in the urine, and hand and face edema, which develop late in pregnancy or soon after. Persistent hypertension compromises the fetus's blood supply and damages the mother's kidneys. Monitoring of blood pressure and weight gain may detect it before symptoms (headaches, visual disturbances, stomach pain) begin. Eclampsia follows in about 5% of cases, with convulsions that pose a serious threat to mother and child. It can usually be prevented by special diets, drugs, and limited activity or early delivery.

prefect, In ancient Rome, any of various high officials with primarily judicial and administrative responsibilities. In the early republic, a prefect of the city (*praefectus urbi*) took over the consul's duties during their absence from Rome. The office lost some importance after the introduction of praetors (mid 4th century BC). Augustus revitalized the office when he appointed five prefects to supervise the city government, the fire brigade, the grain supply, and the Praetorian Guard. The praetorian prefects acquired great power and often became virtual prime ministers.

pregnancy, Process of human gestation that takes place in the female's body as a fetus develops, from fertilization to birth. It begins when a viable sperm from the male and egg from the ovary merge in the fallopian tube. The fertilized egg (zygote) grows by cell division as it moves toward the uterus, where it implants in the lining and grows into an embryo and then a fetus. A placenta and umbilical cord develop for nutrient and waste exchange be-

tween the circulations of mother and fetus. A protective fluid-filled amniotic sac encloses and cushions the fetus. Early in pregnancy, higher estrogen and progesterone levels halt menstruation, cause nausea, often with vomiting (morning sickness), and enlarge the breasts and prepare them for lactation. As the fetus grows, so does the uterus, displacing other organs. Normal weight gain in pregnancy is 20–25 lbs (9–11.5 kg). The fetus's nutritional needs require the mother to take in more calories and especially protein, water, calcium, and iron. Folic-acid supplements are recommended during early pregnancy to prevent neural tube defects. Smoking, alcohol, and many legal and illegal drugs can cause congenital disorders and should be avoided during pregnancy. Ultrasound imaging is often used to monitor structural and functional progress of the growing fetus. The due date is estimated as 280 days from the time of last menstruation; 90% of babies are born within two weeks of the estimated date.

prehistoric religion, Religious practices and beliefs of prehistoric peoples, as inferred from archaeological findings. The oldest burials that attest to a belief in life after death date from 50,000–30,000 BC. Corpses were buried with goods such as stone tools and parts of animals, suggesting an attempt to placate the dead or equip them for the next world. The Middle Paleolithic Period provides the first evidence of animal sacrifices, which may have been offerings to the dead, to a higher power, or to the fertility of the animal species. Prehistoric human sacrifices have also been found, usually of women and children. From the Bronze Age on, weapons and jewelry were often thrown into springs, wells, and other bodies of water as sacrifices (probably of war booty). Animals such as bears were important in prehistoric religion from the Upper Paleolithic Period on, probably seen as guardian spirits and associated with magical powers. Fertility rites were also practiced, as evidenced by small, corpulent female figures, known as Venus statuettes, with highly emphasized breasts and buttocks.

prelude, Musical composition, usually brief, generally played as an introduction to another piece. The prelude originated as short pieces that were improvised by an organist to establish the key of a following piece or to fill brief interludes in a church service. Their improvisatory origins were often reflected in rhythmic freedom and virtuosic runs. A section in this style would often lead to a closing fugal section; in time this turned into a separate movement, and preludes came to be paired with fugues. In the 17th century, preludes began to be frequently written for lute or harpsichord. In later years the term came to be used for short piano pieces, often in sets, by composers such as Frédéric Chopin, Aleksandr Scriabin, and Claude Debussy.

premature birth, Birth less than 37 weeks after conception. Infants born as early as 23–24 weeks may survive but many face lifelong disabilities (e.g., cerebral palsy, blindness, deafness). Premature infants account for 8–9% of live births but two-thirds of infant deaths. 40–50% of cases have no explanation; other cases can be attributed to such causes as maternal hypertension or diabetes, multiple pregnancy, or placental separation. With good care, about 85% of live-born premature infants should survive. Infants born very early (before 32–34 weeks) lack fully developed lungs and often develop respiratory distress syndrome. They also have problems maintaining body temperature and fighting infection. Most deaths result from breathing problems, infections, and brain or lung hemorrhages. Premature infants are characterized by low birth weight, small size, irregular breathing, absence of subcutaneous fat, and thin skin.

premenstrual syndrome (PMS), Variable group of symptoms occurring before menstruation in 40% of women, severe in about 10% of those. Physical symptoms may include headache, cramps, bloating, and constipation or diarrhea. Emotional symptoms range from irritability, lethargy, and mood swings to hostility, confusion, and depression. Theories as to the cause centre on hormones, nutrition, and stress (known to affect severity). Depending on the symptoms, treatment may involve exercise, stress management, nutritional therapy, or drugs. Dietary measures include low sodium and high protein and complex carbohydrate intake and avoidance of xanthines (including caffeine). Increasing calcium intake has been shown to prevent or reduce cramps, which are best treated with ibuprofen.

Presbyterianism, Form of church government based on rule by elders, or presbyters. The presbyters who govern the church are grouped in a hierarchy of courts, the highest of which is the general assembly. They are elected by the members of the congregation for fixed terms, in a system intended to affirm the equality of all Christians. The term Presbyterianism also refers to a denomination, the Presbyterian Church. The modern Presbyterian churches trace their origins to the Calvinist churches of the British Isles; in continental Europe such congregations were known as Reformed churches. The Presbyterian Church is strongest in Scotland, where it was founded by John Knox in 1557, but it is also well established in England, Wales, and the U.S.

president, In government, the officer who serves as head of state and sometimes also as chief executive. In countries where the president is chief of state but not of government, the role is largely ceremonial, with few or no political powers. Presidents may be elected directly or indirectly, for a limited or unlimited number of terms. In the U.S., the president's chief duty is to ensure that the laws are faithfully executed, which he does through various executive agencies and with the aid of his cabinet. He also serves as commander in chief of the armed forces, nominates judges to the Supreme Court, and makes treaties with foreign governments (contingent on Senate approval). The office of president is used in governments in South and Central America, Africa, and elsewhere. In western Europe executive power is generally vested in a prime minister and his cabinet, and the president, where the office exists, has few responsibilities (though France is a significant exception).

pressure, Perpendicular force per unit area, or stress at a point within a confined fluid. A solid object exerts pressure on a floor equal to its weight divided by the area of contact. The weight of the Earth's atmosphere on the surface constitutes atmospheric pressure, which varies from place to place but always decreases with altitude. The pressure exerted by a confined gas results from the average effect of the forces produced on the walls of the container by the continual, numerous collisions by gas molecules. Hydrostatic pressure is the stress, or pressure, exerted equally in all directions at points within a confined fluid. Lithostatic pressure is the stress exerted on a body of rock in the Earth's crust by surrounding rock, which increases with depth below the surface. The SI unit of pressure is the pascal (Pa), which is equal to one newton of force per square metre.

Pretoria, City (pop., 2005 est.: metro. area, 1,282,000), administrative capital of the Republic of South Africa. Founded in 1855, it became the capital of the Transvaal in 1860, the administrative capital of South Africa in 1910, and a city in 1931. In 1899, during the South African War (1899–1902), Winston Churchill was imprisoned there until his escape. Pretoria is primarily a seat of government, and most people are employed in the service sector. It is also an important rail centre, with an industrial economy based on iron and steel. Its educational institutions include the University of South Africa (1873) and the University of Pretoria (1908). Pretoria became part of the Tshwane Metropolitan Municipality in 2000.

Priam, In Greek mythology, the last king of Troy. He succeeded his father Laomedon as king and gradually expanded Troy's control over the Hellespont. By his wife, Hecuba, he had many children, including Hector and Paris. He reigned during the Trojan War; in its final year he lost 13 sons, three of whom were killed by Achilles in a single day. Hector's death broke his spirit, and he

went humbly to Achilles to ask for the corpse. When Troy fell, Achilles' son Neoptolemus killed the elderly Priam on an altar.

prickly pear, Any of a group of flat-stemmed, spiny opuntia

Engelmann prickly pear (Opuntia engelmannii)
Grant Heilman Photography

cacti, native to the Western Hemisphere, or the edible fruit of certain species. Engelmann prickly pear (*Opuntia engelmannii*) and beaver tail cactus (*O. basilaris*) commonly occur in the southwestern U.S. The Indian fig (*O. ficus-indica*) is an important food in tropical and subtropical countries. Because their stems have a high water content, prickly pears can be used as forage crops and emergency stock feed during drought. Some species are cultivated as ornamentals and valued for their large flowers.

priesthood, Office of a spiritual leader expert in the ceremonies of worship and the performance of religious rituals. Though chieftains, kings, and heads of households have sometimes performed priestly functions, in most civilizations the priesthood is a specialized office. The priest's duties are concerned less with magic than with the right performance of ritual acts required by the divine powers. Many African societies, for example, differentiated between shamans and the priests responsible for the worship of tribal ancestors. Sacrifice is often one of the most important duties of the priesthood. Not every highly developed religion possesses a priesthood, the most notable exception being Islam. The idea of the "priesthood of all believers" was also a cardinal doctrine of the Reformation, and the Protestant belief that priests are not needed as intermediaries between church members and the Holy Spirit is seen most clearly in sects such as the Society of Friends.

primate, Any of more than 300 species of the order Primates, including monkeys, apes, humans, and others. Primates are distinguished from other mammals by one or more of the following traits: unspecialized structure, specialized behaviour, a short muzzle, comparatively poor sense of smell, prehensile five-digit hands and feet possessing flat nails instead of claws, acute vision with depth perception due to forward-facing eyes, a large brain, and prolonged pre- and postnatal development. Most species bear a single young and live in troops headed by a male. The primates are one of the most diverse orders of mammals on Earth. They include the lemurs (more than 70 species in six families), the lorises (three or more species in one subfamily), the tarsiers (six or more species in one family), the New World monkeys (almost 100 species in five families), the Old World monkeys (more than 100 species in one family), and the apes and humans (about 20 species in two families). The oldest known fossil remains of primates are about 60 million years old.

prime minister, or PREMIER, Head of government in countries with a parliamentary or semipresidential system of government. The prime minister is the leader of the political party or coalition with a governing majority and is formally appointed by the head of state. Although the origin of the title lies in 17th-century France, where the cardinal de Richelieu was acknowledged in 1624 as *principal* or *premier ministre*, the office essentially developed in Britain in the 18th century. Robert Walpole (1721–42) is generally considered the first British prime minister; the powers of the office were consolidated by William Pitt the Younger. The British prime ministry has served as a model for the heads of government in many Commonwealth countries, Europe, and Japan. The prime minister has appointive powers and is responsible for the government's legislative program, budget, and other policies. His term of office lasts until the next scheduled election or until he loses legislative support. In France and Russia, which have semipresidential systems with both a president and a prime minister, the president wields greater power but the prime minister controls the domestic legislative agenda.

primrose, Any flowering plant of the genus *Primula*, one of 28 genera of the family Primulaceae. *Primula* includes 490–600 species, which occur chiefly in the Northern Hemisphere in cool or mountainous regions. The plants are low-growing, usually perennial herbs; a few are biennials. Most species grow 25–50 cm (10–20 inches) tall, but some are as short as 5 cm and others as tall as 120 cm. Many species are cultivated for their attractive, five-petaled flowers, which may be red, pink, purple, blue, white, or yellow. Pimpernels are also in the primrose family. The evening primrose (family Onagraceae) is not a true primrose.

prince, European title of rank, usually denoting a person exercising complete or almost complete sovereignty or a member of a royal family. The wife of a prince is a princess. In Britain, the title was not used until 1301, when Edward I invested his son, the future Edward II, as prince of Wales. From Edward III's time, the king's (or queen's) eldest son and heir has usually been so invested.

princeps (Latin: "first one," "leader"), Unofficial title used by Roman emperors from Augustus (r. 27 BC–AD 14) to Diocletian (r. 284–305), a period called the principate. The title originated during the Roman republic, when it was held by the leading member of the Senate. Its use by Augustus strengthened his claim to be the restorer of republican institutions and virtues, though he and his successors were in fact autocrats.

printed circuit, Electrical device in which the wiring and certain components consist of a thin coat of electrically conductive material applied in a pattern on an insulating substrate. Printed circuits replaced conventional wiring after World War II in much electronic equipment, greatly reducing size and weight while improving reliability and uniformity over the hand-soldered circuits formerly used. They are commonly used to mount integrated circuits on boards for use as plug-in units in computers, televisions, and other electronic devices. Mass-produced printed circuit boards allow automated assembly of electronic components, considerably reducing their cost.

printing, Process for reproducing text and illustrations, traditionally by applying ink to paper under pressure but today including various other methods. In modern commercial printing, three basic techniques are used. Letterpress printing relies on mechanical pressure to transfer a raised inked image to the surface to be printed. Gravure printing transfers ink from recessed cells of varying depths. In offset printing the printing and nonprinting areas of the plate differ not in height but in wettability.

prion, Disease-causing agent, discovered by Stanley Prusiner, responsible for various fatal neurodegenerative diseases called transmissible spongiform encephalopathies. An abnormal form of a normally harmless protein found in mammals and birds, the disease-causing prion can enter the brain through infection, or it can arise from a mutation in the gene that encodes the protein. Once present in the brain it causes normal proteins to refold into the abnormal shape. As prion proteins multiply, they accumulate within nerve cells, destroying them and eventually causing brain tissue to become riddled with holes. Diseases caused by prions include Creutzfeldt-Jakob disease, mad cow disease, and scrapie. Prions are unlike all other known disease-causing organisms in that they appear to lack nucleic acid (DNA or RNA).

prison, Institution for the confinement of people convicted of crimes. Prisons are administered by state, provincial, or national governments and house inmates for relatively long terms. They

thus differ from jails, which usually are under local jurisidiction and house inmates serving short sentences. Until the late 18th century, prisons were used mainly for the confinement of debtors who could not meet their obligations, of accused persons waiting to be tried, and of convicts who were waiting for their sentences of death or banishment to be put into effect. Later, imprisonment itself came to be accepted as a means of punishing convicted criminals. In early U.S. prisons, prisoners were kept in isolation; in the 19th century, they were permitted to work together, but only in silence. At the end of the 19th century, prison reformers successfully advocated segregation of criminals by type of crime, age, and sex; rewards for good behaviour; indeterminate sentencing; vocational training; and parole. In the late 20th century, prison populations in many countries began to explode as arrests for violent offenses and for possession of small amounts of illegal drugs increased.

prisoner's dilemma, Imaginary situation employed in game theory. One version is as follows. Two prisoners are accused of a crime. If one confesses and the other does not, the one who confesses will be released immediately and the other will spend 20 years in prison. If neither confesses, each will be held only a few months. If both confess, they will each be jailed 15 years. They cannot communicate with one another. Given that neither prisoner knows whether the other has confessed, it is in the self-interest of each to confess himself. Paradoxically, when each prisoner pursues his self-interest, both end up worse off than they would have been had they acted otherwise. *See* egoism.

Pristina, City (pop., 2003 est.: 165,844), capital of Kosovo. Pristina was the capital of the Serbian state before the Turks defeated the Balkan Christian armies in 1389 at the Battle of Kosovo. It is also a cultural centre for Kosovar Albanians. It lost many of its ethnic Albanian inhabitants in 1999 when they were driven out by the Serbian campaign of "ethnic cleansing." Many returned after a peace accord was signed in June 1999.

Pritzker Architecture Prize, World's most prestigious honour in the field of architecture. Established through the philanthropic efforts of the Pritzkers, a prominent Chicago business family, the prize, first awarded in 1979, bestows an annual award of $100,000 on an architect whose built contributions to the field and to society are judged worthiest. The international jury has included architects, artists, historians, academicians, critics, and business executives.

privacy, right of, Right of a person to be free from intrusion into matters of a personal nature. Although not explicitly mentioned in the U.S. Constitution, a right to privacy has been held to be implicit in the Bill of Rights, providing protection from unwarranted government intrusion into areas such as marriage and contraception. A person's right to privacy may be overcome by a compelling state interest. In tort law, privacy is a right not to have one's intimate life and affairs exposed to public view or otherwise invaded. Less broad protections of privacy are afforded public officials and others defined by law as "public figures" (e.g., movie stars).

probability theory, Branch of mathematics that deals with analysis of random events. Probability is the numerical assessment of likelihood on a scale from 0 (impossibility) to 1 (absolute certainty). Probability is usually expressed as the ratio between the number of ways an event can happen and the total number of things that can happen (e.g., there are 13 ways of picking a diamond from a deck of 52 cards, so the probability of picking a diamond is $^{13}/_{52}$, or $^{1}/_{4}$). Probability theory grew out of attempts to understand card games and gambling. As science became more rigorous, analogies between certain biological, physical, and social phenomena and games of chance became more evident (e.g., the sexes of newborn infants follow sequences similar to those of coin tosses). As a result, probability became a fundamental tool of modern genetics and many other disciplines. Probability theory is also the basis of the insurance industry, in the form of actuarial statistics.

probation, Conditional suspension of an offender's sentence upon the promise of good behaviour and agreement to accept supervision and abide by specified requirements. It differs from parole in that the offender is not required to serve any of his sentence. Those convicted of serious offenses and those previously convicted of other offenses are usually not considered for probation. Studies in several countries show that 70 to 80% of probationers successfully complete their probation; additional limited evidence suggests that recidivism may be less than 30%.

procedural law, Law that prescribes the procedures and methods for enforcing rights and duties and for obtaining redress (e.g., in a suit). It is distinguished from substantive law (i.e., law that creates, defines, or regulates rights and duties). Procedural law is a set of established forms for conducting a trial and regulating the events that precede and follow it. It prescribes rules relative to jurisdiction, pleading and practice, jury selection, evidence, appeal, execution of judgments, representation of counsel, costs, registration (e.g., of a stock offer), prosecution of crime, and conveyancing (transference of deeds, leases, etc.), among other matters.

producer goods, or CAPITAL GOODS, or INTERMEDIATE GOODS, Goods manufactured and used in further manufacturing, processing, or resale. Intermediate goods either become part of the final product or lose their distinct identity in the manufacturing stream, while capital goods are the plant, equipment, and inventories used to produce final products. The contribution of intermediate goods to a country's gross domestic product may be determined through the value-added method, which calculates the amount of value added to the final consumer good at each stage of production. This series of values is summed to estimate the total value of the final product.

productivity, In economics, a measure of productive efficiency calculated as the ratio of what is produced to what is required to produce it. Any of the traditional factors of production—land, labour, or capital—can be used as the denominator of the ratio, though productivity calculations are actually seldom made for land or capital since their capacity is difficult to measure. Labour is in most cases easily quantified—for example, by counting workers engaged on a particular product. In industrialized nations, the effects of increasing productivity are most apparent in the use of labour. Productivity can be seen not only as a measure of efficiency but also as an indicator of economic development. Productivity increases as a primitive extractive economy develops into a technologically sophisticated one. The pattern of increase typically exhibits long-term stability interrupted by sudden leaps that represent major technological advances. Productivity in Europe and the U.S. made great strides following the development of such technologies as steam power, the railroad, and the gasoline motor. Later in the 20th century, advances in productivity stemmed from a number of innovations, including assembly lines and automation, computer-integrated manufacturing, database management systems, just-in-time manufacturing, and just-in-time inventory management. Increases in productivity have tended to lead to long-term increases in real wages.

profit, In business usage, the excess of total revenue over total cost during a specific period of time. In economics, profit is the excess over the returns to capital, land, and labour. Since these resources are measured by their opportunity costs, economic profit can be negative. There are various sources of profit: an innovator who introduces a new production technique can earn entrepreneurial profits; changes in consumer tastes may bring some firms windfall profits; or a firm may restrict output to prevent prices from falling to the level of costs (monopoly profit).

profit sharing, System by which employees are paid a share of the profits of the business enterprise in which they are employed, in keeping with a plan outlined in advance. These payments, which may vary according to salary or wage, are in addition to regular earnings. Profit-sharing plans were probably first developed in France in the early 19th century as worker incentives. Today such plans are used by businesses in Western Europe, the U.S., and parts of Latin America. Profit shares may be distributed on a current or deferred basis or through some combination of the two. Under current distribution, profits are paid out to employees immediately in the form of cash or company stock. In deferred-payment plans, profit shares may be paid into a trust fund from which employees can draw annuities in later years.

progesterone, Steroid hormone secreted by the female reproductive system that functions mainly to regulate the condition of the endometrium, preparing it to accept a fertilized egg. If the egg is not fertilized, the level of progesterone drops, the uterine lining breaks down, and menstruation ensues. If the egg is fertilized, the placenta produces progesterone, whose effects include preparing the mammary glands for lactation. Many forms of oral contraception use a synthetic progesterone.

programming language, Language in which a computer programmer writes instructions for a computer to execute. Some languages, such as COBOL, FORTRAN, Pascal, and C, are known as procedural languages because they use a sequence of commands to specify how the machine is to solve a problem. Others, such as LISP, are functional, in that programming is done by invoking procedures (sections of code executed within a program). Languages that support object-oriented programming take the data to be manipulated as their point of departure. Programming languages can also be classified as high-level or low-level. Low-level languages address the computer in a way that it can understand directly, but they are very far from human language. High-level languages deal in concepts that humans devise and can understand, but they must be translated by means of a compiler into language the computer understands.

progressive tax, Tax levied at a rate that increases as the quantity subject to taxation increases. Designed to collect a greater proportion of tax revenue from wealthy people, progressive taxes reflect the view that those who are able to pay more should carry a heavier share of the tax burden. Progressive income taxes may provide for exemption from tax liability for incomes under a specified amount, or they may establish progressively greater rates for larger and larger incomes. The presence of deductions can also make a tax progressive. Progressive taxes are a stabilizing force in periods of inflation or recession because the amount of tax revenue changes more than proportionately with an increase or decrease in income. For example, in an inflationary economy, as prices and incomes rise, a greater percentage of taxpayers' income goes toward taxes. Government revenues increase, and the government has more leverage over the economy. A side effect of this system is that lower-income taxpayers have an especially difficult time making ends meet when inflation is high. To compensate, many economists advocate indexation; several countries adjust their tax rates annually in times of inflation, usually in line with the consumer price index.

Prohibition, Legal prevention of the manufacture, sale, or transportation of alcoholic beverages. In the U.S., the Prohibition movement arose out of the religious revivalism of the 1820s. Maine passed the first state Prohibition law in 1846, ushering in a wave of such state legislation. The drive toward national Prohibition was fueled by the Anti-Saloon League, founded in 1893. With Prohibition already adopted in 33 states, the 18th Amendment to the U.S. Constitution went into effect in 1920. Prohibition was embraced with varying degrees of enthusiasm in different parts of the country, and enforced accordingly. In urban areas, bootlegging gave rise to organized crime, with such gangsters as Al Capone.

In part because of the rise in crime, its supporters gradually became disenchanted with it. The 21st Amendment repealed the 18th in 1933, and by 1966 all states had also abandoned Prohibition.

projective geometry, Branch of mathematics that deals with the relationships between geometric figures and the images (mappings) of them that result from projection. Examples of projections include motion pictures, maps of the Earth's surface, and shadows cast by objects. One stimulus for the subject's development was the need to understand perspective in drawing and painting. Every point of the projected object and the corresponding point of its image must lie on the projection ray, a line that passes through the centre of projection. Modern projective geometry emphasizes the mathematical properties (such as straightness of lines and points of intersection) preserved in projections despite the distortion of lengths, angles, and shapes.

prokaryote, Any cellular organism that lacks a distinct nucleus. Organisms classified in the domains Bacteria (including bluegreen algae, or cyanobacteria) and Archaea are prokaryotes; all other organisms are eukaryotes and are placed in the domain Eukarya. Prokaryotic cells lack a nuclear membrane and most of the components of eukaryotic cells. The cytoplasm includes ribosomes that carry out protein synthesis and a double-stranded DNA chromosome, usually circular. Many prokaryotes also contain additional circular DNA molecules called plasmids. The flagella are distinct from those of eukaryotes in design and movement.

Prometheus, In Greek religion, one of the Titans and a god of fire. He was a master craftsman and a supreme trickster, and he was sometimes associated with the creation of humans. According to legend, Prometheus stole fire from the gods and gave it to humans. In vengeance, Zeus created Pandora, who married Prometheus's brother and set loose all the evils of the world. Another tale held that Zeus had Prometheus chained to a mountain and sent an eagle to devour his liver, which regenerated every night so that he could suffer the same torment the next day.

propaganda, Manipulation of information to influence public opinion. The term comes from Congregatio de Propaganda Fide (Congregation for the Propagation of the Faith), a missionary organization established by the pope in 1622. Propagandists emphasize the elements of information that support their position and deemphasize or exclude those that do not. Misleading statements and even lies may be used to create the desired effect in the public audience. Lobbying, advertising, and missionary activity are all forms of propaganda, but the term is most commonly used in the political arena. Prior to the 20th century, pictures and the written media were the principal instruments of propaganda; radio, television, motion pictures, and the Internet later joined their ranks. Authoritarian and totalitarian regimes use propaganda to win and keep the support of the populace. In wartime, propaganda directed by a country at its own civilian population and military forces can boost morale; propaganda aimed at the enemy is an element of psychological warfare.

propane, Colourless, easily liquefied hydrocarbon gas (C_3H_8 or, more fully, $CH_3CH_2CH_3$). Separated in large quantities from natural gas, light crude oil, and oil-refinery gases, it is available as liquefied propane or as a major constituent of liquefied petroleum gas (LPG). It is an important raw material for the manufacture of ethylene and for the petrochemical industry. It is also used as a refrigerant, extractant, solvent, aerosol propellant, and fuel for portable cooking appliances, torches, and lighters.

propeller, Device with a central hub and radiating blades placed so that each forms part of a helical (spiral) surface, used to propel a vehicle such as a ship or airplane. By its rotation in water or air, the propeller produces thrust on the blades, which gives forward motion to the vehicle.

proper motion, Apparent motion of a star across the celestial sphere at right angles to the observer's line of sight, generally measured in seconds of arc per year. Any radial motion (toward or away from the observer) is not included. Edmond Halley was the first to detect proper motions; the largest known is that of Barnard's star, about 10 seconds yearly.

property, In law, something that is owned or possessed. Concepts of property vary widely among cultures. In the West, property is generally regarded as either tangible (e.g., land or goods) or intangible (e.g., stocks and bonds or a patent). Individual ownership of property is emphasized in Western societies, whereas in many non-Western societies property ownership is deemphasized or conceived on a more strictly communal basis. The use of property is extensively regulated throughout the West. Landowners injured by adjoining land uses may sue in nuisance in Anglo-American countries; similar actions exist in civil-law countries. Throughout the West, landowners may agree to allow others to use their land in ways that would otherwise be actionable, and such agreements may be made to bind those to whom the land is conveyed. Anglo-American law tends to divide these grants of use rights into categories that reflect their common-law origins: easements (such as rights of way), profits (such as the right to take minerals or timber), real covenants (such as a promise to pay a homeowners' association fee), and equitable servitudes (such as a promise to use the property for residential purposes only). The civil law has fewer categories, the general category "servitudes" tending to cover for them all, and is a bit more restrictive. A common means of acquiring property is by transfer from the previous owner or owners. Such transfers include sales, donations, and inheritance.

prophet, Person who speaks by divine inspiration, revealing or interpreting the will of a god. Prophets have appeared in many religions throughout history. The most familiar in the West are such Old Testament leaders as Moses, Isaiah, and Daniel, along with the Prophet Muhammad. In contrast to the diviner or interpreter of omens, who may answer private questions, prophets often address the destiny and moral life of a whole people. Some prophets seek to create a new society that will realize their message and thus found new religions. Others may look only to reform or purify an existing society and religion. The tone of prophecy ranges widely, from ecstasy, inspired utterance, and ethical fervor to passionate social criticism, prediction of the future, and expectation of apocalypse.

Prophet's Mosque, House of worship built on the site of Muhammad's house in Medina, considered one of the three holiest places of Islam. It was originally a simple brick structure surrounding an enclosed courtyard where people gathered to hear Muhammad. Muhammad later built roofed galleries to shelter his visitors, and in 628 a pulpit was added to raise him above the crowd. In 706 Caliph al-Walīd I pulled down the original building and built a mosque on the site, which contains Muhammad's tomb. The mosque served as the model for later Islamic architecture.

proportional representation, Electoral system in which the share of seats held by a political party in the legislature closely matches the share of popular votes it received. It was devised in Europe in the mid-19th century to guarantee minority groups more representation than was possible under the majority or plurality systems. Its supporters claim that it creates a more accurate reflection of public opinion; its opponents argue that by allowing more parties in a legislature, it may result in weaker, less stable governments. Two methods for apportioning seats are the single-transferable-vote method, under which voters rank candidates by preference, and the list system, under which voters select a party's list of candidates rather than individuals. Some countries (e.g., Germany and Russia) use a combination of plurality and proportional methods for allocating seats in the lower house of the national legislature.

proscenium, In a theatre, the frame or arch separating the stage from the auditorium, through which the action of a play is viewed. In ancient Greek theatres, the *proskenion* was an area in front of the skene that eventually functioned as the stage. The first permanent proscenium in the modern sense was built in 1618 at the Farnese Theatre in Parma. Though the arch contained a stage curtain, its main purpose was to provide a sense of spectacle and illusion; scene changes were carried out in view of the audience. Not until the 18th century was the curtain commonly used to hide scene changes. The proscenium opening was of particular importance to 19th-century realist playwrights, for whom it served as a picture frame or an invisible wall through which the audience experienced the illusion of spying on the characters.

prose, Literary medium distinguished from poetry especially by its greater irregularity and variety of rhythm and its closer correspondence to the patterns of everyday speech. Though it is readily distinguishable from poetry in that it does not treat a line as a formal unit, the significant differences between prose and poetry are of tone, pace, and sometimes subject matter.

prosody, Study of the elements of language, especially metre, that contribute to rhythmic and acoustic effects in poetry. The basis of "traditional" prosody in English is the classification of verse according to the syllable stress of its lines. Effects such as rhyme scheme, alliteration, and assonance further influence a poem's "sound meaning." Nonmetrical prosodic study is sometimes applied to modern poetry, and visual prosody is used when verse is "shaped" by its typographical arrangement. Prosody also involves examining the subtleties of a poem's rhythm, its "flow," the historical period to which it belongs, the poetic genre, and the poet's individual style.

prostaglandin, Any of a class of organic compounds that occur in many animal tissues and have diverse hormonelike effects in animals. Their common chemical structure is derived from a fatty acid with 20 carbon atoms. They have important effects on blood pressure, blood clotting, pain sensation, and reproduction mechanisms, but one prostaglandin may have different and even opposite effects in different tissues. They hold promise for treating heart disease and viral diseases and may be useful in contraception. Some substances that inhibit prostaglandin synthesis are useful in controlling pain, asthma attacks, or anaphylactic shock or as anticoagulants.

prostate gland, Chestnut-shaped male reproductive organ, located under the bladder, which adds secretions to the sperm during ejaculation of semen. It surrounds the urethra and is rounded at the top, narrowing to a blunt point. The prostate consists of 30–50 glands, supported by connective tissue, that discharge fluids into the urethra and two ejaculatory ducts. Those ducts, which also carry sperm and fluid discharged by the seminal vesicles, join the urethra inside the prostate. The prostate contributes 15–30% of the seminal fluid. It reaches its mature size at puberty. Around age 50, it commonly shrinks and decreases its secretions; an increase in size after midlife may be due to inflammation or malignancy.

prosthesis, Artificial substitute for a missing part of the body, usually an arm or leg. Prostheses have evolved from wooden legs and hooks that replaced hands to sophisticated plastic, fibreglass, and metal devices designed to fit limbs amputated at different points. They may have working joints and allow motion either by amplification of electric current generated by muscle contractions or by actual attachment to the muscles. Arm prostheses usually allow some degree of grasping and manipulation. External or implanted breast prostheses are used after mastectomy.

prostitution, Practice of engaging in sexual activity, usually with individuals other than a spouse or friend, in exchange for immediate payment in money or other valuables. Prostitutes may be of either sex and may engage in either heterosexual or homosexual activity, but historically most prostitution has been by females with males as clients. Prostitution is a very old and universal phenomenon; also universal is condemnation of the prostitute but relative indifference toward the client. Prostitutes are often set apart in some way. In ancient Rome they were required to wear distinctive dress; under Hebrew law only foreign women could be prostitutes; and in pre-World War II Japan they were required to live in special sections of the city. In medieval Europe prostitution was licensed and regulated by law, but by the 16th century an epidemic of venereal disease and post-Reformation morality led to the closure of brothels. International cooperation to end the traffic in women for the purpose of prostitution began in 1899. In 1921 the League of Nations established the Committee on the Traffic in Women and Children, and in 1949 the UN General Assembly adopted a convention for the suppression of prostitution. In the U.S. prostitution was first curtailed by the Mann Act (1910), and by 1915 most states had banned brothels (Nevada being a notable exception). Prostitution is nevertheless tolerated in most U.S. and European cities. In the Netherlands many prostitutes have become members of a professional service union, and in Scandinavia government regulations emphasize hygienic aspects, requiring frequent medical examination and providing free mandatory hospitalization for anyone found to be infected with venereal disease. Prostitutes are very often poor and lack other skills to support themselves; in many traditional societies there are few other available money-earning occupations for women without family support. In developing African and Asian countries, prostitution has been largely responsible for the spread of AIDS and the orphaning of hundreds of thousands of children.

protectionism, Policy of protecting domestic industries against foreign competition by means of tariffs, subsidies, import quotas, or other handicaps placed on imports. The chief protectionist measures, government-levied tariffs, raise the price of imported articles, making them less attractive to consumers than cheaper domestic products. Import quotas, which limit the quantities of goods that can be imported, are another protectionist device. Wars and economic depressions historically have resulted in increases in protectionism, while peace and prosperity have tended to encourage free trade. Protectionist policies were common in Europe in the 17th–18th centuries under mercantilism. Britain abandoned many of its protectionist laws in the 19th century, and by World War I tariffs were low throughout the Western world. Economic and political dislocation led to rising customs barriers in Europe in the 1920s, and the Great Depression produced a spate of protectionist measures; world trade shrank drastically as a result. The U.S. had a long history of protectionism, with tariffs reaching high points in the 1820s and the Great Depression, but in 1947 it became one of 23 nations to sign the General Agreement on Tariffs and Trade (GATT), which substantially reduced customs tariffs while reducing or eliminating quotas. Despite trade agreements such as GATT and NAFTA, calls for protectionism are still heard in many countries when industries suffer severely from foreign competition.

protectorate, Relationship in which one country exercises some decisive control over another country or region. The degree of control may vary from one in which the protecting state guarantees the safety of the other to one that is a disguised form of annexation. Though the relationship is an ancient one, the use of the term dates only from the 19th century. In modern times most protectorates have been established by treaties requiring the weaker state to surrender management of its international relations, thus losing part of its sovereignty.

protein, Any of numerous organic compounds, complex polymers of amino acids that are involved in nearly every aspect of the physiology and biochemistry of living organisms. Twenty different amino acids are common to proteins, linked in chains of hundreds to thousands of units. An active protein molecule has three important levels of structure: primary (the amino acid sequence), determined by the genes; secondary (the geometric shape, often a helix), determined by the angles of the covalent bonds between and within amino acids; and tertiary (the looped and folded overall shape), determined largely by attraction between oppositely charged groups (and repulsion between like charged groups) on amino-acid side chains and especially by hydrogen bonding. The tertiary structure, which can be globular or sheetlike with ridges, crevices, or pockets, often holds the key to a protein's biological activity. Proteins can serve, e.g., as structural material (as in connective tissue and hair), as enzymes and hormones, as transporters of essential substances such as oxygen, as antibodies, or as regulators of gene expression. Some proteins are simple (amino acids only), some conjugated to other groups, often vitamins or metal atoms needed in tiny amounts in the diet; cofactor). Rhodopsin and hemoglobin are conjugated proteins. Proteins may be covalently linked to other atoms or molecules, as to sugars (glycoproteins), phosphate groups (phosphoproteins), or sulfur (sulfoproteins). Proteins are an essential human nutrient, obtained from both plant and animal foods. Their greatest commercial use is in food products; they are also employed in adhesives, plastics, and fibres.

Proterozoic Eon, Younger of the two divisions of Precambrian time, from 2.5 billion to 542 million years ago. Proterozoic rocks have been identified on all the continents and often constitute important sources of metallic ores, notably of iron, gold, copper, uranium, and nickel. The many small protocontinents formed during early Precambrian time coalesced into a single, large landmass known as Columbia toward the middle of the Proterozoic. Columbia later broke apart, and the fragments recoalesced into the continental assemblage known as Rodinia toward the end of the eon. Rocks of the Proterozoic Eon contain many traces of primitive life-forms, such as the fossil remains of bacteria, blue-green algae, and soft-bodied multicellular organisms.

Protestantism, One of the three major branches of Christianity, originating in the 16th-century Reformation. The term applies to the beliefs of Christians who do not adhere to Roman Catholicism or Eastern Orthodoxy. A variety of Protestant denominations grew out of the Reformation. The followers of Martin Luther established the evangelical churches of Germany and Scandinavia; John Calvin and more radical reformers such as Huldrych Zwingli founded Reformed churches in Switzerland, and Calvin's disciple John Knox established a church in Scotland (Presbyterianism). Another important branch of Protestantism, represented by the Church of England and Episcopal Church, had its origins in 16th-century England and is now the Protestant denomination closest to Roman Catholicism in theology and worship. The doctrines of the various Protestant denominations vary considerably, but all emphasize the supremacy of the Bible in matters of faith and order, justification by grace through faith and not through works, and the priesthood of all believers. In the early 21st century there were nearly 350 million Protestants in the world.

protist, Any member of a kingdom (Protista) of diverse eukaryotes, including algae, protozoans, and lower fungi. Most are single-celled organisms, though the algae tend to be multicellular. Many can move, mainly by using flagella, cilia, or footlike extensions (pseudopodia). The kingdom was developed to accommodate intermediate organisms that, even though they possessed some plant or animal characteristics, did not exhibit the specialized features indicative of those groups. Some protists are considered the ancestors of multicellular plants, animals, and fungi. The term was first suggested in 1866 by Ernst Haeckel. With the development of advanced biochemical, genetic, and imaging techniques, previously established relationships have come under scrutiny, and it is now thought that some groups are less closely related to one another than once believed. As a result, the classification of protists, while convenient, is no longer entirely satisfactory.

protoceratops, Any member of a genus of quadrupedal dinosaurs found as fossils in Gobi deposits of the Cretaceous period (144–65 million years ago). The hind limbs were more strongly developed than the forelimbs; the back was arched. Adults were about 7 ft (2 m) long and probably weighed about 400 lbs (180 kg). The skull was about one-fifth the body length. Bones in the skull grew backward into a perforated frill. The jaws were beaklike and toothed. There may have been a hornlike structure on top of the snout. Long spines on the well-developed tail suggest that protoceratops was semiaquatic.

proton, Stable subatomic particle (one of the baryons) with a unit of positive electric charge and a mass 1,836 times that of the electron. Protons are found in the atomic nucleus along with neutrons. For every nucleus of a given element, the number of protons is always the same; this number is the element's atomic number. A single proton is the nucleus of an atom of ordinary hydrogen; as such, it is identical to the hydrogen ion (H^+). Protons have antimatter counterparts (antiprotons), with the same mass but a negative charge. Protons are used as projectiles in particle accelerators to produce and study nuclear reactions. They are the chief constituent of primary cosmic rays and are among the products of radioactive decay and nuclear reactions.

protozoan, Any of a group of small (usually microscopic) single-celled protists that are nonfilamentous and heterotrophic (using organic carbon as a source of energy). They are found in most soils, fresh water, and oceans. While most are solitary individuals, various colonial forms exist. The taxonomic relationships of protozoans to one another and to other protists continue to be revised. The smallest known protozoans are tiny blood parasites less than 2 micrometres long; the largest may be 16 mm long and visible to the naked eye. Protozoan shapes vary, but all share such eukaryotic features as lipid-protein membranes and membrane-enclosed vacuoles and organelles. They show wide variation in modes of movement, nutrition, and reproduction. Various classification systems exist to group the protozoans. Commonly known protozoans include dinoflagellates, amoebas, and paramecia.

proverb, Succinct and pithy saying that is in general use and expresses commonly held ideas and beliefs. Proverbs are part of every spoken language and folk literature, originating in oral tradition. Often a proverb is found with variations in many different parts of the world. Literate societies dating to the ancient Egyptians have collected proverbs. One of the earliest English proverb collections, *The Proverbs of Alfred*, dates from *c.* 1150–80. In North America the best-known collection is probably *Poor Richard's*, an almanac published 1732–57 by Benjamin Franklin.

Prussia, German PREUSSEN, In European history, any of three areas of eastern and central Europe. The first was the land of the Prussians on the southeastern coast of the Baltic Sea, which came under Polish and German rule in the Middle Ages. The second was the kingdom ruled from 1701 by the German Hohenzollern dynasty, including Prussia and Brandenburg, with Berlin as its capital. It seized much of northern Germany and western Poland in the 18th–19th centuries and united Germany under its leadership in 1871. The third was the state created after the fall of the Hohenzollerns in 1918, which included most of their former kingdom and which was abolished by the Allies in 1947 as part of the political reorganization of Germany after its defeat in World War II.

psalm, Sacred song or poem. The term is most widely known from the book of Psalms in the Bible. Its 150 psalms, ranging in subject from songs of joyous faith and thanksgiving to songs of bitter protest and lamentation, rank among the immortal poems of all time. They have had a profound influence on the liturgies of Judaism and Christianity. Their dating and authorship are highly problematic, and the tradition of assigning them to King David is no longer accepted. In the original Hebrew text the book had no name. When the Hebrew Bible was translated into Greek (the Septuagint), it was titled Psalterion, referring to a stringed instrument that would accompany such songs.

psoriasis, Chronic, recurrent skin disorder with reddish, slightly elevated patches or bumps covered with silvery-white scales. Spots may coalesce into large patches around a normal area. If the nails are involved, they may become pitted, thick, and separated from the nail bed. Skin injury, infection, stress, and certain drugs may trigger psoriasis. Skin cells move at an accelerated rate from the dermis into the epidermis, where they slough off, causing inflammation. In some cases, patients also have arthritis. Psoriasis often becomes less severe in the summer and during pregnancy. There is no cure, but treatment with drugs and ultraviolet light may help.

Psyche, In Greek and Roman mythology, a beautiful princess who won Cupid's love. Her beauty was such that worshipers began to turn away from Venus, and the envious goddess commanded her son Cupid to make Psyche fall in love with the most despicable of men. But Cupid himself fell in love with Psyche and hid her in a remote place, where he visited her secretly under cover of darkness. One night she lit a lamp and discovered her lover's identity. He left angrily, and Psyche wandered the earth searching for him and was captured by Venus. After Cupid rescued Psyche, Jupiter made her immortal and gave her in marriage to Cupid.

Psyche, depicted with wings, classical sculpture; in the Louvre, Paris
Alinari/Art Resource, New York

psychiatry, Branch of medicine concerned with mental disorders. Until the 18th century, mental health problems were considered forms of demonic possession; gradually they came to be seen as illnesses requiring treatment. In the 19th century, research into and classification and treatment of mental illnesses advanced. Sigmund Freud's psychoanalytic theory dominated the field for many years before it was challenged by behavioral and cognitive therapy and humanistic psychology in the mid-20th century. Psychiatrists hold medical degrees and can prescribe drugs and other medical treatments in addition to conducting psychotherapy. The psychiatrist often works as a member of a mental health team that includes clinical psychologists and social workers.

psychoanalysis, Method of treating mental disorders that emphasizes the probing of unconscious mental processes. It is based on the psychoanalytic theory devised by Sigmund Freud in Vienna in the late 19th and early 20th century. It calls for patients to engage in free association of ideas, speaking to therapists about anything that comes to mind. Dreams and slips of the tongue are examined as a key to the workings of the unconscious mind, and the "work" of therapy is to uncover the tensions existing between the instinctual drive of the id, the perceptions and actions of the ego, and the censorship imposed by the morality of the superego. Careful attention is paid to early childhood experiences (especially those with a sexual dimension), the memory of which may have been repressed because of guilt or trauma; recalling and analyzing these experiences is thought to help free patients from the anxiety and neuroses caused by repression as well as from more serious illnesses known as psychoses. Some of Freud's early associates, notably Carl Gustav Jung and Alfred Adler, rejected his theories on many points and devised alternative methods of

analysis. Other important figures in psychoanalysis, including Erik Erikson, Karen Horney, and Erich Fromm, accepted the basic Freudian framework but contributed their own additions or modifications.

psychology, Scientific discipline that studies mental processes and behaviour in humans and other animals. Literally meaning "the study of the mind," psychology focuses on both individual and group behaviour. Clinical psychology is concerned with the diagnosis and treatment of mental disorders. Other specialized fields of psychology include child psychology, educational psychology, sports psychology, social psychology, and comparative psychology. The issues studied by psychologists cover a wide spectrum, including learning, cognition, intelligence, motivation, emotion, perception, personality, and the extent to which individual differences are shaped by genetics or environment. The methods used in psychological research include observation, interviews, psychological testing, laboratory experimentation, and statistical analysis.

psychosis, Any of several serious mental illnesses characterized by defects in judgment and other cognitive processes and by loss of contact with reality. Psychoses can be divided into two major types: functional and organic. Functional psychoses include schizophrenia and affective disorders (also called mood disorders), such as major depressive disorder and bipolar disorder. Organic psychoses arise secondary to a preexisting medical condition such as Alzheimer disease and share important features with functional psychoses. Certain medications, including narcotics (used to treat pain) and levodopa (used to treat Parkinson disease), can cause symptoms of psychoses. The major symptoms, aside from delusions and hallucinations, are disorganized speech and behaviour, lack of emotional expression, and apathy. Treatment usually consists of medication and psychotherapy; severe cases may require permanent hospitalization. *Compare* neurosis.

psychosomatic disorder, Bodily ailment or symptom, caused by mental or emotional disturbance, in which psychological stresses adversely affect physiological (somatic) functioning to the point of distress. Psychosomatic disorders may include hypertension, respiratory ailments, gastrointestinal disturbances, migraine and tension headaches, sexual dysfunctions, and dermatitis. Many patients with psychosomatic conditions respond to a combination of drug therapy and psychotherapy.

psychotherapy, Treatment of psychological, emotional, or behaviour disorders through interpersonal communications between the patient and a trained counselor or therapist. The goal of many modern individual and group therapies is to establish a central relationship of trust in which the client or patient can feel free to express personal thoughts and emotions and thus gain insight into his condition and generally share in the healing power of words. Such therapies include psychoanalysis and its variants, client-centred or nondirective psychotherapy, Gestalt therapy, play and art therapy, and general counseling. In contrast, behaviour therapy focuses on modifying behaviour by reinforcement techniques without concerning itself with internal states.

Ptah, In Egyptian religion, the creator god. The patron of craftsmen, especially sculptors, Ptah was identified by the Greeks with Hephaestus, the divine blacksmith. He was represented as a man in mummy form, wearing a skullcap and a short, straight false beard. He was originally the local deity of Memphis, capital of Egypt from the 1st dynasty onward; the political importance of Memphis caused Ptah's cult to spread across Egypt. With Sekhmet and Nefertem, he was one of the Memphite Triad of deities. See photograph on following page.

Pteranodon, Genus of extinct flying reptiles, descendants of the pterodactyl. Fossils are known from Late Cretaceous (99–65 million years ago) deposits of Europe, Asia, and North America. *Pter-*

Ptah, holding the emblems of life and power, bronze statuette, Memphis, c. 600–100 BCE; in the British Museum, London.

anodon had a wingspan of 23 ft (7 m) or more. The largest specimen had a wingspan of 50 ft (15.5 m). The body was about the size of a modern turkey. *Pteranodon* had a crest at the back of the skull and long, pelicanlike, toothless jaws. They probably made nests and spent much time gliding over the ocean searching for fish. They probably depended on air currents for liftoff rather than on flapping their wings.

pterodactyl, Any member of the pterosaur suborder Pterodactyloidea, known from Late Jurassic and Cretaceous fossils (159–65 million years ago) in eastern Africa and Europe. Members of the typical genus, *Pterodactylus*, ranged from the size of a sparrow to that of an albatross. Pterodactyls had slender, delicate teeth that were angled forward (possibly for use as straining devices), long metacarpal bones, and a short tail. They were probably able gliders but not efficient as active fliers, and they apparently lacked feathers. Unlike the archaeopteryx, the pterodactyl was not an ancestor of the birds.

pterosaur, Any of several extinct flying reptiles (order Pterosauria) that flourished during the Jurassic and Cretaceous periods (206–65 million years ago). Pterosaurs hung by their long, slender hind limbs when at rest. They soared and glided on fragile, membranous wings that were attached to the long fourth finger of each forelimb and extended along the flank. The first three fingers were slender, clawed, clutching structures. Pterosaurs had a long, slender beak and a large brain. *Ramphorhynchus* had strong, sharply pointed teeth, a long tail, and a wingspread of about 3 ft (1 m). It probably obtained food by diving for fish.

puberty, In human physiology, the period of first becoming capable of reproducing sexually. Occurring at about age 12 in girls and age 14 in boys, puberty is characterized by the maturing of the genital organs, development of secondary sex characteristics, and, in girls, onset of menstruation. Both sexes experience a swift increase in body size and changes in body shape and composition. Puberty marks the beginning of adolescence.

public health, Science and art of preventing disease, prolonging life, and promoting health through organized community efforts. These include sanitation, control of contagious infections, hygiene education, early diagnosis and preventive treatment, and adequate living standards. It requires understanding not only of epidemiology, nutrition, and antiseptic practices but also of social science. Historical public health measures included quarantine of leprosy victims in the Middle Ages and efforts to improve sanitation following the 14th-century plague epidemics. Population increases in Europe brought with them increased awareness of infant deaths and a proliferation of hospitals. Britain's Public Health Act of 1848 established a special public health ministry. In the U.S., public health is studied and coordinated on a national level by the Centers for Disease Control and Prevention; internationally, the World Health Organization plays an equivalent role.

public relations (PR), Aspect of communications that involves promoting a desirable image for a person or group seeking public attention. It originated in the U.S. in the early 20th century with pioneers such as Edward L. Bernays and Ivy Ledbetter Lee. Government agencies in Britain and the U.S. soon began hiring publicists to engineer support for their policies and programs, and the public-relations business boomed after World War II. Clients may include individuals such as politicians, performers, and authors, and groups such as business corporations, government agencies, charities, and religious bodies. The audience addressed may be as narrow as male alternative-music fans between the ages of 21 and 30 or as broad as the world at large. A publicist's functions include generating favourable publicity and knowing what kind of story is likely to be printed or broadcast. The task is complicated by the variety of existing media: besides newspapers, magazines, radio, and television, there are publications of professional associations, direct-mail lists, on-site promotional events, and so on. It consists largely of optimizing good news and forestalling bad news; if disaster strikes, the publicist must assess the situation, organize the client's response so as to minimize damage, and marshal and present information to the media.

public utility, Enterprise that provides certain classes of services to the public, including common-carrier transportation (buses, airlines, railroads); telephone and telegraph services; power, heat and light; and community facilities for water and sanitation. In most countries such enterprises are state-owned and state-operated; in the U.S. they are mainly privately owned, but they operate under close regulation. Given the technology of production and distribution, they are considered natural monopolies, since the capital costs for such enterprises are large and the existence of competing or parallel systems would be inordinately expensive and wasteful. Government regulation in the U.S., particularly at the state level, aims to ensure safe operation, reasonable rates, and service on equal terms to all customers. Some states have experimented with deregulation of electricity and natural-gas operations to stimulate price reductions and improved service through competition, but the results have not been universally promising.

publishing, Traditionally, the selection, preparation, and distribution of printed matter—including books, newspapers, magazines, and pamphlets. Contemporary publishing includes the production of materials in digital formats such as CD-ROMs, as well as materials created or adapted for electronic distribution. Publishing has evolved from small, ancient, and law- or religion-bound origins into a vast industry that disseminates every kind of information imaginable. In the modern sense of a copying industry supplying a lay readership, publishing began in Hellenistic Greece, in Rome, and in China. After paper reached the West from China in the 11th century, the central innovation in Western publishing was Johannes Gutenberg's invention of movable type. In the 19th and 20th centuries, technological advances, the rise of literacy and leisure, and ever-increasing information needs contributed to an unprecedented expansion of publishing. Contemporary challenges in publishing include attempts at censorship, copyright laws and plagiarism, royalties for authors and commissions for literary agents, competitive marketing techniques, pressures from advertisers affecting editorial independence, acquisition of independent publishing concerns by conglomerates, and the loss of readers to other media such as television and the Internet.

Puccini, Giacomo (Antonio Domenico Michele Secondo Maria) (b. Dec. 22, 1858, Lucca, Tuscany—d. Nov. 29, 1924, Brussels, Belg.), Italian composer. Born into a family of organists and choirmasters, he was inspired to write operas after hearing Giuseppe Verdi's *Aïda* in 1876. At the Milan Conservatory he studied with Amilcare Ponchielli (1834–86). Puccini entered his first opera, *Le villi* (1883), in a competition; though it lost, a group of his friends subsidized its production, and its premiere took place with immense success. His second, *Edgar* (1889), was a failure, but *Manon Lescaut* (1893) brought him international recognition. His mature operas included *La Bohème* (1896), *Tosca* (1900), *Madam Butterfly* (1904), and *The Girl of the Golden West* (1910). All four are tragic love stories; his use of the orchestra was refined, and he established a dramatic structure that balanced action and conflict with moments of repose, contemplation, and lyricism. They remained exceedingly popular into the 21st century. He was the most popular opera composer in the world at the time of his death; his unfinished *Turandot* was completed by Franco Alfano (1875–1954).

puddling process, Method of converting pig iron into wrought iron by subjecting it to heat and frequent stirring in a furnace in the presence of oxidizing substances. Invented by Henry Cort in 1784 (superseding the finery process), it was the first method that allowed wrought iron to be produced on a large scale.

Puducherry, Union territory (pop., 2008 est.: 1,074,000), India. It was formed in 1962 from the four former French colonies of Pondicherry, Karikal, and Yanam, on the eastern seaboard, and Mahe, on the western seaboard. With a total area of 190 sq mi (492 sq km), it is united by little other than its colonial past and focus on tourism. The city of Puducherry is the administrative capital.

pueblo (Spanish: "town") Community of the Pueblo Indians of the southwestern U.S., consisting of multistoried apartment houses constructed of large adobe blocks beginning *c.* AD 1000. Freestanding structures up to five stories tall were built around a central court. Each floor is set back from the floor under it; the whole structure resembles a stepped pyramid, with terraces formed by the rooftops of the level below. Though rooms often have connecting doorways, movement between levels is by means of ladders through holes in the ceilings. Ground-floor rooms, used for storage, have no outside doors. Each pueblo has at least two kivas. Many of the pueblos are still occupied; Acoma pueblo is believed to be the oldest continuously inhabited place in the U.S. Some of the largest pueblos are at Taos, Isleta, Laguna, and Zuni.

puerperal fever, or CHILDBED FEVER, Infection of the female reproductive system after childbirth or abortion, with fever over 100 °F (38 °C) in the first 10 days. The inner surface of the uterus is most often infected, but lacerations of any part of the genital tract can give bacteria (often *Streptococcus pyogenes*) access to the bloodstream and lymphatic system to cause septicemia, cellulitis (cellular inflammation), and pelvic or generalized peritonitis. Severity varies. Puerperal fever has become very rare in developed countries but is still seen after abortions performed in unhygienic surroundings.

Puerto Rico, officially COMMONWEALTH OF PUERTO RICO, Self-governing island commonwealth of the West Indies, in the northeastern Caribbean Sea; it is associated with the U.S. Area: 3,515 sq mi (9,104 sq km). Population: (2011 est.) 3,716,000. Capital: San Juan. Most of the population is of Spanish descent, with significant minorities of people of African and mixed (African-European) descent. Languages: Spanish, English (both official). Religion: Christianity (predominantly Roman Catholic; also Protestant). Currency: U.S. dollar. The island of Puerto Rico may be divided into three geographic regions: the mountainous interior, the northern plateau, and the coastal plains. It has a developing free-market economy, of which manufacturing, financial services, and trade (mostly with the U.S.) are the main components. Tourism is also an important source of income. Puerto Rico's head of state is the U.S. president, and its head of government is the commonwealth governor. The island was inhabited by Arawak Indians when it was settled by the Spanish in the early 16th century. It remained largely undeveloped economically until the late 18th century. After 1830 it gradually developed a plantation economy based on the export crops of sugarcane, coffee, and tobacco. The independence movement began in the late 19th century, and Spain ceded the island to the U.S. in 1898 after the Spanish-American War. In 1917 Puerto Ricans were granted U.S. citizenship, and in 1952 the island became a commonwealth with autonomy in internal affairs. Voters reaffirmed the island's commonwealth status in plebiscites in 1967, 1993, and (tacitly) 1998, but Puerto Rican statehood remained a political issue into the 21st century.

puffin, or SEA PARROT, Any of three species (family Alcidae) of

diving birds with a large, brightly coloured, triangular beak. Puffins nest in large colonies on seaside and island cliffs. Both parents carry up to 10 fish crosswise in the bill to the nest (a deep burrow); they feed the single chick for about six weeks. They then leave, and the chick waits alone for its flight feathers to grow, living on stored fat, and then flies out to sea by itself. The common, or Atlantic, puffin (*Fratercula arctica*) is about 12 in. (30 cm) long. The Pacific species are the horned puffin (*F. corniculata*) and the tufted puffin (*Lunda cirrhata*).

*Common puffin (*Fratercula arctica*)*
Ben Goldstein/Root Resources

puja, In Hinduism, a form of ceremonial worship. It may range from brief daily rites in the home to an elaborate temple ritual. A typical *puja* offers the image of a deity the honours accorded to a royal guest. The god is gently roused from sleep, ritually bathed and dressed, served three meals during the day, and ceremonially put to bed. Rituals may also include a sacrifice and oblation to the sacred fire. Some *puja*s are performed by the worshiper alone; others require a ritually pure person. A *puja* may be performed for a specific purpose or simply as an act of devotion.

Pulitzer, Joseph (b. April 10, 1847, Makó, Hung.—d. Oct. 29, 1911, Charleston, S.C., U.S.), Hungarian-born U.S. newspaper editor and publisher. He immigrated to the U.S. in 1864 to serve in the American Civil War. After the war he became a reporter and then proprietor at German-language newspapers in St. Louis and entered Missouri politics. In 1878 he merged the *St. Louis Dispatch* (founded 1864) and the *Post* (founded 1875) into the *Post-Dispatch*, which soon became the city's dominant evening newspaper. Shifting his interests to New York City, he purchased the *World* (1883) and founded the *Evening World* (1887). He helped establish the pattern of the modern newspaper by combining exposés of political corruption and crusading investigative reporting with publicity stunts, self-advertising, and sensationalism. In his will he endowed the Columbia University School of Journalism and established the Pulitzer Prizes.

Pulitzer Prize, Any of a series of annual prizes awarded by Columbia University for outstanding public service and achievement in American journalism, letters, and music. Fellowships are also awarded. The prizes, originally endowed with a gift of $500,000 from Joseph Pulitzer, are highly esteemed and have been awarded each May since 1917 on the recommendation of the Pulitzer Prize Board, composed of judges appointed by the university. The numbers and categories of prizes have varied over the years. Today they include 14 awards in journalism, six in letters, one in music, and four fellowships.

pulmonary heart disease, or COR PULMONALE, Enlargement and eventual failure of the right ventricle of the heart due to disorders of the lungs or their blood vessels or chest wall abnormalities. Chronic disease is most often caused by chronic bronchitis or emphysema. Symptoms include chronic cough, trouble in breathing after exertion, wheezing, weakness, leg edema, right upper abdominal pain, and neck vein distension. Pressure in the pulmonary artery rises and the right ventricle enlarges in response, leading, if uncorrected, to heart failure. Treatment includes a respirator, low-sodium diet, diuretics, digitalis, and antibiotics for respiratory infection. Acute disease due to pulmonary embolism is often treated by removal of the blockage.

pulsar, in full PULSATING RADIO STAR, Any of a class of cosmic objects that appear to emit extremely regular pulses of radio waves. A few give off short rhythmic bursts of visible light, X rays, and gamma radiation as well. Thought to be rapidly spinning neutron stars, they were discovered by Antony Hewish and Jocelyn Bell Burnell in 1967 with a specially designed radio telescope. More than 550 have been detected since. All behave similarly, but the intervals between pulses (and thus their rotation periods) range from one-thousandth of a second to four seconds. Charged particles from the surface enter the star's magnetic field, which accelerates them so that they give off radiation, released as intense beams from the magnetic poles. These do not coincide with the pulsar's own axis of rotation, so as the star spins, the radiation beams swing around like lighthouse beams and are seen as pulses. Pulsars have been shown to be slowing down, typically by a millionth of a second per year. It has been calculated that pulsars "switch off" after about 10 million years, when their magnetic fields weaken enough.

pulse, Pressure wave in the arteries from contraction of the heart. It can be felt where arteries are near the skin's surface; it is usually read at the carotid artery in the neck or at the wrist. Its rate, strength, and rhythm and the contour of the wave provide valuable information but must be viewed in context (e.g., rapid pulse occurs with serious heart disease, simple fever, or vigorous exercise). The average adult pulse rate is 70–80 beats per minute; the rate decreases with age and is generally faster in women.

punctuation, Standard set of marks used in written and printed texts to clarify meaning and to separate sentences, words, and parts of words. It often marks discourse features such as intonational contours and pauses. It may also convey information about a word (e.g., hyphens in compound words) unrelated to speech patterns. In English, the period (.) marks the end of a sentence or an abbreviation. The comma (,) usually separates clauses, phrases, or items in a series. The colon (:) often introduces an explanation or series of examples. The semicolon (;) usually separates independent clauses. The em-dash (—) marks an abrupt transition. The exclamation point (!) signals surprise. The question mark (?) signals a question. The apostrophe (') marks the possessive case or the omission of letters. Quotation marks (" ") set off either quoted words or words used with special significance. Interpolations in a sentence are marked by brackets ([ ]) or parentheses ( ).

Punic Wars, or CARTHAGINIAN WARS, Three wars (264–241 BC, 218–201, 149–146) between Rome and Carthage. The first concerned control of Sicily and of the sea lanes in the western Mediterranean; it ended with Rome victorious but with great loss of ships and men on both sides. In 218 Hannibal attacked Roman territory, starting from Spain and marching overland into Italy with troops and elephants. After an initial Carthaginian victory, Fabius Maximus Cunctator harassed him wherever he went without offering battle. Abandoning this tactic resulted in a major Roman loss at the Battle of Cannae (216); that defeat drew the Romans together and, though worn down, they managed to rally, eventually defeating Hannibal and driving him out of Italy (203). The Third Punic War was essentially the siege of Carthage; it led to the destruction of Carthage, the enslavement of its people, and Roman hegemony in the western Mediterranean. The Carthaginian territory became the Roman province of Africa.

Punjab, State (pop., 2008 est.: 26,591,000), northwestern India. Bordered by Pakistan and the states of Jammu and Kashmir, Himachal Pradesh, Haryana, and Rajasthan, it occupies an area of 19,445 sq mi (50,362 sq km). The city of Chandigarh is the joint administrative capital of Punjab and Haryana. In the 18th century the Sikhs built a powerful kingdom in the Punjab region, which came under British rule in 1849. In 1947 the area was split between the new countries of India and Pakistan, the smaller eastern portion going to India. It is the only Indian state with a majority of Sikhs. Hindus make up about one-third of the population, and there are smaller minorities of Christians, Jains, and Muslims. The economy is based on agriculture and small- and medium-scale industry.

Punjabi language, or PANJABI LANGUAGE, Indo-Aryan language of the Punjab in India and Pakistan. Punjabi has about 26 million speakers in India and more than 60 million in Pakistan—nearly half the population of the latter—but linguists have sometimes considered the dialects of southwestern, western, and northern Punjab province in Pakistan a different language. Inhabitants of southern Punjab province have agitated for consideration of their speech, Siraiki (with more than 12 million speakers), as a distinct language, though Siraiki and Punjabi are mutually intelligible.

puppetry, Art of creating and manipulating puppets in a theatrical show. Puppets are figures that are moved by human rather than mechanical aid. They may be controlled by one or several puppeteers, who are screened from the spectators. Varieties include glove (or hand) puppets, rod puppets, shadow puppets, and marionettes (or string puppets). Puppetry had its beginnings in tribal society and has been part of every civilization. By the 18th century it was so popular in Europe that permanent theatres were built for the usually itinerant puppeteers. Companies presented favourite stories of the French Guignol, the Italian Arlecchino, the German Kasperle, and the English Punch and Judy. By the mid 20th century puppetry had reached television with Jim Henson's Muppets.

purdah, Seclusion of women from public observation by means of concealing clothing (including the veil) and walled enclosures as well as screens and curtains within the home. The custom seems to have originated in Persia and was adopted by Muslims during the Arab conquest of what is now Iraq in the 7th century. The Muslim domination of northern India led to its adoption by the Hindu upper classes, but it was discarded by Hindus after the end of British rule in India. The custom of purdah still continues in many Islamic countries.

Pure Land Buddhism, Devotional cult of the buddha Amitabha. It is one of the most popular forms of Mahayana Buddhism in East Asia today. Pure Land Buddhists believe that rebirth in the Western Paradise (the Pure Land) is given to all those who invoke Amitabha's name with sincere devotion. In China the Pure Land cult can be traced back to the 4th century, when the scholar Huiyuan (333–416) formed a society of monks and laymen who meditated on the name of Amitabha. His successors systematized and spread the doctrine in the 6th–7th century. The Pure Land teaching was transmitted to Japan by monks of the Tiantai school.

purgatory, In Roman Catholic doctrine, the condition of those who have died in a state of grace but have not been purged of sin. These remaining sins include unforgiven venial sins or forgiven mortal sins. Souls burdened by such sins must be purified before entering heaven. The church also teaches that souls in purgatory may be aided by efforts of the living faithful through prayers, almsgiving, indulgences, and other works. The existence of purgatory has been denied as unbiblical by Protestant churches and most Eastern Orthodox churches.

purge trials, Soviet trials of critics of Joseph Stalin. After the assassination of Sergey Kirov, prominent Bolsheviks were accused of conspiracy to remove Stalin from power. In three widely publicized show trials (1936–38), which presented confessions obtained under torture or fabricated by the secret police, the accused were found guilty and executed or sent to prison. Numerous closed, unpublicized trials of Soviet military leaders were also held and resulted in a massive purge throughout the armed forces. The trials eliminated such potential rivals and critics of Stalin as Nikolay Bukharin, Lev Kamenev, Aleksey Rykov, Mikhayl Tukhachevsky, Genrikh Yagoda, and Grigory Zinovyev but earned worldwide condemnation.

Purim, Jewish festival celebrating the survival of the Jews marked for death in Persia in the 5th cent BC. According to the Book of Esther, Haman, chief minister of King Ahasuerus, planned a general massacre of the Jews and set the date by casting lots. Ahasuerus' wife Esther interceded for the Jews, and they were allowed to attack their enemies. The ritual observance begins with a day of fasting on the 13th of Adar (in February or March), the day before the actual holiday. The Book of Esther is read in the synagogue, and Jews are enjoined to exchange gifts and make donations to the poor. Purim is a day of merrymaking and feasting.

Puritanism, Movement in the late 16th and 17th century that sought to "purify" the Church of England, leading to civil war in England and to the founding of colonies in North America. Many Puritans joined the Parliamentary party during the English Civil War and gained considerable power, but after the Restoration they were once again a dissenting minority. Believing themselves chosen by God to revolutionize history, some Puritans founded settlements in America, notably the Massachusetts Bay Colony. The Puritans of Massachusetts emphasized the conversion experience, by which the elect experienced the descent of grace. In their theocracy only the elect were allowed to vote and rule, though the privileges of church membership were extended to all baptized and orthodox persons.

purpura, Presence of hemorrhages in the skin, often associated with bleeding from natural cavities and in tissues. Major causes include damage to small artery walls (as in vitamin deficiency or allergic reaction) and platelet deficiency (in association with such disorders as lupus erythematosus and as a complication of leukemia or chemotherapy).

Pusan, or BUSAN, City (pop., 2003 est.: 3,747,369) and port, South Korea, at the southeastern tip of the Korean peninsula. Pusan was opened to Japanese trade in 1876 and to general foreign trade in 1883. It developed into a major port under Japanese rule (1910–45). It served as the country's temporary capital during the Korean War. Pusan is South Korea's largest port and second largest city. Administratively, it has the status of a metropolitan city equal to that of a province. Industries include shipbuilding and manufacturing. Hot springs are located in the northeastern suburbs.

Putin, Vladimir (Vladimirovich) (b. Oct. 7, 1952, Leningrad, U.S.S.R.), Russian president (1999–2008; 2012–) and prime minister (1999; 2008–12). Putin served 15 years with the KGB, including six years in Dresden, E.Ger. In 1990 he retired from active KGB service and returned to Russia to become prorector of Leningrad State University, and by 1994 he had risen to the post of first deputy mayor of the city. In 1996 he moved to Moscow, where he joined the presidential staff as deputy to Pavel Borodin, the Kremlin's chief administrator. In July 1998 President Boris Yeltsin made Putin director of the Federal Security Service (the KGB's domestic successor). In 1999 Yeltsin appointed Putin prime minister, and on December 31 of that year Yeltsin stepped down as president in Putin's favour. Three months later Putin won a resounding electoral victory, partly the result of his success in the battle to keep Chechnya from seceding. In his first term he asserted central control over Russia's 89 regions and republics and moved to reduce the power of Russia's unpopular financiers and media tycoons. The period was also marked by frequent terrorist attacks by Chechen separatists. Putin easily won reelection in 2004. His chosen successor, Dmitry Medvedev, was elected president in March 2008 and, shortly after taking office, appointed Putin prime minister. In 2011 the two men announced that they would be trading posts—pending a victory at the polls—and in the 2012 election, Putin won a third term as president.

PVC, in full POLYVINYL CHLORIDE, Synthetic resin, an organic polymer made by treating vinyl chloride monomers with a peroxide. It may be blended with more rubbery polymers or copolymerized with other vinyls to obtain products with desired properties. PVC resin mixed with plasticizers, stabilizers, and pigments is made into flexible articles (e.g., raincoats, toys, containers). Nonplasticized resin has been used for rigid products (e.g., water pipes, plumbing fittings, phonograph records). Concern over leaching of vinyl chloride into foods has resulted in restrictions on its use in food containers; its decomposition into hydrogen chloride when burned has also raised concerns. Today it is produced in larger quantities than any other plastic except polyethylene.

pyelonephritis, Infection (usually bacterial) and inflammation of kidney tissue and the renal pelvis. Acute pyelonephritis is usually localized and may have no apparent cause. Symptoms include fever, chills, lower-back pain, and bacteria and white blood cells in the urine. Treatment with antibiotics requires one to three weeks. Scar tissue forms, but kidney function is usually not impaired. Chronic pyelonephritis results from repeated bacterial infections, which may have no symptoms but destroy more and more tissue over years. If it is diagnosed before too much function is lost, surgery may help, but uremia, severe infections, and heart and blood-vessel disorders can lead to death. Dialysis or kidney transplant sometimes prolongs life.

Pygmalion, In Greek mythology, a king of Cyprus who fell in love with a statue of Aphrodite. The goddess took pity on him and brought the statue to life, and he married her. In some versions of the myth Pygmalion was a sculptor who carved the statue himself because he was disgusted with the faults of ordinary women, and when it was brought to life he gave it the name Galatea.

Pygmy, Member of any human group whose adult males grow to less than 59 in. (150 cm) in average height. The name is also sometimes loosely applied to the San of southern Africa and the so-called Negrito peoples of Asia (such as the Philippine Ilongot). Besides their short stature, Pygmies are notable in having the highest basal-metabolism rate in the world and a high incidence of sickle-cell anemia. The Bambuti of the Ituri Forest are a well-studied example.

P'yŏngyang, City (pop., 2001 est.: 3,164,000), capital of North Korea, on the Taedong River. Founded in 1122 BC according to legend, it is said to be the oldest city in Korea. In 108 BC the Chinese established a trading colony there. It was the capital of the Koguryŏ kingdom (AD 427–668), then was subjected by Silla. It fell to the Japanese in 1592 and was devastated by the Manchus in the early 17th century. Much of it was destroyed during the Sino-Japanese War (1894–95). During the Japanese occupation of Korea (1910–45), it was built up as an industrial city. Captured by UN forces during the Korean War in 1950, it was retaken by Chinese communist troops. After 1953 it was rebuilt with Soviet and Chinese aid. It is a centre of heavy industry and transportation.

Pyrenees, Mountain range, southwestern Europe. It extends 270 mi (430 km) from the Mediterranean Sea to the Bay of Biscay on the Atlantic Ocean. The Pyrenees form a high wall between France and Spain; generally, the crest of the range marks the boundary between the two countries. The tiny, autonomous principality of Andorra lies among the range's peaks. The highest point is Aneto Peak, elevation 11,169 ft (3,404 m). There are few passes through the mountains. The pass at Roncesvalles was made famous in the 12th-century *La Chanson de Roland*, based on the 778 Battle of Roncesvalles (Roncevaux).

pyrite, or IRON PYRITE, or FOOL'S GOLD, Naturally occurring, gold-coloured iron disulfide mineral. Pyrite has frequently fooled prospectors into thinking they had discovered gold. Pure pyrite (FeS_2) contains 47% iron and 53% sulfur, by weight. Pyrite is used commercially as a source of sulfur, particularly for the production of sulfuric acid. Because there are much better sources of iron, it is not generally used as an iron ore. For many years Spain was the largest producer; other countries include Japan, the U.S., Canada, Italy, Norway, Portugal, and Slovakia.

Pythagoras (b. *c.* 570 BCE, Samos, Ionia—d. *c.* 500–490 BCE, Metapontum, Lucanium), Greek philosopher and mathematician. He established a community of followers in Croton who adhered to a way of life he prescribed. His school of philosophy reduced all meaning to numerical relationships and proposed that all existing objects are fundamentally composed of form and not material substance. The principles of Pythagoreanism, including belief in the immortality and reincarnation of the soul and in the liberating power of abstinence and asceticism, influenced the thought of Plato and Aristotle and contributed to the development of mathematics and Western rational philosophy. The proportions of musical intervals and scales were first studied by Pythagoras, and he was the first influential Western practitioner of vegetarianism. None of his writings survive, and it is difficult to distinguish the ideas he originated from those of his disciples. His memory is kept alive partly by the Pythagorean theorem, probably developed by his school after he died.

Pythagorean theorem, Rule relating the lengths of the sides of a right triangle. It says that the sum of the squares of the lengths of the legs is equal to the square of the length of the hypotenuse (the side opposite the right angle). That is, $a^2 + b^2 = c^2$, where c is the length of the hypotenuse. Triads of whole numbers that satisfy it (e.g., 3, 4, and 5) are called Pythagorean triples.

Pythagoreanism, Philosophical school, probably founded by Pythagoras *c.* 525 BC. It originated as a religious brotherhood or an association for the moral reformation of society; brothers were sworn to strict loyalty and secrecy. The brotherhood had much in common with the Orphic communities, which sought by rites and abstinence to purify the believer's soul and enable it to escape from the "wheel of birth." Pythagoreanism held that reality, at its deepest level, is mathematical, that philosophy can be used for spiritual purification, that the soul can rise to union with the divine, and that certain symbols have mystical significance. It was the first important Western system of thought to advocate vegetarianism. The school became extinct in the mid-4th century.

python, Any of 40 species (family Pythonidae, sometimes a subfamily of Boidae) of sluggish, docile, nonvenomous snakes found in tropical and temperate regions. Except for one Central American species (*Loxocemus bicolor*), pythons are found from western Africa to China, Australia, and the Pacific islands. Pythons feed on birds and mammals, killing them by constriction. Most are found near water; some are arboreal. Unlike boas, pythons lay eggs (15–100, depending on body size). The Asian reticulated python (*Python reticulatus*) may be the world's longest snake (the anaconda is heavier); specimens over 30 ft (9 m) long have been recorded.

Q

qāḍī, Muslim judge who renders decisions according to the Sharīʿah, the canon law of Islam. The *qāḍī* hears only religious cases, such as those involving inheritance, pious bequests, marriage, and divorce, though theoretically his jurisdiction extends to civil and criminal matters. The second caliph, ʿUmar ibn al-Khaṭṭāb, was the first to appoint a *qāḍī* to eliminate the necessity of his personally judging every dispute that arose in the community.

Qaeda, al-, also AL-QĀʿIDAH (Arabic: "the Base"), Broad-based Islamic militant organization founded in Afghanistan by Osama bin Laden. Its members supported Muslim fighters during the Afghan war of 1979–89; afterward the organization dispersed but continued to oppose secularized Muslim regimes and foreign (notably U.S.) presence in Islamic lands. It staged numerous terrorist attacks, including the bombing of the World Trade Center in 1993, the destruction of two U.S. embassies in Africa in 1998, and a suicide bomb attack against the U.S. warship *Cole* in 2000. During that time it merged with other Islamic extremist organizations and eventually reestablished its headquarters in Taliban-controlled Afghanistan, where it trained thousands of Muslim militants. In 2001, 19 such militants staged the September 11 attacks. The U.S. and allied forces responded by attacking Taliban and al-Qaeda forces in Afghanistan, killing and capturing thousands and driving the remainder into hiding. After a nearly decade-long manhunt, bin Laden was killed by U.S. forces in Abbottabad, Pak., in May 2011.

Qaraghandy, or KARAGANDA, City (pop., 2006 est.: 446,139), central Kazakhstan. The first settlement appeared in 1856, and small-scale coal mining began the next year. Mining expanded rapidly in the early 1930s, and the town was made a city in 1934. Kazakhstan's second largest city, it consists of the old town, which grew up haphazardly around more than 20 mining settlements, and the new town, the region's cultural and administrative centre, which includes a university and medical and polytechnic institutes.

Qatar, officially STATE OF QATAR, Country, Middle East, southwestern Asia. It juts out from the east coast of the Arabian Peninsula into the Persian Gulf. Area: 4,468 sq mi (11,571 sq km). Population: (2011 est.) 1,624,000. Capital: Doha. Most of the population is Arab, with South Asian and Iranian minorities who are often migrant workers. Languages: Arabic (official), English. Religions: Islam (official; predominantly Sunni); also Christianity, Hinduism. Currency: Qatar rial. Qatar is mostly stony, sandy, and barren and consists of salt flats, dune desert, and arid plains. Largely because of petroleum and natural gas exports, its gross national product per capita is one of the highest in the world. The government owns all of the agricultural land and generates most of the economic activity; the private sector participates in trade and contracting on a limited scale. Qatar is a constitutional emirate with one advisory body, and its basis of legislation is Islamic law. The head of state and government is the emir, assisted by the prime minister. It was partly controlled by Bahrain from the mid-18th to the mid-19th century and then was nominally part of the Ottoman Empire until World War I (1914–18). In 1916 it became a British protectorate. Oil was discovered in 1939, and Qatar rapidly modernized. It declared independence in 1971, when the British protectorate ended. In 1991 Qatar served as a base for air strikes against Iraq in the Persian Gulf War.

Qazvīn, or KAZVĪN, City (pop., 2006: 355,338), northwestern Iran. It was founded as Shad Shāhpūr in 250 CE and flourished under Muslim rule in the 7th century. Genghis Khan laid waste to the city, but it later revived and was made the capital of Persia (1548–98) under the Ṣafavid dynasty. In the late 18th century it became a base for foreign trade with areas of the Caspian Sea, the Persian Gulf, and Anatolia. A coup was launched from Qazvīn in 1921 that led to Iran's consolidation under Reza Shah Pahlavi. It is a regional communications centre, with some manufacturing.

qi, or CHʿI, In Chinese philosophy, the ethereal substance of which everything is composed. Early Daoist philosophers and alchemists regarded it as a vital force associated with breath and bodily fluids and sought to control its movement within the body in order to achieve longevity and spiritual power. Manipulation of *qi* is central to Chinese meditation, medicine, and martial arts. In the 10th–13th centuries Neo-Confucianism regarded *qi* as emanating from the Great Ultimate by way of *li*, the ordering principle of the universe, transformed into the elements through yin and yang.

Qianlong emperor, or CHʿIEN-LUNG EMPEROR, orig. HONGLI (b. Sept. 25, 1711, China—d. Feb. 7, 1799, Beijing), Fourth emperor of the Qing dynasty in China. His reign (1735–96) was one of the longest in Chinese history. China's boundaries reached their greatest extent, encompassing Mongolia, Tibet, Nepal, Taiwan, and portions of Central Asia. Qianlong sponsored a compilation of the Confucian Classics; the compilation's descriptive catalog is still used today. At the same time, he ordered that all books containing anti-Manchu sentiments be expurgated or destroyed; some 2,600 titles were lost. He enjoyed excellent personal relationships with Jesuit missionaries in Beijing, though Roman Catholic preaching remained officially forbidden. In the first half of his reign, agriculture made great strides and was superior to that in much of Europe. Taxes were light and education was widespread, even among the peasantry. Subsequently, military expeditions and increasing governmental corruption permanently harmed the dynasty, sowing the seeds for its decline in the 19th century.

Qin Jiushao (b. c. 1202, Puzhou, China—d. c. 1261, Meizhou), Chinese mathematician who developed a method of solving simultaneous linear congruences. In 1219 he joined the army as captain of a territorial volunteer unit and helped quash a local rebellion. In 1233 he began his official government service. In his only mathematical book, now known as *Shushu jiuzhang* (1247; "Mathematical Writings in Nine Sections"), he introduced a method of solving systems of linear equations that was rediscovered in Europe about 1802, where it became known as the Ruffini-Horner method. He later became provincial governor of Qiongzhou, but charges of corruption and bribery brought his dismissal in 1258.

Qin tomb, or CHʿIN TOMB, Major Chinese archaeological site near the ancient capital city of Chang'an (now Xi'an), a 20-sq-mi (50-sq-km) funerary compound built by the first sovereign emperor, Qin Shihuangdi. In 1974 workers drilling a well discovered a subterranean chamber that contained an army of some 6,000 life-size terra-cotta soldiers with individually detailed faces, as well as horses, weapons, and other objects. Three nearby chambers containing more than 1,400 figures have also been unearthed; the tomb itself has not yet been excavated. Archaeologists anticipate that it will take many years to unearth the rest of the complex. The mausoleum is a UNESCO World Heritage site.

Qing dynasty, or CHʿING DYNASTY, or MANCHU DYNASTY (1644–1911/12) Last of the imperial dynasties in China. The name Qing was first applied to the dynasty established by the Manchu in 1636 in Manchuria and then applied by extension to their rule in China. During the Qing dynasty, China's territory and population expanded tremendously. Cultural attitudes were strongly conservative and Neo-Confucianism was the dominant philosophy. The arts flourished: literati painting was popular, novels in the vernacular developed substantially, and *jingxi* (Peking opera) developed. Qing porcelain, textiles, tea, paper, sugar, and steel were exported to all parts of the world. Military campaigns in the latter part of the 18th century depleted government finances, and corruption grew. These conditions, combined with population pressures and natural disasters, led to the Opium Wars and the Taiping and Nian rebellions, which in turn so weakened the dynasty that it was unable to rebuff the demands of foreign powers. The dynasty ended with the republican revolution of 1911 and the abdication of the last emperor in 1912.

Qinghai, or CH'ING-HAI, conventional TSINGHAI, Province (pop., 2002 est.: 5,290,000), northwestern China. It is bordered by Gansu and Sichuan provinces and the Tibet and Xinjiang autonomous regions.With an area of 278,400 sq mi (721,000 sq km), it is the fourth largest political subdivision in China. The capital is Xining. Located in a remote region west of the historic provinces of China proper, it forms the northeastern part of the Plateau of Tibet, mostly above 13,000 ft (4,000 m) in elevation. The source of the Huang He (Yellow River) is in one of its mountain ranges. Parts of Qinghai came under Chinese control in the 3rd century BC. For centuries it was sparsely occupied by nomadic herdsmen, chiefly Tibetans and Mongols, and a few Chinese farmers. The Chinese population increased over the years. Qinghai was made a Chinese province in 1928. Economic activities today include farming, herding, mining, lumbering, and manufacturing. It possesses some of China's best pasturelands and is noted for its horse breeding.

Qu Yuan, or CH'Ü YÜAN (b. *c.* 339, Quyi, China—d. 278 BC, Hunan), Chinese poet. Born into the ruling house of Chu, in youth Qu Yuan was a favourite of the region's ruler. Later he was banished and wandered in despair, writing and observing folk customs, which would influence his works. He eventually drowned himself. His most famous poem is the melancholy *Lisao* ("On Encountering Sorrow"). One of the greatest poets of ancient China, he exerted enormous influence on later poets with his highly original verse.

Quadruple Alliance (1718) Alliance between Austria, Britain, the Dutch Republic, and France, formed to prevent Spain from altering the terms of the Peace of Utrecht (1713). When Philip V of Spain seized Sardinia and Sicily, the British fleet brought Austrian troops to Sicily and the French occupied northern Spain, and Philip was forced to renounce his claims in Italy.

Quadruple Alliance (1815) Alliance between Britain, Russia, Austria, and Prussia first formed in 1813 to oppose France in the final phase of the Napoleonic Wars. It was officially renewed in 1815 to enforce the peace settlement concluded at the Congress of Vienna. The allies agreed to meet occasionally to keep European political development within terms of the 1815 settlement. This program was partially carried out by the Congresses of Aix-la-Chapelle (1818), Troppau (1820), Laibach (1821), and Verona (1822).

quality, In philosophy, a property that applies to things taken singly, in contrast to a relation, which applies to things taken in pairs, triples, etc. The distinction drawn by Galileo and John Locke between primary and secondary qualities is motivated by the fact that modern science seems to reveal that unaided sensory perception gives false or incomplete information about the intrinsic qualities of physical objects. In this view, primary qualities, such as shape, quantity, and motion, are genuine properties of things that are describable by mathematics, whereas secondary qualities, such as odour, taste, sound, and colour, exist only in human consciousness.

quantum, In physics, a discrete natural unit, or packet, of energy, charge, angular momentum, or other physical property. Light, for example, which appears in some respects as a continuous electro-

magnetic wave, on the submicroscopic level is emitted and absorbed in discrete amounts, or quanta; for light of a given wavelength, the magnitude of all the quanta emitted or absorbed is the same in both energy and momentum. These particlelike packets of light are called photons, a term also applicable to quanta of other forms of electromagnetic energy such as X rays and gamma rays. Submicroscopic mechanical vibrations in the layers of atoms comprising crystals also give up or take on energy and momentum in quanta called phonons.

quantum computing, Experimental method of computing that makes use of quantum-mechanical phenomena. It incorporates quantum theory and the uncertainty principle. Quantum computers would allow a bit to store a value of 0 and 1 simultaneously. They could pursue multiple lines of inquiry simultaneously, with the final output dependent on the interference pattern generated by the various calculations.

quantum field theory, Theory that brings quantum mechanics and special relativity together to account for subatomic phenomena. In particular, the interactions of subatomic particles are described in terms of their interactions with fields, such as the electromagnetic field. However, the fields are quantized and represented by particles, such as photons for the electromagnetic field. Quantum electrodynamics is the quantum field theory that describes the interaction of electrically charged particles via electromagnetic fields. Quantum chromodynamics describes the action of the strong force. The electroweak theory, a unified theory of electromagnetic and weak forces, has considerable experimental support, and can likely be extended to include the strong force. Theories that include the gravitational force are more speculative.

quantum mechanics, Branch of mathematical physics that deals with atomic and subatomic systems. It is concerned with phenomena that are so small-scale that they cannot be described in classical terms, and it is formulated entirely in terms of statistical probabilities. Considered one of the great ideas of the 20th century, quantum mechanics was developed mainly by Niels Bohr, Erwin Schrödinger, Werner Heisenberg, and Max Born and led to a drastic reappraisal of the concept of objective reality. It explained the structure of atoms, atomic nuclei, and molecules; the behaviour of subatomic particles; the nature of chemical bonds; the properties of crystalline solids; nuclear energy; and the forces that stabilize collapsed stars. It also led directly to the development of the laser, the electron microscope, and the transistor.

quark, Any of a group of subatomic particles thought to be among the fundamental constituents of matter—more specifically, of protons and neutrons. The concept of the quark was first proposed by Murray Gell-Mann and George Zweig (b. 1937); its name was taken from James Joyce's novel *Finnegans Wake*. Quarks include all particles that interact by means of the strong force. They have mass and spin, and they obey the Pauli exclusion principle. They have never been resolved into smaller components, and they never occur alone. Their behaviour is explained by the theory of quantum chromodynamics, which provides a means of calculating their basic properties. There are six types of quarks, called up, down, strange, charm, bottom, and top. Only the up and down quarks are needed to make protons and neutrons; the others occur in heavier, unstable particles.

quartz, Second most abundant mineral (after feldspar) in the Earth's crust, present in many rocks. Quartz, which consists of silica, or silicon dioxide (SiO_2), has great economic importance. Many varieties are gemstones, including amethyst, citrine, smoky quartz, and rose quartz. Sandstone, composed mainly of quartz, is an important building stone. Large amounts of quartz sand (or silica sand) are used in the manufacture of glass and ceramics and for molds in metal casting. Crushed quartz is used as an abrasive in sandpaper; silica sand is employed in sandblasting; and sandstone is used whole to make whetstones, millstones, and grindstones. Silica glass (or fused quartz) is used in optics to transmit ultraviolet light. Tubing and various vessels of fused quartz have important laboratory applications, and quartz fibres are employed in extremely sensitive weighing devices.

quasar, in full QUASI-STELLAR RADIO SOURCE, Any of a class of enigmatic cosmic objects of high luminosity and strong radio emission observed at extremely great distances; also, a closely related object that has the same optical appearance but does not emit radio waves, i.e., a so-called quasi-stellar object (QSO). Most quasars exhibit very large redshifts, suggesting that they are moving away from Earth at tremendous speeds (approaching the speed of light); they thus are some of the most distant known objects in the universe. Quasars are no more than a light-year or two across but as much as 1,000 times more luminous than a giant galaxy having a diameter of 100,000 light-years; their extreme brightness allows them to be observed at distances of more than 10 billion light-years. Many investigators attribute such energy generation to matter spiraling at high velocity into a supermassive black hole (millions or billions of times as much mass as the Sun) at the centre of a distant galaxy.

Quasimodo, Salvatore (b. Aug. 20, 1901, Modica, Italy—d. June 14, 1968, Naples), Italian poet, critic, and translator. He spent 10 years as an engineer for the Italian government while writing poetry in his spare time. He gradually became a leader of Hermeticism after the publication of his first poetry collection, *Waters and Land* (1930). After World War II his social convictions shaped his work, beginning with *Day After Day* (1947). He published an astonishing range of translations, edited anthologies, and wrote essays, including those in *The Poet and the Politician* (1960). He received the Nobel Prize for Literature in 1959.

Quaternary Period, Interval of geologic time, approximately 2.6 million years ago to the present. The Quaternary follows the Neogene Period and is the most recent of the three periods of the Cenozoic Era. The Quaternary is subdivided into the Pleistocene Epoch and the Holocene Epoch and is characterized by major cyclical changes of climate on a global scale. These led to repeated invasions of vast areas by ice sheets. Its major biological feature is the evolution and dispersion of humans. The dramatic changes of climate and environment in the Quaternary led to high rates of evolution and extinction, particularly among the mammals. The extinction of many large mammals toward the end of the last ice age may also be related to the rapid territorial expansion of humans.

Quebec, or QUEBEC CITY, City (pop., 2001: metro. area, 682,757), port and capital of Quebec province, Canada. It lies at the confluence of the St. Lawrence and St. Charles rivers, about 150 mi (240 km) northeast of Montreal, on a rocky promontory above the rivers. Canada's oldest city, it was settled by the French in 1608 as a trading post. It was the capital of New France from 1663 to 1763, when it was lost to the British. It was the capital of Lower Canada 1791–1841 and Canada East 1841–67. It became the provincial capital in 1867. Most of the population is French speaking and Roman Catholic. It is the site of Laval University and other colleges and cultural institutions. Manufactures include newsprint, milled grain, cigarettes, and clothing. Shipbuilding and tourism are important industries.

Quechuan languages, Family of closely related South American Indian languages still spoken by some 12 million people in southern Colombia and Ecuador, Bolivia, and northern Argentina. Southern Peruvian Quechua, one language of the family, was a koine and administrative language within the Inca empire and was spread by Inca colonization.

Queen Anne style, Style of English decorative arts that reached its apex during the reign (1702–14) of Queen Anne. The most distinctive feature of Queen Anne furniture is the cabriole leg, shaped in a double curve (the upper part convex, the lower concave) and ending in either a claw-and-ball or paw foot. The Queen Anne chair is identifiable by a splat back curved to fit the hollow of the spine. The wood used was almost exclusively walnut, often embellished with marquetry, inlay, veneering, and lacquerwork. Ornamentation motifs include scallop shells, scrolls, Asian figures, and animals.

Queensland, State, northeastern Australia. Area: 668,207 sq mi (1,730,648 sq km). Population: (2006) 3,904,532; (2010 est.) 4,513,860. Capital: Brisbane. It is bounded to the north by the Pacific Ocean and the Great Barrier Reef. Its coastal region, the most tropical part of Australia, was designated a UNESCO World Heritage site in 1988; it is a major tourist attraction. Inland from the Great Dividing Range, which runs the entire length of the state, mining and cattle ranching are important. Capt. James Cook charted the coast in 1770. In the 19th century the state housed several penal colonies and drew settlers to mine its gold. It became a constituent state in 1901 when the Commonwealth of Australia was proclaimed.

quenching, Rapid cooling, as by immersion in oil or water, of a metal object from the high temperature at which it is shaped. Quenching is usually done to maintain mechanical properties that would be lost with slow cooling. It is commonly applied to steel objects, to which it gives hardness. The quenching media and the type of agitation during quenching are selected to obtain specified physical properties with minimum internal stresses and distortions. Oil is the mildest medium, and salt brine has the strongest quenching effect. In special cases, steel is cooled and held for some time in a molten salt bath, which is kept at a temperature either just above or just below the temperature where martensite begins to form. These two heat treatments, called martempering and austempering, both result in even less distortion of the metal. Copper objects hardened by hammering or other deformation at ordinary temperatures can be restored to malleability by heating and quenching.

Quetzalcóatl, Feathered Serpent, a major deity of ancient Mexico. Quetzalcóatl began as a god of vegetation in the Teotihuacán civilization. For the Toltecs he was the god of the morning and evening star. The Aztecs revered him as the patron of priests, the inventor of the calendar and of books, and the protector of goldsmiths and other craftsmen. He was also identified with the planet Venus and was a symbol of death and resurrection. One myth held that he was a white priest-king who sailed away on a raft made of snakes. The belief that he would someday return from the east led Montezuma II to regard Hernan Cortes as the fulfillment of the prophecy.

Quetzalcóatl, limestone figure of the Huastec culture, Mexico, AD 900–1250; in The Brooklyn Museum, New York.
Courtesy of The Brooklyn Museum, New York, Henry L. Batterman and Frank S. Benson Funds

Quezon City, City (pop., 2000: 2,173,831), Luzon Island, Philippines, northeast of Manila. Named for Pres. Manuel Quezon, who selected the site in 1939, it replaced Manila as the capital in 1948. Considered part of metropolitan Manila, it began to grow after World War II with the construction of many government buildings. The seat of government moved back to Manila in 1976. The city is home to two major universities.

quicksand, State in which water-saturated sand loses its supporting capacity and acquires the characteristics of a liquid. Quicksand is usually found in a hollow at the mouth of a large river or along a flat stretch of stream or beach where pools of water become partly filled with sand and an underlying layer of stiff clay or other dense material prevents drainage. Mixtures of sand, mud, and vegetation in bogs often act like true quicksands. Any sand may become "quick" if its effective weight is being carried by water between the grains. In that case, even a footstep may collapse the loose structure. The sand-water suspension is denser than an animal or human body, so the body cannot sink below the surface, but struggling may lead to loss of balance and drowning.

quilting, Process of stitching together two layers of fabric, usually with a soft, thick substance placed between them. The layer of wool, cotton, or other stuffing provides insulation; the stitching keeps the stuffing evenly distributed and also provides opportunity for artistic expression. Quilting has long been used for clothing in many parts of the world, especially in the Far and Middle East and the Muslim regions of Africa. It reached its fullest development in the U.S., where it was at first popularly used for petticoats and comforters. By the end of the 18th century the U.S. quilt had distinctive features, such as coloured fabric sewn on the outer layers (appliqué) and stitching that echoed the appliqué pattern. Patchwork patterns proliferated in the 19th and 20th centuries.

quinine, Alkaloid found in the bark of cinchona trees and shrubs. The chemical structure of this heterocyclic compound is large and complex, with several rings. For the 300 years preceding the 1940s, when newer antimalarials were developed, quinine was the only drug known to Western medicine for the prevention and treatment of malaria. The first chemical compound ever used successfully against an infectious disease, it has benefited more people than any other such drug in history and is still used to treat malaria, often in combination with other drugs. Quinine is also a flavouring agent in some carbonated beverages, including tonic water.

Quito, City (pop., 2001: 1,399,378), capital of Ecuador. The city lies at an elevation of 9,350 ft (2,850 m) on the lower slopes of Pichincha, an active volcano, in a narrow valley of the Andes Mountains. A pre-Columbian town, it was captured by the Inca in 1487 and taken by the Spanish in 1534. It is the oldest of all South American capitals, and its old town preserves much of its colonial atmosphere. In 1552 the Franciscans established an art school there, the first of its kind in South America. One of Ecuador's two major industrial centres, it produces textiles and light consumer goods. It is the site of several institutions of higher learning. The old town was designated a UNESCO World Heritage site in 1978.

Qumrān, Site on the northwestern shore of the Dead Sea where the Dead Sea Scrolls were discovered in 1947. Excavations less than a mile from the sea have revealed the ruins of buildings believed by some scholars to have been occupied by Essenes, the probable authors of the scrolls. The buildings include a scriptorium, a potter's workshop, and a flour mill; water was supplied through an aqueduct. The Essenes are thought to have founded a monastic community at Qumrān in the mid-2nd century BC. They temporarily abandoned the settlement after an earthquake and fire in 31 BC but later returned and lived there until Roman legions destroyed the community in AD 68.

Qur'ān, or KORAN, Sacred scripture of Islam, regarded by Muslims as the infallible word of God, revealed to the Prophet Muhammad. The book, first compiled in its authoritative form in the 7th century, consists of 114 chapters (*sūrahs*) of varying length, written in Arabic. The earliest *sūrahs* call for moral and religious obedience in light of the coming Day of Judgment; the ones written later provide directives for the creation of a social structure that will support the moral life called for by God. The Qur'ān also provides detailed accounts of the joys of paradise and the terrors of hell. Muslims believe that the God who spoke to Muhammad is the God worshiped by Jews and Christians but that the revelations received by those religions are incomplete. Emphasis on the stern justice of God is tempered by frequent references to his mercy and compassion. The Qur'ān demands absolute submission (*islam*) to God and his word, and it serves as the primary source of Islamic law. It is regarded as immutable in both form and content; traditionally translation was forbidden. The translations available today are regarded as paraphrases to facilitate understanding of the actual scripture.

qurra, Professional class of reciters of the Qur'ān. Muhammad's early disciples often memorized his divine revelations, and even after the Qur'ān was assembled in written form, it was common for pious Muslims to memorize it in its entirety. Such reciters were often called on by scholars to elucidate points of pronunciation and meaning, and by the 9th century they formed an established class. Religious men employed in mosques still memorize the Qur'ān to aid them in interpreting its revelations to the faithful. In some Arab countries the professional duties of reciting the Qur'ān are usually reserved for blind men.

R

Rabat, Arabic RIBĀṬ, City (pop., 2004: city, 621,480; Rabat-Salé metro. area, 1,622,860), capital of Morocco. It is situated on the Atlantic coast at the mouth of the Bou Regreg River, opposite Salé. One of Morocco's four imperial cities, it was founded in the 12th century by a ruler of the Almohad dynasty, ʿAbd al-Muʾmin, as a *ribāṭ* (camp) quartering troops for his war against Spain. After 1609 the unified community of Rabat-Salé became the home of large numbers of Andalusian Moors who had been driven from Spain and, later, of the Sallee Corsairs, the most dreaded of Barbary Coast pirates. Under the French, it was made the administrative capital of a French protectorate after 1912. Now a centre of the textile industry, it is noted for its carpets, blankets, and leather handicrafts.

rabbi, or REBBE, In Judaism, a person qualified by study of the Hebrew scriptures and the Talmud to serve as spiritual leader of a Jewish community or congregation. Ordination can be conferred by any rabbi, but it usually depends on a written statement issued by the candidate's teacher. Though rabbis are considered teachers rather than priests, they conduct religious services, assist at Bar Mitzvahs, perform marriages, and are present at funerals. In questions of divorce, a rabbi's role depends on an appointment to a special court of Jewish law. The rabbi also counsels and consoles members of his congregation and oversees the religious education of the young.

rabbinic Judaism, Principal form of Judaism that developed after the fall of the Second Temple of Jerusalem (AD 70). It originated in the teachings of the Pharisees, who emphasized the need for critical interpretation of the Torah. Rabbinic Judaism is centered on study of the Talmud and debate about the legal and theological issues it raises. Its mode of worship and life discipline continue to be practiced by Jews worldwide.

rabies, Acute, usually fatal infectious disease of warm-blooded animals that attacks the central nervous system. It is spread by contact with an infected animal's saliva, usually from a bite. The rhabdovirus that causes it spreads along nerve tissue from the wound to the brain. Symptoms usually appear four to six weeks later, often beginning with irritability and aggressiveness. Wild animals lose their fear of humans and are easily provoked to bite, as are pets. Depression and paralysis soon follow. Death usually comes three to five days after symptoms begin. In humans, death can result from a seizure in the early phase even before symptoms of central nervous system depression develop. One name for rabies, hydrophobia ("fear of water"), comes from painful throat contraction on trying to swallow. If not treated in time (within a day or two) with a serum containing antibodies and then a series of vaccinations, rabies in humans is almost always fatal. Immediate cleansing of animal bites with soap and water can remove much of the virus.

Rabin, Yitzhak (b. March 1, 1922, Jerusalem—d. Nov. 4, 1995, Tel Aviv–Yafo, Israel), First native-born prime minister of Israel. He fought in the first Arab-Israeli War and became chief of staff in 1964. His strategies helped win the Six-Day War in 1967. After retiring from the army (1968), he served as ambassador to the U.S. (1968–73). As head of the Israel Labour Party, he twice served as prime minister (1974–77, 1992–95). During his first tenure, he secured a cease-fire with Syria in the Golan Heights and ordered the raid at Entebbe, Ugan.. As defense minister (1984–90) he responded forcefully to the Palestinian first *intifāḍah*. In 1993 secret negotiations with the Palestinians yielded a political settlement that called for limited Palestinian self-rule in the Gaza Strip and the West Bank, for which he shared the 1994 Nobel Prize for Peace with Shimon Peres and Yāsir ʿArafāt. He was assassinated by a right-wing Jewish extremist.

race, Term once commonly used in physical anthropology to denote a division of humankind possessing traits that are transmissible by descent and sufficient to characterize it as a distinct human type (e.g., Caucasoid, Mongoloid, Negroid). Today the term has little scientific standing, as older methods of differentiation, including hair form and body measurement, have given way to the comparative analysis of DNA and gene frequencies relating to such factors as blood typing, the excretion of amino acids, and inherited enzyme deficiencies. Because all human populations today are extremely similar genetically, most researchers have abandoned the concept of race for the concept of the cline, a graded series of differences occurring along a line of environmental or geographical transition. This reflects the recognition that human populations have always been in a state of flux, with genes constantly flowing from one gene pool to another, impeded only by physical or ecological boundaries. While relative isolation does preserve genetic differences and allow populations to maximally adapt to climatic and disease factors over long periods of time, all groups currently existing are thoroughly "mixed" genetically, and such differences as still exist do not lend themselves to simple typologizing. "Race" is today primarily a sociological designation, identifying a class sharing some outward physical characteristics and some commonalities of culture and history.

Rachmaninoff, Sergey (Vassilyevich) (b. April 1, 1873, Oneg, near Semyonovo, Russia—d. March 28, 1943, Beverly Hills, Calif., U.S.), Russian-born U.S. composer and pianist. He studied at the St. Petersburg and Moscow conservatories. After playing his first concerto for his graduation as a piano student (1891), he stayed on to earn a composition degree, writing his first opera, *Aleko* (1892). His first symphony (1897) was such a disaster that he could not compose for three years. Known for his titanic virtuosity as a pianist, he toured widely while returning to composing prolifically. He moved to the U.S. after the 1917 revolution. His works, most of them in a lush late-Romantic style, include three symphonies, four piano concertos, the tone poem *From the Isle of the Dead* (1909), and *Symphonic Dances* (1940).

racism, Any action, practice, or belief that reflects the racial worldview—the ideology that humans are divided into separate and exclusive biological entities called "races," that there is a causal link between inherited physical traits and traits of personality, intellect, morality, and other cultural behavioral features, and that some "races" are innately superior to others. Racism was at the heart of North American slavery and the overseas colonization and empire-building activities of some western Europeans, especially in the 18th century. The idea of race was invented to magnify the differences between people of European origin in the U.S. and those of African descent whose ancestors had been brought against their will to function as slaves in the American South. By viewing Africans and their descendants as lesser human beings, the proponents of slavery attempted to justify and maintain this system of exploitation while at the same time portraying the U.S. as a bastion and champion of human freedom, with human rights, democratic institutions, unlimited opportunities, and equality. The contradiction between slavery and the ideology of human equality, accompanying a philosophy of human freedom and dignity, seemed to demand the dehumanization of those enslaved. By the 19th century racism had matured and the idea spread around the world. Racism differs from ethnocentrism in that it is linked to physical and therefore immutable differences among people. Ethnic identity is acquired, and ethnic features are learned forms of behaviour. Race, on the other hand, is a form of identity that is perceived as innate and unalterable. In the last half of the 20th century several conflicts around the world were interpreted in racial terms even though their origins were in the ethnic hostilities that have long characterized many human societies (e.g., Arabs and Jews, English and Irish). Racism reflects an acceptance of the deepest forms and degrees of divisiveness and carries the implication that differences among groups are so great that they cannot be transcended.

rack and pinion, Mechanical device consisting of a bar of rectangular cross section (the rack), having teeth on one side that mesh with teeth on a small gear (the pinion). If the pinion rotates about a fixed axis, the rack will move in a straight path. Some automobile steering mechanisms have rack-and-pinion drives that use this principle. If the rack is fixed and the pinion is carried in bearings on a table guided on tracks parallel to the rack, rotation of the pinion shaft will move the table parallel to the rack. On machine tools, this principle is used to obtain rapid movements of worktables.

rackets, Game for two or four players with ball and racket on a four-walled court. Rackets is played with a hard ball in a relatively large court (approximately 9 × 18 m), unlike the related games of squash and racquetball. As in these other games, the object of rackets is to bounce, or rebound, the ball off the front and other walls in such a way as to defeat an opponent's attempt to reach and return it. It appears to have developed in England in the early 19th century.

racquetball, Game similar to handball but played with rackets. The game is played on a four-walled court with a short-handled racket and a ball larger than that used in handball. It was invented in 1950 by Joseph G. Sobek (1918–98), who was unhappy with the indoor racket sports then available. By the early 21st century there were some 10 million racquetball players in more than 90 countries.

radar, System that uses electromagnetic echoes to detect and locate objects. It can also measure precisely the distance (range) to an object and the speed at which the object is moving toward or away from the observing unit. Radar (the name is derived from *ra*dio *d*etecting *a*nd *r*anging) originated in the experimental work of Heinrich Hertz in the late 1880s. During World War II British and U.S. researchers developed a high-powered microwave radar system for military use. Radar is used today in identification and monitoring of artificial satellites in Earth orbit, as a navigational aid for airplanes and marine vessels, for air traffic control around major airports, for monitoring local weather systems, and for spotting "speeders."

Radha, In Hindu mythology, mistress of the god Krishna when he lived among the cowherds of Vrindavana. Though Radha was the wife of another cowherd, she was the most beloved of Krishna's consorts and his constant companion. In the bhakti movement of Vaishnavism, Radha symbolizes the human soul and Krishna the divine. The allegorical love of Radha and Krishna has been celebrated in the poetry of many Indian languages, and Radha is often worshiped along with Krishna, especially in northern and eastern India.

radiation, Process by which energy is emitted from a source and propagated through the surrounding medium, or the energy involved in this process. Radiation consists of a flow of atomic or subatomic particles or of waves. Familiar examples are light (a form of electromagnetic radiation) and sound (a form of acoustic radiation). Both electromagnetic and acoustic radiation can be described as waves with a range of frequencies and intensities. Electromagnetic radiation is also often treated as discrete packets of energy, called photons. All matter is constantly bombarded by radiation from cosmic and terrestrial sources, and radioactive elements emit several types of radiation.

radiation therapy, or RADIOTHERAPY, or THERAPEUTIC RADIOLOGY, Use of radiation sources to treat or relieve diseases, usually cancer (including leukemia). The ionizing radiation primarily used to destroy diseased cells works best on fast-growing cancers. However, radiation can also cause cancer and is no longer used for benign conditions. Other complications include nausea, hair loss, weight loss, and weakness. Radioactive substances may be implanted in tumours. External radiation involves 10–20 sessions over several months, either after surgical removal of the growth or when surgery is impossible; it can deliver higher doses to deep tumours than implantation. Infrared radiation and ultraviolet radiation is applied with lamps to relieve inflammation.

radio and radar astronomy, Study of celestial bodies by measuring the energy they emit or reflect at radio wavelengths. It began in 1931 with Karl Jansky's discovery of radio waves from an extraterrestrial source. After 1945, huge dish antennas, improved receivers, and data-processing methods, and radio interferometers let astronomers study fainter sources and obtain greater detail. Radio waves penetrate much of the gas and dust in space, giving a much clearer picture of the centre and structure of the Milky Way Galaxy than optical observation can. This has allowed detailed studies of the interstellar medium in the Galaxy and the discovery of previously unknown cosmic objects (e.g., pulsars, quasars). In radar astronomy, radio signals are sent to near-Earth bodies or phenomena (e.g., meteor trails, the Moon, asteroids, nearby planets) and the reflections detected, providing precise measurement of the objects' distances and surface structure. Because radar waves can penetrate even dense clouds, they have provided astronomers' only maps of the surface of Venus. Radio and radar studies of the Moon revealed its sandlike surface before landings were made. Radio observations have also contributed greatly to knowledge about the Sun.

radio telescope, Combination of radio receiver and antenna, used for observation in radio and radar astronomy. Radio telescopes vary widely, but all have two basic components: a large radio antenna or an antenna array and a radiometer or radio receiver. Because some astronomical radio sources are extremely weak, radio telescopes are usually very large, and only the most sensitive radio receivers are used. The first large fully steerable radio telescope was completed in 1957 at Jodrell Bank, Eng. The world's largest fully steerable radio telescope is the 360 × 330-ft (110 × 100-m) off-axis antenna operated by the National Radio Astronomy Observatory in Green Bank, W.Va. The largest single radio telescope is the 1,000-ft (305-m) fixed spherical reflector at the Arecibo Observatory in Puerto Rico. The world's most powerful radio telescope is the Very Large Array in New Mexico, made up of 27 separate mobile parabolic antennas that together provide the angular resolution of a single antenna 22 mi (35 km) in diameter.

Lovell Telescope, a fully steerable radio telescope at Jodrell Bank, Macclesfield, Cheshire, Eng.
Jodrell Bank Science Centre

radioactivity, Property exhibited by certain types of matter of emitting radiation spontaneously. The phenomenon was first reported in 1896 by Henri Becquerel for a uranium salt, and it was soon found that all uranium compounds are radioactive due to the uranium's radioactivity. In 1898 Marie Curie and her husband discovered two other naturally occurring, strongly radioactive elements, radium and polonium. The radiation is emitted by unstable atomic nuclei as they attempt to become more stable. The main processes of radioactivity are alpha decay, beta decay, and gamma decay. In 1934 it was discovered that radioactivity could be induced in ordinary matter by artificial transmutation.

radiology, Branch of medicine that uses radiation for diagnosis (diagnostic imaging) and treatment (radiation therapy) of disease. Originally, it involved X rays for diagnosis and X rays, gamma rays, and other ionizing radiation for treatment. Diagnostic methods now include isotope scanning, use of nonionizing radiation, as in ultrasound and magnetic resonance imaging, and radioimmunoassay (in which radioactive isotopes in antibodies against hormones detect minute amounts of hormones for diagnosis of endocrine disorders). Radiotherapy now includes, in cancer treatment, radioactive hormones and chemotherapeutic drugs.

radish, Annual or biennial plant (*Raphanus sativus*) of the mustard family, probably of Oriental origin, grown for its large, succulent root. Low in calories and high in bulk, radishes have a sharp taste and are usually eaten raw. The shape of the edible portion of the root varies greatly, as does the color (from white through pink to red, purple, and black). Radishes may weigh only a few ounces (U.S. and European varieties) or, in the case of the Japanese daikon, more than 2 lbs (1 kg).

Radish (Raphanus sativus, variety radicula).
Ingmar Holmasen

radium, Chemical element, heaviest alkaline earth metal, chemical symbol Ra, atomic number 88. It was discovered by Marie Curie and her husband, Pierre Curie, in 1898 and isolated by 1910. All its isotopes are radioactive. Radium does not occur free in nature but occurs in natural ores such as pitchblende as a disintegration product of radioactive decay of heavier elements, including uranium. Chemically it is highly reactive and has valence 2 in all of its compounds. Its use in medicine has declined because of its cost, and its use in consumer goods (to illuminate watch and clock hands and numbers, as well as instrument dials) was halted because it can cause radiation injury. It is still used for some radiography and as a source of neutrons.

radon, Chemical element, chemical symbol Rn, atomic number 86. The heaviest noble gas, it is colourless, odourless, tasteless, radioactive, and almost completely unreactive (forming compounds only with fluorine). It is rare in nature because all its isotopes are short-lived and because radium, its source, is scarce. Radon seeps from certain soils and rocks (such as granite) into the atmosphere and can accumulate in poorly ventilated spaces near ground level, including house basements; in some regions of the world the use of such spaces is believed to increase the risk of lung cancer more than any other common factor except smoking. Radon is used in radiotherapy, radiography, and research.

raga, In the classical music of India, Pakistan, and Bangladesh, a melodic framework for improvisation and composition. A raga is based on a scale with a given set of notes, a typical order in which they appear in melodies, and characteristic musical motifs. There are several hundred ragas in present use, and thousands are possible in theory. The concept of raga, introduced sometime before the 9th century, became influential throughout South Asia, and it remains central to the region's classical music.

Ragnarök, In Scandinavian mythology, the end of the divine and human worlds. As described in the 10th-century Icelandic poem *Völuspá* and other sources, Ragnarök will be preceded by cruel winters and moral chaos. Giants and demons will attack the gods, who will face death like heroes. The sun will be darkened, the stars will vanish, and the earth will sink into the sea. Afterward the earth will rise again, the innocent Balder will return from the dead, and the hosts of the just will live in a hall roofed with gold. The title of Richard Wagner's opera *Götterdämmerung* (*The Twilight of the Gods*) is a German equivalent of Ragnarök.

ragtime, U.S. popular music of the late 19th and early 20th centuries distinguished by its heavily syncopated rhythm. Ragtime found its characteristic expression in formally structured piano compositions, the accented left-hand beat opposed in the right hand by a fast, bouncing melody that gave the music its powerful forward impetus. (The term probably derives from "ragged time," a description of syncopation.) Ragtime compositions typically featured three or four discrete 16-bar strains performed at a moderate tempo. The most celebrated ragtime composer was Scott Joplin. The rhythm and structure of ragtime were important influences on the development of jazz.

ragweed, Any of about 15 species of weedy plants that make up the genus *Ambrosia* in the aster family (Asteraceae), most of which are native to North America. They have rough, hairy stems, mostly lobed or divided leaves, and inconspicuous greenish flowers borne in small heads. Common ragweed (*A. artemisiifolia*) is found across North America. Pollen shed by ragweeds in great abundance in late summer is the principal cause of hay fever in eastern and middle North America. Since ragweeds are annuals, mowing before pollination season eradicates them.

railroad, Mode of land transportation in which flange-wheeled vehicles move over two parallel steel rails or tracks, drawn by a locomotive or propelled by self-contained motors. The earliest railroads were built in European mines in the 16th century, using cars pulled on tracks by men or horses. With the advent of the steam locomotive and construction of the first railway in 1825, the modern railroad developed quickly. Construction was begun on the first U.S. railroad, the Baltimore and Ohio, in 1828. Specialized railroad cars were built to transport freight and passengers, including the sleeping cars developed by George Pullman in 1859. In the 19th century the railroad had an important influence on every country's economic and social development. In the U.S. the transcontinental railroad, completed in 1869, began an era of railroad expansion and consolidation that involved such financial empire builders as Cornelius Vanderbilt, Jay Gould, Edward H. Harriman, James J. Hill, and Leland Stanford. The railroad's importance in the U.S. began to diminish from the early 20th century, but in Europe, Asia, and Africa it continues to provide vital transportation links within and between countries.

rain, Precipitation of liquid water drops with diameters greater than 0.02 in. (0.5 mm). When the drops are smaller, the precipitation is usually called drizzle. Raindrops may form by the coalescence of colliding small water droplets or from the melting of snowflakes and other ice particles as they fall into warm air near the ground. Hawaii's Mount Waialeale, with a 20-year annual average of 460 in. (11,700 mm), is the Earth's wettest known point; the driest areas are in parts of deserts where no appreciable rain has ever been observed. Less than 10 in. (250 mm) and more than 60 in. (1,500 mm) per year represent approximate extremes of rainfall for all the continents.

rain dance, Ceremonial dance performed to bring rain needed to water crops. Rain dances have been customary in many cultures, from the ancient Egyptians to the civilization of the Mayas and the people of the 20th-century Balkans. Rain dances often include dancing in a circle, the participation of young girls, decoration with green vegetation, nudity, the pouring of water, and whirling, meant to act as a wind charm. They may also include phallic and fertility rites.

rainbow, Series of concentric, coloured arcs that may be seen when light from a distant source—usually the Sun—falls on a collection of water drops such as in rain, spray, or fog. The coloured rays of the rainbow are caused by the refraction and internal reflection of light rays that enter the drop, each colour being bent through a slightly different angle. Hence, the combined colours are separated upon emerging from the drop. The most brilliant and most common rainbow is the so-called primary bow, which results from light that emerges from the drop after one internal reflection. The colours of the arc (from outside to inside) are red, orange, yellow, green, blue, indigo, and violet. Occasionally a less-intense secondary bow may be observed; it has its colour sequence reversed.

rainforest, Lush forest, generally composed of tall, broad-leaved trees and usually found in wet tropical regions around the Equator. Despite increased awareness of the rainforests' importance during the late 20th century, they continue to be cleared. Rainforests grow mainly in South and Central America, West and Central Africa, Indonesia, parts of Southeast Asia, and tropical Australia, where the climate is relatively humid with no marked seasonal variation. Depending on the amount of annual rainfall, the trees may be evergreen or mainly deciduous. The former require more water. Temperatures are high, usually about 86 °F (30 °C) during the day and 68 °F (20 °C) at night. Soil conditions vary with location and climate, though most rainforest soils tend to be permanently moist and not very fertile, because the hot, humid weather causes organic matter to decompose rapidly and to be absorbed quickly by tree roots and fungi. Rainforests have several layers. The highest continuous layer, called the canopy, extends across the treetops at a height of 100–165 ft (30–50 m). Most animals live among the leaves and branches. Below the canopy is a thick understory filled with small trees, lianas, and epiphytes. The space directly above the ground can be occupied by tree branches, twigs, and foliage, but, contrary to popular belief, the rainforest floor is not impassable. Rather, it is bare except for a thin layer of humus and fallen leaves. Animals inhabiting this layer (e.g., gorillas, elephants, jaguars, and bears) are adapted to walking or climbing for only short distances. Burrowing animals, such as armadillos and caecilians, are found in the soil, as are microorganisms that help decompose and recycle the organic litter accumulated by other plants and animals from all layers. The climate of the ground layer is unusually stable because the upper stories of tree canopies and the lower branches filter out sunlight, retain heat, and reduce wind speeds, keeping the temperature fairly even.

Rajasthan, State (pop., 2008 est.: 64,641,000), northwestern India. Bordered by Pakistan and the states of Punjab, Haryana, Uttar Pradesh, Madhya Pradesh, and Gujarat, it covers an area of 132,139 sq mi (342,239 sq km); its capital is Jaipur. Archaeological evidence shows continuous human habitation for about 100,000 years. In the 7th–11th centuries CE, several Rajput dynasties arose, reaching their height in the 16th century. The emperor Akbar brought the Rajput states into the Mughal Empire. In the 19th century, the British came into control of the region. After Indian independence (1947), the area was organized as the Union of Rajasthan, then reorganized in 1956. It is dominated by the Aravalli Range and the Thar Desert. Predominantly an agricultural and pastoral state, it is one of the largest producers of wool in India.

Rama, Major Hindu deity. The name became associated with Ramacandra, the seventh incarnation of Vishnu, whose story is told in the *Ramayana*. Conceived as a model of reason, virtue, and right action, Rama was one of the chief objects of the bhakti cults. He is often depicted as a standing figure, holding an arrow in his right hand and a bow in his left. In temples his image is attended by the figures of his wife, Sita, his half brother, Laksmana, and the monkey general, Hanuman.

Ramadan, In Islam, a holy month of fasting, the ninth month of the Muslim year, commemorating the revelation of the Qur'ān to Muhammad. As an act of atonement, Muslims are required to fast and abstain from sexual activity during the daylight hours of Ramadan. Determined according to the lunar calendar, Ramadan can fall in any season of the year. The Ramadan fast is considered one of the Five Pillars of Islam, and the end of the fast is celebrated as one of the important religious holidays of Islam.

Ramakrishna (Paramahamsa), orig. GADADHAR CHATTO-PADHYAYA (b. Feb. 18, 1836, Hooghly, Bengal state, India—d. Aug. 16, 1886, Calcutta), Indian mystic. Born into a poor Brahman family, he worked as a priest in a temple of Kali in Calcutta (now Kolkata), where he had a vision and commenced spiritual practices in a number of different religious traditions. He denounced sexual desire and money as the twin evils that put spiritual enlightenment beyond reach, rejected the caste system, and held that all religions are in essence the same and that all are true. His teachings were spread by his disciples, notably Vivekananda. A religious order bearing his name, with headquarters in Kolkata, sends missionaries throughout the world.

Raman, Sir Chandrasekhara Venkata (b. Nov. 7, 1888, Trichinopoly, India—d. Nov. 21, 1970, Bangalore), Indian physicist influential in the growth of science in India. He received a Nobel Prize in 1930 for discovering that when light passes through a transparent material, some of the light that emerges at a right angle to the original beam is of other frequencies (Raman frequencies) characteristic of the material. He contributed to the building up of nearly every Indian research institution in his time, founded a scholarly physics journal and an academy of sciences, and trained hundreds of students.

Ramanuja (b. *c.* 1017, Shriperumbudur, India—d. 1137, Shrirangam), Indian theologian and philosopher, the most influential thinker of devotional Hinduism. After a long pilgrimage through India, he founded centres to spread devotion to Vishnu and Lakshmi. He provided an intellectual basis for the practice of bhakti in major commentaries on the Vedas, the *Brahma-sutras*, and the *Bhagavadgita*. He was a major figure in the school of Visistadvaita, which emphasized the need for the soul to be united with a personal god. His chief philosophical contributions follow from his conviction that the phenomenal world is real and provides real knowledge and that the exigencies of daily life are not contrary to the life of the spirit.

Ramayana, Indian epic poem, composed in Sanskrit *c.* 300 BCE. With the *Mahabharata*, it is one of the two great epic poems of India. Consisting of 24,000 couplets in seven books, it describes the royal birth of Rama and the loss of his throne. Banished to the forest with his wife, Sita, and his half brother, Laksmana, he spends 14 years in exile. When a demon king carries off Sita, Rama enters into an alliance with Sugriva, king of the monkeys, and Hanuman, the monkey general, who help him rescue her. Rama regains his kingdom, but Sita is banished when her chastity is questioned, and she is swallowed by the earth after proving her innocence.

random variable, In statistics, a function that can take on either a finite number of values, each with an associated probability, or an infinite number of values, whose probabilities are summarized by a density function. Used in studying chance events, it is defined so as to account for all possible outcomes of the event. When these are finite (e.g., the number of heads in a three-coin toss), the random variable is called discrete and the probabilities of the outcomes sum to 1. If the possible outcomes are infinite (e.g., the life expectancy of a light bulb), the random variable is called continuous and corresponds to a density function whose integral over the entire range of outcomes equals 1. Probabilities for specific outcomes are determined by summing probabilities (in the discrete case) or by integrating the density function over an interval corresponding to that outcome (in the continuous case).

Ranger, Any of a series of unmanned probes launched from 1961 to 1965 by NASA. The project was NASA's earliest attempt to explore the Moon's surface. Ranger 4 (1962) became the first U.S. spacecraft to hit the Moon, crash-landing on its surface as planned. The last three probes in the series (1964–65) sent more than 17,000 high-resolution photographs of the Moon before crashing.

Ranjit Singh (b. Nov. 13, 1780, Budrukhan or Gujranwala, India—d. June 27, 1839, Lahore), Founder and maharaja (1801–39) of the Sikh kingdom of the Punjab. He became chief of the Shukerchakias (a Sikh group located in what is now Pakistan) on the death of his father in 1792. In 1799 he seized Lahore, the capital of the Punjab (and now in Pakistan), and in 1801 he proclaimed himself maharaja of the Punjab. In 1802 he captured Amritsar, a city sacred to the Sikhs, and by 1820 he had consolidated his rule over the whole of Punjab between the Sutlej and the Indus rivers. The Sikh state he created, which had included Sikhs, Muslims, and Hindus in both the army and the cabinet, collapsed soon after his death.

rap, Musical style in which rhythmic and/or rhyming speech is chanted ("rapped") to musical accompaniment. This backing music, which can include digital sampling (music and sounds extracted from other recordings), is also called hip-hop, the name used to refer to a broader cultural movement that includes rap, deejaying (turntable manipulation), graffiti painting, and breakdancing. Rap, which originated in African American communities in New York City, came to national prominence with the Sugar Hill Gang's "Rapper's Delight" (1979). Rap's early stars included Grandmaster Flash and the Furious Five, Run-D.M.C., LL Cool J, Public Enemy (who espoused a radical political message), and the Beastie Boys. The late 1980s saw the advent of "gangsta rap," with lyrics that were often misogynistic or that glamorized violence and drug dealing. More recent stars have included Sean "Puffy" Combs, Jay-Z, OutKast, and Eminem.

Rapallo, Treaty of (April 16, 1922) Treaty between Germany and the Soviet Union, signed at Rapallo, Italy. Negotiated by Germany's Walther Rathenau and the Soviet Union's Georgy V. Chicherin, it reestablished normal relations between the two nations. The nations agreed to cancel all financial claims against each other, and the treaty strengthened their economic and military ties. As the first agreement concluded by Germany as an independent agent since World War I, it angered the Western Allies.

rape, Unlawful sexual activity, usually sexual intercourse, carried out forcibly or under threat of injury and against the will of the victim. Though traditionally limited to attacks on women by men, the definition of rape has been broadened to cover same-sex attacks and attacks against those who, because of mental illness, intoxication, or other reasons, are incapable of valid consent. Statutory rape, or intercourse with a person younger than a certain age (generally from 12 to 18 years), has long been a serious crime in most jurisdictions. Rape is widely considered an expression of anger or aggression and a pathological assertion of power by the rapist. The psychological responses of victims vary but usually include feelings of shame, humiliation, confusion, fear, and rage. Many rape victims fail to report the crime, deterred by the prospect of a distressing cross-examination in court and the difficulty of proving a crime for which there usually are no witnesses. In the late 20th century there was a notable increase in the use of rape as a weapon of war, and in the 1990s the tribunal investigating crimes stemming from genocide in Rwanda ruled that rape and sexual violence constituted a form of genocide.

Raphael, orig. RAFFAELLO SANZIO (b. April 6, 1483, Urbino, Duchy of Urbino—d. April 6, 1520, Rome, Papal States), Italian painter and architect. As a member of Perugino's workshop, he established his mastery by 17 and began receiving important commissions. In 1504 he moved to Florence, where he executed many of his famous Madonnas; his unity of composition and suppression of inessentials is evident in *The Madonna of the Goldfinch* (c. 1506). Though influenced by Leonardo da Vinci's chiaroscuro and sfumato, his figure types were his own creation, with round, gentle faces that reveal human sentiments raised to a sublime serenity. In 1508 he was summoned to Rome to decorate a suite of papal chambers in the Vatican. The frescoes in the Stanza della Segnatura are probably his greatest work; the most famous, *The School of Athens* (1510–11), is a complex and magnificently ordered allegory of secular knowledge showing Greek philosophers in an architectural setting. The Madonnas he painted in Rome show him turning away from his earlier work's serenity to emphasize movement and grandeur, partly under Michelangelo's High Renaissance influence. The *Sistine Madonna* (1513) shows the richness of colour and new boldness of compositional invention typical of his Roman period. He became the most important portraitist in Rome, designed 10 large tapestries to hang in the Sistine Chapel, designed a church and a chapel, assumed the direction of work on St. Peter's Basilica at the death of Donato Bramante, and took charge of virtually all the papacy's projects in architecture, painting, and the preservation of antiquities. When he died on his 37th birthday, his last masterpiece, the *Transfiguration* altarpiece, was placed at the head of his bier.

Raphael, In the Bible and the Qur'ān, one of the archangels. In the apocryphal book of Tobit he appears in human disguise and conquers the demon Asmodeus. His name in Hebrew means "God has healed," and in Tobit his business is to heal the earth. Raphael is reckoned among the saints in both Eastern and Western churches, and his feast day is October 24.

Rastafarian, Member of a political and religious movement among blacks in Jamaica and several other countries. Rastafarians worship Haile Selassie, considering him the messiah. They believe that blacks are the Israelites reincarnated, who have been subjected to the evil and inferior white race in divine punishment for their sins; they will eventually be redeemed by repatriation to Africa and will compel the whites to serve them. These beliefs, first enunciated in 1953, can be traced to several independent prophets, particularly Marcus Garvey. As the movement grew, ideas of repatriation tended to give way to either black militancy or mysticism. The Rastafarian life usually includes vegetarianism, the wearing of dreadlocks, and the smoking of marijuana.

rat, Any of more than 500 forms of Asian rodent (genus *Rattus*, family Muridae) that have been introduced worldwide. The black rat (*Rattus rattus*) and the Norway rat (*R. norvegicus*) are the aggressive, omnivorous animals commonly associated with the name. They prefer areas of human habitation, where they can easily find food. They have keen senses and can climb, jump, burrow, or gnaw their way

Norway rat (Rattus norvegicus).
John H. Gerard

into seemingly inaccessible places. They reproduce extremely rapidly (up to 150 offspring a year) and have few natural predators. Rats transmit numerous human diseases and have often destroyed grain supplies. The black rat is about 8 in. (20 cm) long, excluding the slightly longer tail. The Norway rat (also called the brown, barn, sewer, or wharf rat) has proportionately smaller ears and a shorter tail. Laboratory rats are strains of the Norway rat. The name rat is applied, without scientific basis, to other rodents (e.g., kangaroo rat, wood rat).

rationalism, Philosophical view that regards reason as the chief source and test of knowledge. Rationalism has long been the rival of empiricism, the doctrine that all knowledge of matters of fact ultimately derives from, and must be tested by, sense experience. As against this doctrine, rationalism holds reason to be a faculty that can lay hold of truths beyond the reach of sense perception, both in certainty and in generality. In stressing the existence of a "natural light," rationalism also has been the rival of systems claiming esoteric knowledge, whether from mystical experience, revelation, or intuition, and has been opposed to various irrationalisms that tend to stress the biological, the emotional or volitional, the unconscious, or the existential at the expense of the rational.

rationing, Government allocation of scarce resources and consumer goods, usually adopted during wars, famines, or other national emergencies. Rationing according to use prohibits the less important uses of a commodity (e.g., the use of gasoline for pleasure trips as opposed to work-related travel). Rationing by quantity limits the amounts of a commodity available to each claimant (e.g., a pound of butter per month). Rationing by value limits the amount of money consumers can spend on commodities that are difficult to standardize (e.g., clothing). Point rationing assigns a point value to each commodity and allocates a certain number of points to each consumer. These can be tracked through coupons, which are issued to consumers and must be exchanged for the approved amounts of rationed goods. Consumers in a rationed economy are usually encouraged to save their money or invest in government bonds so that unspent money will not be used for unrationed items or purchases on the black market.

rattlesnake, Any of about 30 species in two genera of New

Timber rattlesnake (Crotalus horridus).
Jack Dermid

World pit vipers having a tail rattle that produces a buzzing sound when vibrated. The rattle is composed of horny, loosely connected segments added one at a time with each molt. *Sistrurus* species have large scales on the top of the head. *Crotalus* species have mostly small scales on the head. Species range from 1 to 8 ft (30 to 250 cm) long. Most eat small animals, primarily rodents, birds, and lizards. All bear live young. In hot areas rattlesnakes become nocturnal; in cold areas they hibernate in groups. Heat-sensitive organs on the sides of the head help them locate and strike their prey. A rattlesnake bite is painful and can be fatal if not treated.

Ravana, the 10-headed demon-king, detail from a Guler painting of the Ramayana, c. 1720; in the Cleveland Museum of Art.
Courtesy of the Cleveland Museum of Art, Ohio, gift of George P. Bickford

Ravana, In Hinduism, king of the demons. Ravana is depicted with 10 heads and 20 hands and flying a magic chariot. He ruled in the kingdom of Lanka, from which he had expelled his brother Kubera. His abduction of Sita and defeat by her husband, Rama, are the central events of the epic *Ramayana.* The demon king is also remembered for shaking Mount Kailasa until Shiva intervened and imprisoned him beneath it for 1,000 years. The popular annual Ram Lila festival climaxes with the defeat of Ravana and the burning of huge effigies of demons.

Rawalpindi, City (pop., 2005 est.: urban agglom., 1,770,000), Punjab province, northern Pakistan, just southwest of Islamabad. In ancient times, the locality was included in the Achaemenian Persian Empire. The ruins of the ancient city of Taxila are located nearby to the northwest. Strategically located, it controls the routes to the Kashmir region and was the site of an important British military station. The former capital of Pakistan (1959–69), Rawalpindi is the headquarters of Pakistan's army and an administrative, commercial, and industrial centre. Wheat, barley, corn (maize), and millet are the chief crops grown in the area. Mankial, south of the city, is the site of a Buddhist stupa dating to the 3rd century BC.

ray, Any of 300–350 mostly marine species of cartilaginous fish (order Batoidei) found worldwide and classified as electric rays, sawfishes, skates, and stingrays. Many species are slow-moving bottom-dwellers. The gill openings and mouth are on the underside of the flattened body. Winglike pectoral fins extend along the sides of the head. All but electric rays have a long, slender tail, often with saw-edged, venomous spines, and rough, often spiny, skin.

Ray, Satyajit (b. May 2, 1921, Calcutta, India—d. April 23,

Satyajit Ray.
Camera Press/Globe Photos

1992, Calcutta), Bengali-Indian film director. After studying with Rabindranath Tagore, he became art director of an ad agency and a book illustrator. He sold all his possessions to make his first film, *Pather Panchali* (1955), a story of village life. With *Aparajito* (1956) and *The World of Apu* (1959), he completed the brilliant Apu Trilogy and brought Indian cinema to world attention. He later won acclaim for *Devi* (1960), *Two Daughters* (1961), *The Big City* (1964), *The Lonely Wife* (1964), *The Chess Players* (1977), *The Home and the World* (1984), and *The Visitor* (1990). He wrote all his own screenplays, noted for their humanism and poetry, and often composed the music for his films, though his short stories and novellas became his main source of income.

Re, or RA, In ancient Egyptian religion, the creator god and god of the sun. He was believed to sail across the sky in his solar bark and at night to travel in another bark through the underworld, where he had to vanquish a serpent before he could be born again. As one of the creator gods, he rose from the ocean of chaos, creating himself and then engendering eight other gods. From the 4th dynasty, kings held the title Son of Re, and Re later became part of the throne name they adopted at accession and was appended to the names of such gods as Amon and Sebek.

reaction, heat of, Amount of heat that must be added or removed during a chemical reaction to keep all substances involved at the same temperature. If it is positive (heat must be added), the reaction is endothermic; if it is negative (heat is given off), the reaction is exothermic. Accurate heat of reaction values are needed for proper design of equipment used in chemical processes; they are usually estimated from compiled tables of thermodynamics data (heats of formation and heats of combustion of many known materials). The activation energy is unrelated to the heat of reaction.

Reagan, Ronald W(ilson) (b. Feb. 6, 1911, Tampico, Ill., U.S.—d. June 5, 2004, Los Angeles, Calif.), 40th president of the U.S. (1981–89). He attended Eureka College and worked as a radio sports announcer before going to Hollywood in 1937. In his career as a movie actor, he appeared in more than 50 films and was twice president of the Screen Actors Guild (1947–52, 1959–60). In the mid-1950s he became a spokesman for the General Electric Co.; he hosted its television theatre program from 1954 to 1962. Having gradually changed his political affiliation from liberal Democrat to conservative Republican, he was elected governor of California in 1966 and served two terms. In 1980 he defeated incumbent Pres. Jimmy Carter to become president. Shortly after taking office, he was wounded in an assassination attempt. His administration adopted policies based on supply-side economics in an effort to promote rapid economic growth and reduce the federal deficit. Congress approved many of his proposals (1981), which succeeded in lowering inflation but doubled the national debt by 1986. He began the largest peacetime military buildup in U.S. history; in 1983 he proposed construction of the Strategic Defense Initiative. His administration concluded a treaty with the Soviet Union to restrict intermediate-range nuclear weapons, conducted a proxy war against Nicaragua through its support of the Contras, and invaded Grenada ostensibly to prevent the island nation from becoming a Soviet outpost. He was reelected by a large margin in 1984. Beginning in 1986, the Iran-Contra Affair temporarily weakened his presidency. Though his intellectual capacity for governing was often disparaged by his critics, his affability and artful communication skills enabled him to pursue numerous conservative policies with conspicuous success, and his tough stance toward the Soviet Union is often credited with contributing to the demise of Soviet communism. In 1994 he revealed that he had Alzheimer disease.

realism, In the visual arts, an aesthetic that promotes accurate, detailed, unembellished depiction of nature or of contemporary life. Realism rejects imaginative idealization in favour of close observation of outward appearances. It was a dominant current in French art between 1850 and 1880. In the early 1830s the painters of the Barbizon school espoused realism in their faithful reproduction of the landscape near their village. Gustave Courbet was the first artist to proclaim and practice the realist aesthetic; his *Burial at Ornans* and *The Stone Breakers* (1849) shocked the public and critics with their frank depiction of peasants and labourers. In his satirical caricatures, Honoré Daumier used an energetic linear style and bold detail to criticize the immorality he saw in French society. Realism emerged in the U.S. in the work of Winslow Homer and Thomas Eakins. In the 20th century German artists associated with the Neue Sachlichkeit worked in a realist style to express their disillusionment after World War I. The Depression-era movement known as Social Realism adopted a similarly harsh realism to depict the injustices of U.S. society.

realism, In literature, the theory or practice of fidelity to nature or to real life and to accurate representation without idealization of everyday life. The 18th-century works of Daniel Defoe, Henry Fielding, and Tobias Smollett are among the earliest examples of realism in English literature. It was consciously adopted as an aesthetic program in France in the mid-19th century, when interest arose in recording previously ignored aspects of contemporary life and society; Gustave Flaubert's *Madame Bovary* (1857) established the movement in European literature. The realist emphasis on detachment and objectivity, along with lucid but restrained social criticism, became integral to the novel in the late 19th century. The word has also been used critically to denote excessive minuteness of detail or preoccupation with trivial, sordid, or squalid subjects.

realism, In philosophy, any viewpoint that accords to the objects of human knowledge an existence that is independent of whether they are being perceived or thought about. In the metaphysical debate concerning universals, realism is opposed to nominalism, which denies that universals have any reality at all (except as words), and to conceptualism, which grants universals reality but only as concepts in the mind. Against idealism and phenomenal-

ism, realism asserts the independent existence of material objects and their qualities. Similarly, moral realism holds that the moral qualities of things and actions (such as being good or bad, right or wrong) belong to the things or actions themselves and are not to be explained in terms of the subject's feelings of approval or disapproval. In opposition to conventionalism, realism holds that scientific theories are objectively true (or false) based on their correspondence (or lack of it) to an independently existing reality.

recession, Downward trend in the business cycle characterized by a decline in production and employment, which in turn lowers household income and spending. Even though not all households and businesses experience actual declines in income, they become less certain about the future and consequently delay making large purchases or investments. Consumers buy fewer durable household goods, and businesses are less likely to purchase machinery and equipment and more likely to use up existing inventory instead of adding goods to their stock. This drop in demand leads to a corresponding fall in output and thus worsens the economic situation. Whether a recession develops into a severe and prolonged depression depends on a number of circumstances. Among them are the extent and quality of credit extended during the previous period of prosperity, the amount of speculation permitted, the ability of government monetary and fiscal policies to reverse (or minimize) the downward trend, and the amount of excess productive capacity. *Compare* depression.

recombinant DNA technology, Recombining of DNA molecules from two different species that are inserted into a host organism to produce new genetic combinations that are of value to science, medicine, agriculture, or industry. Using this technology, scientists are able to isolate a gene, determine its nucleotide sequence, study its transcripts, mutate it in highly specific ways, and reinsert the modified sequence into a living organism. The processes of DNA cloning and sequencing are used to compare different organisms for evolutionary relatedness and to determine gene function. Recombinant DNA technology can also be used to study mutations and their biological effects, such as the role of specific mutations in disease or abnormal drug response. Other applications of recombinant DNA technology include gene therapy, reverse genetics, diagnostics, genomics, and protein manufacture (the preparation of large amounts of protein for basic research or medicinal use, such as commercially produced insulin).

recorder, In music, a cylindrical, usually wooden, wind instrument with fingerholes. As a fipple (duct) flute, its rather soft tones are produced by air blown against the sharp edge of an opening in the tube. The large recorder family includes instruments ranging from the sopranino to the contrabass. The recorder emerged in the 14th century and was widely used in ensembles and orchestras in the late Renaissance and throughout the Baroque era. Displaced by the transverse flute after the mid-18th century, it was revived in the 20th century.

Red Brigades, Italian BRIGATE ROSSE, Extreme left-wing terrorist organization in Italy. Its self-proclaimed aim was to undermine the Italian state and pave the way for a Marxist upheaval led by a "revolutionary proletariat." Reputedly founded by Renato Curcio (b. 1945), it began carrying out violent acts with firebombings (1970), escalating to kidnappings (1971) and murders (1974), most notably that of Aldo Moro (1978). At its height, it probably had 400 to 500 full-time members, perhaps 1,000 sporadic members, and a few thousand supporters. Arrest and imprisonment of many leaders and ordinary members greatly weakened the organization in the 1980s. However, a group calling itself the Red Brigades claimed responsibility for several violent attacks in the 1990s and into the 21st century.

Red Cross, officially INTERNATIONAL MOVEMENT OF THE RED CROSS AND RED CRESCENT, formerly INTERNATIONAL RED CROSS, Humanitarian agency with national affiliates worldwide. Established for the care of victims of battle, it now aids in the general prevention and relief of human suffering. It arose out of the work of Jean-Henri Dunant, who proposed the formation of voluntary relief societies in all countries, the first of which came into being in 1864. The name Red Crescent, adopted in 1906 at the insistence of the Ottoman Empire, is used in Muslim countries. In peacetime, the Red Cross aids victims of natural disasters, maintains blood banks, and provides supplementary health care services. In wartime, it serves as an intermediary between belligerents and visits prisoner-of-war camps to provide relief supplies, deliver mail, and transmit information between prisoners and their relatives. Its operating principles are humanity, impartiality, and neutrality. Its headquarters are in Geneva. Individual national organizations run community programs and coordinate natural-disaster relief efforts. The American Red Cross was founded by Clara Barton in 1881 and first chartered by Congress in 1900; it runs the world's largest blood-donor service. In 1901 Dunant received the first Nobel Prize for Peace; the Red Cross itself received the prize in 1917, 1944, and 1963.

red-figure pottery, Type of Greek pottery that flourished from the late 6th to the late 4th century BC. Developed in Athens *c.* 530 BC, the red-figure pottery quickly overtook the older black-figure pottery as the preferred style of vase painting. In red-figure technique, the background was painted black, and the outline details on the figures were also painted (rather than incised) in black, but the rest of each figure was unpainted and so retained the orange-red colour of the natural vase. By comparison with incising, the painting of the details allowed more flexibility in rendering human form, movements, expressions, and perspective. Since most of the ornamentation was narrative, such technical advantages were of utmost importance.

Athenian red-figure cup, detail of a bearded reveler by the Brygos Painter, c. 490 BC; in the Louvre, Paris
J.E. Bulloz

Red River, Chinese YUAN JIANG, Vietnamese SONG HONG, River, Southeast Asia. It rises in central Yunnan province, southwestern China, and flows southeast across northern Vietnam, past Hanoi, into the Gulf of Tonkin. The principal river of northern Vietnam, it is about 750 mi (1,200 km) long and has a wide, fertile delta east of Hanoi.

Red Sea, Narrow inland sea between the Arabian Peninsula and Africa. It extends southeast from Suez, Egypt, for about 1,200 mi (1,930 km) to the Strait of Mandeb, which connects with the Gulf of Aden and then with the Arabian Sea. It separates the coasts of Egypt, The Sudan, and Eritrea from those of Saudi Arabia and Yemen. It contains some of the world's warmest and saltiest seawater. With its connection to the Mediterranean Sea via the Suez Canal, it is one of the most heavily traveled waterways in the world, carrying traffic between Europe and Asia. Its name is derived from the colour changes observed in its waters.

Red Square, Large public square, central Moscow. It lies north of the Moskva River, adjacent to the Kremlin, and covers some 18 acres (7.3 hectares). Dating from the late 15th century, it has long been a busy market area as well as a focal point in Russian history as the scene of executions, demonstrations, riots, and parades. Located around it are the State Historical Museum (1875–81), the nine-towered Cathedral of St. Basil the Blessed (1554–60), the

former state department store GUM, and the tomb of Vladimir Ilich Lenin. The square and Kremlin were designated a UNESCO World Heritage site in 1990.

redshift, Displacement of the spectrum of an astronomical object toward longer wavelengths (visible light shifts toward the red end of the spectrum). In 1929 Edwin Hubble reported that distant galaxies had redshifts proportionate to their distances. Since redshifts can be caused by motion of an object away from the observer (the Doppler effect), Hubble concluded that all galaxies are receding from each other. This became the cornerstone of theories of an expanding universe.

reduction, Any of a class of chemical reactions in which the number of electrons associated with an atom or group of atoms is increased. The electrons taken up by the substance reduced are supplied by another substance, often hydrogen (H_2), which is thereby oxidized.

referendum and initiative, Electoral devices by which voters express their wishes regarding government policy or proposed legislation. Obligatory referenda are those required by law. Optional referenda are put on the ballot when a sufficient number of voters sign a petition demanding that a law passed by the legislature be ratified by the people. Obligatory and optional referenda should be distinguished from the voluntary referenda that legislatures submit to voters to decide an issue or to test public opinion. Initiatives are used to invoke a popular vote on a proposed law or constitutional amendment. Direct initiatives are submitted directly to the public after approval by a required number of voters; indirect initiatives are submitted to the legislature. Switzerland has held about half the world's national referenda. Referenda also are common at the local and state level in the U.S. In the late 20th century, referenda were employed more frequently, particularly in Europe, to decide public policy on voting systems, treaties and peace agreements (e.g., the Maastricht Treaty), and social issues.

reflection, Change in the direction of propagation of a wave that strikes a boundary between different media through which it cannot pass. When a wave strikes such a boundary it bounces back, or is reflected, just as a ball bounces off the floor. The angle of incidence is the angle between the path of the wave and a line perpendicular to the boundary. The angle of reflection is the angle between the same line and the path of the reflected wave. All reflected waves obey the law of reflection, which states that the angle of reflection is equal to the angle of incidence. The reflectivity of a material is the fraction of energy of the oncoming wave that is reflected by it.

Reform Judaism, Religious movement that has modified or abandoned many traditional Jewish beliefs and practices in an effort to adapt Judaism to the modern world. It originated in Germany in 1809 and spread to the U.S. in the 1840s under the leadership of Rabbi Isaac Mayer Wise. Reform Judaism permits men and women to sit together in the synagogue, incorporates choir and organ music in the service, holds a confirmation ceremony for girls parallel to the boys' Bar Mitzvah, and does not observe daily public worship, strict dietary laws, or the restriction of normal activities on the Sabbath. Its principles, initially enunciated in the Pittsburgh Platform (1885), were revised in the Columbus Platform (1937) to support traditional customs and ceremonies and the liturgical use of Hebrew. The Reform movement continues to move toward Orthodox Judaism without embracing all its strictures.

Reformation, or PROTESTANT REFORMATION, Break with Roman Catholicism and the establishment of Protestant churches in the 16th century. Though reformers such as Jan Hus and John Wycliffe attacked abuses in the Roman Catholic church in the late medieval period, the Reformation is usually dated from 1517, when, according to tradition, Martin Luther posted his Ninety-five

Theses on the church door in Wittenberg. Various Protestant denominations were soon founded by more radical reformers, such as Huldrych Zwingli and the Anabaptists. John Calvin established a theocracy in Geneva after his conversion to the Protestant cause. The Reformation spread to other European countries and soon dominated northern Europe. Spain and Italy remained resistant to Protestantism and became centres of the Counter-Reformation. In England, where Henry VIII founded the Church of England in 1534, the Reformation's roots were primarily political rather than religious, motivated by the pope's refusal to grant Henry a divorce. In Scotland the Calvinist John Knox led in the establishment of the Presbyterian church.

Reformed church, Any of several Protestant groups strongly influenced by Calvinism. They are often called by national names (Swiss Reformed, Dutch Reformed, etc.). The name was originally used by all the Protestant churches that arose out of the 16th-century Reformation but was later confined to the Calvinistic churches of continental Europe, most of which use a Presbyterian form of church government. The Calvinistic churches of the British Isles became known as Presbyterian churches.

refraction, Change in direction of a wave as it leaves one medium and enters another. Waves, such as sound and light waves, travel at different speeds in different media. When a wave enters a new medium at an angle of less than 90°, the change in speed occurs sooner on one side of the wave than on the other, causing the wave to bend, or refract. When water waves approach shallower water at an angle, they bend and become parallel to the shore. Refraction explains the apparent bending of a pencil when it is partly immersed in water and viewed from above the surface. It also causes the optical illusion of the mirage.

refrigeration, Process of removing heat from an enclosed space or from a substance in order to lower the temperature. In industrialized nations and prosperous regions in the developing world, refrigeration is used chiefly to store foodstuffs at low temperatures, thus inhibiting the destructive action of bacteria, yeasts, and molds. Many perishable products can be frozen, permitting them to be kept for months and even years with little loss in nutrition or flavour or change in appearance.

refugee, Person involuntarily displaced from his or her homeland. Until the late 19th century and the emergence of fixed and closed national boundaries, refugees were always absorbed by neighbouring countries. Later, immigration restrictions and increasing numbers of refugees necessitated special action to aid them. In 1921 Fridtjof Nansen created a League of Nations Passport to allow refugees to move freely across national boundaries. Refugee status at that time was accorded only if the migrant's departure was involuntary and asylum was sought in another country. In 1938 the definition of refugee was expanded to include persons with a well-founded fear of persecution because of ethnicity, religion, nationality, group membership, or political opinion. Later the definition was expanded again to include persons who have fled from their homes to other places in their own countries. Refugee status ceases to apply when the migrant either is resettled or returns home. At the beginning of the 21st century there were some 16 million refugees, including nearly 4 million Palestinians; much of the rest of the world's refugees were in Asia (particularly Afghanistan) and Africa, though conflict in the former Yugoslavia and elsewhere in post-Cold War Europe significantly increased the number of refugees in those regions.

Régence style, French style in the decorative arts that developed *c.* 1710–1730, when Philippe II, duc d'Orléans, was regent of France. It marks the transition from the massive rectilinear forms of furniture in the Louis XIV style to the Rococo forms of Louis XV style. In reaction against the pomposity of Louis XIV's court, smaller, more intimate rooms replaced formal state apartments and called for a more graceful style. The delicately styled Régence

furniture replaced heavy, carved ornamentation with flat, curving motifs, often foliage and bouquets framed by flowing ribbons and bows. Walnut, rosewood, and mahogany supplied rich but tasteful contrasts in veneering. Intricate tracery in brass and tortoiseshell marquetry on ebony was adapted to the new taste. The commode and writing table were introduced during this period.

Regency style, Style in the decorative arts and architecture produced in England during the regency (1811–20) and reign (1820–30) of George IV. Designers borrowed both structural and ornamental elements from Greek and Roman antiquity. Egyptian motifs, inspired by Napoleon's Egyptian campaign of 1798, became part of the Regency fashion. A resurgence of a taste for chinoiserie is seen in imitation bamboo and in "japanned" lacquerwork. The prince's taste for French furniture popularized pieces ornamented with brass marquetry in the French style. Ornamentation relied on rich contrasts of exotic wood veneers and application of metal or painting rather than extensive carving.

reggae, Jamaican popular music and dance style. It originated in the mid-1960s as a music of the Jamaican poor, reflecting social discontent and the Rastafarian movement. Its instrumentation features an electric bass played at high volume as a lead instrument, around which an ensemble of organ, piano, drums, and lead and rhythm electric guitars plays short ostinato phrases with regular accents on the offbeats. Reggae was popularized in the U.S. by the film *The Harder They Come* (1973), starring the singer Jimmy Cliff, and through tours by Bob Marley and the Wailers and by Toots (Hibbert) and the Maytals, whose influence was felt among white rock musicians.

regiment, In most armies, a body of troops headed by a colonel and divided into companies, battalions, or squadrons. French cavalry units were called regiments as early as 1558. In early U.S. service, as in European armies up to that time, the usual number of companies in a regiment was 10. Early in the 19th century, Napoleon divided the regiments of the French army into three battalions each, and in 1901 the U.S. Army adopted the three-battalion infantry regimental system.

regression, In statistics, a process for determining a line or curve that best represents the general trend of a data set. Linear regression results in a line of best fit, for which the sum of the squares of the vertical distances between the proposed line and the points of the data set are minimized. Other types of regression may be based on higher-degree polynomial functions or exponential functions. A quadratic regression, for example, uses a quadratic function (second-degree polynomial function) to produce a parabola of best fit.

regressive tax, Tax levied at a rate that decreases as its base increases. Regressivity is considered undesirable because poorer people pay a greater percentage of their income in tax than wealthier people. Consumption taxes and sales taxes are usually considered regressive because of their set rate structures. Tobacco, gasoline, and liquor sales taxes, all major sources of tax revenue, are the most regressive taxes. In an effort to limit regressivity, a number of U.S. states have exempted medicine and grocery items from sales tax. Although the property tax is sometimes judged regressive because poorer people spend a larger percentage of their income on housing than wealthier people, property taxes are nonetheless effective in redistributing wealth from higher to lower income groups.

Reign of Terror, French LA TERREUR (1793–94) Period in the French Revolution. It was established by the government on Sept. 5, 1793, to take harsh measures against those suspected of being enemies of the Revolution (including nobles, priests, and hoarders). Controlled by the radical Committee of Public Safety and Maximilien Robespierre, the Terror eliminated enemies on the left (Jacques Hébert and his followers) and the right (Georges Danton and the Indulgents). A law passed in June 1794 that suspended a suspect's right to public trial or legal defense caused the Thermidorian Reaction, and the Terror ended on July 27, 1794, with Robespierre's overthrow. About 300,000 suspects were arrested during the period; about 17,000 were executed, and many others died in prison.

Reims, or RHEIMS, City (pop., 2006 est.: 183,837), northeastern France. The ancient capital of the Gallic tribe of the Remi, it was conquered by the Romans. In the 5th century the Frankish king Clovis was baptized there, and in honour of this occasion most later French kings were crowned in Reims. The city was badly damaged in World Wars I and II and was the scene of Germany's unconditional surrender in May 1945. It is a major wine-producing centre noted especially for champagne. Other industries include aircraft and automobile equipment manufacturing. The 13th-century cathedral of Notre-Dame is one of the most notable Gothic cathedrals in France.

The cathedral of Notre-Dame, Reims, Fr.
Paul Almasy

reincarnation, or TRANSMIGRATION OF SOULS, or METEMPSYCHOSIS, Doctrine of the rebirth of the soul in one or more successive existences, which may be human, animal, or vegetable. Belief in reincarnation is characteristic of Asian religions, especially Hinduism, Jainism, Buddhism, and Sikhism. All hold to the doctrine of karma, the belief that actions in this life will have their effect in the next. In Hinduism, a person may be freed from the cycle of birth and rebirth only by reaching a state of enlightenment. Likewise in Buddhism, discipline and meditation may enable a seeker to reach nirvana and escape the wheel of birth and rebirth. Manichaeism and Gnosticism accepted the concept of reincarnation, as do such modern spiritual movements as Theosophy.

reindeer, Any species of Arctic deer in the genus *Rangifer* (family Cervidae), especially Old World species, some of which are domesticated. New World species are usually called caribou. The reindeer herded by the Sami (Lapps) are used as draft and pack animals and as a source of meat and milk; their skins are used for tents, boots, and other clothing. In Siberia they are used as pack animals and as mounts.

relapsing fever, Infectious disease with recurring fever, caused by several spirochetes of the genus *Borrelia*, transmitted by lice, ticks, and bedbugs. Onset is sudden, with high fever, which breaks within a week with profuse sweating. Symptoms return about a week later. There may be 2 to 10 relapses, usually decreasing in severity. Mortality usually ranges from 0 to 6%, up to 30% in rare epidemics. Central nervous system involvement causes various (usually mild) neurological symptoms. The first microscopic organisms clearly associated with serious human disease (1867–68), the spirochetes mutate repeatedly, changing their antigens so that the host's immunity no longer is effective, which produces the relapses. Antibiotics can be effective, but inadequate therapy may leave spirochetes alive in the brain, and they may reinvade the bloodstream.

relation, In logic, a relation R is defined as a set of ordered pairs, triples, quadruples, and so on. A set of ordered pairs is called a two-place (or dyadic) relation; a set of ordered triples is a three-place (or triadic) relation; and so on. In general, a relation is any set of ordered n-tuples of objects. Important properties of relations include symmetry, transitivity, and reflexivity. Consider a two-place (or dyadic) relation R. R can be said to be symmetrical if, whenever R holds between x and y, it also holds between y and x (symbolically, $(\forall x) (\forall y) [Rxy \supset Ryx]$); an example of a symmetrical relation is "x is parallel to y." R is transitive if, whenever it holds between one object and a second and also between that second object and a third, it holds between the first and the third (symbolically, $(\forall x) (\forall y) (\forall z) [(Rxy \wedge Ryz) \supset Rxz]$); an example is "x is greater than y." R is reflexive if it always holds between any object and itself (symbolically, $(\forall x) Rxx$); an example is "x is at least as tall as y" since x is always also "at least as tall" as itself.

relativity, Concept in physics that measurements change when considered by observers in various states of motion. In classical physics, it was assumed that all observers anywhere in the universe would obtain identical measurements of space and time intervals. According to relativity theory, this is not so; all measurements depend on the relative motions of the observer and the observed. There are two distinct theories of relativity, both proposed by Albert Einstein. The special theory of relativity (1905) developed from Einstein's acceptance that the speed of light is the same in all reference frames, irrespective of their relative motion. It deals with non-accelerating reference frames, and is concerned primarily with electric and magnetic phenomena and their propagation in space and time. The general theory (1916) was developed primarily to deal with gravitation and involves accelerating reference frames. Both theories are major milestones in the history of modern physics.

relief, or RILIEVO (from Italian, *rilievare*: "to raise") In sculpture, any work in which the figures project from a supporting background, usually a plane surface. Bas-reliefs ("low reliefs"), in which the design projects only slightly, were common on the walls of stone buildings in ancient Egypt, Assyria, and elsewhere in the Middle East. High reliefs, in which the forms project at least half or more of their natural circumference, were first employed by the ancient Greeks. Italian Renaissance sculptors combined high and low relief in strikingly illusionistic compositions, as in Lorenzo Ghiberti's bronze doors in Florence. Baroque sculptors continued these experiments, often on a larger scale (e.g., Alessandro Algardi's *Meeting of Attila and Pope Leo*, 1646–53). The dramatic possibilities of the Renaissance concept of relief were later notably employed by François Rude (*The Marseillaise*, 1833–36) and Auguste Rodin (*The Gates of Hell*).

religion, Relation of human beings to God or the gods or to whatever they consider sacred or, in some cases, merely supernatural. Archaeological evidence suggests that religious beliefs have existed since the first human communities. They are generally shared by a community, and they express the communal culture and values through myth, doctrine, and ritual. Worship is probably the most basic element of religion, but moral conduct, right belief, and participation in religious institutions also constitute elements of the religious life. Religions attempt to answer basic questions intrinsic to the human condition (Why do we suffer? Why is there evil in the world? What happens to us when we die?) through the relationship to the sacred or supernatural or (e.g., in the case of Buddhism) through perception of the true nature of reality. Broadly speaking, some religions (e.g., Judaism, Christianity, and Islam) are outwardly focused, and others (e.g., Jainism, Buddhism) are inwardly focused.

Rembrandt (Harmenszoon) van Rijn (b. July 15, 1606, Leiden, Neth.—d. Oct. 4, 1669, Amsterdam), Dutch painter and etcher. As a young man, he was apprenticed to masters in Leiden and in Amsterdam. His early paintings show his interest in the "spotlight effects" of light and shadow that were to dominate his later paintings. Early in his career he began the studies of his own face and the more-formal self-portraits that make up almost a tenth of his painted and etched work. After moving to Amsterdam about 1631, he quickly became the city's most fashionable portrait painter and a popular teacher. In 1632 he produced the celebrated *Anatomy Lesson of Dr. Nicolaes Tulp*. Yearning for recognition as a biblical and mythological painter, in 1635 he produced *The Sacrifice of Isaac* and in 1636 *Danaë*. In 1634 he married Saskia van Uylenburgh (d. 1642), a woman of property. That same year he completed his largest painting, the extraordinary but controversial *The Militia Company of Captain Frans Banning Cocq* (known as *The Night Watch*), which was a watershed in his life and art. For unknown reasons, his portrait commissions thereafter declined, and he began to focus his attention on etching, a medium in which he was self-taught. In 1656, after transferring most of his property to his son, he applied for bankruptcy. In his last decade he treated biblical subjects like portraits and also continued to paint self-portraits. These late works exhibit a lively brushwork and a new treatment of light. In addition to being an innovator, he was an acute observer of life and a sensitive renderer of those observations in his drawings, etchings, and paintings. The human figure, Rembrandt's central subject, contributes to the sense of a shared dialogue between viewer and artist, the foundation of Rembrandt's greatness and of his popularity today.

ren, or JEN, In Confucianism, the most basic of all virtues, variously translated as "humaneness" or "benevolence." It originally denoted the kindness of rulers to subjects. Confucius identified ren as perfect virtue, and Mencius made it the distinguishing characteristic of humanity. In Neo-Confucianism it was a moral quality imparted by Heaven.

Renaissance (French: "Rebirth"), Late medieval cultural movement in Europe. The Renaissance brought renewed interest in Classical learning and values to Italy and subsequently the rest of western and central Europe from the late 13th to the early 17th century. Attracted by the values and rhetorical eloquence of ancient writers, figures such as Petrarch, Giovanni Boccaccio, and Lorenzo Valla rejected medieval Scholasticism in favour of human-centred forms of philosophy and literature. In northern Europe, Desiderius Erasmus cultivated Christian humanism, and writers such as François Rabelais and William Shakespeare produced works that emphasized the intricacies of human character. Inspired by ancient Greece and Rome, Renaissance painters and sculptors took the visible world for their subject and practiced according to mathematical principles of balance, harmony, and perspective. The new aesthetic found expression in the works of Italian artists such as Leonardo da Vinci, Sandro Botticelli, Raphael, Titian, and Michelangelo, and the Italian city of Florence became the centre of Renaissance art. The term has also been applied to cultural revivals in England in the 8th century, the Frankish kingdoms in the 9th century, and Europe in the 12th century.

Renaissance architecture, Style of architecture, reflecting the rebirth of Classical culture, that originated in Florence in the early 15th century and spread throughout Europe, replacing the medieval Gothic style. There was a revival of ancient Roman forms, including the column and round arch, the tunnel vault, and the dome. The basic design element was the order. Knowledge of Classical architecture came from the ruins of ancient buildings and the writings of Vitruvius. As in the Classical period, proportion was the most important factor of beauty; Renaissance architects found a harmony between human proportions and buildings. This concern for proportion resulted in clear, easily comprehended space and mass, which distinguishes the Renaissance style from the more complex Gothic. Filippo Brunelleschi is considered the first Renaissance architect. Leon Battista Alberti's *Ten Books on Architecture*, inspired by Vitruvius, became a bible of Renaissance architecture. From Florence the early Renaissance style spread through Italy. Donato Bramante's move to Rome ushered in the High Renaissance (*c.* 1500–20). Mannerism, the style of the Late Renaissance (1520–1600), was characterized by sophistication, complexity, and novelty rather than the harmony, clarity, and repose of the High Renaissance. The Late Renaissance also saw

much architectural theorizing, with Sebastiano Serlio (1475–1554), Giacomo da Vignola (1507–73), and Andrea Palladio publishing influential books.

renal cell carcinoma, or HYPERNEPHROMA, Malignant tumour of the cells that cover and line the kidney. It usually affects persons over age 50 who have vascular disorders of the kidneys. It seldom causes pain, unless it is advanced. It may metastasize to other organs (e.g., lungs, liver, brain, bone) and go unrecognized until these secondary tumours cause symptoms. Blood can appear in the urine early on but is painless and usually disregarded. Even when the cancer is in the early stages, X-ray films can show deformity in kidney structures.

Renoir, Pierre-Auguste (b. Feb. 25, 1841, Limoges, France—d. Dec. 3, 1919, Cagnes), French painter. His father, a tailor in Limoges, moved with his large family to Paris in 1844. Renoir began working as a decorator of porcelain at 13 and studied painting at night. He formed a close friendship with his fellow student Claude Monet and became a leading member of the Paris Impressionists. His early works were typically Impressionist snapshots of real life, full of sparkling colour and light. By using small, multicoloured strokes, Renoir evoked the vibration of the atmosphere, the sparkling effect of foliage, and especially the luminosity of a young woman's skin in the outdoors. Because of his fascination with the human figure, he was distinctive among the others, who were more interested in landscape. Among his early masterpieces are *Le Moulin de la Galette* (1876) and *The Luncheon of the Boating Party* (1881). A visit to Italy (1881–82) introduced him to Raphael and the expressive force of clear line and smooth painting, and by the mid 1880s he had broken with Impressionism to employ a more disciplined, formal technique. In works such as *Bathers* (1884–87), he emphasized volume, form, contours, and line. In his later works, he departed from the strict rules of Classicism to paint colourful still lifes, portraits, nudes, and landscapes of southern France, where he settled in 1907. Rheumatism confined him to a wheelchair by 1912 but he never ceased to paint, even though often with his brush attached to his hand. The filmmaker Jean Renoir was his son.

reovirus, Any of a small group of animal and plant viruses that appear spheroidal and contain a core of RNA. Among the best-known genera are *Orthoreovirus*, *Orbivirus*, *Rotavirus*, and *Phytoreovirus*. The first three infect animals; the last can destroy rice, corn, and other crops.

reparations, Payment in money or materials by a nation defeated in war. After World War I, reparations to the Allied Powers were required of Germany by the Treaty of Versailles. The original amount of $33 billion was later reduced by the Dawes Plan and the Young Plan and was canceled after 1933. In the 1920s German resentment over reparations was used by ultranationalists to foment political unrest.

representation, In politics, a method or process of enabling a constituency to influence legislation and government policy through deputies chosen by it. The rationale of representative government is that in large modern countries the people cannot all assemble, as they did in the marketplace of democratic Athens. If the public is to participate in government, citizens must select a small number from among themselves to act for them. Political parties have come to act as intermediaries between citizens and their representatives by helping to formulate systematically citizens' demands. Arguments persist about the proper role of representatives; some theories suggest that they should act as delegates carrying out the instructions of the public, whereas others argue that they should serve as free agents, acting in accordance with their best ability and understanding.

reproductive system, human, Organ system by which humans reproduce. In females, the ovaries sit near the openings of the fallopian tubes, which carry eggs from the ovaries to the uterus. The cervix extends from the lower end of the uterus into the vagina, whose opening, as well as that of the urethra, is covered by four folds of skin (the labia); the clitoris, a small erectile organ, is located where the labia join in front. The activity of the ovaries and uterus goes through a monthly cycle of changes throughout the reproductive years except during pregnancy and nursing. In males, the testes lie in a sac of skin (the scrotum). A long duct (the vas deferens) leads from each testis and carries sperm to the ejaculatory ducts in the prostate gland; these join the urethra, which continues through the penis. In the urethra, sperm mixes with secretions from the seminal vesicles, prostate gland, and Cowper gland to form semen. In early embryos, the reproductive systems are undetermined. By birth the organs appropriate to each sex have typically developed but are not yet functioning. They continue to grow, and at puberty their activity increases and maturation occurs, enabling sexual reproduction.

reptile, Any of the approximately 8,700 species of the class Reptilia, the group of air-breathing vertebrates that have internal fertilization and a scaly body and are cold-blooded. Most species have short legs (or none) and long tails, and most lay eggs. Living reptiles include the scaly reptiles (snakes and lizards; order Squamata), the crocodiles (Crocodylia), the turtles (Testudines), and the unique tuatara (Sphenodontida). Being cold-blooded, reptiles are not found in very cold regions; in regions with cold winters, they usually hibernate. They range in size from geckos that measure about 1 in. (3 cm) long to the python, which grows to 30 ft (9 m); the largest turtle, the marine leatherback, weighs about 1,500 lb (680 kg). Extinct reptiles include the dinosaurs, the pterosaurs, and the dolphinlike ichthyosaurs.

republic, Form of government in which a state is ruled by representatives elected by its populace. The term was originally applied to a form of government in which the leader is periodically appointed under a constitution; it was contrasted with governments in which leadership is hereditary. A republic may also be distinguished from direct democracy, though modern representative democracies are by and large republics.

requiem mass, Musical setting of the mass for the dead. (*Requiem,* Latin for "rest," is the first word of the mass.) The requiem's text differs from the standard mass Ordinary in omitting its joyous sections and keeping only the Kyrie, Sanctus, and Agnus Dei, which are combined with other sections, including the sequence *Dies irae* ("Day of Wrath"). The first surviving polyphonic setting is by Johannes Ockeghem; celebrated later requiems include those of Wolfgang Amadeus Mozart, Hector Berlioz, Giuseppe Verdi, Gabriel Fauré, Johannes Brahms, and Benjamin Britten.

resistance, Opposition that a material or electrical circuit offers to the flow of electric current. It is the property of a circuit that transforms electrical energy into heat energy as it opposes the flow of current. The resistance R, the electromotive force or voltage V, and the current I are related by Ohm's law. The resistance of an electrical conductor generally increases with increasing temperature and is utilized in devices such as lamps and heaters. The ohm (Ω) is the common unit of electrical resistance; one ohm is equal to one volt per ampere.

respiratory distress syndrome, or HYALINE MEMBRANE DISEASE, Common complication in newborns, especially after premature birth. Symptoms include very laboured breathing, bluish skin tinge, and low blood oxygen levels. Insufficient surfactant in the pulmonary alveoli raises surface tension, hampering lung expansion. The alveoli collapse, and a "glassy" (hyaline) membrane develops in the alveolar ducts. Once the leading cause of death in premature infants, the syndrome is now usually treated for a few days with a mechanical ventilator, with no aftereffects. An adult respiratory distress syndrome (ARDS) can follow lung injury.

respiratory system, Organ system involved in respiration. In humans, the diaphragm and, to a lesser extent, the muscles between the ribs generate a pumping action, moving air in and out of the lungs through a system of pipes (conducting airways), divided into upper and lower airway systems. The upper airway system comprises the nasal cavity, sinuses, and pharynx; the lower airway system consists of the larynx, trachea, bronchi, bronchioles, and alveolar ducts. The blood and cardiovascular system can be considered elements of a working respiratory system.

restaurant, Establishment where refreshments or meals are served to paying guests. Though inns and taverns served simple fare to travelers for centuries, the first modern restaurant where guests could order from a varied menu is thought to have belonged to A. Boulanger, a soup vendor who opened his business in Paris in 1765. The sign above his door advertised restoratives, or *restaurants,* referring to his soups and broths. By 1804 Paris had more than 500 restaurants, and France soon became internationally famous for its cuisine. Other European restaurants include the Italian *trattorie,* taverns featuring local specialties; the German *Weinstuben,* informal restaurants with a large wine selection; the Spanish tapas bars, which serve a wide variety of appetizers; and the public houses of England. Asian restaurants include the Japanese sushi bars and teahouses serving formal Kaiseki cuisine as well as the noodle shops of China. Most U.S. restaurant innovations have revolved around speed. The cafeteria originated in San Francisco during the 1849 gold rush; cafeterias feature self-service and offer a variety of foods displayed on counters. The U.S. also pioneered fast-food restaurants such as White Castle (founded 1921) and McDonald's, usually operated as chains and offering limited menus.

Restoration, Restoration of the monarchy in England in 1660. It marked the return of Charles II as king (1660–85) following the period of Oliver Cromwell's Commonwealth. The bishops were restored to Parliament, which established a strict Anglican orthodoxy. The period, which also included the reign of James II (1685–88), was marked by an expansion in colonial trade, the Anglo-Dutch Wars, and a revival of drama and literature.

retrograde motion, In astronomy, the actual or apparent motion of a body in a direction opposite to that of the predominant (direct or prograde) motions of similar bodies. Observationally and historically, retrograde motion refers to the apparent reversal of the planets' motion through the stars for several months in each synodic period. This required a complex explanation in Earth-centred models of the universe but was naturally explained in heliocentric models by the apparent motion as Earth passed by a planet in its orbit. It is now known that nearly all bodies in the solar system revolve and rotate in the same counterclockwise direction as viewed from a position in space above Earth's North Pole. This common direction probably arose during the formation of the solar nebula. The relatively few objects with clockwise motions (e.g., the rotation of Venus, Uranus, and Pluto) are also described as retrograde.

retrovirus, Any of a group of viruses that, unlike most other viruses and all cellular organisms, carry their genetic blueprint in the form of RNA. Retroviruses are responsible for some cancers and viral infections of animals, and they cause at least one type of human cancer. The retrovirus HIV is the cause of AIDS in humans. The name signifies that they use RNA to synthesize DNA, the reverse of the usual cell process. This process makes it possible for genetic material from a retrovirus to enter and become a permanent part of the genes of an infected cell.

Réunion, Island and French overseas department, Mascarene Islands, western Indian Ocean. Area: 973 sq mi (2,520 sq km). Population: (2011 est.) 852,000. Capital: Saint-Denis. Located 425 mi (684 km) east of Madagascar, Réunion is about 40 mi (65 km) long and 30 mi (50 km) wide. It consists mainly of rugged mountains dissected by torrential rivers. Most of the population is of mixed ancestry, with African descent predominant. Réunion was settled in the 17th century by the French, who brought slaves from eastern Africa to work on coffee and sugar plantations. It was a French colony until 1946, when it became an overseas department of France. Its economy is based largely on the export of sugar. Other products include meat and milk products, rum, molasses, tobacco, geranium essence, and vanilla.

revelation, Transmission of knowledge from a god or gods to humans. In the Western monotheistic religions of Judaism, Christianity, and Islam, revelation is the basis of religious knowledge. Humans know God and his will because God has chosen to reveal himself to them. He may communicate with his chosen servants through dreams, visions, or physical manifestations and may inspire prophets who relay his message to the people. His will may also be translated directly into writing through the handing down of divine law (e.g., the Ten Commandments) or scripture (e.g., the Bible and the Qurʾān). Other religions emphasize "cosmic" revelation, in which any and all aspects of the world may reveal the nature of a single underlying divine power (e.g., Brahman in the Vedas).

Revelation, Book of, or REVELATIONS, or APOCALYPSE OF JOHN, Last book of the New Testament. It consists of two main parts, the first containing moral admonitions to several Christian churches in Asia Minor, and the second composed of extraordinary visions, allegories, and symbols that have been the subject of varying interpretations throughout history. A popular interpretation is that Revelation deals with a contemporary crisis of faith, possibly the result of Roman persecutions. It exhorts Christians to remain steadfast in their faith and hold firm to the hope that God will ultimately vanquish their enemies. References to "a thousand years" have led some to expect that the final victory over evil will come after the completion of a millennium. Modern scholarship accepts that the book was written not by St. John the Apostle but by various unknown authors in the late 1st century AD.

revenue sharing, Funding arrangement in which one government unit grants a portion of its tax income to another government unit. For example, provinces or states may share revenue with local governments, or national governments may share revenue with provinces or states. Laws determine the formulas by which revenue is shared, limiting the controls that the unit supplying the money can exercise over the receiver and specifying whether matching funds must be supplied by the receiver. Forms of revenue sharing have been used in several countries, including Canada, India, and Switzerland. From 1972 to 1986 the U.S. pursued a revenue-sharing program in which state and local governments received federal funds to spend as they saw fit.

reverberatory furnace, Furnace used for smelting, refining, or melting in which the fuel is not in direct contact with the contents but heats it by a flame blown over it from another chamber. Such furnaces are used in copper, tin, and nickel production, in the production of certain concretes and cements, and in aluminum recycling. In steelmaking, this process (now largely obsolete) is called the open-hearth process. The heat passes over the hearth and then radiates back (reverberates) onto the contents. The roof is arched, with the highest point over the firebox. It slopes downward toward a bridge of flues that deflects the flame so that it reverberates.

revivalism, Reawakening of Christian values and commitment. The spiritual fervour of revival-style preaching, typically performed by itinerant, charismatic preachers before large gatherings, is thought to have a restorative effect on those who have been led away from the right path. Various Protestant sects have experienced periods of revivalism at different times since the 17th century, and many, notably Methodism, came into being during revivalist periods. Common themes are strict interpretation of the Bible,

rejection of literary or historical study of the Bible, emphasis on the conversion experience, and a call to live devoutly. Revivalism can be interpreted as a precursor of 20th-century Christian fundamentalism.

revolution, In politics, fundamental, rapid, and often irreversible change in the established order. Revolution involves a radical change in government, usually accomplished through violence, that may also result in changes to the economic system, social structure, and cultural values. The ancient Greeks viewed revolution as the undesirable result of societal breakdown; a strong value system, firmly adhered to, was thought to protect against it. During the Middle Ages, much attention was given to finding means of combating revolution and stifling societal change. With the advent of Renaissance humanism, there arose the belief that radical changes of government are sometimes necessary and good, and the idea of revolution took on more positive connotations. John Milton regarded it as a means of achieving freedom, Immanuel Kant believed it was a force for the advancement of mankind, and G.W.F. Hegel held it to be the fulfillment of human destiny. Hegel's philosophy in turn influenced Karl Marx.

Revolutions of 1848, Series of republican revolts against European monarchies. The revolutions began in Sicily and spread to France, the German and Italian states, and the Austrian Empire. In France the revolution established the Second Republic, and in central Europe liberal political reform and national unification appeared likely. However, the armies loyal to the monarchies soon reestablished their power and rescinded most of the promised reforms. The revolts eventually ended in failure and repression, and they were followed by widespread disillusionment among liberals.

revolver, Pistol with a revolving cylinder that provides multishot action. Some early versions, known as pepperboxes, had several barrels, but as early as the 17th century pistols were being made with a revolving chamber to load cartridges into a single barrel. The first practical revolver was not designed until 1835, when Samuel Colt patented his version. He established the standard of a cylinder with multiple chambers, each of which successively locked in position behind the barrel and was discharged by pressure on the trigger. In Colt's early single-action revolvers, the cylinder revolved as the hammer was cocked manually. Double-action revolvers, in which the hammer is cocked and the cylinder revolves as the trigger is pulled, were developed soon afterward, along with metal cartridges.

revue, Theatrical production of brief, loosely connected, often satirical skits, songs, and dances. Originally derived from the medieval French street fair, the modern revue dates from the early 19th century with the Parisian *Folies Marigny* and later at the Folies-Bergère. The English revue developed in two forms: one as the costume display and spectacle of the Court Theatre productions in the 1890s and another as the *André Charlot Revues* of the 1920s and the London Hippodrome shows, which emphasized clever repartee and topicality. In the U.S. the *Ziegfeld Follies* began in 1907 and usually featured a star personality. Revues appeared periodically on Broadway and West End stages until competition from movies and television moved the form to small nightclubs and improvisational theatres.

Reye syndrome, Acute neurological illness in children, following influenza, chickenpox, or other viral infections. Vomiting, lethargy, and confusion begin as the child appears to be recovering. These symptoms are followed hours or days later by drowsiness, disorientation, seizures, respiratory arrest, and coma. At worst, the syndrome includes fatty liver degeneration and potentially fatal brain swelling. There is no specific cure, but treatment of imbalances helps over 70% of patients survive (some with brain damage). The incidence has decreased since the recognition that it often follows use of aspirin or other salicylic acid derivatives in children during a viral illness. It can also result from aflatoxin or warfarin poisoning.

Reykjavík, City (pop., 2006 est.: 116,446; urban agglom., 191,431), capital of Iceland. According to tradition, it was founded in 874 by the Norseman Ingólfur Arnarson. Until the 20th century it was a small fishing village at the southeastern corner of Faxa Bay, ruled and largely inhabited by Danes. It became the capital of a self-governing Iceland under the Danish king in 1918 and of the independent Republic of Iceland in 1944. During World War II it was a U.S. naval and air base. In 1986 arms-control talks between the U.S. and U.S.S.R. were held there. It is the commercial, industrial, and cultural centre of the island, its major fishing port, and the site of nearly half of the nation's industries.

Reymont, Władysław (Stanisław), or WŁADYSŁAW STANISŁAW REJMENT (b. May 7, 1867, Kobiele Wielkie, Pol., Russian Empire—d. Dec. 5, 1925, Warsaw, Pol.), Polish novelist. He never finished his schooling and worked in his youth as a shop apprentice, a lay brother in a monastery, a railway official, and an actor. His short stories and novels are written in a naturalistic, factual style with short sentences. His best work, *The Peasants* (1904–09), is a four-volume chronicle of peasant life over the course of a year, written in peasant dialect. Translated into many languages, it won Reymont the 1924 Nobel Prize for Literature.

Reynolds number, In fluid mechanics, a number that indicates whether the flow of a fluid (liquid or gas) is absolutely steady (in streamlined, or laminar flow) or on the average steady with small, unsteady changes (in turbulent flow; *see* turbulence). The Reynolds number, abbreviated N_{Re} or Re, has no dimensions and is defined as the size of the flow—as, for example, the diameter of a tube (D) times the average speed of flow (v) times the mass density of the fluid (ρ)—divided by its absolute viscosity (μ). Osborne Reynolds demonstrated in 1883 that the change from laminar to turbulent flow in a pipe occurs when the value of the Reynolds number exceeds 2,100.

Rh blood-group system, System for classifying blood according to presence or absence of the Rh antigen (factor) in erythrocytes. Rh-negative persons who receive Rh-positive blood transfusions produce antibodies to Rh factor, which attack red blood cells with the factor if they are ever received again, causing serious illness and sometimes death. The antibodies also attack the red cells of an Rh-positive fetus carried by an Rh-negative woman if she has had a previous Rh-positive transfusion or pregnancy. The Rh-negative trait is rare worldwide but more common in some ethnic groups.

rhabdovirus, Any of a group of viruses responsible for rabies and vesicular stomatitis (an acute disease of cattle and horses, characterized by blisters in and about the mouth, that resembles foot-and-mouth disease). The bullet-shaped virus particle is encased in a fatty membrane and contains RNA.

rhesus monkey, Sand-coloured macaque (*Macaca mulatta*), widespread in South and Southeast Asian forests. Rhesus monkeys are 17–25 in. (43–64 cm) long, excluding the furry 8–12-in. (20–30-cm) tail, and weigh 10–24 lb (4.5–11 kg). They eat fruits, seeds, roots, herbs, and insects. They are held sacred in some parts of India. Hardy in captivity, highly intelligent, and lively, they make

Rhesus monkeys (Macaca mulatta).
Ylla—Rapho/Photo Researchers

good pets when young but may become bad-tempered as adults. They have been used frequently in medical research. The determination of the Rh (from rhesus) factor in human blood involves reaction with the blood of this species.

rhetoric, Principles of training communicators. It may entail the study of principles and rules of composition formulated by critics of ancient times, and it can also involve the study of writing or speaking as a means of communication or persuasion. Classical rhetoric probably developed along with democracy in Syracuse (Sicily) in the 5th century BC, when dispossessed landowners argued claims before their fellow citizens. Shrewd speakers sought help from teachers of oratory, called *rhetor*s. This use of language was of interest to philosophers such as Plato and Aristotle because the oratorical arguments called into question the relationships among language, truth, and morality. The Romans recognized separate aspects of the process of composing speeches, a compartmentalization that grew more pronounced with time. Renaissance scholars and poets studied rhetoric closely, and it was a central concern of humanism. In all times and places where rhetoric has been significant, listening and reading and speaking and writing have been the critical skills necessary for effective communication.

rheumatic fever, Generalized disease caused by certain types of streptococcus bacteria. It occurs mostly in children and young adults. Symptoms may be mild or severe. Sudden fever, joint pain, and inflammation may begin days to weeks after a streptococcal infection, usually of the throat. Other symptoms may include skin nodules and rashes, chorea, abdominal pain, nosebleeds, and weight loss. Heart inflammation, with accompanying rapid heartbeat, murmurs, and enlargement, can lead to valve scarring, markedly shortening life. After recovery, survivors are prone to future attacks. Penicillin given when the initial infection is diagnosed can prevent it. Otherwise, salicylic acid derivatives or corticosteroids help the symptoms.

rheumatoid arthritis, Chronic, progressive autoimmune disease causing connective-tissue inflammation, mostly in synovial joints. It can occur at any age, is more common in women, and has an unpredictable course. It usually starts gradually, with pain and stiffness in one or more joints, then swelling and heat. Muscle pain may persist, worsen, or subside. Membrane inflammation and thickening scars joint structures and destroys cartilage. In severe cases, adhesions immobilize and deform the joints, and adjacent skin, bones, and muscles atrophy. If high-dose aspirin, ibuprofen, and other NSAIDs do not relieve pain and disability, low-dose corticosteroids may be tried. Physical medicine and rehabilitation with heat and then range-of-motion exercises reduce pain and swelling. Orthopedic appliances correct or prevent gross deformity and malfunction. Surgery can replace destroyed hip, knee, or finger joints with prostheses. There is also a juvenile form of the disease.

Rhine River, German RHEIN, River, western Europe. Rising in the Swiss Alps, it flows north and west through western Germany to drain through the delta region of the Netherlands into the North Sea. It is 820 mi (1,320 km) long, though in 2010 a length of 765 mi (1,230 km) was proposed; it is navigable for 540 mi (870 km). Its many canals connect it with the Rhône, Marne, and Danube river systems. It has been an international waterway since 1815. It has played a prominent part in German history and legend. During World War II its course was a major line of defense. Major cities along its banks include Basel, Mannheim, Koblenz, Cologne, Duisburg, and Rotterdam.

rhinoceros, Any of five extant African and Asian species (family Rhinocerotidae) of three-toed horned ungulates. One of the largest of all land animals (the white rhinoceros is second only to the elephant), the rhinoceros is particularly distinguished by one or two horns—growths of keratin, a fibrous hair protein—on its upper snout. All have thick, virtually hairless skin that, in the three Asian species, forms platelike folds at the shoulders and thighs. Rhinos grow to 8–14 ft (2.5–4.3 m) long and 3–6.5 ft (1.5–2 m) tall; adults weigh 3–5 tons. Most are solitary inhabitants of open grassland, scrub forest, or marsh, but the Sumatran rhino lives in deep forest. The African black rhino browses on succulent plants, the white and great Indian rhinos graze on short grasses, and the Sumatran and Javan rhinos browse on bushes and bamboo. In the second half of the 20th century, the rhinoceroses were brought to the brink of extinction by hunters, mostly seeking the horn. All five species are threatened or endangered.

rhinovirus, Any of a group of picornaviruses capable of causing common colds in humans. The virus is thought to be transmitted to the upper respiratory tract by airborne droplets. Because of the great number of cold viruses, vaccines against them are virtually impossible to develop.

Rhodes, Greek RÓDHOS, Island of Greece. It is the largest island of the Dodecanese group and the most easterly in the Aegean Sea. Its main city, Rhodes (pop., 2001: 53,709), lies at the northern tip of the island. The earliest known settlers were the Dorians c. 1000 BC. During the Classical period the island's affiliations vacillated between Athens, Sparta, and Persia in attempts to preserve a balance of power. A devastating earthquake c. 225 BC destroyed the Colossus of Rhodes, one of the Seven Wonders of the World. In the medieval period Rhodes was occupied by the Byzantines, Muslims, and Knights of St. John. The knights converted the island into a fortress and held it for two centuries until 1523, when the Turks took control. In 1912 it was taken from Turkey by Italy, and in 1947 it was awarded by treaty to Greece. A year-round tourist industry has brought prosperity to the island.

Rhodes, Cecil (John) (b. July 5, 1853, Bishop's Stortford, Hertfordshire, Eng.—d. March 26, 1902, Muizenberg, Cape Colony), Financier, statesman, and empire builder of British South Africa. Rhodes grew up in the English countryside and in 1871 was sent to assist his brother in business in South Africa, where he became interested in diamond mining. He founded De Beers Consolidated Mines (1888), and by 1891 his company was mining 90% of the world's diamonds. Seeking expansion to the north and dreaming of building a Cape-to-Cairo railway, he persuaded Britain to establish a protectorate over Bechuanaland (1884), clashing with Boer president Paul Kruger. He obtained digging concessions from Lobengula (1889), but in 1893 Rhodes overran him militarily. At his instigation Britain chartered the British South Africa Co. (1889) and put Rhodes in charge. He extended the company's control to two northern provinces, which were eventually named after him as Southern Rhodesia (now Zimbabwe) and Northern Rhodesia (now Zambia). Interested in the mineral-rich Transvaal, he plotted to overthrow Kruger (1895); the attempt was botched by Leander Starr Jameson, and Rhodes was forced to resign as prime minister of Cape Colony and head of the British South Africa Co. His last years were marked by disappointment and scandal brought about by the scheming of Princess Radziwiłł. His will bequeathed most of his fortune to establishing the Rhodes scholarship.

Colossus of Rhodes, constructed c. 294–282 BC, wood engraving reconstruction by Sidney Barclay, c. 1875.
Historical Pictures Service, Chicago

Rhodes, Colossus of, Enormous bronze statue of the sun god Helios that towered more than 100 ft (30 m) over the har-

bour at the city of Rhodes in Greece. The work of Chares of Lindos, the statue commemorated the raising of Demetrios Poliorcetes' long siege of Rhodes (305–304 BC). One of the Seven Wonders of the World, it was toppled by an earthquake c. 225 BC. The fallen Colossus was left in place until AD 653, when raiding Arabs broke up its remains and sold the bronze for scrap.

Rhodesian ridgeback, or AFRICAN LION DOG, South African hound breed characterized by a narrow band of hair growing forward along its back, against the direction of the rest of the coat. The ridge is inherited from a half-wild local hunting dog that was crossbred with European dogs. Strong, active, and of great endurance, it is trim and short-haired, with hanging ears and a glossy brown coat. It stands 24–27 in. (61–69 cm) and weighs 65–75 lbs (30–34 kg). It is an able guard and hunter (especially of lions) and a good companion.

Rhodesian ridgeback.
Walter Chandoha

rhododendron, Any of about 850 diverse species of woody plants that make up the genus *Rhododendron* in the heath family, notable for their attractive flowers and handsome foliage. They are native chiefly to the northern temperate zone, especially South Asia and Malaysia. Some are evergreens, others deciduous. Some are low-growing ground covers; others are tall trees. Flowers are usually tubular to funnel-shaped and occur in a wide range of colours: white, yellow, pink, scarlet, purple, and blue.

Rhodope Mountains, Mountain range, Balkan Peninsula, southeastern Europe. Extending southeast from Bulgaria through Macedonia and Greece, the range is drained by tributaries of the Maritsa River. It forms an important climatic barrier, protecting the Aegean lowlands from cold northerly winds. The mountains were a refuge for Slavic peoples during the period of Turkish rule (15th–19th century), and ancient customs survive. The lakes, river valleys, and extensive forests form the basis of a tourist industry.

Rhône River, River, Switzerland and France. A historic southern gateway, as well as the only major European river flowing directly to the Mediterranean Sea, the Rhône is 505 mi (813 km) long. It is Alpine in character, and its course has been shaped by neighbouring mountain systems. Rising in the Swiss Alps, it flows into Lake Geneva, then crosses into France through the Jura Mountains. It continues south through Lyon, Avignon, and Tarascon to Arles and enters the Mediterranean west of Marseille.

rhubarb, Any of several species of the genus *Rheum* (family Polygonaceae), especially *R. rhaponticum* (or *R. rhabarbarum*), a hardy perennial grown for its large, succulent, edible leafstalks. Rhubarb is best adapted to the cooler parts of the temperate zones. The fleshy, tart, and highly acid leafstalks are used in pies, compotes and preserves, and sometimes as the base of a wine or an aperitif. The roots withstand cold well. The huge leaves that unfold in early spring are toxic to cattle and humans; later in the season a large central flower stalk may bear numerous small, greenish-

Rhubarb (Rheum rhaponticum)
Derek Fell

white flowers and angular, winged fruits. Rhubarb root has long been considered to have cathartic and purgative properties.

rhyme, Type of echoing produced by the close placement of two or more words with similarly sounding final syllables. Rhyme is used in poetry (and occasionally in prose) to produce sounds that appeal to the ear and to unify and establish a poem's stanzaic form. End rhyme (i.e., rhyme used at the end of a line to echo the end of another line) is most common, but internal rhyme (occurring before the end of a line) is frequently used as an embellishment. Types of "true rhyme" include masculine rhyme, in which the two words end with the same vowel-consonant combination (stand/land); feminine rhyme (or double rhyme), in which two syllables rhyme (profession/discretion); and trisyllabic rhyme, in which three syllables rhyme (patinate/latinate).

rhythm and blues (R&B), Any of several closely related musical styles developed by African American artists. The various styles were based on a mingling of European influences with jazz rhythms and tonal inflections, particularly syncopation and the flatted blues chords. They grew out of the blues of the rural South, which blended work chants with songs of deep emotion, and were greatly influenced by gospel music. Three major forms were distinguishable. The earliest, called *race*, was the style of the "jump" band, which emphasized strong rhythm, solo work (especially by saxophones), and vocals in a shout-blues manner. A second form, often called *Chicago blues*, was exemplified by performers such as Muddy Waters and was typically played by a small group with amplified instruments. The third major form was primarily vocal, featuring close, gospel-influenced harmonies often backed by an orchestra. In the mid-1950s the term *rhythm and blues* was adopted by the music industry for music intended for the African American audience; with the gradual disappearance of racial barriers, the Chicago blues style began to seem less a vital form than a folk tradition, while the gospel style was transformed into the soul music of vast appeal. Rhythm and blues was the chief antecedent of rock music.

rhythm and metre, Two aspects of the organization of time in music. Rhythm is the placement of musical sounds in time. Metre, like poetical metre, is usually a regular pattern of beats and provides the context in which rhythm is understood. In Western notated music, metre is indicated by means of a time signature—in which the lower number specifies the basic unit or subunit of the beat (e.g., 8 usually indicates that eighth-notes are the basic subunit) and the upper number specifies the number of beats in a measure—at the beginning of a piece or movement, and by the vertical bar lines that divide the piece into measures.

rhythmic sportive gymnastics, Athletic competition related to gymnastics and dance in which participants, individually or in groups, perform exercise routines with the aid of hand apparatuses such as ropes, hoops, balls, clubs, and ribbons. In scoring points, artistry counts more than acrobatics. The sport dates from the 18th century. Though some gymnasts participated at the Olympic Games from 1948 to 1956, not until 1984 did it become an official Olympic competitive event.

rice, Edible starchy cereal grain and the annual grass (*Oryza sativa*, family Poaceae) that produces it. Roughly one-half of the world's population, including almost all of East and Southeast Asia, depends on rice as its principal staple food. First cultivated in India more than 4,000 years ago, rice was planted gradually westward and is now cultivated widely in flooded fields (paddies) and river deltas of tropical, semitropical, and temperate regions. Growing to about 4 ft (1.2 m) in height, rice has long, flat leaves and an inflorescence made up of spikelets bearing flowers that produce the fruit, or grain. Removal of just the husk produces brown rice, containing 8% protein and iron, calcium, and B vitamins. Removal of the bran layer leaves white rice, greatly diminished in nutrients. Enriched white rice has added B vitamins and

minerals. So-called wild rice (*Zizania aquatica* or *Zizania palustris*) is a coarse annual grass of the same family whose cereal grain, now often considered a delicacy, has long been an important food of North American Indians.

Richard I, known as RICHARD THE LIONHEART(ED), French RICHARD COEUR DE LION (b. Sept. 8, 1157, Oxford, Eng.—d. April 6, 1199, Châlus, Duchy of Aquitaine), Duke of Aquitaine (1168–99) and Poitiers (1172–99) and king of England, duke of Normandy, and count of Anjou (1189–99). He inherited Aquitaine from his mother, Eleanor of Aquitaine. Denied real authority there, he rebelled against his father, Henry II (1173–74) and later enlisted Philip II of France in a successful campaign against Henry (1189). Crowned king of England on Henry's death that year, Richard embarked on the Third Crusade (1190), stopping in Sicily to name Tancred king and conquering Cyprus. He won victories in the Holy Land, but, after failing to gain Jerusalem, he signed a truce (1192) with Saladin. On his way home Richard was captured by Leopold of Austria and turned over to Henry VI of Germany, who imprisoned him until a ransom was paid (1194). Richard returned to England and reclaimed the throne from his brother John, then spent the rest of his life in Normandy fighting against Philip II.

Richard III (b. Oct. 2, 1452, Fotheringhay Castle, Northamptonshire, Eng.—d. Aug. 22, 1485, Bosworth, Leicestershire), Last Yorkist king of England. He was made duke of Gloucester in 1461 after his brother Edward of York had deposed the weak Lancastrian king Henry VI and assumed power as Edward IV. Richard and Edward were driven into exile in 1470 but returned and defeated the Lancastrians in 1471. On Edward's death (1483), Richard became protector for Edward's son, the 12-year-old King Edward V, but he usurped the throne and confined Edward and his little brother to the Tower of London, where they were murdered. Henry Tudor (later Henry VII) raised an army against Richard, who was defeated and killed at the Battle of Bosworth Field. Later Tudor histories and William Shakespeare's play *Richard III* painted Richard as a monster and were gross caricatures motivated by the new dynasty's need to denigrate its predecessor.

Richelieu, Armand-Jean du Plessis, cardinal and duke

de (b. Sept. 9, 1585, Richelieu, Poitou, France—d. Dec. 4, 1642, Paris), French statesman and chief minister to Louis XIII. Born to a minor noble family, he was ordained a priest in 1607 and became bishop of Luçon. As the first bishop in France to implement reforms decreed by the Council of Trent, he brought order to a diocese ruined by the Wars of Religion. In 1614 he was elected a deputy of the clergy in the Estates-General, where he was noted as a conciliatory force. He became an adviser to Marie de Médicis in 1616 and later councillor to her son, Louis XIII. Named a cardinal in 1622, he served as chief minister from 1624 and became

Cardinal de Richelieu, detail of a portrait by Philippe de Champaigne; in the Louvre, Paris
Giraudon/Art Resource, New York

the controlling influence in France's policies. He established royal absolutism in France by suppressing the political power of the Huguenots and reducing the influence of the nobles. In foreign policy, he sought to weaken Habsburg control of Europe and involved France in the Thirty Years' War. Devious and brilliant, he increased the power of the Bourbon dynasty and established orderly government in France. He also founded the Académie Française and rebuilt the Sorbonne.

Richter scale, Widely used measure of the magnitude of an earthquake, introduced in 1935 by U.S. seismologists Beno Gutenberg (1889–1960) and Charles F. Richter (1900–1985). The scale is logarithmic, so that each increase of one unit represents a 10-fold increase in magnitude (amplitude of seismic waves). The magnitude is then translated into energy released. Earthquakes that are fainter than the ones originally chosen to define magnitude zero are accommodated by using negative numbers. Though the scale has no theoretical upper limit, the most severe earthquakes have not exceeded a scale value of 9. The moment magnitude scale, in use since 1993, is more accurate for large earthquakes; it takes into account the amount of fault slippage, the size of the area ruptured, and the nature of the materials that faulted.

rickets, or VITAMIN D DEFICIENCY, Disease of infancy and childhood characterized by defective bone growth due to lack of vitamin D. Calcium phosphate is not properly deposited in the bones, which become soft, curved, and stunted. Early symptoms include restlessness, profuse sweating, lack of limb and abdominal-muscle tone, soft skull bones, and developmental delays. Muscles may cramp and twitch. Without early treatment, effects may include bowlegs, knock-knees, and beadiness where the ribs meet the breastbone. A narrow chest and pelvis can later increase susceptibility to lung diseases and impede childbirth. Treatment is with high-dose vitamin D supplementation, sunlight, and a balanced diet. Adding vitamin D to milk has reduced rickets in high-latitude areas where the skin cannot produce enough.

rickettsia, Any of the rod-shaped bacteria that make up the family Rickettsiaceae (named for Howard Ricketts). They are rod-shaped or variably spherical, and most are gram-negative. Natural parasites of certain arthropods, they can cause serious diseases in humans and other animals, to which they are usually transmitted by a bite from an arthropod carrier. Because certain species can survive considerable drying, rickettsias can also be transmitted when arthropod feces are inhaled or enter the skin through abrasion. Typhus, trench fever, and Rocky Mountain spotted fever are rickettsial infections. The most effective treatment includes timely and prolonged administration of broad-spectrum antibiotics.

riddle, Deliberately enigmatic or ambiguous question requiring a thoughtful and often witty answer. The riddle is a form of guessing game that has been a part of the folklore of most cultures from ancient times. Western scholars generally recognize two main kinds of riddle: the descriptive riddle, usually describing an animal, person, plant, or object in an intentionally enigmatic manner (thus an egg is "a little white house without door or window"); and the shrewd or witty question. A classical Greek example of the latter type is "What is the strongest of all things?"—"Love: iron is strong, but the blacksmith is stronger, and love can subdue the blacksmith."

rifle, Firearm whose barrel is rifled (i.e., has spiral grooves cut inside it to give a spin to the projectile). Though usually applied to a weapon fired from the shoulder, the name can also refer to a rifled cannon. Rifled firearms date to at least the 15th century, when it was discovered that imparting a spin to the bullet improved its range and accuracy. The earliest muzzle-loading rifles were more difficult to load than smoothbore muskets, but the invention of metallic cartridges made possible the development of breech-loading mechanisms. Bolt-action rifles, which use a manually operated cylinder to drive the cartridge into the rifle's chamber, are the most common type for hunting.

rift valley, Elongated trough formed by the subsidence of a segment of the Earth's crust between dip-slip, or normal, faults. Rift valleys are usually narrow and long and have a relatively flat floor. The sides drop away steeply in steps and terraces. Rift valleys are found on the continents and along the crests of oceanic ridges. They occur where two plates that make up the Earth's surface are separating. Submarine rift valleys are usually centres of seafloor spreading, where magma wells up from the mantle. The most extensive continental rift valleys are those of the East African Rift System; other notable examples include Russia's Baikal Rift Valley and Germany's Rhine Rift Valley.

Riga, City (pop., 2000 prelim.: 764,328), capital of Latvia. Riga is situated on both banks of the Western Dvina River, above its mouth on the Gulf of Riga. It was founded as a trading post in 1201 on the site of an ancient Liv settlement and joined the Hanseatic League in 1282. In the Middle Ages it was dominated by the Teutonic Order, and it was fought over by the Poles and Russians in the 16th century. Riga was captured by Sweden in 1621 and granted self-government, but it was ceded to Russia in 1721. The city became the capital of an independent Latvia from 1918 to 1940 but was thereafter incorporated into the U.S.S.R. Riga again became the capital of an independent Latvia in 1991. It is a principal Baltic port and a major administrative, cultural, and industrial centre. Its medieval remains include a 13th-century church and a 14th-century castle.

Riga, Treaty of (1921) Treaty between Poland and Russia signed in Riga, Latvia, that ended the Russo-Polish War of 1919–20 and set their mutual border. The treaty, which gave Poland parts of Byelorussia (Belarus) and Ukraine, lasted until World War II, after which a new treaty established a new border.

Rigveda, or RGVEDA, Oldest religious scripture in the world and most revered of the Vedas, completed by the 12th century BC. Consisting of more than 1,000 hymns addressed to *deva*s (gods), it reflects a polytheism that is mainly concerned with the propitiation of divinities associated with the sky and the atmosphere. It makes reference to such rituals as marriage and funeral rites, which differ little from those practiced today in Hinduism. It is the source of much Indian thought, and many consider its study essential to understanding India.

Ring of Fire, A belt of seismic and volcanic activity roughly surrounding the Pacific Ocean. It includes the Andes Mountains of South America, the coastal regions of western Central America and North America, the Aleutian and Kuril islands, the Kamchatka Peninsula, Japan, the island of Taiwan, eastern Indonesia, the Philippines, New Zealand, and the island arcs of the western Pacific. About three-fourths of all historically recorded active volcanoes have occurred in this belt.

ringworm, Superficial skin changes caused by certain fungi that live on the skin, feeding on keratin. Skin responses vary from slight scaling to blistering and marked disruption of the keratin layer (depending on body area and type of fungus), usually in a ring shape. It includes athlete's foot, jock itch, and fungal infections of the body, hands, nails, and scalp. While the last is very contagious, spread of other types depends on susceptibility and predisposing factors (e.g., excessive perspiration). Ringworm is treated with medications applied to the skin or taken orally.

Rio de Janeiro, City (pop., 2005 est.: city, 6,094,200; metro. area, 11,570,524), capital of Rio de Janeiro state, and port, southeastern Brazil. The site was founded by the Portuguese in the early 16th century and became important in the 18th century as an outlet for mineral exports from gold and diamond mines. Located on one of the largest harbours in the world and known for its scenic views, it was the capital of Brazil from 1822 to 1960, when the national capital was moved to Brasília. It is the country's second largest manufacturing centre, after São Paulo. Major industries include metallurgy, electronics, and food processing. Noted for its wide streets, public buildings, beaches, and public parks and gardens, it is a leading tourist and resort centre.

Rio Grande, in Mexico RÍO BRAVO, River, North America. One of the longest rivers of North America, it flows 1,900 mi (3,000 km) from its sources in the Rocky Mountains of southwestern Colorado, U.S., to the Gulf of Mexico. It rises high in the San Juan

Mountains and flows generally south, passing southeast and forming the entire border between Texas and Mexico. The earliest European settlements were along the lower course of the river in the 16th century, but many of the Pueblo Indian settlements of New Mexico date from before the Spanish conquest. During the Spanish period, the middle and upper portions were called the Río del Norte, and the lower course was called the Río Bravo. It is a major source of irrigation. At the U.S.-Mexican border, it defines the edge of Big Bend National Park, Texas.

Risorgimento (Italian: "Rising Again"), Nineteenth-century movement for Italian unification. Reforms introduced by France into its Italian states in the Napoleonic period remained after the states were restored to their former rulers in 1815 and provided an impetus for the movement. Secret groups such as Young Italy advocated Italian unity, and leaders such as Camillo Cavour, who founded the journal *Il Risorgimento* (1847), Giuseppe Garibaldi, and Giuseppe Mazzini called for liberal reforms and a united Italy. After the failure of the Revolutions of 1848, leadership passed to Cavour and Piedmont, which formed an alliance with France against Austria (1859). The unification of most of Italy in 1861, followed by the annexation of Venetia (1866) and papal Rome (1870), marked the end of the Risorgimento.

river, Natural stream of water that flows in a channel with more or less defined banks. Rivers are a fundamental link in the hydrologic cycle, and they play a major role in shaping the surface features of the Earth. Even apparently arid desert regions are greatly influenced by river action when periodic floodwaters surge down usually dry watercourses. River flow is sustained by the difference between water input and output. Rivers are fed by overland runoff, groundwater seepage, and meltwater released along the edges of snowfields and glaciers. Direct precipitation contributes only very small amounts of water. Losses of river water result from percolation into porous and permeable rock, gravel, or sand; evaporation; and ultimately outflow into the ocean.

river blindness, or ONCHOCERCIASIS, Human disease caused by a filarial worm native to Africa but also found in parts of tropical America and transmitted by several blackflies. It is so called because the flies that transmit the disease breed on rivers and mostly affect riverine populations. Blindness is caused by dead microfilariae—the larvae that can be produced for some 15–18 years by adult worms—inside the eye. River blindness is common in savannah areas of Africa and in Guatemala and Mexico. In 1987 the World Health Organization began to distribute the drug ivermectin (originally developed for use against livestock parasites), which eliminates the microfilariae, though it does not kill the adult parasite.

Rivera, Diego (b. Dec. 8, 1886, Guanajuato, Mex.—d. Nov. 25, 1957, Mexico City), Mexican muralist. After study in Mexico City and Spain, he settled in Paris from 1909 to 1919. He briefly espoused Cubism but abandoned it *c.* 1917 for a visual language of simplified forms and bold areas of colour. He returned to Mexico in 1921, seeking to create a new national art on revolutionary themes in the wake of the Mexican Revolution. He painted many public murals, the most ambitious of which is in the National Palace (1929–57). From 1930 to 1934 he worked in the U.S. His mural for New York's Rockefeller Center aroused a storm of controversy and was ultimately destroyed because it contained the figure of Vladimir Ilich Lenin; he later reproduced it at the Palace of Fine Arts in Mexico City. With José Clemente Orozco and David Alfaro Siqueiros, Rivera created a revival of fresco painting that became Mexico's most significant contribution to 20th-century art. His large-scale didactic murals contain scenes of Mexican history, culture, and industry, with Indians, peasants, conquistadores, and factory workers drawn as simplified figures in crowded, shallow spaces. Rivera was twice married to Frida Kahlo.

Riviera, Coastal region bordering the Mediterranean Sea in southeastern France, Monaco, and northwestern Italy. It extends from Cannes, France, to La Spezia, Italy. The Italian Riviera is divided into the Riviera di Ponente, west of Genoa, and the Riviera di Levante, east of Genoa. The French Riviera is also called the Côte d'Azur. Noted for its scenery and pleasant climate, it is one of the major tourist centres of Europe. Because of its mild winters, many delicate plants flourish there, and flowers are grown out of season for export to northern markets.

Riyadh, City (pop., 2004: 4,087,152), capital of Saudi Arabia. Located in the east-central part of the country, it was chosen as the capital of the Sa'ūd dynasty in 1824. It remained the centre of Sa'ūdī rule until 1881, when the Rashīd family took control of the region. In 1902 Ibn Sa'ūd regained control, and it became the centre for his conquest of the Arabian Peninsula. When the kingdom of Saudi Arabia was proclaimed in 1932, Riyadh became the capital. Discovery of immense petroleum deposits in the kingdom in the 1930s transformed the old provincial town into a showplace of sophisticated technology, modern architecture, and highways. In addition to its administrative role, Riyadh is the kingdom's commercial, education, and transportation centre.

RNA, in full RIBONUCLEIC ACID, One of the two main types of nucleic acid (the other being DNA), which functions in cellular protein synthesis in all living cells and replaces DNA as the carrier of genetic information in some viruses. Like DNA, it consists of strands of repeating nucleotides joined in chainlike fashion, but the strands are single (except in certain viruses), and it has the nucleotide uracil (U) where DNA has thymine (T). Messenger RNA (mRNA), a single strand copied from a DNA strand that acts as its template, carries the message of the genetic code from DNA (in chromosomes) to the site of protein synthesis (on ribosomes). Ribosomal RNA (rRNA), part of the building blocks of ribosomes, participates in protein synthesis. Transfer RNA (tRNA), the smallest type, has fewer than 100 nucleotide units (mRNA and rRNA contain thousands). Each nucleotide triplet on mRNA specifies which amino acid comes next on the protein being synthesized, and a tRNA molecule with that triplet's complement on its protruding end brings the specified amino acid to the site of synthesis to be linked into the protein. Various minor types of RNA also exist; at least some act as catalysts (ribozymes), a function long ascribed only to proteins.

roach, Common European sport fish (*Rutilus rutilus*) of the carp family (Cyprinidae), found in lakes and slow rivers. A highbacked, yellowish green fish with red eyes and reddish fins, the roach is 6–16 in. (15–40 cm) long and weighs up to 4.5 lbs (2 kg). It lives in small schools and eats plants, insects, and small animals. It is sometimes eaten or used as bait. In North America, other fishes are called roach, including the rudd, the golden shiner (both cyprinids), and several members of the sunfish family (Centrarchidae).

road, Traveled way on which people, animals, or wheeled vehicles move. The earliest roads developed from paths and trails and appeared with the invention of wheeled vehicles about 3000 BC. Road systems were developed to facilitate trade in early civilizations; the first major road extended 1,500 mi (2,400 km) from the Persian Gulf to the Mediterranean Sea and was used as early as 3500 BC. The Romans used roads to maintain control of their empire, with over 53,000 mi (85,000 km) of roadways extending across its lands; Roman construction techniques and design remained the most advanced until the late 1700s. In the early 19th century the invention of macadam road construction provided a quick and durable method for building roads, and asphalt and concrete also began to be used. Motorized traffic in the 20th century led to the limited-access highway, the first of which was a parkway in New York City (1925). Superhighways also appeared in

Italy and Germany in the 1930s. In the 1950s the U.S. interstate highway system was inaugurated to link the country's major cities.

Robespierre, Maximilien (François-Marie-Isidore) de

(b. May 6, 1758, Arras, France—d. July 28, 1794, Paris), French revolutionary. A successful lawyer in Arras (1781–89), he was elected to the National Assembly (1789), where he became notorious as an outspoken radical in favour of individual rights. He became a leading member of the Montagnards in the National Convention. After calling for the death of Louis XVI, he led the Jacobins and the Committee of Public Safety (1793) in establishing the Reign of Terror, during which, as virtual dictator of France, he had former friends such as Georges Danton executed. Despite earlier support from the people of Paris, who called him "the Incorruptible," he lost his dominating authority and was overthrown and guillotined in the Thermidorian Reaction. Often regarded as a bloodthirsty dictator, he was later valued for his social ideals of reducing inequality and ensuring work for all.

Robin Hood,

Legendary English outlaw. The hero of ballads dating from as early as the 14th century, Robin Hood was a rebel who robbed and killed landowners and government officials and gave his gains to the poor. He treated women and common people with courtesy, and he ignored the laws of the forest that restricted hunting rights. His greatest enemy was the sheriff of Nottingham. The ballads emerged during a time of agrarian unrest that culminated in the Peasants' Revolt of 1381. There is no evidence of Robin Hood's historical existence, though later tradition places him in the reign of King John. In postmedieval ballads and stories he was a nobleman who took refuge in Sherwood Forest after losing his lands. His men included Little John and Friar Tuck; his beloved was Maid Marion.

Robinson, Mary,

orig. MARY BOURKE (b. May 21, 1944, Ballina, County Mayo, Ire.), Irish politician, the first woman to become president of Ireland (1990–97). She earned a law degree at the University of Dublin, where she became a professor of law (1969–75). She served in the Irish Senate (1969–89) as a Labour Party member. Nominated by the Labour Party and supported by the Green Party and the Workers' Party, she became Ireland's president in 1990 by mobilizing a liberal constituency and merging it with a more conservative constituency opposed to the Fianna Fáil party. In 1997 she left office a few months before her term expired to take up the post of UN high commissioner for human rights (1997–2002).

robot,

Any automatically operated machine that replaces human effort, though it may not look much like a human being or function in a humanlike manner. The term comes from the play *R.U.R.* by Karel Čapek (1920). Major developments in microelectronics and computer technology since the 1960s have led to significant advances in robotics. Advanced, high-performance robots are used today in automobile manufacturing and aircraft assembly, and electronics firms use robotic devices together with other computerized instruments to sort or test finished products.

robotics,

Design, construction, and use of machines (robots) to perform tasks done traditionally by human beings. Robots are widely used in such industries as automobile manufacture to perform simple repetitive tasks, and in industries where work must be performed in environments hazardous to humans. Many aspects of robotics involve artificial intelligence; robots may be equipped with the equivalent of human senses such as vision, touch, and the ability to sense temperature. Some are even capable of simple decision making, and current robotics research is geared toward devising robots with a degree of self-sufficiency that will permit mobility and decision-making in an unstructured environment. Today's industrial robots do not resemble human beings; a robot in human form is called an android.

rock,

In geology, a naturally occurring and coherent aggregate of minerals. The three major classes of rock—igneous, sedimentary, and metamorphic—are based on the processes that formed them. These three classes are further subdivided on the basis of various factors, especially chemical, mineralogical, and textural attributes.

rock art,

Ancient or prehistoric drawing, painting, or similar work on or of stone. Rock art includes pictographs (drawings or paintings), petroglyphs (carvings or inscriptions), engravings (incised motifs), petroforms (rocks laid out in patterns), and geoglyphs (ground drawings). The ancient animals, tools, and human activities depicted often help shed light on daily life in the distant past, though the images are frequently symbolic. Sometimes a single site may have art that dates from several centuries. Rock art may have played a role in prehistoric religion, possibly in connection with ancient myths or the activities of shamans. Important sites occur in southern Africa, Europe, North America, and Australia.

rock music,

or ROCK AND ROLL, Musical style that arose in the U.S. in the mid-1950s and became the dominant form of popular music in the world. Though rock has used a wide variety of instruments, its basic elements are one or several vocalists, heavily amplified electric guitars (including bass, rhythm, and lead), and drums. It began as a simple style, relying on heavy, dance-oriented rhythms, uncomplicated melodies and harmonies, and lyrics sympathetic to its teenage audience's concerns—young love, the stresses of adolescence, and automobiles. Its roots lay principally in rhythm and blues (R&B) and country music. Both R&B and country existed outside the mainstream of popular music in the early 1950s, when the Cleveland disc jockey Alan Freed (1921–65) and others began programming R&B, which until then had been played only to black audiences. Freed's success gave currency to the term *rock and roll*. The highly rhythmic, sensual music of Chuck Berry, Bill Haley and the Comets, and particularly Elvis Presley in 1955–56 struck a responsive chord in newly affluent postwar teenagers. In the 1960s several influences combined to lift rock out of the bland and mechanical format into which it had already declined. In England, where rock's development had been slow, the Beatles and the Rolling Stones were found to have retained the freshness of its very early years, and they achieved enormous success in the U.S., where a new generation had grown up unaware of the musical influences of the new stars. At the same time, Bob Dylan, Joni Mitchell, the Byrds, and others were blending the traditional ballads and verse forms of folk music with rock, and musicians began to explore social and political themes. Performers such as the Grateful Dead, Jim Morrison of the Doors, and Frank Zappa of the Mothers of Invention combined imaginative lyrics with instrumental virtuosity, typically featuring lengthy solo improvisation. Janis Joplin and Jimi Hendrix won large followings with their exotic elaborations on R&B. The 1970s saw the rise of singer-songwriters such as Paul Simon, Neil Young, Elton John, David Bowie, and Bruce Springsteen, and rock assimilated other forms to produce jazz-rock, heavy metal, and punk rock. In the 1980s the disco-influenced rock of Madonna, Michael Jackson, and Prince was balanced by the post-punk "new wave" music of performers such as Laurie Anderson, Talking Heads (led by David Byrne), and the Eurythmics—all of whom illustrated their songs with music videos. By the 1990s rock music had incorporated grunge, rap, techno, and other forms.

rocket,

Type of jet-propulsion device that uses either solid or liquid propellants to provide the fuel and oxidizer needed for combustion. The hot gases provided by combustion are ejected in a jet through a nozzle at the rear of the rocket. The term is also commonly applied to any of various vehicles, including fireworks, skyrockets, guided missiles, and launch vehicles for spacecraft, that are driven by such a propulsive device. Typically, thrust (force causing forward motion) is produced by reaction to a rearward expulsion of hot gases at extremely high speed.

Rocky Mountains, or ROCKIES, Mountain system, western North America. It extends some 3,000 mi (4,800 km) from the Mexican frontier to the Arctic Ocean, through the western U.S. and Canada. The highest peak in the U.S. Rockies is Mount Elbert in Colorado, at 14,433 ft (4,399 m); in the Canadian Rockies it is Mount Robson in British Columbia, at 12,972 ft (3,954 m). The Continental Divide, located in the mountains, separates rivers flowing to the east and to the west. Wildlife includes grizzly bear, brown bear, elk, bighorn sheep, and cougar. The area is rich in deposits of copper, iron ore, silver, gold, lead, zinc, phosphate, potash, and gypsum. Rocky Mountain, Yellowstone, and Grand Teton national parks in the U.S. are major recreational facilities.

Rococo style, or LATE BAROQUE, Style in interior design, the decorative arts, painting, architecture, and sculpture that originated in Paris in the early 18th century. The word Rococo is derived from French *rocaille*, denoting the shell-covered rockwork used to decorate artificial grottoes. Reacting against the ponderous Baroque that had become the official style of Louis XIV's reign, the Rococo was light, elegant, and elaborately ornamented. Several interior designers, painters, and engravers—among them Pierre Le Pautre, Juste-Aurèle Meissonier, Jean Berain, and Nicolas Pineau—developed a lighter and more intimate style of decoration for the new residences of nobles in Paris, and the style was disseminated throughout France by means of engravings. In these designers' work, walls, ceilings, and moldings feature interlacings of curves and countercurves based on S and C shapes as well as on shell forms and other natural shapes. Chinese motifs were also employed. Rococo painting was characterized by easygoing treatments of mythological and courtship themes, delicate brushwork, and sensuous colouring; notable practitioners included Antoine Watteau, François Boucher, and Jean-Honoré Fragonard. The Rococo style spread throughout France and other countries, principally Germany and Austria. Among the finest German examples of Rococo architecture is the church designed by Balthasar Neumann at Vierzehnheiligen, near Lichtenfels, in Bavaria. In Italy the Rococo style was concentrated primarily in Venice, where it was epitomized by the large-scale decorative paintings of Giovanni Battista Tiepolo.

rodent, Any member of the order Rodentia, which contains 50% of all living mammal species. Rodents are gnawing, mostly herbivorous, placental mammals. They have one pair of upper and one pair of lower, continuously growing, incisors. When the lower jaw is pulled back, the cheek teeth connect for grinding; when it is pulled forward and down, the incisors meet at the tips for gnawing. Rodent families include squirrels (Sciuridae); Old World mice and rats (Muridae); deer mice, gerbils, hamsters, lemmings, muskrats, wood rats, and voles (Cricetidae); beaver (Castoridae); gophers (Geomyidae); guinea pigs (Caviidae); pocket mice and kangaroo rats and mice (Heteromyidae); New and Old World porcupines (Erethizontidae and Hystricidae); and hutia (Capromyidae).

rodeo, Sport involving a series of contests derived from North American cowboy skills. Rodeos typically feature competitive or exhibition bronco riding, calf roping, steer wrestling, and Brahma bull riding. The sport developed from informal competitions among cowboys held from the mid-19th century. Denver is traditionally accepted as the birthplace of paid spectator rodeo, in 1887. The oldest surviving annual show is the Frontier Days celebration in Cheyenne, Wyo. (established 1897). The Calgary Stampede has been held annually in Alberta, Can., since 1923. In calf roping and steer wrestling, the contestant seeks to bring down the animal in the shortest possible time. In riding events, contestants seek to stay on their mounts as long as possible and are awarded points for style, control, and other factors.

Rodin, (François-) Auguste (René) (b. Nov. 12, 1840, Paris, France—d. Nov. 17, 1917, Meudon), French sculptor. Insolvent and repeatedly rejected by the École des Beaux-Arts, he earned his living by doing decorative stonework. Not until his late 30s, after a trip to Italy, did he develop a personal style free of academic restraints and establish his reputation as a sculptor with *The Age of Bronze* (exhibited 1878), whose realism was so great that he was accused of forming its mold on a living person. His *Gates of Hell*, a bronze door commissioned in 1880 for a proposed Musée des Arts Décoratifs, remained unfinished at his death, but two of its many figures were the bases of his most famous images, *The Thinker* (1880) and *The Kiss* (1886). His portraits include monumental figures of Victor Hugo and Honoré de Balzac. Though these and many other works caused controversy for their unconventionality, he was successful enough that he could establish a workshop where he executed only molds, leaving the casting of bronze and the carving of marble to assistants. To his sculpture he added book illustrations, etchings, and numerous drawings, mostly of female nudes. He revitalized sculpture as an art of personal expression and has been considered one of its greatest portraitists.

Rolland, Romain (b. Jan. 29, 1866, Clamecy, France—d. Dec. 30, 1944, Vézelay), French novelist, dramatist, and essayist. At age 14 he went to Paris to study and found a society in spiritual disarray, and his life and writings came to reflect his concern with major social, political, and spiritual events. From 1910 he taught music history at the Sorbonne. His best-known novel is *Jean-Christophe* (1904–12), a 10-volume epic whose protagonist is modeled half on Ludwig van Beethoven and half on himself. His pamphlet *Above the Battle* (1915) calls on France and Germany to respect truth and humanity during World War I. In the 1920s he turned to interpreting the mystical philosophy of Asia, especially India, in works such as *Mahatma Gandhi* (1924). He wrote several other major biographies, including *Beethoven* (1910). He was awarded the Nobel Prize for Literature in 1915.

roller-skating, Recreation and sport in which the participants use roller skates (shoes with sets of wheels attached) to move about on special rinks or paved surfaces. The invention of roller skates is traditionally credited to the Belgian Joseph Merlin in the 1760s, but the first practical four-wheel skate was designed in 1863 by James Plimpton of Medford, Mass. Roller-skating speed events became popular in the early 20th century. Later, team competitions in "roller derbies" on banked tracks became a spectator sport. Other roller-skate contests, such as acrobatics and hockey, followed. In the late 20th century, roller skates gave way to in-line (Rollerblade) skates, in which a single row of wheels is used in place of the standard rectangular configuration.

Rolling Stones, British musical group. Its original members were Mick Jagger (b. 1943), Keith Richards (b. 1943), Brian Jones (1944–69), Bill Wyman (b. 1936), and Charlie Watts (b. 1941). The band was formed in 1962 when Jagger, Richards, and Jones, who had been performing sporadically in a blues band, recruited Wyman and formed their own group. Watts joined the band in 1963. Jagger was the lead vocalist, while Jones and Richards played guitars, Wyman played bass, and Watts played drums. The band's name was adopted from a Muddy Waters song. By 1966 a series of outstanding songs had made the band second in popularity only to the Beatles. Jagger and Richards wrote most of the songs, which are marked by a driving backbeat, biting and satirical lyrics, and simple but expressive instrumental accompaniments. The group reached the height of its popularity with albums such as *Beggar's Banquet* (1968) and *Exile on Main Street* (1972). Jones was succeeded by Mick Taylor (b. 1948) in 1969, who was replaced in turn by Ron Wood (b. 1947) in 1976. They continued to perform long after the other classic rock bands of the 1960s disbanded.

Rom, or GYPSY, plural ROMA, Any member of a people originating in northern India but now living worldwide, principally in Europe. Most speak Romany in addition to the local language. It is thought that Roma groups left India in successive migrations, reaching western Europe by the 15th century. In the 20th century they spread to North and South America and Australia. Because of their often nomadic and marginalized lives, population figures are largely guesswork; estimates in the early 21st century range from two to three million. They have often been persecuted and harassed; the Nazis killed about 400,000 Roma in extermination camps. How many Roma retain a nomadic lifestyle is unclear, but those that migrate do so at least seasonally along patterned routes that ignore national boundaries. They pursue occupations compatible with a nomadic life. In the past they were often livestock traders, tinkers, fortune-tellers, and entertainers; today they are often car mechanics, auto-body repairmen, and workers in traveling circuses and amusement parks. Confederations of 10–100 families elect chieftains for life, but their title is not heritable. Women are organized as a group within the confederation and represented by a senior woman. Modern Roma culture faces erosion from urban influences; integrated housing, economic independence, and intermarriage with non-Roma have weakened Roma law.

roman à clef (French: "novel with a key"), Novel that has the extraliterary interest of portraying identifiable people more or less thinly disguised as fictional characters. The tradition dates to 17th-century France, when members of aristocratic literary coteries included in their historical romances representations of well-known figures in the court of Louis XIV. A more recent example is W. Somerset Maugham's *Cakes and Ale* (1930), widely held to portray Thomas Hardy and Hugh Walpole. A more common type of roman à clef is one in which the disguised characters are easily recognized only by a few insiders, as in Simone de Beauvoir's *The Mandarins* (1954).

Roman Catholicism, Largest denomination of Christianity, with more than one billion members. The Roman Catholic Church has had a profound effect on the development of Western civilization and has been responsible for introducing Christianity in many parts of the world. It regards itself as the only legitimate inheritor of the ministry of Jesus, by virtue of an unbroken succession of leaders beginning with St. Peter the Apostle and continuing to the present day. It holds that the pope is the infallible interpreter of divine revelation. Church organization is strictly hierarchical. The pope appoints and presides over the cardinals, whose numbers grew dramatically in the late 20th century, reaching 182 under John Paul II (1978–2005). Each of the church's 500 archbishops is the head of an archdiocese. These in turn are divided into about 1,800 dioceses, each headed by a bishop. Within dioceses are parishes, each served by a church and a priest. Only men can enter the priesthood, but women who wish to enter holy orders can become nuns, who are organized into orders and convents. The basic form of worship is the mass, which celebrates the sacrament of the Eucharist. Theologically, Roman Catholicism differs from Protestantism with regard to its understanding of the sources of revelation and the channels of grace. With Eastern Orthodoxy it asserts that both scripture and church tradition are revelatory of the basis of Christian belief and church polity. It sets the number of sacraments at seven (baptism, reconciliation [formerly known as penance], the Eucharist, matrimony, ordination, confirmation, and anointing of the sick); its rich sacramental life is supplemented by other devotions, chiefly eucharistic services and devotions to the saints. The Second Vatican Council (1962–65) promoted the role of the laity in the church, approved the use of the vernacular in the mass, and strove to improve relations with other religions. Pope John Paul II actively pursued better relations with other faiths, especially Judaism, and remained popular despite various controversies. Although faced with many challenges, the church remained one of the largest and most significant religious bodies in the world at the start of its third millennium.

Roman de la Rose (French: "Romance of the Rose"), One of the most popular French poems of the late medieval period. Modeled on Ovid's *Art of Love*, it survives in more than 300 manuscripts. Its first 4,058 lines were written *c.* 1225–30 by Guillaume

de Lorris; they form a charming dream allegory drawing on traditions of courtly love. About 1280 Jean de Meun wrote the rest of the more than 21,000 lines, incorporating a vast mass of encyclopaedic information and opinions on many contemporary topics, which secured the poem's fame. The *Roman* was translated by Geoffrey Chaucer and was one of the most important literary influences on his writings.

Roman law, Law of the Roman Republic and Empire. Roman law has influenced the development of law in most of Western civilization. It dealt with matters of succession (or inheritance), obligations (including contracts), property (including slaves), and persons. Most laws were passed by assemblies dominated by the patrician families, though the rulings of magistrates were also important. Later emperors bypassed these forms and issued their own decrees. The interpretations of jurists also came to have the weight of law. Though various attempts were made to gather and simplify existing laws (beginning with the Law of the Twelve Tables), by far the most successful effort was that of Justinian I, whose code superseded all previous laws and formed the Roman Empire's legal legacy. Roman legal procedure is the basis for modern procedure in civil-law countries. In the early Republic, the plaintiff was required to call the defendant to court or to bring him by force. A magistrate then decided whether the case should go before a *judex*, or prominent layman. The *judex* heard arguments from advocates and questioned witnesses; he made a decision but had no power to execute it. In the later Republic, much greater power was placed in the hands of the magistrates and courts: the summons was issued by the court, the trial was held only before a magistrate, and the court became responsible for the execution of the sentence.

Roman mythology, Oral and literary traditions of the ancient Romans concerning their gods and heroes and the nature and history of the cosmos. Much of what became Roman mythology was borrowed from Greek mythology at a later date, as Greek gods were associated with their Roman counterparts. As in Greek mythology, legendary Roman heroes (such as Romulus and Remus and Aeneas) were given semidivine status.

Roman numerals, System of representing numbers devised by the ancient Romans. The numbers are formed by combinations of the symbols I, V, X, L, C, D, and M, standing, respectively, for 1, 5, 10, 50, 100, 500, and 1,000 in the Hindu-Arabic numeral system. A symbol placed after another of equal or greater value adds its value; for example, II = 2 and LX = 60. A symbol placed before one of greater value subtracts its value; for example, IV = 4 and XL = 40. A bar over a symbol indicates that its value should be multiplied by 1,000.

Roman religion, Religious beliefs of the Romans from ancient times until official acceptance of Christianity in the 4th century AD. The Romans believed that everything was subordinate to the rule of the gods, and the object of their religion was to secure divine cooperation and benevolence. Prayer and sacrifice were used to propitiate the gods and were often carried out at temples dedicated to particular divinities and presided over by priests. The chief Roman priest, head of the state religion, was known as the *pontifex maximus*; notable among the other groups of priests were the augurs, who practiced divination to determine whether the gods approved of an action. The earliest Roman gods were the sky god Jupiter, the war god Mars, and Quirinus; other important early gods were Janus and Vesta. Many other deities were borrowed from Greek religion or associated with Greek gods, and the stories woven into Roman mythology were often taken directly from Greek mythology. Domestic shrines were devoted to divine ancestors or protectors, the Lares and Penates. Dead Roman emperors were also raised to the status of divinities and were regarded with veneration and gratitude.

Roman Republic and Empire, Ancient state that once ruled the Western world. It centred on the city of Rome from the founding of the republic (509 BC) through the establishment of the empire (27 BC) to the final eclipse of the empire in the west (5th century AD). The republic's government consisted of two consuls, the Senate, and magistrates, originally all patricians, and two popular plebeian assemblies: the military centuriate assembly and the civilian tribal assembly. A written code, the Law of the Twelve Tables (451 BC), became the basis of Roman private law. By the end of the 3rd century BC, Roman territory included all of Italy; by the late republican period it encompassed most of western Europe, northern Africa, and the Near East, organized into provinces. After a period of civil war, Julius Caesar took power as dictator. Following his assassination (44 BC), conflict among the triumvirs—Mark Antony, Lepidus, and Octavian—ultimately resulted in Octavian's victory (31) and his accession as Emperor Augustus (r. 27 BC–AD 14). The imperial government, a principate, combined aspects of the republic and a monarchy. In AD 395 the empire split into eastern and western halves, with the west under severe pressure from the barbarians. Rome was sacked in 410 by the Visigoths, and the western empire fell to German invaders in 476; the east continued as the Byzantine Empire until 1453.

romance, Literary form that developed in the aristocratic courts of mid-12th-century France and had its heyday in France and Germany between the mid-12th and mid-13th century in the works of such masters as Chrétien de Troyes and Gottfried von Strassburg. The staple subject matter is chivalric adventure, though love stories and religious allegories are sometimes interwoven. Most romances draw their plots from classical history and legend, Arthurian legend, and the adventures of Charlemagne and his knights. Written in the vernacular, they share a taste for the exotic, the remote, and the miraculous. Lingering echoes of the form can be found in later centuries, as in the Romanticism of the 18th–19th century and today's popular romantic novels.

Romance languages, Group of related languages derived from Latin, with nearly 920 million native speakers. The major Romance languages—French, Spanish, Portuguese, Italian, and Romanian—are national languages. French is probably the most internationally significant, but Spanish, the official language of 19 American countries and Spain and Equatorial Guinea, has the most speakers. Languages spoken in smaller areas include Catalan, Occitan, Sardinian, and Rhaeto-Romance. The Romance languages began as dialects of Vulgar Latin, which spread during the Roman occupation of Italy, the Iberian Peninsula, Gaul, and the Balkans and developed into separate languages in the 5th–9th centuries. Later, European colonial and commercial contacts spread them to the Americas, Africa, and Asia.

Romanesque architecture, Architecture current in Europe from about the mid-11th century to the advent of Gothic architecture. A fusion of Roman, Carolingian and Ottonian, Byzantine, and local Germanic traditions, it was a product of the great expansion of monasticism in the 10th–11th century. Larger churches were needed to accommodate the numerous monks and priests, as well as the pilgrims who came to view saints' relics. For the sake of fire resistance, masonry vaulting began to replace timber construction. Romanesque churches characteristically incorporated semicircular arches for windows, doors, and arcades; barrel or groin vaults to support the roof of the nave; massive piers and walls, with few windows, to contain the outward thrust of the vaults; side aisles with galleries above them; a large tower over the crossing of nave and transept; and smaller towers at the church's western end. French churches commonly expanded on the early Christian basilica plan, incorporating radiating chapels to accommodate more priests, ambulatories around the sanctuary apse for visiting pilgrims, and large transepts between the sanctuary and nave.

Romanesque art, Sculpture and painting that reached its height in western Europe *c.* 1075–1125, a fusion of Roman, Carolingian and Ottonian, and Byzantine art with local Germanic traditions.

The expansion of monasticism in the 10th–11th centuries revived the art of monumental sculpture after almost 600 years of dormancy. Relief sculpture depicted biblical history and church doctrine on column capitals and around the massive doors of churches. Natural objects were freely transformed into visionary images that derive their power from abstract linear design and expressive distortion. Linear stylization is seen also in the capital letters and marginal decoration of illuminated manuscripts. Romanesque art was concerned with transcendental values, in sharp contrast to the naturalism and humanism of the earlier Classical and later Gothic art traditions. Monumental painting that imitated the sculptural style covered the interior walls of churches. Both sculpture and painting incorporated a broad range of subject matter, including theological works, reflecting the revival of learning.

Romania, or RUMANIA, Country, southeastern Europe. Area: 92,043 sq mi (238,391 sq km). Population: (2011 est.) 21,393,000. Capital: Bucharest. Most of the people are Romanian; a minority are Hungarian. Language: Romanian (official). Religion: Christianity (predominantly Eastern Orthodox; also Protestant, Roman Catholic). Currency: leu. The land is dominated by the great arc of the Carpathian Mountains, whose highest peak, Moldoveanu, reaches an elevation of 8,346 ft (2,544 m). The Danube River forms most of the southern boundary with Bulgaria. Under communist rule (1948–89), Romania had a centrally planned economy that was transformed from an agricultural into an industrial economy. From 1991 the postcommunist government began returning industrial and commercial enterprises to the private sector. Romania is a unitary republic with two legislative houses; its head of state is the president, and the head of government is the prime minister. Romania was formed in 1859 by the de facto unification of Moldavia and Walachia. During World War I it sided with the Allies and doubled its territory in 1918 with the addition of Transylvania, Bukovina, and Bessarabia. Allied with Germany in World War II, Romania was occupied by Soviet troops in 1944 and became a satellite of the U.S.S.R. in 1948. During the 1960s Romania's foreign policy was frequently independent of the Soviet Union's. The communist regime of Nicolae Ceauşescu was overthrown in 1989, and free elections were held in 1990. In the 1990s Romania struggled with rampant corruption, but it entered the 21st century with a stabilizing economy. In 2004 it joined NATO, and in 2007 it became a member of the European Union.

Romanov dynasty, Rulers of Russia from 1613 to 1917. The name derived from Roman Yurev (d. 1543), whose daughter Anastasiya Romanovna was the first wife of Ivan IV the Terrible. Her nephews assumed the surname Romanov, and the dynasty began with the election of Michael Romanov as tsar in 1613. He was succeeded by his son Alexis (r. 1645–76), followed by Alexis's sons Fyodor III and joint rulers Ivan V and Peter I. When Peter was sole ruler, he decreed in 1722 that the monarch could choose his successor, but he was unable to effect the law, so the crown passed to his wife Catherine I, his grandson Peter II, and Ivan V's daughter Anna. The line of descent returned to Peter's daughter Elizabeth (r. 1741–62), her nephew Peter III and his wife Catherine II the Great, and their son Paul I. Paul established a definite order of succession and was followed by his sons Alexander I (r. 1801–25) and Nicholas I (r. 1825–55). Nicholas was succeeded by his son Alexander II, grandson Alexander III, and great-grandson Nicholas II (r. 1894–1917), the last ruler of the Russian monarchy.

Romanticism, Literary, artistic, and philosophical movement that began in Europe in the 18th century and lasted roughly until the mid-19th century. In its intense focus on the individual consciousness, it was both a continuation of and a reaction against the Enlightenment. Romanticism emphasized the individual, the subjective, the irrational, the imaginative, the personal, the spontaneous, the emotional, the visionary, and the transcendental. Among its attitudes were a deepened appreciation of the beauties of nature; a general exaltation of emotion over reason and of the senses over intellect; a turning in upon the self and a heightened examination of human personality; a preoccupation with the genius, the hero, and the exceptional figure; a new view of the artist as a supremely individual creator; an emphasis on imagination as a gateway to transcendent experience and spiritual truth; a consuming interest in folk culture, national and ethnic cultural origins, and the medieval era; and a predilection for the exotic, the remote, the mysterious, the weird, the occult, the monstrous, the diseased, and even the satanic.

Romany language, Indo-Aryan language of the Roma, spoken in many countries of the world, with its greatest concentration of speakers in eastern Europe. Romany is believed to have separated from the northern Indian languages *c.* AD 1000. Its dialects, which include many loanwords from languages where the Roma have lived, are classified according to the languages that influenced them: Greek, Romanian, Hungarian, Czecho-Slovak, German, Polish, Russian, Finnish, Scandinavian, Italian, Serbo-Croatian, Welsh, and Spanish. Romany has no tradition of writing but a rich oral tradition. In the 20th century some collections of Romany poems and folktales were published in eastern Europe.

Rome, Italian ROMA, City (pop., 2007 est.: city, 2,705,603; urban agglom., 3,339,000), capital of Italy. It is situated on the Tiber River in the central part of the country. The historical site of Rome on its seven hills was occupied as early as the Bronze Age (*c.* 1500 BCE), and the city was politically unified by the early 6th century BCE. It became the capital of the Roman Empire. The Romans gradually conquered the Italian peninsula, extended their dominion over the entire Mediterranean basin, and expanded their empire into continental Europe. Under Pompey the Great and Julius Caesar, Rome's influence was extended over Syria, Jerusalem, Cyprus, and Gaul. After the Battle of Actium, all Roman lands were controlled by Octavian (Augustus), the first Roman emperor. As the imperial capital, Rome became the site of magnificent public buildings, including palaces, temples, public baths, theatres, and stadiums. It reached the peak of its grandeur and ancient population during the late 1st and early 2nd centuries CE. It remained the capital of the Roman Empire until Emperor Constantine the Great dedicated Constantinople (now Istanbul) in 330. By the end of the 6th century, the protection of the city was in the hands of the Roman Catholic Church. The papacy achieved absolute rule in the 15th century. The city flourished during the Renaissance and was the seat of the Papal States. In 1870 it became the capital of a united Italy. It was transformed into a modern capital in the 1920s and '30s and is Italy's administrative, cultural, and transportation centre.

Romulus and Remus, Twins of Roman legend who were the legendary founders of Rome. They were the offspring of Mars and

Romulus and Remus with their wolf foster-mother, bronze sculpture; in the Museo Nuovo in the Palazzo dei Conservatori, Rome
Alinari/Art Resource, New York

Rhea Silvia, a Vestal Virgin and princess in Alba Longa. As infants they were thrown into the Tiber River by their great-uncle Amulius, who feared they would lay claim to his title. Suckled by a she-wolf and raised by a shepherd, the twins later deposed Amulius, restored their grandfather Numitor to the throne, and founded a city on the site where they had been saved from the river. When Romulus built a city wall, Remus jumped over it and was killed by his brother. The city was named for Romulus, who ruled until his disappearance in a storm. Believing that he had become a deity, the Romans worshiped him as Quirinus.

Röntgen, Wilhelm Conrad, or WILHELM CONRAD ROENTGEN

Wilhelm Conrad Röntgen.
Historia-Photo

(b. March 27, 1845, Lennep, Prussia—d. Feb. 10, 1923, Munich, Ger.), German physicist. He taught at the Universities of Giessen (1879–88), Würzburg (1888–1900), and Munich (1900–20). In 1895 he discovered rays that did not exhibit properties such as reflection or refraction and mistakenly thought they were unrelated to light. Because of their mysterious nature, he called them X-rays. He later produced the first X-ray photographs, showing the interiors of metal objects and the bones in his wife's hand. He also did important research in a wide variety of other fields. In 1901 he was awarded the first Nobel Prize for Physics.

Roosevelt, Franklin D(elano) (b. Jan. 30, 1882, Hyde Park, N.Y., U.S.—d. April 12, 1945, Warm Springs, Ga.), 32nd president of the U.S. (1933–45). Attracted to politics by the example of his cousin Theodore Roosevelt, he became active in the Democratic Party. In 1905 he married Eleanor Roosevelt, who would become a valued adviser in future years. He served in the New York senate (1910–13) and as U.S. assistant secretary of the navy (1913–20). In 1920 he was nominated by the Democrats as their vice presidential candidate. The next year he was stricken with polio; though unable to walk, he remained active in politics. As governor of New York (1929–33), he set up the first state relief agency in the U.S. In 1932 he won the Democratic presidential nomination with the help of James Farley and easily defeated Pres. Herbert Hoover. In his inaugural address to a nation of more than 13 million unemployed, he pronounced that "the only thing we have to fear is fear itself." Congress passed most of the changes he sought in his New Deal program in the first hundred days of his term. He was overwhelmingly reelected in 1936 over Alf Landon. To solve legal challenges to the New Deal, he proposed enlarging the Supreme Court, but his "court-packing" plan aroused strong opposition and had to be abandoned. By the late 1930s economic recovery had slowed, but Roosevelt was increasingly concerned with the growing threat of war. In 1940 he was reelected to an unprecedented third term, defeating Wendell Willkie. He developed the lend-lease program to aid U.S. allies, especially Britain, in the early years of World War II. In 1941 he met with Winston Churchill to draft the Atlantic Charter. With U.S. entry into war, Roosevelt mobilized industry for military production and formed an alliance with Britain and the Soviet Union; he met with Churchill and Joseph Stalin to form war policy at Tehrān (1943) and Yalta (1945). Despite declining health, he won reelection for a fourth term against Thomas Dewey (1944) but served only briefly before his death.

Roosevelt, Theodore, known as TEDDY ROOSEVELT (b. Oct. 27, 1858, New York, N.Y., U.S.—d. Jan. 6, 1919, Oyster Bay, N.Y.), 26th president of the U.S. (1901–09). He was elected to the

New York legislature (1882), where he became a Republican leader opposed to the Democratic political machine. After political defeats and the death of his wife, he went to the Dakota Territory to ranch. He returned to New York to serve on the U.S. Civil Service Commission (1889–95) and as head of the city's board of police commissioners (1895–97). A supporter of William McKinley, he served as assistant secretary of the navy (1897–98). When the Spanish-American War was declared, he resigned to organize a cavalry unit, the Rough Riders. He returned to New York a hero and was elected governor in 1899. As the Republican vice-presidential nominee, he took office when McKinley was reelected, and he became president on McKinley's assassination in 1901. One of his early initiatives was to urge enforcement of the Sherman Antitrust Act against business monopolies. He won election in his own right in 1904, defeating Alton Parker. At his urging, Congress regulated railroad rates and passed the Pure Food and Drug Act and Meat Inspection Act (1906) to protect public health. He created national forests and set aside mineral, oil, and coal deposits for conservation. He and secretary of state Elihu Root announced the Roosevelt corollary to the Monroe Doctrine, which reasserted the U.S.'s position as protector of the Western Hemisphere. For mediating an end to the Russo-Japanese War, he received the 1906 Nobel Prize for Peace. He secured a treaty with Panama for construction of a trans-isthmus canal. Declining to seek reelection, he secured the nomination for William H. Taft. After traveling in Africa and Europe, he tried to win the Republican presidential nomination in 1912; when he was rejected, he organized the Bull Moose Party and ran on a policy of New Nationalism. Though he lost the election, he secured 88 electoral votes—the most successful third-party candidacy in the 20th century. Throughout his life he continued to write, publishing extensively on history, politics, travel, and nature.

root, In botany, the underground anchoring part of a plant. It grows downward in response to gravity, absorbs water and dissolved minerals, and stores reserve food. Primary root systems have a deep sturdy taproot (in gymnosperms and dicots), plus secondary or lateral smaller roots, and root hairs. Grasses and other monocots produce a shallow diffuse mass of fibrous secondary roots. Additional support (e.g., in corn and orchids) comes from stem offshoots called adventitious, or prop, roots. Fleshy roots that store food may be modified taproots (e.g., carrots, turnips, and beets) or modified adventitious roots (e.g., cassava). Tubers such as the potato are modified, fleshy, underground stems, or rhizomes. Aerial roots arise from the stem and either pass for some distance through the air before reaching the soil or remain hanging in the air.

Rosario, City (metro. area pop., 1999 est.: 1,000,000) and river port, east-central Argentina, on the Paraná River. Founded in 1725, it began to develop into a major city in the late 19th century. In 1819 the city was burned by revolutionaries. In 1860 it welcomed domestic and foreign oceangoing ships to its natural harbour, which became a major port. One of Argentina's largest cities, it exports grain, meat, and lumber. It is also an industrial city, producing steel, automobiles, and agricultural machinery, and it is an educational centre.

rosary, Religious exercise in which prayers are recited and counted on a string of beads or knotted cord, which is also called a rosary. Many of these devices are highly ornamental and incorporate jewels. The practice of using a rosary or "counting beads" occurs widely in world religions, including Christianity, Hinduism, Buddhism, and Islam. In Christianity, the most common rosary is that of the Virgin Mary. Its origin is uncertain, but it is associated with St. Dominic and reached its definitive form in the 15th century.

rose window, In Gothic architecture, a decorated circular window, often glazed with stained glass, that first appeared in mid-12th-century cathedrals. It was used mainly at the western end of the nave and the ends of the transept. The bar tracery of a High Gothic rose window consisted of a series of radiating forms, each tipped by a pointed arch at the outside of the circle. The rose windows of Notre-Dame de Paris are particularly noteworthy. In later Flamboyant-style tracery, the radiating elements consisted of an intricate network of wavy, double-curved bars.

rosemary, Small perennial evergreen shrub (*Rosmarinus officinalis*) of the mint family whose leaves are used to flavour a wide variety of food. The bush grows 3–7.5 ft (1–2.3 m) tall and has short linear leaves that resemble curved pine needles, dark green and shiny above, white beneath. Bluish flowers grow in small clusters. Bees are particularly fond of rosemary. In ancient times rosemary was believed to strengthen memory; in literature and folklore it is an emblem of remembrance and fidelity. Native to the Mediterranean, it has been naturalized throughout Europe and temperate America.

Roses, Wars of the (1455–85) Series of dynastic civil wars between the houses of Lancaster and York for the English throne. The wars were named for the emblems of the two houses, the white rose of York and the red of Lancaster. Both claimed the throne through descent from Edward III. Lancastrians held the throne from 1399, but the country fell into a state of near anarchy during the reign of Henry VI, and during one of Henry's bouts with madness in 1453 the duke of York was declared protector of the realm. Henry reestablished his authority in 1455, and the battle was joined. The Yorkists succeeded in putting Edward IV on the throne in 1461, but the wars continued, and in 1471 they murdered Henry VI in the Tower of London. In 1483 Richard III overrode the claims of his nephew Edward V to seize the throne, alienating many Yorkists. The Lancastrian Henry Tudor (Henry VII) defeated and killed Richard at the Battle of Bosworth Field, ending the wars. He united the houses by marriage and defeated a Yorkist rising in 1487.

Rosetta Stone, Inscribed stone slab, now in the British Museum, that provided an important key to the decipherment of Egyptian hieroglyphs. An irregularly shaped block of black basalt with inscriptions in hieroglyphs, Demotic Egyptian, and Greek, it was discovered by Napoleon's troops near the town of Rosetta (Rashid), northeast of Alexandria, in 1799. The text concerns the deeds of Ptolemy V Epiphanes (205–180 BC) and dates from the ninth year of his reign. Its decipherment was begun by Thomas Young, who isolated the proper names in the Demotic version, and decisively completed by J.-F. Champollion, who grasped that some hieroglyphs were phonetic.

The Rosetta Stone, with Egyptian hieroglyphs in the top section, demotic characters in the middle, and Greek at the bottom; in the British Museum.

Rosh Hashanah, Jewish New Year. Sometimes called the Day of Judgment, Rosh Hashanah falls on Tishri 1 (in September or October) and ushers in a 10-day period of self-examination and penitence that ends with Yom Kippur. The liturgy includes the blowing of the ram's horn, or shofar, a call for spiritual awakening associated with the giving of the Law to Moses on Mount Sinai. It is also called the Day of Remembrance, since it celebrates the creation of the world and the responsibilities of the Jews as God's chosen people. It is a solemn but hopeful holiday; bread and fruit dipped in honey are eaten as omens of sweetness for the year ahead.

Ross Ice Shelf, World's largest body of floating ice. It lies at the head of the Ross Sea, which forms an enormous indentation in Antarctica. Its area is estimated to be about the size of France. The great white barrier wall of the shelf's front, first seen in 1841 by British explorer Capt. James C. Ross, rises in places to 200 ft (60 m). The ice shelf has been an important gateway for explorations of the Antarctic interior, including expeditions (1911–12) to the South Pole by Roald Amundsen and Robert Falcon Scott and Richard E. Byrd's expeditions (1928–41). It is the site of several permanent research stations.

rotary engine, Internal-combustion engine in which the combustion chambers and cylinders rotate with the driven shaft around a fixed control shaft to which pistons are attached. The gas pressures of combustion are used to rotate the shaft. In the Wankel engine, the most fully developed and widely used rotary engine, a triangular rotor rotates with an orbital motion in a specially shaped casing, and forms rotating crescent-shaped combustion chambers between its sides and the curved wall of the casing.

Rotterdam, City (pop., 2001 est.: 593,000) and seaport, western Netherlands. It is situated on both sides of the Nieuwe Maas River (a distributary of the Rhine), near the North Sea. Founded in the 13th century, it developed into a major port and commercial city. From 1795 to 1813 it was occupied by the French. Heavily damaged by the Germans during World War II, it was extensively rebuilt on a new plan. One of the world's busiest cargo-handling ports, it is a major transshipment port for inland Europe, with tens of thousands of Rhine River barges using its facilities. The second largest city in the Netherlands, it has several large oil refineries and produces chemicals, paper, and clothing. It is also a cultural and educational centre.

Rouen, City (pop., 2006 est.: city, 107,904; metro. area, 388,798), northwestern France. Situated on the Seine River, Rouen became important in the 3rd century AD after the arrival of Christianity with St. Mellon. Sacked by the Normans in 876, it became the medieval capital of Normandy. It came under English rule in 1066 and again in 1419. Joan of Arc was imprisoned and executed there in 1431. Rouen was recaptured by the French in 1449. Historic buildings include the 14th-century abbey of Saint Ouen and the great Gothic cathedral, whose oldest parts date to the 11th century. The city was the birthplace of Pierre Corneille and Gustave Flaubert.

roulette, Gambling game. After a small ball is released in the opposite direction of a revolving wheel, players make bets concerning which red or black numbered compartment the ball will enter as it comes to rest. Bets are placed on a table marked to correspond with the compartments of the wheel. Roulette (French: "small wheel") emerged in the late 18th century in the casinos of Europe. All bets are placed against the "house," or casino bank. Bets may be made until the ball slows down and is about to drop from its track into a compartment. Bets may be on a single number or various combinations of numbers that pay off at lesser odds if the winner is among them. Betting that red or black or that an odd or even number will come up are other options.

Rousseau, Jean-Jacques (b. June 28, 1712, Geneva, Switz.—d. July 2, 1778, Ermenonville, France), Swiss-French philosopher. At age 16 he fled Geneva to Savoy, where he became the steward and later the lover of the baronne de Warens. At age 30, having furthered his education and social position under her influence, he moved to Paris, where he joined Denis Diderot at the centre of the philosophes; he wrote on music and economics for Diderot's *Encyclopédie*. His first major work, the *Discourse on the Arts and Sciences* (1750), argued that man is good by nature but has been corrupted by society and civilization; Rousseau's belief in the natural goodness of man set him apart from Roman Catholic writers who, like him, were hostile to the idea of progress. He also wrote music; his light opera *The Cunning-Man* (1752) was

widely admired. In 1752 he became involved in an influential dispute with Jean-Philippe Rameau over the relative merits of French and Italian music; Rousseau championed the latter. In the *Discourse on the Origin and Foundations of Inequality Among Men* (1754), he argued against Thomas Hobbes that human life before the formation of societies was healthy, happy, and free and that vice arose as the result of social organization and especially the introduction of private property. Civil society, he held, comes into being only to ensure peace and to protect property, which not everyone has; it thus represents a fraudulent social contract that reinforces inequality. In the *Social Contract* (1762), which begins with the memorable line, "Man was born free, but he is everywhere in chains," Rousseau argues that a civil society based on a genuine social contract rather than a fraudulent one would provide people with a better kind of freedom for their natural independence, namely, political liberty, which he understands as obedience to a self-imposed law created by the "general will." In 1762 the publication of *Émile*, a treatise on education, produced outrage, and Rousseau was forced to flee to Switzerland. He began showing signs of mental instability *c.* 1767, and he died insane. His *Confessions* (1781–88), which he modeled on the work of the same title by St. Augustine, is among the most famous autobiographies.

rowing, Propulsion of a boat by means of oars. As a sport, it involves one of two kinds of boat: (1) the shell, a narrow, light racing boat propelled by eight rowers pulling single oars under the direction of a coxswain; and (2) the scull, a racing shell propelled by one or two rowers using sculls (pairs of oars). Organized racing began at the Universities of Oxford and Cambridge in the 1820s, culminating in 1839 in the Henley Regatta (from 1851 the Henley Royal Regatta). In the U.S., Harvard and Yale universities first raced in 1851. Rowing events in the Olympic Games have been held for men since 1900 and for women since 1976.

Rowling, J(oanne) K(athleen) (b. July 31, 1965, Chipping Sodbury, near Bristol, Eng.), British author, creator of the popular and critically acclaimed Harry Potter series. The first book in the seven-volume series, *Harry Potter and the Philosopher's Stone* (also published as *Harry Potter and the Sorcerer's Stone*), was published in 1997. Featuring vivid descriptions and an imaginative story line, the book followed the unlikely hero Harry Potter, a lonely orphan who discovers that he is actually a wizard. The book was an immediate success, appealing to both children (its intended audience) and adults. Succeeding volumes—*Harry Potter and the Chamber of Secrets* (1998), *Harry Potter and the Prisoner of Azkaban* (1999), *Harry Potter and the Goblet of Fire* (2000), *Harry Potter and the Order of the Phoenix* (2003), and *Harry Potter and the Half-Blood Prince* (2005)—were also best sellers. In 2007 the final book in the series, *Harry Potter and the Deathly Hallows*, was published. Rowling was credited with renewing children's interest in reading, and in 2001 she was appointed OBE (Officer of the British Empire). That year also marked the release of the film adaptation of the first Harry Potter book. It became one of the top-grossing movies in the world, and subsequent volumes were also made into highly successful films. In 2008 Rowling published *The Tales of Beedle the Bard*, a collection of fairy tales.

Roy, Jamini (b. April 15, 1887, Baliatore, India—d. April 24, 1972, Calcutta), Indian artist. In the late 1920s and early '30s he rejected his academic training and instead developed a linear, decorative, colourful style based on Bengali folk traditions. During the 1930s and '40s the popularity of his paintings represented the passage of modern Indian art from its earlier academic leanings to new nativist predilections. Roy's subject matter ranged from the *Ramayana* to Christ to portraits of contemporary figures such as Mahatma Gandhi. He is one of the best-known Indian artists of the 20th century.

Roy, Ram Mohun (b. May 22, 1772, Radhanagar, Bengal, India—d. Sept. 27, 1833, Bristol, Gloucestershire, Eng.), Indian religious, social, and political reformer. Born to a prosperous Brahman family, he traveled widely in his youth, exposing himself to various cultures and developing unorthodox views of Hinduism. In 1803 he composed a tract denouncing India's religious divisions and superstitions and advocating a monotheistic Hinduism that would worship one supreme God. He provided modern translations of the Vedas and Upanishads to provide a philosophical basis for his beliefs, advocated freedom of speech and of religion, and denounced the caste system and suttee. In 1826 he founded the Vedanta College, and in 1828 he formed the Brahmo Samaj.

Royal Greenwich Observatory, Astronomical observatory, oldest scientific institution in Britain, founded for navigational purposes in 1675 by Charles II at Greenwich, England. Its main contributions have been in navigation, timekeeping, determination of star positions, and almanac publication. In 1767 it began publishing *The Nautical Almanac,* based on the time at the longitude of Greenwich; its popularity among navigators led in part to the Greenwich meridian's being made Earth's prime meridian and the starting point for international time zones in 1884.

rubber, Flexible material that can recover its shape after considerable deformation.The best-known rubber is natural rubber, made from the milky latex of the rubber tree (*Hevea brasiliensis*). Natural rubber is still important industrially, but it now competes with synthetic alternatives (e.g., neoprene, silicone) derived from petroleum, natural gas, and other source materials. Rubber's usefulness is based on the unique elasticity of its constituent polymer molecules (built of thousands of isoprene monomers), which are capable of returning to their original coiled shape after being stretched to great extents; it is made more durable by vulcanization with sulfur or another agent that establishes chemical cross-links between the polymers. Fillers and other additives allow tailoring of properties to the desired use (e.g., by foaming, shaping, and curing). More than half of all rubber goes into making tires; the rest is used principally in belts, hoses, gaskets, shoes, clothing, furniture, and toys.

rubber plant, or INDIA RUBBER TREE, Tropical tree (*Ficus elastica*) of the mulberry family. The rubber plant is large in its native Southeast Asia and other warm areas; elsewhere it is commonly grown indoors as a potted plant. The plant has large, thick, oblong leaves and pairs of figlike fruits along its branches. The milky sap, or latex, was once an important source of an inferior natural rubber. Young plants available in the florist's trade are durable and grow well under less than ideal indoor conditions. Some cultivated varieties have broader, darker green leaves; others are variegated.

rubber tree, South American tropical tree (*Hevea brasiliensis*) of the spurge family. Cultivated on plantations in the tropics and subtropics, especially in Southeast Asia and western Africa, it replaced the rubber plant in the early 20th century as the chief source of natural rubber. It has soft wood, high, branching limbs, and a large area of bark. The milky liquid (latex) that oozes from any wound to the tree bark contains about 30% rubber, which can be coagulated and processed into solid products such as tires. Latex can also be concentrated for producing dipped goods such as surgical gloves.

rubella, or GERMAN MEASLES, Viral disease with a usually mild course, except in women in the first 20 weeks of pregnancy, in whom it can cause fetal birth defects (of eyes, heart, brain, and large arteries) or death. Sore throat and fever are followed by swollen glands and a rash. Up to 30% of infections may have no symptoms. Lifelong immunity follows infection. Encephalitis is a rare complication. Rubella was not distinguished from measles (rubeola) until the early 19th century and was not known to be dangerous until 1941. The virus was isolated in 1962, and a vaccine became available in 1969.

Rubens, Peter Paul (b. June 28, 1577, Siegen, Westphalia —d. May 30, 1640, Antwerp, Spanish Neth.), Flemish painter and diplomat. After apprenticeships in Antwerp, he was admitted to its painters' guild in 1598. He went to Italy in 1600 and until 1608 worked for the duke of Mantua, who in 1603 sent him to Spain to present paintings and other gifts to Philip III, the first of many diplomatic missions he would perform for various courts over three decades. The enormous fame he would achieve made him welcome at royal courts, and sovereigns often discussed affairs of state while they sat for portraits. Returning to the Spanish Netherlands (now Belgium) in 1608, he was appointed court painter to the Spanish Habsburg regents, and over the next decade produced numerous altarpieces. A devout Catholic, he became the Counter-Reformation's chief artistic proponent in northern Europe. In 1620 he contracted to design 39 ceiling paintings for the Jesuit church, to be completed by assistants, including the young Anthony Van Dyck. In France he did 21 large canvases for Marie de Médicis and a tapestry cycle for Louis XIII; for Britain his *Allegory of Peace and War* (1629–30) commemorated the success of his own diplomatic efforts to end hostilities between Britain and Spain, and he decorated the royal Banqueting House for Charles I; in Spain he did more than 60 oil sketches for Philip IV's hunting lodge. Both Charles and Philip knighted him. His output was prodigious. He was the greatest exponent of Baroque painting's dynamism, vitality, and sensual exuberance. His profound stylistic influence extended over three centuries.

Rubicon, Small stream that separated Cisalpine Gaul from Italy in the era of the Roman republic. The movement of Julius Caesar's forces over the Rubicon into Italy in 49 BC violated the law that forbade a general to lead an army out of the province to which he was assigned. Caesar's act thus amounted to a declaration of war against the Roman Senate and resulted in the three-year civil war that left Caesar ruler of the Roman world. "Crossing the Rubicon" became a popular phrase describing a step that irrevocably commits a person to a given course of action.

rubidium, Metallic chemical element that is part of the alkali metal group, chemical symbol Rb, atomic number 37. Rubidium is the second most reactive metal after cesium and is very soft, with a silvery white lustre. It was discovered in 1861, and its name derives from the Latin word for red, in reference to rubidium's prominent red spectral lines. Rubidium is difficult to handle because it ignites spontaneously in air. It is used in photoelectric cells. Rubidium atomic clocks have been constructed.

ruby, Gemstone composed of transparent red corundum. Its colour varies from deep to pale red, in some cases with a tinge of purple, depending on chromium and iron content; the most valued is a pigeon-blood red. When it is cut and polished, ruby is a brilliant (light-deflecting) stone, but it lacks fire (flashes of colour). Ruby is a mineral of very limited distribution. Its best-known source is in Myanmar, and rubies have also been found in Thailand, Sri Lanka, and elsewhere. Rubies have been produced synthetically with much success; those containing 2.5% chromic oxide have the prized pigeon-blood red colour.

rug and carpet, Any decorative textile normally made of a thick material and intended as a floor covering. Floor coverings made of plaited rushes date from the 5th or 4th millennium BCE. Carpets were first made in central and western Asia as coverings for earthen floors; they were also used for blankets, saddle covers, storage bags, tent doorways, and tomb covers. Oriental carpets imported into Europe in the 16th–17th century were considered too valuable to be put on the floor and were often used as wall decoration. They are still popular wall decorations in Russia. Carpet weaving reached its peak of artistry in 16th-century Persia. In the West, outstanding carpets were produced at factories in 17th-century France and 18th-century England. Most handmade carpets are made from sheep's wool. Natural dyes were used until the 19th century, when chemical dyes were introduced.

rugby, Football sport made up of two variant codes—rugby union and rugby league. The sport was first developed in the 1820s at Rugby School in England. In 1895 a dispute over professionalism between the Rugby Football Union and several clubs in northern England led to the creation of rugby league (always a professional sport). Rugby union became fully professional in 1995. The game is played by teams of 15 (union) or 13 (league) members each, using an inflated oval ball. The ball may be kicked, carried, or passed laterally or backward (but not forward). The object is to score goals (worth three points) by kicking the ball between the uprights of the opponent's goal, or tries (worth five points in union play, four in league), by grounding the ball behind the opponent's goal line. A conversion kick (worth two points) is attempted after scoring a try. Both rugby union and rugby league have international play and world cup tournaments. Rugby is most popular in the United Kingdom, South Africa, Australia, and New Zealand.

Ruhr River, River, western Germany. An important tributary of the lower Rhine River, it rises on the northern side of Winterberg and flows 146 mi (235 km) west. The Ruhr valley is a major industrial and mining region; it includes the industrial cities of Essen, Düsseldorf, and Dortmund. The Ruhr coalfield is one of the world's largest and produces the bulk of Germany's bituminous coal. Industries begun by the Krupp and Thyssen families flourished in the 19th–20th centuries. The river was militarily important in World War I, and the river valley was occupied from 1923 to 1925 by France and Belgium. As the industrial heart of Nazi Germany, it was heavily bombed in World War II and occupied by Allied troops in 1945; full control was returned to West Germany in 1954. It is now a centre of steel production and diversified chemical manufacturing.

rummy, Family of card games. The many variants of rummy make it one of the world's best-known and most widely played card games. The basic principle of rummy (also spelled rum, rhum, or romme) is to form sets of three or four cards of the same rank (as four 8s, three 6s) or sequences of three or more cards of the same suit (6–5–4–3, all of diamonds, e.g.). Canasta is an unusual type of rummy, in that sequences are not permitted.

rupa-loka, In Buddhism, any of the 16 planes of existence into which those beings who have renounced sense desires are reborn. It is intermediate between the *kama-loka*, where material beings are born, and the *arupa-loka*, where only the mind exists. Its upper levels are called the Pure Abodes, the birthplace of those beings who do not return to lower planes in subsequent births. The *rupa-loka*, free from sensuous desire but still conditioned by form, is inhabited by gods.

Rushdie, Sir (Ahmed) Salman (b. June 19, 1947, Bombay, India), Anglo-Indian novelist. Educated at the University of Cambridge, he worked as an advertising copywriter in London in the 1970s before winning unexpected success with *Midnight's Children* (1981, Booker Prize), an allegorical novel about modern India. His second novel, *Shame* (1983), is a scathing portrait of politics and sexual morality in Pakistan. *The Satanic Verses* (1988), which includes episodes based on the life of Muhammad, was denounced as blasphemous by outraged Muslim leaders, and in 1989 Iran's Ruhollah Khomeini condemned Rushdie to death. Rushdie became the focus of enormous international attention and was compelled to remain in hiding until 1998, when Iran said it would no longer enforce Khomeini's decree. Rushdie's other novels include *The Moor's Last Sigh* (1995), *Fury* (2001), and *Shalimar the Clown* (2005). He was knighted in 2007.

Russell, Bertrand (Arthur William), 3rd Earl Russell (b. May 18, 1872, Trelleck, Monmouthshire, Eng.—d. Feb. 2, 1970, near Penrhyndeudraeth, Merioneth, Wales), British logician and philosopher. He is best known for his work in mathematical logic and for his advocacy on behalf of a variety of social and political causes, especially pacifism and nuclear disarmament. He was

Bertrand Russell, 1960
Courtesy of the British Broadcasting Corporation, London

born into the British nobility as the grandson of Earl Russell, who was twice prime minister of Britain in the mid-19th century. He studied mathematics and philosophy at Cambridge University, where he came under the influence of the idealist philosopher J.M.E. McTaggart, though he soon rejected idealism in favour of an extreme Platonic realism. In an early paper, "On Denoting" (1905), he solved a notorious puzzle in the philosophy of language by showing how phrases such as "The present king of France," which have no referents, function logically as general statements rather than as proper names. Russell later regarded this discovery, which came to be known as the "theory of descriptions," as one of his most important contributions to philosophy. In *The Principles of Mathematics* (1903) and the epochal *Principia Mathematica* (3 vol., 1910–13), which he wrote with Alfred North Whitehead, he sought to demonstrate that the whole of mathematics derives from logic. For his pacifism in World War I he lost his lectureship at Cambridge and was later imprisoned. (He would abandon pacifism in 1939 in the face of Nazi aggression.) Russell's best-developed metaphysical doctrine, logical atomism, strongly influenced the school of logical positivism. His later philosophical works include *The Analysis of Mind* (1921), *The Analysis of Matter* (1927), and *Human Knowledge: Its Scope and Limits* (1948). His *A History of Western Philosophy* (1945), which he wrote for a popular audience, became a best-seller and was for many years the main source of his income. Among his many works on social and political topics are *Roads to Freedom* (1918); *The Practice and Theory of Bolshevism* (1920), a scathing critique of Soviet communism; *On Education* (1926); and *Marriage and Morals* (1929). In part because of the controversial views he espoused in the latter work, he was prevented from accepting a teaching position at the City College of New York in 1940. After World War II he became a leader in the worldwide campaign for nuclear disarmament, serving as first president of the international Pugwash Conferences on nuclear weapons and world security and of the Campaign for Nuclear Disarmament. In 1961, at the age of 89, he was imprisoned for a second time for inciting civil disobedience. He received the Nobel Prize for Literature in 1950.

Russia, officially RUSSIAN FEDERATION, Country, eastern Europe and northern Asia, formerly the preeminent republic of the Union of Soviet Socialist Republics. Area: 6,601,700 sq mi (17,098,200 sq km). Population: (2011 est.) 142,707,000. Capital: Moscow. The population is primarily Russian; minorities include Tatars and Ukrainians. Languages: Russian (official), various Turkic and Uralic languages. Religions: Christianity (mostly Eastern Orthodox, also Protestant); also Islam. However, about one-third of the people are nonreligious or atheist. Currency: ruble. The land and its environments are varied, including the Ural Mountains and ranges in eastern Siberia, the highest peaks being on the Kamchatka Peninsula. The Russian Plain contains the great Volga and Northern Dvina rivers, and in Siberia are the valleys of the Ob, Yenisey, Lena, and Amur rivers. Tundra covers extensive portions in the north, and in the south there are forests, steppes, and fertile areas. The economy was industrialized from 1917 to 1945 but was in serious decline by the 1980s. In 1992 the government decreed radical reforms to convert the centrally planned economy into a market economy based on private enterprise. Russia is a federal multiparty republic with a bicameral legislative body; its head of state is the president, and the head of government is the prime minister. What is now the territory of Russia was inhabited from ancient times by various peoples, including the Slavs. From the 8th century BCE to the 6th century CE the area was overrun by successive nomadic peoples, including the Sythians, Sarmatians, Goths, Huns, and Avars. Kievan Rus, a confederation of principalities ruling from Kiev, emerged *c.* the 10th century; it lost supremacy in the 11th–12th century to independent principalities, including Novgorod and Vladimir. Novgorod ascended in the north and was the only Russian principality to escape the domination of the Mongol Golden Horde in the 13th century. In the 14th–15th century the princes of Moscow gradually overthrew the Mongols. Under Ivan IV (the Terrible), Russia began to expand. The Romanov dynasty arose in 1613. Expansion continued under Peter I (the Great) and Catherine II (the Great). The area was invaded by Napoleon in 1812; after his defeat, Russia received most of the Grand Duchy of Warsaw (1815). Russia annexed Georgia, Armenia, and Caucasus territories in the 19th century. The Russian southward advance against the Ottoman Empire was of key importance to Europe. Russia was defeated in the Crimean War (1853–56). Chinese cession of the Amur River's left bank in 1858 marked Russia's expansion in East Asia. Russia sold Alaska to the U.S. in 1867. Defeat in the Russo-Japanese War led to an unsuccessful uprising in 1905. In World War I Russia fought against the Central Powers. The popular overthrow of the tsarist regime in 1917 marked the beginning of a government of soviets. The Bolsheviks brought the main part of the former empire under communist control and organized it as the Russian Soviet Federated Socialist Republic (coextensive with present-day Russia). The Russian S.F.S.R. joined other soviet republics in 1922 to form the U.S.S.R. Upon the dissolution of the U.S.S.R. in 1991, the Russian S.F.S.R. was renamed and became the leading member of the Commonwealth of Independent States. It adopted a new constitution in 1993. During the 1990s and into the early 21st century, it struggled on several fronts, beset with economic difficulties, political corruption, and independence movements.

Russian language, East Slavic language spoken by about 170 million people in Russia, former republics of the Soviet Union, and émigré communities. For many non-Russian ethnic groups both within and outside contemporary Russia, it is a common second language and lingua franca. Since the Middle Ages, Russian has gradually expanded its speech area from its historical locus in the upper Volga and Dnieper River drainages northward and eastward. Russian speakers penetrated Siberia in the 16th century and reached the Pacific in the 17th century. Russian became a full-fledged literary language in the 18th century, when it finally displaced Church Slavonic. Dialect differences in Russian are not great, considering the enormous territory over which it is spoken, and the upheavals of the 20th century eroded such distinctions as exist.

Russian Orthodox Church, Eastern Orthodox church of Russia, its de facto national church. In 988 Prince Vladimir of Kiev (later St. Vladimir) embraced Byzantine Orthodoxy and ordered the baptism of his population. By the 14th century, the metropolitan of Kiev and all Russia (head of the Russian church) was residing in Moscow; dissatisfied western Russian principalities obtained temporary separate metropolitans, but authority was later recentralized under Moscow. In the 15th century the church, rejecting Metropolitan Isidore's acceptance of union with the Western church, appointed their own independent metropolitan. Moscow saw itself as the "third Rome" and the last bulwark of true Orthodoxy; in 1589 the head of the Russian church obtained the title patriarch, putting him on a level with the patriarchs of Constantinople, Alexandria, Antioch, and Jerusalem. The reforms of Nikon caused a schism within the church, and Peter I abolished the patriarchate in 1721, making church administration a department of the state. The patriarchate was reestablished in 1917, two months before the Bolshevik revolution, but under the soviets the church was deprived of its legal rights and practically suppressed.

It saw a great resurgence following the collapse of the Soviet Union (1991). The Russian Orthodox Church in the U.S. became independent from Moscow in 1970.

Russian Revolution of 1905, Unsuccessful uprising in Russia against the tsarist regime. After several years of mounting discontent, a peaceful demonstration was crushed by Tsar Nicholas II's troops in the Bloody Sunday massacre. General strikes followed in St. Petersburg and other industrial cities. The revolt spread to non-Russian parts of the empire, including Poland, Finland, and Georgia. Antirevolutionary groups, including the Black Hundreds, opposed the rebellion with violent attacks on socialists and pogroms against Jews. By October 1905, general strikes had spread to all the large cities, and the workers' councils or soviets, often led by the Mensheviks, became revolutionary governments. The strikes' magnitude convinced Nicholas II, advised by Sergey Witte, to issue the October Manifesto, promising an elected legislature. The concessions satisfied most moderates, though the more ardent revolutionaries refused to yield, and pockets of resistance in Poland, Georgia, and elsewhere were harshly suppressed as the regime restored its authority. While most of the revolutionary leaders, including Leon Trotsky, were arrested, the revolution forced the tsar to institute reforms such as a new constitution and a Duma, though he failed to adequately implement various promised reforms.

Russian Revolution of 1917, Revolution that overthrew the imperial government and placed the Bolsheviks in power. Increasing governmental corruption, the reactionary policies of Tsar Nicholas II, and catastrophic Russian losses in World War I contributed to widespread dissatisfaction and economic hardship. In February 1917 riots over food scarcity broke out in Petrograd (St. Petersburg). When the army joined the rebels, Nicholas was forced to abdicate. A provisional government, headed by Georgy Lvov, was appointed in March and tried to continue Russia's participation in World War I, but it was opposed by the powerful Petrograd workers' soviet, which favoured Russian withdrawal from the war. Other soviets were formed in major cities and towns, choosing members from factories and military units. The soviet movement was dominated by the Socialist Revolutionary Party, followed by the Mensheviks and the Bolsheviks. Between March and October, the provisional government was reorganized four times; Aleksandr Kerensky became its head in July; he survived a coup attempt by Lavr Kornilov but was unable to halt Russia's slide into political and military chaos. By September the Bolsheviks, led by Vladimir Lenin, had achieved majorities in the Petrograd and Moscow soviets and won increasing support among the hungry urban workers and soldiers. In October they staged a nearly bloodless coup (the "October Revolution"), occupying government buildings and strategic points. Kerensky tried unsuccessfully to organize resistance, then fled the country. The congress of soviets approved the formation of a new government composed mainly of Bolsheviks.

Russo-Finnish War, or WINTER WAR (1939–40) War waged by the Soviet Union against Finland at the start of World War II, following the signing of the German-Soviet Nonaggression Pact. When Finland refused to grant the Soviets a naval base and other concessions, Soviet troops attacked on several fronts in November 1939. The heavily outnumbered Finns under Carl Gustav Emil Mannerheim put up a skillful defense until February 1940, when heavy Russian bombardments breached the Finns' southern defenses. A peace treaty in March 1940 ceded western Karelia to Russia and allowed construction of a Soviet naval base on the Hanko peninsula.

Russo-Japanese War (1904–05) Conflict between Russia and Japan over territorial expansion in East Asia. After Russia leased the strategically important Port Arthur (now Lüshun, China) and expanded into Manchuria (northeastern China), it faced the increasing power of Japan. When Russia reneged on its agreement with Japan to withdraw troops from Manchuria, the Japanese fleet attacked the Russia naval squadron at Port Arthur and began a siege of the city in February 1904. Japanese land forces cut the Russian army off from coming to aid Port Arthur and pushed it back to Mukden (now Shenyang). The reinforced Russian army took the offensive in October, but poor military leadership blunted its effectiveness. After the long Japanese siege of Port Arthur, in January 1905 the corrupt Russian commander surrendered the garrison without consulting his officers, despite adequate stores and ammunition for its continued defense. Heavy fighting around Mukden ended in March 1905 with the withdrawal of Russian troops under Aleksey Kuropatkin. The decisive naval Battle of Tsushima gave the Japanese the upper hand and brought Russia to the peace table. With the signing of the Treaty of Portsmouth, Russia abandoned its expansionist policy in eastern Asia and Japan gained effective control of Korea and much of Manchuria.

Russo-Turkish Wars, Series of wars fought between Russia and the Ottoman Empire from the 17th to the 19th century. Russia waged the early wars (1676–81, 1686, 1689) in a fruitless attempt to establish a warm-water port on the Black Sea. In the war of 1695–96, however, Peter I captured the fortress of Azov, but subsequent attempts (1710–12, 1735–39) by the Russians to seize the Balkans failed, leading to the Treaty of Belgrade. In Catherine II's reign the first major Russo-Turkish war (1768–74) pushed Russian borders south and gave Russia a vague right of protection over the Ottoman sultan's Christian subjects. Catherine annexed the Crimean Peninsula in 1783. Russia gained the entire western Ukrainian Black Sea coast in the Treaty of Jassy (1792). A subsequent war (1806–12) led to the Treaty of Bucharest. In the 19th century wars were fought over the Dardanelles and Bosporus straits, the Caucasus, and Crimea. The war of 1828–29 ended in the Treaty of Edirne (1829), which ceded large tracts to Russia. The Crimean War (1853–56), however, was a major diplomatic setback for Russia. The 1877–78 Russo-Turkish War pitted Russia and Serbia against Turkey over autonomy for Bosnia and Herzegovina. Russia was victorious, but the gains it achieved under the Treaty of San Stefano (1878) were restricted by the Congress of Berlin (1878), imposed by Britain and Austria-Hungary.

Ruth, Babe, orig. GEORGE HERMAN RUTH (b. Feb. 6, 1895, Baltimore, Md., U.S.—d. Aug. 16, 1948, New York, N.Y.), U.S. baseball player, one of the greatest hitters and most popular figures in the sport's history. He began his career in 1914 as a member of Baltimore's minor league team and joined the Boston Red Sox later that season. He started as a pitcher, compiling an outstanding record (94 wins, 46 losses), but switched to the outfield because of his powerful hitting. Sold to the New York Yankees in 1920, he remained with the team until 1934; he played his last year with the Boston Braves (1935). He coached the Brooklyn Dodgers in 1938, but his reputation for irresponsibility prevented his obtaining a permanent coaching or manager's job. His

Babe Ruth.
UPI/Bettmann Archive

prodigious slugging earned him the nickname "Sultan of Swat." In 1927 he set the most famous of all baseball records when he hit 60 home runs in a single season, a mark that stood until 1961, when broken by Roger Maris. Ruth hit at least 50 home runs in four separate seasons and at least 40 in each of 11 seasons. His career slugging percentage (.690) remains an all-time record; he ranks third in career home runs (714, behind Barry Bonds and Hank Aaron), second in runs batted in (2,213, again behind Aaron), and fourth in runs (2,174, behind Rickey Henderson, Ty Cobb, and Bonds and tied with Aaron).

Rwanda, officially REPUBLIC OF RWANDA, Country, east-central Africa. Area: 10,185 sq mi (26,379 sq km). Population: (2011 est.) 10,943,000. Capital: Kigali. The population is mostly Hutu, with a Tutsi minority; the Twa are also present in small numbers. Languages: Rwanda, French, English (all official). Religions: Christianity (mostly Roman Catholic; also Protestant); also traditional beliefs, Islam. Currency: Rwanda franc. Rwanda is a landlocked mountainous country, most of it at an elevation above 4,000 ft (1,200 m). There are bamboo forests, wooded regions, and grassy savannas with rich and varied wildlife. The developing economy is mainly free-enterprise, based on agriculture. Rwanda is a multiparty republic with two legislative bodies; its head of state and government is the president, assisted by the prime minister. Originally inhabited by the Twa, a Pygmy people, it became home to the Hutu, who were well established there when the Tutsi appeared in the 14th century. The Tutsi conquered the Hutu and in the 15th century founded a kingdom near Kigali. The kingdom expanded steadily, but from 1894 to 1918 Rwanda was part of German East Africa. The Belgians occupied Rwanda in 1916, and the League of Nations created Ruanda-Urundi as a Belgian mandate in 1923. The Tutsi retained their dominance until shortly before Rwanda reached independence in 1962, when the Hutu took control of the government and stripped the Tutsi of much of their land. Many Tutsi fled Rwanda, and the Hutu dominated the country's political system, waging sporadic civil wars until mid-1994, when the death of the country's leader in a plane crash triggered massive violence. The Tutsi-led Rwandan Patriotic Front (RPF) took over the country by force after the massacre of almost one million Tutsi and Tutsi sympathizers by the Hutu. Two million refugees, mostly Hutu, fled to the neighbouring Democratic Republic of the Congo after the RPF's victory. A transitional government was replaced in 2003 following the country's first multiparty elections.

Ryōan Temple, Japanese RYŌAN-JI, Japanese Buddhist temple in Kyōto, famous for its abstract meditation garden (*c.* 1500). An area approximately 30 by 70 ft (10 by 20 m) is covered with raked gravel and set with 15 stones divided into five unequal groups. The pattern of the design may be interpreted as rocky islets in a sea, but the garden's appeal lies essentially in the charm of its relationships and the arrangement of rocks such that all 15 are not visible from any single vantage point.

Ryukyu Islands, Island chain, extreme southern Japan. It extends in an arc 700 mi (1,100 km) long from the southern Japanese island of Kyushu to the northern tip of Taiwan island. The 55 islands and islets have a total land area of 1,193 sq mi (3,090 sq km). In ancient times it was an independent kingdom, but Chinese and Japanese sovereignty were successively imposed on the archipelago from the 14th to the 19th century. In 1879 the Ryukyus became an integral part of Japan. After Japan's defeat in World War II, the U.S. took control of the islands; it returned them all by 1972. The U.S. maintains military bases on Okinawa. The islands are primarily rural, and agriculture is the dominant occupation; tourism has grown in importance.

S

SA, in full STURMABTEILUNG (GERMAN: "ASSAULT DIVISION"), known as STORM TROOPERS, or BROWNSHIRTS, Nazi paramilitary organization that played a key role in Adolf Hitler's rise to power. The SA was founded by Hitler in Munich in 1921 and drew its early membership from the Freikorps. Outfitted in brown uniforms after the fashion of the Italian Fascist Blackshirts, the SA protected Nazi Party meetings and assaulted political opponents. From 1931 it was headed by Ernst Röhm, and by 1932 it had grown to a force of more than 400,000. Röhm wanted to merge the regular army with the SA under his leadership, but Hitler had become wary of the organization's growing power. In 1934 he ordered a "blood purge" of the SA, which became known as the Night of the Long Knives. Thereafter the SA was reduced to a minor political role.

Sabbath, Day of the week set aside for worship and observance of religious duties in Judaism and Christianity. The Jewish Sabbath begins at sunset on Friday and lasts until sunset the next day, during which time no ordinary work or act of labor is performed. For most Christian denominations, the Sabbath is on Sunday; prescribed conduct varies considerably, but attendance at worship services is a feature common to all. In Islam, Friday is the day of worship.

Sabine, Any member of an ancient Italic tribe located east of the Tiber River. According to legend, Romulus invited them to a festival and then carried off ("raped") their women to provide wives for his men. The second king of Rome, Numa Pompilius, probably a Sabine, is credited with creating a great number of the early Roman religious institutions and practices. Later groups displaced the Sabines from Rome. The Romans conquered them and granted them partial citizenship in 290 BC; they became full citizens in 268.

sabre-toothed tiger, or SABRE-TOOTHED CAT, Any of the extinct cat species forming the subfamily Machairodontinae. They had two long, bladelike canine teeth in the upper jaw. They lived from 36.6 million years ago to about 10,000 years ago, arising in North America and Europe and spreading to Asia, Africa, and South America. The best-known, the short-limbed *Smilodon* of the Americas, was bigger than the modern lion. Its "sabres," which grew to 8 in. (20 cm) long, were used to stab and slash prey, including the mastodon, whose pattern of extinction paralleled their own.

saccharin, Synthetic organic compound, $C_7H_5NSO_3$, that is 200–700 times as sweet as cane sugar. The sodium or calcium salt of saccharin is widely used as a diet sweetener. Though approved by the U.S. Food and Drug Administration and other regulatory bodies around the world, its safety is controversial because it appears to be a weak carcinogen.

sacrament, Religious action or symbol in which spiritual power is believed to be transmitted through material elements or the performance of ritual. The concept is ancient; prehistoric people believed that they could advantageously influence events in the natural world, such as weather patterns, through the performance of ritual. The word *sacramentum* was used in Roman law and later became an oath of allegiance soldiers swore in a sacred place. The sacrament is primarily associated with Christianity, and Christian theologians as early as St. Augustine focused on the proper definition of sacrament. Among Christians, sacraments are said to derive from practices instituted by Jesus, such as baptism, the washing of the feet, and the casting out of demons. There are seven sacraments of Roman Catholicism, as codified by St. Thomas Aquinas and promulgated by the Council of Trent: baptism, confirmation, the Eucharist, penance, anointing of the sick, ordination, and matrimony. The Eastern Orthodox church generally accepts seven sacraments, even though no council accepted by the Orthodox church ever defined the number of sacraments. In most Protestant churches, however, only baptism and the Lord's Supper are recognized as sacraments, as the understanding of sacrament differs from that of the Roman Catholic church.

sacrifice, Act of offering objects to a divinity, thereby making them holy. The motivation for sacrifice is to perpetuate, intensify, or reestablish a connection between the human and the divine. It is often intended to gain the favour of the god or to placate divine wrath. The term has come to be applied specifically to blood sacrifice, which entails the death or destruction of the thing sacrificed. The sacrifice of fruits, flowers, or crops (bloodless sacrifice) is more often referred to as an offering.

Sādāt, (Muḥammad) Anwar el- (b. Dec. 25, 1918, Mit Abū al-Kum, Egypt—d. Oct. 6, 1981, Cairo), President of Egypt (1970–81). A graduate of the Cairo Military Academy, he joined Gamal Abdel Nasser's coup that deposed the monarchy in 1950 and later served as vice president (1964–66, 1969–70). He became president when Nasser died in 1970. He led Egypt during the Yom Kippur War (1973) against Israel. A military loss, the war was a political success for Sādāt, bolstering his popularity through the Arab world. At home, he reversed many of Nasser's socialist policies and attempted to garner the support of the country's Islamists. In 1977 he went to Jerusalem to offer peace to Israel, and in 1979 he concluded a peace treaty, the Camp David Accords, with Israeli prime minister Menachem Begin. The two men shared the 1978 Nobel Prize for Peace. His popularity in the Arab world plummeted, and domestic support for his treaty with the Jewish state—especially among Islamists—evaporated. He was killed by a group of Muslim extremists led by Khālid al-Islāmbūlī and associated with the Islamic Jihad Group.

Ṣaddām Ḥussein (b. April 28, 1937, Tikrīt, Iraq—d. Dec. 30, 2006, Baghdad), President of Iraq (1979–2003). He joined the Baʿth Party in 1957. Following participation in a failed attempt to assassinate Iraqi Pres. ʿAbd al-Karīm Qāsim in 1959, Ṣaddām fled to Cairo, where he briefly attended law school. He returned to Iraq when the Baʿthists gained power in 1963. Jailed when the Baʿthists were overthrown, he escaped and helped reinstall the party to power in 1968. He led the nationalization of the oil industry in 1972. He took over the presidency with the aims of replacing Egypt as leader of the Arab world and of gaining hegemony over the Persian Gulf, and he launched wars against Iran (Iran-Iraq War, 1980–88) and Kuwait (Persian Gulf War, 1990–91), both of which he lost. He instituted a brutal dictatorship and directed intensive campaigns against minorities within Iraq, particularly the Kurds. U.S. fears regarding his development of weapons of mass destruction led to Western sanctions against Iraq. Sanctions were followed by a U.S.-led invasion in 2003 (Iraq War) that drove him from power. After several months in hiding, he was captured by U.S. forces. In 2006 the Iraqi High Tribunal sentenced him to death for crimes against humanity. Days after an Iraqi court upheld his sentence in December 2006, Ṣaddām was executed.

Sadducee, Member of a Jewish priestly sect that flourished for about two centuries, until the destruction (AD 70) of the Second Temple of Jerusalem. Sadducees were generally wealthier, more conservative, and better connected politically than their rivals, the Pharisees. They believed in strict interpretation of the Torah and thus rejected such ideas as immortality of the soul, bodily resurrection after death, and the existence of angels. They viewed Jesus' ministry with mistrust and are believed to have played some part in his death. Their wealth and complicity with Roman rulers made them unpopular with the common people.

sadhu and swami, In India, a religious ascetic or holy person. Sadhus are typically wandering ascetics who subsist on alms. They may follow the tenets of a particular belief system, such as Hinduism or Jainism, but are more typically regarded as saintly in their own right. The term swami refers to a sadhu ordained in a specific order and is associated particularly with Vedanta. Sadhus and swamis may live either in communities or in solitude; they typically possess little, eschew conventional and modern dress, and have shaven heads or matted, unkempt hair.

safflower, Flowering annual plant (*Carthamus tinctorius*) of the aster family (Asteraceae). Na-

tive to parts of Asia and Africa, it is now widely grown as an oil crop in the U.S., Canada, Australia, Israel, and Turkey. Oil obtained from the seeds, an ingredient of soft margarines, salad oil, and cooking oil, is valued for its high proportion of polyunsaturated fats. Since the oil does not yellow with age, it is also a useful base for varnish and paint. The plant, which grows 1–4 ft (0.3–1.2 m) high, has flowers in red, orange, yellow, or white, which were formerly a source of textile dyes.

Safflower (Carthamus tinctorius)
J.C. Allen and Son

saffron, Golden-coloured, pungent seasoning and dye obtained

from the dried stigmas of flowers of the saffron crocus (*Crocus sativus*), a bulbous perennial of the iris family. Because 1 lb (0.45 kg) of saffron represents 75,000 blossoms, it is the world's most expensive spice. The colour and flavour are essential ingredients for certain Mediterranean and Asian dishes, as well as for special English, Scandinavian, and Balkan baked goods. Since ancient times, saffron has been the offi-

Saffron (Crocus sativus)
Emil Muench/Ostman Agency

cial colour for the robes of Buddhist priests and for royal garments in several cultures. Greeks and Romans scattered saffron as a perfume in halls, courts, theatres, and baths.

saga, Genre of prose narrative typically dealing with prominent figures and events of the heroic age in Norway and Iceland, especially as recorded in Icelandic manuscripts of the late 12th and 13th century. Once thought to be orally transmitted history that had finally been written down, sagas are now usually regarded as reconstructions of the past, imaginative in varying degrees and created according to aesthetic principles. Important ideals in sagas are heroism and loyalty; revenge often plays a part. Action is preferred to reflection, and description of the inner motives and point of view of protagonists is minimized. Subdivisions of the genre include kings' sagas, recounting the lives of Scandinavian rulers; legendary sagas, treating themes from myth and legend; and Icelanders' sagas.

Sage (Salvia officinalis)
Ingmar Holmasen

sage, Aromatic perennial herb (*Salvia officinalis*) of the mint family, native to the Mediterra-

nean. Its leaves are used fresh or dried as a flavouring in many foods. The stems, 2 ft (60 cm) tall, have rough or wrinkled, downy, gray-green or whitish green oval leaves. The flowers may be purple, pink, white, or red. Since the Middle Ages, sage tea has been brewed as a spring tonic and a stimulant believed to strengthen the memory and promote wisdom.

Sagittarius (Latin: "Archer"), In astronomy, the constellation lying between Capricorn and Scorpio; in astrology, the ninth sign of the zodiac, governing approximately the period November 22–December 21. Its symbol is either a centaur shooting a bow and arrow or an arrow drawn across a bow. The association of this constellation with a mounted archer originated in Babylonia as early as the 11th century BC.

Sagittarius A, Strongest source of cosmic radio waves, lying in the direction of the constellation Sagittarius. It was discovered by Karl Jansky in 1932 and has been identified as the nucleus of the Milky Way Galaxy. The region is relatively small and constitutes an intense source of infrared radiation, thought to be emitted partly by stars and partly by the dust around them. Within the region is a much smaller radio source, Sagittarius (Sgr) A*, which appears to mark the centre of the Galaxy. Observations indicate that the galactic nucleus contains a black hole with a mass 4,310,000 times that of the Sun; they also provide a strong case that Sgr A* is that black hole. The activity at the Galaxy's centre resembles that of an active galactic nucleus but on a much smaller scale.

saguaro, Large, candelabra-shaped, branched cactus (*Carnegiea gigantea*) native to Mexico, Arizona, and California. Slow-growing at first, mature saguaros may eventually reach 50 ft (15 m) in height. They bloom for the first time when 50–75 years old. They may die at 150–200 years (at a weight of up to 10 tons, or 9,000 kg), most commonly by being uprooted by wind or washouts. Shallow, wide-ranging roots gather moisture from a large area of desert to support the weighty top growth. The white, night-blooming flowers, which remain open into the next day, are the Arizona state flower. The red fruits have been an important food of American Indians.

Sahara, Largest desert in the world, encompassing almost all of northern Africa. Covering an area of about 3.3 million sq mi (8.6 million sq km), it is bounded by the Atlantic Ocean, the Atlas Mountains, the Mediterranean Sea, the Red Sea, and the Sahel region. It includes portions of several countries, including Morocco, Algeria, Tunisia, Libya, Egypt, Mauritania, Mali, Niger, Chad, and The Sudan. Principal topographic features include large oasis depressions, extensive stony plains, rock-strewn plateaus, abrupt mountains, sand sheets and dunes, and sand seas. Huge areas of it are uninhabited, but scattered clusters of people survive in fragile ecological balance wherever water sources occur. Sedentary living is restricted to oasis areas..

Saichō, or DENGYŌ DAISHI (b. 767, Ōmi province, Japan—d. 822, Hiei-zan), Monk who established the Tendai (Chinese Tiantai) sect of Buddhism in Japan. Ordained at age 13, he studied in China and returned with the teachings of Tendai Buddhism, which embraced the *Lotus Sutra*. Unlike other Buddhist sects in Japan, it asserted that the material world could hold meaning and value and that the teachings of the Buddha are accessible to all, not just a select few. Saichō enjoyed favour with the government but often incurred the enmity of the leaders of other Japanese Buddhist sects. The monastery he built on Mount Hiei became one of the great centres of Buddhist learning.

sailing, or YACHTING, Sport or pastime of racing or cruising a sailboat or yacht. A modern yacht (from a Dutch word meaning "ship for chasing") is a sailboat used for racing. In the 17th century Dutch royalty sailed early yachts for pleasure; Charles II brought the sport to England. Organized yacht racing on the Thames began in the mid-18th century. In North America yachting began with the Dutch in New York in the 17th century. The first U.S. yacht clubs were founded in the mid-19th century. Sailboat races are held over two kinds of courses, point-to-point and closed. Yacht racing has been part of the Olympic Games since 1900. The America's Cup is the preeminent prize in yachting.

saint, Holy person. In the New Testament, St. Paul used the term to mean a member of the Christian community, but the term more commonly refers to those noted for their holiness and venerated during their lifetimes or after death. In Roman Catholicism and Eastern Orthodoxy, saints are publicly recognized by the church and are considered intercessors with God for the living. They are honoured on special feast days, and their remains and personal effects are venerated as relics. Often Christian saints perform miracles in their lifetime, or miracles occur in their names after their death. In Islam, *wali* ("friend of God") is often translated as "saint"; in Buddhism, arhats and bodhisattvas are roughly equivalent to saints. Hindu sadhus are somewhat similar.

Saint George's, Town (pop., 2004 est.: 4,300), capital of Grenada, in the West Indies. It lies on the island's southwestern coast, on a small peninsula. It was founded by the French in 1650 and became the capital of the Windward Islands (1885–1958). Now a port, it exports cacao, nutmeg, mace, and bananas. It was the scene of fighting in 1983 during the military intervention in Grenada by U.S. and Caribbean forces.

Saint Gotthard Pass, Mountain pass, Lepontine Alps, southern Switzerland. An important route between central Europe and Italy, the pass lies at an elevation of 6,916 ft (2,108 m) and is 16 mi (26 km) long. Though the pass was known to the Romans, it was not generally used until the early 13th century. A long, winding motorway leads across the pass, and rail and road tunnels extend for more than 9 mi (14 km) beneath it. The drilling of a 35-mile (57-km) railway tunnel running well below the existing St. Gotthard tunnels was completed in 2010.

Saint John's, City (pop., 2011 prelim.: 21,475), capital of Antigua and Barbuda, West Indies. It lies on Antigua's northwestern coast. It is a resort and the island's main port, handling sugar, cotton, machinery, and lumber. Nearby Fort St. John's was damaged over the centuries (1690–1847) by earthquakes, fire, and a hurricane.

Saint-John's-wort, Common name for plants in the family Hypericaceae, which contains 560 species of herbs or low shrubs in eight genera. The family is sometimes considered part of the family Guttiferae. The majority of species (about 370) belong to the genus *Hypericum*. Their leaves are opposite or whorled, dotted with glands, and usually have smooth margins. Several species are cultivated in temperate regions for their handsome flowers. *H. perforatum*, a showy golden flower grown in both the Old and New Worlds whose buds contain a red oil, has long been credited with magical and medicinal powers; today it is being widely used and studied for its possible efficacy against depression.

Saint Kitts and Nevis, officially FEDERATION OF SAINT KITTS AND NEVIS, Island country, Leeward Islands, in the eastern Caribbean Sea. Area: 104 sq mi (269 sq km). Population: (2011 est.) 50,300. Capital: Basseterre (on Saint Kitts). Most of the population is of African descent. Language: English (official). Religions: Christianity (predominantly Protestant; also Roman Catholic); also Hinduism. Currency: Eastern Caribbean dollar. The islands—Saint Kitts and Nevis—are of volcanic origin, with mountain ranges rising to 3,792 ft (1,156 m). The climate is tropical, and heavy vegetation covers most of the mountainous interior. The economy is based on agriculture; sugar has long been the mainstay, and tourism is also important. Saint Kitts and Nevis is a constitutional monarchy with one legislative house; its head of state is the British monarch, represented by the governor-general, and the head of government is the prime minister. Saint Kitts became

the first British colony in the West Indies in 1623. Anglo-French rivalry grew in the 17th century and lasted more than a century. In 1783, by the Treaty of Versailles, the islands became wholly British possessions. They were united with Anguilla from 1882 to 1980 but became an independent federation within the British Commonwealth in 1983.

Saint Lucia, Island country, Windward Islands, in the eastern Caribbean Sea. Area: 238 sq mi (617 sq km). Population: (2011 est.) 167,000. Capital: Castries. Most of the population is of African descent. Languages: English (official), French patois. Religions: Christianity (Roman Catholic, Protestant); also Rastafarianism. Currency: Eastern Caribbean dollar. Saint Lucia is of volcanic origin; within the Qualibou Caldera is Sulphur Springs, which continues to emit steam and gases and is a prime tourist attraction. Wooded mountains run north-south, culminating in Mount Gimie (3,145 ft [958.6 m]). The economy is based on agriculture and tourism. Saint Lucia is a constitutional monarchy with a parliament of two legislative houses; its head of state is the British monarch, represented by the governor-general, and the head of government is the prime minister. Caribs replaced early Arawak inhabitants *c.* 800–1300. Settled by the French in 1650, Saint Lucia was ceded to Great Britain in 1814 and became one of the Windward Islands in 1871. It became fully independent in 1979.

Saint Martin, Dutch SINT MAARTEN, Island, Leeward Islands, eastern West Indies. It is located in the northeastern Caribbean Sea northwest of Saint Kitts and Nevis and covers an area of 34 sq mi (88 sq km). Saint Martin was reached by Christopher Columbus in 1493 and was divided in 1648 between the French and the Dutch. The northern section of the island, Saint-Martin, was formerly a dependency of the French overseas department of Guadeloupe but attained separate status as an overseas collectivity of France in 2007; its chief town is Marigot. The island's southern section, Sint Maarten, was administered collectively with five other Dutch dependencies in the West Indies from 1845. From 1954 until its dissolution in 2010 this group was organized as the Federation of the Netherlands Antilles. After the breakup of the federation, Sint Maarten became an autonomous state within the Kingdom of the Netherlands; its capital and main town is Philipsburg. The island's economy is based on tourism.

Saint Paul's Cathedral, Cathedral of the Church of England in London. The present building is a domed church of great openness designed in a restrained style that combines elements of Neoclassical, Gothic, and Baroque architecture. It was designed by Christopher Wren and constructed (1675–1710) of Portland stone. The building replaced Old St. Paul's, destroyed in the Great Fire of 1666. The interior is characterized by ironwork and woodcarving by master craftsworkers. The majestic dome, set on a colonnaded drum, rises 365 ft (111 m). The superbly detailed cathedral that Wren built bears only a slight resemblance to the Classical-Gothic design that had been accepted; why this is so remains a mystery.

Saint Peter's Basilica, Present church of St. Peter's in Rome, begun by Pope Julius II in 1506 and completed in 1615. It is the church of the popes and one of the world's largest churches. It was built to replace Old St. Peter's, erected by Constantine over Peter's traditional burial place. According to the original plan of Donato Bramante, it was to take the form of a Greek cross around a central dome. Successive architects, including Raphael, drew fresh plans after Bramante's death, modifying the original Greek-cross plan to a Latin cross. Antonio da Sangallo the Younger returned to Bramante's symmetrical plan. Michelangelo, who followed Sangallo, nearly completed the drum for the massive dome before his death. Pope Paul V (r. 1605–21) then insisted on a longitudinal plan for liturgical reasons and adopted the plan of Carlo Maderno (1556–1629), which extended the nave to the east. Gian Lorenzo Bernini added the elliptical piazza, lined by colonnades, that serves as the approach to the basilica. The interior is filled with

Renaissance and Baroque masterpieces, including Michelangelo's *Pietà*, Bernini's baldachin, a statue of St. Longinus, the tomb of Urban VIII, and a bronze throne of St. Peter.

Saint Petersburg, Russian SANKT-PETERBURG, formerly (1914–24) PETROGRAD, or (1924–91) LENINGRAD, City (pop., 2006 est.: 4,580,620) and port, northwestern Russia. Located on the delta of the Neva River where it enters the Gulf of Finland, it is Russia's second largest city after Moscow. Founded by Peter I (the Great) in 1703, it was the capital of the Russian Empire from 1712 to 1917. It was the scene of the Decembrist revolt in 1825 and the Bloody Sunday attack on workers in the Russian Revolution of 1905. The original centre of the Bolshevik revolution, it lost its capital status to Moscow in 1918. In World War II it underwent a siege by German forces (September 1941–January 1944), during which hundreds of thousands of people died. From 1990 a reformist city council and mayor helped swing the country from the control of the Communist Party of the Soviet Union. St. Petersburg is a cultural, educational, and industrial centre and Russia's largest seaport. Industries include engineering, printing, manufacturing, and shipbuilding. One of Europe's most beautiful cities, it is strewn with canals and several hundred bridges; its many palaces, cathedrals, museums (including the Hermitage), and historical monuments were designated a UNESCO World Heritage site in 1990.

Saint-Pierre and Miquelon, French overseas territorial collectivity (pop., 2006 est.: 6,125). It consists of an archipelago in the Atlantic Ocean off the southern coast of Newfoundland, Can. The largest island, Miquelon, has an area of 83 sq mi (215 sq km). Saint-Pierre, with an area of 10 sq mi (26 sq km), is the administrative and commercial centre; almost 90% of the population live there. First settled by seafarers from western France early in the 17th century, the islands changed hands several times between France and Britain until an 1814 treaty made French possession final. They were classified as a French territory in 1946, a department in 1976, and a territorial collectivity in 1985. The economy is based on fishing.

Saint Vincent and the Grenadines, Island country, Windward Islands, in the eastern Caribbean Sea. It is composed of Saint Vincent island and the northern Grenadines. Area: 150.3 sq mi (389.3 sq km). Population: (2011 est.) 101,000. Capital: Kingstown. Most of the population is of African descent. Language: English (official). Religions: Christianity (mostly Protestant; also other Christians, Roman Catholic); also Hinduism, Islam. Currency: Eastern Caribbean dollar. The islands are composed of volcanic rock. Thickly wooded volcanic mountains run north-south and are cut by many swift streams. Soufrière (4,048 ft [1,234 m]), the highest of the mountains, has had devastating volcanic eruptions. Agriculture is the mainstay of the economy, and export crops include bananas and arrowroot. Tourism is also important. The country is a constitutional monarchy with one legislative house; its head of state is the British monarch, represented by the governor-general, and the head of government is the prime minister. The French and the British contested for control of Saint Vincent until 1763, when it was ceded to England by the Treaty of Paris. The original inhabitants, the Caribs, recognized British sovereignty but revolted in 1795. Most of the Caribs were deported; many who remained were killed in volcanic eruptions in 1812 and 1902. In 1969 Saint Vincent became a self-governing state in association with the United Kingdom, and in 1979 it achieved full independence.

Sakharov, Andrey (Dmitriyevich) (b. May 21, 1921, Moscow, Russia—d. Dec. 14, 1989, Moscow), Russian nuclear physicist and human rights advocate. He worked with I.Y. Tamm (1895–1971) to develop the Soviet Union's first hydrogen bomb, but in 1961 he opposed Nikita Khrushchev's plan to test a 100-megaton hydrogen bomb in the atmosphere. In 1968 he published in the West "Progress, Coexistence, and Intellectual Freedom," which called for nuclear arms reduction and criticized Soviet repression of dissidents. He and his wife, Yelena G. Bonner, continued to advocate civil liberties and reform in the Soviet Union. In 1975 Sakharov received the Nobel Prize for Peace but was forbidden to travel to Oslo to receive it. In 1980 he was exiled to the closed city Gorky (now Nizhny Novgorod); his wife was exiled there in 1984. They were released in 1986 and returned to Moscow. Elected to the Congress of People's Deputies in April 1989, Sakharov had his honours restored and saw many of the causes for which he had fought and suffered become official policy under Mikhail Gorbachev.

Saladin, byname of ṢALĀḤ AL-DĪN YŪSUF IBN AYYŪB (b. 1137/38, Tikrīt, Mesopotamia—d. March 4, 1193, Damascus, Syria), Kurdish sultan of Egypt, Syria, Yemen, and Palestine and founder of the Ayyūbid dynasty. Though as a youth he preferred religious to military studies, he began his military career under his uncle, a military commander of the Zangid dynasty. On his uncle's death, Saladin became vizier of the Fāṭimid dynasty of Egypt. In 1171 he abolished the Shīʿite Fāṭimid caliphate and announced a return to Sunnite Islam in Egypt. From 1174, as sultan of Egypt and Syria, he succeeded in uniting Egypt, Syria, northern Mesopotamia, and Palestine. His reputation as a generous and virtuous but firm ruler rekindled Muslim resistance to the Crusades. In 1187, turning his full strength against the Latin Crusader states, he captured Jerusalem, which had been in Christian hands for 88 years. Whereas the Christian conquest had been marked by slaughter, Saladin's troops demonstrated courteous and civilized behaviour. His victory deeply shocked the West and led to the call for the Third Crusade (1189–92), which matched him against Richard I (the Lionheart); their stalemate resulted in a peace that gave the Crusaders only a small strip of land from Tyre to Yafo (Jaffa). Many Muslims consider Saladin the paradigm of the pious and virtuous ruler.

sales tax, Levy imposed on the sale of goods and services. A sales tax on the manufacture, purchase, sale, or consumption of a specific commodity is known as an excise tax. Though excise taxes have been used since ancient times, the general sales tax is a comparatively recent innovation. Sales taxes are ad valorem taxes, imposed "according to the value" (i.e., monetary value) of the taxable commodity. They are classified according to the levels of business activity at which they are imposed—production, wholesale, or retail. They account for significant portions of the revenue of most U.S. states and Canadian provinces. A variation of the sales tax, the value-added tax, became popular in western European countries and is widely used. Most sales taxes are borne by the consumer, since even where they are levied on production or wholesale goods, part or all of the cost is shifted to the consumer in the form of higher prices. Because the retail sales tax is considered a regressive tax, essential goods such as food, clothing, or drugs are sometimes exempted or taxed at a lower level.

salmon, Name that originally referred to the Atlantic salmon (*Salmo salar*) and now also refers to six species of Pacific salmon (genus *Oncorhynchus*, family Salmonidae): chum, chinook, pink, and sockeye salmon; coho; and the cherry salmon (*O. masu*) of Japan. Adult salmon live at sea, then migrate, fighting rapids and leaping high falls, to the stream where they hatched to spawn. Pacific salmon die soon after spawning; many Atlantic salmon live to spawn again.

salmonella, Any of the rod-shaped, gram-negative, non-oxygen-requiring bacteria that make up the genus *Salmonella*. Their main habitat is the intestinal tract of humans and other animals. Some of the 2,200 species exist in animals without causing disease; others are serious pathogens. Any of a wide range of mild to serious infections caused by salmonellae are called salmonellosis, including typhoid and paratyphoid fever in humans. Refrigeration prevents their reproduction but does not kill them; as a result, many salmonellae can develop in foods, which, when eaten, can cause gastroenteritis. Chickens are major reservoirs of salmonella, and chicken and eggs are the principal source of human poisoning, whose symptoms include diarrhea, vomiting, chills, and painful headaches. Other food sources include unpasteurized milk, ground meat, and fish.

salmonellosis, Any of several bacterial infections caused by salmonella, including typhoid and similar fevers and gastroenteritis. Meat from diseased animals carries the bacteria, and any food can pick it up from infected feces in the field or during storage or from contaminated food or utensils during food preparation. The source is often hard to trace. Eggs from infected hens can carry it within, not just on the shells. Onset is sudden and sometimes severe, with nausea, vomiting, diarrhea, fatigue, and low fever. Most patients recover within days, with some degree of immunity. Prevention requires care in food handling, especially thorough cooking.

salsa (Spanish: "sauce"), Contemporary Latin American dance music. Salsa developed in Cuba in the 1940s. It drew upon local musical styles, such as *charanga* (featuring primarily strings and flute) and the dance music of the *conjuntos* (bands), and blended them with elements of jazz. In the 1950s salsa began to flourish in New York City, where it incorporated traditional Puerto Rican rhythms, and later, elements from Venezuelan and Colombian music and rhythm and blues. Its stars have included Celia Cruz, Tito Puente, and Willie Colon.

salt, Chemical compound formed when the hydrogen of an acid is replaced by a metal or its equivalent, such as ammonium (NH_4). Typically, an acid and a base react to form a salt and water. Most inorganic salts ionize in water solution. Sodium chloride—common table salt—is the most familiar salt; sodium bicarbonate (bicarbonate of soda), silver nitrate, and calcium carbonate are others.

Salvador, or BAHIA, City (pop., 2002 est.: 2,519,500), port, and capital of Bahia state, northeastern Brazil. Located at the southern tip of a peninsula that separates All Saints Bay from the Atlantic Ocean, it is one of Brazil's oldest cities, founded in 1549 as the Portuguese colonial capital. At the centre of the sugar trade along the bay, it became a prize for privateers, and the Dutch captured it briefly in 1624. Retaken by the Portuguese, it became a major centre for the African slave trade. It has grown continuously since 1940, and its port is one of the country's finest. Important industries include food and tobacco processing, ceramics, and shipbuilding.

salvation, In religion, deliverance from fundamentally negative conditions, such as suffering, evil, death, or samsara, or the restoration or elevation of the natural world to a higher, better state. Eastern religions tend to stress self-help through individual discipline and practice, sometimes over the course of many lifetimes, though in Mahayana Buddhism bodhisattvas and certain buddhas may act as intervening divine agents. In Christianity, Jesus is the source of salvation and faith in his saving power is stressed. Islam emphasizes submission to God. Judaism posits collective salvation for the people of Israel.

Salvation Army, International Christian charitable movement. It was founded in 1865 by William Booth, with the aim of feeding and housing the poor of London. He adopted the name Salvation Army in 1878 and established the organization on a military pattern. Members are called soldiers, and officers earn ranks that range from lieutenant to brigadier. Converts are required to sign Articles of War and to volunteer their services. Doctrines are similar to those of other evangelical Protestant denominations, though Booth saw no need for sacraments. The meetings are characterized by singing and hand clapping, instrumental music, personal testimony, free prayer, and an open invitation to repentance. Headquartered in London, the Salvation Army now provides a wide variety of social services in more than 100 countries.

Salween River, Chinese NU JIANG, River, Southeast Asia. Rising in eastern Tibet, it flows generally south for about 1,500 mi (2,400 km) through Yunnan province, China, and eastern Myanmar (Burma), emptying into the Gulf of Martaban of the Andaman Sea at Moulmein. In its lower course, it forms the frontier between Myanmar and Thailand for about 80 mi (130 km). It is the longest river in Myanmar and is navigable by small craft in certain sections, but dangerous rapids hinder its use as a major waterway.

Salyut, Any of a series of seven Soviet space stations (of two designs) placed into Earth orbit in the 1970s and early '80s that served as living quarters and scientific laboratories or military reconnaissance platforms. Manned Soyuz spacecraft and robotic Progress cargo ferries routinely rendezvoused and docked with the Salyuts to transfer cosmonauts and supplies. Salyut 1 (launched 1971) was the world's first space station; after staying aboard 23 days, the inaugural crew died while returning to Earth. Salyut 6 (1977), the first with an improved design, was a highly successful scientific station that hosted a series of international visitors. Salyut 7 (1982) was succeeded by Mir.

Salzburg, ancient JUVAVUM, City (pop., 2001: city, 142,662; urban agglom., 210,276), north-central Austria. Located on the Salzach River, it began as a Celtic settlement and later became the site of a Roman town. It was made a bishopric by St. Boniface in 739 and was raised to an archbishopric in 798. Its archbishops became princes of the Holy Roman Empire in 1278; Salzburg became the seat of their powerful ecclesiastical principality. A music centre for centuries, it is the birthplace of Wolfgang Amadeus Mozart; the annual Salzburg Festival is held there. Notable buildings include Renaissance and Baroque houses, archiepiscopal palaces, and a 17th-century cathedral.

samadhi, State of intense concentration or absorption of consciousness, the product of meditation. In Hinduism, it is achieved through Yoga, in which the consciousness is absorbed in the object of meditation. In Buddhism, samadhi is the result of mind-development as distinct from insight-development, and is attainable by non-Buddhists as well as Buddhists. In Zen Buddhism, samadhi allows the meditator to overcome dualistic subject-object awareness through unity with the object of meditation.

Samara, formerly (1935–91) KUYBYSHEV, City (pop., 2002: 1,158,100) and river port, western Russia. Located on the left bank of the Volga River at its confluence with the Samara River, it was founded in 1586 as a fortress protecting the Volga trade route. It was the scene of the rebellion of Yemelyan Pugachov against Catherine II in 1773–74. Samara later became a major trade centre. Its growth was stimulated during World War II by the relocation there of numerous government functions when Moscow was threatened by German attack. It is highly industrialized and is the centre of a network of pipelines. Oil and petrochemicals are the major industries.

Samaritan, Member of a now nearly extinct Jewish community. Calling themselves Bene-Yisrael ("Children of Israel") or Shamerim ("Observant Ones"), they claim to be related to those Jews of ancient Samaria who were not deported from Israel by the Assyrians in 722 BC. The Pentateuch (first five books of the Bible) is their sole norm of religious observance. Jews who returned to their homeland after the Babylonian Exile would not accept their help in building the Second Temple of Jerusalem. Consequently, in the 4th century BC the Samaritans built their own temple in Nāblus, at the base of Mount Gerizim, in the present-day West Bank. The modern population (about 500 persons) is distributed between Nāblus and the city of Ḥolon in Israel. All live in semi-isolation, marrying only within their own community. They pray in Hebrew but have adopted Arabic as their vernacular.

Samarkand, or SAMARQAND, City (pop., 2007 est.: 312,863), east-central Uzbekistan. One of the oldest cities in Central Asia, it was known as Maracanda in the 4th century BC and was captured by Alexander the Great in 329. From the 6th century AD it was ruled by various Turkish, Arab, and Persian groups and was an important point on the Silk Road from China to Europe until its destruction by Genghis Khan in 1220. It became the capital of the empire of Timur (Tamerlane) *c.* 1370; he made it the most important economic and cultural centre in the region. The old city contains many fine examples of Central Asian architecture, some dating to the 14th century; this area was designated a UNESCO World Heritage site in 2001. It became a provincial capital of the Russian Empire in 1887, and it grew considerably during the Soviet period.

samba, Ballroom dance of Brazilian origin, popularized in the U.S. and Europe in the 1940s. Danced to music in ⁴/₄ time with a syncopated rhythm, the dance is characterized by simple forward and backward steps and tilting, rocking body movements. In Brazil an older African type of samba is also danced in circles or double lines as a group dance. For decades the samba has dominated Brazilian popular music.

Sami, or LAPP, Any of the descendants of ancient nomadic peoples who inhabited northern Scandinavia. They may be Paleo-Siberian or alpine peoples from central Europe. Reindeer hunting was the basis of their life from earliest times; herding was the basis of their economy until recently. They became nomadic a few centuries ago. The three Sami languages, mutually unintelligible, are sometimes considered dialects of one language of the Finno-Ugric branch of the Uralic family. They number about 70,000.

Samkhya, One of the six orthodox systems (darshans) of Indian philosophy. It adopts a consistent dualism between matter and soul, which are sufficient to account for the existence of the universe; it does not hypothesize the existence of a god. Samkhya also makes a thoroughgoing distinction between psychological and physical functions on the one hand and pure "personhood" on the other.

Samoa, officially INDEPENDENT STATE OF SAMOA, formerly WESTERN SAMOA, Island country, central South Pacific Ocean, among the westernmost of the island nations of Polynesia. Area: 1,075 sq mi (2,785 sq km). Population: (2011 est.) 184,000. Capital: Apia, on Upolu Island. The people are mainly Polynesian, closely akin to Tongans and to New Zealand's Maori. Languages: Samoan, English (both official). Religion: Christianity (mostly Protestant; also Roman Catholic, other Christians). Currency: tala. Samoa is part of the Samoan archipelago and consists of two major islands, Upolu and Savai'i, both of which are volcanic. There are also seven small islands, two of which, Apolima and Manono, are inhabited. Samoa has a developing economy based mainly on agriculture, with some light manufacturing, fishing, lumbering, and tourism. It is a constitutional monarchy with one legislative house, the Legislative Assembly; the head of state is elected by the Legislative Assembly, and the head of government is the prime minister. Polynesians inhabited the islands for thousands of years before Europeans arrived there in the 18th century. The islands were contested by the U.S., Britain, and Germany until 1899, when they were divided between the U.S. and Germany. In 1914 Western Samoa was occupied by New Zealand, which received it as a League of Nations mandate in 1920. After World War II it became a UN trust territory administered by New Zealand. It achieved independence in 1962. In 1997 the word Western was dropped from the country's name.

samsara, In Buddhism and Hinduism, the endless round of birth, death, and rebirth to which all conditioned beings are subject. Samsara is conceived as having no perceptible beginning or end. The particulars of an individual's wanderings in samsara are determined by karma. In Hinduism, moksha is release from samsara. In Buddhism, samsara is transcended by the attainment of nirvana.

The range of samsara stretches from the lowliest insect (sometimes the vegetable and mineral kingdoms are included) to Brahma, the highest of the gods.

samskara, In Hinduism, any of the personal sacraments traditionally observed at every stage of life, from the moment of conception to the scattering of one's funeral ashes. The observance of the samskaras is based on custom and on such texts as the Puranas, and differs considerably according to region, caste, or family. The most generally accepted list of 16 traditional samskaras includes ceremonies for conception, a male birth, name-giving, the upanayana, and marriage. There is also a body of noncanonical samskaras performed by and for the benefit of women.

samurai, Member of the Japanese warrior class. In early Japanese history, culture was associated with the imperial court, and warriors were accorded low status. The samurai became important with the rise in private estates (*shōen*), which needed military protection. Their power increased, and when Minamoto Yoritomo became the first shogun (military ruler) of the Kamakura period (1192–1333), they became the ruling class. They came to be characterized by the ethic of *bushidō*, which stressed discipline, stoicism, and service. Samurai culture developed further under the Ashikaga shoguns of the Muromachi period (1338–1573). During the long interval of peace of the Tokugawa period (1603–1867), they were largely transformed into civil bureaucrats. As government employees, they received a stipend that was worth less and less in the flourishing merchant economy of the 18th–19th centuries in Edo (Tokyo) and Ōsaka. By the mid-19th century, lower-ranking samurai, eager for societal change and anxious to create a strong Japan in the face of Western encroachment, overthrew the shogunal government in the Meiji Restoration of 1868. Feudal distinctions were abolished in 1871. Some samurai rebelled, but most threw themselves into the task of modernizing Japan.

San Andreas Fault, Zone of transform faults at the boundary between two tectonic plates in the western U.S. The fault runs along the coast of northern California for more than 800 mi (1,300 km) and passes seaward in the vicinity of San Francisco. Movement along the fault is characterized by frequent earthquakes, including the major San Francisco quake of 1906, when parts of the fault line moved as much as 21 ft (6.4 m); the less serious earthquake of 1989; and a destructive quake centred in the Los Angeles suburb of Northridge in 1994.

San Francisco, City (pop., 2010: 805,235) and port, northern California, U.S. San Francisco lies on the northern end of a peninsula between the Pacific Ocean and San Francisco Bay. The Golden Gate Bridge spans the strait to the north that separates San Francisco from Marin county. Founded in the 18th century by the Spanish, it came under Mexican control after Mexican independence in 1821. Occupied by U.S. forces in 1846, it grew rapidly after the discovery of gold in nearby areas. San Francisco suffered extensive damage from the earthquake and fire of 1906 and from an earthquake in 1989. The city was prominent in the American cultural revolution of the 1960s. It is a commercial, cultural, educational, and financial centre and one of the country's most cosmopolitan cities.

San Francisco Bay, Large, nearly landlocked bay indenting west-central California, U.S. A drowned river valley paralleling the coastline, it is connected with the Pacific Ocean by the Golden Gate Strait, which is spanned by the Golden Gate Bridge. The bay is one of the world's finest natural harbours. Treasure, Yerba Buena, Angel, and Alcatraz islands are there; the cities of San Francisco, Oakland, and Berkeley are nearby.

San José, City (pop., 2000: 309,672), capital of Costa Rica. Founded *c.* 1736 as Villa Nueva in a broad, fertile valley about 3,800 ft (1,160 m) above sea level, it developed slowly as a tobacco centre in the Spanish colonial era. In 1823 it became the capital and in the 1840s the centre of coffee production, which remained the chief source of the country's income through the 19th century. The political, social, and economic centre of Costa Rica, it grew rapidly throughout the 20th century in both population and area.

San Juan, City (pop., 2000: metro. area, 421,958), seaport, and capital of Puerto Rico. It was visited in 1508 by Juan Ponce de León and founded in the early 16th century by the Spanish. It became heavily fortified and was a starting point for expeditions to unknown parts of the New World. Several times it was attacked by the British, including Francis Drake in 1595. In 1898, during the Spanish-American War, San Juan fell to the U.S. The city expanded rapidly in the 20th century and is one of the major ports and tourist resorts of the West Indies. Industries include petroleum and sugar refining, brewing, and distilling. San Juan is the commonwealth's financial capital and many U.S. banks and corporations maintain offices there. El Morro and San Cristóbal fortifications are among the city's historic remnants.

San Marino, officially REPUBLIC OF SAN MARINO, alternate long-form name MOST SERENE REPUBLIC OF SAN MARINO, Country, central Italian peninsula, southern Europe. It is located near the Adriatic Sea but is surrounded by Italy. Area: 23.63 sq mi (61.2 sq km). Population: (2011 est.) 32,000. Capital: San Marino. Most of the people are Sammarinesi with a significant minority of Italians. Language: Italian (official). Religion: Christianity (predominantly Roman Catholic). Currency: euro. San Marino has an irregular rectangular form with a maximum length of 8 mi (13 km). It is crossed by streams that flow into the Adriatic Sea and is dominated by Mount Titano (2,424 ft [739 m]), on which the capital, the town of San Marino, is located, surrounded by triple walls. The economy is based on private enterprise and includes tourism, commerce, agriculture, crafts, and fine printing, particularly of postage stamps. San Marino is a unitary multiparty republic with one legislative house; its heads of state and government are two captains-regent. According to tradition, it was founded in the early 4th century by St. Marinus. By the 12th century it had developed into a commune and remained independent despite challenges from neighbouring rulers, including the Malatesta family in nearby Rimini. San Marino survived the Renaissance as a relic of the self-governing Italian city-state and remained an independent republic after the unification of Italy in 1861–70. It is one of the smallest republics in the world and may be the oldest one in Europe. At the beginning of the 21st century, its citizens enjoyed a high standard of living.

San Martín, José de (b. Feb. 25, 1778, Yapeyú, Viceroyalty of Río de la Plata—d. Aug. 17, 1850, Boulogne-sur-Mer, Fr.), National hero of Argentina who helped lead the revolutions against Spanish rule in Argentina (1812), Chile (1818), and Peru (1821). Son of a professional soldier and colonial administrator, he was educated in Spain. Initially he fought loyally for Spain against the Moors (1791), the British (1798), and the Portuguese (1801), but in 1812 he returned to the New World to help the revolutionaries. His greatest campaign was the liberation of Lima, without which the independence of the Argentine provinces could not have been secured. His bold strategy was to lead an army over the Andes, a daunting undertaking. In 1817 he liberated Chile, which he turned over to Bernardo O'Higgins, and proceeded to Peru by ship, where he blockaded the chief port until the royalists withdrew. He then entered Lima and declared the independence of Peru, though he lacked adequate forces to subdue the royalists in the interior. The following year he met with Simón Bolívar; what passed between them is unknown, but San Martín soon afterward went into exile in France, leaving Bolívar to complete the liberation of Peru.

San Salvador, City (pop., 2005 est.: city, 507,700; urban area, 2,232,300), capital of El Salvador. Founded near Suchitoto by the Spanish in 1525, it was moved to its present site in 1528 and declared a city in 1546. It became the capital of the country in 1839.

During the late 1970s it became the focus of violence between the government and left-wing political groups. It is the country's financial, commercial, and industrial centre, producing textiles and clothing, leather goods, and wood products. It is also the site of the University of El Salvador. Devasted by earthquakes in 1854, 1873, 1917, and 1986 and by heavy floods in 1934, it has been reconstructed frequently.

San Stefano, Treaty of (1878) Peace settlement imposed on the Ottoman government by Russia at the end of the Russo-Turkish War. It established an independent Bulgarian principality that included most of Macedonia, realigned other European provinces of the Ottoman Empire, and ceded parts of Asian Turkey to Russia. Opposed by Austria-Hungary and Britain, it was modified at the Congress of Berlin.

Sanaa, Arabic ṢANAʿĀʾ, City (pop., 2004: 1,747,627), capital of Yemen. Located in the western part of the country, it was built on the site of an ancient pre-Islamic stronghold that has been traditionally dated to the 1st or 2nd century BC. Its people converted to Islam in 632. Nominally under Ottoman sovereignty from the mid-16th century, it was effectively controlled from the early 17th century until 1872 by the imams (leaders) of the Zaydī Shīʿite sect. It became the capital of an independent Yemen after the Ottoman defeat in World War I (1914–18). In 1990 it became the capital of the unified country. For many centuries it has been the chief economic, political, and religious centre of the Yemen highlands. The old walled city centre was designated a UNESCO World Heritage site in 1986.

sand, Mineral, rock, or soil particles that are 0.0008–0.08 in. (0.02–2 mm) in diameter. Most rock-forming minerals are found in sand, but quartz is by far the most common. Most sands also contain a small quantity of feldspar, as well as white mica. All sands contain small quantities of heavy rock-forming minerals, including garnet, tourmaline, zircon, rutile, topaz, pyroxenes, and amphiboles. In the pottery and glassmaking industries very pure quartz sands are used as a source of silica. Similar sands are used for lining the hearths of steel furnaces. Molds used in foundries for casting metal are made of sand with a clay binder. Quartz and garnet sands are used extensively as abrasives. Among ordinary sand's many uses, it is a basic ingredient of mortar, cement, and concrete.

Sand, George, orig. AMANDINE-AURORE-LUCILE DUPIN (b. July 1, 1804, Paris, France—d. June 8, 1876, Nohant), French writer. During childhood she gained a love of the countryside that would inform most of her works. Married in 1822, she soon tired of her husband, Casimir Dudevant, and began a series of liaisons; her lovers included Prosper Mérimée, Alfred de Musset, and, most importantly, Frédéric Chopin. She became famous (under her pseudonym) with her novel *Indiana* (1832), a protest against conventions that bind an unhappy wife to her husband. *Lélia* (1833) extended her iconoclastic views on social and class associations. Similar themes, along with her sympathy for the poor, are evident in her finest works, the so-called rustic novels, including *The Devil's Pool* (1846), *The Country Waif* (1848), and *Little Fadette* (1849).

George Sand
Courtesy of the Musée Carnavalet, Paris

sand dune, Hill, mound, or ridge of windblown sand or other loose material such as clay particles. Dunes are commonly associated with desert regions and seacoasts, and there are large areas of dunes in nonglacial parts of Antarctica.

sandalwood, Any semiparasitic plant of the genus *Santalum* (family Santalaceae; the sandalwood family), or its wood, especially the wood of the true, or white, sandalwood, *Santalum album*, which is used in making furniture and from which oil used in making perfumes, soaps, candles, and incense is derived. The approximately 10 species of *Santalum* are distributed throughout South Asia and the islands of the South Pacific. The sandalwood family contains more than 400 species of semiparasitic shrubs, herbs, and trees in about 36 genera, found in tropical and temperate regions. In some genera the leaves are reduced to scalelike structures. The green leaves contain some chlorophyll, which allows the plants to make food, but all sandalwoods are parasites to a certain extent, obtaining water and nutrients from their hosts. Most, including *S. album*, are root parasites, but some are stem parasites.

Sandinista, Any member of Nicaragua's Sandinista National Liberation Front (FSLN). Named for César Augusto Sandino, a hero of Nicaraguan resistance to U.S. occupation (1927–33), the group was founded in 1962 to oppose the Somoza family's dictatorship. They organized support among students, workers, and peasants. From bases in Honduras and Costa Rica, they attacked the Nicaraguan National Guard. They split into factions in the mid-1970s but reunited during the revolution of 1978–79 that finally succeeded in overthrowing Pres. Anastasio Somoza. A junta headed by Daniel Ortega led the Sandinista government (1979–90), which implemented literacy and community health programs. In an effort to topple the government, the U.S. imposed a trade embargo, pressured international lending institutions to withhold aid, and trained and supported the contras. The FSLN lost support over time and was voted out of power in 1990. The party regained prominence in 2006, when Ortega won another term as president.

sandstone, Sedimentary rock formed from sand-sized grains (0.0025–0.08 in., or 0.06–2 mm, in diameter). The spaces between grains may be empty or filled with either a chemical cement of silica or calcium carbonate or a fine-grained matrix of silt and clay particles. The principal mineral constituents of the grain framework are quartz, feldspar, and rock fragments. Sandstones are quarried for use as building stone. Because of their abundance, diversity, and mineralogy, sandstones are also important to geologists as indicators of erosional and depositional processes.

sangha, Buddhist monastic order, traditionally composed of four groups: monks, nuns, laymen, and laywomen. Established by the Buddha, it is the world's oldest body of celibate clerics. Together with the Buddha and the dharma, it makes up the Threefold Refuge, a basic creed of Buddhism. Buddha established the bhiksu sangha for men and later the bhiksuni sangha for women. Members depend on alms from the community, since they are discouraged from engaging in commerce or agriculture. They live according to the Vinaya Pitaka.

Sanhedrin, Jewish council that operated in Roman Palestine from the time of the Maccabees (*c.* 165 BC) to the end of the patriarchate (AD 425). While the term refers to the supreme Jewish court, the Sanhedrin's exact composition and powers—religious, judicial, and legislative—are reported variously in different sources. It is mentioned in various books of the Bible (Mark, Luke, Acts) as having taken part in or adjudicated the trials of Jesus, St. Peter the Apostle, and St. John the Baptist. According to Talmudic sources, the Great Sanhedrin was a court of 71 sages that met on fixed occasions in the Temple of Jerusalem, acting as a religious legislative body, trial court, and administrator of rituals.

sannyasi, In Hinduism, one who renounces all ties with family and society and pursues spiritual liberation. Sannyasis are a class of sadhu that do not live in communities, instead leading a mendicant, itinerant life. Those recognized as having achieved full self-knowledge are considered free of all worldly rules and duties, including those pertaining to caste, and are not required to carry out image worship or offerings. After death, their bodies, rather than being cremated, are buried in a seated, meditative posture.

Sanskrit language, Old Indo-Aryan language, the classical literary language of Hinduism. The most ancient form is Vedic, attested in its earliest form in parts of the Rig Veda, dating from the late 2nd millennium BC. Late Vedic Sanskrit was described and codified in a grammar by Panini, dating from about the 5th century BC. Literary activity in so-called Classical Sanskrit, in many respects similar to the language described by Panini, flourished *c.* 500 BC–*c.* AD 1000. Today Sanskrit (now usually written in the Devanagari script) serves as a learned language and lingua franca for Brahman scholars. It is an archaic Indo-European language with an elaborate system of nominal and verbal inflection.

Santa Cruz, City (pop., 2001: 1,116,059), east-central Bolivia. Founded by Spaniards from Paraguay in 1561 at what is now San José de Chiquitos, it was attacked repeatedly by Indians until 1595. It then was moved to its present location and renamed Santa Cruz de la Sierra. In 1811 its inhabitants declared their independence from Spain. Bolivia's largest city, it is a trade centre for crops, including sugarcane and rice, grown in the surrounding area. It has an oil refinery and is the seat of a university.

Santería, Religious movement that originated in Cuba. It combines West African Yoruba beliefs and practices with elements of Roman Catholicism. It includes belief in one supreme being, but worship and rituals centre on *orisha*s, deities or patron saints (with parallels among the Roman Catholic saints) that combine a force of nature and humanlike characteristics. Practices may include trance dancing, rhythmic drumming, spirit possession, and animal sacrifice. Santería has a considerable following in the U.S., particularly in Florida and in other areas with large African and Hispanic populations.

Santiago, City (pop., 2002 prelim.: 4,630,000), capital of Chile. It is located in central Chile, on the Mapocho River at an elevation of about 1,700 ft (520 m). Founded in 1541 by the Spanish, the city has suffered repeatedly from earthquakes, floods, and civil disorder. It was only slightly damaged during the War of Independence (1810–18) and became the capital of an independent Chile at the war's end. It is the country's economic and cultural centre and principal industrial city, producing textiles, footwear, and foodstuffs. The city boasts a cosmopolitan cultural life and is the home of the University of Chile.

Santiago de Cuba, Seaport city (pop., 2002: 423,392), eastern Cuba. The second largest city in Cuba, it was founded in 1514 and moved to its present site in 1522. It commanded a strategic location on the northern Caribbean Sea in the early colonial period and was the capital of Cuba until 1589. It was a focal point of the Spanish-American War, and in 1898 the entire Spanish fleet was destroyed near its coast. In 1953 it was the scene of Fidel Castro's attack against the Moncada army barracks. It is the centre of an agricultural and mining region and exports copper, iron, manganese, sugar, and fruit.

Santo Domingo, City (pop., 2007 est.: 2,154,000), capital of the Dominican Republic. It is situated on the southeastern coast of the island of Hispaniola, at the mouth of the Ozama River. It was founded in 1496 by Christopher Columbus's brother Bartolomeo as the capital of the first Spanish colony in the New World and is the oldest permanent city established by Europeans in the Western Hemisphere. It was under French control from 1795 to 1809, and it was annexed to Spain in 1861. It became the capital of the

Dominican Republic when the country gained independence from Spain in 1865. The city was renamed Ciudad Trujillo in 1936 for Pres. Rafael Trujillo, but it reverted to its original name after his assassination in 1961. It is the commercial and cultural centre of the republic and its principal seaport. Important industries include metallurgy and petrochemicals. It is the reputed site of the tomb of Christopher Columbus.

São Paulo, City (pop., 2005 est.: city, 10,277,500; metro. area, 19,037,487), capital of São Paulo *estado* (state), southeastern Brazil. It is located 30 mi (50 km) from its Atlantic Ocean port of Santos. Founded by Portuguese Jesuits in 1554, it became a base for exploration in the 17th century and a city in 1711. In 1822 it was the scene of the declaration of Brazilian independence by Emperor Pedro I. It developed rapidly from the late 19th century. It is the foremost industrial centre in Latin America, producing steel, motor vehicles, machine tools, and a wide range of consumer goods, including textiles and appliances. It is also Brazil's largest city, an important cultural and publishing centre, and one of the most populous cities in the world.

São Tomé, City (pop., 2001: 49,957), capital of Sao Tome and Principe. It is on the northeastern coast of the island of São Tomé, located on the Equator in the Gulf of Guinea. It is the country's largest city and its major port.

Sao Tome and Principe, officially DEMOCRATIC REPUBLIC OF SAO TOME AND PRINCIPE, Island country, central Africa. It is situated on the Equator in the Gulf of Guinea, west of the African mainland. Area: 386 sq mi (1,001 sq km). Population: (2011 est.) 169,000. Capital: São Tomé. Most of the people are Forro, a mixture of African and European ancestry, or Angolares, the descendants of former Angolan slaves. Languages: Portuguese (official), Creole. Religion: Christianity (predominantly Roman Catholic; also Protestant). Currency: dobra. The country consists of the two main islands, São Tomé and Príncipe, which are separated by about 90 mi (145 km), and a number of islets. The two main islands each have northeastern lowlands, central volcanic highlands, and swift-flowing streams. The economy, partly government-controlled and partly private, has long depended heavily on international assistance; it is based on agriculture and fishing, although petroleum-related earnings have increased since the late 1990s. The country is a multiparty republic with one legislative house; its head of state is the president, and the head of government is the prime minister. First visited by European navigators in the 1470s, the islands were soon colonized by the Portuguese and were used in the trade and transshipment of slaves. Sugar and cocoa were the main cash crops. The islands became an overseas province of Portugal in 1951, and they achieved independence in 1975. Príncipe became autonomous in 1995.

Saoshyans, In Zoroastrianism and Parsiism, the final saviour of the world. He is the foremost of the three saviours who are posthumous sons of Zoroaster. He is expected to appear at the end of the last millennium of the world, miraculously conceived by a virgin who has swum in a lake where Zoroaster's seed is preserved. He will vanquish demonic power and resurrect the bodies of the dead, bestowing eternal perfection on them after all souls have been cleansed.

sapphire, Transparent to translucent natural or synthetic variety of corundum that is highly prized as a gemstone. Its colour is due mainly to the presence of small amounts of iron and titanium and normally ranges from very pale blue to deep indigo. Colourless, gray, yellow, pale pink, orange, green, violet, and brown varieties also are known as sapphire; red varieties are called ruby. Synthetic sapphire has been produced commercially since 1902. Much is used in jewelry, but most is used in the manufacture of jewel bearings, gauges, dies, and other specialized components; some also is used as a high-grade abrasive. It is found in Sri Lanka, Myanmar, India, and Montana in the U.S.

Sappho (fl. 610–*c*. 570 BC, Lesbos, Asia Minor), Greek lyric poet. Although legends about her abound, little is known of her life. She was born on the island of Lesbos and became the leader of a *thiasos*, an informal female community, whose purpose was the education of young women, especially for marriage. The principal themes of her poetry are personal and reflect the activities and atmosphere of the *thiasos*. Her writing, mostly vernacular and not formally literary, is concise, direct, picturesque, and various. It includes nuptial songs and an expression of her love for other women, which produced the word *lesbian* (from the island's name). Though she was much admired in antiquity, most of her work was lost by the early Middle Ages; only an ode to Aphrodite—28 lines long—is complete.

Sapporo, City (pop., 2003 est.: 1,888,953), Hokkaido, Japan. Located on the Ishikari River, the city was laid out in 1871 with wide, tree-lined streets; it became the prefectural capital in 1886. It is a major commercial centre, with Otaru, on the Sea of Japan (East Sea), as its port. Chief industries are lumbering, printing, publishing, and brewing. A popular centre for skiing and winter sports, it was the site of the 1972 Winter Olympic Games. The annual Snow Festival (in February) features giant sculptures carved from packed snow. It is the site of Hokkaido University (1876).

Sarajevo, City (pop., 2007 est.: 304,065), capital of Bosnia and Herzegovina. After the Turks invaded in the late 15th century, it developed as a trading centre and stronghold of Muslim culture. From 1878 it was part of the Austro-Hungarian Empire. In 1914 Archduke Francis Ferdinand was assassinated by a Serbian nationalist, which precipitated World War I. After Bosnia and Herzegovina declared independence from Yugoslavia in 1992, it became a focal point of fierce civil war as Serb militias drove thousands of Bosnian Muslims from the countryside to take refuge in the city. Its pre-civil-war industries included brewing, furniture and automobile manufacturing, and tobacco processing. It was the host of the 1984 Winter Olympic Games and is the centre of a road network. A rail connection to the Adriatic Sea was damaged during fighting in the 1990s but is now operational. Sarajevo retains a Muslim character, with many mosques and an ancient marketplace.

Saramago, José (b. Nov. 16, 1922, Azinhaga, Port.—d. June 18, 2010, Lanzarote, Canary Islands, Spain), Portuguese novelist. From a poor family, Saramago studied part-time while working in a welder's shop. Later he began working as a journalist and translator. He published his first novel, *Country of Sin*, in 1947. His breakthrough work, *Baltasar and Blimunda* (1982), alternates allegorical fantasy with grimly realistic descriptions of the construction of a convent by thousands of labourers pressed into service. Saramago's later novels, in which magic realism is mixed with outspoken political commentary, include *The Stone Raft* (1986), perhaps his best-known work, and *Blindness* (1995). He received the Nobel Prize for Literature in 1998.

Sardinia, Italian SARDEGNA, Island and autonomous region (pop., 2001 prelim.: 1,599,511), Italy. Off the southern Italian coast, Sardinia is the second largest island in the western Mediterranean Sea. It measures 9,194 sq mi (23,813 sq km); its capital is Cagliari. Thousands of structures made of basalt blocks, called *nuraghi*, are a dominating feature of the island. These truncated conic structures of blocks taken from extinct volcanoes were built in prehistoric times without any mortar. Some date to *c*. 1500–400 BC. Phoenicians were Sardinia's first recorded settlers *c*. 800 BC. Greeks and Carthaginians followed; Roman rule began in 238 BC. In the early Middle Ages Pisa and Genoa struggled over its domination. The kingdom of Sardinia, centred on the lands of Piedmont in northwestern Italy and the island of Sardinia, was ruled by the house of Savoy from 1720 until the unification of Italy in 1861. Agriculture, fishing, and mining are economic mainstays of the island.

Sargon (fl. 23rd century BC), Ancient Mesopotamian ruler (r. 2334–2279 BC). What is known of him comes from legends and tales; his capital city, Agade, has never been located. Perhaps originally a royal cupbearer, he came to prominence by defeating a Sumerian king, thereby attaining an empire in southern Mesopotamia and becoming the first emperor whose native tongue was Akkadian rather than Sumerian. He enlarged the empire from Iraq to Anatolia, and trade flourished with the Indus valley, Oman, the Persian Gulf coast, Cappadocia, and perhaps Greece.

SARS, in full SEVERE ACUTE RESPIRATORY SYNDROME, Highly contagious respiratory illness characterized by a persistent fever, headache, and bodily discomfort, followed by a dry cough that may progress to great difficulty in breathing. SARS appeared in November 2002 in Guangdong province, China, and was brought to Hong Kong in February 2003. As it spread from there to other countries of East Asia and the world, health authorities instituted an unprecedented series of control measures, including quarantines and prohibitions on travel, and in June 2003 the global outbreak was declared to be contained. By that time more than 8,000 cases had been reported, and some 800 people had died. SARS is believed to be caused by a mutant coronavirus, a type usually associated with pneumonia and the common cold. A specific vaccine has not been developed. Treatment is usually restricted to easing the patient's symptoms—providing mechanical ventilation if necessary—until the illness has run its course.

Sartre, Jean-Paul (b. June 21, 1905, Paris, France—d. April 15, 1980, Paris), French philos-

Jean-Paul Sartre, photograph by Gisèle Freund, 1968.
Gisèle Freund

opher, novelist, and playwright, the foremost exponent of existentialism. He studied at the Sorbonne, where he met Simone de Beauvoir, who became his lifelong companion and intellectual collaborator. His first novel, *Nausea* (1938), narrates the feeling of revulsion that a young man experiences when confronted with the contingency of existence. Sartre used the phenomenological method of Edmund Husserl with great skill in three successive publications: *Imagination: A Psychological Critique* (1936), *Sketch for a Theory of the Emotions* (1939), and *The Psychology of Imagination* (1940). In *Being and Nothingness* (1943), he places human consciousness, or nothingness (*néant*), in opposition to being, or thingness (*être*); consciousness is nonmatter and thus escapes all determinism. In his postwar treatise *Existentialism and Humanism* (1946) he depicts this radical freedom as carrying with it a responsibility for the welfare of others. In the 1940s and '50s he wrote many critically acclaimed plays—including *The Flies* (1943), *No Exit* (1946), and *The Condemned of Altona* (1959)—the study *Saint Genet, Actor and Martyr* (1952), and numerous articles for *Les Temps Modernes*, the monthly review that he and de Beauvoir founded and edited. A central figure of the French left after the war, he was an outspoken admirer of the Soviet Union—though not a member of the French Communist Party—until the crushing of the Hungarian uprising by Soviet tanks in 1956, which he condemned. His *Critique of Dialectical Reason* (1960) faults Marxism for failing to adapt itself to the concrete circumstances of particular societies and for not respecting individual freedom. His final works include an autobiography, *The Words* (1963), and *Flaubert* (4 vol., 1971–72), a lengthy study of the author. He declined the 1964 Nobel Prize for Literature.

Sarvastivada, One of the 18 schools of Hinayana Buddhism that developed during the first four or five centuries after the Bud-

dha's death. The name literally means the teaching that everything exists, which relates to the notion that the past, present, and future all exist. The Sarvastivada school was particularly influential in northwestern India and portions of Southeast Asia.

satanism, Worship of Satan, or the devil, the personality or principle regarded in the Judeo-Christian tradition as embodying absolute evil, in complete antithesis to God. Cults associated with satanism have been documented, however sketchily, back to the 17th century. Their central feature is the black mass, a corrupted and inverted rendition of the Christian Eucharist. Practices are said to include animal sacrifice and deviant sexual activity. Worship is motivated by the belief that Satan is more powerful than the forces of good, and so is more capable of bringing about the results sought by his adherents.

satellite, Natural object (moon) or spacecraft (artificial satellite) orbiting a larger astronomical body. Most known natural satellites orbit planets; the Earth's Moon is the most obvious example and was the only one known until the discovery of the Galilean satellites of Jupiter in 1610. All the solar system's planets except Mercury and Venus have moons, which vary greatly in size, composition (from rock to mostly ice), and activity (from cold and inert to volcanic). Some asteroids are also known to have their own moons. The first artificial satellite, Sputnik 1, was launched into orbit around Earth in 1957. Since then, thousands have been sent into orbit around Earth as well as the Moon, Venus, Mars, Jupiter, and other bodies. Artificial satellites are used for scientific research and other purposes, such as communication, weather forecasting, Earth resources management, and military intelligence.

satire, Artistic form in which human or individual vices, folly, abuses, or shortcomings are held up to censure by means of ridicule, derision, burlesque, irony, or other methods, sometimes with an intent to bring about improvement. Literature and drama are its chief vehicles, but it is also found in such mediums as film, the visual arts (e.g., caricatures), and political cartoons. Though present in Greek literature, notably in the works of Aristophanes, satire generally follows the example of either of two Romans, Horace or Juvenal. To Horace the satirist is an urbane man of the world who sees folly everywhere but is moved to gentle laughter rather than to rage. Juvenal's satirist is an upright man who is horrified and angered by corruption. Their different perspectives produced the subgenres of satire identified by John Dryden as comic satire and tragic satire.

satrap, Provincial governor in the Achaemenian empire. Darius I (r. 522–486 BC) established 20 satrapies with an annual tribute. Appointed by the king, satraps were usually of the royal family or Persian nobility and held office indefinitely. They collected taxes, were the highest judicial authority, and were responsible for internal security and for raising and maintaining an army. Controls guarded against the abuse of power, but after the mid 5th century BC, with central authority weakened, satrapies became virtually independent. Alexander the Great and his successors retained the satraps.

saturation, State of an organic compound in which all its carbon atoms are linked by single covalent bonds. Saturation also means the state of a solution or vapour in which it has the highest possible concentration of the dissolved or vaporized material at a given pressure and temperature. Though it is sometimes possible to bring about supersaturation (a concentration exceeding the equilibrium value), such solutions or vapours are unstable and spontaneously revert to the saturated state, accompanied by the transformation of the excess material to the solid or liquid form (precipitation).

Saturn, Roman god of agriculture, equated with the Greek deity Cronus. His wife was Ops, the goddess of plenty, and his children included Juno, Neptune, and Ceres. His festival, Saturnalia (beginning December 17), became the most popular Roman festival; its influence is still felt in the celebration of Christmas and the Western New Year. During Saturnalia, all business transactions were suspended, presents were exchanged, and slaves were given token freedom. The remains of Saturn's temple are located in the Forum in Rome. Saturday is named for Saturn.

Saturn, Sixth planet from the Sun, named for the Roman god of sowing and seed. The second largest nonstellar object in the solar system after Jupiter, it is about 95 times as massive as Earth and has more than 700 times its volume. Saturn's outer layers are gaseous, mainly hydrogen. Models of its interior suggest a rock-and-ice core surrounded by a shallow layer of liquid metallic hydrogen encased by an envelope of molecular hydrogen. Its mean density, about 70% that of water, is the lowest of any known object in the solar system. Saturn has over 60 moons (including Titan, the largest) and an extensive ring system, with several main sections visible from Earth with a telescope. Saturn's rings are made up of countless separate particles ranging mainly from inches to many feet in size but also including dust in some regions. Water ice probably constitutes most of the ring material. Galileo discerned the presence of the rings in 1610, though he mistook them for two other planets, owing to the low resolution of his instrument. Saturn's day is about 10.8 hours; its year is approximately 29.5 Earth years. Its rapid rotation, acting on electric currents in the core, generates a strong magnetic field and large magnetosphere. Saturn's fast spin also makes it the most flattened (oblate) of the planets; its polar diameter of 67,560 mi (108,728 km) is 10% smaller than its equatorial diameter. Its average distance from the Sun is 887 million mi (1.43 billion km).

Saturn, Any of a series of space launch vehicles developed by the U.S. beginning in 1958 for the Apollo Moon-landing program. Saturn I, the first U.S. rocket specifically developed for spaceflight (first fired 1961), was a two-stage vehicle that placed unmanned versions of Apollo spacecraft and other satellites into Earth orbit. An upgraded version, Saturn IB, was used for unmanned and manned Apollo Earth-orbital missions and for ferrying crews to the Skylab space station. The three-stage Saturn V, the largest launch vehicle ever built by the U.S., was used for manned Apollo lunar flights and to launch Skylab.

satyagraha, Philosophy of nonviolent protest, or passive resistance. Mohandas K. Gandhi introduced it in South Africa (1906) and, from 1917, developed it in India in the period leading up to independence from Britain. Satyagraha seeks to conquer through submission. It involves refusing to submit to or cooperate with anything perceived as wrong, while adhering to the principle of nonviolence in order to maintain the tranquillity of mind required for insight and understanding. The principle played a significant role in the U.S. civil rights movement led by Martin Luther King.

Saʿūd dynasty, or ĀL SAʿŪD ("SAʿŪD FAMILY"), Rulers of Saudi Arabia. In the 18th century Muḥammad ibn Saʿūd (d. 1765), chief of an Arabian village that had never fallen under control of the Ottoman Empire, rose to power together with the Wahhābī religious movement. He and his son ʿAbd al-ʿAzīz I (r. 1765–1803) conquered much of Arabia; Saʿūd I (r. 1803–14) conquered the holy cities of Mecca and Medina in the early years of his rule. The Ottoman sultan induced the viceroy of Egypt to crush the Saʿūdīs and Wahhābīs, which was accomplished by 1818. A second Saʿūdī state was formed in 1824 by Muḥammad ibn Saʿūd's grandson Turkī (r. 1823–34), who made Riyadh his capital. When Turkī's son Fayṣal (r. 1834–38; 1843–65) died, succession disputes led to civil war. Power did not return to Saʿūdī hands until 1902, when Ibn Saʿūd recaptured Riyadh. He established the kingdom of Saudi Arabia by royal decree in 1932. A number of his sons later ruled the country, including Abdullah (b. *c.* 1923), who assumed the throne in 2005.

Saudi Arabia, officially KINGDOM OF SAUDI ARABIA, Country, Middle East, southwestern Asia. It occupies four-fifths of the Arabian Peninsula and is bounded by the Red Sea and the Persian Gulf. Area: 830,000 sq mi (2,149,690 sq km). Population: (2011 est.) 28,572,000. Capital: Riyadh. The people are predominantly Arab. Language: Arabic (official). Religion: Islam (official; predominantly Sunni). Currency: Saudi riyal. The country is a plateau region, with bands of imposing highlands rising from the narrow Red Sea coast. More than nine-tenths is desert, including the world's largest continuous sand area, the Rubʿ al-Khali ("Empty Quarter"). The largest petroleum producer of the Organization of Petroleum Exporting Countries (OPEC) and one of the leading oil exporters in the world, Saudi Arabia has reserves that represent one-fourth of the world total. Its other products include natural gas, gypsum, dates, wheat, and desalinated water. It is a monarchy; its head of state and government is the king, assisted by the crown prince. Saudi Arabia is the historical home of Islam. During premodern times, local and foreign rulers fought for control of the region; in 1517 the Ottoman Empire attained nominal control of most of the peninsula. In the 18th–19th century an Islamic reform group known as the Wahhābī joined with the Saʿūd dynasty to take control of most of central Arabia; they suffered political setbacks but regained most of their territory by 1904. The British held Saudi lands as a protectorate (1915–27), after which they acknowledged the sovereignty of the Kingdom of the Hejaz and Nejd. The two kingdoms were unified as the Kingdom of Saudi Arabia in 1932. Since World War II (1939–45), the kingdom's rulers have supported the Palestinian cause in the Middle East and maintained close ties with the U.S. In 2000 Saudi Arabia and Yemen settled a long-standing border dispute.

savings and loan association, Financial institution that accepts savings from depositors and uses those funds primarily to make loans to home buyers. Savings and loan associations (S&Ls) originated with 18th-century British building societies, in which workmen banded together to finance the building of their homes. The first U.S. savings and loan was established in Philadelphia in 1831. S&Ls were initially cooperative institutions in which savers were shareholders in the association and received dividends in proportion to profits, but today are mutual organizations that offer a variety of savings plans. They are not obliged to rely on individual deposits for funds but are permitted to borrow from other financial institutions and to market mortgage-backed securities, money-market certificates, and stock. Because high inflation and rising interest rates in the 1970s made fixed-rate mortgages unprofitable, regulations were altered to permit S&Ls to renegotiate mortgages. In the late 1980s, a growing number of S&Ls failed because inadequate regulation had allowed risky investments and fraud to flourish. The government was obliged to cover vast losses in excess of $200 billion, and the Federal Savings and Loan Insurance Corp. (FSLIC) became insolvent in 1989. Its insurance functions were taken over by a new organization supervised by the Federal Deposit Insurance Corp., and the Resolution Trust Corp. was established to handle the bailout of the failed S&Ls.

Savoy, house of, Historic dynasty of Europe and the ruling house of Italy (1861–1946). Its founder was Umberto I the Whitehanded (d. 1048?), who held the county of Savoy and areas east of the Rhône River and south of Lake Geneva. His medieval successors, including Amadeus VI, added territory in the western Alps where France, Italy, and Switzerland converge. In 1416 the house was raised to ducal status in the Holy Roman Empire, after which it declined until the late 16th century. Although under French domination in the 17th century, the house under Victor Amadeus II acquired territory in northeastern Italy and attained the royal title, first of the kingdom of Sicily (1713), which he exchanged for Sardinia (1720). The house was powerful in the Risorgimento, and under the kings Victor Emmanuel I, Victor Emmanuel II, and Charles Albert it contributed to the 19th-century unification of

Italy. It then lost its prominence, and the monarchs Umberto I and Victor Emmanuel III served mainly as figureheads until the vote for a republic in 1946 ended Savoy rule.

saxophone, Single-reed wind instrument with a conical metal tube and finger keys. Though made of brass, it is classified as a woodwind instrument. Its mouthpiece resembles that of the clarinet. The saxophone family includes instruments with at least eight different ranges, the tenor and alto instruments being the most common. The smallest (highest-range) saxophones are straight; the rest have curved necks and their bells are bent up and out. Transposing instruments (producing a higher or lower pitch than indicated in music written for it) in B-flat and E-flat, all have the same written 3^1/$_2$-octave range. The saxophone was patented in 1846 by Adolphe Sax, who created two separate instrument families, for military and orchestral use respectively. Though few composers included saxophones in their orchestral scores, they became centrally important in military, dance, and jazz bands.

scale, In music, primary pitches of a key or mode arranged within an octave. Scales are distinguished by the pattern of the intervals between adjacent notes. A scale can be seen as an abstraction from melody—that is, the pitches of a melody arranged in stepwise order.

scallop, Any of more than 400 species (family Pectinidae) of marine bivalves found worldwide, from the intertidal zone to deep waters. The two halves of the shell (valves) are usually fan-shaped, except for a winglike projection at either side of the straight hinge. The shells are 1–6 in. (2.5–15 cm) long. They may be smooth or ribbed and red, purple, orange, yellow, or white. Cilia filter microscopic plants and animals from the water and move them toward the mouth. Scallops swim by clapping the valves, propelling themselves forward. The muscle that closes the valves is a popular food item.

Scandinavia, Region of northern Europe, usually defined as comprising Norway, Sweden, and Denmark. It is sometimes used more broadly to include Finland and Iceland. Norway and Sweden occupy the Scandinavian Peninsula, though Denmark is part of the North European Plain. The Scandinavian peoples are linked by cultural similarities, and they speak a closely related group of Germanic languages.

Scandinavian Peninsula, Large promontory, northern Europe. Occupied by Norway and Sweden, it is about 1,150 mi (1,850 km) long, with an area of 290,000 sq mi (750,000 sq km), and it extends south from the Barents Sea. It is largely mountainous; its eastern side slopes gently to the Baltic Sea, while the western side has mountains reaching the coast and is deeply dissected by fjords.

scapegoat, In the Old Testament, a goat that was symbolically burdened with the sins of the people and then killed on Yom Kippur to rid Jerusalem of its iniquities. Similar rituals were held elsewhere in the ancient world to transfer guilt or blame. In ancient Greece, human scapegoats were beaten and driven out of cities to mitigate calamities. In early Roman law, an innocent person was allowed to assume the penalty of another; Christianity reflects this notion in its belief that Jesus died to atone for the sins of mankind.

scarlet fever, or SCARLATINA, Acute infectious disease caused by some types of streptococcus bacteria. Fever, sore throat, headache, and, in children, vomiting are followed in two to three days by a rash. The skin peels in about one-third of cases. After a coating disappears, the tongue is swollen, red, and bumpy (strawberry tongue). Glands are usually swollen. Complications frequently involve the sinuses, ears (sometimes with mastoiditis), and neck. Abscesses are common. Nephritis, arthritis, or rheumatic fever may occur later. Treatment involves penicillin, bed rest, and ade-

quate fluid intake. Scarlet fever has become uncommon and much milder since the mid-20th century, independent of the use of antibiotics.

Schelde River, or SCHELDT RIVER, French ESCAUT, River, western Europe. The Schelde rises in northern France, flows through western Belgium to the city of Antwerp, turns northwest, and empties into the North Sea in Dutch territory after a course of 270 mi (435 km). Along with the lower Rhine and the Meuse rivers, it drains one of the world's most densely populated areas. A channel in the western Schelde allows oceangoing vessels to reach Antwerp at full tide.

scherzo (Italian: "joke"), Musical movement in rapid triple time; it replaced the minuet in genres such as the symphony, sonata, and string quartet in the 19th century. The name was first used for light vocal and instrumental pieces of the Baroque era. It formally often resembles the minuet, being in rounded binary form and having a contrasting trio section between two statements of the scherzo proper, but its tempo is often much faster and its style may range from playful to vehement or grotesque.

Schism, Western, or GREAT SCHISM (1378–1417) In Roman Catholic history, a period when there were two, and later three, rival popes, each with his own College of Cardinals. The schism began soon after the papal residence was returned to Rome from Avignon. Urban VI was elected amid local demands for an Italian pope, but a group of cardinals with French sympathies elected an antipope, Clement VII, who took up residence at Avignon. Cardinals from both sides met at Pisa in 1409 and elected a third pope in an effort to end the schism. The rift was not healed until the Council of Constance vacated all three seats and elected Martin V as pope in 1417.

Schism of 1054, or EAST-WEST SCHISM, Event that separated the Byzantine and Roman churches. The Eastern and Western churches had long been estranged over doctrinal issues such as the relationship of the Holy Spirit to the Father and the Son. The Eastern church resented the Roman enforcement of clerical celibacy and the limitation of the right of confirmation to the bishop. There were also jurisdictional disputes between Rome and Constantinople, including Rome's assertion of papal primacy. In 1054 Pope Leo IX, through his representative Humbert of Silva Candida, and the patriarch of Constantinople, Michael Cerularius, excommunicated each other, an event that marked the final break between the two churches. The rift widened in subsequent centuries, and the churches have remained separate, though the excommunications were lifted by the papacy and the patriarch in the 20th century.

schistosomiasis, or BILHARZIASIS, Group of chronic disorders caused by parasitic flatworms of the genus *Schistosoma* (blood flukes). Depending on the infecting species, thousands of eggs released by the females reach either the intestine or the bladder, are excreted in feces or urine, and hatch on contact with fresh water. The larvae invade snails, develop to the next stage, emerge into the water, and invade mammals to feed and breed in the bloodstream. An initial allergic reaction (inflammation, cough, late-afternoon fever, hives, liver tenderness) and blood in the stools and urine give way to a chronic stage, in which eggs impacted in the walls of organs cause fibrous thickening (fibrosis). This condition can lead to serious liver damage in the intestinal types and to bladder stones, fibrosis of other pelvic organs, and urinary-tract bacterial infection. In most cases, early diagnosis and persistent treatment to kill the adult worms ensure recovery.

schizophrenia, Any of a group of severe mental disorders that have in common symptoms such as hallucinations, delusions, blunted emotions, disorganized thinking, and withdrawal from reality. Five main types are recognized: the paranoid, characterized by delusions of persecution or grandeur combined with unrealistic, illogical thinking and frequent auditory hallucinations; the disorganized (hebephrenic), characterized by disordered speech and behaviour and shallow or inappropriate emotional responses; the catatonic, characterized by motor inflexibility or stupor along with mutism, echolalia, or other speech abnormalities; the simple or undifferentiated type, which conforms to basic definitions of schizophrenia but does not exhibit particular behaviours in the aforementioned types; and the residual type, which is a chronic stage indicating advancement toward later-stage schizophrenia. Schizophrenia seems to occur in 0.5–1% of the general population, and more than half of those so diagnosed will eventually recover. There is strong evidence that genetic inheritance plays a role, but no single cause of schizophrenia has been identified. Stressful life experiences may help trigger its onset. Treatment consists of drug therapy and counseling.

Scholasticism, Theological and philosophical movement, beginning in the 11th century, that sought to integrate the secular understanding of the ancient world, as exemplified by Aristotle, with the dogma implicit in the revelations of Christianity. Its aim was a synthesis of learning in which theology surmounted the hierarchy of knowledge. Principal figures in early Scholasticism were Peter Abelard, St. Anselm of Canterbury, St. Albertus Magnus, and Roger Bacon. The movement flourished in the 13th century, drawing on the writings and doctrines of St. Thomas Aquinas. By the 14th century Scholasticism was in decline, but it had laid the foundations for many revivals and revisitations in later centuries, particularly under Pope Leo XIII (1879), who sought to modernize the insights of the medieval scholastics. Modern philosophers influenced by Scholasticism include Jacques Maritain and Étienne Gilson (1884–1978).

schooner, Sailing ship rigged with fore-and-aft sails on its two or more masts. Though apparently developed from a 17th-century Dutch design, the first genuine schooner was built in the American colonies, probably at Gloucester, Mass., in 1713, by Andrew Robinson. Compared to square-rigged ships, they were ideal for coastal sailing; they handled better in the varying coastal winds, had shallower drafts for shallow waters, and required a smaller crew in proportion to their size. By the end of the century, they were the most important North American ship, used for the coastal trade and for fishing. After 1800 they became popular in Europe and around the world. Clipper ships married the schooner design to that of the old three-masted merchantman.

Schrödinger, Erwin (b. Aug. 12, 1887, Vienna, Austria—d. Jan. 4, 1961, Vienna), Austrian physicist. He taught physics in Zürich (1921–27) and Berlin (1927–33), then left Germany, objecting to the persecution of Jews. He settled in Ireland, where he joined the Dublin Institute for Advanced Studies (1940–56). He made fundamental contributions to quantum mechanics, and he shared a 1933 Nobel Prize with P.A.M. Dirac for his development in 1926 of the wave equation now called the Schrödinger equation. In addition to his scientific research, he made contributions to philosophy and the history of science; his books include *What Is Life?* (1944), *Nature and the Greeks* (1954), and *My View of the World* (1961).

Schweitzer, Albert (b. Jan. 14, 1875, Kaysersberg, Upper Alsace, Gcr.—d. Sept. 4, 1965, Lambaréné, Gabon), Alsatian-born German theologian, philosopher, organist, and mission doctor. In his early years he obtained a degree in philosophy (1899) and became an accomplished organist. In his biography of Johann Sebastian Bach (2 vol., 1905), he viewed Bach as a religious mystic. He also wrote on organ construction and produced an edition of Bach's organ works. His books on religion include several on St. Paul; his *Quest of the Historical Jesus* (1910) became widely influential. In 1905 he announced he would become a mission doctor and devote himself to philanthropic work. He and his wife moved in 1913 to Lambaréné in French Equatorial Africa (now Gabon) and with locals built a hospital on the banks of the Ogooué River, to which they later added a leper colony. In 1952 he received

Albert Schweitzer, photograph by Yousuf Karsh.
Karsh—Rapho/Photo Researchers

the Nobel Peace Prize for his efforts on behalf of "the Brotherhood of Nations." Two years before his death, his hospital and leper colony were serving 500 patients. His philosophical books discuss his famous principle of "reverence for life."

science fiction, Fiction dealing principally with the impact of actual or imagined science on society or individuals, or more generally, literary fantasy including a scientific factor as an essential orienting component. Precursors of the genre include Mary Shelley's *Frankenstein* (1818), Robert Louis Stevenson's *The Strange Case of Dr. Jekyll and Mr. Hyde* (1886), and Jonathan Swift's *Gulliver's Travels* (1726). From its beginnings in the works of Jules Verne and H.G. Wells, it emerged as a self-conscious genre in the pulp magazine *Amazing Stories*, founded in 1926. It came into its own as serious fiction in the magazine *Astounding Science Fiction* in the late 1930s and in works by such writers as Isaac Asimov, Arthur C. Clarke, and Robert Heinlein. A great boom in popularity followed World War II, when numerous writers' approaches included predictions of future societies on Earth, analyses of the consequences of interstellar travel, and imaginative explorations of intelligent life in other worlds. Much recent fiction has been written in the "cyberpunk" genre, which deals with the effects of computers and artificial intelligence on anarchic future societies. Radio, film, and television have reinforced the popularity of the genre.

scientific method, Mathematical and experimental techniques employed in the natural sciences. Many empirical sciences, especially the social sciences, use mathematical tools borrowed from probability theory and statistics, together with such outgrowths of these as decision theory, game theory, utility theory, and operations research. Philosophers of science have addressed general methodological problems, such as the nature of scientific explanation and the justification of induction.

Scientology, Church of, International movement established in the U.S. by L. Ron Hubbard in 1954. He introduced his ideas to the general public in *Dianetics: The Modern Science of Mental Health* (1950). Dianetics sought to free subjects from the destructive imprints of past experiences, called engrams. Later Hubbard moved toward a structured system of belief involving the human soul, or thetan (each person's spiritual self), and the origins of life and the universe. The organization has often been the subject of controversy.

scleroderma, or PROGRESSIVE SYSTEMIC SCLEROSIS, Chronic disease that hardens the skin and fixes it to underlying structures. Swelling and collagen buildup lead to loss of elasticity. The cause is unknown. It usually begins at age 25–55, more often in women, with severe inflammation of underlying tissue and stiffness, pain, and skin tautness and thickening. Systemic problems that may arise years later include fever, trouble in breathing, fibrous tissue in the lungs, inflammation of heart muscle or membranes, gastrointestinal disorders, and kidney malfunction. Calcium deposits build up under the skin. The disease may finally stabilize or gradually regress. Steroids may help, and physical medicine and rehabilitation with heat, massage, and passive exercise (movement of the limbs by the therapist) help prevent limb fixation and deformity.

score, In music, the parts of all the instruments or singers of an ensemble notated with simultaneous sounds aligned vertically, on a system of parallel staffs arranged one above another. Polyphonic (multivoiced) music was being composed for some 600 years before the score came into regular use in the 16th–17th centuries. Early examples of scores exist for works of the Notre-Dame school, and early composers may have used temporary scores during composition, perhaps on chalkboards, from which the parts for individual singers were then copied.

Scorpio or SCORPIUS (Latin: "Scorpion"), In astronomy, the constellation lying between Libra and Sagittarius; in astrology, the eighth sign of the zodiac, governing approximately the period October 24–November 21. Its symbol, a scorpion, refers to the Greek myth of the scorpion that stung Orion. The story explains why the constellation of Orion sets as Scorpius rises in the sky. Another Greek myth says that a scorpion caused the horses of the sun to bolt when they were being driven by the inexperienced Phaethon.

scorpion, Any of some 1,300 nocturnal arachnid species (order Scorpionida, subphylum Chelicerata) having a slender body, a segmented tail tipped with a venomous stinger, and six pairs of appendages. The small first pair tear apart insect and spider prey. Strong, clawlike pincers on the large second pair, held horizontally in front, are used as feelers and for grasping prey while sucking the tissue fluids. The last four pairs, each with a pincer, are walking legs. The venom is either a hemotoxin that, in humans, causes swelling, redness, and pain or a neurotoxin that may cause convulsions, paralysis, cardiac irregularities, and death. Most scorpions will sting a human only if provoked. Nocturnal hunters, most species are tropical or subtropical.

Scotland, Northernmost country of the United Kingdom. Area: 30,421 sq mi (78,789 sq km). Population (2001): 5,062,011. Capital: Edinburgh. The population is a blend of Celtic, Angle, and Norman ancestry. Languages: English (official), Scottish Gaelic, and Scots. Religion: Church of Scotland (Presbyterian; official). Currency: pound sterling. Scotland has three major geographic regions. The Highlands, in the north, are occupied by a series of lakes and the Grampian Mountains. The Lowlands, which include some of Scotland's best farmland, comprise the other two major regions: the Midland Valley (Central Lowlands) and the Southern Uplands; the Southern Uplands feature narrow, flat valleys separating table mountains. Scotland has a temperate oceanic climate. Important industries are coal and oil production, electronics, forestry, and marine fishing. Picts inhabited the region when it was invaded by the Romans *c.* 80 CE. In the 5th century it split into four kingdoms under the Picts, Scots, Britons, and Angles. Scottish unification began in the 9th century. It came under a heavy Anglicizing influence from the 11th century, and its ruler was forced to pay homage to the English crown in 1174, leading to numerous future disputes. The Scottish and English kingdoms were united in 1603 when James VI, son of Mary, Queen of Scots, ascended the English throne as James I. Scotland became part of the United Kingdom of Great Britain in 1707, when the parliaments of both governments passed the Act of Union. The English prevailed in two Scottish rebellions in the 18th century, and after 1745 the history of Scotland became part of the history of Great Britain. Scotland has no sovereign executive but retains vestiges of ancient sovereignty in its own legal and educational systems. In 1997 the Scots passed a referendum that allowed them to establish their own parliament in Edinburgh to vote on wide-ranging political issues while remaining part of the United Kingdom. The Scottish Parliament first convened in 1999.

Scotland Yard, officially NEW SCOTLAND YARD, Headquarters of the London Metropolitan Police, and, by extension, the force itself. The London police force was created in 1829 by Sir Robert Peel and housed at 4 Whitehall Place, which had an entrance in Great Scotland Yard. In 1890 it moved to a new building; that location became New Scotland Yard, a name that was kept when it moved again in 1967. In addition to duties common to all metropolitan police forces (including crime detection and prevention and traffic management), it is entrusted with civil defense in times of emergency, and it maintains a special branch for guarding visiting dignitaries, royalty, and political dignitaries. It keeps records on all known criminals in Britain, and other British police forces often seek its assistance. It also helps train the police of Commonwealth nations.

Scott, Sir Walter, 1st Baronet (b. Aug. 15, 1771, Edinburgh,

Sir Walter Scott, detail of an oil painting by Sir Edwin Henry Landseer, 1824; in the National Portrait Gallery, London
Courtesy of The National Portrait Gallery, London

Scot.—d. Sept. 21, 1832, Abbotsford, Roxburgh), Scottish writer, often considered both the inventor and the greatest practitioner of the historical novel. From childhood Scott was familiar with stories of the Border region of Scotland. Apprenticed to his father, a lawyer, in 1786, he later became sheriff depute of Selkirk and clerk to the Court of Session in Edinburgh. His interest in border ballads led to the collection *Minstrelsy of the Scottish Border* (1802–03). His first original poetic romance, *The Lay of the Last Minstrel* (1805), established his reputation; *The Lady of the Lake* (1810) was his most successful contribution to the genre. He produced editions of the works of John Dryden, 18 vol. (1808), and Jonathan Swift, 19 vol. (1814). Troubled with debt, from 1813 he wrote in part to make money. He tired of narrative poetry and turned to prose romances. The extremely popular series now known as the Waverley novels consists of more than two dozen works dealing with Scottish history, including the masterpieces *Old Mortality* (1816), *Rob Roy* (1817), and *The Heart of Midlothian* (1818). He drew on English history and other themes for *Ivanhoe* (1819), *Kenilworth* (1821), and *Quentin Durward* (1823). All his novels were published anonymously until 1827.

screenplay, Written text that provides the basis for a film production. Screenplays usually include not only the dialogue spoken by the characters but also a shot-by-shot outline of the film's action. Screenplays may be adapted from novels or stage plays or developed from original ideas suggested by the screenwriters or their collaborators. They generally pass through multiple revisions, and screenwriters are called on to incorporate suggestions from directors, producers, and others involved in the filmmaking process. Early drafts often include only brief suggestions for planned shots, but by the date of production a screenplay may evolve into a detailed shooting script, in which action and gestures are explicitly stated.

scripture, Sacred writings of religions, comprising a large portion of the literature of the world. Scriptures vary in form, volume, age, and degree of sacredness. Nearly all scriptures were originally oral and were passed down as memorized texts through several generations before being put in writing. In some religions, notably Islam, Hinduism, and Buddhism, there is still strong emphasis on the value of reciting or chanting the scriptures aloud. The Hebrew Bible (Old Testament) is the scripture of Judaism; the Bible (Old and New Testaments together) is the scripture of Christianity; and the Qu'rān is the scripture of Islam. Scriptures of Hinduism include the Vedas and Upanishads.

scuba diving, Swimming done underwater with a self-contained underwater-breathing apparatus (scuba), as opposed to skin diving, which requires only a snorkel, goggles, and flippers. Scuba gear was invented by Jacques-Yves Cousteau and Émile Gagnan in 1943. Diving clubs formed quickly as the technology became widely available. Scuba diving is used in oceanography, in underwater exploration and salvage work, in the study of water pollution, and for recreation.

sculpture, Three-dimensional art produced especially by forming hard or plastic materials into three-dimensional objects, usually by carving or modeling. The designs may be produced in freestanding objects (i.e., in the round), in relief, or in environments, and a variety of media may be used, including clay, wax, stone, metal, fabric, wood, plaster, rubber, and found objects. Materials may be carved, modeled, molded, cast, wrought, welded, sewn, or assembled and combined. Various forms of sculpture have been found in virtually every culture throughout history. Until the 20th century, sculpture was considered a representational art, but, beginning in the early 1900, nonrepresentational works were increasingly produced. The scope of the term became much wider in the second half of the 20th century. Present-day sculptors use any materials and methods of manufacture that will serve their purposes, and so the art of sculpture can no longer be identified with any special materials or techniques.

scurvy, or VITAMIN C DEFICIENCY, Nutritional disorder caused by deficiency of vitamin C. Deficiency interferes with tissue synthesis, causing swollen, bleeding gums; loose teeth; sore, stiff joints and legs; bleeding under the skin and in deep tissues; slow wound healing; and anemia. The scourge of sailors on long sea voyages, scurvy was recognized as diet-related in 1753, when James Lind showed that drinking citrus juice could cure and prevent it, leading to the concept of deficiency diseases. Full-blown scurvy is now rare, and adequate vitamin C usually cures even severe cases in days.

Scythian, Any member of a nomadic people of Iranian stock who migrated from Central Asia to southern Russia in the 8th–7th century BC. Fierce warriors, they were among the first expert horsemen, which enabled them to establish an empire from western Persia through Syria and Judaea to Egypt and to expel the Cimmerians from their territory in the Caucasus and north of the Black Sea. Although driven out of Anatolia by the Medes, they held territory from the Persian border into southern Russia; they repelled an invasion by the Persian Darius I c. 513 BC. Their civilization produced wealthy aristocrats ("Royal Scyths"), whose graves held richly worked articles of gold and other precious materials. The army consisted of freemen; on presentation of an enemy's head, a soldier could share in the booty. They fought with double-curved bows, trefoil-shaped arrows, and Persian swords. Burial called for the sacrifice of the dead man's wife and servants. In the 5th century BC the royal family intermarried with Greeks. The community fell to the Sarmatians in the 2nd century BC.

Sea, Law of the, International law codified in a treaty signed in 1982 covering the status and use of territorial waters, sea lanes, and ocean resources. Originally signed by 117 countries, the treaty had some 140 state parties by the early 21st century. The treaty defines territorial waters as those extending 12 nautical mi (22 km) beyond a country's coast and gives to each country exclusive fishing and mining rights in waters extending to 200 nautical mi (370 km) from its coast.

Sea anemone, Tealia
M. Woodbridge Williams

sea anemone, Any of more than 1,000 cnidarian species in the order Actiniaria, found from the tidal zone of all oceans to depths of more than 30,000 ft (10,000 m) and occasionally in brackish water. Species vary from less than 1 in. (3 cm) to about 5 ft (1.5 m) in diameter. The mouth, at the upper end of the cylindrical body, is surrounded by petal-like, usually colourful tentacles that bear stinging nematocysts for paralyzing prey such as fishes. Some species eat only microorganisms. Most species remain permanently attached to a hard surface such as a rock or the back of a crab.

sea bass, Any of about 400 species (family Serranidae) of carnivorous fishes, most of which inhabit shallow regions of warm and tropical seas. Sea bass have a slender body, small scales, large mouth, and straight-edged or rounded tail. The spiny frontal section and the soft-rayed rear section of the dorsal fin are usually joined but may be separated by a notch. Species range from about 1 in. (3 cm) to 6 ft (1.8 m) long and may weigh 500 lbs (225 kg). About 12 species in the family Moronidae (sometimes considered a subfamily of Serranidae) inhabit temperate waters.

sea cow, or STELLER'S SEA COW, Extinct aquatic mammal (*Hydrodamalis gigas*) that lived around islands in the Bering Sea. It was discovered in 1741 and described by a member of Vitus Bering's expedition. At least 24 ft (7.5 m) long, it had no teeth, a small head, and a broad, horizontal, forked tail fluke; its dark brown skin was sometimes streaked or spotted with white. It browsed on seaweed. Russian sealers hunted it for food and fur; by 1768 the entire population, estimated at about 5,000, had been exterminated. The term also refers to dugongs and manatees.

sea cucumber, Any of 1,100 species of echinoderms constituting the class Holothurioidea, found in all oceans, mostly in shallow water. The soft, cylindrical body is 0.75 in. (2 cm) to 6.5 ft (2 m) long and 0.4–8 in. (1–20 cm) thick. It is usually dull, dark, and often warty. The internal skeleton consists merely of numerous tiny bits in the skin. Most species have five rows of tube feet extending from mouth to anus. The 10 or more retractile tentacles surrounding the mouth are used for taking food (mud containing nutrients or small aquatic animals) or burrowing. Locomotion is sluglike.

sea horse, Any of about 24 species (family Syngnathidae) of fishes that usually live along warm seashores, clinging to plants with their forward-curled, prehensile tail. Species range from 1.5 to 12 in. (4–30 cm) long. Sea horses have bony rings instead of scales, and their eyes can move independently. They swim upright, propelling themselves horizontally with their fins and vertically with their swim bladder. They catch small organisms by sucking them quickly into their small mouths. The female deposits her eggs into a brood pouch beneath the male's tail, and the male expels the newly hatched young.

*Sea horse (*Hippocampus erectus*).*
Des Bartlett/Bruce Coleman Ltd.

sea level, Position of the air-sea boundary, to which all terrestrial elevations and submarine depths are referred. The sea level at any location changes constantly with changes in tides, atmospheric pressure, and wind conditions. Longer-term changes are influenced by changes in the Earth's climates. Consequently, the level is better defined as mean sea level, the height of the sea surface averaged over all stages of the tide over a long period of time.

sea lion, Any of five species (family Otariidae) of eared seals found along coasts on both sides of the Pacific, from Alaska to Australia. Sea lions have short, coarse hair that lacks a distinct undercoat. The males of all but the California sea lion have a mane. Sea lions feed principally on fish, squid, and octopus. They breed in large herds; males establish a harem of 3–20 females. The California sea lion (*Zalophus californianus*) is the trained seal of circuses and zoos. Males of the various species range from 8 to 11 ft (2.5–3.3 m) long and weigh 600–2,200 lbs (270–1,000 kg).

sea otter, or GREAT SEA OTTER, Rare, completely marine otter (*Enhydra lutris*) of the northern Pacific, usually found in kelp beds. Floating on its back, it opens mollusks by smashing them on a stone balanced on its chest. The large hind feet are broad and flipperlike. It is 40–65 in. (100–160 cm) long and weighs 35–90 lbs (16–40 kg). The thick lustrous coat is reddish to dark brown. By 1910 it had been hunted almost to extinction for its fur; now fully protected, it is gradually increasing in numbers.

sea snake, Any of some 50 species (family Hydrophiidae) of venomous, marine snakes with an oarlike tail and flattened body. Most are found along coasts and in estuaries of Australia and Asia, sometimes basking on the surface in a large group, though the yellow-bellied, or pelagic, sea snake ranges throughout the Pacific. The nostrils, usually on top of the snout, have valvelike closings. The body of several species is much thicker than the head and neck. Most species are 3–4 ft (1–1.2 m) long; *Laticauda semifasciata*, a Japanese delicacy, may be twice as long. Though generally slow to strike, their venom may be lethal.

sea urchin, Any of about 700 species (class Echinoidea) of echinoderms found worldwide. Sea urchins have a globular body covered with movable, sometimes poisonous, spines up to 12 in. (30 cm) long. Pores along the internal skeleton accommodate slender, extensible, often sucker-tipped tube feet. Sea urchins live on the seafloor and use their tube feet or spines to move about. The mouth is on the body's underside; teeth are extruded to scrape algae and other food from rocks. Some species excavate hiding places in coral, rock, or even steel. Roe of some species is eaten in certain countries.

*Slate-pencil urchin
(Heterocentrotus
mammillatus)*
Douglas Faulkner

seal, Aquatic carnivore with webbed flippers and a streamlined body. Earless (true, or hair) seals (of the family Phocidae, with 18 species) lack external ears. In water, they propel themselves by side-to-side strokes of the hind limbs and maneuver with their forelimbs. On land, they wriggle on their belly or pull themselves with their forelimbs. Earless species include the elephant seal, harbour seal, harp seal, and leopard seal. The eared seals (family Otariidae, with five species of sea lion and nine of fur seal) have external ears and longer flippers. In water, they propel themselves by a rowing motion of their forelimbs; on land, they use all four limbs to move about.

season, Any of four divisions of the year according to consistent annual changes in the weather. In the Northern Hemisphere, winter formally begins on the winter solstice, December 21 or 22; spring on the vernal equinox, March 20 or 21; summer on the summer solstice, June 21 or 22; and fall (autumn) on the autumnal equinox, September 22 or 23. In the Southern Hemisphere, the dates of onset of summer and winter are reversed, as are those of spring and fall.

seasonal affective disorder (SAD), Cyclical depression occurring in winter, apparently caused by insufficient sunlight. It is most common in places at high latitudes and therefore with long winters and very short daylight hours. Symptoms can include all those of major depression, and there is a risk of suicide. The cause may be related to regulation of the body's temperature and hor-

mones and may involve the pineal gland and melatonin. Exposure to intense full-spectrum light from a set of fluorescent bulbs in a light box with a diffusing screen has proved effective as treatment. Dawn simulation (exposure to low light levels in the final sleep period) and negative-ion therapy can also help.

seaweed, Any of certain species of red, green, and brown marine algae that generally are anchored to the sea bottom or to a solid structure by rootlike holdfasts that perform the sole function of attachment and do not extract nutrients as do the roots of higher plants. The most obvious seaweeds are brown algae; mosslike carpets of red algae are seen at low tides. Seaweeds are often dense in shallow water. Brown algae commonly found as seaweeds include kelp, which include the largest algae, and sargassum. Some seaweeds have hollow, gas-filled floats that keep their fronds at the surface of the water. *Ulva* species, commonly called sea lettuce, are among the relatively few green algae that are seaweeds. Seaweeds are used as food, and brown algae are used in fertilizers. The red alga *Gelidium* is used to make the gelatin-like product called agar.

Second International, or SOCIALIST INTERNATIONAL (1889–1914) Federation of socialist political parties and trade unions that greatly influenced the European labour movement while supporting parliamentary democracy and opposing anarchism. Unlike the centralized First International, it was a loose federation that met in a number of cities at various intervals. By 1912 it represented the socialist parties of all European countries, the U.S., Canada, and Japan, with a membership of about nine million. It reaffirmed Marxist doctrine, but its main concern became the prevention of a general European war. When that failed, the International ended in 1914.

secret society, Any of various oath-bound societies devoted to brotherhood (or sisterhood), moral discipline, and mutual assistance. Such societies usually conduct rituals of initiation to instruct new members in the rules of the group. Greek and Roman mystery religions had their secular counterparts in clandestine social clubs, some of which served as platforms for political dissent. In West Africa secret societies such as Poro (for men) and Sande (for women) serve to translate slight advantages of wealth and prestige into political authority. In parts of New Guinea secret men's societies serve as repositories of tribal knowledge. Fraternal orders such as the Freemasons may be considered secret societies, as may criminal groups such as the Mafia and the Chinese Triads and hate groups such as the Ku Klux Klan.

Secretariat (foaled 1970) U.S. Thoroughbred racehorse. In 1973 he became the first Triple Crown winner since Citation in 1948. At the Belmont Stakes he won by an unprecedented 31 lengths. In his two-year career he came in first 16 times, second 3 times, and third once. He is often regarded as the greatest Thoroughbred in history.

security, In finance, written evidence of ownership conferring the right to receive property not currently in the holder's possession. The most common securities are stocks and bonds. Governments, companies, and financial institutions use securities to raise money. Stocks are securities issued in the form of equity ownership. Bonds are securities that take the form of debt. They constitute promises to pay a specified amount at a specified date and to pay interest at a specified rate in the interim. Most government securities are bonds that pay a fixed amount of interest per year; unlike commercial securities, their repayment is guaranteed. Both stocks and bonds are traded publicly on organized exchanges such as the New York Stock Exchange, the London Stock Exchange, and the Tokyo Stock Exchange. External forces such as international troubles, changes in government policies, and trends in foreign stock markets have an effect on security prices. For individual stocks, the company's current and prospective financial performance plays an important role, as do overall trends within its business sector.

Seder, Ritual meal served on the first night of Passover, commemorating the flight of the Jews from Egypt. Presided over by the head of the family, the Seder follows a liturgy, the Haggadah, that reminds participants of the story of the Exodus. The ritual includes blessings, the pouring of wine, and ritual questions about the meaning of the event ("Why does this night differ from all other nights?") asked by the youngest child present. The meal includes unleavened bread and bitter herbs, the bread symbolizing the haste with which the Israelites left Egypt and the herbs symbolizing the bitterness of slavery. A cup of wine is poured for Elijah, the precursor of the messiah.

sedimentary rock, Rock formed at or near the Earth's surface by the accumulation and lithification of fragments of preexisting rocks or by precipitation from solution at normal surface temperatures. Sedimentary rocks can be formed only where sediments are deposited long enough to become compacted and cemented into hard beds or strata. They are the most common rocks exposed on the Earth's surface but are only a minor constituent of the entire crust. Their defining characteristic is that they are formed in layers. Each layer has features that reflect the conditions during deposition, the nature of the source material (and, often, the organisms present), and the means of transport.

sedition, Crime of creating a revolt, disturbance, or violence against lawful civil authority with the intent to cause its overthrow or destruction. Because it is limited to organizing and encouraging opposition to government rather than directly participating in its overthrow, sedition is regarded as falling one step short of the more serious crime of treason. In the U.S. the display of a certain flag or the advocacy of a particular movement, such as syndicalism, anarchism, or communism, has periodically been declared seditious. More recently, the courts have applied a more stringent test of sedition to ensure that constitutional guarantees regarding freedom of speech are not abridged.

seed, Reproductive structure in plants that consists of a plant embryo, usually accompanied by a supply of food (endosperm, which is produced during fertilization) and enclosed in a protective coat. Seed embryos contain one or more cotyledons. In typical flowering plants, seed production follows pollination and fertilization. As seeds mature, the ovary that enclosed the ovules develops into a fruit containing the seeds. Most seeds are small, weighing less than a gram; the smallest contain no food reserve. At the opposite extreme, the seed of the double coconut palm may weigh up to about 60 lb (27 kg). Seeds are highly adapted to transportation by animals, wind, and water. When circumstances are favorable, water and oxygen penetrate the seed coat, and the new plant begins to grow. The longevity of seeds varies widely: some remain viable for only about a week; others have been known to germinate after hundreds or even thousands of years.

Seferis, George, orig. GIŌRGIOS STYLIANOU SEFERIADĒS, or YEORYIOS STILIANOU SEPHERIADES (b. March 13, 1900, Smyrna, Anatolia, Ottoman Empire—d. Sept. 20, 1971, Athens, Greece), Greek poet, essayist, and diplomat. He studied law in Paris and held various diplomatic posts from 1926 to 1962. His poetry appeared in a number of collections beginning with *Turning Point* (1931). He is considered the leading Greek poet of "the generation of the '30s," which introduced Symbolism to modern Greek literature. He was awarded the Nobel Prize for Literature in 1963.

segregation, racial, Practice of restricting people to certain circumscribed areas of residence or to separate institutions and facilities on the basis of race or alleged race. Racial segregation provides a means of maintaining the economic advantages and higher social status of politically dominant races. Historically, various conquerors—among them Asian Mongols, African Bantu, and American Aztecs—have practiced discrimination involving the segregation of subject races. Racial segregation has appeared in all multiracial communities, except where racial amalgamation has occurred on a large scale, as in Hawaii and Brazil. In such places there has been occasional social discrimination but not legal segregation. In the Southern states of the U.S., public facilities were segregated from the late 19th century into the 1950s, and in South Africa a system of apartheid sanctioned discrimination against nonwhites until it was abolished in the 1990s. The U.S. civil rights movement and Civil Rights Act of 1964 helped end racial segregation in education and public facilities, though other forms of racial discrimination continued.

Seifert, Jaroslav (b. Sept. 23, 1901, Prague, Bohemia, Austria-Hungary—d. Jan. 10, 1986, Prague, Czech.), Czech poet. He made a living as a journalist until 1950. Though his early works reflect youthful expectations for the future of communism in the Soviet Union, he broke with the Communist Party in 1929. More lyrical elements were evident in his later poems, and the history and current events of Czechoslovakia were the most common subjects in his approximately 30 volumes. In the 1980s and '90s many of his works were translated, including *Honeymoon Ride* (1938), *Bozena Nemcova's Fan* (1940), and *Halley's Comet* (1967). He also contributed to journals and wrote children's literature and memoirs. In 1984 he became the first Czech to win the Nobel Prize for Literature.

Seine River, ancient SEQUANA, Second longest river in France. It rises on the Langres plateau, 18 mi (30 km) northwest of Dijon, and flows through Paris before emptying into the English Channel at Le Havre after a course of 485 mi (780 km). Its tributaries include the Marne and Oise rivers. It drains an area of about 30,400 sq mi (78,700 sq km) in northern France; its network carries most of France's inland waterway traffic.

seismic wave, Vibration generated by an earthquake, explosion, or similar phenomenon and propagated within the Earth or along its surface. Earthquakes generate two principal types of waves: body waves, which travel within the Earth, and surface waves, which travel along the surface. Seismograms (recorded traces of the amplitude and frequency of seismic waves) yield information about the Earth and its subsurface structure; artificially generated seismic waves are used in oil and gas prospecting.

Sejong (b. 1397—d. 1450), Monarch of the Chosŏn dynasty in Korea during whose reign (1419–50) Korean cultural achievements reached a high point. Sejong oversaw the creation of hangul, the Korean alphabet, and banned Buddhist monks from Seoul, thereby reducing the power and wealth of the Buddhist hierarchy.

selenium, Semimetallic chemical element, chemical symbol Se, atomic number 34. It is widely distributed, usually in small amounts, occasionally uncombined but more often as selenides of iron, lead, silver, or copper. Selenium has several allotropes; the gray metallic crystalline form is the most stable at room temperature. Its electrical conductivity increases when light strikes it, and it can convert light directly into electricity, so selenium is used in photocells (e.g., in light meters and security alarms), solar cells, and photocopiers. It also has been used in rectifiers to convert alternating to direct electric current. It serves as a red colorant for glass and glazes. Selenium has valence 2, 4, and 6 in its compounds, many of which are toxic though the element is not. Selenium dioxide is an important reagent in organic chemistry. Vital to living cells, it works as an antioxidant in the body and is being studied for a variety of possible beneficial health effects; it is used in nutritional supplements and animal feeds.

Seleucid dynasty, Macedonian Greek dynasty (312–64 BC) founded by Seleucus I Nicator. Carved from the empire of Alexander the Great, the Seleucid domain stretched from Thrace to the border of India and included Babylonia, Syria, and Anatolia. Seleucus was succeeded in 281 by Antiochus I Soter, who reigned until 261. He was followed by Antiochus II (r. 261–246), Seleucus II Callinicus (r. 246–225), Seleucus III (r. 225–223), and Antiochus III (the Great; r. 223–187). Under the last, the empire was at its height. Resistance to the power and spread of Hellenistic culture soon began to manifest itself in the Asian lands. Antiochus III's encounter with the Romans signaled decline, especially after the defeat of 190. The decline accelerated after the death of Antiochus IV (r. 175–164), who lost Judaea to the Maccabees. The efforts of Demetrius I and Antiochus VII could not forestall the dynasty's inevitable end at the hands of the Roman Pompey the Great in 64 BC.

self-determination, Process by which a group of people, usually possessing a degree of political consciousness, form their own state and government. The idea evolved as a byproduct of nationalism. According to the UN charter, a people has the right to form itself into a state or to otherwise determine the form of its association with another state, and every state has the right to choose its own political, economic, social, and cultural systems. Moreover, the administering authorities of dependent territories are enjoined to ensure political advancement and the development of self-government in those territories.

self-esteem, Sense of personal worth and ability that is fundamental to an individual's identity. Family relationships during childhood are believed to play a crucial role in its development. Parents may foster self-esteem by expressing affection and support for the child as well as by helping the child set realistic goals for achievement instead of imposing unreachably high standards. Karen Horney asserted that low self-esteem leads to the development of a personality that excessively craves approval and affection and exhibits an extreme desire for personal achievement. According to Alfred Adler's theory of personality, low self-esteem leads people to strive to overcome their perceived inferiorities and to develop strengths or talents in compensation.

Seljūq dynasty, or SALJŪQ DYNASTY (c. 11th–13th centuries) Muslim Turkmen dynasty that ruled Persia, Iraq, Syria, and Anatolia. Seljūq was the chief of a nomadic Turkish tribe. His grandsons Chaghri Beg and Toghrïl Beg conquered realms in Iran. Under Alp-Arslan and Malik-Shah, the empire came to include all of Iran, Mesopotamia, Syria, and Palestine; Alp-Arslan's victory over the Byzantine Empire at the Battle of Manzikert led to several Crusades. Adherents of Sunnite Islam, the Seljūqs adopted Persian culture, and under them the Persian language partly displaced Arabic as a literary language in Iran. By 1200 Seljūq power remained only in their sultanate of Rūm in Anatolia, which collapsed in a war against the Khwārezm-Shah dynasty in 1230 and was overrun by Mongols in 1243.

semantics, Study of meaning, one of the major areas of linguistic study. Linguists have approached it in a variety of ways. Members of the school of interpretive semantics study the structures of language independent of their conditions of use. In contrast, the advocates of generative semantics insist that the meaning of sentences is a function of their use. Still another group maintains that semantics will not advance until theorists take into account the psychological questions of how people form concepts and how these relate to word meanings.

semiconductor, Class of crystalline solids with electrical conductivity between that of a conductor and an insulator. Such materials can be treated chemically to allow transmission and control of an electric current. Semiconductors are used in the manufacture of electronic devices such as diodes, transistors, and integrated circuits. Intrinsic semiconductors have a high degree of chemical purity, but their conductivity is poor. Extrinsic semiconductors contain impurities that produce much greater conductiv-

ity. Some common intrinsic semiconductors are single crystals of silicon, germanium, and gallium arsenide; such materials can be converted into the technologically more important extrinsic semiconductors by addition of small amounts of impurities, a process called doping. Advances in semiconductor technology in recent years have gone hand in hand with increased operational speed in computers.

seminary, Educational institution, usually for training in theology. In the U.S. the term was formerly also used to refer to institutions of higher learning for women, often teachers' colleges. Since at least the 4th century there have been seminaries for the training of clergy. The first known group of seminarians was gathered by St. Basil of Ancyra. The term dropped out of general use in the Middle Ages, when most theological training was in monasteries, and later, in the universities. After the Reformation and the emergence of new denominations, seminaries again came into use, especially in the U.S. The 16th-century Council of Trent ordered seminaries to be opened in every diocese.

semiotics, or SEMIOLOGY, Study of signs and sign-using behaviour, especially in language. In the late 19th and early 20th century the work of Ferdinand de Saussure and Charles Sanders Peirce led to the emergence of semiotics as a method for examining phenomena in different fields, including aesthetics, anthropology, communications, psychology, and semantics. Interest in the structure behind the use of particular signs links semiotics with the methods of structuralism. Saussure's theories are also fundamental to poststructuralism.

Semite, Person speaking one of a group of related languages, presumably derived from a common language, Semitic. The term came to include Arabs, Akkadians, Canaanites, some Ethiopians, and Aramaean tribes including Hebrews. Semitic tribes migrated from the Arabian Peninsula, beginning c. 2500 BC, to the Mediterranean coast, Mesopotamia, and the Nile River delta. In Phoenicia, they became seafarers. In Mesopotamia, they blended with the civilization of Sumer. The Hebrews settled at last with other Semites in Palestine.

Semitic languages, Family of Afro-Asiatic languages spoken by more than 200 million people in northern Africa and South Asia. No other language family has been attested in writing over a greater time span—from the late 3rd millennium BCE to the present. Both traditional and some recent classifications divide the family into an eastern and western group. Until recently the sole known East Semitic language was Akkadian; now some scholars add Eblaite, the language of a cuneiform archive found at the ancient city of Ebla, with documents dating from c. 2300 to 2250 BCE. West Semitic contains as one major subgroup Northwest Semitic, which includes Ugaritic, known from alphabetic cuneiform texts of c. 1400–1200 BCE; the closely related Canaanite languages (including Moabite, Phoenician, and Ancient Hebrew); and Aramaic. Further subgrouping is controversial; traditionally, Arabic was placed in a distinct South Semitic subgroup of West Semitic, though a more recent classification puts it together with Northwest Semitic. The South Semitic languages include Epigraphic South Arabian; Modern South Arabian (or Modern South Arabic), a group of six languages spoken in eastern Yemen, southwestern Oman, and the island of Socotra; and Ethiopic.

Sen, Amartya (b. Nov. 3, 1933, Santiniketan, India), Indian economist who was awarded the 1998 Nobel Prize in Economic Sciences for his work in welfare economics and social choice. Sen is best known for his work on the causes of famine, and his research led to the development of solutions for limiting the effects of food shortages. After attending Presidency College in Calcutta (now Kolkata), Sen studied at Trinity College, University of Cambridge (B.A., 1955; M.A. and Ph.D., 1959). He taught economics at the Universities of Jadavpur (1956–58) and Delhi (1963–71), the London School of Economics, the University of London

(1971–77), the University of Oxford (1977–88), and Harvard University (1988–98). In 1998 he was appointed master of Trinity College. His *Poverty and Famines: An Essay on Entitlement and Deprivation* (1981) showed that declining wages, unemployment, rising food prices, and inefficient food distribution could lead to starvation. His views encouraged policy makers to maintain stable prices for food.

Senate, In ancient Rome, the governing and advisory council that was the most permanent element in the Roman constitution. Under the monarchy it served as an advisory council, with undefined powers. During the republic it advised the consuls and supposedly stood second to them in power. Senators were appointed by the consuls, but since they served for life, by the late republic the Senate became independent of the consuls, with extensive powers. About 312 BC the selection of senators was transferred from the consuls to the censors. In 81 BC Sulla made selection automatic, routinely admitting all former quaestors. It became the chief governing body and controlled the republic's finances. Julius Caesar increased the number of senators to 900. Augustus dropped the number to 300 and reduced the Senate's power, while giving it new judicial and legislative functions. The number later increased to about 2,000; many were provincials, the most important being the great landowners. The Senate's power faded until it disappeared from the historical record in the 6th century AD.

Senegal, officially REPUBLIC OF SENEGAL, Country, western Africa. Area: 75,955 sq mi (196,722 sq km). Population: (2011 est.) 12,644,000. Capital: Dakar. There are seven major ethnic groups in Senegal—including the Wolof, Fulani, and Malinke, each speaking a separate language—and a number of smaller groups. Language: French (official). Religions: Islam; also traditional beliefs, Christianity. Currency: CFA franc. The climate varies from dry desert to moist tropics. Forests cover about one-third of the total area, and nearly one-third is pasture or rangeland; much of the rest is arable. Agriculture is the main industry; peanuts are the most important cash and export crop. Other important industries are fishing, mining, manufacturing, and tourism. Senegal has large reserves of phosphates and iron ore. It is a multiparty republic with a bicameral legislature; its head of state and government is the president, assisted by the prime minister. Links between the peoples of Senegal and North Africa were established in the early centuries CE. Islam was introduced in the 11th century, although animism retained a hold on the country into the 19th century. The Portuguese explored the coast about 1444, and in 1638 the French established a trading post at the mouth of the Sénégal River. Throughout the 17th and 18th centuries, Europeans exported slaves, ivory, and gold from Senegal. The French gained control over the coast in the early 19th century and moved inland, checking the expansion of the Tukulor empire; in 1895 Senegal became part of French West Africa. Its inhabitants were made French citizens in 1946, and it became an overseas territory of France. It voted for a degree of autonomy in 1958, was federated with Mali in 1959–60, and became an independent state in 1960. In 1982 it entered a confederation with Gambia called Senegambia, which was dissolved in 1989. Separatists fighting in the southern part of the country since the early 1980s signed a peace accord with the government in 2004.

Senghor, Léopold (Sédar) (b. Oct. 9, 1906, Joal, Senegal, French West Africa—d. Dec. 20, 2001, Verson, France), Poet, president of Senegal (1960–80), and cofounder of the Negritude movement in African art and literature. He completed his studies in Paris and became a teacher there. Drafted into the French army in 1939, he was captured and spent two years in Nazi concentration camps, where he wrote some of his finest poems. He was elected to the French National Assembly in 1945. In 1948 he edited *Hosties noires*, an anthology of French-language African poetry that became a seminal Negritude text. That same year he founded the Senegalese Democratic Bloc, which merged with another political party in 1958 to become the Senegalese Progressive Union (known as the Socialist Party since 1976). When Senegal gained independence in 1960, he was unanimously elected president. Advocating a moderate "African socialism," free of atheism and excessive materialism, he became an internationally respected spokesman for Africa and the Third World. In 1984 he became the first black inducted into the French Academy.

sense, or SENSORY RECEPTION, or SENSE PERCEPTION, Mechanism by which information is received about one's external or internal environment. Stimuli received by nerves, in some cases through specialized organs with receptor cells sensitive to one type of stimulus, are converted into impulses that travel to specialized areas of the brain, where they are analyzed. In addition to the "five senses"—sight, hearing, smell, taste, and touch—humans have senses of motion (kinesthetic sense), heat, cold, pressure, pain, and balance. Temperature, pressure, and pain are cutaneous (skin) senses; different points on the skin are particularly sensitive to each.

sentence, In criminal law, a judgment formally pronouncing the punishment to be inflicted on a person convicted of a crime. Among the major types are the concurrent sentence, which runs at the same time as another; the consecutive sentence, which runs before or after another; the mandatory sentence, which is specifically required by statute as punishment for an offense; and the suspended sentence, the imposition or execution of which is suspended by the court.

Seoul, City (pop., 2003 est.: 10,280,503), capital of South Korea since 1948, with the administrative status of a province. Located on the Han River near the centre of the Korean peninsula, Seoul was the capital of the Chosŏn dynasty (1394–1910) and the centre of Japanese rule of Korea (1910–45). During the Korean War it was the capital of the U.S. military government and suffered extensive damage; it has been largely rebuilt since 1953. In 1988 it was the site of the Summer Olympic Games. The commercial, cultural, and industrial heart of South Korea, it is a centre of higher education, with several universities, including Seoul National University (1946).

separation of powers, Division of the legislative, executive, and judicial functions of government among separate and independent bodies. Such a separation limits the possibility of arbitrary excesses by government, since the sanction of all three branches is required for the making, executing, and administering of laws. The concept received its first modern formulation in the work of Charles-Louis de Secondat, baron de La Brède et de Montesquieu, who declared it the best way to safeguard liberty; he influenced the framers of the Constitution of the United States, who in turn influenced the writers of 19th- and 20th-century constitutions.

Sephardi, Any member of the Jewish community, or their descendants, who lived in Spain and Portugal from the Middle Ages until their expulsion in the late 15th century. They fled first to North Africa and other parts of the Ottoman Empire and eventually settled in countries such as France, Holland, England, Italy, and the Balkan states. They differ from the Ashkenazi Jews in their traditional language, Ladino, and in their preservation of Babylonian rather than Palestinian Jewish ritual traditions. Many now live in Israel.

seppuku, or HARA-KIRI, Japanese ritual suicide by disembowelment, practiced by members of the samurai class. Suicide by disembowelment was favoured because it was slow and painful and therefore demonstrated courage, self-control, and strong resolve. Voluntary seppuku was performed to avoid the dishonour of capture, show loyalty to one's lord by following him into death, protest against some policy of a superior, or atone for failure. Obligatory seppuku was a method of capital punishment for a samurai, who would be beheaded by a second once he had made an initial stab wound himself. Obligatory seppuku was abolished in 1873, but voluntary seppuku continued to occur. Notable 20th-century examples included those of army officer Nogi Maresuke and writer Yukio Mishima.

septicemia, or BLOOD POISONING, Invasion of the bloodstream, after surgery or infectious disease, by microorganisms—typically gram-negative bacteria—and the toxins they release. The latter trigger immune responses and widespread coagulation in blood vessels. High fever, chills, weakness, and sweating are followed by a drop in blood pressure. Multiple infections are often present, requiring broad-spectrum antibiotics as well as drainage of foci of infection. Without immediate treatment, septic shock follows, with a mortality rate over 50%. Invasive technology and antibiotic-resistant bacteria in hospitals have made septicemia more severe and more common.

Septuagint, Earliest extant Greek translation of the Hebrew scriptures from the original Hebrew, presumably made for the use of the Jewish community in Egypt when Greek was the lingua franca. The Pentateuch was translated near the middle of the 3rd century BC; the rest of the Hebrew scriptures were translated in the 2nd century BC. The name Septuagint was derived from a legend that 72 translators worked on the project. Its influence was far-reaching. The Septuagint rather than the original Hebrew Bible was the main basis for the Old Latin, Coptic, Ethiopic, Armenian, Georgian, Slavonic, and some Arabic translations of the Bible.

seraph, In Jewish, Christian, and Islamic literature, a celestial being with two or three pairs of wings who guards the throne of God. In Christian angelology, seraphim are the highest-ranking in the hierarchy of angels. In art they are often painted red, symbolizing fire. They appear in the Old Testament in a vision of Isaiah as six-winged creatures praising God.

Serbia, European country located in the west-central Balkans. The autonomous province of Vojvodina is within its borders. Area: 29,922 sq mi (77,498 sq km). Population: (2011 est.) 7,262,000. The capital is Belgrade. Serbia is mountainous, with forests in the central area and low-lying plains in the north. Farming and mining remain important in Serbia, but most workers are employed in manufacturing, which is concentrated in northern industrial zones. The country is a republic with a unicameral legislature; the head of state is the president, and the head of government is the prime minister. Serbs settled the region in the 6th and 7th centuries. In the 9th century the Serbs, nominally under Byzantine suzerainty, converted to Eastern Orthodox Christianity. The Ottoman Empire triumphed at the Battle of Kosovo in 1389; after a long period of resistance, Serbia became part of the empire in 1459. After the Russo-Turkish War of 1828–29, Serbia became an autonomous principality under Ottoman suzerainty and Russian protection. It became completely independent of the Ottoman Empire in 1878. After World War I Serbia became part of the Kingdom of Serbs, Croats, and Slovenes, which was renamed Yugoslavia in 1929. In 1946 Serbia became one of the six federated republics of Yugoslavia. As the Yugoslav economy faltered in the 1980s, the country began to break apart. After an unsuccessful attempt to prevent Slovenia's secession in 1991, Serbian elements of the Yugoslav armed forces began assisting Bosnian Serbs in sweeping Bosniacs (Bosnian Muslims) and Croats from eastern and northern Bosnia and Herzegovina. In 1992, after Yugoslavia's breakup, Serbia joined with Montenegro to form a new Yugoslav federation. The area remained in turmoil. The signing of the Dayton peace accords in 1995 ultimately brought little relief. Slobodan Milošević retained power in Serbia through the end of the century, and the push for more autonomy by Albanian Kosovars provoked another round of fighting in 1998–99. As the violence escalated, NATO responded with a bombing campaign, which led to a peace accord in June 1999. A change in the Yugoslav government late in 2000 brought reinstatement in the UN, and in 2003, though the Montenegrin government threatened to declare independence, the governments of the two constituent states remained united under the name Serbia and Montenegro. By 2006, however, the union was disbanded, and the two were recognized as independent countries. In 2008 Kosovo formally seceded, but Serbia refused to recognize it as an independent country.

Serbo-Croatian language, South Slavic language spoken by some 21 million people in Croatia, Bosnia and Herzegovina, Serbia, and Montenegro. As the dominant language of pre-1991 Yugoslavia, it was used or understood by most ethnic groups of the federation. The Central Neo-Shtokavian dialect forms the basis for both Standard Serbian and Standard Croatian. Historically, Serbia's literary language was the Serbian recension of Church Slavonic. In the 19th century a new literary language based on colloquial Serbian was successfully promulgated by Vuk Stefanović Karadžić. Croatian written in the Latin alphabet first appears in the mid-14th century. In the 19th century the Zagreb-based Illyrian political movement, which aimed at a union of all South Slavs, turned to the Central Neo-Shtokavian dialect as the basis for a literary language that would unite Croatians and bring them closer to their Slavic compatriots. The move toward a unified "Serbo-Croatian" was supported by the politically unified Yugoslav kingdom (1918–41) and communist Yugoslavia (1945–91). With the independence of Bosnia and Herzegovina in 1992, a Bosnian form of the language was recognized of necessity. Vocabulary and pronunciation differences exist among the three but form no real barrier to communication. The Croats and Bosnians use the Roman, or Latin, alphabet; the Serbs and Montenegrins of present-day Serbia and Montenegro use Cyrillic. Most Bosnians, Serbs, and Croats insist that their language is distinct from the others, and, perhaps, from a political perspective this is understandable; but most linguists consider Serbian, Croatian, and Bosnian a single language, which has historically been called Serbo-Croatian.

serfdom, In medieval Europe, condition of a tenant farmer who was bound to a hereditary plot of land and to the will of his landlord. Serfs differed from slaves in that slaves could be bought and sold without reference to land, whereas serfs changed lords only when the land they worked changed hands. From about the 2nd century AD, large privately owned estates in the Roman Empire that had been worked by slaves were broken up and given to peasant farmers. These farmers came to depend on larger landowners for protection in turbulent times, and swearing fealty to a proprietor became common practice. In 332 Constantine I established serfdom legally by requiring tenant farmers to pay labour services to their lords. As serfs, they could not marry, change occupations, or move without the permission of their lords, to whom they were required to give a major portion of their harvest. The development of centralized political power, the labour shortage caused by the Black Death, and endemic peasant uprisings in the 14th and 15th centuries led to the gradual emancipation of serfs in western Europe. In eastern Europe serfdom became more entrenched during that period; the peasants of the Austro-Hungarian Empire were freed in the late 18th century, and Russia's serfs were freed in 1861.

serialism, Use of an ordered set of pitches as the basis of a musical composition. The terms *12-tone music* and *serialism*, though not entirely synonymous, are often used interchangeably. The serial method was worked out by Arnold Schoenberg in 1916–23, though another serial method was being devised simultaneously by Josef Matthias Hauer. To Schoenberg, it represented the culmination of the growth of chromaticism in the late 19th and early 20th centuries. In an attempt to erase the system of tonality, which he regarded as outworn but which frequently asserted itself even in the music of composers who desired to transcend it, Schoenberg's original method stipulated (among several other requirements) that no note be repeated before all 11 other notes of the chromatic scale had been used. *Serialism*, a broader term than *12-tone music*, can be applied to the use of fewer than 12 tones. "Total serialism," a concept that arose in the late 1940s, attempts to organize not only the 12 pitches but also other elements such as rhythm, dynamics, register, and instrumentation into ordered sets.

sesame, Erect, annual plant (*Sesamum indicum*) of numerous types and varieties in the family Pedaliaceae. It has been cultivated since antiquity for its seeds, which are used as food and flavouring and yield a prized oil. The hulled seeds, creamy or pearly white and tiny, have a mild, nutlike aroma and taste. The whole seed is used extensively in the cuisines of the Middle East and Asia. Sesame oil, noted for its stability and its resistance to becoming rancid, is used as a salad or cooking oil, in shortening and margarine, in the manufacture of soaps, pharmaceuticals, and lubricants, and as an ingredient in cosmetics.

Sesame (Sesamum indicum)
Shunji Watari/EB Inc.

set theory, Branch of mathematics that deals with the properties of sets. It is most valuable as applied to other areas of mathematics, which borrow from and adapt its terminology and concepts. These include the operations of union (∪), and intersection (∩). The union of two sets is a set containing all the elements of both sets, each listed once. The intersection is the set of all elements common to both original sets. Set theory is useful in analyzing difficult concepts in mathematics and logic. It was placed on a firm theoretical footing by Georg Cantor, who discovered the value of clearly formulated sets in the analysis of problems in symbolic logic and number theory.

Seth, or SET, Ancient Egyptian god and patron of the 11th nome, or province, of Upper Egypt. A trickster, he was a sky god, lord of the desert, and master of storms, disorder, and warfare. He was the brother of Osiris, whom he killed, and he was antagonistic to Horus, the child of Osiris's sister, Isis. Seth's cult largely died out in the 1st millennium BC, and he was gradually ousted from the Egyptian pantheon. He was later regarded as entirely evil and identified as a god of the Persians and other invaders of Egypt.

SETI, in full SEARCH FOR EXTRATERRESTRIAL INTELLIGENCE, Ongoing effort to seek intelligent extraterrestrial life. SETI focuses on receiving and analyzing signals from space, particularly in the radio and visible-light regions of the electromagnetic spectrum, looking for nonrandom patterns likely to have been sent either deliberately or inadvertently by technologically advanced beings. The first modern SETI search was Project Ozma (1960), which made use of a radio telescope in Green Bank, W.Va. SETI approaches include targeted searches, which typically concentrate on groups of nearby sunlike stars, and systematic surveys covering all directions. The value of SETI efforts has been controversial; programs initiated by NASA in the 1970s were terminated by congressional action in 1993. Subsequently, SETI researchers organized privately funded programs—e.g., the targeted-search Project Phoenix in the U.S. and the survey-type SERENDIP projects in the U.S. and Australia.

Sevastopol, formerly SEBASTOPOL, Seaport city (pop., 2001: 342,000) in the Crimea, southern Ukraine. In 1783 the Russians annexed the Crimea, and, near the ancient Greek colony of Chersonesus, they began construction of a naval base on Sevastopol Bay, an inlet of the Black Sea. It became a commercial port in the early 19th century. It was besieged by Anglo-French forces for 11 months (1854–55) during the Crimean War, an ordeal chronicled by Leo Tolstoy in his *Sevastopol Sketches*. The devastated town

was later rebuilt, and it was the anti-Bolshevik White Army headquarters in the Russian Civil War (1918–20). In World War II it was destroyed after a months-long siege by the Germans, but again it was reconstructed. The chief base of the Russian Black Sea fleet since the early 19th century, it has extensive dockyard facilities and arsenals. The Ukrainian naval forces are also now based in Sevastopol.

Seven Wonders of the World, Preeminent architectural and sculptural achievements of antiquity, as listed by various Greco-Roman observers. Included on the best-known list were the Pyramids of Giza (the oldest of the wonders and the only one substantially in existence today), the Hanging Gardens of Babylon (thought to be a series of landscaped terraces, ascribed to King Nebuchadrezzar II, the semilegendary Queen Sammu-ramat, or the Assyrian king Sennacherib), the Statue of Zeus at Olympia (a large gold-and-ivory figure of the god on his throne by Phidias), the Temple of Artemis at Ephesus (a temple, built in 356 BC, famous for its imposing size and the works of art that adorned it), the Mausoleum of Halicarnassus, the Colossus of Rhodes, and the Pharos of Alexandria (a lighthouse built *c.* 280 BC on the island of Pharos off Alexandria, said to have been more than 350 ft, or 110 m, high). These wonders inspired the compilation of many other lists of seven attractions, or "wonders," by later generations.

Seven Years' War (1756–63) Major European conflict between Austria and its allies France, Saxony, Sweden, and Russia on one side against Prussia and its allies Hanover and Britain on the other. The war arose out of Austria's attempt to win back the rich province of Silesia, taken by Prussia in the War of the Austrian Succession. Early victories by Frederick II the Great in Saxony and Bohemia (1756–58) were offset by a decisive Prussian defeat by Austria and Russia near Frankfurt (1759). After inconclusive fighting in 1760–61, Frederick concluded a peace with Russia (1762) and drove the Austrians from Silesia. The war also involved the overseas colonial struggles between Britain and France in North America and in India. The European conflict was settled with the Treaty of Hubertusburg, by which Frederick confirmed Prussia's stature as a major European power.

Severn, River, Welsh HAFREN, ancient SABRINA, River, eastern Wales and western England. Britain's longest river, it is 180 mi (290 km) long from its source to tidal waters. It rises in east-central Wales and crosses the English border near Shrewsbury, continuing south to the Bristol Channel and the Atlantic Ocean.

Sevilla, English SEVILLE, ancient HISPALIS, City (pop., 2008 est.: city, 690,160), capital of Sevilla province and Andalusia autonomous community (*comunidad autónoma*), Spain. Located on the Guadalquivir River, it is Spain's leading inland port and fourth largest city. Originally an Iberian town, Sevilla prospered under the Romans in the 2nd century BCE. In the 5th–8th centuries CE it was the chief city in southern Spain under the Vandals and the Visigoths. In 711 it fell to the Moors, and under Muslim rule it was a cultural and commercial centre until the 13th century, when Spanish Christians under Ferdinand III captured it. About 1500 Sevilla became the centre of the Spanish colonial trade with the Americas. The French occupied the city (1808–12), and during the Spanish Civil War (1936–39) it was held by the Nationalists. It is one of Spain's main tourist centres, with historic mosques, cathedrals, and the 12th-century Alcázar Palace. It was the site of the Iberoamerican Exposition in 1929 and the Universal Exposition in 1992. The University of Sevilla was founded in 1502.

sewage system, Collection of pipes and mains, treatment works, and discharge lines (sewers) for the wastewater of a community. Early civilizations often built drainage systems in urban areas to handle storm runoff. The Romans constructed elaborate systems that also drained wastewater from the public baths. In the Middle Ages these systems fell into disrepair. As the populations of cities grew, disastrous epidemics of cholera and typhoid fever broke out, the result of ineffective separation of sewage and drinking water. In the mid-19th century the first steps were taken to treat wastewater. The concentration of population and the addition to sewage of manufacturing waste that occurred during the Industrial Revolution increased the need for effective sewage treatment. Sewer pipe is laid following street patterns, and access holes with metal covers allow periodic inspection and cleaning. Catch basins at street corners and along street gutters collect surface runoff of storm water and direct it to the storm sewers. Civil engineers determine the volume of sewage likely, the route of the system, and the slope of the pipe to ensure an even flow by gravity that will not leave solids behind. In flat regions, pumping stations are sometimes needed. Modern sewage systems include domestic and industrial sewers and storm sewers. Sewage treatment plants remove organic matter from waste water through a series of steps. As sewage enters the plant, large objects (such as wood and gravel) are screened out; grit and sand are then removed by settling or screening with finer mesh. The remaining sewage passes into primary sedimentation tanks where suspended solids (sludge) settle out. The remaining sewage is aerated and mixed with microorganisms to decompose organic matter. A secondary sedimentation tank allows any remaining solids to settle out; the remaining liquid effluent is discharged into a body of water. Sludge from the sedimentation tanks may be disposed of in landfills, dumped at sea, used as fertilizer, or decomposed further in heated tanks (digestion tanks) to produce methane gas to power the treatment plant.

sex, Sum of features by which a member of a plant or animal species can be placed into one of two complementary reproductive groups, male or female. In both plants and animals, sex is determined by the reproductive cells (gametes) produced by the organism. The male produces sperm cells, and the female produces egg cells. Males and females may or may not have apparent structural differences, but they always have functional, hormonal, and chromosomal differences. Patterns of behaviour, sometimes elaborate, may also distinguish the sexes in some species.

sextant, Instrument for determining the angle between the horizon and a celestial body—such as the Sun, the Moon, or a star—used in celestial navigation to determine latitude and longitude. It consists of a metal arc, marked in degrees, and a movable radial arm pivoted at the centre of the arc's circle. A telescope, mounted rigidly to the framework, is lined up with the horizon. The radial arm, on which a mirror is mounted, is moved until the star is reflected into a half-silvered mirror in line with the telescope and appears, through the telescope, to coincide with the horizon. The angular distance of the star above the horizon is then read from the graduated arc of the sextant. From this angle, the latitude can be determined (within a few hundred metres) by means of published tables, and by consulting an accurate chronometer the longitude can be established. Invented in 1731, the sextant replaced the octant and became an essential tool of navigation.

sexual dysfunction, Inability to experience arousal or achieve sexual satisfaction under ordinary circumstances, as a result of psychological or physiological problems. The most common sexual dysfunctions have traditionally been referred to as impotence (applied to males) and frigidity (females), but these terms have gradually been replaced by more specific terms. Most sexual dysfunctions can be overcome through use of counseling, psychotherapy, or drug therapy.

sexual harassment, Unsolicited verbal or physical behaviour of a sexual nature. Sexual harassment may embrace any sexually motivated behaviour considered offensive by the recipient. Legal recourse is available in cases that occur in the workplace, though it is very difficult to obtain convictions. In 1994 the Supreme Court of the United States ruled that behaviour can be considered sexual harassment and an abridgment of an individual's civil rights if it creates a hostile and abusive working environment.

sexuality, human, Tendencies and behaviour of human beings with regard to any activity that causes or is otherwise associated with sexual arousal. It is strongly influenced by the genetically inherited sexual response patterns that ensure reproduction, societal attitudes toward sex, and each individual's upbringing. Physiology sets only very broad limits on human sexuality; most of the enormous variation found among humans results from learning and conditioning. What is deviant in one society may be normal in another. Sexuality covers gender identity, sexual orientation, and actual practices, as well as one's acceptance of these aspects of one's personality, which may be more important than their specifics.

sexually transmitted disease (STD), Disease transmitted primarily by direct sexual contact. STDs usually affect the reproductive system and urinary system but can be spread to the mouth or rectum by oral or anal sex. In later stages they may attack other organs and systems. The best-known are syphilis, gonorrhea, AIDS, and herpes simplex. Yeast infections produce a thick, whitish vaginal discharge and genital irritation and itch in women and sometimes irritation of the penis in men. Crab louse infestation can also be considered an STD. The incidence of STDs has been affected by such factors as antibiotics, birth-control methods, and changes in sexual behaviour.

Seychelles, officially REPUBLIC OF SEYCHELLES, Island country, western Indian Ocean. Area: 174 sq mi (452 sq km). Population: (2011 est.) 92,000. Capital: Victoria. The mixed population is of French, African, and Asian ancestry. Languages: Creole, English, French. Religion: Christianity (predominantly Roman Catholic; also Anglican); smaller populations of Hindus and Muslims. Currency: Seychelles rupee. Located east of northeastern Tanzania, Seychelles is composed of two main island groups: the Mahé group of more than 40 central, mountainous, granitic islands and a second group of more than 70 outlying, flat, coralline islands. The country has a developing economy that depends heavily on the service sector in general and the tourism industry in particular. Exports include fish, copra, and cinnamon. It is a multiparty republic with one legislative house; its head of state and government is the president. The first recorded landing on uninhabited Seychelles was made in 1609 by an expedition of the British East India Company. The archipelago was claimed by the French in 1756 and surrendered to the British in 1810. It became a British crown colony in 1903 and a republic within the Commonwealth in 1976. A one-party socialist state since 1979, it held multiparty elections in 1992 and adopted a new constitution in 1993.

Sezession, Name for several groups of progressive artists that broke away from established and conservative artists' organizations in Austria and Germany. The first secession group was formed in Munich in 1892. It was followed by the Berlin Sezession movement, formed by Max Liebermann in 1892, which included such artists as Lovis Corinth. The most famous of the groups, formed in Vienna in 1897 by Gustav Klimt, favoured a highly ornamental Art Nouveau style over the prevailing academicism. Shortly thereafter, murals created by Klimt for the ceiling of the University of Vienna auditorium were rejected as scandalous because of their erotic symbolism. The Sezession movement influenced such artists and architects as Egon Schiele and Josef Hoffmann.

Sfax, or ṢAFĀQIS, Port city (pop., 2004: 265,131), east-central Tunisia. Built on the site of two ancient settlements, the city grew as an Islamic trading centre. It was occupied by the Normans in the 12th century and by the Spanish in the 16th century, and later served as a stronghold of the Barbary Coast pirates. The town was bombarded by the French in 1881 prior to their occupation of Tunisia and again in World War II (1939–45), when it was a base for German forces until taken by the British in 1943. One of Tunisia's largest cities, it is a transportation hub and a major fishing port.

Shaanxi, or SHEN-HSI, conventional SHENSI, Province (pop., 2002 est.: 36,740,000), north-central China. It is bordered by Shanxi, Henan, Hubei, Sichuan, and Gansu provinces, Chongqing municipality, and Ningxia and Inner Mongolia autonomous regions. It has an area of 75,600 sq mi (195,800 sq km). Its capital is Xi'an. Shaanxi has three distinct natural regions: the mountainous southern region, the central Wei River valley, and the northern upland plateau. The valley is especially vulnerable to earthquakes. Its northern parts were some of the earliest settled in China, and the remains of ancient construction projects found there include part of the Great Wall. From 221 BCE until the Tang dynasty, it was wealthy and the centre of much political activity. As its irrigation system deteriorated, the area declined. In the 13th century, under the Mongols, it assumed its present form as a province. Mao Zedong's Long March ended there in 1935. Its ancient irrigation system has been rehabilitated since 1949, and the region is again a rich agricultural area. Crops include corn (maize), winter wheat, fruits, tobacco, and cotton.

Shaivism, or SAIVISM, One of three main forms of modern Hinduism, centred on the worship of Shiva. The earliest of the cults devoted to Shiva date from the 4th century BC. Texts written by devotees of Shiva in the 3rd century AD are the basis of Tantra in Hinduism and other Indian religions. Today Shaivism includes diverse movements, both religious and secular, all of which take Shiva as the supreme and all-powerful deity and teacher and view gaining the nature of Shiva as the ultimate goal of existence. This is believed to be brought about by the performance of complex rituals.

Shaka (b. *c.* 1787—d. Sept. 22, 1828), Zulu chief (1816–28), founder of southern Africa's Zulu kingdom. His life is the subject of numerous colourful and exaggerated stories, many of which are debated by historians. It is generally accepted that Shaka was a highly skilled warrior who established himself as head of the Zulu about 1816. Under his autocratic rule, the Zulu kingdom experienced significant expansion, quickly becoming the dominant power in southeastern Africa. Shaka was murdered by his half-brother.

Shaka, lithograph by W. Bagg, 1836.

Shaker, Member of the United Society of Believers in Christ's Second Appearing, a celibate millenarian sect. Derived from a branch of the radical English Quakers, the movement was brought to the U.S. in 1774 by Ann Lee, an illiterate textile worker whose followers accepted her as the second incarnation of Christ. The Shakers spread throughout New England from their base near Albany, N.Y., and later into Kentucky, Ohio, and Indiana, eventually establishing 19 communities. Communities held property in common, observed celibacy, and pursued a life of productive labour. Although sometimes persecuted for their pacifism and for bizarre beliefs falsely attributed to them, Shakers won admiration for their model farms and orderly, prosperous communities. Their talent for simple, functional design led to numerous inventions and innovations. The movement reached its height in the 1840s and thereafter gradually declined. In the early 21st century only one working Shaker village remained: Sabbathday Lake, near New Gloucester, Maine.

Shakespeare, William (baptized April 26, 1564, Stratford-upon-Avon, Warwickshire, Eng.—d. April 23, 1616, Stratford-upon-Avon), English poet and playwright, often considered the greatest writer in world literature. He spent his early life in Stratford-upon-Avon, receiving at most a grammar-school education, and at age 18 he married a local woman, Anne Hathaway. By 1594 he was apparently a rising playwright in London and an actor in a leading theatre company, the Lord Chamberlain's Men (later King's Men); the company performed at the Globe Theatre from 1599. The order in which his plays were written and performed is highly uncertain. His earliest plays seem to date from the late 1580s to the mid-1590s and include the comedies *Love's Labour's Lost*, *The Comedy of Errors*, *The Taming of the Shrew*, and *A Midsummer Night's Dream*; history plays based on the lives of the English kings, including *Henry VI* (parts 1, 2, and 3), *Richard III*, and *Richard II*; and the tragedy *Romeo and Juliet*. The plays apparently written between 1596 and 1600 are mostly comedies, including *The Merchant of Venice*, *The Merry Wives of Windsor*, *Much Ado About Nothing*, and *As You Like It*, and histories, including *Henry IV* (parts 1 and 2), *Henry V*, and *Julius Caesar*. Approximately between 1600 and 1607 he wrote the comedies *Twelfth Night*, *All's Well That Ends Well*, and *Measure for Measure*, as well as the great tragedies *Hamlet* (probably begun in 1599), *Othello*, *Macbeth*, and *King Lear*, which mark the summit of his art. Among his later works (about 1607 to 1614) are the tragedies *Antony and Cleopatra*, *Coriolanus*, and *Timon of Athens*, as well as the fantastical romances *The Winter's Tale* and *The Tempest*. He probably also collaborated on the plays *Edward III* and *The Two Noble Kinsmen*. In 2010 a case was made for Shakespeare as the coauthor (with John Fletcher) of *Double Falsehood*.

Shakespeare's plays, all of them written largely in iambic pentameter verse, are marked by extraordinary poetry; vivid, subtle, and complex characterizations; and a highly inventive use of English. His 154 sonnets, published in 1609 but apparently written mostly in the 1590s, often express strong feeling within an exquisitely controlled form. Shakespeare retired to Stratford before 1610 and lived as a country gentleman until his death. The first collected edition of his plays, or First Folio, was published in 1623. As with most writers of the time, little is known about his life and work, and other writers, particularly the 17th earl of Oxford, have frequently been proposed as the actual authors of his plays and poems.

shakti, or SAKTI, In Hinduism, the "creative energy" inherent in and proceeding from God. It is exemplified by the female principle, the female reproductive organs, or the goddess Shakti, wife of Shiva. As energy, shakti is viewed as the merging of powers emanating from male gods, and it is possessed by each person. In Tantric Hinduism, the goddess Shakti is associated with the lowest of the chakras, lying dormant within the body as a coiled serpent (Kundalini) that must be aroused to reach spiritual liberation by uniting with Shiva at the top of the head.

Shaktism, or SAKTISM, Worship of the supreme Hindu goddess Shakti. Together with Vaishnavism and Shaivism, it is one of the major forms of Hinduism practiced today. Particularly prominent in Bengal and Assam, Shaktism takes various forms depending on conceptions of Shakti. In popular worship she has many names, and some scholars consider most female deities in Hinduism to be various manifestations of her. Shakti is worshiped and cultivated as a power that can lead to spiritual liberation. Shaktism is inseparably related to the system of practices for the purification of mind and body that are grouped under Tantric Hinduism.

shale, Any of a group of fine-grained, laminated sedimentary rocks consisting of silt- and clay-sized particles. Shale constitutes roughly 60% of the sedimentary rock in the Earth's crust. Shales are commercially important, particularly in the ceramics industry. They are a valuable raw material for tile, brick, and pottery and constitute a major source of alumina for portland cement. In addition, advances in recovery methods may one day make oil shale a practical source for liquid petroleum.

shale oil, Synthetic crude oil that is extracted from oil shale by pyrolysis, or destructive distillation. The oil obtained from oil shale cannot be refined by the methods that have been developed for crude oil, however, because shale oil is low in hydrogen and contains large amounts of nitrogen and sulfur compounds. To be made usable, shale oil must be hydrogenated and then chemically treated to remove the nitrogen and sulfur, a process too expensive to make shale oil commercially competitive with crude oil.

shaman, Person who uses magic to cure the sick, divine the unknown, or control events. Both men and women can be shamans. Shamanism is classically associated with certain Arctic and Central Asian peoples, but today the term is applied to analogous religious and quasi-religious systems throughout the world. As medicine man and priest, the shaman cures illnesses, directs communal sacrifices, and escorts the souls of the dead to the other world. He operates by using techniques of ecstasy, the power to leave his body at will during a trancelike state. In cultures where shamanism occurs, sickness is usually thought of as soul loss; it is thus the shaman's task to enter the spirit world, capture the soul, and reintegrate it in the body. A person becomes a shaman either by inheritance or by self-election.

Shamash, In Mesopotamian religion, the god of the sun, who, with his father, Sin, and the goddess Ishtar, was part of an astral triad of divinities. As the solar god, Shamash was the heroic conqueror of night and death, and he became known as the god of justice and equity. He was said to have presented the Code of Hammurabi to the Babylonian king. At night he served as judge of the underworld. The chief centres of his cult were at Larsa and Sippar.

Shandong, or SHAN-TUNG, conventional SHANTUNG, Coastal province (pop., 2002 est.: 90,820,000), eastern China. It lies on the Yellow Sea and is bordered by Jiangsu, Anhui, Henan, and Hebei provinces. It has an area of 59,200 sq mi (153,300 sq km), and its capital is Jinan. It contains the Shandong Peninsula and an inland zone that includes a fertile, intensely cultivated area that forms part of the Huang He (Yellow River) basin. The peninsula has been occupied since the 3rd millennium BCE, and by the 8th century BCE it had become a centre of political and military activity. It became northern China's leading maritime centre in the 3rd century CE and retained that position for centuries. In the 19th century devastating floods resulted in substantial emigration. It came under German, British, and Japanese influence in the late 19th century. The Japanese occupied it in 1937–45; it came under communist control in 1948. Its products include wheat, corn, iron ore, gold, fish, and silk. Confucius and Mencius were born in Shandong.

Shandong Peninsula, or SHAN-TUNG PENINSULA, conventional SHANTUNG PENINSULA, Peninsula, eastern China. Occupying the eastern section of Shandong province, it extends northeastward between the Bo Hai (Gulf of Chihli) and the Yellow Sea. The terrain is hilly, with elevations around 600 ft (180 m), rising to 3,707 ft (1,130 m) in the Lao Mountains. Fishing is important along the coast, and fruit is grown in the hills. Iron ore, magnesite, and gold are abundant. Some of China's best ports are located along the peninsula's rocky, indented coast.

Shanghai, or SHANG-HAI, Municipality with provincial status (pop., 2006 est.: city, 11,283,714; 2009 est.: municipality, 18,880,000), east-central China. The municipality, on the East China Sea, is bordered by Jiangsu and Zhejiang provinces and has an area of 2,400 sq mi (6,200 sq km). The city is located on the Huangpu River, which gives oceangoing vessels access to it. The site was settled during the Bei (Northern) Song period (960–1127 CE), and later under the Ming dynasty it was an area of intense cot-

ton production. This changed when it became the first Chinese port opened to trade with the West after China's defeat by Britain in the Opium Wars (1842); it came to dominate the nation's commerce. The site of the Chinese Communist Party's founding in 1921, it saw severe fighting in the Sino-Japanese War of 1937–45 and was occupied by Japan during World War II. Since 1949 it has become China's chief industrial and commercial centre and one of its leading centres of higher education and scientific research. In 2010 the city hosted the Expo Shanghai 2010 world exposition.

Shankar, Ravi (b. April 7, 1920, Benares, India), Indian sitar player. He studied music and dance, toured as a member of his brother Uday's dance troupe, and spent years learning the sitar. After serving as music director of All-India Radio (1948–56), he began a series of European and U.S. tours. He wrote the score for Satyajit Ray's *Apu* film trilogy (1955–59). He was a founder of the National Orchestra of India, and in 1962 he founded the Kinnara School of Music in Bombay (now Mumbai) and later in Los Angeles. His performances with Yehudi Menuhin and his association with George Harrison of the Beatles were primarily responsible for bringing Indian music to a broad Western audience.

Ravi Shankar (foreground), 1967.
John Reader—Time Life Pictures/Getty Images

Shannon, River, River, Ireland. The country's longest river, it rises in northwestern County Cavan and flows for about 230 mi (370 km) to enter the Atlantic Ocean below Limerick. It is surrounded by marshes and bogs for much of its course and widens at various points into lakes, many with islands. In the early 19th century it was a vital link in the waterways of Ireland; today it is used by pleasure craft.

Shanxi, or SHAN-HSI, conventional SHÂNSI, Province (pop., 2002 est.: 32,940,000), northern China. It is bordered by Hebei, Henan, and Shaanxi provinces and Inner Mongolia. It has an area of 60,700 sq mi (157,100 sq km). The capital is Taiyuan. Largely a vast plateau covered by great loess deposits, it was the home of early Chinese agriculture. Most of the people are Han Chinese; other ethnic groups include Hui (Chinese Muslims), Mongols, and Manchus. Since ancient times it has been an integral part of the various northern kingdoms of China, serving as a buffer against invaders from the north and as a key trade route. It was one of the major avenues by which Buddhism came to China from India. After the overthrow of the Qing dynasty in 1911–12, the warlord Yan Xishan ruled as absolute dictator until the end of World War II. Japan occupied part of the province during the Sino-Japanese War (1937–45). Communist forces assumed control of Shanxi in 1949. It has vast reserves of coal and iron and the largest titanium and vanadium deposits in China and is a major producer of cotton.

Sharī'ah, Legal and moral code of Islam, systematized in the early centuries of the Muslim era (8th–9th century AD). It rests on four bases: the Qur'ān; the sunna, as recorded in the Ḥadīth; *ijma*, or agreement among scholars; and *qiya*, or analogical reasoning. Sharī'ah differs fundamentally from Western law in that it purports to be grounded in divine revelation. Among modern Muslim countries, Saudi Arabia and Iran retain Sharī'ah as the law of the land, in both civil and criminal proceedings, but the legal codes of most other Muslim countries combine elements of Islamic and

Western law where necessary. Most Islamic fundamentalist groups insist that Muslim countries should be governed by Sharīʿah.

shark, Any of more than 300 species of predatory cartilaginous fish (order Selachii). An ancient animal, it has changed little in 100 million years. The skin typically is dull gray and tough and has toothlike scales. Most sharks have a muscular, asymmetrical, up-turned tail; pointed fins; a pointed snout; and sharp triangular teeth. Sharks have no swim bladder and must swim perpetually to keep from sinking. Most species bear living young. Several species can be dangerous to humans (e.g., great white shark, hammer-head shark, sand shark, tiger shark); smaller ones, called topes, hounds, and dogfishes, are fished commercially.

shaṭḥ, In Sufism, a divinely inspired statement that a practitioner utters in a mystical state. The Sufis claim that there are moments of ecstatic fervour when they are overwhelmed by the divine presence to such a degree that they lose touch with worldly realities. In such moments they utter statements that may seem incoherent or blasphemous if taken literally, so the statements must be interpreted symbolically. Since the state of mystical trance is normally brief, the statements rarely exceed six or seven words, but the Sufis regard all their writings, particularly their poetry, as possessing an element of *shaṭḥ*.

Shatt al-Arab, River, southeastern Iraq, formed by the confluence of the Tigris and Euphrates rivers. It flows southeastward for 120 mi (193 km) and passes the Iraqi port of Al-Baṣrah and the Iranian port of Ābādān before emptying into the Persian Gulf. With dredging, the river is navigable by shallow-draft oceangoing vessels. For about the last half of its course, the river forms the border between Iraq and Iran. In the 1980s it was the scene of prolonged fighting during the Iran-Iraq War.

Shaw, George Bernard (b. July 26, 1856, Dublin, Ire.—d. Nov. 2, 1950, Ayot St. Lawrence, Hertfordshire, Eng.), Irish playwright and critic. After moving to London in 1876, he worked for years as a music and art critic, wrote book and theatre reviews, and was an active member of the socialist Fabian Society. In his first play, *Widowers' Houses* (1892), he emphasized social and economic issues instead of romance, adopting the ironic comedic tone that would characterize all his work. He described his first plays as "unpleasant" because they forced the spectator to face unpleasant

George Bernard Shaw, photograph by Yousuf Karsh.
Karsh/Woodfin Camp and Associates

facts; these plays include *Mrs. Warren's Profession* (1893), which concerns prostitution and was barred from performance until 1902. He then wrote four "pleasant" plays, including the comedies *Arms and the Man* (1894) and *Candida* (1895). His next plays include *Caesar and Cleopatra* (1899) and *Man and Superman* (1905). He used high comedy to explore society's foibles in *Major Barbara* (1905), *The Doctor's Dilemma* (1911), and *Pygmalion* (1913), his comedic masterpiece. Other notable plays include *Androcles and the Lion* (1912), *Heartbreak House* (1919), and *Saint Joan* (1923). His other writings and speeches made him a controversial public figure for much of his life. He received the Nobel Prize in 1925.

Sheba, Queen of (fl. 10th century BC), In Jewish and Islamic traditions, ruler of the Kingdom of Sabaʾ (Sheba) in southwestern Arabia. In an Old Testament story, she visited King Solomon to test his wisdom. In Islamic tradition she is known as Bilqīs and is

converted from worship of the sun to worship of God, marrying either Solomon himself or a Hamdānī tribesman. In Persian folklore she is considered the daughter of a Chinese king and a peri (a type of supernatural being). Ethiopian tradition names her Makeda; her son by Solomon is seen as the founder of the Ethiopian royal dynasty.

sheep, Ruminants (bovid genus *Ovis*) that have scent glands in the face and hind feet. Horns, if present, are more divergent than those of goats. Species range from 80 to 400 lb (35 to 180 kg). The coat of wild species consists of outer hair underlain by wool. Sheep graze in flocks, preferably on short, fine grasses and legumes. They have been domesticated from at least 5000 BC in the Middle East, Europe, and Central Asia. Most domesticated breeds produce fine wool; the few that produce only hair or coarse or long wool are generally raised for meat. The flesh of mature sheep is called mutton; that of immature sheep is called lamb.

Sheffield, City and metropolitan borough (pop., 2001: 513,234), South Yorkshire, England. It is situated at the foot of the Pennines. An Anglo-Saxon village that became the site of a castle and parish church early in the 12th century, it has been known for its cutlery since medieval times. By 1700 it had a monopoly of the English cutlery trade, and it remains the centre of the industry today. It developed a steel industry from the mid-19th century, and several metallurgical innovations, including the process for making stainless steel, originated there. In 1568 Mary, Queen of Scots, was imprisoned in its Norman castle (now in ruins).

sheikh, or SHAYKH, Among Arabic-speaking tribes, especially Bedouin, the male head of the family, as well as of each successively larger social unit making up the tribal structure. The sheikh is generally assisted by an informal tribal council of male elders. Within the broader Arabic-speaking community, the word may also be used as a title or form of respectful address or to designate a religious authority. Its significance may vary from region to region.

Shekhina, In Judaism, the worldly presence of God, sometimes conceived of as a divine light. It is said that the Shekhina descended on the Tabernacle and on Solomon's Temple, though it was one of the five things lacking in the Second Temple of Jerusalem. There is an affinity between the Shekhina and the Holy Spirit; though the two are not identical, both signify divine immanence, are associated with prophecy, can be lost due to sin, and are connected with the study of the Torah.

Shelley, Mary Wollstonecraft, orig. MARY WOLLSTONECRAFT GODWIN (b. Aug. 30, 1797, London, Eng.—d. Feb. 1, 1851, London), English Romantic novelist. The only daughter of William Godwin and Mary Wollstonecraft, she met and eloped with Percy B. Shelley in 1814. They married in 1816 after his first wife committed suicide. Mary Shelley's best-known work is *Frankenstein* (1818), a narrative of the dreadful consequences of a scientist's artificially creating a human being. After her husband's death in 1822, she devoted herself to publicizing his writings and educating their son. Of her several other works, *The Last Man* (1826), is an account of the future destruction of the human race by a plague.

Mary Wollstonecraft Shelley, detail of an oil painting by Richard Rothwell, first exhibited 1840; in the National Portrait Gallery, London.
Courtesy of the National Portrait Gallery, London

shellfish, Any aquatic mollusk, crustacean, or echinoderm that has a shell. Oysters, mussels, scallops, and clams rank among the most commercially important. Certain gastropod mollusks, such as abalone, whelk, and conch, are also marketed. The main crustaceans are shrimp, lobster, and crab. Among echinoderms, sea urchins and sea cucumbers are locally popular. After being harvested, all shellfish are highly perishable. Many types are cooked live to protect the consumer against the effects of spoilage.

Shenyang, or SHEN-YANG, formerly MUKDEN, City (pop., 2003 est.: 3,995,500), capital of Liaoning province, northeastern China. An ancient city, it was the Manchu capital (1625–44) before the establishment of the Qing (Manchu) dynasty. After 1895 it was fought over by Russia and Japan in the struggle for Manchuria. It was occupied by the Japanese (1931–45). Taken by the communist forces in 1948, it was a base for their conquest of the whole of China. It is one of China's leading industrial cities; its manufactures include machinery, wires and cables, textiles, and chemicals. It is also a cultural and educational centre.

Sherpa, Any member of a mountain-dwelling people of the Himalayas. Sherpas are of Tibetan culture and descent and speak a Tibetan dialect. They make a living spinning and weaving wool, along with farming and cattle breeding. They have won international renown as porters in the high Himalayas, and the name Sherpa has come to be used generically for porters there. They number about 50,000.

Shetland Islands, or ZETLAND ISLANDS, Island group (pop., 2001: 21,988), Scotland. The Shetlands comprise some 100 islands located 130 mi (210 km) north of the Scottish mainland and about 400 mi (640 km) south of the Arctic Circle. They form the Shetland administrative region; the region's capital is Lerwick. Fewer than 20 of the islands are inhabited. The northernmost part of Britain, the islands have fjordlike coasts and a climate warmed by the North Atlantic Current. The Norse ruled the Shetlands from the 8th to the 15th century. In 1472 the islands, with Orkney, were annexed to the Scottish crown. They are famous for their livestock, which includes the Shetland pony and the Shetland sheep. The latter's fine wool is used in the distinctive Shetland and Fair Isle knitted patterns. The North Sea oil industry has contributed to the economy.

shigella, Any of the rod-shaped bacteria that make up the genus *Shigella*, which are normal inhabitants of the human intestinal tract and can cause dysentery, or shigellosis. Shigellae are gram-negative, non-spore-forming, stationary bacteria. *S. dysenteriae*, spread by contaminated water and food, causes the most severe dysentery because of its potent toxin, but other species may also be dysentery agents.

shih tzu, Breed of toy dog developed in Tibet from the Pekingese and the Lhasa apso. Sturdily built and short-legged, it stands about 10 in. (26 cm) tall and weighs 18 lb (8 kg) or less. It is longer than it is tall and has a short muzzle, hanging ears, and heavily haired tail, which it carries over its back. Its long, dense coat may be any of several colours and falls over the eyes, forming a beard.

Shīʿite, Member of the Shīʿite branch of Islam, which resulted from the first *fitnah*, or split, within the religion over leadership. Members of the political faction that supported ʿAlī, Muhammad's son-in-law, as the Prophet's heir after the murder of the third caliph, ʿUthmān, the Shīʿites gradually became a religious movement after the murder of ʿAlī. ʿAlī's followers insisted that a caliph, or imam, be a lineal descendant of ʿAlī and his wife, Fāṭimah. Shīʿite legal tradition is distinct from the four major schools of thought in Sunnite Islam and is generally regarded as the most conservative. Though Shīʿites represent only about 10% of Muslims in the world, they are a majority in Iran and Iraq, and there are sizable populations in Yemen, Syria, Lebanon, East Africa, Pakistan, and northern India. The largest subdivision is the Ithnā

ʿAshariyyah, or Twelvers, who recognized 12 historical imams (including ʿAlī); other subsects include the Ismāʿīliyyah and the Zaydiyyah.

Shikoku, Smallest main island (pop., 2004 est.: 4,111,000) of Japan. It is located south of Honshu and east of Kyushu. Much of its 7,065 sq mi (18,298 sq km) is mountainous, and the population is concentrated in urban areas along the coast. Rice, barley, wheat, and mandarin oranges are among the island's major crops. Industries include petroleum refining, textiles, paper, and fishing.

shingles, or HERPES ZOSTER, Acute viral skin and nerve infection. Groups of small blisters appear along certain nerve segments, most often on the back, sometimes after a dull ache at the site; pain becomes more severe when the blisters break out. Caused by the same virus as chickenpox, it probably results from reactivation of seemingly inactive virus in a partially immune person. Spontaneous recovery from the infection usually occurs within two weeks, but neuralgia may last months or even years longer.

Shining Path, Spanish SENDERO LUMINOSO, Maoist movement in Peru dedicated to violent revolution. It was founded in 1970 by a philosophy professor, Abimael Guzmán Reynoso (b. 1934), as a result of a split in the Peruvian Communist Party. The *senderistas* began their campaign among the impoverished Indians of the high Andes, attracting sympathizers by their emphasis on the empowerment of Indians at the expense of Peru's traditional elite. They gained control of large areas of Peru through violence and intimidation. By 1992, when Guzmán was captured and their influence began to wane, they had caused an estimated 25,000 deaths and seriously disrupted the Peruvian economy. Their new leader, Oscar Ramirez Durand, was sentenced to life imprisonment in 1999.

Shintō, Indigenous religion of Japan. Based on the worship of spirits known as *kami*, Shintō has no founder and no official scripture, though its mythology is collected in the *Kojiki* ("Records of Ancient Matters") and *Nihon shoki* ("Chronicles of Japan"), written in the 8th century. The term Shintō ("Way of the Kami") came into use to distinguish indigenous Japanese beliefs from Buddhism, which had been introduced into Japan in the 6th century. At Shintō's core are beliefs in the *kami*'s mysterious creating and harmonizing power. According to Shintō myths, in the beginning a certain number of *kami* simply emerged, and a pair of *kami*, Izanagi and Izanami, gave birth to the Japanese islands, as well as to the *kami* who became ancestors of the various clans. The Japanese imperial family claims descent from Izanagi's daughter, the sun goddess Amaterasu. All *kami* are said to cooperate with one another, and life lived in accordance with their will is believed to produce a mystical power that gains their protection, cooperation, and approval. Through veneration and observation of prescribed rituals at shrines (e.g., ritual purity), practitioners of Shintō can come to understand and live in accordance with divine will. In the early 21st century, Shintō had nearly 2.8 million followers.

shinty, or SHINNY, Game similar to hurling and field hockey. Players (12 per team) use curved sticks to hit a small, hard ball into the opposing team's goal (*hail*). It is considered the national game of Scotland, where it originated before the 17th century.

ship, Large floating vessel capable of crossing open waters. The term formerly was applied to sailing vessels with three or more masts; today it usually denotes a vessel of more than 500 tons' (450 metric tons') displacement. The largest ships today are enormous oil tankers, some of which are 500,000 tons (450,000 metric tons) deadweight. Other specialized ships (containerships) carry general freight in standardized containers that can be easily loaded, unloaded, and transferred.

ship of the line, Type of sailing warship, the principal vessel of the West's great navies from the mid-17th to the mid-19th century. It evolved from a tactic in naval warfare known as the line of battle, in which two opposing columns of ships maneuvered to fire their guns broadside against each other. Since the largest ships carrying the biggest guns usually won these battles, this led to the construction of more big line-of-battle ships, or ships of the line. These three-masted ships were often 200 ft (60 m) long, displaced 1,200–2,000 tons (1,100–1,800 metric tons), and had crews of 600–800 men; they usually had 60–110 cannons and other guns arranged along three decks. They eventually gave way to the steam-powered battleship.

Shīrāz, Industrial and commercial city (pop., 2006: 1,227,331), south-central Iran. It was important during the Seleucid (312–175 BC), Parthian (247 BC–AD 224), and Sāsānian (*c.* AD 224–651) periods but reached its economic and cultural peak later, during the Islamic period. In the late 14th century, Timur twice occupied Shīrāz, which had by that time become a Muslim centre rivaling Baghdad. In 1724 it was sacked by Afghan invaders and later became the capital of the Persian Zand dynasty (1750–94). Famous for its wine, gardens, shrines, and mosques, it was the birthplace of the Persian poets Saʿdī and Ḥāfeẓ, who remain local icons and whose tombs are located there.

shirk, In Islam, idolatry and polytheism, both of which are regarded as heretical. The Qurʾān stresses that God does not share his powers with any partner (*sharik*) and warns that those who believe in idols will be harshly dealt with on the Day of Judgment. The concept of *shirk* has broadened considerably throughout the dogmatic development of Islam, and it has come to be used as the opposite of *tawḥīd* (the oneness of God). Different grades of *shirk* have been distinguished by Islamic law; they include the belief in superstition, belief in the power of created things (e.g., reverencing saints), and belief in those who profess to know the future—all of which pale beside polytheism in seriousness.

Shiva, or SIVA, Major deity of Hinduism, believed to have many

manifestations. Like Vishnu, he is the subject of an elaborate and sometimes contradictory mythology. He is both the destroyer and the restorer, the great ascetic and the symbol of sensuality, the benevolent herdsman of souls and the wrathful avenger. His female consort is known under various manifestations, including Parvati, Durga, and Kali. In Shaivism he is worshiped as the paramount lord.

Shiva, bronze statue, Madras, c. AD 900.
Courtesy of the Government Museum, Chennai; photograph, Royal Academy of Arts, London

shock, State in which the circulatory system fails to supply enough blood to peripheral tissues to meet basic requirements. Symptoms—weak, rapid pulse; low blood pressure; and cold, sweaty skin—are not all present in every case. Causes include low blood volume, caused by bleeding or fluid loss from burns or dehydration; inability of the heart to pump enough blood, due to heart attack, pulmonary embolism, or cardiac tamponade (compression of the heart by fluid in the membrane around it); and blood-vessel dilation as a result of septicemia, allergy (including anaphylaxis), or drugs. All result in reduced capillary blood flow; reflexes increase heart rate and constrict small blood vessels to protect the blood supply to essential organs. Without treatment of the underlying cause, these mechanisms fail; since the cause is not always clear, cases tend to require different and occasionally contradictory treatment (e.g., intravenous fluids can save the life of a patient with massive blood loss but can overload a weakened heart).

Shockley, William B(radford) (b. Feb. 13, 1910, London, Eng.—d. Aug. 12, 1989, Palo Alto, Calif., U.S.), U.S. engineer and teacher. He received a Ph.D. from Harvard University. He joined Bell Labs in 1936, where he began experiments that led to the development of the transistor. During World War II he was director of research for the U.S. Navy's Antisubmarine Warfare Operations Research Group; later (1954–55) he was deputy director of the Defense Department's Weapons Systems Evaluation Group. He established the Shockley Semiconductor Laboratory at Beckman Instruments in 1955. In 1956 he shared a Nobel Prize with John Bardeen and Walter H. Brattain for their work at Bell Labs on the transistor. He taught at Stanford University (1958–74). From the late 1960s he earned notoriety for his outspoken and critical views on the intellectual capacity of blacks.

Shoemaker-Levy 9, Comet that collided with the planet Jupiter in July 1994, discovered by Carolyn and Eugene Shoemaker and David Levy 16 months earlier. The comet was torn apart into more than 20 fragments during a close encounter with Jupiter in July 1992, resulting in a "string of pearls" that collided sequentially with Jupiter two years later over a period of a week, leaving dark spots larger than Earth at their impact sites in Jupiter's atmosphere.

shogun (Japanese: "barbarian-quelling generalissimo"), In Japanese history, a military ruler. The title was first used during the Heian period, when it was occasionally bestowed on a general after a successful campaign. In 1185 Minamoto Yoritomo gained military control of Japan; seven years later he assumed the title of shogun and formed the first *bakufu*, or shogunate. Later Kamakura shoguns lost real power to the Hōjō family while remaining rulers in name. Ashikaga Takauji received the title of shogun in 1338 and established the Ashikaga shogunate, but his successors enjoyed even less control over Japan than had the Kamakura shoguns, and the country gradually fell into civil war. Tokugawa Ieyasu's shogunate proved the most durable, but the Japanese penchant for titular rulers prevailed, and in time a council of elders from the main branches of the Tokugawa clan ruled from behind the scenes. Since the title of shogun ultimately came from the emperor, he became a rallying point for those who brought down the shogunate in the Meiji Restoration.

Sholokhov, Mikhail (Aleksandrovich) (b. May 24, 1905, Veshenskaya, Russia—d. Feb. 21, 1984, Veshenskaya, U.S.S.R.), Russian novelist. A native of the Don River region, he served in the Red Army and joined the Communist Party in 1932. He is best known for the huge novel *The Quiet Don*, translated in two parts as *And Quiet Flows the Don* (1934) and *The Don Flows Home to the Sea* (1940). A portrayal of the struggle between the Cossacks and Bolsheviks, it was heralded in the Soviet Union as a powerful example of Socialist Realism and became the most widely read novel in Russia. It became controversial when Aleksandr Solzhenitsyn and others alleged that it was plagiarized from the Cossack writer Fyodor Kryukov (d. 1920). Sholokhov's later novels include *Virgin Soil Upturned* (1932–60). He received the Nobel Prize for Literature in 1965.

shooting, Sport of gun marksmanship. It typically involves firing at targets with rifles, pistols, and shotguns. World championship competitions are held for the small-bore rifle, free rifle, centre-fire pistol, free pistol, rapid-fire pistol, air rifle, air pistol, and shotgun. Shooting has been an Olympic sport since the modern games began in 1896; women's events were established in 1984.

Shore Temple, Complex of elegant shrines (*c.* 700), one among a number of Hindu monuments at Mahabalipuram, on the coast of Tamil Nadu state, India. It is considered the finest early example of medieval southern Indian temple architecture. Unlike most of its neighbours at the site, it is built of cut stones rather than carved out of caves. It has two shrines, one dedicated to Shiva and the other to Vishnu. Its style is characterized by a pyramidal *kutina-*

*Shore Temple,
Mamallapuram, Tamil Nadu,
India.*
Frederick M. Asher

type tower that consists of stepped stories topped by a cupola and finial, a form quite different from the northern Indian *sikhara.*

short story, Brief fictional prose narrative. It usually presents a single significant episode or scene involving a limited number of characters. The form encourages economy of setting and concise narration; character is disclosed in action and dramatic encounter but seldom fully developed. A short story may concentrate on the creation of mood rather than the telling of a story. Despite numerous precedents, it emerged only in the 19th century as a distinct literary genre in the works of writers such as E.T.A. Hoffmann, Heinrich Kleist, Edgar Allan Poe, Prosper Mérimée, Guy de Maupassant, and Anton Chekhov.

Shostakovich, Dmitry (Dmitriyevich) (b. Sept. 25, 1906, St. Petersburg, Russia—d. Aug. 9, 1975, Moscow, Russia, U.S.S.R.), Russian composer. Shaped by his intellectual parents and the political turmoil of his youth, he was admitted to the St. Petersburg Conservatory at age 13. His *Symphony No. 1* (1924–25) attracted international attention for its convincing command of a large scale and its expressive palette ranging from unaffected lyricism to bitter satire to grand heroics. He experimented with avant-garde trends in his next symphonies and theatre works, such as the opera *Lady Macbeth of Mtsensk* (1932; revised as *Katerina Izmaylova*). The denunciation of *Lady Macbeth* by the Soviet authorities in 1936 led to his adopting a very different style that was serious and elegiac, with a directness that appealed to the public. His wartime *Symphony No. 7* (1941), thought to portray the German invasion, became a symbol of patriotism. After his music was denounced by the government in 1948, he was again devastated and began putting his most personal feelings into chamber works, particularly the remarkable 15 string quartets. With the Cold War "thaw" of the late 1950s, he composed two outspokenly personal late symphonies, including the 13th (1962). He is remembered as the greatest Russian composer to follow Igor Stravinsky.

shot put, Field event in which a metal ball is heaved for distance. It derives from the ancient event of "putting the stone"; later a shot (cannonball) was substituted. A 16-lb (7.3-kg) shot was adopted for men in the first modern Olympic Games (1896); an 8.8-lb (4-kg) weight is used by women.

shotgun, Smoothbore shoulder firearm designed to fire a number of pellets, or shot, that cover a large target area after they leave the muzzle. It is used mainly against small game such as birds. The earliest examples were the fowling pieces that appeared in 16th-century Europe. Repeating shotguns, in which several cartridges could be loaded at once, became available in the 1880s. The range of a modern shotgun is about 50 yards (45 m).

show jumping, Competitive riding of horses through an obstacle course. Horses run the course one at a time, and the winner is judged according to jumping ability and speed. Individual and team jumping events have been part of the Olympic Games since 1912. The President's Cup is the world team championship.

shrapnel, Originally, a type of projectile invented by the British artillery officer Henry Shrapnel (1761–1842), containing small spherical bullets and an explosive charge to scatter the shot and fragments of the shell casing. A time fuse set off the explosive charge late in the shell's flight, when it was near opposing troops. The resulting hail of high-velocity debris was often lethal; it caused most of the artillery-inflicted wounds in World War I. In World War II a high-explosive bursting charge that fragmented the

shell's iron casing made shrapnel balls unnecessary; the term shrapnel came to be used for the shell-casing fragments.

shrew, Any of more than 350 species of small insectivores constituting the family Soricidae. About 40% of these species live in Africa, but shrews are also found throughout the Northern Hemisphere. Shrews are absent from Australia and most of South America. They have tiny eyes and ears, a movable snout, and long, hook-tipped incisors. Typically 2 to 3 in. (6 to 8 cm) long, with a shorter tail, many shrews weigh only about 0.5 oz (14 g). Some are considered the smallest mammals, weighing only a few grams, with bodies less than 2 in. long. Most species live in ground litter, but some live in burrows or trees and a few are semiaquatic. Because they are so small, shrews have the highest metabolic rates of any mammals (with pulses as high as 800 beats per minute). They spend most of their time searching for food, as they can survive only a few hours without eating. Their normal prey is invertebrates such as worms, though some will eat other small animals as well. Some species have toxic saliva (painful to humans). Raptors and snakes eat shrews, but mammals avoid them. Tree shrews (family Tupaiidae) belong to a separate mammalian order (Scandentia) unrelated to true shrews.

shrimp, Any of approximately 2,000 decapod species (suborder Natantia) having a semitrans-

Peneus setiferus, an edible shrimp
Marineland of Florida

parent body flattened from side to side and a flexible abdomen terminating in a fanlike tail. The appendages are modified for swimming, and the antennae are long and whiplike. Shrimps occur in shallow and deep ocean waters and in lakes and streams. Species range from less than an inch (a few millimeters) to about 8 in. (20 cm) long. Larger species are often called prawns. Shrimps swim backward by rapidly flexing the abdomen and tail. They eat small plants and animals; some species eat carrion. Many species are commercially important as food.

Shu, In Egyptian religion, the god of the air and supporter of the sky, created by the god Atum. Shu and his sister Tefnut (goddess of moisture) were the first couple of the group of nine gods called the Ennead of Heliopolis. Of their union were born Geb and Nut. Shu was portrayed in human form with an ostrich feather on his head. He was often represented supporting with uplifted arms the body of Nut arched above him. Later he was frequently termed the son of Re, and he was also identified with Onuris, a warrior god.

Shubrā al-Khaymah, City (pop., 2006: 1,025,569), northeastern Egypt. It is a northern suburb of Cairo, on the eastern bank of the Nile River. It was formerly a marketplace that supplied Cairo with agricultural produce from the rich delta area. After World War I it developed as an industrial centre. The city lies west of the southern terminus of the Ismāʿīliyyah (Ismailia) Canal, which links the Suez Canal with the Nile.

Shudra, or SUDRA, Fourth and lowest of the varnas, or social classes, of Hindu India. Traditionally composed of artisans and labourers, it probably originally included all conquered peoples of the Indus civilization as they were assimilated into the caste system. Members are not permitted to participate in the *upanayana* and thus cannot study the Vedas. The high end of the Shudra includes some landowners; at the low end are untouchables.

shuffleboard, Game in which two or four players use long-handled cues to shove disks into scoring areas of a diagram marked on a flat, smooth surface (6 × 52 ft [1.8 × 15.8 m]). It was popular in England as early as the 15th century, especially with the aristocracy; it later became popular as a deck game among travelers on ocean liners and cruise ships. The current form of the game was defined at St. Petersburg, Fla., U.S., in 1924.

Shujing, or SHU-CHING, One of the Five Classics of Chinese antiquity. Documenting China's ancient history, the *Shujing* contains the oldest Chinese writing of its kind. It consists of 58 chapters, of which 33 are generally considered authentic works of the 4th century BC or earlier. The first 5 chapters purport to preserve the sayings and recall the deeds of emperors who reigned during China's legendary golden age; the next 4 are devoted to the Xia dynasty; the next 17 chapters deal with the Shang dynasty; and the final 32 chapters cover the Western Zhou dynasty.

Siamese cat, Breed of slender, short-haired domestic cat that originated in Thailand (Siam). The Siamese has a pale fawn or gray body with dark points on the ears, face, legs, and tail. The points may be dark brown (seal point), blue-gray (blue point), milk-chocolate brown (chocolate point), pinkish gray (lilac point), or reddish orange (red point). The head is wedge-shaped. The blue eyes are slanted and may be crossed, though crossed eyes and kinked tail are discouraged by breeders of show animals. Siamese are considered highly intelligent and are very vocal, with a distinctive yowling mew.

Siamese fighting fish, Freshwater tropical fish *(Betta splendens*; family Belontiidae or Anabantidae), noted for the males' pugnacity toward one another. A native of Thailand, it was domesticated there for use in contests. Combat consists mainly of fin nipping and is accompanied by a display of extended gill covers, spread fins, and intensified colouring. This slender fish grows to about 2.5 in. (6.5 cm) long. In the wild it is predominantly greenish or brown, with red fins; domesticated, it has been bred with long, flowing fins and in a variety of colours, such as red, green, blue, and lavender.

Siamese fighting fish (Betta splendens).
Douglas Faulkner

Siberia, Region, north-central Asia, largely in Russia. It extends from the Ural Mountains to the Pacific Ocean and from the Arctic Ocean to central Kazakhstan and the boundaries of China and Mongolia; it covers more than 5,000,000 sq mi (13,000,000 sq km). It is notorious for the length and severity of its almost snowless winters. Temperatures of −90 °F (−68 °C) have been recorded. The first settlers probably arrived in southern Siberia in the Paleolithic Period. The area was under Chinese influence from *c.* 1000 BC, followed by the Turkic-Mongols in the 3rd century BC. Russian trappers and Cossack explorers colonized it in the late 16th century, and by the mid-18th century most of Siberia was under Russian rule. It was connected to other parts of Russia by the Trans-Siberian Railroad. Eastern Siberia was the scene of the anti-Bolshevik government of Aleksandr Kolchak (1918–20). It was made part of the Russian S.F.S.R. in 1922. Russia exiled criminals and political prisoners there, and in the 1930s Joseph Stalin set up forced-labour camps that fueled industrial growth. When Russian factories were relocated there during World War II, it played an important role in the war effort. It has deposits of coal, petroleum, natural gas, diamonds, iron ore, and gold; its chief industrial products include steel, aluminum, and machinery. Southern Siberia produces wheat, rye, oats, and sunflowers. Its main cities include Novosibirsk, Omsk, Krasnoyarsk, and Irkutsk.

Sibyl, Prophetess of Greek legend. She was a figure of the mythical past whose prophecies, phrased in Greek hexameters, were handed down in writing. In the late 4th century BC, the number of Sibyls multiplied, and the term *sibyl* was treated as a title. Sibyls were associated with various oracles, especially those of Apollo, who was said to be their inspiration. They were typically depicted as extremely old women who lived in caves and delivered their prophecies in an ecstatic frenzy. A famous collection of prophecies, the *Sibylline Books*, was traditionally kept in the temple of Jupiter, to be consulted only in emergencies.

Sichuan, or SSU-CH'UAN, conventional SZECHWAN, Province (pop., 2002 est.: 86,730,000), upper Yangtze River (Chang Jiang) valley, southwestern China. It is bordered by Qinghai, Gansu, Shaanxi, Guizhou, and Yunnan provinces, Chongqing municipality, and the Tibet Autonomous Region. It has an area of 188,000 sq mi (487,000 sq km) and encompasses the central depression called the Sichuan (or Red) Basin; its capital is Chengdu. Sichuan is one of China's most densely populated and ethnically diverse provinces. It was among the first areas to be settled by the Chinese (5th century BCE). From the Zhou dynasty (1046–256 BCE) until the Song dynasty (960–1279 CE), it was administered through various political subdivisions. It was established as a province during the Qing dynasty (1644–1911/12). It is China's leading producer of rice, corn (maize), sweet potatoes, cattle, and pigs. The most-industrialized province of southwestern China, it is a centre for coal mining, petroleum refining, and chemical production. Sichuan's spicy cuisine is renowned worldwide. A powerful earthquake in the province in 2008 caused massive destruction and the deaths of some 90,000 people.

Sicilian Vespers (1282) Massacre of the French that began a Sicilian revolt against the Angevin king Charles I. Backed by Peter III of Aragon, the rising broke out when Sicilians killed some insulting French soldiers at vespers in the church of Santo Spirito in Palermo. The people of the city followed suit and massacred 2,000 of its French inhabitants. All of Sicily soon revolted and sought help from the Aragonese, and the war became a French-Aragonese struggle for possession of Sicily. The conflict was finally resolved when the Sicilians chose Frederick III, brother of the king of Aragon, as their ruler in 1302.

Sicily, Italian SICILIA, Island, Italy. Sicily is separated from the mainland by the Strait of Messina. The largest island (9,830 sq mi [25,460 sq km]) in the Mediterranean Sea, it is also the site of Europe's highest active volcano, Mount Etna. The capital is Palermo. Sicily's strategic location at the centre of the Mediterranean has made the island a crossroads of history. The Greeks colonized it in the 8th–6th centuries BCE, and in the 3rd century BCE it became the first Roman province. It came under Byzantine rule in the 6th century CE and fell in 965 to Arabs from North Africa. It was taken in 1060 by the Normans. In the 12th–13th centuries and again in the 18th century it formed part of the Kingdom of the Two Sicilies. During the 19th century it was a major centre of revolutionary movements; in 1860 it was liberated from the Bourbons, and in 1861 it was incorporated into the Kingdom of Italy. Agriculture is its economic mainstay; industries include oil refining, food processing, wine making, and shipbuilding. Together with the islands of Egadi, Lipari, Pelagie, and Pantelleria, Sicily forms an autonomous region of Italy (pop., 2007 est.: 5,016,861).

sickle-cell anemia, Blood disorder seen mainly in persons of Sub-Saharan African ancestry and their descendants and in those from the Middle East, the Mediterranean area, and India. About 1 in 400 blacks worldwide has the disease, caused by inheriting two copies of a recessive gene that makes those with one copy (about 1 in 12 blacks worldwide) resistant to malaria. The gene specifies a variant hemoglobin (hemoglobin S or Hb S) that distorts red blood cells (erythrocytes) into a rigid sickle shape. The cells become clogged in capillaries, damaging or destroying various tissues. Symptoms include chronic anemia, shortness of breath, fever, and episodic "crises" (severe pain in the abdomen, bones, or muscles). Hydroxyurea treatment triggers production of fetal hemoglobin (Hb F), which does not sickle, greatly lessening severity of crises and increasing life expectancy, previously about 45 years.

sidereal period, Time required for a celestial body in the solar system to complete one revolution with respect to the fixed stars (as observed from a fixed point outside the system). A planet's sidereal period can be calculated from its synodic period. The sidereal period of the Moon or an artificial satellite of Earth is the time it takes to return to the same position against the background of stars.

Siena, ancient SAENA JULIA, City (pop., 2001: 54,366), western Italy. It is located south of Florence. Founded by the Etruscans, Siena later passed to the Romans and the Lombards; in the 12th century it became a self-governing commune. Rivalry with Florence made Siena the center of pro-imperial Ghibellinism in Tuscany. It was conquered by Charles I (Charles of Anjou), king of Naples and Sicily, in 1270 and joined the Guelph confederation. It was an important banking and commercial centre until surpassed by Florence in the 13th–14th centuries. Conquered by the Holy Roman emperor Charles V in 1555, it was ceded to Florence in 1557. Modern Siena is a market town and tourist centre; historic sites there include the Gothic-Romanesque cathedral, the University of Siena (founded 1240), and the Piazza del Campo, where the Corsa del Palio, a horse race originating in medieval times, is still held.

Sienkiewicz, Henryk (Adam Alexander Pius) (b. May 5, 1846, Wola Okrzejska, Pol.—d. Nov. 15, 1916, Vevey, Switz.), Polish novelist. In 1869 he began to publish critical works showing the influence of positivism. He worked as a newspaperman and published successful short stories before producing the great trilogy consisting of *With Fire and Sword* (1884), *The Deluge* (1886), and *Pan Michael* (1887–88). Describing Poland's struggles against Cossacks, Tatars, Swedes, and Turks, the novels stress Polish heroism in a vivid style of epic clarity and simplicity. The widely translated *Quo Vadis?* (1896), set in Rome under Nero, established his international reputation. He received the Nobel Prize for Literature in 1905.

Sierra Leone, officially REPUBLIC OF SIERRA LEONE, Country, western Africa. Area: 27,699 sq mi (71,740 sq km). Population: (2011 est.) 5,997,000. Capital: Freetown. The Mende and Temne are the largest of about 18 ethnic groups. Languages: English (official), Krio (derived from English and a variety of African languages). Religions: Islam (predominantly Sunni), Christianity, traditional beliefs. Currency: leone. Sierra Leone has four physical regions: the coastal swamp; the Sierra Leone Peninsula, with thickly wooded mountains that rise from the swamps; the interior plains, consisting of grasslands and rolling wooded country; and the interior plateau and mountain regions. Wildlife includes chimpanzees, crocodiles, and many species of birds. The economy is based largely on agriculture and mining; rice, cassava, coffee, cacao, and oil palm are major crops, and diamonds, rutile, and bauxite are mined. Sierra Leone is a republic with one legislative head; the head of state and government is the president. The earliest inhabitants were probably the Bulom and Temne; Mande-speaking peoples began arriving in the 15th century. The coastal region was visited by the Portuguese in the 15th century, who built a fort near the site of modern Freetown. European ships visited the coast regularly to trade for slaves and ivory, and the English built trading posts on offshore islands in the 17th century. British abolitionists and philanthropists founded Freetown in 1787 as a private venture for freed and runaway slaves. In 1808 the coastal settlement became a British colony. The region became a British protectorate in 1896. It achieved independence in 1961 and became a republic in 1971. Since independence Sierra Leone experienced a series of military coups. An 11-year civil war, which was marked by horrific atrocities and further devastated the country, ended in 2002.

Sierra Madre, Principal mountain system, Mexico. It includes the ranges of the Sierra Madre Occidental (to the west), the Sierra Madre Oriental (to the east), and the Sierra Madre del Sur (to the south)—all running roughly northwest-southeast. The Sierra Madre Occidental extends for about 700 mi (1,100 km) parallel with the Gulf of California and the Pacific Ocean; summits reach elevations above 6,000 ft (1,800 m), with some exceeding 10,000 ft (3,000 m). The Sierra Madre Oriental originates near the Rio Grande to the north and extends roughly parallel with the Gulf of Mexico for about 700 mi; it has an average elevation of about 7,000 ft (2,150 m), but some peaks rise above 10,000 ft (Mount Peña Nevada). The Sierra Madre del Sur stretches through the southern Mexican states of Guerrero and Oaxaca, reaching elevations of about 6,500 ft (2,000 m), with a few peaks above 10,000 ft.

Sierra Nevada, Mountain range, eastern California, U.S. The Sierra Nevada range extends more than 250 mi (400 km) from the Mojave Desert to the Cascade Range, and averages about 50 mi (80 km) in width. The peaks of the range are 11,000–14,000 ft (3,350–4,270 m) high; Mount Whitney is the highest mountain. It is a year-round recreation centre and is easily accessed from the state's large urban areas.

sign language, Any means of communication through bodily movements, especially of the hands and arms, rather than through speech. It has long been used by speakers of mutually unintelligible languages—for example, various Plains Indian tribes in 19th-century North America communicated via a sign language—and is widely used for communication by the deaf. Charles-Michel, abbé de l'Épée (1712–89), developed the first sign language for the deaf in the mid-18th century; his system developed into French Sign Language (FSL), still used in France. Transported to the U.S. in 1816 by Thomas Gallaudet (1787–1851), it evolved into American Sign Language (ASL, or Ameslan), now used by more than half a million people. These and other national sign languages generally express concepts rather than elements of words and thus have more in common with each other than with their countries' spoken languages.

Sikh Wars (1845–46, 1848–49) Two wars fought between the Sikhs and the British. In the first war Sikhs invaded British India under the pretext of forestalling a British attack on the Sikh state in the Punjab. They were defeated, the British annexed some of their lands, and British troops and a British resident were stationed in Lahore. The second war was a Sikh national revolt that ended in a British victory and annexation of the Punjab.

Sikhism, Indian religion founded in the late 15th century by Nanak, the first of the Sikh leaders titled Guru. Most of the religion's 25 million members, called Sikhs, live in the Punjab—the site of their holiest shrine, the Golden Temple, and the principal seat of Sikh religious authority, the Akal Takht. The *Adi Granth* is the canonical scripture of Sikhism. Its theology is based on a supreme God who governs with justice and grace. Every human being, irrespective of caste or gender, has the opportunity to become one with God. The basic human flaw of self-centredness can be overcome through proper reverence for God, commitment to hard work, service to humanity, and sharing the fruits of one's labour. Sikhs consider themselves disciples of the 10 human Gurus; the *Adi Granth* assumed the position of Guru after the death of the last human Guru, Gobind Singh (1666–1708). Sikhs accept the Hindu ideas of samsara and karma. The dominant order of Sikhism, into which most Sikh boys and

The Clock Tower and Golden Temple in Amritsar, Punjab, India.
© M. Borchi—IGDA/DeA Picture Library

girls are initiated at puberty, is the Khalsa. The emblems of the Khalsa, called the Five Ks, are *kes* or *kesh* (uncut hair), *kangha* (a comb), *kachha* (long shorts), *kirpan* (a ceremonial sword), and *kara* (a steel bracelet).

Sikkim, State (pop., 2008 est.: 594,000), northeastern India. In the eastern Himalayas, Kanchenjunga, the third highest peak in the world, forms part of its western border with Nepal. It is also bordered by the Tibet Autonomous Region of China, Bhutan, and West Bengal state and has an area of 2,740 sq mi (7,096 sq km); the capital, Gangtok, is the state's largest settlement. As an independent country, it fought prolonged wars in the 18th and 19th centuries with Bhutan and Nepal. It first came under British influence in 1817, though it remained a semiautonomous princely state between British India and Tibet. It became an Indian protectorate in 1950 and, in 1975, a state of India. It is one of India's smallest states. It exports agricultural products and is one of the world's main producers of cardamom. Its mineral resources include copper, lead, zinc, coal, and iron ore.

silicon, Nonmetallic to semimetallic chemical element, chemical symbol Si, atomic number 14. Second only to oxygen in abundance in Earth's crust, it never occurs free but is found in almost all rocks and in sand, clay, and soils, combined with oxygen as silica (silicon dioxide, SiO_2) or with oxygen and metals as silicate minerals. It occurs in many plants and some animals. Pure silicon is a hard, dark gray solid with a metallic lustre and the same crystal structure as diamond. It is an extremely important semiconductor; doped with boron, phosphorus, or arsenic, it is used in various electronic circuit and switching devices, including computer chips, transistors, and diodes. Silicon is also used in metallurgy as a reducing agent and in steel, brass, and bronze. Its usual valence in compounds is 4. Silica is used in the form of sand and clay for many purposes; as quartz, it may be heated to form special glasses. Silicates are used in making glass, enamels, and ceramics; sodium silicates (water glass) are used in soaps, wood treatment, cements, and dyeing.

silicone, or POLYSILOXANE, Any of a diverse class of polymers manufactured as fluids, resins, or elastomers. They are partially organic compounds, but, unlike most polymers, they have a backbone containing no carbon, composed instead of alternating silicon and oxygen atoms. In most silicones, two organic groups, usually methyl or phenyl, are attached to each silicon atom. Silicones in general are exceptionally stable and inert. Silicone fluids are used in hydraulic fluids, emulsion-breaking compositions, and breast implants and as adhesives, lubricants, water repellents, and protective coatings. Silicone rubbers are used as electrical insulators in encapsulations, coatings, and varnishes; as gaskets and caulking material; in specialized tubing; as automobile engine components; as flexible windows in face masks and air locks; for laminating glass cloth; and as surgical membranes and implants.

silicosis, Common pneumoconiosis caused by long-term inhalation of silica mineral dust. Known since the 18th century, it usually occurs after 10–20 years of exposure in jobs such as mining, stonecutting, grinding, or polishing. The smallest particles do the most damage, killing macrophages that engulf them in the pulmonary alveoli. Dead cells accumulate, forming fibrous masses that reduce lung elasticity. Decreased lung volume and poor gas exchange lead to shortness of breath and then to coughing, difficulty in breathing, and weakness. Patients are vulnerable to tuberculosis, emphysema, and pneumonia. In the absence of effective treatment, control of silicosis depends on prevention with face masks, proper ventilation, and X-ray monitoring of workers' lungs.

silk, Animal fibre produced by certain insects as building material for cocoons and webs. In commercial use it refers almost entirely to filament from cocoons produced by the caterpillars of several moth species of the genus *Bombyx*, commonly called silkworms. Silk is a continuous filament around each cocoon. It is freed by softening the cocoon in water and then locating the filament end; the filaments from several cocoons are unwound at the same time, sometimes with a slight twist, to form a single strand. In the process called throwing, several very thin strands are twisted together to make thicker, stronger yarn. Silk was discovered in China sometime before 2700 BC, and the secret of its production was closely guarded for millennia. Along with jade and spices, silk was the primary commodity traded along the Silk Road beginning about 100 BC. Since World War II, nylon and other synthetic fibres have replaced silk in many applications (e.g., parachutes, hosiery, dental floss), but silk remains an important luxury material for clothing and home furnishings. More than 50% of the world's silk is still produced in China.

silkscreen, or SERIGRAPHY, Sophisticated stenciling technique for surface printing, in which a design is cut out of paper or another thin, strong material and then printed by rubbing, rolling, or spraying paint or ink through the cutout areas. It was developed *c.* 1900 and originally used in advertising and display work. In the 1950s fine artists began to use the process. It got its name from the fine-mesh silk that, when tacked to a wooden frame, serves as a support for the cut-paper stencil, which is glued to it. To make a silkscreen print, the wooden frame holding the screen is hinged to a slightly larger wooden board, the printing paper is placed on the board under the screen, and the paint is pressed through the screen with a squeegee (rubber blade) the same width as the screen. Many colours can be used, with a separate screen for each colour.

Sillanpää, Frans Eemil (b. Sept. 16, 1888, Hämeenkyrö, Fin., Russian Empire—d. June 3, 1964, Helsinki, Fin.), Finnish novelist. The son of a farmer, he studied natural science but returned to the country to write. Shocked by the Finnish civil war of 1918, he produced his most substantial novel, *Meek Heritage* (1919), relating how a humble cottager becomes involved with the Red Guards. After several collections of short stories in the late 1920s, he published his best-known work, *The Maid Silja* (1931), about an old peasant family. *People in the Summer Night* (1934) is his most polished and poetic novel. In 1939 he became the first Finnish writer to win the Nobel Prize for Literature.

Silurian Period, Interval of geologic time, 443.7–416 million years ago, the third period of the Paleozoic Era. The Silurian follows the Ordovician Period and precedes the Devonian. It marks the first appearance of land plants and jawed fishes. During most of this period, a vast ocean covered the northern polar region, the supercontinent of Gondwana stretched over the southern polar region, and a ring of at least six continents spanned the Equator and middle latitudes. South America and Africa were likely near the South Pole, with either present-day Brazil or western Africa as the locus of the pole. Large expanses of these continents were flooded by shallow seas which contributed to the building of coral mound reefs. During the Silurian, many faunal groups recovered from the extinctions of Late Ordovician times.

silver, Metallic chemical element, one of the transition elements, chemical symbol Ag, atomic number 47. It is a white, lustrous precious metal, valued for its beauty. It is also valued for its electrical conductivity, which is the highest of any metal. Between copper and gold in their common group of the periodic table, it is intermediate between them in many properties. Widely distributed in nature in small amounts, as the native metal and in ores, it is usually recovered as a by-product of copper and lead production. Its use in bullion and coins was overtaken in the 1960s by demand for industrial purposes, especially photography. It is also used in printed electrical circuits, electronic conductors, and contacts. It is the catalyst for converting ethylene to ethylene oxide, the precursor of many organic chemicals. Its use in alloys in sterling (92.5% silver, 7.5% copper) and plated silverware, ornaments, and jewelry remains important; yellow gold used in jewelry is typically 25% silver, and gold dental alloys are about 10% silver. Silver dental fillings are an amalgam of silver and mercury. Silver in

*Dendritic (branching) silver
from Ontario*
Courtesy of Joseph and Helen
Guetterman Collection; photograph,
John H. Gerard

compounds, the most important of which is silver nitrate, has valence 1. Its chloride, bromide, and iodide are used in photography and its iodide in cloud seeding.

silverfish, Species (*Lepisma saccharina*) of quick-moving, slender, flat, wingless insect having three tail bristles and silvery scales. Silverfish are found worldwide. Females deposit fertilized eggs in cracks and hidden places. The hatched young are scaleless and have short appendages. Silverfish normally live indoors and, because they eat starchy materials (e.g., paste, bookbindings, and wallpaper), can cause much damage. They live two to three years and molt throughout life.

simile, Figure of speech involving a comparison between two unlike entities. In a simile, unlike a metaphor, the resemblance is indicated by the words "like" or "as." Similes in everyday speech reflect simple comparisons, as in "He eats like a bird" or "She is slow as molasses." Similes in literature may be specific and direct or more lengthy and complex. The Homeric, or epic, simile, which is typically used in epic poetry, often extends to several lines.

Simon, Claude (Eugène Henri) (b. Oct. 10, 1913, Tananarive [now Antananarivo], Madag.—d. July 6, 2005, Paris, France), French writer. Captured by the Nazis while fighting in World War II, he escaped to join the French Resistance. He completed his first novel during the war. His works, mixing narration and stream of consciousness in densely constructed prose, are representative of the *nouveau roman* ("new novel"), or French antinovel, that emerged in the 1950s. Perhaps most important is the cycle comprising *The Grass* (1958), *The Flanders Road* (1960), *The Palace* (1962), and *History* (1967), with its recurring characters and events. His other novels include *The Wind* (1957), *Triptych* (1973), *The Acacia* (1989), and *The Trolley* (2001). He received the Nobel Prize for Literature in 1985.

Simon, Herbert (Alexander) (b. June 15, 1916, Milwaukee, Wis., U.S.—d. Feb. 9, 2001, Pittsburgh, Pa.), U.S. social scientist. He received his Ph.D. from the University of Chicago in 1943. At Carnegie-Mellon University (from 1949), he taught psychology and later computer science. In *Administrative Behavior* (1947) Simon argued for recognizing a multiplicity of factors (including psychological ones) in corporate decision making rather than emphasizing the achievement of maximum profits as the primary motivation. He was awarded the Nobel Prize in Economics in 1978. He subsequently worked in the field of artificial intelligence using computer technology.

simony, Buying or selling of church offices or powers. The name is taken from Simon Magus (Acts 8:18), who tried to buy the power of conferring the gifts of the Holy Spirit. Simony was said to have become widespread in Europe in the 10th–11th century, as promotions to the priesthood or episcopate were bestowed by monarchs and nobles, often in exchange for oaths of loyalty. Changes in the understanding of the nature of simony and the relationship between lay and religious orders contributed to the perception of the growth of simony, even though corrupt practices did exist. Rigorously attacked by Pope Gregory VII and the reform

movement associated with him, the practice recurred in the 15th century, but after the 16th century its more flagrant forms disappeared.

simplex method, Standard technique in linear programming for solving an optimization problem, typically one involving a function and several constraints expressed as inequalities. The inequalities define a polygonal region, and the solution is typically at one of the vertices. The simplex method is a systematic procedure for testing the vertices as possible solutions.

Sin, Sumerian NANNA, In Mesopotamian religion, the god of the moon. He was the father of Shamash and, in some myths, of Ishtar. Sin was thought to confer fertility and prosperity on cowherds by governing the rise of waters and the growth of reeds, particularly in the marshes along the lower Euphrates River, where his worship originated. In the 6th century BC, attempts were made to elevate Sin to a supreme position in the Babylonian pantheon.

sin, Wrongdoing, particularly the breaking of moral or religious rules. In the Hebrew scriptures, sin is viewed as a hatred of God or defiance of his commandments. The New Testament regards sinfulness as the inherent state of humanity, which Jesus came into the world to heal. Christian theologians divide sin into actual and original sin. Actual sin, consisting of evil acts, words, and deeds, is in turn divided into mortal sin, in which the perpetrator deliberately turns away from God, and venial sin, a less serious transgression committed without full awareness of wrongdoing. In Islam, sin is a straying from God's path; the prophets were sent to guide people back to the true path. In Hinduism and Buddhism, the good and evil deeds one commits in this life affect one's rebirth in the next.

Sinai, Mount, or MOUNT HOREB, Peak, south-central Sinai Peninsula, Egypt. It rises to 7,497 ft (2,285 m) in elevation and is especially renowned in the Jewish, Christian, and Islamic traditions as the site where Moses received the Ten Commandments. Though not positively identified as the place referred to in biblical texts, it is an important pilgrimage site. St. Catherine's, founded in 527 and thought to be the world's oldest continuously inhabited Christian monastery, is at its northern base.

Sinai Peninsula, Peninsula, northeastern Egypt. Located between the Gulfs of Suez and Aqaba at the northern end of the Red Sea, it covers some 23,500 sq mi (61,000 sq km). Its southern region is mountainous and includes Mount Sinai, while its northern two-thirds is an arid plateau known as the Sinai Desert. Inhabited since prehistoric times, it is famous as the purported route of the Israelite Exodus from Egypt. For centuries its northern coast was the main trade route between Egypt and Palestine. From the 2nd century CE until the rise of Islam in the 7th century, it was part of the Roman Empire and its successor, the Byzantine Empire. It was ruled by various Islamic dynasties until the 16th century, when it became part of the Ottoman Empire. Turned over to Egypt at the end of World War I, in 1918, it was the scene of heavy fighting during the Suez Crisis (1956), the Six-Day War (1967), and the Yom Kippur War (1973); it was occupied by Israel (1967–82) and then was returned to Egypt.

Sint Maarten, Autonomous state within the Kingdom of the Netherlands, on the island of Saint Martin, Leeward Islands, in the northeastern Caribbean Sea. It constitutes the southern third of the island, the northern portion being occupied by Saint-Martin, an overseas collectivity of France. Area: 13 sq mi; (34 sq km). Population: (2011 est.) 38,300. Capital: Philipsburg. Dutch and English are the official languages. The principal religion is Roman Catholicism. The currency is the Netherlands Antillean guilder (to be replaced with the Dutch Caribbean guilder by 2012). The island of Saint Martin was divided between the Dutch and French in 1648, and Sint Maarten became part of the Netherlands Antilles in 1845. The islands of the Netherlands Antilles were granted internal self-government in 1954, and, with the dissolution of the Netherlands Antilles in 2010, Sint Maarten achieved a greater degree of independence while remaining a part of the Netherlands. The economy is based primarily on tourism.

Sinatra, Frank, orig. FRANCIS ALBERT SINATRA (b. Dec. 12, 1915, Hoboken, N.J., U.S.—d. May 14, 1998, Los Angeles, Calif.), U.S. singer and actor. Sinatra began his singing career in the mid-1930s and was "discovered" by trumpeter Harry James, who immediately recruited him. Sinatra achieved sweeping national popularity in 1940–42 while singing with the Tommy Dorsey Orchestra. He sang on the radio program *Your Hit Parade* (1943–45), while becoming a favourite performer in theatres and nightclubs. In the 1940s he costarred in a number of musical films with dancer Gene Kelly. His popularity suddenly declined about 1948, but his performance in *From Here to Eternity* (1953, Academy Award) revived his flagging career, and he later starred in many acclaimed films, including musicals such as *Guys and Dolls* (1955) and dramas such as *The Manchurian Candidate* (1962). After 1953 he performed and recorded, using arrangements by Nelson Riddle, Billy May, and Gordon Jenkins, reaching his peak in albums such as *Only the Lonely* (1958). In 1961 he founded Reprise Records. His masterly performances, alternately swinging and affectingly melancholic, brought him a success unparalleled in the history of American popular music.

Sindh, or SIND, Province (pop., 2006 est.: 35,864,000), southeastern Pakistan. It is bordered by Balochistan and Punjab provinces, India, and, to the south, by the Arabian Sea. The capital is Karachi. The centre of the ancient Indus civilization, it was annexed to the Persian Achaemenian Empire in the 6th century BCE. Conquered by Alexander the Great in 325 BCE, it was part of the Mauryan empire in the 3rd century BCE. It fell to the Arabs *c.* 711 CE. In the 16th–17th centuries it was ruled by the Mughals. It came under British control in 1843. After Pakistan's independence, Sindh was integrated into the province of West Pakistan but in 1970 was reestablished as a separate province. It is arid except in the irrigated Indus River valley, where cotton, wheat, and rice are grown and where the population is concentrated.

Singapore, officially REPUBLIC OF SINGAPORE, Island country, Southeast Asia. Situated off the southern tip of the Malay Peninsula, it comprises Singapore island and 60 islets. Area: 274.2 sq mi (710.2 sq km). Population: (2011 est.) 5,182,000. Capital: Singapore. Three-fourths of the people are of Chinese ethnicity; most of the rest are Malays and Indians. Languages: English, Chinese (Mandarin), Malay, Tamil (all official). Religions: Buddhism, Islam, Christianity, Daoism, Hinduism. Currency: Singapore dollar. Nearly two-thirds of the island's landscape lies below 50 ft (15 m) above sea level. It has a hot, humid climate. Although only about 2% of its land is arable, it is highly productive cropland. The economy is based largely on international trade and finance; there are more than 100 commercial banks, most of which are foreign, and the headquarters of the Asian Dollar Market is located there. The port is one of the largest in the world, and the country is one of the world's leading petroleum refiners. Manufacturing (notably electronic equipment) is also important. Singapore is a unitary parliamentary republic with one legislative house; its head of state is the president, and the head of government is the prime minister. Long inhabited by fishermen and pirates, it was an outpost of the Sumatran empire of Shrivijaya until the 14th century, when it passed to Java and then Ayutthaya (Siam). It became part of the Malacca empire in the 15th century. In the 16th century the Portuguese controlled the area; they were followed by the Dutch in the 17th century. In 1819 it was ceded to the British East India Company, becoming part of the Straits Settlements and the centre of British colonial activity in Southeast Asia. During World War II the Japanese occupied the island (1942–45). In 1946 it became a crown colony. It achieved full internal self-government in 1959, became part of Malaysia in 1963, and gained independence in 1965. Singapore is influential in the affairs of the Association of

Southeast Asian Nations (ASEAN). The country's dominant voice in politics for 30 years after independence was Lee Kuan Yew. Singapore has become a regional economic powerhouse.

Singapore, City (pop., 2005 est.: 4,291,000), capital of the Republic of Singapore. A free port centred on the southern part of Singapore island, it so dominates the island that the republic is now commonly considered a city-state. Known as the Garden City for its many parks and tree-lined streets, it offers glimpses into the cultures brought to it by immigrants from all parts of Asia. It was traditionally founded by a Shrivijayan prince and was an important Malay city in the 13th century. Destroyed by the Javanese in the 14th century, it was refounded by Stamford Raffles of the British East India Company in 1819. It became the capital of the Straits Settlements in 1833 and developed as a port and naval base; today it is one of the world's great commercial centres. Its thriving banking, insurance, and brokerage firms make it the chief trading and financial centre of Southeast Asia. It is home to the National University of Singapore (1980).

Singer, Isaac Bashevis, Yiddish YITSKHOK BASHEVIS ZINGER (b. July 14?, 1904, Radzymin, Pol., Russian Empire—d. July 24, 1991, Surfside, Fla., U.S.), Polish-born U.S. writer of novels, short stories, and essays. He received a traditional Jewish education at the Warsaw Rabbinical Seminary. After publishing his first novel, *Satan in Goray* (1932), he immigrated to the U.S. in 1935 and wrote for the *Jewish Daily Forward*, a Yiddish newspaper in New York. Though he continued to write mostly in Yiddish, he personally supervised the English translations. Depicting Jewish life in Poland and the U.S., his works are a rich blend of irony, wit, and wisdom, flavoured distinctively with the occult and the grotesque. His works include the novels *The Family Moskat* (1950), *The Magician of Lublin* (1960), and *Enemies: A Love Story* (1972; film, 1989); the story collections *Gimpel the Fool* (1957), *The Spinoza of Market Street* (1961), and *A Crown of Feathers* (1973, National Book Award); and the play *Yentl the Yeshiva Boy* (1974; film, 1983). He was awarded the Nobel Prize for Literature in 1978.

Singh, Manmohan (b. Sept. 26, 1932, Gah, West Punjab, India [now in Pakistan]), Prime minister of India (2004–). After earning a doctorate in economics from the University of Oxford, he worked at the Reserve Bank of India, serving as director (1976–80) and governor (1982–85). As India's finance minister (1991–96), he helped revitalize the country's struggling economy by devaluing the rupee and lowering taxes, among other reforms. A member of the Indian National Congress party, he joined the Rajya Sabha (upper house of the Indian parliament) in 1991. In 2004 the party won parliamentary elections. Its leader, Sonia Gandhi, declined the prime ministership and instead recommended Singh for the office. Singh, a Sikh, subsequently formed a government, becoming the first non-Hindu to serve as prime minister.

sinkhole, or SINK, or DOLINE, Depression formed as underlying limestone bedrock is dissolved by groundwater. Sinkholes vary greatly in area and depth and may be very large. The two main varieties are those caused by the collapse of a cavern roof, and those caused by the gradual dissolving of rock under a soil mantle. Collapsed sinkholes generally have steep rock sides and may receive streams that then flow underground. Soil-mantled sinkholes are generally shallower; they may become clogged with clay and hold a small lake.

Sino-Tibetan languages, Superfamily of languages whose two branches are the Sinitic, or Chinese, languages and the Tibeto-Burman family, an assemblage of several hundred very diverse languages spoken by some 65 million people from northern Pakistan east to Vietnam and from the Tibetan Plateau south to the Malay Peninsula. They include Tibetan, Burmese, Karen, and many other languages of Nepal, India, Myanmar (Burma), Bangladesh, China, and Thailand. Tibetan and Burmese are the only Tibeto-Burman languages with long literary traditions. Burmese is written in an adaptation of the Mon script.

sintering, Welding together of small particles of metal by applying heat at temperatures below the melting point. The process is used to form complex shapes, to produce alloys, and to allow work on metals with very high melting points. Sintering is also used in the preliminary molding of ceramic or glass powders into forms that can then be permanently fixed by firing.

sinus, Body cavity or hollow. The paranasal sinuses, which are known commonly simply as the sinuses, are any of four sets of cavities in the bones adjoining the nose: maxillary, the largest, between the eye socket and the palate and upper jaw; frontal, just above and between the eye sockets; ethmoid, consisting of 3–18 thin-walled cavities between the nasal cavities and the eye sockets; and sphenoid, behind the nasal cavity. All are absent or small at birth, enlarge gradually until puberty, and then grow rapidly. They affect the sound of the voice and may help to warm inhaled air. Their lining produces mucus, which drains into the nasal cavity. Blockage of their outlets by swelling (from allergy or infection), polyps, or structural problems hampers breathing through the nose and can lead to serious infection. Severe obstruction may require surgery, which must be done with extreme care to avoid harm to nearby brain structures or the eyes.

sinusitis, Inflammation of the sinuses. Acute sinusitis, usually due to infections such as the common cold, causes localized pain and tenderness, nasal obstruction and discharge, and malaise. Nose drops or inhalations containing drugs that contract blood vessels help drain the sinuses. Antibiotics may be used for bacterial infections. Chronic sinusitis, with frequent colds, pus, obstructed breathing, loss of sense of smell, and sometimes headache, may follow repeated or untreated acute attacks, particularly with impaired breathing or drainage. If antibiotic therapy or repeated lavage (rinsing out) does not help, surgery to open passages for drainage may be needed.

Sioux, A group of related North American Indian peoples living mostly in the Plains and speaking related langauges within the Siouan language stock. They comprise the Dakota-speaking Santee (Eastern Sioux), the Nakota-speaking Yankton, and the Lakota-speaking Teton (Western Sioux), each of which in turn has lesser divisions (e.g., Blackfoot, Oglala). The name Sioux is a French derivation of an Ojibwa name for "enemy" or "snake." Before the 17th century the various groups of Sioux had lived in present Minnesota and around Lake Superior; conflict related to the fur trade displaced them to the Plains. There they adopted a nomadic way of life, hunting buffalo, living in tepees, emphasizing valour in warfare, and practicing the sun dance. The Sioux fought American incursions into their territory in 1862 and again in the 1860s and '70s. Sioux resistance to American colonialism culminated in the Battle of the Little Bighorn in 1876, a great indigenous victory. However, economic pressure eventually caused most Sioux to surrender and move to reservations, where many adopted the Ghost Dance religion. In 1890 the U.S. Seventh Cavalry massacred Sioux civilians at Wounded Knee, also the location of an occupation by the American Indian Movement in 1973. The Sioux numbered about 160,000 in the early 21st century.

Sirius, or DOG STAR, Brightest star in the night sky (apparent magnitude −1.44), a binary star about 8.6 light-years from the Sun in the constellation Canis Major. The bright component of the binary is a blue-white star 23 times as luminous as the Sun, about twice the size, and considerably hotter; its companion was the first white dwarf star discovered. Its name probably comes from a Greek word meaning "sparkling" or "scorching." The ancient Egyptians used its predawn rising to predict the annual flooding

of the Nile. The ancient Romans associated the rising of the Dog Star at dawn with the hottest part of the year, called the "dog days."

Sistine Chapel, Papal chapel in the Vatican Palace, Rome, constructed 1473–81 by Giovanni dei Dolci for Pope Sixtus IV (for whom it is named). It is the site of the principal papal ceremonies. Its exterior is drab and unadorned, but its interior walls and ceiling are decorated with frescoes by Florentine Renaissance masters, including Perugino, Pinturicchio, Sandro Botticelli, Domenico Ghirlandaio, and Luca Signorelli. Portions of the walls were once covered with tapestries designed by Raphael (1515–19). The most important works are the frescoes by Michelangelo on the ceiling and the western wall behind the altar, considered among the greatest achievements of Western painting. The ceiling frescoes, depicting Old Testament scenes, were commissioned by Pope Julius II and painted 1508–12; the *Last Judgment* fresco on the western wall was painted 1536–41 for Pope Paul III. A controversial 10-year cleaning and restoration of the ceiling was completed in 1989, and of the western wall in 1994.

Sisyphus, In Greek mythology, the king of Corinth who was punished in Hades by having to roll a huge stone up a hill over and over again. He was the son of Aeolus and the father of Glaucus. When Death came to fetch him, Sisyphus had him chained up so that no one died until Ares came to free Death. Before being taken to the underworld, Sisyphus asked his wife to leave his body unburied. When he reached Hades he was permitted to go back to earth to punish his wife, and he lived to a ripe old age before dying a second time. His trickery resulted in his punishment in Hades.

Sita, In Hindu mythology, the consort of Rama. She sprang from a furrow when King Janaka was plowing his field, and Rama won her as his bride by bending Shiva's bow. Her abduction by the demon king Ravana and subsequent rescue are described in the *Ramayana*. She kept herself chaste during her long imprisonment, and on her return she proved her purity by undergoing an ordeal by fire. A symbol of the sufferings and strengths of women, she is one of the most revered figures in the Hindu pantheon.

Sita, Mughal painting, c. 1600; in the collection of Bharat Kala Bhavan, Varanasi, India
Pramod Chandra

sitar, Long-necked stringed instrument of the lute family, played primarily in northern India, Pakistan, and Bangladesh. As the dominant instrument in Hindustani music, it is used in ensembles and as a solo instrument with the tamboura (drone-lute) and tabla. It has a deep pear-shaped gourd body, metal strings, front and side tuning pegs, a wide neck, and movable frets. It normally has five melody strings, which are plucked with a plectrum worn on the forefinger; several drone strings; and numerous sympathetic strings (strings caused to vibrate by the other strings' vibrations). A gourd resonator is attached to the top of the neck.

Six, Les (French: "The Six"), Group of young French composers in the 1920s. Named by the critic Henri Collet (1885–1951), the group was made up of Arthur Honegger, Darius Milhaud, Francis Poulenc, Georges Auric (1899–1983), Louis Durey (1888–1979), and Germaine Tailleferre (1892–1983). Their music represents a strong reaction against German Romanticism, as well as against the lush style sometimes termed Impressionism, exemplified by the work of Claude Debussy. Most of Les Six were inspired by the iconoclastic music of Erik Satie, and they benefited from the promotion of Jean Cocteau. They were only active as a group for a few years.

Six-Day War, or ARAB-ISRAELI WAR OF 1967, War between Israel and the Arab countries of Egypt, Syria, and Jordan. Palestinian guerrilla attacks on Israel from bases in Syria led to increased hostility between the two countries. A series of miscalculations by both sides followed. Syria feared that an invasion by Israel was forthcoming and appealed to Egypt for support. Egypt answered by ordering the withdrawal of UN peacekeeping forces from the Sinai Peninsula and by moving troops into the area. Amid increasingly belligerent language from both sides, Egypt signed a mutual defense treaty with Jordan. Israel, surrounded and fearing an Arab attack was imminent, launched what it felt was a preemptive strike against the three Arab states on June 5, 1967. Israeli forces captured the Sinai Peninsula, Gaza Strip, West Bank of the Jordan River, Old City of Jerusalem, and the Golan Heights. The status of these occupied territories subsequently became a major point of contention between the two sides.

skandha, Pali KHANDHA, In Buddhism, any of the five elements that constitute an individual's mental and physical existence. They are *rupa* (physical matter), *vedana* (feeling), *samjna* (perception; Pali *sanna*), *samskara* (mental formations; Pali *sankhara*), and *vijnana* (consciousness; Pali *vinnana*). The four mental aggregates are perceived to be the personality or ego but are in fact only processes in a state of continuous change, subject to the effects of karma. At death the mental *skandha*s dissociate from the *rupa* and find a new physical base, resulting in a new birth.

skate, Any of nine genera (suborder Rajoidea) of rounded to diamond-shaped rays. These bottom-dwellers are found from tropical to near-Arctic waters and from the shallows to depths of more than 9,000 ft (2,700 m). Most have spines on the upper surface, and some have weak electrical organs in their long, slender tails. Skates lay oblong, leathery eggs (called mermaid's purses), which are often found on beaches. Species vary from 20 in. (50 cm) to 8 ft (2.5 m) long. They swim with an undulating movement of their pectoral fins. They trap active mollusk, crustacean, and fish prey by dropping down on them from above. Skates' "wings" are edible.

skateboarding, Form of recreation, popular among youths, in which a person rides standing balanced on a small board mounted on wheels. The skateboard first appeared in the early 1960s on paved areas along California beaches as a makeshift diversion for surfers when the ocean was flat. In the 1970s a faster, polyurethane wheel was developed. Eventually skateboard parks were built, providing a variety of slopes and banked surfaces for sudden turns and flamboyant stunts. The skateboarding craze contributed to the emergence of snowboarding as a winter youth sport.

skating, Sport in which bladelike runners or sets of wheels attached to shoes are used for gliding on ice or on surfaces other than ice. *See* figure skating, ice dancing, ice hockey, roller-skating, speed skating.

skeet shooting, Shooting sport using moving targets. Marksmen use shotguns to shoot at clay targets (pigeons) hurled into the air by spring devices called traps. It differs from trapshooting in that skeet traps are set at two points on the field and targets may be thrown diagonally across the shooter's field of vision. Skeet shooting has been an Olympic event since 1968.

skeleton, Bony framework of the body. It includes the skull, vertebral column, collarbone, shoulder blades, rib cage, pelvic girdle and the bones of the hands, arms, feet, and legs. The skeleton supports the body and protects its internal organs. It is held together by ligaments and moved at the joints by the muscles, which are attached to it. The skeletal system includes both bones and cartilage.

skeleton sledding, Winter sport similar to lugeing in which a small sled is ridden downhill in a headfirst, prone position. The sport of skeleton sledding developed in the 1880s on the famed Cresta Run at Saint Moritz, Switz. The "bony" look of the early sleds gave the sport its name. Riders attain speeds of more than 80 miles (129 km) per hour. It was first contested at the Olympic games in 1928.

skepticism, Philosophical doubting of knowledge claims in various areas. From ancient to modern times, skeptics have challenged accepted views in metaphysics, science, morals, and religion. Pyrrhon of Elis (*c.* 360–272 BCE) sought mental peace by avoiding commitment to any particular view; his approach gave rise in the 1st century BCE to Pyrrhonism, proponents of which sought to achieve suspension of judgment by systematically opposing various knowledge claims. One of its later leaders, Sextus Empiricus (2nd or 3rd century CE), strove for a state of imperturbability. Modern skeptical philosophers include Michel de Montaigne, Pierre Bayle, and David Hume.

skiing, Sport and mode of transportation involving moving over snow on a pair of long flat runners (skis) attached to shoes or boots. Skiing was born in northern Europe; the oldest skis, found in Russia, are some 6,000 years old. The earliest skis were often short and broad. The first written references to skiing come from the Han dynasty (206 BC–AD 220) and describe skiing in northern China. Skiing was used in warfare in Scandinavia from the 13th century or earlier to the 20th century. The earliest mode of skiing developed into the sport now called cross-country skiing. Competitive cross-country skiing began in Norway in the 1840s and had reached California by the 1860s. Improvements on primitive bindings *c.* 1860 led to greater popularity of recreational skiing. Ski-jumping competitions date from the 1870s. Downhill skiing was limited by the need to climb the hill before or after skiing down; the building of ski lifts began in the 1930s. Skis were originally made of a single piece of wood, usually hickory; laminated construction began in the 1930s, plastic running surfaces were introduced in the 1950s, and no wood has been used in the construction of downhill skis for several decades. The business of skiing began its serious growth in the 1930s and became explosive in the 1950s and '60s; huge resorts now dot the Austrian, Swiss, and Italian Alps, the Rocky Mountains, and other mountainous regions.

skin, Surface covering of the body that protects it and receives external sensory stimuli, consisting of an epidermis over a thicker dermis. The epidermis contains cells involved in immune defenses, sensory receptors, pigment cells, and keratin-producing cells. The last harden and migrate to the surface to form a dead, relatively dry outer layer of horny tissue that constantly sloughs away. The dermis contains sensory nerves and blood vessels within connective tissue. Collagen and elastin fibres give skin its tough, elastic quality. Cells scattered through it produce its components and take part in immune and other skin responses. A fat layer under the dermis provides nutritional storage, cushioning, and insulation. Skin disorders range from dermatitis and acne to skin cancer. Changes in skin colour (e.g., jaundice) or texture may be clues to systemic disorders.

Skopje, Albanian SHKUP, Serbian SKOPLJE, City (pop., 2008 est.: 486,600), capital of Macedonia. The old city is located on a terraced riverbank dominated by an ancient fortress, north of which is a Roman aqueduct. Skopje was an important city in the Roman province of Moesia Superior and was a capital of medieval Serbia. It was under Turkish rule from 1392 to 1913 and then was incorporated into Serbia. After an earthquake destroyed 80% of the city in 1963, aid was sent by 78 countries and it was rebuilt. Today it is an industrial, commercial, educational, and administrative centre.

skydiving, Sport of jumping from an airplane at a moderate altitude (e.g., 6,000 ft [1,800 m]) and executing various body maneuvers before pulling the rip cord of a parachute. Competitive events include jumping for style, landing with accuracy, and performing in teams (e.g., making free-fall formations). The sport parachute is designed to be more maneuverable than the safety parachute.

Seven-man freefall hookup.
Guy Sauvage—Agence Vandystadt/Photo Researchers

Skylab, First U.S. space station. Launched into Earth orbit in 1973 on a Saturn V rocket, it used as its main habitat the vehicle's third stage, which had been outfitted as a workshop. Its apparatus included a powerful solar telescope and equipment for Earth- and materials-sciences research and for studies of the human body's adaptation to weightlessness. Three successive astronaut crews conducted research aboard Skylab for a total of 171 days in 1973–74. Because its thermal shielding was damaged during launch, its first crew took up and installed an improvised sunshade to prevent the station from seriously overheating. Although plans called for Skylab to be reused, increased solar activity caused its orbit to degrade faster than expected. In 1979 it entered Earth's atmosphere and broke up, with debris spreading over the southeastern Indian Ocean and a sparsely populated section of Western Australia.

skyscraper, Very tall multistoried building. The term originally applied to buildings of 10–20 stories, but now generally describes high-rises of more than 40–50 stories. James Bogardus (1800–1874) built the pioneering Cast Iron Building, New York (1848), with a rigid iron frame providing the main support for upper-floor and roof loads. The refinement of the Bessemer process for making steel (lighter and stronger than iron) made extremely tall buildings possible. Chicago's Home Insurance Co. Building (1884–85), by William Le Baron Jenney (1832–1907), was the first tall building to use a steel skeleton. Structurally, skyscrapers consist of a substructure supported by a deep foundation of piles or caissons beneath the ground, an aboveground superstructure of columns and girders, and a curtain wall hung on the structural framework. Tube structures, braced tubes, and trussed tubes were developed to give skyscrapers the ability to resist lateral wind and seismic forces. The bundled-tube system, developed by Fazlur Khan (1928–1982), uses narrow steel tubes clustered together to form exceptionally rigid columns, and has been used to build some of the world's tallest skyscrapers (e.g., Sears Tower). Skyscraper design and decoration have passed through several stages: Louis Sullivan emphasized verticality; the firm of McKim, Mead, & White stressed Neoclassicism. The International Style is ideally suited to skyscraper design. Originally a form of commercial architecture, skyscrapers have increasingly been used for residential purposes as well.

slang, Nonstandard vocabulary of extreme informality, usually not limited to any region. It includes newly coined words, short-ened forms, and standard words used playfully out of their usual context. Slang is drawn from the vocabularies of limited groups: cant, the words or expressions coined or adopted by an age, ethnic, occupational, or other group (e.g., college students, jazz musicians); jargon, the shoptalk or technical terminology specific to an occupation; and argot, the cant and jargon used as a secret language by thieves or other criminals. Occupying a middle ground between standard and informal words accepted by the general public and the special words or expressions of these subgroups, slang often serves as a testing ground for words in the latter category. Many prove either useful enough to become accepted as standard or informal words or too faddish for standard use. *Blizzard* and *okay* have become standard, while *conbobberation* ("disturbance") and *tomato* ("girl") have been discarded. Some words and expressions have a lasting place in slang; for instance, *beat it* ("go away"), first used in the 16th century, has neither become standard English nor vanished.

slapstick, Comedy characterized by broad humour, absurd situations, and vigorous, often violent action. It took its name from a paddlelike device, probably introduced by 16th-century commedia dell'arte troupes, that produced a resounding whack when one comic actor used it to strike another. Slapstick comedy became popular in 19th-century music halls and vaudeville theatres and was carried into the 20th century by silent-movie comedians such as Charlie Chaplin, Harold Lloyd, and Mack Sennett's Keystone Kops and later by Laurel and Hardy, the Marx Brothers, and the Three Stooges.

slate, Fine-grained, clayey metamorphic rock that splits readily into thin slabs that have great tensile strength and durability. Some other rocks that occur in thin beds are improperly called slate because they can be used for roofing and similar purposes. True slates generally split not along the bedding plane but along planes of cleavage that may intersect the bedding plane at high angles. Slates may be black, blue, purple, red, green, or gray. Slate may be marketed either as dimension slate, used mainly for electrical panels, laboratory tabletops, roofing, and flooring, or as crushed slate, used on composition roofing, in aggregates, and as a filler.

Slav, Any member of the most numerous ethnic and linguistic body of peoples in Europe. They live chiefly in eastern and southeastern Europe but also extend across northern Asia to the Pacific. Slavs are customarily subdivided into eastern Slavs (Russians, Ukrainians, and Belarusians), western Slavs (Poles, Czechs, Slovaks, and Wends, or Sorbs), and southern Slavs (Serbs, Croats, Bulgarians, Slovenes, and Macedonians). Historically, western Slavs were integrated into western Europe; their societies developed along the lines of other western European nations. Eastern and southern Slavs suffered Mongol and Turkish invasions and evolved more autocratic, state-centred forms of government. Religion (mainly Eastern Orthodoxy and Roman Catholicism) divides Slavs, as does the use of the Cyrillic and Latin alphabets. In the Middle Ages, Slavic polities that left a rich cultural heritage developed in Bohemia, Poland, Croatia, Bosnia, Serbia, and Bulgaria, but, by the end of the 18th century, all these states had been absorbed by powerful neighbours (the Ottoman Empire, Austria, Hungary, Prussia, Russia). Eastern Slavic history often was marked by unsuccessful attempts to repel Asian invaders. In the 16th century, Muscovy (later Russia) embarked on a course of expansion across northern and central Asia that eventually made it the most powerful Slavic state. Pan-Slavism in the 19th century had some influence on the formation of the new Slavic states after World War I, though Czechoslovakia and Yugoslavia—the two attempts to integrate different Slavic peoples into single polities—had both disintegrated by the end of the 20th century, one peacefully and the other violently.

slavery, Condition in which one human being is owned by another. Slavery has existed on nearly every continent, including Asia, Europe, Africa, and the Americas, and throughout most of recorded history. The ancient Greeks and Romans accepted the institution of slavery, as did the Mayas, Incas, Aztecs, and Chinese. Until European involvement in the trade, however, slavery was a private and domestic institution. Beginning in the 16th century, a more public and "racially" based type of slavery was established when Europeans began importing slaves from Africa to the New World. An estimated 11 million people were taken from Africa during the transatlantic slave trade. By the mid-19th century the slave population in the U.S. had risen to more than four million, although slave imports had been banned in 1809. Most of the Africans sent to the United States worked on cotton or rice plantations in the South, their status governed by slave codes. Almost 40% of captives transported from Africa to the Americas were taken to Brazil, where harsh conditions required the constant replenishing of slaves. Following the rise of abolitionism, Britain outlawed slavery in its colonies in 1833, and France did the same in 1848. During the American Civil War, slavery was abolished in the Confederacy by the Emancipation Proclamation (1863), which was decreed by Pres. Abraham Lincoln. Brazil was the last to abolish slavery, doing so in 1888. Official policy notwithstanding, slavery continues to exist in many parts of the world. Many contemporary slaves are women and children forced into prostitution or working at hard labour or in sweatshops. Debt bondage is common, affecting millions of people, and slaves are often traded for material goods.

Slavic languages, or SLAVONIC LANGUAGES, Branch of the Indo-European language family spoken by more than 315 million people in central and eastern Europe and northern Asia. The Slavic family is usually divided into three subgroups: West Slavic (Polish, Slovak, Czech, and Sorbian), East Slavic (Russian, Ukrainian, and Belarusian), and South Slavic (Slovene; Serbian, Bosnian, Croatian, and sometimes Montenegrin [Serbo-Croatian]; Bulgarian; and Macedonian). Polish belongs to the Lekhitic subgroup of West Slavic languages, which also includes Kashubian—now spoken in western Poland by fewer than 150,000 people and regarded in Poland as a Polish dialect—and several now-extinct languages. A distinctive feature of this subgroup is its preservation of the Proto-Slavic nasal vowels. Another remnant language is Sorbian, spoken by 60,000–70,000 people in eastern Germany. Western Lekhitic and Sorbian are all that remains of what was once a much greater Slavic speech area in central Europe; that area was gradually Germanized from about the 9th century. Among Indo-European languages, Slavic is closest to the family of Baltic languages.

Slavic religion, Beliefs and religious practices of the ancient Slavic peoples of East Europe, including the Russians, Ukrainians, Poles, Czechs, Slovaks, Serbs, Croats, and Slovenes. Most Slavic mythologies hold that God ordered the devil to bring up a handful of sand from the bottom of the sea and created the land from it. Slavic religion was often characterized by dualism, with a Black God named in curses and a White God invoked to obtain protection or mercy. Lightning and fire gods were also common. The ancient Russians appear to have erected their idols outdoors, but the Baltic Slavs built temples and enclosed sacred places, where festivals were held and animal and human sacrifices occurred. Such festivals also often included communal banquets at which the flesh of sacrificial animals was consumed.

sleep, Natural periodic suspension of consciousness during which the powers of the body are restored. Humans normally sleep at night, whereas nocturnal species sleep during the day. Adult humans sleep between six and nine hours per night, though increasing numbers of people sleep less than six hours. Sleep is divided into two main types: REM (rapid-eye-movement) and NREM (non-REM), each of which recurs cyclically several times during a normal period of sleep. REM sleep is characterized by increased neuronal activity of the forebrain and midbrain, by depressed muscle tone, and by dreaming, rapid eye movements, and

vascular congestion of the sex organs. NREM sleep is divided into stages, the last of which is the deep, restorative, quiet sleep commonly associated with "a good night's rest."

sleeping sickness, Protozoal disease transmitted by the bite of the tsetse fly. Two forms, caused by different species of the genus *Trypanosoma*, occur in separate regions in Africa. The parasite enters the bloodstream and invades the lymph nodes and spleen, which become swollen, soft, and tender. Irregular fever and delayed pain sensation develop. In the Rhodesian form, the patient soon dies of massive toxemia. The Gambian type progresses to brain and spinal cord invasion, causing severe headache, mental and physical fatigue, spastic or flaccid paralysis, chorea, and profound sleepiness, followed over two or three years by emaciation, coma, and death. Some patients develop a tolerance but still carry the trypanosomes. The earlier drug treatment begins, the greater the chance of recovery. Sleeping sickness is still prevalent in parts of Africa despite efforts to control it.

slime mold, Any of about 500 species of primitive organisms that contain true nuclei and resemble both protists and fungi. Originally grouped within the kingdom Fungi, some classification systems consider slime molds to be in the kingdom Protista. They typically thrive in dark, cool, moist conditions such as on forest floors. Bacteria, yeast, molds, and fungi provide the main source of slime-mold nutrition. The complex life cycle of slime molds, exhibiting complete alternation of generations, may clarify the early evolution of both plant and animal cells. In the presence of water a tiny spore releases a mass of cytoplasm called a swarm cell, which later develops into an amoebalike creeping cell called a myxamoeba. Both swarm cells and myxamoebas can fuse in sexual union; the resulting fertilized cell, or plasmodium, grows through nuclear division and forms a spore case, which, when it dries, disintegrates and releases spores to begin the cycle again.

sloth, Nocturnal, solitary, tree-dwelling mammal (family Bradypodidae), found in South and Central America. About 2 ft (60 cm) long, sloths have a tiny tail, peglike teeth, long curved claws, and long forelimbs. A green alga grows in the shaggy fur. The four species of three-toed sloths, or ais (*Bradypus*), eat only leaves of the trumpet tree. The two species of two-toed sloths, or unaus (*Choloepus*), have two toes on the forelimbs; they eat fruits, stems, and leaves of various plants. Sloths cannot walk. They cling upright to trunks, hang upside down (in which position they sleep some 15 hours a day), or move, extremely slowly (hence their name), by pulling hand over hand. Their natural camouflage is their chief protection from predators.

Three-toed sloth (Bradypus tridactylus)
Des Bartlett/Bruce Coleman Ltd.

Slovakia, officially SLOVAK REPUBLIC, Country, central Europe. Area: 18,932 sq mi (49,034 sq km). Population: (2011 est.) 5,440,000. Capital: Bratislava. More than four-fifths of the population is Slovak; Hungarians form the largest minority. Language: Slovak (official). Religion: Christianity (mostly Roman Catholic; also Protestant, other Christians). Currency: euro. The Carpathian Mountains dominate Slovakia, with lowlands in the southwestern and southeastern regions. The Morava and Danube rivers form parts of the southern and western borders. Grain, sugar beets, and potatoes are grown and pigs, sheep, and cattle are raised, but the economy is based on services and manufacturing. Slovakia is a unitary multiparty republic with one legislative house; its head of state is the president, and the head of government is the prime minister. Slovakia was inhabited in the first centuries CE by Illyrian,

Celtic, and Germanic tribes. Slovaks settled there around the 6th century. In the 9th century, part of what is now Slovakia belonged to Great Moravia, which was conquered by the Magyars in the early 10th century. The Slovak territory then remained in the kingdom of Hungary until the end of World War I, when the Slovaks joined the Czechs to form the new state of Czechoslovakia in 1918. In 1938 Slovakia was declared an autonomous unit within Czechoslovakia; it was nominally independent under German protection from 1939 to 1945. After the expulsion of the Germans, Slovakia joined a reconstituted Czechoslovakia, which came under Soviet domination in 1948. The fall of the communist regime in 1989 led to a revival of interest in autonomy, and Slovakia became an independent nation in 1993. It joined both NATO and the European Union in 2004.

Slovenia, officially REPUBLIC OF SLOVENIA, Country, northwestern Balkans region, central Europe. Area: 7,827 sq mi (20,273 sq km). Population: (2011 est.) 2,052,000. Capital: Ljubljana. The vast majority of the population is Slovene. Language: Slovene (official). Religion: Christianity (predominantly Roman Catholic; also other Christians). Currency: euro. Slovenia is predominantly mountainous and wooded, with deep, fertile valleys and numerous rivers. It is one of the more prosperous regions of the Balkans. Its economy is based largely on services and manufacturing, and forestry, livestock, and crops, including potatoes, grains, and fruits, are also important. Slovenia is a unitary multiparty republic with two legislative houses; its head of state is the president, and the head of government is the prime minister. The Slovenes settled the region in the 6th century CE. In the 8th century it was incorporated into the Frankish empire of Charlemagne, and in the 10th century it came under Germany as part of the medieval empire (later the Holy Roman Empire). Except for the period from 1809 to 1814, when Napoleon ruled the area, most of the lands belonged to Austria until the formation of the Kingdom of Serbs, Croats, and Slovenes in 1918. Slovenia became a constituent republic of Yugoslavia in 1946 and received a section of the former Italian Adriatic coastline in 1947. In 1990 Slovenia held the first contested multiparty elections in Yugoslavia since before World War II. In 1991 Slovenia seceded from Yugoslavia; its independence was internationally recognized in 1992. Subsequently it sought to privatize the economy, build ties with western Europe (becoming a member of both the European Union and the North Atlantic Treaty Organization in 2004), and confront Croatia and Italy over territorial rights.

slug, Any species of gastropod that glides along on a broad tapered foot and has no shell or one that is merely an internal plate or a series of granules. Most slugs use the mantle cavity as a lung. Slugs have a soft, slimy body and live in moist habitats on land (except for one freshwater species). All are hermaphroditic. In temperate regions, the common slugs eat fungi and decaying leaves. Some tropical species eat plants, and some European species eat other snails and earthworms.

slum, Densely populated area of substandard housing, usually in a city, characterized by unsanitary conditions and social disorganization. Rapid industrialization in 19th-century Europe was accompanied by rapid population growth and the concentration of working-class people in overcrowded, poorly built housing. England passed the first legislation for building low-income housing to certain minimum standards in 1851; laws for slum clearance were first enacted in 1868. In the U.S., slum development coincided with the arrival of large numbers of immigrants in the late 19th and early 20th centuries; laws concerning adequate ventilation, fire protection, and sanitation in urban housing were passed in the late 1800s. In the 20th century government and private organizations built low-income housing and appropriated funds for urban renewal and offered low-interest home loans. Shantytowns, which often grow up around urban centres in developing countries

as rural populations migrate to the cities in search of employment, are one type of slum for which alleviating measures have yet to be successfully introduced.

smallpox, or VARIOLA, One of the world's most dreaded plagues before 1980, when it was declared eradicated. It was known in ancient China, India, and Egypt. It came to the Western Hemisphere with Europeans in the 16th century and devastated the native population, which lacked resistance. An infectious viral disease only of humans, it causes fever and then a rash of variable severity that blisters and dries up, leaving scars. It is not spread easily, but the virus can survive for long periods outside the body (e.g., in bedding). Edward Jenner developed a vaccine from cowpox. The World Health Organization's eradication project reduced smallpox deaths from two million in 1967 to zero in 1977–80. The virus now exists only in laboratories; in some countries it may be under development for purposes of biological warfare.

smart bomb, Bomb with a guidance system that directs its path toward a target. It is steered by fins or wings on the bomb that move in response to guidance commands. Guidance systems may be electro-optical, laser, infrared, or inertial. Electro-optical systems send pictures of the area so that the bomb can be guided onto the target. Laser-guided bombs follow the reflections of a laser beam trained onto the target by an aircraft or a spotter on the ground. Infrared guidance responds to radiation generated by warm areas of the target. Inertial navigation is based on inputting coordinates derived from radar systems or from Global Positioning System satellites into the bomb's gyroscopes. Smart bombs, initially used in the Vietnam War, offer far greater accuracy than traditional gravity, or "dumb," bombs.

Smarta, Orthodox Hindu sect consisting of members of higher castes who worship all the gods of the Hindu pantheon and adhere to rules of ritual and conduct laid down in ancient sutras. The sect was founded by Shankara. The head of the monastery he established at Sringeri is the spiritual authority of the Smartas and one of the chief religious personages of India. The Smartas regard five gods as primary: Shiva, Vishnu, Shakti, Surya, and Ganesha. Active in all branches of learning, they have earned the honorary title *sastri* (Sanskrit: "men of learning").

smelting, Process by which a metal is obtained from its ore, either as the element or as a simple compound, usually by heating beyond the melting point, ordinarily in the presence of reducing agents such as coke or oxidizing agents such as air. A metal whose ore is an oxygen compound (e.g., iron, zinc, or lead oxide) is heated (reduction smelting) in a blast furnace to a high temperature; the oxide combines with the carbon in the coke, escaping as carbon monoxide or carbon dioxide. Other impurities are removed by adding flux, with which they combine to form slag. If the ore is a sulfide mineral (e.g., copper, nickel, lead, or cobalt), air or oxygen is blasted through (matte smelting) to oxidize the sulfide to sulfur dioxide and any iron to oxide slag, leaving the metal.

Smith, Adam (baptized June 5, 1723, Kirkcaldy, Fife, Scot.—d. July 17, 1790, Edinburgh), Scottish social philosopher and political economist. The son of a customs official, he studied at the Universities of Glasgow and Oxford. A series of public lectures in Edinburgh (from 1748) led to a lifelong friendship with David Hume and to Smith's appointment to the Glasgow faculty in 1751. After publishing *The Theory of Moral Sentiments* (1759), he became the tutor of the future Duke of Buccleuch (1763–66); with him he traveled to France, where Smith consorted with other eminent thinkers. In 1776, after nine years of work, Smith published *An Inquiry into the Nature and Causes of the Wealth of Nations*, the first comprehensive system of political economy. In it he argued in favour of an economic system based on individual self-interest that would be led, as if by an "invisible hand," to achieve the greatest good for all, and posited the division of labour as the chief factor in economic growth. A reaction to the system of mercantilism then current, it stands as the beginning of classical economics. *The Wealth of Nations* in time won him an enormous reputation and would become virtually the most influential work on economics ever published. Though often regarded as the bible of capitalism, it is harshly critical of the shortcomings of unrestrained free enterprise and monopoly. In 1777 Smith was appointed commissioner of customs for Scotland, and in 1787 rector of the University of Glasgow.

Smith, Joseph (b. Dec. 23, 1805, Sharon, Vt., U.S.—d. June 27, 1844, Carthage, Ill.), Founder of the Church of Jesus Christ of Latter-day Saints (Mormon church). He began experiencing visions as a teenager in Palmyra, N.Y. In 1827 he claimed that an angel had directed him to buried golden plates containing God's revelation; these he translated into the *Book of Mormon* (1830). He led converts to Ohio, Missouri, and Illinois, where he established the town of Nauvoo (1839), which soon became the state's largest town. Imprisoned for treason after his efforts to silence Mormon dissenters led to mob violence, he was murdered by a lynch mob that stormed the jail where he was held. His work was continued by Brigham Young.

Joseph Smith, detail from an oil painting by an unknown artist; in the Community of Christ Temple and Auditorium complex, Independence, Missouri.
Courtesy of the Community of Christ, Independence, Missouri

smog, Polluted air over a community. The term, a combination of "smoke" and "fog," was popularized in the early 20th century and now commonly refers to the pall of automotive or industrial origin that lies over many cities. Sulfurous smog results from the use of sulfur-bearing fossil fuels, particularly coal, and is aggravated by dampness. Photochemical smog requires neither smoke nor fog. Nitrogen oxides and hydrocarbon vapours emitted from automobiles and other sources undergo reactions in the presence of sunlight that produce a light brownish coloration of the atmosphere, reduced visibility, plant damage, irritation of the eyes, and respiratory distress.

smoking, Breathing the fumes of burning plant material, especially tobacco, from a cigarette, cigar, or pipe. Despite social and medical arguments against tobacco use, smoking is widely practiced around the world. Nicotine is an alkaloid in tobacco that is addictive and can have both stimulating and tranquilizing psychoactive effects. The tar (residue) and gases produced by burning tobacco have many negative health effects. They include lung cancer, pancreatic cancer, and laryngeal cancer; heart disease and stroke; and emphysema and chronic bronchitis. Smoking also increases other health-related risk factors. A nonsmoker who breathes secondhand smoke (such as the smoke from a lit cigarette) is at an increased risk of the same diseases that affect smokers. Secondhand smoke also increases the risk of sudden infant death syndrome. Doctor-run programs, along with nicotine patches and gums that provide diminishing doses of nicotine, are among the aids available to help those who wish to quit smoking. Hypnosis, acupuncture, herbal remedies, and other approaches are also widely advertised as ways to quit smoking. Smoking has been greatly reduced in the health-conscious West even as it rises in many less-developed countries.

Smolensk, City (pop., 2006 est.: 317,915), western Russia. One of the oldest and most historic of Russian cities, it was a key stronghold on the Dnieper River by the 9th century and became a commercial centre on the trade route between the Baltic Sea and the Byzantine Empire. Sacked by the Tatars *c.* 1240, it subsequently fell to Lithuania. Sieges led to its capture by Moscow in 1340 and recapture by Lithuania in 1408. It was fought over several times, then was finally taken by Russia in 1654. It was burned during Napoleon's invasion of Russia in 1812. The scene of heavy fighting in World War II, it was occupied by the Germans from 1941 to 1943. It is a light-industry and educational centre.

Smrti, Class of Hindu sacred literature that is based on human memory, as distinct from the Vedas, which are considered to be divinely revealed. Smrti serves to elaborate, interpret, and codify Vedic literature. It is considered less authoritative than Vedic literature but tends to be more widely known. The term has come to refer particularly to texts pertaining to law and social conduct, including the *Kalpa-sutras*, the *Puranas*, the *Bhagavadgita*, the *Ramayana*, and the *Mahabharata*.

smut, Disease of cereals, corn, grasses, onion, and sorghum, caused by many species of fungi. Spores accumulate in sootlike masses (sori) that form within blisters in seeds, leaves, stems, flower parts, and bulbs. The sori usually break up into a black powder that is readily dispersed by wind. Many smut fungi enter embryos or seedling plants, develop throughout the plant, and appear externally only as the plants near maturity. Other smuts are localized, infecting actively growing tissues. Control includes growing resistant varieties in noninfested soil, treating seeds with fungicide, using disease-free transplants, and destroying infected plants or plant parts before the spores are released.

snail, Any species of gastropod that glides along on a broad tapered foot and has a high coiled shell into which it can withdraw. Snails are found in the ocean, in fresh waters, and on land. Most marine snails have gills in the mantle cavity. Most land and freshwater snails have no gills; they use the mantle cavity itself as a lung. Snails may be either scavengers (of dead plant or animal matter) or predators. Some species are used as food, and the shells of some are used as ornaments.

snake, Any member of about 19 reptile families (suborder Serpentes, order Squamata) that has no limbs, voice, external ears, or eyelids, only one functional lung, and a long, slender body. About 2,900 snake species are known to exist, most living in the tropics. Their skin is covered with scales. They have good eyesight, and they continually taste the surrounding air with their tongues. Though they lack any voice, they are capable of hissing. Most live on the ground, but some are arboreal or aquatic, and some are burrowers. They move by muscular contraction, aided by elongated scales on their abdomen. They focus 70% of their mostly solitary existence on tracking, capturing, and digesting their living prey. The construction of their jaws and bodies enables them to swallow large prey whole. Because they are ectotherms (cold-blooded), a single meal can often sustain them for weeks. Mating and laying eggs or bearing live young are brief seasonal activities. About one-tenth of snake species are venomous; some can kill humans with their bite. Others kill their prey by constriction or simply ingesting. Species range from less than 5 in. (12 cm) to over 30 ft (9 m) long. Snakes grow continuously throughout their lives, shedding their outgrown skin at each growth increment. They are found worldwide, but few species are found on islands or in regions with long winters.

snakebite, Wound from the bite of a snake, especially a venomous one. Nonvenomous snakes leave skin tears that may be treated like scratches. A person bitten by a venomous snake needs medical care as soon as possible. Antivenin must be specific to the type of venom, so the snake should be identified or accurately described. Different kinds of venom break down red blood cells or attack the nervous system, causing paralysis. Local tissue destruction may lead to gangrene. First aid for snakebite seeks to keep the venom from spreading to the rest of the body. The bitten limb should be kept still below heart level with a broad, firm (not tight) bandage around it above the bite. Exertion and excitement should be avoided. Cutting, suction, tourniquets, and applying ice are not advised.

snapper, Any of about 250 species of valuable food fishes (family Lutjanidae), found throughout the tropics. These active schooling fishes have slender bodies, large mouths, sharp canine teeth, and blunt or forked tails. Many species grow to 2–3 ft (60–90 cm) long. Snappers eat crustaceans and other fishes. Some species, such as the Atlantic dog snapper, contain a toxin. The red snapper, a bright red fish, inhabits deep Atlantic waters. The emperor snapper is a red-and-white Indo-Pacific fish. The Atlantic yellowtail snapper has a broad yellow stripe from the nose to the wholly yellow tail.

*Red spot snapper (*Lethrinus variegatus*)*
Douglas Faulkner

snooker, Variation of English billiards. It is played with 15 red balls and 6 variously coloured balls. Snooker arose, probably in India, as a game for soldiers in the 1870s. Players try to pocket first the red and then the nonred balls, scoring one point for each red ball and the number value of the others. "Snooker" refers to the position of the cue ball when it cannot hit a required ball.

snow, Solid form of water that crystallizes in the atmosphere and falls to the Earth, covering about 23% of the Earth's surface either permanently or temporarily. Snowflakes are formed by crystals of ice that generally have a hexagonal pattern. Snow cover has a significant effect on climate and on plant, animal, and human life. By increasing the reflection of solar radiation and interfering with the conduction of heat from the ground, it induces a cold climate. The low heat conduction protects small plants from the effects of the lowest winter temperatures; on the other hand, late disappearance of snow in the spring delays the growth of plants.

snow leopard, or OUNCE, Endangered species (*Uncia uncia*) of nocturnal long-haired cat that inhabits the high mountains of Central Asia and India. It is about 6 ft (1.8 m) long, including the 3-ft (1-m) tail, stands about 2 ft (0.5 m) tall, and weighs 60–120 lb (27–55 kg). Its dense, soft coat, consisting of an insulating undercoat and outer coat of 2-in. (5-cm) hairs, is pale grayish with dark rosettes and a dark streak along the spine. The whitish fur of the underparts may be 4 in. (10 cm) long. It preys on marmots, wild sheep and goats, birds, and other animals. It is hunted principally for the market in goods used in Asian traditional medicine.

snowboarding, Sport of sliding downhill over snow on a snowboard, a wide ski ridden in a surfing position. Derived from surfing and influenced also by skateboarding as well as skiing, snowboarding began to burgeon among young people in the U.S. in the mid-1980s. The first Olympic snowboarding competition was held in the 1998 Winter Games. The two main events are giant slalom (similar to Alpine giant slalom) and halfpipe, in which riders use a large, snow-covered trench (halfpipe) to repeatedly launch themselves into the air and perform various acrobatic feats.

soap opera, Broadcast serial drama, characterized by a permanent cast of actors, a continuing story, tangled interpersonal situations, and a melodramatic or sentimental style. Its name derived from the soap and detergent manufacturers who originally often sponsored such programs on radio. Soap operas began in the early 1930s as 15-minute radio episodes and continued on television from the early 1950s as 30-minute and later hour-long episodes. Usually broadcast during the day and aimed at housewives, they

initially focused on middle-class family life, but by the 1970s their content had expanded to include a wider variety of characters and situations and a greater degree of sexual explicitness. In the 1980s similar series began to be aired in prime-time evening hours (e.g., *Dallas* and *Dynasty*).

soaring, or GLIDING, Sport of flying a glider or sailplane. The craft is towed behind a powered airplane to an altitude of about 2,000 ft (600 m) and then released. The glider pilot makes use of rising currents of warm air, such as those above a sunlit field, to maintain or gain altitude. Instruments used include the altimeter, airspeed indicator, compass, and turn-and-bank indicator. National soaring contests, which include events for altitude, speed, distance, and accuracy in returning to a starting point, are held annually.

social contract, Actual or hypothetical compact between the ruled and their rulers. The original inspiration for the notion may derive from the biblical covenant between God and Abraham, but it is most closely associated with the writings of Thomas Hobbes, John Locke, and Jean-Jacques Rousseau. Hobbes argued that the absolute power of the sovereign is justified by a hypothetical social contract in which the people agree to obey him in all matters in return for a guarantee of peace and security, which they lack in the warlike "state of nature" posited to exist before the contract is made. Locke believed that rulers also were obliged to protect private property and the right to freedom of thought, speech, and worship. Rousseau held that in the state of nature people are unwarlike but also undeveloped in reasoning and morality; in surrendering their individual freedom, they acquire political liberty and civil rights within a system of laws based on the "general will" of the governed. The idea of the social contract influenced the shapers of the American Revolution and the French Revolution and the constitutions that followed them.

social Darwinism, Theory that persons, groups, and "races" are subject to the same laws of natural selection as Charles Darwin had proposed for plants and animals in nature. Social Darwinists, such as Herbert Spencer and Walter Bagehot in England and William Graham Sumner in the U.S., held that the life of humans in society was a struggle for existence ruled by "survival of the fittest," in Spencer's words. Wealth was said to be a sign of natural superiority, its absence a sign of unfitness. The theory was used from the late 19th century to support laissez-faire capitalism and political conservatism. Social Darwinism declined as scientific knowledge expanded.

social democracy, Political ideology that advocates a peaceful, evolutionary transition of society from capitalism to socialism, using established political processes. It rejects Marxism's advocacy of social revolution. Social democracy began as a political movement in Germany in the 1870s. Eduard Bernstein argued (1899) that capitalism was overcoming many of the weaknesses Karl Marx had seen in it (including unemployment and overproduction) and that universal suffrage would lead peacefully to a socialist government. After 1945, social-democratic governments came to power in West Germany, Sweden, and Britain (under the Labour Party). Social-democratic thought gradually came to regard state regulation (without state ownership) as sufficient to ensure economic growth and a fair distribution of income.

social insurance, Compulsory public-insurance program that protects against various economic risks (e.g., loss of income due to sickness, old age, or unemployment). Social insurance is considered one type of social security, though the two terms are sometimes used interchangeably. The first compulsory national social-insurance programs were established in Germany under Otto von Bismarck: health insurance in 1883, workers' compensation in 1884, and old-age and disability pensions in 1889. Austria and Hungary soon followed Germany's example. After 1920, social insurance was rapidly adopted throughout Europe and the Western Hemisphere. The U.S. lagged behind until the passage of the Social Security Act in 1935. Social Security in the U.S. now provides retirement benefits, health care for persons over a specific minimum age, and disability insurance. Social-insurance contributions are normally compulsory and may be made by the insured person's employer and the state as well as by the individual. Social insurance is usually self-financing, with contributions being placed in specific funds for that purpose.

social psychology, Branch of psychology concerned with the personality, attitudes, motivations, and behaviour of the individual or group in the context of social interaction. The field emerged in the U.S. in the 1920s. Topics include the attribution of social status based on perceptual cues, the influence of social factors (such as peers) on a person's attitudes and beliefs, the functioning of small groups and large organizations, and the dynamics of face-to-face interactions.

social science, Any discipline or branch of science that deals with the sociocultural aspects of human behaviour. The social sciences generally include cultural anthropology, economics, political science, sociology, criminology, and social psychology. Comparative law and comparative religion (the comparative study of the legal systems and religions of different nations and cultures) are also sometimes regarded as social sciences.

social security, Public provision for the economic security and social welfare of all individuals and their families, especially in the case of income losses due to unemployment, work injury, maternity, sickness, old age, and death. The term encompasses not only social insurance but also health and welfare services and various income maintenance programs designed to improve the recipient's welfare through public services. Some of the first organized cooperative efforts to provide for the economic security of individuals were instituted by workingmen's associations, mutual-benefit societies, and labour unions; social security was not widely established by law until the 19th and 20th centuries, with the first modern program appearing in Germany in 1883. Almost all developed nations now have social security programs that provide benefits or services through several major approaches such as social insurance and social assistance, a needs-based program that pays benefits only to the poor.

social service, also called SOCIAL WORK, Any of various professional activities or methods concerned with providing social services (such as investigatory and treatment services or material aid) to disadvantaged, distressed, or vulnerable persons or groups. The field originated in the charity organizations in Europe and the U.S. in the late 19th century. The training of volunteer workers by these organizations led directly to the founding of the first schools of social work and indirectly to increased government responsibility for the welfare of the disadvantaged. Social service providers may serve the needs of children and families, the poor or homeless, immigrants, veterans, the mentally ill, the handicapped, victims of rape or domestic violence, and persons dependent on alcohol or drugs.

social status, Relative rank that an individual holds, with attendant rights, duties, and lifestyle, in a social hierarchy based on honour and prestige. Status is often ascribed on the basis of sex, age, family relationships, and birth, placing one into a particular social group irrespective of ability or accomplishments. Achieved status, on the other hand, is based on educational attainment, occupational choice, marital status, and other factors involving personal effort. Status groups differ from social classes in being based on considerations of honour and prestige rather than purely economic position. Relative status is a major determinant of people's behaviour toward one another, and competition for status seems to be a prime human motivator.

Social War, or ITALIC WAR, or MARSIC WAR (90–89 BC) Rebellion waged by ancient Rome's Italian allies (Latin, *socii*). The allies in central and southern Italy had aided Rome in its wars, but they were denied the privileges of Roman citizenship. The people of central Italy's hills—the Marsi in the north and the Samnites in the south—organized a confederacy and began an uprising for independence, winning victories over Roman armies in the north and south. After Rome granted citizenship to those who had not revolted and those who would immediately lay down their arms, Italian interest in the struggle declined. Sulla defeated the weakened rebels in the south, and legislation was passed to unify Italy south of the Po River.

socialism, System of social organization in which private property and the distribution of income are subject to social control; also, the political movements aimed at putting that system into practice. Because "social control" may be interpreted in widely diverging ways, socialism ranges from statist to libertarian, from Marxist to liberal. The term was first used to describe the doctrines of Charles Fourier, Henri de Saint-Simon, and Robert Owen, who emphasized noncoercive communities of people working noncompetitively for the spiritual and physical well-being of all. Karl Marx and Friedrich Engels, seeing socialism as a transition state between capitalism and communism, appropriated what they found useful in socialist movements to develop their "scientific socialism." In the 20th century the Soviet Union was the principal model of strictly centralized socialism, while Sweden and Denmark were well known for their noncommunist socialism.

Socialist Realism, Officially sanctioned theory and method of artistic and literary composition in the Soviet Union from 1932 to the mid-1980s. Following the tradition of 19th-century Russian realism, Socialist Realism purported to serve as an objective mirror of life. Instead of critiquing society, however, it took as its primary theme the struggle to build socialism and a classless society and called for the didactic use of art to develop social consciousness. Artists were expected to take a positive view of socialist society and to keep in mind its historical relevance, requisites that seldom coincided with their real experiences and frequently undermined the artistic credibility of their works.

Society Islands, Archipelago (pop., 2002: 214,445), western French Polynesia, South Pacific Ocean. Its chief island is Tahiti. The Society Islands comprise two groups, the Windward Islands and the Leeward Islands. They are volcanic in origin and mountainous. Claimed for Britain in 1767, the islands were visited in 1769 by Capt. James Cook with a scientific expedition of the Royal Society (hence their name). They were claimed by France in 1786 and became a French protectorate in 1842, a French colony in 1881, and a part of French Oceania in 1903. Their chief products are copra and pearls.

sociobiology, Systematic study of the biological basis of social behaviour. The concept was popularized by Edward O. Wilson in his *Sociobiology* (1975) and by Richard Dawkins (b. 1941) in *The Selfish Gene* (1976). Sociobiology attempts to understand and explain animal (and human) social behaviour in the light of natural selection and other biological processes. A central tenet is that the transmission of genes through successful reproduction is the central motivator in animals' struggle for survival, and that animals will behave in ways that maximize their chances of transmitting their genes to succeeding generations. Though sociobiology has contributed insights into animal behaviour (such as altruism in social insects and male-female differences in certain species), it remains controversial when applied to human social behaviour.

sociology, Science of society, social institutions, and social relationships, and specifically the systematic study of the development, structure, interaction, and collective behaviour of organized human groups. It emerged at the end of the 19th century through the work of Émile Durkheim in France, Max Weber and Georg

Simmel in Germany, and Robert E. Park and Albion Small in the U.S. Sociologists use observational techniques, surveys and interviews, statistical analysis, controlled experiments, and other methods to study subjects such as the family, ethnic relations, schooling, social status and class, bureaucracy, religious movements, deviance, the elderly, and social change.

Socrates (b. *c.* 470, Athens—d. 399 BC, Athens), Greek philosopher whose way of life, character, and thought exerted a profound influence on ancient and modern philosophy. Because he wrote nothing, information about his personality and doctrine is derived chiefly from depictions of his conversations and other information in the dialogues of Plato, in the *Memorabilia* of Xenophon, and in various writings of Aristotle. He fought bravely in the Peloponnesian War and later served in the Athenian *boule* (assembly). Socrates considered it his religious duty to call his fellow citizens to the examined life by engaging them in philosophical conversation. His contribution to these exchanges typically consisted of a series of probing questions that cumulatively revealed his interlocutor's complete ignorance of the subject under discussion; such cross-examination used as a pedagogical technique has been called the "Socratic method." Though Socrates characteristically professed his own ignorance regarding many of the (mainly ethical) subjects he investigated (e.g., the nature of piety), he did hold certain convictions with confidence, including that: (1) human wisdom begins with the recognition of one's own ignorance; (2) the unexamined life is not worth living; (3) ethical virtue is the only thing that matters; and (4) a good person can never be harmed, because whatever misfortune he may suffer, his virtue will remain intact. His students and admirers included, in addition to Plato, Alcibiades, who betrayed Athens in the Peloponnesian War, and Critias (*c.* 480–403 BC), who was one of the Thirty Tyrants imposed on Athens after its defeat by Sparta. Because he was connected with these two men, but also because his habit of exposing the ignorance of his fellow citizens had made him widely hated and feared, Socrates was tried on charges of impiety and corrupting the youth and condemned to death by poisoning (the poison probably being hemlock) in 399 BC; he submitted to the sentence willingly. Plato's *Apology* purports to be the speech that Socrates gave in his own defense. As depicted in the *Apology*, Socrates' trial and death raise vital questions about the nature of democracy, the value of free speech, and the potential conflict between moral and religious obligation and the laws of the state.

sodium, Chemical element, one of the alkali metals, chemical symbol Na, atomic number 11. A very soft, silvery white metal, the sixth most abundant element on Earth, it occurs mainly as halite, never free. Extremely reactive, it is used as a chemical reagent and raw material, in metallurgy, as a heat exchanger (in nuclear power generators and certain types of engines), and in sodium-vapour lamps. Sodium is essential for life but rarely deficient in diets; high intake is linked to hypertension. Sodium in compounds, many of great industrial importance (including bicarbonate of soda, caustic soda, sodium nitrate [Chile saltpetre], and sodium chloride), has valence 1. Sodium carbonate, one of the four most important basic chemical commodities, is used in making glass, detergents, and cleansers. Sodium hypochlorite, familiar as household bleach, is also used to bleach paper pulp and textiles, to chlorinate water, and in some medicines. The sulfate is used in the kraft process and also used to make paperboard, glass, and detergents. The thiosulfate (hyposulfite, or "hypo") is used to developed photographs.

Sodom and Gomorrah, Legendary cities of ancient Palestine. According to the Old Testament book of Genesis, the notorious cities were destroyed by "brimstone and fire" because of their wickedness. The site of the cities is unknown but may have been in an area now beneath the waters of the Dead Sea. Archaeological evidence shows that the area may once have been fertile and could have drawn the biblical Lot to graze his flock. The cities' legendary wickedness has inspired many writers, including Jean Giraudoux and Nikos Kazantzakis.

sofer, or SOPHER, In Judaism, a scholar-teacher of the 5th–2nd centuries BC who transcribed, edited, and interpreted the Bible. The first *sofer* was Ezra, who, with his disciples, initiated a tradition of rabbinical scholarship that is still central in Judaism. This tradition of scholarship arose to meet the specific need of applying the idealistic aspirations of the Torah and oral tradition to everyday life, thus in effect codifying Mosaic law. The *soferim* were important historically for having fixed the canon of the Hebrew scriptures. Later the term *sofer* came to refer to one who taught the Bible to children or who was qualified to write Torah scrolls.

Sofia, ancient SERDICA, City (pop., 2001: 1,096,389), capital of Bulgaria. Established as a Thracian settlement *c.* 8th century BC, it flourished under the Romans. Plundered by the Huns in the 5th century AD, it was rebuilt under the Byzantine Empire. In 809 it became a Bulgarian town but reverted to Byzantine rule from 1018 to 1185, when the second Bulgarian empire was established. The Turks held it from 1382 until it was liberated by the Russians in 1878. In 1879 it was made the Bulgarian capital. It is the country's principal transportation and cultural centre and the site of many industries. Among its educational institutions is the University of Sofia (1888), Bulgaria's oldest university. Its historical monuments include the 6th-century church of St. Sofia.

softball, Game resembling baseball but played on a smaller diamond with a larger ball (12 in. [30.5 cm] in circumference), which is pitched underhand. Since the first standard set of rules was published in the 1920s, the game has been popular as an amateur sport in the U.S., and since the 1960s it has grown considerably in popularity outside of North America. In U.S. high schools and colleges it is a popular women's sport; a women's softball competition was added to the Olympic Games in 1996.

soil, The biologically active, porous medium that has developed in the uppermost layer of the Earth's crust. Soil serves as a natural reservoir of water and nutrients, as a medium for the filtration and breakdown of injurious wastes, and as a participant in the cycling of carbon and other elements through the global ecosystem. It has evolved through the weathering of solid materials such as consolidated rocks, sediments, glacial tills, volcanic ash, and organic matter. The bulk of soil consists of mineral particles composed of silicate ions combined with various metal ions. Organic soil content consists of undecomposed or partially decomposed biomass as well as humus, an array of organic compounds derived from broken down biomass.

Soka-gakkai, Lay religious and political group associated with the Buddhist sect Nichiren-sho-shu. The most successful of Japan's new religious movements of the 20th century, it draws on the 13th-century teachings of Nichiren. Like other movements in Nichiren Buddhism, it takes the Lotus Sutra as its chief scripture. Founded in 1930, Soka-gakkai came to prominence in the later 20th century, eventually developing a membership of over 6 million. In 1964 it established the Komeito (Clean Government Party), which by the 1980s was Japan's third-largest political party. It also conducts educational and cultural activities.

Sokoto, City (pop., 2006: local government area, 428,760), northwestern Nigeria. It lies along the Sokoto River on a traditional caravan route that leads north across the Sahara. It was the capital of the Fulani empire. Modern Sokoto is a major trade centre for agriculture and leather crafts. A pilgrimage centre, it is the site of mosques, a sultan's palace, and Usman dan Fodio's tomb and other holy shrines. Usman dan Fodio University was founded in 1975.

Sol, In Roman religion, the name of two distinct sun gods at Rome. The original Sol, or Sol Indiges, had an annual sacrifice and shrines on the Quirinal and in the Circus Maximus. After the importation of various Syrian sun cults, Elagabalus built a temple to Sol Invictus on the Palatine and attempted to make his worship the principal religion at Rome. Aurelian later reestablished the worship and erected a temple to Sol in the Campus Agrippae. The worship of Sol remained the chief imperial cult until the rise of Christianity.

solar cycle, Period in which several important kinds of solar activity repeat, discovered in 1843 by Samuel Heinrich Schwabe (1789–1875). Lasting about 22 years on average, it includes two 11-year cycles of sunspots, whose magnetic polarities alternate between the Sun's northern and southern hemispheres, and two peaks and two declines in the phenomena (e.g., solar prominences, auroras) that vary in the same period. Attempts have been made to connect the solar cycle to various other phenomena, including possible slight variations in the diameter of the Sun, sequences of annual growth rings in trees, and even the stock market's rise and fall.

solar energy, Radiation from the Sun that can produce heat, generate electricity, or cause chemical reactions. Solar collectors collect solar radiation and transfer it as heat to a carrier fluid. It can then be used for heating. Solar cells convert solar radiation directly into electricity by means of the photovoltaic effect. Solar energy is inexhaustible and nonpolluting, but converting solar radiation to electricity is not yet commercially competitive, because of the high cost of producing large-scale solar cell arrays and the inherent inefficiency in converting light to electricity.

solar flare, Sudden intense brightening of a small part of the Sun's surface, often near a sunspot group. Flares develop in a few minutes and may last several hours, releasing intense X-rays and streams of energetic particles. They appear to be connected with changes in the Sun's magnetic fields during the solar cycle. The ejected particles take a day or two to reach the vicinity of Earth, where they can disrupt radio communications and cause auroras, and may pose a radiation hazard to astronauts.

solar nebula, Gaseous cloud from which, in the nebular hypothesis of the origin of the solar system, the Sun and planets formed by condensation. In 1755 Immanuel Kant suggested that a nebula gradually pulled together by its own gravity developed into the Sun and planets. Pierre-Simon, marquis de Laplace, in 1796 proposed a similar model, in which a rotating and contracting cloud of gas—the young Sun—shed concentric rings of matter that condensed into the planets. But James Clerk Maxwell showed that, if all the matter in the known planets had once been distributed this way, shearing forces would have prevented such condensation. Another objection was that the Sun has less angular momentum than the theory seems to require. In the early 20th century most astronomers preferred the collision theory: that the planets formed as a result of a close approach to the Sun by another star. Eventually, however, stronger objections were mounted to the collision theory than to the nebular hypothesis, and a modified version of the latter—in which a rotating disk of matter gave rise to the planets through successively larger agglomerations, from dust grains through planetesimals and protoplanets—became the prevailing theory of the solar system's origin.

solar system, The Sun, its eight major planets, the dwarf planets and small bodies, and interplanetary dust and gas under the Sun's gravitational control. Another component of the solar system is the solar wind. The Sun contains more than 99% of the mass of the solar system; most of the rest is distributed among the planets, with Jupiter containing about 70%. According to the prevailing theory, the solar system originated from the solar nebula.

solar wind, Flux of particles, chiefly protons, electrons, and helium nuclei, accelerated by the hot solar corona's high temperatures to speeds high enough to allow them to escape the Sun. Solar flares increase its intensity. The solar wind deflects planets' magnetospheres and the ion tails of comets away from the Sun. The uninterrupted portion of the solar wind continues to travel to a distance of about 110–170 astronomical units, where it cools and eventually diffuses into interstellar space.

sole, Any of several flatfishes, especially about 100 species in the

*Dover sole (*Solea solea*)*
Jacques Six

family Soleidae. Those found from Europe to Australia and Japan are marine; some New World species live in freshwater. The eyes are on the right side of the head. The Dover sole (*Solea solea*), found from estuaries to offshore waters in the eastern Atlantic and Mediterranean, grows to 20 in. (50 cm) long. The hogchoker (*Trinectes maculatus*), seldom over 10 in. (25 cm) long, is found in shallow coastal waters from New England to Central America and far inland in habitats associated with large rivers.

solid, One of the three basic states of matter. A solid forms from either a liquid or a gas (the other two states of matter) because, as the energy of the atoms decreases, they coalesce in the relatively ordered, three-dimensional structure of a solid. All solids have the ability to support loads applied either perpendicular (normal) or parallel (shear) to a surface. Solids can be crystalline (as in metals), amorphous (as in glass), or quasicrystalline (as in certain metal alloys), depending on the degree of order in the arrangement of the atoms.

soliloquy, Dramatic monologue that gives the illusion of being a series of unspoken reflections. An accepted dramatic convention in the 16th–17th centuries, it was used artfully by William Shakespeare to reveal the minds of his characters. Pierre Corneille emphasized its lyricism, while Jean Racine favoured it for dramatic effect. Overused in English Restoration plays (1660–85), it fell into disfavour. Rejected by prose dramatists such as Henrik Ibsen, it was seldom used in late 19th-century naturalist drama. Many 20th-century dramatists also avoided the soliloquy as artificial, though Tennessee Williams and Arthur Miller, among others, adapted it by introducing narrators who alternately mused on the action and took part in it. It has been used by contemporary playwrights such as John Guare and Brian Friel, and the illusion that the characters are confiding in the audience has proved acceptable to a culture accustomed to the interview and the documentary film.

solmization, or SOLFEGGIO, System of designating musical notes by syllable names. It may have been invented by the 11th-century Italian monk Guido d'Arezzo when training his cathedral singers. The syllables—*ut, re, mi, fa, sol, la*—were derived from the first syllables of the lines of a hymn, each phrase of which began one note higher than the previous phrase. This six-note series, or hexachord, facilitated the sight-reading of music by allowing the singer always to associate a given musical interval with any two syllables. The syllables are still in use, though *ut* is usually replaced by the more singable *do*, and *ti* or *si* has been added for the seventh scale degree.

Solomon (fl. 10th century BC), Son and successor of David. Nearly all that is known about him comes from the Bible (1 Kings 1–11 and 2 Chronicles 1–9). Through the efforts of his mother, Bathsheba, and the prophet Nathan, Solomon was anointed king while David was still alive. On accession to the throne, he liquidated his opponents ruthlessly and installed friends in key posts. He established Israelite colonies outside his kingdom's borders, cooperating with such friendly rulers as the Queen of Sheba to increase commerce. Fortification of his far-flung empire necessitated a vast building program, the crowning achievement of which was the Temple of Jerusalem. He reorganized the nation into 12 tribes with 12 administrative districts. He is said to have had a harem of 700 wives and 300 concubines. After the ascension to the throne of his son Rehoboam, the northern tribes seceded and formed their own kingdom of Israel, bringing an end to Solomon's empire. His legendary wisdom is recorded in the Book of Proverbs, and he is traditionally named as the author of the biblical Song of Solomon. He was regarded as the greatest king of Israel.

Solomon Islands, Island country, southwestern Pacific Ocean. The country includes the islands of Guadalcanal, Malaita, San Cristobal, Choiseul, Santa Isabel, and Rennell; the Russell, Florida, Shortland, Santa Cruz, and New Georgia island groups; and small islands and reefs. The country comprises most of the Solomon Islands chain except for Buka and Bougainville, which are part of Papua New Guinea. Area: 10,954 sq mi (28,370 sq km). Population: (2011 est.) 535,000. Capital: Honiara. The population is largely Melanesian. Languages: English (official), Pijin (an English-based pidgin), and more than 60 indigenous Melanesian languages. Religions: Christianity (predominantly Protestant; also Roman Catholic); also traditional beliefs. Currency: Solomon Islands dollar. The Solomons group comprises numerous volcanic islands arranged in two parallel chains that converge in the southeast. They consist mostly of heavily wooded, mountainous terrain drained by short, swift-flowing rivers. The climate is tropical. The economy is based on agriculture, fishing, and lumbering. Tourism has been developed; cruise ships and visitors to World War II battlefields stop at the islands. The country is a constitutional monarchy with one legislative house; the head of state is the British monarch, represented by the governor-general, and the head of government is the prime minister. The Solomon Islands were probably settled by 2000 BCE by Austronesian people. Visited by the Spanish in 1568, they were subsequently explored and charted by the French and British. They came under British jurisdiction in the 1890s; the British Solomon Islands Protectorate was declared in 1893. The Japanese invasion of 1942 ignited some of the most bitter fighting in the Pacific during the war, particularly on Guadalcanal. The protectorate became self-governing in 1976, and full independence was achieved in 1978. In the late 20th and early 21st centuries, ethnic tensions led to political instability, including a coup in June 2000; a multinational force led by Australia helped restore order.

solstice, Either of the two moments in the year when the Sun's apparent path is farthest north or south from Earth's Equator; also, either of the two points along the ecliptic that the Sun passes through at these times. In the Northern Hemisphere the summer solstice occurs on June 21 or 22; the winter solstice on December 21 or 22. In the Southern Hemisphere the seasons are reversed.

solution, In chemistry, a homogeneous mixture of two or more substances in relative amounts that can vary continuously up to the limit of solubility (saturation), if any, of one in the other. Most solutions are liquids, but solutions also can be of gases or solids—for example, air (composed primarily of oxygen and nitrogen) or brass (composed chiefly of copper and zinc). In solutions that comprise a solid dissolved in a liquid, the liquid is the solvent, and the solid is the solute; if both components are liquids, the one present in a smaller amount is usually considered the solute. If the saturation point is passed, excess solute separates out. Substances with ionic bonds (e.g., salts) and many with covalent bonds (e.g., acids, bases, alcohols) undergo dissociation into ions on dissolving and are called electrolytes. Their solutions can conduct electricity and have other properties that differ from those of nonelectrolytes. Solutions are involved in most chemical reactions, refining and purification, industrial processing, and biological processes.

Solvay process, or AMMONIA-SODA PROCESS, Modern method of manufacturing sodium carbonate (soda ash), devised and commercialized in Belgium by Ernest Solvay (1838–1922). Common salt (sodium chloride) is treated with ammonia and then carbon dioxide, under carefully controlled conditions, to form sodium bicarbonate and ammonium chloride. When heated, the bicarbonate yields sodium carbonate, the desired product; the ammonium chloride is treated with lime to produce ammonia (for reuse) and calcium chloride. The process proved of great commercial value, since large quantities of soda ash are used in making glass, detergents, and cleansers.

Solzhenitsyn, Aleksandr (Isayevich) (b. Dec. 11, 1918, Kislovodsk, Russia—d. Aug. 3, 2008, Troitse-Lykovo, near Moscow), Russian novelist and historian. He fought in World War II but was arrested in 1945 for criticizing Joseph Stalin. He spent eight years in prisons and labour camps and three more in enforced exile. With *One Day in the Life of Ivan Denisovich* (1962), based on his labour-camp experiences, he emerged as an eloquent opponent of government repression. He was forced to publish later works abroad, including *The First Circle* (1968), *Cancer Ward* (1968), and *August 1914* (1971). In 1970 he was awarded the Nobel Prize for Literature. Publication of the first volume of *The Gulag Archipelago* (1973), one of the greatest works in Russian prose, resulted in his being charged with treason. Expelled from the Soviet Union in 1974, he moved to the U.S., at the time enjoying worldwide fame. In the late 1980s glasnost brought renewed access to his work in Russia but also a loss of interest in it and in the prophetic role he claimed for himself in Russian history. In 1994 Solzhenitsyn ended his exile and returned to Russia. From 1998 to 2003 he published installments of his autobiography, "The Little Grain Managed to Land Between Two Millstones," and in 2007 he was awarded Russia's prestigious State Prize.

soma, In ancient Indian religion, an unidentified plant, the juice of which was an offering of the Vedic sacrifices. Its stalks were pressed, and its juice, filtered through wool, was mixed with water and milk. After being offered as a libation to the gods, the remainder of the soma was consumed by the priests and the sacrificer. It was highly valued for its exhilarating, probably hallucinogenic, effect. The plant was believed to have been delivered to the earth from heaven by an eagle. The personified deity Soma was the master of plants, healer of disease, and bestower of riches.

Somali, Any member of a large group of people occupying all of Somalia and parts of Djibouti, Ethiopia, and Kenya. Their language is of the Cushitic branch of the Afroasiatic family. Numbering more than seven million, the Somalis are divided into northern, central, and southern groups. All have been Muslim since at least the 14th century. They are primarily nomadic herdsmen who, because of intense competition for scarce resources, have been extremely individualistic and frequently involved in blood feuds or wars with neighbouring clans or peoples. A second category of Somalis are the townspeople and agriculturalists of the urban centres, especially along the coast of the Horn of Africa, many of whom act as commercial middlemen between the Arab world and the nomads of the interior.

Somalia, Country, eastern Africa. Located in the Horn of Africa, it stretches from just south of the Equator to the Gulf of Aden. Area: 246,201 sq mi (637,657 sq km). Population (2009 est.): 9,133,000 (excluding an estimated 450,000 refugees in other countries). Capital: Mogadishu. Most of the people are nomadic or seminomadic Somali. Languages: Somali, Arabic (both official); also English, Italian. Religion: Islam (official; predominantly Sunni). Currency: Somali shilling. Much of Somalia is semidesert. The central and southern areas are flat, while the northern region rises to form rugged mountain ranges. Only a tiny proportion of its land is arable, though more than half is grazeable. Somalia has a developing mixed economy based largely on livestock and agriculture. It is one of the poorest countries in the world. It has a transitional regime with one legislative body; the head of state and government is the president, assisted by the prime minister. Muslim Arabs and Persians first established trading posts along the coasts in the 7th–10th centuries. By the 10th century Somali nomads occupied the area inland from the Gulf of Aden, and the south and west were inhabited by various groups of pastoral Oromo peoples. Intensive European exploration began after the British occupation of Aden in 1839, and in the late 19th century Britain and Italy set up protectorates in the region. During World War II the Italians invaded British Somaliland (1940); a year later British troops retook the area. Britain administered the region until 1950, when Italian Somaliland became a UN trust territory. In 1960 it was united with the former British Somaliland, and the two became the independent Republic of Somalia. Since then it has suffered political and civil strife, including military dictatorship, civil wars, drought, and famine. No effective central government has existed since the early 1990s. In 1991 a Republic of Somaliland was proclaimed by a breakaway group on territory corresponding to the former British Somaliland, and in 1998 the autonomous region of Puntland in the northeast was self-proclaimed; neither received international recognition, but both were more stable than the rest of Somalia. Several attempts have been made to end the conflict and create a new central government; Somalia's most recent transitional government was approved in 2004, but the country subsequently remained in turmoil. Incidents of piracy increased along the country's coast in the early 21st century and were the focus of international concern.

Somerset, Administrative (pop., 2001: 498,093), geographic, and historic county, southwestern England. Its county seat is Taunton. The remains of prehistoric villages have been found in the region. The Romans mined lead and built villas there; from the 7th century AD, Somerset formed the westernmost part of the kingdom of Wessex. A large part of western Somerset is made up of Exmoor National Park, and long stretches of coastline are protected. It is mainly an agricultural county and is known for its cider. Tourism draws visitors to its Bristol Channel resorts and historic mansions.

Somme River, River, northern France. It rises near St.-Quentin and flows westward 152 mi (245 km) to the English Channel. Canals on its upper valley connect it with navigable waterways that link Paris and Flanders. Its upper basin was the scene of heavy fighting in World War I, particularly that of the Battle of the Somme (1916).

sonar, Technique for detecting and determining the distance and direction of underwater objects by tracking acoustic echoes. The name derives from *so*und *na*vigation *r*anging. Sound waves emitted by or reflected from an object are detected by sonar apparatus and analyzed for information. In active sonar a sound wave is generated that spreads outward and is reflected back by a target object. Passive systems consist simply of receiving sensors that pick up the noise produced by the target (such as a submarine or torpedo). A third kind of sonar, used in communication systems, requires a projector and receiver at both ends. Sonar was first used to detect submarines in 1916. Modern nonmilitary uses include fish finding, depth sounding, mapping of the ocean floor, Doppler navigation, and searching for wrecks or other objects in the oceans.

sonata, Musical form for one or more instruments, usually consisting of three or four movements. The name, Italian for "sounded (on an instrument)," originally simply indicated nonvocal music and was used for a confusing variety of genres into the late 17th century. In the 1650s two types of ensemble sonatas began to be codified, the *sonata da chiesa* (church sonata) and *sonata da camera* (chamber sonata). The former, intended for church performance, was generally in four movements, two of them slow; the latter was usually a suite of dances. The so-called solo sonata (for soloist—usually violin—and continuo) and the trio sonata (for two soloists and continuo) became standard. In the 1740s solo keyboard sonatas began to be written. C.P.E. Bach established the three-movement keyboard sonata as the norm, a status it would retain through the classical era. Duo sonatas in the same form, usually for violin and keyboard, simultaneously became highly popular. Keyboard and duo sonatas have remained the standard types

to the present day. From Bach's time onward, the first movement was generally in allegro tempo and in sonata form. The second movement was usually slow. The last movement was generally a minuet, rondo, or theme and variations. In a four-movement sonata, the third was usually a minuet or scherzo. In these respects the sonata paralleled genres such as the symphony and the string quartet.

sonata form, or SONATA-ALLEGRO FORM, Form of most first movements and often other movements in musical genres such as the symphony, concerto, string quartet, and sonata. The three parts of sonata form evolved from the binary, or two-part, form prominent in the music of the 17th and early 18th centuries. In sonata form the first part, or exposition, presents the basic thematic material of the movement, which is often divided into two thematic groups, the second being in the dominant key or—if the movement is in a minor key—in the relative major key. The second section, or development, generally treats the earlier themes freely, often moving to various different keys. It leads to the final section, or recapitulation, when the tonic key returns and all the thematic material is repeated in the tonic. Sonata form was the most common form for instrumental works in Western art music from *c.* 1760 to the early 20th century.

song, Short and usually simple piece of music for voice, with or without instrumental accompaniment. Folk songs—traditional songs without a known composer transmitted orally rather than in written form—have existed for millennia but have left few traces in ancient sources. Virtually all known preliterate societies have a repertory of songs. Folk songs often accompany religious ceremonies, dancing, labour, or courting; they may tell stories or express emotions; the music follows obvious conventions and is often repetitive. Songs written by a particular composer or poet generally are more sophisticated and are not attached to activities. In the West the continuous tradition of secular art songs began with the troubadours, trouvères, and minnesingers of the 12th–13th centuries. Polyphonic songs, originating in the motet, began to appear in the 13th century. Composers of the 14th century produced a great body of polyphonic songs in the formes fixes. Later the Italian madrigal became the most distinguished genre. Notated accompaniments to solo songs appeared in the 16th century. The Romantic movement made the 19th century a golden age for the art song, notably the German lied. In the 20th century the popular song displaced the more cultivated art song, and popular music is today synonymous with popular song.

Songhai empire, or SONGHAY EMPIRE, Ancient Muslim state, West Africa. Centred on the middle Niger River in what is now central Mali, it eventually extended to the Atlantic coast and into Niger and Nigeria. Established by the Songhai people *c.* AD 800, it reached its greatest extent in the 16th century before falling to Moroccan forces in 1591. Its important cities were Gao and Timbuktu.

sonnet, Fixed verse form having 14 lines that are typically five-foot iambics rhyming according to a prescribed scheme. The sonnet is unique among poetic forms in Western literature in that it has retained its appeal for major poets for five centuries. It seems to have originated in the 13th century among the Sicilian school of court poets. In the 14th century Petrarch established the most widely used sonnet form. The Petrarchan (or Italian) sonnet characteristically consists of an eight-line octave, rhyming *abbaabba*, that states a problem, asks a question, or expresses an emotional tension, followed by a six-line sestet, of varying rhyme schemes, that resolves the problem, answers the question, or resolves the tension. In adapting the Italian form, Elizabethan poets gradually developed the other major sonnet form, the Shakespearean (or English) sonnet. It consists of three quatrains, each with an independent rhyme scheme, and ends with a rhymed couplet.

Soong family, Influential 20th-century Chinese family. Charlie Soong (1866–1918) trained in the U.S. to become a missionary. In China he made his fortune as a publisher, initially of Bibles, and became a supporter of Sun Yat-sen, whose Nationalist Party he helped finance. His first daughter married a businessman who also provided financial support to the Nationalists; his second daughter, Soong Ch'ing-ling (Song Qingling; 1893–1981), married Sun Yat-sen; and his third daughter, Soong Mei-ling (1897–2003), became Chiang Kai-shek's second wife. A son, T.V. Soong (1894–1971), established the Central Bank of China and acted as finance minister for the Nationalist government in the 1920s and foreign minister in the 1930s. The 1949 communist takeover divided the family: Ch'ing-ling, who had earlier denounced the Nationalists for betraying Sun Yat-sen's ideals, remained on the mainland and was named honorary chairman of the People's Republic shortly before her death. Mei-ling accompanied Chiang Kai-shek to Taiwan and publicized his cause in the West; as Madam Chiang, she became extremely popular in the U.S. T.V. Soong, once reputed to be the wealthiest man in the world, moved to the U.S.

sophists, Group of itinerant professional teachers, lecturers, and writers prominent in Greece in the later 5th century BC. The sophistic movement arose at a time when there was much questioning of the absolute nature of familiar values and ways of life. An antithesis arose between nature and custom, tradition, or law, in which custom could be regarded either as artificial trammels on the freedom of the natural state or as beneficial and civilizing restraints on natural anarchy. Both views were represented among the sophists, though the former was the more common. Their first and most eminent representative was Protagoras; other notable sophists include Gorgias of Leontini, Prodicus, Hippias, Antiphon, Thrasymachus, and Critias. A later "second sophistic school" existed in the 2nd century AD.

Sophocles (b. *c.* 496, Colonus, near Athens—d. 406 BC, Athens), Greek playwright. With Aeschylus and Euripides, he was one of the three great tragic playwrights of Classical Athens. A distinguished public figure in Athens, he served successively in important posts as a treasurer, commander, and adviser. He competed in dramatic festivals, where he defeated Aeschylus to win his first victory in 468 BC. He went on to achieve unparalleled success, writing 123 dramas for dramatic competitions and achieving more than 20 victories. Only seven tragedies survive in their entirety: *Antigone, Ajax, Electra, The Trachinian Women, Philoctetes, Oedipus at Colonus,* and *Oedipus the King,* his best-known work. He increased the size of the chorus and was the first to introduce a third actor onstage. For their supple language, vivid characterization, and formal perfection, his works are regarded as the epitome of Greek drama.

soprano, Highest vocal register, ranging from about middle C to the second A above it. Sopranos are normally female but may also include boy sopranos and (previously) castrati. Soprano voices are traditionally classified as dramatic (rich and powerful), lyric (lighter), and coloratura (high and very agile). The mezzo-soprano range is about a third lower.

Soto, Hernando de (b. *c.* 1496/97, Jerez de los Caballeros, Badajoz, Spain—d. May 21, 1542, along the Mississippi River), Spanish explorer and conquistador. He joined the 1514 expedition of Pedro Arias Dávila (1440–1531) to the West Indies, and in Panama he quickly made his mark as a trader and explorer. By 1520 he had accumulated a small fortune through his slave trading in Nicaragua and on the Isthmus of Panama. He joined Francisco Pizarro on an expedition to conquer Peru in 1532, returning to Spain in 1536 with great wealth. Commissioned by the Spanish crown to conquer what is now Florida, he departed in 1538 in command of 10 ships and 700 men. On that expedition he explored the extensive region that was to become the southeastern U.S. and discovered the Mississippi River for Europeans. Overcome by fever, he died in Louisiana and was buried in the Mississippi River.

soul, Immaterial aspect or essence of a person, conjoined with the body during life and separable at death. The concept of a soul is found in nearly all cultures and religions, though the interpretations of its nature vary considerably. The ancient Egyptians conceived of a dual soul, one surviving death but remaining near the body, while the other proceeded to the realm of the dead. The early Hebrews did not consider the soul as distinct from the body, but later Jewish writers perceived the two as separate. Christian theology adopted the Greek concept of an immortal soul, adding the notion that God created the soul and infused it into the body at conception. In Islam the soul is believed to come into existence at the same time as the body but is everlasting and subject to eternal bliss or torment after the death of the body. In Hinduism each soul, or *atman,* was created at the beginning of time and imprisoned in an earthly body; at death the soul is said to pass to a new body according to the laws of karma. Buddhism negates the idea of a soul, asserting that any sense of an individual self is illusory.

soul music, Style of U.S. popular music sung and performed primarily by African American musicians, having its roots in gospel music and rhythm and blues. The term was first used in the 1960s to describe music that combined rhythm and blues, gospel, jazz, and rock music and that was characterized by intensity of feeling and earthiness. In its earliest stages, soul music was found most commonly in the South, but many of the young singers who were to popularize it migrated to cities in the North. The founding of Motown in Detroit, Mich., and Stax-Volt in Memphis, Tenn., did much to encourage the style. Its most popular performers include James Brown, Ray Charles, Sam Cooke, and Aretha Franklin.

sound, Mechanical disturbance that propagates as a longitudinal wave through a solid, liquid, or gas. A sound wave is generated by a vibrating object. The vibrations cause alternating compressions (regions of crowding) and rarefactions (regions of scarcity) in the particles of the medium. The particles move back and forth in the direction of propagation of the wave. The speed of sound through a medium depends on the medium's elasticity, density, and temperature. In dry air at 32 °F (0 °C), the speed of sound is 1,086 feet (331 metres) per second. The frequency of a sound wave, perceived as pitch, is the number of compressions (or rarefactions) that pass a fixed point per unit time. The frequencies audible to the human ear range from approximately 20 hertz to 20 kilohertz. Intensity is the average flow of energy per unit time through a given area of the medium and is related to loudness.

sound barrier, Sharp rise in aerodynamic drag that occurs as an aircraft approaches the speed of sound. At sea level the speed of sound is about 750 miles (1,200 km) per hour, and at 36,000 feet (11,000 metres) it is about 650 miles (1,050 km) per hour. The sound barrier was formerly an obstacle to supersonic flight. If an aircraft flies at somewhat less than sonic speed, the pressure waves (sound waves) it creates outspeed their sources and spread out ahead of it. Once the aircraft reaches sonic speed the waves are unable to get out of its way. Strong local shock waves form on the wings and body; airflow around the craft becomes unsteady, and severe buffeting may result, with serious stability difficulties and loss of control over flight characteristics. Generally, aircraft properly designed for supersonic flight have little difficulty in passing through the sound barrier, but the effect on those designed for efficient operation at subsonic speeds may become extremely dangerous. The first pilot to break the sound barrier was Chuck Yeager (1947), in the experimental X-1 aircraft.

South Africa, officially REPUBLIC OF SOUTH AFRICA, formerly UNION OF SOUTH AFRICA, Southernmost country on the African continent. The Kingdom of Lesotho lies within its boundaries. Area: 471,359 sq mi (1,220,813 sq km). Population: (2011 est.) 50,587,000. Capitals: Pretoria/Tshwane (executive), Cape Town (legislative), Bloemfontein/Mangaung (judicial). Three-fourths of the population are black Africans, including the Zulu, Xhosa, Sotho, and Tswana; nearly all of the remainder are of European or mixed or South Asian descent. Languages: Afrikaans, English, Ndebele, Pedi (North Sotho), Sotho (South Sotho), Swati (Swazi), Tsonga, Tswana, Venda, Xhosa, Zulu (all official). Religions: Christianity (other [mostly independent] Christians, Protestant, Roman Catholic); also traditional beliefs, Hinduism, Islam. Currency: rand. South Africa has three major zones: the broad interior plateau, the surrounding mountainous Great Escarpment, and a narrow belt of coastal plain. It has a temperate subtropical climate. It is one of the world's major producers and exporters of gold, coal, diamonds, platinum, and vanadium. It is a multiparty republic with two legislative houses; its head of state and government is the president. San and Khoekhoe (Khoisan speakers) roamed the area as hunters and gatherers in the Stone Age, and the latter had developed a pastoralist culture by the time of European contact. By the 14th century, peoples speaking Bantu languages had settled in the area and developed gold and copper mining and an active East African trade. In 1652 the Dutch established a colony at the Cape of Good Hope; the Dutch settlers became known as Boers (Dutch: "Farmers") and later as Afrikaners (for their Afrikaans language). In 1795 British forces captured the cape. In 1836 Dutch settlers seeking new land made the Great Trek northward and established (1838) the independent Boer republics of Orange Free State and the South African Republic (later the Transvaal region), which the British annexed as colonies by 1902 following the South African War. In 1910 the British colonies of Cape Colony, Transvaal, Natal, and Orange River were unified into the new Union of South Africa, which became independent and withdrew from the Commonwealth in 1961. Throughout the 20th century, South African politics were dominated by the question of maintaining white European supremacy over the country's black majority, and in 1948 South Africa formally instituted apartheid. Faced by increasing worldwide condemnation, it began dismantling the apartheid laws in 1990. In free elections in 1994, Nelson Mandela became the country's first black president. A permanent nonracial constitution was promulgated in 1997.

South America, Continent, Western Hemisphere. The world's fourth largest continent, it is bounded by the Caribbean Sea to the northwest, the Atlantic Ocean to the northeast, east, and southeast, and the Pacific Ocean to the west. It is separated from Antarctica by the Drake Passage and is joined to North America by the Isthmus of Panama. Area: 6,882,027 sq mi (17,824,370 sq km). Pop., 2008 est.: 378,448,500. Four main ethnic groups have populated South America: Indians, who were the continent's pre-Columbian inhabitants; Spanish and Portuguese who dominated the continent from the 16th to the early 19th century; Africans imported as slaves; and the postindependence immigrants from overseas, mostly Germans and southern Europeans but also Lebanese, South Asians, and Japanese. Nine-tenths of the people are Christian, the vast majority of whom are Roman Catholic. Spanish is the official language everywhere except in Brazil (Portuguese), French Guiana (French), Guyana (English), and Suriname (Dutch); some Indian languages are spoken. South America has three major geographic regions. In the west, the Andes Mountains, which are prone to seismic activity, extend the length of the continent; Mount Aconcagua, at 22,831 ft (6,959 m), is the highest peak in the Western Hemisphere. Highlands lie in the north and east, bordered by lowland sedimentary basins that include the Amazon River, the world's largest drainage basin, and the Pampas of eastern Argentina, whose fertile soils constitute one of South America's most productive agricultural areas. Other important drainage systems include those of the Orinoco and São Francisco rivers and the Paraná–Paraguay–Río de la Plata system. Four-fifths of South America lies within the tropics, but it also has temperate, arid, and cold climatic regions. Less than one-tenth of its land is arable, producing mainly corn (maize), wheat, and rice, and about one-fourth is under permanent pasture. About half is covered by forest, mainly the enormous but steadily diminishing rainforest of the Amazon basin. Almost one-fourth of all the world's known animal species live in the continent's rainforests, plateaus,

rivers, and swamps. South America has one-eighth of the world's total deposits of iron and one-fourth of its copper reserves. Exploitation of these and numerous other mineral resources are important to the economies of many regions. Commercial crops include bananas, citrus fruits, sugar, and coffee; fishing is important along the Pacific coast. Trade in illegal narcotics (mostly for export) is a major source of revenue in some countries. Most countries have free-market or mixed (state and private enterprise) economies. Income tends to be unevenly distributed between large numbers of poor people and a small number of wealthy families, with the middle classes, though growing, still a minority in most countries. Asiatic hunters and gatherers are thought to have been the first settlers, probably arriving less than 12,000 years ago. The growth of agriculture from c. 2500 BCE (it had begun some 6,000 years earlier) initiated a period of rapid cultural evolution whose greatest development occurred in the central Andes region and culminated with the Inca empire. European exploration began when Christopher Columbus landed in 1498; thereafter Spanish and Portuguese adventurers opened it for plunder and, later, settlement. According to terms of the Treaty of Tordesillas, Portugal received the eastern part of the continent, while Spain received the rest. The Indian peoples were decimated by this contact, and most of those who survived were reduced to a form of serfdom. The continent was free of European rule by the early 1800s except for the Guianas. Most of the countries adopted a republican form of government; however, social and economic inequalities or border disputes led to periodic revolutions in many of them, and by the early 20th century most had fallen under some form of autocratic rule. All joined the United Nations after World War II (1938–45), and all joined the Organization of American States in 1948. By the second half of the 20th century most countries had begun to integrate their economies into world markets, and by the 1990s most had embraced democratic rule.

South Asian arts, Literary, performing, and visual arts of India, Pakistan, Bangladesh, and Sri Lanka. Myths of the popular gods, Vishnu and Shiva, in the Puranas (ancient tales) and the *Mahabharata* and *Ramayana* epics, supply material for representational and dramatic arts. The *Ramayana* is often considered the first work in the *kavya* poetic style; *kavya* compositions must convey different *rasa* (sentiments) and also induce the appropriate *rasa* in the audience. The Dravidian languages of the south, including Tamil and Telegu, provided some enduring works, particularly the devotional poems of the Tamil Alvars and Nayannars from the 7th through the 9th century. The introduction of Persian by Muslim conquerors led to the development of Urdu. Following in the Persian tradition, Urdu poets particularly favoured the *ghazal*, a love poem of great metric and rhythmic subtlety. The *Natya-shastra* established the rules for classical dance and drama, the most popular form of which was the heroic tale. From the 14th century onward the heroic tale lost ground to popular folk theatre, but elements of classical drama persist. Dance traditionally requires musical accompaniment, though players and vocalists take their lead from the rhythm of the dancers' feet and not vice versa. Central to South Asian music is the concept of modes known as raga. Rhythm in South Asian music, like the construction of scales, is additive. The music is basically monodic, consisting essentially of a single melody against a drone, though the drum part may virtually constitute another voice. Music is generally for entertainment, but it is nevertheless closely linked to Hinduism. Northern India's most characteristic structure, a temple with a heavily decorated tower, reached its stylistic height in the 7th–11th centuries. The extension of Islam into India in the 11th and 12th centuries introduced typical Islamic architectural forms (e.g., the dome and pointed arch) and decoration. Such masterworks as the Taj Mahal resulted from the rule of the Muslim Mughal dynasty in the 16th–18th centuries. Traditionally, visual artists produced works for patrons, and sacred written canons guided their works' proportions, iconography, and other artistic considerations. Since early in the region's history, wall paintings and miniatures painted on palm leaves or paper were prominent, but sculpture was the favoured medium. Sculptures were largely religious and essentially symbolic and abstract. Works displaying Hindu and Buddhist imagery flourished in the Golden Age of India in the 4th–5th centuries. Islamic influences were incorporated into traditional styles after the Muslim invasions of the 12th century. At the end of the 19th century, rising Indian nationalism led to a conscious revival of native arts traditions, though more recently artists assimilated elements of European art styles.

South Australia, State, south-central Australia. Area: 379,725 sq mi (983,482 sq km). Population: (2006) 1,514,337; (2010 est.) 1,644,582. Capital: Adelaide. The Dutch visited the coast in 1627. British explorers arrived in the early 1800s, and it was colonized as a British province in 1836. Its vast interior, a large part of which is barren, includes Lake Eyre and the Flinders Ranges. It is a major world source of opals and also produces most of the wine and brandy consumed in Australia. It has the country's largest shipyards. It became a state of the Commonwealth of Australia in 1901. Its southeastern part has become industrialized since World War II.

South Indian bronze, Any of the cult images that rank among the finest achievements of Indian visual art. Most of the figures represent Hindu divinities, especially various iconographic forms of the god Shiva and Lord Vishnu, with their consorts and attendants. The images were produced in large numbers from the 8th to the 16th century, principally in the Thanjavur and Tiruchchirappalli districts of modern Tamil Nadu, and maintained a high standard of excellence for almost 1,000 years. The icons range from small household images to almost life-size sculptures intended to be carried in temple processions.

The god Shiva in the garb of a mendicant, South Indian bronze from Tiruvengadu, Tamil Nadu, early 11th century; in the Thanjavur Museum and Art Gallery, Tamil Nadu
P. Chandra

South Island, Island (pop., 2006: 1,022,316), larger and southernmost of the two principal islands of New Zealand. Separated from the North Island by Cook Strait, it has an area of 58,384 sq mi (151,215 sq km). Mountains, including the Southern Alps, occupy almost three-quarters of the island. Its main cities are Christchurch and Dunedin. Fiordland National Park in the southwest contains numerous coastal fjords and high lakes.

South Pole, Southern extremity of the Earth's axis, located at latitude 90° S. It is the southern point from which all meridians of longitude start. The area around it is a lofty plateau in west-central Antarctica, with ice as much as 8,850 ft (2,700 m) thick. It has six months of complete daylight and six months of total darkness each year. It was first reached by the Norwegian explorer Roald Amundsen in 1911, one month before the expedition led by British explorer Robert Falcon Scott; U.S. explorer Richard E. Byrd flew to the pole in 1929. The geographic pole does not coincide with the magnetic South Pole, which in the early 21st century was located on the Adélie Coast about 64°30′ S, 137°50′ E; it moves about 8 mi (13 km) to the northwest each year. The geomagnetic South Pole also moves; during the early 1990s it was located about 79°13′ S, 108°44′ E, in 2000 it was 65°39′ S, 140° 01′ E, and by 2005 it was back to about 79°45′ S, 108°13′ E.

South Sudan, officially REPUBLIC OF SOUTH SUDAN, Country, northeastern Africa. Area: 248,777 sq mi (644,330 sq km). Population: (2011 est.) 9,150,000. Capital: Juba. Languages: English (official working language), indigenous languages, Arabic. Religions: Christianity, traditional beliefs, Islam. Currency: South Sudan pound. It has rainforests and savannas but is dominated by the vast Al-Sudd swamp, located in its centre. A rich variety of wildlife includes lions, elephants, and gazelles. The Nile River flows through the entire length of the country. South Sudan's economy is primarily dependent on oil and agriculture. The chief crops are sorghum and peanuts, and petroleum is the main export. South Sudan is a republic with two legislative bodies; its head of state and government is the president. Settled by many of its current ethnic groups during the 15th–19th centuries, it has long been associated with Sudan, its neighbour to the north, despite the fact that Islam and the Arabic language tended to dominate in the north while older African languages and cultures were predominant in the south. By the end of the 19th century, both the north and the south—collectively considered the Sudan—were under British-Egyptian colonial rule. The existing differences between the two regions, exacerbated by the disparate level of development that occurred under colonial administration, made it difficult for Sudan to be effectively ruled as one country upon achieving independence in 1956. Fears of marginalization of the south by the north led to a civil war that began in 1955, months prior to actual independence. The initial conflict and the fears that fueled it were inflamed by northern leaders who hoped to impose unity upon the nascent country by imposing Islamic law and culture throughout north and south. Fighting subsided with the 1972 Addis Ababa Agreement but resumed in 1983 and continued until 2005, when the Comprehensive Peace Agreement was signed. The agreement fostered a tenuous peace between the north and the south and granted southern Sudan semiautonomous status and the promise of a referendum on independence to be held in six years. The vote took place in January 2011 and was almost unanimous in supporting independence; the country of South Sudan was declared on July 9, 2011.

Southeast Asia, Vast region of Asia lying east of the Indian subcontinent and south of China. It includes a mainland area (also called Indochina) and a string of archipelagoes to the south and east and is generally taken to include Myanmar (Burma), Thailand, Cambodia, Laos, Vietnam, Malaysia, Singapore, Indonesia, Brunei, and the Philippines. For centuries the mainland portion was the site of numerous indigenous dynasties, but in the 19th century all but Thailand (Siam) came under the control of European powers, notably France. All areas became independent after 1945.

Southeast Asia Treaty Organization (SEATO), Regional defense organization (1955–77) comprising Australia, France, New Zealand, Pakistan, the Philippines, Thailand, Britain, and the U.S. It was founded as part of the Southeast Asia Collective Defense Treaty in order to protect the region from communism. Vietnam, Cambodia, and Laos were not considered for membership, and other countries in the region preferred membership in the nonaligned movement. SEATO had no standing forces, but its members engaged in combined military exercises. Pakistan withdrew in 1968, and France suspended financial support in 1975. The organization was disbanded officially in 1977.

Southeast Asian arts, Literary, performing, and visual arts of Myanmar (Burma), Thailand, Laos, Cambodia, Vietnam, Malaysia, Singapore, and the Philippines. The "classical" literatures of Southeast Asia can be divided according to three major regions: the Sanskrit region of Cambodia and Indonesia; the region of Myanmar where Pali was used as a literary and religious language; and the Chinese region of Vietnam. The *Mahabharata, Ramayana, Jataka*s, and local legendary tales are expounded in the performing arts of the region. Dance techniques of the region minimize the mudras (gestures) of Indian classicism to emphasize grace of movement over theme. Regional variations of temple and court dance vie with local developments. Numerous theatrical forms are vehicles for social criticism; most remarkable is *wayang*, or shadow play, in which puppetry has been fused with dance and drama in a unique form of entertainment. Music is generally coordinated with the dramatic arts, resulting in great rhythmic but slight melodic content. The earliest visual arts of the region were wood carvings featuring supernatural and animal imagery developed and shared by the various tribal peoples. A second tradition emerged after Indian artists and artisans followed traders to Southeast Asia in the first centuries CE. Within a short time Southeast Asians were producing their own distinctive local versions of Indian styles, sometimes rivaling Indian artists with their skill, finesse, and invention on a colossal scale. With the introduction of Hinduism and Buddhism, temple building, sculpture, and painting flourished from the 1st through the 13th century. The Indian royal temple, which dominated Southeast Asian culture, typically stood on a terraced plinth, upon which towered shrines could multiply. About 800 CE the Cambodian king Jayavarman II built a brick mountain for a temple group. This plan was furthered when foundations were laid for Angkor, a scheme based on a grid of reservoirs and canals. Successive kings built more temple mountains there, culminating in Angkor Wat. Among Southeast Asia's most impressive sites is the city of Pagan in Myanmar, with many brick and stucco Buddhist temples and stupas built 1056–1287.

Southern Alps, Mountain range, South Island, New Zealand. It extends almost the entire length of the island, and it is the highest range in Australasia. It has elevations from 3,000 ft (900 m) to over 10,000 ft (3,050 m), culminating in Mount Cook at 12,316 ft (3,754 m) high. Glaciers descend from the permanently snow-clad top of the range. The range divides the island climatically: the forested western slopes and narrow coastal plain are much wetter than the eastern slopes and wide Canterbury Plains. Much of the southwest area was designated a UNESCO World Heritage site in 1990.

sovereignty, In political theory, the ultimate authority in the decision-making process of the state and in the maintenance of order. In 16th-century France Jean Bodin used the concept of sovereignty to bolster the power of the king over his feudal lords, heralding the transition from feudalism to nationalism. By the end of the 18th century, the concept of the social contract led to the idea of popular sovereignty, or sovereignty of the people, through an organized government. The Hague Conventions, the Geneva Conventions, and the United Nations all have restricted the actions of sovereign countries in the international arena, as has international law.

soybean, Annual legume (*Glycine max*, or *G. soja*) of the pea

Soybeans (Glycine max)
J.C. Allen and Son

family and its edible seed. The soybean plant has an erect, branching stem, white to purple flowers, and one to four seeds per pod. It was probably derived from a wild plant of East Asia, where it has been cultivated for some 5,000 years. Introduced into the U.S. in 1804, it began to be farmed widely as a livestock feed in the 1930s, and the U.S. is now the world's foremost soybean producer. Economically the world's most important bean, the soybean provides vegetable protein for millions of people and ingredients for hundreds of chemical products, including paints, adhesives, fertilizers, insect sprays, and fire-extinguisher fluids. Because soybeans contain no starch, they are a good source of protein for diabetics. Processed for food, soybean oil is made into margarine, shortening, and vegetarian cheeses and meats. Soybean meal serves as a high-protein meat substitute in many food products, including baby foods. Other food products include soybean milk, tofu, salad sprouts, and soy sauce.

Soyinka, Wole, in full AKINWANDE OLUWOLE SOYINKA (b. July

Wole Soyinka.
Vernon L. Smith

13, 1934, Abeokuta, Nigeria), Nigerian playwright. After studying in Leeds, Eng., he returned to Nigeria to edit literary journals, teach drama and literature at the university level, and found two theatre companies. His plays, written in English and drawing on West African folk traditions, often focus on the tensions between tradition and progress. Symbolism, flashback, and ingenious plotting contribute to a rich dramatic structure. His serious plays reveal his disillusionment with African authoritarian leadership and with Nigerian society as a whole. His works include *A Dance of the Forests* (1960), *The Lion and the Jewel* (1963), *Death and the King's Horseman* (1975), and *From Zia, with Love* (1992). He has written several volumes of poetry; his best-known novel is *The Interpreters* (1965). A champion of Nigerian democracy, he was repeatedly jailed and exiled. In 1986 he became the first black African to be awarded the Nobel Prize for Literature.

Soyuz, Any of several versions of Soviet/Russian manned spacecraft launched since 1967. Originally conceived for the U.S.S.R.'s Moon-landing program, which was canceled in 1974, the modular craft has served mainly as a crew ferry to and from Earth-orbiting space stations, specifically the Salyut stations, Mir, and the International Space Station (ISS). The first version accommodated three persons but was later modified for a crew of two to make room for additional life-support equipment. Soyuz T, introduced in 1979, restored the third crew seat. Soyuz TM, an upgrade featuring a variety of new systems, made its first manned flight in 1987 when it carried Mir's second crew to the then-embryonic station. The Soyuz TMA debuted in 2002 with a manned flight to the ISS; its design incorporated changes to meet certain NASA requirements as an ISS "lifeboat," including eased height and weight restrictions for crew members.

space exploration, Investigation of the universe beyond Earth's atmosphere by means of manned and unmanned spacecraft. Study of the use of rockets for spaceflight began early in the 20th century. Germany's research on rocket propulsion in the 1930s led to development of the V-2 missile. After World War II, the U.S. and the Soviet Union, with the aid of relocated German scientists, competed in the "space race," making substantial progress in high-altitude rocket technology. Both launched their first satellites in the late 1950s (followed by other satellites and unmanned lunar probes) and their first manned space vehicles in 1961. A succession of longer and more complex manned space missions followed, most notably the U.S. Apollo program, including the first manned lunar landing in 1969, and the Soviet Soyuz and Salyut missions. Beginning in the 1960s, U.S. and Soviet scientists also launched unmanned deep-space probes for studies of the planets and other solar system objects, and Earth-orbiting astronomical observatories, which permitted observation of cosmic objects from above the filtering and distorting effects of Earth's atmosphere. In the 1970s and '80s the Soviet Union concentrated on the development of space stations for scientific research and military reconnaissance. After the dissolution of the Soviet Union in 1991, Russia continued its space program, but on a reduced basis owing to economic constraints. In 1973 the U.S. launched its own space station, and since the mid 1970s it devoted much of its manned space efforts to the space shuttle program and, more recently, to developing the International Space Station in collaboration with Russia and other countries.

space shuttle, formally SPACE TRANSPORTATION SYSTEM (STS), Partially reusable rocket-launched vehicle developed by NASA to go into Earth orbit, transport people and cargo between Earth and orbiting spacecraft, and glide to a runway landing on Earth. The first flight of a space shuttle into orbit took place in 1981. The shuttle consisted of: a winged orbiter that carried the crew and cargo; an expendable external tank of liquid fuel and oxidizer for the orbiter's three main rocket engines; and two large, reusable, solid-propellant booster rockets. The orbiter lifted off vertically like an expendable launch vehicle but made an unpowered descent similar to a glider. Each orbiter was designed to be reused up to 100 times. For manipulating cargo and other materials outside the orbiter, astronauts used a remotely controlled robot arm or exited the orbiter wearing space suits. On some missions, the shuttle carried a European-built pressurized research facility called Spacelab in its cargo bay. Between 1981 and 1985 four shuttle orbiters were put into service: *Columbia* (the first in orbit), *Challenger*, *Discovery*, and *Atlantis*. *Challenger* exploded in 1986 during launch, killing all seven astronauts aboard, and was replaced in 1992 by *Endeavour*. From 1995 to 1998 NASA conducted shuttle missions to the Russian space station Mir to prepare for the construction of the International Space Station (ISS). Beginning in 1998, the shuttle was used extensively to ferry components, supplies, and crews to the ISS. In 2003 *Columbia* disintegrated while returning from a space mission, claiming the lives of its seven-person crew. The last space shuttle flight was in 2011.

space station, Manned artificial structure designed to revolve in a fixed orbit as a long-term base for astronomical observations, study of Earth's resources and environment, military reconnaissance, and investigations of materials and biological systems in weightless conditions. As of 2001, nine space stations have been placed in a low Earth orbit and occupied for varying lengths of time. The Soviet Union orbited the world's first space station, Salyut 1, designed for scientific studies, in 1971. From 1974 to 1982 five more Salyut stations—two outfitted for military reconnaissance—were successfully placed in orbit and occupied. In 1986 the U.S.S.R. launched the core module of Mir, a scientific station that was expanded with five additional modules over the next decade. The U.S. orbited its first space station in 1973; called Skylab, it was equipped as a solar observatory and medical laboratory. In 1998 the U.S. and Russia began the in-orbit construction of the International Space Station (ISS), a complex of laboratory and habitat modules that would ultimately involve contributions from at least 16 countries. In 2000 the ISS received its first resident crew.

space-time, Single entity that relates space and time in a four-dimensional structure, postulated by Albert Einstein in his theories of relativity. In the Newtonian universe it was supposed that there was no connection between space and time. Space was thought to be a flat, three-dimensional arrangement of all possible point locations, which could be expressed by Cartesian coordinates; time was viewed as an independent one-dimensional concept. Einstein showed that a complete description of relative motion requires equations that include time as well as the three spatial dimensions. He also showed that space-time is curved, which allowed him to account for gravitation in his general theory of relativity.

spacecraft, Vehicle designed to operate, with or without a crew, in a controlled flight pattern above Earth's lower atmosphere. Since streamlining is not needed in the high vacuum of this environment, a spacecraft's shape is designed according to its mission. Most spacecraft are not self-propelled; they are accelerated to the necessary high velocity by staged rockets, which are jettisoned when their fuel is used up. A major exception, the space shuttle

orbiter, uses three onboard liquid-fuel main engines supplied by a disposable external tank and a pair of solid-fuel boosters to reach space. The spacecraft goes into an orbit around Earth or, if given enough velocity, it continues toward another destination in space. The craft may have its own small rocket engines for orienting and maneuvering. For internal power, Earth-orbiting spacecraft use solar cells and storage batteries, fuel cells, or a combination, whereas craft designed for deep-space missions usually carry thermoelectric generators heated by a radioactive element. The enormous complexity of design, particularly of manned spacecraft with their millions of components, requires a high degree of miniaturization and reliability.

Spain, officially KINGDOM OF SPAIN, Country, southwestern Europe. One of Europe's largest countries, it is located on the Iberian Peninsula and also includes the Balearic and Canary islands. Area: 195,364 sq mi (505,991 sq km). Population: (2011 est.) 47,215,000. Capital: Madrid. The population is a blend of diverse ethnic groups. The country is organized into autonomous communities; each has its own regional customs, and three of them—Catalonia, Galicia, and the Basque Country—have their own official language. There is a small population of Roma (Gypsies or Gitanos) as well. Languages: Castilian Spanish (official), Catalan, Galician, Basque. Religion: Christianity (predominantly Roman Catholic). Currency: euro. Spain's large central plateau is surrounded by the Ebro River valley, the mountainous Catalonia region, the Mediterranean coastal region of Valencia, the Guadalquivir River valley, and the mountainous region extending from the Pyrenees to the Atlantic coast. Spain has a developed market economy based on services, light and heavy industries, and agriculture. Mineral resources include iron ore, mercury, and coal. Agricultural products include grains and livestock. Spain is one of the world's major producers of wine and olive oil. Tourism is also a major industry, especially along the southern Costa del Sol. Spain is a constitutional monarchy with two legislative houses; the head of state is the king, and the head of government is the prime minister.

Remains of Stone Age populations dating back some 35,000 years have been found throughout Spain. Celtic peoples arrived in the 9th century BCE, followed by the Romans, who dominated Spain from *c.* 200 BCE until the Visigoth invasion in the early 5th century CE. In the early 8th century most of the peninsula fell to Muslims (Moors) from North Africa, and it remained under their control until it was gradually reconquered by the Christian kingdoms of Castile, Aragon, and Portugal. Spain was reunited in 1479 following the marriage of Ferdinand II (of Aragon) and Isabella I (of Castile). The last Muslim kingdom, Granada, was reconquered in 1492, and about this time Spain established a colonial empire in the Americas. In 1516 the throne passed to the Habsburgs, whose rule ended in 1700 when Philip V became the first Bourbon king of Spain. His ascendancy caused the War of the Spanish Succession, which resulted in the loss of numerous European possessions and sparked revolution within most of Spain's American colonies. Spain lost its remaining overseas possessions to the U.S. in the Spanish-American War (1898). Spain became a republic in 1931. The Spanish Civil War (1936–39) ended in victory for the Nationalists under Gen. Francisco Franco, who ruled as a dictator until his death in 1975. His successor as head of state, Juan Carlos I, restored the monarchy with his accession to the throne; a new constitution in 1978 established a constitutional monarchy. Spain joined NATO in 1982 and the European Community in 1986. The 1992 quincentennial of Christopher Columbus's first voyage from Spain to the Americas was marked by a fair in Sevilla and the staging of the Olympic Games in Barcelona. In the late 20th century and into the 21st, some Basque separatists continued to resort to violence as they pressed for independence, but it was Islamist militants who were responsible for the March 11, 2004, bombings in Madrid that killed 191 people—the worst terrorist incident in Europe since World War II.

Spanish-American War (1898) Conflict between the U.S. and Spain that ended Spanish colonial rule in the New World. The war originated in Cuba's struggle for independence. The newspapers of William Randolph Hearst fanned U.S. sympathy for the rebels, which increased after the unexplained destruction of the U.S. warship *Maine* on Feb. 15, 1898. Congress passed resolutions declaring Cuba's right to independence and demanding that Spain withdraw its armed forces. Spain declared war on the U.S. on April 24. Commo. George Dewey led the naval squadron that defeated the Spanish fleet in the Philippines on May 1, and Gen.William Shafter led regular troops and volunteers (including future U.S. president Theodore Roosevelt and his Rough Riders) in the destruction of Spain's Caribbean Sea fleet near Santiago, Cuba (July 17). In the Treaty of Paris (December 10), Spain renounced all claim to Cuba and ceded Guam, Puerto Rico, and the Philippines to the U.S., marking the U.S.'s emergence as a world power.

Spanish Civil War (1936–39) Military revolt against the government of Spain. After the 1936 elections produced a Popular Front government supported mainly by left-wing parties, a military uprising began in garrison towns throughout Spain, led by the rebel Nationalists and supported by conservative elements in the clergy, military, and landowners as well as the fascist Falange. The ruling Republican government, led by the socialist premiers Francisco Largo Caballero and Juan Negrín (1894–1956) and the liberal president Manuel Azaña y Díaz, was supported by workers and many in the educated middle class as well as militant anarchists and communists. Government forces put down the uprising in most regions except parts of northwestern and southwestern Spain, where the Nationalists held control and named Francisco Franco head of state. Both sides repressed opposition; together, they executed or assassinated more than 50,000 suspected enemies to their respective causes. Seeking aid from abroad, the Nationalists received troops, tanks, and planes from Nazi Germany and Italy, which used Spain as a testing ground for new methods of tank and air warfare. The Republicans (also called loyalists) were sent matériel mainly by the Soviet Union, and the volunteer International Brigades also joined the Republicans. The two sides fought fierce and bloody skirmishes in a war of attrition. The Nationalist side gradually gained territory and by April 1938 succeeded in splitting Spain from east to west, causing 250,000 Republican forces to flee into France. In March 1939 the remaining Republican forces surrendered, and Madrid, beset by civil strife between communists and anticommunists, fell to the Nationalists on March 28. About 500,000 people died in the war, and all Spaniards were deeply scarred by the trauma. The war's end brought a period of dictatorship that lasted until the mid-1970s.

Spanish language, Romance language spoken in Spain and in large parts of the New World. It has more than 358 million speakers, including more than 85 million in Mexico, more than 40 million in Colombia, more than 35 million in Argentina, and more than 31 million in the U.S. Its earliest written materials date from the 10th century, its first literary works from *c.* 1150. The Castilian dialect, the source of modern standard Spanish, arose in the 9th century in north-central Spain (Old Castile) and had spread to central Spain (New Castile) by the 11th century. In the late 15th century the kingdoms of Castile, León, and Aragon merged, and Castilian became the official language of all of Spain, with Catalan and Galician (effectively a dialect of Portuguese) becoming regional languages and Aragonese and Leonese reduced to a fraction of their original speech areas. Latin American regional dialects are derived from Castilian but differ from it in phonology.

Spanish Succession, War of the (1701–14) Conflict arising from the disputed succession to the throne of Spain after the death of the childless Charles II. The Habsburg Charles had named the Bourbon Philip, duke d'Anjou, as his successor; when Philip took the Spanish throne as Philip V, his grandfather Louis XIV invaded the Spanish Netherlands. The former anti-French alliance from the War of the Grand Alliance was revived in 1701 by Britain, the Dutch Republic, and the Holy Roman emperor, who had been promised parts of the Spanish empire by earlier treaties of partition (1698, 1699). The English forces, led by the duke of Marlborough, won a series of victories over France (1704–09), including the Battle of Blenheim, which forced the French out of the Low Countries and Italy. The imperial general, Eugene of Savoy, also won notable victories. In 1711 conflicts within the alliance led to its collapse, and peace negotiations began in 1712. The war concluded with the Peace of Utrecht (1713), which marked the rise of the power of Britain at the expense of both France and Spain, and the Treaties of Rastatt and Baden (1714).

sparrow, Any of numerous species of small chiefly seed-eating songbirds having a conical bill, particularly the house sparrow, and most members of the New World family Emberizidae. Some species of Emberizidae are common. The trim-looking chipping and tree sparrows have a reddish brown cap. The finely streaked savanna and vesper sparrows inhabit grassy fields. The heavily streaked song and fox sparrows are woodland dwellers. The white-crowned and white-throated sparrows are larger than most species and have black-and-white crown stripes.

White-throated sparrow (Zonotrichia albicollis).
William D. Griffin

Sparta, or LACEDAEMON, Ancient Greek city-state, capital of Laconia and chief city of the Peloponnese. Of Dorian origin, it was founded in the 9th century BC and developed as a strictly militaristic society. In the 8th–5th centuries BC it subdued neighbouring Messenia. From the 5th century BC the ruling class of Sparta devoted itself to war and forged the most powerful army in Greece. After a long contest with Athens in the Peloponnesian War (431–404 BC), it attained dominance over all of Greece. Sparta's power was broken by Thebes at the battle of Leuctra in 371 BC. It lost its independence *c.* 192 BC when it was defeated by and forced to join the Achaean League. It was made part of the Roman province of Achaea in 146 BC. The Visigoths captured and destroyed the city in AD 396. The ruins of its acropolis, agora, theatre, and temples remain.

spearmint, Aromatic herb (*Mentha spicata*) of the mint family, the common garden mint widely used for culinary purposes. It has lax, tapering spikes of reddish lilac flowers similar to peppermint flowers and sharply serrated leaves that are used fresh or dried to flavour many foods. The aroma and taste of spearmint are similar to those of peppermint but not as strong. Native to Europe and Asia, spearmint has been naturalized in North America.

special education, Education for students (such as the physically or mentally disabled) with special needs. An early proponent of education for the blind was Valentin Haüy, who opened a school in Paris in 1784; his efforts were followed by those of Louis Braille. Attempts to educate deaf children predate Haüy, but not until Friedrich Moritz Hill (1805–74) developed an oral method of instruction did teaching to the deaf become established. The development of standardized sign languages further advanced instruction of the deaf. Scientific attempts to educate mentally retarded children began with the efforts of Jean-Marc-Gaspard Itard (1775–1838) to train a feral child known as the Wild Boy of Aveyron; Itard's work influenced such later theorists as Édouard Séguin (1812–80) and Maria Montessori. Children with motor disabilities, once considered subjects for special education, are usually integrated into the standard classroom, often by means of wheelchairs and modified desks. Children with learning disabilities and speech problems usually require specialized techniques, often on an individual basis. For children with behavioral and emotional disorders, special therapeutic and clinical services may be provided.

special effects, Artificial visual or mechanical effects introduced into a movie or television show. The earliest special effects were created through special camera lenses or through tricks such as projecting a moving background behind the actors. Greater flexibility came with the development of the optical printer, which made it possible to combine separate pieces of film and replace part of an image, thus allowing for effects such as characters flying through the air. Special effects have also been created mechanically on the set through the use of devices such as wires, explosives, and puppets and by building miniature models to simulate epic scenes such as battles. The growing use of computer animation and computer-generated imagery has produced increasingly elaborate and realistic visual effects. Though each movie studio formerly had its own special-effects department, effects are now created by private companies such as George Lucas's Industrial Light and Magic, formed to provide the revolutionary effects seen in *Star Wars* (1977) and later movies.

Special Olympics, International sports program for people with intellectual disability. It provides year-round training and athletic competition in a variety of Olympic-type summer and winter sports for participants. Inaugurated in 1968 through the efforts of Eunice Kennedy Shriver and the Chicago Park District, the Special Olympics was officially recognized by the International Olympic Committee in 1988. Games are held every two years, alternating between winter and summer sports. International headquarters are in Washington, D.C.

specific gravity, or RELATIVE DENSITY, Ratio of the density of a substance to that of a standard substance. For solids and liquids, the standard substance is usually water at 39.2 °F (4.0 °C), which has a density of 1.00 kg/liter. Gases are usually compared to dry air, which has a density of 1.29 g/liter at 32 °F (0 °C) and 1 atmosphere pressure. Because it is a ratio of two quantities that have the same dimensions (mass per unit volume), specific gravity has no dimension. For example, the specific gravity of liquid mercury is 13.6, because its actual density is 13.6 kg/liter, 13.6 times that of water.

specific heat, Ratio of the quantity of heat required to raise the temperature of a body one degree to that required to raise the temperature of an equal mass of water one degree. The term is also used to mean the amount of heat, in calories, required to raise the temperature of one gram of a substance by one Celsius degree.

spectroscopy, Study of the absorption and emission of light and other radiation by matter, as related to the dependence of these processes on the wavelength of the radiation. Usually spectroscopy is devoted to identifying elements and compounds and elucidating atomic and molecular structure by measuring the radiant energy absorbed or emitted by a substance at characteristic wavelengths of the electromagnetic spectrum on excitation by an external energy source. However, spectroscopy also includes the study of particles (e.g., electrons, ions) that have been sorted or otherwise differentiated into a spectrum as a function of some property (such as energy or mass). The instruments used are spectrometers. Experiments involve a light source, a disperser to form the spectrum, detectors (visual, photoelectric, radiometric, or photographic) for observing or recording its details, devices for measuring wavelengths and intensities, and interpretation of the measured quantities to identify chemicals or give clues to the structure of atoms and molecules. Specialized techniques include Raman spectroscopy, nuclear magnetic resonance (NMR), nuclear quadrupole resonance (NQR), microwave and gamma-ray spectroscopy, and electron spin resonance (ESR).

speech, Human communication through audible language. Speech sounds are made with air exhaled from the lungs, which passes between the vocal cords in the larynx and out through the vocal tract (pharynx and oral and nasal cavities). This airstream is shaped into different sounds by the articulators, mainly the tongue, palate, and lips. Articulatory phonetics describes each sound in terms of the position and action of the articulators used to make it. Speech is also described in terms of syntax, lexicon (inventory of words or morphemes), and phonology (sounds).

speech recognition, or VOICE RECOGNITION, Ability of computer systems to accept speech input and act on it or transcribe it into written language. Current research efforts are directed toward applications of automatic speech recognition (ASR), where the goal is to transform the content of speech into knowledge that forms the basis for linguistic or cognitive tasks, such as translation into another language. Practical applications include database-query systems, information retrieval systems, and speaker identification and verification systems, as in telebanking. Speech recognition has promising applications in robotics, particularly development of robots that can "hear." *See also* pattern recognition.

speed skating, Sport of racing on ice skates. The blade of the speed skate is longer and thinner than that of the hockey or figure skate. Two types of track are used in international competition. The long track is a 400-m (about one-quarter mile) flattened oval (straight sides and curved ends) on which two skaters race simultaneously. In long track the race is against the clock rather than the opponent. The short track, a more recent development, is a 111-m (364-ft) oval on which four to six skaters race during each heat. Short track is a race to the finish line. Long-track speed skating was included in the first Winter Olympics in 1924; short-track skating was added in 1992.

sperm, or SPERMATOZOON, Male reproductive cell. In mammals, sperm are produced in the testes and travel through the reproductive system. At fertilization, one sperm of the roughly 300 million in an average ejaculation fertilizes an egg to produce an offspring. At puberty, immature cells (spermatogonia) begin a maturation process (spermatogenesis). A mature human sperm has a flat, almond-shaped head, with a cap (acrosome) containing chemicals that help it penetrate an ovum. It is essentially a cell nucleus, with 23 chromosomes (including either the X or Y that determines the child's sex). A flagellum propels the sperm, which may live in a woman's reproductive tract for two to three days after sexual intercourse, to the egg. Sperm may be frozen and stored for artificial insemination.

sperm whale, or CACHALOT, Thickset, blunt-snouted toothed whale (*Physeter catodon*, family Physeteridae) with small, paddlelike flippers and rounded humps on the back. Sperm whales have an enormous head, squarish in profile, and a narrow, underslung lower jaw with large conical teeth that fit into sockets in the toothless upper jaw when the mouth is closed. They are dark blue-gray or brownish. (Herman Melville's Moby-Dick was presumably an albino.) The male grows to 60 ft (18 m). Herds of 15–20 live in temperate and tropical waters worldwide. They commonly dive to 1,200 ft (350 m), feeding primarily on cephalopods. The whales have been hunted for their spermaceti (a waxy substance in the snout, used in ointments and cosmetics) and for ambergris. The pygmy sperm whale (genus *Kogia*) is a black dolphinlike whale, about 13 ft (4 m) long, of the Northern Hemisphere that lacks commercial value.

sphere of influence, In international politics, a state's claim to exclusive or predominant control over a foreign area or territory. Beginning in the late 1880s, European colonial powers undertook legal agreements consisting of promises not to interfere with each other's actions in mutually recognized spheres of influence in Africa and Asia. After colonial expansion ceased, geopolitical rather than legal claims to spheres of influence became common, examples being the U.S. claim to dominance in the Western Hemisphere under the much-earlier Monroe Doctrine and the Soviet Union's expansion of its sphere of influence to eastern Europe following World War II.

sphinx, Mythological creature with a lion's body and a human's head. It figures prominently in Egyptian and Greek art and legend. The winged sphinx of Thebes was said to have terrorized people by demanding the answer to a riddle taught to her by the Muses— What is it that has one voice and yet becomes successively four-footed, then two-footed, then three-footed?—and devoured every person who answered incorrectly. When Oedipus correctly answered "man"—who crawls on all fours in infancy, walks on two feet when grown, and leans on a staff in old age—the sphinx killed herself. The earliest and most famous example in art is the Great Sphinx at Giza in Egypt, built *c.* 2500 BC. The sphinx appeared in the Greek world *c.* 1600 BC and in Mesopotamia *c.* 1500 BC.

The Great Sphinx at Giza, 4th dynasty
E. Streichan/Shostal Associates

spice and herb, Dried parts of various plants cultivated for their aromatic, savory, medicinal, or otherwise desirable properties. Spices are the fragrant or pungent products of such tropical or subtropical species as cardamom, cinnamon, clove, ginger, and pepper; spice seeds include anise, caraway, cumin, fennel, poppy, and sesame. Herbs are the fragrant leaves of such plants as basil, marjoram, mint, rosemary, and thyme. The most notable uses of spices and herbs in very early times were in medicine, in the making of holy oils and unguents, and as aphrodisiacs; they were also used to flavour food and beverages and to inhibit or hide food spoilage. Trade in spices has played a major role in human history. Important early trade routes, including those between Asia and the Middle East and between Europe and Asia, were initially forged to obtain exotic spices and herbs. The 15th-century voyages of discovery were launched largely as a result of the spice trade, and in the 17th century Portugal and the British, Dutch, and French East India companies battled furiously for dominance.

spider, Any of approximately 42,700 predatory arachnid species, mostly terrestrial, in the order Araneida, abundant worldwide except in Antarctica. Spiders have two main body parts, eight legs, two pincerlike venomous appendages, and three pairs of spinnerets. Species range in length from 0.02 to 3.5 in. (0.5 to about 90 mm). The venom of a few species (e.g., brown recluse) is harmful to humans. Most species catch insect prey in a web of silk extruded from the spinnerets. Spiders change little during growth, except in size. Species are classified largely on the basis of the number and arrangement of eyes and the type of web.

spider monkey, Any of four species (family Cebidae) of diurnal, arboreal New World monkeys found from Mexico to Brazil.

Long-limbed and somewhat potbellied, they are 14–26 in. (35–66 cm) long and have thumbless hands and a heavily furred, prehensile 24–36-in. (60–92-cm) tail. The coat is gray, reddish, brown, or black. They swing through branches, using their tails and hands, or leap or drop spread-eagled from tree to tree. They eat fruit, nuts, flowers, and buds. They are used in laboratory studies of malaria, to which they are susceptible. Though sometimes kept as pets, adults are likely to throw tantrums and may be dangerous.

Spielberg, Steven (b. Dec. 18, 1946, Cincinnati, Ohio, U.S.), U.S. film director and producer. About the time of his graduation from California State College, Long Beach (1970), he attracted the attention of Universal Pictures with a short film he made. As a director of television movies, he made the thriller *Duel* (1971), and in 1974 he directed the feature film *The Sugarland Express*. His shark-attack thriller *Jaws* (1975) became one of the highest-grossing movies ever, and he went on to direct huge successes such as *Close Encounters of the Third Kind* (1977), *Raiders of the Lost Ark* (1981) and its sequels, and *E.T.: The Extra-Terrestrial* (1982). He received Academy Awards for directing *Schindler's List* (1993), which tells the story of a group of Polish Jews who avoided Nazi extermination camps through the heroic actions of a German industrialist, and *Saving Private Ryan* (1998), which followed American soldiers in the days after the Normandy invasion of 1944. His other movies include *The Color Purple* (1985), *Empire of the Sun* (1987), *Jurassic Park* (1993), *A.I. Artificial Intelligence* (2001), *Minority Report* (2002), *Munich* (2005), and *War Horse* (2011). In 1994 he cofounded DreamWorks SKG, a film, animation, and television production company; it was sold to Viacom in 2006.

spin, Amount of angular momentum associated with a subatomic particle or nucleus. It is measured in multiples of $\hbar$ (h-bar), equal to Planck's constant divided by 2π. Electrons, neutrons, and protons have a spin of $1/2$, for example, while pions and helium nuclei have zero spin. The spin of a complex nucleus is the vector sum of the orbital angular momentum and intrinsic spins of the constituent nucleons. For nuclei of even mass number, the multiple is an integral; for those of odd mass number, it is a half-integer.

spinal cord, In vertebrates, the body's major nerve tract. In humans it is about 18 in. (45 cm) long, running from the base of the brain through the vertebral column. It is covered by the meninges and cushioned by cerebrospinal fluid. It connects the peripheral nervous system (outside the brain and spinal cord) to the brain. The spinal cord and the brain constitute the central nervous system. Sensory impulses reach the brain via the spinal cord, and impulses from the brain travel down the spinal cord to motor neurons, which reach the body's muscles and glands via the peripheral nerves. The peripheral nerves are connected to the spinal cord via the spinal nerves. In humans there are 31 pairs of spinal nerves containing both sensory and motor fibres, which originate in the spinal cord and pass out between the vertebrae. These nerves branch and relay motor impulses to all parts of the body. Injury to the spinal cord may result in loss of communication between the brain and outlying parts and cause paralysis, loss of sensation, or weakness in the parts of the body served by areas below the injured region. Because nerve cells and fibres are unable to regenerate themselves, the effects are usually permanent.

spirillum, Any of the spiral-shaped bacteria that make up the genus *Spirillum*, which are aquatic except for one species that causes a type of rat-bite fever in humans. The term is used generally for any corkscrewlike species of bacteria. Spirilla are gramnegative and move by means of tufts of flagella at each end.

spiritualism, Belief that the souls of the dead can make contact with the living, usually through a medium or during abnormal mental states such as trances. The basis of spiritualism is the conviction that spirit is the essence of life and that it lives on after the body dies. A medium is a person sensitive to vibrations from the spirit world, who may hold meetings known as séances in order to seek messages from spirits. A "control" is a spirit that gives messages to the human medium, who in turn gives them to other people. Spirits are also thought to manifest themselves through such means as rapping or levitating objects. Some spiritualists claim powers of paranormal healing. Scientific study of spiritualist phenomena has been the focus of the Society for Psychical Research, founded in Britain in 1882.

spirochete, Any of an order (Spirochaetales) of spiral-shaped bacteria. Some are serious pathogens for humans, causing such diseases as syphilis, yaws, and relapsing fever. Spirochetes are gram-negative and motile. They are unique in that their flagella, which number between two and more than 200 per organism, are contained within the cell. Most spirochetes are found in a liquid environment (e.g., mud and water, blood and lymph). Several species are borne by lice and ticks, which transmit them to humans.

Spitteler, Carl (b. April 24, 1845, Liestal, Switz.—d. Dec. 29, 1924, Lucerne), Swiss poet. He was a private tutor in Russia and Finland before he wrote his first great poetic work, the mythical epic *Prometheus und Epimetheus* (1881). His second great work was the epic *The Olympic Spring* (1900–05), in which he found full scope for bold invention and vividly expressive power. Late in life he rewrote his first epic as *Prometheus the Long-Suffering* (1924). Though known for his pessimistic yet heroic verse, he also wrote lyrical poems, stories, novels, and essays. He received the Nobel Prize for Literature in 1919.

spleen, Lymphoid organ, located in the left side of the abdomen behind the stomach. The spleen is the primary filtering element for the blood, and it is a storage site for red blood cells (erythrocytes) and platelets. It is one of four places where reticuloendothelial cells are found. Two types of tissue, red pulp and white pulp, are intermixed. The white pulp is lymphoid tissue containing lymphocyte production centres. The red pulp is a network of channels filled with blood where most of the filtration occurs and is the major site of destruction of deteriorating erythrocytes and recycling of their hemoglobin. Both contain cells that remove foreign material and initiate an antibody-producing process. The spleen becomes enlarged in some infections. Its rupture in high-impact injuries may require surgical removal, which leaves the patient more susceptible to overwhelming infection.

Split, ancient SPALATUM, Seaport (pop., 2001: 188,694), Dalmatia, Croatia. The Romans established the colony of Salonae nearby in 78 BC, and the emperor Diocletian lived at Split until his death in AD 313. After the Avars sacked the town in 615, the inhabitants built a new town within Diocletian's 7-acre (3-hectare) palace compound; this "old town" has been continuously inhabited since that time. Split came under Byzantine rule in the 9th century, shifted to Venetian control in 1420, and was held by Austria in the 18th and 19th centuries. It came under Yugoslavian rule in 1918, finally becoming part of independent Croatia in 1992. The port facilities were destroyed in World War II, but the old city was little-damaged, and repairs were subsequently made. Split is a commercial, educational, and tourist centre. Collectively with the historic royal residences, fortifications, and churches in the city, the palace was designated a UNESCO World Heritage site in 1979.

sponge, Any of some 5,000 species (phylum Porifera) of permanently affixed (sessile), mostly marine, solitary or colonial invertebrates, found from shallow to deep (more than 30,000 ft, or 9,000 m) waters. Simple sponges are hollow cylinders with a large opening at the top through which water and wastes are expelled. A thin, perforated outer epidermal layer covers a porous skeleton, which is composed of interlocking spicules of calcium carbonate, silica, or spongin (found in 80% of all sponges), a proteinaceous material. The body, ranging in diameter or length from 1 in. (2.5 cm) to several yards, may be fingerlike, treelike, or a shapeless mass. Sponges lack organs and specialized tissue; flagellated cells move

water into the central cavity through the perforations, and individual cells digest food (bacteria, other microorganisms, and organic debris), excrete waste, and absorb oxygen. Sponges can reproduce asexually or sexually. Larval forms are free-swimming but all adults are sessile. Since antiquity, sponges have been harvested for use in holding water, bathing, and scrubbing; because of overharvesting and newer technologies, most sponges sold today are synthetic.

spore, Reproductive cell capable of developing into a new individual without fusing with another reproductive cell. Spores thus differ from gametes, which must fuse in pairs in order to create a new individual. Spores are agents of nonsexual reproduction; gametes are agents of sexual reproduction. Spores are produced by bacteria, fungi, and green plants. Bacterial spores serve largely as a resting, or dormant, stage in the life cycle, preserving the bacterium through periods of unfavorable conditions. Many bacterial spores are highly durable and can germinate even after years of dormancy. Fungal spores serve a function similar to that of seeds in plants; they germinate and grow into new individuals under suitable conditions of moisture, temperature, and food availability. Among green plants (all of which have a life cycle characterized by alternation of generations), spores are the reproductive agents of the nonsexual generation (sporophyte), giving rise to the sexual generation (gametophyte).

sports medicine, Medical and paramedical supervision and treatment of athletes. It has four aspects. Preparation (conditioning) uses diet, exercises, and monitoring of practice sessions to improve performance. Prevention identifies any predisposition to injury or illness and covers warmup, stretching, and design and use of protective equipment. Many surgical techniques developed in sports medicine, particularly for knee injuries, are now used for the general population. Rehabilitation prepares an injured or ill athlete to return to activity after initial treatment.

spring, In hydrology, an opening at or near the Earth's surface where water from underground sources is discharged. Springs discharge either at ground level or directly into the bed of a stream, lake, or sea. Water that emerges at the surface without a perceptible current is called a seep.

Sputnik, Any of a series of Earth-orbiting spacecraft whose launching by the Soviet Union inaugurated the space age. Sputnik 1, the world's first artificial satellite (October 1957), remained in orbit until early 1958, when it reentered Earth's atmosphere and burned up. Sputnik 2 carried a dog, Laika, the first living creature to orbit Earth; since Sputnik 2 was not designed to sustain life, Laika did not survive the flight. Eight more missions with similar satellites carried out experiments on various animals to test life-support systems and reentry procedures and to furnish data on space temperatures, pressures, particles, radiation, and magnetic fields.

squash (rackets), Singles or doubles game played in a four-walled court with a long-handled racket and a rubber ball. A descendant of rackets, it probably originated in the mid-19th century at England's Harrow School. The standard international game uses a relatively soft, slow ball; hardball squash, popular in the U.S., is played on a narrower court with a harder, faster ball. The object of squash is to bounce, or rebound, the ball off the front wall in such a way as to defeat an opponent's attempt to reach and return it.

squid, Any of nearly 400 species of 10-armed cephalopods, found in both coastal and oceanic waters, that prey on fishes and crustaceans. They range from less than 0.75 in. (1.5 cm) to more than 65 ft (20 m) long (in the case of the giant squid). Two of the 10 arms are long, slender tentacles; each has an expanded end and four rows of suckers with toothed, hard-edged rings. An internal shell supports the slender tubular body of most species. Squid eyes, almost as complex as human eyes, are usually set into the sides of the head. Squids may be swift swimmers (propelling themselves by contracting and relaxing their mantle or by undulating their two fins) or mere drifters; water expelled from a funnel below the head can propel the squid backward. Like the octopus, the squid may emit an inky cloud from its ink sac when in danger from sperm whales, fishes, or humans, among other predators.

*Squid (*Illex coindeti*) swimming forward*
Douglas P. Wilson

squirrel, Any of about 260 species in 50 genera (family Sciuridae) of mostly diurnal rodents found almost worldwide. Many species are arboreal; some are terrestrial. All species have strong hind legs and a hairy tail. They vary widely in colour and form and range in total length from the 4-in. (10-cm) African pygmy squirrel to the giant squirrels of Asia, about 35 in. (90 cm) long. Tree dwellers live in a tree hollow or nest, and most are active year-round. Ground dwellers live in burrows, and many become dormant in winter (hibernate) or summer (estivate). Most species are primarily vegetarian and are fond of seeds and nuts; some eat insects or supplement their diet with animal protein.

squirrel monkey, Any of several species (genus *Saimiri*, family Cebidae) of arboreal New World monkeys, found in groups of up to several hundred during the day in riverside forests of Central and South America. They eat fruit, insects, and small animals. They are 10–16 in. (25–40 cm) long and have a heavy, nonprehensile, black-tipped tail, 15–19 in. (37–47 cm) long. They have a small white face, large eyes, and large, usually tufted, ears. The short, soft coat is grayish to greenish, with yellow or orange arms, hands, and feet. The crown of the common squirrel monkey (*S. sciureus*) is olive or grayish; the red-backed squirrel monkey (*S. oerstedii*) has a black crown and reddish back.

*Common squirrel monkey (*Saimiri sciureus*).*
© Gerry Ellis Nature Photography

Sraosha, In Zoroastrianism and Parsiism, the divine being who is the messenger of Ahura Mazda and the embodiment of the divine word. He serves as the mediator between the human and the divine. Zoroastrians believe that no ritual is valid without his presence. He is depicted as a strong and holy youth who lives in a celestial thousand-pillared house. He chastises the demons that harass people every night, and he leads the righteous soul through the ordeal of judgment three days after death. At the end of time, he will be the agent of the extermination of evil.

Sri Lanka, officially DEMOCRATIC SOCIALIST REPUBLIC OF SRI LANKA, formerly CEYLON, Island country in the Indian Ocean, off the southeastern coast of India. Area: 25,332 sq mi (65,610 sq km). Population: (2011 est.) 21,045,000. Capitals: Colombo (executive and judicial), Sri Jayewardenepura Kotte (legislative). About three-fourths of the population is Sinhalese; other ethnic groups include Tamils and Muslims. Languages: Sinhala, Tamil (both official); also English. Religions: Buddhism; also Hinduism, Islam, Christianity. Currency: Sri Lanka rupee. Highlands make up Sri Lanka's south-central region and core, with narrow gorges and deep river valleys. The surrounding lowlands include hills and fertile plains. The developing mixed economy is largely based on agriculture, services, and light industries. Clothing, tea, gemstones, and rubber are exported. The island is world-famous for its gemstones, which include sapphires, rubies, and topaz. It is also a major producer of high-grade graphite. Sri Lanka is a republic with one legislative house; its head of state and government is the president, assisted by the prime minister. The Sinhalese people are probably the result of aboriginal inhabitants mixing with Indo-Aryans who began migrating from India *c.* the 5th century BCE. The Tamils were later immigrants from Dravidian India, migrating over a period from the early centuries CE to *c.* 1200. Buddhism was introduced during the 3rd century BCE. As Buddhism spread, the Sinhalese kingdom extended its political control over the island but lost it to invaders from southern India in the 10th century. Between 1200 and 1505, Sinhalese power gravitated to southwestern Sri Lanka, while a southern Indian dynasty seized power in the north and established the Tamil kingdom in the 14th century. Foreign invasions from India, China, and Malaya occurred in the 13th–15th centuries. In 1505 the Portuguese arrived, and by 1619 they controlled most of the island. The Sinhalese enlisted the Dutch to help oust the Portuguese, and the island eventually came under the control of the Dutch East India Company, which relinquished it in 1796 to the British. In 1802 it became the British crown colony of Ceylon, which gained independence in 1948. It became the Republic of Sri Lanka in 1972 and took its present name in 1978. Civil strife between Tamil and Sinhalese groups beset the country beginning in the early 1980s, the Tamils demanding a separate autonomous state in northern Sri Lanka. A prolonged insurrection by the Tamil Tigers guerrilla group was defeated by government forces in 2009. In 2004 Sri Lanka was struck by a tsunami that badly damaged much of the coastline and killed tens of thousands of people.

Srinagar, City (pop., 2001: 898,440), summer capital of Jammu and Kashmir state, northwestern India. It lies on the banks of the Jhelum River in the Vale of Kashmir. Situated amid clear lakes and lofty mountains, it has long had a considerable tourist economy. Seven wooden bridges span the river, and the gondolas of Kashmir ply the adjacent canals and waterways. The floating gardens of Dal Lake are a noted attraction.

The Jhelum River at Srinagar, Jammu and Kashmir state, India.
Richard Abeles—Artstreet

SS, German in full SCHUTZSTAFFEL ("PROTECTIVE ECHELON"), Paramilitary corps of the Nazi Party. Founded in 1925 by Adolf Hitler as a personal bodyguard, it was directed from 1929 by Heinrich Himmler, who enlarged its membership from fewer than 300 to more than 250,000. Wearing black uniforms and special insignia (lightning-like runic S's, death's-head badges, and silver daggers), the SS considered itself superior to the SA, whom they purged on Hitler's orders in 1934. The corps was divided into the General SS (Allgemeine-SS), which dealt with police matters and included the Gestapo, and the Armed SS (Waffen-SS), which included the concentration-camp guards and the 39 regiments in World War II that served as elite combat troops. SS men were schooled in racial hatred and absolute obedience to Hitler. They carried out massive executions of political opponents, Roma (Gypsies), Jews, communists, partisans, and Russian prisoners. In 1946 the SS was declared a criminal organization at the Nürnberg trials.

stadium, Enclosure that provides a broad space for sports events and tiers of seats for a large number of spectators. The name derives from a Greek unit of measurement, the stade (about 607 ft, or 185 m), the length of the footrace in the ancient Olympics. Shapes of stadiums have varied depending on use: Some are rectangular with curved corners; others are elliptical or U-shaped. As a type of long-span structure, the stadium played a significant role in 20th-century construction technology. The building of large stadiums has been greatly facilitated by the use of reinforced concrete, steel, and membrane structures, which have made possible daring new designs. The Houston Astrodome was the first major fully roofed stadium. Cables contributed significantly to speed of construction, lightness of roof, and economy in covered stadiums. The enormous Hubert H. Humphrey Metrodome in Minneapolis (opened 1982) was built using a cable system.

Staël, Germaine de, orig. ANNE-LOUISE-GERMAINE NECKER, BARONESS DE STAËL-HOLSTEIN known as MADAME DE STAËL (b. April 22, 1766, Paris, France—d. July 14, 1817, Paris), French-Swiss writer, political propagandist, and salon hostess. She early gained a reputation as a lively wit. She first became known for *Letters on the Works and the Character of J.-J. Rousseau* (1788). The most brilliant period of her career began in 1794, when she returned to Paris after the Reign of Terror; her salon, known for its literary and intellectual figures, flourished, and she published political and literary essays, notably *A Treatise on the Influence of the Passions upon the Happiness of Individuals and of Nations* (1796), an important document of European Romanticism. In 1803 Napoleon, who resented her opposition, had her banished from Paris, and she made the family residence in Coppet, Switz., her headquarters. Probably her most important work is *Germany* (1810), a serious study of German manners, literature and art, philosophy and morals, and religion. Her other writings include novels, plays, moral essays, history, and memoirs.

Germaine de Staël, portrait by Jean-Baptiste Isabey, 1810; in the Louvre, Paris
Giraudon/Art Resource, New York

stagecraft, Technical aspects of a theatrical production, which include lighting, scenery, costumes, and sound. While elements such as painted screens and wheeled platforms were used in the Greek theatre as early as the 5th century BCE, most innovations in stagecraft were developed in the Italian Renaissance theatre, where painted backdrops, perspective architectural settings, and numerous changes of scenery were common. Italian staging was introduced in England in 1605 by Inigo Jones for court masques. In the late 19th century, staging was influenced by the new naturalism, which called for historically accurate sets. In the 20th century, simplified scenic design focused attention on the actor. Staging techniques and the design of theatres have been greatly affected by advances in lighting, from the use of candles in the Renaissance to oil lamps in the 18th century and gas and electric lights in the 19th century. Modern stage lighting, which employs computerized control boards to achieve complex effects, can unify all the visual elements of a stage production.

stained glass, Coloured glass used to make decorative windows and other objects through which light passes. Stained glass is often made in large, richly detailed panels that are set together in a framework of lead. Like all coloured glass, it acquires its colour by the addition of metallic oxides to molten glass. A purely Western phenomenon, stained glass originated as a fine art of the Christian church, beginning in the 12th–13th century, when it was combined with Gothic architecture to create brilliant, moving effects. A decline set in after the 13th century, when stained-glass artists began to seek the realistic effects sought by Renaissance painters, effects to which the technique was less suited and which diverted artists from exploiting the all-important light-refracting quality of glass. More recently, stained-glass artists again achieved high quality: during the 19th-century Gothic revival, in the Art Nouveau designs of Louis Comfort Tiffany, and in the work of such 20th-century artists as Marc Chagall.

stainless steel, Any of a family of alloy steels usually containing 10–30% chromium. The presence of chromium, together with low carbon content, gives remarkable resistance to corrosion and heat. Other elements, such as nickel, molybdenum, titanium, aluminum, niobium, copper, nitrogen, sulfur, phosphorus, and selenium, may be added to increase corrosion resistance to specific environments, enhance resistance to oxidation, and impart special characteristics.

stalactite and stalagmite, Elongated forms of various minerals deposited from solution by slowly dripping water. A stalactite hangs like an icicle from the ceiling or side of a cavern. A stalagmite rises from the floor of a cavern. The two are not necessarily paired; when they are, continual elongation of one or both may eventually join them into a column. The dominant mineral in such deposits is calcite (calcium carbonate), and the largest displays are formed in caves of limestone and dolomite.

Stalin, Joseph, orig. IOSEB DZHUGASHVILI (b. Dec. 18, 1879, Gori, Georgia, Russian Empire—d. March 5, 1953, Moscow, Russia, U.S.S.R.), Soviet politician and dictator. The son of a cobbler, he studied at a seminary but was expelled for revolutionary activity in 1899. He joined an underground revolutionary group and sided with the Bolshevik faction of the Russian Social-Democratic Workers' Party in 1903. A disciple of Vladimir Lenin, he served in minor party posts and was appointed to the first Bolshevik Central Committee (1912). He remained active behind the scenes and in exile (1913–17) until the Russian Revolution of 1917 brought the Bolsheviks to power. Having adopted the name Stalin (from Russian *stal*, "steel"), he served as commissar for nationalities and for state control in the Bolshevik government (1917–23). He was a member of the Politburo, and in 1922 he became secretary-general of the party's Central Committee. After Lenin's death (1924), Stalin overcame his rivals, including Leon Trotsky, Grigory Zinovyev, Lev Kamenev, Nikolay Bukharin, and Aleksey Rykov, and took control of Soviet politics. In 1928 he inaugurated the Five-Year Plans that radically altered Soviet economic and social structures and resulted in the deaths of many millions. In the 1930s he contrived to eliminate threats to his power through the purge trials and through widespread secret executions and persecution. In World War II he signed the German-Soviet Nonaggression Pact (1939), attacked Finland, and annexed parts of eastern Europe to strengthen his western frontiers. When Germany invaded Russia (1941), Stalin took control of military operations. He allied Russia with Britain and the U.S.; at the Tehrān, Yalta, and Potsdam conferences, he demonstrated his negotiating skill. After the war he consolidated Soviet power in eastern Europe and built up the Soviet Union as a world military power. He continued his repressive political measures to control internal dissent; increasingly paranoid, he was preparing to mount another purge after the so-called Doctors' Plot when he died. Noted for bringing the Soviet Union into world prominence, at terrible cost to his own people, he left a legacy of repression and fear as well as industrial and military power. In 1956 Stalin and his personality cult were denounced by Nikita Khrushchev.

standard of living, Level of material comfort that an individual or group aspires to or may achieve. This includes not only privately purchased goods and services but collectively consumed goods and services such as those provided by public utilities and governments. A standard of living determined for a group such as a country must be examined critically in terms of its constituent values. If the mean value increases over time, but at the same time the rich become richer and the poor poorer, the group may not be collectively better off. Various quantitative indicators can be used as measuring rods, including life expectancy, access to nutritious food and a safe water supply, and availability of medical care.

standard time, Official local time of a region or country. Local mean solar time depends on longitude; it advances by four minutes per degree eastward. The Earth can thus be divided into 24 standard time zones, each approximately 15° in longitude. The actual boundaries of each time zone are determined by local authorities and in many places deviate considerably from 15°. The times in different zones usually differ by an integral number of hours; minutes and seconds are the same.

Stanton, Elizabeth Cady, orig. ELIZABETH CADY (b. Nov. 12, 1815, Johnstown, N.Y., U.S.—d. Oct. 26, 1902, New York, N.Y.), U.S. social reformer and women's suffrage leader. She graduated from Troy Female Seminary (1832), and in 1840 she married the abolitionist Henry B. Stanton and began working to secure passage of a New York law giving property rights to married women. She and Lucretia Mott organized the 1848 Seneca Falls Convention. She joined forces in 1850 with Susan B. Anthony in the woman suffrage movement, and later she coedited the women's-rights newspaper *The Revolution* (1868–70). In 1869 she became the founding president of the National Woman Suffrage Association.

staphylococcus, Any of the spherical bacteria that make up the genus *Staphylococcus*. The best-known species are present in great numbers on the mucous membranes and skin of all humans and other warm-blooded animals. The cells characteristically group together in grapelike clusters. Staphylococci are gram-positive and stationary and do not require oxygen. Of significance to humans is the species *S. aureus*, an important agent of wound infections, boils, and other human skin infections, and one of the most common causes of food poisoning. It also causes udder inflammation in domestic animals and breast infections in women. The largest cause of hospital infections (accounting for almost 15%), "staph" is often difficult to treat because of its increasing resistance to antibiotics.

star, Any massive celestial body of gas that shines by radiant energy generated inside it. The Milky Way Galaxy contains hundreds of billions of stars; only a very small fraction are visible to the unaided eye. The closest star to Earth is the Sun. The closest star to the Sun is about 4.2 light-years away; the most distant are in galaxies billions of light-years away. Single stars such as the Sun are the minority; most stars occur in pairs and multiple systems. Stars also associate by their mutual gravity in larger assemblages called clusters. Constellations consist not of such groupings but of stars in the same direction as seen from Earth. Stars vary greatly in brightness (magnitude), colour, temperature, mass, size, chemical composition, and age. In nearly all, hydrogen is the most abundant element. Stars are classified by their spectra, from blue-white to red, as O, B, A, F, G, K, or M; the Sun is a spectral type G star. Generalizations on the nature and evolution of stars can be made from correlations between certain properties and from statistical results. A star forms when a portion of a dense interstellar cloud of hydrogen and dust grains collapses from its own gravity. As the cloud condenses, its density and internal temperature increase until it is hot enough to trigger nuclear fusion in its core (if not, it becomes a brown dwarf). After hydrogen is exhausted in the core from nuclear burning, the core shrinks and heats up while the star's outer layers expand significantly and cool, and the star becomes a red giant. The final stages of a star's evolution, when it no longer produces enough energy to counteract its own gravity, depend largely on its mass and whether it is a component of a close binary system. Some stars other than the Sun are known to have one or more planets.

starfish, or SEA STAR, Any of 1,800 echinoderm species (class Asteroidea) that have regenerable arms surrounding an indistinct disk and that inhabit all oceans. Species range from 0.4 to 25 in. (1–65 cm) across, but most are 8–12 in. (20–30 cm) across. Their arms, usually five, are hollow and, like the disk, covered with short spines and pincerlike organs; on the lower side are tube feet, sometimes sucker-tipped, used for creeping or clinging to steep surfaces. Some species sweep organic particles into the mouth on the underside of the disk. Others either evert the stomach upon their prey for external digestion or swallow the prey whole.

Stasi, officially STAATSSICHERHEIT ("STATE SECURITY"), Secret police of East Germany (1950–90), established with Soviet help by German communists in Soviet-occupied Germany after World War II. It was responsible for both domestic political surveillance and espionage. At its peak, it employed 85,000 officers full-time. Using hundreds of thousands of informers, it monitored one-third of the population. Most of its foreign operations were focused on West Germany—whose governing circles and military and intelligence services it successfully penetrated—and West Germany's NATO allies. The Stasi was disbanded after German reunification. In 1991 the newly reunified German government passed the Stasi Records Law, under which East German citizens and foreigners were granted the right to view their Stasi files. By the early 21st century, more than 1.5 million individuals had done so.

state, Political organization of society, or the body politic, or, more narrowly, the institutions of government. The state is distinguished from other social groups by its purpose (establishment of order and security), methods (its laws and their enforcement), territory (its area of jurisdiction), and sovereignty. In some countries (e.g., the U.S.), the term also refers to nonsovereign political units subject to the authority of the larger state, or federal union.

states' rights, Rights or powers retained by the regional governments of a federal union under the provisions of a federal constitution. In the U.S., Switzerland, and Australia, the powers of the regional governments are those that remain after the powers of the central government have been enumerated in the constitution. The powers of both the state or regional and national levels of government are defined clearly by specific provisions of the constitutions of Canada and Germany. The concept of states' rights is closely related to that of the 18th-century European concept of state rights, which was invoked to legitimate the powers vested in sovereign national governments. In the U.S. before the mid-19th century, some Southern states claimed the right to annul an act of the federal government within their boundaries, as well as the right to secede from the Union. The constitutional question was resolved against the South by the North's victory in the American Civil War. In the civil rights era, states' rights were invoked by opponents of federal efforts to enforce racial integration in public schools. The federal government can influence state policy even in areas that are constitutionally the purview of the states (e.g., education, local road construction) through withholding funds from states that fail to comply with its wishes. In the late 20th century the term came to be applied more broadly to a variety of efforts aimed at reducing the powers of national governments.

statistics, Branch of mathematics dealing with gathering, analyzing, and making inferences from data. Originally associated with government data (e.g., census data), the subject now has applications in all the sciences. Statistical tools not only summarize past data through such indicators as the mean and the standard deviation but can predict future events using frequency distribution functions. Statistics provides ways to design efficient experiments that eliminate time-consuming trial and error. Double-blind tests for polls, intelligence and aptitude tests, and medical, biological, and industrial experiments all benefit from statistical methods and theories. The results of all of them serve as predictors of future performance, though reliability varies.

steady-state theory, Concept of an expanding universe whose average density remains constant, matter being continuously created throughout it to form new stars and galaxies at the same rate that old ones recede from sight. A steady-state universe has no beginning or end, and its average density and arrangement of galaxies are the same as seen from every point. Galaxies of all ages are intermingled. The theory was first put forward by William Macmillan (1861–1948) in the 1920s and modified by Fred Hoyle to deal with problems that had arisen in connection with the big-bang model. Much evidence obtained since the 1950s contradicts the steady-state theory and supports the big-bang model.

stealth, Any military technology intended to make vehicles or missiles nearly invisible to enemy radar or other electronic detection. Research in antidetection technology began soon after radar was invented. In World War II the Germans coated their U-boat snorkels with radar-absorbent material. By the end of the 20th century the U.S. had developed models of stealth technology, including the F-117 Nighthawk fighter-bomber and the B-2 Spirit strategic bomber. The aircraft featured surface materials and coatings that absorbed radar transmissions, faceted or rounded surfaces that reduced radar reflections, and shielded engine exhausts that reduced infrared radiation. Stealth technology has also been incorporated into the design of naval submarines and surface vessels.

steam engine, Machine that uses steam power to perform mechanical work through the agency of heat (hence a prime mover). In a steam engine, hot steam, usually supplied by a boiler, expands under pressure, and part of the heat energy is converted into work. The rest of the heat may be allowed to escape, or, for maximum engine efficiency, the steam may be condensed in a separate apparatus, a condenser, at comparatively low temperature and pressure. For high efficiency, the steam must decrease substantially in temperature as it expands within the engine. The most efficient performance (i.e., the greatest output of work in relation to the heat supplied) is obtained by using a low condenser temperature and a high boiler pressure.

steamboat, or STEAMSHIP, Watercraft propelled by steam; more narrowly, a shallow-draft paddle-wheel steamboat widely used on rivers in the 19th century, particularly the Mississippi River and its tributaries. Though U.S. experiments with steam-powered boats began in 1787, the first regular steamboat service, operating on the Mississippi, was not established until 1812. Until *c.* 1870 the steamboat dominated the economy, agriculture, and commerce of the middle of the U.S. Because the paddle wheel created turbulence that eroded the banks of narrow channels, river steamboats worked best on broad rivers. The first ocean voyage of a steamboat occurred along the eastern coast of the U.S. in 1809, and Europeans soon developed steamboats capable of crossing Europe's stormy, narrow seas. The first transatlantic steamboat journey was made by the *Savannah* in 1819, and the first commercial shipping line, the Cunard Line, was established in 1840. The screw propeller replaced the paddle wheel in oceanic steamers in the later 19th century.

steel drum, Tuned gong made from the end, and part of the wall, of an oil barrel. The barrel's end surface is hammered into a concave shape, and several areas are outlined by chiseled grooves. It is heated and tempered, and bosses or domes are hammered into the outlined areas; the depth, curvature, and size of each boss de-

termines its pitch. Melodies, complex accompaniments, and counterpoint can be played with rubber-tipped mallets on a single drum. The steel drum originated in Trinidad in the 1940s. It is usually played in ensembles, called steel bands, of widely varying sizes.

steeplechase, Either of two distinct sporting events: (1) a horse race over a closed course with obstacles, including hedges and walls; or (2) a footrace of 3,000 m over hurdles and a water jump. The name derives from impromptu races by fox hunters in 18th-century Ireland over natural country in which church steeples served as course landmarks. Equestrian steeplechase is popular in England, France, and Ireland, and to a lesser extent in the U.S. The most famous equestrian steeplechase is the Grand National. Track-and-field steeplechase dates back to a cross-country race at the University of Oxford in 1850. The course and distance were standardized at the 1920 Olympic Games.

stegosaur, Any of the plated dinosaur species, including *Stegosaurus*, of the Late Jurassic Epoch (159–144 million years ago). Stegosaurs were four-legged herbivores that reached a maximum length of about 30 ft (9 m). The skull and brain were very small. The forelimbs were much shorter than the hind limbs, the back was arched, and the feet were short and broad. Stegosaurs had double rows of large, triangular, bony plates along their backs and tail that may have been a temperature-regulating system. Pairs of long, pointed, bony spikes on the end of the tail were probably defensive weapons.

Steinbeck, John (Ernst) (b. Feb. 27, 1902, Salinas, Calif., U.S.—d. Dec. 20, 1968, New York, N.Y.), U.S. novelist. Steinbeck intermittently attended Stanford University and worked as a manual labourer before his books attained success. He spent much of his life in Monterey county, Calif. His reputation rests mostly on the naturalistic novels on proletarian themes that he wrote in the 1930s. Among them are *Tortilla Flat* (1935), *In Dubious Battle* (1936), *Of Mice and Men* (1937), and the acclaimed *The Grapes of Wrath* (1939, Pulitzer Prize), which aroused widespread sympathy for the plight of migratory farm workers. In World War II he served as a war correspondent. His later novels include *Cannery Row* (1945), *The Pearl* (1947), *The Wayward Bus* (1947), and *East of Eden* (1952). He received the Nobel Prize for Literature in 1962.

John Steinbeck.
Encyclopædia Britannica, Inc.

Stephen, Saint (d. *c.* AD 36, Jerusalem), First Christian martyr. As told in the Acts of the Apostles, he was a foreign-born Jew who lived in Jerusalem and joined the church at an early date. He was one of seven deacons appointed by the Apostles to care for elderly women, widows, and orphans. As a Hellenized Jew, he was strongly opposed to the Temple cult of Judaism. For expressing his opposition, he was brought before the Sanhedrin. His defense of Christianity so outraged his hearers that he was condemned to be stoned to death. One of those who assented to the execution was Saul of Tarsus (St. Paul).

Stephen Báthory, Hungarian ISTVÁN BÁTHORY, Polish STEFAN BATORY (b. Sept. 27, 1533, Szilágysomlyó, Transylvania —d. Dec. 12, 1586, near Grodno, grand duchy of Lith.), Prince of Transylvania (1571–76) and king of Poland (1575–86). In 1571 he was elected prince of Transylvania by the Hungarians, and in 1575, as son-in-law of the late Sigismund I, he was elected king of Poland by the Polish nobility. A forceful and ambitious monarch, he successfully defended Poland's eastern Baltic provinces against Russian incursion and forced the cession of Livonia to Poland in 1582. He planned to unite Poland, Muscovy, and Transylvania and was preparing to renew the war against Russia when he died.

Sterkfontein, One of three neighbouring South African sites (the others being Kromdraai and Swartkrans) at which the remains of fossil hominids have been found. The fossils found include those of *Australopithecus africanus, A. robustus,* and *Homo erectus*. In 1996 researchers uncovered the most complete australopithecine fossil skeleton since Lucy, that of an *A. africanus* individual with a humanlike pelvis but with limb proportions similar to those of a modern chimpanzee. At Makapansgat, 150 mi (240 km) to the north, the remains of about 40 individuals of *A. africanus* have been found.

steroid, Any of a class of natural or synthetic organic compounds with a molecular core, or nucleus, of 17 carbon atoms in a characteristic three-dimensional arrangement of four rings. The configuration of the nucleus, the nature of the groups attached to it, and their positions distinguish different steroids. Hundreds have been found in plants and animals and thousands more synthesized or made by modifying natural steroids. Steroids are important in biology, chemistry, and medicine. Examples include many hormones (including the sex hormones), bile acids, sterols (including cholesterol), and oral contraceptives. Digitalis was the first steroid widely used in Western medicine. Corticosteroids and their synthetic analogs are used to treat rheumatism and other inflammatory ailments.

Stevenson, Robert Louis (Balfour) (b. Nov. 13, 1850, Edinburgh, Scot.—d. Dec. 3, 1894, Vailima, Samoa), Scottish essayist, novelist, and poet. He prepared for a law career but never practiced. He traveled frequently, partly in search of better climates for his tuberculosis, which would eventually cause his death at age 44. He became known for accounts such as *Travels with a Donkey in the Cévennes* (1879) and essays in periodicals, first collected in *Virginibus Puerisque* (1881). His immensely popular novels *Treasure Island* (1883), *Kidnapped* (1886), and *Dr. Jekyll and Mr. Hyde* (1886), and *The Master of Ballantrae* (1889) were written over the course of a few years. *A Child's Garden of Verses* (1885) is one of the most influential children's works of the 19th century. In his last years he lived in Samoa and produced works moving toward a new maturity, including the story "The Beach of Falesá" (1892) and the novel *Weir of Hermiston* (1896), his unfinished masterpiece.

Stieglitz, Alfred (b. Jan. 1, 1864, Hoboken, N.J., U.S.—d. July 13, 1946, New York, N.Y.), U.S. photographer and exhibitor of modern art. He was taken to Europe by his wealthy family to further his education in 1881. In 1883 he abandoned engineering studies in Berlin for a photographic career. Returning to the U.S. in 1890, he made the first successful photographs in snow, in rain, and at night. In 1902 he founded the Photo-Secession group to establish photography as an art. His own best photographs are perhaps two series (1917–27), one of portraits of his wife, Georgia O'Keeffe, and the other of cloud shapes corresponding to emotional experiences. His photographs were the first to be exhibited in major U.S. museums. He also was the

Alfred Stieglitz at his gallery "291" in 1934; behind him is a painting by his wife, Georgia O'Keeffe.
Imogen Cunningham

first to exhibit, at his "291" gallery in New York City, works of modern European and U.S. painters, five years before the Armory Show.

stigmata, In Christian mysticism, bodily marks, scars, or pains suffered in places corresponding to those of the crucified Jesus—on the hands and feet, near the heart, and sometimes on the head (from the crown of thorns) or shoulders and back (from carrying the cross and being whipped). They are often presumed to accompany religious ecstasy and are taken as signs of holiness. The first to experience stigmata was St. Francis of Assisi (1224). Of the more than 330 persons identified with stigmata since the 14th century, more than 60 were canonized or beatified by the Roman Catholic church.

Stijl, De (Dutch: The Style), Group of Dutch artists founded in 1917, including Theo van Doesburg and Piet Mondrian. The group advocated a utopian style: "the universal harmony of life." Its ideal of purity and order in life and society as well as art reflects the Calvinist background of its members. Through its journal, *De Stijl* (1917–31), it influenced painting, the decorative arts (including furniture design), typography, and especially architecture, where its aesthetic found expression at the Bauhaus and in the International Style.

still-life painting, Depiction of inanimate objects for the sake of their qualities of form, colour, texture, composition, and sometimes allegorical or symbolical significance. Still lifes were painted in ancient Greece and Rome. In the Middle Ages they occur in the borders of illuminated manuscripts. The modern still life emerged as an independent genre in the Renaissance. Netherlandish still lifes often depicted skulls, candles, and hourglasses as allegories of mortality, or flowers and fruits to symbolize nature's cycle. Several factors contributed to the rise of still life in the 16th–17th century: an interest in realistic representation, the rise of a wealthy middle class that wanted artworks to decorate its homes, and increased demand for paintings of secular subjects other than portraits in the wake of the Reformation. Dutch and Flemish painters were the masters of still life in the 17th century. From the 18th century until the rise of nonobjective painting after World War II, France was the centre of still-life painting.

stimulant, Any drug that excites any bodily function; usually one that stimulates the central nervous system, inducing alertness, elevated mood, wakefulness, increased speech and motor activity, and decreased appetite. Their mood-elevating effects make some stimulants (e.g., amphetamines, caffeine and its relatives, cocaine, nicotine) potent drugs of abuse. Ritalin, prescribed for attention deficit disorder in children, is a mild stimulant.

stingray, or WHIP-TAILED RAY, Any of various species (family Dasyatidae) of rays noted for their slender, whiplike tail with barbed, usually venomous spines. Most species inhabit warm seas; a few live in the rivers of South America. Species range in width from 10 in. (25 cm) to 7 ft (2 m). Stingrays eat worms, mollusks, and other invertebrates. These bottom-dwellers often lie partially buried in the shallows, lashing their tail when disturbed. Large stingrays can drive their tail spines into a wooden boat. The spines cause serious, extremely painful wounds that, if abdominal, may be fatal.

stock, In finance, the subscribed capital of a corporation or limited-liability company, usually divided into shares and represented by transferable certificates. Many companies have only one class of stock, called common stock. Common stock, as a share of ownership in the company, entitles the holder to an interest in the company's earnings and assets. It carries voting rights that enable the holder to participate in the running of the company (unless such rights are specifically withheld, as in special classes of nonvoting shares). Dividends paid on common stock are often unstable because they vary with earnings; they are also usually less than earnings, the difference being used by the management to expand the firm. To appeal to investors who want to be sure of receiving dividends regularly, some companies issue preferred stock, which has a prior claim to dividends paid by the company and, in most cases, to the company's assets in case of its dissolution. Preferred-stock dividends are usually set at a fixed annual rate that must be paid before dividends are distributed to common stockholders.

stock exchange, or STOCK MARKET, or (in continental Europe) BOURSE, Organized market for the sale and purchase of securities such as stocks and bonds. Trading is done in various ways: it may occur on a continuous auction basis, it may involve brokers buying from and selling to dealers in certain types of stock, or it may be conducted through specialists in a particular stock. Some stock exchanges, such as the New York Stock Exchange (NYSE), sell seats (the right to trade) to a limited number of members who must meet eligibility requirements. Stocks must likewise meet and maintain certain requirements or risk being delisted. Stock exchanges differ from country to country in eligibility requirements and in the degree to which the government participates in their management. The London Stock Exchange, for example, is an independent institution, free from government regulation. In Europe, members of the exchanges are often appointed by government officials and have semigovernmental status. In the U.S., stock exchanges are not directly run by the government but are regulated by law. Technological developments have greatly influenced the nature of trading. In a traditional full-service brokerage, a customer placed an order with a broker or member of a stock exchange, who in turn passed it on to a specialist on the floor of the exchange, who then concluded the transaction. By the 21st century, increased access to the Internet and the proliferation of electronic communications networks (ECNs) altered the investment world. Through e-trading, the customer enters an order directly on-line, and software automatically matches orders to achieve the best price available without the intervention of specialists or market makers. In effect, the ECN is a stock exchange for off-the-floor trading.

Stockholm, City (pop., 2000 est.: city, 750,348; urban agglom.: 1,660,700), capital of Sweden. Built on numerous islands and peninsulas connected by old bridges and modern overpasses, Stockholm is regarded as one of the most beautiful capitals in the world. According to tradition, Swedish ruler Birger Jarl founded Stockholm c. 1250. In the Middle Ages it became Sweden's chief trade port, and in 1436 the capital. After years of conflict between the Swedes and Danes, Gustav I Vasa liberated the city from Danish rule in 1523. It developed rapidly in the mid-17th century as Sweden became a great power, and it was Sweden's cultural centre by the 18th century. It was extensively redeveloped in the 19th century. The second largest port in Sweden (Göteborg being the first), it is the country's leading cultural, commercial, financial, and educational centre.

Stoicism, School of philosophy in Greco-Roman antiquity. Inspired by the teaching of Socrates and Diogenes of Sinope, Stoicism was founded at Athens by Zeno of Citium c. 300 BC and was influential throughout the Greco-Roman world until at least AD 200. It stressed duty and held that, through reason, mankind can come to regard the universe as governed by fate and, despite appearances, as fundamentally rational, and that, in regulating one's life, one can emulate the grandeur of the calm and order of the universe by learning to accept events with a stern and tranquil mind and to achieve a lofty moral worth. Its teachings have been transmitted to later generations largely through the surviving books of Cicero and the Roman Stoics Seneca, Epictetus, and Marcus Aurelius.

stomach, Digestive sac in the left upper abdominal cavity, which expands or contracts with the amount of food in it. It has four regions: the cardia leads down from the esophagus; the fundus curves above it; the body is the largest part; and the antrum nar-

rows to join the duodenum at the pyloric valve. Iron and very fat-soluble substances (e.g., alcohol, some drugs) are absorbed in the stomach. Peristalsis mixes food with enzymes and hydrochloric acid from glands in its lining and moves the resulting chyme toward the small intestine. The vagus nerve and sympathetic nervous system control the stomach's secretions and movements. Emotional stress affects its function. Common disorders include gastritis, peptic ulcer, hiatal hernia, and cancer.

Stone Age, First known period of prehistoric human culture, characterized by the use of stone tools. The term is little used by specialists today. *See* Paleolithic Period; Mesolithic Period; Neolithic Period; stone tool industry.

Stonehenge, Monumental circular arrangement of standing stones built in prehistoric times and located near Salisbury, Wiltshire, Eng. The stones are believed to have been put in place in three main phases c. 3100–c. 1550 BC. The reasons for the building of Stonehenge are unknown, but it is believed to have been a place of worship and ritual. Many theories have been advanced as to its specific purpose (e.g., for the prediction of eclipses), but none has been proved. Stones erected during the second phase of construction (c. 2100 BC) were aligned with the sunrise at the summer solstice, suggesting some ritual connection with that event.

stoneware, Pottery fired at a high temperature (about 2,200 °F, or 1,200 °C) until vitrified (made glasslike and impervious to liquid). Because stoneware is nonporous, glaze is applied only for decoration. Stoneware originated in China c. 1400 BC and was exported to Europe in the 17th century. This red to dark-brown stoneware was copied in Germany, England, and the Netherlands.

Salt-glazed stoneware Bartmannkrug *with applied relief decoration, Cologne, c. 1540; in the Victoria and Albert Museum, London*
Courtesy of the Victoria and Albert Museum, London; photograph, Wilfrid Walter—EB Inc.

stork, Any of 20 species (family Ciconiidae) of voiceless long-necked, mainly Old World birds. Storks are 2–5 ft (60–150 cm) tall, often with a totally or partially bald brightly coloured head and upper neck. They fly by alternately flapping and soaring, with neck outstretched and legs trailing. Most species are diurnal, feeding on small animals in shallow water and fields; some eat carrion. Although they are usually found in flocks, storks pair off during the breeding season, and both parents incubate the eggs. Typical storks have a straight or nearly straight bill; the four species of wood stork have a curved bill. The only U.S. stork, the wood ibis (*Mycteria americana*), is white, with black wings and tail and a curved bill.

strabismus, or SQUINT, or HETEROTROPIA, Failure of the eyes to align properly to focus on an object. The affected eye may deviate in any direction, including inward (cross-eye) or outward (walleye). Problems with photoreception or the nerves that relay images to the brain cause a constant degree of deviation (comitant); defects in the nerves that control the muscles that move the eyes cause deviation that varies with the direction of gaze (noncomitant). Both types impede development of a child's ability to focus the eyes and merge images from the two retinas into one (fusional reflex). The brain suppresses the image from the deviant eye, which may become functionally blind. Treatment may involve exercises to strengthen the weak eye or surgery or both.

strain, In the physical sciences and engineering, a number that describes the relative deformation of elastic, plastic, and fluid materials under applied forces. It arises throughout the material as the particles of the material are displaced from their usual position. Normal strain is caused by forces perpendicular to planes or cross sections of the material, such as in a volume that is under pressure on all sides. Shear strain is caused by forces that are parallel to, and lie in, planes or cross sections, such as in a short metal tube that is twisted about its longitudinal axis.

Strasbourg, German STRASSBURG, City (pop., 2006 est.: 272,975), eastern France. Located on the Franco-German border, Strasbourg was originally a Celtic village; it became a garrison under the Romans. The Franks captured it in the 5th century, and in 842 the Oath of Strasbourg, uniting the western and eastern Franks, was concluded there. It became a free city within the Holy Roman Empire in 1262. It was seized by the French in 1681 and captured by Germany in the Franco-Prussian War (1870–71). It reverted to France after World War I but was occupied by Germany again during World War II, when it suffered considerable damage. A major river port and industrial centre, it is the seat of the Council of Europe and an international communications centre. Notable buildings include the restored medieval cathedral with its 14th-century astronomical clock. The parliament of what is now the European Union has met there since 1979.

Strategic Arms Limitation Talks (SALT), Negotiations between the U.S. and the Soviet Union aimed at curtailing the manufacture of strategic nuclear missiles. The first round of negotiations began in 1969 and resulted in a treaty regulating antiballistic missiles and freezing the number of intercontinental ballistic missiles and submarine-launched ballistic missiles. It was signed by Leonid Brezhnev and Richard Nixon in 1972. A second round of talks (1972–79), known as SALT II, addressed the asymmetry between the two sides' strategic forces and ended with an agreement to limit strategic launchers. Signed by Brezhnev and Jimmy Carter, it was never formally ratified by the U.S. Senate, though its terms were observed by both sides. Subsequent negotiations took the name Strategic Arms Reduction Talks (START).

Strategic Arms Reduction Talks (START), Negotiations between the U.S. and the Soviet Union aimed at reducing those countries' nuclear arsenals and delivery systems. Two sets of negotiations (1982–83, 1985–91) concluded in an agreement signed by George Bush and Mikhail Gorbachev that committed the Soviet Union to a reduction from 11,000 to 8,000 nuclear weapons and the U.S. to a reduction from 12,000 to 10,000. After the Soviet Union's collapse (1991), a supplementary agreement (1992) obligated Ukraine, Belarus, and Kazakhstan to destroy the nuclear weapons on their soil or to give them to Russia. Subsequent U.S. efforts to develop an antimissile defense system threatened new complications for the arms control regime.

Strategic Defense Initiative (SDI), also called STAR WARS, Proposed U.S. strategic defense system against nuclear attacks. Announced as a 20-year, $20 billion effort by Pres. Ronald Reagan in 1983, SDI was intended to defend the U.S. from a full-fledged Soviet attack by intercepting ICBMs in flight. The interception was to be effected by technology not yet developed, including space- and ground-based laser stations and air- and ground-based missiles. The space component of SDI led to its being derisively dubbed "Star Wars" after the popular film. Though the program was roundly criticized by opposition politicians and arms-control advocates as unworkable and as a dangerous violation of the Antiballistic Missile (ABM) Treaty of 1972, Congress granted initial funding for it. Early development efforts were largely unsuccessful, and with the fall of the Soviet Union in 1991 the concept lost urgency. During the Bush and Clinton administrations, ballistic missile defense was scaled back to focus on protecting the U.S. from limited attack by a "rogue" state or a single accidentally launched missile. In 2002 the U.S. withdrew from the ABM treaty to begin active testing of a limited antimissile program.

strategus, In ancient Greece, a general, often functioning as a magistrate with wide powers. Cleisthenes introduced an annual board of 10 *strategi* in Athens to be commanders of the army; one or more, all equal, were responsible for each operation. In the 5th century BC they gained political influence, in part because they were elected and could be reelected, thus were able to entrench themselves in office. In the Hellenistic Age they were the supreme magistrates in most federations and leagues. In Egypt (3rd century BC–4th century AD) they were civil governors.

Stratford-upon-Avon, Town (pop., 2001: 22,187), Warwickshire, England. It is located on the River Avon. The town's first royal charter was granted in 1553. For centuries it was a country market town, but it became a tourist centre because of its association with William Shakespeare, who was born and died there; his grave is in the parish church of Holy Trinity. The Shakespeare Centre in Stratford includes a library and an art gallery (opened 1881) and a theatre (opened 1932). Every year from March until October, Shakespeare's plays are performed in the Royal Shakespeare Theatre.

stratosphere, Layer of the atmosphere that is located above the troposphere. The stratosphere extends from a lower boundary of about 6–11 mi (about 10–17 km) in altitude to an upper boundary (the stratopause) at about 30 mi (50 km). The ozone layer is a part of the stratosphere.

Stravinsky, Igor (Fyodorovich) (b. June 17, 1882, Oranienbaum, Russia—d. April 6, 1971, New York, N.Y., U.S.), Russianborn U.S. composer. Son of an operatic bass, he decided to be a composer at age 20 and studied privately with Nikolay Rimsky-Korsakov (1902–08). His *Fireworks* (1908) was heard by the impresario Sergey Diaghilev, who commissioned Stravinsky to write the *Firebird* ballet (1910); its dazzling success made him Russia's leading young composer. The great ballet score *Petrushka* (1911) followed. His next ballet, *The Rite of Spring* (1913), with its shifting and audacious rhythms and its unresolved dissonances, was a landmark in music history; its Paris premiere caused an actual riot in the theatre, and Stravinsky's international notoriety was assured. In the early 1920s he adopted a radically different style of restrained Neoclassicism—employing often ironic references to older music—in works such as his *Octet* (1923). His major Neoclassical works include *Oedipus rex* (1927) and the *Symphony of Psalms* (1930) and culminate in the opera *The Rake's Progress* (1951). From 1954 he employed serialism, a compositional technique. His later works include *Agon* (1957)—the last of his many ballets choreographed by George Balanchine—and *Requiem Canticles* (1966).

strawberry, Fruit plant of eight main species of the genus *Fragaria* (rose family), the chief cultivated varieties of which are *F. virginiana* and *F. chiloensis*, native to the Americas. The low-growing, herbaceous plant has a fibrous root system and a crown from which basal leaves arise. The leaves are compound, with three leaflets, sawtooth-edged and hairy. Small clusters of white flowers grow on slender stalks. Botanically, the strawberry fruit is not a berry or a single fruit, but is instead a greatly enlarged stem end that contains many partially embedded true fruits (achenes), popularly called seeds. The plant propagates by stolons as it ages. Strawberries are very perishable and require cool, dry storage. They are eaten fresh or prepared for use in desserts or preserves. Rich in vitamin C, they also provide iron and other minerals.

stream of consciousness, Narrative technique in nondramatic fiction intended to render the flow of myriad impressions—visual, auditory, tactile, associative, and subliminal—that impinge on an individual consciousness. To represent the mind at work, a writer may incorporate snatches of thought and grammatical constructions that do not seem coherent because they are based on the free association of ideas and images. The term was first used by William James in *The Principles of Psychology* (1890). In the 20th century, writers attempting to capture the total flow of their characters' consciousness commonly used the techniques of interior monologue, which represents a sequence of thought and feeling. Novels in which stream of consciousness plays an important role include James Joyce's *Ulysses* (1922), William Faulkner's *The Sound and the Fury* (1929), and Virginia Woolf's *The Waves* (1931).

streetcar, or TROLLEY CAR, Passenger-carrying vehicle that runs on rails laid in city streets. Streetcars in the 1830s were pulled by horses. Electric motors later supplied the power, with electricity transmitted by a trolley from overhead electric lines. From the 1890s to the 1940s, streetcars were widely used in cities around the world; they were gradually replaced by the automobile, the bus, and the subway, and by the 1950s few remained. A variant, the cable car, invented in 1873 for use on San Francisco's steep hills, is drawn by a continuous cable set in a slot between the tracks.

streptococcus, Any of the spheroidal bacteria that make up the genus *Streptococcus*. The cells characteristically group together in chains resembling a string of beads. Streptococci are gram-positive and stationary and do not require oxygen. Some species cause infections, including rheumatic fever, scarlet fever, strep throat, and tonsillitis. Others are used in commercial starters for the production of butter, cultured buttermilk, and certain cheeses.

streptomyces, Any of the threadlike bacteria that make up the genus *Streptomyces*, occurring in soil and water. These gram-positive, oxygen-requiring bacteria form a branching net called a mycelium that bears chains of spores at maturity. Many species are important in the decomposition of organic matter in soil, contributing in part to the earthy odour of soil and decaying leaves and to the fertility of soil. Certain species produce antibiotics such as tetracycline and streptomycin.

streptomycin, Antibiotic synthesized by the actinomycete *Streptomyces griseus*, found in soil. It was among the first antibiotics discovered (1943, by Selman Waksman), after penicillin, gramicidin, and tyrocidine. The first antibiotic effective against tuberculosis, it interferes with the tubercle bacillus's ability to synthesize certain vital proteins. It still has some use in combination with penicillin for treating endocarditis and with tetracyclines in the treatment of plague, tularemia, and brucellosis.

Stresemann, Gustav (b. May 10, 1878, Berlin, Ger.—d. Oct. 3, 1929, Berlin), German chancellor and foreign minister of the Weimar Republic. Noted as an expert on municipal affairs and a writer on economics, he was elected to the Reichstag (1907) as a member of the National Liberal Party. In 1918 he founded the German People's Party and sought to form coalitions with other democratic parties. As chancellor (1923) and foreign minister (1923–29), he worked to restore Germany's international status, pursuing a conciliatory policy with the Allied Powers. He negotiated the Pact of Locarno, supported the reparations revisions in the Dawes and Young plans, and secured Germany's admission to the League of Nations. He shared the 1926 Nobel Prize for Peace with Aristide Briand.

Gustav Stresemann.
Bildarchiv Preussischer Kulturbesitz, Berlin

stress, In phonetics, an emphasis given to a syllable of speech by making it louder than the rest of the word. This emphasis may have no meaning; for example, Czech words are regularly stressed on the first syllable. It may, however, distinguish the meanings of similarly spelled but differently pronounced words; for example, *permit* is stressed on the first syllable as a noun and on the second as a verb. It may also be applied to a word to express its importance in a sentence.

stress, In the physical sciences and engineering, the force per unit area within materials that arises from externally applied forces, uneven heating, or permanent deformation. Normal stress refers to the stress caused by forces that are perpendicular to a cross-section area of the material. Shear stress arises from forces that are parallel to the plane of the cross section. Stress is expressed as the quotient of a force divided by an area.

stress, In psychology, a state of bodily or mental tension resulting from factors that tend to alter an existent equilibrium. Stress is an unavoidable effect of living and is an especially complex phenomenon in modern technological society. It has been linked to coronary heart disease, psychosomatic disorders, and various other mental and physical problems. Treatment usually consists of a combination of counseling or psychotherapy and medication.

strike, Collective refusal by employees to work under the conditions set by employers. Strikes may arise from disputes over wages and working conditions. They may also be conducted in sympathy with other striking workers, or for purely political goals. Many strikes are organized by labour unions; strikes not authorized by the union (wildcat strikes) may be directed against union leadership as well as the employer. The right to strike is granted in principle to workers in nearly all industrialized countries, and its use has paralleled the rise of labour unions since the 19th century. Most strikes are intended to inflict a cost to employers for failure to meet specific demands. Among Japanese unions, strikes are not intended to halt production for long periods of time and are more akin to demonstrations. In western Europe and elsewhere, workers have carried out general strikes aimed at winning changes in the political system rather than concessions from employers. The decision to call a strike does not come easily, because union workers risk a loss of income for long periods of time. They also risk the permanent loss of their jobs, especially when replacement workers hired to continue operations during the strike stay on as permanent employees.

string quartet, Ensemble consisting of two violins, viola, and cello, or a work written for such an ensemble. Since *c.* 1775 such works have been perhaps the predominant genre of chamber music. It was principally developed (if not quite invented) by Joseph Haydn, who wrote some 70 quartets between 1757 and 1803. Wolfgang Amadeus Mozart, Ludwig van Beethoven, Franz Schubert, Béla Bartók, and Dmitry Shostakovich are the preeminent subsequent quartet composers. Works called string quartets have traditionally observed the four-movement design of the sonata and symphony. Like most chamber music genres, quartet music was traditionally intended primarily for the private enjoyment of amateur musicians rather than for public performance.

string theory, Any of a number of theories in particle physics that treat elementary particles as infinitesimal one-dimensional "stringlike" objects rather than dimensionless points in space-time. Different vibrations of the strings correspond to different particles. Introduced in the early 1970s in attempts to describe the strong force, string theories became popular in the 1980s when it was shown that they might provide a fully self-consistent quantum field theory that could describe gravitation as well as the weak, strong, and electromagnetic forces. The development of a unified quantum field theory is a major goal in theoretical particle physics, but inclusion of gravity usually leads to difficult problems with infinite quantities in the calculations. The most self-consistent string theories propose 11 dimensions; 4 correspond to the 3 ordinary spatial dimensions and time, while the rest are curled up and not perceptible.

strip mining, Technique for the surface mining of coal by removing the soil and rock overburden above a seam and extracting the exposed mineral. The method is used to best advantage where the coal seam is thin and not deeply buried. (Thicker and deeper seams would be extracted by open-pit or underground mining.) Strip mining is most economical where flat terrain and horizontal seams permit a large area to be stripped. Where deposits occur in rolling or mountainous terrain, a contour method is used that creates a shelf with a slope on one side and an almost vertical wall on the other. A variety of equipment is used, including dozers, scrapers, hydraulic shovels, draglines, and bucket-wheel excavators. Concern over the environmental effects of strip mining have resulted in numerous requirements for the reclamation of excavated land.

stroke, or CEREBROVASCULAR ACCIDENT (CVA), Sudden impairment of brain function due to hypoxia, which may cause death of brain tissue. Hypertension, atherosclerosis, smoking, high cholesterol, diabetes, old age, atrial fibrillation, and genetic defects are risk factors. Strokes due to thrombosis (the most common cause), embolism, or arterial spasm, which cause ischemia (reduced blood supply), must be distinguished from those due to hemorrhage (bleeding), which are usually severe and often fatal. Depending on its site in the brain, a stroke's effects may include aphasia, ataxia, local paralysis, and/or disorders of one or more senses. A massive stroke can produce one-sided paralysis, inability to speak, coma, or death within hours or days. Anticoagulants can arrest strokes caused by clots but worsen those caused by bleeding. If the cause is closure of the major artery to the brain, surgery may clear or bypass the obstruction. Rehabilitation and speech therapy should begin within two days to retain and restore as much function as possible, since survivors may live many more years. Transient ischemic attacks ("mini strokes"), with short-term loss of function, result from blockage of blood flow to small areas. They tend to recur and may worsen, leading to multi-infarct dementia or stroke.

strong force, or STRONG NUCLEAR FORCE, Fundamental force acting between elementary particles of matter, mainly quarks. The strong force binds quarks together in clusters to form protons and neutrons and heavier short-lived particles. It holds together the atomic nucleus and underlies interactions among all particles containing quarks. In strong interactions, quarks exchange gluons, carriers of the strong force, which are massless particles with one unit of intrinsic spin. Within its short range (about 10^{-15} m), the strong force appears to become stronger with distance. At such distances, the strong interaction between quarks is about 100 times greater than the electromagnetic force.

strontium, Chemical element, one of the alkaline earth metals, chemical symbol Sr, atomic number 38. A soft metal, it has a silvery lustre when freshly cut but reacts rapidly with air. In both the metal and the compounds (in which it has valence 2), strontium resembles calcium and barium so closely that it has few uses that the other two elements cannot supply more cheaply. The nitrate and chlorate, very volatile, give off brilliant crimson flames and are used in flares, fireworks, and tracer bullets. The radioactive isotope strontium-90, produced in nuclear explosions, is the principal health hazard in fallout; it can replace some of the calcium in foods, concentrate in bones and teeth, and cause radiation injury.

structuralism, European critical movement of the mid-20th century. It is based on the linguistic theories of Ferdinand de Saussure, which hold that language is a self-contained system of signs, and the cultural theories of Claude Lévi-Strauss, which hold that cultures, like languages, can be viewed as systems of signs and analyzed in terms of the structural relations among their elements. Central to structuralism is the notion that binary oppositions (e.g., male/female, public/private, cooked/raw) reveal the unconscious logic or "grammar" of a system. Literary structuralism views literary texts as systems of interrelated signs and seeks to make explicit their hidden logic. Prominent figures in the structuralist movement are Michel Foucault, Jacques Lacan, Roman Jakobson, and Roland Barthes. Areas of study that have adopted and developed structuralist premises and methodologies include semiotics and narratology.

strychnine, Organic compound, a poisonous alkaloid obtained from seeds of the nux vomica tree of India and related plants of the genus *Strychnos*. It does not dissolve in water nor well in alcohol, and it has an intense bitter taste. It has been used in rodent poisons. Within 20 minutes after ingestion, it causes painful muscle contractions and convulsions, pulling the head back and arching the back; death usually results from respiratory muscle spasms. It is used in small doses by veterinarians as a stimulant.

Stuart, house of, or house of STEWART, or STEUART, Royal house of Scotland (1371–1714) and of England (1603–49, 1660–1714). The earliest members of the family were stewards in 11th-century Brittany; in the 12th century a member entered the service of David I (r. 1124–53) in Scotland and received the title of steward. The 6th steward married the daughter of King Robert I the Bruce, and in 1371 their son became King Robert II, the first Stewart king of Scotland (r. 1371–90). His descendants in the 15th–17th centuries included the Scottish monarchs James I, James II, James III, James IV, Mary, Queen of Scots, and James VI (who inherited the English throne as James I). The Stuarts (who eventually adopted the French-influenced spelling of their name) were excluded from the English throne after Charles I until the restoration of Charles II in 1660. He was followed by James II, William III and Mary II, and Anne. The Stuart royal line ended in 1714, and the British crown passed to the house of Hanover, despite later claims by James II's son James Edward (the Old Pretender) and grandson Charles Edward (the Young Pretender).

studio system, System whereby U.S. movie companies controlled all aspects of production, distribution, and exhibition. In the 1920s film studios such as Paramount and MGM acquired theatre chains to strengthen their vertical control of the industry, and Warner Brothers, RKO, and Twentieth Century-Fox built similar empires soon thereafter. Studio heads exerted control over the types of movies to be made and the directors and actors to be hired; only a few directors maintained some independent control over their films. The studio system also developed the "star system," by which certain actors and actresses were groomed for stardom, with studio executives choosing their roles, publicizing their glamorized offscreen lives, and keeping them under control through long contracts. The system declined after a 1948 Supreme Court decision forced the large studios to sell their theatre chains and increasing competition from television forced studios to limit their staffs, and by the 1960s it had effectively ended.

stupa, Monument erected in memory of the Buddha or a Buddhist saint, often marking a sacred spot, commemorating an event, or housing a relic. Stupas are architectural symbols of the Buddha's death. A simple stupa may consist of a circular earthenware base supporting a massive solid dome from which projects an umbrella, symbolizing protection. This basic design is the inspiration for other types of Buddhist monuments, including pagodas, seen through-

Stupa III and its single gateway, Sanchi, Madhya Pradesh state, India.
Holle Bildarchiv

out Asia. Worship consists of walking clockwise around a stupa. Many important stupas have become places of pilgrimage.

sturgeon, Any of about 20 species (family Acipenseridae) of large, primitive fishes that live mainly in southern Russia, Ukraine, and North America. Most species live in the sea and ascend rivers to spawn; a few live permanently in fresh water. Four tactile barbels near the toothless mouth detect invertebrates and small fishes on the mud bottom. Sturgeon flesh and eggs, or roe (caviar), are sold for food. The swim bladder is used in isinglass, a gelatin. The Baltic sturgeon (*Acipenser sturio*) and several other species are endangered. The Atlantic sturgeon (*A. oxyrhynchus*), however, is common along the eastern coast of North America and generally is about 10 ft (3 m) long and weighs about 500 lb (225 kg).

Sturm und Drang (German: "storm and stress"), German literary movement of the latter half of the 18th century characterized by a revolt against what the writers saw as the Enlightenment cult of rationalism and the sterile imitation of French literature. It exalted nature, intuition, impulse, instinct, emotion, fancy, and inborn genius as the wellsprings of literature. Influenced by Jean-Jacques Rousseau, Johann Gottfried Herder, and others, it took its name from the title of a play by Friedrich von Klinger (1752–1831). Dramatic works were the movement's most characteristic product. Its most gifted representatives were Friedrich Schiller and Johann Wolfgang von Goethe, whose *Sorrows of Young Werther* (1774) epitomizes its spirit.

stuttering, or STAMMERING, or DYSPHEMIA, Speech defect affecting the rhythm and fluency of speech, with involuntary repetition of sounds or syllables and intermittent blocking or prolongation of sounds, syllables, and words. Stutterers consistently have trouble with words starting with consonants, first words in sentences, and multisyllable words. Stuttering has a psychological, not a physiological, basis, tending to appear in children pressured to speak fluently in public. In earlier times, stutterers were subjected to often torturous efforts to cure them. Today it is known that about 80% recover without treatment, usually by early adulthood. This probably results from increased self-esteem, acceptance of the problem, and consequent relaxation.

Stuttgart, City (pop., 2002 est.: city, 587,152; urban agglom., 2,529,675), southwestern Germany. Located on the Neckar River, Stuttgart was originally a 10th-century stud farm. It became a town in the 13th century and passed to the counts of Württemberg, serving as their capital until the 19th century. The Thirty Years' War, French invasions in the 17th century, and heavy bombing during World War II took a toll on the city. Many historic buildings have been rebuilt, including the 13th-century castle. It is a cultural, transportation, industrial, and publishing centre. The University of Stuttgart was founded in 1829.

sty, or HORDEOLUM, Infection of an eyelid gland. An external sty results from infection of a sebaceous gland at the edge of the eyelid; tears flow and the eye feels tender, as if something is in it. The sty reddens and swells. Warm compresses help it break sooner. An internal sty is caused by infection of a meibomian gland under the eyelid lining. More painful than an external sty, it usually breaks through the inner lining of the lid when it discharges and may leave a painless cyst (chalazion) at the site.

Styx, In Greek mythology, a river of the underworld. The name comes from a Greek word that denotes both hatred and extreme cold, and it expresses loathing of death. In the epics of Homer, the gods swore by the water of Styx as their most binding oath. Hesiod personified Styx as the daughter of Oceanus and the mother of Emulation, Victory, Power, and Might. The ancients believed that its water was poisonous and would dissolve any vessel except one made of the hoof of a horse or an ass.

subatomic particle, or ELEMENTARY PARTICLE, Any of various self-contained units of matter or energy. Discovery of the electron in 1897 and of the atomic nucleus in 1911 established that the atom is actually a composite of a cloud of electrons surrounding a tiny but heavy core. By the early 1930s it was found that the nucleus is composed of even smaller particles, called protons and neutrons. In the early 1970s it was discovered that these particles are made up of several types of even more basic units, named quarks, which, together with several types of leptons, constitute the fundamental building blocks of all matter. A third major group of subatomic particles consists of bosons, which transmit the forces of the universe. More than 200 subatomic particles have been detected so far, and most appear to have a corresponding antiparticle.

subbituminous coal, Dark-brown to black coal, intermediate in rank between lignite and bituminous coal. It contains less water and is harder than lignite, making it easier to transport, store, and use. It has lower heating value than bituminous coal, but its sulfur content is often low, so that a number of coal-fired electric-power plants have switched from bituminous to subbituminous coal and lignite (which also tends to have relatively low sulfur). Subbituminous deposits are found in the U.S., Canada, Brazil, Germany, Russia, Ukraine, Australia, and China.

submachine gun, Lightweight automatic small-arms weapon chambered for relatively low-energy pistol cartridges and fired from the hip or shoulder. Submachine guns usually have box-type magazines that hold 10–50 cartridges, or occasionally drums holding more rounds. A short-range weapon, they are rarely effective at more than 200 yards (180 m). They can fire 650 or more rounds per minute and weigh 6–10 lbs (2.5–4.5 kg). Important types include the Thompson submachine gun, or tommy gun (patented 1920), the British Sten gun of World War II, and the later Israeli Uzi.

submarine, Naval vessel capable of operating underwater for sustained periods. In the 18th and 19th centuries, American inventors such as David Bushnell (1742?–1824) and Robert Fulton experimented with hand-powered submarines. In 1898 John P. Holland (1840–1914) launched the *Holland*, which had both a gasoline engine for surface locomotion and a battery-powered electric motor for submerged cruising; it was purchased by the U.S. government in 1900. The innovations of Simon Lake (1866–1945) were adopted first in Europe and later in the U.S. By the eve of World War I, all major navies had diesel-electric submarines. German U-boats were an especially potent threat; through World War II they introduced such innovations as the snorkel, which supplied fresh air to the diesel engine without having to surface the boat. Nuclear-powered submarines began service with the launching of the USS *Nautilus* in 1954. The abundant power provided by uranium-fueled reactors means that nuclear submarines can remain submerged and operate at high speed indefinitely. Only the navies of the U.S., Russia, Britain, France, and China have nuclear-powered submarines; other navies rely on conventional diesel-electric power. Subs may be armed with torpedoes, cruise missiles, or ballistic missiles fitted with nuclear warheads. Because they are so difficult to locate, they are of great importance in the forces of almost all maritime states.

subpoena, In law, a writ commanding the person upon whom it has been served to appear in court or before a congressional committee, grand jury, or some other body, under a penalty for failure to comply. Unlike a summons, a subpoena may command the recipient to produce evidence necessary to the resolution of a legal matter or controversy.

subsidy, Financial assistance, either through direct payments or through indirect means such as price cuts and favourable contracts, to a person or group in order to promote a public objective. Subsidies to transportation, housing, agriculture, mining, and other industries have been instituted on the grounds that their preservation or expansion is in the public interest. Subsidies to the arts, sciences, humanities, and religion also exist in many nations where the private economy is unable to support them. Examples of direct subsidies include payments in cash or in kind, while more-indirect subsidies include governmental provision of goods or services at prices below the normal market price, governmental purchase of goods or services at prices above the market price, and tax concessions. Although subsidies exist to promote the public welfare, they result in either higher taxes or higher prices for consumer goods. Some subsidies, such as protective tariffs, may also encourage the preservation of inefficient producers. A subsidy is desirable only if its effects increase total benefits more than total costs.

subway, Underground railway system used to transport passengers within urban and suburban areas. The first subway line, 3.75 mi (6 km) long, opened in London in 1863 and carried 9½ million passengers in its first year. The first electrified subway opened in 1890 in London (where it is called the underground or tube). Subways opened in Budapest in 1896 (the first on the European continent), Boston in 1897, Paris in 1900 (where it is called the *métro*), Berlin in 1902, New York in 1904, and later in Madrid (1919), Tokyo (1927), and Moscow (1935). Improvements in systems built from the 1970s on (including San Francisco, Washington, D.C., and Los Angeles) include computer technology to run subway trains by remote control, and refinements in track and car construction for faster, smoother, and quieter rides.

succulent, Any plant with fleshy, thick tissues adapted to water storage. Some succulents (e.g., the cactus) store water only in the stem and have no leaves or very small leaves; others (e.g., agaves) store water mainly in the leaves. Most have deep or broad root systems and are native to either deserts or regions that have a semiarid season. In succulents, the stomata close during the day and open at night—the opposite of the usual pattern—in order to minimize transpiration.

Sucre, Judicial capital (pop., 2001: 193,873), Bolivia. Founded by the Spanish (*c.* 1539) on the site of a Charcas Indian village, it became the capital of the Charcas territory of Upper Peru in 1561 and in 1609 the seat of an archdiocese. Many of its colonial churches survive. It was an early scene (1809) of the revolt against Spain. The Bolivian declaration of independence was signed there in 1825, and it became the capital in 1839. An effort to move the capital to La Paz in 1898 precipitated a civil war, which left the two cities sharing capital status. Sucre is also the seat of the national supreme court. It is a growing commercial centre. The University of San Francisco Xavier, one of the oldest universities in South America, was founded there in 1624.

sucrose, or TABLE SUGAR, Organic compound, colourless, sweet-tasting crystals that dissolve in water. Sucrose ($C_{12}H_{22}O_{11}$) is a disaccharide; hydrolysis, by the enzyme invertase, yields "invert sugar" (so called because the hydrolysis results in an inversion of the rotation of plane polarized light), a 50:50 mixture of fructose and glucose, its two constituent monosaccharides. Sucrose occurs naturally in sugarcane, sugar beets, sugar-maple sap, dates, and honey. It is produced commercially in large amounts (especially from sugarcane and sugar beets) and is used almost entirely as food.

Sudan, officially REPUBLIC OF THE SUDAN, Country, northeastern Africa. Area: 712,280 sq mi (1,844,797 sq km). Population: (2011 est.) 36,787,000. Capitals: Khartoum (executive), Omdurman (legislative). People identifying themselves as Arab predominate, but other ethnic groups also live in the country. Languages: Arabic, English (official working languages), Nubian languages, others. Religions: Islam (predominantly Sunni); also Christianity, traditional beliefs. Currency: Sudanese pound. The country encompasses an immense plain with the Sahara Desert in the north-

centre, sand dunes in the west, and semiarid shrublands in the south-central belt. The Nile River flows through the entire length of the country. Wildlife includes lions, leopards, elephants, and giraffes. Sudan has a developing mixed economy based largely on oil and agriculture. One of the largest irrigation projects in the world provides water to farms between the White Nile and the Blue Nile. Chief cash crops are cotton, peanuts, and sesame; livestock is also important. Major industries include food processing and cotton ginning, and petroleum is the main export. The country is ruled by a military-backed regime; the head of state and government is the president, assisted by vice presidents. Evidence of human habitation dates back tens of thousands of years. From the end of the 4th millennium BCE, Nubia (now northern Sudan) periodically came under Egyptian rule, and it was part of the kingdom of Cush from the 11th century BCE to the 4th century CE. Christian missionaries converted the area's three principal kingdoms during the 6th century CE; those black Christian kingdoms coexisted with their Muslim Arab neighbours in Egypt for centuries, until the influx of Arab immigrants brought about their collapse in the 13th–15th centuries. Egypt had conquered all of the Sudan region by 1874 and encouraged British interference there; this aroused Muslim opposition and led to the revolt of the Mahdī, who captured Khartoum in 1885 and established a Muslim theocracy in the Sudan that lasted until 1898, when his forces were defeated by the British. The British ruled, generally in partnership with Egypt, until the region achieved independence in 1956. Since then the country has fluctuated between ineffective parliamentary government and unstable military rule, with the distraction of long-running civil wars (1955–72; 1983–2005) between the northern-based government and southern rebels. Meanwhile, fighting broke out in 2003 in the Darfur region of western Sudan; tens of thousands of people were killed and hundreds of thousands were displaced. In 2011 the southern Sudanese population voted overwhelmingly in favour of independence from the north and seceded on July 9.

sudden infant death syndrome (SIDS), or CRIB DEATH, Unexpected death of an apparently well infant. It occurs almost always during sleep at night and usually at 2–4 months of age. Sleeping facedown and exposure to cigarette smoke have been implicated. It is more common in cases of premature birth, low birth weight, and poor prenatal care. Many cases that would once have been labeled SIDS prove to be due to suffocation in bedding or overheating. Some babies who die of SIDS have been found to have brain stem abnormalities that interfere with their response to high levels of carbon dioxide in the blood.

Suez, Gulf of, Northwestern extension of the Red Sea. It is located between Africa and the Sinai Peninsula and is roughly 195 mi (314 km) long and 12–20 mi (19–32 km) wide. Linked to the Mediterranean Sea by the Suez Canal, it is an important shipping route. In the 1970s and '80s, oil was discovered at numerous locations in the gulf.

Suez Canal, Ship canal, Isthmus of Suez, Egypt. Connecting the Red Sea with the eastern Mediterranean Sea, it extends 101 mi (163 km) from Port Said to the Gulf of Suez and allows ships to sail directly between the Mediterranean and the Indian Ocean. Built by the French-owned Suez Canal Co., it was completed in 1869 after a decade of construction. Its ownership remained largely in French and British hands until Egypt nationalized it in 1956, setting off an international crisis. It has a minimum width of 179 ft (55 m) and a depth of about 40 ft (12 m) at low tide. Though protected by international treaty, the canal has been closed twice. The first closing was during the Suez Crisis. The canal was closed again by the Six-Day War (1967) and remained inoperative until 1975. It is one of the world's most heavily used shipping lanes.

Suez Crisis (1956) International crisis that arose when Egyptian president Gamal Abdel Nasser nationalized the Suez Canal after Western countries withdrew promised financial aid to build the

Aswan High Dam. The French and British, who had controlling interests in the company that owned the canal, sent troops to occupy the canal zone. Their ally Israel seized the Sinai Peninsula. International opposition quickly forced the French and British out, and Israel withdrew in 1957. The incident led to the resignation of Britain's prime minister, Anthony Eden, and was widely perceived as heralding the end of Britain as a major international power. Nasser's prestige, by contrast, soared within the developing world.

Sufism, Mystical movement within Islam that seeks to find divine love and knowledge through direct personal experience of God. It consists of a variety of mystical paths that are designed to ascertain the nature of mankind and God and to facilitate the experience of divine love and wisdom in the world. Sufism arose as an organized movement after the death of Muhammad (632 CE), among different groups who found orthodox Islam to be spiritually stifling. The practices of contemporary Sufi orders and suborders vary, but most include the recitation of the name of God or of certain phrases from the Qu'rān as a way to loosen the bonds of the lower self, enabling the soul to experience the higher reality toward which it naturally aspires. Though Sufi practitioners have often been at odds with the mainstream of Islamic theology and law, the importance of Sufism in the history of Islam is incalculable. Sufi literature, especially love poetry, represents a golden age in Arabic, Persian, Turkish, and Urdu languages.

sugar, Any of numerous sweet, colourless organic compounds that dissolve readily in water and occur in the sap of seed plants and the milk of mammals. Sugars (whose names end in *-ose*) are the simplest carbohydrates. The most common is sucrose, a disaccharide; there are numerous others, including glucose and fructose (both monosaccharides); invert sugar (a 50:50 mixture of glucose and fructose produced by enzyme action on sucrose); and maltose (produced in the malting of barley) and lactose (both disaccharides). Commercial production of sugars is almost entirely for food.

sugar beet, Variety of beet (*Beta vulgaris*) that accounts for about two-fifths of global sugar production, making it second only to sugarcane as a source of the world's sugar. Unlike sugarcane, sugar beets can be grown in temperate or cold climates in Europe, North America, and Asia; that is, within the densely populated, well-developed areas where much of the product is consumed. The sugar beet was grown as a garden vegetable and for fodder long before it was valued for its sugar content.

*Sugar beet (*Beta vulgaris*).*
Grant Heilman/EB Inc.

*Sugarcane (*Saccharum officinarum*)*
Ray Manley/Shostal Associates

sugarcane, Giant, thick, perennial grass belonging to the genus *Saccharum* (family Poaceae), cultivated in tropical and subtropical regions worldwide for its sweet sap, a major source of sugar and molasses. The plant grows in clumps of solid stalks with regularly spaced nodes or joints, each with a bud that can be planted for commercial asexual propagation. Graceful, sword-shaped leaves, similar to those of the corn plant, fold in a sheath around the stem. Mature canes may be 10–20 ft (3–6 m) tall and 1–3 in. (2.5–7.5 cm) in diame-

ter. Molasses, the syrup remaining after sugar is crystallized out of the juice, is used in cooking, in making rum, and as feed for farm animals. Residual cane fibre (bagasse) is burned as fuel or used as filler for paper and particleboard.

Sui dynasty (581–618) Short-lived Chinese dynasty that unified northern and southern China after centuries of division. Under the Sui, the cultural and artistic renaissance that was to reach its height under the succeeding Tang dynasty was set in motion. The first Sui emperor, Wendi, established uniform institutions of government throughout the country, promulgated a new legal system, conducted a census, recruited officials through examinations, and reestablished Confucian rituals. The Sui conducted three costly and unsuccessful campaigns against the Korean kingdom of Koguryŏ. The Sui capital at Chang'an was, in design, six times the size of the modern city of Xi'an at the same site.

suicide, Act of intentionally taking one's own life. Suicide may have psychological origins such as the difficulty of coping with depression or other mental disorders; it may be motivated by the desire to test the affection of loved ones or to punish their lack of support with the burden of guilt. It may also stem from social and cultural pressures, especially those that tend to increase isolation, such as bereavement or estrangement. Attitudes toward suicide have varied in different ages and cultures; convicted criminals in ancient Greece were permitted to take their own lives, and the Japanese custom of seppuku (also called hara-kiri), or self-disembowelment, allowed samurai to commit ritual suicide as a way of protecting honour and demonstrating loyalty. Jews committed suicide rather than submit to ancient Roman conquerors or crusading knights who intended to force their conversion. In the 20th century, members of new religious movements, notably the Peoples Temple and Heaven's Gate, committed mass suicide. Buddhist monks and nuns have also committed sacrificial suicide by self-immolation as a form of social protest. Japan's use of kamikaze suicide bombers during World War II was a precursor to the suicide bombing that emerged in the late 20th century as a form of terrorism, particularly among Islamic extremists. Suicide, however, is generally condemned by Islam, Judaism, and Christianity, and attempts to commit suicide are still punishable by law in many countries. Some communities around the world have sought to legalize physician-assisted suicide for the terminally ill. Euthanasia was legalized in the Netherlands in 2001 and Belgium in 2002, and it is openly practiced in Colombia. Since the 1950s suicide-prevention organizations have been established in many countries, with telephone hotlines serving as a source of readily available counseling.

Sukarno (b. June 6, 1901, Surabaja, Java, Dutch East Indies—d. June 21, 1970, Jakarta, Indon.), First president of Indonesia (1949–67). Son of a Javanese schoolteacher, he excelled in languages, mastering Javanese, Sundanese, Balinese, and modern Indonesian, which he did much to create. He emerged as a charismatic leader in the country's independence movement. When the Japanese invaded in 1942, he served them as a chief adviser, while pressuring them to grant Indonesia independence. Immediately following Japan's defeat, he declared independence; the Dutch did not transfer sovereignty until 1949. Once he became president, Indonesia made gains in health, education, and cultural self-awareness, but democracy and the economy foundered. His government was corrupt, inflation soared, and the country experienced a continuous state of crisis. An attempted coup, purportedly by communists, in 1965 led to a military takeover by Suharto and a purge of alleged communists. Stripped of his power in 1966, Sukarno resigned in 1967 and lived under house arrest until his death.

Sukhothai style, Canonical style for Buddha icons developed probably in the kingdom of Sukhothai (modern Thailand), beginning in the 14th century. The Sukhothai Buddhas—typically either seated in the half-lotus posture with right hand performing the earth-touching gesture or walking with one foot forward and the right hand raised to the chest—have a boneless, weightless elegance. The parts of the body follow abstract ideals based on analogy with natural forms (e.g., shoulders like an elephant's trunk, torso like a lion). The head typically bears a flamelike protuberance above a cranial bump, which the faithful believe contains an extra brain cavity.

sukiya style, Japanese architectural style developed in the Azuchi-Momoyama (1574–1600) and Tokugawa (1603–1867) periods, originally used for teahouses and later also for private residences and restaurants. Based on an aesthetic of naturalness and rustic simplicity, buildings in this style are intended to harmonize with their surroundings. Timber construction is employed, with wood left in a natural state, sometimes with the bark still attached. Walls are typically made of clay. Great attention is paid to detail and proportions, and the effect is one of refined simplicity. The architect Yoshida Isoya (1894–1974) pioneered a modern *sukiya* style using contemporary materials.

Süleyman I, or SÜLEYMAN THE MAGNIFICENT (b. November 1494–April 1495—d. Sept. 5/6, 1566, near Szigetvár, Hung.), Ottoman sultan (r. 1520–66). He became sultan of the Ottoman Empire after serving as a provincial governor under his grandfather Bayezid II and his father, Selim I (r. 1512–20). He immediately began leading campaigns against the Christians, taking Belgrade (1521) and Rhodes (1522). At the Battle of Mohács (1526) he broke the military strength of Hungary. In 1529 he laid siege to Vienna but failed to capture it. Further campaigns in Hungary (1541, 1543) left the region divided between Habsburg- and Ottoman-dominated areas. Iraq and eastern Anatolia were captured during his first campaign (1534–35) against the Persian Ṣafavid dynasty; his second (1548–49) brought conquests in southern Anatolia around Lake Van; but his third (1554–55) was unsuccessful. His navy, under Barbarossa, controlled the Mediterranean Sea. He built mosques, bridges, and aqueducts and surrounded himself with great poets and legal scholars. His reign is considered a high point of Ottoman civilization.

sulfur, Nonmetallic chemical element, chemical symbol S, atomic number 16. It is very reactive but occurs native in deposits, as well as combined in various ores (e.g., pyrite, galena, cinnabar); in coal, petroleum, and natural gas; and in the water in sulfur springs. Sulfur is the third most abundant constituent of minerals and one of the four most important basic chemical commodities. Pure sulfur, a tasteless, odourless, brittle yellow solid, occurs in several crystalline and amorphous allotropes, including brimstone and flowers of sulfur.

Sulfur crystals from Sicily (greatly enlarged)
Courtesy of the Illinois State Museum; photograph, John H. Gerard/EB Inc.

It combines, with valence 2, 4, or 6, with nearly all other elements. Its most familiar compound is hydrogen sulfide, a poisonous gas that smells like rotten eggs. All metals except gold and platinum form sulfides, and many ores are sulfides. The oxides are sulfur dioxide and sulfur trioxide, which when dissolved in water make sulfurous acid and sulfuric acid, respectively. Several sulfur compounds with halogen elements are industrially important. Sodium sulfite (Na_2SO_3) is a reducing agent used to pulp paper and in photography. Organic compounds with sulfur include several amino acids, the sulfa drugs, and many insecticides, solvents, and substances used in making rubber and rayon.

sulfuric acid, or OIL OF VITRIOL, Dense, colourless, oily, corrosive liquid inorganic compound (H_2SO_4). A very strong acid, it forms ions of hydrogen or hydronium (H^+ or H_3O^+), hydrogen sulfate ($HSO_4{}^-$), and sulfate ($SO_4{}^{2-}$). It is also an oxidizing and dehydrating agent and chars many organic materials. It is one of the most important industrial chemicals, used in various concentrations in manufacturing fertilizers, pigments, dyes, drugs, explosives, detergents, and inorganic salts and acids, in petroleum refining and metallurgical processes, and as the acid in lead-acid storage batteries. It is made industrially by dissolving sulfur trioxide (SO_3) in water, sometimes beyond the saturation point to make oleum (fuming sulfuric acid), used to make certain organic chemicals.

Sully Prudhomme, orig. RENÉ-FRANÇOIS-ARMAND PRUDHOMME (b. March 16, 1839, Paris, France—d. Sept. 7, 1907, Châtenay), French poet. Inspired at first by an unhappy love affair, he published fluent and melancholic verse in volumes beginning with *Stances et poèmes* (1865), containing his well-known "Le Vase brise." He later adopted the more objective approach of the Parnassian poets and attempted to represent philosophical concepts in verse. Among his best-known later works are *La Justice* (1878) and *Le Bonheur* (1888). In 1901 he was awarded the first Nobel Prize for Literature, over such greatly admired figures as Leo Tolstoy.

Sully Prudhomme.
H. Roger-Viollet

sumac, Any of certain species of shrubs and small trees in the genus *Rhus* of the family Anacardiaceae (the sumac, or cashew, family), native to temperate and subtropical zones. All sumacs have a milky or resinous sap, which in some species (e.g., poison sumac) can irritate the skin. Used in the past as a source of dyes, medicines, and beverages, sumacs are now valued as ornamentals, soil binders, and cover plants. The sumacs grown for landscape use display a graceful form, spectacular fall colour, or colourful fruit clusters. The smooth, or scarlet, sumac (*R. glabra*), native to the eastern and central U.S., is the most common.

Sumatra, Island (pop., 2000 including adjoining islands: 43,309,707), western Indonesia. It is one of the Sunda Islands and the second largest island of Indonesia. It is 1,060 mi (1,706 km) long and 250 mi (400 km) wide. A chief city is Palembang. Located on the seaborne trade routes, the island had early contact with Hindu civilization. The Srivijaya empire arose in the 7th century and came to dominate much of the island. It fell under the Majapahit empire in the 14th–16th centuries. First the Portuguese, then the Dutch and English established forts there beginning in the 16th century. It was occupied by Japan in World War II and in 1950 became part of the Republic of Indonesia. Its exports include rubber, tobacco, coffee, pepper, and timber products; mineral reserves include petroleum and coal. In 2004 a large tsunami generated by a massive earthquake off the west coast of Sumatra caused widespread death and destruction in coastal areas bordering the Indian Ocean.

Sumer, Region of southern Mesopotamia and site of the earliest known civilization. It was first settled *c.* 4500–4000 BC by a non-Semitic people called the Ubaidians, who drained the marshes for agriculture and developed trade. The Sumerians, who spoke a Semitic language that came to dominate the region, arrived *c.* 3300 BC and established the world's first known cities. These polities evolved into city-states, which eventually developed monarchical systems that later came to be loosely united under a single city, beginning with Kish *c.* 2800 BC. Thereafter, Kish, Erech, Ur, and Lagash vied for ascendancy for centuries; Nippur emerged as a religous centre. The area came under the control of dynasties from outside the region, beginning with Elam (*c.* 2530–2450 BC) and later Akkad, led by the Akkadian king Sargon (r. 2334–2279 BC). After the Akkadian dynasty collapsed, the city-states were largely independent until they were reunified under the 3rd dynasty of Ur (22nd–21st century BC). That final Sumerian dynasty declined after being weakened by foreign invasions, and the Sumerians as a distinct political entity disappeared, becoming part of Babylonia in the 18th century BC. The Sumerian legacy includes a number of technological and cultural innovations, including the first known wheeled vehicles, the potter's wheel, a system of writing (cuneiform), and written codes of law.

summons, In law, written notification that one is required to appear in court. In civil (noncriminal) cases, it notifies a defendant that he or she must appear and defend (e.g., by filing an answer) within a specified time or a default judgment will be rendered for the plaintiff. The summons is also used in cases involving minor criminal offenses (e.g., traffic violations) to call defendants to appear and answer to charges against them.

sumo, Japanese form of wrestling. A contestant loses if he is forced out of the ring (a 15-ft circle) or if any part of his body except the soles of his feet touches the ground. In sumo, a wrestler's weight, size, and strength are of the greatest importance, though speed and suddenness of attack are also useful. The wrestlers, who are fed a special protein diet and may weigh over 300 lbs (136 kg), wear only loincloths and grip each other by the belt. Sumo wrestling is an ancient sport with a complex system of ranking; at the top of the hierarchy is the *yokozuna* ("grand champion"). Lengthy rituals and elaborate posturings accompany the bouts, which are extremely brief, often lasting only a few seconds.

Sun, Star around which the components of the solar system revolve. It is about 4.6 billion years old and is the dominant body of the system, with more than 99% of its mass. It converts about 4.5 million tons of matter into energy every second by nuclear fusion reactions in its core, producing neutrinos and solar radiation. The small amount of this energy that penetrates Earth's atmosphere provides the light and heat that support life. A sphere of luminous gas 1,392,000 km (864,950 mi) in diameter, the Sun has about 330,000 times the mass of Earth. Its core temperature is close to 15,000,000 K (27,000,000 °F) and its surface temperature about 6,000 K (10,000 °F). The Sun, a spectral type G2 V (yellow) star, has fairly average properties for a main-sequence star. It rotates at different rates at different latitudes; one rotation takes 36 days at the poles but only 25 days at the equator. The visible surface, or photosphere, is in constant motion, with the number and position of sunspots changing in a regular solar cycle. External phenomena include magnetic activity extending into the chromosphere and corona, solar flares, solar prominences, and the solar wind. Effects on Earth include auroras and disruption of radio communications and power-transmission lines. Despite its activity, the Sun appears to have remained relatively unchanged for billions of years.

sun worship, Veneration of the sun or its representation as a deity. It appears in several early cultures, notably in ancient Egypt, Indo-Europe, and Mesoamerica, where urban civilizations were combined with a strong ideology of sacred kingship, in which kings ruled by the power of the sun and claimed descent from it. The imagery of the sun as the ruler of both the upper and the lower world, which he visits daily, was prominent. Sun heroes and deities also figure in many mythologies, including Indo-Iranian, Greco-Roman, and Scandinavian. In late Roman history, sun worship was of such importance that it was later called "solar monotheism." *See also* Amaterasu, Re, Shamash, Sol, Surya, Tonatiuh.

Sun Yat-sen, or SUN YIXIAN (b. Nov. 12, 1866, Xiangshan, Guangdong province, China—d. March 12, 1925, Beijing), Leader of the Chinese Nationalist Party, known as the father of modern China. Educated in Hawaii and Hong Kong, Sun em-

Sun Yat-sen
Brown Brothers

barked on a medical career in 1892, but, troubled by the conservative Qing dynasty's inability to keep China from suffering repeated humiliations at the hands of more advanced countries, he forsook medicine two years later for politics. A letter to Li Hongzhang in which Sun detailed ways that China could gain strength made no headway, and he went abroad to try organizing expatriate Chinese. He spent time in Hawaii, England, Canada, and Japan and in 1905 became head of a revolutionary coalition, the Tongmenghui ("Alliance Society"). The revolts he helped plot during this period failed, but in 1911 a rebellion in Wuhan unexpectedly succeeded in overthrowing the provincial government. Other provincial secessions followed, and Sun returned to be elected provisional president of a new government. The emperor abdicated in 1912, and Sun turned over the government to Yuan Shikai. The two men split in 1913, and Sun became head of a separatist regime in the south. In 1924, aided by Soviet advisers, he reorganized his Nationalist Party, admitted three communists to its central executive committee, and approved the establishment of a military academy, to be headed by Chiang Kai-shek. He also delivered lectures on his doctrine, the Three Principles of the People (nationalism, democracy, and people's livelihood), but died the following year without having had the opportunity to put his doctrine into practice.

sunburn, Acute skin inflammation caused by overexposure to ultraviolet radiation from sunlight or other sources. More common and severe in light-skinned people, it ranges from mild redness and tenderness to intense pain, edema, and blistering, sometimes with shock, fever, and nausea. The process begins after 15 minutes in the sun, but redness starts 6–12 hours later and peaks within a day. Pigment cells in the skin increase melanin production ("tan"). Cold compresses and analgesics reduce pain. Limiting sun exposure, using sunscreen, and wearing protective clothing can prevent severe sunburn. Long-term sun exposure can eventually cause skin cancer, as well as skin wrinkling and thickening.

sunna, Body of traditional social and legal custom and practice that constitutes proper observance of Islam. Early Muslims did not concur on what constituted sunna, because of the wide variety of pre-Islamic practices among converted peoples that had to be assimilated, reconciled, or abandoned. In the 8th century the sunna of Muhammad, as preserved in eyewitness records, was codified as the Ḥadīth by Abū ʿAbd Allāh Shāfʿī. Later Muslim scholars strengthened the authority of sunna by devising a system for attesting the authenticity of various practices claimed as descending from Muhammad.

Sunnite, Larger of the two major divisions of Islam, comprising 90% of the world's Muslims. Sunnites regard theirs as the mainstream and traditionalist branch of Islam, as distinguished from the minority branch, the Shīʿites. Sunnites recognize the first four Umayyad caliphs as Muhammad's rightful successors. Because the Sunnites understood Muhammad's theocratic state to have been an earthly, temporal dominion, they were willing to accept unexceptional and even foreign caliphs, provided order and religious orthodoxy were maintained. Sunnite orthodoxy emphasizes consensus based on the views and customs of the majority of the community, thereby enabling them to incorporate various customs and usages that arose historically but that had no roots in the Qurʾān. Sunnites recognize the six authentic books of the Ḥadīth and accept the four major schools of Islamic law. In the early 21st century, Sunnite Muslims numbered about one billion.

sunspot, Cooler-than-average region of gas on the Sun's surface associated with strong local magnetic activity. Sunspots appear as dark spots, but only in contrast with the surrounding photosphere, which is several thousand degrees hotter. Spots several times larger than Earth are visible to the unaided eye (viewed through a filter); very small ones are hard to see even with a telescope. They come and go as part of the solar cycle, usually in pairs or groups, and may last for months; their cause appears to be related to the magnetic field reversals that occur every 11 years. The reality of these apparent flaws in the Sun was generally accepted only *c.* 1611. Periods of high sunspot activity are associated on Earth with brighter auroras and interference with radio signals.

Sunzi, or SUN-TZU (fl. 5th century BC), Chinese military strategist. A general who served the state of Wu late in the Spring and Autumn period (770–476 BC), he is traditionally regarded as the author of the earliest known treatise on war and military science, *The Art of War*, though it was more likely written early in the Warring States period (475–221 BC). A systematic guide to strategy and tactics, it discusses various maneuvers and the effect of terrain, stresses the importance of accurate information about the enemy's forces, and emphasizes the unpredictability of battle and the need for flexible responses. Its insistence on the close relationship between political considerations and military policy influenced modern strategists, notably Mao Zedong.

Super Bowl, Annual championship game of the National Football League. It is played by the winners of the league's American Football Conference and National Football Conference. The first Super Bowl competition was held in 1967. It normally falls in January, usually on the last Sunday, and is watched by more Americans than any other sporting event.

supercomputer, Any of a class of extremely powerful digital computers. The term is commonly applied to the fastest high-performance systems available at a given time; current personal computers are more powerful than the supercomputers of just a few years ago. Supercomputers are used primarily for scientific and engineering work. Unlike conventional computers, they usually have more than one CPU, often functioning in parallel (simultaneously); even higher-performance supercomputers are now being developed through use of massively parallel processing, incorporating thousands of individual processors. Supercomputers have huge storage capacity and very fast input/output capability, and can operate in parallel on corresponding elements of arrays of numbers rather than on one pair of elements at a time.

superconductivity, Almost total lack of electrical resistance in certain materials when they are cooled to a temperature near absolute zero. Superconducting materials allow low power dissipation, high-speed operation, and high sensitivity. They also have the ability to prevent external magnetic fields from penetrating their interiors and are perfect diamagnets. Since it was first discovered in mercury by Heike Kamerlingh Onnes in 1911, similar behaviour has been found in some 25 other chemical elements and in thousands of alloys and compounds. Superconductors have applications in medical imaging, magnetic energy-storage systems, motors, generators, transformers, computer components, and sensitive magnetic-field measuring devices.

superfluidity, Unusual property of liquid helium cooled below −455.75 °F (−270.97 °C). At such low temperatures, helium exhibits an enormous rise in heat conductivity and rapid flow through capillaries or over the rim of its container. To explain such behaviour, the substance is described in terms of a "two-fluid" mixture model consisting of normal helium and superfluid helium. In normal helium the atoms are in excited states, whereas in superfluid helium they are in their ground state. As the temperature is lowered below −455.75 °F, more of the helium becomes super-

fluid. It is assumed that the superfluid component can move through the container without friction, thereby explaining the unusual behaviour.

supergiant star, Star of very great natural luminosity and relatively enormous size, typically several magnitudes brighter and several times larger than a giant star. Like other classes of stars, they are distinguished in practice by examination of certain lines in their spectra. A supergiant may have a diameter several hundred times that of the Sun and a luminosity nearly a million times as great. Supergiants live probably only a few million years, an extremely short life for a star.

supernova, Any of a class of violently exploding stars whose luminosity after eruption suddenly increases many millions of times above its normal level. Like novas, supernovas undergo a tremendous, rapid brightening lasting a few weeks, followed by a slow dimming, and show blue-shifted emission lines on spectroscopy, which implies that hot gases are blown outward. Unlike a nova, a supernova explosion is a catastrophic event for a star, leading to its collapse into a neutron star or black hole. Amounts of its matter equal to the mass of several Suns may be blasted into space with such energy that the exploding star outshines its entire home galaxy. Only seven supernovas are known to have been recorded before the 17th century, the most famous in AD 1054; its remnants are visible today as the Crab Nebula. The closest and most studied supernova in modern times is SN 1987A, which appeared in 1987 in the Large Magellanic Cloud. Supernova explosions release not only tremendous amounts of radio energy and X-rays but also cosmic rays; in addition, they create and fling into interstellar space many of the heavier elements found in the universe, including those forming Earth's solar system.

supply and demand, Relationship between the quantity of a commodity that producers have available for sale and the quantity that consumers are willing and able to buy. Demand depends on the price of the commodity, the prices of related commodities, and consumers' incomes and tastes. Supply depends not only on the price obtainable for the commodity but also on the prices of similar products, the techniques of production, and the availability and costs of inputs. The function of the market is to equalize demand and supply through the price mechanism. If buyers want to purchase more of a commodity than is available on the market, they will tend to bid the price up. If more of a commodity is available than buyers care to purchase, suppliers will bid prices down. Thus, there is a tendency toward an equilibrium price at which the quantity demanded equals the quantity supplied. The measure of the responsiveness of supply and demand to changes in price is their elasticity.

supply-side economics, Theory that focuses on influencing the supply of labour and goods, using tax cuts and benefit cuts as incentives to work and produce goods. It was expounded by the U.S. economist Arthur Laffer (b. 1940) and implemented by Pres. Ronald Reagan in the 1980s. Supporters point to the economic growth of the 1980s as proof of its efficacy; detractors point to the massive federal deficits and speculation that accompanied that growth.

Surabaya, Seaport city (pop., 2003 est.: 2,660,381), northeastern coast of Java, Indonesia. It is Indonesia's second-largest city and has been eastern Java's chief trading centre since the 14th century. The Dutch gained control in the 18th century and built their main East Indies naval base there. Occupied by the Japanese in World War II, it suffered heavy damage; it was damaged again during Indonesia's war for independence (1945–49). It is the site of Indonesia's main naval base and a naval college, and of Airlangga University (1954).

sūrah, or SURA, Any chapter of the Qur'ān. According to Muslim belief, each of the 114 *sūrah*s, which vary in length from several lines (known as *āyah*s) to several pages, encompasses one or more divine revelations of Muhammad. All but three lines are in the form of a direct address from God. The tone of each varies but is generally moralistic, demanding obedience to a transcendent but compassionate God. Except for the opening *sūrah*, known as *fātiḥah* (the "opening"), they are arranged in descending order of length and numbered serially. They carry conventional names (e.g., Cow, Spider, Blood Clot) deriving from some image contained in them that is not necessarily indicative of their meaning or theme.

Surat, City (pop., 2001: 2,433,835), southeastern Gujarat state, west-central India. It is near the mouth of the Tapti River and the Gulf of Khambhat (Cambay). A major seaport from the 16th century, it was conquered by the Mughals in 1573 and was twice sacked by the Marathas in the 17th century. It became a centre for textile manufacturing and shipbuilding. The British established their first factory (trading post) in India there *c.* 1612, marking the beginning of the British imperial presence in India. The city declined in the 18th century but prospered again with the opening of India's railways. Surat's cottons, silks, brocades, and objects of gold and silver are still famous.

surface tension, Property of a liquid surface that causes it to act like a stretched elastic membrane. Its strength depends on the forces of attraction among the particles of the liquid itself and with the particles of the gas, solid, or liquid with which it comes in contact. Surface tension allows certain insects to stand on the surface of water and can support a razor blade placed horizontally on the liquid's surface, even though the blade may be denser than the liquid and unable to float. Surface tension results in spherical drops of liquid, as the liquid tends to minimize its surface area.

surfing, Sport of riding breaking waves toward the shore, especially with a surfboard. The sport originated prehistorically in the South Seas. In 1777 and 1778 Capt. James Cook first reported seeing surfers in Tahiti and on Oahu. In 1821 surfing was banned by missionaries who thought it immoral. It was revived in the 1920s by the Hawaiian swimmer Duke Kahanamoku (1890–1968). Today surfing is enjoyed on beaches with breakers throughout the world, and several international championships are held. The goal is to maneuver on the unbroken face of the wave, preferably as far back toward the curl ("tube") as possible. In addition to surfboards, surfers can use belly-boards, kneeboards, or kayaks, or they can bodysurf using no board at all.

surgery, Branch of medicine concerned with treatment by physical means rather than drugs. In addition to operations requiring access to the inside of the body (open surgery), it includes manipulation from outside the body (e.g., setting of a broken bone, skin grafts). Modern surgery began in the mid-19th century with use of anesthetics and antiseptics. Other important advances have included diagnostic imaging, blood typing, intubation to support breathing, intravenous administration of fluids and drugs, heart-lung machines, endoscopy, and devices that monitor body functions. Specialized instruments used in surgery include scalpels to cut tissue, forceps to hold blood vessels closed or grasp and manipulate structures, clamps to immobilize or crush tissues, gauze sponges to absorb fluids and keep an area dry, retractors to hold incisions open, and curved needles to suture them closed. Pre- and postoperative care is crucial to the success of surgery.

Suriname, officially REPUBLIC OF SURINAME, formerly DUTCH GUIANA, Country, northern coast of South America. Area: 63,251 sq mi (163,820 sq km). Population: (2011 est.) 529,000. Capital: Paramaribo. The population includes South Asians, Creoles, Javanese, and smaller groups of people of African, Chinese, Indian, and Dutch descent. Languages: Dutch (official), English, Sranan (a creole language), Javanese, Sarnami (derived from Hindi and Urdu). Religions: Christianity (mostly Roman Catholic and Moravian), Hinduism, Islam, traditional beliefs. Currency: Suriname

dollar. Suriname has a low, narrow coastal plain, inland savannas, a forested plateau region, and mountain ranges. A number of major rivers, including the Courantyne, Maroni, and Suriname, cross the country to empty into the Atlantic. Bauxite mining, aluminum production, and agriculture are the largest sectors of the economy. Exports include rice, bananas, sugarcane, oranges, and shrimp. Suriname is a multiparty republic with one legislative house; its head of state and government is the president. It was inhabited by various South American Indians prior to European settlement. Spanish explorers claimed Suriname in 1593, but the Dutch began to settle there in 1602, followed by the English in 1651. It was ceded to the Dutch in 1667, and in 1682 the Dutch West India Company introduced coffee and sugarcane plantations and brought over African slaves to cultivate them. Slavery was abolished in Suriname in 1863, and indentured servants were brought from China, Java, and India to work the plantations, adding to the ethnic mix of the population. Except for brief interludes of British rule (1799–1802, 1804–15), Suriname remained a Dutch colony. It gained internal autonomy in 1954 and independence in 1975. A military coup in 1980 ended civilian control until the electorate approved a new constitution in 1987. Military control resumed after a coup in 1990. Elections were held in 1992, and civilian democratic government returned. By the early 21st century a vast criminal economy, including drug trafficking and gold smuggling, had developed. In 2007 the country lost a long-standing maritime border dispute with Guyana.

Surrealism, Movement in the visual arts and literature that flourished in Europe between World Wars I and II. Surrealism grew principally out of the earlier Dada movement, which before World War I produced works of anti-art that deliberately defied reason; Surrealism developed in reaction against the "rationalism" that had led to World War I. The movement was founded in 1924 by André Breton as a means of joining dream and fantasy to everyday reality to form "an absolute reality, a surreality." Drawing on the theories of Sigmund Freud, he concluded that the unconscious was the wellspring of the imagination. Breton was a poet, but Surrealism's major achievements were in painting. Some artists practiced organic, emblematic, or absolute Surrealism, expressing the unconscious through suggestive yet indefinite biomorphic images (e.g., Jean Arp, Max Ernst, André Masson, Joan Miró). Others created realistically painted images, removed from their context and reassembled within a paradoxical or shocking framework (Salvador Dalí, René Magritte). With its emphasis on content and free form, Surrealism provided a major alternative to the contemporary, highly formalistic Cubist movement and was largely responsible for perpetuating in modern painting the traditional emphasis on content.

Surrey, Administrative county (pop., 2001: 1,059,015) and historic county, southern England. Surrey is located southwest of London. Sheep raising was an important medieval activity for the county, and by the 16th century a cloth trade was also growing. Its forested hills were a source of timber for charcoal, construction, and shipbuilding. Transport of these products, originally dependent on rivers, was facilitated in 1801 when the Surrey Iron Railway was established as the first public railway. During the 19th century the world's densest network of suburban railways developed in northern Surrey. Suburban growth continued after World War II, proceeding under planning restraints. The county seat is Guildford.

surrogate motherhood, Practice in which a woman (the surrogate mother) bears a child for a couple unable to produce children, usually because the wife is infertile or unable to carry a pregnancy to term. The surrogate is impregnated either through artificial insemination (usually with the sperm of the husband) or through the implantation of an embryo produced by in vitro fertilization. The surrogate traditionally gives up all parental rights, though this has been subject to legal challenge.

surveying, Method of making relatively large-scale, accurate measurements of the earth's surfaces. Its principal modern uses are in the fields of transportation, building, land use, and communications. Surveying is divided into the categories of plane surveying (mapping small areas) and geodetic surveying (mapping large areas of the globe). The Romans are said to have used the plane table, which consists of a drawing board mounted on a tripod or other support and a straightedge along which lines are drawn. It was the first device capable of recording or establishing angles. With the publication of logarithmic tables in 1620, portable angle-measuring instruments, called topographic instruments, or theodolites, came into use; they included pivoted arms for sighting and could be used for measuring both horizontal and vertical angles. Two revolutionary 20th-century innovations were photogrammetry (mapping from aerial photographs) and electronic distance measurement, including the use of the laser.

Surveyor, Any of a series of seven unmanned U.S. space probes sent to make soft landings on the Moon in 1966–68. Surveyor 2 crashed on the Moon, and radio contact with Surveyor 4 was lost minutes before landing, but the rest sent back thousands of photographs; some were equipped to sample and test lunar soil. Surveyor 6 made the first liftoff from an extraterrestrial body; Surveyor 7 landed in the lunar highlands and returned data showing that the landscape and soil there differ from those of lower areas.

sutra, Pali SUTTA, In Hinduism, a brief aphoristic composition; in Buddhism, a more extended exposition of a subject and the basic form of the scripture of both Theravada and Mahayana traditions. Since the early Indian philosophers did not work with written texts at all, and later philosophers often disdained them, there was a need for very brief explanatory works that could be committed to memory. The earliest sutras were expositions of ritual procedures, but their use spread, and eventually nearly all Indian philosophical systems had their own sutras.

Sutta Pitaka, Major section of the *Tripitaka*, the canon of Theravada Buddhism, largely attributed to the Buddha himself. It is divided into five collections, or *Nikayas*: the *Digha Nikaya* ("Long Collection"), containing 34 lengthy sutras, including some of the most important doctrinal expositions; the *Majjhima Nikaya* ("Medium Collection"), containing 152 sutras dealing with a variety of subjects; the *Samyutta Nikaya* ("Cluster Collection"), with more than 7,000 sutras arranged according to subject; the *Anguttara Nikaya* ("Gradual Collection"), a numerical arrangement, for mnemonic purposes, of 9,557 terse sutras; and the *Khuddaka Nikaya* ("Short Collection").

suttee, or SATI, Indian practice whereby a widow burns herself to death either on the funeral pyre of her husband or soon after his death. The custom may be rooted in ancient beliefs that a husband needed his companions in the afterlife, though opponents point to it as an indication of a value system deeply hostile to women. Developed by the 4th century BC, it became widespread in the 17th–18th centuries but was banned in British India in 1829. Frequent instances of suttee continued to occur for many years thereafter, and occasional instances in remote areas are still reported today.

Suva, Seaport, (pop., 2003 est.: urban area, 210,472), capital of Fiji. Founded in 1849, it was made a city in 1952; it is now one of the largest urban centres in the South Pacific Ocean. With its fine harbour, Suva is Fiji's chief port and commercial centre and the site of educational and cultural institutions.

Svalbard, Archipelago, Norway. Located in the Arctic Ocean, north of the Arctic Circle, Svalbard consists of nine main islands, the largest being Spitsbergen (formerly West Spitsbergen). The islands are mountainous, with glaciers and snowfields covering nearly 60% of the area. The islands were first visited in modern times by the Dutch in 1596. In the early 20th century many coun-

tries, including the U.S., debated ownership of mineral rights there. Officially a Norwegian possession since 1920, the islands have been the site of many scientific polar expeditions (beginning in 1773). The population changes seasonally but numbers about 3,000; there are no indigenous inhabitants. Longyearbyen is the administrative centre.

Swahili language, Bantu language spoken in Tanzania, Kenya, Uganda, and Congo (Kinshasa). It is spoken as a first language by more than 2 million people and as a second language by some 60 million. Standard Swahili is based on the Unguja (kiUnguja) dialect of Zanzibar, which was spread far inland in the 19th century by entrepreneurs seeking ivory and slaves. Its use was perpetuated by the European colonial governments that occupied East Africa toward the end of the century. Modern Swahili is usually written in the Latin alphabet, though Swahili literature in Arabic script dates to the early 18th century. Among Bantu languages, Swahili is remarkable for the number of loanwords it has absorbed, especially from Arabic.

swallow, Any of several species (family Hirundinidae) of songbirds found nearly worldwide.  Swallows are 4–9 in. (10–23 cm) long, with long pointed, narrow wings, a short bill, small, weak feet, and sometimes a forked tail. The dark upper plumage may have a metallic blue or green sheen. Swallows capture insects on the wing. They nest in tree holes, burrow into sandbank, or plaster mud nests to walls. Some species (e.g., the common swallow, *Hirundo rustica*) are long-distance migrants; all have a strong homing instinct. The swallows of California's San Juan Capistrano Mission are cliff swallows (*Petrochelidon pyrrhonota*).

Common swallow (Hirundo rustica).
Stephen Dalton—Natural History Photographic Agency/EB Inc.

swamp, Freshwater wetland ecosystem characterized by poorly drained mineral soils and plant life dominated by trees. Swamps have a sufficient water supply to keep the ground waterlogged, and the water has a high-enough mineral content to stimulate decay of organisms and to prevent the accumulation of organic materials. They are found throughout the world.

swan, Long-necked, heavy-bodied, big-footed waterfowl (genus *Cygnus*, family Anatidae). Among waterfowl, swans are the largest and fastest, both swimming and flying; at about 50 lbs (23 kg), the mute swan (*C. olor*) is the heaviest flying bird. Swans dabble in shallows for aquatic plants. Five all-white, black-legged species live in the Northern Hemisphere; a black and a black-necked species live in the Southern Hemisphere. Males (cobs) and females (pens) look alike. Swans mate for life. The cob keeps guard while the pen incubates, on average, six eggs on a heap of vegetation; the young (cygnets) are tended for several months. Their graceful form when swimming has made swans emblems of beauty for centuries.

Swansea, Welsh ABERTAWE, Seaport and county (pop., 2001: 223,293), southern Wales. Lying along the Bristol Channel, it is the second largest city in Wales. It dates from the 12th century. Until the early 18th century it was a small market town and coal port; thereafter it grew steadily with industry, and by the mid-19th century it was the focus of the world copper trade. The city centre was almost totally destroyed by German bombing in 1941 but has been redeveloped, and Swansea is now the chief shopping and service hub for southwestern Wales. The poet Dylan Thomas was born there.

swastika, Equilateral cross with its arms bent at right angles, all in the same rotary direction, usually clockwise. It is used widely throughout the world as a symbol of prosperity and good fortune. In India, it continues to be the most common auspicious symbol of Hindus and Jains, as well as for Buddhists, for whom it symbolizes the Buddha's feet or footprints. In China and Japan, where it traveled with the spread of Buddhism, it has been used to denote plurality, prosperity, and long life. It occurs as a motif in early Christian and Byzantine art, as well as in Maya and Navajo art. The counterclockwise swastika, suggested as a general anti-Semitic symbol in 1910 by the German poet and nationalist Guido von List, was adopted as the symbol of the Nazi Party at its founding in 1919–20.

Swaziland, officially KINGDOM OF SWAZILAND, Country, southern Africa. Area: 6,704 sq mi (17,364 sq km). Population: (2011 est.) 1,203,000. Capitals: Mbabane (administrative and judicial), Lobamba (legislative), Lozitha and Ludzidzini (royal). Some four-fifths of the population is Swazi and about one-tenth is Zulu, with a small number of other minorities. Languages: Swazi (Swati), English (both official). Religions: Christianity (predominantly other [African, unaffiliated] Christians; also Protestant, Roman Catholic); also traditional beliefs. Currency: lilangeni. The landlocked country is composed of high, middle, and low velds, culminating in the Lubombo escarpment in the east. Fauna includes hippopotamuses, antelopes, zebras, and crocodiles. Four major rivers, including the Komati, flow through the country and irrigate citrus and sugarcane estates. Mineral resources include asbestos and diamonds. Swaziland is a monarchy with two legislative houses; its head of state and government is the king, assisted by the prime minister. Stone tools and rock paintings indicate prehistoric habitation in the region, but it was not settled until the Bantu-speaking Swazi people migrated there in the 18th century and established the nucleus of the Swazi nation. The British gained control in the 19th century after the Swazi king sought their aid against the Zulu. Following the South African War, the British governor of Transvaal administered Swaziland; his powers were transferred to the British high commissioner in 1906. In 1949 the British rejected the Union of South Africa's request to control Swaziland. The country gained limited self-government in 1963 and achieved independence in 1968. In the 1970s new constitutions were framed based on the supreme authority of the king and traditional government. Although the kingdom remained in place in the early 21st century, steps were being taken to establish a constitution. Swaziland has one of the highest rates of HIV infection in the world, with some two-fifths of the population infected.

Sweden, officially KINGDOM OF SWEDEN, Country, eastern Scandinavian Peninsula, northern Europe. Area: 173,860 sq mi (450,295 sq km). Population: (2011 est.) 9,451,000. Capital: Stockholm. The population is largely homogeneous, although there are Finnish and Sami (Lapp) minorities and 10% of the inhabitants are immigrants or their descendents. Language: Swedish (official). Religions: Christianity (predominantly Protestant; also Roman Catholic); also Islam. Currency: Swedish krona. Sweden has three traditional regions: mountainous Norrland covers about three-fifths of the country and has vast forests and large ore deposits; Svealand has undulating glacial ridges and contains most of the country's 90,000 lakes; and Götaland comprises the stony Småland highlands and the rich Skåne plains. About 15% of Sweden lies north of the Arctic Circle. The economy is largely based on services, heavy industries, and international trade. Sweden has large deposits of iron ore; industries include mining, lumbering, steel manufacturing, and tourism. Agricultural products include grains, sugar beets, potatoes, and livestock. One of the world's richest countries, Sweden is known for its comprehensive social welfare system. It is a constitutional monarchy and parliamentary state with one legislative house; its head of state is the king, and the head of government is the prime minister. The first traces of human life in Sweden date from about 9000 BCE. During the Viking era (9th–10th century CE), the Swedes controlled river trade in eastern Europe between the Baltic Sea and the Black Sea; they also raided western European lands. Sweden was loosely united and Christianized in the 11th–12th century. It conquered the Finns in the 12th century, and in the 14th century it united with Norway and Denmark under a single monarchy. Sweden broke away in 1523 under Gustav I Vasa. In the 17th century it emerged as a great European power in the Baltic region, but its dominance declined after its defeat in the Second Northern War (1700–21). It became a constitutional monarchy in 1809 and united with Norway in 1814; it acknowledged Norwegian independence in 1905. Sweden maintained its neutrality during both World Wars. It was a charter member of the UN but abstained from membership in NATO and did not join the European Union until 1995. A new constitution drafted in 1975 reduced the monarch's powers to those of a ceremonial chief of state. In 1997 Sweden began the controversial shutdown of its nuclear power industry. By the early 21st century it had emerged as a European centre of telecommunications and information technology.

sweet potato, Food plant (*Ipomoea batatas*; family Convolvulaceae) native to tropical America and widely cultivated in tropical and warm temperate climates. Botanically unrelated to the white, or Irish, potato or the yam, sweet potatoes are oblong or pointed oval, tuberous roots. Skin colour ranges from light buff to brown to purplish red; the pulp may be white (highest in starch) to orange (also high in carotene) to purple. Long, trailing plant stems bear funnel-shaped flowers tinged with pink or rose violet. Sweet potatoes are served baked or mashed and used as pie filling.

swimming, In recreation and sports, the propulsion of the body through water by combined arm and leg motions. Swimming is popular as an all-around fitness routine and as a competitive sport. It has been included in the modern Olympic Games since their inception in 1896. Events include freestyle (crawl-stroke) races at distances of 50, 100, 200, 400, 800, and 1,500 m; backstroke, breaststroke, and butterfly races at 100 and 200 m; individual medley races at 200 and 400 m; freestyle relays, 4 × 100 m and 4 × 200 m; and the medley relay, 4 × 100 m. Long-distance swimming competitions, usually of 15–37 mi (24–59 km), are generally held on lakes and inland waters.

swing, Jazz played with a steady beat using the harmonic structure of popular songs and the blues as the basis for improvisations and arrangements. The popular music of the U.S. from about 1930 to 1945 (years sometimes called the swing era), swing is characterized by syncopated rhythmic momentum with equal stress accorded to the four beats of a measure. Larger jazz bands required some arranged material, and Fletcher Henderson, Duke Ellington, and Count Basie were the primary innovators of big-band swing. In smaller ensembles, improvised instrumental solos generally follow a rendering of the melody.

switching theory, Theory of circuits made up of ideal digital devices, including their structure, behaviour, and design. It incorporates Boolean logic, a basic component of modern digital switching systems. Switching is essential to telephone, telegraph, data processing, and other technologies in which it is necessary to make rapid decisions about routing information.

Switzerland, officially SWISS CONFEDERATION, Country, central Europe. Area: 15,940 sq mi (41,285 sq km). Population: (2011 est.) 7,913,000. Capitals: Bern (administrative), Lausanne (judicial). The population is German, French, and Italian. Languages: German, French, Italian, Romansh (all official, with Romansh used locally). Religions: Christianity (Roman Catholic, Protestant); also Islam. Currency: Swiss franc. Switzerland is divided into three regions: the meadow-covered Jura Mountains; the central Mittelland, a rich agricultural and urbanized area; and the lofty crags of the Alps. It is one of the world's major financial centres; its economy is based largely on international trade and banking, as well as light and heavy industries. Manufactures include watches, precision instruments, machinery, and chemicals. Tourism and agriculture are also important; products include grains, sugar beets, fruits and vegetables, dairy products, chocolate, and wine. Despite diverse ethnic groups, religions, and languages, Switzerland has maintained the world's oldest democracy for some 700 years. It is a federal state with two legislative houses; its head of state and government is the president of the Federal Council. The original inhabitants were the Helvetians, who were conquered by the Romans in the 1st century BCE. Germanic tribes penetrated the region from the 3rd to the 6th century CE, and Muslim and Magyar raiders ventured in during the 10th century. It came under the rule of the Franks in the 9th century and the medieval empire (later the Holy Roman Empire) in the 11th century. In 1291 three cantons formed an anti-Habsburg league that became the nucleus of the Swiss Confederation. It was a centre of the Reformation, which divided the confederation and led to a period of political and religious conflict. The French organized Switzerland as the Helvetic Republic in 1798. In 1815 the Congress of Vienna recognized Swiss independence and guaranteed its neutrality. A new federal state was formed in 1848 with Bern as the capital. Switzerland remained neutral in both World War I and World War II and has continued to defend this neutrality. It joined the European Free Trade Association in 1960, but it has opted against joining the European Union. It joined the United Nations in 2002.

sword, Hand weapon consisting of a long metal blade fitted with a handle or hilt. Roman swords had a short, flat blade and a hilt distinct from the blade. Medieval European swords were heavy and equipped with a large hilt and a protective guard, or pommel. The blade was straight, double-edged, and pointed. The introduction of firearms did not eliminate the sword but led to new designs; the discarding of body armour required the swordsman to be able to parry, and the rapier, a double-edged sword with a narrow, pointed blade, came into use. Swords with curved blades were used in India and Persia and were introduced into Europe by the Turks, whose scimitar, with its curved, single-edged blade, was modified in the West to the cavalry sabre. Japanese swords are renowned for their hardness and extreme sharpness; they were the weapon of the samurai. Repeating firearms ended the value of the sword as a military weapon, though its continued use in duels led to the modern sport of fencing.

swordfish, Species (*Xiphias gladius*) of prized food and game fish, found in warm and temperate oceans worldwide. A slender, scaleless fish, it has a tall dorsal fin and a long extension of the snout, used for slashing at prey. The "sword" is flat, rather than rounded as in marlins. The swordfish is also distinguished by its lack of teeth and pelvic fins. It is purplish or bluish above, silvery below, and grows as large as 15 ft (4.5 m) and 1,000 lb (450 kg). Though a popular food fish, it may have dangerous levels of mercury concentrated in its flesh.

sycamore, Any of several distinct trees called by the same name though in different genera and families. In the U.S. the term refers to the American plane tree or buttonwood (*Platanus occidentalis*), a hardy street tree. The sycamore maple, or mock plane (*Acer pseudoplatanus*), is sometimes also called simply sycamore. The biblical sycamore, actually the sycamore fig (*Ficus sycomorus*), was used by the ancient Egyptians to make mummy cases.

Sydney, City (pop., 2006: 4,119,191), capital of New South Wales, Australia. Located on Australia's southeastern coast, it is the oldest and largest city in Australia and a major commercial and manufacturing centre. It was founded in 1788 as a penal colony and quickly became a major trading centre. It is built on low hills surrounding one of the world's finest natural harbours, which supports extensive port facilities. It is dominated by Sydney Harbour Bridge, one of the biggest single-span bridges in the world, and the Sydney Opera House. The city is widely known for its water sports, recreational facilities, and cultural life. It is the site of the

Universities of Sydney (1850) and New South Wales (1949) and Macquarie University (1964). Sydney was the host of the 2000 Summer Olympic Games.

Sydney Opera House, Performing-arts centre on the harbour in Sydney, Australia. Its dynamic, imaginative design by Danish architect Jørn Utzon won a competition in 1957 and brought Utzon international fame. Construction posed a variety of problems, many resulting from the bold design consisting of a series of glittering white shell-shaped roofs. After several years of research, Utzon gave the vaults a more spherical geometry, making them easier and more economical to build. The roofs are made up of precast concrete sections held together by cables. The centre finally opened in 1973.

syllable, Segment of speech usually consisting of a vowel with or without accompanying consonant sounds (e.g., *a, I, out, too, cap, snap, check*). A syllabic consonant, like the final *n* sound in *button* and *widen*, also constitutes a syllable. Closed (checked) syllables end in a consonant, open (free) syllables in a vowel. Syllables play an important role in the study of speech and in phonetics and phonology.

symbiosis, Any of several living arrangements between members of two different species, including commensalism, mutualism, and parasitism. The species involved are called symbionts. In commensalism, one species (the commensal) obtains nutrients, shelter, support, or locomotion from the host species, which is substantially unaffected (e.g., remoras obtain locomotion and food from sharks). In mutualism, both species benefit. Many mutualistic relationships are obligative; neither species can live without the other (e.g., protozoans in the gut of termites digest the wood ingested by the termites).

symbol, Element of communication intended to represent or stand for a person, object, group, process, or idea. Symbols may be presented graphically (e.g., the red cross and crescent for the worldwide humanitarian agency) or representationally (e.g., a lion representing courage). They may involve associated letters (e.g., C for the chemical element carbon), or they may be assigned arbitrarily (e.g., the mathematical symbol ∞ for infinity). Symbols are devices by which ideas are transmitted between people sharing a common culture. Every society has evolved a symbol system that reflects a specific cultural logic; and every symbolism functions to communicate information between members of the culture in much the same way as, but more subtly than, conventional language. Symbols tend to appear in clusters and to depend on one another for their accretion of meaning and value.

Symbolism, In art, a loosely organized movement that flourished in the 1880s and '90s and was closely related to the Symbolist movement in literature. In reaction against both Realism and Impressionism, Symbolist painters stressed art's subjective, symbolic, and decorative functions and turned to the mystical and occult in an attempt to evoke subjective states of mind by visual means. Though aspects of Symbolism appear in the work of Paul Gauguin, Vincent van Gogh, and the Nabis, its leading exponents were Gustave Moreau, Odilon Redon, and Pierre Puvis de Chavannes. Though associated primarily with France, it flourished all over Europe, had great international impact, and influenced 20th-century art and literature.

Symbolist movement, Literary movement that originated with a group of French poets in the late 19th century, spread to painting and the theatre, and influenced Russian, European, and American arts of the 20th century. Reacting against the rigid conventions of traditional French poetry, as seen in the precise description favoured by the Parnassian poets, Symbolist poets sought to convey individual emotional experience through the subtle, suggestive use of highly metaphorical language. The arcane and indirect meaning of the symbol is evoked as a substitute for the increasingly attenuated sense of collective and universal meanings. Principal Symbolist poets included the Frenchmen Stéphane Mallarmé, Paul Verlaine, and Arthur Rimbaud, and the Belgian poet Émile Verhaeren. Many Symbolists were also identified with the Decadent movement. Just as Symbolist painters avoided concrete representation in favour of fantasy and imagination, Symbolist dramatists relied on myth, mood, and atmosphere to reveal only indirectly the deeper truths of existence.

symphonic poem, or TONE POEM, Musical work for orchestra inspired by an extramusical story, idea, or "program," to which the title typically refers or alludes. It evolved from the concert overture, an overture not attached to an opera or play yet suggestive of a literary or natural sequence of events. Franz Liszt, who coined the term, wrote 13 such works. Famous symphonic poems include Bedřich Smetana's *The Moldau* (1879), Claude Debussy's *Prelude to the Afternoon of a Faun* (1894), Paul Dukas's *The Sorcerer's Apprentice* (1897), Richard Strauss's *Don Quixote* (1897), and Jean Sibelius's *Finlandia* (1900).

symphony, Long musical composition for orchestra, usually in several movements. The term (meaning "sounding together") came to be the standard name for instrumental episodes, and especially overtures, in early Italian opera. The late 17th-century Neapolitan opera overture, or *sinfonia*, as established especially by Alessandro Scarlatti *c.* 1780, had three movements, their tempos being fast-slow-fast. Soon such overtures began to be performed by themselves in concert settings, like another forerunner of the symphony, the concerto grosso. The two merged in the early 18th century in the symphonies of Giovanni Battista Sammartini (1700/01–1775). German and Viennese composers *c.* 1750 began to add a minuet movement. Joseph Haydn, the "father of the symphony," wrote more than 100 symphonies of remarkable originality, intensity, and brilliance in the years 1755–95, and since Haydn the symphony has been regarded as the most important orchestral genre. Wolfgang Amadeus Mozart wrote about 35 original symphonies. Ludwig van Beethoven's nine symphonies endowed the genre with enormous weight and ambition. Later symphonists include Franz Schubert, Felix Mendelssohn, Robert Schumann, Anton Bruckner, Johannes Brahms, Antonín Dvořák, Pyotr Ilyich Tchaikovsky, and Gustav Mahler. Their 20th-century successors include Ralph Vaughan Williams, Jean Sibelius, Dmitry Shostakovich, and Witold Lutosławski.

synagogue, In Judaism, a community house of worship that also serves as a place for assembly and study. Though their exact origins are uncertain, synagogues flourished side by side with the ancient Temple cult; they existed long before Jewish sacrifice and the established priesthood were terminated with Titus's destruction of the Second Temple (AD 70). Thereafter, synagogues took on even greater importance as the unchallenged focal point of Jewish life. There is no standard synagogue architecture. A typical synagogue contains an ark (where the scrolls of the Law are kept), an "eternal light" burning before the ark, two candelabra, pews, a *bimah*, and sometimes a ritual bath (*mikvah*).

synapse, Site of transmission of electric nerve impulses between two nerve cells or between a nerve cell and a gland or muscle cell. At chemical synapses, impulses are transmitted across microscopic spaces via chemical substances called neurotransmitters. In electric synapses, direct communication between nerve cells whose membranes are fused is possible because ions flow between the cells through channels. Electric synapses are found mainly in invertebrates and lower vertebrates; they transmit messages faster than chemical synapses. Chemical transmission seems to have evolved in large, complex vertebrate nervous systems, in which multiple messages must be transmitted over long distances.

synchronized swimming, Swimming sport in which the movements of one or more swimmers are synchronized with a musical accompaniment. The sport developed in the U.S. in the

1930s and was admitted as an Olympic event (solo and duet only) in 1984; in 1996 the rules were changed to allow only teams of eight women. Teams are judged on compulsory and optional routines.

synchrotron radiation, Electromagnetic radiation emitted by charged particles that are moving at speeds close to that of light when their paths are altered. It is so called because it is produced by high-speed particles in a synchrotron. Such radiation is highly polarized and continuous. Its intensity and frequency depend on the strength of the magnetic field that alters the path of the particles, as well as on the energy of those particles. Synchrotron radiation at radio frequencies is emitted by high-energy electrons as they spiral through magnetic fields in space, such as those around Jupiter. Synchrotron radiation is emitted by a variety of astronomical objects, from planets to supernova remnants to quasars.

synodic period, Time required for a body in the solar system to return to the same or about the same position relative to the Sun as seen from Earth. The Moon's synodic period is the time between successive recurrences of the same phase (e.g., the period between one full moon and the next). A planet's synodic period is the time required for Earth to overtake it as both go around the Sun or (in the case of fast-moving Mercury or Venus) for the other planet to overtake Earth.

syntax, Arrangement of words in sentences, clauses, and phrases, and the study of the formation of sentences and the relationship of their component parts. In English, the main device for showing this relationship is word order; for example, "The boy loves his dog" follows standard subject-verb-object word order, and switching the order of such a sentence would change the meaning or make the sentence meaningless. Word order is much more flexible in languages such as Latin, in which word endings indicate the case of a noun or adjective; such inflections make it unnecessary to rely on word order to indicate a word's function in the sentence.

synthesizer, Machine that electronically generates and modifies sounds, frequently with the use of a digital computer, for use in the composition of electronic music and in live performance. The synthesizer generates wave forms and then subjects them to alteration in intensity, duration, frequency, and timbre. It may use subtractive synthesis (removing unwanted components from a signal containing a fundamental and all related overtones), additive synthesis (building tones from signals for pure sine-wave tones), or other techniques, most importantly whole-sound sampling (digital recording of sounds, usually from acoustic instruments). The first synthesizer was developed *c.* 1955 by RCA. Compact, commercially viable synthesizers, generally with pianolike keyboards, were produced in the 1960s by Robert Moog (born 1934), Donald Buchla (born 1937), and others. With transistor technology, these soon became portable and cheap enough for practical performance use, and such instruments became fixtures in rock bands, often displacing electric pianos and organs. *See also* MIDI.

synthetic biology, Field of research in which the main objective is to create fully operational biological systems (e.g., bacteria) from the smallest constituent parts possible, including DNA, proteins, and other organic molecules. Synthetic biology makes use of many different scientific techniques and approaches. The common goal is to create synthetic systems and organisms that operate like biological "factories" or "computers," producing organic products of value to medicine, agriculture, and other industries. Similar to other biotechnologies, synthetic biology is not without risks; thus, risk assessment and ethical considerations are important components of the field.

syphilis, Sexually transmitted disease caused by the spirochete *Treponema pallidum.* Without treatment, it may progress through three stages: primary, characterized by a chancre and low fever; secondary (weeks to months later; only half of those infected display symptoms), with a skin and mucous-membrane rash, lymph node swelling, and bone, joint, eye, and nervous system involvement; and tertiary. The tertiary stage follows a latency period that can last years, and only one-fourth of those infected display tertiary symptoms. These can be benign or incapacitating and even fatal; almost any part of the body may be attacked. Syphilis can spread to a fetus from an infected mother. Other species of *Treponema* cause similar but milder, nonsexually transmitted forms of syphilis. Several blood tests can detect syphilis, even during latency. Antibiotic treatment is effective.

Syr Darya, ancient JAXARTES RIVER, River, Central Asia, in Uzbekistan, Tajikistan, and Kazakhstan. It is formed by the confluence of two headstreams in the fertile Fergana valley and flows northwest for 1,374 mi (2,212 km) to empty into the Aral Sea. Its lower course is on the eastern edge of the Kyzylkum desert. It is the longest river in Central Asia but carries less water than does the Amu Darya. It is used extensively for hydroelectric power and irrigation, and its waters thus frequently do not reach the Aral.

Syracuse, Italian SIRACUSA, ancient SYRACUSAE, Seaport city (pop., 2001 prelim.: 121,000), eastern coast of Sicily, Italy. Founded in 734 BC by Greeks from Corinth, it was seized by Hippocrates of Gela in 485 BC and ruled by tyrants until a revolution established a democratic government *c.* 465 BC. In 413 BC, during the Peloponnesian War, Syracuse defeated an Athenian invasion force. Under the rule of Dionysius I the Elder (405–367 BC), it became the most powerful of the Greek cities, fighting three wars against rival Carthage. Syracuse fell to Rome in 211 BC. It was sacked by Frankish invaders in AD 280 and captured by Arabs in 878; its importance waned in medieval times. Now the commercial centre for an agricultural district, it also supports the fishing and tourist industries. It has many examples of medieval and Renaissance architecture as well as Greek and Roman ruins. It is the birthplace of Theocritus and Archimedes.

Syria, officially SYRIAN ARAB REPUBLIC, Country, Middle East, along the eastern coast of the Mediterranean Sea. Area: 71,498 sq mi (185,180 sq km). Population: (2011 est.) 20,766,000. Capital: Damascus. Arabs are the main ethnic group, and Kurds are the largest minority. Languages: Arabic (official), Kurdish, Armenian. Religions: Islam (predominantly Sunni); also Christianity, Druze. Currency: Syrian pound. Syria consists of a coastal zone with abundant water supplies, a mountain zone that includes the Anti-Lebanon Mountains, and a portion of the Syrian Desert. The Euphrates River is its most important water source and only navigable river. Syria has a mixed economy based on agriculture, trade, and mining and manufacturing. Crops include cotton, cereals, fruits, tobacco, and livestock. The main mineral resources are petroleum, natural gas, and phosphates; manufactures include textiles, cement, and steel. Syria is a unitary multiparty republic with one legislative house; its head of state and government is the president, who by law must be a Muslim. The legal system is based largely on Islamic law. The area now included within the Syrian republic has been inhabited for several thousand years. From the 3rd millennium BCE it was under the control variously of Sumerians, Akkadians, Amorites, Egyptians, Hittites, Assyrians, and Babylonians. In the 6th century BCE it became part of the Persian Achaemenian Empire, which fell to Alexander the Great in 330 BCE. Seleucid rulers governed it (301–*c.* 164 BCE); then Parthians and Nabataean Arabs divided the region. It flourished as a Roman province (64 BCE–300 CE) and as part of the Byzantine Empire (300–634), until Arab Muslims invaded and established control. Thereafter the region was ruled by various Muslim dynasties. It came under the Ottoman Empire in 1516, which held it, except for brief periods, until the British invaded in World War I (1914–18). After the war it became a French mandate; it was fully independent by 1946. It united with Egypt in the United Arab Republic (1958–61). During the Six-Day War (1967), it lost the Golan Heights to Israel. Syrian troops frequently clashed with Israeli forces in Lebanon during the 1980s and '90s. Ḥāfiẓ al-Assad's long regime (1971–2000) also was marked by antagonism toward Syria's neighbours Turkey and Iraq. Following the death of al-Assad in 2000, his son Bashar al-Assad became president; he was reelected in 2007.

syringomyelia, Disease characterized by the entrance of cerebrospinal fluid into the spinal cord, where it forms a cavity (syrinx). The syrinx can expand and elongate over time, destroying the centre of the spinal cord and causing symptoms that vary with the syrinx's size and location. It is often related to the presence of a congenital malformation of the cerebellum, called a Chiari malformation, but it may also arise as a complication of spinal trauma, meningitis, tumour, or other conditions. Symptoms include loss of sensitivity, especially to temperature, muscle weakness and spasticity, and headaches and chronic pain. Syringomyelia may be diagnosed with magnetic resonance imaging. Surgery to correct the condition that caused the syrinx to form may stabilize or improve a patient's health.

systems analysis, In information processing, a phase of systems engineering. The principal objective of the systems-analysis phase is the specification of what the system needs to do to meet the requirements of end users. In the systems-design phase such specifications are converted to a hierarchy of charts that define the data required and the processes to be carried out on the data so that they can be expressed as instructions of a computer program. Many information systems are implemented with generic software, rather than with such custom-built programs.

systems engineering, Technique of using knowledge from various branches of engineering and science to introduce technological innovations into the planning and development stages of a system. Systems engineering was first applied to the organization of commercial telephone systems in the 1920s and '30s. Many systems-engineering techniques were developed during World War II in an effort to deploy military equipment more efficiently. Postwar growth in the field was spurred by advances in electronic systems and by the development of computers and information theory. Systems engineering usually involves incorporating new technology into complex, man-made systems, in which a change in one part affects many others. One tool used by systems engineers is the flowchart, which shows the system in graphic form, with geometric figures representing various subsystems and arrows representing their interactions. Other tools include mathematical models, probability theory, statistical analysis, and computer simulations.

Szczecin, German STETTIN, Seaport (pop., 2000 est.: 416,500), near the mouth of the Oder River, northwestern Poland. A Slavic fishing and commercial centre for centuries, it was annexed to Poland by Mieszko I in the 10th century. Szczecin joined the Hanseatic League in 1360. It passed to Sweden in 1648 and to Prussia in 1720 and remained under German control until it was transferred to Poland after World War II. During the war the port was completely destroyed and the city greatly depopulated. Under Polish administration the port and city were rebuilt, and Szczecin is now part of Poland's largest port complex. It is a cultural hub of western Poland, and several institutions of higher education are located there.

Szymborska, Wisława (b. July 2, 1923, Bnin, Pol.—d. Feb. 1, 2012, Kraków), Polish poet. From 1953 to 1981 Szymborska was on the staff of the weekly *Życie Literackie* ("Literary Life"), gaining a reputation as a poet, book reviewer, and translator of French poetry. Her first two volumes of poetry were attempts to conform to Socialist Realism. Later poems, notable for their precise and concrete language and ironic detachment, express her dissatisfaction with communism and explore philosophical, moral, and ethical issues. A selection of her poems was published in English translation as *View with a Grain of Sand* (1995). She received the Nobel Prize for Literature in 1996.

T

T cell, With the B cell, one of the two main types of white blood cell, essential parts of the immune system. T cells originate in the bone marrow, mature in the thymus, and travel in the blood to other lymphoid tissues, such as the spleen, tonsils, and lymph nodes. Through receptor molecules on their surfaces, T cells directly attack invaders (antigens) by binding to them and helping remove them from the body. Because the body contains millions of T and B cells, many of which carry unique receptors, it can respond to virtually any antigen.

Tabernacle, In Jewish history, the portable sanctuary constructed by Moses as a place of worship for the Hebrew tribes during the period of wandering that preceded their arrival in the Promised Land. Elaborately described in Exodus, it was divided into an outer room, the "holy place," and an inner room, the Holy of Holies, which housed the Ark of the Covenant. With the erection of the Temple of Jerusalem, the Tabernacle no longer served a purpose. In modern Roman Catholicism and Eastern Orthodoxy, the tabernacle is the receptacle on the church altar in which the consecrated elements of the Eucharist are stored.

tabla, Pair of small drums, the principal percussion in Hindustani music of northern India, Pakistan, and Bangladesh. The higher-pitched *daya*, played with the right hand, is a roughly cylindrical one-skinned drum, usually wooden, normally tuned to the raga's tonic. The *baya*, played with the left hand, is a deep kettledrum usually of copper; its pitch varies with pressure from the heel of the player's hand. A disk of black tuning paste on the membrane of each drum affects pitch and gives it characteristic overtones.

Indian tabla, consisting of two drums, baya (left) and daya, in the James Blades Collection.
James Blades

table tennis, or (trademark) PING-PONG, Game similar to lawn tennis that is played on a tabletop with wooden paddles and a small, hollow, plastic ball. The object is to hit the ball so that it goes over the net and bounces on the opponent's half of the table in such a way as to defeat the opponent's attempt to reach and return it. Both singles and doubles games are played. A match consists of the best of any odd number of games, each game being won by the player or team who first reaches 11 points or who, after 10 points each, gains a two-point lead. Invented in England in the early 20th century, it soon spread throughout the world. Since the mid-1950s, East Asian countries have dominated the sport. It has been an Olympic sport for both men and women since 1988.

taboo, Prohibition against touching, saying, or doing something for fear of immediate harm from a supernatural force. The term is of Polynesian origin and was first noted by Capt. James Cook during his 1771 visit to Tonga, but taboos have been present in virtually all cultures. They may include prohibitions on fishing or hunting at certain seasons, eating certain foods, interacting with members of other social classes, coming into contact with corpses, and (for women) performing certain activities during menstruation. Although some taboos can be traced to evident risks to health and safety, there is no generally accepted explanation of most others; most authorities agree that they tend to relate to objects and actions that are significant for the maintenance of social order.

Tabrīz, City (pop., 2006: 1,398,060), northwestern Iran. Earthquakes have damaged the city numerous times, and it has weathered invasions by Arabs, Turks, and Mongols. The Turkic ruler Timur conquered it in 1392. During the next 200 years control passed several times between Ṣafavid Iran and the Ottoman Empire. During the 19th and 20th centuries it passed between the Ottomans and the Russian Empire, and the same powers fought over it in World War I (1914–18). In the 1850s a schismatic Shīʿite religious leader known as the Bāb ("Gateway") and 40,000 of his followers were executed there. It was damaged during the Iran-Iraq War (1980–88). Notable ancient sites include the 15th-century Blue Mosque, renowned for the splendour of its blue tile decoration, and the remains of the 12-sided tomb of Mongol leader Maḥmūd Ghāzān.

Tabrīz school, School of miniaturist painting founded by the Mongol Il-Khans early in the 14th century. Reflecting the penetration of East Asian traditions into Islamic painting, early Tabrīz works were characterized by light, feathery brush strokes, gentle colouring, and an attempt to create the illusion of spatiality. The school reached its peak just as the Il-Khans were being conquered by the Islamic Timurids (1370–1506). It continued to be active in this period, though it was overshadowed by the workshops in Shiraz and Herat.

tachycardia, Heart rate over 100 (as high as 240) beats per minute. When it is a normal response to exercise or stress, it is no danger to healthy people, but when it originates elsewhere, it is an arrhythmia. Symptoms include fatigue, faintness, shortness of breath, and feeling the heart thumping. It may subside within minutes or hours with no lasting ill effects, but in serious heart, lung, or circulatory disease it can precede atrial fibrillation or heart attack and demands immediate medical attention. Tachycardias can be treated by an electric shock to the heart, by antiarrhythmic drugs, and by pacemakers.

tae kwon do, Korean martial art resembling karate. It is characterized by the use of high standing and jump kicks as well as punches and is practiced for sport, self-defense, and spiritual development. In sparring, blows are stopped just short of contact. Based on earlier forms of Korean self-defense, tae kwon do was formalized and named in 1955. It became an Olympic sport in the year 2000.

Taegu, Metropolitan city (pop., 2003 est.: 2,540,647), capital of North Kyŏngsang province, southeastern South Korea. For centuries the administrative, economic, and cultural centre of South Korea, it developed during the Chosŏn dynasty (1392–1910) into one of the country's three big market cities. It has important textile industries but is best known for the apples grown in the surrounding area, which are exported throughout East and Southeast Asia. The area attracts visitors to its several parks, ancient pagodas, and the 9th-century Buddhist temple containing the Tripitaka. It is home to many universities and colleges.

tafsīr, Science of explanation and interpretation of the Qurʾān. It arose after the death of Muhammad to deal with ambiguity, variant readings, defective texts, and apparent contradictions in the scripture. Starting from mere personal speculation, *tafsīr* developed into a system of systematic exegesis of the Qurʾān's text, proceeding verse by verse and sometimes word by word. Early efforts relied on the Ḥadīth, later giving rise to a more dogmatic type of *tafsīr*. The most comprehensive work was compiled by the scholar al-Ṭabarī. Some Muslim modernists have employed *tafsīr* as a vehicle for reformist ideas.

Tagalog, Any member of the largest cultural-linguistic group in the Philippines. They are the dominant population of Manila and of several provinces near the city. Most are Roman Catholic, and most are farmers; their main cash crops are sugarcane and coconuts. Manila's dominance has given the urban Tagalog economic leadership in the Philippines. The Tagalog language is the basis of Pilipino, the national language.

Tagalog language, Austronesian language of the Philippines, spoken as a first language by about 17 million people on the island of Luzon and by at least half a million immigrant Filipinos. As the language of Manila, the capital and chief city of the Philippines, Tagalog has long had an importance outside its own speech area. With vocabulary enrichment from other Philippine languages, it has been made the basis of Pilipino, the national language; widely used in education and the media, Pilipino is now understood by more than 60% of the Philippine population. Though a script ultimately of South Asian origin was in use for Tagalog in the 16th century, all recent literature in the language has utilized adaptations of the Latin alphabet.

Tagore, Rabindranath (b. May 7, 1861, Calcutta, India—d.

Aug. 7, 1941, Calcutta), Bengali poet, writer, composer, and painter. The son of Debendranath Tagore, he published several books of poetry, including *Manasi*, in his 20s. His later religious poetry was introduced to the West in *Gitanjali* (1912). Through international travel and lecturing, he introduced aspects of Indian culture to the West and vice versa. He spoke ardently in favour of Indian independence; as a protest against the Massacre of Amritsar, he repudiated the knighthood he had received in 1915. He founded an experimental school in Bengal where he sought to blend Eastern and Western philosophies; it became Vishva-Bharati University (1921). He was awarded the 1913 Nobel Prize for Literature.

Rabindranath Tagore.
Encyclopædia Britannica, Inc.

Tagus River, Spanish RÍO TAJO, Portuguese RIO TEJO, Longest waterway of the Iberian Peninsula. It rises in eastern central Spain and flows west across Spain and Portugal for 626 mi (1,007 km) to empty into the Atlantic Ocean near Lisbon. It covers the heart of the two nations, and is of vital economic importance. Dams harness it for irrigation and hydroelectric power, and large artificial lakes have been created. Navigable for about 100 mi (160 km) in its lower courses, it supplies a fine natural harbor at Lisbon.

Tahiti, Island, Society Islands, French Polynesia, central South Pacific Ocean. The largest of the Society Islands, it occupies an area of 402 sq mi (1,042 sq km) in their eastern group. Papeete, the capital of French Polynesia, is on Tahiti. The island's interior is mountainous, rising to 7,339 ft (2,237 m) at Mount Orohena; its towns are located on the coastal plain. Long inhabited by Polynesians, it was visited by British Capt. Samuel Wallis in 1767 and in 1768 by Louis-Antoine de Bougainville, who claimed it for France. The first permanent European settlers were English missionaries who arrived in 1797. It became a French colony in 1880 and is now part of the self-governing overseas territory of French Polynesia. Continued French nuclear testing in the area has angered the inhabitants and brought calls for independence. Tourism is economically important.

Tai, Any member of the dominant group of mainland Southeast Asia. They include the Thai, or Siamese (in Thailand), the Lao (in Laos and Thailand), the Shan (in Myanmar), the Lü (primarily in Yunnan province, China), the Yunnan Tai (in Yunnan), and the tribal Tai (in Vietnam). All speak Tai languages, and most are Buddhists of the Theravada school. The status of Tai women is high. The Tai number about 76 million.

Tai Chi Chuan, Chinese TAIJIQUAN, or T'AI-CHI-CH'ÜAN, Ancient Chinese form of exercise or of attack and defense. As exercise, it is designed to provide relaxation in the process of body conditioning, which it accomplishes partly by harmonizing the principles of yin-yang. It employs flowing, deliberate movements with carefully prescribed stances and positions. As a mode of attack and defense, it resembles kung fu and is properly considered a martial art. Dating to the 3rd century AD, Tai Chi Chuan consists of two major schools, the Wu and the Yang. Depending on the school, the number of exercises varies from 24 to more than 100.

Tai languages, Family of closely related languages spoken in Southeast Asia and southern China by more than 80 million people. According to a widely used classification, Tai comprises three branches. The Southwestern group includes Thai, the national language of Thailand; northeastern Thai and Lao, spoken in eastern Thailand and Laos; Pak Tay (South Thai), spoken in southern Thailand; Shan, spoken in eastern and northern Myanmar; and Tai Dam (Black Tai) and Tai Don (Tai Khaw, or White Tai), spoken mainly in North Vietnam. The Central group includes Nung and South Zhuang, a dialect chain in northern Vietnam and China's Guangxi autonomous region; and Tay (Thô), spoken in the same area. The Northern group includes Buyi and North Zhuang, a dialect chain spoken in Guangxi, Guizhou, and Yunnan, China. All Tai languages are tone languages. Most scholars believe the Tai family is related to a number of other languages spoken by minority peoples of southern China and northern Vietnam. Together with Tai, the entire group has been named the Kadai or Tai-Kadai family.

T'ai-nan, formerly DAINAN, City (pop., 2005 est.: 754,917), southwestern Taiwan. It is one of the oldest urban settlements on the island. The Han Chinese settled there as early as 1590. The Dutch arrived in the city in 1623 and stayed until they were driven out in 1662 by Zheng Chenggong, who made it his capital. It remained the island's capital when the Qing dynasty reestablished Chinese control over Taiwan (1683). Under Chinese rule in the 19th century, it grew into a prosperous city and was the commercial and educational centre of Taiwan. After the transfer of the capital to Taipei in 1891, it became primarily commercial. It expanded during the Japanese occupation (1895–1945). Today it is a major market and tourism centre.

Taipei, City, special (province-level) municipality (pop., 2005 est.: 2,622,472), and seat of government of the Republic of China (Taiwan). Founded in the early 18th century, it became an important centre of overseas trade in the mid-19th century. When Taiwan was proclaimed a province of China in 1886, Taipei was later made the capital, and it retained that designation under Japanese rule (1895–1945). In 1949 it became the administrative centre of the Chinese Nationalist government. It was designated a special municipality in 1967. Taipei is the commercial, financial, industrial, and transportation centre of Taiwan. Its many educational institutions include the National Taiwan University (1928). The city's National Palace Museum houses one of the world's largest collections of Chinese artifacts. The Taipei 101 building became the world's tallest building upon completion of its framework in 2003.

Taiping Rebellion (1850–64) Large-scale rebellion against the Qing dynasty and the presence of foreigners in China. The peasants, having suffered floods and famines in the late 1840s, were ripe for rebellion, which came under the leadership of Hong Xiuquan. Hong's visions convinced him he was the younger brother of Jesus, and he saw it as his duty to free China from Manchu rule. He preached the brotherhood and sisterhood of all people under God; property was to be held in common. His followers' militant faith unified a fiercely disciplined army that swelled to more than a million men and women (women were treated as equals by Taiping rebels). They captured Nanjing in 1853 and renamed it Tianjing ("Heavenly Capital"). Their attempts to capture Beijing failed, but an expedition into the upper Yangtze River (Chang Jiang) valley scored many victories. Hong's idiosyncratic Christianity alienated both Western missionaries and the Chinese scholar-gentry. Without the gentry, the Taiping forces were unable to govern the countryside or supply their cities effectively. The leadership strayed from its original austerity and descended into power struggles that left Hong without competent help. In 1860 an attempt to take Shanghai was repelled by U.S.- and British-led forces, and by 1862 Chinese forces under Zeng Guofan had surrounded Nanjing. The city fell in 1864, but almost 100,000 of the Taiping followers preferred death to capture. Sporadic resistance continued elsewhere until 1868. The rebellion ravaged 17 provinces, took some 20 million lives, and left the Qing government unable to regain an effective hold over the country.

Taiwan, formerly FORMOSA, Island, western Pacific Ocean, off southeastern China, and since 1949 the principal component of the Republic of China (which also includes Matsu and Quemoy islands and the Pescadores). Area: 13,973 sq mi (36,191 sq km), including its outlying islands. Population: (2011 est.) 23,190,000. Seat of government: Taipei. Han Chinese constitute virtually the entire population. Languages: Mandarin Chinese (official); Taiwanese, Fukien, and Hakka dialects also spoken. Religions: Buddhism, Daoism, Confucianism, Christianity. Currency: new Taiwan dollar. Lying 100 mi (160 km) off the Chinese mainland, Taiwan is composed mainly of mountains and hills, with densely populated coastal plains in the west. It has one of the highest population densities in the world and is a leading industrial power of the Pacific Rim, with an economy based on manufacturing industries, international trade, and services. Leading exports include nonelectrical and electrical machinery, electronics, textile products, plastic articles, and transportation equipment. Taiwan is a major producer of Chinese-language motion pictures. It is a multiparty republic with one legislative branch; its head of state is the president, and the head of government is the premier. Known to the Chinese as early as the 7th century, the island of Taiwan was widely settled by them early in the 17th century. In 1646 the Dutch seized control of the island, only to be ousted in 1661 by a large influx of Chinese refugees, supporters of the Ming dynasty. Taiwan fell to the Manchu in 1683 and was not open to Europeans again until 1858. In 1895 it was ceded to Japan following the first Sino-Japanese War. A Japanese military centre in World War II, it was frequently bombed by U.S. planes. After Japan's defeat it was returned to China, which was then governed by the Nationalists. When the communists took over mainland China in 1949, the Nationalist Party government fled to Taiwan and made it their seat of government, with Gen. Chiang Kai-shek as president. Since then, both the Nationalist government and the People's Republic of China (mainland China) have considered Taiwan a province of China. In 1954 Chiang and the U.S. signed a mutual defense treaty, and Taiwan received U.S. support for almost three decades, developing its economy in spectacular fashion. It was recognized as the representative of China in the UN until 1971, when it was replaced there by the People's Republic. Martial law in Taiwan, in effect since 1949, was lifted in 1987, and travel restrictions with mainland China were removed in 1988. In 1989 opposition parties were legalized. The relationship with the mainland grew increasingly close in the 1990s, but it again became strained over the future status of Taiwan after Chen Shui-bian (Ch'en Shui-pian) was elected president in 2000.

Taiwan Strait, or FORMOSA STRAIT, Arm of the northwestern Pacific Ocean. Lying between the coast of China's Fujian province and the island of Taiwan, it is about 100 mi (160 km) wide. The strait connects the South China Sea and East China Sea.

Taiyuan, or T'AI-YÜAN, City (pop., 2003 est.: 1,970,300), capital of Shanxi province, China, lying on the Fen River. Known since the time of the Zhou dynasty, it was a strategic centre and administrative capital in the time of the Mongols (12th–14th century). In 1900 it was the scene of a massacre of foreign missionaries dur-

ing the Boxer Rebellion and was one of the first areas to oppose the emperor in 1911. Invaded by the Japanese in 1937, it was again besieged by communist forces in 1948–49. One of the most important industrial cities in China, it produces cement, iron and steel, and coal. It also is an education and research centre. There are notable cave temples from the Tang and Yuan eras in the area.

Taizong, or T'AI-TSUNG, orig. LI SHIMIN (b. 598, China—d. 649, China), Second emperor of China's Tang dynasty. In his father's campaign against the Sui dynasty, Li Shimin was responsible for the conquest of Luoyang, the eastern capital. There he built up a regional administration and an entourage of talented officials. His brothers are said to have plotted to kill him; he did away with them instead, and his father soon abdicated in his favour. He restored normal civil administration to local government and created a unified civil service. He further developed the state schools created by his father and launched the editing of the Confucian Classics. On the frontiers, he fought eastern and western Turks and began to establish sovereignty over the oasis kingdoms of Xinjiang. An invasion of the Korean Koguryŏ kingdom failed, but he won great prestige for the Tang and came to be widely revered.

Taizu, or T'AI-TSU (b. 927, Luoyang, China—d. Nov. 14, 976, Kaifeng), First emperor of the Song dynasty, who began the unification of China, which his brother would complete. Initially a general for the founder of the Later Zhou dynasty (951–960), he was induced by his troops to take over when the dynasty was left in the hands of a child successor. An upright man, Taizu forgave minor faults while holding his officials accountable in important matters. He had his ministers submit rough drafts of papers for his review, and he frequently traveled about incognito to observe conditions among his people. He reformed the Chinese examination system to prevent favouritism and began to award larger numbers of degrees. He gradually moved the administration of the prefectures from the military to civil officials. At his death, a solid foundation had been laid for the future development of the dynasty.

Taj Mahal, Mausoleum complex on the southern bank of the Yamuna River, outside Agra, India. It was built by the Mughal emperor Shah Jahān in memory of his wife, Mumtāz Maḥal, who died in 1631. The Taj complex, begun *c.* 1632, took 22 years to complete. At its centre lies a square garden area bounded by two smaller, oblong sections, one comprising the mausoleum and the other an entrance gateway. The mausoleum, of pure-white marble inlaid with semiprecious stones, is flanked by two red sandstone buildings, a mosque on one side and an identical building for aesthetic balance on the other. It stands on a high marble plinth with a minaret at each corner. It has four identical facades, each with a massive central arch 108 ft (33 m) high, and is surmounted by a bulbous double dome and four domed kiosks. Its interior, with fine, restrained stone decoration, centres on an octagonal chamber containing the marble tombs, enclosed by a perforated marble screen, with sarcophagi below. Regarded as one of the world's most beautiful buildings, it was designated a UNESCO World Heritage site in 1983. Steps have been taken since the late 1990s to reduce air pollution that has damaged the facade of the building.

Taj Mahal in Agra, Uttar Pradesh, India.
Gavin Hellier—Robert Harding World Imagery/Getty Images ·

Tajikistan, officially REPUBLIC OF TAJIKISTAN, Country, Central Asia. Area: 55,300 sq mi (143,100 sq km). Population: (2011 est.) 7,681,000. Capital: Dushanbe. The majority of the population are Tajiks; Uzbeks make up a large minority. Languages: Tajik (official), Russian. Religion: Islam (predominantly Sunni). Currency: somoni. Tajikistan is a mountainous country; about half of its territory lies at elevations above 10,000 ft (3,000 m), with the Pamirs dominating the east. The entire region is prone to seismic activity. The Amu Darya and Syr Darya rivers cross it and are used for irrigation. Cotton, cattle, fruits, vegetables, and grains are raised. Heavy industries include coal mining, petroleum and natural gas extraction, metalworking, and nitrogen fertilizer production. Notable light industries are cotton milling, food processing, and textiles. Tajikistan is a republic with two legislative houses; the head of state is the president, and the head of government is the prime minister. Settled by Persians *c.* the 6th century BCE, Tajikistan was part of the empires of the Persian Achaemenian dynasty and of Alexander the Great and his successors. In the 7th–8th century CE it was conquered by the Arabs, who introduced Islam. The Uzbeks controlled the region in the 15th–18th centuries. In the 1860s the Russian Empire took over much of Tajikistan. In 1924 it became an autonomous republic under the administration of the Uzbek S.S.R., and it gained union republic status in 1929. It achieved independence with the collapse of the Soviet Union in 1991. Civil war raged through much of the 1990s between government forces and an opposition composed mostly of Islamic militants. A peace agreement was reached in 1997.

Takla Makan Desert, Chinese TAKLIMAKAN SHAMO, or T'A-K'O-LA-MA-KAN SHA-MO, Desert, forming the greater part of the Tarim Basin, west-central China. One of the world's largest sandy wastes, it is about 600 mi (960 km) across, with an area of 123,550 sq mi (320,000 sq km). It is flanked by high mountain ranges, including the Kunlun Mountains, whose rivers penetrate the desert 60–120 mi (100–200 km) before drying up in its sands. Its windblown sand cover is as much as 1,000 ft (300 m) thick and has formed such features as pyramidal dunes that can reach heights of 1,000 ft (300 m).

Taliban, Political and religious faction and militia that came to power in Afghanistan in the mid-1990s. Following the Soviet Union's 1989 withdrawal from Afghanistan, the Taliban (Persian: "Students")—whose name refers to the Islamic religious students who formed the group's main recruits—arose as a popular reaction to the chaos that gripped the country. In 1994–95, under the leadership of Mullah Mohammad Omar, the Taliban extended its control in Afghanistan from a single city to more than half the country, and in 1996 it captured Kabul and instituted a strict Islamic regime. By 1999, the Taliban controlled most of Afghanistan but failed to win international recognition of its regime because of its harsh social policies—which included the almost complete removal of women from public life—and its role as a haven for Islamic extremists. Among these extremists was Osama bin Laden, the expatriate Saudi Arabian leader of Al-Qaeda, a network of Islamic militants that had engaged in numerous acts of terrorism. The Taliban's refusal to extradite bin Laden to the U.S. following the September 11 attacks in 2001 prompted the U.S. to attack Taliban and Al-Qaeda forces in Afghanistan, driving the former from power and sending the leaders of both groups into hiding.

Talleyrand (-Périgord), Charles-Maurice de (b. Feb. 2, 1754, Paris, France—d. May 17, 1838, Paris), French statesman. Ordained a priest, he became bishop of Autun in 1788. Elected to represent the clergy at the Estates-General (1789), he became the "bishop of the Revolution" by calling for confiscation of church property to fund the new government and supporting the Civil Constitution of the Clergy. Excommunicated by the pope in 1790, he was sent to England as an envoy in 1792. He was expelled from France during the Reign of Terror, lived in the U.S. (1794–96), then returned to serve in the Directory as foreign minister (1797–99). He was forced to resign briefly for involvement in bribery scandals, including the XYZ Affair. Adept at political survival, he supported Napoleon and again became foreign minister (1799–1807) and later grand chamberlain (1804–07). He resigned in opposition to Napoleon's policy toward Russia but continued to advise him, arranging his marriage with Marie-Louise of Austria. As Napoleon faced defeat, Talleyrand secretly worked to restore the monarchy; in 1814 he was appointed foreign minister to Louis XVIII and represented France at the Congress of Vienna. Forced by ultraroyalists to resign (1815), he later became involved in the July Revolution of 1830 and served as ambassador to Britain (1830–34).

Tallinn, formerly (until 1918) REVEL, Seaport city (pop., 2003 est.: 400,378), capital of Estonia. It is located on the Gulf of Finland. A fortified settlement existed there from the late 1st millennium BC and a town in the 12th century AD. In 1219 it was captured by the Danes, who built a new fortress. Trade flourished after it joined the Hanseatic League in 1285. In 1346 it was sold to the Teutonic Order, and in 1561 it passed to Sweden. Russia captured it in 1710, and it remained a Russian city until 1918, when it became the capital of independent Estonia. From 1940 to 1991 Estonia was a republic of the U.S.S.R. During World War II the city was occupied by German forces and was severely damaged. Rebuilt, it again became the capital of independent Estonia in 1991. It is a major commercial and fishing port, an industrial centre, and the cultural focus of Estonia, with numerous educational institutions. Historical structures include a medieval city wall and a 13th-century church. Tallinn's historic centre was designated a UNESCO World Heritage site in 1997.

Talmud, In Judaism, the systematic amplification and analysis of passages of the Mishna, the Gemara, and other oral law, including the Tosefta. Two Talmuds exist, produced by two different groups of Jewish scholars: the Babylonian Talmud (*c.* AD 600) and the Palestinian Talmud (*c.* AD 400). The Babylonian Talmud is more extensive and thus more highly esteemed. Both Talmuds formulate their own hermeneutics to convey their theological system by defining the Torah and by demonstrating its perfection and comprehensive character. The Talmud remains a text of central importance, particularly in Orthodox Judaism. Intensive modern Talmudic scholarship is pursued in Israel and the U.S.

Talmud Torah, Religious study of the Torah in search of the God who makes himself known in that work. It focuses on learning God's message for contemporary times through inquiry into the books of Hebrew scripture or those that record the original oral Torah of Sinai, the Mishna, Midrash, and Talmuds. Talmud Torah is also the name given to an elementary school under Jewish auspices that places special emphasis on religious education.

tambourine, Small frame drum with one skin nailed or glued to a shallow circular frame, into which jingles or pellet bells are set. It is held with one hand and struck with the other, or simply shaken. Tambourines were played in ancient Mesopotamia, Greece, and Rome, especially in religious contexts, and they have long been prominent in Middle Eastern folk and religious use. Crusaders took them to Europe in the 13th century.

Tamil language, Dravidian language spoken by more than 63 million people. It is an official language of Tamil Nadu state in India and one of the official languages of Sri Lanka. Large Tamil-speaking communities also reside in Malaysia and Singapore, South Africa, and the Indian Ocean islands of Réunion and Mauritius. The earliest Tamil inscriptions date from *c.* 200 BC; literature in the language has a 2,000-year history. Tamil script is descended from the southern Indian Pallava script. Tamil has several regional dialects, Brahman and non-Brahman caste dialects, and a marked division between literary and colloquial forms.

Tamil Nadu, formerly MADRAS, State (pop., 2008 est.: 66,396,000), southeastern India. Lying on the Indian Ocean, its coastline includes the enclaves of Puducherry and Karaikal (both parts of Puducherry union territory); it is also bordered by Kerala, Karnataka, and Andhra Pradesh states. Tamil Nadu covers an area of 50,216 sq mi (130,058 sq km), and its capital is Chennai (Madras). Its interior includes the fertile Kaveri (Cauvery) River delta. By the 4th century CE the region was occupied by Tamil kingdoms. The Hindu kingdom of Vijayanagar ruled the southern regions from the mid-14th to the mid-16th century. The British established a settlement in present-day Chennai in the 17th century. The settlement expanded to become the separate presidency of Madras, which lasted from 1653 to 1946. The state of Tamil Nadu was formed in 1956. It is one of India's most industrialized states, manufacturing vehicles, electrical equipment, and chemicals.

Tamil Tigers, or LIBERATION TIGERS OF TAMIL EELAM (LTTE), Guerrilla organization seeking to establish an independent Tamil state in northern and eastern Sri Lanka. Formed in 1972, it is considered one of the world's most sophisticated and tightly organized insurgent groups. By 1985 it controlled the port of Jaffna and most of the Jaffna Peninsula in northern Sri Lanka. After losing control of Jaffna in 1987, it carried out several attacks, including the assassinations of the Sri Lankan president and the former Indian prime minister and a suicide bombing that killed 100 people in the capital, Colombo. Negotiations between the Tigers and the government broke down in the mid-1990s, and fighting subsequently intensified until February 2002, when a permanent cease-fire agreement was signed. Sporadic violence continued, however, and in 2006 the European Union added the Tigers to its list of banned terrorist organizations. Soon after, heavy fighting erupted between the rebels and government forces. In January 2008 the government formally abandoned the 2002 cease-fire and began a sustained offensive against the Tigers. By May 2009 government forces had captured the last rebel stronghold and claimed victory over the Tigers.

tamoxifen, Synthetic hormone, marketed as Nolvadex, that prevents the binding of estrogen to estrogen-sensitive breast cancer cells. Initially used to prevent recurrences of breast cancer after successful treatment, it was later found to prevent first occurrences in women at high risk. The most serious side effect is an increased risk of thrombosis, which may require patients to take an anticoagulant as well. Studies on its effectiveness against breast and other cancers continue.

Tana, Lake, Lake, Ethiopia. The country's largest lake, its surface area covers more than 1,400 sq mi (3,620 sq km). It forms the main reservoir for the Blue Nile, which pours from it over a lava barrier, dropping 138 ft (42 m) to form Tisisat Falls. Coptic monasteries were built on two of its islands during the Middle Ages.

Tanagra figure, Any of the small terra-cotta figures dating primarily from the 3rd century BC and named after the site in Boeotia, Greece, where they were found. The statuettes, mostly of well-dressed young women standing or sitting, were all formed from molds and originally were covered with a white coating and then painted. On their discovery in the 19th century, they became enormously popular and were extensively and expertly forged.

Tanganyika, Lake, Lake, central Africa. Located on the boundary between Tanzania and Congo (Kinshasa), it is the longest freshwater lake in the world, 410 mi (660 km) long, and the second deepest, 4,710 ft (1,436 m) deep. Fed by several rivers, it tends to be brackish. Oil palms and rice grow along its steep shores; hippopotamuses and crocodiles abound. It was first visited by Europeans, searching for the source of the Nile, in 1858.

Tangier, French TANGER, Arabic ṬANJAH, ancient TINGIS, Seaport city (pop., 2004: 669,685), northern Morocco, located at the western end of the Strait of Gibraltar. It was first known as an ancient Phoenician trading post and later became a Carthaginian and then a Roman settlement. After five centuries of Roman rule,

it was captured successively by the Vandals, the Byzantines, and the Arabs. It fell to the Portuguese in 1471 and later passed to the British, who gave it up to Morocco in 1684. When the rest of Morocco became a French protectorate in 1912, Tangier was granted special status; in 1923 it officially became an international city, governed by an international commission. It remained an international zone until 1956, when it was integrated with the independent kingdom of Morocco. It became a free port and a royal summer residence in the 1960s. The old town is dominated by a casbah (citadel) and the Great Mosque. It is a busy port and trade centre; industries include tourism, fishing, and textiles, especially carpets.

tango, Spirited dance; also a South American ballroom dance. It evolved in the dance halls and, perhaps, the brothels of poorer districts of Buenos Aires, Arg., possibly influenced by the Cuban habanera. It was made popular in the U.S. by Vernon and Irene Castle, and by 1915 it was being danced throughout Europe. Early versions, danced to music in the prevailing duple metre ($^2/4$), were fast and exuberant; these were later modified to the smoother ballroom step, characterized by long pauses and stylized body positions and danced to music usually in $^4/4$ time. Among those associated with tango are Juan D'Arienzo, Anibal Troilo, Osvaldo Pugliese, Carlos Di Sarli, Francisco Canaro, Astor Piazzolla, and Carlos Gardel.

Tango danced by Rudolph Valentino and partner from the motion picture Four Horsemen of the Apocalypse, *1921*

Courtesy of Metro-Goldwyn-Mayer Inc., © 1921; photograph, from the Museum of Modern Art Film Stills Archive

Tangun, Mythological first king of the Koreans, whose reign began in 2333 BC. According to one legend, Tangun's father descended from heaven to rule earth from a mountaintop. When a bear and a tiger expressed the wish to become human, he ordered them into a cave for 100 days; after the tiger grew impatient and left, the bear was transformed into the beautiful woman who became Tangun's mother. Buddhism and Daoism credited Tangun with establishing a national religion and originating the Korean maxim "Hongik-ingan" ("Love humanity"). His birthday is a school holiday.

tank, Heavily armed and armoured combat vehicle that moves on two continuous metal chains called tracks. It is usually equipped with a cannon mounted in a revolving turret as well as lighter automatic weapons. The British developed tanks during World War I to fill the need for an armoured assault vehicle that could cross the muddy, uneven terrain of the trench battle zone. They first saw combat at the Battle of the Somme (1916). In World War II, Germany's tank force was initially the most effective in Europe because it was organized into fast-moving massed formations with great striking power. After World War II, tanks became larger and more heavily armed. Most modern main battle tanks weigh more than 50 tons yet are capable of road speeds of 30–40 mph (50–70 km/hr). The standard main armament is a 120-mm gun, which fires armour-piercing projectiles; laser range-finders and infrared imaging devices aid in sighting.

tantalum, Metallic chemical element, one of the transition elements, chemical symbol Ta, atomic number 73. It is a dense, hard, unreactive, silvery gray metal with an extremely high melting point (5,425 °F [2,996 °C]). Relatively rare, it occurs native in a few places. It is difficult to separate from niobium, the element above it in the periodic table, with which it shares many properties. The most important uses are in electrolytic capacitors, corrosion-resistant chemical equipment, dental and surgical instruments, tools, catalysts, components of electron tubes, rectifiers, and prostheses. Its compounds are relatively unimportant commercially; tantalum carbide is used in machine tools and dies.

Tantalus, In Greek mythology, the king of Sipylus (or Phrygia). An intimate friend of the gods, he was allowed to dine at their table until he offended them by repeating their secrets on earth. Another version of the myth held that he killed his son Pelops and served him to the gods. In the underworld he was placed up to his neck in water, which flowed away every time he tried to drink, just as the branches overhead swung out of reach whenever he tried to pick the fruit from them.

tantra, In some Indian religions, a text that deals with esoteric aspects of religious teaching. There is considerable tantric literature and practice in Hinduism, Buddhism, and, to a lesser extent, Jainism. Because tantric practices typically represent teachings of relatively late development and incorporate elements of different traditions, they are often eschewed by orthodox practitioners. In Hinduism, tantras deal with popular aspects of the religion, such as spells, rituals, and symbols. Buddhist tantric literature, believed to date from the 7th century or earlier, has reference to numerous practices, some involving sexual activity, that have no basis in canonical literature.

Tanzania, officially UNITED REPUBLIC OF TANZANIA, Country, eastern Africa. It is mostly on the African mainland but also includes the islands of Zanzibar, Pemba, and Mafia in the Indian Ocean. Area: 364,901 sq mi (945,090 sq km). Population: (2011 est.) 45,030,000. Capital: Dar es Salaam; Dodoma, designated. There are more than 120 identifiable ethnic groups; the largest, the Sukuma, are about one-tenth of the population. Languages: Swahili, English (both official). Religions: Christianity (Protestant, Roman Catholic), Islam (mainly Sunni), traditional beliefs. Currency: Tanzanian shilling. Although most of Tanzania consists of plains and plateaus, it has some spectacular relief features, including Kilimanjaro and Ol Doinyo Lengai, an active volcano. All or portions of Lakes Nyasa, Tanganyika, Victoria, and Rukwa lie within Tanzania, as do the headwaters of the Nile, Congo, and Zambezi rivers. Serengeti National Park is the most famous of its extensive game reserves. Important mineral deposits include gold, diamonds, gemstones, coal, and natural gas. The economy is based largely on agriculture; major crops include cotton, coffee, corn, rice, cloves, sisal, cashews, and tobacco. Industries include food processing, textiles, cement, and brewing. Tanzania is a unitary multiparty republic with one legislative house; its head of state and government is the president. Inhabited from the 1st millennium BCE, it was occupied by Arab and Indian traders and Bantu-speaking peoples by the 10th century CE. The Portuguese gained control of the coastline in the late 15th century, but they were driven out by the Arabs of Oman and Zanzibar in the late 18th century. German colonists entered the area in the 1880s, and in 1891 the Germans declared the region a protectorate as part of German East Africa. During World War I, Britain captured the German holdings, which became a British mandate (1920) under the name Tanganyika. Britain retained control of the region after World War II when it became a UN trust territory. Tanganyika gained independence in 1961 and became a republic in 1962. In 1964 it united with Zanzibar, later taking the name Tanzania, and was led by Pres. Julius Nyerere until 1985. The country subsequently experienced both political and economic struggles; it held its first multiparty elections in 1995.

tap dance, Style of American theatrical dance using precise rhythmical patterns of foot movement and audible foot tapping. It is derived from the traditional clog dance of northern England, the jigs and reels of Ireland and Scotland, and the rhythmic foot stamping of African dances. Popular in 19th-century minstrel shows, versions such as "buck-and-wing" (danced vigorously in

wooden-soled shoes) and "soft-shoe" (danced smoothly in soft-soled shoes) developed as separate techniques; by 1925 they had merged, and metal taps were attached to shoe heels and toes to produce a more pronounced sound. The dance was also popular in variety shows and early musicals.

tapas, Ascetic practice carried out to achieve spiritual power or purification. In Hinduism, it is associated with Yoga as a way of purifying the body in preparation for the more exacting spiritual exercises leading to liberation. In Jainism, its practice is a central means of breaking the cycle of rebirths by preventing new karma from forming and by eliminating the old. Tapas can take many forms, including fasting, controlling the breath, and holding difficult and painful body postures. Extreme forms are carried out by sadhus, many of whom earn alms for their unusual abilities or deprivations.

tapestry, Heavy, reversible, patterned or figured handwoven textile, usually in the form of a hanging or upholstery fabric. Tapestries are usually designed as single panels or as sets of panels related by subject and style and intended to be hung together. The earliest known tapestries were made from linen by the ancient Egyptians. Tapestry weaving was well established in Peru by the 6th century, and outstanding silk tapestries were made in China beginning in the Tang dynasty (618–907 CE). In western Europe, tapestry making flourished from the 13th century. Among the greatest European tapestries are the 15th-century set *The Lady and the Unicorn* and the 16th-century Acts of the Apostles set, based on cartoons by Raphael. Tapestry art was revitalized in late 19th-century Britain with the Arts and Crafts Movement. In the 20th century, abstract tapestries were produced at the Bauhaus, and many painters, including Pablo Picasso and Henri Matisse, allowed their paintings to provide the basis for tapestry art.

tapeworm, Any of about 3,000 species (class Cestoda, phylum Platyhelminthes) of bilaterally symmetrical parasitic flatworms found worldwide. Tapeworms range from 0.04 in. (1 mm) to more than 50 ft (15 m) long. The head bears suckers and often hooks for attaching to the liver or digestive tract of the host. Once attached, a tapeworm absorbs food through its body wall. The body is often divided into a head, or scolex, possessing the suckers and hooks, an unsegmented neck, and a series of proglottids (units containing both male and female reproductive organs) that continually form in a growth region at the base of the neck. Following fertilization, each mature proglottid containing thousands of embryos breaks off and is eliminated in the host's feces. If these are ingested by an animal (the intermediate host) grazing on food contaminated with feces, they develop into larvae, which bore through the intestinal wall into the circulatory system and are carried to muscle tissues, which they burrow into, forming a dormant cyst. When meat is inadequately cooked, humans become infested with the larvae, which attach to the intestinal wall. Many species that infest humans belong to the genus *Taenia*; the intermediate host is implied by the name (e.g., beef tapeworm, *T. saginata*). Humans can also acquire tapeworms through fecal contamination of soil or water.

taqlīd, In Islamic canon law, the unquestioning acceptance of legal precedent. The interpretation of *taqlīd* varies widely among the major schools of Islamic law. *Taqlīd* is compulsory for Shīʿites. Of the four Sunnite legal schools, views are mixed; most scholars of the Shāfiʿī, Mālikī, and Ḥanafī schools embrace *taqlīd*, but those of the Ḥanbalī do not view the opinions of earlier scholars as necessarily binding. Support for the practice is based mainly on the belief that early Muslim scholars, being closer in time to Muhammad, were in the best position to derive authoritative legal opinions.

tarantula, Name that originally referred to the wolf spider but now covers any spider in the family Theraphosidae. It is found from the southwestern U.S. to South America. Many species live in a burrow, and most have a hairy body and long, hairy legs. They

Mexican red-kneed tarantula (Brachypelma smithii).
Lynam/Tom Stack & Associates

are nocturnal predators of insects and, occasionally, amphibians and mice. Certain South American tarantulas eat small birds. In the southwestern U.S., tarantulas of the genus *Aphonopelma* may have a body 2 in. (5 cm) long and a leg spread of nearly 5 in. (12 cm). They may inflict a painful bite if provoked. The most common U.S. species, *Eurypelma californicum*, may live up to 30 years.

Targum, Any of several translations of the Hebrew scriptures or its parts into Aramaic. The earliest date from after the Babylonian Exile and were designed to meet the needs of uneducated Jews who did not know Hebrew. After the destruction of the Second Temple of Jerusalem (AD 70), Targums became established in synagogues, where scripture was read aloud with a translation in Aramaic. These readings eventually incorporated paraphrase and commentary. Targums were regarded as authoritative throughout the Talmudic period and began to be committed to writing in the 5th century.

tariff, or CUSTOMS DUTY, Tax levied upon goods as they cross national boundaries, usually by the government of the importing country. The words *tariff, duty,* and *customs* are generally used interchangeably. Usually assessed on imports, tariffs may apply to all foreign goods or only to goods produced outside the borders of a customs union. A tariff may be assessed directly, at the border, or indirectly, by requiring the prior purchase of a license or permit to import specified quantities of the good. Examples of tariffs include transit duties and import or export taxes, which may be levied on goods passing through a customs area en route to another destination. In addition to providing a source of revenue, tariffs can effectively protect local industry by driving up the price of an imported item that competes with domestic products. This practice allows domestic producers either to charge higher prices for their goods or to capitalize on their own lighter taxes by charging lower prices and attracting more customers. Tariffs are often used to protect "infant industries" or to safeguard older industries that are in decline. They are sometimes criticized for imposing hidden costs on domestic consumers and encouraging inefficiency in domestic industries. Tariffs are subject to negotiation and treaties among nations.

Moon, the 18th card of the major arcana.
Mary Evans Picture Library

tarot, Sets of cards used in fortune-telling and in certain card games. The origins of tarot cards are obscure; cards approximating their present form first appeared in Italy and France in the late 14th century. Modern tarot decks consist of 78 cards, of which 22 have pictures representing forces, characters, virtues, and vices. The remaining cards are divided into four suits—(1) wands, batons, or rods, (2) cups, (3) swords, and (4) coins, pentacles, or disks—of 14 cards each. Each suit has 10 numbered cards and 4 court cards (king, queen, knight, and page). Modern playing cards evolved from these suit cards. Initially used as play-

ing cards, tarot cards were imbued with esoteric associations in the 18th century and are now used widely for fortune-telling. Each card's basic meaning is altered by the card's position in the spread of cards laid out by the fortune-teller, by the card's orientation, and by the cards that are near it.

tarragon, Bushy aromatic herb (*Artemisia dracunculus*) of the aster family (Asteraceae), the dried leaves and flowering tops of which are used to add tang to many culinary dishes. Tarragon is a common ingredient in seasoning blends, such as fines herbes. The fresh leaves are used in salads, and vinegar in which fresh tarragon has been steeped is a distinctive condiment. The plant is probably native to Siberia; a French variety is cultivated in Europe and North America.

Tarsus, City (pop., 2000: 216,382), south-central Turkey. It is located near the Mediterranean Sea coast. Settled from Neolithic times, it was razed and rebuilt *c.* 700 BC by the Assyrian king Sennacherib. Later, Achaemenid and Seleucid rule alternated with periods of autonomy. In 67 BC it was absorbed into the new Roman province of Cilicia, becoming one of the principal cities of the Eastern and Byzantine empires. It was the site of the first meeting in 41 BC between Mark Antony and Cleopatra and was the birthplace of St. Paul. It remained a leading industrial and cultural centre through the early Byzantine period. It came under various powers in the 10th–15th century and passed to the Ottoman Empire in the early 16th century. Modern Tarsus is a prosperous agricultural and cotton-milling centre.

Tartarus, In Greek mythology, the lowest depths of the underworld. It was a region of eternal darkness where the evil were punished after death for having offended the gods. Here Zeus confined the Titans, who were prevented from escaping by hundred-armed giants. Later classical authors sometimes used Tartarus interchangeably with Hades to designate the entire underworld.

Tashkent, or TOSHKENT, City (pop., 2007 est.: 1,959,190), capital of Uzbekistan. Dating from about the 1st or 2nd century BCE, it was an important trade centre on the caravan routes to Europe and East Asia. The Arabs conquered it in the early 8th century; it fell to the Mongols in the 13th century and was under Turkish control in the 14th–15th century. Taken by the Russians in 1865, it was made the administrative centre of Turkistan in 1867, and a new European city grew up beside the old native one. The city was heavily damaged by an earthquake in 1966. Today it is the main economic and cultural centre of Central Asia. Its many institutions of higher education include the Uzbek Academy of Sciences (1943).

Tasman Sea, Part of the South Pacific Ocean, between southeastern Australia and western New Zealand. About 1,400 mi (2,250 km) wide, it has maximum depths exceeding 17,000 ft (5,200 m) in the Tasman Basin. Explored by Abel Janszoon Tasman in 1642 and by Capt. James Cook in the 1770s, it is notoriously stormy. Economic resources include fisheries and petroleum deposits.

Tasmania, formerly VAN DIEMEN'S LAND, Island and state, Australia. Area: 26,410 sq mi (68,401 sq km). Population: (2006) 476,481; (2010 est.) 507,643. Capital: Hobart. It is located off the southeastern corner of the continent and separated from it by Bass Strait. The state's area includes numerous smaller islands. Originally inhabited by Australian Aborigines, the island was explored and named Van Diemen's Land by Abel Janszoon Tasman in 1642. Taken by the British in the early 1800s and made a colony in 1825, it was used as an auxiliary penal settlement until the 1850s. It was granted self-government and renamed Tasmania in 1856, and it became a state of the Australian Commonwealth in 1901. Chief economic activities include copper, zinc, lead, and silver mining; livestock raising, especially sheep for wool; and tourism. Several natural areas, collectively called the Tasman Wilderness, were designated a UNESCO World Heritage site in 1982 (extended in 1989).

Tasmanian devil, Marsupial species (*Sarcophilus harrisii* or *S.*

Tasmanian devil (Sarcophilus harrisii).
John Yates/Shostal Associates

ursinus, family Dasyuridae), now extinct on the Australian mainland, that survives in remote rocky areas of Tasmania. It is 30–40 in. (75–100 cm) long, with a stocky body, large head and jaws, and long bushy tail. The coat is usually black and brown with a white-marked breast. Named for its devilish expression and husky snarl, it is mainly a scavenger of wallaby and sheep carcasses but also eats beetle larvae and occasionally poultry. Its three or four young remain in the mother's pouch about five months.

Tathagata, Epithet of the Buddha that he employed primarily when referring to himself. He also used it to refer to other buddhas who preceded him and who would follow. Tathagatha refers to one who has trod the path to full awakening and so reached the end of suffering and escaped samsara. The implication is that the path is open to all who would follow it. In later Mahayana Buddhism, Tathagata came to mean the essential buddha nature found in everyone.

tattoo, Permanent mark or design made on the body by pigment introduced through ruptures in the skin. The term is also loosely applied to the inducement of scars (cicatrization). Tattooing has been practiced in most parts of the world, and examples have been found on Egyptian and Nubian mummies dating from 2000 BC. Decoration is perhaps the most common motive, though designs may also serve to identify rank, status, or membership and are thought by some to provide magical protection against sickness or misfortune. The word comes from Tahiti, where it was recorded by James Cook's expedition in 1769. The first electric tattooing implement was patented in the U.S. in 1891.

Taurus (Latin: "Bull") In astronomy, the constellation lying between Aries and Gemini; in astrology, the second sign of the zodiac, governing approximately the period April 20–May 20. Its symbol is a bull, a reference to the Greek myth in which Zeus transformed himself into a white bull to abduct Europa.

Taurus Mountains, Mountain chain, southern Turkey, running parallel with the Mediterranean Sea coast. The system extends along a curve from Lake Egridir in the west to the upper reaches of the Euphrates River in the east. It has many peaks rising above 12,000 ft (3,700 m) in elevation. The Cilician Gates pass, used by caravans and armies since antiquity, crosses the range north of Tarsus.

tax, Government levy on persons, groups, or businesses. Taxes are a general obligation of taxpayers and are not paid in exchange for any specific benefit. They have existed since ancient times—property taxes and sales taxes were known in ancient Rome—but tariffs were favoured over internal taxes as a source of revenue. In modern economies, there has been a trend away from tariffs in favour of internal taxes, which provide the majority of revenues. Taxes have three functions: to cover government spending, to promote stable economic growth, and to lessen inequalities in the distribution of income and wealth. They have also been used for nonfiscal reasons, such as to encourage or discourage certain activities (e.g., cigarette consumption). Taxes may be classified as direct or indirect. Direct taxes are those that the taxpayer cannot shift onto someone else; they are mainly taxes on persons and are based on an individual's ability to pay as measured by income or net wealth.

Direct taxes include income taxes, taxes on net worth, death duties (i.e., inheritance and estate taxes), and gift taxes. Indirect taxes are those that can be shifted in whole or in part to someone other than the person legally responsible for payment. These include excise taxes, sales taxes, and value-added taxes. Taxes may also be classified according to the effect they have on the distribution of wealth. A proportional tax is one that imposes the same relative burden on all taxpayers, unlike progressive taxes and regressive taxes.

taxidermy, Practice of creating lifelike representations of animals by using their prepared skins and various supporting structures. Taxidermy began with the ancient custom of keeping trophies of the hunt. Beginning in the 18th century, a growing interest in natural history resulted in collections and exhibits of birds, beasts, and curiosities. Chemically preserving skins, hair, and feathers made it possible to recreate the appearance of live animals by stuffing the sewed-up skin with straw or hay. Constructing and sculpting anatomically correct manikins of clay and plaster are the basis of modern taxidermy.

taxonomy, In biology, the classification of organisms into a hier-

Carolus Linnaeus, detail of a portrait by Alexander Roslin, 1775; in the Svenska Porträttarkivet, Stockholm.
Courtesy of the Svenska Porträttarkivet, Stockholm

archy of groupings, from the general to the particular, that reflect evolutionary and usually morphological relationships: kingdom, phylum, class, order, family, genus, species. The black-capped chickadee, for example, is an animal (kingdom Animalia) with a dorsal nerve cord (phylum Chordata) and feathers (class Aves: birds) that perches (order Passeriformes: perching birds) and is small with a short bill (family Paridae), a song that sounds like "chik-a-dee" (genus *Poecile*), and a black-capped head (species *atricapillus*). Most authorities recognize five kingdoms: monerans (prokaryotes), protists, fungi, plants, and animals. Carolus Linnaeus established the scheme of using Latin generic and specific names in the mid-18th century; his work was extensively revised by later biologists.

Tay, River, Longest river in Scotland. It rises on the northern slopes of Ben Lui and flows through Loch Tay to enter the North Sea below Dundee after a course of 120 mi (193 km). It drains 2,400 sq mi (6,200 sq km), the largest drainage area in Scotland.

Tay-Sachs disease, Recessive hereditary metabolic disorder, mostly in Ashkenazi Jews, causing progressive mental and neurologic deterioration and death by age five. A lipid, ganglioside GM_2, accumulates in the brain (because of inadequate activity of the enzyme that breaks it down), with devastating neurological effects. Infants appear normal at birth but soon become listless and inattentive, lose motor abilities, and develop seizures. Blindness and general paralysis usually precede death. Tests can detect the disease in fetuses and the Tay-Sachs gene in carriers. There is no treatment.

Tbilisi, formerly TIFLIS, City (pop., 2010 est.: 1,122,300), capital of Georgia, on the Mtkvari (Kura) River. Founded *c.* 458 CE as the capital of the Georgian kingdom, its strategic position on trade routes between Europe and Asia led to its frequent capture. It endured under successive Persian, Byzantine, Arab, Mongol, and Turkish rulers and came under the control of the Russian Empire *c.* 1801. It was made the capital of the Transcaucasian S.F.S.R. by 1922, of the Georgian S.S.R. in 1936, and of independent Georgia in 1991. Some ancient structures still exist in the city, which is now a major cultural, educational, research, and industrial centre.

Tchaikovsky, Pyotr Ilyich (b. May 7, 1840, Votkinsk, Russia—d. Nov. 6, 1893, St. Petersburg), Russian composer. Sensitive and interested in music from his early childhood, Tchaikovsky turned to serious composition at age 14. In 1862 he began studying at the new St. Petersburg Conservatory; from 1866 he taught at the Moscow Conservatory. His *Piano Concerto No. 1* (1875) was premiered in Boston and became immensely popular. He wrote his first ballet, *Swan Lake* (first performed 1877), on commission from the Bolshoi Ballet. In 1877 he received a commission from the wealthy Nadezhda von Meck (1831–94), who became his patron and longtime correspondent. The opera *Eugene Onegin* (1878) soon followed. Though homosexual, he married briefly; after three disastrous months of marriage, he attempted suicide. His composition was overshadowed by his personal crisis for years. His second ballet, *Sleeping Beauty* (1889), was followed by the opera *The Queen of Spades* (1890) and the great ballet *The Nutcracker* (1892). The *Pathétique Symphony* (1893) premiered four days before his death from cholera; claims that he was forced to commit suicide by noblemen outraged by his sexual liaisons are unfounded. He revolutionized the ballet genre by transforming it from a grand decorative gesture into a staged musical drama. His music has always had great popular appeal because of its tuneful, poignant melodies, impressive harmonies, and colourful, picturesque orchestration.

TCP/IP, in full TRANSMISSION CONTROL PROTOCOL/INTERNET PROTOCOL, Standard Internet communications protocols that allow digital computers to communicate over long distances. The Internet is a packet-switched network, in which information is broken down into small packets, sent individually over many different routes at the same time, and then reassembled at the receiving end. TCP is the component that collects and reassembles the packets of data, while IP is responsible for making sure the packets are sent to the right destination. TCP/IP was developed in the 1970s and adopted as the protocol standard for ARPANET (the predecessor to the Internet) in 1983.

tea, Beverage produced by steeping in freshly boiled water the young leaves and leaf buds of the tea plant, *Camellia sinensis*, a member of the family Theaceae, which contains 40 genera of trees and shrubs. Tea cultivation is first documented in China in AD 350; according to legend, it had been known there since *c.* 2700 BC. It was established in Japan by the 13th century and was spread to Java by the Dutch and to India by the English in the 19th century. Today tea is the most widely consumed drink in the world, drunk (either hot or cold) by half the world's population. Major tea types are classified by processing method: fermented, or black, tea produces an amber-colored, full-flavored beverage without bitterness; semifermented, or oolong, tea yields a slightly bitter, light brownish-green liquid; and unfermented, or green, tea, results in a mild, slightly bitter, pale greenish-yellow beverage. Caffeine is responsible for tea's stimulating effect. Green tea, long regarded as healthful in the Far East, has in recent years attracted much favorable attention in the West for a wide range of possible beneficial effects. Infusions and decoctions of the leaves, bark, and roots of many other, unrelated plants are commonly drunk as herbal or medicinal teas.

tea ceremony, Japanese CHADŌ, or CHA-NO-YU, Ritualized preparation and drinking of tea developed in Japan. It involves a host and one or more guests; the tea, utensils, and movements used in preparing, serving, and drinking the tea are all prescribed. When tea was introduced from Song-dynasty China by the Zen monk Eisai (1141–1215), it was drunk by Zen monks to help them stay awake during meditation. The laity enjoyed tea-tasting competitions that developed into a more refined, meditative form among the warrior aristocracy in the 15th century. The most famous exponent of the tea ceremony was Sen Rikyū (1522–91), tea master to

Toyotomi Hideyoshi, who codified a style known as *wabi*, which favoured rustic, rough-shaped tea bowls and spare, simple surroundings. Three popular schools of the tea ceremony trace their roots to Rikyū, and other schools exist as well; today mastery of the tea ceremony is one accomplishment of a well-bred young woman.

teak, Large deciduous tree (*Tectona grandis*) of the verbena family, and its wood, one of the most valuable and durable timbers. Teak has been widely used in India for more than 2,000 years; some temples contain teak beams more than 1,000 years old. The tree has a straight stem, often thickened at the base, a spreading crown, and four-sided branchlets. The rough leaves are opposite or sometimes whorled, and the branches end in many small white flowers. The unseasoned heartwood has a pleasant, strong aromatic fragrance and a beautiful golden-yellow colour, which on seasoning darkens into brown, mottled with darker streaks. Resistant to the effects of water, teakwood is used for shipbuilding, fine furniture, door and window frames, wharves, bridges, cooling-tower louvers, flooring, and paneling. Its desirability has led to severe overcutting in tropical forests.

tear gas, Any of a group of substances, most often synthetic organic halogen compounds, that irritate the mucous membranes of the eyes, causing a stinging sensation and tears. They may also irritate the upper respiratory tract, causing coughing, choking, and general debility. Tear gas was first used in warfare in World War I, but since its effects are short-lasting and rarely disabling, it came into use by law-enforcement agencies as a means of dispersing mobs, disabling rioters, and flushing out armed suspects without the use of deadly force.

technetium, Metallic chemical element, one of the transition elements, chemical symbol Tc, atomic number 43. All its isotopes are radioactive; some occur in trace amounts in nature as nuclear fission products of uranium. Its isotope technetium-97 was the first element artificially produced (1937; *see* cyclotron). Technetium-99, a fission product of nuclear reactors that emits gamma rays, is the most-used tracer isotope in nuclear medicine. Technetium resembles platinum in appearance and manganese and rhenium in chemical behaviour. It is also used as a metallurgical tracer and in corrosion-resistant products.

Teflon, Trademark for a polymer of tetrafluoroethylene fluorocarbon (polytetrafluoroethylene [PTFE]). Teflon is a tough, waxy, nonflammable organic compound with a slippery surface, attacked by very few chemicals and stable over a wide temperature range. Its qualities make it useful in gaskets, bearings, container and pipe linings, electrical insulation, parts for valves and pumps used for corrosive fluids, and protective nonstick coatings on cooking utensils, saw blades, and other articles. A closely related fluorocarbon polymer, fluorinated ethylene-propylene (FEP), has properties and applications similar to those of Teflon.

Tegucigalpa, City (pop., 2001: 769,061), capital of Honduras. Located on hilly terrain hemmed in by mountains, it was founded in 1578 as a gold- and silver-mining centre. It was made the permanent capital of Honduras in 1880. It produces textiles and sugar. Principal buildings include the presidential and legislative palaces, the National University of Honduras (1847), and an 18th-century cathedral.

Tehrān, or TEHERAN, City (pop., 2006: 7,797,520), capital of Iran. It is situated on the southern slopes of the Elburz Mountains. It was originally a suburb of ancient Rhagae (Rey), which was destroyed by the Mongols in 1220 and was later the home of several Ṣafavid rulers of Persia (16th–18th century). It became prominent after its capture (1785) by Āghā Muḥammad Khan, founder of the Qājār dynasty, who made it his capital. It underwent rapid modernization after 1925 and especially after World War II (1939–45). In 1943 it was the site of the Tehrān Conference. In 1979, following the Islamic revolution in Iran, the U.S. embassy there was seized and its staff taken hostage by Iranian militants. A transportation and industrial centre, Tehrān produces more than half of Iran's manufactured goods. It is the seat of several educational institutions, including the University of Tehrān (1934).

Tel Aviv–Yafo, or TEL AVIV–JAFFA, City (pop., 2005 est.: 371,400) and main port of Israel. The hub of Israel's largest urban centre, it was formed in 1950 by the incorporation of the ancient port of Jaffa with Tel Aviv, its former suburb. Tel Aviv was founded in 1909 and was the capital of Israel (1948–50). It grew with Jewish immigration in the early 20th century and by 1936 was the largest and most important city in Palestine. Jaffa was an old Canaanite city that was taken by Egypt in the 15th century BCE and occupied by the Israelite kings David and Solomon. Over the centuries it was ruled by the Ptolemies, Syrians, and Romans, captured by the Crusaders, and razed by the Mamlūks. The British occupied it in 1917. It surrendered to Jewish military forces during the first Arab-Israeli war (1948). Israel's main business, communications, and cultural centre, it is the site of more than half of Israel's industrial plants, the country's stock exchange, Tel Aviv University (1953), and Bar-Ilan University (1953).

telecommunication, Communication between parties at a distance from one another. Modern telecommunication systems—capable of transmitting telephone, fax, data, radio, or television signals—can transmit large volumes of information over long distances. Digital transmission is employed in order to achieve high reliability with minimal noise, or interference, and because it can transmit any signal type, digital or analog. For digital transmission, analog signals must be subjected to a process of analog-to-digital conversion; most television, radio, and voice communications are analog and must be digitized before transmission. Transmission may occur over cables, wireless radio relay systems, or via satellite links.

teleology, Causality in which the effect is explained by an end (Greek, *telos*) to be realized. Teleology thus differs essentially from efficient causality, in which an effect is dependent on prior events. Aristotle's account of teleology declared that a full explanation of anything must consider its final cause—the purpose for which the thing exists or was produced. Following Aristotle, many philosophers have conceived of biological processes as involving the operation of a guiding end. Modern science has tended to appeal only to efficient causes in its investigations.

telescope, Device that collects light from and magnifies images of distant objects, undoubtedly the most important investigative tool in astronomy. The first telescopes focused visible light by refraction through lenses; later instruments used reflection from curved mirrors. Their invention is traditionally credited to Hans Lippershey (1570?–1619?). Among the earliest telescopes were Galilean telescopes, modeled after the simple instruments built by Galileo, who was the first to use telescopes to study celestial bodies. Since the 1930s radio telescopes have been used to detect and form images from radio waves emitted by celestial objects. More recently, telescopes have been designed to observe objects and phenomena in other parts of the electromagnetic spectrum. Spaceflight has allowed telescopes to be launched into Earth orbit to avoid the light-scattering and light-absorbing effects of the atmosphere (e.g., the Hubble Space Telescope).

Tell, William, German WILHELM TELL, Swiss national hero whose historical existence is disputed. According to tradition, in the 13th or early 14th century he defied Austrian authority and was forced to shoot an apple from his son's head with a crossbow at a distance of 80 paces by the hated Austrian governor. He subsequently ambushed and killed the governor, an event that supposedly led to rebellion against Austrian rule. He is first mentioned in a chronicle from 1470. The marksman's test is widely found in folklore, and the story has resemblances to the founding myths of other nations.

Telugu language, Dravidian language spoken by more than 66 million people in South India and in immigrant communities elsewhere. It is the official language of the state of Andhra Pradesh. The earliest inscription entirely in Telugu is from the 6th century; literary texts begin in the 11th century. The Telugu script, derived from the writing of the Calukya dynasty, is closely akin to Kannada script. Like other major Dravidian languages, Telugu has very marked distinctions between formal or literary and colloquial registers and between social dialects.

temperature, Measure of hotness expressed in terms of any of several arbitrary scales, such as Fahrenheit, Celsius, or Kelvin. Heat flows from a hotter body to a colder one and continues to do so until both are at the same temperature. Temperature is a measure of the average energy of the molecules of a body, whereas heat is a measure of the total amount of thermal energy in a body. For example, whereas the temperature of a cup of boiling water is the same as that of a large pot of boiling water (212 °F, or 100 °C), the large pot has more heat, or thermal energy, and it takes more energy to boil a pot of water than a cup of water. The most common temperature scales are based on arbitrarily defined fixed points. The Fahrenheit scale sets 32 as the freezing point of water and 212 as the boiling point of water (at standard atmospheric pressure). The Celsius scale defines the triple point of water (at which all three phases, solid, liquid, and gas, coexist in equilibrium) at 0.01 and the boiling point at 100. The Kelvin scale, used primarily for scientific and engineering purposes, sets the zero point at absolute zero and uses a degree the same size as those of the Celsius scale.

tempering, Heat-treating of metal alloys, particularly steel, to reduce brittleness and restore ductility. In tempering, steel is slowly heated to a temperature between 300 and 1,300 °F (150 and 700 °C), depending on desired properties, in an oil or salt bath and held for about two hours and then allowed to air cool. As steel is physically worked (e.g., rolling, wiredrawing, hammering), hardening takes place, and it grows progressively more brittle. Similarly, but more deliberately, heating and quenching increase hardness. Combined quench-and-temper heat-treating is applied at many different cooling rates, holding times, and temperatures and is a very important means of controlling the properties of steel.

Templar, or KNIGHT TEMPLAR, Member of a religious military order of knighthood established during the Crusades. At its beginning (*c.* 1119), the group consisted of eight or nine French knights who devoted themselves to protecting from Muslim warriors those on pilgrimage to Jerusalem. They were given quarters near the site of the former Temple of Jerusalem, from which they derived their name. Taking vows of poverty and chastity, they performed courageous service, and their numbers increased rapidly, partly because of the propagandistic writing of St. Bernard de Clairvaux, who also wrote their rule of life. They flourished for two centuries, expanding to other countries, growing in number to 20,000, and acquiring vast wealth and property. By 1304 rumours, probably false, of irreligious practices and blasphemies had made them the target of persecution. In 1307 Philip IV of France and Pope Clement V initiated the offensive that culminated in the Templars' final suppression in 1312, including the confiscation of all their property and the imprisonment or execution of many members; their last leader, Jacques de Molay (1243–1314), was burned at the stake.

Temple of Heaven, Large religious complex in the old outer city of Beijing, considered the supreme achievement of traditional Chinese architecture. Its layout symbolizes the belief that heaven is round and earth square. The three buildings are built in a straight line. The Hall of Prayer for Good Harvests (1420) has three concentric circles of massive wood columns symbolizing the four seasons, 12 months, and 12 daily hours; in a remarkable feat of engineering, they support the three roof levels and, in succession, a huge square brace (earth), circular architrave (heaven), and vast interior cupola. The Imperial Vault of Heaven (1530; rebuilt 1572) is a smaller circular building constructed without crossbeams; its dome is supported by complicated span work. The Circular Mound Altar (1530; rebuilt 1749) is a triple-tiered white stone terrace enclosed by two sets of walls that are square outside and round inside.

Ten Commandments, List of religious precepts sacred in Judaism and Christianity. They include injunctions to honour God, the Sabbath, and one's parents, as well as bans on idolatry, blasphemy, murder, adultery, theft, false witness, and covetousness. In the book of Exodus, they are divinely revealed to Moses on Mount Sinai and engraved on two stone tablets. Most scholars propose a date between the 16th and 13th century BC for the commandments, though some date them as late as 750 BC. They were not regarded with deep reverence by Christians until the 13th century.

tendinitis, or TENDONITIS, Inflammation of a tendon sheath, due to irritation of this thin, filmy tissue by overuse of the tendons, which slide within them, or to bacterial infection. It is often an occupational disease, affecting tendons used in repetitive motions on the job. The tendon becomes swollen and red, with pain that increases on motion. The swelling hampers the tendon's sliding within, causing stiffness. Treatment involves immobilization with a splint, cast, or bandage and gradually increasing motion after inflammation subsides, which may happen sooner with corticosteroid injections. Repeated episodes can permanently thicken the sheath, limiting motion.

tendon, Tissue attaching a muscle to other body parts, usually bones, to transmit the mechanical force of muscle contraction to the other part. Much like ligaments, tendons are composed of dense, fibrous connective tissue with a high collagen content, which makes them remarkably tough and strong, with great tensile strength to withstand the stresses generated by muscle contraction.

tennis, Game played with rackets and a light, elastic ball by two players or pairs of players on a rectangular court divided by a low net. Tennis is played indoors and outdoors, on hard-surface, clay, and grass courts. The object is to hit the ball over the net and into the opponent's half of the court in such a way as to defeat the opponent's attempt to reach and return it. Each player serves for an entire game. Points are scored as 15, 30, 40, and game (the term "love" is used for 0). A tied score ("deuce") requires continued play until a two-point margin is achieved. The first player to win six games, with a lead of two games, takes the set. A match consists of the best two out of three (or three out of five) sets. Since the early 1970s, tiebreakers have been employed to eliminate marathon sets. Tennis developed in the 1870s in Britain from earlier racket-and-ball games. The first world lawn-tennis championship was held in 1877 at Wimbledon; clay- and hard-court competitions emerged later. Current international team tournaments include the Davis Cup for men and the Federation Cup (since 1963) for women's teams. The major tournaments for individual players constitute the "Grand Slam" of tennis: the national championships of Britain (Wimbledon), the U.S., Australia, and France.

Tenochtitlán, Ancient capital of the Aztec empire. Located at the site of modern Mexico City, it was founded c. 1325 in the marshes of Lake Texcoco. It formed a confederacy with Texcoco and Tlacopán and was the Aztec capital by the late 15th century. Originally located on two small islands in Lake Texcoco, it gradually spread through the construction of artificial islands to cover more than 5 sq mi (13 sq km). It was connected to the mainland by several causeways. The population in 1519 was estimated to be about 400,000 people, the largest residential concentration in Mesoamerican history. It contained the palace of Montezuma II, said to consist of 300 rooms, as well as hundreds of temples. It was destroyed by the Spanish conquistadores under Hernán Cortés in 1521.

tenor, High male voice range, extending from about the second B below middle C to the G above it. In the polyphony of the 13th–16th centuries, the tenor was the part that held (Latin, *tenere*: "to hold") the cantus firmus. Tenor voices are often classified as dramatic, lyric, or heroic (heldentenor). In instrument families, tenor refers to the instrument in which the central range is roughly that of the tenor voice (e.g., tenor saxophone).

Tenrikyo, Largest and most successful of the modern Shinto sects in Japan. Its founder, Nakayama Miki (1798–1887), was a charismatic peasant who, at age 40, claimed to be possessed by a god of divine wisdom. She developed a form of worship characterized by ecstatic dancing and shamanistic practices, and a doctrine emphasizing charity and the healing of disease through mental acts of faith. Her writings and deeds were considered divine models. Tenrikyo was one of the most powerful religious movements in Japan immediately after World War II, and its membership reached about 2.5 million in the late 20th century.

tense, In grammar, an inflected form of a verb indicating the time of a narrated event in relation to the time at which the narrator is speaking. Time is often perceived as a continuum with three main divisions, past, present, and future, defined in relation to the time when the event is described. Other categories, including mood and aspect, may further specify the action as definite or indefinite, completed or not completed, lasting or nonlasting, and recurring or occurring once.

Teotihuacán, Largest (though not most populous) city of pre-Columbian central Mexico, about 30 mi (50 km) northeast of modern Mexico City. Teotihuacán wielded its greatest influence in the first 900 years AD, after which it was sacked by the Toltecs. At its height, some 150,000 people lived in the city, which covered about 8 sq mi (21 sq km). Its plazas, temples, and palaces are dominated by the Pyramid of the Moon and the huge Pyramid of the Sun. Teotihuacán was the capital of one of the earliest Mesoamerican civilizations, and some consider it also to have been the centre of Toltec civilization.

Teresa (of Calcutta), Blessed Mother, orig. AGNES GONXHA BOJAXHIU (b. Aug. 27, 1910, Skopje, Maced., Ottoman Empire—d. Sept. 5, 1997, Calcutta, India; beatified Oct. 19, 2003), Roman Catholic nun, founder of the Order of the Missionaries of Charity. The daughter of a grocer, she became a nun and went to India as a young woman. After studying nursing, she moved to the slums of Calcutta (Kolkata); in 1948 she founded her order, which served the blind, the aged, the disabled, and the dying. In 1963 the Indian government awarded her the Padmashri ("Lord of the Lotus") for her services to the people of India, and in 1971 Pope Paul VI awarded her the first Pope John XXIII Peace Prize. In 1979 she received the Nobel Prize for Peace. Although in her later years she suffered from a worsening heart condition, Mother Teresa continued to serve the poor and sick and also spoke out against divorce, contraception, and abortion. Her order included hundreds of centres in more than 90 countries, with some 4,000 nuns and hundreds of thousands of lay workers. She was succeeded by the Indian-born Sister Nirmala. The process to declare her a saint began within two years of her death, and Pope John Paul II issued a special dispensation to expedite the process. She was beatified on Oct. 19, 2003, reaching the ranks of the blessed in the shortest time in the church's history.

Teresa of Ávila, Saint, orig. TERESA DE CEPEDA Y AHUMADA (b. March 28, 1515, Ávila, Spain—d. Oct. 4, 1582, Alba de Tormes; canonized 1622; feast day October 15), Spanish Carmelite nun, mystic, and saint. After entering a convent around the age of 20, she fell seriously ill. She underwent a religious awakening in 1555 and, despite her frail health, initiated the Carmelite Reform, leading the order's return to its original austere practices, including poverty and seclusion from the world. Against some opposition, she opened new convents (the first in 1562) under the reformed order throughout Spain. St. John of the Cross joined her in her efforts, establishing reformed Carmelite monasteries. Her doctrines have been accepted as the classical exposition of the contemplative life, and her spiritual writings are still widely read today, among them *The Interior Castle* (1588). In 1970 she became the first woman elevated to the position of Doctor of the Church.

Tereshkova, Valentina (Vladimirovna) (b. March 6, 1937, Maslennikovo, Russia, U.S.S.R.), Russian cosmonaut. An accomplished parachutist, she was accepted for the cosmonaut program in 1961. In 1963 she became the first woman in space, making 48 orbits in 71 hours aboard Vostok 6. She left the program after her flight and served in various governmental positions until the early 1990s. She was named a hero of the Soviet Union and twice awarded the Order of Lenin.

termite, Any of 2,750 species (order Isoptera) of mostly tropical, social, cellulose-eating insects that are usually soft-bodied and wingless. Intestinal microorganisms enable them to digest cellulose. Termite colonies consist of a fertile queen and king (reproductives), workers (the most numerous), and soldiers. Kings are less than an inch long (1–2 cm), but a queen may grow to more than 4 in. (11 cm). Workers and soldiers are sterile and blind. They survive two to five years; reproductives may live for 60–70 years. Termites live in a sealed, humid nest in wood or underground. Underground nests may be built up into a mound. Periodically, alates (winged, sighted forms) develop and leave the nest to start a new colony. Termites eat chiefly wood. Soil-dwelling termites attack wood that is in contact with the ground; wood-dwelling termites, requiring less humidity than soil-dwellers, attack trees, posts, and wooden buildings.

terra-cotta (Italian: "baked earth"), Fairly coarse, porous clay

that, when fired, assumes a colour ranging from dull ochre to red. Terra-cotta objects are usually left unglazed and are often of a utilitarian kind, because of their cheapness, versatility, and durability. Small terra-cotta figures from 3000 BC have been found in Greece and others throughout the Roman Empire from the 4th century BC. The use of terra-cotta virtually died out when the Roman Empire collapsed, but it was revived in Italy and Germany in the 15th century.

"Virgin and Child," polychromed and gilded terra-cotta relief by Andrea del Verrocchio, c. 1470; in the Metropolitan Museum of Art, New York City.
Courtesy of the (bottom) Rogers Fund, 1909

terrier, Any of several dog breeds developed, mostly in England, to find and kill vermin and for use in the sports of foxhunting and dog fighting. Bred to fight and kill, they often were pugnacious but are now bred for a friendlier temperament. Because terriers had to fit in rodent burrows, most breeds are small and lean and have a rough, wiry coat that requires little maintenance. They have a long head, square jaw, and deep-set eyes. All terriers are vocal and inclined to chase and confront. Most breeds were named for the place where they were developed.

territorial waters, Waters under the sovereign jurisdiction of a nation or state, including both marginal sea and inland waters. The concept originated in the 17th-century controversy over the status of the sea. Though the doctrine that the sea must be free to all was upheld, a nation's jurisdiction over its coastal waters was also recognized. Nations subscribing to the Law of the Sea observe a territorial limit of 12 nautical mi (22 km) from shore. Territorial rights include the airspace above those waters and the seabed below them.

terrorism, Systematic use of violence to create a general climate of fear in a population and thereby to bring about a particular political objective. It has been used throughout history by political organizations of both the left and the right, by nationalist and ethnic groups, and by revolutionaries. Although usually thought of as a means of destabilizing or overthrowing existing political institutions, terror also has been employed by governments against their own people to suppress dissent; examples include the reigns of certain Roman emperors, the French Revolution, Nazi Germany, the Soviet Union under Stalin, and Argentina during the "dirty war" of the 1970s. Terrorism's impact has been magnified by the deadliness and technological sophistication of modern-day weapons and the capability of the media to disseminate news of such attacks instantaneously throughout the world. The deadliest terrorist attack ever occurred in the United States on Sept. 11, 2001, when members of al-Qaeda terrorist network hijacked four commercial airplanes and crashed two of them into the twin towers of the World Trade Center complex in New York City and one into the Pentagon building near Washington, D.C.; the fourth plane crashed near Pittsburgh, Pa. The crashes resulted in the collapse of much of the World Trade Center complex, the destruction of part of the southwest side of the Pentagon, and the deaths of some 3,000 people.

Tertiary Period, Informal division of geologic time spanning the interval between about 65.5 and 2.6 million years ago. Officially, it has been replaced by the Paleogene Period (65.5–23 million years ago) and the Neogene Period (23–2.6 million years ago). It constituted the first of the two periods of the Cenozoic Era, the second being the Quaternary. The Tertiary was made up of five subdivisions: (from oldest to youngest) the Paleocene, Eocene, Oligocene, Miocene, and Pliocene epochs. During most of the Tertiary the spatial distribution of the major continents was largely similar to that of today. Emergence and submergence of land bridges between continents critically affected the distribution of both terrestrial and marine animals and plants. Virtually all the existing major mountain ranges were formed either partly or wholly during the Tertiary.

testosterone, Masculinizing sex hormone produced by the testes. It is responsible for the development of the male sex organs and secondary sex characteristics (e.g., facial hair, masculine musculature, deep voice, and male-pattern baldness). Testosterone can be manufactured by modifying other, less expensive steroids. It is used in the treatment of hypogonadism, undescended testes (cryptorchism), and certain cancers.

tetanus, or LOCKJAW, Acute bacterial disease caused by *Clostridium tetani*. Spores of this organism are common, especially in soil; it thrives away from oxygen in deep wounds, especially punctures. Its toxin stimulates nerves, causing muscle rigidity with frequent spasms. This may occur around the site of the wound or, if the toxin reaches spinal motor ganglia via the bloodstream, throughout the body. The jaw muscles are almost always involved (lockjaw). Vaccination every few years is the best protection; an antitoxin prevents or delays symptoms in cases of suspect wounds but has limited value once they develop. Treatment usually includes antibiotics, sedatives, and muscle relaxants. Recovered patients are not immune.

tetracycline, Any of a class of broad-spectrum antibiotics with a common basic structure, including doxycycline. They may be isolated directly from several species of actinomycetes of the genus *Streptomyces* or modified from the compounds isolated. They are the drugs of choice in the treatment of cholera, rickettsial infections, psittacosis, brucellosis, and tularemia; tetracyclines are also used in the treatment of acne. Overuse of these and other antibiotics has led to drug resistance in microorganisms.

tetrarch (Greek: "ruler of a quarter"), In Greco-Roman antiquity, the ruler of a principality, originally the ruler of one-quarter of a region or province. The first tetrarchs ruled the four tetrarchies of Thessaly under Philip II of Macedonia. Tetrarchs ruled in Galatia (in Asia Minor) before the Roman conquest (169 BC) and still later in Hellenized Syria and Palestine, where the title denoted the semi-independent ruler of a divided kingdom or minor district. Herod the Great's realm after his death (4 BC) was ruled by his three sons, two of whom were called tetrarchs.

Teutonic Order, or TEUTONIC KNIGHTS, officially HOUSE OF THE HOSPITALLERS OF SAINT MARY OF THE TEUTONS, Religious order important in eastern Europe in the late Middle Ages. Founded in 1189–90 to nurse the sick in Palestine during the Third Crusade, it was militarized in 1198 and given land in Jerusalem and Germany. It transferred its base of operations to eastern Europe in the 13th century, gaining control of Prussia by 1283 and making Marienburg the centre of a military principality (1309–1525). The order extended its influence until it was defeated at the Battle of Tannenberg (1410). Another Polish victory in 1466 forced the knights to cede lands to Poland and become vassals of the Polish king. In 1525 the grand master in Prussia converted to Protestantism, dissolved the order in Prussia, and became a duke under Polish suzerainty. In other parts of Europe, especially Austria, the order survived the Reformation. Napoleon declared the order dissolved in 1809 and redistributed most of its remaining lands. In 1834 the Austrian emperor refounded it as a charitable religious order, and it is now headquartered in Vienna.

textile, Any filament, fibre, or yarn that can be made into fabric or cloth, and the resulting material itself. The word originally referred only to woven fabrics but now includes knitted, bonded, felted, and tufted fabrics as well. The basic raw materials used in textile production are fibres, either obtained from natural sources (e.g., wool) or produced from chemical substances (e.g., nylon and polyester). Textiles are used for wearing apparel, household linens and bedding, upholstery, draperies and curtains, wall coverings, rugs and carpets, and bookbindings, in addition to being used widely in industry.

Tezcatlipoca, Omnipotent god of the Aztec pantheon and god of the constellation Ursa Major. The protector of slaves, he severely punished masters who ill-treated them. He is said to have put an end to the Toltecs' golden age. Each year his worshipers selected a handsome prisoner of war who was allowed to live in princely luxury for a year before being sacrificed. Tezcatlipoca is represented in art with an obsidian mirror, in which he sees all, on his chest or in place of a foot.

Thailand, officially KINGDOM OF THAILAND formerly SIAM, Country, mainland Southeast Asia. Area: 198,117 sq mi (513,120 sq km). Population: (2011 est.) 65,856,000. Capital: Bangkok. The population is predominantly Thai, with significant Chinese, Khmer, and Malay minorities. Language: Thai (official). Religions: Buddhism; also Islam. Currency: baht. The country encompasses forested hills and mountains, a central plain containing the Chao Phraya River delta, and a plateau in the northeast. Its market economy is based largely on services (notably trade) and light industries; agriculture employs a large proportion of the workforce. Thailand is a major producer of tungsten and tin. Among its chief agricultural products are rice, corn, rubber, soybeans, and pineapples; manufactures include clothing, canned goods, electronic equipment, and cement. Tourism is also important. Thailand is a constitutional monarchy with two legislative houses; its head of state is the king, and the head of government is the prime minister. The region that is now Thailand was part of the Mon and Khmer kingdoms from the 9th century CE. Thai-speaking peoples

emigrated from China *c.* the 10th century. During the 13th century two Thai states emerged: the Sukhothai kingdom, founded *c.* 1220 after a successful revolt against the Khmer, and Chiang Mai (which evolved into the kingdom of Lan Na with Chiang Mai as its capital), founded in 1296 after defeating the Mon. In 1351 the Tai kingdom of Ayutthaya (Siam) succeeded the Sukhothai. Myanmar (Burma) was its most powerful rival, Burman armies occupying it briefly in the 16th century and destroying it in 1767. The Chakri dynasty came to power in 1782, moved the capital to Bangkok, and extended its empire along the Malay Peninsula and into Laos and Cambodia. The empire was formally named Siam in 1856. Although Western influence increased during the 19th century, Siam's rulers avoided colonization by granting concessions to European countries; it was the only Southeast Asian country able to do so. In 1917 Siam entered World War I on the side of the Allies. Following a military coup in 1932, it became a constitutional monarchy and was officially renamed Thailand in 1939. It was occupied by Japan in World War II. It participated in the Korean War as a member of the UN forces and was allied with South Vietnam in the Vietnam War. The country subsequently became a regional economic powerhouse, though serious social problems also emerged, including a growing gap between rich and poor and a major AIDS epidemic.

Thailand, Gulf of, formerly GULF OF SIAM, Inlet of the South China Sea. Mostly bordering Thailand, though Cambodia and Vietnam form its southeastern shore, it is 300–350 mi (500–560 km) wide and 450 mi (725 km) long. Thailand's main harbours lie along its shores, its waters are important fishing grounds, and beaches along its coast are popular tourist attractions.

thalidomide, Drug formerly used as a sedative and to prevent morning sickness during pregnancy. Synthesized in 1954, it was introduced in almost 50 countries, including West Germany and Britain, where it became popular because it was effective and huge overdoses were not fatal. In 1961 it was found to cause congenital disorders; when it is taken in early pregnancy, some 20% of fetuses have phocomelia (defective development of the limbs) and other deformities; 5,000–10,000 such babies were born. It was never distributed for clinical use in the U.S.. Thalidomide appears effective against inflammatory and autoimmune disorders, including certain late-stage AIDS symptoms, and is licensed for use in such treatments in some countries.

Thames, River, ancient TAMESIS, Principal river of England. It rises in the Cotswolds in Gloucestershire and winds 205 mi (330 km) eastward across south-central England into a great estuary, through which it empties into the North Sea. It is tidal for about 65 mi (104 km). Known by the Romans and by early English chroniclers, it has been celebrated by bards throughout history. One of the world's most important commercial waterways, it is navigable by large vessels to London.

Thanatos, Ancient Greek personification of death. He was the son of Nyx, goddess of night, and brother to Hypnos, god of sleep. He appeared to humans to carry them off to the underworld when the time allotted to them by the Fates had expired. Thanatos was once defeated by Heracles, who wrestled him to save the life of Alcestis, and he was tricked by Sisyphus, who wanted a second chance at life.

Thanksgiving Day, U.S. holiday. It originated in the autumn of 1621 when Plymouth governor William Bradford invited neighbouring Indians to join the Pilgrims for a three-day festival of recreation and feasting in gratitude for the bounty of the season, which had been partly enabled by the Indians' advice. Neither the standard Thanksgiving meal of turkey, cranberry sauce, and pumpkin pie nor the family orientation of the day reflects the Plymouth event, however. Proclaimed a national holiday in 1863, Thanksgiving is celebrated on the fourth Thursday in November (though it was moved back one week in 1939–41 to extend the

Christmas shopping season). Canada adopted Thanksgiving as a national holiday in 1879; since 1957 it has been celebrated on the second Monday in October.

Thar Desert, or GREAT INDIAN DESERT, Region of hot, dry desert, northwestern India and southeastern Pakistan. Its undulating surface is composed of sand dunes separated by sandy plains and low, barren hills. Several saline lakes are found there. Covering some 77,000 sq mi (200,000 sq km), it is bordered by the Indus River plain, the Aravalli Range, and the Punjab plain.

Thatcher, Margaret, Baroness Thatcher (of Kesteven),

Margaret Thatcher, 1983.
AP

orig. MARGARET HILDA ROBERTS (b. Oct. 13, 1925, Grantham, Lincolnshire, Eng.), British politician and prime minister (1979–90). She earned a degree from the University of Oxford, where she was one of the first woman presidents of the Oxford University Conservative Association, then worked as a research chemist. After her marriage to Denis Thatcher (1951), she read for the bar and specialized in tax law. She was elected to Parliament in 1959, and she served as secretary of state for education and science (1970–74). As a member of the Conservative Party's newly energetic right wing, she succeeded Edward Heath as party leader in 1975. In 1979 she became Britain's first woman prime minister. She advocated individual initiative, confronted the labour unions, privatized national industries and utilities and attempted to privatize aspects of health care and education, pursued a strong monetarist policy, and endorsed a firm commitment to NATO. Her landslide victory in 1983 owed partly to her decisive leadership in the Falkland Islands War. A split in party ranks over European monetary and political integration led to her resignation in 1990, by which time she had become Britain's longest continuously serving prime minister since 1827.

theatre, Live performance of dramatic actions in order to tell a story or create a spectacle. The word derives from the Greek *theatron* ("place of seeing"). Theatre is one of the oldest and most important art forms in cultures worldwide. While the script is the basic element of theatrical performance, it also relies in varying degrees on acting, singing, and dancing, as well as on technical aspects of production. Theatre is thought to have had its earliest origins in religious ritual; it often enacts myths or stories central to the belief structure of a culture or creates comedy through travesty of such narratives. In Western civilization, theatre began in ancient Greece and was adapted in Roman times; it was revived in the medieval liturgical dramas and flourished in the Renaissance with the Italian commedia dell'arte and in the 17th–18th century with established companies such as the Comédie-Française. Varying theatrical forms may evolve to suit the tastes of different audiences (e.g., in Japan, the Kabuki of the townspeople and the Noh theatre of the court). In Europe and the U.S. in the 19th and early 20th centuries, theatre was a major source of entertainment for all social classes, with forms ranging from burlesque shows and vaudeville to serious dramas performed in the style of the Moscow Art Theatre. Though the musicals of Broadway and the farces of London's West End retain their popular appeal, the rise of television and movies eroded audiences for live theatre and has tended to limit its spectators to an educated elite.

Theatre of Fact, or DOCUMENTARY THEATRE, Movement to bring social issues to the stage by emphasizing factual information over aesthetic considerations. An outgrowth of the Living Newspaper technique employed in the 1930s by the WPA Federal Theatre Project in the U.S., the form became popular in the 1960s. In Germany Rolf Hochhuth's *The Representative* (1963), Peter Weiss's *The Investigation* (1965), and Heinar Kipphardt's *In the Matter of J. Robert Oppenheimer* (1964) examined recent historical events through authentic documentary sources such as trial transcripts and statistics. The movement influenced later political drama in Europe and the U.S.

Theatre of the Absurd, Body of dramatic works of the 1950s and '60s that expressed the existentialist philosophy of meaninglessness and the absurdity of life. Playwrights such as Arthur Adamov, Edward Albee, Samuel Beckett, Jean Genet, Eugène Ionesco, and Harold Pinter created Absurdist plays without traditional plots and with characters who engaged in circular, purposeless conversations. Beckett's *Waiting for Godot* (1953), in which two tramps wait for a mysterious man who never arrives, is a classic of the genre.

theatricalism, Twentieth-century theatrical movement that emphasized artifice in reaction to 19th-century naturalism. Marked by stylized acting, a stage projecting into the audience, and frank scenic artifices and conventions, it did not strive to create the illusion of reality but rather to remind the audience of their role as viewers and critics of the artwork in progress before them. Theatricalism was found in the Expressionist, Dadaist, and Surrealist drama of the early 20th century and has continued as a current in the modern theatre.

Thebes, Greek THÍVAI, Ancient city, Boeotia, east-central Greece, one of the chief Greek city-states. Traditionally said to have been founded by Cadmus, it was the seat of the legendary Oedipus and the setting for many classic Greek tragedies. The building of its celebrated seven-gated wall is usually attributed to Amphion. It was a centre of Mycenaean power in the Bronze Age (c. 1500–1200 BC). Hostility to Athens led it to side with the Persians in the Persian Wars and with Sparta in the Peloponnesian War. Thebes and Sparta subsequently clashed, and the victorious Spartans occupied it. It revolted c. 380 BC and defeated Sparta at the battles of Tegyra (375 BC) and Leuctra (371 BC). For the next 10 years it was the chief military power in Greece. It joined Athens against Philip II of Macedon and shared the defeat at the Battle of Chaeronea in 338 BC. It was sacked by Alexander the Great in 336 and eventually fell to Rome in the 1st century BC. Among the few ancient remains are remnants of the city walls, the Mycenaean palace (c. 1450–1350 BC), and a temple of Apollo.

Thebes, biblical NO, Ancient city, Egypt. Its remains are located on the Banks of the Nile River. In early times it also included Karnak and Luxor; the Valley of the Kings is situated nearby. The earliest monuments in the city itself date from the 11th dynasty (c. 21st century BC), when the rulers of Thebes united Egypt and made Thebes the capital of Upper Egypt. It remained the capital until the end of the Middle Kingdom (c. 18th century BC). It was obscured for two centuries under the rule of various foreign invaders, after which the kings of Thebes restored Egyptian rule in the 16th century BC and again made it the capital. It flourished as Egypt's political and religious centre throughout the New Kingdom period and was well known for achievements in sculpture and architecture. It began to decline in the 12th century BC and was sacked by Assyrians in the mid-7th century BC, by Persians in the 6th–4th centuries BC, and by Romans c. 30 BC. Its ruins include great temples and tombs, including the Temple of Amon at Karnak (c. 20th century BC), the tomb of Tutankhamen in the Valley of the Kings, and the great mortuary temples of Ramses II and Hatshepsut. The region's antiquities were collectively designated a UNESCO World Heritage site in 1979.

theft, In law, the crime of taking the property or services of another without consent. Under most statutes, theft encompasses the crimes of larceny, robbery, and burglary. Larceny is the crime of taking and carrying away the goods of another with intent to steal. Grand larceny, or larceny of property of substantial value, is a felony, whereas petty larceny, or larceny of less valuable property, is a misdemeanour. The same principle applies to grand theft and petty theft, which need not necessarily involve the "carrying away" of property and may include the theft of services. Robbery is an aggravated form of larceny involving violence or the threat of violence directed against the victim in his presence. Burglary is defined as the breaking and entering of the premises of another with an intent to commit a felony within. Two offenses usually distinguished from theft are embezzlement and fraud.

theism, View that all observable phenomena are dependent on but distinct from one supreme being. The view usually entails the idea that God is beyond human comprehension, perfect and self-sustained, but also peculiarly involved in the world and its events. Theists seek support for their view in rational argument and appeals to experience. Arguments for God's existence are of four principal types: cosmological, ontological, teleological, or moral. A central issue for theism is reconciling God, usually understood as omnipotent and perfect, with the existence of evil.

theocracy, Government by divine guidance or by officials who are regarded as divinely guided. In many theocracies, government leaders are members of the clergy, and the state's legal system is based on religious law. Theocratic rule was typical of early civilizations. The Enlightenment marked the end of theocracy in most Western countries. Contemporary examples of theocracies include Saudi Arabia, Iran, and the Vatican.

theodicy, Argument for the justification of God, concerned with reconciling God's goodness and justice with the observable facts of evil and suffering in the world. Most such arguments are a necessary component of theism. Under polytheism, the problem is solved by attributing evil to a conflict of wills between deities. The solution is less simple in monotheism, and it can take several forms. In some approaches, the perfect world created by God was spoiled by human disobedience or sin. In others, God withdrew after creating the world, which then fell into decay.

Theodora (b. *c.* 497—d. June 28, 548, Constantinople), Byzantine empress, wife of Justinian I. The daughter of a bear keeper at the Hippodrome in Constantinople, she became an actress and the mistress of Justinian. He married her in 525, and when he became emperor in 527 she was proclaimed empress. Probably the most powerful woman in Byzantine history, she was her husband's most trusted adviser, sponsoring legal reforms and wielding great influence in diplomacy, military appointments, and internal politics. Her impassioned speech gave Justinian the strength to order the brutal suppression of the Nika revolt (532) and save his empire. She recognized the rights of women and ended persecution of Monophysite Christians, with whom she sympathized.

Theodora, detail of a Byzantine mosaic in the church of San Vitale, Ravenna, Italy.
Andre Held/J.P. Ziolo

theology, Study of the nature of God and the relationship of the human and divine. The term was first used in the works of Plato and other Greek philosophers to refer to the teaching of myth, but the discipline expanded within Christianity and has found application in all theistic religions. It examines doctrines concerning such subjects as sin, faith, and grace and considers the terms of God's covenant with humankind in matters such as salvation and eschatology. Theology typically takes for granted the authority of a religious teacher or the validity of a religious experience. It is distinguished from philosophy in being concerned with justifying and explicating a faith, rather than questioning the underlying assumptions of such faith, but it often employs quasi-philosophical methods.

theosophy, Religious philosophy with mystical concerns that can be traced to the ancient world. It holds that God, whose essence pervades the universe as an absolute reality, can be known only through mystical experience. It is characterized by esoteric doctrine and an interest in occult phenomena. Theosophical beliefs are found in Neoplatonism, Gnosticism, and among students of the Kabbala, but Jakob Böhme, who developed a complete theosophical system, is often called the father of modern theosophy. Today theosophy is associated with the Theosophical Society, founded by Helena Blavatsky in 1875.

therapeutics, Treatment and care to combat disease or alleviate pain or injury. Its tools include drugs, surgery, radiation therapy, mechanical devices, diet, and psychiatry. Treatment may be active, to cure a disease (requiring no further treatment after recovery), treat it long-term, or heal a wound; symptomatic, to relieve symptoms until the immune system heals the body; supportive, to keep body functions going until the disease clears; or palliative, to minimize discomfort for patients with no chance of recovery. It almost always includes prevention, usually tertiary. Therapeutic measures can be chosen, combined, and tailored based on accurate diagnosis to fit each patient.

Theravada, Major form of Buddhism, prevalent in Myanmar, Sri Lanka, Thailand, Cambodia, and Laos. It is the only survivor among the Hinayana schools of Buddhism, and it is generally regarded as the oldest, most orthodox, and most conservative form of Buddhism. It is relatively uninfluenced by other indigenous belief systems. It is believed to have survived intact from the 500 Elders, who followed in the tradition of the monks of the first Buddhist sangha. Theravada has no hierarchical authority structure, though seniority is respected in the sangha. It accepts the Pali canon as authoritative scripture. Theravadins revere the historical Buddha but do not recognize the various celestial buddhas and ancillary gods associated with Mahayana Buddhism.

thermodynamics, Study of the relationships among heat, work, temperature, and energy. Any physical system will spontaneously approach an equilibrium that can be described by specifying its properties, such as pressure, temperature, or chemical composition. If external constraints are allowed to change, these properties generally change. The three laws of thermodynamics describe these changes and predict the equilibrium state of the system. The first law states that whenever energy is converted from one form to another, the total quantity of energy remains the same. The second law states that, in a closed system, the entropy of the system does not decrease. The third law states that, as a system approaches absolute zero, further extraction of energy becomes more and more difficult, eventually becoming theoretically impossible.

thermoluminescence, Emission of light from certain heated substances as a result of previous exposure to high-energy radiation. The radiation causes displacement of electrons within the crystal lattice of the substance. Upon heating, the trapped electrons return to their normal, lower-energy positions, releasing energy in the process. The longer the substance is exposed to radiation, the greater is the energy released. By measuring the amount of light given off, the duration of exposure to radiation can be determined; thus, thermoluminescence has been used to determine the age of various minerals and archaeological artifacts.

theropod, Any species of bipedal, carnivorous saurischian in the suborder Theropoda. The chicken-sized *Compsognathus*, the smallest known adult dinosaur, probably weighed 2–4 lb (1–2 kg); the tyrannosaurs weighed tons. The theropods also included Allosaurus, Deinonychus, Megalosaurus, Oviraptor, and Velociraptor. Theropod remains recovered have been from the Late Triassic through the Late Cretaceous Epoch (227–65 million years ago) from all continents except Antarctica. Their well-developed hind legs provided support and locomotion; their short forelimbs had mobile hands, probably for grasping and tearing prey. Despite the group's name, which means "beast (i.e., mammal) foot," theropod feet usually resembled those of birds. It is widely believed that all modern birds are descended from one line of small theropods.

Theseus, Hero of ancient Greek legend. He was the son of Ae-

Theseus killing the Minotaur, detail of a vase painting by the Kleophrades Painter, 6th century BC; in the British Museum.
Courtesy of the trustees of the British Museum

geus, king of Athens. On his journey to Athens, he slew many legendary villains, including Sinis, Sciron, and Procrustes. In Athens he found Aegeus married to Medea; she recognized him before her husband did and tried to poison him but failed, and Aegeus declared him heir to the throne. In Crete Theseus met Ariadne and slew the Minotaur; on returning to Athens, he forgot to replace the ship's black sail with a white one signaling his victory, and Aegeus threw himself from the Acropolis in grief. Theseus went on to unite and extend the borders of Attica. He captured the Amazon princess Antiope (Hippolyte), with the result that the Amazons attacked Athens and Antiope was killed while defending it. He abducted the child Helen and attempted to steal Persephone from Hades, but he was confined in the underworld until his rescue by Heracles. He died when the king of Scyros threw him from a cliff.

Thessaloníki, formerly SALONIKA, Seaport (pop., 2001: 363,987), Macedonia, Greece. Founded in 316 BC, it became the capital of the Roman province of Macedonia in 146 BC and grew to great importance. The apostle Paul visited *c.* AD 49–50, and he later addressed epistles to converts there. During the time of the Byzantine Empire, it prospered despite repeated attacks by Avars and Slavs. It was part of the Ottoman Empire from 1430 to 1912. Thessaloníki was the headquarters of the Young Turk movement in 1908 and was returned to Greece in 1913. It was an important Allied base in World War I and was occupied by the Germans in World War II. It is Greece's second largest city.

thiamin, or VITAMIN B$_1$, Organic compound, part of the vitamin B complex, necessary in carbohydrate metabolism. It carries out these functions in its active form, as a component of the coenzyme thiamin pyrophosphate. Its molecular structure includes a substituted pyridine ring and a thiazole ring. Thiamin is found most abundantly in whole cereal grains and certain other seeds. Deficiency leads to beriberi.

Thimphu, City (pop., 2002 est.: 45,000), capital of Bhutan. It lies on the Raidak River in the Himalayas. It was designated the official seat of government in 1962. The Tashi Chho castle, a traditional fortified monastery and one of the finest examples of traditional Bhutanese architecture, houses the offices of the royal government. The local economy is based on agriculture and lumbering.

Third Estate, French TIERS ÉTAT, In French history, one of the three orders (with the nobility and the clergy) of the Estates-General before the French Revolution. The unprivileged order, it represented the great majority of the people. Its transformation with the Tennis Court Oath into a National Assembly in 1789 marked the beginning of the Revolution.

Third Reich, Official designation for the Nazi Party's regime in Germany from January 1933 to May 1945. The name reflects Adolf Hitler's conception of his expansionist regime—which he predicted would last 1,000 years—as the presumed successor of the Holy Roman Empire (800–1806, the First Reich) and the German empire under the Hohenzollern dynasty (1871–1918, the Second Reich).

Third Republic, French government (1870–1940). After the fall of the Second Empire and the suppression of the Paris Commune, the new Constitutional Laws of 1875 were adopted, establishing a regime based on parliamentary supremacy. Despite its series of short-lived governments, the Third Republic was marked by social stability (except for the Alfred Dreyfus affair), industrialization, and establishment of a professional civil service. It ended with the fall of France to the Germans in 1940. Presidents of the Third Republic included Adolphe Thiers (1871–73), Patrice de Mac-Mahon (1873–79), Jules Grévy (1879–87), Sadi Carnot (1887–94), Félix Faure (1895–99), Émile Loubet (1899–1906), Armand Fallières (1906–13), Raymond Poincaré (1913–20), Alexandre Millerand (1920–24), Gaston Doumergue (1924–31), and Albert Lebrun (1932–40). Other notable leaders included Léon Blum, Georges Boulanger, Aristide Briand, Georges Clemenceau, Édouard Daladier, Jules Ferry, Léon Gambetta, Édouard Herriot, Jean Jaurès, Pierre Laval, Philippe Pétain, and Paul Reynaud.

Thirteen Articles of Faith, or THIRTEEN PRINCIPLES OF FAITH, Summary of the basic tenets of Judaism. It was formulated by Moses Maimonides in his commentary on the Mishna, in an effort to put forth true concepts of God and faith as a tool in avoiding error. Though presented as dogma, his statement was a personal concept and has been much debated and revised. The articles state various doctrines concerning the nature of God, the law, and Moses, and they affirm that the messiah is coming and that the dead will rise. All versions include the hymn "Yigdal," which is part of most Jewish prayer services.

Thirty Tyrants (404–403 BC) Spartan-imposed oligarchy that ruled Athens after the Peloponnesian War. Thirty commissioners were appointed to the oligarchy, which had an extremist conservative core, led by Critias. Their oppressive regime fostered a bloody purge, in which perhaps 1,500 residents were killed. Many moderates fled the city; gathering a force, they returned to defeat the tyrants' forces in a battle at Piraeus in 403. The 30 fled and were killed off over the next few years.

Thirty Years' War (1618–48) Series of intermittent conflicts in Europe fought for various reasons, including religious, dynastic, territorial, and commercial rivalries. The overall war was mainly a struggle between the Habsburg-controlled Holy Roman Empire and the Protestant principalities that relied on the chief anti-Catholic powers of Sweden and the Netherlands. It also involved the rivalry of France with the Habsburg powers, which formed anti-French alliances. The conflicts began in 1618 when the future Emperor Ferdinand II tried to impose Roman Catholicism on his domains and the Protestant nobles rebelled; the war was sparked by the Defenestration of Prague. The battlefield centred on the principalities in Germany, which suffered severely from plundering armies. Early successes by the Catholic League were countered by military gains by Sweden. When the bloodshed ended with the Peace of Westphalia (1648), the balance of power in Europe had been radically changed. France emerged as the chief

Western power, and states of the Holy Roman Empire were granted full sovereignty, establishing a framework for a modern Europe of sovereign states.

thistle, Weedy species of *Cirsium, Carduus, Echinops, Sonchus,* and other plant genera of the aster family (Asteraceae). The term usually refers to prickly leaved species of *Carduus* and *Cirsium,* which have dense heads of small, usually pink or purple flowers. Because they have spiny stems and flower heads without ray flowers, *Carduus* species are called plumeless thistles. Canadian thistle (*Cirsium arvense*) is an attractive but troublesome weed in agricultural areas of North America. The thistle is the national emblem of Scotland.

Thomism, Philosophical and theological system developed by St. Thomas Aquinas. It holds that the human soul is immortal and is a unique subsistent form, that human knowledge is based on sensory experience but also depends on the mind's reflective capacity, and that all creatures have a natural tendency to love God that can be perfected and elevated by grace and application. In the 20th century, Thomism was developed by Étienne Gilson (1884–1978) and Jacques Maritain. After World War II, Thomists faced three major tasks: to develop an adequate philosophy of science, to account for phenomenological and psychiatric findings, and to evaluate the ontologies of existentialism and naturalism.

Thomson, Sir J(oseph) J(ohn) (b. Dec. 18, 1856, Cheetham Hill, near Manchester, Eng.—d. Aug. 30, 1940, Cambridge, Cambridgeshire), English physicist. Educated at the University of Cambridge, he taught there at the Cavendish Laboratory (1884–1918), which he developed into a world-renowned institution, and was master of Trinity College (1918–40). In 1897 he showed that cathode rays are rapidly moving particles and, by measuring their displacement by electric and magnetic fields, he determined that these particles were nearly 2,000 times less massive than the lightest known atomic particle. Originally called corpuscles by Thomson, the particles are now known as electrons. His discovery helped revolutionize the knowledge of atomic structure. In 1903 he suggested a discontinuous theory of light, foreshadowing Albert Einstein's later theory of photons. He later discovered isotopes and invented mass spectrometry. In 1906 Thomson received a Nobel Prize for his research into the electrical conductivity of gases. Throughout his life he was noted as an outstanding teacher, and seven of his assistants also became Nobel laureates.

Thor, Deity, common to all the early Germanic peoples, who appeared as a great, red-bearded warrior of tremendous strength. The son of Odin (according to some legends) and Jord, the earth goddess, he was the implacable foe of the harmful race of giants but was benevolent toward humans. His name is the Germanic word for thunder. His great weapon was his hammer, Mjollnir. His greatest enemy was the world serpent Jörmungand, which he was destined to kill, and be killed by, in the Ragnarök. Thursday is named for Thor.

Thor with his hammer, Mjollnir, on his knees, bronze statuette from northern Iceland, c. AD 1000; in the National Museum of Iceland, Reykjavík.

Thor rocket, Missile initially developed by the U.S. Air Force as an intermediate-range ballistic missile. It became operational in 1958 and was later modified to serve as the first stage of launch vehicles for sev-

eral spacecraft. The Thor missile force was withdrawn in 1963. For space launching, three small auxiliary motors were strapped to a Thor rocket, and this resulted in a thrust nearly twice as powerful as the original.

Thoth, Egyptian DJHUTY, also spelled DJHOWTEY, Egyptian god of the moon and of reckoning, learning, and writing. He was the inventor of writing, the creator of languages, the representative of Re, and the scribe, interpreter, and adviser of the gods. In the myth of Osiris, Thoth protected the pregnant Isis and healed the eye of her son Horus. He judged the deceased and reported the results to Osiris. His sacred animals were the ibis and the baboon, millions of which were mummified in his honour. He was often represented in human form with the head of an ibis. The Greeks identified Thoth with Hermes; as Hermes Trismegistos he was regarded as the author of the Hermetic writings.

Thousand and One Nights, The, or ARABIAN NIGHTS' ENTERTAINMENT, Arabic ALF LAYLAH WA LAYLAH, Collection of Oriental stories of uncertain date and authorship. The frame story, in which the vengeful King Shahryar's plan to marry and execute a new wife each day is foiled by the resourceful Scheherazade, is probably Indian; the tales with which Scheherazade beguiles Shahryar, postponing and eventually averting her execution, come from India, Iran, Iraq, Egypt, Turkey, and possibly Greece. It is now believed that the collection is a composite work originally transmitted orally and developed over a period of several centuries. The first published version was an 18th-century European translation; Sir Richard Burton's *Book of the Thousand Nights and a Night* (1885–88) has become the best-known English translation.

Three Emperors' League, German DREIKAISERBUND, Diplomatic alignment of the empires of Germany, Austria-Hungary, and Russia devised by Otto von Bismarck in 1872. Its aim was to neutralize disagreement between Austria-Hungary and Russia over spheres of influence in the Balkans and to isolate Germany's enemy France. After the first Three Emperors' League (1872–78) collapsed, Bismarck succeeded in renewing it (1881, 1884). When Russia declined a third renewal, Bismarck negotiated a separate accord with Russia, the Reinsurance Treaty (1887).

thrombosis, Formation of a blood clot (thrombus) in the heart or a blood vessel. Contributing factors include injury to a blood vessel's lining from inflammation (thrombophlebitis) or atherosclerosis, blood flow that is turbulent (e.g., from an aneurysm) or sluggish (e.g., from prolonged bed rest), or coagulation abnormalities (e.g., from high numbers of platelets or excessive fats in the blood). Thrombosis, especially in deep veins of the leg, is a particular danger after major surgery. A thrombus can block blood flow at the point of clot formation or break free to block it elsewhere (embolism).

thunderbird, In North American Indian mythology, a powerful spirit in the form of a bird that watered the earth and made vegetation grow. Lightning was believed to flash from its eyes or beak, and the beating of its wings was thought to represent rolling thunder. The thunderbird was often portrayed with an extra head on its abdomen, particularly on totem poles, and it was frequently accompanied by lesser bird spirits. Though it is

Wooden thunderbird of the Haida tribe, northwest coast of North America, 19th century; in the British Museum, London.

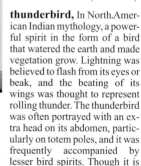

best known in North America, evidence of similar figures has been found throughout Africa, Asia, and Europe.

thunderstorm, Violent, short-lived atmospheric disturbance, almost always associated with cumulonimbus clouds (very tall, dense rain clouds) and accompanied by thunder and lightning. Such storms usually generate strong gusty winds and heavy rain and occasionally hail or tornadoes. Thunderstorms have been known to occur in almost every part of the world, although they are rare in the polar regions. In the U.S. the areas of maximum thunderstorm activity are the Florida peninsula and the coast of the Gulf of Mexico (70–80 days per year).

thyme, Pungent herb (*Thymus vulgaris*) of the mint family, na-

Thyme (Thymus vulgaris)
Walter Chandoha

tive to southern Europe, the Mediterranean, Asia Minor, and Central Asia, and cultivated in North America. A small, low-growing shrub, it has small, curled leaves that give off a fragrant odour when crushed. The dried leaves and flowering tops are used to flavour a wide range of foods. Bees are fond of thyme, and Sicily's thyme honey has been famous for centuries. The essential oil has antiseptic and anesthetic properties and is used as an internal medicine; it is also used in perfumes and toothpastes.

thymus, Pyramid-shaped lymphoid organ between the breastbone and the heart. Starting at puberty, it shrinks slowly. It has no lymphatic vessels draining into it and does not filter lymph; instead, stem cells in its outer cortex develop into different kinds of T cells. Some migrate to the inner medulla and enter the bloodstream; those that do not may be destroyed to prevent autoimmune reactions. This process is most active during infancy. If a newborn's thymus is removed, not enough T cells are produced, the spleen and lymph nodes have little tissue, and the immune system fails, causing a gradual, fatal wasting disease. Thymus removal in adults has little effect.

Tian or T'IEN (Chinese: "Heaven"), In indigenous Chinese religion, the supreme power reigning over humans and lesser gods. The term refers to a deity, to impersonal nature, or to both. As a god, Tian is an impersonal power, in contrast to the supreme ruler Shangdi, but the two are closely identified and their names are sometimes used synonymously. In later references, Tian is likened to nature or fate. Scholars generally agree that Tian was the source of moral law, but they long debated whether Tian responded to pleas and rewarded and punished human actions or whether events merely followed Tian's order and principles.

Tiananmen Square, One of the largest public squares in the world, originally designed and built in Beijing in 1651 and enlarged in 1958. It is named for the massive stone "Gate of Heavenly Peace" (Tiananmen) at its northern end. It contains and is surrounded by halls, museums, and monuments, including the Mao Zedong Memorial Hall, where Mao's body rests in state. Tiananmen Square is the site of numerous parades and other celebrations. It has also been the rallying point for political demonstrations, including events during the May Fourth Movement in 1919 and during May–June 1989.

Tianjin, or T'IEN-CHIN, conventional TIENTSIN, Seaport and municipality with provincial status (pop., 2003 est.: city, 4,933,100; 2002 est.: municipality, 10,070,000), northeastern China. The municipality, on the Bo Hai, is bordered by Hebei province and Beijing municipality and has an area of 4,400 sq mi (11,300 sq km).

The city, China's third largest, lies at the head of the short Hai River, which flows into the Bo Hai. Tianjin is connected to the Yangtze River (Chang Jiang) by the Grand Canal. It has been a major transportation and trading centre since the Yuan dynasty in the 13th century. It was a garrison town during the Ming dynasty (1368–1644). The British and French occupied it during the Second Opium War (1856–60); a treaty signed there in 1858 opened 11 Chinese ports to foreign trade. As a treaty port, it developed rapidly. It was the scene of heavy fighting during the Boxer Rebellion (1900), after which it was placed under an international commission and its walls razed. It is the leading port in northern China and the country's second largest manufacturing centre. Educational institutions include Tianjin University (1895) and Nankai University (1919).

Tiantai, Japanese TENDAI, Buddhist sect founded by Zhiyi in the 6th century AD. Its chief scripture is the Lotus Sutra, and the school is thus known as the Lotus school. Its basic philosophical doctrine is summarized as the Triple Truth: All dharmas lack ontological reality; nevertheless, they have a temporary existence; and they are simultaneously unreal and temporarily existing—an absolute truth that surpasses the others. In Tiantai, all Buddhist learning is arranged in a grand hierarchical scheme. In Japan, Saicho attempted to incorporate Zen meditation, monastic discipline, and esoteric cults. Amalgamation of Shinto and Buddhism was also encouraged.

Tiber River, Italian TEVERE, River, Italy. The country's second-longest river, it rises in the Tuscan Apennines and flows south for 252 mi (405 km), ultimately passing through the city of Rome before entering the Mediterranean at Ostia. It was an important navigation route for trade in Roman times. Despite sporadic dredging over the centuries, its persistent silting has limited its use in modern times.

Tiberias, Hebrew TEVERYA, Town (pop., 2004 est.: 40,100) and resort, northeastern Israel. Located on Lake Tiberias (Sea of Galilee), at 689 ft (210 m) below sea level, it is one of the lowest-lying towns in the world. It was founded *c.* AD 20 by Herod Antipas and named for the Roman emperor Tiberius. After the destruction of Jerusalem by the Romans in AD 70, it became a centre of Jewish learning and later the seat of the Sanhedrin and rabbinical schools. The Talmud was edited there in the 3rd–6th centuries. Saladin took the town from the Crusaders in 1187. The modern town was refounded under the British mandate in 1922 and became part of independent Israel in 1948. Historic sites include the tomb of the great Jewish scholar Moses Maimonides. Along with Hebron, Jerusalem, and Zefat, it is one of the four holy cities of Judaism.

Tiberias, Lake, or SEA OF GALILEE, Freshwater lake, northern Israel. It is 13 mi (21 km) long and 7 mi (11 km) wide; it lies about 700 ft (212 m) below sea level and receives most of its inflow from the Jordan River. The region has been inhabited for millennia: archaeological finds dating to some 500,000 years ago are among the oldest in the Middle East. In the 1st century AD, the region was rich and populated; Christians know it as the scene of many episodes in the life of Jesus. Today the lake's waters irrigate the surrounding agricultural region. Modern health resorts have grown up, and the baths at Tiberias are among Israel's winter resort attractions.

Tibet, Tibetan BOD, Chinese XIZANG, or HSI-TSANG, Autonomous region (pop., 2002 est.: 2,670,000), western China. It is bordered by India (including the Kashmir region), Nepal, Bhutan, and Myanmar (Burma), the provinces of Yunnan, Sichuan, and Qinghai, and Xinjiang autonomous region. It has an area of 471,700 sq mi (1,221,600 sq km), and its capital is Lhasa. Before the 1950s it was a unique entity, with its own Buddhist culture and religion, that sought isolation from the rest of the world. Situated on a plateau averaging 15,000 ft (4,500 m) above sea level, it is the highest region in the world. Its surrounding mountain ranges include the Kunlun Mountains and the Himalayas; Mount Everest (Cho-molungma) rises on its border with Nepal. Tibet emerged as a powerful Buddhist kingdom in the 7th–9th century CE. It came under the control of the Mongols in the 13th century and the Qing (Manchu) dynasty in the 18th century. After the 1911–12 Chinese Revolution, it gained a measure of autonomy. The Chinese People's Liberation Army entered Tibet in 1950 and reestablished Chinese authority. The 14th Dalai Lama, Bstan-'dzin-rgya-mtsho, led an abortive rebellion in 1959, after which he fled to India. The Tibet Autonomous Region was established in 1965. Many of Tibet's cultural treasures were destroyed or badly damaged during the Cultural Revolution, but restoration work has been under way since then.

Tibetan Buddhism, Form of Mahayana Buddhism that evolved from the 7th century in Tibet. Based on Madhyamika and Yogacara philosophies, it incorporates the rituals of Vajrayana, the monastic disciplines of early Theravada, and the shamanistic features of Bon. The predominant Tibetan sect for the past three centuries has been Dge-lugs-pa. Its spiritual head is the Dalai Lama. The Tibetan canon is divided into the *Bka'-'gyur* ("Translation of the Word"), consisting of canonical texts translated mostly from Sanskrit, and *Bstan-'gyur* ("Transmitted Word"), consisting of commentaries by Indian masters. Tibetan Buddhism has become better known worldwide since 1959, when the 14th Dalai Lama went into exile in India.

Tibetan language, Sino-Tibetan language spoken by more than five million people in Tibet (Xizang), Qinghai, Sichuan, and Gansu provinces in China; Bhutan; northern Nepal; and the Kashmir region of India and Pakistan. Since 1960, enclaves of Tibetan speakers have dispersed to India and other parts of the world. Spoken Tibetan comprises a very diverse range of dialects, conventionally divided into several groups: Western, including Balti and Ladakhi in Jammu and Kashmir; Central, including the speech of Lhasa and most of the Nepalese dialects (including Sherpa); Southern, including the dialects of Sikkim and Bhutan; Khams, or Southeastern, including the dialects of the interior plateau, southern Qinghai, eastern Tibet, and parts of western Sichuan; and Amdo or Northeastern, including the dialects of northern Qinghai, southern Gansu, and northern Sichuan. Most Tibetans share a common literary language, written in a distinctive script of disputed origin first attested in the 8th century AD.

tic, Sudden rapid, recurring muscle contraction—usually a blink, sniff, twitch, or shrug—always brief, irresistible, and localized. Frequency decreases from head to foot. Unlike a spasm, a cramp, or the movements of chorea or epilepsy, it does not interfere with other movement and can be held off for a time. It can become ingrained as a habit of which the person (most often a nervous child 5–12 years old) is unaware. Most tics are probably psychological, but similar movements occur in some physical disorders (e.g., late-stage encephalitis). People with tics have some control over the movement but feel impelled to go through with it to feel better. Tension increases the movement's likelihood, and distraction reduces it. Psychotherapy, relaxation training, and biofeedback training have had some success in treating tics.

tide, Regular, periodic rise and fall of the surface of the sea, occurring in most places twice a day. Tides result from differences in the gravitational forces exerted at different points on the Earth's surface by another body (such as the Moon). Although any celestial body (e.g., Jupiter) produces minute tidal effects, the majority of the tidal forces on the Earth are raised by the Sun (because of its enormous mass) and the Moon (because of its proximity to Earth). In fact, the tidal forces from the Moon are about twice as strong as those from the Sun. The largest tides (spring tides, exhibiting very large change in sea level between high and low tides) occur at the new and full moon, when the Earth, the Moon, and the Sun are aligned and the Sun's tidal forces are added to those of the Moon. The smallest tides (neap tides) occur when the Sun and

Moon are at right angles (from Earth), when the tidal forces from the Sun partially cancel those from the Moon. The geometry of the coastline and of the water's basin also affects the range of the tides.

Tien Shan, Chinese TIAN SHAN, or T'IEN SHAN ("CELESTIAL MOUNTAINS"), Mountain chain, Central Asia. Lying mainly in Kyrgyzstan and northwestern China (Xinjiang autonomous region), its ranges and valleys stretch for about 1,500 mi (2,500 km) in an east-west direction. Its highest point is Victory Peak (Pik Pobeda) in Kyrgyzstan, which reaches 24,406 ft (7,439 m); the peak was discovered in 1943 by a Soviet expedition. Most of the area's population lives in the Fergana Valley of Uzbekistan.

Tierra del Fuego, Archipelago at the southern extremity of South America. It is separated from the Antarctic Archipelago by the Drake Passage. The southern and western parts are an extension of the Andes Mountains, with peaks exceeding 7,000 ft (2,100 m). About two-thirds of the islands are in Chile, and the remainder are in Argentina. The main island, Tierra del Fuego, is divided roughly equally between Chile (west) and Argentina (east); the city of Ushuaia, Arg., is the southernmost city in the world. Indigenous peoples were the sole occupants until 1880, when colonization by Chilean and Argentine nationals was prompted by the discovery of gold. Chile's only oil field is there. The region's name (Spanish: "Land of Fire") refers to its many volcanoes.

tiger, Reddish tan, striped great cat (*Panthera tigris*) of forests, grasslands, and swamps in eastern Russia, South Asia, Sumatra, and a few small parts of China. Tigers are solitary, nocturnal hunters, preying on medium-sized mammals (e.g., deer). Locality and subspecies determine size, colour, and stripes. Southern tigers, such as the Bengal tiger (*P. tigris tigris*), are smaller and more brightly coloured than northern ones, such as the rare Siberian tiger (*P. tigris altaica*). Males grow to more than 3 ft (1 m) high and 7 ft (2.2 m) long, excluding the 3-ft (1-m) tail, and may weigh 350–640 lb (160–290 kg). Tigers live about 11 years. The persistent use of tiger parts as tonics or medicines, despite evidence refuting their efficacy, is rooted in the awe that the cat has inspired for millennia. Although internationally protected, tigers are seriously endangered; their populations shrank by more than 90% in the last century, and three subspecies are now extinct.

tiger shark, Potentially dangerous shark (*Galeocerdo cuvieri*, family Carcharhinidae), found worldwide in warm oceans, from the shoreline to the open sea. Up to 18 ft (5.5 m) long, the grayish tiger shark has a long, pointed upper tail lobe, and its large teeth are deeply notched along one side. This voracious shark eats fishes, other sharks, turtles, mollusks, birds, carrion, and garbage, including coal, tin cans, and clothing. It is a source of leather and liver oil.

Tigris River, Arabic DIJLAH, Turkish DICLE, biblical HIDDEKEL, River, Turkey and Iraq. It originates in the Taurus Mountains at Lake Hazar and flows 1,180 mi (1,900 km) southeast through Turkey and past Baghdad to unite with the Euphrates River at Al-Qurnah in southeastern Iraq; there it forms the Shatt al-Arab. With the Euphrates it defined the ancient region of Mesopotamia. Important for its irrigation capacity, it gave rise to sustained civilization. The ruins of many ancient cities lie on its banks, including those of Nineveh, Calah, Ashur, Ctesiphon, and Seleucia.

Tikal, Ancient Maya city, northern Guatemala. First occupied as a small village in a tropical rainforest (*c.* 900–300 BC), it grew into an important ceremonial centre. It flourished *c.* AD 600–900, when its great plazas, pyramids, and palaces were built and when Maya art flowered in monumental sculpture. At its height it was the largest urban centre in the southern Maya lowlands; the core city had a population of perhaps 10,000 residents with an outlying population of about 50,000. Its main structures covered about 1 sq mi (2.5 sq km). It was abandoned by the 10th century. Major excavation began in 1956; it is now a central part of Tikal National Park, which was designated a UNESCO World Heritage site in 1979.

tilapia, Any of numerous, mostly freshwater, fish species (genus *Tilapia*, family Cichlidae), native to Africa. They resemble North American sunfishes; one species grows to 20 lbs (9 kg). *Tilapia* species are easy to raise and harvest for food; they grow rapidly, resist disease, and eat readily abundant algae and zooplankton. They have been used in warm-water aquaculture systems since the early Egyptian civilization and have been introduced into many freshwater habitats.

timbre, Quality of sound that distinguishes one instrument, voice, or other sound source from another. Timbre largely results from a characteristic combination of overtones produced by different instruments. This distinctive combination (which usually varies across the range of pitches) is what principally permits a listener to distinguish a clarinet from a flute, an alto from a tenor, or even a Stradivarius violin from a Guarneri violin, when both are sounding the same pitch. One element of timbre results from the differing methods of producing the sounds (blowing, bowing, striking, etc.), especially audible at the moment a note begins.

Timbuktu, French TOMBOUCTOU, Town (pop., 1998: 31,973), Mali, on the southern edge of the Sahara near the Niger River. Founded *c.* AD 1100 by Tuareg nomads, it became an important post on the trans-Saharan caravan routes. After it was incorporated within the Mali empire, probably in the late 13th century, it became a centre of Islamic culture (*c.* 1400–1600). It reached its apex as a commercial and cultural centre under Songhai rule *c.* 1500 but declined rapidly after being conquered by Moroccan forces in the late 16th century. The French captured it in 1894. It became part of independent Mali in 1960. The town was designated a UNESCO World Heritage site in 1988.

time, Measured or measurable period. More broadly, it is a continuum that lacks spatial dimensions. Philosophers have sought an understanding of time by focusing on the broad questions of the relation between time and the physical world and the relation between time and consciousness. Those who adopt an absolutist theory of time regard it as a kind of container within which the universe exists and change takes place, and believe that its existence and properties are independent of the physical universe. According to the rival relationist theory, time is nothing over and above change in the physical universe. Largely because of Albert Einstein, it is now held that time cannot be treated in isolation from space. Some argue that Einstein's theories of relativity vindicate relationist theories, others that they vindicate the absolutist theory. The primary issue concerning the relation between time and consciousness is the extent, if any, to which time or aspects of time depend on the existence of conscious beings. Events in time are normally thought of in terms of notions of past, present, and future, which some philosophers treat as mind-dependent; others believe that time is independent of perception and hold that past, present, and future are objective features of the world.

time dilation, In the theory of special relativity, the "slowing down" of a clock as perceived by an observer in relative motion with respect to that clock. Time dilation becomes noticeable only at speeds approaching that of light and has been accurately confirmed by the apparent increased lifetime of unstable subatomic particles traveling at nearly the speed of light and by the precise timing of atomic clocks carried on airplanes.

Timişoara, City (pop., 2002: 317,651), western Romania. Located near the Timiş River, it was first settled in Neolithic and Roman times. It was sacked by the Tatars in the 13th century. Its citadel was rebuilt in the 14th century and for a few years became the residence of Charles I of Hungary. The Turks held the town from 1552 until the Austrians took it in 1716. Occupied by Serbia in 1919, Timişoara was allotted to Romania by the 1920 Treaty of

Trianon. Antigovernment demonstrations there in 1989 led to the execution of Pres. Nicolae Ceauşescu and the end of communist rule in Romania. It is a manufacturing, commercial, and cultural centre.

Timor, Island, southern Malay Archipelago. It is the easternmost of the Lesser Sunda Islands. Indonesian-Malay peoples live along the coast and Melanesian aboriginals in the mountains. They speak dozens of Papuan and Malayan languages, as well as Portuguese in the east and Indonesian in the west. The Portuguese began trading with Timor *c.* 1520. In 1613 the Dutch settled at the island's southwestern tip, and the Portuguese moved to the north and east. Treaties in 1860 and 1914 divided the island between them. The island was occupied by the Japanese during World War II. In 1950 Netherlands Timor (West Timor) was transferred to Indonesia. East Timor was held by the Portuguese until 1975, when Indonesian troops invaded and annexed the area; it achieved full sovereignty in 2002.

timpani, or KETTLEDRUMS, Large bowl-shaped drums with pedal mechanisms for altering their pitch by changing the membrane's tension. The timpani are the principal orchestral percussion instruments. Each drum usually has a range of a fifth; they are classically used in pairs. Until *c.* 1800 each drum was tuned to a single pitch (usually tonic or dominant) that could not be altered in performance. Primitive kettledrums, or *naker*s, were played on horseback by Middle Eastern cavalry. In Europe they were primarily associated, in tandem with the trumpets, with court ceremony and the military. They entered the orchestra in the mid-17th century.

Timur, or TAMERLANE, or TAMBURLAINE (b. 1336, Kesh, near Samarkand, Transoxania—d. Feb. 19, 1405, Otrar, near Chimkent), Turkic conqueror of Islamic faith whose conquests reached from India and Russia to the Mediterranean Sea. Timur took part in campaigns in Transoxania with Chagatai, a descendant of Genghis Khan. (Timur Lenk, or Tamerlane, means "Timur the Lame," reflecting the battle wounds he received.) Through machinations and treachery he took over Transoxania and proclaimed himself the restorer of the Mongol empire. In the 1380s he began his conquest of Iran (Persia), taking Khorāsān and eastern Iran in 1383–85 and western Iran as far as Mesopotamia and Georgia in 1386–94. He occupied Moscow for a year. When revolts broke out in Iran, he ruthlessly suppressed them, massacring the populations of whole cities. In 1398 he invaded India, leaving a trail of carnage. Next he marched on Damascus and Baghdad, deporting the artisans of the former to Samarkand and destroying all the monuments of the latter. In 1404 he prepared to march on China but died early in the march. Although Timur strove to make Samarkand the most splendid city in Asia, he himself preferred to be always on the move. His most lasting memorials are the architectural monuments of Samarkand and the dynasty he established, under which Samarkand became a centre of scholarship and science.

tin, Metallic chemical element, chemical symbol Sn, atomic number 50. It is a soft, silvery white metal with a bluish tinge, employed since antiquity in the traditional form of bronze, its alloy with copper. It occurs chiefly as the dioxide (stannic oxide, SnO_2) in cassiterite. Since it is nontoxic, ductile, malleable, and easily worked, it is used to plate steel cans ("tin cans") for use as food containers and to coat and plate other items. Pure tin is too weak to be used alone, but its many alloys include soft solder, pewter, bronze, and low-temperature casting alloys. It has valence 2 or 4 in compounds, including stannous chloride (used in tin galvanizing and manufacturing polymers and dyes), stannous oxide (used to make tin salts for chemical reagents and plating), stannous fluoride (used as an anticavity ingredient in toothpastes), stannic chloride (a stabilizer for perfumes and a source of other tin salts), and stannic oxide (a catalyst and a polishing powder for steel). Tin bonds with carbon to form organotin compounds, used to stabilize PVC and in biocides and fungicides.

Tiranë, or TIRANA, City (pop., 2001: 343,078), capital of Albania. Founded in the early 17th century by a Turkish general, it gradually became a trading centre at the junction of roads and caravan trails. It was named the capital of Albania in 1920. In World War II Tiranë was occupied by Axis forces (1939–44). It is Albania's largest city and main industrial and cultural centre, home to the national library and theatre and site of the University of Tiranë (1957).

tirtha, In Hinduism, a holy river, mountain, or other place made sacred through association with a deity or saint. Such sites are often the destination of pilgrims and the venue for large religious festivals. A Hindu will make such a pilgrimage as an act of devotion, to carry out a vow, to appease a deity, or to seek prosperity. On reaching a tirtha, the pilgrim will usually bathe, circle the temple or shrine, make an offering, have his name recorded by the tirtha priests, and listen to evening music and religious discourses.

Tirthankara, or JINA, In Jainism, a saviour who has succeeded in crossing over life's stream of rebirths and has made a path for others to follow. Each cosmic age produces 24 Tirthankaras; the first are giants, but, as the age proceeds, they decrease in stature and appear after shorter intervals of time. Of the 24 Tirthankaras of the present age, each of whom is represented by a symbolic colour and emblem, only Parshvanatha and Mahavira are considered actual historical figures. The Tirthankaras are not worshiped as gods but rather honoured as exemplars.

tissue culture, Biological research method in which tissue fragments (a cell, a population of cells, or all or part of an organ) are sustained in an artificial environment for examination and manipulation of cell behaviour. It has been used to study normal and abnormal cell structure; biochemical, genetic, and reproductive activity; metabolism, functions, and aging and healing processes; and reactions to physical, chemical, and biological agents (e.g., drugs, viruses). A tiny sample of the tissue is spread on or in a culture medium of biological (e.g., blood serum or tissue extract), synthetic, or mixed origin having the appropriate nutrients, temperature, and pH for the cells being incubated. The results are observed with a microscope, sometimes after treatment (e.g., staining) to highlight particular features. Some viruses also grow in tissue cultures. Work with tissue cultures has helped identify infections, enzyme deficiencies, and chromosomal abnormalities; classify brain tumours; and formulate and test drugs and vaccines.

Titan, Largest moon of Saturn. Titan is the only satellite in the solar system known to have clouds and a dense atmosphere. It makes one rotation on its axis (about every 16 days) for each revolution around Saturn, thus always keeping the same hemisphere toward the planet. With a diameter of 3,200 mi (5,150 km), Titan is the second largest moon in the solar system; only Jupiter's Ganymede is larger. Its density (about 1.9 times that of water) implies that its interior is a mixture of rocky and icy materials, the latter likely being mostly water ice mixed with frozen ammonia and methane. Its atmosphere is about 95% nitrogen. Its surface, veiled in a thick brownish red haze, was largely a mystery until the arrival at Saturn in 2004 of the Cassini-Huygens spacecraft, which revealed a complex topography shaped by rains, winds, flowing liquids, and other processes similar to those acting on Earth's surface.

Titan rocket, Any of a series of U.S. liquid-fueled rockets originally developed as ICBMs but later used as space launch vehicles. The Titan I missile (deployed 1962–65) was designed to deliver a four-megaton nuclear warhead over 5,000 mi (8,000 km) to targets in the Soviet Union. It was replaced by the much larger Titan II, which carried a nine-megaton warhead. Titan II was the principal weapon in the land-based U.S. nuclear arsenal until the 1980s, when it was replaced by solid-fueled ICBMs (e.g., Minuteman missiles). NASA used the Titan II to launch Gemini spacecraft in the 1960s; deactivated Titan II missiles were refurbished

as space launchers. Titan III was a space launcher based on Titan II; much used in the 1970s for space probes, it usually was configured with strap-on boosters and often an upper-stage vehicle. The Titan IV, developed in the late 1980s, was built with larger engines to lift heavy space cargo such as that carried by the space shuttle. Coupled with strap-on boosters and the Centaur upper stage, it was the most powerful expendable launch vehicle in the U.S. until its retirement in 2005.

Titanic, British luxury passenger liner that sank on April 15, 1912, en route to New York from Southampton, England, on its maiden voyage. Over 1,500 of its 2,200 passengers were lost. The largest and most luxurious ship afloat, it had a double-bottomed hull divided into 16 watertight compartments. Because four of these could be flooded without endangering its buoyancy, it was considered unsinkable. Shortly before midnight on April 14, it collided with an iceberg southeast of Cape Race, Newfoundland; five compartments ruptured and the ship sank. As a result, new rules were drawn up requiring that the number of places in lifeboats equal the number of passengers (the *Titanic* had only 1,178 lifeboat places for 2,224 passengers) and that all ships maintain a 24-hour radio watch for distress signals (a ship less than 20 mi [32 km] away had not heard the *Titanic*'s distress signal because no one had been on duty). The International Ice Patrol was established to monitor icebergs in shipping lanes. In 1985 the wreck was found lying upright in two pieces at a depth of 13,000 ft (4,000 m) and was explored by American and French scientists using an unmanned submersible.

The Titanic.
The Bettmann Archive

titanium, Metallic chemical element, one of the transition elements, chemical symbol Ti, atomic number 22. A silvery gray, lightweight, high-strength, low-corrosion structural metal, it is found combined in almost all rocks and soils and in plants and animals, natural waters, and deep-sea dredgings. Its chief commercial ores are ilmenite and rutile. Its alloys are used for parts for high-speed aircraft, spacecraft, missiles, and ships; in electrodes; in chemical, desalination, and food-handling equipment; and in prostheses. Its compounds, in which it has valence 2, 3, or 4, include titanium trichloride (used as a catalyst in polypropylene production), titanium dioxide (extensively used as a pigment—with the greatest hiding power of all white pigments—in paints, enamels, and lacquers), and titanium tetrachloride (used in skywriting, smoke screens, and as a catalyst).

Titicaca, Lake, South American lake, the world's highest lake navigable to large vessels. Located in the Altiplano, a high basin of the Andes Mountains, and on the border between Peru and Bolivia, it lies at an elevation of about 12,500 ft (3,810 m). The second largest lake in South America, it covers some 3,200 sq mi (8,300 sq km) and is 120 mi (190 km) long by 50 mi (80 km) wide. A narrow strait joins the lake's two bodies of water, which have 41 islands, some densely populated. The remains of one of the oldest known American civilizations have been found in the area. Temple ruins on Titicaca Island mark the spot where, according to legend, the founders of the Inca were sent down to earth by the sun.

Tito, Josip Broz, orig. JOSIP BROZ (b. May 7, 1892, Kumrovec, near Zagreb, Croatia, Austria-Hungary—d. May 4, 1980, Ljubljana, Yugos.), Yugoslav politician, premier (1945–53), and president (1953–80). Born to a peasant family, he fought in the Austro-Hungarian army in World War I and was captured by the Russians in 1915. While in Russia, he took part in the July Days demonstrations (1917) and joined the Bolsheviks. In 1920 he returned to Croatia, where he became a local leader of the Communist Party of Yugoslavia. He rose in the party hierarchy, interrupted by a prison term (1928–34), to become its secretary-general in 1939. In World War II, Tito (a pseudonym he adopted about 1935) proved an effective leader of Yugoslav Partisans. As marshal from 1943, he strengthened communist control of Yugoslavia. As premier and president, he developed an independent form of socialist rule in defiance of the Soviet Union, pursued a policy of nonalignment, built ties with other nonaligned states, and improved relations with the Western powers. Within Yugoslavia, he established a system of "symmetrical federalism" (1974) that created equality among the six republics and Serbia's autonomous provinces (including Kosovo), while maintaining tight control to prevent separatist movements. After his death, resentment of Serbian domination led gradually to a dissolution of the federal system.

TNT, in full TRINITROTOLUENE, Pale yellow, solid organic compound made by adding nitrate ($-NO_2$) groups to toluene. Because TNT melts below the boiling point of water but explodes only above 464 °F (240 °C), it can safely be melted and poured into casings. It is relatively insensitive to shock and, for practical purposes, cannot be exploded without a detonator, making it the preferred chemical explosive, used in munitions and for demolition.

tobacco, Any of numerous species of plants in the genus *Nicotiana*, or the cured leaves of several of the species, used after processing in various ways for smoking, snuffing, chewing, and extracting of nicotine. Native to South America, Mexico, and the West Indies, common tobacco (*N. tabacum*) grows 4–6 ft (1–2 m) high and bears usually pink flowers and huge leaves, as long as 2–3 ft (0.6–1 m) and about half as wide. When Christopher Columbus reached the Americas, he reported natives using tobacco as it is used today, as well as in religious ceremonies. Believed to have medicinal properties, tobacco was introduced into Europe and the rest of the world, becoming the chief commodity that British colonists exchanged for European manufactured articles. Awareness of the numerous serious health risks posed by tobacco, including various cancers and a range of respiratory diseases, has led to campaigns against its use, but the number of tobacco users worldwide continues to rise. The World Health Organization estimates that smoking now causes three million deaths annually and within two decades will cause more deaths than any single disease.

tobogganing, Sport of sliding down a snow-covered hill on a toboggan, a long, flat-bottomed sled made of thin boards curved up at the front end. The word is of Algonquian origin and probably refers to a towing sled. Tobogganing as a sport appears to have originated on the slopes of Mount Royal in Montreal in the late 19th century. In the early 20th century many tobogganing chutes (3-ft-wide wood- or ice-sided channels) were built.

Togo, officially TOGOLESE REPUBLIC, Republic, western Africa. Area: 21,853 sq mi (56,600 sq km). Population: (2011 est.) 5,830,000. Capital: Lomé. It has some 30 ethnic groups; the Ewe is the largest. Languages: French (official), Ewe, other indigenous languages. Religions: Christianity (mostly Roman Catholic), traditional beliefs, Islam. Currency: CFA franc. Togo occupies a strip of land about 70 mi (115 km) wide that extends about 320 mi (515 km) inland from the Gulf of Guinea. Regions include a swampy coastal plain, a northern savanna, and a central mountain range. The developing economy is based largely on agriculture. Chief crops are cassava (manioc), yams, corn (maize), cotton, coffee, and cacao. It is one of the world's leading producers of phosphates; food products, beverages, and cement are also important. Togo is a multiparty republic with one legislative house; its head of state is the president, supported by the military, and the head of government is the prime minister. Until 1884 what is now Togo was an intermediate zone between the states of Asante and Dahomey, and its various ethnic groups lived in general isolation from each other. In 1884 it became part of the Togoland German protectorate, which was occupied by British and French forces in 1914. In 1922 the League of Nations assigned eastern Togoland to France and the western portion to Britain. In 1946 the British and French governments placed the territories under UN trusteeship. Ten years later British Togoland was incorporated into the Gold Coast, and French Togoland became an autonomous republic within the French Union. Togo gained independence in 1960. It suspended its constitution from 1967 to 1980. A constitution providing for multiparty government was approved in 1992, but the political situation remained unstable.

Tokyo, Japanese TŌKYŌ, formerly (until 1868) EDO, City (pop., 2003 est.: city, 8,083,980; metro. area, 12,310,000), capital of Japan. The country's largest city, it is located in east-central Honshu at the head of Tokyo Bay. The site has been inhabited since ancient times, and the small fishing village of Edo existed there for centuries before it became the capital of the Tokugawa shogunate in 1603. By the 19th century it was one of the largest cities in the world, with a population exceeding 1,000,000. Under the Meiji Restoration, in 1868 it replaced Kyōto as the imperial capital, and Edo was renamed Tokyo ("Eastern Capital"). A massive earthquake in the region in 1923 destroyed most of the city and killed at least 100,000 people, but most of it had been rebuilt by 1930. Much of it was again devastated by U.S. bombing during World War II and had to be reconstructed. The Summer Olympic Games were held there in 1964. Tokyo is the administrative, cultural, financial, commercial, and educational centre of Japan and the focus of an extensive urban complex that includes Kawasaki and Yokohama. Attractions include the Imperial Palace, encircled by stone-walled moats and broad gardens, and numerous temples and shrines. There are some 150 institutions of higher learning, including the University of Tokyo (1877).

Toledo, ancient TOLETUM, City (pop., 2001: 68,382), capital of Castile–La Mancha autonomous community, south-central Spain. On the Tagus River, it was the stronghold of the Carpentini, a powerful Iberian tribe, when it was conquered by Rome in 193 BC. In the 6th century AD it became the Visigoths' capital in Spain. Under the Moors (712–1085) it became a centre of Hebrew and Arabic culture, and it was noted for the manufacture of swords. Taken by Alfonso VI in 1085, it became the capital of New Castile and, in 1230, of the united kingdom of Castilla y León. Toledo was noted for its policy of religious tolerance toward Jews and Arabs during the 11th–15th centuries. It lost importance after Philip II moved the capital to Madrid in 1560. The French occupied Toledo during the Peninsular War (1808–14), and Nationalist forces besieged it (1936) in the Spanish Civil War. Known for its great wealth of notable architecture, the entire urban area is a national monument. It was the home of El Greco.

toll, Sum levied on users of certain roads, canals, bridges, tunnels, and other such travel and transportation infrastructure, primarily to pay for construction and maintenance. Tolls were known in the ancient world and were widely used in medieval Europe as a means of supporting bridge construction. Canal building, which became extensive in Europe in the 18th–19th centuries, was financed chiefly by tolls, and many major roads were built by private companies with the right to collect tolls. In the U.S. the National Road, built beginning in 1806, was initially financed through the sale of public land, but maintenance problems led Congress to authorize tolls. Toll roads diminished in the latter part of the 19th century, but the idea was revived with the Pennsylvania Turnpike in the 1930s, and after World War II many states built toll expressways. In many countries tolls are also used to finance long-span bridges, major tunnels, and highways. They have also been blamed for both reducing, and abetting, rush-hour traffic congestion. Canal tolls are still charged in some parts of the world, notably on the Suez and Panama canals.

Tolstoy, Leo, Russian LEV NIKOLAYEVICH, COUNT TOLSTOY (b. Sept. 9, 1828, Yasnaya Polyana, Tula province, Russian Empire—d. Nov. 20, 1910, Astapovo, Ryazan province), Russian writer, one of the world's greatest novelists. The scion of prominent aristocrats, Tolstoy spent much of his life at his family estate of Yasnaya Polyana. After a somewhat dissolute youth, he served in the army and traveled in Europe before returning home and starting a school for peasant children. He was already known as a brilliant writer for the short stories in *Sevastopol Sketches* (1855–56) and the novel *The Cossacks* (1863) when *War and Peace* (1865–69) established him as Russia's preeminent novelist. Set during the Napoleonic Wars, the novel examines the lives of a large group of characters, centring on the partly autobiographical figure of the spiritually questing Pierre. Its structure, with its flawless placement of complex characters in a turbulent historical setting, is regarded as one of the great technical achievements in the history of the Western novel. His other great novel, *Anna Karenina* (1875–77), concerns an aristocratic woman who deserts her husband for a lover and the search for meaning by another autobiographical character, Levin. After its publication Tolstoy underwent a spiritual crisis and turned to a form of Christian anarchism. Advocating simplicity and nonviolence, he devoted himself to social reform. His later works include *The Death of Ivan Ilich* (1886), often considered the greatest novella in Russian literature, and *What Is Art?* (1898), which condemns fashionable aestheticism and celebrates art's moral and religious functions. He lived humbly on his great estate, practicing a radical asceticism and in constant conflict with his wife. In November 1910, unable to bear his situation any longer, he left his estate incognito. During his flight he contracted pneumonia, and he was dead within a few days.

Toltec, Nahuatl-speaking people who held sway over what is now central Mexico from the 10th to the 12th century. Whether their urban centre was Tula or Teotihuacán is a matter of dispute. In the 10th century they formed a number of small states of various ethnic origins into an empire. They introduced the cult of Quetzalcóatl, and other Toltec religious and military influences spread through the Yucatán region and were absorbed by the Maya. They were noted as builders and craftsmen; artifacts include fine metalwork, gigantic statues, and carved human and animal standard-bearers. They were succeeded by the Aztec.

tonality, Organization of music around a single pitch; more specifically, the Western system of keys that grew out of the modal music of the Renaissance in the 17th century. The term is often used to refer to the network of relationships implicit in the seven principal tones of a given key, each of which has the potential to become the tonic temporarily by means of modulation, whereby a new network of relationships arises. Because of its capacity to extend pitch relationships to remote lengths in an audibly comprehensible way, the tonal system permits the composition of music of great complexity.

Tonga, officially KINGDOM OF TONGA, Island country, South Pacific Ocean. Area: 289 sq mi (748 sq km). Population: (2011 est.) 104,000. Capital: Nukuʿalofa. The people are of Polynesian ancestry. Languages: Tongan, English (both official). Religions: Christianity (mostly Protestant; also Roman Catholic, other Christians); also Bahāʾī. Currency: paʿanga. Tonga comprises an archipelago of some 170 islands that extends north-south in two parallel chains for roughly 500 mi (800 km). The eastern islands are low and formed of coral limestone; those in the west are mountainous and of volcanic origin, and four of the western islands are active volcanoes. The country has a developing free-market economy based mainly on agriculture. Chief products include fish, coconuts, sweet potatoes, and bananas. Tourism also is important. Tonga is a constitutional monarchy with one legislative house; the head of

state is the king, and the head of government is the prime minister. Tonga was inhabited at least 3,000 years ago by people of the Lapita culture. The Tongans developed a stratified social system headed by a paramount ruler whose dominion by the 13th century extended as far as the Hawaiian Islands. The Dutch visited in the 17th century, but effective European contact dates from 1773, when Capt. James Cook arrived and named the archipelago the Friendly Islands. The modern kingdom was established during the reign (1845–93) of King George Tupou I. It became a British protectorate in 1900. This was dissolved in 1970 when Tonga, the only ancient kingdom surviving from the pre-European period in Polynesia, achieved complete independence within the Commonwealth. Tonga was at the centre of a financial scandal in the early 21st century when money in a government trust fund was lost while under the management of an American investor. This added to the country's ongoing financial problems. A political reform movement brought changes in the country's government in 2008; King George Tupou V ceded much of the monarchy's formerly absolute power and agreed to make most governmental decisions in consultation with the prime minister.

tongue, Muscular organ on the floor of the mouth. It is important in motions of eating, drinking, and swallowing, and its complex movements shape the sounds of speech. Its top surface consists of thousands of raised projections (papillae). The receptors of taste (taste buds) are embedded in the papillae and are sensitive to four basic flavours: sweet, salty, sour, and bitter. More specific flavours are influenced by the sense of smell. The tongue's appearance (e.g., coated or red) can give clues to disease elsewhere. Disorders of the tongue include cancer (often caused by smokeless tobacco), leukoplakia (white patches), fungal infection, and congenital disorders. Different animals use the tongue to serve varied functions; for example, frogs have an elongated tongue adapted to capturing prey, the snake's tongue collects and transfers odours to a specialized sensory structure to help locate prey, and cats use their tongues for grooming and cleaning.

Tonkin, Gulf of, Arm of the South China Sea, between northern Vietnam and Hainan Island, China. It is 300 mi (500 km) long and 150 mi (250 km) wide. In 1964 the Vietnamese reportedly fired on U.S. ships there, leading the U.S. Congress to adopt the Gulf of Tonkin Resolution that supported increased U.S. involvement in the Vietnam War.

tonsil, Small mass of lymphoid tissue in the wall of the pharynx. The term usually refers to the palatine tonsils on each side of the oropharynx. They are thought to produce antibodies to help prevent respiratory and digestive tract infection but often become infected themselves, mostly in children. There are also pharyngeal tonsils, better known as adenoids, and lingual tonsils, at the base of the tongue. The last have more effective drainage than the others and are rarely infected.

tonsillitis, Inflammatory infection of the tonsils, usually with hemolytic streptococci or viruses. The symptoms are sore throat, trouble in swallowing, fever, and enlarged lymph nodes on the neck. The infection, which usually lasts about five days, is treated with bed rest and antiseptic gargling. Sulfa drugs or other antibiotics are prescribed in severe bacterial infections to prevent complications. Streptococcal infection can spread to nearby structures. Complications may include abscess, nephritis, and rheumatic fever. Tonsils that become chronically inflamed and enlarged require surgical removal (tonsillectomy).

tool and die making, Industrial art of manufacturing stamping dies, plastics molds, and jigs and fixtures to be used in the mass production of solid objects. The making of dies for punch presses constitutes most of the work done in tool and die shops, and most such pressworking dies are used in the manufacture of sheet-metal parts such as the panels of an automobile body.

tooth, Any of the hard structures in the mouth used for biting and chewing and in speech. Each consists of a crown above the gum and one or more roots below it, embedded in the jaw. Its inner pulp contains the blood and nerve supply for the bonelike dentin, covered in the crown by enamel, the hardest tissue in the body. Twenty primary (baby) teeth come in by age 2½ and fall out between ages 5 and 13 to be replaced by 32 permanent teeth. The incisors, in front, are shaped mostly for biting, the pointed canines for tearing, and the premolars and molars for grinding food. The teeth are subject to caries (decay), caused by acid from bacteria in plaque, a yellowish film that builds up on teeth. Misalignment of teeth between the upper and lower jaws can grind down the teeth and cause problems in chewing. Elsewhere, it is a cosmetic problem. Both can be treated with braces.

topology, In mathematics, the study of the properties of a geometric object that remains unchanged by deformations such as bending, stretching, or squeezing but not breaking. A sphere is topologically equivalent to a cube because, without breaking them, each can be deformed into the other as if they were made of modeling clay. A sphere is not equivalent to a doughnut, because the former would have to be broken to put a hole in it. Topological concepts and methods underlie much of modern mathematics, and the topological approach has clarified very basic structural concepts in many of its branches.

Torah, or PENTATEUCH, In Judaism, the divine revelations to Israel; specifically, the first five books of the Bible: Genesis, Exodus, Leviticus, Numbers, and Deuteronomy. By tradition their authorship has been ascribed to Moses, but biblical scholarship has shown that they were written and compiled at a much later date, probably in the 9th–5th century BC, though drawing on much older traditions. The Scroll of the Torah (Sefer Torah) is kept in the Synagogue Ark. The term Torah (but not Pentateuch) is often applied to the whole Hebrew Scripture (i.e., the later books of the Old Testament), or, even more generally, to that and other Jewish sacred literature and oral tradition.

Tordesillas, Treaty of (June 7, 1494) Agreement between Spain and Portugal aimed at settling conflicts over lands explored by voyagers of the late 15th century. In 1493 Pope Alexander VI had granted Spain all the lands west of a line 100 leagues (about 320 mi) west of the Cape Verde Islands, in return for an agreement to Christianize the peoples of the New World; Portuguese expeditions were to keep to the east. At Tordesillas (a village in Spain), ambassadors from Spain and Portugal moved that line west, thereby allowing Portugal to claim Brazil when it was discovered in 1500.

Tori style, In Japanese art, a style of sculpture that emerged during the Asuka period (552–645) and lasted into the Nara period (710–784). Derived from the style of the Chinese Northern Wei dynasty (AD 386–534), Tori was named after a sculptor of Chinese descent whose only known piece is a Buddhist triad (623). Works in the Tori style are characterized by slender, elegant bodies, a strong linear interest in drapery, and a tendency toward squatness in the proportion of the faces and also in the relation of the body to the feet.

Bronze triad of Shaka with attendant figures (left figure lost) in the Tori style, Asuka period, 623; in the Hōryū-ji, Nara, Japan
Courtesy of the Horyu-ji, Nara, Japan

tornado, Violent low-pressure storm, relatively small in diameter but with very rapidly rotating winds and an intense updraft near the centre. The relatively low pressure at the centre of a tornado's funnel-like vortex causes cooling and condensation, making the storm visible as a revolving column of cloud, which is called the funnel. Tornadoes normally travel at 30–40 mph (50–65 km/hr). The winds around the vortex may exceed 300 mph (500 km/hr) in extreme events. Tornadoes often occur in groups.

Toronto, City (pop., 2006: city, 2,503,281; metro. area, 5,113,149), capital of Ontario, Canada. Canada's most populous metropolitan area, it lies on the northern shore of Lake Ontario. Originally inhabited by Seneca tribes, its site was occupied by a tiny French fort in the mid-18th century. It was founded in 1793 as York by American colonists loyal to the British. U.S. troops pillaged it during the War of 1812. In 1834 it received its city charter and current name. It became the capital of Ontario in 1867. In 1953–54 it joined neighbouring villages, towns, and townships to form the Municipality of Metropolitan Toronto. In 1967 those 13 municipalities were reduced to six (Toronto, Etobicoke, North York, Scarborough, York, and the borough of East York), which amalgamated to form the City of Toronto in 1998. It is Canada's financial and commercial centre, the seat of the Toronto Stock Exchange, and a major international trading centre, with access to Atlantic shipping via the Saint Lawrence Seaway and to major U.S. ports via the Great Lakes. It produces more than half of Canada's manufactured goods. Extensive immigration (1950s–70s) brought a variety of foreign cultures that transformed it into one of the liveliest cities on the continent. It is the site of the CN Tower (1,815 ft [553 m] tall), the Hockey Hall of Fame, and the annual Canadian National Exhibition. Its educational institutions include the University of Toronto (1827).

torpedo, Cigar-shaped, self-propelled underwater missile, launched from a submarine, surface vessel, or airplane and designed to explode on contact with the hulls of surface vessels and submarines. It contains devices to control depth and direction as well as a detonator for the explosive-filled warhead. Originally the word referred to any explosive charge, including the weapon now known as a submarine mine. The first modern torpedo (1866) carried an 18-lb (8-kg) charge of dynamite in its nose and was powered by a compressed-air engine driving a single propeller; its range was 200–700 yd (180–640 m). Torpedoes were used successfully by submarines in both world wars, when many merchant ships were sunk, mostly by German U-boats. Torpedoes are now usually propelled by battery-powered electric motors.

torque, or MOMENT, In physics, the tendency of a force to rotate the body to which it is applied. Torque is always specified with regard to the axis of rotation. It is equal to the magnitude of the component of the force lying in the plane perpendicular to the axis of rotation, multiplied by the shortest distance between the axis and the direction of the force component. Torque is the force that affects rotational motion; the greater the torque, the greater the change in this motion.

torsion balance, Device used to measure the gravitational acceleration at the Earth's surface. It consists essentially of two small masses at different elevations that are supported at opposite ends of a beam. The latter is suspended from a wire that twists because the masses are affected differently by the force of gravity. When the wire is twisted, an optical system indicates the angle of deflection, and the torque, or twisting force, can be calculated. The torque is correlated with the gravitational force at the point of observation. Torsion balance may also refer to a device used in weighing, a type of equal-arm balance.

tort, Wrongful act, other than a breach of contract, that injures another and for which the law permits a civil (noncriminal) action to be brought. Relief may be obtained in the form of damages or an injunction. The term derives from Latin *tortum,* meaning "something twisted, wrung, or crooked." Assault, defamation, malpractice, negligence, nuisance, product liability, property damage, and trespass are all (apart from their potentially criminal and contractual aspects) torts.

tortoise, Any of some 49 species (family Testudinidae) of slow-moving terrestrial, herbivorous turtles, found in the Old World and New World but chiefly in Africa and Madagascar. Tortoises have a high, domed shell, heavy elephant-like hind legs, and hard-scaled forelegs. The four North American species (genus *Gopherus*) have a brown shell and flattened forelimbs adapted for burrowing and are about 8–14 in. (20–35 cm) long. The common, or European, tortoise (*Testudo graeca*) has a shell about 7–10 in. (18–25 cm) long. Most species of giant tortoises (genus *Geochelone*) on the Galapagos and other islands are now rare or extinct. One captive Galapagos tortoise had a shell 4.25 ft (1.3 m) long and weighed 300 lb (140 kg).

Galapagos tortoise (Geochelone elephantopus).
Francisco Erize/Bruce Coleman Ltd.

torture, Infliction of intolerable physical or psychological pain. Torture has been used by governments throughout history for punishment, coercion, and intimidation and for extracting confessions and information. A common practice in ancient times, it was defended by Aristotle but eloquently opposed by Cicero, Seneca, and St. Augustine. Beginning in the 12th century, torture was increasingly used in Europe; from the mid-14th through the 18th century it was a common part of the legal proceedings of most European countries. The Roman Catholic church supported its use by the Inquisition in cases of heresy. Common instruments of torture were the strappado (for repeatedly hoisting the body by the wrists behind the back and dropping it), the rack (for stretching the limbs and body), and the thumbscrew (for crushing the thumbs). By 1800 torture was illegal in many European countries, but it became common again in the 20th century, notably in Nazi Germany and the Soviet Union, and it is still widely practiced in Latin America, Africa, and the Middle East. In 1984 the United Nations adopted an international convention against torture and other forms of cruel, inhuman, and degrading treatment. By the early 21st century some 130 countries were party to the convention. The belief that only sadists are capable of committing torture was challenged by a study in the 1960s that found that ordinary people could be easily persuaded to inflict pain on others.

totalitarianism, Form of government that subordinates all aspects of its citizens' lives to the authority of the state, with a single charismatic leader as the ultimate authority. The term was coined in the early 1920s by Benito Mussolini, but totalitarianism has existed throughout history throughout the world (e.g., Qin dynasty China). It is distinguished from dictatorship and authoritarianism by its supplanting of all political institutions and all old legal and social traditions with new ones to meet the state's needs, which are usually highly focused. Large-scale, organized violence may be legitimized. The police operate without the constraint of laws and regulations. Where pursuit of the state's goal is the only ideological foundation for such a government, achievement of the goal can never be acknowledged. Hannah Arendt's *Origins of Totalitarianism* (1951) is the standard work on the subject.

totem pole, Carved and painted vertical log, constructed by many Northwest Coast Indian peoples. The poles display mythological images, usually animal spirits, whose significance is their association with the lineage. Each figure represents a type of family crest. Some poles relate a family legend in the form of pictographs. Poles are erected to identify the owner of a house or other property, welcome visitors, indicate a portal or passageway, mark a gravesite, and even to ridicule an important person who failed in some way.

totemism, Complex of ideas and practices based on the belief in kinship or mystical relationship between a group (or individual) and a natural object, such as an animal or plant. The term derives from the Ojibwa word *ototeman*, signifying a blood relationship. A society exhibits totemism if it is divided into an apparently fixed number of clans, each of which has a specific relationship to an animate or inanimate species (totem). A totem may be a feared or respected hunted animal or an edible plant. Very commonly connected with origin myths and with instituted morality, the totem is almost always hedged about with taboos of avoidance or of strictly ritualized contact. Totem, taboo, and exogamy seem to be inextricably intertwined.

toucan, Any of about 35 species (family Ramphastidae) of large-billed, long-tailed Central and South American birds. Many species are black with a bold breast colour; their thick saw-edged bills are brightly and distinctively coloured. Bands of toucans emit loud barks, bugling calls, and harsh croaks. They eat fruit, insects, lizards, and nestling birds. Toucans deposit two to four eggs in an unlined natural tree cavity or an abandoned woodpecker hole. *Ramphastos* species are up to 24 in. (60 cm) long, a third of which may be the bill. Smaller species (toucanets) are 10–14 in. (25–35 cm) long.

touchstone, Black, silica-containing stone used in assaying to determine the purity of gold and silver. The metal to be assayed is rubbed on the touchstone, and then a sample of metal of known purity is rubbed on the stone right next to it. The streaks of metal on the stone are treated with nitric acid, which dissolves impurities, thus increasing the contrast between the two samples when compared. Because other metals, such as copper, can be alloyed to silver without changing its colour significantly, the touchstone method is not usually used now to assay silver, though it is still used to assay gold and provides a reasonably accurate guide to quality.

Toulouse, ancient TOLOSA, City (pop., 2004 est.: 426,700), on the Garonne River in southern France. Founded in ancient times, it was taken from its Celtic inhabitants by the Romans in the 1st century BC. After AD 778 it became the seat of the feudal countship of Toulouse. Protestants were massacred there during the 16th-century Wars of Religion. In 1814 it was the scene of the British victory over the French in the last battle of the Peninsular War. A rail junction and canal port, Toulouse is a centre of the French aviation industry. It has many historic buildings, including a Gothic cathedral and a Romanesque basilica, and the tomb of St. Thomas Aquinas. The university, founded in 1229, is one of the oldest in the world.

Tour de France, World's most prestigious and difficult bicycle race. Staged for three weeks each July—usually in some 20 day-long stages—the Tour typically comprises 20 professional teams of nine riders each and covers some 3,600 km (2,235 mi) of flat and mountainous country, mainly in France, with occasional and brief visits to Belgium, Italy, Germany, and Spain. Each stage of the race is timed, and the rider with the lowest aggregate time for all stages is the winner. Established in 1903 by Henri Desgrange (b. 1865—d. 1940), a French cyclist and journalist, the race has been run every year except during the world wars.

Tourette syndrome, Rare neurological disorder that causes repetitive motor and vocal tics. Named for Georges Gilles de la Tourette, who first described it in 1885, it occurs worldwide, is usually inherited, generally begins at ages 2–15, and is three times more common in males. Motor tics occur first in about 80% of cases, compulsions to utter abnormal sounds in the rest. A compulsion to utter obscenities, once thought characteristic, is often absent. Repetition of words heard and spontaneous repetition of one's own words are two distinctive symptoms. Other vocal tics may include meaningless sounds. Motor tics may be virtually unnoticeable; more complex ones may appear intentional (e.g., hopping, clapping). Sleep, intense concentration, and exertion tend to suppress the tics; emotional stress worsens them. Unlike psychiatric compulsive disorders, Tourette syndrome has a neurological origin and may improve with psychogenic drugs. Brain neurotransmitter abnormalities may be involved, but the underlying cause remains uncertain.

Tours, City (pop., 2006 est.: 136,942), northwest-central France. Gallic tribes inhabited the site before the Roman conquest. In the 3rd century AD it was made an episcopal see, but the Christian community remained small until St. Martin became bishop in the 4th century; a magnificent basilica was raised above his tomb in the late 5th century, attracting pilgrims for hundreds of years. In the 5th century Tours became part of the Frankish dominion; Charles Martel defeated Moorish invaders nearby at the Battle of Tours/Poitiers in 732. Under Alcuin it developed as a centre of learning. Though it prospered in the Middle Ages, it declined with the 17th-century emigration of the Protestant Huguenots. It was the seat of French government during the siege of Paris (1870) in the Franco-Prussian War. The chief tourist hub for the Loire valley, Tours still has the remains of the basilica of St. Martin. Tours is the birthplace of Honore de Balzac.

Toussaint Louverture, orig. FRANÇOIS DOMINIQUE TOUSSAINT (b. c. 1743, Bréda, near Cap-Français, Saint-Domingue—d. April 7, 1803, Fort-de-Joux, Fr.), Leader of the Haitian independence movement during the French Revolution. Born a slave, he was freed in 1777. In 1791 he joined a slave rebellion and soon assembled an army of his own, which he trained in guerrilla warfare. When France and Spain went to war in 1793, he and other black commanders joined the Spaniards, but in 1794 he switched his allegiance to the French because France, unlike Spain, had recently abolished slavery. His revolt created the first independent nation in Latin America. He rose from lieutenant governor to governor-general of Saint-Domingue and gradually rid himself of nominal French superiors. Treaties with the British secured their withdrawal, and he began trade with them and the U.S. In 1801 he turned his attention to Santo Domingo, the Spanish-controlled portion of Hispaniola, driving out the Spanish and freeing the slaves there. He made himself governor-general for life. He was deposed by the French in 1802 and died in custody in France.

Tower of London, Royal fortress on the northern bank of the River Thames. The central keep, or donjon, known as the White Tower because of its limestone, was begun c. 1078 by William I the Conqueror inside the Roman city wall. In the 12th–13th century the fortifications were extended beyond the wall, the White Tower becoming the nucleus of a series of concentric defenses. The only entrance from the land is at the southwestern corner; when the river was still a major highway, the 13th-century water gate was much used. Its nickname, Traitors' Gate, derives from the prisoners brought through it to the Tower, long used as a state prison; many were murdered or executed there.

toxic shock syndrome, Bacterial disease caused by a toxin produced by the bacterium *Staphylococcus aureus*. It was first recognized in 1978 in women using superabsorbent tampons. High fever, diarrhea, vomiting, and rash may progress to abdominal tenderness, drop in blood pressure, shock, respiratory distress, and kidney failure. The syndrome also has other causes, including postsurgical infection. Antibiotics are not effective. With intensive supportive therapy, most patients recover in 7–10 days, but 10–15% die. Many patients have a milder recurrence within eight months.

toxin, Any substance poisonous to an organism; often restricted to poisons produced by living organisms. In addition to those from such microorganisms as bacteria, dinoflagellates, and algae, there are toxins in fungi (mycotoxins; *see* aflatoxin; mushroom poisoning), higher plants (phytotoxins), and animals (zootoxins, or venoms). The plants include nightshade, poison hemlock, foxglove, mistletoe, and poison ivy. Many plant toxins (e.g., pyrethrins, nicotine, rotenone) apparently protect their producers against certain animals (especially insects) or fungi. Similar defensive secretions in animals may be widely distributed or concentrated in certain tissues, often with some sort of delivery system (e.g., spines, fangs). Animals such as spiders and snakes use venoms to catch prey and often for defense. Many normally edible fishes and shellfishes become poisonous after feeding on toxic plants or algae.

tracery, In architecture, bars or ribs used decoratively in windows, especially the ornamental openwork in Gothic windows. In the earliest phase, two or three narrow, arched windows were placed close together under a single large arch, with the section of wall between the small and large arches pierced by a circular or four-lobed opening. The complexity of this plate tracery increased, reaching a climax in the magnificent windows of Chartres Cathedral. After c. 1220 windows began to be subdivided by mullions, or upright bars, that continued at the head of the window to branch and form the patterns of bar tracery. Elaborate bar tracery soon became one of the most important elements of Gothic architecture and one of its finest achievements, as in the rose windows of the French Rayonnant style. The bar tracery of the parallel English Decorated style formed netlike patterns based on the circle, arch, trefoil, and quatrefoil. By the late 14th century, the Perpendicular style replaced curvilinear tracery with straight mullions extending to the top of the main arch, connected at intervals by horizontal bars.

tracheitis, Inflammation and infection of the trachea. Inhaled irritants can injure the tracheal lining and increase the chance of infection (bacterial or viral). Acute infections, usually bacterial, produce fever, fatigue, and swelling of the tracheal lining but generally do no great damage. Chronic infections, promoted by irritants such as heavy smoking and alcohol abuse, cause progressive tissue degeneration and scarring.

Trade, Board of, Organized market for the exchange of commodity contracts. The Toronto Board of Trade, one of the earliest, was incorporated in 1845. The first grain-futures exchange in the U.S. was organized in Chicago in 1848. The Chicago Board of Trade (CBOT) began as a voluntary association of prominent Chicago grain merchants and was chartered by the Illinois legislature in 1859. Initially it sold grain by sample; later it introduced a system of inspection and grading to standardize the market and facilitate trading. By 1858 access to the trading floor was limited to members with seats on the exchange. It became the world's largest commodity exchange in terms of volume and value of business.

trademark, Mark used by a manufacturer or merchant to identify the origin or ownership of goods and to distinguish them from others. Trademarks may be words or groups of words, letters, numerals, devices, names, the shape or other presentation of products or their packages, or combinations of colours. A trademark (indicated by ^TM or, when registered, by the symbol ®) is considered the property of the holder and is protected by law from unauthorized use by others. In most countries, registration is a prerequisite for ownership and protection of the mark. In the U.S., however, the trademark right is granted by the mere use of the mark, though registration often proves legally advantageous.

Trafalgar, Battle of (Oct. 21, 1805) Naval engagement in the Napoleonic Wars that established British naval supremacy in Europe. It was fought west of Cape Trafalgar, Spain, between a Franco-Spanish fleet of 33 ships under Pierre de Villeneuve (1763–1806) and a British fleet of 27 ships under Horatio Nelson. As Villeneuve tried to slip out of the besieged port of Cádiz, he was caught by Nelson. The French ships formed a single line and were attacked by the English at two points. After sending the famous signal "England expects that every man will do his duty," Nelson broke through the centre of the French line and in the pell-mell battle captured Villeneuve and 20 ships. Near the end of the battle, Nelson was mortally wounded by a sniper. No British ships were lost, and Napoleon abandoned his plan to invade England.

tragedy, Drama of a serious and dignified character that typically describes the development of a conflict between the protagonist and a superior force (such as destiny, circumstance, or society) and reaches a sorrowful or disastrous conclusion. Tragedy of a high order has been created in three periods and locales, each with a characteristic emphasis and style: Attica, in Greece, in the 5th century BCE; Elizabethan and Jacobean England (1558–1625); and 17th-century France. The idea of tragedy also found embodiment in other literary forms, especially the novel.

tragicomedy, Literary genre consisting of dramas that combine elements of tragedy and comedy. Plautus coined the Latin word *tragicomoedia* to denote a play in which gods and mortals, masters and slaves reverse the roles traditionally assigned to them. In the Renaissance and after, tragicomedy was mainly comic, though Elizabethan and Jacobean tragedies almost always include some comic or grotesque elements. Modern tragicomedy is sometimes used synonymously with absurdist drama, which suggests that laughter is the only response left to people faced with an empty and meaningless existence.

trampoline, Resilient sheet or web (often of nylon) supported by springs in a metal frame and used as a springboard and landing area in tumbling. Trampolining is an individual sport of acrobatic movements performed after rebounding into the air from the trampoline. As a competitive sport, it was included in the Pan-American Games for the first time in 1955, and a world championship was established in 1964; competitors are scored on difficulty, execution, and form.

tranquilizer, Drug used to reduce anxiety, fear, tension, agitation, and related disturbed mental states. Major tranquilizers (antipsychotic agents, or neuroleptics) are used to treat schizophrenia and other psychoses; phenothiazines, including chlorpromazine, are the best known. They are thought to block the activity of the neurotransmitter dopamine in the brain. Minor tranquilizers (antianxiety agents, or anxiolytics) are used to treat anxiety and tension; they are usually benzodiazepines, including diazepam (Valium) and chlordiazepoxide (Librium). They have a calming effect and reduce both physical and psychological effects of anxiety, fear, and stress by enhancing the action of the neurotransmitter gamma-aminobutyric acid (GABA) in the brain.

Transcendental Meditation (TM), Spiritual development technique developed and promoted by Maharishi Mahesh Yogi, a former Hindu ascetic. A movement that became popular in the West in the 1960s, it is based on specific meditation techniques and is not strictly connected with any religious tradition, though the perspective behind it has roots in Vedanta. Practice entails the mental repetition of a mantra in order to still the activity of thought and experience a deeper level of consciousness. Through this process, the practitioner finds deep relaxation, which can lead to inner joy, vitality, and creativity.

Transcendentalism, Movement of 19th-century New England philosophers and writers. The Transcendentalists were loosely bound together by adherence to an idealistic system of thought based on a belief in the essential unity of all creation, the innate goodness of humankind, and the supremacy of vision over logic and experience for the revelation of the deepest truths. Part of the Romantic movement, it developed around Concord, Mass., attracting individualistic figures such as Ralph Waldo Emerson, Henry David Thoreau, Margaret Fuller, and Bronson Alcott. Transcendentalist writers and their contemporaries signaled the emer-

gence of a new national culture based on native materials, and they were a major part of the American Renaissance in literature. They advocated reforms in church, state, and society, contributing to the rise of free religion and the abolition movement and to the formation of various utopian communities, such as Brook Farm. Some of the best writings by minor Transcendentalists appeared in *The Dial* (1840–44), a literary magazine.

transducer, Device that converts one form of energy to another. A microphone is an acoustic transducer, converting sound waves into electrical signals. Different types of transducers act on heat, radiation, sound, strain, vibrations, pressure, and acceleration; they may output mechanical, electrical, pneumatic, or hydraulic signals. Examples include strain gauges, loudspeakers, photocells, transformers, and thermocouples.

transistor, Solid-state semiconductor device for amplifying, controlling, and generating electrical signals. Invented at Bell Labs (1947) by John Bardeen, Walter H. Brattain, and William B. Shockley, it displaced the vacuum tube in many applications. Transistors consist of layers of different semiconductors produced by addition of impurities (such as arsenic or boron) to silicon. These impurities affect the way electric current moves through the silicon. Transistors were pivotal in the advancement of electronics because of their small size, low power requirements, low heat generation, modest cost, reliability, and speed of operation. Single transistors were superseded in the 1960s and '70s by integrated circuits; present-day computer chips contain billions of transistors. Today transistors perform many different functions in nearly every type of electronic equipment.

transpiration, Loss of water from a plant, mainly through the stomata of leaves. Darkness, internal water deficit, and extremes of temperature tend to close stomata and decrease transpiration; illumination, ample water supply, and optimum temperature cause stomata to open and increase transpiration. Its exact significance is disputed; its roles in providing the energy to transport water in the plant and in aiding dissipation of the sun's heat (by cooling through evaporation of water) have been challenged. Since stomatal openings are necessary for the exchange of gases, transpiration has been considered by some to be merely an unavoidable phenomenon that accompanies the real functions of the stomata.

transplant, or GRAFT, Partial or complete organ or other body part removed from one site and attached at another. It may come from the same or a different person or an animal. One from the same person—most often a skin graft—is not rejected. Transplants from another person or, especially, an animal are rejected unless they are unusually compatible or have no blood vessels (e.g., the cornea), or if the recipient's immune reaction is suppressed by lifelong drug treatment. Transplanted tissues must match (by blood tests) more closely than blood transfusions. Monoclonal antibodies targeting the cells that cause rejection hold great promise. Tests are now under way with monoclonal antibodies that react with antigens present only on T cells that are participating in rejection, sparing the rest. Rejection matters less in skin grafts, which may need to last only weeks, and bone grafts, whose structure remains after the cells die. In bone marrow transplants, the donor's marrow cells may attack the recipient's tissues, often fatally. Lung transplants have greater chance of success as part of a heart-and-lung transplant.

transsexualism, Self-identification with one sex by a person who has the external genitalia and secondary sexual characteristics of the other sex. Early in life, such a person adopts the behaviour characteristic of the opposite sex. Surgery and hormone therapy now allow permanent sex change, a procedure first performed in 1952. The male-to-female operation is more common because the genital reconstruction is more satisfactory. The male transsexual's penis and testes are removed and an artificial vagina created; breasts are created with implants or female sex hormones. Female transsexuals may undergo mastectomy and hormone treatments to produce male secondary sexual characteristics, but attempts to create an artificial penis have not been satisfactory.

transubstantiation, In Christianity, the change by which the bread and wine of the Eucharist become in substance the body and blood of Jesus, though their appearance is not altered. This transformation is thought to bring the literal truth of Christ's presence to the participants. The doctrine was first elaborated by theologians in the 13th century and was incorporated into documents of the Council of Trent. In the mid-20th century, some Roman Catholic theologians interpreted it as referring to a change of meaning rather than a change of substance, but in 1965 Paul VI called for the retention of the original dogma.

trapshooting, Shooting sport with moving targets. A shotgun (usually 12-gauge) is used. The targets are clay disks (called pigeons) that are sprung into the air from a trap. A later variant is skeet shooting. Trapshooting's origins date to the 18th century, when marksmen shot at live pigeons released from cages or box traps. The modern clay-pigeon variety has been included in Olympic Games competition since 1900. A single trap throws 25 targets at varying angles; each competitor fires four 25-target rounds.

Trasimeno, Lake, Lake, Umbria, central Italy. The largest lake of the Italian peninsula, it has an area of 49 sq mi (128 sq km) and is shallow, with a maximum depth of 20 ft (6 m). It is fed by small streams and has an artificial subterranean outlet (opened 1898) to the Tiber River. In 217 BC Hannibal defeated a Roman army led by Flaminius there in the Second Punic War. In World War II it was the scene of severe fighting (1944) between the British and German armies.

treason, Offense of attempting to overthrow the government of one's country or of assisting its enemies in war. In the U.S., the framers of the Constitution defined treason narrowly—as the levying of war against the U.S. or the giving of aid and comfort to its enemies—in order to lessen the possibility that those in power might falsely or loosely charge their political opponents with treason.

treaty, Contract or other written instrument binding two or more states under international law. The term is generally reserved for the more important international agreements, usually requiring, in addition to the signatures of authorized persons, ratification by the governments involved. A treaty may be bilateral or multilateral; it usually contains a preamble, an enumeration of the issues agreed on, and clauses that discuss its ratification procedures, lifespan, and terms for termination. Treaties may be political, commercial, constitutional, or administrative, or they may relate to criminal and civil justice or codify international law.

Treblinka, German Nazi concentration camp during World War II. Located near the village of Treblinka, Pol., it opened in 1941 as a forced-labour camp. A larger and ultrasecret second camp a mile away, called T.II, opened in 1942 as an extermination camp for Jews. Victims were stripped and marched into "bathhouses," where they were gassed with carbon monoxide from ceiling pipes. Ukrainian guards and up to 1,500 Jewish prisoner-workers performed the executions. The total number killed has been estimated at 700,000 to 900,000. In 1943 a group of prisoner-workers rose in revolt and escaped, but most were soon killed or recaptured. The T.II camp was closed in October 1943, the labour camp in July 1944.

tree frog, or TREE TOAD, Any of some 550 species (family Hylidae) of mostly arboreal frogs, found worldwide but primarily in the New World. Most species are small, slender, and long-legged and have suckerlike adhesive disks on the finger and toe tips. Some do not climb well and live in water, on land, or in a burrow.

European green tree frogs (Hyla arborea).
Jane Burton/Bruce Coleman Ltd.

Most species lay eggs in water. Young marsupial frogs (genus *Gastrotheca*), of South America, develop in a brood pouch on the female's back.

Trent, Council of (1545–63) 19th ecumenical council of the Roman Catholic church, which made sweeping reforms and laid down dogma clarifying nearly all doctrines contested by the Protestants. Convened by Pope Paul III at Trento in northern Italy, it served to revitalize Roman Catholicism in many parts of Europe. In its first period (1545–47) it accepted the Nicene Creed as the basis of Catholic faith, fixed the canon of the Old and New Testaments, set the number of sacraments at seven, and defined the nature and consequences of original sin; it also ruled against Martin Luther's doctrine of justification by faith. In its second period (1551–52) it confirmed the doctrine of transubstantiation and issued decrees on episcopal jurisdiction and clerical discipline. In the final period (1562–63) it defined the mass as a true sacrifice and issued statements on several other doctrinal issues. By the end of the 16th century, many of the abuses that had motivated the Protestant Reformation had disappeared, and the church had reclaimed many of its European followers.

trespass, In law, unlawful entry onto land. Trespass was formerly defined as wrongful conduct causing injury or loss; today it is generally confined to issues involving real property. Once a trespass is proved, the trespasser is usually held liable for any damages resulting, regardless of whether the trespasser was negligent or the damage was foreseeable. Criminal trespass, trespass to property that is forbidden by statute, is punishable as a crime.

triage, Division of patients for priority of care, usually into three categories: those who will not survive even with treatment; those who will survive without treatment; and those whose survival depends on treatment. If triage is applied, the treatment of patients requiring it is not delayed by useless or unnecessary treatment of those in the other groups. Triage originated in military medicine, when limited resources faced many wounded soldiers. It is used in civilian settings during disasters or epidemics and in emergency rooms. Triage decisions are made after relatively quick examination; patients in lower-priority groups should be reexamined periodically.

trial, In law, a judicial examination of issues of fact or law for the purpose of determining the rights of the parties involved. Attorneys for the plaintiff and the defendant make opening statements to a judge or jury, then the attorney for the plaintiff makes his case by calling witnesses, whom the defense attorney may cross-examine. Unless the case is then dismissed for lack of sufficient evidence, the defense attorney next takes a turn calling witnesses, whom the plaintiff's attorney cross-examines. Both sides make closing arguments. In a trial before a jury, the judge instructs the jury on the applicable laws, and the jury retires to reach a verdict. If the defendant is found guilty, the judge then hands down a sentence.

Trianon, Treaty of (June 4, 1920) Treaty at the end of World War I between Hungary and the Allied Powers, signed at the Trianon Palace at Versailles, France. By its terms, Hungary lost two-thirds of its former territory, which was divided among Czechoslovakia, Austria, the future Yugoslavia, and Romania. Hungary's armed forces were restricted to 35,000 lightly armed men, to be used only to maintain internal order.

Triassic Period, Interval of geologic time, *c.* 251–199.6 million years ago, that marks the beginning of the Mesozoic Era. Many new vertebrates emerged during the Triassic, heralding the major changes that were to occur in both terrestrial and marine life forms during the Mesozoic Era. The seas became inhabited by large marine reptiles. On land, ancestral forms of various modern amphibians arose, as did reptiles such as turtles and crocodilians. By the Late Triassic, archosaurs were becoming more and more dominant, and the first true mammals, small shrewlike omnivores, evolved. Seed ferns dominated the flora of southern Gondwana, and gymnosperms, including conifers, cycads, and ginkgos, were common throughout much of Pangea.

triathlon, Endurance contest involving swimming, cycling, and running. Triathlons originated in California in the 1970s and became an Olympic event in 2000. Olympic and world championship triathlons consist of a 1.5-km open water swim, a 40-km bicycle ride, and a 10-km run. The sport's most famous event, the Ironman triathlon, is held annually in Hawaii and consists of a 3.8-km (2.4-mi) swim, a 180-km (112-mi) bicycle ride, and a 42.2-km (26.2-mi) marathon run.

tribe, Any of a variety of social units, including some defined by unilineal descent and some defined by ethnic origin. Cultural anthropologists now usually apply the term to a unit of social organization that is culturally homogeneous and consists of multiple kinship groups—such as the family, lineage, or clan—that prohibit marriages within themselves but endorse or require marriages with persons of the other kinship groups. Most tribes are organized as unitary political entities, within which people share a common language and culture. Some tribes are spread across large territories, and individual members may never meet or know all of the others. Some are small groups, confined to a limited territory, sometimes a single small island, within which everyone knows everyone else very well. What unites societies of such diverse scales as being "tribal" is their own internal sense of "being a single people," but—anthropologists would add—a people that lacks the equipment of citizenship, a constitution, or a formalized legal system that would define them as a nation-state. Throughout most of the history of modern cultural anthropology, the terms *tribe* and *primitive* were usually linked; however, in recent years *primitive* has been avoided by most anthropologists because it appears to carry with it an unintended judgment of the moral or technological development of a people.

tribe (Greek, *phylai*; Roman, *tribus*) In ancient Greece and Rome, any of a group of political and demographic subdivisions of the population. In Greece the groups divided into tribes were distinct by location, dialect, and tradition, and they included the Ionians, Dorians, Achaeans, and Aetolians. In Attica, Cleisthenes replaced the 4 Ionian tribes with 10 new tribes, each of which was named after a local hero; these came to develop political and civic functions, including the election of magistrates. The demes developed out of the tribal system. In Rome the tribes formed the 3 (later 4, and still later 35) original divisions of Roman citizens. These were the basis of military levies, property tax, census taking, and voting units in political assemblies.

tribune, In ancient Rome, any of various military and civil officials. Military tribunes were originally infantry commanders. In the early republic there were six to a legion; some were appointed by consuls or military commanders, others elected by the people. During the Roman empire (from 27 BC), the emperor nominated military tribunes, the office of which was considered preliminary to a senatorial or equestrian career. Of the civil tribunes, the most important were the tribunes of the plebs, who were elected in the plebeian assembly. By 450 BC there were 10 plebeian tribunes, who

were elected annually with the right to intervene in cases of unjust acts of consuls or magistrates by saying "Veto" (meaning "I forbid it"). The office became powerful; its powers were curtailed by Sulla but restored by Pompey. Under the empire the powers of the plebeian tribunes passed to the emperor.

tricarboxylic acid cycle, or KREBS CYCLE, or CITRIC-ACID CYCLE, Last stage of the chemical processes by which living cells obtain energy from foodstuffs. Described by Hans Adolf Krebs in 1937, the reactions of the cycle have been shown in animals, plants, microorganisms, and fungi, and it is thus a feature of cell chemistry shared by all types of life. It is a complex series of reactions beginning and ending with the compound oxaloacetate. In addition to re-forming oxaloacetate, the cycle produces carbon dioxide and the energy-rich compound ATP. The enzymes that catalyze each step are located in mitochondria in animals, in chloroplasts in plants, and in the cell membrane in microorganisms. The hydrogen atoms and electrons that are removed from intermediate compounds formed during the cycle are channeled ultimately to oxygen in animal cells or to carbon dioxide in plant cells.

Triceratops, Genus of large, plant-eating ornithischian dinosaurs of the Late Cretaceous Epoch (100–65.5 million years ago). *Triceratops* had a very long skull (some more than 6 ft [1.8 m] long); a large bony frill about the neck; a relatively short, pointed horn on the nose; a beaklike mouth; and two pointed horns, more than 3.3 ft (1 m) long, above the eyes. Adults weighed 4–5 tons (3.6–4.5 metric tons) and grew up to 30 ft (9 m) long. The limbs were very stout, and the hind limbs were more massive than the forelimbs.

trichinosis, Disorder caused by the roundworm trichina, commonly acquired from undercooked infested pork. Larval worms invade the small intestine, maturing within a week. Fertilized females deposit new larvae, which are carried by the blood, notably to the muscles (most often the diaphragm, eyes, throat, and tongue), where they encapsulate and may remain alive for years. Though trichinosis usually eventually subsides, it may be fatal if the heart and brain are involved. Few infected persons have sufficient parasites to produce symptoms (including diarrhea, nausea, and fever, followed by pain, stiffness, and swelling of various muscular structures). Anti-inflammatory drugs can relieve symptoms; thiabendazole may effectively destroy parasites in the intestine. There is no practical way to detect trichinous pork; the surest safeguard remains thorough cooking.

trigonometry, Mathematical discipline dealing with the relationships between the sides and angles of triangles. Literally, it means triangle measurement, though its applications extend far beyond geometry. It emerged as a rigorous discipline in the 15th century, when the demand for accurate surveying techniques and navigational methods led to its use for the "solution" of right triangles, or the calculation of the lengths of two sides of a right triangle given one of its acute angles and the length of one side. The solution can be found by using ratios in the form of the trigonometric functions.

trikaya, In Mahayana Buddhism, the concept of the three bodies, or modes of being, of the Buddha: the *dharmakaya* ("body of essence"), the unmanifested mode; the *sambhogakaya* ("body of enjoyment"), the heavenly mode; and the *nirmanakaya* ("body of transformation"), the earthly mode, or the Buddha as he appeared on earth in any form. The concept of *trikaya* applies to the Buddha Gautama and all other buddhas.

trilobite, Any of a group of ovate arthropods (subphylum Trilobita) that came to dominate the seas *c.* 540 million years ago and became extinct *c.* 245 million years ago. Trilobites had a chitinous exoskeleton and three body lobes: a raised middle lobe with a lower lobe on each side. The head, thorax, and tail were segmented; each segment bore two appendages. The forwardmost appendages were sense and feeding organs. Most species had two compound eyes, though some were eyeless. Some were predators, others were scavengers, and still others probably ate plankton. *Paradoxides harlani*, found near Boston, grew to 18 in. (45 cm) long and may have weighed 10 lbs (4.5 kg). Other species were small.

Trimble, David, orig. WILLIAM DAVID TRIMBLE (b. Oct. 15, 1944, Belfast, N.Ire.), Former first minister of Northern Ireland and corecipient with John Hume of the Nobel Prize for Peace in 1998. Trimble was elected to the British Parliament in 1990 and became leader of the Ulster Unionist Party (UUP) in 1995. He represented the UUP in multiparty peace talks beginning in September 1997. These talks, which included members of Sinn Féin, the political wing of the Irish Republican Army (IRA), culminated in the Good Friday Agreement of April 1998, which aimed to restore self-government in Northern Ireland. Defying opposition from hard-line unionists, he signed the agreement and successfully campaigned for its acceptance in referenda in Northern Ireland and in Ireland. In subsequent elections to the new Northern Ireland Assembly, he was elected first minister. He resigned as first minister in 2001, following a conflict with the IRA over decommissioning (disarmament), though he returned to government later that year after decommissioning commenced; the post of first minister was suspended the following year. In 2005 he lost his seat in the British Parliament and subsequently resigned as leader of the UUP.

trimurti, In Hinduism, the triad of the three great gods: Brahma, Vishnu, and Shiva. Scholars consider the trimurti doctrine an attempt to reconcile different monotheistic approaches with one another and with the philosophic doctrine of ultimate reality. In trimurti symbolism, the three gods are collapsed into a single form with three faces. Each god is in charge of an aspect of creation, with Brahma as creator, Vishnu as preserver, and Shiva as destroyer; however, some sects ascribe all aspects of creation to their deity of choice. Though sometimes called the Hindu Trinity, trimurti has little similarity to the Holy Trinity of Christianity.

Trinidad and Tobago, officially REPUBLIC OF TRINIDAD AND TOBAGO, Island country, West Indies. The islands of Trinidad and Tobago—the two southernmost links in the Antilles island chain—lie northeast of Venezuela and northwest of Guyana. Area: 1,990 sq mi (5,155 sq km). Population: (2011 est.) 1,325,000. Capital: Port of Spain. The people are mainly of South Asian or African ancestry. Language: English (official). Religions: Christianity (Protestant, Roman Catholic), Hinduism, Islam. Currency: Trinidad and Tobago dollar. The islands are mostly flat or rolling, with narrow belts of mountainous highlands and luxuriant rain forests. The Caroni Swamp, an important bird sanctuary on Trinidad, supports flamingo, egret, and scarlet ibis populations. The country has large reserves of petroleum and natural gas, as well as one of the world's largest supplies of natural asphalt. Other industries include agriculture, fishing, and tourism. Chief crops include sugarcane, citrus fruits, cocoa, and coffee. It is a republic with two legislative houses; its head of state is the president, and the head of government is the prime minister. When Christopher Columbus visited Trinidad in 1498, it was inhabited mostly by Arawak Indians, though there were probably some Carib speakers as well; Caribs inhabited Tobago. The islands were settled by the Spanish in the 16th century. In the 17th–18th centuries African slaves were imported for plantation labour to replace the original Indian population, which had been decimated by the impact of slavery and diseases introduced by the Europeans. Trinidad was surrendered to the British in 1797. The British attempted to settle Tobago in 1721, but the French captured the island in 1781 and transformed it into a sugar-producing colony. The British acquired it in 1802. After slavery ended in the islands (1834–38), immigrants from India were brought in to work the plantations. Trinidad and Tobago were administratively combined in 1889. Granted limited self-government in 1925, the islands became an independent state within the Commonwealth in 1962 and a republic in 1976. There occurred some political unrest and in 1990 a failed Muslim-fundamentalist coup against the government.

Trinity, Holy, In Christian doctrine, the unity of the Father, Son, and Holy Spirit as one God in three persons. The word Trinity does not appear in the Bible. It is a doctrine formulated in the early church to interpret the way God revealed himself, first to Israel, then in Jesus as Saviour, and finally as Holy Spirit, preserver of the church. The doctrine of the Trinity developed in the early centuries of the church and was explicitly stated at the Council of Nicaea in 325.

trio sonata, Principal chamber music genre of the Baroque era. Despite its name, it requires four performers: two melody instruments and continuo (usually a keyboard instrument and a bass instrument). It arose early in the 17th century as an instrumental version of the Italian vocal-duet ensemble. The two upper instruments, usually violins, generally wove their melodic, quasi-vocal lines high above the accompanying parts. Two standard forms emerged after 1750: the *sonata da chiesa*, or church sonata, standardized as a four-movement form (in slow-fast-slow-fast order); and the suite-like *sonata da camera*, or chamber sonata. By 1770 the genre had been abandoned in favour of the solo sonata.

Tripitaka, Pali TIPITAKA, Collective term for the three major divisions of the Pali canon, the canon of Theravada Buddhism. (The term means "Triple Basket.") It consists of the Abhidhamma Pitaka, the Sutta Pitaka, and the Vinaya Pitaka, which were transmitted orally by the sangha until they were committed to writing about 500 years after the Buddha's death. The texts appeared in two languages, Sanskrit and Pali, the Pali version being the better preserved. Sanskrit versions were translated into Tibetan, Chinese, and other languages.

Triple Alliance (1882) Secret agreement between Germany, Austria-Hungary, and Italy. It provided that Germany and Austria-Hungary would support Italy if it was attacked by France, that Italy would similarly assist Germany, and that Italy would remain neutral if Austria-Hungary was attacked by Russia. The alliance advanced Otto von Bismarck's efforts to isolate France. Conflicts between Italy and Austria-Hungary over their interests in the Balkans led Italy to reach an understanding of neutrality with France in 1902, which effectively nullified Italy's pledge to the members of the Triple Alliance, though the alliance was renewed in 1907 and 1912.

Triple Alliance, War of the, or PARAGUAYAN WAR (1864/65–70) Bloodiest conflict in Latin American history, fought between Paraguay and the allied countries of Argentina, Brazil, and Uruguay. The Paraguayan dictator Francisco Solano López (1827–70), objecting to Brazil's interference in the politics of neighbouring Uruguay, declared war on Brazil in 1864. The next year Argentina organized the Triple Alliance with Brazil and Uruguay. After three years of fighting, the allies annihilated the Paraguayan forces, but Solano López carried on a guerrilla war until he was killed. Paraguay was devastated by the war; its population was reduced by half, and territory covering some 55,000 sq mi (140,000 sq km) was annexed by Brazil and Argentina.

Triple Entente (1907) Association between Britain, France, and Russia. It developed from the Franco-Russian Alliance of 1894, the Anglo-French Entente Cordiale of 1904, and the Anglo-Russian Entente of 1907. Formed to settle mutual colonial disputes, the alignment became the nucleus of the Allied Powers in World War I.

triple jump, or HOP, STEP, AND JUMP, Track-and-field distance jump. It incorporates three distinct, continuous movements: a hop, in which the athlete takes off and lands on the same foot; a step, in which he lands on the other foot; and a jump, in which the athlete lands in any manner, usually with both feet together. It has been a modern Olympic event since the first games in 1896.

Tripoli, Arabic ṬARĀBULUS AL-SHĀM, Seaport city (pop., 2003 est.: 212,900), northwestern Lebanon. Founded *c.* 700 BCE, it became the capital of a federation of three Phoenician city-states: Sidon, Tyre, and Arvad. It was controlled by the Seleucids and Romans and taken by the Muslims in the mid-7th century CE. Besieged and partially destroyed by Crusaders in the early 12th century, it was rebuilt by the later Crusaders. It was occupied by the Egyptians in the 1830s, the British in 1918, and the British and Free French in 1941. It became part of the Republic of Lebanon in 1946. It has sometimes been a centre of Christian-Muslim conflict during Lebanon's history. It was also the scene of a siege in 1983 by Palestine Liberation Organization (PLO) rebels against PLO leader Yāsir ʿArafāt. It is a major port, a commercial and industrial centre, and a popular beach resort. At the terminus of an oil pipeline from Iraq, it is an important oil storage and refining centre.

Tripoli, Arabic ṬARĀBULUS AL-GHARB, City (pop. 2003 est.: city, 1,150,000; urban agglom., 2,006,000), capital of Libya. Located on the Mediterranean Sea, it is the country's largest city and chief seaport. Founded by the Phoenicians *c.* 7th century BC, it was known as Oea in ancient times and was one of the three cities of the region of Tripolitania. It was controlled by the Romans from the 1st century BC and later by the Byzantines. It was taken by the Arabs in 645. Conquered by the Ottoman Empire in 1551, it was made an Ottoman colonial capital. It was under Italy's control (1911–43), after which it was occupied by the British until Libya's independence in 1951. U.S. warplanes bombed targets within the city in 1983 in response to Libya's alleged support of terrorist activity. Historical structures include numerous mosques and a Roman triumphal arch. In 1973 Al-Fateh University replaced the former University of Libya.

Tripura, State (pop., 2008 est.: 3,510,000), northeastern India. It is bordered to the north, west, and south by Bangladesh and to the east by Mizoram and Assam states; it has an area of 4,049 sq mi (10,486 sq km), and its capital is Agartala. It was an independent Hindu kingdom before it became part of the Mughal Empire in the 17th century. After 1808 it was under the influence of the British. Tripura became a union territory in 1956 and acquired full status as a state in 1972. The main economic activity is agriculture, with rice and jute the major crops.

tritium, Isotope of hydrogen, chemical symbol written as ^{3}H or T, with atomic number 1 but atomic weight approximately 3. Its nucleus contains one proton and two neutrons. Tritium is radioactive, with a half-life of 12.32 years. Its occurrence in natural water in an amount 10^{-18} that of ordinary hydrogen is believed to be due to the action of cosmic rays. Some tritium is used in self-luminous materials (e.g., for watch dials) and as a radioactive tracer in chemical and biochemical studies. Nuclear fusion of deuterium and tritium at high temperatures releases enormous amounts of energy. Such reactions have been used in nuclear weapons and experimental power reactors.

Triton, Largest of Neptune's moons. Its diameter is about 1,680 mi (2,700 km), nearly 80% that of Earth's Moon. Unique among the large moons of the solar system, Triton moves in a retrograde orbit, opposite the direction of Neptune's rotation. Its orbital period of 5.9 Earth days is the same as its rotation period; as a result it always keeps the same face toward Neptune. It has a very thin atmosphere of nitrogen and methane and a surface temperature of −390 °F (−235 °C). Its surface is covered with enormous expanses of ice sculpted with fissures, puckers, and ridge-crossed depressions. Geyser-like plumes observed by the Voyager 2 spacecraft may be gas venting through fissures when the surface is warmed

by sunlight. Triton appears to have formed elsewhere in the solar system and to have been gravitationally captured by Neptune in the planet's early history.

triumph, Ancient Roman ritual procession honouring a general who had won a major battle and killed at least 5,000 of the enemy. Senators and magistrates were followed by sacrificial animals, captured loot, and captives in chains. The general, in a purple-and-gold tunic, rode in a chariot, holding a laurel branch in his right hand and an ivory sceptre in his left, while a slave held a golden crown over his head. Lastly came the soldiers, who sang songs. Under the empire only the emperor and members of his family celebrated triumphs.

triumvirate, In ancient Rome, usually a board of three officials who assisted higher magistrates in judicial functions, oversaw festival banquets, or ran the mint. The First Triumvirate (60 BC) of Pompey, Julius Caesar, and Crassus was an informal group of three strong leaders with no sanctioned powers. The Second Triumvirate (43 BC), consisting of Mark Antony, Lepidus, and Octavian (later Augustus)—formally *tresviri rei publicae constituendae* ("triumvirate for organizing the state")—held absolute dictatorial power.

Trojan War, Mostly legendary conflict between the Greeks and the people of Troy in western Asia Minor. It was dated by later Greeks to the 12th or 13th century BC. It is celebrated in Homer's *Iliad* and *Odyssey*, in Greek tragedy, and in Roman literature. In Homer's account the Trojan prince Paris ran off with the beautiful Helen, wife of Menelaus of Sparta, whose brother Agamemnon then led a Greek expedition to retrieve her. The war lasted 10 years; its participants included Hector, Achilles, Priam, Odysseus, and Ajax. Its end resulted from a ruse: The Greeks built a large wooden horse in which a raiding party hid. When the Greeks pretended to leave, the Trojans brought the horse into the walled city and the Greeks swarmed out, opening the gates to their comrades and sacking Troy, killing the men and enslaving the women. The extent of the legend's actual historical content is not known; excavations have revealed human habitation from 3000 BC to AD 1200, and there is evidence of violent destruction about 1250 BC.

trombone, Brass instrument with an extendable slide with which the length of its tubing can be increased. It has a mostly cylindrical bore and a cup-shaped mouthpiece. The slide performs the same function as the valves in other brass instruments. Valve trombones, both with and without slides, were developed in the early 19th century; they provide increased agility but diminished tone quality. The trombone exists in several sizes; the tenor trombone in B-flat is the standard instrument, but the bass trombone is also used orchestrally. The trombone (long known as the sackbut) developed in the 15th century and has changed little over 400 years. By the 16th century it had been adopted by town, court, church, and military bands; it was employed in early opera orchestras, but it only began to be used in the symphony orchestra *c.* 1800. In the 20th century it became important in dance and jazz bands.

Tropic of Cancer, Parallel of latitude approximately 23°27′ north of the terrestrial Equator. It is the northern boundary of the tropics and marks the northernmost latitude at which the Sun can be seen directly overhead at noon.

Tropic of Capricorn, Parallel of latitude approximately 23°27′ south of the terrestrial Equator. It is the southern boundary of the tropics and marks the southernmost latitude at which the Sun can be seen directly overhead at noon.

tropical cyclone, Severe atmospheric disturbance in tropical oceans. Tropical cyclones have very low atmospheric pressures in the calm, clear centre (the eye) of a circular structure of rain, cloud, and very high winds. In the Atlantic and Caribbean they are called hurricanes; in the Pacific they are known as typhoons. Because of the Earth's rotation, tropical cyclones rotate clockwise in the

Southern Hemisphere and counterclockwise in the Northern. They may be 50–500 mi (80–800 km) in diameter, and sustained winds in excess of 100 mph (160 km/hr) are common. In the eye, however, the winds drop abruptly to light breezes or even complete calm. The lowest sea-level pressures on Earth occur in or near the eye.

troposphere, Lowest region of the atmosphere, bounded by the Earth below and the stratosphere above, with the upper boundary being about 6–8 mi (10–13 km) above the Earth's surface. The troposphere is marked by decreasing temperature with height, which distinguishes it from the stratosphere. Most clouds and weather systems occur in the troposphere.

Trotsky, Leon, orig. LEV DAVIDOVICH BRONSHTEIN (b. Nov. 7,

1879, Yanovka, Ukraine, Russian Empire—d. Aug. 21, 1940, Coyoacán, near Mexico City, Mex.), Russian communist leader. Born to Russian Jewish farmers, he joined an underground socialist group and was exiled to Siberia in 1898 for his revolutionary activities. He escaped in 1902 with a forged passport using the name Trotsky. He fled to London, where he met Vladimir Lenin.

Leon Trotsky.
H. Roger-Viollet

In 1903, when the Russian Social-Democratic Workers' Party split, Trotsky became a Menshevik, allying himself with Lenin's opponents. He returned to St. Petersburg to help lead the Russian Revolution of 1905. Arrested and again exiled to Siberia, he wrote *Results and Prospects*, setting forth his theory of "permanent revolution." He escaped to Vienna in 1907, worked as a journalist in the Balkan Wars (1912–13), and moved around Europe and the U.S. until the Russian Revolution of 1917 brought him back to St. Petersburg (then Petrograd), where he became a Bolshevik and was elected leader of the workers' soviet. He played a major role in the overthrow of the provisional government and the establishment of Lenin's communist regime. As commissar of war (1918–24), Trotsky rebuilt and brilliantly commanded the Red Army during the Russian Civil War. Although favoured by Lenin to succeed him, Trotsky lost support after Lenin's death (1924) and was forced out of power by Joseph Stalin. After a campaign of denunciation, he was expelled from the Politburo (1926) and Central Committee (1927), then banished from Russia (1929). He lived in Turkey and France, where he wrote his memoirs and a history of the revolution. Under Soviet pressure, he was forced to move around Europe and eventually found asylum in 1936 in Mexico, where, falsely accused in the purge trials as the chief conspirator against Stalin, he was murdered in 1940 by a Spanish communist.

Trotskyism, Marxist ideology based on the theory of permanent revolution first expounded by Leon Trotsky. Trotsky believed that because all national economic development was affected by the laws of the world market, a revolution depended on revolutions in other countries for permanent success, a position that put him at odds with Joseph Stalin's "socialism in one country." After Trotsky's exile in 1929, Trotskyists continued to attack the Soviet bureaucracy as "Bonapartist" (based on the dictatorship of one man). In the 1930s Trotskyists advocated a united front with trade unions against fascism. After Trotsky's murder (1940), Trotskyism became a generic term for various revolutionary doctrines that opposed the Soviet form of communism.

Troy, or ILIUM, Ancient city in Troas, northwestern Anatolia. It holds an enduring place in both literature and archaeology. In literature, it is well known as the location of the Trojan War. The archaeological site, a huge mound at modern Hisarlık, Tur., on the Menderes (Scamander) River, was first excavated by archaeolo-

gist Heinrich Schliemann (1870–90). It consists of nine major layers dating from the early Bronze Age to Roman times (*c.* 3000 BCE–4th century CE). In Greek legend, the city was besieged by the Greeks for 10 years and finally destroyed. Its story is told in Homer's *Iliad* and *Odyssey* and in Virgil's *Aeneid*. Whether the site is the actual city of these works is still debated, but the archaeological evidence indicates that a city (Troy VIIa) was destroyed at that location *c.* 1260–40 BCE and likely was the Homeric Troy. The ruins were designated a UNESCO World Heritage site in 1998.

truck, or LORRY, Motor vehicle designed to carry freight or heavy articles. The first truck was built in Germany in 1896 by Gottlieb Daimler. By the 1920s trucks had become a major means of freight transport. Gasoline engines for trucks were common until the 1940s, when diesel engines generally replaced them. Trucks may be either straight (all axles attached to the frame) or articulated (two or more frames connected by couplings); large articulated trucks consist of a towing tractor and a connected semitrailer. Air brakes were added to trucks in 1918 and four-wheel brakes in 1925; later improvements included power steering.

truffle, Edible underground fungus in the genus *Tuber* (order

Pezizales, phylum Ascomycota) that has been prized as a food delicacy since antiquity. Native mainly to temperate regions, truffles flourish in open woodlands on calcium-rich soil. The different species range from pea-sized to orange-sized. Truffles usually are associated with tree roots and are found up to about 1 ft (30 cm) below the soil surface. Experienced gatherers occasionally detect mature truffles by scent or by the morning

English truffle (Tuber aestivum).
S.C. Porter/Bruce Coleman Inc.

and evening presence of hovering columns of small yellow flies but more often with the help of trained pigs or dogs. The truffle is important in French cookery, and truffle gathering is an important industry in France. Truffles are among the most highly valued foods in the world. False truffles (genus *Rhizopogon*, order Boletales, phylum Basidiomycota) form small, underground, potato-like structures under coniferous trees in parts of North America.

Truman, Harry S. (b. May 8, 1884, Lamar, Mo., U.S.—d. Dec. 26, 1972, Kansas City, Mo.), 33rd president of the U.S. (1945–53). He worked at various jobs before serving with distinction in World War I. He became a partner in a Kansas City haberdashery; when the business failed, he entered Democratic Party politics with the help of Thomas Pendergast. He was elected county judge (1922–24), and he later became presiding judge of the county court (1926–34). His reputation for honesty and good management gained him bipartisan support. In the U.S. Senate (1935–45), he led a committee that exposed fraud in defense production. In 1944 he was chosen to replace the incumbent Henry Wallace as the Democratic Party vice presidential nominee, and he won election with Pres. Franklin D. Roosevelt. After only 82 days as vice president, he became president on Roosevelt's death (April 1945). He quickly made final arrangements for the San Francisco charter-writing meeting of the UN, helped arrange Germany's unconditional surrender on May 8, which ended World War II in Europe, and in July attended the Potsdam Conference. The Pacific war ended officially on September 2, after he ordered atomic bombs dropped on Hiroshima and Nagasaki; his justification was a report that 500,000 U.S. troops would be lost in a conventional invasion of Japan. He announced what would become known as the Truman Doctrine, which entailed aid for Greece and Turkey (1947); established the Central Intelligence Agency; and pressed for passage of the Marshall Plan to aid the economic recovery of western Europe. In the 1948 presidential election he defeated Thomas Dewey despite widespread expectation of his own defeat. On July

26, 1948, Truman issued an executive order banning segregation in the armed forces. He initiated a foreign policy of containment to restrict the Soviet Union's sphere of influence, pursued his Point Four Program, and initiated the Berlin airlift and the NATO pact of 1949. He sent troops under Gen. Douglas MacArthur to fight in the Korean War. Problems of pursuing the war occupied his administration until he retired. Though he was often criticized during his presidency, his reputation grew steadily in later years.

trumpet, Brass instrument with tubing twice-folded in an elongated shape. (In its broad sense, trumpet may refer to any lip-vibrated instrument.) The modern trumpet has a mostly cylindrical bore, three valves, and a cup-shaped mouthpiece, and it is usually a B-flat or C instrument. The trumpet had taken its basic modern shape, with its ovoid loop, by *c.* 1500. In the 17th–18th centuries it employed crooks (removable lengths of tubing) to enable playing in different keys. The valved trumpet was developed in the 1820s. The trumpet has been associated with ceremonial and military uses since the 16th century. It joined the standard orchestra by *c.* 1700, though it was only selectively used, usually with the timpani. Its brilliant sound has since made it indispensable in a wide variety of ensembles.

trust, In law, a relationship between parties in which one, the trustee or fiduciary, has the power to manage property, and the other, the beneficiary, has the privilege of receiving the benefits from that property. Trusts are used in a variety of contexts, most notably in family settlements and in charitable gifts. The traditional requirements of a trust are a named beneficiary and trustee, an identified property (constituting the principal of the trust), and delivery of the property to the trustee with the intent to create a trust. Trusts are often created for the sake of advantageous tax treatment (including exemption). A charitable trust, unlike most trusts, does not require definite beneficiaries and may exist in perpetuity.

trust company, Company, often a commercial bank, acting as trustee for individuals and businesses and providing related financial or estate-planning services. Trust services for individuals commonly include the administration of estates, living trusts (trusts that become effective during the lifetimes of their makers, or settlors), and testamentary trusts (trusts originating in a will). Services for businesses include the administration of corporate bond indentures and corporate pension funds. Trust companies may also serve as corporate stock registrars and as paying agents for the distribution of dividends.

truth, In philosophy, the property of statements, thoughts, or propositions that are said, in ordinary discourse, to agree with the facts or to state what is the case. At least four major types of truth theory have been proposed: correspondence theories, coherence theories, pragmatic theories, and deflationary theories. The latter group encompasses a wide variety of views, including the redundancy theory, the disquotation theory, and the prosentential theory.

tsar, or CZAR, Byzantine or Russian emperor. The title, derived from *caesar*, was used in the Middle Ages to refer to a supreme ruler, particularly the Byzantine emperor. With the fall of the Byzantine Empire in 1453, the Russian monarch became the only remaining Orthodox monarch, and the Russian Orthodox clergy considered him a possible new supreme head of Orthodox Christianity. Ivan IV (the Terrible) was the first to be crowned tsar, in 1547. Though theoretically wielding absolute power, he and his successors were limited by the power of the Orthodox church, the Boyar Council, and the successive legal codes of 1497, 1550, and 1649. In 1721 Peter I changed his title to "Emperor of All Russia," but he and his successors continued to be popularly called tsars.

tsetse fly, Any of about 21 species (genus *Glossina*, family Muscidae) of African bloodsucking dipterans that are robust, sparsely bristled, and usually larger than a housefly. They have stiff, piercing mouthparts. Only two species commonly transmit the protozoan parasites (trypanosomes) that cause human sleeping sickness: *G. palpalis*, found primarily in dense streamside vegetation, and *G. morsitans*, found in more open woodlands. The female requires a sufficient blood meal to produce viable larvae, but both sexes suck blood almost daily.

tsunami, or SEISMIC SEA WAVE, or TIDAL WAVE, Catastrophic ocean wave, usually caused by a submarine earthquake. Underwater or coastal landslides or volcanic eruptions also may cause tsunamis. The term *tsunami* is Japanese for "harbour wave." The term *tidal wave* is a misnomer, because the wave has no connection with the tides. Perhaps the most destructive tsunami ever occurred in 2004 in the Indian Ocean, after an earthquake struck the seafloor off the Indonesian island of Sumatra. More than 200,000 people were killed in Indonesia, Thailand, India, Sri Lanka and other countries as far away as Somalia on the Horn of Africa.

tuba, Deep-pitched valved brass instrument with a widely expanding conical bore. Tubas vary in size and pitch. The tubing is coiled in an oblong shape, and the bell points upward or forward. Patented in Berlin in 1835, the tuba displaced the ophicleide to become the foundation of the brass section in the orchestra and in military and brass bands.

tuber, Short, thickened, mostly underground stem that constitutes the resting stage of certain seed plants. It is often an organ of food storage, reproduction, or both. It bears minute scale leaves, each with a bud that has the potential for developing into a new plant. The common potato is a typical tuber; the much-reduced leaves and associated buds form its "eyes." The term is also used imprecisely but widely for fleshy roots or rhizomes that resemble tubers (e.g., the "tuber" of the dahlia, actually a tuberous root).

tuberculosis (TB), formerly CONSUMPTION, Bacterial disease caused by some species of mycobacterium (tubercle bacillus). Mentioned in ancient Egyptian records and by Hippocrates, it has occurred throughout history worldwide. In the 18th–19th centuries it reached near-epidemic proportions in the rapidly industrializing and urbanizing Western world, where it was the leading cause of death until the early 20th century. TB resurged in the 1980s, spreading from AIDS patients to others, especially in prisons, homeless shelters, and hospitals, since enclosed settings promote spread. It occurs worldwide and is still a major cause of death in many countries. The body isolates the bacilli by forming tiny tubercles (nodules) around them. This often arrests TB's progress and no symptoms occur, but if the disease is not treated, it may become active—and contagious—later in life, most often when the immunity of the infected individual is suppressed (e.g., AIDS, after organ transplant). The original tubercle breaks down, releasing still viable bacilli into the bloodstream to cause a new infection, which starts with loss of energy and weight and persistent cough. Health deteriorates, with increasing cough and possibly pleurisy and spitting up blood. Growing tubercle masses may destroy so much lung tissue that respiration cannot supply the body with enough oxygen. Other organs can be affected, with complications including meningitis. A vaccine with weakened bacteria has helped control infection, but preventing exposure by recognizing and treating active TB early is more effective. Because many strains are resistant to drugs, treatment requires at least two drugs to which the patient's strain is sensitive and at least six months; inadequate treatment lets resistant bacilli multiply. The acute disease caused by multidrug-resistant strains is very hard to cure and usually fatal.

tudi, or T'U-TI, Type of Chinese god whose nature and functions are determined by local residents. Its chief characteristic is the limitation of its jurisdiction to a single place, such as a bridge, temple, or home. A tudi is subservient to the chenghuang, or municipal god. In most cases, a tudi originates as a person who in life aided the community. By deifying and offering sacrifices to them, residents hope to move them to show similar solicitude after death. If misfortunes visit a locality, the tudi is determined to have lost interest and a new patron is chosen.

Tudor, house of, English royal dynasty that gave five sovereigns to England (1485–1603). The Tudors originated in the 13th century, but the dynasty's fortunes were established by Owen Tudor (*c.* 1400–61), a Welsh adventurer who took service with Henry V and married Henry's widow, Catherine of Valois (1401–37). Owen and Catherine's son Edmund Tudor (*c.* 1430–56) was created earl of Richmond and married Lady Margaret Beaufort (1443–1509), a descendant of John of Gaunt of the house of Lancaster. Their son Henry Tudor claimed the English throne as Henry VII in 1485 and cemented his claim with his marriage to Elizabeth of the house of York, daughter of Edward IV. The Tudor rose symbolized the union between the red rose of the Lancastrians and the white rose of the Yorkists. The Tudor dynasty continued in the 16th century with the reigns of Henry VIII and his children Edward VI, Mary I, and Elizabeth I. In 1603 the dynasty was succeeded by the house of Stuart.

Tudor style, Architectural style in England (1485–1558) that made lavish use of half-timbering, as well as oriels, gables, decorative brickwork, and rich plasterwork. Exposed diagonal bracing usually occurs at building corners, with the second story often sporting a picturesque overhang; this cantilevered construction partially counterbalances the load carried by the spanning portions of the beams.

Tula, Ancient city in Mexico, the capital of the Toltecs, which flourished in the 9th–12th centuries. Its exact location is uncertain; the archaeological site now designated Tula, near the town of that name in Hidalgo state, has been the choice of historians. The Tula site suggests a city that had a population in the tens of thousands. The major civic centre consists of a plaza bordered by a five-stepped pyramid, two other pyramids, and two ball courts. Tula's art and architecture are strikingly similar to those of the Aztec capital, Tenochtitlán, and its artistic themes suggest that the Aztecs' concept of themselves as warrior-priests of the sun god was borrowed directly from Tula.

tumour, or NEOPLASM, Mass of abnormal tissue that arises from normal cells, has no useful function, and tends to grow. Cell abnormalities may include increased size or number or loss of characteristics that differentiate their tissue of origin. Cells in malignant tumours have a distorted size, shape, and/or structure. Less differentiated cells tend to grow faster. Malignant tumours invade tissues locally and spread (metastasize) in blood or lymph: the stronger the tendency to metastasize, the more malignant the tumour. Tumours may not cause pain until they press on or invade nerves. Both benign and malignant tumours can press on nearby structures, block vessels, or produce excess hormones, all of which can cause death. Benign tumours remain as a solid mass that can be removed by surgery if accessible; they can consist of various tissues and may become malignant; malignant tumours, though they may remain quiescent for a time, never become benign.

tuna, Any of seven species (genus *Thunnus*, family Scombridae) of commercially valuable food fishes. Species range from the 80-lb (36-kg) albacore to the bluefin tuna (*T. thynnus*), which grows to 14 ft (4.3 m) long and weighs up to 1,800 lb (800 kg). Tunas have a slender, streamlined body and a forked or crescent-shaped tail. They are unique among fishes in having a vascular system modified to maintain a body temperature above the water temperature. Though slow swimmers, they migrate long distances over all the world's oceans. They eat fishes, squid, shellfish, and plankton.

tundra, Treeless, level or rolling ground above the taiga in polar regions (Arctic tundra) or on high mountains (alpine tundra), char-

acterized by bare ground and rock or by such vegetation as mosses, lichens, small herbs, and low shrubs. Animal species are limited by harsh environmental conditions. In the Arctic tundra they include lemmings, the Arctic fox, the Arctic wolf, caribou, reindeer, and musk-oxen. In the alpine tundra many animals, including mountain sheep and wildcats, descend to warmer zones during winter. The climate of alpine tundra is more moderate and has a higher amount of rainfall than does Arctic tundra. The freezing climate of the Arctic produces a layer of permanently frozen soil (permafrost). An overlying layer of soil alternates between freezing and thawing with seasonal temperature variations. Alpine tundras have a freeze-thaw layer but no permafrost. Because Arctic tundras receive extremely long periods of daylight and darkness (lasting between one and four months), biological rhythms tend to be adjusted more to variations in temperature than to variations in sunlight. Arctic tundra covers about one-tenth of the earth's surface. Alpine tundras begin above the timberline of spruce and firs. Because of the small number of plant and animal species and the fragility of the food chains in tundra regions, natural or mechanical damage to any element of the habitat affects the whole ecosystem.

tungsten, or WOLFRAM, Metallic chemical element, one of the transition elements, chemical symbol W, atomic number 74. Exceptionally strong, white to grayish, and brittle, it has the highest melting point (6,170 °F [3,410 °C]), greatest high-temperature strength, and lowest thermal expansion coefficient of any metal. Its chief uses are in steels to increase hardness and strength and in lightbulb filaments. It is also used in electrical contacts, rocket nozzles, chemical apparatus, high-speed rotors, and solar-energy devices. Tungsten is relatively inert, but compounds (in which it has various valences) are known. The most important, tungsten carbide, noted for its hardness, is used to increase the wear-resistance of cast iron and of tools' cutting edges.

Tunis, City (pop., 2004: 728,453), capital of Tunisia. It is situated on Tunis Lake, an inlet of the Gulf of Tunis; its port, La Goulette (Ḥalq al-Wādī), is 6 mi (10 km) to the northeast. Founded by Libyans, it was later a small town under Carthage; it became important after the Muslim conquest in the 7th century AD. It was a religious centre during the Aghlabid dynasty (9th century) and reached its greatest prosperity under the Ḥafṣid dynasty (13th century). The Spanish and Ottomans controlled it during the 16th century, and it was occupied by the Germans in 1942. It was made the national capital when Tunisia gained independence from France in 1956. It produces textiles, carpets, and olive oil and has metallurgical industries. Tourism is also important. The city's historic centre was designated a UNESCO World Heritage site in 1979.

Tunisia, officially TUNISIAN REPUBLIC, Country, North Africa. Area: 63,170 sq mi (163,610 sq km). Population: (2011 est.) 10,594,000. Capital: Tunis. The population is of Arab and Amazigh ancestry. Languages: Arabic (official), French. Religion: Islam (official; predominantly Sunni). Currency: Tunisian dinar. Tunisia comprises a coastal region, mountains, an extensive hilly steppe, a marshy area with shallow salt lakes, and a tract of the Sahara. The Majardah is its longest (about 290 mi [460 km]) and only perennial river. Tunisia contains some of the largest phosphate and natural gas reserves in Africa, as well as substantial oil reserves. Major economic activities are services, agriculture, light industries, and the production and export of petroleum and phosphates. Tourism, focusing on Tunisia's beaches and Roman ruins, is also important. Tunisia is a republic with two legislative houses; its head of state is the president, and the head of government is the prime minister. From the 12th century BCE the Phoenicians had a series of trading posts on the North African coast. By the 6th century BCE the Carthaginian kingdom encompassed most of present-day Tunisia. The Romans ruled from 146 BCE. It was part of the Byzantine Empire until the Muslim Arab invasions in the mid-7th century CE. The area was fought over, won, and lost by many, including the ʿAbbāsid dynasty, the Almohad dynasty, Spain, and the Ottoman Empire, which conquered it in 1574 and held it until the late 19th century. For a time it maintained autonomy as the French, British, and Italians contended for the region. In 1881 it became a French protectorate. During World War II (1939–45) U.S. and British forces captured it (1943), putting an end to a brief German occupation. France granted it full independence in 1956; Habib Bourguiba assumed power and remained in power until he was forced from office in 1987. His successor, Zine al-Abidine Ben Ali, continued with a similar authoritarian-style rule until 2011, when he stepped down amid an unprecedented level of unrest in the country.

tunnel, Horizontal or nearly horizontal underground or underwater passageway. Tunnels are used for mining, as passageways for trains and motor vehicles, for diverting rivers around damsites, for housing underground installations such as power plants, and for conducting water. Ancient civilizations used tunnels to carry water for irrigation and drinking, and in the 22nd century BCE the Babylonians built a tunnel for pedestrian traffic under the Euphrates River. The Romans built aqueduct tunnels through mountains by heating the rock face with fire and rapidly cooling it with water, causing the rock to crack. The introduction of gunpowder blasting in the 17th century marked a great advance in solid-rock excavation. For softer soils, excavation is accomplished using devices such as the tunneling mole, with its rotating wheel that continuously excavates material and loads it onto a conveyor belt. Railroad transportation in the 19th–20th century led to a tremendous expansion in the number and length of tunnels. Brick and stone were used for support in early tunnels, but in modern tunneling steel is generally used until a concrete lining can be installed. A common method of lining involves spraying shotcrete onto the tunnel crown immediately after excavation.

tunneling, or BARRIER PENETRATION, In physics, the passage of a particle through a seemingly impassable energy barrier. Though a particle's energy may be too low to surmount a barrier in classical physics, the particle may still cross the barrier as a consequence of its quantum-mechanical wave properties. An important application of this phenomenon is in the operation of the scanning tunneling microscope.

Túpac Amaru, Peruvian revolutionary group. Founded in 1983, the group is best known for holding 490 people hostage in the Japanese embassy in Lima (1996) in an effort to gain the release of jailed comrades. After a standoff of several weeks, Peruvian troops stormed the embassy and killed all the guerrillas. Defections have apparently since decreased its membership. The group takes its name from the Indian revolutionary Túpac Amaru II (orig. José Gabriel Condorcanqui, 1742?–81), who in 1780 led Peruvian Indian peasants in the last widespread rebellion against Spain before independence. The Indians identified him with his ancestor Túpac Amaru, the last leader of the Inca, who was executed by the Spaniards in 1572.

Turin, Italian TORINO, City (pop., 2001 prelim.: 857,433), Piedmont region, northwestern Italy. Located on the Po River, it was founded by the Taurini. It was partly destroyed by Hannibal in 218 BC. It was made a Roman military colony under Emperor Augustus. A part of the Lombard duchy in the 6th century AD, it became the seat of government under Charlemagne (742–814). It passed to the house of Savoy in 1046. The capital of the kingdom of Sardinia in 1720, Turin was occupied by the French during the Napoleonic Wars. The political and intellectual centre of the Risorgimento movement, it served as the first capital of united Italy (1861–65). During World War II Turin sustained heavy damage from Allied air raids but was rebuilt. It is the focus of Italy's automotive industry and an international fashion centre. The Shroud of Turin has been housed in the 15th-century cathedral there since the 16th century.

Turin, Shroud of, Linen fragment said to be the burial garment of Jesus. It has been preserved since 1578 in the royal chapel of the Cathedral of San Giovanni Battista in Turin, Italy. Measuring 14.5 by 3.7 ft (4.42 by 1.13 m), it appears to portray images of the back and front of a gaunt, sunken-eyed man. The images contain markings that correspond to the stigmata and stains presumed to be blood. The cloth emerged historically in 1354 and went on exhibition in 1389, first as a representation of the shroud and eventually as the shroud itself. In 1988 independent tests using radiocarbon dating techniques indicated that the cloth had been made *c.* 1260–1390. Subsequent chemical analyses and other tests, however, suggested a much older date, possibly even the 1st century.

Turing machine, Hypothetical computing device proposed by Alan M. Turing (1936). Not actually a machine, it is an idealized mathematical model that reduces the logical structure of any computing device to its essentials. It consists of an infinitely extensible tape, a tape head that is capable of performing various operations on the tape, and a modifiable control mechanism in the head that can store instructions. As envisaged by Turing, it performs its functions in a sequence of discrete steps. His extrapolation of the essential features of information processing was instrumental in the development of modern digital computers, which share his basic scheme of an input/output device (tape and tape reader), central processing unit (CPU, or control mechanism), and stored memory.

Turkey, officially REPUBLIC OF TURKEY, Country, western Asia and southeastern Europe. Area: 303,224 sq mi (785,347 sq km), nearly all of which lies in Asia. Population: (2011 est.) 74,306,000. Capital: Ankara. Ethnic groups include the Turks and Kurds. Languages: Turkish (official), Kurdish, Arabic. Religion: Islam (mostly Sunni). Currency: Turkish lira. Turkey is a mountainous country with an extensive plateau covering central Anatolia. The highest peak is Mount Ararat (16,945 ft [5,165 m]). The Taurus Mountains lie in the south. Rivers include the Tigris, Euphrates, Kızıl, and Menderes. Turkey is a major producer and exporter of chromite and also mines iron ore, coal, lignite, bauxite, and copper. It is the Middle East's leading steel producer. Chief agricultural products include wheat, barley, olives, and tobacco. Tourism also is important. Turkey is a multiparty republic with one legislative house; its head of state is the president, and the head of government is the prime minister. Turkey's early history corresponds to that of Anatolia, the Byzantine Empire, and the Ottoman Empire. Byzantine rule emerged when Constantine the Great made Constantinople (Istanbul) his capital. The Ottoman Empire, begun in the 12th century, dominated for more than 600 years; it ended in 1918 after the Young Turk revolt (1908) precipitated its demise. Under the leadership of Mustafa Kemal Atatürk, a republic was proclaimed in 1923. Turkey remained neutral throughout most of World War II (1939–45), siding with the Allied powers in 1945. Since the war it has alternated between civil and military governments and has had several conflicts with Greece over Cyprus. The country has developed a strong, diversified economy, but it has also experienced periods of political and civic turmoil between Islamists and secularists and ongoing ethnic tension with Kurdish separatists.

turkey, Either of two species of birds assigned to either of two families, Phasianidae or Meleagrididae. The North American common turkey (*Meleagris gallopavo*) has been domesticated since pre-Columbian times. The adult male has a featherless bright-red head, a fleshy red ornament (snood) growing over the bill, and a similar wattle on the throat. The male (gobbler or tom) may be 50 in. (1.3 m) long and may weigh over 20 lb (10 kg). Wild turkeys inhabit woodlands near water, eating seeds, insects, and an occasional frog or lizard. Males assemble a harem, and each hen lays 8–15 eggs in a hollow in the ground. An excellent source of meat and easily shot, the wild turkey was practically exterminated by European settlers; conservation efforts have reestablished it in much of its former range. The ocellated turkey (*Agriocharis*, or *Meleagris, ocellata*) of Central America has never been domesticated.

Turkic languages, Family of more than 20 Altaic languages spoken by some 135 million people from the Balkans to central Siberia. The traditional division of Turkic is into four groups. The southeastern or Uighur group comprises Uighur, spoken mainly in Xinjiang, China; and Uzbek, spoken mainly in Uzbekistan, other Central Asian republics, and northern Afghanistan. The southwestern, or Oguz, group includes Turkish; Azerbaijani (Azeri), spoken in Azerbaijan and northwestern Iran; Crimean Tatar, spoken mostly in Ukraine and Uzbekistan; and Turkmen, used in Turkmenistan, northern Iran, and northern Afghanistan. The northwestern, or Kipchak, group includes Kazakh, spoken in Kazakhstan, other Central Asian republics, and western China and Mongolia; Kyrgyz, spoken in Kyrgyzstan, other Central Asian republics, and western China; Tatar; Baskhir, spoken in Bashkortostan and adjacent areas in Russia; Karachay-Balkar and Kumyk, spoken in the Russian Caucasus; and Karaim, with a few speakers in Lithuania and parts of southwestern Ukraine. The northeastern, or Altai, group comprises languages and dialects spoken in Siberia northeast of the Irtysh River and in adjacent parts of Mongolia, including Altai, Khakas, Shor, and Tuvan; and Sakha, spoken in Sakha (Yakutia) republic of Russia and adjacent areas. Distinct from all the other languages is Chuvash, spoken in Russia's Chuvash republic and adjacent areas. The earliest attestations of Turkic are a group of 8th-century funerary inscriptions of northern Mongolia, in a distinctive writing system called runic script, or Turkic runes. With the Islamization of nearly all Turkic peoples southwest of the Irtysh beginning *c.* 900, Turkic languages began to adopt the Arabic alphabet. Today the Latin alphabet and Cyrillic alphabet are more extensively used.

Turkish bath, Bath originating in the Middle East, combining exposure to warm air, steam immersion, massage, and a cold bath or shower. The Turkish bath (*ḥammām*) reflects the fusion of the massage and cosmetic aspects of the Eastern bath tradition and the plumbing and heating techniques of the Romans. Turkish baths were smaller than the Roman thermae and more sparsely lit. The baths at Constantinople were domed, and rooms were richly decorated with marble or mosaics. Used for socializing and relaxation as well as bathing, the *ḥammām* was popular throughout the Islamic world; some baths are still in use. In the 19th century, the Turkish bath was adapted and exported to Europe and the U.S.

Turkish language, Turkic language of Turkey, spoken by about 90% of its population. Turkish has about 59 million speakers, with many enclaves in the Balkans and Cyprus (dating from Ottoman times) and in western Europe. Turkish was introduced into Anatolia with the invasion of Turkmen tribes in the 13th–14th centuries. Anatolian Turkish, written in the Arabic alphabet, is first attested in the 13th century. Ottoman Turkish was so heavily influenced by Persian and Arabic that it lost some of its Turkic characteristics and was incomprehensible to lower social strata. Efforts to re-Turkicize the language began in the 18th century but did not make serious gains until the 20th century and the founding of the Turkish republic. Much Perso-Arabic vocabulary was removed, and the Latin alphabet was adopted with the addition of diacritics to symbolize sounds peculiar to Turkish.

Turkistan, or TURKESTAN, Historical region, Central Asia. This somewhat broad geographic region—situated between Siberia (Russia) to the north and Tibet (China), India, Afghanistan, and Iran to the south—derived its name from its inhabitants, who were predominantly of Turkic ancestry. The total area of more than 1,000,000 sq mi (2,600,000 sq km) was bisected by the Pamir and Tien Shan ranges, forming West and East Turkistan. West Turkistan, which included what is now Turkmenistan, Uzbekistan, Tajikistan, Kyrgyzstan and southern Kazakhstan, came under Russian rule in the 19th century. East Turkistan came to be included in what is now the Uygur Autonomous Region of Xinjiang.

Turkmen, Member of a Central Asian people belonging to the southwestern branch of the Turkic linguistic group. At the beginning of the 21st century, they numbered more than six million, and most lived in Turkmenistan and adjacent parts of Central Asia. A significant number also live in Iran and parts of Turkey and Afghanistan, and there are pockets of Turkmen in northern Iraq and Syria. Initially a nomadic pastoral people living in tent villages, many took up agriculture while under Soviet rule. Most are Muslim, and they have traditionally divided themselves by economic function. They are patrilineal, and each family or tribal group is headed by a khan.

Turkmenistan, officially TÜRKMENISTAN, Country, Central Asia. Area: 189,657 sq mi (491,210 sq km). Population: (2011 est.) 4,998,000. Capital: Ashgabat. Turkmen make up three-fourths of the population, with small groups of Uzbeks, Russians, Kazakhs, and Tatars. Language: Turkmen (official). Religions: Islam (predominantly Sunni); also Eastern Orthodox. Currency: (new) manat. There are some hills and low mountains. About nine-tenths of Turkmenistan is desert, chiefly the Karakum. The main rivers are the Amu Darya and Morghāb. Many irrigation canals and reservoirs have been built, including the Karakum Canal, which runs 870 mi (1,400 km) between the Amu Darya and the Caspian Sea. The country's chief products are petroleum and natural gas, cotton, silk, carpets, fish, and fruit. It is a unitary single-party republic with one legislative body, and its head of state and government is the president. The earliest traces of human settlement in Central Asia, dating to Paleolithic times, have been found in Turkmenistan. The nomadic tribal Turkmen probably entered the area in the 11th century CE. They were conquered by the Russians in the early 1880s, and the region became part of Russian Turkistan. It was organized as the Turkmen S.S.R. in 1924 and became a constituent republic of the U.S.S.R. in 1925. The country gained full independence from the Soviet Union in 1991 under the name Turkmenistan. It experienced years of economic difficulty until oil and gas production was more fully developed and was subject to the highly authoritarian rule of Saparmurad Niyazov.

Turks and Caicos Islands, British dependency (pop., 2002 est.: 18,738), West Indies. It comprises two small island groups at the southeastern end of The Bahamas. The Turks group includes Grand Turk, Salt Cay, and lesser cays. The Caicos group includes South Caicos, East Caicos, Middle (or Grand) Caicos, North Caicos, Providenciales, West Caicos, and several smaller cays. The seat of government is at Cockburn Town on Grand Turk Island. When Spanish explorer Juan Ponce de León visited in 1512, the

*Turmeric (*Curcuma longa*).*
W.H. Hodge

islands were inhabited by Indians. British colonists from Bermuda arrived in 1678. The islands were at first placed under the government of The Bahamas, but in 1874 they were annexed to the colony of Jamaica. The Turks and Caicos Islands became a crown colony in 1962 and shared a governor with The Bahamas from 1965 to 1973. A new constitution was adopted in 1988. The chief industries are tourism and offshore financial services.

turmeric, Perennial herbaceous plant (*Curcuma longa*; family Zingiberaceae), native to southern India and Indonesia. Its tuberous rhizomes have been used from antiquity as a condiment, as a textile dye, and medically as an aromatic stimulant. The rhizome has a pepperlike aroma and a somewhat bitter, warm taste. It colours and flavours prepared mustard and is used in curry powder, relishes, pickles, spiced butters, and numerous culinary dishes. Paper tinged with turmeric turns from yellow to reddish brown when an alkali is added to it, thus providing a test for alkalinity.

Turner syndrome, Chromosomal disorder (from the presence of only one sex chromosome, X, in all or some of the body's cells) that causes abnormal sexual development in females. The syndrome may include absent or undeveloped ovaries, underdeveloped secondary sex characteristics, low hairline, webbed neck, shield-shaped chest with wide-spaced nipples, and kidney and heart malformations with coarctation (narrowing) of the aorta. It may not be recognized until a girl fails to undergo puberty at a normal age. Estrogen treatment results in puberty, adult appearance, and normal sex drive but not fertility. Surgery can correct malformations.

turquoise, Hydrated copper and aluminum phosphate mineral, $CuAl_6(PO_4)_4(OH)_8 \cdot 4H_2O$, that is used extensively as a gemstone. The colour of turquoise ranges from blue through various shades of green to greenish and yellowish gray. A delicate sky-blue, which provides an attractive contrast with precious metals, is most valued for gem purposes. Numerous deposits of turquoise in the southwestern U.S. have been worked for centuries by American Indians. The mineral also occurs in Iran, northern Africa, Australia, and Siberia.

turtle, Any of approximately 300 species (order Testudines) of reptiles that have a bony shell overlaid with horny shields and are found in most parts of the world. Turtles have existed for 200 million years, making them the oldest of all surviving reptiles. Most species are aquatic or semiaquatic; some are terrestrial. Turtles eat plants, animals, or both. They are toothless, have a horny beak, and range from less than 4 in. (10 cm) to more than 5 ft (1.5 m) long. They have sturdy, sprawling limbs with short feet or paddlelike flippers (marine turtles). Some species bend the neck sideways, but most pull the head and neck backward into the shell. Almost half of the known turtle species are rare, threatened, or endangered.

Tutankhamen, orig. TUTANKHATEN (fl. 14th century BC), Egyptian pharaoh (r. 1333–23 BC) of the 18th dynasty. When he took the throne at about age eight, he was advised to move back to Memphis from Akhetaton, the city of his father-in-law and predecessor, Akhenaton. During his reign the traditional religion was restored after the changes made by Akhenaton. Shortly before he died, while still in his teens, he sent troops to Syria to aid an ally against a group connected with the Hittites. Because his name was among those stricken from the royal lists during the 19th dynasty, his tomb's location was forgotten and his burial chamber was not opened until 1922, when it was discovered by Howard Carter (1873–1939). Its treasures made Tutankhamen perhaps the best-known of the pharaohs despite his early death and limited accomplishments.

Tutankhamen, gold funerary mask found in the king's tomb, 14th century BCE; in the Egyptian Museum, Cairo.
© Lee Boltin

Tutsi, People of Rwanda and Burundi who are traditionally considered Nilotic. They speak Rundi or Rwanda (mutually intelligible languages of the Niger-Congo family) and number some 1.5 million. The Tutsi represent a traditional aristocratic minority, which has dominated the more populous Hutu. Originally warrior-herders, the Tutsi entered the area in the 14th or 15th century and later, assisted by German and Belgian colonial regimes, cultivated a lord-vassal relationship with the Hutu. At the head of the pyramidal political structure was the *mwami* ("king"), considered to be of divine origin. Today Hutu and Tutsi cultures have largely become integrated. In addition to sharing languages, they both adhere to similar traditional and/or Christian religious beliefs. The Tutsi retained their dominant position over the Hutu in Rwanda until 1961, when the monarch was overthrown. An unsuccessful Hutu revolt in Burundi in 1972 led to 100,000 deaths, mostly Hutu. In 1993 in Burundi and in 1994 in Rwanda, further clashes occurred, the latter including a genocidal campaign by Hutu militia and civilians in which more than a million Tutsi and their Hutu allies were killed and one to two million Hutu fled to refugee camps in Congo (Kinshasa; then Zaire) and Tanzania.

Tutu, Sir Desmond (Mpilo) (b. Oct. 7, 1931, Klerksdorp, S.Af.), South African Anglican cleric. He studied theology at the University of South Africa and King's College, London. He became an Anglican priest in 1961 and bishop of Lesotho in 1976. In 1978 he became general secretary of the South African Council of Churches and an eloquent and outspoken advocate for the rights of black South Africans. He emphasized nonviolent protest and encouraged other countries to apply economic pressure to South Africa. In 1984 he received the Nobel Prize for Peace for his role in opposing apartheid. In 1986 he was elected the first black archbishop of Cape Town and titular head of South Africa's 1.6-million-member Anglican Church. He retired from the primacy in 1996 and became chairman of the Truth and Reconciliation Commission, charged with hearing evidence of human-rights violations under white rule. In 1988 he was named chancellor of the University of the Western Cape in Bellville, S.Af. In 2010 he retired from public life.

Tuvalu, Island country, west-central South Pacific Ocean. Area: 9.9 sq mi (25.6 sq km). Population: (2011 est.) 11,200. Capital: Vaiaku, Fongafale islet (of Funafuti atoll). The majority of the people are Polynesian. Languages: Tuvaluan; English is widely used. Religion: Christianity (predominantly Protestant). Currency: Tuvalu dollar (equivalent to the Australian dollar). Tuvalu is an island group comprising five atolls and four coral islands, all of them low-lying, with maximum elevations below 20 ft (6 m), and covered mainly with coconut palms, breadfruit trees, and grasses. The economy is based on subsistence agriculture and livestock raising. Tuvalu is a constitutional monarchy with one legislative house; its head of state is the British monarch, represented by the governor-general, and the head of government is the prime minister. The original Polynesian settlers probably came mainly from Samoa or Tonga. The islands were sighted by the Spanish in the 16th century. Europeans settled there in the 19th century and intermarried with Tuvaluans. During this period Peruvian slave traders known as "blackbirders" decimated the population. In 1856 the U.S. claimed the four southern islands for guano mining. Missionaries from Europe arrived in 1865 and rapidly converted the islanders to Christianity. In 1892 Tuvalu, then known as the Ellice Islands, joined the British Gilbert Islands, a protectorate that became the Gilbert and Ellice Islands colony in 1916. Tuvaluans voted in 1974 for separation from the Gilberts (now Kiribati), whose people are Micronesian. Tuvalu gained independence in 1978, and in 1979 the U.S. relinquished its claims. Elections were held in 1981, and a revised constitution was adopted in 1986. The government subsequently has tried to improve Tuvalu's economy, including finding overseas job opportunities for its citizens. In the early 21st century, rising sea levels in the South Pacific began to degrade

Tuvalu's coasts and to contaminate its freshwater aquifers, leading to fears that the islands might become uninhabitable within several decades.

Twain, Mark, orig. SAMUEL LANGHORNE CLEMENS (b. Nov. 30, 1835, Florida, Mo., U.S.—d. April 21, 1910, Redding, Conn.), U.S. humorist, writer, and lecturer. He grew up in Hannibal, Mo., on the Mississippi River and was apprenticed in 1848 to a local printer. He received a riverboat pilot's license in 1859 and later moved on to Nevada and California. In 1863 he took his pseudonym, the riverman's term for water 2 fathoms (12 ft [3.7 m]) deep. In a California mining camp he heard the story that he first published in 1865 and made famous as the title story of his first book, *The Celebrated Jumping Frog of Calaveras County and Other Sketches* (1867). He traveled widely, using his travels as subject matter for lectures and books, from the humorous narratives *The Innocents Abroad* (1869) and *Roughing It* (1872) to *Life on the Mississippi* (1883), his reflections on being a riverboat captain. He won a worldwide audience for his adventure stories of boyhood, especially *Tom Sawyer* (1876) and *Huckleberry Finn* (1885), one of the masterpieces of American fiction. The satirical *A Connecticut Yankee in King Arthur's Court* (1889) and increasingly grim works including *Pudd'nhead Wilson* (1894) and *The Man Who Corrupted Hadleyburg* (1899) followed. In the 1890s financial speculations bankrupted him. His eldest daughter died in 1896, his wife in 1904, and another daughter in 1909. He expressed his pessimism about human character in such late works as the posthumously published *Letters from the Earth* (1962).

Twelve Tables, Law of the, Earliest codification of ancient Roman law, traditionally dated to 451–450 BC. They were purportedly written at the demand of the plebeians, who felt that their legal rights were hampered by the fact that court judgments were rendered according to unwritten custom preserved only within a small group of learned patricians. The Twelve Tables were not a reform or a liberalizing of old custom; they recognized the prerogatives of the patrician class and of the patriarchal family, the validity of enslavement for unpaid debt, and the interference of religious custom in civil cases. Because only random quotations from the Twelve Tables are extant, knowledge about their contents is largely derived from references in later juridical writings. Venerated by the Romans as a prime legal source, the Twelve Tables were superseded by later changes in Roman law but were never formally abolished.

Two Sicilies, Kingdom of the, Former kingdom, Italy. It united the southern part of the Italian peninsula with the island of Sicily. The region was conquered by the Normans in the 11th century; the two areas were divided in 1282 between the Angevin (French) dynasty on the mainland and the Aragonese (Spanish) dynasty on the island, both of which claimed the title of King of Sicily. In 1442 Alfonso V of Aragon reunited the two areas and took the title of King of the Two Sicilies. This title was sometimes used during the Spanish and Bourbon rule of the region in the 16th–19th centuries; it became official in 1816, when the administration of both areas was combined and Sicily lost its autonomy. Conquered by Giuseppe de Garibaldi in 1860, the Two Sicilies became part of the Kingdom of Italy.

Tyne and Wear, Metropolitan county (pop., 2001: 1,075,979), northeastern England. It was named for its two main rivers, the Tyne and the Wear. Settled since prehistoric times, the area was occupied by the Romans, who built Hadrian's Wall. Saxon, then Norman settlement followed. From the 13th century to recent times, the economy was based on local coal reserves and on such coal-dependent industries as glass, pottery, and chemicals. The main industries now include shipbuilding and heavy electrical engineering.

typhoid, or TYPHOID FEVER, Acute infectious disease resembling typhus (and distinguished from it only in the 19th century).

Salmonella typhi, usually ingested in food or water, multiplies in the intestinal wall and then enters the bloodstream, causing septicemia. Symptoms begin with headache, aching, and restlessness. High fever gradually develops, with delirium. A rash appears on the trunk. The sites where the bacilli multiplied become inflamed and may ulcerate, leading to intestinal bleeding or peritonitis. Patients become exhausted and emaciated; up to 25% die if not treated. Antibiotic treatment is effective. Patients can carry typhoid for weeks to months or years. Carriers can contaminate the food they handle. Prevention depends mainly on water and sewage treatment and excluding carriers from food-handling jobs.

typhus, Any of a group of related diseases caused by various species of rickettsia that release toxins into the blood. Headache, chills, fever, and general pains begin suddenly and a rash soon after. The bacteria are transmitted by lice, fleas, mites, and ticks. Epidemic typhus, spread by the body louse, is the most severe. It is one of the great scourges of history, associated with crowded, filthy conditions. Improved hygiene has nearly eliminated it from the Western world, but it persists in many countries, despite modern vaccines and pesticides. Endemic typhus, spread by fleas on rats and other rodents, is milder (mortality under 5%). Scrub typhus, carried by mites, is usually classed as a separate disease.

typography, Design or selection of letter forms to be organized into words and sentences and printed or displayed electronically. Typography originated after the invention of printing from movable type in the mid 15th century. The three major type families in the history of Western printing are roman, italic, and black letter (Gothic). All had their origin in the scripts of the calligraphers whose work was ultimately replaced by printing. In the succeeding centuries typographers have created some 10,000 typefaces (a complete set of letter forms of a particular design). Depending on the style of their letters, typefaces are categorized as old style, transitional, and modern. Commonly used typefaces include Caslon, Baskerville, Bodoni, Garamond, and Times New Roman. The selection of a typeface is an important part of the aesthetic process in graphic design.

tyrannosaur, Any of a group of related predatory dinosaurs with large, high skulls, powerful jaws and legs, and large, sharp teeth shaped for biting through flesh and bone. *Tyrannosaurus rex* is the largest and best-known, found as fossils in North American deposits from the latest part of the Cretaceous Period (about 65 million years ago). Tyrannosaurs walked with the body horizontal and the long tail held off the ground as a counterweight. In that posture, large adults, weighing more than six tons, would have been more than 40 ft (12 m) long. In some forms the hands had only two digits. A nearly complete skeleton of *T. rex* called "Sue" is on display at the Field Museum in Chicago. Other tyrannosaurs include *Albertosaurus* and *Tarbosaurus*.

Tyrrhenian Sea, Italian MARE TIRRENO, Arm of the Mediterranean Sea. It is located between the western coast of Italy and the islands of Corsica, Sardinia, and Sicily. It is connected with the Ligurian Sea on the northwest through the Tuscan Archipelago and with the Ionian Sea on the southeast through the Strait of Messina. Chief inlets include the Bay of Naples.

tzaddiq, or ZADDIK, One who embodies the religious ideals of Judaism. The term is used repeatedly in the Old Testament and in the Talmud, which asserts that the continued existence of the world is due to the merits of 36 righteous men. In Hasidism it came to refer to a religious leader who was viewed as a mediator between humankind and God. Initially the zaddikim traveled widely and engaged in social activities to strengthen the community's spiritual life. Toward the end of the 18th century, they ceased this practice and became available at home for those seeking advice.

U

U-boat, German UNTERSEEBOOT ("UNDERSEA BOAT"), German submarine. The first German submarine, the U-1, was built in 1905. During World War I Germany became the first country to employ submarines in war, and during World War II its U-boats dominated the Battle of the Atlantic until the Allies developed new antisubmarine tactics. The principal German U-boat was the type VII; the VIIC variant was 220.25 ft (66 m) long, displaced 769 tons on the surface, carried one 90-mm deck gun and five torpedo tubes, and was manned by a crew of 44. Modern German U-boats are built for the German navy and navies of allied countries; their sophisticated structures, electronics, and propulsion systems allow them to be used for intelligence gathering and special operations in addition to defending sea lanes and threatening enemy forces.

ʿūd, Stringed instrument prominent in medieval and modern Islamic music, forerunner of the European lute. Dating from the 7th century, it has a pear-shaped body, a fretless fingerboard, a short neck, and a bent-back pegbox with the tuning pegs set in the sides. The gut strings, of which there are often four pairs, are plucked with a plectrum.

Ufa, City (pop., 2006 est.: 1,029,616), western Russia. Lying at the confluence of the Belaya and Ufa rivers, it was founded as a fortress in 1574 to protect the trade route across the Ural Mountains from Kazan to Tyumen. It became a town in 1586. It developed as an industrial centre from the late 19th century and especially after World War II. Chief industries include electrical equipment, lumber and veneer, and oil refining.

Uffizi Gallery, Art museum in Florence, housing the world's finest collection of Italian Renaissance painting. The core collection derives from the Medici family of Tuscany. In 1559 Cosimo I hired Giorgio Vasari to design the Uffizi Palace (1560–80), originally for use as government offices (*uffizi*). In 1565 Vasari built the corridor over the Ponte Vecchio connecting the Uffizi with the Pitti Palace. In 1737 Maria Ludovica, last of the Medici, bequeathed the family collections to Tuscany; the collection was given museum status and opened to the public in 1769. The building was restored and enlarged after bomb damage in World War II and flooding in 1966. In addition to Florentine paintings, the Uffizi houses outstanding works of other Italian and non-Italian schools, antique sculpture, a gallery of self-portraits, and 100,000 prints and drawings.

Uganda, officially REPUBLIC OF UGANDA, Country, eastern Africa. Area: 93,263 sq mi (241,551 sq km). Population: (2011 est.) 34,509,000. Capital: Kampala. Uganda is home to dozens of African ethnic groups, as well as a small Asian community. Languages: English (official), Swahili. Religions: Christianity (mostly Roman Catholic; also Protestant); also Islam, traditional beliefs. Currency: Uganda shilling. A landlocked country on the Equator, Uganda is largely situated on a plateau, with volcanic mountains edging its eastern and western borders; Margherita Peak, at 16,795 ft (5,119 m), is the highest mountain. Part of Lake Victoria occupies virtually all of southeastern Uganda; other major lakes are Lakes Albert, Kyoga, Edward, George, and Bisina. The Nile River traverses the country. Huge tracts of land are devoted to national parks and game reserves. The economy is based largely on agriculture and food processing. Livestock raising and fishing are also important, and there is some manufacturing and mining. Uganda is a multiparty republic with one legislative house; its head of state and government is the president, assisted by the prime minister. By the 19th century the region was divided into several separate local kingdoms inhabited by various Bantu- and Nilotic-speaking peoples. Arab traders reached the area in the 1840s. The kingdom of Buganda was visited by the first European explorers in 1862. Protestant and Catholic missionaries arrived in the 1870s, and the development of religious factions led to persecution and civil strife. In 1894 Buganda was formally proclaimed a British protectorate. As Uganda, it gained independence in 1962, and in 1967 it adopted a republican constitution. The civilian government was overthrown in 1971 and replaced by a military regime under Idi Amin. His invasion of Tanzania in 1978 resulted in the collapse of his regime. The civilian government was again deposed by the military in 1985, but the military government was in turn overthrown in 1986. A constituent assembly enacted a new constitution in 1995.

ukiyo-e (Japanese: "pictures of the floating world"), Dominant art movement of the Edo culture in Japan. Screen paintings were the first works to be done in the style, which depicted aspects of the entertainment quarters ("floating world") of Edo (modern Tokyo) and other cities. Ukiyo-e artists switched their focus to woodblock prints, which were mass-produced for an eager public. Favourite ukiyo-e subjects included famous courtesans and prostitutes, kabuki actors in famous roles, and erotica; they were executed in flat, decorative colours and expressive patterns. Hishikawa Moronobu is generally accredited as the first master of ukiyo-e. The transition from single- to two-colour prints was made by Okumura Masanobu; in 1765 polychrome prints using numerous blocks were introduced by Suzuki Harunobu. The essence of the ukiyo-e style was embodied in the works of Utamaro, Hokusai, and Hiroshige. The prints attracted much attention in Europe in the 19th century and had a great influence on avant-garde French artists such as the Impressionists and Post-Impressionists.

Ukraine, Country, eastern Europe. Area: 233,062 sq mi (603,628 sq km). Population: (2011 est.) 45,672,000. Capital: Kiev (Kyiv). Ukrainians make up more than three-fourths of the population; there is a significant minority of Russians. Languages: Ukrainian (official), Russian, Romanian, Polish, Hungarian, Belarusian, Bulgarian. Religions: Christianity (mostly Eastern Orthodox; also other Christians, Roman Catholic, Protestant), Islam. Currency: hryvnia. Ukraine consists of level plains and the Carpathian Mountains, which extend through the western region for more than 150 mi (240 km). The Dnieper (Dnipro), Southern Buh (Pivdennyy Buh), Donets, and Dniester (Dnistro) are the major rivers. The Donets Basin in the east-central region is one of the major heavy-industrial and mining-metallurgical complexes of Europe. There iron ore and coal are mined, and natural gas, petroleum, iron, and steel are produced. Ukraine is a major producer of winter wheat and sugar beets. It is a unitary multiparty republic with one legislative body; its head of state is the president, and the head of government is the prime minister. Different parts of the area were invaded and occupied in the 1st millennium BCE by the Cimmerians, Scythians, and Sarmatians and in the 1st millennium CE by the Goths, Huns, Bulgars, Avars, Khazars, and Magyars (Hungarians). Slavic tribes settled there after the 4th century. Kiev was the chief town. The Mongol conquest in the mid-13th century decisively ended Kievan power. From the 14th to the 18th century, portions of Ukraine were ruled by Lithuania, Poland, and Russia. In addition, Cossacks controlled a largely self-governing territory known as the Hetmanate. Most of Ukraine fell to Russian rule in the 18th century. In the aftermath of World War I and the Russian Revolution of 1917, most of the Ukrainian region became a republic of the Soviet Union, though parts of western Ukraine were divided between Poland, Romania, and Czechoslovakia. Ukraine suffered a severe famine in 1932–33 under Soviet leader Joseph Stalin. Overrun by Axis armies in 1941 during World War II, it was further devastated before being retaken by the Soviets in 1944. By the end of the war, the borders of the Ukrainian S.S.R. had been redrawn to include the western Ukrainian territories. Ukraine was the site of the 1986 Chernobyl accident at a Soviet-built nuclear power plant. In 1991 Ukraine declared independence. The turmoil it experienced in the 1990s as it attempted to implement economic and political reforms culminated in the disputed presidential election of 2004; mass protests over the results came to be known as the Orange Revolution. The effects of the revolution were short-lived, however, and political differences continued to rend the country.

ukulele, Small Hawaiian four-stringed guitar. It developed out of a similar Portuguese instrument introduced to Hawaii by sailors in the 1870s. It became highly popular in the U.S. after World War I, when it was used in jazz and bluegrass ensembles and more widely as an amateur solo instrument.

Ulaanbaatar, or ULAN BATOR, City (pop., 2002 est.: mun., 812,500), capital of Mongolia. Situated on a windswept plateau, it was founded in the mid-17th century as the residence of the *bod-go-gegen*, the high priest of Tibetan Buddhism. It subsequently became a trading centre on caravan routes between Russia and China; it remains the principal junction of Mongolian transportation routes. The Outer Mongolian revolt for independence was centred there in 1911. Ulaanbaatar became the capital when the Mongolian People's Republic was established in 1924 and remained the capital when the country's name was changed to Mongolia in 1992. It is the country's main industrial centre.

ulcer, Concave sore on the skin or lining of an organ, with well-defined, sometimes raised edges. Erosion of surface tissue may extend to deeper layers. The main symptom is pain. The term most often refers to peptic ulcer but also includes skin ulcer, common on legs with varicose veins and the feet of people with diabetes mellitus (when nerve damage has reduced sensation), and decubitus ulcer (bedsore or pressure sore). Other causes include infection, trauma (e.g., burn, frostbite), improper nutrition (e.g., thiamine deficiency), and cancer (likely in ulcers hard to the touch). Skin ulcers over a month old should be checked for cancer, especially after middle age.

ulcerative colitis, Inflammation of the colon, especially of its mucous membranes. The inflamed membranes develop patches of tiny ulcers, and the diarrhea contains blood and mucus. It often becomes chronic, with sustained fever and weight loss; complications and death may result. Specific causes, such as amoebic or bacillary dysentery, are rarer than unknown or multiple causes. If treatment with sulfasalazine, corticosteroids, immunosuppressive drugs, or antibiotics does not control it, part or all of the colon may have to be removed.

ultrasonics, Vibrational or stress waves in elastic media that have a frequency above 20 kilohertz, the highest frequency of sound waves that can be detected by the human ear. They can be generated or detected by piezoelectric transducers. High-power ultrasonics produce distortion in a medium; applications include ultrasonic welding, drilling, irradiation of fluid suspensions (as in wine clarification), cleaning of surfaces (such as jewelry), and disruption of biological structures. Low-power ultrasonic waves do not cause distortions; uses include sonar, structure testing, and medical imaging and diagnosis. Some animals, including bats, employ ultrasonic echolocation for navigation.

ultrasound, or ULTRASONOGRAPHY, Use of ultrasonic waves to produce images of body structures. The waves travel through tissues and are reflected back where density differs (e.g., the border between a hollow organ's wall and its inside). The reflected echoes are received by an electronic apparatus that measures their intensity level and the position of the tissue reflecting them. The results can be displayed as still images or as a moving picture of the inside of the body. Unlike X-rays or other ionizing radiation, ultrasound carries minimal, if any, risk. Most often used during pregnancy to examine the fetus, ultrasound imaging is also used

on internal organs and on the eye, breast, and major blood vessels. It can often show whether a growth is benign or malignant.

ultraviolet astronomy, Study of astronomical objects and phenomena by observing the ultraviolet radiation (UV radiation) they emit. It has yielded much information about chemical abundances and processes in interstellar matter, the Sun, and other stellar objects, such as hot young stars and white dwarf stars. Ultraviolet astronomy became feasible once rockets could carry instruments above Earth's atmosphere, which absorbs most electromagnetic radiation of UV wavelengths. Since the early 1960s, a number of unmanned space observatories carrying UV telescopes, including the Hubble Space Telescope, have collected UV data on objects such as comets, quasars, nebulae, and distant star clusters. The Extreme Ultraviolet Explorer, launched in 1992, was the first orbiting observatory to map the sky in the shortest UV wavelengths, at the boundary with the X-ray region of the electromagnetic spectrum.

ultraviolet radiation, Portion of the electromagnetic spectrum extending from the violet end of visible light to the X-ray region. Ultraviolet (UV) radiation lies between wavelengths of about 400 nanometres and 10 nanometres, corresponding to frequencies of 7.5×10^{14} Hz to 3×10^{16} Hz. Most UV rays from the Sun are absorbed by the Earth's ozone layer. UV has low penetrating power, so its effects on humans are limited to the skin. These effects include stimulation of production of vitamin D, sunburn, suntan, aging signs, and carcinogenic changes. UV radiation is also used to treat jaundice in newborns, to sterilize equipment, and to produce artificial light.

Uluru/Ayers Rock, Rock outcrop, southwestern Northern Territory, Australia. Called Uluru by the Australian Aborigines and located in Uluru–Kata Tjuta National Park, it is 1,100 ft (335 m) high and may be the world's largest monolith. Its arkosic sandstone changes colour according to the height of the sun. Shallow caves at the base of the rock are sacred to several Aboriginal tribes and contain carvings and paintings. In 1985 ownership of Uluru/Ayers Rock was officially returned to the Aborigines. The park was designated a UNESCO World Heritage site in 1987.

Underground Railroad, Secret system in northern U.S. states to help escaping slaves. Its name derived from the need for secrecy and the railway terms used in the conduct of the system. Various routes in 14 states, called lines, provided safe stopping places (stations) for the leaders (conductors) and their charges (packages) while fleeing north, sometimes to Canada. The system developed in defiance of the Fugitive Slave Acts and was active mainly from 1830 to 1860. An estimated 40,000 to 100,000 slaves used the network. Assistance was provided mainly by free blacks, including Harriet Tubman, and philanthropists, church leaders, and abolitionists. Its existence aroused support for the antislavery cause and convinced Southerners that the North would never allow slavery to remain unchallenged.

Undset, Sigrid (b. May 20, 1882, Kalundborg, Den.—d. June 10, 1949, Lillehammer, Nor.), Norwegian novelist. Her father was an archaeologist, and her home life was steeped in legend, folklore, and Norwegian history. Her early novels deal with the position of women in the contemporary lower middle class. She then turned to the distant past and created her masterpiece, the trilogy *Kristin Lavransdatter* (1920–22), which is set in medieval Norway and depicts the spiritual growth of a strong woman. Undset converted to Roman Catholicism in 1924. Her later works, including the historical novel *The Master of Hestviken* (1925–27) and novels on contemporary themes, reflect her interest in religion. She received the Nobel Prize for Literature in 1928.

unemployment, Condition of a person who is able to work, is actively seeking work, but is unable to find any. Statistics on unemployment are collected and analyzed by government labour offices in most countries and are considered an important indicator of economic health. Since World War II full employment has been a stated goal of many governments. Full employment is not necessarily synonymous with a zero unemployment rate, since at any given time the unemployment rate will include some people who are between jobs and not unemployed in any long-term sense. Underemployment is the term used to describe the situation of those who are able to find employment only for shorter than normal periods—for example, part-time workers and seasonal workers—and may also describe the condition of workers whose education or training makes them overqualified for their jobs.

UNESCO, in full UNITED NATIONS EDUCATIONAL, SCIENTIFIC AND CULTURAL ORGANIZATION, Specialized agency of the UN, created in 1946 to aid peace by promoting international cooperation in education, science, and culture. It supports member states' efforts to eliminate illiteracy, encouraging the extension of free education, and acts as a clearinghouse for the exchange of ideas and knowledge. In 1972 it sponsored an international agreement to establish a World Heritage list of cultural sites and natural areas that would enjoy government protection. In 1984 the U.S. withdrew from UNESCO to protest what it considered the agency's anti-Western approach to cultural issues; the United Kingdom and Singapore withdrew a year later. The United Kingdom rejoined in 1997, and the U.S. followed suit in 2003.

UNICEF, in full UNITED NATIONS CHILDREN'S FUND, formerly (1946–53) UNITED NATIONS INTERNATIONAL CHILDREN'S EMERGENCY FUND, Special United Nations program for aiding national efforts to improve the health, nutrition, education, and general welfare of children. Its original purpose was to provide relief to children in countries devastated by World War II. After 1950 it turned to general programs for the improvement of children's welfare. It was awarded the Nobel Prize for Peace in 1965. UNICEF has focused its efforts on areas in which relatively small expenditures can have a significant impact on the lives of the most disadvantaged children, such as the prevention and treatment of disease. UNICEF also provides funding for health services, educational facilities, and other welfare services. It is headquartered in New York City.

unicorn, Mythological animal resembling a white horse with a single horn on its forehead. The unicorn was depicted in Mesopotamian art and was referred to in the ancient myths of India and China. Its earliest description in Greek literature dates from *c.* 400 BC and probably refers to the Indian rhinoceros. The unicorn was believed to be fierce and difficult to capture, but if a virgin were brought before it, it would lay its head in the virgin's lap. Its horn was thought to offer protection against poison. Medieval writers associated the unicorn with Jesus, and the hunt for the unicorn was often represented in medieval art.

Unicorn, detail from "The Lady and the Unicorn" tapestry, late 15th century; in the Musée de Cluny, Paris
Giraudon/Art Resource, New York

unidentified flying object (UFO), Aerial object or optical phenomenon not readily explainable to the observer. Interest in UFOs increased with developments in aeronautics and astronautics after World War II. A U.S. government panel investigating sightings in the 1950s reported that 90% coincided with astronomical or meteorological phenomena or sightings of aircraft, birds, or hot gases, sometimes under unusual weather conditions. Some remained unexplained, however, and in the mid-1960s a few scientists concluded that a small percentage indicated the presence of extraterrestrial visitors. This sensational hypothesis, promoted in the press, met with prompt resistance from other scientists. A U.S. Air Force UFO study begun in 1968 firmly rejected the extraterrestrial hypothesis, but a large fraction of the public, and a few scientists, continued to support it. UFO reports vary widely in reliability. The unaided eye is easily fooled; radar sightings of UFOs, more reliable in some ways, may fail to distinguish physical objects from meteor trails, rain, or thermal discontinuities and are subject to radio interference.

Unification Church, officially HOLY SPIRIT ASSOCIATION FOR THE UNIFICATION OF WORLD CHRISTIANITY, Religious movement founded (1954) in South Korea by Sun Myung Moon. Influenced by yin-yang principles and Korean shamanism, it seeks to establish divine rule on earth through the restoration of the family, based on the union of the Lord and Lady of the Second Advent (believed to be Moon and his wife, Hak Ja Han). It strives to fulfill what it asserts to be the uncompleted mission of Jesus—procreative marriage. The church has been criticized for its recruitment policies (said to include brainwashing) and business practices. Its mass marriage ceremonies have gained press attention. Its worldwide membership is about 200,000 in more than 100 countries.

unified field theory, Attempt to describe all fundamental interactions between elementary particles in terms of a single theoretical framework (a "theory of everything") based on quantum field theory. So far, the weak force and the electromagnetic force have been successfully united in electroweak theory, and the strong force is described by a similar quantum field theory called quantum chromodynamics. However, attempts to unite the strong and electroweak theories in a grand unified theory have failed, as have attempts at a self-consistent quantum field theory of gravitation.

Union, Act of (May 1, 1707) Treaty that effected the union of England (and Wales) and Scotland under the name of Great Britain. The union benefited England's need for political safeguards against a possible Jacobite restoration through Scotland, and it gave Scotland economic security by freedom of trade with England. Under the treaty, initiated by Queen Anne, the two kingdoms adopted the Protestant succession, preserved Scots law and the law courts, and agreed to uniform taxation.

Union, Act of (Jan. 1, 1801) Legislative agreement uniting Great Britain and Ireland under the name of the United Kingdom of Great Britain and Ireland. After the unsuccessful Irish revolt of 1798, the British prime minister, William Pitt the Younger, decided that the best solution to the Irish problem was a union to strengthen the connection between the two countries. The Irish parliament resisted the proposal, which called for its abolition, but votes bought by cash or honours ensured passage of the agreement in 1800. The union remained until the recognition of the Irish Free State (excluding six of the counties of the northern province of Ulster) by the Anglo-Irish treaty concluded on Dec. 6, 1921; the union officially ended on Jan. 15, 1922.

Union of Soviet Socialist Republics (U.S.S.R.), or SOVIET UNION, Former republic, eastern Europe and northern and central Asia. It consisted, in its final years, of 15 soviet socialist republics that gained independence at its dissolution: Armenia, Azerbaijan, Belorussia (now Belarus), Estonia, Georgia, Kazakhstan, Kirgiziya (now Kyrgyzstan), Latvia, Lithuania, Moldavia (now Moldova), Russia, Tajikistan, Turkmenistan, Ukraine, and Uzbekistan. It also contained 20 autonomous soviet socialist republics: 16 within Russia, 2 within Georgia, 1 within Azerbaijan, and 1 within Uzbekistan. Capital: Moscow. Stretching from the Baltic and Black seas to the Pacific Ocean and encompassing some 8,650,000 sq mi (22,400,000 sq km), the Soviet Union constituted the largest country on Earth, having a maximum east-west extent of about 6,800 mi (10,900 km) and a maximum north-south extent of about 2,800 mi (4,500 km). It encompassed 11 time zones and had common boundaries with six European countries and six Asian countries. Its regions contained fertile lands, deserts, tundra, high mountains, some of the world's longest rivers, and large inland waters, including most of the Caspian Sea. The coastline on the Arctic Ocean extended 3,000 mi (4,800 km), while that on the Pacific was 1,000 mi (1,600 km) long. The U.S.S.R. was an agricultural, mining, and industrial power. Following the Russian Revolution of 1917, four socialist republics were established on the territory of the former Russian Empire: the Russian Soviet Federated Socialist Republic, the Transcaucasian Soviet Federated Socialist Republic, the Ukrainian Soviet Socialist Republic, and the Belorussian Soviet Socialist Republic. These four constituent republics established the Union of Soviet Socialist Republics in 1922, to which other republics subsequently were added. A power struggle begun in 1924 with the death of communist leader Vladimir Lenin ended in 1927 when Joseph Stalin gained victory. Implementation of the first of the Five-Year Plans in 1928 centralized industry and collectivized agriculture. A purge in the late 1930s resulted in the imprisonment or execution of millions of persons considered dangerous to the state. After World War II, with their respective allies, the U.S.S.R. and the U.S. engaged in the Cold War. In the late 1940s the U.S.S.R. helped to establish communist regimes throughout most of eastern Europe. The U.S.S.R. exploded its first atomic bomb in 1949 and its first hydrogen bomb in 1953. Following Stalin's death, it experienced limited political and cultural liberalization under Nikita Khrushchev. It launched the first manned orbital spaceflight in 1961. Under Leonid Brezhnev liberalization was partially reversed, but in the mid-1980s Soviet leader Mikhail Gorbachev instituted the liberal policies called glasnost and perestroika. By the end of 1990 the communist government had toppled, and a program to create a market economy had been implemented. The U.S.S.R. was officially dissolved on Dec. 25, 1991.

Unitarianism, Religious movement that stresses free use of reason in religion, holds that God exists in only one person, and denies the divinity of Jesus and the doctrine of the Holy Trinity. Its modern roots are traced to several liberal, radical, and rationalist thinkers of the Protestant Reformation, who were in turn inspired by Arius. The mainstream of British and American Unitarianism grew out of Calvinist Puritanism. The scientist Joseph Priestley was a founder of the English Unitarians, who became a force in Parliament and were noted advocates of social reform. In the U.S., Unitarianism developed out of New England Congregationalism that rejected the 18th-century revival movement. Transcendentalism injected Unitarianism with a new interest that attracted many more followers.

United Arab Emirates (UAE), formerly TRUCIAL STATES, Country, Middle East, southwestern Asia. It is a federation of seven states on the eastern coast of the Arabian Peninsula. They are the emirates of Abū Ẓaby (Abu Dhabi), Dubayy (Dubai), ʿAjmān, Al-Shāriqah (Sharjah), Umm al-Qaywayn, Raʾs al-Khaymah, and Al-Fujayrah. Area: 32,280 sq mi (83,600 sq km). Population: (2011 est.) 7,891,000. Capital: Abu Dhabi. The indigenous inhabitants are Arabs, but there are a large number of South Asian and Iranian migrant workers. Languages: Arabic (official), English, Persian, Urdu, Hindi. Religions: Islam (official; predominantly Sunni); also Christianity, Hinduism. Currency: UAE dirham. The UAE's low-lying desert plain is broken by the Ḥajar Mountains along the Musandam Peninsula. Three natural deepwater harbours are located along the Gulf of Oman. The UAE (mainly Abū Ẓaby) has roughly one-tenth of the world's petroleum reserves and significant natural gas deposits, the production of which are the federation's principal industries. Other important economic activities include fishing, livestock herding, and date production. The federation has one advisory board; its head of

state is the president, and the head of government is the prime minister. In 1820 the British signed a peace treaty with the region's coastal rulers. The area, formerly called the Pirate Coast, became known as the Trucial Coast. In 1892 the rulers agreed to entrust foreign relations to Britain, but the British never assumed sovereignty; each state maintained full internal control. The states formed the Trucial States Council in 1960 and in 1971 terminated defense treaties with Britain and established the six-member federation. Raʾs al-Khaymah joined it in 1972. The UAE aided coalition forces against Iraq in the Persian Gulf War (1990–91).

United Kingdom of Great Britain and Northern Ireland, or UNITED KINGDOM, or GREAT BRITAIN, Island country, western Europe, North Atlantic Ocean. It comprises Great Britain (England, Scotland, and Wales) and Northern Ireland. Area: 93,851 sq mi (243,073 sq km). Population: (2011 est.) 62,675,000. Capital: London. The population is composed of English (major ethnic group), Scots, Irish, and Welsh and immigrants and their descendants from India, the West Indies, Pakistan, Bangladesh, and Africa. Languages: English (official); also Welsh, Scottish Gaelic. Religions: Christianity (Protestant [Church of England—established; Church of Scotland—national], Roman Catholic, other Christians); also Islam, Hinduism, Sikhism, Judaism. Currency: pound sterling. The country has hill, lowland, upland, highland, and mountain regions. Tin and iron ore deposits, once central to the economy, have become exhausted or uneconomical, and the coal industry, long a staple of the economy, began a steady decline in the 1950s that worsened with pit closures in the 1980s. Offshore petroleum and natural gas reserves are significant. Chief crops are barley, wheat, sugar beets, and potatoes. Major manufactures include motor vehicles, aerospace equipment, electronic data-processing and telecommunication equipment, and petrochemicals. Fishing and publishing also are important economic activities. The U.K. is a constitutional monarchy with two legislative houses; its head of state is the sovereign, and the head of government is the prime minister.

The early pre-Roman inhabitants of Britain were Celtic-speaking peoples, including the Brythonic people of Wales, the Picts of Scotland, and the Britons of Britain. Celts also settled in Ireland *c.* 500 BCE. Julius Caesar invaded and took control of the area in 55–54 BCE. The Roman province of Britannia endured until the 5th century CE and included present-day England and Wales. Germanic tribes, including Angles, Saxons, and Jutes, invaded Britain in the 5th century. The invasions had little effect on the Celtic peoples of Wales and Scotland. Christianity began to flourish in the 6th century. During the 8th and 9th centuries, Vikings, particularly Danes, raided the coasts of Britain. In the late 9th century Alfred the Great repelled a Danish invasion, which helped bring about the unification of England under Athelstan. The Scots attained dominance in Scotland, which was finally unified under Malcolm II (1005–34). William of Normandy took England in 1066. The Norman kings established a strong central government and feudal state. The French language of the Norman rulers eventually merged with the Anglo-Saxon of the common people to form the English language. From the 11th century, Scotland came under the influence of the English throne. Henry II conquered Ireland in the late 12th century. His sons Richard I and John had conflicts with the clergy and nobles, and eventually John was forced to grant the nobles concessions in the Magna Carta (1215). The concept of community of the realm developed during the 13th century, providing the foundation for parliamentary government. During the reign of Edward I (1272–1307), statute law developed to supplement English common law, and the first Parliament was convened. In 1314 Robert the Bruce won independence for Scotland. The house of Tudor became the ruling family of England following the Wars of the Roses (1455–85). Henry VIII (1509–47) established the Church of England and incorporated Wales as part of England.

The reign of Elizabeth I (1558–1603) began a period of colonial expansion; in 1588 British forces defeated the "invincible" Spanish Armada. In 1603 James VI of Scotland ascended the English throne, becoming James I, and established a personal union of the two kingdoms. The English Civil Wars erupted in 1642 between Royalists and Parliamentarians, ending in the execution of Charles I (1649). After 11 years of Puritan rule under Oliver Cromwell and his son (1649–60), the monarchy was restored with Charles II. In 1689, following the Glorious Revolution, Parliament proclaimed the joint sovereigns William III and Mary II, who accepted the British Bill of Rights. In 1707 England and Scotland assented to the Act of Union, forming the kingdom of Great Britain. The Hanoverians ascended the English throne in 1714, when George Louis, elector of Hanover, became George I of Great Britain. During the reign of George III, Great Britain's North American colonies won independence (1783). This was followed by a period of war (1789–1815) with Revolutionary France and later with the empire of Napoleon. In 1801 legislation united Great Britain with Ireland to create the United Kingdom of Great Britain and Ireland. Britain was the birthplace of the Industrial Revolution in the late 18th century, and it remained the world's foremost economic power until the late 19th century. During the reign of Queen Victoria (1837–1901), Britain's colonial expansion reached its zenith, though the older dominions, including Canada and Australia, were granted independence (1867 and 1901, respectively).

The U.K. entered World War I allied with France and Russia in 1914. Following the war, revolutionary disorder erupted in Ireland, and in 1921 the Irish Free State was granted dominion status. Six counties of Ulster, however, remained in the U.K. as Northern Ireland. The U.K. entered World War II in 1939. Following the war, the Irish Free State became the Irish republic and left the Commonwealth. India also gained independence from the U.K. Throughout the postwar period and into the 1970s, the U.K. continued to grant independence to its overseas colonies and dependencies. With UN forces, it participated in the Korean War (1950–53). In 1956 it intervened militarily in Egypt during the Suez Crisis. It joined the European Economic Community, a forerunner of the European Union, in 1973. In 1982 it defeated Argentina in the Falkland Islands War. As a result of continuing social strife in Northern Ireland, it joined with Ireland in several peace initiatives, which eventually resulted in an agreement to establish an assembly in Northern Ireland. In 1997 referenda approved in Scotland and Wales devolved power to both countries, though both remained part of the U.K. In 1991 the U.K. joined an international coalition to reverse Iraq's conquest of Kuwait. In 2003 the U.K. and the U.S. attacked Iraq and overthrew the government of Ṣaddām Ḥussein. Terrorist bombings in London in July 2005 killed more than 50 people.

United Nations (UN), International organization founded (1945) at the end of World War II to maintain international peace and security, develop friendly relations among nations on equal terms, and encourage international cooperation in solving intractable human problems. A number of its agencies have been awarded the Nobel Prize for Peace, and the UN was the corecipient, with Kofi Annan, of the prize in 2001. The term originally referred to the countries that opposed the Axis powers. An international organization was discussed at the Yalta Conference in February 1945, and the UN charter was drawn up two months later at the UN Conference on International Organization. The UN has six principal organs: the Economic and Social Council, the United Nations General Assembly, the International Court of Justice, the Secretariat, the United Nations Security Council, and the United Nations Trusteeship Council. It also has several specialized agencies—some inherited from its predecessor, the League of Nations (e.g., the International Labour Organization)—and a number of special offices (e.g., the Office of the United Nations High Commissioner for Refugees), programs, and funds (e.g., UNICEF). The UN is involved in economic, cultural, and humanitarian activities and the coordination or regulation of international postal services, civil aviation, meteorological research, telecommunications, international shipping, and intellectual property. Its

peacekeeping troops have been deployed in several areas of the world, sometimes for lengthy periods. The UN's world headquarters are in New York City. In 2005 the UN had 192 member countries. The principal administrative officer of the UN is the secretary-general, who is elected to a five-year renewable term by the General Assembly on the recommendation of the Security Council. The secretaries-general of the UN have been Trygve Lie (1946–53), Dag Hammarskjöld (1953–61), U Thant (1961–71), Kurt Waldheim (1972–81), Javier Pérez de Cuéllar (1982–91), Boutros Boutros-Ghali (1992–96), Kofi Annan (1997–2006), and Ban Ki-moon (2007–).

United Nations Conference on Trade and Development (UNCTAD), Organ of the United Nations General Assembly, created in 1964 to promote international trade. Its highest policy-making body, the Conference, meets every four years; when the Conference is not in session, the organization is run by its executive body, the Trade and Development Board. UNCTAD's principal functions include the promotion of trade between countries in different stages of development and with different economic systems, initiation of negotiations for trade agreements, and the formulation of international trade policies. In the late 20th and early 21st centuries, UNCTAD's efforts were directed toward the problems created in developing countries by economic globalization, and special attention was given to measures to help the poorest and least-developed countries become integrated into the world economy.

United Nations Development Programme (UNDP), UN organization formed in 1965 to promote environmentally sustainable human development in low-income countries. Based in New York City, the UNDP is headed by an administrator who oversees a 36-member Executive Board representing both developing and developed countries. Recent programs have focused on reducing poverty, developing strategies to treat and combat the spread of HIV/AIDS, promoting environmentally sound energy and economic policies, and expanding communications and technology infrastructure. UNDP resident representatives in more than 125 developing countries help to coordinate the local activities of other UN agencies and programs, as well as those of nongovernmental organizations.

United Nations General Assembly, One of six principal components of the United Nations and the only one in which all UN members are represented. It meets annually or in special sessions. It acts primarily as a deliberative body; it may discuss and make recommendations about any issue within the scope of the UN charter. Its president is elected annually on a rotating basis from five geographic groups of members.

United Nations High Commissioner for Refugees, Office of the (UNHCR), Office established in 1951 to give legal, social, economic, and political aid to refugees. The UNHCR is the successor of the International Refugee Organization. Its first efforts focused on Europeans displaced by World War II; it has since assisted refugees in Africa, Asia, Latin America, and Yugoslavia. It is based in Geneva and is financed by voluntary government contributions. The office won the Nobel Prize for Peace in 1954 and 1981.

United Nations Relief and Rehabilitation Administration, Administrative body (1943–47) for an extensive social-welfare program for war-ravaged nations. It distributed relief supplies and services, including shelter, food, and medicine, and helped with agricultural and economic rehabilitation. Its functions were later taken over by the International Refugee Organization, the World Health Organization, and UNICEF.

United Nations Security Council, Division of the United Nations whose primary purpose is to maintain international peace and security. The Security Council originally consisted of five permanent members—China (represented by the government on Taiwan until 1971), France, the United Kingdom, the U.S., and the Soviet Union (succeeded in 1991 by Russia)—and six rotating members elected by the United Nations General Assembly for two-year terms. In 1965 the number of nonpermanent members was increased to 10. UN members agree to abide by the Security Council's resolutions when they join. The Security Council investigates disputes that threaten international peace and advises on how to resolve them. To prevent or halt aggression, it may impose diplomatic or economic sanctions or authorize the use of military force. Each of the permanent members holds veto power in decisions on substantive matters, such as the application of sanctions. Decisions on both substantive and procedural matters require nine affirmative votes, including the affirmative vote of all five permanent members (though in practice a permanent member may abstain without impairing the validity of a decision).

United States, officially UNITED STATES OF AMERICA, Country, North America. It comprises 48 conterminous states occupying the mid-continent, Alaska at the northwestern extreme of North America, and the island state of Hawaii in the mid-Pacific Ocean. Area, including inland water area and the U.S. share of the Great Lakes: 3,678,190 sq mi (9,526,468 sq km). Population: (2011 est.) 313,387,000. Capital: Washington, D.C. The population includes people of European and Middle Eastern ancestry, African Americans, Hispanics, Asians, Pacific Islanders, American Indians (Native Americans), and Alaska Natives. Languages: English (predominant), Spanish. Religions: Christianity (Protestant, Roman Catholic, other Christians, Eastern Orthodox); also Judaism, Islam, Buddhism, Hinduism. Currency: U.S. dollar. The country encompasses mountains, plains, lowlands, and deserts. Mountain ranges include the Appalachians, Ozarks, Rockies, Cascades, and Sierra Nevada. The lowest point is Death Valley, Calif. The highest point is Alaska's Mount McKinley; within the conterminous states it is Mount Whitney, Calif. Chief rivers are the Mississippi system, the Colorado, the Columbia, and the Rio Grande. The Great Lakes, the Great Salt Lake, Iliamna Lake, and Lake Okeechobee are the largest lakes. The U.S. is among the world's leading producers of several minerals, including copper, silver, zinc, gold, coal, petroleum, and natural gas; it is the chief exporter of food. Its manufactures include iron and steel, chemicals, electronic equipment, motor vehicles, computers, and textiles. Other important industries are tourism, dairying, livestock raising, fishing, and lumbering. The U.S. is a federal republic with two legislative houses; its head of state and government is the president.

The territory was originally inhabited for several thousand years by numerous American Indian peoples who had probably migrated from Asia. European exploration and settlement from the 16th century began displacement of the Indians. The first permanent European settlement, by the Spanish, was at Saint Augustine, Fla., in 1565. The English settled Jamestown, Va. (1607); Plymouth, Mass. (1620); Maryland (1634); and Pennsylvania (1681). The English took New York, New Jersey, and Delaware from the Dutch in 1664, a year after English noblemen had begun to colonize the Carolinas. The British defeat of the French in 1763 assured Britain political control over its 13 colonies. Political unrest caused by British colonial policy culminated in the American Revolution (1775–83) and the Declaration of Independence (1776). The U.S. was first organized under the Articles of Confederation (1781), then finally under the Constitution (1787) as a federal republic. Boundaries extended west to the Mississippi River, excluding Spanish Florida. Land acquired from France by the Louisiana Purchase (1803) nearly doubled the country's territory. The U.S. fought the War of 1812 against the British and acquired Florida from Spain in 1819. In 1830 it legalized the removal of American Indians to lands west of the Mississippi River. Settlement expanded into the Far West in the mid-19th century, especially after the discovery of gold in California in 1848. Victory in the Mexican War (1846–48) brought the territory of seven more future states (including California and Texas) into U.S. hands. The north-

western boundary was established by treaty with Britain in 1846. The U.S. acquired southern Arizona by the Gadsden Purchase (1853). It suffered disunity during the conflict between the slavery-based plantation economy in the South and the industrial and agricultural economy in the North, culminating in the American Civil War and the abolition of slavery under the 13th Amendment. After Reconstruction (1865–77) the U.S. experienced rapid growth, urbanization, industrial development, and heightened European immigration. In 1887 it authorized allotment of American Indian reservation land to individual tribesmen, resulting in widespread loss of land to whites. Victory in the Spanish-American War brought the U.S. the overseas territories of the Philippines, Guam, and Puerto Rico. By the end of the 19th century, it had further developed foreign trade and acquired other outlying territories, including Alaska, Midway Island, the Hawaiian Islands, Wake Island, American Samoa, and the Panama Canal Zone.

The U.S. participated in World War I in 1917–18. It granted suffrage to women in 1920 and citizenship to American Indians in 1924. The stock market crash of 1929 led to the Great Depression, which New Deal legislation combated by increasing the federal government's role in the economy. The U.S. entered World War II after the Japanese bombing of Pearl Harbor (Dec. 7, 1941). The explosion by the U.S. of an atomic bomb on Hiroshima (Aug. 6, 1945) and another on Nagasaki (Aug. 9, 1945), Japan, brought about Japan's surrender. Thereafter the U.S. was the military and economic leader of the Western world. In the first decade after the war, it aided the reconstruction of Europe and Japan and became embroiled in a rivalry with the Soviet Union known as the Cold War. It participated in the Korean War from 1950 to 1953. In 1952 it granted autonomous commonwealth status to Puerto Rico. Racial segregation in schools was declared unconstitutional in 1954. Alaska and Hawaii were made states in 1959. In 1964 Congress passed the Civil Rights Act and authorized U.S. entry into the Vietnam War. The mid- to late 1960s were marked by widespread civil disorder, including race riots and antiwar demonstrations. The U.S. accomplished the first manned lunar landing in 1969. All U.S. troops were withdrawn from Vietnam in 1973. With the dissolution of the Soviet Union in 1991, the U.S. assumed the status of sole world superpower. The U.S. led a coalition of forces against Iraq in the Persian Gulf War (1990–91). Administration of the Panama Canal was turned over to Panama in 1999. After the September 11 attacks on the U.S. in 2001 destroyed the World Trade Center and part of the Pentagon, the U.S. attacked Afghanistan's Taliban government for harbouring and refusing to extradite the mastermind of the terrorism, Osama bin Laden. In 2003 the U.S. attacked Iraq, with British support, and overthrew the government of Ṣaddām Ḥussein; the U.S. then found itself engaged in protracted wars in both Iraq and Afghanistan. In 2008 the U.S. economy was rocked by a financial crisis brought about largely by the collapse of the housing market. As the crisis rippled worldwide, recession and a slow recovery followed in the U.S.

United States Virgin Islands, Organized unincorporated U.S. island territory, West Indies. Part of the Virgin Islands chain, it consists of the islands of Saint Croix, Saint John, and Saint Thomas and about 50 small islets. Area: 136 sq mi (352 sq km). Population: (2011 est.) 119,000. Capital: Charlotte Amalie. The great majority of the population is of African descent; most of the remainder are Hispanic (mainly Puerto Rican) or recent immigrants from the U.S. The people are U.S. citizens and elect a nonvoting representative to the U.S. House of Representatives, but they do not vote in U.S. national elections. Languages: English (official), French, Spanish. Religion: Christianity (mainly Protestant; also Roman Catholic, other Christians). The islands are hilly and surrounded by coral reefs. Tourism dominates the economy. The islands probably were originally settled by Arawak Indians but were inhabited by the Carib by the time Christopher Columbus landed on St. Croix in 1493. St. Croix was occupied by the Dutch, English, French, and Spanish and at one time was owned by the Knights of Malta. Denmark occupied St. Thomas, St. John, and St. Croix and established them as a Danish colony in 1754. The U.S. purchased the Danish West Indies in 1917 for $25 million and changed the name to the Virgin Islands. They were administered by the U.S. Department of the Interior from 1931. In 1954 the Organic Act of the Virgin Islands created the current governmental structure, and in 1970 the first popularly elected governor took office. The area suffered extensive damage by a major hurricane in 1995.

universal, In metaphysics, epistemology, and logic, a general category, such as a property or relation, considered as distinct from the particular things that instantiate or exemplify it. The problem of universals concerns the question of what sort of being should be ascribed to such categories (e.g., is there any such thing as redness apart from particular red things?). The debate over the status of universals stems from Plato's theory of forms. Whereas Plato held that forms (universals) exist independently of particulars, Aristotle argued that forms exist only in the particulars in which they are exemplified.

Universal Declaration of Human Rights, Declaration adopted by the United Nations General Assembly in 1948. Drafted by a committee chaired by Eleanor Roosevelt, it was adopted without dissent but with eight abstentions. Among its 30 articles are definitions of civil and political rights (including the rights to life, liberty, and a fair trial) as well as definitions of economic, social, and cultural rights (including the right to social security and to participation in the cultural life of one's community), all of which are owed by UN member states to those under their jurisdiction. It has acquired more juridical status than originally intended and has been widely used, even by national courts, as a means of judging compliance with member states' human-rights obligations. The declaration has been the foundation of the work of nongovernmental organizations such as Amnesty International.

Universalism, Belief in the salvation of all souls. Arising as early as the time of Origen and at various points in Christian history, the concept became an organized movement in North America in the mid-18th century. It maintains the impossibility that a loving God would bestow salvation on only a portion of humankind while dooming the rest to eternal punishment. It stresses the use of reason in religion and the modification of belief in light of the discoveries of science. Thus, the miraculous elements of traditional Christianity are rejected, and Jesus, while a worthy teacher and model, is not held to be divine. Universalist and Unitarian churches in the U.S. merged in 1961.

universe, Whole cosmic system of matter and energy of which Earth is a part. Its main constituents are the galaxies, within which are stars and stellar groupings and nebulae. Earth's Sun is one star among the billions of stars in the Milky Way Galaxy. All atoms, subatomic particles, and everything they compose are also part of the universe. The universe is governed by four fundamental forces: the strong force, the weak force, the electromagnetic force, and gravitation. Numerous theories have been proposed for the origin and structure of the universe.

UNIX, Operating system for digital computers, developed by Ken Thompson of Bell Laboratories in 1969. It was initially designed for a single user (the name was a pun on the earlier operating system Multics). The C language was subsequently developed specifically for UNIX, and the system was rewritten almost entirely in C; it was improved by the addition of multiprogramming and time-sharing capabilities and enhanced portability. UNIX is very popular in universities, where it is used mostly on scientific and engineering workstations, and it is used on most of the servers of Internet service providers. Because its modular construction allows it to be easily modified, it has been improved in many ways by academic and industrial institutions.

untouchable, Former classification of various low-status persons and those outside the Hindu caste system in Indian society. The term Dalit has been used for such people (in preference to Mohandas K. Gandhi's earlier term, Harijan, which is now considered condescending by the Dalit themselves), and their plight is recognized by the Indian constitution and by legislation. The groups traditionally considered untouchable included people whose occupations or habits of life involved activities considered to be polluting, such as taking life for a living (e.g., fishermen); killing or disposing of dead cattle or working with their hides; coming into contact with human waste (e.g., sweepers); and eating flesh of cattle, pigs, or chickens. Many untouchables converted to other religions to escape discrimination. Indian law now categorizes the Dalit under the official term Scheduled Castes and accords them certain special privileges.

upanayana, Hindu initiation ritual, restricted to the three upper varnas. It marks a male's entrance into the life of a student and his acceptance as a full member of the religious community. After a ritual bath, the boy, aged 5–24, is dressed as an ascetic and brought before his guru, who invests him with various symbolic articles. The initiate receives a sacred thread, worn throughout his life, that identifies him as twice-born, the second birth being effected by receipt of a mantra. Observance of upanayana is decreasing and is now largely confined to the Brahman class.

Upanishad, Any of 108 speculative texts of the Vedas that contain elaborations in poetry and verse. They are believed to have been composed since 500 BC, based on teachings circulated since 1000 BC. They represent the final stage in the tradition of the Vedas, and the teaching based on them is called Vedanta. Generally the Upanishads are concerned with the nature of reality, the individual soul (atman), and the universal soul (Brahman) and with the theory of the transmigration of souls and the nature of morality.

upasaka, Lay devotee of the Buddha. Originally the term applied to followers of the Buddha who were not ordained as *bhiksus*; today it is normally applied, mainly in Southeast Asia, to pious individuals who visit the local monastery on the weekly holy days and who undertake special vows. They support the sangha with regular offerings and observe the five precepts expected of all Buddhists: to abstain from killing, stealing, sexual misconduct, lying, and using intoxicants.

Uppsala, City (pop., 2001 est.: 191,110), Sweden. Located north of Stockholm, it lies near a village which was originally the capital of the ancient pre-Christian kingdom of Svea. By the 13th century it was an important commercial centre. Relinquishing its political primacy to Stockholm, it remained the seat of the archbishop of Sweden; its Gothic cathedral (erected from the 13th–15th centuries) is Sweden's largest. It is also an educational centre, the site of Sweden's oldest university, Uppsala University (founded 1477). It is now an industrial city and transportation hub. Carolus Linnaeus lived there.

Ur, Ancient city and district, Sumer, southern Mesopotamia. It was situated on a former channel of the Euphrates River in what is

Northeastern facade (the ascents partly restored) of the ziggurat at Ur, southern Iraq.
Hirmer Fotoarchiv, Munich

now southern Iraq. One of the oldest cities of Mesopotamia, it was settled sometime in the 4th millennium BC. In the 25th century BC it was the capital of southern Mesopotamia under its first dynasty. Though it later declined, it again became important around the 22nd century BC. It is mentioned in the Bible (as Ur of the Chaldees) as the early home of Hebrew patriarch Abraham (*c.* 2000 BC). In subsequent centuries it was captured and destroyed by many groups, including the Elamites and Babylonians. Nebuchadrezzar II restored it in the 6th century BC. Excavations, especially in the 1920s and '30s, uncovered remains of great archaeological value.

Ural Mountains, Mountain range, Russia and Kazakhstan. Generally held to constitute the boundary between Europe and Asia, the range extends north-south for some 1,550 mi (2,500 km) from just south of the Kara Sea to the Ural River; a southward spur extends into northwestern Kazakhstan. The mountains average 3,300–3,600 ft (1,000–1,100 m) in elevation; the highest peak is Mount Narodnaya at 6,217 ft (1,895 m). The Central and Southern Urals contain one of the largest industrial regions of Russia, producing metal goods, chemicals, and machinery; that region developed rapidly during World War II (1939–45), when many industrial plants were moved from the western part of the Soviet Union to prevent their destruction by the Germans.

Ural River, River, Russia and Kazakhstan. Rising at the southern end of the Ural Mountains, it flows southwest to cross through western Kazakhstan to the Caspian Sea at Atyrau. It is 1,509 mi (2,428 km) long and drains an area of 91,500 sq mi (237,000 sq km). Its lower course is navigable.

Uralic languages, Family of more than 20 languages spoken by some 25 million people in central and northern Eurasia. A primary division is between the Finno-Ugric languages, which account for most of the languages and speakers, and the Samoyedic languages. The latter languages have historically been spoken in the forest region of northern Siberia and in the tundra and coastal zones from the Ob to the White Sea and east into the Taymyr Peninsula. The known languages are Nganasan, Enets, Nenets, Selkup, Kamas (which became extinct in the late 20th century), and Mator (which became extinct in the 19th century). Of the other languages that are still spoken, Nenets, which has 25,000 speakers and is still being learned by children, is the most viable. The Samoyedic languages share little vocabulary with Finno-Ugric. At its very earliest stages Uralic most probably included the ancestors of the Yukaghir languages, still sometimes included with the Paleo-Siberian languages.

uranium, Chemical element of the actinoid series (with many transition element properties), chemical symbol U, atomic number 92. A dense, hard, silvery white metal that tarnishes in air, it is isolated from such ores as pitchblende. Until the discovery of the first transuranium element in 1940, uranium was believed to be the heaviest element. Radioactivity was discovered in uranium by A.-H. Becquerel. All its isotopes are radioactive; several have half-lives long enough to permit determination of the age of the Earth by uranium-thorium-lead dating and uranium-234–uranium-238 dating. Nuclear fission was discovered in 1938 in uranium bombarded with neutrons, and the self-sustaining nuclear chain reaction, the atomic bomb, and the generation of nuclear power followed. Uranium has various valences in compounds, some of which have been used as colours in ceramic glazes, in lightbulb filaments, in photography, and as dyes and mordants.

Uranus, or OURANUS, Ancient Greek personification of heaven. When Gaea emerged from Chaos, she produced Uranus, the mountains, and the sea. Her subsequent union with Uranus produced the Titans, the Cyclopes, and the Hecatoncheires. Uranus despised his offspring and hid them in Gaea's body. In response to her appeal for vengeance, Cronus castrated Uranus. From the drops of blood that fell on Earth were born the Furies, the Giants, and the ash-tree nymphs called Meliai. His severed genitals floated on the sea, producing a white foam from which sprang Aphrodite. Uranus also consorted with Clymene, Hemera, Hestia, and Nyx.

Uranus, Seventh planet from the Sun. It was discovered in 1781 by William Herschel and named for the Greek god personifying heaven. A blue-green gas giant, it has almost 15 times the mass of Earth and over 50 times its volume. It is less dense than Earth; the gravity at the top of its atmosphere is 11% weaker. Its equatorial diameter is 31,800 mi (51,100 km). Uranus has 10 sharply defined narrow, dark rings, with broad dust bands between them; the rings consist mainly of boulder-size chunks of dark material. Uranus also has at least 27 moons (most named after Shakespearean characters) and a magnetic field about as strong as Earth's. The planet rotates once every 17 hours around an axis that, unusually, is almost parallel to the ecliptic; from Earth it appears to spin on its side. It takes 84 years to orbit the Sun, at a mean distance of 1.78 billion mi (2.87 billion km). It has no solid surface; its fluid interior is thought to consist of a mixture of rock, ices, and gas, with little or no rocky core. Its upper atmosphere is mostly hydrogen and helium; the blue-green colour comes from absorption of red light by the small amount of methane present.

Urban II, orig. ODO OF CHÂTILLON-SUR-MARNE (b. *c.* 1035, Châtillon-sur-Marne or Lagery or Lagny, Champagne, France—d. July 29, 1099, Rome), Pope (1088–99). The prior of a Cluniac monastery, he was made cardinal by Pope Gregory VII, whose reforms he furthered. Elected pope in 1088, Urban secured his authority against the antipope Clement III and strengthened the role of the papacy in the reform movement. He called for the First Crusade at the Council of Clermont (1095) in response to the appeal of Alexius I Comnenus, promoted the union of the Eastern and Western churches, and supported the Christian reconquest of Spain from the Moors.

urban planning, Programs pursued as a means of improving the urban environment and achieving certain social and economic objectives. Evidence of urban planning can be found in the ruins of ancient cities, including orderly street systems and conduits for water and sewage. During the Renaissance, European city areas were consciously planned to achieve circulation of the populace and provide fortification against invasion. Such concepts were exported to the New World, where William Penn, in founding the city of Philadelphia, developed the standard gridiron plan—the laying out of streets and plots of land adaptable to rapid change in land use. Modern urban planning and redevelopment arose in response to the disorder and squalor of the slums created by the Industrial Revolution. The urban planner best known for his transformation of Paris was Georges-Eugène Haussmann. City planners imposed regulatory laws establishing standards for housing, sanitation, water supply, sewage, and public health conditions, and introduced parks and playgrounds into congested city neighbourhoods. In the 20th century, zoning—the regulation of building activity according to use and location—came to be a key tool for city planners.

Urdu language, Indo-Aryan language used by Muslims in India and Pakistan. In the sociopolitical realm, Urdu and Hindi are different languages, but the colloquial basis of both is identical, and as a written language Urdu differs from Hindi principally in its greater acceptance of Persian-Arabic vocabulary and in some syntactic features. It is written in the Arabic alphabet with modification of some letters to denote specifically Indo-Aryan sounds. As Pakistan's official language, Urdu has been promoted as a token of national unity, though less than 8% of Pakistanis—mainly immigrants and descendants of immigrants from India after the 1947 partition—speak it as a first language.

uremia, Excess nitrogenous waste products in the blood and their toxic effects. Kidney impairment or disorders that hinder urine excretion (e.g., prostatic disorders) allow urea and other protein waste products to accumulate. Symptoms usually start with fatigue and loss of concentration. They may include itching and muscle twitches; dry, flaky, yellowish skin; dry mouth, metallic taste, and ammonia breath; and nausea, vomiting, diarrhea, and constipation. Advanced stages affect the nervous, cardiovascular, and respiratory systems and can lead to hypertension, seizures, heart failure, and death. If the underlying disorder cannot be treated, dialysis or kidney transplant may be required.

urinary system, or RENAL SYSTEM, System that produces and discharges urine to rid the body of waste products. It consists of the kidneys, which balance electrolytes in blood, retaining and adding needed ones and removing unneeded or dangerous ones for excretion; the ureters, two thin muscular tubes 10–12 in. (25–30 cm) long that move the urine by peristalsis; the hollow, muscular bladder, which receives and stores it; and the urethra, through which it leaves the body. In women the urethra is 1.5 in. (4 cm) long. In men it is longer (since it passes through the penis), about 8 in. (20 cm), and carries semen from the prostate gland as well as urine. Urinary disorders, which can lead to dehydration or edema and to a dangerous buildup of waste and toxic substances, include kidney failure, tumours, and bladder and kidney stones.

Urmia, Lake, Persian DARYĀCHEH-YE ORŪMIYYEH, Shallow, saline lake, northwestern Iran. The largest lake in the Middle East, it covers an area that varies from 2,000 to 2,300 sq mi (5,200 to 6,000 sq km). It is about 87 mi (140 km) long and 25–35 mi (40–55 km) wide, with a maximum depth of 53 ft (16 m). There is a cluster of about 50 tiny islands at its southern part. Fed by three rivers, it has no outlet. It has been protected since 1967.

Uruguay, officially ORIENTAL REPUBLIC OF URUGUAY, Country, southeastern South America. Area: 68,679 sq mi (177,879 sq km). Population: (2011 est.) 3,380,000. Capital: Montevideo. People of European ancestry (mostly Spanish and Italian) make up about nine-tenths of the population; most of the remainder are mestizos or people of African-European descent. Few Indians remain. Language: Spanish (official). Religions: Christianity (predominantly Roman Catholic; also other Christians, Protestant), Judaism. Currency: Uruguayan peso. Uruguay is the only South American country lying entirely outside the tropics. Its topography consists mainly of low plateaus and low hilly regions. The principal waterway is the Negro River; the Uruguay River forms the country's entire western border with Argentina. Mineral and energy resources are limited. Pastures, covering almost four-fifths of the land area, support large herds of livestock raised for meat, leather goods, and wool. Chief crops include rice, sugarcane, oranges, wheat, and corn. Other important economic activities are tourism, fishing, and the manufacture of textiles and chemicals. Uruguay is a republic with two legislative houses; its head of state and government is the president. Prior to European settlement, it was inhabited mainly by the Charrúa and Guaraní Indians. The Spanish navigator Juan Díaz de Solís sailed into the Río de la Plata estuary in 1516. The Portuguese established Colonia in 1680. Subsequently the Spanish established Montevideo in 1726, driving the Portuguese from their settlement; 50 years later Uruguay became part of the Viceroyalty of the Río de la Plata. It gained independence from Spain in 1811. The Portuguese regained it in 1821, incorporating it into Brazil as a province. A revolt against Brazil in 1825 led to its being recognized as an independent country in 1828. It sided with Brazil and Argentina against Paraguay in the War of the Triple Alliance (1864/65–70). The economy benefited from a demand for raw material during World War II (1939–45) and the Korean War (1950–53). The office of the president was abolished in 1951 and replaced with a nine-member council. The country adopted a new constitution and restored the presidential system in 1966. A military coup occurred in 1973, but the country returned to civilian rule in 1985. The 1990s brought a general upturn in the economy, largely the result of reform measures and membership in Mercosur, the Southern Common Market (1991).

Uruguay River, River, southeastern South America. Rising in southern Brazil, it forms the border between Argentina and Brazil and between Argentina and Uruguay. Above Buenos Aires, it combines with the Paraná River to form the great estuary of the Río de la Plata. Its 990-mi (1,593-km) course is interrupted by rapids, but it is navigable by ocean vessels for about 130 mi (210 km) upriver from its mouth.

Ürümqi, or URUMCHI, or WU-LU-MU-CH'I, City (pop., 2003 est.: 1,401,990), capital of Xinjiang autonomous region, northwestern China. Situated along the northern face of the Tien Shan, it first came under Chinese control in the 7th–8th century and became an important centre for caravans en route to Turkistan. The Uighurs had control from c. 750 until the resumption of Chinese rule in the 18th century. The city was held by Muslim rebels in 1864–76. When the province of Xinjiang was established in 1884, Ürümqi became its capital. It grew rapidly into the province's most important city and the centre of trade in Central Asia. It is located in a coal-mining and petroleum-producing area; its chief manufactures include iron and steel, agricultural machinery, and chemicals.

USB, in full UNIVERSAL SERIAL BUS, Type of serial bus that allows peripheral devices (disks, modems, printers, digitizers, data gloves, etc.) to be easily connected to a computer. A "plug-and-play" interface, it allows a device to be added without an adapter card and without rebooting the computer (the latter is known as hot-plugging). The USB standard, developed by several major computer and telecommunications companies, supports data-transfer speeds up to 12 megabits per second, multiple data streams, and up to 127 peripherals.

usury, In law, the crime of charging an unlawfully high rate of interest. In Old English law, the taking of any compensation whatsoever was termed usury. With the expansion of trade in the 13th century, the demand for credit increased, necessitating a modification in the definition of the term. In 1545 England fixed a legal maximum interest, a practice later followed by other Western nations.

uterus, or WOMB, Inverted-pear-shaped organ of the female reproductive system, in which the embryo and fetus develop during pregnancy. Lying over and behind the bladder, it is 2.5–3 in. (6–8 cm) long and about 2.5 in. (6 cm) across at the top, where the fallopian tubes enter it; at the other end, the cervix extends down into the vagina. The uterine lining (endometrium), a moist mucous membrane, changes in thickness during the menstrual cycle, being thickest at ovulation in readiness for a fertilized egg. The uterine wall, about 1 in. (2.5 cm) thick, expands and becomes thinner as a fetus develops inside. The cervix expands to about 4 in. (10 cm) for delivery. Disorders of the uterus include infections, benign and malignant tumours, prolapse, endometriosis, and fibroids (leiomyomas; *see* muscle tumour).

ʿUthmān ibn ʿAffān (d. June 17, 656, Medina, Arabia), Third caliph to rule after the death of the Prophet. Born into the powerful Umayyad clan of Mecca, he became a wealthy merchant before converting to Islam; he was the first convert of high social and economic standing. He married a daughter of Muhammad. On the death of ʿUmar ibn al-Khaṭṭāb (644), ʿUthmān was chosen as his successor. His reign as caliph was marked by nepotism and personal profit, and he made many enemies. His accomplishments included centralizing the administration of the caliphate and establishing an official version of the Qu'rān. His death at the hands of rebels marked the beginning of the first *fitnah*.

utilitarianism, Ethical principle according to which an action is right if it tends to maximize happiness, not only that of the agent but also of everyone affected. Thus, utilitarians focus on the consequences of an act rather than on its intrinsic nature or the motives of the agent. Classical utilitarianism is hedonist, but values other than, or in addition to, pleasure (ideal utilitarianism) can be employed, or—more neutrally, and in a version popular in economics—anything can be regarded as valuable that appears as an object of rational or informed desire (preference utilitarianism). The test of utility maximization can also be applied directly to single acts (act utilitarianism), or to acts only indirectly through some other suitable object of moral assessment, such as rules of conduct (rule utilitarianism). Jeremy Bentham's *Introduction to the Principles of Morals and Legislation* (1789) and John Stuart Mill's *Utilitarianism* (1863) are major statements of utilitarianism.

utopian socialism, Political and social idea of the mid-19th century. Adapted from such reformers as Robert Owen and Charles Fourier, utopian socialism drew from early communist and socialist ideas. Advocates included Louis Blanc, noted for his theory of worker-controlled "social workshops," and John Humphrey Noyes, founder of the Oneida Community in the U.S. Utopian settlements were also attempted by religious groups such as the Mennonites, Shakers, and Mormons.

Utrecht, City (pop., 2001 est.: 256,420), central Netherlands. The site of successive Roman, Frisian, and Frankish fortresses, it became an episcopal see in 696 under St. Willibrord. It was most prosperous during the 11th and 12th centuries, when it was an important commercial centre. In 1527 it was transferred to Holy Roman Emperor Charles V and became part of the Habsburg dominions. It was ruled by Spain until the 1570s, when it became a centre of Protestant resistance. It was the site of the signing of the Union of Utrecht (1579), which established a league of northern Dutch provinces against Spain; the league was the basis of the future Netherlands kingdom. Occupied by the French (1795–1813), it was the residence of Louis Bonaparte, king of Holland (1806–10). The only Dutch pope, Adrian VI, was born in Utrecht. It is a transportation, financial, and insurance centre.

Utrecht school, Principally a group of three Dutch painters from Utrecht—Dirck van Baburen (*c.* 1590–1624), Gerrit van Honthorst, and Hendrik Terbrugghen—who were greatly influenced by Caravaggio's art during travels to Rome. They used their newly learned technique in artwork with primarily religious subject matter, but also produced brothel scenes and pictures in sets, such as five works devoted to the senses. The numerous candles, lanterns, and other sources of artificial light in their paintings also differentiate them from Caravaggio, who never used such devices. Honthorst enjoyed the widest reputation at the time, but Terbrugghen is now considered the most talented and versatile of the group.

Uttar Pradesh, formerly UNITED PROVINCES, State (pop., 2008 est.: 190,891,000), north-central India. It is bordered by Nepal; the states of Bihar, Jharkhand, Chhattisgarh, Madhya Pradesh, Rajasthan, Haryana, and Uttarakhand; and Delhi national capital territory. Uttar Pradesh covers an area of 93,933 sq mi (243,286 sq km). Its capital is Lucknow. The state is the most populous in the country. It lies largely in the plains formed by the Ganges and Yamuna rivers. The region was the setting of two great Sanskrit epics, the *Mahabharata* and the *Ramayana*, and was the scene of the rise of Buddhism after the 6th century BCE. It was ruled by the Mauryan emperor Ashoka in the mid-3rd century BCE, the Gupta dynasty in the 4th–6th centuries CE, and King Harsha in 606–647. The Mughals gained control in the 16th century, at which time the city of Agra became a chief centre. The British arrived in the late 18th century; by the 1830s they held sway and organized the region as the North-Western Provinces (later renamed the United Provinces of Agra and Oudh; eventually shortened to the United Provinces). The area was the main scene of the Indian Mutiny of

1857–58. Following Indian independence in 1947, the United Provinces became the state of Uttar Pradesh. In 2000 the state's northern portion was made into the new state of Uttaranchal (now Uttarakhand). Agriculture is the most important economic sector. Noted tourist meccas are Agra and Varanasi.

Uttarakhand, State (pop., 2008 est.: 9,497,000), northern India. It is bordered by the Tibet Autonomous Region of China, Nepal, and the states of Uttar Pradesh, Haryana, and Himachal Pradesh and covers an area of 19,739 sq mi (51,125 sq km); its capital is Dehra Dun. The state lies in the Himalayas, and some of India's highest peaks rise in its northern areas. The upper reaches of the Ganges (Ganga) and Yamuna rivers flow southward through the state. In the south are hill resorts such as Mussoorie, Nainital, and Ranikhet. The area now constituting Uttarakhand was a part of Uttar Pradesh state after Indian independence in 1947 until it was made into a separate state, Uttaranchal, in 2000. In 2007 it became the state of Uttarakhand. The population is mostly engaged in agriculture, although tourism is also important.

uveitis, Inflammation of the uvea, the middle coat of the eyeball. Anterior uveitis, involving the iris or ciliary body (containing the muscle that adjusts the lens) or both, can lead to glaucoma and blindness. Posterior uveitis, involving the choroid (which contains the eye's blood supply), can cause bleeding, lens clouding, and eyeball atrophy. Granulomatous uveitis (persistent inflammation with a grainy surface) causes vision impairment, pain, watery eyes, and sensitivity to light; nongranulomatous uveitis causes less pain and sensitivity, with a better chance of recovery. Causes include generalized infections and other diseases, allergic reactions, and injury. Rarely, the uninjured eye also has symptoms, with a risk of blindness in both eyes. Treatment aims to eliminate infection, reduce inflammation, and preserve vision.

Uzbekistan, officially REPUBLIC OF UZBEKISTAN, Country, Central Asia. The autonomous republic of Qoraqalpoghiston (Karakalpakstan) is within its borders. Area: 171,469 sq mi (444,103 sq km). Population: (2011 est.) 28,129,000. Capital: Tashkent. The Uzbeks constitute three-fourths of the population; Russians, Tajiks, Kazakhs, Tatars, and Karakalpaks make up the remainder. Languages: Uzbek (official), Russian, Tajik, Kazakh. Religions: Islam (predominantly Sunni); also Eastern Orthodox. Currency: sum. Uzbekistan lies largely between the Amu Darya and Syr Darya rivers. Although it contains fertile oases and high mountain ranges in the south and east, almost four-fifths of the country consists of flat, sunbaked lowlands. Two-thirds of the Aral Sea extends into Uzbekistan. It is a major producer and exporter of natural gas and has sizable reserves of petroleum, coal, and various metallic ores. It is a leading grower of cotton and also produces fruits and vegetables and Karakul sheep. It is the main manufacturer of machinery and heavy equipment in Central Asia. It is a republic with two legislative bodies; its head of state and government is the president, assisted by the prime minister. A grandson of Mongol leader Genghis Khan received the territory as his inheritance in the 13th century. The Mongols ruled over a number of Turkic tribes, who would eventually intermarry with the Mongols to form the Uzbeks and other Turkic peoples of Central Asia. In the early 16th century a federation of Mongol-Uzbeks invaded and occupied settled regions, including an area called Transoxania that would become the permanent Uzbek homeland. By the early 19th century the region was dominated by the khanates of Khiva, Bukhara, and Kokand, all of which eventually succumbed to Russian domination. The Uzbek S.S.R. was created in 1924. In June 1990 Uzbekistan became the first Central Asian republic to declare sovereignty. It achieved full independence from the Soviet Union in 1991. Its economy subsequently became the strongest in Central Asia.

V-2 missile, German liquid-fueled ballistic missile of World War II, forerunner of modern space launch vehicles and long-range missiles. Developed starting in 1936 under Wernher von Braun, it was fired against Paris, Great Britain, and Belgium in 1944 and 1945. After the war, the U.S. and the Soviet Union captured large numbers of V-2s and used them in research that led to the development of their missile and space-exploration programs.

vaccine, Preparation containing either killed or weakened live microorganisms or their toxins, introduced by mouth, by injection, or by nasal spray to stimulate production of antibodies against an infectious agent. This confers immunity to that agent, since the B lymphocytes remain sensitized to it and respond to later infection by producing more antibodies. The first vaccine, against smallpox, was introduced by Edward Jenner in 1798. Vaccines have been developed against diseases caused by bacteria (e.g., typhoid, whooping cough, tuberculosis) and by viruses (e.g., measles, influenza, rabies, poliomyelitis). Effectiveness varies, and a small percentage of people have adverse reactions. Those with immunodeficiency disorders should not receive live vaccines.

vacuum, Space in which there is no matter or in which the pressure is so low that any particles in the space do not affect any processes being carried on there. It is a condition well below normal atmospheric pressure and is measured in units of pressure (the pascal). A vacuum can be created by removing air from a space using a vacuum pump or by reducing the pressure using a fast flow of fluid, as in Bernoulli's principle.

vaginitis, Inflammation of the vagina. The chief symptom is a whitish or yellowish vaginal discharge. Treatment depends on the cause: appropriate drugs for sexually transmitted diseases (often from *Gardnerella* bacteria or trichomonads) or yeast infections; estrogen cream for atrophy of the vaginal lining, which may dry out after menopause; and avoidance of any chemicals found to trigger irritation or allergy.

vagrancy, Act of wandering about without employment or identifiable means of support. Traditionally a vagrant was thought to be one who was able to work for his maintenance but preferred instead to live idly, often as a beggar. Punishment ranged from branding and whipping to conscription into the military services and transportation to penal colonies. In the U.S., laws against vagrancy were used by police and prosecutors to proscribe a wide range of behaviours. Many such laws were struck down as unconstitutionally vague, thus largely decriminalizing vagrancy, though in the 1990s many local laws were implemented to curtail aggressive panhandling, begging, and other activities by vagrants on city streets.

Vairocana, In Mahayana and tantric Buddhism, the supreme buddha who is the cosmic counterpart of Sakyamuni in his teaching mode. He is the most prominent of the five self-born buddhas, those who were born as humans to propagate the dharma. Though without canonical basis, Vairocana holds a special place in Tibetan Buddhism and has a special role in the Avatamsaka-sutra, in which he is the solar buddha who is both the ultimate reality of the cosmos and the one who pervades its component parts.

Vaishnavism, Worship of Vishnu as the supreme deity, as well as of his incarnations, mainly Rama and Krishna. Vaishnavism is one of the major forms of modern Hinduism, along with Shaivism and Shaktism, and is probably the most popular and most widely practiced. Characterized by an emphasis on bhakti, its goal is to escape from the cycle of birth and death in order to enjoy the presence of Vishnu. The philosophical schools into which Vaishnavism is divided are distinguished by their varying interpretations of the relationship between individual souls and God, and include aspects of monism and dualism.

Vaishya, Third highest of the four varnas of India. Traditionally described as commoners, Vaishyas are connected with productive labour, such as trade, agriculture, and pastoralism. According to legend, they sprang from the thighs of Prajapati, after the Brahmans and the Kshatriyas but before the Shudras. Like the two higher classes, they are "twice-born". They are credited historically with favouring the rise of the reformist religious beliefs of Buddhism and Jainism. In modern times they have become a symbol of middle-class prestige, and many rise to higher classes.

Vajpayee, Atal Bihari (b. Dec. 15, 1924, Gwalior, Madhya Pradesh, India), Leader of India's pro-Hindu Bharatiya Janata Party (BJP) and prime minister of India in 1996 and from 1998 to 2004. Politically active as a teenager, he was briefly jailed by British colonial authorities. He was first elected to parliament in 1957 as a member of the Bharatiya Jana Sangh, a forerunner of the BJP. He served as foreign minister in the late 1970s and helped formally establish the BJP in 1980. In 1992 he was one of the few Hindu leaders to speak out against the destruction of the historic Babri Masjid mosque by anti-Muslim extremists. Elected prime minister in May 1996, he was unable to form a government and resigned after 13 days. In 1998 and 1999 he was again elected prime minister as head of a BJP-led coalition. In May 1998 nuclear weapons tests ordered by Vajpayee drew international condemnation and economic sanctions. In 2000 his government began an extensive program of divestment of public funds from several key state-run industries. Under his leadership India achieved steady economic growth and became a world leader in information technology. In 2004 his coalition was defeated in parliamentary elections, and he resigned from office.

vajra, Five-pronged ritual object extensively employed in the ceremonies of Tibetan Buddhism. It is fashioned out of brass or bronze, the four prongs at each end curving around the central fifth to form a lotus-bud shape. In Sanskrit the word means both thunderbolt and diamond: like a thunderbolt it cuts through ignorance, and like a diamond it destroys but is itself indestructible. Originally a symbol of Indra, it was used to conquer the non-Buddhist deities of Tibet. In ritual use, it is often employed in conjunction with a bell in the execution of mudras.

Vajrayana, Form of tantric Buddhism that emerged in India in the first millennium AD and spread to Tibet, where it is the predominant tradition in Tibetan Buddhism. Philosophically, Vajrayana is a blend of the Yogacara and Madhyamika disciplines. It aims to recapture the enlightenment experience of the Buddha Gautama, and it places special emphasis on the notion that enlightenment arises from the realization that seemingly opposite principles are in truth one. It introduced innovations involving the use of mantras and mandalas as aids to meditation, and, in rare cases, the use of yogically disciplined sexual activities.

valence, Number of bonds an atom can form. Hydrogen (H) always has valence 1, so other elements' valences equal the number of hydrogen atoms they combine with. Thus, oxygen (O) has valence 2, as in water (H_2O); nitrogen (N) has valence 3, as in ammonia (NH_3); and chlorine (Cl) has valence 1, as in hydrochloric acid (HCl). The valence depends on the number of unpaired electrons in the outermost (and, in transition elements, the next) shell of the atom's structure. The sharing of the unpaired (valence) electrons in a bond mimics the stable configuration of the noble gases, whose outer shells are full. Elements that can achieve stable configurations by various combinations have more than one valence.

Valencia, City (pop., 2001: city, 738,441; metro. area, 1,397,809), capital of the autonomous community of Valencia, eastern Spain. First mentioned as a Roman settlement in 138 BC, it was later taken by the Visigoths in AD 413 and the Moors in 714. It became the seat of the newly established independent Moorish kingdom of Valencia in 1021. After 1238 it was part of the dominions of Aragon. The first Spanish printing press was established in Valencia in 1474; during the next two centuries the city was the seat of the Valencian school of painting. It was severely damaged in the Peninsular War, during the Spanish Civil War, and by flood in 1957. Its port ships agricultural produce and manufactured items.

Valencia, City (pop., 2000 est.: 1,338,833), northwestern Venezuela. It is located near the western shore of Lake Valencia. Founded in 1555, it rivaled Caracas as the region's major city well into the 19th century. In 1814, during the struggle for Venezuela's independence, it was the site of a bloody battle between Spanish and opposition forces. It served as national capital in 1812, 1830, and 1858. One of Venezuela's principal industrial and transportation centres, it produces textiles, pharmaceuticals, and automobiles.

Valentine's Day, Lovers' holiday celebrated on February 14, the feast day of St. Valentine, one of two 3rd-century Roman martyrs of the same name. St. Valentine is considered the patron of lovers and especially of those unhappily in love. The feast day became a lovers' festival in the 14th century, probably as an extension of pagan love festivals and fertility rites celebrated in mid-February. Today it is marked by the exchange of romantic cards (valentines), flowers, and other gifts.

Valhalla, In Germanic religion, the hall of slain warriors who live blissfully under the leadership of Odin. Valhalla is depicted as a splendid palace, roofed with shields, where the warriors feast on the flesh of a boar slaughtered daily and made whole again each evening. They drink liquor that flows from the udders of a goat, and their sport is to fight one another every day, with the slain being revived in the evening. Thus, they will live until the Ragnarok, when they will leave Valhalla to fight at the side of Odin against the Giants.

validity, In logic, the property of an argument consisting in the fact that the truth of the premises logically guarantees the truth of the conclusion. Whenever the premises are true, the conclusion must be true, because of the form of the argument. Some arguments that fail to be valid are acceptable on grounds other than formal logic (e.g., inductively strong arguments), and their conclusions are supported with less than logical necessity. Where the support yields high probability of the conclusion relative to the premises, such arguments are sometimes called inductively valid. In other purportedly persuasive arguments, the premises actually provide no rational grounds for accepting the conclusion; such defective forms of argument are called fallacies.

Valkyrie, In Germanic religion, any of a group of maidens sent by Odin to select slain warriors worthy of a place in Valhalla. They rode to the battlefield on horses or, in some accounts, flew through the air and sea. Some had the power to cause the death of warriors they disliked; others guarded the lives and ships of those they favoured. According to various myths, they were either purely supernatural or human with supernatural powers; they were associated with fairness, brightness, and gold as well as with bloodshed.

Valladolid, City (pop., 2001: 316,580), capital of the autonomous community of Castile-León, Spain. First mentioned in 1074, it was the seat of the Castilian court until c. 1600. The Catholic Monarchs, Isabella of Castile and Ferdinand of Aragon, were married there in 1469. It suffered heavy damage by fire in 1561 and by the French during the Peninsular War. Industry and commerce are economic mainstays. It has many medieval buildings, and its university (founded 1346) is one of Spain's oldest. Christopher Columbus died in Valladolid in 1506.

Valletta, Seaport city (pop., 2007 est.: 6,154), capital of Malta. It is located on a rocky promontory with harbours on either side. Built after the Great Siege of Malta (1565), which checked the advance of Ottoman power in southern Europe, it was named after Jean Parisot de la Valette, grand master of the Knights of Malta. It became the Maltese capital in 1570. After 1814 it was made the principal base of the British Mediterranean naval fleet and remained important through World War II, during which it suffered heavy damage from bombing raids. Several 16th-century buildings still exist. The city's economy relies mainly on trade and tourism.

valley, Elongate depression of the Earth's surface. Valleys are commonly drained by rivers and may be in a relatively flat plain or between ranges of hills or mountains. Valleys formed by rivers and slope denudation are typically V-shaped; those formerly occupied by glaciers are characteristically U-shaped. Valley evolution is controlled mainly by climate and rock type. Very narrow, deep valleys cut in resistant rock and having steep, almost vertical sides are called canyons. Smaller valleys of similar appearance are called gorges.

Valparaíso, City (pop., 2002 est.: 262,000) and port, central Chile. It was founded by the Spanish in 1536; few of its colonial buildings have survived a succession of pirate raids, storms, fires, floods, and earthquakes. After Chilean independence in 1818, the city's port developed with the growth of the Chilean navy. In 1884 a treaty was signed there by which Bolivia ceded to Chile a coastal region containing principal nitrate deposits. As Chile's principal seaport, it handles the bulk of the country's imports, and it is still a naval facility. It also produces chemicals and textiles. Chile's bicameral parliament, the National Congress, has been situated there since it was reestablished in 1990.

value-added tax (VAT), Government levy on the amount a firm adds to the price of a goods or services as value is added—that is, at each step of their production and distribution. In the most common method of calculation, the seller subtracts the sum of taxes paid on items being purchased from the sum of all taxes that have been collected on the items being sold; the net tax liability is the difference between the tax collected and the tax paid. The burden of the value-added tax, like that of other sales taxes, tends to be passed on to the consumer. To limit the VAT's regressiveness, most countries set lower rates for consumer necessities than for luxury items. In 1954 France became the first country to adopt the value-added tax on a large scale. Though complex to calculate, the tax served as an improvement on earlier systems by which a product was taxed repeatedly at every stage of production and distribution. It has since been adopted throughout much of Europe and in many countries in South America, Asia, and Africa. All European Union member countries have a VAT.

vampire, In popular legend, a bloodsucking creature that rises

Bela Lugosi with Frances Dade in Dracula *(1931).*
Courtesy of Universal Pictures; photograph, The Bettmann Archive

from its burial place at night, sometimes in the form of a bat, to drink the blood of humans. By daybreak it must return to its grave or to a coffin filled with its native earth. Tales of vampires are part of the world's folklore, most notably in Hungary and the Balkan Peninsula. The disinterment in Serbia in 1725 and 1732 of several fluid-filled corpses that villagers claimed were behind a plague of vampirism led to widespread interest and imaginative treatment of vampirism throughout western Europe. Vampires are supposedly dead humans (originally suicides, heretics, or criminals) who maintain a kind of life by biting the necks of living humans and sucking their blood; their victims also become vampires after death. These "undead" creatures cast no shadow and are not reflected in mirrors. They can be warded off by crucifixes or wreaths of garlic and can be killed by exposure to the sun or by an oak stake driven through the heart. The most famous vampire is Count Dracula from Bram Stoker's novel *Dracula* (1897).

vampire bat, Any of three species (family Desmodontidae) of tailless, brown, blood-eating bats native to the New World tropics. They grow to 2–3.5 in. (6–9 cm) long and weigh 0.5–2 oz (15–50 g). They run swiftly and leap with agility. They live in colonies in caves, hollow trees, and culverts, leaving after dark to forage low on the ground. They feed on quietly resting birds and mammals, including the occasional human, making a small cut with their sharp incisor teeth, often without disturbing the prey, and lapping the blood. The wounds are not serious but may transmit rabies or other diseases.

Van, City (pop., 2007: 331,986), eastern Turkey, on the eastern shore of Lake Van. The ruins of stone buildings there date from the 8th century BCE, when it was the chief centre of the kingdom of Urartu. After the fall of Nineveh (612 BCE), it was occupied in succession by the Medes, the kings of Pontus, the Arabs (7th century CE), and the Armenians (8th century CE). It fell to the Seljūq dynasty after 1071 CE and to the Ottoman Empire in 1543. Russian forces held it (1915–17) during World War I. It has a large Kurdish population. It once had a large Armenian population, but it was brutally expelled following the war. Van is a shipping point for hides, grains, fruits, and vegetables.

Van, Lake, Salt lake, eastern Anatolia. The largest lake in Turkey, it covers an area of 1,434 sq mi (3,713 sq km) and is more than 74 mi (119 km) across at its widest point. Its greatest depth exceeds 330 ft (100 m). It is fed by precipitation and meltwater as well as by several small tributaries. It has no apparent outlet, and its brackish waters are unsuitable for either drinking or irrigation.

Van Allen radiation belts, Two doughnut-shaped zones of highly energetic charged particles trapped at high altitudes in Earth's magnetic field. Named for James A. Van Allen (1914–2006), who discovered them in 1958, they are most intense over the Equator and effectively absent above the poles. The two zones merge gradually, with the flux of charged particles showing two regions of maximum density. The inner one, mostly protons thought to be produced by primary cosmic rays striking the atmosphere, is centred about 3,700 mi (6,000 km) above Earth's surface. The outer region includes some helium ions from the solar wind and is centred about 12,500 mi (20,000 km) above Earth's surface. Intense solar activity causes disruptions of the belts, linked in turn with such phenomena as auroras and magnetic storms.

vanadium, Metallic chemical element, one of the transition elements, chemical symbol V, atomic number 23. A silvery white, soft metal found (always combined) in various minerals, coal, and petroleum, it is used in alloys with steel and iron for high-speed tool steel, high-strength low-alloy steel, and wear-resistant cast iron. Unalloyed, it is used in high-temperature applications, as a target in X-ray applications, and as a catalyst. Its compounds, in which it has various valences, have many beautiful colours in solution and are used as catalysts and mordants.

Vancouver, City (pop., 2006: city, 578,041; metro. area, 2,116,581), southwestern British Columbia, Canada. Located on a fine natural harbour, Vancouver originated as a lumber-processing settlement in the 1870s. It recovered from a disastrous fire (1886) to become Canada's principal seaport. Its development was aided by completion of the transcontinental railroad in 1887 and the opening of the Panama Canal in 1914, which made it economically feasible to export grain and lumber from Vancouver to the North American east coast and Europe. Economic activities include producing lumber and plywood, oil refining, fishing, shipbuilding, and film and television production. Vancouver's picturesque natural setting and cultural amenities helped land the city the 2010 Winter Olympic Games.

Vancouver Island, Island (pop., 2001: 705,000) off southwestern British Columbia, Canada. It is the largest island (12,079 sq mi [31,285 sq km]) on the Pacific coast of North America. It has several peaks of more than 7,000 ft (2,100 m), as well as several fine harbours. The chief city is Victoria. It was inhabited by coastal Indians for several millennia before it was visited by early Spanish and English explorers, including Capt. James Cook in 1778. It was surveyed in 1792 by George Vancouver and was held by the Hudson's Bay Co. until it was made a British crown colony in 1849. It united with British Columbia in 1866. The island's main industries include lumbering, fishing, agriculture, and tourism.

Vandal, Any member of a Germanic people who ruled a kingdom in North Africa from 429 to 534 and who sacked Rome in 455. Fleeing westward from the Huns, they invaded Gaul before settling in Spain (409). Under King Gaiseric (r. 428–477) they migrated to North Africa and became federates of Rome (435). Four years later Gaiseric threw off Roman overlordship and captured Carthage. The Vandals later annexed Sardinia, Corsica, and Sicily, and their pirate fleets controlled much of the western Mediterranean. When they invaded Italy and captured Rome (455), they plundered the city and its artworks, and their name has remained a synonym for willful desecration and destruction. The Vandals were Arian Christians who persecuted Roman Catholics in Africa. They were conquered when the Byzantines invaded North Africa (533–534).

Vanguard, Any of three unmanned U.S. experimental satellites. Vanguard I (1958), the second U.S. satellite placed in orbit around Earth (after Explorer 1), was a tiny 3.25-lb (1.47-kg) sphere with two radio transmitters. Its flight path revealed that Earth is almost imperceptibly pear-shaped, confirming earlier theories. Vanguard II (1959) carried light-sensitive photocells to provide information about Earth's cloud cover, but its tumbling motion rendered the data unreadable. Vanguard III (1959) was used to map Earth's magnetic field.

vanilla, Any member of a group of tropical climbing orchids that make up the genus *Vanilla*, and the flavouring agent extracted from its seedpods. The plant has a long, fleshy climbing stem that attaches itself by aerial rootlets to trees; roots also penetrate the soil. Numerous flowers open a few at a time and last only a day. The fruit, a bean pod about 8 in. (20 cm) long at maturity, is harvested as soon as it turns golden green at the base. Curing and processing turn the pods a deep chocolate brown. Vanilla is used in a variety of sweet foods and beverages as well as in perfumery.

Vanuatu, officially REPUBLIC OF VANUATU, Island country, South Pacific Ocean. It consists of a chain of 13 principal and many smaller islands. Area: 4,707 sq mi (12,190 sq km). Population: (2011 est.) 251,000. Capital: Port-Vila. The population is nearly all indigenous Melanesian. Languages: Bislama, English, French (all official); Melanesian languages and dialects. Religions: Christianity (mostly Protestant; also Roman Catholic); also traditional beliefs and cargo cults. Currency: vatu. Extending north-south some 400 mi (650 km), Vanuatu includes the islands of Vanua Lava, Santa Maria, Espiritu Santo, Aoba, Maéwo, Pentecost, Malakula, Ambrym, Épi, Éfaté, Erromango, Tanna, and Anatom. The larger islands are volcanic in origin and mountainous; there are several active volcanoes. Some of them, especially Éfaté and Malakula, have good harbours. The highest point is Tabwémasana (6,165 ft [1,879 m]) on Espiritu Santo. The developing

free-market economy is based mainly on agriculture, cattle raising, and fishing. Tourism is increasingly important. Vanuatu is a
republic with a single legislative house; its head of state is the president, and the head of government is the prime minister. The islands were inhabited for some 3,000 years by Melanesian peoples
before European contact in 1606 by the Portuguese. They were
visited by French navigator Louis-Antoine de Bougainville in
1768, then explored by English mariner Capt. James Cook in
1774, who named the islands the New Hebrides. Sandalwood merchants and European missionaries arrived in the mid-19th century;
they were followed by British and French planters of cotton and
other crops. Control of the islands was sought by both the French
and British, who agreed in 1906 to form a condominium government. During World War II a major Allied naval base was on Espiritu Santo; Vanuatu escaped Japanese invasion. New Hebrides became the independent Republic of Vanuatu in 1980. Much of its
history since then has been marked by frequent changes of government but relative political stability.

Varanasi, or BENARES, City (pop., 2001 prelim.: 1,100,748), Uttar Pradesh, India. Located on the Ganges River in southeastern
Uttar Pradesh, it is one of the oldest continuously inhabited cities
in the world and was the site of an Aryan settlement before the 2nd
millennium BC. It is one of the seven sacred cities of Hinduism and
has numerous shrines, temples, and palaces and miles of steps for
ritual bathing. More than a million Hindus visit the city each year.
Just north of Varanasi is Sarnath, where the Buddha delivered his
first sermon.

varicose vein, or VARIX, Twisted vein distended with blood.
Varix also covers arteries and lymphatic vessels. Varicose veins
occur mostly in the legs, when malfunctioning valves let blood
pool in veins near the skin. Causes include hereditary valve and
vein wall weakness and internal or external pressure on veins.
Varices are common in pregnancy, suggesting that hormone abnormalities play a role. Symptoms include a heavy feeling, with
leg cramps and swelling after standing a long time. Complications
include skin ulcers and thrombosis. Treatment involves strong
support hose, injection therapy, or surgery. Varices in the esophagus, which often occur in liver disease, can ulcerate and bleed.

Varna, Seaport city (pop., 2001: 314,539), Bulgaria, on the Black
Sea coast. Founded as Odessus by Milesian Greeks in the 6th century BC, it later was Thracian, Macedonian, and Roman. In AD 681
it became part of the first Bulgarian empire (c. 679–1018) and was
named Varna. It came under Ottoman domination in 1391. In 1444
it was the scene of a battle between Turkish and Hungarian armies
in which Władysław III, king of Poland and Hungary, was killed.
Varna was ceded to Bulgaria by the 1878 Treaty of Berlin. It is an
important administrative, economic, cultural, and resort centre.
Shipbuilding and manufacturing are important industries.

varna, Any of the four traditional social classes of Hindu India.
One of the hymns of the Rigveda declares that the Brahman, the
Kshatriya, the Vaishya, and the Shudra issued forth at creation
from the mouth, arms, thighs, and feet of Prajapati. Traditional
lawmakers specified a set of obligations, observed mainly in theory only, to each varna: the Brahman, to study and advise; the
Kshatriya, to protect; the Vaishya, to cultivate; and the Shudra, to
serve. An unofficial fifth class, the *pancama*, was created to include certain untouchables and tribal groups falling outside this
system. The relationship of the caste system to the class system is
complex; individual castes, of which there are dozens, have sought
to raise their social rank by identifying with a particular varna,
demanding the associated privileges of rank and honour.

Vasa dynasty, Swedish (and Polish) royal dynasty. Its founder
was Gustav Eriksson Vasa, regent of Sweden (1521) and king
(1523) as Gustav I Vasa. His descendants reigned in Sweden until
1818, the last being Charles XIII. A grandson of Gustav became
king of Poland (1587–1632) as Sigismund III Vasa, also ruling

Sweden in the years 1592–99. He was succeeded as king of Poland
by his sons, Wladyslaw IV Vasa (r. 1632–48) and John II Casimir
Vasa (r.1648–68), after which the dynasty ended in Poland.

vascular plant, or TRACHEOPHYTE, Any plant that has a specialized conducting system consisting mostly of phloem (food-conducting tissue) and xylem (water-conducting tissue), collectively
called vascular tissue. Ferns, gymnosperms, and flowering plants
are all vascular plants. In contrast to the nonvascular bryophytes,
the more conspicuous generation among vascular plants is the
sporophyte. Because they have vascular tissues, these plants have
true stems, leaves, and roots, modifications of which enable species of vascular plants to survive in a variety of habitats under
diverse, even extreme, environmental conditions. This ability to
flourish in so many different habitats is the primary reason that
vascular plants have become dominant among terrestrial plants.

vasectomy, Severing of the vas deferens, which carries sperm
from the testes to the prostate gland, to cause sterility or prevent
infection. This relatively simple procedure, which can be performed in a doctor's office with local anesthetics, removes the
ability to father children without affecting ability to achieve erection or orgasm. The vas is cut near its beginning, in the scrotum.
The cut ends may be sealed off or left open. Reversal is more likely
to succeed in the latter case; microsurgery has improved the success rate.

Vatican City, in full STATE OF THE VATICAN CITY, Independent
papal state, southern Europe, within the commune of Rome, Italy.
Area: 109 acres (44 hectares). Population: (2009 est.) 800. Its medieval and Renaissance walls form its boundaries except on the
southeast at St. Peter's Square. Within the walls is the world's
smallest independent nation-state, with its own diplomatic missions, newspaper, post office, radio station, banking system, army
of 100 Swiss Guards, and publishing house. Extraterritoriality of
the state extends to Castel Gandolfo and to several churches and
palaces in Rome proper. Its independent sovereignty was recognized in the Lateran Treaty of 1929. The pope has absolute executive, legislative, and judicial powers within the city. He appoints
the members of the Vatican's government organs, which are separate from those of the Holy See, the name given to the government of the Roman Catholic Church. The many imposing buildings include St. Peter's Basilica, the Vatican Palace, and the
Vatican Museums. Frescoes by Michelangelo in the Sistine
Chapel, by Pinturicchio in the Borgia Apartment, and by Raphael
in the Stanze (rooms in the papal apartments) are also there. The
Vatican Library contains a priceless collection of manuscripts
from the pre-Christian and Christian eras. The pope and other representatives of the papal state travel widely to maintain international relations.

Vatican Council, Second (1962–65) 21st ecumenical council
of the Roman Catholic church, announced by Pope John XXIII. It
has come to symbolize the church's readiness to acknowledge the
circumstances of the modern world. Among the most notable of
the 16 documents enacted were the "Dogmatic Constitution on the
Church," which treats church hierarchy and provides for greater
involvement of laypeople in the church; the "Dogmatic Constitution of Divine Revelation," which maintains an open attitude toward scholarly study of the Bible; the "Constitution on the Sacred
Liturgy," which provides for the use of vernacular languages in the
mass in place of Latin; and the "Pastoral Constitution on the
Church in the World of Today," which acknowledges the profound
changes humanity has experienced in the modern world and attempts to relate the church to contemporary culture. Observers
from other Christian churches were invited to the council in a gesture of ecumenism.

Vatican Museums and Galleries, Institutions and papal palaces in Vatican City housing the art collections of the popes since
the beginning of the 15th century. Among the many separate muse-

ums are the 18th-century Pio-Clementino Museum, which exhibits the collection of Classical sculpture that originated in 1503–13 with Julius II; the exhibition rooms in the Vatican Library; and the Sistine Chapel. The Vatican collections are most famous for their Classical statues (including *Apollo Belvedere*, *Belvedere Torso*, and *Laocoön*) but also contain important examples of Egyptian and early Christian art. The Pinacoteca ("Picture Gallery"), founded by Pius VI in 1797, contains Italian religious paintings and Russian and Byzantine art. In 1956 a modern-art collection was begun with secular works by such artists as Pierre-Auguste Renoir, Georges Seurat, Vincent van Gogh, Henri Matisse, and Pablo Picasso. The Vatican collections are among the largest and most important in the world.

Vatican Palace, Pope's residence since the late 14th century, located north of St. Peter's Basilica in the Vatican. First enclosed in 850, the irregularly walled compound contains gardens (begun by Nero), courtyards, living quarters, galleries, the Vatican Museums and Library, and other facilities. The residence, with more than 1,400 rooms, was begun in the 13th century by Pope Nicholas III. Nicholas V founded the Vatican Library. Under Julius II, Giovanni dei Dolci built the Sistine Chapel, noted for its spectacular interior artwork including Michelangelo's ceiling; Donato Bramante completed the palace's northern facade and planned the immense Belvedere court; and Raphael painted his masterpieces in the palace. Antonio da Sangallo the Younger, employed by Paul III, designed the Sala Regia (Royal Hall) and Pauline Chapel, decorated by Michelangelo. Several chapels, along with Ottaviano Mascherino's famous Gallery of Maps, date from the late 16th century. Domenico Fontana added a wing of apartments and the present library building under Sixtus V. In the Baroque period, Urban VIII built the Matilda Chapel and, under Alexander VII, Gian Lorenzo Bernini built the Scala Regia (Royal Stairway).

vaudeville, Light entertainment popular in the U.S. in the late 19th and early 20th centuries. It consisted of 10–15 unrelated acts featuring magicians, acrobats, comedians, trained animals, singers, and dancers. The form developed from the coarse variety shows held in beer halls for a primarily male audience. Tony Pastor established a successful "clean variety show" at his New York City theatre in 1881 and influenced other managers to follow suit. By 1900 chains of vaudeville theatres around the country included Martin Beck's Orpheum Circuit, of which New York's Palace Theatre was the most famous (1913–32). Among the many entertainers who began in vaudeville were Mae West, W.C. Fields, Will Rogers, Buster Keaton, Charlie Chaplin, the Marx Brothers, Bud Abbott and Lou Costello, Milton Berle, and Bob Hope.

Veda, Any of a group of sacred hymns and verses composed in archaic Sanskrit, probably in the period 1500–1200 BC. Together they form a body of liturgical literature that grew up around the cult of the soma ritual. They extol the hereditary deities that personified various natural and cosmic phenomena. The entire corpus of Vedic literature, including the Upanishads, was considered the product of divine revelation. The Vedas were handed down orally for many generations before being committed to writing. Even today, several are recited with intonation and rhythm associated with the early days of Vedic religion.

Vedanta, One of the six orthodox systems (darshans) of Indian philosophy and the one that forms the basis of most modern schools of Hinduism. Its three fundamental texts are the Upanishads, the Bhagavadgita, and the Brahma Sutras, which are very brief interpretations of the doctrine of the Upanishads. Several schools of Vedanta have developed, differentiated by their conception of the relationship between the self (atman) and the absolute (Brahman). They share beliefs in samsara and the authority of the Vedas as well as the conviction that Brahman is both the material and instrumental cause of the world and that the atman is the agent of its own acts and therefore the recipient of the consequences of action.

Vedic religion, or VEDISM, Ancient religion of India that was contemporary with the composition of the Vedas and was the precursor of Hinduism. The religion of the Indo-European-speaking peoples who entered India *c.* 1500 BCE from the region of present-day Iran, it was a polytheistic system in which Indra was the highest-ranked god. It involved the worship of numerous male divinities connected with the sky and natural phenomena. Ceremonies centred on ritual sacrifice of animals and on the use of soma to achieve trancelike states. These ceremonies, simple in the beginning, grew to be so complex that only trained Brahmans could carry them out correctly. Out of Vedism developed the philosophical concepts of atman and Brahman. The spread (8th–5th century BCE) of the related concepts of reincarnation, karma, and release from the cycle of rebirth through meditation rather than sacrifice marked the end of the Vedic period and the rise of Hinduism. The Hindu initiation ceremony, *upanayana*, is a direct survivor of Vedic tradition.

vegetable, In the broadest sense, all plant life and plant products (vegetable matter); in common, narrow usage, the fresh edible portion of herbaceous plants (roots, stems, leaves, flowers, or fruit), either eaten fresh or prepared in some way. Almost all current vegetables were cultivated in ancient Old or New World civilizations, though some have been greatly modified. Vegetables are good sources of minerals (especially calcium and iron), vitamins (especially A and C), and dietary fiber. All the amino acids needed to synthesize protein are available in vegetables. Fresh vegetables quickly age and spoil, but their storage life can be extended by such preservation methods as dehydration, canning, freezing, fermenting, and pickling.

vegetarianism, Theory or practice of eating only plants. The vegetarian diet includes grains, vegetables, fruits, and nuts; it excludes meat, poultry, and fish, but some vegetarians eat dairy products (lactovegetarians), egg products (ovovegetarians), or both (ovolactovegetarians). Those who eat no animal products (including honey) are called vegans. Motivations vary and include ethics (both unwillingness to kill animals and abhorrence of modern methods of raising animals for meat), self-denial or religious taboo, ecology (including concern about the wastefulness and environmental costs of beef farming), and health. Vegetarians point to the many health benefits of their diet, including low rates of heart disease, diabetes, colon cancer, and obesity. While obtaining sufficient protein is seldom a problem in affluent societies, vegetarians must be careful to consume enough iron and, especially for vegans, calcium and vitamins D and B_{12}. The most influential early proponent of vegetarianism was Pythagoras, in the 6th century BC. Many Hindu sects and most Buddhists are vegetarian, and much of the world eats hardly any meat because it is unavailable. The Enlightenment led to a humane concern for animals; in the 19th century Britain became a major centre of vegetarianism, and vegetarian movements soon arose in Germany, the U.S., and other countries.

Velociraptor, Genus of clawed theropod dinosaur (family Dromaeosauridae) that flourished in central and eastern Asia during the Late Cretaceous Epoch (99–65 million years ago). It was related to an Early Cretaceous (144–99 million years ago) North American genus, *Deinonychus*. Both genera had a sickle-shaped claw on each foot and ossified tendon reinforcements in the tail that enabled them to keep their balance while striking and slashing at prey. Swift, agile predators of small herbivores, they grew up to 6 ft (1.8 m) long and weighed up to 100 lb (45 kg).

velocity, Quantity that designates the speed and direction in which a body moves. It can be represented graphically by an arrow (pointing in the direction of the motion), the length of which is proportional to the magnitude, or speed. For an object in circular motion, the direction at any instant is tangential to the circle at that point, and so is perpendicular to the radius at that point. The instantaneous speed of a vehicle, such as an automobile, can be determined by a speedometer, or mathematically by differential calculus. The average speed is the ratio of the distance traveled in any given time interval divided by the time taken.

vena cava, Either of two major veins that deliver oxygen-depleted blood to the right side of the heart. The superior vena cava drains the upper body, and the inferior vena cava drains the lower body.

Vendée, Wars of the (1793–96) Insurrections in the west of France during the French Revolution. In the religious and impoverished area known as the Vendée, discontent with the new government grew after it instituted strict controls over the Catholic church (1790). An uprising began in opposition to the conscription acts (1793) and spread throughout the region, where peasants were joined by royalists to form the Catholic and Royal Army. Led by the nobleman François Charette de La Contrie (1763–1796), the Vendéan army of 65,000 occupied several towns, but was defeated at Cholet by government troops and forced to retreat. After further defeats at Le Mans (about 15,000 rebels killed) and at Savenay, the general warfare ended in December 1793. Vicious reprisals by the government provoked further resistance, until an amnesty was announced (1794) and the Vendée was granted freedom from conscription (1795). Charette joined a British-backed landing of exiled French nobles in Brittany (1795), but after their defeat and his execution (1796) the counterrevolutionary struggle ended.

Venera, Any of a series of unmanned Soviet planetary probes sent to Venus 1965–83. Venera 2 flew to within 25,000 mi (40,000 km) of Venus in 1966; a few days later, Venera 3 crash-landed on its surface, becoming the first spacecraft to strike another planet. Later missions analyzed Venus's atmosphere, made soft landings, detected certain long-lived radioactive isotopes (chiefly uranium and thorium), sent back the first close-up photographs of the planet's surface, and mapped the surface of the northern hemisphere with radar (by Venera 15 and 16, the last two of the series).

Venetian glass, Variety of glassware made in Venice from the 13th century to the present. In the 15th century efforts were concentrated on the perfection of *cristallo* (clear glass that approximated rock crystal in appearance). By the 16th century Venetian glassmakers mastered techniques of adding colour and of removing the smoky tint produced by metal in the glass material. These and other secrets were guarded closely, and defecting workers were severely punished. But eventually many Venetian glassmakers did defect, and the techniques became common knowledge in France, Germany, the Netherlands, and England.

Venetian school, Renaissance artists of Venice whose work is characterized by a love of light and colour. Jacopo Bellini was the first in this influential line, followed by his son Gentile Bellini, the instructor of Venice's great High Renaissance painters, including Giorgione and Titian. In due course Titian became the dominant force in Venetian painting, and his rich colours and painterly technique were widely imitated. Other 16th-century masters included Veronese, known for his vast, brilliantly coloured, pageantlike canvases, and Tintoretto, who combined the Mannerists' rapidly receding diagonals and dramatic foreshortenings with the Venetian love of light as a means of defining form and heightening drama. Giovanni Battista Tiepolo was the last important Venetian figure painter and one of the greatest artists of the Rococo period.

Venezuela, officially BOLIVARIAN REPUBLIC OF VENEZUELA, Country, northern South America. Area: 353,841 sq mi (916,445 sq km). Population: (2011 est.) 29,437,000. Capital: Caracas. About two-thirds of the people are mestizos; most of the rest are of European or African descent. Languages: Spanish (official), some 25 Indian languages. Religion: Christianity (predominantly Roman Catholic). Currency: bolívar. Mountain ranges and plains dominate Venezuela's geography. In the west, a northeastern spur

of the Andes Mountains rises to Bolívar Peak. The Llanos (plains) occupy one-third of the country's central region. The Orinoco River system drains almost the entire country and has an extensive and thickly wooded delta. The highest waterfall in the world, Angel Falls, is in Venezuela. Lakes include Maracaibo and Valencia. Principal mineral resources are petroleum and natural gas. Other mineral reserves include iron, bauxite, gold, and diamonds. Industries include steel, chemicals, textiles, and oil refining. Agricultural products—notably sugar, coffee, corn, bananas, and cacao—are important. Venezuela is a federal multiparty republic with a unicameral legislature; its head of state and government is the president. Venezuela has been inhabited by indigenous peoples for millennia. In 1498 Christopher Columbus sighted it; European explorers named the region Venezuela (Spanish: "Little Venice") after observing local Indian houses on stilts along the shores of Lake Maracaibo. A Spanish missionary established the first European settlement at Cumana c. 1523. In 1717 it was included in the Viceroyalty of New Granada. Venezuelan Creoles led by Francisco de Miranda and Simón Bolívar spearheaded the South American independence movement, and, though Venezuelans had declared independence from Spain as early as 1797, it was not assured until the last royalist forces surrendered in 1823. Military dictators generally ruled the country from 1830 until the overthrow of Marcos Pérez Jiménez in 1958. A new constitution adopted in 1961 marked the beginning of democracy. As a founding member of OPEC (Organization of Petroleum Exporting Countries), Venezuela enjoyed relative economic prosperity from oil production during the 1970s, but its economy has remained dependent on fluctuations in the world petroleum market. The government of Hugo Chávez promulgated a new constitution in 1999, the year in which a devastating rainstorm killed thousands in and around Caracas—one of the deadliest events in Venezuelan history. Despite an increase in oil prices in the early 21st century, the country experienced great political turmoil.

Venice, Italian VENEZIA, City (pop., 2008 est.: 268,993), capital of Veneto region, northern Italy. Built on a lagoon, Venice encompasses some 118 islands, the whole 90-mi (145-km) perimeter of the lagoon, and two industrial mainland boroughs. Refugees from northern invasions of the mainland founded settlements in the 5th century that were built uniquely on islands as protection against raids. Venice was a vassal of the Byzantine Empire until the 10th century. Beginning with control of a trade route to the Levant, Venice emerged from the Fourth Crusade (1202–04) as ruler of a colonial empire which included Crete, Euboea, the Cyclades, the Ionian Islands, and footholds in Morea and Epirus. In 1381 it defeated Genoa after a century-long struggle for commercial supremacy in the Levant and eastern Mediterranean. In the 15th century, with the acquisition of neighbouring regions, the Republic of Venice became an extensive Italian state. It gradually lost its eastern possessions to Ottoman Turks, with whom Venice fought intermittently from the 15th to the 18th century; it gave up its last hold in the Aegean in 1715. The republic dissolved and the territory was ceded to Austria in 1797. Incorporated into Napoleon's Kingdom of Italy in 1805, it was restored to Austria in 1815. A revolt against Austria (1848–49) eventually resulted in Venice being ceded to Italy in 1866. It suffered little damage during World War II, but flooding along its many miles of canals caused severe damage in 1966. The waters of the lagoon rise and flood the city on a regular basis, complicating efforts to preserve its architecture, which includes Italian, Arabic, Byzantine, and Renaissance forms. There are some 450 palaces and homes of major historic importance in Venice. Notable among its 400 bridges is the Bridge of Sighs (built c. 800) and among its churches St. Mark's Basilica. Most of the city's workers find employment in tourism and related industries, though Venice also plays a key market role within the vibrant economic system of the Veneto region.

venom, Poison secreted by an animal, produced by specialized glands often associated with spines, teeth, or stings. It may be primarily for paralyzing or killing prey or may be purely defensive. Some venoms also function as digestive fluids. Their effects can range from localized skin inflammation to almost immediate death; they include nervous-system excitation (cramps, vomiting, convulsions) or depression (paralysis, respiratory or cardiac depression or arrest), hemorrhage, red-blood-cell breakdown, circulatory collapse, and allergic reactions (including hives and inflammation). Many major groups of animals contain venomous species: snakes (cobras, mambas, vipers, pit vipers); fish (stingrays, spiny sharks, certain catfish, puffers); lizards (Gila monsters, beaded lizards); scorpions; spiders (black widow spiders, brown recluse spiders); social insects (bees, wasps, some ants); and marine invertebrates (sea anemones, fire corals, jellyfish, sea urchins).

ventriloquism, Art of "throwing" one's voice in such a way that the sound seems to come from a source other than the speaker. A dummy or doll is commonly used to assist in the deception, with the ventriloquist moving the dummy's mouth while speaking through closed lips. Ventriloquists date from ancient times and include Eurycles of Athens. Such peoples as the Maoris, Zulus, and Eskimos are adept ventriloquists. The art was long a feature of puppet shows as well as of variety entertainment such as vaudeville. Notable ventriloquists included Edgar Bergen in the U.S. and Robert Lamouret in France.

venue, In law, the place or county in which the events giving rise to a legal action take place and from which a jury may be drawn to try the case. Venue statutes usually specify that a trial must take place in the district that has jurisdiction over the matter. The grounds for a change of venue are also specified; they include fear of biased jurors due to media coverage, danger of violence, and racial prejudice.

Venus, Roman goddess of cultivated fields and gardens, later associated with Aphrodite. She was the daughter of Jupiter and Dione, the wife of Vulcan, and the mother of Cupid. She was famous for her romantic intrigues and affairs with both gods and mortals, and she became associated with many aspects of femininity. The planet Venus, originally the star of Ishtar, came to be named for Venus through her association with Ishtar. She has been a favourite subject in art since ancient times, notably in the statue known as *Venus de Milo* (*c.* 150 BC)and in Sandro Botticelli's painting *The Birth of Venus* (*c.* 1485).

Venus, Second major planet from the Sun. Named for the Roman goddess, Venus is, after the Moon, the most brilliant natural object in the night sky. Venus comes closer to Earth—about 26 million mi (42 million km)—than any other planet. Its orbit around the Sun is nearly circular at a distance of about 67 million mi (108 million km) and takes 225 days; its rotation, in retrograde motion, takes even longer (243 days). As viewed from Earth, Venus undergoes phase changes similar to the Moon's, going through one cycle of phases in 584 days. It is seen only near sunrise or sunset and has long been known as both the morning star and the evening star. Venus is a near twin of Earth in size and mass but is completely enveloped by thick clouds of concentrated sulfuric acid droplets. Its surface gravity is about 90% that of Earth. Its atmosphere is over 96% carbon dioxide, with a pressure about 95 times Earth's. The dense atmosphere and thick cloud layers trap incoming solar energy so efficiently that Venus has the highest surface temperature of any of the Sun's planets, more than 860 °F (460 °C). Radar imaging indicates that the surface is dry and rocky, consisting mostly of gently rolling plains, broad depressions, and two large elevated regions analogous to continents on Earth; Venus also has impact craters, extensive lava fields, and massive shield volcanos. The interior is thought to be similar to that of Earth, with a metal core, a dense rocky mantle, and a less-dense rocky crust. Unlike Earth, Venus has no intrinsic magnetic field.

Venus's-flytrap (Dionaea muscipula)
Jack Dermid

Venus's-flytrap, or VENUS FLYTRAP, Flowering perennial plant (*Dionaea muscipula*), sole member of its genus, in the sundew family, notable for its unusual habit of catching and eating insects and other small animals. Native to a small region of North and South Carolina, it is common in damp, mossy areas. Growing from a bulblike rootstock, the plant bears hinged leaves with spiny teeth along their margins and a round cluster of small white flowers at the tip of an erect stem 8–12 in. (20–30 cm) tall. When an insect alights on a leaf and stimulates its sensitive hairs, the leaf snaps shut in about half a second. Leaf glands secrete a red sap that digests the insect's body and gives the entire leaf a red, flowerlike appearance. After 10 days of digestion, the leaf reopens. The trap dies after capturing three or four insects.

Verdi, Giuseppe (Fortunato Francesco) (b. Oct. 9/10, 1813, Roncole, near Busseto, duchy of Parma—d. Jan. 27, 1901, Milan, Italy) Italian composer. He was the son of an innkeeper, and he showed talent early. While earning a living as an organist, he began to write operas in Milan; in 1839 his *Oberto* was successfully performed at La Scala, and it initiated Verdi's long association with the publisher Giulio Ricordi. His next opera, *Un giorno di regno* (1840), was a failure. Much worse, Verdi's two young daughters and his wife died. He overcame his despair by composing *Nabucco* (1842); it was a sensational success and was followed by the equally successful *I Lombardi* (1843). For the rest of the decade he wrote a hit opera every year. Rejecting the prevailing structure of Italian opera—a patchwork of open-ended scenes and inserted arias, duets, and trios—he began conceiving of an opera as a series of integrated scenes, then as unified acts. Specializing in stories in which people's private and public lives come into conflict, he produced a series of masterworks, including *Rigoletto* (1851), *Il trovatore* (1853), *La traviata* (1853), *Don Carlos* (1867), and *Aïda* (1871). A fervent nationalist, he was regarded as a great national figure. After composing his *Requiem* (1874), he retired, but when Ricordi brought him together with the poet and composer Arrigo Boito, initially to revise *Simon Boccanegra*, their mutual esteem led to the two great operas of Verdi's old age, *Otello* (1886) and *Falstaff* (1890).

Verdun, Battle of (Feb. 21–July 1916) Major engagement of World War I between Germany and France. As part of its strategy of war by attrition, Germany selected the fortress of Verdun as the site it believed France would defend to the last man. After a massive bombardment, the Germans advanced with little opposition for four days before the reinforced French army under Philippe Pétain slowed their advance. For two months the hills west of the Meuse River and north of Verdun were bombarded, attacked, and counterattacked. By July, Germany, which was also engaged in the Battle of the Somme, had abandoned its strategy of attrition, and France gradually regained its forts and territory. The devastating losses included more than 400,000 French casualties and nearly as many German casualties.

Verdun, Treaty of (843) Treaty partitioning the Carolingian empire among the three surviving sons of Louis I (the Pious). It marked a first stage in the dissolution of Charlemagne's empire and a step toward the formation of the modern countries of western Europe. The treaty was signed following three years of civil war between the three brothers. Lothar I received the imperial title and Francia Media, which included much of Italy as well as parts of several other present-day European countries. Louis the German received Francia Orientalis, the land east of the Rhine River, and Charles II (the Bald) received Francia Occidentalis, the remainder of modern France.

verifiability principle, Criterion of meaningfulness associated with logical positivism and the Vienna Circle. Moritz Schlick's formulation "The meaning of a [declarative sentence] is the method of its verification" was close to the view held in pragmatism, and later in operationalism, that an assertion has factual meaning only if there is a difference in principle, open to test by observation, between the affirmation and the denial of the assertion. Thus, the statements of ethics, metaphysics, religion, and aesthetics were held to be meaningless. The verifiability criterion of meaningfulness was in part inspired by Albert Einstein's abandonment of the ether hypothesis and the notion of absolute simultaneity.

Vermeer, Johannes (b. Oct. 31, 1632, Delft, Neth.—d. Dec. 15, 1675, Delft), Dutch painter. His parents were tavern keepers. He twice served as head of the Delft artists' guild but seems to have depended on his activities as an art dealer to support his family. He painted mainly interior genre subjects, depicting members of aristocratic and upper-middle-class society. About half of these paintings show solitary figures of women absorbed in some ordinary, everyday activity. His interiors combine a microscopic observation of objects with a meticulous depiction of the gradations of daylight on varied shapes and surfaces. His masterpieces (none dated) include *View of Delft*, *Young Woman Reading a Letter*, and *Allegory of Painting*, his most symbolically complex work. He manages to be unique within a typically Dutch genre. Few foreign influences can be sensed in his work. His work was not widely appreciated in his own time, and he remained in obscurity until 1866, when Théophile Thoré celebrated his work and attributed 76 paintings to him; later authorities have reduced the number to between 30 and 35, while proclaiming him one of the greatest painters of all time.

Verona, City (pop., 2001 prelim.: 243,474), northern Italy. Located on the Adige River, it became a Roman colony in 89 BC and was the birthplace of the poet Catullus. It was captured by the Goths after the fall of the Roman Empire and was the site of Odoacer's defeat by the Ostrogothic king Theodoric in 489. It was occupied by Charlemagne in 774. Verona came under the della Scala family (1260–1387), the era recalled in William Shakespeare's *Romeo and Juliet*. It passed in 1405 to Venice, which held it almost continuously until 1797, when it was ceded to Austria. It became part of the Kingdom of Italy in 1866. It is noted for its ancient Roman amphitheatre (1st century AD), now used for opera, and for Romanesque and Gothic buildings.

Versailles, Palace of, Baroque palace southwest of Paris built chiefly under Louis XIV. It was the principal residence of the French kings and the seat of government from 1682 to 1789, with some 1,000 courtiers and 4,000 attendants residing there. Originally a hunting lodge, it was enlarged by Louis XIII and Louis XIV. Louis Le Vau (1612–70), with Charles Le Brun and André Le Nôtre, began work on the palace in the 1660s. A masterpiece of formal grandeur intended as the visible expression of the glory of France, Versailles became the palatial ideal throughout Europe and the Americas. Le Nôtre's inventive arrangement of earth forms, plantings, and fountains created vistas, terraces, formal gardens, and wooded areas that celebrated the delights of both open and intimate space. After Le Vau's death, Jules Hardouin-Mansart (1646–1708) was commissioned to triple the size of the palace and built the northern and southern wings, the Orangerie, and the Grand Trianon. Later additions include the Classically restrained Petit Trianon, built 1761–64 for Louis XV and Madame de Pompadour. The first scenes of the French Revolution were enacted at Versailles, which had become a symbol of royal extravagance. In 1837 Louis-Philippe restored the palace and turned it into a museum.

Versailles, Treaty of, International agreement, signed in 1919 at the Palace of Versailles, that concluded World War I. It was negotiated primarily by the U.S., Britain, and France, without participation by the war's losers. Germany was forced to accept blame for Allied losses and to pay major reparations. Its European territory was reduced by about 10%, its overseas possessions were confiscated, and its military establishment was reduced. Although some of the treaty's terms were eased in the 1920s, the bitterness it created helped to foster an environment that led to the growth of fascism in Italy and the rise of the Nazi Party in Germany. The treaty also established the League of Nations, the International Labour Organization, and the Permanent Court of International Justice (later the International Court of Justice).

vertebrate, Any animal of the chordate subphylum Vertebrata, which includes the fishes, amphibians, reptiles, birds, and mammals. Vertebrates have an internal skeleton formed of cartilage, bone, or both. The skeleton consists of a backbone (vertebral column), which partly encloses a spinal cord; a skull, which encloses the brain; and usually two pairs of limbs. Nerves extending from the spinal cord and brain permeate the skin, muscles, and internal organs. The muscular system consists primarily of bilaterally paired masses attached to bones or cartilage. Skin and scales, feathers, fur, or hair cover the outer surface..

vertigo, Feeling that one is spinning or that one's surroundings are spinning around one, causing confusion and difficulty keeping one's balance, sometimes accompanied by nausea and vomiting. Vertigo is normal after actual spinning, since inner-ear fluid continues to move once the body has stopped, producing a mismatch between visual and internal sensations. Lack of a stable visual reference point also contributes to this effect. Other causes include concussion and abnormalities of the inner ear (e.g., labyrinthitis; *see* otitis), of the nerves that carry signals from it, or of the brain centers that receive them (e.g., stroke). Vertigo is often confused with a feeling of faintness, since both are called dizziness.

Very Large Array (VLA), Radio telescope system consisting of 27 parabolic dishes. The most powerful radio telescope in the world, it has been operated on the plains of San Agustin near Socorro, N.M., U.S., by the National Radio Astronomy Observatory since 1980. Each dish is 82 ft (25 m) in diameter and can be moved independently by transporter along rails laid out in an enormous Y pattern whose arms are about 13 mi (21 km) long. The radio signals received by the dishes are integrated by computer, so the entire array acts as a single radio antenna (an interferometer). The VLA, which has a maximum angular resolution better than a tenth of an arc second, has been responsible for producing many of the most detailed radio images of quasars; galaxies; supernovas; and the Milky Way Galaxy's nucleus.

Vesta, In Roman religion, the goddess of the hearth, identified with the Greek Hestia. Because maintaining a hearth fire was important in ancient times, she was worshiped in every household. Her state worship was elaborate: her temple in Rome had a perpetual fire that was attended by the Vestal Virgins. The fire was officially extinguished and renewed annually on March 1st; its extinction at any other time was viewed as a portent of disaster to Rome.

Vesta (seated on the left) with Vestal Virgins, classical relief sculpture; in the Palermo Museum, Italy
Courtesy of the Palermo Museum, Italy

Vestal Virgin, In Roman religion, any of six priestesses, representing the daughters of the royal house, who tended the state cult of Vesta. Chosen between the ages of 6 and 10, they served for 30 years, during which time they had to remain virgins; violation of the vow of chastity was punishable by burial alive. Their duties included tending the perpetual fire in the Temple of Vesta, fetching water from a sacred spring, preparing ritual food, caring for objects in the temple's inner sanctuary, and officiating at the public worship of Vesta. They enjoyed many honours and privileges, including emancipation from their fathers' rule.

Vesuvius, Active volcano, eastern side of the Bay of Naples, southern Italy. It originated about 200,000 years ago; its current height of 4,198 ft (1,280 m) has varied considerably after each of its major eruptions; in 1900 it was 4,275 ft (1,303 m) high; in 1906, 3,668 ft (1,118 m) high; and in the 1960s, 4,203 ft (1,281 m) high. The cone is half-encircled on the northern side by Mount Somma, part of the wall of a large crater in which the present cone has formed. There have been numerous destructive eruptions; in AD 79 Pompeii and Herculaneum were destroyed, and in 1631 about 3,000 people were killed. The last major eruption occurred in 1944. More than two million people live in the area of Vesuvius, whose fertile slopes are covered with vineyards and orchards.

veterinary medicine, Medical field dealing with animals and with diseases that are transmissible between animals and humans. It was practiced as a specialty in ancient Egypt and Babylonia; the first veterinary schools in Europe were founded in the mid-18th century. Veterinarians practice internal medicine, surgery, and preventive medicine, using the same techniques used on humans. They serve worldwide in private and corporate clinical practice, academic programs, private industry, government service, public health, and military services. Many specialize in either small animals (pets) or large ones (livestock); a few specialize in wild animals.

vibraphone, or VIBRAHARP, Percussion instrument with tuned metal bars, arranged keyboard-style like the xylophone. Felt or wool beaters are used to strike the bars, giving a soft, mellow tone quality. Each bar has a resonating tube suspended vertically below it to sustain the tone; small electrically powered spinning disks at the top of the resonators produce a vibrato effect by rapidly closing and opening the resonators. Invented *c.* 1920, it soon became a popular jazz instrument.

vibration, Periodic back-and-forth motion of the particles of an elastic body or medium. It is usually a result of the displacement of a body from an equilibrium condition, followed by the body's response to the forces that tend to restore equilibrium. Free vibrations occur when a system is disturbed but immediately allowed to move without restraint, as when a weight suspended by a spring is pulled down and then released. Forced vibrations occur when a system is continuously driven by an external agency, as when a child's swing is pushed on each downswing. Because all systems are subject to friction, they are also subject to damping. In the example of free vibration, damping would cause the amplitudes of the spring's vibrations to diminish until eventually the system came to rest.

vibrio, Any of a group of aquatic, comma-shaped bacteria in the family Vibrionaceae. Some species cause serious diseases in humans and other animals. They are gram-negative, highly capable of movement (with one to three flagella at one end), and do not require oxygen. Their cells are curved rods, single or strung together in S-shapes or spirals. Two species are of significance to humans: one causes cholera, the other acute bacterial diarrhea.

Victoria, orig. ALEXANDRINA VICTORIA (b. May 24, 1819, Kensington Palace, London, Eng.—d. Jan. 22, 1901, Osborne, near Cowes, Isle of Wight), Queen of the United Kingdom of Great Britain and Ireland (1837–1901) and Empress of India (from 1876). The only child of Edward, duke of Kent, she succeeded her uncle, William IV, in 1837. She was first guided as queen by the Whig prime minister Lord Melbourne and then by her husband, Prince Albert, whom she married in 1840. Devoted to him, she accepted his decisions on all issues in the period sometimes called the "Albertine monarchy." They had nine children, through whose marriages descended many of the royal families of Europe. From 1861 Victoria deeply mourned Albert's death and thereafter made royal decisions as she believed he would have advised. She was frequently at odds with Prime Minister William E. Gladstone and welcomed his replacement by Benjamin Disraeli in 1874. Her reign, called the Victorian Age, was marked by a period of British expansion and a restoration of dignity and popularity to the monarchy, as shown by her Jubilees of 1887 and 1897. She remains the longest-reigning monarch in British history.

Victoria, State, southeastern Australia. Area: 87,806 sq mi (227,416 sq km). Population: (2006) 4,932,422; (2009 est.) 5,443,228. Capital: Melbourne. The state's western and northwestern parts are sandy desert and lowland, while the central and eastern parts are highlands forming the southern end of the Australian Alps. The southwestern coastal region is known as Gippsland. The Murray River forms almost the entire boundary between the state and New South Wales. Australian Aboriginal peoples had lived in the region for at least 40,000 years before contact with Europeans. Some 60 years after Capt. James Cook first sighted its coastline (1770), the area was settled by immigrants from Tasmania. European diseases decimated much of the Aboriginal population. Victoria became a separate colony in 1851. In 1901 it became a state of the Commonwealth of Australia. Boosting its economy is a highly productive agricultural hinterland.

Victoria, City (pop., 2001: metro. area, 311,902), capital of British Columbia, Canada. It is located on the southeastern tip of Vancouver Island, overlooking Juan de Fuca Strait. It was founded in 1843 by the Hudson's Bay Co. as a fur-trading post known as Fort Camosun; it was later renamed Fort Victoria to honour the English queen. It was selected as the capital in 1866 when Vancouver Island united with British Columbia. It is now one of the province's largest business centres and a tourist resort and retirement community. A major port, it is the Pacific headquarters of the Canadian navy.

Victoria, Seaport, urban district, administrative centre of Hong Kong special administrative region, China. It lies on the northern shore of Hong Kong Island (pop., 2001: 1,335,469). It has extensive wharves and is connected to the mainland by ferry and by automobile and railway tunnels. It is the chief administrative, commercial, and cultural centre of Hong Kong and is the headquarters for numerous international banks and corporations.

Victoria, Town (pop., 2004 est.: 25,500), capital of the Republic of Seychelles. Located on the northeastern coast of Mahé Island in the Indian Ocean, it is the only port of the archipelago and the only town of any size in Seychelles. It is the country's business and cultural centre.

Victoria, Lake, or VICTORIA NYANZA, Largest lake in Africa and chief reservoir of the Nile River, east-central Africa. The southern half lies in Tanzania, the northern half in Uganda; it borders Kenya in the northeast. With an area of 26,828 sq mi (69,484 sq km), it is the second largest freshwater lake in the world (after Lake Superior in North America). It is about 210 mi (337 km) long, 150 mi (240 km) wide, and up to 270 ft (82 m) deep. Though the Kagera River is its largest tributary, the most important source of water for the lake is rainfall. Its only outlet is the Victoria Nile. John Hanning Speke, searching for the source of the Nile in 1858, was the first European to sight it. He named it for Queen Victoria; the Arabs had called it Ukerewe. Henry Morton Stanley circumnavigated it in 1875. It became a reservoir when the water level was raised after completion of Owen Falls Dam (now the Nalubaale Dam) in 1954.

Victoria Falls, Waterfall, at the border between Zambia and Zimbabwe. Approximately twice as wide and twice as deep as Niagara Falls, the falls span the entire breadth of the Zambezi River at one of its widest points (more than 5,500 ft [1,700 m]). There the river plunges over a precipice, split by islands and promontories, to a drop of 355 ft (108 m). Two national parks, Victoria Falls in Zimbabwe and Mosi-oa-Tunya in Zambia, are adjacent to the falls. Victoria Falls was designated a World Heritage site in 1989. The first European sighting of the falls was in 1855 by David Livingstone, who named them after Queen Victoria.

Victoria Nile, River, Uganda. It forms the upper section of the Nile River. Some 300 mi (480 km) long, it issues from the northern end of Lake Victoria and then flows over the Nalubaale and Kiira dams at Owen Falls, through Lake Kyoga, and over Kabalega Falls (118 ft [36 m]) before entering the northeastern corner of Lake Albert.

Vienna, German WIEN, City (pop., 2007 est.: 1,664,146; metro. area, 1,954,964), capital of Austria, on the Danube River. It was founded by the Celts; it became a Roman military station in the 1st century BCE. Ruled by many—including the Franks in the 6th century CE and the Magyars in the 10th century—Vienna was an important trade centre during the Crusades. It was the seat of the Holy Roman Empire (1558–1806), the Austrian (and Habsburg) Empire (1806–67), and the Austro-Hungarian Empire until 1918. In 1814–15 it was the seat of the Congress of Vienna. The administrative centre of German Austria (1938–45), it was frequently bombed during World War II by the Allies, and the city was taken by Soviet troops in 1945. It was under joint Soviet-Western Allied occupation from 1945 to 1955. The Strategic Arms Limitation Talks (SALT) between the U.S. and Soviet Union took place in Vienna in the 1970s. Vienna is not only the commercial and industrial centre of Austria but also a cultural centre renowned for its architecture and music. It was the birthplace of composers Franz Schubert, Johann Strauss (the Younger), and Arnold Schoenberg and the home of Wolfgang Amadeus Mozart, Ludwig van Beethoven, Johannes Brahms, and Gustav Mahler. It also was the home of Sigmund Freud, Gustav Klimt, Oskar Kokoschka, and Josef Hoffmann. Vienna is the headquarters of many international organizations, including the International Atomic Energy Agency, the UN Industrial Development Organization, and the Organization of Petroleum Exporting Countries (OPEC).

Vienna, Congress of (1814–15) Assembly that reorganized Europe after the Napoleonic Wars. The powers of the Quadruple Alliance had concluded the Treaty of Chaumont just before Napoleon's first abdication and agreed to meet later in Vienna. There they were joined by Bourbon France as a major participant and by Sweden and Portugal; many minor states also sent representatives. The principal negotiators were Klemens, prince von Metternich, representing Francis II (Austria); Alexander I (Russia); Frederick William III and Karl August, prince von Hardenberg (Prussia); Viscount Castlereagh (Britain); and Charles-Maurice de Talleyrand (France). The Congress reduced France to its 1789 borders. A new kingdom of Poland, under Russian sovereignty, was established. To check possible future aggression by France, its neighbours were strengthened: the Kingdom of the Netherlands acquired Belgium, Prussia gained territory along the Rhine River, and the Italian kingdom acquired Genoa. The German states were joined loosely in a new German Confederation, subject to Austria's influence. For its part in the defeat of Napoleon, Britain acquired valuable colonies, including Malta, the Cape of Good Hope, and Ceylon. The Vienna settlement was the most comprehensive treaty that Europe had ever seen, and the configuration of Europe established at the congress lasted for more than 40 years.

Vienna Circle, German WIENER KREIS, Group of philosophers, scientists, and mathematicians formed in the 1920s that met regularly in Vienna to investigate scientific language and scientific method. It formed around Moritz Schlick (1882–1936), who

taught at the University of Vienna; its members included Gustav Bergmann, Philipp Frank, Rudolf Carnap, Kurt Godel, Friedrich Waismann, Otto Neurath, Herbert Feigl, and Victor Kraft. The movement associated with the Circle has been called logical positivism. Its members' work was distinguished by their attention to the form of scientific theories, their formulation of a verifiability principle of meaning, and their espousal of a doctrine of unified science. The group dissolved after the Nazis invaded Austria in 1938.

Vientiane, Laotian VIANGCHAN, City (pop., 2003 est.: city, 194,200; 2005 est.: urban agglom., 702,000), capital of Laos. It is located northeast of the Mekong River. Founded in the late 13th century, it was made the administrative centre of an early Laotian kingdom in the mid-16th century. In 1778 it came under Siamese (Thai) control; in 1828 it was destroyed when the Laotian king revolted against the Siamese. The French made it the capital of their colony on their takeover of the region in the 1890s; it remained the administrative centre after Laos gained independence in 1953. It is the commercial centre of the region and Laos's principal port of entry.

Viet Cong in full VIET NAM CONG SAN (English: "Vietnamese Communists"), Guerrilla force that sought to reunify North and South Vietnam under communist leadership from the late 1950s through 1975. Originally a collection of various groups opposed to the government of South Vietnam's Pres. Ngo Dinh Diem, the Viet Cong became the military arm of the National Liberation Front (1960) and later of the Provisional Revolutionary Government (PRG; 1969). Members were recruited largely from South Vietnam, but they received guidance, weapons, and reinforcements from the north. The Viet Cong's guerrilla war against the South Vietnamese government and its powerful U.S. allies was successful; the U.S. withdrew its troops from Vietnam between 1969 and 1973, and the PRG assumed power in South Vietnam in 1975, following a full-scale invasion. It became part of a National United Front the following year.

Vietnam, officially SOCIALIST REPUBLIC OF VIETNAM, Country, Southeast Asia. Area: 127,882 sq mi (331,212 sq km). Population: (2011 est.) 88,145,000. Capital: Hanoi. The great majority of the population is Vietnamese; minorities include Chinese, Hmong, Thai, Khmer, and Cham. Languages: Vietnamese (official), French, Chinese, English, Khmer. Religions: Buddhism, new religions, traditional beliefs, Christianity. Currency: dong. Vietnam is about 1,025 mi (1,650 km) long, 210–340 mi (340–550 km) wide at its widest parts, and 30 mi (50 km) wide at its narrowest part. Northern Vietnam is mountainous; Fan Si Peak, the country's highest mountain, rises to 10,312 ft (3,143 m). The Red River is the principal river. Southern Vietnam is dominated by the Mekong River delta. A long, relatively narrow coastal plain connects the two major river deltas. The densely forested Annamese Cordillera extends through west-central Vietnam. Northern Vietnam is rich in mineral resources, especially anthracite coal and phosphates. Some petroleum deposits exist off the southern coast. Significant food crops include rice, sugarcane, coffee, tea, and bananas. Food processing and fishing are important industries, as are the manufacture of steel and phosphates. Vietnam is a socialist republic with one legislative house; its head of state is the president, and its head of government is the prime minister.

A distinct Vietnamese group began to emerge *c.* 200 BCE in the independent kingdom of Nam Viet, which was later annexed to China in the 1st century BCE. The Vietnamese were under continuous Chinese control until the 10th century. The southern region was gradually overrun by Vietnamese from the north in the late 15th century. The area was divided into northern and southern dynasties in the early 17th century, and in 1802 these two parts were unified under a single dynasty. Following several years of attempted French colonial expansion in the region, the French captured Saigon (now Ho Chi Minh City) in 1859 and later the rest of the area, controlling it until World War II. The Japanese occupied

Vietnam in 1940–45 and allowed the Vietnamese to declare independence at the end of the war, a move the French opposed. The First Indochina War ensued and lasted until French forces with U.S. financial backing were defeated by the Vietnamese at Dien Bien Phu in 1954; evacuation of French troops followed. After an international conference at Geneva (April–July 1954), Vietnam was partitioned along latitude 17° N, with the northern part under the communist leadership of Ho Chi Minh and the southern part under the U.S.-supported former emperor Bao Dai; the partition was to be temporary, but the reunification elections scheduled for 1956 were never held. An independent South Vietnam (Republic of Vietnam) was declared, while the communists established North Vietnam (Democratic Republic of Vietnam). The activities of North Vietnamese guerrillas and procommunist rebels in South Vietnam led to U.S. intervention and the Vietnam War. A cease-fire agreement was signed in 1973 and U.S. troops withdrawn, but the civil war soon resumed; in 1975 North Vietnam invaded South Vietnam, and the South Vietnamese government collapsed. In 1976 the two Vietnams were united as the Socialist Republic of Vietnam. From the mid-1980s the government enacted a series of economic reforms and began to open up to Asian and Western nations. In 1995 the U.S. officially normalized relations with Vietnam.

Vietnam War (1954–75) Protracted conflict between South Vietnam (with its principal ally, the U.S.) and North Vietnam, in which South Vietnam was fighting to prevent being united with North Vietnam under communist leadership. After the First Indochina War, Vietnam was partitioned to separate the warring parties until free elections could be held in 1956. Ho Chi Minh's popular—and communist-sympathizing—Viet Minh party from the North was expected to win the elections, which the leader in the South, Ngo Dinh Diem, refused to hold. In the war that ensued, fighters trained by North Vietnam (the Viet Cong) fought a guerrilla war against U.S.-supported South Vietnamese forces; North Vietnamese forces later joined the fighting. At the height of U.S. involvement, there were more than half a million U.S. military personnel in Vietnam. The Tet Offensive of 1968, in which the Viet Cong and North Vietnamese attacked 36 of 44 South Vietnamese provincial capitals and 64 district capitals, marked a turning point in the war. Many in the U.S. had come to oppose the war on moral and practical grounds, and Pres. Lyndon B. Johnson decided to shift to a policy of "de-escalation." Peace talks were begun in Paris. Between 1969 and 1973 U.S. troops were withdrawn from Vietnam, but the war was expanded to Cambodia and Laos in 1970. Peace talks, which had reached a stalemate in 1971, started again in 1973, producing a cease-fire agreement. Fighting continued, and there were numerous truce violations. In 1975 the North Vietnamese launched a full-scale invasion of the South. The South surrendered later that year, and in 1976 the country was reunited as the Socialist Republic of Vietnam. More than 3,000,000 people (including 58,000 Americans) died over the course of the war, more than half of them civilians.

Vietnamese language, Mon-Khmer language, the native language of 60–65 million people in Vietnam and a second language for many members of Vietnam's more than 50 minority ethnic groups, with some 2 million speakers outside the country. For much of Vietnam's history, Classical Chinese was the dominant literary language, and Chinese vocabulary gave a Vietnamese pronunciation ("Sino-Vietnamese") remains a significant part of the language's lexicon. By the 13th century Chinese characters were adapted to write native Vietnamese words. In the 17th century Roman Catholic missionaries introduced a system of writing Vietnamese in the Latin alphabet with diacritics distinguishing vowel qualities and tones, a system that was widely adopted only in the 20th century.

Viking, Either of two unmanned U.S. spacecraft launched by NASA in 1975. After nearly yearlong journeys, Vikings 1 and 2 entered orbits around Mars and released landers that touched

Viking 2 lander (foreground) on Mars, photographed by one of the spacecraft's own cameras, 1976.
LaRC/NASA

down on the planet and relayed measurements of properties of its atmosphere and soil, as well as colour photographs of its surface. Experiments designed to detect evidence of living organisms provided no convincing evidence of life on the surface. The orbiters transmitted photographs of large expanses of the Martian surface.

Viking, or NORSEMAN, Member of the Scandinavian seafaring warriors who raided and colonized wide areas of Europe from the 9th to the 11th century. Overpopulation at home, ease of conquest abroad, and their extraordinary capacity as shipbuilders and sailors inspired their adventures. In 865 Vikings conquered East Anglia, Northumbria, and much of Mercia. Wessex under Alfred the Great made a truce in 878 that led to Danish control of much of England. Alfred defeated fresh Viking armies (892–899), and his son continued his reconquest, recovering lands in Mercia and East Anglia by 924; Viking Northumbria fell in 954. Renewed raids in 980 brought England into the empire of Canute, and it remained as such until 1042, when native rule was restored. The Vikings permanently affected English social structure, dialect, and names. In the western seas, Vikings had settled in Iceland by 900, whence they traveled to Greenland and North America. They invaded Ireland in 795, establishing kingdoms at Dublin, Limerick, and Waterford. The Battle of Clontarf (1014) ended the threat of Scandinavian rule. France suffered periodic Viking raids but no domination. In Russia Vikings briefly dominated Novgorod, Kiev, and other centres, but they were quickly absorbed by the Slav population. As traders they made commercial treaties with the Byzantines (912, 945), and they served as mercenaries in Constantinople. Viking activity ended in the 11th century.

Vila, or PORT-VILA, Seaport, capital, and largest town (pop., 2003 est.: 33,987) of Vanuatu, southwestern South Pacific Ocean. Although French in appearance, the town has a multinational population including British, French, and Vietnamese. It served as a base for the U.S. in World War II and subsequently became the commercial centre of Vanuatu.

Villa, Pancho, orig. DOROTEO ARANGO (b. June 5, 1878, Hacienda de Río Grande, San Juan del Río, Mex.—d. June 20, 1923, Parral), Mexican guerrilla leader. He was orphaned at a young age and spent his adolescence as a fugitive, having murdered a landowner in revenge for an assault on his sister. An advocate of radical land reform, he joined Francisco Madero's uprising against Porfirio Díaz. His División del Norte joined forces with Venustiano Carranza to overthrow Victoriano Huerta (1854–1916), but he soon broke with the moderate Carranza and in 1914 was forced to flee with Emiliano Zapata. In 1916, to demonstrate that Carranza did not control the north, he raided a town in New Mexico. A U.S. force led by Gen. John Pershing was sent against him, but his popularity and knowledge of his home territory made him impossible to capture. He was granted a pardon after Carranza's overthrow (1920) but was assassinated three years later.

Vilnius, City (pop., 2004 est.: 553,038), capital of Lithuania. Founded in the 10th century, it became the capital of Lithuania in 1323. It was destroyed in 1377 by the Teutonic Knights but was rebuilt. Vilnius passed to Russia in 1795 and for several centuries was a noted European centre for Jewish learning. It was occupied by the Germans in World Wars I and II and suffered heavy damage. From 1920 to 1939 it was part of Poland; taken by Soviet troops in 1939, it was restored to Lithuania, which the Soviets annexed in 1940. One result of the World War II German occupation was the decimation of the city's Jewish population, which dropped from 80,000 in 1941 to 6,000 in 1945. In 1991 it became the capital of the newly independent Lithuania. An important industrial centre, it also has many historic buildings representing Gothic, Renaissance, and Baroque styles of architecture. The historic centre of Vilnius was designated a UNESCO World Heritage site in 1994.

Vinaya Pitaka, Oldest and smallest division of the Tripitaka. It lays out the 227 rules of monastic life for bhiksus, along with an account of the occasion that led the Buddha to formulate the rule. It varies less from school to school than does the Sutta Pitaka or the Abhidhamma Pitaka. It includes an exposition of the rules, which are divided into classes according to the severity of the punishment for breaking them; texts that deal with such matters as admission to and expulsion from the order; and a classified digest of the rules in the other Vinaya texts.

viola, Stringed instrument, the tenor member of the violin family. In appearance it is almost identical to the violin but slightly larger; its strings are tuned a fifth lower. It is a member of many chamber music ensembles, and the modern orchestra uses 6 to 10 violas. Its tone is darker, warmer, and less powerful than the violin's, and it is rarely employed as a solo instrument. The viola d'amore is an 18th-century instrument with six or seven melody strings, under which are strung several sympathetic strings that resonate in concord with the sounded pitches.

violin, Bowed stringed instrument. The violin is the highest-pitched member of a family of instruments that includes the viola, cello, and double bass. It has a fretless fingerboard, four strings, and a distinctively shaped wooden body whose "waist" permits freedom of bowing. The violin is held on the shoulder and bowed with the right hand. It has a wide range of more than four octaves. It evolved in Italy in the 16th century from the medieval fiddle and other instruments. Its average proportions were settled by the 17th century, but innovations in the 18th–19th centuries increased its tonal power. With its brilliance, agility, and singing tone, the violin has been immensely important in Western art music, and it has the largest and most distinguished repertoire of any stringed instrument. From the mid-17th century it has been the foundation of the symphony orchestra, which today usually includes 20–26 violins, and it is also widely used in chamber music and as a solo instrument. It is played as a folk instrument in many countries, folk violins being often called fiddles.

viper, Any of about 200 species (family Viperidae) of venomous snakes in two subfamilies: Viperinae (Old World vipers of Europe, Asia, and Africa) and Crotalinae (pit vipers). Two long, hollow, venom-injecting fangs attached to the movable bones of the viper's upper jaw can be folded back in the mouth when not in use. Vipers range in length from less than 12 in. (30 cm) to more than 10 ft (3 m). They eat small animals and hunt by striking, then trailing, their prey. Many Old World vipers are terrestrial; a few are arboreal or burrowers. Most bear live young.

Virgil, or VERGIL, orig. PUBLIUS VERGILIUS MARO (b. Oct. 15, 70 BCE, Andes, near Mantua—d. Sept. 21, 19 BCE, Brundisium), Greatest of Roman poets. The well-educated son of a prosperous provincial farmer, Virgil led a quiet life, though he eventually became a member of the circle around Octavian (later Caesar Augustus) and was patronized by Maecenas. His first major work, the 10 pastoral *Eclogues* (42–37), may be read as a prophecy of tranquility, and one has even been read as a prophecy of Christianity. The *Georgics* (37–30) point toward a Golden Age in the form of practical goals: the repopulation of rural lands and the rehabilitation of agriculture. His great epic, the *Aeneid* (begun c. 29, but unfinished at his death), is one of the masterpieces of world literature. A celebration of the founding of Rome by the legendary Aeneas at the request of Augustus, whose consolidation of power in 31–30

unified the Roman world, it also explores the themes of war and the pathos of unrequited love. In later centuries his works were regarded in the Roman Empire as virtually sacred. He was taken up reverently by Christians as well, including Dante, who, in his poem *The Divine Comedy*, made Virgil his guide through hell and purgatory.

Virgin Birth, Fundamental doctrine of orthodox Christianity that Jesus had no natural father but was conceived by Mary through the power of the Holy Spirit. Based on the infancy narratives in the Gospels of Matthew and Luke, the doctrine was universally accepted in the Christian church by the 2nd century. It remains a basic article of belief in Roman Catholicism, Eastern Orthodoxy, most Protestant churches, and Islam. A corollary of its dogma is the doctrine of Mary's perpetual virginity, accepted by the Orthodox and Roman Catholic churches and by some Lutheran and Anglican theologians.

Virgin Islands, British, British overseas territory (pop., 2005 est.: 27,200), West Indies. Part of the Virgin Islands chain, it consists of the islands of Tortola, Anegada, Virgin Gorda, and Jost Van Dyke and 32 smaller, mostly uninhabited islands. The chief town and port is Road Town on Tortola. The majority of British Virgin Islanders are of African or African-European descent. English is the chief language. Religion: Christianity (predominantly Protestant). The islands are generally hilly, and many have lagoons with coral reefs and barrier beaches. Tourism is the mainstay of the economy. The Virgin Islands probably were originally settled by Arawak Indians but were inhabited by Caribs by the time Christopher Columbus visited in 1493. The islands were a haunt for pirates, and Tortola was held by Dutch buccaneers until it was taken by English planters in 1666; it was annexed by the British-administered Leeward Islands in 1672. The British sugar plantations declined after slavery was abolished in the 19th century. The islands were part of the Colony of the Leeward Islands from 1872 until 1956, when the British Virgin Islands became a separate colony. Its status was changed to an overseas territory in 2002.

virginal, or VIRGINALS, Small rectangular harpsichord with a

single set of strings and a single manual. The derivation of its name is uncertain. The virginal's strings run parallel to the keyboard, which occupies only a portion of the longer side. Combination virginals include a smaller portable virginal that can be placed on top of the larger keyboard to create a two-manual instrument. The virginal was particularly popular in 16th–17th-century England, where much music was written for it by William Byrd, Thomas Morley, Thomas Weelkes, and others.

English virginal (with jack rail removed) made by Robert Hatley, London, 1664; in the Benton-Fletcher Collection, the National Trust, Hampstead, London

From the Benton-Fletcher Collection at the National Trust Property, Fenton House, Hampstead, London

Virgo (Latin: "Virgin" or "Maiden"), In astronomy, the constellation lying between Leo and Libra; in astrology, the sixth sign of the zodiac, governing approximately the period August 23–September 22. Its symbol is a maiden carrying a sheaf of wheat. She has been identified with fertility goddesses such as Ishtar or with Persephone.

virion, Entire virus particle, consisting of an outer protein shell (called a capsid) and an inner core of nucleic acid (either RNA or DNA). The core gives the virus infectivity, and the capsid provides specificity (i.e., determines which organisms the virus can infect). In virions whose capsids are further encased by a fatty membrane, the virion can be inactivated by exposure to a solvent such as ether or chloroform. Many virions have capsids with 20 triangular faces and the nucleic acid densely coiled within; others have capsids consisting of surface spikes, with the nucleic acid loosely coiled within. Virions of most plant viruses are rod-shaped.

viroid, Infectious particle that is smaller than any of the known viruses. The particle consists of an extremely small circular RNA molecule that lacks the protein coat of a virus. Viroids appear to be transmitted mechanically from one cell to another through cellular debris. They are of much interest because of their subviral nature and their unknown mode of action. Viroids are agents of certain plant diseases; whether they occur in animal cells is uncertain.

virtual reality, Use of computer modeling and simulation to enable a person to interact with an artificial three-dimensional visual or other sensory environment. A computer-generated environment simulates reality by means of interactive devices that send and receive information and are worn as goggles, headsets, gloves, or body suits. The illusion of being in the created environment (telepresence) is accomplished by motion sensors that pick up the user's movements and adjust his or her view accordingly, usually in real time. The basis of the technology emerged in the 1960s in simulators that taught how to fly planes, drive tanks, shoot artillery, and generally perform in combat. It came of commercial age in the 1980s and is now used in games, exhibits, and aerospace simulators. It has potential for use in many fields, including entertainment, medicine and biotechnology, engineering, design, and marketing.

virtue, Practical dispositions in conformity with standards of excellence or with principles of practical reason. The seven cardinal virtues of the Christian tradition include the four "natural," or cardinal, virtues, those inculcated in the old pagan world that spring from the common endowment of humanity, and the three "theological" virtues, those specifically prescribed in Christianity and arising as special gifts from God. The natural virtues are prudence, temperance, fortitude, and justice; this enumeration, said to go back to Socrates, is found in Plato and Aristotle. To these St. Paul added the theological virtues of faith, hope, and love—virtues which, in Christian teaching, do not originate naturally in humanity but are instead imparted by God through Christ and then practiced by the believer.

Virunga Mountains, Volcanic range, east-central Africa. Located north of Lake Kivu, it extends for about 50 mi (80 km) along the borders of Congo (Kinshasa), Rwanda, and Uganda. Of its eight major volcanic peaks, the highest is Karisimbi, while Nyiragongo is at the western end of the chain; in 1861 John Hanning Speke was the first European to spot them. Parts of the range are in Virunga National Park, Volcanoes National Park (Rwanda), and Gorilla National Park (Uganda).

virus, Microscopic, simple infectious agent that can multiply only in living cells of animals, plants, or bacteria. Viruses are much smaller than bacteria and consist of a single- or double-stranded nucleic acid (DNA or RNA) surrounded by a protein shell called a capsid; some viruses also have an outer envelope composed of lipids and proteins. They vary in shape. The two main classes are RNA viruses and DNA viruses. Outside of a living cell, a virus is an inactive particle, but within an appropriate host cell it becomes active, capable of taking over the cell's metabolic machinery for the production of new virus particles (virions). Some animal viruses produce latent infections, in which the virus persists in a quiet state, becoming periodically active in acute episodes, as in the case of the herpes simplex virus. An animal can respond to a viral infection in various ways, including fever, secretion of interferon, and attack by the immune system. Many human diseases, including influenza, the common cold, and AIDS, as well as many economically important plant and animal diseases, are caused by viruses. Successful vaccines have been developed to combat such viral diseases as measles, mumps, poliomyelitis, smallpox, and rubella. Drug therapy is generally not useful in controlling established viral infections, since drugs that inhibit viral development also inhibit the functions of the host cell.

viscosity, Resistance of a fluid to a change in shape, or movement of neighbouring portions relative to one another. Viscosity denotes opposition to flow. It may also be thought of as internal friction between the molecules. Viscosity is a major factor in determining the forces that must be overcome when fluids are used in lubrication or transported in pipelines. It also determines the liquid flow in spraying, injection molding, and surface coating. The viscosity of liquids decreases rapidly with an increase in temperature, while that of gases increases with an increase in temperature. The SI unit for viscosity is the newton-second per square metre ($N-s/m^2$).

Vishnu, Principal Hindu deity worshiped as the protector and preserver of the world and restorer of dharma. He is known chiefly through his avatars, particularly Rama and Krishna. In theory, he manifests himself anytime he is needed to fight evil, and his appearances are innumerable, but in practice 10 are most common. His various names, numbering about 1,000, are repeated as acts of devotion by his worshipers.

Vishnu on the serpent Shesha, Badami, India.
Frederick M. Asher

Visigoth, Western division of the Goths. Separated from the Ostrogoths (Eastern Goths) in the 4th century AD, the Visigoths were driven from Dacia by the Huns (376) and crossed the Danube into the Roman empire. Oppressed by Roman taxation, they revolted and plundered the Balkan provinces, defeating Valens and his army at the Battle of Adrianople (378). Theodosius I settled them in Moesia (382) to defend the frontier. Converted to Arian Christianity, they left Moesia in 395 under Alaric and invaded Greece and Italy, sacking Rome (410) and settling in southern Gaul and Spain (415). Recalled from Spain by Constantius III, they lost their first king, Theodoric I, in a battle against Attila (451). They were federates of Rome until King Euric declared independence (475). He extended their kingdom from the Loire to the Pyrenees and the lower Rhône, including most of Spain. In 507 they were defeated by the Franks under Clovis; retaining only Septimania (a strip from the Pyrenees to the Rhône), they held it and much of Spain until defeated by the Muslims in 711.

Vistula River, Polish WISŁA, River, the largest in Poland. It rises on the northern slope of the Carpathian Mountains in southwestern Poland, flows in a curve through Warsaw and Torun, then empties into the Baltic Sea at Gdańsk. Most of its 651 mi (1,047 km) are navigable. Its tributaries include the Bug and Dunajec rivers.

vitamin, Organic compound required in small amounts in the diet to maintain normal metabolic functions. The term *vitamine* (1911) was changed to *vitamin* when it was realized that not all vitamins are amines (i.e., not all contain nitrogen). Many vitamins act as or are converted to coenzymes. They neither provide energy nor are incorporated into tissues. Water-soluble vitamins (vitamin B complex, vitamin C) are excreted quickly. Fat-soluble vitamins (vitamin A, vitamin D, vitamin E, and vitamin K) require bile salts for absorption and are stored in the body. The normal functions of many vitamins are known. Deficiency of specific vitamins can lead to diseases (including beriberi, neural tube defect, pernicious anemia, rickets, and scurvy). Excess amounts, especially of fat-soluble vitamins, can also be dangerous: e.g., too much vitamin A causes liver damage, an effect not seen with beta-carotene, which the body converts into vitamin A. Several vitamins are now known to support the immune system. Most vitamins are adequately supplied by a balanced diet, but people with higher requirements may need supplements.

vitiligo, or LEUKODERMA, Skin disorder manifested by smooth, white spots on various parts of the body. Though the pigment-making cells of the skin, or melanocytes, are structurally intact, they have lost the ability to synthesize the pigment. The reason for the condition is unclear. Individuals with vitiligo (about 1% of the adult population) are usually in good general health, but vitiligo presents a cosmetic problem that can be serious in dark-skinned individuals. Normal skin color rarely returns, and there is no known cure.

Vivekananda, orig. NARENDRANATH DATTA (b. Jan. 12, 1863, Calcutta—d. July 4, 1902, Calcutta), Hindu spiritual leader and reformer. He received a Western education. He later joined the Brahmo Samaj and became the most notable disciple of Ramakrishna. By stressing the universal and humanistic aspects of the Veda and emphasizing service over dogma, he attempted to infuse vigour into Hinduism. He was a motivating force behind the Vedānta movement in the U.S. and England, lecturing and proselytizing in both countries. In 1897 he founded the Ramakrishna Mission, which carries out extensive educational and philanthropic work in India and expounds Vedānta in Western countries.

vivisection, Operation on a living animal for experimental rather than healing purposes; more broadly, all experimentation on live animals. It is opposed by many as cruelty and supported by others on the ground that it advances medicine; a middle position is to oppose unnecessarily cruel practices, use alternatives when possible, and restrict experiments to necessary medical research (as opposed, for example, to cosmetics testing). Surgery on animals without anesthesia was once common; many people, most significantly René Descartes, claimed that animals did not really feel pain. The testing of certain chemicals on animals to find the lethal dose still occurs; however, the development of alternative methods (computer simulations, tissue culture tests) has led some funding agencies and research organizations to ban these tests. An anti-vivisection movement in the late 19th century broadened its scope to include prevention of all cruelty to animals and later gave rise to the animal rights movement.

vizier, Arabic WAZĪR, Chief minister of the ʿAbbāsid caliphs and later a high government official in various Muslim countries. The office was originally held and defined by the Barmakids in the 8th century; they acted as the caliph's representative to the public, later serving a similar function for various sultans. In the Ottoman Empire the title could be held by several people at once; under Mehmed II the position of grand vizier, the absolute representative of the sultan, was created.

Vladimir I, Saint, Russian VLADIMIR SVYATOSLAVICH (b. 956, Kiev, Kievan Rus—d. July 15, 1015, Berestova, near Kiev; feast day July 15), Grand prince of Kiev (980–1015). He became prince of Novgorod in 970, and after his father's death in 972 he seized Kiev from his brother. He consolidated the Kievan realm from Ukraine to the Baltic Sea by 980 and fortified its frontiers against Baltic and Eastern nomads. Originally a pagan, Vladimir made a pact (c. 987) with Basil II, providing him with military aid in exchange for marriage to Basil's sister and promising to convert to Christianity. He adopted the Byzantine rite for his realm, forcibly converting Kiev and Novgorod and ordering pagan idols cast into the Dnieper River.

Vladivostok, Seaport city (pop., 2006 est.: 583,673), southeastern Russia, in Asia. Founded in 1860 as a Russian military outpost, it became the main Russian naval base on the Pacific Ocean in 1872. It became a free commercial port about 1900 and grew rapidly as a military base after the Russian Revolution of 1917. During the Soviet era it was the home of the Pacific fleet; its military importance was such that it was closed to foreign shipping from the late 1950s. After the collapse of the U.S.S.R. in 1991, it reemerged as a commercial port, with industries such as ship repair and fish and meat processing. A cultural centre, it is the eastern terminus of the Trans-Siberian Railroad.

Vltava River, German MOLDAU, River, Czech Republic. The Czech Republic's longest river, it flows 270 mi (435 km). The river rises in southwestern Bohemia from two headstreams in the Bohemian Forest. It flows first southeast, then north across Bohemia and empties into the Elbe River.

Vodou, or VOODOO, National folk religion of Haiti. It combines theological and magical elements of African religions and ritual elements of Roman Catholicism. Practitioners profess belief in a supreme God but give more attention to a large number of spirits called the loa, which can be identified as local or African gods, deified ancestors, or Catholic saints. The loa demand ritual service and attach themselves to individuals or families. In turn, they act as helpers, protectors, and guides. In ritual services, a priest or priestess leads devotees in ceremonies involving song, drumming, dance, prayer, food preparation, and animal sacrifice. The loa possess worshipers during services, dispensing advice, performing cures, or displaying special physical feats. A well-known aspect of Vodou is the zombie.

voice, In grammar, the form of a verb indicating the relation between the participants (subject, object) in a narrated event and the event itself. English grammar distinguishes between the active voice ("The hunter killed the bear") and the passive voice ("The bear was killed by the hunter"). In the active voice, the emphasis is on the subject of the active verb (the agent performing the action named), whereas the passive voice indicates that the subject receives the action.

voir dire (Anglo-French: "to speak the truth"), In law, the act or process of questioning prospective jurors to determine whether they are qualified and suitable for service on a jury. The questioning attorneys may dismiss a juror for cause, such as when bias or preconceived notions of guilt or innocence are in evidence; they also have a limited number of peremptory challenges that they can use to dismiss a juror for any or no reason.

volcano, Vent in the crust of the Earth from which molten rock, hot rock fragments, ash, gas, and steam issue. Most volcanoes are found on the boundaries of the enormous plates that make up the Earth's surface. Some of the most violent eruptions take place along convergent boundaries where one plate margin is forced beneath another. The most famous such boundary is the circum-Pacific belt bordering the Pacific Ocean; the island arcs and mountain ranges of this "Ring of Fire" have seen gigantic explosions, among them the eruptions of Mount Pinatubo in the Philippines in 1991, Mount Saint Helens in the U.S. state of Washington in 1980, and Krakatoa (Krakatau) in Indonesia in 1883. Volcanic activity is also common at divergent boundaries, where two plates slowly pull apart and allow molten rock to escape to the surface; the most prominent example is the Mid-Atlantic Ridge, site of volcanic islands such as Iceland, the Azores, Ascension, Saint Helena, and Tristan da Cunha. Yet another type of volcanic activity is found on the island of Hawaii, located on a "hot spot" near the middle of the Pacific Plate where plumes of partially melted rock rise from below the Earth's crust; there the volcanoes Kilauea and Mauna Loa frequently eject streams and fountains of lava. Some of the best-known volcanism takes place around the Mediterranean Sea, where the eruptions of Mount Etna, Vesuvius, the islands of

Stromboli and Vulcano, and other volcanoes have been observed for millennia. Some volcanoes have cultural or religious significance for the peoples around them; these include Misti Volcano in Peru, Mount Fuji in Japan, and Ol Doinyo Lengai in Tanzania.

Volga River, River, western Russia. Europe's longest river and the principal waterway of western Russia, it rises in the Valdai Hills northwest of Moscow and flows 2,193 mi (3,530 km) southeastward to empty into the Caspian Sea. It is used for power production, irrigation, flood control, and transportation. The river has played an important part in the life of the Russian people, and in Russian folklore it is characteristically named "Mother Volga."

Volgograd, formerly (until 1925) TSARITSYN (1925–61) STALIN-GRAD, City (pop., 2006 est.: 999,122), southwestern Russia. Located on the Volga River, it was founded as the fortress of Tsaritsyn in 1589. During the Russian Civil War (1918–20), Joseph Stalin organized the city's defense against the White Russian armies, and it was later renamed in his honour. During World War II it was reduced to rubble in the Battle of Stalingrad; it was rebuilt in the postwar era. Its manufactures include steel and aluminum, engineering products, timber goods, building materials, and foodstuffs. A major railroad junction and river port, it is the eastern terminus of the Volga-Don Ship Canal.

volleyball, Game played by two teams of six players each, in which an inflated ball is volleyed over a high net. Each team tries to make the ball touch the court within the opposing side's playing areas before it can be returned. A team is allowed to touch the ball three times before returning it. The team that first scores 15 points wins the game. Volleyball was invented in 1895 by William G. Morgan in Holyoke, Mass. It soon proved to have wide appeal for both sexes in schools, playgrounds, the armed forces, and other settings. International competition began in 1913, and volleyball became an Olympic sport in 1964. Beach volleyball, a variation with two players on a side, has grown increasingly popular and became an Olympic sport in 1996.

Volta River, River, Ghana, western Africa. The nation's chief river, it flows from Lake Volta and receives the Black Volta and the White Volta rivers. It flows southward through Ghana to the Bight of Benin in the Gulf of Guinea. The river system is 1,000 mi (1,600 km) long.

vomiting, Forcible ejection of the stomach contents from the mouth, usually following nausea. Causes include illness, motion sickness, certain drugs, inner ear disorders, and head injury. Vomiting may occur without nausea (e.g., after extreme exertion). Two centres in the brain's medulla oblongata are believed to control it; the vomiting centre initiates and controls a series of muscle contractions beginning at the small intestine and moving through the stomach and esophagus. This reaction may be set off by the chemoreceptor trigger zone, stimulated by many toxins and drugs, to rid the body of them, or by stimuli from various parts of the body that may be stressed or diseased. Severe vomiting may cause dehydration, malnutrition, or esophageal wall rupture. Vomiting of blood may be a sign of bleeding ulcer or other upper digestive tract disorders.

Vostok, Any of a series of six manned Soviet spacecraft launched from 1961 to 1963. Vostok 1 (1961) carried the first human (Yury A. Gagarin) into space. Vostok 3 set a new time record in space of 94 hours. Vostoks 5 and 6 were launched two days apart and traveled very close together, at times only 3 mi (5 km) apart, setting the stage for future dockings between orbiting vehicles. The first woman in space, Valentina Tereshkova, flew aboard Vostok 6.

vowel, Speech sound in which air from the lungs passes through the mouth with minimal obstruction and without audible friction, like the *i* in *fit*. The word also refers to a letter representing such a sound (*a, e, i, o, u,* and sometimes *y*). In articulatory phonetics, vowels are classified by tongue and lip position; for example, high vowels like the *i* in *machine* and the *u* in *flute* are both pronounced with the tongue arched high in the mouth, but in *u* the lips are also rounded. Single vowel sounds are monophthongs; two vowel sounds pronounced as one syllable, like the *ou* in *round*, are diphthongs.

Voyager, Either of two unmanned U.S. interplanetary probes launched in 1977 to gather information about the Sun's outer planets. Voyager 1 flew by Jupiter in 1979 and reached Saturn in 1980. Voyager 2 traveled more slowly, flying by Jupiter, Saturn, and Uranus to reach Neptune in 1989. Data and photographs from both probes revealed new details about these giant planets, their moons, and their rings. In 1998 Voyager 1 became the most distant human-made object in space (overtaking Pioneer 10). Both Voyagers were expected to remain operable through the first or second decade of the 21st century, periodically transmitting data on the heliopause.

Vulcan, Ancient Roman god of fire. He was the counterpart of the Greek Hephaestus. Vulcan was especially associated with the destructive aspects of fire, such as volcanoes or conflagrations, and for this reason his temples were usually located outside the city. His chief festival, the Volcanalia, was marked by a rite in which the heads of Roman families threw fish into the fire. Often invoked to avert fire, he was addressed with epithets such as Mulciber ("Fire Allayer").

vulcanization, Chemical process, discovered by Charles Goodyear (1839), by which the physical properties of natural or synthetic rubber are improved. It consists principally of heating rubber with sulfur; other substances (accelerators, carbon black, antioxidants, etc.) are also added. The sulfur does not simply dissolve or disperse in the rubber, but rather combines chemically, mostly in the form of cross-links (bridges) between the long-chain molecules; however, the reactions are not fully understood. Vulcanized rubber has higher tensile strength and resistance to swelling and abrasion, and is elastic over a greater range of temperatures.

vulture, A bare-headed, keen-sighted bird of prey in any of 22 species found mainly in warm regions. New World vultures (family Cathartidae, related to storks) are 24–31 in. (60–80 cm) long. Old World vultures (family Accipitridae, related to eagles) include the smallest (20 in. [50 cm] long) and the largest vulture species. The cinereous, or black, vulture (*Aegypius monachus*), one of the largest flying birds, grows to about 40 in. (100 cm) long, weighs almost 30 lb (13 kg), and has a 9-ft (2.7-m) wingspan. Most species eat carrion, garbage, and excrement, but some will occasionally eat a live animal.

vulvitis, Inflammation of the vulva (female external genitalia), with red, swollen, itchy skin that may turn white, crack, or blister. The vulva provides a moist, warm breeding ground for microorganisms, particularly for yeast but also for other fungi, bacteria, or viruses, especially if underwear is tight, nonporous, and nonabsorbent and if hygiene is poor. Pantyhose, synthetic underwear, detergents, vaginal sprays, and deodorants may cause allergy or irritation. Drying and thinning of tissues after menopause makes them more susceptible to irritation and infection. Treatment ranges from wearing loose, absorbent cotton underwear to creams that kill the infective microorganisms.

Wagner, (Wilhelm) Richard (b. May 22, 1813, Leipzig, Ger.—d. Feb. 13, 1883, Venice, Italy), German composer. His childhood was divided between Dresden and Leipzig, where he had his first composition lessons; his teacher refused payment because of his talent. His first opera, *The Fairies* (1834), was followed by *The Ban on Love* (1836); the premiere performance was so unprepared that the event was a fiasco, and he henceforth determined not to settle for modest productions. The success of *Rienzi* (1840) led him to be more adventurous in *The Flying Dutchman* (1843) and even more so in *Tannhäuser* (1845). Caught up in the political turmoil of 1848, he was forced to flee Dresden for Zürich. During this enforced vacation, he wrote influential essays, asserting (following G.W.F. Hegel) that music had reached a limit after Ludwig van Beethoven and that the "artwork of the future" would unite music and theatre in a *Gesamtkunstwerk* ("total artwork"). In 1850 he saw *Lohengrin* produced. He had begun his most ambitious work, *The Ring of the Nibelung*, a four-opera cycle. The need for large-scale unity brought him to the concept of the leitmotiv. He ceased work on the *Ring*'s third opera, *Siegfried*, in the throes of an adulterous love with Mathilde Wesendonk and wrote an opera of forbidden love, *Tristan und Isolde* (1859), which also seemed to break the bonds of tonality. He published the *Ring* librettos in 1863, with a plea for financial support, and Louis II of Bavaria responded, inviting Wagner to complete the work in Munich. From the late 1860s to the early 1880s, Wagner completed work on *Die Meistersinger*, *Siegfried*, *Götterdämmerung*, and the long-deferred *Parsifal*, as he also oversaw the building of the great festival theatre at Bayreuth (1872–76) that would be dedicated to his operas. His astonishing works made Wagner one of the most influential and consequential figures in the history of Western music and, indeed, of Western culture. In the late 20th century his undoubted musical stature was challenged somewhat by the strongly racist and anti-Semitic views expressed in his writings, and evidence of anti-Semitism in his operas was increasingly documented.

Wahhāb, Muḥammad ibn ʿAbd al- (b. 1703, ʿUyaynah, Arabia—d. 1792, Al-Dirʿīyah), Islamic theologian and founder of the Wahhābī movement. Educated in Medina, he spent several years teaching in Iraq and Iran. He reacted against what he perceived as the extremism of various sects of Sufism, setting out his ideas in the *Book of Unity* (1736). He stressed a conservative observation of Islam, rejecting polytheism and condemning reverence of saints and the decoration of mosques. His views were controversial; eventually he settled in Nejd, where, in alliance with Ibn Saʿūd, his teachings found favour and grew dominant.

Wahhābī, Member of a Muslim puritan movement founded in the 18th century by Muḥammad ibn ʿAbd al-Wahhāb. Members call themselves al-Muwaḥḥidūn, a name derived from their emphasis on the absolute oneness of God. They reject all acts implying polytheism, including the veneration of saints, and advocate a return to the original teachings of Islam as found in the Quʾrān and the Ḥadīth. They supported the establishment of a Muslim state based on Islamic canon law. Adopted by the ruling Saudi family in 1744, the movement controlled all of Nejd by the end of the 18th century. It was assured of dominance on the Arabian Peninsula with the creation of the kingdom of Saudi Arabia in 1932, and in the 20th century—supported by Saudi wealth—it engaged in widespread missionary work throughout the Islamic world.

Walcott, Derek (Alton) (b. Jan. 23, 1930, Castries, Saint Lucia), West Indian poet and playwright. Walcott was educated in Saint Lucia and Jamaica, and after 1958 he lived in Trinidad and the U.S. Many of his works explore the Caribbean cultural experience. He is best known for his poetry; in volumes such as *In a Green Night* (1962), *The Gulf* (1969), *The Star-Apple Kingdom* (1979), *The Fortunate Traveller* (1981), *The Bounty* (1997), and *White Egrets* (2010), Walcott's erudition is submerged in sweeping rhythmic and sensuous sonorities. His book-length poems include *Omeros* (1990), a retelling of Homer's *Iliad* and *Odyssey* in a 20th-century Caribbean setting, and *The Prodigal* (2004). *Tiepolo's Hound* (2000) is a poetic biography of West Indian-born French painter Camille Pissarro. Of Walcott's approximately 30 plays, the best-known are *Ti-Jean and His Brothers* (1958), *Dream on Monkey Mountain* (produced 1967), and *Pantomime* (1978). In 1992 he was awarded the Nobel Prize for Literature.

Waldenses, French VAUDOIS, Italian VALDESI, Members of a Christian movement that originated in 12th-century France. Devotees sought to follow the example of Jesus and the Apostles by adopting lives of preaching and poverty. The movement's founder, Valdes, was condemned by the archbishop of Lyon for continuing to preach without church permission. Although placed under a ban in 1184 by Pope Lucius III (1181–85), Valdes remained orthodox and hoped for eventual acceptance by the church. His followers, however, gradually departed from Roman Catholicism by rejecting the clergy's right to administer the sacraments, the notion of purgatory, and the veneration of saints. Rome responded by actively persecuting the Waldenses, and their numbers diminished by the end of the 15th century. In the 16th century they adopted some aspects of Protestant doctrine and the church organization of Genevan Protestantism. Intermittently persecuted in later centuries, they have remained a small movement within Christianity. They survive today in Argentina, Uruguay, and the U.S.

Wales, Welsh CYMRU, Principality, constituting an integral part of the United Kingdom. It occupies a peninsula on the western side of the island of Great Britain. Area: 8,015 sq mi (20,758 sq km). Population (2001): 2,903,085. Capital: Cardiff. The population is of Celtic, Anglo-Saxon, and Anglo-Norman ancestry. Languages: English, Welsh. Religion: Methodism. Wales is almost entirely an upland area the core of which is the Cambrian Mountains. The highest peak in England and Wales, Mount Snowdon, is found in Snowdonia National Park. The Severn, Wye, and Dee are the longest rivers. Economic activities include mining coal (though coal mining suffered a sharp decline in the late 20th century), slate, and lead; importing and refining petroleum; and manufacturing consumer electronics. Tourism is an important industry. In prehistoric times, tribal divisions of the British Celtic speakers who dominated all of Britain south of the Firth of Forth and the Firth of Clyde inhabited the region. The Romans ruled from the 1st century CE until the 4th–5th century. Welsh Celts fought off incursions from the Anglo-Saxons. A number of kingdoms arose there, but none was successful in uniting the area. The Norman conquerors of England brought all of southern Wales under their rule in 1093. English King Edward I conquered northern Wales and made it a principality in 1284. Since 1301 the heir to the English throne has carried the title Prince of Wales. Wales was incorporated with England in the reign of Henry VIII. It became a leading international coal-mining centre during the 19th century. The Plaid Cymru, or Welsh Nationalist Party, was founded in 1925, but its influence did not gather force until the 1960s, when Welsh nationalist aspirations rose. In 1997 a referendum approved the devolution of power to an elected assembly, which first convened in 1999.

Wales, Prince of, Title of the heir apparent to the British throne. In 1301 Edward I of England granted it to his son Edward after conquering Wales and executing the last native Welsh prince (1283). Since that time most of the eldest sons of English sovereigns have been given the title. The title ceases to exist when a Prince of Wales becomes king, until a monarch bestows it on a son.

Walęsa, Lech (b. Sept. 29, 1943, Popowo, near Włocławek, Pol.), Polish labour leader and president of Poland (1990–95). An electrician, he worked in the Lenin Shipyard at Gdańsk, Pol. (1967–76), but he was fired for his antigovernment activities. In 1980 he joined workers in a strike and soon became leader of the Solidarity trade union. The union was banned in 1981, and he was detained into 1982. In 1983 he was awarded the Nobel Prize for Peace; fearing involuntary exile, he remained in Poland while his wife, Danuta, traveled to Norway to accept the prize on his behalf. He continued to direct the outlawed union until it received legal recognition in 1988. Solidarity won an overwhelming victory in free elections in June 1989, and after Walęsa refused to form a coalition government with the communists, the Parliament was forced to accept a Solidarity-led government, though Walęsa himself refused to serve as premier. In 1990 he won Poland's first direct presidential election by a landslide, and he helped guide Poland into a free-market economy. His confrontational style eroded his popularity, and he was narrowly defeated in his bid for reelection in 1995.

Wallis and Futuna, Island group, west-central Pacific Ocean. It is a self-governing overseas collectivity (pop., 2003: 14,944) of France, which includes Uvea (Wallis Island), the Horne (Futuna) Islands (Futuna and Alofi), and a number of islets. The administrative seat is the village of Matâ'utu on Uvea. Until 1961 Wallis and Futuna was a protectorate under French authority attached to New Caledonia.

walrus, Only living species (*Odobenus rosmarus*) of the pinniped family Odobenidae.  Larger than the related seals, walrus males grow up to 12 ft (3.7 m) long and weigh up to 2,800 lbs (1,270 kg). Both sexes have long, downward-pointing tusks that may grow to 3 ft (1 m) long and weigh 12 lbs (5.4 kg) each. They have no external ears. The grayish skin is deeply folded over the shoulders. They live on ice floes, in groups of up to 100, on relatively shallow water in arctic seas of Eurasia and North America. They may dive to great depths in search of food, mostly shellfish. On land and ice, they move on all four limbs. They generally follow the ice line south in winter and north in summer. Traditionally important to native humans as sources of food and clothing, they have also been hunted commercially for centuries, which has resulted in serious depletion of their numbers. Commercial hunting is now generally banned.

Walrus (Odobenus rosmarus).
© Corbis

waltz, Ballroom turning dance evolved from the *Ländler* in the 18th century. It is characterized by a step, slide, and step in 3/4 time. It was highly popular in the 19th and early 20th century. Variations include the rapid, whirling Viennese waltz and the slower, dipping Boston waltz, modified by Vernon and Irene Castle as the hesitation waltz. Many 19th-century composers wrote waltz music, most notably Franz Peter Schubert, Frédéric Chopin, Johannes Brahms, and Johann Strauss.

Wang Hui (b. 1632, Jiangsu province, China—d. 1717), Chinese artist who was the paramount member of the group of Chinese painters known as the Four Wangs (including Wang Shimin, Wang Jian, and Wang Yuanqi). Wang Hui, much like the other Wangs, primarily painted landscapes. In his best works he built up an intense web of rhythmic brushwork, while at the same time maintaining a composition's sense of unity and clarity. His fame reached the court in Beijing, and in 1691–98 he was commissioned to supervise the production of a series of hand scrolls commemorating the Kangxi emperor's tour of the South.

Wang Jingwei, or WANG CHING-WEI (b. May 4, 1883, Sanshui, Guangdong province, China—d. Nov. 10, 1944, Nagoya, Japan), Chinese Nationalist Party figure, later head of the puppet regime established by the Japanese in 1940 to govern their conquests in China. A leading polemicist for Sun Yat-sen's revolutionary party, in 1910 he tried to assassinate the imperial regent and was caught; his courage in the face of execution resulted in his sentence being reduced. He was released the following year, after the republican revolution. In the 1920s he served as a major official in the Nationalist Party. After Sun's death, he chaired the party while Chiang Kai-shek allied with the communists in the Northern Expedition against China's warlords. Chiang and Wang vied for party control; in a compromise in 1932, Wang became president and Chiang headed the military. After war erupted with Japan, Wang flew to Hanoi, Viet., and issued a statement calling on the Chinese to stop resisting. In 1940, in collaboration with the Japanese, he became head of a regime that governed the Japanese-occupied areas centred on Nanjing. Though Wang had hoped to be granted virtual autonomy, the Japanese continued to exercise military and economic dominance. He died while undergoing medical treatment in Japan.

Wang Mang (b. 45 BC, China—d. Oct. 6, AD 23, Chang'an), Founder of the short-lived Xin dynasty (AD 9–25), an interlude between the two halves of the Han dynasty in China. Wang's family was well connected to the Han imperial family, and in 8 BC Wang was appointed regent, only to lose the position when the emperor died. When the new emperor died in 1 BC, Wang was reappointed regent and married his daughter to the subsequent emperor, Ping, who died in AD 6. Wang picked the youngest of more than 50 eligible heirs to follow Ping and was named acting emperor. In AD 9 he ascended the throne and proclaimed the Xin dynasty. His dynasty might have endured had the Huang He (Yellow River) not changed course twice before AD 11, causing massive devastation and attendant famines, epidemics, and social unrest. Peasants banded together in ever larger units. In AD 23 rebel forces set the capital, Chang'an (modern Xi'an), on fire, forced their way into the palace, and killed him.

Wannsee Conference (Jan. 20, 1942) Meeting of Nazi officials in the Berlin suburb of Wannsee to plan the "final solution" to the "Jewish question." It was attended by 15 Nazi senior bureaucrats led by Reinhard Heydrich, head of the SS and Gestapo, and included Adolf Eichmann, chief of Jewish affairs for the Reich Central Security Office. It marked a turning point in Nazi policy toward the Jews. An earlier idea, to deport all of Europe's Jews to Madagascar, was abandoned as impractical in wartime. Instead, the newly planned final solution would entail rounding up all Jews throughout Europe, transporting them eastward, and organizing them into labour gangs. The final protocol of the Wannsee Conference never explicitly mentioned extermination, but, within a few months after the meeting, the first gas chambers were installed at Auschwitz and Treblinka.

war, State of conflict, generally armed, between two or more entities. It is characterized by intentional violence on the part of large bodies of individuals organized and trained for that purpose. On the national level, some wars are fought internally between rival political factions (civil war); others are fought against an external enemy. Wars have been fought in the name of religion, in self-defense, to acquire territory or resources, and to further the political aims of the aggressor state's leadership.

war crime, Any violation of the laws of war, as laid down by international customary law and certain international treaties. At the end of World War II, the part of the London Agreement signed by the U.S., Britain, the Soviet Union, and France established three categories of war crime: conventional war crimes (including murder, ill treatment, or deportation of the civilian population of occupied territories), crimes against peace, and crimes against humanity (political, racial, or religious persecution against any civilian population). The charter also provided for an international military tribunal to try major Axis war criminals. It further stated that a defendant's position as head of state would not free him from accountability, nor would having acted on orders or out of military necessity. German and Japanese war criminals were tried before Allied tribunals in Nürnberg and Tokyo in 1945–46 and 1946–48, respectively, and in the 1990s tribunals were created for the prosecution of war crimes committed in Rwanda and the territory of the former Yugoslavia.

War of 1812, U.S.-British conflict arising from U.S. grievances over oppressive British maritime practices in the Napoleonic Wars. To enforce its blockade of French ports, the British boarded U.S. and other neutral ships to check cargo they suspected was being sent to France and to impress seamen alleged to be British navy deserters. The U.S. reacted by passing legislation such as the Embargo Act (1807); Congress's War Hawks called for expulsion of the British from Canada to ensure frontier security. When the U.S. demanded an end to the interference, Britain refused, and the U.S. declared war on June 18, 1812. Despite early U.S. naval victories, notably the duel between the *Constitution* and the *Guerrière*, Britain maintained its blockade of eastern U.S. ports. A British force burned public buildings in Washington, D.C., including the White House, in retaliation for similar U.S. acts in York (Toronto), Can. The war became increasingly unpopular, especially in New England, where a separatist movement originated at the Hartford Convention. On Dec. 24, 1814, both sides signed the Treaty of Ghent, which essentially restored territories captured by each side. Before news of the treaty reached the U.S., its victory in the Battle of New Orleans led it to later proclaim the war a U.S. victory.

warbler, Any songbird of almost 350 Old World species (family Sylviidae) or about 120 New World species (families Parulidae and Peucedramidae). Old World warblers, found in gardens, woodlands, and marshes, have a slender bill adapted for gleaning insects from foliage. They occur mainly from Europe and Asia to Africa and Australia, but a few (e.g., the gnatcatcher) live in the Americas. They are drab greenish, brownish, or black and 3.5–10 in. (9–26 cm) long.

warrant, In law, authorization in writing empowering a person to perform an act or execute an office. Arrest warrants are necessary (except in certain circumstances) for an arrest to be considered legal. Search warrants entitle the holder to enter and search a property. Both are classes of judicial warrants. To obtain them, a complainant must provide an affidavit setting forth facts sufficient to satisfy the belief that a crime has been committed and that the accused is the guilty party (or, in the case of the search warrant, that the place to be searched will yield the expected evidence). Nonjudicial warrants include tax warrants (which provide the authority to collect taxes) and land warrants (which entitle the holder to a specific tract of public land).

Warsaw, City (pop., 2009 est.: 1,709,781), capital of Poland, on the Vistula River. Founded *c.* 1300, it flourished as a trade centre, came under Polish control in 1526, and became the capital in 1596. During the late 18th century it expanded rapidly, but it was destroyed in 1794 by the Russians. In 1807 it was made the capital of the Duchy of Warsaw by Napoleon. Taken by the Russians in 1813, it was the centre of Polish insurrections in 1830–31 and 1860. It was occupied by the Germans in World War I and again in World War II, when its large Jewish population revolted in the Warsaw Ghetto Uprising (1943). The Warsaw Uprising in 1944 was unsuccessful, and the Germans virtually destroyed the city. Modern Warsaw, rebuilt after the war, now houses government bodies, including the Sejm (parliament); it is also an industrial and educational centre. Among its historic buildings are a 14th-century Gothic cathedral and a medieval castle.

Warsaw Pact, or WARSAW TREATY ORGANIZATION, Military alliance of the Soviet Union, Albania (until 1968), Bulgaria, Czechoslovakia, East Germany, Hungary, Poland, and Romania, formed in 1955 in response to West Germany's entry into NATO. Its terms included a unified military command and the stationing of Soviet troops in the other member states. Warsaw Pact troops were called into action to suppress uprisings in Poland (1956), Hungary (1956), and Czechoslovakia (1968). The alliance was dissolved in 1991 after the collapse of the Soviet bloc, and Soviet troops departed. Several Warsaw Pact members later joined NATO.

wart, or VERRUCA, Well-defined growth on the skin, usually caused by a papillomavirus, which triggers overproduction of epidermal cells. This may lead to a single long-standing wart, profuse local spread (especially in moist areas), or warts in various parts of the body. The most common type is a round bump with a dry, rough surface. Warts are usually painless except in pressure areas, such as the sole of the foot (plantar wart). Genital warts are merely a nuisance unless they become large or numerous enough to interfere with urination, defecation, or childbirth, but some viral strains are associated with cervical cancer. Warts are considered contagious. They may be removed by applying acids, cryotherapy, electrocautery, or surgery; they sometimes disappear spontaneously.

warthog, Large-headed species (*Phacochoerus aethiopicus*) of pig (ungulate family Suidae), inhabiting open and lightly forested areas of Africa. Warthogs, about 30 in. (76 cm) high, are blackish or brown, with a coarse mane from the neck to the midback. The male has two pairs of bumps (warts) on the face. Both sexes have tusks. The tusks on the lower jaw are weapons; those on the upper jaw curve upward and inward in a semicircle, growing to more than 24 in. (60 cm) in some males. The long tufted tail is held high when the animal runs. Warthogs live in groups, feeding on grass and other vegetation.

Warthog (Phacochoerus aethiopicus)
Karl H. Maslowski

Washington, D.C., City (pop., 2008 est.: 591,833), capital of the U.S. It is coextensive with the District of Columbia. Situated at the navigational head of the Potomac River, between Maryland and Virginia, it has an area of 68 sq mi (176 sq km). The site was chosen by George Washington in 1790 as a political compromise that satisfied both Northern and Southern states. Designed by Pierre-Charles L'Enfant, it is one of the few cities in the world planned expressly as a national capital. The federal government occupied it in 1800. British troops burned the city (1814) during the War of 1812. With the annexation of Georgetown in 1871, the city became coterminous with the District of Columbia. Significant buildings include the Capitol, the White House, and the Library of Congress. The Washington Monument, Lincoln Memorial, Jefferson Memorial, and Vietnam Veterans Memorial are among the most famous of the city's hundreds of memorials and statues. The Smithsonian Institution is in Washington, as are numerous other cultural and educational institutions and foreign embassies. The economy is based on national and international political activities, scientific research, and tourism.

Washington, George (b. Feb. 22, 1732, Westmoreland county, Va.—d. Dec. 14, 1799, Mount Vernon, Va., U.S.), American Revolutionary commander-in-chief (1775–83) and first president of the U.S. (1789–97). Born into a wealthy family, he was educated privately. In 1752 he inherited his brother's estate at Mount Vernon, including 18 slaves; their ranks grew to 49 by 1760, though he disapproved of slavery. In the French and Indian War he was commissioned a colonel and sent to the Ohio Territory. After Edward Braddock was killed, Washington became commander of all Virginia forces, entrusted with defending the western frontier (1755–58). He resigned to manage his estate and in 1759 married Martha Dandridge Custis (1731–1802), a widow. He served in the House of Burgesses (1759–74), where he supported the colonists' cause, and later in the Continental Congress (1774–75). In 1775 he was elected to command the Continental Army. In the ensuing American Revolution, he proved a brilliant commander and a stalwart leader, despite several defeats. With the war effectively ended by the capture of Yorktown (1781), he resigned his commission and returned to Mount Vernon (1783). He was a delegate to and presiding officer of the Constitutional Convention (1787) and helped secure ratification of the Constitution in Virginia. When the state electors met to select the first president (1789), Washington was the unanimous choice. He formed a cabinet to balance sectional and political differences but was committed to a strong central government. Elected to a second term, he followed a middle course between the political factions that later became the Federalist Party and the Democratic Party. He proclaimed a policy of neutrality in the war between Britain and France (1793) and sent troops to suppress the Whiskey Rebellion (1794). He declined to serve a third term (thereby setting a 144-year precedent) and retired in 1797 after delivering his "Farewell Address." Known as the "father of his country," he is universally regarded as one of the greatest figures in U.S. history.

Washington Conference, officially INTERNATIONAL CONFERENCE ON NAVAL LIMITATION, Conference held in Washington, D.C. (1921–22), to limit the naval arms race and negotiate Pacific security agreements. Several major and minor treaty agreements were drafted and signed: the Four-Power Pact (signed by Britain, Japan, France, and the U.S.) stipulated mutual consultation regarding any issue in the Pacific and affirmed respect for the Pacific territories of signatory nations. The Five-Power Naval Limitation Treaty (which Italy also signed) imposed proportional limits on the number of warships each signatory nation could maintain and mandated some actual disarmament; it lapsed in 1936 when Japan was refused equality with the U.S. and Britain. Another agreement regulated the use of submarines and outlawed poison gas in warfare. A Nine-Power Pact (with the Netherlands, Portugal, Belgium, and China) affirmed China's sovereignty.

wasp, Any of more than 20,000, usually winged, insect species in the order Hymenoptera. The abdomen is attached to the thorax by a slender petiole, or "waist," and the female's abdomen has a formidable stinger. Most species are solitary; about 1,000 species are highly social; and some may be either social or solitary. Adults feed primarily on nectar. Most solitary wasps nest in tunnels in the ground and feed larvae with paralyzed insects or spiders. The paperlike nest of social wasps (family Vespidae) consists of chewed plant material mixed with saliva and arranged in adjacent hexagonal cells. The female lays one egg in each cell and provisions it with a macerated caterpillar. Successive generations may enlarge the nest and care for the young.

water, Inorganic compound composed of hydrogen and oxygen (H_2O), existing in liquid, gas (steam, water vapour), and solid (ice) states. At room temperature, water is a colourless, odourless, tasteless liquid. One of the most abundant compounds, water covers about 75% of Earth's surface. Life depends on water for virtually every process, its ability to dissolve many other substances being perhaps its most essential quality. Life is believed to have originated in water (the world's oceans or smaller bodies), and living organisms use aqueous solutions (including blood and digestive juices) as mediums for carrying out biological processes. Because water molecules are asymmetric and therefore electric dipoles, hydrogen bonding between molecules in liquid water and in ice is important in holding them together. Many of water's complex and anomalous physical and chemical properties (high melting and boiling points, viscosity, surface tension, greater density in liquid than in solid form) arise from this extensive hydrogen bonding. Water undergoes dissociation to the ions H^+ (or H_3O^+) and OH^-, particularly in the presence of salts and other solutes; it may act as an acid or as a base. Water occurs bound (as water of hydration) in many salts and minerals. It has myriad industrial uses, including as a suspending agent (papermaking, coal slurrying), solvent, diluting agent, coolant, and source of hydrogen; it is used in filtration, washing, steam generation, hydration of lime and cement, textile processing, sulfur mining, hydrolysis, and hydraulics, as well as in beverages and foods.

water buffalo, or INDIAN BUFFALO, Any of three subspecies of oxlike bovid (species *Bubalus bubalis*). Two have been domesticated in Asia since the earliest recorded history. The animal is named for its ability to work on waterlogged land and in humid climates. The largest breeds stand 5–6 ft (1.5–1.8 m), is up to 9 ft (2.8 m) long, and may weigh over 2,000 lb (900 kg). The dull black or dark gray body has little hair. The horns spread outward and upward, measuring up to 7 ft (2 m) across. One subspecies, the swamp buffalo, is the principal draft animal of southern China and South and Southeast Asia. Another, the river buffalo, is used for dairy and meat production and draft work in southern and South Asia and Egypt. The third subspecies is the wild water buffalo, of which only a few dozen herds remain. It is larger than domestic buffaloes and is sometimes referred to as a separate species (*B. arnee*).

water hyacinth, Any of about five species of aquatic plants that

Common water hyacinth (Eichhornia crassipes)
W.H. Hodge

make up the genus *Eichhornia* of the pickerelweed family (Pontederiaceae). They are native mainly to the New World tropics. Some species float in shallow water; others are rooted in muddy streambanks and lakeshores. All have slender rootstocks, feathery roots, rosettes of stalked leaves, and flowers arranged in spikes or clusters. The common water hyacinth (*E. crassipes*) is the most widespread. The leafstalk is spongy and inflated, and the upper lobes of its purple flowers have blue and yellow markings. It reproduces quickly, often clogging slow-flowing streams. It is used as an ornamental in outdoor pools and aquariums.

water lily, Any of the freshwater plants in eight genera that make

Santa Cruz water lily (Victoria cruziana)
Gottlieb Hampfler

up the family Nymphaeaceae, native to temperate and tropical regions. All are perennial except those in the genus *Euryale*. Most have rounded, floating, waxy-coated leaves growing atop long stalks that contain many air spaces. Thick, fleshy, creeping underwater stems are buried in the mud. In some species the leaves are also submerged. Showy, solitary, cuplike flowers with numerous spirally arranged petals are borne at or above the water surface on the long stalks. The genus *Nymphaea* includes the water lilies proper (or water nymphs). The common North

American white water lily, pond lily, or toad lily is *N. odorata*. The lotus of ancient Egyptian art was usually the blue lotus (*N. caerulea*). The largest water lilies are two species that make up the tropical South American genus *Victoria*; the Santa Cruz water lily (*V. cruziana*) has leaves 2–6 ft (60–180 cm) in diameter. Water lilies provide food for fish and wildlife but sometimes cause drainage problems because of their rapid growth. Many varieties have been developed for ornamental use in garden pools and conservatories.

water moccasin, or COTTONMOUTH, Either of two species of pit viper that inhabits marshy lowlands of the southeastern U.S. and Mexico. The U.S. species (*Agkistrodon piscivorus*) is called a cottonmouth because it threatens with the mouth open, showing the white interior. It is up to 5 ft (1.5 m) long and is completely black or brown with darker crossbands. A dangerous snake with a potentially lethal bite, it tends to stand its ground or move slowly away when alarmed. It will eat almost any small animal, including turtles, fishes, and birds.

water polo, Sport played in a swimming pool by teams of seven with a buoyant ball resembling a football (soccer ball). The ball may be carried or thrown, and a point is scored when the ball is placed in the opposing team's goal. The name derives from a mid-19th-century version of the sport in which players rode barrels and struck the ball with sticks. A rough and demanding game, it is played by both men and women. Modern water polo was introduced as an Olympic sport in 1900.

water table, or GROUNDWATER TABLE, Surface of a body of underground water below which the soil or rocks are permanently saturated with water. The water table separates the groundwater zone (zone of saturation) that lies below it from the zone of aeration that lies above it. The water table fluctuates both with the seasons and from year to year because it is affected by climatic variations and by the amount of precipitation used by vegetation. It also is affected by withdrawing excessive amounts of water from wells or by recharging them artificially.

watercolour, Painting made with a pigment ground in gum, usually gum arabic, and applied with brush and water to a surface, usually paper. The pigment is ordinarily transparent but can be made opaque by mixing with a whiting to produce gouache. Transparent watercolour allows for freshness and luminosity. Whereas oil paintings achieve their effects by a building up of colour, watercolours rely on what is left out, with empty, unpainted spaces being an integral part of the work.

watercress, Perennial plant (*Nasturtium officinale*) of the mustard family, native to Eurasia and naturalized throughout North America. It grows submerged, floating on the water, or spread over mud surfaces in cool, flowing streams. White flowers are followed by small, beanlike seedpods. Watercress is often cultivated in tanks for its young shoots, which are used in salads. The delicate, light green, peppery-flavoured leaves are rich in vitamin C. Since watercress grown near cattle and sheep feedlots can become contaminated by feces containing cysts of the liver fluke, agent of the illness fascioliasis (liver rot), regulations specify that commercial watercress beds be protected from such pollution.

waterfall, Area where flowing river water drops abruptly and nearly vertically. A waterfall may also be termed a falls, or, when large volumes of water are involved, a cataract. Waterfalls of small height and less steepness or a series of small falls are called cascades. Still gentler stretches of river that exhibit turbulent flow and white water are called rapids.

Waterford glass, Heavy cut glassware, produced in Waterford, Ire., from the 1720s to the present, characterized by thick walls, deeply incised geometric cutting, and brilliant polish. Characteristic Waterford products include Rococo chandeliers, wall lamps, sconces, bowls, and vases. After *c.* 1770 Waterford glassmakers gradually abandoned the Rococo style in favour of the more restrained Neoclassical style popular in England.

Watergate scandal (1972–74) Political scandal involving illegal activities by Pres. Richard Nixon's administration. In June 1972 five burglars were arrested after breaking into the Democratic Party's national headquarters at the Watergate Hotel complex in Washington, D.C. Within a few days of their arrest at the Watergate, charges of burglary and wiretapping were brought against the five and two others, including a former White House aide and G. Gordon Liddy, general counsel for the Committee to Reelect the President. Nixon and his aides steadfastly denied that anyone in the administration had been involved, despite persistent press reports to the contrary, and in November 1972 Nixon was easily reelected. In January 1973 the trial of the burglars was held before Judge John Sirica; five pleaded guilty and two were convicted by a jury. Sirica's direct questioning of witnesses revealed details of a cover-up by H.R. Haldeman, John D. Ehrlichman, and John W. Dean. They and Attorney General Richard G. Kleindienst resigned in April. The new attorney general, Elliot L. Richardson (1920–98), appointed Archibald Cox (1912–2004) as special prosecutor. A Senate committee under Samuel Ervin held televised hearings in which the existence of tapes of conversations in the president's office was disclosed. Cox and Ervin subpoenaed the tapes, but Nixon refused to relinquish them and ordered Cox fired (Oct. 20, 1973). Richardson resigned in protest, and the public outcry eventually forced Nixon to surrender the tapes (December 8), which revealed clear signs of his involvement in the cover-up. In July 1974 the Judiciary Committee of the House of Representatives passed three articles of impeachment against Nixon. On August 5 Nixon supplied three tapes that clearly implicated him in the cover-up. Though Nixon continued to insist that he had not committed any offenses, he resigned on Aug. 8, 1974. He was pardoned a month later by his successor, Gerald Ford.

Waterloo, Battle of (June 18, 1815) Final defeat of Napoleon and French forces in the Napoleonic Wars. The battle was fought near Waterloo village, south of Brussels, during the Hundred Days of Napoleon's restoration, by Napoleon's 72,000 troops against the duke of Wellington's combined Allied army of 68,000 aided by 45,000 Prussians under Gebhard von Blücher. After the French defeated the Prussians at Ligny and held Wellington at Quatre-Bras in secondary battles on June 16, Napoleon's marshals, including Michel Ney, failed to eliminate either enemy while they were separated. Napoleon delayed his attack at Waterloo until midday, to allow the ground to dry, which enabled Blücher's main force to escape the pursuing French and join Wellington. Four French attacks on the Allied centre failed to break through, and Napoleon had to move troops to meet the Prussian flanking attack. When Ney succeeded in capturing a farmhouse at the centre of the Allied line, his call to Napoleon for reinforcements was refused. Wellington and his forces, though vulnerable after heavy losses, repulsed the final French assault and turned to advance against the French, forcing them into a disorganized retreat. The French suffered 25,000 killed and wounded, and 9,000 were captured; Wellington's casualties were 15,000, and Blücher's were about 8,000. Four days later, Napoleon abdicated for the last time.

watermelon, Succulent fruit of *Citrullus lanatus* (formerly *C. vulgaris*), in the gourd family, native to tropical Africa and cultivated on every continent except Antarctica. The vines spread across the ground with branched tendrils, deeply cut leaves, and light-yellow flowers. Each vine bears 2–15 large, reddish, white, or yellow, sweet, very juicy fruits with flat black seeds. Varieties differ in flesh color, shape, and rind thickness. The rind may be preserved as a pickle.

waterpower, Power produced by a stream of water as it turns a wheel or similar device. The waterwheel, probably invented in the 1st century BC, was widely used throughout the Middle Ages and into modern times for grinding grain, operating bellows for furnaces, and other purposes. The more compact water turbine, which passes water through a series of fixed and rotating blades, was introduced in 1827. Water turbines, used originally for direct mechanical drive for irrigation, now are used almost exclusively to generate hydroelectric power.

waterskiing, Sport of planing and jumping on water skis, broad skilike runners that a rider wears while being towed by a motorboat. The sport originated in the U.S. in the 1920s. International competitions have been held since 1946. Single-ski slalom competition is held on a course consisting of a specified number of buoys around which the skier must negotiate. Jumping competitions employ a ramp; skiers are judged for distance and style. Barefoot and trick skiing are also part of some competitions. A later development in waterskiing, wakeboarding began in the U.S. in the 1980s when surfers began riding their boards as they were pulled behind boats. Since the mid 1990s wakeboarding has been an event at both the Gravity Games and the X Games and has become the fastest-growing water sport worldwide.

Watson, James D(ewey) (b. April 6, 1928, Chicago, Ill., U.S.), U.S. geneticist and biophysicist. He earned his Ph.D. at Indiana University in 1950. Using X-ray diffraction techniques, he began work in Britain with Francis Crick on the problem of DNA structure. In 1952 he determined the structure of the protein coat surrounding the tobacco mosaic virus. In early 1953 he determined that the essential DNA components, four organic bases, must be linked in definite pairs, a discovery that enabled Watson and Crick to formulate a double-helix molecular model for DNA. In 1962 the two scientists and Maurice Wilkins shared the Nobel Prize. Watson's *The Double Helix* (1968), a best-selling personal account of the DNA discovery, aroused controversy. He taught at Harvard University (1955–76) and served as director of the Carnegie Institute's laboratory at Cold Spring Harbor (1968–94).

wave, Propagation of disturbances from place to place in a regular and organized way. Most familiar are surface waves that travel on water, but sound, light, and the motion of subatomic particles all exhibit wavelike properties. In the simplest waves, the disturbance oscillates periodically with a fixed frequency and wavelength. Mechanical waves, such as sound, require a medium through which to travel, while electromagnetic waves do not require a medium and can be propagated through a vacuum. Propagation of a wave through a medium depends on the medium's properties.

wave, In oceanography, a ridge or swell on the surface of a body of water, normally having a forward motion distinct from the motions of the particles that compose it. Ocean waves are fairly regular, with an identifiable wavelength between adjacent crests and with a definite frequency of oscillation. Waves result when a generating force (usually the wind) displaces surface water and a restoring force returns it to its undisturbed position. Surface tension alone is the restoring force for small waves. For large waves, gravity is more important.

wave-particle duality, Principle that subatomic particles possess some wavelike characteristics, and that electromagnetic waves, such as light, possess some particlelike characteristics. In 1905, by demonstrating the photoelectric effect, Albert Einstein showed that light, which until then had been thought of as a form of electromagnetic wave, must also be thought of as localized in packets of discrete energy. In 1924 Louis-Victor Broglie proposed that electrons have wave properties such as wavelength and frequency; their wavelike nature was experimentally established in 1927 by the demonstration of their diffraction. The theory of quantum electrodynamics combines the wave theory and the particle theory of electromagnetic radiation.

wavelength, Distance between corresponding points of two consecutive waves. "Corresponding points" refers to two points or particles that have completed identical fractions of their periodic motion. In transverse waves, wavelength is measured from crest to crest or from trough to trough. In longitudinal waves, it is measured from compression to compression or from rarefaction to rarefaction. Wavelength, λ, is equal to the speed v of a wave in a medium divided by its frequency f, or $\lambda = v/f$.

weak force, or WEAK NUCLEAR FORCE, Fundamental interaction that underlies some forms of radioactivity and certain interactions between subatomic particles. It acts on all elementary particles that have a spin of $1/2$. The particles interact weakly by exchanging particles that have integer spins. These particles have masses about 100 times that of a proton, and it is this relative massiveness that makes the weak force appear weak at low energies. For example, in radioactive decay, the weak force has a strength about 1/100,000 that of the electromagnetic force. However, it is now known that the weak force has intrinsically the same strength as the electromagnetic force, and the two are believed to be only different manifestations of a single electroweak force.

weather, State of the atmosphere at a particular place during a short period of time. It involves day-to-day changes in such atmospheric phenomena as temperature, humidity, precipitation (type and amount), air pressure, wind, and cloud cover. Most weather occurs in the troposphere, but phenomena of the higher regions of the atmosphere, such as jet streams, and geographic features, most notably mountains and large bodies of water, also affect it.

weather forecasting, Prediction of the weather through application of the principles of physics and meteorology. Weather forecasting predicts atmospheric phenomena and changes on the Earth's surface caused by atmospheric conditions (snow and ice cover, storm tides, floods, etc.). Scientific weather forecasting relies on empirical and statistical techniques, such as measurements of temperature, humidity, atmospheric pressure, wind speed and direction, and precipitation, and computer-controlled mathematical models.

weather modification, Deliberate or inadvertent alteration of atmospheric conditions by human activity, sufficient to modify the weather on a local or regional scale. Deliberate alterations include covering plants to keep them warm at night, seeding clouds to induce or augment precipitation, and firing silver-iodide particles into clouds to suppress or mitigate hail and to reduce fog at airports. Inadvertent alterations are the result of industrialization and urbanization, which have added billions of tons of carbon dioxide and other gases to the atmosphere.

weathering, Physical disintegration and chemical decomposition of rocks, minerals, and immature soils at or near the Earth's surface. Physical, chemical, and biological processes induced or modified by wind, water, and climate cause the changes. Weathering is distinguished from erosion in that no transportation of material is involved. A broader application of erosion, however, includes weathering as a component. Weathering is also distinguished from metamorphism, which usually takes place deep in the crust at much higher temperatures and elevated pressures.

Wedgwood ware, English stoneware made by Staffordshire factories originally established by Josiah Wedgwood. Creamware appealed to the middle class because of its high quality, durability, and affordability. Black basaltes (from 1768), unglazed stoneware of fine texture that was ideal for imitating antique and Renaissance objects, appealed to antiquarians. Also in the Neoclassical tradition was jasperware (from 1775), a white, matte, unglazed stoneware that could be stained. White ornaments were applied to the coloured body, achieving the look of an antique

Wedgwood jasperware vase, Staffordshire, England, c. 1785; in the Victoria and Albert Museum, London

Courtesy of the Victoria and Albert Museum, London; photograph, Wilfrid Walter

cameo. With the help of such artists as John Flaxman, Wedgwood copied many antique designs. Production of fine Wedgwood ware continues to the present day.

weight, Gravitational force of attraction on an object, caused by the presence of a massive second object, such as the Earth or Moon. It is a consequence of Isaac Newton's universal law of gravitation, which states that the force of attraction between two objects is proportional to the product of their masses and inversely proportional to the square of the distance between them. For this reason, objects of greater mass weigh more on the surface of the Earth. On the other hand, an object's weight on the Moon is about one-sixth of its weight on Earth, even though its mass remains the same, because the Moon has less mass and a smaller radius than the Earth and therefore exerts less gravitational force. Weight W is the product of an object's mass m and the acceleration of gravity g at the location of the object, or $W = mg$. Since weight is a measure of force rather than mass, the units of weight in the International System of Units are newtons (N). In common usage, weight is measured by the gram in the metric system and by the ounce and pound in the U.S. and British systems.

weight lifting, Sport in which barbells are lifted competitively or as an exercise. The two main events are (1) the snatch, in which the barbell is lifted from the floor to arm's length overhead in a single, continuous motion; and (2) the clean and jerk, in which it is lifted first to the shoulders and then, after a pause, to arm's length overhead. Contestants are divided into 10 body-weight categories ranging from flyweight to superheavyweight. Lifts may range to over 1,000 lbs (455 kg) in the heavyweight divisions. The origins of modern competition are to be found in 18th- and 19th-century strongman contests. The first three Olympic Games (1896, 1900, 1904) included weight lifting, as have all games after 1920.

weights and measures, Standard quantities by which comparisons are made between an object to be measured and a known quantity of the same kind. Weights and measures are fundamental to the sciences, to engineering, building, and other technical matters, and to much everyday activity.

Weimar Republic, Government of Germany 1919–33, so named because the assembly that adopted its constitution met at Weimar in 1919. In its early years, the Weimar Republic was troubled by postwar economic and financial problems and political instability, but it had recovered considerably by the late 1920s. Its major political leaders included presidents Friedrich Ebert (1919–25) and Paul von Hindenburg (1925–34), as well as Gustav Stresemann, who was chancellor (1923) and foreign minister (1923–29). With the Great Depression, its political and economic collapse enabled Adolf Hitler to rise to power and become chancellor (1933), after which he suspended the Weimar constitution.

welding, Technique for joining metallic parts, usually through the application of heat. Discovered in the 1st millennium AD during attempts to manipulate iron into useful shapes, the technique produced a strong, tough blade. Welding traditionally involved interlayering relatively soft and tough iron with high-carbon material, followed by hammer forging. Modern welding processes include gas welding, arc welding, and resistance welding. More recently, electron-beam welding, laser welding, and several solid-phase processes such as diffusion bonding, friction welding, and ultrasonic joining have been developed.

Welf dynasty, Dynasty of German nobles and rulers. They descended from Count Welf of Bavaria (early 9th century), whose daughters married Louis I the Pious and Louis the German. The Welfs were linked to the House of Este in the 11th century. They supported the papal party against Emperor Henry IV and were rivals of the Hohenstaufens in central Europe and in Italy (where their name was Guelpho; *see* Guelphs and Ghibellines). As part of the House of Hanover, they became rulers of Britain.

welfare, or SOCIAL WELFARE, Any of a variety of governmental programs that provide assistance to those in need. Programs include pensions, disability and unemployment insurance, family allowances, survivor benefits, and national health insurance. The earliest modern welfare laws were enacted in Germany in the 1880s, and by the 1920s and '30s most Western countries had adopted similar programs. Most industrialized countries require firms to insure workers for disability so that they have income if they are injured, whether temporarily or permanently. For disability from illness unrelated to occupational injury, most industrial states pay a short-term benefit followed by a long-term pension. Many countries pay a family allowance to reduce the poverty of large families or to increase the birth rate. Survivor benefits, provided for widows below pension age who are left with a dependent child, vary considerably among nations and generally cease if the woman remarries. Among the world's wealthy countries, only the U.S. fails to provide national health insurance other than for the aged and the poor.

welfare state, Concept of government in which the state plays a key role in protecting and promoting the economic and social well-being of its citizens. It is based on the principles of equality of opportunity, equitable distribution of wealth, and public responsibility for those who lack the minimal provisions for a good life. The term may be applied to a variety of forms of economic and social organization. A basic feature of the welfare state is social insurance, intended to provide benefits during periods of greatest need (e.g., old age, illness, unemployment). The welfare state also usually includes public provision of education, health services, and housing. Such provisions are less extensive in the U.S. than in many European countries, where comprehensive health coverage and state-subsidized university-level education have been common. In countries with centrally planned economies, the welfare state also covers employment and administration of consumer prices. Most nations have instituted at least some of the measures associated with the welfare state; Britain adopted comprehensive social insurance in 1948, and in the U.S., social-legislation programs such as the New Deal and the Fair Deal were based on welfare-state principles. Scandinavian countries provide state aid for the individual in almost all phases of life.

Wellington, City (pop., 2006: city, 178,500; urban agglom., 397,714), port, and capital of New Zealand. It is located at the southern shore of the North Island, on Port Nicholson. Founded in 1840, it became a municipality in 1853. In 1865 the capital was transferred there from Auckland. It is the financial, commercial, and transportation centre of New Zealand. Wellington produces transportation equipment, machinery, metal products, textiles, and printed materials. It is the site of the major government buildings and the headquarters of many cultural, scientific, and agricultural organizations.

Wen Jiabao (b. Sept. 1942, Tianjin, China), Premier of China (from 2003). While studying at the Beijing Institute of Geology, Wen joined the Chinese Communist Party (CCP). In 1985 he was named deputy director of the General Office of the CCP Central Committee and the following year became director. While at the General Office, Wen also served as chief of staff to several general secretaries of the CCP, including Zhao Ziyang. The two men faced criticism after visiting Beijing's Tiananmen Square during demonstrations there in 1989. Although Zhao was placed under house arrest, Wen escaped any lasting political damage. In 1993 he became a full member of the Secretariat of the CCP Central Committee and four years later a member of the Political Bureau. In 1998 he was appointed one of China's four vice-premiers. Aided by his experience in shaping agricultural policy, Wen succeeded Zhu Rongji as premier in 2003.

werewolf, In European folklore, a man who changes into a wolf

Lon Chaney, Jr., as a werewolf in The Wolf Man *(1941).*
Courtesy of Universal Pictures; photograph, Lincoln Center Library of the Performing Arts, New York Public Library

at night and devours animals, people, or corpses, returning to human form by day. Some werewolves are thought to change shape at will; others, who inherited the condition or acquired it by being bitten by a werewolf, are transformed involuntarily under the influence of a full moon. Belief in werewolves is found throughout the world and was especially common in 16th-century France. Humans who believe they are wolves suffer from a mental disorder called lycanthropy.

West Bank, Area (pop., 2009 est.: 2,733,000 [including 305,000 Israeli Jews]), west of the Jordan River and east of Jerusalem. Covering an area of about 2,278 sq mi (5,900 sq km), excluding east Jerusalem, the territory is also known within Israel by its biblical names, Judaea and Samaria. It is a region with deep history, forming the heart of historic Palestine. Populated areas include Nāblus, Hebron, Bethlehem, and Jericho. Under a 1947 UN agreement, most of what is now the West Bank was to become part of a Palestinian state. When the State of Israel was formed, the Arabs attacked Israel, and the partition plan was never adopted. Following a truce, Jordan remained in control of the area and annexed it in 1950. Israel subsequently occupied it during the Six-Day War of 1967. During the 1970s and '80s Israel established settlements there, provoking resentment among the Arab population and protest from the international community. Arab uprisings began in 1987 in the Gaza Strip and spread to the West Bank. Jordan relinquished its claims in 1988, and the Palestine Liberation Organization (PLO) assumed power. Secret meetings between the PLO and Israel in 1993 led to an end of violence and an agreement granting Palestinian self-rule in parts of the West Bank and Gaza Strip. Further negotiations to resolve outstanding issues proceeded intermittently in the 1990s but broke down amid renewed violence in late 2000. In 2007, clashes between leading Palestinian parties Ḥamās and Fatah and the failure of a coalition government led to Ḥamās's taking control of the Gaza Strip and a Fatah-led emergency cabinet taking control of the West Bank.

West Bengal, State (pop., 2011 prelim.: 91,347,736), eastern India. It is bordered by the countries of Nepal, Bhutan, and Bangladesh and the states of Orissa, Jharkhand, Bihar, Sikkim, and Assam and has an area of 34,267 sq mi (88,752 sq km); the capital is Kolkata (Calcutta). It encompasses two broad natural regions, the Gangetic Plain in the south and the sub-Himalayan and Himalayan area in the north. From the 3rd century BCE the broader region of Bengal formed part of Ashoka's empire. In the 4th century CE it was absorbed into the Gupta empire. From the 13th century it was under Muslim rule until it came under the British in the 18th cen-

Workers picking tea leaves near Darjiling, West Bengal, India.
Gerald Cubitt

tury. At Indian independence in 1947, Bengal was partitioned, the eastern sector becoming East Pakistan (later Bangladesh) and the western sector becoming India's West Bengal. Agriculture is the main economic activity in the state. It is noted for its artistic endeavours, including filmmaking.

West Indies, Islands, enclosing the Caribbean Sea. Lying between southeastern North America and northern South America, they may be divided into the following groups: the Greater Antilles, including Cuba, Jamaica, Hispaniola (Haiti and the Dominican Republic), and Puerto Rico; the Lesser Antilles, including the Virgin Islands, Windward Islands, Leeward Islands, Barbados, and the islands in the southern Caribbean Sea north of Venezuela (generally considered to include Trinidad and Tobago); and the Bahamas. Although physiographically not a part of the West Indies, Bermuda is often included.

West Nile virus, Virus, belonging to the family Flaviviridae, that can cause encephalitis (inflammation of the brain). West Nile is predominantly a fatal infection of birds but can be transmitted to humans by mosquitoes. Most human infections are inapparent or mild, causing a flu-like illness that lasts only a few days. A minority develop encephalitis, characterized by headache, fever, neck stiffness, and muscle weakness, that has proved fatal in some cases. There is no cure. In severe cases, intensive medical care, involving intravenous fluids and respiratory support, is necessary. The virus was originally confined to Africa, the Middle East, and Southeast Asia but has spread to Europe and North America.

western, Genre of novels and short stories, motion pictures, and television and radio shows set in the American West, usually during 1850–1900, when the area was opened to white settlement. Though basically an American creation, it has counterparts in the gaucho literature of Argentina and in tales of the settlement of the Australian Outback. Conflicts between white pioneers and Native Americans and between cattle ranchers and fence-building farmers form two basic themes. Cowboys, the town sheriff, and the U.S. marshal are staple figures, and lawlessness and gun violence are standard. Owen Wister's *The Virginian* (1902) is regarded as the seminal western novel; the popularity of the genre peaked in the early and middle decades of the 20th century and declined somewhat thereafter.

Western Australia, State, western Australia. Area: 976,790 sq mi (2,529,875 sq km). Population: (2006) 1,959,088; (2010 est.) 2,293,510. Capital: Perth. It constitutes one-third of the continent's area but has only about one-tenth of Australia's population. The extensive interior region has three deserts: Great Sandy, Gibson, and Great Victoria. The coast along the Timor Sea and Indian Ocean has only a few good harbours; notable inlets are Joseph Bonaparte and Exmouth gulfs. Australian Aboriginal peoples have occupied Western Australia for about 40,000 years. The western coast was first visited in 1616 by the Dutch. It was later explored by Englishman William Dampier in 1688 and 1699. In 1829 Capt. James Stirling led the first group of settlers there to establish Australia's first nonconvict colony. The discovery of gold in 1886 prompted a movement for constitutional autonomy, which was granted in 1890. In 1900 it was the last state to ratify the newly constituted Commonwealth of Australia. Initially it suffered from slow growth, but since 1960 its economy, fueled by agriculture and mining (notably of fossil fuels), has been expanding.

Western Dvina River, Russian ZAPADNAYA DVINA, Latvian DAUGAVA, River, north-central Europe. It rises in Russia's Valdai Hills and flows 632 mi (1,020 km) in a great arc south through Russia and into Belarus and then northwest across Latvia. It discharges into the Gulf of Riga on the Baltic Sea. An important water route since early times, connected in its upper reaches by easy portages to the Dnieper, Volga, and Lovat-Volkhov river systems, it constituted part of the great trade route from the Baltic region to Byzantium and to the Arabic east. Rapids and the presence of dams have restricted navigation on it.

Western European Union (WEU), Association of 10 European countries to coordinate matters of European security and defense. The WEU was formed in 1955 as an outgrowth of the Brussels Treaty of 1948. Composed of Belgium, France, Germany, Greece, Italy, Luxembourg, the Netherlands, Portugal, Spain, and Britain, it works in cooperation with NATO and the European Union and is administered by a council of the foreign affairs and defense ministers of the member countries. There are also several associate members, observers, and associate partners. It is headquartered in Brussels.

Western Hemisphere, Part of Earth comprising North and South America and the surrounding waters. Longitudes 20° W and 160° E are often considered its boundaries.

Western Indian bronze, Style of metal sculpture that flourished in India from the 6th to the 12th century and later, mainly in the area of modern Gujarat and Rajasthan states. Most of the bronzes are associated with Jainism; they include representations of saviour figures and ritual objects such as incense burners and lamp bearers. Most are small, as they were intended for private worship. They were made by lost-wax casting, and the eyes and ornaments are frequently inlaid with silver and gold.

Rsabhanatha, Western Indian bronze from Chahardi, western Khandesh, Maharashtra state, 9th century AD; in a private collection.
P. Chandra

Western Sahara, formerly SPANISH SAHARA, Territory, northwestern Africa. Area: 97,344 sq mi (252,120 sq km). Population: (2011 est.) 507,000. Capital: Laayoune. Little is known of the area's prehistory, though rock engravings in southern locations suggest a succession of nomadic groups. In the 4th century BCE there was trade across the Mediterranean Sea between the region and Europe, but there was little European contact afterward, until the 19th century. In 1884 Spain claimed a protectorate over the Río de Oro region. Boundary agreements with France were concluded in 1900 and 1912. Spain formally united the area's northern and southern parts into the overseas province of the Spanish Sahara in 1958. The Polisario Front, a Saharawi separatist group formed in 1973, led an insurgency against Spanish colonial rule. In 1976 Spain relinquished its claim; the region then was divided between Mauritania and Morocco. That same year, the Polisario Front declared a government-in-exile, the Saharan Arab Democratic Republic. Sporadic fighting between Moroccan and Mauritanian forces and the Polisario Front began in the mid-1970s. Although Mauritania relinquished its claim in 1979, Morocco promptly annexed their portion. Despite a 1991 cease-fire and a number of United Nations-sponsored talks between the Polisario Front and the Moroccan government, at the beginning of the 21st century the issue of Western Sahara's status remained unresolved. Western Sahara has vast phosphate deposits and some potash and iron ore.

Western Wall, or WAILING WALL, Place of prayer in the Old City of Jerusalem sacred to the Jewish people. It is the only remnant of the Second Temple of Jerusalem. Because it now forms part of a larger area—known as the Temple Mount by Jews and as al-Ḥaram al-Sharīf by Muslims—surrounding the Muslim Dome of the Rock and al-Aqṣā Mosque, the two groups have often vied for control of it. When Israel captured the Old City in the Six-Day War (1967), the Jews once more gained authority over the site.

Westminster, Statute of (1931) Parliamentary statute that effected the equality of Britain and the then-dominions of Canada, Australia, New Zealand, South Africa, Ireland, and Newfoundland. It confirmed declarations made at British imperial conferences in 1926 and 1930 that the self-governing dominions were to be regarded as "autonomous communities within the British Empire." United in their allegiance to the crown, the countries individually controlled their own domestic and foreign affairs as equal members of the British Commonwealth of Nations.

Westminster Abbey, Church in London. It was originally a Benedictine monastery. Edward the Confessor built a Norman-style church (consecrated 1065) on the site of an older church there; this was pulled down in 1245 by Henry III (except for the nave) and replaced with the present Gothic-style abbey church. The rebuilding of the nave was begun by 1376 and continued intermittently until Tudor times. The chapel of Henry VII (begun *c.* 1503) is noted for its exquisite fan vaulting. Elizabeth I refounded the church as the Collegiate Church of St. Peter in Westminster (1560). The western towers (1745), by Nicholas Hawksmoor and John James, were the last addition. Every British sovereign since William the Conqueror has been crowned in the abbey except Edward V and Edward VIII. Many are also buried there, and it is crowded with the tombs and memorials to other famous Britons. Part of the southern transept is known as the Poets' Corner, while the northern transept has memorials to statesmen.

Westphalia, Peace of (1648) European settlements that ended the Thirty Years' War, negotiated in the Westphalian towns of Münster and Osnabrück. The deliberations began in 1644 and ended in 1648 with two assemblies that produced the treaty between Spain and the Dutch (signed January 30) and another between Emperor Ferdinand III, the other German princes, France, and Sweden (signed October 24). Territorial changes gave Sweden control of the Baltic Sea, ensured France a firm frontier west of the Rhine River, and provided their allies with additional lands. Independence was confirmed for the United Provinces of the Netherlands and for the Swiss Confederation. The treaties also confirmed the Peace of Augsburg and extended the religious toleration of Lutherans to include toleration of the Reformed (Calvinist) Church. The Holy Roman Empire was forced to recognize its German princes as absolute sovereigns in their own dominions, which greatly weakened its central authority.

whale, Any of dozens of species of exclusively aquatic mammals found in oceans, seas, rivers, and estuaries worldwide but especially numerous in the Antarctic Ocean. Whales are commonly distinguished from the smaller porpoises and dolphins and sometimes from narwhals, but they are all cetaceans.

whaling, Hunting of whales for food, oil, or both. Whaling dates to prehistoric times, when Arctic peoples used stone tools to hunt whales. They used the entire animal, a feat not accomplished by Western commercial whalers until the advent of floating factories in the 20th century. The Basque were the first Europeans to hunt whales commercially; when seaworthy oceangoing vessels began to be made, they took to the open seas (14th–16th century). They were followed by the Dutch and the Germans in the 17th century and the British and their colonists in the 18th century. In 1712 the first sperm whale was killed; its oil proved more valuable than that of the right whale, which had hitherto been the object of whaling ventures. Whaling expeditions in pursuit of the free-ranging sperm whale could last for four years. The discovery of petroleum (1859), overfishing, the use of vegetable oil, and the substitution of steel for whalebones in corsets led to a steep decline in whaling in the later 19th century, but Norwegian innovations made hunting the hitherto "wrong" whales (rorquals, including the blue whale and the sei whale; so called because they sank when killed) commercially feasible, and the number of whales killed rose from under 2,000 to over 20,000 between 1900 and 1911. The Norwegians and the British dominated whaling into the mid 20th century, when overfishing again made it unprofitable for most nations, though not Japan and the Soviet Union, which became the chief whaling nations. Concern over the near extinction of many species led to the establishment in 1946 of the International Whaling Commission. Commercial whaling was prohibited altogether in 1986, but several nations refused to comply. At the beginning of the 21st century, Norway and Japan continued to hunt hundreds of nonendangered whales annually.

wheel, Circular frame of hard material capable of turning on an axle. Wheels may be solid, partly solid, or spoked. The oldest known wheel was a wooden disk of planks held together by crosspieces. A pottery wheel or turntable was developed *c.* 3500 BC in Mesopotamia. The spoked wheel appeared *c.* 2000 BC on chariots in Asia Minor. Later developments included iron hubs that turned on greased axles. Perhaps the most important invention in human history, the wheel was essential to developing civilizations, and has remained essential to power generation, transportation, industrial manufacturing, and countless other applications.

whiskey, or WHISKY, Any of several distilled liquors made from a fermented mash of cereal grains. Whiskeys are distinctive because of differences in raw materials and production methods. All are aged in wooden containers. The earliest direct account of whiskey making is found in Scottish records from 1494. Scotch whisky (this spelling is also used by Canadians) is usually somewhat light in body, with a distinctive smoky malt flavour; it is made primarily from malted barley that has been heated over a peat fire, fermented, distilled, and blended with similar whiskies made by different distillers. Irish whiskeys, lighter-bodied and lacking any smoky flavor, are not malt-fired and may be mixed with neutral grain spirits. Canadian whisky, light in colour and flavour, is a blend of highly flavoured and neutral grain whiskies. In the U.S., the largest producer and consumer of whiskey, both straight (at least 51% single-mash) and blended whiskeys are produced, derived from both sour and sweet mashes. (Sour mashes are fermented with both fresh and previously fermented yeast; sweet mashes employ only fresh yeast.) Bourbon, first produced in Bourbon Co., Ky., is a full-bodied unblended whiskey derived from a sour mash of corn grain. Whiskeys are consumed both unmixed and in cocktails, punches, and other beverages.

White, Patrick (Victor Martindale) (b. May 28, 1912, London, Eng.—d. Sept. 30, 1990, Sydney, N.S.W., Austrl.), Australian writer. As a youth White moved between Australia and England, where he attended Cambridge University. After serving in the Royal Air Force during World War II, he returned to Australia, which he saw as a country in a volatile process of growth and self-definition. His somewhat misanthropic novels often explore the possibilities of savagery in that context; they include *The Tree of Man* (1955), *Voss* (1957), *Riders in the Chariot* (1961), and *The Twyborn Affair* (1979). His other works include plays and short stories, the latter collected in *The Burnt Ones* (1964) and *The Cockatoos* (1974). He was awarded the Nobel Prize for Literature in 1973.

white dwarf star, Any of a class of small, faint stars representing the end point of the evolution of stars without enough mass to become neutron stars or black holes. Named for the white colour of the first ones discovered, they actually occur in a variety of colours depending on their temperature. They are extremely dense, typically containing the mass of the Sun within the volume of the Earth. White dwarfs have exhausted all their nuclear fuel and cannot produce heat by nuclear fusion to counteract their own gravity, which compresses the electrons and nuclei of their atoms until they prevent further gravitational contraction. When a white dwarf's reservoir of thermal energy is exhausted (after several billion years), it stops radiating and becomes a cold, inert stellar remnant, sometimes called a black dwarf. White dwarf stars are predicted to have an upper mass limit, known as the Chandrasekhar limit, of about 1.4 times the Sun's mass. Dying stars that are more massive undergo a supernova explosion. As members of binary stars, white dwarf stars play an essential role in the outbursts of novas.

White House, Official residence of the U.S. president, in Washington, D.C. It has been the home of every president since John Adams. In 1791 James Hoban (1762–1831) won the commission to build the presidential residence with his plan for a Georgian mansion in the style of Andrea Palladio. The structure, to be built of gray sandstone, was to have more than 100 rooms. The British burned it in 1814, but it was rebuilt and enlarged under Hoban's direction. In the 1820s, Hoban added eastern and western terraces as well as a semicircular southern portico and a colonnaded northern portico. The later addition of the West Wing (1902) and East Wing (1942) provided additional office space. Theodore Roosevelt adopted "White House" as the building's official name in 1902. Its public areas are toured by about 1.5 million people every year.

White Sea, Sea, extension of the Arctic Ocean, northwestern Russia. Almost landlocked, it is connected to the more northerly Barents Sea by a long, narrow strait known as the Gorlo. It covers an area of approximately 35,000 sq mi (90,000 sq km) and has a maximum depth of 1,115 ft (340 m). Rivers, including the Northern Dvina and Onega, flow into it. An important transportation route, it remains navigable year-round with the help of icebreakers in winter. Arkhangelsk is one of the principal ports.

white-tailed deer, or VIRGINIA DEER, Common reddish brown  deer (*Odocoileus virginianus*), an important game animal found alone or in small groups from southern Canada to South America. The tail, white on the underside, is held aloft when the deer is alarmed or running. The male has forwardly curved antlers with several unbranched tines. Northern white-tailed deer grow up to 3.5 ft (107 cm) tall and weigh up to 400 lbs (180 kg). The white-tailed deer lives in open woodlands (young and cutover forests) and on the fringes of urban areas and farmlands, and eats leaves, twigs, fruits, nuts, lichen, and fungi.

White-tailed deer buck (Odocoileus virginianus)
Karl H. Maslowski

Whitney, Eli (b. Dec. 8, 1765, Westboro, Mass., U.S.—d. Jan. 8, 1825, New Haven, Conn.), U.S. inventor, engineer, and manufacturer. He is best remembered as the inventor of the cotton gin (1793), which led to greatly increased production of the short-staple cotton grown in much of the South, making the region prosperous. The most important innovation credited to Whitney may be the concept of mass production of interchangeable parts. His idea of manufacturing quantities of identical parts for assembly into muskets, after undertaking in 1797 to supply the U.S. government with 10,000 muskets in two years, helped inaugurate the vastly important American System of manufacture.

whooping cough, or PERTUSSIS, Acute, very contagious childhood disease, typically with bouts of coughing followed by a long, loud inhalation (whoop) and ending with mucus expulsion and often vomiting. Caused by the bacterium *Bordetella pertussis*, it initially resembles a cold with a short dry cough. Within one or two weeks, coughing bouts begin; this phase usually lasts four to six weeks. Serious complications include bronchopneumonia (pneumonia involving the bronchi), asphyxia, seizures, and signs of brain damage. Treatment is with antibiotics. The pertussis vaccine is usually combined with tetanus and diphtheria toxoids as part of routine childhood immunizations.

whooping crane, Migratory North American bird (*Grus americana*) and one of the world's rarest birds, on the verge of extinction. The tallest North American bird, it is almost 5 ft (150 cm) tall and has a wingspread of about 7 ft (210 cm). It is white with black-tipped wings, black legs, and a bare red face and crown. Its shrill, whooping call can be heard for 2 miles (3 km). Almost exterminated in the early 20th century, it became the object of intensive conservation efforts; by century's end there were still fewer than 300 wild and captive individuals.

*Whooping crane (*Grus americana*).*
H. William Belknap

Wicca, Modern Western witchcraft movement. Some practitioners consider Wicca the religion of pre-Christian Europe, forced underground by the Christian church. That thesis is not accepted by historians, and modern Wicca is usually dated to the work of Gerald B. Gardner (1884–1964) and Doreen Valiente (1922–1999), who, after the repeal of the last Witchcraft Act in England (1951), went public with their cult of witchcraft, which centered on a horned god of fertility and a great earth goddess. Gardner is credited with introducing the term Wicca. So-called "Dianic" Wicca focuses on the Goddess as the supreme being and usually excludes men. Wiccans share a belief in the importance of the feminine principle, a deep respect for nature, and a pantheistic and polytheistic worldview. They practice some form of ritual magic, almost always considered good or constructive. Some are solitary practitioners; others belong to covens.

Wiesbaden, City (pop., 2002 est.: 271,276), capital of Hesse, southern Germany. It is situated on the Rhine River. The Romans fortified it in the 1st century AD; it has been noted since then for its hot saline springs. Made an imperial city in 1241, it passed to the counts of Nassau in 1255. It was capital of the duchy of Nassau from 1806 to 1866, when it passed to Prussia. After World War I it was the seat of the Rhineland Commission under French and British occupation (1918–29). In 1946 Wiesbaden became the capital of the newly created state of Hesse. It was particularly noted for its spa in the 18th and 19th centuries, when it was frequented by Johann W. von Goethe, Johannes Brahms, and Fyodor Dostoyevsky. It continues to be a popular resort. It has printing firms, publishing houses, and film studios, and it is noted for its *Sekt* (sparkling wine).

Wiesel, Elie, orig. ELIEZER WIESEL (b. Sept. 30, 1928, Sighet, Rom.), Romanian-born U.S. novelist. Living in a small Hasidic community, Wiesel and his family were deported in 1944 to Auschwitz and then to Buchenwald; his parents and sister were killed. All his works reflect his experiences as a survivor of the Holocaust and his attempt to resolve the ethical torment of why it happened and what it reveals about human nature. They include *Night* (1958), *A Beggar in Jerusalem* (1968), *The Testament* (1980), and *The Forgotten* (1989). A noted lecturer, he was awarded the 1986 Nobel Prize for Peace for his universal condemnation of violence, hatred, and oppression.

Wight, Isle of, Island and unitary authority (pop., 2001: 132,719), part of the historic county of Hampshire, in the English Channel off the southern coast of England. Separated from mainland Hampshire by the Solent, the island has an area of 147 sq mi (381 sq km). Its main town is Newport. The backbone of the Isle of Wight is a chalk ridge that extends across its entire breadth, the thickest bed of chalk in the British Isles. The Needles are three detached masses of chalk that lie off the island's westernmost point and rise to about 100 ft (30 m). Three rivers, the Eastern Yar, the Medina, and the Western Yar, flow northward into the Solent. A major British maximum security prison is located at Parkhurst. Boatbuilding, marine engineering, and the aerospace, plastics, and electronics industries are economically important. The island's warm, sunny climate has made it a popular vacation spot.

wildcat, Wild species (*Felis silvestris*) of cat (family Felidae) native to Eurasian forests. Very similar to the domestic yellowish tabby, it will interbreed with domestic cats (of which it is presumably an ancestor). It is 20–32 in. (50–80 cm) long, excluding the 10–14-in. (25–35-cm) tail. It stands 14–16 in. (35–40 cm) and weighs 6–20 lbs (3–10 kg). Solitary and nocturnal, it preys on birds and small animals. In North America the name is used for the bobcat and lynx; in Africa it refers to the Caffre cat.

Wilde, Oscar (Fingal O'Flahertie Wills) (b. Oct. 16, 1854, Dublin, Ire.—d. Nov. 30, 1900, Paris, France), Irish poet and dramatist. Son of an eminent surgeon, Wilde attended Trinity College, Dublin, and later Oxford University, becoming widely known for his wit while still an undergraduate. A spokesman for Aestheticism, in the early 1880s he gave a lecture tour in the U.S. and established himself in London circles by his wit and flamboyance. His only novel, *The Picture of Dorian Gray* (1891), combines gothic elements with mockery of bourgeois morality. His macabre play *Salomé* (1893) was later adapted as the libretto of Richard Strauss's opera; his other plays, all successes, include *Lady Windermere's Fan* (1893), *A Woman of No Importance* (1893), and *An Ideal Husband* (1895). His greatest work was the comedy *The Importance of Being Earnest* (1899), a satire of Victorian social hypocrisy. Two critical dialogues, "The Decay of Lying" and "The Critic as Artist," are admired as equally brilliant. Though happily married, in 1891 he began an intimate relationship with the young Lord Alfred Douglas, son of the marquess of Queensberry. Accused by Queensberry of being a sodomite, Wilde sued for libel and lost, then was arrested for sodomy and convicted in a trial that became internationally notorious. Imprisoned at Reading Gaol (1895–97), he wrote a recriminatory letter to his lover that was edited and published as *De Profundis* (1905). After his release, he moved to Paris; his only later work was *The Ballad of Reading Gaol* (1898), on inhumane prison conditions. He died suddenly of acute meningitis.

Oscar Wilde, 1882.
Courtesy of the William Andrews Memorial Library of the University of California, Los Angeles

wildlife conservation, Regulation of wild animals and plants in such a way as to provide for their continuance. Efforts are aimed at preventing the depletion of present populations and ensuring the continued existence of the habitats targeted species need to survive. Techniques involve establishment of sanctuaries and controls on hunting, use of land, importation of exotic species, pollution, and use of pesticides.

Wilkins, Maurice (Hugh Frederick) (b. Dec. 15, 1916, Pongaroa, N.Z.—d. Oct. 6, 2004, London, Eng.), New Zealand-born British biophysicist. Educated in Birmingham and Cambridge, he participated in the Manhattan Project, working on the separation of uranium isotopes for use in the atomic bomb. On his return to Britain, he began a series of investigations that led ultimately to his studies of DNA. His X-ray diffraction studies of DNA proved crucial to the determination of DNA's molecular structure by James D. Watson and Francis Crick, for which the three were awarded a 1962 Nobel Prize. He later applied X-ray diffraction techniques to the study of RNA.

will, In law, a formal declaration, usually in the form of an executed document, of a person's wishes regarding the disposal of his or her property after death. It is valid if it meets the formalities of the law, which usually requires that it be witnessed. It may be considered invalid if, among other instances, the testator was mentally incapable of disposing of his or her property, if it imposes unreasonable or cruel demands as a condition of inheritance, or if the testator did not have clear title to the bequeathed assets. Any party who contests a will must bring the claim within a time specified by statute and must bear the burden of proof in demonstrating that the will is faulty.

William I, known as WILLIAM THE CONQUEROR (b. *c.* 1028, Falaise, Normandy—d. Sept. 9, 1087, Rouen), Duke of Normandy (1035–87) and king of England (1066–87). Though born out of wedlock, he succeeded his father as duke of Normandy, subduing rebellions and becoming the mightiest noble in France. In 1051 Edward the Confessor promised to make him heir to the English throne, but on Edward's death in 1066, Harold Godwineson, earl of Wessex (Harold II), was accepted as king. Determined to assert his right to the throne, William sailed from Normandy with an invasion force, defeated Harold at the Battle of Hastings, and was crowned king. The Norman Conquest was thus completed, though English rebellions continued until 1071. To secure England's frontiers, William invaded Scotland (1072) and Wales (1081). In 1086 he ordered the survey summarized in the Domesday Book. He divided his lands between his sons, giving Normandy and Maine to Robert II and England to William II.

Wilson, (Thomas) Woodrow (b. Dec. 28, 1856, Staunton, Va., U.S.—d. Feb. 3, 1924, Washington, D.C.), 28th president of the U.S. (1913–21). He earned a law degree and later received his doctorate from Johns Hopkins University. He taught political science at Princeton University (1890–1902). As its president (1902–10), he introduced various reforms. With the support of progressives, he was elected governor of New Jersey. His reform measures attracted national attention, and he became the Democratic Party presidential nominee in 1912. His campaign emphasized his progressive New Freedom policy, and he defeated Theodore Roosevelt and William H. Taft to win the presidency. As president, he approved legislation that lowered tariffs, created the Federal Reserve System, established the Federal Trade Commission, and strengthened labour unions. In foreign affairs he promoted self-government for the Philippines and sought to contain the Mexican civil war. From 1914 he maintained U.S. neutrality in World War I, offering to mediate a settlement and initiate peace negotiations. After the sinking of the *Lusitania* (1915) and other unarmed ships, he obtained a pledge from Germany to stop its submarine campaign. Campaigning on the theme that he had "kept us out of war," he was narrowly reelected in 1916, defeating Charles Evans Hughes. Germany's renewed submarine attacks on unarmed passenger ships caused Wilson to ask for a declaration of war in April 1917. In a continuing effort to negotiate a peace agreement, he presented the Fourteen Points (1918). He led the U.S. delegation to the Paris Peace Conference. The Treaty of Versailles faced opposition in the Senate from the Republican majority led by Henry Cabot Lodge. In search of popular support for the treaty and its provision creating the League of Nations, Wilson began a cross-country speaking tour, during which he collapsed. He returned to Washington, D.C. (September 1919), where he suffered a massive stroke that left him partially paralyzed. In the months that followed, his wife Edith controlled access to him, made some decisions by default, and engineered a cover-up of his condition. He rejected any attempts to compromise his version of the League of Nations and urged his Senate followers to vote against ratification of the treaty, which was defeated in 1920. He was awarded the 1919 Nobel Prize for Peace.

Wilson disease, or HEPATOLENTICULAR DEGENERATION, Recessive hereditary defect that impairs one's ability to metabolize copper. In affected persons, copper accumulates in the basal ganglia of the brain (involved in control of movement), causing progressive degeneration; forms a brownish ring at the margin of the cornea of the eye; and is deposited in the liver, gradually leading to cirrhosis. Other symptoms include tremor, lack of coordination, and personality changes. The disease usually appears in the person's teen years or twenties. Early diagnosis and treatment with a high-protein, low-copper diet and a substance to chelate copper can reverse the effects and prevent permanent brain and liver damage.

Wimbledon, Municipal center in the Greater London borough of Merton, known as the site of the annual lawn-tennis All-England Championships. Held in late June and early July, the tournament is the oldest (founded 1877) and most prestigious in the world. It is one of four tournaments that make up the Grand Slam of tennis, and the only one still played on natural grass. Competition was opened to professionals in 1968.

wind, Movement of air relative to the surface of the Earth. Wind is an important factor in determining and controlling climate and weather. It is also the generating force of most ocean and freshwater waves. Wind occurs because of horizontal and vertical differences in atmospheric pressure. The general pattern of winds over the Earth is known as the general circulation, and specific winds are named for the direction from which they originate (e.g., a wind blowing from west to east is a westerly). Wind speeds are often classified according to the Beaufort scale.

wind chill, Still-air temperature that would have the same cooling effect on exposed skin as a given combination of temperature and wind speed. As the wind speed increases, the wind chill equivalent temperature decreases; e.g., an air temperature of 30 °F (–1.1 °C) with a wind speed of 20 mph (32.2 kph) produces a wind chill of 17 °F (–8 °C). Wind chill is often included in weather reports to describe how cold it feels.

wind power, Use of the energy in winds to produce power. Though wind is irregular and spread out, it contains tremendous amounts of energy. Sophisticated wind turbines have been developed to convert this energy to electric power. The use of wind-energy systems grew considerably in the 1980s and '90s. Germany today produces more wind energy than any other country. Some 15,000 wind turbines are now in operation in California.

wind shear, Rate of change of wind velocity with distance perpendicular to the wind direction. A very narrow zone of abrupt velocity change is known as a shear line. Wind shear is observed near the ground and in jet streams, where it may be associated with clear-air turbulence. Vertical wind shear is closely associated with the vertical flux of momentum, heat, and water vapour.

Windsor, house of, formerly (1901–17) HOUSE OF SAXE-COBURG-GOTHA, Royal house of Britain, which succeeded the house of Hanover on the death of its last monarch, Queen Victoria. The dynastic name of Saxe-Coburg-Gotha was that of Victoria's German-born husband, Prince Albert. The dynasty has included Edward VII, George V, Edward VIII, George VI, and Elizabeth II. In view of the anti-German atmosphere of World War I, George V proclaimed in 1917 that all British male descendants of Queen Victoria would adopt the surname of Windsor.

windsurfing, Sport of riding a sailboard, a modified surfboard with a movable mast. Steered from a standing position, sailboards are capable of moderately high speeds and are usually used on lakes, or close to shore—sometimes within the surf zone—on the ocean. The sport originated in the U.S. in the late 1960s and quickly grew in popularity. It was introduced at the Olympic Games in 1984.

wine, Alcoholic beverage made from the fermented juice of grapes. Wine may also be made from various fruits and plant parts. Though known by the ancients, wine was not drunk in its matured form until the development of the bottle and cork in the late 17th century. In wine manufacture, grapes are crushed and strained, and the juice (called must) is sealed in vats along with yeast (*Saccharomyees ellipsoideus*) and often sulfur dioxide, which suppresses wild yeasts and organisms. Fermentation continues for several weeks, and then the wine is drawn off ("racked") into wooden barrels or other containers for a second fermentation ("aging"). It is clarified and bottled before undergoing final maturation. Wines may be classified according to colour as red, rosé (pink), or white; colour depends on whether the skins of red grapes are allowed to ferment with the juice. Wine taste is described as sweet or dry, sweet wines being high in sugar content and dry wines containing little or no sugar. Sparkling wines, such as champagne, contain suspended carbon dioxide, the result of bottling the wine before fermentation is complete. Fortified wines, such as port and sherry, contain added brandy. The leading wine-producing countries are France, Italy, Spain, the U.S., Argentina, Germany, Australia, South Africa, Portugal, and Romania.

wing, In zoology, one of the paired structures certain animals use for flying. Bat and bird wings are modifications of the vertebrate forelimb. In birds, the fingers are reduced and the forearm is lengthened. The primary flight feathers propel the bird forward, and the secondaries (on the upper wing) provide lift. Bat wings consist of a membrane stretched over slender, elongated arm and hand bones. Insect wings are folds of integument ("skin"). Most insects have two pairs of wings; dipterans (flies) have only one developed pair, and beetles have two but use only one for flying. The two wings on a side usually move together, but dragonfly wings work independently.

Winnipeg, City (pop., 2001: metro. area, 671,274), capital of Manitoba, Canada. Located at the confluence of the Red River of the North and the Assiniboine River, Winnipeg was settled as a French fur-trading post in 1738. In the early 19th century Thomas Douglas founded a Scottish settlement there. Development ensued with the arrival of Canada's first transcontinental railroad in 1885. Following disastrous floods in 1950, much of the city was rebuilt. It is a cultural, financial, commercial, industrial, and government centre.

wireless communications, System using radio-frequency, infrared, microwave, or other types of electromagnetic or acoustic waves in place of wires, cables, or fibre optics to transmit signals or data. Wireless devices include cell phones, two-way radios, remote garage-door openers, television remote controls, and GPS receivers. Wireless modems, microwave transmitters, and satellites make it possible to access the Internet from anywhere in the world. A Wireless Markup Language (WML) based on XML is intended for use in such narrow-band devices as cellular phones and pagers for the transfer and display of text.

witchcraft and sorcery, Use of alleged supernatural powers, usually to control people or events. Sorcery is sometimes distinguished from witchcraft in that sorcery may be practiced by anyone with the appropriate knowledge, using charms, spells, or potions, whereas witchcraft is considered to result from inherent mystical power and to be practiced by invisible means. Modern witches, however, claim that their craft is learned, and therefore another distinction between witchcraft and sorcery is that sorcery is always used with evil intent. Controversies over witchcraft and sorcery have been especially prevalent in close-knit communities experiencing decline or misfortune and embroiled in petty social conflict and scapegoating. In ancient Greece, witchcraft was mentioned as early as Homer. The best-known sorceress in Classical times was the legendary Medea. The Roman Horace describes two witches in his *Satires*. The Bible contains several references to witches, notably the Witch of Endor consulted by Saul (1 Samuel 28). The early Church Fathers held that witchcraft was a delusion and denounced its practice. In the Middle Ages, witchcraft was believed to involve demonic possession. It was also associated with heresy and so came within the scope of the Inquisition. In the witch-hunts of the 16th–17th centuries, European courts frequently regarded witches and sorcerers alike as candidates for burning. Although estimates of the number killed vary widely, it is likely that between 40,000 and 60,000 people were executed and many more were tortured and imprisoned during the witch-hunts. In the 20th century the modern witchcraft movement, Wicca, established and promoted respect for nature and a pantheistic worldview. Belief in witchcraft is apparent in traditional societies throughout the world. The Navajo protect themselves against witches with sand or pollen paintings, and in African societies people seek aid from medical doctors and witch doctors, the former for treatment of the "external" causes of the illness and the latter for the "internal."

wolf, Any of three extant species of canine. The gray, or timber, wolf (*Canis lupus*) is the ancestor of all domestic dogs. It once had the largest distribution of any mammal except human beings, but it is now found primarily in Canada, Alaska, the Balkans, and Russia. Wolves are intelligent and social. Their primary prey are deer, moose, and caribou, though they feed on many smaller animals as well. Because wolves have killed livestock, they have been persecuted by farmers and ranchers. A male gray wolf may be 7 ft (2 m) long and weigh up to 175 lb (80 kg); it is the largest living wild canid. Gray wolves live in hierarchical packs whose territories cover at least 38 sq mi (100 sq km) and hunt mostly at night. The

Mary Wollstonecraft (Godwin), detail, oil on canvas by John Opie, c. 1797; in the National Portrait Gallery, London.
National Portrait Gallery, London

much smaller red wolf (*C. rufus*), once widespread in the south-central U.S., has been bred in captivity and reintroduced. The Abyssinian wolf (*C. simensis*) of Ethiopia was formerly considered a jackal.

Wollstonecraft, Mary (b. April 27, 1759, London, Eng.—d. Sept. 10, 1797, London), English writer. She taught school and worked as a governess and as a translator for a London publisher. Her early *Thoughts on the Education of Daughters* (1787) foreshadowed her mature work on the place of women in society, *A Vindication of the Rights of Woman* (1792), whose core is a plea for equality in the education of men and women. The *Vindication* is widely regarded as the founding document of modern feminism. In 1797 she married the philosopher William Godwin; she died days after the birth of their daughter, Mary, that same year.

wolverine, or SKUNK BEAR, Solitary, voracious, nocturnal carni-

Wolverine (Gulo gulo).
Alan G. Nelson/Root Resources

vore (*Gulo gulo*) that inhabits northern timberlands worldwide. Wolverines are 26–36 in. (65–90 cm) long and 14–18 in. (36–45 cm) high, and weigh 20–65 lbs (9–30 kg); the bushy tail is 5–10-in. (13–26-cm) long. They have short bowed legs, hairy soles, and long, sharp claws. Their long, coarse hair, used to trim parkas, is blackish brown, with a light horizontal strip. The anal glands secrete an unpleasant-smelling fluid. A cunning, fearless predator, the wolverine will attack almost any animal, including sheep, deer, and small bears.

wombat, Either of two species (family Vombatidae) of noctur-

*Common wombat (*Vombatus ursinus).*
Warren Garst/Tom Stack and Associates

nal Australian marsupials that are heavily built, 28–47 in. (70–120 cm) long, and tailless. The single newborn develops in the mother's pouch for about five months. Wombats eat grasses, tree bark, and shrub roots. They make a grassy nest at the end of a long burrow. The common wombat (*Vombatus ursinus*) of southeastern Australia and Tasmania, considered a pest, has coarse dark hair and short ears. The rare Queensland hairynosed wombat (*Lasiorhinus barnardi*) has fine fur and longer ears; protected by law, the population lives principally in a national park.

women's movement, Diverse social movement, largely based in the U.S., seeking equal rights and opportunities for women in their economic activities, personal lives, and politics. It is recognized as the "second wave" of the larger feminist movement. While first-wave feminism of the 19th and early 20th centuries focused on women's legal rights, such as the right to vote, the second-wave feminism of the "women's movement" peaked in the 1960s and '70s and touched on every area of women's experience—including family, sexuality, and work. A variety of U.S. women's groups, including the National Organization for Women, sought to overturn laws that enforced discrimination in matters such as contract and property rights and employment and pay. The movement also sought to broaden women's self-awareness and challenge traditional stereotypes of women as passive, dependent, or irrational. An effort in the 1970s to pass the Equal Rights Amendment failed, but its aims had been largely achieved by other means by the end of the 20th century.

woodpecker, Any of about 180 species (family Picidae) of mostly nonmigratory, solitary birds found nearly worldwide. Woodpeckers spiral up tree trunks, probing for insects, and chisel nest holes in dead wood by means of rapidly repeating blows of the beak. Though they spend their entire life in trees, only the few ground-feeding species can perch. Some species eat fruits and berries or tree sap. Woodpeckers are usually silent, except in spring, when males call loudly and drum on hollow wood. Species range from 6 to 18 in. (15 to 46 cm) long. All have a straight, chisel-like bill, and most are patterned in black, white, or yellow and bright colours.

Woods, Tiger, orig. ELDRICK WOODS (b. Dec. 30, 1975, Cypress, Calif., U.S.), U.S. golfer. The child of a Thai mother and an African American father, Woods was a golf prodigy and won the first of three consecutive U.S. Junior Amateur Championships (1991–93) when he was 15 years old. In 1994 at age 18 he became the youngest winner of the U.S. Amateur competition, which he also won in 1995 and 1996. In 1997 Woods at age 21 became the youngest player and the first of African or Asian descent ever to win the Masters Tournament, winning by a record margin of 12 strokes. Winner of five other PGA tournaments in 1997, Woods became the youngest player ever ranked first in world golf competition. On July 23, 2000, Woods became the fifth player—after Gene Sarazen, Jack Nicklaus, Ben Hogan, and Gary Player—in golf history, and the youngest, to achieve a career grand slam of the four major championships (the Masters, U.S. Open, British Open, and PGA Championship). In 2005 he completed his second career grand slam.

Woolf, (Adeline) Virginia, orig. ADELINE VIRGINIA STEPHEN (b. Jan. 25, 1882, London, Eng.—d. March 28, 1941, near Rodmell, Sussex), British novelist and critic. Daughter of Leslie Stephen, she and her sister became the early nucleus of the Bloomsbury group. She married Leonard Woolf in 1912; in 1917 they founded the Hogarth Press. Her best novels—including *Mrs. Dalloway* (1925) and *To the Lighthouse* (1927)—are experimental; in them she examines the human experience of time, the indefinability of character, and external circumstances as they impinge on consciousness. *Orlando* (1928) is a historical fantasy about a single character who experiences England from the Elizabethan era to the early 20th century, and *The Waves* (1931), perhaps her most radically experimental work, uses interior monologue and recurring images to trace the inner lives of six characters. Such works confirmed her place among the major figures of literary modernism. Her best critical studies are collected in *The Common Reader* (1925, 1932). Her long essay *A Room of One's Own* (1929) addressed the status of women, and women artists in particular. Her other novels include *Jacob's Room* (1922), *The Years* (1937), and *Between the Acts* (1941). She also wrote a biography of Roger Fry. Her health and mental stability were delicate throughout her life; in a recurrence of mental illness, she drowned herself. Her diaries and correspondence have been published in several editions.

word processing, Preparation of textual documents on computer. A word-processing system typically consists of simply of a personal computer linked to a computer printer, but it may instead employ a terminal linked to a mainframe computer. Word processing differs from typewriter typing in numerous ways. Electronic text can be moved around at will; misspelled terms can be corrected throughout the document by means of a single command; spelling and grammar checkers can automatically alert the user to apparent errors of spelling, punctuation, and syntax; and the document's format, layout, and type fonts and sizes can be changed repeatedly until a satisfactory design is achieved. Since all editing ideally occurs on-screen, word processing can result in decreased paper usage and simplified editing. When the final draft is ready, the document can be printed out (in multiple copies if necessary), sent as an e-mail attachment, shared on a computer network, or simply stored as an electronic file.

Wordsworth, William (b. April 7, 1770, Cockermouth, Cumberland, Eng.—d. April 23, 1850, Rydal Mount, Westmorland), English poet. Orphaned at age 13, Wordsworth attended Cambridge University, but he remained rootless and virtually penniless until 1795, when a legacy made possible a reunion with his sister Dorothy Wordsworth. He became friends with Samuel Taylor Coleridge, with whom he wrote *Lyrical Ballads* (1798), the collection often considered to have launched the English Romantic movement. Wordsworth's contributions include "Tintern Abbey" and many lyrics controversial for their common, everyday language. About 1798 he began writing *The Prelude* (1850), the epic autobiographical poem that would absorb him intermittently for the next 40 years. His second verse collection, *Poems, in Two Volumes* (1807), includes many of the rest of his finest works, including "Ode: Intimations of Immortality." His poetry is perhaps most original in its vision of the organic relation between man and the natural world, a vision that culminated in the sweeping metaphor of nature as emblematic of the mind of God. The most memorable poems of his middle and late years were often cast in elegiac mode; few match the best of his earlier works. By the time he became widely appreciated by the critics and the public, his poetry had lost much of its force and his radical politics had yielded to conservatism. In 1843 he became England's poet laureate. He is regarded as the central figure in the initiation of English Romanticism.

work, In economics and sociology, the activities and labour necessary for the survival of society. As early as 40,000 BC, hunters worked in groups to track and kill animals, while younger or weaker members of the tribe gathered food. When agriculture replaced hunting and gathering, the resulting surplus of food allowed early societies to develop and some of its members to pursue crafts such as pottery, weaving, and metallurgy. Historically, rigid social hierarchies caused nobles, clergy, merchants, artisans, and peasants to pursue occupations defined largely by hereditary social class. Craft guilds, influential in the economic development of medieval Europe, limited the supply of labour in each profession and controlled production. The establishment of towns led to the creation of new occupations in commerce, law, medicine, and defense. The coming of the Industrial Revolution, spurred by technological advances such as steam power, changed working life profoundly. Factories divided the work once done by a single craftsman into a number of distinct tasks performed by unskilled or semiskilled workers. Manufacturing firms grew larger in the 19th century as standardized parts and machine tools came into use, and ever-more-specialized positions for managers, supervisors, accountants, engineers, technicians, and salesmen became necessary. The trend toward specialization continued into the 21st century, giving rise to a number of disciplines concerned with the management and design of work, including production management, industrial relations, personnel administration, and systems engineering. By the turn of the 21st century, automation and technology had spurred tremendous growth in service industries.

work, In physics, the measure of energy transfer that occurs when an object is moved over a distance by an external force, some component of which is applied in the direction of displacement. For a constant force, work W is equal to the magnitude of the force F times the displacement d of the object, or $W = Fd$. Work is also done by compressing a gas, by rotating a shaft, and by causing invisible motions of particles within a body by an external magnetic force. No work is accomplished by simply holding a heavy stationary object, because there is no transfer of energy and no displacement. Work done on a body is equal to the increase in energy of the body. Work is expressed in units called joules (J). One joule is equivalent to the energy transferred when a force of one newton is applied over a distance of one metre.

World Bank, Specialized agency of the United Nations system, established at the Bretton Woods Conference for postwar reconstruction. It is the principal international development institution. Its five divisions are the International Bank for Reconstruction and Development (IBRD; its main component), the International Development Association (IDA), the International Finance Corporation (IFC), the Multilateral Investment Guarantee Agency (MIGA), and the International Center for Settlement of Investment Disputes (ICSID). The IDA (founded 1960) makes interest-free loans to the bank's poorest member countries. The IFC (founded 1956) lends to private businesses in developing countries. The MIGA (founded 1985) supports national and private agencies that encourage foreign direct investment by offering insurance against noncommercial risks. The ICSID (founded 1966) was developed to relieve the IBRD of the burden of settling investment disputes.

World Council of Churches (WCC), Christian ecumenical organization founded in 1948 in Amsterdam. It functions as a forum for Protestant and Eastern Orthodox denominations, which cooperate through the WCC on a variety of undertakings and explore doctrinal similarities and differences. It grew out of two post-World War I ecumenical efforts, the Life and Work Movement (which concentrated on practical activities) and the Faith and Order Movement (which focused on doctrinal issues and the possibility of reunion). The impetus for these two organizations sprang from the International Missionary Conference in Edinburgh in 1910, the first such cooperative effort since the Reformation. The Roman Catholic church, though not a member of the WCC, sends representatives to its conferences. The more fundamentalist Protestant denominations have also refused to join.

World Cup, Major international football (soccer) competition. The tournament brings together 32 qualifying national teams from around the world, culminating in a match between the two top teams. It has been held every fourth year since 1930 (except during World War II). Followed and watched by billions of people worldwide, it has by far the greatest audience of any single sporting event in the world. Several competitions in other sports also use the name "world cup."

World Health Organization (WHO), Public-health agency of the UN, established in Geneva in 1948 to succeed two earlier agencies. Its mandate is to promote "the highest possible level of health" in all peoples. Its work falls into three categories. It provides a clearinghouse for information on the latest developments in disease and health care and establishes international sanitary standards and quarantine measures. It sponsors measures for the control of epidemic and endemic disease (including immunization campaigns and assistance in providing sources of pure water). Finally, it encourages the strengthening of public-health programs in member nations. Its greatest success to date has been the worldwide eradication of smallpox (1980).

World Heritage site, Any of various areas or objects designated as having "outstanding universal value" under the Convention Concerning the Protection of the World Cultural and Natural Heritage. This convention, adopted by UNESCO in 1972, provides for international cooperation in preserving and protecting cultural and natural treasures throughout the world. Each site on the list is under strict legal protection by the government of the nation in which it is situated. Among the cultural sites are many of the world's most famous buildings. The ratio of cultural to natural sites on the list is roughly three to one.

world music, Musical genre incorporating diverse styles from Africa, eastern Europe, Asia, South and Central America, the Caribbean, and nonmainstream Western folk sources. The term was first coined largely in response to the sudden increase of recordings in non-English languages that were released in Great Britain and the United States in the 1980s, but by the early 1990s world music had become a bona fide musical genre and counterpoint to the increasingly synthetic sounds of Western pop music. Initially, African popular music and world music were virtually synonymous, and the genre's biggest stars included the Nigerians King Sunny Ade and Fela Anikulapo Kuti and the Senegalese Youssou N'Dour. Moreover, one of its earliest advocates was the Cameroonian-born Frenchman Francis Bebey. By the 21st century world music encompassed everything from Pakistani singer Nusrat Fateh Ali Khan and the pop-flamenco of the French group the Gipsy Kings to "ambient-global" projects that merged so-called ethnic voice samples with state-of-the-art rhythm programming.

World Series, Annual championship of U.S. major league baseball, played between the top team of the American League (AL) and that of the National League (NL). First held in 1903, it was canceled the following year after the New York Giants (NL) refused to play Boston (AL). The series resumed in 1905 and continued annually until a players' strike in 1994 forced its cancellation that year. A seven-game series has been standard since 1922.

World Trade Center, Complex formerly consisting of seven buildings around a central plaza, near the southern tip of Manhattan. Its huge twin towers (completed 1970–72) were designed by Minoru Yamasaki (1912–86). At 1,368 ft (417 m) and 1,362 ft (415 m) tall, they were the world's tallest buildings until surpassed in 1973 by the Sears Tower in Chicago. The towers were notable for the relationship of their simple, light embellishment to their underlying structure. In 1993 a bomb planted by terrorists exploded in the underground garage, killing several people and injuring some 1,000. A much more massive attack occurred on Sept. 11, 2001, when first One World Trade Center and then Two World Trade Center were struck by hijacked commercial airliners that were deliberately flown into them. Shortly thereafter both of the heavily damaged towers, as well as adjacent buildings, collapsed into enormous piles of debris. The attacks claimed the lives of some 2,750 people. Thousands more were injured.

World Trade Organization (WTO), International organization based in Geneva that supervises world trade. It was created in 1995 to replace the General Agreement on Tariffs and Trade (GATT). Like its predecessor, it aims to lower trade barriers and encourage multilateral trade. It monitors members' adherence to GATT agreements and negotiates and implements new agreements. Critics of the WTO, including many opponents of economic globalization, have charged that it undermines national sovereignty by promoting the interests of large multinational corporations and that the trade liberalization it encourages leads to environmental damage and declining living standards for low-skilled workers in developing countries. By the early 21st century, the WTO had more than 145 members.

world tree, Centre of the world, a widespread motif in myths and folktales among various peoples, especially in Asia, Australia, and North America. There are two main forms. In the vertical tradition, the tree extends between and connects earth, heaven, and the underworld; oracles, judgments, and other prophetic activities are performed at its base. In the horizontal tradition, the tree is planted at the centre of the world and is protected by supernatural guardians; it is the source of terrestrial fertility and life.

World War I, or FIRST WORLD WAR (1914–18) International conflict between the Central Powers—Germany, Austria-Hungary, and Turkey—and the Allied Powers—mainly France, Britain, Russia, Italy, Japan, and (from 1917) the U.S. After a Serbian nationalist assassinated Archduke Francis Ferdinand of Austria in June 1914, a chain of threats and mobilizations resulted in a general war between the antagonists by mid-August. Prepared to fight a war on two fronts, based on the Schlieffen Plan, Germany first swept through neutral Belgium and invaded France. After the First Battle of the Marne (1914), the Allied defensive lines were stabilized in France, and a war of attrition began. Fought from lines of trenches and supported by modern artillery and machine guns, infantry assaults gained little ground and were enormously costly in human life, especially at the Battles of Verdun and the Somme (1916). On the Eastern Front, Russian forces initially drove deep into East Prussia and German Poland (1914) but were stopped by German and Austrian forces at the Battle of Tannenberg and forced back into Russia (1915). After several offensives, the Russian army failed to break through the German defensive lines. Russia's poor performance and enormous losses caused widespread domestic discontent that led to the Russian Revolution of 1917. Other fronts in the war included the Dardanelles Campaign, in which British and Dominion forces were unsuccessful against

Turkey; the Caucasus and Iran (Persia), where Russia fought Turkey; Mesopotamia and Egypt, where British forces fought the Turks; and northern Italy, where Italian and Austrian troops fought the costly Battles of the Isonzo. At sea, the German and British fleets fought the inconclusive Battle of Jutland, and Germany's use of the submarine against neutral shipping eventually brought the U.S. into the war in 1917. Though Russia's armistice with Germany in December 1917 released German troops to fight on the Western Front, the Allies were reinforced by U.S. troops in early 1918. Germany's unsuccessful offensive in the Second Battle of the Marne was countered by the Allies' steady advance, which recovered most of France and Belgium by October 1918 and led to the November Armistice. Total casualties were estimated at 10 million dead, 21 million wounded, and 7.7 million missing or imprisoned.

World War II, or SECOND WORLD WAR (1939–45) International conflict principally between the Axis powers—Germany, Italy, and Japan—and the Allied powers—France, Britain, the U.S., the Soviet Union, and China. Political and economic instability in Germany, combined with bitterness over its defeat in World War I and the harsh conditions of the Treaty of Versailles, allowed Adolf Hitler and the Nazi Party to rise to power. In the mid-1930s Hitler began secretly to rearm Germany, in violation of the treaty. He signed alliances with Italy and Japan to oppose the Soviet Union and intervened in the Spanish Civil War in the name of anticommunism. Capitalizing on the reluctance of other European powers to oppose him by force, he sent troops to occupy Austria in 1938 and to annex Czechoslovakia in 1939. After signing the German-Soviet Nonaggression Pact, Germany invaded Poland on Sept. 1, 1939. Two days later France and Britain declared war on Germany. Poland's defeat was followed by a period of military inactivity on the Western Front. At sea Germany conducted a damaging submarine campaign by U-boat against merchant shipping bound for Britain. By early 1940 the Soviet Union had divided Poland with Germany, occupied the Baltic states, and subdued Finland in the Russo-Finnish War. In April 1940 Germany overwhelmed Denmark and began its conquest of Norway. In May German forces swept through the Netherlands and Belgium on their blitzkrieg invasion of France, forcing it to capitulate in June and establish the Vichy France regime. Germany then launched massive bombing raids on Britain in preparation for a cross-Channel invasion, but, after losing the Battle of Britain, Hitler postponed the invasion indefinitely. By early 1941 Hungary, Romania, and Bulgaria had joined the Axis, and German troops quickly overran Yugoslavia and Greece in April. In June Hitler abandoned his pact with the Soviet Union and launched a massive surprise invasion of Russia, reaching the outskirts of Moscow before Soviet counterattacks and winter weather halted the advance. In East Asia Japan expanded its war with China and seized European colonial holdings. In December 1941 Japan attacked U.S. bases at Pearl Harbor and in the Philippines. The U.S. declared war on Japan, and the war became truly global when the other Axis powers declared war on the U.S. Japan quickly invaded and occupied most of Southeast Asia, Burma, the Netherlands East Indies, and many Pacific islands. After the crucial U.S. naval victory at the Battle of Midway (1942), U.S. forces began to advance up the chains of islands toward Japan. In the North Africa campaigns the British and Americans defeated Italian and German forces by 1943. The Allies then invaded Sicily and Italy, forcing the overthrow of the Fascist government in July 1943, though fighting against the Germans continued in Italy until 1945. In the Soviet Union the Battle of Stalingrad (1943) marked the end of the German advance, and Soviet reinforcements in great numbers gradually pushed the German armies back. The massive Allied invasion of western Europe began with the Normandy Campaign in western France (1944), and the Allies' steady advance ended in the occupation of Germany in 1945. After Soviet troops pushed German forces out of the Soviet Union, they advanced into Poland, Czechoslovakia, Hungary, and Romania and had occupied the eastern third of Germany by the time the surrender of Germany was signed on May 8, 1945. In the Pacific an Allied invasion of the Philippines (1944) was followed by the successful Battle of Leyte Gulf and the costly Battles of Iwo Jima and Okinawa (1945). Atomic bombs were dropped on Hiroshima and Nagasaki in August 1945, and Japan's formal surrender on September 2 ended the war. Estimates of total military and civilian casualties varied from 35 million to 60 million killed, including about 6 million Jews who died in the Holocaust. Millions more civilians were wounded and made homeless throughout Europe and East Asia.

World Wide Web (WWW), or WEB, Leading information-exchange service of the Internet. It was created by Tim Berners-Lee and his colleagues at CERN and introduced to the world in 1991. The Web gives users access to a vast array of documents that are connected to each other by means of hypertext or hyperlinks. A hypertext document with its corresponding text and hyperlinks is written in HTML and is assigned an on-line address, or URL. The Web operates within the Internet's basic client-server architecture. Individual HTML files with unique electronic addresses are called Web pages, and a collection of Web pages and related files (such as graphics files, scripted programs, and other resources) sharing a set of similar addresses is called a Web site. The main or introductory page of a Web site is usually called the site's home page. Users may access any page by typing in the appropriate address, search for pages related to a topic of interest by using a search engine, or move quickly between pages by clicking on hyperlinks incorporated into them. Though introduced in 1991, the Web did not become truly popular until the introduction of Mosaic, a browser with a graphical interface, in 1993. Subsequently, browsers produced by Netscape and Microsoft have become predominant.

World Wildlife Fund, or WORLD WIDE FUND FOR NATURE, Largest privately supported international conservation organization in the world. Founded in 1961 by a small group of European scientists, naturalists, and business and political leaders, including Peter Markham Scott, the organization raises funds and channels them to other conservation groups. It directs its efforts toward protecting endangered environments such as coral reefs, saving endangered species, and addressing global threats such as pollution. It has helped establish and manage parks and reserves, and was instrumental in saving the giant panda (whose image it uses as its symbol) and other endangered species.

worm, Any of thousands of species of unrelated invertebrate animals that typically have a soft, slender, elongated body with no appendages. The major phyla are Platyhelminthes (flatworms), Annelida (annelids, or segmented worms), Nemertea (ribbon worms), Acanthocephala (spiny-headed worms), and Aschelminthes (nematodes and others). There are several minor phyla. Length ranges from microscopic (e.g., some aschelminths) to more than 100 ft (30 m) (some ribbon worms). Worms are found worldwide on land and in water. They may be parasitic or free-living and are important as soil conditioners, parasites, and a link in the food chain in all ecosystems.

Worms, Concordat of (1122) Compromise between Pope Calixtus II and Emperor Henry V (r. 1106–25) to settle the Investiture Controversy, reached at Worms, Germany. It marked the end of the first phase of conflict between Rome and what was becoming the Holy Roman Empire and made a clear distinction between the spiritual side of a prelate's office and his position as a landed magnate and vassal of the crown. Bishops and abbots were to be chosen by the clergy, but the emperor was to decide contested elections. Those selected were to be invested first with the powers and privileges of their office as vassal (granted by the emperor) and then with their ecclesiastical powers and lands (granted by church authority).

Worms, Diet of, Meeting of the Diet (assembly) of the Holy Roman Empire at Worms, Ger., in 1521, where Martin Luther defended the principles of the Reformation. Luther had already been excommunicated by Pope Leo X, but Emperor Charles V granted him safe conduct to a hearing at the Diet. On April 17, 1521, Luther refused to recant his views. Disorder broke out, the emperor adjourned the proceedings, and Luther was obliged to go into hiding. In May the Diet issued the Edict of Worms, declaring Luther an outlaw and a heretic and banning his writings.

wound, or TRAUMA, Break in any body tissue due to external action (including surgery). It may be closed (blunt trauma) or open (penetrating trauma). Blood vessels, nerves, muscles, bones, joints, and internal organs may be damaged. A closed wound can be caused by impact, twisting, bending, or deceleration (as in a car crash). It can range from a minor bruise or sprain to a skull fracture with brain damage or a spinal-cord injury with paralysis. In an open wound, foreign matter such as bacteria, dirt, and clothing fragments entering through broken skin or mucous membrane may result in infection. Other factors affecting severity include depth, surface area, degree of tearing, and structures damaged. Minor wounds need only first aid. For others, after examination and perhaps diagnostic imaging and exploratory surgery, treatment may include fluid replacement or drainage, sterilization and antibiotics, tetanus antitoxin, and repair of damaged structures. A closed wound may need to be opened or an open one sutured closed.

Wren, Sir Christopher (b. Oct. 20, 1632, East Knoyle, Wiltshire, Eng.—d. Feb. 25, 1723, London), British architect, astronomer, and geometrician. He taught astronomy at Gresham College, London (1657–61) and Oxford (1661–73), and did not turn to architecture until 1662, when he was engaged to design the Sheldonian Theatre at Oxford. Though Classical in form, the theatre was roofed with novel wood trusses that were the product of Wren's scholarly and empirical approach. As King's Surveyor of Works (1669–1718), he had a hand in the rebuilding of more than 50 churches destroyed in the Great Fire of London. Meanwhile, he was evolving designs for Saint Paul's Cathedral, a work that occupied him until its completion in 1710. Other works, generally in the English Baroque style, include the classical Trinity College library, Cambridge (1676–84), additions to Hampton Court (begun 1689), and Greenwich Hospital (begun 1696). Wren was buried in Saint Paul's; nearby is the famous inscription: "Reader, if you seek a monument, look around."

Sir Christopher Wren, detail of an oil painting by Sir Godfrey Kneller, 1711; in the National Portrait Gallery, London.
Courtesy of the National Portrait Gallery, London

wrestling, Sport in which two competitors grapple with and strive to trip or throw each other down or off-balance. It is practiced in various styles, including freestyle wrestling, in which contestants can use holds above and below the waist, and Greco-Roman wrestling, which allows only holds above the waist. Sambo is a style of Russian origin employing judo techniques. Sumo wrestling is a specialized Japanese variety. U.S. professional wrestling is today among the most popular of all spectator sports, though it principally involves wildly flamboyant showmanship, including such nonclassical moves as kicks to the head that would be lethal if they were not actually pulled.

Wright, Frank Lloyd (b. June 8, 1867, Richland Center, Wis., U.S.—d. April 9, 1959, Phoenix, Ariz.), U.S. architect. After studying engineering briefly at the University of Wisconsin, he worked for the firm of Dankmar Adler (1844–1900) and Louis Sullivan in Chicago before opening his own practice there in 1893. Wright became the chief practitioner of the Prairie school, building about 50 Prairie houses from 1900 to 1910. Early nonresidential buildings include the forward-looking Larkin Building in Buffalo, N.Y. (1904; destroyed 1950), and Unity Temple in Oak Park, Ill. (1906). In 1911 he began work on his own house, Taliesin, near Spring Green, Wis. The lavish Imperial Hotel in Tokyo (1915–22, dismantled 1967) was significant for its revolutionary floating cantilever construction, which made it one of the only large buildings to withstand the earthquake of 1923. In the 1930s he designed his low-cost Usonian houses, but his most admired house, Fallingwater, in Bear Run, Pa. (1936), is an extravagant country retreat cantilevered over a waterfall. His Johnson Wax Building (1936–39), an example of humane workplace design, touched off an avalanche of major commissions. Of particular note is the Guggenheim Museum (1956–59), which has no separate floor levels but instead uses a spiral ramp, realizing Wright's ideal of a continuous space. Throughout his career he retained the use of ornamental detail, earthy colours, and rich textural effects. His sensitive use of materials helped to control and perfect his dynamic expression of space, which opened a new era in American architecture. Often considered the greatest U.S. architect of all time, his greatest legacy is "organic architecture," or the idea that buildings harmonize both with their inhabitants and with their environment.

Wright, Wilbur; and Wright, Orville (b. April 16, 1867, near Millville, Ind., U.S.—d. May 30, 1912, Dayton, Ohio), (b. Aug. 19, 1871, Dayton, Ohio, U.S.—d. Jan. 30, 1948, Dayton), U.S. inventors who achieved the first powered, sustained, and controlled airplane flight. The brothers first worked in printing-machinery design and later in bicycle manufacturing, which financed their early experiments in airplane design. To test flight control, essential to successful powered flight, they built and flew three biplane gliders (1900–02). Propeller and engine innovations led to their first powered airplane, which Orville flew successfully for 12 seconds and Wilbur later flew for 59 seconds at Kill Devil Hills, N.C. (near the village of Kitty Hawk), on Dec. 17, 1903. Their flyer of 1905 could turn, bank, circle, and remain airborne for over 35 minutes. They demonstrated their planes in Europe and the U.S.; in 1908 Wilbur gave over 100 exhibition flights in France, setting a duration record of 2 hours and 20 minutes. They established an aircraft company and produced planes for the U.S. Army. After Wilbur's death from typhoid, Orville sold his interest in the company, which later merged with the company of Glenn H. Curtiss.

writ, In common law, an order issued in the name of a sovereign or court commanding a person to perform or refrain from performing a specified act. It was a vital official instrument in Old English law. A plaintiff would commence a suit by choosing the proper form of action and obtaining a writ appropriate to the remedy sought; its issuance forced the defendant to comply or to appear in court. Writs were also constantly in use for financial and political purposes of government. Though the writ no longer governs civil pleading and has lost many of its applications, the extraordinary writs, especially of habeas corpus, mandamus (commanding the performance of a ministerial act), prohibition (commanding an inferior court to stay within its jurisdiction), and certiorari, reflect its historical importance as an instrument of judicial authority.

writing, System of human visual communication using signs or symbols associated by convention with units of language—meanings or sounds—and recorded on materials such as paper, stone, or clay. Its precursor was pictography. Logography, in which symbols stand for individual words, typically develops from pictography. Logography requires thousands of symbols for all possible words and names. In phonographic systems, the symbol associated with a word also stands for similar- or identical-sounding words. Phonographic systems may evolve to the point where symbols represent syllables, constituting a syllabary. An alphabet provides symbols for all the consonants and vowels.

Wrocław, German BRESLAU, City (pop., 2000 est.: 633,857), southwestern Poland. Located on the Oder River, it originated in the 10th century at the crossroads of the trade route linking the Black Sea to western Europe. In 1138 it became the first capital of Silesia. The Tartars destroyed Wrocław in 1241. Rebuilt, it passed to Bohemia with the rest of Silesia in 1335 and to the Habsburgs in 1526. In 1741 it fell to Prussia under the rule of Frederick II (the Great), and it eventually became part of Germany. During World War II Wrocław was besieged (1945) by Soviet troops. The city was assigned to Poland by the Potsdam Conference of 1945. Heavily damaged during the war, it was rebuilt and is now a major commercial city.

wu, Fundamental Daoist philosophical concept. *Wu* ("not-being"), *you* ("being"), *wuming* ("the nameless"), and *youming* ("the named") are interdependent and grow out of one another. *Wu* and *you* are two aspects of the *dao*. Not-being does not mean nothingness but rather the absence of perceptible qualities; in Laozi's view, it is superior to being. It is the void that harbours in itself all potentialities and without which even being lacks its efficacy. According to the scholar He Yan (d. 249), *wu* is beyond name and form and hence is absolute, complete, and capable of accomplishing anything.

Wuwang, or WU-WANG (fl. 11th century BC, China), Founder and first ruler of the Zhou dynasty. After establishing the Zhou dynasty, Wuwang, assisted by his brother, Zhougong, consolidated his rule by establishing a feudalistic form of government in which territory was bestowed on relatives and vassals willing to acknowledge Zhou suzerainty. He was regarded by later Confucians as a wise king.

XYZ

X-ray, Electromagnetic radiation of extremely short wavelength (100 nanometres to 0.001 nanometre) produced by the deceleration of charged particles or the transitions of electrons in atoms. X-rays travel at the speed of light and exhibit phenomena associated with waves, but experiments indicate that they can also behave like particles. On the electromagnetic spectrum, they lie between gamma rays and ultraviolet radiation. They were discovered in 1895 by Wilhelm Conrad Röntgen, who named them X-rays for their unknown nature. They are used in medicine to diagnose bone fractures, dental cavities, and cancer; to locate foreign objects in the body; and to stop the spread of malignant tumours. In industry, they are used to analyze and detect flaws in structures.

X-ray astronomy, Study of astronomical objects and phenomena that emit radiation at X-ray wavelengths. Because Earth's atmosphere absorbs most X-rays, X-ray telescopes and detectors are taken to high altitudes or into space by balloons and spacecraft. In 1949 detectors aboard sounding rockets showed that the Sun gives off X-rays, but it is a weak source; it took 30 more years to clearly detect X-rays from other ordinary stars. Beginning with the Uhuru X-ray satellite (launched 1970), a succession of space observatories carried increasingly sophisticated instruments into Earth orbit. Astronomers discovered that most types of stars emit X-rays but usually as a tiny fraction of their energy output. Supernova remnants are more powerful X-ray sources; the strongest sources known in the Milky Way Galaxy are certain binary stars in which one star is probably a black hole. In addition to myriad point sources, astronomers have found a diffuse background of X-ray radiation emanating from all directions; unlike cosmic background radiation, it appears to have many distant individual sources. The Chandra X-Ray Observatory and XMM-Newton X-ray satellite (both launched 1999) have made numerous discoveries relating to the nature and quantity of black holes in the universe, the evolution of stars and galaxies, and the composition and activity of supernova remnants.

xenon, Chemical element, chemical symbol Xe, atomic number 54. One of the noble gases, it is colourless, odourless, tasteless, and nearly inert, combining only with fluorine and oxygen and in complexes. Xenon occurs in slight traces in Earth's atmosphere and in rocks. Obtained by fractional distillation of liquefied air, it is used in luminescent tubes, flash lamps, lasers, and tracer studies and as an anesthetic.

Xenophon (b. 431, Attica, Greece—d. shortly before 350 BC, Attica), Greek historian. Born of a well-to-do Athenian family, Xenophon was critical of extreme democracy and for a time was exiled as a traitor. He served with the Greek mercenaries of the Persian prince Cyrus, an experience on which he based his best-known work, the *Anabasis*. Its prose was highly regarded in antiquity and exerted a strong influence on Latin literature. His other works include *On Horsemanship*; *On Hunting*; *Cyropaedia*, a historical novel about Cyrus II; *Oeconomicus*, a treatise on estate management; and his completion of a work by the historian Thucydides.

xerography, Image-forming process that relies on a photoconductive substance whose electrical resistance decreases when light falls on it. Xerography is the basis of the most widely used document-copying machines. The process was invented in the 1930s by U.S. physicist Chester F. Carlson (1906–1968) and developed in the 1940s and '50s by Xerox Corp. (then called Haloid). Light passing through or reflected from a document reaches a selenium-coated drum surface onto which negatively charged particles of ink (toner) are sprayed, forming an image of the document on the drum. As a sheet of paper is passed close to the drum, a positive electric charge under the sheet attracts the negatively charged ink particles, transferring the image to the copy paper. Heat briefly applied fuses the ink particles to the paper. The first commercially successful xerographic copier was introduced in 1959.

Xi River system, Chinese XI JIANG, or HSI CHIANG, English WEST RIVER, River system, southern China. Known as the Nanpan and then the Hongshui in its upper course, the Xi proper begins as it enters Guangdong province from eastern Guangxi autonomous region. It flows east through Guangdong and then through the vast Pearl River Delta before entering the South China Sea west of Hong Kong near Macau; the city of Guangzhou (Canton) is in its delta. The Xi is 1,216 mi (1,957 km) long, shorter than other important Chinese rivers, but its volume of flow is second only to that of the Yangtze River (Chang Jiang). It is the great commercial waterway of southern China, linking the delta cities with the interior.

Xia Gui, or HSIA KUEI (fl. 1195–1224, Qiantang, Zhejiang province, China), Chinese master of landscape painting. Xia served in the Imperial Painting Academy, and most sources agree that he followed the stylistic tradition of an earlier landscapist in the academy, Li Tang. Xia and his contemporary, Ma Yuan, were the most influential members of the academy, and a school of painting inspired by them came to be known as the Ma-Xia school. Most of Xia's surviving works are album leaves painted on silk. A typical work by him is exquisitely calculated and perfectly balanced, conveying with great precision a scene glimpsed through haze, sharply focused at a few points but obscured at others. Chinese writers spoke of his use of a "split brush" (i.e., the brush tip divided so as to make two or more strokes at once) in painting tree foliage and of his freehand drawing "without employing a ruler." While his influence was considerable, it was only in modern times that he came to be recognized as one of the leading masters of Chinese landscape painting and one of art's great interpreters of nature.

Xi'an, or HSI-AN, conventional SIAN, City (pop., 2003 est.: 2,657,900), capital of Shaanxi province, central China. Located on the Wei River, the site served as the capital of several dynasties beginning in the 11th century BCE. It became one of the most splendid cities of the ancient world during the Tang dynasty (618–907 CE) and was a thriving commercial centre. Marco Polo visited in the 13th century. It was an entry point in the 1920s for communist ideology from the Soviet Union. In 1936, after Nationalist leader Chiang Kai-shek had been kidnapped there, the communists and Nationalists formed a united front against Japanese invaders. It is the site of several educational institutions and numerous temples and pagodas. It became an important tourist destination after the discovery of the nearby tomb of Emperor Shihuangdi, with its army of 6,000 life-size terra-cotta warriors (designated a UNESCO World Heritage site in 1987).

Xinjiang, or HSIN-CHIANG, conventional SINKIANG, in full UYGUR AUTONOMOUS REGION OF XINJIANG, Autonomous region (pop., 2002 est.: 19,050,000), northwestern China. It is bordered by the Kashmir region, Afghanistan, Tajikistan, Kyrgyzstan, Kazakhstan, Russia, and Mongolia, Gansu and Qinghai provinces, and Tibet. China's largest political unit, it covers some 635,900 sq mi (1,646,900 sq km). The capital is Ürümqi. Inhabited since early times by nomad tribes, it is an area of rugged mountains and desert basins. The Silk Road traversed the region. It came under the control of local leaders with the fall of the Han dynasty in the 3rd century AD and was regained by China in the 7th century. It was successively subject to the Tibetans, Uighurs, and Arabs and was conquered by Genghis Khan in the 13th century. Again under Chinese rule during the Manchu dynasty, it was established as Xinjiang province c. 1884. It came under Chinese communist rule in

1949. It was reconstituted as an autonomous region in 1955. It has mineral resources, heavy industry (including iron and steel works), and some agricultural production.

Xiwangmu, or HSI WANG-MU, In ancient Chinese Daoist mythology, the queen of the female immortals. A former mountain spirit who had been transformed into a beautiful woman, she ruled a paradise called West Flower, while her husband, Mu Gong, guarded males in his East Flower paradise. Her garden contained rare flowers and the peach of immortality, which blooms once in 3,000 years.

XML, in full EXTENSIBLE MARKUP LANGUAGE, Markup language developed to be a simplified and more structural version of SGML. It incorporates features of HTML (e.g., hypertext linking), but is designed to overcome some of HTML's limitations. For example, it is designed to be extensible (i.e., designed to allow the creation of customized markup tags), which HTML is not. It is also designed to represent data by meaning rather than by layout (as it is represented in HTML). Like SGML, it is a metalanguage (a language for dealing with languages); it allows users to create a language tailored specifically to their needs.

Xu Yue (b. *c.* 185, Donglai, China—d. *c.* 227, China), Chinese astronomer and mathematician. He wrote several books, of which only *Shushu jiyi* ("Memoir on the Methods of Numbering") is extant; some scholars question its authenticity. The treatise was used as an auxiliary mathematics textbook in the Tang (618–907) and Song (960–1279) state universities. Its first part provides three methods of assigning the powers of 10 up to $10^{4,096}$ to traditionally established terms for "large numbers" and alludes to a method of indefinite generation of even larger numbers. The second part contains descriptions of various devices for representing, if not actually manipulating, large numbers. Among them the book mentions a device resembling the abacus, which some scholars believe originated in China.

Xuanzang, or HSÜAN-TSANG (b. 600, Guoshi, China—d. 664, Chang'an), Chinese Buddhist monk and pilgrim to India. He received a classical Confucian education before converting to Buddhism. Troubled by discrepancies in the sacred texts, he left for India in 629 to study the religion at its source. He traveled by foot across Central Asia and reached India in 633. After study at the famous Nalanda monastery, he returned home in 645 to a hero's welcome, bringing back hundreds of Buddhist texts, including some of the most important Mahayana scriptures, and spent the rest of his life translating. Influenced by the Yogacara school, he established the Weishi ("Ideation Only") school of Buddhism, which won many followers in Japan as the Hossō school. The classic novel *Xiyou ji* was inspired by his life.

xylophone, Percussion instrument consisting of a set of tuned wooden bars that are struck with mallets. Primitive xylophones may consist of logs of graded length laid across two supporting logs; a pit may be dug underneath to serve as a resonator. The xylophone has long been one of the principal instruments of African music; it is also important in the Indonesian gamelan. The marimba is a Latin American xylophone. In the modern orchestral xylophone, the bars are laid out on a stand in keyboard arrangement, with vertical resonating tubes suspended under each bar.

African log amadinda *xylophone; property of the Uganda Museum, Kampala*
Hillegeist/Kubik

yacht, Sail- or motor-driven vessel used for racing or recreation. The term is popularly applied to large recreational engine-powered boats; the sailboats known as yachts and used for racing are usually light and comparatively small. Until the mid-19th century, yachts were designed along the lines of naval craft such as schooners and cutters. Yacht design was greatly affected by the 1851 success of the *America* in the race that established the America's Cup. In the 20th century, notably after World War II, smaller racing and recreational craft became more common.

yahrzeit, or JAHRZEIT, In Judaism, the anniversary of the death of a parent or close relative, commonly observed by burning a candle for an entire day. On that day, the Kaddish is recited in the synagogue, and the Torah is read. Some mark the anniversary by studying portions of the Mishna, choosing those sections from the sixth division that begin with letters from the name of the deceased. Yahrzeit developed from an early Jewish custom of fasting on the anniversaries of deaths of certain leaders, and some Jews still fast on yahrzeit.

yak, Massive ox (*Bos grunniens mutus*) of high Tibetan plateaus.

*Yak (*Bos grunniens*).*
Russ Kinne/Photo Researchers

Bulls grow to 6 ft (1.8 m) at the shoulder hump. The wild yak's hair is black and short, except for a long, shaggy fringe on the flanks and tail. The horns spread outward and upward; the head is held low. Wild females and young live in large herds; mature bulls form smaller groups. Yaks graze on grass and require much water, eating snow in winter. Wild yaks are now endangered. Domestic yaks, which breed freely with domestic cattle, are used as pack, draft, milk, and beef animals. The hide provides leather; the tail, fly whisks; the fringe hair, ropes; the dried dung, fuel.

Yale University, Private university in New Haven, Conn., a traditional member of the Ivy League. Founded in 1701, it is the third-oldest institution of higher learning in the U.S. Yale's initial curriculum emphasized classical studies and strict adherence to orthodox Puritanism. Medical, divinity, and law schools were added in 1810, 1822, and 1824. The geologist Benjamin Silliman (1779–1864), who taught at Yale from 1802 to 1853, did much to expand the experimental and applied sciences. Beginning in the mid 19th century, schools of architecture, art, drama, forestry, graduate studies, management, music, and nursing were organized. Yale's library, with more than 10 million volumes, is one of the largest in the U.S. Its extensive art galleries were established in 1832. The Peabody Museum of Natural History houses important collections of paleontology, archaeology, and ethnology. Yale is one of the most highly regarded schools in the nation; its graduates have included several U.S. presidents.

Yalta, City (pop., 2001: 82,000), southern Crimea, Ukraine. It faces the Black Sea on the southern shore of the Crimean Peninsula. Settlement on the site dates from prehistoric times, but modern Yalta developed only in the early 19th century, becoming a town in 1838. Its mild winters and scenic location between sea and mountains have made it one of the most popular vacation and health resorts of Ukraine. In 1945 during World War II it was the site of the Allied leaders' Yalta Conference.

Yalta Conference (Feb. 4–11, 1945) Conference of Allied leaders at Yalta to plan Germany's defeat in World War II. Franklin Roosevelt, Winston Churchill, and Joseph Stalin discussed the postwar occupation of Germany, postwar assistance to the German people, German disarmament, war-crimes trials, the fate of the defeated or liberated states of eastern Europe, voting in the future

United Nations Security Council, and German reparations. Stalin agreed to enter the war against Japan after the German surrender. Roosevelt died two months later, and Stalin broke his promise to allow democratic elections in eastern Europe.

yam, Any of several plant species of the genus *Dioscorea* (family Dioscoreaceae, or yam family), native to warmer regions of both hemispheres. A number of species are cultivated for food in the tropics; in certain tropical cultures, notably of West Africa and New Guinea, the yam is the primary agricultural commodity and the focal point of elaborate ritual. The edible tuberous roots, which vary in taste from sweet to bitter to tasteless, are eaten as cooked starchy vegetables. Often boiled and then mashed, they may also be fried, roasted, or baked. True yams are botanically distinct from the sweet potato, though in the U.S. the names are commonly interchanged. *Dioscorea mexicana* contains a chemical that can suppress ovulation in humans and is used as the basis for birth-control pills. The so-called yam bean is the legume jicama.

Yamagata Aritomo (b. Aug. 3, 1838, Hagi, Japan—d. Feb 1, 1922, Tokyo), First prime minister under Japan's parliamentary regime (1889–91, 1898–1900). As a samurai youth in Chōshū province, Yamagata was among those who answered the foreign threat with the slogan "Sonnō jōi" ("Revere the emperor, expel the barbarians"). In 1864 Western gunboats bombarded the Chōshu coast, convincing him of the need for modern armaments. After participating in the Meiji Restoration, he went abroad to research military institutions, returning to become commander of an imperial force of 10,000 troops. When he introduced conscription, bearing arms ceased to be the exclusive prerogative of a warrior class. His forces defeated Saigō Takamori's rebellion in 1877. In politics he was more conservative than his contemporary Itō Hirobumi, favouring a strong executive. As prime minister, his policies were expansionist; Japan sent the largest of all foreign forces to China to quell the Boxer Rebellion. He increased the autonomy of the military and tried to suppress an incipient social-labour movement. After retirement, he continued to wield power as a genro (elder statesman).

Yamoussoukro, Town (pop., 2003 est.: 185,600), capital designate of Côte d'Ivoire. From 1960 to 1993 it served as the country's "second capital" because it was the birthplace, home, and unofficial headquarters of Pres. Félix Houphouët-Boigny. It was designated the official capital in 1983 and shares some of the functions of the former national capital, Abidjan. Fishing and forestry are important to its economy. It is the site of the basilica of Notre-Dame de la Paix, the world's largest Christian church, an almost exact replica of St. Peter's in Rome.

Yangon, formerly RANGOON, City (pop., 2007 prelim.: 4,090,000), principal port, and historical capital of Myanmar (Burma), on the Yangon River. It was a fishing village until the present city was founded in the mid-1750s by King Alaungpaya; he developed it as a port. The British occupied it in 1824–26 during the First Anglo-Burmese War and again took it in 1852 during the Second Anglo-Burmese War. After the British annexation of all of Burma in 1886, Rangoon became the capital city. During World War II the Japanese advanced on and occupied the city, and it suffered considerable damage. It handles more than four-fifths of Myanmar's foreign commerce. In 2005 Myanmar government offices began to be moved to Pyinmana, some 200 mi (320 km) north of Yangon. Subsequently they were transferred to a new city, Nay Pyi Taw, which is located near Pyinmana and was declared the country's official capital in 2006.

Yangtze River, Chinese CHANG JIANG, or CH'ANG CHIANG, River, China. It is the world's third longest river, 3,915 mi (6,300 km) long. Rising in the Tanggula Mountains in west-central China, it flows southeast before turning northeast and then generally east across south-central and east-central China to the East China Sea near Shanghai. It is known as the Jinsha in its upper course. Its

chief tributaries are the Yalong, Min, Jialing, Han, and Wu rivers. Several large cities, including Shanghai, Nanjing, Wuhan, and Chongqing, lie in the river's basin, which is known as the granary of China. Large ships can sail to Wuhan, and smaller vessels can reach Yichang; it becomes harder to navigate above Yichang because of the gorges that occur between Chongqing and Yichang. Work on the Three Gorges Dam project—first discussed in the 1920s and promoted in the 1950s by Mao Zedong—was inaugurated in 1993; the dam was completed in 2006. Located west of Yichang, it will enable freighters to navigate 1,400 mi (2,250 km) inland from the East China Sea to Chongqing.

Yao, In Chinese mythology, one of three legendary emperors, along with Shun and Dayu, of the golden age of antiquity (c. 24th century BC). All three were exalted by Confucius as models of virtue, righteousness, and unselfish devotion.

Yao, imaginative portrait by an artist of the Qianlong period (1735–96); in the Metropolitan Museum of Art, New York City.
Courtesy of the Metropolitan Museum of Art, New York, gift of Mrs. Edward S. Harkness, 1947

Yaoundé, City (pop., 2004 est.: 1,434,700), capital of Cameroon. It was founded in 1888 while Cameroon was a German protectorate. The area came under French control, and it was declared the capital of French Cameroun in 1922. In 1940–46 it was replaced as the capital by Douala, but, after Cameroon achieved independence in 1960, it again became the capital. It contains several small manufacturing and processing industries (sawmills and printing presses), and it is the area's agricultural market.

yard, Unit of length equal to 36 in., or 3 ft, in the U.S. Customary System or 0.9144 m in the International System of Units. A cloth yard, used to measure cloth, is 37 in. long; it was also the standard length for arrows. In casual speech, a yard (e.g., of concrete, gravel, or topsoil) may refer to a cubic yard.

yaws, or FRAMBESIA, Contagious tropical disease, caused by a variant of the spirochete that causes syphilis. Yaws spreads mainly by discharge from skin sores, not sexual activity. It is common in children, who usually become immune. In the first stage, a skin sore starts as a wartlike thickening, cracks open, leaks fluid, and bleeds easily. A month or more later, multiple sores erupt. The third stage (much rarer than in syphilis) involves destruction of skin, mucous membranes, and bones. Penicillin cures early-stage yaws. Prevention requires isolation and prompt treatment and personal and group hygiene.

year, Time required for the Earth to travel once around the Sun, slightly less than 365 $1/4$ days. This fractional number makes necessary the periodic adjustment of days in any calendar that is to be kept in step with the seasons. In the Gregorian calendar, a common year contains 365 days, and every fourth year is a leap year of 366 days except for any year that is divisible by 100 but not divisible by 400 (e.g., 1900 was not a leap year).

yeast, Any of certain economically important and usually single-celled fungi, most of which are classified as ascomycetes. Found worldwide in soils and on plant surfaces, yeasts are especially abundant in sugary mediums such as flower nectar and fruits. The types commonly used in the production of bread, beer, and wine are selected strains of *Saccharomyces cerevisiae*; the small cakes and packets used contain billions of individual yeast cells, each of which can ferment approximately its own weight of glucose per hour. Dried yeast is 50% protein and is rich in B vitamins; brewer's yeast is sometimes taken as a vitamin supplement. Some yeasts are mild to dangerous pathogens of humans and other animals. *Candida albicans*, for example, irritates oral and vaginal linings, and *Histoplasma* and *Blastomyces* cause persistent lung infections.

Yeats, William Butler (b. June 13, 1865, Sandymount, Dublin, Ire.—d. Jan. 28, 1939, Roquebrune-Cap-Martin, France), Irish poet, dramatist, and prose writer. The son of a well-known painter, Yeats early developed an interest in mysticism and visionary traditions as well as in Irish folklore, and both interests would continue to be sources of poetic imagery for him. His early volumes include the poetry volume *The Wanderings of Oisin* (1889) and the essay collection *The Celtic Twilight* (1893). In 1889 he fell in love with Maud Gonne, a brilliant, beautiful Irish patriot who inspired his involvement in Irish nationalism but did not reciprocate his feelings. With Lady Augusta Gregory and others, he founded the theatre that became the Abbey Theatre; throughout his life he would remain one of its directors. He contributed plays to its repertoire, including *The Countess Cathleen* (1899), *On Baile's Strand* (1905), and *Deirdre* (1907). His poetry changed decisively in the years 1909–14: the otherworldly, ecstatic atmosphere of the early lyrics cleared and his work gained in concreteness and complexity, often dealing with political themes, though his interest in mysticism and his passion for Maud Gonne continued unabated. With *Responsibilities* (1914) and *The Wild Swans at Coole* (1917) he began the period of his highest achievement. Some of his greatest verse appears in *The Tower* (1928), *The Winding Stair* (1929), and *Last Poems* (1939). The individual poems of the latter are largely held together by the system of symbolism he developed in *A Vision* (1925), which used astrological images to link individual psychology with the larger patterns of history. Yeats was a member of the Irish Senate (1922–28). He won the Nobel Prize for Literature in 1923, and he is regarded by some as the greatest English-language poet of the 20th century.

Yekaterinburg, formerly (1924–91) SVERDLOVSK, City (pop., 2006 est.: 1,308,441), west-central Russia. An ironworks was established in 1721, and a fortress, named for Empress Catherine I, was founded there in 1722. It grew as the centre for all the ironworks of the Ural Mountains region, and its importance increased with the building of a highway (1783) and the Trans-Siberian Railroad. It achieved notoriety as the place where Tsar Nicholas II and his family were held prisoner and executed by the Bolsheviks in 1918. In 1924 it was renamed Sverdlovsk in honour of Yakov Sverdlov. The city reverted to its original name after the breakup of the U.S.S.R. in 1991. It is a major industrial centre, especially for heavy machinery.

yellow fever, Acute infectious tropical disease, sometimes occurring in temperate zones. Abrupt onset of headache, backache, fever, nausea, and vomiting is followed by either recovery with immunity or by higher fever, slow pulse, and vomiting of blood. Patients may die in a week. Jaundice is common (hence the name). One of the world's great plagues for 300 years, it is caused by a virus transmitted by several species of mosquitoes. Carlos Finlay suggested and Walter Reed proved this means of spread, leading to near elimination of the disease through mosquito control. Treatment consists of supportive care, particularly fever reduction. Control of mosquitoes near cities and live-virus vaccines—developed by Max Theiler (1899–1972), who won a 1951 Nobel Prize for his work—have made yellow fever completely preventable.

Yellow Sea, Chinese HUANG HAI, Large inlet of the western North Pacific Ocean, between northeastern China and the Korean peninsula. Renowned for its fishing grounds, it connects with the East China Sea on the south; the Shandong Peninsula extends into it from the west. Two major arms of it are the Bo Hai (northwest) and Korea Bay (north). Excluding the Bo Hai, it has an area of about 146,700 sq mi (380,000 sq km) and a maximum depth of roughly 500 ft (152 m). It derives its name from the colour of the silt-laden water discharged into it by major Chinese rivers, including the Huang He (Yellow River), which flows into the Bo Hai, and the Yangtze. Leading port cities include Qingdao and Dalian in China, Inch'ŏn in South Korea, and Namp'o in North Korea.

Yellowstone National Park, National preserve in northwestern Wyoming, southern Montana, and eastern Idaho, U.S. The oldest national park in the U.S.—and in the world—it was established by the U.S. Congress in 1872. It covers 3,472 sq mi (8,987 sq km). The Gallatin, Absaroka, and Teton mountain ranges extend into it. Yellowstone has unusual geologic features, including fossil forests and eroded basaltic lava flows, and some 10,000 hydrothermal features, including hot springs, steam vents, fumaroles, and geysers. Old Faithful, the park's most famous geyser, erupts about every 60 to 110 minutes, the average being roughly 90 minutes. Notable among the park's many lakes and rivers are Yellowstone Lake, Shoshone Lake, the Snake River, and the Yellowstone River. In 1988 an extensive series of forest fires temporarily laid waste to large areas of the park, but the tree cover gradually returned.

Yeltsin, Boris (Nikolayevich) (b. Feb. 1, 1931, Sverdlovsk, Russia, U.S.S.R.—d. April 23, 2007, Moscow, Russia), Russian politician and president of Russia (1990–99). After attending the Urals Polytechnic Institute, he worked at construction projects in western Russia (1955–68). He became Communist Party leader in Sverdlovsk in 1976, and he was an ally of Mikhail Gorbachev. Gorbachev later charged Yeltsin with eliminating corruption in the Moscow party organization, and as first secretary (mayor) of Moscow (1985–87) he proved a determined reformer. His criticism of the slow pace of reform led to a break with Gorbachev, and Yeltsin lost his position. In 1989 he was elected to the new Soviet parliament by a landslide, then became president of the Russian Republic (1990) and resigned from the Communist Party. In 1991 he won the presidency again in the first popular election in Russian history. When communist hard-liners staged a coup against Gorbachev, Yeltsin successfully opposed it, facing down its leaders with a dramatic outdoor speech in Moscow. He led the establishment of the Commonwealth of Independent States (1991) and began to transform Russia's economy into one based on free markets and private enterprise. Hard-liners staged an unsuccessful coup against Yeltsin in 1993. When Chechnya unilaterally declared independence, Yeltsin sent troops to fight the rebels (1994). The Chechnya situation and Russia's deepening economic distress lessened his popularity, but he won reelection over a Communist Party challenger in 1996. After suffering a heart attack, he spent several months recovering. Continuing poor health led to his resignation on Dec. 31, 1999. He was succeeded by Vladimir Putin.

Boris Yeltsin, 1991.
Vario Press—Camera Press/Globe Photos

Yemen, officially REPUBLIC OF YEMEN, Country, Middle East, southwestern Asia. It occupies the southern tip of the Arabian Peninsula and also includes the island of Socotra in the Indian Ocean and the Kamaran island group in the Red Sea. Area: 203,891 sq mi (528,076 sq km). Population: (2011 est.) 24,800,000. Capital: Sanaa. The population is mainly Arab. Language: Arabic (official). Religion: Islam (official; mostly Sunni). Currency: Yemeni rial. From the Gulf of Aden and the Red Sea, a narrow coastal plain leads to highlands that cover most of the country. The northern region extends into the southern and southwestern Rub' al-Khali desert. Mineral resources include iron ore, salt, petroleum, and natural gas, all of which are exploited. Agriculture is important; industries include petroleum and salt production. Yemen is a multiparty republic with two legislative houses; its head of state is the president, and the head of government is the prime minister. Tribal affiliations remain strong and directly affect local and national policy. Yemen was the home of ancient Minaean, Sabaean, and Ḥimyārite kingdoms. The Romans invaded the region in the 1st century CE. In the 6th century it was conquered by Ethiopians and Persians. Following the adoption of Islam in the 7th century, it was ruled nominally under a caliphate. The Egyptian Ayyūbid dynasty ruled there in the late 12th–early 13th century, after which the region passed to the Rasūlids. From *c.* 1520 through 1918 the Ottoman Empire maintained varying degrees of control, especially in the northwestern section. A boundary agreement was reached in 1934 between the northwestern territory (controlled by a local religious leader), which subsequently became the Yemen Arab Republic (North Yemen), and the southeastern British-controlled territory, which subsequently became the People's Democratic Republic of Yemen (South Yemen). Relations between the two Yemens remained tense and were marked by conflict throughout the 1970s and '80s. The two officially united as the Republic of Yemen in 1990. Its 1993 elections were the first free, multiparty general elections held in the Arabian Peninsula, and they were the first in which women participated. In 1994, after a two-month civil war, a new constitution was approved. Desire for political and economic reform led to a popular uprising of unprecedented proportions in 2011.

Yenisey River, River, central Russia. One of the longest rivers in Asia, it rises in the borderland of south-central Russia and Mongolia and flows generally north along the edge of the West Siberian Plain to empty into the Kara Sea. Along its course it receives numerous tributaries, including the Angara River. Approximately 1,900 mi (3,000 km) of the river's 2,540-mi (4,090-km) course (calculated from the Great Yenisey River) are navigable.

Yerevan, formerly ERIVAN, City (pop., 2004 est.: 1,101,900), capital of Armenia. Fortified since the 8th century BC and part of Armenia since the 6th century BC, it developed as an important centre of the caravan trade. Over the centuries, its rulers have included the Romans, Arabs, Turks, and Russians; it fell to the latter in 1827. In 1920 it became the capital of independent Armenia and remained so during the period of Soviet rule and after independence was restored. Its industries include those producing chemicals, aluminum, automobiles, and electrical machinery.

yeshiva, Academy of higher Talmudic learning. Through its biblical and legal exegesis and application of scripture, the yeshiva has defined and regulated Judaism for centuries. Traditionally, it is the setting for the training and ordination of rabbis. Following the destruction of the Second Temple of Jerusalem, a series of yeshivas were set up around the Levant to codify and explain centuries of Jewish scholarship. In medieval times, yeshivas flourished in Europe wherever there were large populations of Jews. The first yeshiva in the U.S., ʿEtz Ḥayyim (1886), later became Yeshiva University (1945).

yew, Any of about eight species of ornamental evergreens in the genus *Taxus*, family Taxaceae (the yew family), distributed throughout the Northern Hemisphere. Two species are always shrubby, but the others may reach heights of 77 ft (25 m). The plants have many branches, covered with needlelike leaves. Yew wood is hard, fine-grained, and heavy, with white or creamy sapwood and amber to brown heartwood. Once popular for cabinetwork, implements, and archery bows, it is used more today for articles either carved or turned on a lathe. Other trees called yew but not in this family are the plum-yew (family Cephalotaxaceae) and Prince Albert yew (family Podocarpaceae).

Yggdrasill, In Norse mythology, the world tree. One of its roots extended into the underworld, another into the land of the giants, and the third into Asgard. At its base were three wells: the Well of Fate, from which the tree was watered by the Fates; the Roaring Kettle, in which dwelt Nidhogg, the monster that gnawed the tree's roots; and Mimir's Well, the source of wisdom, for whose water Odin sacrificed an eye. After the Ragnarok, Yggdrasill, though badly shaken, is to be the source of new life.

Yi Song-gye, or T'AEJO (b. 1335—d. 1408), Founder of the Korean Chosŏn dynasty (1392–1910). A military leader in the Koryŏ dynasty, he rose through the ranks by battling invading forces. He defeated his rivals and drove out the last king of the Koryŏ dynasty, taking the throne in 1392. He established his capital at Hanyang (now Seoul). He and his successors redistributed land, which had been concentrated in the hands of a few high-ranking bureaucrats, throughout the various levels of officialdom. In a break with the past, he made Neo-Confucianism the state religion, replacing Buddhism. Farming was made the centre of the economy. In foreign relations, he maintained a close relationship with China's Ming dynasty.

Yiddish language, Language of Ashkenazic Jews and their descendants, written in the Hebrew alphabet. Yiddish developed from southeastern dialects of Middle High German carried into central and eastern Europe beginning in the 12th century; it has been strongly influenced by Hebrew and Aramaic, from which it draws 12–20% of its lexicon. The isolation of eastern European speakers from High German and their exposure to Slavic languages, particularly Polish and Ukrainian, led to a primary distinction between West and East Yiddish dialects. From the late 18th century most Jews remaining in central Europe gave up Yiddish in favour of German; it has now virtually died out. East Yiddish dialects differ markedly in realization of vowels; there are central, northeastern, and southeastern dialects. A flourishing literary language in the 19th and early 20th century, Yiddish declined dramatically due to suppression, massive migration, assimilation, and Nazi genocide. The language nevertheless continues to flourish among the ultra-Orthodox Hasidim in numerous countries and among secular students of Yiddish at leading universities, including Columbia University (New York), Hebrew University (Jerusalem), McGill University (Montreal), the University of Oxford, and the University of Paris. Yiddish is spoken by three million people worldwide.

Yijing or I CHING (Chinese: "Book of Changes"), Ancient Chinese text, one of the Five Classics of Confucianism. The main body of the work, traditionally attributed to Wenwang, contains a discussion of the divinatory system used by wizards in the Zhou dynasty. A supplementary section of "commentaries," believed to date from the Warring States period (475–221 BC), is a philosophical exposition that attempts to explain the world and its ethical principles. The book's cosmology, which involves humans and nature in a single system, has made it universally popular.

yin-yang, In East Asian thought, the two complementary forces or principles that make up all aspects and phenomena of life. Yin is earth, female, dark, passive, and absorbing; it is present in even numbers and in valleys and streams and is represented by the tiger, the colour orange, and a broken line. Yang is heaven, male, light, active, and penetrating; it is present in odd numbers and mountains and is represented by the dragon, the colour azure, and an unbroken line. Together they express the interdependence of opposites.

Yinchuan, or YIN-CH'UAN, City (pop., 2003 est.: 535,743), capital of Ningxia autonomous region, north-central China. It is located near the western end of the Great Wall. Originally a county in the 1st century BC, it became the capital of the Xi (Western) Xia dynasty in AD 907. In 1227 it came under the Yuan dynasty and was later ruled by the Ming and the Qing dynasties. In 1928 it became the capital of the newly formed Ningxia province. In

1954, when Ningxia province was abolished, the city became part of Gansu province. With the establishment of the Ningxia autonomous region in 1958, Yinchuan once again became the capital. Largely nonindustrial, it is the chief agricultural market and distribution centre for the area.

Yoga, One of the six orthodox systems (darshans) of Indian philosophy, which has had widespread influence on many schools of Indian thought. It is better known through its practical aspect than its intellectual content, which is largely based on the philosophy of Samkhya. Holding that the evolution of the world occurred in stages, Yoga attempts to reverse this order so that a person reenters his or her state of purity and consciousness. Generally, the Yoga process involves eight stages, which may require several lifetimes to pass through. The first two stages are ethical preparations emphasizing morality, cleanliness, and devotion to God. The next two stages are physical preparations that condition the body to make it supple, flexible, and healthy; the physical aspects of Yoga have been most successfully popularized in the West. The fifth stage involves control of the mind and senses to withdraw from outward objects. The remaining three stages entail the cultivation of increasingly concentrated states of awareness, which will ultimately lead to release from the cycle of rebirth.

Yogacara, or VIJNANAVADA, Idealistic school of Mahayana Buddhism. It rejects the complete realism of Theravada Buddhism and the practical realism of the Madhyamika school, preferring a more complicated position in which the reality perceived by humans does not exist but only appears to do so by virtue of the capacity of the mind to perceive patterns of continuity and regularity. Yogacara emerged in India about the 2nd century and was introduced into China in the 7th century by Xuanzang. It was transmitted to Japan in the mid-7th century as Hossō.

yogurt, Semisolid, fermented, often flavoured milk food. Yogurt is known and consumed in almost all parts of the world. It is traditionally made by adding common strains of *Streptococcus* and *Lactobacillus* bacteria to raw milk. The culture is produced by taking a portion of a previous batch. In modern commercial yogurt making, a blend of concentrated sterilized milk and milk solids is inoculated with the two bacteria; sometimes *L. acidophilus* or a lactose-fermenting yeast is also added. The product is then incubated four or five hours at 110–112 °F (43–44 °C) until curd forms. Various flavours and sweetening may be added.

Yokohama, Seaport city (pop., 2003 est.: 3,466,875), east-central Honshu, Japan. The country's principal port and second largest city, it is located on the western shore of Tokyo Bay and is part of the Tokyo urban-industrial complex. It was a small fishing village when U.S. naval officer Matthew Perry visited in 1854 to negotiate Japanese trading possibilities. In 1859 it was opened for foreign settlement and trade. Yokohama was destroyed by earthquake and fire in 1923 and severely damaged by U.S. air raids in 1945 during World War II, but it was rebuilt both times. It produces textiles, chemicals, ships, machinery, petroleum products, and automobiles.

Yom Kippur, English DAY OF ATONEMENT, Jewish religious holiday, observed on the 10th day of the lunar month of Tishri (in late September or early October). It concludes the 10 days of repentance that begin with Rosh Hashanah. Its purpose is to purify the individual and community by forgiving the sins of others and by repenting one's own sins against God. Before the destruction of the Temple of Jerusalem, the high priest performed a sacrificial ceremony that concluded with the death of a scapegoat. Today it is marked by fasting and abstention from sex. Its eve, when the Kol Nidre is recited, and the entire day of Yom Kippur, are spent in prayer and meditation.

yoni, In Hinduism, a representation of the female sexual organ and feminine generative power, the symbol of the goddess Shakti.

The yoni is often associated with the phallic linga, the symbol of the god Shiva. The linga is depicted in art as resting in the yoni, their union representing the eternal process of creation and regeneration.

York, ancient EBORACUM, City and unitary authority (pop., 2001: 181,131), geographic county of North Yorkshire, historic county of Yorkshire, England. Located at the confluence of the Ouse and Foss rivers, it is the cathedral city of the archbishop of York and was historically the ecclesiastical capital of northern England. It was also the seat of the historic county of Yorkshire. York was a Celtic and then a Roman settlement. Constantine I was proclaimed Roman emperor in York in AD 306. It was conquered by the Danes in 867. York suffered severely in the Norman conquest of northern England in the 11th century. During the Middle Ages it was a prosperous wool-trading town and the performance site of the York plays. It has a manufacturing economy and a tourist industry fostered by its medieval sites.

York, house of, Younger branch of the Plantagenet dynasty, descended from Edward III's fifth son, Edmund of Langley (1341–1402), 1st duke of York. In the 15th century the Yorkists took the throne from the house of Lancaster; the Yorkist kings were Edward IV, Edward V, and Richard III. The Wars of the Roses between the two houses continued until Richard's death at the Battle of Bosworth Field in 1453. The marriage of Henry VII, the first Tudor king, to the daughter of Edward IV, merged the house of York with the house of Tudor.

Yoruba, One of Nigeria's three largest ethnic groups, numbering more than 22 million. The many dialects comprising the Yoruba language belong to the Benue-Congo branch of the Niger-Congo family. The Yoruba states, including the Oyo empire, were built in the 11th–16th centuries. Yorubaland remains divided into politically autonomous kingdoms, each centred on a capital city or town and headed by a hereditary king (*oba*), traditionally considered sacred. Most Yoruba men are farmers, growing yams, corn, and millet as staples; cocoa is a cash crop. Yoruba women control much of the complex market system. Craftsmen work in blacksmithing, weaving, leatherworking, glassmaking, bronze casting, and ivory- and wood-carving. Though some Yoruba are now Christians or Muslims, belief in their traditional religion continues, and it remains alive, too, in the New World countries to which many Yoruba were transported to work as slaves. The Yoruba language has an extensive literature of poetry, short stories, myths, and proverbs.

yttrium, Metallic chemical element, one of the transition elements, chemical symbol Y, atomic number 39. It was the first rare earth metal to be discovered (1794) and was named after Ytterby, the Swedish town where it was discovered. Yttrium is used in alloys and in metallurgical operations. Yttrium compounds are used in optical glasses and in special ceramics, as catalysts, and in electronic and optical devices including phosphors and lasers.

Yuan Shikai, or YÜAN SHIH-KAI (b. Sept. 16, 1859, Xiangcheng, Henan province, China—d. June 6, 1916, Beijing), Chinese army leader and president of the Republic of China (1912–16). He began his military career serving in Korea in the 1880s. In 1885 he was made Chinese commissioner at Seoul; his promotion of China's interests contributed to the outbreak of the Sino-Japanese War (1894–95). The war destroyed China's navy and army, and the task of training a new army fell to Yuan. When his division was the only one to survive the Boxer Rebellion (1900), his political stature increased. He played a decisive part in China's modernization and defense programs and enjoyed the support of the empress dowager Cixi. On her death he was dismissed, only to be called back following the overthrow of the Qing dynasty in 1911–12, when he became the first president of the new republic; Sun Yat-sen had previously served as the provisional president. Impatient with the new National Assembly, he ordered the assassination of Song

Jiaoren, leader of the Nationalist Party in 1913. He quelled a subsequent revolt, but his efforts to found his own dynasty (1915–16) failed.

Yucatán Peninsula, Peninsula, northeastern Central America. It lies between the Gulf of Mexico and the Caribbean Sea; its 76,300-sq-mi (197,600-sq-km) territory includes the Mexican states of Campeche, Quintana Roo, and Yucatán and, in the south, large parts of Belize and Guatemala. It is about 200 mi (320 km) wide and has a coastline of about 700 mi (1,100 km). The area had long been home to many pre-Columbian civilizations before Spanish explorer Hernán Cortés traversed its inland portion in 1525. Spanish rule was subsequently established, but since that time many independent Maya Indians have kept to its inland rural areas and resisted the authority of the central government. Its coastal area, with many beaches and resorts, and its ancient archaeological sites, including Chichén Itzá, Uaxactún, and Uxmal, are major tourist destinations, as is the resort city of Cancún.

yucca, Any of about 40 species of succulent plants (genus *Yucca*) of the agave family, native to southern North America. Most species lack a stem and have a rosette of stiff, sword-shaped leaves at the base and clusters of waxy white flowers. The Joshua tree (*Y. brevifolia*) has a stem more than 33 ft (10 m) high. Commonly cultivated as ornamentals for their unusual appearance and attractive flower clusters are the aptly named Spanish bayonet (*Y. aloifolia*), Spanish dagger (*Y. gloriosa*), and Adam's needle, or bear grass (*Y. filamentosa*). Yucca moths (genus *Tegeticula*) inhabit yucca bushes, and each moth species is adapted to a particular yucca species. The yucca can be fertilized by no other insect, and the moth can use no other plant to raise its larvae.

Yucca
Courtesy of the New Mexico
Department of Development

yuga, Unit of the cosmic cycle in Hindu cosmology. Each yuga is progressively shorter than the preceding one, corresponding to a decline in the moral and physical state of humanity. Four such yugas make up a mahayuga; 2,000 mahayugas make up the basic cosmic cycle, the kalpa. The first yuga was an age of perfection that lasted 1,728,000 years. The fourth and most degenerate yuga began in 3102 BC and will last 432,000 years. At the close of this yuga, the world will be destroyed, to be recreated after a period of quiescence as the cycle resumes.

Yugoslavia, Former federated country situated on the west-central Balkan Peninsula of southern Europe. Between 1929 and 2003 three federations bore the name Yugoslavia ("Land of the South Slavs"). After the Balkan Wars of 1912–13 ended Turkish rule in the Balkan Peninsula and Austria-Hungary was defeated in World War I, a Kingdom of Serbs, Croats, and Slovenes was established, comprising the former kingdoms of Serbia and Montenegro (including Serbian-held Macedonia) as well as Croatia, Bosnia and Herzegovina, Austrian territory in Dalmatia and Slovenia, and Hungarian land north of the Danube River. The Kingdom of Yugoslavia, officially proclaimed in 1929 by King Alexander I and lasting until World War II, covered 95,576 sq mi (247,542 sq km). The postwar Socialist Federal Republic of Yugoslavia covered 98,766 sq mi (255,804 sq km) and had a population of about 24 million by 1991; it consisted of six republics (Serbia, Croatia, Slovenia, Macedonia, Montenegro, and Bosnia and Herzegovina) as well as two autonomous provinces (Vojvodina and Kosovo). After the violent breakup of federal Yugoslavia and the declarations of independence of Slovenia, Croatia, Bosnia, and Macedonia, the "third

Yugoslavia" was inaugurated on April 27, 1992. It had roughly 45% of the population and 40% of the area of its predecessor and consisted of the republics of Serbia and Montenegro. In 2003 the name Yugoslavia was abandoned, and the country was renamed Serbia and Montenegro. In 2006 Montenegro declared its independence, and the Republic of Serbia became a country in its own right. After serious violence, NATO intervention, and nine years of UN administration, Kosovo declared its independence in 2008.

Yukon River, River system, northwestern North America. Its length, measured from the headwaters of the McNeil River in south-central Yukon, Can., is 1,980 mi (3,190 km), making it the third longest river and fourth longest river system in North America. It flows northwest across the Yukon border into the U.S. state of Alaska and then generally southwest across central Alaska to the Bering Sea. Its entire course of 1,265 mi (2,035 km) in Alaska is navigable. It attracted attention following the rich gold strikes in 1896, notably the Klondike gold rush on one of its Canadian tributaries, the Klondike River.

Yunnan, or YÜN-NAN, Province (pop., 2002 est.: 43,330,000), southern China. It is bordered by Vietnam, Laos, and Myanmar, Sichuan and Guizhou provinces, and Guangxi and Tibet autonomous regions. It has an area of 168,400 sq mi (436,200 sq km), and its capital is Kunming. Its population is one of China's most ethnically mixed, comprising more than 20 nationalities. The terrain is largely mountainous, especially in the north and west. It is crossed by three major river systems—the Yangtze (Chang; there known as the Jinsha), the Mekong, and the Salween—and is the source of two others—the Xi (there known as the Nanpan and Hongshui) and the Yuan. Because of its isolation, the region was independent during the historical development of China. The Mongols overran it in the 13th century. In 1855–73 it was the scene of the great Panthay (Muslim) rebellion. Part of the province was seized by the Japanese in World War II. Yunnan is now noted for its agricultural production, especially of rice, as well as for its extensive mining industry.

Zagreb, City (pop., 2001: 691,724), capital of Croatia. It was first mentioned in 1093, when a Roman Catholic bishopric was established there. In medieval times the area contained a civil and an ecclesiastical settlement. Rivals until the 19th century, they were joined when a spate of new building occurred and expanded onto the Sava River floodplain. At the time of the Croatian national revival in the 19th century, Zagreb was the centre of both a pan-Yugoslav movement and a Croatian independence movement. During the civil war following Croatia's secession from Yugoslavia in 1991, Zagreb sustained heavy damage. It is Croatia's principal industrial centre. It is also the seat of the Academy of Sciences and Arts and of the University of Zagreb (1669).

Zambezi River, River, south-central Africa. It rises in northwestern Zambia, flows south across eastern Angola and western Zambia to the border of Botswana, then turns east and forms the Zambia-Zimbabwe border. It then crosses central Mozambique and empties into the Mozambique Channel at Chinde. About 2,200 mi (3,540 km) long, it is navigable in three long stretches, separated by rapids and by Victoria Falls. It drains the entire south-central region of the continent. Its many tributaries include the Kwando, the Kafue, and the Shire. It was explored by David Livingstone in the early 1850s.

Zambia, officially REPUBLIC OF ZAMBIA, formerly NORTHERN RHODESIA, Landlocked country, south-central Africa. Area: 290,585 sq mi (752,612 sq km). Population: (2011 est.) 13,306,000. Capital: Lusaka. The population is composed almost entirely of Bantu-speaking African ethnic groups. Languages: English (official); numerous local languages are also spoken. Religions: Christianity (Protestant, other Christians, Roman Catholic); also traditional beliefs, Islam. Currency: kwacha. The country consists of a high plateau through which the Zambezi (including

Victoria Falls), Kafue, and Luangwa rivers flow. Lakes Mweru and Tanganyika touch Zambia's northern boundaries, and Lake Bangweulu and the Bangweulu Swamps form extensive wetlands farther to the south. The Muchinga Mountains in the east and the ranges along the eastern border have the highest elevations in the country. There are forests of Zambezi teak in the southwest. Zambia's economy depends on the production and export of copper. Other important mineral resources include lead, zinc, cobalt, coal, and gold. Agriculture also is important. There is some manufacturing. Zambia is a multiparty republic with one legislative house; its head of state and government is the president. Ancestors of the Tonga reached the region early in the 2nd millennium CE, but other peoples from the Democratic Republic of the Congo and Angola reached the country only in the 17th–18th century. Portuguese trading missions were established early in the 18th century. Emissaries of Cecil Rhodes and the British South Africa Company concluded treaties with most of the Zambian chiefs during the 1890s. The company administered the region known as Northern Rhodesia until 1924, when it became a British protectorate. It was part of the Central African Federation of Rhodesia and Nyasaland in 1953–63. In 1964 Northern Rhodesia became independent as the Republic of Zambia. A constitutional amendment enacted in 1991 allowed opposition parties.

Zande, or AZANDE, People of central Africa who live in South Sudan, the Democratic Republic of the Congo, and the Central African Republic. They speak an Adamawa-Ubangi language of the Niger-Congo family. They occupy widely scattered family homesteads, subsisting through agriculture and hunting. Patrilineal clans are numerous. Witchcraft, magic, and divination are major features of social life. The Zande number about 3.8 million.

Zanzibar, Chief island (pop., 2002: 622,459) of Tanzania. Located in the Indian Ocean off the coast of east-central Africa, it has an area of 637 sq mi (1,651 sq km). Zanzibar city (pop., 2002: 205,870), the island's principal port and commercial centre, is on the western side. Both Zanzibar and Pemba islands are believed to have once formed part of the African continent. In the late 17th century, Zanzibar came under the control of Omani Arabs, and the sultan of Oman made Zanzibar city his capital in 1832. In 1861 Zanzibar was separated from Oman and became an independent sultanate. Under Sultan Barghash (r. 1870–88), most of the mainland territories were lost to European powers. In 1890 the British proclaimed a protectorate over Zanzibar and Pemba islands. In 1963 the sultanate regained its independence and became a member of the Commonwealth. The sultanate was overthrown in 1964, and a republic was established. It then joined with Tanganyika to form the Republic of Tanzania. The economy depends on agriculture and fishing.

Zapata, Emiliano (b. Aug. 8, 1879, Anenecuilco, Mex.—d. April 10, 1919, Morelos), Mexican revolutionary and champion of the rural poor. A mestizo peasant, he was orphaned at age 17 and took responsibility for his brothers and sisters. He led his neighbours in protests against the hacienda that had appropriated their land and eventually led them in taking the land by force. He organized a small force to help Francisco Madero unseat Porfirio Díaz. Dissatisfied with the pace of land reform under Madero, Zapata led a guerrilla campaign that took land back from the haciendas and returned it to the communal Indian *ejido*s. He was instru-

Zapata, 1912
Archivo Casasola

mental in the defeat of Gen. Victoriano Huerta after Huerta deposed and assassinated Madero. With Pancho Villa he occupied Mexico City and began to implement land reform, but he was tricked, ambushed, and killed by the forces of Venustiano Carranza, whom the U.S. had recognized as president.

Zapotec, Indian population living in the state of Oaxaca, southern Mexico. Early Zapotec civilization, centred on Monte Albán (near the modern city of Oaxaca), produced the first writing in Mesoamerica and devised the 52-year round calendar later borrowed by other groups. Present-day traditional Zapotec society is largely agricultural, and members practice shifting cultivation. The major crafts include pottery and weaving. The Zapotecs profess Roman Catholicism, but belief in spirits and myths persists.

Zaragoza, or SARAGOSSA, City (pop., 2001: 614,905), northeastern Spain. The capital of the Aragon autonomous community (*comunidad autónoma*), Zaragoza is located on the southern bank of the Ebro River. The Celtiberian town of Salduba at the site was taken by the Romans at the end of the 1st century BC and made a colony named Caesaraugusta, from which its present name derives. It became an episcopal see in the 3rd century AD, and it was taken by the Moors *c.* 714. It was the capital of the kingdom of Aragon from the 12th to the 15th century. It underwent two sieges (1808–09) by the French, which were commemorated in Lord Byron's *Childe Harold*. It is an industrial centre and the site of the annual National Trade Fair. Notable buildings include Romanesque and Gothic churches and palaces. Its university was founded in 1474.

zazen, Sitting meditation as practiced in Zen Buddhism. The disciple sits in a quiet room, breathing rhythmically and easily, with legs fully or half crossed, spine and head erect, hands folded one palm above the other, and eyes open. Logical, analytic thinking is suspended, as are all desires, attachments, and judgments, leaving the mind in a state of relaxed attention. The practice was brought to prominence by Dogen, who considered it not only to be a method of moving toward enlightenment but also, if properly experienced, to constitute enlightenment itself.

Zealand, Danish SJÆLLAND, Island, Denmark. Located between the Kattegat strait and the Baltic Sea, Zealand is the largest (2,715 sq mi [7,031 sq km]) and most populous island (pop., 2003 est.: 2,096,449) of Denmark. Copenhagen is its major city. Two fjords break the irregular coastline of the island, and fine beaches line its northern shore. It has many Stone Age and Viking relics, including the Viking fortress of Trælleborg (*c.* 1000), as well as medieval churches, castles, and manor houses. Grain and livestock farming, fishing, and tourism are major industries.

zebra, Any of three species of black-and-white-striped equines that subsist almost entirely on grass. Zebras stand 47–55 in. (120–140 cm) tall. The Burchell's zebra, or bonte quagga (*Equus quagga*), of eastern and southern African grasslands, has wide, widely spaced stripes. Grevy's zebra (*E. grevyi*), of arid areas in Kenya, Ethiopia, and Somalia, has narrow, closely spaced stripes and a white belly. The small mountain zebra (*E. zebra*), of dry upland plains in Namibia and western South Africa, has a gridlike pattern on the rump. Small zebra groups consisting of a stallion and several mares and foals may coalesce into large herds but retain their identity. See photograph on following page.

Zen, Important school of Buddhism that claims to transmit the experience of enlightenment achieved by the Buddha Gautama. Arising as Chan in China in the 6th century (introduced by Bodhidharma), it divided into two schools, the Southern school, which believed in sudden enlightenment, and the Northern school, which believed in gradual enlightenment. By the 8th century only the Northern school survived. Zen developed fully in Japan by the 12th century and had a significant following in the West by the later 20th century. Zen teaches that the potential to achieve en-

A group of plains zebras (Equus quagga) *near a stream.*
Leonard Lee Rue III

lightenment is inherent in everyone but lies dormant because of ignorance. It is best awakened not by the study of scripture, the practice of good deeds, rites and ceremonies, or worship of images, but by breaking through the boundaries of mundane logical thought. Methods employed vary among different schools and may emphasize the practice of zazen (in the Soto school), the use of koans (in the Rinzai school), or the continual invocation of Amida (in the Obaku school; *see* Amitabha).

zeolite, Any member of a family of hydrated aluminosilicate minerals that have a framework structure enclosing interconnected cavities occupied by large metal cations (positively charged ions)—generally sodium, potassium, magnesium, calcium, and barium—and water molecules. The ease of movement of ions and water within the framework allows reversible dehydration and cation exchange, properties that are exploited in water softeners and molecular sieves for pollution control, among other uses.

Zeus, In Greek religion, the chief deity of the pantheon, a sky and weather god. His Roman counterpart was Jupiter. Zeus was regarded as the bearer of thunder and lightning, rain, and winds, and his traditional weapon was the thunderbolt. The son of Cronus and Rhea, he was fated to dethrone his father. He divided dominion over the world with his brothers Poseidon and Hades. As ruler of heaven, Zeus led the gods to victory against the Titans. From his home atop Mount Olympus, he dispensed justice and served as protector. Known for his amorousness—a source of perpetual discord with his wife, Hera—he had many love affairs with mortal and immortal women, giving rise to numerous offspring, including Apollo, Ares, Artemis, Athena, Dionysus, Helen, Hephaestus, and Persephone. In art he was represented as a bearded, dignified, and mature man.

Zeus hurling a thunderbolt, bronze statuette from Dodona, Greece, early 5th century BC; *in the Staatliche Museen zu Berlin, Germany*
Antikenabteilung, Staatliche Museen zu Berlin—Preussischer Kulturbesitz

Zhang Daoling, or CHANG TAO-LING (b. AD 34?, Pei, Jiangsu province, China—d. 156?, Hanzhong), Founder and first patriarch of organized religious Daoism. Zhang composed a Daoist work that attracted many followers among Chinese and indigenous groups in Sichuan. Like contemporary Daoists, he promised longevity and physical immortality, but, unlike others, he emphasized the importance of religious organization. He founded the Five Pecks of Rice movement. Zhang, his son, and his grandson are known as the Three Zhangs. While the *Daodejing* was the basic text, Zhang's *Xiang'er* commentary interpreted it to suit the organization's needs.

Zhejiang, or CHE-CHIANG, conventional CHEKIANG, Province (pop., 2002 est.: 46,470,000), eastern China. With an area of 39,300 sq mi (101,800 sq km), it is bounded by the East China Sea, Shanghai municipality, and Fujian, Jiangxi, Anhui, and Jiangsu provinces; its capital is Hangzhou. It is one of China's smallest provinces and one of the most densely populated. Its northern part lies just south of the Yangtze River (Chang Jiang) delta. Occupying parts of various kingdoms until the 13th century, it was divided into eastern and western regions. Foreign penetration began in the 1840s, and it was devastated during the Taiping Rebellion (1850–64). After the Chinese revolution (1911–12), it became a power base for the Nationalist Party of Chiang Kai-shek, who was born in the province. Occupied by the Japanese during World War II, it was little affected by the 1946–49 civil war. In addition to its agricultural importance, it has a thriving fishing industry. Its hydroelectric power plants have spurred more growth.

Zhengzhou, or CHENG-CHOU, formerly (1913–49) ZHENGXIAN, or CHENG-HSIEN, City (pop., 2003 est.: 1,770,800), capital of Henan province, east-central China. Located south of the Huang He (Yellow River), it is an important rail centre. There were Neolithic settlements in the area, and the Shang Bronze Age culture (fl. *c.* 1500 BC) was centred there on a walled city. Zhou-dynasty tombs have also been discovered. The city was first called Zhengzhou in AD 605, and it has been known by that name virtually ever since. It achieved its greatest importance in the 6th–12th century, when it was the terminus of a canal that joined the Huang to the north. In the early 20th century it became a rail junction and a regional agricultural centre. Since 1949 its industrial base has greatly expanded, and its population has grown considerably.

Zhiyi, or CHIH-I (b. 538, Hunan province, China—d. 597, Mount Tiantai, Zhejiang province), Chinese Buddhist monk who founded the eclectic Tiantai sect. Orphaned at age 17, he studied with the Buddhist master Huisi for seven years. He was associated with the imperial governments of the Chen dynasty in southern China and the Sui dynasty, which reunified China. He reconciled the various strains of Buddhism by regarding all Buddhist doctrines as true and present in the mind of the enlightened Buddha, who unfolded his teachings in periods to accommodate his listeners' capacities. He considered the *Lotus Sutra* the highest teaching and helped establish it as the most popular scripture in East Asia.

Zhoukoudian, or CHOU-K'OU-TIEN, Archaeological site some 26 mi (42 km) southwest of Beijing, China, where fossil remains of the extinct hominin *Homo erectus* have been found. So-called Peking man was identified as a new fossil human by Canadian anthropologist Davidson Black in 1927 and variously classified as *Pithecanthropus* and *Sinanthropus* before being assigned to *H. erectus*. Partial remains of about 40 individuals along with more than 100,000 artifacts have been uncovered, making Zhoukoudian one of the most important *H. erectus* sites in the world. Its strata date to 770,000–230,000 years ago. It was named a World Heritage site in 1987.

Zhu Rongji, or CHU JUNG-CHI (b. Oct. 23, 1928, Changsha, Hunan province, China), Premier of the State Council of China (1998–2003). In the 1950s he was denounced as a rightist, and he was purged again in the 1970s, but, once his Communist Party membership was restored, he rose rapidly. In 1988 he became mayor of Shanghai and in 1991 a deputy premier of the State Council. He was governor of the People's Bank of China (1993–95) and became director of the Institute for Economic Management at Qinghua University in 1994. He was appointed premier in 1998. In the face of the Asian economic crisis at the end of the 1990s, he worked to drastically cut back the size of the government bureaucracy. Zhu, whose economic policies have been both praised and criticized, stepped down as premier in 2003 and was replaced by Wen Jiabao.

Zhu Shijie (fl. 1300, China), Chinese mathematician who stood at the pinnacle of traditional Chinese mathematics. Zhu is known for having unified the southern and northern Chinese mathematical traditions. His fame rests on two publications, *Suanxue qimeng* (1299; "Introduction to Mathematical Science") and *Siyuan yujian* (1303; "Precious Mirror of Four Elements"). The former is an introductory mathematics textbook; following the southern Chinese tradition, it presents many rules and problems in the form of verses to facilitate their memorization. It played a central role in the development of the *wasan* ("Japanese calculation") tradition. "Precious Mirror" corresponds to the final stage in the generalization of the northern Chinese technique of *tian yuan* ("method of the celestial unknown"), a kind of algebraic computation performed with counting rods to solve problems.

Zhuangzi, or CHUANG-TZU (b. *c.* 369, Meng, China—d. 286 BCE). Most significant early Chinese interpreter of Daoism and the purported author of the Daoist classic that bears his name. A minor official and a contemporary of Mencius, he drew on the sayings of Laozi but took a broader perspective. He taught that enlightenment comes from the realization that everything is one, the *dao*, but that the *dao* has no limitations or demarcations and whatever can be known or said of the *dao* is not the *dao*. He held that things should be allowed to follow their own course and that no situation should be valued over any other.

ziggurat, Pyramidal, stepped temple tower characteristic of the major cities of Mesopotamia between 2200 and 500 BC. It was built with a core of mud brick and an exterior covered with baked brick. It had no internal chambers and was usually square or rectangular. Some 25 ziggurats are known, located in Sumer, Babylonia, and Assyria. The best-preserved ziggurat is at Ur, and the largest is at Elam. The legendary Tower of Babel has been associated with the ziggurat of the great temple of Marduk in Babylon.

Zimbabwe, officially REPUBLIC OF ZIMBABWE formerly RHODESIA, Landlocked country, southern Africa. Area: 150,872 sq mi (390,757 sq km). Population: (2011 est.) 12,084,000. Capital: Harare. The Shona make up more than two-thirds of the population; most of the rest are Ndebele, Chewa, and people of European ancestry. Languages: English (official); Bantu languages of the Shona and Ndebele are much more widely spoken. Religions: Christianity (other [mostly independent] Christians, Protestant, Roman Catholic), traditional beliefs. Currency: Zimbabwe dollar. A broad ridge running southwest-northeast, reaching elevations of 4,000–5,000 ft (1,200–1,500 m), dominates Zimbabwe's landscape. The Zambezi River forms the country's northwestern boundary and contains Victoria Falls as well as the Kariba Dam (completed 1959); Lake Kariba, created by the dam, covers some 2,000 sq mi (5,200 sq km). The Limpopo and Save river basins are in the southeast. Agricultural products, livestock, and mineral reserves, including gold, are all economically important. Zimbabwe's current form of government is a transitional coalition regime that is a multiparty republic with two legislative houses; the head of state and government is the president, assisted by the prime minister and cabinet. Remains of Stone Age cultures dating to 500,000 years ago have been found in the area. The first Bantu-speaking peoples reached Zimbabwe during the 5th–10th centuries CE, driving the San inhabitants into the desert. A second migration of Bantu speakers began *c.* 1830. During that period the British and Afrikaners moved up from the south, and the area came under the administration of the British South Africa Company (1889–1923). Called Southern Rhodesia (1911–64), it became a self-governing British colony in 1923. The colony united in 1953

with Nyasaland (Malawi) and Northern Rhodesia (Zambia) to form the Central African Federation of Rhodesia and Nyasaland. The federation dissolved in 1963, and Southern Rhodesia reverted to its former colonial status. In 1965 it issued a unilateral declaration of independence considered illegal by the British government, which led to economic sanctions against it. The country, which proclaimed itself a republic in 1970, called itself Rhodesia from 1964 to 1979. In 1979 it instituted limited majority rule and changed its name to Zimbabwe Rhodesia. It was granted independence by Britain in 1980 and became Zimbabwe. A multiparty system was established in 1990. The economy began to experience a decline in the 1990s that accelerated dramatically in the 2000s. In 2008 long-simmering political tensions between the ruling party and the opposition led to a hotly contested presidential election that sparked a protracted political crisis and exacerbated the country's economic troubles and deteriorating health and welfare conditions. An agreement for a power-sharing government, reached in September 2008, was implemented in February 2009.

zinc, Metallic chemical element, chemical symbol Zn, atomic number 30. Zinc is a bluish silver metal, ductile when very pure but brittle otherwise. It forms brass (with copper) and many other alloys. Its major use is in galvanizing iron, steel, and other metals. Zinc is an essential trace element, particularly in red blood cells; in snails, it corresponds to iron in the blood of vertebrates. Zinc oxide is used as a pigment, ultraviolet light absorber (to prevent sunburn), dietary supplement and seed treatment, and photoconductor. Zinc's many other compounds (in which it has valence 2 or, rarely, 1) are used in industrial and consumer applications, including as pesticides, pigments, mordants, fluxes, and wood preservatives.

zinnia, Any of about 22 species of herbaceous plants and shrubs

Zinnia elegans
Kenneth and Brenda Formanek/EB Inc.

that make up the genus *Zinnia* in the aster family (Asteraceae), native mainly to North America. Where native, they are perennial; elsewhere they are annual. Zinnias have stiff, hairy stems and oval or lance-shaped leaves arranged opposite each other and often clasping the stem. The numerous garden varieties grown for their showy solitary flowers come from the species *Z. violacea* (*Z. elegans*). Garden zinnias range from dwarf compact plants (less than 1 ft, or 30 cm, tall), with flowers 1 in. (2.5 cm) in diameter, to giant forms (up to 3 ft, or 1 m, tall), with flowers up to 6 in. (15 cm) across.

Zion, Easternmost of the two hills of ancient Jerusalem, where David established his royal capital. In the Old Testament, the name Zion frequently refers to Jerusalem as a whole; it is overwhelmingly a poetic and prophetic designation. Mount Zion is the place where Yahweh (God) dwells and is the scene of his messianic salvation. The name came to mean the Jewish homeland, symbolic of Judaism or Jewish national aspirations, and thus was the source of the term Zionism. Though the name is rare in the New Testament, it has been frequently used in Christian literature and hymns as a designation for the heavenly city or for the earthly city of Christian faith and fraternity.

Zionism, Jewish nationalism movement with the goal of establishing a Jewish state in Palestine. In the 16th–17th century, a number of "messiahs" tried to persuade the Jews to return to Palestine, but by the late 18th century interest had largely faded. Pogroms in Eastern Europe led to formation of the "Lovers of Zion," which promoted the settlement of Jewish farmers and artisans in Palestine. In the face of persistent anti-Semitism, Theodor Herzl advocated a Jewish state in Palestine. He held the first Zionist Congress in Basel in 1897. After World War I the movement picked up momentum with the issuing of the Balfour Declaration. The Jewish population in Palestine increased from 90,000 in 1914 to 238,000 in 1933. The Arab population resisted Zionism, and the British tried unsuccessfully to reconcile Jewish and Arab demands. Zionism achieved its goal with the creation of Israel in 1948.

zircon, Silicate mineral, zirconium silicate, $ZrSiO_4$, the principal source of zirconium. Zircon is widespread as an accessory mineral in acid igneous rocks; it also occurs in metamorphic rocks and, fairly often, in detrital deposits. It occurs in beach sands in many parts of the world, particularly Australia, India, Brazil, and Florida, and is a common heavy mineral in sedimentary rocks. Gem varieties occur in stream gravels and detrital deposits, particularly in Indochina and Sri Lanka, but also in Myanmar, Australia, and New Zealand. Zircon forms an important part of the syenite of southern Norway and occurs in large crystals in Quebec.

Zircon with quartz from Cheyenne Canyon, Colorado
Courtesy of the Field Museum of Natural History, Chicago; photograph, John H. Gerard/EB Inc.

zirconium, Metallic chemical element, one of the transition elements, chemical symbol Zr, atomic number 40. The metal is hard and brittle when impure, soft and ductile when highly purified. It is relatively abundant, occurring as zircon (also marketed as a natural gemstone) and baddeleyite. Highly transparent to neutrons, zirconium became important in the 1940s in nuclear energy applications such as fuel cladding. Other uses are in alloys, fireworks, and flashbulbs and as a scavenger for oxygen and other gases. Its compounds, in most of which it has valence 4, are important industrial materials. Zirconia (the oxide) is used in piezoelectric crystals, high-frequency induction coils, coloured glazes and glasses, and heat-resistant fibres; zirconium carbonate is employed in preparations to treat the rash of poison ivy.

zither, Plucked or struck stringed instrument with a shallow soundbox. The common Austrian zither is roughly rectangular and has 30–40 strings; it is placed on the player's knees or on a table. Several melody strings pass over a fretted fingerboard; the player's left hand stops these strings, while the right hand plucks with the fingers and a thumb plectrum. Zither is also a generic term for stringed instruments, the strings of which are fastened across a frame that lacks any projecting neck or arms. The larger zither family thus includes instruments such as the Aeolian harp, autoharp, cimbalom, dulcimer, koto, and even the clavichord, harpsichord, and piano.

zodiac, Belt around the heavens extending about 9° on either side of the ecliptic. The orbits of the Moon and the major planets lie entirely within the zodiac. In astrology, each of 12 constellations along this circle is considered to occupy 1/12 (30°) of it. The positions of the Sun and planets when a person is born and their motion through these constellations are said to exert influence on his or her life, though precession of the equinoxes has shifted the constellations eastward, and the Sun no longer passes through them on the traditional dates: Aries, the ram (March 21–April 19); Taurus, the bull (April 20–May 20); Gemini, the twins (May 21–June 21); Cancer, the crab (June 22–July 22); Leo, the lion (July 23–August 22); Virgo, the virgin (August 23–September 22); Libra, the balance (September 23–October 23); Scorpius, the scorpion (October 24–November 21); Sagittarius, the archer (November 22–December 21); Capricornus, the goat (December 22–January 19); Aquarius, the water bearer (January 20–February 18); Pisces, the fish (February 19–March 20).

Zoe (b. *c.* 978, Constantinople—d. 1050, Constantinople), Byzantine empress. The daughter of Constantine VIII, she married Romanus III Argyrus in 1028. He died in 1034, perhaps poisoned by her, and she married her lover and chamberlain, who became Michael IV. After his death in 1041, his successor, Michael V, banished Zoe to a convent; she was recalled by public outcry, and Michael was deposed, blinded, and exiled (1042). Zoe and her sister became uneasy corulers, and she married Constantine IX Monomachus to secure her throne.

Zola, Émile (-Édouard-Charles-Antoine) (b. April 2, 1840, Paris, France—d. Sept. 28, 1902, Paris), French novelist and critic. Raised in straitened circumstances, Zola worked at a Paris publishing house for several years during the 1860s while establishing himself as a writer. In the gruesome novel *Thérèse Raquin* (1867), he put his "scientific" theories of the determination of character by heredity and environment into practice for the first time. These ideas established him as the founder of naturalism in literature. In 1870 he began the ambitious project for which he is best known, the *Rougon-Macquart Cycle* (1871–93), a sequence of 20 novels documenting French life through the lives of the violent Rougon family and the passive Macquarts. It includes *L'Assommoir* (1877), a study of alcoholism that is among his most successful and popular novels; *Nana* (1880); *Germinal* (1885), his masterpiece; and *La Bête humaine* (1890). Among his other works are two shorter novel cycles and treatises explaining his theories on art, including *The Experimental Novel* (1880). He is also notable for his involvement in the Alfred Dreyfus affair, especially for his open letter, "J'accuse" (1898), denouncing the French army general staff. He died under suspicious circumstances, overcome by carbon-monoxide fumes in his sleep.

Zollverein (German: "Customs Union") Free-trade area throughout much of Germany established in 1834 under Prussian leadership. The customs union developed from the 1818 Prussian tariff law that abolished internal customs dues and the customs union set up in 1828 in southern Germany by Bavaria and Württemberg. By 1834 other German states had joined, for a total of 18 members; more joined in subsequent years. The Zollverein represented an important step in German unification.

zombi, In Vodou, a dead person who is revived after burial and compelled to do the bidding of the reviver, including criminal acts and heavy manual labour. It is believed that actual zombis are living persons under the influence of powerful drugs, including burundanga (a drug reportedly used by Colombian criminals) and drugs derived from poisonous toads and puffer fish.

zone melting, Any of a group of techniques used to purify an element or a compound or to control its composition by melting a short region (called a zone) and causing this liquid zone to travel slowly through a relatively long ingot, or charge, of the solid. In zone refining, the most important of the zone-melting techniques, a solid is refined by multiple molten zones being passed through it in one direction. Each zone carries a fraction of the impurities to the end of the solid charge, thereby purifying the remainder. Zone refining is particularly important as a method of purifying crystals, especially for use in semiconductor devices.

zoning, Legislative method of controlling land use by regulating considerations such as the type of buildings that may be erected and population density. German and Swedish cities first applied zoning regulations in the late 19th century to address the problems of urban congestion and building height. The earliest U.S. zoning ordinances, which date from the beginning of the 20th century, were motivated by the need to regulate the location of commercial and industrial activities. In 1916 New York City adopted the first comprehensive zoning law; it and other early regulations were designed to protect property values and preserve light and air. Modern zoning regulations divide land use into three types: residential, commercial, and industrial. Within each designation, more specific aspects of development (e.g., building proximity, height, and type) are also determined. Zoning is often used to maintain the distinctive character of a town or city; an adverse consequence of such zoning is economic segregation. The Supreme Court of the United States ruled against such laws in 1977 when it declared the zoning regulations of one Chicago suburb discriminatory.

zoo, or ZOOLOGICAL GARDEN, Place where wild and sometimes domesticated animals are exhibited in captivity. Aquatic zoological gardens are called aquariums. The first zoos were perhaps associated with domestication. Pigeons were kept in captivity as early as 4500 BC; other animals (e.g., elephants and antelopes) have also been kept in captivity since antiquity. Animal collections were kept by Charlemagne and other European monarchs. Hernán Cortés described a zoo in Mexico (1519) so large that it required a staff of 300. Modern zookeeping started in 1752 with the founding of the Imperial Menagerie at Vienna's Schönbrunn Palace. Open-range zoos were first established in the early 1930s, some so large that visitors drive through in cars, as on an African safari. There are now more than 1,000 animal collections open to the public throughout the world (e.g., in the U.S., the Bronx Zoo and San Diego Zoo).

zoology, Branch of biology concerned with members of the animal kingdom and with animal life in general. The science originated in the works of Hippocrates, Aristotle, and Pliny. The contributions of individuals such as William Harvey (the circulation of blood), Carolus Linnaeus (system of nomenclature), Georges-Louis de Buffon (natural history), Georges Cuvier (comparative anatomy), and Claude Bernard (homeostasis) greatly advanced the field. The 1859 publication of Charles Darwin's *On the Origin of Species by Means of Natural Selection* was a major turning point. Since that time the study of genetics has become essential in zoological studies.

Zoroastrianism and Parsiism, Ancient religion that originated in Iran based on the teachings of Zoroaster. Founded in the 6th century BCE, it influenced the monotheistic religions Judaism, Christianity, and Islam. It rejects polytheism, accepting only one supreme God, Ahura Mazdā. In early Zoroastrianism, the struggle between good and evil was seen as an eternal rivalry between Ahura Mazdā's twin sons, Spenta Mainyu (good) and Angra Mainyu (evil). Later Zoroastrian cosmology made the rivalry between Ahura Mazdā himself (by then called Ormizd) and Angra Mainyu (Ahriman). This later cosmology identifies four periods of history; the last began with the birth of Zoroaster. Zoroastrian practice includes an initiation ceremony and various rituals of purification intended to ward off evil spirits. Fire worship, a carryover from an earlier religion, survives in the sacred fire that must be kept burning continually and be fed at least five times a day. The chief ceremony involves a sacrifice of haoma, a sacred liquor, accompanied by recitation of large parts of the Avesta, the primary scripture. Zoroastrianism enjoyed status as an official religion at various times before the advent of Islam, but Zoroastrians were persecuted in the 8th–10th centuries, and some left Iran to settle in India. By the 19th century these Indian Zoroastrians, or Parsis, were noted for their wealth and education. The small group of Zoroastrians remaining in Iran are known as the Gabars.

Zu Chongzhi (b. 429, Jiankang, China—d. 500, China), Chinese astronomer, mathematician, and engineer. About 462 he proposed a new calendar system that would provide a more precise number of lunations per year and take into consideration the precession of the equinoxes. His Daming calendar was finally adopted in 510 through the efforts of his son, Zu Geng. Li Chunfeng called Zu Chongzhi the best mathematician ever and gave him credit for three approximations of π: $^{22}/_7$, $^{355}/_{113}$, and the interval $3.1415926 < \pi < 3.1415927$; the third result remained the best in the world until improved by the Arab mathematician al-Kashi (fl. *c.* 1400). He also worked on the mathematical theory of music and metrology, and he constructed several devices, such as a semilegendary "south-pointing carriage." The carriage was topped by a symbolic figure that, once properly aligned, would always point to the south.

Zuma, Jacob (b. April 12, 1942, Inkandla, S.Af.), President of South Africa from 2009. He joined the African National Congress (ANC) in 1959 and its military wing, Umkhonto we Sizwe ("Spear of the Nation"), in 1962. He was arrested the next year and sentenced to 10 years in prison. In 1975 he fled the country, and he continued to work for the ANC while based in neighbouring countries; he returned in 1990. In December 1997 he was elected deputy president of the ANC, and in June 1999 he was appointed deputy president of the country. He was dismissed from both positions in 2005 following charges of corruption, which were eventually dropped. He was elected president of the ANC in 2007 and president of the country in 2009.

Zürich, or ZURICH, City (pop., 2006 est.: 347,517), northern Switzerland. Located at the northwestern end of Lake Zürich, the site was occupied first by prehistoric lake dwellers and later by the Celtic Helvetii before the Romans conquered the area *c.* 58 BCE. It subsequently was held by the Alemanni and the Franks. Zürich grew as a trade centre, and in 1218 it became a free imperial city. In 1351 it joined the Swiss Confederation. Under the leadership of Huldrych Zwingli, Zürich became the centre of the Swiss Reformation in the 16th century. Attracting refugees from the Counter-Reformation, it established a liberal democratic order during the 1830s. Long an industrial centre and Switzerland's largest city, Zürich is also an important financial centre and a major tourist destination. The city's cultural treasures include the Swiss National Museum (1898) and the Zürich Opera House (1891).